OPEN A WINDOW

PRENTICE HALL

LITERATURE

Where Great Ideas Happen

OPEN A WINDOW...

TO EXCEPTIONAL LITERATURE

Lead your students to appreciate literature across time and cultures with an unparalleled collection of classic and contemporary selections.

OPEN A WINDOW…

TO LANGUAGE ARTS INTEGRATION

*U*se literature
as a bridge
to teaching
skills mastery:
critical reading,
writing, grammar,
speaking
and listening…
solid instruction
at the teachable
moment.

OPEN A WINDOW...

TO GROUND-BREAKING TECHNOLOGY

Discover a remarkable multimedia Writing Studio that integrates literature and writing:

writing software, hand–held Electronic Grammar Handbook, Literature Videodiscs, Transparencies for Writing, Audio Prose Library.

OPEN A WINDOW...

TO PRENTICE HALL LITERATURE

WHERE GREAT IDEAS HAPPEN

Student Text

Annotated Teacher's Edition

Teaching Portfolio
(with Computer Test Bank)

Multicultural Library

Great Works Library

Study Guides

Library of Video Classics

Listening to Literature
Audiocassettes

**The Prentice Hall Literature
Writing Studio:**

Bank Street Writer Software

Writer's Helper Software

Franklin Language Master 6000

Literature Videodiscs

Audio Prose Library Audiocassettes

Transparencies for Writing

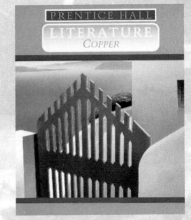

Annotated Teacher's Edition

PRENTICE HALL

LITERATURE
GOLD

PARAMOUNT EDITION

OVERSEAS HIGHWAY
Ralston Crawford
The Regis Collection, Minneapolis, Minnesota

PRENTICE HALL
Englewood Cliffs, New Jersey
Needham, Massachusetts

ISBN 0-13-722505-9

10 9 8 7 6 5 4 3 2 1   97 96 95 94 93

 PRENTICE HALL
A Division of Simon & Schuster
Englewood Cliffs, New Jersey 07632

ACKNOWLEDGMENTS

Grateful acknowledgment is made to the following for permission to reprint copyrighted material.

National Council of Teachers of English
From *SLATE Starter Sheet*, June 1987, "Guidelines for Using Journals in School Settings." Approved by the NCTE Commission on Composition, November 28, 1986. Reprinted with permission of the National Council of Teachers of English.

Weidenfeld & Nicolson Ltd.
From "The Novel From Dickens to the Present" from *A Short History of English Literature* by Ifor Evans. Copyright © B. Ifor Evans, 1940, 1963, 1970.

CONTENTS

WHAT IS INTEGRATED LANGUAGE ARTS?

Sharon Sorenson
formerly with Evansville-Vanderburgh School Corporation
Evansville, Indiana

Those of us who have been in the classroom for more than a few years recall the time when there were separate literature, composition, and grammar classes. We were reasonably satisfied teaching literature. We lectured, occasionally asking questions and seeking discussion. The students listened, and, for the most part, were successful on the tests we gave on literature. Beyond that, however, we could say little about our students' understanding and even less about their enthusiasm. We were frustrated, for instance, by students who, even though they were superior literature students, wrote miserably poor compositions chock full of grammatical errors. Why, we stormed, couldn't students see the connection between all those grammar rules and their own writing? Why couldn't they write successful, thoughtful, coherent essays about literature? Some of us even cast blame on one another. "If the teacher across the hall really did a good job of teaching grammar last semester, students would know where to put commas this semester," we fumed behind closed doors.

Later, we took a bold step: We decided to do away with some of those separate classes and teach grammar and composition together. We believed integrated grammar and composition classes would be the answer to our prayers. Now, at last, we could have the same students for grammar and composition and know full well that students had been taught the rules and could apply those rules to their writing. Unfortunately, in spite of our hopes, combined grammar and composition classes weren't the answer, either. For the most part, student writing was little improved.

The Writing Process

Next, the writing process took the language arts teaching profession by storm. We began working more carefully with students, taking them through prewriting activities, giving them supervised time to write, modeling the revising process, and talking about proofreading in terms of grammar, usage, and mechanics rules. We increased classroom emphasis on peer editing, cooperative learning, and editorial boards, moving away from transmission of information to transaction, from a teacher-centered classroom to a student-centered one. Suddenly, those old grammar handbooks came off the shelves as students struggled to find rules to support whatever error a proofreader found. Grammar, usage, and mechanics became a relevant part of the writing process as students began to see the purpose behind the rules.

The research had been there all along. "Don't teach grammar in isolation," studies said. "It has no meaning to students if not couched in the context of something useful—like writing."

Let's face it. Would anybody except an English teacher expect Ernest Hemingway to describe the use of gerund phrases in his writing? Would Mark Twain have passed a test that asked him to identify the tense and form of verb phrases such as *could have been revising*? What, then, is the relationship between understanding grammar and writing well? That was the question research posed. Of course, we know now that a student's thorough understanding of grammar is no guarantee that he or she will write well. Accurately, maybe, but not well. Writing, the researchers said, is far more than nouns, commas, and participles that don't dangle.

What Makes Good Writing?

Ah, that was the rub! If writing well takes more than applying grammar rules, what makes good writing? We know the answer: We expect our students to say something when they write! But, we argued, given the tools of grammar, usage, and mechanics, shouldn't they be able to just say it? Apparently not. The problem is that grammar rules don't teach students to think like writers. Or to create sentences, paragraphs, and pages like writers. In fact, to think like writers, students need to study writers. Regularly. Daily. All kinds of writers. Then students can identify with the process of writing as a form of thinking. To write is to think. Bingo! This was the first step toward recognizing the importance of integrated language arts.

Integrated Language Arts and Whole Language

About the same time that this first step started marching in the minds of middle-school and high-school language arts teachers, our colleagues in elementary schools began talking about whole language. Depending on whose definition you acept, whole language can be a thematically structured curriculum or a literature-driven curriculum. In either case, all content areas—language arts, science, social studies, math, art, music—spring from a central theme or a central piece of literature. A story about an ugly duckling, for instance, will lead to a science lesson about why duck feathers repel moisture, a math lesson about the incubation of their eggs, a social studies lesson about their semiannual migratory routes, a language arts lesson about using quotation marks when writing narrative, and similar music and art lessons.

However, we middle- and high-school teachers teach mainly language arts, so the term *whole language* didn't seem entirely appropriate. As a result, most of us began talking about integrated language arts. We followed the same philosophy as our elementary-school colleagues—that the parts should come from the whole—but we framed it in the context of our own teaching world. Thus, the term *integrated language arts* has come to refer to a literature-driven language arts curriculum. We start with a piece of literature—a short story, poem, play, essay, or novel—and incorporate instruction in all of the other language arts skills within its framework: reading, writing, grammar, usage, mechanics, spelling, vocabulary, critical thinking, and speaking and listening. We rely heavily on the teachable moment, teaching, for instance, a vocabulary word the moment it pops up in the literature, teaching critical thinking skills as part of the response to literature, teaching grammar as it springs from the discussion of the writer's style, teaching writing as students prepare written responses to the literature, and teaching usage and mechanics during the proofreading process of that written response.

A Changed Classroom

The result is a changed classroom. Some of the changes are hard for us; all of them are proving successful for students. For instance, lesson plans are harder to write because content pops up at unexpected and unanticipated moments, changing the direction of the best laid plans. Curriculum guides must necessarily become more flexible because we address skills within the context of the literature and at the teachable moment. Classroom strategies and management techniques change because we focus on student-centered activities that meet varying ability levels and respond to individual needs. While the changes are sometimes hard for veteran teachers, the results are changed classrooms that excite students, promote learning, and improve test scores.

What does an integrated language arts classroom look like and sound like? Here's a mythical classroom. As students settle in their seats, they find a learning log prompt on the overhead projector. Its purpose is to serve as a prereading activity. The prompt asks students to think about an experience they have had in nature. Maybe they have watched a sunset, hiked in the desert, crossed a glacier, or witnessed a severe storm. What did they see? Students begin writing in response to the prompt. The teacher roams the room reading over shoulders, checking for prior knowledge and individual interests, while also preparing students for the experience they will have reading M. Scott Momaday's poem "New World." A few minutes later, the teacher asks students to name the five senses, to give examples of each, and then to return to their learning logs to add the other senses to their descriptions. The teacher gives them three minutes. Afterward, students are asked to reason logically about what the term *sensory language* must mean, and, without discussion, to write a one-sentence definition in their logs. The teacher is setting students up for the literary focus of Momaday's poem, using another kind of prereading activity but also employing critical thinking skills. Simultaneously, the teacher is engaging students as active learners. To write is to think. And everyone is participating.

Next it is time for an initial choral reading of the poem. Students simply listen for overall impression. On a second reading, however, the teacher stops—at the teachable moment—to ask students to define an unusual word. It is the vocabulary lesson for the day.

Then, to begin getting at the poem's meaning, students do what they were prepared to do before the reading: look for sensory words, an activity completed individually, cooperatively, or in a whole-class setting. After the choral reading of the poem (to say is to think), students read about the author and indicate how understanding his background helps them understand the poem. After further discussion, moving through as complicated an analysis of the literature as makes sense with the given class, the teacher surprises students by asking them to name the verbs in the poem and to identify their tense. After students identify the verbs as present tense, the teacher asks them to substitute the past tense as he or she rereads the poem. Many students recognize that the change in verb tense affects the meaning of the poem—dramatically. So there's the grammar lesson for the day: Use consistent verb tense and use it to convey your message.

Now, back to those learning logs. The prereading activity also functions as a prewriting activity, because the teacher now asks students to use their learning log ideas (with the sensory language already in place) to create one or two products: a poem modeled after "New World" or a narrative description of their experience. In the course of students developing their written products, the teacher may refer to the poem to model structure, sensory language, punctuation, even grammar. Not only does that teaching technique reiterate the elements of the author's style, but it stimulates students' thinking. In the course of revising, students cope with unity, coherence, supporting details, transitions, and the other techniques of clear writing. In the course of proofreading, peer editors tackle grammar, usage, and mechanics problems and find their solutions. Students who are writing at computers may even use a style checker to analyze their sentence lengths, sentence structure, and readability indices. The lesson is finished in about two days.

What Happens in the Integrated Classroom?

What happened during that integrated language arts lesson? Students addressed all of the language arts skills within the context of the literature. All of the parts came out of the whole. They studied literature—a poem—and literary concepts, including sensory language. They practiced active reading skills —predicting, analyzing, clarifying, visualizing, summarizing. They wrote—in their learning logs to promote active learning and in response to the literature to produce a formal written product. They studied grammar—the use of consistent verb tense and its effect on meaning. They referred to usage and mechanics rules, employed critical thinking skills, and engaged in speaking and listening activities.

Integrated language arts classrooms are as varied as the teachers and students who inhabit them, and the activities are equally varied. They are exciting places where skills, not drills, are taught when the students need them. Some teachers, however, feel frustration because they believe that the teachable moment lacks structure. There is no guarantee, they say, that we will actually cover everything we're supposed to cover; it's just too hit or miss.

Those of us who are highly structured will continue to feel this tugging at our professional consciences.

However, look at it this way: If the student isn't using dangling participles, why teach him not to? If he is using them, then teach him, not his classmates, at the teachable moment, referring to his own writing. Or if most of the students face the same problem, do a five-minute minilesson, and then let the practice come in their own writing. Remind yourself what the research tells us: Students don't learn skills in isolation. We can best approach skills from the context or their use—in the literature and in the student's own writing at the moment the student needs them.

The Test

Two teachers told me recently that they put these integrated language arts ideas to the test. They had evenly matched classes, so one teacher taught the traditional grammar units and intersperesed them with writing, and the other teacher taught the integrated language arts approach, letting all of the language arts skills spring from the literature. At the end of the year, both classes took the same test (it happened to be a state-mandated one). The class whose teacher had used the integrated approach attained much higher scores than those whose teacher had pounded rules and skills all year.

"Why do you think that happened?" I asked. "Simple," was one teacher's response. "The kids learn best at the moment they have a need for the knowledge. That's when it makes sense to them, and that's why they remember it." "You know," she went on, "it's like someone telling you how to change a flat tire. Only when you really need to know do those instructions matter. I just applied that little analogy to my language arts classroom."

Lots of teachers who faced flat tires in their classrooms have turned to an integrated language arts approach. They like what they find. "It's refreshing," one teacher said, "to find students who really have something to say. The literature discussions provoke thought, the literature itself provides for structure and style, and the writing process makes sense after students see how other writers put it into effect. It's the complete cycle. We read writing to write reading."

Right!

The Prentice Hall Literature Program
OVERVIEW

The *Prentice Hall Literature* program is an integrated language arts program, offering high-quality, appealing, traditional and contemporary literarature, writing instruction and activities, and study aids that will guide students into, through, and beyond the literature.

The Student Book Organization

The selections are organized by genre to encourage comprehensive study of the types of literature. The following list shows the units and the sections within each unit into which the selections are organized:

The Short Story: Plot, Character, Point of View, Setting, Theme
Drama: Two full-length plays, including a Shakespearean Play
Nonfiction: Biographies and Personal Accounts, Types of Essays, Essays in the Arts and Sciences
Poetry: Narrative Poetry, Dramatic Poetry and the Speaker, Lyric Poetry, Word Choice and Tone, Imagery, Figurative Language, Musical Devices, Structure
The Epic
The Novel: Two complete novels

The number and variety of selections offer choice and flexibility in meeting curriculum requirements as well as student needs and interests.

Unique Features

Because the *Prentice Hall Literature* program puts emphasis on the reading and appreciation of literature, it offers several unique features to help students become active readers.

Reading Preparation and Support

Reading Actively Each unit begins with a feature called Reading Actively, which includes a set of strategies for effectively reading the literature in the unit. The strategies involve the reader in the text before reading and while reading. Such involvement and reaction are necessary if students are to learn.

In the short story, nonfiction, and poetry units, this feature is followed by a Model. This Model is annotated by a student to demonstrate how a good reader might use the active reading strategies to understand a selection. Students are encouraged to use these strategies as they read other selections in the unit. This feature provides a method of scaffolding—giving students help and support while they acquire the skills to become successful readers of literature. To give students further practice with this process, there is an additional selection in the Teaching Portfolio, that students can annotate themselves.

Guide for Reading All other selections begin with a Guide for Reading. This page, which precedes the selection, contains useful prereading information. The Guide for Reading prepares students for successful reading in four ways:

- A biography of the author provides insight into how the author came to write the selection.
- A literary focus section introduces the literary concept that is taught with the selection.
- A reading focus feature activates students' prior knowledge, involves them in the reading process, and provides a specific goal for reading.
- A vocabulary list presents, in glossary format, words from the selection that might present difficulty in reading.

This Guide for Reading provides background to encourage comprehension, motivate students to read, and give them technical support to read successfully.

Theme Bar At the top of the beginning of each selection, you will find a label identifying the theme. This feature makes it easy to thumb through the book and connect selections with similar themes.

Reading and Responding The short story, nonfiction, and poetry units also end with a feature called Reading and Responding. This feature serves as a summary for reading and analyzing the particular types of literature and comprehending the literary elements and devices that are in them. For example, the Reading and Responding for short stories shows a student responding to plot, character, theme, and setting, and analyzes the application of these elements in a particular story. In the Teaching Portfolio, there is an additional selection that the students can annotate themselves.

Each selection is self-contained and complete so that you can use the selections in any order.

After Reading

Features at the end of the selection are designed to foster comprehension and encourage constructive response, either personal or literary. They also encourage the growth of skills needed by students to become independent readers. They comprise five areas:

Responding to the Selection These study questions are built upon four levels of comprehension: the personal response, the literal, the interpretive, and the applied. The questions are grouped by four levels of increasing complexity: your response, recalling (literal), interpreting (inference, analysis), and applying (generalization, extension, judgment). The different levels may be used as appropriate for different ability levels, or may be used to take all students through different levels of thinking.

Analyzing Literature This section develops and reinforces the literary concept or skill introduced on the Guide for Reading page and applies it to the selection. It helps students to understand literary concepts and appreciate writers' techniques, thereby enabling them to respond appropriately to literature.

Critical Thinking and Reading This section introduces students to those critical thinking and critical reading skills that are necessary for understanding literature. It gives them an opportunity to apply these skills to the literary selections.

Thinking and Writing This is a composition assignment arising from the selection. This assignment, which may be creative or analytical, is process-oriented, suggesting steps for prewriting, drafting, and revising.

Learning Options This section provides activities that address a variety of learning styles and helps facilitate a student-centered approach.

Other Special Features

One Writer's Process This feature is always connected to a selection in the anthology. The process used by the writer of that selection is explained,

allowing students to gain insight into how writers think and write and to see the writing process in action.

Multicultural Connection Using a literature selection as a springboard, this feature helps students to appreciate connections among cultures.

End of Unit

Your Writing Process Each unit ends with two complete writing lessons. Each lesson focuses on a form of writing and guides students through the writing process.

End of Book

Three handbooks are provided at the end of *Prentice Hall Literature:* Handbook of the Writing Process, Handbook of Grammar and Revising Strategies, and Handbook of Literary Terms and Techniques.

Handbook of the Writing Process This handbook presents three lessons focusing on the writing process. One lesson concentrates on prewriting, another on drafting and revising, and the third on proofreading and publishing.

Handbook of Grammar and Revising Strategies This handbook presents strategies for revising common writing problems, with examples of good usage from the literature selections. It also contains a brief overview of the grammar of a sentence, punctuation rules, and correct usage.

Handbook of Literary Terms and Techniques This handbook provides an alphabetical guide to the literary terms introduced on the Guide for Reading pages and taught in the Analyzing Literature activities at the end of selections. Each entry provides a full definition of the term or technique with one or more examples. The handbook can be used for preteaching, for review, or as a support for students as they work on individual Analyzing Literature activities.

TEACHING SUPPORT

The Annotated Teacher's Edition

The annotated teacher's edition of *Prentice Hall Literature* is designed to be used both for planning and for actual in-class teaching. It offers planning aids and specific teaching suggestions for all selections. This planning and teaching material appears in the side columns next to the reduced student pages of each selection. These annotations, which correspond

to the student material on that page, help you give your students positive and relevant experiences with literature by asking the right questions at the right time and by pointing out what is significant.

Preparation

The annotations in the margin next to the Guide for Reading page help you prepare your students to read.

These annotations provide the groundwork for reading, help you deal with different ability levels, and often call upon students' prior knowledge. You will find the following notes:

More About the Author These notes extend the information about the author given in the student book. Often they contain a quotation, anecdote, or question that helps personalize the writer.

Literary Focus These notes provide tips for teaching the literary element introduced on the Guide for Reading page.

Prereading Focus These notes provide tips for Focus activity on the Guide for Reading page.

Vocabulary These notes provide tips for teaching the vocabulary words. When appropriate, a **Spelling Tip** also accompanies the vocabulary words.

Objectives This boxed material lists the instructional objectives for the selection. These objectives are keyed in to the end-of-selection material.

Support Material This section lists all the support material for the selection found in the Teaching Portfolio and other program components.

Presentation

You may use the notes throughout the pages of the selection to direct your discussion in class. As you and your students read the selection, you will find additional notes that enable you to customize the lesson for your class. They let you increase your students' involvement in the work and enrich their reading of it, while enabling them to deal with the particular genres. The following kinds of notes may direct your class discussions:

Motivation/Prior Knowledge These notes contain questions and tips for calling upon students' prior knowledge in order to motivate them to read the selections.

Purpose-Setting Question These notes provide a focus for reading.

Master Teacher Notes These classroom tips from master teachers give an approach, a strategy, or a very special bit of information that enlivens the selection or increases appreciation.

Thematic Focus These notes connect to the Theme Bar at the top of every selection. They provide suggestions for teaching the theme.

Making Connections These notes connect the particular selection with other selections in the anthology having a similar theme or topic.

Humanities Notes For each piece of fine art in the student book, there is a humanities note giving information on the work of art and the artist. These notes generally point out features of the piece of art that relate it to the work of literature with which it is presented. Additionally, the humanities note concludes with questions that you may use if you wish to discuss the art as part of your discussion of the work.

Enrichment Enrichment notes provide additional information on points of interest that arise in the selection. You may use this information to enrich your students' knowledge of the background of a selection and appreciation of it.

Reading Strategies Strategies to promote student comprehension of the literary text reinforce the emphasis on enabling students to read literature.

Clarification Words, phrases, or ideas that might be obstacles to student understanding are clarified to ensure comprehension.

Discussion Throughout the selection, you will find additional questions and points for discussion. These help you proceed through the selection with students, eliciting their understanding and appreciation of significant passages.

Literary Focus To promote understanding of the writer's techniques, literary focus annotations direct attention to those aspects of the selection that reflect the literary concept presented with it.

Critical Thinking and Reading These notes reinforce the critical thinking and reading skills developed throughout the program.

ESL Teaching Strategy These notes suggest ways to make the selection accessible to students.

Multicultural Focus These notes connect cultural information in the selections with other cultures and the students' own experiences. At times, they contain tips on teaching sensitive material.

Alternative Assessment These notes provide alternative assessment suggestions for most selections. At times they provide strategies for assessing students' understanding of the selection; at other times they are tied to end-of-selection activities.

Technology Notes These notes show when and how to use the components of the Prentice Hall Literature Writing Studio. An icon, printed in blue, indicates which component would be useful at this point.

Cooperative Learning These notes provide cooperative activities that help students better understand the selection and move beyond the selection.

Thematic Response These notes ask students to respond to the theme of the selection. This theme was identified in the Theme Bar.

Reader's Response These notes ask a question designed to prompt students' personal response to the selection.

Grammar in Action Grammar in Action notes integrate language arts skills. These notes demonstrate the writer's use of particular grammatical or style points. They present a direct link between grammar and writing.

Occasional **Commentary** and **Primary Source** notes add background or insight to the selection.

There are probably more notes than you need for presenting any given selection. We emphasize the importance of selecting those annotations that are best suited to your classes and course of instruction.

Closure and Extension

Answers are provided for all questions in each feature following the selections. Where questions are open-ended, we present a suggested response or suggest points that students should note in their answers.

The annotations after the selection also include the following:

Challenge These questions take students beyond those given with the instruction.

Publishing Student Writing For many selections, additional notes suggest ways to publish the writing students have done in the Thinking and Writing.

Writing Across the Curriculum Where appropriate, you will see suggestions for additional assignments or suggestions for relating the Thinking and Writing assignment to student's work in another discipline.

Learning Options These activities address various learning styles.

In addition, you will find teaching suggestions for the special features in the student book.

The Teaching Portfolio

The Teaching Portfolio provides support for teaching and testing all of the selections and skills in *Prentice Hall Literature.*

Fine Art Transparencies

Twenty fine art transparencies with blackline masters are provided in the Teaching Portfolio. These can be used to introduce selections and motivate students to read, or they may be used as additional writing assignments in response to art. The fine art is keyed in to the selections through Master Teacher Notes in the Annotated Teacher's Edition. In the Portfolio, each transparency is accompanied by a writing assignment for students and a lesson plan for that assignment.

Beginning of Unit

Each unit begins with a list of objectives and a skills chart listing literary elements and skills covered in the unit. The skills chart also identifies all the blackline masters in the Teaching Portfolio that correlate to each selection.

The Selections

Full teaching support is provided for each selection. This support material is organized by selection for your convenience. The support for each selection consists of the following: Teacher Backup, Grammar in Action Worksheet, Usage and Mechanics Worksheet, Vocabulary Check, Analyzing Literature Worksheet*, Critical Thinking and Reading Worksheet*, Language Worksheet* (there are always two of the starred three), and a Selection Test.

Teacher Backup Teacher Backup material is provided for each selection. This material consists of more information about the author, a critical quotation about the author, a summary of the selection, and a list of other works by the author. In addition, there is a Check Test that you can use to check if students have read the selection. Help in teaching and evaluating the writing assignment in the student text is provided as well as three alternative composition assignments for the students. One of these is less challenging than the assignment in the student text, one is more challenging, and one requires the student to write in response to literary criticism. Finally, answers to all worksheets and tests are provided.

Grammar in Action Worksheets These worksheets provide additional instruction and practice on the topic presented with a selection in the Annotated Teacher's Edition.

Usage and Mechanics The Usage and Mechanics Worksheets provide sentences dealing with the selection that contain errors in usage and mechanics. They provide additional practice with the skill presented in the Grammar in Action worksheet. Such common problems as run-on sentences, sentence fragments, and subject-verb agreement are incorporated into these sentences as well as errors in spelling and punctuation. We suggest you have your students correct these sentences and discuss each problem.

Vocabulary Check The Vocabulary Check tests mastery of the vocabulary words listed on the Guide for Reading page before each selection. This blackline master can be used as a test or as an in-class or at-home assignment.

Worksheets The Analyzing Literature Worksheet, Critical Thinking and Reading Worksheet, and Language Worksheet support and expand upon the skills taught at the end of the selection in the student book.

Selection Test A Selection Test is provided for each selection. This test requires students to demonstrate comprehension and interpretation of the selection and to apply the skills taught at the end of the selection. The test includes an essay question and a reader's response question.

Annotated Models For each selection that is annotated as a model in the student book (at the beginning and end of the short story, nonfiction, and poetry units), a selection is provided in the Teaching Portfolio for students to annotate themselves.

End of Unit

Each unit ends with two unit tests: a short-answer test and an essay test, with guidelines for evaluating student responses to the essay test questions. In addition, a list of suggested projects, a bibliography, and list of audio-visual aids are included.

End of Portfolio

At the end of the Teaching Portfolio are models of strong and weak student writing, a guide to evaluating student writing, and writing process activities.

Computer Test Bank

Information about the Computer Test Bank and instructions for ordering the appropriate version are included in the Teaching Portfolio. The Computer Test Bank provides the selection tests and unit tests from the Teaching Portfolio on a computer disk. The program allows you to modify the selection tests by deleting items from the short-answer selection tests, choosing a different essay question, and writing your own test questions. You can save your test for future use.

Study Guides

Study Guides for major novels and plays are available with *Prentice Hall Literature*. These guides will help you teach many of the works of your choice as part of your total literature program. Each guide contains an overview of the novel or play, chapter-by-chapter lessons, assignments leading to essays and imaginative writing, guidelines for dealing with provocative themes, a bibliography, and blackline masters of skills and a test for the work.

Multicultural Library

This library contains twenty young adult novels by acclaimed writers from diverse backgrounds. The books will have particular appeal in Grades 6–10. Each title is accompanied by a Study Guide.

Great Works Library

This library contains unabridged editions of time-honored classics by major writers. The books will have particular appeal to high-school students. Each title is accompanied by a Study Guide.

Listening to Literature Audiocassettes

A series of audiocassettes is available for each level of *Prentice Hall Literature*. The audiocassettes provide professional readings of selections to enliven classroom learning. Each level is accompanied by a teacher's guide.

Library of Video Classics

The Library of Video Classics provides videotapes of films made of major works in this level. Each tape is accompanied by a Viewing Guide, which gives background on the film or director; a planning overview for the film; and pre-viewing and after-viewing questions and activities.

Prentice Hall Literature Writing Studio

The Writing Studio provides tools that help the teacher integrate writing instruction with the literature program and facilitate the writing process. Tips on how and when to use the Writing Studio are provided in the Annotated Teacher's Edition for *Prentice Hall Literature*. We suggest teachers customize their program from the following components:

Bank Street Writer software
Writer's Helper software
Franklin Language Master 6000
Literature Videodiscs
Audio Prose Library audiocassettes
Transparencies for Writing

Skills Chart For Selections In Each Unit

The following chart shows the literary elements and the integrated language arts skills covered with each selection. An asterisk (*) indicates that a worksheet appears in the Teaching Portfolio.

SHORT STORIES

Selection	Analyzing Literature	Critical Thinking and Reading	Thinking and Writing	Learning Options	Grammar in Action	Understanding Language
READING ACTIVELY						
"The Cask of Amontillado," Edgar Allan Poe, p. 3	Understanding setting	Analyzing the effect of setting*	Creating a setting	Speaking and listening Art	Using action verbs*	Using word roots*
PLOT						
"The Most Dangerous Game," Richard Connell, p. 13	Understanding plot*	Analyzing sequence in a story*	Writing about plot	Cross-curricular connection	Using dashes* Writing suspense*	
"The Interlopers," Saki, p. 33	Understanding conflict*	Identifying causes and effects	Writing about conflict	Performance Cross-curricular connection	Using participles*	Using context clues*
"Rules of the Game," Amy Tan, p. 39	Understanding generational and cultural conflict*	Inferring meaning from the title*	Extending the story	Art Cross-curricular connection	Achieving emphasis with varied sentence length*	
"The Lady or the Tiger?" Frank R. Stockton, p. 49	Analyzing a dilemma	Analyzing solutions*	Writing an ending	Performance Cross-curricular connection	Varying sentence length*	Using context clues*
CHARACTER						
"All the Years of Her Life," Morley Callaghan, p. 57	Understanding characterization*	Recognizing stereotypes	Writing about a person	Speaking and listening	Using active and passive voice*	Understanding phonetic spelling*
"Uncle Marcos," Isabel Allende, p. 63	Recognizing character traits	Understanding magical realism*	Writing about a memorable person		Recognizing adverb clauses*	Recognizing hyperbole*
"The Red-headed League," Sir Arthur Conan Doyle, p. 71	Understanding motivation Recognizing character traits*	Contrasting characters' abilities*	Analyzing a detective's methods	Art Writing	Using single quotation marks* Examining deductive reasoning*	
"Blues Ain't No Mockin Bird," Toni Cade Bambara, p. 91	Understanding verisimilitude*	Noting relevant details*	Responding to meaning	Art		

Selection	Analyzing Literature	Critical Thinking and Reading	Thinking and Writing	Learning Options	Grammar in Action	Understanding Language
POINT OF VIEW						
"The Invalid's Story," Mark Twain, p. 99	Understanding first-person narration	Identifying exaggeration*	Writing a tall tale	Performance	Recognizing dialect*	Understanding idioms*
"Before the End of Summer," Grant Moss, Jr., p. 107	Recognizing limited point of view	Using narration to draw conclusions*	Writing about characters	Art Writing	Writing dialogue* Recognizing introductory adverb clauses*	Choosing the meaning to fit the context*
"The Harvest," Tomás Rivera, p. 121	Understanding omniscient narration*	Making inferences about a character*	Writing from another perspective	Cross-curricular connection	Recognizing introductory elements*	
"Autumn Gardening," Siu Wai Anderson, p. 127	Understanding perspective*	Determining cultural perspective*	Writing a human-interest news story	Performance Speaking and listening Cross-curricular connection	Recognizing subordinate clauses*	
SETTING						
"To Da-duh, in Memoriam," Paule Marshall, p. 139	Understanding setting and conflict*	Understanding symbolism*	Describing a setting	Multicultural activity	Capturing the sounds of speech* Using compound-complex sentences*	
"The Man to Send Rain Clouds," Leslie Marmon Silko, p. 151	Recognizing the cultural setting*	Understanding cultural conflict*	Writing about cultural practices	Cross-curricular connection Multicultural activity		
"If I Forget Thee, Oh Earth . . ." Arthur C. Clarke, p. 157	Responding to setting in science fiction*	Understanding plausibility	Writing science fiction	Art	Using adjective clauses*	Using vivid words*
THEME						
"A Very Old Man with Enormous Wings," Gabriel García Márquez, p. 165	Understanding theme*	Identifying different interpretations	Writing from a different perspective	Writing Art Speaking and listening	Illustrating and giving examples* Using different sentence openers*	Using context clues*
"The Gift of the Magi," O. Henry, p. 175	Understanding key statements	Paraphrasing*	Writing about theme	Performance	Determining author's tone*	Tracing word histories*

Selection	Analyzing Literature	Critical Thinking and Reading	Thinking and Writing	Learning Options	Grammar in Action	Understanding Language
"The Scarlet Ibis," James Hurst, p. 181	Interpreting symbols*	Recognizing emotive language	Writing about symbols	Art Cross-curricular connection	Using concrete details* Recognizing infinitives and infinitive phrases*	Identifying simile and metaphor*
"The Necklace," Guy de Maupassant, p. 193	Understanding irony*	Making inferences about characters	Repsonding to criticism		Varying sentences*	Choosing the meaning that fits the context*

READING AND RESPONDING

Selection	Analyzing Literature	Critical Thinking and Reading	Thinking and Writing	Learning Options	Grammar in Action	Understanding Language
"The Secret Life of Walter Mitty," James Thurber, p. 201	Understanding point of view*	Identifying wishful thinking	Continuing the story	Art	Writing dialogue*	Understanding prefixes*

DRAMA

Selection	Analyzing Literature	Critical Thinking and Reading	Thinking and Writing	Learning Options	Grammar in Action	Understanding Language
The Miracle Worker, Act I, p. 219	Recognizing protagonist and antagonist	Comparing and contrasting characters*	Writing about characters	Speaking and listening Writing	Recognizing sentence fragments*	Using specific words*
The Miracle Worker, Act II, p. 243	Understanding conflict in drama	Recognizing causes and effects*	Writing a scene		Using dashes* Writing directions*	Recognizing and forming compound words*
The Miracle Worker, Act III, p. 267	Understanding the theme of a play	Summarizing a play*	Writing a review of a play		Using direct objects and subject complements*	Recognizing the prefix *dis-**

Selection	Analyzing Literature	Critical Thinking and Reading	Thinking and Writing	Learning Options	Grammar in Action	Understanding Language
Romeo and Juliet, Act I, p. 287	Appreciating blank verse	Interpreting the effect of imagery*	Writing a speech in blank verse	Language	Using commas in poetry*	Understanding words from Elizabethan times*
Romeo and Juliet, Act II, p. 313	Understanding the dramatic foil*		Modernizing dialogue	Performance Language	Understanding antecedents* Determining author's tone*	Interpreting personification*
Romeo and Juliet, Act III, p. 335	Understanding dramatic speeches	Inferring tone in a monologue*	Writing a soliloquy	Performance Writing Community connections	Using imagery* Using quotation marks with end punctuation*	Understanding allusions*
Romeo and Juliet, Act IV, p. 361	Understanding dramatic irony*	Predicting outcomes	Writing an ending for the play		Using apostrophes*	Appreciating puns*
Romeo and Juliet, Act V, p. 375	Understanding tragedy and theme	Interpreting metaphorical language*	Responding to criticism		Using a noun of direct address*	Using the context to find the meaning*

NONFICTION

Selection	Analyzing Literature	Critical Thinking and Reading	Thinking and Writing	Learning Options	Grammar in Action	Understanding Language
READING ACTIVELY						
From *Jacob Lawrence: American Painter*, Ellen Harkins Wheat, p. 397	Understanding a biographical profile*	Reading an essay about art*	Writing a biographical profile	Cross-curricular connection		
BIOGRAPHIES AND PERSONAL ACCOUNTS						
From *A Lincoln Preface*, Carl Sandburg, p. 405	Understanding a biography*	Evaluating the subject of a biography*	Writing a biographical sketch	Performance Cross-curricular connection	Recognizing main idea and supporting details*	
"Of Dry Goods and Black Bow Ties," Yoshiko Uchida, p. 413	Understanding characterization*	Separating fact from opinion	Writing about characterization	Speaking and listening	Using transitions*	Understanding synonyms*

Selection	Analyzing Literature	Critical Thinking and Reading	Thinking and Writing	Learning Options	Grammar in Action	Understanding Language
"Across the Big Water," from *Black Elk Speaks,* John Neihardt, p. 421	Understanding cultural viewpoints*	Making inferences about cultural beliefs*	Writing from another point of view		Recognizing infinitives*	
From *Kon-Tiki,* Thor Heyerdahl, p. 429	Understanding suspense*	Understanding the sequence of events*	Writing about autobiography	Cross-curricular connection Performance	Appreciating narrative writing* Using semicolons*	

TYPES OF ESSAYS

Selection	Analyzing Literature	Critical Thinking and Reading	Thinking and Writing	Learning Options	Grammar in Action	Understanding Language
"Nameless, Tennessee," from *Blue Highways,* William Least Heat Moon, p. 441	Understanding the narrative essay*	Summarizing an essay*	Writing a narrative essay	Language Art	Recognizing supporting information*	
"A Celebration of Grandfathers," Rudolfo A. Anaya, p. 447	Understanding the reflective essay*	Understanding an author's tone*	Writing a reflective essay	Speaking and listening	Using commas to separate sentence parts*	
"The Loch Ness Monster," John McPhee, p. 457	Understanding the expository essay*	Finding relevant evidence	Writing an expository essay	Performance Art	Writing description* Varying sentence openers*	Understanding words with the suffix *-ity*
"I Have a Dream," Martin Luther King, Jr., p. 467	Understanding the persuasive essay*	Recognizing persuasive techniques	Writing about persuasion	Performance Speaking and listening	Using parallel structure*	Understanding synonyms and antonyms*

ESSAYS IN THE ARTS AND SCIENCES

Selection	Analyzing Literature	Critical Thinking and Reading	Thinking and Writing	Learning Options	Grammar in Action	Understanding Language
"But a Watch in the Night," James C. Rettie, p. 475	Understanding the central idea*	Recognizing an implied central idea*			Recognizing active and passive voice*	
"Georgia O'Keeffe," Joan Didion, p. 481	Character analysis*	Evaluating conclusions about art*	Writing about art	Writing	Using coordination*	
"Single Room, Earth View," Sally Ride, p. 487	Understanding scientific observation*	Finding the main idea of a paragraph*	Writing up an observation	Speaking and listening	Using *like* and *as**	
"The Spreading '*You* Know,'" James Thurber, p. 493	Understanding illustration	Inferring a writer's purpose*	Writing about spoken language	Performance Language		Understanding words with the prefix *over-**

Selection	Analyzing Literature	Critical Thinking and Reading	Thinking and Writing	Learning Options	Grammar in Action	Understanding Language
From *Shakespeare of London*, Marchette Chute, p. 497	Understanding historical inference*	Evaluating historical inferences	Writing about inference	Speaking and listening Art	Understanding infinitives*	Understanding theater terms*

READING AND RESPONDING

Selection	Analyzing Literature	Critical Thinking and Reading	Thinking and Writing	Learning Options	Grammar in Action	Understanding Language
"Butch Cassidy," from *In Patagonia*, Bruce Chatwin, p. 503	Understanding anecdotes*	Appreciating tone*	Writing a travel narrative		Using the semicolon*	

POETRY

Selection	Analyzing Literature	Critical Thinking and Reading	Thinking and Writing	Learning Options	Grammar in Action	Understanding Language

READING ACTIVELY

Selection	Analyzing Literature	Critical Thinking and Reading	Thinking and Writing	Learning Options	Grammar in Action	Understanding Language
"Sympathy," Paul Laurence Dunbar, p. 517	Understanding symbols*		Writing an extended definition	Art Speaking and listening		Understading shades of difference*

NARRATIVE POETRY

Selection	Analyzing Literature	Critical Thinking and Reading	Thinking and Writing	Learning Options	Grammar in Action	Understanding Language
"Casey at the Bat," Ernest Lawrence Thayer, p. 521	Enjoying narrative poetry	Paraphrasing poetry*	Writing narrative verse	Language Performance		Recognizing jargon*
"The Raven," Edgar Allan Poe, p. 527	Understanding repetition and refrain*	Making inferences about the speaker*	Responding to criticism		Using alliteration*	
"The Charge of the Light Brigade," Alfred Lord Tennyson, p. 533	Understanding rhythm in poetry*		Writing a news report			Using concise language for effect*

DRAMATIC POETRY AND THE SPEAKER

Selection	Analyzing Literature	Critical Thinking and Reading	Thinking and Writing	Learning Options	Grammar in Action	Understanding Language
"Incident in a Rose Garden," Donald Justice, p. 539	Understanding dramatic poetry*	Interpreting personification	Continuing a poem	Speaking and listening Art		Effective word choices*

Selection	Analyzing Literature	Critical Thinking and Reading	Thinking and Writing	Learning Options	Grammar in Action	Understanding Language
"The Seven Ages of Man," William Shakespeare, p. 543	Appreciating poems from plays*		Imitating Shakespeare	Art Writing		Understanding synonyms and antonyms*
"The Runaway" Robert Frost, p. 548 "There Is a Longing . . ." Chief Dan Geroge, p. 550 "George Gray," Edgar Lee Masters, p. 552	Understanding point of view Understanding a speaker's point of view*	Inferring the speaker's meaning Recognizing assertions		Cross-curricular connection		Language of contrast*
LYRIC POETRY						
"Winter," William Shakespeare, "The Dark Hills," Edwin Arlington Robinson, p. 558 "The Funeral," Gordon Parks, p. 559 "Uphill," Christina Rosetti, p. 560 "I Hear an Army," James Joyce, p. 561	Understanding lyric poetry	Interpreting connotative meaning Interpreting symbols in lyric poetry* Interpreting sensory words	Writing a lyric poem Writing about a lyric poem Writing about fine art	Writing Art		Using general and specific words*
WORD CHOICE AND TONE						
"Meeting at Night," Robert Browning, p. 566 "Jabberwocky," Lewis Carroll, p. 568 "Macavity: The Mystery Cat," T.S. Eliot, p. 570 "Astonishment," Wisława Szymborska, p. 574	Understanding word choice* Understanding made-up words Using exaggeration Understanding tone		Writing a poem using made-up words Writing about tone	Writing Cross-curricular connection Performance Speaking and listening Language	Using coordinating conjunctions*	Understanding made-up words*

Selection	Analyzing Literature	Critical Thinking and Reading	Thinking and Writing	Learning Options	Grammar in Action	Understanding Language
IMAGERY						
"Memory," Maragret Walker, p. 578	Studying imagery*		Writing your own "memory"		Using commas*	Appreciating vivid verbs*
"The Meadow Mouse," Theodore Roethke, p. 579	Understanding imagery		Writing about imagery			
"To be of use," Marge Piercy, p. 581						
"The Space," Gary Soto, p. 582		Appreciating the effects of imagery				
"The Creation," James Weldon Johnson; p. 583			Writing a poem with imagery	Art		
FIGURATIVE LANGUAGE						
"The Eagle," Alfred, Lord Tennyson, p. 590	Understanding similes			Writing	Using punctuation*	Using context clues*
"I Wandered Lonely as a Cloud," William Wordsworth, p. 592			Writing a poem using a simile			
"Dream Deferred," Langston Hughes, p. 594			Analyzing a poem			
"Dreams," Langston Hughes, p. 595	Understanding metaphors					
"The Sky Is Low," Emily Dickinson, p. 596	Understanding personification		Responding to criticism	Writing		
"Splinter," Carl Sandburg, p. 598	Understanding figurative language*		Writing a poem	Speaking and listening Art		
MUSICAL DEVICES						
"The Listeners," Walter de la Mare, p. 602	Recognizing alliteration			Speaking and listening Writing	Using precise words*	Identifying synonyms*
"The Bells," Edgar Allan Poe, p. 604	Recognizing forms of repetition			Speaking and listening	Using denotation and connotation*	
Ecclesiates 3:1–8, King James Bible, p. 609	Understanding parallelism					

Selection	Analyzing Literature	Critical Thinking and Reading	Thinking and Writing	Learning Options	Grammar in Action	Understanding Language
"I Hear America Singing," Walt Whitman, p. 611	Understanding free verse Recognizing musical devices and parallelism*		Responding to criticism	Writing		

STRUCTURE

Selection	Analyzing Literature	Critical Thinking and Reading	Thinking and Writing	Learning Options	Grammar in Action	Understanding Language
"There Will Come Soft Rains," Sara Teasdale, p. 616 "maggie and milly and molly and may," E.E. Cummings, p. 617 "Sea-Fever," John Masefield, p. 618 "My Father's Song," Simon J. Ortiz, p. 620 "Meciendo," Gabriela Mistral, p. 621	Understanding structure* Understanding meter		Comparing structures Writing a critical evaluation			Recognizing related words*
"The Sound of the Sea," Henry Wadsworth Longfellow, p. 624 Sonnet 30, William Shakespeare, p. 625	Understanding a Petrarchan sonnet Understanding a Shakespearean sonnet Understanding the forms of a sonnet*					Exploring word origins*
Three Haiku, p. 628 Hokku Poems, Richard Wright, p. 629 "Pendulum," John Updike, p. 630	Understanding haiku* Understanding concrete		Writing haiku Writing a concrete poem	Art Multicultural acitivity		Appreciating concrete words*

READING AND RESPONDING

Selection	Analyzing Literature	Critical Thinking and Reading	Thinking and Writing	Learning Options	Grammar in Action	Understanding Language
"A Red, Red Rose," Robert Burns, p. 633	Analyzing musical devices*	Analyzing the effect of musical devices	Writing a lyric	Speaking and listening		Interpreting dialect*

THE EPIC

Selection	Analyzing Literature	Critical Thinking and Reading	Thinking and Writing	Learning Options	Grammar in Action	Understanding Language
The *Odyssey* Part 1, Homer, p. 645	Understanding the epic hero*	Interpreting epithets	Writing about the epic hero	Art Speaking and listening Writing	Using figurative language* Using appositives and appositive phrases*	Recognizing allusions*
The *Odyssey*, Part 2, Homer, p. 680	Understanding the plot of an epic	Reading a map Inferring customs and beliefs*	Responding to criticism	Writing	Using parenthetical expressions* Using vivid verbs*	Interpreting Homeric similes*
"Siren Song," Margaret Atwood p. 711	Understanding interpretations of the *Odyssey**					Recognizing modern allusions to the *Odyssey**
"Ithaca," Constantine Cavafy, p. 712	Understanding interpretations		Interpreting the *Odyssey* creatively	Performance Art		
"Homeric Chorus," Derek Walcott, p. 714	Understanding historical context		Writing a dialogue	Speaking and listening Multicultural activity		

THE NOVEL

Selection	Analyzing Literature	Critical Thinking and Reading	Thinking and Writing	Learning Options	Grammar in Action	Understanding Language
Great Expectations						
Chapters 1–8, p. 725	Understanding point of view*		Writing from another point of view	Writing Art Art	Using direct quotations* Using gerunds*	Appreciating word histories*
Chapters 9–15, p. 753	Understanding characterization*	Drawing conclusions about characters	Writing about art		Writing dialogue* Appreciating details of setting that suggest time*	Understanding context clues*
Chapters 16–23, p. 777	Understanding plot and subplot	Predicting outcomes*	Extending the story	Art Writing	Using *who* and *whom** Using participial phrases*	Understanding the Latin root *spect**
Chapters 24–31, p. 803	Understanding setting and atmosphere*	Identifying details that create setting	Comparing and contrasting settings	Art Art	Using prepositional phrases* Using parallelism*	Exploring connotations*

THE NOVEL (continued)

Selection	Analyzing Literature	Critical Thinking and Reading	Thinking and Writing	Learning Options	Grammar in Action	Understanding Language
Chapters 32–44, p. 825	Understanding theme	Paraphrasing key statements*	Responding to the theme of a novel	Art Writing Cross-curricular connection Art Art	Using subordination* Appreciating dialect*	Completing analogies*
Chapters 45–58, p. 869	Understanding the novel as a whole	Using criteria to evaluate the novel*	Evaluating the novel		Using repetition* Understanding referents*	Recognizing dialect*
Dragon Song						
Chapters 1–3, p. 915	Understanding imaginary settings Understanding setting	Inferring the meanings of words*	Creating an imaginary place	Writing Art	Varying sentence beginnings* Using phrases in a series*	
Chapters 4–6, p. 941	Understanding motivation*	Recognizing cause and effect*	Writing about cause and effect	Writing Writing Cross-curricular connection	Recognizing infinitive phrases* Recognizing participial phrases*	
Chapters 7–10, p. 967	Recognizing atmosphere*	Comparing and contrasting atmospheres*	Describing atmospheres	Writing Art	Using adverb clauses* Using noun clauses*	
Chapters 11–13, p. 1001	Understanding universal themes*	Evaluating a novel*	Writing a critique	Writing Writing	Using adjective clauses* Using prepositional phrases*	

THE READER'S RESPONSE JOURNAL
Dr. Charles R. Cooper

University of California
San Diego, California

A Reader's Response Journal can be a very important component of a literature course using *Prentice Hall Literature*. Along with a wide range of other writing activities catalogued later in this section, many of the writing activities in the text can be collected in a student's Reader's Response Journal. For example, students could enter into their Reader's Response Journals the text's writing-prior-to-reading activities; the Critical Thinking and Reading activities requiring writing; prewriting, notes, and drafts of revised essays written for the Your Writing Process assignments.

A Reader's Response Journal is a place for students to write often and informally about their reading. They may write nearly every day. Each time, they may write only a few sentences, a page, or more. The writing must be legible, so that you and other students can read it; but it does not have to be entirely correct. It is rarely revised. It is usually not planned carefully. Instead, students start writing quickly and let their ideas or examples develop *as they write*. This kind of writing can best be considered exploratory. Though it should be honest and engage the reading seriously, it can also be playful.

A collection of journal entries can provide the basis for later, carefully planned formal essays, of course, but that does not have to be its primary purpose. Most teachers who assign Reader's Response Journals consider their primary benefits to be engagement with literature, testing and clarifying of responses and ideas through writing, experimentation with various kinds of writing about literature, a record of students' progress through the course, and a repository of material to be used in later assignments.

Though many school and college teachers assign Reader's Response Journals—they are also called reader's logs or learner's journals or academic journals—some teachers remain skeptical. It is not unreasonable to assume that unplanned, exploratory, unrevised writing leads only in circles, rather than toward shaped, formal essays. A teacher might ask: Doesn't casual writing involve only casual thinking? If students' errors are accepted in any of their assigned writing, won't they be practicing error rather than perfecting their prose? How can time be found in an already full course for a major new strand of work? How will reluctant student writers respond to demands for still more writing? How can time be found to evaluate such large amounts of writing? If all students keep journals, what unforeseen problems of classroom management result?

Some of these appropriately skeptical questions can be answered here, the answers coming from reported practices of many classroom teachers. (Perhaps the best source is *The Journal Book*, edited by Toby Fulwiler and published by Heineman Educational Books, 70 Court Street, Portsmouth, N.H. 03801. Teachers' journals, like *English Journal*, now regularly report teachers' experiences with Reader's Response Journals.) Teachers who advocate the use of Reader's Response Journals rely on a fundamentally important idea about writing: Writing fulfills two different but complementary functions—exploratory and expository (or expressive and transactional). These teachers, supported by current researchers and theorists of language, believe that better expository writing results from the kind of exploratory writing that fills students' journals. These teachers also believe that even brief journal writings require critical thinking. They know that over several months of personal choice and assigned journal writings, students will practice a wide range of thinking and writing activities.

Getting Your Students Started

The most representative advice for getting started comes from the Commission on Composition of the National Council of Teachers of English (NCTE). Here are their "Guidelines for Using Journals in the School Setting," published in 1986:

1. Explain that journals are neither "diaries" nor "class notebooks," but borrow features from each: Like the diary, journals are written in the first person about issues the writer cares about; like the class notebook, journals are concerned with the content of a particular course.
2. Ask students to buy looseleaf notebooks. This way students can hand in to you only that which pertains directly to your class, keeping more intimate entries private.
3. Suggest that students divide journals in several sections, one for your course, one for another

course, another for private entries. When you collect the journal, you need only collect that which pertains to your own course.

4. Ask students to do short journal writes in class; write with them; and share your writing with the class. Since you don't grade journals, the fact that you write too gives the assignment more value.

5. Every time you ask students to write in class, do something active and deliberate with what they have written: Have volunteers read whole entries aloud; have everyone read one sentence to the whole class; have neighbors share one passage with each other, etc. (In each case, students who do not like what they have written should have the right to pass.) Sharing the writing like this also gives credibility to a nongraded assignment.

6. Count but do not grade student journals. While it's important not to qualitatively evaluate specific journal entries—for here students must be allowed to take risks—good journals should count in some quantitative way: a certain number of points, a plus added to a grade, as an in-class resource for taking tests.

7. Do not write back to every entry; it will burn you out. Instead, skim-read journals and write responses to entries that especially concern you.

8. At the end of the term, ask students to put in (a) page numbers, (b) a title for each entry, (c) a table of contents, and (d) an evaluative conclusion. This synthesizing activity asks journal writers to treat these documents seriously and to review what they have written over a whole term of study.

Some teachers ask students to keep a spiralbound notebook, which can be more easily carried around by the student, gathered up in quantity by the teacher at evaluation time, or filed more readily somewhere in the classroom for classes or students reluctant to do homework. Other teachers prefer looseleaf notebooks (recommended in Point 2 of the NCTE guidelines) because they can take up and evaluate just a few pages at a time.

Write with your students at first: They may never have seen anyone writing in a journal. You can help them see what you expect in a journal entry by reading yours aloud. They will be reading some of their entries aloud in class, but you may also want to duplicate exemplary entries for the class to examine more carefully. You could share with them selections from published journals.

Evaluation

To persist at the frequent writing required in a Reader's Response Journal, students will need rewards and encouragement. Let them know at the start how you will read and evaluate their journals. Inform them of the contribution of their journal work to their total grades.

Some teachers make a certain grade (perhaps a "C") contingent on completion of all Reader's Response Journal assignments. Some give points for completing each entry, with bonus points for especially insightful entries. Some teachers base as much as half of the course grade on journals.

It is important to look fairly soon at the journals for the first time so that you can ensure that everyone is off to a good start.

Reader's Response Journal Activities

Following are several classroom-proven journal writing activities. You can choose from among them to devise an appropriate Reader's Response Journal plan for any of your classes.

Prewriting for Essays A Reader's Response Journal can be a valuable repository of students' prewriting for essays and other writing activities. The early writing activities up to the draft could be entered into the journal, where they are immediately available for class or small-group sharing and discussion.

Answering Prepared Questions During or after reading a work, students can answer specific questions that you assign. These can be especially valuable frequent journal assignments when students are reading a longer novel or play. These questions can very well be designed as prewriting for essays, or they can have the purpose of exploring and clarifying important passages in the reading, perhaps as preparation for class discussion.

Students must understand that answering questions in the Reader's Response Journal is different from answering questions on a test. In the journal, they should write in an exploratory (even playful) way. They should be taking risks, expecting to be surprised by what they write, knowing they will make discoveries *during* the writing. They do not have to find the answer and plan their response carefully before writing, as though they are answering an essay question in a test. They should just start writing and let the writing lead them to an answer.

Occasionally you may want students to revise their answers to important questions. At the beginning of class, in small groups, students can compare and discuss their answers to a question. They can then bring problems and questions to the teacher and other students in the class for discussion. Students then revise their original answers as homework.

Writing Questions About Puzzling Passages

Students can list questions they have about puzzling passages. This activity can encourage students to be active, questioning readers. The questions are good discussion starters.

Predicting What Comes Next

From research on the process we know that skilled readers are always making predictions about what comes next. You can encourage students to make predictions by asking them, especially with longer works, to write down their predictions in the Reader's Response Journal. You can assign predictions at timely points in the reading of a work.

Writing Alternative Beginnings and Endings to Stories

Students may be asked to write alternative beginnings and endings to stories or chapters in novels, alternatives based on a careful reading of the story and relying on the story's characters and plot. Students may also usefully be asked to write a justification (an argument with reasons) for their alternative beginnings and endings.

This activity leads to productive class discussions about the structure of stories. Students invariably enjoy sharing their alternative beginnings and endings for a story read in common.

Participating in Class Meetings

The Reader's Response Journal can be useful in class. Students can write to focus their energy and attention at the beginning of class. They can write at various moments during class—to summarize a discussion, quietly argue a point in a debate too hot for further rowdy class discussion, react to part of a work read aloud, analyze the style of a brief passage, or contrast two brief passages just before small-group or whole-class discussion. They can reflect on a class meeting. In all of these ways, the Reader's Response Journal becomes a valuable adjunct to class discussion.

Copying and Commenting on Favorite Passages

Students can copy out brief passages and comment on the passages in any way they like. They can explain why they like a passage (its style or art), or they can write about what it evokes in their personal experience. Copying (old-fashioned as it seems) remains a useful way of learning about syntax and style.

A variation on copy/comment is an activity Phillis Brooks at the University of California at Berkeley calls "persona paraphrase." In this activity, students imitate a sentence or a paragraph in their reading by supplying their own content to the exact syntax of the original.

Making Personal Responses

Personal response and evaluation are central to literary study. Personal response to literature is a natural first step toward analysis and interpretation. A Reader's Response Journal gives response a prominent place in your course. The various activities that follow are valuable in their own right, and they can also lead to personal or reflective essays on assigned readings. All of these activities are generic: They can be used repeatedly in just the form below with any kind of literary work. Consequently, you could select a few of them to use as continuing response activities in a course.

Responding to the Most Important Word, Sentence, and Passage

Ask students to select what seems to *them* to be the most important word, sentence, and brief passage in a work. They copy their choices into the journal and then explain why they chose them. The choices are theirs, but they must have reasons for their choices. These journal entries can lead to interesting class discussions.

Associating Personal Experiences

Students can connect what they've read to their own experience. You tell them, "Briefly describe a part of the work that reminds you of something in your own experience. Tell the story of what you were reminded of."

Expressing Identification With Characters

Identifying with characters is central to the process of reading fiction. Two teachers in British Columbia have suggested the following questions to help students express responses to characters in the Reader's Response Journal (G. L. Sampson and N. Carlman, "A Hierarchy of Student Responses to Literature," *English Journal*, 71 [January 1982], 54–57).

Questions to initiate student responses:

1. What do you think of the main character?
2. Why do you like or dislike him or her?
3. What do you think of the antagonist?
4. Why do you like or dislike him or her?

Questions for reflection on overt characteristics:

1. What similarities are there among the characters you like?
2. What similarities are there among the characters you dislike?
3. What generalizations can you make now about why you like or dislike certain characters?

Questions for reflection on inferred characteristics:

1. What are the values of the characters you like?
2. How do these values compare with your values?
3. What are the values of the characters you dislike?
4. How do these values compare with your values?
5. What generalizations can you make now about how characters' values affect the way you feel about them?

Giving Unguided Responses You can simply invite students to write about anything at all in response to the reading, perhaps giving them guidelines as general as "Write at least a half [or one] page." Or you can offer suggestions for students' unguided responses. A California teacher (D. Cookston, "This Guy Can Really Write," in M. Barr, P. D'Arcy, M. K. Healy, eds., *What's Going On*, Boynton/Cook, 1982, pp. 196–217) provides suggestions like the following for Part II of John Steinbeck's *East of Eden*.

You might respond to
—nostalgia for the past.
—hope for the future.
—Adam's blindness to Cathy's flaws.
—the decency of the Hamilton family.
—Kate's plot against Eve.
—Samuel's advice to Adam: "Act out being alive, like a play. And after awhile, a long while, it will be true."
—"And I guess a man's importance in the world can be measured by the quality and number of his glories."

Reflecting on Earlier Journal Entries In this variation, sometimes called "double-entry" or "dialectical" journal writing, students write only on the right of two facing pages about their reading as they read, reserving the left page for commentary, reflection, and interpretation afterward. Here are one teacher's instructions about what to put on the right page.

1. Times when your reading changes:
   You see something you didn't see before.
   You recognize a pattern—the images start to overlap, gestures or phrases recur, some details seem associated with each other.
   The story suddenly seems to you to be about something different from what you thought.
   You discover that you were misreading.
   The writer introduces a new context or new perspective.
2. Times when you are surprised or puzzled:
   Something just doesn't fit.

Things don't make sense—pose explicitly the question or problem that occurs to you.
3. Details that seem important and that make you look again.
4. Way in which the story makes you speculate about life.
5. Your first impression of the ending—what "ended"?

And on the left page:

Whereas the right-hand pages involve your direct reactions to the text, your first gestures at making meanings out of it, the left-hand pages are for a completely different activity. When you finish a story or a group of stories by the same writer, go back and use the facing pages to comment on your original observations and to make something of them. Is there a pattern to the changes you experienced? Does the ending tie them together? Why did you misread when you did? Then reflect on yourself as a reader—what do you focus on? What do you care most about? What do you disregard? Where do you have to strain to follow the story sympathetically? Finally, as you make these reflections on your reading experience, discuss your emerging sense of how the story works and what it's about. (Gary Lindberg, "The Journal Conference: From Dialectic to Dialogue," in Toby Fulwiler, *The Journal Book*.)

Some teachers rely solely on the double-entry journal, giving no specific assignments like those in many other activities catalogued here.

Reflecting on the Course Students can use the Reader's Response Journal for a very important task —reflecting on their own learning. They can describe and evaluate their development as readers and writers in the course. Questions like these would be appropriate:

—Do your own personal reading interests seem to be changing? If so, explain how.
—At what moment during the reading [of a particular text] did you feel your own attitudes most challenged? How did you react to that moment? What do you make of your reaction?
—As a result of your reading [of a particular text] have you changed any of your beliefs, attitudes, or values? If so, explain what happened and how it happened.
—What have you learned about reading literature (as a special form of reading) during this course? Describe what you have learned.
—Think about the way your Reader's Response

Journal influenced your development as a reader and writer during this unit. Describe what you learned by keeping a Reader's Response Journal.

—What kinds of writing about literature have you most enjoyed in this course? Least enjoyed? Describe specific writings and say why you feel as you do about them.

—As a reader and writer, what can you do now that you couldn't do before this course began?

—What one writing assignment was most valuable to you during this course? Describe this assignment and what you wrote. Explain why it was valuable.

Summary of Reader's Response Journal Activities

You will want students to vary the writing in the Reader's Response Journal. This summary of writing activities can be a checklist to help you evaluate the variety of journal assignments you are giving.

Prewriting for Essays
Answering Prepared Questions
Writing Questions About Puzzling Passages
Predicting What Comes Next
Writing Alternative Beginnings and Endings to Stories
Participating in Class Meetings
Copying and Commenting on Favorite Passages
Making Personal Responses
Responding to the Most Important Word, Sentence, and Passage
Associated Personal Experiences
Expressing Identification with Characters
Giving Unguided Responses
Reflecting on Earlier Journal Entries
Reflecting on the Course

The Reader's Response Journal activities may be summarized in another way—as specific thinking and writing strategies. The following list illustrates the surprisingly wide range of intellectual activity required in a Reader's Response Journal. (Mary Weber, a high-school English teacher and curriculum consultant in the San Diego schools, prepared this summary.)

Listing of
  actions or events in a plot sequence
  different versions of a story
  differing points of view
Responding to prepared questions on content
Questioning a puzzling passage

Summarizing
  a class discussion about a work
  plot in a work
  findings in log writings
  information or ideas in an article or book about a literary work
Predicting development in a longer work
Imitating the style of a passage
Commenting on a passage copied from
  the work
  its style
  its art
  its relevance to its historical context
  its relevance to the present
Reacting personally to
  a passage (as a key scene, as illustrative of the writer's art, theme, etc.)
  a character or characters (values, personality, actions)
  a work's content, theme, structure, etc.
  a group or class discussion on a work
Categorizing
  characters by qualities they have in common
  actions in a plot
  different works by elements they have in common
Analyzing an aspect of a work
  style
  characterization
  plot
  theme
  setting
  meanings of selected quotations
Analyzing similarities and differences in
  literary works
  characters
  events
  settings
  passages
Justifying the selection of a
  word
  line
  sentence
  passage
Arguing about ideas in a work
Reflecting on learning accomplished in
  reading a work or several works
  writing about literature
Evaluating
  a work as a whole
  the theme, characterization, language, etc., of a work
  writing about literature as an activity

SUCCESS STRATEGIES FOR THE AT-RISK STUDENT

Dr. Ellen Lees Backstrom
Former English Department Chair
Wm. F. Hart Union High School District
Santa Clarita, California

Who is the at-risk student? How will we have to adapt to meet the needs of this student? For example, will we have to alter our lesson plans to facilitate the at-risk student's learning in our classrooms? Will expectations and/or assessment have to change in order to accommodate at-risk students? In order to examine possible answers to these questions, we must develop a working vocabulary: When you think of an at-risk student, what characteristics come to mind? What characteristics would you add to the list below?

Characteristics of At-Risk Students

Bored—short attention span
Excessive absenteeism
Fears failure
Low self-esteem
Discipline problem
Health problems
Inattentive—lack of motivation
Less able
Language impaired
Disadvantaged
Prone to drop out
Dependent

These characteristics describe certain behaviors. They are not necessarily the causes of the student's being at risk. These behaviors can be changed. We all know of individuals who have overcome these behaviors. We know of specific teachers who have motivated students to change and schools that have dedicated themselves to the success of all. Therefore, our working definition of an at-risk student is simple: The at-risk student is anyone who is not working up to potential.

A Suitable Environment

The story of the at-risk student can be turned into a tale of success, not failure. Student success will be achieved if there is a supportive learning environment that takes into consideration the following:

Appropriate learning outcomes
Specific content that engages students
Communication of expectations
Model task related thinking and problem solving
Lesson strategies that address individual needs
Learning activities that address learning styles
Instructional materials that motivate
Authentic assessment that links assessment with curriculum and instruction

How can we provide a supportive environment? To start, teachers must believe that underachievers can achieve. They must provide learning options that will help the underachievers succeed. These options are keys to success.

Creating a Program for Success

Keeping in mind the qualities of a supportive learning environment, the teacher can create a program for success by setting realistic, attainable goals and by utilizing authentic assessment strategies such as performance-based assessment and portfolio assessment. In addition, the teacher can help students to recognize the connection between effort and outcome. All too often, students do not see that they can turn failure into success simply by working a little "smarter," not necessarily a little harder. Rewards also help. The teacher can motivate students by supplying both extrinsic and intrinsic rewards.

Extrinsic Motivators

Provide rewards/incentives
Positive postcards home or phone calls
Time in class to pursue special interests
Provide prizes
Play money to bank for prizes
Raffle tickets
Free homework passes
Create an atmosphere of healthy competition

Intrinsic Motivators

Adapt tasks to interests
Vary activities
Allow choices, individual responses, and decisions
Provide immediate feedback
Allow enough time to finish projects
Include higher-level objectives always

As teachers, we must stimulate students to learn. If we show interest in learning, students can and will use our behavior as a model. If we project enthusiasm, students will believe we have something interesting and valuable to teach. If we clearly communicate our expectations, students will strive to meet those expectations. In our classrooms, we must minimize anxiety, or fear of failure, and stimulate creativity and curiosity by making students feel safe enough to make mistakes. All too often, students don't try because they feel their answers will be wrong. In addition, we must make students responsible for their own learning by collaborating on goals and objectives and maintaining a balance between teacher-centered and student-centered learning.

Special Problems

We find at-risk students everywhere. They run the gamut from AP classes to regular classes to remediation classes. Whatever the placement, we find that at-risk students usually have academic and/or social difficulties. Disorganization may be the first weakness to strengthen. Providing strategies for students to become organized will lead to improvement in their academic performance. For example, some teachers have students use a daily planner to get themselves organized. Others have them create "To Do" lists at the end of each day and then refer to these lists at the start of the next day. They can create their own "To Do" list on the computer. The idea is to empower the students so that they take responsibility for themselves. Another strategy is to have students take a partner to keep each other on track, especially if one partner is absent.

Another problem is dependency. At-risk students often grow dependent on the teacher or on the class routine. They may not have had enough successful experiences to enable them to rely on and trust their own abilities. Collaborative learning strategies often help students build their confidence and overcome feelings of dependency. And breaking the routine or doing something unexpected not only stimulates interest but also weans students away from dependency.

At-risk students also may process information differently—and their way of processing information may be in direct opposition to the ways in which you structure your lessons. Rather than focusing on what these students cannot accomplish, it might be easier to concentrate on a methodology that will help these students grasp the material. Whatever methods you choose, keep in mind that one of your objectives should include activities that meet the needs of all learning modalities (visual, auditory, and kinesthetic). Remember that a 100% diet of one item may be deadly. The activities must balance with the instruction. There is a big difference between looking at students as a problem and labeling them, and looking at your classroom as part of the problem and finding ways to improve the classroom through a balance of heterogeneous groupings, equal interactions, and student-centered activities.

Activities for Success

Here is a list of sample activities that create success in the classroom. Many of these activities can be based on literature, using as a springboard the plot and characters of selections students have read.

Writing and Illustrating
For a specific audience
 young readers
 older readers
 cross-generational
For television and/or movies
Letters to famous people, authors, or penpals in other countries
Surveys
Questionnaires and interview guides
Advertisements and commercials
Diary entries
Cartoons
Obituaries
Headlines
Bumper stickers
Maps
Timelines
Adapted classics and mixed-up classics
Songs, rap music
Storyboards
Dear Abby columns
Postcards
Literary report cards
Wanted posters
Crossword puzzles
Collages
Mobiles
Time capsules
Murals
Fine-art re-creations

Creative Dramatics
Skits
Readers theater
Scenarios
Inventions
Role-playing
Soap operas
Singing telegrams
Videotapes
Audio tapes
Scavenger hunts
Five senses
Debates
Mime
Puppets
Dance
Poses
Simulations
Line ups
Hot Seat (Twenty Questions)
Who Am I?
Pictionary
Win, Lose, or Draw
Charades

Activities like the ones above allow teachers to move in three directions. First, they allow the teacher to create an environment of active learning. Next, they allow the teacher to link active learning with higher-level thinking skills. Third, they provide the opportunity for the teacher to tie it all together with cooperative learning. Thus the teacher can provide choice, balance, and control in order to create a classroom with a learning environment that invites student success.

ASSESSMENT AND EVALUATION IN PRENTICE HALL LITERATURE
Ruth Townsend
former English Teacher and Teacher Coordinator
Yorktown High School
Yorktown Heights, New York

> Education . . . Helping the child realize
> his [her] potentialities.
> —Erich Fromm

There are many valid ways to educate students, to help them achieve success as readers and writers, speakers and listeners. However, the way students' learning is assessed and evaluated often determines the quality of that learning. *Prentice Hall Literature* offers a variety of assessment and evaluation strategies to promote students' progress toward mastery of language arts outcomes.

LEARNING OUTCOMES

The goal of language arts instruction is to make students successful readers, writers, speakers, and thinkers who can demonstrate the following learning outcomes:

1. As readers, students
   - respond personally, aesthetically, and critically to diverse texts
   - collect facts and ideas, discover relationships, and make inferences
   - make critical judgments, analyze, evaluate, and draw conclusions.
2. As writers, students
   - express personal feelings and ideas in a variety of modes
   - communicate information, ideas, and beliefs to a variety of audiences
   - express their ideas critically and evaluatively express their ideas persuasively and provide support for those ideas.
3. As speakers and listeners, students
   - express themselves orally to entertain and to inform
   - interpret information and apply it
   - evaluate ideas according to personal and/or objective criteria.

ASSESSMENT AND EVALUATION OPTIONS

Measuring student growth begins with assessment, an ongoing process of gathering information to meet many different evaluation purposes. *Prentice Hall Literature* provides a wide range of assessment strategies and procedures, including testing.

Testing Options

Selection Tests

1. Part A of the Selection Tests contains multiple-choice questions. These types of test items play a role in the initial stages of the assessment and evaluation of your students' growth toward mastery of the learning outcomes. You may use tests on content knowledge as reading checks and as the basis of discussions; you may also use them for collaborative reviews of reading and to prompt personal and critical responses. You may choose to have students work independently or collaboratively to frame their answers to each question and to justify them with textual evidence. You may want students to extend their discussion of the story beyond the printed questions to develop their own questions and to evaluate the universal relevance of the story.

2. Part B of the Selection Test is an essay question. Essay questions offer your students the opportunity to go beyond the limited responses of the multiple-choice items to explore an idea in some depth.

3. Part C of the Selection Test is a reader's response question. This type of question elicits a personal reaction to literature.

Other Testing Options

Prentice Hall Literature offers a number of assignments and activities that may be used as tests to assess and evaluate your students' mastery of the learning outcomes.

ALTERNATIVE ASSESSMENT OPTIONS

Testing is only one way to measure comprehension of ideas, reasoning processes, or problem-solving skills. Assessment is a continuing process linked with curriculum and instruction.

In a student-centered classroom, you assess and evaluate growth in many ways, each of which motivates your students to use language for effective communication. The student-centered classroom enables students to perceive themselves as partners with you in the learning process. That process includes their ability to assess their own competence, determine goals for their own achievement, and judge their own performance. As your students learn to assess and evaluate their own work, they become empowered to take increasing responsibility for their own learning.

You can assist your students in developing these self-assessment skills by involving them in the following activities:

Reader's Response Journals
Alternative and Expressive Assignments
Protocols
Peer Review
Collaborative Assessment

Reader's Response Journals

Reader's response journals help students become conscious of their own thinking processes by asking them to make observations of what they read and to respond personally based on those observations. Making observations about a text requires readers to be as objective as possible. Of course some personal judgment is involved in deciding which details of the text are relevant and appropriate to "observe." However, when making observations students concentrate on factual information and cite concrete details of language or description to back up their observations.

Responding personally to a text is also an important part of active reading. After students have recorded each observation, they react personally, making inferences and predictions, evaluating details, and raising questions. They may question the significance of details they have observed, the meaning of events they have recorded, or the reasons for human behavior they have noted. They may also explore the implications of the connections between what they have read and their own experiences, other pieces of literature, and the world in which they live. Because students' questions are generated by their personal responses to what is otherwise objective and concrete, they can see the relationship between logical inferences and concrete details.

A student's response journal may look like this sample based on a reading of Gabriel García Márquez's story "A Very Old Man With Enormous Wings."

Observations	*Personal Responses*
Three days of rain had brought many crabs into the house. Pelayo threw them into the sea because he felt they caused the child to have a fever.	Gross! Crabs in the house. What does that have to do with the child being sick? The opening is strange and frightening. "The world had been sad since Tuesday." I like that even though I can't understand the use of "sad."
Pelayo discovers an old man lying face down in the mud. He can't get up because he has "huge buzzard wings, dirty and half plucked."	Come on—a man with wings? Am I supposed to believe this? I wonder why he's described as so dirty and like a buzzard. A neighbor tells them the old man is an angel who had been coming for the sick child. How can they kill an angel?

Alternative and Expressive Assignments

Alternative assignments challenge students to present their critical reading responses imaginatively. They make judgments about character development, the significance of plot details and stylistic techniques, including characteristics of diction, imagery, and syntax. Judgments about literary elements may lend support to students' ideas of theme and the universal significance of a text or they may cause students to rethink or re-envision their initial responses to the reading. These are sample alternative assignments:

Writing letters to real and imagined audiences
Writing in the persona of a character in the text
Comparing literary figures to real people
Writing investigative reports
Writing editorials
Writing human interest stories
Creating speeches in various personae
Creating commercials or advertisements

You will find examples of alternative assignments throughout the student text under Thinking and Writing, in the Annotated Teachers' Edition, and in the Teaching Portfolio. For example, here is an alternative assignment in the Annotated Teacher's Edition for "A Very Old Man With Enormous Wings":

> Assume the persona of a news reporter sent to Pelayo's home to investigate reports of the appearance of an angel. Your editor has instructed you to interview Pelayo's family, his neighbors, Father Gonzaga, and the old man, reputed to be an angel. After you have collected your data, write a report, confirming or discrediting the claim that the old man is an angel. Be sure to include direct quotes from those people you interview.

Expressive assignments stimulate creativity by encouraging students to re-envision the text and to recreate portions of it. Here are some examples of expressive assignments:

> Writing a new ending for a selection
> Adding scenes
> Changing the point of view
> Writing a modern version or a parody
> Conducting a trial of a character
> Holding elections for literary characters
> Inventing a newspaper or magazine based on a selection
> Writing a poem based on the selection
> Making a video

You will find examples of expressive assignments throughout the student text, in the Teaching Portfolio, and in the Annotated Teacher's Edition. For example, here is an expressive assignment for "A Very Old Man With Enormous Wings":

> In "A Very Old Man With Enormous Wings" García Márquez describes the old man's apperance and the villagers' reaction to him, but we learn very little about what the old man thinks and feels. Imagine that you were the old man in García Márquez's story and rewrite the story from your perspective as the old man. Try to penetrate the old man's personality, thoughts, and feelings.

Protocols

Protocols are descriptions of the thinking and writing process. They enable your students to assess their own learning by providing them with the opportunity to describe the processes they follow in writing, reading, and speaking. Thus students begin to monitor their progress toward mastery. To prompt the writing of protocols, students answer questions such as these:

> What were your content and stylistic goals in this piece?
> How successful do you feel you were in meeting those goals?
> What gave you difficulty in this assignment?
> What new learning came out of writing this piece?

You may adapt this basic protocol to fit your specific assignments. For example, if students are writing a response to the expressive assignment for "A Very Old Man With Enormous Wings," they will be rewriting the story from the point of view of the old man and might respond in a protocol to questions like these:

> What personality did you give the old man?
> How did you convey that personality?
> What feelings did you wish to convey?
> What effect did changing the point of view have on the meaning of the story?
> What did you learn about point of view from this assignment?

Peer Review

Peer review offers your students another opportunity to develop their metacognition skills as they learn from each other. Working in pairs or in small groups, students review each other's work and make suggestions for revision of content, form, and mechanics. However, the emphasis of the review changes, depending on what stage in the writing process the peer critique occurs. For example, in the drafting stage students focus on content and development, answering questions like these:

> What do you see as the writer's purpose?
> For what audience is this piece intended?
> What specific details did the writer include to accomplish that purpose?
> What additional information would enhance the piece?
> What, if anything, would you suggest the writer delete?

In the editing stage the review questions may focus more on form and mechanics. Your students may consider these questions:

> What is the topic of each paragraph?
> Are the supporting details presented logically?

Are the verb tenses appropriate and consistent?
What corrections do you suggest for improving the language and mechanics of the piece?

You may tailor the peer reviews to fit specific assignments. For example, if your students have written a response to the assignment for "A Very Old Man With Enormous Wings," the peer review might include questions like these:

What personality did the writer give the old man? How successfully did the writer convey that personality?
What details did the writer add?
What effect did those details have on your view of the old man?
What did the change in point of view do to your understanding of the story?
What concrete suggestions do you have for the writer to make the story more effective?

To validate the peer review, you may have your students revise their work, incorporating those suggestions they believe will enhance their final product. Thoughtful peer reviews have a value not only for the students whose pieces are reviewed but for the reviewers who in the process of assessing other students' work are practicing their active reading skills.

Collaborative Assessment

Collaborative assessment offers yet another opportunity for your students to develop an awareness of their thinking and writing processes, enabling you and your students to work together to determine the criteria for evaluating student performance. These criteria, usually identified in the initial stages of an assignment, may change as your students develop their competence as language users. Because they have helped define the criteria for evaluation, your students have a clearer understanding of how to complete the assignment successfully. These criteria form the basis for the writing of their protocols and for peer reviews. Criteria vary but may include these factors:

Accuracy of content
Relevance of detail
Appropriateness of form
Consistency of voice
Variety of sentence structure
Correctness of language mechanics

Collaborative assessment helps your students gain confidence in their ability to participate in evaluating their individual mastery of the learning outcomes.

Student Portfolios

One of the most powerful assessment options available to you and your students is the portfolio. Portfolios are collections of students' work. You may choose to have portfolios contain various drafts of students' work so that you can assess growth during the process of writing a paper, examples of students' best work so that you can assess growth during the year, or a combination of both. For portfolios to be effective learning tools, students must be trained to take responsibility for their own learning. That means they must develop skills for self-assessment.

Once students have taken responsibility for their own learning by working through reader response and critical response activities, they have developed the skills necessary to create portfolios. What makes portfolios effective is that they involve students even further in the assessment and evaluation process. To prepare their portfolios, students review a body of their work and select those performance pieces they believe best represent their growth toward mastery of the learning outcomes. They may create several different kinds of portfolios.

Individual Performance Portfolios Your students may create individual portfolios reflecting their performance on a particular unit of study. Students collaborate with you in determining the number and type of pieces to include in the portfolio. Your students also help establish the criteria for evaluation of the portfolio. Individual portfolios may be a collection of videotaped dramatic presentations or speeches, stories, memoirs, poems and/or responses to poems, and personal and analytical essays on a particular theme or literary work.

A sample portfolio for "A Very Old Man With Enormous Wings" might include student responses to the following assignments: the Reader's Response Journal, the Thinking and Writing Assignment, the Selection Test, the Essay Question in the Teaching Portfolio, the news story assignment in the Annotated Teacher's Edition.

From these five assignments, you and your students may decide to include three pieces. By selecting those pieces, students reveal their ability to assess their own work. You may also give your students the opportunity to revise any of their selections and to enhance their portfolio with additional pieces that reflect their appreciation and understanding of the text.

Project Portfolios Working collaboratively, your students may create project portfolios that reflect their performance on a particular project. Here too students help define the direction and scope of the product or activity. They work together with you to establish the criteria for evaluation of the project. Project portfolios may be written products such as newspapers, news magazines, or handbooks based on a particular literary work, or they may be performance oriented such as trials, elections, game shows, interview shows, or videos.

Mastery Portfolios At the end of a course your students may compile a mastery portfolio that reflects their best work in the course. You and your students may decide how many pieces to include, what modes to have represented, and whether to include early pieces as well as later pieces to demonstrate growth. Creating the portfolio also offers your students an opportunity to revise any work in order to demonstrate mastery.

Portfolio Protocols The most valuable step in the creation of a portfolio is the writing of the protocol in which students describe the rationale behind their portfolio selections, the learning demonstrated in each piece, and their awareness of their strengths and weaknesses as language users. To prompt the writing of the protocols, your students may consider questions like these:

What pieces did you include in your portfolio?
Why did you select these particular pieces?
What learning does each piece reflect?
What insights did you gain about yourself as a reader, writer, speaker, and listener from creating this portfolio?

Evaluating Portfolios

Even though students have been active participants in the creation and assessment of their portfolios, ultimately it is your responsibility to evaluate the work and assign a grade. Just as your students are guided by clearly defined criteria as they develop their portfolios, you are guided by these same criteria as you evaluate their performance. In general, these criteria reflect concern for content, form, and presentation.

Evaluation of content focuses on the students' abilities to reflect their understanding of or insight into the literature studied, the concepts explored, the issues considered as well as their facility with modes of writing. Mastery is characterized by each student's demonstration of skill in analytical thinking, that is, the ability to summarize, compare, and synthesize.

Evaluation of form focuses on students' mastery of the modes of response, including logical and appropriate organization and sequence, coherence, unity, sophistication of style, and control of language use.

Evaluation of presentation deals with the appearance of the final product—its neatness, its attractiveness, and its appropriateness for the focus of the content.

MASTERY OF LEARNING OUTCOMES

Evaluation of student mastery requires consideration of the desired outcomes for reading, writing, speaking, and listening. The extent to which your students meet the desired outcomes determines their level of mastery of English/language arts skills.

Competent: The students who demonstrate competence in reading, writing, speaking, and listening can deal with a wide range of subject matter in a variety of forms. They reveal an ability to see relationships; they can emulate models; they can apply knowledge in a limited number of contexts.

Excellent: Students who demonstrate excellence in reading, writing, speaking, and listening can deal with complex and sophisticated subject matter. They discriminate among language forms for specific purposes and make appropriate stylistic judgments. They synthesize their insights in a variety of contexts.

Superior: Superior students are characterized by their orginality and creativity. They reveal depth of perception, imaginative insights, and authority in all aspects of language use.

CONCLUSION

As an English/language arts teacher you have a wide variety of assessment and evaluation options available to you in *Prentice Hall Literature*. These assessment and evaluation strategies, including testing, alternative assessment options, and student portfolios, offer you and your students choices for measuring growth toward mastery of the learning outcomes. Even more important, these strategies afford you the opportunity to respond to the individual needs of your students.

Bibliography

Benson, Barbara. "Effective Tests: Let Them Write!" *The English Journal*, Feb. 1991.

DeFabio, Roseanne. "Outcomes Project." State Education Department. Albany, N.Y., 1991.

English Language Arts Syllabus K-12. State Education Department. Bureau of Curriculum Development. Albany, N.Y., 1988.

Johnson, D.W., and Johnson, R. *Circles of Learning: Cooperation in the Classroom.* Alexandria, Va.: ASCD, 1984. New York State English Language Arts Syllabus.

Neubert, Gloria and McNelis, Sally. "Peer Response: Teaching Specific Revision Suggestions." *The English Journal*, Sept. 1990.

Perrone, Vito. *Expanding Student Assessment.* Alexandria, Va.: ASCD, 1991.

Rosenblatt, L. *The Reader, the Text, and the Poem.* Cambridge, Ma.: Harvard University Press, 1978.

Schwartz, Jeffrey. "Let Them Assess Their Own Learning." *The English Journal*, Feb. 1991.

Shaughnessy, Mina. *Errors and Expectations.* New York: Oxford University Press, 1977.

Tchudi, Stephen. *Planning and Assessing the Curriculum in English Language Arts.* Alexandria, Va.: ASCD, 1991.

Tierney, Robert J., Carter, Mark, and Desai, Laura. *Portfolio Assessment in the Reading-Writing Classroom.* Norwood, Ma.: Christopher Gordon Publishers, 1991.

Wiggins, Grant. "A True Test: Toward More Authentic and Equitable Assessment." *Phi Delta Kappan*, May, 1989.

Wolf, Denny P. "Portfolio Assessment: Sampling Student Work." *Educational Leadership*, April, 1989.

MULTICULTURALISM AND THE LANGUAGE ARTS CLASSROOM
Dr. Rose Duhon-Sells
Founder and President of National Association for Multicultural Education

Why Do We Need Multicultural Education?

Increasingly, the nation's classrooms are becoming more culturally diverse. The 1990 census revealed that one of every four people who live in the United States is a person of color; by the turn of the century that figure will be one out of every three. Students of color constitute a majority in twenty-five of the nation's largest school districts and in California, our most populous state. Furthermore, people of color will make up nearly half (46 percent) of the nation's school-age youth by the year 2020 and about 27 percent of these students will be victims of poverty. The percentage of people of color in our schools will continue to rise throughout the early decades of the next century.

In a nation as culturally, racially, and linguistically diverse as ours, the need for intergroup knowledge, understanding, and respect is critical. Multicultural education is a fundamental element in the restructuring of our educational systems. We need to prepare our young people to meet these goals:

- to understand the pluralistic nature of our country
- to recognize and appreciate connections between cultures
- to view our nation's diversity as a rich resource

Recognizing and appreciating the richness, rareness, and similarities and differences of each cultural group contributing to the American mosaic benefits us all. With this in mind, multicultural education endeavors to actualize the concept of "*e pluribus unum*," while encouraging a society that recognizes and respects the cultures of its diverse groups.

Teachers Are the Key

Teachers can lead students to celebrate the diversity of our nation. As teachers help students understand the cultures of different groups, they break down students' hostility toward those unlike themselves. We all remember what it was like to be young—the awkwardness, the insecurity. To the young, to be different is wrong. The young need their teachers' support, not only to accept diversity but to celebrate it. Multicultural education helps students in these ways:

- They affirm their own culture.
- They free themselves from cultural boundaries.
- They widen their own perspective.

- They accept individuals whose views are different from theirs.

The Language Arts Classroom

The language arts classroom is the ideal arena for celebrating diversity. Literature teaches us to walk in another's shoes and see through that person's eyes. As students read, they see the similarities among people of various cultures across time and place. They identify with characters whose backgrounds are quite unlike their own and see that we are together striving to find answers to the human predicament. They come to acknowledge that whatever they have felt or feared or hoped, someone else has experienced similar fears and dreams. Literature teaches us that in this vast world, we are all connected: We are not alone.

In your language arts classroom, encourage students to see literature as a window on life. As they talk about literature, have them make connections with their own experiences. Try book talks: Establish weekly discussion sessions where students from varying cultures read and review books about each other's culture. By guiding students to see cultural connections, you will help them move from a simple awareness of diversity to acceptance and support.

Infusing Multicultural Education in the Curriculum

The following stages will help to infuse multicultural education in the school curriculum:

Stage 1: At the university level, the teacher education curriculum must reflect the quality and value of cultural diversity of this country. Student teachers should have opportunities to participate in field experiences, such as classroom observations and peer training in schools with mixed-group student populations. Professors in colleges of education must be required to be knowledgeable about the contributions to this nation by people of varous cultures. There is a critical need for educators to accept and understand the value of multicultural education and its significance to the survival of all Americans.

Stage 2: Our educational policymakers must emphasize the need for multicultural education and accept no delays. They must evaluate programs effectively; for example, a project funded in the name of multicultural education that deals only with food and dress practices does not further multicultural goals. Kroeber and Kluckman (1952) emphasize stressing the intangible aspects of culture in a multicultural program—ideas, ways of thinking, values, symbols, etc. It is these factors that distinguish cultural groups in the United States.

Stage 3: Teachers and the general public must appreciate the pyschological cost on human beings who are forced to assimilate in order to be accepted by the dominant culture. Assimilation may lead to self-denial and rejection of family and ethnic ties. The demands of assimilation run counter to democratic goals and equality of opportunity (Banks, Cortes, Gay, Garcia, Ochoa). On the other hand, multicultual education fosters self-esteem by appreciating differences and celebrating diversity.

As teachers come to understand the historical development of stereotypes of various ethnic groups, they can recognize them in written works and popular culture and take practical steps to help students avoid reinforcing or perpetuating these stereotypes. For example, when studying Native Americans, supplementing works written in the 1800's with contemporary portraits will help students form a more balanced picture (Charles, 1991).

Literature helps readers build self-respect and encourages the development of positive values. However, in the past, not all groups have been presented well. For example, African Americans have not always been presented in a positive fashion. Fortunately, books today are bringing about more positive outlooks.

It is anticipated, or at least hoped that the goals of multicultural education will be reached as teachers and others responsible for educating our children include multiculturalism in their plans as they restructure our education system.

References

Banks, James. "Curriculum Guidelines for Multicultural Education." Prepared by the NCSS Task Force on Ethnic Studies Guidelines. Adopted by NCSS Board of Directors, 1976.

Caldwell-Wood, Naomi, and Mitten, Lisa A. " 'I' Is Not for Indian: The Portrayal of Native Americans in Books for Young People." *Multicultural Review*, Vol. 1, Number 2, April 1992.

Charles, Jesus. "Combating American Indian Stereotypes Through Literature Study." In Carl A. Grant (ed.), *Toward Education That Is Multicultural*, Proceedings of the First Annual Meeting of the National Association for Multicultural Education, 1991.

Garcia, Jesus. "Multicultural Education Teacher Preparation Programs: A Political or an Educational Concept?" *Phi Delta Kappan*, November 1991.

Gay, Geneva. "Culturally Diverse Students and Social Studies." In James P. Shaver (ed.), *Handbook of Research on Social Studies Teaching and Learning* (pp. 144–156). New York: Macmillan, 1991.

Kroeber, Alfred, and Kluckman, Clyde. *Cultures: A Critical Review of Concepts and Definitions.* New York: Vintage, 1952.

Prentice Hall Literature

"Literature—the mystery of the human heart moving through time."
Hugh Dinwiddy

Prentice Hall Literature is firmly committed to the goals of multicultural education. We believe these goals can be accomplished when students and teachers are provided with literary selections that are sensitively chosen to reflect the diversity of our nation and to move students to an appreciation and acceptance of cultures other than their own. Key elements of the *Prentice Hall Literature* program are

- A Multicultural Review Board to advise on the appropriateness of selections
- Literature written by authors from a broad spectrum of times, cultures, and backgrounds
- Literature reflecting the diversity of our nation and of the world
- Multicultural Connection features in the student anthologies that help students see connections between cultures and appreciate cultures other than their own
- Multicultural Focus notes in the Annotated Teacher's Editions that create an awareness of cultural connections with almost every selection
- Questioning strategy that helps students apply literature to their own lives and that leads to deeper understanding and affirmation
- *Prentice Hall Literature* Multicultural Library of fine young adult literature
- *Prentice Hall Literature* Audio Prose Library containing interviews with authors from a variety of backgrounds and cultures and readings by those authors

TECHNOLOGY IN THE LANGUAGE ARTS CLASSROOM

Bonita C. LaBelle

Director of English
Shrewsbury High School
Shrewsbury, Massachusetts

English teachers want to share their enthusiasm for reading and writing with students. That is why looking through the table of contents of a literary anthology excites the feelings and intellect of a truly committed English teacher. When teachers see Cather's short stories and Hughes's poetry, for example, they imagine stimulating classroom discussions and enlightening analyses of writing form and style. But even the most dedicated and creative classroom teacher runs up against the students of the 1990's: young people who like stories but don't necessarily want to read and write about literature. How, then, does today's English teacher actively involve students in reading and writing?

Involving Students by Using Technology

We know that students learn best when they are actively involved in the learning process, interacting with each other, and when they have opportunities to show what they already know. Students today are visual learners who have been brought up in a world of technology. At home, many use computers, calculators, VCRs, CD players, camcorders, video games, and a variety of advanced appliances and machines. After school or in the summers, students work with database inventories at the local lumberyard or doctor's office. Today's typical young person comes to school with good technological skills and a real interest in video, graphics, and sound. Why not capitalize on these skills and interests by teaching reading and writing using the tools of technology?

By using technology, ranging from writing software to multimedia databases, English teachers can maximize student involvement and bring literature and writing to life. The ideal English teaching environment is a classroom with an area for student discussion and sharing, and another space equipped with a computer for each student. More realistically, however, effective integration of technology often takes place in school-shared writing labs. Even one to five computers in any individual classroom provide English teachers with the opportunity to teach with technology. Writing software, hand-held grammar checks, laserdiscs, videos, and audio tapes can all contribute to improved student understanding of writing and literature.

Writing Software

When writing software was first introduced into schools, no one could have anticipated the impact technology would have on writing programs across the country. Writing software packages now provide teachers with a way to teach writing. There is no better way to improve student writing than by sharing student examples with the class, focusing on mechanical issues under study, and discussing style and content with actual student examples. By using a liquid crystal display (LCD) unit attached to one computer, with the flick of a switch, an English instructor can easily project any sample student writing. No longer is it necessary to stand in a long line to make multiple copies of student writing on duplicating machines. With just one LCD and a box of students' disks, the teacher has a writing lesson at his or her fingertips. This technology helps create a writing workshop atmosphere where students gain confidence in their writing skills and grow adept at discussing writing techniques. They love to see their own work projected up on the screen; shared writing motivates them to try harder and to improve. As one lower-level student wrote in an evaluation of his ninth-grade English class: "Computers helped me become a better writer. Sharing my work in front of the class and seeing how other kids liked my ideas and images made me realize I'm a pretty good writer—and knowing that is half the battle."

Similarly, tenth-grader Joanne Schnare reflected back on the experiences of tenth-grade English class this way: "I walked into Room 319 on the first day of school, shy and still looking for the piece of self-esteem I lost along the way. Even though I had heard many good things about both the English teacher and the computer lab, I still had a clear vision of a class like I had last year . . . boring. But this year's English class made me think about what I read and pushed me to read more carefully and write more effectively. We used word processors and shared our writings and reading responses frequently on 'the big screen.' I gained so much confidence because kids wanted to see my thoughts . . . they'd say, 'Read Jo Jo's!!' I may have walked in shy, but I walked out . . . Jo-Jo Schnare."

Computers make the writing process possible. English teachers who take students to writing labs to create rough drafts provide kids with an "on disk" copy of their writing that will ultimately go through multiple editing changes based on peer editing and teacher conferencing. Word processing has made editing easier by providing tools for correcting spelling, reorganizing and rearranging sentences and paragraphs, running grammar checks, etc. Before word processing, students were hesitant to spend time editing their work. By word processing first drafts, students see first attempts as simply beginnings and willingly progress through additional drafts until they complete an acceptable final piece.

Therefore, students are eager to word process and edit their writing; they like to write with computers, becoming very focused on their work. Students who hate to hand write compositions become avid word processor writers who enjoy creating and sharing their ideas and feelings. The student with atrocious handwriting can finally understand his or her own thoughts and successfully share them with others. Spelling improves. Self-esteem improves. Also, students become more concerned about accuracy and correctness. Learning-disabled students carry work begun in English class on disk to the resource room where support staff continue and expand upon lessons in writing and mechanics. If an electronic network exists in the school, special and regular education teachers can communicate about students' process and share examples of work and assignments.

Laserdiscs

Laserdisc technology provides the English teacher with focused looks at specific video footage. Thousands of movies and plays are available on laserdiscs, and many excellent historical presentations. *Letter From the Birmingham Jail* and *The Gettysburg Address* are now available. Given the limited class time in a typical high school, sharing full-length films has become virtually impossible. While students might be given videos to take home and review for homework, spending two to three hours of classroom time watching a movie or documentary is counterproductive.

What laserdisc technology allows the teacher to do is key in on selected segments of a given presentation. By using a remote control and a publisher-provided segment guide, the teacher can focus in on a specific passage by simply inputting chapter or track numbers. Without winding and rewinding videotape, the teacher has immediate control of the presentation. This technique provides students with key passages for analysis, comparison, and contrast. (For *Prentice Hall Literature*, bar code access through the Annotat-

ed Teacher's Edition is provided for all laserdiscs in the *Prentice Hall Literature* Writing Studio.

For example, when reading Shakespeare's *Romeo and Juliet*, students are able to read descriptions of certain characters and events and, then, with laserdisc technology, key in on just those passages that help illustrate specific ideas or descriptions. Mercutio's street fight and death scene are difficult for students to imagine; they are often confused as to how Romeo was involved. Keying in on the corresponding videodisc footage clarifies the scene and brings Shakespeare's words to life.

Laserdisc technology helps teachers promote thinking skills, particularly comparison and contrast. In reading *Great Expectations,* for example, students need not watch the entire film to write a comparison and contrast paper. Using the laserdisc, the students can focus on and analyze specific portions of the novel and film versions. They can note parallel scenes, changes in chronology, and deliberate changes by the filmmaker to highlight their own understanding of Dickens's purpose.

Integrating Technology in Your Lesson Plans

Technology helps students get actively involved in reading and writing. The following paragraphs delineate the integration of technology in teaching Fitzgerald's *The Great Gatsby.* Before reading the novel, students view an art transparency of life in the 1920's, and, then, using the details they see in the painting, write descriptive pieces of what life might have been like at that time. Using the LCD and the student writing, the teacher then shares sample writing, highlighting quality student work and recognizing good uses of mechanical points studied in class.

Continuing to ready students for a reading of the book, the teacher shows students Chapter 2 of the *History in Motion* videodisc (easily available through many media centers), comparing daily life in the 1920's with their own speculations written the day before. They gain additional real-life details from audio tapes, including jazz performances and speeches from the 1920's. Students now have a feel for the time period of the novel, and their minds have been activated to become more intensely involved in Fitzgerald's book.

After reading Chapters 1 and 2 of the novel, cooperative learning groups of students (four students in a group works well) gather around a common computer and generate lists of character descriptions. Each group is responsible for a single character: Daisy, Tom, Myrtle, Nick, or Wilson. In presenting their character to the rest of the class, each group is responsible for reviewing information given by Fitzgerald and speculating on the character's future actions.

As students progress through the novel and the teacher continues to emphasize the interrelationship between history and literature, students might use a piece of software like the "Mac TimeLiner" to bring Gatsby's life and the events of the 1920's together. By creating their own timelines of Gatsby's life, students are forced to use the text to verify dates and chronology. Printouts are available on a single page or banner-length display. However, before printing, students might call up some of the events of the 1920's that appear on the prepared American History timeline available in the software package. By creating a merge between their own Gatsby timeline and the prepared events of 1920's, students see clearly the interrelationship of history and literature.

Multimedia projects can be used as a culmination activity for studying a piece of literature such as *The Great Gatsby,* or they may be interjected at any point in the unit. Using software packages like "Point of View" or "Media Text," students can expand their knowledge base of the 1920's by doing additional research. For many students, writing the traditional research paper is not a valuable experience. Students frequently plagiarize and often lose their own voice, writing in a style that is clearly not their own. English teachers have to wonder if the weeks and weeks spent on form and documentation are worth the effort. The multimedia research project allows students to integrate information from printed materials, various videodiscs, and audio sources, and to become more personally involved.

For example, after reading *The Great Gatsby,* students brainstorm for ideas to research. Fitzgerald's book is loaded with wonderful topics, from Prohibition to the movies. After brainstorming, students might choose to investigate something like the World Series of 1919. Using details about the fictional character of Meyer Wolfshiem from *The Great Gatsby* as an opening, students could go on to write about the importance of baseball in America by adding an audio portion from Lou Gehrig's or Babe Ruth's farewell to baseball speeches (*Great Speeches of the 20th Century*). They could include primary sources based on oral history in both textual and audio formats. Students could then go on to Eliot Asinof's *Eight Men Out* for more textual material and scan any related still photos into the report. Finally, they would share the project with the rest of the class. Other students and teachers would assess the relevance of the included multimedia materials and comment on the effectiveness of the piece. By compiling such a research project, students become actively involved thinkers: They must read

new material; they must watch and listen to audio and visual materials; and, above all, they must make critical decisions about the selection of appropriate textual, audio, and visual components.

Personalizing Students' Experiences

Contrary to popular opinion, the integration of technology into the English curriculum personalizes students' reading and writing experiences. Rather than distancing students from their teacher and classmates, technological learning tools foster interactive experiences.

Several years ago, a student of mine created a multimedia project that was an outgrowth of an oral history project she had completed: a ten-page biography about her grandfather. Because her grandfather had fought in World War II, Rachel decided to investigate further some history about the war, specifically the bombing of Hiroshima. Using a multimedia database that supplied information through timelines, texts, pictures, and video sequences, Rachel gave her grandfather's memories accurate and expanded historical perspective. As part of the presentation, Rachel recorded her grandfather's comments, integrating them into the report; she scanned in original photographs of her grandfather in uniform with his battalion. Her presentation of the project to the class was a moving experience. As Rachel described it, the multimedia approach was rigorous but fun and "I learned more about World War II, my grandfather, and me than I ever dreamed I would. The class's response to my work made me feel like I really accomplished something important in school."

Preparing Students for the Twenty-first Century

As we prepare students for the twenty-first century, we must think about our current teaching and learning paradigm. The teacher-centered classroom must be viewed as a model of the past. Student interaction, collaborative learning groups, and the tools of technology are important parts of today's learning styles. Students today need individualized approaches to learning; it is no longer possible to maximize student learning without using technology. Because English teachers most directly prepare students for successful communication in the technologically advanced world beyond high school, we must capitalize upon the feelings, goals, and skills students bring to our classrooms. We can do so by integrating technology into the English curriculum.

HOW SCIENCE, PHYSICAL EDUCATION, MATH, AND HISTORY CAN MAKE YOUR STUDENTS LOVE ENGLISH

Terri Fields

English Teacher
Sunnyslope High School
Phoenix, Arizona

The bell rings before you can answer a student's question about a story the class has been reading, so you're pleased to see the student in the hallway after school. You walk over to him and begin to explain the point about which he'd asked earlier in the day. He looks at you blankly. "Uhh, let's see; which story was that?" he finally mumbles.

You remind him that the class has been discussing the same short story for the past three days.

"Oh, yeah, right," he says sheepishly. "Well, it's been a long time since English this morning. . . ."

As a teacher you have probably asked yourself how you can get students to remember what they have learned in English. You've also asked an even more basic question: How do you get them to care about learning the literature at all?

A solution to both questions may be found in bringing other content material into the English classroom, for literature is not something separate from life but instead an integral part of life. As an English teacher, you can see this truth so vividly that you may not realize how many students have never made the connection. In fact, few students see any application of their literature study to any other class work.

Therefore, if you really want literature to matter to your students, if you really want to involve them in its study, it is your responsibility to relate literature to the rest of the curriculum and to current events. The more knowledge students apply to their reading, the more they can enjoy the reading. By the same token, the more they learn to apply the details, themes, and characters of literature to life and its problems, the more they can develop insightful answers.

If you believe that an interdisciplinary approach makes sense, you must ask how you can best make it a reality in your classroom. The answer begins in mapping out your literature units by asking yourself, "How might these stories/poems/plays/novels apply to other classes students are taking?"

For example, suppose you are going to cover a story in which the protagonists endure bitter cold to survive. Consider assigning the story while the students' science teacher is talking about the effects of temperature on the body. If you can't coordinate timing precisely, you can assign the story some time after the science teacher's unit on body temperature. Then you can tell students you expect them to use their science books and notes to explain how the author of this story used scientific knowledge to make the story both suspenseful and believable. Not only will this assignment allow students to see that there is relationship between science and English, but it will also help them to appreciate the research a writer undertakes.

Suppose you are going to study a poem in which the theme centers on oppression. You might ask students to select a person they have studied in history class and write a short paper discussing how that historical figure would have reacted to the meaning and mood of the poem. Such an assignment allows students a variety of learning experiences. They must reread and interpret the poem. They must review their history notes to decide on a particular figure. They must review what the figure believed and then decide how that would affect their interpretation of the poem.

You might present copies of some of the best papers to the history teacher. Imagine this teacher's surprise on discovering that another teacher is helping to review the history material with students. You may find the teacher saying, "Thanks! Is there something I can do in my class to help you with English?"

At that point, you have a perfect opportunity to suggest that the teacher intersperse a few of your vocabulary words in lectures. You might also offer to provide a list of all the selections your students will be reading. If the teacher remembers any of them, you would appreciate the teacher mentioning his or her enjoyment of them during class.

In interdisplinary learning's most ideal form, teachers from all disciplines would reinforce one another's teaching. Teachers would plan units together so that students could see the same concept covered from historical, literary, and scientific viewpoints.

While that may not be feasible at your school, you can get a taste of the idea and its impact on student learning by planning even one unit with a teacher from a different discipline. If logistics prevent that, you can still bring interdisciplinary learning to your classroom by helping students apply the material they are learning in other classes to your literature units and the literature they are learning in English to material being covered in other classes. The more purpose students see in knowing material, the more likely it is that they will learn, retain, and apply it.

PRENTICE HALL
LITERATURE

COPPER

BRONZE

SILVER

GOLD

PLATINUM

THE AMERICAN EXPERIENCE

THE BRITISH TRADITION

WORLD MASTERPIECES

ii

PRENTICE HALL
LITERATURE
GOLD

PARAMOUNT EDITION

OVERSEAS HIGHWAY
Ralston Crawford
The Regis Collection, Minneapolis, Minnesota

PRENTICE HALL
Englewood Cliffs, New Jersey
Needham, Massachusetts

Humanities Note

Fine art, *Overseas Highway*, 1939, by Ralston Crawford. American Ralston Crawford's paintings are in the style of European modernism, yet they have a personal and distinctly American twist. This is his contribution to American modern art.

Born in 1906, Crawford left his native Buffalo, New York, after high school to take a job on a freighter. He eventually landed in Los Angeles, California, where he enrolled for two terms at the Otis Art Institute. Crawford then returned to the East and attended both the traditional Pennsylvania Academy of the Fine Arts in Philadelphia and the Barnes Foundation, a school devoted to modern art in Merion, Pennsylvania. This diverse education led Crawford to view painting as a purely intellectual pursuit rather than an emotional expression.

Ralston Crawford's early paintings can be classified as Precisionist, a style characterized by a pristine and well-ordered geometricized view of the industrial landscape. Crawford abruptly stopped painting in the Precisionist style after he witnessed the first tests of the atomic bomb at Bikini Atoll in 1946. His subsequent works were detached, non-objective abstracts of cool flat broken shapes and erratic disjointed black lines that did not betray his emotional response to the devastation he had witnessed.

Overseas Highway is the most famous painting done in Crawford's early Precisionist style. In 1939, it was featured in *Life* magazine to great acclaim. The clean, concrete causeway suspended between sea and sky captured the imagination of the American public. It is the very embodiment of wanderlust, the open highway that leads beyond the horizon to new places, freedom and adventure.

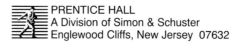

PRENTICE HALL
A Division of Simon & Schuster
Englewood Cliffs, New Jersey 07632

STAFF CREDITS FOR PRENTICE HALL LITERATURE

Publisher: Eileen Thompson

Editorial: Ellen Bowler, Douglas McCollum, Philip Fried, Kelly Ackley, Eric Hausmann, Lauren Weidenman

Multicultural/ESL: Marina Liapunov, Barbara T. Stone

Marketing: Mollie Ledwith, Belinda Loh

National Language Arts Consultants: Ellen Lees Backstrom, Ed.D., Craig A. McGhee, Karen Massey Riley, Vennisa Travers, Gail Witt

Permissions: Doris Robinson

Design: Susan Walrath, Carmela Pereira, Leslie Osher, AnnMarie Roselli

Visual Research: Libby Forsyth, Emily Rose, Martha Conway

Production: Suse Bell, Joan McCulley, Elizabeth Torjussen, Amy E. Fleming, Lynn Contrucci, Garret Schenck, Lorraine Moffa

Publishing Technology: Andrew Black, Deborah J. Jones, Monduane Harris, Cleasta Wilburn, Greg Myers

Pre-Press Production: Laura Sanderson, Natalia Bilash, Denise Herckenrath

Print and Bind: Rhett Conklin, Gertrude Szyferblatt

ACKNOWLEDGMENTS

Grateful acknowledgment is made to the following for permission to reprint copyrighted material:

Margaret Walker Alexander
"Memory" from *For My People* by Margaret Walker, copyright 1942 Yale University Press. Reprinted by permission of Margaret Waler Alexander.

Rudolfo A. Anaya
"A Celebration of Grandfathers," copyright by Rudolfo Anaya, from *New Mexico Magazine,* March 1983. Reprinted by permission of the author.

Arte Público Press
"The Harvest" from *La Cosecha* by Tomás Rivera, translated by Julián Olivares. Copyright © 1989 Tomás Rivera Archives/Concepción Rivera. Lines from "piñones" by Leroy V. Quintana, originally published in *Revista Chicano-Riqueña* (now titled *The Americas Review*), Vol.2, No. 2, 1974. Reprinted by permission of Arte Público Press.

(Continued on page 1094.)

CONTENTS

SHORT STORIES

DRAMA

NONFICTION

POETRY

vii

viii

THE EPIC

ix

THE NOVEL

ADDITIONAL FEATURES

PRENTICE HALL
LITERATURE
GOLD

A journey of a thousand miles must begin with a single step.
—Lao Tzu

Humanities Note

Fine art, *The Gulf Stream,* 1899, Winslow Homer. The painter and illustrator Winslow Homer (1836–1910), is known today for the marine, genre, and landscape paintings he produced in profusion.

In *The Gulf Stream* Homer explores the conflict of man against nature. This is a grim view of a man adrift in a disabled vessel surrounded by sharks. The ominous mood of the painting is emphasized by the inexplicable red splotches in the water. The hopelessness of the situation is emphasized by the ship passing out of sight in the upper left unseen by the man. This painting speaks of nature's impersonal power and man's weakness in the face of it. It leaves the viewer wondering what will become of the forlorn figure in the boat.

THE GULF STREAM
Winslow Homer
The Metropolitan Museum of Art

SHORT STORIES

The writer Edgar Allan Poe defined the short story as a brief tale that can be read in one sitting. Poe believed that such a story could have a more powerful effect and give greater pleasure than a longer tale read at different sittings. The pleasure you will get from the short stories in this book is the special kind of pleasure that fiction offers.

Fiction is literature based on the writer's imagination and so contains made-up characters and events. However, although fiction is made up, it has its roots in life. Virginia Woolf has written,". . . fiction is like a spider's web, attached ever so lightly perhaps, but still attached to life at four corners."

The short stories in this unit are arranged according to the elements of plot, character, point of view, setting, and theme. Plot is the pattern of action in the story, while characters are the people who take part in the action. Point of view is the angle or perspective from which the story is told. Setting consists of where and when the action takes place, and theme is the insight into life revealed by the story.

Science fiction, action and adventure, mysteries—you will encounter these types of stories and others in this unit. You will also learn strategies that will help you read short stories with greater appreciation and understanding.

Reading Actively The process outlined on this page is based on research into the ways that good readers construct meaning from fiction. These strategies make students aware of their own reading process, enabling them to monitor and improve their comprehension.

The model on the following pages, "The Cask of Amontillado" by Edgar Allan Poe, shows an active reader's questions, predictions, visualizations, and responses. As you present this process to students, it is important that they understand that the application of these strategies is continued throughout the story. Questions do not necessarily lead to final answers but often to other questions; predictions may be incorrect and require modification; connections help elucidate the text. Point out that not all readers ask the same questions, make the same predictions and connections, or visualize the same material.

The process may seem risky to some students who are eager to ask the "right" questions and make the earliest accurate predictions. With these students, emphasize the use of the strategies rather than the content that generates them.

To give students further practice with this process, use the selection on page 9 in the Teaching Portfolio, "Stranger on the Night Train," which students can annotate themselves. Encourage students to continue to use these strategies when they read other short stories in this unit.

READING ACTIVELY

Short Stories

A short story is fiction—a work of literature in which the characters and events are imagined by the author. Fiction allows you to explore new worlds, share joys and sorrows of characters, and learn from the invented experiences of others.

Reading short stories is an active process. It is a process in which you visualize what is happening in the story and derive meaning from the picture you are visualizing. You do this through the following active-reading strategies:

QUESTION What questions come to mind as you are reading? For example, why do characters act as they do? What causes events to happen? Why does the writer include certain information? Look for answers to your questions as you read on.

VISUALIZE Use details from the story to create a picture in your mind. As you read along, change your picture as the story unfolds and your understanding grows. If you find yourself confused, try to state your confusion. Use your visualization to clarify whatever may not at first seem clear to you.

PREDICT What do you think will happen? Look for hints in the story that seem to lead to a certain outcome. As you read on, you will see if your predictions are correct.

CONNECT Bring your own experience and knowledge to the story. Make connections with what you know about similar situations or people in your own life.

Also, make connections between one event and another in the story. Try to summarize how all the pieces of the story fit together.

RESPOND Think about what the story means. What does it say to you? What feelings does it evoke in you as you read? What has the story added to your understanding of people and events?

Try to use these strategies as you read the stories in this unit. They will help you increase your enjoyment and understanding of literature.

On pages 3–10 you can see an example of active reading by Scott Reilly of Cibola High School in Albuquerque, New Mexico. The notes in the side columns include Scott's thoughts and comments while reading "The Cask of Amontillado." Your own thoughts as you read may be different, because each reader brings something different to a story and takes away something different.

2   Short Stories

Objectives

1 To understand setting
2 To analyze the effect of setting
3 To create a setting
4 To express individual interests and abilities through optional activities

Support Material

Teaching Portfolio
Teacher Backup, p. 5
Reading Actively, "Stranger on the Night Train," by Mary Hocking, p. 9
Grammar in Action Worksheet, *Using Action Verbs*, p. 13
Usage and Mechanics Worksheet, p. 15
Vocabulary Check, p. 16

Critical Thinking and Reading Worksheet, *Analyzing the Effect of Setting*, p. 17
Language Worksheet, *Using Word Roots*, p. 18
Selection Test, p. 19

Library of Video Classics
The Cask of Amontillado and The Necklace

Listening to Literature
"The Cask of Amontillado"

The Cask of Amontillado[1]

Edgar Allan Poe

1   The thousand injuries of Fortunato I had borne as I best could, but when he ventured upon insult I vowed revenge. You, who so well know the nature of my soul, will not suppose, however, that I gave utterance to a threat. *At length* I would be avenged; this was a point definitely settled—but the very definitiveness with which it was resolved precluded[2] the idea of risk. I must not only punish but punish with impunity.[3] A wrong is unredressed when retribution overtakes its redresser. It is equally unredressed when the avenger fails to make himself felt as such to him who has done the wrong.

   It must be understood that neither by word nor deed had I given Fortunato cause to doubt my good will. I continued, as was my wont, to smile in his face, and he did not perceive that my smile *now* was at the thought of his immolation.[4]

2   He had a weak point—this Fortunato—although in other regards he was a man to be respected and even feared. He prided himself on his connoisseurship[5] in wine. Few Italians have the true virtuoso spirit.[6] For the most part their enthusiasm is adopted to suit the time and opportunity, to practice imposture[7] upon the British and Austrian millionaires. In painting and gemmary,[8] Fortunato, like his countrymen, was a quack, but in the matter of old wines he was sincere. In this respect I did not differ from him materially; I was skillful in the Italian vintages myself, and bought largely whenever I could.

   It was about dusk, one evening during the supreme madness of the carnival season, that I encountered my friend. He accosted me with excessive warmth, for he had been drinking

Question: *What insult is the author speaking of?*

Connect: *By what the author is saying, the insult would seem to be great.*

Predict: *The narrator seems to be foreshadowing. He has a plan.*

Connect: *We now realize that the narrator is telling of the events after they occurred.*

---

1. Amontillado (ə män′ tə lä′ dō) *n.*: A pale, dry sherry.
2. precluded (prē klōōd′ id) *v.*: Made impossible in advance.
3. impunity (im pyōō′ nə tē) *n.*: Freedom from punishment.
4. immolation (im′ ə lā shən) *n.*: Sacrifice.
5. connoisseurship (kän′ ə sɐr′ ship) *n.*: Expert judgment.
6. virtuoso (vɐr′ chōō ō′ sō) **spirit:** Knowledge of the arts.
7. practice imposture (im päs′ chər): Deceive.
8. gemmary (jem′ ə rē′) *n.*: Knowledge of precious stones.

**Prentice Hall Literature Writing
Studio**

Presentation

Motivation/Prior Knowledge
Ask students what qualities make a person a good actor. Then tell them that the narrator of this story uses his acting ability to gain revenge.

Thematic Focus Every choice has a consequence. Ask the students what kinds of consequences might result from the choice to seek revenge.

Making Connections Other selections in which revenge is an important motivation are *Romeo and Juliet,* page 287, and the *Odyssey,* page 645.

Purpose-Setting Question Do you think that the narrator is sane?

1 **Discussion** What kind of insult could have motivated thoughts of revenge?

2 **Discussion** What do you think Fortunato's name means? What might be ironic about this meaning?

3 **Discussion** Why does the narrator use a cask of wine to lure Fortunato?

4 **Critical Thinking and Reading** Why do you think the narrator praises Fortunato's expertise as a wine-taster?

Visualize: *Whatever plan the narrator has devised, this Amontillado seems to be the bait.*

Connect: *Obviously the narrator knew that Fortunato would not refuse.*

much. The man wore motley.[9] He had on a tight-fitting parti-striped dress, and his head was surmounted by the conical cap and bells. I was so pleased to see him that I thought I should never have done wringing his hand.

I said to him, "My dear Fortunato, you are luckily met. How remarkably well you are looking today. But I have received a pipe[10] of what passes for Amontillado, and I have my doubts."

"How?" said he. "Amontillado? A pipe? Impossible! And in the middle of the carnival!"

"I have my doubts," I replied: "and I was silly enough to pay the full Amontillado price without consulting you in the matter. You were not to be found, and I was fearful of losing a bargain."

"Amontillado!"

"I have my doubts."

"Amontillado!"

"And I must satisfy them."

"Amontillado!"

"As you are engaged, I am on my way to Luchresi. If any one has a critical turn it is he. He will tell me——"

"Luchresi cannot tell Amontillado from sherry."

"And yet some fools will have it that his taste is a match for your own."

"Come, let us go."

"Whither?"

"To your vaults."

"My friend, no; I will not impose upon your good nature. I perceive you have an engagement. Luchresi——"

"I have no engagement—come."

"My friend, no. It is not the engagement, but the severe cold with which I perceive you are afflicted. The vaults are insufferably damp. They are encrusted with niter."

"Let us go, nevertheless. The cold is merely nothing. Amontillado! You have been imposed upon. And as for Luchresi, he cannot distinguish sherry from Amontillado."

Thus speaking, Fortunato possessed himself of my arm; and putting on a mask of black silk and drawing a *roquelaure*[11] closely about my person, I suffered him to hurry me to my palazzo.

---

9. motley (mät′ lē) *n.*: A clown's multicolored costume.
10. pipe (pīp) *n.*: A large barrel.
11. roquelaure (räk′ ə lôr′) *n.*: Knee-length cloak.

4   *Short Stories*

Audiocassette If you wish students to hear the story, either while they are reading it or after reading it, play the reading of "The Cask of Amontillado" from the **Listening to Literature** Audiocassettes, Side 1.

Videocassette The **Library of Video Classics** work "The Cask of Amontillado and The Necklace" provides a visual presentation of "The Cask of Amontillado" along with a reading to enhance the students' understanding of the story. You might use it effectively after students have read the story. Playing parts of it at intervals during their reading of the story both increases their comprehension and provides opportunities for visualizing and predicting.

ESL Strategy Students who are not native English speakers may have difficulty with Poe's language. Using either the **Listening to Literature** Audiocassette or the **Library of Video Classics** Videocassette of "The Cask of Amontillado" will benefit these students.

There were no attendants at home; they had absconded to make merry in honor of the time. I had told them that I should not return until the morning, and had given them explicit orders not to stir from the house. These orders were sufficient, I well knew, to insure their immediate disappearance, one and all, as soon as my back was turned.

I took from their sconces two flambeaux,[12] and giving one to Fortunato, bowed him through several suites of rooms to the archway that led into the vaults. I passed down a long and winding staircase, requesting him to be cautious as he followed. We came at length to the foot of the descent, and stood together upon the damp ground of the catacombs[13] of the Montresors.

The gait of my friend was unsteady, and the bells upon his cap jingled as he strode.

"The pipe," he said.

"It is farther on," said I; "but observe the white webwork which gleams from these cavern walls."

He turned towards me, and looked into my eyes with two filmy orbs that distilled the rheum of intoxication.

"Niter?" he asked, at length.

"Niter," I replied. "How long have you had that cough?"

"Ugh! ugh! ugh!—ugh! ugh! ugh!—ugh! ugh! ugh!—ugh! ugh! ugh!—ugh! ugh! ugh!"

My poor friend found it impossible to reply for many minutes.

"It is nothing," he said, at last.

"Come," I said, with decision, "we will go back; your health is precious. You are rich, respected, admired, beloved; you are happy, as once I was. You are a man to be missed. For me it is no matter. We will go back; you will be ill, and I cannot be responsible. Besides, there is Luchresi——"

"Enough," he said; "the cough is a mere nothing; it will not kill me. I shall not die of a cough."

"True—true," I replied; "and, indeed, I had no intention of alarming you unnecessarily—but you should use all proper caution. A draft of this Medoc will defend us from the damps."

Here I knocked off the neck of a bottle which I drew from a long row of its fellows that lay upon the mold.

---

12. flambeaux (flam' bōz) *n.*: Lighted torches.
13. catacombs (kat' ə kōmz) *n.*: Vaults or passages in an underground burial place.

Question: *Why were his orders to his servants explicit? What did he expect?*

Connect: *We learn the narrator's name.*

Predict: *Odd how the narrator seems to show concern and refers to Fortunato as friend. I think he is planning something evil.*

The Cask of Amontillado 5

5 **Discussion** Do you think it is an accident that the servants happen to be away at this time?

6 **Discussion** Why does the narrator continually throw the name of Luchresi at Fortunato? How does this affect Fortunato?

7 **Master Teacher Note** Point out to students the irony of Fortunato's statement, "I shall not die of a cough," and the narrator's reply, "True—true." Have students look for other similar examples of irony.

Commentary

Poe's idea for "The Cask of Amontillado" was based on a true incident. According to Emily and David Kales in their book *All About the Boston Harbor Islands,* Poe enlisted in the army in 1827 under the assumed name of Edgar A. Perry. He was assigned to Battery H of the First Artillery, which was stationed at Castle Island, in Boston Harbor. While there, Poe heard a macabre tale that he would one day retell as "The Cask of Amontillado."

Ten years earlier, two army officers had fought a duel over a card game. One of the officers, Lieutenant Robert Massie, was killed in the duel. His friends decided to avenge his death. They got Massie's killer drunk and led him to the fort's lowest dungeons. There they chained him to the floor, sealed the entrance, and left him to die.

In 1905, workers renovating the fort found the skeleton, clad in the remains of his army uniform.

How are the Montresor coat of arms and its motto significant to the story?

Humanities Note

Fine Art, *Keying Up—The Court Jester,* 1875, by William Merritt Chase. Chase (1849–1916) was born in what is now Ninevah, Indiana. After a brief stint in the U.S. Navy, he studied in New York with artist Joseph O. Eaton. He also took classes at the National Academy of Design. When Chase visited family in St. Louis, Missouri, local businessmen raised money for him to study in Munich. *Keying Up—The Court Jester* was Chase's first highly acclaimed work. It won the Medal of Honor at the Centennial Exhibition in Philadelphia, although many critics objected to the "overpowering" color used. Nevertheless, the painting attracted the attention necessary to establish Chase's credibility, and he enjoyed a successful career as artist and teacher for the rest of his life.

You might use these questions for discussion:
1. Which of the two story characters could this figure portray?
2. The jester in this painting is wearing clothing similar to the motley that Fortunato is wearing. What effect does this kind of clothing have on the effect of the story?
3. What elements of the setting in this painting convey an appropriate mood for the story?

Connect: *Again Montresor is speaking against what he is really thinking.*

Connect: *There is irony in the connection between the family's arms and what Montresor is planning.*

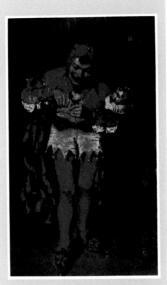

KEYING UP—THE COURT JESTER, 1875
William Merritt Chase
Pennsylvania Academy of Fine Arts

"Drink," I said, presenting him the wine.

He raised it to his lips with a leer. He paused and nodded to me familiarly, while his bells jingled.

"I drink," he said "to the buried that repose around us."

"And I to your long life."

He again took my arm, and we proceeded.

"These vaults," he said, "are extensive."

"The Montresors," I replied, "were a great and numerous family."

"I forget your arms."[14]

"A huge human foot d'or, in a field azure; the foot crushes a serpent rampant whose fangs are imbedded in the heel."[15]

"And the motto?"

"*Nemo me impune lacessit.*"[16]

"Good!" he said.

The wine sparkled in his eyes and the bells jingled. My own fancy grew warm with the Medoc. We had passed through long walls of piled skeletons, with casks and puncheons[17] intermingling, into the inmost recesses of the catacombs. I paused again, and this time I made bold to seize Fortunato by an arm above the elbow.

"The niter!" I said; "see, it increases. It hangs like moss upon the vaults. We are below the river's bed. The drops of moisture trickle among the bones. Come, we will go back ere it is too late. Your cough——"

"It is nothing," he said; "let us go on. But first, another draft of the Medoc."

I broke and reached him a flagon of De Grâve. He emptied it at a breath. His eyes flashed with a fierce light. He laughed and threw the bottle upwards with a gesticulation I did not understand.

I looked at him in surprise. He repeated the movement—a grotesque one.

"You do not comprehend?" he said.

"Not I," I replied.

"Then you are not of the brotherhood."

"How?"

---

14. arms: Coat of arms, a design and motto used by a family.
15. A huge . . . in the heel: A large golden foot crushing a snake, shown against a blue background.
16. *Nemo me impune lacessit:* Latin for "No one attacks me with impunity."
17. puncheons (pun' chənz) n.: Large barrels.

Grammar in Action

There are two main kinds of verbs: action verbs and linking verbs. An **action verb** is a verb that tells what action someone or something is performing. The action may be mental as well as physical:

> The kites *soared* in the March wind. (physical action)
> Dad *remembered* newspaper kites. (mental action)

Careful use of action verbs can make writing seem lively. The following sentences show how Edgar Allan Poe uses action verbs:

> I *broke* and *reached* him a flagon of De Grâve. He *emptied* it at a breath. His eyes *flashed* with a fierce light. He *laughed* and *threw* the bottle upwards with a gesticulation I did not *understand.*

The action verbs, appearing one right after another, add power-

"You are not of the masons."[18]

"Yes, yes," I said; "yes, yes."

"You? Impossible! A mason?"

"A mason," I replied.

"A sign," he said, "a sign."

"It is this," I answered, producing from beneath the folds of my *roquelaure* a trowel.

"You jest," he exclaimed, recoiling a few paces. "But let us proceed to the Amontillado."

"Be it so," I said, replacing the tool beneath the cloak and again offering him my arm. He leaned upon it heavily. We continued our route in search of the Amontillado. We passed through a range of low arches, descended, passed on, and descending again, arrived at a deep crypt, in which the foulness of the air caused our flambeaux rather to glow than flame.

At the most remote end of the crypt there appeared another less spacious. Its walls had been lined with human remains, piled to the vault overhead, in the fashion of the great catacombs of Paris. Three sides of this interior crypt were still ornamented in this manner. From the fourth side the bones had been thrown down, and lay promiscuously upon the earth, forming at one point a mound of some size. Within the wall thus exposed by the displacing of the bones, we perceived a still interior crypt or recess, in depth about four feet, in width three, in height six or seven. It seemed to have been constructed for no especial use within itself, but formed merely the interval between two of the colossal supports of the roof of the catacombs, and was backed by one of their circumscribing walls of solid granite.

It was in vain that Fortunato, uplifting his dull torch, endeavored to pry into the depth of the recess. Its termination the feeble light did not enable us to see.

"Proceed," I said: "herein is the Amontillado. As for Luchresi——"

"He is an ignoramus," interrupted my friend, as he stepped unsteadily forward, while I followed immediately at his heels. In an instant he had reached the extremity of the niche, and finding his progress arrested by the rock, stood stupidly bewildered. A moment more and I had fettered him to the granite. In its surface were two iron staples, distant from each other about two feet, horizontally. From one of these depended a short chain, from the other a padlock. Throwing the links about his

18. **masons:** The Freemasons, an international secret society.

9

Predict: *Why is he carrying a trowel? It possibly foreshadows what he is planning.*

Visualize: *The description adds to the mood and suspense.*

Visualize: *The final phase of the plan is becoming evident.*

The Cask of Amontillado 7

fully to the sense of menace and horror. Note, too, that almost all of the actions described by these verbs are physical.

Student Activity 1. Indicate which of the following verbs are action verbs:

1. We *continued,* our route in search of the Amontillado.
2. We *passed* through a range of low arches, *descended, passed* on, and descending again, *arrived* at a deep crypt. . . .
3. At the most remote end of the crypt there *appeared* another less spacious.
4. We *perceived* a still interior crypt or recess. . . .

Student Activity 2. Using vivid action verbs, write four sentences about revenge.

Electronic Handbook You might want students to review verbs before completing the Grammar in Action activities. If students have access to the Language Master 6000, have them enter *verb* and press the GRAMMAR key.

10 Discussion In what tone of voice does the narrator make this comment? Explain.

11 Discussion Does the narrator discover these materials by accident? Explain.

Multicultural Focus Explain that the theme of revenge in Poe's story is a major theme in many great works of Western literature. Revenge plays an important role, for example, in the great American novel *Moby-Dick* by Herman Melville. Captain Ahab leads his whaling ship on a desperate hunt for the great white whale who took Ahab's leg. Revenge was a favorite theme of Elizabethan playwrights in sixteenth century England. The greatest example is *Hamlet* by William Shakespeare, about a Danish prince who seeks the murderer of his father.

Ask students to find a story that uses the theme of revenge and share it with the class.

Connect: *The narrator is making fun of Fortunato, for he had given Fortunato so many chances to turn back, and now it is too late.*

Connect: *The need for the trowel is now known.*

Visualize: *Montresor seems on edge and nervous.*

waist, it was but the work of a few seconds to secure it. He was too much astounded to resist. Withdrawing the key I stepped back from the recess.

"Pass your hand," I said, "over the wall; you cannot help feeling the niter. Indeed, it is *very* damp. Once more let me *implore* you to return. No? Then I must positively leave you. But I must first render you all the little attentions in my power." 10

"The Amontillado!" ejaculated my friend, not yet recovered from his astonishment.

"True," I replied; "the Amontillado."

As I said these words I busied myself among the pile of bones of which I have before spoken. Throwing them aside, I soon uncovered a quantity of building stone and mortar. With these materials and with the aid of my trowel, I began vigorously to wall up the entrance of the niche. 11

I had scarcely laid the first tier of the masonry when I discovered that the intoxication of Fortunato had in a great measure worn off. The earliest indication I had of this was a low moaning cry from the depth of the recess. It was *not* the cry of a drunken man. There was then a long and obstinate silence. I laid the second tier, and the third, and the fourth; and then I heard the furious vibrations of the chain. The noise lasted for several minutes, during which, that I might hearken to it with the more satisfaction, I ceased my labors and sat down upon the bones. When at last the clanking subsided, I resumed the trowel, and finished without interruption the fifth, the sixth, and the seventh tier. The wall was now nearly upon a level with my breast. I again paused, and holding the flambeaux over the masonwork, threw a few feeble rays upon the figure within.

A succession of loud and shrill screams, bursting suddenly from the throat of the chained form, seemed to thrust me violently back. For a brief moment I hesitated, I trembled. Unsheathing my rapier,[19] I began to grope with it about the recess; but the thought of an instant reassured me. I placed my hand upon the solid fabric of the catacombs, and felt satisfied. I reapproached the wall; I replied to the yells of him who clamored. I reechoed, I aided, I surpassed them in volume and in strength. I did this, and the clamorer grew still.

It was now midnight, and my task was drawing to a close. I had completed the eighth, the ninth, and the tenth tier. I had

19. rapier (rā′ pē ər) *n.*: A slender, two-edged sword.

finished a portion of the last and the eleventh; there remained but a single stone to be fitted and plastered in. I struggled with its weight; I placed it partially in its destined position. But now there came from out the niche a low laugh that erected the hairs upon my head. It was succeeded by a sad voice, which I had difficulty in recognizing as that of the noble Fortunato. The voice said—

"Ha! ha! ha!—he! he! he!—a very good joke, indeed—an excellent jest. We will have many a rich laugh about it at the palazzo—he! he! he!—over our wine—he! he! he!"

"The Amontillado!" I said.

"He! he! he!—he! he! he!—yes, the Amontillado. But is it not getting late? Will not they be awaiting us at the palazzo, the Lady Fortunato and the rest? Let us be gone."

"Yes," I said, "let us be gone."

"*For the love of God, Montresor!*"

"Yes," I said, "for the love of God!"

But to these words I hearkened in vain for a reply. I grew impatient. I called aloud—

"Fortunato!"

No answer. I called again—

"Fortunato!"

No answer still. I thrust a torch through the remaining aperture and let it fall within. There came forth in return only a jingling of the bells. My heart grew sick; it was the dampness of the catacombs that made it so. I hastened to make an end of my labor. I forced the last stone into its position; I plastered it up. Against the new masonry I reerected the old rampart of bones. For the half of a century no mortal has disturbed them. *In pace requiescat!*[20]

Connect: *Fortunato does not realize—or want to accept—what is happening to him.*

Respond: *Montresor might be having second thoughts.*

Respond: *Montresor actually left him there to die. Sick! I guess that's what I expected from Poe.*

12

---

20. *In pace requiescat!:* Latin for "May he rest in peace!"

Edgar Allan Poe (1809–1849) was born in Boston to a family of traveling actors. After losing both parents before he was three, Poe was raised by John Allan of Richmond, Virginia. He attended the University of Virginia and the United States Military Academy at West Point. Despite his recognized talent for writing, he was unable to succeed in his jobs or his personal life. Poe is perhaps best known for his horror stories, like "The Cask of Amontillado," which have the eerie atmosphere of nightmares.

The Cask of Amontillado 9

Montresor extensively, hoping that he would make a slip.

12 Discussion What else might be making the narrator ill? Explain.

Reader's Response What did you think was most horrifying about this story?

Thematic Response Each of the characters in the story made choices. Which choices would have affected the story most if they had been made differently? Which choice made the ending of the story inevitable?

More About the Author Edgar Allan Poe is considered one of the originators of both the modern short story itself and the detective story. Ask students why they think the short story has been such a successful literary form in the modern world.

ANSWERS TO ANALYZING LITERATURE

1. Suggested Response: They are in the street at dusk during carnival time.
2. Montresor takes Fortunato to the crypt under his house. It is dark, damp, dreary, and oppressive. This setting contrasts with the revelry, excitement, and "madness" of the carnival.

ANSWERS TO CRITICAL THINKING AND READING

1. Suggested Response: At the carnival, he can pretend to meet Fortunato casually. Also, he can count on the fact that Fortunato will be drunk and distracted.
2. Suggested Response: If Montresor's wine cellar had not been in the catacombs, he would have had to lure Fortunato by some other means, or he would have had to devise some other method of disposing of him.
3. Answers will differ. Most students will realize that the daytime is less suited to the mood of the story. Also, night provides a cover for Montresor's plan.

---

prospect of sampling it.
3. He points out the niter which is used as a preservative. He tells Fortunato that he is a man to be missed. He shows Fortunato a trowel when asked if he is a mason. Montresor fails to understand these hints.

Interpreting

4. Answers will differ. Students may respond that Montresor is so strange that he might have imag-

ined the insult. The possibility that there was no insult makes the "punishment," and Montresor's careful planning of it, even more horrible.
5. Suggested Response: The coat of arms and motto are appropriate because they reflect the same spirit of unforgiving revenge that Montresor displays.
6. Suggested Response: He is an easy prey because he is vain and somewhat foolish.

7. Suggested Response: Montresor's urging Fortunato in turn back is reverse psychology. The more he encourages him to turn back, the more it makes Fortunato want to go on.
8. Suggested Response: Fifty years have passed since the crime occurred. He still feels the effect of the horror that he experienced.

Applying

9. Answers will differ. Students might respond that they would interview

4. Suggested Response: The crypt, which is a tomb, and the presence of bones contribute to the horror.

THINKING AND WRITING

Writing Transparency
Graphic organizers are a helpful tool when writing descriptions. Before students write, have them brainstorm for ideas using the Sensory Language Chart in **Transparencies for Writing.**

Alternative Assessment Based on the settings your students have created in the Thinking and Writing assignment, ask them to write the story that will take place in that setting. Encourage them to model their story on "The Cask of Amontillado," noting that the story takes place in a short period of time—only an hour or two, that there are only two characters in the story, one of whom is the narrator who shares his feelings with the reader, and that Poe relies on dialogue between Fortunato and Montresor to develop the conflict and to help create suspense.
Peer Review In pairs or groups of four, have your students assess each other's stories by responding to the following questions:
What is the setting and how does it contribute to the atmosphere?
What does the writer reveal about each character? How?
What is the conflict? How does the interaction between the characters contribute to it?
How does the writer create suspense?
What additional details would you suggest the writer add to enhance the story?
What, if anything, would you suggest the writer delete?

RESPONDING TO THE SELECTION

Your Response

1. Is guilt more intense if the wrongdoing is undiscovered? Explain.

Recalling

2. Find three hints that Montresor gives to Fortunato of what he intends to do. How does Fortunato interpret each hint?
3. What happens to Fortunato at the end?

Interpreting

4. The nature of the insult Fortunato offered Montresor is never clear. Do you think it really happened or occurred only in Montresor's mind? Explain your answer. How does not knowing make the horror even greater?
5. Explain how the Montresors' family motto and coat of arms are appropriate.
6. What character traits make Fortunato such an easy prey for Montresor?
7. Why does Montresor keep urging Fortunato to turn back?
8. How long ago did the crime Montresor relates occur? What does this fact tell you about the effect of the crime on Montresor?

Applying

9. Suppose you were a police detective in Italy when this story took place and you suspected that Montresor had killed Fortunato. How might you get proof of the crime?

ANALYZING LITERATURE

Understanding Setting

The **setting** of a story is the place and the time of the action. Often a setting, such as that in "The Cask of Amontillado," is central to the story, as important as the characters and events.

1. Describe the setting at the beginning of the story, when Montresor meets Fortunato.

2. Where does Montresor take Fortunato? Describe this setting, contrasting it with the first.

CRITICAL THINKING AND READING

Analyzing the Effect of Setting

In "The Cask of Amontillado" Poe has created every detail of setting to contribute to his intended effect. When you examine the details carefully, you can see how each detail fits his plan.

1. Give two reasons why the carnival setting is appropriate for Montresor's plan and therefore for the plot.
2. Suppose that Montresor's wine cellar were not in the catacombs. How would the plot change?
3. Could the story have taken place during the day? Why or why not?
4. What details of the setting contribute to the horror of the story?

THINKING AND WRITING

Creating a Setting

You are planning to write a horror story in the style of Edgar Allan Poe. You want to set the scene so that your reader gets a physical sense of it. Since it is dark, you cannot use visual details; you must use only details of hearing and touch. Brainstorm for ideas. Then write a paragraph describing your setting. Revise it, adding words that suggest sounds and feelings.

LEARNING OPTIONS

1. **Speaking and Listening.** Prepare a scene from this story as a radio presentation. Read it dramatically and incorporate sound effects. You might tape record it and play the tape for your classmates.
2. **Art.** On page 6, Montresor describes his family's coat of arms. Illustrate this coat of arms. You may wish to do research to see examples of coats of arms.

Writing Across the Curriculum
You might have students illustrate their writing assignments. If you do, consider informing the art department so that art teachers can provide assistance and materials.

LEARNING OPTIONS

1. This activity will appeal to students who enjoy performing. You may wish to suggest appropriate music to be played as an introduction to the reading.
2. Artistic students will enjoy this activity. You may wish to suggest that students design their own personal coat of arms also.

Plot

ANGST
Edvard Munch
Three Lions

Humanities Notes

Fine art, *Angst,* 1894, Edvard Munch. Edvard Munch (1863–1944), was a Norwegian painter and graphic artist who attended the School of Arts and Crafts in Oslo and studied in Paris. Munch's unique and complex psychological style is considered to be one of the first manifestations of Expressionism, the nonobjective use of symbols, stylizations, and so on, to give objective expression to emotion and inner experience. The power of Munch's art was based on his obsession with depression, fear, and death. His exploration of these morbid subjects lent expressive weight to his art.

Angst, or "anxiety," along with other paintings, was prepared by Munch as a motif for use in a series of large decorative murals entitled "The Frieze of Life." The frozen, haunted figures in this painting seem to be gripped with the overwhelming emotion of fear. The sky, caught by the forces of nature, swirls and twists above them, adding to the tension of the scene.

Preparation

More About the Author Richard Connell started to earn money for his writing when he was ten years old, receiving ten cents for each baseball story he covered. He worked as city editor of a local newspaper when he was sixteen and in college he was editor of the school newspaper and magazine. Ask students how job experience gained when growing up is a good way to learn about a profession.

Literary Focus You might want to explain to students that the climax is usually the most dramatic point in the story. Tell students that when they reach this point, they will feel that the conflict is about to be resolved.

Prereading Focus You may wish to have students identify their positions for and against hunting at the beginning of the debate. During the debate you may want to have a volunteer record the individual arguments on the chalkboard.

Vocabulary Have less advanced students work in pairs to learn the meanings and pronunciations of the vocabulary words.

Spelling Tip Students may have trouble spelling the /sk/ sound in *grotesque*. Point out that this sound is spelled by *sque* not only in *grotesque* but also in *brusquely* (page 56).

Richard Connell

(1893–1949) was born in Dutchess County, New York. His love of writing began early: At ten, he was covering basketball games for his father's newspaper and at sixteen he was editing the paper. After serving in World War I, Connell lived in various cities in Europe and the United States, finally settling in Beverly Hills, California. The author of more than a hundred short stories, Connell drew upon his firsthand knowledge of life-and-death conflict when he wrote his gripping masterpiece—"The Most Dangerous Game."

The Most Dangerous Game

Plot

The **plot** of a story is made up of a series of related events that include the conflict, the climax, and the resolution. The conflict is a struggle between opposing people or forces. The climax is the turning point in the story, the point at which the conflict comes to a head. The resolution shows how the situation turns out and ties up loose ends. At the beginning of the story, the author may provide background information, called exposition, which sets the scene for the conflict. As the story proceeds, this information may introduce complications that keep the plot from moving too smoothly toward its resolution.

Focus

"The Most Dangerous Game" raises questions about the ethics of hunting wild animals for sport. With your classmates, engage in an informal debate about the issue of hunting. Consider questions like the following: What is the value, if any, of hunting? Does hunting for sport interfere with the effort to preserve our natural environment? Why or why not? After you have debated this issue, read this story of a hunter who becomes the hunted.

Vocabulary

Knowing the following words will help you as you read "The Most Dangerous Game."

palpable (pal′ pə b′l) *adj.*: Able to be touched or felt (p. 13)

indolently (in′ də lənt lē) *adv.*: Lazily; idly (p. 14)

bizarre (bi zär′) *adj.*: Odd in appearance (p. 17)

naive (nä ēv′) *adj.*: Unsophisticated (p. 22)

scruples (skrōō′ pəlz) *n.*: Misgivings about something one feels is wrong (p. 22)

blandly (bland′ lē) *adv.*: In a mild and soothing manner (p. 22)

grotesque (grō tesk′) *adj.*: Having a bizarre design (p. 24)

futile (fyōōt′ ′l) *adj.*: Useless; hopeless (p. 26)

Objectives

1 To understand plot in a short story
2 To analyze the sequence of events in a short story
3 To write about plot
4 To express individual interests and abilities through an optional activity

Support Material

Teaching Portfolio
Teacher Backup, p. 21
Grammar in Action Worksheets, *Using Dashes*, p. 24; *Writing Suspense*, p. 26
Usage and Mechanics Worksheet, p. 28
Vocabulary Check, p. 29
Analyzing Literature Worksheet, *Understanding Plot*, p. 31

Critical Thinking and Reading Worksheet, *Analyzing Sequence in a Story*, p. 32
Selection Test, p. 33
Art Transparency 1: *Evening by the Sea*, by Karl Schmidt-Rottluff

Prentice Hall Literature Writing Studio

The Most Dangerous Game

Richard Connell

1 "Off there to the right—somewhere—is a large island," said Whitney. "It's rather a mystery—"

"What island is it?" Rainsford asked.

"The old charts call it 'Ship-Trap Island,'" Whitney replied. "A suggestive name, isn't it? Sailors have a curious dread of the place. I don't know why. Some superstition—"

"Can't see it," remarked Rainsford, trying to peer through the dank tropical night that was palpable as it pressed its thick warm blackness in upon the yacht.

"You've good eyes," said Whitney, with a laugh, "and I've seen you pick off a moose moving in the brown fall bush at four hundred yards, but even you can't see four miles or so through a moonless Caribbean[1] night."

"Not four yards," admitted Rainsford. "Ugh! It's like moist black velvet."

2 "It will be light in Rio," promised Whitney. "We should make it in a few days. I hope the jaguar guns have come from Purdey's. We should have some good hunting up the Amazon.[2] Great sport, hunting."

"The best sport in the world," agreed Rainsford.

"For the hunter," amended Whitney. "Not for the jaguar."

---

1. Caribbean (kar' ə bē' ən): The Caribbean Sea, a part of the Atlantic Ocean bounded by South America, Central America, and the West Indies.
2. Amazon (am' ə zän'): A large river in South America.

"Don't talk rot, Whitney," said Rainsford. "You're a big-game hunter, not a philosopher. Who cares how a jaguar feels?"

"Perhaps the jaguar does," observed Whitney.

"Bah! They've no understanding."

"Even so, I rather think they understand one thing—fear. The fear of pain and the fear of death."

"Nonsense," laughed Rainsford. "This hot weather is making you soft, Whitney. Be a realist. The world is made up of two classes—the hunters and the huntees. Luckily, you and I are the hunters. Do you think we've passed that island yet?"

"I can't tell in the dark. I hope so."

"Why?" asked Rainsford.

"The place has a reputation—a bad one."

"Cannibals?" suggested Rainsford.

"Hardly. Even cannibals wouldn't live in such a God-forsaken place. But it's gotten into sailor lore, somehow. Didn't you notice that the crew's nerves seemed a bit jumpy today?"

"They were a bit strange, now you mention it. Even Captain Nielsen—"

"Yes, even that tough-minded old Swede, who'd go up to the devil himself and ask him for a light. Those fishy blue eyes held a look I never saw there before. All I could get out of him was: 'This place has an evil name among sea-faring men, sir.' Then he said to me, very gravely: 'Don't you feel anything?'— as if the air about us was actually poisonous.

The Most Dangerous Game 13

Presentation

Motivation/Prior Knowledge You might want to ask students to name the most dangerous sport they can imagine. Have them compare and contrast the dangers of the sports that are suggested. Then tell them that they will read about an even riskier activity.

Master Teacher Note Review with students the meaning of irony and an ironic situation. Tell them that there is a central irony in the plot of this story.

Thematic Focus Conflict is an inescapable part of life. Landing on the ominously named "Ship Trap Island," plunges the protagonist of this story into mortal conflict with a deadly enemy. Have students discuss movies and television programs they have seen in which characters became involved in mortal conflicts. How did the characters react to these conflicts? What were the outcomes?

Making Connections Other selections that focus on a time for courage are "A Lincoln Preface," page 405; the excerpt from *Kon-Tiki*, page 429; and the excerpts from the *Odyssey*, page 645.

Purpose-Setting Question What is the meaning of the title?

1 Enrichment Discuss the fact that ships and planes have sometimes disappeared mysteriously. Cite the example of the Bermuda Triangle, whose vertices touch Bermuda, Miami, and Puerto Rico. What might account for increased dangers in that area?

2 Discussion Whitney claims animals understand fear—the fear of death and the fear of pain. Does Rainsford agree? Ask students with whom they agree or disagree.

Alternative Assessment To promote active reading, have students keep a reader's response journal as they read the story. Ask them to focus their observations on the words and phrases that convey mood as well as the details that reveal the personalities of Rainsford and Zaroff. Encourage students to respond personally to Zaroff's idea that "Life is for the strong" and Rains- ford's demonstration of the ability of the "weak" to prevail.

Their observations will enable you to assess their understanding of the issues in the story.

3 **Discussion** Compare Whitney's feelings upon passing the island to Rainsford's statement about superstition.

4 **Discussion** Whitney believes that sailors possess an "extra sense" to detect danger. Do you think that this notion might be true?

5 **Reading Strategy** Up to this point, the descriptions of the island and the atmosphere should suggest a particular mood. Given that mood, predict what might happen next.

Now, you mustn't laugh when I tell you this—I did feel something like a sudden chill.

"There was no breeze. The sea was as flat as a plate-glass window. We were drawing near the island then. What I felt was a—a mental chill; a sort of sudden dread."

"Pure imagination," said Rainsford. "One superstitious sailor can taint the whole ship's company with his fear."

"Maybe. But sometimes I think sailors have an extra sense that tells them when they are in danger. Sometimes I think evil is a tangible thing—with wave lengths, just as sound and light have. An evil place can, so to speak, broadcast vibrations of evil. Anyhow, I'm glad we're getting out of this zone. Well, I think I'll turn in now, Rainsford."

"I'm not sleepy," said Rainsford. "I'm going to smoke another pipe on the after deck."

"Good night, then, Rainsford. See you at breakfast."

"Right. Good night, Whitney."

There was no sound in the night as Rainsford sat there, but the muffled throb of the engine that drove the yacht swiftly through the darkness, and the swish and ripple of the wash of the propeller.

Rainsford, reclining in a steamer chair, indolently puffed on his favorite brier. The sensuous drowsiness of the night was on him. "It's so dark," he thought, "that I could sleep without closing my eyes; the night would be my eyelids—"

An abrupt sound startled him. Off to the right he heard it, and his ears, expert in such matters, could not be mistaken. Again he heard the sound, and again. Somewhere, off in the blackness, someone had fired a gun three times.

Rainsford sprang up and moved quickly to the rail, mystified. He strained his eyes in the direction from which the reports had

come, but it was like trying to see through a blanket. He leaped upon the rail and balanced himself there, to get greater elevation; his pipe, striking a rope, was knocked from his mouth. He lunged for it; a short, hoarse cry came from his lips as he realized he had reached too far and had lost his balance. The cry was pinched off short as the blood-warm waters of the Caribbean Sea closed over his head.

Grammar in Action

Skillful writers can use a single **dash** to emphasize a particular word or phrase, or to indicate a summary statement. A pair of dashes can set off a dramatic interrupting idea.

Notice how Richard Connell uses dashes in the following sentences:

Even so, I rather think they understand one thing—fear.
The world is made up of two classes—the hunters and the huntees.

Ten minutes of determined effort brought another sound to his ears—the most welcome he had ever heard—the muttering and growling of the sea breaking on a rocky shore.

In these examples, Connell takes full advantage of the possibilities of the dash. The slight pause that the dash introduces in the first two examples gives added emphasis to the following word or phrase. In the third example, the phrase set off by dashes is extremely dramatic.

Student Activity 1. Identify three additional sentences from "The Most Dangerous Game" in which Connell uses dashes. For each

He struggled up to the surface and tried to cry out, but the wash from the speeding yacht slapped him in the face and the salt water in his open mouth made him gag and strangle. Desperately he struck out with strong strokes after the receding lights of the yacht, but he stopped before he had swum fifty feet. A certain cool-headedness had come to him; it was not the first time he had been in a tight place. There was a chance that his cries could be heard by someone aboard the yacht, but that chance was slender, and grew more slender as the yacht raced on. He wrestled himself out of his clothes, and shouted with all his power. The lights of the yacht became faint and ever-vanishing fireflies; then they were blotted out entirely by the night.

6 **Discussion** How does Rainsford feel after falling overboard? What does he decide to do?

sentence, explain the purpose of the dash or dashes. Also, tell why this punctuation mark is or is not effective in each sentence.

Student Activity 2. Using Connell's sentences as models, write three original sentences in which dashes emphasize a word or phrase, indicate a summary, or set off a dramatic interruption.

Electronic Handbook You might want to have students review sentence fragments before completing the Grammar in Action activities. If the students have access to the Language Master 6000, have them use the access word *fragment* and press the GRAMMAR key to get information on sentence fragments.

7 Discussion This section describing Rainsford's struggle demonstrates his strength and will to survive. Which phrases illustrate these qualities?

8 Discussion Rainsford's examination of the area of crushed jungle leads him to several conclusions. What are they?

Multicultural Focus Connell's story focuses on hunting—an activity that is part of the heritage of all cultures. While farming has been practiced for about one percent of human history, hunting was humankind's occupation for more than half a million years. Anthropologists think hunting may have encouraged many traits common to human beings in modern societies, including cooperation, organization, and aggression. There are few hunting and gathering societies left in the world. The only people who still exist solely by hunting are the Mbuti Pygmies of the Central African rain forest and the disappearing Bushmen of the Kalahari in Southern Africa. Societies that combine hunting with other means of sustenance include the Eskimos, the Pacific Northwest Indians, some Plains Indians, the Siriono Indians of Bolivia, and the Aborigines of Australia. These hunting societies are quite egalitarian: cooperation is paramount for successful hunting, and individualism and authoritarianism are discouraged. Identification with the environment is very strong, as reflected in such religious ceremonies as the Mbuti songs to the forest god, Eskimo poetry celebrating the sea goddess, and the giraffe dance of the Kalahari Bushmen.

Ask students to read further about one of the above groups or about the history of hunting in various cultures.

Rainsford remembered the shots. They had come from the right, and doggedly he swam in that direction, swimming with slow, deliberate strokes, conserving his strength. For a seemingly endless time he fought the sea. He began to count his strokes; he could do possibly a hundred more and then—

Rainsford heard a sound. It came out of the darkness, a high screaming sound, the sound of an animal in an extremity of anguish and terror.

He did not recognize the animal that made the sound; he did not try to; with fresh vitality he swam toward the sound. He heard it again; then it was cut short by another noise, crisp, staccato.

"Pistol shot," muttered Rainsford, swimming on.

Ten minutes of determined effort brought another sound to his ears—the most welcome he had ever heard—the muttering and growling of the sea breaking on a rocky shore. He was almost on the rocks before he saw them; on a night less calm he would have been shattered against them. With his remaining strength he dragged himself from the swirling waters. Jagged crags appeared to jut into the opaqueness, he forced himself upward, hand over hand. Gasping, his hands raw, he reached a flat place at the top. Dense jungle came down to the very edge of the cliffs. What perils that tangle of trees and underbrush might hold for him did not concern Rainsford just then. All he knew was that he was safe from his enemy, the sea, and that utter weariness was on him. He flung himself down at the jungle edge and tumbled headlong into the deepest sleep of his life.

When he opened his eyes he knew from the position of the sun that it was late in the afternoon. Sleep had given him new vigor; a

sharp hunger was picking at him. He looked about him, almost cheerfully.

"Where there are pistol shots, there are men. Where there are men, there is food," he thought. But what kind of men, he wondered, in so forbidding a place? An unbroken front of snarled and ragged jungle fringed the shore.

He saw no sign of a trail through the closely knit web of weeds and trees; it was easier to go along the shore, and Rainsford floundered along by the water. Not far from where he had landed, he stopped.

Some wounded thing, by the evidence a large animal, had thrashed about in the underbrush; the jungle weeds were crushed down and the moss was lacerated; one patch of weeds was stained crimson. A small, glittering object not far away caught Rainsford's eye and he picked it up. It was an empty cartridge.

"A twenty-two," he remarked. "That's odd. It must have been a fairly large animal too. The hunter had his nerve with him to tackle it with a light gun. It's clear that the brute put up a fight. I suppose the first three shots I heard was when the hunter flushed his quarry[3] and wounded it. The last shot was when he trailed it here and finished it."

He examined the ground closely and found what he had hoped to find—the print of hunting boots. They pointed along the cliff in the direction he had been going. Eagerly he hurried along, now slipping on a rotten log or a loose stone, but making headway; night was beginning to settle down on the island.

Bleak darkness was blacking out the sea and jungle when Rainsford sighted the lights. He came upon them as he turned a

---

3. **flushed his quarry** (kwôr′ ē): Drove his prey into the open.

crook in the coast line, and his first thought was that he had come upon a village, for there were many lights. But as he forged along he saw to his great astonishment that all the lights were in one enormous building—a lofty structure with pointed towers plunging upward into the gloom. His eyes made out the shadowy outlines of a palatial château;[4] it was set on a high bluff, and on three sides of it cliffs dived down to where the sea licked greedy lips in the shadows.

"Mirage," thought Rainsford. But it was no mirage, he found, when he opened the tall spiked iron gate. The stone steps were real enough; the massive door with a leering gargoyle[5] for a knocker was real enough; yet about it all hung an air of unreality.

He lifted the knocker, and it creaked up stiffly, as if it had never before been used. He let it fall, and it startled him with its booming loudness. He thought he heard steps within; the door remained closed. Again Rainsford lifted the heavy knocker, and let it fall. The door opened then, opened as suddenly as if it were on a spring, and Rainsford stood blinking in the river of glaring gold light that poured out. The first thing Rainsford's eyes discerned was the largest man Rainsford had ever seen—a gigantic creature, solidly made and black-bearded to the waist. In his hand the man held a long-barreled revolver, and he was pointing it straight at Rainsford's heart.

Out of the snarl of beard two small eyes regarded Rainsford.

"Don't be alarmed," said Rainsford, with a smile which he hoped was disarming. "I'm no robber. I fell off a yacht. My name is Sanger Rainsford of New York City."

The menacing look in the eyes did not change. The revolver pointed as rigidly as if the giant were a statue. He gave no sign that he understood Rainsford's words, or that he had even heard them. He was dressed in uniform, a black uniform trimmed with gray astrakhan.[6]

"I'm Sanger Rainsford of New York," Rainsford began again. "I fell off a yacht. I am hungry."

The man's only answer was to raise with his thumb the hammer of his revolver. Then Rainsford saw the man's free hand go to his forehead in a military salute, and he saw him click his heels together and stand at attention. Another man was coming down the broad marble steps, an erect, slender man in evening clothes. He advanced to Rainsford and held out his hand.

In a cultivated voice marked by a slight accent that gave it added precision and deliberateness, he said: "It is a very great pleasure and honor to welcome Mr. Sanger Rainsford, the celebrated hunter, to my home."

Automatically Rainsford shook the man's hand.

"I've read your book about hunting snow leopards in Tibet, you see," explained the man. "I am General Zaroff."

Rainsford's first impression was that the man was singularly handsome; his second was that there was an original, almost bizarre quality about the general's face. He was a tall man past middle age, for his hair was a vivid white; but his thick eyebrows and pointed military mustache were as black as the night from which Rainsford had come. His eyes, too, were black and very bright. He had high cheek bones, a sharp-cut nose, a

---

4. palatial château (pə lā′ shəl sha tō′): A mansion as luxurious as a palace.
5. gargoyle (gär′ goil) *n.*: A strange and distorted animal form projecting from a building.

6. astrakhan (as′ trə kan′) *n.*: Fur made from young lambs.

The Most Dangerous Game 17

14 Discussion The general says that Ivan is ". . . like all his race, a bit of a savage." He adds that he and Ivan are of the same race. What does this indicate about the general?

15 Critical Thinking and Reading From the description of the dining room, what conclusions can you draw about the general's personality?

16 Discussion Why do you think the general is appraising Rainsford?

spare, dark face, the face of a man used to giving orders, the face of an aristocrat. Turning to the giant in uniform, the general made a sign. The giant put away his pistol, saluted, withdrew.

"Ivan is an incredibly strong fellow," remarked the general, "but he has the misfortune to be deaf and dumb. A simple fellow, but, I'm afraid, like all his race, a bit of a savage."

"Is he Russian?"

"He is a Cossack,"[7] said the general, and his smile showed red lips and pointed teeth. "So am I."

"Come," he said, "we shouldn't be chatting here. We can talk later. Now you want clothes, food, rest. You shall have them. This is a most restful spot."

Ivan had reappeared, and the general spoke to him with lips that moved but gave forth no sound.

"Follow Ivan, if you please, Mr. Rainsford," said the general. "I was about to have my dinner when you came. I'll wait for you. You'll find that my clothes will fit you, I think."

It was to a huge, beam-ceilinged bedroom with a canopied bed big enough for six men that Rainsford followed the silent giant. Ivan laid out an evening suit, and Rainsford, as he put it on, noticed that it came from a London tailor who ordinarily cut and sewed for none below the rank of duke.

The dining room to which Ivan conducted him was in many ways remarkable. There was a medieval magnificence about it; it suggested a baronial hall of feudal times with its oaken panels, its high ceiling, its vast refectory table where twoscore men could sit down to eat. About the hall were the mounted heads of many animals—lions, tigers, elephants, moose, bears; larger or more perfect specimens Rainsford had never seen. At the great table the general was sitting, alone.

"You'll have a cocktail, Mr. Rainsford," he suggested. The cocktail was surpassingly good; and, Rainsford noted, the table appointments were of the finest—the linen, the crystal, the silver, the china.

They were eating *borsch*, the rich, red soup with whipped cream so dear to Russian palates. Half apologetically General Zaroff said: "We do our best to preserve the amenities of civilization here. Please forgive any lapses. We are well off the beaten track, you know. Do you think the champagne has suffered from its long ocean trip?"

"Not in the least," declared Rainsford. He was finding the general a most thoughtful and affable host, a true cosmopolite.[8] But there was one small trait of the general's that made Rainsford uncomfortable. Whenever he looked up from his plate he found the general studying him, appraising him narrowly.

"Perhaps," said General Zaroff, "you were surprised that I recognized your name. You see, I read all books on hunting published in English, French, and Russian. I have but one passion in my life, Mr. Rainsford, and it is the hunt."

"You have some wonderful heads here," said Rainsford as he ate a particularly well cooked filet mignon. "That Cape buffalo is the largest I ever saw."

"Oh, that fellow. Yes, he was a monster."

"Did he charge you?"

"Hurled me against a tree," said the gen-

---

7. Cossack (käs′ ak): A member of a people from southern Russia, famous for their fierceness.

8. cosmopolite (käz mäp′ ə līt′) *n.*: A person at home in all parts of the world.

eral. "Fractured my skull. But I got the brute."

"I've always thought," said Rainsford, "that the Cape buffalo is the most dangerous of all big game."

For a moment the general did not reply; he was smiling his curious red-lipped smile. Then he said slowly: "No. You are wrong, sir. The Cape buffalo is not the most dangerous big game." He sipped his wine. "Here in my preserve on this island," he said in the same slow tone, "I hunt more dangerous game."

Rainsford expressed his surprise. "Is there big game on this island?"

The general nodded. "The biggest."

"Really?"

"Oh, it isn't here naturally, of course. I have to stock the island."

"What have you imported, general?" Rainsford asked. "Tigers?"

The general smiled. "No," he said. "Hunting tigers ceased to interest me some years ago. I exhausted their possibilities, you see. No thrill left in tigers, no real danger. I live for danger, Mr. Rainsford."

The general took from his pocket a gold cigarette case and offered his guest a long black cigarette with a silver tip; it was perfumed and gave off a smell like incense.

"We will have some capital hunting, you and I," said the general. "I shall be most glad to have your society."

"But what game—" began Rainsford.

"I'll tell you," said the general. "You will be amused, I know. I think I may say, in all modesty, that I have done a rare thing. I have invented a new sensation. May I pour you another glass of port, Mr. Rainsford?"

"Thank you, general."

The general filled both glasses, and said: "God makes some men poets. Some He makes kings, some beggars. Me He made a hunter. My hand was made for the trigger, my father said. He was a very rich man with a quarter of a million acres in the Crimea,[9] and he was an ardent sportsman. When I was only five years old he gave me a little gun, specially made in Moscow for me, to shoot sparrows with. When I shot some of his prize turkeys with it, he did not punish me; he complimented me on my marksmanship. I killed my first bear in the Caucasus[10] when I was ten. My whole life has been one prolonged hunt. I went into the army—it was expected of noblemen's sons—and for a time commanded a division of Cossack cavalry, but my real interest was always the hunt. I have hunted every kind of game in every land. It would be impossible for me to tell you how many animals I have killed."

The general puffed at his cigarette.

"After the debacle[11] in Russia I left the country, for it was imprudent for an officer of the Czar to stay there. Many noble Russians lost everything. I, luckily, had invested heavily in American securities, so I shall never have to open a tea room in Monte Carlo or drive a taxi in Paris. Naturally, I continued to hunt—grizzlies in your Rockies, crocodiles in the Ganges, rhinoceroses in East Africa. It was in Africa that the Cape buffalo hit me and laid me up for six months. As soon as I recovered I started for the Amazon to hunt jaguars, for I had heard they were unusually cunning. They weren't." The Cossack sighed. "They were no match at all for a hunter with his wits about him, and a high-powered rifle. I was bitterly disappointed. I was lying in my tent with a split-

---

9. Crimea (krī mē′ ə): A region in southwestern Russia on the Black Sea.
10. Caucasus (kô′ kə səs): A mountain range in southern Russia.
11. debacle (di bäk′ 'l) n.: Bad defeat; Zaroff is referring to the Russian Revolution of 1917, a defeat for upper-class Russians like himself.

The Most Dangerous Game 19

17 **Discussion** How does Zaroff's reply create suspense?

18 **Reading Strategy** Have students summarize the important events to this point. Are there any clues that indicate what the "most dangerous game" might be?

19 **Discussion** How have the general's earlier experiences influenced his attitude toward hunting?

Cooperative Learning Arrange the class in groups of four. Assign each group member a number from 1 to 4. Tell students that they are to work together to come up with predictions about the kind of game General Zaroff hunts. Tell students to look for clues in the author's description of Zaroff and in Zaroff's words. When students have had sufficient time, call a number for each team and ask for the team's response.

Humanities Note

Illustration, *Hat, Knife, and Gun in Woods*, David Mann. Mann (1940-   ), who was born in Kansas City, Missouri, now lives in California. He has painted since he was a child under the guidance of his father, who was also an artist. *Hat, Knife, and Gun in Woods* was done as an illustration for a book cover. In addition to being a book cover illustrator, Mann is an artist for *Easy Rider* magazine.

You might use the following questions for discussion:

1. What is the mood of the painting? How does the artist create the mood?
2. Explain why this is an effective and appropriate illustration for this story.

HAT, KNIFE, AND GUN IN WOODS
David Mann
Sal Barracca & Associates

ting headache one night when a terrible thought pushed its way into my mind. Hunting was beginning to bore me! And hunting, remember, had been my life. I have heard that in America business men often go to pieces when they give up the business that has been their life."

"Yes, that's so," said Rainsford.

The general smiled. "I had no wish to go to pieces," he said. "I must do something. Now, mine is an analytical mind, Mr. Rainsford. Doubtless that is why I enjoy the problems of the chase."

"No doubt, General Zaroff."

"So," continued the general, "I asked myself why the hunt no longer fascinated me. You are much younger than I am, Mr. Rainsford, and have not hunted as much, but you perhaps can guess the answer."

"What was it?"

"Simply this: hunting had ceased to be what you call 'a sporting proposition.' It had become too easy. I always got my quarry. Always. There is no greater bore than perfection."

The general lit a fresh cigarette.

"No animal had a chance with me any more. That is no boast; it is a mathematical certainty. The animal had nothing but his legs and his instinct. Instinct is no match for reason. When I thought of this it was a tragic moment for me, I can tell you."

Rainsford leaned across the table, absorbed in what his host was saying.

"It came to me as an inspiration what I must do," the general went on.

"And that was?"

The general smiled the quiet smile of one who has faced an obstacle and surmounted it with success. "I had to invent a new animal to hunt," he said.

"A new animal? You're joking."

"Not at all," said the general. "I never joke about hunting. I needed a new animal. I found one. So I bought this island, built this house, and here I do my hunting. The island is perfect for my purposes—there are jungles with a maze of trails in them, hills, swamps—"

"But the animal, General Zaroff?"

"Oh," said the general, "it supplies me with the most exciting hunting in the world. No other hunting compares with it for an instant. Every day I hunt, and I never grow bored now, for I have a quarry with which I can match my wits."

Rainsford's bewilderment showed in his face.

"I wanted the ideal animal to hunt," explained the general. "So I said: 'What are the attributes of an ideal quarry?' And the answer was, of course: 'It must have courage, cunning, and, above all, it must be able to reason.' "

"But no animal can reason," objected Rainsford.

"My dear fellow," said the general, "there is one that can."

"But you can't mean—" gasped Rainsford.

"And why not?"

"I can't believe you are serious, General Zaroff. This is a grisly joke."

"Why should I not be serious? I am speaking of hunting."

"Hunting? General Zaroff, what you speak of is murder."

The general laughed with entire good nature. He regarded Rainsford quizzically. "I refuse to believe that so modern and civilized a young man as you seem to be harbors romantic ideas about the value of human life. Surely your experiences in the war—"

"Did not make me condone cold-blooded murder," finished Rainsford stiffly.

Laughter shook the general. "How extraordinarily droll you are!" he said. "One

20 Discussion Why did the general look for a more cunning animal to hunt? What does Zaroff fear?

21 Discussion How does the general's statement about the hunt add to the drama and suspense of the story?

22 Discussion What does the general mean by his assertion that "Instinct is no match for reason"? Why did that thought mark a tragic moment for him?

23 Discussion What does Rainsford think the general means by "a new animal"?

24 Discussion Has Rainsford guessed what the "new animal" is?

25 Discussion What animal is the general talking about?

26 Critical Thinking and Reading When the general refers to Rainsford's experiences in the war, what point is he making?

27 Discussion How does this image illustrate what the general means?

28 Discussion Compare the general's assertion that "Life is for the strong. . . ." with Rainsford's statement, at the beginning of the story, that "The world is made up of two classes—the hunters and the huntees." How are these two statements similar? Yet how do the two men differ?

29 Discussion What is ironic about General Zaroff's statement that he treats his "visitors with every consideration"?

does not expect nowadays to find a young man of the educated class, even in America, with such a naive, and, if I may say so, mid-Victorian point of view.[12] It's like finding a snuff-box in a limousine. Ah, well, doubtless you had Puritan ancestors. So many Americans appear to have had. I'll wager you'll forget your notions when you go hunting with me. You've a genuine new thrill in store for you, Mr. Rainsford."

"Thank you, I'm a hunter, not a murderer."

"Dear me," said the general, quite unruffled, "again that unpleasant word. But I think I can show you that your scruples are quite ill founded."

"Yes?"

"Life is for the strong, to be lived by the strong, and, if need be, taken by the strong. The weak of the world were put here to give the strong pleasure. I am strong. Why should I not use my gift? If I wish to hunt, why should I not? I hunt the scum of the earth—sailors from tramp ships—lascars,[13] blacks, Chinese, whites, mongrels—a thoroughbred horse or hound is worth more than a score of them."

"But they are men," said Rainsford hotly.

"Precisely," said the general. "That is why I use them. It gives me pleasure. They can reason, after a fashion. So they are dangerous."

"But where do you get them?"

The general's left eyelid fluttered down in a wink. "This island is called Ship-Trap," he answered. "Sometimes an angry god of the high seas sends them to me. Sometimes, when Providence is not so kind, I help Providence a bit. Come to the window with me."

---

12. mid-Victorian point of view: A point of view emphasizing proper behavior and associated with the time of Queen Victoria of England (1819–1901).

13. lascars (lăs′ kərz)*n.*: Oriental sailors, especially natives of India.

Rainsford went to the window and looked out toward the sea.

"Watch! Out there!" exclaimed the general, pointing into the night. Rainsford's eyes saw only blackness, and then, as the general pressed a button, far out to sea Rainsford saw the flash of lights.

The general chuckled. "They indicate a channel," he said, "where there's none: giant rocks with razor edges crouch like a sea monster with wide-open jaws. They can crush a ship as easily as I crush this nut." He dropped a walnut on the hardwood floor and brought his heel grinding down on it. "Oh, yes," he said, casually, as if in answer to a question, "I have electricity. We try to be civilized here."

"Civilized? And you shoot down men?"

A trace of anger was in the general's black eyes, but it was there for but a second, and he said, in his most pleasant manner: "Dear me, what a righteous young man you are! I assure you I do not do the thing you suggest. That would be barbarous. I treat these visitors with every consideration. They get plenty of good food and exercise. They get into splendid physical condition. You shall see for yourself tomorrow."

"What do you mean?"

"We'll visit my training school," smiled the general. "It's in the cellar. I have about a dozen pupils down there now. They're from the Spanish bark San Lucar that had the bad luck to go on the rocks out there. A very inferior lot, I regret to say. Poor specimens and more accustomed to the deck than to the jungle."

He raised his hand, and Ivan, who served as waiter, brought thick Turkish coffee. Rainsford, with an effort, held his tongue in check.

"It's a game, you see," pursued the general blandly. "I suggest to one of them that we go hunting. I give him a supply of food

PEERING THROUGH THE JUNGLE
Larry Noble
Sal Barracca & Associates

The Most Dangerous Game 23

Illustration, *Peering Through the Jungle,* 1987, Larry Noble. Noble (1948-   ), who was born in Tampa, Florida, now lives in Crestline, California. For many years Noble has been a free-lance artist for movie posters, advertising campaigns, book covers, and magazine covers, including *Forbes, World Tennis, Field and Stream,* and *Children's Digest.* He has done the cover illustration for and has been featured in *American Artists* magazine and *Step by Step* magazine. *Peering Through the Jungle* was originally the book cover for *Life During Wartime.*

You might use the following questions for discussion:

1. What emotions do you see in this soldier's gaze that might be the emotions of Sanger Rainsford in the story?

2. What similarities are there between Rainsford and a soldier of war? Why is this an appropriate illustration for the story? Explain.

3. Does this illustration reflect the setting of "The Most Dangerous Game"? Explain.

30 Discussion Connell uses several descriptions in this paragraph. How do they add to the mood and tone of the story?

31 Literary Focus What is ironic about the general humming a tune from the Folies Bergère?

32 Discussion What mood does this passage call up? Which words and phrases contribute to this mood?

and an excellent hunting knife. I give him three hours' start. I am to follow, armed only with a pistol of the smallest caliber and range. If my quarry eludes me for three whole days, he wins the game. If I find him"—the general smiled—"he loses."

"Suppose he refuses to be hunted?"

"Oh," said the general, "I give him his option, of course. He need not play the game if he doesn't wish to. If he does not wish to hunt, I turn him over to Ivan. Ivan once had the honor of serving as official knouter[14] to the Great White Czar, and he has his own ideas of sport. Invariably, Mr. Rainsford, invariably they choose the hunt."

"And if they win?"

The smile on the general's face widened. "To date I have not lost," he said.

Then he added, hastily: "I don't wish you to think me a braggart, Mr. Rainsford. Many of them afford only the most elementary sort of problem. Occasionally I strike a tartar.[15] One almost did win. I eventually had to use the dogs."

"The dogs?"

"This way, please. I'll show you."

30 The general steered Rainsford to a window. The lights from the windows sent a flickering illumination that made grotesque patterns on the courtyard below, and Rainsford could see moving about there a dozen or so huge black shapes; as they turned toward him, their eyes glittered greenly.

31 "A rather good lot, I think," observed the general. "They are let out at seven every night. If anyone should try to get into my house—or out of it—something extremely regrettable would occur to him." He hummed a snatch of song from the Folies Bergère.[16]

"And now," said the general, "I want to show you my new collection of heads. Will you come with me to the library?"

"I hope," said Rainsford, "that you will excuse me tonight, General Zaroff. I'm really not feeling at all well."

"Ah, indeed?" the general inquired solicitously. "Well, I suppose that's only natural, after your long swim. You need a good, restful night's sleep. Tomorrow you'll feel like a new man, I'll wager. Then we'll hunt, eh? I've one rather promising prospect—"

Rainsford was hurrying from the room.

"Sorry you can't go with me tonight," called the general. "I expect rather fair sport—a big, strong black. He looks resourceful—Well, good night, Mr. Rainsford; I hope you have a good night's rest."

The bed was good, and the pajamas of the softest silk, and he was tired in every fiber of his being, but nevertheless Rainsford could not quiet his brain with the opiate of sleep. He lay, eyes wide open. Once he thought he heard stealthy steps in the corridor outside his room. He sought to throw open the door; it would not open. He went to the window and looked out. His room was high up in one of the towers. The lights of the château were out now, and it was dark and silent, but there was a fragment of sallow moon, and by its wan light he could see, dimly, the courtyard; there, weaving in and out in the pattern of shadow, were black, noiseless forms; the hounds heard him at the window and looked up, expectantly, with their green eyes. Rainsford went back to the bed and lay down. By many methods he tried to put himself to sleep. He had achieved a

32

---

14. **knouter** (nout′ ər) n.: Someone who beats criminals with a leather whip, or knout.
15. **tartar** (tär′ tər) n.: A stubborn, violent person.

16. **Folies Bergère** (fô lē ber zħär′): A musical theater in Paris.

Grammar in Action

Suspense is that quality in a work of literature that makes us read on to see what will happen next. Writers create suspense with details that arouse curiosity in the reader and details that foreshadow, or hint at, what is to come. Richard Connell begins to build suspense in the first paragraphs of "The Most Dangerous Game":

"Off there to the right—somewhere—is a large island," said Whitney. "It's rather a mystery—"

"What island is it?" Rainsford asked.

"The old charts call it 'Ship-Trap Island,'" Whitney replied. A suggestive name, isn't it? Sailors have a curious dread of the place. I don't know why. Some superstition—"

Notice that in the passage, Whitney twice brings up the mystery that surrounds the island and both times lets his thoughts trail off before he says anything specific about this mystery. Additional suspense is created by the island's name.

Connell continues to use details to build suspense. What details can you find in this passage?

[Rainsford] sought to throw open the door; it would not open. He went to the window and looked out. His room was

doze when, just as morning began to come, he heard, far off in the jungle, the faint report of a pistol.

General Zaroff did not appear until luncheon. He was dressed faultlessly in the tweeds of a country squire. He was solicitous about the state of Rainsford's health.

"As for me," sighed the general, "I do not feel so well. I am worried, Mr. Rainsford. Last night I detected traces of my old complaint."

To Rainsford's questioning glance the general said: "Ennui. Boredom."

Then, taking a second helping of crêpes suzette, the general explained: "The hunting was not good last night. The fellow lost his head. He made a straight trail that offered no problems at all. That's the trouble with these sailors; they have dull brains to begin with, and they do not know how to get about in the woods. They do excessively stupid and obvious things. It's most annoying. Will you have another glass of Chablis, Mr. Rainsford?"

"General," said Rainsford firmly, "I wish to leave this island at once."

The general raised his thickets of eyebrows; he seemed hurt. "But, my dear fellow," the general protested, "you've only just come. You've had no hunting—"

"I wish to go today," said Rainsford. He saw the dead black eyes of the general on him, studying him. General Zaroff's face suddenly brightened.

He filled Rainsford's glass with venerable Chablis from a dusty bottle.

"Tonight," said the general, "we will hunt—you and I."

Rainsford shook his head. "No, general," he said. "I will not hunt."

The general shrugged his shoulders and delicately ate a hothouse grape. "As you wish, my friend," he said. "The choice rests entirely with you. But may I not venture to suggest that you will find my idea of sport more diverting than Ivan's?"

He nodded toward the corner to where the giant stood, scowling, his thick arms crossed on his hogshead of chest.

"You don't mean—" cried Rainsford.

"My dear fellow," said the general, "have I not told you I always mean what I say about hunting? This is really an inspiration. I drink to a foeman worthy of my steel—at last."

The general raised his glass, but Rainsford sat staring at him.

"You'll find this game worth playing," the general said enthusiastically. "Your brain against mine. Your woodcraft against mine. Your strength and stamina against mine. Outdoor chess! And the stake is not without value, eh?"

"And if I win—" began Rainsford huskily.

"I'll cheerfully acknowledge myself defeated if I do not find you by midnight of the third day," said General Zaroff. "My sloop will place you on the mainland near a town."

The general read what Rainsford was thinking.

"Oh, you can trust me," said the Cossack. "I will give you my word as a gentleman and a sportsman. Of course you, in turn, must agree to say nothing of your visit here."

"I'll agree to nothing of the kind," said Rainsford.

"Oh," said the general, "in that case— But why discuss that now? Three days hence we can discuss it over a bottle of Veuve Cliquot, unless—"

The general sipped his wine.

Then a businesslike air animated him. "Ivan," he said to Rainsford, "will supply you with hunting clothes, food, a knife. I suggest you wear moccasins; they leave a poorer trail. I suggest too that you avoid the big

33

34

35

33 **Discussion** Why do you think the writer includes this detail?

34 **Discussion** How is this activity like "Outdoor chess"?

35 **Discussion** Why does General Zaroff believe Rainsford's refusal to keep silent about the island is not important enough to discuss now?

---

high up in one of the towers. The lights of the chateau were out now, and it was dark and silent, but there was a fragment of sallow moon, and by its wan light he could see, dimly, the courtyard; there, weaving in and out in the pattern of shadow, were black, noiseless forms; the hounds heard him at the window and looked up, expectantly, with their green eyes.

Note how details in the passage rule out each avenue of escape that Rainsford explores.

Student Activity 1. Find three other suspense-filled passages and copy these. Exchange papers with a partner and discuss why you chose the passages you did.

Student Activity 2. With a small group of classmates, decide on a plot and setting for a suspense-filled story. Then brainstorm a list of details that might be used to create suspense in that story. Use items from the list to help you draft the first paragraph of the story.

◆ **Software** If students are using computers, you might want them to use the **Writer's Helper** activity Brainstorms to generate ideas for their suspenseful paragraphs.

36 Reading Strategy Ask students to review Rainsford's remarks about hunting at the beginning of the story and to explain the irony of his present situation.

37 Discussion What does Rainsford mean when he says he is "in a picture with a frame of water"?

38 Critical Thinking and Reading What can you deduce about Rainsford from this passage?

swamp in the southeast corner of the island. We call it Death Swamp. There's quicksand there. One foolish fellow tried it. The deplorable part of it was that Lazarus followed him. You can imagine my feelings, Mr. Rainsford. I loved Lazarus; he was the finest hound in my pack. Well, I must beg you to excuse me now. I always take a siesta after lunch. You'll hardly have time for a nap, I fear. You'll want to start, no doubt. I shall not follow till dusk. Hunting at night is so much more exciting than by day, don't you think? Au revoir,[17] Mr. Rainsford, au revoir."

36 General Zaroff, with a deep, courtly bow, strolled from the room.

From another door came Ivan. Under one arm he carried khaki hunting clothes, a haversack of food, a leather sheath containing a long-bladed hunting knife; his right hand rested on a cocked revolver thrust in the crimson sash about his waist. . . .

Rainsford had fought his way through the bush for two hours. "I must keep my nerve. I must keep my nerve," he said through tight teeth.

He had not been entirely clear-headed when the château gates snapped shut behind him. His whole idea at first was to put distance between himself and General Zaroff, and, to this end, he had plunged along, spurred on by the sharp rowels of something very like panic. Now he had got a grip on himself, had stopped, and was taking stock of himself and the situation.

37 He saw that straight flight was futile; inevitably it would bring him face to face with the sea. He was in a picture with a frame of water, and his operations, clearly, must take place within that frame.

"I'll give him a trail to follow," muttered

---

17. au revoir (ō′ rə vwär′): French for "until we meet again."

Rainsford, and he struck off from the rude paths he had been following into the trackless wilderness. He executed a series of intricate loops; he doubled on his trail again and again, recalling all the lore of the fox hunt, and all the dodges of the fox. Night found him leg-weary, with his hands and face lashed by the branches, on a thickly wooded ridge. He knew it would be insane to blunder on through the dark, even if he had the strength. His need for rest was imperative and he thought: "I have played the fox, now I must play the cat of the fable." A big tree with a thick trunk and outspread branches was nearby, and, taking care to leave not the slightest mark, he climbed up into the crotch, and stretching out on one of the broad limbs, after a fashion, rested. Rest brought him new confidence and almost a feeling of security. Even so zealous a hunter as General Zaroff could not trace him there, he told himself; only the devil himself could follow that complicated trail through the jungle after dark. But, perhaps, the general was a devil—

An apprehensive night crawled slowly by like a wounded snake, and sleep did not visit Rainsford, although the silence of a dead world was on the jungle. Toward morning when a dingy gray was varnishing the sky, the cry of some startled bird focused Rainsford's attention in that direction. Something was coming through the bush, coming slowly, carefully, coming by the same winding way Rainsford had come. He flattened himself down on the limb, and through a screen of leaves almost as thick as tapestry, he watched. The thing that was approaching was a man.

It was General Zaroff. He made his way along with his eyes fixed in utmost concentration on the ground before him. He paused, almost beneath the tree, dropped to his knees and studied the ground. Rainsford's impulse was to hurl himself down like

THE RED CEDAR
Emily Carr
Vancouver Art Gallery

Fine art, *The Red Cedar,* Emily Carr. Carr (1871–1945), who was born in Victoria, British Columbia, was one of Canada's most gifted artists. Even as a child, Carr showed a strong desire to commit her life to art. Before she was twenty, Carr persuaded her parents to allow her to attend art school. She studied art in San Francisco, London, and Paris. Throughout her travels, Carr longed to return home. It was her homeland that provided the strongest influence in her artwork. Once home, Carr traveled to remote areas of British Columbia where she found the inspiration for some of her finest work. Here Carr painted native villages and dramatic images of the vast forests of the area, as illustrated in *The Red Cedar.*

You might use the following questions for discussion:
1. List the words that come to mind when you look at this painting.
2. Does this painting capture the mood of the story? Explain.

The Most Dangerous Game   27

39 Discussion Considering General Zaroff's behavior, do you think he is aware of Rainsford's presence?

40 Discussion Why is Rainsford filled with terror?

41 Discussion How does the comparison of the two men to a cat and mouse suggest the barbarity of the hunt?

42 Discussion How do you think Rainsford feels as he hears these words?

a panther, but he saw the general's right hand held something metallic—a small automatic pistol.

The hunter shook his head several times, as if he were puzzled. Then he straightened up and took from his case one of his black cigarettes; its pungent incense-like smoke floated up to Rainsford's nostrils.

Rainsford held his breath. The general's eyes had left the ground and were traveling inch by inch up the tree. Rainsford froze there, every muscle tensed for a spring. But the sharp eyes of the hunter stopped before they reached the limb where Rainsford lay; a smile spread over his brown face. Very deliberately he blew a smoke ring into the air; then he turned his back on the tree and walked carelessly away, back along the trail he had come. The swish of the underbrush against his hunting boots grew fainter and fainter.

The pent-up air burst hotly from Rainsford's lungs. His first thought made him feel sick and numb. The general could follow a trail through the woods at night; he could follow an extremely difficult trail; he must have uncanny powers; only by the merest chance had the Cossack failed to see his quarry.

Rainsford's second thought was even more terrible. It sent a shudder of cold horror through his whole being. Why had the general smiled? Why had he turned back?

Rainsford did not want to believe what his reason told him was true, but the truth was as evident as the sun that had by now pushed through the morning mists. The general was playing with him! The general was saving him for another day's sport! The Cossack was the cat; he was the mouse. Then it was that Rainsford knew the full meaning of terror.

"I will not lose my nerve. I will not."

He slid down from the tree, and struck off again into the woods. His face was set and he forced the machinery of his mind to function. Three hundred yards from his hiding place he stopped where a huge dead tree leaned precariously on a smaller, living one. Throwing off his sack of food, Rainsford took his knife from its sheath and began to work with all his energy.

The job was finished at last, and he threw himself down behind a fallen log a hundred feet away. He did not have to wait long. The cat was coming again to play with the mouse.

Following the trail with the sureness of a bloodhound, came General Zaroff. Nothing escaped those searching black eyes, no crushed blade of grass, no bent twig, no mark, no matter how faint, in the moss. So intent was the Cossack on his stalking that he was upon the thing Rainsford had made before he saw it. His foot touched the protruding bough that was the trigger. Even as he touched it, the general sensed his danger and leaped back with the agility of an ape. But he was not quite quick enough; the dead tree, delicately adjusted to rest on the cut living one, crashed down and struck the general a glancing blow on the shoulder as it fell; but for his alertness, he must have been smashed beneath it. He staggered, but he did not fall; nor did he drop his revolver. He stood there, rubbing his injured shoulder, and Rainsford, with fear again gripping his heart, heard the general's mocking laugh ring through the jungle.

"Rainsford," called the general, "if you are within the sound of my voice, as I suppose you are, let me congratulate you. Not many men know how to make a Malay man-catcher. Luckily, for me, I too have hunted in Malacca. You are proving interesting, Mr. Rainsford. I am going now to have my wound dressed; it's only a slight one. But I shall be back. I shall be back."

28 **Short Stories**

When the general, nursing his bruised shoulder, had gone, Rainsford took up his flight again. It was flight now, a desperate, hopeless flight, that carried him on for some hours. Dusk came, then darkness, and still he pressed on. The ground grew softer under his moccasins; the vegetation grew ranker, denser; insects bit him savagely. Then, as he stepped forward, his foot sank into the ooze. He tried to wrench it back, but the muck sucked viciously at his foot as if it were a giant leech. With a violent effort, he tore his foot loose. He knew where he was now. Death Swamp and its quicksand.

His hands were tight closed as if his nerve were something tangible that some one in the darkness was trying to tear from his grip. The softness of the earth had given him an idea. He stepped back from the quicksand a dozen feet or so, and, like some huge prehistoric beaver, he began to dig.

Rainsford had dug himself in in France[18] when a second's delay meant death. That had been a placid pastime compared to his digging now. The pit grew deeper; when it was above his shoulders, he climbed out and from some hard saplings cut stakes and sharpened them to a fine point. These stakes he planted in the bottom of the pit with the points sticking up. With flying fingers he wove a rough carpet of weeds and branches and with it he covered the mouth of the pit. Then, wet with sweat and aching with tiredness, he crouched behind the stump of a lightning-charred tree.

He knew his pursuer was coming; he heard the padding sound of feet on the soft earth, and the night breeze brought him the perfume of the general's cigarette. It seemed to Rainsford that the general was coming with unusual swiftness; he was not feeling

---

18. **dug himself in in France:** Had dug a foxhole to protect himself during World War I.

his way along, foot by foot. Rainsford, crouching there, could not see the general, nor could he see the pit. He lived a year in a minute. Then he felt an impulse to cry aloud with joy, for he heard the sharp crackle of the breaking branches as the cover of the pit gave way; he heard the sharp scream of pain as the pointed stakes found their mark. He leaped up from his place of concealment. Then he cowered back. Three feet from the pit a man was standing, with an electric torch in his hand.

"You've done well, Rainsford," the voice of the general called. "Your Burmese tiger pit has claimed one of my best dogs. Again you score. I think, Mr. Rainsford, I'll see what you can do against my whole pack. I'm going home for a rest now. Thank you for a most amusing evening."

At daybreak Rainsford, lying near the swamp, was awakened by a sound that made him know that he had new things to learn about fear. It was a distant sound, faint and wavering, but he knew it. It was the baying of a pack of hounds.

Rainsford knew he could do one of two things. He could stay where he was and wait. That was suicide. He could flee. That was postponing the inevitable. For a moment he stood there, thinking. An idea that held a wild chance came to him, and, tightening his belt, he headed away from the swamp.

The baying of the hounds drew nearer, then still nearer, nearer, ever nearer. On a ridge Rainsford climbed a tree. Down a watercourse, not a quarter of a mile away, he could see the bush moving. Straining his eyes, he saw the lean figure of General Zaroff; just ahead of him Rainsford made out another figure whose wide shoulders surged through the tall jungle weeds; it was the giant Ivan, and he seemed pulled forward by some unseen force; Rainsford knew that Ivan must be holding the pack in leash.

The Most Dangerous Game 29

43 Discussion What is Rainsford learning that he did not know when he first expressed his ideas about hunting?

44 Critical Thinking and Reading How does the author increase the suspense in the story at this point?

45 Discussion Why does Zaroff say that Rainsford "hadn't played the game"?

46 Enrichment Tell students that Marcus Aurelius believed that the world is governed by the benevolent force of Reason, and that each individual should be guided by reason and not by his or her passions. It is ironic for Zaroff to read Aurelius because the general is dominated by his passion for hunting, to the exclusion of reason. There is further irony in his admiration for Aurelius since the philosopher believed it was important for individuals to help one another.

47 Literary Focus How does the writer use the structure of the last sentence to maintain suspense until the end?

Reader's Response Would you have liked to be in Rainsford's position? Why or why not?

Thematic Response In what other ways could the conflict between Zaroff and Rainsford have been resolved?

Master Teacher Note Use the overhead projector to show students Art Transparency 1, *Evening by the Sea,* by Karl Schmidt-Rottluff. Ask students to describe the setting. Have them speculate about the identity and purpose, if any, of the man in the foreground. Also, have them explain whether he is like Rainsford in any way. Does the mood of this painting correspond to that of the story.

They would be on him any minute now. His mind worked frantically. He thought of a native trick he had learned in Uganda. He slid down the tree. He caught hold of a springy young sapling and to it he fastened his hunting knife, with the blade pointing down the trail; with a bit of wild grapevine he tied back the sapling. Then he ran for his life. The hounds raised their voices as they hit the fresh scent. Rainsford knew now how an animal at bay feels.

He had to stop to get his breath. The baying of the hounds stopped abruptly, and Rainsford's heart stopped too. They must have reached the knife.

He shinnied excitedly up a tree and looked back. His pursuers had stopped. But the hope that was in Rainsford's brain when he climbed died, for he saw in the shallow valley that General Zaroff was still on his feet. But Ivan was not. The knife, driven by the recoil of the springing tree, had not wholly failed.

"Nerve, nerve, nerve!" he panted, as he dashed along. A blue gap showed between the trees dead ahead. Ever nearer drew the hounds. Rainsford forced himself on toward that gap. He reached it. It was the shore of the sea. Across a cove he could see the gloomy gray stone of the château. Twenty feet below him the sea rumbled and hissed. Rainsford hesitated. He heard the hounds. Then he leaped far out into the sea. . . .

When the general and his pack reached the place by the sea, the Cossack stopped. For some minutes he stood regarding the blue-green expanse of water. He shrugged his shoulders. Then he sat down, took a drink of brandy from a silver flask, lit a perfumed cigarette, and hummed a bit from *Madame Butterfly.*[19]

General Zaroff had an exceedingly good dinner in his great paneled dining hall that evening. With it he had a bottle of Pol Roger and half a bottle of Chambertin. Two slight annoyances kept him from perfect enjoyment. One was the thought that it would be difficult to replace Ivan; the other was that his quarry had escaped him; of course the American hadn't played the game—so thought the general as he tasted his after-dinner liqueur. In his library he read, to soothe himself, from the works of Marcus Aurelius.[20] At ten he went up to his bedroom. He was deliciously tired, he said to himself, as he locked himself in. There was a little moonlight, so, before turning on his light, he went to the window and looked down at the courtyard. He could see the great hounds, and he called: "Better luck another time," to them. Then he switched on the light.

A man, who had been hiding in the curtains of the bed, was standing there.

"Rainsford!" screamed the general. "How in God's name did you get here?"

"Swam," said Rainsford. "I found it quicker than walking through the jungle."

The general sucked in his breath and smiled. "I congratulate you," he said. "You have won the game."

Rainsford did not smile. "I am still a beast at bay," he said, in a low, hoarse voice. "Get ready, General Zaroff."

The general made one of his deepest bows. "I see," he said. "Splendid! One of us is to furnish a repast for the hounds. The other will sleep in this very excellent bed. On guard, Rainsford. . . ."

He had never slept in a better bed, Rainsford decided.

---

19. ***Madame Butterfly:*** An opera by Giacomo Puccini.

20. **Marcus Aurelius** (ô rē′ lē əs): A Roman emperor and philosopher (121–180 A.D.).

Closure and Extension

ANSWERS TO RESPONDING TO THE SELECTION
Your Response
1. Discuss with students the idea that education should have a civilizing influence on a person. Ask if Zaroff's behavior is that of a civilized human being.

Recalling
2. The island is called by that name because ships have mysteriously disappeared near it.
3. He falls overboard from a yacht while sailing near the island, and he swims to shore.
4. Zaroff treats Rainsford as a respected equal and guest at first. Later, he is put off by Rainsford's protests and makes him the

RESPONDING TO THE SELECTION

Your Response

1. General Zaroff is an educated, cultivated man. Do you think that education served its true purpose in his case? Why or why not?

Recalling

2. Why is the island called Ship-Trap Island?
3. How does Rainsford come to the island?
4. Explain how Zaroff's treatment of Rainsford changes during the story.
5. What three tricks does Rainsford use to elude Zaroff? What is the outcome of each trick?

Interpreting

6. Why does Zaroff think of himself as "civilized"? In what ways is he "uncivilized"?
7. Compare and contrast Rainsford's attitude toward hunting with Zaroff's.
8. Why does Rainsford call himself "a beast at bay"?
9. What are two possible meanings of the title?

Applying

10. Do you think Rainsford will continue to hunt? Explain your answer.

ANALYZING LITERATURE

Understanding Plot

The **plot** of a story is a sequence of related events. It often begins with some **exposition** that provides important background information. It then presents a **conflict,** with the action rising to a **climax** and falling to a **resolution.**

Study the plot diagram below.

1. Identify the exposition and tell how it sets the scene for coming events.

2. Explain how the plot involves conflicts between two men, and between two different views of life.
3. At what point is the climax reached?
4. How are the conflicts resolved?

CRITICAL THINKING AND READING

Analyzing Sequence in a Story

A writer **sequences,** or orders, events to create a certain effect. For example, by having Rainsford learn of the mystery surrounding Ship-Trap Island at the beginning of the story, the writer creates suspense—the quality of a story that keeps you wondering and turning pages.

1. Why do you think the writer had Rainsford sit down to an elegant dinner with Zaroff before learning of the hunt?
2. Why do you think the writer had Zaroff relax and have dinner before discovering the surprise awaiting him in his room?

THINKING AND WRITING

Writing About Plot

Write a review of "The Most Dangerous Game" for a school literary magazine. Imagine that your readers have not read the story. First diagram the plot of the story. Make a list of the plot segments you particularly liked or disliked. Then write one or two paragraphs explaining why you liked or disliked the story, using the items on your list as examples. In revising, make sure you have included enough information to give your readers a sense of the story.

LEARNING OPTION

Cross-curricular Connection. Imagine that you have been commissioned to design a video game based on this story. Describe the game, give it a name, and tell how it would be played. You might even accompany your explanation with one or more sketches.

The Most Dangerous Game 31

Applying

10. Answers will differ but most students will realize that Rainsford's experience will probably change his attitude towards hunting.

ANSWERS TO ANALYZING LITERATURE

1. Suggested Response: The exposition includes the discussion between Whitney and Rainsford, the description of the island, Rainsford's fall from the boat, and his arrival on the island. It sets the scene by creating a suspenseful mood and stressing Rainsford's opinions and abilities.
2. Suggested Response: Rainsford and Zaroff fight a life-and-death battle. Also, they have different views about hunting humans. Finally, Rainsford must contend with the jungle and the sea to beat Zaroff.
3. Suggested Response: The climax is reached when Rainsford confronts Zaroff in the bedroom.
4. Suggested Response: The conflicts are resolved when Rainsford kills Zaroff.

ANSWERS TO CRITICAL THINKING AND READING

1. Suggested Response: The elegant dinner prolongs the tension.
2. Suggested Response: This delay also heightens the suspense by making us wonder about Rainsford.

THINKING AND WRITING

Writing Transparency Students often find graphic organizers helpful. To help students diagram the plot, you might want to show them the Story Map in the **Transparencies for Writing.**

LEARNING OPTION

This activity will appeal to students who enjoy using their imaginations. You may extend the activity for analytic learners by having students invent a board game. Their final product should include instructions and rules for the game.

---

quarry. During the hunt, he shows a kind of mocking respect and then disappointment as Rainsford refuses to play the game.
5. Rainsford creates a winding, difficult trail, but Zaroff finds him; Rainsford builds a Malay mancatcher trap, but the general is only slightly wounded; Rainsford

digs a Burmese tiger pit, but one of Zaroff's dogs falls into it, not the general; and Rainsford uses a hunting trick from Uganda which kills Ivan, not the general.

Interpreting

6. Suggested Response: He thinks he is civilized because he lives comfortably. He is uncivilized because he is a murderer.

7. Suggested Response: Both love hunting and, at first, Rainsford shares Zaroff's contempt for the hunted. Rainsford won't commit murder, however, while Zaroff will.
8. Suggested Response: A beast at bay is one that is cornered and has turned to defend itself, even if that means its death.
9. Suggested Response: The title refers to the general's human quarry and to the actual hunt itself.

Munro (Saki) had a strong interest in politics and often wrote about the public figures of his time. As Lewis Carroll did in *Alice in Wonderland,* he sometimes disguised these public figures as animals or other imaginative characters. Ask students why such disguise might have been necessary.

Literary Focus You many want to point out to students that the conflict is the focus of a story. The story usually moves toward a resolution of the conflict.

Prereading Focus You may wish to suggest specific scenarios to students as reasons for the dislike between the individuals. For example, one person might have quarreled with another over the result of a game or because of some annoying behavior. Suggest that people might dislike each other because of differing political views.

Vocabulary Have your **less advanced** students read these words, and when the words appear in the story, ask students to substitute a synonym for each.

Spelling Tip Point out the double *c* in *succor.* Some students may misspell this word *suckor.*

GUIDE FOR READING

Saki

(1870–1916) is the pen name of H. H. Munro, an English writer who was born in Burma, where his father was inspector general of the police force. In England Saki worked as a journalist, writing political satire and serving as a correspondent to Russia and France. Saki served in the army during World War I and was killed in France. He wrote many short stories that, like "The Interlopers," end with some surprising twists.

The Interlopers

Conflict

Most plots are built on **conflict,** or the struggle between opposing forces. An **external conflict** occurs between two or more characters or between a character and the forces of nature. An **internal conflict** occurs within a character who possesses opposing ideas or feelings. The two characters in "The Interlopers" inherited an external conflict from grandparents.

Focus

Imagine that you are stranded on a desert island with someone you have quarreled with or do not like. You would probably need this person's help and cooperation in order to survive until you are rescued, but that would mean resolving your differences with him or her. How would you go about doing this? Do you think it would be easy or difficult? Why? Make a list of things you would do or say to clear the air between yourself and this person. Trade lists with a classmate and compare strategies. Then read "The Interlopers" to find out how two lifelong enemies respond to a similar set of circumstances.

Vocabulary

Knowing the following words will help you as you read "The Interlopers."

precipitous (pri sip′ ə təs) *adj.*: Steep; sheer (p. 33)
marauders (mə rôd′ ərz) *n.*: Raiders; people who take goods by force (p. 34)
medley (med′ lē) *n.*: A mixture of things not usually found together (p. 34)

condolence (kən dō′ ləns) *n.*: An expression of sympathy with a grieving person (p. 35)
languor (laŋ′ gər) *n.*: A lack of vigor; weakness (p. 35)
succor (suk′ ər) *n.*: Aid; help; relief (p. 36)

Objectives

1 To understand conflict
2 To identify the causes and effects of conflict
3 To write about conflict
4 To express individual interests and abilities through optional activities

Support Material

Teaching Portfolio
Teacher Backup, p. 35
Grammar in Action Worksheet, *Using Participles,* p. 38
Usage and Mechanics Worksheet, p. 40
Vocabulary Check, p. 41
Analyzing Literature Worksheet, *Understanding Conflict,* p. 42

Language Worksheet, *Using Context Clues,* p. 43
Selection Test, p. 44

Prentice Hall Literature Writing Studio

The Interlopers

Saki

In a forest of mixed growth somewhere on the eastern spurs of the Carpathians,[1] a man stood one winter night watching and listening, as though he waited for some beast of the woods to come within the range of his vision, and, later, of his rifle. But the game for whose presence he kept so keen an outlook was none that figured in the sportsman's calendar as lawful and proper for the chase: Ulrich von Gradwitz[2] patrolled the dark forest in quest of a human enemy.

The forest lands of Gradwitz were of wide extent and well stocked with game; the narrow strip of precipitous woodland that lay on its outskirt was not remarkable for the game it harbored or the shooting it afforded, but it was the most jealously guarded of all its owner's territorial possessions. A famous lawsuit, in the days of his grandfather, had wrested it from the illegal possession of a neighboring family of petty landowners; the dispossessed party had never acquiesced in the judgment of the Courts, and a long series of poaching affrays[3] and similar scandals had embittered the relationships between the families for three generations. The neighbor feud had grown into a personal one since Ulrich had come to be head of his family; if there was a man in the world whom he detested and wished ill to it was Georg Znaeym,[4] the inheritor of the quarrel and the tireless game-snatcher and raider of the disputed border-forest. The feud might, perhaps, have died down or been compromised if the personal ill will of the two men had not stood in the way: as boys they had thirsted for one another's blood, as men each prayed that misfortune might fall on the other, and this wind-scourged winter night Ulrich had banded together his foresters to watch the dark forest, not in quest of four-footed quarry, but to keep a lookout for the prowling thieves whom he suspected of being afoot from across the land boundary. The roebuck,[5] which usually kept in the sheltered hollows during a storm wind, were running like driven things tonight, and there was movement and unrest among the creatures that were wont to sleep through the dark hours. Assuredly there was a disturbing element in the forest, and Ulrich could guess the quarter from whence it came.

He strayed away by himself from the watchers whom he had placed in ambush on the crest of the hill, and wandered far down the steep slopes amid the wild tangle of undergrowth, peering through the tree trunks and listening through the whistling and skirling

---

1. Carpathians (kär pā′ thē ənz): Mountains in central Europe.
2. Ulrich von Gradwitz (ool′ rik fôn gräd′ vitz)
3. poaching affrays (pōch′ iŋ ə frāz′): Disputes about hunting on someone else's property.

---

4. Georg Znaeym (gā′ ôrg znä′ im)
5. roebuck (rō′ buk′) n.: Male deer.

Making Connections Another selection that deals with a long-standing feud is *Romeo and Juliet*, by Shakespeare, page 287. You might have students compare the resolution of each of these feuds.

Thematic Focus The characters in this story are challenged to solve a conflict with each other that is due to external forces over which they have no control. Their dawning friendship is their response to the challenge. Ask students if they have ever become friends with someone because of a shared problem. Can adversity draw people together? Why or why not?

Presentation

Motivation/Prior Knowledge Ask students if they know of the Hatfields and the McCoys. If they do not, explain that these two families from Kentucky and West Virginia, engaged in a bloody, long-standing feud. Tell them that such feuds often begin with an insult or injury, real or imagined, that must be avenged. The act of vengeance then prompts a response, resulting in a never-ending cycle. Feuds appear frequently in literature. For example, a feud is central to the plot of Shakespeare's *Romeo and Juliet*. Tell students that a feud plays an important part in this story as well.

Master Teacher Note Point out to students that the forest plays an important role in this story, almost as if it were a character itself. Ask students to look for evidence of this as they read.

Purpose-Setting Question Who are "the interlopers" in the title, and why do they deserve that name?

1 Clarification The word *interloper* is made of the prefix *inter-* (between or among) and the root word *lope* (to run or leap along). The original meaning of the word is "to interfere with another's trading rights or privileges." The word has developed a more general meaning as well—"to intrude in the affairs of others."

2 Discussion The disputed land was not particularly desirable. What does this fact reveal about the families who contested its ownership for so many years?

3 Discussion What do you learn about the depth of feeling between these two men?

Fine art, *Winter in the Rockies,* Thomas Moran. Moran (1837-1926) was born in England and came to the United States with his family when he was seven. A very popular painter, he is best known for the romantic power of his portrayals of Western scenery. Moran traveled through the United States with government expeditions, for magazines, and on his own to document the landscape scientifically and artistically. Much of his work is watercolor because watercolor materials were very easy to carry while traveling and were suited to quick sketching, but Moran also painted highly detailed oils based on his sketches. *Winter in the Rockies* shows his ability to capture the details and the feeling of a landscape.

You might use these questions for discussion:
1. What is the mood in this landscape? How does the artist create the mood?
2. Does this landscape reflect the setting in "The Interlopers"? Explain.

4 Literary Focus What does the wild night foreshadow?

5 Reading Strategy Ask students to predict what will happen.

6 Discussion What is ironical about this event?

7 Critical Thinking and Reading What does the action of each man in this situation tell you about him?

WINTER IN THE ROCKIES
Thomas Moran
Three Lions

4 of the wind and the restless beating of the branches for sight or sound of the marauders. If only on this wild night, in this dark, lone spot, he might come across Georg Znaeym, man to man, with none to witness—that was the wish that was uppermost in his thoughts. And as he stepped round the trunk of a huge beech he came face to face with the man he sought.

5 The two enemies stood glaring at one another for a long silent moment. Each had a rifle in his hand, each had hate in his heart and murder uppermost in his mind. The chance had come to give full play to the passions of a lifetime. But a man who has been brought up under the code of a restraining

34   Short Stories

civilization cannot easily nerve himself to shoot down his neighbor in cold blood and without word spoken, except for an offense against his hearth and honor. And before the moment of hesitation had given way to action a deed of Nature's own violence overwhelmed them both. A fierce shriek of the storm had been answered by a splitting crash over their heads, and ere they could leap aside a mass of falling beech tree had thundered down on them. Ulrich von Gradwitz found himself stretched on the ground, one arm numb beneath him and the other held almost as helplessly in a tight tangle of forked branches, while both legs were pinned beneath the fallen mass. His heavy shooting-boots had saved his feet from being crushed to pieces, but if his fractures were not as serious as they might have been, at least it was evident that he could not move from his present position till some one came to release him. The descending twigs had slashed the skin of his face, and he had to wink away some drops of blood from his eyelashes before he could take in a general view of the disaster. At his side, so near that under ordinary circumstances he could almost have touched him, lay Georg Znaeym, alive and struggling, but obviously as helplessly pinioned down as himself. All round them lay a thick-strewn wreckage of splintered branches and broken twigs.

Relief at being alive and exasperation at his captive plight brought a strange medley of pious thank-offerings and sharp curses to Ulrich's lips. Georg, who was nearly blinded with the blood which trickled across his eyes, stopped his struggling for a moment to listen, and then gave a short, snarling laugh.

"So you're not killed, as you ought to be, but you're caught, anyway," he cried; "caught fast. Ho, what a jest, Ulrich von Gradwitz snared in his stolen forest. There's real justice for you!"

6

7

Grammar in Action

A **participle** is a verb form that can function as an adjective to modify a noun or pronoun. Present participles end in *-ing* while regular past participles end in *-ed*. The participial endings of irregular verbs can vary: *chosen,* for example, is the past participle of *choose.*

Since the same participle can serve as a verb or an adjective, you should not confuse these two functions. Here are some examples:

The wind was *whistling* through the trees. (present participle as verb)
The *whistling* wind shook the trees. (present participle as adjective)
The news had *startled* her. (past participle as verb)
Startled, she hardly knew how to react to the news. (past participle as adjective)

Because it is a verb form, a participle used as an adjective seems to show action. Writers therefore use participles to make their

And he laughed again, mockingly and savagely.

"I'm caught in my own forest land," retorted Ulrich. "When my men come to release us you will wish, perhaps, that you were in a better plight than caught poaching on a neighbor's land, shame on you."

Georg was silent for a moment; then he answered quietly:

"Are you sure that your men will find much to release? I have men, too, in the forest tonight, close behind me, and *they* will be here first and do the releasing. When they drag me out from under these branches it won't need much clumsiness on their part to roll this mass of trunk right over on the top of you. Your men will find you dead under a fallen beech tree. For form's sake I shall send my condolences to your family."

"It is a useful hint," said Ulrich fiercely. "My men had orders to follow in ten minutes' time, seven of which must have gone by already, and when they get me out—I will remember the hint. Only as you will have met your death poaching on my lands I don't think I can decently send any message of condolence to your family."

"Good," snarled Georg, "good. We fight this quarrel out to the death, you and I and our foresters, with no cursed interlopers to come between us. Death and damnation to you, Ulrich von Gradwitz."

"The same to you, Georg Znaeym, forest-thief, game-snatcher."

Both men spoke with the bitterness of possible defeat before them, for each knew that it might be long before his men would seek him out or find him; it was a bare matter of chance which party would arrive first on the scene.

Both had now given up the useless struggle to free themselves from the mass of wood that held them down; Ulrich limited his endeavors to an effort to bring his one partially free arm near enough to his outer coat pocket to draw out his wine flask. Even when he had accomplished that operation it was long before he could manage the unscrewing of the stopper or get any of the liquid down his throat. But what a heaven-sent draft it seemed! It was an open winter, and little snow had fallen as yet, hence the captives suffered less from the cold than might have been the case at that season of the year; nevertheless, the wine was warming and reviving to the wounded man, and he looked across with something like a throb of pity to where his enemy lay, just keeping the groans of pain and weariness from crossing his lips.

"Could you reach this flask if I threw it over to you?" asked Ulrich suddenly; "there is good wine in it, and one may as well be as comfortable as one can. Let us drink, even if tonight one of us dies."

"No, I can scarcely see anything; there is so much blood caked round my eyes," said Georg, "and in any case I don't drink wine with an enemy."

Ulrich was silent for a few minutes, and lay listening to the weary screeching of the wind. An idea was slowly forming and growing in his brain, an idea that gained strength every time that he looked across at the man who was fighting so grimly against pain and exhaustion. In the pain and languor that Ulrich himself was feeling the old fierce hatred seemed to be dying down.

"Neighbor," he said presently, "do as you please if your men come first. It was a fair compact. But as for me, I've changed my mind. If my men are the first to come you shall be the first to be helped, as though you were my guest. We have quarreled like devils all our lives over this stupid strip of forest, where the trees can't even stand upright in a breath of wind. Lying here tonight, thinking, I've come to think we've been rather fools; there are better things in life than

8 Discussion How does each man envision his rescue?

9 Discussion To whom is George referring when he says, ". . . with no cursed interlopers to come between us"?

10 Discussion How do Ulrich's remarks about the wine signal a change in his attitude and a possible end to the conflict?

11 Literary Focus What do you think motivates Ulrich's change of heart? Does this change reflect internal or external conflict?

descriptions more lively. The following participles, for instance, add to the drama of "The Interlopers":

A fierce shriek of the storm had been answered by a *splitting* crash over their heads, . . .
The descending twigs had slashed the skin of his face, . . .
Georg . . . then gave a short, *snarling* laugh.

Student Activity 1. Substitute an adjective for each of the participles from "The Interlopers." Explain whether the participle or the adjective creates the more vivid description.

Student Activity 2. Write five sentences of your own using participles as adjectives.

Electronic Handbook To help students understand participles, you may wish to review conjugation of verbs. You may also wish to review the punctuation of participial phrases. If students have access to the Language Master 6000, have them enter the access words *tense* and *participial* and press the GRAMMAR key to get information on conjugating verbs and on the punctuation of participial phrases.

12 Master Teacher Note Point out the reappearance of the word *interlopers* to the students. Explain that each time a writer repeats a key word, its meaning or context may change. Clarify the difference between this use of the word and its previous use. Explain that a writer may repeat a word and vary its context in much the same way as a composer will repeat and vary a melodic theme throughout a musical piece.

13 Reading Strategy Ask students to predict how the story will end.

14 Discussion How does the writer build suspense in this passage?

15 Discussion How is the last word of the story related to the title?

16 Discussion With his surprise ending, what comment does the writer seem to be making about the role of human plans and wishes? Throughout the story, the conflict is between two men, who come together at the end. What is the writer teaching us about the importance of humans in the scheme of nature?

Reader's Response Would you have acted as Ulrich did and tried to end the feud? Explain.

Thematic Response In the end of the story the conflict is resolved, but the final challenge, facing death, is not. How do you think that the two men faced this challenge?

---

getting the better of a boundary dispute. Neighbor, if you will help me to bury the old quarrel I—I will ask you to be my friend."

Georg Znaeym was silent for so long that Ulrich thought, perhaps, he had fainted with the pain of his injuries. Then he spoke slowly and in jerks.

"How the whole region would stare and gabble if we rode into the market square together. No one living can remember seeing a Znaeym and a von Gradwitz talking to one another in friendship. And what peace there would be among the forester folk if we ended our feud tonight. And if we choose to make peace among our people there is none other to interfere, no interlopers from outside. . . . You would come and keep the Sylvester night beneath my roof, and I would come and feast on some high day at your castle. . . . I would never fire a shot on your land, save when you invited me as a guest; and you should come and shoot with me down in the marshes where the wildfowl are. In all the countryside there are none that could hinder if we willed to make peace. I never thought to have wanted to do other than hate you all my life, but I think I have changed my mind about things too, this last half-hour. And you offered me your wine flask. . . . Ulrich von Gradwitz, I will be your friend."

For a space both men were silent, turning over in their minds the wonderful changes that this dramatic reconciliation would bring about. In the cold, gloomy forest, with the wind tearing in fitful gusts through the naked branches and whistling round the tree trunks, they lay and waited for the help that would now bring release and succor to both parties. And each prayed a private prayer that his men might be the first to arrive, so that he might be the first to show honorable attention to the enemy that had become a friend.

Presently, as the wind dropped for a moment, Ulrich broke silence.

"Let's shout for help," he said; "in this lull our voices may carry a little way."

"They won't carry far through the trees and undergrowth," said Georg, "but we can try. Together, then."

The two raised their voices in a prolonged hunting call.

"Together again," said Ulrich a few minutes later, after listening in vain for an answering halloo.

"I heard something that time, I think," said Ulrich.

"I heard nothing but the pestilential wind," said Georg hoarsely.

There was silence again for some minutes, and then Ulrich gave a joyful cry.

"I can see figures coming through the wood. They are following in the way I came down the hillside."

Both men raised their voices in as loud a shout as they could muster.

"They hear us! They've stopped. Now they see us. They're running down the hill toward us," cried Ulrich.

"How many of them are there?" asked Georg.

"I can't see distinctly," said Ulrich; "nine or ten."

"Then they are yours," said Georg; "I had only seven out with me."

"They are making all the speed they can, brave lads," said Ulrich gladly.

"Are they your men?" asked Georg. "Are they your men?" he repeated impatiently as Ulrich did not answer.

"No," said Ulrich with a laugh, the idiotic chattering laugh of a man unstrung with hideous fear.

"Who are they?" asked Georg quickly, straining his eyes to see what the other would gladly not have seen.

"*Wolves.*"

Closure and Extension

ANSWERS TO RESPONDING TO THE SELECTION
Your Response

1. Ask students what each character said that revealed his personality. Discuss whether students disliked both men at first and then gradually found them more sympathetic.

2. Ask students if they prefer only happy endings to stories or films. Discuss how this story might have ended happily.

Recalling

3. He is searching for poachers—specifically, his enemy Georg Znaeym.
4. The feud continued because the new generations of both families were brought up to believe that

the forest lands belonged to them. The feud has become personal because Ulrich and Georg have hated each other since they were young; they are no longer fighting because of the land dispute.

5. They hate each other. They will not shoot each other because they are both civilized men and cannot simply murder a person in cold blood.
6. They become trapped when a

RESPONDING TO THE SELECTION

Your Response

1. With whom did you sympathize, Ulrich, Georg, neither, or both? Why?
2. Were you satisfied by the story's ending? Why or why not?

Recalling

3. What is Ulrich doing in the forest?
4. What has kept the feud between the families going for three generations? How has the feud between Ulrich and Georg become personal?
5. How do Ulrich and Georg feel toward each other when they meet in the forest? Why can they not shoot each other?
6. How do they become trapped? Why does each hope that his men will come to the rescue?

Interpreting

7. Why doesn't Georg consider himself a poacher?
8. Why do you think Ulrich's and Georg's attitudes toward each other change?
9. Give two interpretations of the story's title.

Applying

10. If the two men had been saved, how would they have behaved toward each other years later?

ANALYZING LITERATURE

Understanding Conflict

A **conflict** is a struggle between opposing forces. An **external conflict** pits characters against each other or against the forces of nature. An **internal conflict** pits a character against himself or herself. For example, when Ulrich is trying to decide whether or not to share his wine with Georg, he is undergoing an internal conflict.

Find an example of each of the following types of conflict in "The Interlopers" and explain the nature of the conflict.

1. A character in conflict with another character
2. A character in conflict with nature
3. A character in conflict with himself

CRITICAL THINKING AND READING

Identifying Causes and Effects

Conflicts generally have causes. For example, the conflict between Ulrich's and Georg's grandfathers occurred because they both wanted the same piece of land. Conflicts also have effects. One effect of this conflict is that, generations later, Ulrich and Georg are enemies.

1. Identify one cause of the conflict between Ulrich and Georg and the tree.
2. Identify two effects of the conflict between Ulrich and Georg and the tree.

THINKING AND WRITING

Writing About Conflict

Imagine that you were a friend of both Ulrich's and Georg's grandfathers when the feud began. Write a brief speech directed toward one of the two men trying to bring about a reconciliation. First describe the conflict in objective, or factual, terms. Then tell what effects it will have on the participants and on their friends and family. Finally, explain your ideas for a solution.

LEARNING OPTIONS

1. **Performance.** Prepare a dramatic interpretation of the story to perform for the class. In a small group, review the story and the dialogue, and, if necessary, write additional lines for the characters. Then decide who will play the parts of Ulrich, Georg, and the narrator. Other students can be in charge of simple sets, props, costumes, and sound effects. Try to re-create the drama and tension of "The Interlopers" in your play.
2. **Cross-curricular Connection.** Interview a wildlife expert or zookeeper, or watch the movie *Never Cry Wolf* to learn more about wolves. Find out when and why wolves attack people, why they travel in packs, and how they track down their prey. Compare your findings with the information provided in the story.

Challenge Would other endings to the story have been more satisfying? Explain.

ANSWERS TO CRITICAL THINKING AND READING

1. Suggested Response: The wind is blowing violently.
2. Suggested Response: Ulrich and Georg become friends; they are unable to escape from the wolves.

THINKING AND WRITING

Writing Transparency To help students understand how to structure their persuasive speeches, you may wish to show them Model 6: Persuasive Essay in the **Transparencies for Writing.**

Alternative Assessment *Peer Review:* Have students work in groups of four to evaluate one another's stories by responding to these questions:

What description of the conflict does the writer include in the speech?

What does the writer say the effect of that conflict will be?

What ideas for reconciliation does the writer include?

How effectively does the writer communicate his or her point of view?

What, if anything, would you suggest the writer add or delete?

Have students revise their work, incorporating those suggestions they believe will enhance their speeches.

LEARNING OPTIONS

1. This activity will appeal to kinesthetic learners. If you wish, this activity may be extended for visual learners by having students write reviews of the dramatization.
2. This activity will challenge students who enjoy doing research. The activity can be extended for visual learners by having them either create drawings of wolves or find pictures of wolves in books, magazines, or encyclopedias.

---

tree falls on them. Each man wants his own men to rescue him and kill his enemy.

Interpreting

7. Suggested Response: Georg does not consider himself a poacher because he believes that he is hunting on land that belongs to him.
8. Answers may differ. Students may indicate that life-threatening situations tend to make people think more seriously about the way they conduct their lives.
9. Answers will differ but might include: Each of the men regards the other as an interloper; the wolves are interlopers.

Applying

10. Answers will differ but might depict Georg and Ulrich as best friends, or as having reverted to hating each other once they were rescued.

ANSWERS TO ANALYZING LITERATURE

1. Suggested Response: An example is the conflict between Ulrich and Georg.
2. Suggested Response: Both Ulrich and Georg are victims of the fallen tree.
3. Suggested Response: Both Ulrich and Georg experience an internal conflict as they decide whether to become friends.

Preparation

More About the Author Having turned to fiction writing as a self-imposed therapy for her work-aholic condition, Amy Tan produced memorable stories that clearly identified Chinese American women. Of the many complimentary reviews of her material, several pointed out her "ear for authentic dialogue."

Literary Focus Most students will be able to identify with the generational conflict, so ask students to find parallels between their own generational conflicts and those of Meimei's. To help students better identify with cultural conflicts, ask them to imagine how they would feel if tomorrow they were transplanted into a foreign country and expected to adapt to that culture. What problems might they encounter?

Prereading Focus The maturation process inevitably produces generational conflict. Ask students to list the typical kinds of conflicts that younger and older generations often experience. Are generational conflicts likely to differ in different cultures?

Vocabulary Have students use the vocabulary words to design a crossword puzzle, including the clues.

Electronic Handbook If your students are using the Language Master 6000, you may want them to use the electronic thesaurus to find synonyms.

Teaching to Ability Levels Less advanced students with access to the Language Master 6000 should listen to the pronunciation of the words, repeating them aloud as they listen.

Spelling Tip Remind students that the letter *g* sounds like *j* when it is followed by a vowel, as in *pungent* and *prodigy*.

GUIDE FOR READING

Amy Tan

(1952–   ) displayed promising literary talent at the age of eight, when she won a writing contest. As an adult she worked as a business writer and as a consultant to programs for disabled children before she turned to writing fiction full time. In 1985 she wrote "Rules of the Game," which later became part of her best-selling novel, *The Joy Luck Club* (1989). This novel is a set of interrelated stories about four Chinese women and their daughters in America. Tan has since written a second novel about a mother and daughter, called *The Kitchen God's Wife*.

Rules of the Game

Generational and Cultural Conflict

The plot of a short story usually grows out of a conflict, or struggle. In "Rules of the Game," the conflict is **generational,** because it takes place between a mother and her daughter. Like most daughters, Meimei wants to make her mother proud, but she also rebels against the pressure her mother puts on her. In another sense the conflict between Meimei and her mother is **cultural,** because Meimei is growing up in America and Mrs. Jong grew up in China. The differences in their backgrounds sometimes lead them to view things differently.

Focus

In "Rules of the Game," Mrs. Jong shares with her family expressions of Chinese philosophy. In the beginning of the story, she tells Meimei, "Wise guy, he not go against wind. In Chinese we say, Come from South, blow with wind—poom!—North will follow. Strongest wind cannot be seen." With a group of two or three classmates, discuss what the saying might mean. Then work independently to write a saying in your own words that expresses the same idea. When you are finished, share your version with your group or with your whole class. As you read, see whether your interpretation of this saying is close to Mrs. Jong's meaning.

Vocabulary

Knowing the following words will help you as you read "Rules of the Game."

pungent (pun′ jənt) *adj.*: Producing a sharp sensation of smell (p. 39)

benevolently (bə nev′ ə lent lē) *adv.*: In a kind and well-meaning way (p. 43)

retort (ri tôrt′) *n.*: Sharp or clever reply (p. 43)

prodigy (präd′ ə jē) *n.*: A person who is amazingly talented or intelligent (p. 44)

malodorous (mal ō′ dər əs) *adj.*: Having a bad smell (p. 45)

concessions (kən sesh′ ənz) *n.*: Things given or granted, as privileges (p. 45)

Objectives

1 To understand generational and cultural conflict
2 To infer meaning from the title
3 To write an extension of the story
4 To express individual interests and abilities through optional activities

Support Material

Teaching Portfolio
Teacher Backup, p. 47
Grammar in Action Worksheet, *Achieving Emphasis With Varied Sentence Length,* p. 51
Usage and Mechanics Worksheet, p. 53
Vocabulary Check, p. 54
Analyzing Literature Worksheet, *Appreciating Generational and Cultural Conflict,* p. 55

Critical Thinking and Reading Worksheet,
Inferring Meaning From the Title, p. 56
Selection Test, p. 57

Prentice Hall Literature Writing Studio

Audio Prose Library
Maxine Hong Kingston: Interview

Rules of the Game
from *The Joy Luck Club*
Amy Tan

1 I was six when my mother taught me the art of invisible strength. It was a strategy for winning arguments, respect from others, and eventually, though neither of us knew it at the time, chess games.

2 "Bite back your tongue," scolded my mother when I cried loudly, yanking her hand toward the store that sold bags of salted plums. At home, she said, "Wise guy, he not go against wind. In Chinese we say, Come from South, blow with wind—poom!—North will follow. Strongest wind cannot be seen."

3 The next week I bit back my tongue as we entered the store with the forbidden candies. When my mother finished her shopping, she quietly plucked a small bag of plums from the rack and put it on the counter with the rest of the items.

4 My mother imparted her daily truths so she could help my older brothers and me rise above our circumstances. We lived in San Francisco's Chinatown. Like most of the other Chinese children who played in the back alleys of restaurants and curio shops,[1] I didn't think we were poor. My bowl was always full, three five-course meals every day, beginning with a soup full of mysterious things I didn't want to know the names of.

We lived on Waverly Place, in a warm, clean, two-bedroom flat that sat above a small Chinese bakery specializing in steamed pastries and dim sum.[2] In the early morning, when the alley was still quiet, I could smell fragrant red beans as they were cooked down to a pasty sweetness. By daybreak, our flat was heavy with the odor of fried sesame balls and sweet curried chicken crescents. From my bed, I would listen as my father got ready for work, then locked the door behind him, one-two-three clicks.

5 At the end of our two-block alley was a small sandlot playground with swings and slides well-shined down the middle with use. The play area was bordered by wood-slat benches where old-country people sat cracking roasted watermelon seeds with their golden teeth and scattering the husks to an impatient gathering of gurgling pigeons. The best playground, however, was the dark alley itself. It was crammed with daily mysteries and adventures. My brothers and I would peer into the medicinal herb shop, watching old Li dole out onto a stiff sheet of white paper the right amount of insect shells, saffron-colored[3] seeds, and pungent leaves for his ailing customers. It was said that he once cured a woman dying of an ancestral curse that had eluded the best of American doctors. Next to the pharmacy was a printer who spe-

6

---

1. curio (kyoor′ ē ō′) **shops:** Shops that sell unusual or rare items.

2. dim sum (dim′ tsoom′): Shells of dough filled with meat and vegetables and served as a light meal.
3. saffron-colored (saf′ rən): Orange-yellow.

Rules of the Game 39

Presentation

Motivation/Prior Knowledge Find out if any student has visited a Chinatown in a big city, eaten Chinese food, or otherwise experienced any segment of Chinese culture. What differences did they notice between Chinese culture and their local culture? What similarities did they notice?

Thematic Focus Part of growing up is learning the unwritten, and often unspoken, rules that are part of one's culture. What rules must Meimei learn as part of her rite of passage?

Making Connections The short story "All the Years of Her Life," by Morley Callaghan, p. 57, also deals with the influence of a parent on her offspring.

Purpose-Setting Question The title "Rules of the Game" refers to several kinds of rules and more than one game. As you read, can you figure out what they are?

1 **Reading Strategy** What do you think the narrator means by "invisible strength"?

2 **Critical Thinking and Reading** What rule is Mrs. Jong imposing? How does it relate to the title of the story?

3 **Reading Strategy** What inference can you make about this detail?

4 **Literary Focus: Conflict** Why does Meimei not think they are poor, yet Mrs. Jong wants the children to rise above their circumstances?

5 **Reading Strategy** What inference can you draw about their living conditions?

6 **Reading Strategy** Visualize the setting.

Master Teacher Note Find out if any of your students play chess. Ask them to explain the game and, perhaps, demonstrate certain moves, explaining the decision-making process for those moves. If no student is able to describe and demonstrate, perhaps a member of a local chess club will share this basic information with the class.

7 **Literary Focus: Conflict** What does this detail tell you about tourists?

8 **Reading Strategy** Visualize the setting. Try to see color and motion.

9 **Literary Focus: Conflict** What conflict does Meimei experience with the American cultures?

10 **Literary Focus: Conflict** What conflict does Meimei have with her mother? What cultural conflict is apparent?

11 **Reading Strategy** What connections can you make with this scene? Have you ever been part of a similar activity?

ESL Teaching Strategy Students who have not yet mastered the language may have difficulty understanding Mrs. Jong's dialect. You may wish to ask heterogeneous groups to rewrite the dialogue in standard English.

Alternative Assessment To promote active reading, have students keep a reader's response journal as they read the story. Ask them to focus their observations on the details that reveal the generational and cultural conflict between Meimei and her mother. Encourage students to respond personally to the conflict between parents and children. What similar conflicts have they experienced?

You may use students' response journals to assess their understanding of the conflict in this story.

cialized in gold-embossed wedding invitations and festive red banners.

Farther down the street was Ping Yuen Fish Market. The front window displayed a tank crowded with doomed fish and turtles struggling to gain footing on the slimy green-tiled sides. A hand-written sign informed tourists, "Within this store, is all for food, not for pet." Inside, the butchers with their bloodstained white smocks deftly gutted the fish while customers cried out their orders and shouted, "Give me your freshest," to which the butchers always protested, " All are freshest." On less crowded market days, we would inspect the crates of live frogs and crabs which we were warned not to poke, boxes of dried cuttlefish, and row upon row of iced prawns, squid, and slippery fish. The sanddabs made me shiver each time; their eyes lay on one flattened side and reminded me of my mother's story of a careless girl who ran into a crowded street and was crushed by a cab. "Was smash flat," reported my mother.

At the corner of the alley was Hong Sing's, a four-table café with a recessed stairwell in front that led to a door marked "Tradesmen." My brothers and I believed the bad people emerged from this door at night. Tourists never went to Hong Sing's, since the menu was printed only in Chinese. A Caucasian man[4] with a big camera once posed me and my playmates in front of the restaurant. He had us move to the side of the picture window so the photo would capture the roasted duck with its head dangling from a juice-covered rope. After he took the picture, I told him he should go into Hong Sing's and eat dinner. When he smiled and asked me what they served, I shouted, "Guts and duck's feet and octopus gizzards!" Then I ran off with my friends, shrieking with laughter as we scam-

pered across the alley and hid in the entryway grotto[5] of the China Gem Company, my heart pounding with hope that he would chase us.

My mother named me after the street that we lived on: Waverly Place Jong, my official name for important American documents. But my family called me Meimei,[6] "Little Sister," I was the youngest, the only daughter. Each morning before school, my mother would twist and yank on my thick black hair until she had formed two tightly wound pigtails. One day, as she struggled to weave a hard-toothed comb through my disobedient hair, I had a sly thought.

I asked her, "Ma, what is Chinese torture?" My mother shook her head. A bobby pin was wedged between her lips. She wetted her palm and smoothed the hair above my ear, then pushed the pin in so that it nicked sharply against my scalp.

"Who say this word?" she asked without a trace of knowing how wicked I was being. I shrugged my shoulders and said, "Some boy in my class said Chinese people do Chinese torture."

"Chinese people do many things," she said simply. "Chinese people do business, do medicine, do painting. Not lazy like American people. We do torture. Best torture."

My older brother Vincent was the one who actually got the chess set. We had gone to the annual Christmas party held at the First Chinese Baptist Church at the end of the alley. The missionary ladies had put together a Santa bag of gifts donated by members of another church. None of the gifts had names on them. There were separate sacks for boys and girls of different ages.

One of the Chinese parishioners had

---

4. Caucasian (kô kā′ zhən) **man** *adj.*: A man of European ancestry.

5. entryway grotto (grät′ ō) *n.*: The entryway resembled a cave.
6. Meimei (mā′ mā′)

Grammar in Action

Skillful writers like Amy Tan **vary sentence length** to create emphasis. Often a series of long sentences will be followed by an abrupt, short sentence. Sometimes a single long sentence will be followed by a strong, short one. Consider these examples from "Rules of the Game."

At the end of our two-block alley was a small sandlot playground with swings and slides well-shined down the middle with use. [22 words] The play area was bordered by wood-slat benches where old-country people sat cracking roasted watermelon seeds with their golden teeth and scattering the husks to an impatient gathering of gurgling pigeons. [31 words] The best playground, however, was the dark alley itself. [9 words] The sanddabs made me shiver each time; their eyes lay on one flattened side and reminded me of my mother's story of a careless girl who ran into a crowded street and was crushed by a cab. [37 words] "Was smash flat," reported my mother. [6 words]

In the first example, the varied lengths emphasize the alley as a playground by first elaborating upon the setting of the "formal"

donned a Santa Claus costume and a stiff paper beard with cotton balls glued to it. I think the only children who thought he was the real thing were too young to know that Santa Claus was not Chinese. When my turn came up, the Santa man asked me how old I was. I thought it was a trick question; I was seven according to the American formula and eight by the Chinese calendar. I said I was born on March 17, 1951. That seemed to satisfy him. He then solemnly asked if I had been a very, very good girl this year and did I believe in Jesus Christ and obey my parents. I knew the only answer to that. I nodded back with equal solemnity.

Having watched the other children opening their gifts, I already knew that the big gifts were not necessarily the nicest ones. One girl my age got a large coloring book of biblical characters, while a less greedy girl who selected a small box received a glass vial of lavender toilet water. The sound of the box was also important. A ten-year-old boy had chosen a box that jangled when he shook it. It was a tin globe of the world with a slit for inserting money. He must have thought it was full of dimes and nickels, because when he saw that it had just ten pennies, his face fell with such undisguised disappointment that his mother slapped the side of his head and led him out of the church hall, apologizing to the crowd for her son who had such bad manners he couldn't appreciate such a fine gift.

As I peered into the sack, I quickly fingered the remaining presents, testing their weight, imagining what they contained. I chose a heavy, compact one that was wrapped in shiny silver foil and a red satin ribbon. It was a twelve-pack of Life Savers and I spent the rest of the party arranging and rearranging the candy tubes in the order of my favorites. My brother Winston chose wisely as well. His present turned out to be a box of intricate plastic parts; the instructions on the box proclaimed that when they were properly assembled he would have an authentic miniature replica of a World War II submarine.

Vincent got the chess set, which would have been a very decent present to get at a church Christmas party, except it was obviously used and, as we discovered later, it was missing a black pawn and a white knight. My mother graciously thanked the unknown benefactor, saying, "Too good. Cost too much." At which point, an old lady with fine white, wispy hair nodded toward our family and said with a whistling whisper, "Merry, merry Christmas."

When we got home, my mother told Vincent to throw the chess set away. "She not want it. We not want it," she said, tossing her head stiffly to the side with a tight, proud smile. My brothers had deaf ears. They were already lining up the chess pieces and reading from the dog-eared instruction book.

I watched Vincent and Winston play during Christmas week. The chess board seemed to hold elaborate secrets waiting to be untangled. The chessmen were more powerful than Old Li's magic herbs that cured ancestral curses. And my brothers wore such serious faces that I was sure something was at stake that was greater than avoiding the tradesmen's door to Hong Sing's.

"Let me! Let me!" I begged between games when one brother or the other would sit back with a deep sigh of relief and victory, the other annoyed, unable to let go of the outcome. Vincent at first refused to let me play, but when I offered my Life Savers as replacements for the buttons that filled in for the missing pieces, he relented. He chose the flavors: wild cherry for the black pawn and peppermint for the white knight. Winner could eat both.

---

12 Literary Focus: Conflict What inference can you make about Chinese culture and Christmas?

13 Reading Strategy What inference can you make about Meimei as a result of this response?

14 Discussion Do you think she is truthful?

15 Discussion What reaction do you have to Meimei's obvious pleasure in receiving the Life Savers?

16 Literary Focus: Generational and Cultural Conflict Although Mrs. Jong is properly polite, she seems to resent the chess set. Why? What does this say about her culture?

17 Critical Thinking and Reading How does this detail connect with the title?

18 Discussion Why does Meimei see the chess board in this way?

19 Reading Strategy What inference can you draw from this detail?

---

playground and then flatly stating that the alley is best. In the second example, the varied lengths create emphasis by building details about the fish, comparing it to the girl, emphasizing the flatness in the final sentence.

Student Activity 1. Search "Rules of the Game" to find five more examples of varied sentence lengths that create emphasis. How many words are in each sentence? What kind of emphasis does the sentence variety create?

Student Activity 2. Write a paragraph in which you describe an imaginary chess match for Meimei. Vary your sentence lengths to create emphasis.

◆ **Software** If students have access to computers, use the **Writer's Helper** revising tool Sentence Lengths to quickly measure and graph the length of every sentence in students' paragraphs.

20 Critical Thinking and Reading How does this detail relate to the title?

21 Critical Thinking and Reading What further connection can you make with the meaning of the story's title?

22 Discussion What parallels does Mrs. Jong draw between chess and life?

23 Reading Strategy What does this detail tell you about Meimei? Why do you think she sees the game in this way?

24 Reading Strategy Compare this sentence with the first paragraph. Have you changed your mind about what the invisible strength is?

25 Critical Thinking and Reading Why does Meimei enjoy a game of power, of secrets? How does that interpretation affect the message in the title?

26 Discussion What does this mean?

Multicultural Focus The game of chess has intrigued and challenged players across cultures and over many centuries. Though its precise beginning is shrouded in mystery, chess is believed to have evolved from a game first played in India in the sixth century A.D. The pastime was known as *chaturanga*, a name that referred to the four parts of an army in that time: elephants, horses, chariots, and foot soldiers. The game spread to neighboring Persia, where, according to legend, it was introduced by an envoy from India who challenged the ruling shah to solve and play the game. He did—with the help of a wise man. The modern word chess comes from the Persian word *shah*, which means "king."

After Arab invaders conquered Persia in the seventh century, they introduced chess in the lands they captured around the Mediterranean Sea. In Europe during medieval times, chess blossomed into a social mixer, affording knights and ladies the chance to meet over a game. Later in the eighteenth and nineteenth centuries, the game flourished in fashionable coffee houses, where writers and artists came to play and match wits.

As our mother sprinkled flour and rolled out small doughy circles for the steamed dumplings that would be our dinner that night, Vincent explained the rules, pointing to each piece. "You have sixteen pieces and so do I. One king and queen, two bishops, two knights, two castles, and eight pawns. The pawns can only move forward one step, except on the first move. Then they can move two. But they can only take men by moving crossways like this, except in the beginning, when you can move ahead and take another pawn."

"Why?" I asked as I moved my pawn. "Why can't they move more steps?"

"Because they're pawns," he said.

"But why do they go crossways to take other men. Why aren't there any women and children?"

"Why is the sky blue? Why must you always ask stupid questions?" asked Vincent. "This is a game. These are the rules. I didn't make them up. See. Here. In the book." He jabbed a page with a pawn in his hand. "Pawn. P-A-W-N. Pawn. Read it yourself."

My mother patted the flour off her hands. "Let me see book," she said quietly. She scanned the pages quickly, not reading the foreign English symbols, seeming to search deliberately for nothing in particular.

"This American rules," she concluded at last. "Every time people come out from foreign country, must know rules. You not know, judge say, Too bad, go back. They not telling you why so you can use their way go forward. They say, Don't know why, you find out yourself. But they knowing all the time. Better you take it, find out why yourself." She tossed her head back with a satisfied smile.

I found out about all the whys later. I read the rules and looked up all the big words in a dictionary. I borrowed books from the Chinatown library. I studied each chess piece, trying to absorb the power each contained.

I learned about opening moves and why it's important to control the center early on; the shortest distance between two points is straight down the middle. I learned about the middle game and why tactics between two adversaries are like clashing ideas; the one who plays better has the clearest plans for both attacking and getting out of traps. I learned why it is essential in the endgame[7] to have foresight, a mathematical understanding of all possible moves, and patience; all weaknesses and advantages become evident to a strong adversary and are obscured to a tiring opponent. I discovered that for the whole game one must gather invisible strengths and see the endgame before the game begins.

I also found out why I should never reveal "why" to others. A little knowledge withheld is a great advantage one should store for future use. That is the power of chess. It is a game of secrets in which one must show and never tell.

I loved the secrets I found within the sixty-four black and white squares. I carefully drew a handmade chessboard and pinned it to the wall next to my bed, where at night I would stare for hours at imaginary battles. Soon I no longer lost any games or Life Savers, but I lost my adversaries. Winston and Vincent decided they were more interested in roaming the streets after school in their Hopalong Cassidy[8] cowboy hats.

On a cold spring afternoon, while walking home from school, I detoured through the playground at the end of our alley. I saw a group of old men, two seated across a folding table playing a game of chess, others smok-

---

7. endgame (end′ gām′): The final stage of a chess game in which each player has only a few pieces left on the board.
8. Hopalong Cassidy: A character in cowboy movies during the 1950's.

Over the years its intense tournaments have been dominated by brilliantly masterful players of the former Soviet Union.

Suggest that students find out about some leading chess players of the past: Jose Raoul Capablanca, the Cuban prodigy who held the world's chess championship from 1921 to 1927; the American prodigy Bobby Fischer; and the formidable masters of the former Soviet Union.

Today the broad appeal of chess is manifested by its global acceptance and its many local variations. In the East, Chinese chess and Japanese chess both use boards, pieces, and rules that, though similar, are different from those that evolved in the West.

Official worldwide chess competition, however, is governed by the strict rules of the International Chess Federation.

CHESS MATES, 1992
Pamela Chin Lee
Courtesy of the Artist

ing pipes, eating peanuts, and watching. I ran home and grabbed Vincent's chess set, which was bound in a cardboard box with rubber bands. I also carefully selected two prized rolls of Life Savers. I came back to the park and approached a man who was observing the game.

"Want to play?" I asked him. His face widened with surprise and he grinned as he looked at the box under my arm.

27

"Little sister, been a long time since I play with dolls," he said, smiling benevolently. I quickly put the box down next to him on the bench and displayed my retort.

Lau Po, as he allowed me to call him, turned out to be a much better player than my brothers. I lost many games and many

Life Savers. But over the weeks, with each diminishing roll of candies, I added new secrets. Lau Po gave me the names. The Double Attack from the East and West Shores. Throwing Stones on the Drowning Man. The Sudden Meeting of the Clan. The Surprise from the Sleeping Guard. The Humble Servant Who Kills the King. Sand in the Eyes of Advancing Forces. A Double Killing Without Blood.

28

There were also the fine points of chess etiquette. Keep captured men in neat rows, as well-tended prisoners. Never announce "Check" with vanity, lest someone with an unseen sword slit your throat. Never hurl pieces into the sandbox after you have lost a game, because then you must find them again, by yourself, after apologizing to all around you. By the end of the summer, Lau Po had taught me all he knew, and I had become a better chess player.

29

A small weekend crowd of Chinese people and tourists would gather as I played and defeated my opponents one by one. My mother would join the crowds during these outdoor exhibition games. She sat proudly on the bench, telling my admirers with proper Chinese humility, "Is luck."

30

A man who watched me play in the park suggested that my mother allow me to play in local chess tournaments. My mother smiled graciously, an answer that meant nothing. I desperately wanted to go, but I bit back my tongue. I knew she would not let me play among strangers. So as we walked home I said in a small voice that I didn't want to play in the local tournament. They would have

31

32

Rules of the Game 43

27 Discussion What does the man think?

28 Critical Thinking and Reading How does this reference to the rules affect the interpretation of the story's title?

29 Critical Thinking and Reading She learns more and more rules about chess. What parallel can you draw between her experience and life?

30 Reading Strategy What inferences can you draw about the culture?

31 Critical Thinking and Reading What rule is Meimei following? How does that relate to the title?

32 Discussion Why does Meimei say this when it isn't true?

Humanities Note

Fine art, *Chess Mates*, 1992, Pamela Chin. Painter and illustrator Pamela Chin Lee was born in Kingston, Jamaica, in 1953. She earned a Bachelor of Fine Arts degree from the Rhode Island School of Design and now lives in New York City.

Pamela Chin has painted *Chess Mates* in a brightly colored and patterned style that could be described as neo-impressionistic. The figures in the foreground are shown in simple but clear detail while the background is a profusion of patchy color indicating sunlit parkland. The solid mass created by the figures in the foreground offsets the rhythmic patterns of the chess board and the background. The young girl, intent on unlocking the secrets of the game, leans forward to make her move. Her features are sensitively portrayed and convey her concentration. The arc formed by her arm draws the eye to the chessboard, which is the center of interest. Pamela Chin Lee's narrative paintings of the Chinese American community are a delightful insight into one of the diverse parts of American life.

Consider using these questions for discussion:

1. How would you describe the expression of the man in this painting?
2. Who do you think is winning this game?
3. What "rules" can you see in effect in this painting?

33 Reading Strategy What inference can you draw about the culture?

34 Discussion What does Mrs. Jong mean?

35 Discussion What happened that Meimei is playing in a tournament? Why did her mother agree?

36 Discussion How does this explain the first and second paragraphs?

37 Reading Strategy What inference can you make about Mrs. Jong?

38 Literary Focus: Conflict Why couldn't Meimei say anything?

39 Critical Thinking and Reading Why are some American rules acceptable? How does this detail add further meaning to the title?

American rules. If I lost, I would bring shame on my family.

"Is shame you fall down nobody push you," said my mother.

During my first tournament, my mother sat with me in the front row as I waited for my turn. I frequently bounced my legs to unstick them from the cold metal seat of the folding chair. When my name was called, I leapt up. My mother unwrapped something in her lap. It was her *chang*,[9] a small tablet of red jade which held the sun's fire. "Is luck," she whispered, and tucked it into my dress pocket. I turned to my opponent, a fifteen-year-old boy from Oakland. He looked at me, wrinkling his nose.

As I began to play, the boy disappeared, the color ran out of the room, and I saw only my white pieces and his black ones waiting on the other side. A light wind began blowing past my ears. It whispered secrets only I could hear.

"Blow from the South," it murmured. "The wind leaves no trail." I saw a clear path, the traps to avoid. The crowd rustled. "Shhh! Shhh!" said the corners of the room. The wind blew stronger. "Throw sand from the East to distract him." The knight came forward ready for the sacrifice. The wind hissed, louder and louder. "Blow, blow, blow. He cannot see. He is blind now. Make him lean away from the wind so he is easier to knock down."

"Check," I said, as the wind roared with laughter. The wind died down to little puffs, my own breath.

My mother placed my first trophy next to a new plastic chess set that the neighborhood Tao society[10] had given to me. As she wiped each piece with a soft cloth, she said, "Next time win more, lose less."

"Ma, it's not how many pieces you lose," I said. "Sometimes you need to lose pieces to get ahead."

"Better to lose less, see if you really need."

At the next tournament, I won again, but it was my mother who wore the triumphant grin.

"Lost eight piece this time. Last time was eleven. What I tell you? Better off lose less!" I was annoyed, but I couldn't say anything.

I attended more tournaments, each one farther away from home. I won all games, in all divisions. The Chinese bakery downstairs from our flat displayed my growing collection of trophies in its window, amidst the dust-covered cakes that were never picked up. The day after I won an important regional tournament, the window encased a fresh sheet cake with whipped-cream frosting and red script saying, "Congratulations, Waverly Jong, Chinatown Chess Champion." Soon after that, a flower shop, headstone engraver, and funeral parlor offered to sponsor me in national tournaments. That's when my mother decided I no longer had to do the dishes. Winston and Vincent had to do my chores.

"Why does she get to play and we do all the work," complained Vincent.

"Is new American rules," said my mother. "Meimei play, squeeze all her brains out for win chess. You play, worth squeeze towel."

By my ninth birthday, I was a national chess champion. I was still some 429 points away from grand-master status, but I was touted as the Great American Hope, a child prodigy and a girl to boot. They ran a photo of me in *Life* magazine next to a quote in which Bobby Fischer[11] said, "There will never be a

---

9. *chang* (chän)
10. Tao (dou) society: A group of people who believe in Taoism, a Chinese religion that stresses simplicity and unselfishness.

---

11. Bobby Fischer: Born in 1943, this American chess prodigy attained the high rank of grand master in 1958.

44   Short Stories

Primary Source

"Rules of the Game" is one of sixteen interconnected stories that make up Amy Tan's best-selling novel *The Joy Luck Club.* According to *Contemporary Literary Criticism,* the stories are told by four immigrants from China and their four American-born daughters. . . . [The novel] illuminates the nature of mother-daughter relationships in both cultures. The theme of Tan's novel is the impact of past generations on the present, and the structure, in which the daughters' eight stories are enveloped by those of the mothers, implies that the older generation may hold a key to resolving the problems of the young. Critics praised Tan's striking metaphors, her wry wit, and her avoidance of sentimentality. The diverse voices related in *The Joy Luck Club* demonstrate Tan's ability to capture both the fractured English of Chinese immigrants and the abrupt, colloquial English of the Americanized daughters.

Student Activity. Write an essay in which you describe the mother-daughter relationship as it is revealed in "Rules of the Game." Try to present both sides of the relationship.

woman grand master." "Your move, Bobby," said the caption.

The day they took the magazine picture I wore neatly plaited braids clipped with plastic barrettes trimmed with rhinestones. I was playing in a large high school auditorium that echoed with phlegmy coughs and the squeaky rubber knobs of chair legs sliding across freshly waxed wooden floors. Seated across from me was an American man, about the same age as Lau Po, maybe fifty. I remember that his sweaty brow seemed to weep at my every move. He wore a dark, malodorous suit. One of his pockets was stuffed with a great white kerchief on which he wiped his palm before sweeping his hand over the chosen chess piece with great flourish.

In my crisp pink-and-white dress with scratchy lace at the neck, one of two my mother had sewn for these special occasions, I would clasp my hands under my chin, the delicate points of my elbows poised lightly on the table in the manner my mother had shown me for posing for the press. I would swing my patent leather shoes back and forth like an impatient child riding on a school bus. Then I would pause, suck in my lips, twirl my chosen piece in midair as if undecided, and then firmly plant it in its new threatening place, with a triumphant smile thrown back at my opponent for good measure.

I no longer played in the alley of Waverly Place. I never visited the playground where the pigeons and old men gathered. I went to school, then directly home to learn new chess secrets, cleverly concealed advantages, more escape routes.

But I found it difficult to concentrate at home. My mother had a habit of standing over me while I plotted out my games. I think she thought of herself as my protective ally. Her lips would be sealed tight, and after each move I made, a soft "Hmmmmph" would escape from her nose.

"Ma, I can't practice when you stand there like that," I said one day. She retreated to the kitchen and made loud noises with the pots and pans. When the crashing stopped, I could see out of the corner of my eye that she was standing in the doorway. "Hmmmmph!" Only this one came out of her tight throat.

My parents made many concessions to allow me to practice. One time I complained that the bedroom I shared was so noisy that I couldn't think. Thereafter, my brothers slept in a bed in the living room facing the street. I said I couldn't finish my rice; my head didn't work right when my stomach was too full. I left the table with half-finished bowls and nobody complained. But there was one duty I couldn't avoid. I had to accompany my mother on Saturday market days when I had no tournament to play. My mother would proudly walk with me, visiting many shops, buying very little. "This my daughter Wave-ly Jong," she said to whoever looked her way.

One day, after we left a shop I said under my breath, "I wish you wouldn't do that, telling everybody I'm your daughter." My mother stopped walking. Crowds of people with heavy bags pushed past us on the sidewalk, bumping into first one shoulder, then another.

"Aiii-ya. So shame be with mother?" She grasped my hand even tighter as she glared at me.

I looked down. "It's not that, it's just so obvious. It's just so embarrassing."

"Embarrass you be my daughter?" Her voice was cracking with anger.

"That's not what I meant. That's not what I said."

"What you say?"

I knew it was a mistake to say anything more, but I heard my voice speaking. "Why do you have to use me to show off? If you want to

Rules of the Game 45

Audiocassette You might wish to explore the Chinese American culture further through the **Audio Prose Library** interview with Maxine Hong Kingston, another Chinese American writer. Students might compare Amy Tan with Maxine Hong Kingston.

40 Reading Strategy What can you predict at this point?

41 Reading Strategy Visualize the setting and the activity.

42 Literary Focus: Conflict Why does Mrs. Jong hover? Why is her throat tight when she returns?

43 Critical Thinking and Reading How does this detail add meaning to the story's title?

44 Literary Focus: Conflict What is the underlying cause of this serious generational conflict?

Cooperative Learning If some students have difficulty reading this long selection, divide the class into groups of five. Then divide the selection into five approximately equal parts. Assign each part to one person in each group. After each student reads his or her assigned part, have each group of experts meet— i.e., all the students who read part one meet, those who read part two meet, etc. After each panel of experts clarifies with each other the contents of that part of the story, they return to their original groups to "teach" their peers about their respective parts. Evaluate by using the selection test for everyone.

Speaking and Listening Have pairs of students imagine that they are two of the characters in the story: Meimei and her mother, her two brothers, Meimei and a brother, Meimei's parents, etc. Tell students to imagine a conversation the characters might have that gives added background to the story. Students should list the kinds of things they might talk about, and then role-play in front of the class or in front of smaller groups. Ask listeners to respond with at least one question about each character played.

45 **Reading Strategy** How does this detail relate to the first and second paragraphs of the story?

46 **Discussion** Why do the alleys contain no escape routes? Are the escape routes literal or figurative?

47 **Discussion** How can smoke be cold? Why does the author use this description?

48 **Discussion** What is the significance of this simile?

49 **Discussion** What does Mrs. Jong's comment mean?

50 **Discussion** Who is described here?

51 **Discussion** In her imagination, what is happening to Meimei? Who is her opponent in this unrealistic game? Why does she blow away?

Reader's Response What should Meimei's next move be?

Thematic Response How are Meimei's rites of passage similar to ones you have experienced? How are they different?

Challenge What generational conflicts does Meimei confront? Does she have more conflicts with certain members of the older generation than with others? Explain.

---

show off, then why don't you learn to play chess."

My mother's eyes turned into dangerous black slits. She had no words for me, just sharp silence.

I felt the wind rushing around my hot ears. I jerked my hand out of my mother's tight grasp and spun around, knocking into an old woman. Her bag of groceries spilled to the ground.

"Aii-ya! Stupid girl!" my mother and the woman cried. Oranges and tin cans careened down the sidewalk. As my mother stooped to help the old woman pick up the escaping food, I took off.

I raced down the street, dashing between people, not looking back as my mother screamed shrilly, "Meimei! Meimei!" I fled down an alley, past dark curtained shops and merchants washing the grime off their windows. I sped into the sunlight, into a large street crowded with tourists examining trinkets and souvenirs. I ducked into another dark alley, down another street, up another alley. I ran until it hurt and I realized I had nowhere to go, that I was not running from anything. The alleys contained no escape routes.

My breath came out like angry smoke. It was cold. I sat down on an upturned plastic pail next to a stack of empty boxes, cupping my chin with my hands, thinking hard. I imagined my mother, first walking briskly down one street or another looking for me, then giving up and returning home to await my arrival. After two hours, I stood up on creaking legs and slowly walked home.

The alley was quiet and I could see the yellow lights shining from our flat like two tiger's eyes in the night. I climbed the sixteen steps to the door, advancing quietly up each so as not to make any warning sounds. I turned the knob; the door was locked. I heard

a chair moving, quick steps, the locks turning—click! click! click!—and then the door opened.

"About time you got home," said Vincent. "Boy, are you in trouble."

He slid back to the dinner table. On a platter were the remains of a large fish, its fleshy head still connected to bones swimming upstream in vain escape. Standing there waiting for my punishment, I heard my mother speak in a dry voice.

"We not concerning this girl. This girl not have concerning for us."

Nobody looked at me. Bone chopsticks[12] clinked against the insides of bowls being emptied into hungry mouths.

I walked into my room, closed the door, and lay down on my bed. The room was dark, the ceiling filled with shadows from the dinnertime lights of neighboring flats.

In my head, I saw a chessboard with sixty-four black and white squares. Opposite me was my opponent, two angry black slits. She wore a triumphant smile. "Strongest wind cannot be seen," she said.

Her black men advanced across the plane, slowly marching to each successive level as a single unit. My white pieces screamed as they scurried and fell off the board one by one. As her men drew closer to my edge, I felt myself growing light. I rose up into the air and flew out the window. Higher and higher, above the alley, over the tops of tiled roofs, where I was gathered up by the wind and pushed up toward the night sky until everything below me disappeared and I was alone.

I closed my eyes and pondered my next move.

---

12. chopsticks (chäp′ stiks′): Two small sticks of wood, bone, or ivory, held together in one hand and used as utensils for eating, cooking, and serving food.

Closure and Extension

ANSWERS TO RESPONDING TO THE SELECTION
Your Response

1. Students who believe that the effort was worth the price may suggest that Meimei has taken a great step toward rising above her circumstances. Those who believe otherwise may suggest that Meimei would be better off preparing for a future job market.

2. Students who think Meimei's anger is justified may say that the mother knows nothing about chess and therefore should not hover or offer advice about the game. Also, to be shown off to strangers in public is demeaning. Students who criticize Meimei's anger may say that the mother is justifiably proud of her daughter, for the daughter's success is also her success.

Recalling

3. Meimei does not see the family as poor and finds the neighborhood a source of adventure.

4. She learns the formal rules from books; she learns strategic moves from Lau Po.

Interpreting

5. Suggested Response: She maintains silence in order to get a bag of plums.

6. Suggested Response: They are

RESPONDING TO THE SELECTION

Your Response

1. Do you feel that Meimei's anger toward her mother was justified? Why or why not?

Recalling

2. Meimei learns different aspects of the game of chess from different sources. What does she learn from books? What does she learn from Lau Po?

Interpreting

3. How does Meimei show that she understands the use of strategy even before she starts playing chess?
4. How are Meimei and her mother alike? How are they different?
5. In what ways is chess more than just a game in this story?

Applying

6. Referring to chess, Meimei says that "for the whole game one must gather invisible strengths and see the endgame before the game begins." In what other more general situations does this idea apply? Explain.

ANALYZING LITERATURE

Understanding Generational and Cultural Conflict

Generational conflict exists when beliefs and values change from one generation to another. The "generation gap" becomes even wider, however, when parents have a **cultural** background that is different from the one in which they are raising their children.

1. Scanning the chess rule book, Mrs. Jong says, "This American rules. . . . Every time people come out from foreign country, must know rules."
   a. What does Mrs. Jong mean by "American rules" in this statement?
   b. Why is Meimei in a better position to understand "American rules" than her mother?

2. What does Mrs. Jong want for her daughter that she doesn't have herself?
3. What does Meimei resent about her mother's behavior when they are shopping together?

CRITICAL THINKING AND READING

Inferring Meaning From the Title

The title often provides clues to a story's meaning. When you recognize details in a story that refer to the title, stop and think: What ideas are common to the details and the title? How do these ideas relate to the story as a whole?

1. Review "Rules of the Game" to find references to rules and games. Is there more than one type of game in the story? Explain.
2. Mrs. Jong gives Meimei rules of behavior in the form of Chinese sayings. How does Meimei use these rules to win at chess? How does she use them in her struggle with her mother?
3. Why do you think Amy Tan chose this title?

THINKING AND WRITING

Extending the Story

Write an extension of "Rules of the Game "that tells what happens the next day in the Jong household. Explain how Meimei and her mother behave toward each other. Include their dialogue. Share your draft with a classmate for helpful comments.

LEARNING OPTIONS

1. **Art.** Design your own chess set. You can draw or paint your design, or use modeling clay to sculpt your chess set. Label each piece.
2. **Cross-curricular Connection.** Work with a partner to invent a game with its own rules. Begin by brainstorming about favorite games. What features would you like your game to include? Once you decide how your game is played, make a model of it with your partner. When you are finished, teach your game to your classmates and have a class tournament.

Rules of the Game 47

---

differ in that Meimei is becoming Americanized; her mother is not.
5. Suggested Response: It is the symbol of the maturation process for Meimei, learning the rules of life.

Applying

6. Suggested Response: It applies to life planning, for in order to attain a goal—a successful ca-

reer, for instance—one must understand all that goes into it: education, work, social skills, whatever.

ANSWERS TO ANALYZING LITERATURE

Suggested Responses:

1. a. Because the rules are written in English, which she cannot read, she calls them "American rules."

b. Meimei was born in the United States and has learned American culture at school and in the streets. Her mother, reared in China, makes no effort to leave Chinatown or to have contact with American culture.
2. Mrs. Jong wants her daughter to rise above their circumstances, to have knowledge and wealth.
3. Meimei resents her mother's "showing her off" to strangers in the street.

ANSWERS TO CRITICAL THINKING AND READING

Suggested Responses:

1. Yes. There is the game of chess and the game of growing up, of learning what is and is not accepted behavior for a proper Chinese girl.
2. Meimei uses the rules as personal mottos for concentration. With her mother, she bites her tongue or minimizes the importance of things in order to give her mother the feeling that she is in control of her daughter and also to get what she herself wants.
3. She chose the title to draw a parallel between Meimei's struggle for success in playing chess and in moving through rites of passage to learn "rules" of social and family interaction.

THINKING AND WRITING

Writing Transparency Before students write, you may want to use the Paragraph Exercise for Transitions to model kinds of connectors that students can use in their story extensions. This exercise is in **Transparencies for Writing.**

Software For students working at computers, you may want to suggest that they use the **Writer's Helper** revising tools to help them to maintain a style similar to Tan's as they extend the story. To do so, enter segments of "Rules of the Game," run the revising summaries, and compare the summaries with those run on the students' work.

Publishing Student Writing When students have finished their story extensions, have them share their work with groups of four or five. Then ask each group to select one extension they want to share with the entire class.

LEARNING OPTIONS

1. This option will appeal particularly to artistic students.
2. This activity will help visual and kinesthetic learners appreciate Meimei's character.

47

Stockton's writing is said to reflect his unusual and witty personality. Ask students whether they think an author's writing usually reflects his or her personality.

Literary Focus Discuss with students the expression "on the horns of a dilemma." The "horns" are the two equally positive or equally negative choices that create the dilemma. Sometimes a dilemma can be solved by a compromise. Tell students that in this story, however, the king's justice does not allow for such a solution.

Prereading Focus Suggest to students that their dilemmas might involve issues that are difficult to resolve, such as the need to protect both the environment and people's need for natural resources. Point out that many political questions pose dilemmas for those who must solve them.

Vocabulary You might want to ask **more advanced** students to look up the etymologies of the vocabulary words.

Spelling Tip Point out the *or* ending in *ardor*. Some students may misspell this word *arder*.

GUIDE FOR READING

Frank R. Stockton

(1834–1902) was born in Philadelphia, the third of nine children. An ancestor, Richard Stockton, was one of the signers of the Declaration of Independence. Stockton was an engraver by trade, but he spent much of his time writing stories. His earliest stories were for children, but later he began writing for adults. "The Lady or the Tiger?" is Stockton's best-known work. When it was published in 1882, it caused much excitement as readers debated what the ending should be.

The Lady or the Tiger?

Dilemma

A **dilemma** is a situation in which a person must choose between two equal alternatives. There is no objective way to determine that one alternative is better than the other. Most often, the word *dilemma* is used in regard to situations in which both alternatives are equally unpleasant. You can learn something about the characters in stories by seeing how they react to dilemmas. For example, when the princess is faced with a dilemma in "The Lady or the Tiger?" the choice she makes depends upon the kind of person she is.

Focus

In a group brainstorm to think of a difficult dilemma. For ideas think of news stories you have read or viewed on television, books you have read, and movies you have seen. Once you have chosen a dilemma, discuss the pros and cons of both alternatives in the dilemma. Then arrange yourselves into two teams, one for each alternative. Have a member from each team present the dilemma and explain why his or her alternative is a better solution. Then, as you read, see how the dilemma you chose compares to the one in the story.

Vocabulary

Knowing the following words will help you as you read "The Lady or the Tiger?"

exuberant (ig zōō′ bər ənt) *adj.*: Very great; extreme (p. 49)
bland (bland) *adv.*: Pleasantly smooth; agreeable (p. 49)
dire (dīr) *adv.*: Dreadful; terrible (p. 50)
retribution (ret′ rə byōō′ shən) *n.*: Deserved punishment (p. 60)
fervent (fur′ vənt) *adj.*: Burning; passionate (p. 51)

imperious (im pir′ ē əs) *adj.*: Overbearing; arrogant; domineering (p. 51)
ardor (är′ dər) *n.*: Emotional warmth; passion (p. 51)
aesthetic (es thet′ ik) *adj.*: Sensitive to art and beauty (p. 51)

Objectives

1 To analyze a dilemma
2 To analyze solutions
3 To write an ending to a story
4 To express individual interests and abilities through optional activities

Support Material

Teaching Portfolio
Teacher Backup, p. 59
Grammar in Action Worksheet, *Varying Sentence Length*, p. 63
Usage and Mechanics Worksheet, p. 65
Vocabulary Check, p. 66
Critical Thinking and Reading Worksheet, *Analyzing Solutions*, p. 68

Language Worksheet, *Using Context Clues*, p. 69
Selection Test, p. 70

Prentice Hall Literature Writing Studio

The Lady or the Tiger?

Frank R. Stockton

In the very olden time, there lived a semi-barbaric king, whose ideas, though somewhat polished, were still large, florid, and untrammeled,[1] as became the half of him which was barbaric. He was a man of exuberant fancy, and of an authority so irresistible that, at his will, he turned his varied fancies into facts. He was greatly given to self-communing, and when he and himself agreed upon anything, the thing was done. When every member of his domestic and political systems moved smoothly, his nature was bland and genial; but whenever there was a little hitch, he was blander and more genial still, for nothing pleased him so much as to make the crooked straight, and crush down uneven places.

Among the borrowed notions by which his barbarism had become modified was that of the public arena, in which, by exhibitions of manly and beastly valor, the minds of his subjects were refined and cultured.

But even here the exuberant and barbaric fancy asserted itself. The arena of the king was built to widen and develop the mental energies of the people. This vast amphitheater[2] with its encircling galleries, its mysterious vaults, and its unseen passages, was an agent of poetic justice, in which crime was punished, or virtue rewarded, by the decrees of an impartial and incorruptible chance.

When a subject was accused of a crime of sufficient importance to interest the king, public notice was given that on an appointed day the fate of the accused person would be decided in the king's arena. And this structure well deserved that name: for, although its form and plan were borrowed from afar, its purpose emanated[3] solely from the brain of this man.

When all the people had assembled in the galleries, and the king, surrounded by his court, sat high up on his throne of royal state on one side of the arena, he gave a signal, a door beneath him opened, and the accused subject stepped out into the amphitheater. Directly opposite him, on the other side of the enclosed space, were two doors, exactly alike and side by side. It was the duty and the privilege of the person on trial to walk directly to these doors and open one of them. He could open either door he pleased. He was subject to no guidance or influence but that of the aforementioned impartial and incorruptible chance. If he opened the one, there came out of it a hungry tiger, the fiercest and most cruel that could be procured, which immediately sprang upon him, and tore him to pieces, as a punishment for

---

1. florid (flôr′ id), **and untrammeled** (un tram′ ′ld): Showy and bold.
2. amphitheater (am′ fə thē′ ə tər) n.: An open space surrounded by rising rings of seats.

3. emanated (em′ ə nāt′ id) v.: Came.

The Lady or the Tiger? 49

Presentation

Motivation/Prior Knowledge
Ask students whether they know of anyone who has been punished unjustly. Why was the punishment unjust? Ask them to consider the problem of choosing a just punishment for any crime. Tell them that the selection deals with these issues.

Thematic Focus As the princess in this story discovers, the choices people make can have consequences both for themselves and for others. Have students discuss the consequences of some difficult choices they have made. How were their own lives affected by their choices? How were other people's lives affected?

Making Connections Another selection that deals with the consequences of forbidden love is *Romeo and Juliet,* page 287.

Master Teacher Note This story has achieved wide renown because of the clever ending, which does not provide readers with a resolution of the conflict. Tell students to be prepared to invent their own ending—and to back up their choice with details from the story.

Purpose-Setting Question What is the answer to the question in the title?

1 **Discussion** If students have read "The Most Dangerous Game," page 13, have them compare General Zaroff to the king. What is similar about the two characters?

2 **Clarification** The ancient Romans punished enemies or criminals by confining them in an arena with wild beasts.

TIGER
Samuel Marsden Brookes
The Oakland Museum
Kahn Collection

3

his guilt. The moment that the case of the criminal was thus decided, doleful iron bells were clanged, great wails went up from the hired mourners posted on the outer rim of the arena, and the vast audience, with bowed heads and downcast hearts, wended slowly their homeward way, mourning greatly that one so young and fair, or so old and respected, should have merited so dire a fate.

But if the accused person opened the other door, there came forth from it a lady, the most suitable to his years and station that His Majesty could select among his fair subjects; and to this lady he was immediately married, as a reward of his innocence. It mattered not that he might already possess a wife and family, or that his affections might be engaged upon an object of his own selection. The king allowed no such subordi-

nate arrangements to interfere with his great scheme of retribution and reward. The exercises, as in the other instance, took place immediately, and in the arena. Another door opened beneath the king, and a priest, followed by a band of choristers, and dancing maidens blowing joyous airs on golden horns and treading an epithalamic measure,[4] advanced to where the pair stood side by side, and the wedding was promptly and cheerily solemnized. Then the gay brass bells rang forth their merry peals, the people shouted glad hurrahs, and the innocent man, preceded by children strewing flowers on his path, led his bride to his home.

This was the king's semibarbaric method of administering justice. Its perfect fairness is obvious. The criminal could not know out of which door would come the lady. He opened either he pleased, without having the slightest idea whether, in the next instant, he was to be devoured or married. On some occasions the tiger came out of one door, and on some out of the other. The decisions of this tribunal[5] were not only fair, they were positively determinate.[6] The accused person was instantly punished if he found himself guilty; and if innocent, he was rewarded on the spot, whether he liked it or not. There was no escape from the judgments of the king's arena.

The institution was a very popular one. When the people gathered together on one of the great trial days, they never knew whether they were to witness a bloody slaughter or a hilarious wedding. This element of uncertainty lent an interest to the occasion which it could not otherwise have attained. Thus, the masses were entertained and pleased, and the thinking part of the community

4

5

6

---

4. **epithalamic** (ep' ə thə lā' mik) **measure:** Marriage dance.
5. **tribunal** (trī byoo' n'l) *n.*: Court.
6. **determinate** (di tur' mi nit) *adj.*: Final.

could bring no charge of unfairness against this plan; for did not the accused person have the whole matter in his own hands?

This semibarbaric king had a daughter as blooming as his most florid fancies, and with a soul as fervent and imperious as his own. As is usual in such cases, she was the apple of his eye, and was loved by him above all humanity. Among his courtiers was a young man of that fineness of blood and lowness of station common to the conventional heroes of romance who love royal maidens. This royal maiden was well satisfied with her lover, for he was handsome and brave to a degree unsurpassed in all this kingdom, and she loved him with an ardor that had enough of barbarism in it to make it exceedingly warm and strong. This love affair moved on happily for many months, until, one day, the king happened to discover its existence. He did not hesitate nor waver in regard to his duty. The youth was immediately cast into prison, and a day was appointed for his trial in the king's arena. This, of course, was an especially important occasion, and His Majesty, as well as all the people, was greatly interested in the workings and development of this trial. Never before had such a case occurred—never before had a subject dared to love the daughter of a king. In after years such things became commonplace enough, but then they were, in no slight degree, novel and startling.

The tiger cages of the kingdom were searched for the most savage and relentless beasts, from which the fiercest monster might be selected for the arena, and the ranks of maiden youth and beauty throughout the land were carefully surveyed by competent judges, in order that the young man might have a fitting bride in case fate did not determine for him a different destiny. Of course, everybody knew that the deed with which the accused was charged had been done. He had loved the princess, and neither he, she, nor anyone else thought of denying the fact. But the king would not think of allowing any fact of this kind to interfere with the workings of the tribunal, in which he took such great delight and satisfaction. No matter how the affair turned out, the youth would be disposed of, and the king would take an aesthetic pleasure in watching the course of events, which would determine whether or not the young man had done wrong in allowing himself to love the princess.

The appointed day arrived. From far and near the people gathered, and thronged the great galleries of the arena, while crowds, unable to gain admittance, massed themselves against its outside walls. The king and his court were in their places, opposite the twin doors—those fateful portals, so terrible in their similarity!

All was ready. The signal was given. A door beneath the royal party opened, and the lover of the princess walked into the arena.

Original illustration from STORIES FROM THE ARABIAN NIGHTS
Edmund Dulac

10 Discussion How does this youth's appearance add drama to the story?

11 Reading Strategy Have students read this section carefully for clues about the princess's decision. Ask them to predict what might happen to the youth.

Tall, beautiful, fair, his appearance was greeted with a low hum of admiration and anxiety. Half the audience had not known so grand a youth had lived among them. No wonder the princess loved him! What a terrible thing for him to be there!

As the youth advanced into the arena, he turned, as the custom was, to bow to the king. But he did not think at all of that royal personage; his eyes were fixed upon the princess, who sat to the right of her father. Had it not been for the portion of barbarism in her nature, it is probable that lady would not have been there. But her intense and fervid soul would not allow her to be absent on an occasion in which she was so terribly interested. From the moment that the decree had gone forth that her lover should decide his fate in the king's arena, she had thought of nothing, night or day, but this great event and the various subjects connected with it. Possessed of more power, influence, and force of character than anyone who had ever before been interested in such a case, she had done what no other person had done— she had possessed herself of the secret of the doors. She knew in which of the two rooms behind those doors stood the cage of the tiger, with its open front, and in which waited the lady. Through these thick doors, heavily curtained with skins on the inside, it was impossible that any noise or suggestion should come from within to the person who should approach to raise the latch of one of them. But gold, and the power of a woman's will, had brought the secret to the princess.

Not only did she know in which room stood the lady, ready to emerge, all blushing and radiant, should her door be opened, but she knew who the lady was. It was one of the fairest and loveliest of the damsels of the court who had been selected as the reward of the accused youth, should he be proved innocent of the crime of aspiring to one so far above him; and the princess hated her. Often had she seen, or imagined that she had seen, this fair creature throwing glances of admiration upon the person of her lover, and sometimes she thought these glances were perceived and even returned. Now and then she had seen them talking together. It was but for a moment or two, but much can be said in a brief space. It may have been on unimportant topics, but how could she know that? The girl was lovely, but she had dared to raise her eyes to the loved one of the princess, and, with all the intensity of the savage blood transmitted to her through long lines of wholly barbaric ancestors, she hated the woman who blushed and trembled behind that silent door.

When her lover turned and looked at her, and his eye met hers as she sat there paler and whiter than anyone in the vast ocean of anxious faces about her, he saw, by that power of quick perception which is given to those whose souls are one, that she knew behind which door crouched the tiger, and behind which stood the lady. He had expected her to know it. He understood her nature, and his soul was assured that she would never rest until she had made plain to herself this thing, hidden to all other lookers-on, even to the king. The only hope for the youth in which there was any element of certainty was based upon the success of the princess in discovering this mystery, and the moment he looked upon her, he saw she had succeeded.

Then it was that his quick and anxious glance asked the question, "Which?" It was as plain to her as if he shouted it from where he stood. There was not an instant to be lost. The question was asked in a flash; it must be answered in another.

Her right arm lay on the cushioned parapet before her. She raised her hand, and made a slight, quick movement toward the

Grammar in Action

Writers **vary their sentences** to maintain reader interest, eliminate choppy passages, and build suspense. The following paragraph by Frank R. Stockton illustrates this technique:

All was ready. The signal was given. A door beneath the royal party opened, and the lover of the princess walked into the arena. Tall, beautiful, fair, his appearance was greeted with a low hum of admiration and anxiety. Half the audience had not known so grand a youth had lived among them. No wonder the princess loved him! What a terrible thing for him to be there!

The paragraph opens with two short, almost staccato sentences. Following are three descriptive, smooth-flowing sentences of nearly equal length. The final two sentences are relatively short exclamations. Thus, the sentence length emphasizes the paragraph's three parts: the quick beginning signal, the audience's observation, and their emotional reaction.

right. No one but her lover saw her. Every eye but his was fixed on the man in the arena.

He turned, and with a firm and rapid step he walked across the empty space. Every heart stopped beating, every breath was held, every eye was fixed immovably upon that man. Without the slightest hesitation, he went to the door on the right, and opened it.

Now, the point of the story is this: Did the tiger come out of that door, or did the lady?

The more we reflect upon this question, the harder it is to answer. It involves a study of the human heart which leads us through devious mazes of passion, out of which it is difficult to find our way. Think of it, fair reader, not as if the decision of the question depended upon yourself, but upon that hot-blooded, semibarbaric princess, her soul at a white heat beneath the combined fires of despair and jealousy. She had lost him, but who should have him?

How often, in her waking hours and in her dreams, had she started in wild horror and covered her face with her hands as she thought of her lover opening the door on the other side of which waited the cruel fangs of the tiger!

But how much oftener had she seen him at the other door! How in her grievous reveries had she gnashed her teeth and torn her hair when she saw his start of rapturous delight as he opened the door of the lady! How her soul had burned in agony when she had seen him rush to meet that woman, with her flushing cheek and sparkling eye of triumph; when she had seen him lead her forth, his whole frame kindled with the joy of recovered life; when she had heard the glad shouts from the multitude, and the wild ringing of the happy bells; when she had seen the priest, with his joyous followers, advance to the couple, and make them man and wife before her very eyes; and when she had seen them walk away together upon their path of flowers, followed by the tremendous shouts of the hilarious multitude, in which her one despairing shriek was lost and drowned!

Would it not be better for him to die at once, and go to wait for her in the blessed regions of semibarbaric futurity?

And yet, that awful tiger, those shrieks, that blood!

Her decision had been indicated in an instant, but it had been made after days and nights of anguished deliberation. She had known she would be asked, she had decided what she would answer, and, without the slightest hesitation, she had moved her hand to the right.

The question of her decision is one not to be lightly considered, and it is not for me to presume to set up myself as the one person able to answer it. So I leave it with all of you: Which came out of the opened door—the lady or the tiger?

The Lady or the Tiger? 53

12 Discussion What effect does the writer create by shifting away from the narration at this point?

13 Master Teacher Note When this story first appeared in a major magazine, the question the writer poses was hotly debated throughout the country. Ask students if they think the story would have such an effect today.

14 Critical Thinking and Reading Discuss the ending of the story with the class. Consider whether or not the story would have been better if Stockton had completed the narrative. Explore possible decisions that the princess might have made. Tell students that their predictions should depend on their interpretations of the princess's character. What clues to her character does Stockton give? Also explain that their predictions may also reflect their own ideas about human nature.

15 Critical Thinking and Reading Think carefully about the last paragraph. What larger, more universal, issue is Stockton addressing here?

Reader's Response Which door would you choose?

Thematic Response The princess had two very difficult choices. What did she choose? What do you think were the consequences of her choices?

Student Activity 1. Read Stockton's paragraph again. Explain why Stockton might have returned to short sentences at the end of this passage.

Student Activity 2. Using Stockton's paragraph as a model, write a paragraph of your own. Vary your sentence length, as Stockton does, to build suspense and keep your readers interested in your description. Share your paragraph with your classmates when you are finished.

Electronic Handbook Before beginning these activities, you might want to have students review complex sentences, conjunctions, and phrases and clauses. If they have access to the Language Master 6000, have them enter the access words *conjunctions, complex, phrase and clause* and press the GRAMMAR key for information on these topics.

ANSWERS TO RESPONDING TO THE SELECTION
Your Response

1. In understanding the princess's nature, the young man might be condemning himself. Ask students what they think about the risk the young man took.

Recalling

2. The king tried accused people by having their fate decided in his arena. The accused person had two doors to choose from in the arena. Behind one was a tiger and behind the other was a beautiful maiden. The accused was either killed or married, depending on which door he choose.
3. The young man dares to love the king's daughter.
4. She moves her hand quickly to the right.

Interpreting

5. Answers may differ but might include the fact that the trials are dramatic and provide entertainment.
6. Suggested Response: The king's justice is considered "perfectly fair" because it is based on chance. This form of justice is barbaric because it is unrelated to guilt or innocence. Because it has an aesthetic quality, however, the writer calls it and the king semibarbaric.
7. Suggested Response: The princess has a fiery, passionate temperament, and this might have made her wish her lover dead, rather than see him in the arms of another lady.

Applying

8. Answers may differ but should show students' awareness that such a system of punishment has no relationship to the crime, and is, therefore, not fair or just.

ANSWERS TO ANALYZING LITERATURE

1. Suggested Response: The princess's dilemma is a choice between losing the person she loves through death, or losing the per-

RESPONDING TO THE SELECTION
Your Response

1. The author tells us that the young man "understood her nature," speaking of the princess. Do you agree or disagree? Why?

Recalling

2. What is the king's method of trying accused criminals?
3. Of what crime is the young man accused?
4. How does the princess signal the young man when he is in the arena?

Interpreting

5. Why are public trials in the arena so popular with the people of the kingdom?
6. In what way is the king's system of justice considered perfectly fair? Why does the author describe it and the king as semibarbaric?
7. How does the author describe the nature of the princess? How might this quality influence her decision?

Applying

8. Imagine a modern equivalent of the king's arena—a lottery in which the accused picks a "to jail" ticket or a "go free" ticket. Would such a lottery be fair? Why or why not?

ANALYZING LITERATURE
Analyzing a Dilemma

A character who is confronted with a **dilemma** must choose between two equally balanced (and usually unpleasant) alternatives. In "The Lady or the Tiger?" each person sent into the arena was faced with a dilemma—either choice he made would have an unpleasant consequence.

1. Describe the dilemma the princess faces.
2. Describe the dilemma the young man faces.

CRITICAL THINKING AND READING
Analyzing Solutions

Characters in stories usually have problems to solve. The solutions involve making choices. Because you are able to see the big picture, you are often in a better position to weigh the choices than the character is.

If you were the young man, would you follow the princess's direction? Explain your answer.

THINKING AND WRITING
Writing an Ending

Write an ending for "The Lady or the Tiger?" Decide how you think the characters would behave. Think about which solution to "The Lady or the Tiger?" would be most satisfying to your readers and how you personally would like the story to turn out. When you revise your ending, be sure the suspense builds until the moment of revelation.

LEARNING OPTIONS

1. **Performance.** With your class conduct a mock trial in which the king is tried for his barbarous way of administering justice. Now you, his subjects, are going to judge him. After assigning the roles of the king and the judge, jurors, and attorneys, prepare arguments for and against the king. Have classmates prepare to act as key witnesses, such as the princess or the lady behind the door. As you enact your trial, think about how your concept of justice differs from the king's.
2. **Cross-curricular Connection.** Write the lyrics to a song that tells the story of the princess who had to choose between losing her beloved to another woman or losing him to death. Include details from the story in your lyrics. You may even want to compose or find music to accompany them. When you are finished, recite or sing your song to the class.

son she loves through his marrying the maiden.
2. Suggested Response: The young man's dilemma is deciding which door he should choose. He must also decide whether the princess's advice is reliable.

ANSWERS TO CRITICAL THINKING AND READING

Answers will differ but should include a direct yes or no answer to the first question and an expla-

nation supported by details concerning the princess's character found in, or inferred from, the story.

THINKING AND WRITING

Writing Transparency You might want to show Model 3: Short Story in **Transparencies for Writing** before students begin the Thinking and Writing activity.

LEARNING OPTIONS

1. This activity is especially appropriate for kinesthetic learners.
2. Auditory learners and students with an interest in music will particularly enjoy this activity. You might wish to extend the activity by having students record their songs.

Character

PASSING BY, 1924
E. Martin Hennings
Museum of Fine Arts, Houston

Humanities Note

Fine Art, *Passing By*, E. Martin Hennings. E. Martin Hennings (1886-1956), an American painter of Western scenes, was educated in academic art at the Art Institute of Chicago and the National Academy in Munich, Germany. He worked for a time as a commercial artist and muralist before moving to the artist's colony of Taos, New Mexico.

Passing By is a pleasant Western scene painted with technical proficiency. The dappled light coming through the trees creates a bright decorative pattern on the figures. The subject is obvious and is intended to appeal to a wide audience.

Preparation

More About the Author Morley Callaghan describes his "tangled friendships" with Ernest Hemingway, F. Scott Fitzgerald, and others in *That Summer in Paris.* Ask students to discuss some of the particular difficulties authors might encounter in their friendships with other authors.

Literary Focus Point out to students that writers can also reveal a character's personality through what he or she does *not* do in a situation. Tell students that they may want to consider this idea when evaluating the personality of Mrs. Higgins in this story.

Prereading Focus You might have students work with partners to complete their charts. You may also want to establish specific points in the story at which students should interrupt their reading in order to fill in their charts.

Electronic Handbook You might suggest that students use the Language Master 6000 to find synonyms for *contempt.*

Vocabulary Explain to **less advanced** students that these vocabulary words describe mannerisms or feelings. Ask them to study the list and write a sentence using each word.

Morley Callaghan

(1903–1990) was born in Toronto, Canada, and graduated from the University of Toronto. He worked as a reporter on the *Daily Star,* where he met Ernest Hemingway, who helped him publish his stories in literary magazines. After some success as a writer, Callaghan gave up his earlier intention to become a lawyer and devoted all his time to writing stories and novels. His works often focus on questions involving personal loyalty and conscience, as in "All the Years of Her Life."

All the Years of Her Life

Direct and Indirect Characterization

Characterization refers to a character's personality or the method by which the writer reveals this personality. With **direct characterization** the writer tells you directly about the character. With **indirect characterization** the writer lets you learn about the characters through the dialogue and action. You might also learn about characters through their thoughts or through what other characters think about them. In "All the Years of Her Life" Callaghan allows the characters to reveal themselves through their thoughts and dialogue.

Focus

The two main characters in "All the Years of Her Life" sometimes "put on an act" in order to conceal their true thoughts and feelings. Completing a chart like the one below as you read will help you identify the differences between how Alfred and his mother act and how they feel. An example has been entered for you.

WHAT CHARACTER DOES AND SAYS	WHAT CHARACTER PRETENDS TO THINK AND FEEL	WHAT CHARACTER REALLY THINKS AND FEELS
Alfred responds to Mr. Carr's accusation by saying "What do you mean? Do you think I'm crazy?"	Alfred is pretending to be indignant.	Alfred is really frightened.

Vocabulary

Knowing the following words will help you as you read "All the Years of Her Life."

brusquely (brusk′ lē) *adv.*: In an abrupt and curt manner (p. 57)
blustered (blus′ tərd) *v.*: Spoke in a noisy, swaggering manner (p. 57)
indignation (in′ dig nā′ shən) *n.*: Anger resulting from injustice (p. 57)

contempt (kən tempt′) *n.*: The feeling or attitude toward a person one considers unworthy (p. 58)
humility (hyoo mil′ ə tē) *n.*: Humbleness; lack of pride (p. 59)

Objectives

1 To understand characterization
2 To recognize stereotypes
3 To write about a person
4 To express individual interests and abilities through optional activities

Support Material

Teaching Portfolio
Teacher Backup, p. 73
Grammar in Action Worksheet, *Using Active and Passive Voice,* p. 76
Usage and Mechanics Worksheet, p. 78
Vocabulary Check, p. 79
Analyzing Literature Worksheet, *Understanding Characterization,* p. 80

Language Worksheet, *Understanding Phonetic Spelling,* p. 81
Selection Test, p. 82
Art Transparency 2: *Tocito Waits for the Boarding School Bus,* by Grey Cohoe

Prentice Hall Literature Writing Studio

All the Years of Her Life

Morley Callaghan

They were closing the drugstore, and Alfred Higgins, who had just taken off his white jacket, was putting on his coat and getting ready to go home. The little gray-haired man, Sam Carr, who owned the drugstore, was bending down behind the cash register, and when Alfred Higgins passed him, he looked up and said softly, "Just a moment, Alfred. One moment before you go."

The soft, confident, quiet way in which Sam Carr spoke made Alfred start to button his coat nervously. He felt sure his face was white. Sam Carr usually said, "Good night," brusquely, without looking up. In the six months he had been working in the drugstore Alfred had never heard his employer speak softly like that. His heart began to beat so loud it was hard for him to get his breath. "What is it, Mr. Carr?" he asked.

"Maybe you'd be good enough to take a few things out of your pocket and leave them here before you go," Sam Carr said.

"What things? What are you talking about?"

"You've got a compact and a lipstick and at least two tubes of toothpaste in your pockets, Alfred."

"What do you mean? Do you think I'm crazy?" Alfred blustered. His face got red and he knew he looked fierce with indignation. But Sam Carr, standing by the door with his blue eyes shining brightly behind his glasses and his lips moving underneath his gray moustache, only nodded his head a few times, and then Alfred grew very frightened and he didn't know what to say. Slowly he raised his hand and dipped it into his pocket, and with his eyes never meeting Sam Carr's eyes, he took out a blue compact and two tubes of toothpaste and a lipstick, and he laid them one by one on the counter.

"Petty thieving, eh, Alfred?" Sam Carr said. "And maybe you'd be good enough to tell me how long this has been going on."

"This is the first time I ever took anything."

"So now you think you'll tell me a lie, eh? What kind of a sap do I look like, huh? I don't know what goes on in my own store, eh? I tell you you've been doing this pretty steady," Sam Carr said as he went over and stood behind the cash register.

Ever since Alfred had left school he had been getting into trouble wherever he worked. He lived at home with his mother and his father, who was a printer. His two older brothers were married and his sister had got married last year, and it would have been all right for his parents now if Alfred had only been able to keep a job.

While Sam Carr smiled and stroked the side of his face very delicately with the tips of his fingers, Alfred began to feel that familiar terror growing in him that had been in him every time he had got into such trouble.

"I liked you," Sam Carr was saying. "I liked you and would have trusted you, and

All the Years of Her Life 57

Multicultural Focus Adolescence is a time of change, when a person is no longer a child but not yet an adult. In some cultures, formal ceremonies and rituals clearly mark the beginning of adulthood. In modern Westernized societies, the beginning is less clear. Expectations of society for behavior and responsibilities can be contradictory and frustrating, such as having to serve in the military before being able to vote. Anthropologists have also noted that, while some parent-child conflict is universal, it is less common in traditional types of societies because the child knows that his or her bonds with the family and community must last for life. In many Western societies, adolescents know that soon they must strike out on their own, while at the same time having relatively little preparation for the coming responsibilities. The resulting tension often leads to rebellion against parents.

Students might reflect on the above ideas and decide if they agree. Have them read about family life in another culture and compare it with their own.

Presentation

Motivation/Prior Knowledge Tell students that *petty larceny* involves the theft of relatively inexpensive items. Ask them whether and how such criminals ought to be punished. Then tell them that, in this story, a young man commits petty larceny.

Thematic Focus Awakenings occur at many stages in our lives. We cannot grow without them. Have students share any awakenings they have experienced. What types of awakenings do they imagine they may experience in the future?

Making Connections Another selection that deals with passages and transformations is "Before the End of Summer" by Grant Moss, Jr., page 107.

Purpose-Setting Question What important change does Alfred experience in this story?

1 **Critical Thinking and Reading** How do Alfred's reactions to Mr. Carr's remarks indicate that Alfred knows something is wrong?

2 **Discussion** What does the word *blustered* reveal about Alfred's reaction?

3 **Discussion** Which character do you believe? Why?

4 **Discussion** Does this passage reveal any motives Alfred might have for stealing? Explain.

Fine art, *Self Portrait,* 1944–45, Charley Toorop. Toorop (named Annie Caroline Pontifex but nicknamed "Charley") was born in 1891 in Holland and died in Norway in 1955. She was trained as a musician but began to paint as a young woman under the influence of her father, Jan. He was a painter as well, and had considerable impact on Dutch art at the turn of the century. Charley Toorop painted still lifes and portraits and purposely distorted figurative reality to communicate an inner vision. In this sense she was an expressionist painter, one who transforms nature rather than imitates it. You might discuss these questions with your students:

1. What "inner vision" do you think the artist might be communicating in this portrait?
2. What emotions do you see in this woman's face that might be the emotions of Mrs. Higgins in this story?

5 Critical Thinking and Reading What does Mr. Carr's uncertainty about what to do reveal about his feelings for Alfred?

6 Literary Focus What does the difference between what Alfred says and what he feels indicate about his character?

7 Critical Thinking and Reading Why do you think his expectations are so specific?

8 Literary Focus What is Alfred's greatest concern? What does this reveal about him?

9 Critical Thinking and Reading What do you think is going through the mind of each character?

10 Discussion Contrast Mrs. Higgins's manner with Alfred's expectations about the way she would behave.

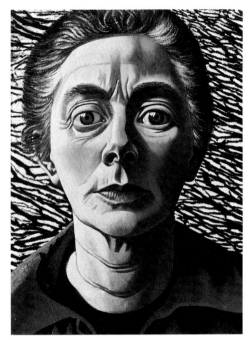

SELF-PORTRAIT 1944–5
Charley Toorop
Stedelijk Van Abbedmuseum, Eindhoven

now look what I got to do." While Alfred watched with his alert, frightened blue eyes, Sam Carr drummed with his fingers on the counter. "I don't like to call a cop in point-blank,"[1] he was saying as he looked very worried. "You're a fool, and maybe I should call your father and tell him you're a fool. Maybe I should let them know I'm going to have you locked up."

"My father's not at home. He's a printer. He works nights," Alfred said.

"Who's at home?"

"My mother, I guess."

"Then we'll see what she says." Sam Carr went to the phone and dialed the number.

---

1. point-blank: Right away.

Alfred was not so much ashamed, but there was that deep fright growing in him, and he blurted out arrogantly, like a strong, full-grown man, "Just a minute. You don't need to draw anybody else in. You don't need to tell her." He wanted to sound like a swaggering, big guy who could look after himself, yet the old, childish hope was in him, the longing that someone at home would come and help him. "Yeah, that's right, he's in trouble," Mr. Carr was saying. "Yeah, your boy works for me. You'd better come down in a hurry." And when he was finished Mr. Carr went over to the door and looked out at the street and watched the people passing in the late summer night. "I'll keep my eye out for a cop," was all he said.

Alfred knew how his mother would come rushing in; she would rush in with her eyes blazing, or maybe she would be crying, and she would push him away when he tried to talk to her, and make him feel her dreadful contempt; yet he longed that she might come before Mr. Carr saw the cop on the beat passing the door.

While they waited—and it seemed a long time—they did not speak, and when at last they heard someone tapping on the closed door, Mr. Carr, turning the latch, said crisply, "Come in, Mrs. Higgins." He looked hard-faced and stern.

Mrs. Higgins must have been going to bed when he telephoned, for her hair was tucked in loosely under her hat, and her hand at her throat held her light coat tight across her chest so her dress would not show. She came in, large and plump, with a little smile on her friendly face. Most of the store lights had been turned out and at first she did not see Alfred, who was standing in the shadow at the end of the counter. Yet as soon as she saw him she did not look as Alfred thought she would look: she smiled, her blue eyes never wavered, and with a calm-

Grammar in Action

Voice is the form of the verb that shows whether the subject is performing or receiving the action. Verbs have two voices: active and passive. The verb in the following sentence, for instance, is in the active voice, because the subject performs the action: Gavin's classmates *sent* their congratulations. In the passive voice, the subject is acted upon; for example, Gavin *was sent* congratulations. Writers usually use verbs in the **active voice** to make their writing vivid, strong, and emphatic.

ness and dignity that made them forget that her clothes seemed to have been thrown on her, she put out her hand to Mr. Carr and said politely, "I'm Mrs. Higgins. I'm Alfred's mother."

Mr. Carr was a bit embarrassed by her lack of terror and her simplicity, and he hardly knew what to say to her, so she asked, "Is Alfred in trouble?"

"He is. He's been taking things from the store. I caught him red-handed. Little things like compacts and toothpaste and lipsticks. Stuff he can sell easily," the proprietor said.

As she listened Mrs. Higgins looked at Alfred sometimes and nodded her head sadly, and when Sam Carr had finished she said gravely, "Is it so, Alfred?"

"Yes."

"Why have you been doing it?"

"I been spending money, I guess."

"On what?"

"Going around with the guys, I guess," Alfred said.

Mrs. Higgins put out her hand and touched Sam Carr's arm with an understanding gentleness, and speaking as though afraid of disturbing him, she said, "If you would only listen to me before doing anything." Her simple earnestness made her shy; her humility made her falter and look away, but in a moment she was smiling gravely again, and she said with a kind of patient dignity, "What did you intend to do, Mr. Carr?"

"I was going to get a cop. That's what I ought to do."

"Yes, I suppose so. It's not for me to say, because he's my son. Yet I sometimes think a little good advice is the best thing for a boy when he's at a certain period in his life," she said.

Alfred couldn't understand his mother's quiet composure, for if they had been at home and someone had suggested that he was going to be arrested, he knew she would be in a rage and would cry out against him. Yet now she was standing there with that gentle, pleading smile on her face, saying, "I wonder if you don't think it would be better just to let him come home with me. He looks a big fellow, doesn't he? It takes some of them a long time to get any sense," and they both stared at Alfred, who shifted away with a bit of light shining for a moment on his thin face and the tiny pimples over his cheekbone.

But even while he was turning away uneasily Alfred was realizing that Mr. Carr had become aware that his mother was really a fine woman; he knew that Sam Carr was puzzled by his mother, as if he had expected her to come in and plead with him tearfully, and instead he was being made to feel a bit ashamed by her vast tolerance. While there was only the sound of the mother's soft, assured voice in the store, Mr. Carr began to nod his head encouragingly at her. Without being alarmed, while being just large and still and simple and hopeful, she was becoming dominant there in the dimly lit store. "Of course, I don't want to be harsh," Mr. Carr was saying. "I'll tell you what I'll do. I'll just fire him and let it go at that. How's that?" and he got up and shook hands with Mrs. Higgins, bowing low to her in deep respect.

There was such warmth and gratitude in the way she said, "I'll never forget your kindness," that Mr. Carr began to feel warm and genial himself.

"Sorry we had to meet this way," he said. "But I'm glad I got in touch with you. Just wanted to do the right thing, that's all," he said.

"It's better to meet like this than never, isn't it?" she said. Suddenly they clasped hands as if they liked each other, as if they had known each other a long time. "Good night, sir," she said.

All the Years of Her Life 59

---

11 Critical Thinking and Reading How do you think Mr. Carr expected Mrs. Higgins to behave?

12 Literary Focus What can you infer about Alfred based on his responses?

13 Discussion Do you think that Mrs. Higgins is doing the right thing by convincing Mr. Carr not to call the police? Explain your answer.

14 Reading Strategy How do you think Alfred's awareness will affect him?

15 Discussion Why is Mrs. Higgins's patience and dignity more effective than anger or pleading would have been?

The following passage from "All the Years of Her Life" illustrates both active and passive voice:

Most of the store lights *had been turned out* and at first she *did* not *see* Alfred, who *was standing* in the shadow. . . . Yet as soon as she *saw* him she *did* not *look* as Alfred *thought* she *would look;* she *smiled,* her blue eyes never *wavered,* and . . . she *put out* her hand to Mr. Carr. . . .

The verb *turn* is in the passive voice; all the other verbs are active. Why? Good writers use the passive voice only when the doer is either unknown or unimportant. (It really does not matter who turned out the lights.) Otherwise, the active voice is preferable, because it makes writing more lively and direct.

Student Activity. Write four sentences of your own about Alfred, Mr. Carr, or Mrs. Higgins. Decide whether your verbs are in the active or passive voice. If you have used the passive voice, rewrite your sentence so that the verb is in the active voice.

Electronic Handbook You might wish to have students review active and passive verbs before completing the Grammar in Action activity. If students have access to the Language Master 6000, have them enter the access word *active* and press the GRAMMAR key for information on active verbs.

16 **Critical Thinking and Reading** Do Alfred's feelings indicate that he understands the seriousness of his crime or feels remorse for committing it? Explain.

17 **Literary Focus** Why do you think Mrs. Higgins responds angrily to Alfred's assurances that he will not misbehave again? What accounts for the difference between her apparent tolerance for Alfred in the store and her bitter anger at him now?

18 **Literary Focus** What do Alfred's thoughts at this moment reveal about him?

19 **Discussion** What accounts for the change in Mrs. Higgins?

20 **Critical Thinking and Writing** What does Alfred understand about his mother for the first time? Why does his new understanding signal the fact that his youth is over?

Master Teacher Note Place Art Transparency 2, *Tocito Waits for the Boarding School Bus*, by Grey Cohoe on the overhead projector. Ask students to comment on the relationship between the woman and the boy. Also have them comment on the mood of the picture. Then have them compare this mood with that of the story.

Reader's Response How would you have reacted if you were Alfred's mother? Explain.

Thematic Response Alfred's "awakening" leads him to an understanding of his mother's character. How do you think he feels about his discovery? Why?

"Good night, Mrs. Higgins. I'm truly sorry," he said.

The mother and son walked along the street together, and the mother was taking a long, firm stride as she looked ahead with her stern face full of worry. Alfred was afraid to speak to her, he was afraid of the silence that was between them, so he only looked ahead too, for the excitement and relief was still pretty strong in him; but in a little while, going along like that in silence made him terribly aware of the strength and the sternness in her; he began to wonder what she was thinking of as she stared ahead so grimly; she seemed to have forgotten that he walked beside her; so when they were passing under the Sixth Avenue elevated and the rumble of the train seemed to break the silence, he said in his old, blustering way, "Thank God it turned out like that. I certainly won't get in a jam like that again."

"Be quiet. Don't speak to me. You've disgraced me again and again," she said bitterly.

"That's the last time. That's all I'm saying."

"Have the decency to be quiet," she snapped. They kept on their way, looking straight ahead.

When they were at home and his mother took off her coat, Alfred saw that she was really only half-dressed, and she made him feel afraid again when she said, without even looking at him, "You're a bad lot. God forgive you. It's one thing after another and always has been. Why do you stand there stupidly? Go to bed, why don't you?" When he was going, she said, "I'm going to make myself a cup of tea. Mind, now, not a word about tonight to your father."

While Alfred was undressing in his bedroom, he heard his mother moving around the kitchen. She filled the kettle and put it on the stove. She moved a chair. And as he listened there was no shame in him, just wonder and a kind of admiration of her strength and repose. He could still see Sam Carr nodding his head encouragingly to her; he could hear her talking simply and earnestly, and as he sat on his bed he felt a pride in her strength. "She certainly was smooth," he thought. "Gee, I'd like to tell her she sounded swell."

And at last he got up and went along to the kitchen, and when he was at the door he saw his mother pouring herself a cup of tea. He watched and he didn't move. Her face, as she sat there, was a frightened, broken face utterly unlike the face of the woman who had been so assured a little while ago in the drugstore. When she reached out and lifted the kettle to pour hot water in her cup, her hand trembled and the water splashed on the stove. Leaning back in the chair, she sighed and lifted the cup to her lips, and her lips were groping loosely as if they would never reach the cup. She swallowed the hot tea eagerly, and then she straightened up in relief, though her hand holding the cup still trembled. She looked very old.

It seemed to Alfred that this was the way it had been every time he had been in trouble before, that this trembling had really been in her as she hurried out half-dressed to the drugstore. He understood why she had sat alone in the kitchen the night his young sister had kept repeating doggedly that she was getting married. Now he felt all that his mother had been thinking of as they walked along the street together a little while ago. He watched his mother, and he never spoke, but at that moment his youth seemed to be over; he knew all the years of her life by the way her hand trembled as she raised the cup to her lips. It seemed to him that this was the first time he had ever looked upon his mother.

60   Short Stories

Closure and Extension

ANSWERS TO RESPONDING TO THE SELECTION
Your Response
1. Encourage students to share their experiences with the class and to explain what led them to their discoveries.

Recalling
2. Mr. Carr catches Alfred stealing items from the drug store.

3. Mr. Carr expects Mrs. Higgins to be upset and is prepared for an emotional reaction. Mrs. Higgins's quiet dignity in this situation both embarrasses and calms Mr. Carr.
4. Mrs. Higgins is so angry at Alfred that she cannot even speak to him.

Interpreting
5. Suggested Response: Mrs. Higgins is very angry and disappointed in Alfred, and though she seemed calm at the store, she was really very upset by Alfred's actions.
6. Suggested Response: Alfred sees his mother's strength disintegrate as she sits in the kitchen. He sees the disappointments she has experienced through the years. For the first time, he realizes that she has suffered because of his irresponsibility. The statement suggests that Alfred is now an aware adult rather than a thoughtless boy.

RESPONDING TO THE SELECTION

Your Response

1. Has there ever been a time when you suddenly saw a familiar person in a new light? Explain.

Recalling

2. Explain the situation that brings Alfred's mother to the store.
3. How does her manner surprise Sam Carr? Describe the effect of her manner on him.
4. How does Alfred's mother behave after she leaves the store?

Interpreting

5. Why does Alfred's mother refuse to talk to him on the walk home?
6. As Alfred watches his mother sip tea, the writer says, "at that moment his youth seemed to be over." What does this statement suggest?
7. What, if anything, does Alfred learn from this incident?

Applying

8. How do you think Alfred will behave on the next job he gets?
9. If you were Alfred, what might you have done to resolve the situation with Sam?

ANALYZING LITERATURE

Understanding Characterization

With **direct characterization** writers state what the characters are like. With **indirect characterization** they show you indirectly what the characters are like through what the characters say and do. Very often writers use both methods to reveal characters. In "All the Years of Her Life" most of the characterization occurs indirectly through the words, actions, and thoughts of the characters. For example, the writer states directly that Sam "usually said 'Good night,' brusquely." Later, as the story develops, Sam behaves in a brusque manner, saying, "I'll keep my eye out for a cop."

The following are direct statements about the characters in "All the Years of Her Life." Find an

example in the story of the character's actions, thoughts, or words that shows the character trait indirectly. Explain your example.

1. Alfred's mother cares very much about him.
2. Sam is not as tough as he appears.
3. Alfred tends to be irresponsible.

CRITICAL THINKING AND READING

Recognizing Stereotypes

A **stereotype** is a fixed and oversimplified idea of what a type of person or group of people is like. A stereotyped image includes certain traits, characteristics, or behavior that are assumed to be typical. For example, one stereotype of women is that they are very emotional. However, Alfred's mother, who behaves in a very calm, reasoned manner, proves this stereotype false.

Show how the character named proves or disproves the following stereotypes.

1. Alfred: Bad kids don't care about anybody but themselves.
2. Sam: People in business think only about money.

THINKING AND WRITING

Writing About a Person

Think of someone you know and respect. Imagine that this person is about to hire a friend of yours. Write a letter to your friend telling what the prospective employer is like. Stress in your letter what kind of employer you think this person would be. When you revise your letter, try to add at least two strong adverbs to describe the person's behavior.

LEARNING OPTION

Speaking and Listening. Imagine that you have traveled through time and you find yourself ten years into the future. Find out where Alfred Higgins is and go and see him. After your return to the present, tell the class about your visit with Alfred.

---

7. Suggested Response: Alfred realizes that his actions have an effect on other people, specifically his mother. He realizes that she has suffered because of them.

Applying

8. Answers will differ. Some students may believe that Alfred has learned a lesson from this experience. Others may believe that Alfred will forget the lesson and act irresponsibly again. Students should support their answers with examples from the story.
9. Answers will differ. Some students might respond that they would have asked for forgiveness.

Challenge How might the story have been different if Mrs. Higgins had allowed Mr. Carr to call the police? What might have happened if she had told Alfred's father what had happened?

3. Suggested Response: Alfred steals the items and then tries to bluster his way out of trouble.

ANSWERS TO CRITICAL THINKING AND READING

1. Suggested Response: Alfred's awareness of his mother's pain at the end of this story disproves this stereotype.
2. Suggested Response: Mr. Carr never mentions the money Alfred's stealing cost him, nor does he ask Alfred to pay for the articles. Also he is concerned enough about the boy's future to call his mother instead of the police. These actions refute this stereotype.

THINKING AND WRITING

Software If your students have access to computers, have them use the **Bank Street Writer** to incorporate material they generated during the Prereading Focus into this assignment. As students revise, they can use the program's on-line thesaurus to come up with strong adverbs describing the prospective employer's behavior.

Alternative Assessment For Alternative Composition Assignments to assess students' learning, see page 73 of the Teaching Portfolio.

Publishing Student Writing Ask for student volunteers to share their letters with the class. Have students decide for which employer they would most enjoy working.

LEARNING OPTION

This activity will appeal to creative and imaginative students. You might want to expand this activity by having students speculate about what they will be like ten years from now.

ANSWERS TO ANALYZING LITERATURE

1. Suggested Response: That she comes so quickly indicates that she cares about Alfred.
2. Suggested Response: Mr. Carr threatens to call the police, but calls Alfred's mother instead. Rather than firing Alfred immediately, he tells Alfred's mother, "I'll just fire him and let it go at that. How's that?"

Preparation

More About the Author As a young girl, Isabel Allende lived with her grandmother. In an interview, Allende recalled that "I had a very lonely life when I was a child but very interesting—only adults around me, very extravagant people, a very extravagant family, really."

At 16, Allende left school and became a secretary in the Food and Agricultural Organization at the United Nations in Chile. She worked with journalists and soon became one herself. In a short period of time, she had her own television program, wrote for a radical women's magazine, and wrote plays and short stories for children. *The House of the Spirits* is her first novel, which captures and immortalizes the spirits of her extravagant family. Ask students how her uncle's death may have affected Allende's writing.

Literary Focus You might lead a discussion about eccentricity. Ask students to describe eccentric people they have known.

Prereading Focus You might assist the students' brainstorming by suggesting some possible career area, such as the circus, outer space, or undersea exploration. When the students have finished their diagrams, ask them to share the more unusual occupations with the class.

GUIDE FOR READING

Isabel Allende

(1942–   ), the niece of the former Chilean president Salvador Allende, was born in Lima, Peru. As a girl she lived with her grandparents, who became the models for Esteban and Clara in her novel *The House of the Spirits.* In 1973, after General Pinochet overthrew her uncle's government, Allende fled to Venezuela with her husband and children, where they now live in exile. Allende's novel is her memorial to "the house that I lost, the people that are dead, those that disappeared, the friends that were scattered all around the world."

Uncle Marcos
from *The House of the Spirits*

Character Traits

Character traits are all of those qualities that make a person unique. Authors give their characters a number of different traits that together form their personalities.

Focus

In this story, Uncle Marcos is one of the many eccentric characters Allende brings to life in her novel. Clara describes him in a journal, from which her granddaughter narrates some fifty years later.

Uncle Marcos is a man of great imagination and energy. He is constantly turning his hand to some new enterprise, and each undertaking he attempts is more unusual than the one before. With a partner, brainstorm for unusual occupations that you know of or can imagine. You might do it in the form of a diagram like the one below:

As you read the story, compare these occupations with Uncle Marcos's undertakings and ask: If he were living today, which of the ones you suggested would he try?

Vocabulary

Knowing the following words will help you as you read "Uncle Marcos."

vanquished (vaŋ′ kwis h't) *adj.*: Defeated (p. 63)

fetid (fet′ id) *adj.*: Rancid; rank; smelly (p. 63)

impassive (im pas′ iv) *adj.*: Showing no emotion (p. 64)

disconsolately (dis kän′ sə lit lē) *adv.*: Unhappily (p. 66)

Unrequited (un ri kwīt′ id) *adj.*: Not returned; unreciprocated (p. 68)

Objectives

1 To recognize character traits
2 To write about a memorable person

Support Material

Teaching Portfolio
Teacher Backup, p. 85
Grammar in Action Worksheet, *Recognizing Adverb Clauses,* p. 88
Usage and Mechanics Worksheet, p. 90
Vocabulary Check, p. 91
Critical Thinking and Reading Worksheet, *Understanding Magical Realism,* p. 92

Language Worksheet, *Recognizing Hyperbole,* p. 93
Selection Test, p. 94

Prentice Hall Literature Writing Studio

Uncle Marcos
from *The House of the Spirits*
Isabel Allende

... It had been two years since Clara had last seen her Uncle Marcos, but she remembered him very well. His was the only perfectly clear image she retained from her whole childhood, and in order to describe him she did not need to consult the daguerreotype[1] in the drawing room that showed him dressed as an explorer leaning on an old-fashioned double-barreled rifle with his right foot on the neck of a Malaysian tiger, the same triumphant position in which she had seen the Virgin standing between plaster clouds and pallid angels at the main altar, one foot on the vanquished devil. All Clara had to do to see her uncle was close her eyes and there he was, weather-beaten and thin, with a pirate's mustache through which his strange, sharklike smile peered out at her. It seemed impossible that he could be inside that long black box that was lying in the middle of the courtyard.

Each time Uncle Marcos had visited his sister Nívea's home, he had stayed for several months, to the immense joy of his nieces and nephews, particularly Clara, causing a storm in which the sharp lines of domestic order blurred. The house became a clutter of trunks, of animals in jars of formaldehyde,[2] of Indian lances and sailor's bundles. In every part of the house people kept tripping over his equipment, and all sorts of unfamiliar animals appeared that had traveled from remote lands only to meet their death beneath Nana's irate broom in the farthest corners of the house. Uncle Marcos's manners were those of a cannibal, as Severo put it. He spent the whole night making incomprehensible movements in the drawing room; later they turned out to be exercises designed to perfect the mind's control over the body and to improve digestion. He performed alchemy[3] experiments in the kitchen, filling the house with fetid smoke and ruining pots and pans with solid substances that stuck to their bottoms and were impossible to remove. While the rest of the household tried to sleep, he dragged his suitcases up and down the halls, practiced making strange, high-pitched sounds on savage instruments, and taught Spanish to a parrot whose native language was an Amazonic dialect. During the day, he slept in a hammock that he had strung between two columns in the hall, wearing only a loincloth that put Severo in a terrible mood but that Nívea forgave because Marcos had convinced her that it was the same costume in which Jesus of Nazareth had preached. Clara remembered perfectly, even though she had been only a tiny child, the first time her Uncle Marcos came to the house after one of his voyages. He settled in as if he planned to stay forever. After a short time, bored with having to appear at ladies' gatherings where the mistress of the house played the piano, with playing cards, and

---

1. **daguerreotype** (də ger′ ō tïp′) *n.*: An early type of photograph.
2. **formaldehyde** (fôr mal′ də hīd′) *n.*: A solution used as a preservative.

3. **alchemy** (al′ kə mē) *n.*: An early form of chemistry, with philosophic and magical associations.

Uncle Marcos 63

Presentation

Motivation/Prior Knowledge Ask students to think about people who have become legends in their own families. Invite the class to share family stories that may have become exaggerated or taken on elements of fantasy over the years. Tell students that the author shares such family legends in the selection they are about to read.

Purpose-Setting Question How does the author blend fantasy and reality to paint a vivid picture of a character?

1 **Literary Focus** From this introduction, try to predict some of Uncle Marcos's character traits.

2 **Clarification** The majority of this selection is a flashback in which Clara is remembering her Uncle Marcos.

3 **Discussion** What is meant by "the sharp lines of domestic order blurred"? What are some lines of domestic order in your home or classroom?

4 **Clarification** Nana is the housekeeper and takes care of Clara; Severo is Clara's father; Nivea is Clara's mother and the sister of Uncle Marcos.

5 **Clarification** Uncle Marcos is practicing some sort of meditation technique, such as yoga.

6 **Enrichment** The principal goal of alchemy was to turn "base" metals such as lead into gold. In Asian countries, alchemists sought to make an elixir that would give immortality to the one who drank it.

7 **Reading Strategy** Go back to the beginning of this paragraph and list all of Uncle Marcos's eccentric traits you have learned so far.

Master Teacher Note Tell students to notice that the excerpt they are about to read is divided into four anecdotes, each of which illustrates aspects of Uncle Marcos's personality. Suggest that, as they read, they note which character traits are illustrated by each anecdote. You might also suggest that students take note of how the author makes transitions from one anecdote to the next so that the piece holds together as a unit.

Thematic Focus Often the most imaginative and adventurous people are not appreciated by their family. They are frequently looked upon as irresponsible by their more conventional relatives. Ask students whether such colorful characters make an important contribution to family life and to society.

Making Connections You may wish to pair this selection with "A Very Old Man with Enormous Wings," page 165, another work by a South American author who incorporates fantastic details with realistic ones to create a magical effect.

8 Discussion How might this feat be possible?

9 Literary Focus What character trait of Uncle Marcos does this belief reveal?

10 Literary Focus What does Antonieta's reaction to Uncle Marcos reveal about her character?

11 Enrichment The goosestep is an exaggerated style of marching practiced by Prussian soldiers, known for being the best drilled and disciplined in the German Army during World War I.

Multicultural Focus Point out that while many North American family units are limited to parents and children, an extended family is typical of Hispanic cultures. In addition to parents and children, it often includes grandparents, aunts, uncles, cousins, and even close family friends (compadres) living in the same house or neighborhood. Even when they do not live in the same house, but far away like Uncle Marcos, they often visit and depend upon one another.

Find examples in the selection that show how family members depend upon one another.

Ask students whom they would like to live with if they could create their own extended family.

with dodging all his relatives' pressures to pull himself together and take a job as a clerk in Severo del Valle's law practice, he bought a barrel organ and took to the streets with the hope of seducing his Cousin Antonieta and entertaining the public in the bargain. The machine was just a rusty box with wheels, but he painted it with seafaring designs and gave it a fake ship's smokestack. It ended up looking like a coal stove. The organ played either a military march or a waltz, and in between turns of the handle the parrot, who had managed to learn Spanish although he had not lost his foreign accent, would draw a crowd with his piercing shrieks. He also plucked slips of paper from a box with his beak, by way of selling fortunes to the curious. The little pink, green, and blue papers were so clever that they always divulged the exact secret wishes of the customers. Besides fortunes there were little balls of sawdust to amuse the children. The idea of the organ was a last desperate attempt to win the hand of Cousin Antonieta after more conventional means of courting her had failed. Marcos thought no woman in her right mind could remain impassive before a barrel-organ serenade. He stood beneath her window one evening and played his military march and his waltz just as she was taking tea with a group of female friends. Antonieta did not realize the music was meant for her until the parrot called her by her full name, at which point she appeared in the window. Her reaction was not what her suitor had hoped for. Her friends offered to spread the news to every salon[4] in the city, and the next day people thronged the downtown streets hoping to see Severo del Valle's brother-in-law playing the organ and selling little sawdust balls with a moth-eaten parrot, for the sheer pleasure of proving that even in the best of families there

could be good reason for embarrassment. In the face of this stain to the family reputation, Marcos was forced to give up organ grinding and resort to less conspicuous ways of winning over his Cousin Antonieta, but he did not renounce his goal. In any case, he did not succeed, because from one day to the next the young lady married a diplomat who was twenty years her senior; he took her to live in a tropical country whose name no one could recall, except that it suggested negritude,[5] bananas, and palm trees, where she managed to recover from the memory of that suitor who had ruined her seventeenth year with his military march and his waltz. Marcos sank into a deep depression that lasted two or three days, at the end of which he announced that he would never marry and that he was embarking on a trip around the world. He sold his organ to a blind man and left the parrot to Clara, but Nana secretly poisoned it with an overdose of cod-liver oil, because no one could stand its lusty glance, its fleas, and its harsh, tuneless hawking of paper fortunes and sawdust balls.

That was Marcos's longest trip. He returned with a shipment of enormous boxes that were piled in the far courtyard, between the chicken coop and the woodshed, until the winter was over. At the first signs of spring he had them transferred to the parade grounds, a huge park where people would gather to watch the soldiers file by on Independence Day, with the goosestep they had learned from the Prussians. When the crates were opened, they were found to contain loose bits of wood, metal, and painted cloth. Marcos spent two weeks assembling the contents according to an instruction manual written in English, which he was able to decipher thanks to his invincible imagination and a small dictionary. When the job was finished, it turned out to be a

---

4. salon (sə län´) *n.*: A regular gathering of distinguished guests that meets in a private home.

5. negritude (neg´ rə tōōd´) *n.*: Blacks and their cultural heritage.

Grammar in Action

Adverb clauses, like adverbs, tell where, when, in what manner, to what extent, under what condition, or why. An adverb clause begins with a subordinating conjunction and includes a subject and verb. It may include complements and modifiers. In the sentence, *"When we finally reached home,* we were exhausted,"* the italicized words form an adverb clause telling when. The clause includes the subordinating conjunction *when,* the subject

we, the verb *reached,* and the complement *home.* Because the clause precedes the verb, it is followed by a comma.

Writers use adverb clauses to vary their sentences, make their descriptions more specific, and clarify relationships between ideas. Note, for example, the following adverb clauses from "Uncle Marcos":

"Antonieta did not realize the music was meant for her *until the parrot called her by her full name . . ."*

"*When the job was finished,* it turned out to be a bird of prehistoric dimensions . . ."

Each clause begins with a subordinating conjunction; each has a subject; each includes a verb.

bird of prehistoric dimensions, with the face of a furious eagle, wings that moved, and a propeller on its back. It caused an uproar. The families of the oligarchy[6] forgot all about the barrel organ, and Marcos became the star attraction of the season. People took Sunday outings to see the bird; souvenir vendors and strolling photographers made a fortune. Nonetheless, the public's interest quickly waned. But then Marcos announced that as soon as the weather cleared he planned to take off in his bird and cross the mountain range. The news spread, making this the most talked-about event of the year. The contraption lay with its stomach on terra firma,[7] heavy and sluggish and looking more like a wounded duck than like one of those newfangled airplanes they were starting to produce in the United States. There was nothing in its appearance to suggest that it could move, much less take flight across the snowy peaks. Journalists and the curious flocked to see it. Marcos smiled his immutable[8] smile before the avalanche of questions and posed for photographers without offering the least technical or scientific explanation of how he hoped to carry out his plan. People came from the provinces to see the sight. Forty years later his great-nephew Nicolás, whom Marcos did not live to see, unearthed the desire to fly that had always existed in the men of his lineage. Nicolás was interested in doing it for commercial reasons, in a gigantic hot-air sausage on which would be printed an advertisement for carbonated drinks. But when Marcos announced his plane trip, no one believed that his contraption could be put to any practical use. The appointed day dawned full of clouds, but so many people had turned out

that Marcos did not want to disappoint them. He showed up punctually at the appointed spot and did not once look up at the sky, which was growing darker and darker with thick gray clouds. The astonished crowd filled all the nearby streets, perching on rooftops and the balconies of the nearest houses and squeezing into the park. No political gathering managed to attract so many people until half a century later, when the first Marxist candidate attempted, through strictly democratic channels, to become President. Clara would remember this holiday as long as she lived. People dressed in their spring best, thereby getting a step ahead of the official opening of the season, the men in white linen suits and the ladies in the Italian straw hats that were all the rage that year. Groups of elementary-school children paraded with their teachers, clutching flowers for the hero. Marcos accepted their bouquets and joked that they might as well hold on to them and wait for him to crash, so they could take them directly to his funeral. The bishop himself, accompanied by two incense bearers, appeared to bless the bird without having been asked, and the police band played happy, unpretentious music that pleased everyone. The police, on horseback and carrying lances, had trouble keeping the crowds far enough away from the center of the park, where Marcos waited dressed in mechanic's overalls, with huge racer's goggles and an explorer's helmet. He was also equipped with a compass, a telescope, and several strange maps that he had traced himself based on various theories of Leonardo da Vinci and on the polar knowledge of the Incas.[9] Against all logic, on the second try the bird lifted off without mishap and with a certain elegance, accompanied by

6. **oligarchy** (äl′ i gär′ kē) n.: Government ruled by a few.
7. **terra firma** (ter′ ə fur′ mə) n.: Firm earth; solid ground.
8. **immutable** (im myoo̅t′ ə bəl) adj.: Never changing.

9. **Leonardo da Vinci** (lē′ ə när′ dō də vin′ chē) . . . **Incas:** Leonardo da Vinci (1452–1519) was an Italian painter, sculptor, architect, and scientist. The Incas were native Americans who dominated ancient Peru until the Spanish conquest.

Uncle Marcos 65

12 **Reading Strategy** Describe the onlookers' reactions. Why did the public's interest wane so quickly? Tell students to take note of how the public's reactions change throughout Uncle Marcos's flight.

13 **Enrichment** The author is referring to the Andes Mountains. Stretching the entire west coast of South America, the Andes are the longest chain of mountains in the world, and second highest to the Himalayas of India and Tibet. It is about 500 miles across the widest part of the Andes.

14 **Discussion** Why is it typical of Marcos's character to withhold an explanation of how he is to carry out his plan?

15 **Enrichment** The author is referring to a blimp. Blimps are filled with helium, a lighter-than-air gas that keeps them aloft. They are still used for advertising purposes.

16 **Enrichment** The author is referring to her uncle, Salvador Allende, who was President of Chile from 1970 to 1973.

17 **Literary Focus** What character traits of Uncle Marcos does this sentence reveal?

18 **Reading Strategy** Try to visualize Uncle Marcos in detail as described by the narrator in this scene. What effect does the description achieve?

Student Activity 1. Locate the adverb clauses in the following sentences from the story. Identify the subordinating conjunction, the subject, the verb, and any complements or modifiers in each clause.

1. But when Marcos announced his plane trip, no one believed that his contraption could be put to any practical use.

2. Clara continued to stare at the sky long after her uncle had become invisible.

Student Activity 2. Write two original sentences using adverb clauses. In one sentence, place the adverb clause at the beginning of the sentence.

Electronic Handbook You might want students to review adverb clauses before completing the Grammar in Action activities. If students have access to the Language Master 6000, have them enter *adverb, interruption,* or *clause* and press the GRAMMAR key.

19 Discussion What comment on human nature in general is the author making? Do you agree that this is a typical public reaction to an important event? Can you think of any parallels in recent news reports?

20 Reading Strategy How does the word *ignorant* in this sentence achieve a humorous effect? Is it more ridiculous to suggest that Uncle Marcos reached the moon than to speculate that he disappeared into outer space?

21 Discussion Why is Severo sad? Why is he relieved?

22 Discussion Why doesn't Clara weep? Why is she watching the sky? What does it mean that she has "the patience of an astronomer"?

23 Discussion Does Uncle Marcos believe that he owes his survival to the prayers of the women and children? Why does he say that he believes this?

the creaking of its skeleton and the roar of its motor. It rose flapping its wings and disappeared into the clouds, to a send-off of applause, whistlings, handkerchiefs, drumrolls, and the sprinkling of holy water. All that remained on earth were the comments of the amazed crowd below and a multitude of experts, who attempted to provide a reasonable explanation of the miracle. Clara continued to stare at the sky long after her uncle had become invisible. She thought she saw him ten minutes later, but it was only a migrating sparrow. After three days the initial euphoria that had accompanied the first airplane flight in the country died down and no one gave the episode another thought, except for Clara, who continued to peer at the horizon.

After a week with no word from the flying uncle, people began to speculate that he had gone so high that he had disappeared into outer space, and the ignorant suggested he would reach the moon. With a mixture of sadness and relief, Severo decided that his brother-in-law and his machine must have fallen into some hidden crevice of the *cordillera*,[10] where they would never be found. Nívea wept disconsolately and lit candles to

10. **cordillera** (kôr′ dil yer′ə) *n.*: A system or chain of mountains.

66   *Short Stories*

San Antonio, patron of lost objects. Severo opposed the idea of having masses said, because he did not believe in them as a way of getting into heaven, much less of returning to earth, and he maintained that masses and religious vows, like the selling of indulgences, images, and scapulars,[11] were a dishonest business. Because of his attitude, Nívea and Nana had the children say the rosary[12] behind their father's back for nine days. Meanwhile, groups of volunteer explorers and mountain climbers tirelessly searched peaks and passes, combing every accessible stretch of land until they finally returned in triumph to hand the family the mortal remains of the deceased in a sealed black coffin. The intrepid traveler was laid to rest in a grandiose funeral. His death made him a hero and his name was on the front page of all the papers for several days. The same multitude that had gathered to see him off the day he flew away in his bird paraded past his coffin. The entire family wept as befit the occasion, except for Clara, who continued to watch the sky with the patience of an astronomer. One week after he had been buried, Uncle Marcos, a bright smile playing behind his pirate's mustache, appeared in person in the doorway of Nívea and Severo del Valle's house. Thanks to the surreptitious[13] prayers of the women and children, as he himself admitted, he was alive and well and in full possession of his faculties, including his sense of humor. Despite the noble lineage of his aerial maps, the flight had been a failure. He had lost his airplane and had to return on foot, but he had not broken any bones and his adventurous

11. **indulgences, images, and scapulars** (skap′ yə lərz): Indulgences are pardons for sins, images are pictures or sculptures of religious figures, and scapulars are garments worn by Roman Catholics as tokens of religious devotion.
12. **say the rosary:** Use a set of beads to say prayers, as Roman Catholics do.
13. **surreptitious** (sur′ əp tish′ əs) *adj.*: Secretive.

Primary Source: The House of the Spirits

Allende's novel, *The House of the Spirits*, begins as Alba, the granddaughter of Clara, writes from exile to keep alive the memory of her past. It is not difficult to see that the character of Alba is based on the author herself. "When I left Chile," says Allende, "I didn't dare tell my grandfather. . . . I couldn't find the words." Years later when her grandfather, nearly a hundred years old, telephoned to tell her that he was dying, "I wanted to tell my grandfather that I was never going to forget him, he would never die, just as my grandmother had never died. . . . And I started writing a letter, telling him the same things he had told me when I was a child." The letter, never sent, evolved into *The House of the Spirits*.

spirit was intact. This confirmed the family's eternal devotion to San Antonio, but was not taken as a warning by future generations, who also tried to fly, although by different means. Legally, however, Marcos was a corpse. Severo del Valle was obliged to use all his legal ingenuity to bring his brother-in-law back to life and the full rights of citizenship. When the coffin was pried open in the presence of the appropriate authorities, it was found to contain a bag of sand. This discovery ruined the reputation, up till then untarnished, of the volunteer explorers and mountain climbers, who from that day on were considered little better than a pack of bandits.

Marcos's heroic resurrection made everyone forget about his barrel-organ phase. Once again he was a sought-after guest in all the city's salons and, at least for a while, his name was cleared. Marcos stayed in his sister's house for several months. One night he left without saying goodbye, leaving behind his trunks, his books, his weapons, his boots, and all his belongings. Severo, and even Nívea herself, breathed a sigh of relief. His visit had gone on too long. But Clara was so upset that she spent a week walking in her sleep and sucking her thumb. The little girl, who was only seven at the time, had learned to read from her uncle's storybooks and been closer to him than any other member of the family because of her prophesying powers. Marcos maintained that his niece's gift could be a source of income and a good opportunity for him to cultivate his own clairvoyance.[14] He believed that all human beings possessed this ability, particularly his own family, and that if it did not function well it was simply due to a lack of training. He bought a crystal ball in the Persian bazaar, insisting that it had magic powers and was from the East (although it was later found to be part of a buoy from a fishing boat), set it down on a background of black velvet, and announced that he could tell people's fortunes, cure the evil eye, and improve the quality of dreams, all for the modest sum of five centavos.[15] His first customers were the maids from around the neighborhood. One of them had been accused of stealing, because her employer had misplaced a valuable ring. The crystal ball revealed the exact location of the object in question: it had rolled beneath a wardrobe. The next day there was a line outside the front door of the house. There were coachmen, storekeepers, and milkmen; later a few municipal employees and distinguished ladies made a discreet appearance, slinking along the side walls of the house to keep from being recognized. The customers were received by Nana, who ushered them into the waiting room and collected their fees. This task kept her busy throughout the day and demanded so much of her time that the family began to complain that all there ever was for dinner was old string beans and jellied quince.[16] Marcos decorated the carriage house with some frayed curtains that had once belonged in the drawing room but that neglect and age had turned to dusty rags. There he and Clara received the customers. The two divines wore tunics "color of the men of light," as Marcos called the color yellow. Nana had dyed them with saffron powder, boiling them in pots usually reserved for rice and pasta. In addition to his tunic, Marcos wore a turban around his head and an Egyptian amulet around his neck. He had grown a beard and let his hair grow long and he was thinner than ever before. Marcos and Clara were utterly convincing, especially because the child had no need to look into the crystal ball

14. **clairvoyance** (kler voi′ ans) *n.*: The ability to perceive things that are not in sight or can't be seen.

15. **centavos** (sen tä′ vōs) *n.*: Brazilian currency equal to $\frac{1}{100}$ of a cruzeiro.
16. **quince** (kwins): A golden or greenish-yellow, hard, apple-shaped fruit.

Uncle Marcos 67

24 **Discussion** What might have motivated the explorers and mountain climbers to claim that they had found Uncle Marcos's body?

25 **Discussion** Why is Uncle Marcos's name cleared? What does this reaction reveal about human nature?

26 **Enrichment** This passage describes what the author herself had to do when she left Chile and fled to Venezuela after the overthrow of her uncle's government.

27 **Clarification** In the novel, *The House of the Spirits,* from which this selection is an excerpt, Clara is born with the supernatural abilities to move objects without touching them and to foretell the future.

28 **Discussion** Why do the municipal employees and distinguished ladies want to be unrecognized?

29 **Discussion** Why is it necessary for Uncle Marcos to look the part of a fortune teller? What does this detail reveal about his character?

30 **Reading Strategy** What words and phrases does the author use to suggest that Uncle Marcos and Clara are frauds? What does this fact reveal about Uncle Marcos's character? Tell students to look for more proof on the following page.

Commentary: Chile

Chile is the southernmost country of South America, lying between the snow-capped peaks of the Andes Mountains and the Pacific Ocean. Chile has a long history of political upheaval, beginning in 1817 when it won its independence from the Spanish who had controlled the country since the sixteenth century. In 1970, Salvador Allende Gossens became president of Chile. Allende was the first Marxist to be democratically elected to head any country in the Western Hemisphere. In 1973, the military, led by General Augusto Pinochet Ugarte, forcibly took over Allende's government and arrested his supporters. Reports suggested that Allende had committed suicide during the coup, although many believe he was assassinated. Pinochet became the military dictator of the new government. In 1989, he allowed democratic elections to be held, but retained control of the military.

31 Discussion What is the reason for Clara's and Uncle Marcos's success as fortune tellers? Why do some people find comfort in visiting fortune tellers?

32 Literary Focus What character traits of Clara, Uncle Marcos, and Nana does this passage reveal?

33 Clarification Students may be unfamiliar with the word *macaws*. Tell them that macaws are a type of parrot that is indigenous to South and Central America.

34 Enrichment A lama is a high monk of Lamaism, a religion practiced in Tibet, Bhutan, Kashmir, Sikim, and Mongolia. Yak lard is a butter made from the milk of the yak, a stocky, long-haired wild ox.

35 Enrichment This passage describes a similar happening in the author's own life: Allende's grandmother kept journals of the family and daily life.

36 Clarification The author is referring to an event that occurs later in the novel.

37 Reading Strategy To what other trips in a coffin is the author referring?

to guess what her clients wanted to hear. She would whisper in her Uncle Marcos's ear, and he in turn would transmit the message to the client, along with any improvisations of his own that he thought pertinent. Thus their fame spread, because all those who arrived sad and bedraggled at the consulting room left filled with hope. Unrequited lovers were told how to win over indifferent hearts, and the poor left with foolproof tips on how to place their money at the dog tracks. Business grew so prosperous that the waiting room was always packed with people, and Nana began to suffer dizzy spells from being on her feet so many hours a day. This time Severo had no need to intervene to put a stop to his brother-in-law's venture, for both Marcos and Clara, realizing that their unerring guesses could alter the fate of their clients, who always followed their advice to the letter, became frightened and decided that this was a job for swindlers. They abandoned their carriage-house oracle and split the profits, even though the only one who had cared about the material side of things had been Nana.

Of all the del Valle children, Clara was the one with the greatest interest in and stamina for her uncle's stories. She could repeat each and every one of them. She knew by heart words from several dialects of the Indians, was acquainted with their customs, and could describe the exact way in which they pierced their lips and earlobes with wooden shafts, their initiation rites, the names of the most poisonous snakes, and the appropriate antidotes for each. Her uncle was so eloquent that the child could feel in her own skin the burning sting of snakebites, see reptiles slide across the carpet between the legs of the jacaranda[17] room divider, and hear the shrieks of macaws behind the drawing-room drapes. She did not

hesitate as she recalled Lope de Aguirre's search for El Dorado,[18] or the unpronounceable names of the flora and fauna her extraordinary uncle had seen; she knew about the lamas who take salt tea with yak lard and she could give detailed descriptions of the opulent women of Tahiti, the rice fields of China, or the white prairies of the North, where the eternal ice kills animals and men who lose their way, turning them to stone in seconds. Marcos had various travel journals in which he recorded his excursions and impressions, as well as a collection of maps and books of stories and fairy tales that he kept in the trunks he stored in the junk room at the far end of the third courtyard. From there they were hauled out to inhabit the dreams of his descendants, until they were mistakenly burned half a century later on an infamous pyre.

Now Marcos had returned from his last journey in a coffin. He had died of a mysterious African plague that had turned him as yellow and wrinkled as a piece of parchment. When he realized he was ill, he set out for home with the hope that his sister's ministrations and Dr. Cuevas's knowledge would restore his health and youth, but he was unable to withstand the sixty days on ship and died at the latitude of Guayaquil,[19] ravaged by fever and hallucinating about musky women and hidden treasure. The captain of the ship, an Englishman by the name of Longfellow, was about to throw him overboard wrapped in a flag, but Marcos, despite his savage appearance and his delirium, had made so many friends on board and seduced so many women that the passengers prevented him from doing so, and Longfellow

---

17. jacaranda (jak′ ə ran′ də): A type of tropical American tree.

18. Lope de Aguirre's (lō′ pā thä ag ē′ räz) . . . **El Dorado:** Lope de Aguirre was a Spanish adventurer (1510–1561) in colonial South America who searched for a legendary country called El Dorado, which was supposedly rich in gold.
19. Guayaquil (gwī′ ä kēl′): A seaport in western Ecuador.

Closure and Extension
ANSWERS TO RESPONDING TO THE SELECTION

Your Response
1. Have the students share their opinions with the class. Remind them that since Clara had an unusual quality herself—clairvoyance—Uncle Marcos was probably the only family member who understood her and with whom she had something in common.

Interpreting
2. Nana dislikes Uncle Marcos's untidy habits and his animals, but likes him enough to become his fortune-telling partner; Severo finds him irresponsible and uncivilized, but feels responsible for him; Nivea finds his eccentric habits unsettling but loves him; Clara loves him and is enchanted by him.
3. The following evidence refutes Severo's claim: Uncle Marcos can

was obliged to store the body side by side with the vegetables of the Chinese cook, to preserve it from the heat and mosquitoes of the tropics until the ship's carpenter had time to improvise a coffin. At El Callao[20] they obtained a more appropriate container, and several days later the captain, furious at all the troubles this passenger had caused the shipping company and himself personally, unloaded him without a backward glance,

38

---

20. El Callao (kə yä′ ō): A seaport in western Peru.

surprised that not a soul was there to receive the body or cover the expenses he had incurred. Later he learned that the post office in these latitudes was not as reliable as that of far-off England, and that all his telegrams had vaporized en route. Fortunately for Longfellow, a customs lawyer who was a friend of the del Valle family appeared and offered to take charge, placing Marcos and all his paraphernalia in a freight car, which he shipped to the capital to the only known address of the deceased: his sister's house. . . .

39

RESPONDING TO THE SELECTION

Your Response

1. What difference do you think Uncle Marcos made in Clara's life?

Interpreting

2. What is each character's attitude toward Uncle Marcos? How do the other characters' attitudes differ from Clara's attitude?

3. Severo says, "Uncle Marcos's manners were those of a cannibal." What evidence from this story refutes Severo's claim?

Applying

4. Uncle Marcos is the embodiment of curiosity and imagination. He broadens Clara's view of the world, but he is often misunderstood by his family and the townspeople. How does a society value seemingly strange and innovative ideas? How does a society or culture benefit from such people and their innovations?

5. Allende immortalizes those who were dear to her by modeling her novel's characters after them. In what other ways might we immortalize those who are memorable?

ANALYZING LITERATURE

Recognizing Character Traits

Any quality that is part of a character's personality is a **character trait.** Some character traits are essential to the development of a story; others are not but may help to make the character seem true to life. In Clara's journal she described the qualities of her uncle that captured her attention as a child—those qualities that seemed to her extravagant and enchanting.

1. List five of Uncle Marcos's character traits. What details in the story support your answer?

2. As a child, why might Clara have tended to focus on her uncle's extravagant aspects?

3. Close your eyes and envision Uncle Marcos. What instructions would you give to an artist who was drawing a portrait of him? What actor would you cast to play him? Compare your vision with those of your classmates.

THINKING AND WRITING

Writing About a Memorable Person

Think about someone who is especially meaningful to you and whose spirit you would like to keep alive. Make a list of that person's character traits, including any extravagant or particularly unforgettable characteristics. Write about one memorable incident in which you and this person were involved. Weave into the story details that illustrate what this person means to you, in much the same way as Allende does in "Uncle Marcos." You may wish to add some fantastic details, but they should tell your readers something about the person's character.

Uncle Marcos **69**

---

38 Literary Focus Is this account of Uncle Marcos's death sad or humorous? How would Uncle Marcos have reacted to it?

39 Literary Focus Why was Nivea's house Uncle Marcos's only known address? Which of Uncle Marcos's character traits does this final sentence emphasize?

Reader's Response Which character's response to Uncle Marcos is most like your own?

Thematic Response Clara appreciated her Uncle Marcos, but do you think others appreciated him as well? Find evidence in the story that Uncle Marcos was appreciated by many whose lives he touched.

THINKING AND WRITING

Alternative Assessment *Protocol for Thinking and Writing Assignment:* Ask your students to assess their own work by responding to the following questions:

Whose memory do you wish to keep alive? Why?

What memorable incident involving you and this person did you describe?

What characteristics of this person are revealed in this incident?

What insight did you gain about this person and yourself from this assignment?

What aspect of this assignment was most difficult for you? Why?

You may have your students use the information gained from their protocols as a guide for revising this assignment.

Publishing Student Writing Compile students' work in a classroom book that students illustrate and name. Display it in the classroom or library for others to read and enjoy.

---

make the airplane fly, has a keen sense of humor, owns many books, knows stories from all over the world, charms the passengers on the ship.

Applying

4. Answers may differ. Suggested Response: New ideas are usually met with suspicion; such people pave the way for change and progress.

5. Suggested Responses: We might commemorate them in other media, tell others about them, work for causes they supported, try to emulate them, erect memorials, or establish holidays in their honor.

ANSWERS TO ANALYZING LITERATURE

1. Answers may differ. Suggested Response: (1) adventurous—traveled to exotic places all over the world (2) romantic—tried to win Antonieta's hand by playing the barrel organ (3) storyteller—told Clara captivating stories of his adventures (4) daring—flew the airplane with his stories (5) charming—was popular aboard ship.

2. Uncle Marcos brought Clara a taste of the exotic and romantic.

3. Students might refer to the photograph of Uncle Marcos at the beginning of the selection. They might choose actors who have played parts of eccentrics or adventurers in movies or television shows.

Preparation

More About the Author Sir Arthur Conan Doyle claimed that the character of Sherlock Holmes was based on his anatomy teacher, whose diagnostic skills he had greatly admired. Ask students whether they believe most fictional characters are based on real people.

Literary Focus You might have students reinforce their understanding of character traits by listing some that they think a detective should possess.

Prereading Focus You might want to suggest some television or film detectives, such as Columbo and Inspector Clouseau, to students to get them started on the exercise. It might also be helpful to model the creation of a Venn diagram if students are unfamiliar with them.

Vocabulary Have your **less advanced** students study these words and use as many of them as possible in a single paragraph.

Spelling Tip Point out the two words that end in *x: hoax, vex*. Tell students that *x* can spell the sound /ks/ as in *box* and *coax*.

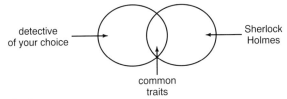

GUIDE FOR READING

Sir Arthur Conan Doyle

(1859–1930) was born in Edinburgh, Scotland. He became a doctor, but he practiced medicine for only eight years. Three years after he wrote his first story about Sherlock Holmes, he gave up medicine to write full time. All of the Holmes stories are narrated by a medical man, the somewhat naive Doctor Watson. "The Red-headed League" was first published in *Strand* magazine in 1891. In it, as in other Holmes stories, Watson is amazed at Holmes's feats of deduction.

The Red-headed League

Motivation

Motivation is a character's reason or reasons for saying or doing something. What motivates a character to act may be a feeling or a goal. A character is likely to have many motives, both emotional and rational, for a particular action. When reading a detective story, motives are of particular interest because they reveal why the criminal committed the crime.

Focus

Think about detectives you have read about or know of from television and film. Do they share traits common to good sleuths, such as keen powers of observation and deduction? How are they different from one another? Do they have personalities or styles that are unique or even eccentric? As you read "The Red-headed League," compare one of these detectives with Sherlock Holmes. List common traits in the intersection of the circles of a Venn diagram like the one below. Then, in the remaining parts of the circles, list traits that are unique to each character.

detective of your choice → ⟨ ⟩ ← Sherlock Holmes

common traits

Vocabulary

Knowing the following words will help you as you read "The Red-headed League."

singular (siŋ′ gyə lər) *adj.*: Extraordinary; rare (p. 71)
avail (ə vāl′) *v.*: Be of help (p. 78)
hoax (hōks) *n.*: A deceitful trick (p. 78)
introspective (in′ trə spek′ tiv) *adj.*: Causing one to look into one's own thoughts and feelings (p. 80)

vex (veks) *v.*: Annoy (p. 82)
conundrums (kə nun′ drəmz) *n.*: Puzzling questions or problems (p. 82)
astuteness (ə stoot′ nis) *n.*: Shrewdness (p. 82)
formidable (fôr′ mə də b'l) *adj.*: Awe-inspiring (p. 82)

Objectives

1 To understand motivation
2 To contrast characters' abilities
3 To analyze a detective's methods
4 To express individual interests and abilities through optional activities

Support Material

Teaching Portfolio
Teacher Backup, p. 99
Grammar in Action Worksheets, *Using Single Quotation Marks,* p. 101; *Examining Deductive Reasoning,* p. 103
Usage and Mechanics Worksheet, p. 105
Vocabulary Check, p. 106
Analyzing Literature Worksheet, *Recognizing Character Traits,* p. 108
Critical Thinking and Reading Worksheet, *Contrasting Characters' Abilities,* p. 109
Selection Test, p. 110

Prentice Hall Literature Writing Studio

The Red-headed League

Sir Arthur Conan Doyle

I had called upon my friend, Mr. Sherlock Holmes, one day in the autumn of last year and found him in deep conversation with a very stout, florid-faced, elderly gentleman with fiery red hair. With an apology for my intrusion, I was about to withdraw when Holmes pulled me abruptly into the room and closed the door behind me.

"You could not possibly have come at a better time, my dear Watson," he said cordially.

"I was afraid that you were engaged."

"So I am. Very much so."

"Then I can wait in the next room."

"Not at all. This gentleman, Mr. Wilson, has been my partner and helper in many of my most successful cases, and I have no doubt that he will be of the utmost use to me in yours also."

The stout gentleman half rose from his chair and gave a bob of greeting, with a quick little questioning glance from his small, fat-encircled eyes.

"Try the settee,"[1] said Holmes, relapsing into his armchair and putting his finger tips together, as was his custom when in judicial moods. "I know, my dear Watson, that you share my love of all that is bizarre and outside the conventions and humdrum routine of everyday life. You have shown your relish for it by the enthusiasm which has prompted you to chronicle, and, if you will

excuse my saying so, somewhat to embellish so many of my own little adventures."

"Your cases have indeed been of the greatest interest to me," I observed.

"You will remember that I remarked the other day, just before we went into the very simple problem presented by Miss Mary Sutherland, that for strange effects and extraordinary combinations we must go to life itself, which is always far more daring than any effort of the imagination."

"A proposition which I took the liberty of doubting."

"You did, Doctor, but none the less you must come round to my view, for otherwise I shall keep on piling fact upon fact on you until your reason breaks down under them and acknowledges me to be right. Now, Mr. Jabez Wilson here has been good enough to call upon me this morning, and to begin a narrative which promises to be one of the most singular which I have listened to for some time. You have heard me remark that the strangest and most unique things are very often connected not with the larger but with the smaller crimes, and occasionally, indeed, where there is room for doubt whether any positive crime has been committed. As far as I have heard it is impossible for me to say whether the present case is an instance of crime or not, but the course of events is certainly among the most singular that I have ever listened to. Perhaps, Mr. Wilson, you would have the great kindness to

---

1. **settee** (se tē´) n.: Small sofa.

Presentation

Motivation/Prior Knowledge
Write the heading, "World's Most Famous Detective," on the chalkboard and ask students to name characters they think might fit this title. Explain that many readers consider Sherlock Holmes the world's most famous detective because of his superior powers of deduction. Then ask students to consider whether his reputation is deserved as they read this story.

Thematic Focus The gullible nature of Jabez Wilson and the amazement of Doctor Watson show readers the lighter side of crime detection. Have students discuss whether they have ever seen the funny side of something that was supposed to be serious.

Making Connections Another selection in which the protagonist displays intelligence and courage is "The Most Dangerous Game," by Richard Connell, page 13.

Purpose-Setting Question How is Holmes able to make inferences from facts that seem puzzling or disconnected to others?

1 **Clarification** This is another way of saying that truth is stranger than fiction.

2 **Reading Strategy** Ask students to make predictions about the story based on this remark.

Alternative Assessment To promote active reading, have students keep a reader's response journal as they read the story. Ask them to focus their observations on the details that Sherlock Holmes uses to solve the mystery. Encourage students to respond personally to the characters and events in the story. With which character can they more readily identify—Holmes or Watson? Their observations will enable you to assess their understanding of the issues in the story.

3   recommence your narrative. I ask you not merely because my friend Dr. Watson has not heard the opening part but also because the peculiar nature of the story makes me anxious to have every possible detail from your lips. As a rule, when I have heard some slight indication of the course of events, I am able to guide myself by the thousands of other similar cases which occur to my memory. In the present instance I am forced to admit that the facts are, to the best of my belief, unique."

The portly client puffed out his chest with an appearance of some little pride and pulled a dirty and wrinkled newspaper from the inside pocket of his great coat. As he glanced down the advertisement column, with his head thrust forward and the paper flattened out upon his knee, I took a good look at the man and endeavored, after the fashion of my companion, to read the indications which might be presented by his dress or appearance.

I did not gain very much, however, by my inspection. Our visitor bore every mark of being an average commonplace British tradesman, obese, pompous, and slow. He wore rather baggy gray shepherd's check trousers, a not over-clean black frock coat, unbuttoned in the front, and a drab waistcoat with a heavy brassy Albert chain, and a square pierced bit of metal dangling down as an ornament. A frayed top hat and a faded brown overcoat with a wrinkled velvet collar lay upon a chair beside him. Altogether, look as I would, there was nothing remarkable about the man save his blazing red head, and the expression of extreme chagrin and discontent upon his features.

Sherlock Holmes's quick eye took in my occupation, and he shook his head with a smile as he noticed my questioning glances. "Beyond the obvious facts that he has at some time done manual labor, that he takes snuff,[2] that he is a Freemason,[3] that he has been in China, and that he has done a considerable amount of writing lately, I can deduce nothing else."

Mr. Jabez Wilson started up in his chair, with his forefinger upon the paper, but his eyes upon my companion.

"How, in the name of good fortune, did you know all that, Mr. Holmes?" he asked. "How did you know, for example, that I did manual labor? It's as true as gospel, for I began as a ship's carpenter."

---

2. **snuff:** Powdered tobacco.
3. **Freemason:** Member of a secret society.

"Your hands, my dear sir. Your right hand is quite a size larger than your left. You have worked with it, and the muscles are more developed."

"Well, the snuff, then, and the Freemasonry?"

"I won't insult your intelligence by telling you how I read that, especially as, rather against the strict rules of your order, you use an arc-and-compass breastpin."

"Ah, of course, I forgot that. But the writing?"

"What else can be indicated by that right cuff so very shiny for five inches, and the left one with the smooth patch near the elbow where you rest it upon the desk?"

"Well, but China?"

"The fish that you have tattooed immediately above your right wrist could only have been done in China. I have made a small study of tattoo marks and have even contributed to the literature of the subject. That trick of staining the fishes' scales of a delicate pink is quite peculiar to China. When, in addition, I see a Chinese coin hanging from your watch-chain, the matter becomes even more simple."

Mr. Jabez Wilson laughed heavily. "Well, I never!" said he. "I thought at first that you had done something clever, but I see that there was nothing in it, after all."

"I begin to think, Watson," said Holmes, "that I make a mistake in explaining. '*Omne ignotum pro magnifico,*'[4] you know, and my poor little reputation, such as it is, will suffer shipwreck if I am so candid. Can you not find the advertisement, Mr. Wilson?"

"Yes, I have got it now," he answered with his thick red finger planted halfway down the column. "Here it is. This is what began it all. You just read it for yourself, sir."

---

4. *Omne ignotum pro magnifico* (äm′ nä ig nō′ t'm prō mag nē′ fē kō): Latin for "Whatever is unknown is magnified."

---

4 **Discussion** What does this statement indicate about Sherlock Holmes's methods of deduction?

5 **Discussion** Compare and contrast Watson's deductions with those of Holmes.

6 **Discussion** Holmes's deduction about Mr. Wilson has nothing to do with the crime that will be committed. Why did the author include it?

7 **Clarification** After Holmes explains his methods of deduction, Mr. Wilson dismisses his talent saying, ". . . there was nothing in it, after all." Holmes then shares a joke with Watson in Latin, a language that Mr. Wilson would not understand; he explains that it would be better for his reputation not to explain his deductive methods to someone who cannot appreciate his ability.

---

pects' personalities and psychology as he does following clues.

Why do students think detective stories are so popular? What detective stories do students prefer? Have them give a reason for their preference.

8 **Literary Focus** Why is Holmes in such high spirits? What does this indicate about his personality?

9 **Reading Strategy** Ask students to listen to Mr. Wilson's story as Holmes would and try to predict which details will provide a clue to the mystery.

10 **Critical Thinking and Reading** Why do you think Holmes makes this comment?

11 **Discussion** Why do you think Spaulding is taking such an active part in getting Mr. Wilson this position?

Cooperative Learning Arrange the class in groups of four. Hand each group a sheet of paper. Explain that the groups are to come up with predictions about the real purpose of the advertisement. Ask: Who might have put the advertisement in the newspaper? Could there be a sinister purpose behind it?

Have a representative from each group share its prediction with the class.

I took the paper from him and read as follows:

To the Red-headed League:
On account of the bequest of the late Ezekiah Hopkins, of Lebanon, Pennsylvania, U.S.A., there is now another vacancy open which entitles a member of the League to a salary of £4[5] a week for purely nominal services. All red-headed men who are sound in body and mind, and above the age of twenty-one years, are eligible. Apply in person on Monday, at eleven o'clock, to Duncan Ross, at the offices of the League, 7 Pope's Court, Fleet Street.

"What on earth does this mean?" I ejaculated after I had twice read over the extraordinary announcement.

Holmes chuckled and wriggled in his chair, as was his habit when in high spirits. "It is a little off the beaten track, isn't it?" said he. "And now, Mr. Wilson, off you go at scratch and tell us all about yourself, your household, and the effect which this advertisement had upon your fortunes. You will first make a note, Doctor, of the paper and the date."

"It is *The Morning Chronicle* of April 27, 1890. Just two months ago."

"Very good. Now, Mr. Wilson?"

"Well, it is just as I have been telling you, Mr. Sherlock Holmes," said Jabez Wilson, mopping his forehead; "I have a small pawnbroker's business at Coburg Square, near the City. It's not a very large affair, and of late years it has not done more than just give me a living. I used to be able to keep two assistants, but now I only keep one; and I would have a job to pay him but that he is willing to come for half wages so as to learn the business."

"What is the name of this obliging youth?" asked Sherlock Holmes.

"His name is Vincent Spaulding, and he's not such a youth, either. It's hard to say his age. I should not wish a smarter assistant, Mr. Holmes; and I know very well that he could better himself and earn twice what I am able to give him. But, after all, if he is satisfied, why should I put ideas in his head?"

"Why, indeed? You seem most fortunate in having an employee who comes under the full market price. It is not a common experience among employers in this age. I don't know that your assistant is not as remarkable as your advertisement."

"Oh, he has his faults, too," said Mr. Wilson. "Never was such a fellow for photography. Snapping away with a camera when he ought to be improving his mind, and then diving down into the cellar like a rabbit into its hole to develop his pictures. That is his main fault, but on the whole he's a good worker. There's no vice in him."

"He is still with you, I presume?"

"Yes, sir. He and a girl of fourteen, who does a bit of simple cooking and keeps the place clean—that's all I have in the house, for I am a widower and never had any family. We live very quietly, sir, the three of us; and we keep a roof over our heads and pay our debts, if we do nothing more.

"The first thing that put us out was that advertisement. Spaulding, he came down into the office just this day eight weeks, with this very paper in his hand, and he says:

" 'I wish to the Lord, Mr. Wilson, that I was a red-headed man.'

" 'Why that?' I asks.

" 'Why,' says he, 'here's another vacancy on the League of the Red-headed Men. It's worth quite a little fortune to any man who

---

5. **£4:** Four pounds in British money—a large amount at the time in which the story is set.

gets it, and I understand that there are more vacancies than there are men, so that the trustees are at their wits' end what to do with the money. If my hair would only change color, here's a nice little crib all ready for me to step into.'

" 'Why, what is it, then?' I asked. You see, Mr. Holmes, I am a very stay-at-home man, and as my business came to me instead of my having to go to it, I was often weeks on end without putting my foot over the doormat. In that way I didn't know much of what was going on outside, and I was always glad of a bit of news.

" 'Have you never heard of the League of the Red-headed Men?' he asked with his eyes open.

" 'Never.'

" 'Why, I wonder at that, for you are eligible yourself for one of the vacancies.'

" 'And what are they worth?' I asked.

" 'Oh, merely a couple of hundred a year, but the work is slight, and it need not interfere very much with one's other occupations.'

"Well, you can easily think that that made me prick up my ears, for the business has not been over-good for some years, and an extra couple of hundred would have been very handy.

" 'Tell me all about it,' said I.

" 'Well,' said he, showing me the advertisement, 'you can see for yourself that the League has a vacancy, and there is the address where you should apply for particulars. As far as I can make out, the League was founded by an American millionaire, Ezekiah Hopkins, who was very peculiar in his ways. He was himself red-headed, and he had a great sympathy for all red-headed men; so when he died it was found that he had left his enormous fortune in the hands of trustees, with instructions to apply the interest to the providing of easy berths to men whose hair is of that color. From all I hear it is splendid pay and very little to do.'

" 'But,' said I, 'there would be millions of red-headed men who would apply.'

" 'Not so many as you might think,' he answered. 'You see it is really confined to Londoners, and to grown men. This American had started from London when he was young, and he wanted to do the old town a good turn. Then, again, I have heard it is no use your applying if your hair is light red, or dark red, or anything but real bright, blazing, fiery red. Now, if you cared to apply, Mr. Wilson, you would just walk in; but perhaps it would hardly be worth your while to put yourself out of the way for the sake of a few hundred pounds.'

"Now, it is a fact, gentlemen, as you may see for yourselves, that my hair is of a very full and rich tint, so that it seemed to me that if there was to be any competition in the matter I stood as good a chance as any man that I had ever met. Vincent Spaulding seemed to know so much about it that I thought he might prove useful so I just ordered him to put up the shutters for the day and to come right away with me. He was very willing to have a holiday,[6] so we shut the business up and started off for the address that was given us in the advertisement.

"I never hope to see such a sight as that again, Mr. Holmes. From north, south, east, and west every man who had a shade of red in his hair had tramped into the city to answer the advertisement. Fleet Street was choked with red-headed folk, and Pope's Court looked like a coster's orange barrow.[7] I should not have thought there were so many in the whole country as were brought together by that single advertisement. Every

---

6. **holiday:** A day off from work; a vacation.
7. **coster's orange barrow:** Pushcart of a seller of oranges.

12 **Reading Strategy** Summarize Mr. Wilson's description of the Red-headed League. Make special note of the facts that seem suspicious.

13 **Discussion** Why does Mr. Wilson take Spaulding with him when he applies for the job?

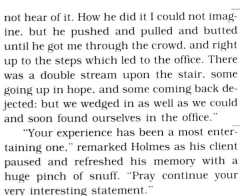

14 Critical Thinking and Reading
Do you think Mr. Spaulding's interest in getting Mr. Wilson to the office is unusual? Support your answer.

ESL Teaching Strategy Have ESL students connect the various shades of red described by Conan Doyle with those depicted in this picture. You might want to have ESL students work with native-speaking partners to make these connections.

shade of color they were—straw, lemon, orange, brick, Irish-setter, liver, clay: but, as Spaulding said, there were not many who had the real vivid flame-colored tint. When I saw how many were waiting, I would have given it up in despair: but Spaulding would

not hear of it. How he did it I could not imagine, but he pushed and pulled and butted until he got me through the crowd, and right up to the steps which led to the office. There was a double stream upon the stair, some going up in hope, and some coming back dejected: but we wedged in as well as we could and soon found ourselves in the office."

"Your experience has been a most entertaining one." remarked Holmes as his client paused and refreshed his memory with a huge pinch of snuff. "Pray continue your very interesting statement."

"There was nothing in the office but a couple of wooden chairs and a deal table, behind which sat a small man with a head that was even redder than mine. He said a few words to each candidate as he came up, and

then he always managed to find some fault in them which would disqualify them. Getting a vacancy did not seem to be such a very easy matter, after all. However, when our turn came the little man was much more favorable to me than to any of the others, and he closed the door as we entered, so that he might have a private word with us.

" 'This is Mr. Jabez Wilson,' said my assistant, 'and he is willing to fill a vacancy in the League.'

" 'And he is admirably suited for it,' the other answered. 'He has every requirement. I cannot recall when I have seen anything so fine.' He took a step backward, cocked his head on one side, and gazed at my hair until I felt quite bashful. Then suddenly he plunged forward, wrung my hand, and congratulated me warmly on my success.

" 'It would be injustice to hesitate,' said he. 'You will, however, I am sure, excuse me for taking an obvious precaution.' With that he seized my hair in both his hands, and tugged until I yelled with the pain. 'There is water in your eyes,' said he as he released me. 'I perceive that all is as it should be. But we have to be careful, for we have twice been deceived by wigs and once by paint. I could tell you tales of cobbler's wax which would disgust you with human nature.' He stepped over to the window and shouted through it at the top of his voice that the vacancy was filled. A groan of disappointment came up from below, and the folk all trooped away in different directions until there was not a red head to be seen except my own and that of the manager.

" 'My name,' said he, 'is Mr. Duncan Ross, and I am myself one of the pensioners upon the fund left by our noble benefactor. Are you a married man, Mr. Wilson? Have you a family?'

"I answered that I had not.

"His face fell immediately.

" 'Dear me!' he said gravely, 'that is very serious indeed! I am sorry to hear you say that. The fund was, of course, for the propogation and spread of the red-heads as well as for their maintenance. It is exceedingly unfortunate that you should be a bachelor.'

"My face lengthened at this, Mr. Holmes, for I thought that I was not to have the vacancy after all; but after thinking it over for a few minutes he said that it would be all right.

" 'In the case of another,' said he, 'the objection might be fatal, but we must stretch a point in favor of a man with such a head of hair as yours. When shall you be able to enter upon your new duties?'

" 'Well, it is a little awkward, for I have a business already,' said I.

" 'Oh, never mind about that, Mr. Wilson!' said Vincent Spaulding. 'I should be able to look after that for you.'

" 'What would be the hours?' I asked.

" 'Ten to two.'

"Now a pawnbroker's business is mostly done of an evening, Mr. Holmes, especially Thursday and Friday evening, which is just before pay-day; so it would suit me very well to earn a little in the mornings. Besides, I knew that my assistant was a good man, and that he would see to anything that turned up.

" 'That would suit me very well,' said I. 'And the pay?'

" 'Is £4 a week.'

" 'And the work?'

" 'Is purely nominal.'

" 'What do you call purely nominal?'

" 'Well, you have to be in the office, or at least in the building, the whole time. If you leave, you forfeit your whole position forever. The will is very clear upon that point. You don't comply with the conditions if you budge from the office during that time.'

" 'It's only four hours a day, and I should not think of leaving,' said I.

The Red-headed League 77

15 **Critical Thinking and Reading** What is unusual about the manner in which Mr. Wilson is treated by the head of the League?

16 **Discussion** What qualifications does Mr. Wilson have for the job at the League?

17 **Discussion** Do you think that Mr. Spaulding might be motivated by something other than kindness?

18 **Discussion** Why do you think the man stresses these conditions?

19 Critical Thinking and Reading
What inferences can you make about the Red-headed League based on what you have read about it so far?

20 Reading Strategy Summarize Mr. Wilson's experience at the Red-headed League, stressing the points you think most significant.

" 'No excuse will avail,' said Mr. Duncan Ross; 'neither sickness nor business nor anything else. There you must stay, or you lose your billet.'[8]

" 'And the work?'

" 'Is to copy out the Encyclopedia Britannica. There is the first volume of it in that press. You must find your own ink, pens, and blotting-paper, but we provide this table and chair. Will you be ready tomorrow?'

" 'Certainly,' I answered.

" 'Then, good-bye, Mr. Jabez Wilson, and let me congratulate you once more on the important position which you have been fortunate enough to gain.' He bowed me out of the room, and I went home with my assistant, hardly knowing what to say or do, I was so pleased at my own good fortune.

"Well, I thought over the matter all day, and by evening I was in low spirits again; for I had quite persuaded myself that the whole affair must be some great hoax or fraud, though what its object might be I could not imagine. It seemed altogether past belief that anyone could make such a will, or that they would pay such a sum for doing anything so simple as copying out the Encyclopedia Britannica. Vincent Spaulding did what he could to cheer me up, but by bedtime I had reasoned myself out of the whole thing. However, in the morning I determined to have a look at it anyhow, so I bought a penny bottle of ink, and with a quill-pen, and seven sheets of foolscap paper,[9] I started off for Pope's Court.

"Well, to my surprise and delight, everything was as right as possible. The table was set out ready for me, and Mr. Duncan Ross was there to see that I got fairly to work. He started me off upon the letter A, and then he

---

8. **billet** (bil' it) *n.*: Position, job.
9. **foolscap paper:** Writing paper.

left me; but he would drop in from time to time to see that all was right with me. At two o'clock he bade me good-day, complimented me upon the amount that I had written, and locked the door of the office after me.

"This went on day after day, Mr. Holmes, and on Saturday the manager came in and planked down four golden sovereigns for my week's work. It was the same next week, and the same the week after. Every morning I was there at ten, and every afternoon I left at two. By degrees Mr. Duncan Ross took to coming in only once of a morning, and then, after a time, he did not come in at all. Still, of course, I never dared to leave the room for an instant, for I was not sure when he might come, and the billet was such a good one, and suited me so well, that I would not risk the loss of it.

"Eight weeks passed away like this, and I had written about Abbots and Archery and Armor and Architecture and Attica, and hoped with diligence that I might get on to the B's before very long. It cost me something in foolscap, and I had pretty nearly filled a shelf with my writings. And then suddenly the whole business came to an end."

"To an end?"

"Yes, sir. And no later than this morning. I went to my work as usual at ten o'clock, but the door was shut and locked, with a little square of cardboard hammered on to the middle of the panel with a tack. Here it is, and you can read for yourself."

He held up a piece of white cardboard about the size of a sheet of notepaper. It read in this fashion:

THE RED-HEADED LEAGUE

IS

DISSOLVED.

October 9, 1890.

Grammar in Action

Single quotation marks show a quotation within a quotation and never appear without being accompanied by double quotation marks. Dialogue sometimes requires single quotation marks when a speaker is repeating the exact words of another speaker. Note the following example from "The Red-headed League":

" 'Oh,' said he, 'his name was William Morris . . . He moved out yesterday.'

" 'Where could I find him?'

" 'Oh, at his new offices. He did tell me the address. Yes. 17 King Edward Street, near St. Paul's.'

"I started off, Mr. Holmes, but when I got to that address . . . no one in it had ever heard of either Mr. William Morris or Mr. Duncan Ross."

"And what did you do then?" asked Holmes.

In the above passage, Jabez Wilson is reporting to Sherlock

Sherlock Holmes and I surveyed this curt announcement and the rueful face behind it, until the comical side of the affair so completely overtopped every other consideration that we both burst out into a roar of laughter.

"I cannot see that there is anything very funny," cried our client, flushing up to the roots of his flaming head. "If you can do nothing better than laugh at me, I can go elsewhere."

"No, no," cried Holmes, shoving him back into the chair from which he had half risen. "I really wouldn't miss your case for the world. It is most refreshingly unusual. But there is, if you will excuse my saying so, something just a little funny about it. Pray what steps did you take when you found the card upon the door?"

"I was staggered, sir. I did not know what to do. Then I called at the offices round, but none of them seemed to know anything about it. Finally, I went to the landlord, who is an accountant living on the ground floor, and I asked him if he could tell me what had become of the Red-headed League. He said that he had never heard of any such body. Then I asked him who Mr. Duncan Ross was. He answered that the name was new to him.

" 'Well,' said I, 'the gentleman at No. 4.'

" 'What, the red-headed man?'

" 'Yes.'

" 'Oh,' said he, 'his name was William Morris. He was a solicitor[10] and was using my room as a temporary convenience until his new premises were ready. He moved out yesterday.'

" 'Where could I find him?'

" 'Oh, at his new offices. He did tell me

---
10. **solicitor:** A member of the legal profession.

the address. Yes, 17 King Edward Street, near St. Paul's.'

"I started off, Mr. Holmes, but when I got to that address it was a manufactory of artificial kneecaps, and no one in it had ever heard of either Mr. William Morris or Mr. Duncan Ross."

"And what did you do then?" asked Holmes.

"I went home to Saxe-Coburg Square, and I took the advice of my assistant. But he could not help me in any way. He could only say that if I waited I should hear by post. But that was not quite good enough, Mr. Holmes. I did not wish to lose such a place without a struggle, so, as I had heard that you were good enough to give advice to poor folk who were in need of it, I came right away to you."

"And you did very wisely," said Holmes. "Your case is an exceedingly remarkable one, and I shall be happy to look into it. From what you have told me I think that it is possible that graver issues hang from it than might at first sight appear."

"Grave enough!" said Mr. Jabez Wilson. "Why, I have lost four pound a week."

"As far as you are personally concerned," remarked Holmes, "I do not see that you have any grievance against this extraordinary league. On the contrary, you are, as I understand, richer by some £30, to say nothing of the minute knowledge which you have gained on every subject which comes under the letter A. You have lost nothing by them."

"No, sir. But I want to find out about them, and who they are, and what their object was in playing this prank—if it was a prank—upon me. It was a pretty expensive joke for them, for it cost them two and thirty pounds."

"We shall endeavor to clear up these

21 **Discussion** After the League is dissolved, what circumstances lead Mr. Wilson to question its validity?

22 **Literary Focus** What attitude does Holmes take about this case? What is his attitude toward Mr. Wilson? What does this indicate about Holmes's character?

Holmes a conversation that he, Wilson, had with the landlord. Single quotation marks are used to set off the exact words of that earlier conversation. The double quotation marks indicate the conversation in the present with Holmes. Note that double quotation marks begin each new paragraph but end only in the fourth and fifth paragraphs, marking a change of speaker.

Student Activity 1. Read paragraphs 6-10 in the second column of page 74. Note each set of quotation marks. Decide who is speaking. How did you recognize that the speaker changed?

Student Activity 2. Write a brief dialogue between two speakers in which one speaker repeats the exact words of a third speaker. Use single quotation marks to show the quotation within the quotation.

Electronic Handbook You might want students to review quotation marks before completing the Grammar in Action activities. If students have access to the Language Master 6000, have them enter the access symbol " and press the GRAMMAR key for information on quotation marks.

23 Discussion Why do you think Holmes is interested in the assistant?

24 Critical Thinking and Reading Why do you think Holmes is so excited when he hears this description of Spaulding?

25 Discussion Why does Holmes say that more bizarre crimes are easier to figure out than "commonplace, featureless crimes"?

26 Master Teacher Note Notice the techniques that Holmes uses to help him concentrate. In other stories, he plays a violin. Tell students that people use many different devices to help them concentrate. Some take a walk or pace a room, while others prefer to sit still like Holmes. Have students describe the techniques that they use to focus their attention on a problem. Ask them why such devices are helpful.

27 Critical Thinking and Reading What does *introspective* mean? How do you think that going to a concert will help Holmes solve this case?

points for you. And, first, one or two questions, Mr. Wilson. This assistant of yours who first called your attention to the advertisement—how long had he been with you?"

"About a month then."

"How did he come?"

"In answer to an advertisement."

"Was he the only applicant?"

"No, I had a dozen."

"Why did you pick him?"

"Because he was handy and would come cheap."

"At half-wages, in fact."

"Yes."

"What is he like, this Vincent Spaulding?"

"Small, stout-built, very quick in his ways, no hair on his face, though he's not short of thirty. Has a white splash of acid upon his forehead."

Holmes sat up in his chair in considerable excitement. "I thought as much," said he. "Have you ever observed that his ears are pierced for earrings?"

"Yes, sir. He told me that a gypsy had done it for him when he was a lad."

"Hum!" said Holmes, sinking back in deep thought. "He is still with you?"

"Oh, yes, sir; I have only just left him."

"And has your business been attended to in your absence?"

"Nothing to complain of, sir. There's never very much to do of a morning."

"That will do, Mr. Wilson. I shall be happy to give you an opinion upon the subject in the course of a day or two. Today is Saturday, and I hope that by Monday we may come to a conclusion."

"Well, Watson," said Holmes when our visitor had left us, "what do you make of it all?"

"I make nothing of it," I answered frankly. "It is a most mysterious business."

"As a rule," said Holmes, "the more bizarre a thing is the less mysterious it proves to be. It is your commonplace, featureless crimes which are really puzzling, just as a commonplace face is the most difficult to identify. But I must be prompt over this matter."

"What are you going to do, then?" I asked.

"To smoke," he answered. "It is quite a three pipe problem, and I beg that you won't speak to me for fifty minutes." He curled himself up in his chair, with his thin knees drawn up to his hawk-like nose, and there he sat with his eyes closed and his black clay pipe thrusting out like the bill of some strange bird. I had come to the conclusion that he had dropped asleep, and indeed was nodding myself, when he suddenly sprang out of his chair with the gesture of a man who has made up his mind and put his pipe down upon the mantelpiece.

"Sarasate[11] plays at the St. James's Hall this afternoon," he remarked. "What do you think, Watson? Could your patients spare you for a few hours?"

"I have nothing to do today. My practice is never very absorbing."

"Then put on your hat and come. I am going through the City first, and we can have some lunch on the way. I observe that there is a good deal of German music on the program, which is rather more to my taste than Italian or French. It is introspective, and I want to introspect. Come along!"

We traveled by the Underground as far as Aldersgate: and a short walk took us to Saxe-Coburg Square, the scene of the singular story which we had listened to in the morning. It was a poky, little, shabby-genteel place, where four lines of dingy two-storied brick houses looked out into a small railed-

---

11. Sarasate (sä rä sä′ tä): Spanish violinist and composer.

in enclosure, where a lawn of weedy grass and a few clumps of faded laurel bushes made a hard fight against a smoke-laden and uncongenial atmosphere. Three gilt balls and a brown board with "JABEZ WILSON" in white letters, upon a corner house, announced the place where our red-headed client carried on his business. Sherlock Holmes stopped in front of it with his head on one side and looked it all over, with his eyes shining brightly between puckered lids. Then he walked slowly up the street, and then down again to the corner, still looking keenly at the houses. Finally he returned to the pawnbroker's, and, having thumped vigorously upon the pavement with his stick two or three times, he went up to the door and knocked. It was instantly opened by a bright-looking, clean-shaven young fellow, who asked him to step in.

"Thank you," said Holmes, "I only wished to ask you how you would go from here to the Strand."

"Third right, fourth left," answered the assistant promptly, closing the door.

"Smart fellow, that," observed Holmes as we walked away. "He is, in my judgment, the fourth smartest man in London, and for daring I am not sure that he has not a claim to be third. I have known something of him before."

"Evidently," said I, "Mr. Wilson's assistant counts for a good deal in this mystery of the Red-headed League. I am sure that you inquired your way merely in order that you might see him."

"Not him."

"What then?"

"The knees of his trousers."

"And what did you see?"

"What I expected to see."

"Why did you beat the pavement?"

"My dear doctor, this is a time for observation, not for talk. We are spies in an en-

emy's country. We know something of Saxe-Coburg Square. Let us now explore the parts which lie behind it."

The road in which we found ourselves as we turned round the corner from the retired Saxe-Coburg Square presented as great a contrast to it as the front of a picture does to the back. It was one of the main arteries which conveyed the traffic of the City to the north and west. The roadway was blocked with the immense stream of commerce flowing in a double tide inward and outward, while the footpaths were black with the hurrying swarm of pedestrians. It was difficult to realize as we looked at the line of fine

28 **Critical Thinking and Reading** Why does Holmes thump his walking stick on the pavement outside Mr. Wilson's house?

29 **Discussion** Discuss what possible clues might be found by examining the knees of Mr. Spaulding's trousers.

30 **Reading Strategy** Summarize the observations Holmes has made since he arrived at Saxe-Coburg Square.

31 Discussion Which building do you think will be significant for this case?

32 Enrichment *Conundrum* originally meant "a riddle whose answer is a pun, or play on words." However, the meaning of this word has expanded to include "any puzzling question or problem." The assumption, however, is that a conundrum always has a clear solution. This is not always the case with a mystery.

33 Master Teacher Note Holmes's violin, like his pipe, is one of his trademarks. What are some of Holmes's other trademarks? Ask students why writers sometimes give their characters certain trademarks. Have them recall trademarks of other characters in fiction or film. If students were to create a detective of their own, what trademarks would they give him or her?

34 Reading Strategy Summarize what Watson says about Holmes's "dual nature."

35 Critical Thinking and Reading Why might the fact that it is Saturday complicate matters?

36 Discussion How has the lighter mood of the story changed?

shops and stately business premises that they really abutted on the other side upon the faded and stagnant square which we had just quitted.

"Let me see," said Holmes, standing at the corner and glancing along the line, "I should like just to remember the order of the houses here. It is a hobby of mine to have an exact knowledge of London. There is Mortimer's, the tobacconist, the little newspaper shop, the Coburg branch of the City and Suburban Bank, the Vegetarian Restaurant, and McFarlane's carriage-building depot. That carries us right on to the other block. And now, Doctor, we've done our work, so it's time we had some play. A sandwich and a cup of coffee, and then off to violin land, where all is sweetness and delicacy and harmony, and there are no red-headed clients to vex us with their conundrums."

My friend was an enthusiastic musician, being himself not only a very capable performer but a composer of no ordinary merit. All the afternoon he sat in the stalls wrapped in the most perfect happiness, gently waving his long, thin fingers in time to the music, while his gently smiling face and his languid, dreamy eyes were as unlike those of Holmes, the sleuthhound, Holmes the relentless, keen-witted, ready-handed criminal agent, as it was possible to conceive. In his singular character the dual nature alternately asserted itself, and his extreme exactness and astuteness represented, as I have often thought, the reaction against the poetic and contemplative mood which occasionally predominated in him. The swing of his nature took him from extreme languor to devouring energy; and, as I knew well, he was never so truly formidable as when, for days on end, he had been lounging in his armchair amid his improvisations and his black-letter editions. Then it was that the lust of the chase would suddenly come upon

him, and that his brilliant reasoning power would rise to the level of intuition, until those who were unacquainted with his methods would look askance at him as on a man whose knowledge was not that of other mortals. When I saw him that afternoon so enwrapped in the music at St. James's Hall I felt that an evil time might be coming upon those whom he had set himself to hunt down.

"You want to go home, no doubt, Doctor," he remarked as we emerged.

"Yes, it would be as well."

"And I have some business to do which will take some hours. This business at Coburg Square is serious."

"Why serious?"

"A considerable crime is in contemplation. I have every reason to believe that we shall be in time to stop it. But today being Saturday rather complicates matters. I shall want your help tonight."

"At what time?"

"Ten will be early enough."

"I shall be at Baker Street at ten."

"Very well. And, I say, Doctor, there may be some little danger, so kindly put your army revolver in your pocket." He waved his hand, turned on his heel, and disappeared in an instant among the crowd.

I trust that I am not more dense than my neighbors, but I was always oppressed with a sense of my own stupidity in my dealings with Sherlock Holmes. Here I had heard what he had heard, I had seen what he had seen, and yet from his words it was evident that he saw clearly not only what had happened but what was about to happen, while to me the whole business was still confused and grotesque. As I drove home to my house in Kensington I thought over it all, from the extraordinary story of the red-headed copier of the Encyclopedia down to the visit to Saxe-Coburg Square, and the ominous words with which he had parted from me. What was this nocturnal expedition, and why should I go armed? Where were we going, and what were we to do? I had the hint from Holmes that this smooth-faced pawnbroker's assistant was a formidable man—a man who might play a deep game. I tried to puzzle it out, but gave it up in despair and set the matter aside until night should bring an explanation.

It was a quarter past nine when I started from home and made my way across the Park, and so through Oxford Street to Baker Street. Two hansoms[12] were standing at the door, and as I entered the passage I heard the sound of voices from above. On entering his room I found Holmes in animated conversation with two men, one of whom I recognized as Peter Jones, the official police agent, while the other was a long, thin, sad-faced man, with a very shiny hat and oppressively respectable frock coat.

"Ha! our party is complete," said Holmes, buttoning up his pea-jacket and taking his heavy hunting crop from the rack. "Watson, I think you know Mr. Jones, of Scotland Yard? Let me introduce you to Mr. Merryweather, who is to be our companion in tonight's adventure."

"We're hunting in couples again, Doctor, you see," said Jones in his consequential way. "Our friend here is a wonderful man for starting a chase. All he wants is an old dog to help him to do the running down."

"I hope a wild goose may not prove to be the end of our chase," observed Mr. Merryweather gloomily.

"You may place considerable confidence in Mr. Holmes, sir," said the police agent loftily. "He has his own little methods, which

are, if he won't mind my saying so, just a little too theoretical and fantastic, but he has the makings of a detective in him. It is not too much to say that once or twice, as in that business of the Sholto murder and the Agra treasure, he has been more nearly correct than the official force."

"Oh, if you say so, Mr. Jones, it is all right," said the stranger with deference. "Still, I confess that I miss my rubber.[13] It is the first Saturday night for seven-and-twenty years that I have not had my rubber."

"I think you will find," said Sherlock Holmes, "that you will play for a higher stake tonight than you have ever done yet, and that the play will be more exciting. For you, Mr. Merryweather, the stake will be some £30,000; and for you, Jones, it will be the man upon whom you wish to lay your hands."

"John Clay, the murderer, thief, smasher, and forger. He's a young man, Mr. Merryweather, but he is at the head of his profession, and I would rather have my bracelets on him than on any criminal in London. He's a remarkable man, is young John Clay. His grandfather was a royal duke, and he himself has been to Eton[14] and Oxford.[15] His brain is as cunning as his fingers, and though we meet signs of him at every turn, we never know where to find the man himself. He'll crack a crib[16] in Scotland one week, and be raising money to build an orphanage in Cornwall the next. I've been on his track for years and have never set eyes on him yet."

"I hope that I may have the pleasure of introducing you tonight. I've had one or two

---

12. hansoms: Two-wheeled covered carriages for two passengers.

13. rubber: Card games.
14. Eton: A famous British secondary school for boys.
15. Oxford: The oldest university in Great Britain.
16. crack a crib: Break into and rob a house.

The Red-headed League 83

37 Critical Thinking and Reading You might review some of the questions raised by Holmes in the course of the investigation. Can you answer any of the questions that Dr. Watson poses?

38 Reading Strategy Does the fact that 30,000 pounds are at stake help you to predict the crime that will be committed?

39 Discussion What character already introduced might fit this brief description of John Clay?

40 Discussion Why do you think that Mr. Merryweather, a bank director, has been invited to go along?

41 Critical Thinking and Reading Contrast what Holmes says about Jones's talents with what Jones has said about Holmes's ability.

42 Reading Strategy Predict where Holmes and the others are going, basing your answer on the buildings listed by Holmes on page 82.

43 Discussion How has Conan Doyle prepared us for Merryweather's discovery of the hollow sound?

little turns also with Mr. John Clay, and I agree with you that he is at the head of his profession. It is past ten, however, and quite time that we started. If you two will take the first hansom, Watson and I will follow in the second."

Sherlock Holmes was not very communicative during the long drive and lay back in the cab humming the tunes which he had heard in the afternoon. We rattled through an endless labyrinth of gas-lit streets until we emerged into Farrington Street.

40
41
"We are close there now," my friend remarked. "This fellow Merryweather is a bank director, and personally interested in the matter. I thought it as well to have Jones with us also. He is not a bad fellow, though an absolute imbecile in his profession. He has one positive virtue. He is as brave as a bulldog and as tenacious as a lobster if he gets his claws upon anyone. Here we are, and they are waiting for us."

42
We had reached the same crowded thoroughfare in which we had found ourselves in the morning. Our cabs were dismissed, and, following the guidance of Mr. Merryweather, we passed down a narrow passage and through a side door, which he opened for us. Within there was a small corridor, which ended in a very massive iron gate. This also was opened, and led down a flight of winding stone steps, which terminated at another formidable gate. Mr. Merryweather stopped to light a lantern, and then conducted us down a dark, earth-smelling passage, and so, after opening a third door, into a huge vault or cellar, which was piled all round with crates and massive boxes.

"You are not very vulnerable from above," Holmes remarked as he held up the lantern and gazed about him.

43
"Nor from below," said Mr. Merryweather, striking his stick upon the flags which lined the floor. "Why, dear me, it sounds quite hollow!" he remarked, looking up in surprise.

"I must really ask you to be a little more quiet!" said Holmes severely. "You have already imperiled the whole success of our expedition. Might I beg that you would have the goodness to sit down upon one of those boxes, and not to interfere?"

The solemn Mr. Merryweather perched himself upon a crate, with a very injured expression upon his face, while Holmes fell upon his knees upon the floor and, with the lantern and a magnifying lens, began to examine minutely the cracks between the stones. A few seconds sufficed to satisfy him, for he sprang to his feet again and put his glass in his pocket.

"We have at least an hour before us," he remarked, "for they can hardly take any steps until the good pawnbroker is safely in bed. Then they will not lose a minute, for the sooner they do their work the longer time they will have for their escape. We are at present, Doctor—as no doubt you have divined—in the cellar of the City branch of one of the principal London banks. Mr. Merryweather is the chairman of directors, and he will explain to you that there are reasons why the more daring criminals of London should take a considerable interest in this cellar at present."

"It is our French gold," whispered the director. "We have had several warnings that an attempt might be made upon it."

"Your French gold?"

"Yes. We had occasion some months ago to strengthen our resources and borrowed for that purpose 30,000 napoleons from the Bank of France. It has become known that we have never had occasion to unpack the money, and that it is still lying in our cellar. The crate upon which I sit contains 2,000

Grammar in Action

Sherlock Holmes's success as a detective lies in his skill at **deduction,** or arriving at a conclusion based on a set of observable facts. Holmes is a skilled observer, noting details that those around him—especially Watson—often overlook. He is then able to see in these details, each based on reliable observation, an overall pattern. The pattern—how all the details fit together, how they are related—provides him with the solution to the mystery.

Note the details that Holmes has so far learned about this case.

Spaulding, Mr. Wilson's assistant, works for half the current wage.

Spaulding spends a great deal of time developing photographs in the basement of the shop.

Spaulding sends Wilson to the League of Red-headed Men.

Wilson spends four hours in the middle of the day at the League.

Without warning, the League is dissolved.

When Holmes and Watson call on Spaulding, Holmes checks the knees of that man's trousers.

napoleons packed between layers of lead foil. Our reserve of bullion is much larger at present than is usually kept in a single branch office, and the directors have had misgivings upon the subject."

"Which were very well justified," observed Holmes. "And now it is time that we arranged our little plans. I expect that within an hour matters will come to a head. In the meantime, Mr. Merryweather, we must put the screen over that dark lantern."

"And sit in the dark?"

"I am afraid so. I had brought a pack of cards in my pocket, and I thought that, as we were a *partie carrée*,[17] you might have your rubber after all. But I see that the enemy's preparations have gone so far that we cannot risk the presence of a light. And, first of all, we must choose our positions. These are daring men, and though we shall take them at a disadvantage, they may do us some harm unless we are careful. I shall stand behind this crate, and do you conceal yourselves behind those. Then, when I flash a light upon them, close in swiftly. If they fire, Watson, have no compunction about shooting them down."

I placed my revolver, cocked, upon the top of the wooden case behind which I crouched. Holmes shot the slide across the front of his lantern and left us in pitch darkness—such an absolute darkness as I have never before experienced. The smell of hot metal remained to assure us that the light was still there, ready to flash out at a moment's notice. To me, with my nerves worked up to a pitch of expectancy, there was something depressing and subduing in the sudden gloom, and in the cold dank air of the vault.

---

17. *partie carrée* (pär tē′ cä rā′): French for "group of four."

"They have but one retreat," whispered Holmes. "That is back through the house into Saxe-Coburg Square. I hope that you have done what I asked you, Jones?"

"I have an inspector and two officers waiting at the front door."

"Then we have stopped all the holes. And now we must be silent and wait."

What a time it seemed! From comparing notes afterwards it was but an hour and a quarter, yet it appeared to me that the night must have almost gone, and the dawn be breaking above us. My limbs were weary and stiff, for I feared to change my position; yet my nerves were worked up to the highest pitch of tension, and my hearing was so acute that I could not only hear the gentle breathing of my companions, but I could distinguish the deeper, heavier in-breath of the bulky Jones from the thin, sighing note of the bank director. From my position I could look over the case in the direction of the floor. Suddenly my eyes caught the glint of a light.

At first it was but a lurid spark upon the stone pavement. Then it lengthened out until it became a yellow line, and then, without any warning or sound, a gash seemed to open and a hand appeared; a white, almost womanly hand, which felt about in the center of the little area of light. For a minute or more the hand, with its writhing fingers, protruded out of the floor. Then it was withdrawn as suddenly as it appeared, and all was dark again save the single lurid spark which marked a chink between the stones.

Its disappearance, however, was but momentary. With a rending, tearing sound, one of the broad, white stones turned over upon its side and left a square, gaping hole, through which streamed the light of a lantern. Over the edge there peeped a clean-cut, boyish face, which looked keenly about it,

44 **Critical Thinking and Reading** How does the description of their preparations heighten the suspense?

45 **Discussion** How does Watson's description of what he was feeling and hearing add to the suspense?

46 **Discussion** Why do you think that it is so effective to describe the criminal's hand as it first appears from the tunnel?

Holmes taps with his cane on the street outside the pawnshop.
Holmes visits the busy commercial street that lies behind the pawnshop.
Holmes learns that the Coburg branch of the City and Suburban Bank has a great deal of gold in its vaults.

Student Activity 1. With a small group of classmates, briefly review the story, and add any additional information to the list of observations. Then discuss each item on the list. Can you see a pattern? What conclusion might be drawn from these facts?

Student Activity 2. Report your conclusion to the rest of the class, comparing and contrasting it with those arrived at by other groups.

47 Critical Thinking and Reading
Can you identify the two men
who climb out of the tunnel?

ESL Teaching Strategy Again,
encourage ESL students to connect the events depicted in the
picture with those Conan Doyle
describes in his story. Have them
study the picture, noting the details it includes.

and then, with a hand on either side of the
aperture, drew itself shoulder-high and
waist-high, until one knee rested upon the
edge. In another instant he stood at the side
of the hole and was hauling after him a companion, lithe and small like himself, with a
pale face and a shock of very red hair.

"It's all clear," he whispered. "Have you
the chisel and the bags? Great Scott! Jump,
Archie, jump, and I'll swing for it."

Sherlock Holmes had sprung
out and seized the intruder by
the collar. The other

dived down the hole, and I heard the sound
of rending cloth as Jones clutched at his
skirts. The light flashed upon the barrel of a
revolver, but Holmes's hunting crop came
down on the man's wrist,
and the pistol clinked
upon the stone floor.

"It's no use, John Clay," said Holmes blandly. "You have no chance at all."

"So I see," the other answered with the utmost coolness. "I fancy that my pal is all right, though I see you have got his coat-tails."

"There are three men waiting for him at the door," said Holmes.

"Oh, indeed! You seem to have done the thing very completely. I must compliment you."

"And I you," Holmes answered. "Your red-headed idea was very new and effective."

"You'll see your pal again presently," said Jones. "He's quicker at climbing down holes than I am. Just hold out while I fix the der-bies."[18]

"I beg that you will not touch me with your filthy hands," remarked our prisoner as the handcuffs clattered upon his wrists. "You may not be aware that I have royal blood in my veins. Have the goodness, also, when you address me always to say 'sir' and 'please.' "

"All right," said Jones with a stare and a snigger. "Well, would you please, sir, march upstairs, where we can get a cab to carry your Highness to the police station?"

"That is better," said John Clay serenely. He made a sweeping bow to the three of us and walked quietly off in the custody of the detective.

"Really, Mr. Holmes," said Mr. Merry-weather as we followed them from the cellar, "I do not know how the bank can thank you or repay you. There is no doubt that you have detected and defeated in the most complete manner one of the most determined attempts at bank robbery that have ever come within my experience."

"I have had one or two little scores of my own to settle with Mr. John Clay," said

_____
18. **derbies:** Handcuffs.

Holmes. "I have been at some small expense over this matter, which I shall expect the bank to refund, but beyond that I am amply repaid by having had an experience which is in many ways unique, and by hearing the very remarkable narrative of the Red-headed League."

"You see, Watson," he explained in the early hours of the morning as we sat over a glass of whisky and soda in Baker Street, "it was perfectly obvious from the first that the only possible object of this rather fantastic business of the advertisement of the League, and the copying of the Encyclopedia, must be to get this not over-bright pawnbroker out of the way for a number of hours every day. It was a curious way of managing it, but, really, it would be difficult to suggest a better. The method was no doubt suggested to Clay's ingenious mind by the color of his accomplice's hair. The £4 a week was a lure which must draw him, and what was it to them, who were playing for thousands? They put in the advertisement, one rogue has the temporary office, the other rogue incites the man to apply for it, and together they manage to secure his absence every morning in the week. From the time that I heard of the assistant having come for half wages, it was obvious to me that he had some strong motive for securing the situation."

"But how could you guess what the motive was?"

"Had there been women in the house, I should have suspected a mere vulgar intrigue. That, however, was out of the question. The man's business was a small one, and there was nothing in his house which could account for such elaborate preparations, and such an expenditure as they were at. It must, then, be something out of the house. What could it be? I thought of the assistant's fondness for photography, and his

48 **Critical Thinking and Reading** What do John Clay's remarks reveal about his personality?

49 **Discussion** How does Holmes reveal his opinion of John Clay's intelligence?

50 **Discussion** Are you satisfied by Holmes's explanation of the case? Were you able to predict some of the developments?

51 **Literary Focus** *Ennui* means "boredom." What do Holmes's remarks about ennui reveal about his personality?

52 **Master Teacher Note** One critic has written that, in a good detective story, the reader should always have the same information as the detective. Otherwise, the detective has an unfair advantage. Have students evaluate "The Red-headed League" according to this criterion. Then have them discuss whether it is a fair standard by which to measure a detective story.

Reader's Response With whom do you more easily identify, Sherlock Holmes or Doctor Watson? Explain.

Thematic Response What devices does the author use to "lighten" this story?

---

trick of vanishing into the cellar. The cellar! There was the end of this tangled clue. Then I made inquiries as to this mysterious assistant and found that I had to deal with one of the coolest and most daring criminals in London. He was doing something in the cellar—something which took many hours a day for months on end. What could it be, once more? I could think of nothing save that he was running a tunnel to some other building.

"So far I had got when we went to visit the scene of action. I surprised you by beating upon the pavement with my stick. I was ascertaining whether the cellar stretched out in front or behind. It was not in front. Then I rang the bell, and, as I hoped, the assistant answered it. We have had some skirmishes, but we had never set eyes upon each other before. I hardly looked at his face. His knees were what I wished to see. You must yourself have remarked how worn, wrinkled, and stained they were. They spoke of those hours of burrowing. The only remaining point was what they were burrowing for. I walked round the corner, saw that the City and Suburban Bank abutted on our friend's premises, and felt that I had solved my problem. When you drove home after the concert I called upon Scotland Yard and upon the chairman of the bank directors, with the result that you have seen."

"And how could you tell that they would make their attempt tonight?" I asked.

"Well, when they closed their League offices that was a sign that they cared no longer about Mr. Jabez Wilson's presence—in other words, that they had completed their tunnel. But it was essential that they should use it soon, as it might be discovered, or the bullion might be removed. Saturday would suit them better than any other day, as it would give them two days for their escape. For all these reasons I expected them to come tonight."

"You reasoned it out beautifully," I exclaimed in unfeigned admiration. "It is so long a chain, and yet every link rings true."

"It saved me from ennui,"[19] he answered, yawning. "Alas! I already feel it closing in upon me. My life is spent in one long effort to escape from the commonplaces of existence. These little problems help me to do so."

"And you are a benefactor of the race," said I.

He shrugged his shoulders. "Well, perhaps, after all, it is of some little use," he remarked. " 'L'homme c'est rien—l'oeuvre c'est tout,'[20] as Gustave Flaubert wrote to George Sand."[21]

---

19. ennui (än' wē): Boredom.
20. L'homme c'est rien—l'oeuvre c'est tout (lum sä rē''n lœvr sä tōō): French for "Man is nothing—the work is everything."
21. Gustave Flaubert (gūs täv' flō bär') . . . **George Sand:** Notable French novelists of the nineteenth century.

Closure and Extension

ANSWERS TO RESPONDING TO THE SELECTION
Your Response
1. Encourage students to share the specific clues that led them to their solutions.

Recalling
2. Wilson wants Holmes to find out what happened to the Red-headed League.
3. He thumps the pavement in front of Wilson's house to hear if it is hollow; he knocks on Wilson's door in order to check the assistant's appearance for clues; and he checks the back of Wilson's house to see what buildings it faces.
4. The true purpose of the Red-headed League was to remove Mr. Wilson from his house so that a tunnel could be dug from the house to the bank's vault.
5. Holmes, Watson, Jones, and Merryweather hide in the dark, waiting for the appearance of John Clay and his accomplice. When Clay comes up from the tunnel, Holmes grabs him by the collar and knocks Clay's pistol out of his hand with a hunting crop. Jones tears the coat of Clay's accomplice as he makes a temporary getaway.

RESPONDING TO THE SELECTION

Your Response

1. Did you solve the mystery before Holmes revealed his solution? If so, how? If not, did the story's solution satisfy you?

Recalling

2. Explain the mystery that Jabez Wilson wants Sherlock Holmes to solve.
3. What three actions does Holmes take when he first visits Saxe-Coburg Square? What is the reason behind each of these actions?
4. Explain the true purpose of the Red-headed League.
5. Describe what happens in the bank's cellar on Saturday night.

Interpreting

6. From what clues does Holmes know the real identity of Spaulding?
7. Find three deductions Holmes makes from what he learns at Saxe-Coburg Square. Explain the reasoning behind each.

Applying

8. Would a real detective be able to solve a crime using Holmes's methods? Explain.

ANALYZING LITERATURE

Understanding Motivation

Motivation is a character's reasons for behaving in a certain way. In a detective story, when you understand a character's motives, you better understand the character and his or her reasons for committing the crime. At the end of this story, Holmes directly reveals the criminals' motives for committing the crime.

Explain the criminals' motives for the following actions:

1. Establishing the Red-headed League
2. Digging a tunnel between the pawn shop and the bank
3. Working for Mr. Wilson for half wages

CRITICAL THINKING AND READING

Contrasting Characters' Abilities

Both Sherlock Holmes and Dr. Watson examine Mr. Wilson's appearance. From their observations only Holmes reasons correctly to make conclusions about Wilson's past activities.

1. What is the difference between their powers of observation?
2. What observations does Holmes make in Saxe-Coburg Square that Watson does not?
3. Give two examples to show that Holmes is a better observer than Watson.
4. Give an example of Holmes's logical reasoning that Watson is unable to perform.

THINKING AND WRITING

Analyzing a Detective's Methods

Write instructions for someone who wants to become a detective like Holmes. Analyze the steps that Holmes takes to solve the mystery of the Red-headed League. Then tell how the steps can be applied to other mysteries. Revise your instructions so they will be clear to someone who has not read the story.

LEARNING OPTIONS

1. **Art.** Review the parts of the story that describe Saxe-Coburg Square, where Mr. Wilson keeps his pawn shop. Then draw a cross-sectional diagram of the site. Include the shop, the City and Suburban Bank situated directly behind the shop, and the tunnel through which John Clay attempts to rob the bank. Present your diagram to the class and explain the details of John Clay's plan.
2. **Writing.** Sherlock Holmes stories are narrated by Dr. Watson. Rewrite the story using Mr. Wilson as the narrator instead. Writing in the first person as Wilson, include perceptions of Holmes and Watson in your story. Do they strike you as an odd pair? Does Holmes seem brilliant and eccentric? What about Watson?

The Red-headed League 89

Interpreting

6. Suggested Response: He knows the assistant is Clay when he is described as small and stoutly built, with a hairless face, a white mark on his forehead, and pierced ears.
7. Suggested Response: He deduces that Mr. Wilson's cellar extends behind the house, because the pavement in front does not sound hollow when he strikes it. He deduces that Clay has been digging a tunnel, because the knees of his trousers are worn and stained. He deduces that the prospective crime is robbery, because a bank is right next to Mr. Wilson's property.

Applying

8. Answers will differ, depending upon whether students believe that Holmes's methods are sound or whether the stories are overly contrived by the author.

ANSWERS TO ANALYZING LITERATURE

Suggested Responses:
1. He establishes the Red-headed League to get the pawnbroker out of the way for a few hours every day.
2. The tunnel is a secret passageway into the bank.
3. By asking for half the wages, he is sure of securing the position above the other applicants.

More About the Author After graduating from Queens College in 1959, Toni Cade Bambara attended universities in Florence, Paris, and New York. She studied dance and film making, and worked as a social investigator for the New York State Department of Welfare. Her writing centers on the emerging identity of the black woman. How might Bambara's background have influenced her writing?

Literary Focus You might ask students to think of characteristic gestures, expressions, or speech habits of people they know. Lead a discussion about how a writer might use one or more such mannerisms to make a character more realistic.

Prereading Focus Have students discuss various dialects with which they are familiar. What are some of the key characteristics of each? How did students become familiar with these dialects?

Audiocassette You may wish to play Toni Cade Bambara's reading of "The Organizer's Wife" in the **Audio Prose Library** before students read this story.

GUIDE FOR READING

Toni Cade Bambara

(1939–   ) was born and raised in New York City. She grew up reading the stories of black heroes. Her interest in her Afro-American heritage is shown by her last name— a name she assumed after finding it on a sketchbook in her great-grandmother's trunk. Bambara is the name of an African tribe known for its intricate wood carvings. She has published two collections of short stories—*Gorilla, My Love,* from which "Blues Ain't No Mockin Bird" was taken, and *The Sea Birds Are Still Alive*—and a novel, *The Salt Eaters.*

Blues Ain't No Mockin Bird

Verisimilitude

When reading a work of fiction, often we expect the characters to be true to life or realistic. **Verisimilitude,** which literally means "similar to the truth," is the appearance of truth or reality in a work of fiction. A writer creates verisimilitude by giving characters the mannerisms, speech, and character traits of real people. In "Blues Ain't No Mockin Bird," Bambara creates characters who have the qualities, characteristics, and actions of people who are believable and true to life. Because they are true to life, we respond to them as we do toward people we know.

Focus

"Blues Ain't No Mockin Bird" is written in dialect, a way of speaking that is common to people in a particular region. The result is informal, intimate language that sounds like the spoken voice. Do the following activity to see how powerful the use of dialect can be. As you read the story, jot down sentences that you like. Rewrite each in standard English and compare it to the original. Which is more effective? Would the story be as authentic and interesting if it had been written in standard English?

DIALECT	STANDARD ENGLISH
"And the frozen patch splinterin every which way kinda spooky."	"And the frozen patch, splintering in all directions, was kind of spooky."

Vocabulary

Knowing the following words will help you as you read "Blues Ain't No Mockin Bird."

lassoed (las′ ōd) *v.*: Wrapped around (p. 91)

formality (fôr mal′ ə tē) *n.*: Established rules or customs (p. 94)

Objectives

1 To understand verisimilitude
2 To note relevant details
3 To respond to meaning
4 To express individual interests and abilities through optional activities

Support Material

Teaching Portfolio
Teacher Backup, p. 113
Usage and Mechanics Worksheet, p. 116
Vocabulary Check, p. 117
Analyzing Literature Worksheet, *Understanding Verisimilitude,* p. 118
Critical Thinking and Reading Worksheet, *Noting Relevant Details,* p. 114

Selection Test, p. 120

Audio Prose Library
Toni Cade Bambara reads "The Organizer's Wife"

Prentice Hall Literature Writing Studio

Blues Ain't No Mockin Bird

Toni Cade Bambara

The puddle had frozen over, and me and Cathy went stompin in it. The twins from next door, Tyrone and Terry, were swingin so high out of sight we forgot we were waitin our turn on the tire. Cathy jumped up and came down hard on her heels and started tap-dancin. And the frozen patch splinterin every which way underneath kinda spooky. "Looks like a plastic spider web," she said. "A sort of weird spider, I guess, with many mental problems." But really it looked like the crystal paperweight Granny kept in the parlor. She was on the back porch, Granny was, making the cakes drunk. The old ladle dripping rum into the Christmas tins, like it used to drip maple syrup into the pails when we lived in the Judson's woods, like it poured cider into the vats when we were on the Cooper place, like it used to scoop buttermilk and soft cheese when we lived at the dairy.

"Go tell that man we ain't a bunch of trees."

"Ma'am?"

"I said to tell that man to get away from here with that camera." Me and Cathy look over toward the meadow where the men with the station wagon'd been roamin around all mornin. The tall man with a huge camera lassoed to his shoulder was buzzin our way.

"They're makin movie pictures," yelled Tyrone, stiffenin his legs and twistin so the tire'd come down slow so they could see.

"They're makin movie pictures," sang out Terry.

"That boy don't never have anything original to say," say Cathy grown-up.

By the time the man with the camera had cut across our neighbor's yard, the twins were out of the trees swingin low and Granny was onto the steps, the screen door bammin soft and scratchy against her palms. "We thought we'd get a shot or two of the house and everything and then—"

"Good mornin," Granny cut him off. And smiled that smile.

"Good mornin," he said, head all down the way Bingo does when you yell at him about the bones on the kitchen floor. "Nice place you got here, aunty. We thought we'd take a—"

"Did you?" said Granny with her eyebrows. Cathy pulled up her socks and giggled.

"Nice things here," said the man, buzzin his camera over the yard. The pecan barrels, the sled, me and Cathy, the flowers, the printed stones along the driveway, the trees, the twins, the toolshed.

"I don't know about the thing, the it, and the stuff," said Granny, still talkin with her eyebrows. "Just people here is what I tend to consider."

Camera man stopped buzzin. Cathy giggled into her collar.

"Mornin, ladies," a new man said. He

Presentation

Motivation/Prior Knowledge
Have students imagine that a camera crew was sent to film their school for a documentary. What reasons might they have for not wanting their school to be filmed?

Purpose-Setting Question Why doesn't Granny want her family and house filmed?

1 Literary Focus Why did the author choose first person narration for this story? Why does she write in dialect?

2 Critical Thinking and Reading What do these details reveal about the two characters in this dialogue?

3 Discussion What does Granny mean by this statement?

4 Critical Thinking and Reading What does this dialogue reveal about each twin?

5 Reading Strategy Why does the narrator describe Cathy as a grown-up? Watch for other descriptions of Cathy in the story.

6 Discussion How would you describe Granny's expression?

7 Discussion By enumerating the "things" in the yard, what does the narrator reveal about the cameraman's attitude toward the family?

8 Discussion What does Granny's statement imply about her attitude toward the cameramen?

Alternative Assessment To promote active reading, have students keep a reader's response journal as they read the story. Encourage personal responses to the situations in the story. Students' observations will enable you to assess their understanding of the issues in the story.

Thematic Focus This story allows us to see part of Granny and Granddaddy Cain's life journey. Ask students if a difficult life can affect a person's sense of self-worth. Have the times they have suffered added to their self-esteem or taken away from it?

Master Teacher Note Explain to students that blues music was developed from the work songs that black slaves improvised as a form of communication. Many blues lyrics express loneliness or sorrow, while others reflect a humorous or defiant attitude to life's troubles.

The mockingbird is able to imitate the songs of other birds. In American folklore, it sings to mourn for a lost love.

Making Connections You might group this selection with "Uncle Marcos," page 63, and "Before the End of Summer," page 107, two stories in which strong family relationships and vivid characterization are central.

9 Discussion How has the twins' attitude toward the men changed? Why has it changed?

10 Reading Strategy What might Cathy's giggling and smiling foreshadow?

11 Discussion How does Granny feel about being called "aunty"? Why?

12 Clarification Food stamps are given by the government to people who cannot afford to buy sufficient food for themselves and their families. The stamps can be exchanged for food at grocery stores.

13 Reading Strategy What might Smilin man hope Granny will say? How might he have finished his sentence? What does this show about his attitude?

14 Clarification According to certain religious doctrines, a mortal sin is a sin of the most severe type.

15 Critical Thinking and Reading What do you learn about Granny from this anecdote?

16 Discussion For what purpose was the person in the story saving the end of the film?

17 Discussion Why has the author waited to reveal Cathy's relationship to the family? Why do you think she had to be "picked up"? How does this change or add to your feelings about the Cain family?

18 Critical Thinking and Reading Who are Mr. Judson and Mrs. Cooper? Why do they make Granny angry? How does this reinforce what you have already learned about Granny?

19 Literary Focus How would you describe Granddaddy Cain's facial expression when he has "rocks all in his jaw"?

had come up behind us when we weren't lookin. "And gents," discoverin the twins givin him a nasty look. "We're filmin for the county," he said with a smile. "Mind if we shoot a bit around here?"

"I do indeed," said Granny with no smile. Smilin man was smiling up a storm. So was Cathy. But he didn't seem to have another word to say, so he and the camera man backed on out the yard, but you could hear the camera buzzin still. "Suppose you just shut that machine off," said Granny real low through her teeth, and took a step down off the porch and then another.

"Now, aunty," Camera said, pointin the thing straight at her.

"Your mama and I are not related."

Smilin man got his notebook out and a chewed-up pencil. "Listen," he said movin back into our yard, "we'd like to have a statement from you . . . for the film. We're filmin for the county, see. Part of the food stamp campaign. You know about the food stamps?"

Granny said nuthin.

"Maybe there's somethin you want to say for the film. I see you grow your own vegetables," he smiled real nice. "If more folks did that, see, there'd be no need—"

Granny wasn't sayin nuthin. So they backed on out, buzzin at our clothesline and the twins' bicycles, then back on down to the meadow. The twins were danglin in the tire, lookin at Granny. Me and Cathy were waitin, too, cause Granny always got somethin to say. She teaches steady with no let-up. "I was on this bridge one time," she started off. "Was a crowd cause this man was goin to jump, you understand. And a minister was there and the police and some other folks. His woman was there, too."

"What was they doin?" asked Tyrone.

"Tryin to talk him out of it was what they was doin. The minister talkin about how it was a mortal sin, suicide. His woman takin bites out of her own hand and not even knowin it, so nervous and cryin and talkin fast."

"So what happened?" asked Tyrone.

"So here comes . . . this person . . . with a camera, takin pictures of the man and the minister and the woman. Takin pictures of the man in his misery about to jump, cause life so bad and people been messin with him so bad. This person takin up the whole roll of film practically. But savin a few, of course."

"Of course," said Cathy, hatin the person. Me standin there wonderin how Cathy knew it was "of course" when I didn't and it was *my* grandmother.

After a while Tyrone say, "Did he jump?"

"Yeh, did he jump?" say Terry all eager.

And Granny just stared at the twins till their faces swallow up the eager and they don't even care any more about the man jumpin. Then she goes back onto the porch and lets the screen door go for itself. I'm lookin to Cathy to finish the story cause she knows Granny's whole story before me even. Like she knew how come we move so much and Cathy ain't but a third cousin we picked up on the way last Thanksgivin visitin. But she knew it was on account of people drivin Granny crazy till she'd get up in the night and start packin. Mumblin and packin and wakin everybody up sayin, "Let's get on away from here before I kill me somebody." Like people wouldn't pay her for things like they said they would. Or Mr. Judson bringin us boxes of old clothes and raggedy magazines. Or Mrs. Cooper comin in our kitchen and touchin everything and sayin how clean it all was. Granny goin crazy, and Granddaddy Cain pullin her off the people, sayin, "Now, now, Cora." But next day loadin up the truck, with rocks all in his jaw, madder than Granny in the first place.

ESL Teaching Strategy In addition to dialect, Bambara uses colloquial expressions to make the dialogue more real and the language more colorful. Students who speak English as a second language may find the numerous colloquial expressions in the story difficult to understand. They may need help with expressions such as *aunty,* as a familiar form of address for an older woman; *with no let-up,* meaning "constantly"; *all eager,* meaning "eagerly"; and *so their faces swallow up the eager,* meaning "the eagerness fades from their faces."

You might wish to pair your ESL students with another student from the class. As students read the story, the partners can help ESL students understand the colloquial expressions.

SHARECROPPER
Elizabeth Catlett
Courtesy Evan Tibbs Collection

"I read a story once," said Cathy soundin like Granny teacher. "About this lady Goldilocks who barged into a house that wasn't even hers. And not invited, you understand. Messed over the people's groceries and broke up the people's furniture. Had the nerve to sleep in the folks' bed."

"Then what happened?" asked Tyrone. "What they do, the folks, when they come in to all this mess?"

"Did they make her pay for it?" asked Terry, makin a fist. "I'd've made her pay me."

I didn't even ask. I could see Cathy actress was very likely to just walk away and leave us in mystery about this story which I heard was about some bears.

"Did they throw her out?" asked Tyrone, like his father sounds when he's bein extra nasty-plus to the washin-machine man.

"Woulda," said Terry. "I woulda gone upside her head with my fist and—"

"You woulda done whatcha always do—go cry to Mama, you big baby," said Tyrone. So naturally Terry starts hittin on Tyrone,

Blues Ain't No Mockin Bird 93

Humanities Note

Fine art, *Sharecropper,* 1966, Elizabeth Catlett. Catlett (1919–), who was born in Washington, D.C., is a sculptor and printmaker. Her typical subject matter is the struggles and achievements of black people.

Catlett's work has been strongly influenced by the American artist Grant Wood (1892–1942), who is best known for *American Gothic,* a rather stark painting of an American farm couple. "Grant Wood," Catlett said, "insisted that we work with the subject matter that we know best. What I know best is black people, especially black women."

Sharecropper is a linocut—a print made from a design cut into the surface of a linoleum block. Because this medium allows for little shading, transitions from black to white are abrupt, with little subtlety of line or tone. It is particularly well-suited to simple, direct expression in which lines and areas are strong and bold.

1. How does *Sharecropper* reflect the struggles and achievements of black people?
2. How does Toni Cade Bambara in "Blues Ain't No Mockin Bird" achieve this same goal?
3. Describe the woman in Catlett's print. How is she similar to Granny Cain?

20 **Discussion** How does Cathy's rendition of the story of the three bears differ from the traditional telling of the tale?

21 **Discussion** If Cathy walked away without finishing the story, whom would she be imitating? Why does the narrator call her "Cathy actress"?

22 **Literary Focus** Does this piece of dialogue advance the plot? Why does the author include it?

Cooperative Learning A group of students may enjoy visiting a museum to look for other prints, drawings, and paintings that depict people who remind them of the characters in this story. As an alternative to visiting a museum, you might consider having students look through art books. Suggest that students choose a piece of art they particularly like and write a research report on the artist and his or her work.

23 Critical Thinking and Reading
What do we learn about Granny from this passage?

24 Critical Thinking and Reading
What is your first impression of Granddaddy Cain? How do the colors in this scene contribute to your impression of the character?

25 Discussion What does the narrator think Smilin and Camera are going to do?

26 Discussion What does Cathy mean by this? Do you believe that her explanation is correct? How has the author prepared you to trust her judgment?

27 Literary Focus What word would you use to describe this scene? What might be the author's purpose in making it so strong?

28 Critical Thinking and Reading
What do Granny's words and tone tell the reader about the relationship between her and Granddaddy Cain?

29 Literary Focus What specific details in this paragraph make the scene seem real to the reader?

30 Critical Thinking and Reading
How does this passage characterize Camera and Smilin? How does it show the contrast between the two men and Granddaddy Cain?

31 Literary Focus What is making the "low groaning music"? Why is this detail important to the story?

and next thing you know they tumblin out the tire and rollin on the ground. But Granny didn't say a thing or send the twins home or step out on the steps to tell us about how we can't afford to be fightin amongst ourselves. She didn't say nuthin. So I get into the tire to take my turn. And I could see her leanin up against the pantry table, starin at the cakes she was puttin up for the Christmas sale, mumblin real low and grumpy and holdin her forehead like it wanted to fall off and mess up the rum cakes.

Behind me I hear before I can see Granddaddy Cain comin through the woods in his field boots. Then I twist around to see the shiny black oilskin cuttin through what little left there was of yellows, reds, and oranges. His great white head not quite round cause of this bloody thing high on his shoulder, like he was wearin a cap on sideways. He takes the shortcut through the pecan grove, and the sound of twigs snapping overhead and underfoot travels clear and cold all the way up to us. And here comes Smilin and Camera up behind him like they was goin to do somethin. Folks like to go for him sometimes. Cathy say it's because he's so tall and quiet and like a king. And people just can't stand it. But Smilin and Camera don't hit him in the head or nuthin. They just buzz on him as he stalks by with the chicken hawk slung over his shoulder, squawkin, drippin red down the back of the oilskin. He passes the porch and stops a second for Granny to see he's caught the hawk at last, but she's just starin and mumblin, and not at the hawk. So he nails the bird to the toolshed door, the hammerin crackin through the eardrums. And the bird flappin himself to death and droolin down the door to paint the gravel in the driveway red, then brown, then black. And the two men movin up on tiptoe like they was invisible or we were blind, one.

"Get them persons out of my flower bed, Mister Cain," say Granny moanin real low like at a funeral.

"How come your grandmother calls her husband 'Mister Cain' all the time?" Tyrone whispers all loud and noisy and from the city and don't know no better. Like his mama, Miss Myrtle, tell us never mind the formality as if we had no better breeding than to call her Myrtle, plain. And then this awful thing—a giant hawk—come wailin up over the meadow, flyin low and tilted and screamin, zigzaggin through the pecan grove, breakin branches and hollerin, snappin past the clothesline, flyin every which way, flyin into things reckless with crazy.

"He's come to claim his mate," say Cathy fast, and ducks down. We all fall quick and flat into the gravel driveway, stones scrapin my face. I squinch my eyes open again at the hawk on the door, tryin to fly up out of her death like it was just a sack flown into by mistake. Her body holdin her there on that nail, though. The mate beatin the air overhead and clutchin for hair, for heads, for landin space.

The camera man duckin and bendin and runnin and fallin, jigglin the camera and scared. And Smilin jumpin up and down swipin at the huge bird, tryin to bring the hawk down with just his raggedy ole cap. Granddaddy Cain straight up and silent, watchin the circles of the hawk, then aimin the hammer off his wrist. The giant bird fallin, silent and slow. Then here comes Camera and Smilin all big and bad now that the awful screechin thing is on its back and broken, here they come. And Granddaddy Cain looks up at them like it was the first time noticin, but not payin them too much mind cause he's listenin, we all listenin, to that low groanin music comin from the porch. And we figure any minute, somethin in my back tells me any minute now, Granny

94

Multicultural Focus Considered to be a forerunner of American Jazz and rock, the blues first became popular in the early part of this century with such performers as W. C. Handy, known as the Father of the Blues, Ma Rainey, and later, the immortal Bessie Smith. No one knows when or how the blues began. The best guess is that the blues developed from work songs called *field hollers* that were sung by African Americans who worked in the fields as slaves. The blues used the call-and-response pattern of African music. Eventually, these songs were accompanied by instruments, and a highly individualized musical form developed. Some blues lyrics are very sad, others quite humorous—but all seem to address the hardships faced by African Americans in this country.

Have students find out about performers of the blues, including W. C. Handy, Muddy Waters, B. B. King, Janis Joplin, and Elvis Presley—and musicians who were influenced by them. Also, suggest that they explore blues-type music in other countries, such as Greek *bouzouki* or Spanish *flamenco*.

gonna bust through that screen with somethin in her hand and murder on her mind. So Granddaddy say above the buzzin, but quiet, "Good day, gentlemen." Just like that. Like he'd invited them in to play cards and they'd stayed too long and all the sandwiches were gone and Reverend Webb was droppin by and it was time to go.

They didn't know what to do. But like Cathy say, folks can't stand Granddaddy tall and silent and like a king. They can't neither. The smile the men smilin is pullin the mouth back and showin the teeth. Lookin like the wolf man, both of them. Then Granddaddy holds his hand out—this huge hand I used to sit in when I was a baby and he'd carry me through the house to my mother like I was a gift on a tray. Like he used to on the trains. They called the other men just waiters. But they spoke of Granddaddy separate and said, The Waiter. And said he had engines in his feet and motors in his hands and couldn't no train throw him off and couldn't nobody turn him round. They were big enough for motors, his hands were. He held that one hand out all still and it gettin to be not at all a hand but a person in itself.

"He wants you to hand him the camera," Smilin whispers to Camera, tiltin his head to talk secret like they was in the jungle or somethin and come upon a native that don't speak the language. The men start untyin the straps, and they put the camera into that great hand speckled with the hawk's blood all black and crackly now. And the hand don't even drop with the weight, just the fingers move, curl up around the machine. But Granddaddy lookin straight at the men. They lookin at each other and everywhere but at Granddaddy's face.

"We filmin for the county, see," say Smilin. "We puttin together a movie for the food stamp program . . . filmin all around these parts. Uhh, filmin for the county."

"Can I have my camera back?" say the tall man with no machine on his shoulder, but still keepin it high like the camera was still there or needed to be. "Please, sir."

Then Granddaddy's other hand flies up like a sudden and gentle bird, slaps down fast on top of the camera and lifts off half like it was a calabash[1] cut for sharing.

"Hey," Camera jumps forward. He gathers up the parts into his chest and everything unrollin and fallin all over. "Whatcha tryin to do? You'll ruin the film." He looks down into his chest of metal reels and things like he's protectin a kitten from the cold.

"You standin in the misses' flower bed," say Granddaddy. "This is our own place."

The two men look at him, then at each other, then back at the mess in the camera man's chest, and they just back off. One sayin over and over all the way down to the meadow, "Watch it, Bruno. Keep ya fingers off the film." Then Granddaddy picks up the hammer and jams it into the oilskin pocket, scrapes his boots, and goes into the house. And you can hear the squish of his boots headin through the house. And you can see the funny shadow he throws from the parlor window onto the ground by the string-bean patch. The hammer draggin the pocket of the oilskin out so Granddaddy looked even wider. Granny was hummin now—high, not low and grumbly. And she was doin the cakes again, you could smell the molasses from the rum.

"There's this story I'm goin to write one day," say Cathy dreamer. "About the proper use of the hammer."

"Can I be in it?" Tyrone say with his hand up like it was a matter of first come, first served.

"Perhaps," say Cathy, climbin onto the tire to pump us up. "If you there and ready."

_____
1. calabash (kal′ ə bash′) n.: A large gourdlike fruit.

32 **Literary Focus** Why did the author include this anecdote? How does it change your feelings about Granddaddy Cain?

33 **Discussion** How do you interpret the men's words and actions? How would you describe their feelings right now?

34 **Discussion** Why does Smilin repeat that they are filming "for the county"?

35 **Discussion** Why has Camera's tone changed?

36 **Discussion** Why does Granddaddy Cain say, "This is our own place"?

37 **Discussion** How do you think the two men would describe this experience?

38 **Discussion** Does the narrator believe that Cathy will write a story? What might Cathy mean by, "the proper use of the hammer"?

39 **Critical Thinking and Reading** How does Tyrone's question and gesture reinforce the author's previous characterization of him?

40 **Discussion** What will Tyrone have to do in order to be in Cathy's story?

Reader's Response How did you react when you read the scene involving Granddaddy Cain and the two hawks?

Thematic Response The story presents an elderly couple who have had a hard journey through life. How did their struggles affect them? Have they triumphed over—or been overwhelmed by —life's journey?

Enrichment For a different perspective on photographers and the media, you might present to the class the following quotations from interviews with two war photographers. Then lead a discussion about responsible journalism.

W. Eugene Smith: "My camera, my intentions stopped no man from falling. Photographs could cause compassionate horror within the viewer, they might also prod the conscience of that viewer into taking action."

Don McCullin: "Someone may have been killed . . . and I'm going to photograph it.

. . . People think that because a person has been killed he's no longer useful. Of course he's useful. He's useful to say, 'Look what's happened to that young man.'

. . . We need something very quick to understand that we as human beings are not permitted to allow this."

Closure and Extension

ANSWERS TO RESPONDING TO THE SELECTION

Your Response

1. Encourage students to share their responses with the class. Use the responses as a springboard for a general discussion of the issue of privacy.

Recalling

2. They are making a documentary film about people who use food stamps.

Interpreting

3. They see the family as types, not as individuals.
4. The cameramen are like the photographer: they see people only as news items.
5. Like Goldilocks, the two men are intruders. She invades the privacy of the bears' home.
6. Granddaddy's killing of the mate reveals that he will take strong, even harsh, measures to accomplish his ends.
7. The male hawk tries to defend his mate; Granddaddy Cain defends granny.
8. The Cains have suffered sorrow and hardships; thus they are "singing the blues." Their song, however, is one of life and survival.

Applying

9. Some may feel that individual privacy is sacred; others, that an informed public is more important; some, that it depends on how sensitively media people handle such situations.

ANSWERS TO ANALYZING LITERATURE

1. Students will admire Granny's resilience, courage, assertiveness, pride, sensitivity, generosity, and love for her family.
2. Students will admire Granddaddy Cain's courage, strength, pride, loyalty, gentleness, and love for his family. Some may find his treatment of the hawk inhumane.
3. Most will share the narrator's response that the reporters are insensitive, ignorant, and cowardly. Students who see the story from the reporters' point of view may respond more sympathetically.

96

RESPONDING TO THE SELECTION

Your Response

1. How would you feel if you caught a stranger videotaping you without your permission? Would you feel angry or intruded upon? Why or why not?

Recalling

2. Why are the two men filming the Cain family and their home?

Interpreting

3. What is the cameraman's attitude toward the Cain family?
4. What is the main point of Granny's story about the man who attempted suicide?
5. How is the story of Goldilocks similar to the Cain's predicament?
6. What does killing the hawk's mate reveal about Granddaddy Cain's character?
7. How do the two hawks resemble Granny and Granddaddy Cain?
8. The title of the story indicates that the sound of the blues is not similar to the bittersweet music of a mocking bird, which according to legend sings of death. How is the blues different? Why is this an appropriate title for this story?

Applying

9. In part, this story examines the ethics (standards of conduct and moral judgment) of the news media. Do you believe the media have a right to intrude in others' lives to achieve their goals? Why or why not?

ANALYZING LITERATURE

Understanding Verisimilitude

Verisimilitude means creating characters that are believable and realistic—characters that make us respond to them as real people.

1. Describe Granny's chief qualities. How do you respond to her?
2. Describe Granddaddy's chief qualities. How do you respond to him?

96   Short Stories

---

3. Describe the reporters' chief qualities. How do you respond to them?

CRITICAL THINKING AND READING

Noting Relevant Details

Authors often fill their stories with details that give readers a feeling for the world in which the story takes place. Some details move the plot forward or provide insight into the characters. In "Blues Ain't No Mockin Bird," Bambara provides a wealth of details that, taken together, reveal significant information about the characters and their way of life.

1. What details in the first paragraph provide insight into Granny and the family?
2. What about the family is revealed in Smilin man's simple comment, "I see you grow your own vegetables"?

THINKING AND WRITING

Responding to Meaning

Like Granny, Cathy is able to tell stories that are entertaining yet also prove a point. At the end of the story, Cathy says she is going to write a story about the proper use of a hammer. Imagine you are Cathy and write this story. What is the "proper use of the hammer" and how was it improperly or properly used in "Blues Ain't No Mockin Bird"? Let a classmate read and respond to your story before you write a final draft.

LEARNING OPTION

Art. Design a book jacket for "Blues Ain't No Mockin Bird." For the front you may wish to illustrate a scene in the story, draw a portrait of the narrator or Granny, or create an abstract design that captures the story's mood. For the flaps and the back, include the following kinds of information: a blurb telling the reader about the story, information about the author, and invented excerpts from reviews. Look at book jackets in the library for ideas. When you are finished, display your book jacket in the classroom.

ANSWERS TO CRITICAL THINKING AND READING

1. The children are swinging on a tire, (they are country people who do not have swings in their yard); Cathy compares the cracks in the ice with a plastic spider web, (she has an active imagination); Granny made maple syrup when they lived in the Judson's woods, cider on the Cooper place, and buttermilk and cheese at the dairy, (the family has moved around a lot; Granny is resourceful).
2. They are resourceful, hardworking, proud, and independent.

THINKING AND WRITING

Software If students are working on computers, have them use **Bank Street Writer** to complete all stages of the assignment. Using the program's cut and paste features, students will easily be able to make revisions based on their peer reviewer's comments.

LEARNING OPTION

This activity will appeal to visual learners. You might vary the activity by having students provide one another with their own original reviews of the story.

Point of View

OPEN DOORWAY ON THE BEACH
K. Rodko
Three Lions

Humanities Note

Fine art, *Open Doorway on the Beach,* by Karl Rodko. Karl Rodko is an American artist. This charming view of sunlight and sea is given added interest by the perspective through a doorway. The contrast between the inside and outside world makes the viewer yearn to step through the doorway into the sunlit air, filled with the sound of gulls and the surf and the smells of the sea. The cheerful colors and simplified forms of this painting add to its pleasing effect.

More About the Author Mark Twain was the best known and most successful author of his generation. He took pride in his ability to publish books that appealed to the public. Ask students to discuss what subjects a contemporary author might choose to capture the attention of readers.

Literary Focus Point out to students that, although this is a first-person narration, the narrator tells the story long after the incident occurred. This enables him to share with the reader the joke that events played on him.

Prereading Focus If students have trouble coming up with a story, you might wish to point out that many situation comedies center on mistakes or misunderstandings. Remind students that many of the classic "I Love Lucy" episodes involve misunderstandings of this sort.

Vocabulary Have your **less advanced** students read these words aloud so that they can be sure of the pronunciation.

Electronic Handbook You might wish to have students use the Language Master 6000 to hear the pronunciations of *deleterious* and *desultory*.

Spelling Tip Point out the four words ending in *ous: prodigious, deleterious, ominous, judicious.*

GUIDE FOR READING

Mark Twain

(1835–1910) was born Samuel Langhorne Clemens in Florida, Missouri, and grew up in the river town of Hannibal. He worked as a steamboat pilot on the Mississippi River, and he took his pen name from a sounding cry used on Mississippi steamboats—*by the mark, twain* means "two fathoms deep." Twain also worked as a printer, prospector, reporter, editor, and lecturer. Writing, however, was his true calling. A talented humorist, Twain's special brand of wit is clearly seen in "The Invalid's Story."

The Invalid's Story

First-Person Narration

Authors may write stories from a number of **points of view,** or perspectives. With **first-person narration,** the story is told by one of the characters in it, with the character referring to himself or herself as "I." The character who tells the story in this way is called the narrator.

By using the first-person point of view, the author makes the story seem immediate. However, first-person point of view has some limitations. Since the author can reveal only what the narrator would know or observe, you get only one side of the story. You have to make inferences based on what other characters say and do to get a wider picture.

Focus

Misunderstandings can be funny. Think of a story or joke in which a silly mistake grows into a humorous situation. The story or joke can come from film, television, literature, or your own experience. Briefly tell this story or joke to a classmate. Have your partner listen critically for ways in which you can make your telling more entertaining. After you have commented on each other's stories or jokes, revise them and retell them. Then read "The Invalid's Story" to see how Mark Twain tells a tale about a humorous misunderstanding.

Vocabulary

Knowing the following words will help you as you read "The Invalid's Story."

prodigious (prə dij′ əs) *adj.:* Enormous (p. 99)

deleterious (del′ ə tir′ ē əs) *adj.:* Injurious; harmful to health or well-being (p. 100)

ominous (äm′ ə nəs) *adj.:* Threatening (p. 100)

judicious (jōō dish′ əs) *adj.:*

Showing good judgment (p. 102)

placidly (plas′ id lē) *adv.:* Calmly; quietly (p. 102)

desultory (des′ əl tôr′ ē) *adj.:* Random (p. 103)

stifling (stī′ fliŋ) *adj.:* Suffocating (p. 104)

Objectives

1 To understand first-person narration
2 To identify exaggeration
3 To write a tall tale
4 To express individual interests and abilities through optional activities

Support Material

Teaching Portfolio
Teacher Backup, p. 123
Grammar in Action Worksheet, *Recognizing Dialect,* p. 127
Usage and Mechanics Worksheet, p. 129
Vocabulary Check, p. 130
Critical Thinking and Reading Worksheet, *Identifying Exaggeration,* p. 131

Language Worksheet, *Understanding Idioms,* p. 132
Selection Test, p. 133

Prentice Hall Literature Writing Studio

The Invalid's Story

Mark Twain

I seem sixty and married, but these effects are due to my condition and sufferings, for I am a bachelor, and only forty-one. It will be hard for you to believe that I, who am now but a shadow, was a hale, hearty man two short years ago—a man of iron, a very athlete!—yet such is the simple truth. But stranger still than this fact is the way in which I lost my health. I lost it through helping to take care of a box of guns on a two-hundred-mile railway journey one winter's night. It is the actual truth, and I will tell you about it.

I belong in Cleveland, Ohio. One winter's night, two years ago, I reached home just after dark, in a driving snowstorm, and the first thing I heard when I entered the house was that my dearest boyhood friend and schoolmate, John B. Hackett, had died the day before, and that his last utterance had been a desire that I would take his remains home to his poor old father and mother in Wisconsin. I was greatly shocked and grieved, but there was no time to waste in emotions; I must start at once. I took the card, marked "Deacon Levi Hackett, Bethlehem, Wisconsin," and hurried off through the whistling storm to the railway station. Arrived there I found the long white-pine box which had been described to me; I fastened the card to it with some tacks, saw it put safely aboard the express car, and then ran into the eating room to provide myself with a sandwich and some cigars. When I returned, presently, there was my coffin-box *back again*, apparently, and a young fellow examining around it, with a card in his hands, and some tacks and a hammer! I was astonished and puzzled. He began to nail on his card, and I rushed out to the express car, in a good deal of a state of mind, to ask for an explanation. But no—there was my box, all right, in the express car; it hadn't been disturbed. [The fact is that without my suspecting it a prodigious mistake had been made. I was carrying off a box of *guns* which that young fellow had come to the station to ship to a rifle company in Peoria, Illinois, and *he* had got my corpse!] Just then the conductor sang out "All aboard," and I jumped into the express car and got a comfortable seat on a bale of buckets. The expressman was there, hard at work—a plain man of fifty, with a simple, honest, good-natured face, and a breezy, practical heartiness in his general style. As the train moved off a stranger skipped into the car and set a package of peculiarly mature and capable Limburger cheese[1] on one end of my coffin-box—I mean my box of guns. That is to say, I know *now* that it was Limburger cheese, but at that time I never had heard of the article in my life, and of course was wholly ignorant of its character. Well, we sped through the wild night, the bitter storm raged on, a cheerless

---

1. **Limburger cheese:** A cheese with a strong odor.

Presentation

Motivation/Prior Knowledge
Ask students if they have ever participated in or seen a confusing situation that later became clear when they learned a key fact. Tell them that just such a situation occurs in this story.

Thematic Focus By presenting a character's absurd mistake, Twain's story captures the lighter side of matters that are usually quite serious. Discuss with students how something serious can become absurd. Ask them if they have ever encountered absurdity in a situation that seemed serious.

Making Connections Another humorous selection that you might teach with this one is "The Secret Life of Walter Mitty," page 201.

Purpose-Setting Question How is the humor in this story based on irony?

1 **Discussion** What humorous comment on marriage does the author make in this passage?

2 **Critical Thinking and Reading** The author chooses to share this information with you at the beginning of the story. How might this knowledge add to the humor?

3 Critical Thinking and Reading
Why do you think Twain includes these details?

4 Discussion How might your response to this detail be different if you did not know about the cheese?

5 Discussion Why might a warm fire affect the smell coming from the cheese? How does this description heighten the humor of the story?

3 misery stole over me, my heart went down, down, down! The old expressman made a brisk remark or two about the tempest and the arctic weather, slammed his sliding doors to, and bolted them, closed his window down tight, and then went bustling around, here and there and yonder, setting things to rights, and all the time contentedly humming "Sweet By and By " in a low tone, and flatting a good deal. Presently I began to detect a most evil and searching odor stealing about on the frozen air. This depressed my spirits still more, because of course I at-**4** tributed it to my poor departed friend. There was something infinitely saddening about his calling himself to my remembrance in this dumb, pathetic way, so it was hard to keep the tears back. Moreover, it distressed me on account of the old expressman, who, I was afraid, might notice it. However, he went humming tranquilly on, and gave no sign; and for this I was grateful. Grateful, yes, but still uneasy; and soon I began to feel more and more uneasy every minute, for every minute that went by that odor thickened up the more, and got to be more and more gamy and hard to stand. Presently, having got things arranged to his satisfaction, the expressman got some wood and made up a tremendous fire in his stove. This distressed **5** me more than I can tell, for I could not but

feel that it was a mistake. I was sure that the effect would be deleterious upon my poor departed friend. Thompson—the expressman's name was Thompson, as I found out in the course of the night—now went poking around his car, stopping up whatever stray cracks he could find, remarking that it didn't make any difference what kind of a night it was outside, he calculated to make *us* comfortable, anyway. I said nothing, but I believed he was not choosing the right way. Meantime he was humming to himself just as before; and meantime, too, the stove was getting hotter and hotter, and the place closer and closer. I felt myself growing pale and qualmish,[2] but grieved in silence and said nothing. Soon I noticed that the "Sweet By and By" was gradually fading out; next it ceased altogether, and there was an ominous stillness. After a few moments Thompson said—

"Pfew! I reckon it ain't no cinnamon 't I've loaded up thish-year stove with!"

He gasped once or twice, then moved toward the cof—gun-box, stood over that Limburger cheese part of a moment, then

---

2. qualmish (kwäm´ ish) *adj.*: Slightly ill.

Grammar in Action

To present a realistic portrait of a character, writers have the character speak in **dialect.** This type of speech is characterized by words, pronunciations, and sentence structure not common in standard English. To capture the flavor of dialect, writers may purposely misspell words to show unusual pronunciations, use contractions and poor grammar, and insert colorful language. The following passage from "The Invalid's Story" shows how Twain uses dialect:

". . . One day you're hearty and strong . . . and next day he's *cut down like the grass,* and the *places which knowed him* then knows him no more forever, as *Scriptur'* says. *Yes'ndeedy,* it's awful solemn and *cur'us;* but we've all got to go, one time or another; *they ain't no getting around it.*"

Twain indicates unusual pronunciations with words like "Yes'ndeedy" and "cur'us"; he purposely uses incorrect grammar in phrases like "places which knowed him" and "they ain't no getting around it"; and he inserts colorful figures of speech based on the Bible, such as "cut down like the grass." By

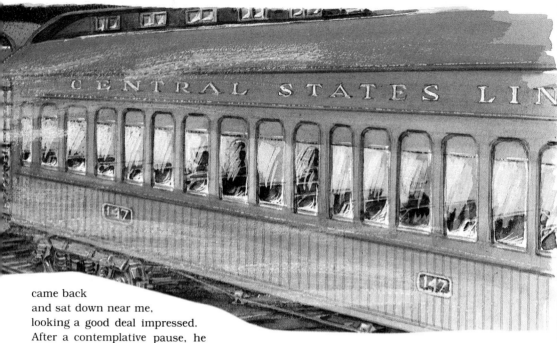

6 **Discussion** Why is Thompson so sure that this particular corpse is really dead?

7 **Critical Thinking and Reading** How does Thompson's way of speaking contribute to the humor of the story?

8 **Discussion** What is humorous about this apparently serious remark?

came back
and sat down near me,
looking a good deal impressed.
After a contemplative pause, he
said, indicating the box with a gesture—

"Friend of yourn?"

"Yes," I said with a sigh.

"He's pretty ripe, *ain't* he!"

Nothing further was said for perhaps a couple of minutes, each being busy with his own thoughts; then Thompson said, in a low, awed voice—

"Sometimes it's uncertain whether they're really gone or not—*seem* gone, you know—body warm, joints limber—and so, although you *think* they're gone, you don't really know. I've had cases in my car. It's perfectly awful, becuz *you* don't know what minute they'll rise up and look at you!" Then, after a pause, and slightly lifting his elbow toward the box,—"But *he* ain't in no trance! No, sir, I go bail for *him!*"

We sat some time, in meditative silence, listening to the wind and the roar of the train; then Thompson said, with a good deal of feeling:

"Well-a-well, we've all got to go, they ain't no getting around it. Man that is born of woman is of few days and far between, as Scriptur'[3] says. Yes, you look at it any way you want to, it's awful solemn and cur'us: they ain't *nobody* can get around it; *all's* got to go—just *everybody*, as you may say. One day you're hearty and strong"—here he scrambled to his feet and broke a pane and stretched his nose out at it a moment or two, then sat down again while I struggled up and thrust my nose out at the same place, and this we kept on doing every now and then—"and next day he's cut down like the grass, and the places which knowed him then knows him no more forever, as Scriptur' says. Yes'ndeedy, it's awful solemn and cur'us; but we've all got to go, one time or another; they ain't no getting around it."

There was another long pause; then—

_____

3. Scriptur': Scripture, the Bible.

The Invalid's Story   101

accurately reproducing Thompson's dialect, Twain makes his story both humorous and realistic.

Student Activity 1. Identify a similar passage from the story. Point out each technique Twain uses to write dialect. Note any misspellings, unusual contractions, examples of poor grammar, and colorful figures of speech.

Student Activity 2. Rewrite a dialect passage from "The Invalid's Story" in standard English, omitting all dialect. Read the original passage and the revised passage aloud. Discuss the differences between the two. Which is more effective? Why?

Electronic Handbook You might want students to review colloquialisms, slang, jargon, and idioms before completing this exercise on dialect. If students have access to the Language Master 6000, have them enter the access words *informal* and *idiom* and press the GRAMMAR key to obtain information on these topics.

9 Discussion What does this statement mean?

10 Master Teacher Note Twain's tone in this story is chatty and conversational. Ask students to give some examples of the way Twain achieves this effect.

11 Discussion How would you paraphrase this passage without using dialect?

12 Critical Thinking and Reading Whenever Thompson mentions the odor, he talks as though the corpse is deliberately causing the situation. How does this add to the humor of the story?

"What did he die of?"

I said I didn't know.

"How long has he ben dead?"

9 ⎡ It seemed judicious to enlarge the facts to fit the probabilities: so I said:

"Two or three days."

But it did no good; for Thompson received it with an injured look which plainly said, "Two or three *years*, you mean." Then he went right along, placidly ignoring my statement, and gave his views at considerable length upon the unwisdom of putting off burials too long. Then he lounged off toward the box, stood a moment, then came back on a sharp trot and visited the broken pane, observing:

" 'Twould 'a' ben a dum sight better, all around, if they'd started him along last summer."

Thompson sat down and buried his face in his red silk handkerchief, and began to slowly sway and rock his body like one who is doing his best to endure the almost unendurable. By this time the fragrance—if you may call it fragrance—was just about suffocating, as near as you can come at it. Thompson's face was turning gray; I knew mine hadn't any color left in it. By and by Thompson rested his forehead in his left hand, with his elbow on his knee, and sort of waved his red handkerchief toward the box with his other hand, and said:

11 ⎡ "I've carried a many a one of 'em—some of 'em considerable overdue, too—but, lordy, he just lays over 'em all!—and does it *easy*. Cap, they was heliotrope[4] to *him!*"

This recognition of my poor friend gratified me, in spite of the sad circumstances, because it had so much the sound of a compliment.

Pretty soon it was plain that something

had got to be done.

I suggested cigars. Thompson thought it was a good idea. He said:

"Likely it'll modify him some."

We puffed gingerly along for a while, and tried hard to imagine that things were improved. But it wasn't any use. Before very long, and without any consultation, both cigars were quietly dropped from our nerveless fingers at the same moment. Thompson said, with a sigh:

"No, Cap, it don't modify him worth a cent. Fact is, it makes him worse, becuz it appears to stir up his ambition. What do you reckon we better do, now?"

I was not able to suggest anything; indeed, I had to be swallowing and swallowing all the time, and did not like to trust myself

---

4. **heliotrope** (hē′ lē ə trōp′) *n*.: A sweet-smelling plant.

Multicultural Focus Mark Twain's story is an excellent example of the Western regional humor that was popular in the United States during the late 1800's. As Twain's story illustrates, certain types of humor tend to be associated with particular regions, countries, or cultures. For example, the Spanish are known for their pessimistic humor, while the English are known for their dry irony.

Humor also serves different purposes from society to society. In some cultures, humor is a social tool, and the clown or fool is a secretly powerful or influential person, like the court jester of medieval Europe. The Greenland Eskimos use humor in a distinctive way with a "laughter duel" in which opponents insult each other with derisive jokes and the loser, who gets the least laughs from the onlookers, is deeply shamed. In the United States, there are roasts, an entertainment at which the celebrity honored is playfully ridiculed.

Suggest that students try to see a foreign comedy film and report on the humor they observed.

to speak.

Thompson fell to maundering,[5] in a desultory and low-spirited way, about the miserable experiences of this night; and he got to referring to my poor friend by various titles—sometimes military ones, sometimes civil ones; and I noticed that as fast as my poor friend's effectiveness grew, Thompson promoted him accordingly—gave him a bigger title. Finally he said:

"I've got an idea. Suppos'n' we buckle down to it and give the Colonel a bit of a shove toward t'other end of the car?—about ten foot, say. He wouldn't have so much influence, then, don't you reckon?"

I said it was a good scheme. So we took in a good fresh breath at the broken pane, calculating to hold it till we got through; then we went there and bent over that deadly cheese and took a grip on the box. Thompson nodded "All ready," and then we threw ourselves forward with all our might; but Thompson slipped, and slumped down with his nose on the cheese, and his breath got loose. He gagged and gasped, and floundered up and made a break for the door, pawing the air and saying hoarsely, "Don't hender me!—gimme the road! I'm a-dying; gimme the road!" Out on the cold platform I sat down and held his head awhile, and he revived. Presently he said:

"Do you reckon we started the Gen'rul any?"

I said no; we hadn't budged him.

"Well, then, *that* idea's up the flume. We got to think up something else. He's suited wher' he is, I reckon; and if that's the way he feels about it, and has made up his mind that he don't wish to be disturbed, you bet he's a-going to have his own way in the business. Yes, better leave him right wher' he is, long as he wants it so; becuz he holds all the trumps, don't you know, and so it stands to reason that the man that lays out to alter his plans for him is going to get left."

But we couldn't stay out there in that mad storm; we should have frozen to death. So we went in again and shut the door, and began to suffer once more and take turns at the break in the window. By and by, as we were starting away from a station where we had stopped a moment Thompson pranced in cheerily, and exclaimed:

"We're all right, now! I reckon we've got the Commodore this time. I judge I've got the stuff here that'll take the tuck out of him."

It was carbolic acid. He had a carboy[6] of

---

5. maundering (môn′ dər iŋ) *v.*: Talking in an unconnected way.

6. carboy (kär′ boi) *n.*: A large glass bottle enclosed in basketwork to prevent it from breaking.

13 Discussion Why does Thompson change the titles he gives to the corpse?

14 Discussion What is the irony in the use of the adverb "deadly" to describe the cheese?

15 Discussion How does the increasing strength of the odor correlate with the powers that Thompson attributes to the corpse?

16 Reading Strategy Recall the titles that Thompson has given the dead man.

The Invalid's Story 103

104

17 Critical Thinking and Reading
How is this statement ironical?

18 Critical Thinking and Reading
What "work" is Thompson referring to when he says, "I never did see one of 'em warm up to his work so . . ."?

19 Discussion How is this description ironical?

20 Clarification Mr. Thompson believes that he has contracted typhoid fever because of his exposure to the stench of the corpse. Typhoid fever is a general infection that includes a high fever and rose-colored spots on the chest and abdomen. It can lead to serious complications and can be fatal.

21 Discussion Why does the author refer to "imagination" as the cause of his ruined health?

Reader's Response Has there ever been a time when you let your imagination run away with you? Explain.

Thematic Response Humor plays an important role in this story. What technique does Twain use to let the reader in on the joke?

---

it. He sprinkled it all around everywhere: in fact he drenched everything with it, rifle-box, cheese and all. Then we sat down, feeling pretty hopeful. But it wasn't for long. You see the two perfumes began to mix, and then—well, pretty soon we made a break for the door; and out there Thompson swabbed his face with his bandanna and said in a kind of disheartened way:

"It ain't no use. We can't buck agin *him*. He just utilizes everything we put up to modify him with, and gives it his own flavor and plays it back on us. Why, Cap, don't you know, it's as much as a hundred times worse in there now than it was when he first got a-going. I never *did* see one of 'em warm up to his work so, and take such a dumnation interest in it. No, sir, I never did, as long as I've ben on the road; and I've carried a many a one of 'em, as I was telling you."

We went in again after we were frozen pretty stiff; but my, we couldn't *stay* in, now. So we just waltzed back and forth, freezing, and thawing, and stifling, by turns. In about an hour we stopped at another station; and as we left it Thompson came in with a bag, and said—

"Cap, I'm a-going to chance him once more—just this once; and if we don't fetch him this time, the thing for us to do, is to just throw up the sponge and withdraw from the canvass.⁷ That's the way *I* put it up."

He had brought a lot of chicken feathers, and dried apples, and leaf tobacco, and rags, and old shoes, and sulphur, and asafetida,⁸

---

7. withdraw from the canvass (kan' vəs): Give up the attempt.
8. asafetida (as' ə fet' ə də) *n*.: A bad-smelling substance from certain plants, used as medicine.

---

and one thing or another; and he piled them on a breadth of sheet iron in the middle of the floor, and set fire to them.

When they got well started, I couldn't see, myself, how even the corpse could stand it. All that went before was just simply poetry to that smell—but mind you, the original smell stood up out of it just as sublime as ever—fact is, these other smells just seemed to give it a better hold; and my, how rich it was! I didn't make these reflections there—there wasn't time—made them on the platform. And breaking for the platform, Thompson got suffocated and fell; and before I got him dragged out, which I did by the collar, I was mighty near gone myself. When we revived, Thompson said dejectedly:

"We got to stay out here, Cap. We got to do it. They ain't no other way. The Governor wants to travel alone, and he's fixed so he can outvote us."

And presently he added:

"And don't you know, we're *pisoned*. It's *our* last trip, you can make up your mind to it. Typhoid fever is what's going to come of this. I feel it a-coming right now. Yes, sir, we're elected, just as sure as you're born."

We were taken from the platform an hour later, frozen and insensible, at the next station, and I went straight off into a virulent fever, and never knew anything again for three weeks. I found out, then, that I had spent that awful night with a harmless box of rifles and a lot of innocent cheese; but the news was too late to save *me*; imagination had done its work, and my health was permanently shattered; neither Bermuda nor any other land can ever bring it back to me. This is my last trip; I am on my way home to die.

Closure and Extension
ANSWERS TO RESPONDING TO THE SELECTION
Your Response
1. Encourage students to support their responses by citing the passages they found most or least entertaining.

Recalling
2. The purpose of his journey is to take his friend's corpse to his par-

ents in Wisconsin.
3. The narrator confuses the coffin box with an identical box of rifles. He takes the box of rifles by mistake. A stranger enters the car and leaves a package of Limburger cheese on top of the coffin.
4. It is a gloomy, bitterly cold, and stormy night. By lighting the stove, the expressman heats the car and the cheese, making the odor stronger.
5. Because of the journey, his health was permanently ruined.

RESPONDING TO THE SELECTION

Your Response

1. Did you find the story entertaining? Why or why not?

Recalling

2. What is the purpose of the narrator's journey?
3. Describe the mistake the narrator makes at the train station. How does the stranger complicate the mistake?
4. How do weather conditions make the narrator's journey particularly uncomfortable? Why do Thompson's efforts to make the car comfortable have the opposite effect?
5. According to the narrator, what long-term effect does the journey have on him?

Interpreting

6. Compare what the narrator and Thompson believe to be true with what is really true.
7. How would the experience have differed if they had known the source of the odor?

Applying

8. Think of a joke you have heard whose humor depends on the difference between appearance and reality. Share it with your classmates.

ANALYZING LITERATURE

Understanding First-Person Narration

With **first-person narration,** one of the characters in the story relates the events. This character, who uses the pronoun *I* or *we,* tells the story from his or her **point of view,** or perspective. In "The Invalid's Story" the narrator tells about events long after they happened, and he knows more than he did when the events occurred.

1. What two facts does the narrator learn after the events of the story took place?
2. How does the fact that the narrator takes the events so seriously add to the humor?
3. Retell the part of the story in which the odor first surfaces (end of paragraph 1, page 100) from Thompson's point of view.

CRITICAL THINKING AND READING

Identifying Exaggeration

An **exaggeration** is an overstatement. It is often used for humor. For example, in this story the narrator exaggerates the effects of the trip when he says, "I seem sixty and married, but these effects are due to my condition and sufferings, for I am a bachelor, and only forty-one."

1. Why does the narrator exaggerate the length of time his friend has been dead? How does Thompson respond to this exaggeration?
2. Find the military terms Thompson uses to refer to the corpse. Why does he promote the corpse as the story goes on?
3. Explain how the narrator's statement at the end brings the story to a humorous conclusion.

THINKING AND WRITING

Writing a Tall Tale

Write a tall tale of your own. The plot should hinge on an absurd exaggeration, such as having the main character climb Mount Everest in one hour. Brainstorm to form a list of possible exaggerated events for your tall tale. Select a character and have this character narrate the events in the first person. When you revise the tale, be sure the events follow logically from your exaggeration. Proofread your tall tale and share it with your classmates.

LEARNING OPTION

Performance. Find other stories by Mark Twain that have first-person narrators and perform them for the class. If the stories have dialect, try to speak the words as they would actually be said. In rehearsing your performance, you may want to listen to tapes or compact disks of the actor Hal Holbrook portraying Mark Twain.

Interpreting

6. Suggested Response: The narrator and the expressman both believe that the odor is coming from the decaying corpse. The true source of the odor is the Limburger cheese.
7. Answers will differ. Students may respond that if the men had known that the cheese was the source of the odor, they could have thrown it away and spent the journey comfortably warm in the train.

Applying

8. Answers will differ. Students should share examples that depend on the difference between appearance and reality.

Challenge The phrase "grisly humor" refers to humor based on topics that are usually considered unpleasant or repellent. How is this story an example of grisly humor?

ANSWERS TO ANALYZING LITERATURE

1. Suggested Response: The narrator learns that he had spent the night with a "harmless box of rifles and a lot of innocent cheese."
2. Suggested Response: The narrator's solemnity would have been appropriate if the box contained a corpse. Because we know that the box contains rifles and the smell is caused by cheese, the narrator's seriousness seems ridiculous.

3. Answers will differ. Students may indicate that Thompson would begin to wonder about the odor and then realize it was coming from the corpse.

ANSWERS TO CRITICAL THINKING AND READING

1. Suggested Response: The narrator exaggerates the length of time the corpse has been dead because of the strength of the odor. Thompson responds in disbelief because he thinks the odor is strong enough for the corpse to have been dead for a much longer period.
2. Suggested Response: The military terms Thompson uses to refer to the corpse are Colonel, Gen'rul, and Commodore. The corpse gets promoted as the odor grows stronger.
3. Suggested Response: The narrator humorously exaggerates the harmful effects of the trip.

THINKING AND WRITING

Writing Transparency Students often find it helpful to use graphic organizers before writing. Before they begin this exercise, you may wish to show them the Story Map in the **Transparencies for Writing.**

Alternative Assessment *Protocol* Have students assess their own work by responding to these questions:

What exaggeration forms the basis for your tall tale?

What events do you include to develop your exaggeration?

What is the climax of your story?

What characteristics of the narrator are revealed in the tale?

Suggest that students use the information from their protocols to help them revise their tall tales.

LEARNING OPTION

This activity will appeal to auditory learners. You might want to expand the activity by having students record their performances on audiotape.

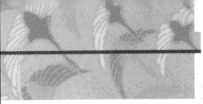

Preparation

More About the Author Grant Moss, Jr., is presently teaching at Grambling College in Louisiana. Ask students why they think college teaching is a good profession for a writer.

Literary Focus Discuss with students the various points of view from which a story may be told. Have students give examples of other stories written from the third-person point of view. Explain to students that the author's use of limited third-person narration helps readers see how difficult Bennie's problem is for him and how much he grows in the course of the story.

Prereading Focus To help students appreciate how Bennie might feel, encourage them to role-play his situation. Have one student assume the role of Bennie, and one or more students assume the role of friends or relatives trying to offer comfort.

Vocabulary Have your **less advanced** students use each word in a sentence that reflects its meaning.

GUIDE FOR READING

Before the End of Summer

Third-Person Narration

When authors use **third-person narration,** the narrator is a voice outside the story who refers to all the characters as *he, she,* or *they.* Sometimes the narrator relates the events from the **point of view,** or perspective, of one of the characters. This method is referred to as **limited third-person narration.** With limited third-person narration, the reader sees events through the eyes of one character and knows only what that character knows. In "Before the End of Summer" the narrator relates the events as Bennie, the ten-year-old hero, learns them. The child's limited experience and understanding give the story its special slant.

Focus

"Before the End of Summer" is a story about a boy, Bennie, who is forced to deal with his fear of his grandmother's impending death. In small groups discuss how Bennie must feel. Brainstorm ways in which Bennie might work on overcoming his fear. Then, as you read the story, compare the way Bennie deals with his fear to the ways suggested by your group.

Vocabulary

Knowing the following words will help you as you read "Before the End of Summer."

rawboned (rô′ bōnd′) *adj.*: Having little flesh or fat covering the bones; lean (p. 111)

plaits (plāts) *n.*: Braids (p. 112)

glistened (glis′ ′nd) *v.*: Shone or sparkled with reflected light (p. 117)

Grant Moss, Jr., has written short stories that appeared in such magazines as *The New Yorker, Essence,* and *Opportunity* during the 1960's. "Before the End of Summer" was first published in the October 15, 1960, issue of *The New Yorker,* and it has since appeared in many anthologies. The story offers a vivid depiction of life among blacks in the rural South as well as a touching portrayal of a close-knit and loving family.

Objectives

1 To recognize limited point of view
2 To use narration to draw conclusions
3 To write an essay about characters in a story
4 To express individual interests and abilities through optional activities

Support Material

Teaching Portfolio
Teacher Backup, p. 135
Grammar in Action Worksheets, *Writing Dialogue,* p. 139; *Recognizing Introductory Adverb Clauses,* p. 141
Usage and Mechanics Worksheet, p. 143
Vocabulary Check, p. 144

Critical Thinking and Reading Worksheet, *Using Narration to Draw Conclusions,* p. 145
Language Worksheet, *Choosing the Meaning to Fit the Context,* p. 146
Selection Test, p. 147

Prentice Hall Literature Writing Studio

Before the End of Summer

Grant Moss, Jr.

When Dr. Frazier came, Bennie's grandmother told him to run down to the spring and wade in the stream that flowed from it across the pasture field to Mr. Charley Miller's pond, or play under the big oak tree that stood between her field and Mr. Charley Miller's. He started along the path, but when he was about midway to the spring he stopped. He had waded in the stream and caught minnows all that morning. He had played under the oak tree all yesterday afternoon. He had asked his grandmother to let him walk the mile and a half down the road to James and Robert Lee Stewart's to play, but she had not let him go. There was nothing he wanted to do alone. He wanted someone to play with. He turned and went back and crept under the window of his grandmother's room. Their voices floated low and quiet out into the cool shade that lay over the house.

"How long will it be?" he heard his grandmother say.

"Before the end of summer."

"Are you sure?"

"Yes. You should have sent for me long ago."

"I've passed my threescore and ten years. I'm eighty-four."

What did they mean? Perhaps he ought not to be listening.

"How will it come? Tell me, Doctor. I can stand it."

"There will be sharp, quick pains like the ones you've been having. Your heart cannot stand many more attacks. It grows weaker with each one, even though you're able to go about your work as you did before the attack came. I'm going to leave you a prescription for some pills that will kill the pain almost instantly. But that's about all they will do. When an attack comes, take two with a glass of water. They'll make you drop off to sleep. One time you won't wake up."

Now Bennie understood. But he could not turn and run away.

There was a brief silence. Then his grandmother said, "Don't tell Birdie nor anybody else."

"But you can't stay here alone with the child all day long. Why, he's only ten years old."

"I know. . . . Doctor, there ain't anyone to come stay with me. Birdie must go to the Fieldses' to work. You know it's just Birdie, the boy, and me. I got no close kin. My husband, my three sons, and my other daughter's been dead for years now. You see, I know death, Doctor. I know it well. I'm just not use to it."

"No one is," Dr. Frazier said.

"Here's what I want to do. I'll go on just like before. There ain't nothin' else for me to do. When an attack comes, I'll take the two pills and I'll send Bennie runnin' down the road for May Mathis. She'll come. May will come. I know nobody I'd rather have set beside me than May. I knowed her all my life.

Presentation

Motivation/Prior Knowledge
Have students discuss how people react when they find out someone they care for is moving away or dying. Tell them that this story deals with such a situation.

Thematic Focus The rites of passage that lead people toward adulthood are often difficult or unpleasant. In the story, Bennie's rite of passage occurs when he becomes aware of his grandmother's impending death. Ask students if they have experienced such a rite of passage in their lives. How did it affect them? How did it affect people close to them?

Master Teacher Note The focus of the story is the way that the boy confronts and deals with his grandmother's imminent death. Have students look for details that show the boy trying to understand death.

Purpose-Setting Question What character traits does Bennie reveal as he lives with the secret of his grandmother's approaching death?

1 Critical Thinking and Reading Most of this story is told from the point of view of a child. How does this paragraph reveal a young boy's perceptions?

2 Reading Strategy Have students predict what they think might happen as a result of Bennie's eavesdropping.

3 Discussion What does Bennie finally understand? Why is he unable to move?

4 Discussion What does Bennie's grandmother mean when she says she knows death but is not used to it?

Alternative Assessment To promote active reading, have students keep a reader's response journal as they read the story. Ask them to focus their observations on the details that reveal the personalities of the characters as well as those that show growth in Bennie. Encourage students to respond personally to Bennie's experience with death. What relevance does the story have to their lives and experiences?

Their observations will enable you to assess their understanding of the issues in the story.

Making Connections Another selection that deals with a grandson's relationship with a beloved grandparent is "A Celebration of Grandfathers" by Rudolfo Anaya, page 447.

5 **Discussion** Did you realize before this point in the story that the narrator and his family were black? If so, what made you realize it?

6 **Discussion** How does Bennie react to his secret knowledge?

7 **Discussion** Why does Bennie want to be by himself?

8 **Discussion** Why do you think Bennie stays outdoors most of the day? How might these actions reflect Bennie's thoughts about his grandmother's death?

Me and her done talked about this thing many times. It's July now. July the seventh. Then August—then September. But here I go runnin' on and on. Let me get your money. You've got to be paid. You've got to live."

"Please," Dr. Frazier said.

"No harm meant."

In a moment, Bennie heard them walking out onto the porch through the door of her room. Then he could see them as they crossed the yard to the gate, where Dr. Frazier's horse and buggy stood. He was a little man, with a skin that was almost black. He climbed into his buggy and started up the road toward the town, which was three miles away, and she stood and looked after him. Her back was to the house. People said that Bennie's grandmother had Indian blood in her veins, for she had high cheekbones and her nose was long and straight, but her mouth was big. Her eyes seemed as though they were buried way back in her head, in a mass of wrinkles. They danced and twinkled whenever they looked at him. She was a big woman, and she wore long full skirts that came all the way to the ground.

She closed the gate and started back to the house, and it came to Bennie that he was alone with her, and that she was going to die soon. He turned and ran noiselessly across the back yard, through the back gate, and down the path to the spring.

When he reached the spring, he kept running. He ran across the pasture field and up the hill to the barbed-wire fence that divided his grandmother's land from Mr. Charley Miller's. He threw himself to the ground and rolled under the fence, picked himself up on the other side, and ran through Mr. Charley Miller's field of alfalfa and into the woods, until at last he fell exhausted in the cool damp grass of a shaded clearing.

His grandmother was going to die. She might even be dead now. She was going to lie cold and still, in a long black casket that would be put into a hearse that would take her to church in town. The Reverend Isaiah Jones would preach her funeral. People would cry, because people liked his grandmother. His mother would cry. He would cry. And now he was crying, and he could not stop crying.

But at last he did, and he sat up and took from his pocket the clean white rag that his grandmother had given him to use as a handkerchief and dried his eyes. He must get up and go back to the house. He would have to be alone with his grandmother until his mother came home from the Fieldses' after she had cooked their supper. And he must tell no one what he had heard Dr. Frazier say to his grandmother.

He found her sitting in her big rocking chair, her hands clasped in her lap. "You been gone a long time," she said. "The water bucket's empty. Take it and go fill it at the spring. Time for me to be gettin' up from here and cookin' supper."

When he got back from the spring, he found her laying a fire in the kitchen stove.

It was nearly dark when he saw his mother coming, and he ran to meet her. She looked at him closely and said, "Bennie, why on earth did you run so fast?"

He could only say breathlessly. "I don't know." He added quickly, "What did you bring me?" Sometimes she brought him a piece of cake or pie, or the leg of a chicken from the Fieldses'. Today she did not have anything.

It was a long time before he went to sleep that night.

The next day, he stayed outdoors and only went into the house when his grandmother called him to do something for her. She did not notice.

On Sunday, his mother did not go to the Fieldses'. In the morning, they went to church. That afternoon. Mr. Joe Bailey drove

Multicultural Focus This story focuses on death and mourning, two of humankind's most universal experiences. Yet attitudes toward death vary greatly among cultures. Many psychologists feel that industrialized, Western societies do little to prepare people to face and accept death, and ignore the subject instead. The rituals of more traditional societies seem striking in contrast. For example, a traditional Chinese funeral is full of color; the mourners wear white and the coffin is highly decorated. At a Hindu funeral, the body is cremated and the ashes thrown in the Ganges or another sacred river—a gesture of farewell to a soul that has moved on to a new life.

Have students research societies where grieving is more expressive than it is in the West, such as rural Greece with its tradition of lamentation, and rural Egypt where women perform a grieving dance in which they slap their own faces to show pain. Do students think ceremonies of mourning and those to end a mourning period are a good idea?

NEGRO BOY
Eastman Johnson
National Academy of Design

up to the house in his horse and buggy to take Bennie's mother for a buggy ride. She had put on her pretty blue-flowered dress and her big wide-brimmed black straw hat with the red roses around its crown and the black ribbon that fell over the brim and down her back. She looked very pretty and as pleased as she could be. Bennie wanted to go riding with them. Once, he had asked Mr. Joe if he could go along, and Mr. Joe had grinned and said yes, but Bennie's mother had not been pleased at all, for some reason. This Sunday, after they had gone, his grand-

mother let him walk the mile and a half down the road to play with James and Robert Lee Stewart.

He knew that his grandmother was preparing to die. He came upon her kneeling in prayer beside her bed with its high headboard that almost touched the ceiling. As she sat in her rocking chair, she said the Twenty-third Psalm. He knew only the first verse: "The Lord is my shepherd; I shall not want."

Now he felt toward his grandmother the way he felt toward certain people, only more

Before the End of Summer 109

10 Discussion What do you think Bennie means when he says that his grandmother made him stand away from her?

11 Clarification In the world of this story, whites are distant figures.

12 Discussion What do you think Bennie means?

10 so. There was a feeling that made people seem strange—a feeling that came from them to you—that made you stand away from them. There was Miss Sally Cannon, his teacher. You did not go close to Miss Sally. She made you sit still and always keep your reader or your spelling book open on your desk, or do your arithmetic problems. If she caught you whispering or talking, she called you up to the front of the room and gave you several stinging lashes on your legs or across your back with one of the long switches that always lay across her desk. You did not go close to Miss Sally unless you had to. You did not go close to Dr. Frazier or the Reverend Isaiah Jones. Teachers, doctors, and preachers were special people.

11 You did not go close to white people, either. Sometimes when he and his grandmother went to town, they would stop at the Fieldses'. They would walk up the long green yard and go around the big red brick house, with its tall white columns, to the kitchen, where his mother was; it always seemed a nice place to be, even on a hot summer day. His mother and his grandmother would chuckle over something that Miss Marion Fields or Mr. Ridley Fields had done. They would stop smiling the minute Miss Marion came into the **12** room, and they would become like people waiting in the vestibule of a church for the prayer to be finished so they could go in. He knew that he acted the same way.

Miss Marion had light-brown hair and light-brown eyes. His grandmother said that she was like a sparrow, for she was a tiny woman. She always wore a dress that was pretty enough to wear to church. The last time he was at the Fieldses', Miss Marion came into the kitchen. After she had spoken to his grandmother, she turned to him. He was sitting in a chair near the window, and he felt himself stiffen both inside and outside. She said, "I declare, Birdie, Bennie's the prettiest colored child I ever did see. Lashes long as a girl's. Is he a good boy, Hannah?"

"He's a quiet child," his grandmother said. "Sometimes I think he's too quiet, but he's a good child—at least when I got my eyes on him." They all laughed.

"I'm sure Bennie's good," Miss Marion said. "Be a good boy, Bennie. Eat plenty and grow strong, and when you're big enough to work, Mr. Ridley will be glad to give you work here on his place. We're so glad to have your mother here with us. Now, be good, won't you?"

"Yes, Ma'am," he answered.

"Birdie, give him a piece of that lemon pie you baked for supper. Well, Hannah, it's been nice talking with you again. Always stop on your way to town."

Two weeks to the day after Dr. Frazier's visit, Miss May Mathis came to see his grandmother. She was much shorter than his grandmother—a plump woman, who always wore long black-and-white checked gingham[1] dresses that fell straight down from her high full breasts to her knees and then flared outward. Her chin was sharp, with folds of flesh around it. Her nose was wide and flat. She had small, snapping black eyes. Her skin was like cream that had been kept too long and into which hundreds of tiny black specks had fallen.

As she came into the yard, she asked Bennie if his grandmother was at home. She said she would sit on the porch, where it was cool. He ran into the house to tell his grandmother that she was there.

His grandmother put away her sewing

---

1. gingham (giŋ' əm) *adj.*: A cotton cloth, usually woven in stripes, checks, or plaids (most often, a noun).

Grammar in Action

Knowing how to write **dialogue** will make your own short stories fun to write and interesting to read. Dialogue, or conversation between characters in a work of literature, is enclosed in quotation marks. A new paragraph is started each time the speaker changes. Read these lines of dialogue from the story:

His grandmother put away her sewing and went out on the porch. "May, I'm glad you come. I've been lookin' for you," she said.

"I'd been here sooner, but my stomach's been givin' me trouble lately. Sometimes I think my time ain't long."
"Hush—hush! You'll live to see me put under the ground."
"Well, the day before yesterday I spent half the day in bed. I thought I'd have to send John for you." Miss May answered, and she went into a long account of the illness that troubled her.

Notice that in this excerpt the two middle paragraphs are made up entirely of quoted material, with no words or phrases that identify the speaker. How can you tell who is speaking?

The context of the work helps you keep track of the speaker in dialogue such as this: In the first paragraph, readers are told

and went out on the porch. "May, I'm glad you come. I've been lookin' for you," she said.

"I'd been here sooner, but my stomach's been givin' me trouble lately. Sometimes I think my time ain't long."

"Hush—hush! You'll live to see me put under the ground."

"Well, the day before yesterday I spent half the day in bed. I thought I'd have to send John for you," Miss May answered, and she went into a long account of the illness that troubled her.

Bennie got up from the edge of the porch and ran around the house. The two old women paid no attention to his going. He knew what his grandmother would say to Miss May. She would tell Miss May how she wanted to be dressed for burial. She would name the song she wanted to be sung over her. He had heard the same conversation many times. Now it was different. What they were talking about would soon "come to pass," as his grandmother would say. Miss May did not know, but he knew.

He went out of the back gate and down the path to the spring. He waded in the stream awhile, catching minnows in his hands and then letting them go. He went across the pasture field. He broke off a persimmon bush to use as a switch, and he chased his grandmother's cow about the pasture a bit. But the cow was old and soon grew tired of moving when he hit her with the switch. Then he went to the big oak tree that stood between the fields and sat down. He stayed there until he saw Miss May Mathis going out of the front gate.

The July days went slowly by, one much like another. It grew hotter and hotter.

One day when he walked into the house after playing a long time in the stream and the pasture field, he found his grandmother quietly sleeping in her big rocking chair. He saw a bottle full of big white pills on the dresser. It had not been there when he left the house. An empty glass stood beside the pills. He felt too frightened to move. Her breast was rising and falling evenly. She stirred and then opened her eyes.

She seemed dazed and not to see him for a moment. Then her lips curved into a queer smile, and a twinkle came into her eyes. "Must have dropped off to sleep like a baby," she said. "Run outdoors and play. I'll set here awhile and then I'll get up and start supper."

Later on, she called him and asked if he could make out with milk and cold food from dinner. She left the milking for his mother to do when she came home from the Fieldses'. But the next morning his grandmother was all right, and he thought that she was not going to die that summer, after all.

One morning, a little after his mother had gone to the Fieldses', Mr. John Mathis drove up. He turned his horse and buggy around to face the way he had come. Then he walked up the path to the house. He was a tall, rawboned man with a bullet-shaped head, and he looked exactly like what he was—a deacon[2] in a church.

"What is it, John?" Bennie's grandmother asked.

"It's May. She was sick all day yesterday. Last night I had to get the doctor for her. Jennie Stewart's there now."

"I'll be ready to go in a minute," his grandmother said.

On the way to the Mathises', Bennie sat on the back of the buggy. His grandmother and Mr. John said only a few words. When they reached the house, his grandmother told him to keep very quiet and to be good,

---

2. **deacon** (dēk''n) *n*.: A church officer who helps the minister.

13 **Discussion** Why is he frightened?

14 **Discussion** Why does Bennie's grandmother smile strangely?

that Grandmother is talking. In the next, context makes it clear that Miss May answers her. Grandmother then responds, and Miss May answers by telling about her illness.

Student Activity 1. In the story, find another passage of dialogue in which the speaker is not always identified. Share this passage with a partner, discussing who is speaking each line.

Student Activity 2. Choose one of the passages and practice reading the speech of the characters aloud with your partner. Present your reading to the class.

Student Activity 3. Write a brief conversation between two people. Use punctuation and paragraphs to help you indicate who is speaking.

Electronic Handbook You may wish to review with students the mechanics of writing dialogue before having students complete Student Activity 3. If students have access to the Language Master 6000, have them enter the access symbol " or the access word *quotation* and press the GRAMMAR key to get information about the punctuation of dialogue.

15 **Discussion** What does his grandmother mean?

16 **Discussion** How do you think she feels?

17 **Discussion** Do you think this passage indicates a change in Bennie's attitude toward his grandmother's death? Explain.

and she went inside at once. There were people on the porch, and people continued to come and go. It was midafternoon, and still his grandmother had not come from within the house. A Ford car drove up to the gate. In it were Philomena Jones and her mother. Philomena was a year younger than Bennie. She had a sharp little yellow face, big black eyes that went everywhere, and she wore her hair in two long plaits. "Come on," she said, "and let's play something." When they were out of hearing of the grown-up people, she said, "Miss May going to die."

"How do you know?"

"I heard my mama say she was. She's old. When you're old you have to die."

Next, Philomena said, "Your mama's tryin' to catch Mr. Joe Bailey for a husband. Mama said it's time she's getting another husband if she's ever going to get one."

"You stop talkin'!" Bennie told her.

"She said your pa's been dead nine years now and if your mama don't hurry and take Mr. Joe Bailey—that is, if she can get him— she may never get a chance to marry again."

"If you don't stop talking', I'll hit you!"

"No, you won't. I'm not scared of you, even if you are a boy, and I'll say what I want to. Mama said, 'Birdie Wilson's in her forties, if she a day, and if a woman lets herself get into her forties without marryin', her chance are mighty slim after that.' I'm goin' to marry when I'm twenty."

"Nobody'd want you. You talk too much."

"I don't, neither."

"I won't play with you. I'm goin' back to the porch," he said.

Philomena stayed in the yard a little longer. She carried on an imaginary conversation with a person who seemed as eager to talk as she. After a while, she ran back to the porch and sat down and gave her attention to what the grown-up people were saying, now and then putting in a word herself.

Then his grandmother came out from the house. People stopped talking at the sight of her face. "May's gone," she said.

The people on the porch bowed their heads, and their faces became as though they were already at Miss May Mathis's funeral.

His grandmother looked very tired. After a moment, she said, "The Lord giveth and the Lord taketh. Blessed be the name of the Lord." There was a silence. Then she spoke again. "I thought May would do for me what I have to do for her now." She turned and went back into the house. Some of the women rose and followed her.

The people who remained on the porch spoke in low voices. Someone wondered when the funeral would be. Someone wondered if Miss May's sister Ethel, who lived in St. Louis, would come. Someone hoped that it would not rain the day of the funeral.

Then Mr. John Mathis and Bennie's grandmother came out on the porch. Mr. John said, "Hannah, you done all you could do. May couldn't have had a better friend. You're tired now. I'll send you home."

At home, his grandmother seemed not to notice him. Her eyes seemed to be taking a great sad rest. She sent him to the spring to get water to cook supper.

As he walked down the path, he thought about his grandmother. He felt more sorry for her than he felt fear of her. Miss May Mathis was dead; he could not run and get her now.

On Sunday afternoon at two o'clock at the Baptist Church, Miss May Mathis's funeral service was held. There was a procession of buggies, surreys,[3] and even a few automobiles from the house to the church. Mr. Joe Bailey came and took Bennie's

3. **surreys** (sʉr′ ēz) *n.pl.*: Light, horse-drawn carriages.

mother, his grandmother, and him to church. The funeral was a long one. He sat beside his grandmother and listened to the prayers, the songs, and the sermon, all the time dreading the moment when the flowers would be taken from the gray casket, the casket would be opened, and the people would file by to see the body for the last time.

The Reverend Isaiah Jones described Heaven as a land flowing with milk and honey, a place where people ate fruit from the tree of life, wore golden slippers, long white robes, and starry crowns, and rested forever. The Reverend Isaiah Jones was certain that Miss May Mathis was there, resting in the arms of Jesus, done with the sins and sorrows of this world. Bennie wondered why Mr. John covered his face with his hands, and why Miss May's sister Ethel, who had come all the way from St. Louis, cried out, and why people cried, if Miss May was so happy in this land. It seemed that they should be glad for her, so glad they would not cry. Or did they cry because they were glad? He could not understand. The Reverend Jones said that they would see Miss May on the Resurrection morning.[4] Bennie could not understand this, either.

At last the gray casket was opened, and people began to file by it. And at last he was close. His mother went by, and then Mr. Joe. Now his grandmother. The line of people stopped, waiting expectantly. His grandmother stood and looked down on Miss May for a long time. She did not cry out. She simply stood there and looked down, and finally she moved on. Now he was next. Miss May Mathis looked as though she had simply combed her hair and piled it on top of her head, put on her best black silk dress, pinned her big old pearl brooch to its lace

4. **the Resurrection** (rez′ ə rek′ shən) **morning:** In Christian teaching, the time when the dead come back to life.

collar, picked up a white handkerchief with one hand, and then decided that instead of going to church she would sleep a little while. As he looked down on her, he was not as afraid as he'd thought he would be.

Outside the church, as the procession was forming to go to the graveyard, Dr. Frazier came up to his grandmother and asked how she was.

"As well as could be expected, Doctor," his grandmother said. And then, in a low voice, "I've had only one."

"You got through it all right."

"Yes."

"And this?"

"I've managed to get through it."

"You will be careful."

"Yes."

"Now?"

"He'll have to go to the Stewarts'."

They did not know that he understood what they were talking about, even if none of the other people around them did. He heard two women whispering. One said to the other, "It's wonderful the way Aunt Hannah took it." He felt very proud of his grandmother.

Now his grandmother's footsteps were slower as she moved about the house and yard. He kept the garden and the flower beds along the yard fences weeded, the stove box full of wood, the water bucket full all the time, without her having to ask him to do these things for her. He overheard her say to his mother, "Child does everything without being told. It ain't natural."

"Reckon he's not well?" his mother asked anxiously.

"Don't think so. He eats well. Maybe the trouble is the child don't have nobody to play with every day. He'll be all right when fall comes and school starts."

Before the End of Summer 113

---

18 Discussion Why is Bennie confused? How is his confusion typical of young people who tend to interpret everything literally?

19 Discussion What do you think Bennie's grandmother is thinking as she stands and looks down at Miss May?

20 Discussion How might the death of Miss May have affected Bennie's feelings about his grandmother's death?

21 Critical Thinking and Reading What do you know about Bennie from the fact that he keeps the garden and flower beds weeded and the water bucket full without being told?

Humanities Note

Fine art, *Anna Washington Derry*, 1927, by Laura Wheeler Waring. Waring was an American painter, illustrator, and teacher with a straightforward, harmonious style and a flair for depicting strong personalities. There is warmth in her attitudes toward her subjects, and she took great care to portray people as they appeared to her in life. Daughter of a minister, she painted many prominent blacks and whites of her day, including W.E.B. Du Bois, the most important black protest leader of the first half of the twentieth century.

Waring painted *Anna Washington Derry* when she was on the faculty of a Pennsylvania teacher's college, and this picture won her an award for distinguished achievement in the arts.

Have students compare this portrait with the previous one, *Negro Boy*, and point out the lack of a background in this portrait.

1. How does the absence of a background add to the definition of this woman's personality?
2. How could other objects or a landscape detract from a clear vision of who she is?
3. How would you describe this woman?

22 Discussion Why is this simile an effective way to describe the summer sun in the South?

ANNA WASHINGTON DERRY, 1927
Laura Wheeler Waring
National Museum of American Art
The Smithsonian Institution

22 August came, and it grew hotter. The sun climbed up the sky in the morning and down the sky in the evening like a tired old man with a great load on his back going up and down a hill. Then one hot mid-August day dawned far hotter and sultrier than the one just past. It grew still hotter during the early part of the morning, but by midday there was a change, for there was a breeze, and in the west a few dark clouds gathered in the sky. His grandmother said, "I believe the rain will come at last."

About three o'clock, the wind rose suddenly. It bent the top of the big oak tree that stood in the yard. There were low rumbles of thunder.

"Bennie, Bennie, come! Let's get the chickens up!" his grandmother called to him.

By the time all the chickens were safe in the henhouse and chicken coops, it was time to go into the house and put the windows down. The wind lifted the curtains almost to the ceiling. They got the windows down. His grandmother went into the kitchen. He went out on the porch. He wanted to watch the clouds, for he had never seen any bigger or blacker or quite so low to the earth—he was sure they must be touching the ground somewhere. He wanted to see what the wind did to the trees, the corn, and the grass.

At last the rain fell, first in great drops that were blown onto the edge of the porch by the wind and felt cool and good as they touched his face. They made him want to run out into the yard. Then the rain came so quickly and so heavily, and with it so much wind, that it came up on the porch and almost pushed him back into the house. The thunder roared and there were flashes of lightning.

"Bennie, Bennie, where are you?" his grandmother called, and when he went inside she said, "Set down—set down in the big chair there or come into my room if you want to. I'm goin' to just set in my rocker."

"I'll stay here," he said, and he went to the big chair near the fireplace and sat down.

"There—there—just set there. I'll leave the door open."

He tried to keep from thinking what might happen if his grandmother had one of her spells, but he could not. He went to the fireplace. The back of the fireplace was wet; water stood on it in drops that looked like tears on a face. He stood and looked at it awhile, then he sat down in the big chair. There was nothing else to do but to sit there.

He heard her cry out. The cry was sharp and quick. Then it was cut off.

She called him. "Bennie! Bennie!" Her voice was thick.

He could not move.

"Bennie!"

He went into the room where she was.

She sat on the side of her bed. She was breathing hard, and in one hand she had the bottle of white pills. "Get me a glass of water. One of my spells done come over me."

He went into the kitchen and got a glass from the kitchen safe and filled it with water from the bucket that sat on the side table. Then he went back to her and gave her the water.

She took it and put two pills in her mouth and gulped them down with the water. She was breathing hard. "Pull off my shoes," she said.

As he was unlacing the high-top shoes she always wore, she gave a little cry. He felt her body tremble. "Just a bit of pain. Don't worry. I'm all right," she said. "It's gone," she added a moment later.

When he got her shoes off, he lifted her legs onto the bed, and she lay back and closed her eyes. "Go into the front room," she said, "and close the door behind you and stay there until the storm is past. I'm goin' to drop off to sleep—and if I'm still asleep when the storm is over, just let me sleep until your mama comes. Don't come in here. Don't try to wake me. 'Twon't do me no harm to take me a long good sleep."

He could not move. He could only stand there and stare at her.

"Hear me? Go on, I tell you. Go on— don't, I'll get up from here and skin you alive."

He crept from the room, closing the door after him.

He went to the big chair and sat down. He must not cry. Crying could not help him. There was nothing to do but to sit there until the storm was past.

The rain and the wind came steadily now. He sat back in the big chair. He wondered about his mother. Was she safe at the Fieldses'? He wondered if the water had flowed into the henhouse and under the chicken coops, where the little chickens were. If it had, some of the little chickens might get drowned. The storm lasted so long that it began to seem to him that it had always been there.

At last he became aware that the room

Before the End of Summer 115

23 **Discussion** Why is this an effective simile?

24 **Discussion** Why does she tell him not to disturb her?

25 **Discussion** Why is Bennie unable to move?

26 **Discussion** How does the felling of the oak relate to the grand-mother's imminent death?

27 **Discussion** Why do you think she cannot continue?

28 **Discussion** What does Bennie's grandmother mean?

was growing lighter and the rain was not so hard. The thunder and lightning were gone. Then, almost as suddenly as it had begun, the storm was over.

He got up and went out on the porch. Everything was clean. Everything looked new. There were little pools of water everywhere, and it was cool. There were a few clouds in the sky, but they were white and light gray. He looked across the field toward Mr. Charley Miller's, and he opened his eyes wide when he saw that the storm had blown down the big oak tree. He started to run back into the house to tell his grandmother that the storm had blown the tree down, and then he stopped. After a minute, he stepped down from the porch. The wet grass felt good on his bare feet.

He felt his grandmother in the doorway even before he heard her call. He turned and looked at her. She had put on her shoes and the long apron she always wore. She came out on the porch, and he decided that she looked as though her sleep had done her good.

26 He remembered the tree, and he cried, "Look—look, Grannie! The storm blowed down the tree between your field and Mr. Charley Miller's."

27 "That tree was there when me and your grandpa came here years and years ago," she said. "The Lord saw fit to let it be blowed down in this storm. I— I—" She broke off and went back into the house.

He ran into the house and said to her, "I'm goin' down to the spring. I bet the stream's deep as a creek."

"Don't you get drowned like old Pharaoh's army,"[5] she said.

---

5. **drowned like old Pharaoh's** (fer′ ōz) **army:** Pharaoh was the title of the kings of Egypt; the Biblical story (Exodus 14:28) tells that the Egyptian army was drowned while chasing the Israelites across the Red Sea.

116   Short Stories

The storm drove away the heat, for the days were now filled with cool winds that came and rattled the cornstalks and the leaves on the oak tree in the yard. There were showers. The nights were long and cool; the wind came into the rooms, gently pushing aside the neat white curtains to do so.

One morning when he went into the kitchen to get hot water and soap to take to the back porch to wash his face and hands, he found his mother and grandmother busy talking. They stopped the moment they saw him. His mother's face seemed flushed and uncomfortable, but her eyes were very bright.

"Done forgot how to say good mornin' to a body?" his grandmother said.

"Good mornin', Grannie. Good mornin', Mama."

"That's more like it."

"Good mornin', Bennie," his mother said. She looked at him, and he had a feeling that she was going to come to him and take him in her arms the way she used to do when he was a little boy. But she did not.

28 His grandmother laughed. "Well, son, Mr. Joe Bailey went and popped the question to your mama last night."

His mother blushed. He did not know what to say to either of them. He just stood and looked at them.

"What you goin' to say to that?" his mother said.

All he could think to say was "It's all right."

His grandmother laughed again, and his mother smiled at him the way she did when he ran down the road to meet her and asked her to let him carry the packages that she had.

"When will they be married?" he asked.

"Soon," his mother said.

"Where will they live—here?"

"That ain't been settled yet," his grandmother said. "Nothin' been settled. They just

---

Grammar in Action

Adverb clauses modify verbs, adjectives, adverbs, or verbals by telling where, when, in what manner, to what extent, under what condition, or why. An **introductory adverb clause** appears at the beginning of a sentence. Like other adverb clauses, this one begins with a subordinating conjunction and includes a subject and verb. It may also include complements and modifiers.

Read the following passage from the story. Notice how the writer begins each of the first four sentences with a subject.

Then, to vary his sentences, he begins the last one with an adverb clause:

His mother was going to marry Mr. Joe Bailey. He did mind a little. He knew that was what she wanted. He liked Mr. Joe. *When Mr. Joe smiled at him,* he always had to smile back at him; something seemed to make him do so.

By inserting an introductory adverb clause, he varies the rhythm and length of his sentences.

Student Activity 1. Identify the introductory adverb clauses in the following sentences. Indicate the word that each clause modifies.

got engaged last night while they were settin' in the front room and you was sleepin' in your bed. Things can be settled later." She gave a sigh that his mother did not hear. But he heard it.

He poured water from the teakettle into the wash pan and took the pan out on the back porch and washed and dried his hands. He looked across the fields and hills. The sun had not come up yet, but the morning lay clear and soft and quiet as far as his eyes could see.

His mother was going to marry Mr. Joe Bailey. He did mind a little. He knew that was what she wanted. He liked Mr. Joe. When Mr. Joe smiled at him, he always had to smile back at him; something seemed to make him do so.

After his mother had gone to the Fieldses', he and his grandmother sat down to breakfast at the table in the kitchen. His grandmother never ate a meal without saying grace. Usually she gave thanks just for the food that they were about to eat. This morning she asked the Lord to bless his mama, Mr. Joe, and him, and she thanked the Lord for answering all her prayers.

As they ate, she talked to him. She spoke as though she were talking to herself, expecting no answer from him, but he knew that she meant for him to listen to her words, and he knew why she was talking to him. "Joe Bailey will make your mama a good husband and you a good father to take the place of your father who you never knew. The Lord took your father when your father was still young, but that was the Lord's will. Joe Bailey will be good to you, for he is a good man. Mind him. Don't make trouble between him and your mama. Hear me?"

"Yes, Ma'am."

"Don't you worry about where you'll stay. You'll be with your mama. Hear me?"

"Yes'm."

She sat silent for a moment, and then she added, "Well, no matter if your mama is going to marry Mr. Joe Bailey. We got to work today just like we always has. No matter what comes, we have to do the little things that our hands find to do. Soon as you finish eatin', go to the spring and get water and fill the pot and the tubs."

August drew toward its close, but the soft cool days stayed on, and they were calm and peaceful. His grandmother cooked the meals, and washed and ironed their own clothes and those that his mother brought home from the Fieldses' and Mr. Charley Miller's. Sometimes Bennie wondered if she had put from her mind the things that Dr. Frazier had said to her that day he listened under the window. Sometimes it seemed to him that he had never crept close to the window and listened to her and Dr. Frazier. The summer seemed just like last summer and the summer before that.

One day near the end of the month, Mr. John Mathis stopped by the house on his way to town. He was on horseback, riding a big black horse whose sides glistened. He hailed Bennie's grandmother, and she came out on the porch to pass the time of day with him.

"Ever see such a fine summer day, John?" she said.

"It's not a summer day, Hannah. It's a fall day. It's going to be an early fall this year."

"Think so?" his grandmother asked. Her face changed, but Mr. John did not notice.

"I can feel it. I can feel it in the air. The smell of fall is here already." Then they fell to talking about the church and people they knew.

She stood on the porch and watched Mr. John ride up the road on his big black horse. Often that day, she came out on the porch and stood and looked across the fields and hills.

Before the End of Summer 117

29 **Discussion** What do you think bothers Bennie about his mother marrying Joe Bailey?

30 **Discussion** Why does Bennie doubt that he eavesdropped?

31 **Discussion** Why do you think Bennie's grandmother's face changes?

1. Although the sleet and wind tore at his shattered leg, Rob continued the struggle to get help.
2. While Amanda waited anxiously in the next room, the doctor studied the test results.
3. If we hurry, we can catch the last bus.

Student Activity 2. Write a paragraph modeled on the one by Grant Moss, Jr. Use four sentences with the same structure and length. Then add a longer fifth sentence that begins with an adverb clause.

Electronic Handbook You might want to review skills related to adverb clauses before having students complete the activities. If students have access to the Language Master 6000, have them enter the access words *adverb, interruption,* or *clause* and then press the GRAMMAR key for information on these topics.

32 **Discussion** Why do you think Bennie is no longer afraid? What events in the story may have helped him to change? How do you think he feels?

33 **Discussion** What makes Bennie start to run as fast as he can?

Reader's Response If you were Bennie, would you have acted as he did? Why or why not?

Thematic Response Bennie discovers that his mother will marry again. Do you think that this event will involve another rite of passage for Bennie? Why or why not?

When Bennie went outside for the first time the next morning and looked around him, he did not see a single cloud in the sky. The quiet that lay about him felt like a nice clean sheet you pull over your head before you go to sleep at night that shuts out everything to make a space both warm and cool just for you. The day grew warm. A little after midday, clouds began to float across the sky, but for the most part it remained clear and very blue. He played in the yard under the oak tree, and then he went down to the spring and played. In the afternoon, he rolled his hoop up and down the road in front of the house. He grew tired of this and went and sat under the tree.

He was still sitting under the tree when his grandmother cried out. She gave a sharp sudden cry, like the cry people make when they've been stung by a bee or a wasp. He got to his feet. Then he heard her call. "Bennie! Bennie!"

He ran into the house and into her room.

She sat in her big rocking chair, leaning forward a little, her hands clutching the arms of the chair. She was breathing hard. He had never seen her eyes as they were now. "Water—the pills—in the dresser."

He ran into the kitchen and got a glass of water and ran back to the room and gave it to her and then went to the dresser and got the bottle of pills. He unscrewed the top and took out two of them and gave them to her.

She put the pills in her mouth and gulped them down with water. Then she leaned back and closed her eyes. At last she breathed easier, and in a few moments she opened her eyes. "Run and get—get Miss— No, go get your mama. Hurry! Your grandmother is very sick."

It was a long way to the Fieldses'— even longer than to the Stewarts'! He stood still and looked at her. She was a big woman, and the chair was a big chair. Now she seemed smaller—lost in the chair.

"Hurry—hurry, child."

"Grannie, I'll stay with you until you go to sleep, if you want me to," he heard himself say.

"No! No! Hurry!"

"I heard you and Dr. Frazier talking that day."

"Child! Child! You knew all the time?"

"Yes, Grannie."

"When I drop off to sleep, I won't wake up. Your grandmother won't wake up here."

"I know."

"You're not afraid?"

He shook his head.

She seemed to be thinking hard, and at last she said, "Set down, child. Set down beside me."

He pulled up the straight chair and sat down facing her.

"Seems like I don't know what to say to you, Bennie. Be a good boy. Seems like I can't think any more. Everything leavin' me—leavin' me."

"I'll set here until you go to sleep, and then I'll go and get mama."

"That's a good boy," she said, and she closed her eyes.

He sat still and quiet until her breath came softly and he knew that she was asleep. It was not long. Then he got up and walked from the room and out of the house.

He did not look back, and he did not run until he was a good way down the road. Then suddenly he began to run, and he ran as fast as he could.

32

33

Closure and Extension

ANSWERS TO RESPONDING TO THE SELECTION
Your Response

1. Encourage students to share their responses with the class.

Recalling

2. The doctor tells Bennie's grandmother that she will die before the end of summer. Bennie eavesdrops and finds this out.

3. At first he is very frightened by the seizures. After Miss May's funeral, he seems to accept them better.

4. He learns to accept death and takes more responsibility for his actions.

Interpreting

5. Suggested Response: Grandmother feels that Bennie's mother has enough to worry about.

6. Suggested Response: He probably does not know exactly what to say, or he does not want them to know that he had been eavesdropping.

7. Suggested Response: Her death enables Bennie to experience the

death of someone he has known but whom he is not as close to. He comes to realize that the experience is not necessarily frightening and terrible. He thinks that Miss May looks as if she had dressed for church and then had decided to lie down a while. He is not as afraid as he had expected to be.

8. Suggested Response: When Bennie first hears that his grand-

RESPONDING TO THE SELECTION

Your Response

1. Does Bennie have qualities that you would like to develop in yourself? If so, which qualities are they? If not, why not?

Recalling

2. What does Dr. Frazier tell Bennie's grandmother? How does Bennie learn what is said?
3. How does Bennie react to his grandmother's seizures?
4. In what two ways does Bennie's life change by the end of the story?

Interpreting

5. Why doesn't Bennie's grandmother share the doctor's conclusions with Bennie's mother?
6. Why doesn't Bennie discuss what he has learned with his mother or his grandmother?
7. How does May Mathis's funeral help Bennie prepare for his grandmother's death?
8. Compare Bennie's reactions to death at the beginning and at the end of the selection.

Applying

9. Explain what a person can gain from the experience of losing someone close.

ANALYZING LITERATURE

Recognizing Limited Point of View

In **third-person narration,** the narrator uses the pronouns *he, she,* and *they* to identify the characters. With **limited third-person narration,** the narrator tells the story from the **point of view** of one of the characters, and the reader learns only what that character knows or sees. For example, if "Before the End of Summer" were told from the mother's point of view, you would not learn that the grandmother is going to die or that Bennie is aware of her condition.

1. Explain what Bennie does not understand about Miss May's funeral.
2. How might the story change if it were told from the grandmother's point of view?

3. Do you think the story is more effective for being told from Bennie's point of view? Explain your answer.

CRITICAL THINKING AND READING

Using Narration to Draw Conclusions

When authors use limited third-person narration, they do not give you an objective picture of a character from the outside. You must draw conclusions about the character from his or her thoughts and feelings. You know that Bennie is considered to be a "good boy," for example, because he hears the adults say he is.

What evidence in the story supports or refutes each of the following conclusions?

1. Bennie is a loving grandson.
2. Bennie does not have many friends.

THINKING AND WRITING

Writing About Characters

In "Before the End of Summer" Bennie acts as your eyes and ears: You observe his world through him. Bennie is also deeply affected by the events. List all the details you learn about Bennie. Then write an essay explaining what you think of Bennie and how he behaves. When you revise, think about how well you have shown that you understand Bennie's point of view.

LEARNING OPTIONS

1. **Art.** Illustrate a scene from the story or create a collage that reveals Bennie's relationship with his grandmother. Keep in mind the setting of the story as you work. Display your illustration in the classroom when you are finished.
2. **Writing.** Pretend that you are Bennie and write a poem to your grandmother expressing how you feel about her. Review the story for clues about Bennie's feelings to include in your poem. When you are finished, share your poem with your class.

Before the End of Summer 119

mother is going to die. He is proud of his grandmother for the way she handles herself at Miss May's funeral. He does his chores before his grandmother has to ask him to.
2. Suggested Response: Evidence to support this conclusion includes the fact that Bennie plays by himself throughout the story. He is also referred to as a quiet boy. His only friends seem to be two boys who live down the road.

THINKING AND WRITING

Writing Transparency You might want to show students a model to help them in this writing assignment. Model 5: Expository Essay in the **Transparencies for Writing** will be of help to them in this exercise.

Publishing Student Writing Call on volunteers to read aloud one or two main points from their reports. List the most frequently made points on the chalkboard.

Alternative Assessment *Peer Review* Have students work in groups of four and assess each other's essays by responding to these questions:

What does the writer think of Bennie's behavior?

What specific details does the writer use to support his or her view?

What additional details would improve the writer's work?

What, if anything, would you suggest the writer delete?

Encourage students to incorporate the group's suggestions into the revisions of their stories.

LEARNING OPTIONS

1. This activity is appropriate for visual learners. Students with other learning styles might find it challenging. You might want to vary the activity by having students include a line or two of dialogue as a caption for the illustration.
2. Creative students will appreciate this activity. You might want to vary this activity by having students illustrate their poems.

mother is going to die, he runs until he is exhausted, throws himself on the ground, and cries. At the end of the story, he refuses to leave his grandmother's side, talks with her, and sits with her until he knows that she is asleep. He is no longer afraid and is able to accept her death.

Applying

9. Answers will differ. Students may respond that a person can discover resources of strength in himself or herself.

ANSWERS TO ANALYZING LITERATURE

1. Suggested Response: Bennie cannot understand why people cry when they know that she is happy wherever she is.
2. Answers will differ. Students may respond that Bennie's growth would not be as clear to the reader.

3. Answers will differ. Students could support either side of this question. They should use examples from the story and sound arguments to back up their answers.

ANSWERS TO CRITICAL THINKING AND READING

1. Suggested Response: Evidence to support this conclusion includes the following: He cries when he hears that his grand-

More about the Author Tomás Rivera told one reviewer, "Up to the time I started teaching, I was part of the migrant labor stream that went from Texas to the Midwest. I lived and worked in Iowa, Minnesota, Wisconsin, Michigan, and North Dakota." After having left that life, why do you suppose Rivera chose that subject for his lifelong writing topic?

Literary Focus Ask students to imagine what it would be like to know what everyone around them is thinking and how they view events. Remind students that because authors know everything about the characters they have created, they can use an omniscient narrator who shares selected information with readers.

Prereading Focus Prior to having students brainstorm with classmates about times when they made inferences about others, you might take a few minutes to have students prepare for the cooperative task by freewriting for three or four minutes on the topic.

Vocabulary Have some students act out the vocabulary words while other students guess the word. The activity will appeal to kinesthetic and visual learners.

Electronic Handbook If students are using the Language Master 6000, you may want them to use the electronic thesaurus to find suitable synonyms.

Teaching to Ability Levels Your less advanced students with access to the Language Master 6000 should listen to the pronunciation of the words, repeating them aloud as they listen.

Spelling Tip Point out to students the various sounds of the vowel *a* in the vocabulary words.

GUIDE FOR READING

Tomás Rivera

(1935–1984), born in Crystal City, Texas, was one of the most renowned Mexican American writers in the United States of recent years. As a young man Rivera had to alternate his schooling with migrant labor, yet he pursued his education tirelessly, eventually earning a Ph.D. in Spanish Literature. His concern for the education of his people and other minorities led Rivera to seek a career in education, which left him limited time for his writing. Rivera's work is uniquely Mexican American, most often focusing on the experiences of the migrant farm worker, as in "The Harvest."

The Harvest

Omniscient Narrator

A story told by a third-person narrator is told by a voice outside the story. When this voice is all-seeing and all-knowing, it is called an **omniscient narrator.** An omniscient narrator can tell us things that the characters in the story do not know. This narrator can also enter the minds of the characters, telling us what they think and feel and how they view events. In theory the omniscient narrator presents all characters' thoughts but, in practice, does so selectively. In "The Harvest" the narrator chooses not to tell us what one very particular character is thinking.

Focus

The characters in "The Harvest" make inferences, or draw conclusions, about a character named Don Trine based on his actions. With a small group of classmates, brainstorm about times when you made inferences about others based on their actions. Did your guesses turn out to be accurate? How did you feel after you found out more about the person? Did you feel that you treated this person fairly? Why or why not? As you read the story, list the inferences the characters make about Don Trine and the evidence for these inferences. At the end of the story, compare your list with what you find out about Don Trine.

Vocabulary

Knowing the following words will help you as you read "The Harvest."

aura (ô′ rə) *n.*: Atmosphere (p. 121)

harrowed (har′ ō'd) *v.*: Broken up and leveled by a harrow, a frame with spikes or disks, drawn by a horse or tractor (p. 123)

allusions (ə lōō′ zhənz) *n.*: Indirect references (p. 123)

astutely (ə stōōt′ lē) *adv.*: Cleverly or cunningly (p. 123)

procedure (prō sē′ jər) *n.*: An established way of carrying out an act (p. 123)

caressing (kə res′ iŋ) *v.*: Touching or stroking lovingly or affectionately (p. 123)

120   Short Stories

The Harvest

Tomás Rivera

1 The end of September and the beginning of October. That was the best time of the year. First, because it was a sign that the work was coming to an end and that the return to Texas would start. Also, because there
2 was something in the air that the folks created, an aura of peace and death. The earth also shared that feeling. The cold came more frequently, the frosts that killed by night, in the morning covered the earth in whiteness. It seemed that all was coming to an end. The folks felt that all was coming to rest. Everyone took to thinking more. And they talked more about the trip back to Texas, about the har-
3 vests, if it had gone well or bad for them, if they would return or not to the same place next year. Some began to take long walks around the grove. It seemed like in these last days of work there was a wake over the earth. It made you think.

That's why it wasn't very surprising to see Don Trine take a walk by himself through the grove and to walk along the fields every after-
4 noon. This was at the beginning, but when some youngsters asked him if they could tag along, he even got angry. He told them he didn't want anybody sticking behind him.

"Why would he want to be all by himself, anyway?"
"To heck with him; it's his business."
"But, you notice, it never fails. Every time, why, sometimes I don't even think he eats supper, he takes his walk. Don't you think that's a bit strange?"
"Well, I reckon. But you saw how he got real mad when we told him we'd go along with him. It wasn't anything to make a fuss over. This ain't his land. We can go wherever we take a liking to. He can't tell us what to do."
"That's why I wonder, why'd he want to walk by hisself?"

And that's how all the rumors about Don Trine's walks got started. The folks couldn't figure out why or what he got out of taking off by himself every afternoon. When he would leave, and somebody would spy on him, somehow or other he would catch on, then
5 take a little walk, turn around and head right back to his chicken coop. The fact of the matter is that everybody began to say he was hiding the money he had earned that year or that he had found some buried treasure and every day, little by little, he was bringing it back to his coop. Then they began to say that when he was young he had run around with a gang in Mexico and that he always carried around a lot of money with him. They said, too, that even if it was real hot, he carried a belt full of money beneath his undershirt. Practically all the speculation centered on the idea that he
6 had money.

"Let's see, who's he got to take care of? He's an old bachelor. He ain't

The Harvest 121

Presentation

Motivation/Prior Knowledge
Ask students to think of someone who does not "fit the mold," who behaves differently from most people. What reasons might he or she have for different behavior?

Purpose-Setting Question Why is Don Trine's behavior such a matter of curiosity to his fellow workers?

Thematic Focus The earth means different things to different people. Why would a man like Don Trine view our living earth with such reverence?

1 **Reading Strategy** What inference can you draw about the time, place, and characters?

2 **Discussion** Why are death and peace equated?

3 **Reading Strategy** What do you think these characters are thinking about?

4 **Critical Thinking and Reading** What inferences can you draw about the character of Don Trine?

5 **Critical Thinking and Reading** What inferences can you make about Don Trine's living conditions?

6 **Critical Thinking and Reading** Why is money so important to those who started the rumors?

Master Teacher Note Students who respond well to Rivera's work may enjoy reading about him and other Mexican American authors in Juan Bruce-Novoa's *Chicano Authors: Inquiry by Interview* (University of Texas Press, 1980) or editor Luis Davila's *Chicano Literature and Tomás Rivera* (University of Indiana Press, 1974).

ESL Teaching Strategy ESL students may have difficulty sorting out the details in this story. To help them, make a photocopy of the story, and use five different-colored highlighter pens to mark the who, what, why, when, and where details on the copy so that they can more readily understand the content.

Making Connections To examine connections to the earth, students might compare Don Trine's love of the land with that of Da-duh in "To Da-Duh, In Memoriam," page 139. You might also compare it with another person's love of the sea, in "Sea-Fever," by John Masefield, page 618.

Humanities Note

Fine art, *Farmworker de Califas*, by Tony Ortega. Ortega's work is a rich reflection of the Mexican American experience—even his titles are often a mixture of English and Spanish. His bright colors and pulsating shapes recreate impressions of places he knows intimately—barrios, the Southwest, Latin America.

Color is the dominating element in Ortega's work. He considers himself a colorist—someone who defines objects by color rather than line. This characteristic is evident in *Farmworker de Califas*. Spots of color indicate the workers with lines of color radiating from them.

You might use the following questions for discussion:

1. What impressions do you have looking at this piece? What do you think the artist is trying to do with this particular use of color?
2. What connection can you make between the vibrancy of this painting and the subject matter of "The Harvest"?
3. What connections do you see between this work and *Campesino* on page 124?

7 Critical Thinking and Reading
What additional inferences can you make about Don Trine?

8 Discussion Do these seem like reasonable plans? Why or why not?

9 Reading Strategy From these details, what can you predict about the cause of Don Trine's behavior?

FARMWORKER DE CALIFAS
Tony Ortega
Courtesy of the Artist

7 never married or had a family. So, with him working so many years . . . Don't you think he's bound to have money? And then, what's that man spend his money on? The only thing he buys is his bit of food every Saturday. Once in a while, a beer, but that's all."

"Yeah, he's gotta have a pile of money, for sure. But, you think he's going to bury it around here?"

8 "Who said he's burying anything? Look, he always goes for his food on Saturday. Let's check close where he goes this week, and on Saturday,

when he's on his errand, we'll see what he's hiding. Whadda you say?"

"Good'nuff. Let's hope he doesn't catch on to us."

That week the youngsters closely watched Don Trine's walks. They noticed that he would disappear into the grove, then come out on the north side, cross the road then cross the field until he got to the irrigation ditch. There he dropped from sight for a while, then he reappeared in the west field. It was there where he would disappear and linger the most. They noticed also that, so as to throw people off his track, he would take a 9

122   Short Stories

Grammar in Action

Writers may begin sentences with a variety of **introductory elements.** In "The Harvest," Tomás Rivera uses words, phrases, and clauses to begin sentences. All introductory elements are followed by a comma. The introductory elements are in italics in the following examples:

"*Yeah*, he's gotta have a pile of money, for sure." (introductory word)

". . . *[W]ith him working so many years*, . . . don't you think he's bound to have money?" (introductory phrase)

When that day arrived, the boys were filled with anticipation. (introductory clause)

Remember that a clause has a subject and a verb; a phrase does not.

Student Activity 1. Identify the introductory word, phrase, or clause in each of these sentences from "The Harvest."

1. Look, he always goes for his food on Saturday.
2. Well, it's bound to be Don Trine.
3. In reality, they thought Don Trine was crazy.

different route, but he always spent more time around the ditch that crossed the west field. They decided to investigate the ditch and that field the following Saturday.

When that day arrived, the boys were filled with anticipation. The truck had scarcely left and they were on their way to the west field. The truck had not yet disappeared and they had already crossed the grove. What they found they almost expected. There was nothing in the ditch, but in the field that had been harrowed after pulling the potatoes they found a number of holes.

"You notice all the holes here? The harrow didn't make these. Look, here's some foot prints, and notice that the holes are at least a foot deep. You can stick your arm in them up to your elbow. No animal makes these kind of holes. Whadda you think?"

"Well, it's bound to be Don Trine. But, what's he hiding? Why's he making so many holes? You think the land-owner knows what he's up to?"

"Naw, man. Why, look, you can't see them from the road. You gotta come in a ways to notice they're here. What's he making them for? What's he using them for? And, look, they're all about the same width. Whadda you think?"

"Well, you got me. Maybe we'll know if we hide in the ditch and see what he does when he comes here."

"Look, here's a coffee can. I bet you this is what he digs with."

"I think you're right."

The boys had to wait until late the following Monday to discover the reason for the holes. But the word had spread around so that everybody already knew that Don Trine had a bunch of holes in that field. They tried not to let on but the allusions they made to the holes while they were out in the fields during the day were very obvious. Everybody thought there had to be a big explanation. So, the youngsters spied more carefully and astutely.

That afternoon they managed to fool Don Trine and saw what he was doing. They saw, and as they had suspected, Don Trine used the coffee can to dig a hole. Every so often, he would measure with his arm the depth of the hole. When it went up to his elbow, he stuck in his left arm, then filled dirt in around it with his right hand, all the way up to the elbow. Then he stayed like that for some time. He seemed very satisfied and even tried to light a cigarette with one hand. Not being able to, he just let it hang from his lips. Then he dug another hole and repeated the process. The boys could not understand why he did this. That was what puzzled them the most. They had believed that, with finding out what it was he did, they would understand everything. But it didn't turn out that way at all. The boys brought the news to the rest of the folks in the grove and nobody there understood either. In reality, when they found out that the holes didn't have anything to do with money, they thought Don Trine was crazy and even lost interest in the whole matter. But not everybody.

The next day one of the boys who discovered what Don Trine had been up to went by himself to a field. There he went through the same procedure that he had witnessed the day before. What he experienced and what he never forgot was feeling the earth move, feeling the earth grasp his fingers and even caressing them. He also felt the warmth of the earth. He sensed he was inside someone. Then he understood what Don Trine was doing. He was not crazy, he simply liked to feel the earth when it was sleeping.

That's why the boy kept going to the field

The Harvest   123

10 **Literary Focus: Omniscient Narrator** What evidence here indicates the omniscient narrator?

11 **Reading Strategy** What predictions can you make based on these details?

12 **Critical Thinking and Reading** What inferences can you make about Don Trine's character?

13 **Literary Focus: Omniscient Narrator** How can you tell this segment is written from the point of view of an omniscient narrator?

14 **Reading Strategy** Try to visualize what Don Trine is doing. Can you demonstrate?

15 **Reading Strategy** How do these details add to the mystery?

16 **Literary Focus: Omniscient Narrator** What evidence do you find here that proves the story is written from the point of view of an omniscient narrator?

17 **Critical Thinking and Reading** What inferences can you make about the rest of the characters?

18 **Reading Strategy** Do you agree with the people's evaluation of Don Trine? What can you predict from the line, "But not everybody"?

19 **Discussion** What advantage does this boy have over the others?

20 **Literary Focus: Omniscient Narrator** Can you pinpoint here another characteristic of the omniscient narrator's point of view?

21 **Discussion** What image of the earth is given here? How does it compare with that in the first paragraph?

4. When they found out the holes didn't have anything to do with money, they lost interest in the whole matter.

Student Activity 2. Write a paragraph telling how you feel about the boy who followed in Don Trine's footsteps. Include three kinds of sentences: one with an introductory word, one with an introductory phrase, and one with an introductory clause.

Electronic Handbook You may want students to review phrases and clauses before completing the Grammar in Action activities. If students have access to the Language Master 6000, have them enter *phrase, verbal,* and *clause* and press the GRAMMAR key.

22 Discussion Why does the boy feel this way?

Reader's Response Why does Don Trine try to conceal his actions from others?

Thematic Response What effect does the final comparison—the last two sentences—have on your attitude toward the living earth?

Humanities Note

Fine art, *Campesino*, 1976, by Daniel DeSiga. DeSiga (1948–), is very involved in the Mexican American art movement in the United States. He was born in Washington State to migrant worker parents, who early on discovered and encouraged his artistic talent. He graduated with a fine arts degree from the University of Washington in 1975 and became involved with the Royal Chicano Airforce, an art collective.

DeSiga's purpose in *Campesino* is to bring attention to the undocumented farm worker, who often worked in unrelenting hot sun. The now illegal short hoe seen in this painting forced the laborer to work in a backbreaking position.

DeSiga's pride in his heritage is evident. His parents worked hard and now own a ranch in Washington State. Much of DeSiga's work now concentrates on the American cowboy, who was often Mexican or black, and his paintings travel often with Southwestern art exhibits.

You might use these questions for discussion:
1. How would a worker like this one come to feel a kinship with the land?
2. What is the artist's attitude toward his subject? Is it similar to the writer's attitude toward his? Explain.
3. What might be the purpose of not showing the worker's face?

every afternoon, until one night a hard freeze came on so that he could no longer dig any holes in the ground. The earth was fast asleep. Then he thought of next year, in October at harvest time, when once again he could repeat what Don Trine did. It was like when someone died. You always blamed yourself for not loving him more before he died.

CAMPESINO, 1976
Daniel DeSiga
Wight Art Gallery, University of California, Los Angeles

Multicultural Focus Agriculture, the raising of crops and livestock, started fairly recently in human history—only 8,000 to 10,000 years ago. Until then, people hunted and gathered food for survival. Agriculture gradually allowed for stable settlement and, eventually, the growth of societies and civilizations. It is no wonder that the land was once considered almost sacred by most peoples and that this reverence is reflected in the many harvest festivals that exist around the world.

Have students research different celebrations of harvest. Some possibilities are Thanksgiving, the New Yam festival of the Nigerian Yorubas, the Posviceni festival of the Czechs, the Zulu festival of the first fruits, or the Jewish festival of Sukkot. Students might also explore the various attitudes of different cultures toward the land, such as the widespread Native American belief that no one can own land or the European notion of inherited property.

RESPONDING TO THE SELECTION

Your Response

1. What did you think of Don Trine?

Recalling

2. What does Don Trine do every afternoon that arouses the curiosity of his fellow workers?
3. How does one boy come to understand Don Trine's behavior?

Interpreting

4. How does the opening paragraph foreshadow, or anticipate, the ending of the story?
5. What do the boys' speculations about Don Trine reveal about them?
6. What does the narrator mean when he says at the end of the story: "It was like when someone died. You always blamed yourself for not loving him more before he died"?
7. Why are most of the workers satisfied with speculating about Don Trine's afternoon walk, whereas only one boy tries to understand it.

Applying

8. Think of times in history or in current events in which people and their actions were misinterpreted. How might we try in the future to understand people and their actions better?

ANALYZING LITERATURE

Understanding Omniscient Narration

An **omniscient narrator** can reveal anything a character knows, thinks, and feels. In "The Harvest" the narrator reveals most of the characters' thoughts and actions yet withholds information about Don Trine. The motivation behind Don Trine's unusual behavior is kept from other characters in the story as well as from the reader.

1. (a) What reason might the author have for using an omniscient narrator who withholds information? (b) What effect does this create?
2. Describe how the story would be different if the omniscient narrator had revealed more information about Trine's thoughts and actions.

CRITICAL THINKING AND READING

Making Inferences About a Character

The narrator of "The Harvest" describes Don Trine's actions but not his thoughts or feelings. We therefore make **inferences** about his thoughts and feelings based on the information the narrator gives us, including the story's mood and setting.

1. Read the following passage and answer the questions about it.

> It seemed like in these last days of work there was a wake over the earth. It made you think. That's why it wasn't very surprising to see Don Trine take a walk by himself through the grove and to walk along the fields every afternoon.

 a. What mood is created by the phrase "a wake over the earth"?
 b. What does this mood suggest about Don Trine's thoughts and feelings?
2. Later in the story, the narrator tells us that Don Trine "seemed very satisfied" with his arm snug in the earth. What inference can you make about his reason for doing such a thing?

THINKING AND WRITING

Writing From Another Perspective

By the end of "The Harvest," you have a clearer sense of Don Trine's character and motivations. Rewrite the story using Trine as your first-person narrator. As you tell the story from his perspective, expand upon the inferences you have already made about his character.

LEARNING OPTION

Cross-curricular Connection. Go for a walk in a nearby park or preserve and sit quietly. What effect does the natural world have on you? Then write a short piece describing your experience. How did your experience compare to Don Trine's?

The Harvest 125

Preparation

More About the Author In a letter to her daughter, Chinese American author Siu [shoō] Wai [wā] Anderson says of her adoptive white mother, "Lacking a mirror image in the mother who raised me, I had to seek my identity as a woman on my own." She turned to music and writing to seek that identity. How does "Autumn Gardening" show a similar kind of search for identity?

Literary Focus Ask less advanced students to think about how perspective affects point of view. You may wish to lead a discussion in which students compare their own point of view about a relevant issue, like curfew, dating, homework, grades, or after-school jobs, with that of a parent or other supervisory adult. Ask more advanced students to identify specific clues in "Autumn Gardening" that suggest a character's perspective.

Prereading Focus To clarify the differences in perspective, use the Focus activity as the basis for role-playing. Discuss the problems encountered in playing the roles accurately.

Vocabulary To clarify meanings and render the words part of students' vocabularies, make a game of the vocabulary words. Ask these questions: Who or what is _____ [insert a verb or adjective from the vocabulary list. Use the past participial form of a verb or the adjective form of the adverb]? Who or what is in _____ [insert a noun from the vocabulary list]? Students should strive to think of as many answers as make sense.

Spelling Tip Remind students that when adding a suffix, they should double the last consonant of the base word if the vowel is short: *remission, allotted.* If the vowel is long, use a single consonant: *dilapidated, improvised.*

GUIDE FOR READING

Siu Wai Anderson

(1958–   ), although born in Hong Kong, was adopted and raised by a family in the United States. During the late 1970's, Anderson lived in the Asian American community in San Francisco. There she found a link to her heritage and identity as an Asian American, which has become a central theme in much of her writing. Anderson currently teaches at the University of Massachusetts/Boston's Summer Enrichment Program, whose students come from a diversity of cultural backgrounds.

Autumn Gardening

Perspective

A person's **perspective** on an issue or event is shaped by many factors, including his or her gender, age, cultural heritage, and personal experiences. "Autumn Gardening" is written from the perspective of a Japanese American survivor of the U.S. atomic bombing of Hiroshima during World War II. The character's direct experience of the bombing and her Japanese ancestry give her a unique understanding of this historical event. As you read the story, put yourself in her place and try to see the events as she does. Imagine how that experience would affect your own perspective.

Focus

Looking at a situation from another person's perspective can broaden your understanding of all the facets of an event or issue. You can demonstrate this truth, for example, by getting together with a group of classmates to make recommendations about a school dress code. First state your own views on the issue. Then imagine that you are making recommendations as a teacher or the principal. Is your perspective similar to or different from theirs? What accounts for these differences or similarities?

Vocabulary

Knowing the following words will help you as you read "Autumn Gardening."

dilapidated (də lap' ə dat' id) *adj.*: Broken down; neglected (p. 127)

remission (ri mish' ən) *n.*: Lessening of the symptoms of a disease (p. 128)

shards (shardz) *n.*: Fragments or broken pieces (p. 129)

cynical (sin' i kəl) *adj.*: Sneering (p. 129)

pervasive (pər vā' siv) *adj.*: Spread throughout (p. 129)

allotted (ə lät' id) *adj.*: Assigned (p. 131)

reminisce (rem' ə nis') *v.*: To think about remembered events (p. 131)

paradoxically (par' ə däks' i kəl lē) *adv.*: In a contradictory way (p. 132)

improvised (im' prə vīz'd) *adj.*: Made at the spur of the moment with materials at hand (p. 132)

Objectives

1 To understand perspective
2 To write a human-interest news story
3 To determine cultural perspective
4 To express individual interests and abilities through optional activities

Support Material

Teaching Portfolio
Teacher Backup, p. 161
Grammar in Action Worksheet, *Recognizing Subordinate Clauses,* p. 165
Usage and Mechanics Worksheet, p. 167
Vocabulary Check, p. 168
Analyzing Literature Worksheet, *Understanding Perspective,* p. 169

Critical Thinking and Reading Worksheet, *Determining Cultural Perspective,* p. 170
Selection Test, p. 171

Prentice Hall Literature Writing Studio

Autumn Gardening

Siu Wai Anderson

It was a mild morning for early November, sunny and cool with only a hint of frost. The heavy rains that had flooded the gutters for the past week were gone now. Patches of mud amid sparse wet spikes of grass made the yard treacherous. Along the cyclone fence clusters of sun-dappled brown and yellow leaves rustled in the light breeze. They drifted to the ground and skittered across the small yard, coming to rest against the splintered white wall of the dilapidated garage. The breeze became a steady wind.

Mariko Abe[1] opened the screen door and shuffled onto her back porch, blinking in the bright sunlight. She moved over to a rusty lawn chair and sat down heavily, gasping from the effort. When she had caught her breath she sniffed the air, enjoying the tangy scent that made her think of dry crackling leaves and wood-burning stoves—the heady smell of autumn in New England.

As she exhaled with a long sigh, a sharper, more pungent smell intruded on her senses. It seemed to come from the laundry snapping on the line strung across her next-door-neighbor's porch. Mariko wrinkled her nose. Whatever kind of detergent that was, it reminded her of the starched uniforms of American soldiers.

As she settled herself in the chair and drew her sweater closer about her shoulders, she glanced at the porch railing and noticed that the paint was peeling badly. Better tell Paul to buy some sandpaper so he could scrape off the old paint before putting on a fresh coat. If he let it go until spring, it would probably never get done.

There never seemed to be enough time to do all the tedious little upkeep tasks that an old house required. Now that her asthma was worse, she found it even harder to manage. Paul was a big help, but he had his own family to mind on the weekends. Sometimes when he did odd jobs for Mariko he brought the children along, but not often. They were too wild for her, these *Sansei*.[2] She and Paul had been raised with old-fashioned Japanese manners, but he seemed to have forgotten his when it came time to raising his own kids.

These days it was a rare luxury to just sit and think as she was doing now. Usually she preferred it that way. If she kept busy during the daytime hours she was more likely to sleep soundly at night, instead of tossing and turning with nervous thoughts or waking up screaming from a nightmare.

The sharp edges of folded paper in her pocket reminded Mariko of the letter. Slowly she withdrew it and smoothed it out on her lap, staring at the flowing handwriting until the words blurred and ran together. A

---

1. Mariko Abe (mär ē'kō ä'bā)

2. Sansei (sän'sā') *n.*: Third generation of Japanese ancestry.

Presentation

Motivation/Prior Knowledge Ask students to imagine that they are among only a few survivors of some tragedy—a flood, an airplane crash, an explosion. Ask them to freewrite for four or five minutes about how they would feel and then to share their ideas with their peers.

Thematic Focus Sometimes a traumatic situation causes a person to awaken to a new knowledge about him or herself. Ask students to think of people they know or have read about who have had a traumatic experience —lost all of their possessions in a natural disaster, were seriously injured in an accident, or struggled with a fatal disease. Have students discuss what awakening these people may have experienced about themselves.

Purpose-Setting Question What awakening does Mariko experience?

1 Reading Strategy Visualize the setting, perhaps sketching the significant parts.

2 Reading Strategy What inferences can you make about Mariko?

3 Reading Strategy What sensory details clarify the setting?

4 Literary Focus: Perspective What can you infer about Mariko's perspective—her age, cultural heritage, and personal perspective?

5 Literary Focus: Perspective What more do you learn here about her perspective?

6 Reading Strategy What inference can you make about her state of mind?

Alternative Assessment To promote active reading, have students keep a reader's response journal as they read the story. Ask them to focus their observations on the details that reveal the lasting effect of the bombing on Mariko's life. Encourage students to respond personally to the bombing of Hiroshima as well as to the internment of Japanese American citizens during the war. What feelings do they have about those events?

Students' responses will enable you to assess their grasp of the concerns in this story.

ESL Teaching Strategy To help students better understand the story, share with them as a pre-reading activity the summary found in the Teaching Portfolio, page 161.

Making Connections James Joyce's poem "I Hear an Army," page 561, shows another view of war's destruction. Students may read *Farewell to Manzanar* in the **Prentice Hall Literature Multicultural Library** to understand the experiences and feelings of an interned Japanese family.

7 Clarification Many survivors of the bombings of Hiroshima and Nagasaki have suffered from a variety of diseases caused by radiation. Leukemia is one of the more common.

8 Reading Strategy To what scars do you think she is referring?

9 Literary Focus: Perspective What makes her react as she does?

10 Discussion Why do you think the two women have never talked about what happened to them?

11 Discussion What parallel does the author draw between the weather and Mariko's inner self?

12 Clarification Early Japanese American parents sometimes sent their American-born daughters back to Japan to receive a traditional, old-fashioned education in an attempt to avoid Westernized ideas of personal freedom and independence.

Master Teacher Note Have students read about the bombing of Hiroshima and Nagasaki in newspaper or magazine accounts from 1945 or from significant anniversary years. Have other students read accounts in history books or encyclopedias. Ask them to discuss the perspective from which each publication addresses the topic.

sudden gust of wind threatened to pull the letter from her grasp. Her fingers tightened automatically and she rubbed her thumb across the slightly rough surface of the paper as she re-read the first page.

> Dear Mariko:
> How have you been this fall? I hope you've managed to stay well. I'm doing much better since my leukemia[3] went into remission. Here's hoping it stays that way.
> Recently I joined a group of hibakusha[4] who meet once a month to talk about our problems. It's not as terrible as it sounds! Sometimes we talk about the Bomb, but mostly we think about ways to make people aware of us.
> They want me to speak at the next Hiroshima[5] anniversary event and tell about my life. It's going to be on television. Imagine that!

Mariko smiled and shook her head. Her friend Mitsuye[6] was never one to turn down a chance to be in the spotlight. Mariko had told her many times that she should have been an actress. Mitsuye brought a dramatic flair to everything she did. And her scars were hardly noticeable.

The sound of a distant plane caused Mariko to raise her head and peer nervously at the sky. Scanning the milky blue expanse, she instinctively shielded her eyes from the

---

3. leukemia (lo͞o kē′mē ə) n.: A disease that increases the production of cells in the blood, lymph, and tissues that are important in the body's defenses against infection.
4. hibakusha (hē bäk′shä′) n.: Survivors of the atomic destruction of Hiroshima or of Nagasaki in 1945.
5. Hiroshima (hir′ə shē′mə): An important military site, this large Japanese city was the first of two cities to be bombed by the United States in an effort to end World War II.
6. Mitsuye (mit so͞o′ä)

sun's glare. A black dot appeared in the east. She followed the jet's white trail as it passed overhead, probably heading for the Air Force base twenty miles out of town. Only when the faint whine had completely faded did she sit down again and rub her eyes wearily.

"Stop this nonsense," she scolded herself. "You've been in America for nearly forty years. The war is over. Are you going to jump like a rabbit every time an airplane passes overhead?" For several minutes a painful tightness gripped her chest, then gradually subsided. Slowly her breathing returned to normal and she resumed reading the letter.

> The group asked me if I knew of any other hibakusha who would talk. I thought of you right away. You and I have never talked about what happened to us, but I have never forgotten and I know you haven't either. Marichan,[7] will you join me?

A chill passed through Mariko; she shut her eyes and shivered. The wind had grown stronger, picking up the leaves by the fence and relentlessly spinning them through the air. Fast-moving clouds obscured the sun and cast shadows across the yard. The mild sunny morning was rapidly turning into a gloomy afternoon, but Mariko hardly noticed the sudden change in weather conditions. Her discomfort came from within.

Mitsuye knew her too well. The two women had been friends since childhood. Both had lived on farms in California's San Joaquin Valley back in the thirties. Until they turned thirteen, the two girls were almost inseparable. Then their *Issei*[8] parents had sent the girls back to Hiroshima to get a "good" Japanese education.

---

7. Marichan (mär′ē chän): Nickname for Mariko.
8. Issei (ē′sā′) adj. (usually a noun): First generation Japanese who emigrated to the United States.

Multicultural Focus As seen in this account, survivors of the atomic bomb dropped on Hiroshima present us with a morally sensitive issue in American history. In a different way, Japanese Americans also suffered in this country during World War II. In 1942, approximately 250,000 Japanese living in the United States—two thirds of whom were American citizens—were put in concentration camps simply because of their ancestry. Most lived in California and the government feared they would somehow assist Japan in an attack on the West Coast, a belief never substantiated. Whole communities were uprooted and forced to sell their property and businesses at low prices or simply lose them through confiscation.

Despite the intense anti-Japanese feeling during the war and the unprecedented loss of civil rights, 17,000 Japanese American soldiers fought bravely against the Germans on the European front. Their families, who had been detained in concentration camps, were all released by the end of the war, but many never returned to California. Only a third of their losses were made

LAUNDRYMAN'S DAUGHTER, 1988
Tomie Arai
Courtesy of the Artist

of radiation sickness, that she began to suffer symptoms of leukemia.

Mariko had just begun her day at the clinic on the outskirts when the *pika*[11] flashed over downtown, two miles away. Falling debris knocked her to the ground and flying shards of glass left her with several cuts on her face. There was no time to wonder what had happened. She and the few surviving doctors and nurses were soon caught up with taking care of others who had been more badly injured.

Like Mitsuye, she seemed to have survived the Bomb with no serious effects. Then when she was forty-two she began to experience sharp pains in her face. Tiny pieces of glass had worked their way through her skin and had to be picked out. Several facial nerves were damaged by the emerging glass. When they healed, her mouth was stretched to one side, giving it a permanent cynical twist.

Lately, her health had taken a turn for the worse. The asthma she'd had since childhood was becoming more severe. She often woke up in the morning gasping for breath. Whether it was in any way related to the Bomb, she could only speculate. Her trips to the doctor were much more frequent these days, and she dared not tell him the full truth. She knew she would lose her medical benefits if it were known she was an A-bomb survivor.

After the war Mariko had returned to the United States. She was unprepared for the all-pervasive hatred of the Japanese in California. Her family had been interned[12] in one of the so-called relocation camps ordered by President Roosevelt to contain all the "traitorous" Japanese American citizens. Her parents and brothers were released in 1944

The girls ended up in different schools and seldom saw one another. After graduating from high school, Mariko had gone to Tokyo to receive training as a nurse. She moved back to Hiroshima in 1940 when a position opened at Taruya[9] Surgical Clinic. Meanwhile, Mitsuye had married a restaurant owner and settled in the nearby town of Fukuyama.[10] Mariko managed to visit her friend on occasion.

Mariko and Mitsuye were on opposite sides of Hiroshima the day the Bomb was dropped. Mitsuye had come to do some shopping at Fukuya's less than a mile from the explosion. Miraculously she managed to escape with only a few small burns. Aside from a persistent feeling of tiredness, she seemed to have no obvious problems. It wasn't until thirty years later, after her husband had died

---

9. Taruya (tär o͞o'yə)
10. Fukuyama (fo͞o'ko͞o yä'mə)

11. *pika* (pi'kə) *n.*: A blinding light that appears before the atomic bomb explodes.
12. interned (in turnd') *v.*: Detained or confined.

up by the government.

Do students think the internment was justified? Have them ponder how to prevent it from happening again to another ethnic group.

Enrichment If students would like to explore further the lives of survivors of Hiroshima, direct them to *Children of the Atomic Bomb,* compiled by Dr. Arata Osada, published in the United States by Midwest Publishers International, Ann Arbor, Michigan. This is a collection of compositions by grade school, high school, and university students sharing their experiences as survivors of the bomb.

Humanities Note

Fine art, *Laundryman's Daughter,* 1988, by Tomie Arai. Arai did this silkscreen as part of her "Memory-in-Progress: A Mother/ Daughter Project," shown in 1989 at the Chinatown History Project in New York City. The intent of this major undertaking was "to create a sense of place through positive images of Asian American women." Fans, tenements, Oriental objects, and writing spin restlessly through the air behind the formally posed figures. Although Arai is *sansei,* or third-generation Japanese American, she defines herself through the immigrant experience, saying "the sojourner, forever foreign, uprooted and marginal, is a central character in Asian American art."

Consider using these questions for discussion:
1. In what ways does the formality of the women's poses remind you of Mariko Abe?
2. What might the images behind the women represent?

13 Literary Focus: Perspective
What is the effect of such long-term suffering?

14 Literary Focus: Perspective
How do you think Mariko feels about this experience and the resulting disfigurement?

15 Clarification According to Anderson, Congress has never formally apologized to American A-bomb survivors, nor has it offered to pay for the medical care they have needed over the years. The Japanese government, on the other hand, provides free treatment to *all* bomb survivors. Some American *hibakusha,* then, have to go back to Japan for medical care. Japanese American survivors risk losing their medical insurance, which pays for emergencies but not ongoing illnesses. Anderson adds, "I built the story around this dilemma."

Humanities Note

Photograph of Hiroshima, by Shunkichi Kikuchi. Hiroshima was Japan's seventh largest city at the beginning of World War II, with a population of 350,000. In 1945, the atomic bomb was a recent development. In an attempt to end the war quickly, U.S. forces dropped the bomb near the center of Hiroshima at 8:15 A.M. on August 6. This historic photograph shows Hiroshima after it was bombed. Everything within 8,000 feet of the explosion was totally destroyed. More than 70,000 people were killed immediately. Within the next five years, nearly 200,000 died as a result of direct exposure to radiation. The *hibakusha*, or survivors, still suffer today from radiation-induced illnesses.

Although 98 percent of the city was destroyed by the atomic bomb, Hiroshima today is a thriving industrial city dedicated to peace. Peace Memorial Park contains a museum and monuments dedicated to the victims.

You might use these questions for discussion:
1. What is your reaction to this image?
2. Does this photograph help you to understand Mariko's complex emotions and feelings? In what ways?

16 Discussion Speculate about what life has been like for Mariko.

17 Discussion Why is Mitsuye doing this?

18 Discussion Why does Mariko decide to say no?

and sent east to Boston and New York. Mariko joined them shortly after her return from Japan. After her parents died she settled in Boston near her brother Paul and his family.

Mariko never married. She was always aware of the scars on her face and blamed them for making her unattractive. They were also a constant reminder of what she'd been through. Over the years the memories had never faded. When an occasional man did show interest in her, she quickly backed off from getting involved. She was afraid to get too close to anyone, not wishing to burden anyone with her memories and her nightmares. Her only real friend was Mitsuye, whose silent understanding helped Mariko feel she was not totally alone.

Through some cousins in New York Mariko had learned that Mitsuye had also returned from Hiroshima and was living in Queens. They quickly renewed their old friendship, although they seldom talked about their years in Hiroshima. Every two or three months Mariko would visit Mitsuye in New York, or Mitsuye would come up to Boston.

And now Mitsuye was asking her to get up in front of a TV camera and relive the awful events she had spent years trying to forget. She would also risk losing her insurance. Brave, foolish Mitsuye . . . how could she even think of doing such a thing since her bout with leukemia? What purpose would it serve?

With difficulty Mariko got to her feet and put the letter back in her pocket. She pursed her lips as she made her way down the porch steps and towards the garage. Mitsuye was a dear friend but there were limits to what one could do, even for a friend. Tomorrow she would write back and say no.

Today was for chores, raking the leaves and perhaps some weeding. She didn't want

Grammar in Action

Writers use **subordinate clauses** to create sentence variety and to show supporting or modifying ideas. By definition, a clause includes a subject and a verb. Subordinate clauses are introduced by subordinating conjunctions like *when, as, so, if, that,* and *who.* While an independent clause can stand alone, a subordinate clause must support an independent clause. A sentence that includes an independent clause and one or more subordinate clauses is called a complex sentence. Study these examples from Siu Wai Anderson's "Autumn Gardening."

The heavy rains were gone now. (subject: *rains;* verb: *were gone;* independent clause) . . . that had flooded the gutters for the past week (subject: *that;* verb, *had flooded;* subordinate clause): The heavy rains that had flooded the gutters for the past week were gone now. (independent clause + subordinate clause = complex sentence)

Anderson uses many subordinate clauses. Most of the clauses she uses modify or add explanation.

Student Activity 1. Find the subordinate clauses in these sentences. One sentence has two.

to think anymore. As she tugged open the creaking garage door just wide enough to squeeze through, she felt a growing irritation. How could Mitsuye consider speaking about such private things? The guilt for still being alive when so many had died. The horror of crawling half-naked and bloody through rubble that only moments before had been a gleaming modern clinic, the pride and joy of its staff. And all the years since then. She often felt as if she were neither dead nor alive, only an organism living out her allotted timespan because fate had chosen not to take her life that day.

Mariko groped about the dim interior of the garage and put on an old jacket and a pair of gardening gloves. Now where had Paul left the rake last Saturday? She found she was trembling and suddenly anxious to get out of the small dark room. In her haste, she tripped over something and nearly fell. It was the long handle of the rake. Paul must have carelessly tossed it there. Suddenly she was unreasonably angry with him. Didn't he care whether his sister got hurt?

The sudden upwelling of emotion caused Mariko to gasp for breath. She forced herself to calm down and breathe more slowly. It would do no good to have an asthma attack in this miserable shed where no one could hear her or come to her aid. A survivor of something as catastrophic as the atom bomb deserved a more dignified end. She shook free of her self-pity long enough to smile at her own joke. Then she picked up the rake and went outside.

The cool fresh air cleared her head. The wind had died down and scattered its hapless burden of leaves across the wet grass. Mariko began to rake them into a neat pile. The slow mechanical action of swinging the rake helped further to calm her down. For a while, her mind was at ease.

Calmly, she began to reminisce about her years as a nursing student at Tokyo's General Hospital. How she had enjoyed the lively debates she had engaged in with her girlfriends! They cheerfully argued medical ethics in what little spare time they could find between nursing rounds and academic studies. Their favorite topic was what one would call "lifeboat ethics"—making choices in dire circumstances. Playing God—or Buddha, as it were—with their patients' lives.

If you were trapped in a bomb shelter with a very sick child and a feeble old man and you only had enough food and medicine for one of them, whom should you try to save? Was it more important to honor one's elders and preserve a life that was a dying ember, or should one invest in the future and fight to keep alive the newer spark? Whose life was more valuable? Did mere human beings have the right to decide such a thing?

Mariko shook her head ruefully as she recalled the ease with which she and her friends had argued the question, arrogantly confident that they would be able to make such a decision if forced to. None of them ever expected to encounter such a situation in real life. Yet she had, during the nightmarish aftermath of the Bomb. She was haunted by the faces of those she had passed by because their wounds looked far too difficult to deal with.

Mariko stopped raking. She leaned on the handle and bowed her head. Oh, Mitsuye, you are asking too much of me. How could I tell strangers what I did—leaving people to die because I couldn't deal with their awful injuries? She wasn't sure if there were words to describe the stunned faces, some with lips locked against pain, others contorted in anguish. She had felt overwhelmed and frustrated as a lone nurse working with meager supplies salvaged from the ruins of the hospital. She did what she could to stem a never-ending tide of burns and wounds and dysentery.[13]

The bandages and ointments were de-

Autumn Gardening 131

19 **Literary Focus: Perspective** What emotions does Mariko experience? Why?

20 **Discussion** Why does she suddenly feel anxious?

21 **Discussion** Why is she now at ease?

22 **Enrichment** Some students may be able to compare Mariko's experiences with similar documented cases in Vietnam. They may wish to discuss the ramifications of the moral dilemma of living as a severely handicapped veteran or dying from battle wounds. Which is better for the victim? For the family? What considerations are involved?

1. As she exhaled with a long sigh, a sharper, more pungent smell intruded on her senses.
2. If he let it go until spring, it would probably never get done.
3. You and I have never talked about what happened to us.
4. When the nerves healed, her mouth was stretched to one side.
5. She often felt as if she were neither dead nor alive, only an organism living out her allotted timespan because fate had chosen not to take her life that day.

Student Activity 2. In the story find five more sentences which include subordinate clauses.

Student Activity 3. From the two previous activities, use any five sentences as models by which to write your own five sentences. Include an independent clause and one or more subordinate clauses in each sentence.

Electronic Handbook You may want students to review complex sentences before completing the Grammar in Action activities. If students have access to the Language Master 6000, have them enter *complex* and *clause* and press the GRAMMAR key.

pleted within an hour after the Bomb was dropped and still the people came, clutching their torn bleeding faces and carrying dying family members, friends or co-workers on their backs. She had to resort to treating burns with cooking oil, animal fat, and even sliced cucumbers. All through that first night and for the next two days, she and the few surviving nurses and doctors had struggled to ease the pain of those who came begging for help. It was a losing battle.

23 | Paradoxically, some of the victims with the worst injuries eventually recovered, while

---

13. dysentery (dis′ən ter′ē) *n*.: An intestinal inflammation characterized by abdominal pain and frequent and intense diarrhea.

FALLOUT SHELTER
Akemi Takeda
Courtesy of the Trustees of the British Museum

others who appeared unscathed suddenly died. Making decisions based on conventional medical knowledge became impossible in the face of this strange radiation sickness. Mariko knew she had done her best in the horrifying circumstances, but her feelings of guilt lingered nonetheless.

It had been almost a relief when the last of her improvised bandages and salves had run out and she could no longer even attempt to treat the many victims that still came seeking help. Though it was agonizing to have to abandon people in pain, the burden of choosing who would live and who would die had been lifted from her shoulders.

Exhausted by her round-the-clock nursing and in pain from the cuts on her face, Mariko had finally left the clinic and caught a ride on an army truck to her uncle's house in Tomo Village several miles away. Her cuts became infected and refused to heal for months. She was ashamed to show herself in public. The villagers thought she brought bad luck with her, and avoided her whenever she went out. At last her skin healed enough for her to return to work. As soon as she had saved the money to return to America she left Japan with a sigh of relief.

Mariko was brought back to the present by the loud barking of her neighbor's German Shepherd on the other side of the wire fence. She glanced at her watch—it was nearly two. The dog always barked at the jabbering groups of schoolchildren streaming past on their way home from the bus stop. You could set your clock by that foolish dog's daily howling and pawing at the fence.

She was surprised to see that she had been outside since eleven-thirty. Her bones were beginning to feel the autumn dampness. Winter would be coming soon, but the flowerbeds could use some weeding. She looked forward to spring when she would plant chrysanthemums along the side of the

---

house. They reminded her of her father's garden.

As she put the wire rake in a corner of the garage, making sure that no one would trip over it, she paused to deliberate. Should she start working in the flowerbeds today? The rest of the afternoon stretched before her and she felt a need to fill it with activity. Her friend's letter had unsettled her. She needed time to push aside the ghosts of the past. Something fell from her pocket and fluttered to the floor. Huffing with the effort, Mariko stooped to pick it up. Her hand trembled. Somehow the folded letter had opened up as it fell to the ground. The words "speak for the dead" caught her eye, and she shivered as she straightened up. She read the rest of the letter.

. . . I know I'm asking a lot of you. These things are painful to remember. But we hibakusha *are the only ones who've seen firsthand what the* gembaku[14] *can do to human beings. The world needs to hear from us, but we're getting old. Pretty soon there won't be anyone left who was actually there.*

You and I owe it to all those people who lost their lives. They can't speak for themselves. I firmly believe that that is why some of us have survived. If we don't speak for the dead, none of it will mean anything to anyone anymore. Does that make sense?

"We can speak for the dead . . . " Mariko had never thought of it in that light before. Was that why her life had been spared? Could she find a purpose to her seemingly empty existence? The letter blurred before her eyes.

---

14. *gembaku* (gem bä´kōō): The atom bomb.

I guess you could call this "bearing witness," as the Jewish people did to get through the concentration camps. Oh Mari, I can't tell you how much better I feel to be doing something like this. After all those years of wishing I'd never survived, now I feel I'm doing something worthwhile.

Well, please think about it. Call me when you can, or I'll call you. I miss you. My love to Paul.

Sayonara,[15]
Mitsuye

Mariko slowly squatted in front of her empty flowerbeds and began pulling weeds, her mind turning over her friend's words. She said aloud, "*Kuri kaesa-nai*[16] . . . it should never be repeated." She saw once again the child who had died in her arms, his bewildered eyes asking her how it had come to pass that one minute he was playing in the street, the next he lay dying. The young mother who tried in vain to keep her baby alive by nursing it even as she herself was bleeding to death. And the man whose entire body was one raw burn. There were more faces than she could count. Perhaps with Mitsuye's help, Mariko could pass on their memories.

She folded the letter and put it carefully back in the pocket of her work pants. Her hands in their thick cotton gloves cleared away the weeds with smooth, strong motions, deftly untangling them and tossing them aside. The mid-afternoon sun reappeared and warmed her back as she patted the rich moist soil and prepared it for the flowers that she would plant there next spring.

---

15. **Sayonara** (sä´yŏ nä´rä): Literally, if it is to be that way; farewell.
16. **Kuri kaesa-nai** (kōō´rē kä ē´sə nī)

26 Discussion Why does the author include a reference to spring and at the same time a reference to her past?

27 Reading Strategy Why does she need the activity?

28 Reading Strategy What can you predict from this detail?

29 Literary Focus: Perspective What effect does this additional burden have on Mariko?

30 Literary Focus: Perspective What effect do these memories have?

31 Reading Strategy Based on this final reference to the autumn garden and the spring flowers, what can you predict about Mariko's future?

Reader's Response Mariko is obviously not wealthy; she is ill; she risks losing her health benefits by going public with her story. Do you think Mitsuye was right in persuading the quiet Mariko to join her in the public forum?

Thematic Response Spring is a time of awakening. How is Mariko's life moving, figuratively, from autumn to spring, to an awakening? Has she gone through winter? Or is that yet to come?

Autumn Gardening 133

133

ANSWERS TO RESPONDING TO THE SELECTION

Your Response

1. Since responses will differ, lead students to discuss what is to be gained by her sacrifice.

Recalling

2. She is reluctant because she wants to put the experience behind her.

3. She gains hope and reassurance from Mitsuye's letter asking her to "speak for the dead."

Interpreting

4. Suggested Response: Mariko is in the "autumn" of her life but now has an opportunity for reawakening, for cultivating a new purpose in life. Autumn is also the time to get rid of the dead leaves, the debris of the mind.

5. Suggested Response: She probably wanted to escape further reminders of death and destruction and return to her family.

6. Suggested Response: Mitsuye's letter asks her to speak for the dead or "none of it will mean anything to anyone anymore."

7. Suggested Response: Both women will convey the message that that kind of bombing should never again occur.

Applying

8. Suggested Response: The story conveys the message that war hurts everyone, even the innocent.

ANSWERS TO ANALYZING LITERATURE

1. a. It presents the perspective of the administrator of the destruction.
   b. The perspective acknowledges the responsibility of loss of lives and property, but recognizes the dilemma in which the Japanese placed the United States, refusing to surrender even in the light of possible destruction.

2. Suggested Response: Mariko probably would have accepted the logic but would have been critical of anyones saying they understood the responsibility involved.

RESPONDING TO THE SELECTION

Your Response

1. Do you think it is important for people to hear Mariko's story? Explain.

Recalling

2. Why is Mariko reluctant to share her feelings and experiences about the bombing of Hiroshima even with her best friend?

3. What gives Mariko hope and reassurance that her life had been saved for a reason?

Interpreting

4. With its suggestion of both dead leaves and new growth, why is "Autumn Gardening" an appropriate title for this story?

5. Why do you think Mariko wanted to return to the United States as soon as she had saved enough money?

6. What causes the changes in Mariko's attitude about sharing her experiences as a *hibakusha*?

7. Mariko says to herself aloud, "It should never be repeated." What message do you think Mariko will convey to her audience when she and Mitsuye are televised?

Applying

8. Although "Autumn Gardening" is written from one person's perspective, what universal message is the story conveying?

ANALYZING LITERATURE

Understanding Perspective

A person's **perspective** is his or her unique way of looking at and understanding an issue or event. "Autumn Gardening" presents Mariko's perspective on the bombing of Hiroshima. Another perspective appeared in the August 7, 1945, issue of *The New York Times*:

> There was an element of elation in the realization that we had perfected this devastating weapon for employment against an enemy who started the war

and has told us she would rather be destroyed than surrender, but it was grim elation. There was sobering awareness of the tremendous responsibility involved.

1. (a) What perspective on the bombing does the passage present? (b) What factors influenced this perspective?

2. How might Mariko have responded to this passage?

THINKING AND WRITING

Writing a Human-Interest News Story

Good journalists often incorporate elements of literature in their human-interest news stories. They narrate events as though they were telling a story. Also, they often portray events from a variety of perspectives. Write a human-interest news story about an event that follows the ending of "Autumn Gardening": Mariko's appearance at the Hiroshima anniversary. Include story elements such as dialogue to help make your account come alive for the reader. You may even want to use dialogue and quotations to provide different perspectives on the events you describe.

LEARNING OPTIONS

1. **Performance.** With a partner act out a scene in which Mariko and Mitsuye, or two other Japanese American survivors, tell their accounts before a television audience. Use information from the story to help you develop a script. Convey emotion through the tone and volume of your voice and through the use of gestures and pauses.

2. **Speaking and Listening.** In small groups select a current event that can be examined from two or more perspectives. In an oral presentation or mock debate, have your group explain these perspectives to the class.

3. **Cross-curricular Connection.** Find out more about why Japan and the United States were in conflict during World War II. Report your findings to the class.

Challenge How does the weeding of the garden work symbolically to characterize Mariko?

THINKING AND WRITING

Cooperative Learning If students are working at computers, place three students at a terminal so that they can develop a group written response to the Thinking and Writing Activity.

Software For students working at the computer, suggest that they use the **Writer's Helper** revising tools that lead to Audience Summary to help them with revising techniques.

Publishing Student Writing Compile the news stories to represent the many avenues such an ending can take.

Writing Across the Curriculum Mitsuye's letter refers to bearing witness, "as the Jewish people did to get through the concentration camps." Ask for volunteers who will work with a social studies teacher to develop further parallels between Mariko, Mitsuye, and the Jews.

ONE WRITER'S PROCESS

Siu Wai Anderson and "Autumn Gardening"

PREWRITING

Keeping an Open Ear In 1985 while she was a student at Vermont College's Adult Degree Program, Siu Wai Anderson attended a memorial service marking the fortieth anniversary of the bombing of Hiroshima. There she heard a middle-aged *hibakusha*, or survivor of the bombing, describe his experiences that fateful August morning in 1945. He had been riding on a streetcar when the bomb fell on the unsuspecting city at 8:15 A.M.

Anderson recalls being spellbound as the survivor described the mighty flash, the shaking of the ground, and the mushroom cloud of smoke that rose over Hiroshima. Dazed and bleeding from a few cuts but otherwise unhurt, the boy found himself the *only* survivor on a charred street. He resolved that as a survivor of this nuclear nightmare, he must tell others his story, warning them in a personal way about the disastrous effects of nuclear warfare.

A Creative Response At the time Anderson heard the *hibakusha*'s eyewitness account, she was pregnant with her son. "What would the future hold for our children?" she wondered. Inspired by the survivor's moving story, Anderson "decided to write a story that would help spread the *hibakusha*'s story and his urgent call for lasting peace."

"Read Before Writing!" Though inspired to write about the bombing, Anderson did not feel she knew enough about the event to make her fictional account sufficiently realistic. Before she began drafting, she followed the advice she gives her students in her writing workshops. "Before writing a word," Anderson reports, "I spent four months reading everything I could find about the Hiroshima-Nagasaki bombings."

"If you are going to write about an event that really happened," Anderson advises, "you need to know your facts. Was there really a Teruya Surgical Clinic? How far was it from the center of the bomb's blast?" To these and other questions, Anderson felt she "couldn't just make up the answers" even though she was writing fiction.

DRAFTING

Easier Said Than Done Armed with all the "gruesome details" that her reading yielded, Anderson felt overwhelmed. "How do you write about such an awesome tragedy, one that involved millions of people?" she asked herself. "I tried several approaches, but nothing seemed to work." Then, on a November morning, she had a breakthrough. "I gazed out my living room window and simply began to write down what I saw," Anderson remembers. "The entire setting of the story, right down to the leaves stuck in the cyclone fence and the dog who barks at passersby, is drawn from what I saw in my yard that day."

A Movie in Her Mind Writing is "a magic craft," Anderson believes. It "allows you to become anyone and go anywhere." While drafting "Autumn Gardening" and shaping the character of Mariko, Anderson says she felt as if she were under a spell. "I settled back to watch the movie in my mind," Anderson admits. "I was as curious as anyone to see what would happen next." Giving free rein to her imagination, Anderson says she

One Writer's Process **135**

ANSWERS TO THINKING ABOUT THE PROCESS

Suggested Responses:

1. (a) Students should recognize that Anderson thinks that facts must be accurate and that factual detail (like the distance of the Teruya Surgical Clinic from the center of the bomb's blast) make a story more convincing. (b) Responses will differ; ask students to explain their answers.

2. (a) Anderson used her own house and yard as the setting for her story. (b) Suggested response: Reflecting on his or her own life might give the writer a sense of historical perspective that would be useful to the story.

3. Answers will differ. Ask students to explain their own writing process and compare it to Anderson's.

was "able to step into the heart and mind of a woman very different from me."

REVISING

Computer Magic Anderson says she is glad we live in an age of word processors that make revising easier. "I would have been very frustrated in the days of typewriters, or worse, quills on parchment scrolls." Nevertheless, whenever she first begins to write, Anderson uses a pen. "I like the sensation of words rushing from my brain, down my arm, and through my hand onto fresh blank paper." As soon as her handwritten pages become "an unreadable scrawl," however, Anderson moves to her word processor. "Then I can revise to my heart's content. That's when you can be a critical judge of your work." Anderson advises every would-be story writer to "take the time to master word processing—it's well worth it! Thanks to computer magic, you can revise each page, save your changes, and print out a nice clean manuscript (which you can then scribble all over because you've seen a dozen more things that need changing)."

Consulting With a Qualified Editor Anderson spent six weeks writing and rewriting "Autumn Gardening" while she was a student at Vermont College. One of her professors "read and commented on each draft of the story, just as an editor would do."

The professor's own background unexpectedly proved to be an invaluable help to Anderson in developing a realistic portrait of Mariko. As it turned out, Anderson's professor "was born in the Warsaw ghetto in Poland and her family narrowly escaped the Nazi death camps. She was well qualified to advise me on the experiences of a World War II survivor!"

PUBLISHING

The Diversity of America Today One reason Anderson is pleased about publishing her short stories is that she feels it is important for American readers to learn about the diverse cultural background of America today. "America has many voices from many cultures who until now have been overlooked or suppressed."

Just as Anderson has been inspired by the writings of the Japanese American history professor Hisaye Yamamoto and the African American writer Zora Neale Hurston, her own published writing might well inspire future writers who are hoping to add their voices to American literature.

THINKING ABOUT THE PROCESS

1. (a) Why does Siu Wai Anderson think that doing background research is a helpful prewriting activity, even when she is writing fiction? (b) Do you agree with her? Why or why not?

2. (a) What details from Anderson's own life found their way into "Autumn Gardening"? (b) Why might a writer reflect upon his or her own life while writing a story based on historical fact?

3. When Siu Wai Anderson begins drafting a story, she starts with pen and paper but then transfers her work onto a word processor to continue her drafting and revising. (a) How different is this strategy from your own writing process? (b) Do you think that Anderson's approach could help you with your writing? Explain.

4. **Brainstorming Activity** With several classmates, decide on a historical event that could serve as the core of a short story. Then brainstorm to develop possible characters, actions, and a setting. When you have finished brainstorming, select a spokesperson for your group and share your plot outline with the rest of the class.

136 Short Stories

Setting

SUNKEN FOREST
Rebecca Grutzik, Student, Stevens Point, Wisconsin
Courtesy of the Artist

Humanities Note

Sunken Forest by Rebecca Grutzik. Rebecca Ann Grutzik, a student at Stevens Point Area Senior High School in Stevens Point, Wisconsin, was exposed to painting at an early age by an artistic tenant of her parent's house and by her grandmother, a painter.

Rebecca was fourteen when she painted *Sunken Forest.* The inspiration for it came from a spot she visited on a canoe trip one summer. She sought to capture her memory of the nighttime peace and harmony of nature in this place. Her rendering of the moonlit clouds and their reflection in the water shows developing artistic skill. The medium, oil paint, is well suited to the smooth surface of the water and the even color changes in the clouds and trees. The artist's portrayal of this woodland setting creates a mood of quiet contemplation in the viewer.

1. Do you think this painting successfully conveys the sense of nature at peace that the artist intended? Explain.
2. How does this artist's creation of a mood by showing this setting compare to a writer's use of setting?

More About the Author Paule Marshall has earned critical and popular acclaim for three novels. Her first, *Brown Girls, Brownstones* (1959) tells of a Barbadian immigrant girl whose parents are caught in the conflict between assimilation and ethnic autonomy. Her second, *The Chosen Place, the Timeless People* (1969), is a symbolic novel about the inhabitants of a small, underdeveloped Caribbean island and their refusal to accept modernization. *Praisesong for the Widow* (1983) is the story of an unhappy, affluent American woman who experiences a spiritual rebirth while vacationing in the West Indies. In what ways are the themes of these novels present in "To Da-duh, in Memoriam"?

Literary Focus One might see the conflict in this story as being between two characters: the narrator and her grandmother. The conflict might also be between two settings, or two ways of life. How would you name the two settings that are in conflict?

Prereading Focus As students create their web diagrams around the word *grandmother,* encourage them to use a wide range of experience as their source. They needn't be limited to their own grandmothers; for example, they can think about grandmothers in books, in fairy tales, in films; they can include their friends' grandmothers, grandmothers in advertising, on television shows, and even in cartoons.

Electronic Handbook/Vocabulary Most of the words on this list contain prefixes, and/or suffixes. Use the words to review these word parts: *-able, -ent, -ably, -ous, -ial, -ous, pro-, re-,* and *in-.* Encourage students who have access to the Language Master 6000 to discover alternative definitions and synonyms.

138

GUIDE FOR READING

Paule Marshall

(1929–) grew up in a Barbadian emigrant community in Brooklyn, New York, the setting for her first novel, *Brown Girls, Brownstones* (1959). When she was nine years old, Marshall visited her parents' native land, the island of Barbados in the West Indies. "To Da-duh, in Memoriam," included in Marshall's book *Reena and Other Stories* (1983), is based on her trip. Besides writing novels and short stories, Marshall has worked as a librarian and a lecturer on African American literature at several universities.

138   *Short Stories*

To Da-duh, in Memoriam

Setting and Conflict

Setting, the time and place in which a story occurs, often has a direct bearing on other elements in the story. For example, writers sometimes heighten the conflict or central problem in a story by describing differences in settings. In "To Da-duh, in Memoriam," the narrator's home is New York City, whereas her grandmother lives on an island in the Caribbean. Paule Marshall uses these settings to develop conflict in the story by contrasting the lush natural world of Barbados with life in a large, modern city in the United States.

Focus

"To Da-duh, in Memoriam" is a story about a girl's relationship with her grandmother, whom she calls "Da-duh." Make a web diagram with the word *grandmother* in the center, as shown below. Include words, ideas, and feelings you associate with *grandmother.* Make another web centering on the name *Da-duh,* and, as you read, fill it out for the narrator in the story. Then compare the two. What similarities and differences do you find?

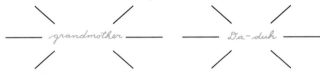

Vocabulary

Knowing the following words will help you as you read "To Da-duh, in Memoriam."

reconciled (rek' ən sil'd') *v.:* Made compatible; brought into harmony (p. 140)

scrutiny (skroot' ən ē) *n.:* Close examination or inspection (p. 140)

formidable (fôr' mə də bəl) *adj.:* Impressive; awe-inspiring (p. 140)

truculent (truk' yoo lənt) *adj.:* Fierce; savage (p. 140)

inexplicably (in eks pli' kə blē) *adv.:* In an incomprehensible manner; mysteriously (p. 144)

tremulous (trem' yoo ləs) *adj.:* Trembling; quivering (p. 144)

perennial (pər en' ē əl) *adj.:* Lasting for a long time (p. 144)

incredulous (in krej' oo ləs) *adj.:* Disbelieving (p. 146)

protracted (prō trakt' id) *adj.:* Lengthy; prolonged (p. 148)

Objectives

1 To understand setting and conflict
2 To understand symbolism
3 To write a description of setting
4 To express individual interests and abilities through an optional activity

Support Material

Teaching Portfolio
Teacher Backup, p. 173
Grammar in Action Worksheets, *Capturing the Sounds of Speech,* p. 177
Using Compound-Complex Sentences, p. 179
Usage and Mechanics Worksheet, p. 181
Vocabulary Check, p. 182

Analyzing Literature Worksheet, *Understanding Setting and Conflict,* p. 183
Critical Thinking and Reading Worksheet, *Understanding Symbolism,* p. 184
Selection Test, p. 185

Prentice Hall Literature Writing Studio

Audio Prose Library
Paule Marshall: Interview

To Da-duh, in Memoriam[1]

Paule Marshall

1
". . . Oh Nana! all of you is not involved in this evil
   business Death,
Nor all of us in life."
—From "At My Grandmother's Grave," by Lebert Bethune

2   I did not see her at first I remember. For not only was it dark inside the crowded disembarkation shed[2] in spite of the daylight flooding in from outside, but standing there waiting for her with my mother and sister I was still somewhat blinded from the sheen of tropical sunlight on the water of the bay which we had just crossed in the landing boat, leaving behind us the ship that had 3 brought us from New York lying in the offing.[3] Besides, being only nine years of age at the time and knowing nothing of islands I was busy attending to the alien sights and sounds of Barbados,[4] the unfamiliar smells.

I did not see her, but I was alerted to her approach by my mother's hand which suddenly tightened around mine, and looking up I traced her gaze through the gloom in the shed until I finally made out the small, purposeful, painfully erect figure of the old 4 woman headed our way.

Her face was drowned in the shadow of an ugly rolled-brim brown felt hat, but the details of her slight body and of the struggle taking place within it were clear enough—an intense, unrelenting struggle between her back which was beginning to bend ever so 5 slightly under the weight of her eighty-odd years and the rest of her which sought to deny those years and hold that back straight, keep it in line. Moving swiftly toward us (so swiftly it seemed she did not intend stopping when she reached us but would sweep past us out the doorway which opened onto the sea and like Christ walk upon the water!), she was caught between the sunlight at her end of the building and the darkness inside— and for a moment she appeared to contain them both: the light in the long severe old-fashioned white dress she wore which brought the sense of a past that was still alive into our bustling present and in the snatch of white at her eye; the darkness in her black 6 high-top shoes and in her face which was visible now that she was closer.

---

1. **in Memoriam** (mə môr' ē əm'): A Latin phrase, meaning "in memory of," often appearing on gravestones.
2. **disembarkation** (dıs'em bär kā'shən) **shed:** Place for unloading of passengers from a ship.
3. **in the offing:** A position at a distance from the shore.
4. **Barbados** (bär bā'dōs): A country on the easternmost island of the West Indies; it became independent from Great Britain in 1966.

To Da-duh, in Memoriam   139

Presentation

Motivation/Prior Knowledge
Have students explore their own notions about living in an urban center such as New York City and living in a rural area such as a sugarcane farm. Have them construct a four-part chart with *City* and *Country* on one side and *Advantages* and *Disadvantages* on top.

Purpose-Setting Question In how many different ways can you express the conflict that is at the heart of this story?

1 **Enrichment** An epigraph is a quotation at the beginning of a book, story, or chapter. This epigraph is a quotation from a poem by the Jamaican-born poet Lebert Bethune (1937–).

2 **Reading Strategy** Help students to see how much essential information is embedded in this first paragraph.

3 **Reader's Response** Ask students to try to remember something important that happened to them when they were nine years old.

4 **Discussion** Why does the narrator call her grandmother "painfully erect"? What does this phrase make you think of?

5 **Reading Strategy** This paragraph is an excellent choice for reading aloud; it is rich with poetry and beautifully ornate sentences. Help students to see how it sets up the oppositions in the story: light and darkness, past and present, young and old.

6 **Discussion** In good literature, clothing is always a way to show a character's personality. Is this also true in life?

Thematic Focus Appreciation of another person may come with understanding over time. The narrator of this story, in conflict with her grandmother, comes to appreciate her only years later. What qualities of her grandmother do you think the narrator appreciates most? Give evidence to support your answer.

Making Connections Students can easily compare the syntax and rhythms of "To Da-duh, in Memoriam" with Poe's in "The Cask of Amontillado" (page 3) and Márquez's in "A Very Old Man with Enormous Wings" (p. 165). They might also enjoy comparing and contrasting the subject of this story with that of Toni Cade Bambara's "Blues Ain't No Mockin Bird" (page 91).

7 Discussion Notice the words used to describe Da-duh's face: *fleshless, death mask, maggots, ruined.* How do these words make you feel about Da-duh?

8 Reader's Response Fourteen children! Ask students to respond to this fact.

9 Discussion *Reconciled* means "brought into harmony," but is Da-duh portrayed as a harmonious character? In other words, is this word used seriously or ironically?

10 Discussion Why might Da-duh prefer boys?

11 Discussion Da-duh, like most people, reacts to the color of other people's skin. This passage suggests that even within races, shades of skin color are important to people. Why do you think that Da-duh liked her grandchildren to be "fair-skinned"?

12 Literary Focus A major conflict in the story begins here: Da-duh finds the narrator disturbing and threatening. In this first confrontation, Da-duh "loses" the stare down.

13 Discussion Does the word "won" here seem strange? What does it mean to "win an encounter"?

14 Discussion Why does Da-duh call her granddaughter "soul"?

ESL Teaching Strategy Students with limited English proficiency may have difficulty with the complexity of Paule Marshall's prose. Help them by reading the story aloud, stopping after long paragraphs and asking students to recall, summarize, and ask questions. Read slowly and reread challenging sections after students have the general idea.

It was as stark and fleshless as a death mask, that face. The maggots might have already done their work, leaving only the framework of bone beneath the ruined skin and deep wells at the temple and jaw. But her eyes were alive, unnervingly so for one so old, with a sharp light that flicked out of the dim clouded depths like a lizard's tongue to snap up all in her view. Those eyes betrayed a child's curiosity about the world, and I wondered vaguely seeing them, and seeing the way the bodice of her ancient dress had collapsed in on her flat chest (what had happened to her breasts?), whether she might not be some kind of child at the same time that she was a woman, with fourteen children, my mother included, to prove it. Perhaps she was both, both child and woman, darkness and light, past and present, life and death—all the opposites contained and reconciled in her.

"My Da-duh," my mother said formally and stepped forward. The name sounded like thunder fading softly in the distance.

"Child," Da-duh said, and her tone, her quick scrutiny of my mother, the brief embrace in which they appeared to shy from each other rather than touch, wiped out the fifteen years my mother had been away and restored the old relationship. My mother, who was such a formidable figure in my eyes, had suddenly with a word been reduced to my status.

"Yes, God is good," Da-duh said with a nod that was like a tic. "He has spared me to see my child again."

We were led forward then, apologetically because not only did Da-duh prefer boys but she also liked her grandchildren to be "white," that is, fair-skinned; and we had, I was to discover, a number of cousins, the outside children of white estate managers and the like, who qualified. We, though, were as black as she.

My sister being the oldest was presented first. "This one takes after the father," my mother said and waited to be reproved.

Frowning, Da-duh tilted my sister's face toward the light. But her frown soon gave way to a grudging smile, for my sister with her large mild eyes and little broad winged nose, with our father's high-cheeked Barbadian cast to her face, was pretty.

"She's goin' be lucky," Da-duh said and patted her once on the cheek. "Any girl child that takes after the father does be lucky."

She turned then to me. But oddly enough she did not touch me. Instead leaning close, she peered hard at me, and then quickly drew back. I thought I saw her hand start up as though to shield her eyes. It was almost as if she saw not only me, a thin truculent child who it was said took after no one but myself, but something in me which for some reason she found disturbing, even threatening. We looked silently at each other for a long time there in the noisy shed, our gaze locked. She was the first to look away.

"But Adry," she said to my mother and her laugh was cracked, thin, apprehensive. "Where did you get this one here with this fierce look?"

"We don't know where she came out of, my Da-duh," my mother said, laughing also. Even I smiled to myself. After all I had won the encounter. Da-duh had recognized my small strength—and this was all I ever asked of the adults in my life then.

"Come, soul," Da-duh said and took my hand. "You must be one of those New York terrors you hear so much about."

She led us, me at her side and my sister and mother behind, out of the shed into the sunlight that was like a bright driving summer rain and over to a group of people clustered beside a decrepit lorry.[5] They were our

---

5. **lorry** (lôr′ē) *n.:* A British word for a motor truck.

Such students may have trouble with the Barbadian dialect. You might help them by "translating" some of the dialogue into standard English or asking them to do so.

Multicultural Focus Tensions between generations are somewhat inevitable in almost all societies. Yet certain situations seem to increase them: the stress experienced by immigrants and their children, or changes in the occupation or social class between children and parents. In this story, the conflict seems to spring from the threat the old-fashioned, countrified grand-

GRANDMOTHER
AND CHILD, 1989
Carlton Murrell
*Courtesy of
the Artist*

relatives, most of them from St. Andrews although Da-duh herself lived in St. Thomas,[6] the women wearing bright print dresses, the colors vivid against their darkness, the men rusty black suits that encased them like straitjackets. Da duh, holding fast to my hand, became my anchor as they circled round us like a nervous sea, exclaiming, touching us with their calloused hands, embracing us shyly. They laughed in awed bursts: "But look Adry got big-big children!"/

---

6. St. Andrews . . . St. Thomas: In Barbados, two districts of local government.

To Da-duh, in Memoriam   141

---

mother feels from her citified granddaughter. American anthropologist Margaret Mead wrote about three kinds of societies that she felt exist in the world. One is completely traditional, in which the ways of the past will also become the ways of the future. In these societies, elders are important and highly valued for the information they possess. Another type of society has values and behavior that are increasingly based on one's adult peers, not the past. The changing world of the first half of the twentieth century produced many of these kinds of societies. In a third type of society, unprecedented change created new divisions: The younger generations began to experience things that their grandparents and even their parents never had, and would live in a future that their elders could not have imagined. This was the kind of society that Mead considered the whole world to be heading toward and saw it as an explanation for the phenomenon widely called the generation gap.

Do students agree with this? Have them investigate whether there is more conflict between generations now than in the past.

Fine art, *Selling Fruit, Highway 1 Barbados*, by Jill Walker. Jill Crockford Walker was born in England in 1927 and studied art at the Regent Street Polytechnic and the Royal Academy Schools. She subsequently worked on theater productions at the Old Vic, Stratford Memorial, and other theaters around the West End in London. She first traveled to the West Indies in the early 1950's; there she met and married architect Jimmy Walker. The couple traveled the Caribbean by schooner and finally settled in Barbados. During this time Walker painted many of the Caribbean islands and is best known for her original oil, watercolor, and prints of West Indian life.

Consider the following questions for discussion:

1. What "alien sights and sounds" might the girl in the story have experienced in this image of Barbados?

2. Does this picture fit your idea of what Da-duh's world was like? Explain.

15 Reading Strategy Alert students to the use of dialect in this story. Ask them to notice words such as *sheself* that they may not have seen or heard before and syntax such as "Why you all got to get on like you never saw people from 'Away' before?"

16 Reading Strategy This paragraph is ideal for reading aloud and careful study.

SELLING FRUIT, HIGHWAY 1 BARBADOS
Jill Walker
Savacou Gallery, New York

15 "And see the nice things they wearing, wrist watch and all!"/ "I tell you, Adry has done all right for sheself in New York. . . ."

Da-duh, ashamed at their wonder, embarrassed for them, admonished them the while. "But oh Christ," she said, "why you all got to get on like you never saw people from 'Away' before? You would think New York is the only place in the world to hear wunna. That's why I don't like to go anyplace with you St. Andrews people, you know. You all ain't been colonized."[7]

We were in the back of the lorry finally, packed in among the barrels of ham, flour, cornmeal and rice and the trunks of clothes that my mother had brought as gifts. We made our way slowly through Bridgetown's[8] clogged streets, part of a funereal procession of cars and open-sided buses, bicycles and donkey carts. The dim little limestone shops and offices along the way marched with us, at the same mournful pace, toward the same grave ceremony—as did the people, the women balancing huge baskets on top their heads as if they were no more than hats they wore to shade them from the sun. Looking over the edge of the lorry I watched as their

16

---

7. colonized (käl' ə nīzd') *v*.: In this context, it means civilized.

8. Bridgetown: The capital of Barbados.

142   *Short Stories*

Grammar in Action

Remind students that writers often express many ideas by combining clauses in different ways into long sentences. In doing so, they create the following kinds of sentence structures:

Compound: Two or more independent clauses joined by coordinating conjunctions or semicolons
I was only nine years old, **and** *I knew nothing about Barbados.*

Complex: One independent clause and one or more subordinate clauses
I knew nothing of Barbados **until** *I was nine years old.*

In addition, writers can combine these two kinds of structures to create a **compound-complex sentence,** a sentence that consists of two or more independent clauses and one or more subordinate clauses. The following example from "To Da-duh, in Memoriam" consists of three independent clauses and one subordinate clause:

I did not see her, **but** *I was alerted to her approach by my mother's hand which suddenly tightened around mine,* **and** *looking up, I traced her gaze through the gloom in the*

feet slurred the dust. I listened, and their voices, raw and loud and dissonant in the heat, seemed to be grappling with each other high overhead.

Da-duh sat on a trunk in our midst, a monarch amid her court. She still held my hand, but it was different now. I had suddenly become her anchor, for I felt her fear of the lorry with its asthmatic motor (a fear and distrust, I later learned, she held of all machines) beating like a pulse in her rough palm.

As soon as we left Bridgetown behind though, she relaxed, and while the others around us talked she gazed at the canes standing tall on either side of the winding marl road. "C'dear," she said softly to herself after a time. "The canes this side are pretty enough."

They were too much for me. I thought of them as giant weeds that had overrun the island, leaving scarcely any room for the small tottering houses of sunbleached pine we passed or the people, dark streaks as our lorry hurtled by. I suddenly feared that we were journeying, unaware that we were, toward some dangerous place where the canes, grown as high and thick as a forest, would close in on us and run us through with their stiletto blades. I longed then for the familiar: for the street in Brooklyn where I lived, for my father who had refused to accompany us ("Blowing out good money on foolishness," he had said of the trip), for a game of tag with my friends under the chestnut tree outside our aging brownstone house.

"Yes, but wait till you see St. Thomas canes," Da-duh was saying to me. "They's canes father, bo," she gave a proud arrogant nod. "Tomorrow, God willing, I goin' take you out in the ground and show them to you."

True to her word Da-duh took me with her the following day out into the ground. It was a fairly large plot adjoining her weathered board and shingle house and consisting of a small orchard, a good-sized canepiece and behind the canes, where the land sloped abruptly down, a gully. She had purchased it with Panama money sent her by her eldest son, my uncle Joseph, who had died working on the canal. We entered the ground along a trail no wider than her body and as devious and complex as her reasons for showing me her land. Da-duh strode briskly ahead, her slight form filled out this morning by the layers of sacking petticoats she wore under her working dress to protect her against the damp. A fresh white cloth, elaborately arranged around her head, added to her height, and lent her a vain, almost roguish air.

Her pace slowed once we reached the orchard, and glancing back at me occasionally over her shoulder, she pointed out the various trees.

"This here is a breadfruit," she said. "That one yonder is a papaw. Here's a guava. This is a mango. I know you don't have anything like these in New York. Here's a sugar apple." (The fruit looked more like artichokes than apples to me.) "This one bears limes. . . ." She went on for some time, intoning the names of the trees as though they were those of her gods. Finally, turning to me, she said, "I know you don't have anything this nice where you come from." Then, as I hesitated: "I said I know you don't have anything this nice where you come from. . . ."

"No," I said and my world did seem suddenly lacking.

Da-duh nodded and passed on. The orchard ended and we were on the narrow cart road that led through the canepiece, the canes clashing like swords above my cowering head. Again she turned and her thin muscular arms spread wide, her dim gaze embracing the small field of canes, she said— and her voice almost broke under the weight

17 **Discussion** How is this a reversal of an idea that comes before?

18 **Connection** Call attention to Da-duh's fear of machines.

19 **Clarification** The "canes" are sugarcane plants of Barbados.

20 **Literary Focus: Setting** Help students to see how even the fine details of setting contribute to the conflict.

21 **Reader's Response** What does the image of stiletto blades make you think of?

22 **Enrichment** Marshall's first novel *Brown Girls, Brownstones* (1959) uses this image of the tall brick row houses typical of Brooklyn's neighborhoods in the 1930's.

23 **Enrichment** The building of the Panama Canal lasted from 1904 to 1914. About three quarters of the more than 40,000 workers were from the West Indies.

24 **Literary Focus: Setting** This line ". . . you don't have anything this nice . . ." becomes a kind of refrain in the story that builds in intensity until the end. Each time we read it, we know that the two characters are going to engage in their verbal comparisons of New York and Barbados.

25 **Critical Thinking and Reading** Students will probably notice that the image of the sugarcane is repeated in the story and that it is accumulating meaning with each mention.

---

shed **until** *I finally made out the small, purposeful, painfully erect figure of the old woman headed our way.*

Reassure students that they will write such sentences unconsciously as they gain more experience reading and writing. Alert them to the beauty of the structure by pointing out some good student-written examples when you discover them.

Student Activity 1. In "To Da-duh, in Memoriam," find an example of a simple sentence, a compound sentence, a complex sentence, and another compound-complex sentence.

Student Activity 2. Write three compound-complex sentences by filling in the following blanks with independent clauses about "To Da-duh, in Memoriam."

1. _____, and _____ because _____.
2. When _____, _____, but _____.
3. _____; if _____, _____.

Electronic Handbook Have students review complex sentences and coordinating conjunctions before completing the Grammar in Action activities. If they have access to the Language Master 6000, have them enter the access words *complex* and *coordinating* and then press the GRAMMAR key to get information on each.

---

26 Literary Focus: Setting The gully is described as both "violent" and "peaceful." How can it be both at the same time? Is this contradiction believable?

27 Clarification What Da-duh is asking here is, "Does your chestnut tree flower and grow chestnuts?" In other words, "Is it fertile?"

28 Visualization How do you imagine the narrator dramatizing her description of snow?

29 Discussion Think about the words *bare* and *buried* in this passage? What do the words have to do with snow? What do they have to do with Da-duh?

30 Clarification In the 1930's, Shirley Temple became one of the most famous child performers in the world. She made her debut at the age of three in the motion picture *Stand Up and Cheer* (1932).

of her pride, "Tell me, have you got anything like these in that place where you were born?"

"No."

"I din' think so. I bet you don't even know that these canes here and the sugar you eat is one and the same thing. That they does throw the canes into some machine at the factory and squeeze out all the little life in them to make sugar for you all so in New York to eat. I bet you don't know that."

"I've got two cavities and I'm not allowed to eat a lot of sugar."

But Da-duh didn't hear me. She had turned with an inexplicably angry motion and was making her way rapidly out of the canes and down the slope at the edge of the field which led to the gully below. Following her apprehensively down the incline amid a stand of banana plants whose leaves flapped like elephants' ears in the wind, I found myself in the middle of a small tropical wood—a place dense and damp and gloomy and tremulous with the fitful play of light and shadow as the leaves high above moved against the sun that was almost hidden from view. It was a violent place, the tangled foliage fighting each other for a chance at the sunlight, the branches of the trees located in what seemed an immemorial struggle, one both necessary and inevitable. But despite the violence, it was pleasant, almost peaceful in the gully, and beneath the thick undergrowth the earth smelled like spring.

This time Da-duh didn't even bother to ask her usual question, but simply turned and waited for me to speak.

"No," I said, my head bowed. "We don't have anything like this in New York."

"Ah," she cried, her triumph complete. "I din' think so. Why, I've heard that's a place where you can walk till you near drop and never see a tree."

"We've got a chestnut tree in front of our house," I said.

"Does it bear?" She waited. "I ask you, does it bear?"

"Not anymore," I muttered. "It used to, but not anymore."

She gave the nod that was like a nervous twitch. "You see," she said. "Nothing can bear there." Then, secure behind her scorn, she added, "But tell me, what's this snow like that you hear so much about?"

Looking up, I studied her closely, sensing my chance, and then I told her, describing at length and with as much drama as I could summon not only what snow in the city was like, but what it would be like here, in her perennial summer kingdom.

". . . And you see all these trees you got here," I said. "Well, they'd be bare. No leaves, no fruit, nothing. They'd be covered in snow. You see your canes. They'd be buried under tons of snow. The snow would be higher than your head, higher than your house, and you wouldn't be able to come down into this here gully because it would be snowed under. . . ."

She searched my face for the lie, still scornful but intrigued. "What a thing, huh?" she said finally, whispering it softly to herself.

"And when it snows you couldn't dress like you are now," I said. "Oh no, you'd freeze to death. You'd have to wear a hat and gloves and galoshes and ear muffs so your ears wouldn't freeze and drop off, and a heavy coat. I've got a Shirley Temple coat with fur on the collar. I can dance. You wanna see?"

Before she could answer I began, with a dance called the Truck which was popular back then in the 1930's. My right forefinger waving, I trucked around the nearby trees and around Da-duh's awed and rigid form. After the Truck I did the Suzy-Q, my lean hips swishing, my sneakers sidling zigzag over the ground. "I can sing," I said and did so, starting with "I'm Gonna Sit Right Down and Write Myself a Letter," then without pausing, "Tea For Two," and ending with "I Found a

Grammar in Action

Paule Marshall has used certain techniques to help readers "hear" the sounds of speech, that is, the two spoken voices contained in quotation marks in the story: the narrator as a child and her grandmother, Da-duh.

First, Marshall uses contractions beyond the ones we usually read in English. As you read these examples, ask yourself what letters are omitted:

"C'dear," she said softly to herself.

"I din' think so."

"What d'ya mean," I said.

Second, Marshall uses ellipses (. . .) to remind us that real speaking people do not always finish their thoughts or sentences, sometimes on purpose.

"and you wouldn't be able to come down into this here gully because it would be snowed under . . ."

Third, Marshall uses sentence fragments within her characters' dialogue because people often speak in incomplete sentences.

GOING HOME
Carlton Murrell
Courtesy of the Artist

Fine art, *Going Home,* by Carlton Murrell. Murrell has lived in New York since 1968 but travels back to his native Barbados once or twice a year, where galleries carry prints and reproductions of his work. He is highly regarded by critics and fellow artists. He also teaches painting to children at the Brooklyn Truth Center.

In this oil painting, Murrell wanted to capture old memories as well as Barbadian homes of the past, many of which have been replaced by modern concrete structures.

You may use the following questions for discussion:
1. How does this scene compare to the Brooklyn Street in the painting on page 147? Can you find any similarities?
2. The narrator of this story and the artist of this painting are both looking back over many years. How might their perceptions have changed?

31 Discussion What is significant about Da-duh having to reach way under layers of petticoats to get to her money?

32 Literary Focus Think about the word *surrender* here. If the "battle" takes place with words, does it makes sense that the "surrender" is silence?

Million Dollar Baby in a Five and Ten Cent Store."

For long moments afterwards Da-duh stared at me as if I were a creature from Mars, an emissary[9] from some world she did not know, but which intrigued her and whose power she both felt and feared. Yet something about my performance must have pleased her, because bending down she slowly lifted her long skirt and then, one by one, the layers of petticoats until she came to a drawstring purse dangling at the end of a long strip of cloth tied round her waist. Opening the purse she handed me a penny. "Here," she said half-smiling against her will. "Take this

---

9. emissary (em'i ser'ē) *n.*: A person sent on a specific mission.

to buy yourself a sweet at the shop up the road. There's nothing to be done with you, soul."

From then on, whenever I wasn't taken to visit relatives, I accompanied Da-duh out into the ground, and alone with her amid the canes or down in the gully I told her about New York. It always began with some slighting remark on her part: "I know they don't have anything this nice where you come from," or "Tell me, I hear those foolish people in New York does do such and such. . . ." But as I answered, re-creating my towering world of steel and concrete and machines for her, building the city out of words, I would feel her give way. I came to know the signs of her surrender: the total stillness that would come over her little hard dry form, the probing gaze

To Da-duh, in Memoriam 145

"No leaves, no fruit, nothing."
"Beating up white people!"

Encourage students to use these three techniques when writing dialogue of their own. In doing so, they can capture the sound and flavor of speech, not just the meaning of what is said.

Student Activity 1. Have students locate three other examples of ways in which Paule Marshall has captured the sound of speech in the story. Have them read the examples aloud.

Student Activity 2. Have students write short dialogues between themselves and one of the characters in the story in which they use all three techniques to capture the sounds of speech. Ask them to read their dialogues aloud with a partner.

Electronic Handbook Have students review contractions, ellipses, and fragments before completing the Grammar in Action activities. If they have access to the Language Master 6000, have them enter the access word *fragment* or the symbol for apostrophe (') and press the GRAMMAR key to get information on each.

33 Discussion How is the "incredibly tall royal palm" like Da-duh herself?

34 Discussion Do you think this is the turning point of the story—"All the fight went out of her . . ."? Is this where the conflict is resolved?

that like a surgeon's knife sought to cut through my skull to get at the images there, to see if I were lying; above all, her fear, a fear nameless and profound, the same one I had felt beating in the palm of her hand that day in the lorry.

Over the weeks I told her about refrigerators, radios, gas stoves, elevators, trolley cars, wringer washing machines, movies, airplanes, the cyclone at Coney Island,[10] subways, toasters, electric lights: "At night, see, all you have to do is flip this little switch on the wall and all the lights in the house go on. Just like that. Like magic. It's like turning on the sun at night."

"But tell me," she said to me once with a faint mocking smile, "do the white people have all these things too or it's only the people looking like us?"

I laughed. "What d'ya mean," I said. "The white people have even better." Then: "I beat up a white girl in my class last term."

"Beating up white people!" Her tone was incredulous.

"How you mean!" I said, using an expression of hers. "She called me a name."

For some reason Da-duh could not quite get over this and repeated in the same hushed, shocked voice, "Beating up white people now! Oh, the lord, the world's changing up so I can scarce recognize it anymore."

One morning toward the end of our stay, Da-duh led me into a part of the gully that we had never visited before, an area darker and more thickly overgrown than the rest, almost impenetrable. There in a small clearing amid the dense bush, she stopped before an incredibly tall royal palm which rose cleanly out of the ground, and drawing the eye up with it, soared high above the trees around it into the sky. It appeared to be touching the blue

dome of sky, to be flaunting its dark crown of fronds right in the blinding white face of the late morning sun.

Da-duh watched me a long time before she spoke, and then she said, very quietly, "All right, now, tell me if you've got anything this tall in that place you're from."

I almost wished, seeing her face, that I could have said no. "Yes," I said. "We've got buildings hundreds of times this tall in New York. There's one called the Empire State building[11] that's the tallest in the world. My class visited it last year and I went all the way to the top. It's got over a hundred floors. I can't describe how tall it is. Wait a minute. What's the name of that hill I went to visit the other day, where they have the police station?"

"You mean Bissex?"

"Yes, Bissex. Well, the Empire State Building is way taller than that."

"You're lying now!" she shouted, trembling with rage. Her hand lifted to strike me.

"No, I'm not," I said. "It really is, if you don't believe me I'll send you a picture postcard of it soon as I get back home so you can see for yourself. But it's way taller than Bissex."

All the fight went out of her at that. The hand poised to strike me fell limp to her side, and as she stared at me, seeing not me but the building that was taller than the highest hill she knew, the small stubborn light in her eyes (it was the same amber as the flame in the kerosene lamp she lit at dusk) began to fail. Finally, with a vague gesture that even in the midst of her defeat still tried to dismiss me and my world, she turned and started back through the gully, walking slowly, her steps groping and uncertain, as if she were

---

10. the cyclone at Coney Island: A famous roller coaster in a New York City amusement park.

11. Empire State building: At the time of the story, the tallest building in the United States. Now it is the third tallest; the Sears Tower in Chicago and the World Trade Center in New York City are taller.

Primary Source

"My work asks that you become involved, that you think," Paule Marshall once commented in the *Los Angeles Times* (May 18, 1983). "On the other hand, . . . I'm first trying to tell a story, because I'm always about telling a good story." Marshall received her first training in storytelling from her mother, a native of Barbados, and her mother's West Indian friends, all of whom gathered for daily talks in Marshall's home after a hard day of "scrubbing floors." Marshall pays tribute to these "poets in the kitchen" in a *New York Times Book Review* essay where she describes the women's gatherings as a form of inexpensive therapy and an outlet for their enormous creative energy. She writes, "They taught me my first lessons in the narrative art. They trained my ear. They set a standard of excellence. This is why the best of my work must be attributed to them; it stands as testimony to the rich legacy of language and culture they so freely passed on to me in the wordshop of the kitchen."

CLASSON AVE., BROOKLYN
Carlton Murrell
Courtesy of the Artist

35

36

suddenly no longer sure of the way, while I followed triumphant yet strangely saddened behind.

The next morning I found her dressed for our morning walk but stretched out on the Berbice chair in the tiny drawing room where she sometimes napped during the afternoon heat, her face turned to the window beside her. She appeared thinner and suddenly indescribably old.

"My Da-duh," I said.

"Yes, nuh," she said. Her voice was listless and the face she slowly turned my way was, now that I think back on it, like a Benin[12] mask, the features drawn and almost distorted by an ancient abstract sorrow.

"Don't you feel well?" I asked.

"Girl, I don't know."

"My Da-duh, I goin' boil you some bush tea,"[13] my aunt, Da-duh's youngest child, who lived with her, called from the shed roof kitchen.

"Who tell you I need bush tea?" she cried, her voice assuming for a moment its old authority. "You can't even rest nowadays without some malicious person looking for you to be dead. Come girl," she motioned me to a place beside her on the old-fashioned lounge chair, "give us a tune."

I sang for her until breakfast at eleven, all

---

12. **Benin** (be nēn'): A native kingdom in West Africa that flourished during the period 1300–1600.

13. **bush tea:** Tea made from a particular weed or wild plant.

To Da-duh, in Memoriam   147

---

35 Discussion The narrator feels "triumphant"—is she?

36 Discussion How does Da-duh change in the eyes of the narrator?

Cooperative Learning "To Da-duh, in Memoriam" is filled with specific details with which students may not be familar: imagery from tropical flora, literary and historical allusions, references to popular culture in the 1930's, geographical and historical facts about Barbados. (Brief information is sometimes offered in the footnotes.) First, have students list details that they don't know much about (i.e., Christ walking on the water, St. Thomas and St. Andrew, papaw, guava, Shirley Temple, the Empire State Building, Coney Island, Benin, van Gogh). Then, have pairs of students research the various topics and report back to the class, answering the following questions:
1. What exactly is this?
2. How is the detail used in the story?
3. Why do you think Paule Marshall chose this image?
4. Does the image have any symbolic possibilities?
     Encourage students to share photographs or drawings if possible or any other visual or aural aids that might help their classmates' understanding. Encourage discussion and questions after each short report.

Humanities Note

Fine art, *Classon Ave., Brooklyn,* by Carlton Murrell. Murrell's first influences were the artists of his native Barbados. His techniques changed, however, after he moved to the United States in 1968 and studied the work of van Gogh and Monet. More contemporary influences include John Pike, a watercolorist, and George Wilson, an African American artist who painted children. This oil painting is a scene near Murrell's mother's home in Brooklyn, New York. Use the following questions for discussion:
1. Would Da-duh feel comfortable in this setting? Explain.
2. How does the artist use perspective (depth and distance) in this work?
3. Does this neighborhood scene help you to visualize the contrasting settings in this story? Explain.

37 Reading Strategy Have a volunteer read this paragraph aloud. In some ways, it capsulizes the entire story. Help students to understand the paragraph first literally then figuratively. For example, you might suggest that Da-duh is just like one of the ripened mangoes in her orchard, shaken from her branch by the intense downdraft.

38 Reading Strategy Have a volunteer read this last paragraph aloud so that students can hear its music and savor its rich imagery.

39 Discussion Why does the narrator paint these pictures? Why are the factory machines "mocking"?

Reader's Response What are your feelings about the conflict between the narrator and her grandmother?

Thematic Response Why do you think it sometimes takes a long time to appreciate another person who has a powerful influence on our lives?

🎧 **Audiocassette** To help students further appreciate Paule Marshall, play for them the interview with her in the **Audio Prose Library**. In this interview Marshall discusses her childhood and the creative process. Have students draw parallels between her life and information in this story.

---

my brash irreverent Tin Pan Alley[14] songs, and then just before noon we went out into the ground. But it was a short, dispirited walk. Da-duh didn't even notice that the mangoes were beginning to ripen and would have to be picked before the village boys got to them. And when she paused occasionally and looked out across the canes or up at her trees it wasn't as if she were seeing them but something else. Some huge, monolithic[15] shape had imposed itself, it seemed, between her and the land, obstructing her vision. Returning to the house she slept the entire afternoon on the Berbice chair.

She remained like this until we left, languishing away the mornings on the chair at the window gazing out at the land as if it were already doomed; then, at noon, taking the brief stroll with me through the ground during which she seldom spoke, and afterwards returning home to sleep till almost dusk sometimes.

On the day of our departure she put on the austere, ankle length white dress, the black shoes and brown felt hat (her town clothes she called them), but she did not go with us to town. She saw us off on the road outside her house and in the midst of my mother's tearful protracted farewell, she leaned down and whispered in my ear, "Girl, you're not to forget now to send me the picture of that building, you hear."

37 | By the time I mailed her the large colored picture postcard of the Empire State building she was dead. She died during the famous '37 strike[16] which began shortly after we left.

On the day of her death England sent planes flying low over the island in a show of force—so low, according to my aunt's letter, that the downdraft from them shook the ripened mangoes from the trees in Da-duh's orchard. Frightened, everyone in the village fled into the canes. Except Da-duh. She remained in the house at the window so my aunt said, watching as the planes came swooping and screaming like monstrous birds down over the village, over her house, rattling her trees and flattening the young canes in her field. It must have seemed to her lying there that they did not intend pulling out of their dive, but like the hardback beetles which hurled themselves with suicidal force against the walls of the house at night, those menacing silver shapes would hurl themselves in an ecstasy of self-immolation[17] onto the land, destroying it utterly.

When the planes finally left and the villagers returned they found her dead on the Berbice chair at the window.

She died and I lived, but always, to this day even, within the shadow of her death. For a brief period after I was grown I went to live alone, like one doing penance, in a loft above a noisy factory in downtown New York and there painted seas of sugar-cane and huge swirling Van Gogh suns[18] and palm trees striding like brightly-plumed Tutsi[19] warriors across a tropical landscape, while the thunderous tread of the machines downstairs jarred the floor beneath my easel, mocking my efforts.

3[
3[

---

14. Tin Pan Alley: A district in New York City where there were and are many musicians, songwriters, and publishers of popular music.
15. monolithic (män′ ə lith′ ik) *adj.*: Like a huge, unyielding block of stone.
16. famous '37 strike: In 1937, worsening economic conditions caused riots in Barbados.

17. self-immolation (im′ ə lā′ shən) *n.*: Self-sacrifice.
18. Van Gogh (van gō′) **suns:** Refers to the brilliant yellow and orange suns painted by the nineteenth-century Dutch artist Vincent van Gogh.
19. Tutsi (to͞ot′sē): A nickname for the Watusi (wä to͞o′sē), an African people known for their great height.

148 Short Stories

Closure and Extension

ANSWERS TO RESPONDING TO THE SELECTION
Your Response

1. Many students will say that the narrator "wins" because Da-duh loses heart and stops the battle. Some may suggest that Da-duh wins because her spirit haunts her granddaughter after she is dead.

148

Recalling

2. When they meet, the narrator senses a struggle in Da-duh between life and death. She is someone who is very old but whose eyes are still very young and alive.
3. Suggested Response: When they meet, Da-duh scrutinizes her daughter and only briefly embraces her. When Da-duh first sees the narrator, she stares at her and seems to be threatened.
4. The story of the Empire State

Building's great height has the most effect.

Interpreting

5. Suggested Response: The narrator's sister is pretty, but the narrator is more like Da-duh herself: fierce.
6. Da-duh is frightened by machines and technology.
7. Suggested Response: Somehow, her knowledge of New York prevents her from feeling as close to the land as she did before.

8. Suggested Response: She paints island scenes because she is haunted by the spirit of Da-duh. It is as if she is, in part, her grandmother now.

Applying

9. Answers will differ. Suggested Response: City and country life pose very different challenges. If you don't grow up in one, you may never develop the skills it takes to live there successfully.

RESPONDING TO THE SELECTION

Your Response

1. Who do you think "wins" in the rivalry between Da-duh and the narrator? Explain.

Recalling

2. What is the narrator's impression of Da-duh when they first meet?
3. What details in the story reveal the conflict between the narrator's mother and Da-duh? Between the narrator and Da-duh?
4. Which of the narrator's stories has the greatest effect on Da-duh?

Interpreting

5. Why do you think Da-duh is drawn to the narrator rather than to the narrator's sister?
6. What frightens Da-duh about the narrator's stories of New York City?
7. Referring to her grandmother, the narrator states: "Some huge, monolithic shape had imposed itself, it seemed, between her and the land, obstructing her vision." What do you think the narrator means?
8. At the end of the story, why does the narrator paint island scenes, although she lives in a big city?

Applying

9. Why do you think that some people raised in the country cannot adjust to city life, or vice versa?

ANALYZING LITERATURE

Understanding Setting and Conflict

In "To Da-duh, in Memoriam," Paule Marshall uses the differences between two settings—New York City and Barbados—to help develop the conflict between the narrator and her grandmother. For example, after the narrator describes a non-bearing chestnut tree that stands in front of her house in the city, her grandmother responds, "Nothing can bear there."

1. List three examples in which Da-duh and the narrator compete with each other by describing aspects of their homelands.
2. Why do you think Da-duh keeps comparing Barbados with New York City?
3. What details does the writer use in the last paragraph to emphasize conflict through setting?

CRITICAL THINKING AND READING

Understanding Symbolism

A **symbol** is anything that stands for or represents something else. Often an object from nature is used to symbolize an abstract idea or a feeling; for example, the sun can be used to represent knowledge. Writers sometimes use symbolism to help convey concepts, attitudes, and themes. In "To Da-duh, in Memoriam," for example, Marshall uses images of light and darkness to symbolize her ambivalent attitude toward Da-duh and Barbados.

1. How might the Empire State Building be seen as a symbol in the story?
2. What symbolism can you find in the narrator's description of her paintings?
3. What other symbols do you think Marshall uses in the story? Explain.

THINKING AND WRITING

Describing a Setting

In response to her grandmother's description of Barbados, the narrator tells Da-duh about New York City by "building the city out of words." Think of a distinctive place. Briefly describe the setting and tell why it is special. If appropriate, you may wish to include conflicting attributes, as Paule Marshall does in describing Barbados.

LEARNING OPTION

Multicultural Activity. Organize an exhibit on the culture of Barbados or of other Caribbean islands. Displays could range from native foods and crafts to music and history.

To Da-duh, in Memoriam 149

ANSWERS TO ANALYZING LITERATURE

1. Suggested Responses: The narrator describes snow, which Da-duh has never seen. Da-duh describes how sugarcane is turned into sugar. The narrator sings and dances the way they do in New York. Da-duh takes her granddaughter into a gully, thick with tangled foliage.
2. Suggested Response: Barbados is the only place she's ever lived and New York is where her granddaughter lives; both settings are wondrous in their own ways.
3. Answers may differ. Suggested Responses: The palm trees are like *warriors*. The machines downstairs are like *thunder;* they *jar* the floor and *mock* her efforts.

ANSWERS TO CRITICAL THINKING AND READING

1. Suggested Response: The Empire State Building might represent a modern urban way of life—all of New York City, its technology, and Da-duh's inability to imagine it.
2. Suggested Responses: The van Gogh suns may symbolize her knowledge of Barbados. The palm trees might represent Da-duh herself.

3. Suggested Responses: The gully may represent Barbados and tropical beauty, the way that the Empire State Building represents New York and technology. The airplanes may symbolize the violence and intrusion of the high-tech world.

THINKING AND WRITING

Writing Transparency Review descriptive writing techniques by working through the Spatial Order Paragraph Exercise in **Transparencies for Writing.** The graphic organizer Sensory Language Chart will help students to develop sensory details for their writing.

Software If students are working on computers, have them use the *Develop a Paragraph* Activity in the **Writer's Helper** to write their descriptions of settings.

Alternative Assessment *Protocol* Ask your students to assess their own work by responding to the following questions:

What details of this special place do you include?

What conflicting attributes of this place have you included?

What aspect of this assignment did you find most difficult?

What have you learned about writing a description of a place?

You may have your students use the information from their protocols to help them revise their descriptions.

LEARNING OPTION

Perhaps your class could combine with a social studies or foreign language class in such an exhibit. If possible, have someone who has visited Barbados or the West Indies come in to answer questions and tell stories. You could also send students to a local travel agency for information and brochures.

More About the Author As a child at the Laguna Pueblo, Leslie Marmon Silko heard tribal stories from her great-grandmother and great-aunts. She has said that these stories "incorporate you into them. There have to be stories. It's stories that make this a community." Ask students to discuss why these stories might be important for Native Americans.

Literary Focus You might want to review with students the meaning of the word *culture.* Explain to them that it refers to a people's beliefs, rituals, and ways of life. Have students identify important elements of their own culture.

Prereading Focus Before students begin this activity, you may wish to discuss the sorts of clues they will look for in their neighborhood. Are there eating places that reflect cultural influences? Are there places of worship that indicate the religious beliefs of the community? Do the store owners decorate their windows for such holidays as Kwanzaa, Hanuka, Christmas?

Vocabulary Have more advanced students use a thesaurus to find synonyms and antonyms for the vocabulary words. Have less advanced students work in groups of two to practice pronouncing the words and to learn their meanings.

The Man to Send Rain Clouds

Setting and Culture

The **setting** of a story is not only the place and time in which the events occur, but it is also the cultural background against which the action takes place. The customs, ideas, values, and beliefs of the society in which the story occurs provide what might be called the cultural setting. In "The Man to Send Rain Clouds," these aspects of setting form an even more important background than the physical background.

Focus

How can you learn about a group of people from the place where they live? Structures, spaces, and objects all reveal something about the people who make and use them. Review your route to or from school. List the places you pass, and make notes about the roles they play in the culture of your area. What customs, rituals, and attitudes do the places reflect? Then, as you read the following selection, look for details that relate to the beliefs of the Pueblo Indians.

Vocabulary

Knowing the following words will help you as you read "The Man to Send Rain Clouds."

arroyo (ə roi′ ō) *n.:* A dry gully (p. 151)

cloister (klois′ tər) *n.:* A place devoted to religious seclusion (p. 153)

pagans (pā′ gənz) *n.:* People who are not Christians, Muslims, or Jews (p. 154)

perverse (pər vurs′) *adj.:* Persisting in error (p. 154)

Leslie Marmon Silko

(1948–   ) was born in Albuquerque, New Mexico, and raised on the Laguna Pueblo reservation. In works such as *Ceremony* and *Storyteller,* she explores the power of the myths and traditional ritual she learned as a child. Silko has been described as "a child of more than one culture" because she is a descendant of English- and Spanish-speaking settlers as well as of Pueblo Indians. The conflicting demands of different cultures dominate "The Man to Send Rain Clouds."

150   Short Stories

Objectives

1 To recognize a cultural setting
2 To understand cultural conflict
3 To write about cultural practices
4 To express individual interests and abilities through optional activities

Support Material

Teaching Portfolio
Teacher Backup, p. 187
Usage and Mechanics Worksheet, p. 190
Vocabulary Check, p. 191
Analyzing Literature Worksheet, *Recognizing the Cultural Setting,* p. 192
Critical Thinking and Reading Worksheet, *Understanding Cultural Conflict,* p. 193

Selection Test, p. 194
Art Transparency 3: *Arizona Corral,* by Millard Sheets

Prentice Hall Literature Writing Studio

The Man to Send Rain Clouds

Leslie Marmon Silko

They found him under a big cottonwood tree. His Levi jacket and pants were faded light blue so that he had been easy to find. The big cottonwood tree stood apart from a small grove of winterbare cottonwoods which grew in the wide, sandy arroyo. He had been dead for a day or more, and the sheep had wandered and scattered up and down the arroyo. Leon and his brother-in-law, Ken, gathered the sheep and left them in the pen at the sheep camp before they returned to the cottonwood tree. Leon waited under the tree while Ken drove the truck through the deep sand to the edge of the arroyo. He squinted up at the sun and unzipped his jacket—it sure was hot for this time of year. But high and northwest the blue mountains were still in snow. Ken came sliding down the low, crumbling bank about fifty yards down, and he was bringing the red blanket.

Before they wrapped the old man, Leon took a piece of string out of his pocket and tied a small gray feather in the old man's long white hair. Ken gave him the paint. Across the brown wrinkled forehead he drew a streak of white and along the high cheekbones he drew a strip of blue paint. He paused and watched Ken throw pinches of corn meal and pollen into the wind that fluttered the small gray feather. Then Leon painted with yellow under the old man's broad nose, and finally, when he had painted green across the chin, he smiled.

"Send us rain clouds, Grandfather." They laid the bundle in the back of the pickup and covered it with a heavy tarp before they started back to the pueblo.

They turned off the highway onto the sandy pueblo road. Not long after they passed the store and post office they saw Father Paul's car coming toward them. When he recognized their faces he slowed his car and waved for them to stop. The young priest rolled down the car window.

"Did you find old Teofilo?" he asked loudly.

Leon stopped the truck. "Good morning, Father. We were just out to the sheep camp. Everything is O.K. now."

"Thank God for that. Teofilo is a very old man. You really shouldn't allow him to stay at the sheep camp alone."

"No, he won't do that any more now."

"Well, I'm glad you understand. I hope I'll be seeing you at Mass[1] this week—we missed you last Sunday. See if you can get old Teo-

---

1. **mass** (mas): A church service celebrated by Roman Catholics.

The Man to Send Rain Clouds 151

Thematic Focus In "The Man to Send Rain Clouds," the death of an old man causes several other characters to experience a rite of passage. Have students discuss rites of passage that they have experienced as a result of a pivotal event in the life of someone close to them.

Making Connections Another selection that deals with differences between cultures is "Rules of the Game," page 39.

Presentation

Motivation/Prior Knowledge Tell students that Silko once said that she wrote, "because I love the stories, the feelings, the words." Point out to them that the story they are about to read reflects Silko's deep feeling for Native American culture.

Master Teacher Note Use an overhead projector to show students Art Transparency 3, *Arizona Corral*, by Millard Sheets. Have students discuss the feelings that this landscape calls up. Then tell them that the story takes place in a similar environment.

You might also want to point out that the Pueblo Indians, whose beliefs and customs are described in the story, have lived in this region for many hundreds of years. Pueblo Indians have the oldest civilization north of Mexico. When the Spanish first came to America during the sixteenth century, for example, they found Pueblo villages that were already old. With the arrival of the Spanish, many Pueblos converted to Christianity. Tell students that in this story they will see how Native Americans and Christian beliefs coexist.

Purpose-Setting Question How does this story show the clash of Native American and Christian beliefs?

1 Discussion Why do the men take care of the sheep first?

2 Literary Focus What Native American customs are revealed in this passage?

3 Enrichment Tell students that the term *pueblo* refers to a village of Pueblo Indians.

4 Discussion Why does Leon not tell the young priest that Teofilo is dead?

5 Literary Focus Do you think their lack of outward grief may reveal cultural differences? Explain.

6 Literary Focus What Native American customs does this passage describe?

7 Literary Focus Why do you think Louise sprinkled corn meal around the body? Can you think of any customs observed by other groups of people that are similar?

8 Literary Focus How does this request reflect the coexistence of two cultures?

Alternative Assessment To promote active reading, have your students keep a reader's response journal as they read the story. Ask them to focus on the details that reveal the customs and beliefs of Native Americans. Encourage students to respond personally to the story by relating the customs associated with death in their own culture.

Their observations will enable you to assess their understanding of the issues in the story.

filo to come with you." The priest smiled and waved at them as they drove away.

Louise and Teresa were waiting. The table was set for lunch, and the coffee was boiling on the black iron stove. Leon looked at Louise and then at Teresa.

"We found him under a cottonwood tree in the big arroyo near sheep camp. I guess he sat down to rest in the shade and never got up again." Leon walked toward the old man's bed. The red plaid shawl had been shaken and spread carefully over the bed, and a new brown flannel shirt and pair of stiff new Levi's were arranged neatly beside the pillow. Louise held the screen door open while Leon and Ken carried in the red blanket. He looked small and shriveled, and after they dressed him in the new shirt and pants he seemed more shrunken.

It was noontime now because the church bells rang the Angelus.[2] They ate the beans with hot bread, and nobody said anything until after Teresa poured the coffee.

Ken stood up and put on his jacket. "I'll see about the gravediggers. Only the top layer of soil is frozen. I think it can be ready before dark."

Leon nodded his head and finished his coffee. After Ken had been gone for a while, the neighbors and clanspeople came quietly to embrace Teofilo's family and to leave food on the table because the gravediggers would come to eat when they were finished.

The sky in the west was full of pale yellow light. Louise stood outside with her hands in the pockets of Leon's green army jacket that was too big for her. The funeral was over, and the old men had taken their candles and

medicine bags[3] and were gone. She waited until the body was laid into the pickup before she said anything to Leon. She touched his arm, and he noticed that her hands were still dusty from the corn meal that she had sprinkled around the old man. When she spoke, Leon could not hear her.

"What did you say? I didn't hear you."

"I said that I had been thinking about something."

"About what?"

"About the priest sprinkling holy water for Grandpa. So he won't be thirsty."

Leon stared at the new moccasins that Teofilo had made for the ceremonial dances in the summer. They were nearly hidden by the red blanket. It was getting colder, and the wind pushed gray dust down the narrow pueblo road. The sun was approaching the long mesa where it disappeared during the winter. Louise stood there shivering and watching his face. Then he zipped up his jacket and opened the truck door. "I'll see if he's there."

Ken stopped the pickup at the church, and Leon got out; and then Ken drove down the hill to the graveyard where people were waiting. Leon knocked at the old carved door with its symbols of the Lamb.[4] While he waited he looked up at the twin bells from the king of Spain with the last sunlight pouring around them in their tower.

The priest opened the door and smiled when he saw who it was. "Come in! What brings you here this evening?"

The priest walked toward the kitchen, and Leon stood with his cap in his hand, playing with the earflaps and examining the

---

2. **Angelus** (an′ ja ləs): A bell rung at morning, noon, and evening to announce a prayer.

3. **medicine bags:** Bags containing objects that were thought to have special powers.
4. **the Lamb:** Jesus Christ, as the sacrificial Lamb of God.

Multicultural Focus The Pueblo Indians, whose beliefs and customs are described in this story, have lived in the southwestern United States for nearly 3,000 years. In fact, they have the oldest civilization north of Mexico. Their original name was the Anasazi, which means "ancient ones" in the language of their neighbors, the Navajo. Their culture reached its height by 1000 A.D., when they had build vast complexes of cliff dwellings and structures that had as many as a thousand rooms. They had also built a fine system of roads and irrigation, and understood much about astronomy. When the Spanish came to the area in the 1500's, they were so impressed by the Anasazi buildings that they called their inhabitants the "pueblo" people, using the Spanish word for town.

Have students read about the history of the Pueblo people, their first encounters with the Spanish, and their status in today's society. Ask individual students to do additional research on different aspects of the Pueblo culture such as religion, government, food, clothing, and so on. Have them present their findings to the class in brief oral reports.

FEAST DAY, SAN JUAN PUEBLO, 1921
William Penhallow Henderson
National Museum of American Art
Smithsonian Institution

9 living room—the brown sofa, the green armchair, and the brass lamp that hung down from the ceiling by links of chain. The priest dragged a chair out of the kitchen and offered it to Leon.

"No thank you, Father. I only came to ask you if you would bring your holy water to the graveyard."

The priest turned away from Leon and looked out the window at the patio full of shadows and the dining-room windows of the nuns' cloister across the patio. The curtains were heavy, and the light from within faintly penetrated; it was impossible to see the nuns inside eating supper. "Why didn't you tell me he was dead? I could have brought the Last Rites[5] anyway." 10

---

5. the Last Rites: A religious ceremony for a dying person or for someone who has just died.

The Man to Send Rain Clouds   153

Humanities Note

Fine Art, *Feast Day, San Juan Pueblo,* 1921, by William Penhallon Henderson. After Henderson (1877–1943), who was an easterner, settled in Santa Fe, he quickly adapted to the dramatic landscape and was fascinated by the Spanish and Indian cultures. He traveled to Indian Pueblos by horseback, carefully memorizing the color and movement of the rituals and dances and sketching them when he returned home. Whether painting with soft pastels or bold oils, he caught the spirit and air of his adopted home. Discuss with the students the texture and feeling of this work. Have them identify the people that are gathered, their expressions, the church, and the hills in the background.

1. What seems to be the mood of the setting?
2. Do you believe that this picture is an appropriate accompaniment to the story? Why or why not?

9 **Discussion** How does Leon seem to feel about making his request? Do you think he would have made this request on his own? Why or why not?

10 **Reading Strategy** How do you think Father Paul will respond to Leon's request?

11 Discussion Why does Leon believe that last rites were not necessary?

12 Literary Focus Have students compare Leon's reasons for wanting the father to sprinkle holy water and Father Paul's reasons for doing so. What does this indicate about the conflict between Christian and Native American traditions?

13 Discussion Why do you think the priest has decided to sprinkle holy water on the grave?

14 Literary Focus The headlights on the highway emphasize that this story takes place in relatively modern times. Why is this detail important?

Reader's Response What did you find most interesting about Native American beliefs in this story? Most surprising? Explain.

Thematic Response Leon and Ken, though following their culture and tradition, persuade the priest to add part of his own ritual to Teofilo's burial. Which element of this rite of passage was most meaningful to Teofilo's family?

Leon smiled. "It wasn't necessary, Father."

The priest stared down at his scuffed brown loafers and the worn hem of his cassock. "For a Christian burial it was necessary."

His voice was distant, and Leon thought that his blue eyes looked tired.

"It's O.K. Father, we just want him to have plenty of water."

The priest sank down into the green chair and picked up a glossy missionary magazine. He turned the colored pages full of lepers and pagans without looking at them.

"You know I can't do that, Leon. There should have been the Last Rites and a funeral Mass at the very least."

Leon put on his green cap and pulled the flaps down over his ears. "It's getting late, Father. I've got to go."

When Leon opened the door Father Paul stood up and said, "Wait." He left the room and came back wearing a long brown overcoat. He followed Leon out the door and across the dim churchyard to the adobe steps in front of the church. They both stooped to fit through the low adobe entrance. And when they started down the hill to the graveyard only half of the sun was visible above the mesa.

The priest approached the grave slowly, wondering how they had managed to dig into the frozen ground; and then he remembered that this was New Mexico, and saw the pile of cold loose sand beside the hole. The people stood close to each other with little clouds of steam puffing from their faces. The priest looked at them and saw a pile of jackets, gloves, and scarves in the yellow, dry tumbleweeds that grew in the graveyard. He looked at the red blanket, not sure that Teofilo was so small, wondering if it wasn't some perverse Indian trick—something they did in March to ensure a good harvest—wondering

if maybe old Teofilo was actually at sheep camp corraling the sheep for the night. But there he was, facing into a cold dry wind and squinting at the last sunlight, ready to bury a red wool blanket while the faces of his parishioners were in shadow with the last warmth of the sun on their backs.

His fingers were stiff, and it took him a long time to twist the lid off the holy water. Drops of water fell on the red blanket and soaked into dark icy spots. He sprinkled the grave and the water disappeared almost before it touched the dim, cold sand; it reminded him of something—he tried to remember what it was, because he thought if he could remember he might understand this. He sprinkled more water; he shook the container until it was empty, and the water fell through the light from sundown like August rain that fell while the sun was still shining, almost evaporating before it touched the wilted squash flowers.

The wind pulled at the priest's brown Franciscan robe[6] and swirled away the corn meal and pollen that had been sprinkled on the blanket. They lowered the bundle into the ground, and they didn't bother to untie the stiff pieces of new rope that were tied around the ends of the blanket. The sun was gone, and over on the highway the eastbound lane was full of headlights. The priest walked away slowly. Leon watched him climb the hill, and when he had disappeared within the tall, thick walls, Leon turned to look up at the high blue mountains in the deep snow that reflected a faint red light from the west. He felt good because it was finished, and he was happy about the sprinkling of the holy water; now the old man could send them big thunderclouds for sure.

---

6. **Franciscan** (fran sis′ kən) **robe:** The robe worn by a member of the Franciscan religious order, founded in 1209 by Saint Francis of Assisi.

Closure and Extension

ANSWERS TO RESPONDING TO THE SELECTION
Your Response

1. Discuss with students the idea that the priest was "bending the rules" by participating in what was, for him, an unorthodox rite. Suggest that both the young men

and Father Paul demonstrated respect for one another's beliefs.

Recalling

2. They find the body of the old man.
3. Father Paul asks them if they found Teofilo and they say yes, but do not tell him that Teofilo is dead.
4. Louise asks Leon to have Father Paul come and sprinkle holy water on the body.

RESPONDING TO THE SELECTION

Your Response

1. Why do you think that Father Paul decides to honor Leon's request?

Recalling

2. What do Leon and Ken find at the opening of the story?
3. Explain what happens when Leon and Ken meet Father Paul on the highway.
4. Why does Leon ask Father Paul for holy water?

Interpreting

5. Why doesn't Leon tell Father Paul about Teofilo's death?
6. Why is Father Paul upset about the burial ceremony?
7. What insight into the Pueblo people does Father Paul gain during the ceremony?

Applying

8. If you were Father Paul, what would you have done in response to Leon's request?

ANALYZING LITERATURE

Recognizing the Cultural Setting

The customs and cultural attitudes of the society in which a story takes place form a part of its setting. There are two cultures at play in "The Man to Send Rain Clouds," both of whose customs and beliefs affect the story. For example, the rituals related to death are important aspects of the story's cultural setting.

1. Point out two details that illustrate the Pueblo Indian customs or beliefs.
2. Point out three details that give evidence of the Christian rituals or beliefs.

CRITICAL THINKING AND READING

Understanding Cultural Conflict

When two cultures meet, the different customs and values of the groups can lead to conflict. For example, the Pueblo Indians in "The Man to Send Rain Clouds" have become members of Father Paul's church but cling to their Indian beliefs and customs.

Describe a situation you have read about or know about personally in which two cultures have clashed. What customs, values, or ways of behaving were involved in the clash? How did the conflict conclude?

THINKING AND WRITING

Writing About Cultural Practices

Choose a holiday or another celebration that people in your community observe. You might select Independence Day or a wedding, for example. Describe this event in an article for publication in a magazine from a foreign country. Include details to help your readers understand your customs and culture. When you revise your article, make clear the significance of the details you have described.

LEARNING OPTIONS

1. **Cross-curricular Connection.** Find out more about other rituals, arts, beliefs, or customs of the Pueblo Indians; for example, the use of the medicine bag, as mentioned in the story.
2. **Multicultural Activity.** Imagine that you are Father Paul writing a letter to your bishop about your work with the local Native Americans. Using the story as a guide, address the cultural differences you have encountered and how you have dealt with them.

The Man to Send Rain Clouds 155

More About the Author You might tell students that Arthur C. Clarke writes articles about science as well. A number of years ago, he wrote an article predicting the development of communications satelites. Ask students what breakthroughs in technology they think will occur in the next ten years.

Literary Focus Point out to students that even though writers like Clarke often set their stories in the future, they include details that will seem realistic to readers.

Prereading Focus You might wish to stimulate the students' thinking by pointing out that people in a protected space colony would not have the same relationship with nature as that enjoyed by people on Earth. Also remind students that space vessels have no room for nonessential items. Tell them to keep this fact in mind as they consider what they would miss.

Vocabulary Have less advanced students write a sentence for each word. Then have students read each of their sentences to a partner, leaving a blank for the word. The partner should try to identify the missing word by referring to the vocabulary list.

Electronic Handbook You might want students to use the Language Master 6000 to hear the pronunciation of *crepitation* and *benison.*

Spelling Tip Write the word *phosphorescence* on the board. Remind students that the sound /f/ can be spelled by the letters *ph.*

GUIDE FOR READING

Arthur C. Clarke

(1917–   ), born in Somerset, England, has been fascinated with science fiction and science since childhood. While in the Air Force during World War II, he wrote and published his first science-fiction stories. Since then, he has written many stories. His most famous work is a collaboration with Stanley Kubrick on the screenplay for *2001: A Space Odyssey,* a film based on his story "The Sentinel." "'If I Forget Thee, Oh Earth . . . ,'" like much science fiction, deals with the future consequences of today's technological advances.

"If I Forget Thee, Oh Earth . . ."

Setting in Science Fiction

The **setting** of science-fiction stories is usually the future. Using ideas of science or space travel, science-fiction writers may take you to places that do not now exist or that are currently beyond reach. For example, "'If I Forget Thee, Oh Earth . . . ,'" opens in a space colony. When a setting like this one is part of a story, you might ask yourself what bearing the setting has on the plot.

Focus

Much science fiction deals with life in outer space. The following selection describes what it would be like to live in a space colony protected from the vacuum outside. Imagine that you are going to participate in an experiment that involves living in outer space for several months. What would you miss most about Earth? With a small group of classmates, discuss this situation and write down your ideas. Then compare your responses with the memories of life on Earth as described in the story.

Vocabulary

Knowing the following words will help you as you read "'If I Forget Thee, Oh Earth . . .'"

crepitation (krep′ ə tā shən) *n.*: A crackling sound (p. 159)

benison (ben′ ə zən) *n.*: A blessing (p. 160)

exile (eg′ zīl) *n.*: Enforced removal from one's native land (p. 160)

phosphorescence (fäs′ fə res′ 'ns) *n.*: Emission of light resulting from exposure to radiation (p. 160)

pyre (pīr) *n.*: A pile of wood on which a body is burned at a funeral (p. 160)

benison (ben′ ə zən) *n.*: A blessing (p. 160)

perennial (pə ren′ ē əl) *adj.*: Lasting through the year or for a long time (p. 160)

pilgrimage (pil′ grəm ij) *n.*: A journey to a sacred place or shrine; a special trip to a place of personal significance (p. 160)

156   Short Stories

Objectives

1 To respond to setting in science fiction
2 To understand plausibility
3 To write a science-fiction story
4 To express individual interests and abilities through an optional activity

Support Material

Teaching Portfolio
Teacher Backup, p. 197
Grammar in Action Worksheet, *Using Adjective Clauses,* p. 201
Usage and Mechanics Worksheet, p. 203
Vocabulary Check, p. 204
Analyzing Literature Worksheet, *Responding to Setting in Science Fiction,* p. 206

Language Worksheet, *Using Vivid Words,* p. 207
Selection Test, p. 208

Prentice Hall Literature Writing Studio

"If I Forget Thee, Oh Earth . . ."

Arthur C. Clarke

When Marvin was ten years old, his father took him through the long, echoing corridors that led up through Administration and Power, until at last they came to the uppermost levels of all and were among the swiftly growing vegetation of the Farmlands. Marvin liked it here: it was fun watching the great, slender plants creeping with almost visible eagerness toward the sunlight as it filtered down through the plastic domes to meet them. The smell of life was everywhere, awakening inexpressible longings in his heart: no longer was he breathing the dry, cool air of the residential levels, purged of all smells but the faint tang of ozone.[1] He wished he could stay here for a little while, but Father would not let him. They went onward until they had reached the entrance to the Observatory, which he had never visited: but they did not stop, and Marvin knew with a sense of rising excitement that there could be only one goal left. For the first time in his life, he was going Outside.

There were a dozen of the surface vehicles, with their wide balloon tires and pressurized cabins, in the great servicing chamber. His father must have been expected, for they were led at once to the little scout car waiting by the huge circular door

of the airlock. Tense with expectancy, Marvin settled himself down in the cramped cabin while his father started the motor and checked the controls. The inner door of the lock slid open and then closed behind them: he heard the roar of the great air pumps fade slowly away as the pressure dropped to zero. Then the "Vacuum" sign flashed on, the outer door parted, and before Marvin lay the land which he had never yet entered.

He had seen it in photographs, of course: he had watched it imaged on television screens a hundred times. But now it was lying all around him, burning beneath the fierce sun that crawled so slowly across the jet-black sky. He stared into the west, away from the blinding splendor of the sun—and there were the stars, as he had been told but had never quite believed. He gazed at them for a long time, marveling that anything could be so bright and yet so tiny. They were intense unscintillating points, and suddenly he remembered a rhyme he had once read in one of his father's books:

> Twinkle, twinkle, little star,
> How I wonder what you are.

Well, *he* knew what the stars were. Whoever asked that question must have been very stupid. And what did they mean by

---

1. **ozone** (ō' zōn) n.: A form of oxygen with a sharp odor.

4 Reading Strategy Where do you think Marvin's father is taking him?

"twinkle"? You could see at a glance that all the stars shone with the same steady, unwavering light. He abandoned the puzzle and turned his attention to the landscape around him.

4 | They were racing across a level plain at almost a hundred miles an hour, the great balloon tires sending up little spurts of dust behind them. There was no sign of the Colony: in the few minutes while he had been gazing at the stars, its domes and radio towers had fallen below the horizon. Yet there were other indications of man's presence, for about a mile ahead Marvin could see the curiously shaped structures clustering round the head of a mine. Now and then a puff of

MULTICULTURAL CONNECTION

World Ecology

As you read this selection, keep in mind the ecological problems that endanger our planet.

Economic considerations. Economic considerations are the biggest obstacles keeping the peoples of the world from working together to tackle ecological problems. In every nation, governments have been reluctant to shut down polluting factories for fear of putting too many citizens out of work.

In the United States, experts believe that cutting back on auto use would significantly improve the environment. Major cutbacks, however, would be economically painful for millions of people who depend on cars for a living. In India overgrazing by cattle leads to sickly herds and soil erosion; nevertheless, poor farmers need to keep cows. Even a scrawny bull can pull plows, produce manure for fertilizer and fuel, and, when it dies, provide leather to be sold for cash.

In general, residents of Europe, North America, and Japan resist making changes that might lower their high standard of living. Few want to give up the cars, refrigerators, and climate-controlled malls that consume a great deal of energy and natural resources. At the same time, the peoples of the poorer nations see no reason why they should not seek the same luxuries, or why they should not cut down a jungle, for example, to obtain lumber or minerals.

Overpopulation. Economic factors might not be so ecologically damaging were it not for overpopulation. Projections show that the world's five billion people will double by the middle of the next century, requiring that even more land be cleared for farms, roads, and urban sprawl.

Hope for the future. As bleak as it may seem, the future is by no means lost. Already, several European countries are imposing carbon taxes on polluters, and international lending agencies are taking the environment into account when they finance projects. Also, businesses are seeking profits from environment-friendly goods like biodegradable plastic, windmills, and electric cars. Finally, scientists are devising ways to use solar energy as a source of power.

Suggesting Solutions

Find articles in newspapers and magazines about environmental problems in different parts of the world. For each article, write a few lines suggesting how the problem discussed in the article may be solved.

Grammar in Action

An **adjective clause** is a subordinate clause that modifies a noun or pronoun by telling what kind or which one. It begins with a relative pronoun or relative adverb, includes a subject and verb, and may have complements and modifiers:

The book *that is bound in red leather* belongs to me.

Notice that the clause is next to the noun it modifies, *book.* The relative pronoun *that* introduces the clause and is its subject. The verb, *is bound,* is modified by *in red leather,* a prepositional phrase.

Writers use adjective clauses to add detail to their descriptions. In the following sentences, Arthur Clarke uses adjective clauses for this purpose:

The ground fell sharply away beneath them in a dizzying slope *whose lower stretches were lost in shadow.*
For hours they drove through valleys and past the foot of mountains *whose peaks seemed to comb the stars. . . .*

vapor would emerge from a squat smoke-stack and would instantly disperse.

They were past the mine in a moment: Father was driving with a reckless and exhilarating skill as if—it was a strange thought to come into a child's mind—he were trying to escape from something. In a few minutes they had reached the edge of the plateau on which the Colony had been built. The ground fell sharply away beneath them in a dizzying slope whose lower stretches were lost in shadow. Ahead, as far as the eye could reach, was a jumbled wasteland of craters, mountain ranges, and ravines. The crests of the mountains, catching the low sun, burned like islands of fire in a sea of darkness: and above them the stars still shone as steadfastly as ever.

There could be no way forward—yet there was. Marvin clenched his fists as the car edged over the slope and started the long descent. Then he saw the barely visible track leading down the mountainside, and relaxed a little. Other men, it seemed, had gone this way before.

Night fell with a shocking abruptness as they crossed the shadow line and the sun dropped below the crest of the plateau. The twin searchlights sprang into life, casting blue-white bands on the rocks ahead, so that there was scarcely need to check their speed. For hours they drove through valleys and past the foot of mountains whose peaks seemed to comb the stars, and sometimes they emerged for a moment into the sunlight as they climbed over higher ground.

And now on the right was a wrinkled, dusty plain, and on the left, its ramparts and terraces rising mile after mile into the sky, was a wall of mountains that marched into the distance until its peaks sank from sight below the rim of the world. There was no sign that men had ever explored this land, but once they passed the skeleton of a crashed rocket, and beside it a stone cairn[2] surmounted by a metal cross.

It seemed to Marvin that the mountains stretched on forever: but at last, many hours later, the range ended in a towering, precipitous headland[3] that rose steeply from a cluster of little hills. They drove down into a shallow valley that curved in a great arc toward the far side of the mountains: and as they did so, Marvin slowly realized that something very strange was happening in the land ahead.

The sun was now low behind the hills on the right: the valley before them should be in total darkness. Yet it was awash with a cold white radiance that came spilling over the crags beneath which they were driving. Then, suddenly, they were out in the open plain, and the source of the light lay before them in all its glory.

It was very quiet in the little cabin now that the motors had stopped. The only sound was the faint whisper of the oxygen feed and an occasional metallic crepitation as the outer walls of the vehicle radiated away their heat. For no warmth at all came from the great silver crescent that floated low above the far horizon and flooded all this land with pearly light. It was so brilliant that minutes passed before Marvin could accept its challenge and look steadfastly into its glare, but at last he could discern the outlines of continents, the hazy border of the atmosphere, and the white islands of cloud. And even at this distance, he could see the glitter of sunlight on the polar ice.

It was beautiful, and it called to his heart across the abyss of space. There in that shining crescent were all the wonders that

---

2. **cairn** (kern) *n.*: A pile of stones left as a monument.
3. **precipitous headland:** Steep cliff.

5 Critical Thinking and Reading
On what planet or satellite are they?

6 Discussion How does this description heighten the suspense?

. . . the range ended in a towering, precipitous headland *that rose steeply from a cluster of little hills.*
They drove down into a shallow valley *that curved in a great arc toward the far side of the mountains.* . . .

Student Activity 1. Analyze the four adjective clauses in Clarke's description of the lunar landscape. Find the relative pronoun or relative adverb, the subject and verb, and any modifiers or complements in each. Then decide which noun or pronoun each adjective clause modifies.

Student Activity 2. Using Clarke's sentences as models, write your own description of an unusual landscape. You may use other relative pronouns *(which, who, whom),* or relative adverbs *(before, since, when, where, why)* to introduce your adjective clauses.

Electronic Handbook Before having students complete the Grammar in Action activities, you may wish them to review adjectives and clauses. If students have access to the Language Master 6000, have them enter the access words *adjective* or *clause* and press the GRAMMAR key to obtain information on these topics.

7 Discussion At what planet are they looking?

8 Reading Strategy Ask students to summarize the story that Marvin's father tells him.

9 Discussion Why will Marvin someday bring his son to the same place and tell him the same story that his father told him?

Reader's Response What do you think the future will be like?

Thematic Response Marvin's venture into the unknown gave him insight into his father's reasons for the pilgrimage. What emotions do you think Marvin was feeling as he went to rejoin his people in "their long exile"?

7 he had never known—the hues of sunset skies, the moaning of the sea on pebbled shores, the patter of falling rain, the unhurried benison of snow. These and a thousand others should have been his rightful heritage, but he knew them only from the books and ancient records, and the thought filled him with the anguish of exile.

Why could they not return? It seemed so peaceful beneath those lines of marching cloud. Then Marvin, his eyes no longer blinded by the glare, saw that the portion of the disk that should have been in darkness was gleaming faintly with an evil phosphorescence: and he remembered. He was looking upon the funeral pyre of a world—upon the radioactive aftermath of Armageddon.[4] Across a quarter of a million miles of space, the glow of dying atoms was still visible, a perennial reminder of the ruinous past. It would be centuries yet before that deadly glow died from the rocks and life could return again to fill that silent, empty world.

8 And now Father began to speak, telling Marvin the story which until this moment had meant no more to him than the fairy tales he had once been told. There were many things he could not understand: it was impossible for him to picture the glowing, multicolored pattern of life on the planet he had never seen. Nor could he comprehend the forces that had destroyed it in the end, leaving the Colony, preserved by its isolation, as the sole survivor. Yet he could share the agony of those final days, when the Colony had learned at last that never again would the supply ships come flaming down through the stars with gifts from home. One

---

4. Armageddon (är' mə ged' 'n): In the Bible, the place where the final battle between good and evil was to be fought.

---

by one the radio stations had ceased to call: on the shadowed globe the lights of the cities had dimmed and died, and they were alone at last, as no men had ever been alone before, carrying in their hands the future of the race.

Then had followed the years of despair, and the long-drawn battle for survival in their fierce and hostile world. That battle had been won, though barely: this little oasis of life was safe against the worst that Nature could do. But unless there was a goal, a future toward which it could work, the Colony would lose the will to live, and neither machines nor skill nor science could save it then.

So, at last, Marvin understood the purpose of this pilgrimage. He would never walk beside the rivers of that lost and legendary world, or listen to the thunder raging above its softly rounded hills. Yet one day—how far ahead?—his children's children would return to claim their heritage. The winds and the rains would scour the poisons from the burning lands and carry them to the sea, and in the depths of the sea they would waste their venom until they could harm no living things. Then the great ships that were still waiting here on the silent, dusty plains could lift once more into space, along the road that led to home.

9 That was the dream: and one day, Marvin knew with a sudden flash of insight, he would pass it on to his own son, here at this same spot with the mountains behind him and the silver light from the sky streaming into his face.

He did not look back as they began the homeward journey. He could not bear to see the cold glory of the crescent Earth fade from the rocks around him, as he went to rejoin his people in their long exile.

"If I Forget Thee, Oh Earth . . ." 161

Closure and Extension

(Questions begin on p. 162.)

ANSWERS TO RESPONDING TO THE SELECTION
Your Response

1. Encourage students to extend their responses by comparing Clarke's vision of the future with their own.

Recalling

2. Marvin's father takes him from the moon colony and across the lunar landscape in a surface vehicle. After many hours they reach a place where they can view Earth from the moon. There Marvin's father tells him about the end of life on Earth.
3. Marvin discovers that his homeland, Earth, has been made uninhabitable by nuclear pollution.
4. They share a dream that one day Marvin's children's children will return to a cleansed Earth to reclaim their heritage.

Interpreting

5. Suggested Response: Marvin's father had waited to take him Outside until Marvin was old enough to fully understand and share his dream of humans returning to Earth.
6. Suggested Response: The people of the colony cannot return to Earth because no one can live in the atmosphere poisoned by radioactivity.
7. Suggested Response: His father seems to regard the journey almost as a sacred rite. He wants to pass on to his son a love of Earth and a wish to have their descendants live there again.
8. Suggested Response: The "anguish of exile" refers to the pain of not being able to return to one's home.
9. Suggested Response: A pilgrimage is a journey to a holy place. Marvin and his father travel to a place where they can view their homeland. The goal of returning there seems almost sacred to Marvin's father.

Applying

10. Suggested Response: Marvin's father thinks that this goal gives life in the Colony a meaning and higher purpose.

11. Answers will differ. Most students will respond that they would pass on the story and sense of mission to their child.

ANSWERS TO ANALYZING LITERATURE

1. Suggested Response: The colony is located on the moon. They drive through a lunar landscape. The author also states that Earth is a quarter of a million miles away—the distance from Earth to the moon.

2. Suggested Response: Marvin sees that the valley ahead, which should have been dark, is "awash with a cold white radiance." Then he sees a "great silver crescent that floated low above the far horizon."

3. Answers will differ. Most students will respond that people in the colony do not venture out very much. Earth is seen and remembered as a place of wonder where people can experience the miracles of nature.

ANSWERS TO CRITICAL THINKING AND READING

1. Suggested Response: Men have already been to the moon, and it is possible for them to land there and return to Earth. Lunar craft have been developed to travel over the moon's landscape. Colonies may be established on the moon in the next century.

2. Suggested Response: Current knowledge of growing food in protected environments could lead to the type of agriculture described in the moon colony. Current nuclear technology makes it possible to destroy life on Earth.

3. Answers will differ. Students may respond that those who have seen films of the moon landings would recognize the lunar landscape. Also, astronauts have taken pictures of the Earth from outer space.

RESPONDING TO THE SELECTION

Your Response

1. Do you think that Clarke's vision of life in the future is believable? Explain.

Recalling

2. Describe the journey Marvin's father takes him on when he is ten years old.
3. What does Marvin discover on the journey?
4. What is the dream that Marvin and his father share?

Interpreting

5. Why had Marvin never been Outside before?
6. Why are the people of the Colony unable to return to Earth?
7. How does Marvin's father feel about the journey?
8. What is meant by the phrase "the anguish of exile" (page 160)?
9. Why does the author use the word *pilgrimage* to describe Marvin's journey?

Applying

10. How do you think the dream of returning to Earth affects everyday life in the Colony?
11. Imagine that you are Marvin. You are now grown up and have a ten-year-old child. What will you tell your child?

ANALYZING LITERATURE

Responding to Setting in Science Fiction

The **setting** of science-fiction stories is usually the future, a future affected by developments in science and technology. Scientific developments make the setting of "'If I Forget Thee, Oh Earth . . .'" both possible and necessary.

1. Where is the Colony located? Give clues from the story to support your answer.
2. "Marvin slowly realized that something very strange was happening in the land ahead." Identify two descriptions that contribute to Marvin's awareness that there is something strange about the land ahead.

---

3. Contrast life in the Colony with the vision and memory of life on Earth.

CRITICAL THINKING AND READING

Understanding Plausibility

Although the setting of "'If I Forget Thee, Oh Earth . . .'" does not exist in reality, Clarke describes it with enough familiar details to make it seem plausible, that is, true or likely while you are reading about it, and perhaps at some actual time in the future. Such details make this imagined setting of the future real to readers.

1. What aspects of the setting of "'If I Forget Thee, Oh Earth . . .'" are based on real or possible scientific developments?
2. What current scientific knowledge could lead to the future Clarke imagines?
3. What aspects of the setting would be entirely familiar to somebody living today?
4. Despite realistic details, why is the story still outside the realm of reality?
5. If Arthur C. Clarke had lived one hundred years ago and written "'If I Forget Thee, Oh Earth . . .'" then, would the details of the story's setting be considered largely realistic or largely fantastic? Explain.

THINKING AND WRITING

Writing Science Fiction

Write your own science-fiction story. Brainstorm with your classmates about what some recent scientific developments you have read or heard about might lead to. Build the plot of your story around these consequences. Revise your story, adding realistic details of setting that your readers will be able to relate to.

LEARNING OPTION

Art. Create a model space colony like the one depicted in the story. You may wish to use futuristic illustrations to help you imagine what such an environment might be like.

---

4. Suggested Response: The story remains outside the realm of reality because we do not have the technology to establish a permanent colony on the moon.

5. Suggested Response: One hundred years ago this story would have seemed fantastic because no one had escaped Earth's gravitational pull and journeyed in space. Also, the destruction of life on Earth would have been almost inconceivable.

THINKING AND WRITING

Writing Transparency Students find models helpful when creating their own stories. You might want to show them Model 3: Short Story in the **Transparencies for Writing** before they begin this activity.

LEARNING OPTION

This activity will appeal to kinesthetic learners. You might wish to extend the activity for visual learners by having students write about life in their colony.

Theme

MEN EXIST FOR THE SAKE OF ONE ANOTHER. TEACH THEM THEN OR BEAR WITH THEM, 1984
Jacob Lawrence
National Museum of American Art, Washington, D.C.

Humanities Note

Fine art, *Men Exist For The Sake of One Another, Teach Them Then or Bear With Them,* by Jacob Lawrence.

The African American painter and educator Jacob Armstead Lawrence was born in Atlantic City, New Jersey in 1917. He grew up in Harlem (New York City) during the Great Depression where he took advantage of art lessons sponsored by the Works Progress Administration. Lawrence later won a scholarship to attend the American Artists School. His paintings of scenes from African American experience and history are often portrayed in serial form. Until his retirement in 1987, Jacob Lawrence was a full professor at the School of Art, University of Washington, and served for six years as commissioner of the National Council of the Arts.

Men Exist For The Sake of One Another, Teach Them Then or Bear With Them is painted in Jacob Lawrence's bold, expressive style. The deliberate reduction of the figures to flat patterns of color gives the painting a primitive strength. The distortions of the head size and hands on the figures gives them an exaggerated importance. All of the paintings of Jacob Lawrence are strongly narrative. The story told by this painting reflects his unceasing appeal to the conscience of all people to enhance the human condition. (See the essay "Jacob Lawrence: American Painter" on page 397.)

1. What message does this painting communicate?
2. How does this artist's attempt to convey a theme compare to a writer's in a short story?

Preparation

More About the Author After studying law briefly at the National University of Colombia, Gabriel García Márquez worked in several Colombian cities as a journalist, in Europe as a correspondent for a Colombian newspaper, and in New York City for a Cuban news agency. Before publishing his fiction, he supplemented his income by writing film scripts.

Ask students how they think that García Márquez's legal and journalistic training might have contributed to his way of seeing and describing his world.

Literary Focus To help students understand the concept of theme, ask them to consider what larger meaning lies beyond the simple events of a well-known fairy tale or myth. Explain that writers often use events in the lives of characters to represent a truth about the larger world.

Prereading Focus Discuss with students the human tendency to make facts fit their preconceptions. Ask if their reaction to the situation in this activity would be disbelief. Discuss whether fear of the unknown would make them hostile or curious.

Teaching to the Ability Levels Point out to less advanced students that theme is not what happens in the story, although theme may be revealed by the action. Emphasize that what happens to the characters in a short story has significance that results in the theme.

Vocabulary Because these are difficult words, you may wish to put these words and others in the selection on flash cards. Have pairs of students periodically test each other on the words.

GUIDE FOR READING

Gabriel García Márquez

(1928–   ) was born in Aracataca, Colombia, and now lives in Mexico City. Growing up in a land of sharp contrasts, he saw hunger side by side with great wealth, and everyday people cohabit a land of strange and unusual creatures. He was awarded the Nobel Prize for Literature in 1982 for his novel *One Hundred Years of Solitude.* "A Very Old Man with Enormous Wings," from his short story collection *Leaf Storm,* shows a deep understanding of the magical reality of the people of his native land.

A Very Old Man with Enormous Wings

Theme

The **Theme** of a story is the general idea or insight into life that the story presents. To understand the theme of a story, it is sometimes necessary to understand the literary style of the piece. Magical realism—popular among recent Latin American writers—reveals the mysterious and miraculous elements that are hidden in everyday life. In this story, the theme, or the realization about life, stems from the fusion of a fantastic event—in this case, an angel's appearance—with the reality of the characters' everyday lives.

Focus

In this selection, an old man with enormous wings inexplicably appears in the home of an unsuspecting couple, upsetting their lives. Imagine that an alien creature showed up in your living room. How would you respond? Would you try to find out what the creature was doing in your home? Would you tell yourself you were seeing things and dismiss the creature as a daydream? Talk with your classmates about what you would do in such a situation, and make a collective list of your ideas. As you read the story, notice the ways in which the characters respond to the old man. Compare their responses to the ones you have listed.

Vocabulary

Knowing the following words will help you as you read "A Very Old Man with Enormous Wings."

celestial (sə les′ chəl) *adj.*: Of heaven; divine (p. 165)

magnanimous (mag nan′ ə məs) *adj.*: Noble in mind; high-souled, especially in overlooking injury or insult (p. 167)

impertinences (im pʉrt′ 'n əns əs) *n.*: Examples of insolence or lack of respect (p. 168)

terrestrial (tə res′ trē əl) *adj.*: Of this world; earthly (p. 168)

prudence (proōd′ 'ns) *n.*: Practical, sound judgment (p. 168)

proliferated (prō lif′ ər āt′ id) *v.*: Grew rapidly (p. 169)

providential (präv′ ə den′ shəl) *adj.*: As if decreed by God (p. 169)

Objectives

1 To recognize possible themes in a short story
2 To identify multiple interpretations of an event
3 To write a story from a different perspective
4 To express individual interests and abilities through optional activities

Support Material

Teaching Portfolio
Teacher Backup, p. 211
Grammar in Action Worksheets, *Illustrating and Giving Examples,* p. 215; *Using Different Sentence Openers,* p. 217
Usage and Mechanics Worksheet, p. 219
Vocabulary Check, p. 220
Analyzing Literature Worksheet,

Understanding Theme, p. 221
Language Worksheet, *Using Context Clues,* p. 222
Selection Test, p. 223

Listening to Literature
"A Very Old Man with Enormous Wings"

Prentice Hall Literature Writing Studio

A Very Old Man with Enormous Wings

A Tale for Children

Gabriel García Márquez

On the third day of rain they had killed so many crabs inside the house that Pelayo had to cross his drenched courtyard and throw them into the sea, because the newborn child had a temperature all night and they thought it was due to the stench. The world had been sad since Tuesday. Sea and sky were a single ash-gray thing and the sands of the beach, which on March nights glimmered like powdered light, had become a stew of mud and rotten shellfish. The light was so weak at noon that when Pelayo was coming back to the house after throwing away the crabs, it was hard for him to see what it was that was moving and groaning in the rear of the courtyard. He had to go very close to see that it was an old man, a very old man, lying face down in the mud, who, in spite of his tremendous efforts, couldn't get up, impeded by his enormous wings.

Frightened by that nightmare, Pelayo ran to get Elisenda, his wife, who was putting compresses on the sick child, and he took her to the rear of the courtyard. They both looked at the fallen body with mute stupor. He was dressed like a ragpicker. There were only a few faded hairs left on his bald skull and very few teeth in his mouth, and his pitiful condition of a drenched great-grandfather had taken away any sense of grandeur he might have had. His huge buzzard wings, dirty and half-plucked, were forever entangled in the mud. They looked at him so long and so closely that Pelayo and Elisenda very soon overcame their surprise and in the end found him familiar. Then they dared speak to him, and he answered in an incomprehensible dialect with a strong sailor's voice. That was how they skipped over the inconvenience of the wings and quite intelligently concluded that he was a lonely castaway from some foreign ship wrecked by the storm. And yet, they called in a neighbor woman who knew everything about life and death to see him, and all she needed was one look to show them their mistake.

"He's an angel," she told them. "He must have been coming for the child, but the poor fellow is so old that the rain knocked him down."

On the following day everyone knew that a flesh-and-blood angel was held captive in Pelayo's house. Against the judgment of the wise neighbor woman, for whom angels in those times were the fugitive survivors of a celestial conspiracy, they did not have the heart to club him to death. Pelayo watched over him all afternoon from the kitchen, armed with his bailiff's club, and before going to bed he dragged him out of the mud

A Very Old Man with Enormous Wings 165

Presentation

Motivation/Prior Knowledge
Put the following statement on the chalkboard: "Seeing is believing." Ask students if, from their experience, this is an accurate statement. Have their perceptions ever misled them? How do people react to the unknown, the mysterious, or the bizarre? What in human nature makes these reactions necessary?

Tell students that the characters in "A Very Old Man with Enormous Wings" have a variety of reactions to the sudden appearance of an old man. Have students note how these reactions change during the course of the story.

Purpose-Setting Question How are the lives of Pelayo and Elisenda changed by the old man with enormous wings?

1 Reading Strategy Ask students to make inferences about the story based on its subtitle.

2 Enrichment Students may be interested to know that the author based many of the settings of his short stories and novels on the Atlantic seacoast town where he was born.

3 Discussion How does the physical description of the old man with wings contradict the typical image of an angel?

4 Critical Thinking and Reading Why and how does Pelayo and Elisenda's initial reaction of nightmare and mute stupor change to one of familiarity?

5 Discussion Why is the neighbor woman sure that the old man is an angel who has come for the child?

6 Discussion Describe the way in which Pelayo treats the old man. Why does he treat someone who is supposed to be an angel in this manner?

Alternative Assessment To promote active reading, have students keep a reader's response journal as they read the story. Have them respond personally to the humor in the story and to the gullibility of the humans. Their journal entries will help you to assess their understanding of the story.

Thematic Focus Have students share experiences in which they feared something unknown to them. For example, maybe they feared changing schools, moving to a new town, or meeting new people. Were they able to overcome their fears? If so, how?

Making Connections Magical realism, in which the imaginary often outweighs the laws of logic, is popular among South American writers. You might consider pairing this story with "Uncle Marcos" by Isabel Allende, page 63. Ask students to compare and contrast the authors' purposes in using fantastic details and the effects of the details on the stories.

166   *Short Stories*

Primary Source

In the following quotation from *Harper's* magazine, Earl Shorris illustrates the way in which history and the social and cultural climates at the time influence the fiction that writers produce.

It is also necessary to consider García Márquez as a moralist, a political man; for myth, though it negates history by making circles of time and events, relates to the way we live; it is not made in a vacuum, but in the depths of experience. García Márquez writes of exploitation, colonialism, and revolution from the point of view of a man who was influenced in his childhood by a grandfather who lived out his days as one of the leavings of a revolution in a town called Aracataca, which was exploited and then abandoned by banana barons from the United States.

You might discuss with students how "A Very Old Man with Enormous Wings" supports Shorris' claim.

and locked him up with the hens in the wire chicken coop. In the middle of the night, when the rain stopped, Pelayo and Elisenda were still killing crabs. A short time afterward the child woke up without a fever and with a desire to eat. Then they felt magnanimous and decided to put the angel on a raft with fresh water and provisions for three days and leave him to his fate on the high seas. But when they went out into the courtyard with the first light of dawn, they found the whole neighborhood in front of the chicken coop having fun with the angel, without the slightest reverence, tossing him things to eat through the openings in the wire as if he weren't a supernatural creature but a circus animal.

Father Gonzaga arrived before seven o'clock, alarmed at the strange news. By that time onlookers less frivolous than those at dawn had already arrived and they were making all kinds of conjectures concerning the captive's future. The simplest among them thought that he should be named mayor of the world. Others of sterner mind felt that he should be promoted to the rank of five-star general in order to win all wars. Some visionaries[1] hoped that he could be put to stud in order to implant on earth a race of winged wise men who could take charge of the universe. But Father Gonzaga, before becoming a priest, had been a robust woodcutter. Standing by the wire, he reviewed his catechism[2] in an instant and asked them to open the door so that he could take a close look at that pitiful man who looked more like a huge decrepit hen among the fascinated chickens. He was lying in a corner drying his open wings in the sunlight

---

1. **visionaries** (vizh′ ən er′ ēz) n.: People whose ideas, plans, and so on, are impractical, too idealistic, or fantastic; dreamers.
2. **catechism** (kat′ ə kiz′ əm) n.: A handbook of questions and answers for teaching the principles of a religion.

A Very Old Man with Enormous Wings   167

7 **Reading Strategy** What miracle occurs because of the angel? Tell students to look for other miracles throughout the story.

8 **Discussion** What do the villagers' reactions to the captive angel reveal about them?

9 **Discussion** Chickens are a common and essential element in the daily lives of Latin Americans. Why does Pelayo put the old man in the chicken coop? What might this act represent?

ESL Teaching Strategy Students with limited English proficiency might have difficulty with some of the words in this selection. Suggest that pairs of students work toegther to look up the definitions of unfamiliar words and write original sentences in which they use the words correctly.

Master Teacher Note You may want to remind students of Icarus, the Greek hero, who defied the gods by flying too close to the sun. From the heat of the sun, the wax that held Icarus' wings together melted, and he plummeted into the sea. Ask students how the old man with wings is an ironic reversal of the Greek myth. You might point out that the angel of García Márquez's story can be interpreted as a symbol of modern alienation that contrasts sharply with a more heroic and poetic past.

Commentary: Interpreting "A Very Old Man with Enormous Wings"

"A Very Old Man with Enormous Wings" is particularly intriguing because it can be read on several levels. It is a delightful fantasy for children, filled with strange and fantastic situations, humorous details, and a distinctive blend of surrealism and innocence.

On a more complex level, however, the story presents some interesting themes that appear frequently in the work of South American writers. The angel's decrepitude and his fall from his former home suggest physical decay and loss of innocence while his uncommunicative nature and isolation suggest alienation. The weakness of the church is conveyed in the preposterous ecclesiastical investigation of the angel. The absurd attempts to explain the angel's appearance logically and to discover his reasons for being there demonstrate the limits of human reason. The respected authorities of the village—the doctor and the priest—can reach no agreement on what is real and what is fantastic. Finally, the angel's reduction to being a sideshow freak for the monetary gain of Pelayo and Elisenda implies a condemnation of capitalistic exploitation.

Using their observations about the various themes in the short story, students might comment on the picture of South American society that the author portrays in "A Very Old Man with Enormous Wings."

168

10 Discussion On the basis of what facts does the parish priest determine that the angel is an imposter? In what way is his approach logical or illogical?

11 Literary Focus Why does the priest seek a verdict from the church authorities?

12 Reading Strategy Have students summarize the nature and the reactions of the pilgrims who visit the angel. What types of people do they represent?

13 Literary Focus Point out to students García Márquez's use of an accumulation of precise detail around an impossible event. Ask them how these details add or detract from the believability of the situation.

among the fruit peels and breakfast leftovers that the early risers had thrown him. Alien to the impertinences of the world, he only lifted his antiquarian[3] eyes and murmured something in his dialect when Father Gonzaga went into the chicken coop and said good morning to him in Latin. The parish priest had his first suspicion of an imposter when he saw that he did not understand the language of God or know how to greet His ministers. Then he noticed that seen close up he was much too human: he had an unbearable smell of the outdoors, the back side of his wings was strewn with parasites and his main feathers had been mistreated by terrestrial winds, and nothing about him measured up to the proud dignity of angels. Then he came out of the chicken coop and in a brief sermon warned the curious against the risks of being ingenuous. He reminded them that the devil had the bad habit of making use of carnival tricks in order to confuse the unwary. He argued that if wings were not the essential element in determining the difference between a hawk and an airplane, they were even less so in the recognition of angels. Nevertheless, he promised to write a letter to his Bishop so that the latter would write to his primate so that the latter would write to the Supreme Pontiff in order to get the final verdict from the highest courts.

His prudence fell on sterile hearts. The news of the captive angel spread with such rapidity that after a few hours the courtyard had the bustle of a marketplace and they had to call in troops with fixed bayonets to disperse the mob that was about to knock the house down. Elisenda, her spine all twisted from sweeping up so much marketplace trash, then got the idea of fencing in the yard and charging five cents admission to see the angel.

---

3. antiquarian (an′ ti kwer′ ē ən) *adj.*: Old-fashioned: outdated.

168   Short Stories

The curious came from far away. A traveling carnival arrived with a flying acrobat who buzzed over the crowd several times, but no one paid any attention to him because his wings were not those of an angel but, rather, those of a sidereal bat. The most unfortunate invalids on earth came in search of health: a poor woman who since childhood had been counting her heartbeats and had run out of numbers; a Portuguese man who couldn't sleep because the noise of the stars disturbed him; a sleepwalker who got up at night to undo the things he had done while awake; and many others with less serious ailments. In the midst of that shipwreck disorder that made the earth tremble, Pelayo and Elisenda were happy with fatigue, for in less than a week they had crammed their rooms with money and the line of pilgrims waiting their turn to enter still reached beyond the horizon.

The angel was the only one who took no part in his own act. He spent his time trying to get comfortable in his borrowed nest, befuddled by the hellish heat of the oil lamps and sacramental candles that had been placed along the wire. At first they tried to make him eat some mothballs, which, according to the wisdom of the wise neighbor woman, were the food prescribed for angels. But he turned them down, just as he turned down the papal[4] lunches that the penitents[5] brought him, and they never found out whether it was because he was an angel or because he was an old man that in the end he ate nothing but eggplant mush. His only supernatural virtue seemed to be patience. Especially during the first days, when the hens pecked at him, searching for the stellar

---

4. papal (pā′ pəl) *adj.*: Appropriate for the pope or the papacy.

5. penitents (pen′ i tənts) *n.*: People receiving or intending to receive the sacrament of penance, which involves the confession and repentance of sin or wrongdoing.

Grammar in Action

Skillful writers **illustrate and give examples** in addition to making statements. In "A Very Old Man with Enormous Wings," for example, García Márquez sets the scene and tone of the story by making a statement about the sad world in which the characters live and backs it up with examples that create an image in the reader's mind:

The world had been sad since Tuesday. Sea and sky were a single ash-gray thing and the sands of the beach, which on March nights glimmered like powdered light, had become a stew of mud and rotten shellfish. The light was so weak at noon that when Pelayo was coming back to the house after throwing away the crabs, it was hard for him to see what it was that was moving and groaning in the rear of the courtyard.

Similarly, when García Márquez describes Father Gonzaga's observations about how human and how unlike an angel the old man looks, he supports his claim with examples:

Then he noticed that seen close up he was much too human: he had an unbearable smell of the outdoors, the back side of his wings was strewn with parasites and his main feathers had been mistreated by terrestrial winds,

parasites that proliferated in his wings, and the cripples pulled out feathers to touch their defective parts with, and even the most merciful threw stones at him, trying to get him to rise so they could see him standing. The only time they succeeded in arousing him was when they burned his side with an iron for branding steers, for he had been motionless for so many hours that they thought he was dead. He awoke with a start, ranting in his hermetic[6] language and with tears in his eyes, and he flapped his wings a couple of times, which brought on a whirlwind of chicken dung and lunar dust and a gale of panic that did not seem to be of this world. Although many thought that his reaction had been one not of rage but of pain, from then on they were careful not to annoy him, because the majority understood that his passivity was not that of a hero taking his ease but that of a cataclysm[7] in repose.

Father Gonzaga held back the crowd's frivolity with formulas of maidservant inspiration while awaiting the arrival of a final judgment on the nature of the captive. But the mail from Rome showed no sense of urgency. They spent their time finding out if the prisoner had a navel, if his dialect had any connection with Aramaic,[8] how many times he could fit on the head of a pin, or whether he wasn't just a Norwegian with wings. Those meager letters might have come and gone until the end of time if a providential event had not put an end to the priest's tribulations.

It so happened that during those days, among so many other carnival attractions, there arrived in town the traveling show of the woman who had been changed into a spider for having disobeyed her parents. The admission to see her was not only less than the admission to see the angel, but people were permitted to ask her all manner of questions about her absurd state and to examine her up and down so that no one would ever doubt the truth of her horror. She was a frightful tarantula the size of a ram and with the head of a sad maiden. What was most heartrending, however, was not her outlandish shape but the sincere affliction with which she recounted the details of her misfortune. While still practically a child she had sneaked out of her parents' house to go to a dance, and while she was coming back through the woods after having danced all night without permission, a fearful thunderclap rent the sky in two and through the crack came the lightning bolt of brimstone that changed her into a spider. Her only nourishment came from the meatballs that charitable souls chose to toss into her mouth. A spectacle like that, full of so much human truth and with such a fearful lesson, was bound to defeat without even trying that of a haughty angel who scarcely deigned to look at mortals. Besides, the few miracles attributed to the angel showed a certain mental disorder, like the blind man who didn't recover his sight but grew three new teeth, or the paralytic[9] who didn't get to walk but almost won the lottery, and the leper whose sores sprouted sunflowers. Those consolation miracles, which were more like mocking fun, had already ruined the angel's reputation when the woman who had been changed into a spider finally crushed him completely. That was how Father Gonzaga was cured forever of his insomnia[10] and Pelayo's courtyard went back

---

6. hermetic (hər met′ ik) *adj.*: Obscure; hard to understand.
7. cataclysm (kat′ ə kliz′ əm) *n.*: A violent upheaval.
8. Aramaic (ar′ ə mā′ ik) *n.*: A Semitic language that was the common language throughout the Near East from *c.* 300 B.C. to *c.* A.D. 650; one of its dialects was spoken by Jesus and his disciples.

---

9. paralytic (par′ ə lit′ ik) *n.*: A person having paralysis.
10. insomnia (in säm′ nē ə) *n.*: Chronic inability to sleep.

A Very Old Man with Enormous Wings 169

---

14 Discussion Have students describe the angel's responses during his captivity. Are his responses those that one might expect from an angel? Explain.

15 Discussion What is significant about the way in which Rome reacts to the appearance of an angel?

16 Discussion Why does the author include the story about the woman who had been changed into a tarantula? Contrast the townspeople's reactions to her with their reaction to the angel.

17 Discussion Why is the angel a disappointment to the townspeople?

---

and nothing about him measured up to the proud dignity of angels.

Student Activity 1. Find two more passages in "A Very Old Man with Enormous Wings" in which García Márquez illustrates character traits, setting and tone, or ideas. Identify the words which seem most vivid.

Student Activity 2. Write a brief passage of your own in which you illustrate someone's youth, inexperience, physical dexterity, musical ability, comic behavior, or some other personality trait. Do not mention the specific trait. When you finish, read the passage aloud and ask your listeners to identify the trait you are highlighting.

Software If students are working on computers, have them use the **Writer's Helper** activity Develop a Paragraph to assist them in completing Student Activity 2.

18 **Discussion** What does this statement reveal about human nature?

19 **Discussion** Have students discuss the meaning of the sentence. What does this detail reveal about the old man? Does it further affirm or disprove that he is an angel? Why?

20 **Clarification** Point out to students that the angel, portrayed as a lonely, proud individual, asserts a sense of dignity in spite of his treatment by a brutal society.

21 **Reading Strategy** Compare and contrast the doctor's reaction to the angel with that of the priest. Which reaction seems more accurate? Why?

22 **Discussion** How have Pelayo and Elisenda's reactions and behavior changed since they discovered the angel?

to being as empty as during the time it had rained for three days and crabs walked through the bedrooms.

The owners of the house had no reason to lament. With the money they saved they built a two-story mansion with balconies and gardens and high netting so that crabs wouldn't get in during the winter, and with iron bars on the windows so that angels wouldn't get in. Pelayo also set up a rabbit warren close to town and gave up his job as bailiff for good, and Elisenda bought some satin pumps with high heels and many dresses of iridescent silk, the kind worn on Sunday by the most desirable women in those times. The chicken coop was the only thing that didn't receive any attention. If they washed it down with creolin[11] and burned tears of myrrh[12] inside it every so often, it was not in homage[13] to the angel but to drive away the dungheap stench that still hung everywhere like a ghost and was turning the new house into an old one. At first, when the child learned to walk, they were careful that he not get too close to the chicken coop. But then they began to lose their fears and got used to the smell, and before the child got his second teeth he'd gone inside the chicken coop to play, where the wires were falling apart. The angel was no less standoffish with him than with other mortals, but he tolerated the most ingenious infamies with the patience of a dog who had no illusions. They both came down with chicken pox at the same time. The doctor who took care of the child couldn't resist the temptation to listen to the angel's heart, and he found so much whistling in the heart and so many sounds in his kidneys that it seemed impossible for him to be alive. What surprised him most, however, was the logic of his wings. They seemed so natural on that completely human organism that he couldn't understand why other men didn't have them too.

When the child began school it had been some time since the sun and rain had caused the collapse of the chicken coop. The angel went dragging himself about here and there like a stray dying man. They would drive him out of the bedroom with a broom and a moment later find him in the kitchen. He seemed to be in so many places at the same time that they grew to think that he'd been duplicated, that he was reproducing himself all through the house, and the exasperated and unhinged Elisenda shouted that it was awful living in that hell full of angels. He could scarcely eat and his antiquarian eyes had also become so foggy that he went about bumping into posts. All he had left were the bare cannulae[14] of his last feathers. Pelayo threw a blanket over him and

---

11. creolin (krē′ ə lin) *n.*: Possibly an antiseptic.
12. myrrh (mʉr) *n.*: A fragrant, bitter-tasting perfume.
13. homage (häm′ ij) *n.*: Anything done to show reverence, honor, or respect.

14. cannulae (kan′ yōo lē′) *n.*: Tubes that are inserted into the body.

170 Short Stories

Grammar in Action

Authors avoid monotony in their writing by varying their sentence patterns. One way to vary a sentence is to use different **sentence openers.**

In addition to its subject, a sentence can begin with one-word modifiers, phrases, clauses, or a combination of these openers.

García Márquez uses a variety of sentence openers in "A Very Old Man with Enormous Wings." Examine the following sentences and notice the type of sentence openers García Márquez used:

In the middle of the night, when the rain stopped, Pelayo and Elisenda were still killing crabs.

Standing by the wire, he reviewed his catechism in an instant and asked them to open the door so that he could take a close look at that pitiful man who looked more like a decrepit hen among the fascinated chickens.

Alien to the impertinences of the world, he only lifted his antiquarian eyes and murmured something in his dialect when Father Gonzaga went into the chicken coop and said good morning to him in Latin.

A Very Old Man with Enormous Wings 171

Cooperative Learning According to García Márquez, the most important influences on his works are probably the short stories of Ernest Hemingway (for his succinct mode of expression) and William Faulkner (for his creation of a single microcosmic universe populated by eccentric people). You might have students read several Hemingway or Faulkner short stories and then work together in small groups to discuss how these two writers influenced García Márquez.

Multicultural Focus People from cultures throughout the world share a belief in angels. In the Jewish and Christian religions, angels are considered to be spirits that serve as God's messengers. Angels also figure in the beliefs of other important religions—including Islam, Buddhism, Taoism, and Zoroastrianism. Although, as spirits, angels are believed to be invisible, they are traditionally shown in art as human beings with wings, usually dressed according to the custom of the culture that depicts them and resembling people of that culture.

Have students investigate the teachings of various religions about angels. Suggest that they find examples of art and sculpture with angels, representative of different cultures.

In the first sentence García Márquez uses both a prepositional phrase and an adverbial clause; in the second he uses a participial phrase; and in the third he uses an adjective with its modifiers.

Student Activity 1. Find three other sentences with differing sentence openers from the story. Name the type of opener each sentence uses.

Student Activity 2. Write a paragraph about your impressions of this story. Use at least four different sentence openers. Exchange papers with a partner and name the sentence openers in your partner's paper.

Electronic Handbook You may wish students to review phrases, clauses, prepositional phrases, and verbal phrases before completing the activities. If students have access to the Language Master 6000, have them enter the access words *phrase, clause, preposition,* or *verbal* and press the GRAMMAR key for information on these topics.

23 Discussion For what reasons might the angel be getting better? Why should he be careful that no one notice the changes?

24 Reading Strategy In what ways was the old man an annoyance to Elisenda? What does this reaction to the old man reveal about her?

Reader's Response Would you have held the angel captive and treated him as unkindly as Pelayo and Elisenda did? Why or why not?

Thematic Response The unknown must have been very frightening for the angel. How do you think he was feeling as he saw the strange actions of some of his human "watchers"?

Speaking and Listening Divide students into pairs and have them develop questions that they might use to interview an angel who suddenly appeared in their neighborhood. Give each student the opportunity to play the roles of angel and interviewer. Students might then present their results to the class in the format of a news report or a talk-show interview.

Challenge The author gives us no indication that Pelayo, Elisenda, or the villagers have learned anything from the angel. What "human truth" or "fearful lesson" might the old man with wings have taught them? How might their lives differ after his departure?

Closure and Extension

ANSWERS TO RESPONDING TO THE SELECTION
Your Response
1. Encourage students to discuss the concept of fairness. Ask them to state what they think is fair and what is not fair.

extended him the charity of letting him sleep in the shed, and only then did they notice that he had a temperature at night, and was delirious with the tongue twisters of an old Norwegian. That was one of the few times they became alarmed, for they thought he was going to die and not even the wise neighbor woman had been able to tell them what to do with dead angels.

And yet he not only survived his worst winter, but seemed improved with the first sunny days. He remained motionless for several days in the farthest corner of the courtyard, where no one would see him, and at the beginning of December some large, stiff feathers began to grow on his wings, the feathers of a scarecrow, which looked more like another misfortune of decrepitude. But he must have known the reason for those changes, for he was quite careful that no one should notice them, that no one should hear the sea chanteys that he sometimes sang under the stars. One morning Elisenda was cutting some bunches of onions for lunch when a wind that seemed to come from the high seas blew into the kitchen. Then she went to the window and caught the angel in his first attempt at flight. They were so clumsy that his fingernails opened a furrow in the vegetable patch and he was on the point of knocking the shed down with the ungainly flapping that slipped on the light and couldn't get a grip on the air. But he did manage to gain altitude. Elisenda let out a sigh of relief, for herself and for him, when she saw him pass over the last houses, holding himself up in some way with the risky flapping of a senile vulture. She kept watching him even when she was through cutting the onions and she kept on watching until it was no longer possible for her to see him, because then he was no longer an annoyance in her life but an imaginary dot on the horizon of the sea.

RESPONDING TO THE SELECTION

Your Response
1. Do you think the old man with enormous wings was treated fairly? Why or why not?

Recalling
2. Describe the old man.
3. According to the wise neighbor woman, why has the old man come to Pelayo and Elisenda's house?
4. For what two reasons does Father Gonzaga suspect the old man is not an angel?

Interpreting
5. What inferences do you make about the people who come to see the old man?
6. Why do the villagers' attitudes toward the angel change? For example, why do the villagers treat the old man first "without the slightest reverence" and then want to name him the "mayor of the world"?
7. In what way is the woman who was turned into a tarantula "full of so much human truth and with such a fearful lesson"?
8. Explain Elisenda's reaction at the end of the story.
9. How do you interpret the character of the old man? Support your answer.

Applying
10. Throughout the course of human history, people have tried to make meaning out of their world. For example, long ago people interpreted thunder as an angry god hurling thunder bolts. Even today, when a terrible disaster occurs, some people say, "There must be a reason why this occurred." Why do you think it is important to humans to find meaning in amazing occurrences? How has this drive led to the development of science?

Recalling
2. The old man is bald and practically toothless. Dressed like a rag-picker, he has dirty, half-plucked wings that are covered with mud. He has a strong sailor's voice but speaks an incomprehensible dialect.
3. The wise neighbor believes that the angel has come for Pelayo and Elisenda's sick child. She says that the angel is so old that he was knocked down by the rain.
4. Father Gonzaga suspects that the old man is an imposter because he does not know the language of God (Latin) and because he looks too human, lacking the dignity of angels.

Interpreting
5. Answers will differ. Suggested Response: The people who come to see the old man are sensation seekers or those pursuing their own gain, such as cures for their ailments or forgiveness for their sins.
6. Answers will differ. Suggested Response: At first they treat the angel harshly like a curiosity or a caged animal there for their amusement. They then regard him as a major, general, or stud —just in case he truly is a messenger from God.
7. Answers will differ. Suggested Response: The tarantula story is much easier for the villagers to understand. Her punishment for disobeying her parents was

ANALYZING LITERATURE

Understanding Theme

The **theme** of a story is an insight into life, or the point the story is making. In the context of magical realism, the theme lies in what happens when the magical or fantastic enters the ordinary, everyday lives of the characters.

1. What important insight does this story convey to you about life?
2. Imagine that you were telling friends what this story meant to you. One of your friends says, "I didn't see that." How would you respond? Which details would you point out?
3. The subtitle of the story is "A Tale for Children." Why?

CRITICAL THINKING AND READING

Identifying Different Interpretations

When you make an **interpretation,** you explain the meaning of something, make something understandable, or express your perception of something. In "A Very Old Man with Enormous Wings," for example, each character has his or her own interpretation or perception of who the old man is. Pelayo and Elisenda believe he is "a castaway from some foreign ship," the neighbor woman claims he is an angel, and Father Gonzaga thinks he is an imposter.

1. What other interpretations of who the old man is do the villagers propose?
2. García Márquez wrote this story in response to critics' interpretations of his novel *One Hundred Years of Solitude.* In what way does this tale send a cautionary note to critics who interpret the symbols used in literature?

THINKING AND WRITING

Writing From a Different Perspective

In "A Very Old Man with Enormous Wings," García Márquez describes the old man's appearance and the villagers' reactions to him, but we learn very little about what the old man thinks and feels. Imagine that you were the old man in García Márquez's story and rewrite the story from your perspective as the old man. Try to penetrate the old man's personality, thoughts, and feelings. Review your work with a classmate, asking your partner if you adequately and accurately portray the old man. Does your partner get a real sense of who the old man is? Write a final draft.

LEARNING OPTIONS

1. **Writing.** Whereas the woman who was turned into a spider explains the circumstances of this miracle, the old man never explains why he has wings or what circumstances brought him to Pelayo's courtyard. Review the part of the story in which the tarantula-woman recounts her tale of woe. Then write a short account of how the old man came to have wings and explain the events that led up to his appearance in the couple's home.
2. **Art.** With a group of classmates, invent a card game based on the story "A Very Old Man with Enormous Wings." On index cards, draw or paint images that represent characters or events from the story. Then use the cards as you work out the details of how the game is played. Referring to the story as you work may give you ideas about rules and strategies for your game.
3. **Speaking and Listening.** Prepare and deliver a human-interest story for the television evening news about the very old man with enormous wings. Describe the events of the story as if they are happening in the present or have happened recently. Include in your report interviews with Pelayo and Elisenda, Father Gonzaga, and other eyewitnesses. When you have finished writing your story, deliver it to your class.

A Very Old Man with Enormous Wings 173

---

mysterious, they have predominantly selfish motives. Other students may note that there are certain things that no one can explain and that it is absurd to try. Still others may note how people respond indifferently to the miraculous.

2. Answers will differ. Students should cite numerous examples to support their interpretation.
3. Answers will differ. Suggested Response: The subtitle implies that his short story resembles a fairy tale in its simplicity, its humor, its mixture of the real with the supernatural, its universality, and its theme.

ANSWERS TO CRITICAL THINKING AND READING

1. Answers will differ. Other interpretations of the old man's identity include a healer, a side-show freak, a prisoner, and a human.
2. Answers will differ. Suggested Response: The author may have been trying to indicate that one interpretation of a symbol or a circumstance is just that—one perception. García Márquez may have been cautioning critics that to hold up one interpretation as valid is to do a disservice both to readers and authors.

THINKING AND WRITING

◆ **Software** If students are working on computers, you might wish to have them use the **Writer's Helper** activity Sentence Length to help them revise their stories.

LEARNING OPTIONS

1. Creative students will enjoy this activity. You might wish to extend the activity for visual learners by asking them to illustrate their accounts.
2. Kinesthetic learners will appreciate this activity. You might wish to extend the activity for visual learners by having them think up a name for the game and by having students write the instructions and rules for playing the games.
3. This activity is especially appropriate for extroverted students.

---

straightforward and readily apparent. There are understandable reasons for her state and for her appearance—there are no such reasons for the angel's appearance.
8. Elisenda seems to lack any gratefulness for the angel's part in bringing her money and an easier life. She is annoyed and even infuriated by the angel's intrusion into her home. She greets his departure with relief.
9. Answers will differ. Suggested

Response: The old man serves as a symbol rather than as a fully developed character. Uncommunicative, coldly indifferent, he seems to represent a loss of innocence and a fall from grace into an unhappy earthly existence.

Applying

10. Answers will differ. Most students will understand the human need for comprehending and

mastering the unknown. The desire to know what lies beyond Earth has led to space travel. The desire to cure and control disease has led to advances in medicine, and so forth.

ANSWERS TO ANALYZING LITERATURE

1. Answers will differ. Some students will interpret the story pessimistically: that although people want to understand the unknown or the

Preparation

More About the Author O. Henry had little formal education. He drew his themes and plots from his experiences as a pharmacist, cowboy, draftsman, bank teller, and convicted embezzler. Ask students whether they think a fiction writer must have a wide experience of life.

Literary Focus Have students work in small groups and brainstorm for ideas that might be used as the theme of a story. Ask them to select the idea they find the most interesting and consider the kind of story in which that theme could be developed. What kind of characters would the story have and what would be the situation? Have each group report to the class the problem that the characters would resolve in its story and see if other students can predict what the theme might be.

Prereading Focus Sacrifice is a purposeful act that one person does for another, for a group, or for an ideal or cause. The sacrifices in "The Gift of the Magi" are done in the name of love. As students begin the activity, ask them to think of a personal sacrifice they might make that would have great meaning for the person to whom they give their gift. Point out that a gift is more precious when the receiver is aware that the giver has made a sacrifice.

Vocabulary Ask less advanced students how *ravages* might *depreciate* something, how someone could *instigate* something in a *discreet* way, how *chaste* and *meretricious* might be used as antonyms, and how *cascade* might be used to describe a person's hair.

Spelling Tip Point out the second *e* in *meretricious*. Some students may misspell this word *meritricious*.

GUIDE FOR READING

O. Henry

(1862–1910) was born William Sydney Porter in Greensboro, North Carolina. As a young man, he moved to Texas where he worked as a bank teller. Convicted of embezzling funds from the bank, he served time in prison. While in prison he began writing short stories. After his release O. Henry moved to New York, which is the setting for many of his stories. He is most famous for his use of surprise or twist endings. "The Gift of the Magi," one of his most popular works, has an unexpected twist at the end.

The Gift of the Magi

Key Statements as a Clue to Theme

The **theme** of a story is an insight into life that the author presents through characters and action. This insight may be about problems, conditions, or situations in human life. Often an author will include key statements that point to the theme, as O. Henry does in "The Gift of the Magi."

Focus

In this story two people make great sacrifices in order to give each other holiday gifts. Think of a person you love, to whom you would like to give a special gift. Write a brief description of a gift this person would especially enjoy and also tell why the present would make such a hit. Then, as you read the story, note how the characters choose gifts for each other. What guides them in their choices?

Vocabulary

Knowing the following words will help you as you read "The Gift of the Magi."

instigates (in' stə gāts') *v.*: Urges on; stirs up (p. 175)

depreciate (di prē' shē āt') *v.*: Reduce in value (p. 176)

cascade (kas kād') *n.*: A waterfall (p. 176)

chaste (chāst) *adj.*: Pure or clean in style; not ornate (p. 176)

meretricious (mer' ə trish' əs) *adj.*: Attractive in a cheap, flashy way (p. 176)

ravages (rav' ij iz) *n.*: Ruins; devastating damages (p. 176)

discreet (dis krēt') *adj.*: Tactful; respectful (p. 177)

The Gift of the Magi

O. Henry

One dollar and eighty-seven cents. That was all. And sixty cents of it was in pennies. Pennies saved one and two at a time by bulldozing the grocer and the vegetable man and the butcher until one's cheeks burned with the silent imputation of parsimony[1] that such close dealing implied. Three times Della counted it. One dollar and eighty-seven cents. And the next day would be Christmas.

There was clearly nothing to do but flop down on the shabby little couch and howl. So Della did it. Which instigates the moral reflection that life is made up of sobs, sniffles, and smiles, with sniffles predominating.

While the mistress of the home is gradually subsiding from the first stage to the second, take a look at the home. A furnished flat[2] at $8 per week. It did not exactly beggar description,[3] but it certainly had that word on the lookout for the mendicancy squad.[4]

In the vestibule below was a letter-box into which no letter would go, and an electric button from which no mortal finger could coax a ring. Also appertaining thereunto was a card bearing the name "Mr. James Dillingham Young."

The "Dillingham" had been flung to the breeze during a former period of prosperity when its possessor was being paid $30 per week. Now, when the income was shrunk to $20, the letters of "Dillingham" looked blurred, as though they were thinking seriously of contracting to a modest and unassuming D. But whenever Mr. James Dillingham Young came home and reached his flat above he was called "Jim" and greatly hugged by Mrs. James Dillingham Young, already introduced to you as Della. Which is all very good.

Della finished her cry and attended to her cheeks with the powder rag. She stood by the window and looked out dully at a gray cat walking a gray fence in a gray backyard. Tomorrow would be Christmas Day, and she had only $1.87 with which to buy Jim a present. She had been saving every penny she could for months, with this result. Twenty dollars a week doesn't go far. Expenses had been greater than she had calculated. They always are. Only $1.87 to buy a present for Jim. Her Jim. Many a happy hour she had spent planning for something nice for him. Something fine and rare and sterling—something just a little bit near to being worthy of the honor of being owned by Jim.

There was a pier glass[5] between the windows of the room. Perhaps you have seen a pier glass in an $8 flat. A very thin and very agile person may, by observing his reflection

---

1. **silent imputation** (im pyoo tā′ shən) **of parsimony** (pär′ sə mō′ nē): Silent accusation of stinginess.
2. **flat** (flat) *n.*: Apartment.
3. **beggar description:** Resist description.
4. **mendicancy** (men′ di kən′ sē) **squad:** Police who arrested beggars.

5. **pier** (pir) **glass:** A tall mirror.

The Gift of the Magi 175

Thematic Focus In this story, Jim and Della both make sacrifices to show how much they love and appreciate each other. Ask students how they show their appreciation for the people they love. What makes a person feel appreciated more, words or actions?

Making Connections You might want to have students contrast the generosity of Della and Jim with the selfishness and vanity of the protagonist in "The Necklace," page 193.

4 Critical Thinking and Reading Ask students to infer what two emotions these descriptive details might suggest. What clue do they see to a possible solution to Della's problem?

5 Discussion Ask students to discuss the possible importance of this descriptive paragraph to the telling of the story. What does O. Henry establish here?

6 Discussion How does the writer hint at what is going on in Della's mind?

7 Discussion What further clue to Della's intentions does the writer give?

8 Clarification Point out to students that at the time this story is set, women used heated metal rods called *curling irons* to curl their hair.

in a rapid sequence of longitudinal strips, obtain a fairly accurate conception of his looks. Della, being slender, had mastered the art.

Suddenly she whirled from the window and stood before the glass. Her eyes were shining brilliantly, but her face had lost its color within twenty seconds. Rapidly she pulled down her hair and let it fall to its full length.

Now, there were two possessions of the James Dillingham Youngs in which they both took a mighty pride. One was Jim's gold watch that had been his father's and his grandfather's. The other was Della's hair. Had the Queen of Sheba[6] lived in the flat across the airshaft, Della would have let her hair hang out the window some day to dry just to depreciate Her Majesty's jewels and gifts. Had King Solomon been the janitor, with all his treasures piled up in the basement, Jim would have pulled out his watch every time he passed, just to see him pluck at his beard from envy.

So now Della's beautiful hair fell about her rippling and shining like a cascade of brown waters. It reached below her knee and made itself almost a garment for her. And then she did it up again nervously and quickly. Once she faltered for a minute and stood still while a tear or two splashed on the worn red carpet.

On went her old brown jacket; on went her old brown hat. With a whirl of skirts and with the brilliant sparkle still in her eyes, she fluttered out the door and down the stairs to the street.

Where she stopped the sign read: "Mme. Sofronie. Hair Goods of All Kinds." One flight up Della ran, and collected herself, panting. Madame, large, too white, chilly, hardly looked the "Sofronie."

"Will you buy my hair?" asked Della.

"I buy hair," said Madame. "Take yer hat off and let's have a sight at the looks of it."

Down rippled the brown cascade.

"Twenty dollars," said Madame, lifting the mass with a practiced hand.

"Give it to me quick," said Della.

Oh, and the next two hours tripped by on rosy wings. Forget the hashed metaphor. She was ransacking the stores for Jim's present.

She found it at last. It surely had been made for Jim and no one else. There was no other like it in any of the stores, and she had turned all of them inside out. It was a platinum fob chain[7] simple and chaste in design, properly proclaiming its value by substance alone and not by meretricious ornamentation—as all good things should do. It was even worthy of The Watch. As soon as she saw it she knew that it must be Jim's. It was like him. Quietness and value—the description applied to both. Twenty-one dollars they took from her for it, and she hurried home with the 87 cents. With that chain on his watch Jim might be properly anxious about the time in any company. Grand as the watch was he sometimes looked at it on the sly on account of the old leather strap that he used in place of a chain.

When Della reached home her intoxication gave way a little to prudence and reason. She got out her curling irons and lighted the gas and went to work repairing the ravages made by generosity added to love. Which is always a tremendous task, dear friends—a mammoth task.

Within forty minutes her head was covered with tiny, close-lying curls that made her look wonderfully like a truant schoolboy. She looked at her reflection in the mirror long, carefully, and critically.

---

6. Queen of Sheba: In the Bible, the beautiful queen who visited King Solomon to test his wisdom.

7. fob (fäb) **chain:** A small chain connecting a watch to its pocket.

Grammar in Action

Tone refers to the author's attitude toward his or her subject. Readers determine tone from the way a subject is presented and described. The tone of a work of literature can often be stated in one or two words, such as *admiring, very sarcastic, highly respectful, angry,* and so forth. What is O. Henry's attitude toward the characters and situation in this story? Read this passage:

Now there were two possessions of the James Dillingham Youngs in which they both took a great and mighty pride. One was Jim's gold watch that had been his father's and his grandfather's. The other was Della's hair. Had the queen of Sheba lived in the flat across the airshaft, Della would have let her hair hang out the window some day to dry just to depreciate Her Majesty's jewels and gifts. Had King Solomon been the janitor, with all his treasures piled up in the basement, Jim would have pulled out his watch every time he passed, just to see him pluck at his beard with envy.

The author's amused fondness for the young couple is shown in a description in which even their vanity is treated with affection.

"If Jim doesn't kill me," she said to herself, "before he takes a second look at me, he'll say I look like a Coney Island[8] chorus girl. But what could I do—oh! what could I do with a dollar and eighty-seven cents?"

At 7 o'clock the coffee was made and the frying-pan was on the back of the stove hot and ready to cook the chops.

Jim was never late. Della doubled the fob chain in her hand and sat on the corner of the table near the door that he always entered. Then she heard his step on the stair away down on the first flight, and she turned white for just a moment. She had a habit of saying little silent prayers about the simplest everyday things, and now she whispered: "Please God, make him think I am still pretty."

The door opened and Jim stepped in and closed it. He looked thin and very serious. Poor fellow, he was only twenty-two—and to be burdened with a family! He needed a new overcoat and he was without gloves.

Jim stopped inside the door, as immovable as a setter at the scent of quail. His eyes were fixed upon Della, and there was an expression in them that she could not read, and it terrified her. It was not anger, nor surprise, nor disapproval, nor horror, nor any of the sentiments that she had been prepared for. He simply stared at her fixedly with that peculiar expression on his face.

Della wriggled off the table and went for him.

"Jim, darling," she cried, "don't look at me that way. I had my hair cut off and sold it because I couldn't have lived through Christmas without giving you a present. It'll grow out again—you won't mind, will you? I just had to do it. My hair grows awfully fast. Say 'Merry Christmas!' Jim, and let's be happy. You don't know what a nice—what a

───────────

8. **Coney Island:** A beach and amusement park in Brooklyn, New York.

beautiful, nice gift I've got for you."

"You've cut off your hair?" asked Jim, laboriously, as if he had not arrived at that patent fact yet even after the hardest mental labor.

"Cut it off and sold it," said Della. "Don't you like me just as well, anyhow? I'm me without my hair, ain't I?"

Jim looked about the room curiously.

"You say your hair is gone?" he said, with an air almost of idiocy.

"You needn't look for it," said Della. "It's sold, I tell you—sold and gone, too. It's Christmas Eve, boy. Be good to me, for it went for you. Maybe the hairs of my head were numbered," she went on with a sudden serious sweetness, "but nobody could ever count my love for you. Shall I put the chops on, Jim?"

Out of his trance Jim seemed quickly to wake. He enfolded his Della. For ten seconds let us regard with discreet scrutiny some inconsequential object in the other direction. Eight dollars a week or a million a year—what is the difference? A mathematician or a wit would give you the wrong answer. The Magi brought valuable gifts, but that was not among them. This dark assertion will be illuminated later on.

Jim drew a package from his overcoat pocket and threw it upon the table.

"Don't make any mistake, Dell," he said, "about me. I don't think there's anything in the way of a haircut or a shave or a shampoo that could make me like my girl any less. But if you'll unwrap that package you may see why you had me going a while at first."

White fingers and nimble tore at the string and paper. And then an ecstatic scream of joy; and then, alas! a quick feminine change to hysterical tears and wails, necessitating the immediate employment of all the comforting powers of the lord of the flat.

For there lay The Combs—the set of

The Gift of the Magi 177

9 Discussion What more practical gift might Della have purchased for Jim? Do you agree or disagree with Della's choice? Why?

10 Reading Strategy Ask students to predict what Jim might have purchased for her.

11 Master Teacher Note Authors at times use allusions to characters and situations from other stories or from history. Through the use of an allusion an author can bring to the reader's mind ideas and emotions from another situation. Ask students to consider what the allusion to the Magi might contribute to this story.

Student Activity 1. Find two other passages in the story that convey the author's tone and discuss these with your classmates.

Student Activity 2. Discuss with a partner your own attitude about a particular subject, and then write a paragraph about it. Exchange drafts and discuss ways to improve compositions.

Software If students are working on computers, have them use the **Writer's Helper** activity Develop a Paragraph to guide them through Student Activity 2.

12 Literary Focus How can the couple be both "foolish" and "wisest"? How does this apparent contradiction suggest the theme?

Reader's Response What is the most precious gift you have ever received? What made it so special?

Thematic Response The appreciation that Jim and Della have for each other is made very clear by the surprise gifts they give each other for Christmas. How does this make you feel about their relationship? What does it say about each of them?

Multicultural Focus Customs regarding gift giving around the world are a true measure of cultural diversity. The Japanese, with their complex society and emphasis on ceremony, have different categories of gift giving—from obligatory business gifts (exchanged twice a year) to those given for personal reasons. Wrapping the gift is also very important, so that the recipient is free to open it in private. In Arab countries, great generosity is expected and returned, as a matter of pride and status. In Latin American countries, gift giving is less formal and seems to be enjoyed for its own sake, without a sense of obligation. In some countries, associations and symbols make certain gifts taboo. Flowers are given around the world, but chrysanthemums are associated with funerals in France and Belgium; red roses would be given only to lovers in France and Germany. Clocks are a symbol of death and bad luck in China.

Have students explore different gift-giving customs and occasions around the world.

178

combs, side and back, that Della had worshipped for long in a Broadway window. Beautiful combs, pure tortoise shell, with jeweled rims—just the shade to wear in the beautiful vanished hair. They were expensive combs, she knew, and her heart had simply craved and yearned over them without the least hope of possession. And now, they were hers, but the tresses that should have adorned the coveted adornments were gone.

But she hugged them to her bosom, and at length she was able to look up with dim eyes and a smile and say: "My hair grows so fast, Jim!"

And then Della leaped up like a little singed cat and cried, "Oh, oh!"

Jim had not yet seen his beautiful present. She held it out to him eagerly upon her open palm. The dull precious metal seemed to flash with a reflection of her bright and ardent spirit.

"Isn't it a dandy, Jim? I hunted all over town to find it. You'll have to look at the time a hundred times a day now. Give me your

watch. I want to see how it looks on it."

Instead of obeying, Jim tumbled down on the couch and put his hands under the back of his head and smiled.

"Dell," said he, "let's put our Christmas presents away and keep 'em a while. They're too nice to use just at present. I sold the watch to get the money to buy your combs. And now suppose you put the chops on."

The Magi, as you know, were wise men—wonderfully wise men—who brought gifts to the Babe in the manger. They invented the art of giving Christmas presents. Being wise, their gifts were no doubt wise ones, possibly bearing the privilege of exchange in case of duplication. And here I have lamely related to you the uneventful chronicle of two foolish children in a flat who most unwisely sacrificed for each other the greatest treasures of their house. But in a last word to the wise of these days let it be said that of all who give gifts these two were the wisest. Of all who give and receive gifts, such as they are wisest. Everywhere they are wisest. They are the magi.

178   Short Stories

Closure and Extension

ANSWERS TO RESPONDING TO THE SELECTION
Your Response

1. Ask students to share their feelings about a time when they received something unexpected, but appreciated. Encourage them to talk about special verbal compliments they have received. Ask them if they thought of these as gifts.

Recalling

2. They prize Jim's watch and Della's long hair.

3. Jim loved Della's long hair and bought her expensive combs to wear in her hair.

4. Jim is dismayed at receiving the gift of a watch fob because he has sold his watch to buy the combs for Della.

Interpreting

5. Suggested Response: They love

each other very much. Each was willing to sacrifice his or her most precious possession to buy a gift for the other.

6. Suggested Response: The fact that Della cannot use her combs because she sold her hair and Jim cannot use his watch fob because he has sold his watch, makes the end of the story ironic.

7. Suggested Response: The Magi were wise men who gave precious gifts to the infant Christ. Della and

RESPONDING TO THE SELECTION

Your Response

1. What makes a gift special? Is it the monetary value, or something else? Explain your answer.

Recalling

2. At the beginning of the story, what possessions do Jim and Della prize the most?
3. Why is Jim particularly sorry that Della has cut her hair?
4. Why is Jim dismayed when he opens Della's gift to him?

Interpreting

5. How do Della and Jim feel toward each other? Give evidence from the story that shows their feelings.
6. An ironic situation is one in which actions lead to an unexpected outcome. Explain how the ending of this story is an ironic situation.
7. Why does the author compare Della and Jim to the Magi?

Applying

8. If you were either Jim or Della, how would you feel about the gift you received?

ANALYZING LITERATURE

Understanding Key Statements

The **theme** of a story is a general statement about life. Usually a theme is implied through the characters and action of the story. You can often find key statements in a story that serve as clues to the theme. For example, the statement, "I'm me without my hair, ain't I?" makes the point that people's characters are more important than their superficial appearance.

1. What point does each of the following key statements make?
   a. ". . . two foolish children in a flat who most unwisely sacrificed for each other the greatest treasures of their house."
   b. "Of all who give and receive gifts, such as they are wisest."

2. In your own words, state the theme of "The Gift of the Magi."

CRITICAL THINKING AND READING

Paraphrasing

When you paraphrase a statement or a passage in a text, you restate it in your own words. For example, you might paraphrase the sentence "Quietness and value—the description applied to both [the watch chain and Jim]" as follows: "Both Jim and the watch chain showed quality in an inconspicuous way."

Paraphrase each of these statements.

1. ". . . repairing the ravages made by generosity added to love . . . is always a tremendous task."
2. "I don't think there's anything in the way of a haircut or a shave or a shampoo that could make me like my girl any less."

THINKING AND WRITING

Writing About Theme

Write an essay about the theme of "The Gift of the Magi." First, state the theme in your own words. Then make notes about how the characters, the setting, and the events contribute to it. Organize your notes into an outline and draft your essay, showing how O. Henry has used the story elements to illustrate the theme. Finally, revise your essay, checking that each of your points supports your statement of the theme.

LEARNING OPTION

Performance. "The Gift of the Magi" has been adapted for the stage. Find the play in the library or write a stage version of your own. Then, with a small group of classmates, perform the play for the class. You may wish to make simple props for the watch fob chain and the jeweled comb using aluminum foil, glitter, and the like. Other classmates may choose to contribute ideas for set design, costumes, staging, lighting, and background music for your production.

The Gift of the Magi 179

Preparation

More About the Author James Hurst himself wrote, "The ancient Egyptians worshiped the ibis because they believed it destroyed the crocodiles. In their liturgy, it took second place only to the phoenix. So I chose as my symbol a scarlet ibis, the most beautiful and rare member of the ibis family . . . I wanted a bird to represent Doodle—not Doodle's physical self, but his spirit. Certainly, Doodle inside had much more to admire than his outside . . . This bird must be destined to die as Doodle was to die." Ask students why writers use symbols in their stories.

Literary Focus Symbols are often visible representations of something invisible, such as a concept, idea, or hidden truth. Although the ibis is a symbol for Doodle and both are visible, the bird represents a quality within Doodle that is not evident from his appearance.

Prereading Focus You might have students work in pairs as they complete this exercise. It might also be helpful if you establish in advance at which points in the story students should interrupt their reading in order to discuss the story and to add details to the diagram.

Vocabulary You might have your students organize a vocabulary baseball game. They should divide into two teams with one student serving as umpire. The pitcher of one team throws out a vocabulary word to a batter from the other team and asks that student to define the word or to use the word in a sentence. The student can advance to first base by responding correctly. Any member of the pitcher's team can challenge the answer, and the umpire must rule if the student is safe or out.

James Hurst

(1922–   ) was born and raised on a farm in North Carolina. He studied chemical engineering but preferred music and took voice lessons at New York's Juilliard School of Music. When he realized that he was not meant to have a career in opera, he took a job as a bank clerk and wrote in the evenings. He has published several stories in small magazines and has achieved recognition with "The Scarlet Ibis," published in *The Atlantic* in 1960.

The Scarlet Ibis

Symbol

A **symbol** is an object, person, idea, or action that represents something other than itself. Authors may use symbols to make a point, create a mood, or reinforce a theme. Many common symbols have fixed or universal meanings; for example, the season of autumn frequently symbolizes a time of dying. Within a given work, a symbol takes much of its meaning from the work itself. It exists as an integral part of the story but represents something larger or more significant beyond the events of the story. "The Scarlet Ibis" has many symbols, but one stands out—the ibis. What might it symbolize?

Focus

This story is about two brothers who, despite differences in age, personality, and ability, are inseparable. Think about how two such dissimilar siblings could have such a close relationship. Then, as you read "The Scarlet Ibis," fill in a Venn diagram like the one below with the traits of each brother. What traits do the brothers share? Would you say that their relationship is shaped more by their similarities or by their differences? Why?

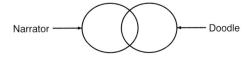

Narrator ⟶ ⟵ Doodle

Vocabulary

Knowing the following words will help you as you read "The Scarlet Ibis."

imminent (im′ ə nent) *adj.*: Likely to happen soon (p. 184)

iridescent (ir′ ə des′ 'nt) *adj.*: Having shifting, rainbowlike colors (p. 186)

vortex (vôr′ teks) *n.*: The center of a situation, which draws all that surrounds it (p. 186)

infallibility (in fal′ ə bil′ ə tē) *n.*: The condition of being unable to fail (p. 186)

entrails (en′ trālz) *n.*: Internal organs, specifically intestines (p. 186)

precariously (prē′ ker′ ē əs lē) *adv.*: Insecurely (p. 187)

evanesced (ev ə nest′) *v.*: Faded away (p. 190)

Objectives

1. To interpret symbols
2. To recognize emotive language
3. To write about symbols

Support Material

Teaching Portfolio
Teacher Backup, p. 237
Grammar in Action Worksheets, *Using Concrete Details*, p. 241; *Using Infinitive Phrases*, p. 243
Usage and Mechanics Worksheet, p. 245
Vocabulary Check, p. 246
Analyzing Literature Worksheet, *Interpreting Symbols*, p. 247

Language Worksheet, *Identifying Simile and Metaphor*, p. 248
Selection Test, p. 249

Prentice Hall Literature Writing Studio

The Scarlet Ibis

James Hurst

It was in the clove of seasons, summer was dead but autumn had not yet been born, that the ibis lit in the bleeding tree. The flower garden was stained with rotting brown magnolia petals and ironweeds grew rank amid the purple phlox. The five o'clocks by the chimney still marked time, but the oriole nest in the elm was untenanted and rocked back and forth like an empty cradle. The last graveyard flowers were blooming, and their smell drifted across the cotton field and through every room of our house, speaking softly the names of our dead.

It's strange that all this is still so clear to me, now that the summer has long since fled and time has had its way. A grindstone stands where the bleeding tree stood, just outside the kitchen door, and now if an oriole sings in the elm, its song seems to die up in the leaves, a silvery dust. The flower garden is prim, the house a gleaming white, and the pale fence across the yard stands straight and spruce. But sometimes (like right now), as I sit in the cool, green-draped parlor, the grindstone begins to turn, and time with all its changes is ground away— and I remember Doodle.

Doodle was just about the craziest brother a boy ever had. Of course, he wasn't a crazy crazy like old Miss Leedie, who was in love with President Wilson and wrote him a letter every day, but was a nice crazy, like someone you meet in your dreams. He was born when I was six and was, from the out-

set, a disappointment. He seemed all head, with a tiny body which was red and shriveled like an old man's. Everybody thought he was going to die—everybody except Aunt Nicey, who had delivered him. She said he would live because he was born in a caul[1] and cauls were made from Jesus' nightgown. Daddy had Mr. Heath, the carpenter, build a little mahogany coffin for him. But he didn't die, and when he was three months old Mama and Daddy decided they might as well name him. They named him William Armstrong, which was like tying a big tail on a small kite. Such a name sounds good only on a tombstone.

I thought myself pretty smart at many things, like holding my breath, running, jumping, or climbing the vines in Old Woman Swamp, and I wanted more than anything else someone to race to Horsehead Landing, someone to box with, and someone to perch with in the top fork of the great pine behind the barn, where across the fields and swamps you could see the sea. I wanted a brother. But Mama, crying, told me that even if William Armstrong lived, he would never do these things with me. He might not, she sobbed, even be "all there." He might as long as he lived, lie on the rubber sheet in the center of the bed in the front bedroom where the white marquisette cur-

---

1. **caul** (kôl) *n.*: The membrane enclosing a baby at birth.

The Scarlet Ibis 181

5 **Discussion** What sides of the narrator's character are revealed in this paragraph?

6 **Reading Strategy** Ask students to summarize Doodle's progress and to predict what further progress he might make.

7 **Discussion** Is Doodle a good name for William Armstrong? Why?

8 **Discussion** What character traits does the narrator's behavior reveal?

9 **Discussion** What kind of unspoken pact develops between the brothers?

tains billowed out in the afternoon sea breeze, rustling like palmetto fronds.[2]

It was bad enough having an invalid brother, but having one who possibly was not all there was unbearable, so I began to make plans to kill him by smothering him with a pillow. However, one afternoon as I watched him, my head poked between the irons posts of the foot of the bed, he looked straight at me and grinned. I skipped through the rooms, down the echoing halls, shouting, "Mama, he smiled. He's all there! He's all there!" and he was.

When he was two, if you laid him on his stomach, he began to try to move himself, straining terribly. The doctor said that with his weak heart this strain would probably kill him, but it didn't. Trembling, he'd push himself up, turning first red, then a soft purple, and finally collapse back onto the bed like an old worn-out doll. I can still see Mama watching him, her hand pressed tight across her mouth, her eyes wide and unblinking. But he learned to crawl (it was his third winter), and we brought him out of the front bedroom, putting him on the rug before the fireplace. For the first time he became one of us.

As long as he lay all the time in bed, we called him William Armstrong, even though it was formal and sounded as if we were referring to one of our ancestors, but with his creeping around on the deerskin rug and beginning to talk, something had to be done about his name. It was I who renamed him. When he crawled, he crawled backwards, as if he were in reverse and couldn't change gears. If you called him, he'd turn around as if he were going in the other direction, then he'd back right up to you to be picked up. Crawling backward made him look like a

doodle-bug, so I began to call him Doodle, and in time even Mama and Daddy thought it was a better name than William Armstrong. Only Aunt Nicey disagreed. She said caul babies should be treated with special respect since they might turn out to be saints. Renaming my brother was perhaps the kindest thing I ever did for him, because nobody expects much from someone called Doodle.

Although Doodle learned to crawl, he showed no signs of walking, but he wasn't idle. He talked so much that we all quit listening to what he said. It was about this time that Daddy built him a go-cart and I had to pull him around. At first I just paraded him up and down the piazza, but then he started crying to be taken out into the yard and it ended up by my having to lug him wherever I went. If I so much as picked up my cap, he'd start crying to go with me and Mama would call from wherever she was, "Take Doodle with you."

He was a burden in many ways. The doctor had said that he mustn't get too excited, too hot, too cold, or too tired and that he must always be treated gently. A long list of don'ts went with him, all of which I ignored once we got out of the house. To discourage his coming with me, I'd run with him across the ends of the cotton rows and career him around corners on two wheels. Sometimes I accidentally turned him over, but he never told Mama. His skin was very sensitive, and he had to wear a big straw hat whenever he went out. When the going got rough and he had to cling to the sides of the go-cart, the hat slipped all the way down over his ears. He was a sight. Finally, I could see I was licked. Doodle was my brother and he was going to cling to me forever, no matter what I did, so I dragged him across the burning cotton field to share with him the only beauty I knew, Old Woman Swamp. I pulled the go-cart through the saw-tooth fern, down into the green dimness where the pal-

---
2. palmetto fronds: Palm leaves.

Grammar in Action

When a writer uses **concrete details,** readers can see, hear, smell, taste, and feel what the writer is describing. For instance, if a writer merely says "dog," the reader will only have a vague or general idea of the type of animal the writer has in mind. If a writer specifies "German shepherd," however, readers will have a much more specific picture.

Notice how James Hurst uses concrete, specific details to enliven the following description:

. . . I dragged him across the *burning cotton field* to share with him the only beauty I knew, Old Woman Swamp. I pulled the go-cart through the *saw-tooth fern,* down into the *green dimness* where the *palmetto fronds* whispered by the stream, lifted him out and set him down in the *soft rubber grass* beside a *tall pine.* His eyes were round with wonder as he gazed about him, and his little hands began to stroke the *rubber grass.* Then he began to cry.

Without the concrete details, this passage would be much less effective:

metto fronds whispered by the stream. I lifted him out and set him down in the soft rubber grass beside a tall pine. His eyes were round with wonder as he gazed about him, and his little hands began to stroke the rubber grass. Then he began to cry.

"For heaven's sake, what's the matter?" I asked, annoyed.

"It's so pretty," he said. "So pretty, pretty, pretty."

After that day Doodle and I often went down into Old Woman Swamp. I would gather wildflowers, wild violets, honeysuckle, yellow jasmine, snakeflowers, and water lilies, and with wire grass we'd weave them into necklaces and crowns. We'd bedeck ourselves with our handiwork and loll about thus beautified, beyond the touch of the everyday world. Then when the slanted rays of the sun burned orange in the tops of the pines, we'd drop our jewels into the stream and watch them float away toward the sea.

There is within me (and with sadness I have watched it in others) a knot of cruelty borne by the stream of love, much as our blood sometimes bears the seed of our destruction, and at times I was mean to Doodle. One day I took him up to the barn loft and showed him his casket, telling him how we all had believed he would die. It was covered with a film of Paris green[3] sprinkled to kill the rats, and screech owls had built a nest inside it.

Doodle studied the mahogany box for a long time, then said, "It's not mine."

"It is," I said. "And before I'll help you down from the loft, you're going to have to touch it."

"I won't touch it," he said sullenly.

"Then I'll leave you here by yourself," I threatened, and made as if I were going down.

Doodle was frightened of being left.

---

3. **Paris green:** A poisonous green powder.

"Don't go leave me, Brother," he cried, and he leaned toward the coffin. His hand, trembling, reached out, and when he touched the casket he screamed. A screech owl flapped out of the box into our faces, scaring us and covering us with Paris green. Doodle was paralyzed, so I put him on my shoulder and carried him down the ladder, and even when we were outside in the bright sunshine, he clung to me, crying, "Don't leave me. Don't leave me."

When Doodle was five years old, I was embarrassed at having a brother of that age who couldn't walk, so I set out to teach him. We were down in Old Woman Swamp and it was spring and the sick-sweet smell of bay flowers hung everywhere like a mournful song. "I'm going to teach you to walk, Doodle," I said.

He was sitting comfortably on the soft grass, leaning back against the pine. "Why?" he asked.

I hadn't expected such an answer. "So I won't have to haul you around all the time."

"I can't walk, Brother," he said.

"Who says so?" I demanded.

"Mama, the doctor—everybody."

"Oh, you can walk," I said, and I took him by the arms and stood him up. He collapsed onto the grass like a half-empty flour sack. It was as if he had no bones in his little legs.

"Don't hurt me, Brother," he warned.

"Shut up. I'm not going to hurt you. I'm going to teach you to walk." I heaved him up again, and again he collapsed.

This time he did not lift his face up out of the rubber grass. "I just can't do it. Let's make honeysuckle wreaths."

"Oh yes you can, Doodle," I said. "All you got to do is try. Now come on," and I hauled him up once more.

It seemed so hopeless from the beginning that it's a miracle I didn't give up. But

The Scarlet Ibis 183

15 Discussion Why is this an important moment in the story?

16 Discussion Why does the narrator feel this was his accomplishment as well as Doodle's? Does he have a right to share in Doodle's glory?

17 Discussion Do you agree that the narrator was a slave to pride? Why? How does this statement relate to his earlier confession about having "a knot of cruelty"?

18 Reading Strategy Ask students to summarize all the progress Doodle has made since birth. Ask them to predict what might happen to him in the future.

19 Discussion What do you think the narrator means by "lies"?

Multicultural Focus The central symbol of Hurst's story is a bird, one of the most common symbols in stories and tales from all over the world. Because they can fly, birds have most often been associated with freedom and the heavens. Birds also represent the human soul in flight in ancient Egyptian, Hebrew, Native American, and Hindu mythology. In myths across the world, they are believed to be able to talk to people. The eagle, in particular, was worshiped by many Native American groups and came to symbolize royalty and dynastic authority for empires from Babylon to Czarist Russia. Other birds, like the raven and the owl, were feared by many cultures as harbingers of evil, death, and bad fortune. The ibis was sacred to the Egyptians, who associated it with Thoth, their god of wisdom and the arts. Perhaps the most fascinating bird symbol is the mythological phoenix, which supposedly burns itself up every 500 years to rise again from its ashes.

Have students find out about the symbolic meaning of a particular bird from any mythology about which they are curious.

all of us must have something or someone to be proud of, and Doodle had become mine. I did not know then that pride is a wonderful, terrible thing, a seed that bears two vines, life and death. Every day that summer we went to the pine beside the stream of Old Woman Swamp, and I put him on his feet at least a hundred times each afternoon. Occasionally I too became discouraged because it didn't seem as if he was trying, and I would say, "Doodle, don't you *want* to learn to walk?"

He'd nod his head, and I'd say, "Well, if you don't keep trying, you'll never learn." Then I'd paint for him a picture of us as old men, white-haired, him with a long white beard and me still pulling him around in the go-cart. This never failed to make him try again.

Finally one day, after many weeks of practicing, he stood alone for a few seconds. When he fell, I grabbed him in my arms and hugged him, our laughter pealing through the swamp like a ringing bell. Now we knew it could be done. Hope no longer hid in the dark palmetto thicket but perched like a cardinal in the lacy toothbrush tree, brilliantly visible. "Yes, yes," I cried, and he cried it too, and the grass beneath us was soft and the smell of the swamp was sweet.

With success so imminent, we decided not to tell anyone until he could actually walk. Each day, barring rain, we sneaked into Old Woman Swamp, and by cotton-picking time Doodle was ready to show what he could do. He still wasn't able to walk far, but we could wait no longer. Keeping a nice secret is very hard to do, like holding your breath. We chose to reveal all on October eighth, Doodle's sixth birthday, and for weeks ahead we mooned around the house, promising everybody a most spectacular surprise. Aunt Nicey said that, after so much talk, if we produced anything less tremen-

dous than the Resurrection,[4] she was going to be disappointed.

At breakfast on our chosen day, when Mama, Daddy, and Aunt Nicey were in the dining room, I brought Doodle to the door in the go-cart just as usual and had them turn their backs, making them cross their hearts and hope to die if they peeked. I helped Doodle up, and when he was standing alone I let them look. There wasn't a sound as Doodle walked slowly across the room and sat down at his place at the table. Then Mama began to cry and ran over to him, hugging him and kissing him. Daddy hugged him too, so I went to Aunt Nicey, who was thanks praying in the doorway, and began to waltz her around. We danced together quite well until she came down on my big toe with her brogans, hurting me so badly I thought I was crippled for life.

Doodle told them it was I who had taught him to walk, so everyone wanted to hug me, and I began to cry.

"What are you crying for?" asked Daddy, but I couldn't answer. They did not know that I did it for myself; that pride, whose slave I was, spoke to me louder than all their voices, and that Doodle walked only because I was ashamed of having a crippled brother.

Within a few months Doodle had learned to walk well and his go-cart was put up in the barn loft (it's still there) beside his little mahogany coffin. Now, when we roamed off together, resting often, we never turned back until our destination had been reached, and to help pass the time, we took up lying. From the beginning Doodle was a terrible liar and he got me in the habit. Had anyone stopped to listen to us, we would have been sent off to Dix Hill.

My lies were scary, involved, and usually

4. **the Resurrection** (rez′ ə rek′ shən): The rising of Jesus Christ from the dead after his death and burial.

TWO BOYS IN A PUNT
N. C. Wyeth
Courtesy of Dr. and Mrs. William A. Morton, Jr.

The Scarlet Ibis 185

Humanities Note

Fine art, *Boys in a Punt,* by N. C. Wyeth. Newel Convers Wyeth (1882–1945), who was born in Needham, Massachusetts, lived during the time that is now known as the Golden Age of American Illustration—the time from the mid-1870's to approximately the 1920's. The age was so named because of the number of creative and well-known illustrators whose work was published during that period, including Winslow Homer, Howard Pyle, and N. C. Wyeth.

By the time he was a teenager, Wyeth knew he wanted to be an artist and enrolled in the Howard Pyle School of Illustration in Philadelphia, where he was taught by Howard Pyle.

While in school, Wyeth frequently took trips to Pyle's home at Chadds Ford, Pennsylvania, to roam the hills and woods of the Brandywine Valley. He later permanently moved to this area to raise his own family. Much of Wyeth's finest work, including *Boys in a Punt,* was inspired by the rural life around him.

You might use the following questions for discussion.
1. The tone of a painting is the painter's attitude toward the subject. It may be established through the colors the artist chose or the composition. What is the tone of this painting? How does the tone of the painting complement the tone of the story?
2. Do you think Wyeth's illustration is appropriate for this story? Explain.

20 **Critical Thinking and Reading**
Discuss this story with students. What emotions does it evoke? What does it indicate about Doodle?

21 **Discussion** Are the narrator's goals sensible? Explain.

22 **Discussion** What mood does this passage call up?

23 **Clarification** World War I ended in November of 1918. During the summer, major battles were being fought in France.

24 **Discussion** Why does the author include this passage? How does it relate to the story?

20 pointless, but Doodle's were twice as crazy. People in his stories all had wings and flew wherever they wanted to go. His favorite lie was about a boy named Peter who had a pet peacock with a ten-foot tail. Peter wore a golden robe that glittered so brightly that when he walked through the sunflowers they turned away from the sun to face him. When Peter was ready to go to sleep, the peacock spread his magnificent tail, enfolding the boy gently like a closing go-to-sleep flower, burying him in the gloriously iridescent, rustling vortex. Yes, I must admit it. Doodle could beat me lying.

Doodle and I spent lots of time thinking about our future. We decided that when we were grown we'd live in Old Woman Swamp and pick dog-tongue for a living. Beside the stream, he planned, we'd build us a house of whispering leaves and the swamp birds would be our chickens. All day long (when we weren't gathering dog-tongue) we'd swing through the cypresses on the rope vines, and if it rained we'd huddle beneath an umbrella tree and play stickfrog. Mama and Daddy could come and live with us if they wanted to. He even came up with the idea that he could marry Mama and I could marry Daddy. Of course, I was old enough to know this wouldn't work out, but the picture he painted was so beautiful and serene that all I could do was whisper Yes, yes.

21 Once I had succeeded in teaching Doodle to walk, I began to believe in my own infallibility and I prepared a terrific development program for him, unknown to Mama and Daddy, of course. I would teach him to run, to swim, to climb trees, and to fight. He, too, now believed in my infallibility, so we set the deadline for these accomplishments less than a year away, when, it had been decided, Doodle could start to school.

That winter we didn't make much progress, for I was in school and Doodle suffered from one bad cold after another. But when spring came, rich and warm, we raised our sights again. Success lay at the end of summer like a pot of gold, and our campaign got off to a good start. On hot days, Doodle and I went down to Horsehead Landing and I gave him swimming lessons or showed him how to row a boat. Sometimes we descended into the cool greenness of Old Woman Swamp and climbed the rope vines or boxed scientifically beneath the pine where he had learned to walk. Promise hung about us like the leaves, and wherever we looked, ferns unfurled and birds broke into song.

That summer, the summer of 1918, was blighted. In May and June there was no rain and the crops withered, curled up, then died under the thirsty sun. One morning in July a hurricane came out of the east, tipping over the oaks in the yard and splitting the limbs of the elm trees. That afternoon it roared back out of the west, blew the fallen oaks around, snapping their roots and tearing them out of the earth like a hawk at the entrails of a chicken. Cotton bolls were wrenched from the stalks and lay like green walnuts in the valleys between the rows, while the cornfield leaned over uniformly so that the tassels touched the ground. Doodle and I followed Daddy out into the cotton field, where he stood, shoulders sagging, surveying the ruin. When his chin sank down onto his chest, we were frightened, and Doodle slipped his hand into mine. Suddenly Daddy straightened his shoulders, raised a giant knuckly fist, and with a voice that seemed to rumble out of the earth itself began cursing heaven, hell, the weather, and the Republican Party. Doodle and I, prodding each other and giggling, went back to the house, knowing that everything would be all right.

And during that summer, strange names were heard through the house: Château Thierry, Amiens, Soissons, and in her bless-

Grammar in Action

Knowing how to use infinitives correctly will avoid confusion and will make your writing clear and accurate. An **infinitive** is the form of a verb that comes after the word *to* and acts as a noun, adjective, or adverb. When an infinitive has modifiers or a complement, it is called an **infinitive phrase.** Read the following sentences in which James Hurst uses infinitives and infinitive phrases.

"Of course, I was old enough *to know this wouldn't work out."*

"*I would teach him to run, to swim, to climb trees,* and *to fight."*

Notice that the first sentence contains an infinitive phrase, whereas the second contains infinitives.

It is important not to confuse infinitives and infinitive phrases with prepositional phrases that can also begin with the word *to.*

Writers need to be aware of several rules governing the use of infinitives. First, when using several infinitives in a series, the same form of the verb must be used each time. Sometimes writers are careless and combine infinitives with the *ing* form of

ing at the supper table, Mama once said, "And bless the Pearsons, whose boy Joe was lost at Belleau Wood."[5]

So we came to that clove of seasons. School was only a few weeks away, and Doodle was far behind schedule. He could barely clear the ground when climbing up the rope vines and his swimming was certainly not passable. We decided to double our efforts, to make that last drive and reach our pot of gold. I made him swim until he turned blue and row until he couldn't lift an oar. Wherever we went, I purposely walked fast, and although he kept up, his face turned red and his eyes became glazed. Once, he could go no further, so he collapsed on the ground and began to cry.

"Aw, come on, Doodle," I urged. "You can do it. Do you want to be different from everybody else when you start school?"

"Does it make any difference?"

"It certainly does," I said. "Now, come on," and I helped him up.

As we slipped through dog days, Doodle began to look feverish, and Mama felt his forehead, asking him if he felt ill. At night he didn't sleep well, and sometimes he had nightmares, crying out until I touched him and said, "Wake up, Doodle. Wake up."

It was Saturday noon, just a few days before school was to start. I should have already admitted defeat, but my pride wouldn't let me. The excitement of our program had now been gone for weeks, but still we kept on with a tired doggedness. It was too late to turn back, for we had both wandered too far into a net of expectations and had left no crumbs behind.

Daddy, Mama, Doodle, and I were seated at the dining-room table having lunch. It

---

5. **Château Thierry** (shȧ tō tye rē'), **Amiens** (a myan'), **Soissons** (swä sôn'), . . . **Belleau** (be lō') **Wood:** Places in France where battles were fought during World War I.

was a hot day, with all the windows and doors open in case a breeze should come. In the kitchen Aunt Nicey was humming softly. After a long silence, Daddy spoke. "It's so calm, I wouldn't be surprised if we had a storm this afternoon."

"I haven't heard a rain frog," said Mama, who believed in signs, as she served the bread around the table.

"I did," declared Doodle. "Down in the swamp."

"He didn't," I said contrarily.

"You did, eh?" said Daddy, ignoring my denial.

"I certainly did," Doodle reiterated, scowling at me over the top of his iced-tea glass, and we were quiet again.

Suddenly, from out in the yard, came a strange croaking noise. Doodle stopped eating, with a piece of bread poised ready for his mouth, his eyes popped round like two blue buttons. "What's that?" he whispered.

I jumped up, knocking over my chair, and had reached the door when Mama called, "Pick up the chair, sit down again, and say excuse me."

By the time I had done this, Doodle had excused himself and had slipped out into the yard. He was looking up into the bleeding tree. "It's a great big red bird!" he called.

The bird croaked loudly again, and Mama and Daddy came out into the yard. We shaded our eyes with our hands against the hazy glare of the sun and peered up through the still leaves. On the topmost branch a bird the size of a chicken, with scarlet feathers and long legs, was perched precariously. Its wings hung down loosely, and as we watched, a feather dropped away and floated slowly down through the green leaves.

"It's not even frightened of us," Mama said.

"It looks tired," Daddy added. "Or maybe sick."

Doodle's hands were clasped at his

The Scarlet Ibis 187

25 Reading Strategy Ask students to note the connection between this sentence and the first sentence of the story. Help students to understand that they are now at the same point of time as indicated in the first paragraph of the story.

26 Discussion Is the narrator pushing his brother too hard to achieve their goals? Why?

27 Discussion What does Doodle's question reveal about his changing mood?

28 Discussion How is Doodle's failing health related to his changed mood?

29 Discussion What keeps the narrator so determined to push ahead with their plans?

30 Literary Focus What qualities of the ibis does the author stress?

Electronic Handbook You might want students to review infinitives and infinitive phrases before completing the activities. If students have access to the Language Master 6000, have them enter the access words *tense* and *verbal* and press the GRAMMAR key to obtain information on these topics.

the verb. Note in the following sentence the confusion that can arise when the wrong verb form is used:

I would teach him to run, to swim, to climb trees, and fighting.

Secondly, writers should never split an infinitive by inserting an adverb between the word *to* and the verb. For example, never write:

I would teach him to quickly run.

The sentence should read:

I would teach him to run quickly.

Student Activity 1. Identify the infinitives and infinitive phrases in the following sentences. Revise any sentences that use the wrong form of the verb.
1. "He began to move himself, straining terribly."
2. "Doodle, don't you want to learn walking?"
3. "Black clouds began to gather in the southwest."

Student Activity 2. Write three original sentences in which you use infinitives or infinitive phrases.

Humanities Note

Fine art, *Scarlet Ibis,* by John James Audubon. Audubon (1785–1851) was born in Santo Domingo (Haiti). Throughout Audubon's childhood on the island, his interest in birds and drawing birds developed. When he was an adult this interest was insatiable and he thought of little else.

Audubon is recognized as one of the first to study and paint the birds of America. His paintings are most noted for their life-size depiction of birds in their natural habitat. For example, in the original painting of the scarlet ibis, this South American bird is depicted in its natural habitat: wading along a tropical beach where the water is shallow and close to a swampy area. It is here the scarlet ibis will hunt for its food and build its nest.

You might use the following questions for discussion.
1. Why do you think it was important to Audubon to paint birds in their natural surroundings?
2. Why might Hurst in this story have displaced the scarlet ibis from its natural surroundings?
3. The scarlet ibis dies in an unfamiliar place. Why is this an important detail in the story?

31 Literary Focus How does the fact that the bird is out of place relate to Doodle?

SCARLET IBIS
John James Audubon
New York Historical Society

throat, and I had never seen him stand still so long. "What is it?" he asked.

Daddy shook his head. "I don't know, maybe it's—"

At that moment the bird began to flutter, but the wings were uncoordinated, and amid much flapping and a spray of flying feathers, it tumbled down, bumping through the limbs of the bleeding tree and landing at our feet with a thud. Its long, graceful neck jerked twice into an S, then straightened out, and the bird was still. A white veil came over the eyes and the long white beak unhinged. Its legs were crossed and its clawlike feet were delicately curved at rest. Even death did not mar its grace, for it lay on the earth like a broken vase of red flowers, and we stood around it, awed by its exotic beauty.

"It's dead," Mama said.

"What is it?" Doodle repeated.

"Go bring me the bird book," said Daddy.

I ran into the house and brought back the bird book. As we watched, Daddy thumbed through its pages. "It's a scarlet ibis," he said, pointing to a picture. "It lives in the tropics—South America to Florida. A storm must have brought it here."

Sadly, we all looked back at the bird. A scarlet ibis! How many miles it had traveled to die like this, in *our* yard, beneath the bleeding tree.

"Let's finish lunch," Mama said, nudging us back toward the dining room.

"I'm not hungry," said Doodle, and he knelt down beside the ibis.

"We've got peach cobbler for dessert," Mama tempted from the doorway.

Doodle remained kneeling. "I'm going to bury him."

"Don't you dare touch him," Mama warned. "There's no telling what disease he might have had."

"All right," said Doodle. "I won't."

Daddy, Mama, and I went back to the dining-room table, but we watched Doodle through the open door. He took out a piece of string from his pocket and, without

188   *Short Stories*

touching the ibis, looped one end around its neck. Slowly, while singing softly *Shall We Gather at the River*, he carried the bird around to the front yard and dug a hole in the flower garden, next to the petunia bed. Now we were watching him through the front window, but he didn't know it. His awkwardness at digging the hole with a shovel whose handle was twice as long as he was made us laugh, and we covered our mouths with our hands so he wouldn't hear.

When Doodle came into the dining room, he found us seriously eating our cobbler. He was pale and lingered just inside the screen door. "Did you get the scarlet ibis buried?" asked Daddy.

Doodle didn't speak but nodded his head.

"Go wash your hands, and then you can have some peach cobbler," said Mama.

"I'm not hungry," he said.

"Dead birds is bad luck," said Aunt Nicey, poking her head from the kitchen door. "Specially *red* dead birds!"

As soon as I had finished eating, Doodle and I hurried off to Horsehead Landing. Time was short, and Doodle still had a long way to go if he was going to keep up with the other boys when he started school. The sun, gilded with the yellow cast of autumn, still burned fiercely, but the dark green woods through which we passed were shady and cool. When we reached the landing, Doodle said he was too tired to swim, so we got into a skiff and floated down the creek with the tide. Far off in the marsh a rail was scolding, and over on the beach locusts were singing in the myrtle trees. Doodle did not speak and kept his head turned away, letting one hand trail limply in the water.

After we had drifted a long way, I put the oars in place and made Doodle row back against the tide. Black clouds began to gather in the southwest, and he kept watching them, trying to pull the oars a little faster. When we reached Horsehead Landing, lightning was playing across half the sky and thunder roared out, hiding even the sound of the sea. The sun disappeared and darkness descended, almost like night. Flocks of marsh crows flew by, heading inland to their roosting trees, and two egrets, squawking, arose from the oyster-rock shallows and careened away.

Doodle was both tired and frightened, and when he stepped from the skiff he collapsed onto the mud, sending an armada of fiddler crabs rustling off into the marsh grass. I helped him up, and as he wiped the mud off his trousers, he smiled at me ashamedly. He had failed and we both knew it, so we started back home, racing the storm. We never spoke (What are the words that can solder cracked pride?), but I knew he was watching me, watching for a sign of mercy. The lightning was near now, and from fear he walked so close behind me he kept stepping on my heels. The faster I walked, the faster he walked, so I began to run. The rain was coming, roaring through the pines, and then, like a bursting Roman candle, a gum tree ahead of us was shattered by a bolt of lightning. When the deafening peal of thunder had died, and in the moment before the rain arrived, I heard Doodle, who had fallen behind, cry out, "Brother, Brother, don't leave me! Don't leave me!"

The knowledge that Doodle's and my plans had come to naught was bitter, and that streak of cruelty within me awakened. I ran as fast as I could, leaving him far behind with a wall of rain dividing us. The drops stung my face like nettles, and the wind flared the wet glistening leaves of the bordering trees. Soon I could hear his voice no more.

I hadn't run too far before I became tired, and the flood of childish spite evanesced as

The Scarlet Ibis 189

32 Discussion Why is Doodle's reaction to the bird's death different from that of the rest of the family?

33 Discussion How might Aunt Nicey's remark foreshadow what will happen in the story?

34 Discussion Why do the narrator and Doodle seem to be in different worlds?

35 Discussion What is the meaning of the phrase in parentheses?

36 Reading Strategy When has Doodle said this before? How are the situations similar?

37 Discussion Why does the narrator's cruelty emerge at this moment?

Literary Focus Compare the description of Doodle to that of the ibis after it had fallen from the tree. How does that incident foreshadow the end of the story?

Reader's Response How did your feelings change as you read this story?

Thematic Response Brother's rite of passage was very painful for him. In what way do you think Brother will be affected by Doodle's death?

---

well. I stopped and waited for Doodle. The sound of rain was everywhere, but the wind had died and it fell straight down in parallel paths like ropes hanging from the sky. As I waited, I peered through the downpour, but no one came. Finally I went back and found him huddled beneath a red nightshade bush beside the road. He was sitting on the ground, his face buried in his arms, which were resting on his drawn-up knees. "Let's go, Doodle," I said.

He didn't answer, so I placed my hand on his forehead and lifted his head. Limply, he fell backwards onto the earth. He had been bleeding from the mouth, and his neck and the front of his shirt were stained a brilliant red.

"Doodle! Doodle!" I cried, shaking him, but there was no answer but the ropy rain. He lay very awkwardly, with his head thrown far back, making his vermilion neck appear unusually long and slim. His little legs, bent sharply at the knees, had never before seemed so fragile, so thin.

I began to weep, and the tear-blurred vision in red before me looked very familiar. "Doodle!" I screamed above the pounding storm and threw my body to the earth above his. For a long long time, it seemed forever, I lay there crying, sheltering my fallen scarlet ibis from the heresy[6] of rain.

---

6. **heresy** (her′ ə sē): An idea opposed to the beliefs of a religion or philosophy.

RESPONDING TO THE **S**ELECTION

Your Response

1. Do you think the narrator was in any way responsible for his brother's death? Why or why not?

Recalling

2. How does Doodle disappoint his brother?
3. What motivates the narrator to teach Doodle to walk?
4. What other plans does he make for Doodle?
5. The narrator says, "There is within me . . . a knot of cruelty borne by the stream of love. . . ." Give two examples of his cruelty to Doodle.
6. Summarize the circumstances leading to Doodle's death.

Interpreting

7. What does each of the following show about Doodle?
   a. his reactions to his brother's plans for him
   b. his favorite "lies"
   c. his response to the scarlet ibis

8. Why does the narrator set such demanding goals for Doodle?
9. The narrator states that ". . . pride is a wonderful, terrible thing, a seed that bears two vines, life and death." Explain how the story demonstrates the truth of this statement.
10. What larger meaning might be read into Doodle's cry, ". . . Brother, don't leave me! . . ."?

Applying

11. The story opens with the narrator, now an adult, remembering the events from long ago. How does the passage of time change people and their feelings about past events?
12. Do you think that many people have mixed feelings about sisters and brothers? Explain.

ANALYZING **L**ITERATURE

Interpreting Symbols

A **symbol** is something that represents something beyond itself. Writers may use symbols to present or reinforce a theme. For instance, throughout "The Scarlet Ibis," James Hurst refers

---

Closure and Extension

ANSWERS TO RESPONDING TO THE SELECTION

Your Response

1. Ask students to discuss Brother's motives for helping Doodle. Have them consider these motives as they respond to the question of whether Brother was in any way responsible for Doodle's death.

Recalling

2. The narrator wanted someone to race, box, and climb trees with, but Doodle could do none of these.
3. The narrator said he was embarrassed to have a brother who could not walk.
4. The narrator also planned to teach Doodle to run, swim, climb trees, and fight.
5. The narrator demonstrated his cruelty when he forced Doodle to touch the coffin and when he left

him behind during the rainstorm.
6. After the ibis had died, the narrator made a final attempt to get Doodle to achieve the physical goals set for him. Doodle was too tired to try. As they ran home during a rainstorm, Doodle got left behind, collapsed, and died.

Interpreting

7. Suggested Response:
   a. Doodle was not enthusiastic about the plans, but to please his brother he demonstrated

courage and tried his best.
   b. Doodle had a vivid imagination.
   c. Doodle felt a kinship with this exotic outsider.
8. Suggested Response: His pride caused him to want a brother who could accomplish these goals.
9. Suggested Response: Because of the narrator's pride in achieving a goal, he worked tenaciously to teach Doodle to walk. Because of this same pride, he

to things that are red. The color red commonly symbolizes blood, or courage, or tragedy. This is an appropriate symbol in a story that deals with the tragic death of a courageous boy.

A character, thing, setting, or action may suggest a larger meaning or idea within the story. The narrator sees a great similarity between Doodle and the scarlet ibis, the major symbol in this story.

1. In what ways is Doodle like the scarlet ibis?
2. Compare Doodle's appearance in death with the appearance of the scarlet ibis.
3. What does the scarlet ibis symbolize?

CRITICAL THINKING AND READING

Recognizing Emotive Language

Writers may use **emotive language** in describing a mood or feeling. Such language can cause you to laugh, cry, feel fear or other emotions along with the characters. "The Scarlet Ibis" contains many emotive passages. For example, the very first paragraph sets the somber mood for the story with words like *dead, bleeding tree, stained, rotting,* and *graveyard.*

1. What emotions does the paragraph beginning "It was bad . . ." (page 190) communicate? What words convey this emotion?
2. What words and phrases convey the feeling of exhilaration in the paragraph in which Doodle first walks (page 193)?

THINKING AND WRITING

Writing About Symbols

Suppose that you wanted an artist to draw an illustration that captured the feelings of the narrator in "The Scarlet Ibis." Identify an emotion he feels at a particular point, and think of a symbol for that emotion. Write a note to the artist that tells why the symbol is appropriate and how it should appear. When you revise, check that your explanation will be clear to the reader, and that you have given details about the symbol to guide the illustrator in drawing it.

LEARNING OPTIONS

1. **Art.** Create a drawing, painting, collage, or other work of art to illustrate the scene described in this passage from "The Scarlet Ibis":

> After that day Doodle and I often went down into Old Woman Swamp. I would gather wildflowers, wild violets, honeysuckle, yellow jasmine, snakeflowers, and water lilies, and with wire grass we'd weave them into necklaces and crowns. We'd bedeck ourselves with our handiwork and loll about thus beautified, beyond the touch of the everyday world. Then when the slanted rays of the sun burned orange in the tops of the pines, we'd drop our jewels into the stream and watch them float away toward the sea.

Display your finished art work in the classroom.

2. **Cross-curricular Connection.** Find out more about the scarlet ibis in an encyclopedia or a reference book on birds. Think about why the author chose this particular animal as a symbol for Doodle. What qualities do the bird and Doodle share? As you learn more about the scarlet ibis, do you think that the bird is an appropriate choice as a symbol for Doodle? Why or why not?

The Scarlet Ibis 191

2. Suggested Response: Doodle's neck was stained red; his head thrown back made his neck appear long and slim; his little legs were bent sharply at the knees. These descriptions all suggest the ibis's appearance at the foot of the tree.
3. Suggested Response: The scarlet ibis was a beautiful, delicate, and wounded bird that symbolized the inner beauty, delicate nature, and imminent death of Doodle. They were both unusual and lovely, but out of place in their worlds.

ANSWERS TO CRITICAL THINKING AND READING

1. Suggested Response: This paragraph conveys the emotions of depression and anger through the words "invalid," "not all there," "unbearable," "kill," and "smothering." The paragraph also conveys exhilaration, hope, and anticipation through the words "grinned," "skipped," "shouting," "smiled," and "he's all there."
2. Suggested Response: The words and phrases that convey a feeling of exhilaration are "hugged," "laughter pealing," "ringing bell," "perched like a cardinal," "brilliantly visible," "soft," and "sweet."

THINKING AND WRITING

 Writing Transparency
Graphic organizers are a good tool for helping students to translate abstract ideas into visual symbols. Before students write, have them brainstorm for ideas using the sensory Language Chart in **Transparencies for Writing.**

LEARNING OPTIONS

1. This activity will appeal to visually learners and artistically gifted students.
2. You might want to extend the activity by having students bring in and share photographs of the scarlet ibis.

forced Doodle to overtax himself in achieving new goals, and Doodle died.
10. Answers will differ. Doodle may have realized that he would soon die.

Applying

11. Answers will differ. Students may respond that, although adults have memories of how they felt as children, they can view childhood from an adult's perspective. Also, certain events stand out more clearly, while others fade as time passes.
12. Answers will differ. Students may respond that, although siblings often feel a family kinship and enjoy a close relationship, they can also feel competitive at times.

ANSWERS TO ANALYZING LITERATURE

1. Suggested Response: Doodle was as beautiful inside as the ibis was in appearance. The ibis was crippled and could not fly; Doodle was crippled and could not do many things. The ibis struggled against a great storm until its strength gave out and it died. Doodle also struggled with all his strength until he died.

Preparation

More About the Author Guy de Maupassant (gē də mō pə sänt) is more highly regarded outside his own country than in France. For some critics, his popular success is reason enough to devalue his work. Ask students to discuss the relationship between popular success and literary merit. In what way can popular success be a drawback for a serious writer?

Literary Focus Irony can be shown in many ways. In this story it is shown through dramatic contrasts and a surprise ending. Point out that irony is quite common in everyday speech. Nicknames often have an ironic intent.

Prereading Focus Before students begin this activity, you might lead them in a brief discussion about fate. What is it? How do they see it affecting their lives? You might have them hypothesize about how even a small change in a person's circumstances can affect his or her life in major ways. Then have them apply this idea to their own lives through a brief writing.

Vocabulary Have your **less advanced** students read these words aloud so that you can be sure they know them.

Spelling Tip Write the words *resplendent* and *exorbitant* on the board. Tell students that the suffixes *-ent* and *-ant* are both used to form adjectives. There is no satisfactory rule for determining which to use.

Guy de Maupassant

(1850–1893) was born and grew up in the province of Normandy, France. After serving in the Franco-Prussian War, he worked in a poorly paid job as a government clerk. During this period, though, he practiced writing and became the literary apprentice of the renowned nineteenth-century writer Gustave Flaubert. Maupassant is considered the best-known short story writer in the world. "The Necklace" reflects his first-hand knowledge of the world of civil servants and the bourgeoisie, or middle class.

The Necklace

Irony

Irony is a contrast between an expected outcome and the actual outcome or between appearance and reality. For example, a man may court rich and famous people as a way of furthering his career. However, he may find that the friend he abandoned on his climb to the top becomes a wealthy industrialist who holds the key to his success in her hands. We call this turn of events *ironic*. By using irony, a writer may suggest that life is more complicated than it may at first appear.

Focus

In "The Necklace" the author suggests in the very first paragraph that the main character is the victim of an "error of fate." The idea is that the character was given the wrong destiny. If she had been born into a wealthier family, her life would have come out the way it should have. What if some major factor in your life were changed? Suppose you were born to a royal family or possessed extraordinary athletic ability. Think of some important fact about your life that could be different. Write briefly about how the change would affect you. Then, as you read the story, think about the effect of fate on Madame Loisel.

Vocabulary

Knowing the following words will help you as you read "The Necklace."

déclassée (dā′ klä sā′) *adj.*: lowered in social status (p. 193)
rueful (r$\overline{oo}$′ fəl) *adj.*: causing sorrow or pity (p. 193)
anguish (an′ gwish) *n.*: great suffering (p. 196)
resplendent (ri splen′ dənt) *adj.*: shining brightly (p. 196)
dejection (di jek′ shən) *n.*: lowness of spirits (p. 197)

exorbitant (ig zôr′ bə tənt) *adj.*: exceeding the appropriate limits (p. 197)
coarse (kôrs) *adj.*: rough, crude, unrefined (p. 198)
disheveled (di shev′ 'ld) *adj.*: disarranged and untidy (p. 198)
profoundly (prə found′ lē) *adv.*: deeply and intensely (p. 198)

192   Short Stories

Objectives

1 To understand irony
2 To make inferences about characters
3 To respond to criticism

Support Material

Teaching Portfolio
Teacher Backup, p. 251
Grammar in Action Worksheet, *Varying Sentences,* p. 255
Usage and Mechanics Worksheet, p. 257
Vocabulary Check, p. 258
Analyzing Literature Worksheet, *Understanding Irony,* p. 259
Language Worksheet, *Choosing the Meaning That Fits the Context,* p. 260

Selection Test, p. 261
Art Transparency 5: *Sunday Afternoon on the Island of La Grande Jatte,* by Georges Seurat

Library of Video Classics
The Cask of Amontillado and The Necklace

Prentice Hall Literature Writing Studio

The Necklace

Guy de Maupassant

She was one of those pretty, charming young women who are born, as if by an error of Fate, into a petty official's family. She had no dowry,[1] no hopes, not the slightest chance of being appreciated, understood, loved, and married by a rich and distinguished man; so she slipped into marriage with a minor civil servant at the Ministry of Education.

Unable to afford jewelry, she dressed simply; but she was as wretched as a *déclassée*, for women have neither caste nor breeding—in them beauty, grace, and charm replace pride of birth. Innate refinement, instinctive elegance, and suppleness of wit give them their place on the only scale that counts, and these qualities make humble girls the peers of the grandest ladies.

She suffered constantly, feeling that all the attributes of a gracious life, every luxury, should rightly have been hers. The poverty of her rooms—the shabby walls, the worn furniture, the ugly upholstery—caused her pain. All these things that another woman of her class would not even have noticed, tormented her and made her angry. The very sight of the little Breton girl who cleaned for her awoke rueful thoughts and the wildest dreams in her mind. She dreamt of thick-carpeted reception rooms with Oriental hangings, lighted by tall, bronze torches, and with two huge footmen in knee breeches, made drowsy by the heat from the stove, asleep in the wide armchairs. She dreamt of great drawing rooms upholstered in old silks, with fragile little tables holding priceless knickknacks, and of enchanting little sitting rooms redolent of perfume, designed for tea-time chats with intimate friends—famous, sought-after men whose attentions all women longed for.

When she sat down to dinner at her round table with its three-day-old cloth, and watched her husband opposite her lift the lid of the soup tureen and exclaim, delighted: "Ah, a good homemade beef stew! There's nothing better . . ." she would visualize elegant dinners with gleaming silver amid tapestried walls peopled by knights and ladies and exotic birds in a fairy forest; she would think of exquisite dishes served on gorgeous china, and of gallantries whispered and received with sphinx-like smiles[2] while eating the pink flesh of trout or wings of grouse.

She had no proper wardrobe, no jewels, nothing. And those were the only things that she loved—she felt she was made for them. She would have so loved to charm, to be envied, to be admired and sought after.

She had a rich friend, a schoolmate from the convent she had attended, but she didn't like to visit her because it always made her so miserable when she got home again. She would weep for whole days at a time from sorrow, regret, despair, and distress.

---

1. **dowry** (dou′ rē) *n.*: The property that a woman brought to her husband at marriage.

2. **gallantries whispered and received with sphinx** (sfiṇks)-**like smiles:** Flirtatious compliments whispered and received with mysterious smiles.

The Necklace 193

Presentation

Motivation/Prior Knowledge Have students imagine they have received an invitation to a fancy-dress ball. Among the guests will be actors, politicians, and some of the wealthiest people in the country. Would they feel excited? Would their excitement be tempered by nervousness or fear? Why? How would they prepare for the party?

Master Teacher Note This story, which was written 1884, takes place in Paris. Set the period for this story by bringing in paintings by some of the great French artists of the time: Renoir, Seurat, Monet, and Cezanne. Show students Art Transparency 5, Georges Seurat's *Sunday Afternoon on the Island of La Grande Jatte* (Teaching Portfolio) to give students a sense of the time and place.

Purpose-Setting Question How does fate provide surprises for the characters in this story?

1 **Discussion** What do you learn about the character of this woman? Contrast her imagined life with her real life.

2 **Clarification** *Breton* refers to a person who comes from Brittany, a province in France.

3 **Discussion** What have you learned about the values of this woman?

4 **Critical Thinking and Reading** Maupassant chose to adopt a third-person point of view in his writing. However, he strove to describe characters in such detail from without, that readers would be able to infer what was going on inside them.

Thematic Focus All choices have consequences, and often these consequences are not the ones we anticipate. Ask students whether a person's "fate" might be simply the consequence of a series of good or bad choices.

Making Connections Another selection that deals with the role of fate in people's lives is "The Interlopers" by Saki, page 33. You might also have students compare Madame Loisel's expectations for her future with those of Pip in *Great Expectations,* page 723.

Alternative Assessment To promote active reading, have your students keep a reader's response journal as they read "The Necklace." Suggest that they focus their observations on the examples of materialism exhibited by Madame Loisel. Encourage them to respond personally to the relevance of her attitude to the materialism they see around them. You may use their response journals to assess their appreciation of the story.

Then one evening her husband arrived home looking triumphant and waving a large envelope.

"There," he said, "there's something for you."

She tore it open eagerly and took out a printed card which said:

5 "The Minister of Education and Madame Georges Ramponneau[3] request the pleasure of the company of M. and Mme. Loisel[4] at an evening reception at the Ministry on Monday, January 18th."

Instead of being delighted, as her husband had hoped, she tossed the invitation on the table and muttered, annoyed:

"What do you expect me to do with that?"

6 "Why, I thought you'd be pleased, dear. You never go out and this would be an occasion for you, a great one! I had a lot of trouble getting it. Everyone wants an invitation; they're in great demand and there are only a few reserved for the employees. All the officials will be there."

She looked at him, irritated, and said impatiently:

"I haven't a thing to wear. How could I go?"

It had never even occurred to him. He stammered:

"But what about the dress you wear to the theater? I think it's lovely. . . ."

7 He fell silent, amazed and bewildered to see that his wife was crying. Two big tears escaped from the corners of her eyes and rolled slowly toward the corners of her mouth. He mumbled:

"What is it? What is it?"

But, with great effort, she had overcome her misery; and now she answered him calmly, wiping her tear-damp cheeks:

---

3. Madame Georges Ramponneau (ma dam′ zhôrzh ram pə nō′)
4. Loisel (lwa zel′)

"It's nothing. It's just that I have no evening dress and so I can't go to the party. Give the invitation to one of your colleagues whose wife will be better dressed than I would be."

He was overcome. He said:

"Listen, Mathilde,[5] how much would an evening dress cost—a suitable one that you could wear again on other occasions, something very simple?"

She thought for several seconds, making her calculations and at the same time estimating how much she could ask for without eliciting an immediate refusal and an exclamation of horror from this economical government clerk.

At last, not too sure of herself, she said:

8 "It's hard to say exactly but I think I could manage with four hundred francs."

He went a little pale, for that was exactly the amount he had put aside to buy a rifle so that he could go hunting the following summer near Nanterre, with a few friends who 9 went shooting larks around there on Sundays.

However, he said:

"Well, all right, then. I'll give you four hundred francs. But try to get something really nice."

As the day of the ball drew closer, Madame Loisel seemed depressed, disturbed, worried—despite the fact that her dress was ready. One evening her husband said:

"What's the matter? You've really been very strange these last few days."

And she answered:

"I hate not having a single jewel, not one stone, to wear. I shall look so dowdy.[6] I'd almost rather not go to the party."

He suggested:

"You can wear some fresh flowers. It's

---

5. Mathilde (ma tēld′)
6. dowdy (dou′ dē) *adj.:* Shabby.

THE NEW NECKLACE, 1910
William McGregor Paxton
Museum of Fine Arts, Boston

considered very chic[7] at this time of year. For ten francs you can get two or three beautiful roses."

That didn't satisfy her at all.

"No . . . there's nothing more humiliating than to look poverty-stricken among a lot of rich women."

Then her husband exclaimed:

"Wait—you silly thing! Why don't you go and see Madame Forestier[8] and ask her to lend you some jewelry. You certainly know her well enough for that, don't you think?"

She let out a joyful cry.

"You're right. It never occurred to me."

The next day she went to see her friend and related her tale of woe.

7. **chic** (shēk) *n.*: Fashionable.
8. **Forestier** (fô rə styā′)

Madame Forestier went to her mirrored wardrobe, took out a big jewel case, brought it to Madame Loisel, opened it, and said:

"Take your pick, my dear."

Her eyes wandered from some bracelets to a pearl necklace, then to a gold Venetian cross set with stones, of very fine workmanship. She tried on the jewelry before the mirror, hesitating, unable to bring herself to take them off, to give them back. And she kept asking:

"Do you have anything else, by chance?"

"Why yes. Here, look for yourself. I don't know which ones you'll like."

All at once, in a box lined with black satin, she came upon a superb diamond necklace, and her heart started beating with overwhelming desire. Her hands trembled as

11

12

The Necklace 195

13 **Reading Strategy** Have students summarize the story to this point, emphasizing what they have learned about Mme. Loisel.

14 **Reading Strategy** Have students predict what might happen to Mme. Loisel as a result of the ball.

15 **Literary Focus** Her triumph at the ball contrasts with her life to come.

16 **Discussion** Contrast Mme. Loisel's beauty and splendor with her husband's dullness.

17 **Literary Focus** Point out the irony in the naming of their street (Street of Martyrs). How does the name hint at their life to come?

she picked it up. She fastened it around her neck over her high-necked dress and stood there gazing at herself ecstatically.

Hesitantly, filled with terrible anguish, she asked:

"Could you lend me this one—just this and nothing else?"

"Yes, of course."

She threw her arms around her friend's neck, kissed her ardently, and fled with her treasure.

The day of the party arrived. Madame Loisel was a great success. She was the prettiest woman there—resplendent, graceful, beaming, and deliriously happy. All the men looked at her, asked who she was, tried to get themselves introduced to her. All the minister's aides wanted to waltz with her. The minister himself noticed her.

She danced enraptured—carried away, intoxicated with pleasure, forgetting everything in this triumph of her beauty and the glory of her success, floating in a cloud of happiness formed by all this homage, all this admiration, all the desires she had stirred up—by this victory so complete and so sweet to the heart of a woman.

When she left the party, it was almost four in the morning. Her husband had been sleeping since midnight in a small, deserted sitting room, with three other gentlemen whose wives were having a wonderful time.

He brought her wraps so that they could leave and put them around her shoulders—the plain wraps from her everyday life whose shabbiness jarred with the elegance of her evening dress. She felt this and wanted to escape quickly so that the other women, who were enveloping themselves in their rich furs, wouldn't see her.

Loisel held her back.

"Wait a minute. You'll catch cold out there. I'm going to call a cab."

But she wouldn't listen to him and went hastily downstairs. Outside in the street, there was no cab to be found; they set out to look for one, calling to the drivers they saw passing in the distance.

They walked toward the Seine,[9] shivering and miserable. Finally, on the embankment, they found one of those ancient nocturnal broughams[10] which are only to be seen in Paris at night, as if they were ashamed to show their shabbiness in daylight.

It took them to their door in the Rue des Martyrs, and they went sadly upstairs to their apartment. For her, it was all over. And he was thinking that he had to be at the Ministry by ten.

She took off her wraps before the mirror so that she could see herself in all her glory once more. Then she cried out. The necklace was gone; there was nothing around her neck.

Her husband, already half undressed, asked:

"What's the matter?"

She turned toward him in a frenzy:

"The . . . the . . . necklace—it's gone."

He got up, thunderstruck.

"What did you say? . . . What! . . . Impossible!"

And they searched the folds of her dress, the folds of her wrap, the pockets, everywhere. They didn't find it.

He asked:

"Are you sure you still had it when we left the ball?"

"Yes. I remember touching it in the hallway of the Ministry."

"But if you had lost it in the street, we would have heard it fall. It must be in the cab."

"Yes, most likely. Do you remember the number?"

"No. What about you—did you notice it?"

"No."

---

9. **Seine** (sān): A river flowing through Paris.
10. **broughams** (brŏŏms) *n.*: Horse-drawn carriages.

Grammar in Action

Authors **vary sentence structure** to keep readers' interest and add drama to their writing. The three basic sentence types are *simple*—a single, independent clause; *compound*—two or more independent clauses; and *complex*—an independent clause and one or more subordinate clauses. By using a mixture of simple, compound, and complex sentences, authors make their writing lively and clear.

In the following passage from "The Necklace," for example, Guy de Maupassant uses a variety of sentence types:

They walked toward the Seine, shivering and miserable. Finally, on the embankment, they found one of those ancient nocturnal broughams which are only to be seen in Paris at night, as if they were ashamed to show their shabbiness in daylight.

It took them to their door in the Rue des Martyrs, and they

They looked at each other in utter dejection. Finally Loisel got dressed again.

"I'm going to retrace the whole distance we covered on foot," he said, "and see if I can't find it."

And he left the house. She remained in her evening dress, too weak to go to bed, sitting crushed on a chair, lifeless and blank.

Her husband returned at about seven o'clock. He had found nothing.

He went to the police station, to the newspapers to offer a reward, to the offices of the cab companies—in a word, wherever there seemed to be the slightest hope of tracing it.

She spent the whole day waiting, in a state of utter hopelessness before such an appalling catastrophe.

Loisel returned in the evening, his face lined and pale; he had learned nothing.

"You must write to your friend," he said, "and tell her that you've broken the clasp of the necklace and that you're getting it mended. That'll give us time to decide what to do."

She wrote the letter at his dictation.

By the end of the week, they had lost all hope.

Loisel, who had aged five years, declared: "We'll have to replace the necklace."

The next day they took the case in which it had been kept and went to the jeweler whose name appeared inside it. He looked through his ledgers:

"I didn't sell this necklace, madame. I only supplied the case."

Then they went from one jeweler to the next, trying to find a necklace like the other, racking their memories, both of them sick with worry and distress.

In a fashionable shop near the Palais Royal, they found a diamond necklace which they decided was exactly like the other. It was worth 40,000 francs. They could have it for 36,000 francs.

They asked the jeweler to hold it for them for three days, and they stipulated that he should take it back for 34,000 francs if the other necklace was found before the end of February.

Loisel possessed 18,000 francs left him by his father. He would borrow the rest.

He borrowed, asking a thousand francs from one man, five hundred from another, a hundred here, fifty there. He signed promissory notes,[11] borrowed at exorbitant rates, dealt with usurers and the entire race of moneylenders. He compromised his whole career, gave his signature even when he wasn't sure he would be able to honor it, and horrified by the anxieties with which his future would be filled, by the black misery about to descend upon him, by the prospect of physical privation and moral suffering, went to get the new necklace, placing on the jeweler's counter 36,000 francs.

When Madame Loisel went to return the necklace, Madame Forestier said in a faintly waspish tone:

"You could have brought it back a little sooner! I might have needed it."

She didn't open the case as her friend had feared she might. If she had noticed the substitution, what would she have thought? What would she have said? Mightn't she have taken Madame Loisel for a thief?

Madame Loisel came to know the awful life of the poverty-stricken. However, she resigned herself to it with unexpected fortitude. The crushing debt had to be paid. She would pay it. They dismissed the maid; they moved into an attic under the roof.

She came to know all the heavy household chores, the loathsome work of the kitchen. She washed the dishes, wearing down her pink nails on greasy casseroles and the bottoms of saucepans. She did the

---

11. **promissory** (präm' i sôr' ē) **notes:** Written promises to pay back borrowed money.

The Necklace 197

18 **Discussion** Have students evaluate Loisel's plan. What complications could arise from it?

19 **Discussion** What will replacing the necklace mean to them?

20 **Reading Strategy** The author raises a doubt in the reader's mind about the necklace. Why would someone buy a very expensive necklace from one jeweler and a case from another? Ask students if this provides them with any indication of what might happen. What is their prediction?

21 **Master Teacher Note** Many of the most exclusive shops in Paris are near the Palais Royal. Ask students to name equivalent shopping areas in the United States, for example New York's Fifth Ave., Chicago's Michigan Ave., Los Angeles's Rodeo Dr., Dallas's Galleria.

22 **Clarification** At the time of this story 36,000 francs was worth about $7,200. The effects of inflation since then would increase the value of the necklace tremendously.

23 **Discussion** Have students discuss the degree of sacrifice Loisel was willing to make to follow his plan. What labels would they put on his actions—wise, honorable, foolish, stubborn, short-sighted, practical?

24 **Discussion** Contrast Mathilde's way of life now with a kind of life she thought she deserved. What is surprising about her behavior?

went sadly upstairs to their apartment. For her, it was all over. And he was thinking that he had to be at the Ministry by ten.

Notice that the first sentence is simple; the second, complex; the third, compound; the fourth, simple; and the fifth, complex. This variety of sentence structures produces an interesting rhythm and keeps the passage from being choppy.

Student Activity 1. Choose another passage of at least ten lines from "The Necklace" and analyze the structure of the sentences.

Student Activity 2. Using de Maupassant's passage as a model, write about an experience you had as you left a friend's house. Vary the structure of your sentences as de Maupassant does.

Electronic Handbook You may want to have students review the ways in which they can vary sentences before completing the Grammar in Action activities. If students have access to the Language Master 6000, have them enter *subject, conjunction, complex, phrase,* or *clause* and press the GRAMMAR key with each entry.

25 Reading Strategy Have students summarize what the lost necklace has cost the Loisels, not in money but in their way of life, in their expectations and hopes for the future. Ask them to predict what lies ahead for the couple.

26 Discussion Ask students to discuss the truth of this statement. To what degree was it fate and to what degree the Loisels' own actions that created the situation? Is this the theme of the story? Support your answer.

27 Discussion Contrast this Mme. Loisel with the one who went to the ball. Did she deserve what happened to her? Why or why not?

28 Literary Focus Have students contrast the way the situation appeared to the Loisels with the facts. In what way is this contrast ironic? Ask students to discuss whether or not they were surprised at the end of the story. How does this add to the story's irony?

29 Discussion Ask students to discuss how Mathilde's choice of the imitation necklace is symbolic of her character. What might the necklace symbolize?

Reader's Response Describe a situation in which you learned a lesson similar to the one Mathilde Loisel learned in this story.

Thematic Response What choices might Madame Loisel have made differently? What might have been the consequences of those choices?

laundry, washing shirts and dishcloths which she hung on a line to dry; she took the garbage down to the street every morning, and carried water upstairs, stopping at every floor to get her breath. Dressed like a working-class woman, she went to the fruit store, the grocer, and the butcher with her basket on her arm, bargaining, outraged, contesting each sou[12] of her pitiful funds.

Every month some notes had to be honored and more time requested on others.

Her husband worked in the evenings, putting a shopkeeper's ledgers in order, and often at night as well, doing copying at twenty-five centimes a page.

And it went on like that for ten years.

After ten years, they had made good on everything, including the usurious rates and the compound interest.

Madame Loisel looked old now. She had become the sort of strong woman, hard and coarse, that one finds in poor families. Disheveled, her skirts askew, with reddened hands, she spoke in a loud voice, slopping water over the floors as she washed them. But sometimes, when her husband was at the office, she would sit down by the window and muse over that party long ago when she had been so beautiful, the belle of the ball.

How would things have turned out if she hadn't lost that necklace? Who could tell? How strange and fickle life is! How little it takes to make or break you!

Then one Sunday when she was strolling along the Champs Elysées[13] to forget the week's chores for a while, she suddenly caught sight of a woman taking a child for a walk. It was Madame Forestier, still young, still beautiful, still charming.

---

12. **sou** (sōō) n.: A former French coin, worth very little; the centime (sän' tēm), mentioned later, was also of little value.
13. **Champs Elysées** (shän zā lē zā'): A fashionable street in Paris.

198   *Short Stories*

Madame Loisel started to tremble. Should she speak to her? Yes, certainly she should. And now that she had paid everything back, why shouldn't she tell her the whole story?

She went up to her.

"Hello, Jeanne."

The other didn't recognize her and was surprised that this plainly dressed woman should speak to her so familiarly. She murmured:

"But . . . madame! . . . I'm sure . . . You must be mistaken."

"No, I'm not. I am Mathilde Loisel."

Her friend gave a little cry.

"Oh! Oh, my poor Mathilde, how you've changed!"

"Yes, I've been through some pretty hard times since I last saw you and I've had plenty of trouble—and all because of you!"

"Because of me? What do you mean?"

"You remember the diamond necklace you lent me to wear to the party at the Ministry?"

"Yes. What about it?"

"Well, I lost it."

"What are you talking about? You returned it to me."

"What I gave back to you was another one just like it. And it took us ten years to pay for it. You can imagine it wasn't easy for us, since we were quite poor. . . . Anyway, I'm glad it's over and done with."

Madame Forestier stopped short.

"You say you bought a diamond necklace to replace that other one?"

"Yes. You didn't even notice then? They really were exactly alike."

And she smiled, full of a proud, simple joy.

Madame Forestier, profoundly moved, took Mathilde's hands in her own.

"Oh, my poor, poor Mathilde! Mine was false. It was worth five hundred francs at the most!"

Closure and Extension

ANSWERS TO RESPONDING TO THE SELECTION

Your Response
1. Suggest to students that Madame Loisel's "fate" might have been avoided at several key decision points in the story.
2. Discuss the idea that telling the truth to Madame Forestier would have been the best solution.

Recalling
3. The invitation displeases her because she believes that she has no dress as beautiful as those the other women will wear so she cannot go to the ball.
4. Although dissatisfied, Mathilde had a comfortable bourgeois life. Now the Loisels have to live in poverty, working night and day to pay their debt.

Interpreting
5. Suggested Response: She is dissatisfied because she feels she

RESPONDING TO THE SELECTION

Your Response

1. Do you feel sorry for Madame Loisel, or do you think she brought her "fate" on herself? Explain.
2. If you had been in Madame Loisel's situation, how would you have solved the problem of the lost necklace? Explain.

Recalling

3. How do the lives of the Loisels change after the necklace is lost?

Interpreting

4. At the beginning of the story, why is Madame Loisel dissatisfied with her life?
5. In what way are the borrowed necklace and Madame Loisel's dreams of life in high society the same?
6. How does Madame Loisel change during the course of the story?

Applying

7. To resolve her problem, Madame Loisel resorted to deceit. What are the harmful consequences of deceit? Can deceit ever produce beneficial consequences? Give examples.

ANALYZING LITERATURE

Understanding Irony

Irony is the contrast between the expected outcome and the actual outcome or between appearance and reality. For example, in "The Necklace," Madame Loisel is a pretty, proud young woman who feels that the attributes of a gracious life should rightly be hers. It is ironic that because of her pride, she comes to know not splendor and wealth, but "the awful life of the poverty stricken."

1. After her great success at the ball, Madame Loisel creeps slowly upstairs, because for her, she thinks, all is over. How does this thought turn out to be truer than she expected?
2. The street the Loisels live on is the Rue des Martyrs, or Avenue of the Martyrs. Why is the name of this street ironic?
3. In what way is the ending of the story ironic?
4. Madame Loisel thinks, "How strange and fickle life is! How little it takes to make or break you!" What do this statement and the ironic tone of the story suggest about the complexity of life?

CRITICAL THINKING AND READING

Making Inferences About Characters

When you make inferences about characters, you decide what they are like based on evidence in the story. For example, when you read the beginning of "The Necklace," you probably inferred that Monsieur Loisel is content with his station in life. You based your inference on evidence: his pleasure in the homemade beef stew, his feeling of triumph in receiving the invitation, and his bewilderment at his wife's dissatisfaction.

1. Which of the following adjectives fits Madame Loisel: *self-centered, generous, warm, envious?* Support your answer.
2. How are the things Madame Loisel values different from the things her husband values?
3. In what essential way are Madame and Monsieur Loisel alike? Support your answer.

THINKING AND WRITING

Responding to Criticism

The critic Theophil Spoerri has written that Maupassant's stories are "the perfected expression of an age which had lost itself amid things." Do you think the Loisels are or are not representative of a materialistic age? Jot down reasons that support your answer. Next, imagine you are writing for a high-school literary magazine. Using "The Necklace" as your example, write an essay supporting or refuting Spoerri's comment. Revise your essay, making sure that your argument is clear and that you have provided adequate support. Finally, prepare a final draft.

should have a gracious, luxurious life rather than only an ordinary middle-class existence.
6. Suggested Response: Both are glittering and both are not what they seem to be.
7. Suggested Response: She goes from a vain and dissatisfied young woman to a hard-working drudge. She loses her looks and becomes old before her time. She still lapses into unreality, however, and dreams about the ball. She blames her friend for her troubles.

Applying

8. Answers will differ. Students may respond that deceit often results in punishment or, at least, guilty feelings. Some students may suggest that there can be beneficial consequences from deceit. Discuss the probability that such benefits may be short-lived.

Challenge How do you think Maupassant wants you to feel toward Madame Loisel? Find evidence that supports your answer.

ANSWERS TO ANALYZING LITERATURE

1. Suggested Response: Her former middle-class life of comfort and security is also over because she has lost the necklace.
2. Suggested Response: The name of the street mirrors the Loisels' fate—they must endure great suffering.

3. Suggested Response: The Loisels endure poverty and hard work for ten years to replace a diamond necklace that turns out to be a cheap imitation.
4. Suggested Response: Conditions in life continually change and you cannot be sure what the future will hold. No matter how carefully you may plan, fate can move your life in an entirely different direction.

ANSWERS TO CRITICAL THINKING AND READING

1. Suggested Response: She is self-centered and envious. Her reactions to her living conditions and to the invitation to the ball show that she thinks only of herself. Her reactions to her friend and to the other women at the ball reveal that she is envious.
2. Suggested Response: She values the life of the rich. Her husband is content with his own station in life. Madame Loisel places her own happiness above all things. Her husband is willing to deny himself in order to make his wife happy.
3. Suggested Response: Both are proud. They do not tell Madame Forestier about the lost necklace but instead replace it and slave for ten years to repay the debts incurred.

THINKING AND WRITING

Alternative Assessment For alternative composition assignments, see page 254 of the Teaching Portfolio.

Publishing Student Writing Ask for student volunteers to read their essays aloud. Have students in the audience record at least one noteworthy feature of each essay.

Writing Across the Curriculum You might want students to research and report about the middle class in France during the 1880's. If you do, perhaps inform the social studies department. Social studies teachers might provide guidance for students in conducting research.

Reading Actively The reading process outlined on this page is based on research into the ways that good readers construct meaning from fiction. This approach makes students aware of their reading habits, enabling them to monitor and improve their comprehension.

Although most good readers use these techniques unconsciously or intuitively, students can learn to become highly effective readers by making a conscious effort to follow this process until it becomes internalized.

Active reading means interacting with a text. Questioning not only keeps readers turning pages but, more important, forces them to explore the meaning of the text. By reflecting on what is happening within a story, what might happen as the story proceeds, and how the writer conveys this information, readers can become more sensitive and literate.

Introduce the strategies listed here and explain that they will help students become more effective readers. The model on the following pages contains the types of questions, predictions, clarifications, and summaries that an active reader might make while reading. It also shows the way an active reader might pull together these details after reading.

Ask students to pay attention to these annotations as they read. Also ask them to create their own questions, predictions, clarifications, and summaries, and, finally, to react to the story.

For further practice with the process, use "You Need to Go Upstairs"—in the Teaching Portfolio, page 266, following the Teacher Backup for this selection—which students can annotate themselves. Encourage students to continue to use these strategies when reading other stories.

READING AND RESPONDING

The Short Story

As an active reader, you involve yourself in a story and derive meaning from it. You apply your active reading strategies to the plot, characters, setting, and theme—the elements that work together to create an effective whole. Your response is what you think and feel about the story and its elements.

RESPONDING TO PLOT The **plot** of a short story is what happens as that story unfolds. Knowing how a plot is structured can help you make connections and predictions as you read. Involving yourself in the plot can enhance your response to the resolution of the conflict. The more involved you are, the more satisfaction you derive from a good ending.

RESPONDING TO CHARACTERS **Characters** are the people in a story. Like real people, characters have traits and personalities that determine the way they behave. When you read, let yourself identify with the characters: Share their emotions, and think about what you would do in their place.

RESPONDING TO SETTING **Setting** is the time and the place in which the story events occur. As you read actively, you respond to the details of the setting. What kind of atmosphere or mood do these details create? How does the setting affect the plot and the characters? How does it affect you?

RESPONDING TO POINT OF VIEW **Point of view** is the vantage point from which the story is narrated. Is it told in the first person or the third person? Are you in the mind of one character, or more? How does the point of view affect the way you understand what is happening?

RESPONDING TO THEME **Theme** is the general idea about life presented in a story, or what the story means to you. As you read actively, you will notice how the author has constructed the story to reveal the theme. Does the main character learn something about life? Is the theme stated or implied? What does the story say to you?

On pages 201–208 you can see an example of active reading and responding by Mark Devine of Anderson High School in Cincinnati, Ohio. The notes in the side column include Mark's thoughts and comments as he read "The Secret Life of Walter Mitty." Your own thoughts as you read may be different because you bring your own experiences to your reading.

200   Short Stories

Support Material

Teaching Portfolio
Teacher Backup, p. 263
Reading Actively, "You Need to Go Upstairs," page 266
Grammar in Action Worksheet, *Writing Dialogue,* p. 270
Usage and Mechanics Worksheet, p. 272
Analyzing Literature Worksheet, *Understanding Point of View,* p. 273

Language Worksheet, *Understanding Prefixes,* p. 274
Selection Test, p. 275

Prentice Hall Literature Writing Studio

MODEL

The Secret Life of Walter Mitty

James Thurber

"We're going through!" The Commander's voice was like thin ice breaking. He wore his full-dress uniform, with the heavily braided white cap pulled down rakishly over one cold gray eye. "We can't make it, sir. It's spoiling for a hurricane, if you ask me." "I'm not asking you, Lieutenant Berg," said the Commander. "Throw on the power lights! Rev her up to 8,500! We're going through!" The pounding of the cylinders increased: ta-pocketa-pocketa-pocketa-*pocketa-pocketa.* The Commander stared at the ice forming on the pilot window. He walked over and twisted a row of complicated dials. "Switch on No. 8 auxiliary!" he shouted. "Switch on No. 8 auxiliary!" repeated Lieutenant Berg. "Full strength in No. 3 turret!" shouted the Commander. "Full strength in No. 3 turret!" The crew, bending to their various tasks in the huge, hurtling eight-engined Navy hydroplane,[1] looked at each other and grinned. "The Old Man'll get us through," they said to one another. "The Old Man ain't afraid of Hell!" . . .

"Not so fast! You're driving too fast!" said Mrs. Mitty. "What are you driving so fast for?"

"Hmm?" said Walter Mitty. He looked at his wife, in the seat beside him, with shocked astonishment. She seemed grossly unfamiliar, like a strange woman who had yelled at him in a crowd. "You were up to fifty-five," she said. "You know I don't like to go more than forty. You were up to fifty-five." Walter Mitty drove on toward Waterbury in silence, the roaring of the SN202 through the worst storm in twenty years of Navy flying fading in the remote, intimate airways of his mind. "You're tensed up again," said Mrs. Mitty. "It's one of your days. I wish you'd let Dr. Renshaw look you over."

---

1. **hydroplane** (hī′ drə plăn) *n.*: A seaplane.

Title: *The idea of a secret life is interesting. What secret life does this Walter Mitty lead?*

Plot: *It sounds like these characters are preparing to go into a huge naval battle.*

Character: *Who is the Old Man? Could he be Walter Mitty?*

Plot: *What in the world just happened? Did the hydroplane suddenly turn into a car?*

Character: *Oh, here is Walter Mitty. So who were the characters in the beginning of the story?*

Plot: *Now it's clear that Mitty was daydreaming in the beginning of the story, and was jogged out of his daydream when his wife scolded him.*

The Secret Life of Walter Mitty 201

Presentation

Motivation/Prior Knowledge
Ask students if they have imagined experiences in which they are great heroes in dramatic situations. Tell them that everyone tends to have these daydreams but that for Walter Mitty, the main character of Thurber's story, fantasy is a way of life.

Purpose-Setting Question
What is Walter Mitty's "secret life"?

Thematic Focus Walter Mitty seems to have become lost in his search for his real self. Ask the students whether they ever daydream about what they might like to be in the future. Ask if they think such daydreams can help them reach their goals.

Making Connections You might want to use "George Gray," page 552, with this selection. Although this poem is more serious in tone than Thurber's story, it also focuses on a character who is afraid to take real risks.

Master Teacher Note One way to use this model is either to read aloud the first page yourself or to have a student read it. Then discuss the annotations. You might elicit students' own responses and compare them with the notes on the page.

Humanities Note

Fine art, *The Man with Three Masks*, by John Rush. Rush (1948–   ) is a painter, illustrator, and printmaker. Born in Indianapolis, Indiana, he received his artistic training at the Art Center in Pasadena, California. When asked who has influenced his work, he has commented, "My heroes are long dead." The greatest single influence on his work is Michaelangelo, who has shaped his figure design.

This painting was done in *gouache*—a technique in which the artist mixes watercolors with white paint to achieve an opaque effect.

You might use the following questions to discuss the painting:

1. What is the significance of the masks in this painting? Why do you think the figure holds one mask up to his face and has others nearby?
2. Can it be said that Walter Mitty wears a mask? Why or why not?
3. Does everyone wear a mask at one time or another? Explain.

Character: *Mitty's wife seems to nag him and treat him like a baby. Mitty doesn't like it, but he doesn't fight back.*

Walter Mitty stopped the car in front of the building where his wife went to have her hair done. "Remember to get those overshoes while I'm having my hair done," she said. "I don't need overshoes," said Mitty. She put her mirror back into her bag. "We've been all through that," she said, getting out of the car. "You're not a young man any longer." He raced the engine a little. "Why don't you wear your gloves? Have you lost your gloves?" Walter Mitty reached in a pocket and brought out the gloves. He put them on, but after she had turned and gone into the building and he had driven on to a red light, he took them off again. "Pick it up, brother!" snapped a cop as the light changed, and Mitty hastily pulled on his gloves and lurched ahead. He drove around the streets aimlessly for a time, and then he drove past the hospital on his way to the parking lot.

THE MAN WITH THREE MASKS
John Rush
Courtesy of the Artist

... "It's the millionaire banker, Wellington McMillan," said the pretty nurse. "Yes?" said Walter Mitty, removing his gloves slowly. "Who has the case?" "Dr. Renshaw and Dr. Benbow, but there are two specialists here, Dr. Remington from New York and Mr. Pritchard-Mitford from London. He flew over." A door opened down a long, cool corridor and Dr. Renshaw came out. He looked distraught and haggard. "Hello, Mitty," he said. "We're having the devil's own time with McMillan, the millionaire banker and close personal friend of Roosevelt. Obstreosis of the ductal tract.[2] Tertiary. Wish you'd take a look at him." "Glad to," said Mitty.

In the operating room there were whispered introductions: "Dr. Remington, Dr. Mitty. Mr. Pritchard-Mitford, Dr. Mitty." "I've read your book on streptothricosis," said Pritchard-Mitford, shaking hands. "A brilliant performance, sir." "Thank you," said Walter Mitty. "Didn't know you were in the States, Mitty," grumbled Remington. "Coals to Newcastle,[3] bringing Mitford and me up here for tertiary." "You are very kind," said Mitty. A huge, complicated machine, connected to the operating table, with many tubes and wires, began at this moment to go pocketa-pocketa-pocketa. "The new anesthetizer is giving way!" shouted an intern. "There is no one in the East who knows how to fix it!" "Quiet, man!" said Mitty, in a low, cool voice. He sprang to the machine, which was now going pocketa-pocketa-queep-pocketa-queep. He began fingering delicately a row of glistening dials. "Give me a fountain pen!" he snapped. Someone handed him a fountain pen. He pulled a faulty piston out of the machine and inserted the pen in its place. "That will hold for ten minutes," he said. "Get on with the operation." A nurse hurried over and whispered to Renshaw, and Mitty saw the man turn pale. "Coreopsis has set in," said Renshaw nervously. "If you would take over, Mitty?" Mitty looked at him and at the craven figure of Benbow, who drank, and at the grave, uncertain faces of the two great specialists. "If you wish," he said. They slipped a white gown on him; he adjusted a mask and drew on thin gloves; nurses handed him shining ...

2. **obstreosis of the ductal tract:** Thurber has invented this and other medical terms.
3. **coals to Newcastle:** The proverb, "bringing coals to Newcastle," means bringing things to a place unnecessarily—Newcastle, England, was a coal center and so did not need coal brought to it.

The Secret Life of Walter Mitty   203

Plot: *Now where is Mitty? What important role does he play in this daydream?*

Theme: *The doctors in Mitty's daydream treat him with respect, whereas his wife reprimands him and orders him around. No wonder he likes to daydream!*

Plot: *Of course Walter Mitty saves the day.*

Critical Thinking and Reading Have students contrast Mitty's real personality with his imagined versions of himself. What connection might there be between them?

Speaking and Listening You might want to have student volunteers read aloud from the three paragraphs that begin with "... 'It's the millionaire banker ...'" on page 203. Ask one of the students to be the narrator and have the others take the roles of Mrs. Mitty, the cop, the nurse, the doctor, and of course, Mitty himself.

Character: *Mrs. Mitty isn't the only one who treats Walter as though he were an incompetent fool.*

Setting: *The setting and the pace of the story go from exciting and quick, to dull and sluggish whenever Mitty comes out of a daydream.*

Point of View: *This story is told from Mitty's perspective. In this paragraph you find out exactly what he thinks and how he feels about people thinking he is incompetent.*

Plot: *I bet the newsboy's shouting is going to set off another one of Mitty's daydreams.*

Electronic Handbook You might want students to review quotation marks before completing the activities. If students have access to the Language Master 6000, have them enter the access symbol " or the access word *quotation* and press the GRAMMAR key for information on this topic.

"Back it up, Mac! Look out for that Buick!" Walter Mitty jammed on the brakes. "Wrong lane, Mac," said the parking-lot attendant, looking at Mitty closely. "Gee. Yeh," muttered Mitty. He began cautiously to back out of the lane marked "Exit Only." "Leave her sit there," said the attendant. "I'll put her away." Mitty got out of the car. "Hey, better leave the key." "Oh," said Mitty, handing the man the ignition key. The attendant vaulted into the car, backed it up with insolent skill, and put it where it belonged.

They're so cocky, thought Walter Mitty, walking along Main Street; they think they know everything. Once he had tried to take his chains off, outside New Milford, and he had got them wound around the axles. A man had had to come out in a wrecking car and unwind them, a young, grinning garageman. Since then Mrs. Mitty always made him drive to a garage to have the chains taken off. The next time, he thought, I'll wear my right arm in a sling; they won't grin at me then. I'll have my right arm in a sling and they'll see I couldn't possibly take the chains off myself. He kicked at the slush on the sidewalk. "Overshoes," he said to himself, and he began looking for a shoe store.

When he came out into the street again, with the overshoes in a box under his arm, Walter Mitty began to wonder what the other thing was his wife had told him to get. She had told him, twice, before they set out from their house for Waterbury. In a way he hated these weekly trips to town—he was always getting something wrong. Kleenex, he thought, Squibb's, razor blades? No. Toothpaste, toothbrush, bicarbonate, carborundum, initiative and referendum?[4] He gave it up. But she would remember it. "Where's the what's-its-name?" she would ask. "Don't tell me you forgot the what's-its-name." A newsboy went by shouting something about the Waterbury trial.

. . . "Perhaps this will refresh your memory." The District Attorney suddenly thrust a heavy automatic at the quiet figure on the witness stand. "Have you ever seen this before?" Walter

---

4. **carborundum** (kär′ ə run′ dəm), **initiative** (i nish′ē ə tiv) **and referendum** (ref′ ə ren′ dəm): Thurber is purposely making a nonsense list; carborundum is a hard substance used for scraping, initiative is the right of citizens to introduce ideas for laws, and referendum is the right of citizens to vote on laws.

Grammar in Action

Writing **dialogue** can add an exciting element to your short stories. Dialogue, or conversation between characters in a work of literature, is usually punctuated like this:

"Back it up, Mac," the young parking attendant shouted.
"I'll do that." Mitty began to back up the exit ramp.

Notice that the exact words spoken are enclosed in quotation marks, and words or phrases that identify the speaker (*the young parking attendant shouted* and Mitty *began to back up the exit ramp*) are set off from the dialogue either with commas or end punctuation. To minimize confusion about who is speaking, most writers start a new paragraph for each change in speaker. Sometimes, however, a writer chooses a different style. Look at this passage from "The Secret Life of Walter Mitty."

". . . Perhaps this will refresh your memory." The District Attorney suddenly thrust a heavy automatic at the quiet figure on the witnesses stand. "Have you ever seen this before?" Walter Mitty took the gun and examined it expertly. "This is my Webley-Vickers 50.80," he said calmly. An excited buzz ran around the courtroom. The Judge rapped

Mitty took the gun and examined it expertly. "This is my Webley-Vickers 50.80," he said calmly. An excited buzz ran around the courtroom. The Judge rapped for order. "You are a crack shot with any sort of firearms, I believe?" said the District Attorney, insinuatingly. "Objection!" shouted Mitty's attorney. "We have shown that the defendant could not have fired the shot. We have shown that he wore his right arm in a sling on the night of the fourteenth of July." Walter Mitty raised his hand briefly and the bickering attorneys were stilled. "With any known make of gun," he said evenly, "I could have killed Gregory Fitzhurst at three hundred feet *with my left hand*." Pandemonium broke loose in the courtroom. A woman's scream rose above the bedlam and suddenly a lovely, dark-haired girl was in Walter Mitty's arms. The District Attorney struck at her savagely. Without rising from his chair, Mitty let the man have it on the point of the chin. "You miserable cur!" . . .

Theme: *Before, Mitty thought that if he wore a fake sling on his arm people would excuse him for his shortcomings. It's interesting how the sling comes up again in his daydream—but now, not only is it real, but it presents no handicap for the Mitty in the daydream.*

NEW ORLEANS FANTASY, 1985
Max Papart
Nahan Galleries, New York

The Secret Life of Walter Mitty 205

for order. "You are a crack shot with any sort of firearm, I believe?" said the District Attorney, insinuatingly. "Objection!" shouted Mitty's attorney. "We have shown that the defendant could not have fired the shot. . . ."

Notice how this passage departs from the conventional way of presenting dialogue. A new paragraph is not begun each time the speaker changes. Readers must rely on material outside the quotation marks to determine who says what.

Student Activity 1. Discuss with classmates the purpose and the effect of Thurber's way of presenting dialogue. In what way does the style suit the content of the story? Do you think the style is effective? Explain.

Student Activity 2. With a small group of classmates, brainstorm and list other situations in which a writer might choose an unconventional way of presenting dialogue. Then select one of these situations and write a passage of dialogue for it. Be prepared to discuss how the style you have chosen is related to the content of the passage.

"Puppy biscuit," said Walter Mitty. He stopped walking and the buildings of Waterbury rose up out of the misty courtroom and surrounded him again. A woman who was passing laughed. "He said 'Puppy biscuit,'" she said to her companion. "That man said 'Puppy biscuit' to himself." Walter Mitty hurried on. He went into an A. & P., not the first one he came to but a smaller one farther up the street. "I want some biscuit for small, young dogs," he said to the clerk. "Any special brand, sir?" The greatest pistol shot in the world thought a moment. "It says 'Puppies Bark for It' on the box," said Walter Mitty.

His wife would be through at the hairdresser's in fifteen minutes, Mitty saw in looking at his watch, unless they had trouble drying it; sometimes they had trouble drying it. She didn't like to get to the hotel first; she would want him to be there waiting for her as usual. He found a big leather chair in the lobby, facing a window, and he put the overshoes and the puppy biscuit on the floor beside it. He picked up an old copy of *Liberty* and sank down into the chair. "Can Germany Conquer the World Through the Air?" Walter Mitty looked at the pictures of bombing planes and of ruined streets.

. . . "The cannonading has got the wind up in young Raleigh,[5] sir," said the sergeant. Captain Mitty looked up at him through tousled hair. "Get him to bed," he said wearily. "With the others. I'll fly alone." "But you can't, sir," said the sergeant anxiously. "It takes two men to handle that bomber and the Archies[6] are pounding hell out of the air. Von Richtman's circus[7] is between here and Saulier." "Somebody's got to get that ammunition dump," said Mitty. "I'm going over. Spot of brandy?" He poured a drink for the sergeant and one for himself. War thundered and whined around the dugout and battered at the door. There was a rending of wood and splinters flew through the room. "A bit of a near thing," said Captain Mitty carelessly. "The box barrage is closing in," said the sergeant. "We only live once, Sergeant," said Mitty, with his faint,

---

5. has got the wind up in young Raleigh: Has made young Raleigh nervous.

6. Archies: A slang term for antiaircraft guns.

7. Von Richtman's circus: A German airplane squadron.

fleeting smile. "Or do we?" He poured another brandy and tossed it off. "I never see a man could hold his brandy like you, sir," said the sergeant. "Begging your pardon, sir." Captain Mitty stood up and strapped on his huge Webley-Vickers automatic. "It's forty kilometers through hell, sir," said the sergeant. Mitty finished one last brandy. "After all," he said softly, "what isn't?" The pounding of the cannon increased; there was the rat-tat-tatting of machine guns, and from some-

UNTITLED
John P. Maggard III
Courtesy of the Artist

The Secret Life of Walter Mitty   207

Setting: *Certain sounds are repeated from daydream to daydream, such as "pocketa-pocketa-pocketa." Maybe the author wants to keep certain details the same when so much in the story changes so often.*

Plot: *Being yelled at is what brings Mitty out of his daydream each time.*

Theme: *Facing a firing squad is the ultimate escape. By retreating into his daydreams all the time, that's what Mitty does: he escapes.*

where came the menacing pocketa-pocketa-pocketa of the new flame-throwers. Walter Mitty walked to the door of the dugout humming "Auprès de Ma Blonde."[8] He turned and waved to the sergeant. "Cheerio!" he said. . . .

Something struck his shoulder. "I've been looking all over this hotel for you," said Mrs. Mitty. "Why do you have to hide in this old chair? How did you expect me to find you?" "Things close in," said Walter Mitty vaguely. "What?" Mrs. Mitty said. "Did you get the what's-its-name? The puppy biscuit? What's in that box?" "Overshoes," said Mitty. "Couldn't you have put them on in the store?" "I was thinking," said Walter Mitty. "Does it ever occur to you that I am sometimes thinking?" She looked at him. "I'm going to take your temperature when I get you home," she said.

They went out through the revolving doors that made a faintly derisive whistling sound when you pushed them. It was two blocks to the parking lot. At the drugstore on the corner she said, "Wait here for me. I forgot something. I won't be a minute." She was more than a minute. Walter Mitty lighted a cigarette. It began to rain, rain with sleet in it. He stood up against the wall of the drugstore, smoking. . . . He put his shoulders back and his heels together. "To hell with the handkerchief," said Walter Mitty scornfully. He took one last drag on his cigarette and snapped it away. Then, with that faint, fleeting smile playing about his lips, he faced the firing squad; erect and motionless, proud and disdainful, Walter Mitty the Undefeated, inscrutable to the last.

8. "Auprès de Ma Blonde" (ō pre′ də mä blôn′ d): "Next to My Blonde," a popular French song.

James Grover Thurber (1894–1961) was born and grew up in Columbus, Ohio. He began his writing career as a reporter for the *Columbus Evening Dispatch*. It was through his later work on *The New Yorker* magazine, however, that he became well known as a writer and a cartoonist. "The Secret Life of Walter Mitty," Thurber's most famous story, reveals his characteristic style of wit, mixing sadness with humor.

208   Short Stories

RESPONDING TO THE SELECTION

Your Response

1. In what ways do your daydreams differ from your real life?

Recalling

2. Describe each of the five characters Mitty daydreams himself to be.
3. What triggers Mitty's second, third, and fourth daydreams? How is he pulled out of each one?

Interpreting

4. Compare and contrast Mitty in real life with Mitty in his daydreams.
5. Explain the significant difference between the way people treat Mitty in real life and the way they treat him in his daydreams.
6. How does Mrs. Mitty's personality trigger Mitty's last daydream? In what way is this daydream an apt comment upon his fate in real life?

Applying

7. Mark Twain wrote, "The secret source of humor is not joy but sorrow." Why do you think that humor and sorrow go hand in hand?

ANALYZING LITERATURE

Understanding Point of View

Point of view is the angle of vision from which a story is told. In "The Secret Life of Walter Mitty" the author takes you inside the mind of Walter Mitty and tells the story from his point of view. By telling a story from the point of view of one character, the author encourages you to sympathize with this character. You know what this character thinks or feels in a way you never can with people in real life.

1. How do you come to feel about Mitty as a result of seeing the world through his eyes?
2. Why is it especially effective for this story to be told from the point of view of Walter Mitty?
3. How would the story have been different if Mrs. Mitty had told it?

CRITICAL THINKING AND READING

Identifying Wishful Thinking

Wishful thinking is a way of escaping from unpleasant situations into a more appealing world. The kinds of situations in which characters imagine themselves sometimes tell more about them than their words or actions do. If a character is meek and retiring like Walter Mitty is, his wishful thinking can reveal things about him that he otherwise tries to conceal.

Explain what wish or desire each of the following daydreams reveals.

1. "'I've read your book on strepthotricosis,' said Pritchard-Mitford, shaking hands. 'A brilliant performance, sir.'"
2. "A woman's scream rose above the bedlam and suddenly a lovely, dark-haired girl was in Walter Mitty's arms."
3. "Without rising from his chair, Mitty let the man have it on the point of the chin."

THINKING AND WRITING

Continuing the Story

Make up another daydream for Walter Mitty. First brainstorm to list possible situations in which Mitty might find himself. Remember that for Walter Mitty, at least in his daydreams, anything is possible! Then select one situation you would like to develop. Write the first draft of an episode relating this event. Whatever adventure you create, try to tell it in a humorous way, as Thurber does. When you revise your episode, make sure it is true to Mitty's personality. Proofread your episode.

LEARNING OPTION

Art. Suppose that Walter Mitty were a teenager in the 1990's. Create a collage of the glamorous occupations or activities that he might daydream about. Possibilities include being an astronaut, a computer whiz, or a rock star. When you have finished, share your work with the class.

The Secret Life of Walter Mitty 209

Interpreting

4. Suggested Response: While Mitty is strong, brave, and capable in his daydreams, he is bumbling, absent-minded, and timid in real life.
5. Suggested Response: Mitty is treated as a respected hero in his daydreams and as an incompetent fool in real life.

6. Suggested Response: Mrs. Mitty's patronizing treatment of her husband is so demoralizing that the firing squad daydream may represent a final escape. Also, Mitty has stood up to her for the first time, and he may be anticipating what will happen to him when they get home.

Applying

7. Answers will differ. Students may respond that often we laugh instead of cry.

ANSWERS TO ANALYZING LITERATURE

1. Answers will differ, but most readers, remembering their own daydreams, will empathize with Mitty.
2. Suggested Response: Readers would have no insight into Mitty's secret life otherwise.

---

3. Suggested Response: It would be the story of an incompetent, bumbling, absent-minded fool. It would be difficult to empathize with Mitty because he would have no redeeming qualities.

ANSWERS TO CRITICAL THINKING AND READING

1. Suggested Response: Mitty wishes he were a brilliant, respected doctor, scientist, researcher, and writer.
2. Suggested Response: Mitty wishes beautiful women were attracted to him.
3. Suggested Response: Mitty wishes he were a strong and able fighter so that people could not take advantage of him.

THINKING AND WRITING

◆ **Software** If your students have access to computers, have them use the **Writer's Helper** activity Brainstorms to assist them in finding a situation to write about.

Alternative Assessment *Protocol:* Ask your students to assess their own work by responding to these questions:

What daydream have you chosen for Walter Mitty?

What details have you used to develop the incident?

What is the humor of the situation?

Is your episode true to Walter Mitty's personality?

Have the students use insights from their protocols to revise their work.

LEARNING OPTION

Kinesthetic learners will enjoy this activity. You might want to extend the activity for visual learners by asking the students to illustrate their Walter Mitty episode.

Preparation

Motivation/Prior Knowledge
Lead students in a discussion about extraordinary individuals —actual and fictional. Guide the students in discovering the variety of characteristics and actions that can make a person extraordinary. Examples may include unusual demonstrations of courage, intelligence, perseverance, optimism, creativity, and so on.

Focus Review the stated purpose of the assignment on student page 210. Direct students to give special emphasis to the details that will bring the character to life for the reader.

Presentation

Prewriting The following group activity may help to stimulate students in surfacing details about their chosen characters. One student acts as the "mystery character." The other students in the group ask questions, in an effort to determine the identity of the character. Instruct the students to use specific questions that will elicit revealing details about the character. At the conclusion of the activity, the students can discuss which responses were most helpful in giving dimension and life to the character.

Skills Practice If you wish to give your students practice in writing description, use the worksheet *Writing a Descriptive Paragraph* in the Writing Process Activities section of the **Teaching Portfolio, Volume II.**

Drafting Urge the students to enhance the authenticity of their account by using conversations. They should also include specific details about the setting and the appearance of the character. Point out to the students that describing their own internal reactions at the meeting will induce

"The secret of good writing is to say an old thing a new way or a new thing an old way."

Richard Harding Davis

YOUR WRITING PROCESS

WRITING ABOUT AN EXTRAORDINARY PERSON

Magazines often feature articles written about encounters with famous or extraordinary people. The short stories in this unit contain many interesting characters, each of whom would be an appropriate subject for such an article.

Focus

Assignment: Write a magazine article describing an encounter with a character from one of the short stories in this unit.
Purpose: To convey a vivid impression of this character's appearance, conversation, and traits.
Audience: Readers of the magazine.

Prewriting

1. Choose a character. Review the short stories in this unit to find a character you would enjoy meeting.

2. Visualize the character. Note how the author describes the character you have chosen. Much of what you write will be based on the author's description. Where the author does not provide details, however, you are free to invent them for yourself. Use the details from the book and the ones you invent to create a face chart for the character.

Student Model
Sherlock Holmes

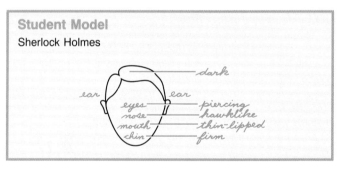

3. List the character's traits. As you review the story, look for indications of the character's personality traits. In addition to relying on the author's descriptions, try to infer traits from the character's behavior.

the reader to become actively involved.

Software If your students have access to computers, you may wish to use the guided lesson on *Description,* in **Bank Street Writer,** to model the effective use of descriptive details.

Revising and Editing Refer your students back to their face

charts and character notes. Have they included enough realistic details to bring the character to life for the reader? Assist students in finding appropriate places to insert any details that have been omitted. Demonstrate how the use of modifiers and specific language can communicate a character trait or physical attribute in places where a separate sentence might interrupt the flow of the account.

Grammar Tip/Electronic Handbook Students frequently make errors when punctuating interrupted dialogue. Demonstrate the proper method. If your students have access to the Language Master 6000, have them enter the access word *quotation* and press the GRAMMAR key for a review of the correct punctuation in dialogue.

4. Set up a believable situation. Your article will relate what happened at an imaginary meeting. Decide where and when you met the character. What did you discuss?

Drafting

1. Explain the circumstances. Begin by explaining how you happened to meet the character. Tell your readers about your feelings and impressions at the meeting.

2. Keep the character "in character." Be sure that your character is the same person that the author describes. The character's conversation must reflect the time, place, and circumstances of the short story.

Revising and Editing

1. Add details. To convince the reader that you have actually met the character, you must include realistic details.

2. Exchange articles with a partner. Evaluate each other's articles for accuracy and imaginative use of detail.

3. Proofread your article for publication.

Grammar Tip

If you have included dialogue in your article, review the rules for punctuating it to make sure you have not made any errors.

Options for Publishing

- Together with other members of the class, bind your articles into a magazine. Have one of your classmates illustrate the cover of the magazine.
- Read your magazine article aloud to the class.

Reviewing Your Writing Process

1. How did you select a character to write about?

2. Was it easier to describe the person, tell what happened at the meeting, or make up what you and the person said to one another? Explain.

Closure and Extension

Guidelines for Evaluation You may wish to consider the following questions as you evaluate each student's article:

1. Does the article demonstrate a knowledge of the character's personality traits and physical appearance?
2. Does the student include de-tails that lend a realistic tone to the article?
3. Is the account of the meeting clearly written and easy to follow?
4. Is the article free of errors in spelling, punctuation, grammar, and usage?

Reviewing Your Writing Process The following Protocol will help students reflect on and internalize their writing process:

1. What character from a short story have you chosen for your imaginary meeting? What are the circumstances of this meeting?
2. What details of appearance do you include to make your character vivid to your readers?
3. What is the subject of the conversation? What words and phrases have you included that are typical of your character?
4. What suggestions from your classmates did you include to improve your imaginary conversation?
5. What insight into this fictional character have you gained from this assignment?

Publishing You may wish to allow the students to work with partners in preparing a dramatic reenactment of the meetings described in their articles.

Student Portfolios You may wish to have your students keep their articles in their writing portfolios.

Enrichment Set aside a class session to "meet the stars." Allow time for each student to be interviewed, as his or her chosen character, by the class. You may also wish to have students explore an interaction between two characters.

Preparation

Lead a discussion about court-room dramas. Students may draw upon what they've seen on television and in movies. Have them pinpoint what attorneys do in summarizing testimony and arguments for the jury.

Focus Summarize students' observations about how attorneys make their points. Emphasize the need for strong evidence in making a closing argument effective. Have students keep this information in mind as they prepare their own arguments for or against a character.

Presentation

Prewriting You might urge students to organize their information graphically, showing their supporting evidence in a chart or outline. Urge them to be sure to anticipate what the opposing side will say in response to their evidence. They should be prepared to rebut the opposing side's arguments.

Drafting Organization is particularly important in this assignment. You might wish to review order of importance, suggesting that students present their arguments from the weakest to the strongest. This organization will present their case most dramatically and effectively.

Software If your students are working on computers, they might find it helpful to use the **Writer's Helper** activity *Debating an Issue* for help in preparing and organizing their material.

YOUR WRITING PROCESS

WRITING A CLOSING ARGUMENT

"It is better to risk saving a guilty person than to condemn an innocent one."
Voltaire

Guilty—or not guilty? A person's life hangs in the balance! The attorneys for the defense and the prosecution make their closing arguments. Then it's up to the jury to decide. Imagine that you're an attorney preparing a closing argument and that a character from a short story is the prisoner on trial.

Focus

Assignment: Write a closing argument defending or prosecuting a character from a story.
Purpose: To convince jurors that the person is innocent or guilty.
Audience: Jurors who will decide the case.

Prewriting

1. Review the stories. Scan the stories you have read to find a character already in trouble with the law or a character who may commit a crime in the future.

2. Organize your defense or prosecution team. Find two or three other students who are interested in defending or prosecuting the character you have chosen. Then sit down with them and create a chart showing the evidence.

3. Brainstorm an argument. After reviewing the reasons and evidence your legal team has gathered, brainstorm ideas for a closing argument. Be sure your closing argument anticipates what the opposing attorney may say.

Student Model

Prisoner: Sanger Rainsford of "The Most Dangerous Game"
Charge: Murder of General Zaroff

Guilty	Innocent
Rainsford was found asleep in Zaroff's bed; Zaroff's body was on the floor. <u>Evidence</u>: Signed statement of witness who found the body—Ivan's wife, on weekly visit to her husband (who has mysteriously disappeared).	Rainsford killed in self-defense. Zaroff tried to kill him first. <u>Evidence</u>: Rainsford's statement. Police photos showing signs of struggle; bedroom furniture broken.

---

212   Short Stories

Drafting

1. Grab the jury's attention. Think of a dramatic beginning that will capture the jury's attention and make them receptive to your point of view. If possible, your opening should include a statement of what you want the jury to believe.

> **Student Model**
>
> Ladies and gentlemen of the jury: There is a murderer in this room. Sanger Rainsford hunted down his victim and killed him in cold blood.

2. Organize your argument. You may find it helpful to refer to your chart of evidence as you present the facts of the case, briefly describe the crime, and tell why you are sure of your client's guilt or innocence.

3. Appeal to both reason and emotions. As you put together your argument, include the most powerful ideas that your team came up with when it brainstormed. Use clear, persuasive language that will appeal to the jurors' reason. Don't be afraid to appeal to the jurors' emotions by using vivid, specific details, but don't antagonize any of your listeners.

Revising and Editing

1. Listen to the argument. Take turns reading aloud or taping and listening to the argument each person on your legal team has composed on paper. Before you make changes, have your team answer the following questions:
- Is my argument easy to follow?
- Am I dramatic enough—or have I overdone the drama?
- Do I back up reasons with evidence?

2. Be tough on your own work. Make sure every word counts. Cut out details that distract from your argument.

> **Student Model**
>
> Rainsford steps from behind the curtain. He had a sword in his hand. General Zaroff, waking up suddenly, could not defend himself. Rainsford leaps at him and stabbed him.

Grammar Tip
Proofread for **consistent tense.** When you describe the crime, you should keep the same tense throughout. Shifting tenses unnecessarily from present to past sounds awkward and can be confusing.

Options for Publishing

- Take turns presenting your closing arguments to a jury of your classmates.
- Find another legal team that has worked on arguments that oppose your team's position. Choose a judge and jury. Then stage a trial for your class.
- Make a bulletin board display for your classroom. Ask someone to draw a picture of the character and put it in a central place on the display. Write "Guilty or Innocent?" above the picture. Then arrange on the board, where students can read them, the closing arguments from opposing legal teams.

Reviewing Your Writing Process

1. What was the most helpful thing about working with a "legal team"? The least helpful?

2. Did listening to arguments read aloud help you to determine their strengths and weaknesses? Explain.

Revising Emphasize to students the effectiveness of reading their drafts aloud. Have listeners suggest ways to revise for dramatic effect.

Grammar Tip Suggest that students refer to the Handbook of Grammar and Revising Strategies for additional guidance in correcting problems with tense consistency.

Closure and Extension

Guidelines for Evaluation You might use the following guidelines in evaluating students' closing arguments.

1. Does the argument include sound evidence?
2. Does the beginning grab attention?
3. Is the argument organized for dramatic effect?
4. Is the essay free of grammar, spelling, and punctuation problems?

Publishing Your students might enjoy staging a trial of characters. Set aside a class period for the presentation of arguments in a mock courtroom setting. Select a judge and jury to rule on the arguments.

Reflecting on the Process Urge students to apply what worked most effectively for them in their next writing assignment. For example, if they found it helpful to work with a partner or a team, they should take the initiative to work that way on future assignments.

Humanities Note

Fine art, *The Sheridan Theatre,*
1937, by Edward Hopper. Edward Hopper (1882–1967), an
American painter, studied painting in New York City with Robert
Henri and on his own in Paris.
Hopper, a realist, painted rural,
urban, and suburban American
scenes. He portrayed with simple honesty the beauty and the
ugliness of everyday surroundings. He took the mundane and
the ordinary and turned them into
something unforgettable.

The Sheridan Theatre is
painted with the objective observation that is Hopper's hallmark.
Hopper was fascinated with the
interiors of theaters and painted
them many times. This scene, a
theater in darkness half lit at the
rear, is a challenge that he met
successfully. The mood of mystery and loneliness may result
from the artist's detachment and
the stark, direct, architectural
rendering of the forms of a darkened theater.

THE SHERIDAN THEATRE, 1937
Edward Hopper
Collection of the Newark Museum

DRAMA

Drama is literature that is meant to be performed before an audience. Like a short story, it may contain the elements of plot, character, setting, and theme. In drama, actors take the parts of the characters. The story is unfolded through their words, which we call dialogue, and their actions. Usually the playwright includes stage directions that tell the actors how to behave upon the stage. Drama has other elements, too—lighting, sets, props, costumes—that bring the play alive on the stage.

Some of the earliest forms of drama were parts of religious rituals and festivals in ancient times. They were performed out-of-doors in huge amphitheaters. Today, you may see drama performed in a theater, or you may see a play produced as a movie. You may see plays performed on television, or you may have drama come into your home through radio or even audiocassettes.

One type of dramatic work is tragedy. The word *tragedy* comes from a Greek word meaning "goat song." Although scholars do not agree on the explanations for the name, most agree that its origin has some connection to a religious rite. A tragedy is a dramatic work in which a person of noble birth is brought down by a single weakness or fatal flaw. Another type of dramatic composition is comedy. The word *comedy* is based on an ancient Greek word that means "a merrymaker; a singer." Obviously, comedy is very different from tragedy. In comedy, the protagonist usually triumphs over his or her limitations so that the play has a happy ending. Today, the dividing line between comedy and tragedy has become blurred, with most plays having elements of each.

In this unit you will read a contemporary play and a classic play.

215

Drama

Drama, as a form of literature, contains one-act plays and full-length plays. As a story, a play shows a character in conflict—facing a problem that gets progressively worse until it reaches a crisis. At this crisis the character acts decisively to solve the problem. His or her action speedily brings about the end of the story.

A play is told mostly through dialogue, the speech of the characters. This convention does not allow the audience to look directly into the minds of the characters to see from the inside what they are thinking and feeling. The audience must infer a character's thoughts and feelings from the dialogue. A second way in which the audience infers thoughts and feelings is from physical movements and gestures.

Plays are meant to be performed. When you read a play, you are reading a script. The stage directions, printed in italics and in brackets, are intended to show the actors when and how to move and to suggest to the director what kinds of sound effects and lighting are needed and what the stage should look like. Stage directions use a particular vocabulary. *Right, left, up, down,* and *center* refer to areas of the stage as the actors see it. Picture the stage like this:

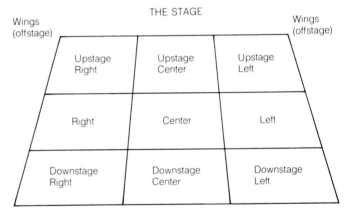

Just as you read stories actively, you should also read drama actively. Reading actively involves seeing the play in your mind while you continually question the meaning of what the actors are saying and doing.

The following strategies will help you read drama actively. Reading actively will help you to enjoy and appreciate the plays in this unit.

VISUALIZE   Picture the stage and the characters in action. Use the directions and information supplied by the playwright to create the scene in your mind. Hear the characters speak; listen to their tones of voice. Let them show you what is happening.

QUESTION   What is each character like? What situation does each character face? What is the conflict? What motives and traits does each character reveal by his or her words and actions?

PREDICT   Building on the play's conflict and the characters' motives, predict what you think will happen. How will the conflict be resolved? What will become of each character?

CLARIFY   Be sure that you can make sense of the characters' words or actions. If something is not clear to you, perhaps you need to review to find a clue in earlier words or actions. Look for answers to your questions, and check your predictions.

CONNECT   Occasionally pause to review what has happened. What is the conflict? What is happening toward its resolution? Try to summarize how the characters' actions and words fit together. Bring your own knowledge and experience into play to make connections between events and real life.

RESPOND   Finally, think about all the elements of the play. What does the play mean? What has it revealed about life? What does it say to you?

You will be a more effective reader if you use these strategies when you read drama. You will be better able to understand the conflict and resolution of a play and apply your understanding to your world.

Reading Actively   217

Reading Actively Point out that a play requires a different kind of reading from a story in prose. Reading a play involves learning to interpret stage directions and to visualize scenes. The creative reader also practices what Coleridge called "the willing suspension of disbelief"; that is, the reader accepts the conventions of the drama and judges the play on its own terms.

Master Teacher Note Close reading of a play helps students to understand the author's intentions. While the class is reading any of the plays in this unit, you might use part of a class period to have students look through a play and find lines that were written to achieve any of the following purposes:
(1) to reveal a character trait of the speaker
(2) to advance the action of the plot
(3) to create mood
(4) to show the speaker's attempt to persuade by appealing to another's needs or wishes

William Gibson

(1914–　) was born in New York City. In his first successful play, *Two for the Seesaw,* a character says, ". . . after the verb to love, to help is the sweetest in the tongue." These words express a major theme in Gibson's work, one that is clearly seen in his most famous play, *The Miracle Worker,* which is based on the real-life story of the teacher Annie Sullivan and her student Helen Keller, a seven-year-old girl who is unable to see, hear, or speak. The original title of this play was *After the Verb to Love.*

The Miracle Worker, Act I

Protagonist and Antagonist

The **protagonist** is the central character of a play. He or she will be engaged in a struggle or conflict with another character or group of characters. This other character, or group of characters, is the **antagonist.** In traditional drama, the conflict between the protagonist and the antagonist develops and intensifies until it reaches a climax, the high point of the play. At that point the conflict is settled by the victory of one of the characters.

Focus

The Miracle Worker is about the efforts of a young woman to help a girl unable to see, hear, or speak. Ordinarily, if a child's sight is impaired, he or she can be taught using the Braille alphabet and audio tapes. Or, if a child is deaf, he or she can be taught sign language in order to communicate and learn. However, if a child is unable to see, hear, or speak, the challenge of finding an effective form of communication becomes even greater. With a partner or small group, write down possible methods you would use to try to communicate with such a child. As you read *The Miracle Worker,* compare your group's ideas with the methods the teacher in the play uses to communicate with her pupil.

Vocabulary

Knowing the following words will help you as you read Act I of *The Miracle Worker.*

vigil (vij′ əl) *n.*: A watchful staying awake (p. 219)
vivacious (vi vā′ shəs) *adj.*: Lively (p. 220)
pantomime (pan′ tə mīm′) *n.*: Wordless actions or gestures

as a means of expression (p. 221)
obstinate (äb′ stə nət) *adj.*: Stubborn (p. 225)
bristling (bris′′liŋ) *v.*: Becoming tense with fear or anger (p. 226)

The Miracle Worker

William Gibson

<table>
<tr><td colspan="4" align="center">**CHARACTERS**</td></tr>
<tr><td>A Doctor</td><td>Helen</td><td>James</td><td></td></tr>
<tr><td>Kate</td><td>Martha</td><td>Anagnos (an ag′ nŏs)</td><td>Blind Girls</td></tr>
<tr><td>Keller</td><td>Percy</td><td>Annie Sullivan</td><td>A Servant</td></tr>
<tr><td></td><td>Aunt Ev</td><td>Viney</td><td>Offstage Voices</td></tr>
</table>

TIME. *The 1880's*
PLACE. *In and around the Keller homestead in Tuscumbia, Alabama; also, briefly, the Perkins Institution for the Blind, in Boston.*

ACT I

[*It is night over the Keller homestead. Inside, three adults in the bedroom are grouped around a crib, in lamplight. They have been through a long vigil, and it shows in their tired bearing and disarranged clothing. One is a young gentlewoman with a sweet girlish face,* KATE KELLER; *the second is an elderly* DOCTOR, *stethoscope at neck, thermometer in fingers; the third is a hearty gentleman in his forties with chin whiskers,* CAPTAIN ARTHUR KELLER.]

DOCTOR. She'll live.

KATE. Thank God.

[*The* DOCTOR *leaves them together over the crib, packs his bag.*]

DOCTOR. You're a pair of lucky parents. I can tell you now, I thought she wouldn't.

KELLER. Nonsense, the child's a Keller, she has the constitution of a goat. She'll outlive us all.

DOCTOR. [*Amiably*] Yes, especially if some of you Kellers don't get a night's sleep. I mean you, Mrs. Keller.

KELLER. You hear, Katie?

KATE. I hear.

KELLER. [*Indulgent*] I've brought up two of them, but this is my wife's first, she isn't battle-scarred yet.

KATE. Doctor, don't be merely considerate, will my girl be all right?

DOCTOR. Oh, by morning she'll be knocking down Captain Keller's fences again.

KATE. And isn't there anything we should do?

KELLER. [*Jovial*] Put up stronger fencing, ha?

DOCTOR. Just let her get well, she knows how to do it better than we do.

[*He is packed, ready to leave.*]

The Miracle Worker   219

Presentation

Motivation/Prior Knowledge
Have students imagine how difficult it would be to communicate with someone who can neither see nor hear. How would they tell that person when to go to bed? How would they teach him or her to do arithmetic? Tell students that Helen Keller's teacher, Annie Sullivan, faced such a challenge.

Purpose-Setting Question
What problems does Annie face as she tries to teach her young student?

Making Connections Another selection that deals with courage and the teaching of a physically challenged child is "The Scarlet Ibis," page 181. This short story, however, has a tragic ending, while *The Miracle Worker* ends triumphantly.

1 Clarification The title of the play comes from Mark Twain's description of Annie Sullivan. He said she was a "miracle worker."

2 Master Teacher Note The stage directions in this play are difficult to read. Yet they are more important in some scenes than the dialogue. You may want to encourage students to use these directions to visualize the setting and action.

3 Discussion Who do you think is the object of concern?

4 Discussion What do you learn from this speech about Keller and Kate's marriage?

5 Critical Thinking and Reading You might want to ask students to compare and contrast Kate's and Keller's concerns. How do they reveal their different temperaments?

Master Teacher Note Use the overhead projector to show students Art Transparency 6, *Reine Lefebvre and Margot Before a Window,* by Mary Cassatt. Tell students that the colors and mood of the picture, as well as the body language of the subjects, can convey a great deal of information about the relationship between the subjects. Have students comment on this relationship.

Then tell students that a dramatist establishes relationships between characters by means of their words and behavior on stage. Explain that, in the first act of this three-act play, the playwright introduces the protagonist and antagonist, provides background material on them, and shows the beginnings of their conflict.

Less advanced students may have trouble identifying Annie Sullivan as the protagonist. Point out to them that the title of the play refers to Annie.

Such students may also have trouble seeing that there are several antagonists. To help students understand this point, ask them to look for the problems that Annie encounters with family members other than Helen.

Main thing is the fever's gone, these things
come and go in infants, never know why.
Call it acute congestion of the stomach and
brain.

KELLER. I'll see you to your buggy, Doctor.

DOCTOR. I've never seen a baby, more vitality, that's the truth.

[*He beams a good night at the baby and*
KATE, *and* KELLER *leads him downstairs
with a lamp. They go down the porch steps,
and across the yard, where the* DOCTOR
goes off left; KELLER *stands with the lamp
aloft.* KATE *meanwhile is bent lovingly over
the crib, which emits a bleat; her finger is
playful with the baby's face.*]

KATE: Hush. Don't you cry now, you've been
trouble enough. Call it acute congestion, indeed, I don't see what's so cute about a congestion, just because it's yours. We'll have
your father run an editorial in his paper, the
wonders of modern medicine, they don't
know what they're curing even when they
cure it. Men, men and their battle scars, we
women will have to—

[*But she breaks off, puzzled, moves her
finger before the baby's eyes.*]

Will have to—Helen?

[*Now she moves her hand, quickly.*]

Helen.

[*She snaps her fingers at the baby's eyes
twice, and her hand falters; after a moment she calls out, loudly.*]

Captain, Captain, will you come—

[*But she stares at the baby, and her next
call is directly at her ears.*]

Captain!

[*And now, still staring,* KATE *screams.* KEL-
LER *in the yard hears it, and runs with the
lamp back to the house.* KATE *screams*

again, *her look intent on the baby and terrible.* KELLER *hurries in and up.*]

KELLER. Katie? What's wrong?

KATE. Look.

[*She makes a pass with her hand in the
crib, at the baby's eyes.*]

KELLER. What, Katie? She's well, she needs
only time to—

KATE. She can't see. Look at her eyes.

[*She takes the lamp from him, moves it before the child's face.*]

She can't see!

KELLER. [*Hoarsely*] Helen.

KATE. Or hear. When I screamed she didn't
blink. Not an eyelash—

KELLER. Helen. Helen!

KATE. She can't *hear* you!

KELLER. *Helen!*

[*His face has something like fury in it, crying the child's name;* KATE *almost fainting
presses her knuckles to her mouth, to stop
her own cry.*

The room dims out quickly.

*Time, in the form of a slow tune of distant
belfry chimes which approaches in a crescendo and then fades, passes; the light
comes up again on a day five years later,
on three kneeling children and an old dog
outside around the pump.*

The dog is a setter named BELLE, *and she
is sleeping. Two of the children are Ne-
groes,* MARTHA *and* PERCY. *The third child is*
HELEN, *six and a half years old, quite unkempt, in body a vivacious little person
with a fine head, attractive, but noticeably
blind, one eye larger and protruding; her
gestures are abrupt, insistent, lacking in*

220   Drama

human restraint, and her face never smiles. She is flanked by the other two, in a litter of paper-doll cutouts, and while they speak HELEN'S *hands thrust at their faces in turn, feeling baffledly at the movements of their lips.]*

MARTHA. [*Snipping*] First I'm gonna cut off this doctor's legs, one, two, now then—

PERCY. Why you cuttin' off that doctor's legs?

MARTHA. I'm gonna give him a operation. Now I'm gonna cut off his arms, one, two. Now I'm gonna fix up—

[*She pushes* HELEN'S *hand away from her mouth.*]

You stop that.

PERCY. Cut off his stomach, that's a good operation.

MARTHA. No, I'm gonna cut off his head first, he got a bad cold.

PERCY. Ain't gonna be much of that doctor left to fix up, time you finish all them opera—

[*But* HELEN *is poking her fingers inside his mouth, to feel his tongue; he bites at them, annoyed, and she jerks them away.* HELEN *now fingers her own lips, moving them in imitation, but soundlessly.*]

MARTHA. What you do, bite her hand?

PERCY. That's how I do, she keep pokin' her fingers in my mouth, I just bite 'em off.

MARTHA. What she tryin' do now?

PERCY. She tryin' *talk.* She gonna get mad. Looka her tryin' talk.

[HELEN *is scowling, the lips under her fingertips moving in ghostly silence, growing more and more frantic, until in a bizarre rage she bites at her own fingers. This*

sends PERCY *off into laughter, but alarms* MARTHA.]

MARTHA. Hey, you stop now.

[*She pulls* HELEN'S *hand down.*]

You just sit quiet and—

[*But at once* HELEN *topples* MARTHA *on her back, knees pinning her shoulders down, and grabs the scissors.* MARTHA *screams.* PERCY *darts to the bell string on the porch, yanks it, and the bell rings.*

Inside, the lights have been gradually coming up on the main room, where we see the family informally gathered, talking, but in pantomime: KATE *sits darning socks near a cradle, occasionally rocking it;* CAPTAIN KELLER *in spectacles is working over newspaper pages at a table; a benign visitor in a hat,* AUNT EV, *is sharing the sewing basket, putting the finishing touches on a big shapeless doll made out of towels; an indolent young man,* JAMES KELLER, *is at the window watching the children.*

With the ring of the bell, KATE *is instantly on her feet and out the door onto the porch, to take in the scene; now we see what these five years have done to her, the girlish playfulness is gone, she is a woman steeled in grief.*]

KATE. [*For the thousandth time*] Helen.

[*She is down the steps at once to them, seizing* HELEN'S *wrists and lifting her off* MARTHA; MARTHA *runs off in tears and screams for momma, with* PERCY *after her.*]

Let me have those scissors.

[*Meanwhile the family inside is alerted,* AUNT EV *joining* JAMES *at the window;* CAPTAIN KELLER *resumes work.*]

JAMES. [*Blandly*] She only dug Martha's eyes out. Almost dug. It's always almost, no point worrying till it happens, is there?

The Miracle Worker 221

9 Discussion What does Helen seem to sense about the importance of lips and mouths?

10 Discussion Why do you think the playwright has the lights gradually come up on this scene while Helen fights with Martha?

11 Discussion What do you think has changed Kate over the past five years?

12 Discussion How do you know this incident has occurred before?

Speaking and Listening You might want to have students volunteer to read aloud the first major family scene in which the Baltimore doctor is discussed. This scene clearly reveals the family members' character traits. If you wish, individual students may read the parts of Keller, Kate, James, and Aunt Ev. One volunteer should read aloud the stage directions, which are very important in this play.

13 Discussion What is Kate trying to tell Helen? Does Helen understand?

14 Discussion Why is it important to know this background information about the Kellers' attempts to have Helen treated?

15 Discussion What does Helen suddenly realize about the doll?

KELLER. A refreshing suggestion. What?

[KATE *entering turns* HELEN *to* AUNT EV, *who gives her the towel doll.*]

AUNT EV. Why, this very famous oculist[1] in Baltimore I wrote you about, what was his name?

KATE. Dr. Chisholm.

AUNT EV. Yes, I heard lots of cases of blindness people thought couldn't be cured he's cured, he just does wonders. Why don't you write to him?

KELLER. I've stopped believing in wonders.

KATE. [*Rocks the cradle*] I think the Captain will write to him soon. Won't you, Captain?

KELLER. No.

JAMES. [*Lightly*] Good money after bad, or bad after good. Or bad after bad—

AUNT EV. Well, if it's just a question of money, Arthur, now you're marshal you have this Yankee money. Might as well—

KELLER: Not money. The child's been to specialists all over Alabama and Tennessee, if I thought it would do good I'd have her to every fool doctor in the country.

KATE. I think the Captain will write to him soon.

KELLER. Katie. How many times can you let them break your heart?

KATE. Any number of times.

[HELEN *meanwhile sits on the floor to explore the doll with her fingers, and her hand pauses over the face: this is no face, a blank area of towel, and it troubles her. Her hand searches for features, and taps questioningly for eyes, but no one notices.*]

[*They gaze out, while* KATE *reaches for the scissors in* HELEN'S *hand. But* HELEN *pulls the scissors back, they struggle for them a moment, then* KATE *gives up, lets* HELEN *keep them. She tries to draw* HELEN *into the house.* HELEN *jerks away.* KATE *next goes down on her knees, takes* HELEN'S *hands gently, and using the scissors like a doll, makes* HELEN *caress and cradle them; she points* HELEN'S *finger housewards.* HELEN'S *whole body now becomes eager; she surrenders the scissors,* KATE *turns her toward the door and gives her a little push,* HELEN *scrambles up and toward the house, and* KATE *rising follows her.*]

13

AUNT EV. How does she stand it? Why haven't you seen this Baltimore man? It's not a thing you can let go on and on, like the weather.

JAMES. The weather here doesn't ask permission of me, Aunt Ev. Speak to my father.

AUNT EV. Arthur. Something ought to be done for that child.

---

1. oculist (äk′ yə list)*n*.: An old-fashioned term for an eye specialist.

222   Drama

Grammar in Action

A **fragment** is a group of words that does not express a complete thought. It is usually advisable to avoid fragments in writing; however, dramatists and fiction writers often use fragments in dialogue to make conversation seem realistic. These fragments are usually understandable from the context:

"What made you leave the scene of the accident?" (Sentence)

"Fear." (Fragment)
"Of what?" (Fragment)
"I don't know. I was just scared." (Sentences)

Notice the mixture of complete sentences and fragments in the following passage from *The Miracle Worker*.

KATE.   As long as there's the least chance. For her to see. Or hear, or—

KELLER.   There isn't. Now I must finish here.

She then yanks at her AUNT'S *dress, and taps again vigorously for eyes.*]

AUNT EV. What, child?

[*Obviously not hearing,* HELEN *commences to go around, from person to person, tapping for eyes, but no one attends or understands.*]

KATE. [*No break*] As long as there's the least chance. For her to see. Or hear, or—

KELLER. There isn't. Now I must finish here.

KATE. I think, with your permission, Captain, I'd like to write.

KELLER. I said no, Katie.

AUNT EV. Why, writing does no harm, Arthur, only a little bitty letter. To see if he can help her.

KELLER. He can't.

KATE. We won't know that to be a fact, Captain, until after you write.

KELLER. [*Rising, emphatic*] Katie, he can't.

[*He collects his papers.*]

JAMES. [*Facetiously*] Father stands up, that makes it a fact.

KELLER. You be quiet! I'm badgered enough here by females without your impudence.

[JAMES *shuts up, makes himself scarce.* HELEN *now is groping among things on* KELLER'S *desk, and paws his papers to the floor.* KELLER *is exasperated.*]

Katie.

[KATE *quickly turns* HELEN *away, and retrieves the papers.*]

I might as well try to work in a henyard as in this house—

JAMES. [*Placating*] You really ought to put her away, Father.

KATE. [*Staring up*] What?

JAMES. Some asylum. It's the kindest thing.

AUNT EV. Why, she's your sister, James, not a nobody—

JAMES. Half sister, and half—mentally defective, she can't even keep herself clean. It's not pleasant to see her about all the time.

KATE. Do you dare? Complain of what you *can* see?

KELLER. [*Very annoyed*] This discussion is at an end! I'll thank you not to broach it again, Ev.

[*Silence descends at once.* HELEN *gropes her way with the doll, and* KELLER *turns back for a final word, explosive.*]

I've done as much as I can bear, I can't give my whole life to it! The house is at sixes and sevens from morning till night over the child, it's time some attention was paid to Mildred here instead!

KATE. [*Gently dry*] You'll wake her up, Captain.

KELLER. I want some peace in the house, I don't care how, but one way we won't have it is by rushing up and down the country every time someone hears of a new quack. I'm as sensible to this affliction as anyone else, it hurts me to look at the girl.

KATE. It was not our affliction I meant you to write about, Captain

[HELEN *is back at* AUNT EV, *fingering her dress, and yanks two buttons from it.*]

AUNT EV. Helen! My buttons.

[HELEN *pushes the buttons into the doll's face.* KATE *now sees, comes swiftly to kneel, lifts* HELEN'S *hand to her own eyes in question.*]

KATE. Eyes?

The Miracle Worker 223

16 Critical Thinking and Reading What can you infer about James and his relationship with his father?

17 Critical Thinking and Reading Why does Helen rip off Aunt Ev's buttons and push them into the doll's face?

17

KATE. I think, with your permission, Captain, I'd like to write.
KELLER. I said no, Katie.
AUNT EV. Why, writing does no harm, Arthur, only a little bitty letter. To see if he can help her.

Student Activity 1. Identify the fragments in this passage. Explain how each manages to express a complete thought.

Student Activity 2. Rewrite the passage from *The Miracle Worker* eliminating all the fragments. Then explain which passage sounds most like normal speech.

Electronic Handbook You might wish to have students review sentence fragments before completing Grammar in Action activities. If students have access to Language Master 6000, have them enter the access word *fragment* and press the GRAMMAR key to find information on recognition of sentence fragments.

18 **Critical Thinking and Reading**
How does this remark conflict with his earlier statement that "the least she can have are the little things she wants"? What are Keller's divided feelings about his daughter?

19 **Discussion** What evidence is there that Helen is intelligent even though she cannot understand what is going on?

[HELEN *nods energetically.*]

She wants the doll to have eyes.

[*Another kind of silence now, while* KATE *takes pins and buttons from the sewing basket and attaches them to the doll as eyes.* KELLER *stands, caught, and watches morosely.* AUNT EV *blinks, and conceals her emotion by inspecting her dress.*]

AUNT EV. My goodness me, I'm not decent.

KATE. She doesn't know better, Aunt Ev. I'll sew them on again.

JAMES. Never learn with everyone letting her do anything she takes it into her mind to—

KELLER. You be quiet!

JAMES. What did I say now?

KELLER. You talk too much.

JAMES. I was agreeing with you!

KELLER. Whatever it was. Deprived child, the least she can have are the little things she wants.

[JAMES, *very wounded, stalks out of the room onto the porch; he remains here, sulking.*]

AUNT EV. [*Indulgently*] It's worth a couple of buttons, Kate, look.

[HELEN *now has the doll with eyes, and cannot contain herself for joy; she rocks the doll, pats it vigorously, kisses it.*]

This child has more sense than all these men Kellers, if there's ever any way to reach that mind of hers.

[*But* HELEN *suddenly has come upon the cradle, and unhesitatingly overturns it; the swaddled baby tumbles out, and* CAPTAIN KELLER *barely manages to dive and catch it in time.*]

KELLER. Helen!

[*All are in commotion, the baby screams, but* HELEN *unperturbed is laying her doll in its place.* KATE *on her knees pulls her hands off the cradle, wringing them;* HELEN *is bewildered.*]

KATE. Helen, Helen, you're not to do such things, how can I make you understand—

KELLER. [*Hoarsely*] Katie.

KATE. How can I get it into your head, my darling, my poor—

KELLER. Katie, some way of teaching her an iota of discipline has to be—

KATE. [*Flaring*] How can you discipline an afflicted child? Is it her fault?

[HELEN'S *fingers have fluttered to her* MOTHER'S *lips, vainly trying to comprehend their movements.*]

KELLER. I didn't say it was her fault.

KATE. Then whose? I don't know what to do! How can I teach her, beat her—until she's black and blue?

KELLER. It's not safe to let her run around loose. Now there must be a way of confining her, somehow, so she can't—

KATE. Where, in a cage? She's a growing child, she has to use her limbs!

KELLER. Answer me one thing, is it fair to Mildred here?

KATE. [*Inexorably*] Are you willing to put her away?

[*Now* HELEN'S *face darkens in the same rage as at herself earlier, and her hand strikes at* KATE'S *lips.* KATE *catches her hand again, and* HELEN *begins to kick, struggle, twist.*]

KELLER. Now what?

KATE. She wants to talk, like—*be* like you and me.

[*She holds* HELEN *struggling until we hear from the child her first sound so far, an inarticulate weird noise in her throat such as an animal in a trap might make; and* KATE *releases her. The second she is free* HELEN *blunders away, collides violently with a chair, falls, and sits weeping.* KATE *comes to her, embraces, caresses, soothes her, and buries her own face in her hair, until she can control her voice.*]

Every day she slips further away. And I don't know how to call her back.

AUNT EV. Oh, I've a mind to take her up to Baltimore myself. If that doctor can't help her, maybe he'll know who can.

KELLER. [*Presently, heavily*] I'll write the man, Katie.

[*He stands with the baby in his clasp, staring at* HELEN'S *head, hanging down on* KATE'S *arm.*]

[*The lights dim out, except the one on* KATE *and* HELEN. *In the twilight,* JAMES, AUNT EV, *and* KELLER *move off slowly, formally, in separate directions;* KATE *with* HELEN *in her arms remains, motionless, in an image which overlaps into the next scene and fades only when it is well under way.*

Without pause, from the dark down left we hear a man's voice with a Greek accent speaking.]

ANAGNOS. —who could do nothing for the girl, of course. It was Dr. Bell who thought she might somehow be taught. I have written the family only that a suitable governess, Miss Annie Sullivan, has been found here in Boston—

[*The lights begin to come up, down left, on a long table and chair. The table contains equipment for teaching the blind by touch— a small replica of the human skeleton, stuffed animals, models of flowers and plants, piles of books. The chair contains a girl of 20,* ANNIE SULLIVAN, *with a face which in repose is grave and rather obstinate, and when active is impudent, combative, twinkling with all the life that is lacking in* HELEN'S, *and handsome; there is a crude vitality to her. Her suitcase is at her knee.* ANAGNOS, *a stocky bearded man, comes into the light only toward the end of his speech.*]

ANAGNOS. —and will come. It will no doubt be difficult for you there, Annie. But it has been difficult for you at our school too, hm? Gratifying, yes, when you came to us and could not spell your name, to accomplish so much here in a few years, but always an Irish battle. For independence.

[*He studies* ANNIE, *humorously; she does not open her eyes.*]

This is my last time to counsel you, Annie, and you do lack some—by some I mean *all*— what, tact or talent to bend. To others. And what has saved you on more than one occasion here at Perkins is that there was nowhere to expel you to. Your eyes hurt?

ANNIE. My ears, Mr. Anagnos.

[*And now she has opened her eyes; they are inflamed, vague, slightly crossed, clouded by the granular growth of trachoma,[2] and she often keeps them closed to shut out the pain of light.*]

ANAGNOS. [*Severely*] Nowhere but back to Tewksbury,[3] where children learn to be saucy. Annie, I know how dreadful it was there, but that battle is dead and done with, why not let it stay buried?

---

2. trachoma (trə kō′ mə)*n.*: A disease of the eyelid and eyeball.
3. Tewksbury: A town in Massachusetts, the location of an institution for the poor.

The Miracle Worker 225

20 Discussion Why do you think Helen is becoming more of a problem?

21 Discussion Why do you think the playwright has the characters exit in this manner, leaving Kate and Helen behind? What mood does he create by ending the scene like this?

22 Critical Thinking and Reading What can you infer about Annie from the stage directions and from Anagnos's words?

23 Reading Strategy You might want to ask students to look for references to this phase of Annie's life as the play unfolds.

ANNIE. [*Cheerily*] I think God must owe me a resurrection.

ANAGNOS. [*A bit shocked*] What?

ANNIE. [*Taps her brow*] Well, He keeps digging up that battle!

ANAGNOS. That is not a proper thing to say, Annie. It is what I mean.

ANNIE. [*Meekly*] Yes. But I know what I'm like, what's this child like?

ANAGNOS. Like?

ANNIE. Well—Bright or dull, to start off.

ANAGNOS. No one knows. And if she is dull, you have no patience with this?

ANNIE. Oh, in grownups you have to, Mr. Anagnos. I mean in children it just seems a little—precocious, can I use that word?

ANAGNOS. Only if you can spell it.

ANNIE. Premature. So I hope at least she's a bright one.

24 | **ANAGNOS.** Deaf, blind, mute—who knows? She is like a little safe, locked, that no one can open. Perhaps there is a treasure inside.

ANNIE. Maybe it's empty, too?

ANAGNOS. Possible. I should warn you, she is much given to tantrums.

25 | **ANNIE.** Means something is inside. Well, so am I, if I believe all I hear. Maybe you should warn *them*.

ANAGNOS. [*Frowns*] Annie. I wrote them no word of your history. You will find yourself among strangers now, who know nothing of it.

ANNIE. Well, we'll keep them in a state of blessed ignorance.

26 | **ANAGNOS.** Perhaps *you* should tell it?

ANNIE. [*Bristling*] Why? I have enough trouble with people who don't know.

ANAGNOS. So they will understand. When you have trouble.

ANNIE. The only time I have trouble is when I'm right.

[*But she is amused at herself, as is* ANAGNOS.]

Is it my fault it's so often? I won't give them trouble, Mr. Anagnos, I'll be so ladylike they won't notice I've come.

ANAGNOS. Annie, be—humble. It is not as if you have so many offers to pick and choose. You will need their affection, working with this child.

ANNIE. [*Humorously*] I hope I won't need their pity.

ANAGNOS. Oh, we can all use some pity.

[*Crisply*]

So. You are no longer our pupil, we throw you into the world, a teacher. *If* the child can be taught. No one expects you to work miracles, even for twenty-five dollars a month. Now, in this envelope a loan, for the railroad, which you will repay me when you have a bank account. But in this box, a gift. With our love.

[ANNIE *opens the small box he extends, and sees a garnet ring. She looks up, blinking, and down.*]

I think other friends are ready to say goodbye.

[*He moves as though to open doors.*]

ANNIE. Mr. Anagnos.

[*Her voice is trembling.*]

Dear Mr. Anagnos, I—

[*But she swallows over getting the ring on her finger, and cannot continue until she finds a woebegone joke.*]

Well, what should I say, I'm an ignorant

opinionated girl, and everything I am I owe to you?

ANAGNOS. [*Smiles*] That is only half true, Annie.

ANNIE. Which half? I crawled in here like a drowned rat, I thought I died when Jimmie died, that I'd never again—come alive. Well, you say with love so easy, and I haven't *loved* a soul since and I never will, I suppose, but this place gave me more than my eyes back. Or taught me how to spell, which I'll never learn anyway, but with all the fights and the trouble I've been here it taught me what help is, and how to live again, and I don't want to say goodbye. Don't open the door, I'm crying.

ANAGNOS. [*Gently*] They will not see.

[*He moves again as though opening doors, and in comes a group of girls, 8-year-olds to 17-year-olds; as they walk we see they are blind.* ANAGNOS *shepherds them in with a hand.*]

A CHILD. Annie?

ANNIE: [*Her voice cheerful.*] Here, Beatrice.

[*As soon as they locate her voice they throng joyfully to her, speaking all at once;* ANNIE *is down on her knees to the smallest, and the following are the more intelligible fragments in the general hubbub.*]

CHILDREN. There'a a present. We brought you a going-away present, Annie!

ANNIE. Oh, now you shouldn't have—

CHILDREN. We did, we did, where's the present?

SMALLEST CHILD. [*Mournfully*] Don't go, Annie, away.

CHILDREN. Alice has it. Alice! Where's Alice? Here I am! Where? Here!

[*An arm is aloft out of the group, waving a present;* ANNIE *reaches for it.*]

ANNIE. I have it. I have it, everybody, should I open it?

CHIDREN. Open it! Everyone be quiet! Do, Annie! She's opening it. Ssh!

[*A settling of silence while* ANNIE *unwraps it. The present is a pair of smoked glasses, and she stands still.*]

Is it open, Annie?

ANNIE. It's open.

CHILDREN. It's for your eyes, Annie. Put them on, Annie! 'Cause Mrs. Hopkins said your eyes hurt since the operation. And she said you're going where the sun is *fierce*.

ANNIE. I'm putting them on now.

SMALLEST CHILD. [*Mournfully*] Don't go, Annie, where the sun is fierce.

CHILDREN. Do they fit all right?

ANNIE. Oh, they fit just fine.

CHILDREN. Did you put them on? Are they pretty, Annie?

ANNIE. Oh, my eyes feel hundreds of per cent better already, and pretty, why, do you know how I look in them? Splendiloquent. Like a race horse!

CHILDREN. [*Delighted*] There's another present! Beatrice! We have a present for Helen, too! Give it to her, Beatrice. Here, Annie!

[*This present is an elegant doll, with movable eyelids and a momma sound.*]

It's for Helen. And we took up a collection to buy it. And Laura dressed it.

ANNIE. It's beautiful!

CHILDREN. So, don't forget, you be sure to give it to Helen from us, Annie!

ANNIE. I promise it will be the first thing I give her. If I don't keep it for myself, that is, you know I can't be trusted with dolls!

The Miracle Worker 227

28 Reading Strategy Have students summarize what they know about Annie up to this point.

29 Discussion How do the girls feel about Annie?

Master Teacher Note Students often make the mistake of viewing *The Miracle Worker* as simply a play "about Helen Keller." The play is actually the story of a teacher who is challenged by and refuses to surrender to seemingly insurmountable obstacles.

Discuss with students Annie Sullivan's background, the core of which is told in Act I scenes with Dr. Anagnos and the meeting of Annie and Kate: Annie Sullivan had lived a wretched life as a poor blind child, had arrived at the Perkins Institute unaware that the alphabet even existed, and had graduated as valedictorian of her class.

Impress upon students that this play is a dramatization of a true story. Annie Sullivan and Helen Keller were real people.

30 Discussion What does this scene reveal about Annie?

31 Clarification This change in the color of the light signals a scene from the past. Such a scene is usually called a flashback.

32 Literary Focus Consider pointing out to students the effective staging here. Three scenes—one from the past and two in the present—are tied together with the three words, "Annie! Annie?" and "Coming!"

SMALLEST CHILD. [*Mournfully*] Don't go, Annie, to her.

ANNIE. [*Her arm around her.*] Sarah, dear, I don't *want* to go.

SMALLEST CHILD. Then why are you going?

ANNIE. [*Gently*] Because I'm a big girl now, and big girls have to earn a living. It's the only way I can. But if you don't smile for me first, what I'll just have to do is—

[*She pauses, inviting it.*]

SMALLEST CHILD. What?

ANNIE. Put *you* in my suitcase, instead of this doll. And take *you* to Helen in Alabama!

[*This strikes the children as very funny, and they begin to laugh and tease the smallest child, who after a moment does smile for* ANNIE.]

ANAGNOS. [*Then*] Come, children. We must get the trunk into the carriage and Annie into her train, or no one will go to Alabama. Come, come.

[*He shepherds them out and* ANNIE *is left alone on her knees with the doll in her lap. She reaches for her suitcase, and by a subtle change in the color of the light, we go with her thoughts into another time. We hear a boy's voice whispering; perhaps we see shadowy intimations of these speakers in the background.*]

BOY'S VOICE. Where we goin', Annie?

ANNIE. [*In dread*] Jimmie.

BOY'S VOICE. Where we goin'?

ANNIE. I said—I'm takin' care of you—

BOY'S VOICE. Forever and ever?

MAN'S VOICE. [*Impersonal*] Annie Sullivan, aged nine, virtually blind. James Sullivan, aged seven—What's the matter with your leg, Sonny?

ANNIE. Forever and ever.

MAN'S VOICE. Can't he walk without that crutch?

[ANNIE *shakes her head, and does not stop shaking it.*]

Girl goes to the women's ward. Boy to the men's.

BOY'S VOICE. [*In terror*] Annie! Annie, don't let them take me—Annie!

ANAGNOS. [*Offstage*] Annie! Annie?

[*But this voice is real, in the present, and* ANNIE *comes up out of her horror, clearing her head with a final shake; the lights begin to pick out* KATE *in the* KELLER *house, as* ANNIE *in a bright tone calls back.*]

ANNIE. Coming!

[*This word catches* KATE, *who stands half turned and attentive to it, almost as though hearing it. Meanwhile* ANNIE *turns and hurries out, lugging the suitcase.*

The room dims out; the sound of railroad wheels begins from off left, and maintains itself in a constant rhythm underneath the following scene; the remaining lights have come up on the* KELLER *homestead.* JAMES *is lounging on the porch, waiting. In the upper bedroom which is to be* ANNIE'S, HELEN *is alone, puzzledly exploring, fingering and smelling things, the curtains, empty drawers in the bureau, water in the pitcher by the washbasin, fresh towels on the bedstead. Downstairs in the family room* KATE *turning to a mirror hastily adjusts her bonnet, watched by a Negro servant in an apron,* VINEY.]

VINEY. Let Mr. Jimmy go by hisself, you been pokin' that garden all day, you ought to rest your feet.

KATE. I can't wait to see her, Viney.

VINEY. Maybe she ain't gone be on this train neither.

KATE. Maybe she is.

VINEY. And maybe she ain't.

KATE. And maybe she is. Where's Helen?

VINEY. She upstairs, smellin' around. She know somethin' funny's goin' on.

KATE. Let her have her supper as soon as Mildred's in bed, and tell Captain Keller when he comes that we'll be delayed tonight.

VINEY. Again.

KATE. I don't think we need say *again.* Simply delayed will do.

[*She runs upstairs to* ANNIE'S *room,* VINEY *speaking after her.*]

VINEY. I mean that's what he gone say. "What, again?"

[VINEY *works at setting the table. Upstairs* KATE *stands in the doorway, watching* HELEN'S *groping explorations.*]

KATE. Yes, we're expecting someone. Someone for my Helen.

[HELEN *happens upon her skirt, clutches her leg;* KATE *in a tired dismay kneels to tidy her hair and soiled pinafore.*]

Oh, dear, this was clean not an hour ago.

[HELEN *feels her bonnet, shakes her head darkly, and tugs to get it off.* KATE *retains it with one hand, diverts* HELEN *by opening her other hand under her nose.*]

Here. For while I'm gone.

[HELEN *sniffs, reaches, and pops something into her mouth, while* KATE *speaks a bit guiltily.*]

I don't think one peppermint drop will spoil your supper.

[*She gives* HELEN *a quick kiss, evades her*

hands, and hurries downstairs again. Meanwhile CAPTAIN KELLER *has entered the yard from around the rear of the house, newspaper under arm, cleaning off and munching on some radishes; he sees* JAMES *lounging at the porch post.*]

KELLER. Jimmie?

JAMES. [*Unmoving*] Sir?

KELLER. [*Eyes him*] You don't look dressed for anything useful, boy.

JAMES. I'm not. It's for Miss Sullivan.

KELLER. Needn't keep holding up that porch, we have wooden posts for that. I asked you to see that those strawberry plants were moved this evening.

JAMES. I'm moving your—Mrs. Keller, instead. To the station.

KELLER. [*Heavily*] Mrs. Keller. Must you always speak of her as though you haven't met the lady?

[KATE *comes out on the porch, and* JAMES *inclines his head.*]

JAMES. [*Ironic*] Mother.

[*He starts off the porch, but sidesteps* KELLER'S *glare like a blow.*]

I said mother!

KATE. Captain.

KELLER. Evening, my dear.

KATE. We're off to meet the train, Captain. Supper will be a trifle delayed tonight.

KELLER. What, again?

KATE. [*Backing out*] With your permission, Captain?

[*And they are gone.* KELLER *watches them offstage, morosely.*]

[*Upstairs* HELEN *meanwhile has groped for her mother, touched her cheek in a mean-*

The Miracle Worker 229

33 Discussion How do you think Helen knows that something unusual is happening?

34 Discussion Why does Helen want to take off Kate's bonnet? What does she realize?

35 Critical Thinking and Reading Compare and contrast James with Keller. Why do you think there is so much tension between them?

36 Discussion How has Helen worked out a language of her own?

37 Discussion What does this speech reveal about Keller?

38 Discussion Why do you think that people constantly give Helen snacks? What does this practice suggest about their attitude toward her?

39 Discussion How does James seem to feel about Annie? Why do you think he feels this way?

ingful gesture, waited, touched her cheek, waited, then found the open door, and made her way down. Now she comes into the family room, touches her cheek again; VINEY *regards her.*]

VINEY. What you want, honey, your momma?

[HELEN *touches her cheek again.* VINEY *goes to the sideboard, gets a tea-cake, gives it into* HELEN'S *hand;* HELEN *pops it into her mouth.*]

Guess one little tea-cake ain't gone ruin your appetite.

[*She turns* HELEN *toward the door.* HELEN *wanders out onto the porch, as* KELLER *comes up the steps. Her hands encounter him, and she touches her cheek again, waits.*]

KELLER. She's gone.

[*He is awkward with her; when he puts his hand on her head, she pulls away.* KELLER *stands regarding her, heavily.*]

She's gone, my son and I don't get along, you don't know I'm your father, no one likes me, and supper's delayed.

[HELEN *touches her cheek, waits.* KELLER *fishes in his pocket.*]

Here. I brought you some stick candy, one nibble of sweets can't do any harm.

[*He gives her a large stick candy;* HELEN *falls to it.* VINEY *peers out the window.*]

VINEY. [*Reproachfully*] Cap'n Keller, now how'm I gone get her to eat her supper you fill her up with that trash?

KELLER. [*Roars*] Tend to your work!

[VINEY *beats a rapid retreat.* KELLER *thinks better of it, and tries to get the candy away from* HELEN, *but* HELEN *hangs on to it; and when* KELLER *pulls, she gives his leg a kick.* KELLER *hops about,* HELEN *takes ref-*

uge with the candy down behind the pump, and KELLER *then irately flings his newspaper on the porch floor, stamps into the house past* VINEY *and disappears.*

The lights half dim on the homestead, where VINEY *and* HELEN *going about their business soon find their way off. Meanwhile, the railroad sounds off left have mounted in a crescendo to a climax typical of a depot at arrival time, the lights come up on stage left, and we see a suggestion of a station. Here* ANNIE *in her smoked glasses and disarrayed by travel is waiting with her suitcase, while* JAMES *walks to meet her; she has a battered paper-bound book, which is a Perkins report,[4] under her arm.*]

JAMES. [*Coolly*] Miss Sullivan?

ANNIE. [*cheerily*] Here! At last, I've been on trains so many days I thought they must be backing up every time I dozed off—

JAMES. I'm James Keller.

ANNIE. James?

[*The name stops her.*]

I had a brother Jimmie. Are you Helen's?

JAMES. I'm only half a brother. You're to be her governess?

ANNIE. [*Lightly*] Well. Try!

JAMES. [*Eying her*] You look like half a governess.

[KATE *enters.* ANNIE *stands moveless, while* JAMES *takes her suitcase.* KATE'S *gaze on her is doubtful, troubled.*]

Mrs. Keller, Miss Sullivan.

[KATE *takes her hand.*]

---

4. Perkins report: One of the annual reports by Dr. Samuel G. Howe, founder of the Perkins Institution, describing his methods for teaching blind and deaf children.

230 *Drama*

KATE. [*Simply*] We've met every train for two days.

[ANNIE *looks at* KATE's *face, and her good humor comes back.*]

ANNIE. I changed trains every time they stopped, the man who sold me that ticket ought to be tied to the tracks—

JAMES. You have a trunk, Miss Sullivan?

ANNIE. Yes.

[*She passes* JAMES *a claim check, and he bears the suitcase out behind them.* ANNIE *holds the battered book.* KATE *is studying her face, and* ANNIE *returns the gaze; this is a mutual appraisal, southern gentlewoman and working-class Irish girl, and* ANNIE *is not quite comfortable under it.*]

You didn't bring Helen, I was hoping you would.

KATE. No, she's home.

[*A pause.* ANNIE *tries to make ladylike small talk, though her energy now and then erupts; she catches herself up whenever she hears it.*]

ANNIE. You—live far from town, Mrs. Keller?

KATE. Only a mile.

ANNIE. Well. I suppose I can wait one more mile. But don't be surprised if I get out to push the horse!

KATE. Helen's waiting for you, too. There's been such a bustle in the house, she expects something, heaven knows what.

[*Now she voices part of her doubt, not as such, but* ANNIE *understands it.*]

I expected—a desiccated[5] spinster. You're very young.

ANNIE. [*Resolutely*] Oh, you should have

---
5. desiccated (des′ i kāt′ id): Dried up.

seen me when I left Boston. I got much older on this trip.

KATE. I mean, to teach anyone as difficult as Helen.

ANNIE. *I* mean to try. They can't put you in jail for trying!

KATE. Is it possible, even? To teach a deaf-blind child *half* of what an ordinary child learns—has that ever been done?

ANNIE. Half?

KATE. A tenth.

ANNIE. [*Reluctantly*] No.

[KATE's *face loses its remaining hope, still appraising her youth.*]

Dr. Howe did wonders, but—an ordinary child? No, never. But then I thought when I was going over his reports—

[*She indicates the one in her hand.*]

—he never treated them like ordinary children. More like—eggs everyone was afraid would break.

KATE. [*A pause*] May I ask how old you are?

ANNIE. Well, I'm not in my teens, you know! I'm twenty.

KATE. All of twenty.

[ANNIE *takes the bull by the horns, valiantly.*]

ANNIE. Mrs. Keller, don't lose heart just because I'm not on my last legs. I have three big advantages over Dr. Howe that money couldn't buy for you. One is his work behind me, I've read every word he wrote about it and he wasn't exactly what you'd call a man of few words. Another is to *be* young, why, I've got energy to do anything. The third is, I've been blind.

[*But it costs her something to say this.*]

The Miracle Worker   231

40 Discussion Is Annie eager to meet Helen? How do you know?

41 Discussion Why is it hard for Annie to tell Kate that she has been blind?

42 Discussion Why do you think Kate is surprised by Annie's answer?

43 Literary Focus Consider telling students that the main conflict in this drama occurs between the protagonist and the antagonist; however, conflicts also occur *within* Annie Sullivan, the protagonist. Ask them what these lines reveal about Annie's divided feelings.

44 Literary Focus You might want to tell students that playwrights sometimes use props—movable articles that are part of the setting—to reveal a relationship between characters. Since Helen cannot speak, this device is especially important in *The Miracle Worker*. Ask students to follow the action involving the suitcase and consider what this action suggests about the developing relationship between Annie and Helen.

KATE. [*Quietly*] Advantages.

ANNIE. [*Wry*] Well, some have the luck of the Irish, some do not.

[KATE *smiles; she likes her.*]

KATE. What will you try to teach her first?

ANNIE. First, last, and—in between, language.

KATE. Language.

ANNIE. Language is to the mind more than light is to the eye. Dr. Howe said that.

KATE. Language.

[*She shakes her head.*]

We can't get through to teach her to sit still. You *are* young, despite your years, to have such—confidence. Do you, inside?

[ANNIE *studies her face; she likes her, too.*]

ANNIE. No, to tell you the truth I'm as shaky inside as a baby's rattle!

[*They smile at each other, and* KATE *pats her hand.*]

KATE. Don't be.

[JAMES *returns to usher them off.*]

We'll do all we can to help, and to make you feel at home. Don't think of us as strangers, Miss Annie.

ANNIE. [*Cheerily*] Oh, strangers aren't so strange to me. I've known them all my life!

[KATE *smiles again,* ANNIE *smiles back, and they precede* JAMES *offstage.*

The lights dim on them, having simultaneously risen full on the house; VINEY *has already entered the family room, taken a water pitcher, and come out and down to the pump. She pumps real water. As she looks offstage, we hear the clop of hoofs, a carriage stopping, and voices.*]

VINEY. Cap'n Keller! Cap'n Keller, they comin'!

[*She goes back into the house, as* KELLER *comes out on the porch to gaze.*]

She sure 'nuff came, Cap'n.

[KELLER *descends, and crosses toward the carriage; this conversation begins offstage and moves on.*]

KELLER. [*Very courtly*] Welcome to Ivy Green, Miss Sullivan. I take it you are Miss Sullivan—

KATE. My husband, Miss Annie, Captain Keller.

ANNIE. [*Her best behavior*] Captain, how do you do.

KELLER. A pleasure to see you, at last. I trust you had an agreeable journey?

ANNIE. Oh, I had several! When did this country get so big?

JAMES. Where would you like the trunk, father?

KELLER. Where Miss Sullivan can get at it, I imagine.

ANNIE. Yes, please. Where's Helen?

KELLER. In the hall, Jimmie—

KATE. We've put you in the upstairs corner room, Miss Annie, if there's any breeze at all this summer, you'll feel it—

[*In the house the setter* BELLE *flees into the family room, pursued by* HELEN *with groping hands; the dog doubles back out the same door, and* HELEN *still groping for her makes her way out to the porch; she is messy, her hair tumbled, her pinafore now ripped, her shoelaces untied.* KELLER *acquires the suitcase, and* ANNIE *gets her hands on it too, though still endeavoring to* live up to the general air of propertied manners.[6]]

KELLER. *And* the suitcase—

ANNIE. [*Pleasantly*] I'll take the suitcase, thanks.

KELLER. Not at all, I have it, Miss Sullivan.

ANNIE. I'd like it.

KELLER. [*Gallantly*] I couldn't think of it, Miss Sullivan. You'll find in the south we—

ANNIE. Let me.

KELLER. —view women as the flowers of civiliza—

ANNIE. [*Impatiently*] I've got something in it for Helen!

[*She tugs it free;* KELLER *stares.*]

Thank you. When do I see her?

KATE. There. There is Helen.

[ANNIE *turns, and sees* HELEN *on the porch. A moment of silence. Then* ANNIE *begins across the yard to her, lugging her suitcase.*]

KELLER. [*Sotto voce*[7]] Katie—

[KATE *silences him with a hand on his arm. When* ANNIE *finally reaches the porch steps she stops, contemplating* HELEN *for a last moment before entering her world. Then she drops the suitcase on the porch with intentional heaviness,* HELEN *starts with the jar, and comes to grope over it.* ANNIE *puts forth her hand, and touches* HELEN'S. HELEN *at once grasps it, and commences to explore it, like reading a face. She moves her hand on to* ANNIE'S *forearm, and dress; and* ANNIE *brings her face within reach of* HELEN'S

---

6. the general air of propertied manners: Atmosphere of refinement and wealth.

7. sotto voce (sät′ ō vō′ chē): In a low voice.

fingers, which travel over it, quite without timidity, until they encounter and push aside the smoked glasses. ANNIE'S *gaze is grave, unpitying, very attentive. She puts her hands on* HELEN'S *arms, but* HELEN *at once pulls away, and they confront each other with a distance between. Then* HELEN *returns to the suitcase, tries to open it, cannot.* ANNIE *points* HELEN'S *hand overhead.* HELEN *pulls away, tries to open the suitcase again;* ANNIE *points her hand overhead again.* HELEN *points overhead, a question, and* ANNIE, *drawing* HELEN'S *hand to her own face, nods.* HELEN *now begins tugging the suitcase toward the door; when* ANNIE *tries to take it from her, she fights her off and backs through the doorway with it.* ANNIE *stands a moment, then follows her in, and together they get the suitcase up the steps into* ANNIE'S *room.*]

KATE. Well?

KELLER. She's very rough, Katie.

KATE. I like her, Captain.

KELLER. Certainly rear a peculiar kind of young woman in the north. How old is she?

KATE. [*Vaguely*] Ohh— Well, she's not in her teens, you know.

KELLER. She's only a child. What's her family like, shipping her off alone this far?

KATE. I couldn't learn. She's very close-mouthed about some things.

KELLER. Why does she wear those glasses? I like to see a person's eyes when I talk to—

KATE. For the sun. She was blind.

KELLER. Blind.

KATE. She's had nine operations on her eyes. One just before she left.

KELLER. Blind, good heavens, do they expect one blind child to teach another? Has she

The Miracle Worker 233

45

46 Discussion If you were auditioning young actresses for Helen's part, what qualities would you look for?

47 Enrichment You might want to explain to students that the finger alphabet is a system in which each letter is represented by a different position of the fingers. To communicate, a person forms the letters in another person's palm.

Deaf people who are sighted can also communicate by signing—making hand signals that stand for letters and ideas. Ask students if they have seen speeches on television being translated into sign language.

Students may also be interested to learn that scientists have tried to teach chimpanzees the sign language of the deaf, with some success.

experience at least, how long did she teach there?

KATE. She was a pupil.

KELLER. [*Heavily*] Katie, Katie. This is her first position?

KATE. [*Bright voice*] She was valedictorian—

KELLER. Here's a houseful of grownups can't cope with the child, how can an inexperienced half-blind Yankee schoolgirl manage her?

[JAMES *moves in with the trunk on his shoulder.*]

JAMES. [*Easily*] Great improvement. Now we have two of them to look after.

KELLER. You look after those strawberry plants!

[JAMES *stops with the trunk.* KELLER *turns from him without another word, and marches off.*]

JAMES. Nothing I say is right.

KATE. Why say anything?

[*She calls.*]

Don't be long, Captain, we'll have supper right away—

[*She goes into the house, and through the rear door of the family room.* JAMES *trudges in with the trunk, takes it up the steps to* ANNIE'S *room, and sets it down outside the door. The lights elsewhere dim somewhat.*

Meanwhile, inside, ANNIE *has given* HELEN *a key; while* ANNIE *removes her bonnet,* HELEN *unlocks and opens the suitcase. The first thing she pulls out is a voluminous shawl. She fingers it until she perceives what it is; then she wraps it around her, and acquiring* ANNIE'S *bonnet and smoked glasses as well, dons the lot: the shawl swamps her, and the bonnet settles down*

upon the glasses, but she stands before a mirror cocking her head to one side, then to the other, in a mockery of adult action. AN-NIE *is amused, and talks to her as one might to a kitten, with no trace of company manners.*]

ANNIE. All the trouble I went to and that's how I look?

[HELEN *then comes back to the suitcase, gropes for more, lifts out a pair of female drawers.*]

Oh, no. Not the drawers!

[*But* HELEN *discarding them comes to the elegant doll. Her fingers explore its features, and when she raises it and finds its eyes open and close, she is at first startled, then delighted. She picks it up, taps its head vigorously, taps her own chest, and nods questioningly.* ANNIE *takes her finger, points it to the doll, points it to* HELEN, *and touching it to her own face, also nods.* HELEN *sits back on her heels, clasps the doll to herself, and rocks it.* ANNIE *studies her, still in bonnet and smoked glasses like a caricature of herself, and addresses her humorously.*]

All right, Miss O'Sullivan. Let's begin with doll.

[*She takes* HELEN'S *hand; in her palm* AN-NIE'S *forefinger points, thumb holding her other fingers clenched.*]

D.

[*Her thumb next holds all her fingers clenched, touching* HELEN'S *palm.*]

O.

[*Her thumb and forefinger extend.*]

L.

[*Same contact repeated.*]

L.

48

[*She puts* HELEN's *hand to the doll.*]

Doll.

JAMES. You spell pretty well.

[ANNIE *in one hurried move gets the drawers swiftly back into the suitcase, the lid banged shut, and her head turned, to see* JAMES *leaning in the doorway.*]

Finding out if she's ticklish? She is.

[ANNIE *regards him stonily, but* HELEN *after a scowling moment tugs at her hand again, imperious.* ANNIE *repeats the letters, and* HELEN *interrupts her fingers in the middle, feeling each of them, puzzled.* ANNIE *touches* HELEN's *hand to the doll, and begins spelling into it again.*]

JAMES. What is it, a game?

ANNIE. [*Curtly*] An alphabet.

JAMES. Alphabet?

ANNIE. For the deaf.

[HELEN *now repeats the finger movements in air, exactly, her head cocked to her own hand, and* ANNIE's *eyes suddenly gleam.*]

Ho. How *bright* she is!

49

JAMES. You think she knows what she's doing?

[*He takes* HELEN's *hand, to throw a meaningless gesture into it; she repeats this one too.*]

The Miracle Worker **235**

50 Literary Focus How do James's comments add to the drama of the encounter between Annie and Helen?

51 Clarification It is thought that Spanish monks invented the finger alphabet so they could communicate without speaking, thereby keeping their vows of silence.

52 Discussion Why does Annie remove the cake?

She imitates everything, she's a monkey.

ANNIE. [*Very pleased*] Yes, she's a bright little monkey, all right.

[*She takes the doll from* HELEN, *and reaches for her hand;* HELEN *instantly grabs the doll back.* ANNIE *takes it again, and* HELEN'S *hand next, but* HELEN *is incensed now; when* ANNIE *draws her hand to her face to shake her head no, then tries to spell to her,* HELEN *slaps at* ANNIE'S *face.* ANNIE *grasps* HELEN *by both arms, and swings her into a chair, holding her pinned there, kicking, while glasses, doll, bonnet fly in various directions.* JAMES *laughs.*]

JAMES. She wants her doll back.

ANNIE. When she spells it.

JAMES. Spell, she doesn't know the thing has a name, even.

ANNIE. Of course not, who expects her to, now? All I want is her fingers to learn the letters.

50 **JAMES.** Won't mean anything to her.

[ANNIE *gives him a look. She then tries to form* HELEN'S *fingers into the letters, but* HELEN *swings a haymaker instead, which* ANNIE *barely ducks, at once pinning her down again.*]

Doesn't like that alphabet, Miss Sullivan. You invent it yourself?

[HELEN *is now in a rage, fighting tooth and nail to get out of the chair, and* ANNIE *answers while struggling and dodging her kicks.*]

51 **ANNIE.** Spanish monks under a—vow of silence. Which I wish *you'd* take!

[*And suddenly releasing* HELEN'S *hands, she comes and shuts the door in* JAMES'S *face.* HELEN *drops to the floor, groping around for the doll.* ANNIE *looks around*

desperately, sees her purse on the bed, rummages in it, and comes up with a battered piece of cake wrapped in newspaper; with her foot she moves the doll deftly out of the way of* HELEN'S *groping, and going on her knee she lets* HELEN *smell the cake. When* HELEN *grabs for it,* ANNIE *removes the cake and spells quickly into the reaching hand.*]

Cake. From Washington up north, it's the best I can do.

[HELEN'S *hand waits, baffled.* ANNIE *repeats it.*]

C, a, k, e. Do what my fingers do, never mind what it means.

[*She touches the cake briefly to* HELEN'S *nose, pats her hand, presents her own hand.* HELEN *spells the letters rapidly back.* ANNIE *pats her hand enthusiastically, and gives her the cake;* HELEN *crams it into her mouth with both hands.* ANNIE *watches her, with humor.*]

Get it down fast, maybe I'll steal that back too. Now.

[*She takes the doll, touches it to* HELEN'S *nose, and spells again into her hand.*]

D, o, l, l. Think it over.

[HELEN *thinks it over, while* ANNIE *presents her own hand. Then* HELEN *spells three letters.* ANNIE *waits a second, then completes the word for* HELEN *in her palm.*]

L.

[*She hands over the doll, and* HELEN *gets a good grip on its leg.*]

Imitate now, understand later. End of the first les—

[*She never finishes, because* HELEN *swings the doll with a furious energy, it hits* ANNIE *squarely in the face, and she falls back* with a cry of pain, her knuckles up to her mouth. HELEN *waits, tensed for further combat. When* ANNIE *lowers her knuckles she looks at blood on them; she works her lips, gets to her feet, finds the mirror, and bares her teeth at herself. Now she is furious herself.*]

You little wretch, no one's taught you any manners? I'll—

[*But rounding from the mirror she sees the door slam,* HELEN *and the doll are on the outside, and* HELEN *is turning the key in the lock.* ANNIE *darts over, to pull the knob; the door is locked fast. She yanks it again.*]

Helen! Helen, let me out of—

[*She bats her brow at the folly of speaking, but* JAMES, *now downstairs, hears her and turns to see* HELEN *with the key and doll groping her way down the steps;* JAMES *takes in the whole situation, makes a move to intercept* HELEN, *but then changes his mind, lets her pass, and amusedly follows her out onto the porch. Upstairs* ANNIE *meanwhile rattles the knob, kneels, peers through the keyhole, gets up. She goes to the window, looks down, frowns.* JAMES *from the yard sings gaily up to her:*]

JAMES.
> *Buffalo girl, are you coming out tonight,*
> *Coming out tonight,*
> *Coming out—*

[*He drifts back into the house.* ANNIE *takes a handkerchief, nurses her mouth, stands in the middle of the room, staring at door and window in turn, and so catches sight of herself in the mirror, her cheek scratched, her hair disheveled, her handkerchief bloody, her face disgusted with herself. She addresses the mirror, with some irony.*]

ANNIE. Don't worry. They'll find you, you're not lost. Only out of place.

[*But she coughs, spits something into her palm, and stares at it, outraged.*]

And toothless.

[*She winces.*]

Oo! It hurts.

[*She pours some water into the basin, dips the handkerchief, and presses it to her mouth. Standing there, bent over the basin in pain—with the rest of the set dim and unreal, and the lights upon her taking on the subtle color of the past—she hears again, as do we, the faraway voices, and slowly she lifts her head to them; the boy's voice is the same, the others are cracked old crones in a nightmare, and perhaps we see their shadows.*]

BOY'S VOICE. It hurts. Annie, it hurts.

FIRST CRONE'S VOICE. Keep that brat shut up, can't you, girlie, how's a body to get any sleep in this damn ward?

BOY'S VOICE. It hurts. It hurts.

SECOND CRONE'S VOICE. Shut up, you!

BOY'S VOICE. Annie, when are we goin' home? You promised!

ANNIE. Jimmie—

BOY'S VOICE. Forever and ever, you said forever—

[ANNIE *drops the handkerchief, averts to the window, and is arrested there by the next cry.*]

Annie? Annie, you there? Annie! It *hurts!*

THIRD CRONE'S VOICE. Grab him, he's fallin'!

BOY'S VOICE. *Annie!*

DOCTOR'S VOICE. [*A pause, slowly*] Little girl.

The Miracle Worker **237**

53 Literary Focus How does James's action, or lack of action, heighten conflict?

54 Discussion Why do you think Annie remembers the past at this particular moment?

Little girl, I must tell you your brother will be going on a—

[*But* ANNIE *claps her hands to her ears, to shut this out; there is instant silence.*]

As the lights bring the other areas in again, JAMES *goes to the steps to listen for any sound from upstairs.* KELLER *re-entering from left crosses toward the house; he passes* HELEN *on route to her retreat under the pump.* KATE *re-enters the rear door of the family room, with flowers for the table.*]

KATE. Supper is ready, Jimmie, will you call your father?

JAMES. Certainly.

[*But he calls up the stairs, for* ANNIE'S *benefit.*]

Father! Supper!

KELLER. [*At the door*] No need to shout, I've been cooling my heels for an hour. Sit down.

JAMES. Certainly.

KELLER. Viney!

[VINEY *backs in with a roast, while they get settled around the table.*]

VINEY. Yes, Cap'n, right here.

KATE. Mildred went directly to sleep, Viney?

VINEY. Oh yes, that babe's a angel.

KATE. And Helen had a good supper?

VINEY. [*Vaguely*] I dunno, Miss Kate, somehow she didn't have much of a appetite tonight—

55 **KATE.** [*A bit guilty*] Oh. Dear.

KELLER. [*Hastily*] Well, now. Couldn't say the same for my part, I'm famished. Katie, your plate.

KATE. [*Looking*] But where is Miss Annie?

[*A silence*]

JAMES. [*Pleasantly*] In her room.

KELLER. In her room? Doesn't she know hot food must be eaten hot? Go bring her down at once, Jimmie.

JAMES. [*Rises*] Certainly. I'll get a ladder.

KELLER. [*Stares*] What?

JAMES. I'll need a ladder. Shouldn't take me long.

KATE. [*Stares*] What shouldn't take you—

KELLER. Jimmie, do as I say! Go upstairs at once and tell Miss Sullivan supper is getting cold—

JAMES. She's locked in her room.

KELLER. Locked in her—

KATE. What on earth are you—

JAMES. Helen locked her in and made off with the key.

KATE. [*Rising*] And you sit here and say nothing?

JAMES. Well, everyone's been telling me not to say anything.

[*He goes serenely out and across the yard, whistling.* KELLER *thrusting up from his chair makes for the stairs.*]

KATE. Viney, look out in back for Helen. See if she has that key.

VINEY. Yes, Miss Kate.

[VINEY *goes out the rear door.*]

KELLER. [*Calling down*] She's out by the pump!

[KATE *goes out on the porch after* HELEN, *while* KELLER *knocks on* ANNIE'S *door, then rattles the knob, imperiously.*]

Miss Sullivan! Are you in there?

ANNIE. Oh, I'm in here, all right.

KELLER. Is there no key on your side?

ANNIE. [*With some asperity*] Well, if there was a key in here, *I* wouldn't be in here. Helen took it, the only thing on my side is me.

KELLER. Miss Sullivan, I—

[*He tries, but cannot hold it back.*]

Not in the house ten minutes, I don't see *how* you managed it!

[*He stomps downstairs again, while* ANNIE *mutters to herself.*]

56 **ANNIE.** And even I'm not on my side.

KELLER. [*Roaring*] Viney!

VINEY. [*Reappearing*] Yes, Cap'n?

KELLER. Put that meat back in the oven!

[VINEY *bears the roast off again, while* KELLER *strides out onto the porch.* KATE *is with* HELEN *at the pump, opening her hands.*]

KATE. She has no key.

KELLER. Nonsense, she must have the key. Have you searched in her pockets?

KATE. Yes. She doesn't have it.

KELLER. Katie, she must have the key.

KATE. Would you prefer to search her yourself, Captain?

KELLER. No, I would not prefer to search her! She almost took my kneecap off this evening, when I tried merely to—

[JAMES *reappears carrying a long ladder, with* PERCY *running after him to be in on things.*]

Take that ladder back!

JAMES. Certainly.

[*He turns around with it.* MARTHA *comes skipping around the upstage corner of the house to be in on things, accompanied by the setter* BELLE.]

KATE. She could have hidden the key.

KELLER. Where?

KATE. Anywhere. Under a stone. In the flower beds. In the grass—

KELLER. Well, I can't plow up the entire grounds to find a missing key! Jimmie!

JAMES. Sir?

KELLER. Bring me a ladder!

JAMES. Certainly.

[VINEY *comes around the downstage side of the house to be in on things; she has* MIL-DRED *over her shoulder, bleating.* KELLER *places the ladder against* ANNIE'S *window and mounts.* ANNIE *meanwhile is running about making herself presentable, washing the blood off her mouth, straightening her clothes, tidying her hair. Another Negro servant enters to gaze in wonder, increasing the gathering ring of spectators.*]

KATE. [*Sharply*] What is Mildred doing up?

VINEY. Cap'n woke her, ma'am, all that hollerin'.

KELLER. Miss Sullivan!

[ANNIE *comes to the window, with as much air of gracious normality as she can manage;* KELLER *is at the window.*]

ANNIE. [*Brightly*] Yes, Captain Keller?

KELLER. Come out!

ANNIE. I don't see how I can. There isn't room.

KELLER. I intend to carry you. Climb onto my shoulder and hold tight.

ANNIE. Oh, no. It's—very chivalrous of you, but I'd really prefer to—

56 Discussion What does Annie mean?

Reader's Response If you were Annie, how would you have handled Helen's tantrums and seeming unwillingness to learn? Explain.

Thematic Response What is the greatest challenge facing Annie?

Closure and Extension

ANSWERS TO RESPONDING TO THE SELECTION
Your Response

1. Encourage students to remember the descriptions of Annie by Dr. Anagnos and by herself and to compare them to Helen's character and spirit. Ask students if they think Annie can do for Helen what was done for her.

Recalling

2. She is like a wild, untrained animal—violent, seemingly unteachable, and undisciplined.

3. Mrs. Keller is willing to continue her search for help for Helen, regardless of how often the news is heartbreaking. Captain Keller

---

240

KELLER. Miss Sullivan, follow instructions! I will not have you also tumbling out of our windows.

[ANNIE *obeys, with some misgivings.*]

I hope this is not a sample of what we may expect from you. In the way of simplifying the work of looking after Helen.

ANNIE. Captain Keller, I'm perfectly able to go down a ladder under my own—

KELLER. I doubt it, Miss Sullivan. Simply hold onto my neck.

[*He begins down with her, while the spectators stand in a wide and somewhat awe-stricken circle, watching.* KELLER *half-misses a rung, and* ANNIE *grabs at his whiskers.*]

My *neck,* Miss Sullivan!

ANNIE. I'm sorry to inconvenience you this way—

KELLER. No inconvenience, other than having that door taken down and the lock replaced, if we fail to find that key.

ANNIE. Oh, I'll look everywhere for it.

KELLER. Thank you. Do not look in any rooms that can be locked. There.

[*He stands her on the ground.* JAMES *applauds.*]

ANNIE. Thank you very much.

[*She smooths her skirt, looking as composed and ladylike as possible.* KELLER *stares around at the spectators.*]

KELLER. Go, go, back to your work. What are you looking at here? There's nothing here to look at.

[*They break up, move off.*]

Now would it be possible for us to have supper, like other people?

240 *Drama*

[*He marches into the house.*]

KATE. Viney, serve supper. I'll put Mildred to sleep.

[*They all go in.* JAMES *is the last to leave, murmuring to* ANNIE *with a gesture.*]

JAMES. Might as well leave the l, a, d, d, e, r, hm?

[ANNIE *ignores him, looking at* HELEN; JAMES *goes in too. Imperceptibly the lights commence to narrow down.* ANNIE *and* HELEN *are now alone in the yard,* HELEN *seated at the pump, where she has been oblivious to it all, a battered little savage, playing with the doll in a picture of innocent contentment.* ANNIE *comes near, leans against the house, and taking off her smoked glasses, studies her, not without awe. Presently* HELEN *rises, gropes around to see if anyone is present;* ANNIE *evades her hand, and when* HELEN *is satisfied she is alone, the key suddenly protrudes out of her mouth. She takes it in her fingers, stands thinking, gropes to the pump, lifts a loose board, drops the key into the well, and hugs herself gleefully.* ANNIE *stares. But after a moment she shakes her head to herself, she cannot keep the smile from her lips.*]

ANNIE. You *devil.*

[*Her tone is one of great respect, humor, and acceptance of challenge.*]

You think I'm so easily gotten rid of? You have a thing or two to learn, first. I have nothing else to do.

[*She goes up the steps to the porch, but turns for a final word, almost of warning.*]

And nowhere to go.

[*And presently she moves into the house to the others, as the lights dim down and out, except for the small circle upon* HELEN *solitary at the pump, which ends the act.*]

57
58
5

---

feels that they have exhausted every resource and that there is no point in being disappointed again.

4. Annie Sullivan was a young orphan, nearly blind, who grew up in a poorhouse. After her brother died, she went to the Perkins School for the Blind. Several operations restored some of her sight. She is a strong person, obstinate, not willing to give up. But she is also haunted by her past and feels guilty because she feels she let her brother down.

5. She feels Helen must learn language. There is no limit to what a person can learn if he or she has a knowledge of language. She wants to teach Helen to associate words with things through the use of finger language.

Interpreting

6. Suggested Response: Annie's persistence, strength, obstinacy, and willingness to accept a challenge will be important. Annie has

---

been blind herself so she can sympathize with some of Helen's problems.

7. Suggested Response: Annie felt responsible for her brother, but she could not save him. She might feel that she is getting a second chance to save someone.

8. Suggested Response: The family is continually disrupted by Helen and her unruly behavior. No meal is ever peaceful, and there is always the danger of violence, as when Helen attacks Martha with the scissors.

RESPONDING TO THE SELECTION

Your Response

1. Do you think Annie will be able to teach Helen? Explain your answer.

Recalling

2. What is Helen like at age six when Annie comes to teach her?
3. How do Captain and Mrs. Keller differ in their views of what to do for Helen?
4. Describe Annie Sullivan's background, personality, and physical condition.
5. What does Annie consider the most important thing to teach Helen? How does she plan to teach this to Helen?

Interpreting

6. Which of Annie's qualities are likely to play an important role in her relationship with Helen? What advantages does Annie have?
7. What is the link between Annie's memories of her brother and her present situation?
8. What effect has Helen had on the life of her family?

Applying

9. Annie says, "Language is to the mind more than light is to the eye." What does her remark imply about the importance of language?

ANALYZING LITERATURE

Recognizing Protagonist and Antagonist

The **protagonist** is the central character of a play. The **antagonist** is the character or characters in conflict with him or her. As you read a play, you wonder how events will turn out. Will the protagonist meet with success or failure?

1. Is Annie or Helen the protagonist of the play? Give reasons for your opinion.
2. What problems do you expect the protagonist to encounter?

CRITICAL THINKING AND READING

Comparing and Contrasting Characters

Comparing and **contrasting** characters means noting the similarities and differences between them. Noticing these similarities and differences will increase your understanding of the characters and of what the playwright may be suggesting about life.

Compare and contrast the characters in each of the following pairs.

1. Kate and Captain Keller
2. Annie and Helen
3. Annie and Captain Keller

THINKING AND WRITING

Writing About Characters

Imagine that you have been visiting the Kellers. Write a letter to a friend in which you give specific descriptions of Captain Keller, Mrs. Keller, James, and Helen. First decide what words or actions of the characters illustrate their traits. Then write a short paragraph about each person. When you revise your letter, ask, "How can I make this description more clear, vivid, and exact?"

LEARNING OPTIONS

1. **Speaking and Listening.** People unable to speak or hear often use sign language to communicate. Find out about sign language and report your research orally to the class. In your presentation, include visual illustrations of the signs and, if possible, demonstrations.
2. **Writing.** Take a "trust walk" with a partner. Cover the eyes of your partner and guide him or her around an unfamiliar setting, being sure to avoid any obstacles. Then exchange places with your partner. When you have finished your trust walks, write a poem or paragraph about what it is like to be without the use of your sight.

The Miracle Worker 241

Preparation

Literary Focus You might re-mind students that the charac-ters in a play can experience internal conflicts. However, the playwright must find the means to communicate these internal conflicts to the audience. Ask students how Gibson dramatizes Annie's internal conflict.

Prereading Focus The conflicts that exist within the Keller family are not all caused by Helen. Many of them existed before she was born. The purpose of this activity is to focus student atten-tion on both the internal and ex-ternal conflicts in the play. You might want to discuss the individ-ual characters with the students to remind them of the many diffi-culties in this troubled family. Suggest that students compare and discuss their charts.

Vocabulary Have more ad-vanced students create ques-tions that elicit the meaning of these words; for example, "What word would you use to say that a person could not speak well?" "How could you describe some-one who did not show any emo-tion?" Then have students ex-change papers and answer each other's questions with the correct word.

Spelling Tip Remind students that *wrath* is spelled with a *w*.

GUIDE FOR READING

The Miracle Worker, Act II

Conflict in Drama

Conflict is so basic to drama that drama may be defined as the story of a conflict told primarily in dialogue and presented before an audience. Conflict may be classified as external or internal. External conflicts include those between one individual and another, between an individual and society, and between an individual and a force such as destiny or fate. An internal conflict is between an individual and himself or herself. The character is torn by conflicting feelings or wants.

Focus

The Miracle Worker dramatizes a number of different conflicts, both external and internal. Based on what you have read so far, think of all the conflicts that are already suggested and likely to develop in Act II. For example, imagine what further difficulties Annie Sulli-van will have to face in trying to teach Helen. There are also indi-cations of conflicts within the Keller family. On a piece of paper, write down the names of the characters in the play and draw arrows con-necting characters who seem to be in conflict. Then circle the names of characters you think are experiencing internal conflicts and write down a phrase describing that conflict. As you read Act II, compare your thoughts with the developments in the play.

Vocabulary

Knowing the following words will help you as you read Act II of *The Miracle Worker*.

impassively (im pas′ iv lē) *adv.*: In an unfeeling or unemo-tional manner (p. 243)

inarticulate (in′ är tik′ yə lit) *adj.*: Not able to speak well (p. 243)

deferential (def′ ə ren′ shəl) *adj.*: Very respectful (p. 245)

wrath (ratħ) *n.*: Intense anger (p. 248)

ire (īr) *n.*: Anger (p. 248)

sullen (sul′ ən) *adj.*: Showing resentment (p. 250)

242   *Drama*

Objectives

1 To understand conflict in drama
2 To recognize causes and effects when reading a drama
3 To write a scene extend-ing Act II of *The Miracle Worker*

Support Material

Teaching Portfolio
Teacher Backup, p. 307
Grammar in Action Worksheets, *Using Dashes*, p. 310; *Writing Directions*, p. 312
Usage and Mechanics Work-sheet, p. 314
Vocabulary Check, p. 315
Critical Thinking and Reading Worksheet, *Recognizing Caus-es and Effects*, p. 315

Language Worksheet, *Recogniz-ing and Forming Compound Words*, p. 317
Selection Test, p. 318

Library of Video Classics
The Miracle Worker

Prentice Hall Literature Writing Studio

ACT II

[It is evening.

1 The only room visible in the KELLER house is ANNIE's, where by lamplight ANNIE in a shawl is at a desk writing a letter; at her bureau HELEN in her customary unkempt state is tucking her doll in the bottom drawer as a cradle, the contents of which she has dumped out, creating as usual a fine disorder.

ANNIE mutters each word as she writes her letter, slowly, her eyes close to and almost touching the page, to follow with difficulty her penwork.]

ANNIE. ". . . and, nobody, here, has, attempted, to, control, her. The, greatest, problem, I, have, is, how, to, discipline, her, without, breaking, her, spirit."

[Resolute voice]

"But, I, shall, insist, on, reasonable, obedience, from, the, start—"

2 [At which point HELEN, groping about on the desk, knocks over the inkwell. ANNIE jumps up, rescues her letter, rights the inkwell, grabs a towel to stem the spillage, and then wipes at HELEN's hands; HELEN as always pulls free, but not until ANNIE first gets three letters into her palm.]

Ink.

[HELEN is enough interested in and puzzled by this spelling that she proffers her hand again; so ANNIE spells and impassively dunks it back in the spillage.]

Ink. It has a name.

[She wipes the hand clean, and leads HELEN to her bureau, where she looks for something to engage her. She finds a sewing card, with needle and thread, and going to her knees, shows HELEN's hand how to connect one row of holes.]

Down. Under. Up. And be careful of the needle—

[HELEN gets it, and ANNIE rises.]

3 Fine. You keep out of the ink and perhaps I can keep out of—the soup.

[She returns to the desk, tidies it, and resumes writing her letter, bent close to the page.]

"These, blots, are, her, handiwork. I—"

[She is interrupted by a gasp: HELEN has stuck her finger, and sits sucking at it, darkly. Then with vengeful resolve she seizes her doll, and is about to dash its brains out on the floor when ANNIE diving catches it in one hand, which she at once shakes with hopping pain but otherwise ignores, patiently.]

All right, let's try temperance.

[Taking the doll, she kneels, goes through the motion of knocking its head on the floor, spells into HELEN's hand:]

Bad, girl.

[She lets HELEN feel the grieved expression on her face. HELEN imitates it. Next she makes HELEN caress the doll and kiss the hurt spot and hold it gently in her arms, then spells into her hand:]

Good, girl.

[She lets HELEN feel the smile on her face, HELEN sits with a scowl, which suddenly clears; she pats the doll, kisses it, wreathes her face in a large artificial smile, and bears the doll to the washstand, where she carefully sits it. ANNIE watches, pleased.]

Very good girl—

[Whereupon HELEN elevates the pitcher and dashes it on the floor instead. ANNIE leaps to her feet, and stands inarticulate; HELEN

The Miracle Worker 243

4 **Discussion** Why does Annie continue spelling to Helen?

5 **Discussion** Why does Annie compare Helen's head to a mousetrap?

6 **Discussion** Do you think Annie is being cruel? Explain.

Videocassette You might want to show the breakfast scene from the film adaptation of *The Miracle Worker* in the Prentice Hall **Library of Video Classics** so that students may see the extension of the battle of wits between Helen and Annie into physical struggle. It might be beneficial to have students read this scene carefully first, using a student narrator, and then to compare the author's directions with the filmed scene.

Alternative Assessment To promote active reading, have students keep a reader's response journal as they read Act II of the play. Ask them to focus their observations on the details that reveal the conflict between Helen and Annie. Encourage students to respond personally to the situation. How well do they feel Annie is handling things? To what in their own lives can they relate this story?

Their observations will enable you to assess their understanding of the issues in the play.

calmly gropes back to sit to the sewing card and needle.

ANNIE *manages to achieve self-control. She picks up a fragment or two of the pitcher, sees* HELEN *is puzzling over the card, and resolutely kneels to demonstrate it again. She spells into* HELEN'S *hand.*

KATE *meanwhile coming around the corner with folded sheets on her arm, halts at the doorway and watches them for a moment in silence; she is moved, but level:]*

KATE. [*Presently*] What are you saying to her?

[ANNIE *glancing up is a bit embarrassed, and rises from the spelling, to find her company manners.*]

ANNIE. Oh, I was just making conversation. Saying it was a sewing card.

KATIE. But does that—

[*She imitates with her fingers.*]

—mean that to her?

ANNIE. No. No, she won't know what spelling is till she knows what a word is.

KATE. Yet you keep spelling to her. Why?

ANNIE. [*Cheerily*] I like to hear myself talk!

KATE. The Captain says it's like spelling to the fence post.

ANNIE. [*A pause*] Does he, now.

KATE. Is it?

4 **ANNIE.** No, it's how I watch you talk to Mildred.

KATE. Mildred.

ANNIE. Any baby. Gibberish, grown-up gibberish, babytalk gibberish, do they understand one word of it to start? Somehow they begin to. If they hear it, I'm letting Helen hear it.

KATE. Other children are not—impaired.

ANNIE. Ho, there's nothing impaired in that head, it works like a mousetrap! 5

KATE. [*Smiles*] But after a child hears how many words, Miss Annie, a million?

ANNIE. I guess no mother's ever minded enough to count.

[*She drops her eyes to spell into* HELEN'S *hand, again indicating the card;* HELEN *spells back, and* ANNIE *is amused.*]

KATE. [*Too quickly*] What did she spell?

ANNIE. I spelt card. She spelt cake!

[*She takes in* KATE'S *quickness, and shakes her head, gently.*]

No, it's only a finger-game to her, Mrs. Keller. What she has to learn first is that things have names.

KATE. And when will she learn?

ANNIE. Maybe after a million and one words.

[*They hold each other's gaze;* KATE *then speaks quietly.*]

KATE. I should like to learn those letters, Miss Annie.

ANNIE. [*Pleased*] I'll teach you tomorrow morning. That makes only half a million each!

KATE. [*Then*] It's her bedtime.

[ANNIE *reaches for the sewing card,* HELEN *objects,* ANNIE *insists, and* HELEN *gets rid of* ANNIE'S *hand by jabbing it with the needle.* ANNIE *gasps, and moves to grip* HELEN'S *wrist; but* KATE *intervenes with a proffered sweet, and* HELEN *drops the card, crams the sweet into her mouth, and scrambles up to search her mother's hands for more.* ANNIE *nurses her wound, staring after the sweet.*] 6

I'm sorry, Miss Annie.

ANNIE. [*Indignantly*] Why does she get a re-ward? For stabbing me?

KATE. Well—

[*Then, tiredly*]

We catch our flies with honey, I'm afraid. We haven't the heart for much else, and so many times she simply cannot be compelled.

ANNIE. [*Ominous*] Yes. I'm the same way my-self.

[KATE *smiles, and leads* HELEN *off around the corner.* ANNIE *alone in her room picks up things and in the act of removing* HELEN's *doll gives way to unmannerly temptation: she throttles it. She drops it on her bed, and stands pondering. Then she turns back, sits decisively, and writes again, as the lights dim on her.*]

[*Grimly*] "The, more, I, think, the, more, cer-tain, I, am, that, obedience, is, the, gateway, through, which, knowledge, enters, the, mind, of, the, child—"

[*On the word "obedience" a shaft of sun-light hits the water pump outside, while* AN-NIE's *voice ends in the dark, followed by a distant cockcrow; daylight comes up over another corner of the sky, with* VINEY's *voice heard at once.*]

VINEY. Breakfast ready!

[VINEY *comes down into the sunlight beam, and pumps a pitcherful of water. While the pitcher is brimming we hear conversation from the dark; the light grows to the family room of the house where all are either en-tering or already seated at breakfast, with* KELLER *and* JAMES *arguing the war.[1]* HELEN *is wandering around the table to explore the contents of the other plates. When* ANNIE *is in her chair, she watches* HELEN.]

---

1. **the war:** The Civil War (1861–1865) between the North (Union) and the South (Confederacy).

VINEY *re-enters, sets the pitcher on the ta-ble;* KATE *lifts the almost empty biscuit plate with an inquiring look,* VINEY *nods and bears it off back, neither of them interrupt-ing the men.* ANNIE *meanwhile sits with fork quiet, watching* HELEN, *who at her mother's plate pokes her hand among some scrambled eggs.* KATE *catches* ANNIE's *eyes on her, smiles with a wry gesture.* HELEN *moves on to* JAMES's *plate, the male talk continuing,* JAMES *deferential and* KELLER *overriding.*]

JAMES. —no, but shouldn't we give the devil his due, father? The fact is we lost the South two years earlier when he outthought us be-hind Vicksburg.[2]

KELLER. Outthought is a peculiar word for a butcher.

JAMES. Harness maker, wasn't he?

KELLER. I said butcher. his only virtue as a soldier was numbers and he led them to slaughter with no more regard than for so many sheep.

JAMES. But even if in that sense he was a butcher, the fact is he—

KELLER. And a drunken one, half the war.

JAMES. Agreed, father. If his own people said he was I can't argue he—

KELLER. Well, what is it you find to admire in such a man, Jimmie, the butchery or the drunkenness?

JAMES. Neither, father, only the fact that he beat us.

KELLER. He didn't.

JAMES. Is it your contention we won the war, sir?

---

2. **Vicksburg:** A Mississippi city attacked during the Civil War by Ulysses S. Grant (1822–1885), the Union general to whom James is referring.

The Miracle Worker 245

7 Critical Thinking and Reading Contrast Annie's and Kate's views of the "reward." Why do their views differ?

8 Reading Strategy What do you think Annie's ominous tone im-plies?

9 Literary Focus Why do you think Gibson includes a scene with the whole family after a scene with only a few characters?

10 Clarification In numerous plac-es two or even three actions may be taking place at once. Notice Helen's activities as Keller and James have been speaking. No one, except Annie, seems to be aware of them.

11 Reading Strategy As students read this discussion between James and Keller, have them no-tice the unspoken parallels be-tween Annie and General Grant. Both invaded the South, were obstinate, and so forth. Ask stu-dents to look for other references to the Civil War as they read.

KELLER. He didn't beat us at Vicksburg. We lost Vicksburg because Pemberton gave Bragg five thousand of his cavalry and Loring, whom I knew personally for a nincompoop before you were born, marched away from Champion's Hill with enough men to have held them, we lost Vicksburg by stupidity verging on treason.

JAMES. I would have said we lost Vicksburg because Grant was one thing no Yankee general was before him—

KELLER. Drunk? I doubt it.

JAMES. Obstinate.

KELLER. Obstinate. Could any of them compare even in that with old Stonewall?[3] If he'd been there we would still have Vicksburg.

JAMES. Well, the butcher simply wouldn't give up, he tried four ways of getting around Vicksburg and on the fifth try he got around. Anyone else would have pulled north and—

KELLER. He wouldn't have got around if we'd had a Southerner in command, instead of a half-breed Yankee traitor like Pemberton—

[*While this background talk is in progress,* HELEN *is working around the table, ultimately toward* ANNIE's *plate. She messes with her hands in* JAMES's *plate, then in* KELLER's, *both men taking it so for granted they hardly notice. Then* HELEN *comes groping with soiled hands past her own plate, to* ANNIE's; *her hand goes to it, and* ANNIE, *who has been waiting, deliberately lifts and removes her hand.* HELEN *gropes again,* ANNIE *firmly pins her by the wrist, and removes her hand from the table.* HELEN *thrusts her hands again,* ANNIE *catches them, and* HELEN *begins to flail and make noises; the interruption brings* KELLER's *gaze upon them.*]

---

3. old Stonewall: The nickname of Thomas J. Jackson (1824–1863), a Confederate general.

What's the matter there?

KATE. Miss Annie. You see, she's accustomed to helping herself from our plates to anything she—

ANNIE. [*Evenly*] Yes, but *I'm* not accustomed to it.

KELLER. No, of course not. Viney!

KATE. Give her something, Jimmie, to quiet her.

JAMES. [*Blandly*] But her table manners are the best she has. Well.

[*He pokes across with a chunk of bacon at* HELEN's *hand, which* ANNIE *releases; but* HELEN *knocks the bacon away and stubbornly thrusts at* ANNIE's *plate,* ANNIE *grips her wrists again, the struggle mounts.*]

KELLER. Let her this time, Miss Sullivan, it's the only way we get any adult conversation. If my son's half merits that description.

[*He rises.*]

I'll get you another plate.

ANNIE. [*Gripping Helen*] I have a plate, thank you.

KATE. [*Calling*] Viney! I'm afraid what Captain Keller says is only too true, she'll persist in this until she gets her own way.

KELLER. [*At the door*] Viney, bring Miss Sullivan another plate—

ANNIE. [*Stonily*] I have a plate, nothing's wrong with the *plate*, I intend to keep it.

[*Silence for a moment, except for* HELEN's *noises as she struggles to get loose; the* KELLERS *are a bit nonplussed, and* ANNIE *is too darkly intent on* HELEN's *manners to have any thoughts now of her own.*]

JAMES. Ha. You see why they took Vicksburg?

KELLER. [*Uncertainly*] Miss Sullivan. One

plate or another is hardly a matter to struggle with a deprived child about.

ANNIE. Oh, I'd sooner have a more—

[HELEN *begins to kick*, ANNIE *moves her ankles to the opposite side of the chair.*]

—heroic issue myself, I—

KELLER. No, I really must insist you—

[HELEN *bangs her toe on the chair and sinks to the floor, crying with rage and feigned injury;* ANNIE *keeps hold of her wrists, gazing down, while* KATE *rises.*]

Now she's hurt herself.

ANNIE. [*Grimly*] No, she hasn't.

KELLER. Will you please let her hands go?

KATE. Miss Annie, you don't know the child well enough yet, she'll keep—

ANNIE. I know an ordinary tantrum well enough, when I see one, and a badly spoiled child—

JAMES. Hear, hear.

KELLER. [*Very annoyed*] Miss Sullivan! You would have more understanding of your pupil if you had some pity in you. Now kindly do as I—

ANNIE. Pity?

[*She releases* HELEN *to turn equally annoyed on* KELLER *across the table; instantly*

The Miracle Worker 247

13 Discussion Compare and contrast Keller's and Annie's views.

13

14 Discussion What does Annie mean by this statement?

15 Discussion Is James beginning to change his mind about what Annie is trying to do? Explain.

[HELEN *scrambles up and dives at* ANNIE'S *plate. This time* ANNIE *intercepts her by pouncing on her wrists like a hawk, and her temper boils.*]

For this *tyrant?* The whole house turns on her whims, is there anything she wants she doesn't get? I'll tell you what I pity, that the sun won't rise and set for her all her life, and every day you're telling her it will, what good will your pity do her when you're under the strawberries, Captain Keller?

KELLER. [*Outraged*] Kate, for the love of heaven will you—

KATE. Miss Annie, please, I don't think it serves to lose our—

14 **ANNIE.** It does you good, that's all. It's less trouble to feel sorry for her than to teach her anything better, isn't it?

KELLER. I fail to see where you have taught her anything yet, Miss Sullivan!

ANNIE. I'll begin this minute, if you'll leave the room, Captain Keller!

KELLER. [*Astonished*] Leave the—

ANNIE. Everyone, please.

[*She struggles with* HELEN, *while* KELLER *endeavors to control his voice.*]

KELLER. Miss Sullivan, you are here only as a paid teacher. Nothing more, and not to lecture—

ANNIE. I can't *un*teach her six years of pity if you can't stand up to one tantrum! Old Stonewall, indeed. Mrs. Keller, you promised me help.

KATE. Indeed I did, we truly want to—

ANNIE. Then leave me alone with her. Now!

KELLER. [*In a wrath*] Katie, will you come outside with me? At once, please.

[*He marches to the front door.* KATE *and*

JAMES *follow him. Simultaneously* ANNIE *releases* HELEN'S *wrists, and the child again sinks to the floor, kicking and crying her weird noises;* ANNIE *steps over her to meet* VINEY *coming in the rear doorway with biscuits and a clean plate, surprised at the general commotion.*]

VINEY. Heaven sakes—

ANNIE. Out, please.

[*She backs* VINEY *out with one hand, closes the door on her astonished mouth, locks it, and removes the key.* KELLER *meanwhile snatches his hat from a rack, and* KATE *follows him down the porch steps.* JAMES *lingers in the doorway to address* ANNIE *across the room with a bow.*]

JAMES. If it takes all summer, general.

[ANNIE *comes over to his door in turn, removing her glasses grimly; as* KELLER *outside begins speaking,* ANNIE *closes the door on* JAMES, *locks it, removes the key, and turns with her back against the door to stare ominously at* HELEN, *kicking on the floor.*

JAMES *takes his hat from the rack, and going down the porch steps joins* KATE *and* KELLER *talking in the yard,* KELLER *in a sputter of ire.*]

KELLER. This girl, this—cub of a girl—*presumes!* I tell you, I'm of half a mind to ship her back to Boston before the week is out. You can inform her so from me!

KATE. [*Eyebrows up*] I, Captain?

KELLER. She's a *hireling!* Now I want it clear, unless there's an apology and complete change of manner she goes back on the next train! Will you make that quite clear?

KATE. Where will you be, Captain, while I am making it quite—

KELLER. At the office!

248 *Drama*

Grammar in Action

When characters are engaged in a conflict, their strong emotions may cause them to interrupt one another's speech. Playwrights indicate such interruptions with **dashes.** The following lines from *The Miracle Worker* illustrate this technique:

KELLER. [*Outraged*] Kate for the love of heaven will you—

KATE. Miss Annie, please. I don't think it serves to lose our—

ANNIE. It does you good, that's all. It's less trouble to feel sorry for her than to teach her anything better, isn't it?

KELLER. I fail to see where you have taught her anything yet, Miss Sullivan!

ANNIE. I'll begin this minute, if you'll leave the room, Captain Keller!

KELLER. [*Astonished*] Leave the—

ANNIE. Everyone, please.

[*He begins off left, finds his napkin still in his irate hand, is uncertain with it, dabs his lips with dignity, gets rid of it in a toss to* JAMES, *and marches off.* JAMES *turns to eye* KATE.]

JAMES. Will you?

[KATE'S *mouth is set, and* JAMES *studies it lightly.*]

I thought what she said was exceptionally intelligent. I've been saying it for years.

KATE. [*Not without scorn*] To his face?

[*She comes to relieve him of the white napkin, but reverts again with it.*]

6 Or will you take it, Jimmie? As a flag?

[JAMES *stalks out, much offended, and* KATE *turning stares across the yard at the house; the lights narrowing down to the following pantomime in the family room leave her motionless in the dark.*

7 ANNIE *meanwhile has begun by slapping both keys down on a shelf out of* HELEN'S *reach; she returns to the table, upstage,* HELEN'S *kicking has subsided, and when from the floor her hand finds* ANNIE'S *chair empty she pauses.* ANNIE *clears the table of* KATE'S, JAMES'S, *and* KELLER'S *plates; she gets back to her own across the table just in time to slide it deftly away from* HELEN'S *pouncing hand. She lifts the hand and moves it to* HELEN'S *plate, and after an instant's exploration,* HELEN *sits again on the floor and drums her heels.* ANNIE *comes around the table and resumes her chair. When* HELEN *feels her skirt again, she ceases kicking, waits for whatever is to come, renews some kicking, waits again.* ANNIE *retrieving her plate takes up a forkful of food, stops it halfway to her mouth, gazes at it devoid of appetite, and half-lowers it; but after a look at* HELEN *she*

sighs, dips the forkful toward* HELEN *in a for-your-sake toast, and puts it in her own mouth to chew, not without an effort.*

HELEN *now gets hold of the chair leg, and half-succeeds in pulling the chair out from under her.* ANNIE *bangs it down with her rear, heavily, and sits with all her weight.* HELEN'S *next attempt to topple it is unavailing, so her fingers dive in a pinch at* ANNIE'S *flank.* ANNIE *in the middle of her mouthful almost loses it with startle, and she slaps down her fork to round on* HELEN. *The child comes up with curiosity to feel what* ANNIE *is doing, so* ANNIE *resumes eating, letting* HELEN'S *hand follow the movement of her fork to her mouth; whereupon* HELEN *at once reaches into* ANNIE'S *plate.* ANNIE *firmly removes her hand to her own plate.* HELEN *in reply pinches* ANNIE'S *thigh, a good mean pinchful that makes* ANNIE *jump.* ANNIE *sets the fork down, and sits with her mouth tight.* HELEN *digs another pinch into her thigh, and this time* ANNIE *slaps her hand smartly away;* HELEN *retaliates with a roundhouse fist that catches* AN-NIE *on the ear, and* ANNIE'S *hand leaps at once in a forceful slap across* HELEN'S *cheek;* HELEN *is the startled one now.* AN-NIE'S *hand in compunction falters to her own face, but when* HELEN *hits at her again,* ANNIE *deliberately slaps her again.* HELEN *lifts her fist irresolute for another round-house,* ANNIE *lifts her hand resolute for another slap, and they freeze in this posture, while* HELEN *mulls it over. She thinks better of it, drops her fist, and giving* ANNIE *a wide berth, gropes around to her* MOTHER'S *chair, to find it empty; she blunders her way along the table upstage, and encountering the empty chairs and missing plates, she looks bewildered; she gropes back to her* MOTHER'S *chair, again touches her cheek and indicates the chair, and waits for the world to answer.*

The Miracle Worker 249

16 **Discussion** Why does Kate refer to the white napkin as a flag?

17 **Discussion** Why does Annie put the keys away?

18 **Literary Focus** You might point out to students that this conflict takes place in silence. How might the lack of dialogue make this scene even more effective?

19 **Literary Focus** You might have students act out this scene or a portion of it.

20 **Discussion** Do you think Helen has ever been slapped before? Explain.

21 **Discussion** Whom does Helen seek out and wait for? Why?

The dashes help set the fast pace for the speeches and keep the audience interested in the building argument. Actors and actresses delivering these lines must make the interruptions seem as lifelike as possible.

Student Activity 1. Reread the passage from *The Miracle Worker*. Decide which words have been omitted from the sentences interrupted by dashes. Explain how you reached your conclusions.

Student Activity 2. Write a brief dialogue between two people engaged in a conflict. Use dashes to show dramatic interruptions. Ask your classmates to read the dialogue and guess which words are missing.

Electronic Handbook You might wish to have students review the use of dashes before they complete Grammar in Action activities. If students have access to Language Master 6000, have them enter the access word *fragment* and press the GRAMMAR key to obtain information on the use of dashes.

22 **Discussion** Do you think Annie
is being unnecessarily cruel?

23 **Discussion** What does Annie
want Helen to do? Why?

24 **Reading Strategy** Ask students
to predict what will happen.

ANNIE *now reaches over to spell into her hand, but* HELEN *yanks it away; she gropes to the front door, tries the knob, and finds the door locked, with no key. She gropes to the rear door, and finds it locked, with no key. She commences to bang on it.* ANNIE *rises, crosses, takes her wrists, draws her resisting back to the table, seats her, and releases her hands upon her plate; as* ANNIE *herself begins to sit,* HELEN *writhes out of her chair, runs to the front door, and tugs and kicks at it.* ANNIE *rises again, crosses, draws her by one wrist back to the table, seats her, and sits;* HELEN *escapes back to the door, knocking over her* MOTHER'S *chair en route.* ANNIE *rises again in pursuit, and this time lifts* HELEN *bodily from behind and bears her kicking to her chair. She deposits her, and once more turns to sit.* HELEN *scrambles out, but as she passes* ANNIE *catches her up again from behind and deposits her in the chair;* HELEN *scrambles out on the other side, for the rear door, but* ANNIE *at her heels catches her up and deposits her again in the chair. She stands behind it.* HELEN *scrambles out to her right, and the instant her feet hit the floor* ANNIE *lifts and deposits her back; she scrambles out to her left, and is at once lifted and deposited back. She tries right again and is deposited back, and tries left again and is deposited back, and now feints* ANNIE *to the right but is off to her left, and is promptly deposited back. She sits a moment, and then starts straight over the tabletop, dishware notwithstanding;* ANNIE *hauls her in and deposits her back, with her plate spilling in her lap, and she melts to the floor and crawls under the table, laborious among its legs and chairs; but* ANNIE *is swift around the table and waiting on the other side when she surfaces, immediately bearing her aloft;* HELEN *clutches at* JAMES'S *chair for anchorage, but it comes with her, and halfway back she abandons it to the floor.*

ANNIE *deposits her in her chair, and waits.* HELEN *sits tensed motionless. Then she tentatively puts out her left foot and hand,* ANNIE *interposes her own hand, and at the contact* HELEN *jerks hers in. She tries her right foot,* ANNIE *blocks it with her own, and* HELEN *jerks hers in. Finally, leaning back, she slumps down in her chair, in a sullen biding.*

ANNIE *backs off a step, and watches;* HELEN *offers no move.* ANNIE *takes a deep breath. Both of them and the room are in considerable disorder, two chairs down and the table a mess, but* ANNIE *makes no effort to tidy it; she only sits on her own chair, and lets her energy refill. Then she takes up knife and fork, and resolutely addresses her food.* HELEN'S *hand comes out to explore, and seeing it* ANNIE *sits without moving; the child's hand goes over her hand and fork, pauses—*ANNIE *still does not move—and withdraws. Presently it moves for her own plate, slaps about for it, and stops, thwarted. At this,* ANNIE *again rises, recovers* HELEN'S *plate from the floor and a handful of scattered food from the deranged tablecloth, drops it on the plate, and pushes the plate into contact with* HELEN'S *fist. Neither of them now moves for a pregnant moment—until* HELEN *suddenly takes a grab of food and wolfs it down.* ANNIE *permits herself the humor of a minor bow and warming of her hands together; she wanders off a step or two, watching.* HELEN *cleans up the plate.*

After a glower of indecision, she holds the empty plate out for more. ANNIE *accepts it, and crossing to the removed plates, spoons food from them onto it; she stands debating the spoon, tapping it a few times on* HELEN'S *plate; and when she returns with the plate she brings the spoon, too. She puts the spoon first into* HELEN'S *hand, then sets the plate down.* HELEN *discarding the spoon* reaches with her hand, and ANNIE stops it by the wrist; she replaces the spoon in it. HELEN impatiently discards it again, and again ANNIE stops her hand, to replace the spoon in it. This time HELEN throws the spoon on the floor. ANNIE after considering it lifts HELEN bodily out of the chair, and in a wrestling match on the floor closes her fingers upon the spoon, and returns her with it to the chair. HELEN again throws the spoon on the floor. ANNIE lifts her out of the chair again; but in the struggle over the spoon HELEN with ANNIE on her back sends her sliding over her head; HELEN flees back to her chair and scrambles into it. When AN-NIE comes after her she clutches it for dear life; ANNIE pries one hand loose, then the other, then the first again, then the other again, and then lifts HELEN by the waist, chair and all, and shakes the chair loose. HELEN wrestles to get free, but ANNIE pins her to the floor, closes her fingers upon the spoon, and lifts her kicking under one arm; with her other hand she gets the chair in place again, and plunks HELEN back on it. When she releases her hand, HELEN throws the spoon at her.

ANNIE now removes the plate of food. HELEN grabbing finds it missing, and commences to bang with her fists on the table. ANNIE collects a fistful of spoons and descends

with them and the plate on HELEN; *she lets her smell the plate, at which* HELEN *ceases banging, and* ANNIE *puts the plate down and a spoon in* HELEN's *hand.* HELEN *throws it on the floor.* ANNIE *puts another spoon in her hand.* HELEN *throws it on the floor.* AN-NIE *puts another spoon in her hand.* HELEN *throws it on the floor. When* ANNIE *comes to her last spoon she sits next to* HELEN, *and gripping the spoon in* HELEN's *hand compels her to take food in it up to her mouth.* HELEN *sits with lips shut,* ANNIE *waits a stolid moment, then lowers* HELEN's *hand. She tries again;* HELEN's *lips remain shut.* ANNIE *waits, lowers* HELEN's *hand. She tries again; this time* HELEN *suddenly opens her mouth and accepts the food.* ANNIE *lowers the spoon with a sigh of relief, and* HELEN *spews the mouthful out at her face.* ANNIE *sits a moment with eyes closed, then takes the pitcher and dashes its water into* HELEN's *face, who gasps astonished.* ANNIE *with* HELEN's *hand takes up another spoonful, and shoves it into her open mouth.* HELEN *swallows involuntarily, and while she is catching her breath* ANNIE *forces her palm open, throws four swift letters into it, then another four, and bows toward her with devastating pleasantness.*]

ANNIE. Good girl.

[ANNIE *lifts* HELEN's *hand to feel her face nodding;* HELEN *grabs a fistful of her hair, and yanks. The pain brings* ANNIE *to her knees, and* HELEN *pummels her; they roll under the table, and the lights commence to dim out on them.*

Simultaneously the light at left has been rising, slowly, so slowly that it seems at first we only imagine what is intimated in the yard: a few ghostlike figures, in silence, motionless, waiting. Now the distant belfry chimes commence to toll the hour, also very slowly, almost—it is twelve—interminably; the sense is that of a long time passing. We

can identify the figures before the twelfth stroke, all facing the house in a kind of watch: KATE *is standing exactly as before, but now with the baby* MILDRED *sleeping in her arms, and placed here and there, unmoving, are* AUNT EV *in her hat with a hanky to her nose, and the two Negro children,* PERCY *and* MARTHA *with necks outstretched eagerly, and* VINEY *with a knotted kerchief on her head and a feather duster in her hand.*

The chimes cease, and there is silence. For a long moment none of the group moves.]

VINEY. [*Presently*] What am I gone do, Miss Kate? It's noontime, dinner's comin', I didn't get them breakfast dishes out of there yet.

[KATE *says nothing, stares at the house.* MARTHA *shifts* HELEN's *doll in her clutch, and it plaintively says momma.*]

KATE. [*Presently*] You run along, Martha.

[AUNT EV *blows her nose.*]

AUNT EV. [*Wretchedly*] I can't wait out here a minute longer, Kate, why, this could go on all afternoon, too.

KATE. I'll tell the captain you called.

VINEY. [*To the children*] You hear what Miss Kate say? Never you mind what's going on here.

[*Still no one moves.*]

You run along tend your own bizness.

[*Finally* VINEY *turns on the children with the feather duster.*]

Shoo!

[*The two children divide before her. She chases them off.* AUNT EV *comes to* KATE, *on her dignity.*]

AUNT EV. Say what you like, Kate, but that child is a *Keller.*

Grammar in Action

One of the most basic forms of descriptive writing is **writing directions.** Playwrights, such as William Gibson, rely on writing accurate instructions to tell directors and actors what actions they are to take. Writing directions involves telling how to do something in a series of logical steps. Writers of everything from cookbooks to plays are required to write directions, and the success of their work depends to a great extent on how easy it is to follow the directions they write. Look at these stage directions from *The Miracle Worker.*

. . . ANNIE lowers the spoon with a sigh of relief, and HELEN spews the mouthful out at her face. ANNIE sits for a moment with eyes closed, then takes the pitcher and dashes its water into HELEN's face, who gasps astonished. ANNIE with HELEN's hand takes up another spoonful, and shoves it into her open mouth. HELEN swallows involuntarily, and while she is catching her breath ANNIE forces her palm open, throws four swift letters into it, then another four, and bows toward her with devastating pleasantness.

[*She opens her parasol, preparatory to leaving.*]

I needn't remind you that all the Kellers are cousins to General Robert E. Lee.[4] I don't know *who* that girl is.

[*She waits; but* KATE *staring at the house is without response.*]

The only Sullivan I've heard of—from Boston too, and I'd think twice before locking her up with that kind—is that man John L.[5]

[*And* AUNT EV *departs, with head high. Presently* VINEY *comes to* KATE, *her arms out for the baby.*]

VINEY. You give me her, Miss Kate, I'll sneak her in back, to her crib.

[*But* KATE *is moveless, until* VINEY *starts to take the baby;* KATE *looks down at her before relinquishing her.*]

KATE. [*Slowly*] This child never gives me a minute's worry.

VINEY. Oh yes, this one's the angel of the family, no question bout *that*.

[*She begins off rear with the baby, heading around the house; and* KATE *now turns her back on it, her hand to her eyes. At this moment there is the slamming of a door, and when* KATE *wheels* HELEN *is blundering down the porch steps into the light, like a ruined bat out of hell.* VINEY *halts, and* KATE *runs in;* HELEN *collides with her mother's knees, and reels off and back to clutch them as her savior.* ANNIE *with smoked glasses in hand stands on the porch, also much undone, looking as though she had indeed just taken Vicksburg.* KATE *taking in* HELEN's *ravaged state becomes steely in her gaze up at* ANNIE.]

---

4. General Robert E. Lee: (1807–1870), leader of the Confederate forces in the Civil War.
5. John L.: John L. Sullivan (1858–1918), a champion boxer.

KATE. What happened?

[ANNIE *meets* KATE's *gaze, and gives a factual report, too exhausted for anything but a flat voice.*]

ANNIE. She ate from her own plate.

[*She thinks a moment.*]

She ate with a spoon. Herself.

[KATE *frowns, uncertain with thought, and glances down at* HELEN.]

And she folded her napkin.

[KATE's *gaze now wavers, from* HELEN *to* ANNIE, *and back.*]

KATE. [*Softly*] Folded—her napkin?

ANNIE. The room's a wreck, but her napkin is folded.

[*She pauses, then:*]

I'll be in my room, Mrs. Keller.

[*She moves to re-enter the house; but she stops at* VINEY's *voice.*]

VINEY. [*Cheery*] Don't be long, Miss Annie. Dinner be ready right away!

[VINEY *carries* MILDRED *around the back of the house.* ANNIE *stands unmoving, takes a deep breath, stares over her shoulder at* KATE *and* HELEN, *then inclines her head graciously, and goes with a slight stagger into the house. The lights in her room above steal up in readiness for her.*

KATE *remains alone with* HELEN *in the yard, standing protectively over her, in a kind of wonder.*]

KATE. [*Slowly*] Folded her napkin.

[*She contemplates the wild head in her thighs, and moves her fingertips over it, with such a tenderness, and something like a fear of its strangeness, that her own eyes close; she whispers, bending to it.*]

The Miracle Worker 253

26 **Discussion** How do differences between the North and South surface again?

27 **Discussion** Why does Kate's gaze become "steely"?

28 **Critical Thinking and Reading** Why do you think Annie does not go into all the details of the battle?

29 **Discussion** Why does this particular detail seem to mean so much to Kate?

Notice that these, like most, directions are given in chronological, or time, order. The steps to be taken are organized according to which is to be done first, second, third, and so on, to the completion of the task. The test of how well directions are written is how well those directions can be followed.

Student Activity 1. With a small group of classmates, select another passage of stage directions from the play. Discuss these, noting which directions apply to the actors themselves and which refer to how the stage set itself is to look. Then take parts and practice reading the scene according to the stage directions. Review the directions and try again. Are the directions easy to follow? What makes you feel as you do?

Student Activity 2. Write directions on how to do something. Choose an activity that has at least four or five steps. Exchange papers with a classmate and discuss whether the directions are easy to understand and to follow. Revise your directions based on this conference.

30 Literary Focus Kate's inner conflict of hope and fear has finally surfaced. Ask students to explain why she is crying?

31 Discussion Why has Annie gone to her suitcase?

32 Reading Strategy Ask students to predict how these memories will influence Annie.

My Helen—folded her napkin—

30 [*And still erect, with only her head in surrender,* KATE *for the first time that we see loses her protracted war with grief; but she will not let a sound escape her, only the grimace of tears comes, and sobs that shake her in a grip of silence. But* HELEN *feels them, and her hand comes up in its own wondering, to interrogate her mother's face, until* KATE *buries her lips in the child's palm.*

Upstairs, ANNIE *enters her room, closes the door, and stands back against it; the lights, growing on her with their special color, commence to fade on* KATE *and* HELEN. *Then*

31 ANNIE *goes wearily to her suitcase, and lifts it to take it toward the bed. But it knocks an object to the floor, and she turns back to regard it. A new voice comes in a cultured murmur, hesitant as with the effort of remembering a text:*]

32 **MAN'S VOICE.** This—soul—

[ANNIE *puts the suitcase down, and kneels to the object; it is the battered Perkins report, and she stands with it in her hand, letting memory try to speak:*]

This—blind, deaf, mute—woman—

[ANNIE *sits on her bed, opens the book, and finding the passage, brings it up an inch from her eyes to read, her face and lips following the overheard words, the voice quite factual now.*]

Can nothing be done to disinter this human soul? The whole neighborhood would rush to save this woman if she were buried alive by the caving in of a pit, and labor with zeal until she were dug out. Now if there were one who had as much patience as zeal, he might awaken her to a consciousness of her immortal—

[*When the boy's voice comes,* ANNIE *closes her eyes, in pain.*]

254 Drama

BOY'S VOICE. Annie? Annie, you there?

ANNIE. Hush.

BOY'S VOICE. Annie, what's that noise?

[ANNIE *tries not to answer; her own voice is drawn out of her, unwilling.*]

ANNIE. Just a cot, Jimmie.

BOY'S VOICE. Where they pushin' it?

ANNIE. To the deadhouse.

BOY'S VOICE. Annie. Does it hurt to be dead?

[ANNIE *escapes by opening her eyes, her hand works restlessly over her cheek; she retreats into the book again, but the cracked old crones interrupt, whispering,* ANNIE *slowly lowers the book.*]

FIRST CRONE'S VOICE. There is schools.

SECOND CRONE'S VOICE. There is schools outside—

THIRD CRONE'S VOICE. —schools where they teach blind ones, worse'n you—

FIRST CRONE'S VOICE. To read—

SECOND CRONE'S VOICE. To read and write—

THIRD CRONE'S VOICE. There is schools outside where they—

FIRST CRONE'S VOICE. There is schools—

[*Silence.* ANNIE *sits with her eyes shining, her hand almost in a caress over the book. Then:*]

BOY'S VOICE. You ain't goin' to school, are you, Annie?

ANNIE. [*Whispering*] When I grow up.

BOY'S VOICE. You ain't either, Annie. You're goin' to stay here take care of me.

ANNIE. I'm goin' to school when I grow up.

BOY'S VOICE. You said we'll be together, forever and ever and ever—

ANNIE. [*Fierce*] I'm goin' to school when I grow up!

DOCTOR'S VOICE. [*Slowly*] Little girl. Little girl, I must tell you. Your brother will be going on a journey, soon.

[ANNIE *sits rigid, in silence. Then the boy's voice pierces it, a shriek of terror.*]

BOY'S VOICE: *Annie!*

[*It goes into* ANNIE *like a sword, she doubles onto it; the book falls to the floor. It takes her a racked moment to find herself and what she was engaged in here; when she sees the suitcase she remembers, and lifts it once again toward the bed. But the voices are with her, as she halts with suitcase in hand.*]

FIRST CRONE'S VOICE. Goodbye, Annie.

DOCTOR'S VOICE. Write me when you learn how.

SECOND CRONE'S VOICE. Don't tell anyone you came from here. Don't tell anyone—

THIRD CRONE'S VOICE. Yeah, don't tell anyone you came from—

FIRST CRONE'S VOICE. Yeah, don't tell anyone—

SECOND CRONE'S VOICE. Don't tell any—

[*The echoing voices fade. After a moment* ANNIE *lays the suitcase on the bed; and the last voice comes faintly, from far away.*]

BOY'S VOICE. Annie. It hurts, to be dead. Forever.

[ANNIE *falls to her knees by the bed, stifling her mouth in it. When at last she rolls blindly away from it, her palm comes down on the open report; she opens her eyes, regards it dully, and then, still on her knees, takes in the print.*]

MAN'S VOICE. [*Factual*] —might awaken her to a consciousness of her immortal nature.

The chance is small indeed; but with a smaller chance they would have dug desperately for her in the pit; and is the life of the soul of less import than that of the body?

[ANNIE *gets to her feet. She drops the book on the bed, and pauses over her suitcase; after a moment she unclasps and opens it. Standing before it, she comes to her decision; she at once turns to the bureau, and taking her things out of its drawers, commences to throw them into the open suitcase.*] | 33

In the darkness down left a hand strikes a match, and lights a hanging oil lamp. It is KELLER'S *hand, and his voice accompanies it, very angry; the lights rising here before they fade on* ANNIE *show* KELLER *and* KATE *inside a suggestion of a garden house, with a bay-window seat toward center and a door at back.*]

KELLER. Katie, I will not *have* it! Now you did not see when that girl after supper tonight went to look for Helen in her room—

KATE. No.

KELLER. The child practically climbed out of her window to escape from her! What kind of teacher *is* she? I thought I had seen her at her worst this morning, shouting at me, but I come home to find the entire house disorganized by her—Helen won't stay one second in the same room, won't come to the table with her, won't let herself be bathed or undressed or put to bed by her, or even by Viney now, and the end result is that *you* have to do more for the child than before we hired this girl's services! From the moment she stepped off the train she's been nothing but a burden, incompetent, impertinent, ineffectual, immodest— | 34

KATE. She folded her napkin, Captain.

KELLER. What?

The Miracle Worker 255

33 Discussion What has Annie decided to do?

34 Discussion How would you answer Keller's arguments?

35 **Discussion** What has Helen's folded napkin come to symbolize to Kate?

36 **Literary Focus** As Annie knocks on the door, she is faced with external conflicts—opposition from Keller—as well as internal ones—fears about her ability to help Helen.

37 **Critical Thinking and Reading** Why do you think Keller is nervous?

38 **Clarification** *Vexedly* means "in an irritated or annoyed manner."

39 **Discussion** Why do you think Keller changes his mind about firing Annie?

40 **Discussion** Why is Annie cheerful?

35

KATE. Not ineffectual. Helen did fold her napkin.

KELLER. What in heaven's name is so extraordinary about folding a napkin?

KATE. [*With some humor*] Well. It's more than you did, Captain.

KELLER. Katie. I did not bring you all the way out here to the garden house to be frivolous. Now, how does Miss Sullivan propose to teach a deaf-blind pupil who won't let her even touch her?

KATE. [*A pause*] I don't know.

KELLER. The fact is, today she scuttled any chance she ever had of getting along with the child. If you can see any point or purpose to her staying on here longer, it's more than—

KATE. What do you wish me to do?

KELLER. I want you to give her notice.

KATE. I can't.

KELLER. Then if you won't, I must. I simply will not—

[*He is interrupted by a knock at the back door.* KELLER *after a glance at* KATE *moves to open the door;* ANNIE *in her smoked glasses is standing outside.* KELLER *contemplates her, heavily.*]

Miss Sullivan.

36

ANNIE. Captain Keller.

[*She is nervous, keyed up to seizing the bull by the horns again, and she assumes a cheeriness which is not unshaky.*]

Viney said I'd find you both over here in the garden house. I thought we should—have a talk?

KELLER. [*Reluctantly*] Yes, I— Well, come in.

[ANNIE *enters, and is interested in this room; she rounds on her heel, anxiously,*

256 Drama

studying it. KELLER *turns the matter over to* KATE, *sotto voce.*]

Katie.

KATE. [*Turning it back, courteously*] Captain.

[KELLER *clears his throat, makes ready.*]

KELLER. I, ah—wanted first to make my position clear to Mrs. Keller, in private. I have decided I—am not satisfied—in fact, am deeply dissatisfied—with the manner in which—

ANNIE. [*Intent*] Excuse me, is this little house ever in use?

KELLER. [*With patience*] In the hunting season. If you will give me your attention, Miss Sullivan.

[ANNIE *turns her smoked glasses upon him; they hold his unwilling stare.*]

I have tried to make allowances for you because you come from a part of the country where people are—women, I should say—come from who—well, for whom—

[*It begins to elude him.*]

—allowances must—be made. I have decided, nevertheless, to—that is, decided I—

[*Vexedly*]

Miss Sullivan, I find it difficult to talk through those glasses.

ANNIE. [*Eagerly, removing them*] Oh, of course.

KELLER. [*Dourly*] Why do you wear them, the sun has been down for an hour.

ANNIE. [*Pleasantly, at the lamp*] Any kind of light hurts my eyes.

[*A silence;* KELLER *ponders her, heavily.*]

KELLER. Put them on. Miss Sullivan, I have decided to—give you another chance.

ANNIE. [*Cheerfully*] To do what?

KELLER. To—remain in our employ.

[ANNIE'S *eyes widen.*]

But on two conditions. I am not accustomed to rudeness in servants or women, and that is the first. If you are to stay, there must be a radical change of manner.

ANNIE. [*A pause*] Whose?

KELLER. [*Exploding*] Yours, young lady, isn't it obvious? And the second is that you persuade me there's the slightest hope of your teaching a child who flees from you now like the plague, to anyone else she can find in this house.

ANNIE. [*A pause*] There isn't.

[KATE *stops sewing, and fixes her eyes upon* ANNIE.]

KATE. What, Miss Annie?

ANNIE. It's hopeless here. I can't teach a child who runs away.

KELLER. [*Nonplussed*] Then—do I understand you—propose—

ANNIE. Well, if we all agree it's hopeless, the next question is what—

KATE. Miss Annie.

[*She is leaning toward* ANNIE, *in deadly earnest; it commands both* ANNIE *and* KELLER.]

I am not agreed. I think perhaps you—underestimated Helen.

ANNIE. I think everybody else here does.

KATE. She did fold her napkin. She learns, she learns, do you know she began talking when she was six months old? She could say "water." Not really—"wahwah." "Wahwah," but she meant water, she knew what it meant, and only six months old, I never saw a child so—bright, or outgoing—

[*Her voice is unsteady, but she gets it level.*]

It's still in her, somewhere, isn't it? You should have seen her before her illness, such a good-tempered child—

ANNIE. [*Agreeably*] She's changed.

[*A pause,* KATE *not letting her eyes go; her appeal at last is unconditional, and very quiet.*]

KATE. Miss Annie, put up with it. And with us.

KELLER. Us!

KATE. Please? Like the lost lamb in the parable, I love her all the more.

ANNIE. Mrs. Keller, I don't think Helen's worst handicap is deafness or blindness. I think it's your love. And pity.

KELLER. Now what does that mean?

ANNIE. All of you here are so sorry for her you've kept her—like a pet, why, even a dog you housebreak. No wonder she won't let me come near her. It's useless for me to try to teach her language or anything else here. I might as well—

KATE. [*Cuts in*] Miss Annie, before you came we spoke of putting her in an asylum.

[ANNIE *turns back to regard her. A pause*]

ANNIE. What kind of asylum?

KELLER. For mental defectives.

KATE. I visited there. I can't tell you what I saw, people like—animals, with—*rats*, in the halls, and—

[*She shakes her head on her vision.*]

What else are we to do, if you give up?

ANNIE. Give up?

KATE. You said it was hopeless.

ANNIE. Here. Give up, why, I only today saw what has to be done, to begin!

The Miracle Worker 257

41 **Clarification** *Nonplussed* means "perplexed and unable to speak or act."

42 **Discussion** Why does Annie think Helen's worst handicap is her parents' love and pity?

43 Discussion Evaluate Annie's idea.

44 Discussion Why do you think Annie chooses this moment to tell the Kellers about her past?

Speaking and Listening You might want to have student volunteers read aloud the garden house scene between Keller, Kate, and Annie. It is here that confrontations among the three take place, positions become clear, and Annie's background —which was hazily suggested by her "ghost voices"—are explained. If you wish, individual students may read the parts of Keller, Kate, and Annie.

[*She glances from* KATE *to* KELLER, *who stare, waiting; and she makes it as plain and simple as her nervousness permits.*]

I—want complete charge of her.

KELLER. You already have that. It has resulted in—

ANNIE. No, I mean day and night. She has to be dependent on me.

KATE. For what?

ANNIE. Everything. The food she eats, the clothes she wears, fresh—

[*She is amused at herself, though very serious.*]

—air, yes, the air she breathes, whatever her body needs is a—primer, to teach her out of. It's the only way, the one who lets her have it should be her teacher.

[*She considers them in turn; they digest it,* KELLER *frowning,* KATE *perplexed.*]

Not anyone who *loves* her, you have so many feelings they fall over each other like feet, you won't use your chances and you won't let me.

KATE. But if she runs from you—*to us*—

ANNIE. Yes, that's the point. I'll have to live with her somewhere else.

KELLER. What!

ANNIE. Till she learns to depend on and listen to me.

KATE. [*Not without alarm*] For how long?

ANNIE. As long as it takes.

[*A pause. She takes a breath.*]

I packed half my things already.

KELLER. Miss—Sullivan!

[*But when* ANNIE *attends upon him he is speechless, and she is merely earnest.*]

258 Drama

ANNIE. Captain Keller, it meets both your conditions. It's the one way I can get back in touch with Helen, and I don't see how I can be rude to you again if you're not around to interfere with me.

KELLER. [*Red-faced*] And what is your intention if I say no? Pack the other half, for home, and abandon your charge to—to—

ANNIE. The asylum?

[*She waits, appraises* KELLER'S *glare and* KATE'S *uncertainty, and decides to use her weapons.*]

I grew up in such an asylum. The state almshouse.

[KATE'S *head comes up on this, and* KELLER *stares hard;* ANNIE'S *tone is cheerful enough, albeit level as gunfire.*]

Rats—why, my brother Jimmie and I used to play with the rats because we didn't have toys. Maybe you'd like to know what Helen will find there, not on visiting days? One ward was full of the—old women, crippled, blind, most of them dying, but even if what they had was catching there was nowhere else to move them, and that's where they put us. There were younger ones across the hall, with T.B., and epileptic fits, and some insane. The room Jimmie and I played in was the deadhouse, where they kept the bodies till they could dig—

KATE. [*Closes her eyes*] Oh, my dear—

ANNIE. —the graves.

[*She is immune to* KATE'S *compassion.*]

No, it made me strong. But I don't think you need send Helen there. She's strong enough.

[*She waits again; but when neither offers her a word, she simply concludes.*]

No, I have no conditions, Captain Keller.

KATE. [*Not looking up*] Miss Annie.

258

ANNIE. Yes.

KATE. [A pause] Where would you—take Helen?

ANNIE. Ohh—

[Brightly]

Italy?

KELLER. [Wheeling] What?

ANNIE. Can't have everything, how would this garden house do? Furnish it, bring Helen here after a long ride so she won't recognize it, and you can see her every day. If she doesn't know. Well?

KATE. [A sigh of relief] Is that all?

ANNIE. That's all.

KATE. Captain.

[KELLER turns his head; and KATE's request is quiet but firm.]

With your permission?

KELLER. [Teeth in cigar] Why must she depend on you for the food she eats?

ANNIE. [A pause] I want control of it.

KELLER. Why?

ANNIE. It's a way to reach her.

KELLER. [Stares] You intend to starve her into letting you touch her?

ANNIE. She won't starve, she'll learn. All's fair in love and war, Captain Keller, you never cut supplies?

KELLER. This is hardly a war!

ANNIE. Well, it's not love. A siege is a siege.

KELLER. [Heavily] Miss Sullivan. Do you like the child?

ANNIE. [Straight in his eyes] Do you?

[A long pause]

KATE. You could have a servant here—

ANNIE. [Amused] I'll have enough work without looking after a servant! But that boy Percy could sleep here, run errands—

KATE. [Also amused] We can let Percy sleep here, I think, Captain?

ANNIE. [Eagerly] And some old furniture, all our own—

KATE. [Also eager] Captain? Do you think that walnut bedstead in the barn would be too—

KELLER. I have not yet consented to Percy! Or to the house, or to the proposal! Or to Miss Sullivan's—staying on when I—

[But he erupts in an irate surrender.]

Very well, I consent to everything!

[He shakes the cigar at ANNIE.]

For two weeks. I'll give you two weeks in this place, and it will be a miracle if you get the child to tolerate you.

KATE. Two weeks? Miss Annie, can you accomplish anything in two weeks?

KELLER. Anything or not, two weeks, then the child comes back to us. Make up your mind, Miss Sullivan, yes or no?

ANNIE. Two weeks. For only one miracle?

[She nods at him, nervously.]

I'll get her to tolerate me.

[KELLER marches out, and slams the door. KATE on her feet regards ANNIE, who is facing the door.]

KATE. [Then] You can't think as little of love as you said.

[ANNIE glances questioning.]

Or you wouldn't stay.

ANNIE. [A pause] I didn't come here for love. I came for money!

The Miracle Worker 259

45 Literary Focus The conflict between Annie and Keller reaches its high point here, as they trade questions about liking Helen. Why is the question important?

46 Discussion How is Keller's use of the word *miracle* an example of foreshadowing?

47 Discussion What may Kate know about Annie's feelings that Annie has not yet realized?

48 **Discussion** Explain Annie's gesture.

49 **Literary Focus** We know James's external conflict with his father. What inner conflict does he reveal to Annie here?

[KATE *shakes her head to this, with a smile; after a moment she extends her open hand.* ANNIE *looks at it, but when she puts hers out it is not to shake hands, it is to set her fist in* KATE'S *palm.*]

KATE. [*Puzzled*] Hm?

ANNIE. A. It's the first of many. Twenty-six!

[KATE *squeezes her fist, squeezes it hard, and hastens out after* KELLER. ANNIE *stands as the door closes behind her, her manner so apprehensive that finally she slaps her brow, holds it, sighs, and, with her eyes closed, crosses herself for luck.*

The lights dim into a cool silhouette scene around her, the lamp paling out, and now, in formal entrances, persons appear around ANNIE *with furniture for the room:* PERCY *crosses the stage with a rocking chair and waits;* MARTHA *from another direction bears in a stool,* VINEY *bears in a small table, and the other Negro servant rolls in a bed partway from left; and* ANNIE, *opening her eyes to put her glasses back on, sees them. She turns around in the room once, and goes into action, pointing out locations for each article; the servants place them and leave, and* ANNIE *then darts around, interchanging them. In the midst of this—while* PERCY *and* MARTHA *reappear with a tray of food and a chair, respectively—*JAMES *comes down from the house with* ANNIE'S *suitcase, and stands viewing the room and her quizzically;* ANNIE *halts abruptly under his eyes, embarrassed, then seizes the suitcase from his hand, explaining herself brightly.*]

ANNIE. I always wanted to live in a doll's house!

[*She sets the suitcase out of the way, and continues;* VINEY *at left appears to position a rod with drapes for a doorway, and the other servant at center pushes in a wheel-*

barrow loaded with a couple of boxes of HELEN'S *toys and clothes.* ANNIE *helps lift them into the room, and the servant pushes the wheelbarrow off. In none of this is any heed taken of the imaginary walls of the garden house, the furniture is moved in from every side and itself defines the walls.*

ANNIE *now drags the box of toys into center, props up the doll conspicuously on top; with the people melted away, except for* JAMES, *all is again still. The lights turn again without pause, rising warmer.*]

JAMES. You don't let go of things easily, do you? How will you—win her hand now, in this place?

ANNIE. [*Curtly*] Do I know? I lost my temper, and here we are!

JAMES. [*Lightly*] No touching, no teaching. Of course, you *are* bigger—

ANNIE. I'm not counting on force, I'm counting on her. That little imp is dying to know.

JAMES. Know what?

ANNIE. Anything. Any and every crumb in God's creation. I'll have to use that appetite too.

[*She gives the room a final survey, straightens the bed, arranges the curtains.*]

JAMES. [*A pause*] Maybe she'll teach you.

ANNIE. Of course.

JAMES. That she isn't. That there's such a thing as—dullness of heart. Acceptance. And letting go. Sooner or later we all give up, don't we?

ANNIE. Maybe you all do. It's my idea of the original sin.

JAMES. What is?

ANNIE. [*Witheringly*] Giving up.

JAMES. [*Nettled*] You won't open her. Why

can't you let her be? Have some—pity on her, for being what she is—

ANNIE. If I'd ever once thought like that, I'd be dead!

JAMES. [*Pleasantly*] You will be. Why trouble?

[ANNIE *turns to glare at him; he is mocking.*]

Or will you teach me?

[*And with a bow, he drifts off.*

Now in the distance there comes the clopping of hoofs, drawing near, and nearer, up to the door; and they halt. ANNIE *wheels to face the door. When it opens this time, the* KELLERS—KATE *in traveling bonnet,* KELLER *also hatted—are standing there with* HELEN *between them; she is in a cloak.* KATE *gently cues her into the room.* HELEN *comes in groping, baffled, but interested in the new surroundings;* ANNIE *evades her exploring hand, her gaze not leaving the child.*]

ANNIE. Does she know where she is?

KATE. [*Shakes her head*] We rode her out in the country for two hours.

KELLER. For all she knows, she could be in another town—

[HELEN *stumbles over the box on the floor and in it discovers her doll and other battered toys, is pleased, sits to them, then becomes puzzled and suddenly very wary. She scrambles up and back to her mother's thighs, but* ANNIE *steps in, and it is hers that* HELEN *embraces.* HELEN *recoils, gropes, and touches her cheek instantly.*]

KATE. That's her sign for me.

ANNIE. I know.

[HELEN *waits, then recommences her groping, more urgently.* KATE *stands indecisive,*

and takes an abrupt step toward her, but ANNIE'S *hand is a barrier.*]

In two weeks.

KATE. Miss Annie, I— Please be good to her. These two weeks, try to be very good to her—

ANNIE. I will.

[KATE, *turning then, hurries out. The* KELLERS *cross back of the main house.*

ANNIE *closes the door.* HELEN *starts at the door jar, and rushes it.* ANNIE *holds her off.* HELEN *kicks her, breaks free, and careens around the room like an imprisoned bird, colliding with furniture, groping wildly, repeatedly touching her cheek in a growing panic. When she has covered the room, she commences her weird screaming.* ANNIE *moves to comfort her, but her touch sends* HELEN *into a paroxysm of rage: she tears away, falls over her box of toys, flings its contents in handfuls in* ANNIE'S *direction, flings the box too, reels to her feet, rips curtains from the window, bangs and kicks at the door, sweeps objects off the mantelpiece and shelf, a little tornado incarnate, all destruction, until she comes upon her doll and, in the act of hurling it, freezes. Then she clutches it to herself, and in exhaustion sinks sobbing to the floor.* ANNIE *stands contemplating her, in some awe.*]

Two weeks.

[*She shakes her head, not without a touch of disgusted bewilderment.*]

What did I get into now?

[*The lights have been dimming throughout, and the garden house is lit only by moonlight now, with* ANNIE *lost in the patches of dark.*

KATE, *now hatless and coatless, enters the family room by the rear door, carrying a lamp.* KELLER, *also hatless, wanders si-*

The Miracle Worker 261

51 Discussion Why does Keller react so violently?

52 Discussion What does James mean?

53 Critical Thinking and Reading Earlier Keller asked Annie if she *liked* Helen; here Kate asks the same question. Why do you think she asks?

54 Literary Focus How is this moment a turning point in Annie's internal conflict?

multaneously around the back of the main house to where JAMES *has been waiting, in the rising moonlight, on the porch.*]

KELLER. I can't understand it. I had every intention of dismissing that girl, not setting her up like an empress.

JAMES. Yes, what's her secret, sir?

KELLER. Secret?

JAMES. [*Pleasantly*] That enables her to get anything she wants out of you? When I can't.

[JAMES *turns to go into the house, but* KELLER *grasps his wrist, twisting him half to his knees.* KATE *comes from the porch.*]

KELLER. [*Angrily*] She does *not* get anything she—

JAMES. [*In pain*] Don't—don't—

KATE. Captain.

KELLER. He's afraid.

[*He throws* JAMES *away from him, with contempt.*]

What *does* he want out of me?

JAMES. [*An outcry*] My God, don't you know?

[*He gazes from* KELLER *to* KATE.]

Everything you forgot, when you forgot my mother.

KELLER. What!

[JAMES *wheels into the house.* KELLER *takes a stride to the porch, to roar after him.*]

One thing that girl's secret is not, she doesn't fire one shot and disappear!

[KATE *stands rigid, and* KELLER *comes back to her.*]

Katie. Don't mind what he—

KATE. Captain, *I* am proud of you.

KELLER. For what?

262   Drama

KATE. For letting this girl have what she needs.

KELLER. Why can't my son be? He can't bear me, you'd think I treat him as hard as this girl does Helen—

[*He breaks off, as it dawns in him.*]

KATE. [*Gently*] Perhaps you do.

KELLER. But he has to learn some respect!

KATE. [*A pause, wryly*] Do you like the child?

[*She turns again to the porch, but pauses, reluctant.*]

How empty the house is, tonight.

[*After a moment she continues on in.* KELLER *stands moveless, as the moonlight dies on him.*

The distant belfry chimes toll, two o'clock, and with them, a moment later, comes the boy's voice on the wind, in a whisper.]

BOY'S VOICE. Annie. Annie.

[*In her patch of dark* ANNIE, *now in her nightgown, hurls a cup into a corner as though it were her grief, getting rid of its taste through her teeth.*]

ANNIE. No! No pity, I won't have it.

[*She comes to* HELEN, *prone on the floor.*]

On either of us.

[*She goes to her knees, but when she touches* HELEN'S *hand the child starts up awake, recoils, and scrambles away from her under the bed.* ANNIE *stares after her. She strikes her palm on the floor, with passion.*]

I *will* touch you!

[*She gets to her feet, and paces in a kind of anger around the bed, her hand in her hair, and confronting* HELEN *at each turn.*]

How, how? How do I—

[ANNIE *stops. Then she calls out urgently, loudly.*]

Percy! Percy!

[*She moves swiftly to the drapes, at left.*]

Percy, wake up!

[PERCY'S *voice comes in a thick sleepy mumble, unintelligible.*]

Get out of bed and come in here, I need you.

[ANNIE *darts away, finds and strikes a match, and touches it to the hanging lamp; the lights come up dimly in the room, and* PERCY *stands bare to the waist in torn overalls between the drapes, with eyes closed, swaying.* ANNIE *goes to him, pats his cheeks vigorously.*]

Percy. You awake?

PERCY. No'm.

ANNIE. How would you like to play a nice game?

PERCY. Whah?

ANNIE. With Helen. She's under the bed. Touch her hand.

[*She kneels* PERCY *down at the bed, thrusting his hand under it to contact* HELEN'S; HELEN *emits an animal sound and crawls to the opposite side, but commences sniffing.* ANNIE *rounds the bed with* PERCY *and thrusts his hand again at* HELEN; *this time* HELEN *clutches it, sniffs in recognition, and comes scrambling out after* PERCY, *to hug him with delight.* PERCY *alarmed struggles, and* HELEN'S *fingers go to his mouth.*]

PERCY. Lemme go. Lemme go—

[HELEN *fingers her own lips, as before, moving them in dumb imitation.*]

She tryin' talk. She gonna hit me—

ANNIE. [*Grimly*] She *can* talk. If she only knew, I'll show you how. She makes letters.

[*She opens* PERCY'S *other hand, and spells into it.*]

This one is C. C.

[*She hits his palm with it a couple of times, her eyes upon* HELEN *across him;* HELEN *gropes to feel what* PERCY'S *hand is doing, and when she encounters* ANNIE'S *she falls back from them.*]

She's mad at me now, though, she won't play. But she knows lots of letters. Here's another, A. C. a. C. a.

[*But she is watching* HELEN, *who comes groping, consumed with curiosity;* ANNIE *makes the letters in* PERCY'S *hand, and* HELEN *pokes to question what they are up to. Then* HELEN *snatches* PERCY'S *other hand, and quickly spells four letters into it.* ANNIE *follows them aloud.*]

C, a, k, e! She spells cake, she gets cake.

[*She is swiftly over to the tray of food, to fetch cake and a jug of milk.*]

She doesn't know yet it means this. Isn't it funny she knows how to spell it and doesn't *know* she knows?

[*She breaks the cake in two pieces, and extends one to each;* HELEN *rolls away from her offer.*]

Well, if she won't play it with me, I'll play it with you. Would you like to learn one she doesn't know?

PERCY. No'm.

[*But* ANNIE *seizes his wrist, and spells to him.*]

ANNIE. M, i, l, k. M is this. I, that's an easy one, just the little finger. L is this—

[*And* HELEN *comes back with her hand, to*

The Miracle Worker 263

55

55 Critical Thinking and Reading
Why do you think Annie starts playing with Percy? What strategy might she have in mind?

56 **Discussion** Why has Annie's strategy succeeded?

57 **Discussion** What does Annie mean by this statement?

58 **Discussion** Do you think Annie has a new understanding of love? Explain.

Reader's Response Try to imagine what life would be like if you were Helen. What do you think you would miss most? Why?

Thematic Response It is a victory for Annie to have Helen with no outside influences for two weeks; the first night, she wins Helen's need for her. Do you think that this victory will be lasting or temporary? Why?

Closure and Extension

ANSWERS TO RESPONDING TO THE SELECTION
Your Response

1. Discuss the concept of the "spoiled" person who knows the methods of manipulation to obtain a desired end. Ask students if this person really becomes what Annie calls "a tyrant" on whose whims the entire house turns. Have them discuss reasons for their answers.

Recalling

2. Her chief problem is how to discipline Helen without breaking her spirit. She will insist on reasonable obedience.

3. Annie hopes that by spelling the names of things into Helen's hand, she can teach Helen to connect the object with the name.

4. Annie is convinced she cannot teach Helen if she does not have complete control over her actions. She feels she cannot be successful in a place where Helen can go to family members for love and pity when things do not go her way.

feel the new word. ANNIE *brushes her away, and continues spelling aloud to* PERCY. HELEN'S *hand comes back again, and tries to get in;* ANNIE *brushes it away again.* HELEN'S *hand insists, and* ANNIE *puts it away rudely.*]

No, why should I talk to you? I'm teaching Percy a new word. L. K is this—

[HELEN *now yanks their hands apart; she butts* PERCY *away, and thrusts her palm out insistently.* ANNIE'S *eyes are bright, with glee.*]

Ho, you're *jealous,* are you!

[HELEN'S *hand waits, intractably waits.*]

All *right.*

[ANNIE *spells into it,* milk; *and* HELEN *after a moment spells it back to* ANNIE. ANNIE *takes her hand, with her whole face shining. She gives a great sigh.*]

56 Good! So I'm finally back to where I can touch you, hm? Touch and go! No love lost, but here we go.

[*She puts the jug of milk into* HELEN'S *hand and squeezes* PERCY'S *shoulder.*]

You can go to bed now, you've earned your sleep. Thank you.

[PERCY *stumbling up weaves his way out through the drapes.* HELEN *finishes drinking, and holds the jug out, for* ANNIE; *when* ANNIE *takes it,* HELEN *crawls onto the bed, and makes for sleep.* ANNIE *stands, looks down at her.*]

57 Now all I have to teach you is—one word. Everything.

[*She sets the jug down. On the floor now* ANNIE *spies the doll, stoops to pick it up, and with it dangling in her hand, turns off the lamp. A shaft of moonlight is left on* HELEN *in the bed, and a second shaft on the rocking chair; and* ANNIE, *after putting off her*

264   Drama

smoked glasses, sits in the rocker with the doll. She is rather happy, and dangles the doll on her knee, and it makes its momma sound.* ANNIE *whispers to it in mock solicitude.*]

Hush, little baby. Don't—say a word—

[*She lays it against her shoulder, and begins rocking with it, patting its diminutive behind; she talks the lullaby to it, humorously at first.*]

Momma's gonna buy you—a mockingbird: If that—mockingbird don't sing—

[*The rhythm of the rocking takes her into the tune, softly, and more tenderly.*]

Momma's gonna buy you a diamond ring: If that diamond ring turns to brass—

[*A third shaft of moonlight outside now rises to pick out* JAMES *at the main house, with one foot on the porch step; he turns his body, as if hearing the song.*]

Momma's gonna buy you a looking-glass: If that looking-glass gets broke—

[*In the family room a fourth shaft picks out* KELLER *seated at the table, in thought; and he, too, lifts his head, as if hearing.*]

Momma's gonna buy you a billy goat: If that billy goat won't pull—

[*The fifth shaft is upstairs in* ANNIE'S *room, and picks out* KATE, *pacing there; and she halts, turning her head, too, as if hearing.*]

Momma's gonna buy you a cart and bull: If that cart and bull turns over, Momma's gonna buy you a dog named Rover; If that dog named Rover won't bark—

[*With the shafts of moonlight on* HELEN, *and* JAMES, *and* KELLER, *and* KATE, *all moveless, and* ANNIE *rocking the doll, the curtain ends the act.*]

58

Interpreting

5. **Suggested Response:** While Annie and Kate are friends, they disagree about the treatment of Helen. Annie also has a conflict with James, who feels that her efforts will not be successful. Finally, Annie has a conflict with Keller, who finds it difficult to give up his role as decision-maker. Also, he feels that Annie is too harsh with Helen.

6. **Suggested Response:** Annie believes that Helen should be taught to sit quietly and eat from her own plate with her own utensils. Her parents have allowed her to help herself with her hands from anyone's plate. Keller says that giving Helen this freedom is the only way they can have any adult conversation at mealtime.

7. **Suggested Response:** The events of the play take place not very long after the Civil War.

Also, the Kellers are cousins of Robert E. Lee, the leader of the Southern forces during the war. Annie, as a Northerner seems like an outsider and James humorously compares her to General Grant. Annie's struggle to teach Helen is therefore associated with the Civil War.

8. **Suggested Response:** Annie's brother did not want her to go to school. He wanted her to take care of him "forever." When he

RESPONDING TO THE SELECTION

Your Response

1. Do you think Helen's parents have treated her with too much love and pity, as Annie believes? Explain your answer.

Recalling

2. According to the letter she is writing at the start of Act II, what is Annie's chief problem with Helen, and what will Annie insist on?
3. What is the idea behind the hand-spelling Annie uses with Helen?
4. Why does Annie want to live alone with Helen in the garden house?

Interpreting

5. Describe Annie's conflicts with other people.
6. Contrast the views of Annie and Helen's parents regarding Helen's behavior at meals.
7. Explain the connection between the references to Civil War battles and generals and the action of the play.
8. Summarize Annie's past as it is revealed in Act II and explain how it affects her work with Helen.
9. In her letter, Annie writes, ". . . obedience, is, the, gateway, through, which, knowledge, enters, the, mind, of, the, child—." Explain how the events of the play illustrate the truth of this statement.

Applying

10. What is the difference between authority and self-control? Explain why each is necessary for education.

ANALYZING LITERATURE

Understanding Conflict in Drama

Conflict, whether external or internal, is the essence, or heart, of drama. If you understand the basic conflict of a play and why it concludes as it does, you understand the play.

1. Describe the basic conflict of *The Miracle Worker.*

2. At this point in your reading, how do you think that the conflict will conclude? Give reasons for your opinion.
3. An underlying conflict in this play is that between James and Captain Keller. Describe this conflict.

CRITICAL THINKING AND READING

Recognizing Causes and Effects

A **cause** is an action, event, or situation that produces a result. An **effect** is the result produced by a cause. One way to understand a play or other kind of story is to analyze the chain of causes and effects that advances the plot. This means noticing how one event causes another event, which is the effect, and how that effect becomes the cause of yet another event, and so on to the end.

1. According to Annie, what is the cause of Helen's bad behavior?
2. In Act II, Annie picks up Helen's doll and throttles it. What is the cause of her anger?
3. By the end of the first two acts, what effect have Annie's efforts had on Helen?

THINKING AND WRITING

Writing a Scene

Extend Act II by writing a brief scene in which Annie, at the end of her lullaby, falls asleep and dreams. In this dream scene, characters from either her past or her present life would appear to her. The scene would end with Annie waking up.

Before you write, imagine the kind of dream Annie might have. Think of how it might express her activities, fears, or hopes. What characters would appear? What would they say or do?

When you have answered such questions as these, write the scene as it might appear in the printed version of the play, with dialogue and stage directions. When you revise, concentrate on improving the scene as an expression of Annie's hidden thoughts and feelings.

The Miracle Worker 265

---

2. Students' answers will differ. Most students will probably feel that once Annie has complete control over Helen, she may be able to teach her. Some may feel, however, that Annie will not be able to accomplish her goal in two weeks.
3. Suggested Response: James is angry at his father because he has remarried. James feels ignored and unloved. Keller resents James's attitude, feels he is weak, and treats him as if he were a child.

ANSWERS TO CRITICAL THINKING AND READING

1. Suggested Response: Annie feels that the family encourages Helen's bad table manners by giving in to any and all of her actions. She says, about this situation–"It's less trouble to feel sorry for her than to teach her anything better . . .".
2. Suggested Response: Annie is angry because Kate, rather than letting Annie discipline Helen, has given her a piece of candy, almost as a reward for her actions.
3. Suggested Response: By the end of this act, Helen will let Annie touch her again. Also, Helen has learned to spell words with finger language, but still does not connect the word to the thing. Finally, Helen has–once at least–eaten from her own plate and folded her napkin.

THINKING AND WRITING

Writing Transparency Students often find the use of a graphic organizer helpful in preparing for a writing assignment. Before students write, you may wish to show them the Story Map graphic organizer in the **Transparencies for Writing.**

---

died, Annie felt as if she let him down by telling him that she wanted to go to school. Her guilt about not being able to save her brother increases her determination to help Helen.

9. Suggested Response: Only when Annie makes Helen obey her at the breakfast table, can she begin to teach her to eat with a spoon and fold her napkin.

Applying

10. Students' answers will differ. Suggested Response: Authority is the right of someone in charge to determine goals and set limits. Self-control is a person's ability to perform these same functions for himself or herself. Without discipline and authority, no learning could take place at all. However, students who do not have inner discipline cannot learn on their own.

Challenge Have students prepare a brief summary of Annie's life up to the time she leaves for Alabama.

ANSWERS TO ANALYZING LITERATURE

1. Suggested Response: The basic conflict is Annie's struggle to reach and unlock the mind of Helen. To achieve this goal, Annie must battle against Helen herself and other members of her family.

Writing Across the Curriculum
Ask students to research and report on some of the Civil War references in the play—the battle of Vicksburg, Ulysses S. Grant, Stonewall Jackson, and Robert E. Lee. Consider informing the social studies department of this assignment, so that social studies teachers can provide guidance for students.

GUIDE FOR READING

Preparation

Literary Focus Sometimes themes are presented as direct and thoughtful statements. Sometimes they must be inferred. In this play, Annie's statement at the beginning of the act suggests the theme: "There's only one way out, for you, and it's language."

Prereading Focus The purpose of this brief exercise is to focus student attention on the difficulty of trying to make a connection between abstract symbols and some other knowledge. Helen must connect the letters of the alphabet to physical reality. Students will connect the letters of the cryptogram to the alphabet they know. Assist them by suggesting that they substitute words like *is, to,* and *the* to the smaller words in the cryptogram. Explain that solving cryptograms is a matter of trial and error. The answer to the cryptogram is "Language is the key to understanding."

Vocabulary Have your **less advanced** students read the words and their meanings several times. Then have them write a short paragraph about a real incident. They must write at least four sentences and use all the words in the list.

Spelling Tip Point out the silent *b* in *subtle.*

Electronic Handbook You might want students to use the Language Master 6000 to hear the pronunciation of *subtle.*

The Miracle Worker, Act III

Theme in Drama

The **theme** of a play is the central idea, or insight into life, that the play expresses. Since conflict is the heart of drama, understanding why the conflict of a play develops and concludes as it does brings you close to an understanding of the play's theme. Imagine, for example, that a young woman wants to be a dancer. She is told that she lacks talent. She does poorly at auditions. She suffers injuries in training. However, she keeps practicing and eventually joins a dance company. You could say that the triumph of discipline and effort over failure and discouragement is the theme of this story. Such a statement explains why the conflict is resolved as it is.

Focus

Without language, Helen Keller is trapped in a world where few of her experiences have meaning. In order to break out of this world, she must make the connection between the alphabet Annie Sullivan is teaching her and the objects that the spelled-out words represent. This is not an easy task. Suppose that you were to wake up one morning and discover that someone had changed the alphabet overnight. The letters no longer correspond to the sounds you had been taught. A message left on your bedside table reads:

KZMFTZFD HR SGD JDX SN TMCDQRSZMCHMF.

In order to read the message, you will have to find a connection between the sounds you know and new symbols for those sounds. Solving the puzzle will be easy if you can make a single breakthrough, as Helen Keller does in the final act of *The Miracle Worker.*

Vocabulary

Knowing the following words will help you as you read Act III of *The Miracle Worker.*

interminable (in tʉr′ mi nə b′l) *adj.*: Lasting or seeming to last forever (p. 267)

haggard (hag′ ərd) *adj.*: Worn, as from lack of sleep (p. 268)

painstakingly (pānz′ tā′ kiŋ lē) *adv.*: Acting very carefully (p. 271)

subtly (sut′ lē) *adv.*: In a delicately suggestive way (p. 274)

aversion (ə vʉr′ zhən) *n.*: Intense dislike (p. 278)

266   Drama

Objectives

1 To understand the theme of a play
2 To summarize a play
3 To write a review of a play

Support Material

Teaching Portfolio
Teacher Backup, p. 321
Grammar in Action Worksheet, *Using Direct Objects and Subject Complements,* p. 324
Usage and Mechanics Worksheet, p. 326
Vocabulary Check, p. 327
Critical Thinking and Reading Worksheet, *Summarizing a Play,* p. 328

Language Worksheet, *Recognizing the Prefix -dis,* p. 329
Selection Test, p. 330

Library of Video Classics
The Miracle Worker

Prentice Hall Literature Writing Studio

ACT III

[*The stage is totally dark, until we see* AN-NIE *and* HELEN *silhouetted on the bed in the garden house.* ANNIE'S *voice is audible, very patient, and worn; it has been saying this for a long time.*]

ANNIE. Water, Helen. This is water. W, a, t, e, r. It has a *name*.

[*A silence. Then:*]

Egg, e, g, g. It has a *name*, the name stands for the thing. Oh, it's so simple, simple as birth, to explain.

[*The lights have commenced to rise, not on the garden house but on the homestead. Then:*]

Helen, Helen, the chick *has* to come out of its shell, sometime. You come out, too.

[*In the bedroom upstairs, we see* VINEY *un-hurriedly washing the window, dusting, turning the mattress, readying the room for use again; then in the family room a dimin-ished group at one end of the table—*KATE, KELLER, JAMES*—finishing up a quiet break-fast; then outside, down right, the other Negro servant on his knees, assisted by* MARTHA, *working with a trowel around a new trellis and wheelbarrow. The scene is one of everyday calm, and all are oblivious to* ANNIE'S *voice.*]

There's only one way out, for you, and it's language. To learn that your fingers can talk. And say anything, anything you can name. This is mug. Mug, m, u, g. Helen, it has a *name*. It—has—a—*name*—

[KATE *rises from the table.*]

KELLER. [*Gently*] You haven't eaten, Katie.

KATE. [*Smiles, shakes her head*] I haven't the appetite. I'm too—restless, I can't sit to it.

KELLER. You should eat, my dear. It will be a long day, waiting.

JAMES. [*Lightly*] But it's been a short two weeks. I never thought life could be so—noiseless, went much too quickly for me.

[KATE *and* KELLER *gaze at him, in silence.* JAMES *becomes uncomfortable.*]

ANNIE. C, a, r, d. Card. C, a—

JAMES. Well, the house has been practically normal, hasn't it?

KELLER. [*Harshly*] Jimmie.

JAMES. Is it wrong to enjoy a quiet breakfast, after five years? And you two even seem to enjoy each other—

KELLER. It could be even more noiseless, Jimmie, without your tongue running every minute. Haven't you enough feeling to imag-ine what Katie has been undergoing, ever since—

[KATE *stops him, with her hand on his arm.*]

KATE. Captain.

[*To* JAMES]

It's true. The two weeks have been normal, quiet, all you say. But not short. Intermin-able.

[*She rises, and wanders out; she pauses on the porch steps, gazing toward the garden house.*]

ANNIE. [*Fading*] W, a, t, e, r. But it means *this*. W, a, t, e, r. *This*. W, a, t—

JAMES. I only meant that Miss Sullivan is a boon. Of contention, though, it seems.[1]

KELLER. [*Heavily*] If and when you're a par-ent, Jimmie, you will understand what sepa-ration means. A mother loses a—protector.

---

1. **a boon. Of contention:** A boon, or gift, but also a bone of contention—the subject of a dispute.

The Miracle Worker **267**

3 Discussion What does Keller mean? About whom is he talking?

4 Discussion What conflict seems to be ending?

JAMES. [*Baffled*] Hm?

KELLER. You'll learn, we don't just keep our children safe. They keep us safe.

[*He rises, with his empty coffee cup and saucer.*]

There are of course all kinds of separation, Katie has lived with one kind for five years. And another is disappointment. In a child.

[*He goes with the cup out the rear door.* JAMES *sits for a long moment of stillness. In the garden house the lights commence to come up;* ANNIE, *haggard at the table, is writing a letter, her face again almost in contact with the stationery;* HELEN, *apart on the stool, and for the first time as clean and neat as a button, is quietly crocheting an endless chain of wool, which snakes all around the room.*]

ANNIE. "I, feel, every, day, more, and, more, in—"

[*She pauses, and turns the pages of a dictionary open before her; her finger descends the words to a full stop. She elevates her eyebrows, then copies the word.*]

"—adequate."

[*In the main house* JAMES *pushes up, and goes to the front doorway, after* KATE.]

JAMES. Kate?

[KATE *turns her glance.* JAMES *is rather weary.*]

I'm sorry. Open my mouth, like that fairy tale, frogs jump out.

KATE. No. It has been better. For everyone.

[*She starts away, up center.*]

ANNIE. [*Writing*] "If, only, there, were, someone, to, help, me, I, need, a, teacher, as, much, as, Helen—

JAMES. Kate.

[KATE *halts, waits.*]

What does he want from me?

KATE. That's not the question. Stand up to the world, Jimmie, that comes first.

JAMES. [*A pause, wryly*] But the world is him.

KATE. Yes. And no one can do it for you.

JAMES. Kate.

[*His voice is humble.*]

At least we— Could you—be my friend?

KATE. I am.

[KATE *turns to wander, up back of the garden house.* ANNIE'S *murmur comes at once; the lights begin to die on the main house.*]

ANNIE. " my, mind, is, undisiplined, full, of, skips, and, jumps, and—"

[*She halts, rereads, frowns.*]

Hm.

[ANNIE *puts her nose again in the dictionary, flips back to an earlier page, and fingers down the words;* KATE *presently comes down toward the bay window with a trayful of food.*]

Disinter—disinterested—disjoin—dis—

[*She backtracks, indignant.*]

Disinterested, disjoin— Where's disipline?

[*She goes a page or two back, searching with her finger, muttering.*]

What a dictionary, have to know how to spell it before you can look up how to spell it, disciple, *discipline!* Diskipline.

[*She corrects the word in her letter.*]

Undisciplined.

[*But her eyes are bothering her, she closes them in exhaustion and gently fingers the* eyelids. KATE *watches her through the window.*]

KATE. What are you doing to your eyes?

[ANNIE *glances around; she puts her smoked glasses on, and gets up to come over, assuming a cheerful energy.*]

ANNIE. It's worse on my vanity! I'm learning to spell. It's like a surprise party, the most unexpected characters turn up.

KATE. You're not to overwork your eyes, Miss Annie.

ANNIE. Well.

[*She takes the tray, sets it on her chair, and carries chair and tray to* HELEN.]

Whatever I spell to Helen I'd better spell right.

KATE. [*Almost wistful*] How—serene she is.

ANNIE. She learned this stitch yesterday. Now I can't get her to stop!

[*She disentangles one foot from the wool chain, and sets the chair before* HELEN. HELEN, *at its contact with her knee feels the plate, promptly sets her crocheting down, and tucks the napkin in at her neck, but* ANNIE *withholds the spoon; when* HELEN *finds it missing, she folds her hands in her lap, and quietly waits.* ANNIE *twinkles at* KATE *with mock devoutness.*]

Such a little lady, she'd sooner starve than eat with her fingers.

[*She gives* HELEN *the spoon, and* HELEN *begins to eat, neatly.*]

KATE. You've taught her so much, these two weeks. I would never have—

ANNIE. Not enough.

[*She is suddenly gloomy, shakes her head.*]

Obedience isn't enough. Well, she learned

two nouns this morning, key and water, brings her up to eighteen nouns and three verbs.

KATE. [*Hesitant*] But—not—

ANNIE. No. Not that they mean things. It's still a finger-game, no meaning.

[*She turns to* KATE, *abruptly.*]

Mrs. Keller—

[*But she defers it; she comes back, to sit in the bay and lift her hand.*]

Shall we play our finger-game?

KATE. How will she learn it?

ANNIE. It will come.

[*She spells a word;* KATE *does not respond.*]

KATE. How?

ANNIE. [*A pause*] How does a bird learn to fly?

[*She spells again.*]

We're born to use words, like wings, it has to come.

KATE. How?

ANNIE. [*Another pause, wearily*] All right. I don't know how.

[*She pushes up her glasses, to rub her eyes.*]

I've done everything I could think of. Whatever she's learned here—keeping herself clean, knitting, stringing beads, meals, setting-up exercises each morning, we climb trees, hunt eggs, yesterday a chick was born in her hands all of it I spell, everything we do, we never stop spelling. I go to bed with—writer's cramp from talking so much!

KATE. I worry about you, Miss Annie. You must rest.

ANNIE. Now? She spells back in her *sleep*,

The Miracle Worker 269

5 **Discussion** On what other occasions has Annie displayed humor? How has her sense of humor helped her?

6 **Critical Thinking and Reading** Paraphrase Annie's reason for believing Helen will learn language.

7 **Critical Thinking and Reading** Why do you think Annie keeps spelling to Helen?

8 Discussion Why is Kate unwilling to give Annie more time with Helen?

her fingers make letters when she doesn't know! In her bones those five fingers know, that hand aches to—speak out, and something in her mind is asleep, how do I—nudge that awake? That's the one question.

KATE. With no answer.

ANNIE. [*Long pause*] Except keep at it. Like this.

[*She again begins spelling—I, need—and* KATE's *brows gather, following the words.*]

KATE. More—time?

[*She glances at* ANNIE, *who looks her in the eyes, silent.*]

Here?

ANNIE. Spell it.

[KATE *spells a word—no—shaking her head;* ANNIE *spells two words—why, not—back, with an impatient question in her eyes; and* KATE *moves her head in pain to answer it.*]

KATE. Because I can't—

8

270 *Drama*

270

ANNIE. Spell it! If she ever learns, you'll have a lot to tell each other, start now.

[KATE *painstakingly spells in air. In the midst of this the rear door opens, and* KELLER *enters with the setter* BELLE *in tow.*]

KELLER. Miss Sullivan? On my way to the office, I brought Helen a playmate—

ANNIE. Outside please, Captain Keller.

KELLER. My dear child, the two weeks are up today, surely you don't object to—

ANNIE. [*Rising*] They're not up till six o'clock.

KELLER. [*Indulgent*] Oh, now. What difference can a fraction of one day—

ANNIE. An agreement is an agreement. Now you've been very good, I'm sure you can keep it up for a few more hours.

[*She escorts* KELLER *by the arm over the threshold; he obeys, leaving* BELLE.]

KELLER. Miss Sullivan, you are a tyrant.

ANNIE. Likewise, I'm sure. You can stand there, and close the door if she comes.

KATE. I don't think you know how eager we are to have her back in our arms—

ANNIE. I do know, it's my main worry.

KELLER. It's like expecting a new child in the house. Well, she *is*, so—composed, so—

[*Gently*]

Attractive. You've done wonders for her, Miss Sullivan.

ANNIE. [*Not a question*] Have I.

KELLER. If there's anything you want from us in repayment tell us, it will be a privilege to—

ANNIE. I just told Mrs. Keller. I want more time.

KATE. Miss Annie—

ANNIE. Another week.

[HELEN *lifts her head, and begins to sniff.*]

KELLER. We miss the child. *I* miss her, I'm glad to say, that's a different debt I owe you—

ANNIE. Pay it to Helen. Give *her* another week.

KATE. [*Gently*] Doesn't she miss us?

KELLER. Of course she does. What a wrench this unexplainable—exile must be to her, can you say it's not?

ANNIE. No. But I—

[HELEN *is off the stool, to grope about the room; when she encounters* BELLE, *she throws her arms around the dog's neck in delight.*]

KATE. Doesn't she need affection too, Miss Annie?

ANNIE. [*Wavering*] She—never shows me she needs it, she won't have any—caressing or—

KATE. But you're not her mother.

KELLER. And what would another week accomplish? We are more than satisfied, you've done more than we ever thought possible, taught her constructive—

ANNIE. I can't promise anything. All I can—

KELLER. [*No break*] —things to do, to behave like—even look like—a human child, so manageable, contented, cleaner, more—

ANNIE. [*Withering*] Cleaner.

KELLER. Well. We say cleanliness is next to godliness, Miss—

ANNIE. Cleanliness is next to nothing, she has to learn that everything has its name! That words can be her *eyes*, to everything in the world outside her, and inside too, what is she without words? With them she can

The Miracle Worker 271

9 **Discussion** Why does Annie insist Kate do finger spelling?

10 **Discussion** Why is this a worry to Annie?

11 **Discussion** Why do you think that Helen does not show physical affection for Annie?

12 **Discussion** Compare Annie's and Keller's feelings about what has been accomplished in two weeks. Which one is satisfied?

13 **Reading Strategy** Ask students to predict whether Annie's fears will be borne out.

14 **Discussion** How does Keller feel about Annie's hopes for Helen?

15 **Discussion** What does Keller imply when he asks, "Is the opposite true, for you?"

16 **Discussion** Why does Annie, who is normally so combative, surrender in this case?

Speaking and Listening You might want to have student volunteers read aloud the final portion of Act III from the point when the entire family is silent because they notice that Helen has begun to test them. Here, all the conflicts—both internal and external—are finally confronted and resolved. If you wish, individual students may read the parts of Aunt Ev, Helen, Annie, Kate, Keller, Jimmy, and the narrator who will read stage directions.

think, have ideas, be reached, there's not a thought or fact in the world that can't be hers. You publish a newspaper, Captain Keller, do I have to tell you what words are? And she has them already—

KELLER. Miss Sullivan.

ANNIE. —eighteen nouns and three verbs, they're in her fingers now, I need only time to push *one* of them into her mind! One, and everything under the sun will follow. Don't you see what she's learned here is only clearing the way for that? I can't risk her unlearning it, give me more time alone with her, another week to—

KELLER. Look.

[*He points, and* ANNIE *turns.* HELEN *is playing with* BELLE'S *claws; she makes letters with her fingers, shows them to* DELLE, *waits with her palm, then manipulates the dog's claws.*]

What is she spelling?

[*A silence.*]

KATE. Water?

[ANNIE *nods.*]

KELLER. Teaching a dog to spell.

[*A pause*]

The dog doesn't know what she means, any more than she knows what you mean, Miss Sullivan. I think you ask too much, of her and yourself. God may not have meant Helen to have the—eyes you speak of.

ANNIE. [*Toneless*] I mean her to.

KELLER. [*Curiously*] What is it to you?

[ANNIE'S *head comes slowly up.*]

You make us see how we indulge her for our sake. Is the opposite true, for you?

ANNIE. [*Then*] Half a week?

KELLER. An agreement is an agreement.

ANNIE. Mrs. Keller?

KATE. [*Simply*] I want her back.

[*A wait;* ANNIE *then lets her hands drop in surrender, and nods.*]

KELLER. I'll send Viney over to help you pack.

ANNIE. Not until six o'clock. I have her till six o'clock.

KELLER. [*Consenting*] Six o'clock. Come, Katie.

[KATE *leaving the window joins him around back, while* KELLER *closes the door; they are shut out.*

Only the garden house is daylit now, and the light on it is narrowing down. ANNIE *stands watching* HELEN *work* BELLE'S *claws. Then she settles beside them on her knees, and stops* HELEN'S *hand.*]

ANNIE. [*Gently*] No.

[*She shakes her head, with* HELEN'S *hand to her face, then spells.*]

Dog, D, o, g. Dog.

[*She touches* HELEN'S *hand to* BELLE. HELEN *dutifully pats the dog's head, and resumes spelling to its paw.*]

Not water.

[ANNIE *rolls to her feet, brings a tumbler of water back from the tray, and kneels with it, to seize* HELEN'S *hand and spell.*]

Here. Water. *Water.*

[*She thrusts* HELEN'S *hand into the tumbler.* HELEN *lifts her hand out dripping, wipes it daintily on* BELLE'S *hide, and taking the tumbler from* ANNIE, *endeavors to thrust* BELLE'S *paw into it.* ANNIE *sits watching, wearily.*]

I don't know how to tell you. Not a soul in the world knows how to tell you. Helen, Helen.

[*She bends in compassion to touch her lips to* HELEN'S *temple, and instantly* HELEN *pauses, her hands off the dog, her head slightly averted. The lights are still narrowing, and* BELLE *slinks off. After a moment* ANNIE *sits back.*]

Yes, what's it to me? They're satisfied. Give them back their child and dog, both housebroken, everyone's satisfied. But me, and you.

[HELEN'S *hand comes out into the light, groping.*]

Reach. *Reach!*

[ANNIE *extending her own hand grips* HELEN'S; *the two hands are clasped, tense in the light, the rest of the room changing in shadow.*]

I wanted to teach you—oh, everything the earth is full of, Helen, everything on it that's ours for a wink and it's gone, and what we are on it, the—light we bring to it and leave behind in—words, why, you can see five thousand years back in a light of words, everything we feel, think, know—and share, in words, so not a soul is in darkness, or done with, even in the grave. And I know, I *know*, one word and I can—put the world in your hand—and whatever it is to me, I won't take less! How, how, how do I tell you that *this*—

[*She spells.*]

—means a *word*, and the word means this *thing*, wool?

[*She thrusts the wool at* HELEN'S *hand;* HELEN *sits, puzzled.* ANNIE *puts the crocheting aside.*]

Or this—s, t, o, o, l—means this *thing*, stool?

[*She claps* HELEN'S *palm to the stool.* HELEN *waits, uncomprehending.* ANNIE *snatches up her napkin, spells:*]

Napkin!

[*She forces it on* HELEN'S *hand, waits, discards it, lifts a fold of the child's dress, spells.*]

Dress!

[*She lets it drop, spells.*]

F, a, c, e, face!

[*She draws* HELEN'S *hand to her cheek, and pressing it there, staring into the child's responseless eyes, hears the distant belfry begin to toll, slowly: one, two, three, four, five, six.*]

On the third stroke the lights stealing in around the garden house show us figures waiting: VINEY, *the other servant,* MARTHA, PERCY *at the drapes, and* JAMES *on the dim porch.* ANNIE *and* HELEN *remain, frozen. The chimes die away. Silently* PERCY *moves the drape-rod back out of sight;* VINEY *steps into the room—not using the door—and unmakes the bed; the other servant brings the wheelbarrow over, leaves it handy, rolls the bed off;* VINEY *puts the bed linens on top of a waiting boxful of* HELEN'S *toys, and loads the box on the wheelbarrow;* MARTHA *and* PERCY *take out the chairs, with the trayful, then the table; and* JAMES, *coming down and into the room, lifts* ANNIE'S *suitcase from its corner.* VINEY *and the other servant load the remaining odds and ends on the wheelbarrow, and the servant wheels it off.* VINEY *and the children departing leave only* JAMES *in the room with* ANNIE *and* HELEN. JAMES *studies the two of them, without mockery, and then, quietly going to the door and opening it, bears the suitcase out, and housewards. He leaves the door open.*

17 Literary Focus How does this speech relate to the play's theme?

18 Discussion Compare this action with the move into the garden house. What feelings does the move back to the main house call up?

The Miracle Worker 273

19 Discussion Compare Helen's display of affection for her mother with Annie's statement about Helen's need on page 271.

20 Discussion How do these voices from the past sum up Annie's inner conflict?

21 Discussion Why is Keller pleased while Annie is not?

KATE *steps into the doorway, and stands.* ANNIE *lifting her gaze from* HELEN *sees her; she takes* HELEN'S *hand from her cheek, and returns it to the child's own, stroking it there twice, in her mother-sign, before spelling slowly into it:*]

M, o, t, h, e, r. Mother.

[HELEN *with her hand free strokes her cheek, suddenly forlorn.* ANNIE *takes her hand again.*]

M, o, t, h—

[*But* KATE *is trembling with such impatience that her voice breaks from her, harsh.*]

KATE. Let her *come!*

[ANNIE *lifts* HELEN *to her feet, with a turn, and gives her a little push. Now* HELEN *begins groping, sensing something, trembling herself; and* KATE *falling one step in onto her knees clasps her, kissing her.* HELEN *clutches her, tight as she can.* KATE *is inarticulate, choked, repeating* HELEN'S *name again and again. She wheels with her in her arms, to stumble away out the doorway;* ANNIE *stands unmoving, while* KATE *in a blind walk carries* HELEN *like a baby behind the main house, out of view.*

ANNIE *is now alone on the stage. She turns, gazing around at the stripped room, bidding it silently farewell, impassively, like a defeated general on the deserted battlefield. All that remains is a stand with a basin of water; and here* ANNIE *takes up an eyecup, bathes each of her eyes, empties the eyecup, drops it in her purse, and tiredly locates her smoked glasses on the floor. The lights alter subtly; in the act of putting on her glasses* ANNIE *hears something that stops her, with head lifted. We hear it too, the voices out of the past, including her own now, in a whisper:*]

274 Drama

BOY'S VOICE. You said we'd be together, forever— You promised, forever and—*Annie!*

ANAGNOS' VOICE. But that battle is dead and done with, why not let it stay buried?

ANNIE'S VOICE. [*Whispering*] I think God must owe me a resurrection.

ANAGNOS' VOICE. What?

[*A pause, and* ANNIE *answers it herself, heavily.*]

ANNIE. And I owe God one.

BOY'S VOICE. Forever and ever—

[ANNIE *shakes her head.*]

—forever, and ever, and—

[ANNIE *covers her ears.*]

—forever, and ever, and ever—

[*It pursues* ANNIE; *she flees to snatch up her purse, wheels to the doorway, and* KELLER *is standing in it. The lights have lost their special color.*]

KELLER. Miss—Annie.

[*He has an envelope in his fingers.*]

I've been waiting to give you this.

ANNIE. [*After a breath*] What?

KELLER. Your first month's salary.

[*He puts it in her hand.*]

With many more to come, I trust. It doesn't express what we feel, it doesn't pay our debt. For what you've done.

ANNIE. What have I done?

KELLER. Taken a wild thing, and given us back a child.

ANNIE. [*Presently*] I taught her one thing, no. Don't do this, don't do that—

Grammar in Action

A **complement** is word or a group of words that completes the meaning of the predicate of a sentence. There are two broad kinds of complements. Direct objects complete the meaning of sentences with action verbs. Predicate nominatives or predicate adjectives complete the meaning of sentences with linking verbs.

The driver raced his *engine.* (direct object of the action verb *raced*)

Our team was the *winner.* (predicate nominative after the linking verb *was*)

The speech team has usually been *victorious.* (predicate adjective after the linking verb *has been*)

Writers use many different complements to complete basic sentence patterns. The following sentences from *The Miracle Worker* illustrate a variety of complements:

KELLER. It's more than all of us could, in all the years we—

ANNIE. I wanted to teach her what language is. I wanted to teach her yes.

KELLER. You will have time.

ANNIE. I don't know how. I know without it to do nothing but obey is—no gift, obedience without understanding is a—blindness, too. Is that all I've wished on her?

KELLER. [*Gently*] No, no—

ANNIE. Maybe. I don't know what else to do. Simply go on, keep doing what I've done, and have—faith that inside she's— That inside it's waiting. Like water, underground. All I can do is keep on.

KELLER. It's enough. For us.

ANNIE. You can help, Captain Keller.

KELLER. How?

ANNIE. Even learning no has been at a cost. Of much trouble and pain. Don't undo it.

KELLER. Why should we wish to—

ANNIE. [*Abruptly*] The world isn't an easy place for anyone, I don't want her just to obey but to let her have her way in everything is a lie, to *her*, I can't—

[*Her eyes fill, it takes her by surprise, and she laughs through it.*]

And I don't even love her, she's not my child! Well. You've got to stand between that lie and her.

KELLER. We'll try.

ANNIE. Because *I* will. As long as you let me stay, that's one promise I'll keep.

KELLER. Agreed. We've learned something too, I hope.

[*A pause*]

Won't you come now, to supper?

ANNIE. Yes.

[*She wags the envelope, ruefully.*]

Why doesn't God pay His debts each month?

KELLER. I beg your pardon?

ANNIE. Nothing. I used to wonder how I could—

[*The lights are fading on them, simultaneously rising on the family room of the main house, where* VINEY *is polishing glassware at the table set for dinner.*]

—earn a living.

KELLER. Oh, you do.

ANNIE. I really do. Now the question is, can I survive it!

[KELLER *smiles, offers his arm.*]

KELLER. May I?

[ANNIE *takes it, and the lights lose them as he escorts her out.*

Now in the family room the rear door opens, and HELEN *steps in. She stands a moment, then sniffs in one deep grateful breath, and her hands go out vigorously to familiar things, over the door panels, and to the chairs around the table, and over the silverware on the table, until she mets* VINEY; *she pats her flank approvingly.*]

VINEY. Oh, we glad to have you back too, prob'ly.

[HELEN *hurries groping to the front door, opens and closes it, removes its key, opens and closes it again to be sure it is unlocked, gropes back to the rear door and repeats the procedure, removing its key and hugging herself gleefully.*]

AUNT EV *is next in by the rear door, with a relish tray; she bends to kiss* HELEN's *cheek.*]

The Miracle Worker 275

22 Discussion What does Annie think is "waiting" inside Helen?

23 Reading Strategy Have students predict whether Keller will keep his promise.

24 Discussion At what other time has a key been an important prop? How is the key also a symbol?

Electronic Handbook You might wish to have students review direct and indirect objects and subject complements before they complete Grammar in Action activities. If students have access to Language Master 6000, have them enter the access words *direct* and *linking* and press the GRAMMAR key to obtain information on direct and indirect objects and subject complements.

Annie is now *alone* on the stage. She turns, gazing around at the stripped room. . . . All that remains is a *stand* with a basin of water; and here Annie takes up an *eyecup*, bathes *each* of her eyes, empties the *eyecup*, drops *it* in her purse, and tiredly locates her smoked *glasses* on the floor.

Alone is a predicate adjective; *stand* is a predicate nominative; and the other italicized words are direct objects. Notice that each complement answers the question *what?* after the verb.

Student Activity 1. Find the verb to which each complement in the passage belongs. Identify it as an action verb or a linking verb.

Student Activity 2. Write six sentences describing an important scene in a real or imaginary play. Use different types of complements in your sentences.

25 Discussion What do James' action and words signify?

26 Discussion Why does James mention this particular story from the Bible when saying grace?

HELEN *finds* KATE *behind her, and thrusts the keys at her.*]

KATE. What? Oh.

[*To* EV]

Keys.

[*She pockets them, lets* HELEN *feel them.*]

Yes, *I'll* keep the keys. I think we've had enough of locked doors, too.

[JAMES, *having earlier put* ANNIE'S *suitcase inside her door upstairs and taken himself out of view around the corner, now reappears and comes down the stairs as* ANNIE *and* KELLER *mount the porch steps. Following them into the family room, he pats* ANNIE'S *hair in passing, rather to her surprise.*]

JAMES. Evening, general.

[*He takes his own chair opposite.*

VINEY *bears the empty water pitcher out to the porch. The remaining suggestion of garden house is gone now, and the water pump is unobstructed;* VINEY *pumps water into the pitcher.*

KATE *surveying the table breaks the silence.*]

KATE. Will you say grace, Jimmie?

[*They bow their heads, except for* HELEN, *who palms her empty plate and then reaches to be sure her mother is there.* JAMES *considers a moment, glances across at* ANNIE, *lowers his head again, and obliges.*]

JAMES. [*Lightly*] And Jacob was left alone, and wrestled with an angel until the breaking of the day; and the hollow of Jacob's thigh was out of joint, as he wrestled with him; and the angel said, Let me go, for the day breaketh. And Jacob said, I will not let thee go, except thou bless me. Amen.

276 *Drama*

[ANNIE *has lifted her eyes suspiciously at* JAMES, *who winks expressionlessly and inclines his head to* HELEN.]

Oh, you angel.

[*The others lift their faces;* VINEY *returns with the pitcher, setting it down near* KATE, *then goes out the rear door; and* ANNIE *puts a napkin around* HELEN.]

AUNT EV. That's a very strange grace, James.

KELLER. Will you start the muffins, Ev?

JAMES. It's from the Good Book, isn't it?

AUNT EV. [*Passing a plate*] Well, of course it is. Didn't you know?

JAMES. Yes, I knew.

KELLER. [*Serving*] Ham, Miss Annie?

ANNIE. Please.

AUNT EV. Then why ask?

JAMES. I meant it *is* from the Good Book, and therefore a fitting grace.

AUNT EV. Well. I don't know about *that.*

KATE. [*With the pitcher*] Miss Annie?

ANNIE. Thank you.

AUNT EV. There's an awful *lot* of things in the Good Book that I wouldn't care to hear just before eating.

[*When* ANNIE *reaches for the pitcher,* HELEN *removes her napkin and drops it to the floor.* ANNIE *is filling* HELEN'S *glass when she notices it; she considers* HELEN'S *bland expression a moment, then bends, retrieves it, and tucks it around* HELEN'S *neck again.*]

JAMES. Well, fitting in the sense that Jacob's thigh was out of joint, and so is this piggie's.

AUNT EV. I declare, James—

KATE. Pickles, Aunt Ev?

AUNT EV. Oh, I should say so, you know my opinion of your pickles—

KATE. This is the end of them, I'm afraid. I didn't put up nearly enough last summer, this year I intend to—

[*She interrupts herself, seeing* HELEN *deliberately lift off her napkin and drop it again to the floor. She bends to retrieve it, but* ANNIE *stops her arm.*]

KELLER. [*Not noticing*] Reverend looked in at the office today to complain his hens have stopped laying. Poor fellow, *he* was out of joint, all he could—

[*He stops too, to frown down the table at* KATE, HELEN, *and* ANNIE *in turn, all suspended in midmotion.*]

JAMES. [*Not noticing*] I've always suspected those hens.

AUNT EV. Of what?

JAMES. I think they're Papist. Has he tried—

[*He stops, too, following* KELLER's *eyes.* ANNIE *now stops to pick the napkin up.*]

AUNT EV. James, now you're pulling my—lower extremity, the first thing you know we'll be—

[*She stops, too, hearing herself in the silence.* ANNIE, *with everyone now watching, for the third time puts the napkin on* HELEN. HELEN *yanks it off, and throws it down.* ANNIE *rises, lifts* HELEN's *plate, and bears it away.* HELEN, *feeling it gone, slides down and commences to kick up under the table; the dishes jump.* ANNIE *contemplates this for a moment, then coming back takes* HELEN's *wrists firmly and swings her off the chair.* HELEN *struggling gets one hand free, and catches at her mother's skirt; when* KATE *takes her by the shoulders,* HELEN *hangs quiet.*]

KATE. Miss Annie.

ANNIE. No.

KATE. [*A pause*] It's a very special day.

ANNIE. [*Grimly*] It will be, when I give in to that.

[*She tries to disengage* HELEN's *hand;* KATE *lays hers on* ANNIE's.]

KATE. Please. I've hardly had a chance to welcome her home—

ANNIE. Captain Keller.

KELLER. [*Embarrassed*] Oh. Katie, we—had a little talk, Miss Annie feels that if we indulge Helen in these—

AUNT EV. But what's the child done?

ANNIE. She's learned not to throw things on the floor and kick. It took us the best part of two weeks and—

AUNT EV. But only a napkin, it's not as if it were breakable!

ANNIE. And everything she's learned *is*? Mrs. Keller, I don't think we should—play tug-of-war for her, either give her to me or you keep her from kicking.

KATE. What do you wish to do?

ANNIE. Let me take her from the table.

AUNT EV. Oh, let her stay, my goodness, she's only a child, she doesn't have to wear a napkin if she doesn't want to her first evening—

ANNIE. [*Level*] And ask outsiders not to interfere.

AUNT EV. [*Astonished*] Out—outsi— I'm the child's *aunt!*

KATE. [*Distressed*] Will once hurt so much, Miss Annie? I've—made all Helen's favorite foods, tonight.

[*A pause*]

KELLER. [*Gently*] It's a homecoming party, Miss Annie.

The Miracle Worker 277

27 Discussion What does each person slowly realize is happening?

28 Literary Focus How does the old conflict resurface?

29 **Discussion** What does James mean as he repeats his statement?

30 **Discussion** Have students infer what Kate must be thinking as she tells Annie to take Helen.

30

[ANNIE *after a moment releases* HELEN. *But she cannot accept it, at her own chair she shakes her head and turns back, intent on* KATE.]

ANNIE. She's testing you. You realize?

JAMES. [*To Annie*] She's testing you.

KELLER. Jimmie, be quiet.

[JAMES *sits, tense.*]

Now she's home, naturally she—

ANNIE. And wants to see what will happen. At your hands. I said it was my main worry, is this what you promised me not half an hour ago?

KELLER. [*Reasonably*] But she's *not* kicking, now—

ANNIE. And not learning not to. Mrs. Keller, teaching her is bound to be painful, to everyone. I know it hurts to watch, but she'll live up to just what you demand of her, and no more.

29 | **JAMES.** [*Palely*] She's testing *you.*

KELLER. [*Testily*] Jimmie.

JAMES. I have an opinion, I think I should—

KELLER. No one's interested in hearing your opinion.

ANNIE. *I'm* interested, of course she's testing me. Let me keep her to what she's learned and she'll go on learning from me. Take her out of my hands and it all comes apart.

[KATE *closes her eyes, digesting it;* ANNIE *sits again, with a brief comment for her.*]

Be bountiful, it's at her expense.

[*She turns to* JAMES, *flatly.*]

Please pass me more of—her favorite foods.

[*Then* KATE *lifts* HELEN'S *hand, and turning*

her toward ANNIE, *surrenders her;* HELEN *makes for her own chair.*]

KATE. [*Low*] Take her, Miss Annie.

ANNIE. [*Then*] Thank you.

[*But the moment* ANNIE *rising reaches for her hand,* HELEN *begins to fight and kick, clutching to the tablecloth, and uttering laments.* ANNIE *again tries to loosen her hand, and* KELLER *rises.*]

KELLER. [*Tolerant*] I'm afraid you're the difficulty, Miss Annie. Now I'll keep her to what she's learned, you're quite right there—

[*He takes* HELEN'S *hands from* ANNIE, *pats them;* HELEN *quiets down.*]

—but I don't see that we need send her from the table, after all, she's the guest of honor. Bring her plate back.

ANNIE. If she was a seeing child, none of you would tolerate one—

KELLER. Well, she's not, I think some compromise is called for. Bring her plate, please.

[ANNIE'S *jaw sets, but she restores the plate, while* KELLER *fastens the napkin around* HELEN'S *neck; she permits it.*]

There. It's not unnatural, most of us take some aversion to our teachers, and occasionally another hand can smooth things out.

[*He puts a fork in* HELEN'S *hand;* HELEN *takes it. Genially*]

Now. Shall we start all over?

[*He goes back around the table, and sits.* ANNIE *stands watching.* HELEN *is motionless, thinking things through, until with a wicked glee she deliberately flings the fork on the floor. After another moment she plunges her hand into her food, and crams a fistful into her mouth.*]

278 *Drama*

JAMES. [*Wearily*] I think we've started all over—

[KELLER *shoots a glare at him, as* HELEN *plunges her other hand into* ANNIE's *plate.* ANNIE *at once moves in, to grasp her wrist, and* HELEN *flinging out a hand encounters the pitcher; she swings with it at* ANNIE; AN-NIE *falling back blocks it with an elbow, but the water flies over her dress.* ANNIE *gets her breath, then snatches the pitcher away in one hand, hoists* HELEN *up bodily under the other arm, and starts to carry her out, kicking.* KELLER *stands.*]

ANNIE. [*Savagely polite*] Don't get up!

KELLER. Where are you going?

ANNIE. Don't smooth anything else out for me, don't interfere in any way! I treat her like a seeing child because I *ask* her to see, I *expect* her to see, don't undo what I do!

KELLER. Where are you taking her?

ANNIE. To make her fill this pitcher again!

[*She thrusts out with* HELEN *under her arm, but* HELEN *escapes up the stairs and* ANNIE *runs after her.* KELLER *stands rigid.* AUNT EV *is astounded.*]

AUNT EV. You let her speak to you like that, Arthur? A creature who *works* for you?

KELLER. [*Angrily*] No. I don't.

[*He is starting after* ANNIE *when* JAMES, *on his feet with shaky resolve, interposes his chair between them in* KELLER's *path.*]

JAMES. Let her go.

KELLER. What!

JAMES. [*A swallow*] I said—let her go. She's right.

(KELLER *glares at the chair and him.* JAMES *takes a deep breath, then headlong:*]

She's right, Kate's right, I'm right, and you're wrong. If you drive her away from here it will be over my dead—chair, has it never occurred to you that on one occasion you might be consummately wrong?

[KELLER's *stare is unbelieving, even a little fascinated.* KATE *rises in trepidation, to mediate.*]

KATE. Captain.

[KELLER *stops her with his raised hand; his eyes stay on* JAMES's *pale face, for a long hold. When he finally finds his voice, it is gruff.*]

KELLER. Sit down, everyone.

[*He sits.* KATE *sits.* JAMES *holds onto his chair.* KELLER *speaks mildly.*]

Please sit down, Jimmie.

[JAMES *sits, and a moveless silence prevails;* KELLER's *eyes do not leave him.*

ANNIE *has pulled* HELEN *downstairs again by one hand, the pitcher in her other hand, down the porch steps, and across the yard to the pump. She puts* HELEN's *hand on the pump handle, grimly.*]

ANNIE. All right. Pump.

[HELEN *touches her cheek, waits uncertainly.*]

No, she's not here. Pump!

[*She forces* HELEN's *hand to work the handle, then lets go. And* HELEN *obeys. She pumps till the water comes, then* ANNIE *puts the pitcher in her other hand and guides it under the spout, and the water tumbling half into and half around the pitcher douses* HELEN's *hand.* ANNIE *takes over the handle to keep water coming, and does automatically what she has done so many times before, spells into* HELEN's *free palm:*]

The Miracle Worker 279

31 **Discussion** Both Keller and James have used the term *start all over.* Does each mean the same thing? Explain.

32 **Discussion** Why is Aunt Ev shocked?

31

32

Water. W, a, t, e, r. *Water*. It has a—*name*—

[*And now the miracle happens.* HELEN *drops the pitcher on the slab under the spout, it shatters. She stands transfixed.* ANNIE *freezes on the pump handle: there is a change in the sundown light, and with it a change in* HELEN'S *face, some light coming into it we have never seen there, some struggle in the depths behind it; and her lips tremble, trying to remember something the muscles around them once knew, till at last it finds its way out, painfully, a baby sound buried under the debris of years of dumbness.*]

HELEN. Wah. Wah.

[*And again, with great effort*]

Wah. Wah.

[HELEN *plunges her hand into the dwindling water, spells into her own palm. Then she gropes frantically,* ANNIE *reaches for her hand, and* HELEN *spells into* ANNIE'S *hand.*]

ANNIE. [*Whispering*] Yes.

[HELEN *spells into it again.*]

Yes!

[HELEN *grabs at the handle, pumps for more water, plunges her hand into its spurt and grabs* ANNIE'S *to spell it again.*]

Yes! Oh, my dear—

[*She falls to her knees to clasp* HELEN'S *hand, but* HELEN *pulls it free, stands almost bewildered, then drops to the ground, pats it swiftly, holds up her palm, imperious.* ANNIE *spells into it:*]

Commentary

Helen Keller learned to talk when she was ten years old. When Helen attended Radcliffe College, Annie translated the lectures in her hand. Helen graduated with honors.

Annie Sullivan married—and later divorced—John Macy, a literary critic who helped Helen write *The Story of My Life,* which was published in 1902.

Helen Keller became a famous public figure. She lectured around the world and knew personally many world leaders. Annie Sullivan translated everything that happened around, or was said to, Helen. The two women were constant companions until Annie Sullivan's death in 1936.

Ground.

[HELEN *spells it back.*]

Yes!

[HELEN *whirls to the pump, pats it, holds up her palm, and* ANNIE *spells into it.*]

Pump.

[HELEN *spells it back.*]

Yes! Yes!

34 [*Now* HELEN *is in such an excitement she is possessed, wild, trembling, cannot be still, turns, runs, falls on the porch steps, claps it, reaches out her palm, and* ANNIE *is at it instantly to spell:*]

Step.

[HELEN *has no time to spell back now, she whirls groping, to touch anything, encounters the trellis, shakes it, thrusts out her palm, and* ANNIE *while spelling to her cries wildly at the house.*]

Trellis. Mrs. Keller! *Mrs. Keller!*

35 [*Inside,* KATE *starts to her feet.* HELEN *scrambles back onto the porch, groping, and finds the bell string, tugs it; the bell rings, the distant chimes begin tolling the hour, all the bells in town seem to break into speech while* HELEN *reaches out and* ANNIE *spells feverishly into her hand.* KATE *hurries out, with* KELLER *after her;* AUNT EV *is on her feet, to peer out the window; only* JAMES *remains at the table, and with a napkin wipes his damp brow. From up right and left the servants—*VINEY, *the two Negro children, the other servant—run in, and stand watching from a distance as* HELEN, *ringing the bell, with her other hand encounters her mother's skirt; when she throws a hand out,* ANNIE *spells into it:*]

Mother.

[KELLER *now seizes* HELEN's *hand, she tou-* ches him, gestures a hand, and ANNIE *again spells:*]

Papa—She *knows!*

[KATE *and* KELLER *go to their knees, stammering, clutching* HELEN *to them, and* ANNIE *steps unsteadily back to watch the threesome,* HELEN *spelling wildly into* KATE's *hand, then into* KELLER's, KATE *spelling back into* HELEN's; *they cannot keep their hands off her, and rock her in their clasp.*] 36

34 **Enrichment** Most of us might find it hard to imagine Helen's excitement. But ask students to think back to a time in their lives when they found the key to understanding a math process or a science experiment—when suddenly it was all so clear.

35 **Clarification** Helen cannot hear the bell, but its clamor proclaims her understanding.

36 **Discussion** What do you think Kate and Keller are feeling as Helen uses language for the first time?

Discussion How does this scene signal a resolution of the main conflict?

Discussion The symbolism of the keys has become apparent. Why does Helen give the keys to Annie? How are the keys related to a theme of the play?

39 Discussion How does the silence relate to the resolution of Annie's inner conflict?

40 Discussion How does the action here summarize the end of the conflicts within the family? How is everyone now able to see more clearly?

◖◗ Videocassette You might wish to show the final portion of *The Miracle Worker* videocassette from the Prentice Hall **Library of Video Classics** after students have read the scene.

Reader's Response How did you feel after reading this play? Explain.

Thematic Response What was Helen's awakening in this act?

Then HELEN *gropes, feels nothing, turns all around, pulls free, and comes with both hands groping, to find* ANNIE. *She encounters* ANNIE'S *thighs,* ANNIE *kneels to her,* HELEN'S *hand pats* ANNIE'S *cheek impatiently, points a finger, and waits; and* ANNIE *spells into it:*]

37 Teacher.

[HELEN *spells it back, slowly;* ANNIE *nods.*]

Teacher.

[*She holds* HELEN'S *hand to her cheek. Presently* HELEN *withdraws it, not jerkily, only with reserve, and retreats a step. She stands thinking it over, then turns again and stumbles back to her parents. They try to embrace her, but she has something else in mind, it is to get the keys, and she hits* KATE'S *pocket until* KATE *digs them out for her.*

ANNIE *with her own load of emotion has retreated, her back turned, toward the pump, to sit;* KATE *moves to* HELEN, *touches her hand questioningly, and* HELEN *spells a word to her.* KATE *comprehends it, their first act of verbal communication, and she can hardly utter the word aloud, in wonder, gratitude, and deprivation; it is a moment in which she simultaneously finds and loses a child.*]

KATE. Teacher?

[ANNIE *turns; and* KATE, *facing* HELEN *in her direction by the shoulders, holds her back, holds her back, and then relinquishes her.* HELEN *feels her way across the yard, rather shyly, and when her moving hands touch* ANNIE'S *skirt she stops. Then she holds out the keys and places them in* ANNIE'S *hand.* 38 *For a moment neither of them moves. Then* HELEN *slides into* ANNIE'S *arms, and lifting away her smoked glasses, kisses her on the cheek.* ANNIE *gathers her in.*]

282 Drama

KATE *torn both ways turns from this, gestures the servants off, and makes her way into the house, on* KELLER'S *arm. The servants go, in separate directions.*

The lights are half down now, except over the pump. ANNIE *and* HELEN *are here, alone in the yard.* ANNIE *has found* HELEN'S *hand, almost without knowing it, and she spells slowly into it, her voice unsteady, whispering:*]

ANNIE. I, love, Helen.

[*She clutches the child to her, tight this time, not spelling, whispering into her hair.*]

Forever, and—

[*She stops. The lights over the pump are taking on the color of the past, and it brings* ANNIE'S *head up, her eyes opening, in fear; and as slowly as though drawn she rises, to listen, with her hand on* HELEN'S *shoulders. She waits, waits, listening with ears and eyes both, slowly here, slowly there: and hears only silence. There are no voices. The color passes on, and when her eyes come back to* HELEN *she can breathe the end of her phrase without fear:*]

—ever.

[*In the family room* KATE *has stood over the table, staring at* HELEN'S *plate, with* KELLER *at her shoulder; now* JAMES *takes a step to move her chair in, and* KATE *sits, with head erect, and* KELLER *inclines his head to* JAMES; *so it is* AUNT EV, *hesitant, and rather humble, who moves to the door.*

Outside HELEN *tugs at* ANNIE'S *hand, and* ANNIE *comes with it.* HELEN *pulls her toward the house; and hand in hand, they cross the yard, and ascend the porch steps, in the rising lights, to where* AUNT EV *is holding the door open for them.*

The curtain ends the play.]

Closure and Extension

ANSWERS TO RESPONDING TO THE SELECTION
Your Response

1. Encourage students to reveal their feelings. Ask students whether the ending left them feeling that there was more to come, that it was really a beginning.

Recalling

2. The Kellers miss her, and they feel she needs their affection.
3. She makes them promise that they will uphold her behavior standards. She is afraid their love and pity will undo all she has achieved.
4. Helen realizes that the word Annie is spelling in her palm stands for the water she feels on her fingers. Anie prepared for this "miracle" by constantly spelling out words for Helen.

Interpreting

5. Suggested Response: She means that through words you can learn about the world and its history.
6. Suggested Response: Helen is challenging Annie and the family to see if they will make her obey the rules Annie has established.
7. Suggested Response: As a baby, Helen had said "wah-wah," meaning "water." This memory enables her to connect that spoken word with the water flowing over her hands and the word Annie has spelled.

RESPONDING TO THE SELECTION

Your Response

1. How does the conclusion of the play make you feel? Explain your answer.

Recalling

2. Give two reasons for the Kellers' insistence that Helen be returned to them when the two weeks have ended.
3. What does Annie make the Kellers promise when she and Helen return? Explain the reason for her request.
4. What is the "miracle" that occurs at last? How is it the result of hard work?

Interpreting

5. At one point Annie says, "—words, why, you can see five thousand years back in a light of words. . . ." What does she mean?
6. Why does Helen's behavior change when she returns to her home?
7. Explain why Helen can connect the feel of water with the baby sound wah-wah.
8. At the end, why does Kate feel "wonder, gratitude, and deprivation"? How does she simultaneously find and lose her child?

Applying

9. If you had to work with a seriously handicapped or disabled person, what lesson could you draw from the example of Annie Sullivan?

ANALYZING LITERATURE

Understanding the Theme of a Play

The **theme** of a play is its central idea or insight into life. A statement of the theme should reflect why the conflict concludes as it does. Another way to approach the theme is to ask, "What accounts for the way the characters' lives have changed by the end of the play?" An accurate answer to this question would also touch upon the play's central idea or insight.

1. Annie's attempt to teach Helen might have ended in failure. Why did it succeed?

2. Tell how and why each of the following characters has changed by the end of the play: Annie, Captain Keller, Mrs. Keller, and James.
3. State in a sentence the theme of *The Miracle Worker*. You might try expressing it in this form: "The theme of the play is that _____ can triumph over _____."

CRITICAL THINKING AND READING

Summarizing a Play

Summarizing a play means retelling briefly its plot, or story. Summarizing can help you understand a play, novel, or complex short story. Moreover, a summary that tells not only what happened but also why it happened shows how well you have understood motives, cause-and-effect relationships, and other elements that propel the story from its beginning to its end.

1. Without explaining why they occur, list the main events of each of the three acts.
2. For each event you listed, tell what caused it and what it led to.
3. Now retell the story of the play in a clear, complete summary that makes clear why the events occurred as they did.

THINKING AND WRITING

Writing a Review of a Play

A **review** of a play gives the reader a clear idea of what the play is about. It also tells why the reviewer liked or did not like it. Ultimately, a review should help the reader to answer the question, "Shall I go see this play?"

Write a review of *The Miracle Worker* as if it were going to appear in your school newspaper. Base the first part of your review on the summary you wrote for Critical Thinking and Reading, but do not tell how the play ends or give away too much of the plot. In evaluating the play, try to be objective. Tell what is good or bad about it.

When you revise your review, make sure that it is fair to the play and would be useful to someone who was trying to decide whether to see it.

The Miracle Worker 283

Romeo and Juliet

Of all the love stories ever written, that of Romeo and Juliet is the most famous. To many people Shakespeare's tragic lovers represent the essence of romantic love. When Shakespeare wrote *The Tragedy of Romeo and Juliet,* he was a young man, and the play is a young man's play about young love.

THE THEATER IN SHAKESPEARE'S DAY

Romeo and Juliet, like most of Shakespeare's plays, was produced in a public theater. Public theaters were built around roofless courtyards without artificial light. Performances, therefore, were given only during daylight hours. Surrounding the courtyard were three levels of galleries with benches where wealthier playgoers sat. Poorer spectators, called groundlings, stood and watched a play from the courtyard, which was called the pit.

Most of Shakespeare's plays were performed in the Globe Theatre. No one is certain exactly what the Globe looked like, though Shakespeare tells us it was round or octagonal. We know that it was open to the sky and held between 2,500 and 3,000 people. Scholars disagree about its actual dimensions and size. The discovery of its foundation in 1990 was exciting because the eventual excavation will reveal clues about the plays, actors, and the audience. The tiny part of the foundation initially uncovered yielded a great number of hazelnut shells. Hazelnuts were Elizabethan popcorn; people munched on them all during the performance.

The stage was a platform that extended into the pit. Actors entered and left the stage from doors located behind the platform. The portion of the galleries behind and above the stage was used primarily as dressing and storage rooms. The second-level gallery right above the stage, however, was used as an upper stage. It would have been here that the famous balcony scene in *Romeo and Juliet* was enacted.

There was no scenery in the theaters of Shakespeare's day. Settings were indicated by references in the dialogue. As a result, one scene could follow another in rapid succession. The actors wore elaborate clothing. It was, in fact, typical Elizabethan clothing, not costuming. Thus, the plays produced in Shakespeare's day were fast-paced, colorful productions. Usually a play lasted two hours.

One other difference between Shakespeare's theater and today's is that acting companies of the sixteenth century were made up only of men and boys. Women did not perform on the stage. This was not considered proper for a woman. Boys of eleven, twelve, or thirteen—before their voices changed—performed the female roles, and no one in the audience thought it the least bit odd because it was what they were used to.

Although Shakespeare did not have the advantages of the modern theater to draw on, the theaters of his day must be considered highly sophisticated. The greatest dramas in our language were produced on the sixteenth-century English stage. This fact alone suggests how advanced the theater arts were when Shakespeare was writing his masterpieces.

SOME COMMON ELIZABETHAN WORDS

As you read *Romeo and Juliet,* most of the unfamiliar words and phrases you will encounter are explained in footnotes. The following, however, appear so frequently that learning them now will make your reading of the play easier.

against: For, in preparation for
alack: Alas (an exclamation of sorrow)
an, and: If
anon: Soon
aye: Yes
but: Only, except
e'en: Even
e'er: Ever
haply: Perhaps
happy: Fortunate
hence: Away, from here
hie: Hurry
hither: Here
marry: Indeed
whence: Where
wilt: Will
withal: In addition, notwithstanding
would: Wish

SWAN, THEATRE, LONDON, c. 1596
Drawing by Johannes DeWitt

The Shakespearean Theater 285

Humanities Note

Johannes De Witt's drawing of the Swan Theatre, London, c. 1596. Johannes De Witt, a priest from Utrecht, was visiting London in 1596. In addition to making notes, he made this unique sketch of the interior of a theater. His notes translated from Latin, include the following description: "Of all the theatres, however, the largest and most magnificent is that one of which the sign is a swan, called in the vernacular the Swan Theatre; for it accommodates in its seats three thousand persons, and it is built of a mass of flint stones (of which there is a prodigious supply in London), and supported by wooden columns painted in such excellent imitation of marble that it is able to deceive even the most cunning. Since its form resembles that of a Roman work, I have made a sketch of it above."

The Swan, which had opened its doors to the public by the summer of 1596, had the features of a typical theater of the Elizabethan period, where Shakespeare and his company would have played.

More About The Author You might want to tell students that Shakespeare worked very close-ly with a successful troupe of actors in London. In addition to writing plays for them, he acted in their productions and was a shareholder in their earnings. Ask students why such a close association with a theater company might be advantageous for a playwright.

Literary Focus To help students understand the rhythm of blank verse, suggest they intone an iambic foot as de-DUMM. An iamb is an unstressed syllable followed by a stressed one. Have them read aloud the first four lines of the prologue to feel the meter.

Prereading Focus *The Tragedy of Romeo and Juliet* begins with the chorus's announcement of the long-standing feud between the Capulets and the Monta-gues, which forms the basis of the tale. The purpose of the activ-ity is to focus students' attention on ingrained hatreds spawned by feuds. Tell students that the initial reason for such feuds often becomes lost over time. Remind students that feuds are difficult to end because the emotions that feed them are as ingrained and senseless as bigotry.

Vocabulary Have your **less ad-vanced** students read the words and their meanings several times. Then have them write sen-tences, using one of the words in each sentence.

Electronic Handbook You might want students to use the Language Master 6000 to hear the pronunciations of the vocab-ulary words.

GUIDE FOR READING

William Shakespeare

(1564–1616) was born in Stratford-on-Avon, in England. As a young man he went to London, where he wrote and acted in plays. Considered the greatest playwright in the Eng-lish language, before he re-tired to Stratford in 1610, he wrote thirty-seven plays, 154 sonnets, and several longer poems. *Romeo and Juliet* is based on a story that first ap-peared in Italy many years be-fore. Shakespeare's genius, however, transformed this story of star-crossed lovers into the most famous love story the world has ever known.

The Tragedy of Romeo and Juliet, Act I

Blank Verse

Blank verse is unrhymed verse written in iambic pentameter, or ten-syllable lines in which every second syllable is stressed. For ex-ample, when Romeo sees Juliet appear at her window, he exclaims,

> But sóft! What líght through yónder wíndow bréaks?
> It ís the eást, and Júliet ís the sún!

Much of *Romeo and Juliet* is written in blank verse. This meter is well suited to serious subjects and has been used in many of the greatest poems and verse dramas of British and American literature.

Focus

Romeo and Juliet is the tragic story of a feud between two fam-ilies: the Montagues and the Capulets. What circumstances could make two families hate each other for generations? With a group of classmates, discuss other family feuds you have heard or read about. One example from American history is the longstanding feud be-tween the Hatfields and the McCoys in West Virginia. What starts such feuds and why are they so hard to end?

Vocabulary

Knowing the following words will help you as you read Act I of *Romeo and Juliet*.

pernicious (pər nish′ əs) *adj.*: Causing great injury or ruin (p. 291)

augmenting (ôg ment′ iŋ) *v.*: Increasing; enlarging (p. 292)

grievance (grē′ vəns) *n.*: Injus-tice; complaint (p. 293)

transgression (trans gresh′ ən) *n.*: Wrongdoing; sin (p. 294)

heretics (her′ ə tiks) *n.*: Those who hold to a belief opposed to the established teachings of a church (p. 298)

Objectives

1 To appreciate blank verse
2 To interpret the effect of imagery
3 To write a speech in blank verse
4 To express individual in-terests and abilities through an optional ac-tivity

Support Material

Teaching Portfolio
Teacher Backup, p. 333
Grammar in Action Worksheet, *Using Commas in Poetry*, p. 337
Usage and Mechanics Work-sheet, p. 340
Vocabulary Check, p. 341
Critical Thinking and Reading Worksheet, *Interpreting the Ef-fect of Imagery*, p. 342
Language Worksheet, *Under-*

standing Words from Elizabe-than Times, p. 343
Selection Test, p. 344
Library of Video Classics
Romeo and Juliet; Shakespeare in Rehearsal: Romeo and Juliet; Shakespeare in Conversation
Literature Videodiscs *Shake-speare in Rehearsal; Romeo and Juliet; Shakespeare in Con-versation*

Prentice Hall Literature Writing Studio

The Tragedy of Romeo and Juliet

William Shakespeare

CHARACTERS

Chorus
Escalus, Prince of Verona
Paris, a young count, kinsman to the Prince
Montague
Capulet
An old Man, of the Capulet family
Romeo, son to Montague
Mercutio, kinsman to the Prince and friend to Romeo
Benvolio, nephew to Montague and friend to Romeo
Tybalt, nephew to Lady Capulet
Friar Lawrence } Franciscans
Friar John

Balthasar, servant to Romeo
Sampson } servants to Capulet
Gregory
Peter, servant to Juliet's nurse
Abram, servant to Montague
An Apothecary
Three Musicians
An Officer
Lady Montague, wife to Montague
Lady Capulet, wife to Capulet
Juliet, daughter to Capulet
Nurse to Juliet
Citizens of Verona, Gentlemen and Gentlewomen of both houses, Maskers, Torchbearers, Pages, Guards, Watchmen, Servants, and Attendants

---

Scene: Verona; Mantua

THE PROLOGUE

[*Enter* CHORUS]

CHORUS. Two households, both alike in dignity,[1]
 In fair Verona, where we lay our scene,
 From ancient grudge break to new mutiny,[2]
 Where civil blood makes civil hands unclean.[3]
5 From forth the fatal loins of these two foes
 A pair of star-crossed[4] lovers take their life;
 Whose misadventured piteous overthrows[5]
 Doth with their death bury their parents' strife.
 The fearful passage of their death-marked love,

1. dignity: High social rank.
2. mutiny: Violence.
3. Where . . . unclean: In which the blood of citizens stains citizens' hands.
4. star-crossed: Ill-fated by the unfavorable positions of the stars.
5. Whose . . . overthrows: Whose unfortunate sorrowful destruction.

The Tragedy of Romeo and Juliet, Prologue 287

Videocassette You might wish to show the beginning of the film adaptation of *Romeo and Juliet* in the Library of Video Classics to familiarize the students with the youthful and emotional characters of Romeo and Juliet, who live amid a very active family feud.

Thematic Focus The awakening of love between Romeo and Juliet is beautiful, but their lives are overshadowed by their families' hatred for each other. Ask students if love can flourish amid hatred. Are such awakening feelings too fragile to withstand disapproval, or are they stronger than the force of others' opinions?

Making Connections Another selection that deals with the consequences of love that goes against parental wishes is "The Lady or the Tiger?," page 49. You might also have students compare the roles of fate in this tragedy and in "The Necklace," page 193.

Alternative Assessment To promote active reading, have your students keep a reader's response journal as they read Act I of the play. Ask them to focus their observations on the details that reveal the conflict between the Montagues and the Capulets as well as those that reveal the personalities of Romeo and Juliet. Encourage students to respond personally to the situation. What effect might a family feud have on their relationship with a boy or girl in that family?

Their observations will enable you to assess their understanding of the issues in the play.

Videocassette The films *Shakespeare in Rehearsal: Romeo and Juliet* and *Shakespeare in Conversation* from the **Library of Video Classics** will offer your students valuable insights that will enhance their reading of the play. Each film is brief enough to be shown in a single class period either before or after students begin reading the play.

Videodisc If you have *Shakespeare in Rehearsal: Romeo and Juliet* and *Shakespeare in Conversation* on Videodisc, you can easily show students brief segments of the films that connect directly to scenes from the play. The Videodisc notes throughout the play will suggest key points at which you may want to incorporate a Videodisc segment into your lesson.

288 *Drama*

10 And the continuance of their parents' rage,
      Which, but[6] their children's end, naught could remove,
      Is now the two hours' traffic[7] of our stage;
      The which if you with patient ears attend,
      What here shall miss, our toil shall strive to mend.[8]

[*Exit.*]

Act I

Scene i. *Verona. A public place.*

[*Enter* SAMPSON *and* GREGORY, *with swords and bucklers,[1] of the house of Capulet.*]

SAMPSON. Gregory, on my word, we'll not carry coals.[2]

GREGORY. No, for then we should be colliers.[3]

SAMPSON. I mean, and we be in choler, we'll draw.[4]

GREGORY. Ay, while you live, draw your neck out of collar.[5]

5 **SAMPSON.** I strike quickly, being moved.

GREGORY. But thou art not quickly moved to strike.

SAMPSON. A dog of the house of Montague moves me.

GREGORY. To move is to stir, and to be valiant is to stand. Therefore, if thou art moved, thou run'st away.

10 **SAMPSON.** A dog of that house shall move me to stand. I will take the wall[6] of any man or maid of Montague's.

GREGORY. That shows thee a weak slave; for the weakest goes to the wall.

SAMPSON. 'Tis true; and therefore women, being the
15 weaker vessels, are ever thrust to the wall. Therefore I will push Montague's men from the wall and thrust his maids to the wall.

GREGORY. The quarrel is between our masters and us their men.

20 **SAMPSON.** 'Tis all one. I will show myself a tyrant. When I have fought with the men, I will be civil with the maids—I will cut off their heads.

GREGORY. The heads of the maids?

SAMPSON. Ay, the heads of the maids or their maiden-
25 heads. Take it in what sense thou wilt.

The Tragedy of Romeo and Juliet, Act I, Scene i   289

---

6. but: Except.
7. two hours' traffic: Two hours' business.
8. What . . . mend: What is not clear in this prologue we actors shall try to clarify in the course of the play.

1. bucklers: Small shields.

2. carry coals: Endure insults.
3. colliers: Sellers of coal.
4. and . . . draw: If we are angered, we'll draw our swords.
5. collar: The hangman's noose.

6. take the wall: Assert superiority by walking nearest the houses and therefore farthest from the gutter.

---

4 Reading Strategy Summarize what this play is about.

5 Clarification These plays had no scenery to speak of but costumes indicated whether an actor was playing a noble or a servant. Servants wore the coats of arms of the families for whom they worked so the audience would not be confused.

6 Clarification The first scene of every Shakespearean tragedy was planned to get the attention of the groundlings, people of the lower classes who stood in the pit to watch the plays. Shakespeare used comedy, the supernatural, or violence to get their interest. Why might this scene have appealed to the groundlings?

Videodisc Introduce students to the play by showing the opening segment of the *Shakespeare in Rehearsal: Romeo and Juliet* Videodisc. Urge students not to read along with the actors, but rather to watch and listen. The fact is, we do not know exactly how Shakespeare's acting company rehearsed. We can determine that they probably rehearsed at night since performances were held every afternoon except on Sunday. Therefore, they probably did *not* rehearse on the stage itself because they would not have been able to see well enough at night.

Frames 1150 to 4600

7 Discussion Does this exchange have a childish quality? Explain.

GREGORY. They must take it in sense that feel it.

SAMPSON. Me they shall feel while I am able to stand; and 'tis known I am a pretty piece of flesh.

30 **GREGORY.** 'Tis well thou art not fish; if thou hadst, thou hadst been Poor John. Draw thy tool![7] Here comes two of the house of Montagues.

[Enter two other Servingmen, ABRAM *and* BALTHASAR.*]*

SAMPSON. My naked weapon is out. Quarrel! I will back thee.

GREGORY. How? Turn thy back and run?

35 **SAMPSON.** Fear me not.

GREGORY. No, marry. I fear thee!

SAMPSON. Let us take the law of our sides;[8] let them begin.

GREGORY. I will frown as I pass by, and let them take it as they list.[9]

40 **SAMPSON.** Nay, as they dare. I will bite my thumb[10] at them, which is disgrace to them if they bear it.

ABRAM. Do you bite your thumb at us, sir?

SAMPSON. I do bite my thumb, sir.

ABRAM. Do you bite your thumb at us, sir?

45 **SAMPSON.** *[Aside to* GREGORY*]* Is the law of our side if I say ay?

GREGORY. *[Aside to* SAMPSON*]* No.

SAMPSON. No, sir, I do not bite my thumb at you, sir; but I bite my thumb, sir.

50 **GREGORY.** Do you quarrel, sir?

ABRAM. Quarrel, sir? No, sir.

SAMPSON. But if you do, sir, I am for you. I serve as good a man as you.

ABRAM. No better.

55 **SAMPSON.** Well, sir.

[Enter BENVOLIO.*]*

GREGORY. Say "better." Here comes one of my master's kinsmen.

7. tool: Weapon.

8. take . . . sides: Make sure the law is on our side.

9. list: Please.

10. bite . . . thumb: Make an insulting gesture.

290 *Drama*

SAMPSON. Yes, better, sir.

ABRAM. You lie.

60   **SAMPSON.** Draw, if you be men. Gregory, remember thy
    swashing[11] blow.   *[They fight.]*

  BENVOLIO. Part, fools!
    Put up your swords. You know not what you do.

[Enter TYBALT.*]*

  TYBALT. What, art thou drawn among these heartless
    hinds?[12]
65   Turn thee, Benvolio; look upon thy death.

  BENVOLIO. I do but keep the peace. Put up thy sword,
    Or manage it to part these men with me.

  TYBALT. What, drawn, and talk of peace? I hate the word
    As I hate hell, all Montagues, and thee.
70   Have at thee, coward!   *[They fight.]*

[Enter an OFFICER, *and three or four Citizens with clubs or
partisans.[13]]*

  OFFICER. Clubs, bills,[14] and partisans! Strike! Beat them
    down!
    Down with the Capulets! Down with the Mon-
    tagues!

[Enter old CAPULET *in his gown, and his* WIFE.*]*

  CAPULET. What noise is this? Give me my long sword, ho!

  LADY CAPULET. A crutch, a crutch! Why call you for a
    sword?

75   **CAPULET.** My sword, I say! Old Montague is come
    And flourishes his blade in spite[15] of me.

[Enter old MONTAGUE *and his* WIFE.*]*

  MONTAGUE. Thou villain Capulet!— Hold me not; let me go.

  LADY MONTAGUE. Thou shalt not stir one foot to seek a foe.

[Enter PRINCE ESCALUS, *with his Train.[16]]*

  PRINCE. Rebellious subjects, enemies to peace,
80   Profaners[17] of this neighbor-stainèd steel—
    Will they not hear? What, ho! You men, you beasts,
    That quench the fire of your pernicious rage
    With purple fountains issuing from your veins!

---

11. swashing: Hard downward swordstroke.

12. heartless hinds: Cowardly servants. **Hind** also meant "a female deer."

13. partisans: Spearlike weapons with broad blades.
14. bills: Weapons consisting of hook-shaped blades with long handles.

15. spite: Defiance.

16. Train: Attendants.

17. Profaners: Those who show disrespect or contempt.

The Tragedy of Romeo and Juliet, Act I, Scene i   291

8 **Enrichment** Tybalt's name comes from a word that means "bold." Benvolio is from Latin words that mean "I wish" and "well." From what you know about them so far, how appropriate are their names?

9 **Discussion** What makes this scene humorous and serious at the same time?

On pain of torture, from those bloody hands
85 Throw your mistempered[18] weapons to the ground
And hear the sentence of your movèd prince.
Three civil brawls, bred of an airy word
By thee, old Capulet, and Montague,
Have thrice disturbed the quiet of our streets
90 And made Verona's ancient citizens
Cast by their grave beseeming ornaments[19]
To wield old partisans, in hands as old,
Cank'red with peace, to part your cank'red hate.[20]
If ever you disturb our streets again,
95 Your lives shall pay the forfeit of the peace.
For this time all the rest depart away.
You, Capulet, shall go along with me;
And, Montague, come you this afternoon,
To know our farther pleasure in this case,
100 To old Freetown, our common judgment place.
Once more, on pain of death, all men depart.

[*Exit all but* MONTAGUE, *his* WIFE, *and* BENVOLIO.]

MONTAGUE. Who set this ancient quarrel new abroach?[21]
Speak, nephew, were you by when it began?

BENVOLIO. Here were the servants of your adversary
105 And yours, close fighting ere I did approach.
I drew to part them. In the instant came
The fiery Tybalt, with his sword prepared;
Which, as he breathed defiance to my ears,
He swung about his head and cut the winds,
110 Who, nothing hurt withal, hissed him in scorn.
While we were interchanging thrusts and blows,
Came more and more, and fought on part and part,[22]
Till the Prince came, who parted either part.

LADY MONTAGUE. O, where is Romeo? Saw you him today?
115 Right glad I am he was not at this fray.

BENVOLIO. Madam, an hour before the worshiped sun
Peered forth the golden window of the East,
A troubled mind drave me to walk abroad;
Where, underneath the grove of sycamore
120 That westward rooteth from this city side,
So early walking did I see your son.
Towards him I made, but he was ware[23] of me
And stole into the covert[24] of the wood.
I, measuring his affections[25] by my own,

18. **mistempered:** Hardened for a wrong purpose; bad-tempered.

19. **Cast . . . ornaments:** Put aside their dignified and appropriate clothing.
20. **Cank'red . . . hate:** Rusted from lack of use, to put an end to your malignant feuding.

21. **Who . . . abroach?:** Who reopened this old fight?

22. **on . . . part:** On one side and the other.

23. **ware:** Aware; wary.
24. **covert:** Hidden place.
25. **measuring . . . affections:** Judging his feelings.

Grammar in Action

Poetry is one of the most concentrated and difficult forms of literature. It is therefore especially important for poets to use **commas** to set apart modifiers, signify series, and clarify which groups of words should be read together.

Notice how Shakespeare uses commas to clarify meaning in the following passage from *Romeo and Juliet:*

Montague. Many a morning hath he there been seen,

With tears augmenting the fresh morning's dew.
Adding to clouds more clouds with his deep sighs;
But all so soon as the all-cheering sun
Should in the farthest East begin to draw
The shady curtains from Aurora's bed
Away from light steals home my heavy son
And private in his chamber pens himself,
Shuts up his windows, locks fair daylight out,
And makes himself an artificial night.

Which then most sought where most might not be
    found,[26]
125   Being one too many by my weary self,
Pursued my humor not pursuing his,[27]
And gladly shunned who gladly fled from me.

MONTAGUE. Many a morning hath he there been seen,
130   With tears augmenting the fresh morning's dew,
Adding to clouds more clouds with his deep sighs;
But all so soon as the all-cheering sun
Should in the farthest East begin to draw
The shady curtains from Aurora's[28] bed,
135   Away from light steals home my heavy[29] son
And private in his chamber pens himself,
Shuts up his windows, locks fair daylight out,
And makes himself an artificial night.
Black and portentous[30] must this humor prove
140   Unless good counsel may the cause remove.

BENVOLIO. My noble uncle, do you know the cause?

MONTAGUE. I neither know it nor can learn of him.

BENVOLIO. Have you importuned[31] him by any means?

MONTAGUE. Both by myself and many other friends;
145   But he, his own affections' counselor,
Is to himself—I will not say how true—
But to himself so secret and so close,
So far from sounding[32] and discovery,
As is the bud bit with an envious worm
150   Ere he can spread his sweet leaves to the air
Or dedicate his beauty to the sun.
Could we but learn from whence his sorrows grow,
We would as willingly give cure as know.

[*Enter* ROMEO.]

BENVOLIO. See, where he comes. So please you step aside;
155   I'll know his grievance, or be much denied.

MONTAGUE. I would thou wert so happy by thy stay
To hear true shrift.[33] Come, madam, let's away.
                [*Exit* MONTAGUE *and* WIFE.]

BENVOLIO. Good morrow, cousin.

ROMEO.   Is the day so young?

BENVOLIO. But new struck nine.

The Tragedy of Romeo and Juliet, Act I, Scene i   293

26. Which . . . found: Which wanted to be where there was no one else.
27. Pursued . . . his: Followed my own mind by not following after Romeo.

28. Aurora: Goddess of the dawn.
29. heavy: Sad, moody.

30. portentous: Promising bad fortune.

31. importuned: Questioned deeply.

32. sounding: Understanding.

33. I . . . shrift: I hope you are lucky enough to hear him confess the truth.

11 **Discussion** Why do you think Romeo has been behaving strangely?

12 **Enrichment** Elizabethan audiences were familiar with Roman and Greek gods and goddesses, so Shakespeare often referred to them.

13 **Literary Focus** Shakespeare used blank verse even in brief conversations. These interchanges make up two lines of blank verse.

Electronic Handbook You might want students to review the use of commas in poetry before completing the Grammar in Action activities. If students have access to the Language Master 6000, have them enter the access symbol , and press the GRAMMAR key to obtain information on the use of commas in poetry.

The commas at the end of lines 1 and 2 help show that lines 2 and 3 contain participial phrases to describe Romeo, the subject in line 1. (In line 2, Shakespeare has inverted the natural word order, which should read: Augmenting with tears. . . .) The absence of commas at the end of lines 4 and 5 tells the reader to connect the thoughts from line to line. Indeed, the subject *sun* in line 4 has its verb in line 5 and its direct object in line 6. The series of four verbs in lines 8, 9, and 10 is clearly separated by commas.

Student Activity 1. Select another passage of similar length from *Romeo and Juliet* and study the use of commas in it. What do the commas tell you about how to read the passage with meaning?

Student Activity 2. Work in pairs, each of you selecting a speech of at least eight lines. Copy the passage, omitting commas. Then read the passage your partner copied. Explain whether or not the lack of commas affected your ability to understand the speech.

14 Discussion What does Romeo mean by this statement?

15 Discussion Explain the reason for Romeo's strange actions.

16 Critical Thinking and Reading What images does Romeo use to describe love? How do these images reflect his agitated state of mind?

ROMEO.   Ay me! Sad hours seem long.
160   Was that my father that went hence so fast?

BENVOLIO. It was. What sadness lengthens Romeo's
       hours?

ROMEO. Not having that which having makes them short.

BENVOLIO. In love?

ROMEO. Out—

165 **BENVOLIO.** Of love?

ROMEO. Out of her favor where I am in love.

BENVOLIO. Alas that love, so gentle in his view,[34]
       Should be so tyrannous and rough in proof![35]

ROMEO. Alas that love, whose view is muffled still,[36]
170   Should without eyes see pathways to his will!
       Where shall we dine? O me! What fray was here?
       Yet tell me not, for I have heard it all.
       Here's much to do with hate, but more with love.[37]
       Why then, O brawling love, O loving hate,
175   O anything, of nothing first created!
       O heavy lightness, serious vanity,
       Misshapen chaos of well-seeming forms,
       Feather of lead, bright smoke, cold fire, sick health,
       Still-waking sleep, that is not what it is!
180   This love feel I, that feel no love in this.
       Dost thou not laugh?

BENVOLIO.   No, coz,[38] I rather weep.

ROMEO. Good heart, at what?

BENVOLIO.   At thy good heart's oppression.

ROMEO. Why, such is love's transgression.
       Griefs of mine own lie heavy in my breast,
185   Which thou wilt propagate, to have it prest
       With more of thine.[39] This love that thou hast shown
       Doth add more grief to too much of mine own.
       Love is a smoke made with the fume of sighs;
       Being purged, a fire sparkling in lovers' eyes;
190   Being vexed, a sea nourished with loving tears.
       What is it else? A madness most discreet,[40]
       A choking gall,[41] and a preserving sweet.
       Farewell, my coz.

BENVOLIO.   Soft![42] I will go along.

294   Drama

34. **view:** Appearance.
35. **in proof:** When experienced.

36. **whose . . . still:** Cupid is traditionally represented as blindfolded.

37. **but . . . love:** Loyalty to family and love of fighting. In the following lines Romeo speaks of love as a series of contradictions—a union of opposites.

38. **coz:** Cousin.

39. **Which . . . thine:** Which griefs you will increase by adding your own sorrow to them.

40. **discreet:** Intelligently sensitive.
41. **gall:** A bitter liquid.

42. **Soft!:** Hold on a minute.

And if you leave me so, you do me wrong.

195 **ROMEO.** Tut! I have lost myself; I am not here;
This is not Romeo, he's some other where.

BENVOLIO. Tell me in sadness,[43] who is that you love?

43. in sadness: Seriously.

ROMEO. What, shall I groan and tell thee?

BENVOLIO.   Groan? Why, no;
But sadly tell me who.

200 **ROMEO.** Bid a sick man in sadness make his will.
Ah, word ill urged to one that is so ill!
In sadness, cousin, I do love a woman.

BENVOLIO. I aimed so near when I supposed you loved.

ROMEO. A right good markman. And she's fair I love.

205 **BENVOLIO.** A right fair mark, fair coz, is soonest hit.

ROMEO. Well, in that hit you miss. She'll not be hit
With Cupid's arrow. She hath Dian's wit,[44]
And, in strong proof[45] of chastity well armed,
From Love's weak childish bow she lives uncharmed.
210 She will not stay[46] the siege of loving terms,
Nor bide th' encounter of assailing eyes,
Nor ope her lap to saint-seducing gold.
O, she is rich in beauty; only poor
That, when she dies, with beauty dies her store.[47]

44. Dian's wit: The mind of Diana, goddess of chastity.
45. proof: Armor.
46. stay: Endure, put up with.

47. That ... store: In that her beauty will die with her if she does not marry and have children.

BENVOLIO. Then she hath sworn that she will still live
215 chaste?

ROMEO. She hath, and in that sparing make huge waste;
For beauty, starved with her severity,

17 Enrichment You might want to point out to students that Elizabethan audiences enjoyed this type of word-play.

7

18 **Discussion** What has Romeo's love sworn not to do?

19 **Critical Thinking and Reading** Compare and contrast Romeo and Benvolio.

20 **Enrichment** Tell students that scenery was not used very much in Elizabethan plays. Changes of scene were not usually indicated by changes in scenery.

21 **Discussion** What does Capulet think the chances are for keeping the peace?

22 **Clarification** Girls married at a younger age because the average life span was shorter.

Cuts beauty off from all posterity.[48]

She is too fair, too wise, wisely too fair

220 To merit bliss by making me despair.[49]

She hath forsworn to[50] love, and in that vow

Do I live dead that live to tell it now.

BENVOLIO. Be ruled by me; forget to think of her.

ROMEO. O, teach me how I should forget to think!

225 **BENVOLIO.** By giving liberty unto thine eyes.

Examine other beauties.

ROMEO.   'Tis the way

To call hers, exquisite, in question more.[51]

These happy masks that kiss fair ladies' brows,

Being black puts us in mind they hide the fair.

230 He that is strucken blind cannot forget

The precious treasure of his eyesight lost.

Show me a mistress that is passing fair:

What doth her beauty serve but as a note

Where I may read who passed that passing fair?[52]

235 Farewell. Thou canst not teach me to forget.

BENVOLIO. I'll pay that doctrine, or else die in debt.[53]

[*Exit.*]

Scene ii. *A street.*

[*Enter* CAPULET, COUNTY PARIS, *and the* CLOWN, *his Servant.*]

CAPULET. But Montague is bound as well as I,

In penalty alike; and 'tis not hard, I think,

For men so old as we to keep the peace.

PARIS. Of honorable reckoning[1] are you both,

5 And pity 'tis you lived at odds so long.

But now, my lord, what say you to my suit?

CAPULET. But saying o'er what I have said before:

My child is yet a stranger in the world,

She hath not seen the change of fourteen years;

10 Let two more summers wither in their pride

Ere we may think her ripe to be a bride.

PARIS. Younger than she are happy mothers made.

CAPULET. And too soon marred are those so early made.

Earth hath swallowed all my hopes[2] but she;

15 She is the hopeful lady of my earth.[3]

But woo her, gentle Paris, get her heart;

48. in . . . posterity: By denying herself love and marriage, she wastes her beauty, which will not live on in future generations.
49. She . . . despair: She is being too good—she'll earn happiness in heaven by dooming me to live without her love.
50. forsworn to: Sworn not to.

51. 'Tis . . . more: That way will only make her beauty more strongly present in my mind.

52. who . . . fair: Who surpassed in beauty that very beautiful woman.
53. I'll . . . debt: I'll teach you to forget, or else die trying.

1. reckoning: Reputation.

2. hopes: Children.
3. She . . . earth: My hopes for the future rest in her; she will inherit all that is mine.

296   *Drama*

My will to her consent is but a part.
And she agreed, within her scope of choice
Lies my consent and fair according voice,[4]
20 This night I hold an old accustomed feast,
Whereto I have invited many a guest,
Such as I love; and you among the store,
One more, most welcome, makes my number more.
At my poor house look to behold this night
25 Earth-treading stars[5] that make dark heaven light.
Such comfort as do lusty young men feel
When well-appareled April on the heel
Of limping Winter treads, even such delight
Among fresh fennel buds shall you this night
30 Inherit at my house. Hear all, all see,
And like her most whose merit most shall be;
Which, on more view of many, mine, being one,
May stand in number, though in reck'ning none.[6]
Come, go with me. [*To* SERVANT, *giving him a paper*]
Go, sirrah, trudge about
35 Through fair Verona; find those persons out
Whose names are written there, and to them say
My house and welcome on their pleasure stay.[7]

[*Exit with* PARIS.]

SERVANT. Find them out whose names are written here?
It is written that the shoemaker should meddle with his
40 yard and the tailor with his last, the fisher with his pencil and the painter with his nets;[8] but I am sent to find
those persons whose names are here writ, and can
never find what names the writing person hath here
writ. I must to the learned. In good time![9]

[*Enter* BENVOLIO *and* ROMEO.]

45 **BENVOLIO.** Tut, man, one fire burns out another's
burning;
One pain is less'ned by another's anguish;
Turn giddy, and be holp by backward turning;[10]
One desperate grief cures with another's languish.
Take thou some new infection to thy eye,
50 And the rank poison of the old will die.

ROMEO. Your plantain leaf[11] is excellent for that.

BENVOLIO. For what, I pray thee?

ROMEO.   For your broken shin.

BENVOLIO. Why, Romeo, art thou mad?

The Tragedy of Romeo and Juliet, Act I, Scene ii 297

4. and . . . voice: If she agrees, I will consent to and agree with her choice.

5. Earth-treading stars: Young ladies.

6. Which . . . none: If you look at all the young girls, you may see her as merely one among many, and not worth special admiration.

7. stay: Await.

8. shoemaker . . . nets: The servant is confusing workers and their tools. He intends to say that people should stick with what they know.
9. In good time!: Just in time! The servant has seen Benvolio and Romeo, who can read.

10. Turn . . . turning: If you're dizzy from turning one way, turn the other way.

11. plantain leaf: A leaf used to stop bleeding.

23

23 Discussion How does this speech represent a continuation of the previous discussion between Benvolio and Romeo?

24 Discussion Who is welcome to come to Capulet's traditional party?

25 Discussion Chance plays an important part in the events of the play. How do you think this chance meeting will advance the plot?

ROMEO. Not mad, but bound more than a madman is;
55 Shut up in prison, kept without my food,
Whipped and tormented and—God-den,[12] good fellow.

12. God-den: Good afternoon; good evening.

SERVANT. God gi' go-den. I pray, sir, can you read?

ROMEO. Ay, mine own fortune in my misery.

SERVANT. Perhaps you have learned it without book.
60 But, I pray, can you read anything you see?

ROMEO. Ay, if I know the letters and the language.

SERVANT. Ye say honestly. Rest you merry.[13]

13. Rest you merry: May God keep you happy—a way of saying farewell.

ROMEO. Stay, fellow; I can read.   [*He reads the letter.*]
"Signior Martino and his wife and daughters;
65 County Anselm and his beauteous sisters;
The lady widow of Vitruvio;
Signior Placentio and his lovely nieces;
Mercutio and his brother Valentine;
Mine uncle Capulet, his wife and daughters;
70 My fair niece Rosaline; Livia;
Signior Valentio and his cousin Tybalt;
Lucio and the lively Helena."
A fair assembly. Whither should they come?

SERVANT. Up.

75 **ROMEO.** Whither? To supper?

SERVANT. To our house.

ROMEO. Whose house?

SERVANT. My master's.

ROMEO. Indeed I should have asked you that before.

24
80 **SERVANT.** Now I'll tell you without asking. My master is the
great rich Capulet; and if you be not of the house of
Montagues, I pray come and crush a cup of wine. Rest
you merry.   [*Exit*]

BENVOLIO. At this same ancient[14] feast of Capulet's
85 Sups the fair Rosaline whom thou so loves;
With all the admirèd beauties of Verona.

14. ancient: Long-established, traditional.

25
Go thither, and with unattainted[15] eye
Compare her face with some that I shall show,
And I will make thee think thy swan a crow.

15. unattainted: Unprejudiced.

90 **ROMEO.** When the devout religion of mine eye
Maintains such falsehood, then turn tears to fires:

298 *Drama*

And these, who, often drowned, could never die,
Transparent heretics, be burnt for liars![16]
One fairer than my love? The all-seeing sun
95 Ne'er saw her match since first the world begun.

BENVOLIO. Tut! you saw her fair, none else being by,
Herself poised with herself in either eye;[17]
But in that crystal scales[18] let there be weighed
Your lady's love against some other maid
100 That I will show you shining at this feast,
And she shall scant show well that now seems best.

ROMEO. I'll go along, no such sight to be shown,
But to rejoice in splendor of mine own.[19]   [*Exit.*]

Scene iii. *A room in* CAPULET'S *house.*

[*Enter* CAPULET'S WIFE, *and* NURSE.]

LADY CAPULET. Nurse, where's my daughter? Call her
    forth to me.

NURSE. Now, by my maidenhead at twelve year old,
I bade her come. What, lamb! What, ladybird!
5 God forbid, where's this girl? What, Juliet!

[*Enter* JULIET.]

JULIET. How now? Who calls?

NURSE.   Your mother.

JULIET.   Madam, I am here.
What is your will?

LADY CAPULET. This is the matter—Nurse, give leave[1]
    awhile;
We must talk in secret. Nurse, come back again.
10 I have rememb'red me; thou's hear our counsel.[2]
Thou knowest my daughter's of a pretty age.

NURSE. Faith, I can tell her age unto an hour.

LADY CAPULET. She's not fourteen.

NURSE.   I'll lay fourteen of my teeth—
And yet, to my teen[3] be it spoken, I have but four—
15 She's not fourteen. How long is it now
To Lammastide?[4]

LADY CAPULET.   A fortnight and odd days.[5]

NURSE. Even or odd, of all days in the year,

16. When . . . liars!:
When I see Rosaline as just
a plain-looking girl, may my
tears turn to fire and burn
my eyes out!

17. Herself . . . eye: Rosaline compared with no
one else.
18. crystal scales: Your
eyes.

19. mine own: My own
love, Rosaline.

1. give leave: Leave us
alone.

2. thou's . . . counsel:
You shall hear our con-
ference.

3. teen: Sorrow.

4. Lammastide: August
1, a holiday celebrating the
summer harvest.
**5. A fortnight and odd
days:** Two weeks plus a few
days.

26 Discussion Contrast the reasons that Benvolio and Romeo
offer for attending the party.

Enrichment Tell students that
The Tragedy of Romeo and Juliet
first appeared in print in 1597.
The play was popular among
critics and the general public
even though it was a pirated version, put together from actors'
memories as a way of cashing in
on the play's success. The second edition, which was published in 1599 and considered a
superior version to the first, was
apparently printed from Shakespeare's working papers.

27 Discussion What does Nurse's manner of speaking reveal about her?

Come Lammas Eve at night shall she be fourteen.
Susan and she (God rest all Christian souls!)

20 Were of an age.[6] Well, Susan is with God;
She was too good for me. But, as I said,
On Lammas Eve at night shall she be fourteen;
That shall she, marry; I remember it well.
'Tis since the earthquake now eleven years.

25 And she was weaned (I never shall forget it),
Of all the days of the year, upon that day;
For I had then laid wormwood to my dug,
Sitting in the sun under the dovehouse wall.
My lord and you were then at Mantua.

30 Nay, I do bear a brain. But, as I said,
When it did taste the wormwood on the nipple
Of my dug and felt it bitter, pretty fool,
To see it tetchy and fall out with the dug!
Shake, quoth the dovehouse! 'Twas no need, I
    trow,

35 To bid me trudge.
And since that time it is eleven years,
For then she could stand high-lone; nay, by th'
    rood,
She could have run and waddled all about;
For even the day before, she broke her brow;

40 And then my husband (God be with his soul!
'A was a merry man) took up the child.
"Yea," quoth he, "dost thou fall upon thy face?
Thou wilt fall backward when thou hast more wit;
Wilt thou not, Jule?" and, by my holidam,

45 The pretty wretch left crying and said, "Ay."
To see now how a jest shall come about!
I warrant, and I should live a thousand years,
I never should forget it. "Wilt thou not, Jule?"
    quoth he,
And, pretty fool, it stinted and said, "Ay."

50 **LADY CAPULET.** Enough of this. I pray thee hold thy
    peace.

NURSE. Yes, madam. Yet I cannot choose but laugh
To think it should leave crying and say, "Ay."
And yet, I warrant, it had upon it brow

55 A bump as big as a young cock'rel's stone;
A perilous knock; and it cried bitterly.
"Yea," quoth my husband, "fall'st upon thy face?
Thou wilt fall backward when thou comest to age,

6. Susan . . . age: Susan, the Nurse's child, and Juliet were the same age.

300 Drama

Commentary: Lammas Day

The date of Juliet's birthday, Lammas Eve, marked a time of great celebration for Elizabethans. Lammas (loaf mass) Day, an annual August celebration of the summer harvest, was honored with a day of feasting and game playing. The day usually began by thanking God for a good harvest and blessing the grains and breads and was followed by a glorious feast.

The Lammas feast featured breads and pastries of all types that were paraded through the feast hall or prominently displayed. The highlight of the day was the bread making. Bakers baked bread in all shapes and sizes, including geometric, animal, and celestial shapes. They also sculptured bread into castles and multi-decked warships. The meal was served on bread, or the courses themselves consisted of types of bread, such as currant buns, shortbread, gingerbread, and cucumber bread.

After the meal, feasters participated in a playlet called "Bringing Home the Bacon," that reminded them that true love is hard work. Traditionally, since the fourteenth century, a prize—half a pig—was given to any couple who, after a year and a day

Wilt thou not, Jule?" It stinted and said, "Ay."

JULIET. And stint thou too, I pray thee, nurse, say I.

60 **NURSE.** Peace, I have done. God mark thee to His grace!
Thou wast the prettiest babe that e'er I nursed.
And I might live to see thee married once,
I have my wish.

LADY CAPULET. Marry, that "marry" is the very theme
65 I came to talk of. Tell me, daughter Juliet,
How stands your dispositions to be married?

JULIET. It is an honor that I dream not of.

NURSE. An honor? Were not I thine only nurse,
I would say thou hadst sucked wisdom from thy
teat.

LADY CAPULET. Well, think of marriage now. Younger than
70 you,
Here in Verona, ladies of esteem,
Are made already mothers. By my count,
I was your mother much upon these years
That you are now a maid.[7] Thus then in brief;
75 The valiant Paris seeks you for his love.

NURSE. A man, young lady! Lady, such a man
As all the world—Why, he's a man of wax.[8]

LADY CAPULET. Verona's summer hath not such a flower.

NURSE. Nay, he's a flower, in faith—a very flower.

LADY CAPULET. What say you? Can you love the
80 gentleman?
This night you shall behold him at our feast.
Read o'er the volume of young Paris' face,
And find delight writ there with beauty's pen;
Examine every married lineament,
85 And see how one another lends content;[9]
And what obscured in this fair volume lies
Find written in the margent[10] of his eyes.
This precious book of love, this unbound lover,
To beautify him only lacks a cover.[11]
90 The fish lives in the sea, and 'tis much pride
For fair without the fair within to hide.
That book in many's eyes doth share the glory,
That in gold clasps locks in the golden story;
So shall you share all that he doth possess,
95 By having him making yourself no less.

The Tragedy of Romeo and Juliet, Act I, Scene iii 301

7. I . . . maid: I was your mother when I was as old as you are now.

8. he's . . . wax: He's a model of a man.

9. Examine . . . content: Examine every harmonious feature of his face, and see how each one enhances every other. Throughout this speech, Lady Capulet compares Paris to a book.

10. margent: margin. Paris's eyes are compared to the margin of a book, where whatever is not clear in the text (the rest of his face) can be explained by notes.

11. cover: A metaphor for wife.

28 **Clarification** In Shakespeare's time, the word *marry* was also used as an exclamation. Shakespeare is playing on both meanings in this passage.

29 **Discussion** How does Juliet feel about marriage?

30 **Critical Thinking and Reading** Is this extended metaphor effective? Explain.

of marriage, could swear that they did not have any regrets about being married. Couples—real or pretend—who asserted they had no regrets were placed on trial, at which they had to prove their claim. Twelve guests (the jury) and a judge questioned the couples to try to disprove their claim. The result was usually a humorous dialogue of "What if . . ." questions and ingenious responses. For example, the judge might ask the wife: "What if your husband chased the dog into the banquet hall, which spooked the cat, which leapt into the bowl of cream, which splashed the guest of honor?" The wife then had to give an immediate response to prove her gladness that her husband caused these unfortunate events. After the couples were questioned, the jury would then decide the verdict and name the couple that would "bring home the bacon."

The last event of the day was a candlelight procession around the feast hall. Everyone carried a small loaf of bread in which a candle was placed. Afterward, they would set aside three quarters of the bread to be eaten the following day. They preserved the remaining quarter for the next year's celebration, at which time the bread would be made into crumbs and fed to the birds to indicate the beginning of the new festival.

31 Discussion How can Romeo and his friends go to the party and not be recognized?

NURSE. No less? Nay, bigger! Women grow by men.

LADY CAPULET. Speak briefly, can you like of Paris' love?

JULIET. I'll look to like, if looking liking move;[12]
But no more deep will I endart mine eye
100   Than your consent gives strength to make it fly.[13]

[*Enter* SERVINGMAN.]

SERVINGMAN. Madam, the guests are come, supper served up, you called, my young lady asked for, the nurse cursed in the pantry, and everything in extremity. I must hence to wait. I beseech you follow straight.   [*Exit.*]

105 **LADY CAPULET.** We follow thee. Juliet, the County stays.[14]

NURSE. Go, girl, seek happy nights to happy days. [*Exit.*]

Scene iv. *A street*

31 [*Enter* ROMEO, MERCUTIO, BENVOLIO, *with five or six other* MASKERS; TORCHBEARERS.]

ROMEO. What, shall this speech[1] be spoke for our excuse?
Or shall we on without apology?

BENVOLIO. The date is out of such prolixity.[2]
We'll have no Cupid hoodwinked with a scarf,
5   Bearing a Tartar's painted bow of lath,

302   *Drama*

12. I'll . . . move: If looking favorably at someone leads to liking him, I'll look at Paris in a way that will lead to liking him.
13. But . . . fly: But I won't look harder than you want me to.

14. the County stays: The Count, Paris, is waiting.

1. this speech: Romeo asks whether he and his companions, being uninvited guests, should follow custom by announcing their arrival in a speech.

2. The . . . prolixity: Such wordiness is outdated. In the following lines, Benvolio says, in sum: "Let's forget about announcing our entrance with a show. The other guests can look us over as they see fit. We'll dance a while, then leave."

Scaring the ladies like a crowkeeper,
Nor no without-book prologue, faintly spoke
After the prompter, for our entrance;
But, let them measure us by what they will,
10   We'll measure them a measure and be gone.

ROMEO. Give me a torch. I am not for this ambling.
Being but heavy,[3] I will bear the light.

MERCUTIO. Nay, gentle Romeo, we must have you dance.

ROMEO. Not I, believe me. You have dancing shoes
15   With nimble soles; I have a soul of lead
So stakes me to the ground I cannot move.

MERCUTIO. You are a lover. Borrow Cupid's wings
And soar with them above a common bound.

ROMEO. I am too sore enpiercèd with his shaft
20   To soar with his light feathers; and so bound
I cannot bound a pitch above dull woe.
Under love's heavy burden do I sink.

MERCUTIO. And, to sink in it, should you burden love—
Too great oppression for a tender thing.

25   **ROMEO.** Is love a tender thing? It is too rough,
Too rude, too boist'rous, and it pricks like thorn.

MERCUTIO. If love be rough with you, be rough with love.
Prick love for pricking, and you beat love down.
Give me a case to put my visage[4] in.
30   A visor for a visor![5] What care I
What curious eye doth quote deformities?[6]
Here are the beetle brows shall blush for me.

BENVOLIO. Come, knock and enter; and no sooner in
But every man betake him to his legs.[7]

35   **ROMEO.** A torch for me! Let wantons light of heart
Tickle the senseless rushes[8] with their heels;
For I am proverbed with a grandsire phrase,[9]
I'll be a candleholder and look on;
The game was ne'er so fair, and I am done.[10]

MERCUTIO. Tut! Dun's the mouse, the constable's own
40   word![11]
If thou art Dun,[12] we'll draw thee from the mire
Of this sir-reverence love, wherein thou stickest
Up to the ears. Come, we burn daylight, ho!

ROMEO. Nay, that's not so.

3. heavy: Weighed down with sadness.

4. visage: Mask.

5. A visor . . . visor!: A mask for a mask—which is what my real face is like!

6. quote deformities: Notice my ugly features.

7. betake . . . legs: Start dancing.

8. Let . . . rushes: Let fun-loving people dance on the floor coverings.

9. proverbed . . . phrase: Directed by an old saying.

10. The game . . . done: No matter how much enjoyment may be had, I won't have any.

11. Dun's . . . word!: Lie low like a mouse—that's what a constable waiting to make an arrest might say.

12. Dun: Proverbial name for a horse.

The Tragedy of Romeo and Juliet, Act I, Scene iv   303

32 Discussion What does Benvolio's plan suggest about his personality?

33 Discussion Why do you think Mercutio teases Romeo?

34 Enrichment Mercutio's name comes from that of the Roman god Mercury, who was known for eloquence, cleverness, and thievery.

35 Discussion What does this speech reveal about Mercutio? To what extent does he resemble the god after whom he was named?

MERCUTIO.   I mean, sir, in delay

45   We waste our lights in vain, like lights by day.
      Take our good meaning, for our judgment sits
      Five times in that ere once in our five wits.[13]

ROMEO. And we mean well in going to this masque,
      But 'tis no wit to go.

MERCUTIO.   Why, may one ask?

ROMEO. I dreamt a dream tonight.

50   **MERCUTIO.**   And so did I.

ROMEO. Well, what was yours?

MERCUTIO.   That dreamers often lie.

ROMEO. In bed asleep, while they do dream things true.

MERCUTIO. O, then I see Queen Mab[14] hath been with you.
      She is the fairies' midwife, and she comes
55   In shape no bigger than an agate stone
      On the forefinger of an alderman,
      Drawn with a team of little atomies[15]
      Over men's noses as they lie asleep;
      Her wagon spokes made of long spinners'[16] legs,
60   The cover, of the wings of grasshoppers;
      Her traces, of the smallest spider web;
      Her collars, of the moonshine's wat'ry beams;
      Her whip, of cricket's bone; the lash, of film;[17]
      Her wagoner, a small gray-coated gnat,
65   Not half so big as a round little worm
      Pricked from the lazy finger of a maid;
      Her chariot is an empty hazelnut,
      Made by the joiner squirrel or old grub,[18]

13. Take . . . wits: Understand my intended meaning. That shows more intelligence than merely following what your senses perceive.

14. Queen Mab: The queen of fairyland.

15. atomies: Creatures.

16. spinners: Spiders.

17. film: Spider's thread.

18. old grub: An insect that bores holes in nuts.

Commentary: The Power of the Stars and Planets

Reread Romeo's statement at the end of Act I, Scene iv, ll. 106, in which he says he is fearful that his life will be cut short as determined by the stars. Point out to students that belief in the stars' influence on humankind and in astrology were common in the sixteenth century.

Many Elizabethans believed in astrology—the notion that the positions of the moon, sun, and planets—were responsible for their general dispositions. For example, they believed that the zodiac sign under which a person was born and the position of the planets at that time determined his or her general character.

Elizabethans also believed that the planetary influences that determined a person's character were separate from the control the stars had on humankind. They believed the stars determined a person's fate. For example, it was the stars that determined if a person would live a long and happy life or a short life wrought with unhappiness. It is this belief that causes Romeo to be fearful that his life will be cut short as the stars have fated.

Time out o' mind the fairies' coachmakers.
70 And in this state she gallops night by night
Through lovers' brains, and then they dream of love;
On courtiers' knees, that dream on curtsies straight;
O'er lawyers' fingers, who straight dream on fees;
O'er ladies' lips, who straight on kisses dream,
75 Which oft the angry Mab with blisters plagues,
Because their breath with sweetmeats¹⁹ tainted are.
Sometimes she gallops o'er a courtier's nose,
And then dreams he of smelling out a suit;²⁰
And sometime comes she with a tithe pig's²¹ tail
80 Tickling a parson's nose as 'a lies asleep,
Then he dreams of another benefice.²²
Sometime she driveth o'er a soldier's neck,
And then dream he of cutting foreign throats,
Of breaches, ambuscadoes,²³ Spanish blades,
85 Of healths²⁴ five fathom deep; and then anon
Drums in his ear, at which he starts and wakes,
And being thus frighted, swears a prayer or two
And sleeps again. This is that very Mab
That plats²⁵ the manes of horses in the night
90 And bakes the elflocks²⁶ in foul sluttish hairs,
Which once untangled much misfortune bodes.
This is the hag, when maids lie on their backs,
That presses them and learns them first to bear,
Making them women of good carriage.²⁷
This is she—

95 **ROMEO.**   Peace, peace, Mercutio, peace!
Thou talk'st of nothing.

MERCUTIO.   True, I talk of dreams;
Which are the children of an idle brain,
Begot of nothing but vain fantasy;
Which is as thin of substance as the air,
100 And more inconstant than the wind, who woos
Even now the frozen bosom of the North
And, being angered, puffs away from thence,
Turning his side to the dew-dropping South.

BENVOLIO. This wind you talk of blows us from ourselves.
105 Supper is done, and we shall come too late.

ROMEO. I fear, too early; for my mind misgives
Some consequence yet hanging in the stars
Shall bitterly begin his fearful date
With this night's revels and expire the term

The Tragedy of Romeo and Juliet, Act I, Scene v   305

19. sweetmeats: Candy.
20. smelling . . . suit: Finding someone who has a petition (suit) for the king and who will pay the courtier to gain the king's favor for the petition.
21. tithe pig: A pig donated to a parson.
22. benefice: A church appointment that included a guaranteed income.
23. ambuscadoes: Ambushes.
24. healths: Toasts ("To your health!").

25. plats: Tangles.
26. elflocks: Tangled hair.

27. carriage: Posture.

38 Critical Thinking and Reading
How does Mercutio's imagery reflect his personality?

39 Reading Strategy Have students identify where else in this act "the stars" and fate have been mentioned.

Because many Elizabethans feared the stars determined their fate, they sought astrologers to tell them their horoscopes. To determine the horoscopes, astrologers would track the stars and the movements of the sun, moon, and planets and predict the effect these would have on humankind. Elizabethan astrologers, it seems, were unaware of Copernicus' theory of planetary order, which was published in 1543, fifty-two years before *Romeo and Juliet* was written. Astrologers believed that the Earth was at the center of the universe and that the sun, moon, and planets revolved around it.

Ask students why Romeo and Juliet might have been referred to as "star-crossed lovers" and their love said to be "death-mark'd" in the play's prologue (p. 287).

40 Discussion Why do you think Shakespeare included this exchange?

41 Discussion What is Capulet's mood?

42 Discussion What is the atmosphere of the party?

110 Of a despisèd life, closed in my breast,
By some vile forfeit of untimely death.[28]
But he that hath the steerage of my course
Direct my sail! On, lusty gentlemen!

BENVOLIO. Strike, drum.

[*They march about the stage, and retire to one side.*]

Scene v. *A hall in* CAPULET'S *house.*

[SERVINGMEN *come forth with napkins.*]

FIRST SERVINGMAN. Where's Potpan, that he helps not to take away? He shift a trencher![1] He scrape a trencher!

SECOND SERVINGMAN. When good manners shall lie all in one or two men's hands, and they unwashed too, 'tis a
5 foul thing.

FIRST SERVINGMAN. Away with the join-stools, remove the court cupboard, look to the plate. Good thou, save me a piccc of marchpane,[2] and, as thou loves me, let the porter let in Susan Grindstone and Nell. Anthony, and
10 Potpan!

SECOND SERVINGMAN. Ay, boy, ready.

FIRST SERVINGMAN. You are looked for and called for, asked for and sought for, in the great chamber.

THIRD SERVINGMAN. We cannot be here and there too.
15 Cheerly, boys! Be brisk awhile, and the longer liver take all. [*Exit.*]

[*Enter* CAPULET, *his* WIFE, JULIET, TYBALT, NURSE, *and all the* GUESTS *and* GENTLEWOMEN *to the* MASKERS.]

CAPULET. Welcome, gentlemen! Ladies that have their toes
Unplagued with corns will walk a bout[3] with you.
Ah, my mistresses, which of you all
20 Will now deny to dance? She that makes dainty,[4]
She I'll swear hath corns. Am I come near ye now?
Welcome, gentlemen! I have seen the day
That I have worn a visor and could tell
A whispering tale in a fair lady's ear,
25 Such as would please. 'Tis gone, 'tis gone, 'tis gone.
You are welcome, gentlemen! Come, musicians, play.
[*Music plays, and they dance.*]
A hall,[5] a hall! Give room! And foot it, girls.
More light, you knaves, and turn the tables up,

28. my mind . . . death: My mind is fearful that some future event, fated by the stars, shall start to run its course tonight and cut my life short.

1. trencher: Wooden platter.

2. marchpane: Marzipan, a confection made of sugar and almonds.

3. walk a bout: Dance a turn.

4. makes dainty: Hesitates, acts shy.

5. A hall: Clear the floor, make room for dancing.

Literary Element: Imagery

Images are words and phrases that appeal to the senses—sight, sound, smell, touch, and taste. Imagery is the use of images throughout any given work to form an overall picture, tone, or impression.

In *Romeo and Juliet,* a dominant image is light. Have students read Romeo's description of Juliet in Act I, Scene v.

Then ask them to read aloud the lines that contain images of light, for example, "O, she doth teach the torches to burn bright!"

Afterward, read the quotation that follows by Caroline Spurgeon, from *Shakespeare's Imagery and What It Tells Us,* in which she comments on the light imagery in *Romeo and Juliet:*

> To Juliet, Romeo is "day in night"; to Romeo, Juliet is the sun rising from the east, and when they soar to love's ecstasy, each alike pictures the other as stars in heaven, shedding such brightness as puts to shame the heavenly bodies themselves. (p. 310)

Ask students what tone or impression the light imagery elicits.

In contrast to his light imagery, Shakespeare also uses

And quench the fire; the room is grown too hot.
30　Ah, sirrah, this unlooked-for sport comes well.
Nay, sit; nay, sit, good cousin Capulet;
For you and I are past our dancing days.
How long is't now since last yourself and I
Were in a mask?

SECOND CAPULET. By'r Lady, thirty years.

35　**CAPULET.** What, man? 'Tis not so much, 'tis not so much;
'Tis since the nuptial of Lucentio,
Come Pentecost as quickly as it will,
Some five-and-twenty years, and then we masked.

SECOND CAPULET. 'Tis more, 'tis more. His son is elder, sir;
His son is thirty.

40　**CAPULET.**　　　Will you tell me that?
His son was but a ward[6] two years ago.

ROMEO. [*To a* SERVINGMAN] What lady's that which doth
enrich the hand
Of yonder knight?

SERVINGMAN.　　　I know not, sir.

45　**ROMEO.** O, she doth teach the torches to burn bright!
It seems she hangs upon the cheek of night
As a rich jewel in an Ethiop's ear—
Beauty too rich for use, for earth too dear!
So shows a snowy dove trooping with crows
50　As yonder lady o'er her fellows shows.
The measure done, I'll watch her place of stand
And, touching hers, make blessèd my rude hand.
Did my heart love till now? Forswear[7] it, sight!
For I ne'er saw true beauty till this night.

55　**TYBALT.** This, by his voice, should be a Montague.
Fetch me my rapier, boy. What! Dares the slave
Come hither, covered with an antic face,[8]
To fleer[9] and scorn at our solemnity?
Now, by the stock and honor of my kin,
60　To strike him dead I hold it not a sin.

CAPULET. Why, how now, kinsman? Wherefore storm you
so?

TYBALT. Uncle, this is a Montague, our foe,
A villain, that is hither come in spite
To scorn at our solemnity this night.

6. ward: A minor.

7. Forswear: Deny.
8. antic face: Strange,
fantastic mask.
9. fleer: Mock.

The Tragedy of Romeo and Juliet, Act I, Scene v　307

43 Discussion How does this good-natured argument reflect the advanced age of the participants?

44 Literary Focus Romeo's description of Juliet is written in iambic pentameter couplets rather than blank verse. This change of form makes the speech stand out.

45 Critical Thinking and Reading What can you infer about Tybalt from this speech?

Master Teacher Note Because much of Act I, Scene v, takes place during the Capulet's party, you might want to give students a taste of Elizabethan music and food. For example, you might play *Robin Is to the Greenwood Gone,* performed by Paul O'Dette (Book of the Month Club recording number 67–6553); *The Scholars: The Silver Swan and Other Elizabethan and Jacobean Madrigals* (Book of the Month Club recording number 97–6556); or any similar recordings. You might also look for recordings of Elizabethan music performed by Julian Bream or composed by John Dowland.

For a taste of Elizabethan food, you or your students might prepare some Elizabethan dishes from *To the Queen's Taste* by Lorna Sass, published by The Metropolitan Museum of Art, 1976.

images of darkness, which generate a different tone or impression. Have students compare the images of darkness in the following passages from *Romeo and Juliet* with the light imagery on the preceding quotation. For example, what tone or impression do the following lines from Act III, Scene v, containing imagery of darkness and rain present the reader?

When the sun sets, the air doth drizzle dew;
But for the sunset of my brother's son
It rains downright. (Act III, Sc. v, 11. 127–129)

More light and light: more dark and dark our woes!
(Act III, Sc. v, 11. 36)

Student Activity. In addition to images of light and dark, Shakespeare also includes images of poison, graves, dreams, and color, each of which creates its own tone and impression for the reader. In a notebook, trace one of these recurring images through the play as follows: Divide a sheet of paper into four columns. In one column copy the lines; in the second, indicate the location of the lines; in the third, state who said them; and in the fourth, note what impression or tone the lines convey. Then as a class discuss the role of these images and their importance to the play.

46 Discussion Give two reasons why Capulet restrains Tybalt.

47 Discussion Why is Capulet so angry at Tybalt?

48 Reading Strategy Have students predict what Tybalt will do.

CAPULET. Young Romeo is it?

65 **TYBALT.**   'Tis he, that villain Romeo.

CAPULET. Content thee, gentle coz,[10] let him alone.
    'A bears him like a portly gentleman,[11]
    And, to say truth, Verona brags of him
    To be a virtuous and well-governed youth.
70 I would not for the wealth of all this town
    Here in my house do him disparagement.[12]
    Therefore be patient; take no note of him.
    It is my will, the which if thou respect,
    Show a fair presence and put off these frowns,
75 An ill-beseeming semblance[13] for a feast.

TYBALT. It fits when such a villain is a guest.
    I'll not endure him.

CAPULET.   He shall be endured.
    What, goodman[14] boy! I say he shall. Go to![15]
    Am I the master here, or you? Go to!
80 You'll not endure him, God shall mend my soul![16]
    You'll make a mutiny among my guests!
    You will set cock-a-hoop.[17] You'll be the man!

TYBALT. Why, uncle, 'tis a shame.

CAPULET.   Go to, go to!
    You are a saucy boy. Is't so, indeed?
85 This trick may chance to scathe you.[18] I know what.
    You must contrary me! Marry, 'tis time—
    Well said, my hearts!—You are a princox[19]—go!
    Be quiet, or—More light, more light!—For shame!
    I'll make you quiet. What!—Cheerly, my hearts!

90 **TYBALT.** Patience perforce with willful choler meeting[20]
    Makes my flesh tremble in their different greeting.
    I will withdraw; but this intrusion shall,
    Now seeming sweet, convert to bitt'rest gall.   [*Exit.*]

ROMEO. If I profane with my unworthiest hand
95   This holy shrine,[21] the gentle sin is this:
    My lips, two blushing pilgrims, ready stand
        To smooth that rough touch with a tender kiss.

JULIET. Good pilgrim, you do wrong your hand too much,
        Which mannerly devotion shows in this;
100   For saints have hands that pilgrims' hands do touch,
        And palm to palm is holy palmers'[22] kiss.

ROMEO. Have not saints lips, and holy palmers too?

10. coz: Here *coz* is used as a term of address for any relative.
11. 'A ... gentleman: He behaves like a dignified gentleman.
12. disparagement: Insult.

13. ill-beseeming semblance: Inappropriate appearance.

14. goodman: A term of address for someone below the rank of gentleman.
15. Go to!: An expression of angry impatience.
16. God ... soul!: An expression of impatience, equivalent to *God save me!*
17. You will set cock-a-hoop: You want to swagger like a barnyard rooster.

18. This ... you: This trait of yours may turn out to hurt you.
19. princox: Rude youngster, wise guy.

20. Patience ... meeting: Enforced self-control mixing with strong anger.

21. shrine: Juliet's hand.

22. palmers: Pilgrims, who at one time carried palm branches from the Holy Land.

JULIET. Ay, pilgrim, lips that they must use in prayer.

ROMEO. O, then, dear saint, let lips do what hands do!
105   They pray; grant thou, lest faith turn to despair.

JULIET. Saints do not move,²³ though grant for prayers'
    sake.

ROMEO. Then move not while my prayer's effect I take.
    Thus from my lips, by thine my sin is purged.
                             [*Kisses her.*]

JULIET. Then have my lips the sin that they have took.

110 **ROMEO.** Sin from my lips? O trespass sweetly urged!²⁴
    Give me my sin again.   [*Kisses her.*]

JULIET.   You kiss by th' book.²⁵

NURSE. Madam, your mother craves a word with you.

ROMEO. What is her mother?

NURSE.   Marry, bachelor,
    Her mother is the lady of the house,
115   And a good lady, and a wise and virtuous.
    I nursed her daughter that you talked withal.
    I tell you, he that can lay hold of her
    Shall have the chinks.²⁶

ROMEO.   Is she a Capulet?
    O dear account! My life is my foe's debt.²⁷

120 **BENVOLIO.** Away, be gone; the sport is at the best.

23. move: Initiate involvement in earthly affairs.

24. O . . . urged!: Romeo is saying, in substance, that he is happy. Juliet calls his kiss a sin, for now he can take it back—by another kiss.

25. by th' book: As if you were following a manual of courtly love.

26. chinks: Cash.

27. My life . . . debt: Since Juliet is a Capulet, Romeo's life is at the mercy of the enemies of his family.

Reader's Response If you were Juliet's or Romeo's best friend, what advice would you give to the "star-crossed lover" at the end of Act I? For example, would you discourage or encourage him or her from falling in love? Why?

Thematic Response Both Romeo and Juliet awaken to the dangers that threaten their love. Which do you think will be stronger in the end, their love or their families' hatred?

ROMEO. Ay, so I fear: the more is my unrest.

CAPULET. Nay, gentlemen, prepare not to be gone:
We have a trifling foolish banquet towards.[28]
Is it e'en so?[29] Why then, I thank you all.
125 I thank you, honest gentlemen. Good night.
More torches here! Come on then; let's to bed.
Ah, sirrah, by my fay,[30] it waxes late;
I'll to my rest.   [*Exit all but* JULIET *and* NURSE.]

JULIET. Come hither, nurse. What is yond gentleman?

130 **NURSE.** The son and heir of old Tiberio.

JULIET. What's he that now is going out of door?

NURSE. Marry, that, I think, be young Petruchio.

JULIET. What's he that follows here, that would not dance?

NURSE. I know not.

135 **JULIET.** Go ask his name—If he is married,
My grave is like to be my wedding bed.

NURSE. His name is Romeo, and a Montague,
The only son of your great enemy.

140 **JULIET.** My only love, sprung from my only hate!
Too early seen unknown, and known too late!
Prodigious[31] birth of love it is to me
That I must love a loathèd enemy.

NURSE. What's this? What's this?

JULIET.   A rhyme I learnt even now.
Of one I danced withal.   [*One calls within,* "Juliet."]

145 **NURSE.**   Anon, anon!
Come, let's away; the strangers all are gone.   [*Exit.*]

28. **towards:** Being prepared.
29. **Is . . . so?:** Is it the case that you really must leave?

30. **fay:** Faith.

31. **Prodigious:** Monstrous; foretelling misfortune.

RESPONDING TO THE **SELECTION**

Your Response

1. If you were Romeo or Juliet, would you continue on the path of your relationship? Why or why not?
2. Why do you think tales of forbidden love have appealed to people throughout history?

Recalling

3. Explain what you learn from the Prologue about the fate of Romeo and Juliet and the feud between the two families.
4. Why does the Prince want to settle the feud? With what penalty does he threaten the Montagues and Capulets for fighting?
5. Why is Romeo filled with melancholy in the

Closure and Extension

ANSWERS TO RESPONDING TO THE SELECTION
Your Response

1. Encourage students to consider the question of family loyalty *versus* personal desires. Discuss whether the young lovers have a right to challenge their families' senseless hatred.
2. Discuss the elements of danger and of tasting the "forbidden fruit" as attractive to young people. Suggest that the full knowledge of danger in this relationship may well be part of its attraction.

Recalling

3. The death of Romeo and Juliet will end the feud between the families.
4. The feud has upset the community three times and the citizens are tired of it. The next time it erupts, the guilty party will be sentenced to death.
5. He says he is in love with someone who is not in love with him. Benvolio says he should forget her and look for someone else.
6. She is rather indifferent and uninterested.
7. He thinks she is more beautiful than all the others there, and he falls in love with her.
8. He feels his life is at the mercy of his enemy. She thinks it is a cruel twist of fate to love an enemy.

first scene? How does Benvolio react to his mood?

6. Describe Juliet's response to her mother's announcement that Paris wishes to marry her.
7. Describe Romeo's reaction when he first sees Juliet.
8. Describe Romeo's and Juliet's reactions upon learning each other's identity.

Interpreting

9. Compare and contrast the personalities of Romeo and Juliet in Act I. Explain what is unusual about the way they speak to each other when they first meet.
10. Explain the possible threats to their love that are already present in Act I.
11. How does Juliet's comment when she asks her nurse to find out Romeo's name echo back to the Prologue? Find lines Romeo spoke earlier in the scene that have the same effect.

Applying

12. Romeo and Juliet fall in love at first sight. Do you believe love at first sight is possible? Explain your answer.

ANALYZING LITERATURE

Appreciating Blank Verse

Blank verse is unrhymed iambic pentameter. Normally, a line of such verse will consist of ten syllables with every second syllable stressed. However, poets and playwrights like Shakespeare often depart from the normal pattern for a number of reasons: to avoid monotony, to imitate the rhythms of real speech, to vary the "music" of the verse, and so on.

On a separate piece of paper, indicate the pattern of unaccented and accented syllables in lines 52–57 of Mercutio's Queen Mab speech (Scene iv). Use the mark ˘ for an unaccented syllable and the mark ´ for an accented one. This is how the first line should look:

Ŏ, thén Ĭ séé Quĕen Máb hăth beén wĭth yoú.

CRITICAL THINKING AND READING

Interpreting the Effect of Imagery

Throughout the play, imagery creates mood, reveals character, suggests ideas, and otherwise affects your response. In Scene v reread lines 94–111, which Romeo and Juliet speak when they first meet. Then answer the following questions about them.

1. What kind of imagery is introduced by the words "shrine," "sin," and "saints"?
2. How does this imagery affect your view of Romeo and Juliet?
3. Explain what the imagery suggests about Romeo and Juliet's love.

THINKING AND WRITING

Writing a Speech in Blank Verse

Write a speech to stop the fighting between two feuding families. Use Escalus's speech as a model for content and organization. Then rewrite your speech in blank verse. You can do so by changing individual words and phrases to fit the thought content into the blank-verse pattern.

When you revise your speech, read it aloud to hear how it sounds. See if you can increase its force and persuasiveness. Deliver your speech to a group of your classmates, and ask their opinion of its effectiveness.

LEARNING OPTION

Language. An allusion is a reference to something in another work of literature, mythology, or history. For example, in Scene i Romeo alludes to Cupid and Diana, both figures from Roman mythology. An allusion will enrich or reinforce a statement by drawing on the ideas, feelings, or images associated with the reference.

To better understand Romeo's feelings at the beginning of the play, look up Cupid and Diana in an encyclopedia or dictionary of mythology. Keep a list of other allusions you find in the play.

The Tragedy of Romeo and Juliet, Act I   311

Interpreting

9. Answers will differ. Most students will realize that Romeo is moody, impulsive, and romantic. Also, his wayward behavior is a source of concern to his parents. Juliet, by contrast, is a dutiful young girl who, before meeting Romeo, does not seem to have given much thought to love.

When they meet, they are so in tune with each other that their

words create a sonnet. Also, they use religious imagery.
10. Suggested Response: Tybalt threatens retaliation against Romeo. Juliet's family is considering her marriage to someone else.
11. Suggested Response: She says her only love has sprung from her only hate, an echo of the prologue's line, "From forth the fatal loins of these two foes." Romeo says, "My life is my foe's debt."

Applying

12. Answers will differ. Some students will agree; most will probably feel that true love comes after two people have come to know and enjoy being with each other.

ANSWERS TO ANALYZING LITERATURE

Ŏ, thén, Ĭ seé Quĕen Máb hăth beén wĭth yoú.

She ĭs thĕ faíriĕs' mídwĭfe, ănd shĕ comĕs
In shápe nŏ bíggĕr thán ăn ágătĕ stónĕ
On thĕ fórefíngĕr ŏf ăn áldĕrmăn,
Dráwn wĭth ă teám ŏf líttlĕ átŏmiĕs
Ovĕr mén's nósĕs ăs thĕy liĕ aśleép;

Challenge Have students compare the meter of this play with the meter of *The Song of Hiawatha* by Longfellow.

ANSWERS TO CRITICAL THINKING AND READING

1. Suggested Response: These words portray images associated with religious worship.
2. Answers will differ. Many students will respond that this imagery makes them take more seriously the love between Romeo and Juliet.
3. Suggested Response: This imagery suggests that their love is in some way holy and pure.

Writing Transparency Students often find it helpful to see a model of their writing assignment. Before students write, you may wish to show them Model 6: *Persuasive Essay* in the **Transparencies for Writing** and then review with them Escalus's speech as a model for content and organization.

Alternative Assessment Ask students to predict what will happen after this first encounter between Romeo and Juliet. How will they develop their relationship given the problem between their two families?

For Alternate Composition Assignments to assess your students' learning, see pages 364–365 of the Teaching Portfolio.

LEARNING OPTION

Visual learners will appreciate this activity. You might extend the activity by having students write brief versions of the myths alluded to in the play as they encounter them.

Preparation

Literary Focus Suggest to students that the "straight man" in a comedy team is a kind of dramatic foil for the comic. Have students think of comedy teams that function in this way.

Prereading Focus The purpose of this activity is to focus student attention on the differences between love and infatuation. Discuss the idea that love involves commitment, long-term effort, and self-sacrifice. Infatuation is usually a fleeting and superficial emotion. Ask students to consider whether infatuation can deepen into true love.

Vocabulary Have less advanced students read the words and their definitions several times.

GUIDE FOR READING

The Tragedy of Romeo and Juliet, Act II

The Dramatic Foil

A dramatic foil is a character who highlights or brings out the personality traits of another character in a play. Usually the foil contrasts with the other character, and the contrast serves to emphasize the other character's traits. For example, in Act I of *Romeo and Juliet,* Benvolio, who tries to quiet the brawling servants, is a dramatic foil to the fiery Tybalt. More important, by his calm and sensible disposition, he is a dramatic foil to the moody, emotional Romeo.

Focus

In Act I Romeo attends the party at the Capulet's house to see the girl with whom he is infatuated, Rosaline. He leaves the house believing he is deeply in love with Juliet. Do you think his feelings for Juliet represent true love or merely infatuation? Divide a piece of paper into two columns. Label one column "Love" and the other column "Infatuation." Under the appropriate headings, write down some of the signs and characteristics that indicate love and some of those that indicate infatuation. As you continue reading the play, see if Romeo and Juliet display the traits you have identified in either column.

Vocabulary

Knowing the following words will help you as you read Act II of *Romeo and Juliet.*

kinsmen (kinz′ mən) *n.*: Relatives (p. 316)

cunning (kun′ iŋ) *n.*: Cleverness; slyness (p. 317)

variable (ver′ ē ə b'l) *adj.*: Changeable; inconstant (p. 318)

procure (prō kyoor′) *v.*: Get; obtain (p. 319)

vile (vīl) *adj.*: Worthless; cheap; low (p. 320)

sallow (sal′ ō) *adj.*: Of a sickly pale-yellowish complexion (p. 322)

waverer (wā′ vər ər) *n.*: One who changes or is unsteady (p. 322)

lamentable (lam′ ən tə b'l) *adj.*: Distressing; sad (p. 323)

unwieldy (un wēl′ dē) *adj.*: Awkward; clumsy (p. 329)

312 Drama

Objectives

1 To understand the dramatic foil
2 To modernize dialogue
3 To express individual interests and abilities through optional activities

Support Material

Teaching Portfolio
Teacher Backup, p. 347
Grammar in Action Worksheets, *Understanding Antecedents,* p. 350; *Determining Author's Tone,* p. 352
Usage and Mechanics Worksheet, p. 354
Vocabulary Check, p. 355
Analyzing Literature, *Understanding the Dramatic Foil,* p. 357

Language Worksheet, *Interpreting Personification,* p. 358
Selection Test, p. 359

Library of Video Classics
Romeo and Juliet; Shakespeare in Rehearsal: Romeo and Juliet; Shakespeare in Conversation

Literature Videodiscs
Shakespeare in Rehearsal: Romeo and Juliet; Shakespeare in Conversation

Prentice Hall Literature Writing Studio

Act II

PROLOGUE

[*Enter* CHORUS.]

CHORUS. Now old desire¹ doth in his deathbed lie,
  And young affection gapes to be his heir;²
  That fair³ for which love groaned for and would die,
  With tender Juliet matched, is now not fair.
5 Now Romeo is beloved and loves again,
  Alike bewitchèd⁴ by the charm of looks;
  But to his foe supposed he must complain,⁵
  And she steal love's sweet bait from fearful hooks.
  Being held a foe, he may not have access
10   To breathe such vows as lovers use to swear,
  And she as much in love, her means much less
   To meet her new belovèd anywhere;
  But passion lends them power, time means to meet,
  Temp'ring extremities with extreme sweet.⁶   [*Exit.*]

Scene i. *Near* CAPULET'S *orchard.*

[*Enter* ROMEO *alone.*]

ROMEO. Can I go forward when my heart is here?
  Turn back, dull earth,¹ and find thy center² out.

[*Enter* BENVOLIO *with* MERCUTIO. ROMEO *retires.*]

BENVOLIO. Romeo! My cousin Romeo! Romeo!

MERCUTIO.   He is wise
  And, on my life, hath stol'n him home to bed.

5 **BENVOLIO.** He ran this way and leapt this orchard wall.
  Call, good Mercutio.

MERCUTIO.   Nay, I'll conjure³ too.
  Romeo! Humors! Madman! Passion! Lover!
  Appear thou in the likeness of a sigh;
  Speak but one rhyme, and I am satisfied!
10 Cry but "Ay me!" pronounce but "love" and "dove";
  Speak to my gossip⁴ Venus one fair word,
  One nickname for her purblind son and heir,
  Young Abraham Cupid, he that shot so true
  When King Cophetua loved the beggar maid!
15 He heareth not, he stirreth not, he moveth not;
  The ape is dead,⁵ and I must conjure him.
  I conjure thee by Rosaline's bright eyes,

---

1. old desire: Romeo's love for Rosaline.
2. young . . . heir: Romeo's new love for Juliet is eager to replace his love for Rosaline.
3. fair: Beautiful woman (Rosaline).
4. Alike bewitchèd: Both Romeo and Juliet are enchanted.
5. complain: Address his words of love.

6. Temp'ring . . . sweet: Easing their difficulties with great delights.

1. dull earth: Lifeless body.
2. center: Heart, or possibly soul (Juliet).

3. conjure: Recite a spell to make Romeo appear.

4. gossip: Merry old lady.

5. The ape is dead: Romeo, like a trained monkey, seems to be playing dead.

The Tragedy of Romeo and Juliet, Act II, Scene i   313

Thematic Focus Each of the two lovers goes through a rite of passage in this act. Romeo discovers the difference between infatuation and love. Juliet realizes that there is more to life than being a dutiful daughter. Ask students if they have experienced such rites of passage. Did their experiences involve a great inward struggle? Were they changed as a result of their experiences?

Presentation

Motivation/Prior Knowledge
Have students predict whether Romeo will try to see Juliet. If he decides to see her again, what difficulties will he face?

Master Teacher Note Tell students that a tragic character's flaw is the weakness that will lead to his tragic downfall. Have them speculate about the nature of Romeo's flaw. Then ask them to look for evidence of it as they read this act.

Purpose-Setting Question How are Mercutio and the Nurse foils for Romeo and Juliet?

1 Discussion Does the prologue provide a useful introduction to each act, or is it unnecessary? Explain.

2 Reading Strategy Have students paraphrase these lines.

3 Literary Focus How does Mercutio's attitude toward love contrast with Romeo's?

4 Enrichment Elizabethan audiences were noisy and often called out to the actors. What do you think they might have called out to Mercutio when he mentioned Rosaline?

313

5 Discussion Why is it ironic that Mercutio teases Romeo about Rosaline?

6 Discussion Explain the metaphor that Romeo uses to describe Juliet. How does this figure of speech reveal Romeo's feelings about her?

Alternative Assessment To promote active reading, have your students continue their reader's response journal as they read Act II. Ask them to focus their observations on the details that complicate the plot as well as those that show the personalities of Benvolio, Mercutio, and Tybalt. Encourage students to respond personally to the events. How do they feel about the hasty secret marriage? What would they have done in a similar situation?

Their observations will enable you to assess their understanding of the issues in the play.

By her high forehead and her scarlet lip,
By her fine foot, straight leg, and quivering thigh,
20 And the demesnes that there adjacent lie,
That in thy likeness thou appear to us!

BENVOLIO. And if he hear thee, thou wilt anger him.

MERCUTIO. This cannot anger him. 'Twould anger him
To raise a spirit in his mistress' circle
25 Of some strange nature, letting it there stand
Till she had laid it and conjured it down.
That were some spite; my invocation
Is fair and honest; in his mistress' name,
I conjure only but to raise up him.

30 **BENVOLIO.** Come, he hath hid himself among these trees
To be consorted[6] with the humorous[7] night.
Blind is his love and best befits the dark.

MERCUTIO. If love be blind, love cannot hit the mark.
Now will he sit under a medlar tree
35 And wish his mistress were that kind of fruit
As maids call medlars[8] when they laugh alone.
O, Romeo, that she were, O that she were
An open *et cetera*, thou a pop'rin pear!
Romeo, good night. I'll to my truckle bed;[9]
40 This field bed is too cold for me to sleep.
Come, shall we go?

BENVOLIO.   Go then, for 'tis in vain
To seek him here that means not to be found.

[*Exit with others.*]

6. consorted: Associated.
7. humorous: Humid; moody, like a lover.

8. medlars: An applelike fruits.

9. truckle bed: A trundle-bed, placed under a larger bed when not in use.

Scene ii. CAPULET'S *orchard.*

ROMEO. [*Coming forward*] He jests at scars that never felt a wound.

[*Enter* JULIET *at a window.*]

But soft! What light through yonder window breaks?
It is the East, and Juliet is the sun!
5 Arise, fair sun, and kill the envious moon,
Who is already sick and pale with grief
That thou her maid art far more fair than she.
Be not her maid, since she is envious.
Her vestal livery[1] is but sick and green,
10 And none but fools do wear it. Cast it off.
It is my lady! O, it is my love!

1. livery: Clothing or costume worn by a servant.

314 Drama

Grammar in Action

Pronouns get their meaning from the words they stand for. These words are called **antecedents.** Personal pronouns agree with their antecedents in number, person, and gender, as follows:

Jerri paid for *her* mother's new ring. (*Her* refers to *Jerri,* both the pronoun and its antecedent are singular, third person, feminine.)
Holmes and *his* client ate *their* meal in silence. (*His* refers to *Holmes;* both are singular, third person, masculine. *Their*

refers to *Holmes . . . and client,* both the antecedent and the pronoun are plural, third person.)

Since poetry is such a concentrated literary form, poets must be especially careful in their use of pronouns and antecedents. Note the following examples from *Romeo and Juliet:*

1. But soft! What light through yonder window breaks?
2. *It* is the East, and Juliet is the sun!
3. Arise, fair sun, and kill the envious moon,
4. *Who* is already sick and pale with grief
5. That *thou her* maid art far more fair than *she.*
6. Be not *her* maid, since *she* is envious.

O, that she knew she were!
She speaks, yet she says nothing. What of that?
Her eye discourses; I will answer it.
15 I am too bold; 'tis not to me she speaks.
Two of the fairest stars in all the heaven,
Having some business, do entreat her eyes
To twinkle in their spheres² till they return.   **2. spheres:** Orbits.
What if her eyes were there, they in her head?
20 The brightness of her cheek would shame those stars
As daylight doth a lamp; her eyes in heaven
Would through the airy region stream so bright
That birds would sing and think it were not night.
See how she leans her cheek upon that hand,
25 O, that I were a glove upon that hand,
That I might touch that cheek!

JULIET.   Ay me!

ROMEO.   She speaks.
O, speak again, bright angel, for thou art
As glorious to this night, being o'er my head,
As is a wingèd messenger of heaven
30 Unto the white-upturnèd wond'ring eyes
Of mortals that fall back to gaze on him
When he bestrides the lazy puffing clouds
And sails upon the bosom of the air.

JULIET. O Romeo, Romeo! Wherefore art thou Romeo?³   **3. Wherefore . . . Romeo?**
35 Deny thy father and refuse thy name;   Why are you Romeo—a
Or, if thou wilt not, be but sworn my love,   Montague?
And I'll no longer be a Capulet.

ROMEO. [*Aside*] Shall I hear more, or shall I speak at this?

JULIET. 'Tis but thy name that is my enemy.
40 Thou art thyself, though not⁴ a Montague.   **4. though not:** Even if you
What's Montague? It is nor hand, nor foot,   were not.
Nor arm, nor face. O, be some other name
Belonging to a man.
What's in a name? That which we call a rose
45 By any other name would smell as sweet.
So Romeo would, were he not Romeo called,
Retain that dear perfection which he owes⁵   **5. owes:** Owns, possesses.
Without that title. Romeo, doff⁶ thy name;   **6. doff:** Remove.
And for thy name, which is no part of thee,
Take all myself.

50 **ROMEO.**   I take thee at thy word.

The Tragedy of Romeo and Juliet, Act II, Scene ii   315

In line 2, the pronoun *it* refers to *window*. *Who* in line 4 refers to *moon*. *Thou* in line 5 refers to *sun* (or Juliet). *Her* and *she* in lines 5 and 6 both refer to *moon*. If Shakespeare had not used pronouns and antecedents correctly, readers would have been unable to unravel the meaning.

Student Activity 1. Identify the antecedents of the italicized pronouns in the following passage:

Juliet (to Romeo). Well, do not swear. Although I joy in *thee*,
I have no joy of this contract tonight.
It is too rash, too unadvised, too sudden;
Too like the lightning, which doth cease to be
Ere one can say *it* lightens . . .

Student Activity 2. Write a brief description of your reaction to Romeo or Juliet. Underline each pronoun and circle its antecedent.

Electronic Handbook You may wish students to review antecedents before completing the Grammar in Action activities. If students have access to the Language Master 6000, have them enter the access words *pronoun* and *each* and press the GRAMMAR key to obtain information on antecedents.

315

Call me but love, and I'll be new baptized;
Henceforth I never will be Romeo.

9 **JULIET.** What man art thou, thus bescreened in night,
So stumblest on my counsel?[7]

7. **counsel:** Secret thoughts.

10 **ROMEO.**   By a name
55 I know not how to tell thee who I am.
My name, dear saint, is hateful to myself
Because it is an enemy to thee.
Had I it written, I would tear the word.

JULIET. My ears have yet not drunk a hundred words
60 Of thy tongue's uttering, yet I know the sound.
Art thou not Romeo, and a Montague?

ROMEO. Neither, fair maid, if either thee dislike.

JULIET. How camest thou hither, tell me, and wherefore?
The orchard walls are high and hard to climb,
65 And the place death, considering who thou art,
If any of my kinsmen find thee here.

11 **ROMEO.** With love's light wings did I o'erperch[8] these walls;
For stony limits cannot hold love out,
And what love can do, that dares love attempt.
70 Therefore thy kinsmen are no stop to me.

8. **o'erperch:** Fly over.

JULIET. If they do see thee, they will murder thee.

ROMEO. Alack, there lies more peril in thine eye
Than twenty of their swords! Look thou but sweet,
And I am proof[9] against their enmity.

75 **JULIET.** I would not for the world they saw thee here.

ROMEO. I have night's cloak to hide me from their eyes;
And but[10] thou love me, let them find me here.
My life were better ended by their hate
Than death prorogued,[11] wanting of thy love.

80 **JULIET.** By whose direction found'st thou out this place?

ROMEO. By love, that first did prompt me to inquire.
He lent me counsel, and I lent him eyes.
I am no pilot; yet, wert thou as far
As that vast shore washed with the farthest sea,
85 I should adventure[12] for such merchandise.

JULIET. Thou knowest the mask of night is on my face;
Else would a maiden blush bepaint my cheek
For that which thou hast heard me speak tonight.
Fain would I dwell on form[13]—fain, fain deny
90 What I have spoke; but farewell compliment![14]
Dost thou love me? I know thou wilt say "Ay";
And I will take thy word. Yet, if thou swear'st,
Thou mayst prove false. At lovers' perjuries,
They say Jove laughs. O gentle Romeo,
95 If thou dost love, pronounce it faithfully.
Or if thou thinkest I am too quickly won,
I'll frown and be perverse[15] and say thee nay,
So thou wilt woo; but else, not for the world.
In truth, fair Montague, I am too fond,[16]
100 And therefore thou mayst think my havior light;[17]
But trust me, gentleman, I'll prove more true
Than those that have more cunning to be strange.[18]
I should have been more strange, I must confess,
But that thou overheard'st, ere I was ware,
105 My truelove passion. Therefore pardon me,
And not impute this yielding to light love,
Which the dark night hath so discovered.[19]

ROMEO. Lady, by yonder blessèd moon I vow,
That tips with silver all these fruit-tree tops—

110 **JULIET.** O, swear not by the moon, th' inconstant moon,
That monthly changes in her circle orb,

The Tragedy of Romeo and Juliet, Act II, Scene ii   317

9. **proof:** Protected, as by armor.

10. **And but:** Unless.

11. **prorogued:** Postponed.

12. **adventure:** Risk a long journey, like a sea adventurer.

13. **Fain . . . form:** Eagerly would I follow convention (by acting reserved).
14. **compliment:** Conventional behavior.

15. **be perverse:** Act contrary to my true feelings.
16. **fond:** Affectionate.
17. **my havior light:** My behavior immodest or unserious.
18. **strange:** Distant and cold.

19. **discoverèd:** Revealed.

12 **Enrichment** Point out to students the "t" alliteration in this line. Then have them make the "t" sound, noticing the position of their tongue. How does this alliteration contribute to the meaning of the line?

13 **Discussion** Why does Juliet call the moon inconstant?

14 Discussion Why is Juliet concerned about this love? How does the imagery she uses reflect her concern?

15 Discussion How has Juliet changed as a result of her love?

Lest that thy love prove likewise variable.

ROMEO. What shall I swear by?

JULIET.   Do not swear at all;
115   Or if thou wilt, swear by thy gracious self,
        Which is the god of my idolatry,
        And I'll believe thee.

ROMEO.   If my heart's dear love—

JULIET. Well, do not swear. Although I joy in thee,
        I have no joy of this contract[20] tonight.   **20. contract:** Betrothal.
        It is too rash, too unadvised, too sudden;
120   Too like the lightning, which doth cease to be
        Ere one can say it lightens. Sweet, good night!
        This bud of love, by summer's ripening breath,
        May prove a beauteous flow'r when next we meet.
        Good night, good night! As sweet repose and rest
125   Come to thy heart as that within my breast!

ROMEO. O, wilt thou leave me so unsatisfied?

JULIET. What satisfaction canst thou have tonight?

ROMEO. Th' exchange of thy love's faithful vow for mine.

JULIET. I gave thee mine before thou didst request it;
130   And yet I would it were to give again.

ROMEO. Wouldst thou withdraw it? For what purpose,
        love?

JULIET. But to be frank[21] and give it thee again.   **21. frank:** Generous.
        And yet I wish but for the thing I have.
        My bounty[22] is as boundless as the sea,   **22. bounty:** What I have
135   My love as deep; the more I give to thee,   to give.
        The more I have, for both are infinite.
        I hear some noise within. Dear love, adieu!

                    [NURSE *calls within.*]
        Anon, good nurse! Sweet Montague, be true.
        Stay but a little, I will come again.   [*Exit.*]

140 **ROMEO.** O blessèd, blessèd night! I am afeard,
        Being in night, all this is but a dream,
        Too flattering-sweet to be substantial.[23]   **23. substantial:** Real.

                    [*Enter* JULIET *again.*]

JULIET. Three words, dear Romeo, and good night indeed.
        If that thy bent[24] of love be honorable,   **24. bent:** Purpose, in-
145   Thy purpose marriage, send me word tomorrow,   tention.

Grammar in Action

Tone refers to the author's attitude toward his or her subject. Readers determine tone from the way a subject is presented and described. Within a work of literature, writers may show different attitudes toward the various characters. These attitudes are indicated in the same way that attitude toward the subject is.

In drama, tone is conveyed by what characters say and do and by what other characters say about them. At this point in the play, readers know that Juliet is a dutiful daughter who has not yet considered the possibility of love or marriage. We have learned that Romeo—until he saw Juliet—has been in love with Rosaline. Romeo's friends seem not to take this love for Rosaline seriously, suggesting that it is an infatuation that will last only until Romeo sees a more beautiful woman.

What do these lines suggest about Shakespeare's attitude toward Juliet?

JULIET: Well do not swear. Although I joy in thee,
        I have no joy of this contract tonight.
        It is too rash, too unadvised, too sudden . . .
JULIET: My bounty is as boundless as the sea,

By one that I'll procure to come to thee,
Where and what time thou wilt perform the rite;
And all my fortunes at thy foot I'll lay
And follow thee my lord throughout the world.

150 **NURSE.** [*Within*] Madam!

JULIET. I come anon.—But if thou meanest not well,
I do beseech thee—

NURSE. [*Within*] Madam!

JULIET.   By and by²⁵ I come.—
To cease thy strife²⁶ and leave me to my grief.
Tomorrow will I send.

ROMEO.   So thrive my soul—

155 **JULIET.** A thousand times good night!   [*Exit.*]

ROMEO. A thousand times the worse, to want thy light!
Love goes toward love as schoolboys from their books;
But love from love, toward school with heavy looks.

[*Enter* JULIET *again.*]

JULIET. Hist! Romeo, hist! O for a falc'ner's voice
160 To lure this tassel gentle²⁷ back again!
Bondage is hoarse²⁸ and may not speak aloud,
Else would I tear the cave where Echo²⁹ lies
And make her airy tongue more hoarse than mine
With repetition of "My Romeo!"

165 **ROMEO.** It is my soul that calls upon my name.
How silver-sweet sound lovers' tongues by night,
Like softest music to attending ears!

JULIET. Romeo!

ROMEO.   My sweet?

JULIET.   What o'clock tomorrow
Shall I send to thee?

ROMEO.   By the hour of nine.

170 **JULIET.** I will not fail. 'Tis twenty year till then.
I have forgot why I did call thee back.

ROMEO. Let me stand here till thou remember it.

JULIET. I shall forget, to have thee still stand there,
Rememb'ring how I love thy company.

175 **ROMEO.** And I'll stay, to have thee still forget,

25. By and by: At once.
26. strife: Efforts.

27. tassel gentle: Male falcon.
28. Bondage is hoarse: Being bound in by my family restricts my speech.
29. Echo: In classical mythology the nymph Echo, unable to win the love of Narcissus, wasted away in a cave until nothing was left of her but her voice.

The Tragedy of Romeo and Juliet, Act II, Scene ii   319

16 Clarification Explain to students that falconry, or the art of training falcons to hunt, was familiar to Elizabethans. Falconers would call out commands to their birds.

17 Enrichment Point out to students that there are many references to names in this scene. Why is this subject so important for these lovers?

My love as deep; the more I give to thee,
The more I have; for both are infinite. . . .
If that thy bent of love be honorable,
Thy purpose marriage, send me word tomorrow . . .

These passages suggest that Juliet is fickle. In the first passage, although Juliet uses the word *joy* twice, she is not joyful; she is, in fact, confused and despondent. In the second passage, Juliet's tone is more cheerful as she is reveling in her love of Romeo.

Student Activity 1. Find two passages that suggest Shakespeare's attitude toward Juliet. Discuss these with your classmates and teacher.

Student Activity 2. Work with a partner to find passages that show Shakespeare's attitude toward Romeo. Compare and contrast these with the attitude toward Juliet.

Forgetting any other home but this.

JULIET. 'Tis almost morning. I would have thee gone—
And yet no farther than a wanton's³⁰ bird,
That lets it hop a little from his hand,
180   Like a poor prisoner in his twisted gyves,³¹
And with a silken thread plucks it back again,
So loving-jealous of his liberty.

ROMEO. I would I were thy bird.

JULIET.   Sweet, so would I.
Yet I should kill thee with much cherishing.
185   Good night, good night! Parting is such sweet sorrow
That I shall say good night till it be morrow.   [*Exit.*]

ROMEO. Sleep dwell upon thine eyes, peace in thy breast!
Would I were sleep and peace, so sweet to rest!
Hence will I to my ghostly friar's³² close cell,³³
190   His help to crave and my dear hap³⁴ to tell.   [*Exit.*]

30. **wanton's:** Spoiled, playful child's.
31. **gyves** (jīvz): Chains.

32. **ghostly friar's:** Spiritual father's.
33. **close cell:** Small room.
34. **dear hap:** Good fortune.

18 | **Scene iii.** FRIAR LAWRENCE'S *cell.*

[*Enter* FRIAR LAWRENCE *alone, with a basket.*]

FRIAR. The gray-eyed morn smiles on the frowning night,
Check'ring the eastern clouds with streaks of light;
And fleckèd¹ darkness like a drunkard reels
From forth day's path and Titan's burning wheels.²
5   Now, ere the sun advance his burning eye
The day to cheer and night's dank dew to dry,
I must upfill this osier cage³ of ours
With baleful⁴ weeds and precious-juicèd flowers.
The earth that's nature's mother is her tomb.
10   What is her burying grave, that is her womb;
And from her womb children of divers kind⁵
We sucking on her natural bosom find,
Many for many virtues excellent,
None but for some, and yet all different.
15   O, mickle⁶ is the powerful grace⁷ that lies
In plants, herbs, stones, and their true qualities;
For naught so vile that on the earth doth live
But to the earth some special good doth give;
Nor aught so good but, strained⁸ from that fair use,
20   Revolts from true birth,⁹ stumbling on abuse.
Virtue itself turns vice, being misapplied,

1. **flecked:** Spotted.
2. **Titan's burning wheels:** The wheels of the sun god's chariot.

3. **osier cage:** Willow basket.
4. **baleful:** Poisonous.

5. **divers kind:** Different kinds.

6. **mickle:** Great.
7. **grace:** Divine power.

8. **strained:** Turned away.
9. **Revolts . . . birth:** Conflicts with its real purpose.

And vice sometime by action dignified.

[*Enter* ROMEO.]

Within the infant rind[10] of this weak flower
Poison hath residence and medicine power;[11]
For this, being smelt, with that part cheers each
    part;[12]
25 Being tasted, stays all senses with the heart.[13]
Two such opposèd kings encamp them still[14]
In man as well as herbs—grace and rude will;
And where the worser is predominant,
30 Full soon the canker[15] death eats up that plant.

ROMEO. Good morrow, father.

FRIAR.   *Benedicite!*[16]
What early tongue so sweet saluteth me?
Young son, it argues a distemperèd head[17]
So soon to bid good morrow to thy bed.
35 Care keeps his watch in every old man's eye,
And where care lodges, sleep will never lie;
But where unbruisèd youth with unstuffed[18] brain
Doth couch his limbs, there golden sleep doth reign.
Therefore thy earliness doth me assure
40 Thou art uproused with some distemp'rature;[19]
Or if not so, then here I hit it right—
Our Romeo hath not been in bed tonight.

ROMEO. That last is true. The sweeter rest was mine.

FRIAR. God pardon sin! Wast thou with Rosaline?

45 **ROMEO.** With Rosaline, my ghostly father? No.
I have forgot that name and that name's woe.

FRIAR. That's my good son! But where hast thou been
    then?

ROMEO. I'll tell thee ere thou ask it me again.
I have been feasting with mine enemy,
50 Where on a sudden one hath wounded me
That's by me wounded. Both our remedies
Within thy help and holy physic[20] lies.
I bear no hatred, blessèd man, for, lo,
My intercession likewise steads my foe.[21]

55 **FRIAR.** Be plain, good son, and homely in thy drift.[22]
Riddling confession finds but riddling shrift.[23]

ROMEO. Then plainly know my heart's dear love is set

The Tragedy of Romeo and Juliet, Act II, Scene iii   321

---

10. **infant rind:** Tender skin.
11. **and medicine power:** And medicinal quality has power.
12. **with . . . part:** With that quality—odor—revives each part of the body.
13. **stays . . . heart:** Kills (stops the working of the five senses along with the heart).
14. **still:** Always.
15. **canker:** A destructive caterpillar.
16. *Benedicite!:* God bless you!
17. **distempered head:** Troubled mind.
18. **unstuffed:** Not filled with cares.
19. **distemp'rature:** Illness.
20. **physic** (fiz′ ik): Medicine.
21. **My . . . foe:** My plea also helps my enemy (Juliet, a Capulet).
22. **and . . . drift:** And simple in your speech.
23. **Riddling . . . shrift:** A confusing confession will get you uncertain forgiveness. The Friar means that unless Romeo speaks clearly he will not get clear and direct advice.

21 **Discussion** How does Friar Lawrence's knowledge of herbs influence his ideas about people?

22 **Literary Focus** Contrast Friar Lawrence and Romeo.

23 Reading Strategy Have students summarize Friar Lawrence's concern about Romeo's change of heart. Why does he mistrust it?

24 Discussion Do you think Romeo's argument makes sense? Explain.

25 Discussion Why does Friar Lawrence finally agree to marry the couple? Do you think his reason is justified? Explain.

26 Literary Focus How do these last two lines of the scene sum up the difference between these two characters?

On the fair daughter of rich Capulet;
As mine on hers, so hers is set on mine,
60   And all combined, save[24] what thou must combine
By holy marriage. When and where and how
We met, we wooed, and made exchange of vow,
I'll tell thee as we pass; but this I pray,
That thou consent to marry us today.

65   **FRIAR.** Holy Saint Francis! What a change is here!
Is Rosaline, that thou didst love so dear,
So soon forsaken? Young men's love then lies
Not truly in their hearts, but in their eyes.
Jesu Maria! What a deal of brine[25]
70   Hath washed thy sallow cheeks for Rosaline!
How much salt water thrown away in waste
To season love, that of it doth not taste!
The sun not yet thy sighs from heaven clears,
Thy old groans ring yet in mine ancient ears.
75   Lo, here upon thy cheek the stain doth sit
Of an old tear that is not washed off yet.
If e'er thou wast thyself, and these woes thine,
Thou and these woes were all for Rosaline.
And art thou changed? Pronounce this sentence then:
80   Women may fall[26] when there's no strength[27] in men.

ROMEO. Thou chidst me oft for loving Rosaline.

FRIAR. For doting,[28] not for loving, pupil mine.

ROMEO. And badst[29] me bury love.

FRIAR.   Not in a grave
To lay one in, another out to have.

85   **ROMEO.** I pray thee chide me not. Her I love now
Doth grace[30] for grace and love for love allow.[31]
The other did not so.

FRIAR.   O, she knew well
Thy love did read by rote, that could not spell.[32]
But come, young waverer, come go with me.
90   In one respect I'll thy assistant be;
For this alliance may so happy prove
To turn your households' rancor[33] to pure love.

ROMEO. O, let us hence! I stand on[34] sudden haste.

FRIAR. Wisely and slow. They stumble that run fast.   [*Exit.*]

24. And . . . save: And we are united in every way, except for (save).

25. brine: Salt water (tears).

26. fall: Be weak or inconstant.
27. strength: Constancy, stability.
28. doting: Being infatuated.
29. badst: Urged.

30. grace: Favor.
31. allow: Give.

32. Thy . . . spell: Your love was someone who recites words from memory with no understanding of them.

33. rancor: Hatred.

34. stand on: Insist on.

Literary Element: Character Traits

Tell students that **character traits** are all of those qualities that make a person unique. Authors give their characters a number of different traits that work together to form their personalities. Often characters will share the same traits. In *Romeo and Juliet,* for example, Mercutio and the Nurse share similar character traits.

Compare and contrast with students the character traits of Mercutio and the Nurse. Ask them in what ways Mercutio and the Nurse are alike. Students might mention, for example, that the nurse is Juliet's best friend and Mercutio is Romeo's. In addition, both characters are comical. On the other hand, Mercutio is young and the Nurse is old. In addition, Mercutio is also eloquent in speech, whereas the Nurse is long-winded and repetitive.

To aid your discussion, have students make a Venn diagram. In Mercutio's circle, students should list his character traits that are different from the Nurse's. Similarly, in the Nurse's circle, students should list her traits that are different from Mercutio's. In the intersecting section of both circles, students should list the traits that the two characters share. Use the following example as a guide.

Scene iv. *A street.*

[*Enter* BENVOLIO *and* MERCUTIO.]

MERCUTIO. Where the devil should this Romeo be?
    Came he not home tonight?

BENVOLIO. Not to his father's. I spoke with his man.

MERCUTIO. Why, that same pale hardhearted wench, that
    Rosaline,
5   Torments him so that he will sure run mad.

BENVOLIO. Tybalt, the kinsman to old Capulet,
    Hath sent a letter to his father's house.

MERCUTIO. A challenge, on my life.

BENVOLIO. Romeo will answer it.

10 **MERCUTIO.** Any man that can write may answer a letter.

BENVOLIO. Nay, he will answer the letter's master, how he
    dares, being dared.

MERCUTIO. Alas, poor Romeo, he is already dead: stabbed
15   with a white wench's black eye; run through the ear
    with a love song; the very pin of his heart cleft with the
    blind bow-boy's butt-shaft;[1] and is he a man to en-
    counter Tybalt?

BENVOLIO. Why, what is Tybalt?

MERCUTIO. More than Prince of Cats.[2] O, he's the coura-
20   geous captain of compliments.[3] He fights as you sing
    pricksong[4]—keeps time, distance, and proportion; he
    rests his minim rests,[5] one, two, and the third in your
    bosom! The very butcher of a silk button,[6] a duelist, a
    duelist! A gentleman of the very first house,[7] of the first
25   and second cause.[8] Ah, the immortal *passado!* The
    punto reverso! The hay![9]

BENVOLIO. The what?

MERCUTIO. The pox of such antic, lisping, affecting fantas-
    ticoes—these new tuners of accent![10] By Jesu, a very
30   good blade! A very tall man! A very good whore! Why,
    is not this a lamentable thing, grandsir, that we
    should be thus afflicted with these strange flies, these
    fashionmongers, these pardon-me's,[11] who stand so
    much on the new form that they cannot sit at ease on

1. pin . . . butt-shaft:
Center of his heart pierced
by Cupid's blunt arrow.
2. Prince of Cats: Tybalt, or a variation of it, is
the name of the cat in medieval stories of Reynard
the Fox.
**3. captain of compli-
ments:** Master of formal
behavior.
**4. as you sing prick-
song:** That is to say, with
attention to precision and
correctness.
5. rests . . . rests:
Observes all formalities.
6. button: An exact spot
on his opponent's shirt.
7. first house: Finest
school of fencing.
**8. the first and second
cause:** The reasons that
would cause a gentleman to
challenge another to a duel.
**9. passado! . . . punto
reverso! . . . hay!:** Lunge
. . . backhanded stroke . . .
home thrust.
10. The pox . . . accent:
May the plague strike these
absurd characters with
their phony manners—
these men who speak in
weird, newfangled ways!
11. these pardon-me's:
These men who are always
saying "Pardon me" (adopt-
ing ridiculous manners).

The Tragedy of Romeo and Juliet, Act II, Scene iv **323**

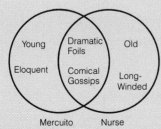

Mercuito   **Nurse**

Young / Eloquent
Dramatic Foils / Comical Gossips
Old / Long-Winded

Student Activity. Using the same procedure, select two other characters from the play to compare and contrast. You might want to compare and contrast Montague and Capulet, for example.

35 the old bench? O, their bones, their bones!

[*Enter* ROMEO.]

BENVOLIO. Here comes Romeo! Here comes Romeo!

MERCUTIO. Without his roe, like a dried herring.[12] O flesh, flesh, how art thou fishified! Now is he for the num-
40 bers[13] that Petrarch flowed in. Laura,[14] to his lady, was a kitchen wench (marry, she had a better love to be-rhyme her), Dido a dowdy, Cleopatra a gypsy, Helen and Hero hildings and harlots, Thisbe a gray eye or so, but not to the purpose. Signior Romeo, *bon jour!* There's a French salutation to your French slop. You
45 gave us the counterfeit fairly last night.

ROMEO. Good morrow to you both. What counterfeit did I give you?

MERCUTIO. The slip,[15] sir, the slip. Can you not conceive?

ROMEO. Pardon, good Mercutio. My business was great,
50 and in such a case as mine a man may strain courtesy.

MERCUTIO. That's as much as to say, such a case as yours constrains a man to bow in the hams.[16]

ROMEO. Meaning, to curtsy.

MERCUTIO. Thou hast most kindly hit it.

55 **ROMEO.** A most courteous exposition.

MERCUTIO. Nay, I am the very pink of courtesy.

ROMEO. Pink for flower.

MERCUTIO. Right.

ROMEO. Why, then is my pump[17] well-flowered.

60 **MERCUTIO.** Sure wit, follow me this jest now till thou hast worn out thy pump, that, when the single sole of it is worn, the jest may remain, after the wearing, solely singular.[18]

ROMEO. O single-soled jest, solely singular for the single-
65 ness![19]

MERCUTIO. Come between us, good Benvolio! My wits faints.

ROMEO. Swits and spurs, swits and spurs; or I'll cry a match.[20]

12. Without . . . herring: Worn out.
13. numbers: Verses of love poems.
14. Laura: Laura and the other ladies mentioned are all notable figures of European love literature. Mercutio is saying that Romeo thinks that none of them compare with Rosaline.

15. slip: Escape. *Slip* is also a term for counterfeit coin.

16. hams: Hips.

17. pump: Shoe.

18. when . . . singular: The jest will outwear the shoe and will then be all alone.
19. O . . . singleness!: O thin joke, unique for only one thing—weakness!
20. Swits . . . match: Drive your wit harder to beat me or else I'll claim victory in this match of word-play.

70 **MERCUTIO.** Nay, if our wits run the wild-goose chase, I
    am done; for thou hast more of the wild goose in one of
    thy wits than, I am sure, I have in my whole five. Was I
    with you there for the goose?

    ROMEO. Thou wast never with me for anything when thou
75 wast not there for the goose.

    MERCUTIO. I will bite thee by the ear for that jest.

    ROMEO. Nay, good goose, bite not!

    MERCUTIO. Thy wit is a very bitter sweeting;[21] it is a most   **21. sweeting:** A kind of
    sharp sauce.   apple.

80 **ROMEO.** And is it not, then, well served in to a sweet
    goose?

    MERCUTIO. O, here's a wit of cheveril,[22] that stretches from   **22. cheveril:** Easily
    an inch narrow to an ell broad!   stretched kid leather.

    ROMEO. I stretch it out for that word "broad," which added
85 to the goose, proves thee far and wide a broad goose.

    MERCUTIO. Why, is not this better now than groaning for
    love? Now art thou sociable, now art thou Romeo; now
    art thou what thou art, by art as well as by nature. For
    this driveling love is like a great natural[23] that runs   **23. natural:** Idiot.
90 lolling[24] up and down to hide his bauble[25] in a hole.   **24. lolling:** With tongue
                                                                        hanging out.
    BENVOLIO. Stop there, stop there!   **25. bauble:** Toy.

    MERCUTIO. Thou desirest me to stop in my tale against the   **26. the hair:** Natural in-
    hair.[26]   clination.

33 Discussion Why is Mercutio especially pleased by Romeo?

BENVOLIO. Thou wouldst else have made thy tale large.

95 **MERCUTIO.** O, thou art deceived! I would have made it short; for I was come to the whole depth of my tale, and meant indeed to occupy the argument[27] no longer.

ROMEO. Here's goodly gear![28]

[*Enter* NURSE *and her Man,* PETER.]

A sail, a sail!

100 **MERCUTIO.** Two, two! A shirt and a smock.[29]

NURSE. Peter!

PETER. Anon.

NURSE. My fan, Peter.

MERCUTIO. Good Peter, to hide her face; for her fan's the
105 fairer face.

NURSE. God ye good morrow, gentlemen.

MERCUTIO. God ye good-den, fair gentlewoman.

NURSE. Is it good-den?

MERCUTIO. 'Tis no less, I tell ye; for the bawdy hand of the
110 dial is now upon the prick of noon.

NURSE. Out upon you! What a man are you!

ROMEO. One, gentlewoman, that God hath made, himself to mar.

NURSE. By my troth, it is well said. "For himself to mar,"
115 quoth 'a? Gentlemen, can any of you tell me where I may find the young Romeo?

ROMEO. I can tell you; but young Romeo will be older when you have found him than he was when you sought him. I am the youngest of that name, for fault[30] of a
120 worse.

NURSE. You say well.

MERCUTIO. Yea, is the worst well? Very well took,[31] i' faith! Wisely, wisely.

34 ⎡ **NURSE.** If you be he, sir, I desire some confidence[32] with
125 ⎣ you.

BENVOLIO. She will endite him to some supper.

MERCUTIO. A bawd, a bawd, a bawd! So ho!

326 *Drama*

27. occupy the argument: Talk about the matter.
28. goodly gear: Good stuff for joking (Romeo sees the Nurse approaching).

29. A shirt and a smock: A man and a woman.

30. fault: Lack.

31. took: Understood.

32. confidence: The Nurse means *conference*.

Primary Source

Shakespeare based this play on *The Tragical History of Romeus and Juliet,* a narrative poem written in 1562 by Arthur Brooke. Following is a portion of Brooke's poem, in which Romeus tells the nurse of his plan to marry Juliet.

After you read these lines aloud, discuss with students how Romeo and the nurse in Shakespeare's play are similar to and different from the same characters in Brooke's poem.

"On Saturday," quoth he,
   "if Juliet come to shrift,
She shall be shrived and marrièd;
   how like you, Nurse, this drift?"
"Now, by my troth," quoth she,
   "God's blessing have your heart,

For yet in all my life I have
   not heard of such a part.
Lord, how you young men can
   such crafty wiles devise,
If that you love the daughter well,
   to blear the mother's eyes.
An easy thing it is,
   with cloak of holiness,
To mock the silly mother that
   suspecteth nothing less.
But that it pleasèd you
   to tell me of the case,

For all my many years perhaps
   I should have found it scarce.
Now for the rest let me
   and Juliet alone;
To get her leave, some feat[1] excu
   I will devise anon:
For that her golden locks
   by sloth have been unkempt,
Or for unwares some wanton drea
   the youthful damsel dreamt,
Or for in thoughts of love

---
[1]neat.

ROMEO. What hast thou found?

MERCUTIO. No hare, sir; unless a hare, sir, in a lenten pie,
130   that is something stale and hoar ere it be spent.

[He walks by them and sings.]

An old hare hoar,
And an old hare hoar,
Is very good meat in Lent;
But a hare that is hoar
135   Is too much for a score
When it hoars ere it be spent.

Romeo, will you come to your father's? We'll to dinner
thither.

ROMEO. I will follow you.

140 **MERCUTIO.** Farewell, ancient lady. Farewell, [*singing*]
"Lady, lady, lady."[33]   [*Exit* MERCUTIO, BENVOLIO.]

NURSE. I pray you, sir, what saucy merchant was this that
was so full of his ropery?[34]

ROMEO. A gentleman, nurse, that loves to hear himself talk
145   and will speak more in a minute than he will stand to
in a month.

NURSE. And 'a[35] speak anything against me, I'll take him
down, and 'a were lustier than he is, and twenty such
Jacks; and if I cannot, I'll find those that shall. Scurvy
150   knave! I am none of his flirt-gills;[36] I am none of his
skainsmates.[37] And thou must stand by too, and suffer
every knave to use me at his pleasure!

PETER. I saw no man use you at his pleasure. If I had, my
weapon should quickly have been out, I warrant you. I
155   dare draw as soon as another man, if I see occasion in
a good quarrel, and the law on my side.

NURSE. Now, afore God, I am so vexed that every part about
me quivers. Scurvy knave! Pray you, sir, a word; and,
as I told you, my young lady bid me inquire you out.
160   What she bid me say, I will keep to myself; but first let
me tell ye, if ye should lead her in a fool's paradise, as
they say, it were a very gross kind of behavior, as they
say; for the gentlewoman is young; and therefore, if
you should deal double with her, truly it were an ill
165   thing to be off'red to any gentlewoman, and very
weak[38] dealing.

33. "Lady . . . lady": A line from an old ballad, "Chaste Susanna."

34. ropery: The nurse means *roguery*, the talk and conduct of a rascal.

35. 'a: He.

36. flirt-gills: Common girls.
37. skainsmates: Criminals, cutthroats.

38. weak: Unmanly.

35 Discussion How does the Nurse reveal unladylike qualities in this passage?

The Tragedy of Romeo and Juliet, Act II, Scene iv   327

---

her idle time she spent,
Or otherwise within her heart
  deservèd to be shent.
I know her mother will
  in no case say her nay,
I warrant you she shall not fail
  to come on Saturday."
And then she swears to him,
  the mother loves her well;
And how she gave her suck in youth
  she leaveth not to tell.
"A pretty babe," quoth she,

"it was when it was young;
Lord, how it could full prettily
  have prated with its tongue!
A thousand times and more
  I laid her on my lap,
And clapped her on the buttock soft
  and kissed where I did clap.
And gladder then was I
  of such a kiss forsooth,
Than I had been to have a kiss
  of some old lecher's mouth."
And thus of Juliet's youth

began this prating nurse,
And of her present state to make
  a tedious long discourse.
For though he pleasure took
  in hearing of his love,
The message answer seemed him
  to be of more behoove.
But when these beldams sit
  at ease upon their tale,
The day and eke the candlelight
  before their talk shall fail,
And part they say is true,

and part they do devise,
Yet boldly do they that of both
  when no man checks their lies.
Then he six crowns of gold
  out of his pocket drew,
And gave them her, "A slight
  reward," quoth he,
  "and so, adieu."

36 **Discussion** What message does Romeo give the Nurse for Juliet?

37 **Discussion** Do you think the Nurse is good at keeping secrets? Explain.

38 **Clarification** *Rosemary* is "an herb that was considered the emblem of fidelity and remembrance."

ROMEO. Nurse, commend[39] me to thy lady and mistress.
    I protest unto thee—

NURSE. Good heart, and i' faith I will tell her as much.
170   Lord, Lord, she will be a joyful woman.

ROMEO. What wilt thou tell her, nurse? Thou dost not
    mark me.

NURSE. I will tell her, sir, that you do protest, which, as I
    take it, is a gentlemanlike offer.

175 **ROMEO.** Bid her devise
    Some means to come to shrift[40] this afternoon;
    And there she shall at Friar Lawrence' cell
    Be shrived and married. Here is for thy pains.

NURSE. No, truly, sir; not a penny.

180 **ROMEO.** Go to! I say you shall.

NURSE. This afternoon, sir? Well, she shall be there.

ROMEO. And stay, good nurse, behind the abbey wall.
    Within this hour my man shall be with thee
    And bring thee cords made like a tackled stair.[41]
185   Which to the high topgallant[42] of my joy
    Must be my convoy[43] in the secret night.
    Farewell. Be trusty, and I'll quit[44] thy pains.
    Farewell. Commend me to thy mistress.

NURSE. Now God in heaven bless thee! Hark you, sir.

190 **ROMEO.** What say'st thou, my dear nurse?

NURSE. Is your man secret? Did you ne'er hear say,
    Two may keep counsel, putting one away?[45]

ROMEO. Warrant thee my man's as true as steel.

NURSE. Well, sir, my mistress is the sweetest lady. Lord,
195   Lord! When 'twas a little prating[46] thing—O, there is a
    nobleman in town, one Paris, that would fain lay knife
    aboard;[47] but she, good soul, had as lieve[48] see a toad,
    a very toad, as see him. I anger her sometimes, and tell
    her that Paris is the properer man; but I'll warrant
200   you, when I say so, she looks as pale as any clout[49] in
    the versal world.[50] Doth not rosemary and Romeo be-
    gin both with a letter?

ROMEO. Ay, nurse; what of that? Both with an *R*.

NURSE. Ah, mocker! That's the dog's name.[51] *R* is for the—

39. commend: Convey my respect and best wishes.

40. shrift: Confession.

41. tackled stair: Rope ladder.
42. topgallant: Summit.
43. convoy: Conveyance.
44. quit: Reward, pay you back for.

45. Two . . . away: Two can keep a secret if one is ignorant, or out of the way.

46. prating: Babbling.
47. fain . . . aboard: Eagerly seize Juliet for himself.
48. had as lieve: Would as willingly.

49. clout: Cloth.
50. versal world: Universe.

51. dog's name: *R* sounds like a growl.

328 *Drama*

Primary Source

Tell students that various actresses who have played Juliet have brought their own interpretation of the character to the role. One such actress was Sarah Siddons (1755–1831), who critics claim was the greatest Shakespearean actress of her time.

Siddons began her acting career at the age of eight, playing the spirit Ariel in an adaptation of Shakespeare's *The Tempest*. During her acting career, Siddons played almost every female character in Shakespeare's plays.

Although her greatest achievement was her role as Lady Macbeth, Siddons's portrayal of Juliet was also beautiful and convincing. The *Bath Journal* published the following letter in reference to Siddons's March 4, 1779, performance as Juliet:

I think I never beheld a Juliet till Mrs. Siddons showed me one at that time, and yet for these 30 years past I scarce ever miss'd this favourite play, both in London and elsewhere.

The following diary entry written by Mrs. Thrale, a long-standing follower and admirer of Siddons, gives a slightly different critique of Siddons's portrayal as Juliet:

205 No; I know it begins with some other letter; and she
hath the prettiest sententious[52] of it, of you and rosemary, that it would do you good to hear it.

ROMEO. Commend me to thy lady.

NURSE. Ay, a thousand times. [*Exit* ROMEO.] Peter!

210 **PETER.** Anon.

NURSE. Before, and apace.[53]   [*Exit, after* PETER.]

Scene v. CAPULET'S *orchard.*

[*Enter* JULIET.]

JULIET. The clock struck nine when I did send the nurse;
In half an hour she promised to return.
Perchance she cannot meet him. That's not so.
O, she is lame! Love's heralds should be thoughts,
5   Which ten times faster glides than the sun's beams
Driving back shadows over low'ring[1] hills.
Therefore do nimble-pinioned doves draw Love,[2]
And therefore hath the wind-swift Cupid wings.
Now is the sun upon the highmost hill
10 Of this day's journey, and from nine till twelve
Is three long hours; yet she is not come.
Had she affections and warm youthful blood,
She would be as swift in motion as a ball;
My words would bandy her[3] to my sweet love,
15 And his to me.
But old folks, many feign[4] as they were dead—
Unwieldy, slow, heavy and pale as lead.

[*Enter* NURSE *and* PETER.]

O God, she comes! O honey nurse, what news?
Hast thou met with him? Send thy man away.

20 **NURSE.** Peter, stay at the gate.   [*Exit* PETER.]

JULIET. Now, good sweet nurse—O Lord, why lookest thou
sad?
Though news be sad, yet tell them merrily;
If good, thou shamest the music of sweet news
By playing it to me with so sour a face.

25 **NURSE.** I am aweary, give me leave[5] awhile.
Fie, how my bones ache! What a jaunce[6] have I!

JULIET. I would thou hadst my bones, and I thy news.
Nay, come, I pray thee speak. Good, good nurse, speak.

52. sententious: The
Nurse means *sentences*—
clever, wise sayings.

53. Before, and apace:
Go ahead of me, and
quickly.

1. low'ring: Darkening.

2. Therefore . . . Love:
Therefore, doves with quick
wings pull the chariot of
Venus, goddess of love.

3. bandy her: Send her
rapidly.

4. feign: Act.

5. give me leave: Excuse
me; give me a moment's
rest.
6. jaunce: Rough trip.

The Tragedy of Romeo and Juliet, Act II, Scene v   329

39 **Discussion** If you were a director, what instructions would you
give Juliet about the way to
speak these lines?

40 **Discussion** Do you think the
Nurse is teasing Juliet, or is she
behaving as she usually does?
Explain.

Master Teacher Note In order to
present a story on stage, playwrights use dramatic conventions to indicate time and location. In *Romeo and Juliet*,
Shakespeare used many dramatic conventions. One important element established through
such conventions was the time of
day. Since there was no lighting,
plays were performed during the
day. If a scene took place at
night, the time and setting were
indicated through dialogue. In
Act I, Scene iv, ll. 11, for example, Romeo calls for a torch. The
audience accepts, therefore,
that it is night. Ask students to
look for other examples in Act II
in which dialogue establishes
time and setting.

Mrs Siddons acted Juliet last night.—She does it so
naturally says someone, so artificially rather said I; but she
is a great Performer. . . . The pouting Scene with the old
Nurse was the cleverest thing I ever saw—so pretty, so
Babyish, *so* charming. . . .

Student Activity. Reread Act II, Scene v, of *Romeo and Juliet.* In
groups, discuss how Sarah Siddons might have played this
scene. What gestures, expressions, and movements might she
have used to appear "so babyish and so charming"? Write the
stage comments for this scene that Siddons might have noted in
her script. Share and discuss your stage directions with your
classmates. Then as a class, discuss how Siddons's performance might be different from other actresses' interpretations of
Juliet, such as Olivia Hussey's Juliet in Franco Zeffirelli's film
version of the play.

41 Literary Focus How is the Nurse a dramatic foil in this scene, pointing up Juliet's concerns and state of mind?

NURSE. Jesu, what haste? Can you not stay awhile?
30   Do you not see that I am out of breath?

JULIET. How art thou out of breath when thou hast breath
To say to me that thou art out of breath?
The excuse that thou dost make in this delay
Is longer than the tale thou dost excuse.
35   Is thy news good or bad? Answer to that.
Say either, and I'll stay the circumstance.[7]
Let me be satisfied, is't good or bad?

NURSE. Well, you have made a simple[8] choice; you know
not how to choose a man. Romeo? No, not he. Though
40   his face be better than any man's, yet his leg excels all
men's; and for a hand and a foot, and a body, though
they be not to be talked on, yet they are past compare.
He is not the flower of courtesy, but, I'll warrant him,
as gentle as a lamb. Go thy ways, wench; serve God.
45   What, have you dined at home?

JULIET. No, no. But all this did I know before.
What says he of our marriage? What of that?

NURSE. Lord, how my head aches! What a head have I!
It beats as it would fall in twenty pieces.
50   My back a[9] t' other side—ah, my back, my back!
Beshrew[10] your heart for sending me about
To catch my death with jauncing up and down!

JULIET. I' faith, I am sorry that thou art not well.
Sweet, sweet, sweet nurse, tell me, what says my love?

NURSE. Your love says, like an honest gentleman, and a
55   courteous, and a kind, and a handsome, and, I warrant, a virtuous—Where is your mother?

JULIET. Where is my mother? Why, she is within.
Where should she be? How oddly thou repliest!
60   "Your love says, like an honest gentleman,
'Where is your mother?' "

NURSE.   O God's Lady dear!
Are you so hot?[11] Marry come up, I trow.[12]
Is this the poultice[13] for my aching bones?
Henceforward do your messages yourself.

65 **JULIET.** Here's such a coil![14] Come, what says Romeo?

NURSE. Have you got leave to go to shrift today?

7. stay the circumstance: Wait for the details.

8. simple: Foolish; simpleminded.

9. a: On.

10. Beshrew: Shame on.

11. hot: Impatient; hot-tempered.
12. Marry . . . trow: Indeed, cool down, I say.
13. poultice: Remedy.
14. coil: Disturbance.

Commentary: Elizabethan Weddings

Tell students that unlike Romeo and Juliet's secret marriage, most Elizabethan weddings were all-day extravaganzas in which almost the whole village or town participated.

Traditionally, the formal betrothal or engagement of the couple was done privately. Afterward, the law required that the banns of marriage be made public. At this time, the priest would announce in church on three consecutive Sundays the couple's engagement and call for any person who knew any cause why the marriage should not be performed to come forward and declare it.

A wedding celebration was usually an all-day event. It began early in the morning when the bridesmaids awakened and dressed the bride. Shortly thereafter, the groom, his groomsmen, friends, relatives, and musicians would arrive at the bride's house to claim her. The entire wedding party then paraded through the town to the church. The bride in her white gown and loose-flowing hair was the center of attraction.

After the ceremony, the wedding party went to the groom's

JULIET. I have.

NURSE. Then hie you hence to Friar Lawrence' cell;
There stays a husband to make you a wife.
70 Now comes the wanton[15] blood up in your cheeks:
They'll be in scarlet straight at any news.
Hie you to church; I must another way,
To fetch a ladder, by the which your love
Must climb a bird's nest soon when it is dark.
75 I am the drudge, and toil in your delight;
But you shall bear the burden soon at night.
Go; I'll to dinner; hie you to the cell.

JULIET. Hie to high fortune! Honest nurse, farewell. [*Exit.*]

Scene vi. *Friar Lawrence's cell.*

[*Enter* FRIAR LAWRENCE *and* ROMEO.]

FRIAR. So smile the heavens upon this holy act
That afterhours with sorrow chide us not![1]

ROMEO. Amen, amen! But come what sorrow can,
It cannot countervail[2] the exchange of joy
5 That one short minute gives me in her sight.
Do thou but close our hands with holy words,
Then love-devouring death do what he dare—
It is enough I may but call her mine.

FRIAR. These violent delights have violent ends
10 And in their triumph die, like fire and powder,[3]
Which, as they kiss, consume. The sweetest honey
Is loathsome in his own deliciousness
And in the taste confounds[4] the appetite.
Therefore love moderately: long love doth so;
15 Too swift arrives as tardy as too slow.

[*Enter* JULIET.]

Here comes the lady. O, so light a foot
Will ne'er wear out the everlasting flint.[5]
A lover may bestride the gossamers[6]
That idles in the wanton summer air,
20 And yet not fall; so light is vanity.[7]

JULIET. Good even to my ghostly confessor.

FRIAR. Romeo shall thank thee, daughter, for us both.

JULIET. As much to him,[8] else is his thanks too much.

15. wanton: Excited.

1. That . . . not!: That the future does not punish us with sorrow.
2. countervail: Equal.

3. powder: Gunpowder.

4. confounds: Destroys.

5. flint: Stone.
6. gossamers: Spider webs.

7. vanity: Foolish things that cannot last.

8. As . . . him: The same greeting to him.

The Tragedy of Romeo and Juliet, Act II, Scene vi   331

42 Literary Focus How does Friar Lawrence serve as a dramatic foil for Romeo, pointing up his traits and state of mind?

house for a great feast and celebration. The party lasted the rest of the day with plenty of food, dances, and games.

Sometime during the evening, the bride and groom left the party with their attendants, who would prepare the couple for the night. Later the attendants rejoined the other guests and continued to celebrate until late into the night or early morning.

In the morning on the following day, musicians awakened the couple with a song at their bedroom window. Thereafter, the village considered the couple to be among the married folk. Newlyweds did not have a honeymoon.

Student Activity. Shakespeare chose to have Romeo and Juliet's wedding performed in secret and offstage. Imagine you are the director of a new adaptation of this play and want to perform the marriage on stage. In groups, write the script for this scene, developing the dialogue and writing the stage directions for the wedding ceremony as it might have been staged in the sixteenth century. What will Romeo and Juliet's vows be? Who will attend? What events will occur as a result of the marriage? Perform your scenes for your classmates.

Reading Strategy Paraphrase the speeches of Romeo and Juliet.

Reader's Response If you were Romeo, would you renounce your family name for the love of a woman? Explain.

Thematic Response Romeo and Juliet each grow as they experience rites of passage. Which of the two seems to have acquired greater maturity? Explain.

43

ROMEO. Ah, Juliet, if the measure of thy joy
25   Be heaped like mine, and that thy skill be more
        To blazon it,[9] then sweeten with thy breath
        This neighbor air, and let rich music's tongue
        Unfold the imagined happiness that both
        Receive in either by this dear encounter.

30 **JULIET.** Conceit, more rich in matter than in words,
        Brags of his substance, not of ornament.[10]
        They are but beggars that can count their worth;
        But my true love is grown to such excess
        I cannot sum up sum of half my wealth.

35 **FRIAR.** Come, come with me, and we will make short work;
        For, by your leaves, you shall not stay alone
        Till Holy Church incorporate two in one.   [*Exit.*]

9. and . . . it: And if you are better able to proclaim it.

10. Conceit . . . ornament: Understanding does not need to be dressed up in words.

Closure and Extension

ANSWERS TO RESPONDING TO THE SELECTION
Your Response

1. Encourage students to discuss the motives of Friar Lawrence in agreeing to marry the young people. Ask students why they think age is not a barrier to the marriage of Romeo and Juliet.

Recalling

2. She wonders why Romeo has to be a Montague.
3. She fears for his life at the hands of her relatives. She fears that his love is shallow and that he may have a change of heart and turn out to be a liar. She doubts whether he can be sincere in so short a time.

4. He says that Romeo has been too impulsive in falling out of love with one woman and in love with another. Romeo says that Rosaline did not return his love while Juliet does.
5. Friar Lawrence feels the marriage may end in the feuding. The Nurse is Juliet's confidante and will do whatever makes Juliet happy.
6. Romeo now seems to be his old self. He is relaxed, happy, and sociable.

Interpreting

7. Suggested Response: Darkness keeps Juliet's relatives from finding Romeo, who has come to be near her. It also hides him from view as she reveals her love for him, a circumstance which leads them to pledge their love for each other.
8. Suggested Response: She is excited and impatient as she waits for the Nurse to return. She is even more impatient and exasperated as she tries to prod

RESPONDING TO THE SELECTION

Your Response

1. Do you think Friar Lawrence is right in agreeing to marry Romeo and Juliet? Explain.

Recalling

2. Why does Juliet cry out in Scene ii, "O Romeo, Romeo! Wherefore [Why] art thou Romeo?"
3. What doubts and fears does Juliet express even as she realizes that Romeo loves her?
4. What weakness in Romeo's character does Friar Lawrence point out before agreeing to assist the lovers in their plan to wed? How does Romeo defend himself?
5. Why does Friar Lawrence finally agree to marry Romeo and Juliet? Why does the Nurse help them carry out their plan?
6. In Scene iv, what change in Romeo's behavior causes Mercutio to say, "Now art thou sociable, now art thou Romeo . . ."?

Interpreting

7. Explain the role that darkness plays in helping Romeo and Juliet learn of their love for each other.
8. Describe Juliet's feelings in Scene v as she waits for the Nurse and then as she waits for the Nurse to reveal Romeo's message.
9. Juliet is thirteen years old and Romeo not much older. In what way is their love typical of adolescence, and in what way is it not?

Applying

10. Why do you think the love scene in Capulet's garden is the most famous one in all of literature?

ANALYZING LITERATURE

Understanding the Dramatic Foil

A **dramatic foil** contrasts with another character and helps to highlight this character's traits.

Explain how the first character in each of the following pairs is a foil for the other.

1. Mercutio and Romeo
2. the Nurse and Juliet

THINKING AND WRITING

Modernizing Dialogue

Rewriting passages of Shakespeare's dialogue in contemporary language is a good way to test your comprehension. Rewrite the dialogue that Romeo and Juliet speak in lines 53–84 of Scene ii. (This is the famous balcony scene.) Juliet's first lines might be rewritten as follows:

JULIET: Who are you who, under cover of night, overhears my secret thoughts?

Before you begin, make sure you understand Shakespeare's words. Use the marginal notes, and look up in a dictionary any words you still do not know. When you revise your work, try to make the language sound natural enough for actors to speak on stage. Ask two classmates to read your dialogue aloud. How does it sound to you?

LEARNING OPTIONS

1. **Performance.** Bring Romeo and Juliet into the twentieth century. Write and deliver a rap song that describes their situation. You may work with a partner, if you wish.
2. **Language.** Personification is a figure of speech in which a quality, idea, or any nonhuman being is represented as having human traits. In the following quotation from Act II, the sun and moon are personified: "Arise, fair sun, and kill the envious moon,/ Who is already sick and pale with grief. . . ." List other examples of personification in the play. Are there recurring images in these examples?

The Tragedy of Romeo and Juliet, Act II 333

---

the Nurse into giving her the message.
9. Answers will differ, but students may suggest that adolescents make up their minds and rush into things very quickly. In this way, their actions would be typical of others their age. On the other hand, most adolescents are not yet interested in marriage, so in this respect their actions would not be typical.

Applying

10. Answers will differ, but students may indicate that the romantic words and images, the vivid descriptions, and the expressions of devotion are extremely effective.

Challenge Some of your **more advanced** students may wish to read the passages from Chaucer's *Canterbury Tales* that describe the Wife of Bath. Have

them compare her with the Nurse in this play.

ANSWERS TO ANALYZING LITERATURE

1. Suggested Response: Mercutio is a carefree, outgoing, and optimistic person to whom almost everything is a joke. He is a good dramatic foil for Romeo, who is sensitive, moody, pessimistic, and romantic.

2. Suggested Response: The Nurse's crude comments and idle chatter make her a good foil for the romantic young Juliet. The Nurse's ramblings, usually in prose, contrast with Juliet's passages in verse. The Nurse is practical in her approach to love while Juliet is romantic. (Neither Mercutio nor the Nurse can understand the serious commitment the lovers have made to each other.)

THINKING AND WRITING

 Software

working on computers, have them use the **Writer's Helper** activity Readability as they revise their dialogues.

Alternative Assessment: *Peer Review:* In pairs or in groups of four, have your students assess each other's stories by responding to the following questions:

What is the content of the scene the writer has rewritten?

How accurately has the writer transmitted the meaning of the scene through his/her modernized dialogue?

What specific devices has the writer included to make the language sound natural?

What specific changes do you suggest the writer make to enhance the effectiveness of the scene and its faithfulness to the meaning and tone of the original?

To validate the peer review, ask students to incorporate those suggestions they find helpful in a revision of their essays.

Publishing Student Writing You might ask volunteers to present their modernized dialogue to the class.

LEARNING OPTIONS

1. Visual learners will enjoy this activity.
2. You might wish to extend this activity by having students add these examples of personification to the list of allusions that they made in the Act I optional activities. Both lists could be extended as they continue their study of imagery.

Preparation

Literary Focus You might have students compare the *soliloquy* and *aside* as methods of revealing a character's thoughts with the techniques a novelist uses for this purpose.

Prereading Focus The purpose of this activity is to have students make logical predictions based on what they have read so far. Have them consider the personalities of the characters. Discuss the impetuosity of the lovers, the angry disposition of Tybalt, the hatred between the older Montagues and Capulets. Guide students to draw conclusions about the probable results of interaction between such emotionally volatile characters.

Vocabulary Have your **less advanced** students review the meanings of these words by seeing how many of them they can use in a paragraph.

Electronic Handbook You might suggest that students use the Language Master 6000 to hear the pronunciations of *martial*, *agile*, and *abhors*.

GUIDE FOR READING

The Tragedy of Romeo and Juliet, Act III

Soliloquy, Aside, and Monologue

A **soliloquy** is a speech in which a character, alone on stage, expresses his or her thoughts to the audience. An **aside** is a remark made to the audience, unheard by the other characters. There are two differences between these devices. One is that a soliloquy is usually lengthy, whereas an aside is brief. The second is that a soliloquy is usually spoken when no other characters are present, whereas an aside is delivered with other characters present but unable to hear. Both devices, however, let the audience know what a character is really thinking or feeling. Shakespeare uses soliloquies and asides to reveal character and advance the plot.

Similar to a soliloquy is a **monologue,** which is a lengthy speech. Unlike a soliloquy, however, a monologue is addressed to other characters, not to the audience.

Focus

At the end of Act II, Friar Lawrence warns Romeo: "These violent delights have violent ends. . . ." From what you have read so far, predict what you think some of the "violent ends" might be in Act III. To record these predictions, use a chart like the following:

Causes	"Violent ends"

Vocabulary

Knowing the following words will help you as you read Act III of *Romeo and Juliet.*

gallant (gal' ənt) *adj.*: Brave and noble (p. 338)

fray (frā) *n.*: Noisy fight (p. 339)

martial (mär' shəl) *adj.*: Military (p. 340)

agile (aj' əl) *adj.*: Quick and easy of movement (p. 340)

exile (eg' zil) *v.*: Banish (p. 340)

tedious (tē' dē əs) *adj.*: Tiresome and boring (p. 341)

eloquence (el' ə kwəns) *n.*: Speech that is vivid, forceful, graceful, and persuasive (p. 341)

fickle (fik' əl) *adj.*: Changeable (p. 352)

abhors (əb hôrz') *v.*: Detests; intensely dislikes (p. 353)

334   Drama

Objectives

1 To understand dramatic speeches
2 To infer tone in a monologue
3 To write a soliloquy
4 To express individual interests and abilities through optional activities

Support Material

Teaching Portfolio
Teacher Backup, p. 361
Grammar in Action Worksheets, *Using Imagery*, p. 364; *Using Quotation Marks with Other Punctuation,* p. 366
Usage and Mechanics Worksheet, p. 368
Vocabulary Check, p. 369
Critical Thinking and Reading, *Inferring Tone in a Monologue*, p. 371

Language Worksheet, *Understanding Allusions*, p. 372
Selection Test, p. 373

Library of Video Classics
Romeo and Juliet; Shakespeare in Rehearsal: Romeo and Juliet; Shakespeare in Conversation

Literature Videodisc
Shakespeare in Rehearsal: Romeo and Juliet; Shakespeare in Conversation

Prentice Hall Literature Writing Studio

Act III

Scene i. *A public place.*

[*Enter* MERCUTIO, BENVOLIO, *and* MEN.]

BENVOLIO. I pray thee, good Mercutio, let's retire.
    The day is hot, the Capels are abroad,
    And, if we meet, we shall not 'scape a brawl,
    For now, these hot days, is the mad blood stirring.

5 **MERCUTIO.** Thou art like one of these fellows that, when he
    enters the confines of a tavern, claps me his sword
    upon the table and says, "God send me no need of
    thee!" and by the operation of the second cup draws
    him on the drawer,[1] when indeed there is no need.

10 **BENVOLIO.** Am I like such a fellow?

MERCUTIO. Come, come, thou art as hot a Jack in thy
    mood as any in Italy; and as soon moved to be moody,
    and as soon moody to be moved.[2]

BENVOLIO. And what to?

15 **MERCUTIO.** Nay, and there were two such, we should have
    none shortly, for one would kill the other. Thou! Why,
    thou wilt quarrel with a man that hath a hair more or
    a hair less in his beard than thou hast. Thou wilt
    quarrel with a man for cracking nuts, having no other
20   reason but because thou hast hazel eyes. What eye but
    such an eye would spy out such a quarrel? Thy head
    is as full of quarrels as an egg is full of meat; and
    yet thy head hath been beaten as addle[3] as an egg for
    quarreling. Thou hast quarreled with a man for cough-
25   ing in the street, because he hath wakened thy dog
    that hath lain asleep in the sun. Didst thou not fall out
    with a tailor for wearing his new doublet[4] before Eas-
    ter? With another for tying his new shoes with old rib-
    and?[5] And yet thou wilt tutor me from quarreling![6]

30 **BENVOLIO.** And I were so apt to quarrel as thou art, any
    man should buy the fee simple[7] of my life for an hour
    and a quarter.[8]

MERCUTIO. The fee simple? O simple![9]

[*Enter* TYBALT, PETRUCHIO, *and others.*]

BENVOLIO. By my head, here comes the Capulets.

35 **MERCUTIO.** By my heel, I care not.

---

1. and . . . drawer: And by the effect of the second drink draws his sword against the waiter.

2. and . . . moved: And as quickly stirred to anger as you are eager to be so stirred.

3. addle: Scrambled, crazy.

4. doublet: Jacket.

5. riband: Ribbon.
6. tutor . . . quarreling: Instruct me not to quarrel.
7. fee simple: Complete possession.
8. an hour and a quarter: The length of time that a man with Mercutio's fondness for quarreling may be expected to live.
9. O simple!: O stupid!

The Tragedy of Romeo and Juliet, Act III, Scene i   335

Thematic Focus Conflicts can change the course of life and love. Ask students if they have ever experienced a conflict that changed their lives. Could the conflict have been prevented? If they had known beforehand what the results would be, would they have acted differently?

Presentation

Motivation/Prior Knowledge Ask students what consequences might arise from the secret marriage of Romeo and Juliet.

Master Teacher Note You might tell students that the third act in a five-act play is often a turning point. Have them summarize the conflicts that have been simmering and may boil over in this act.

Purpose-Setting Question How do the monologues and soliloquies advance the plot and reveal the characters' feelings?

1 Discussion How does Benvolio's advice reflect his general approach to life?

2 Discussion Do you agree with Mercutio's description of Benvolio? Explain.

Alternative Assessment To promote active reading, have your students continue their **reader's response journal** as they read Act III. Ask them to focus their observations on the details that contribute to the increasing complexity of Romeo's relationship with Juliet. Encourage students to respond to Mercutio's death and Romeo's violent revenge on Tybalt. How do they feel about Romeo at this point? What would they suggest he do now?

Their observations will enable you to assess their understanding of the issues of the play.

3 **Discussion** How does Mercutio interpret Tybalt's phrase "Here comes my man"?

4 **Discussion** Why does Romeo try to call off the duel?

TYBALT. Follow me close, for I will speak to them.
　　　Gentlemen, good-den. A word with one of you.

MERCUTIO. And but one word with one of us? Couple it
　　　with something; make it a word and a blow.

40 **TYBALT.** You shall find me apt enough to that, sir, and you
　　　will give me occasion.[10]

MERCUTIO. Could you not take some occasion without
　　　giving?

TYBALT. Mercutio, thou consortest[11] with Romeo.

45 **MERCUTIO.** Consort?[12] What, dost thou make us min-
　　　strels? And thou make minstrels of us, look to hear
　　　nothing but discords.[13] Here's my fiddlestick; here's
　　　that shall make you dance. Zounds,[14] consort!

BENVOLIO. We talk here in the public haunt of men.
50 　　Either withdraw unto some private place,
　　　Or reason coldly of your grievances,
　　　Or else depart. Here all eyes gaze on us.

MERCUTIO. Men's eyes were made to look, and let them
　　　gaze.
　　　I will not budge for no man's pleasure, I.

[*Enter* ROMEO.]

55 **TYBALT.** Well, peace be with you, sir. Here comes my
　　　man.[15]

MERCUTIO. But I'll be hanged, sir, if he wear your livery.[16]
　　　Marry, go before to field,[17] he'll be your follower!
　　　Your worship in that sense may call him man.

TYBALT. Romeo, the love I bear thee can afford
60 　　No better term than this: thou art a villain.[18]

ROMEO. Tybalt, the reason that I have to love thee
　　　Doth much excuse the appertaining[19] rage
　　　To such a greeting. Villain am I none.
　　　Therefore farewell. I see thou knowest me not.

65 **TYBALT.** Boy, this shall not excuse the injuries
　　　That thou hast done me; therefore turn and draw.

ROMEO. I do protest I never injured thee,
　　　But love thee better than thou canst devise[20]
　　　Till thou shalt know the reason of my love;
70 　　And so, good Capulet, which name I tender[21]
　　　As dearly as mine own, be satisfied.

10. occasion: Cause, reason.

11. consortest: Associate with.
12. Consort: Associate with; *consort* also meant a group of musicians.
13. discords: Harsh sounds.
14. Zounds: An exclamation of surprise or anger ("By God's wounds").

15. man: The man I'm looking for; *man* also meant "manservant."
16. livery: Servant's uniform.
17. field: Dueling place.

18. villain: A low, vulgar person.

19. appertaining: Appropriate.

20. devise: Understand; imagine.

21. tender: Value.

336 *Drama*

MERCUTIO. O calm, dishonorable, vile submission!
  Alla stoccata[22] carries it away.   [*Draws.*]
  Tybalt, you ratcatcher, will you walk?

75 **TYBALT.** What wouldst thou have with me?

MERCUTIO. Good King of Cats, nothing but one of your
  nine lives. That I mean to make bold withal,[23] and, as
  you shall use me hereafter, dry-beat[24] the rest of the
  eight. Will you pluck your sword out of his pilcher[25] by
80 the ears? Make haste, lest mine be about your ears ere
  it be out.

TYBALT. I am for you.   [*Draws.*]

ROMEO. Gentle Mercutio, put thy rapier up.

MERCUTIO. Come, sir, your *passado!*   [*They fight.*]

85 **ROMEO.** Draw, Benvolio; beat down their weapons.
  Gentlemen, for shame! Forbear this outrage!
  Tybalt, Mercutio, the Prince expressly hath
  Forbid this bandying in Verona streets.
  Hold, Tybalt! Good Mercutio!

[TYBALT *under* ROMEO's *arms thrusts* MERCUTIO *in, and flies.*]

MERCUTIO.   I am hurt.
90 A plague a[26] both houses! I am sped.[27]
  Is he gone and hath nothing?

BENVOLIO.   What, art thou hurt?

MERCUTIO. Ay, ay, a scratch, a scratch. Marry, 'tis enough.
  Where is my page? Go, villain, fetch a surgeon.
                                    [*Exit* PAGE.]

ROMEO. Courage, man. The hurt cannot be much.

95 **MERCUTIO.** No, 'tis not so deep as a well, nor so wide as a
  church door; but 'tis enough, 'twill serve. Ask for me
  tomorrow, and you shall find me a grave man. I am
  peppered,[28] I warrant, for this world. A plague a both
  your houses! Zounds, a dog, a rat, a mouse, a cat, to
100 scratch a man to death! A braggart, a rogue, a villain,
  that fights by the book of arithmetic![29] Why the devil
  came you between us? I was hurt under your arm.

ROMEO. I thought all for the best.

MERCUTIO. Help me into some house, Benvolio,
105 Or I shall faint. A plague a both your houses!

The Tragedy of Romeo and Juliet, Act III, Scene i   337

22. *Alla stoccata*: At the thrust—an Italian fencing term that Mercutio uses as a nickname for Tybalt.

23. make bold withal: Make bold with; take.
24. dry-beat: Thrash.
25. pilcher: Scabbard.

26. a: On.
27. sped: Wounded, done for.

28. peppered: Finished off.

29. by . . . arithmetic: By formal rules.

5 Discussion How does Mercutio interpret Romeo's reluctance to fight?

6 Discussion How are Mercutio's comments about his wound in keeping with his character?

7 Discussion What does Mercutio mean by "a plague a both your houses"?

They have made worms' meat of me. I have it,[30]
And soundly too. Your houses!

            [Exit MERCUTIO *and* BENVOLIO.]

30. I have it: I've got my
deathblow.

ROMEO. This gentleman, the Prince's near ally,[31]
My very friend, hath got his mortal hurt
110 In my behalf—my reputation stained
With Tybalt's slander—Tybalt, that an hour
Hath been my cousin. O sweet Juliet,
Thy beauty hath made me effeminate
And in my temper soft'ned valor's steel!

31. ally: Relative.

[Enter BENVOLIO.]

115 **BENVOLIO.** O Romeo, Romeo, brave Mercutio is dead!
That gallant spirit hath aspired[32] the clouds,
Which too untimely here did scorn the earth.

32. aspired: Climbed to.

ROMEO. This day's black fate on moe[33] days doth
    depend;[34]
This but begins the woe others must end.

33. moe: More.
34. depend: Hang over.

[Enter TYBALT.]

120 **BENVOLIO.** Here comes the furious Tybalt back again.

8

ROMEO. Alive in triumph, and Mercutio slain?
Away to heaven respective lenity,[35]
And fire-eyed fury be my conduct[36] now!
Now, Tybalt, take the "villain" back again
125 That late thou gavest me; for Mercutio's soul
Is but a little way above our heads,
Staying for thine to keep him company.
Either thou or I, or both, must go with him.

35. respective lenity:
Thoughtful mercy.
36. conduct: Guide.

TYBALT. Thou, wretched boy, that didst consort him
    here,
Shalt with him hence.

130 **ROMEO.**   This shall determine that.

             [They fight. TYBALT *falls.*]

BENVOLIO. Romeo, away, be gone!
The citizens are up, and Tybalt slain.
Stand not amazed. The Prince will doom thee death
If thou art taken. Hence, be gone, away!

ROMEO. O, I am fortune's fool![37]

37. fool: Plaything.

135 **BENVOLIO.**   Why dost thou stay?

                 [Exit ROMEO.]

Primary Source

Historians and scholars generally believe that stage directions in Elizabethan plays were the author's notations and not the director's or prompter's. We can assume, therefore, that the stage directions, which were found in the original first and second quartos of *Romeo and Juliet*, were written by Shakespeare himself. A quarto is a published manuscript made up of sheets each of which is folded twice to form four leaves, or eight pages. The first quarto for *Romeo and Juliet* was printed in London in

1597, approximately two years after Shakespeare wrote the play.

Read the following passages from the introduction of *Shakespeare, The Complete Works*, edited by G. B. Harrison, to your students. The stage directions from the first quarto are shown in italics and single quotation marks; those from the second quarto are shown in italics and double quotation marks. The other directions are purely conjectural; Harrison is showing how the rest of the scene might have been staged. "RIGHT" means as the actor faces the audience—the viewer's left.

Act III, Scene i:
"Enter Mercutio, Benvolio and men," by the LEFT door. By the RIGHT door, enter Tybalt and others. Romeo enters through the RECESS curtains. Tybalt draws attention to his

[*Enter* CITIZENS.]

CITIZEN. Which way ran he that killed Mercutio?
Tybalt, that murderer, which way ran he?

BENVOLIO. There lies that Tybalt.

CITIZEN. Up, sir, go with me.
I charge thee in the Prince's name obey.

9 [*Enter* PRINCE, *old* MONTAGUE, CAPULET, *their* WIVES, *and all.*]

140 **PRINCE.** Where are the vile beginners of this fray?

BENVOLIO. O noble Prince, I can discover[38] all   **38. discover:** Reveal.
The unlucky manage[39] of this fatal brawl.   **39. manage:** Course.
There lies the man, slain by young Romeo,
That slew thy kinsman, brave Mercutio.

145 **LADY CAPULET.** Tybalt, my cousin! O my brother's child!
O Prince! O cousin! Husband! Oh, the blood is spilled
Of my dear kinsman! Prince, as thou art true,
For blood of ours shed blood of Montague.
O cousin, cousin!

150 **PRINCE.** Benvolio, who began this bloody fray?

BENVOLIO. Tybalt, here slain, whom Romeo's hand did
slay.
Romeo, that spoke him fair, bid him bethink

The Tragedy of Romeo and Juliet, Act III, Scene i **339**

entry with "Here comes my man." Tybalt and Mercutio fight; *'Tybalt under Romeo's arm thrusts Mercutio, in and flies'* through the RIGHT door. The page goes out by the LEFT door. Mercutio, supported by Benvolio, goes out through the LEFT door, whence Benvolio emerges to say that Mercutio is dead. Tybalt reenters by the RIGHT door. Romeo and Tybalt fight and Tybalt is slain. Romeo runs out by the LEFT door. The citizens enter through the curtains of the RECESS, followed by the Prince. Capulet and his wife enter by the RIGHT door. Montague and his wife enter by the LEFT. At the end of the scene, all go out by the ways in which they have entered, the body of Tybalt being carried out through the RIGHT door.

Act III, Scene ii
The curtains of the CHAMBER above are opened, revealing Juliet alone. *'Enter Nurse, wringing her hands, with the ladder of the cords in her lap.'* At the end of the scene the curtains of the CHAMBER are closed.

Student Activity. Choose a scene from the play and write the stage directions for it, keeping in mind the structure and layout of the Elizabethan theater (see pages 284–285 in the student edition).

10 Literary Focus Benvolio's monologue reviews the previous events. Do you think his account is accurate? Why or why not?

11 Critical Thinking and Reading Contrast the views of Lady Capulet and Montague. Why do you think they differ?

12 Clarification Today Romeo would be tried for murder. In earlier times, however, revenge was more common and accepted. Montague says that Romeo only did what the law would have done anyway.

13 Critical Thinking and Reading Why do you think the Prince does not impose the death penalty, as he threatened in Act I?

How nice[40] the quarrel was, and urged withal
Your high displeasure. All this—utterèd
155 With gentle breath, calm look, knees humbly bowed—
Could not take truce with the unruly spleen[41]
Of Tybalt deaf to peace, but that he tilts[42]
With piercing steel at bold Mercutio's breast;
Who, all as hot, turns deadly point to point,
160 And, with a martial scorn, with one hand beats
Cold death aside and with the other sends
It back to Tybalt, whose dexterity
Retorts it. Romeo he cries aloud,
"Hold, friends! Friends, part!" and swifter than his tongue,
165 His agile arm beats down their fatal points,
And 'twixt them rushes; underneath whose arm
An envious[43] thrust from Tybalt hit the life
Of stout Mercutio, and then Tybalt fled;
But by and by comes back to Romeo,
170 Who had but newly entertained[44] revenge,
And to't they go like lightning; for, ere I
Could draw to part them, was stout Tybalt slain;
And, as he fell, did Romeo turn and fly.
This is the truth, or let Benvolio die.

175 **LADY CAPULET.** He is a kinsman to the Montague;
Affection makes him false, he speaks not true.
Some twenty of them fought in this black strife,
And all those twenty could but kill one life.
I beg for justice, which thou, Prince, must give.
180 Romeo slew Tybalt; Romeo must not live.

PRINCE. Romeo slew him; he slew Mercutio.
Who now the price of his dear blood doth owe?

MONTAGUE. Not Romeo, Prince; he was Mercutio's friend;
His fault concludes but what the law should end,
The life of Tybalt.[45]

185 **PRINCE.**   And for that offense
Immediately we do exile him hence.
I have an interest in your hate's proceeding.
My blood[46] for your rude brawls doth lie a-bleeding;
But I'll amerce[47] you with so strong a fine
190 That you shall all repent the loss of mine.
I will be deaf to pleading and excuses;
Nor tears nor prayers shall purchase out abuses.
Therefore use none. Let Romeo hence in haste,

40. nice: Trivial.

41. spleen: Angry nature.
42. tilts: Thrusts.

43. envious: Full of hatred.

44. entertained: Considered.

45. His fault . . . Tybalt: By killing Tybalt, he did what the law would have done.

46. My blood: Mercutio was related to the Prince.
47. amerce: Punish.

Grammar in Action

Writers use **images** to create pictures for the readers. Using images in your own work will make your writing interesting and come alive for your audience. An image is a word or phrase that appeals to one of the five senses—sight, hearing, touch, taste, smell. By appealing to the reader's senses, use of image, or **imagery,** allows that reader to experience what is being described. Study these lines from the play:

JULIET: Come, night; come, Romeo; come, thou day in night;
For thou wilt lie upon the wings of night
Whiter than new snow upon a raven's back.
Come gentle night; come, loving, black-browed night;
Give me my Romeo; and, when he shall die,
Take him and cut him out in little stars,
And he will make the face of heaven so fine
That all the world will be in love with night
And pay no worship to the garish sun.

Images in these lines appeal to the sense of sight. Notice the number and variety of these images: Romeo is compared to snow on a raven's back (lines 2 and 3). Night is given the

Else, when he is found, that hour is his last.
195   Bear hence this body and attend our will.[48]
   Mercy but murders, pardoning those that kill.

                  [*Exit with others.*]

Scene ii. CAPULET'S *orchard.*

[*Enter* JULIET *alone.*]

   JULIET. Gallop apace, you fiery-footed steeds,[1]
   Towards Phoebus' lodging![2] Such a wagoner
   As Phaëton[3] would whip you to the west
   And bring in cloudy night immediately.
5   Spread thy close curtain, love-performing night,
   That runaways' eyes may wink,[4] and Romeo
   Leap to these arms untalked of and unseen.
   Lovers can see to do their amorous rites,
   And by their own beauties; or, if love be blind,
10   It best agrees with night. Come, civil night,
   Thou sober-suited matron all in black,
   And learn me how to lose a winning match,
   Played for a pair of stainless maidenhoods.
   Hood my unmanned blood, bating in my cheeks,[5]
15   With thy black mantle till strange[6] love grow bold,
   Think true love acted simple modesty,
   Come, night; come, Romeo; come, thou day in night;
   For thou wilt lie upon the wings of night
   Whiter than new snow upon a raven's back.
20   Come, gentle night; come, loving, black-browed night;
   Give me my Romeo; and, when I shall die,
   Take him and cut him out in little stars,
   And he will make the face of heaven so fine
   That all the world will be in love with night
25   And pay no worship to the garish sun.
   O, I have bought the mansion of a love,
   But not possessed it; and though I am sold,
   Not yet enjoyed. So tedious is this day
   As is the night before some festival
30   To an impatient child that hath new robes
   And may not wear them. O, here comes my nurse,

[*Enter* NURSE, *with cords.*]

   And she brings news; and every tongue that speaks
   But Romeo's name speaks heavenly eloquence.
   Now, nurse, what news? What hast thou there, the
     cords
   That Romeo bid thee fetch?

48. attend our will: Await my decision.

1. fiery-footed steeds: Horses of the sun god, Phoebus.
2. Phoebus' lodging: Below the horizon.
3. Phaëton: Phoebus' son, who tried to drive his father's horses but was unable to control them.
4. That runaways' eyes may wink: So that the eyes of busybodies may not see.

5. Hood . . . cheeks: Hide the untamed blood that makes me blush.
6. strange: Unfamiliar.

4

The Tragedy of Romeo and Juliet, Act III, Scene ii   341

14 Literary Focus This soliloquy gives the audience a glimpse into Juliet's thoughts. Ask students to describe her mood. Why is this soliloquy especially touching after the dramatic events that have just occurred?

qualities of a person—"gentle," "loving, black-browed" (line 4). The image of the stars (lines 5–8) indicates the intensity of Juliet's love. And the use of the word *garish* to describe the sun (line 9) allows readers to not only visualize it but also to see it as Juliet does.

Student Activity 1. Find another passage that contains imagery, and discuss your choice with a classmate. Talk about which sense is appealed to and the effect of the image. (If more than one sense is appealed to, be sure to discuss each one.)

Student Activity 2. Write several sentences that contain imagery. Read these aloud to a partner, and discuss ways in which they are effective and how they might be improved.

15 **Critical Thinking and Reading**
These next two scenes show
how Juliet and Romeo act in the
face of bad news. As students
read, have them compare and
contrast the ways in which the
two handle their grief.

35 **NURSE.**   Ay, ay, the cords.

JULIET. Ay me! What news? Why dost thou wring thy
hands?

15

NURSE. Ah, weraday![7] He's dead, he's dead, he's dead!
We are undone, lady, we are undone!
Alack the day! He's gone, he's killed, he's dead!

7. Ah, weraday!: Alas!

JULIET. Can heaven be so envious?

40 **NURSE.**   Romeo can,
Though heaven cannot. O Romeo, Romeo!
Who ever would have thought it? Romeo!

JULIET. What devil art thou that dost torment me thus?
This torture should be roared in dismal hell.
45 Hath Romeo slain himself? Say thou but "Ay,"
And that bare vowel "I" shall poison more
Than the death-darting eye of cockatrice.[8]
I am not I, if there be such an "Ay,"[9]
Or those eyes' shot[10] that makes thee answer "Ay."
50 If he be slain, say "Ay"; or if not, "No."
Brief sounds determine of my weal or woe.

8. cockatrice: A serpent
that, in fables, could kill
with its glance.
9. "Ay": Yes.
10. eyes' shot: The
nurse's glance.

NURSE. I saw the wound, I saw it with mine eyes,
(God save the mark![11]) here on his manly breast.
A piteous corse,[12] a bloody piteous corse;
55 Pale, pale as ashes, all bedaubed in blood,
All in gore-blood. I sounded[13] at the sight.

11. God save the mark!:
May God save us from evil!
12. corse: Corpse.
13. sounded: Swooned,
fainted.

JULIET. O, break, my heart! Poor bankrout,[14] break at
once!
To prison, eyes; ne'er look on liberty!
Vile earth, to earth resign;[15] end motion here,
60 And thou and Romeo press one heavy bier![16]

14. bankrout: Bankrupt.

15. Vile . . . resign: Let
my body return to the
earth.
16. bier: A platform on
which a corpse is displayed
before burial.

NURSE. O Tybalt, Tybalt, the best friend I had!
O courteous Tybalt! Honest gentleman!
That ever I should live to see thee dead!

JULIET. What storm is this that blows so contrary?[17]
65 Is Romeo slaught'red, and is Tybalt dead?
My dearest cousin, and my dearer lord?
Then, dreadful trumpet, sound the general doom![18]
For who is living, if those two are gone?

17. contrary: In opposite
directions.

18. dreadful . . . doom:
Let the trumpet that an-
nounces doomsday be
sounded.

NURSE. Tybalt is gone, and Romeo banishèd;
70 Romeo that killed him, he is banishèd.

JULIET. O God! Did Romeo's hand shed Tybalt's blood?

NURSE. It did, it did! Alas the day, it did!

JULIET. O serpent heart, hid with a flow'ring face!
    Did ever dragon keep so fair a cave?
75   Beautiful tyrant! Fiend angelical!
    Dove-feathered raven! Wolvish-ravening lamb!
    Despisèd substance of divinest show!
    Just opposite to what thou justly seem'st—
    A damnèd saint, an honorable villain!
80   O nature, what hadst thou to do in hell
    When thou didst bower the spirit of a fiend
    In mortal paradise of such sweet flesh?
    Was ever book containing such vile matter
    So fairly bound? O, that deceit should dwell
    In such a gorgeous palace!

85 **NURSE.**   There's no trust,
    No faith, no honesty in men; all perjured,
    All forsworn,[19] all naught, all dissemblers.[20]
    Ah, where's my man? Give me some *aqua vitae*.[21]
    These griefs, these woes, these sorrows make me old.
    Shame come to Romeo!

90 **JULIET.**   Blistered be thy tongue
    For such a wish! He was not born to shame.
    Upon his brow shame is ashamed to sit;
    For 'tis a throne where honor may be crowned
    Sole monarch of the universal earth.
95   O, what a beast was I to chide at him!

NURSE. Will you speak well of him that killed your cousin?

JULIET. Shall I speak ill of him that is my husband?
    Ah, poor my lord, what tongue shall smooth thy name
    When I, thy three-hours wife, have mangled it?
100   But wherefore, villain, didst thou kill my cousin?
    That villain cousin would have killed my husband.
    Back, foolish tears, back to your native spring!
    Your tributary[22] drops belong to woe,
    Which you, mistaking, offer up to joy.
105   My husband lives, that Tybalt would have slain;
    And Tybalt's dead, that would have slain my husband.
    All this is comfort; wherefore weep I then?
    Some word there was, worser than Tybalt's death,
    That murd'red me. I would forget it fain;
110   But O, it presses to my memory
    Like damnèd guilty deeds to sinners' minds!
    "Tybalt is dead, and Romeo—banishèd."

The Tragedy of Romeo and Juliet, Act III, Scene ii   **343**

19. forsworn: Are liars.
20. dissemblers: Hypocrites.
21. *aqua vitae*: Brandy.

22. tributary: In tribute.

16 Discussion How do Juliet's words reflect her divided feelings?

17 Discussion What word would Juliet like to forget but cannot?

That "banishèd," that one word "banishèd,"
Hath slain ten thousand Tybalts. Tybalt's death
115   Was woe enough, if it had ended there;
Or, if sour woe delights in fellowship
And needly will be ranked with[23] other griefs,
Why followed not, when she said "Tybalt's dead,"
Thy father, or thy mother, nay, or both,
120   Which modern[24] lamentation might have moved?
But with a rearward[25] following Tybalt's death,
"Romeo is banishèd"—to speak that word
Is father, mother, Tybalt, Romeo, Juliet,
All slain, all dead. "Romeo is banishèd"—
125   There is no end, no limit, measure, bound,
In that word's death; no words can that woe sound.
Where is my father and my mother, nurse?

NURSE. Weeping and wailing over Tybalt's corse.
Will you go to them? I will bring you thither.

JULIET. Wash they his wounds with tears? Mine shall be
130   spent,
When theirs are dry, for Romeo's banishment.
Take up those cords. Poor ropes, you are beguiled,
Both you and I, for Romeo is exiled.
He made you for a highway to my bed;
135   But I, a maid, die maiden-widowèd.
Come, cords; come, nurse. I'll to my wedding bed;
And death, not Romeo, take my maidenhead!

NURSE. Hie to your chamber. I'll find Romeo
To comfort you. I wot[26] well where he is.
140   Hark ye, your Romeo will be here at night.
I'll to him; he is hid at Lawrence' cell.

JULIET. O, find him! Give this ring to my true knight
And bid him come to take his last farewell.

[Exit with NURSE.]

Scene iii. FRIAR LAWRENCE'S *cell.*

[Enter FRIAR LAWRENCE.]

FRIAR. Romeo, come forth; come forth, thou fearful man.
Affliction is enamored of thy parts.[1]
And thou art wedded to calamity.

[Enter ROMEO.]

23. **needly . . . with:** Must be accompanied by.

24. **modern:** Ordinary.
25. **rearward:** Follow up; literally, a rear guard.

26. **wot:** Know.

1. **Affliction . . . parts:** Misery is in love with your attractive qualities.

344   *Drama*

ROMEO. Father, what news? What is the Prince's doom?[2]

5   What sorrow craves acquaintance at my hand
    That I yet know not?

FRIAR.   Too familiar
    Is my dear son with such sour company.
    I bring thee tidings of the Prince's doom.

ROMEO. What less than doomsday[3] is the Prince's doom?

10 **FRIAR.** A gentler judgment vanished[4] from his lips—
    Not body's death, but body's banishment.

ROMEO. Ha, banishment? Be merciful, say "death";
    For exile hath more terror in his look,
    Much more than death. Do not say "banishment."

15 **FRIAR.** Here from Verona art thou banishèd.
    Be patient, for the world is broad and wide.

ROMEO. There is no world without[5] Verona walls,
    But purgatory, torture, hell itself.
    Hence banishèd is banished from the world,
20 And world's exile is death. Then "banishèd"
    Is death mistermed. Calling death "banishèd,"
    Thou cut'st my head off with a golden ax
    And smilest upon the stroke that murders me.

FRIAR. O deadly sin! O rude unthankfulness!
25 Thy fault our law calls death;[6] but the kind Prince,
    Taking thy part, hath rushed[7] aside the law,
    And turned that black word "death" to "banishment."
    This is dear mercy, and thou seest it not.

ROMEO. 'Tis torture, and not mercy. Heaven is here,
30 Where Juliet lives; and every cat and dog
    And little mouse, every unworthy thing,
    Live here in heaven and may look on her;
    But Romeo may not. More validity,[8]
    More honorable state, more courtship lives
35 In carrion flies than Romeo. They may seize
    On the white wonder of dear Juliet's hand
    And steal immortal blessing from her lips,
    Who, even in pure and vestal modesty,
    Still blush, as thinking their own kisses sin;
40 But Romeo may not, he is banishèd.
    Flies may do this but I from this must fly;
    They are freemen, but I am banishèd.
    And sayest thou yet that exile is not death?

2. doom: Final decision.

3. doomsday: My death.

4. vanished: Escaped, came forth.

5. without: Outside.

6. Thy fault . . . death: For what you did our law demands the death penalty.
7. rushed: Pushed.

8. validity: Value.

The Tragedy of Romeo and Juliet, Act III, Scene iii   345

20 Discussion Is Romeo's reaction to his punishment unreasonable? Explain.

21 Clarification Verona and Mantua are only about twenty-five miles apart, less than a day's walk.

22 Discussion Why does Friar Lawrence disagree with Romeo?

23 Literary Focus How does this monologue reveal a flaw in Romeo's character?

24 Critical Thinking and Reading
If you were directing this scene, how would you instruct the actors to move and behave?

25 Critical Thinking and Reading
How would you describe Romeo's tone of voice in this speech?

Hadst thou no poison mixed, no sharp-ground knife,
45   No sudden mean[9] of death, though ne'er so mean,[10]
      But "banishèd" to kill me—"banishèd"?
      O friar, the damnèd use that word in hell;
      Howling attends it! How hast thou the heart,
      Being a divine, a ghostly confessor,
50   A sin-absolver, and my friend professed,
      To mangle me with that word "banishèd"?

24

FRIAR. Thou fond mad man, hear me a little speak.

ROMEO. O, thou wilt speak again of banishment.

FRIAR. I'll give thee armor to keep off that word;
55   Adversity's sweet milk, philosophy,
        To comfort thee, though thou art banishèd.

25

ROMEO. Yet "banishèd"? Hang up philosophy!
        Unless philosophy can make a Juliet,
        Displant a town, reverse a prince's doom,
60   It helps not, it prevails not. Talk no more.

FRIAR. O, then I see that madmen have no ears.

ROMEO. How should they, when that wise men have no eyes?

FRIAR. Let me dispute[11] with thee of thy estate.[12]

9. mean: Method.
10. mean: Humiliating.

11. dispute: Discuss.
12. estate: Condition, situation.

346   Drama

Grammar in Action

The placement of **quotation marks with other punctuation** causes some confusion among beginning writers. The question mark or exclamation mark is placed *inside* the final quotation mark if the end mark is part of the quotation:

> The teacher asked, "Have you done your homework?"
> He exclaimed, "I can't believe I won; I really won!"

The question mark or exclamation mark is placed *outside* the final quotation mark if the end mark is *not* part of the quotation:

> Who said: "I'm going to do better next time"?
> I was ecstatic when he droned, "Nam Hee Chin, first place"!

Notice how Shakespeare observes these rules in the following excerpts from *Romeo and Juliet:*

> But "banished" to kill me—"banishèd"?
> . . . How hast thou the heart,/To mangle me with that word 'banishèd'?
> Yet "banishèd"? Hang up philosophy!

The quotation marks around *banished* show the exact wording of the Prince's sentence. The questions are Romeo's; therefore, the question marks appear outside the quotation marks.

ROMEO. Thou canst not speak of that thou dost not feel.
65   Wert thou as young as I, Juliet thy love,
    An hour but married, Tybalt murderèd,
    Doting like me, and like me banishèd,
    Then mightst thou speak, then mightst thou tear thy
       hair,
    And fall upon the ground, as I do now,
70   Taking the measure of an unmade grave.

[*Enter* NURSE *and knock.*]

FRIAR. Arise, one knocks. Good Romeo, hide thyself.

ROMEO. Not I; unless the breath of heartsick groans
    Mistlike infold me from the search of eyes.   [*Knock.*]

FRIAR. Hark, how they knock! Who's there? Romeo, arise;
75   Thou wilt be taken.—Stay awhile!—Stand up; [*Knock.*]
    Run to my study.—By and by![13]—God's will,
    What simpleness[14] is this.—I come, I come!   [*Knock.*]
    Who knocks so hard? Whence come you? What's your
      will?

[*Enter* NURSE.]

NURSE. Let me come in, and you shall know my errand.
    I come from Lady Juliet.

80 **FRIAR.**   Welcome then.

NURSE. O holy friar, O, tell me, holy friar,
    Where is my lady's lord, where's Romeo?

FRIAR. There on the ground, with his own tears made
    drunk.

NURSE. O, he is even in my mistress' case,
85   Just in her case! O woeful sympathy!
    Piteous predicament! Even so lies she,
    Blubb'ring and weeping, weeping and blubb'ring.
    Stand up, stand up! Stand, and you be a man.
    For Juliet's sake, for her sake, rise and stand!
90   Why should you fall into so deep an O?[15]

ROMEO. [*Rises.*] Nurse—

NURSE. Ah sir, ah sir! Death's the end of all.

ROMEO. Spakest thou of Juliet? How is it with her?
    Doth not she think me an old murderer,
95   Now I have stained the childhood of our joy
    With blood removed but little from her own?

13. By and by!: In a minute! (said to the person knocking).
14. simpleness: Silly behavior (Romeo does not move).

15. O: Cry of grief.

26 Discussion Do you think Romeo's argument is valid? Explain.

The Tragedy of Romeo and Juliet, Act III, Scene iii   347

Student Activity 1. Add end marks either inside or outside the quotation marks in the following sentences:
1. Did he say, "I'm planning a weekend party"
2. At the final buzzer, he screamed, "We did it"
3. Mr. Gaddis asked, "Who's on the newspaper staff"
4. Did you read "The Interlopers" and "The Necklace"

Student Activity 2. Write four sentences, two using end marks inside quotation marks and two using them outside.

Electronic Handbook You may wish students to review the use of quotation marks with other punctuation before completing the Grammar in Action activities. If students have access to the Language Master 6000, have them enter the access symbol " or the access word *quotation* and press the GRAMMAR key to obtain information on the use of quotation marks with other punctuation.

27 Discussion Does Romeo really intend to stab himself?

Where is she? And how doth she? And what says
My concealed lady[16] to our canceled love?

NURSE. O, she says nothing, sir, but weeps and weeps;
100 And now falls on her bed, and then starts up,
And Tybalt calls; and then on Romeo cries,
And then down falls again.

ROMEO.   As if that name,
Shot from the deadly level[17] of a gun,
Did murder her; as that name's cursèd hand
105 Murdered her kinsman. O, tell me, friar, tell me,
In what vile part of this anatomy
Doth my name lodge? Tell me, that I may sack[18]
The hateful mansion.

27
[*He offers to stab himself, and* NURSE
snatches the dagger away.]

110 **FRIAR.**   Hold thy desperate hand.
Art thou a man? Thy form cries out thou art;
Thy tears are womanish, thy wild acts denote
The unreasonable fury of a beast.
Unseemly[19] woman in a seeming man!
And ill-beseeming beast in seeming both![20]
Thou hast amazed me. By my holy order,
115 I thought thy disposition better tempered.
Hast thou slain Tybalt? Wilt thou slay thyself?
And slay thy lady that in thy life lives,
By doing damnèd hate upon thyself?
Why railest thou on thy birth, the heaven, and earth?
120 Since birth and heaven and earth, all three do meet
In thee at once; which thou at once wouldst lose.
Fie, fie, thou shamest thy shape, thy love, thy wit,[21]
Which, like a usurer,[22] abound'st in all,
And usest none in that true use indeed
125 Which should bedeck[23] thy shape, thy love, thy wit.
Thy noble shape is but a form of wax,
Digressing from the valor of a man;
Thy dear love sworn but hollow perjury,
Killing that love which thou hast vowed to cherish;
130 Thy wit, that ornament to shape and love,
Misshapen in the conduct[24] of them both,
Like powder in a skilless soldier's flask,[25]
Is set afire by thine own ignorance,
And thou dismemb'red with thine own defense.[26]
135 What, rouse thee, man! Thy Juliet is alive,

16. concealed lady: Secret bride.

17. level: Aim.

18. sack: Plunder.

19. Unseemly: Inappropriate (because unnatural).
20. And . . . both!: That is, Romeo inappropriately has lost his human nature because he seems like a man and woman combined.

21. wit: Mind, intellect.
22. Which, like a usurer: Who, like a rich money-lender.
23. bedeck: Do honor to.

24. conduct: Management.
25. flask: Powder flask.
26. And thou . . . defense: The friar is saying that Romeo's mind, which is now irrational, is destroying rather than aiding him.

348 Drama

For whose dear sake thou wast but lately dead.[27]
There art thou happy.[28] Tybalt would kill thee,
But thou slewest Tybalt. There art thou happy.
The law, that threat'ned death, becomes thy friend
140 And turns it into exile. There art thou happy.
A pack of blessings light upon thy back;
Happiness courts thee in her best array;
But, like a misbehaved and sullen wench,[29]
Thou puts up[30] thy fortune and thy love.
145 Take heed, take heed, for such die miserable.
Go get thee to thy love, as was decreed,
Ascend her chamber, hence and comfort her.
But look thou stay not till the watch be set,[31]
For then thou canst not pass to Mantua,
150 Where thou shalt live till we can find a time
To blaze[32] your marriage, reconcile your friends,
Beg pardon of the Prince, and call thee back
With twenty hundred thousand times more joy
Than thou went'st forth in lamentation.
155 Go before, nurse. Commend me to thy lady,
And bid her hasten all the house to bed,
Which heavy sorrow makes them apt unto.[33]
Romeo is coming.

NURSE. O Lord, I could have stayed here all the night
160 To hear good counsel. O, what learning is!
My lord, I'll tell my lady you will come.

ROMEO. Do so, and bid my sweet prepare to chide.[34]
[NURSE *offers to go in and turns again.*]

NURSE. Here, sir, a ring she bid me give you, sir.
Hie you, make haste, for it grows very late. [*Exit.*]

165 **ROMEO.** How well my comfort is revived by this!

FRIAR. Go hence; good night; and here stands all your
state:[35]
Either be gone before the watch be set,
Or by the break of day disguised from hence.
Sojourn[36] in Mantua. I'll find out your man,
170 And he shall signify[37] from time to time
Every good hap to you that chances here.
Give me thy hand. 'Tis late. Farewell; good night.

ROMEO. But that a joy past joy calls out on me,
It were a grief so brief to part with thee.
175 Farewell. [*Exit.*]

The Tragedy of Romeo and Juliet, Act III, Scene iii **349**

---

27. but lately dead: Only recently declaring yourself dead.
28. happy: Fortunate.

29. wench: Low, common girl.
30. puts up: Pouts over.

31. watch be set: The watchmen go on duty.

32. blaze: Announce publicly.

33. apt unto: Likely to do.

34. chide: Rebuke me (for slaying Tybalt).

35. here . . . state: This is your situation.

36. Sojourn: Remain.
37. signify: Let you know.

---

28 Reading Strategy Ask students to predict whether these events will occur.

29 Discussion What are Friar Lawrence's instructions to Romeo?

30 **Critical Thinking and Reading** Why does Capulet think that Juliet is grieving?

31 **Reading Strategy** Have students predict how Juliet will react to this news.

Scene iv. *A room in* CAPULET'S *house.*

[*Enter old* CAPULET, *his* WIFE, *and* PARIS.]

CAPULET. Things have fall'n out, sir, so unluckily
That we have had no time to move[1] our daughter.
Look you, she loved her kinsman Tybalt dearly,
And so did I. Well, we were born to die.
5 'Tis very late; she'll not come down tonight.
I promise you, but for your company,
I would have been abed an hour ago.

PARIS. These times of woe afford no times to woo.
Madam, good night. Commend me to your daughter.

10 **LADY.** I will, and know her mind early tomorrow;
Tonight she's mewed up to her heaviness.[2]

CAPULET. Sir, Paris, I will make a desperate tender[3]
Of my child's love. I think she will be ruled
In all respects by me; nay more, I doubt it not.
15 Wife, go you to her ere you go to bed;
Acquaint her here of my son[4] Paris' love
And bid her (mark you me?) on Wednesday next—
But soft! What day is this?

PARIS.   Monday, my lord.

CAPULET. Monday! Ha, ha! Well, Wednesday is too soon.
20 A[5] Thursday let it be—a Thursday, tell her,
She shall be married to this noble earl.
Will you be ready? Do you like this haste?
We'll keep no great ado[6]—a friend or two;
For hark you, Tybalt being slain so late,
25 It may be thought we held him carelessly,[7]
Being our kinsman, if we revel much.
Therefore we'll have some half a dozen friends,
And there an end. But what say you to Thursday?

PARIS. My lord, I would that Thursday were tomorrow.

30 **CAPULET.** Well, get you gone. A Thursday be it then.
Go you to Juliet ere you go to bed;
Prepare her, wife, against[8] this wedding day.
Farewell, my lord.—Light to my chamber, ho!
Afore me,[9] it is so very late
35 That we may call it early by and by.
Good night.   [*Exit.*]

1. move: Discuss your proposal with.

2. mewed . . . heaviness: Locked up with her sorrow.
3. desperate tender: Risky offer.

4. son: Son-in-law.

5. A: On.

6. We'll . . . ado: We won't make a great fuss.
7. held him carelessly: Did not respect him enough.

8. against: For.

9. Afore me: Indeed (a mild oath).

Scene v. CAPULET'S *orchard.*

[*Enter* ROMEO *and* JULIET *aloft.*]

JULIET. Wilt thou be gone? It is not yet near day.
It was the nightingale, and not the lark,[1]
That pierced the fearful hollow of thine ear.
Nightly she sings on yond pomegranate tree.
5   Believe me, love, it was the nightingale.

ROMEO. It was the lark, the herald of the morn;
No nightingale. Look, love, what envious streaks
Do lace the severing[2] clouds in yonder East.
Night's candles[3] are burnt out, and jocund day
10   Stands tiptoe on the misty mountaintops.
I must be gone and live, or stay and die.

JULIET. Yond light is not daylight; I know it, I.
It is some meteor that the sun exhales[4]
To be to thee this night a torchbearer
15   And light thee on thy way to Mantua.
Therefore stay yet; thou need'st not to be gone.

ROMEO. Let me be ta'en, let me be put to death.
I am content, so thou wilt have it so.
I'll say yon gray is not the morning's eye,
20   'Tis but the pale reflex of Cynthia's brow;[5]
Nor that is not the lark whose notes do beat
The vaulty heaven so high above our heads.
I have more care to stay than will to go.
Come, death, and welcome! Juliet wills it so.
25   How is't, my soul? Let's talk; it is not day.

JULIET. It is, it is! Hie hence, be gone, away!
It is the lark that sings so out of tune,
Straining harsh discords and unpleasing sharps.[6]
Some say the lark makes sweet division;[7]
30   This doth not so, for she divideth us.
Some say the lark and loathèd toad change eyes;[8]
O, now I would they had changed voices too,
Since arm from arm that voice doth us affray,[9]
Hunting thee hence with hunt's-up[10] to the day.
35   O, now be gone! More light and light it grows.

ROMEO. More light and light—more dark and dark our
        woes.

[*Enter* NURSE.]

1. nightingale . . . lark:
The nightingale was associated with the night, the lark with dawn.

2. severing: Parting.
3. Night's candles: The stars.

4. exhales: Sends out.

5. reflex . . . brow: Reflection of the moon (Cynthia was a name for the moon goddess).

6. sharps: Shrill high notes.
7. division: Melody.

8. change eyes: Exchange eyes (because the lark has a beautiful body with ugly eyes and the toad has an ugly body with beautiful eyes).
9. affray: Frighten.
10. hunt's-up: A morning song for hunters.

32 Critical Thinking and Reading
Contrast the different feelings that night and day inspire.

The Tragedy of Romeo and Juliet, Act III, Scene v   351

33 **Discussion** Compare their fare-wells. Who seems to be more optimistic about the future now?

34 **Reading Strategy** As students read the rest of the scene, have them look for the irony in the exchanges between Juliet and her parents.

Speaking and Listening You might want to have student volunteers read aloud the dialogue in Act III, Scene i. Have another volunteer read the stage directions in the script. Then have them discuss the difficulties of actually playing the scene.

NURSE. Madam!

JULIET. Nurse?

NURSE. Your lady mother is coming to your chamber.
40   The day is broke; be wary, look about.   [*Exit.*]

JULIET. Then, window, let day in, and let life out.

ROMEO. Farewell, farewell! One kiss, and I'll descend.
               [*He goeth down.*]

JULIET. Art thou gone so, love-lord, ay husband-friend?
    I must hear from thee every day in the hour,
45   For in a minute there are many days.
    O, by this count I shall be much in years[11]
    Ere I again behold my Romeo!

ROMEO. Farewell!
    I will omit no opportunity
50   That may convey my greetings, love, to thee.

JULIET. O, think'st thou we shall ever meet again?

ROMEO. I doubt it not; and all these woes shall serve
    For sweet discourses[12] in our times to come.

JULIET. O God, I have an ill-divining[13] soul!
55   Methinks I see thee, now thou art so low,
    As one dead in the bottom of a tomb.
    Either my eyesight fails, or thou lookest pale.

ROMEO. And trust me, love, in my eye so do you.
    Dry sorrow drinks our blood.[14] Adieu, adieu!   [*Exit.*]
60 **JULIET.** O Fortune, Fortune! All men call thee fickle.
    If thou art fickle, what dost thou[15] with him
    That is renowned for faith? Be fickle, Fortune,
    For then I hope thou wilt not keep him long
    But send him back.

[*Enter* MOTHER.]

65 **LADY CAPULET.** Ho, daughter! Are you up?

JULIET. Who is't that calls? It is my lady mother.
    Is she not down so late,[16] or up so early?
    What unaccustomed cause procures her hither?[17]

LADY CAPULET. Why, how now, Juliet?

JULIET.   Madam, I am not well.

70 **LADY CAPULET.** Evermore weeping for your cousin's death?

11. much in years: Much older.

12. discourses: Conversations.
13. ill-divining: Predicting evil.

14. Dry sorrow . . . blood: It was once believed that sorrow drained away the blood.
15. dost thou: Do you have to do.

16. Is she . . . late: Has she stayed up so late?
17. What . . . hither?: What unusual reason brings her here?

352   *Drama*

Multicultural Focus In *Romeo and Juliet,* Shakespeare showed how the stubbornness of two feuding families can bring tragedy. In our own country, the terrible feud between the Hatfield and McCoy families in the 1880's resulted in the death of as many as 200 people before the authorities took action. (Curiously, the worst of it erupted when a Hatfield boy tried to elope with a McCoy girl, almost imitating Shakespeare's play.) Generational feuding, known as blood feuds, is also expressed as continuing conflicts between different neighboring ethnic and religious groups, such as the Catholics and Protestants of Northern Ireland, or the Serbs and the Croats. This kind of feuding can lead to civil war, as in Lebanon, Yugoslavia, or Somalia, or national conflict, as with the Israelis and the Arab states.

Have students find out about other feuds in the past or in the world today.

What, wilt thou wash him from his grave with tears?
And if thou couldst, thou couldst not make him live.
Therefore have done. Some grief shows much of love;
But much of grief shows still some want of wit.

75 **JULIET.** Yet let me weep for such a feeling[18] loss.   **18. feeling:** Deeply felt.

LADY CAPULET. So shall you feel the loss, but not the friend
Which you weep for.

JULIET.   Feeling so the loss,
I cannot choose but ever weep the friend.

LADY CAPULET. Well, girl, thou weep'st not so much for his
death
80 As that the villain lives which slaughtered him.

JULIET. What villain, madam?

LADY CAPULET.   That same villain Romeo.

JULIET. [*Aside*] Villain and he be many miles asunder.[19]—   **19. asunder:** Apart.
God pardon him! I do, with all my heart;
And yet no man like he doth grieve my heart.

85 **LADY CAPULET.** That is because the traitor murderer lives.

JULIET. Ay, madam, from the reach of these my hands.
Would none but I might venge my cousin's death!

LADY CAPULET. We will have vengeance for it, fear thou
not.
Then weep no more. I'll send to one in Mantua,
90 Where that same banished runagate[20] doth live,   **20. runagate:** Renegade;
Shall give him such an unaccustomed dram[21]   runaway.
That he shall soon keep Tybalt company;   **21. unaccustomed dram:**
And then I hope thou wilt be satisfied.   Unexpected dose of poison.

JULIET. Indeed I never shall be satisfied
95 With Romeo till I behold him—dead[22]—   **22. dead:** Juliet is deliber-
Is my poor heart so for a kinsman vexed.   ately ambiguous here. Her
Madam, if you could find out but a man   mother thinks *dead* refers
To bear a poison, I would temper[23] it;   to Romeo. But Juliet is us-
That Romeo should, upon receipt thereof,   ing the word with the fol-
100 Soon sleep in quiet. O, how my heart abhors   lowing line, in reference to
To hear him named and cannot come to him,   her heart.
To wreak[24] the love I bore my cousin   **23. temper:** Mix; weaken.
Upon his body that hath slaughtered him!   **24. wreak** (rēēk): Avenge;
express.

LADY CAPULET. Find thou the means, and I'll find such a
man.
105 But now I'll tell thee joyful tidings, girl.

The Tragedy of Romeo and Juliet, Act III, Scene v   353

35 **Literary Focus** Why is an *aside* an especially effective device when a character says one thing but means another?

36 **Discussion** Why is Lady Capulet so intent on revenge?

37 **Clarification** Have students read this sentence aloud, pausing before the word *dead,* to show what Juliet really means; then read it again, pausing after the word *dead,* to indicate what her mother thinks she is saying.

38 Discussion How does this speech reflect the growth in Juliet's character since the beginning of the play?

39 Clarification Young girls were expected to obey their parents and to accept their choice of husbands without question.

JULIET. And joy comes well in such a needy time.
What are they, beseech your ladyship?

LADY CAPULET. Well, well, thou hast a careful[25] father, child;
One who, to put thee from thy heaviness,
110 Hath sorted out[26] a sudden day of joy
That thou expects not nor I looked not for.

JULIET. Madam, in happy time![27] What day is that?

LADY CAPULET. Marry, my child, early next Thursday morn
The gallant, young, and noble gentleman,
115 The County Paris, at Saint Peter's Church,
Shall happily make thee there a joyful bride.

JULIET. Now by Saint Peter's Church, and Peter too,
He shall not make me there a joyful bride!
I wonder at this haste, that I must wed
120 Ere he that should be husband comes to woo.
I pray you tell my lord and father, madam,
I will not marry yet; and when I do, I swear
It shall be Romeo, whom you know I hate,
Rather than Paris. These are news indeed!

LADY CAPULET. Here comes your father. Tell him so yourself,
125 And see how he will take it at your hands.

[*Enter* CAPULET *and* NURSE.]

CAPULET. When the sun sets the earth doth drizzle dew,
But for the sunset of my brother's son
It rains downright.
130 How now? A conduit,[28] girl? What, still in tears?
Evermore show'ring? In one little body
Thou counterfeits a bark,[29] a sea, a wind:
For still thy eyes, which I may call the sea,
Do ebb and flow with tears; the bark thy body is,
135 Sailing in this salt flood; the winds, thy sighs,
Who, raging with thy tears and they with them,
Without a sudden calm will overset
Thy tempest-tossèd body. How now, wife?
Have you delivered to her our decree?

LADY CAPULET. Ay, sir; but she will none, she gives you thanks.[30]
140 I would the fool were married to her grave!

CAPULET. Soft! Take me with you,[31] take me with you, wife.

25. **careful:** Considerate.

26. **sorted out:** Selected.

27. **in happy time:** Just in time.

28. **conduit:** Water pipe.

29. **bark:** Boat.

30. **she . . . thanks:** She'll have nothing to do with it, thank you.
31. **Soft! Take . . . you:** Wait a minute. Let me understand you.

How? Will she none? Doth she not give us thanks?
Is she not proud?[32] Doth she not count her blest,
145 Unworthy as she is, that we have wrought[33]
So worthy a gentleman to be her bride?

JULIET. Not proud you have, but thankful that you have.
Proud can I never be of what I hate,
But thankful even for hate that is meant love.

CAPULET. How, how, how, how, chopped-logic?[34] What is
150 this?
"Proud"—and "I thank you"—and "I thank you not"—
And yet "not proud"? Mistress minion[35] you,
Thank me no thankings, nor proud me no prouds,
But fettle[36] your fine joints 'gainst Thursday next
155 To go with Paris to Saint Peter's Church,
Or I will drag thee on a hurdle[37] thither.
Out, you greensickness carrion![38] Out, you baggage![39]
You tallow-face![40]

LADY CAPULET.   Fie, fie! What, are you mad?

32. proud: Pleased.
33. wrought: Arranged.

34. chopped-logic: Contradictory, unsound thought and speech.

35. Mistress minion: Miss Uppity.

36. fettle: Prepare.

37. hurdle: Sled on which prisoners were taken to their execution.
38. greensickness carrion: Anemic lump of flesh.
39. baggage: Naughty girl.
40. tallow-face: Wax-pale face.

40 Discussion How is this speech similar to Capulet's outburst at Tybalt at the party? What do both speeches reveal about Capulet?

355

41 Discussion Ask students to consider how events might have turned out differently if Capulet had been more patient and understanding.

42 Discussion Many analyses of this play mention the rashness of the adolescents, Romeo and Juliet. What does this speech suggest about the rashness of an adult character?

JULIET. Good father, I beseech you on my knees,
160　Hear me with patience but to speak a word.

CAPULET. Hang thee, young baggage! Disobedient wretch!
I tell thee what—get thee to church a Thursday
Or never after look me in the face.
Speak not, reply not, do not answer me!
165　My fingers itch. Wife, we scarce thought us blest
That God had lent us but this only child;
But now I see this one is one too much,
And that we have a curse in having her.
Out on her, hilding!⁴¹

41. hilding: Worthless person.

NURSE.　　　　　　　God in heaven bless her!
170　You are to blame, my lord, to rate⁴² her so.

42. rate: Scold, berate.

CAPULET. And why, my Lady Wisdom? Hold your tongue,
Good Prudence. Smatter with your gossips, go!⁴³

43. Smatter . . . go: Go chatter with the other old women.

NURSE. I speak no treason.

CAPULET.　　　　　　　O, God-i-god-en!

NURSE. May not one speak?

CAPULET.　　　　　　Peace, you mumbling fool!
175　Utter your gravity⁴⁴ o'er a gossip's bowl,
For here we need it not.

44. gravity: Wisdom.

LADY CAPULET.　　　　　You are too hot.

CAPULET. God's bread!⁴⁵ It makes me mad.
Day, night; hour, tide, time; work, play;
Alone, in company; still my care hath been
180　To have her matched; and having now provided
A gentleman of noble parentage,
Of fair demesnes,⁴⁶ youthful, and nobly trained,
Stuffed, as they say, with honorable parts,⁴⁷
Proportioned as one's thought would wish a man—
185　And then to have a wretched puling⁴⁸ fool,
A whining mammet,⁴⁹ in her fortune's tender,⁵⁰
To answer "I'll not wed, I cannot love;
I am too young, I pray you pardon me"!
But, and you will not wed, I'll pardon you!
190　Graze where you will, you shall not house with me.
Look to't, think on't; I do not use to jest.
Thursday is near; lay hand on heart, advise:⁵¹
And you be mine, I'll give you to my friend;
And you be not, hang, beg, starve, die in the streets,
195　For, by my soul, I'll ne'er acknowledge thee,

45. God's bread: By the holy Eucharist!

46. demesnes: Property.
47. parts: Qualities.
48. puling: Whining.
49. mammet: Doll.
50. tender: When good fortune is offered her.

51. advise: Consider.

Nor what is mine shall never do thee good.
Trust to't. Bethink you. I'll not be forsworn.[52]   [*Exit.*]

52. forsworn: Made to violate my promise.

JULIET. Is there no pity sitting in the clouds
That sees into the bottom of my grief?
200   O sweet my mother, cast me not away!
Delay this marriage for a month, a week;
Or if you do not, make the bridal bed
In that dim monument where Tybalt lies.

LADY CAPULET. Talk not to me, for I'll not speak a word.
205   Do as thou wilt, for I have done with thee.   [*Exit.*]

JULIET. O God!—O nurse, how shall this be prevented?
My husband is on earth, my faith in heaven.[53]
How shall that faith return again to earth
Unless that husband send it me from heaven
210   By leaving earth?[54] Comfort me, counsel me.
Alack, alack, that heaven should practice stratagems[55]
Upon so soft a subject as myself!
What say'st thou? Hast thou not a word of joy?
Some comfort, nurse.

53. my faith in heaven: My marriage vow is recorded in heaven.

54. leaving earth: Dying.
55. stratagems: Tricks, plots.

NURSE.   Faith, here it is.
215   Romeo is banished; and all the world to nothing[56]
That he dares ne'er come back to challenge[57] you;
Or if he do, it needs must be by stealth.
Then, since the case so stands as now it doth,
I think it best you married with the County.
220   O, he's a lovely gentleman!
Romeo's a dishclout to him.[58] An eagle, madam,
Hath not so green, so quick, so fair an eye
As Paris hath. Beshrew my very heart,
I think you are happy in this second match,
225   For it excels your first; or if it did not,
Your first is dead—or 'twere as good he were
As living here and you no use of him.

56. all . . . nothing: The odds are overwhelming.
57. challenge: Claim.

58. A dishclout to him: A dishcloth compared with him.

JULIET. Speak'st thou from thy heart?

NURSE. And from my soul too; else beshrew them both.

JULIET. Amen!

NURSE. What?

JULIET. Well, thou hast comforted me marvelous much.
Go in; and tell my lady I am gone,
Having displeased my father, to Lawrence' cell,
235   To make confession and to be absolved.[59]

59. absolved: Receive forgiveness for my sins.

The Tragedy of Romeo and Juliet, Act III, Scene v   357

43 Discussion What does the Nurse's change of heart reveal about her approach to life?

44 Clarification When Nurse says she speaks from the heart and from the soul or else they are both cursed, Juliet's *"Amen,"* is a curse of the Nurse.

45 **Literary Focus** Juliet's final soliloquy is really addressed to the absent Nurse. Why can she no longer confide in the Nurse?

46 **Critical Thinking and Reading** How does her decision not to confide in the Nurse mark a change in her character? How might her reliance on Friar Lawrence affect the plot?

Reader's Response Do you think that the Nurse and Friar Lawrence have acted responsibly and appropriately? If so, why? If not, what would you have done differently?

Thematic Response Could Romeo have avoided his conflict with Tybalt? If so, how? What will be the result of this conflict?

Closure and Extension

ANSWERS TO RESPONDING TO THE SELECTION
Your Response
1. Encourage students to discuss the idea of fate as immutable versus the belief that people control their own destinies through their own personal decisions and actions.

Recalling
2. Romeo controls his anger and tries to make light of the challenge to a duel. Mercutio becomes angry and begins to fight with Tybalt. As Romeo tries to separate them, Tybalt kills Mercutio and runs away. When Tybalt returns, Romeo avenges his friend's death by killing Tybalt. Romeo runs away. The Prince banishes Romeo.
3. At first Juliet believes Romeo is evil and begins to speak against him although she can only half-curse him. But when the Nurse also attacks Romeo, Juliet defends him, feeling guilty that she had even thought he was villainous. She is upset for both Tybalt

358

NURSE. Marry, I will; and this is wisely done.   [*Exit.*]

45
46
240

JULIET. Ancient damnation![60] O most wicked fiend!
Is it more sin to wish me thus forsworn,
Or to dispraise my lord with that same tongue
Which she hath praised him with above compare
So many thousand times? Go, counselor!
Thou and my bosom henceforth shall be twain.[61]
I'll to the friar to know his remedy.
If all else fail, myself have power to die.   [*Exit.*]

60. Ancient damnation: Old devil.

61. Thou ... twain: You will from now on be separated from my trust.

RESPONDING TO THE SELECTION

Your Response
1. Do you think Romeo is a victim of fate or of his own character? Explain.

Recalling
2. Trace the sequence of events that begins with Tybalt's insult to Romeo and ends with Tybalt's death and Romeo's banishment.
3. Describe the clashing emotions Juliet feels when the Nurse reports Tybalt's death and Romeo's banishment.
4. In his long speech to Romeo, Friar Lawrence mentions three things for which Romeo should consider himself fortunate. What are they?
5. What decision concerning Paris and Juliet does Lord Capulet make in Scene iv? Describe Juliet's reaction to this plan.
6. As Romeo and Juliet are about to part, how do they differ in their views of the future? What advice does the Nurse give Juliet at the end of Act III? Describe Juliet's reaction to this advice.

Interpreting
7. What does Romeo mean when he says, after killing Tybalt, "O, I am fortune's fool!"?

358   Drama

8. Why did Escalus not sentence Romeo to death, in keeping with his speech in Act I?
9. Explain why you think Romeo and Juliet's troubles do or do not result primarily from fate. Support your answer with details from the play.

Applying
10. Up to this point, the Nurse has acted as a counselor for Juliet. What qualities should a counselor have?

ANALYZING LITERATURE

Understanding Dramatic Speeches
A **soliloquy** is a speech in which a character, alone on stage, speaks directly to the audience. An **aside** is a brief remark to the audience, uttered while other characters are nearby but unable to hear. A **monologue** is a lengthy speech addressed to other characters, rather than to the audience.

1. What thoughts and feelings does Juliet reveal in her soliloquy that opens Scene ii?
2. When Lady Capulet, in Scene v, refers to Romeo as a villain, Juliet utters the aside "Villain and he be many miles asunder." In your own words, what is Juliet saying? Why is it im-

---

and Romeo because one is dead and the other is banished.
4. Friar Lawrence thinks Romeo should feel fortunate because Juliet is alive, he is alive, and he has only been banished—not sentenced to death.
5. Capulet has decided that Paris and Juliet will marry in two days. Juliet's reaction is explosive and definite. She will not marry Paris.
6. Juliet is pessimistic, Romeo more positive. She is wondering if they will ever see each other

again. Romeo assures her that they will and then all their sorrows will be gone. The Nurse advises Juliet to forget Romeo and marry Paris. Juliet reacts by secretly rejecting the Nurse as a confidante.

Interpreting
7. Suggested Response: Romeo feels he is a victim of fate.
8. Suggested Response: The Prince was more lenient because Romeo killed a person who had

himself killed the Prince's relative.
9. Answers will differ, but many students will conclude that most of the troubles arise from the fact that their families have been feuding; as a result, their love is dangerous and bound to lead to trouble. Tybalt's anger at Romeo and the need to keep the marriage a secret are the result of the feud. Capulet might easily have approved a marriage to Romeo instead of Paris, if there

portant that the audience, but not Lady Capulet, hear this remark?

3. Reread Friar Lawrence's monologue in Scene iii beginning "Hold thy desperate hand." What criticisms is he addressing to Romeo?

CRITICAL THINKING AND READING

Inferring Tone in a Monologue

Tone in a monologue refers to the feelings and emotions that accompany the words. When you attend a play, the tone of a speech is conveyed by the voice of the speaker. When you read a play, however, you must infer the tone. When reading Shakespeare, first do your best to understand what the words and sentences mean. Read again Benvolio's monologue in Scene i beginning "Tybalt, here slain, whom Romeo's hand did slay" (lines 151–174). Then answer the following questions:

1. What situation is the speaker in?
2. To whom is he speaking?
3. Why is Benvolio uttering these words?
4. In view of the answers to these three questions, what feelings and emotions seem appropriate to the monologue?

THINKING AND WRITING

Writing a Soliloquy

At the end of Act III, Juliet delivers a brief soliloquy. She expresses anger with the Nurse for suggesting that she should forget Romeo and marry Paris. Then she announces that she will go to the Friar to see how he might help her.

Write a brief soliloquy either in prose or blank verse such as Juliet might speak just before she meets with the Friar. First think of the thoughts that might be on her mind. What might she be thinking about all that has happened since she met Romeo? What might be her thoughts of the future? What feelings would her words convey? Try to suggest the personality and emotional state of a thirteen-year-old girl in such a situation. When you revise your soliloquy, check that it is in harmony with the events of the play to this point and with Juliet's character. Read your finished soliloquy to some of your classmates and ask them if it sounds like the kind of speech Juliet might give.

LEARNING OPTIONS

1. **Performance.** With a partner, choose a brief scene in Act III that involves two characters and perform the scene for the class. Rehearse the scene carefully to learn the pronunciations of words and to develop appropriate tones of voice, volume, and gestures.
2. **Writing.** Imagine there was a teen advice column to which Romeo or Juliet could write. Write a letter in which one of these characters asks for advice about his or her problems. Then write a plausible response from the writer of the column.
3. **Community Connections.** As a class, work with the librarian at your community library to create a Shakespeare display that you could share with the public. In your display, consider including resources such as biographies and various editions of the plays, as well as student compositions and drawings.

The Tragedy of Romeo and Juliet, Act III 359

Preparation

Literary Focus You might point out other examples of dramatic irony. For example, when Tybalt and Romeo fight, they are kinsmen—though Tybalt is unaware of this fact.

Prereading Focus The purpose of this exercise is to focus student attention on issues with which they may be unfamiliar. Ask students to discuss whether they think that they now are mature enough to choose a spouse. Remind them that Juliet is thirteen years old and Romeo is fourteen or fifteen years of age.

Vocabulary Have your **less advanced** students read the words and their meanings. Then have them write a paragraph using all the words on the list.

Electronic Handbook You might suggest that students use the Language Master 6000 to find synonyms for *pensive* and *loathsome.*

GUIDE FOR READING

The Tragedy of Romeo and Juliet, Act IV

Dramatic Irony

Dramatic irony is a device whereby a character's words or actions have one meaning for the character and a quite different meaning for the audience or reader. For example, in Act III, Scene iv, Lord Capulet decides to have Juliet wed Paris on Thursday. He does not know what you know—that Juliet is already married. Such dramatic irony is a powerful device. It adds suspense or tension. It involves us emotionally in the action. It can even make us want to step into the world of the play and give the characters a correct understanding of the situation they are in.

Focus

In the past, marriages were often arranged by parents. They still are in many societies today. With a group of classmates, list some of the points that might be presented in favor of an arranged marriage. Then list some of the objections to it. You might proceed by asking yourselves, "What problems might an arranged marriage eliminate (or create)? What benefits might it bring (or prevent)?" As you read the play, consider how your responses to these questions might apply to the situation of Romeo and Juliet.

Vocabulary

Knowing the following words will help you as you read Act IV of *Romeo and Juliet.*

pensive (pen' siv) *adj.*: Thinking deeply or seriously (p. 362)
vial (vī' əl) *n.*: A small bottle containing medicine or other liquids (p. 363)
enjoined (en joind') *v.*: Ordered (p. 365)

dismal (diz' məl) *adj.*: Causing gloom or misery (p. 366)
loathsome (lōth' səm) *adj.*: Disgusting (p. 367)
pilgrimage (pil' grəm ij) *n.*: Long journey (p. 370)

360   Drama

Objectives

1 To understand dramatic irony
2 To predict outcomes
3 To write an ending for a play

Support Material

Teaching Portfolio
Teacher Backup, p. 375
Grammar in Action Worksheet, *Using Apostrophes,* p. 378
Usage and Mechanics Worksheet, p. 380
Vocabulary Check, p. 381
Analyzing Literature Worksheet, *Understanding Dramatic Irony,* p. 382
Language Worksheet, *Appreciating Puns,* p. 383

Selection Test, p. 384

Library of Video Classics
Romeo and Juliet; Shakespeare in Rehearsal: Romeo and Juliet; Shakespeare in Conversation

Literature Videodisc
Shakespeare in Rehearsal: Romeo and Juliet; Shakespeare in Conversation

Prentice Hall Literature Writing Studio

Act IV

Scene i. FRIAR LAWRENCE'S *cell.*

[*Enter* FRIAR LAWRENCE *and* COUNTY PARIS.]

FRIAR. On Thursday, sir? The time is very short.

PARIS. My father[1] Capulet will have it so,
And I am nothing slow to slack his haste.[2]

FRIAR. You say you do not know the lady's mind.
5   Uneven is the course;[3] I like it not.

PARIS. Immoderately she weeps for Tybalt's death,
And therefore have I little talked of love;
For Venus smiles not in a house of tears.
Now, sir, her father counts it dangerous
10   That she do give her sorrow so much sway,
And in his wisdom hastes our marriage
To stop the inundation[4] of her tears,
Which, too much minded[5] by herself alone,
May be put from her by society.
15   Now do you know the reason of this haste.

FRIAR. [*Aside*] I would I knew not why it should be
    slowed.—
Look, sir, here comes the lady toward my cell.

[*Enter* JULIET.]

PARIS. Happily met, my lady and my wife!

JULIET. That may be, sir, when I may be a wife.

20 **PARIS.** That "may be" must be, love, on Thursday next.

JULIET. What must be shall be.

FRIAR.   That's a certain text.[6]

PARIS. Come you to make confession to this father?

JULIET. To answer that, I should confess to you.

PARIS. Do not deny to him that you love me.

25 **JULIET.** I will confess to you that I love him.

PARIS. So will ye, I am sure, that you love me.

JULIET. If I do so, it will be of more price,[7]
Being spoke behind your back, than to your face.

PARIS. Poor soul, thy face is much abused with tears.

---

1. **father:** Future father-in-law.
2. **I . . . haste:** I won't slow him down by being slow myself.
3. **Uneven . . . course:** Irregular is the plan.

4. **inundation:** Flood.
5. **minded:** Thought about.

6. **That's . . . text:** That's a certain truth.

7. **price:** Value.

The Tragedy of Romeo and Juliet, Act IV, Scene i   361

Videocassette You might wish to show the scene between Friar Lawrence and Juliet (Act IV, Scene i) in the film adaptation of *Romeo and Juliet* in the **Library of Video Classics**. The segment will help students appreciate Juliet's emotional state as she faces her dilemma.

Thematic Focus In refusing to marry Paris and in agreeing to Friar Lawrence's plan, Juliet has made a choice that will lead to a very serious consequence. Ask students whether Juliet could have made better choices. What choices would they have made in her place? What would have been the consequences?

4 Reading Strategy Have students predict what Juliet might do if there is no way to postpone the wedding.

5 Discussion How do Juliet's words echo an earlier speech by Romeo?

30 **JULIET.** The tears have got small victory by that,
For it was bad enough before their spite.[8]

PARIS. Thou wrong'st it more than tears with that report.

JULIET. That is no slander, sir, which is a truth;
And what I spake, I spake it to my face.

35 **PARIS.** Thy face is mine, and thou hast sland'red it.

JULIET. It may be so, for it is not mine own.
Are you at leisure, holy father, now,
Or shall I come to you at evening mass?

FRIAR. My leisure serves me, pensive daughter, now.
40 My lord, we must entreat the time alone.[9]

PARIS. God shield[10] I should disturb devotion!
Juliet, on Thursday early will I rouse ye.
Till then, adieu, and keep this holy kiss. [*Exit.*]

JULIET. O, shut the door, and when thou hast done so,
45 Come weep with me—past hope, past care, past help!

FRIAR. O Juliet, I already know thy grief;
It strains me past the compass of my wits.[11]
I hear thou must, and nothing may prorogue[12] it,
On Thursday next be married to this County.

50 **JULIET.** Tell me not, friar, that thou hearest of this,
Unless thou tell me how I may prevent it.
If in thy wisdom thou canst give no help,
Do thou but call my resolution wise
And with this knife I'll help it presently.[13]
55 God joined my heart and Romeo's, thou our hands;
And ere this hand, by thee to Romeo's sealed,
Shall be the label to another deed,[14]
Or my true heart with treacherous revolt
Turn to another, this shall slay them both.
60 Therefore, out of thy long-experienced time,
Give me some present counsel; or, behold,
'Twixt my extremes and me[15] this bloody knife
Shall play the umpire, arbitrating[16] that
Which the commission of thy years and art
65 Could to no issue of true honor bring.[17]
Be not so long to speak. I long to die
If what thou speak'st speak not of remedy.

FRIAR. Hold, daughter. I do spy a kind of hope,
Which craves[18] as desperate an execution
70 As that is desperate which we would prevent.

8. before their spite: Before the harm that the tears did.

9. entreat . . . alone: Ask to have this time to ourselves.
10. shield: Forbid.

11. past . . . wits: Beyond the ability of my mind to find a remedy.
12. prorogue: Delay.

13. presently: At once.

14. Shall . . . deed: Shall give the seal of approval to another marriage contract.

15. 'Twixt . . . me: Between my misfortunes and me.
16. arbitrating: Deciding.
17. Which . . . bring: Which the authority that derives from your age and ability could not solve honorably.
18. craves: Requires.

362 Drama

Commentary: The Role of Friar Lawrence

Discuss with students Friar Lawrence's role in *Romeo and Juliet*. Point out that literary critics see Friar Lawrence in basically two opposing ways: In one view, the Friar is a surrogate father figure to Romeo who aids and counsels him—he is Romeo's confidant. In the other view, the Friar is a well-meaning but incompetent counselor who leads Romeo and Juliet to their deaths.

Critic Edward Dowden is one who regards Friar Lawrence as an interfering, middle-aged busybody. He states in the introduction of the Arden publication of *Romeo and Juliet* that "the amiable critic of life as seen from the cloister does not understand life or hate or love . . . [he is] an actor whose wisdom is of a kind which may easily lead himself and others astray."

Ask students with which view of Friar Lawrence they agree. Is he a middle-aged busybody who knows nothing about life or love, or does he give Romeo good advice? Or does chance and fate determine the deaths of the "star-crossed lovers"? Students should back up their statements with evidence from the play.

Also ask students if they think that Romeo and Juliet would have been better off had they not followed the advice of Friar Lawrence. What other options were open to Romeo and Juliet? Could their deaths have been avoided? How?

If, rather than to marry County Paris,
Thou hast the strength of will to slay thyself,
Then is it likely thou wilt undertake
A thing like death to chide away this shame,
75　That cop'st with death himself to scape from it;[19]
And, if thou darest, I'll give thee remedy.

JULIET. O, bid me leap, rather than marry Paris,
From off the battlements of any tower,
Or walk in thievish ways,[20] or bid me lurk
80　Where serpents are; chain me with roaring bears,
Or hide me nightly in a charnel house,[21]
O'ercovered quite with dead men's rattling bones,
With reeky[22] shanks and yellow chapless[23] skulls;
Or bid me go into a new-made grave
85　And hide me with a dead man in his shroud—
Things that, to hear them told, have made me
　　tremble—
And I will do it without fear or doubt,
To live an unstained wife to my sweet love.

FRIAR. Hold, then. Go home, be merry, give consent
90　To marry Paris. Wednesday is tomorrow.
Tomorrow night look that thou lie alone;
Let not the nurse lie with thee in thy chamber.
Take thou this vial, being then in bed,
And this distilling liquor drink thou off;
95　When presently through all thy veins shall run
A cold and drowsy humor;[24] for no pulse
Shall keep his native[25] progress, but surcease;[26]
No warmth, no breath, shall testify thou livest;
The roses in thy lips and cheeks shall fade
100　To wanny ashes,[27] thy eyes' windows[28] fall
Like death when he shuts up the day of life;
Each part, deprived of supple government,[29]
Shall, stiff and stark and cold, appear like death;
And in this borrowed likeness of shrunk death
105　Thou shalt continue two-and-forty hours,
And then awake as from a pleasant sleep.
Now, when the bridegroom in the morning comes
To rouse thee from thy bed, there art thou dead.
Then, as the manner of our country is,
110　In thy best robes uncovered on the bier[30]
Thou shalt be borne to that same ancient vault
Where all the kindred of the Capulets lie.
In the meantime, against[31] thou shalt awake,

19. That cop'st . . . it: That bargains with death itself to escape from it.

20. thievish ways: Roads where criminals lurk.

21. charnel house: Vault for bones removed from graves to be reused.
22. reeky: Foul-smelling.
23. chapless: Jawless.

24. humor: Fluid, liquid.
25. native: Natural.
26. surcease: Stop.

27. wanny ashes: To the color of pale ashes.
28. eyes' windows: Eyelids.
29. supple government: Ability for maintaining motion.

30. uncovered on the bier: Displayed on the funeral platform.

31. against: Before.

6 **Discussion** Why does Friar Lawrence suggest such a desperate solution?

7 **Critical Thinking and Reading** How does this speech reflect a change in Juliet?

8 **Discussion** Is Friar Lawrence's plan a good one? Why or why not?

The Tragedy of Romeo and Juliet, Act IV, Scene i　363

Student Activity. At some point in time we all need to confide in someone and seek advice and counsel. Imagine that Romeo or Juliet approaches you with his or her problem. What advice would you give? In a letter to either Romeo or Juliet, express how you believe he or she should handle the situation.

115 Shall Romeo by my letters know our drift;[32]
And hither shall he come; and he and I
Will watch thy waking, and that very night
Shall Romeo bear thee hence to Mantua.
And this shall free thee from this present shame,
If no inconstant toy[33] nor womanish fear
120 Abate thy valor[34] in the acting it.

JULIET. Give me, give me! O, tell not me of fear!

FRIAR. Hold! Get you gone, be strong and prosperous
In this resolve. I'll send a friar with speed
To Mantua, with my letters to thy lord.

JULIET. Love give me strength, and strength shall help
125   afford.
Farewell, dear father.   [*Exit with* FRIAR.]

Scene ii. *Hall in* CAPULET's *house.*

[*Enter* FATHER CAPULET, MOTHER, NURSE, *and* SERVINGMEN, *two or three.*]

CAPULET. So many guests invite as here are writ.
              [*Exit a* SERVINGMAN.]
9   Sirrah, go hire me twenty cunning[1] cooks.

SERVINGMAN. You shall have none ill, sir; for I'll try[2] if
they can lick their fingers.

5 **CAPULET.** How canst thou try them so?

SERVINGMAN. Marry, sir, 'tis an ill cook that cannot lick
his own fingers.[3] Therefore he that cannot lick his
fingers goes not with me.

CAPULET. Go, begone.   [*Exit* SERVINGMAN.]
10 We shall be much unfurnished[4] for this time.
What, is my daughter gone to Friar Lawrence?

NURSE. Ay, forsooth.[5]

CAPULET. Well, he may chance to do some good on her.
A peevish self-willed harlotry it is.[6]

[*Enter* JULIET.]

15 **NURSE.** See where she comes from shrift with merry look.

CAPULET. How now, my headstrong? Where have you been
gadding?

32. **drift:** Purpose, plan.

33. **inconstant toy:** Passing whim.
34. **Abate thy valor:** Lessen your courage.

1. **cunning:** Skillful.
2. **try:** Test.

3. **'tis . . . fingers:** It's a bad cook that won't taste his own cooking.

4. **unfurnished:** Unprepared.

5. **forsooth:** In truth.

6. **A peevish . . . harlotry:** It is the ill-tempered, selfish behavior of a woman without good breeding.

364   *Drama*

JULIET. Where I have learnt me to repent the sin
Of disobedient opposition
20   To you and your behests,[7] and am enjoined
By holy Lawrence to fall prostrate[8] here
To beg your pardon. Pardon, I beseech you!
Henceforward I am ever ruled by you.

CAPULET. Send for the County. Go tell him of this.
25   I'll have this knot knit up tomorrow morning.

JULIET. I met the youthful lord at Lawrence' cell
And gave him what becomèd[9] love I might,
Not stepping o'er the bounds of modesty.

CAPULET. Why, I am glad on't. This is well. Stand up.
30   This is as't should be. Let me see the County.
Ay, marry, go, I say, and fetch him hither.
Now, afore God, this reverend holy friar,
All our whole city is much bound[10] to him.

JULIET. Nurse, will you go with me into my closet[11]
35   To help me sort such needful ornaments[12]
As you think fit to furnish me tomorrow?

LADY CAPULET. No, not till Thursday. There is time
enough.

CAPULET. Go, nurse, go with her. We'll to church
tomorrow.   [*Exit* JULIET *and* NURSE.]

LADY CAPULET. We shall be short in our provision.[13]
'Tis now near night.

40 **CAPULET.**   Tush, I will stir about,
And all things shall be well, I warrant thee, wife.
Go thou to Juliet, help to deck up her.[14]
I'll not to bed tonight; let me alone.
I'll play the housewife for this once. What, ho![15]
45   They are all forth; well, I will walk myself
To County Paris, to prepare up him
Against tomorrow. My heart is wondrous light,
Since this same wayward girl is so reclaimed.
                    [*Exit with* MOTHER.]

Scene iii. JULIET'S *chamber.*

[*Enter* JULIET *and* NURSE.]

JULIET. Ay, those attires are best; but, gentle nurse,
I pray thee leave me to myself tonight;

The Tragedy of Romeo and Juliet, Act IV, Scene iii   365

7. behests: Requests.
8. fall prostrate: Lie face down in humble submission.

9. becomèd: Suitable, proper.

10. bound: Indebted.

11. closet: Private room.
12. ornaments: Clothes.

13. short . . . provision: Lacking time for preparation.

14. deck her up: Dress her; get her ready.

15. What, ho!: Capulet is calling for his servants.

10 Literary Focus How is Capulet's bustle and activity an example of dramatic irony?

For I have need of many orisons[1]
To move the heavens to smile upon my state,[2]
5   Which, well thou knowest, is cross[3] and full of sin.

[*Enter* MOTHER.]

LADY CAPULET. What are you busy, ho? Need you my help?

JULIET. No, madam; we have culled[4] such necessaries
As are behoveful[5] for our state tomorrow.
So please you, let me now be left alone,
10   And let the nurse this night sit up with you;
For I am sure you have your hands full all
In this so sudden business.

LADY CAPULET.   Good night.
Get thee to bed, and rest; for thou hast need.
[*Exit* MOTHER *and* NURSE.]

JULIET. Farewell! God knows when we shall meet again.
15   I have a faint cold fear thrills through my veins
That almost freezes up the heat of life.
I'll call them back again to comfort me.
Nurse!—What should she do here?
My dismal scene I needs must act alone.
20   Come, vial.
What if this mixture do not work at all?
Shall I be married then tomorrow morning?
No, no! This shall forbid it. Lie thou there.
[*Lays down a dagger.*]
What if it be a poison which the friar
25   Subtly hath minist'red[6] to have me dead,
Lest in this marriage he should be dishonored
Because he married me before to Romeo?
I fear it is; and yet methinks it should not,
For he hath still been tried[7] a holy man.
30   How if, when I am laid into the tomb,
I wake before the time that Romeo
Come to redeem me? There's a fearful point!
Shall I not then be stifled in the vault,
To whose foul mouth no healthsome air breathes in,
35   And there die strangled ere my Romeo comes?
Or, if I live, is it not very like
The horrible conceit[8] of death and night,
Together with the terror of the place—
As in a vault, an ancient receptacle
40   Where for this many hundred years the bones

1. **orisons:** Prayers.
2. **state:** Condition.
3. **cross:** Selfish, disobedient.

4. **culled:** Chosen.
5. **behoveful:** Desirable,
appropriate.

6. **minist'red:** Given me.

7. **tried:** Proved.

8. **conceit:** Idea, thought.

Of all my buried ancestors are packed;
Where bloody Tybalt, yet but green in earth,[9]
Lies fest'ring in his shroud; where, as they say,
At some hours in the night spirits resort—
45 Alack, alack, is it not like[10] that I,
So early waking—what with loathsome smells,
And shrieks like mandrakes[11] torn out of the earth,
That living mortals, hearing them, run mad—
O, if I wake, shall I not be distraught,[12]
50 Environèd[13] with all these hideous fears,
And madly play with my forefathers' joints,
And pluck the mangled Tybalt from his shroud,
And, in this rage, with some great kinsman's bone
As with a club dash out my desp'rate brains?
55 O, look! Methinks I see my cousin's ghost
Seeking out Romeo, that did spit his body
Upon a rapier's point. Stay, Tybalt, stay!
Romeo, Romeo, Romeo, I drink to thee.

[*She falls upon her bed within the curtains.*]

Scene iv. *Hall in* CAPULET'S *house.*

[*Enter* LADY OF THE HOUSE *and* NURSE.]

LADY CAPULET. Hold, take these keys and fetch more
spices, nurse.

9. green in earth: Newly entombed.

10. like: Likely.

11. mandrakes: Plants with forked roots that resemble human legs. The mandrake was believed to shriek when uprooted and cause the hearer to go mad.
12. distraught: Insane.
13. Environèd: Surrounded.

12 **Discussion** is Juliet's drinking of the potion foolhardy or courageous? Explain.

13 **Literary Focus** Point out to students that this scene is a powerful example of dramatic irony. The excitement of the household and the humor between Capulet and his wife contrast sharply with the desperation of the true situation.

Cooperative Learning Arrange the class in groups of four. Hand each group a sheet of paper. Ask students to take turns writing a response to this question: What will happen to Juliet as a result of taking the potion? When students have had enough time to think of responses, call on a member of each team to read the group's responses.

NURSE. They call for dates and quinces[1] in the pastry.[2]

[*Enter old* CAPULET.]

CAPULET. Come, stir, stir, stir! The second cock hath
crowed,

5   The curfew bell hath rung, 'tis three o'clock.
Look to the baked meats, good Angelica;[3]
Spare not for cost.

NURSE.   Go, you cotquean,[4] go,
Get you to bed! Faith, you'll be sick tomorrow
For this night's watching.[5]

10 **CAPULET.** No, not a whit. What, I have watched ere now
All night for lesser cause, and ne'er been sick.

LADY CAPULET. Ay, you have been a mouse hunt[6] in your
time;
But I will watch you from such watching now.

[*Exit* LADY *and* NURSE.]

CAPULET. A jealous hood,[7] a jealous hood!

[*Enter three or four* FELLOWS *with spits and logs and baskets.*]

Now, fellow,

15   What is there?

FIRST FELLOW. Things for the cook, sir; but I know not
what.

CAPULET. Make haste, make haste.   [*Exit first* FELLOW.]
Sirrah, fetch drier logs.
Call Peter; he will show thee where they are.

20 **SECOND FELLOW.** I have a head, sir, that will find out logs
And never trouble Peter for the matter.

CAPULET. Mass,[8] and well said; a merry whoreson, ha!
Thou shalt be loggerhead.[9] [*Exit second* FELLOW, *with
the others.*] Good faith, 'tis day.
The County will be here with music straight,
For so he said he would.   [*Play music.*]

25   I hear him near.
Nurse! Wife! What, ho! What, nurse, I say!

[*Enter* NURSE.]

Go waken Juliet; go and trim her up.
I'll go and chat with Paris. Hie, make haste,
Make haste! The bridegroom he is come already:

30   Make haste, I say.   [*Exit.*]

1. **quinces:** Golden, apple-shaped fruit.
2. **pastry:** Baking room.

3. **Angelica:** This is probably the Nurse's name.

4. **cotquean** (kät′ kwēn): Man who does housework.
5. **watching:** Staying awake.

6. **mouse hunt:** Woman chaser.

7. **jealous hood:** Jealousy.

8. **Mass:** By the Mass (an oath).
9. **loggerhead:** Blockhead.

Scene v. JULIET'S *chamber.*

NURSE. Mistress! What, mistress! Juliet! Fast,[1] I warrant
    her, she.
    Why, lamb! Why, lady! Fie, you slugabed.[2]
    Why, love, I say! Madam; Sweetheart! Why, bride!
    What, not a word? You take your pennyworths now;
5   Sleep for a week; for the next night, I warrant,
    The County Paris hath set up his rest
    That you shall rest but little. God forgive me!
    Marry, and amen. How sound is she asleep!
    I needs must wake her. Madam, madam, madam!
10   Ay, let the County take you in your bed;
    He'll fright you up, i' faith. Will it not be?
    I needs must wake her. Madam, madam, madam!
                      [Draws aside the curtains.]
    What, dressed, and in your clothes, and down again?[3]
    I must needs wake you. Lady! Lady! Lady!
15   Alas, alas! Help, help! My lady's dead!
    O weraday that ever I was born!
    Some *aqua vitae,* ho! My lord! My lady!

[Enter MOTHER.*]*

LADY CAPULET. What noise is here?

NURSE.   O lamentable day!

LADY CAPULET. What is the matter?

NURSE.   Look, look! O heavy day!

20 LADY CAPULET. O me, O me! My child, my only life!
    Revive, look up, or I will die with thee!
    Help, help! Call help.

[Enter FATHER.*]*

CAPULET. For shame, bring Juliet forth; her lord is come.

NURSE. She's dead, deceased; she's dead, alack the day!

LADY CAPULET. Alack the day, she's dead, she's dead, she's
25   dead!

CAPULET. Ha! Let me see her. Out alas! She's cold,
    Her blood is settled, and her joints are stiff;
    Life and these lips have long been separated.
    Death lies on her like an untimely frost
30   Upon the sweetest flower of all the field.

NURSE. O lamentable day!

---

1. Fast: Fast asleep.

2. slugabed: Sleepy head.

3. down again: Back in bed.

---

14 Critical Thinking and Reading
Contrast the ways in which Lady Capulet and her husband verify that Juliet is dead.

The Tragedy of Romeo and Juliet, Act IV, Scene v   369

16 **Critical Thinking and Reading** Have students compare and contrast these speeches of lament.

LADY CAPULET.   O woeful time!

CAPULET. Death, that hath ta'en her hence to make me wail,
Ties up my tongue and will not let me speak.

[*Enter* FRIAR LAWRENCE *and the* COUNTY PARIS, *with Musicians.*]

15   **FRIAR.** Come, is the bride ready to go to church?

35 **CAPULET.** Ready to go, but never to return.
O son, the night before thy wedding day
Hath Death lain with thy wife. There she lies,
Flower as she was, deflowerèd by him.
Death is my son-in-law, Death is my heir;
40   My daughter he hath wedded. I will die
And leave him all. Life, living, all is Death's.

PARIS. Have I thought, love, to see this morning's face,
And doth it give me such a sight as this?

LADY CAPULET. Accursed, unhappy, wretched, hateful day!
45   Most miserable hour that e'er time saw
In lasting labor of his pilgrimage!
But one, poor one, one poor and loving child,
But one thing to rejoice and solace[4] in,
And cruel Death hath catched it from my sight.

50 **NURSE.** O woe! O woeful, woeful, woeful day!
Most lamentable day, most woeful day
That ever ever I did yet behold!
O day, O day, O day! O hateful day!
Never was seen so black a day as this.
16 55   O woeful day! O woeful day!

PARIS. Beguiled,[5] divorcèd, wrongèd, spited, slain!
Most detestable Death, by thee beguiled,
By cruel, cruel thee quite overthrown.
O love! O life!—not life, but love in death!

60 **CAPULET.** Despised, distressèd, hated, martyred, killed!
Uncomfortable[6] time, why cam'st thou now
To murder, murder our solemnity?[7]
O child, O child! My soul, and not my child!
Dead art thou—alack, my child is dead,
65   And with my child my joys are burièd!

FRIAR. Peace, ho, for shame! Confusion's cure lives not
In these confusions.[8] Heaven and yourself

4. solace: Find comfort.

5. Beguiled: Cheated.

6. Uncomfortable: Painful, upsetting.
7. solemnity: Solemn rites.

8. Confusion's . . . confusions: The remedy for this calamity is not to be found in these outcries.

Grammar in Action

Apostrophes are used with nouns to show possession, or ownership. To form the possessive of most singular nouns, add an apostrophe and -*s*. To form the possessive of plural nouns ending in -*s* or -*es,* add an apostrophe.

Possessive, singular: *Martin's* garage, my best *friend's* car
Possessive, plural: *teachers'* grading scales, *boys'* teams

Apostrophes also show where a letter is left out in a contraction.

Contractions: can't (cannot), we'd (we would)

Shakespeare uses the apostrophe both to show ownership and to show where letters are left out. Because of the poetic form of *Romeo and Juliet,* he uses contractions often. Many of the contractions are uncommon in modern English. The following lines illustrate his use of apostrophes:

Death, that hath *ta'en* her hence to make me wail . . .
Life, living, all is *Death's*
Most miserable hour that *e'er* time saw . . .

Had part in this fair maid—now heaven hath all,
And all the better is it for the maid.
70 Your part in her you could not keep from death,
But heaven keeps his part in eternal life.
The most you sought was her promotion,
For 'twas your heaven she should be advanced;
And weep ye now, seeing she is advanced
75 Above the clouds, as high as heaven itself?
O, in this love, you love your child so ill
That you run mad, seeing that she is well.[9]
She's not well married that lives married long,
But she's best married that dies married young.
80 Dry up your tears and stick your rosemary[10]
On this fair corse, and, as the custom is,
And in her best array bear her to church;
For though fond nature[11] bids us all lament,
Yet nature's tears are reason's merriment.[12]

85 **CAPULET.** All things that we ordainèd festival[13]
Turn from their office to black funeral—
Our instruments to melancholy bells,
Our wedding cheer to a sad burial feast;
Our solemn hymns to sullen dirges[14] change;
90 Our bridal flowers serve for a buried corse;
And all things change them to the contrary.

FRIAR. Sir, go you in; and, madam, go with him;
And go, Sir Paris. Everyone prepare
To follow this fair corse unto her grave.
95 The heavens do low'r[15] upon you for some ill;
Move them no more by crossing their high will.

[*Exit, casting rosemary on her and shutting the curtains.
The* NURSE *and* MUSICIANS *remain.*]

FIRST MUSICIAN. Faith, we may put up our pipes and be
gone.

NURSE. Honest good fellows, ah, put up, put up!
For well you know this is a pitiful case.[16]   [*Exit.*]

100 **FIRST MUSICIAN.** Ay, by my troth, the case may be
amended.

[*Enter* PETER.]

PETER. Musicians, O, musicians, "Heart's ease," "Heart's
ease"! O, and you will have me live, play "Heart's ease."

The Tragedy of Romeo and Juliet, Act IV, Scene v 371

---

9. well: Blessed in heaven.

10. rosemary: An evergreen signifying love and remembrance.

11. fond nature: Mistake-prone human nature.
12. Yet . . . merriment: While human nature causes us to weep for Juliet, reason should cause us to be happy (since she is in heaven).
13. ordainèd festival: Planned to be part of a celebration.
14. dirges: Funeral hymns.

15. low'r: Frown.

16. case: Situation; instrument case.

---

17 **Discussion** What knowledge might help Friar Lawrence offer this consolation?

18 **Reading Strategy** Have students predict whether Friar Lawrence's plan will succeed.

Electronic Handbook You might want to have students review the use of apostrophes before completing the Grammar in Action activities. If students have access to the Language Master 6000, have them enter the access symbol ' or the access word *possessive* and press the GRAMMAR key to obtain information on the use of apostrophes.

For *'twas* your heaven she should be advanced. . . .
The heavens do *low'r* upon you for some ill. . . .
Musicians, O, musicians, *"Heart's* ease," *"Heart's* ease"!

Two instances above show possession: *Death's* and *Heart's.* The others are all contractions, which Shakespeare used to make his verse run smoothly.

Student Activity 1. Study each of the contractions in the illustration above. Decide which letter or letters each apostrophe represents.

Student Activity 2. Write a series of sentences in which you use both possessive nouns and contractions. Be sure to put apostrophes in the right places.

Discussion Why do you think Shakespeare ends this act with a comic scene?

Reader's Response To what lengths would you go for a loved one? Explain.

Thematic Response Juliet has made one truly important choice immediately preceding Act IV: to remain faithful to Romeo. Everything she does in this act is colored by that choice. Do you think the choice is a wise one? Why or why not? Would you have made that choice, and why? Compare the cost to Juliet with the cost to you.

FIRST MUSICIAN. Why "Heart's ease"?

PETER. O, musicians, because my heart itself plays "My
105 heart is full." O, play me some merry dump[17] to comfort
me.

FIRST MUSICIAN. Not a dump we! 'Tis no time to play now.

PETER. You will not then?

FIRST MUSICIAN. No.

PETER. I will then give it you soundly.

110 **FIRST MUSICIAN.** What will you give us?

PETER. No money, on my faith, but the gleek.[18] I will give
you[19] the minstrel.[20]

FIRST MUSICIAN. Then will I give you the serving-creature.

PETER. Then will I lay the serving-creature's dagger on
115 your pate. I will carry no crotchets.[21] I'll *re* you, I'll *fa*
you. Do you note me?

FIRST MUSICIAN. And you *re* us and *fa* us, you note us.

SECOND MUSICIAN. Pray you put up your dagger, and put
out your wit. Then have at you with my wit!

120 **PETER.** I will dry-beat you with an iron wit, and put up my
iron dagger. Answer me like men.

"When griping grief the heart doth wound,
And doleful dumps the mind oppress,
Then music with her silver sound"—

125 Why "silver sound"? Why "music with her silver
sound"? What say you, Simon Catling?

FIRST MUSICIAN. Marry, sir, because silver hath a sweet
sound.

PETER. Pretty! What say you, Hugh Rebeck?

130 **SECOND MUSICIAN.** I say "silver sound" because musicians
sound for silver.

PETER. Pretty too! What say you, James Soundpost?

THIRD MUSICIAN. Faith, I know not what to say.

PETER. O, I cry you mercy,[22] you are the singer. I will say
135 for you. It is "music with her silver sound" because musicians have no gold for sounding.

17. dump: Sad tune.

18. gleek: Scornful speech.
19. give you: Call you.
20. minstrel: A contemptuous term (as opposed to *musician*).

21. crotchets: Whims; quarter notes.

22. cry you mercy: Beg your pardon.

372 *Drama*

Closure and Extension

ANSWERS TO RESPONDING TO THE SELECTION
Your Response

1. Encourage students to consider the possibilities as well as the probabilities. Ask students what could unexpectedly happen to ruin Friar Lawrence's plan.

Recalling

2. Friar Lawrence will give her a potion to make her fall into a coma for forty-two hours. She will be placed in the tomb. Friar Lawrence will call Romeo and they will be in the tomb when she wakes. Romeo will then take her back to Mantua.
3. The potion may not work; it may kill her; she may wake up before Romeo comes.
4. Everyone is happy, busy, full of good humor, and ready to meet the bridegroom.

Interpreting

5. Suggested Response: Juliet has developed a more mature and serious outlook. She is no longer a little girl, but a woman in love and determined not to be married to someone other than Romeo.
6. Suggested Response: Friar Lawrence is well-meaning but unrealistic and perhaps in a way as rash as the young couple. He hopes to unite the families through the marriage of Romeo and Juliet, but he

"Then music with her silver sound
With speedy help doth lend redress."   [*Exit.*]

FIRST MUSICIAN. What a pestilent knave is this same!

140 **SECOND MUSICIAN.** Hang him, Jack! Come, we'll in here,
tarry for the mourners, and stay dinner.

[*Exit with others.*]

RESPONDING TO THE SELECTION

Your Response
1. Should Romeo and Juliet have followed Friar Lawrence's advice? What other actions could they have taken?

Recalling
2. Describe Friar Lawrence's plan for Juliet.
3. What three fears rise up in Juliet just before she drinks the potion?
4. Describe the atmosphere in Capulet's house in Scene iv.

Interpreting
5. How has Juliet's character developed since the start of the play?
6. Describe Friar Lawrence's character. Why do you think he concocts his plan rather than tell the Capulets of Romeo and Juliet's marriage?

Applying
7. Compare and contrast marriage in the society that Romeo and Juliet belonged to and marriage in contemporary society.

ANALYZING LITERATURE

Understanding Dramatic Irony

Dramatic irony is a device whereby an audience's understanding of a character's words or actions is quite different from the character's understanding. The audience's special knowledge enables it to view the characters with superior understanding.

1. How is Juliet's meeting with Paris in Friar Lawrence's cell an example of dramatic irony?

2. Review Scene iv, in which Capulet is preparing for Juliet's wedding to Paris. What makes this scene an example of dramatic irony?
3. Find at least one other example of dramatic irony in the first four acts.

CRITICAL THINKING AND READING

Predicting Outcomes

To predict a story's outcome you need to be alert to **foreshadowings**—the hints and preparations for later events. In *Romeo and Juliet,* foreshadowings appear from the very start. In the Prologue to Act I, for example, Romeo and Juliet are described as "star-crossed," their love as "death-marked."

1. What foreshadowings are present in Act IV?
2. Find two other examples of foreshadowing in the first four acts.

THINKING AND WRITING

Writing an Ending for the Play

If you were to write your own ending to *Romeo and Juliet,* what would it be? Write a narrative of the events that would occur in your version of Act V. First answer such questions as these: Will Romeo and Juliet live and be reunited? Or will one—or both—die? What events will lead up to and bring about the happy (or tragic) ending? What will be the settings of these events? When you revise the narrative, make sure that it develops naturally out of Acts I–IV.

Then ask some classmates if your ending is convincing.

The Tragedy of Romeo and Juliet, Act IV   373

Juliet has taken the drug and that the wedding will turn into a funeral.
3. Answers will differ. One possibility is the scene at the beginning of Act II, when Romeo goes to the orchard to be near Juliet and Mercutio teases him by talking about Rosaline.

ANSWERS TO CRITICAL THINKING AND READING

1. Answers will differ, but some possibilities are: Juliet's fears concerning Friar Lawrence's plan may foreshadow real difficulties; the lament over Juliet's supposed death may hint at her real death at the end of the play.
2. Answers will differ, but two possibilities from Act I are: Tybalt's promise that he will challenge Romeo, and the fears that Romeo and Juliet express when they learn each other's identities.

THINKING AND WRITING

Writing Transparency Students often find it helpful to see a model of their writing assignment. Before students write, you may wish to show them Model 1: *Narrative Essay* in the **Transparencies for Writing.**

Collaborative Assessment After your students complete the Thinking and Writing assignment, have them work collaboratively with a partner. Ask students to read their partner's ending of *Romeo and Juliet* and then to write an essay in which they compare their ending with that of their partner. Students should defend the plausibility of their own versions of the ending. Their defense should include an explanation of their views on the final reunification of the two lovers, the events that lead up to this ending, and the reasons why their ending is inevitable, given the circumstances so far.

Publishing Student Writing Have volunteers present their endings to the class.

---

does not foresee the difficulties. He might concoct his plan to have Juliet drink the potion because he is afraid of revealing the marriage and his part in it.

Applying
7. Answers will differ, but most students will realize that today marriages are no longer arranged and people tend to marry when they are older. As in the time of Romeo

and Juliet, however, we often celebrate marriages with religious rituals and feasts.

Challenge Romeo does not appear in this act. Have students plan a scene set in Mantua. This outline or plan should indicate how Romeo is spending his time and what he is thinking and feeling.

ANSWERS TO ANALYZING LITERATURE

1. Suggested Response: When Juliet goes to Friar Lawrence for help in avoiding a marriage with Paris, she finds him there arranging for the ceremony.
2. Suggested Response: The entire household is busy and in good humor, getting ready for a large and happy wedding. They do not know, as the audience does, that

Preparation

Literary Focus You may want to ask students to consider, as they read the final act, what distinguishes a tragedy from a story that is merely sad. For example, what are the differences between this tragedy and a newspaper story about a fire or an automobile crash?

Prereading Focus The purpose of making this list is to focus students' attention on the combination of plot elements that drive Shakespeare's tragedy to its inevitable conclusion. You might want to review some of the key points with the students before having them complete the activity.

Vocabulary Have your **less advanced** students study the words carefully. Then have them look up synonyms for each word in a thesaurus.

Electronic Handbook You might want students to use the Language Master 6000 to find synonyms and antonyms for *haughty*.

GUIDE FOR READING

The Tragedy of Romeo and Juliet, Act V

Tragedy and Theme

A **tragedy** is a drama in which the central character meets with disaster or great misfortune. In the great tragedies of the past, including Shakespeare's, the central character's downfall is usually the result of fate or a serious character flaw or a combination of the two. Other causes, however, may also be involved. Though flawed, the tragic hero or heroine is usually of noble stature and basically good. The downfall, therefore, always seems worse than what the character deserves. Yet a great tragedy is not depressing. It uplifts the audience by showing what greatness of spirit human beings are capable of.

A **theme** is the central idea or insight about life revealed in a work of literature. In a tragedy, the theme will concern the downfall of the hero or heroine—or both, as in *Romeo and Juliet*. It will be an idea or insight that explains why the central character suffers a downfall.

Focus

Time is a crucial factor among the forces that bring about the downfall of Romeo and Juliet. However, there are many other factors that shape their fate. Divide a paper into three columns as follows:

Character Traits	Chance	Other Causes and Circumstances

In the appropriate columns, briefly note the various factors that have conspired against Romeo and Juliet. As you read the final act, observe the consequences of the factors you have identified.

Vocabulary

Knowing the following words will help you as you read Act V of *Romeo and Juliet*.

remnants (rem′ nənts) *n.*: Remaining persons or things (p. 376)

penury (pen′ yə rē) *n.*: Extreme poverty (p. 376)

haughty (hôt′ ē) *adj.*: Arrogant (p. 380)

sepulcher (sep′ əl kər) *n.*: Tomb (p. 383)

ambiguities (am′ bə gyoo̅′ ə tēz) *n.*: Statements or events whose meanings are unclear (p. 386)

scourge (skʉrj) *n.*: Whip or other instrument for inflicting punishment (p. 388)

374   Drama

Objectives

1 To understand tragedy and theme
2 To interpret metaphorical language
3 To respond to literary criticism

Support Material

Teaching Portfolio
Teacher Backup, p. 387
Grammar in Action Worksheet, *Using Nouns of Direct Address,* p. 390
Usage and Mechanics Worksheet, p. 392
Vocabulary Check, p. 393
Critical Thinking and Reading Worksheet, *Interpreting Metaphorical Language,* p. 394
Language Worksheet, *Using the*

Context to Find the Meaning, p. 395
Selection Test, p. 396

Library of Video Classics
Romeo and Juliet; Shakespeare in Rehearsal: Romeo and Juliet; Shakespeare in Conversation

Literature Videodisc
Shakespeare in Rehearsal: Romeo and Juliet; Shakespeare in Conversation

Prentice Hall Literature Writing Studio

Act V

Scene i. *Mantua. A street.*

[*Enter* ROMEO.]

1

ROMEO. If I may trust the flattering truth of sleep,[1]
My dreams presage[2] some joyful news at hand.
My bosom's lord[3] sits lightly in his throne,
And all this day an unaccustomed spirit
5 Lifts me above the ground with cheerful thoughts.

2

I dreamt my lady came and found me dead
(Strange dream that gives a dead man leave to think!)
And breathed such life with kisses in my lips
That I revived and was an emperor.
10 Ah me! How sweet is love itself possessed,
When but love's shadows[4] are so rich in joy!

[*Enter* ROMEO'S MAN, BALTHASAR, *booted.*]

News from Verona! How now, Balthasar?
Dost thou not bring me letters from the friar?
How doth my lady? Is my father well?
15 How fares my Juliet? That I ask again,
For nothing can be ill if she be well.

MAN. Then she is well, and nothing can be ill.
Her body sleeps in Capels' monument,[5]
And her immortal part with angels lives.
20 I saw her laid low in her kindred's vault
And presently took post[6] to tell it you.
O, pardon me for bringing these ill news,
Since you did leave it for my office,[7] sir.

ROMEO. Is it e'en so? Then I defy you, stars!
25 Thou knowest my lodging. Get me ink and paper
And hire post horses. I will hence tonight.

MAN. I do beseech you, sir, have patience.
Your looks are pale and wild and do import
Some misadventure.[8]

ROMEO.   Tush, thou art deceived.
30 Leave me and do the thing I bid thee do.
Hast thou no letters to me from the friar?

MAN. No, my good lord.

3

ROMEO.   No matter. Get thee gone.
And hire those horses. I'll be with thee straight.

[*Exit* BALTHASAR.]

---

1. flattering . . . sleep: Pleasing illusions of dreams.
2. presage: Foretell.
3. bosom's lord: Heart.

4. shadows: Dreams; unreal images.

5. Capels' monument: The Capulets' burial vault.

6. presently took post: Immediately set out on horseback.
7. office: Duty.

8. import/Some misadventure: Suggest some misfortune.

The Tragedy of Romeo and Juliet, Act V, Scene i   375

4 **Discussion** What is Romeo about to do? How is this in keeping with his nature?

5 **Discussion** Have students explain why he picked this particular apothecary.

6 **Discussion** Why does the apothecary not wish to sell the poison? What argument does Romeo use to convince him?

Enrichment Point out to students that early in his career, Shakespeare developed his acting talents, working for perhaps more than one theater company at a time. His shift from acting to writing may have been because of the outbreak of the plague in 1592. The plague—which also lurks in Verona in *Romeo and Juliet*—almost entirely closed all of London's theaters and forced actors to find other employment. Some of London's theaters remained open for a few performances each week.

4

35 Well, Juliet, I will lie with thee tonight.
 Let's see for means. O mischief, thou art swift
 To enter in the thoughts of desperate men!
 I do remember an apothecary,[9]
 And hereabouts 'a dwells, which late I noted
 In tatt'red weeds, with overwhelming brows,
40 Culling of simples.[10] Meager were his looks,
 Sharp misery had worn him to the bones;
 And in his needy shop a tortoise hung,
 An alligator stuffed, and other skins
 Of ill-shaped fishes; and about his shelves
45 A beggarly account[11] of empty boxes,
 Green earthen pots, bladders, and musty seeds,
 Remnants of packthread, and old cakes of roses[12]
 Were thinly scattered, to make up a show.
 Noting this penury, to myself I said,
50 "And if a man did need a poison now
 Whose sale is present death in Mantua,
 Here lives a caitiff[13] wretch would sell it him."

5

 O, this same thought did but forerun my need,
 And this same needy man must sell it me.
55 As I remember, this should be the house.
 Being holiday, the beggar's shop is shut.
 What, ho! Apothecary!

[*Enter* APOTHECARY.]

APOTHECARY.   Who calls so loud?

ROMEO. Come hither, man. I see that thou art poor.
 Hold, there is forty ducats.[14] Let me have
60 A dram of poison, such soon-speeding gear[15]
 As will disperse itself through all the veins
 That the life-weary taker may fall dead,
 And that the trunk[16] may be discharged of breath
 As violently as hasty powder fired
65 Doth hurry from the fatal cannon's womb.

APOTHECARY. Such mortal drugs I have; but Mantua's law
 Is death to any he that utters[17] them.

ROMEO. Art thou so bare and full of wretchedness

6

70 And fearest to die? Famine is in thy cheeks,
 Need and oppression starveth in thy eyes,
 Contempt and beggary hangs upon thy back:
 The world is not thy friend, nor the world's law;
 The world affords no law to make thee rich;
 Then be not poor, but break it and take this.

9. apothecary: One who prepares and sells drugs and medicines.

10. In tatt'red . . . simples: In torn clothing, with overhanging eyebrows, sorting out herbs.

11. beggarly account: Small number.

12. cakes of roses: Pressed rose petals (used for perfume).

13. caitiff: Miserable.

14. ducats: Gold coins.

15. soon-speeding gear: Fast-working stuff.

16. trunk: Body.

17. utters: Sells.

Primary Source

Tell students that playing a part in one of Shakespeare's plays can present some problems for the actor. One problem for Sir Laurence Olivier (1907–1989)—a well-known stage and screen actor—was in delivering Shakespeare's lines in verse. Olivier wrote in his autobiography, *Laurence Olivier On Acting*, that it was always his intention to modernize Shakespeare's language —in other words, deemphasize the verse. Critics, however, attacked Olivier, claiming that he could not speak the verse.

Olivier did not buckle under the critics' reviews and stuck to his "modern" speech, always hoping, however, the critics would soon accept him.

In his autobiography, Olivier wrote the following about the production of *Romeo and Juliet* he did with Sir John Gielgud— also a well-known stage and screen actor.

It's very easy, looking back, to criticize, but in those days there was a way of doing things. That was how they were done, and that was what the public came to see. They wanted their verse spoken beautifully, and if that was not how you delivered it, you were considered an upstart, an outsider. . . .

75 **APOTHECARY.** My poverty but not my will consents.

ROMEO. I pay thy poverty and not thy will.

APOTHECARY. Put this in any liquid thing you will
 And drink it off, and if you had the strength
 Of twenty men, it would dispatch you straight.

80 **ROMEO.** There is thy gold—worse poison to men's souls,
 Doing more murder in this loathsome world,
 Than these poor compounds[18] that thou mayst not sell.
 I sell thee poison; thou hast sold me none.
 Farewell. Buy food and get thyself in flesh.
85 Come, cordial[19] and not poison, go with me
 To Juliet's grave; for there must I use thee.   [*Exit.*]

18. compounds:
Mixtures.

19. cordial: Health-giving
drink.

Scene ii. FRIAR LAWRENCE'S *cell.*

[*Enter* FRIAR JOHN *to* FRIAR LAWRENCE.]

JOHN. Holy Franciscan friar, brother, ho!

[*Enter* FRIAR LAWRENCE.]

LAWRENCE. This same should be the voice of Friar John.
 Welcome from Mantua. What says Romeo?
 Or, if his mind be writ, give me his letter.

JOHN. Going to find a barefoot brother out,
5 One of our order, to associate[1] me
 Here in this city visiting the sick,
 And finding him, the searchers[2] of the town,
 Suspecting that we both were in a house
 Where the infectious pestilence did reign,
10 Sealed up the doors, and would not let us forth,
 So that my speed to Mantua there was stayed.

1. associate: Accom-
pany.

2. searchers: Health officers who search for victims of the plague.

LAWRENCE. Who bare my letter, then, to Romeo?

JOHN. I could not send it—here it is again—
 Nor get a messenger to bring it thee,
15 So fearful were they of infection.

LAWRENCE. Unhappy fortune! By my brotherhood,
 The letter was not nice,[3] but full of charge,
 Of dear import;[4] and the neglecting it
 May do much danger. Friar John, go hence,
20 Get me an iron crow and bring it straight
 Unto my cell.

3. nice: Trivial.

**4. full of charge, Of
dear import:** Urgent and
important.

JOHN.   Brother, I'll go and bring it thee.   [*Exit.*]

The Tragedy of Romeo and Juliet, Act V, Scene ii   377

7 **Literary Focus** There are many unfortunate coincidences in this act that could change the end of the play. As students read, have them keep track of these mis-chances.

8 **Clarification** Bubonic plague was a feared disease. In the Mid-dle Ages, it had killed millions of people in Europe. By Shake-speare's time, people still had not realized that the plague was transmitted from rats to humans by fleas. In a misguided attempt to prevent the spread of the dis-ease, houses and whole towns were closed off or quarantined. The quarantine of humans, of course, did not hinder the move-ment of rats and fleas!

[John Gielgud's] voice, of course was musical enough to sell his performance to the people on the old grounds. He was giving the familiar tradition fresh life, whereas I was completely disregarding the old in favor of something new. . . . By the time we did Romeo, I was considered by the Establishment to be his opponent. Everybody was in his favor, while I might have been from another planet. I can still remember some of the awful headlines. You always do, don't you? The good ones dance through your head and are forgotten in a day; the bad ones become indelibly stamped forever. Here's one from the *Evening News:* "A beautiful Juliet but . . ." Another said, "Mr. Olivier can play many parts; Romeo is not one of them. His blank verse is the blankest I've ever heard."

I made a terrible flop as Romeo because they said I couldn't speak verse. . . .

Student Activity. In small groups, select a scene in Act V to perform for the class. Half of the groups should modernize the verse; the other half should read the lines in verse as written. Perform your scenes for your classmates. Then, as a class compare and contrast the performances. What difficulties did each way present? What are the pros and cons of each way?

9
25

LAWRENCE. Now must I to the monument alone.
Within this three hours will fair Juliet wake.
She will beshrew[5] me much that Romeo
Hath had no notice of these accidents;[6]
But I will write again to Mantua,
And keep her at my cell till Romeo come—
Poor living corse, closed in a dead man's tomb!   [*Exit.*]

5. **beshrew:** Blame.
6. **accidents:** Happenings.

10
Scene iii. *A churchyard; in it a monument belonging to the* CAPULETS.

11
[*Enter* PARIS *and his* PAGE *with flowers and sweet water.*]

PARIS. Give me thy torch, boy. Hence, and stand aloof.[1]
Yet put it out, for I would not be seen.
Under yond yew trees lay thee all along,[2]
Holding thy ear close to the hollow ground.
5 So shall no foot upon the churchyard tread
(Being loose, unfirm, with digging up of graves)
But thou shalt hear it. Whistle then to me,
As signal that thou hearest something approach.
Give me those flowers. Do as I bid thee, go.

1. **aloof:** Apart.
2. **lay . . . along:** Lie down flat.

10 PAGE. [*Aside*] I am almost afraid to stand alone
Here in the churchyard; yet I will adventure.[3]   [*Retires.*]

3. **adventure:** Chance it.

12

PARIS. Sweet flower, with flowers thy bridal bed I strew
(O woe! thy canopy is dust and stones)
Which with sweet[4] water nightly I will dew;
15 Or, wanting that, with tears distilled by moans.
The obsequies[5] that I for thee will keep
Nightly shall be to strew thy grave and weep.
                    [*Whistle* BOY.]
The boy gives warning something doth approach.
What cursèd foot wanders this way tonight
20 To cross[6] my obsequies and true love's rite?
What, with a torch? Muffle me, night, awhile.   [*Retires.*]

4. **sweet:** Perfumed.
5. **obsequies:** Memorial ceremonies.
6. **cross:** Interrupt.

[*Enter* ROMEO, *and* BALTHASAR *with a torch, a mattock, and a crow of iron.*]

ROMEO. Give me that mattock and the wrenching iron.
Hold, take this letter. Early in the morning
See thou deliver it to my lord and father.
25 Give me the light. Upon thy life I charge thee,
Whate'er thou hearest or seest, stand all aloof
And do not interrupt me in my course.
Why I descend into this bed of death

378 *Drama*

Is partly to behold my lady's face,
30 But chiefly to take thence from her dead finger
A precious ring—a ring that I must use
In dear employment.[7] Therefore hence, be gone.
But if thou, jealous,[8] dost return to pry
In what I farther shall intend to do,
35 By heaven, I will tear thee joint by joint
And strew this hungry churchyard with thy limbs.
The time and my intents are savage-wild,
More fierce and more inexorable[9] far
Than empty[10] tigers or the roaring sea.

40 **BALTHASAR.** I will be gone, sir, and not trouble ye.

ROMEO. So shalt thou show me friendship. Take thou
    that.
Live, and be prosperous; and farewell, good fellow.

BALTHASAR. [*Aside*] For all this same, I'll hide me
    hereabout.
His looks I fear, and his intents I doubt.   [*Retires.*]

45 **ROMEO.** Thou detestable maw,[11] thou womb of death,
Gorged with the dearest morsel of the earth,
Thus I enforce thy rotten jaws to open,
And in despite[12] I'll cram thee with more food.
        [ROMEO *opens the tomb.*]

7. dear employment:
Important business.
8. jealous: Curious.

9. inexorable: Uncontrollable.
10. empty: Hungry.

11. maw: Stomach.

12. despite: Scorn.

13 Critical Thinking and Reading
What do you think Balthasar fears?

14 Critical Thinking and Reading
This play contains many examples of metaphorical language. What rotten jaws is Romeo opening? What is the food he will cram in them?

Enrichment You might want to tell students that David Garrick and Spranger Barry, both eighteenth-century actors, simultaneously played Romeo in competing theaters in London. At each of twelve shows, each actor tried to outdo the other's performance. Critics coined the two actors the rivaling Romeos. "Such a contest had never been known before in the history of the stage, and merits of the rival Romeos were discussed and compared for many years afterwards," Margaret Barton wrote in *David Garrick,* her biography of the actor.

My kind propitious stars o'erpay me now
For all my sorrows past. Rise, rise, my Juliet,
And from this cave of death, this house of horror,
Quick let me snatch thee to thy Romeo's arms.
There breathe a vital spirit in thy lips,
And call thee back to life and love! (*Takes her hand.*)—
Author Margaret Barton wrote in *David Garrick,* her biography of the actor, this description of the changes he made in his production of *Romeo and Juliet:*

'No play ever received greater advantage from alteration than this tragedy,' wrote Francis Gentleman, a distinguished critic of the day, 'especially in the last act. Bringing Juliet to life before Romeo dies is undoubtedly a change of infinite merit. The whole dying scene does Mr. Garrick great credit.' And generation after generation of playgoers agreed with him. It was not until 1845 that Garrick's additions to the play were scrapped.

Student Activity. Form two debating teams: One team will argue that Shakespeare's plays can and should be "refashioned"; the other team will argue that the plays cannot and should not be altered for any reason. After you have prepared and organized your arguments, hold a debate.

15 **Discussion** Why is this statement ironical?

16 **Literary Focus** Romeo's weakness is his rash and impulsive nature, but he is not bent on murder. Have students recall how he tried to avoid a fight with Tybalt in Act III.

17 **Discussion** How has Romeo ironically fulfilled his promise to give the tomb "more food"?

15

PARIS. This is that banished haughty Montague
50   That murd'red my love's cousin—with which grief
    It is supposed the fair creature died—
    And here is come to do some villainous shame
    To the dead bodies. I will apprehend[13] him.
    Stop thy unhallowèd toil, vile Montague!
55   Can vengeance be pursued further than death?
    Condemnèd villain, I do apprehend thee.
    Obey, and go with me; for thou must die.

    13. apprehend: Seize, arrest.

ROMEO. I must indeed; and therefore came I hither.
    Good gentle youth, tempt not a desp'rate man.
60   Fly hence and leave me. Think upon these gone;
    Let them affright thee. I beseech thee, youth,
16   Put not another sin upon my head
    By urging me to fury. O, be gone!
    By heaven, I love thee better than myself,
65   For I come hither armed against myself.
    Stay not, be gone. Live, and hereafter say
    A madman's mercy bid thee run away.

PARIS. I do defy thy conjurations.[14]
    And apprehend thee for a felon[15] here.

    14. conjurations: Solemn appeals.
    15. felon: Criminal.

70 **ROMEO.** Wilt thou provoke me? Then have at thee, boy!

                                    [*They fight.*]

PAGE. O Lord, they fight! I will go call the watch.

                          [*Exit.* PARIS *falls.*]

PARIS. O, I am slain! If thou be merciful,
    Open the tomb, lay me with Juliet.   [*Dies.*]

ROMEO. In faith, I will. Let me peruse[16] this face.
75   Mercutio's kinsman, noble County Paris!
    What said my man when my betossèd[17] soul
    Did not attend[18] him as we rode? I think
    He told me Paris should have married Juliet.
    Said he not so, or did I dream it so?
80   Or am I mad, hearing him talk of Juliet,
    To think it was so? O, give me thy hand,
    One writ with me in sour misfortune's book!
17   I'll bury thee in a triumphant grave.
    A grave? O, no, a lanthorn,[19] slaught'red youth,
85   For here lies Juliet, and her beauty makes
    This vault a feasting presence[20] full of light.
    Death, lie thou there, by a dead man interred.

                         [*Lays him in the tomb.*]

    16. peruse: Look over.

    17. betossèd: Upset.
    18. attend: Give attention to.

    19. lanthorn: Windowed structure on top of a room to admit light; also, a lantern.
    20. feasting presence: Chamber fit for a celebration.

380   *Drama*

Grammar in Action

A noun of direct address is the name of the person being spoken to, or addressed. Daily conversation regularly includes nouns of direct address:

    "Fred, did you phone in our order?"
    "Come on, *Valda,* we'll catch the first bus."
    "So I ask you, *fellow classmates,* to vote for me tomorrow."
    "Is this, *Madam Chairman,* in keeping with our bylaws?"

Notice that the noun of direct address may be a proper name (*Fred, Valda*), a common noun (*classmates*), or a title (*Madam Chairman*). In each case, the noun of direct address is set apart from the rest of the sentence with commas.

Shakespeare uses the noun of direct address regularly. The following examples illustrate:

    Condemnèd villain, I do apprehend thee.
    Good gentle youth, tempt not a desp'rate man.

18 Discussion If Romeo had been thinking more calmly, what would he have realized from Juliet's appearance?

How oft when men are at the point of death
Have they been merry! Which their keepers²¹ call
90 A lightning before death. O, how may I
Call this a lightning? O my love, my wife!
Death, that hath sucked the honey of thy breath,
Hath had no power yet upon thy beauty.
Thou art not conquered. Beauty's ensign²² yet
95 Is crimson in thy lips and in thy cheeks,
And death's pale flag is not advancèd there.
Tybalt, liest thou there in thy bloody sheet?
O, what more favor can I do to thee
Than with that hand that cut thy youth in twain
100 To sunder²³ his that was thine enemy?
Forgive me, cousin!, Ah, dear Juliet,

21. keepers: Jailers.

22. ensign: Banner.

23. sunder: Cut off.

The Tragedy of Romeo and Juliet, Act V, Scene iii   *381*

Let them affright thee. I beseech thee, *youth.* . . .
Death, lie thou there, by a dead man interred.
Tybalt, liest thou there in thy bloody sheet?
Forgive me, *cousin!* Ah, *dear Juliet,* . . .

Shakespeare uses a variety of nouns of direct address. Each is set off with commas.

Student Activity 1. Suggest possible substitute nouns for each noun of address that Shakespeare uses in the quoted lines.

Student Activity 2. Write five sentences, each with a noun of address. Vary the kinds of nouns you use. Be sure to set each off with commas.

Electronic Handbook You might want students to review the use of the noun of direct address before completing the Grammar in Action activities. If students have access to the Language Master 6000, have them enter the access words *noun* or *capital* and press the GRAMMAR key to obtain information on the use of the noun of direct address.

19 Literary Focus How is Friar Lawrence's late arrival another example of chance contributing to this tragedy?

Why art thou yet so fair? Shall I believe
That unsubstantial Death is amorous,[24]
And that the lean abhorrèd monster keeps
105   Thee here in dark to be his paramour?
For fear of that I still will stay with thee
And never from this pallet[25] of dim night
Depart again. Here, here will I remain
With worms that are thy chambermaids. O, here
110   Will I set up my everlasting rest
And shake the yoke of inauspicious[26] stars
From this world-wearied flesh. Eyes, look your last!
Arms, take your last embrace! And, lips, O you
The doors of breath, seal with a righteous kiss
115   A dateless[27] bargain to engrossing[28] death!
Come, bitter conduct;[29] come, unsavory guide!
Thou desperate pilot,[30] now at once run on
The dashing rocks thy seasick weary bark!
Here's to my love! [*Drinks.*] O true apothecary!
120   Thy drugs are quick. Thus with a kiss I die.   [*Falls.*]

[*Enter* FRIAR LAWRENCE, *with lanthorn, crow, and spade.*]

19

    FRIAR. Saint Francis be my speed![31] How oft tonight
    Have my old feet stumbled[32] at graves! Who's there?

BALTHASAR. Here's one, a friend, and one that knows you
    well.

FRIAR. Bliss be upon you! Tell me, good my friend,
125   What torch is yond that vainly lends his light
To grubs[33] and eyeless skulls? As I discern,
It burneth in the Capels' monument.

BALTHASAR. It doth so, holy sir; and there's my master,
One that you love.

FRIAR.   Who is it?

BALTHASAR.   Romeo.

FRIAR. How long hath he been there?

130 **BALTHASAR.**   Full half an hour.

FRIAR. Go with me to the vault.

BALTHASAR.   I dare not, sir.
My master knows not but I am gone hence,
And fearfully did menace me with death
If I did stay to look on his intents.

24. **amorous:** Full of love.

25. **pallet:** Bed.

26. **inauspicious:** Promising misfortune.

27. **dateless:** Eternal.
28. **engrossing:** All-encompassing.
29. **conduct:** Guide (poison).
30. **pilot:** Captain (Romeo himself).

31. **speed:** Help.
32. **stumbled:** Stumbling was thought to be a bad omen.

33. **grubs:** Worms.

135 **FRIAR.** Stay then; I'll go alone. Fear comes upon me.
O, much I fear some ill unthrifty[34] thing.

BALTHASAR. As I did sleep under this yew tree here,
I dreamt my master and another fought,
And that my master slew him.

FRIAR.   Romeo!
140 Alack, alack, what blood is this which stains
The stony entrance of this sepulcher?
What mean these masterless[35] and gory swords
To lie discolored by this place of peace?
                         [*Enters the tomb.*]
Romeo! O, pale! Who else? What, Paris too?
145 And steeped in blood? Ah, what an unkind[36] hour
Is guilty of this lamentable chance!
The lady stirs.   [JULIET *rises.*]

JULIET. O comfortable[37] friar! Where is my lord?
I do remember well where I should be,
150 And there I am. Where is my Romeo?

FRIAR. I hear some noise. Lady, come from that nest
Of death, contagion, and unnatural sleep.
A greater power than we can contradict
Hath thwarted our intents. Come, come away.
155 Thy husband in thy bosom there lies dead;
And Paris too. Come, I'll dispose of thee
Among a sisterhood of holy nuns.
Stay not to question, for the watch is coming.
Come, go, good Juliet. I dare no longer stay.

160 **JULIET.** Go, get thee hence, for I will not away.   [*Exit* FRIAR.]
What's here? A cup, closed in my truelove's hand?
Poison, I see, hath been his timeless[38] end.
O churl![39] Drunk all, and left no friendly drop
To help me after? I will kiss thy lips.
165 Haply some poison yet doth hang on them
To make me die with a restorative.[40]   [*Kisses him.*]
Thy lips are warm!

CHIEF WATCHMAN. [*Within*] Lead, boy. Which way?

JULIET. Yea, noise? Then I'll be brief. O happy[41] dagger!
                  [*Snatches* ROMEO's *dagger.*]
This is thy sheath; there rust, and let me die.
                  [*She stabs herself and falls.*]

The Tragedy of Romeo and Juliet, Act V, Scene iii   383

34. unthrifty: Unlucky.

35. masterless: Discarded (without masters).

36. unkind: Unnatural.

37. comfortable: Comforting.

38. timeless: Untimely; too soon.
39. churl: Rude fellow.

40. restorative: Medicine.

41. happy: Convenient; opportune.

20 **Discussion** What is Friar Lawrence's final solution for Juliet?

21 **Critical Thinking and Reading** Why do you think that Friar Lawrence is so quick to leave at the appearance of the watch?

22 **Discussion** How does this passage echo lines 85–100?

[*Enter* PARIS' BOY *and* WATCH.]

170 **BOY.** This is the place. There, where the torch doth burn.

CHIEF WATCHMAN. The ground is bloody. Search about the
churchyard.
Go, some of you; whoe'er you find attach.[42]   **42: attach:** Arrest.
                  [*Exit some of the* WATCH.]
Pitiful sight! Here lies the County slain;
And Juliet bleeding, warm, and newly dead,
175 Who here hath lain this two days burièd.
Go, tell the Prince; run to the Capulets;
Raise up the Montagues; some others search.
                  [*Exit others of the* WATCH.]

384 Drama

Commentary: The Rose Theater

Tell students that although scholars and historians have been able to piece together a fairly accurate picture of Elizabethan theater, it was not until in June, 1989, when archaeologists discovered the actual Rose Theater—believed to be where Shakespeare first performed—that they could confirm and update their information and conjectures. Scholars, for example, had believed that 2,000 people could fit into the standing area of the Globe Theater. Based on the size of the Rose, however, they now think that their estimate is too high; it appears that the Rose could only accommodate a few hundred people.

What is confirmed is that the Rose and Globe theaters were within close proximity of each other. Because of this, the two theaters competed for their audiences. At the height of the competition, the Rose brought in a packed house every day with its production of *The Spanish Tragedy* by Thomas Kyd. As an attempt to cash in on the success of the Rose's monopoly of the most popular play of the age, Shakespeare wrote for the Globe a tragedy—which appears to have been lost—entitled *Hamlet, Revenge!*

Once the popularity of *The Spanish Tragedy* began to wane, audiences began noticing that the theater was decaying and

We see the ground whereon these woes do lie,
But the true ground[43] of all these piteous woes
180 We cannot without circumstance descry.[44]

43. **ground:** Cause.
44. **without circum-stance descry:** See clearly without details.

[*Enter some of the* WATCH, *with* ROMEO'S MAN, BALTHASAR.]

SECOND WATCHMAN. Here's Romeo's man. We found him in the churchyard.

CHIEF WATCHMAN. Hold him in safety till the Prince come hither.

[*Enter* FRIAR LAWRENCE *and another* WATCHMAN.]

THIRD WATCHMAN. Here is a friar that trembles, sighs, and
185   weeps.
We took this mattock and this spade from him
As he was coming from this churchyard's side.

CHIEF WATCHMAN. A great suspicion! Stay the friar too.

[*Enter the* PRINCE *and Attendants.*]

PRINCE. What misadventure is so early up,
That calls our person from our morning rest?

[*Enter* CAPULET *and his* WIFE *with others.*]

190 **CAPULET.** What should it be, that is so shrieked abroad?

LADY CAPULET. O, the people in the street cry "Romeo,"
Some "Juliet," and some "Paris"; and all run
With open outcry toward our monument.

PRINCE. What fear is this which startles in your ears?

CHIEF WATCHMAN. Sovereign, here lies the County Paris
195   slain;
And Romeo dead; and Juliet, dead before,
Warm and new killed.

PRINCE. Search, seek, and know how this foul murder
comes.

CHIEF WATCHMAN. Here is a friar, and slaughtered Romeo's
man,
200 With instruments upon them fit to open
These dead men's tombs.

CAPULET. O heavens! O wife, look how our daughter
bleeds!
This dagger hath mista'en, for, lo, his house[45]
Is empty on the back of Montague,
205 And it missheathèd in my daughter's bosom!

45. **house:** Sheath.

The Tragedy of Romeo and Juliet, Act V, Scene iii 385

24 **Master Teacher Note** Consider telling students that at this point everyone is brought on stage for the denouement (the outcome or final solution of a complex sequence of events). All the pieces come together and, for the first time, everyone knows the whole story. Have students think of instances, at the end of modern film and television mysteries, where similar scenes are enacted.

25 **Discussion** What does Capulet think has happened?

was too small to accommodate the number of people wanting to see its productions. The Globe, on the other hand, offered audiences the latest in theatrical architecture and a larger capacity.

In the end, the Globe won the competition, leaving the Rose in a state of neglect and decay. In 1613 the Globe burned down.

Student Activity. Research Elizabethan audiences and give an oral presentation of your findings. You might, for example, report on the occupations of those who attended the theater or report on the class status of those who went to the theater and where each class was expected to sit. Present your research to the class.

LADY CAPULET. O me, this sight of death is as a bell
    That warns my old age to a sepulcher.

[*Enter* MONTAGUE *and others.*]

PRINCE. Come, Montague; for thou art early up
    To see thy son and heir more early down.

210 **MONTAGUE.** Alas, my liege,[46] my wife is dead tonight!
    Grief of my son's exile hath stopped her breath.
    What further woe conspires against mine age?

PRINCE. Look, and thou shalt see.

MONTAGUE. O thou untaught! What manners is in this,
215   To press before thy father to a grave?

PRINCE. Seal up the mouth of outrage[47] for a while,
    Till we can clear these ambiguities
    And know their spring, their head, their true descent;
    And then will I be general of your woes[48]
220   And lead you even to death. Meantime forbear,
    And let mischance be slave to patience.[49]
    Bring forth the parties of suspicion.

FRIAR. I am the greatest, able to do least,
    Yet most suspected, as the time and place
225   Doth make against me, of this direful[50] murder;
    And here I stand, both to impeach and purge[51]
    Myself condemnèd and myself excused.

PRINCE. Then say at once what thou dost know in this.

FRIAR. I will be brief, for my short date of breath[52]
230   Is not so long as is a tedious tale.
    Romeo, there dead, was husband to that Juliet;
    And she, there dead, that's Romeo's faithful wife.
    I married them; and their stol'n marriage day
    Was Tybalt's doomsday, whose untimely death
235   Banished the new-made bridegroom from this city;
    For whom, and not for Tybalt, Juliet pined.
    You, to remove that siege of grief from her,
    Betrothed and would have married her perforce
    To County Paris. Then comes she to me
240   And with wild looks bid me devise some mean
    To rid her from this second marriage,
    Or in my cell there would she kill herself.
    Then gave I her (so tutored by my art)
    A sleeping potion; which so took effect
245   As I intended, for it wrought on her

26 Literary Focus How does this development suggest the idea that the tragedy involves the whole city rather than two unfortunate adolescents?

46. liege (lēj): Lord.

47. mouth of outrage: Violent cries.

48. general . . . woes: Leader in your sorrowing.

49. let . . . patience: Be patient in the face of misfortune.

50. direful: Terrible.
51. impeach and purge: Accuse and declare blameless.

52. date of breath: Term of life.

386 Drama

The form of death. Meantime I writ to Romeo
That he should hither come as[53] this dire night
To help to take her from her borrowed grave,
Being the time the potion's force should cease,
250   But he which bore my letter, Friar John,
Was stayed by accident, and yesternight
Returned my letter back. Then all alone
At the prefixèd hour of her waking
Came I to take her from her kindred's vault;
255   Meaning to keep her closely[54] at my cell
Till I conveniently could send to Romeo.
But when I came, some minute ere the time
Of her awakening, here untimely lay
The noble Paris and true Romeo dead.
260   She wakes; and I entreated her come forth
And bear this work of heaven with patience;
But then a noise did scare me from the tomb,
And she, too desperate, would not go with me,
But, as it seems, did violence on herself.
265   All this I know, and to the marriage
Her nurse is privy;[55] and if aught in this
Miscarried by my fault, let my old life
Be sacrificed some hour before his time
Unto the rigor[56] of severest law.

270   **PRINCE.** We still have known thee for a holy man.
Where's Romeo's man? What can he say to this?

BALTHASAR. I brought my master news of Juliet's death;
And then in post he came from Mantua
To this same place, to this same monument.
275   This letter he early bid me give his father,
And threat'ned me with death, going in the vault,
If I departed not and left him there.

PRINCE. Give me the letter. I will look on it.
Where is the County's page that raised the watch?
280   Sirrah, what made your master[57] in this place?

BOY. He came with flowers to strew his lady's grave;
And bid me stand aloof, and so I did.
Anon comes one with light to ope the tomb;
And by and by my master drew on him;
285   And then I ran away to call the watch.

PRINCE. This letter doth make good the friar's words,
Their course of love, the tidings of her death;
And here he writes that he did buy a poison

53. **as:** On.

54. **closely:** Hidden; secretly.

55. **privy:** Secretly informed about.

56. **rigor:** Strictness.

57. **made your master:** Was your master doing.

The Tragedy of Romeo and Juliet, Act V, Scene iii   387

28 **Discussion** Why does the Prince blame himself? How has he been punished?

29 **Discussion** How does the trage-dy resolve the feud?

30 **Discussion** If you were the Prince, whom would you pardon or punish? What types of punish-ment would you decree?

Reader's Response Do you be-lieve Romeo and Juliet's ending was due to fate—as the stars predicted? Explain.

Thematic Response Do you think that the journey through life of the young lovers would have been better if they had never met? Give reasons for your an-swer.

Of a poor pothecary and therewithal
290   Came to this vault to die and lie with Juliet.
Where be these enemies? Capulet, Montague,
See what a scourge is laid upon your hate,
That heaven finds means to kill your joys with love.
And I, for winking at[58] your discords too,
295   Have lost a brace[59] of kinsmen. All are punished.

CAPULET. O brother Montague, give me thy hand.
This is my daughter's jointure,[60] for no more
Can I demand.

MONTAGUE.   But I can give thee more:
For I will raise her statue in pure gold,
300   That whiles Verona by that name is known,
There shall no figure at such rate[61] be set
As that of true and faithful Juliet.

CAPULET. As rich shall Romeo's by his lady's lie—
Poor sacrifices of our enmity![62]

305 **PRINCE.** A glooming[63] peace this morning with it brings.
The sun for sorrow will not show his head.
Go hence, to have more talk of these sad things;
Some shall be pardoned, and some punishèd;
For never was a story of more woe
310   Than this of Juliet and her Romeo.   [*Exit all.*]

58. **winking at:** Closing my eyes to.
59. **brace:** Pair (Mercutio and Paris).
60. **jointure:** Wedding gift; marriage settlement.
61. **rate:** Value.
62. **enmity:** Hostility.
63. **glooming:** Cloudy, gloomy.

■ RESPONDING TO THE SELECTION

Your Response

1. Were you in any way surprised by the way in which this play ends? Why or why not?

Recalling

2. At the start of Scene i, why is Romeo happy and expecting joyful news?
3. Why does the Friar go to Juliet's tomb?
4. What causes Paris and Romeo to fight?
5. How do Romeo and Juliet die?
6. How does the relationship of the feuding fam-ilies change at the end of the play?

Interpreting

7. Hearing Balthasar's report of Juliet's death (Scene i), Romeo exclaims, "Then I defy you, stars!" What might he mean by this? How are his words consistent with what you know of his character?

8. Explain why the following words of Romeo over Juliet's body are ironic:

Death, that hath sucked the honey of
    thy breath,
Hath had no power yet upon thy beauty.
Thou art not conquered. Beauty's en-
    sign yet
Is crimson in thy lips and in thy cheeks,
And death's pale flag is not advanced
    there.

9. Tell why you think that either character or chance plays the greater role in bringing about the deaths of Romeo and Juliet.

Closure and Extension

ANSWERS TO RESPONDING TO THE SELECTION
Your Response

1. Encourage students to discuss the predictability of such chance events as Romeo's not receiving Friar Lawrence's message.

Recalling

2. Throughout the play, Romeo has believed in dreams. He says that his dreams have predicted some joyful news.
3. He wants to be there when she wakes up so he can take her to his cell until he can send for Romeo.
4. Paris believes that Juliet died be-cause she was heartbroken about Tybalt, who was killed by Romeo. He suspects that Romeo has come to vandalize the tomb.
5. Believing Juliet dead, Romeo takes poison. Juliet wakes up and sees the dead Romeo, so

Applying

10. In a good play, the ending develops from the preceding action. How would preceding events have to be changed so that *Romeo and Juliet* could have a happy ending?

ANALYZING LITERATURE

Understanding Tragedy and Theme

A **tragedy** is a drama in which the central character or characters suffer disaster or great misfortune. In many tragedies, the downfall results from fate, a serious character flaw, or a combination of the two. Other contributing causes may be present as well. The **theme** of a tragedy is the central idea or insight about life that explains why the downfall occurred.

1. What character traits of the lovers may have led to their destruction?
2. What events reveal the tragic influence of fate or chance?
3. What other causes or conditions are important to the way events turn out?
4. Using your answers to the preceding questions, write a one-sentence statement of the theme of *Romeo and Juliet*. You might put your sentence in a form like the following: "The theme of the play is that _____ leads to the destruction of _____."

CRITICAL THINKING AND READING

Interpreting Metaphorical Language

Metaphorical language involves a comparison of unlike things. For example, when Paris is standing over the apparently lifeless body of Juliet, he says, "Sweet flower, with flowers thy bridal bed I strew . . ." He is comparing Juliet to a flower and her tomb to a bridal bed. Such metaphorical language deepens meaning and expresses feelings and emotions in a way that ordinary, plain language often cannot.

To interpret metaphorical language, first clarify what the subject of the comparison is—what is the writer writing about? Then clarify what the subject is being compared to. Finally ask yourself, "What ideas, feelings, and emotions are suggested by the comparison?"

Interpret the following examples of metaphorical language from Act V.

1. "My bosom's lord sits lightly in his throne . . ." (Romeo, Scene i, line 3)
2. "There is thy gold—worse poison to men's souls . . ." (Romeo to the Apothecary, Scene i, line 80)
3. "Thou detestable maw, . . . /Gorged with the dearest morsel of the earth . . ." (Romeo opening Juliet's tomb, Scene iii, lines 45–46)

THINKING AND WRITING

Responding to Criticism

A well-known poet and critic, W. H. Auden, has said of *Romeo and Juliet* that it "is not simply a tragedy of two individuals, but the tragedy of a city. Everybody in the city is in one way or another involved in and responsible for what happens."

Write a brief essay in which you explain why you agree or disagree with this statement. First think about the many characters that appear in the play: the Prince, the Friar, Lords Capulet and Montague, their wives, relatives, and servants, and so on. Are all such characters "involved in and responsible for what happens"? Then decide in what sense the play can be thought the tragedy of a city, since the city does not lie slain at the end.

When you write your essay, deal directly with such issues as these to support your opinion of Auden's criticism. When you revise, check that you have included enough references to what is actually in the play to make your own views convincing.

---

she stabs herself with his dagger.
6. The fathers shake hands and end their feud. Each says he will erect a monument in memory of the other man's child.

Interpreting

7. Suggested Response: Romeo says he is challenging fate, that nothing can keep him from Juliet. They are the angry words of a rash and impulsive person.

8. Suggested Response: Romeo sees the evidence that Juliet is not really dead, but ironically he is too distracted to understand what he himself sees and says.
9. Answers will differ. Students should select episodes from the play to prove their point. There are many mischances that suggest the role of fate in the tragedy. However, there are also instances of rash and impulsive behavior, especially on Romeo's part.

Applying

10. Answers will differ. Students might respond that if the Friar's plan had not gone amiss, the ending could have been happy.

ANSWERS TO ANALYZING LITERATURE

1. Suggested Response: The lovers are impulsive, quick to act, stub-

---

born, and insistent on having their way.
2. Answers will differ. Some events might be: the chance meeting of Romeo and Juliet as he overhears her speaking from the balcony, or the circumstances that keep Friar John from delivering the letter.
3. Answers will differ. A key cause is: the feud between the two families.
4. Answers will differ. Students may respond that a combination of fate and character flaws leads to the destruction of the hero and heroine.

ANSWERS TO CRITICAL THINKING AND READING

1. Suggested Response: My heart feels light in my breast—I am happy.
2. Suggested Response: Gold is a more powerful corrupter of men's souls than poison is a destroyer of their bodies.
3. Suggested Response: The tomb is like a mouth or stomach into which Juliet has been placed. This metaphor suggests Romeo's feelings of disgust and horror.

THINKING AND WRITING

Writing Transparencies Students often find it helpful to see a model of their writing assignment. Before students write, you may wish to show them both Model 6: *Persuasive Essay* and Model 8: *Literary Analysis* in the Transparencies for Writing.

Alternative Assessment You may vary the Thinking and Writing assignment as follows: Have your students review their responses to the Thinking About the Selection and Analyzing Literature exercises. Then ask them to decide on a theme reflected by this tragedy and write a modern version of the story around that theme. Students may develop their contemporary story around an irrational conflict caused by racial, religious, ethnic, or other differences and organize the story in terms of the effect of that conflict on the lives of a man and woman in love.

Preparation

Motivation/Prior Knowledge If you have access to the video *West Side Story*, show students the dance scene in *West Side Story* and have them compare it to the masked ball in *Romeo and Juliet.*

Your students may be interested to know that Shakespeare's play is itself an adaptation of an adaptation! Shakespeare's main source was a long, narrative poem called *The Tragical History of Romeus and Juliet*, written by Arthur Brooke, in 1562. (See the Primary Source note on page 326 in this Annotated Teacher's Edition.) Brooke's poem was based on several Italian plays, written between 1540 and 1560. These plays were, in turn, adaptations of a popular legend. Have your students identify Shakespeare's counterparts of these characters from the Italian versions: Montecchi, Cappelletti, Friar Lorenzo and Guilietta.

Focus Explain to your students that a play like *Romeo and Juliet* can be successfully updated because it has a timeless theme and reveals truths about human nature that are relevant in any age. As the students create their updated versions, instruct them to focus on the theme of the play and the motivations of the characters.

Presentation

Prewriting As students consider possible scenes for adaptation, have them jot down notes on the characters involved in each scene and the motives for their actions. Identifying the influences of loyalty, fear, bitterness, rivalry, pride, and love will help your students translate the action of *Romeo and Juliet* into a contemporary situation.

You may want to allow time for students to research the situation that they choose. Suggest

---

> *"To change your language, you must change your life."*
>
> **Derek Walcott**

WRITING A NEW VERSION OF A SCENE

Imagine *Romeo and Juliet* set in contemporary times. How would the characters differ from those in the original play? How would society differ? Perhaps the most famous adaptation of *Romeo and Juliet* is the Broadway musical *West Side Story*. In it, Shakespeare's Italian Renaissance setting with its two feuding families becomes a poor New York City neighborhood during the 1950's where rival gangs clash.

Focus

Assignment: Update a scene from *Romeo and Juliet.*
Purpose: To demonstrate that the play can serve as a basis for a television drama set in the present.
Audience: A potential producer of the show.

Prewriting

1. Select a scene. Look back over the play and select a scene with plenty of action or emotional impact.

2. Brainstorm contemporary settings and situations. With a partner or small group, brainstorm possibilities. Could the scene be played out in some part of today's world where factions are in conflict? Jot down every possibility, no matter how far-fetched.

Student Model

Act III, Scene 1: Deaths of Mercutio and Tybalt.
Possible settings
1. A Muslim section in Bosnia during the Serbian siege.
2. A neighborhood in Belfast, Northern Ireland.
3. An American high school with rival gangs.

Possible situations
1. The Capulets and Montagues are rival militias in Bosnia.
2. Catholics and Protestants are battling.
3. Tensions are mounting between two gangs.

Romeo is
1. A Bosnian freedom fighter.
2. A militant Irish Protestant.
3. A member of one gang.

---

that, for the purposes of this assignment, fictional treatments, as well as factual accounts, may provide insights into setting and character.

Drafting It may help students, in visualizing the scene, to write a brief narrative account of the action, using their updated setting and characters. The account may include reflections on the thoughts and feelings of the characters.

Urge students to get the basic framework of the scene written quickly. The scene can later be enriched with revisions in diction and the addition of specific stage directions.

◆ **Software** If your students have access to computers, you may have them use the *Diction Level* activity in **Writer's Helper** to assist in updating their dialogue.

Revising and Editing When working with peer editors, have the writers watch their scenes performed by other students. This will help reveal areas where the dialogue may be flat or the scene may be static. Student writers may solicit suggestions from the actors about how to improve problem areas.

Drafting

1. Update Shakespeare's language. Turning Shakespeare's Elizabethan English into contemporary speech should be a really interesting challenge. Use the original play as a guide, but change the language to make it accessible to today's audiences. Make your characterizations as realistic as possible within your chosen setting and situation. What about your characters' names? They probably need to be changed to reflect the time and place of your new play.

Student Model

Shakespeare's language:
TYBALT. Romeo, the hate I bear thee can afford
No better term than this, thou art a villain.
Updated version:
CARLOS. Matthew! You turn my stomach. You're nothing but a vile maggot.

---

2. Add stage directions. Visualize what your characters are doing as they speak their lines. Add stage directions to your dialogue to convey a vivid picture of the action.

Student Model

CARLOS. *[shaking his fist and speaking through clenched teeth]* Matthew! You turn my stomach. You're nothing but a vile maggot. *[He turns his head and spits on the ground.]*

Revising and Editing

1. Bring your characters' personalities into focus. Think about the various motives that your characters have for speaking and acting as they do. Fine-tune your dialogue to reveal each character's distinct personality.

2. Consult with your peers. Read your scene to a small group of classmates. You might ask them questions like these to help you improve your draft:

- Is my language appropriate for a modern setting?
- Can any of the stage directions be beefed up to make the action more dramatic?
- Can you still recognize Shakespeare's original characters and situations in my updated version?

Reviewing Your Writing Process

1. Did working with peers help you to come up with good ideas for contemporary situations? Why or why not?

2. Did you find it easy or difficult to replace Shakespeare's Elizabethan language with the language of contemporary characters? Explain.

Closure and Extension

Guidelines for Evaluation You may wish to consider the following questions as you evaluate each student's updated scene:

1. Is the action in the new scene consistent with the action in Romeo and Juliet?
2. Do the personalities and motivations of the new characters reflect an understanding of the personalities and motives of the original characters?
3. Are the setting and situation well researched?
4. Is the diction of the characters in the scene appropriate for the setting?
5. Does the student make effective use of stage directions?
6. Is the written scene free of errors in spelling and mechanics?

Reviewing Your Writing Process The following Protocol will help students to further reflect on and internalize their own writing process:

1. What is the scene you have chosen to update? In what contemporary situation have you set the scene?
2. What character details from Shakespeare's play have you included?
3. What details from your research into the contemporary situation have you included?
4. How do you conclude your scene? What do your characters do that is consistent with their behavior in Shakespeare's play?
5. What have you learned from completing this assignment?

Student Portfolios You may wish to have students keep their adaptations in their writing Portfolios.

Publishing Encourage the students to take their final drafts home and share them with their families. Parents might relate situations from the social and political climate of their own youth, which could also be appropriate settings for the scene. Students may wish to share their parents' suggestions with the class.

Enrichment *West Side Story* demonstrates that music can help set the mood and tone of a scene. Have your students choose appropriate music for the setting and situation in their scenes and find places in the script to incorporate the music. Invite the class to comment on their emotional reactions to the various musical selections.

Preparation

Motivation/Prior Knowledge

You may wish to begin by role-playing the encounter between Prince Escalus and his advisor, with you taking the role of the prince, and student volunteers taking turns as the advisor. As the prince, interrupt the report at any point where opinions are expressed, and instruct your advisor to relate only the facts.

Allow time for other students to comment on sections of the advisor's oral report that are not clear.

Focus

Remind the students that Escalus is not familiar with the events leading up to the tragedy. In order for him to understand the report, the students will need to meticulously place the events in chronological order and clearly establish the cause and effect relationships.

Presentation

Prewriting

It may help students, in organizing the events, to create a two column page by drawing a ruled line down the center of the page or folding the paper in half. In the left column, students can list the main events chronologically, leaving several spaces above and below each entry. Where two events occur simultaneously, they can be recorded on the same line, with one in each column.

As students explore the cause and effect of each event, they will probably discover that they have overlooked some circumstances. They can insert these into the appropriate blank space without disturbing the sequence of events.

In reviewing their lists, students may find that they have included some facts that are not directly related to the cause and effect chain of events. Help students to identify and eliminate these irrelevant incidents.

> *"Facts are stubborn things, and whatever may be our wishes, our inclinations, or the dictates of our passions, they cannot alter the state of facts and evidence."*
> **John Adams**

YOUR WRITING PROCESS

WRITING A REPORT

Prince Escalus of Verona appears only three times in *Romeo and Juliet*—at the beginning and end to restore peace and after Tybalt's death to banish Romeo. By the end of the play, he is apparently not yet fully aware of the tangle of events that resulted in the deaths of the young lovers. Imagine that you are an advisor to Prince Escalus. He has asked you to brief him on the events leading up to the deaths of Romeo and Juliet. How would you unravel all the twists and turns that resulted in the tragedy?

Focus

Assignment: Write an official report of the events leading up to Romeo's and Juliet's deaths.
Purpose: To show how a linked chain of causes and effects resulted in tragedy.
Audience: Prince Escalus.

Prewriting

1. Summarize the plot. First, you will need to review the play. Lay out all the links in the chain—all the interrelated events from beginning to end—starting with the street fight in Act I. At this point, concentrate only on the sequence of events, listing events in the order in which they occurred.

2. Identify causes and effects. Once you have laid out the series of events, you can begin determining the causes and effects that link one event to the next. Try asking yourself questions. For example, you might ask, what is the effect of Romeo's trying to stop the duel between Mercutio and Tybalt? A possible answer is that Tybalt seizes the advantage and fatally stabs Mercutio.

Remember, an effect often becomes the cause of another event. By working backward and forward along the chain of events, you can place each link in its proper chronological place.

392   Drama

Drafting Offer students guidelines for achieving a respectful, dignified tone in their reports. Suggest that they avoid using contractions and colloquial expressions. The passive voice may also lend an air of formality to their account of the events.

◆ **Software** If your students are using computers, you may wish to have them use the *Transitions* and *Sweet or Stuffy?* activities in **Writer's Helper** for assistance in improving the clarity and style of their report.

Revising and Editing Call the students' attention to the chart of transitional words and phrases on page 343. Emphasize the importance of using them appropriately.

Remind students to check once more that their report is free of opinions, irrelevant facts, and informal language.

Drafting

1. Settle on an appropriate tone. You might begin your report with a brief overview of your findings. Since you are writing an official report at the request of the Prince, a respectful, dignified tone is in order.

Student Model

Your Highness, a thorough investigation into the deaths of Juliet Capulet and Romeo Montague has revealed that the two had been secretly married. That this marriage was kept secret resulted, in my estimation, in a series of intrigues and miscalculations ending in their untimely deaths. Certain parties, however, had knowledge of the marriage and may share responsibility for the tragedy.

---

2. Focus on the facts. It is likely that you will become involved in this tragedy as you recount it for the Prince. It's important, however, that you keep your emotional responses out of the report. Simply present the facts.

Revising and Editing

1. Use transitions to connect your thoughts. Use transitional words and phrases to clarify your ideas.

Student Model

Friar Lawrence secretly sent Friar John to Mantua with a letter revealing the scheme, but a quarantine prevented him from delivering the news to Romeo.
Consequently,
The young husband believed that Juliet was dead.

---

2. Consult with your peers. Read your report to a partner or editing group. You might ask them questions like these to help you improve your draft:

• Have I included all the important events? Are there any events I can omit?
• Is the report clear and straightforward? Would it make sense to someone unfamiliar with all the facts?
• Do I reveal the underlying causes leading up to the final tragedy?
• Is my tone appropriately formal without being stuffy?

Publishing If class time is too limited to allow a session for a "Grand Jury," post the reports and allow students to vote by ballot on the indictment of characters.

In addition to the reports, you may wish to display a copy of Prince Escalus' closing speech, possibly printed in calligraphy on parchment.

Writer's Hint

Following are some transitional words and phrases that might prove useful. Time relationships—*first, next, finally, before;* cause-and-effect relationships—*thus, therefore, because of.*

Options for Publishing

• Read your official report before the class. Ask for reactions.
• Present your report before a "Grand Jury" made up of students from another class. On the basis of your findings, would they bring charges against any of the characters in the play?

Reviewing Your Writing Process

1. Did working backward and forward along the chain of events in the play help you to see how effects can sometimes become causes? Explain.
2. In what specific ways was the peer editing process helpful to you?

Closure and Extension

Guidelines for Evaluation You may wish to consider the following questions as you evaluate each student's report:
1. Does the report demonstrate an accurate knowledge of the events leading up to the tragedy?
2. Is the report objective?
3. Is the report written in an appropriately formal style?
4. Is the report free of errors in spelling, grammar, and punctuation?

Reviewing Your Writing Process The following Protocol will help students reflect on and internalize their writing process.
1. What major events leading up to the deaths of Romeo and Juliet do you cover in your report to Prince Escalus?
2. What words and phrases do you use to help you connect the details and to show a cause and effect relationship between events?
3. What words and phrases from the play do you include to suggest the Renaissance setting of events?
4. What suggestions from your peer reviewer did you include to improve your report?
5. From writing this cause and effect report, what conclusion have you come to about who is responsible for the tragedy of Romeo and Juliet?

Student Portfolios You may wish to have students keep their reports in their writing portfolios.

Enrichment Have students bring in examples of biased reporting from newspapers and magazines. Hold a class meeting to discuss these examples.

Humanities Note

Fine art, *Office in a Small City,* 1953, by Edward Hopper. Edward Hopper (1882–1967) painted evocative urban scenes and rural landscapes in a simple, realistic style. Hopper studied painting in New York City with the important realist painter Robert Henri. Despite the influence of this teacher, Hopper developed his own unique style. His objective paintings are diffused with mood and colored by harsh light.

Edward Hopper would have insisted that the mood created by *Office in a Small City* was unintentional. He claimed that he painted buildings and rooms merely to study the effects of light, space, and color. However, this poignant, stark painting of a modern office looking out on the older architecture of a small city is more than that to the viewer, who must wonder about the life of the lone figure in the painting. The scene might also prompt a viewer to contemplate human isolation and the impersonality of the business world as well. Hopper's compelling paintings show American scenes with uncompromising truth and clarity.

OFFICE IN A SMALL CITY, 1953
Edward Hopper
The Metropolitan Museum of Art

NONFICTION

Nonfiction is concerned with real life, rather than with people and events drawn from the imagination. Autobiographies and biographies tell about the lives of people who once lived or who are now living. An autobiography is written by the person whose life is being related, whereas a biography is written by someone other than the subject. An essay is a type of musing upon a subject. The form gives a writer the opportunity to think aloud on paper and explore one or even all aspects of the topic.

Nonfiction is written for a variety of purposes. Its purpose may be to inform, to describe, to persuade, and even to entertain. It also comes in a variety of types, called forms of discourse. Narrative essays relate stories, whereas descriptive essays primarily describe and present sensory impressions. Expository essays set forth information, whereas persuasive essays influence people and may even change the course of their actions.

In this unit you will encounter each of these types of essays as well as autobiographies and biographies. In addition, you will take a special look at essays on subjects in the arts and sciences.

395

Reading Actively The strategies outlined here for reading actively help students monitor their own reading process. These strategies are based on research into the ways in which effective readers derive meaning from nonfiction.

Introduce these strategies to the students, pointing out that they are similar to those used in reading fiction. You might emphasize the importance of interacting with the text while reading. Remind students that the sample annotations are those of a student like themselves. Their own thoughts while interacting with the text may differ.

Encourage students to use these strategies when reading the other nonfiction selections in this unit. To give them further practice with these strategies, you might use the selection on page 416 of the Teaching Portfolio, "Talent," by Annie Dillard, which students can annotate themselves.

Teaching to Ability Levels Less advanced students may need help with the detailed reading most nonfiction requires. Prior to their reading, share with them the Summary for this selection (in the Teaching Portfolio, p. 413) to preview the material. **More advanced** students may enjoy reading more of Lawrence's complete biography.

READING ACTIVELY

Nonfiction

Nonfiction is a type of literature that gives information about real people, events, and ideas. Nonfiction may instruct you, entertain you, inform you, or satisfy your curiosity.

Reading nonfiction actively means interacting with and responding to the information the author presents. You do this by using the following strategies:

QUESTION What questions come to mind as you preview the selection? What additional questions arise as you read it? For example, before you read, you may wonder what the title means. As you read, you might wish to know what the author's purpose is, or why he or she includes certain information. Look for the answers to your questions as you continue to read.

PREDICT Predict what the author will say about the topic. How will the author support his or her points? Make new predictions as you go.

CONNECT Think of what you already know about the topic and make connections to what the author is saying. Take in new facts and ideas as you read and connect these to what you know. Doing so will help you to understand the information presented.

EVALUATE What do you think of the author's conclusions? What have you learned?

RESPOND Think about what the author has said. Allow yourself to respond personally. How do you feel about the topic? What will you do with this information?

Try to use these strategies as you read the selections in this unit. They will help you increase your enjoyment and understanding of nonfiction.

On pages 397–401 you can see an example of active reading by Brendan Lippman of Medfield High School in Medfield, Massachusetts. The notes in the side column include Brendan's thoughts and comments as he read "Jacob Lawrence: American Painter." Your own thoughts as you read may be different because you bring your own experiences to your reading.

396 Nonfiction

Objectives

1 To understand a biographical profile
2 To discover how to read an essay about art
3 To write a biographical profile
4 To express individual interests and abilities through an optional activity

Support Material

Teaching Portfolio
Teacher Backup, p. 413
Reading Actively, "Talent," by Annie Dillard, p. 416
Usage and Mechanics Worksheet, p. 418
Analyzing Literature Worksheet, *Understanding a Biographical Profile,* p. 419
Critical Thinking and Reading

Worksheet, *Reading an Essay About Art,* p. 420
Selection Test, p. 421
Art Transparency 13, *War Series: Casualty—The Secretary of War Regrets,* by Jacob Lawrence

Prentice Hall Literature Writing Studio

MODEL

from Jacob Lawrence: American Painter

Ellen Harkins Wheat

The work of Jacob Lawrence is social, in content and in consciousness. Lawrence's paintings consistently portray the lives and struggles of the people he knows best, black Americans. In a career spanning five decades, his art has maintained an unbroken coherence.[1] Lawrence has manifested a persistent concern with everyday reality and the dignity of the poor, and all human effort toward freedom and justice, and he deals with these themes while extolling[2] the value and diversity of human existence. Because of the universality of his themes as well as his accessible, colorful style, Lawrence's work has always interested a wide audience.

Jacob Lawrence received almost overnight acclaim when his *Migration of the Negro* series was shown at New York's prestigious Downtown Gallery in November 1941. With this exhibition, Lawrence became the first black artist to be represented by a New York gallery. He was only twenty-four years old. That same month, *Fortune* magazine reproduced twenty-six of the series' sixty panels in color in a lengthy article. Since these events, Lawrence's life story has been a record of achievements and accolades;[3] his career has been singularly free of disappointment and controversy. By the time he was thirty, he had become widely known as the foremost black artist in the country, and his paintings have been exhibited throughout the world—from the Soviet Union, to Nigeria, to Brazil. For over thirty years he has also distinguished himself as a teacher of drawing, painting, and design. He is currently Professor

---

1. maintained an unbroken coherence (kō hir′ əns): Displayed an unbroken consistency, or similarity.
2. extolling (eks tōl′ iŋ) v.: Praising highly.
3. accolades (ak′ ə lādz′) n.: Praise; recognition.

from *Jacob Lawrence: American Painter* 397

Question: *What types of paintings does Jacob Lawrence paint?*

Connect: *The title says "American Painter," so I figured that the subject of his paintings was American. Specifically, he paints about the hardships experienced by African Americans.*

Predict: *Perhaps he is able to paint about these themes— the dignity of the poor and the fight for freedom and justice—so well because of his own life experiences.*

Predict: *This national publicity probably started him well on his way to becoming a leading artist.*

Making Connections "Dreams," page 595, by Langston Hughes, another member of the Harlem Renaissance movement, deals with a similar kind of struggle for success in spite of the odds. Joan Didion's "Georgia O'Keeffe," page 481, discusses another famous painter who, like Lawrence, developed a style all her own.

ESL Teaching Strategy To heighten comprehension for ESL students, use the following strategy: On a photocopy of the selection, highlight in different colors the details that tell who, what, why, when, and where.

You may also wish to ask ESL students to share paintings from their own culture, telling what they can about the artist and why the work is particularly meaningful to them.

Presentation

Motivation/Prior Knowledge
Ask students to think about paintings they have seen, perhaps in classrooms, restaurants, homes, offices, libraries, or museums. Ask students to speculate about the artists' purpose. Why do they paint? Why do they paint what they do?

Purpose-Setting Question Why is artist Jacob Lawrence so widely acclaimed?

Thematic Focus While Jacob Lawrence is an inspiration to aspiring young artists, he himself was inspired and encouraged by many of the Harlem Renaissance artists. Who is someone you admire and look up to as a role model? How do you think having an inspirational voice to follow may influence you?

Master Teacher Note Use Fine Art Transparency 13, *War Series: Casualty—The Secretary of War Regrets*, to give students an additional example of Jacob Lawrence's work. Have students study the painting and identify the artistic features characteristic of Lawrence's style. Ask them to compare this painting with the two paintings that accompany the selection. What similarities and differences do they find?

Reading Strategy The opening paragraph introduces Lawrence's goals as an artist. Keep these goals in mind as you read the selection and study the paintings that accompany it. Ask yourself whether you think Lawrence's artwork achieves these goals.

Respond: *I would have thought that growing up in Harlem in the 1930's would have influenced his career negatively because of poverty. But, instead, it was as though he was in the right place at the right time.*

Connect: *The Depression must have been an especially hard time to earn a living as an artist because people couldn't afford nonessential things such as paintings.*

Respond: *Lawrence was lucky to have such supportive and talented friends. They must have helped to inspire him and motivate him to succeed.*

Emeritus[4] of Art, University of Washington, Seattle, where he is widely regarded with respect and affection.

Jacob Lawrence grew up in Harlem during the Depression,[5] an experience that figured significantly in his evolution as an artist. That epoch of social awareness and burgeoning[6] black consciousness, economic hard times, and government support of the arts nurtured this developing young painter. Harlem was a cultural nucleus of the nation in the 1920's and early 1930's. Lawrence felt the persistent influence of what was called the "Harlem Renaissance"[7] all around him, in the artistic concentration thriving in Harlem, in his teachers, and in the people he met and the pursuits they shared. Lawrence's mother, a single parent, tried to support her three children with domestic work but was often on welfare. While juggling odd jobs to help out, Lawrence committed himself to painting as a young teenager and has never wavered in his disciplined productivity.

During his formative years, Lawrence was fortunate in being encouraged by artists in his community. He has said, "I never saw an art gallery until I was eighteen years old," so his awareness of art came from teachers and from books, local exhibitions, and frequent trips to the Metropolitan Museum. He took his first art lessons at a Harlem Art Workshop in the early 1930's, from painter Charles Alston. At Alston's studio, he met many of the cultural figures of the era, including Claude McKay, Countee Cullen, Alain Locke, and Langston Hughes, as well as artists Aaron Douglas, Henry Bannarn, and Augusta Savage. Sculptor Augusta Savage was one of the many community artists who believed in him. It was at her studio as a young teenager he met one of her students, Gwendolyn Knight. Their friendship led to marriage, and their long relationship has been a vital factor in Lawrence's career.

Some of the artist's first major works were produced during the period that Lawrence was a member of the Works Progress

---

4. Professor Emeritus (ē mer′ i təs) *adj.*: Retired but keeping the title of professor.
5. Depression: The period of economic hard times that began in 1929 and lasted through most of the 1930's.
6. burgeoning (bur′ jən in) *v.*: Flourishing; expanding.
7. Harlem Renaissance: A cultural movement that emerged in Harlem during the 1920's. Artists, writers, and musicians in this movement expressed pride in black life and in their African heritage.

THE STUDIO, 1977
Jacob Lawrence
Seattle Art Museum

Humanities Note

Fine art, *The Studio,* 1977, by Jacob Lawrence. This is a self-portrait of the artist in his studio. The most striking features of this painting are the use of bright colors, applied in broad planes, the use of bold lines and crisp edges, and the reduction of organic and inorganic forms to abstract, geometric shapes. Even the human figure is represented by a series of triangles and ovals. These qualities, found in most of Lawrence's paintings, are what make his work so direct, immediate, and accessible.

You might use the following questions for discussion:
1. Lawrence is quoted as saying about his work, "I want the idea to strike right away." What idea strikes you as you look at this painting?
2. What artistic techniques described in the selection can you recognize in *The Studio*?

Administration (WPA) Federal Art Project—for example, the Frederick Douglass and Harriet Tubman series, created between 1938 and 1940. Lawrence considers "the Project" to have been a school for him in many ways: the interchange with many diverse artists, the opportunity to concentrate on work with all materials provided, and the dignity in having a good job in hard times.

When Lawrence began his career in the mid-1930's, his work assumed the character of what is broadly called Social Realism, the predominant style of that period in this country. His content was presented through the modes of historical narrative and genre, and always by means of representational imagery. Remarkably, Lawrence's work, having exhibited diverse manners and subtle influences of intervening styles, today

Connect: *I know what "social" means, and I know what "realism" means. "Social Realism" must be showing social conditions as they really are, without romanticizing what is going on.*

from *Jacob Lawrence: American Painter* 399

Primary Source

As a widely acclaimed artist, Jacob Lawrence is the subject of numerous books, reference works, exhibition catalogs, and articles and reviews. One of the most interesting bibliographical lists is that of the books he has illustrated. They include *Aesop's Fables,* Harlem Renaissance poet Langston Hughes's *One Way Ticket,* and Lawrence's own book, *Harriet and the Promised Land*.

Ellen Harkins Wheat's book *Jacob Lawrence: American Painter,* from which this selection came, is a principal source of information about the artist. Shortly after its publication in 1990, a reviewer wrote:

As this study points out, Lawrence's unique style of dramatic, dynamic figures and bold colors has remained consistent through the years, as has his recurrent theme of the black experience in America.

Fine art, *Harriet Tubman Series, No. 4,* by Jacob Lawrence. This painting is one of the works Lawrence produced during his membership in the Works Progress Administration. Given his interest in portraying the struggles of African Americans, it is not surprising that he would choose Harriet Tubman as a subject for a series. Tubman was a slave who escaped in 1849 and traveled north on the Underground Railroad. Over the years she risked her life to guide her family and over 300 others to freedom. This painting, the fourth in a series of thirty-one, shows the young Harriet Tubman leaping and tumbling with other slave children.

You might use the following questions for discussion:

1. In what ways do the figures in the painting embody the spirit of freedom?
2. What overall emotion is expressed in the painting?
3. The spiky, angular figures give the image of children at play a disturbing quality. What might Lawrence be suggesting about this seemingly innocent scene?

4 Discussion In what ways does Lawrence's work "[transcend] historical documentation"? What qualities of his work are responsible for this effect?

5 Enrichment Francisco Goya (1746–1828) was a leading Spanish painter who produced, among other works, a series of biting social satires. Like Lawrence, he used brilliant colors and was skilled in capturing dramatic moments. José Clemente Orozco (1883–1949) was a Mexican painter who was known for murals that use themes from Mexico's history. Orozco's style is similar to Lawrence's in that it emphasizes human figures portrayed with bold lines and dramatic angles. His paintings express his reaction to the sufferings of the common people. Käthe Kollwitz (1867–1945) was a German printmaker whose powerful, roughly cut works championed the cause of the poor.

HARRIET TUBMAN SERIES NO. 4
Jacob Lawrence
Hampton University Museum, Hampton, Virginia

remains unique and very much as it was when he began as a painter. It focuses on the human figure, presented in tableaux[8] of expressive forms. His subjects range from simple street scenes to emotional renderings of social inequities. Much of his art approaches but transcends historical documentation in its depiction of significant events and its poignant portrayal of lives. Lawrence's distinctive formal approach is dominated by an attempt to capture the feeling obtained from his subject. In his pictorial indictments of man's cruelty and injustice, Lawrence has frequently been compared to such artists as Francisco Goya, José Clemente Orozco, and Käthe Kollwitz. His discreet but often strong messages are readily apparent, obtained through distortion of shape, space, and color. His chosen ico-

8. tableaux (tab′ lōz) *n.*: Striking, dramatic scenes or pictures.

nography[9] always clearly supports his aim of personal emotive expression. Lawrence's painstakingly crafted works, characteristically executed in water-base media, are notable for their vivid pure color and compelling design and pattern. He said about his work in a 1945 interview:

> The human subject is the most important thing. My work is abstract in the sense of having been designed and composed, but it is not abstract in the sense of having no human content. . . . [I] want to communicate. I want the idea to strike right away.

While he has also produced drawings, prints, book illustrations, large murals, and even costume designs, Lawrence commonly makes small easel paintings. Although his work is meant to be viewed closely and experienced intimately, the impact of its form and content is often monumental.

The career of Jacob Lawrence is characterized by a continuing allegiance to his cultural heritage. In his work, Lawrence not only acknowledges an awareness of the influence of his environment, he celebrates it, by focusing on the history and hopes of his community members. Although his work always speaks of the black experience from an emotionally autobiographical position, his imagery has universal appeal. Lawrence is a humanist with a moral vision, whose deep involvement with the struggles of mankind reminds us of the perpetual validity of the human story.

---

9. iconography (ī′ kə näg′ rə fē) *n.*: The collection of symbols or images of a particular artist.

Respond: *Lawrence seems to have a great love of humanity, which is interesting, considering the fact that most of his work is about social injustice.*

Question: *How does Lawrence achieve intimacy and powerful impact at the same time? Maybe it has something to do with his style and what he calls "human content."*

Evaluate: *I agree that the images in Lawrence's paintings have universal appeal. Although his work focuses on the hardships experienced by African Americans, it also focuses on the hopes for a better future, sending a positive message to all people.*

Ellen Harkins Wheat (1941–   ) is an art historian who has taught for many years at the University of Washington in Seattle. While working toward her advanced degrees, she focused on the art of Jacob Lawrence, and she is considered a leading authority on Lawrence's work. Wheat has lectured throughout the United States on Lawrence's paintings, as well as on other aspects of African American art. Wheat teaches nonfiction writing at the University of Washington and is planning her third book, which will be on Native American art of the Pacific Northwest Coast.

from *Jacob Lawrence: American Painter*   401

ANSWERS TO RESPONDING TO THE SELECTION

Your Response

1. Since student responses will differ, discuss ways of looking at both the subject matter and the artist's technique.
2. Encourage students to think about what is important to them and what message they may want to convey about the subject in their artwork.

Recalling

3. Lawrence was influenced by the new black consciousness and Harlem Renaissance leaders as well as by government programs, such as the WPA.
4. Lawrence's main concerns are recording, partly in historical aspect, the experiences of African Americans.

Interpreting

5. Suggested Response: Lawrence's work is universal in that it focuses on the human figure and "extols the value and diversity of all human existence."
6. Suggested Response: His Harriet Tubman series tells a story from history in which a social injustice is corrected: slaves are led to freedom. His self-portrait shows how the artist interprets the social reality he sees, expressing it in bold shapes and vivid color.
7. Suggested Response: By focusing on human struggles, Lawrence's work reminds us of the dignity and the endurance of the human spirit.

Applying

8. Suggested Response: Students who argue that it is good may point out that Lawrence's consistency of vision has worked to drive his message home. Those who argue that it is not good may suggest that such consistency of vision suggests artistic stagnation.

ANSWERS TO ANALYZING LITERATURE

1. Suggested Response: This profile highlights the aspects of Lawrence's life that deal with his artis-

---

RESPONDING TO THE SELECTION

Your Response

1. What feelings do Jacob Lawrence's paintings create in you?
2. If you were an artist, what subject would you choose for your artwork? Why?

Recalling

3. What aspects of the Depression influenced Lawrence as a young painter?
4. In your own words, describe Lawrence's main concerns as a painter.

Interpreting

5. In what ways is Lawrence's work universal?
6. What elements in the paintings that accompany this selection show the social and historical content of Lawrence's work?
7. What does the author mean when she says that Lawrence is a "humanist"?

Applying

8. The author says that Lawrence's style remains very much today as it was when he began to paint. Is it good for an artist to have such a consistent vision throughout his or her career? Explain your answer.

ANALYZING LITERATURE

Understanding a Biographical Profile

In a **biography** a writer tells the life story of another person. The author may use the subject's writings, personal interviews, and other reference materials to present the subject to the reader. A full-length biography often explores the psychology of the subject, examining his or her formative experiences. A **biographical profile,** however, does not give as full a picture of the subject. In a biographical profile, the writer limits his or her focus by stressing only key moments in the subject's life or career.

1. What aspects of Jacob Lawrence's life does this biographical profile highlight?

---

2. What is missing from this selection that you might find in a full-length biography?

CRITICAL THINKING AND READING

Reading an Essay About Art

An essay about art is more than a reading experience. In order to clearly understand the ideas presented in this kind of essay, you need to become familiar with the art being described. When reading an essay about art, it is helpful to preview the material carefully. Look at the examples of art that accompany the essay. Read the captions, and then read the text. In the course of reading the essay, stop and reexamine each example of art as the writer discusses it. When you have finished reading, you can look again at the art with a new understanding.

1. How did your perceptions of Lawrence's art change as you previewed the essay, then read about his work?
2. Evaluate one of Wheat's comments about Lawrence's art after examining his work.

THINKING AND WRITING

Writing a Biographical Profile

Write a biographical profile about someone you admire. The person may be someone you know or a well-known public figure. Gather information on your subject. If possible, interview the subject. If you are writing about a public figure, look in *Who's Who* or a similar reference book for information. Include the subject's date of birth, education, and major accomplishments in your essay. Revise your first draft and share your essay with the class.

LEARNING OPTION

Cross-curricular Connection. Investigate Lawrence's art by consulting sources at the library or a local art museum. Share your findings with the class.

---

tic development and his career as an artist.
2. Suggested Response: Some students may suggest that the article omits details about specific paintings and exhibitions. Other students may point out that only sketchy information is included about his formative years.

ANSWERS TO CRITICAL THINKING AND READING

1. Suggested Response: Students may feel that Lawrence's work became more interesting and meaningful to them after they read about his artistic goals and his "moral vision."
2. Suggested Response: Wheat says that Lawrence's messages are "discreet but often strong" and come about through "distortion of shape, space, and color."

The paintings clearly show this kind of emotional strength and visual distortion.

THINKING AND WRITING

Software For students working at computers, suggest the **Writer's Helper** tool *Questioner* to help them generate intriguing content for their biographical profiles.

Biographies and Personal Accounts

MY WIFE, SACKVILLE RIVER,
NOVA SCOTIA, 1918
Arthur Lismer
Art Gallery of Ontario, Toronto

Humanities Note

Fine Art, *My Wife, Sackville River,* by Arthur Lismer. Arthur Lismer (1885–1969) emigrated to Canada from England. He became a part of the Group of Seven, Canadian nationalist artists who sought to glorify the rugged beauty of their country in a modern painting style. Lismer and these other artists changed the face of Canadian painting.

My Wife, Sackville River, was painted on one of the many sketching trips Lismer made into the Canadian wilderness. Painted in a decorative Fauve-like style, the painting serves as a partial account of the trip. Later in his career, Lismer became an innovative teacher of art to children. His innovative techniques are still in use today to open children's eyes and imaginations to beauty.

Writing Transparencies Before students write, you may want to have them use the Graphic Organizer *Flow Chart* in **Transparencies for Writing** to help organize their ideas.

Before students revise, you may want them to work in cooperative groups to complete the Paragraph Exercise *Transitions* in **Transparencies for Writing.**

The corrected exercise can then serve as a model for peer editor response.

Alternative Assessment *Collaborative Assessment* After students have completed the Thinking and Writing assignment, have them work in groups of four to assess their biographical profiles. Ask them to revise their work and bind their final copies in a class book. Students may

wish to illustrate their collection with pictures of their subjects.

Cross-curricular Activity Art, music, and history teachers may be willing to share with students additional information about activities and work associated with the Harlem Renaissance movement. Students who are interested should be encouraged to seek additional information in the library, perhaps sharing an oral

report of their findings with the class.

LEARNING OPTION

Students who are visual and kinesthetic learners will respond well to this activity. Their reports should help the rest of the class become better visual learners.

More About the Author Carl Sandburg's biography of Abraham Lincoln required thirty years of research. Ask students what might motivate an author to spend thirty years researching another person's life.

Literary Focus You might point out to students that Sandburg uses many anecdotes, or stories, to convey Lincoln's personality.

Prereading Focus During Abraham Lincoln's own time, he was a very controversial figure. Since his assassination, however, memories of him often have been glorified. The purpose of the brief writing exercise is to call students' attention to any prior knowledge and attitudes they have about Lincoln. Have students share and discuss the information on their lists. Ask them to recall where they learned certain facts. Have students identify and explain qualities they associate with Lincoln and speculate about whether they think Sandburg's biography will confirm or alter their ideas.

Vocabulary For the benefit of **less advanced** students, assign each of several students a vocabulary word. Ask each student to define the word for the class and to use the word in a sentence.

Electronic Handbook You might suggest that students use the Language Master 6000 to hear the pronunciation of any vocabulary words that are unfamiliar to them.

Carl Sandburg

(1878–1967) was born in Galesburg, Illinois, of Swedish immigrant parents. He won Pulitzer prizes both for his poetry and for his biography of Abraham Lincoln, from which this preface comes. His six-volume biography describes Lincoln's life from his early years in the West to his presidency during the Civil War. Sandburg believed that this war was our nation's most desperate crisis and Lincoln our greatest leader.

GUIDE FOR READING

from A Lincoln Preface

Biography

The word *biography* comes from two Greek words, *bios* (life) and *graphein* (to write). These Greek words are reflected in the meaning of **biography**: an account of a person's life written by someone else.

Anyone can be the subject of a biography, from a world leader to the person next door. Writers of biography, called **biographers,** carefully research the facts of their subjects' lives. However, biographers also present their own interpretation of these facts. They explain both the reasons for their subjects' actions and the meaning of their lives. In "A Lincoln Preface," for example, Sandburg weaves together insights and stories to present Lincoln's many-sided personality.

Focus

Anyone who has studied United States history knows some facts about Abraham Lincoln. Like other famous figures in history, he is the subject of many legends, as well. What do you remember about Lincoln? Make a list of all the facts you know about the man, as well as the qualities you associate with him. As you read, compare your impression of Lincoln with Sandburg's account.

Vocabulary

Knowing the following words will help you as you read "A Lincoln Preface."

despotic (des pät′ ik) *adj.*: Absolute; unlimited (p. 405)

chattel (chat′′l) *n.*: A movable item of personal property (p. 405)

cipher (sī′ fər) *adj.*: Code (usually a noun or verb) (p. 407)

slouching (slouch′ iŋ) *adj.* Drooping (usually a verb) (p. 407)

censure (sen′ shər) *n.*: Strong disapproval (p. 408)

gaunt (gônt) *adj.*: Thin and bony (p. 410)

droll (drōl) *adj.*: Comic and amusing in an odd way (p. 410)

raillery (rāl′ ər ē) *n.*: Good-natured teasing (p. 410)

Objectives

1 To understand the features of biography
2 To evaluate the subject of a biography
3 To write a biographical sketch
4 To express individual interests and abilities through optional activities

Support Material

Teaching Portfolio
Teacher Backup, p. 423
Grammar in Action Worksheet, *Recognizing Main Idea and Supporting Details*, p. 427
Usage and Mechanics Worksheet, p. 429
Vocabulary Check, p. 430
Analyzing Literature Worksheet, *Understanding Biography*, p. 431

Critical Thinking and Reading Worksheet, *Evaluating the Subject of a Biography*, p. 432
Selection Test, p. 433

Prentice Hall Literature Writing Studio

from **A Lincoln Preface**

Carl Sandburg

In the time of the April lilacs in the year 1865, a man in the City of Washington, D. C., trusted a guard to watch at a door, and the guard was careless, left the door, and the man was shot, lingered a night, passed away, was laid in a box, and carried north and west a thousand miles: bells sobbed; cities wore crepe[1]; people stood with hats off as the railroad burial car came past at midnight, dawn or noon.

During the four years of time before he gave up the ghost, this man was clothed with despotic power, commanding the most powerful armies till then assembled in modern warfare, enforcing drafts of soldiers, abolishing the right of habeas corpus[2], directing politically and spiritually the wild, massive forces loosed in civil war.

Four billion dollars' worth of property was taken from those who had been legal owners of it, confiscated, wiped out as by fire, at his instigation and executive direction; a class of chattel property recognized as lawful for two hundred years went to the scrap pile.

When the woman who wrote *Uncle Tom's Cabin*[3] came to see him in the White House, he greeted her, "So you're the little woman who wrote the book that made this great war," and as they seated themselves at a fireplace, "I do love an open fire: I always had one at home." As they were finishing their talk of the days of blood, he said, "I shan't last long after it's over."

An Illinois Congressman looked in on him as he had his face lathered for a shave in the White House, and remarked, "If anybody had told me that in a great crisis like this the people were going out to a little one-horse town and pick out a one-horse lawyer for president, I wouldn't have believed it." The answer was, "Neither would I. But it was a time when a man with a policy would have been fatal to the country. I never had a policy. I have simply tried to do what seemed best each day, as each day came."

"I don't intend precisely to throw the Constitution overboard, but I will stick it in a hole if I can," he told a Cabinet officer. The enemy was violating the Constitution to destroy the Union, he argued, and therefore, "I will violate the Constitution, if necessary, to save the Union." He instructed a messenger to the Secretary of the Treasury, "Tell him not to bother himself about the Constitution. Say that I have that sacred instrument here at the White House, and I am guarding it with great care."

When he was renominated, it was by the device of seating delegates from Tennessee,

---

1. crepe (krāp) n · Thin, black cloth worn to show mourning.
2. habeas corpus (hā′ bē əs kôr′ pəs): Right of an imprisoned person to have a court hearing.
3. woman . . . Cabin: Harriet Beecher Stowe (1811–1896), whose novel stirred up opinion against slavery.

Presentation

Motivation/Prior Knowledge Ask students what qualities a national leader must possess during a time of crisis. Then tell them that, by reading this selection, they can learn whether Abraham Lincoln displayed any of the qualities they have mentioned.

Master Teacher Note You might remind students that Abraham Lincoln was born in Kentucky on February 12, 1809. A Republican candidate, he was elected President of the United States in November 1860. The first battle of the Civil War was fought at Bull Run in July 1861. Lincoln was elected to a second term in November 1864. The Civil War officially ended on April 9, 1865, and on April 15, 1865, Lincoln was assassinated by John Wilkes Booth at Ford's Theater in Washington, D.C.

Making Connections Another selection that deals with a great and original personality is "Georgia O'Keeffe," page 481.

Purpose-Setting Question What qualities made Lincoln the right man to lead our country during one of its worst crises?

1 Clarification The expression *gave up the ghost* means "died or passed away."

2 Clarification During Lincoln's presidency, the right to own slaves, a practice that had existed for 200 years, was abolished.

3 Discussion How would you characterize Lincoln's attitude toward the Constitution?

Thematic Focus Times of crisis often give rise to the inspirational voices of individuals who can influence great masses of people. Ask students to name some leaders who inspired the nation. What qualities make a leader inspiring? Can a person with such qualities inspire people to do evil as well as good?

Alternative Assessment To promote active reading, have your students keep a reader's response journal as they read this selection. Ask them to focus their observations on the details that reveal Lincoln's contradictory personality. Encourage them to respond personally by reflecting on the insights they gain about Lincoln as a human being and as a leader. How do they feel about him after reading this selection?

Their observations will enable you to assess their understanding of the essay.

LINCOLN PROCLAIMING THANKSGIVING
Dean Cornwell
Louis A. Warren Lincoln Library and Museum, Fort Wayne, Indiana

which gave enough added votes to seat favorable delegates from Kentucky, Missouri, Louisiana, Arkansas, and from one county in Florida. Until late in that campaign of 1864, he expected to lose the November election; military victories brought the tide his way; the vote was 2,200,000 for him and 1,800,000 against him. Among those who bitterly fought him politically, and accused him of blunders or crimes, were Franklin Pierce, a former president of the United States; Horatio Seymour, the Governor of New York; Samuel F. B. Morse, inventor of the telegraph; Cyrus H. McCormick, inventor of the farm reaper; General George B. Mc-

Clellan, a Democrat who had commanded the Army of the Potomac; and the Chicago *Times,* a daily newspaper. In all its essential propositions the Southern Confederacy had the moral support of powerful, respectable elements throughout the North, probably more than a million votes believing in the justice of the cause of the South as compared with the North.

While propagandas raged, and the war winds howled, he sat in the White House, the Stubborn Man of History, writing that the Mississippi was one river and could not belong to two countries, that the plans for railroad connection from coast to coast must

white kid gloves broke into tatters while shaking hands at a White House reception, he remarked, "This looks like a general bustification." When he talked with an Ohio friend one day during the 1864 campaign, he mentioned one public man and murmured, "He's a thistle! I don't see why God lets him live." Of a devious senator, he said, "He's too crooked to lie still!" And of a New York editor, "In early life in the West, we used to make our shoes last a great while with much mending, and sometimes, when far gone, we found the leather so rotten the stitches would not hold. Greely is so rotten that nothing can be done with him. He is not truthful; the stitches all tear out." As he sat in the telegraph

be pushed through and the Union Pacific[4] realized.

His life, mind and heart ran in contrasts. When his white kid gloves broke into tatters while shaking hands at a White House reception, he remarked, "This looks like a general bustification." When he talked with an Ohio friend one day during the 1864 campaign, he mentioned one public man, and murmured, "He's a thistle! I don't see why God lets him live." Of a devious Senator, he said, "He's too crooked to lie still!" And of a New York editor, "In early life in the West, we used to make our shoes last a great while with much mending, and sometimes, when far gone, we found the leather so rotten the stitches would not hold. Greeley is so rotten that nothing can be done with him. He is not truthful; the stitches all tear out." As he sat in the telegraph office of the War Department, reading cipher dispatches, and came to the words, Hosanna and Husband, he would chuckle, "Jeffy D.,"[5] and at the words, Hunter and Happy, "Bobby Lee."[6]

While the luck of war wavered and broke and came again, as generals failed and campaigns were lost, he held enough forces of the Union together to raise new armies and supply them, until generals were found who made war as victorious war has always been made, with terror, frightfulness, destruction, and valor and sacrifice past words of man to tell.

A slouching, gray-headed poet,[7] haunting the hospitals at Washington, characterized him as "the grandest figure on the crowded canvas of the drama of the nineteenth century—a Hoosier Michael Angelo."[8]

His own speeches, letters, telegrams and official messages during that war form the most significant and enduring document from any one man on why the war began, why it went on, and the dangers beyond its end. He mentioned "the politicians," over and again "the politicians," with scorn and blame. As the platoons filed before him at a review of an army corps, he asked, "What is to become of these boys when the war is over?"

He was a chosen spokesman; yet there were times he was silent; nothing but silence could at those times have fitted a chosen spokesman; in the mixed shame and blame of the immense wrongs of two crashing civilizations, with nothing to say, he said nothing, slept not at all, and wept at those times in a way that made weeping appropriate, decent, majestic.

His hat was shot off as he rode alone one night in Washington; a son he loved died as he watched at the bed; his wife was accused of betraying information to the enemy, until denials from him were necessary; his best companion was a fine-hearted and brilliant son with a deformed palate and an impediment of speech; when a Pennsylvania Congressman told him the enemy had declared they would break into the city and hang him to a lamppost, he said he had considered "the violent preliminaries" to such a scene; on his left thumb was a scar where an ax had nearly chopped the thumb off when he was a boy; over one eye was a scar where he had been hit with a club in the hands of a man trying to steal the cargo off a Mississippi River flatboat; he threw a cashiered[9]

---

4. **Union Pacific:** Railroad chartered by Congress in 1862 to form part of a transcontinental system.
5. **"Jeffy D.":** Jefferson Davis (1808–1889), president of the Confederacy.
6. **"Bobby Lee":** Robert E. Lee (1807–1870), commander in chief of the Confederate army.
7. **slouching . . . poet:** Walt Whitman (1819–1892).

8. **Michael Angelo:** Michelangelo (mī′ k'l an′ jə lō′), a famous Italian artist (1475–1564).
9. **cashiered** (ka shird′) v.: Dishonorably discharged.

4 **Enrichment** Walt Whitman's poem "When Lilacs Last in the Dooryard Bloom'd" mourns Lincoln's death.

5 **Literary Focus** Sandburg portrays Lincoln as a man of contrasts. Ask students what contrast in Lincoln's personality is revealed in this passage.

6 **Discussion** We rarely think of the President as someone who weeps. Ask students how their knowledge that Lincoln wept affects their opinion of him.

---

office of the War Department, reading cipher dispatches, and came to the words Hosanna and Husband, he would chuckle, "Jeffy D.," and at the words Hunter and Happy, "Bobby Lee." Notice that the first sentence states that Lincoln's character "ran to contrasts." The rest of the paragraph supports this statement with specific examples from Lincoln's life. These examples serve as **supporting details,** details provided to prove the accuracy of the main idea. Notice that the supporting details show on the one hand a gentle, almost playful side to the man's character and on the other, an indignation and anger that is aweinspiring—and perhaps a bit frightening—in its righteousness.

Student Activity 1. With your classmates, examine the supporting details in the paragraph, and then classify them according to which side of Lincoln's character they describe.

Student Activity 2. Discuss the overall effect of this paragraph. Do the details adequately support the main idea? Explain your opinion.

Software If students are working on computers, you may wish to have them use the *Paragraph Development* activity from the **Writer's Helper** to help them revise their paragraphs.

8 **Discussion** Abraham Lincoln is often referred to as "Honest Abe." Does the information in these two paragraphs undercut that nickname? Do you think that rules should be bent to benefit an important cause? Why or why not?

Multicultural Focus Tell students that unlike modern presidents, Abraham Lincoln never traveled to a foreign country, either before or during his presidency. He was, however, a voracious reader and through books was able to learn about different cultures. Point out that students can do the same thing, perhaps even more effectively than Lincoln could, since media technology is so much more advanced today.

Ask students to pick a country they would like to visit. Have them research and compile a bibliography of resources about that country, including fiction and nonfiction books. Then have them read one of the books on their list and report to the class what they learned from it.

officer out of his room in the White House, crying, "I can bear censure, but not insult. I never wish to see your face again."

As he shook hands with the correspondent of the London *Times*, he drawled, "Well, I guess the London *Times* is about the greatest power on earth—unless perhaps it is the Mississippi River." He rebuked with anger a woman who got on her knees to thank him for a pardon that saved her son from being shot at sunrise; and when an Iowa woman said she had journeyed out of her way to Washington just for a look at him, he grinned, "Well, in the matter of looking at one another, I have altogether the advantage."

He asked his Cabinet to vote on the high military command, and after the vote, told them the appointment had already been made; one Cabinet officer, who had been governor of Ohio, came away personally baffled and frustrated from an interview, to exclaim, to a private secretary, "That man is the most cunning person I ever saw in my life"; an Illinois lawyer who had been sent on errands carrying his political secrets, said, "He is a trimmer[10] and such a trimmer as the world has never seen."

He manipulated the admission of Nevada as a state in the Union, when her votes were needed for the Emancipation Proclamation,[11] saying, "It is easier to admit Nevada than to raise another million of soldiers." At the same time he went to the office of a former New York editor, who had become Assistant Secretary of War, and said the votes of three congressmen were wanted for the required three-quarters of votes in the House of Representatives, advising, "There are

---

10. trimmer (trim′ ər) *n.*: Person who changes his opinion to suit the circumstances.
11. Emancipation Proclamation: Document issued by President Lincoln freeing the slaves in all territories still at war with the Union.

three that you can deal with better than anybody else. . . . Whatever promise you make to those men, I will perform it." And in the same week, he said to a Massachusetts politician that two votes were lacking, and, "Those two votes must be procured. I leave it to you to determine how it shall be done; but remember that I am President of the United States and clothed with immense power, and I expect you to procure those votes." And while he was thus employing every last resource and device of practical politics to constitutionally abolish slavery, the abolitionist[12] Henry Ward Beecher attacked him with javelins of scorn and detestation in a series of editorials that brought from him the single comment, "Is thy servant a dog?"

When the King of Siam sent him a costly sword of exquisite embellishment, and two elephant tusks, along with letters and a photograph of the King, he acknowledged the gifts in a manner as lavish as the Orientals. Addressing the King of Siam as "Great and Good Friend," he wrote thanks for each of the gifts, including "also two elephant's tusks of length and magnitude, such as indicate they could have belonged only to an animal which was a native of Siam." After further thanks for the tokens received, he closed the letter to the King of Siam with strange grace and humor, saying, "I appreciate most highly your Majesty's tender of good offices in forwarding to this Government a stock from which a supply of elephants might be raised on our soil. . . . Our political jurisdiction, however, does not reach a latitude so low as to favor the multiplication of the elephant, and steam on land as well as water has been our best agent of transportation. . . . Meantime, wishing for your Majesty a long and happy life, and, for the

---

12. abolitionist (ab′ ə lish′ ən ist) *n.*: Person in favor of doing away with slavery in the United States.

PECULIARSOME ABE
N. C. Wyeth
The Free Library of Philadelphia

from *A Lincoln Preface* 409

9 Discussion What does Lincoln's preference for this story reveal about him?

10 Reading Strategy Ask students to summarize this paragraph in their own words.

Reader's Response If you were to write a biography of a famous political figure you admired, who would it be? Why?

Thematic Response In what ways was this biographical selection about Abraham Lincoln inspirational? How were your previous impressions of Lincoln affected?

Closure and Extension

ANSWERS TO RESPONDING TO THE SELECTION
Your Response

1. Discuss the fact that the Constitution had already been violated by the South when it seceded from the Union. Ask whether the ends Lincoln sought justified the means he used.

Recalling

2. As the luck of the war changed, Lincoln managed to hold enough forces of the union together to raise new armies until effective generals could be found.

3. Lincoln had a number of family tragedies—his son died, his wife was accused of giving information to the enemy, and another son had a speech impediment and a deformed palate.

generous and emulous people of Siam, the highest possible prosperity, I commend both to the blessing of Almighty God."

He sent hundreds of telegrams, "Suspend death sentence" or "Suspend execution" of So-and-So, who was to be shot at sunrise. The telegrams varied oddly at times, as in one, "If Thomas Samplogh, of the First Delaware Regiment, has been sentenced to death, and is not yet executed, suspend and report the case to me." And another, "Is it Lieut. Samuel B. Davis whose death sentence is commuted? If not done, let it be done."

While the war drums beat, he liked best of all the stories told of him, one of two Quakeresses[13] heard talking in a railway car. "I think that Jefferson will succeed." "Why does thee think so?" "Because Jefferson is a praying man." "And so is Abraham a praying man." "Yes, but the Lord will think Abraham is joking."

An Indiana man at the White House heard him say, "Voorhees, don't it seem strange to you that I, who could never so much as cut off the head of a chicken, should be elected, or selected, into the midst of all this blood?"

A party of American citizens, standing in the ruins of the Forum in Rome, Italy, heard there the news of the first assassination of the first American dictator, and took it as a sign of the growing up and the aging of the civilization on the North American continent. Far out in Coles County, Illinois, a beautiful, gaunt old woman in a log cabin said, "I knowed he'd never come back."

Of men taking too fat profits out of the war, he said, "Where the carcass is there will the eagles be gathered together."

---

13. Quakeresses (kwăk′ ər es əz) n.: Female members of the religious group known as the Society of Friends, or Quakers.

An enemy general, Longstreet, after the war, declared him to have been "the one matchless man in forty millions of people," while one of his private secretaries, Hay, declared his life to have been the most perfect in its relationships and adjustments since that of Christ.

Between the days in which he crawled as a baby on the dirt floor of a Kentucky cabin, and the time when he gave his final breath in Washington, he packed a rich life with work, thought, laughter, tears, hate, love.

With vast reservoirs of the comic and the droll, and notwithstanding a mastery of mirth and nonsense, he delivered a volume of addresses and letters of terrible and serious appeal, with import beyond his own day, shot through here and there with far, thin ironics, with paragraphs having raillery of the quality of the Book of Job,[14] and echoes as subtle as the whispers of wind in prairie grass.

Perhaps no human clay pot has held more laughter and tears.

The facts and myths of his life are to be an American possession, shared widely over the world, for thousands of years, as the tradition of Knute or Alfred, Lao-tse or Diogenes, Pericles or Caesar,[15] are kept. This because he was not only a genius in the science of neighborly human relationships and an artist in the personal handling of life from day to day, but a strange friend and a friendly stranger to all forms of life that he met.

He lived fifty-six years of which fifty-two were lived in the West—the prairie years.

---

14. Book of Job (jōb): Book of the Old Testament in which a man named Job is tested by God.
15. Knute (k' nōōt′) **or Alfred, Lao-tse** (lou′dzu′) **or Diogenes** (dī äj′ ə nēz′), **Pericles** (per′ ə klēz′) **or Caesar** (sē′ zər): Well-known thinkers and leaders from different eras and places.

4. "He manipulated the admission of Nevada as a state in the Union" in order to obtain votes for the Emancipation Proclamation. He also procured additional Congressional votes by exercising his great power as President.

Interpreting

5. Suggested Response: Lincoln's most important goal during the Civil War was to hold the country together.

6. Answers will differ, but most students will realize that Sandburg portrays Lincoln as an active, thoughtful, sensitive, many-sided man. Lincoln's life was eventful before he became President, and afterward he was at the center of the greatest crisis in the history of the United States.

7. Suggested Response: Sandburg describes Lincoln as a man of contrasts. He could be angry and compassionate, sad and humor-ous. Also, he was a "man of the people" who exercised an almost despotic power.

Applying

8. Answers may differ. A positive response would be that no limits should be placed on achieving a goal that results in a greater common good. A negative response would be that certain laws and restrictions are necessary and that adherence to these rules prevents

RESPONDING TO THE SELECTION

Your Response

1. Do you think Lincoln was justified in violating the Constitution? Why or why not?

Recalling

2. How did he show his leadership as "the luck of war" changed?
3. Describe the family tragedies he experienced.
4. How did he use "practical politics" to end slavery?

Interpreting

5. What was Lincoln's most important goal during the Civil War?
6. How does Sandburg show that Lincoln "packed a rich life with work, thought, laughter, tears, hate, love"?
7. In what ways does Sandburg describe Lincoln as a complex man?

Applying

8. Do you think the ends ever justify the means? Support your answer with evidence from current events or history.

ANALYZING LITERATURE

Understanding Biography

A **biography** is the story of a person's life written by someone else. In "A Lincoln Preface," Sandburg combines facts, anecdotes, and his own insights to produce a vivid portrait of Lincoln.

1. Why is Lincoln a good subject for a biography?
2. Sandburg tells you that Lincoln was shot in 1865. Find three other key facts about Lincoln that he includes.
3. Select three of the many anecdotes that he tells about his subject. Why did you find each of these anecdotes effective?
4. Summarize Sandburg's opinion of Lincoln. On the basis of this biography, do you agree with it? Explain your answer.

CRITICAL THINKING AND READING

Evaluating the Subject of a Biography

Sandburg tells many little stories about Lincoln that reveal different sides of his personality. For example, you learn that he once said when reviewing troops, "What is to become of these boys when the war is over?" This indicates that he was a thoughtful person, concerned about others.

1. Sandburg tells how Lincoln obtained votes to pass the Emancipation Proclamation. What do these stories reveal about him?
2. What can you learn about him from the story of Harriet Beecher Stowe's visit?
3. Why has Lincoln been called many-sided? Do you agree with this estimation? Why?

THINKING AND WRITING

Writing a Biographical Sketch

Imagine that your school newspaper wants you to write a biographical sketch. First select your subject. It could be someone you know or someone you have read about. List the facts and anecdotes that readers should know about your subject. Then write a short biography of your subject that your schoolmates will enjoy. As you revise, check to see that you have included your own insights into your subject's life.

LEARNING OPTIONS

1. **Performance.** Write a dramatic monologue in which you re-create the personality of Lincoln. Have him speak about one or more of the experiences Sandburg describes. Perform the monologue for your classmates.
2. **Cross-curricular Connection.** According to legend Lincoln drafted the Gettysburg Address on the back of an envelope. On an envelope jot down the key concepts and phrases that Lincoln may have written in a first draft of this address.

from A Lincoln Preface 411

---

about Lincoln's methods of obtaining votes to pass the Emancipation Proclamation reveal that he was relentless in the pursuit of his goals.
2. Suggested Response: His meeting with Stowe reveals his wit, sentimentality, and sense of mortality.
3. Answers will differ. However, most students will realize that Lincoln was a person of contrasts. For example, he could pardon a soldier out of compassion and then rebuke the soldier's mother for thanking him on her knees. He could write a proclamation freeing the slaves and then use every trick of practical politics to get it adopted.

THINKING AND WRITING

◆ **Software** Students sometimes need help revising their work. You might wish to have them use the *Paragraph Coherence* activity from the **Writer's Helper** as they revise their biographies.

Alternative Assessment *Peer Review* In pairs or in groups of four, have students assess each other's stories by responding to the following questions:

What facts about the subject does the writer cite?

What insights into the person's character are revealed through facts and anecdotes?

What concrete suggestions do you have for the writer to make the account more informative and more enjoyable?

To validate the peer reviews, you might ask students to incorporate those suggestions they find helpful in a revision of their stories.

LEARNING OPTIONS

1. This activity will appeal to visual learners. You may wish to extend the activity for analytical learners by having each performer develop a short list of performance skills by which he or she wishes to be judged.
2. Analytical learners will enjoy this activity.

---

the abuse of power. Students may consider such historical and current events as the rise and fall of Hitler, the Bay of Pigs invasion, Watergate, and the Iran-Contra scandal to support their answers.

ANSWERS TO ANALYZING LITERATURE

1. Suggested Response: Lincoln is a good subject for a biography because of his complex personality and central role in American history.

2. Suggested Response: Sandburg also tells us that Lincoln was born in Kentucky and lived in a log cabin, lived to be fifty-six years old, and won the 1864 election with 2,200,000 votes.
3. Answers may differ but might include the meeting between Lincoln and Harriet Beecher Stowe (this anecdote shows his humility and foreshadows his death); Lincoln's response to the woman whose son he had pardoned (this anecdote shows the contradictions in his nature); and the opin-

ions of the Quaker women (this anecdote shows his ability to laugh at himself).
4. Answers will differ. Most students will realize that Sandburg thinks Lincoln was one of the greatest men in history. Many students will also realize that Sandburg tends to present facts that support his thesis.

ANSWERS TO CRITICAL THINKING AND READING

1. Suggested Response: The stories

More About the Author One of Uchida's goals as a writer is "to dispel the stereotype image still held by many non-Asians about . . . Japanese Americans. . . ." Ask students why stereotypes—simplified or distorted images of a people or group—can be harmful. What can a writer do to correct such false images?

Literary Focus You might have students consider the advantages and disadvantages of the different methods of characterization.

Prereading Focus The United States has always been a nation of immigrants. Over the years, people from different cultures have faced some surprisingly similar challenges as they established new lives in an unfamiliar land. As students relate stories of immigrants they know, help them integrate their own knowledge of history and of other cultures with the details they recall about the immigration experiences of specific people. Then draw their attention to challenges common to all immigration experience.

Vocabulary For the benefit of **less advanced** students, assign students to work in pairs to write a brief story that includes all the listed vocabulary words.

Electronic Handbook You might suggest that students use the Language Master 6000 to find synonyms for *confidant* and *repository*.

GUIDE FOR READING

Yoshiko Uchida

(1921–1992) was born in Alameda, California, the daughter of a Japanese businessman. As a girl, she made books out of brown wrapping paper and filled them with her own stories. Today she is known for her prize-winning collections of Japanese folk tales and her descriptions of the Japanese experience in the United States. Uchida once stated that she hoped "to give young Asians a sense of their own history." She also wanted to write about Japanese Americans so that non-Asians would see them "as real people."

Of Dry Goods and Black Bow Ties

Biography: Characterization

Characterization refers to the way that writers make people in their narratives come alive for readers. Biographers use many of the same methods as fiction writers do to accomplish this goal. Often they will describe how a character looks and behaves, letting you draw your own conclusions about his or her personality. Sometimes they will tell you directly that the person has certain traits, such as pride or intelligence. Finally, they might show how other characters react to this person. In "Of Dry Goods and Black Bow Ties," Yoshiko Uchida uses all these techniques to create a touching portrait of Mr. Shimada.

Focus

In the selection that follows, Mr. Shimada comes to the United States with dreams for the future. His way of living has a profound effect on many characters in the story. Recall any stories you know of people coming to this country for the first time. How did they make their way in this new place? What personal qualities did they possess to help them succeed? Write briefly about their experiences. Then compare their dreams of a new life with Mr. Shimada's story.

Vocabulary

Knowing the following words will help you as you read "Of Dry Goods and Black Bow Ties."

expediency (ek spē′ dē ən sē) *n.*: Practicality (p. 413)

confidant (kän′ fə dant′) *n.*: A close friend to whom one tells secrets (p. 414)

repository (ri päz′ ə tôr′ ē) *n.*: Place for safekeeping (p. 414)

tycoon (tī kōōn′) *n.*: Wealthy and powerful person (p. 415)

awe (ô) *n.*: Mixed feeling of fear and wonder (p. 415)

exhilarated (ig zil′ ə rāt′ əd) *adj.*: Lively (p. 416)

typhoon (tī fōōn′) *n.*: Violent tropical storm (p. 417)

Objectives

1 To understand characterization in biography
2 To separate fact from opinion in biography
3 To write about characterization in biography
4 To express individual interests and abilities through an optional activity

Support Material

Teaching Portfolio
Teacher Backup, p. 435
Grammar in Action Worksheet, *Using Transitions*, p. 439
Usage and Mechanics Worksheet, p. 441
Vocabulary Check, p. 442
Analyzing Literature Worksheet, *Understanding Characterization*, p. 443

Language Worksheet, *Understanding Synonyms*, p. 444
Selection Test, p. 445

Prentice Hall Literature Writing Studio

Of Dry Goods[1] and Black Bow Ties

Yoshiko Uchida

Long after reaching the age of sixty, when my father was persuaded at last to wear a conservative four-in-hand tie,[2] it was not because of his family's urging, but because Mr. Shimada (shi mä' də) (I shall call him that) had died. Until then, for some forty years, my father had always worn a plain black bow tie, a formality which was required on his first job in America and which he had continued to observe as faithfully as his father before him had worn his samurai[3] sword.

My father came to America in 1906 when he was not yet twenty-one. Sailing from Japan on a small six-thousand-ton ship which was buffeted all the way by rough seas, he landed in Seattle on a bleak January day. He revived himself with the first solid meal he had enjoyed in many days, and then allowed himself one day of rest to restore his sagging spirits. Early on the second morning, wearing a stiff new bowler,[4] he went to see Mr. Shozo Shimada to whom he carried a letter of introduction.

At that time, Shozo Shimada was Seat-tle's most successful Japanese businessman. He owned a chain of dry goods stores which extended not only from Vancouver to Portland, but to cities in Japan as well. He had come to America in 1880, penniless but enterprising, and sought work as a laborer. It wasn't long, however, before he saw the futility of trying to compete with American laborers whose bodies were twice his in muscle and bulk. He knew he would never go far as a laborer, but he did possess another skill that could give him a start toward better things. He knew how to sew. It was a matter of expediency over masculine pride. He set aside his shovel, bought a second-hand sewing machine, and hung a dressmaker's sign in his window. He was in business.

In those days, there were some Japanese women in Seattle who had neither homes nor families nor sewing machines, and were delighted to find a friendly Japanese person to do some sewing for them. They flocked to Mr. Shimada with bolts of cloth, elated to discover a dressmaker who could speak their native tongue and, although a male, sew western-styled dresses for them.

Mr. Shimada acquainted himself with the fine points of turning a seam, fitting sleeves, and coping with the slippery folds of satin, and soon the women ordered enough dresses to keep him thriving and able to es-

---

1. **dry goods:** Cloth, lace, thread, buttons, and so forth.
2. **four-in-hand tie:** Necktie.
3. **samurai** (sam' ə ri'): Members of a military class in feudal Japan who wore two swords.
4. **bowler** (bōl' ər) n.: Derby hat.

Presentation

Motivation/Prior Knowledge Have students imagine that their family is moving to another country for a year. What fears would they have? What would they look forward to? What customs from home would they want to preserve?

Thematic Focus Mr. Shimada's life's journey included risks, choices, rough seas, and progress. Ask students how they measure a successful journey through life. Is it measured in the amount of wealth one accumulates, or can success be measured by other values, such as dignity and self-respect?

Master Teacher Note You might tell students that a symbol is anything that stands for something beyond itself. The bald eagle, for example, has become the symbol of the United States. Tell them that the black bow ties, mentioned in the title, are also a symbol. Have them decide, as they read, what meanings are associated with these bow ties.

Making Connections Another selection that deals with new Americans is "Rules of the Game," page 39.

Purpose-Setting Question Why does the writer's father look up to Mr. Shimada?

1 **Discussion** What does this statement mean?

Alternative Assessment To promote active reading, have students keep a reader's response journal as they read this selection. Ask them to focus their observations on the details that reveal the reasons for Mr. Shimada's success and those that reflect his admirable nature. Encourage students to respond personally to Mr. Shimada's handling of his personal reversal. How do they feel about him? What would they have done in a similar situation?

Students' observations will help you to assess their understanding of the essay.

tablish a healthy bank account. He became a trusted friend and confidant to many of them and soon they began to bring him what money they earned for safekeeping.

"Keep our money for us, Shimada-san,"[5] they urged, refusing to go to American banks whose tellers spoke in a language they could not understand.

---

5. -san (sän): Respectful Japanese suffix added to names and titles.

At first the money accumulated slowly and Mr. Shimada used a pair of old socks as a repository, stuffing them into a far corner of his drawer beneath his union suits. But after a time, Mr. Shimada's private bank began to overflow and he soon found it necessary to replenish his supply of socks.

He went to a small dry goods store downtown, and as he glanced about at the buttons, threads, needles and laces, it occurred to him that he owed it to the women to in-

414   Nonfiction

Grammar in Action

A smooth writing style results from making clear connections between ideas. Words that make connections are called **transitions.** They clarify relationships such as time, contrast, result, and addition. Subordinating and coordinating conjunctions are specific kinds of transitions.

Afterward, we walked home. (transition showing time)
After the game ended, we walked home. (subordinate clause)

Some drove home, *but we walked.* (coordinating conjunction)

The following illustrate transitions in Uchida's work:

At first the money accumulated slowly *and* Mr. Shimada used a pair of old socks as a repository . . . (transition indicating time; coordinator)

By the time my father appeared, Mr. Shimada had long since abandoned his sewing machine . . . (subordinate clause)

vest their savings in a business venture with more future than the dark recesses of his bureau drawer. That night he called a group of them together.

"Think, ladies," he began. "What are the two basic needs of the Japanese living in Seattle? Clothes to wear and food to eat," he answered himself. "Is that not right? Every man must buy a shirt to put on his back and pickles and rice for his stomach."

The women marveled at Mr. Shimada's cleverness as he spread before them his fine plans for a Japanese dry goods store that would not only carry everything available in an American dry goods store, but Japanese foodstuff as well. That was the beginning of the first Shimada Dry Goods Store on State Street.

By the time my father appeared, Mr. Shimada had long since abandoned his sewing machine and was well on his way to becoming a business tycoon. Although he had opened cautiously with such stock items as ginghams, flannel, handkerchiefs, socks, shirts, overalls, umbrellas and ladies' silk and cotton stockings, he now carried tins of salt rice crackers, bottles of soy sauce, vinegar, ginger root, fish-paste cakes, bean paste, Japanese pickles, dried mushrooms, salt fish, red beans, and just about every item of canned food that could be shipped from Japan. In addition, his was the first Japanese store to install a U.S. Post Office Station, and he therefore flew an American flag in front of the large sign that bore the name of his shop.

When my father first saw the big American flag fluttering in front of Mr. Shimada's shop, he was overcome with admiration and awe. He expected that Mr. Shozo Shimada would be the finest of Americanized Japanese gentlemen, and when he met him, he was not disappointed.

Although Mr. Shimada was not very tall,

he gave the illusion of height because of his erect carriage. He wore a spotless black alpaca suit, an immaculate white shirt and a white collar so stiff it might have overcome a lesser man. He also wore a black bow tie, black shoes that buttoned up the side and a gold watch whose thick chain looped grandly on his vest. He was probably in his fifties then, a ruddy-faced man whose hair, already turning white, was parted carefully in the center. He was an imposing figure to confront a young man fresh from Japan with scarcely a future to look forward to. My father bowed, summoned as much dignity as he could muster, and presented the letter of introduction he carried to him.

Mr. Shimada was quick to sense his need. "Do you know anything about bookkeeping?" he inquired.

"I intend to go to night school to learn this very skill," my father answered.

Mr. Shimada could assess a man's qualities in a very few minutes. He looked my father straight in the eye and said, "Consider yourself hired." Then he added, "I have a few basic rules. My employees must at all times wear a clean white shirt and a black bow tie. They must answer the telephone promptly with the words, 'Good morning or good afternoon, Shimada's Dry Goods,' and they must always treat each customer with respect. It never hurts to be polite," he said thoughtfully. "One never knows when one might be indebted to even the lowliest of beggars."

My father was impressed with these modest words from a man of such success. He accepted them with a sense of mission and from that day was committed to white shirts and black bow ties, and treated every customer, no matter how humble, with respect and courtesy. When, in later years, he had his own home, he never failed to answer the phone before it could ring twice if at all possible.

Of Dry Goods and Black Bow Ties 415

2 Discussion Why do you think this privilege was important to Mr. Shimada?

3 Enrichment What symbols of success does Mr. Shimada display? Compare and contrast them with current status symbols.

4 Discussion Is it wise to make quick decisions on a person's character? Explain.

. . . he *therefore* flew an American flag . . . (transition indicating result)
He *also* wore a black bow tie . . . (transition indicating addition)
In spite of his phenomenal success, however, Mr. Shimada never forgot his early friends . . . (transitions indicating contrast)

By using a variety of transitions, you will allow readers to understand the relationships among your ideas.

Student Activity 1. Tell whether the following transitions show time, contrast, result, or addition:
1. moreover
2. consequently
3. nevertheless
4. because
5. on the other hand
6. earlier

Student Activity 2. Write a paragraph of at least six sentences. Use transitions to join your ideas. Mark each transition.

My father worked with Mr. Shimada for ten years, becoming first the buyer for his Seattle store and later, manager of the Portland branch. During this time Mr. Shimada continued on a course of exhilarated expansion. He established two Japanese banks in Seattle, bought a fifteen-room house outside the dreary confines of the Japanese community and dressed his wife and daughter in velvets and ostrich feathers. When his daughter became eighteen, he sent her to study in Paris, and the party he gave on the eve of her departure, with musicians, as well as caterers to serve roast turkey, venison,

416 Nonfiction

Multicultural Focus Begin a discussion of the portrayal of Japanese Americans in this story by asking students if they know what *stereotype* means. Explain that a stereotype is a fixed notion about something—a person, a group, a place, or an idea—that is widely held and that allows for no individuality or variation. For example, according to one common stereotype, the Japanese businessman is always successful, wealthy, and hard-working to the point of obsession. Point out that these traits are not in themselves negative but that their blanket application to an entire group of people keeps us from seeing the members of that group as individuals.

Ask students whether Mr. Shimada was a real person or simply a stereotype, and have them give reasons for their responses. You may want to broaden the discussion by eliciting other common examples of positive ethnic stereotyping. Help them realize that whether a stereotype is positive or negative, and even if in some instances it fits, it is destructive and unfair to apply it to every member of a group.

Have students research the wave of Japanese immigration to California during the nineteenth century. Ask them to find out how many people came and when,

baked ham and champagne, seemed to verify rumors that he had become one of the first Japanese millionaires of America.

In spite of his phenomenal success, however, Mr. Shimada never forgot his early friends nor lost any of his generosity, and this, ironically enough, was his undoing. Many of the women for whom he had once sewn dresses were now well established, and they came to him requesting loans with which they and their husbands might open grocery stores and laundries and shoe repair shops. Mr. Shimada helped them all and never demanded any collateral. He operated his banks on faith and trust and gave no thought to such common prudence as maintaining a reserve.

When my father was called to a new position with a large Japanese firm in San Francisco, Mr. Shimada came down to Portland to extend personally his good wishes. He took Father to a Chinese dinner and told him over the peanut duck and chow mein that he would like always to be considered a friend.

"If I can ever be of assistance to you," he said, "don't ever hesitate to call." And with a firm shake of the hand, he wished my father well.

That was in 1916. My father wrote regularly to Mr. Shimada telling him of his new job, of his bride, and later, of his two children. Mr. Shimada did not write often, but each Christmas he sent a box of Oregon apples and pears, and at New Year's a slab of heavy white rice paste from his Seattle shop.

In 1929 the letters and gifts stopped coming and Father learned from friends in Seattle that both of Mr. Shimada's banks had failed.[6] He immediately dispatched a letter to Mr. Shimada, but it was returned unopened. The next news he had was that Mr.

6. **In 1929 . . . failed:** This was the year that the Great Depression began.

Shimada had had to sell all of his shops. My father was now manager of the San Francisco branch of his firm. He wrote once more asking Mr. Shimada if there was anything he could do to help. The letter did not come back, but there was no reply, and my father did not write again. After all, how do you offer help to the head of a fallen empire? It seemed almost irreverent.

It was many years later that Mr. Shimada appeared one night at our home in Berkeley.[7] In the dim light of the front porch my mother was startled to see an elderly gentleman wearing striped pants, a morning coat[8] and a shabby black hat. In his hand he carried a small black satchel. When she invited him inside, she saw that the morning coat was faded, and his shoes badly in need of a shine.

"I am Shimada," he announced with a courtly bow, and it was my mother who felt inadequate to the occasion. She hurriedly pulled off her apron and went to call my father. When he heard who was in the living room, he put on his coat and tie before going out to greet his old friend.

Mr. Shimada spoke to them about Father's friends in Seattle and about his daughter who was now married and living in Denver. He spoke of a typhoon that had recently swept over Japan, and he drank the tea my mother served and ate a piece of her chocolate cake. Only then did he open his black satchel.

"I thought your girls might enjoy these books," he said, as he drew out a brochure describing *The Book of Knowledge*.

"Fourteen volumes that will tell them of the wonders of this world." He spread his arms in a magnificent gesture that recalled his eloquence of the past. "I wish I could give

7. **Berkeley** (bʉr′ klē): City in California, on San Francisco Bay.
8. **morning coat:** Jacket with tails, used for formal occasions.

Of Dry Goods and Black Bow Ties   417

---

5 **Reading Strategy** Ask students to predict whether the writer's father and Mr. Shimada will continue to be close friends.

6 **Clarification** The expression *almost irreverent* means "almost disrespectful."

7 **Critical Thinking and Reading** How has Mr. Shimada's appearance changed? What does this change indicate?

how they made their living, what life was like for them in this country, and so forth. Have students share their findings.

8 **Discussion** Why was Mr. Shimada able to take the extra fifty dollars from the author's father without feeling he was taking charity?

9 **Discussion** What does the author's father mean when he says, "I am still one of the Shimada men"?

Readers Response What lesson did you learn from this story? How might you apply this lesson to your own life?

Thematic Response Mr. Shimada tried many new ventures over his lifetime. What measures could you use to decide whether Mr. Shimada's life's journey was successful or unsuccessful?

them to your children as a personal gift," he added softly.

Without asking the price of the set, my father wrote a check for one hundred dollars and gave it to Mr. Shimada.

Mr. Shimada glanced at the check and said, "You have given me fifty dollars too much." He seemed troubled for only a moment, however, and quickly added, "Ah, the balance is for a deposit, is it? Very well, yours will be the first deposit in my next bank."

"Is your home still in Seattle then?" Father asked cautiously.

"I am living there, yes," Mr. Shimada answered.

And then, suddenly overcome with memories of the past, he spoke in a voice so low he could scarcely be heard.

"I paid back every cent," he murmured. "It took ten years, but I paid it back. All of it. I owe nothing."

"You are a true gentleman, Shimada-san," Father said. "You always will be." Then he pointed to the black tie he wore, saying, "You see, I am still one of the Shimada men."

That was the last time my father saw Shozo Shimada. Some time later he heard that he had returned to Japan as penniless as the day he set out for America.

It wasn't until the Christmas after we heard of Mr. Shimada's death that I ventured to give my father a silk four-in-hand tie. It was charcoal gray and flecked with threads of silver. My father looked at it for a long time before he tried it on, and then fingering it gently, he said, "Well, perhaps it is time now that I put away my black bow ties."

MULTICULTURAL CONNECTION

Coming to America

When Mr. Shimada came to the United States in 1880, he was one of many Asian immigrants arriving in this country. These immigrants, mostly Chinese and Japanese men, had left their families behind until they could afford to bring them over.

Today, new groups of immigrants are coming to our shores from Southeast Asian countries like Vietnam, Cambodia, Thailand, and Laos.

In the decades after the Civil War, a record number of immigrants left Europe for the United States. Before the 1880's, about 85 percent of these immigrants came from Great Britain, Canada, Ireland, Germany, and Scandinavia. From 1881 to 1890, however, more and more immigrants came from southern and eastern Europe.

The port of entry for most European immigrants was tiny Ellis Island in New York Harbor.

In the years since World War II, many immigrants have come to America from Caribbean islands like Puerto Rico, Haiti, the Dominican Republic, Jamaica, and Cuba.

All the new immigrants—from Asia, Europe, and the Caribbean—have helped the American economy to expand. They have also enriched American culture. Each group brought traditional foods, songs, theater, and literature that added variety and vitality to American life.

Interview

Interview someone who recently immigrated to the United States. What were his or her reasons for immigrating? What was it like to arrive in the United States? Share your findings with the class.

418 Nonfiction

Closure and Extension

ANSWERS TO RESPONDING TO THE SELECTION
Your Response
1. Encourage students to share their responses.

Recalling
2. Mr. Shimada helped all the people who came to him for loans, neither asking for collateral nor maintaining a reserve of funds.
3. Mr. Shimada has lost his business

empire and now must sell encyclopedias to support himself.

Interpreting
4. Suggested Response: Mr. Shimada symbolized the possibility of achieving success in America and retaining one's Japanese identity.
5. Suggested Response: Mr. Shimada gave Uchida's father a start in business as well as a sense of pride in himself.

6. Suggested Responses: (a) Uchida's father feels Shimada is "a true gentleman" because he treats everyone with respect and courtesy. (b) Uchida's father means that he still upholds the virtues that Shimada had taught him.
7. Suggested Response: She gave him the tie after Shimada's death because it symbolized the end of an era in his life. He would no longer wear bow ties exclusively.

Applying
8. Answers will differ. Students may respond that people need direction in their lives. It is easier to imitate a real person than to live by abstract standards.

Challenge What do you think are the main concerns of immigrants who have just arrived in the United States? If possible, give examples to support your answer.

RESPONDING TO THE SELECTION

Your Response

1. What qualities do you think make Mr. Shimada a memorable character?

Recalling

2. Why does Mr. Shimada's generosity lead to his downfall?
3. In what ways is he a changed man when he visits the Uchidas years later?

Interpreting

4. What did Mr. Shimada symbolize for Uchida's father when they first met?
5. In what important ways did Mr. Shimada affect the life of Uchida's father?
6. (a) Why does Uchida's father consider Mr. Shimada "a true gentleman"? (b) What does he mean when he says, "You see, I am still one of the Shimada men"?
7. Why did Uchida give her father a four-in-hand tie only after Mr. Shimada died?

Applying

8. Uchida's father looked up to Mr. Shimada as a model. Why do you think people search out models to imitate?

ANALYZING LITERATURE

Understanding Characterization

Characterization refers to the way that writers make a person in a narrative come alive for the reader. In "Of Dry Goods and Black Bow Ties," the writer creates a portrait of a man who deeply influenced her father. She tells you directly what Mr. Shimada was like, recounts his history, and shows how others reacted to him.

1. Find two examples where Uchida tells you directly what Mr. Shimada was like.
2. Explain how Mr. Shimada demonstrates pride, cleverness, and generosity.
3. Compare and contrast Mr. Shimada in his first and last meetings with Uchida's father.

4. The Japanese add -san to the end of a name to show respect. Explain how the writer has created a character who is worthy of being called "Shimada-san."

CRITICAL THINKING AND READING

Separating Fact From Opinion

A **statement of fact** can be proved to be true or false. For example, Uchida says that her "father came to America in 1906." You could verify this fact through research. A **statement of opinion,** however, expresses a person's belief. Such a statement can be supported by arguments, but it cannot be proved absolutely true or false. When Uchida says that Mr. Shimada was generous, she is expressing an opinion. Are the following statements facts or opinions?

1. ". . . his was the first Japanese store to install a U.S. Post Office Station. . . ."
2. "Mr. Shimada could assess a man's qualities in a very few minutes."
3. "My father worked with Mr. Shimada for ten years. . . ."

THINKING AND WRITING

Writing About Characterization

Imagine that a friend of yours is writing a biographical sketch for a class assignment and has asked for your advice. First, list the methods that Uchida uses to make Mr. Shimada such a memorable character. Then use this list to write a note to your friend explaining how to make a subject come alive. In revising your note, check to see that your advice is clear and specific.

LEARNING OPTION

Speaking and Listening. Write an obituary for Mr. Shimada. Include all the important information about his life that you find in the selection. Then read your work aloud as though delivering it for a local television newscast.

Of Dry Goods and Black Bow Ties 419

Preparation

More About the Authors Much of what **Black Elk** recounts of his life experiences in the book *Black Elk Speaks* is about the demise of the Sioux nation. Ask students what happened to change the Sioux way of life.

Although **John Neihardt** devoted his life to writing about the Old West, he gained considerable attention when psychologist Carl Jung took an interest in how Neihardt had portrayed Black Elk's mystical qualities. How does Neihardt help readers understand the experiences of a medicine man? In what ways do the beliefs and concerns of Black Elk reflect the beliefs and concerns of the Sioux people?

Literary Focus Point out to students that although Neihardt was not a Native American, he was able to convey a clear understanding of the Sioux culture in part because he lived with the members of that nation for many years.

Prereading Focus Lead students into the activity by holding a class discussion in which students share their prior knowledge of Native American life and culture during the nineteenth century. Then have them contrast their impressions of Native American life with their impressions of life in England during the 1800's.

Vocabulary Because the language in "Across the Big Water" is simple, no vocabulary list appears. Use the Vocabulary Check in the **Teaching Portfolio** to work with Black Elk's figurative expressions.

GUIDE FOR READING

Black Elk

(1863–1950) was a medicine man of the Oglala Lakota Sioux people, buffalo hunters of the Western Dakotas and Nebraska. Black Elk's life story is recounted in the book *Black Elk Speaks*, a compilation of anecdotes told to the writer John Neihardt.

John Neihardt (Flaming Rainbow)

(1881–1973) is known for his fiction and poetry about Native Americans. From 1901 to 1907, Neihardt lived with the Omaha Indians in Nebraska, and his works reflect his experiences with these people and other Native American peoples of the Great Plains. *Black Elk Speaks,* is Neihardt's most popular book.

Across the Big Water

Cultural Point of View

Every story or essay is written from a **cultural point of view** because every writer is influenced by his or her own culture. The assumptions that a writer makes about the world and the way it works are based on the attitudes and beliefs that the writer learned while growing up. As cultures vary greatly, so do the literary works of people from these cultures. Humor is very different from one culture to another, and what one culture considers tragic, another might view in a more matter-of-fact way. When you read a work that is written from a cultural viewpoint other than your own, inferring the assumptions and beliefs of the writer will often help you appreciate the story more fully.

Focus

"Across the Big Water" is about a nineteenth-century Native American who travels from the United States to England. He has lived all his life on the prairie and has never seen a big city or an ocean. Put yourself in the place of the narrator of the story you are about to read. What problems do you think he might encounter? With a group of two or three students, brainstorm to compile a list of the manners and customs that will seem strange to him. As you read "Across the Big Water," compare the narrator's reactions with your predictions about them.

420 Nonfiction

Objectives

1 To understand cultural viewpoints
2 To make inferences about cultural viewpoints
3 To write from another point of view

Support Material

Teaching Portfolio
Teacher Backup, p. 447
Grammar in Action Worksheet, *Recognizing Infinitives,* p. 451
Usage and Mechanics Worksheet, p. 453
Vocabulary Worksheet, p. 454
Analyzing Literature Worksheet, *Understanding Cultural Viewpoints,* p. 455
Critical Thinking and Reading

Worksheet, *Making Inferences About Cultural Beliefs,* p. 456
Selection Test, p. 457

Prentice Hall Literature Writing Studio

Across the Big Water

from *Black Elk Speaks*

as told through John G. Neihardt

As I told you, it was in the summer of my twentieth year (1883) that I performed the ceremony of the elk. That fall, they say, the last of the bison herds was slaughtered by the Wasichus.[1] I can remember when the bison were so many that they could not be counted, but more and more Wasichus came to kill them until there were only heaps of bones scattered where they used to be. The Wasichus did not kill them to eat; they killed them for the metal that makes them crazy, and they took only the hides to sell. Sometimes they did not even take the hides, only the tongues; and I have heard that fire-boats came down the Missouri River loaded with dried bison tongues. You can see that the men who did this were crazy. Sometimes they did not even take the tongues; they just killed and killed because they liked to do that. When we hunted bison, we killed only what we needed. And when there was nothing left but heaps of bones, the Wasichus came and gathered up even the bones and sold them.

All our people now were settling down in square gray houses, scattered here and there across this hungry land, and around them the Wasichus had drawn a line to keep them in. The nation's hoop was broken, and there was no center any longer for the flowering tree. The people were in despair. They seemed heavy to me, heavy and dark; so heavy that it seemed they could not be lifted; so dark that they could not be made to see any more. Hunger was among us often now, for much of what the Great Father in Washington[2] sent us must have been stolen by Wasichus who were crazy to get money. There were many lies, but we could not eat them. The forked tongue made promises.

I kept on curing the sick for three years more, and many came to me and were made over; but when I thought of my great vision, which was to save the nation's hoop and make the holy tree to bloom in the center of it, I felt like crying, for the sacred hoop[3] was broken and scattered. The life of the people was in the hoop, and what are many little lives if the life of those lives be gone?

But late in my twenty-third summer (1886), it seemed that there was a little hope. There came to us some Wasichus who wanted a band of Ogalalas[4] for a big show that the other Pahuska[5] had. They told us this show

---

1. Wasichus (wä shē′ chōōz): White people.

2. Great Father in Washington: Chester A. Arthur, President of the United States from 1881 to 1885.
3. sacred hoop: Among the Sioux nations, the circle, or hoop, is a sacred symbol that has special powers. It represents harmony and life, which has no beginning and no end. When the circle is broken, there is disharmony and tragedy.
4. Ogalalas (ōg′ə lä′läz): A Teton tribe of the Dakota (Sioux) Indians.
5. Pahuska (pä ōōs′kə): Native American term for "long hair," referring to Buffalo Bill Cody (1846– 1917), United States frontier scout and showman.

Across the Big Water 421

Presentation

Motivation/Prior Knowledge
Have students discuss how members of the various Native American nations must have felt when they were forced to live on reservations. Tell them they are about to read one man's account of how he sought a better way of life for his people.

Purpose-Setting Question
What vision did Black Elk have and how did it affect him?

Making Connections For another Native American point of view on cross-cultural experience, read "The Man to Send Rain Clouds," by Leslie Marmon Silko, page 151.

1 **Literary Focus: Cultural Viewpoints** In what ways is the attitude of Black Elk's people toward the bison herds different from the attitude of the Wasichus?

2 **Literary Focus: Cultural Viewpoints** How does the narrator feel about the gray houses and the line that the Wasichus had drawn?

3 **Discussion** What do you think the "nation's hoop" and the "flowering tree" represent?

4 **Discussion** What emotional and physical states do the images of heaviness and darkness convey?

5 **Discussion** What does Black Elk mean by "the life of those lives"? What is the meaning of the question he asks?

ESL Teaching Strategy Suggest that ESL students draw a comparison between themselves and Black Elk. Ask them to describe what American customs and behaviors seem strange to them. Have them look for similarities and differences between their own experiences and those of Black Elk.

Thematic Focus Some historians have said that Black Elk's life was a journey across centuries and across cultures. In what ways is Black Elk's story universal to all people, regardless of the period of history or the cultural background from which they come?

Alternative Assessment To promote active reading, have your students keep a reader's response journal as they read the selection. Ask them to focus their observations on the details that reveal the concerns and values of the Ogalala Sioux people. Encourage them to respond personally to what Black Elk experiences in his search for a way to help his people.

Students' observations and comments will enable you to assess their understanding of the issues in this selection.

6 **Discussion** Do you think that Black Elk will succeed in learning a "secret" about the Wasichu that will help his people? Why or why not?

7 **Literary Focus: Cultural Viewpoints** What is the significance of Black Elk's vision? Why, from the point of view of the Ogalalas, would his vision be any more important than anyone else's?

8 **Literary Focus: Cultural Viewpoints** What might be the origin of the terms "red road" and "black road"? What is the difference between the two roads, according to Black Elk?

9 **Discussion** Why does Black Elk not heed the advice of his relatives?

10 **Discussion** What does this admission reveal about Black Elk?

11 **Reading Strategy** Have students make inferences about what Black Elk saw in Chicago.

12 **Literary Focus: Cultural Viewpoints** Why might the different Native American peoples be so glad to see each other?

13 **Discussion** What does this admission tell you about Black Elk's feelings about his experience so far?

6 would go across the big water to strange lands, and I thought I ought to go, because I might learn some secret of the Wasichu that would help my people somehow. In my great vision, when I stood at the center of the world, the two men from the east had brought me the daybreak-star herb and they had told me to drop it on the earth; and where it touched the ground it took root and 7 bloomed four-rayed. It was the herb of understanding. Also, where the red man of my vision changed into a bison that rolled, the same herb grew and bloomed when the bison had vanished, and after that the people in my vision found the good red road again. Maybe if I could see the great world of the Wasichu, I could understand how to bring the sacred hoop together and make the tree to bloom again at the center of it.

I looked back on the past and recalled my people's old ways, but they were not living 8 that way anymore. They were traveling the black road, everybody for himself and with little rules of his own, as in my vision. I was in despair, and I even thought that if the Wasichus had a better way, then maybe my people should live that way. I know now that this was foolish, but I was young and in despair.

9 My relatives told me I should stay at home and go on curing people, but I would not listen to them.

The show people sent wagons from Rushville on the iron road to get us, and we were about a hundred men and women. Many of our people followed us half way to the iron road and there we camped and ate together. Afterward we left our people crying there, for we were going very far across the big water.

That evening where the big wagons were waiting for us on the iron road, we had a dance. Then we got into the wagons. When 10 we started, it was dark, and thinking of my home and my people made me very sad. I wanted to get off and run back. But we went roaring all night long, and in the morning we ate at Long Pine. Then we started again and went roaring all day and came to a very big town in the evening.[6]

Then we roared along all night again and came to a much bigger town.[7] There we stayed all day and all night; and right there I could compare my people's ways with Wasichu ways, and this made me sadder than before. I wished and wished that I had not gone away from home.

Then we went roaring on again, and afterwhile we came to a still bigger town—a very big town.[8] We walked through this town to the place where the show was. Some Pawnees and Omahas[9] were there, and when they saw us they made war-cries and charged, couping[10] us. They were doing this for fun and because they felt glad to see us. I was surprised at the big houses and so many people, and there were bright lights at night, so that you could not see the stars, and some of these lights, I heard, were made with the power of thunder.

We stayed there and made shows for many, many Wasichus all that winter. I liked the part of the show we made, but not the part the Wasichus made. Afterwhile I got used to being there, but I was like a man who had never had a vision. I felt dead and my people seemed lost and I thought I might never find them again. I did not see anything to help my people. I could see that the Wasichus did not care for each other the way our people did before the nation's hoop was

---

6. a very big town: Omaha, Nebraska.
7. a much bigger town: Chicago, Illinois.
8. a very big town: New York City.
9. Pawnees (pô nēz´) and **Omahas** (ō´ mə hôz): Members of a North American Plains Indian nation and members of the Sioux nation, respectively.
10. couping (kōō´ piŋ): Playfully imitating a display of valor in which a warrior approaches an enemy, touches him with a stick, and escapes without injury.

Grammar in Action

Black Elk's speech includes many infinitives. An **infinitive** is a verb form that generally appears with the word *to* and acts as a noun, adjective, or adverb. Note the following example:

The Wasichus did not kill the buffalo *to eat.*

To avoid confusing an infinitive with a prepositional phrase, remember that *to* followed by a noun or pronoun makes a prepositional phrase but that *to* followed by a verb makes an infinitive. Compare these two sentences:

The people seemed heavy *to me.* (*to* and a pronoun; prepositional phrase)

I thought of my great vision *to save* the nation's hoop. (*to* and a verb; infinitive)

Student Activity 1. In the following sentences from "Across the Big Water," identify the italicized words as prepositional phrases or infinitives:

1. Some of our people went home and wanted me *to go* with them.
2. Maybe across the big water there was something *to see.*
3. Grandmother England came *to the show* in a big shining wagon.

broken. They would take everything from each other if they could, and so there were some who had more of everything than they could use, while crowds of people had nothing at all and maybe were starving. They had forgotten that the earth was their mother. This could not be better than the old ways of my people. . . .

In the spring it got warmer, but the Wasichus had even the grass penned up. We heard then that we were going to cross the big water to strange lands. Some of our people went home and wanted me to go with them, but I had not seen anything good for my people yet; maybe across the big water there was something to see, so I did not go home, although I was sick and in despair.

They put us all on a very big fire-boat, so big that when I first saw, I could hardly believe it; and when it sent forth a voice, I was frightened. There were other big fire-boats sending voices, and little ones too.

Afterwhile I could see nothing but water, water, water, and we did not seem to be going anywhere, just up and down; but we were told that we were going fast. If we were, I thought that we must drop off where the water ended; or maybe we might have to stop where the sky came down to the water. There was nothing but mist where the big town used to be and nothing but water all around.

We were all in despair now and many were feeling so sick that they began to sing their death-songs.

When evening came, a big wind was roaring and the water thundered. We had things that were meant to be hung up while we slept in them. This I learned afterward. We did not know what to do with these, so we spread them out on the floor and lay down on them. The floor tipped in every direction, and this got worse and worse, so that we rolled from one side to the other and could not sleep. We were frightened, and now we were all very

DISTINGUISHED VISITORS TO BUFFALO BILL'S
WILD WEST, LONDON, 1887
Buffalo Bill Historical Center, Cody, Wyoming

sick too. At first the Wasichus laughed at us; but very soon we could see that they were frightened too, because they were running around and were very much excited. Our women were crying and even some of the men cried, because it was terrible and they could do nothing. Afterwhile the Wasichus came and gave us things to tie around us so that we could float. I did not put on the one they gave me. I did not want to float. Instead, I dressed for death, putting on my best clothes that I wore in the show, and then I sang my death song. Others dressed for death too, and sang, because if it was the end of our lives and we could do nothing, we wanted to die brave. We could not fight this that was going to kill us, but we could die so that our spirit relatives would not be ashamed of us. It was harder for us because we were all so sick. Everything we had eaten came right up, and then it kept on trying to come up when there was nothing there.

We did not sleep at all, and in the morning the water looked like mountains, but the

Across the Big Water 423

19

Humanities Note

Graphic art, *Distinguished Visitors to Buffalo Bill's Wild West, London,* 1887. This original color lithograph poster is an advertisement for the traveling show that Black Elk joined. Buffalo Bill, its star, is shown in the center, surrounded by portraits of the royal and noble personages who attended the show in London in 1887. Queen Victoria ("Grandmother England") is the figure above Buffalo Bill. The likeness is probably accurate because lithograph prints are generally faithful to the artist's original drawing.

You might use the following questions for discussion:
1. Does the portrait of Queen Victoria match Black Elk's description? Why or why not?
2. Do you think that the Wild West show accurately represented American culture to its European audience? Explain.

14 Reading Strategy Have students make connections between Black Elk's observation here and today's social climate in the United States.

15 Discussion What do you think Black Elk is referring to in his description of grass as "penned up"?

16 Reading Strategy What inference can you make about Black Elk's understanding of physical geography?

17 Literary Focus: Cultural Viewpoints What does this detail reveal about the Sioux people's view of death?

18 Reading Strategy What do you think these things were?

19 Reading Strategy Have students discuss whether Black Elk's description of seasickness is exaggerated. On what do they base their answers?

4. We liked Grandmother England, because she was good *to us.*
5. Many were so sick that they began *to sing* their death-songs.

Student Activity 2. Write five sentences of your own. Use a prepositional phrase beginning with *to* in the first two sentences. Use an infinitive in the next two. Use both a prepositional phrase beginning with *to* and an infinitive in the last sentence.

Electronic Handbook You may want students to review prepositions before completing the Grammar in Action activities. If students have access to the Language Master 6000, have them enter *preposition* and press the GRAMMAR key.

20 Literary Focus: Cultural Viewpoints What does Black Elk's reaction reveal about his culture?

21 Enrichment In 1877, Sitting Bull, a Sioux chief, led his people to Canada to escape the United States government's law ordering the Sioux to live on reservations. Crazy Horse and the Ogalalas did not go with him. That same year, Crazy Horse was captured and killed by American soldiers. According to Black Elk's account, some of the Ogalala people must have followed Sitting Bull into Canada after the death of their leader.

22 Reading Strategy Have students visualize this scene. Draw their attention to how the sensory details make the images vivid. What effect does the repetition have?

Reader's Response In what ways does Black Elk's story affect your understanding of Native American culture? Explain.

Thematic Response Identify the different journeys, both literal and figurative, that Black Elk takes in "Across the Big Water."

Audiocassette To familiarize students with works of other Native Americans, you may wish to play N. Scott Momaday's interview and reading and William Least Heat Moon's reading in the **Audio Prose Library**. Ask students to look for cultural viewpoints that the various Native American peoples share.

wind was not so strong. Some of the bison and elk that we had with us for the show died that day, and the Wasichus threw them in the water. When I saw the poor bison thrown over, I felt like crying, because I thought right **20** there they were throwing part of the power of my people away.

After we had been on the fire-boat a long while, we could see many houses and then many other fire-boats tied close together along the bank. We thought now we could get off very soon, but we could not. There was a little fire-boat that had come through the gate of waters and it stopped beside us, and the people on it looked at everything on our fire-boat before we could get off. We went very slowly nearly all day, I think, and afterwhile we came to where there were many, many houses close together, and more fire-boats than could be counted. These houses were different from what we had seen before. The Wasichus kept us on the fire-boat all night and then they unloaded us, and took us to a place where the show was going to be. The name of this very big town was London. We were on land now, but we still felt dizzy as though we were still on water, and at first it was hard to walk.

We stayed in this place six moons; and many, many people came to see the show.

One day we were told that Majesty was coming. I did not know what that was at first, but I learned afterward. It was Grandmother **21** England (Queen Victoria), who owned Grandmother's Land[11] where we lived awhile after the Wasichus murdered Crazy Horse.[12]

She came to the show in a big shining wagon, and there were soldiers on both sides of her, and many other shining wagons came too. That day other people could not come to

the show—just Grandmother England and some people who came with her.

Sometimes we had to shoot in the show, but this time we did not shoot at all. We danced and sang, and I was one of the dancers chosen to do this for the Grandmother, because I was young and limber then and could dance many ways. We stood right in front of Grandmother England. She was little but fat and we liked her, because she was good to us. After we had danced, she spoke to us. She said something like this: "I am sixty-seven years old. All over the world I have seen all kinds of people; but today I have seen the best-looking people I know. If you belonged to me, I would not let them take you around in a show like this." She said other good things too, and then she said we must come to see her, because she had come to see us. She shook hands with all of us. Her hand was very little and soft. We gave a big cheer for her, and then the shining wagons came in and she got into one of them and they all went away.

In about a half-moon after that we went to see the Grandmother. They put us in some of those shining wagons and took us to a very beautiful place where there was a very big house with sharp, pointed towers on it. There were many seats built high in a circle, and these were just full of Wasichus who were all pounding their heels and yelling: "Jubilee! Jubilee! Jubilee!"[13] I never heard what this meant.

They put us together in a certain place at the bottom of the seats. First there appeared a beautiful black wagon with two black horses, and it went all around the show place. I heard that the Grandmother's grandson, a little boy, was in that wagon. Next came a beautiful black wagon with four gray horses. On each of the two right-hand horses

---

11. Grandmother's Land: Canada.
12. Crazy Horse: Dakota (Sioux) Indian chief (c. 1842–1877).

13. Jubilee (jōō'bə lē'): The fiftieth anniversary of Queen Victoria's rule, celebrated in 1887.

there was a rider, and a man walked, holding the front left-hand horse. I heard that some of Grandmother's relatives were in this wagon. Next came eight buckskin horses, two by two, pulling a shining black wagon. There was a rider on each right-hand horse and a man walked, holding the front left-hand horse. There were soldiers, with bayonets, facing outward all around this wagon. Now all the people in the seats were roaring and yelling "Jubilee!" and "Victoria!" Then we saw Grandmother England again. She was sitting in the back of the wagon and two women sat in the front, facing her. Her dress was all shining and her hat was all shining and her wagon was all shining and so were the horses. She looked like a fire coming.

Afterward I heard that there was yellow and white metal all over the horses and the wagon.

When she came to where we were, her wagon stopped and she stood up. Then all those people stood up and roared and bowed to her; but she bowed to us. We sent up a great cry and our women made the tremolo.[14] The people in the crowd were so excited that we heard some of them got sick and fell over. Then when it was quiet, we sang a song to the Grandmother.

That was a very happy time.

We liked Grandmother England, because we could see that she was a fine woman, and she was good to us. Maybe if she had been our Grandmother, it would have been better for our people. | 23

---

14. **tremolo** (trem′ə lō′) *n.*: A high-pitched, repetitive cry.

▮ RESPONDING TO THE SELECTION

Your Response
1. How would you feel if you had to live and work among people who did not share any of your beliefs? Explain.

Recalling
2. Why were the narrator's people hungry?
3. What did the narrator do as a member of the Oglala nation?

Interpreting
4. What do the terms *iron road* and *fire-boat* mean?
5. What does the narrator mean by the statement that the "nation's hoop was broken"?
6. (a) Did joining the Wild West show enable Black Elk to achieve the goal he sought? Explain. (b) What, if anything, did he gain from his trip?

Applying
7. The narrator says that white people "had forgotten that the earth was their mother." Does this statement hold true today? Why or why not?

▮ ANALYZING LITERATURE

Understanding Cultural Viewpoints
If a story's narrator is part of a culture that is different from yours, the story will reflect attitudes that may be unfamiliar or difficult to understand. Generally, however, you can make inferences about the narrator's culture by reflecting on what he or she says and does.

1. In what ways does the narrator contrast his culture with that of the Wasichus?
2. How does the narrator's response to the possible sinking of the ship reveal his attitudes and beliefs?

▮ THINKING AND WRITING

Writing From Another Point of View
Imagine that you are a farmer in eighteenth-century America and that you have just been placed in the middle of a twentieth-century city. Write an account of your impressions of the people, the technology, and the spirit of the city.

Across the Big Water 425

Native American Visions

by Joseph Bruchac

A Lakota holy man. Black Elk was a Lakota holy man who was born in 1863 and died in 1950. In his long lifetime, he saw the sweeping changes that took his people from a free life as buffalo hunters on the plains to poverty and starvation on government-controlled reservations. In 1931 he told his life story to a poet named John Neihardt. The result of those interviews was the book called *Black Elk Speaks*.

A series of visions. Although Black Elk spoke of his travels, of the defeat of Custer and the massacre of Lakota people at Wounded Knee, the center of his story was always his religious experience. Black Elk's life was shaped by a series of visions sent to him by Wakan Tanka, The Great Mystery. His first vision, which came to him when he was five years old, was of two men coming down like arrows from the sky, singing a sacred song.

His second vision, when he was nine, was the great vision of his life, one he would not understand until years later. After hearing a voice saying "It is time; now they are calling you," Black Elk became gravely ill and lay in a coma for twelve days. During that time he was shown many things by the beings he called The Five Grandfathers.

Dreams and visions. Visionary experience was an important part of the lives of most of the native peoples of North America. A personal connection with the sacred was regarded as normal and natural. Dreams were as meaningful a part of existence as daily activities. In many cases, in fact, dreams and visions were more real and more important than everyday life. Dream interpretation, which paralleled some of the methods used in modern psychiatry, was practiced among many native nations. Understanding his or her dreams could help a sick person grow well, especially if that sickness was a sickness of the mind and spirit.

When someone had a vision, he or she would usually seek out an experienced old person, a medicine man or woman, to obtain help in interpreting the vision. Among the Iroquois and other peoples of the northeastern woodlands, a boy would go out in the woods and fast for many days until he received a strong vision. The Ojibwa tell the story of a boy whose father came each morning to hear what vision his son had the night before. Each day, however, the father, who wanted his son to be better than all the other boys, said the vision was not strong enough and the boy should wait for a better vision. Finally, after seven days, the boy's father found the boy gone. In his place was a robin, the first bird of spring. From that time on, the bird's song would remind the people not to be overly ambitious. Seeking a vision should be done in the right frame of mind and always with great humility.

Some people, like Black Elk, begin having visions in early childhood, even without seeking out a visionary experience. Such people are usually regarded as holy persons, chosen by The Great Mystery to act as priests. Not everyone receives a vision in that

Presentation

Motivation/Prior Knowledge

Before students read this feature, you may want to have a group of volunteers research Native American culture and religion and share their findings with the class. Use the group's presentation as a springboard for a discussion of similarities and differences between Native American religions and Western religions, including Christianity, Judaism, and Islam. Use the discussion to lead into this feature on Native American visions. Then follow up the students' reading of the feature by having them discuss instances in which important figures from other religions had visions.

BLACK ELK UNDER THE TREE
OF LIFE
Standing Bear
*Western Historical Manuscript
Collection—Columbia and The
John C. Neihardt Trust*

fashion, however. Usually, people must work hard to prove themselves worthy of a visionary experience.

Seeking a vision. From the extreme northeast of the continent to the far west, it was common practice for young people (in some cultures, only the boys; in others, boys and girls) about to enter adulthood to go and seek a vision. Among the Lakota this seeking of a guiding vision is called *hanblechaya,* "crying for a vision."

"All alone on the hill." In order to better understand the great vision given to him at such an early age to help his people, Black Elk engaged in hanblechaya. With the guidance of a wise old medicine man named Few Tails, Black Elk fasted for four days and cleansed himself in a sweat lodge, a small dome-shaped structure where water is poured over red-hot stone to create a steam bath. He took the sacred pipe in his hand and stood all night on a high hill near Grass Creek, crying and praying for understanding, "all alone on the hill with the spirits and the dying light."

Exploring on Your Own

Find out about other cultures that put great emphasis on the spiritual aspects of life and share the results of your research with the class.

Joseph Bruchac is a storyteller and writer of Abenaki, English, and Slovak descent. He is coauthor, with Michael Caduto, of Keepers of the Earth, and his poems, articles, and stories have appeared in hundreds of publications, from Cricket to National Geographic.

Multicultural Connection   427

More About the Author Heyerdahl also sailed a boat made of papyrus reeds from Morocco to the West Indies. The purpose of this trip was to prove that the ancient Egyptians could have made similar voyages. Ask students why such a voyage would have been even more daring for an ancient Egyptian than it was for Heyerdahl.

Literary Focus You may want to have students note the passages in which Heyerdahl describes the dangers that lie ahead.

Prereading Focus To prepare students for the activity, you might want to hold a class discussion in which students share personal experiences related to the sea. Encourage students who have gone boating to share the sensations they experienced during their excursions on the sea. What did they see, hear, touch, smell, and taste during their voyage? Which sensations had the greatest impact on them? Why?

Vocabulary For the benefit of **less advanced** students, assign each of several students a vocabulary word. Ask students to define the word and then use it in proper context within a sentence.

Electronic Handbook You might suggest that students use the Language Master 6000 to find synonyms for *laconic*.

GUIDE FOR READING

Thor Heyerdahl

(1914–   ), born in Larvik, Norway, has won fame as an anthropologist and explorer. His expeditions have taken him to many different parts of the globe, from the Polynesian Islands in the Pacific Ocean to Africa and Asia. One of the many honors he has received for his work is membership in the Royal Norwegian Academy of Sciences. This selection comes from his book *Kon-Tiki,* an account of his daring trip across the Pacific on a specially designed raft.

from Kon-Tiki

Suspense in Autobiography

Suspense is the quality of a work that makes you wonder what will happen next. The two ingredients of suspense are uncertainty—the Latin word from which *suspense* comes means "uncertain"—and danger. You tend to feel suspense, therefore, when someone is in a dangerous situation and you do not know how events will turn out. In this episode from *Kon-Tiki,* Heyerdahl and his crew face the dangers of shipwreck.

Focus

The following selection is an account of Thor Heyerdahl's brush with death as he voyaged across the Pacific on the *Kon-Tiki.* Adventurers and explorers like Heyerdahl frequently take great risks to accomplish their goals. Imagine that you are on a small boat or raft traveling across the Pacific. Get together with a group of classmates and imagine what you would see, hear, feel, taste, and smell. Also, what dangers might you face? Then, as you read the selection, compare your imagined experiences with Heyerdahl's real ones.

Vocabulary

Knowing the following words will help you as you read this selection from *Kon-Tiki.*

ominous (äm′ ə nəs) *adj.*: Threatening; dangerous (p. 429)
idyllic (ī dil′ ik) *adj.*: Pleasing and simple; peaceful (p. 430)
laconic (lə kän′ ik) *adj.*: Not speaking much (p. 432)
lagoon (lə gōōn′) *n.*: Water enclosed by a circular coral reef (p. 433)

elation (i lā′ shən) *n.*: Feeling of great joy (p. 434)
plaiting (plāt′ iŋ) *n.*: Braiding (p. 436)

Objectives

1 To understand suspense in autobiography
2 To understand the sequence of events in autobiography
3 To write about autobiography
4 To express individual interests and abilities through optional activities

Support Material

Teaching Portfolio
Teacher Backup, p. 459
Grammar in Action Worksheets, *Appreciating Narrative Writing,* p. 463; *Using Semicolons,* p. 465
Usage and Mechanics Worksheet, p. 467
Vocabulary Check, p. 468
Analyzing Literature Worksheet,

Understanding Suspense, p. 469
Critical Thinking and Reading Worksheet, *Understanding the Sequence of Events,* p. 470
Selection Test, p. 471
Art Transparency 7: *The Lookout "All's Well,"* by Winslow Homer

Prentice Hall Literature Writing Studio

from Kon-Tiki

Thor Heyerdahl

For three days we drifted across the sea without a sight of land.

We were drifting straight toward the ominous Takume and Raroia reefs, which together blocked up forty to fifty miles of the sea ahead of us. We made desperate efforts to steer clear, to the north of these dangerous reefs, and things seemed to be going well till one night the watch came hurrying in and called us all out.

The wind had changed. We were heading straight for the Takume reef. It had begun to rain, and there was no visibility at all. The reef could not be far off.

In the middle of night we held a council of war. It was a question of saving our lives now. To get past on the north side was now hopeless; we must try to get through on the south side instead. We trimmed the sail, laid the oar over, and began a dangerous piece of sailing with the uncertain north wind behind us. If the east wind came back before we passed the whole façade of the fifty-mile-long reefs, we should be hurled in among the breakers, at their mercy.

We agreed on all that should be done if shipwreck was imminent. We would stay on board the *Kon-Tiki* at all costs. We would not climb up the mast, from which we should be shaken down like rotten fruit, but would cling tight to the stays[1] of the mast when the

seas poured over us. We laid the rubber raft loose on the deck and made fast to it a small watertight radio transmitter, a small quantity of provisions, waterbottles, and medical stores. This would be washed ashore independently of us if we ourselves should get over the reef safe but empty-handed. In the stern of the *Kon-Tiki* we made fast a long rope with a float which also would be washed ashore, so that we could try to pull in the raft if she were stranded out on the reef. And so we crept into bed and left the watch to the helmsman out in the rain.

As long as the north wind held, we glided slowly but surely down along the façade of the coral reefs which lay in ambush below the horizon. But then one afternoon the wind died away, and when it returned it had gone round into the east. According to Erik's position we were already so far down that we now had some hope of steering clear of the southernmost point of the Raroia reef. We would try to get round it and into shelter before going on to other reefs beyond it.

When night came, we had been a hundred days at sea.

Late in the night I woke, feeling restless and uneasy. There was something unusual in the movement of the waves. The *Kon-Tiki*'s motion was a little different from what it usually was in such conditions. We had become sensitive to changes in the rhythm of the logs. I thought at once of suction from a coast, which was drawing near, and was

---

1. **stays** (stāz) *n*.: A heavy rope or cable used for support.

from *Kon-Tiki* 429

Motivation/Prior Knowledge Heyerdahl risked his life to prove that ancient Peruvians could have migrated to Pacific islands in small boats. Tell the students that the risks he took are especially evident in this excerpt.

Master Teacher Note Use the overhead projector to show students Art Transparency 7, *The Lookout "All's Well,"* by Winslow Homer. Ask them how this picture conveys the sense of an ocean voyage.

Tell students that Heyerdahl traveled on a much smaller craft than the one suggested in Homer's picture. It was a raft made of nine fresh balsa logs fastened together with hemp ropes. This raft was named in memory of an Incan god.

Purpose-Setting Question What different types of danger do Heyerdahl and his crew encounter?

Making Connections You might want to teach the *Odyssey*, page 645, with this selection. Like Heyerdahl, Odysseus had to face the dangers of a long sea voyage.

1 Literary Focus How does this passage create suspense?

2 Clarification *Facade* means "the main face or front."

3 Reading Strategy Heyerdahl has given a vivid sense of impending danger and vulnerability. Ask students to predict what is in store for the crew of the *Kon-Tiki*.

Thematic Focus The earth is constantly changing and often contradictory. Its forces can be both life-giving and destructive. Discuss with students why people place themselves at the mercy of nature by climbing mountains, exploring unmapped regions, or crossing the ocean on a raft.

Alternative Assessment To promote active reading, have students keep a reader's response journal as they read this selection. Ask them to focus their observations on the details that provide the suspense in this adventure as well as those that reveal the courage of Heyerdahl and his crew. Encourage students to respond personally to the events in this story. What

similar acts of courage have they heard about or experienced?

Students' observations will help you assess their understanding of the essay.

continually out on deck and up the mast. Nothing but sea was visible. But I could get no quiet sleep. Time passed.

At dawn, just before six, Torstein came hurrying down from the masthead.[2] He could see a whole line of small palm-clad islands far ahead. Before doing anything else we laid the oar over to southward as far as we could. What Torstein had seen must be the small coral islands which lay strewn like pearls on a string behind the Raroia reef. A northward current must have caught us.

4   At half-past seven palm-clad islets had appeared in a row all along the horizon to westward. The southernmost lay roughly ahead of our bow, and thence there were islands and clumps of palms all along the horizon on our starboard[3] side till they disappeared as dots away to northward. The nearest were four or five sea miles away.

A survey from the masthead showed that, even if our bow pointed toward the bottom island in the chain, our drift sideways was so great that we were not advancing in the direction in which our bow pointed. We were drifting diagonally right in toward the reef. With fixed centerboards[4] we should still have had some hope of steering clear. But sharks were following close astern, so that it was impossible to dive under the raft and tighten up the loose centerboards with fresh guy[5] ropes.

5   We saw that we had now only a few hours more on board the *Kon-Tiki*. They must be used in preparation for our inevitable wreck on the coral reef. Every man learned what he had to do when the moment

came: each one of us knew where his own limited sphere of responsibility lay, so that we should not fly round treading on one another's toes when the time came and seconds counted. The *Kon-Tiki* pitched up and down, up and down, as the wind forced us in. There was no doubt that here was the turmoil of waves created by the reef—some waves advancing while others were hurled back after beating vainly against the surrounding wall.

We were still under full sail in the hope of even now being able to steer clear. As we gradually drifted nearer, half sideways, we saw from the mast how the whole string of palm-clad isles was connected with a coral reef, part above and part under water, which lay like a mole where the sea was white with foam and leaped high into the air. The Raroia atoll[6] is oval in shape and has a diameter of twenty-five miles, not counting the adjoining reefs of Takume. The whole of its longer side faces the sea to eastward, where we came pitching in. The reef itself, which runs in one line from horizon to horizon, is only a few hundred yards clear, and behind it idyllic islets lie in a string round the still lagoon inside.

It was with mixed feelings that we saw the blue Pacific being ruthlessly torn up and hurled into the air all along the horizon ahead of us. I knew what awaited us; I had visited the Tuamotu group before and had stood safe on land looking out over the immense spectacle in the east, where the surf from the open Pacific broke in over the reef. New reefs and islands kept on gradually appearing to southward. We must be lying off the middle of the façade of the coral wall.

On board the *Kon-Tiki* all preparations for the end of the voyage were being made. Everything of value was carried into the

---

2. **masthead:** The top part of the mast.
3. **starboard:** The right-hand side of a ship, as opposed to *port*, the left-hand side.
4. **centerboards:** Boards lowered through the bottom of a sailing vessel to prevent drifting.
5. **guy** (gī) *adj.*: Used for steadying or guiding.

6. **atoll** (a' tôl) *n.*: A ring-shaped coral island.

430 *Nonfiction*

Multicultural Focus Explain that Heyerdahl undertook the Kon-Tiki expedition to show that by migrating across the Pacific on rafts, Peruvians could have been the first humans to populate the Polynesian Islands fifteen hundred years ago. Point out that many early cultures were famous for their seafaring skills, citing the Egyptians, the Phoenicians and the early Greeks, and the Vikings as examples. Students should know that the ancient Egyptians made some of the greatest advances in the development of ships, discovering sails and constructing boats from planks of wood about 3000 B.C. Beginning in the late fourteenth century, Europeans gained mastery of the Atlantic, starting with the Portuguese and followed by first the Spanish and then the English. Elicit from students the fact that all these peoples lived on islands or in coastal regions.

Have students work in small groups to research the types of vessels that were used by early seafarers, including the Phoenician galley, the Viking longboat, and the ships of the Portuguese, Spanish, and English explorers —as well as early Asian and African seagoing vessels. Ask each group to present its findings to the rest of the class.

cabin and lashed fast. Documents and papers were packed into watertight bags, along with films and other things which would not stand a dip in the sea. The whole bamboo cabin was covered with canvas, and especially strong ropes were lashed across it. When we saw that all hope was gone, we opened up the bamboo deck and cut off with machete knives all the ropes which held the centerboards down. It was a hard job to get

6 **Critical Thinking and Reading**
Why do you think the men put on their shoes?

7 **Literary Focus** Why is the quoting of entries from the log an effective way to build suspense?

the centerboards drawn up, because they were all thickly covered with stout barnacles. With the centerboards up the draft[7] of our vessel was no deeper than to the bottom of the timber logs, and we would therefore be more easily washed in over the reef. With no centerboards and with the sail down, the raft lay completely sideways on and was entirely at the mercy of wind and sea.

We tied the longest rope we had to the homemade anchor and made it fast to the step of the port mast, so that the *Kon-Tiki* would go into the surf stern first when the anchor was thrown overboard. The anchor itself consisted of empty water cans filled with used radio batteries and heavy scrap, and solid mangrove-wood sticks projected from it, set crosswise.

Order number one, which came first and last, was: Hold on to the raft! Whatever happened, we must hang on tight on board and let the nine great logs take the pressure from the reef. We ourselves had more than enough to do to withstand the weight of the water. If we jumped overboard, we should become helpless victims of the suction which would fling us in and out over the sharp corals. The rubber raft would capsize in the steep seas or, heavily loaded with us in it, it would be torn to ribbons against the reef. But the wooden logs would sooner or later be cast ashore, and we with them, if we only managed to hold fast.

6 | Next, all hands were told to put on their shoes for the first time in a hundred days and to have their life belts ready. The last precaution, however, was not of much value, for if a man fell overboard he would be battered to death, not drowned. We had time, too, to put our passports and such few dollars as we had left into our pockets. But it was not lack of time that was troubling us.

---
7. draft *n.*: The depth of water that a ship displaces.

Those were anxious hours in which we lay drifting helplessly sideways, step after step, in toward the reef. It was noticeably quiet on board; we all crept in and out from cabin to bamboo deck, silent or laconic, and carried on with our jobs. Our serious faces showed that no one was in doubt as to what awaited us, and the absence of nervousness showed that we had all gradually acquired an unshakable confidence in the raft. If it had brought us across the sea, it would also manage to bring us ashore alive.

Inside the cabin there was a complete chaos of provision cartons and cargo, lashed fast. Torstein had barely found room for himself in the radio corner, where he had got the shortwave transmitter working. We were now over 4,000 sea miles from our old base at Callao,[8] where the Peruvian Naval War School had maintained regular contact with us, and still farther from Hal and Frank and the other radio amateurs in the United States. But, as chance willed, we had on the previous day got in touch with a capable radio "ham" who had a set on Rarotonga in the Cook Islands,[9] and the operators, quite contrary to all our usual practice, had arranged for an extra contact with him early in the morning. All the time we were drifting closer and closer in to the reef, Torstein was sitting tapping his key and calling Rarotonga.

Entries in the *Kon-Tiki's* log ran:

—8:15: We are slowly approaching land. We can now make out with the naked eye the separate palm trees inside on the starboard side.
—8:45: The wind has veered into a still more unfavorable quarter for us, so

---
8. Callao (kä yä' ô) *n.*: A seaport in western Peru.
9. Cook Islands: A group of islands of New Zealand, in the South Pacific.

Grammar in Action

Narrative writing relates an event or tells a story. Most fiction is narrative, but the narrative form can also be used to develop a topic in a work of nonfiction. Some subjects for works of nonfiction lend themselves particularly well to the narrative form. When a nonfiction work is about an event, as *Kon-Tiki* is, the logical form to use is the form of the narrative, or story. Look at this passage from the selection:

A few minutes later the anchor rushed overboard and caught hold of the bottom, so that the *Kon-Tiki* swung around and turned her stern inward toward the breakers. It held us for a few valuable minutes, while Thorstein sat hammering like mad on the key. He had got Rarotonga now. The breakers thundered in the air and the sea rose and fell furiously. All hands were at work on deck, and now Thorstein got his message through. He said we were drifting toward the Raroia reef. He asked Rarotonga to listen in on the same wave length every hour. If we were silent for more than thirty-six hours, Rarotonga must let the

we have no hope of getting clear. No nervousness on board, but hectic preparations on deck. There is something lying on the reef ahead of us which looks like the wreck of a sailing vessel, but it may be only a heap of driftwood.

—9:45: The wind is taking us straight toward the last island but one we see behind the reef. We can now see the whole coral reef clearly; here it is built up like a white and red speckled wall which barely sticks up out of the water as a belt in front of all the islands. All along the reef white foaming surf is flung up toward the sky. Bengt is just serving up a good hot meal, the last before the great action!

It *is* a wreck lying in there on the reef. We are so close now that we can see right across the shining lagoon behind the reef and see the outlines of other islands on the other side of the lagoon.

As this was written, the dull drone of the surf came near again; it came from the whole reef and filled the air like thrilling rolls of the drum, heralding the exciting last act of the *Kon-Tiki.*

—9:50: Very close now. Drifting along the reef. Only a hundred yards or so away. Torstein is talking to the man on Rarotonga. All clear. Must pack up log now. All in good spirits; it looks bad, *but we shall make it!*

A few minutes later the anchor rushed overboard and caught hold of the bottom, so that the *Kon-Tiki* swung around and turned her stern inward toward the breakers. It held us for a few valuable minutes, while Torstein sat hammering like mad on the key. He had got Rarotonga now. The breakers thundered in the air and the sea rose and fell furiously. All hands were at work on deck, and now Torstein got his message through. He said we were drifting toward the Raroia reef. He asked Rarotonga to listen in on the same wave length every hour. If we were silent for more than thirty-six hours, Rarotonga must let the Norwegian Embassy in Washington know. Torstein's last words were:

"O.K. Fifty yards left. Here we go. Good-by."

Then he closed down the station, Knut sealed up the papers, and both crawled out on deck as fast as they could to join the rest of us, for it was clear now that the anchor was giving way.

The swell grew heavier and heavier, with deep troughs between the waves, and we felt the raft being swung up and down, up and down, higher and higher.

Again the order was shouted: "Hold on, never mind about the cargo, hold on!"

We were now so near the waterfall inside that we no longer heard the steady continuous roar from all along the reef. We now heard only a separate boom each time the nearest breaker crashed down on the rocks.

All hands stood in readiness, each clinging fast to the rope he thought the most secure. Only Erik crept into the cabin at the last moment; there was one part of the program he had not yet carried out—he had not found his shoes!

No one stood aft, for it was there the shock from the reef would come. Nor were the two firm stays which ran from the masthead down to the stern safe. For if the mast fell they would be left hanging overboard, over the reef. Herman, Bengt, and Torstein had climbed up on some boxes which were lashed fast forward of the cabin wall, and, while Herman clung on to the guy ropes

from Kon-Tiki 433

8 Discussion What are some of the camera shots you would use if you were filming this episode of the story?

8

Writing Transparency Before students begin writing, you might work with them on **Transparencies for Writing,** Model 1: *Narrative Essay.* The model will suggest a form for their work.

Norwegian Embassy in Washington know. Torstein's final words were:

"O.K. Fifty yards left. Here we go. Good-bye"
Note that events are told as a narrative in chronological order, the order in which they actually happen. Use of the narrative form allows readers to experience the events as the crew of the raft does. At this point in the narrative, what is the effect of the description in the fourth sentence? What is the effect of Thorstein's message?

Student Activity 1. Find two other narrative passages from the selection and share them with a classmate. Discuss whether you think the narrative conveys the events as Heyerdahl and the crew experienced them.

Student Activity 2. Write a brief narrative about an event that you or someone you know experienced. Include in the narrative details that will help your readers experience the event. Share your composition with the class.

9 **Clarification** *Ramshackle* means "shoddily constructed or rickety."

10 **Discussion** What can you infer about the crew based on their behavior?

from the ridge of the roof, the other two held on to the ropes from the masthead by which the sail at other times was hauled up. Knut and I chose the stay running from the bow up to the masthead, for, if mast and cabin and everything else went overboard, we thought the rope from the bow would nevertheless remain lying inboard, as we were now head on to the seas.

When we realized that the seas had got hold of us, the anchor rope was cut and we were off. A sea rose straight up under us, and we felt the *Kon-Tiki* being lifted up in the air. The great moment had come; we were riding on the wave back at breathless speed, our ramshackle craft creaking and groaning as she quivered under us. The excitement made one's blood boil. I remember that, having no other inspiration, I waved my arm and bellowed "Hurrah!" at the top of my lungs; it afforded a certain relief and could do no harm anyway. The others certainly thought I had gone mad, but they all beamed and grinned enthusiastically. On we ran with the seas rushing in behind us; this was the *Kon-Tiki's* baptism of fire. All must and would go well.

But our elation was soon dampened. A new sea rose high up astern of us like a glittering, green glass wall. As we sank down it came rolling after us, and, in the same second in which I saw it high above me, I felt a violent blow and was submerged under floods of water. I felt the suction through my whole body, with such great power that I had to strain every single muscle in my frame and think of one thing only—hold on, hold on! I think that in such a desperate situation the arms will be torn off before the brain consents to let go, evident as the outcome is. Then I felt that the mountain of water was passing on and relaxing its devilish grip of my body. When the whole mountain had

rushed on, with an ear-splitting roaring and crashing, I saw Knut again hanging on beside me, doubled up into a ball. Seen from behind, the great sea was almost flat and gray. As it rushed on, it swept over the ridge of the cabin roof which projected from the water, and there hung the three others, pressed against the cabin roof as the water passed over them.

We were still afloat.

In an instant I renewed my hold, with arms and legs bent round the strong rope. Knut let himself down and with a tiger's leap joined the others on the boxes, where the cabin took the strain. I heard reassuring exclamations from them, but at the same time I saw a new green wall rise up and come towering toward us. I shouted a warning and made myself as small and hard as I could where I hung. In an instant the *Kon-Tiki* disappeared completely under the masses of water. The sea tugged and pulled with all the force it could bring to bear at the poor little bundles of human bodies. The second sea rushed over us, to be followed by a third like it.

Then I heard a triumphant shout from Knut, who was now hanging on to the rope ladder:

"Look at the raft—she's holding!"

After three seas only the double mast and the cabin had been knocked a bit crooked. Again we had a feeling of triumph over the elements, and the elation of victory gave us new strength.

Then I saw the next sea coming towering up, higher than all the rest, and again I bellowed a warning aft to the others as I climbed up the stay, as high as I could get in a hurry, and hung on fast. Then I myself disappeared sideways into the midst of the green wall which towered high over us. The others, who were farther aft and saw me dis-

Grammar in Action

A **semicolon** can be used to separate closely related independent clauses not joined by a coordinating conjunction. The semicolon is sometimes preferable to a period because it stresses the close relationship between two clauses and does not break the flow as a period would. You should not use a semicolon to connect clauses, however, unless they are closely related.

Notice Heyerdahl's effective use of the semicolon in the following sentences from *Kon-Tiki:*

The great moment had come; we were riding on the wave back at breathless speed, our ramshackle craft creaking and groaning as she quivered under us.

The vessel we knew from weeks and months at sea was no more; in a few seconds our pleasant world had become a shattered wreck.

In each of these passages, a period would have introduced too sharp a break, slowing the dramatic action.

appear first, estimated the height of the wall of water at twenty-five feet, while the foaming crest passed by fifteen feet above the part of the glassy wall into which I had vanished. Then the great wave reached them, and we had all one single thought—hold on, hold on, hold, hold, hold!

We must have hit the reef that time. I myself felt only the strain on the stay, which seemed to bend and slacken jerkily. But whether the bumps came from above or below I could not tell, hanging there. The whole submersion lasted only seconds, but it demanded more endurance than we usually have in our bodies. There is greater strength in the human mechanism than that of the muscles alone. I determined that, if I was to die, I would die in this position, like a knot on the stay. The sea thundered on, over and past, and as it roared by it revealed a hideous sight. The *Kon-Tiki* was wholly changed, as by the stroke of a magic wand. The vessel we knew from weeks and months at sea was no more; in a few seconds our pleasant world had become a shattered wreck.

I saw only one man on board besides myself. He lay pressed flat across the ridge of

11

11 Discussion What does this statement mean?

from *Kon-Tiki*   435

Student Activity 1. Find two other examples where Heyerdahl uses semicolons to connect related independent clauses. Explain why each sentence is effective.

Student Activity 2. Write a paragraph describing a dramatic action. Use at least two sentences with semicolons.

Electronic Handbook You might want students to review semicolons before completing the Grammar in Action activities. If students have access to the Language Master 6000, have them enter the access symbol *;* and press the GRAMMAR key to get information on use of the semicolon.

the cabin roof, face downward with his arms stretched out on both sides, while the cabin itself was crushed in, like a house of cards, toward the stern and toward the starboard side. The motionless figure was Herman. There was no other sign of life, while the hill of water thundered by, in across the reef. The hardwood mast on the starboard side was broken like a match, and the upper stump, in its fall, had smashed right through the cabin roof, so that the mast and all its gear slanted at a low angle over the reef on the starboard side. Astern, the steering block was twisted round lengthways and the crossbeam broken, while the steering oar was smashed to splinters. The splashboards at the bow were broken like cigar boxes, and the whole deck was torn up and pasted like wet paper against the forward wall of the cabin, along with boxes, cans, canvas, and other cargo. Bamboo sticks and rope ends stuck up everywhere, and the general effect was of complete chaos.

12   I felt cold fear run through my whole body. What was the good of my holding on? If I lost one single man here, in the run in, the whole thing would be ruined, and for the moment there was only one human figure to be seen after the last buffet. In that second Torstein's hunched-up form appeared outside the raft. He was hanging like a monkey in the ropes from the masthead and managed to get on to the logs again, where he crawled up on to the debris forward of the cabin. Herman, too, now turned his head and gave me a forced grin of encouragement, but did not move. I bellowed in the faint hope of locating the others and heard Bengt's calm voice call out that all hands were aboard. They were lying holding on to the ropes behind the tangled barricade which the tough plaiting from the bamboo deck had built up.

All this happened in the course of a few seconds, while the *Kon-Tiki* was being drawn out of the witches' caldron by the backwash, and a fresh sea came rolling over her. For the last time I bellowed "Hang on!" at the top of my lungs amid the uproar, and that was all I myself did; I hung on and disappeared in the masses of water which rushed over and past in those endless two or three seconds. That was enough for me. I saw the ends of the logs knocking and bumping against a sharp step in the coral reef without going over it. Then we were sucked out again. I also saw the two men who lay stretched out across the ridge of the cabin roof, but none of us smiled any longer. Behind the chaos of bamboo I heard a calm voice call out:

"This won't do."

I myself felt equally discouraged. As the masthead sank farther and farther out over the starboard side, I found myself hanging on to a slack line outside the raft. The next sea came. When it had gone by I was dead tired, and my only thought was to get up on to the logs and lie behind the barricade. When the backwash retreated, I saw for the first time the rugged red reef naked beneath us and perceived Torstein standing, bent double, on gleaming red corals, holding on to a bunch of rope ends from the mast. Knut, standing aft, was about to jump. I shouted that we must all keep on the logs, and Torstein, who had been washed overboard by the pressure of water, sprang up again like a cat.

Two or three more seas rolled over us with diminishing force, and what happened then I do not remember, except that water foamed in and out and I myself sank lower and lower toward the red reef over which we were being lifted in. Then only crests of foam full of salt spray came whirling in, and I was able to work my way in on to the raft, where we all made for the after end of the logs which was highest up on the reef.

At the same moment Knut crouched down and sprang up on to the reef with the line which lay clear astern. While the backwash was running out, he waded through the whirling water some thirty yards in and stood safely at the end of the line when the next sea foamed in toward him, died down, and ran back from the flat reef like a broad stream.

Then Erik came crawling out of the collapsed cabin, with his shoes on. If we had all done as he did, we should have got off cheaply. As the cabin had not been washed overboard but had been pressed down pretty flat under the canvas, Erik lay quietly stretched out among the cargo and heard the peals of thunder crashing above him while the collapsed bamboo walls curved downward. Bengt had had a slight concussion when the mast fell but had managed to crawl under the wrecked cabin alongside Erik. We should all of us have been lying there if we had realized in advance how firmly the countless lashings and plaited bamboo sheets would hang on to the main logs under the pressure of the water.

Erik was now standing ready on the logs aft, and when the sea retired he, too, jumped up on to the reef. It was Herman's turn next, and then Bengt's. Each time the raft was pushed a bit farther in, and, when Torstein's turn and my own came, the raft already lay so far in on the reef that there was no longer any ground for abandoning her. All hands began the work of salvage.

13

13 Reading Strategy Ask students to summarize the sequence of events from the moment the raft hits the reef.

Reader's Response What do you think was the most suspenseful part of this story? the most exciting? Why?

Thematic Response This selection tells about a life-threatening struggle between men and forces of nature. How do you think the struggle affected the men's feelings about the natural world?

The Voyage of the *Kon-Tiki*

NORTH AMERICA

Hawaii

PACIFIC OCEAN

EQUATOR

Galapagos Is.   ECUADOR

Marquesas Is.   Travel time: 101 days   PERU   SOUTH AMERICA

Samoa Is.   Callao Lima

Papeete, *Tahiti*   Puka Puka

AUSTRALIA

Easter Is.

NEW ZEALAND

| 0 | 750 | 1500 Miles |
| 0 | 750 | 1500 Kilometers |

from *Kon-Tiki*   437

ANSWERS TO RESPONDING TO THE SELECTION

Your Response

1. Accept all reactions as legitimate, whether they reflect courage or fear. Ask students to identify parts of the selection they think most affected their reactions.

Recalling

2. The raft was drifting toward a forty-to-fifty-mile expanse of reefs with coral and tumultuous waves.
3. After the anchor rope was cut, the *Kon-Tiki* was caught by the waves and tossed about. The men managed to hang on. The *Kon-Tiki* was shattered and carried in over the reef, and all the men survived.

Interpreting

4. Answers will differ, but should include the necessity of hanging on to the raft and a knowledge of their responsibilities so that order would be maintained.
5. Suggested Response: Heyerdahl demonstrates courage and determination.
6. Suggested Response: Heyerdahl creates an impression of the sea as an awesome and powerful adversary.

Applying

7. Answers will differ, but most students will realize that this goal suggests a courageous pursuit of adventure. It applies to Heyerdahl because he set out to prove his theory and nothing, not even powerful natural forces, deterred him.

Challenge Describe an act of courage that does *not* involve facing physical danger.

ANSWERS TO ANALYZING LITERATURE

1. Suggested Response: The description of the emergency preparations keeps you wondering what will happen.
2. Suggested Response: This explanation creates suspense by vividly describing the dangers that the crew faces.

RESPONDING TO THE SELECTION

Your Response

1. How might you have reacted to the events that occurred on the *Kon-Tiki*?

Recalling

2. Explain the danger toward which the raft was drifting.
3. Briefly summarize what happens after the men cut the anchor rope.

Interpreting

4. In your own words, explain the men's plan for surviving the shipwreck.
5. Identify two character traits that Heyerdahl demonstrates in this account.
6. Explain the overall impression that Heyerdahl creates of the sea.

Applying

7. One of the most famous adventurers is Odysseus, a Greek king who wandered the seas for ten years in search of home. (See Homer's *Odyssey*, page 644.) In his poem about Odysseus, Tennyson has him express his goal as "To strive, to seek, to find, and not to yield." Discuss the meaning of this goal. Then explain how it applies to Heyerdahl as well.

ANALYZING LITERATURE

Understanding Suspense

Suspense is the quality of a work that makes you wonder what will happen next. In this selection from *Kon-Tiki,* for example, Heyerdahl builds suspense by describing the crew's repeated "efforts to steer clear" of the reef. This account makes you think about the danger and wonder whether the men will escape it.

Explain how each of the following elements also adds to the suspense.

1. The description of the emergency "preparations for the end of the voyage. . . ."

2. The explanation of the reason for "Order number one . . . Hold on to the raft!"
3. The minute-by-minute entries from the ship's log.

CRITICAL THINKING AND READING

Understanding the Sequence of Events

To appreciate the suspense of a narrative, you must understand the sequence of events. Following are some of the key events from this selection. Arrange them so that they appear in the order in which they occurred.

1. The anchor rope is cut and the *Kon-Tiki* rides "at breathless speed."
2. The cabin of the raft is destroyed.
3. Sharks make it impossible to fix the centerboards under the raft.
4. They try to steer north of the reefs.

THINKING AND WRITING

Writing About Autobiography

Autobiographies often appear on bestseller lists. Do you read autobiographies? Do your friends? Why or why not? Jot down the ingredients that make an autobiography valuable and interesting. Then use this list to write an essay explaining why people enjoy reading autobiographies. When revising, make sure that you have provided adequate support for your opinion.

LEARNING OPTIONS

1. **Cross-curricular Connection.** Look at the map of Heyerdahl's voyage on page 437. Using the distance scale and the number of days the voyage lasted, calculate the average distance the *Kon-Tiki* traveled each day.
2. **Performance.** With a group of classmates, dramatize the episode in which the crew tries to steer clear of the reefs. Create sets, props, and sound effects for your performance.

3. Suggested Response: The minute-by-minute accounts give readers a sense of living through the dangerous situation. Readers can feel like crew members, wondering what will happen.

ANSWERS TO CRITICAL THINKING AND READING

The sentence order would be 4, 3, 1, 2.

THINKING AND WRITING

Writing Transparency Students often find it helpful to see a model of their writing assignment. Before students write, you may wish to show them Model 5: *Expository Essay* in the **Transparencies for Writing.**

Alternative Assessment You may vary the Thinking and Writing assignment as follows: Have students read the *Odyssey,* beginning on page 645, and then write an essay showing how Heyerdahl's adventure and the courage he shows are similar to Odysseus's experiences. Students should use observations from their reader's response journals for specifics to support their comparisons.

Types of Essays

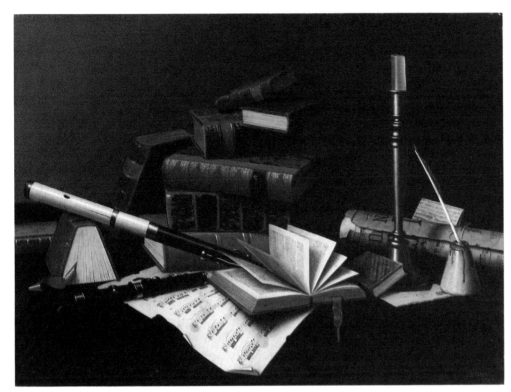

MUSIC AND LITERATURE, 1878
William Harnett
Albright-Knox Art Gallery,
Buffalo, New York

More About the Author William Least Heat Moon left a teaching position at a major university to set out on a journey through America. Ask students whether it would be worth leaving a good job to go on such a trip.

Literary Focus You might want to ask students to consider, as they read, how the narrative element creates suspense and interest. How would a descriptive or expository essay about Nameless differ from this piece of writing?

Prereading Focus In this selection the writer describes his visits with the residents of a tiny, out-of-the-way town who value an older, vanishing way of life. Before reading, ask students to share their knowledge of these older times by recalling stories told by family members portraying what life was like for their own families long ago. You may want to suggest that students bring in family artifacts that have been passed from one generation to another and that reflect some special aspect of life long ago. Have students give short histories of the items and explain why their families value them.

Vocabulary Have less advanced students work in pairs to test each other on the vocabulary words.

Electronic Handbook You might suggest that students use the Language Master 6000 to hear the pronunciation of *solve*.

GUIDE FOR READING

William Least Heat Moon

(1939–   ) is the Sioux pen name of William Trogdon, a Native American teacher and author. In 1978 he toured the country in his van, traveling back roads in search of the "real" America. The book he wrote about his trip is entitled *Blue Highways* because these smaller roads are colored blue on highway maps. One of the places he stopped was "Nameless, Tennessee," a tiny town he visited out of simple curiosity about its name.

Nameless, Tennessee

Narrative Essay

An **essay** is a work of nonfiction in which a writer expresses a personal view of a topic. In a **narrative essay,** a writer tells a story. The narrative essay "Nameless, Tennessee," for example, recounts William Least Heat Moon's visit to a town that is little more than "a dozen houses along the road." Within this narrative there are other stories as well. The residents of Nameless entertain the writer with their own tales, including a recital of "how Nameless come to be Nameless."

Focus

As you read the selection, you will notice that the stories told by the residents of Nameless, Tennessee, recall an older—now vanishing—United States. Have you heard older family members tell stories about how life has changed since they were young? What qualities of this former way of life are special to them? With a small group of classmates, share these stories and see if there are any similarities among them. Then notice the details in "Nameless, Tennessee" that indicate how life was different years ago.

Vocabulary

Knowing the following words will help you as you read "Nameless, Tennessee."

salves (savz) *n.*: Ointments that soothe or heal skin irritations, burns, or wounds (p. 442)

blight (blīt) *n.*: A plant disease (p. 442)

lore (lôr) *n.*: Knowledge of a particular subject (p. 443)

gaunt (gônt) *adj.*: Thin and bony (p. 443)

Objectives

1 To understand the narrative essay
2 To summarize an essay
3 To write a narrative essay
4 To express individual interests and abilities through optional activities

Support Material

Teaching Portfolio
Teacher Backup, p. 473
Grammar in Action Worksheet, *Recognizing Supporting Information,* p. 476
Usage and Mechanics Worksheet, p. 478
Vocabulary Check, p. 479
Analyzing Literature Worksheet, *Understanding the Narrative Essay,* p. 480

Critical Thinking and Reading Worksheet, *Summarizing an Essay,* p. 481
Selection Test, p. 482

Prentice Hall Literature Writing Studio

Nameless, Tennessee

from **Blue Highways**

William Least Heat Moon

Nameless, Tennessee, was a town of maybe ninety people if you pushed it, a dozen houses along the road, a couple of barns, same number of churches, a general merchandise store selling Fire Chief gasoline, and a community center with a lighted volleyball court. Behind the center was an open-roof, rusting metal privy with PAINT ME on the door. From the houses, the odor of coal smoke.

Next to a red tobacco barn stood the general merchandise with a poster of Senator Albert Gore, Jr., smiling from the window. I knocked. The door opened partway. A tall, thin man said, "Closed up. For good," and started to shut the door.

"Don't want to buy anything. Just a question for Mr. Thurmond Watts."

The man peered through the slight opening. He looked me over. "What question would that be?"

"If this is Nameless, Tennessee, could he tell me how it got that name?"

The man turned back into the store and called out, "Miss Ginny! Somebody here wants to know how Nameless come to be Nameless."

Miss Ginny edged to the door and looked me and my truck over. Clearly, she didn't approve. She said, "You know as well as I do, Thurmond. Don't keep him on the stoop in the damp to tell him." Miss Ginny, I found out, was Mrs. Virginia Watts, Thurmond's wife.

I stepped in and they both began telling the story, adding a detail here, the other correcting a fact there, both smiling at the foolishness of it all. It seems the hilltop settlement went for years without a name. Then one day the Post Office Department told the people if they wanted mail up on the mountain they would have to give the place a name you could properly address a letter to. The community met; there were only a handful, but they commenced debating. Some wanted patriotic names, some names from nature, one man recommended in all seriousness his own name. They couldn't agree, and they ran out of names to argue about. Finally, a fellow tired of the talk; he didn't like the mail he received anyway. "Forget the durn Post Office," he said. "This here's a nameless place if I ever seen one, so leave it be." And that's just what they did.

Watts pointed out the window. "We used to have signs on the road, but the Halloween boys keep tearin' them down.

"You think Nameless is a funny name," Miss Ginny said. "I see it plain in your eyes. Well, you take yourself up north a piece to Difficult or Defeated or Shake Rag. Now them are silly names."

Nameless, Tennessee, from *Blue Highways* 441

The old store, lighted only by three fifty-watt bulbs, smelled of coal oil and baking bread. In the middle of the rectangular room, where the oak floor sagged a little, stood an iron stove. To the right was a wooden table with an unfinished game of checkers and a stool made from an apple-tree stump. On shelves around the walls sat earthen jugs with corncob stoppers, a few canned goods, and some of the two thousand old clocks and clockworks Thurmond Watts owned. Only one was ticking; the others he just looked at. I asked how long he'd been in the store.

"Thirty-five years, but we closed the first day of the year. We're hopin' to sell it to a churchly couple. Upright people. No athians."[1]

---

1. athians: Atheists, people who do not believe in God.

442   *Nonfiction*

"Did you build this store?"

"I built this one, but it's the third general store on the ground. I fear it'll be the last. I take no pleasure in that. Once you could come in here for a gallon of paint, a pickle, a pair of shoes, and a can of corn."

"Or horehound candy," Miss Ginny said. "Or corsets and salves. We had cough syrups and all that for the body. In season, we'd buy and sell blackberries and walnuts and chestnuts, before the blight got them. And outside, Thurmond milled corn and sharpened plows. Even shoed a horse sometimes."

"We could fix up a horse or a man or a baby," Watts said.

"Thurmond, tell him we had a doctor on the ridge in them days."

"We had a doctor on the ridge in them days. As good as any doctor alivin'. He'd cut a crooked toenail or deliver a woman. Dead these last years."

Grammar in Action

Writers clarify their ideas and enliven their descriptions by using **supporting information.** The basic kinds of supporting information include examples, details, facts, reasons, and incidents.

The following passages illustrate William Least Heat Moon's use of this technique:

1. In the middle of the rectangular room, where the oak floor sagged a little, stood an iron stove. To the right was a wooden table with an unfinished game of checkers and a stool made from an apple tree stump. (details, facts)

2. "Once you could come in here for a gallon of paint, a pickle, a pair of shoes, and a can of corn." (example)

3. "I got some bad ham meat one day . . . and took to vomitin'. . . . I said to Thurmond, 'Thurmond unless you want shut of me, call the doctor.'" (incident)

Without specific details, William Least Heat Moon's passages may have sounded as general and uninteresting as this:

"I got some bad ham meat one day," Miss Ginny said, "and took to vomitin'. All day, all night. Hangin' on the drop edge of yonder. I said to Thurmond, 'Thurmond, unless you want shut of me, call the doctor.' "

"I studied on it," Watts said.

"You never did. You got him right now. He come over and put three drops of iodeen[2] in half a glass of well water. I drank it down and the vomitin' stopped with the last swallow. Would you think iodeen could do that?"

"He put Miss Ginny on one teaspoon of spirits of ammonia in well water for her nerves. Ain't nothin' works better for her to this day."

"Calms me like the hand of the Lord."

Hilda, the Wattses' daughter, came out of the backroom. "I remember him," she said. "I was just a baby. Y'all were talkin' to him, and he lifted me up on the counter and gave me a stick of Juicy Fruit and a piece of cheese."

"Knew the old medicines," Watts said. "Only drugstore he needed was a good kitchen cabinet. None of them antee-beeotics[3] that hit you worsen your ailment. Forgotten lore now, the old medicines, because they ain't profit in iodeen."

Miss Ginny started back to the side room where she and her sister Marilyn were taking apart a duck-down mattress to make bolsters. She stopped at the window for another look at Ghost Dancing.[4] "How do you sleep in that thing? Ain't you all cramped and cold?"

"How does the clam sleep in his shell?" Watts said in my defense.

"Thurmond, get the boy a piece of buttermilk pie afore he goes on."

---

2. iodeen: Iodine.
3. antee-beeotics: Antibiotics (an' ti bī ät' iks), medicines like penicillin.
4. Ghost Dancing: The name of the author's van.

"Hilda, get him some buttermilk pie." He looked at me. "You like good music?" I said I did. He cranked up an old Edison phonograph, the kind with the big morning-glory blossom for a speaker, and put on a wax cylinder. "This will be 'My Mother's Prayer,' " he said.

While I ate buttermilk pie, Watts served as disc jockey of Nameless, Tennessee. "Here's 'Mountain Rose.' " It was one of those moments that you know at the time will stay with you to the grave: the sweet pie, the gaunt man playing the old music, the coals in the stove glowing orange, the scent of kerosene and hot bread. "Here's 'Evening Rhapsody.' " The music was so heavily romantic we both laughed. I thought: It is for this I have come.

Feathered over and giggling, Miss Ginny stepped from the side room. She knew she was a sight. "Thurmond, give him some lunch. Still looks hungry."

Hilda pulled food off the woodstove in the backroom: home-butchered and canned whole-hog sausage, home-canned June apples, turnip greens, cole slaw, potatoes, stuffing, hot cornbread. All delicious.

Watts and Hilda sat and talked while I ate. "Wish you would join me."

"We've ate," Watts said. "Cain't beat a woodstove for flavorful cookin'."

He told me he was raised in a one-hundred-fifty-year-old cabin still standing in one of the hollows. "How many's left," he said, "that grew up in a log cabin? I ain't the last surely, but I must be climbin' on the list."

Hilda cleared the table. "You Watts ladies know how to cook."

"She's in nursin' school at Tennessee Tech. I went over for one of them football games last year there at Coevul." To say *Cookeville*, you let the word collapse in upon itself so that it comes out "Coevul."

"Do you like football?" I asked.

Nameless, Tennessee, from *Blue Highways*   443

4 **Discussion** What effect does the writer's visit seem to be having on the Watts family?

5 **Critical Thinking and Reading** In your own words, explain the purpose of the writer's visit.

Multicultural Focus Ask students if they know of any towns with funny or unusual names, and discuss their responses. You might want to write the following names of actual towns on the chalkboard and ask students how they might have gotten their names: Paint, Pennsylvania; Hungry Horse, Montana; Recluse, Wyoming; Meddybemps, Maine.

Point out that every country undoubtedly has its equivalent of Nameless, Tennessee. Make an ongoing bulletin board display of unusual names of towns from all over the world. Encourage students to collect names, remembering any names they hear on television or read in the newspaper. They might also interview friends, neighbors, or relatives.

1. The old store was rather primitive and plain.
2. They used to carry a wide variety of things.
3. "One day I got sick and needed a doctor."

The use of specific supporting detail is a sign of good writing.

Student Activity 1. Find four more pieces of supporting information in this selection. Decide whether each is an example, fact, detail, reason, incident, or a combination of these types of support.

Student Activity 2. Write two sentences that lack supporting information. Then expand each with examples, facts, details, reasons, incidents, or a combination of specifics.

6 **Discussion** Which words help you to visualize this book?

7 **Discussion** Why do you think Watts wants to take the writer downstairs?

8 **Critical Thinking and Reading** The author is allowing Watts to speak for himself here. How does this device of Moon's allow the reader to "know" Watts better?

Reader's Response If you were to write a narrative essay about an unusual place, what would it be? Why?

Thematic Response Have students discuss how the town in the selection has shaped the residents' lives. Then have them discuss how the place where they live has shaped their own lives up to this point.

"Don't know. I was so high up in that stadium, I never opened my eyes."

Watts went to the back and returned with a fat spiral notebook that he set on the table. His expression had changed. "Miss Ginny's *Deathbook.*"

The thing startled me. Was it something I was supposed to sign? He opened it but said nothing. There were scads of names written in a tidy hand over pages incised to crinkliness by a ballpoint. Chronologically, the names had piled up: wives, grandparents, a stillborn infant, relatives, friends close and distant. Names, names. After each, the date of *the* unknown finally known and transcribed. The last entry bore yesterday's date.

"She's wrote out twenty years' worth. Ever day she listens to the hospital report on the radio and puts the names in. Folks come by to check a date. Or they just turn through the books. Read them like a scrapbook."

Hilda said, "Like Saint Peter at the gates inscribin' the names."

Watts took my arm. "Come along." He led me to the fruit cellar under the store. As we went down, he said, "Always take a newborn baby upstairs afore you take him downstairs, otherwise you'll incline him downwards."

The cellar was dry and full of cobwebs and jar after jar of home-canned food, the bottles organized as a shopkeeper would: sausage, pumpkin, sweet pickles, tomatoes, corn relish, blackberries, peppers, squash, jellies. He held a hand out toward the dusty bottles. "Our tomorrows."

Upstairs again, he said, "Hope to sell the store to the right folk. I see now, though, it'll be somebody offen the ridge. I've studied on it, and maybe it's the end of our place." He stirred the coals. "This store could give a comfortable livin', but not likely get you rich. But just gettin' by is dice rollin' to people nowadays. I never did see my day guaranteed."

When it was time to go, Watts said, "If you find anyone along your way wants a good store—on the road to Cordell Hull Lake—tell them about us."

I said I would. Miss Ginny and Hilda and Marilyn came out to say goodbye. It was cold and drizzling again. "Weather to give a man the weary dismals," Watts grumbled. "Where you headed from here?"

"I don't know."

"Cain't get lost then."

Miss Ginny looked again at my rig. It had worried her from the first as it had my mother. "I hope you don't get yourself kilt in that durn thing gallivantin' around the country."

"Come back when the hills dry off," Watts said. "We'll go lookin' for some of them round rocks all sparkly inside."

I thought a moment. "Geodes?"

"Them's the ones. The county's properly full of them."

Closure and Extension

ANSWERS TO RESPONDING TO THE SELECTION
Your Response
1. Encourage students who give positive responses to also consider some of the things they would have to give up if they lived in Nameless. Encourage students who give negative responses to also consider some of the things they might gain.

Recalling
2. He wants to know how the town got its name.
3. The Post Office Department requested that the people name their community so that letters could be properly addressed and delivered. People met and debated about a name but could not agree on one. Finally, one person said they should forget the Post Office since it was a nameless place anyway. The people left it that way.
4. In an earlier time, people were more inclined to trust home remedies and indeed preferred them to manufactured medicines.
5. Mr. Watts plays old songs on an old-fashioned record player. He also shows Moon the rows and rows of canned goods in his cellar.

Interpreting
6. Suggested Response: He is able to meet long-time residents of the town, talk with them, and gain insight into an older way of life.
7. Suggested Response: His interest in the town reveals his curiosity. His behavior toward the Watts family shows that he is respectful and capable of warmth.

RESPONDING TO THE SELECTION

Your Response

1. Would you like to live in Nameless, Tennessee? Why or why not?

Recalling

2. What question brings the writer to the little town of Nameless, Tennessee?
3. Recount the story that Mr. and Mrs. Watts tell to answer this question.
4. How does the story about the doctor show the customs of an older time?
5. Find two ways other than storytelling in which Mr. Watts reveals his past.

Interpreting

6. Why does the writer find his visit to this tiny town so satisfying?
7. What clues to the writer's personality can you find in this essay?

Applying

8. What features of a past way of life would you like to preserve or imitate? Explain.

ANALYZING LITERATURE

Understanding the Narrative Essay

An **essay** is a work of nonfiction in which a writer expresses a personal view of a topic. In a **narrative essay,** a writer tells a story. "Nameless, Tennessee" is the story of a writer's visit to a small town for which no one could agree on a name.

1. Why is telling a story an effective way of involving readers in this essay?
2. What do the stories told by the people in the town add to the writer's account?

CRITICAL THINKING AND READING

Summarizing an Essay

Summarizing means briefly stating the main points and key details of a work in your own words. A summary of a narrative essay would in-clude the important events, the narrator's principal thoughts or comments, and a few essential descriptions of people and places. For example, the following is a summary of the first five paragraphs of "Nameless, Tennessee": The writer visits the general store in Nameless, Tennessee, a town that is not much more than a few houses. He tells a tall, thin man who comes to the door that he wants to ask Thurmond Watts how the town got its name.

1. Summarize the next five paragraphs.
2. Review your summary to make sure it captures the main points.

THINKING AND WRITING

Writing a Narrative Essay

Recall a time when your curiosity led you to visit a person or a place. Write what you wanted to find out, and list the events that occurred during your visit. Then, using these notes, write a narrative essay like "Nameless, Tennessee" about this experience. In revising your essay, make sure that you have explained whether your curiosity about this person or place was satisfied. Also, you may want to add details—like the description of the store in "Nameless, Tennessee"—to make your account more vivid. When you are finished, share your essay with your classmates.

LEARNING OPTIONS

1. **Language.** Dialect is a form of spoken language used in a certain region. William Least Heat Moon conveys the flavor of rural Tennessee by including the dialect the Wattses use. Make a dictionary of the expressions used in this selection that are forms of dialect. Use the proper dictionary form for entries.
2. **Art.** Create artwork representing the Wattses' collection of clocks and other items on the shelves of their store. Use the details in the story as a guide. You might make drawings, models, or collages.

Nameless, Tennessee, from *Blue Highways* 445

Preparation

More About the Author Rudolfo Anaya (a nī′ ə) says that "Writing novels seems to be the medium which allows me to bring together all the questions I ask about life, the characters I have met, the haunting beauty of the people and the land."

Although this selection is an essay and not a novel, ask students to consider how the people Anaya has met could influence the questions he asks about life.

Literary Focus Anaya was very close to his grandfather. Lead your students to discuss how such a close, personal tie could lead someone to reflect about old people and the treatment of them.

Prereading Focus Students may also consider stories or movies in which grandparents are main characters. Ask why having an older person as a main character was important to the story. Students may use this character for their lists.

Vocabulary Some of these words may be difficult for students. You might use the Vocabulary Check as a practice sheet.

Electronic Handbook You may suggest that students use the Language Master 6000 to hear how *animate* is pronounced differently when it is used as a verb and when it is used as an adjective.

Rudolfo Anaya

(1937–   ) was born in Pastura, New Mexico, and his writing reflects his Mexican American heritage. Anaya says: "For those of us who listen to the Earth, and to the old legends and the myths of the people, the whispers of the blood draw us to our past." It is the past that concerns Anaya in much of his writing. His first novel, *Bless Me, Ultima* (1972), won national acclaim for its moving depiction of the culture and history of New Mexico. In the years since, Anaya has published *The Heart of Aztlan* (1976) and *Tortuga* (1979), as well as many short stories and articles. His essay "A Celebration of Grandfathers" reflects on the "old ones" he remembers from his childhood.

A Celebration of Grandfathers

Reflective Essay

Reading a **reflective essay** is like listening to a person talk about something that he or she finds interesting and has thought about deeply. As the author explores the many facets of a topic, he or she often reveals personal feelings and experiences. The pace of the essay is usually unhurried, and the reader is not urged to action. The purpose of the reflective essay is to present an idea or issue so that the reader can share the author's personal perspective.

Focus

What are grandfathers like? That question has as many answers as there are grandfathers. Each grandfather is unique. Make a list of the personality traits of a grandfather you know—your own or someone else's. Then write briefly describing this grandfather. Include his appearance, his occupation, and the qualities that make him an interesting person. You might also include examples of his actions that illustrate your points. As you read "A Celebration of Grandfathers," compare the grandfather you have described to the grandfathers the author describes in the essay.

Vocabulary

Knowing the following words will help you as you read "A Celebration of Grandfathers."

nurturing (nʉr′ chər iŋ) *n.*: The act or process of raising or guiding (p. 447)

animate (an′ i mit) *adj.*: Having life, particularly animal life (p. 447)

perplexes (pʉr′ pleks′ iz) *v.*: Confuses or makes hard to understand (p. 447)

authentic (ô then′ tik) *adj.*: Genuine; of true value (p. 448)

permeate (pʉr′ mē āt) *v.*: To spread or flow throughout (p. 448)

epiphany (ē pif′ ə nē) *n.*: A moment of sudden understanding (p. 448)

pungent (pun′ jənt) *adj.*: Producing a sharp sensation of smell (p. 450)

romanticize (rō man′ tə sīz) *v.*: To treat or regard in an ideal way rather than a realistic one (p. 451)

Objectives

1 To understand the reflective essay
2 To understand an author's tone
3 To write a reflective essay
4 To express individual interests and abilities through optional activities

Support Material

Teaching Portfolio
Art Transparency 3: *Arizona Corral,* by Millard Sheets
Teacher Backup, p. 485
Grammar in Action Worksheet, *Using Commas to Separate Sentence Parts,* p. 489
Usage and Mechanics Worksheet, p. 491
Vocabulary Check, p. 492

Analyzing Literature Worksheet, *Understanding the Reflective Essay,* p. 493
Critical Thinking and Reading Worksheet, *Understanding an Author's Tone,* p. 494
Selection Test, p. 495

Audio Prose Library Rudolfo Anaya: Interview

Prentice Hall Literature Writing Studio

A Celebration of Grandfathers

Rudolfo A. Anaya

"Buenos días le de Dios, abuelo."[1] God give you a good day, grandfather. This is how I was taught as a child to greet my grandfather, or any grown person. It was a greeting of respect, a cultural value to be passed on from generation to generation, this respect for the old ones.

The old people I remember from my childhood were strong in their beliefs, and as we lived daily with them we learned a wise path of life to follow. They had something important to share with the young, and when they spoke the young listened. These old abuelos and abuelitas[2] had worked the earth all their lives, and so they knew the value of nurturing, they knew the sensitivity of the earth. The daily struggle called for cooperation, and so every person contributed to the social fabric, and each person was respected for his contribution.

The old ones had looked deep into the web that connects all animate and inanimate forms of life, and they recognized the great design of the creation.

These ancianos[3] from the cultures of the Río Grande, living side by side, sharing, growing together, they knew the rhythms and cycles of time, from the preparation of the earth in the spring to the digging of the acequias[4] that brought the water to the dance of harvest in the fall. They shared good times and hard times. They helped each other through the epidemics and the personal tragedies, and they shared what little they had when the hot winds burned the land and no rain came. They learned that to survive one had to share in the process of life.

Hard workers all, they tilled the earth and farmed, ran the herds and spun wool, and carved their saints and their kachinas[5] from cottonwood late in the winter nights. All worked with a deep faith which perplexes the modern mind.

Their faith shone in their eyes; it was in the strength of their grip, in the creases time wove into their faces. When they spoke, they spoke plainly and with few words, and they meant what they said. When they prayed, they went straight to the source of life. When there were good times, they knew how to dance in celebration and how to prepare the foods of the fiestas.[6] All this they passed on to

---

1. **Buenos días le de Dios, abuelo** (bwe'nôs dē'äs lā dä dē'ôs ä bwä'lō)
2. **abuelitas** (a bwä lē'täs): Grandmothers.
3. *ancianos* (än cē ä'nōs): Old people; ancestors.

4. **acequias** (ä sā'kē əs): Irrigation ditches.
5. **kachinas** (kə chē'nəz): Small wooden dolls, representing the spirit of an ancestor or a god.
6. **fiestas** (fē es'təs): Celebrations; feasts.

A Celebration of Grandfathers 447

Presentation

Motivation/Prior Knowledge
Ask for volunteers to tell stories about their grandparents. Discuss what it is in stories about our grandparents that we find so appealing.

Purpose-Setting Question
What was it about his grandfather that prompted Anaya to write this essay?

Master Teacher Note Use Fine Art Transparency 3, *Arizona Corral,* to give students a sense of the southwestern terrain. It suggests the area in which the *ancianos* Anaya writes about lived and worked. Ask students to consider how such a terrain would affect the lives of farmers and ranchers.

1 **Discussion** What does this opening indicate about the writer's background?

2 **Literary Focus: Reflection** What facts about the author's past are revealed in this paragraph? Why do you think he mentions them at the beginning of his essay?

3 **Discussion** What is the web that Anaya refers to?

4 **Evaluation** Do you agree with the author's conclusion?

5 **Reading Strategy** In this sentence, Anaya sets up a tension between the old ones and "the modern mind." As you read, see if he develops this tension.

Thematic Focus A reflective essay may frequently be one of appreciation—of a person, a place, a situation, or anything else. Anaya shows appreciation for his grandfather and all old people. Ask students to think about someone they appreciate.

Making Connections You may wish to use this selection in conjunction with "Blues Ain't No Mockin Bird," p. 91, or "To Da-

Duh, In Memoriam," p. 139. In both these stories, grandparents figure as important characters. You might also wish to have students read *Bless Me, Ultima* in the Prentice Hall Literature Multicultural Library.

Alternate Assessment To promote active reading, have your students keep a reader's response journal as they read this

essay. Ask them to focus their observations on the details that reveal the values of the grandfathers. Encourage them to respond personally to what is lost by modern society's celebration of youth at the expense of age. Their observations and comments will enable you to assess their comprehension and appreciation of this essay.

6 Discussion Is the author implying that this doesn't happen any more? Explain.

7 Reader's Response What, in your opinion, is an "authentic life"?

8 Reading Strategy This transition marks the beginning of the second section of the essay. Summarize the first section. From the first sentence of this paragraph, what do you predict the author will discuss in this section?

9 Critical Thinking and Reading How strong would something have to be to make time stand still? What does this imply about the author's attitude toward his subject?

10 Enrichment Tell students that in *Bless Me, Ultima,* the young Antonio grapples with Spanish, Indian, and Anglo traditions to forge his own identity. His tutor, Ultima, shows him that "individual choice is the way of knowledge."

11 Discussion What is the blue bowl?

12 Reading Strategy This transition marks the beginning of the third section of the essay. From this paragraph, what do you predict the author will discuss in this section?

13 Discussion How is it possible for someone who is five feet tall to be a giant?

14 Reader's Response What place is magical for you? Why?

the young, so that a new generation would know what they had known, so the string of life would not be broken.

Today we would say that the old abuelitos lived authentic lives.

Newcomers to New Mexico often say that time seems to move slowly here. I think they mean they have come in contact with the inner strength of the people, a strength so solid it causes time itself to pause. Think of it. Think of the high, northern New Mexico villages, or the lonely ranches on the open llano.[7] Think of the Indian pueblo[8] which lies as solid as rock in the face of time. Remember the old people whose eyes seem like windows that peer into a distant past that makes absurdity of our contemporary world. That is what one feels when one encounters the old ones and their land, a pausing of time.

We have all felt time stand still. We have all been in the presence of power, the knowledge of the old ones, the majestic peace of a mountain stream or an aspen grove or red buttes rising into blue sky. We have all felt the light of dusk permeate the earth and cause time to pause in its flow.

I felt this when first touched by the spirit of Ultima, the old *curandera*[9] who appears in my first novel, *Bless Me, Ultima.* This is how the young Antonio describes what he feels:

> When she came the beauty of the llano unfolded before my eyes, and the gurgling waters of the river sang to the hum of the turning earth. The magical time of childhood stood still, and the pulse of the living earth pressed its mystery into my living blood. She took my hand, and the silent, magic powers she possessed made beauty from the raw, sun-baked llano, the green river valley, and the blue bowl which was the white sun's home. My bare feet felt the throbbing earth, and my body trembled with excitement. Time stood still . . .

At other times, in other places, when I have been privileged to be with the old ones, to learn, I have felt this inner reserve of strength upon which they draw. I have been held motionless and speechless by the power of curanderas. I have felt the same power when I hunted with Cruz, high on the Taos[10] mountain, where it was more than the incredible beauty of the mountain bathed in morning light, more than the shining of the quivering aspen, but a connection with life, as if a shining strand of light connected the particular and the cosmic. That feeling is an epiphany of time, a standing still of time.

But not all of our old ones are curanderos or hunters on the mountain. My grandfather was a plain man, a farmer from Puerto de Luna[11] on the Pecos River. He was probably a descendent of those people who spilled over the mountain from Taos, following the Pecos River in search of farmland. There in that river valley he settled and raised a large family.

Bearded and walrus-mustached, he stood five feet tall, but to me as a child he was a giant. I remember him most for his silence. In the summers my parents sent me to live with him on his farm, for I was to learn the ways of a farmer. My uncles also lived in that valley, the valley called Puerto de Luna, there where only the flow of the river and the whispering of the wind marked time. For me it was a magical place.

I remember once, while out hoeing the fields, I came upon an anthill, and before I

---

7. llano (yä'nō): Plain.
8. pueblo (pweb'lō): Village or town.
9. *curandera* (kōō'rän dä' rä): Medicine woman.

10. Taos (tä'ōs)
11. Puerto de Luna (pwer' tō dä lōō'nə): Port of the Moon, the name of a town.

Grammar in Action

One reason for Anaya's clarity of ideas is his use of commas. **Commas** are used to separate certain basic elements in sentences. Three of the most common uses of the comma are to separate independent clauses in a compound sentence, to separate items in a series, and to separate coordinate adjectives. These three uses of commas can be found in this sentence from "A Celebration of Grandfathers."

"She took my hand, and the silent, magic powers she possessed made beauty from the raw, sun-baked llano, the green river valley, and the blue bowl which was the white sun's home."

The first comma separates two independent clauses that have been joined by the coordinating conjunction *and.* The second and third commas separate coordinate adjectives, or adjectives of equal rank: *silent* and *magic* modify *powers; raw* and *sun-baked* modify *llano.* The last two commas separate nouns in a series: the llano, the valley, and the bowl.

Student Activity 1. The following sentences are from the essay. Here, however, some of the commas have been left out. Tell

knew it I was badly bitten. After he had covered my welts with the cool mud from the irrigation ditch, my grandfather calmly said: "Know where you stand." That is the way he spoke, in short phrases, to the point.

One very dry summer, the river dried to a trickle, there was no water for the fields. The young plants withered and died. In my sadness and with the impulses of youth I said, "I wish it would rain!" My grandfather touched me, looked up in the sky and whispered, "Pray for rain." In his language there was a difference. He felt connected to the cycles that brought the rain or kept it from us. His prayer was a meaningful action, because he was a participant with the forces that filled our world, he was not a bystander.

A young man died at the village one summer. A very tragic death. He was dragged by his horse. When he was found I cried, for the boy was my friend. I did not understand why death had come to one so young. My grandfather took me aside and said: "Think of the death of the trees and the fields in the fall.

FARM WORKER
Armando Hinojosa
Courtesy of DagenBela Graphics, Inc.

A Celebration of Grandfathers   449

15 Discussion What does the grandfather mean about the difference between wishing and praying?

16 Evaluation According to the author, what is wrong with being a bystander?

Humanities Note

Fine Art, *Farm Worker,* by Armando Hinojosa. Hinojosa is an award-winning painter and sculptor. His many honors include Official State Artist of Texas, 1982–1983; Artist of the Year Award, Los Angeles; and Gold Medal for Watercolor, Texas Ranger Hall of Fame. Hinojosa's monumental outdoor sculptures appear throughout Texas. In his paintings, he has labored to create works whose minute details and respect for subject reflect the richness of our environment. Have students notice the details in this work. Ask the following:

1. What is your reaction to this painting? Does it fit the tone of the essay? Do you think the artist respects his subject? Explain.
2. Would you say that the man in the painting has lived an "authentic life"? Do you detect an inner reserve of strength? Explain.

where commas should be placed. Give the reason for each comma.

1. The magical time of childhood stood still and the pulse of the living earth pressed its mystery into my living blood.
2. *Paciencia,* how soothing a word coming from this old man who could still sling hundred-pound bags over his shoulder chop wood for hours on end and hitch up his own horses and ride to town and back in one day.
3. He could mount a wild horse and break it and he could ride as far as any man.
4. Family neighbors and friends gathered: they all agreed he had led a rich life.
5. It is only the healthy pink-cheeked outgoing older persons we are shown in the media.

Student Activity 2. Write a sentence modeled on each sentence in Activity 1. Use commas correctly.

Electronic Handbook You may want students to review commas before completing the Grammar in Action activities. If students have access to the Language Master 6000, have them enter , (the comma symbol on the keyboard) and press GRAMMAR to review the use of the comma.

17 Reading Strategy Summarize the examples of the grandfather's few words. Why might his economy of speech have been important to his grandson?

18 Reader's Response How would you characterize education today?

19 Discussion *Venerable* means "worthy of respect by virtue of age." What can you conclude about a society that accords respect to people simply because they are old?

20 Discussion What is the effect of these sensory details?

21 Reading Strategy This paragraph marks the next transition in the essay. What do you predict the author will discuss in this section?

22 Discussion What final transformation does the author refer to?

23 Reader's Response Was the grandfather's advice good?

24 Connection Is the author speaking only of agricultural societies like the one his grandfather lived in, or does he mean something else? How do you know?

25 Critical Thinking and Reading What is the mood of this passage?

The leaves fall, and everything rests, as if dead. But they bloom again in the spring. Death is only this small transformation in life."

These are the things I remember, these fleeting images, few words.

I remember him driving his horse-drawn wagon into Santa Rosa in the fall when he brought his harvest produce to sell in the town. What a tower of strength seemed to come in that small man huddled on the seat of the giant wagon. One click of his tongue and the horses obeyed, stopped or turned as he wished. He never raised his whip. How unlike today when so much teaching is done with loud words and threatening hands.

I would run to greet the wagon, and the wagon would stop. "Buenos días le de Dios, abuelo," I would say. This was the prescribed greeting of esteem and respect. Only after the greeting was given could we approach these venerable old people. "Buenos días le de Dios, mi hijo,"[12] he would answer and smile, and then I could jump up on the wagon and sit at his side. Then I, too, became a king as I rode next to the old man who smelled of earth and sweat and the other deep aromas from the orchards and fields of Puerto de Luna.

We were all sons and daughters to him. But today the sons and daughters are breaking with the past, putting aside los abuelitos. The old values are threatened, and threatened most where it comes to these relationships with the old people. If we don't take the time to watch and feel the years of their final transformation, a part of our humanity will be lessened.

I grew up speaking Spanish, and oh! how difficult it was to learn English. Sometimes I would give up and cry out that I couldn't learn. Then he would say, "Ten paciencia."[13]

---

12. mi hijo (mē ē'hō): My son.
13. Ten paciencia (ten pä sēn'sē ä)

Have patience. *Paciencia,* a word with the strength of centuries, a word that said that someday we would overcome. *Paciencia,* how soothing a word coming from this old man who could still sling hundred-pound bags over his shoulder, chop wood for hours on end, and hitch up his own horses and ride to town and back in one day.

"You have to learn the language of the Americanos,"[14] he said. "Me, I will live my last days in my valley. You will live in a new time, the time of the gringos."[15]

A new time did come, a new time is here. How will we form it so it is fruitful? We need to know where we stand. We need to speak softly and respect others, and to share what we have. We need to pray not for material gain, but for rain for the fields, for the sun to nurture growth, for nights in which we can sleep in peace, and for a harvest in which everyone can share. Simple lessons from a simple man. These lessons he learned from his past which was deep and strong as the currents of the river of life, a life which could be stronger than death.

He was a man; he died. Not in his valley, but nevertheless cared for by his sons and daughters and flocks of grandchildren. At the end, I would enter his room which carried the smell of medications and Vicks, the faint pungent odor of urine, and cigarette smoke. Gone were the aroma of the fields, the strength of his young manhood. Gone also was his patience in the face of crippling old age. Small things bothered him; he shouted or turned sour when his expectations were not met. It was because he could not care for himself, because he was returning to that state of childhood, and all those wishes and desires were now wrapped in a crumbling old body.

---

14. Americanos (ä mer'ē kä'nōs): Americans.
15. gringos (griŋ'gōs): Foreigners, North Americans.

Commentary: Quinto Sol

Rudolfo Anaya belonged to a group of writers associated with Quinto Sol (kēn' tō säl) Publications, which began publishing in 1967. These writers were determined to remain faithful to both their Mexican and Indian heritages. *The Columbia History of the United States* says, "The Quinto Sol writers were experimenters, using multiple narrators, combining poetry and prose in single works, and obliterating boundaries between fiction and nonfiction. Such innovations helped to generate new vitality and excitement among Mexican-American writers. . . ."

"By the mid-1970's, when the Quinto Sol house began to wane, its major objectives had been achieved. It had nurtured a group of writers who helped to determine the literary agenda for years to come . . . Anaya . . . demonstrates the inexhaustible vitality of oral tradition—Spanish, Indian, and Anglo—as a basis of elaborate, sophisticated fictions."

Ask students to look for evidence of both Mexican and Indian cultures in Anaya's essay.

DON NEMESIO, 1977
Esperanza Martínez

"Ten paciencia," I once said to him, and he smiled. "I didn't know I would grow this old," he said. "Now, I can't even roll my own cigarettes." I rolled a cigarette for him, placed it in his mouth and lit it. I asked him why he smoked, the doctor had said it was bad for him. "I like to see the smoke rise," he said. He would smoke and doze, and his quilt was spotted with little burns where the cigarettes dropped. One of us had to sit and watch to make sure a fire didn't start.

I would sit and look at him and remember what was said of him when he was a young man. He could mount a wild horse and break it, and he could ride as far as any man. He could dance all night at a dance, then work the acequia the following day. He helped neighbors, they helped him. He married, raised children. Small legends, the kind that make up everyman's life.

He was 94 when he died. Family, neighbors, and friends gathered; they all agreed he had led a rich life. I remembered the last years, the years he spent in bed. And as I remember now, I am reminded that it is too easy to romanticize old age. Sometimes we forget the pain of the transformation into old age, we forget the natural breaking down of the body. Not all go gentle into the last years, some go crying and cursing, forgetting the names of those they loved the most, withdrawing into an internal anguish few of us can know. May we be granted the patience and care to deal with our ancianos.

A Celebration of Grandfathers 451

Humanities Note

Fine art, *Don Nemesio*, 1977, by Esperanza Martinez. Martinez credits her parents for instilling in her a love of their Mexican heritage. She began art training at seven years of age, and at thirteen painted a mural on the wall of her school. The school has since been rebuilt, but the mural stands as a tribute to her talent.

Martinez attended the Academia de San Carlos in Mexico City. Today she lives in a suburb of Los Angeles. She has traveled throughout Mexico, visiting cities and villages. Martinez specializes in sensitive portrayal of the Indo-Hispanic. "I could not live without painting," she says, ". . . Es mi vida (It's my life)."

Ask the following:
1. What words from the essay might describe this painting?
2. How can stopping to reflect on our lives give us strength? What else can we learn from *ancianos* like this one?

26 Critical Thinking and Reading Why do you think the author put this touch of humor immediately after the preceding paragraph?

27 Literary Focus: Essay In this essay, Anaya usually employs long sentences. Here, in the middle of his reverie about his grandfather's young life, he switches to shorter sentences. Have students discuss the technique he is using to build to his first sentence in the next paragraph.

28 Connection What small legends make up the life of someone you respect?

29 Discussion What does the phrase "romanticize old age" mean?

30 Enrichment Tell students that this is an allusion to Dylan Thomas's famous lines: "Do not go gentle into that good night,/Old age should burn and rave at close of day;/Rage, rage against the dying of the light."

Multicultural Focus Grandfathers—and grandmothers—are highly respected family members not only in Hispanic cultures, as can be seen in this essay, but in other cultures as well. The older members of a traditional Chinese family are considered wise; their advice is sought on important family matters. Grandfathers are often given the best chair in the house when visiting and can expect the largest portion of food at dinner. Among the Hopi people of the southwestern United States, the oldest woman is the head of the family because women are at the center of Hopi family life.

Discuss with students what role their own grandparents play in their family life. Does the emphasis that is placed on youth in the United States distract from the respect and admiration for older people?

31 Evaluation Do you agree with the author? Explain.

32 Reader's Response Do you know an old person who is young at heart? Describe him or her. In Anaya's terms, is this person real or Hollywood?

33 Critical Thinking and Reading What does the neglected adobe symbolize?

34 Discussion The author asks a question but does not answer it. Instead, he says the answers are not simple. How would you answer the question for him?

35 Reading Strategy Compare the ending of this essay with the first sentence. What was the author's purpose in doing this?

Reader's Response Who is the most memorable person you know? What qualities make him or her memorable?

Thematic Response There are more old people in our society than ever before, and their numbers are growing. Are they appreciated? Do you think the increase in the number of old people will change the way they are viewed and valued? Explain.

ESL Teaching Strategy Tell students that although Anaya writes in English, he was raised in a Spanish-speaking community. He read a lot when he was growing up and learned to translate Spanish thoughts into English phrases.

If you have Spanish-speaking students in your class, ask them to teach the rest of the class the pronunciations of the Spanish words and expressions.

For some time we haven't looked at these changes and needs of the old ones. The American image created by the mass media is an image of youth, not of old age. It is the beautiful and the young who are praised in this society. If analyzed carefully, we see that same damaging thought has crept into the way society views the old. In response to the old, the mass media have just created old people who act like the young. It is only the healthy, pink-cheeked, outgoing, older persons we are shown in the media. And they are always selling something, as if an entire generation of old people were salesmen in their lives. Commercials show very lively old men, who must always be in excellent health according to the new myth, selling insurance policies or real estate as they are out golfing; older women selling coffee or toilet paper to those just married. That image does not illustrate the real life of the old ones.

Real life takes into account the natural cycle of growth and change. My grandfather pointed to the leaves falling from the tree. So time brings with its transformation the often painful, wearing-down process. Vision blurs, health wanes; even the act of walking carries with it the painful reminder of the autumn of life. But this process is something to be faced, not something to be hidden away by false images. Yes, the old can be young at heart, but in their own way, with their own dignity. They do not have to copy the always-young image of the Hollywood star.

My grandfather wanted to return to his valley to die. But by then the families of the valley had left in search of a better future. It is only now that there seems to be a return to the valley, a revival. The new generation seeks its roots, that value of love for the land moves us to return to the place where our ancianos formed the culture.

I returned to Puerto de Luna last summer, to join the community in a celebration of the founding of the church. I drove by my grandfather's home, my uncles' ranches, the neglected adobe[16] washing down into the earth from whence it came. And I wondered, how might the values of my grandfather's generation live in our own? What can we retain to see us through these hard times? I was to become a farmer, and I became a writer. As I plow and plant my words, do I nurture as my grandfather did in his fields and orchards? The answers are not simple.

"They don't make men like that anymore," is a phrase we hear when one does honor to a man. I am glad I knew my grandfather. I am glad there are still times when I can see him in my dreams, hear him in my reverie. Sometimes I think I catch a whiff of that earthy aroma that was his smell, just as in lonely times sometimes I catch the fragrance of Ultima's herbs. Then I smile. How strong these people were to leave such a lasting impression.

So, as I would greet my abuelo long ago, it would help us all to greet the old ones we know with this kind and respectful greeting: "Buenos días le de Dios."

---

16. adobe (ä dō′bē): Sun-dried clay brick.

Audiocassette You may want to have your students listen to the **Audio Prose Library** interview with Rudolfo Anaya, in which Anaya talks about his place in the Chicano tradition and mentions the success of *Bless Me, Ultima.*

Alternative Assessment *Portfolio Assignment:* To enable you and your students to assess their learning, you may ask them to create a portfolio of their written responses to "A Celebration of Grandfathers." They may select the three best pieces from among the following assignments: the reader's response journal, the Thinking and Writing Assignment, the Alternative Composition Assignment (Teaching Portfolio, p. 486), the Selection Test, Part A (Teaching Portfolio, p. 495), and the Selection Test Essay question (Teaching Portfolio, p. 496).

RESPONDING TO THE SELECTION

Your Response

1. What quality of the author's grandfather do you admire most? Give reasons for your answer.

Recalling

2. What did the grandfather say whenever the author wanted to give up and stop trying to learn something?

Interpreting

3. What does the author mean when he says that the old people's eyes "peer into a distant past that makes absurdity of our contemporary world"?
4. In what way does the presence of the old people make "time stand still"?
5. How does the author feel old people should be portrayed in the mass media?
6. How do the author's values differ from those of his grandfather?

Applying

7. The author's grandfather said, "Know where you stand." In what way could you apply these words to your own life?

ANALYZING LITERATURE

Understanding the Reflective Essay

A **reflective essay** is a personal, thoughtful exploration of a topic or an issue. The essay often touches upon many facets of the topic, and it frequently reveals the past experiences or impressions of the author.

1. What details of "A Celebration of Grandfathers" reveal the personal aspects of this reflective essay?
2. What details reveal the writer's serious thoughts about the subject?
3. What is the main theme of this essay?

CRITICAL THINKING AND READING

Understanding an Author's Tone

Tone is the attitude toward the subject and audience that is conveyed by the language of the speaker in a literary work. The author's use of language is an important key to understanding the tone of a work. A descriptive essay, for example, may contain vivid words that paint a picture in the reader's mind. A persuasive essay may contain language that expresses anger or urgency. In a reflective essay, the writer's language and details express his considered feelings and opinions.

1. What is the tone of "A Celebration of Grandfathers"?
2. How does the author achieve this tone? Give specific examples from the essay.

THINKING AND WRITING

Writing a Reflective Essay

What is important to you? What have you thought deeply about? Write a reflective essay on something that is important to you. It may be a person, a place, an object, or an idea; it need not be very dramatic. What is important is that you share your thoughts and supply details to illustrate them. Ask a classmate to give you feedback on your first draft. Then revise your essay. You may wish to share it with the class.

LEARNING OPTION

Speaking and Listening. Interview a grandfather—either your own or someone else's. Ask the person what he remembers about his own grandfather. Find out what the person's grandfather did for a living. Ask him what he learned from his grandfather and whether he would want to teach the same things to his grandchildren. Write down the person's responses so that you may share them with your class.

A Celebration of Grandfathers 453

Rudolfo Anaya and "Grandfathers"

PREWRITING

Inspiration Knocks An idea for a reflective essay can come from just about anywhere: something the writer reads, a scene observed, a conversation overheard, or the writer's own thoughts and memories. Rudolfo Anaya says, "I was inspired to write the piece on grandfathers because I felt too many young adults weren't paying attention to their elders." Clearly, his inspiration came from his observations of life around him and his memories of how one aspect of life was very different when he was growing up.

What's the Big Idea? Even an essay that reflects a writer's thinking needs to focus on one main idea. Otherwise, readers are left wondering, "What's the point?" Rudolfo Anaya says, "When I write an essay, I think of the main idea I want to communicate." Focusing on one main idea helps the writer choose the specific details to include.

Time to Get Organized Essay writers in particular have to organize their ideas and present them in a logical order. Rudolfo Anaya's favorite method for getting organized is outlining. "Sometimes," he says, "I just jump right in and start writing, but without a plan I find I have to do a lot of revising. Making an outline of what you want to say is the best way to start."

DRAFTING

Jump In With a topic chosen, a main idea firmly established, and an outline completed, where do the first words come from? Every writer would probably answer that question differently. For Rudolfo Anaya the first step is concentrating completely on the topic. "I sit in front of my computer and think. Thinking about your subject is important. Then I jump in and start writing."

Details and More Details An outline is the bare bones of an essay. The details are what makes an essay come alive and speak to readers' personal feelings. Writing "A Celebration of Grandfathers" was not difficult for Rudolfo Anaya because the details came to him readily. "I thought back to the things I had seen my grandfather do, how he spoke, how he walked, the way he smelled. I tried to bring him to life for the reader, and so I had to go to my memory for all the details and sensory images."

And Nothing But the Truth Rudolfo Anaya likes writing both essays and short stories, but he stresses that writing an essay is different from writing a short story. "In a short story I could 'make up' a grandfather. I wouldn't feel obligated to stay with the facts. When a character comes to my mind and I want to write a story, I can develop that character any way I want. That's the challenge, to create a character the reader will think is real." In an essay the challenge is to make the ideas come alive while staying true to the facts.

When It's Hard For Anaya, "the hardest thing about writing is thinking people may not be interested in what you have to say. You have to be very positive and tell yourself your life is worth telling. Don't freeze up, just plow ahead."

Preparation

Before students read this feature, have them discuss how Anaya might have written his essay "A Celebration of Grandfathers." Have them speculate on where he got his ideas and how he decided which details to use. You might have them jot down their thoughts in their journals, or you might put them on the chalkboard for reference.

Prereading Focus Point out to students that every writer works differently. The way an individual writer approaches each stage of the writing process varies, just as every student writes differently. You might suggest that while reading this, students keep a chart in which they note the similarities and differences between Anaya's process and their own.

Presentation

Discussion questions:
1. What does Anaya find distracting when he writes?
2. What differences does Anaya see between writing about people in fiction and writing about them in an essay?
3. What advice from Anaya or what tips about his working can you apply in your writing? Explain why you think they will be useful to you.

REVISING

Another Opinion When you have finished plowing ahead, it is time to stop and reflect. Do the words say what I want to say? Will my ideas be clear and interesting to readers? Rudolfo Anaya finds it helpful to ask these questions of another person. So he shows everything he writes to his wife. "She makes suggestions, sometimes she corrects my spelling, and she helps me see when it is clear or not clear."

Sticking With It Even when he writes from an outline, Anaya knows that the revising stage is important. "A writer always has to revise his work," he says. "You can't be lazy and hand in the first draft. I reread my work a lot because I am constantly revising it. I always want to make my work as clear as possible." Anaya also knows there are other benefits to revising. "When you revise your work, you get more ideas. The work becomes better."

PUBLISHING

Why He Writes Rudolfo Anaya likes to see his writing in print. Writers "write to communicate," he says. "A Celebration of Grandfathers" first appeared in *New Mexico Magazine*, which, according to Anaya, is read by many older people. "They liked it because it reminded them of their grandfathers. It also reminded them how much things have changed. When readers identify with what you have written, then it makes the writer happy. My grandfather may not be at all like yours, but there are certain similarities. When the reader recognizes those similarities, the reader's emotions are touched.

That's what I want to do, to touch the reader's emotions."

What's Next? After publishing "A Celebration of Grandfathers," Anaya considered a sequel. It would be about grandmothers. "The older women of the small town where I grew up were hard workers. They kept the families together, and they knew a lot. In my novel *Bless Me, Ultima,* I describe such a woman, so maybe I already have written a tribute to those older women of my community."

Whatever he writes next, Rudolfo Anaya will probably never stop writing. As he puts it, "The best way to learn to write is to write. Look at it this way: How does a plumber learn about plumbing? By doing it. Or a bricklayer to lay bricks? By doing it. Or an electrician to wire a house? By doing it. Writing is a process of doing it."

THINKING ABOUT THE PROCESS

1. Rudolfo Anaya says that if he doesn't outline, he spends a lot more time revising. Why do you think this might be so?
2. **Writing.** Imagine that the postal service is awarding a prize for the best design of a stamp honoring grandfathers or grandmothers. Write a brief memorandum to the postmaster describing a design you have created and arguing that this design should win the prize. (You may also want to include a drawing of your design.) Recalling Anaya's advice about outlining, plan your memo before you write it. You may even want to experiment with different types of outlines, including graphic organizers like a flowchart.

Preparation

More About the Author John McPhee's interests are varied and include history, art, and tennis. Ask students if they think that the study of one discipline helps deepen the understanding of others.

Literary Focus In this essay, McPhee alternates voice frequently. For instance, he combines more objective descriptions with recollections of incidents from his own past. The juxtaposition of these styles is striking.

Prereading Focus You may want to encourage students to consult their science teachers about various investigative strategies they can include in their charts. Once students have completed their charts, you may want to have them share the charts with the class.

Vocabulary Ask students to write a meaningful sentence for each word. Talk with them about any words that they find difficult to use in a sentence. Then remind them to watch for the vocabulary words as they are reading "The Loch Ness Monster."

Electronic Handbook You might suggest that students use the Language Master 6000 to hear the pronunciation of *milieu*.

John McPhee

(1931–   ) was a television writer from 1955 to 1957, during the early years of that medium. After that experience he became an associate editor for *Time* magazine. However, he is best known as an essayist for *The New Yorker,* a weekly magazine famous for its excellent writing. McPhee has also written books on various subjects, including Alaska and the Pine Barrens of New Jersey. In "The Loch Ness Monster," he turns his attention to a creature that some believe is a throwback to the dinosaurs.

The Loch Ness Monster

Expository Essay

The purpose of an **expository essay** is to explain a concept, event, or process by presenting information. Such essays usually contain details, examples, and facts conveyed in an informative tone. As "The Loch Ness Monster" shows, however, an expository piece can be personal and entertaining as well as informative. In this essay, John McPhee tells about an organization that gathers data on a shy forty-foot monster living in a deep Scottish lake.

Focus

Here is the problem: A large but elusive "monster" has been sighted in a very big lake. You are the head of a scientific expedition that has been commissioned to find this creature. How would you go about it? Enter your ideas on a chart like the following, and as you read about the Loch Ness Monster, add to your list.

Strategy	Advantages	Disadvantages

Vocabulary

Knowing the following words will help you as you read "The Loch Ness Monster."

panorama (pan' ə ram' ə) *n.*: Unlimited view in all directions (p. 458)

depot (dē' pō) *n.*: Railroad or bus station (p. 458)

milieu (mēl yoo') *n.*: Environment; setting (p. 459)

fanatical (fə nat' i k'l) *adj.*: Unreasonably enthusiastic (p. 460)

hoax (hōks) *n.*: Trick; fraud (p. 461)

nocturnal (näk tur' n'l) *adj.*: Happening in the night (p. 462)

undulates (un' joo lāts') *v.*: Moves in waves (p. 464)

impediment (im ped' ə mənt) *n.*: Obstruction; hindrance (p. 464)

Objectives

1 To understand the expository essay
2 To find relevant evidence
3 To write an expository essay
4 To express individual interests and abilities through optional activities

Support Material

Teaching Portfolio
Teacher Backup, p. 497
Grammar in Action Worksheets, *Writing Description,* p. 501, and *Varying Sentence Openers,* p. 503
Usage and Mechanics Worksheet, p. 505
Vocabulary Check, p. 506
Analyzing Literature Worksheet,

Understanding the Expository Essay, p. 508
Language Worksheet, *Understanding Words With the Suffix* ity, p. 509
Selection Test, p. 510

Prentice Hall Literature Writing Studio

The Loch Ness Monster

John McPhee

The road—the A-82—stayed close to the lake, often on ledges that had been blasted into the mountainsides. The steep forests continued, broken now and again, on one shore or the other, by fields of fern, clumps of bright-yellow whin,[1] and isolated stands of cedar. Along the far shore were widely separated houses and farms, which to the eyes of a traveller appeared almost unbelievably luxuriant after the spare desolation of some of the higher glens.[2] We came to the top of the rise and suddenly saw, on the right-hand side of the road, on the edge of a high meadow that sloped sharply a considerable distance to the lake, a cluster of caravans[3] and other vehicles, arranged in the shape of a C, with an opening toward the road— much like a circle of prairie schooners, formed for protection against savage attack. All but one or two of the vehicles were painted bright lily-pad green. The compound, in its compact half acre, was surrounded by a fence, to keep out, among other things, sheep, which were grazing all over the slope in deep-green turf among buttercups, daisies, and thistles. Gulls above beat hard into the wind, then turned and planed toward the south. Gulls are inland birds in Scotland, there being so little dis-

---

1. **whin** (hwin) *n.*: Prickly, evergreen shrub.
2. **glens** *n.*: Narrow, secluded, mountain valleys.
3. **caravans** *n.*: In Great Britain, camping trailers.

Presentation

Motivation/Prior Knowledge
Ask students whether they have heard of the Loch Ness Monster. If not, tell them a little about its legend. Then tell them that, in this essay, John McPhee describes efforts to solve the mystery surrounding the monster.

Master Teacher Note You might tell students that McPhee's purpose is not simply one of reporting, although his use of detail is extremely effective. It is not until the end of the essay, with the inclusion of the garden snake incident, that McPhee's purpose becomes clear. With this episode, McPhee gives the reader his reaction to the brief visit. Some students will grasp McPhee's strategy relatively easily, but others will need guidance from the teacher

Purpose-Setting Question
What does the search for the Loch Ness Monster reveal aoubt *human* nature?

Making Connections Another selection that deals with unexplained phenomena is "A Very Old Man With Enormous Wings," page 165. Both selections confront human responses to the unfamiliar.

1 **Critical Thinking and Reading** Why do you think McPhee begins the essay with this description of the approach to Loch Ness?

Thematic Focus Since the beginning of time, people have been exploring the unknown and codifying their findings. Yet there are many discoveries still to be made right here on earth. Ask students what would happen to the Loch Ness Monster if it were discovered. Would it benefit from being found, or would fear of the unknown cause people to destroy it?

Alternative Assessment To promote active reading, have students keep a reader's response journal as they read the selection. Ask them to focus their observations on the details that reveal the narrator's and Skelton's attempts to resolve the mystery of the Loch Ness Monster. Encourage personal responses to the investigation. Do they believe there is a Loch Ness Monster? Of what other stories does this selection remind them?

Students' observations will help you assess their understanding of the essay.

2 **Clarification** A *gargoyle* is "a bizarre or grotesque figure carved from stone and projecting outward from a building."

3 **Discussion** Which details in the opening description are the most vivid?

4 **Critical Thinking and Reading** Does this account read like a newspaper story? How is it similar to and different from such a story?

5 **Discussion** Why do you think McPhee includes the titles of some of the books he saw?

tance from anywhere to the sea. A big fireplace had been made from rocks of the sort that were scattered all over the meadow. And on the lakeward side a platform had been built, its level eminence[4] emphasizing the declivity[5] of the hill, which dropped away below it. Mounted on the platform was a thirty-five-millimeter motion-picture camera with an enormous telephoto lens. From its point of view, two hundred feet above the lake and 2 protruding like a gargoyle, the camera could take in a bedazzling panorama that covered thousands of acres of water.

This was Expedition Headquarters, the principal field station of the Loch Ness Phenomena Investigation Bureau—dues five pounds per annum,[6] life membership one hundred pounds, tax on donations recoverable under covenant.[7] Those who join the bureau receive newsletters and annual reports, and are eligible to participate in the fieldwork if they so desire. I turned into the compound and parked between two bright-green reconditioned old London taxis. The central 3 area had long since been worn grassless, and was covered at this moment with fine-grain dust. People were coming and going. The place seemed rather public, as if it were a depot. No one even halfway interested in the natural history of the Great Glen would think of driving up the A-82 without stopping in there. Since the A-82 is the principal route between Glasgow and Inverness,[8] it is not surprising that the apparently amphibious creature as yet unnamed, the so-called Loch Ness Monster, has been seen not only from the highway but on it.

---

4. eminence (em′ə nəns) *n.*: High or lofty place.
5. declivity (di kliv′ə tē) *n.*: Downward slope.
6. dues five pounds per annum: Amount of British money per year that it costs to belong.
7. tax on donations recoverable by covenant: Taxes paid on donations will be refunded.
8. Glasgow and Inverness: Cities in southern and northern Scotland.

The atmosphere around the headquarters suggested a scientific frontier and also a boom town, much as Cape Canaveral and Cocoa Beach do. There were, as well, cirrus[9] wisps of show business and fine arts. Probably the one word that might have been applied to everyone present was adventurer. There was, at any rate, nothing emphatically laboratorial about the place, although the prevailing mood seemed to be one not of holiday but of matter-of-fact application and patient dedication. A telephone call came in that day, to the caravan that served as an office, from a woman who owned an inn south of Inverarigaig, on the other side of the lake. She said that she had seen the creature that morning just forty yards offshore—three humps, nothing else to report, and being very busy just now, thank you very much, good day. This was recorded, with no particular display of excitement, by an extremely attractive young woman who appeared to be in her late twenties, an artist from London who had missed but one summer at Loch Ness in seven years. She wore sandals, dungarees, a black pullover, and gold earrings. Her name was Mary Piercy, and her toes were painted pink. The bulletin board where she recorded the sighting resembled the kind used in railway stations for the listing of incoming trains.

The office walls were decorated with photographs of the monster in various postures—basking,[10] cruising, diving, splashing, looking up inquisitively. A counter was covered with some of the essential bibliography: the bureau's annual report (twenty-nine sightings the previous year), J. A. Carruth's *Loch Ness and Its Monster* (The Abbey Press, Fort Augustus), Tim Dinsdale's *Loch Ness Monster* (Routledge and Kegan

---

9. cirrus (sir′əs) *adj.*: Feathery.
10. basking (bask′iŋ) *n.*: Warming oneself pleasantly, as in sunlight.

Grammar in Action

Descriptive writing gives the reader a picture of a person, a thing, or a place. Look at this passage from "The Loch Ness Monster":

> The atmosphere around the headquarters suggested a scientific frontier and also a boom town, much as Cape Canaveral and Cocoa Beach do. There were, as well, cirrus wisps of show business and fine arts. Probably the word that might have been applied to everyone present

was adventurer. There was, at any rate, nothing emphatically laboratorial about the place, although the prevailing mood seemed to be one not of holiday but of matter-of-fact application and patient dedication.

In the passage John McPhee describes the Expedition Headquarters of the Loch Ness Phenomena Investigation Bureau. Notice that he describes both the physical detail of the place as well as its mood, or emotional atmosphere.

Now read this description:

> This [call] was recorded, with no particular display of excitement, by an extremely attractive young woman who appeared to be in her late twenties, an artist from London

Paul, London), and a report by the Joint Air Reconnaissance Center of the Royal Air Force on a motion picture of the monster swimming about half a mile on the lake's surface. These books and documents could, in turn, lead the interested reader to less available but nonetheless highly relevant works such as R. T. Gould's *The Loch Ness Monster and Others* and Constance Whyte's *More Than a Legend.*

My children looked over the photographs with absorption but not a great deal of awe, and they bought about a dozen postcards with glossy prints of a picture of the monster—three humps showing, much the same sight that the innkeeper had described—that had been taken by a man named Stuart, directly across the lake from Urquhart Castle. The three younger girls then ran out into the meadow and began to pick daisies and buttercups. Their mother and sister sat down in the sun to read about the creature in the lake, and to write postcards. We were on our way to Inverness, but with no need to hurry. "Dear Grammy, we came to see the monster today."

From the office to the camera-observation platform to the caravan that served as a pocket mess hall, I wandered around among the crew, was offered and accepted tea, and squinted with imaginary experience up and down the lake, where the whitecaps had, if anything, increased. Among the crew at the time were two Canadians, a Swede, an Australian, three Americans, two Englishmen, a Welshman, and one Scot. Two were women. When I asked one of the crew members if he knew what some of the others did, vocationally, when they were not at Loch Ness, he said, "I'm not sure what they are. We don't go into that." This was obviously a place where now was all that mattered, and in such a milieu it is distinctly pleasant to accept that approach to things. Nonetheless, I found that I couldn't adhere completely to this principle, and I did find out that one man was a medical doctor, another a farmer, another a retired naval officer, and that several, inevitably, were students. The daily watch begins at four in the morning and goes on, as one fellow put it, "as long as we can stand up." It has been the pattern among the hundreds of sightings reported that the early-morning hours are the most promising ones. Camera stations are manned until ten at night, dawn and sunset being so close to midnight at that latitude in summer, but the sentries tend to thin out with the lengthening of the day. During the autumn, the size of the crew reduces precipitously[11] toward one.

One man lives at the headquarters all year long. His name is Clem Lister Skelton. "I've been staring at that piece of water since five o'clock," he said, while he drank tea in the mess caravan.

"Is there a technique?" I asked him.

"Just look," he said. "Look. Run your eye over the water in one quick skim. What we're looking for is not hard to see. You just sit and sort of gaze at the loch, that's all. Mutter a few incantations.[12] That's all there is to do. In wintertime, very often, it's just myself. And of course one keeps a very much more perfunctory[13] watch in the winter. I saw it once in a snowstorm, though, and that was the only time I've had a clear view of the head and neck. The neck is obviously very mobile. The creature was quite big, but it wasn't as big as a seventy-foot MFV. Motor fishing vessel. I'd been closer to it, but I hadn't seen as much of it before. I've seen it eight times. The last time was in September. Only the

---

11. **precipitously** (pri sip′ə təs lē) *adv.*: Steeply.
12. **incantations** (in′kan tā′shəns) *n.*: Spells.
13. **perfunctory** (pər fuŋk′tər ē) *adj.*: Routine; superficial.

The Loch Ness Monster 459

6 **Discussion** Why do you think McPhee includes this personal information?

7 **Literary Focus** How does McPhee heighten a reader's interest by letting Skelton speak for himself? Why might this passage have been less interesting if McPhee had summarized Skelton's words?

---

who had missed but one summer at Loch Ness in seven years. She wore sandals, dungarees, a black pullover, and gold earrings. Her name was Mary Piercy, and her toes were painted pink.

Keep in mind that these passages of description are from an expository essay, one written to explain a concept or event by providing information. Why might the author have included the descriptive passages? What do they add to the essay?

Student Activity 1. Find several other passages of descriptive writing in the essay, and share them with a partner. Discuss what they add to the essay.

Student Activity 2. Write a paragraph in which you describe a person, an object, or a place. Try to convey in this composition your own feelings about the subject.

Electronic Handbook You might want students to review nouns and adjectives before completing the Grammar in Action activities. If students have access to the Language Master 6000, have them enter the access words *noun* and *adjective* and press the GRAMMAR key to get information on these topics.

back. Just the sort of upturned boat, which is the classic view of it."

Skelton drank some more tea, and refilled a cup he had given me. "I must know what it is," he went on. "I shall never rest peacefully until I know what it is. Some of the largest creatures in the world are out there, and we can't name them. It may take ten years, but we're going to identify the genus.[14] Most people are not as fanatical as I, but I would like to see this through to the end, if I don't get too broke first."

Skelton is a tall, offhand[15] man, English, with reddish hair that is disheveled[16] in long strings from the thinning crown of his head. In outline, Skelton's life there in the caravan on the edge of the high meadow over the lake, in a place that must be uncorrectably gloomy during the wet rains of winter, seemed cagelike and hopeless to me—unacceptably lonely. The impression he gave was of a man who had drawn a circle around himself many hundreds of miles from the rest of his life. But how could I know? He was saying that he had flown Supermarine Spitfires for the R.A.F.[17] during the Second World War. His father had been a soldier, and when Skelton was a boy, he lived, as he put it, "all over the place." As an adult, he became first an actor, later a writer and director of films. He acted in London in plays like *March Hare* and *Saraband for Dead Lovers.* One film he directed was, in his words, "a dreadful thing called *Saul and David.*" These appearances on the surface apparently did not occur so frequently that he needed to do nothing else for a livelihood. He also directed, in the course of many years, several hundred educational films. The publisher who distributed some of these films was David James, a friend of Skelton's, and at that time a Member of Parliament.[18] James happened to be, as well, the founder of the Loch Ness Phenomena Investigation Bureau—phenomena, because, for breeding purposes, there would have to be at least two monsters living in the lake at any one time, probably more, and in fact two had on occasion been sighted simultaneously. James asked Skelton if he would go up to the lake and give the bureau the benefit of his technical knowledge of movie cameras. "Anything for a laugh," Skelton had said to James. This was in the early nineteen-sixties. "I came for a fortnight,"[19] Skelton said now, in the caravan. "And I saw it. I wanted to know what it was, and I've wanted to know what it was ever since. I thought I'd have time to write up here, but I haven't. I don't do anything now except hunt this beast."

Skelton talked on about what the monster might be—a magnified newt,[20] a long-necked variety of giant seal, an unextinct *Elasmosaurus.* Visitors wandered by in groups outside the caravan, and unexplained strangers kept coming in for tea. In the air was a feeling, utterly belied by the relative permanence of the place, of a country carnival on a two-night stand. The caravans themselves, in their alignment, suggested a section of a midway. I remembered a woman shouting to attract people to a big caravan on a carnival midway one night in May in New Jersey. That was some time ago. I must have been nineteen. The woman, who was standing on a small platform, was fifty or sixty, and she was trying to get people to go

---

14. genus (jē' nəs) *n.*: Main subdivision of a family of closely related species.
15. offhand *adj.*: Casual; informal.
16. disheveled (di shev' 'ld) *adj.*: Untidy; tousled.
17. Supermarine Spitfires for the R.A.F.: Fighter planes for the British Royal Air Force.

18. Parliament (pär' lə mənt) *n.*: The national legislative body of Great Britain.
19. fortnight (fôrt' nīt') *n.*: Two weeks.
20. newt (nōot) *n.*: Salamander.

into the caravan to see big jungle cats, I suppose, and brown bears—"Ferocious Beasts," at any rate, according to block lettering on the side of the caravan. A steel cage containing a small black bear had been set up on two sawhorses outside the caravan—a fragment to imply what might be found on a larger scale inside.

So young that it was no more than two feet from nose to tail, the bear was engaged in desperate motion, racing along one side of the cage from corner to corner, striking the steel bars bluntly with its nose. Whirling then, tossing its head over its shoulder like a racing swimmer, it turned and bolted crazily for the opposite end. Its eyes were deep red, and shining in a kind of full-sighted blindness. It had gone mad there in the cage, and its motion, rhythmic and tortured, never ceased, back and forth, back and forth, the head tossing with each jarring turn. The animal abraded its flanks on the steel bars as it ran. Hair and skin had scraped from its sides so that pink flesh showed in the downpour of the carnival arc lights. Blood drained freely through the thinned hair of its belly and dropped onto the floor of the cage. What had a paralyzing effect on me was the animal's almost perfect and now involuntary rhythm—the wild toss of the head after the crash into the corner, the turn, the scraping run, the crash again at the other end, never stopping, metronomic—the exposed interior of some brutal and organic timepiece.

Beside the cage, the plump, impervious woman, red-faced, red-nosed, kept shouting to the crowds, but she said to me, leaning down, her own eyes bloodshot, "Why don't you move on, sonny, if you ain't going to buy a ticket? Beat it. Come on, now. Move on."

"We argue about what it is," Skelton said. "I'm inclined to think it's a giant slug, but there is an amazingly impressive theory for its being a worm. You can't rule out that it's one of the big dinosaurs, but I think this is more wishful thinking than anything else." In the late nineteen-thirties, a large and exotic footprint was found along the shore of Loch Ness. It was meticulously studied by various people and was assumed, for a time, to be an impression from a foot or flipper of the monster. Eventually, the print was identified. Someone who owned the preserved foot of a hippopotamus had successfully brought off a hoax that put layers of mockery and incredibility over the creature in the lake for many years. The Second World War further diverted any serious interest that amateurs or naturalists might have taken. Sightings continued, however, in a consistent pattern, and finally, in the early nineteen-sixties, the Loch Ness Phenomena Investigation Bureau was established. "I have no plans whatever for leaving," Skelton said. "I am prepared to stay here ad infinitum.[21] All my worldly goods are here."

A dark-haired young woman had stepped into the caravan and poured herself a cup of tea. Skelton, introducing her to me, said, "If the beast has done nothing else, it has brought me a wife. She was studying Gaelic[22] and Scottish history at Edinburgh University, and she walked into the glen one day, and I said, 'That is the girl I am going to marry.' " He gestured toward a window of the caravan, which framed a view of the hills and the lake. "The Great Glen is one of the most beautiful places in the world," he continued. "It is peaceful here. I'd be happy here all my life, even if there were nothing in the loch. I've even committed the unforgivable

---

21. ad infinitum (ad in′ fə nīt′ əm): Latin phrase meaning *forever*.
22. Gaelic (gāl′ ik) *adj.*: A Celtic language spoken in Scotland and Ireland.

The Loch Ness Monster 461

10 Critical Thinking and Reading How do you think this memory relates to the rest of the essay?

11 Clarification Some students, particularly those who have taken piano lessons, will know that a *metronome* is a "mechanical device for establishing the regular intervals of a rhythm."

12 Discussion How does the inclusion of the information about Skelton's wife add to the reader's understanding of Skelton's character?

and to investigate the monster legends of other cultures, such as Native American, Scandinavian, African, and Indian. Help students make a bulletin board display of legendary monsters.

13 Literary Focus How does Mc-Phee shift the focus of the essay in this section?

14 Discussion How reliable is this older report? Explain.

sin of going to sleep in the sun during a flat calm. With enough time, we could shoot the beast with a crossbow and a line, and get a bit of skin. We could also shoot a small transmitter into its hide and learn more than we know now about its habits and characteristics."

13　The creature swims with remarkable speed, as much as ten or fifteen knots when it is really moving. It makes no noise other than seismic splashes, but it is apparently responsive in a highly sensitive way to sound. A shout, an approaching engine, any loud report, will send it into an immediate dive, and this shyness is in large part the cause of its inaccessibility, and therefore of its mystery. Curiously, though, reverberate sound was what apparently brought the creature widespread attention, for the first sequence of frequent sightings occurred in 1933, when the A-82 was blasted into the cliffsides of the western shore of the lake. Immense boulders kept falling into the depths, and shock waves from dynamite repeatedly ran through the water, causing the creature to lose confidence in its environment and to alter, at least temporarily, its shy and preferentially nocturnal life. In that year it was first observed on land, perhaps attempting to seek a way out forever from the detonations that had alarmed it. A couple named Spicer saw it, near Inverarigaig, and later described its long, serpentine neck, followed by an ungainly hulk of body, lurching toward the lake and disappearing into high undergrowth as they approached.

14　With the exception of one report recorded in the sixth century, which said that a monster (fitting the description of the contemporary creatures in the lake) had killed a man with a single bite, there have been no other examples of savagery on its part. To the contrary, its sensitivity to people seems

to be acute, and it keeps a wide margin between itself and mankind. In all likelihood, it feeds on fish and particularly on eels, of which there are millions in the lake. Loch Ness is unparalleled in eel-fishing circles, and has drawn commercial eel fishermen from all over the United Kingdom. The monster has been observed with its neck bent down in the water, like a swan feeding. When the creatures die, they apparently settle into the seven-hundred-foot floor of the lake, where the temperature is always forty-

462　Nonfiction

Grammar in Action

Good writers vary their sentence structure, and one means of doing so is to use different **sentence openers.** If all sentences begin the same way, readers soon tire of the repetition.

　In addition to its subject, a sentence can begin with one-word modifiers, phrases, clauses, or a combination of these openers:

Exhausted, the racer collapsed. (one-word modifier)

Sensing danger, the snake coiled. (phrase)

Yesterday, when the mail arrived, the check was missing. (one-word modifier and clause)

Variety results from the many kinds of one-word modifiers, phrases, and clauses writers can use: adjectives, adverbs, participles, infinitives, gerunds, prepositional phrases, adverb clauses, adjective clauses, and so forth.

　John McPhee uses many different types of sentence openers in "The Loch Ness Monster":

two degrees Fahrenheit—so cold that the lake is known for never giving up its dead. Loch Ness never freezes, despite its high latitude, so if the creature breathes air, as has seemed apparent from the reports of observers who have watched its mouth rhythmically opening and closing, it does not lose access to the surface in winter. It clearly prefers the smooth, sunbaked waterscapes of summer, however, for it seems to love to bask in the sun, like an upturned boat, slowly rolling, plunging, squirming around

with what can only be taken as pleasure. By observers' reports, the creature has two pairs of lateral[23] flippers, and when it swims off, tail thrashing, it leaves behind it a wake as impressive as the wake of a small warship. When it dives from a still position, it inexplicably[24] goes down without leaving a bubble. When it dives as it swims, it leaves on the surface a churning signature of foam.

Skelton leaned back against the wall of the caravan in a slouched and nonchalant posture. He was wearing a dark blue tie that was monogrammed in small block letters sewn with white thread—L.N.I. (Loch Ness Investigation). Above the monogram and embroidered also in white thread was a small depiction of the monster—humps undulant, head high, tail extending astern. Skelton gave the tie a flick with one hand. "You get this with a five-pound membership," he said.

The sea-serpent effect given by the white thread on the tie was less a stylization than an attempt toward a naturalistic sketch. As I studied it there, framed on Skelton's chest, the thought occurred to me that there was something inconvenient about the monster's actual appearance. In every sense except possibly the sense that involves cruelty, the creature in Loch Ness is indeed a monster. An average taken from many films and sightings gives its mature length at about forty feet. Its general appearance is repulsive, in the instant and radical sense in which reptiles are repulsive to many human beings, and any number of people might find difficulty in accepting a creature that looks like the one that was slain by St. George. Its neck, about six feet long, columnar, powerfully muscled, is the neck of a serpent. Its

---

23. lateral (lat' ər əl) *adj.*: On the side.
24. inexplicably (in eks' pli kə blē) *adv.*: Unexplainably.

15 Reading Strategy Ask students to summarize the important information about the monster.

16 Clarification St. George was a Christian martyr who died in the year 303. He became the patron saint of England, and during the Middle Ages his name became associated with many legends. According to one tale, he slew a great dragon.

The *sea-serpent* effect given by the white thread . . . (subject with adjective modifier)

As I studied it there, framed on Skelton's chest, the thought occurred to me . . . (clause, participial phrase)

In every sense except possibly the sense that involves cruelty, the creature . . . (prepositional phrase, prepositional phrase that includes an adjective clause)

Good writers like McPhee rarely begin two successive sentences with the same kind of opener.

Student Activity 1. Select three other successive sentences from this selection. Name the kind of sentence opener used in each.

Student Activity 2. Write a paragraph describing your thoughts about the Loch Ness Monster. Use a different opener for each sentence.

Electronic Handbook You might wish students to review varying sentence openers before completing the Grammar in Action activities. If students have access to the Language Master 6000, have them enter the access the words *phrase, clause, prepositional,* and *verbal* and press the GRAMMAR key to get information on varying sentence openers.

17 **Critical Thinking and Reading**
Why is the resemblance of the monster to the creature of legend an impediment to the investigation?

18 **Discussion** Ask students to identify the parallels between the incident with the garden snake and the investigation of the Loch Ness Monster.

Reader's Response Do you believe the Loch Ness Monster exists? Explain.

Thematic Response Do you think that the author's account of the killing of the snake reflects human attitudes toward the unknown? Why or why not?

head, scarcely broader than the neck, is a serpent's head, with uncompromising, lenticular[25] eyes. Sometimes as it swims it holds its head and neck erect. The creature's mouth is at least a foot wide. Its body undulates. Its skin glistens when wet and appears coarse, mottled, gray, and elephantine when exposed to the air long enough to become dry. The tail, long and columnar, stretches back to something of a point. It seemed to me, sitting there at Headquarters, that the classical, mythical, dragon likeness of this animate thing—the modified dinosaur, the fantastically exaggerated newt—was an impediment to the work of the investigation bureau, which has no pertinent interest in what the monster resembles or calls to mind but a great deal in what it actually is, the goal being a final and positive identification of the genus.

"What we need is a good, lengthy, basking sighting," Skelton said. "We've had one long surfacing—twenty-five minutes. I saw it. Opposite Urquhart Castle. We only had a twelve-inch lens then, at four and a half miles. We have thirty-six-inch lenses now. We need a long, clear, close-up—in color."

My children had watched, some months earlier, the killing of a small snake on a lawn in Maryland. About eighteen inches long, it came out from a basement-window well, through a covering lattice of redwood, and

25. lenticular (len tik′ yoo lər) *adj.*: Shaped like a lentil bean.

was noticed with shouts and shrieks by the children and a young retriever that barked at the snake and leaped about it in a circle. We were the weekend guests of another family, and eight children in all crowded around the snake, which had been gliding slowly across the lawn during the moments after it had been seen, but had now stopped and was turning its head from side to side in apparent indecision. Our host hurried into his garage and came running back to the lawn with a long shovel. Before he killed the snake, his wife urged him not to. She said the snake could not possibly be poisonous. He said, "How do you know?" The children, mine and theirs, looked back and forth from him to her. The dog began to bark more rapidly and at a higher pitch.

"It has none of the markings. There is nothing triangular about its head," she told him.

"That may very well be," he said. "But you can't be sure."

"It is *not* poisonous. Leave it alone. Look at all these children."

"I can't help that."

"It is *not* poisonous."

"How do you know?"

"I know."

He hit the snake with the flat of the shovel, and it writhed. He hit it again. It kept moving. He hit it a third time, and it stopped. Its underside, whitish green, segmental, turned up. The children moved in for a closer look.

Closure and Extension

ANSWERS TO RESPONDING TO THE SELECTION
Your Response
1. Accept all responses as valid whether students believe in or reject the existence of the monster. Encourage students to support their positions by citing information from this and other articles.

Recalling
2. The bureau conducts field work to investigate the monster's behavior and appearance; it also publishes a newsletter and annual reports about its findings.
3. A caravan serves as the headquarters' office; the atmosphere suggests both a scientific frontier and a boom town.

RESPONDING TO THE SELECTION

Your Response

1. Do you believe that the Loch Ness Monster actually exists? Why or why not?

Recalling

2. What is the purpose of the Loch Ness Phenomena Investigation Bureau?
3. Describe the layout and atmosphere of the organization.
4. Summarize what is known about the Loch Ness Monster's habits and appearance.

Interpreting

5. How are the crew members being adventurers even though they are not risking their lives?
6. What does McPhee mean by calling the bureau a place "where now was all that mattered"?
7. Why does he include the story about "the killing of a small snake"?

Applying

8. How can investigators find out more about the Loch Ness Monster?

ANALYZING LITERATURE

Understanding the Expository Essay

The purpose of an **expository essay** is to explain a concept, event, or process by presenting information. Skilled writers can make an expository essay fun to read as well as informative. In "The Loch Ness Monster," for instance, McPhee creates interest by dealing with a fascinating topic, holding back information until the end, and introducing personal details.

1. How does McPhee's delay in describing the monster make the essay more interesting?
2. Identify three ways in which he gives the essay a personal flavor.
3. Why do personal details create interest?

CRITICAL THINKING AND READING

Finding Relevant Evidence

Relevant evidence is pertinent to or supports the matter being studied. For example, a photograph of the Loch Ness Monster is relevant to proving its existence.

Make a list of five pieces of evidence you think would be relevant to proving or disproving the existence of this creature.

THINKING AND WRITING

Writing an Expository Essay

Think of a company, club, team, or any other organization that you know about. List facts about this group, including its goal, its location, and the type of people who work for it. Then, using this list, write an expository essay about the group. Remember that such an essay does not tell a story but presents information in an interesting way. You will find it helpful to give the main ideas in your first paragraph, with the other paragraphs providing further details. In revising, you may want to include some of your experiences with the group, as McPhee does in his piece.

LEARNING OPTIONS

1. **Performance.** Create a talk show about the Loch Ness Monster. Invite three classmates to participate in the show, playing the roles of John McPhee, Clem Lister Skelton, and a tourist who has seen the monster. As the "host," ask each guest questions about the monster. Have your classmates ask additional questions.
2. **Art.** No one has ever gotten a clear picture of "Nessie." Using information from the selection, draw a picture of the monster as you think it may look.

McPhee keeps readers wondering about it.

2. Suggested Response: McPhee talks about his children and their response to the visit. He also describes the incident with the garden snake and he describes the carnival incident that he recalls from his youth.
3. Suggested Response: Personal details allow the reader to identify more closely with the writer.

ANSWERS TO CRITICAL THINKING AND READING

Answers will differ, but students might include the following in their list of evidence: a footprint or other trace; a clear film or videotape; the dead body of a monster; a diver's clear sighting of the monster; the actual capture of one of these creatures.

THINKING AND WRITING

Software If students have access to computers, have them use the **Writer's Helper** activity *Paragraph Coherence* in revising their expository essays.

Alternative Assessment For Alternate Composition Assignments to assess students' learning, see pages 528–529 of the Teaching Portfolio.

LEARNING OPTIONS

1. This activity will appeal to auditory learners. You may wish to extend the activity for visual learners by having students write a news article about the show.
2. Visual learners will enjoy this activity. You may wish to vary the activity for kinesthetic learners by having them create models of the monster.

---

4. The Loch Ness Monster is about forty feet long with two fins, a long tail that stretches to a point, and a mouth at least a foot wide. Its appearance is repulsive. The skin is coarse and gray. The monster prefers summer to winter and seems to like to bask in the sun. It is highly sensitive to sound, seems to be shy, and swims with remarkable speed.

Interpreting

5. Suggested Response: They do not know what will happen next or when it will happen. Like adventurers, they must be prepared for anything.
6. Suggested Response: Everyone is united in the task of looking for current evidence of the monster's activity.
7. Suggested Response: The fascination, fear, and repulsion that the snake calls up are the same feelings evoked by the monster.

Applying

8. Answers will differ, but students might suggest that divers look for the creature.

Challenge What do you think would happen if the monster were captured?

ANSWERS TO ANALYZING LITERATURE

1. Suggested Response: By not describing the monster immediately,

More About the Author Martin Luther King, Jr., an American clergyman and civil-rights leader, was awarded the Nobel Peace Prize in 1964. At thirty-five, he was the youngest man and only the third black man to be awarded this prestigious honor. Ask students why they think Dr. King received this award. You might also ask students whether Dr. King's goals have been achieved.

Literary Focus In a persuasive essay, the writer must choose examples carefully to appeal to the reader in particular ways. In his speech, King shows the same concern as the persuasive essayist. He appeals to the audience's respect for the Bible, their traditional American values, and their familiarity with a song well-known to most from their school days. Collectively, these make a powerful appeal to the American reader or listener.

Prereading Focus Martin Luther King had a vision of the kind of world in which he wanted to live. His vision was not only for himself and those close to him, but also for all people. The purpose of the brief writing exercise is to focus students' attention on their own visions for the future. Encourage students to keep broadening their thinking to include more and more people beyond their own circles of friends and family. Challenge them to create a vision of the kind of world in which they want to live.

Vocabulary Have students read the list of words and their definitions. Ask them to use each one in a sentence that indicates its meaning and compare their use of the word with King's.

Martin Luther King, Jr.,

(1929–1968) was a minister and civil rights leader who struggled to bring African Americans into the political and economic mainstream of American life. He was born in Atlanta, Georgia, the son of a minister. Inspired by Christian ideals and the philosophy of the Indian leader Mohandas K. Gandhi, King led marches and sit-ins to protest discrimination against black people. "I Have a Dream" comes from a speech he gave to a massive civil rights demonstration in Washington, D.C., in 1963.

"I Have a Dream"

Persuasive Essay

The purpose of a **persuasive essay** is to convince an audience to accept or consider an opinion or recommended course of action. Usually the writer states the opinion or recommendation at the start of the essay and then supports it with convincing evidence. While Martin Luther King, Jr.'s speech, "I Have a Dream," is not strictly a persuasive essay, it does share qualities with this type of writing. Like an essayist, for example, King tries to convince his audience to accept and work for his dream of equality.

Focus

Martin Luther King, Jr., was a powerful and persuasive speaker. In the following speech, King expresses his vision of what the future should be like, especially in terms of human equality. What are your dreams for the future? Do they involve just yourself? Or do they also involve your family, your community, the country, or the whole world? Which of your dreams do you think will be realized? How will you go about achieving them? Write your thoughts in a journal or notebook. Then compare your personal dreams of the future with the vision that King describes in his speech.

Vocabulary

Knowing the following words will help you as you read "I Have a Dream."

creed (krēd) *n.*: Statement of belief (p. 467)

oppression (ə presh′ ən) *n.*: Keeping others down by the unjust use of power (p. 467)

oasis (ō ā′ sis) *n.*: Fertile place in the desert (p. 467)

exalted (eg zôlt′ əd) *v.*: Lifted up (p. 467)

prodigious (prə dij′ əs) *adj.*: Wonderful; of great size (p. 468)

hamlet (ham′ lit) *n.*: Very small village (p. 468)

Objectives

1 To understand the persuasive essay
2 To recognize persuasive techniques
3 To write about persuasion
4 To express individual interests and abilities through optional activities

Support Material

Teaching Portfolio
Teacher Backup, p. 513
Grammar in Action Worksheet, *Using Parallel Structure*, p. 516
Usage and Mechanics Worksheet, p. 518
Vocabulary Check, p. 519
Analyzing Literature Worksheet, *Understanding the Persuasive Essay*, p. 520
Language Worksheet, *Under-standing Synonyms and Antonyms,* p. 521
Selection Test, p. 522

Listening to Literature
"I Have a Dream"

Literature Videodisc
American Documents: Martin Luther King, Jr.: Letter From Birmingham Jail

Prentice Hall Literature Writing Studio

"I Have a Dream"

Martin Luther King, Jr.

. . . I say to you today, my friends, that in spite of the difficulties and frustrations of the moment I still have a dream. It is a dream deeply rooted in the American dream.

I have a dream that one day this nation will rise up and live out the true meaning of its creed: "We hold these truths to be self-evident; that all men are created equal."

I have a dream that one day on the red hills of Georgia the sons of former slaves and the sons of former slaveowners will be able to sit down together at the table of brotherhood.

I have a dream that one day even the state of Mississippi, a desert state sweltering with the heat of injustice and oppression, will be transformed into an oasis of freedom and justice.

I have a dream that my four little children will one day live in a nation where they will not be judged by the color of their skin but by the content of their character.

I have a dream today.

I have a dream that one day the state of Alabama, whose governor's lips are presently dripping with the words of interposition and nullification,[1] will be transformed into a situation where little black boys and black girls will be able to join hands with little white boys and white girls and walk together as sisters and brothers.

I have a dream today.

I have a dream that one day every valley shall be exalted, every hill and mountain shall be made low, the rough places will be made plains, and the crooked places will be made straight, and the glory of the Lord shall be revealed, and all flesh shall see it together.[2]

This is our hope. This is the faith with which I return to the South. With this faith we will be able to transform the jangling discords of our nation into a beautiful symphony of brotherhood. With this faith we will be able to work together, to pray together, to struggle together, to go to jail together, to stand up for freedom together, knowing that we will be free one day.

This will be the day when all of God's children will be able to sing with new meaning "My country 'tis of thee, sweet land of liberty, of thee I sing. Land where my fathers died, land of the pilgrim's pride, from every mountainside, let freedom ring."

---

1. **interposition** (in′ tər pə zish ən) **and nullification** (nul′ ə fi kā′ shən): The disputed doctrine that a state can reject federal laws considered to be violations of its rights.

2. **every valley . . . all flesh shall see it together:** Refers to a Biblical passage (Isaiah 40:4 and 5).

"I Have a Dream" 467

Alternative Assessment To promote active reading, have students keep a reader's response journal as they read the selection. Ask students to focus their observations on details that reveal King's dream and on the persuasive techniques he uses. Encourage them to respond personally to his dream. What dream for a better world do they have?

Students' responses will enable you to assess their understanding of the speech.

Thematic Focus Martin Luther King's inspirational voice spoke of equality and justice for all people. He influenced great numbers of seemingly powerless people to join together in order to effectively work for change. Discuss with students the resistance King met as he tried to change conditions of inequality and injustice.

4 Clarification *Prodigious* means "wonderful; enormous."

5 Critical Thinking and Reading Where else does King use vivid words like *curvaceous*? Why are these words effective?

6 Literary Focus Is King's use of the phrase "let freedom ring" similar to the earlier use of the phrase "I have a dream"? Explain.

7 Critical Thinking and Reading Why do you think King suggests that other groups will not be truly free until black people are?

8 Discussion Explain how the conclusion of the speech—"Free at last"—relates to the beginning—"I have a dream. . . ."

Reader's Response Do you think King's dream will come true? Why or why not?

Thematic Response Martin Luther King gave this speech over thirty years ago. In what ways is he still an inspirational voice today?

Videodisc To extend students' knowledge about Martin Luther King's life and works, you may want to show them the *"American Documents: Letter From the Birmingham Jail"* videodisc. Have students discuss how the videodisc enhances their appreciation of King's "I Have a Dream" speech.

And if America is to be a great nation this must become true. So let freedom ring from the prodigious hilltops of New Hampshire. Let freedom ring from the mighty mountains of New York. Let freedom ring from the heightening Alleghenies of Pennsylvania!

Let freedom ring from the snowcapped Rockies of Colorado!

Let freedom ring from the curvaceous peaks of California!

But not only that; let freedom ring from Stone Mountain of Georgia!

Let freedom ring from every hill and molehill of Mississippi. From every mountainside, let freedom ring.

When we let freedom ring, when we let it ring from every village and every hamlet, from every state and every city, we will be able to speed up that day when all of God's children, black men and white men, Jews and Gentiles, Protestants and Catholics, will be able to join hands and sing in the words of that old Negro spiritual, "Free at last! Free at last! Thank God almighty, we are free at last!"

468   *Nonfiction*

Grammar in Action

Parallelism is the repetition of similar grammatical structures to create emphasis and show the equality of ideas. Martin Luther King, Jr., used parallel structures in different sentences to create a rousing speech. The parallelism helps listeners hear the emphasis:

Let freedom ring from the mighty mountains of New York. Let freedom ring from the heightening Alleghenies of Pennsylvania! Let freedom ring from the snowcapped Rockies of Colorado! Let freedom ring from the curvaceous peaks of California! But not only that: let freedom ring from Stone Mountain of Georgia!

Each sentence begins with the words "Let freedom ring." In each sentence, two prepositional phrases follow: "from" followed by an adjective and a noun, and "of" followed by a state's name. Variation in the last sentence underscores the parallelism.

Student Activity 1. Find another series of parallel structures in the speech.

Student Activity 2. Write three sentences, each of which includes parallelism. Vary the parts of the sentences that are parallel.

RESPONDING TO THE SELECTION

Your Response

1. What is your definition of equality? Explain.

Recalling

2. In your own words, briefly state King's dream.
3. What are the roots, or sources, of this dream?
4. What will the hope of realizing his dream enable him to do?

Interpreting

5. Why does King mention the names of so many states in his speech?
6. Explain the effect of repeating the phrase, "I have a dream."

Applying

7. Discuss the following statement by John F. Kennedy: "All of us do not have equal talent, but all of us should have equal opportunity to develop our talents."

ANALYZING LITERATURE

Understanding the Persuasive Essay

The purpose of a **persuasive essay** is to convince an audience to accept or consider an opinion or recommended course of action. In "I Have a Dream," King urges his audience to accept his dream of the United States transformed "into a beautiful symphony of brotherhood."

1. King paints many vivid word pictures of his dream, in addition to calling brotherhood a "symphony." Find two examples of the powerful images that he uses.
2. The success of a persuasive essay depends on its effect on its audience. Does King convince you to share his dream? Explain.

CRITICAL THINKING AND READING

Recognizing Persuasive Techniques

One technique that writers of persuasive essays or speeches use is to associate their goals with a familiar and honored document, phrase, or person. In "I Have a Dream," for instance, Martin Luther King, Jr., describes his dream using words from the Bible: ". . . every valley shall be exalted . . ." He wants the audience to transfer to his cause their positive feelings about the Bible.

1. Identify two other examples where King quotes from honored and familiar sources.
2. In each case explain whether King has chosen inspiring words to identify with his cause.

THINKING AND WRITING

Writing About Persuasion

Imagine that two of your good friends have had an argument. List some of the ways in which you could persuade them to settle their dispute. For instance, you might want to consider appealing to a source or an authority they respect, or showing them the benefits of making up. Then, using your list, write an essay further detailing your persuasive techniques. In revising the essay, make sure that you have explained why your persuasive techniques would be effective.

LEARNING OPTIONS

1. **Performance.** Form groups of three or four students and practice delivering "I Have a Dream." Listen to one another carefully and offer suggestions for improvements. Then have each group select a speaker to deliver a portion of the speech to the class. When delivering a speech, speak in a natural way rather than in a singsong voice. Also, try to adjust the volume and pitch of your voice according to the meaning and importance of the words. Keep in mind, however, that even the words you speak softly should be audible to your listeners.
2. **Speaking and Listening.** Recordings of King's speech are available at many libraries. If possible, listen to this speech on your own. Then explain to the class the additional insights into the speech you gained by listening to it.

"I Have a Dream" 469

Motivation/Prior Knowledge
Before students read this feature, have them imagine what it
might have been like to be in
King's place as he prepared for
and delivered his famous
speech. What realities did African Americans face at the time?
What resistance did King face as
a leader of the civil-rights movement? What personal qualities
did he have to possess to overcome this resistance? What
might King have hoped to accomplish through his speech?
How might his purpose have affected how he crafted his
speech?

Prereading Focus Tell students
that this feature will offer them
invaluable insights into the process that King went through in
preparing and delivering his
speech. As students read, have
them think about what they might
learn that they could apply to
their own writing.

Presentation

Discussion Questions
1. How did King's audience and
   purpose affect how he wrote
   his speech?
2. How did King's speech reflect
   the influence of the Bible?
3. What revisions did he make
   as he was delivering his
   speech?

ONE WRITER'S PROCESS

Martin Luther King, Jr., and His "Dream"

PREWRITING

The Problem That King Faced For
those involved in the civil rights movement,
the struggles were difficult and the outcome
unknown. Many uncertainties surrounded
an event that is now regarded as the high-
water mark of the movement: the August 28,
1963, March on Washington. That march
was organized to call attention to the wrongs
suffered by African Americans and to push
for federal legislation to correct these
wrongs. Never had there been so large a
gathering in Washington, D.C., however, and
federal officials were worried about the possibility of violence.

Fears of Violence The organizers of the
march had to avoid violence at all costs. Otherwise they would not win the support of
white Americans for their cause. To ensure
that people remained calm during the
march, its planners arranged for the instal-
lation of first-aid stations, portable bath-
rooms, and drinking fountains.

A Seven-Minute Limit This planning extended even to the time allowed the speakers who would address the crowd. Seven
minutes would be the absolute limit for each.
After all, if the orators talked on and on,
there was a chance that the marchers would
not leave before nightfall. That, in turn,
would increase the risk of violence.

It may not seem difficult to write a seven-
minute speech; however, Martin Luther
King, Jr., was a busy man and did not have
time to start writing until the night before
the march. In addition, he knew that he
faced a difficult problem: His speech had to
inspire his listeners to take action, but it had
to keep them from taking violent action.

Given this pressure, what kind of a
speech was King able to write?

DRAFTING

Partly New and Partly Old Working late
in his Washington hotel room, King fash-
ioned a speech that was partly new and
partly old.

What Was New

King dramatized the plight of African Americans by using an extended comparison from
the business world: "In a sense we have come
to our nation's Capitol to **cash a check.** When
the architects of our republic wrote the magnificent words of the Constitution and the Declaration of Independence, they were signing a
promissory note to which every American was
to **fall heir.** This **note** was a promise that all
men would be granted the unalienable rights of
life, liberty, and the pursuit of happiness . . .
[When African Americans tried to cash this
check, however, it came] "back marked 'insuf-
ficient funds.' But we refuse to believe that the
bank of justice is bankrupt. . . ."

What Was Old

As a minister, King was influenced by the
Bible's use of repeated phrases to tie passages together:

The Bible	King's Speech
"And God said, 'Let there be a firmament' . . . And God said, 'Let the waters under heaven' . . ." (Genesis 1:1)	"And so today, let us go back . . . And so today, let us go back . . ." "With this faith . . . With this faith . . ."

King worked all night on the speech and, in the early morning, gave it to an aide for distribution. In the words of historian Taylor Branch, this prepared text "was politically sound but far from historic. . . ." Also, it did not contain the famous "I have a dream" passage.

How did this good speech become the great one that is remembered today?

REVISING AND PUBLISHING

A Patchwork That Succeeded The address that King delivered was not identical to the one he had prepared. King's actual speech was a patchwork of newly written material, passages from former speeches, and remarks made up during delivery. What is most important, however, is that it worked beautifully. Its success was indicated by the positive response of the listening crowd and the later publication of the speech in newspapers and books.

We should remember, too, that it was not unusual for King to create a speech in this patchwork fashion. African American ministers often made up sermons as they went along, responding to the emotions of their listeners. They also memorized, and repeatedly used, sermons and speeches that had worked well for them on other occasions.

The Crowd and Its Mood The crowd waiting to hear King's speech extended back from the Lincoln Memorial, where the speakers stood, and flanked the sides of the half-mile-long reflecting pool. Altogether there were enough people to fill a large football stadium several times. Few orators in history had faced such a massive gathering.

King was the last in a series of speakers, and although the day had gone well, the crowd was restlessly anticipating his address. Finally, he was introduced as "the moral leader of our nation."

In his stately baritone voice, King read his prepared speech and was interrupted by occasional applause and voices shouting out "Yes!" and "Right on!" Such audience response was a traditional part of African American sermons and religious gatherings.

Revising While Speaking The crowd responded even more enthusiastically when, five minutes into his address, King read a line paraphrasing the Biblical prophet Amos: "We will not be satisfied until justice runs down like waters and righteousness like a mighty stream." The next sentence in his speech must have seemed out of tune with the growing excitement of the crowd: "And so today, let us go back to our communities as members of the international association for the advancement of creative dissatisfaction."

King decided to put aside his prepared speech and respond to the mood of his audience. He expressed the idea contained in the rejected sentence, but he did so with greater force and directness: "Go back to Mississippi. Go back to Alabama. . . ."

When he discarded his prepared text, King made a series of quick decisions about how to end his speech. You can trace the sequence of these decisions in the chart that follows.

One Writer's Process 471

Reader's Response What do the revisions King made while speaking reveal about his abilities as a speaker? Does it take a gifted speaker to make such revisions? Why or why not? Do students feel that King's revisions made his speech stronger? Why or why not?

Closure and Extension

ANSWERS TO THINKING ABOUT THE PROCESS

1. Suggested Response: King's revisions highlight how important it is for persuasive speakers to be attuned to the mood of their audiences.
2. Suggested Response: King was prepared to improvise because he had delivered many earlier speeches that he could draw from, and he had an excellent knowledge of other sources from which he could draw material.
3. Suggested Response: King varied the traditional stages in the writing process by making revisions while presenting his speech.
4. Students should observe the point at which King turns away from his prepared speech and begins to improvise.

Original Speech

And so today, let us go back to our communities as members of the international association for the advancement of creative dissatisfaction. Let us go back and work with all the strength we can muster to get strong civil rights legislation in this session of Congress. Let us go down from this place to ascend the other peaks of purpose. Let us descend from this mountaintop to climb other hills of hope. . . .

With this faith we will be able to transform the jangling discords of our nation into a beautiful symphony of brotherhood.

. . . Free at last! Free at last! Thank God almighty, we are free at last!

He replaced the rest of his text with an oration he had used months before. The phrase that tied this oration together was "I have a dream."

For a moment he returned to his written speech.

Then, however, he started improvising new material, using words from a famous patriotic song: "My country 'tis of thee . . . let freedom ring."

Again he returned to his original text, which concluded with a quotation from an African American spiritual.

New Material

I say to you today, my friends, so even though we face the difficulties of today and tomorrow, I still have a dream. It is a dream deeply rooted in the American dream. I have a dream that one day this nation will rise up and live out the true meaning of its creed—we hold these truths to be self-evident, that all men are created equal. . . .

. . . So let freedom ring from the prodigious hilltops of New Hampshire. Let freedom ring from the mighty mountains of New York. . . .

THINKING ABOUT THE PROCESS

1. What does King's departure from his prepared text indicate about the role of the audience in the process of persuasion?
2. How was King prepared to improvise a new ending, even though he had not planned to do it?
3. Sometimes the writing process is presented as an unchanging sequence of prewriting, writing, revising, and publishing. How does the story behind King's speech show that this description is not always correct?
4. **Cross-curricular Activity** View a film of Martin Luther King, Jr., delivering his "I Have a Dream" speech. Observe what occurs when he begins to revise his prepared address, and present your findings to the class.

472 Nonfiction

Essays in the Arts and Sciences

WOMAN WITH VIOLIN
Henri Matisse
Musée de l'Orangerie, Paris

Essays in the Arts and Sciences   473

Humanities Note

Fine art, *Woman With Violin,* by Henri Matisse. The French painter Henri Matisse (1869–1954) was the leader of the Fauvist movement in painting, which glorified line and rhythm and the free use of vibrant color. His work created a new way of thinking in twentieth-century art and had a lasting influence on subsequent trends.

In *Woman With Violin,* Matisse uses distortion of form to attain a decorative effect. The color has no relation to reality but is expressive of the way the artist feels about his subject. The color combinations are unusual but are made to work through sensitive handling. As in all of his works, detail is kept at a minimum. Matisse felt that any element included in a composition that did not contribute to the overall decorative effect was, in fact, a detriment.

Preparation

More About the Author James Rettie wrote this essay originally for *The Land,* a journal published by a group called Friends of the Land, which supported defensive husbandry of our living earth. The group was absorbed in 1961 by the Izaak Walton League, an organization that also serves to spread knowledge about the care of the earth. Why would Rettie have chosen the format of a fable in writing for a friendly audience?

Literary Focus Lead students to understand that fables, while often seemingly frivolous, have a serious message that is conveyed through the central idea. As in this selection, the central idea is often implied rather than stated.

Prereading Focus To help students recall incidents that should be recorded on their timelines, suggest that they work in cooperative groups. After the timelines are completed, explain to students that they are about to read a selection in which the timeline is for one year, each month of which represents sixty-two million years.

Vocabulary Have students write a definition of these words for someone from another planet.

Electronic Handbook If students are using the Language Master 6000, you may want them to use the electronic thesaurus to find suitable synonyms.

Teaching to Ability Levels To help less advanced students understand the geological and biological time periods, divide the class into twelve pairs or groups. Assign a month to each group, and explain that students in each group must become the experts who will explain and illustrate that month's events to their classmates.

474

James C. Rettie

was a member of the National Forest Service in Upper Darby, Pennsylvania. In his profession he had many opportunities to observe the damaging effects of industrial development and increased recreational use on the nation's forests. What he saw inspired him to write essays on the importance of conservation. Rettie wrote "But a Watch in the Night" in 1950, long before the current wave of interest in the environment; yet its message has perhaps even greater relevance today.

474   Nonfiction

But a Watch in the Night

The Central Idea

In order to understand the **central idea,** or main point, of an essay, it is often helpful to view the work as a whole. Although some writers directly state their main idea at the beginning of an essay, other writers depend on the cumulative effect of their writing to communicate a message. When you read an essay of this type, review the piece so that you can examine the methods the author has used to develop the central idea. Such methods include imaginative storytelling, a device that Rettie uses in this essay.

Focus

In "But a Watch in the Night," James C. Rettie describes the life history of the Earth as a film made by beings from another planet. The film takes one year to watch, and during each month various geological and biological events are described. For example, in April multicellular organisms first appear. Create a time line of your own life history, showing the major events that happened to you. Use the time line that follows, with its sample entries, as a model.

Event	I am born						I enter school							
Age	1	2	3	4	5	6	7	8	9	10	11	12	13	14

Vocabulary

Knowing the following words will help you as you read "But a Watch in the Night."

advent (ad′ vent) *n.*: Arrival (p. 476)

succession (sək sesh′ ən) *n.*: Act of coming after another in a series (p. 476)

aquatic (ə kwat′ ik) *adj.*: Living in water (p. 476)

embryo (em′ brē ō′) *n.*: Animal in the earliest stage of development (p. 477)

unpretentious (un prē ten′ shəs) *adj.*: Not making an extravagant outward show (p. 477)

precarious (prē ker′ ē əs) *adj.*: Uncertain; insecure (p. 478)

domesticated (do mes′ ti kāt′ əd) *v.*: Tamed and bred for human use (p. 478)

Objectives

1 To understand central idea
2 To recognize an implied central idea
3 To write a letter

Support Material

Teaching Portfolio
Teacher Backup, p. 525
Grammar in Action Worksheet, *Recognizing Active and Passive Voice,* p. 529
Usage and Mechanics Worksheet, p. 531
Vocabulary Worksheet, p. 532
Analyzing Literature Worksheet, *Understanding the Central Idea,* p. 533

Critical Thinking and Reading Worksheet, *Recognizing an Implied Central Idea,* p. 534
Selection Test, p. 535

Prentice Hall Literature Writing Studio

"But a Watch in the Night"
A Scientific Fable
James C. Rettie

Out beyond our solar system there is a planet called Copernicus.[1] It came into existence some four or five billion years before the birth of our Earth. In due course of time it became inhabited by a race of intelligent people.

About 750 million years ago, the Copernicans had developed the motion-picture machine to a point well in advance of the stage that we have reached. Most of the cameras that we now use in motion-picture work are geared to take twenty-four pictures per second on a continuous strip of film. When such film is run through a projector, it throws a series of images on the screen, and these change with a rapidity that gives the visual impression of normal movement. If a motion is too swift for the human eye to see it in detail, it can be captured and artificially slowed down by means of the slow-motion camera. This one is geared to take many more shots per second—ninety-six or even more than that. When the slow-motion film is projected at the normal speed of twenty-four pictures per second, we can see just how the jumping horse goes over the hurdle.

What about motion that is too slow to be seen by the human eye? That problem has been solved by the use of the time-lapse camera. In this one, the shutter is geared to take

1. **Copernicus** (kō pur′ni kəs): This fictitious planet is named after the Polish astronomer (1473–1543) who discovered that the Earth orbits the sun.

only one shot per second, or one per minute, or even one per hour—depending upon the kind of movement that is being photographed. When the time-lapse film is projected at the normal speed of twenty-four pictures per second, it is possible to see a bean sprout growing up out of the ground. Time-lapse films are useful in the study of many types of motion too slow to be observed by the unaided human eye.

The Copernicans, it seems, had time-lapse cameras some 757 million years ago, and they also had superpowered telescopes that gave them a clear view of what was happening upon this Earth. They decided to make a film record of the life history of Earth and to make it on the scale of one picture per year. The photography has been in progress during the last 757 million years.

In the near future, a Copernican interstellar expedition will arrive upon our Earth and bring with it a copy of the time-lapse film. Arrangements will be made for showing the entire film in one continuous run. This will begin at midnight on New Year's Eve and continue day and night without a single stop until midnight of December 31. The rate of projection will be twenty-four pictures per second. Time on the screen will thus seem to move at the rate of twenty-four years per second; 1,440 years per minute; 86,400 years per hour; approximately two million years per day; and sixty-two million years per month.

"But a Watch in the Night" 475

The normal life span of human beings will occupy about three seconds. The full period of Earth history that will be unfolded on the screen (some 757 million years) will extend from what geologists call Precambrian times up to the present. This will, by no means, cover the full time span of the Earth's geological history, but it will embrace the period since the advent of living organisms.

During the months of January, February, and March, the picture will be desolate and dreary. The shape of the land masses and the oceans will bear little or no resemblance to those that we know. The violence of geological erosion will be much in evidence. Rains will pour down on the land and promptly go booming down into the seas. There will be no clear streams anywhere except where the rains fall upon hard rock. Everywhere on the steeper ground the stream channels will be filled with boulders hurled down by rushing waters. Raging torrents and dry stream beds will keep alternating in quick succession. High mountains will seem to melt like so much butter in the sun. The shifting of land into the seas, later to be thrust up as new mountains, will be going on at a grand scale.

Early in April there will be some indication of the presence of single-celled living organisms in some of the warmer and sheltered coastal waters. By the end of the month, it will be noticed that some of these organisms have become multicellular. A few of them, including the trilobites, will be encased in hard shells.

Toward the end of May, the first vertebrates[2] will appear, but they will still be aquatic creatures. In June about 60 percent of the land area that we know as North America will be under water. One broad channel will occupy the space where the Rocky Mountains

now stand. Great deposits of limestone[3] will be forming under some of the shallow seas. Oil and gas deposits will be in the process of formation—also under shallow seas. On land there will still be no sign of vegetation. Erosion will be rampant, tearing loose particles and chunks of rock and grinding them into sand and silt[4] to be spewed out by the streams into bays and estuaries.[5]

About the middle of July, the first land plants will appear and take up the tremendous job of soil building. Slowly, very slowly, the mat of vegetation will spread, always battling for its life against the power of erosion. Almost foot by foot, the plant life will advance, lacing down with its root structures whatever pulverized rock material it can find. Leaves and stems will be giving added protection against the loss of the soil foothold. The increasing vegetation will pave the way for land animals that will live upon it.

Early in August the seas will be teeming with fish. This will be what geologists call the Devonian period. Some of the races of these fish will be breathing by means of lung tissue instead of through gill tissues. Before the month is over, some of the lung fish will go ashore and take on a crude lizardlike appearance. Here are the first amphibians.[6]

In early September the insects will put in their appearance. Some will look like huge dragonflies and will have a wingspread of twenty-four inches. Large portions of the land masses will now be covered with heavy vegetation that will include the primitive spore-propagating[7] trees. Layer upon layer of

---

2. vertebrates (vur′tə brāts′) n.: Animals with a backbone, or spinal column.

3. limestone (līm′stōn) n.: Rock composed of the organic remains of sea animals.
4. silt (silt) n.: Tiny particles that accumulate on the bottom of bodies of water.
5. estuaries (es′tyoo er ēz) n.: Inlets or arms of the sea, especially the wide mouths of rivers.
6. amphibians (am fib′ē ənz): Coldblooded, scaleless animals with a backbone, such as frogs and toads.
7. spore-propagating (spōr prăp′ə gāt′iŋ) adj.: Producing seeds for the purpose of reproducing.

Grammar in Action

Writers use verbs in **active or passive voice** to focus reader attention on important ideas. A sentence written in active voice focuses on who or what acts. A sentence written in passive voice focuses on who or what is acted upon. Passive voice is made by adding some form of the verb to be (is, am, are, was, were, be, been, being) to the past participle. Compare these sentences:

The Copernicans had developed the motion-picture machine. (the Copernicans acted; active voice)

A motion too slow for the human eye to see can be captured by means of the slow-motion camera. (a motion is acted upon; constructed of a form of to be and the past participle; passive voice)

Student Activity 1. Decide whether the italicized verbs in the following sentences are in the active or passive voice. Be able to identify the form of to be and the past participle in passive-voice verbs. Note that in some sentences more than one verb is italicized.

1. When such a film is run through a projector, it throws a series of images on the screen.
2. This slow-motion camera is geared to take many more shots per second.

this plant growth will build up, later to appear as coal deposits. About the middle of this month, there will be evidence of the first seed-bearing plants and the first reptiles. Heretofore, the land animals will have been amphibians that could reproduce their kind only by depositing a soft egg mass in quiet waters. The reptiles will now be freed from the aquatic bond because they can reproduce by means of a shelled egg in which the embryo and its nurturing liquids are sealed and thus protected from destructive evaporation. Before September is over, the first dinosaurs will be seen—creatures destined to dominate the animal realm for about 140 million years and then to disappear.

In October there will be a series of mountain uplifts along what is now the eastern coast of the United States. A creature with feathered limbs—half bird and half reptile in appearance—will take itself into the air. Some small and rather unpretentious animals will be seen to bring forth their young in a form that is a miniature replica of the parents and to feed these young on milk from the female parent. The emergence of this mammalian form of animal life will be recognized as one of the great events in geologic time. October will also witness the high-water mark of the dinosaurs—creatures ranging in size from that of the modern goat to monsters like Brontosaurus that weighed some forty tons. Most of them will be placid vegetarians, but a few will be hideous-looking carnivores,[8] like Allosaurus and Tyrannosaurus. Some of the herbivorous[9] dinosaurs will be clad in bony armor for protection against their flesh-eating comrades.

---

8. carnivores (kär'nə vôrz'): Flesh-eating animals.
9. herbivorous (hər biv'ər əs) *adj.*: Feeding chiefly on plants.

10 **Discussion** How do scientists know about the biological progression described here?

Speaking and Listening Have students research a specific environmental issue and deliver a persuasive speech encouraging some action of which Rettie would approve. Ask listeners to respond with questions.

Cooperative Learning After students complete the Speaking and Listening activity, assign groups of four to develop a composite plan for community action.

Amphibians · Insects · Early Fish · Mammals · Trilobites · Dinosaurs · Land Plants · First Vertebrates · Cellular Life · Humans

JAN.	FEB.	MAR.	APR.	MAY	JUNE	JULY	AUG.	SEPT.	OCT.	NOV.	DEC.

3. When the time-lapse film *is projected* at normal speed, it *is* possible to see a bean sprout growing up out of the ground.
4. The Copernicans also *had* superpowered telescopes that *gave* them a clear view of what *was happening* upon this Earth.
5. The photography *has been* in progress during the last 757 million years.

Student Activity 2. Write five sentences of your own about the scientific fable. Use passive voice in two of them, and use active voice in three of them. Your sentences, like those above, may have more than one verb. Underline and identify the voice of all verbs you use.

Electronic Handbook You may want students to review active and passive voice before completing the Grammar in Action activities. If students have access to the Language Master 6000, have them enter *active* and press the GRAMMAR key for information on active and passive voice.

November will bring pictures of a sea extending from the Gulf of Mexico to the Arctic in space now occupied by the Rocky Mountains. A few of the reptiles will take to the air on batlike wings. One of these, called Pteranodon, will have a wingspread of fifteen feet. There will be a rapid development of the modern flowering plants, modern trees, and modern insects. The dinosaurs will disappear. Toward the end of the month, there will be a tremendous disturbance in which the Rocky Mountains will rise out of the sea to assume a dominating place in the North American landscape.

As the picture runs on into December, it will show the mammals in command of the animal life. Seed-bearing trees and grasses will have covered most of the land with a heavy mantle of vegetation. Only the areas newly thrust up from the sea will be barren. Most of the streams will be crystal clear. The turmoil of geologic erosion will be confined to localized areas. About December 25 will begin the cutting of the Grand Canyon of the Colorado River. Grinding down through layer after layer of sedimentary strata,[10] this stream will finally expose deposits laid down in Precambrian times. Thus in the walls of that canyon will appear geological formations dating from recent times to the period when the earth had no living organisms upon it.

The picture will run through the latter days of December and even up to its final day with still no sign of humankind. The spectators will become alarmed in the fear that human beings have somehow been left out. But not so; sometime about noon on December 31 (one million years ago) will appear a stooped, massive creature of human proportions. This will be Pithecanthropus. For tools and weapons it will have nothing but crude stone and wooden clubs. Its children will live a precarious existence threatened on the one side by hostile animals and on the other by tremendous climatic changes. Ice sheets—in places 4,000 feet deep—will form in the northern parts of North America and Eurasia.[11] Four times this glacial ice will push southward to cover half the continents. With each advance the plant and animal life will be swept under or pushed southward. With each recession of ice, life will struggle to reestablish itself in the wake of the retreating glaciers. The woolly mammoth, the musk ox, and the caribou will all fight to maintain themselves near the ice line. Sometimes they will be caught and put into cold storage—skin, flesh, blood, bones, and all.

The picture will run on through suppertime with still very little evidence of human presence on the Earth. It will be about 11:00 P.M. when the Neanderthals appear. Another half hour will go by before the appearance of Cro-Magnon man and woman, living in caves and painting crude animal pictures on the walls of their dwelling. Fifteen minutes more will bring Neolithic man and woman, knowing how to chip stone and thus produce sharp cutting edges for spears and tools. In a few minutes more it will appear that man and woman have domesticated the dog, the sheep, and possibly other animals. They will then learn the arts of basket weaving and the making of pottery and dugout canoes.

The dawn of civilization will not come until about five or six minutes before the end of the picture. The story of the Egyptians, the Babylonians, the Greeks, and the Romans will unroll during the fourth, the third, and the second minute before the end. At 58 minutes and 43 seconds past 11:00 P.M. (just 1 minute and 17 seconds before the end) will come the beginning of the Christian era. Co-

---

10. sedimentary strata (sed′ə men′tər ē strāt′ə): Layers of rock deposits, or silt.

11. Eurasia (yōō rā′zhə): Land mass made up of the continents of Europe and Asia.

lumbus will encounter the "new world" 20 seconds before the end. The Declaration of Independence will be signed just 7 seconds before the final curtain comes down.

In those few moments of geologic time will be told the story of all that has happened since we became a nation. And what a story it will be! A human swarm will sweep across the face of the continent and take it away from the Native American. They will change it far more radically than it has ever been changed before in a comparable time. The great virgin forests will be seen going down before ax and fire. The soil, covered for eons[12] by its protective mantle of trees and grasses, will be laid bare to the ravages of water and wind erosion. Streams that had been flowing clear will, once again, take up a load of silt and push it toward the seas. Humus[13] and mineral salts, both vital elements of productive soil, will be seen to vanish at a terrifying rate.

---

12. **eons** (e′ənz) *n.*: Thousands of years.
13. **Humus** (hyo͞o′məs) *n.*: A rich layer of the soil.

The railroads and highways and cities that will spring up may divert attention, but they cannot cover up the blight of human activity. In great sections of Asia, it will be seen that people must utilize cow dung and every scrap of available straw or grass for fuel to cook their food. The forests that once provided wood for this purpose will be gone without a trace. The use of these agricultural wastes for fuel, in place of returning them to the land, will be leading to increasing soil impoverishment. Here and there will be seen a dust storm darkening the landscape over an area of thousands of miles across. Human beings will be shown counting their wealth in terms of bits of printed paper representing other bits of a scarce but comparatively useless yellow metal that is kept buried in strong vaults. Meanwhile, the soil, the only real wealth that can keep humankind alive on the face of this Earth, is savagely being cut loose from its ancient moorings and washed into the seven seas.

We have just arrived upon this Earth. How long will we stay?

RESPONDING TO THE SELECTION

Your Response
1. Does this essay make you feel optimistic about the Earth's future? Explain.

Recalling
2. During which "month" does life first appear?

Interpreting
3. What is the author's attitude toward humans' effect on the environment?
4. Why does the author say that soil is the only real wealth?

Applying
5. Does Rettie make you want to take action to save the Earth? Explain.

READING IN THE ARTS AND SCIENCES

Understanding the Central Idea

In "But a Watch in the Night," the author takes the time to create an imaginary situation so that the reader can understand the vastness of his subject. The central idea of the essay becomes apparent only at the end. The description of the Copernicans' film, however, is necessary if the reader is to understand the author's message fully.

1. How does the film make the Earth's geological and biological history more understandable to the reader?
2. What is the central idea of the essay?

"But a Watch in the Night" 479

17 Reading Strategy Have students consider the use of the word *swarm* in this sentence. What connotations does it have? What judgment is the author making about the treatment of the Native American?

18 Discussion What inference can be drawn from this sentence?

19 Discussion To what is Rettie referring?

20 Discussion What is causing the loss of soil?

Reader's Response If you could talk to Rettie today, more than forty years after he wrote this essay, what do you think he would recommend?

Thematic Response Rettie's scientific fable looks at the earth from the distance of time and place. If you were a Copernican, what would you predict for our living planet for the following January?

Closure and Extension

ANSWERS TO RESPONDING TO THE SELECTION
Your Response
1. Most students will probably say that the essay does not make them feel optimistic because it demonstrates such rapid destruction.

Recalling
2. Single-celled living organisms appear in April.

Interpreting
3. Suggested Response: The author believes human activity is destroying so much vegetation that the soil will disappear.
4. Suggested Response: All forms of life depend on the soil.

Applying
5. Most students will probably want to take action to save the earth after reading about the devastating effect humans have had in such a short time.

ANSWERS TO ANALYZING LITERATURE

1. Suggested Response: By using the film, Rettie sets up a time analogy in which 750 million years is represented by one year. The historical events can be more easily understood in terms of one year than in terms of 750 million.
2. Suggested Response: Even though humans have been on Earth for only a few seconds of film time, they have destroyed what took 750 million years to build.

THINKING AND WRITING

For a Thinking and Writing assignment, see the Teaching Portfolio, page 526.

479

Preparation

More About the Author Joan Didion's second novel, *Play It As It Lays*, was made into a movie. Also, Didion and her husband collaborated on the script for the Barbra Streisand version of *A Star Is Born*. Ask students to discuss the differences between writing a novel and writing a script for a film.

Literary Focus Help students understand how one might begin to formulate ideas in order to write a character analysis. Have students suggest a famous person whom most students know. Then have them suggest adjectives that describe this person and tell anecdotes about this person to illustrate these characteristics. Help students understand how this brainstorming of ideas can help in the writing of a character analysis.

Prereading Focus You may want to encourage students to expand their understanding of individual words by extending the word cluster activity to other words. For example, the word *open* might be further described with the words *ideas, colors, subjects, mediums, materials,* and *forms* to identify some of the areas in which an artist often takes new approaches.

Vocabulary Have your less advanced students read the words and their definitions. Then have them use the words in a conversation with two or three other classmates.

GUIDE FOR READING

Joan Didion

(1934–   ) descends from a long line of pioneers. Her great-great-grandmother went West in a covered wagon in 1846. Didion grew up in California and, as a young woman, won a writing contest sponsored by *Vogue*. Eventually she rose to become an editor of that well-known magazine. Her reputation in the literary world, however, is based on her novels and collections of essays. The essay "Georgia O'Keeffe," which comes from *The White Album,* pays tribute to an artist who displayed a strong pioneer spirit.

Georgia O'Keeffe

Character Analysis

In a **character analysis,** the writer tries to reveal the key traits that give a person his or her identity. This type of essay is different from a biography in several ways. It is usually briefer and more focused than an account of a person's life, and it does not necessarily follow a chronological sequence. In "Georgia O'Keeffe," for example, Joan Didion begins by identifying an important quality of the artist Georgia O'Keeffe: "Hardness." Didion then gives examples from O'Keeffe's work and life to clarify what she means by this descriptive word.

Focus

In painting her word portrait of the artist Georgia O'Keeffe, Joan Didion uses terms such as "hard," "open," and "aggressive." Make a word cluster showing the qualities *you* think an artist needs to possess. Place the word *artist* in the center of the cluster and add descriptive words and phrases around it. Then read the selection and see if O'Keeffe fits your definition.

Vocabulary

Knowing the following words will help you as you read "Georgia O'Keeffe."

condescending (kän′ də sen′ diŋ) *adj.*: Characterized by looking down on someone (p. 481)

tonic (tän′ ik) *adj.*: Stimulating; invigorating (p. 482)

indulged (in dulj′d′) *v.*: Accepted in a belittling way (p. 482)

sentimental (sen′ tə men′ t'l) *adj.*: Foolishly emotional (p. 482)

genesis (jen′ ə sis) *n.*: Birth; origin; beginning (p. 482)

derisive (di rī′ siv) *adj.*: Scornful; mocking (p. 482)

rancor (raŋ′ kər) *n.*: Hatred; spite (p. 484)

contempt (kən tempt′) *n.*: Scorn; disrespect (p. 484)

immutable (i myoot′ ə b'l) *adj.*: Never changing (p. 484)

Objectives

1 To appreciate character analysis
2 To evaluate conclusions about art
3 To write about art
4 To express individual interests and abilities through an optional activity

Support Material

Teaching Portfolio
Teacher Backup, p. 537
Grammar in Action Worksheet, *Using Coordination,* p. 541
Usage and Mechanics Worksheet, p. 543
Vocabulary Check, p. 544
Analyzing Literature Worksheet, *Character Analysis,* p. 546
Critical Thinking and Reading

Worksheet, *Evaluating Conclusions About Art,* p. 547
Selection Test, p. 548
Art Transparency 9: *Self-portrait,* by Joan Miró

Prentice Hall Literature Writing Studio

Georgia O'Keeffe

Joan Didion

"Where I was born and where and how I have lived is unimportant," Georgia O'Keeffe told us in the book of paintings and words published in her ninetieth year on earth. She seemed to be advising us to forget the beautiful face in the Stieglitz[1] photographs. She appeared to be dismissing the rather condescending romance that had attached to her by then, the romance of extreme good looks and advanced age and deliberate isolation. "It is what I have done with where I have been that should be of interest." I recall an August afternoon in Chicago in 1973 when I took my daughter, then seven, to see what Georgia O'Keeffe had done with where she had been. One of the vast O'Keeffe "Sky Above Clouds" canvases floated over the back stairs in the Chicago Art Institute that day, dominating what seemed to be several stories of empty light, and my daughter looked at it once, ran to the landing, and kept on looking. "Who drew it," she whispered after a while. I told her. "I need to talk to her," she said finally.

My daughter was making, that day in Chicago, an entirely unconscious but quite basic assumption about people and the work they do. She was assuming that the glory she saw in the work reflected a glory in its maker, that the painting was the painter as the poem is the poet, that every choice one made alone—every word chosen or rejected, every brush stroke laid or not laid down—betrayed one's character. *Style is character.* It seemed to me that afternoon that I had

---

1. **Stieglitz:** Alfred Stieglitz (1864–1946). U.S. photographer and husband of Georgia O'Keeffe.

THE WHITE TRUMPET FLOWER, 1932
Georgia O'Keeffe
San Diego Museum of Art

Georgia O'Keeffe 481

Presentation

Motivation/Prior Knowledge
Ask students to mention artists, writers, or musicians whose style they would recognize. Ask them what qualities make a style distinctive. Then tell them that Georgia O'Keeffe, the artist they will read about, developed an inimitable style of her own.

Master Teacher Note Use the overheard projector to show students Art Transparency 9, *Self-portrait,* by Joan Miró. Ask them what qualities the artist has revealed. Have them specify the details that suggest these qualities. Then tell them that Didion's essay is like a portrait in words of the artist Georgia O'Keeffe. Have them look for the way Didion uses words and phrases to reveal O'Keeffe's important qualities.

Purpose-Setting Question
What does Didion mean when she attributes the quality of "hardness" to O'Keeffe?

Making Connections Another selection that deals with a person of integrity is "A Lincoln Preface," page 405.

1 **Discussion** What insights into O'Keeffe's personality does Didion convey in this first paragraph?

2 **Enrichment** *Sky Above Clouds,* which O'Keeffe began in 1965 at the age of seventy-seven, was 28 feet by 8 feet. It was her largest painting.

3 **Critical Thinking and Reading** The author italicized *"Style is character"* to draw attention to and emphasize the importance of that statement. What do you think she meant by it?

Thematic Focus We usually think of certain writers and speakers as inspirational voices. Ask students if visual works can also be sources of inspiration. Can an artist evoke deep emotions in those who view his or her work? Can art stir people to look inward or move them to take action against injustice?

Humanities Note

Fine art, *The White Trumpet Flower,* by Georgia O'Keeffe (1887–1986). Georgia O'Keeffe's inspiration speaks most powerfully through her paintings. Her giant flower paintings were inspired by skyscrapers built all around her in New York City during the 1920's. She observed that she made her flowers "big like the huge buildings going up. People will be startled: they'll *have* to look."

1. Why do you think O'Keeffe chose to focus on a single flower?
2. What kinds of shapes and lines did O'Keeffe emphasize in this painting?
3. What associations or feelings does this painting call up?

4 **Discussion** What does this paragraph reveal about O'Keeffe? Refer to lines in the paragraph to support your answer.

5 **Discussion** Who are the "city men"? What words and phrases in this paragraph tell you how O'Keeffe feels about the "city men"?

Multicultural Focus Didion says that "hardness has not been in our century a quality much admired in women." Ask students if they agree with this statement and why or why not. Discuss what qualities they think are admired in women in American society today; have them back up their opinions with specific examples. You can stimulate discussion by asking students what people might think of a woman who is, for example, strong, clever, gentle, ambitious, intelligent, compassionate, shy, or aggressive.

Point out that in other cultures, the qualities most valued in a woman might be quite different from those valued in the United States. Have students choose another culture and research the role of women and attitudes toward women in that culture. Try to have a broad range of Western and non-Western societies represented. Have students present their finding to the class.

rarely seen so instinctive an application of this familiar principle, and I recall being pleased not only that my daughter responded to style as character but that it was Georgia O'Keeffe's particular style to which she responded: this was a hard woman who had imposed her 192 square feet of clouds on Chicago.

"Hardness" has not been in our century a quality much admired in women, nor in the past twenty years has it even been in official favor for men. When hardness surfaces in the very old we tend to transform it into "crustiness" or eccentricity, some tonic pepperiness to be indulged at a distance. On the evidence of her work and what she has said about it, Georgia O'Keeffe is neither "crusty" nor eccentric. She is simply hard, a straight shooter, a woman clean of received wisdom and open to what she sees. This is a woman who could early on dismiss most of her contemporaries as "dreamy," and would later single out one she liked as "a very poor painter." (And then add, apparently by way of softening the judgment: "I guess he wasn't a painter at all. He had no courage and I believe that to create one's own world in any of the arts takes courage.") This is a woman who in 1939 could advise her admirers that they were missing her point, that their appreciation of her famous flowers was merely sentimental. "When I paint a red hill," she observed coolly in the catalogue for an exhibition that year, "you say it is too bad that I don't always paint flowers. A flower touches almost everyone's heart. A red hill doesn't touch everyone's heart." This is a woman who could describe the genesis of one of her most well-known paintings—the "Cow's Skull: Red, White and Blue" owned by the Metropolitan[2]—as an act of quite deliberate and derisive orneriness. "I thought of the city men I had been seeing in the East," she wrote. "They talked so often of writing the Great American Novel—the Great American Play—the Great American Poetry. . . . So as I was painting my cow's head on blue I thought to myself, 'I'll make it an American painting. They will not think it great with the red stripes down the sides—Red, White and Blue—but they will notice it.' "

The city men. The men. They. The words crop up again and again as this astonishingly aggressive woman tells us what was on her mind when she was making her astonishingly aggressive paintings. It was those city men who stood accused of sentimentalizing her flowers: "I made you take time to look at what I saw and when you took time to really notice my flower you hung all your associations with flowers on my flower and you write about my flower as if I think and see what you think and see—and I don't." *And I don't.* Imagine those words spoken, and the sound you hear is *don't tread on me.*[3] "The men" believed it impossible to paint New York, so Georgia O'Keeffe painted New York. "The men" didn't think much of her bright color, so she made it brighter. The men yearned toward Europe so she went to Texas, and then New Mexico. The men talked about Cézanne,[4] "long involved remarks about the 'plastic quality' of his form and color," and took one another's long involved remarks, in the view of this angelic rattlesnake in their midst, altogether too seriously. "I can paint one of those dismal-colored paintings like the men," the woman who regarded herself always as an outsider remembers thinking one day in 1922, and she did: a painting of a shed "all low-toned

---

2. **Metropolitan:** Metropolitan Museum of Art in New York City.

3. **Don't tread on me:** Motto of the first official American flag that was first flown by a naval vessel on December 3, 1775.
4. **Cézanne:** Paul Cézanne (1839–1906), French Impressionist and Postimpressionist painter.

Grammar in Action

Coordination is the use of conjunctions to connect equally important ideas smoothly and clearly. Among the most common coordinating conjunctions are *and, but, or, nor, for, yet,* and *so.* By using conjunctions, writers can avoid choppy sentences and clarify the relationship between ideas:

Unconnected: Mother wants a cat. She knows it may sometimes claw on furniture.

With coordination: Mother wants a cat, *yet* she knows it may sometimes claw on furniture.

The following sentences from "Georgia O'Keeffe" illustrate effective coordination:

Imagine those words spoken, *and* the sound you hear is *don't tread on me.* "The men" believed it impossible to paint New York, *so* Georgia O'Keeffe painted New York. "The

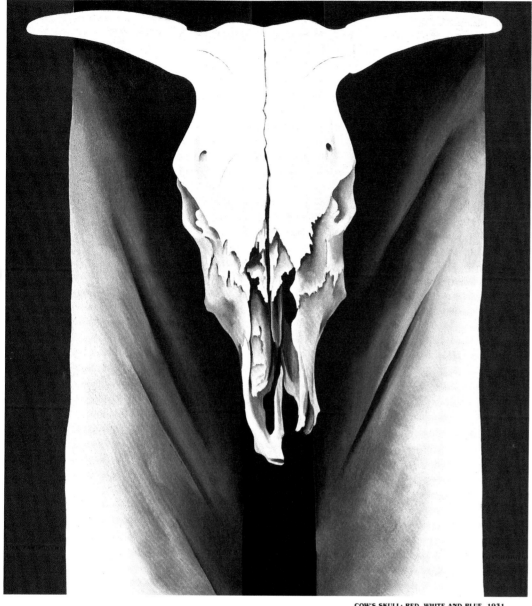

COW'S SKULL: RED, WHITE AND BLUE, 1931
Georgia O'Keeffe
The Metropolitan Museum of Art

Georgia O'Keeffe 483

men" didn't think much of her bright color, so she made it brighter.

"The men" yearned toward Europe, so she went to Texas, *and* then New Mexico. . . . "I can paint one of those dismal-colored paintings like the men," the woman who regarded herself always as an outsider remembers thinking one day in 1922, *and* she did: a painting of a shed. . . .

Student Activity 1. Find three other sentences in "Georgia O'Keeffe" that use coordination.

Student Activity 2. Write three sentences using coordination. Try to use a different coordinating conjunction in each, but be sure the meaning is clear and the relationship between the clauses or phrases logical.

Electronic Handbook You might want students to review coordination before completing the Grammar in Action activities. If students have access to the Language Master 6000, have them enter the access words *conjunction* and *parallel* and press the GRAMMAR key to get information on the use of coordination.

and dreary with the tree beside the door." She called this act of rancor "The Shanty" and hung it in her next show. "The men seemed to approve of it," she reported fifty-four years later, her contempt undimmed. "They seemed to think that maybe I was beginning to paint. That was my only low-toned dismal-colored painting."

Some women fight and others do not. Like so many successful guerrillas in the war between the sexes, Georgia O'Keeffe seems to have been equipped early with an immutable sense of who she was and a fairly clear understanding that she would be required to prove it. On the surface her upbringing was conventional. She was a child on the Wisconsin prairie who played with china dolls and painted watercolors with cloudy skies because sunlight was too hard to paint and, with her brother and sisters, listened every night to her mother read stories of the Wild West, of Texas, of Kit Carson and Billy the Kid. She told adults that she wanted to be an artist and was embarrassed when they asked what kind of artist she wanted to be: she had no idea "what kind." She had no idea what artists did. She had never seen a picture that interested her, other than a pen-and-ink Maid of Athens in one of her mother's books, some Mother Goose illustrations printed on cloth, a tablet cover that showed a little girl with pink roses, and the painting of Arabs on horseback that hung in her grandmother's parlor. At thirteen, in a Dominican convent, she was mortified when the sister corrected her drawing. At Chatham Episcopal Institute in Virginia she painted lilacs and sneaked time alone to walk out to where she could see the line of the Blue Ridge Mountains on the horizon. At the Art Institute in Chicago she was shocked by the presence of live models and wanted to abandon anatomy lessons. At the Art Students League in New York one of her fellow students advised her that, since he would be a great painter and she would end up teaching painting in a girls' school, any work of hers was less important than modeling for him. Another painted over her work to show her how the Impressionists did trees. She had not before heard how the Impressionists did trees and she did not much care.

At twenty-four she left all these opinions behind and went for the first time to live in Texas, where there were no trees to paint and no one to tell her how not to paint them. In Texas there was only the horizon she craved. In Texas she had her sister Claudia with her for a while, and in the late afternoons they would walk away from town and toward the horizon and watch the evening star come out. "That evening star fascinated me," she wrote. "It was in some way very exciting to me. My sister had a gun, and as we walked she would throw bottles into the air and shoot as many as she could before they hit the ground. I had nothing but to walk into nowhere and the wide sunset space with the star. Ten watercolors were made from that star." In a way one's interest is compelled as much by the sister Claudia with the gun as by the painter Georgia with the star, but only the painter left us this shining record. Ten watercolors were made from that star.

Closure and Extension

ANSWERS TO RESPONDING TO THE SELECTION
Your Response

1. Encourage students to comment on how they think the traits they admire most about O'Keeffe affected the quality on her own life and her relationships with others.

Recalling

2. O'Keeffe is described as a direct, open, and original person.
3. O'Keeffe retained her individuality, painting only those things she wanted to paint, regardless of what others thought or said about her work.
4. In growing up, she decided early that she wanted to be an artist and stuck to her decision.

Interpreting

5. Answers will differ, but students

---

6 Critical Thinking and Reading What do you think the first sentence of the paragraph means? What is the relationship between this sentence and the one that follows it?

7 Enrichment The O'Keeffe family lived near Sun Prairie in the southern part of Wisconsin. Georgia lived there with her family until she was thirteen; at thirteen she was enrolled in Sacred Heart Academy, a convent boarding school outside Madison, Wisconsin.

8 Reading Strategy Ask students to summarize O'Keeffe's development as an artist.

9 Discussion Why does Didion end the essay with this image? What does the image suggest about O'Keeffe and her sister?

Reader's Response Conduct your own character analysis. What one word would you use to describe yourself? Why is this word appropriate?

Thematic Response In what ways do you think Georgia O'Keeffe might inspire other women? In what ways might she also inspire men?

RESPONDING TO THE SELECTION

Your Response

1. Which of O'Keeffe's qualities do you admire most? Why?

Recalling

2. Describe O'Keeffe's character as it is portrayed in this essay.
3. How did O'Keeffe assert herself among the male artists whom she knew?
4. What signs of her character did she show in growing up?

Interpreting

5. Explain what Didion means by saying O'Keeffe had "an immutable sense of who she was."
6. What do you think O'Keeffe found attractive about Texas?

Applying

7. O'Keeffe said "that to create one's own world in any of the arts takes courage." Comment on this remark.

READING IN THE ARTS AND SCIENCES

Character Analysis

In a **character analysis,** the writer tries to reveal the key traits that give a person his or her identity. According to Joan Didion, one of Georgia O'Keeffe's important traits was "hardness." An example of this quality was her insistence on using bright colors when other artists favored dull ones.

1. Explain how O'Keeffe demonstrated this trait in two other ways.
2. What is the difference between hardness and crustiness?
3. Explain how O'Keeffe's hardness was the opposite of sentimentality.

CRITICAL THINKING AND READING

Evaluating Conclusions About Art

You can evaluate a writer's conclusions about a painting by carefully studying the work yourself. For example, you will want to look at O'Keeffe's *The White Trumpet Flower* (page 481) before evaluating Didion's remark that O'Keeffe's flowers are not "sentimental." Here are some questions you might ask yourself before reaching a conclusion: Why did O'Keeffe focus in on just one flower? Why did she stress the curved lines?

1. After considering these matters, explain some of the usual feelings about flowers that Didion might be referring to as "sentimental."
2. Is O'Keeffe's flower sentimental? Explain.

THINKING AND WRITING

Writing About Art

Imagine that you have to write about the painting *Cow's Skull: Red, White and Blue* (page 483) for a catalog. Before beginning, reread what Didion says about this painting and look at it carefully. List the points that you want to make. For instance, you might want to tell readers why O'Keeffe used red, white, and blue. You might also discuss the choice of subject. In revising make sure that your catalog entry will help readers to understand the work. When you are done, share your essay with your classmates.

LEARNING OPTION

Writing. The illustrations of the artist's paintings included in this selection give you an opportunity to respond to her work. Examine O'Keeffe's paintings and think about how they make you feel. Write a brief poem for each one in which you convey the impression the painting creates for you. You might wish to arrange the words to duplicate the artist's forms.

Georgia O'Keeffe 485

might say that O'Keeffe was not very influenced by what others thought about her or by what others wanted for her.
6. Answers will differ, but students might say that she was attracted to the open spaces of the prairie.

Applying

7. Answers will differ. Students may realize, however, that art involves two main risks: failing to express one's vision adequately and hav-

ing one's vision rejected by others.

Challenge Georgia O'Keeffe has said, "Still—in a way—nobody sees a flower—really—it is so small—we haven't time—and to see takes time, like to have a friend takes time." Have students comment on the meaning of this quote.

ANSWERS TO READING IN THE ARTS AND SCIENCES

1. Suggested Response: She demonstrated this trait in her comments regarding *Cow's Skull: Red, White and Blue* and in her criticism of her contemporaries and their art.
2. Suggested Response: Crustiness is more often associated with older people. It implies eccentricity and rigidity.
3. Suggested Response: Sentimentality is associated with soft and

conventional emotions like an easy "love" of flowers and other "beautiful" objects. O'Keeffe, however, was hard and unconventional. She did not pretend to experience what others expected her to experience.

ANSWERS TO CRITICAL THINKING AND READING

1. Suggested Response: Flowers are usually thought of as soft, gentle, pleasing, and beautiful in a conventional way.
2. Answers will differ, but students might suggest that O'Keeffe's flowers are bold, arresting, and vibrant—characteristics not often associated with sentimentality.

THINKING AND WRITING

Software If students have access to computers, have them use **Bank Street Writer** to complete all stages of the assignment. Using the program's cut and paste features, students will be able to easily incorporate ideas from their prewriting lists into their compositions.

Alternative Assessment For Alternate Composition Assignments to assess students' learning, see pages 568–569 of the Teaching Portfolio.

Publishing Student Writing Have students design a catalogue. Once it is designed, have students incorporate their writing into it.

Writing Across the Curriculum Have students research and report on criticism of O'Keeffe's work. Consider informing the art department of this assignment, so that teachers can provide guidance for students.

LEARNING OPTION

This activity will appeal to visual learners. You may wish to vary the activity by having some students write haiku, others concrete poems, others lyric poems, and so forth.

Sally Ride

(1951–   ) graduated from Stanford University in 1973 with a bachelor's degree in English and physics. She went on to earn a doctorate in physics from Stanford, specializing in X-ray astronomy and lasers. In June 1983 she became the third woman to orbit the Earth and the first American woman to travel in a spacecraft. Ride tells how our planet looks from 200 miles up in her essay "Single Room, Earth View."

Single Room, Earth View

Scientific Observation

Scientific observation is the act of carefully noting facts and events. This manner of observing is a skill that scientists must learn. It is more precise and systematic than the way we usually look at people and events in everyday life.

When Sally Ride became the first American woman in space, she was already a trained scientist. In this selection her descriptions of the Earth from orbit show her skill as a scientific observer.

Focus

In this selection astronaut Sally Ride indicates that it is difficult to describe the experience of traveling so far above the Earth. Ride's use of comparisons to "earthly" situations, however, help make her descriptions come alive. Imagine that you are an astronaut orbiting the Earth. What is space travel like? What does the planet look like from space? Write comparisons that would be meaningful to someone who has never experienced space flight. Then read Ride's descriptions of life in space.

Vocabulary

Knowing the following words will help you as you read "Single Room, Earth View."

articulate (är tik′ yə lit) *adj.*: Expressing oneself well (p. 487)

surreal (sə rē′ əl) *adj.*: Strange (p. 487)

ominous (äm′ ə nəs) *adj.*: Threatening (p. 487)

novice (näv′ is) *adj.*: Beginner (p. 487)

muted (myо̄ot əd) *adj.*: Weaker; less intense (p. 489)

subtle (sut′′l) *adj.*: Small (p. 489)

eddies (ed′ ēz) *n.*: Circular currents (p. 489)

eerie (ir′ ē) *adj.*: Mysterious (p. 489)

diffused (di fyо̄ozd′) *v.*: Spread out (p. 490)

extrapolating (ik strap′ ə lāt′ iŋ) *v.*: Arriving at a conclusion by making inferences based on known facts (p. 490)

Single Room, Earth View

Sally Ride

Everyone I've met has a glittering, if vague, mental image of space travel. And naturally enough, people want to hear about it from an astronaut: "How did it feel. . . ?" "What did it look like. . . ?" "Were you scared?" Sometimes, the questions come from reporters, their pens poised and their tape recorders silently reeling in the words; sometimes, it's wide-eyed, ten-year-old girls who want answers. I find a way to answer all of them, but it's not easy.

Imagine trying to describe an airplane ride to someone who has never flown. An articulate traveler could describe the sights but would find it much harder to explain the difference in perspective provided by the new view from a greater distance, along with the feelings, impressions, and insights that go with the new perspective. And the difference is enormous: Space flight moves the traveler another giant step farther away. Eight and one-half thunderous minutes after launch, an astronaut is orbiting high above the Earth, suddenly able to watch typhoons form, volcanoes smolder, and meteors streak through the atmosphere below.

While flying over the Hawaiian Islands, several astronauts have marveled that the islands look just as they do on a map. When people first hear that, they wonder what should be so surprising about Hawaii looking the way it does in the atlas. Yet, to the astronauts it is an absolutely startling sensation: The islands really *do* look as if that part of the world has been carpeted with a big page torn out of Rand-McNally,[1] and all we can do is try to convey the surreal quality of that scene.

In orbit, racing along at five miles per second, the space shuttle circles the Earth once every 90 minutes. I found that at this speed, unless I kept my nose pressed to the window, it was almost impossible to keep track of where we were at any given moment—the world below simply changes too fast. If I turned my concentration away for too long, even just to change film in a camera, I could miss an entire land mass. It's embarrassing to float up to a window, glance outside, and then have to ask a crewmate, "What continent is this?"

We could see smoke rising from fires that dotted the entire east coast of Africa, and in the same orbit only moments later, ice floes jostling for position in the Antarctic. We could see the Ganges River dumping its murky, sediment-laden water into the Indian Ocean and watch ominous hurricane clouds expanding and rising like biscuits in the oven of the Caribbean.

Mountain ranges, volcanoes, and river deltas appeared in salt-and-flour relief, all leading me to assume the role of a novice geologist. In such moments, it was easy to imagine the dynamic upheavals that created jutting mountain ranges and the internal

---

1. **Rand-McNally:** Publishers of atlases.

Single Room, Earth View 487

Presentation

Motivation/Prior Knowledge
Have students imagine what it might be like to travel to outer space. Have them consider the speed at which they would be traveling and the distance they would be from Earth. Ask students what they think they would be able to see in outer space and on the surface of the Earth.

Master Teacher Note You might want to tell students that Sally Kristen Ride, the first American woman astronaut, traveled in space in June of 1983 and again in October of 1984. On her first six-day flight on the *Challenger*, she and four other astronauts successfully launched communications satellites and conducted experiments. On her second flight, she assisted in launching a satellite to measure the sun's effect on the earth's weather.

Making Connections Another selection that stresses the importance of observation is "The Loch Ness Monster," page 457.

Purpose-Setting Question
What are Ride's most important observations from orbit?

1 **Discussion** Is Ride successful in explaining the difficulty of describing space flight? Why or why not?

2 **Discussion** How does Ride use humor to make her point?

3 **Clarification** You might tell students that a *relief map* "shows the different heights of land forms."

Thematic Focus In recent times, one of the most important sources of information about our planet has been space travel. Ask students whether the knowledge gained from space travel is worth the risks and the cost. Is it important for us to know what is happening to the rain forests and the polar ice caps?

4 Discussion What does Sally Ride mean when she says that "the view . . . makes theory come alive"?

5 Discussion What land forms would you be most interested in observing from orbit?

6 Discussion Why is the term "signatures" especially appropriate for what Ride means?

Multicultural Focus Remind students that on April 12, 1961, Yuri A. Gagarin of the former Soviet Union became the first person to travel in space. Less than a month later, Alan B. Shepard, Jr., became the first American space traveler. In 1963, a Russian cosmonaut, Valentina Tereshkova, was the first woman in space. When Sally Ride made her first trip in a spacecraft in 1983, she was the first American woman to do so.

Have students find out more about America's astronauts. Ask students to choose astronauts from different ethnic backgrounds and research their life and work. You might want to have students write biographical essays or present their findings informally to the class.

wrenchings that created rifts and seas. I also became an instant believer in plate tectonics:[2] India really *is* crashing into Asia, and Saudi Arabia and Egypt really *are* pulling apart, making the Red Sea wider. Even though their respective motion is really no more than mere inches a year, the view from overhead makes theory come alive.

Spectacular as the view is from 200 miles up, the Earth is not the awe-inspiring "blue marble" made famous by the photos from the moon. From space shuttle height, we can't see the entire globe at a glance, but we can look down the entire boot of Italy, or up the East Coast of the United States from Cape Hatteras to Cape Cod. The panoramic view inspires an appreciation for the scale of some of nature's phenomena. One day, as I scanned the sandy expanse of Northern Af-

---

2. plate tectonics: The theory that the earth's surface consists of plates whose constant motion explains continental drift, mountain building, large earthquakes, and so forth.

rica, I couldn't find any of the familiar landmarks—colorful outcroppings of rock in Chad, irrigated patches of the Sahara. Then I realized they were obscured by a huge dust storm, a cloud of sand that enveloped the continent from Morocco to the Sudan.

Since the space shuttle flies fairly low (at least by orbital standards; it's more than 22,000 miles lower than a typical TV satellite), we can make out both natural and manmade features in surprising detail. Familiar geographical features like San Francisco Bay, Long Island, and Lake Michigan are easy to recognize, as are many cities, bridges, and airports. The Great Wall of China is *not* the only manmade object visible from space.

The signatures of civilization are usually seen in straight lines (bridges or runways) or sharp delineations (abrupt transitions from desert to irrigated land, as in California's Imperial Valley). A modern city like New York doesn't leap from the canvas of its surround-

---

Grammar in Action

Skillful writers usually avoid common usage problems like the **confusion between *like* and *as*.** *Like* is a preposition meaning "similar to" or "such as." Except in informal usage, it should not be used in place of the conjunction *as* or *as if*. (*As* can also be an adverb.)

   Nonstandard: She walks *like* she talks—quickly.
   Standard: She walks *as* she talks—quickly.

   Nonstandard: The students looked *like* they were bored.
   Standard: The students looked *as if* they were bored.

Notice how Sally Ride uses the two words:

   Familiar geographical features *like* San Francisco Bay, Long Island, and Lake Michigan are easy to recognize. . . . (*like* used correctly as a preposition)

ings, but its straight piers and concrete runways catch the eye—and around them, the city materializes. I found Salina, Kansas (and pleased my in-laws, who live there) by spotting its long runway amid the wheat fields near the city. Over Florida, I could see the launch pad where we had begun our trip, and the landing strip, where we would eventually land.

Some of civilization's more unfortunate effects on the environment are also evident from orbit. Oil slicks glisten on the surface of the Persian Gulf, patches of pollution-damaged trees dot the forests of central Europe. Some cities look out of focus, and their colors muted, when viewed through a pollutant haze. Not surprisingly, the effects are more noticeable now than they were a decade ago. An astronaut who has flown in both Skylab and the space shuttle reported that the horizon didn't seem quite as sharp, or the colors quite as bright, in 1983 as they had in 1973.

Of course, informal observations by individual astronauts are one thing, but more precise measurements are continually being made from space: The space shuttle has carried infrared film to document damage to citrus trees in Florida and in rain forests along the Amazon. It has carried even more sophisticated sensors in the payload bay. Here is one example: sensors used to measure atmospheric carbon monoxide levels, allowing scientists to study the environmental effects of city emissions and land-clearing fires.

Most of the Earth's surface is covered with water, and at first glance it all looks the same: blue. But with the right lighting conditions and a couple of orbits of practice, it's possible to make out the intricate patterns in the oceans—eddies and spirals become visible because of the subtle differences in water color or reflectivity.

Observations and photographs by astronauts have contributed significantly to the understanding of ocean dynamics, and some of the more intriguing discoveries prompted the National Aeronautics and Space Administration to fly an oceanographic observer for the express purpose of studying the ocean from orbit. Scientists' understanding of the energy balance in the oceans has increased significantly as a result of the discoveries of circular and spiral eddies tens of kilometers in diameter, of standing waves hundreds of kilometers long, and of spiral eddies that sometimes trail into one another for thousands of kilometers. If a scientist wants to study features on this scale, it's much easier from an orbiting vehicle than from the vantage point of a boat.

Believe it or not, an astronaut can also see the wakes of large ships and the contrails[3] of airplanes. The sun angle has to be just right, but when the lighting conditions are perfect, you can follow otherwise invisible oil tankers on the Persian Gulf and trace major shipping lanes through the Mediterranean Sea. Similarly, when atmospheric conditions allow contrail formation, the thousand-mile-long condensation trails let astronauts trace the major air routes across the northern Pacific Ocean.

Part of every orbit takes us to the dark side of the planet. In space, night is very, very black—but that doesn't mean there's nothing to look at. The lights of cities sparkle; on nights when there was no moon, it was difficult for me to tell the Earth from the sky—the twinkling lights could be stars or they could be small cities. On one nighttime pass from Cuba to Nova Scotia, the entire East Coast of the United States appeared in twinkling outline.

When the moon is full, it casts an eerie light on the Earth. In its light, we see ghostly

---

3. **contrails** (kän' trāls) n.: White trails of condensed water vapor that sometimes form in the wake of aircraft.

7 **Critical Thinking and Reading** What are the implications of this observation?

8 **Literary Focus** What do Ride's comments suggest about the way to become a better observer?

. . . the horizon didn't seem quite *as* sharp, or the colors quite *as* bright, in 1983 *as* they had in 1973. (*as* used correctly as an adverb—twice—and then as a conjunction)

Student Activity 1. Choose the correct word in the following sentences:
1. Kaylen wrote (like, as) a veteran reporter.
2. Misunderstandings (like, as) those he illustrated can cause serious public-relations problems.
3. Gnats were flying (like, as if) they were guided toward my eyes.
4. Report cards went out (like, as) teachers planned.

Student Activity 2. Write two sentences correctly using *like* and two correctly using *as* or *as if*.

Electronic Handbook You might want students to review the standard use of *like* and *as* before completing the Grammar in Action activities. If students have access to the Language Master 6000, have them enter the access word *simile* and press the GRAMMAR key to get information on the standard uses of *like* and *as*.

9 Discussion How does Ride make her description lively and dramatic?

10 Critical Thinking and Reading Ride contends that one cannot liken the experience of space flight to familiar experiences. What are some examples from her essay that support this view?

Reader's Response Would you like to travel in space? Why or why not?

Thematic Response In what ways do you think space travel enhanced astronaut Ride's appreciation of the earth? In what ways do you think space travel made her more concerned about the earth?

clouds and bright reflections on the water. One night, the Mississippi River flashed into view, and because of our viewing angle and orbital path, the reflected moonlight seemed to flow downstream—as if Huck Finn[4] had tied a candle to his raft.

Of all the sights from orbit, the most spectacular may be the magnificent displays of lightning that ignite the clouds at night. On Earth, we see lightning from below the clouds; in orbit, we see it from above. Bolts of lightning are diffused by the clouds into bursting balls of light. Sometimes, when a storm extends hundreds of miles, it looks like a transcontinental brigade is tossing fireworks from cloud to cloud.

As the shuttle races the sun around the Earth, we pass from day to night and back again during a single orbit—hurtling into darkness, then bursting into daylight. The sun's appearance unleashes spectacular blue

and orange bands along the horizon, a clockwork miracle that astronauts witness every 90 minutes. But, I really can't describe a sunrise in orbit. The drama set against the black backdrop of space and the magic of the materializing colors can't be captured in an astronomer's equations or an astronaut's photographs.

I once heard someone (not an astronaut) suggest that it's possible to imagine what spaceflight is like by simply extrapolating from the sensations you experience on an airplane. All you have to do, he said, is mentally raise the airplane 200 miles, mentally eliminate the air noise and the turbulence, and you get an accurate mental picture of a trip in the space shuttle.

Not true. And while it's natural to try to liken space flight to familiar experiences, it can't be brought "down to Earth"—not in the final sense. The environment is different, the perspective is different. Part of the fascination with space travel is the element of the unknown—the conviction that it's different from earthbound experiences. And it is.

---

4. Huck Finn: Hero of Mark Twain's novel *The Adventures of Huckleberry Finn.*

490   *Nonfiction*

Closure and Extension

ANSWERS TO RESPONDING TO THE SELECTION
Your Response
1. Discuss with students some of the experiences that one could have only in space.

Recalling
2. Ride was able to see mountain ranges, volcanoes, river deltas, ice floes, rocks, deserts, and oceans.
3. Ride was able to see bridges, piers, runways, oil slicks, and patches of pollution-damaged trees.

4. Observation and photographs have increased our understanding of ocean dynamics.

Interpreting
5. Answers will differ, but students might relate the title to a typical expression referring to a hotel room—"single room, ocean view." The single room in this case, of course, is the shuttle.

RESPONDING TO THE SELECTION

Your Response

1. What would interest you most about taking a space flight? Why?

Recalling

2. Name three natural features that Ride saw from orbit.
3. Identify three examples that she observed of humans' effect on the environment.
4. How have observations and photographs by astronauts contributed to science?

Interpreting

5. What does the essay's title mean?
6. Why do you think that Ride found it easier to imagine the forces of geology when she was in orbital flight?
7. An astronaut reported that colors did not seem as bright in 1983 as in 1973. What conclusion does this fact suggest?

Applying

8. How have Ride's descriptions of the Earth affected your thoughts about our planet?

READING IN THE ARTS AND SCIENCES

Understanding Scientific Observation

Scientific observation is the act of carefully noting facts and events. Sally Ride made such observations as she orbited around the Earth. For example, she was able to see some of the effects of pollution on the environment—"Oil slicks . . . on the surface of the Persian Gulf."

1. How does Ride show her talent for observation in finding civilization's "signatures"?
2. How does she prove herself to be a careful observer of the Earth's oceans?

CRITICAL THINKING AND READING

Finding the Main Idea of a Paragraph

The **main idea** of a paragraph is the most im-portant idea about the subject on which the paragraph focuses. This idea is stated in the **topic sentence,** which can appear at the beginning, end, or middle of the paragraph. For example, in the paragraph beginning, "The signatures of civilization are usually seen in straight lines . . . ," Ride places the topic sentence at the start of the paragraph. The other sentences contain examples of this idea.

Identify the topic sentence in each of the following paragraphs from the essay. (The quoted words indicate the beginning of each paragraph.)

1. "Some of civilization's . . ." (page 489)
2. "Observations and photographs . . ." (page 489)
3. "Believe it or not . . ." (page 489)

THINKING AND WRITING

Writing Up an Observation

Recall a person, an object, or a scene that fascinated you and that you observed carefully. List some of your observations. Then using this list, write a description of what you saw for your classmates. Try to be as careful an observer as Sally Ride. For example, do not simply say that a person's shirt was red. Tell exactly what shade of red it was. In revising you may want to include some vivid images, like Ride's description of lightning as "fireworks." When you are done, share your observation with your classmates.

LEARNING OPTIONS

1. **Speaking and Listening.** For a mock radio newscast, prepare an interview with three astronauts (classmates) who have just returned from a thirty-year visit to another star system. Before conducting the newscast, prepare imaginative questions and answers for the interview.
2. **Art.** Create a board game whose object is to travel through space to Pluto and back to Earth. Include obstacles that players must avoid for success. Then play your game with the class.

Single Room, Earth View 491

2. "Observations and photographs by astronauts have contributed significantly to the understanding of ocean dynamics. . . ."
3. ". . . an astronaut can also see the wakes of large ships and the contrails of airplanes."

THINKING AND WRITING

Software If students have access to computers, have them use **Bank Street Writer** to complete the assignment. To provide students with additional guidance, have them follow the guided lessons on describing a scene or on describing a real-life character in the *Bank Street Writer* binder (if you have the IBM version) or in the *Writer's Survival Kit* (if you have the Macintosh version).

Alternative Assessment

Protocol Ask students to assess their own work by responding to the following questions:

What person, object, or scene did you observe?

What specific details do you include to describe what you saw?

What vivid images do you create to help your reader see what you observed?

In what sequence do you present your details?

What have you learned from completing this assignment about making careful observations?

Ask students to use information from their protocols to help them revise their descriptions.

LEARNING OPTIONS

1. Auditory learners will find this activity enjoyable. You may want to extend the activity for analytic learners by recording the students' interview, playing it back, and having students make suggestions about how they might make their radio broadcast sound more realistic.
2. This activity will appeal to visual and tactile learners. You may extend the activity for analytic learners by having them write the rules of the game.

---

6. Answers will differ. Many students will realize that from the vantage point of outer space, Ride could better see the effects of such forces.
7. Suggested Response: Pollution has increased.

Applying

8. Responses will differ, but students might say that the essay has given them a new sense of the unity of our planet.

Challenge Start a notebook in which you record daily observations of a familiar place or pet.

ANSWERS TO READING IN THE ARTS AND SCIENCES

1. Suggested Response: She was able to spot the straight lines of bridges and runways.

2. Suggested Response: Ride says that at first glance the ocean is blue. But with experience and the right lighting, Ride is able to report more intricate patterns like eddies and spirals.

ANSWERS TO CRITICAL THINKING AND READING

1. "Some of civilization's more unfortunate effects on the environment are also evident from orbit."

James Thurber

(1894–1961) became famous as a humorous writer for *The New Yorker* magazine. Many of his amusing essays are collected in books such as *My Life and Hard Times* and *The Middle-Aged Man on the Flying Trapeze*. In addition to being a witty writer and a talented cartoonist, Thurber earned a reputation as an author who chose his words with care. "The Spreading '*You* Know'" is a humorous essay about the importance of choosing words carefully in conversation.

More About the Author James Thurber became blind in one eye from an accident he suffered in childhood. However, he did not let this injury slow him down. Ask students what qualities a person must have to overcome such a handicap.

Literary Focus Suggest to students a topic sentence—for example, "The United States has an abundance of beautiful land formations." Have students give examples related to the topic sentence. Have them use descriptive language that clearly illustrates the topic sentence.

Prereading Focus James Thurber was a skilled writer who used precise language. He was also a master at using humor to question conventional thought and behavior. The prereading exercise focuses students' attention on both humor and language. It gives students practice in using humor to communicate their ideas about the careless uses of language today. Before students read the essay, ask them to observe the use of popular words, phrases, and expressions in their own circles of friends and family. Have them share their thoughts about why certain expressions are overused and where they think the expressions originated.

Vocabulary Have your **less advanced** students read the words and their definitions. Have them write a paragraph that incorporates all three words, demonstrating their understanding of the words' meanings.

The Spreading "*You Know*"

Illustration

Illustration is the process by which writers clarify and support their ideas through examples. This practice of introducing a well-timed example to support a more general argument is so natural that most skilled writers do it almost automatically. They know from experience that the mention of an actual case or situation can enliven a discussion and increase a reader's interest. James Thurber, for instance, uses this technique in "The Spreading '*You* Know'" to ridicule the mindless repetition of a phrase.

Focus

In the following selection, James Thurber expresses annoyance at the overuse of the phrase "*you* know" in conversation. To make his point, he uses exaggeration. For example, he calls the overuse of "*you* know" a "blight" and a "curse." With a small group of classmates, make a list of words, phrases, and expressions that you think are overused or irritating in conversation, for instance, the word *like*. Then create a cartoon using exaggeration to make your case against the overuse of a word or phrase. After sharing lists and cartoons in class, read Thurber's humorous attack on "*you* know."

Vocabulary

Knowing the following words will help you as you read "The Spreading '*You* Know.'"

blight (blīt) *n.*: Anything that destroys (p. 493)

reiteration (rē it′ ər ā′ shən) *n.*: Repetition (p. 493)

hapless (hap′ lis) *adj.*: Unlucky (p. 493)

Objectives

1 To understand illustration
2 To infer a writer's purpose
3 To write about spoken language
4 To express individual interests and abilities through optional activities

Support Material

Teaching Portfolio
Teacher Backup, p. 563
Usage and Mechanics Worksheet, p. 566
Vocabulary Check, p. 567
Critical Thinking and Reading Worksheet, *Inferring a Writer's Purpose,* p. 568
Language Worksheet, *Understanding Words with the Prefix* over, p. 569

Selection Test, p. 570

Prentice Hall Literature Writing Studio

The Spreading "You Know"

James Thurber

The latest blight to afflict the spoken word in the United States is the rapidly spreading reiteration of the phrase "*you know*." I don't know just when it began moving like a rainstorm through the language, but I tremble at its increasing garbling[1] of meaning, ruining of rhythm, and drumming upon my hapless ears. One man, in a phone conversation with me last summer, used the phrase thirty-four times in about five minutes, by my own count; a young matron in Chicago got seven "*you knows*" into one wavy sentence, and I have also heard it as far west as Denver, where an otherwise charming woman at a garden party in August said it almost as often as a whippoorwill says, "Whippoorwill." Once, speaking of whippoorwills, I was waked after midnight by one of those feathered hellions[2] and lay there counting his chants. He got up to one hundred and fifty-eight and then suddenly said, "Whip—" and stopped dead. I like to believe that his mate, at the end of her patience, finally let him have it.

_____

1. garbling (gär'b'liŋ) *n*.: Confusion, mix-up.

2. hellions (hel' yənz) *n*.: Mischievous troublemakers.

*Copyright © **1961 JAMES THURBER.** From* Lanterns and Lances, *published by Harper & Row*

The Spreading "You Know" 493

Presentation

Motivation/Prior Knowledge Have students use the words "you know" in sentences. As students suggest sentences in which "you know" is used as a filler, point this out to them. Tell them that James Thurber has written about our use of the expression.

Master Teacher Note You might want to tell students that to Thurber language and culture were synonymous. Whatever was happening in the culture would be reflected in the use of language. The mindless repetition of the expression "you know" indicated to Thurber that our culture was deteriorating.

Thematic Focus Thurber often wrote humorously about the minor annoyances of life. Ask students if they generally find people's quirks irritating or amusing. Does it take a special frame of mind to appreciate the lighter side?

Making Connections Another humorous piece by Thurber that you might want to teach with this one is "The Secret Life of Walter Mitty," page 201.

Purpose-Setting Question How does Thurber use humor to make his point more effective?

1 Discussion What does Thurber believe the use of an expression like "you know" does to language and meaning?

2 Discussion What is Thurber attempting to convey in referring to the use of "you know" in Chicago and Denver?

3 Clarification A *whippoorwill* is "a North American nocturnal bird whose distinctive call sounds like its name."

4 Literary Focus How does this humorous illustration contribute to Thurber's argument? _____

Alternative Assessment To promote active reading, have students keep a reader's response journal as they read the selection. Encourage them to respond personally to Thurber's criticisms. What overused expressions bother them?

Humanities Note

Illustration by James Thurber for this essay. Thurber was a cartoonist and illustrator as well as a writer. Many of his essays are illustrated with his own cartoons. Like many of Thurber's cartoons, this drawing accomplishes much with a few lines and conveys a humorous sense of menace.

You may want to have students look carefully at this cartoon before answering the following questions.
1. What mood does this cartoon call up?
2. How does it convey Thurber's attitude toward the misuse of the language?

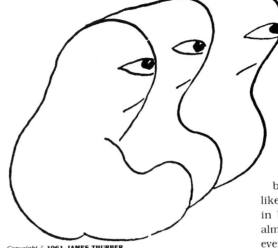

Copyright © **1961 JAMES THURBER.**
From Lanterns and Lances, published by Harper & Row

My unfortunate tendency to count "*you* knows" is practically making a female whippoorwill out of me. Listening to a radio commentator, not long ago, discussing the recent meeting of the United Nations, I thought I was going mad when I heard him using "you know" as a noun, until I realized that he had shortened United Nations Organizations to UNO and was pronouncing it, you know, as if it were "*you* know."

A typical example of speech *you*-knowed to death goes like this. "The other day I saw, you know, Harry Johnson, the, you know, former publicity man for, you know, the Charteriss Publishing Company, and, you know, what he wanted to talk about, strangely enough, was, you know, something you'd never guess. . . ."

5 This curse may have originated simultaneously on Broadway and in Hollywood, where such curses often originate. About twenty-five years ago, or perhaps longer, theater and movie people jammed their sentences with "you know what I mean?" which was soon shortened to "you *know*?" That had followed the overuse, in the 1920s, of

"you see?" or just plain "see?" These blights often disappear finally, but a few have stayed and will continue to stay, such as "Well" and "I mean to say" and "I mean" and "The fact is." Others seem to have mercifully passed out of lingo into limbo,[3] such as, to go back a long way, "Twenty-three, skiddoo" and "So's your old man" and "I don't know nothin' from nothin'" and "Believe you me." About five years ago both men and women were saying things like "He has a new Cadillac job with a built-in bar deal in the back seat" and in 1958 almost everything anybody mentioned, or even wrote about, was "triggered." Arguments were triggered, and allergies, and divorces, and even love affairs. This gun-and-bomb verb seemed to make the jumpiest of the jumpy even jumpier, but it has almost died out now, and I trust that I have not triggered its revival.

It was in Paris, from late 1918 until early 1920, that there was a glut—an American glut, to be sure—of "You said it" and "You can say that again," and an American Marine I knew, from Montana, could not speak any sentence of agreement or concurrence without saying, "It *is*, you *know*." Fortunately, that perhaps original use of "*you* know" did not seem to be imported into America.

6 I am reluctantly making notes for a possible future volume to be called *A Farewell to Speech* or *The Decline and Fall of the King's English*. I hope and pray that I shall not have to write the book. Maybe everything, or at least the language, will clear up before it is too late. Let's face it, it better had, that's for sure, and I don't mean maybe.

---

3. out of lingo (liŋ'gō) **into limbo** (lim'bō): From substandard language into neglect and nonuse.

RESPONDING TO THE SELECTION

Your Response

1. Do you think English needs language "watch-dogs" like Thurber? Why or why not?

Recalling

2. What does Thurber object to about the repetition of the phrase "*you know*"?
3. Find an example he gives to show the overuse of this phrase.
4. According to Thurber, how might this bad habit have started?

Interpreting

5. Explain the techniques Thurber uses to make this essay humorous.
6. Why does Thurber say he is taking notes for a book to be called *A Farewell to Speech*?
7. Explain the joke in the final sentence.
8. What is the true topic of this essay? What main idea does Thurber express about this topic?

Applying

9. Someone once wrote that there are fashions in language just as in clothing. Comment on this remark.

READING IN THE ARTS AND SCIENCES

Understanding Illustration

Illustration is the process by which writers clarify and support their ideas through examples. In "The Spreading '*You* Know,'" Thurber ridicules the overuse of the phrase "*you* know" by giving examples of this bad habit. He tells, for instance, about the man who used this "phrase thirty-four times in about five minutes."

1. What is the effect of Thurber's giving three quick examples of this habit in the very first paragraph?
2. Why does he save his longest example for later in the essay?
3. How might this essay have been different if Thurber had not used any examples?

CRITICAL THINKING AND READING

Inferring a Writer's Purpose

Inferring means reaching a conclusion based on evidence. You can often infer a writer's purpose by paying close attention to his or her opening and closing statements. For example, if a writer begins by criticizing companies that pollute the air, you can infer that the writer's purpose is to halt this form of pollution.

Carefully reread the first and last paragraphs of "The Spreading '*You* Know.'" State Thurber's purpose in your own words.

THINKING AND WRITING

Writing About Spoken Language

Write a humorous essay like Thurber's for your classmates, making fun of an overused word or phrase. First, choose the word or phrase that you want to focus on. The list of words that you compiled with your group will assist you. Note some ways in which people mindlessly repeat this word or phrase. Then, using your notes, write an essay poking fun at this speech habit. Remember to include examples, as Thurber does. In revising your essay, you might want to exaggerate these examples to make them more humorous.

LEARNING OPTIONS

1. **Performance.** Create a brief script for a telephone conversation in which the speakers constantly use the same words and phrases. Use exaggeration to make your script humorous. With a partner perform the script for the class.
2. **Language.** Make a dictionary of some of the slang expressions that you and your friends use. For each entry copy the format used in your own dictionary, showing pronunciation, part of speech, and different meanings. Show your dictionary to your friends to see whether or not they agree with your definitions.

The Spreading "You Know" 495

Applying

9. Answers will differ. Students might agree that words, expressions, and phrases become popular for a time and then drop out of common usage.

Challenge Ask an adult to list some of the colloquial expressions that were popular when he or she was younger.

ANSWERS TO READING IN THE ARTS AND SCIENCES

1. Suggested Response: The three quick examples give readers a clear example of the habit and make it seem that it is overrunning the country.
2. Answers will differ, but students might say that Thurber waits to engage and interest the reader, before giving a longer example.
3. Answers will differ, but students may say that the essay might have been less humorous and persuasive.

ANSWER TO CRITICAL THINKING AND READING

Suggested Response: Thurber wants to convince the reader that the spoken word is on the decline. He wants to stop this deterioration, if possible.

THINKING AND WRITING

Software If students have access to computers, have them use the *Transitions* activity in **Writer's Helper** to help them revise their essays.

LEARNING OPTIONS

1. You might extend the activity for analytic learners by taping the performances and having students identify the techniques the performers used to create humour.
2. This activity is especially appropriate for visual learners. You might wish to extend the activity by having students include examples from speech and written material that clearly illustrate current usage of each expression included in their dictionaries.

Closure and Extension

ANSWERS TO RESPONDING TO THE SELECTION

Your Response

1. Encourage students to speculate about what will happen to the English language with and without language "watchdogs."

Recalling

2. Thurber objects to the phrase because it is overused and garbles meaning.

3. Student responses might include the man in a phone conversation who used it thirty-four times; the two women, one from Chicago and one from Denver; the radio commentator; and the conversation about Harry Johnson.
4. The "curse," according to Thurber, may have started on Broadway or in Hollywood.

Interpreting

5. Suggested Response: Thurber exaggerates the effect of the habit

and provides humorous examples of it.
6. Suggested Response: Thurber believes that language is deteriorating.
7. Suggested Response: The joke is that Thurber uses the types of phrases that he hates.
8. Suggested Response: The true topic of the essay is Thurber's belief that improper or careless use of language reflects imprecise and careless thought.

More About the Author In addition to biographies and historical accounts of famous and important English literary figures, Marchette Chute also writes children's poetry. Ask students to discuss what would motivate a writer to produce such different types of work.

Literary Focus Have students consider how they would find information about a historical period of particular interest to them. Ask them to evaluate the usefulness of the following resources for this purpose: old newspapers, books by scholars of our own time, paintings, records of births, marriages, and deaths, diaries, and accounts by travelers. Have them suggest additional resources as well.

Prereading Focus To prepare students for this activity, you may want to work through the creation of a Venn diagram as a class. Students can compare and contrast two selections they have recently read. Have individual students identify specific similarities and differences, and have a volunteer record them on a Venn diagram on the chalkboard. Students can then use the diagram on the board as a model for their own Venn diagrams.

Vocabulary Have your **less advanced** students read the words and their definitions. Have them use each of the words in a sentence about an historical person or period.

Electronic Handbook You might wish students to use the Language Master 6000 to hear the pronunciation of *sleight of hand*.

GUIDE FOR READING

Marchette Chute

(1909–   ) was born in Minnesota and attended the Minneapolis School of Art and the University of Minnesota. She is primarily known as a writer of biographies and historical studies. Among her award-winning books about great English authors are *Geoffrey Chaucer of England* and *Ben Jonson of Westminster*. In these and in *Shakespeare of London*, she shows her ability to re-create the flavor of an era.

from Shakespeare of London

Historical Inference

Historical inference is the technique of arriving at conclusions about a person or time in history based on limited evidence. In making their inferences, or educated guesses, historians use such sources as district records, pamphlets, books, and written accounts by travelers. They assemble as much information as possible and then draw conclusions from it to paint a more complete picture of the person or time they are studying. In this excerpt from *Shakespeare of London*, Chute uses historical inference to portray the greatest poet and playwright in the English language, William Shakespeare.

Focus

In this essay Marchette Chute discusses some of the qualities that a successful actor needed in Shakespeare's time. What skills must an actor have today? As you read, make a Venn diagram like the following to illustrate similarities and differences between the skills needed for acting then and now.

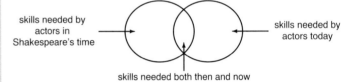

skills needed by actors in Shakespeare's time

skills needed by actors today

skills needed both then and now

Vocabulary

Knowing the following words will help you as you read "Shakespeare of London."

strenuous (stren′ yōō əs) *adj.*: Requiring great effort (p. 497)
parrying (par′ ē iŋ) *v.*: Warding off a sword-thrust (p. 497)
entrails (en′ trālz) *n.*: Intestines; guts (p. 498)
sleight of hand (slīt): Skill in deceiving onlookers (p. 498)
susceptible (sə sep′ tə b'l) *adj.*: Receptive (p. 499)

intricate (in′ tri kit) *adj.*: Complex (p. 499)
supple (sup′'l) *adj.*: Flexible; adaptable (p. 500)
collaborated (kə lab′ ə rāt′ ed) *v.*: Worked together (p. 500)
exacting (ig zakt′ iŋ) *adj.*: Demanding (p. 500)

Objectives

1 To understand historical inference
2 To evaluate historical inferences
3 To write about inference
4 To express individual interests and abilities through optional activities

Support Material

Teaching Portfolio
Teacher Backup, p. 573
Grammar in Action Worksheet, *Understanding Infinitives*, p. 577
Usage and Mechanics Worksheet, p. 579
Vocabulary Check, p. 580
Analyzing Literature Worksheet, *Understanding Historical Inference*, p. 582

Language Worksheet, *Understanding Theater Terms*, p. 583
Selection Test, p. 584

Literature Videodisc
Shakespeare in Conversation

Prentice Hall Literature Writing Studio

from Shakespeare of London

Marchette Chute

Acting was not an easy profession on the Elizabethan[1] stage or one to be taken up lightly. An actor went through a strenuous period of training before he could be entrusted with an important part by one of the great city companies. He worked on a raised stage in the glare of the afternoon sun, with none of the softening illusions that can be achieved in the modern theater, and in plays that made strenuous demands upon his skill as a fencer, a dancer and an acrobat.

Many of the men in the London companies had been "trained up from their childhood" in the art, and an actor like Shakespeare, who entered the profession in his twenties, had an initial handicap that could only be overcome by intelligence and rigorous discipline. Since he was a well-known actor by 1592 and Chettle[2] says he was an excellent one, he must have had the initial advantages of a strong body and a good voice and have taught himself in the hard school of the Elizabethan theater how to use them to advantage.

One of the most famous of the London companies, that of Lord Strange, began its career as a company of tumblers, and a standard production like "The Forces of Hercules" was at least half acrobatics. Training of this kind was extremely useful to the actors, for the normal London stage consisted of several different levels. Battles and sieges were very popular with the audiences, with the upper levels of the stage used as the town walls and turrets, and an actor had to know how to take violent falls without damaging either himself or his expensive costume.

Nearly all plays involved some kind of fighting, and in staging hand-to-hand combats the actor's training had to be excellent. The average Londoner was an expert on the subject of fencing, and he did not pay his penny to see two professional actors make ineffectual dabs at each other with rapiers[3] when the script claimed they were fighting to the death. A young actor like Shakespeare must have gone through long, grueling hours of practice to learn the ruthless technique of Elizabethan fencing. He had to learn how to handle a long, heavy rapier in one hand, with a dagger for parrying in the other, and to make a series of savage, calculated thrusts at close quarters from the wrist and forearm, aiming either at his opponent's eyes or below the ribs. The actor had to achieve the brutal reality of an actual Elizabethan duel without injuring himself or his opponent, a problem that required a high degree of training and of physical coordination. The theaters and the inn-yards were frequently rented by the fencing societies to

---

1. **Elizabethan** (i liz′ ə bē′ thən) *adj.*: Concerning the period 1558 to 1603, when Elizabeth I ruled England.
2. **Chettle:** Henry Chettle (died 1607?), an English playwright, publisher, and poet.

3. **rapiers** (rā′ pē ərz) *n.*: Slender, two-edged swords with cuplike handles.

from Shakespeare of London   497

Presentation

Motivation/Prior Knowledge Ask students what sources of information future historians might use in writing about our own era. Have them consider which of these sources would be most valuable in giving people of the future the true flavor of our times. Then tell them that, in this essay, Marchette Chute tries to recreate one aspect of Elizabethan life—the experience of actors.

Master Teacher Note You might want to tell students that Shakespeare owned a financial share of the theater company for which he acted and wrote plays. In the early 1600's he was able to retire to Stratford, his place of birth, with the money he had earned.

Purpose-Setting Question What do you learn about William Shakespeare from this essay?

Making Connections Another selection that deals with a journey to personal fulfillment through the arts is "Georgia O'Keeffe," page 481.

1 Discussion What does the writer mean by the phrase "trained up from their childhood"?

2 Enrichment The opening of Laurence Olivier's movie, *Henry V*, presents the stage and players as an Elizabethan might have seen them.

3 Discussion You might want to have students compare such "combats" with stunts and special effects in today's movies. Are contemporary audiences just as demanding in this respect as Elizabethan audiences were?

Thematic Focus Throughout history, actors have used their skills to translate the writer's inspiration to the stage. Discuss with students whether a play can be inspiring in the hands of poor actors. How does the performance of a skilled actor affect the audience's perception of the writer's message?

Fine art, *Reconstruction of the Second Globe Theatre at London.* This drawing shows a view of the stage of the Globe Theatre. The stage juts out into the yard, surrounded on three sides by seats and standing room for spectators. Over the stage and supported by pillars is the "shadow," which protected players from the rain. Behind the stage is an inner recess, often called the "tiring house," used for indoor scenes. On the second level is the "chamber," with a balcony. This chamber was used to represent a bedchamber in a dwelling or the walls of a castle or town. On the third level is another chamber, usually used by musicians. The fourth level is the turret, known as "the heavens," containing a bell and other means of creating sound effects.

In this scene, actors are performing a play by Christopher Marlowe, a contemporary of Shakespeare.

1. Notice how the stage extends into the section where some of the audience stands. What advantages does this extended stage give the performer?

2. How might the fact that the audience surrounds the actor affect the way that an actor would portray his character?

4 **Discussion** Does advanced technology—for example, computerized lighting, visual projections, and audio tapes—make it unnecessary for actors to have such skills today?

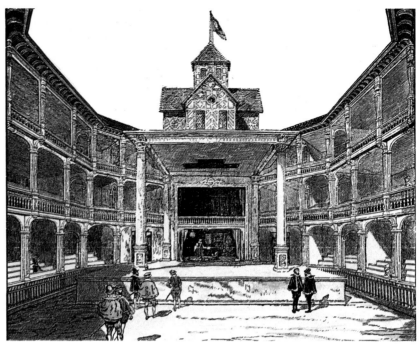

RECONSTRUCTION OF THE SECOND GLOBE THEATRE AT LONDON
The Granger Collection

put on exhibition matches, and on one such occasion at the Swan[4] a fencer was run through the eye and died, an indication of the risks this sort of work involved even with trained, experienced fencers. The actors had to be extremely· skilled, since they faced precisely the same audience. Richard Tarleton, a comic actor of the 80's who was the first great popular star of the Elizabethan theater, was made Master of Fence the year before he died and this was the highest degree the fencing schools could award.

Not being content with savage, realistic fights in its theater productions, the London audience also expected to see bloody deaths and mutilations; and it was necessary to find some way to run a sword through an actor's head or tear out his entrails without impair-

ing his usefulness for the next afternoon's performance. This involved not only agility but a thorough knowledge of sleight of hand, since the players were working close to the audience and in broad daylight. Elizabethan stage management was not slavishly interested in realism but it was always concerned with good stage effects and when bloodshed was involved it gave the audience real blood. It had been found by experience that ox blood was too thick to run well, and sheep's blood was generally used. To stage a realistic stabbing one actor would use a knife with a hollow handle into which the blade would slip back when it was pressed home, and his fellow actor would be equipped with a bladder of blood inside his white leather jerkin,[5] which could be painted to look like skin.

4

---

4. the Swan: A London theater of the time.

---

5. jerkin (jŭr′ kin) *n.*: Short, closefitting jacket.

498 *Nonfiction*

Grammar in Action

An **infinitive** is a form of a verb that generally appears with the word *to* and acts as a noun, adjective, or adverb:

To win the gold medal is his goal. (noun, subject)
Paula planned *to visit her aunt.* (noun, direct object)
The plan is *to work until noon.* (noun, predicate nominative)
The name *to call* appears below. (adjective, modifies *name*)
He spoke *to be understood.* (adverb, modifies *spoke*)

The sentence variety achieved with the use of infinitives helps add interest to a piece of writing. Note how Chute uses them:

It had been found by experience that ox blood was too thick *to run well,* and sheep's blood was generally used. *To stage a realistic stabbing* one actor would use a knife with a hollow handle . . . and his fellow actor would be equipped with a bladder of blood . . . painted *to look like skin.*

. . . beginning actors were expected *to handle several roles in an afternoon* instead of only one. A major company . . .

When the bladder was pricked and the actor arched himself at the moment of contact, the blood spurted out in a most satisfactory manner.

Another test of an actor's physical control was in dancing. Apart from the dances that were written into the actual texts of the plays, it was usual to end the performance with a dance performed by some of the members of the company. A traveler from abroad who saw Shakespeare's company act *Julius Caesar* said that "when the play was over they danced very marvelously and gracefully together," and when the English actors traveled abroad special mention was always made of their ability as dancers. The fashion of the time was for violent, spectacular dances and the schools in London taught intricate steps like those of the galliard,[6] the exaggerated leap called the "capriole" and the violent lifting of one's partner high into the air that was the "volte." A visitor to one of these dancing schools of London watched a performer do a galliard and noted how "wonderfully he leaped, flung and took on"; and if amateurs were talented at this kind of work, professionals on the stage were expected to be very much better.

In addition to all this, subordinate or beginning actors were expected to handle several roles in an afternoon instead of only one. A major company seldom had more than twelve actors in it and could not afford to hire an indefinite number of extra ones for a single production. This meant that the men who had short speaking parts or none were constantly racing about and leaping into different costumes to get onstage with a different characterization as soon as they heard their cues. In one of Alleyn's[7] productions a single actor played a Tartar[8] noble-

man, a spirit, an attendant, a hostage, a ghost, a child, a captain and a Persian; and while none of the parts made any special demands on his acting ability he must have had very little time to catch his breath. The London theater was no place for physical weaklings; and, in the same way it is safe to assume that John Shakespeare must have had a strong, well-made body or he would not have been appointed a constable in Stratford, it is safe to assume that he must have passed the inheritance on to his eldest son.

There was one more physical qualification an Elizabethan actor had to possess, and this was perhaps more important than any of the others. He had to have a good voice. An Elizabethan play was full of action, but in the final analysis it was not the physical activity that caught and held the emotions of the audience; it was the words. An audience was an assembly of listeners and it was through the ear, not the eye, that the audience learned the location of each of the scenes, the emotions of each of the characters and the poetry and excitement of the play as a whole. More especially, since the actors were men and boys and close physical contact could not carry the illusion of love-making, words had to be depended upon in the parts that were written for women.

An Elizabethan audience had become highly susceptible to the use of words, trained and alert to catch their exact meaning and full of joy if they were used well. But this meant, as the basis of any successful stage production, that all the words had to be heard clearly. The actors used a fairly rapid delivery of their lines and this meant that breath control, emphasis and enunciation had to be perfect if the link that was being forged between the emotions of the audience and the action on the stage was not to be broken. When Shakespeare first came to London, the problem of effective stage de-

---

6. **galliard** (gal' yərd) *n.*: Lively French dance.
7. **Alleyn's:** Edward Alleyn (1566–1626), an English actor and theater owner.
8. **Tartar** (tär' tər): Turk or Mongol.

from Shakespeare of London 499

5 **Enrichment** Jerome Robbins created jazzy dances for the teenage gangs in *West Side Story*, a contemporary musical version of *Romeo and Juliet*. Ask students how dance numbers can contribute to a drama.

6 **Clarification** There are well over twelve speaking parts in Shakespeare's *Julius Caesar*. The practice of giving actors more than one role in this and other plays was called *doubling*.

7 **Master Teacher Note** Elizabethan actors often spoke twenty-five or more lines per minute in performing a play. Have students consider what kinds of problems this might have created for actors. You might want to give students a Shakespearean script of twenty-five lines to read so that they can appreciate the demands of this task.

8 **Discussion** What does Chute mean by this statement?

could not afford *to hire an indefinite number of extra ones for a single production*

The first infinitive functions as an adverb (modifies *thick*), the second as an adverb (modifies *use*), the third as an adverb (modifies *painted*), the fourth as a noun (direct object), and the fifth as a noun (direct object).

Student Activity 1. Identify the use of the following infinitives:
1. They raced *to get onstage as a different character.*
2. It is safe *to assume that John Shakespeare was big.*
3. An Elizabethan actor had *to have a good voice.*
4. Elizabethan audiences were trained *to catch the words' exact meaning.*

Student Activity 2. Write four sentences using infinitives in a variety of ways.

Electronic Handbook You might want students to review infinitives before completing the Grammar in Action activities. If students have access to the Language Master 6000, have them enter the access words *tense* and *verbal* and press the GRAMMAR key to get information on these topics related to the use of infinitives.

9 Enrichment Shakespeare himself commented on the competitiveness in the acting profession in his day in the tragedy *Hamlet*. In Act II, Scene ii, Rosencrantz tells Hamlet that it is much more difficult for actors today because of a new fad—companies of child actors! Rosencrantz says, "But there is, sir, an eyrie of children . . . that cry out on the top of question and are most tyranically clapped for't."

10 Critical Thinking and Reading Throughout this historical essay, Chute seems to imply that acting today is much less demanding than it was in Elizabethan times. Compare and contrast the difficulties faced by modern and Elizabethan actors.

11 Literary Focus Explain the process of inference by which Chute arrives at her conclusion.

Reader's Response How do you think Chute's essay would differ if she were writing about contemporary actors and acting?

Thematic Response In what ways are actors—regardless of the time period in which they live—in a unique position to inspire others?

Multicultural Focus Explain that every country has its great theaters and every culture its own theatrical traditions. In England, for instance, the Royal Shakespeare Company and the National Theater carry on the classical tradition. Point out that, unlike many other countries, the United States has never had a national theater but instead has a tradition of excellent regional, city, and state theater groups. The Negro Ensemble Company, the Ballet Hispánico, the Public Theater in New York, and the Steppenwolf Theater in Chicago are just a few well-known American groups. Ask students why they

livery was made somewhat easier by the use of a heavily end-stopped line,[9] where the actor could draw his breath at regular intervals and proceed at a kind of jog-trot. But during the following decade this kind of writing became increasingly old-fashioned, giving way to an intricate and supple blank verse[10] that was much more difficult to handle intelligently; and no one was more instrumental in bringing the new way of writing into general use than Shakespeare himself.

Even with all the assistance given him by the old way of writing, with mechanical accenting and heavy use of rhyme, an Elizabethan actor had no easy time remembering his part. A repertory system[11] was used and no play was given two days in succession. The actor played a different part every night and he had no opportunity to settle into a comfortable routine while the lines of the part became second nature to him. He could expect very little help from the prompter, for that overworked individual was chiefly occupied in seeing that the actors came on in proper order, that they had their properties available and that the intricate stage arrangements that controlled the pulleys from the "heavens"[12] and the springs to the trap doors were worked with quick, accurate timing. These stage effects, which naturally had to be changed each afternoon for each new play, were extremely complicated. A single play in which Greene and Lodge[13] collaborated required the descent of a prophet and an angel let down on a throne, a woman blackened by a thunder stroke, sailors coming in wet from the sea, a serpent devouring a vine, a hand with a burning sword emerging from a cloud and "Jonah the prophet cast out of the whale's belly upon the stage." Any production that had to wrestle with as many complications as this had no room for an actor who could not remember his lines.

Moreover, an actor who forgot his lines would not have lasted long in what was a highly competitive profession. There were more actors than there were parts for them, judging by the number of people who were listed as players in the parish registers.[14] Even the actor who had achieved the position of a sharer in one of the large London companies was not secure. Richard Jones, for instance, was the owner of costumes and properties and playbooks worth nearly forty pounds, which was an enormous sum in those days, and yet three years later he was working in the theater at whatever stray acting jobs he could get. "Sometimes I have a shilling a day and sometimes nothing," he told Edward Alleyn, asking for help in getting his suit and cloak out of pawn.

The usual solution for an actor who could not keep his place in the competitive London theater was to join one of the country companies, where the standards were less exacting, or to go abroad. English actors were extravagantly admired abroad and even a second-string company with poor equipment became the hit of the Frankfort[15] Fair, so that "both men and women flocked wonderfully" to see them. An actor like Shakespeare who maintained his position on the London stage for two decades could legitimately be praised, as Chettle praised him, for being "excellent in the quality he professes." If it had been otherwise, he would not have remained for long on the London stage.

---

9. end-stopped line: Line of poetry read with a pause at the end.
10. blank verse: Unrhymed iambic pentameter (see Handbook of Literary Terms and Techniques).
11. repertory system: The alternate presentation of several plays by the same theater company.
12. the "heavens": A canopy above the stage.
13. Greene and Lodge: Robert Greene (1558–1592) and Thomas Lodge (1557–1625), English playwrights.

---

14. parish registers: District records.
15. Frankfort: Frankfurt, Germany.

think the small, independent, regional theater system is so strong in this country. Help them understand that this kind of theater grows out of cultural diversity.

Ask students to suppose that they will be attending the theater as a class. Have them bring in newspapers to find out what is playing in your community or in a nearby city. Have other students get theater reviews from the local library. Discuss the op-

tions as a class, and call on students to tell what they would be most interested in seeing. Have them give reasons for their choices.

Closure and Extension

ANSWERS TO RESPONDING TO THE SELECTION
Your Response

1. Discuss the idea that every person's life contains elements of drama and comedy.

Recalling

2. Among the required skills were fencing, acrobatics, dance, and the ability to speak well and mem-

RESPONDING TO THE SELECTION

Your Response

1. Shakespeare said that "all the world's a stage." Comment on this thought.

Recalling

2. Identify three skills that an Elizabethan actor had to learn. Explain why each of these skills was important.
3. What evidence is there that Shakespeare had these skills?

Interpreting

4. Basing your answer on this essay, what can you infer about the tastes of Elizabethan theater goers?
5. What can you infer about Elizabethan life in general?

Applying

6. Would you like to have lived during the Elizabethan Age? Explain.

READING IN THE ARTS & SCIENCES

Understanding Historical Inference

Historical inference is the technique of arriving at reasonable conclusions about a person or time in history based on limited evidence. In "Shakespeare of London," for example, Chute infers that, during Elizabethan times, acting "was . . . highly competitive." One piece of evidence for this conclusion is the fact that many people were listed as actors in district records, "more actors than there were parts for them."

1. What conclusion does Chute reach about Shakespeare and other Elizabethan actors in the paragraph beginning, "Nearly all plays. . ."? (page 497)
2. What evidence does she give to support her inference?

CRITICAL THINKING AND READING

Evaluating Historical Inferences

You can evaluate a historical inference by asking yourself whether the evidence suggests other possible conclusions. Then you can decide which of these conclusions is the most reasonable. For instance, Chute infers that acting was competitive because so many actors were listed in district records. Another possible conclusion is that the records were inaccurate. However, in the absence of information about the inaccuracy of the records, Chute's conclusion seems correct.

Examine the following inferences from the essay and determine whether each is reasonable.

1. "The London theater was no place for physical weaklings. . . ." (page 499)
2. "John Shakespeare must have had a strong, well-made body. . . ." (page 499)

THINKING AND WRITING

Writing About Inference

Recall a time in your life when you had to make an inference, or educated guess, based on limited evidence. Briefly note the evidence that was available and the conclusion you reached. Then, using these notes, write an essay describing this situation. Make sure that you explain in detail the way in which you evaluated the evidence and reached your conclusion. In revising check to see that you have told your readers whether your inference was correct.

LEARNING OPTIONS

1. **Speaking and Listening.** Many Elizabethan actors had the skills of today's stunt performers. Learn more about what stunt performers do in movies and present your findings to the class in an oral report.
2. **Art.** Make a model of the Globe Theatre, where Shakespeare's plays were first performed.

2. Suggested Response: Many of the plays involved fighting. Also, the average Londoner knew a great deal about fencing, having witnessed exhibitions. Finally, one comic actor received the highest ranking that fencing schools could bestow.

ANSWERS TO CRITICAL THINKING AND READING

1. Suggested Response: The physical demands of the profession seem to have been great. Chute's case is reasonable.
2. Answers will differ. This conclusion has a certain probability, but Chute does not discuss the duties of a constable. This statement seems a bit speculative, in the absence of further evidence.

THINKING AND WRITING

◆ **Software** If students have access to computers, have them use **Bank Street Writer** to complete all stages of the assignment.

Alternative Assessment *Peer Review* In pairs or in groups of four, have students assess each other's stories by responding to the following questions:

What situation does the writer describe?

What inference does the writer make?

What evidence does the writer cite to explain the inference?

What does the writer say is the reason for the inference?

What suggestions do you have for the writer to clarify the process by which he/she arrived at the inference?

Ask students to incorporate those suggestions they find helpful in a revision of the stories.

LEARNING OPTIONS

1. Visual learners will appreciate this activity.
2. Visual, analytic, and kinesthetic learners will find this activity enjoyable.

---

orize many parts. These skills were important because actors had to fence, dance, speak lines quickly, and often take more than one part in a play.

3. Shakespeare probably had these skills because he maintained his position on the London stage for two decades.

Interpreting

4. Answers will differ. Most students will realize that Elizabethan theatergoers liked action, had a taste

for "bloody deaths and mutilations," enjoyed song and dance, and also were very "susceptible to the use of words."

5. Answers will differ. Students might infer that Elizabethans were dramatic and active, loved novelty, and were more callous about bloodshed than we are.

Applying

6. Answers will differ; however, students should provide reasons to justify their responses.

Challenge Which of our customs might seem strange to people living 100 years from now? Explain.

ANSWERS TO READING IN THE ARTS AND SCIENCES

1. Suggested Response: Chute concludes that actors had to be skilled fencers.

Reading and Responding The purpose of this page is to review the major elements of nonfiction and to show how a writer uses them in constructing a work of nonfiction. Students should be able to use the points outlined on this page to "put together" the elements of nonfiction.

The selection on the following pages, an excerpt from *In Patagonia* by Bruce Chatwin, is a model for "putting it together." The notes in the side column show how one reader might analyze the elements of this essay and then put them together to understand the work as a whole.

To give students further practice with this process, use the essay "On Excellence" by Cynthia Ozick in the **Teaching Portfolio** on page 591, which students can annotate themselves.

READING AND RESPONDING

Nonfiction

Nonfiction deals with people, places, things, and events. The nonfiction writer usually keeps several things in mind while writing: an idea to present (the topic), a purpose for presenting the idea, and an audience. Responding to the elements of nonfiction and the writer's techniques will help you appreciate nonfiction more fully.

RESPONDING TO PURPOSE The purpose is the reason for writing. The general purpose may be to explain, inform, describe, persuade, or entertain. The specific purpose may be to make a particular point about the topic. If the general purpose is to inform the reader about rain forests, for example, the specific purpose may be to persuade the reader to conserve our natural resources. Your understanding of the writer's purpose will affect your response to the work.

RESPONDING TO IDEAS AND SUPPORT The main ideas are the most important points the writer is making. Main ideas can be facts or opinions. Support is the information the writer uses to develop or illustrate the main ideas. Support includes facts to back up opinions, reasons to explain events, examples to illustrate ideas, and descriptive details to give the reader a vivid picture of the topic. Your response to a selection is determined in part by your response to its main ideas and supporting information.

RESPONDING TO ORGANIZATION The writer organizes the ideas and support in such a way as to accomplish the purpose and move the reader's thinking in the intended direction. The information may be arranged in chronological order, spatial order, order of importance, or any other order that serves the author's needs. How does the order help you grasp the writer's ideas?

RESPONDING TO TECHNIQUES Writers may use a variety of techniques to accomplish their purpose. They may use description, argumentation, or comparison and contrast. They may use emotional language to arouse your feelings. How do the author's techniques affect you as you read?

On pages 503–508 you can see an example of active reading and responding by Stephanie Huang of Pershing School in San Diego, California. The notes in the side column include Stephanie's thoughts and comments as she read "Butch Cassidy." Your own thoughts as you read may be different because you bring your own experiences to your reading.

502   Nonfiction

Butch Cassidy
from *In Patagonia*
Bruce Chatwin

He was a nice boy, a lively friendly-faced boy, who loved his Mormon family and the cabin in the cottonwoods. Both his parents came out from England as children and trekked the Plains, with Brigham Young's[1] handcart companies, from Iowa City to the Salt Lake. Anne Parker was a nervous and highly strung Scotswoman; her husband, Max, a simple soul, who had a hard time squeezing a living from the homestead and made a little extra in timber haulage.

The two-room cabin is still standing at Circleville, Utah. The corrals are there, and the paddock where Robert Leroy rode his first calf. The poplars he planted still line the irrigation ditch between the orchard and the sage. He was the oldest of eleven children, a boy of precise loyalties and a sense of fair play. He dreamed of being a cowboy and, in dime novels, read the ongoing saga of Jesse James.

At eighteen he identified as his natural enemies the cattle companies, the railroads and the banks, and convinced himself that right lay the wrong side of the law. One June morning in 1884, awkwardly and ashamed, he told his mother he was going to work in a mine at Telluride. She gave him her father's blue traveling blanket and a pot of blueberry preserves. He kissed his baby sister, Lula, crying in her cradle, and rode out of their lives. The truth came out when Max Parker returned to the homestead. His son had rustled some cattle with a young outlaw called Mike Cassidy. The law was after them both.

Bob Parker took the name Cassidy and rode into a new life of wide horizons and the scent of horse leather. (Butch was the name of a borrowed gun.) His apprentice years, the 1880's, were years of the Beef Bonanza; of Texas longhorns peppering the range; of the Cattle Barons who paid mi-

---

1. **Brigham Young:** 1801–1877: United States Mormon leader.

Purpose: *I think that the author is going to describe Butch Cassidy and inform us of his deeds in order to make us understand why his life was the way it was.*

Ideas and Support: *The author makes the point that Butch Cassidy was a nice boy and backs it up with details describing young Robert Leroy and his family.*

Techniques: *The author includes the detail about young Butch reading the saga of Jesse James. This gives you a hint of the direction his life is heading in.*

Organization: *The author has arranged the information in chronological order.*

Presentation

Motivation/Prior Knowledge
Ask students to name famous historical figures about whom they would like to know more. Have them imagine that they have the opportunity to interview people who knew this person. What questions would they ask? Tell the class that Chatwin's travels to Argentina gave him the opportunity to delve into the life of the famous outlaw, Butch Cassidy.

Purpose-Setting Question
What is Chatwin's attitude toward Butch Cassidy—sympathetic, condemning, or nonjudgmental?

Enrichment Patagonia is a section of Argentina in the southwestern part of South America.

Discussion What would you imagine Robert Leroy Parker's life in Circleville, Utah, to have been like?

Enrichment Jesse James was the leader of a band of bank and train robbers. He was born in Clay County, Missouri, in 1847, and, like Butch Cassidy, grew up on a farm.

Reading Strategy Can you predict the effect the novels about Jesse James might have on young Robert Parker?

Enrichment Telluride is a mining town in Colorado.

Literary Focus What does the anecdote about how Butch Cassidy left home reveal about his character? What function does the anecdote serve with regard to plot?

Discussion How would you compare Cassidy's new life with his old life?

Thematic Focus As a young man, Butch Cassidy made what he probably thought was a minor, momentary choice. It turned out, however, that this choice greatly affected all the other options available to him as he continued on his life's journey. Discuss whether decisions made in youth are irrevocable. Can a person's journey through life be determined by a single foolish act, or is it possible to change course?

Master Teacher Note Ask students to name famous outlaws. (You might suggest Jesse James, Billy the Kid, Bonnie and Clyde.) Ask the class to conjecture why people who committed crimes such as robbery and murder would become romantic folk heroes. Why do we find such figures appealing?

Making Connections Another story that deals with a young man who makes a mistake early in life is "All the Years of Her Life," page 57. You might want to compare Alfred's fate with that of Butch Cassidy.

Enrichment With the completion of the Union Pacific and Central Pacific railroad lines in 1869 and the end of the Civil War came the period of the "cattle kingdom." Ranchers could drive their cattle to the railroads and ship them north.

Critical Thinking and Reading What does the author mean by saying that Cassidy's prison sentence "soured him to any further dealing with the law"?

Enrichment Mormons are members of the Church of Jesus Christ of Latter-day Saints. Some Mormons practiced polygamy as a religious principle during the mid-1800's, but the church outlawed the practice in 1890 after the Supreme Court ruled it illegal.

Discussion Why does Chatwin say that today Cassidy would be classed as a revolutionary? According to Chatwin's description, with what character in folklore could Cassidy be compared?

Techniques: *The quotation gives you a feel for how real cowboys sounded. It also shows how violence was an accepted part of these cowboys' lives.*

Techniques: *The author has you going back and forth about Butch Cassidy. First you think he's a bad guy because he robbed banks. Then you feel sorry for him because he had to go to jail for a crime he didn't commit. You think it was nice of him to pay the widow's rent, but then you think he's bad again when you learn that he robbed the rent man. The author probably wants you to understand that Butch Cassidy had many different sides to his character.*

Ideas and Support: *The fact that Butch Cassidy never killed a man but would hang out with a bunch of killers supports the main idea of the previous paragraph (that he had many sides to his character).*

serly wages and dividends of 40 per cent to their shareholders; of champagne breakfasts at the Cheyenne Club and the English dukes who called their cowboys "cow-servants" and whose cowboys called them "dudes." There were plenty of Englishmen knocking round the West; one cowboy wrote to his Yankee employer: "That Inglishman yu lef in charge at the other ranch got to fresh and we had to kil him. Nothing much has hapened since yu lef . . ."

Then the great white winter of 1886–7 wiped out three-quarters of the stock. Greed combined with natural catastrophe to breed a new type, the cowboy-outlaw, men driven by unemployment and blacklisting into criminal hideouts and the rustling game. At Brown's Hole or Hole-in-the-Wall they joined up with professional desperadoes; men like Black Jack Ketchum, or the psychopath Harry Tracy, or Flat-Nose George Curry, or Harvey Logan, the diarist of his own murders.

Butch Cassidy, in those years, was drover, horse-wrangler, mavericker,[2] part-time bank-robber, and leader of men; the sheriffs feared him most for the last of these accomplishments. In 1894 they gave him two years in the Wyoming State Penitentiary for stealing a horse he hadn't stolen, valued at five dollars. The sentence soured him to any further dealing with the law. And, from 1896 to 1901, his Train Robbers' Syndicate, better known as The Wild Bunch, performed the string of perfect hold-ups that kept lawmen, Pinkerton detectives and the railroad in perpetual jitters. The stories of his antics are endless; breathless rides along the Outlaw Trail; shooting glass conductors from telegraph poles; or paying a poor widow's rent by robbing the rent man. The homesteaders loved him. Many were Mormons, outlawed themselves for polygamy.[3] They gave him food, shelter, alibis, and occasionally their daughters. Today, he would be classed as a revolutionary. But he had no sense of political organization.

Butch Cassidy never killed a man. Yet his friends were seasoned killers; their murders drove him to fits of remorse. He hated having to rely on the deadly aim of Harry Longabaugh, the Pennsylvania German with evil blue eyes and a foul temper. He tried to go straight, but there was too much on his

---

2. mavericker (mav′ ər ik ər) *n*.: A Texas rancher who did not brand his cattle.

3. polygamy (pə lig′ ə mē) *n*.: The state or practice of having two or more spouses at the same time.

Grammar in Action

Writers rely on the **semicolon** to separate closely related independent clauses not joined by a coordinating conjunction such as *and, but, or, for.* While a period interrupts the flow of ideas and distances the connection between clauses, a semicolon shows the close relationship between two independent clauses. Examine, for example, the following sentence from "Butch Cassidy":

Butch Cassidy, in those years, was drover, horsewrangler, mavericker, part-time bank-robber, and leader of men; the sheriffs feared him most for the last of these accomplishments.

By connecting the two independent clauses with a semicolon, Chatwin shows the close relationship between Cassidy's talent as a leader and the fear that he instilled in the sheriffs. If the author had chosen to use a period instead of a semicolon, the connection would not have been as strong. In addition, the period would have created too sharp a break in the narration.

A semicolon may also separate longer phrases in a series. The following sentence from the selection demonstrates this use of the semicolon:

Pinkerton card and his pleas for amnesty went unheard. Each new robbery spawned another and added years to his sentence. The costs of operating became unbearable. The story goes that the Wild Bunch frittered their hauls on women and the gaming table, but this is only half true. They had another, far greater expense: horseflesh.

The art of the hold-up depends on a quick getaway and Butch Cassidy's hold-ups depended on relays of fine thoroughbreds. His horse dealer was a man called Cleophas Dowd, the son of Irish immigrants to San Francisco, dedicated to the Jesuit priesthood, and forced as a boy to grovel to altar and confessional. Immediately after his ordination,[4] Dowd startled his parents and the Fathers by riding past on his new racehorse, a brace of six-shooters strapped over his cassock. That night, in Sausalito, he had the pleasure—a pleasure he had long savored—of giving last rites to the first man he shot. Dowd fled from California and settled at Sheep Creek Canyon, Utah, where he raised horses for outlaws. A Dowd horse was ready for sale when its rider could balance a gun between its ears and fire. The necessary speed he purchased from the Cavendish Stud at Nashville, Tennessee, and relayed the cost to his clients.

Around 1900 law and order settled in on the last American frontier. The lawmen bought their own fine bloodstock, solved the problem of outpacing the outlaws, and organized crime hid in the cities. Posses flushed out Brown's Hole; the Pinkertons put mounted rangers in box cars, and Butch saw his friends die in saloon brawls, picked off by hired gunmen, or disappear behind bars. Some of the gang signed on in the U.S. Armed Forces and exported their talents to Cuba and the Philippines. But for him the choices were a stiff sentence—or Argentina.

Word was out among the cowboys that the land of the gaucho[5] offered the lawless freedom of Wyoming in the 1870's. The artist-cowboy Will Rogers wrote: "They wanted North American riders for foremen over the natives. The natives was too slow." Butch believed he was safe from extradition[6] there, and his last two hold-ups were to raise funds for the journey.

---

4. **ordination** (ôr' d'n ā' shən) n.: The ceremony during which a person is admitted to the priesthood.
5. **gaucho** (gou' chō) n.: A South American cowboy.
6. **extradition** (eks' trə dish' ən) n.: Being turned over to stand trial in the United States where the crimes were committed.

Techniques: *The character Cleophas Dowd is funny. He is like a more extreme version of Butch Cassidy. Both characters are mixtures of good and bad, but Dowd goes from really good to really bad, all in one day.*

Techniques: *The way this sentence is written makes you think that Butch Cassidy is definitely going to Argentina.*

Enrichment Allan Pinkerton (1819–1884) established one of the first detective agencies in the United States. After the Civil War, Pinkerton organized groups of armed men who were available for hire.

Reading Strategy Summarize Cassidy's reasons for going to Argentina.

Enrichment Will Rogers (1879–1935) was an American humorist and social critic. In 1902, Rogers went to seek adventure in Argentina (two years after Cassidy) and then to South Africa to join Texas Jack's Wild West Show doing rope tricks. He returned to the United States in 1904 and began his career as a vaudeville humorist, gaining fame as "the cowboy philosopher."

Critical Thinking and Reading Compare the tone of the quotation from Will Rogers with Chatwin's tone in this selection. How are they similar?

Butch Cassidy 505

The stories of his antics are endless: breathless rides along the Outlaw Trail; shooting glass conductors from telegraph poles; or paying a poor widow's rent by robbing the rent man.

Student Activity 1. Find one example in "Butch Cassidy" in which Chatwin uses a semicolon to join closely related independent clauses. Also find one example in which he uses a semicolon to separate phrases in a series.

Student Activity 2. Write a paragraph about a person whose life interests you. Use at least two sentences in which you use a semicolon to join closely related independent clauses or to separate phrases in a series.

Electronic Handbook You might want students to review the semicolon before completing the Grammar in Action activities. If students have access to the Language Master 6000, have them enter the access symbol ; and press the GRAMMAR key to get information on the use of semicolons.

Seated, left to right: Harry Longabaugh (The Sundance Kid), Ben Kilpatrick (The Tall Texan), and Robert Leroy Parker (Butch Cassidy). Standing: Will Carver, Harvey Logan (Kid Curry).

Techniques: *This quote is funny, considering that the people who are talking are bandits themselves.*

Ideas and Support: *The fact that Ryan was more sociable and joined in the festivities of the settlement supports an idea presented earlier: that Butch Cassidy was more human than any of his outlaw friends.*

After the Winnemucca raid, the five ringleaders, in a mood of high spirits, had their group portrait taken in Fort Worth and sent a copy to the manager. (The photo is still in the office.)

In the fall of 1901 Butch met the Sundance Kid and his girl, Etta Place, in New York. She was young, beautiful and intelligent, and she kept her men to heel. Her Pinkerton card says she was a school teacher in Denver; one rumor has it she was the daughter of an English remittance man called George Capel, hence Place. Under the names of James Ryan and Mr. and Mrs. Harry A. Place, the "family of 3" went to operas and theaters. (The Sundance Kid was a keen Wagnerian.[7]) They bought Etta a gold watch at Tiffany's and sailed for Buenos Aires on S.S. *Soldier Prince*. On landing they stayed at the Hotel Europa, called on the Director of the Land Department, and secured 12,000 acres of rough camp in Chubut.

"Are there any bandits?" they asked. They were glad to hear there were none.

A few weeks later, Milton Roberts, the Welsh police commissioner from Esquel, found them under canvas at Cholila; their fine light thoroughbreds, already saddled up, struck him as rather odd. Butch, as we know from the letter, was alone the first winter. He stocked the farm with sheep bought from an English neighbor. The cabin, modeled on Circleville but bigger, was up by June.

In the following year, a Pinkerton detective, Frank Dimaio, tracked them to Cholila with the Winnemucca photograph, but was put off going to Patagonia by stories of snakes and jungles, perhaps invented for his benefit. The "family of 3" used Cholila as a base for five years without interference. They built a brick house and a country store (now owned by an Arab trader) and put "another North American" in charge.

The locals thought they were peaceable citizens. At Cholila I met the grandchildren of their neighbor, Señora Blanca de Gérez, who left this note when she died three years ago:

> They were not good mixers, but whatever they did was correct. They often slept in our house. Ryan was more sociable than Place and joined in the festivities of the settlement. On the first visit of Governor Lezana, Place

---

7. **Wagnerian** (väg nir′ ē ən) *adj.*: An admirer or follower of Richard Wagner's music and theories.

played the samba on his guitar and Ryan danced with the daughter of Don Ventura Solís. No one suspected they were criminals.

The Pinkerton Agency wrote to the Chief of Police in Buenos Aires: "It is only a question of time until these men commit some desperate robbery in the Argentine Republic." They were right. Apart from running low in funds, "the family of 3" were addicted to the art of the hold-up, without which life itself became a bore. Perhaps they were spurred on by the arrival of their friend Harvey Logan. In 1903 he had wormed his way out of jail in Knoxville, Tennessee, after all but throttling his warder with the coil of wire he kept hidden in his boot. He turned up in Patagonia under the name of Andrew Duffy, an alias he had already used in Montana.

In 1905 the reconstituted Wild Bunch broke out and robbed a bank in Southern Santa Cruz. They repeated the performance on the *Banco de la Nación* at Villa Mercedes in San Luis in the summer of 1907. It seems that Harvey Logan shot the manager through the head. Etta was there, dressed as a man—a fact obliquely confirmed by Blanca de Gérez: "The Señora cropped her hair short and wore a wig."

In December 1907 they sold Cholila, in a hurry, to a beef syndicate, and scattered into the Cordillera. None of their neighbors ever heard of them again. I have heard a number of reasons for their departure. But the most usual explanation is that Etta was bored, had a grumbling appendix and insisted on going to Denver for the operation. There is another possibility: that appendix was a euphemism for baby and that the father was a young Englishman, John Gardner, who was ranching in Patagonia for his health. The story goes that Harvey Logan had to get him out of the Kid's way, back to his family estate in Ireland.

Etta was apparently living in Denver in 1924. (Her daughter may have been a competitive girl called Betty Weaver, who pulled fifteen spectacular bank robberies before her arrest and jail-sentence at Belleplaine, Kansas, in 1932.) In the Ashley Valley in Utah, I met an old man, rocking on his porch, who remembered Butch Cassidy in 1908. But if they did come back that summer, the pace was too hot; for by December both outlaws were in Bolivia working for a man called Siebert at the Concordia tin mine.

Techniques: *The author uses the words "art of the hold-up" and "performance" when talking about robbery. This puts you in the mind of Butch Cassidy so that you can see robbery the way he does.*

Butch Cassidy 507

Enrichment The word *cordillera* refers to the principal mountain group of a continent. It comes from the Spanish word, *cuerda*, which means "cord" or "chain." Chatwin is referring to the Andes Mountains, which stretch the entire west coast of South America.

Critical Thinking and Reading Why does Chatwin call Etta's daughter Betty a "competitive girl"? With whom would she have been competing? What is the author's tone in this sentence?

Organization: *The author gives you four different versions of Butch Cassidy's death. He saves the most ordinary version for last. Maybe he does this to remind the reader that Butch Cassidy was, in some ways, just a regular guy.*

The classic account of their death, at San Vicente, Bolivia, in December 1909, following their theft of a mine payroll, was first set down in *Elk's Magazine* for 1930 by the Western poet, Arthur Chapman. It was an ideal scenario for the moviemakers: the brave cavalry captain shot while trying to arrest the gringos[8]: the mud-walled courtyard full of dead mules: the impossible odds: the Kid first wounded, then shot through the head by Butch, who, having now killed a man, reserves the last bullet for himself. The episode ends with the Bolivian soldiers finding Etta's Tiffany watch on one of the bodies.

No one knows where Chapman got the story: Butch Cassidy could have invented it himself. His aim, after all, was to "die" in South America and re-emerge under a new name. The shooting at San Vicente was investigated by the late President René Barrientos, Ché Guevara's killer, himself an ardent Western history buff. He put a team on to solving the mystery, grilled the villagers personally, exhumed corpses in the cemetery, checked the army and police files, and concluded that the whole thing was a fabrication. Nor did Pinkertons believe it. They have their own version, based on the skimpiest evidence, that the "family of 3" died together in a shoot-out with the Uruguayan police in 1911. Three years later they assumed Butch Cassidy dead—which, if he were alive, was exactly what he wanted.

"Bunkum!" his friends said when they heard the stories coming out of South America. Butch didn't go in for shoot-outs. And from 1915 on, hundreds of people saw—or thought they saw—him: running guns for Pancho Villa in Mexico: prospecting with Wyatt Earp in Alaska: touring the West in a Model T Ford: calling on old girlfriends (who remember him as gotten rather fat): or turning up at a Wild West Show in San Francisco.

I went to see the star witness to his return: his sister, Mrs. Lula Parker Betenson, a forthright and energetic woman in her nineties, with a lifetime of service to the Democratic Party. She has no doubts: her brother came back and ate blueberry pie with the family at Circleville in the fall of 1925. She believes he died of pneumonia in Washington State in the late 1930's. Another version puts his death in an Eastern city, a retired railroad engineer with two married daughters.

---

8. gringos (grin̄′ gōs) *n.*: In Latin America, a contemptuous term for a foreigner, especially an American or Englishman.

from Aaron Copland's ballet, *Billy the Kid*.

Cooperative Learning A group of students might do a research project on other outlaws of the American West and present a report to the class.

Thematic Response What did you learn from Butch Cassidy's life journey that you can apply to your own?

Closure and Extension

ANSWERS TO RESPONDIN **TO THE SELECTION**
Your Response

1. Some students may say that Cassidy's lawlessness gave him a certain amount of freedom that law-abiding citizens surrender when they choose to obey laws.

Bruce Chatwin (1940–1989), who was born in England, traveled extensively. His travels took him all over the world, from Afghanistan to Argentina and Brazil. *In Patagonia*—Chatwin's most highly acclaimed travel book—is a South American quest story. The book revolves around the narrator's search for a giant sloth skin and his encounters with other people whose stories, such as this one about Butch Cassidy, delay his journey. His last travel book, *Songlines*, is a study of Australia's nomadic aborigines.

More About the Author After graduating from a private secondary school in England, Chatwin did not continue his education at a university but went to work as a porter for Sotheby and Company, a prestigious art dealer in London. He became an art auctioneer and then director of Sotheby's Impressionist department. He subsequently became an archeology student, newspaper writer, world traveler, and author. From what you know of Chatwin's life, why might a figure such as Butch Cassidy have captured his imagination?

RESPONDING TO THE SELECTION

Your Response

1. Chatwin applies the phrase "lawless freedom" to Cassidy's life. Comment on this idea.

Interpreting

2. Why did the sheriffs fear Cassidy more for being a "leader of men" than for the crimes he committed?
3. Describe Cassidy's life in Argentina. How did it parallel his life in America?

Applying

4. Cassidy and many other outlaws believed that "right lay the wrong side of the law." Why might they have adopted this philosophy? What happens when civilians take the law into their own hands?

ANALYZING LITERATURE

Understanding Anecdotes

An anecdote is a brief story about an interesting, amusing, or strange event. In "Butch Cassidy," Chatwin writes about the outlaw's life in Argentina and the events that led up to his arrival there. Chatwin effectively embellishes the account of Cassidy's life with anecdotes from many sources. These anecdotes are what give the reader a sense of who Butch Cassidy was.

1. Describe three anecdotes Chatwin uses to reveal the character of Butch Cassidy.
2. What does each anecdote illustrate?

CRITICAL THINKING AND READING

Appreciating Tone

A writer's style reflects the tone, or the writer's attitude toward a subject. The tone of a literary piece might be described as formal, informal, serious, playful, bitter, or ironic. *In Patagonia*, Chatwin's travel narrative, could have been written much like a travel brochure or a history textbook. Instead, he wrote in a humorous, informal tone that makes this book light and interesting to read.

1. Compare and contrast the tone of Chatwin's essay with that of another essay in the unit.
2. List two passages in which Chatwin conveys a light, humorous touch. Is the humor appropriate? Why or why not? What effect do these passages have on the reader?

THINKING AND WRITING

Writing a Travel Narrative

Think of a specific incident that occurred during one of your travels. The incident could have occurred during a vacation, an excursion to a new part of your hometown, a field trip, and so on. Then think of several anecdotes, or brief stories, that relate an interesting, amusing, or strange event that led up to, followed, or occurred during the incident you chose. These anecdotes should either entertain, make a point, or tell more about you or someone else who was involved in the incident.

Butch Cassidy 509

ANSWERS TO CRITICAL THINKING AND READING

1. Students might choose the reverential tone of "A Lincoln Preface," the dramatic tone of the excerpt from *Kon Tiki*, or the eloquence of "I Have a Dream."
2. Students might select Chatwin's description of Cassidy's "apprentice years" (pp. 533–534), his anecdote about Cleophas Dowd (p. 535), or the account of the bank robberies of the summer of 1907 (p. 537). Some may feel that the tone is inappropriate for writing about violence; others may feel that it is appropriate to the author's purpose, which is to entertain rather than moralize.

THINKING AND WRITING

Writing Transparency Students often find it helpful to see a model of their writing assignment. Before students write, you may wish to show them Model 1: *Narrative Essay* in **Transparencies for Writing.**

Alternative Assessment After completing the Responding to the Selection questions and the Analyzing Literature activities, have students write a character sketch of Butch Cassidy's personality, supporting their views with specific details of Cassidy's escapades as described in the selection.

Interpreting

2. A leader influences many people and is therefore more dangerous than an individual acting alone.
3. As in America, Cassidy started his life in Argentina as a law-abiding citizen, then became bored, and commenced a life of crime.

Applying

4. Students might answer that the law often seems to support the interests of those in power, failing to provide for the poor and powerless. Many will recognize that violence and corruption often result when individuals take the law into their own hands.

ANSWERS TO ANALYZING LITERATURE

1. Answers might include how Cassidy left home, his life in New York, and the Winnemucca raid.

2. Cassidy's farewell to his family shows that he was capable of love and tenderness; his life in New York shows that he enjoyed wealth and luxury; the story of the Winnemucca raid shows that he had a sense of humor.

Preparation

Motivation/Prior Knowledge

Stimulate a class discussion on some current social problems. You should have no difficulty getting students to air their views! Some students, however, may not feel comfortable with controversial issues, and all students should be cautioned to respect the views and feelings of others when expressing their own opinions. Guide students in keeping the tone of the discussion objective and practical.

You may wish to provide students with several samples of fliers, illustrating style and format.

Focus

Call the students' attention to the abbreviated format used for fliers. Emphasize the importance of focusing the reader's attention on the main ideas and using the limited space to present only the facts and figures that most effectively support their claims.

Presentation

Prewriting Instruct students to research potential solutions to the problem, as well as the causes and effects.

Writing Transparency Assist students in organizing their research needs by using the *Outline* graphic organizer in **Transparencies for Writing.**

You may wish to allow students who are addressing similar problems to form research teams. Using their outlines as a guide, the team members can divide the main issues among themselves. Assign a time for team members to meet and discuss their findings.

Drafting Refer students to their prewriting outlines for guidance in setting up the flier. Suggest that students express the main headings in their bulleted list.

> *"It has been said that writing comes more easily if you have something to say."*
> **Sholem Asch**

WRITING A FLIER

Essays like "But a Watch in the Night" and "I Have a Dream" are valuable sources of information about some problems that society faces. What other problems are there in today's world that cry out for a solution? Consider what you can do as a writer to inform readers about these issues.

Focus

Assignment: Develop a flier for a cause or an issue that interests you.

Purpose: To explain an issue and promote a point of view.

Audience: General public.

Prewriting

1. Choose a topic. What cause will you write about? There are many issues to choose from because every community has problems that must be solved.

2. Gather information. Once you have a topic, do some research. Read newspaper and magazine articles to come up with ideas for solving the problem. Take notes when you encounter important facts or statistics.

3. Create a chart. Suppose that you are interested in preserving the environment. You want to stop the building of a garbage incinerator in your community. After you have gathered information, you might want to make a cause-and-effect chart to organize your facts and develop an alternative to the proposed incinerator.

Student Model

Cause:	**Cause:**
Building an Incinerator to Burn Garbage	Recycling Garbage
Effects	**Effects**
Neurological damage from lead and mercury in air	Disposal of nearly 85% of garbage
Smog produced by nitrogen oxides in air	Cost effective

The subheadings and research notes will provide the support arguments to be included in the remainder of the file.

Software If students have access to computers, they can experiment with the effects that different fonts and font appearance attributes have on drawing attention to their key points.

Using the cut and paste features in **Bank Street Writer** will allow students to try different layouts as well.

Revising and Editing Because of the structure of the flier, students need to be especially careful in reviewing their work for inappropriate changes in tense and voice. Suggest that they read each item on their bulleted

list as a separate sentence to be sure that they have remained consistent throughout.

Allow peer groups to meet and discuss the questions on page 511. The students may assist each other in making a brief and emphatic statement by identifying words and phrases that could be replaced with more powerful language.

4. Design the flier. Remember that fliers are usually a single sheet of paper that can be folded and placed in an envelope for mailing. The size of the lettering is important. You want the reader to pay attention to your message even if he or she does not want to take the time to read it, so the words must be very obvious. Visuals are important as well. Show a picture of the problem—or of the solution.

Drafting

1. Make the first paragraph count. The first thing that your reader will see is the top of your flier. The message has to be clear and, above all, brief and to the point. A bulleted list is effective because it draws attention to your main ideas.

Student Model

THE NEW INCINERATOR WILL
- ENDANGER YOUR HEALTH
- FOUL THE AIR
- DESTROY RESOURCES
- RAISE YOUR TAXES
WHAT CAN BE DONE ABOUT IT?

---

2. Back up your claims. The remainder of your flier should provide facts and figures to back up your claims. Remember also that you cannot simply point out a problem. You must come up with a solution. Use your cause-and-effect chart to help present your arguments clearly and persuasively.

Revising and Editing

1. Keep it brief. Read your flier to make sure that you have not been overly wordy. People tend to read fliers and advertising "on the run." They want the facts, and they are not prepared to wade through dense paragraphs to find them.

2. Remember your audience. Make sure that your arguments make sense and that they appeal to the self-interest of the reader. Have you stated the issue so that your readers know how the problem affects them?

3. Give your flier to a peer editor. Following are questions you can ask your peer editor:
- Have I used vivid language?
- Are most of my sentences short and simple?
- Have I organized information so that it can be read and understood quickly?

Grammar Tip

Use the active voice to give a dynamic quality to your message. Remember that in the active voice, the subject performs the action, whereas in the passive voice, the subject is acted upon. Examples: PASSIVE VOICE: It was said that the new incinerator will foul the air and pollute the neighborhood. ACTIVE VOICE: Experts said that the new incinerator will foul the air and pollute the neighborhood.

Options for Publishing

- Make photocopies of your flier and distribute them to your classmates.
- Read your flier aloud to the class. Ask them if they have any arguments to add to either side of the issue.
- Give your flier to neighbors and discuss with them the problem you have described.

Reviewing Your Writing Process

1. Was this kind of writing very different from the writing you normally do? How did it differ?
2. Did doing this assignment make you more conscious of the techniques that special-interest groups use in their advertising? Explain.

Closure and Extension

Guidelines for Evaluation You may find the following questions helpful in evaluating each student's flier:
1. Is the main idea of the flier clearly stated?
2. Are the key points listed concisely for quick reading?
3. Are accurate facts and figures used to support the main idea?
4. Is the flier designed to catch the attention of the reader?
5. Is the flier free of errors in spelling and grammar?

Reviewing Your Writing Process The following Protocol will help students reflect on and internalize their own writing process:
1. What cause or issue have you selected to explain to the general public?
2. What have you put in the first paragraph to capture your reader's attention?
3. What action do you urge your readers to take on this issue?
4. What reasons do you present to your readers to take this action?
5. What details do you offer to support those reasons?
6. What reactions did your classmates have to your flier?

Publishing Your students may enjoy creating poster-size versions of their fliers to be displayed throughout the school.

Enrichment Students can use the information they have gathered for their fliers to write a well-informed letter to the editor of the local paper. Encourage students to retain the powerful language they have used in their fliers.

Presentation

Motivation/Prior Knowledge
Hold a mini "job fair" in the classroom. Have on hand a selection of materials to prompt ideas as students consider their options. The employment section of the local newspaper is one good source of ideas. There are also several employment guides available, which give an overview of the opportunities in various companies. The guidance counselor at your school may have pamphlets and fliers about student internships and part-time employment. As students peruse the literature, stimulate discussion about which opportunities seem best suited to each student's interests and abilities.

Focus Remind students that the purpose of the self-evaluation is to convince a prospective employer that the applicant is the best person to fill a position. They must communicate their enthusiasm for the job and demonstrate that they have the ability to do the job effectively. Tell students to think of the evaluations as advertisements of themselves.

Presentation

Prewriting Students may require some assistance in analyzing broadly stated job requirements and breaking them down into specific skills. Help students to determine which skills are most essential to performing the job well. Instruct students to direct the focus of the self-evaluation to relating their experience and accomplishments in these areas.

Drafting You might want to introduce the draft as a simple three-step process. Tell students that each job-related skill they possess should be mentioned three times. It should be listed with the other skills in the introductory paragraph, supported with examples in the body of the evalua-

YOUR WRITING PROCESS

WRITING A SELF-EVALUATION

In essays like "Georgia O'Keeffe" by Joan Didion, a writer evaluates the work and life of another person. At times you may have to write an evaluation of your own life in order to obtain a job. When you write such a statement, your aim is to persuade a prospective employer that you are just the person he or she has been looking for!

"What is written without effort is in general read without pleasure."
Samuel Johnson

Focus

Assignment: Write a self-evaluation.
Purpose: To highlight important aspects of your background in order to win a job.
Audience: The employer.

Prewriting

1. Do some research. To present yourself effectively to a prospective employer, you must know what qualities the employer is looking for. Find out about the company or the type of company you are interested in and the job that you would like. If it is possible, talk to some people who work for such a company.

2. Make a list. Think of all the educational and work experiences that you have had. Make a list of everything that might attract a potential employer.

Student Model

Goal: A position as a cashier in a restaurant.

Qualifications needed	Experience
Math skills	• Earned an A in math
Sense of responsibility	• Baby-sit for two families
Ability to deal with the public	• Volunteer worker in hospital

---

tion, and included in the summarizing final paragraph. Show students how this three-step process was followed in the student model.

Revising and Editing Instruct students to compare the job skills required to the experience they have listed. Is there an example of experience given for each skill? Does each example of experience relate directly to

the job? Encourage peer editors to comment on how effectively the self-evaluation makes the connection between each qualification and the experience described.

Remind students that their self-evaluation is directed at a prospective employer. The tone should be confident and positive, while at the same time remaining appropriately formal.

Software If students have access to computers, you may want to have them use the *Readability* activity in **Writer's Helper** to revise their work for clarity and focus.

Grammar Tip Students' efforts to connect their experience with job qualifications may result in run-on sentences and sentence fragments. Instruct students to care-

Drafting

1. Begin with an attention-getter. Keep in mind that you are not the only person applying for the job. You want your application to be read and remembered.

Student Model

What qualities make a good cashier? Above-average math skills, a responsible nature, and the ability to deal with the public are certainly the key skills—and I possess all these qualities. A brief look at my background will back up that claim.

---

2. Stick to the important facts. The employer will not be interested to know that you won an award in summer camp for winning a canoe race unless you are applying for a job as a camp counselor. Emphasize the experience that is relevant to the job you want. This is where your prewriting list becomes helpful. Write about each point in turn, and make the connection between your experience and the requirements of the job.

Student Model

I am an A student in math and a member of the math club in my school. I have competed successfully in many high school math contests, and I am the current regional math champion. My speed and accuracy in computation is, I believe, a valuable asset.

Revising and Editing

1. Have a peer editor check for coherence. In order to be coherent, your narrative must be well organized. Exchange narratives with another student and evaluate each other's work for organization and coherence. After your classmate reads your self-evaluation, have him or her answer the following questions.
- Is my message clear?
- Do my accomplishments really fit the employer's needs?
- Does my closing paragraph repeat the ideas in the opening paragraph?

2. Check your spelling and punctuation. If you want to win the job, your self-evaluation must be as close to perfect as you can make it.

Grammar Tip
Run-on sentences and sentence fragments will make a poor impression on a prospective employer. Review all your sentences to make sure that they stop where they should and that they express a complete thought.

Options for Publishing
- Join with your classmates in posting your self-evaluations in the classroom. Have a contest to determine the "Person Most Likely to Get the Job."
- Apply for a part-time job. See what response your self-evaluation receives from an actual employer.

Reviewing Your Writing Process
1. Did you find it difficult to write about yourself? Why or why not?
2. Did writing this self-evaluation give you any new thoughts about the kind of job you would like to have? Explain.

---

fully check their work for this weakness. Then direct the students to the Handbook of Grammar and Revising Strategies for guidance in correcting these problems.

Enrichment Invite a career counselor to visit your class. He or she might comment on the self-evaluations, answer questions from the class, and offer tips on presenting oneself well in an interview situation.

Closure and Extension

Guidelines for Evaluation You may wish to consider the following questions as you assess each student's self-evaluation:
1. Does the introductory paragraph clearly outline the qualities that suit the student for the job?
2. Does the self-evaluation address each quality and offer specific examples of related experience?
3. Does the closing paragraph effectively summarize the qualities covered in the self-evaluation?
4. Does the tone of the self-evaluation reflect the writer's confidence in his or her own abilities?
5. Is the self-evaluation free of errors in spelling, punctuation, grammar, and mechanics?

Reviewing Your Writing Process The following questions will help students reflect on and internalize their writing process:
1. What kind of job or position do you say you would like?
2. What specific personal qualities, educational accomplishments, and work experience do you say qualify you for this job?
3. What do you do in the beginning of your evaluation to get your potential employer's attention?
4. What suggestions from your classmates did you include to improve your self-evaluation?

Student Portfolios You might want students to keep their self-evaluations in their writing portfolios.

Humanities Note

Fine art, *Mist Fantasy*, J.E.H. MacDonald. James Edward Harvey MacDonald (1873-1932), a Canadian painter and illustrator, was an important member of the band of Canadian nationalist artists known as the "Group of Seven." Their aim was to capture the magnificence of the landscape of their country on canvas. Their works, modern in approach, were considered radical and brought about far-reaching changes in Canadian art.

The Canadian countryside provided endless subjects for MacDonald to paint. *Mist Fantasy* is painted in thick, pure color. The simplified shapes of the boats riding on the reflective surface of the water, beneath the swirling mist, is bold and evocative, suggesting a poetic image. This is J.E.H. MacDonald's rugged version of impressionism. He sought to express the power and raw beauty of his country in terms that could not be confused with the art of any other country on earth.

MIST FANTASY
J.E.H. MacDonald
Art Gallery of Ontario, Toronto

514 Poetry

514

POETRY

"If I read a book," wrote the poet Emily Dickinson, "and it makes my whole body so cold no fire can ever warm me, I know that is poetry. If I feel physically as if the top of my head were taken off, I know that is poetry."

Poetry is a highly charged form of literature in which every word is packed with meaning. It has a musical quality that may be achieved through the use of rhythm and rhyme or through repetition. A poem is written in lines, which do not always signal the end of sentences, and the lines are arranged in stanzas.

There are several types of poetry. Narrative poetry tells a story, while dramatic poetry is poetry in which one or more characters speak. Lyric poetry expresses a strong emotional response toward its subject.

In this unit you will encounter poems on a variety of subjects and in a variety of forms. You will also develop strategies for gaining the fullest appreciation of each poem.

515

Reading Actively The instruction on this page introduces students to skills important in the active reading of a poem. This process is similar to that used in reading other types of literature. The special requirements of poetry, however, call for a few differences in approach.

Because poetry is more musical than prose, it is important to read it slowly and to read it several times—aloud as well as silently. You might tell students that the sound of a poem—its music—often reinforces its meaning. A poem like "The Charge of the Light Brigade," for example, has a galloping rhythm, which emphasizes the action in the poem.

You might also emphasize the strategy of paraphrasing. Students are sometimes intimidated by poetry. If they can put a poem into their own words, they will feel more comfortable with it. Caution them, however, that a paraphrase is not a substitute for a poem. A paraphrase can be useful in understanding meaning, but it ignores the poem's music.

After discussing these strategies with students, turn to the poem, "Sympathy," on the next page. It is a model for active reading. The annotations show how an active reader might construct meaning from this poem.

Ask students to pay attention to these annotations as they read. Suggest that they also add their own comments and responses as they read.

For further practice with this process, use the poem on page 624 of the **Teaching Portfolio,** "Your World," which students can annotate themselves.

READING ACTIVELY

Poetry

Poetry is different from other forms of writing in its appearance, its use of language, and its musical qualities. The poet Walt Whitman wrote, "To have great poetry, there must be great audiences, too." How do you participate as an audience? Do you approach each poem actively? The following strategies will help you become an active reader of poetry:

QUESTION What is the poem saying? What questions come to mind as you are reading? Why does the writer include certain words and details? Look for answers to your questions as you read.

USE YOUR SENSES What images is the poet creating? How are these images created? Let your imagination see the pictures in your mind, and let your senses take in the poet's language.

LISTEN Much poetry is musical. Read the poem aloud so that you can hear the sound of it and feel its rhythm. Often the sound of the words and the rhythm they create suggest a mood or feeling. How do the sound and the rhythm affect you?

CONNECT Bring your own experience and knowledge to the poem. What images are familiar? Which are new to you?

PARAPHRASE Put the poem in your own words. When you express a poem in your own words, you can better understand its meaning.

RESPOND Think about how the poem makes you feel as you read. What thoughts and emotions do the poet's words evoke in you? What does the poem say to you?

Try to use these strategies as you read the poems in this unit. They will help you increase your enjoyment and understanding of poetry.

On page 517 you can see an example of active reading by Tuan Quoc Pham of Garden Grove High School in Garden Grove, California. The notes in the side column include Tuan's thoughts and comments as he read "Sympathy." Your own thoughts as you read may be different because you bring your own experiences to your reading.

516   Poetry

Objectives

1 To learn to read poetry actively
2 To understand symbols
3 To write an extended definition
4 To express individual interests and abilities through optional activities

Support Material

Teaching Portfolio
Teacher Backup, p. 621
Reading Actively, "Your World," by Georgia Douglas Johnson, p. 624
Usage and Mechanics Worksheet, p. 625
Analyzing Literature Worksheet, *Understanding Symbols,* p. 626
Language Worksheet, *Under-*
standing Shades of Difference, p. 627
Selection Test, p. 628

Library of Video Classics
I Know Why the Caged Bird Sings

Listening to Literature
"Sympathy"

Prentice Hall Literature Writing Studio

Sympathy

Paul Laurence Dunbar

I know what the caged bird feels, alas!
    When the sun is bright on the upland slopes;
When the wind stirs soft through the springing grass,
And the river flows like a stream of glass;
5   When the first bird sings and the first bud opes,
And the faint perfume from its chalice[1] steals—
I know what the caged bird feels!

I know why the caged bird beats his wing
    Till its blood is red on the cruel bars;
10 For he must fly back to his perch and cling
When he fain[2] would be on the bough a-swing;
    And a pain still throbs in the old, old scars
And they pulse again with a keener sting—
I know why he beats his wing!

15 I know why the caged bird sings, ah me,
    When his wing is bruised and his bosom sore,—
When he beats his bars and he would be free;
It is not a carol of joy or glee,
    But a prayer that he sends from his heart's deep core,
20 But a plea, that upward to Heaven he flings—
I know why the caged bird sings!

---

1. chalice (chăl' is) *n.*: A cup or goblet; here, the cup-shaped part of a budding flower.
2. fain (fān) *adv.*: Gladly; eagerly.

Side annotations:

Question: Why is the poem called "Sympathy"?

Senses: These lines create images of things moving about freely: The wind stirs, the river flows, the bird sings, and the bud opens.

Connect: These images show, by contrast, how horrible it feels to be locked up.

Connect: The title refers to the poet's knowing how the bird feels.

Respond: I think Dunbar might be talking from his own experience.

Listen: This poem sounds like a song. Maybe it is the caged bird's song.

Paraphrase: The bird has beat its wings until they are bloody trying to get out. All it can do beyond that is to hope and pray for freedom.

Paul Laurence Dunbar (1872–1906) was born in Dayton, Ohio, the son of former slaves who had been freed before the outbreak of the Civil War. He was the first African American writer to support himself entirely through his writing. He wrote poems, short stories, and novels. In "Sympathy," Dunbar expresses the frustration of not being free.

Presentation

Motivation/Prior Knowledge Have students discuss the true meaning of the word *sympathy*. Ask students what situations elicit this emotion from them.

Thematic Focus Have students discuss why a caged bird might serve as an inspirational voice for someone. What characteristics do we normally associate with birds? Why would a caged bird sing? Would hearing its voice inspire someone to imagine what the bird is trying to communicate?

Purpose-Setting Question Let the model question with the title set the purpose for reading.

Making Connections You might have students compare Dunbar's message with that of Martin Luther King in "I Have a Dream," page 467.

Enrichment You might tell students that the writer Maya Angelou used a line from this poem for the title of her autobiography, *I Know Why the Caged Bird Sings*. What might she be suggesting about her autobiography with this title?

Reader's Response What thoughts does this poem evoke?

Thematic Response Sympathy implies shared feelings. What similar feelings did the voice of the caged bird inspire in the poet?

More About the Author Paul Laurence Dunbar's first collection of poems was published in 1893 and was followed by a steady stream of novels, short stories, and more than 500 poems. Have students discuss how the demands of composing poetry might influence the style of a writer who also writes novels and short stories.

ANSWERS TO RESPONDING TO THE SELECTION

Your Response

1. Encourage students to use their senses as they visualize the images in each stanza. Ask students to describe how their mental picture changes from one stanza to the next.

Recalling

2. The speaker identifies with the bird in these five situations: "When the sun is bright on the upland slopes," "When the wind stirs soft through the springing grass," when "the river flows like a stream of glass," "When the first bird sings and the first bud" opens, and when the perfume from the bud is released.
3. The bird beats its wings on the cage because it wants desperately to be free but is imprisoned in its cage.
4. The caged bird's song is a prayer or plea for freedom.

Interpreting

5. Suggested Response: The poet describes the beauty of life by depicting scenes of spring. The bird, however, trapped in its cage, is unable to experience this beauty.
6. Suggested Response: The "old, old scars" refer to the bird's previous injuries from attempts to escape. For the speaker, the scars refer to past injustices and slavery. Time has neither erased nor soothed the pain of these memories, and the speaker remembers them with increased emotion.
7. Answers will differ. Most students will realize that the speaker feels sympathy with the bird because they have both experienced similar emotions as a result of their lack of freedom.

Applying

8. Answers will differ. Students may respond that a feeling of frustration comes from wanting something you cannot have. Seeing others that are free gives the bird and the speaker a vision of what they want and cannot have.

RESPONDING TO THE SELECTION

Your Response

1. Describe your response to the images created in the first stanza. Compare your feelings as you read the first stanza with your feelings as you read the second and third stanzas.

Recalling

2. In the first stanza, the speaker identifies with, or knows, how the caged bird feels, in what five situations?
3. In the second stanza, why does the caged bird beat his wings?
4. In the last stanza, why does the caged bird sing?

Interpreting

5. In the first stanza, compare the circumstances of the bird with the situations the poet describes.
6. In the second stanza, what do you think are the "old, old scars"? Why do they "pulse again with a keener sting"?
7. Why does the poet call this poem "Sympathy"?

Applying

8. Do you think the caged bird's frustration is greater because it sees creatures that aren't caged? Explain your answer.

ANALYZING LITERATURE

Understanding Symbols

A **symbol** is something that has its own meaning but that also represents something else. For example, an oak tree is a thing in itself, but it can also serve as a symbol of strength and endurance.

1. What do you think the cage represents? Explain your answer.
2. What do you think the woodland scenes represent? Explain your answer.

3. What do you think the bird represents? Explain your answer.
4. Keeping these symbols in mind, what insight into life do you think the poem provides?

THINKING AND WRITING

Writing an Extended Definition

An extended definition both provides the meaning of a word and describes its distinguishing characteristics. Some abstract words require more than a simple dictionary definition. For example, think about the word *sympathy*. First jot down the dictionary definition of the word. Then freewrite about what the word means to you. Explore your thoughts about what sympathy is and is *not*, why it is important, and how you can recognize it. Then write the first draft of an extended definition. Start by defining the word as a dictionary would. Then use the ideas in your freewriting to expand on your definition by describing the word, or getting at the heart of its meaning. When you revise your definition, make sure you have included enough details to make its meaning clear. Proofread your definition and compare it with the definitions of your classmates.

LEARNING OPTIONS

1. **Art.** Illustrate the first stanza of "Sympathy" by drawing or painting a scene in which all the elements described by the poet are present. As you create your scene, imagine that you are a caged bird, denied the right to experience such a beautiful place. When you are finished, share your artwork with the class.
2. **Speaking and Listening.** Practice reading "Sympathy" aloud to yourself. As you read, try to convey the meaning behind the poet's words as well as your own response to the poem. Modify your tone of voice and pacing to fit the content of each stanza. When you are ready, read the poem aloud to the class.

ANSWERS TO ANALYZING LITERATURE

1. Suggested Response: The cage represents restrictions in life. Often social, political, and economic conditions result in such restrictions and constraints.
2. Suggested Response: The woodland scenes represent the beauty of life. We are surrounded by life's gifts and joys, but if we are not free to enjoy them we can only feel frustrated, not blessed.

3. Suggested Response: The bird represents people who encounter restrictions. Social, political, and economic constraints deprive people of their freedom and are like the bars of a cage.
4. Answers will differ. Many students may respond that life offers many exciting possibilities, but people must be free to pursue and enjoy them or they feel as frustrated as a caged bird.

THINKING AND WRITING

Software If students are working on computers, have them use **Bank Street Writer** to complete all stages of the assignment.

Alternative Assessment After students complete the Thinking and Writing activity, ask them to assume the role of Paul Laurence

Narrative Poetry

BUFFALO CHASE WITH BOWS AND LANCES
George Catlin
National Museum of American Art, Smithsonian Institution

Humanities Note

Fine art, *Buffalo Chase,* by George Catlin. George Catlin (1796–1872), a self-taught American painter and anthropologist, enjoyed some success in Philadelphia as a portraitist. Seeing a traveling "Wild West" show convinced him to leave the settled East and pursue his lifelong interest in recording the features, customs, and dwellings of Native Americans. He is one of the foremost painters of Native American tribes.

Catlin's epic journey through the West to paint the various tribes necessitated concessions in equipment to portability. His paints were premixed in large batches, which gives his paintings a uniform color quality. The canvases themselves were painted ahead with general landscape backgrounds upon which he could superimpose details and action scenes from Native American life. These backgrounds, usually of rolling green hills, at times create a strangely unrealistic effect in some of his scenes.

This type of background can be seen in *Buffalo Chase;* however, in this case, it becomes subordinate to the action of the painting. Done in characteristic rapid, sketchy brushwork, this scene has a brisk immediacy that suits the subject.

Dunbar and write to his publisher explaining the relationship of his caged bird image to his experience as an African American. Refer students to the biographical note on page 517 for information about Dunbar's life.

LEARNING OPTIONS

1. Kinesthetic learners will find this activity inspirational. You might extend the activity by having students create a scene for each stanza.
2. You might vary the activity by having the whole class read as a chorus the last two lines of each stanza.

 Audiocassette Before students practice reading aloud, you might wish to have them listen to the reading of "Sympathy" in the **Listening to Literature** Audiocassettes. Ask them to concentrate on tone and pacing.

Preparation

More About the Author Ernest Thayer has become famous for his unforgettable picture of the flawed hero who struck out. Ask students why they think the poem is so popular.

Literary Focus You might tell students that a narrative poem has other characteristics of fiction besides the ones mentioned on the Guide for Reading page. For example, it is told from a point of view. "Casey at the Bat" is written in the third person—an observer of the action narrates the story. There is also a conflict between the two baseball teams, rising action as Flynn and Blake get on base and Casey takes his first two strikes, a climax when Casey takes his third swing, and a resolution when the Mudville team loses the game.

Prereading Focus You might want to have students work in groups of three or four to complete this activity. After the students in each group have shared exciting sports stories among themselves, have them choose two or three to share with the entire class.

Vocabulary Ask less advanced students to find an antonym for each of the words except *wreathed.* Have them write each antonym in a sentence.

Electronic Handbook You might want to have students use the Language Master 6000 to find antonyms and to hear the correct pronunciation of the vocabulary words.

Ernest Lawrence Thayer

(1863–1940) was born in California. He worked there and in New York as a newspaper writer and often published his poems in the newspapers on which he worked. Today, Thayer is remembered best for one work, "Casey at the Bat." This humorous poem grew out of his love of baseball, with its style at least partly reflecting Thayer's work as a reporter. In fact, you could almost read it as a sports story in verse. "Casey at the Bat" was popularized by a comedian, De Wolf Hopper,

GUIDE FOR READING

Casey at the Bat

Narrative Poetry

Narrative poetry is poetry that tells a story. Like a short story, a narrative poem has a plot, characters, a setting, and a theme. Unlike a short story, it is written in verse, language with a definite rhythm, or "beat." In many, but not all, narrative poems, the verses rhyme. Narrative poems, like other kinds of poetry, are often divided into stanzas, or groups of lines that form a unit, rather like paragraphs in prose. The stanzas of a poem usually have the same number of lines and the same rhyme pattern.

Focus

What sport do you most enjoy watching? Get together with other students who also enjoy this sport and recall the most suspenseful moments you ever witnessed. What made these moments so exciting? Then read "Casey at the Bat" to see what happens in the ninth inning of a hotly contested baseball game.

Vocabulary

Knowing the following words will help you as you read "Casey at the Bat."

pallor (pal′ ər) *n.*: Paleness (p. 521)

wreathed (rēthd) *v.*: Curled around (p. 521)

writhing (rīth′ iŋ) *v.*: Twisting, turning (p. 522)

tumult (tōō′ məlt) *n.*: Noisy commotion (p. 522)

Objectives

1 To enjoy narrative poetry
2 To paraphrase poetry
3 To write narrative verse
4 To express individual interests and abilities through optional activities

Support Material

Teaching Portfolio
Teacher Backup, p. 631
Usage and Mechanics Worksheet, p. 634
Vocabulary Check, p. 635
Critical Thinking and Reading Worksheet, *Paraphrasing Poetry,* p. 636

Language Worksheet, *Recognizing Jargon,* p. 637
Selection Test, p. 638

Listening to Literature
"Casey at the Bat"

Prentice Hall Literature Writing Studio

Casey at the Bat

Ernest Lawrence Thayer

1
It looked extremely rocky for the Mudville nine that day;
The score stood two to four, with but an inning left to play.
So, when Cooney died at second, and Burrows did the
    same,
A pallor wreathed the features of the patrons of the game.

2
5 A straggling few got up to go, leaving there the rest,
With that hope which springs eternal within the human
    breast.
For they thought: "If only Casey could get a whack at that,"
They'd put even money now, with Casey at the bat.
But Flynn preceded Casey, and likewise so did Blake,
10 And the former was a pudd'n, and the latter was a fake.
So on that stricken multitude a deathlike silence sat;
For there seemed but little chance of Casey's getting to the
    bat.

3
But Flynn let drive a "single," to the wonderment of all.
And the much-despised Blakey "tore the cover off the ball."
15 And when the dust had lifted, and they saw what had
    occurred,
There was Blakey safe at second, and Flynn a-huggin' third.

Then from the gladdened multitude went up a joyous yell—
It rumbled in the mountaintops, it rattled in the dell;[1]
It struck upon the hillside and rebounded on the flat;
20 For Casey, mighty Casey, was advancing to the bat.

There was ease in Casey's manner as he stepped into his
    place,
There was pride in Casey's bearing and a smile on Casey's
    face;
And when responding to the cheers he lightly doffed[2] his
    hat,
No stranger in the crowd could doubt 'twas Casey at the
    bat.

---

1. dell (del) *n.*: Small, secluded valley.
2. doffed (däft) *v.*: Lifted.

Casey at the Bat 521

4 **Critical Thinking and Reading**
What can you infer about
Casey's past performance?

5 **Discussion** How does the crowd
feel about Casey? What evidence is there of Casey's power
over the crowd?

6 **Reading Strategy** Ask students
to predict what will happen next.

25 Ten thousand eyes were on him as he rubbed his hands
        with dirt,
    Five thousand tongues applauded when he wiped them on
        his shirt;
    Then when the writhing pitcher ground the ball into his
        hip,
    Defiance glanced in Casey's eye, a sneer curled Casey's lip.

    And now the leather-covered sphere came hurtling through
        the air,
30 And Casey stood a-watching it in haughty grandeur there.
    Close by the sturdy batsman the ball unheeded sped;
    "That ain't my style," said Casey. "Strike one," the umpire
        said.

    From the benches, black with people, there went up a
        muffled roar,
    Like the beating of the storm waves on the stern and
        distant shore.
35 "Kill him! kill the umpire!" shouted someone on the stand;
    And it's likely they'd have killed him had not Casey raised
        his hand.

    With a smile of Christian charity great Casey's visage[3]
        shone;
    He stilled the rising tumult, he made the game go on;
    He signaled to the pitcher, and once more the spheroid
        flew;
40 But Casey still ignored it, and the umpire said, "Strike
        two."

    "Fraud!" cried the maddened thousands, and the echo
        answered "Fraud!"
    But one scornful look from Casey and the audience was
        awed;
    They saw his face grow stern and cold, they saw his
        muscles strain,
    And they knew that Casey wouldn't let the ball go by again.

---

3. visage (viz′ ij) *n.*: Face.

BASEBALL PLAYERS PRACTICING, 1875
Thomas Eakins
Museum of Art, Rhode Island School of Design

45   The sneer is gone from Casey's lips, his teeth are clenched
        in hate,
    He pounds with cruel vengeance his bat upon the plate:
    And now the pitcher holds the ball, and now he lets it go,
    And now the air is shattered by the force of Casey's blow.

    Oh, somewhere in this favored land the sun is shining
        bright,
50 The band is playing somewhere, and somewhere hearts are
        light;
7 And somewhere men are laughing, and somewhere children
        shout,
    But there is no joy in Mudville: Mighty Casey has struck
        out.

Casey at the Bat   523

RESPONDING TO THE SELECTION

Your Response

1. Do you think that Casey's striking out was a result of overconfidence? Explain.

Recalling

2. Describe the crowd's response to Casey's coming up to bat. How does the crowd respond after each of the first two pitches to him?
3. How does the game conclude?

Interpreting

4. Describe Casey's personality.
5. Describe the tone and style of the poem. How is it different from a typical sports report?
6. Explain how the poet heightens suspense in this poem.

Applying

7. Why do you think baseball has become our national pastime? What is it about the game that captures our imagination?

ANALYZING LITERATURE

Enjoying Narrative Poetry

A **narrative poem** offers two kinds of pleasure, that of a story and that of poetry. To get the most out of a narrative poem, you might have to read it over more than once to make sure you understand what all the lines mean. You also need to read with attention to the rhythm and rhyme.

1. What do you think is the chief source of pleasure in the poem, the suspenseful story or the rhythm, rhyme, and colorful language? Explain.
2. If this poem were retold as a story, what kinds of details would probably be added to it?

CRITICAL THINKING AND READING

Paraphrasing Poetry

A **paraphrase** is a restatement of a poem in the reader's own words. Paraphrasing is the best way to clarify passages that are hard to understand because of unfamiliar words, unusual sentence structure, or other difficulties presented by poetical language. The following is a paraphrase of the first stanza: The Mudville team's situation was bad. They were losing 4–2 in the ninth inning. When two of their baserunners were called out at second base, their fans became pale with gloom.

Paraphrase stanzas 5, 8, 9, and 10.

THINKING AND WRITING

Writing Narrative Verse

Write a stanza or two that presents your own ending "Casey at the Bat". You may change Thayer's ending if you wish, or you may add to it. (For example, you might want to describe Casey after he has struck out.) Follow Thayer's stanza pattern: four lines, with six or seven "beats" per line and rhymes in the pattern *day/play, same/game*. When you revise, try to make your verses sound as much as possible like those in the poem.

LEARNING OPTIONS

1. **Language.** Sports jargon is special words and phrasing used by athletes and sports reporters to refer to specific aspects of a sport. It is used in sports writing and broadcasts, often adding color to a sports story. For example, the phrase "the hot corner" is baseball jargon meaning "third base" as a fielding position. Make a list of sports jargon you know, including that found in "Casey at the Bat." Set up each word or phrase like a standard dictionary entry and exchange entries with a classmate.
2. **Performance.** Have you ever heard sportcasters comment on a game or race? What techniques did they use to make their coverage seem interesting? Read this poem aloud to the class as if you were delivering a sportscast.

524   *Poetry*

Closure and Extension

ANSWERS TO RESPONDING TO THE SELECTION
Your Response
1. Encourage students to find context clues that can help them respond.

Recalling
2. When Casey comes to bat, the crowd gives out a joyous yell that reverberates over the surrounding landscape. After the first strike, the crowd roars angrily; after the second strike, the crowd cries, "Fraud!"
3. Casey strikes out and the Mudville team loses, four to two.

Interpreting
4. Suggested Response: Casey is proud, defiant, and overconfident.
5. Answers will differ, but most students will realize that the tone is personal and involved and the style humorously lyrical. In these respects, it is unlike a typical newspaper sports story.
6. Suggested Response: The poet builds suspense by reflecting the anticipation of the crowd, first for Flynn, then for Blake, and finally for Casey. The descriptions of Casey's manner also build suspense.

Applying
7. Answers will differ, but many students will say that baseball involves skill and strategy, is suspenseful, and can be played by people who are not physical giants.

ANSWERS TO ANALYZING LITERATURE

1. Answers will differ, but many students will probably point to the suspenseful story. Especially insightful students may mention the humor.
2. Answers will differ, but most students will say that there would be more exposition in the beginning to set the scene.

MULTICULTURAL CONNECTION
Baseball: National and International

When "Casey at the Bat" first appeared, baseball was rapidly becoming the national pastime of the United States. The game probably evolved from the game of rounders, which also involved hitting a ball with a bat. In rounders, however, a fielder put a runner out by actually hitting him with the ball.

Brought by English colonists. English colonists brought rounders with them to the American colonies in the 1700's. By the mid-nineteenth century, rounders had become baseball, largely through the efforts of the sportsman Alexander Cartwright. In 1845, he founded the first organized baseball club—the Knickerbocker Base Ball Club of New York. He also set down the first rules for the game.

In 1846 the first official baseball game was played in Hoboken, New Jersey, by Cartwright's team and the New York Nine. The man who wrote the rulebook had the unpleasant experience of seeing his team lose, 23 to 1!

From local game to national pastime. The Civil War made the game a national diversion. Confederate prisoners watched with fascination as Union soldiers from the Northeast played baseball in camp. After the war, soldiers from other parts of the country brought the game home with them.

In 1869 the Cincinnati Red Stockings became the first truly professional ball team with every team member paid for his efforts. For the next fifty years, baseball was played somewhat differently from the way it is today because the ball was heavier and had less bounce. Unable to hit the ball long distances, batters tried to place it strategically. Base stealing and bunting were therefore more common than they are today.

Given the importance of base running, it is not surprising that the real-life player who rivaled the fictional Casey in popularity was a champion base runner, King Kelly. Fans of the late 1800's cheered him on to home plate with cries of "Slide, Kelly, slide!"

The Negro leagues. There were no cheers for black ballplayers, however, who were banned from the game's first league in 1867. Black players formed their own teams and by 1920 had their own national league. The teams of the Negro Leagues had a grim, unglamorous life. Players traveled around the country in rundown buses, often sleeping in the same ballparks they played in, because segregated hotels would not rent them rooms. They often had to play two or three games a day and played year round, even traveling to Cuba in the winter.

Major league baseball was finally integrated in 1947 when Jackie Robinson was hired by the all-white Brooklyn Dodgers.

An international pastime. Today, baseball is played around the world. It is a major sport in Puerto Rico, home of the legendary baseball player Roberto Clemente, as well as in the Dominican Republic and Cuba. It is also popular in Italy, Canada, the Netherlands, and South Africa.

In Japan baseball is as popular as sumo wrestling. Japanese teams have even hired seasoned American ballplayers to improve the performance of their home-grown players.

Research and Discuss

Find out how baseball is played in another country and present your findings to the class.

Multicultural Connection 525

GUIDE FOR READING

Preparation

More About the Author Edgar Allan Poe's life was plagued by numerous personal and professional conflicts, as well as illness. "The Raven," which is considered one of the most popular poems in the English language, is memorable for its haunting and eerie tone. Ask students how Poe's personal life may have influenced his literary preference for the supernatural.

Literary Focus The concept of repetition in literature should be familiar to students from their earliest experiences with stories and poems. From the "I'll huff and I'll puff, and I'll blow your house down" of the *Three Little Pigs* to the final line of each stanza in "The Raven," students have anticipated the ringing of familiar sounds as they read. When their expectancy is fulfilled, readers have a satisfied feeling. Repetition is a key in making some stories and poems memorable.

Prereading Focus You may want to lead into the activity by having a class discussion about books, movies, and television programs in which characters experience a great loss. What are some of the ways in which the characters react to the loss? How do they attempt to cope with it?

Vocabulary Have less advanced students write a sentence for each of the words on the list.

Edgar Allan Poe

(1809–1849) was born in Boston, Massachusetts. As a young man, he drifted for a while before he found a home with an aunt, Maria Poe Clemm, whose young daughter, Virginia, he secretly married in 1835. Virginia died in 1847. Misfortunes such as Poe's young wife's death and his own poverty and illnesses at least partly inspired his haunting, sometimes mournful poems. Of these, "The Raven" is perhaps the most unforgettable.

The Raven

Repetition and Refrain

Repetition in poetry is the use, again and again, of a word or phrase. When the word or phrase appears in the same position in all or many of the stanzas of a poem, it is termed a **refrain**. In "The Raven," for example, the words "Lenore" and "Nevermore" are prominently repeated. Repetitions and refrains can create powerful effects. They contribute to the music of poetry, emphasize ideas and feelings, and establish mood and tone.

Focus

"The Raven" is largely about the effects of the loss of a loved one. Think of a book or story you have read or a movie you have seen in which someone experienced a permanent loss. The loss can involve a person, an animal, an object, or an ideal. How did the person react during the time just after the loss? What thoughts and feelings did the person have? With your classmates brainstorm about the effects of great loss on a person's state of mind. Then read the poem and see how the speaker reacts to his situation.

Vocabulary

Knowing the following words will help you as you read "The Raven."

quaint (kwānt) *adj.*: Strange; unusual (p. 527, l. 2)

beguiling (bi gīl' iŋ) *v.*: Tricking; charming (p. 529, l. 67)

respite (res' pit) *n.*: Rest; relief (p. 530, l. 82)

desolate (des' ə lit) *adj.*: Deserted; abandoned (p. 530, l. 87)

pallid (pal' id) *adj.*: Pale (p. 530, l. 104)

Objectives

1 To understand the use of repetition and refrain in poetry
2 To make inferences about the speaker of a poem
3 To respond to criticism of a poem

Support Material

Teaching Portfolio
Teacher Backup, p. 641
Grammar in Action Worksheet, *Using Alliteration*, p. 644
Usage and Mechanics Worksheet, p. 646
Vocabulary Check, p. 647
Analyzing Literature Worksheet, *Understanding Repetition and Refrain*, p. 648
Critical Thinking and Reading

Worksheet, *Making Inferences About the Speaker*, p. 649
Selection Test, p. 650
Art Transparency 10: *Crows and Sycamores*, by James Cook

Prentice Hall Literature Writing Studio

The Raven

Edgar Allan Poe

1

Once upon a midnight dreary, while I pondered, weak and weary,
Over many a quaint and curious volume of forgotten lore,[1]
While I nodded, nearly napping, suddenly there came a tapping,
As of someone gently rapping, rapping at my chamber door.
5 " 'Tis some visitor," I muttered, "tapping at my chamber door—
        Only this, and nothing more."

2

Ah, distinctly I remember it was in the bleak December,
And each separate dying ember wrought its ghost upon the floor.
Eagerly I wished the morrow—vainly I had tried to borrow
10 From my books surcease[2] of sorrow—sorrow for the lost Lenore—
For the rare and radiant maiden whom the angels name Lenore—
        Nameless here for evermore.

3

And the silken, sad, uncertain rustling of each purple curtain
Thrilled me—filled me with fantastic terrors never felt before;
15 So that now, to still the beating of my heart, I stood repeating
" 'Tis some visitor entreating entrance at my chamber door—
Some late visitor entreating entrance at my chamber door—
        This it is and nothing more."

Presently my soul grew stronger; hesitating then no longer,
20 "Sir," said I, "or Madam, truly your forgiveness I implore;
But the fact is I was napping, and so gently you came rapping,
And so faintly you came tapping, tapping at my chamber door,
That I scarce was sure I heard you"—here I opened wide the door—
        Darkness there, and nothing more.

25 Deep into that darkness peering, long I stood there wondering, fearing,
Doubting, dreaming dreams no mortal ever dared to dream before;
But the silence was unbroken, and the darkness gave no token,[3]
And the only word there spoken was the whispered word, "Lenore!"
This I whispered, and an echo murmured back the word, "Lenore!"
30   Merely this, and nothing more.

---

1. quaint . . . lore: Strange book of ancient learning.
2. surcease (sur sēs') *n.*: End.
3. token (tō' k'n) *n.*: Sign.

The Raven 527

4 **Discussion** Do you agree with the narrator's solution to the mystery?

5 **Discussion** Describe the raven based on the evidence provided in this stanza.

6 **Reading Strategy** Have students note the first question the narrator puts to the raven. What is its answer? Ask students to predict other questions the narrator will ask the raven. What will be the raven's responses?

7 **Master Teacher Note** Point out to students the two allusions in these stanzas—Pallas and Plutonian shore. Discuss with them the irony of a bird speaking from above the goddess of wisdom and the effect on the poem's atmosphere of referring to the underworld.

8 **Reading Strategy** Have students note the literal acceptance by the narrator of the raven's response to his question. What predictions can they make about the narrator's responses to the raven?

9 **Discussion** Do you think that the raven is responding to the narrator's thought? Explain.

4
35
Then into the chamber turning, all my soul within me burning,
Soon I heard again a tapping somewhat louder than before.
"Surely," said I, "surely that is something at my window lattice;[4]
Let me see, then, what thereat[5] is, and this mystery explore—
Let my heart be still a moment and this mystery explore—
'Tis the wind, and nothing more!"

5
40
Open here I flung the shutter, when, with many a flirt[6] and flutter,
In there stepped a stately raven of the saintly days of yore;
Not the least obeisance[7] made he; not an instant stopped or stayed he;
But, with mien[8] of lord or lady, perched above my chamber door—
Perched upon a bust of Pallas[9] just above my chamber door—
Perched, and sat, and nothing more.

6
7
45
Then this ebony bird beguiling my sad fancy[10] into smiling,
By the grave and stern decorum of the countenance[11] it wore,
"Though thy crest be shorn and shaven, thou," I said, "art sure no craven,[12]
Ghastly grim and ancient raven wandering from the Nightly shore—
Tell me what thy lordly name is on the Night's Plutonian[13] shore!"
Quoth[14] the raven, "Nevermore."

8
50
Much I marveled this ungainly fowl to hear discourse so plainly,
Though its answer little meaning—little relevancy bore;
For we cannot help agreeing that no sublunary[15] being
Ever yet was blessed with seeing bird above his chamber door—
Bird or beast upon the sculptured bust above his chamber door,
With such name as "Nevermore."

9
55
60
But the raven, sitting lonely on the placid bust, spoke only
That one word, as if his soul in that one word he did outpour.
Nothing farther then he uttered—not a feather then he fluttered—
Till I scarcely more than muttered, "Other friends have flown before—
On the morrow *he* will leave me, as my hopes have flown before."
Quoth the raven, "Nevermore."

4. lattice (lat′ is) *n*.: Framework of wood or metal.
5. thereat (*th*er at′) *adv*.: There.
6. flirt (flʉrt) *n*.: Quick, uneven movement.
7. obeisance (ō bā′ s'ns) *n*.: A bow or another sign of respect.
8. mien (mēn) *n*.: Manner.
9. bust of Pallas (pal′ əs): Sculpture of the head and shoulders of Pallas Athena (ə thē′ nə), the ancient Greek goddess of wisdom.
10. fancy (fan′ sē) *n*.: Imagination.
11. countenance (koun′ tə nəns) *n*.: Facial appearance.
12. craven (krā′ vən) *n*.: Coward (usually an adjective).
13. Plutonian (plo͞o tō′ nē ən) *adj*.: Like the underworld, ruled over by the ancient Roman god Pluto.
14. quoth (kwōth) *v*.: Said.
15. sublunary (sub′ lo͞o ner′ ē) *adj*.: Earthly.

528   Poetry

Grammar in Action

Alliteration is the repetition of initial consonant sounds. Writers, and especially poets, use this device to give emphasis to particular words, to imitate sounds, and to create musical effects. Poe makes use of alliteration throughout "The Raven." Look at the repetition of the initial *fl* and *s* sounds in these lines:

Open here I *fl*ung the shutter, when, with many a *fl*irt and *fl*utter,
In there stepped a *s*tately raven of the *s*aintly days of yore;

Now look at this stanza from the poem. How many different initial sounds are repeated? (The best way to begin determining this is either to read the stanza aloud to yourself or listen as it is read aloud.)

Then this ebony bird beguiling my sad fancy into smiling,
By the grave and stern decorum of the countenance it wore,
"Though thy crest be shorn and shaven, thou," I said, "art sure no craven.
Ghastly, grim, and ancient raven wandering from the Nightly shore—
Tell me what thy lordly name is on the Night's Plutonian shore!"

Wondering at the stillness broken by reply so aptly spoken,
"Doubtless," said I, "what it utters is its only stock and store,
Caught from some unhappy master whom unmerciful Disaster
Followed fast and followed faster—so, when Hope he would adjure,[16]
65 Stern Despair returned, instead of the sweet Hope he dared adjure—
      That sad answer, "Nevermore!"

But the raven still beguiling all my sad soul into smiling,
Straight I wheeled a cushioned seat in front of bird, and bust, and door;
Then upon the velvet sinking, I betook myself to linking
70 Fancy unto fancy, thinking what this ominous bird of yore—
What this grim, ungainly, ghastly, gaunt, and ominous bird of yore
      Meant in croaking "Nevermore."

This I sat engaged in guessing, but no syllable expressing
To the fowl whose fiery eyes now burned into my bosom's core;
75 This and more I sat divining,[17] with my head at ease reclining
On the cushion's velvet lining that the lamplight gloated o'er,
But whose velvet violet lining with the lamplight gloating o'er,
      She shall press, ah, nevermore!

---

16. adjure (ə joor´) *v.*: Appeal to.
17. divining (də vīn´ iŋ) *v.*: Guessing.

THE RAVEN
Edouard Manet
Museum of Fine Arts, Boston

10 **Discussion** What is the mood of the narrator in these lines?

11 **Reading Strategy** Ask students to predict how the narrator's questions will be resolved.

12 **Discussion** Who is the woman that comes to the narrator's mind? Why is it the narrator, rather than the bird, who says "nevermore"?

Humanities Note

Fine art, *The Raven,* by Edouard Manet. Manet (1832–1883) broke with tradition by emphasizing the pictorial qualities of his paintings rather than their storytelling aspects. He is often linked with the impressionists, whom he influenced and learned from.
    You might use the following questions:
1. Does this picture capture the mood of the poem? Explain.
2. Which adjectives applied to the speaker and the raven in the poem might also fit the picture?

Speaking and Listening To help with comprehension, you might have students read the poem aloud. If you wish, assign individual students a stanza. Ask each reader to concentrate on tone of voice and rhythm. Have the class discuss differences in oral interpretations.

Quoth the raven, "Nevermore."
The sounds of initial *b, s, q, th,* and *sh* are repeated throughout the lines. This repetition, together with the rhythm of the lines, creates a unique and musical effect.

Student Activity 1. Find three additional examples of alliteration in the poem and share these with a small group of classmates. Discuss the effect of the alliteration.

Student Activity 2. Work with a classmate to compose four lines of verse in which you use at least two different alliterative sounds.

Electronic Handbook You might want students to review the use of alliteration before completing the Grammar in Action activities. If students have access to the Language Master 6000, have them enter the access word *symbol* to get information on using alliteration.

13 **Discussion** Is the raven merely repeating this word like a parrot, or is it really responding to the narrator?

14 **Discussion** In what way does the raven serve as a part of the narrator's own personality?

Reader's Response Why do you think this poem is considered an American classic?

Thematic Response How does the speaker's encounter with the unknown realm of death affect him? Do students sympathize with him? Why or why not?

Multicultural Focus Ask students why they think Poe chose a raven to represent the supernatural. Ask what feelings the raven evokes, such as dread, mystery, and fear. Discuss whether this reaction to a raven is universal or whether various cultures might see a raven differently. Students might be interested to know that in the mythology of the Native Americans of the Pacific Northwest, the raven is a prominent figure whose character combines both mischievousness and beneficence. Discuss other birds and what they represent. In our culture the stork, for example, brings newborn babies. In Dutch folk tales, a stork who builds its nest on the roof of your house brings good luck to your house and your village.

Ask students to find out more about bird symbolism of various cultures. Suggest that they choose a bird, such as an eagle, an owl, a dove, crow, swan, nightingale, falcon, or goose, and research its place in the folklore of different cultures. Use students' findings to make a bulletin board display.

Then, methought, the air grew denser, perfumed from an unseen censer[18]
80 Swung by angels whose faint footfalls tinkled on the tufted floor.
"Wretch," I cried, "thy God hath lent thee—by these angels he hath sent thee
Respite—respite and Nepenthe[19] from thy memories of Lenore!
Let me quaff[20] this kind Nepenthe and forget this lost Lenore!"
        Quoth the raven, "Nevermore."

85 "Prophet!" said I, "thing of evil!—prophet still, if bird or devil!—
Whether Tempter[21] sent, or whether tempest tossed thee here ashore,
Desolate, yet all undaunted, on this desert land enchanted—
On this home by Horror haunted—tell me truly, I implore—
Is there—*is* there balm in Gilead?[22]—tell me—tell me, I implore!"
90   Quoth the raven, "Nevermore."

"Prophet!" said I, "thing of evil!—prophet still, if bird or devil!
By that Heaven that bends above us—by that God we both adore—
Tell this soul with sorrow laden if, within the distant Aidenn,[23]
It shall clasp a sainted maiden whom the angels name Lenore—
95 Clasp a rare and radiant maiden whom the angels name Lenore."
        Quoth the raven, "Nevermore."

"Be that word our sign of parting, bird or fiend!" I shrieked, upstarting—
"Get thee back into the tempest and the Night's Plutonian shore!
Leave no black plume as a token of that lie thy soul hath spoken!
100 Leave my lonelines unbroken!—quit the bust above my door!
Take thy beak from out my heart, and take thy form from off my door!"
        Quoth the raven, "Nevermore."

And the raven, never flitting, still is sitting, still is sitting
On the pallid bust of Pallas just above my chamber door;
105 And his eyes have all the seeming of a demon that is dreaming,
And the lamplight o'er him streaming throws his shadow on the floor;
And my soul from out that shadow that lies floating on the floor
        Shall be lifted—nevermore!

---

18. censer (sen′ sər) *n.*: Container for burning incense.
19. Nepenthe (ni pen′ thē) *n.*: A drug used in ancient times to cause forgetfulness of sorrow.
20. quaff (kwäf) *v.*: Drink.
21. Tempter: The Devil.
22. balm (bäm) **in Gilead** (gil′ ē əd): Cure for suffering; the Bible refers to a medicinal ointment, or balm, made in a region called Gilead.
23. Aidenn: A name meant to suggest Eden or paradise.

530   *Poetry*

Closure and Extension

ANSWERS TO RESPONDING TO THE SELECTION
Your Response

1. Encourage students to share personal experiences in which they were startled by the unusual. Lead them to see how they can apply this knowledge when answering the question.

Recalling

2. The speaker is in his study at midnight nearly going to sleep reading an old book.
3. He thinks it is a visitor knocking at his door.
4. At first the speaker thinks the raven is merely repeating a word it had been taught, but later he accuses it of being a prophet and a thing of evil.
5. At the end of the poem, the raven still is sitting on the statue above the speaker's chamber door.

RESPONDING TO THE SELECTION

Your Response

1. If you were the poem's speaker how would you have responded to the raven's presence?

Recalling

2. Describe the speaker's situation at the start of the poem.
3. What are his thoughts when he hears the noise at his door and window?
4. Describe his changing thoughts as the raven keeps repeating "Nevermore."
5. Describe the situation at the end of the poem.

Interpreting

6. "Lenore" and "Nevermore" rhyme. By the end of the poem, what meaning connects the two words?
7. What can you infer about Lenore and the speaker's relationship with her?
8. Describe how your impression of the raven changes as the poem progresses. What is your first impression? What is your final one?
9. Summarize "The Raven," including the speaker's changing thoughts and feelings.
10. When Poe set out to write this poem, he thought of having a parrot repeat the word "Nevermore." Do you think this poem would have been as effective if Poe had used a parrot instead of a raven? Explain your answer.

Applying

11. Might the raven be a figment of the speaker's imagination? Give reasons for your opinion.

ANALYZING LITERATURE

Understanding Repetition and Refrain

In poetry **repetition** refers to the repeated use of a word or phrase. A **refrain** is a repeated word or phrase that occurs in the same position in each stanza. These devices emphasize ideas and feelings and establish mood and tone.

1. What ideas and feelings are expressed by the refrain "Nevermore"?

2. What mood does it create or deepen?
3. Choose two other important examples of repetition in "The Raven" and tell what they contribute to its meaning and mood.

CRITICAL THINKING AND READING

Making Inferences About the Speaker

Making inferences about the speaker of a poem like "The Raven" means seeing what is suggested about him by his own words. When, for example, the speaker says, "Eagerly I wished the morrow—vainly I had tried to borrow/From my books surcease of sorrow . . . ," you can infer that he is sorrowful and that he is trying in vain to escape from sorrow by reading.

1. What can you infer about the speaker's breeding, education, or social class by the way he speaks throughout the poem?
2. What do you infer about him from the line "Let me quaff this kind Nepenthe and forget this lost Lenore!"?
3. What else could you infer about him from other details of the poem?

THINKING AND WRITING

Responding to Criticism

The poet and critic W. H. Auden once said, "The trouble with 'The Raven' . . . is that the thematic interest and the prosodic [rhythmic] interest . . . do not combine and are even often at odds." In other words, the rhythm of the poem is not suitable to the subject matter. Write an essay in which you tell why you agree or disagree with Auden's statement. Before you write, answer such questions as these: What is the subject matter of "The Raven"? What mood or spirit should a work have that deals with such a subject? What mood or spirit is created by the rhythm of "The Raven"? Is the rhythm suitable or not? When you write your essay, give full and complete reasons in support of your view.

The Raven 531

GUIDE FOR READING

More About the Author Alfred, Lord Tennyson had strong political convictions that are expressed in "The Charge of the Light Brigade." Ask students whether they think poetry is an effective medium for expressing a person's political ideas and opinions. Why or why not? Would the answers for the nineteenth and twentieth centuries be different?

Literary Focus Rhythm is a familiar concept to most students because of the music they listen to. It may help them to understand rhythm in poetry by comparing the musical beat of the percussionist to the pattern of stresses in a line of poetry.

Prereading Focus You might want to lead students into this activity by having them discuss the qualities necessary to be a soldier. How important is it for soldiers to be dutiful and obedient? Should they put aside concerns about their own safety for the good of their regiment? Why or why not? In what, if any, circumstances are they justified in disobeying orders?

Vocabulary Ask less advanced students to add these words to the paragraph they wrote for the writing assignment. They might insert them appropriately as they revise the paragraph, or they might extend the paragraph with sentences that include these words.

Alfred, Lord Tennyson

(1809–1892) was born in Lincolnshire, England. He studied at Cambridge, where he formed a close friendship with Arthur Hallam. Hallam's sudden death in 1833 inspired Tennyson's great elegy, *In Memoriam*. Tennyson was intensely concerned with the vital issues of his day. His political responsibility and interests led him to write "The Charge of the Light Brigade," based on a newspaper account of a battle between British cavalrymen and Russian artillery forces.

The Charge of the Light Brigade

Rhythm in Poetry

In poetry, **rhythm** is the arrangement, or pattern, of accented and unaccented syllables—in a word, "the beat." For example, if you read the following lines from Tennyson's poem aloud, you will hear the forceful rhythm of the lines.

> Theirs not to make reply,
> Theirs not to reason why,
> Theirs but to do and die.

Like songs, different poems have different rhythms. Usually a poet will use a rhythm that is appropriate to the subject and the poet's feelings about it. When you read a poem, your first concern should be with understanding what the lines mean. Your next concern should be with "catching the beat" and responding to it.

Focus

Review the famous lines from "The Charge of the Light Brigade" quoted above. The word *theirs* in these lines refers to soldiers, so the lines speak of soldiers' obedience, without question, to authority and to their duty. Form a group of four students. Discuss possible situations in which a soldier should *not* be ready to "do and die" without being given a good reason by his or her superiors. As you read the poem, reflect on your discussion.

Vocabulary

Knowing the following words will help you as you read "The Charge of the Light Brigade."

dismayed (dis mād') *v.*: Discouraged; made afraid (p. 533, l. 10)

volleyed (väl' ēd) *v.*: Fired at the same time (p. 533, l. 21)

reeled (rēld) *v.*: Fell back; staggered (p. 533, l. 35)

sundered (sun' dərd) *v.*: Broken apart (p. 533, l. 36)

Support Material

Teaching Portfolio
Teacher Backup, p. 653
Usage and Mechanics Worksheet, p. 656
Vocabulary Check, p. 657
Analyzing Literature Worksheet, *Understanding Rhythm in Poetry*, p. 658

Language Worksheet, *Using Concise Language for Effect*, p. 660
Selection Test, p. 661

Listening to Literature
"The Charge of the Light Brigade"

Prentice Hall Literature Writing Studio

The Charge of the Light Brigade[1]

Alfred, Lord Tennyson

1

Half a league,[2] half a league,
Half a league onward,
All in the valley of Death
  Rode the six hundred.
"Forward the Light Brigade!
Charge for the guns!" he said.
Into the valley of Death
  Rode the six hundred.

2

"Forward, the Light Brigade!"
Was there a man dismayed?
Not though the soldier knew
  Someone had blundered.
1 Theirs not to make reply,
Theirs not to reason why,
Theirs but to do and die.
Into the valley of Death
  Rode the six hundred.

3

2 Cannon to right of them,
Cannon to left of them,
Cannon in front of them
  Volleyed and thundered;
Stormed at with shot and shell,
Boldly they rode and well,
Into the jaws of Death,
Into the mouth of hell
  Rode the six hundred.

4

Flashed all their sabers bare,
Flashed as they turned in air
Sab'ring the gunners there,
Charging an army, while
  All the world wondered.
Plunged in the battery[3] smoke
Right through the line they broke;
Cossack[4] and Russian
Reeled from the saber stroke
  Shattered and sundered.
Then they rode back, but not,
  Not the six hundred.

5

Cannon to right of them,
Cannon to left of them,
Cannon behind them
  Volleyed and thundered;
Stormed at with shot and shell,
While horse and hero fell.

1. During the Crimean War (1854–1856), six hundred lightly armed British cavalrymen charged a heavily armed Russian fortification. The charge was the result of a confusion in orders. Three-fourths of the cavalrymen were killed.
2. league (lēg) *n.*: Three miles.

3. battery: A fortification equipped with heavy guns.
4. Cossack (käs' ak): A people of southern Russia famous as horsemen and cavalrymen.

Presentation

Motivation/Prior Knowledge Have students recall any war movies they have seen in which soldiers participated in a dangerous action. Then tell students that the cavalry charge described in this poem was particularly perilous.

Master Teacher Note Have students consider what kind of rhythm would be most appropriate to describe a cavalry charge. To reinforce this point, also have them consider inappropriate rhythms.

Purpose-Setting Question What was the author's purpose in writing this poem?

Thematic Focus Writers often compare life to a journey that takes unexpected turns. How people react to these unforeseen twists is a sign of their character. The Light Brigade is given an order they know is a mistake. They obey it. Did they do the right thing? Are courage and devotion to duty necessary even if they lead to the end of life?

1 **Discussion** Ask students to paraphrase and discuss the significance of these lines.

2 **Discussion** What is the effect of the repetition of these lines?

Audiocassette You might first read the poem to the class in a monotone. Ask students to discuss the effect this has on its emotional appeal. Then have them listen to the reading of the poem in the **Listening to Literature** Audiocassettes. Have them note the words the reader stresses and the inflections used. Ask them to explain why the reader chose these emphases. Discuss how the reading might change if the interpretation was that the soldiers acted foolishly.

4 **Discussion** Ask students to discuss the poet's attitude toward the men of the light brigade? Do they agree or disagree with his evaluation? Why?

Reader's Response If Tennyson were alive today, whom do you think he would want to honor as he does the Light Brigade in this poem? Explain.

Thematic Response Life's journey is filled with unexpected turns. What emotions do you think the few survivors of the charge felt?

Humanities Note

Fine art, *Charge of the Light Brigade at the Battle of Balaclava,* artist unknown.

As students look at the action in this painting, you might ask the following questions:
1. What is happening in this picture?
2. What attitude toward the charge does the artist seem to take?
3. How is the artist's point of view different from or similar to that of the poet?

Closure and Extension

ANSWERS TO RESPONDING TO THE SELECTION
Your Response
1. During the discussion, lead students to realize that actions have consequences. Encourage them to suggest possible outcomes that might have resulted if the soldiers had refused to obey the order.

Recalling
2. They go into battle because they believe that their role as soldiers is to follow orders.
3. The outcome was that only a few of the cavalrymen survived.

Interpreting
4. Suggested Response: The cavalrymen go boldly forth without

---

45 They that had fought so well
Came through the jaws of Death,
3 Back from the mouth of hell,
All that was left of them,
Left of six hundred.

6

50 When can their glory fade?
O the wild charge they made!
All the world wondered.
4 Honor the charge they made!
Honor the Light Brigade,
55 Noble six hundred!

CHARGE OF THE LIGHT BRIGADE AT THE BATTLE OF
BALAKLAVA, 1854
Unknown Artist

RESPONDING TO THE SELECTION

Your Response
1. Should the soldiers who fought in this battle have questioned their orders? Why or why not?

Recalling
2. Although the soldiers realize someone had blundered, why do they still go into battle?
3. What is the outcome of the battle?

Interpreting
4. What is the spirit of the cavalrymen as they make their charge?
5. Describe the speaker's feelings about them.
6. Describe the rhythm of the poem. Does it suggest any aspect of the battle?

Applying
7. Could a poem like this be written about a battle in a modern-day war? Why or why not?

ANALYZING LITERATURE

Understanding Rhythm in Poetry
Rhythm is the pattern of accented and un-

accented syllables in a poem—its beat. Rhythm can reinforce a poem's meaning by creating an appropriate spirit and by affecting a reader's response.

1. Read any stanza of the poem aloud. Tell how many accented syllables each line has.
2. What does the rhythm suggest about the speaker's feelings toward the cavalrymen and their charge?

THINKING AND WRITING

Writing a News Report
"The Charge of the Light Brigade" is based on a newspaper report of the Battle of Balaklava. Write your own newspaper report based on the poem. First find the facts contained in the poem. Then consult an encyclopedia for more information about the battle, which was part of the Crimean War. Write your report as a reporter might. Begin with a one-sentence "lead" that presents the most important fact. Then present the supporting details. When you revise, check that you have included all the facts from the poem.

534 Poetry

---

question and do what they were told to do.
5. Suggested Response: The speaker thinks that their brave deed is worth celebrating.
6. Suggested Response: The rhythm of the poem is punctuated with a heavily accented syllable at the beginning of each line. It reflects the cannon fire of the battle and the stirring spirit of a cavalry charge.

Applying
7. Answers will differ, but most students will realize that modern warfare relies more on air power and on the "super weapons" of the atomic age. Cavalrymen do not play a major role. Bloody hand-to-hand skirmishes and sniper attacks, however, still play a role in remote areas like the southeast Asian jungles. Nevertheless, a frontal attack against a heavily armed position probably would not occur today.

ANSWERS TO ANALYZING LITERATURE

1. Suggested Response: Answers will differ. Each stanza contains three-beat and two-beat lines.
2. Suggested Response: The galloping rhythm suggests that the speaker is inspired by the cavalry charge.

ONE WRITER'S PROCESS

Alfred, Lord Tennyson and "The Charge of the Light Brigade"

PREWRITING

Responding to a Newspaper Story Like many of his fellow Britons, Tennyson eagerly read newspaper accounts of the Crimean War (1853–1856). In this war, Great Britain, France, and Turkey were fighting against Russia.

In December 1854, Tennyson was inspired to write his famous poem after reading war stories two weeks before. These stories described how a British cavalry unit bravely charged against Russian gun positions. One of these articles declared, "The British soldier will do his duty, even to certain death, and is not paralyzed by feeling that he is the victim of some hideous blunder." These words must have been echoing in Tennyson's mind when he wrote the famous line "Someone had blunder'd."

DRAFTING

In the Poet's Own Hand The earliest complete copy of the poem is a handwritten manuscript not very different from the final version. It is missing only the first four and the last six lines. This manuscript appears to be a clean copy of earlier drafts that no longer exist.

REVISING AND EDITING

Evidence of Revision A second manuscript of the poem was copied down by Tennyson's wife. This manuscript had six new lines and some corrections in Tennyson's handwriting, indicating that he revised the poem.

Help From an Editor In making further revisions, Tennyson had help from John Forster, the editor of a newspaper called the *Examiner*. Tennyson sent the corrected manuscript to Forster on December 6, 1854, and asked for help in establishing the correct number of men involved in the charge. Early accounts reported that 600 men participated; later accounts put the number at 700. Tennyson asked Forster to insert the correct number.

He also asked Forster if the first four lines of the poem, beginning "Half a league . . . " should be left in (these lines were crossed out on the manuscript Forster received). The editor must have liked these lines because they appeared in the published poem.

Forster sent Tennyson several printed versions of the poem while the poet changed his mind about the indentation of lines and various additions and deletions. (See examples of his revisions on page 536.) Finally, Tennyson settled on a version he liked, and the poem was seen by the public for the very first time in the December 9, 1854, edition of the *Examiner*.

PUBLISHING

Revising the Published Poem The *Examiner* version of the poem appeared with only the initials "A. T." printed at the bottom because Tennyson wanted to avoid controversy. As the poet laureate, or national poet of Great Britain, he did not want to be seen as critical of the military. In fact, a colleague did interpret the phrase "Someone had blunder'd" as a criticism, and Tennyson deleted it from a later version of the poem.

One Writer's Process 535

1. Answers will differ. Have students explain their reasons for citing a specific passage.
2. After students have finished revising their responses, have them share them with the class.

THE CHARGE OF THE LIGHT BRIGADE.*

1

Half a league, half a league,
　Half a league onward,
All in the valley of Death
　Rode the six hundred.

Into the valley of Death
　Rode the six hundred,
For up came an order which
　Some one had blunder'd.
'Forward, the Light Brigade!
'Take the guns, Nolan said:
Into the valley of Death
　Rode the six hundred.

2

'Forward the Light Brigade!'
No man was there dismay'd?
Not, tho' the soldier knew
　Some one had blunder'd:
Theirs not to make reply,
Theirs not to reason why,
Theirs but to do and die,
Into the valley of Death
　Rode the six hundred.

3

Cannon to right of them,
Cannon to left of them,
Cannon in front of them
　Volley'd and thunder'd;
Storm'd at with shot and shell,
Boldly they rode and well,
Into the jaws of Death,
Into the mouth of Hell
　Rode the six hundred.

Flash'd all their sabres bare,
Flash'd all at once in air
Sabring the gunners there,
Charging an army, while
　All the world wonder'd:
Plunged in the battery smoke
Fiercely the line they broke;
Cossack and Russian
Reel'd from the sabrestroke
　Shatter'd and sunder'd.
Then they rode back, but not
Before they rode onward,
Half a league back, but not
　Not the six hundred.

Cannon to right of them,
Cannon to left of them,
Cannon behind them
　Volley'd and thunder'd;
Storm'd at with shot and shell,
While horse and hero fell,
Those that had fought so well
Came from the jaws of Death,
Back from the mouth of Hell,
All that was left of them,
　Left of six hundred.

When can their glory fade?
O the wild charge they made!
　All the world wonder'd.
Honour the charge they made!
Honour the Light Brigade,
　Noble six hundred!

A. T.

*Written after reading the first report of the *Times'* correspondent, where only 607 sabres are mentioned as having taken part in the charge.

An Audience of Soldiers In August 1855, Tennyson was asked to send copies of the poem to the British soldiers in the Crimea. Many of the enlisted men already loved the original version of the poem—with the line "Someone had blunder'd"—and had even taken to singing it to boost their morale. After learning of this, Tennyson realized that the original version was best, and he had 2,000 copies of it sent to the front. From that point on, he published only the version preferred by the soldiers.

THINKING ABOUT THE PROCESS

1. Compare the revised manuscript on this page with the finished poem. Then select a revision Tennyson made and explain why it does or does not improve the poem.
2. **Writing** Find a newspaper story that causes you to react strongly. Write a response to the article, in prose or poetry; then share your response with the class. Finally, use your classmates' responses to revise your writing and make it more effective.

Dramatic Poetry and the Speaker

PORTRAIT OF MME. MATISSE
Henri Matisse
The Hermitage, Leningrad

Humanities Note

Fine Art, *Portrait of Mme. Matisse,* by Henri Matisse. In 1890 Henri Matisse (1869–1954), gave up the practice of law to study painting at the Académie Julien in Paris. During his early years, he associated with modern artists working in Paris, while he traveled and worked as a decorator. With the painter Derain, Matisse led the Fauve movement —characterized by the unorthodox and free use of vibrant color. His paintings are personal expressions that display a remarkable sensitivity for color relationships.

In this portrait of his wife, Matisse does not rely on shadow and light to model the features of his subject. Rather, in the innovative way that is unique to him, he uses color variations to describe the forms of the features. The feelings of the artist for his subject are also apparent in his expressive use of color. Color was art to Henri Matisse, and through it he expressed harmony and order in a bright, unusual way.

Master Teacher Note Use an overhead projector to show students Art Transparency 11, *The Postman Joseph Roulin,* by Vincent Van Gogh. It is a portrait of a ninotoonth contury Fronch poct man in his uniform. Tell students that just as artists attempt to portray the character of their subjects, poets also strive to make fictional characters come alive for their readers. Have students discuss this postman's personality as Van Gogh depicted it. What qualities do they see in his face? What message does his body language communicate? Why do they think that he has posed in his uniform?

Preparation

More About the Author Donald Justice selected an ancient dialogue form for his poem "Incident in a Rose Garden." It seems surprising to hear the speakers in the poem being so polite and civil when discussing death. Ask students why it is effective for Justice to use an old poetic form in a surprising way.

Literary Focus Readers of dramatic poetry should bring with them the skills they apply to the reading of plays. All conclusions about character and situation must be inferred from what characters say in the dialogue. The poet cannot describe characters directly and tell the reader they are brave or fun-loving or cruel. The alert reader must learn all this from a careful study of the dialogue.

Prereading Focus "Incident in a Rose Garden" uses irony to show how our perceptions of an event can differ from its real meaning. The purpose of this exercise is to help students see how written works can often be read on two levels. Guide them toward an understanding of the real point of the tale. Encourage them to express the moral in their own words.

Vocabulary Ask less advanced students if they have heard the expression "grim reaper." To whom does it refer? Why is it an appropriate expression? Have them write a sentence or two explaining why the "grim reaper" is usually pictured carrying a scythe.

Donald Justice

(1925–   ), a native of Florida, has experimented with different types of poetry and sometimes takes ancient poetic forms and uses them in startling new ways. "Incident in a Rose Garden" is such a poem. It is written in the very old dialogue form. Though all the speakers in the poem are polite and civil, the poem conveys the dread of death.

GUIDE FOR READING

Incident in a Rose Garden

Dramatic Poetry

Dramatic poetry is poetry in which the speaker is clearly someone other than the poet. Some of the best dramatic poetry consists of dialogue in which more than one character speaks.

Focus

Read the following folk tale:

A servant was shopping in a marketplace when he saw Death staring at him intently from a short distance. The terrified man ran home to his master. He asked for his pay, saying that he had seen Death staring at him in the marketplace and that he was going to hide from him in the distant town of Samara. Upon hearing this, the master let him go. However, to satisfy his curiosity he visited the marketplace himself. Looking about, he discovered the dreaded figure. He asked Death why he had been staring at his servant. Death replied, "I was staring because I was surprised to see him here. You see, I have an appointment with him tonight in Samara."

Discuss the point of this folk tale with your classmates. Keep it in mind as you read "Incident in a Rose Garden." What do the folk tale and the poem have in common?

Vocabulary

Knowing the following word will help you as you read "Incident in a Rose Garden."
scythe (si*th*) *n.*: A tool used for cutting down tall grass (p. 539, l. 3)

Objectives

1 To understand dramatic poetry
2 To interpret personification
3 To continue a poem
4 To express individual interests and abilities through optional activities

Support Material

Teaching Portfolio
Teacher Backup, p. 663
Usage and Mechanics Worksheet, p. 666
Analyzing Literature Worksheet, *Understanding Dramatic Poetry,* p. 667
Language Worksheet, *Effective Word Choices,* p. 668
Selection Test, p. 669

Listening to Literature
"Incident in a Rose Garden"

Prentice Hall Literature Writing Studio

THE RACE TRACK OR DEATH ON A PALE HORSE
Albert Pinkham Ryder
The Cleveland Museum of Art

Incident in
a Rose Garden

Donald Justice

Gardener: Sir, I encountered Death
　　　　　Just now among our roses.
　　　　　Thin as a scythe he stood there.

　　　　　I knew him by his pictures.
5　　　　　He had his black coat on,
　　　　　Black gloves, a broad black hat.

Humanities Note

Fine Art, *The Race Track or Death on a Pale Horse,* by Albert Pinkham Ryder. Ryder (1847–1917) is an American artist known for his original, often mystical paintings. He used simple designs and applied paint thickly on his canvases. Ryder said that he got the idea for *The Race Track* in a dream.

　　You might ask students the following questions:
1. What might have prompted Ryder to paint Death on a racetrack?
2. Compare and contrast the gardener's description of Death with the image of Death in the painting.

Presentation

Motivation/Prior Knowledge Death is an event or process that occurs to all living beings. Poets and artists, however, sometimes personify Death. Ask students to imagine that they are casting a movie in which Death is a character. What actor or actress might they choose for this role? What would Death look like? Invite them to compare their description with the character of Death in this poem.

Purpose-Setting Question How does the poet create suspense?

1 **Discussion** Ask students to discuss the effectiveness of this simile. How does it contribute to the picture of Death? How does it match their image of Death? Why is the word *scythe* appropriate?

Thematic Focus We do not have to venture into space to explore the unknown. The unknown is an inescapable part of life. Have students discuss some of the unknown elements of life. How do people try to cope with the unknown?

Making Connections Another selection that deals with the inescapability of death is "The Seven Ages of Man," by Shakespeare, page 543.

Master Teacher Note Help students understand why a poet might choose this topic. Through discussion the class might suggest that the poet could be fearing his or her own death, that the poet might have experienced the death of someone close, that the poet has an awareness of death's final claim on all of us, and that the poet has an appreciation of the dramatic possibilities of the subject.

2
3
> I think he would have spoken,
> Seeing his mouth stood open.
> Big it was, with white teeth.

10
4
> As soon as he beckoned, I ran.
> I ran until I found you.
> Sir, I am quitting my job.

15
> I want to see my sons
> Once more before I die.
> I want to see California.

5
> *Master:* Sir, you must be that stranger
> Who threatened my gardener.
> This is my property, sir.

6
20
> I welcome only friends here.
> *Death:* Sir, I knew your father.
> And we were friends at the end.

7
> As for your gardener,
> I did not threaten him.
> Old men mistake my gestures.

8
25
> I only meant to ask him
> To show me to his master.
> I take it you are he?

RESPONDING TO THE SELECTION

Your Response

1. If you were to create your own character of Death, how would your portrayal differ from Donald Justice's? Explain your answer.

Recalling

2. How does the gardener recognize Death?
3. Why does he run away?
4. According to Death why was the gardener mistaken in running away?

Interpreting

5. Describe Death's personality.
6. Interpret the lines "Sir, I knew your father./And we were friends at the end."
7. What is implied by the final line?
8. In what way is the ending of the poem ironic, or the opposite of what was expected?

Applying

9. If the poet had continued the poem, what might the master's reply to Death be?

ANALYZING LITERATURE

Understanding Dramatic Poetry

In **dramatic poetry** the speaker is someone other than the poet—a character, like one in a play or story. In many dramatic poems, not only is there a speaker, but there may be indications of other characters, a setting, and even a developing situation.

1. Tell how Justice's poem illustrates the characteristics of dramatic poetry.
2. What developing situation is suggested?

CRITICAL THINKING AND READING

Interpreting Personification

Personification is a figure of speech in which human qualities are given to nonhuman objects

or ideas. In "Incident in a Rose Garden," death is personified as a man.

1. Why is it appropriate that Death is wearing black?
2. Why is it appropriate that Death is "Thin as a scythe . . ."?
3. How would you personify death?

THINKING AND WRITING

Continuing a Poem

Using your answer to the Applying question, write one or two three-line stanzas in which the master replies to Death. Then write another stanza or two in which Death speaks. If Death has the last word, what might he say? When you write your continuation, try to follow the poet's verse pattern: short lines, with three accented syllables, or beats, in each line. When you revise and polish your work, try to make the speakers sound as they do in the poem as Justice wrote it. Compare your continuation with those written by your classmates.

LEARNING OPTIONS

1. **Speaking and Listening.** Read aloud "Incident in a Rose Garden" with two of your classmates. Each of you can read the part of one speaker. As you read, try to match your voice tone and quality to the character traits or circumstances of your speaker. For example, the gardener is agitated and would probably speak quickly and excitedly. When you are finished rehearsing, read the poem aloud to the class.
2. **Art.** Draw or paint a picture of the character Death. Refer to the gardener's description in "Incident in a Rose Garden" and the painting on page 539 for ideas. When you are finished, share your artwork with the class.

Incident in a Rose Garden   541

Closure and Extension

ANSWERS TO RESPONDING TO THE SELECTION
Your Response

1. Lead students to discuss traditional representations of death that they have seen.

Recalling

2. The stranger looks like the pictures of Death he has seen.
3. The gardener runs away because he assumes that Death wants to

take him, and he wants to see his sons once more before he dies.
4. Death says that old men frequently mistake his gestures. They assume that Death has come for them.

Interpreting

5. Suggested Response. Death is calm and polite and has a keen sense of irony.
6. Suggested Response Death met the master's father when the father died. The father was glad to die at the end.

7. Suggested Response: Death has come to take the master.
8. Suggested Response: The ending is ironic because at first it seemed that Death had come for the servant, and the master is so sure of himself in protecting his servant and his property.

Applying

9. Answers will differ, but students might reason that the master would try to run off like the gardener.

ANSWERS TO ANALYZING LITERATURE

1. Suggested Response: The title of the poem indicates the setting. As in plays, there is an indication of who speaks each line. The situation is made clear through the exposition in the gardener's lines. The action rises in the dialogue between the master and Death until the climax is reached in the last line. The reader is left to infer the resolution.
2. Suggested Response: Death has come for the master, who at first assumes that Death came to threaten his gardener.

ANSWERS TO CRITICAL THINKING AND READING

1. Black is the color of mourning.
2. Death is often pictured carrying a scythe.
3. Answers will differ, but students should be able to justify their choices.

THINKING AND WRITING

Software If students are working on computers, you may want to have them use the **Writer's Helper** activity *Sweet or Stuffy?* to help them revise and polish their continuation of the poem.

LEARNING OPTIONS

1. This activity will appeal to auditory learners. You might extend the activity by having the class discuss differences in interpretation.
2. Visual and kinesthetic learners will find this exercise stimulating. You might extend the activity for visual learners by having them create a book of poems about death, with a different illustration for each poem.

Publishing Student Writing You might want to have volunteers read their stanzas to the class.

Preparation

More About the Author When Shakespeare retired to Stratford in the early 1600's, he gave up writing entirely and did not even try to publish his complete works. Ask students to consider why the greatest English poet and playwright would behave in such a manner.

Literary Focus It may be easier for students to understand the concept of a dramatic monologue interrupting the flow of action in a play if it is compared to a song in a musical play. The action may come to a halt briefly, but the character's feelings and attitudes are expressed and given emphasis through the lyrics. The same reasons justify the use of dramatic monologues in plays.

Prereading Focus Lead students into the activity by having them share examples of people they know who are at various stages of life. What can they infer, or conclude, about the various stages of life from their encounters with these people?

Vocabulary Ask less advanced students to predict how these two words might be used in describing seven ages of life.

Spelling Tip Point out the *e* in *woeful*.

William Shakespeare

(1564–1616) came to maturity when the English language was rapidly developing into a rich and powerful means of expression. Theater goers were eager to hear impressive, fully developed speeches modeled on those in classical drama. Shakespeare's genius, therefore, was perfectly suited for his era. All of his plays include speeches in which thought and feeling are expressed with a brilliance unequaled by any other poet or dramatist. "The Seven Ages of Man" is one of the best of them.

GUIDE FOR READING

The Seven Ages of Man

Dramatic Monologue

Another kind of dramatic poetry is the **dramatic monologue**: a speech in which a fictional character expresses his or her thoughts and feelings within a developing situation. The word *monologue* is based on the root *mono*, meaning "one"—in other words, only one character speaks. Some of the best dramatic monologues come from verse plays, such as Shakespeare's, and can stand by themselves as complete poems.

Focus

In this famous monologue, Shakespeare describes life as having seven ages or phases. What do you think the seven ages of life might be? Consider the significant points in your life so far. If each of these points marks a phase, how many phases do you think you have already experienced? Work with your classmates to list all seven ages of life on a chart like the following. (Then read the selection and see how Shakespeare divided up the different periods in a person's life.)

Vocabulary

Knowing the following words will help you as you read "The Seven Ages of Man."

woeful (wō′ fəl) *adj.*: Full of sorrow (p. 543, l. 10)

treble (treb′ ′l) *n.*: High-pitched voice (p. 544, l. 24)

Objectives

1 To appreciate poems from plays
2 To write an essay modeled on Shakespeare
3 To express individual interests and abilities through optional activities

Support Material

Teaching Portfolio
Teacher Backup, p. 671
Usage and Mechanics Worksheet, p. 674
Analyzing Literature Worksheet, *Appreciating Poems From Plays*, p. 675
Language Worksheet, *Understanding Synonyms and Antonyms*, p. 676
Selection Test, p. 677

Listening to Literature
"The Seven Ages of Man"

Prentice Hall Literature Writing Studio

The Seven Ages of Man

William Shakespeare

All the world's a stage,
And all the men and women merely players:[1]
They have their exits and their entrances;
And one man in his time plays many parts,
His acts being seven ages.[2] At first the infant,
Mewling[3] and puking in the nurse's arms.
And then the whining schoolboy, with his satchel,
And shining morning face, creeping like snail
Unwillingly to school. And then the lover,
Sighing like furnace, with a woeful ballad
Made to his mistress' eyebrow. Then a soldier,
Full of strange oaths, and bearded like the pard,[4]
Jealous in honor,[5] sudden and quick in quarrel,
Seeking the bubble reputation
Even in the cannon's mouth. And then the justice,[6]
In fair round belly with good capon[7] lined,
With eyes severe and beard of formal cut,
Full of wise saws and modern instances;[8]
And so he plays his part. The sixth age shifts
Into the lean and slippered pantaloon,[9]
With spectacles on nose and pouch on side,
His youthful hose[10] well saved, a world too wide

1. **players:** Actors.
2. **ages:** Periods of life.
3. **mewling** (myo͞ol' iŋ) v.: Whimpering, crying like a baby.
4. **pard** (pärd) n.: A leopard or panther.
5. **Jealous in honor:** Very concerned about his honor.
6. **justice:** A judge.
7. **capon** (kā' pän) n.: A roasted chicken. The speaker is implying that the judge has been bribed with the present of a fat chicken.
8. **wise saws and modern instances:** Wise sayings and modern examples that show the truth of the sayings.
9. **pantaloon** (pan' t'l o͞on') n.: A thin, foolish old man—originally a character in old comedies.
10. **hose** (hōz) n.: Stockings.

Presentation

Motivation/Prior Knowledge Ask students to summarize the main stages they have passed through in their own lives so far. Tell them that Shakespeare describes the stages of human life in this poem.

Making Connections Another selection you might want to use with this one is Marchette Chute's essay from *Shakespeare of London,* page 497. This essay describes the kind of training that Shakespeare received.

Purpose-Setting Question How accurate is the description of each stage of life?

1 **Discussion** How can one person play many parts?

2 **Reading Strategy** Ask students to predict what the stages will be.

3 **Discussion** Ask students to identify the simile in this description. Is the comparison a good one?

4 **Discussion** Ask students to identify the simile in line 10. Is it effective?

5 **Discussion** What does Shakespeare mean by the phrase "the bubble reputation"?

6 **Discussion** How does this phase of life relate to an earlier phase?

Audiocassette To help students distinguish characteristics of the various ages, you might wish to have them listen to the reading of the poem on the **Listening to Literature** Audiocassettes. Have students compare and contrast differences in pitch, speed, and volume of the voice associated with each age.

Thematic Focus Writers often compare life with a journey. The road takes unexpected turns, but there are signposts that mark our progress. Ask students what helps them to recognize that they are moving from one stage of their lives to the next. Are such changes just physical or are interests and knowledge important signposts as well?

Master Teacher Note You might want to tell students that Shakespeare frequently compared life to acting. In this speech, however, he extends the comparison for many lines. Explain to students that "The Seven Ages of Man" is an excerpt from Shakespeare's play *As You Like It,* and its opening lines are frequently quoted.

Speaking and Listening You might wish to select student volunteers to act the part of each age. Have them read their parts aloud and stay in character as they listen to the other readings. Remind the volunteers to change pitch, speed, and tone of voice as appropriate when reading.

Thematic Response What can students learn about life's journey from this poem? Why?

Reader's Response In "The Seven Ages of Man" Shakespeare states, "And one man in his time plays many parts." What parts have you played in your life so far?

Humanities Note

Stained glass window depicting the "Seven Ages of Man," by Nicola D'Ascenzo. D'Ascenzo was born in Torricella, Peligna, Italy, in 1871 and came with his parents to the United States in 1882. He was educated at the Pennsylvania Academy of Fine Arts and the New York School of Design. He was the director of The D'Ascenzo Studios in Philadelphia, artists of stained glass, mosaics, and murals. In addition to the "Seven Ages of Man" windows, completed around 1930 for the Folger Shakespeare Library in Washington, D.C., D'Ascenzo received commissions for numerous other prestigious locations, including the chapel at Princeton University.

You might use the following questions for discussion:
1. How true are the windows to Shakespeare's verse?
2. In which of the seven windows does the artist depict the prime of life? Does seeing the windows help you understand the theme of the poem?

7
25
For his shrunk shank;[11] and his big manly voice,
Turning again toward childish treble, pipes
And whistles in his sound. Last scene of all,
That ends this strange eventful history,
Is second childishness, and mere oblivion,
Sans[12] teeth, sans eyes, sans taste, sans everything.

---

11. **shank** (shank) *n*.: Leg.
12. **sans** (sanz) *prep*.: Without, lacking.

THE SEVEN AGES OF MAN
(stained glass window)
Folger Shakespeare Library
Washington, D.C.

544   Poetry

RESPONDING TO THE SELECTION

Your Response

1. Do you agree with the speaker's assessments about the seven ages of life? Why or why not?

Recalling

2. List the seven types of persons the speaker uses to represent the seven ages of life.

Interpreting

3. What period of life does each of these persons represent?
4. If the speaker compares the world to a stage and people to actors, then what might people's "exits and . . . entrances" represent?
5. What are the qualities or characteristics of the periods of life represented by the soldier and the judge?
6. How does the last age bring us back full circle to the start?
7. What attitude toward life does the speaker seem to be expressing? Support your answer.

Applying

8. Do you think that most people who live long lives pass through seven periods similar to those described in the poem? Give reasons for your opinion.

ANALYZING LITERATURE

Appreciating Poems From Plays

Poems from plays are speeches, songs, or other passages that can be read and enjoyed by themselves. Shakespeare's plays are filled with such passages, and many consider them to be his finest poetry. Such poems are dramatic in that they are found in dramas. Many, however, are dramatic in another sense: They depict a character reacting to other characters in the midst of a developing situation or conflict.

1. "The Seven Ages of Man" is from Shakespeare's play *As You Like It*. Tell why you think the poem is or is not clear and complete by itself, apart from the rest of the play.
2. Describe the organization of the poem. How are the various details arranged in relation to one another?

THINKING AND WRITING

Imitating Shakespeare

Write an essay titled "The Stages of Life." Like Shakespeare, choose a type of person (or, if you wish, a kind of activity) to represent each stage of life. Into how many stages will you divide life? What characteristics will each stage have? When you write your essay, use a systematic organization like the one in "The Seven Ages of Man." When you revise, make sure that each person or activity you have selected is described in a way that clearly suggests a stage of life. Compare your essay with your classmates'. Into how many stages did they divide life? How are their stages similar to or different from yours?

LEARNING OPTIONS

1. **Art.** Shakespeare used vivid images to describe each of the seven ages of a person's life. Using the poet's descriptions as a guide, illustrate three of the seven ages. Then share your work with your classmates.
2. **Writing.** The speaker of this monologue seems to have an ironic, somewhat pessimistic view of life. Rewrite the poem so that the tone is more optimistic. Use images that appeal to the senses in a positive way. For example, instead of "mewling" or "puking," the infant in your version might be "cooing." When you are finished, exchange poems with a classmate.

Applying

8. Answers will differ, but most students will say that people do pass through phases similar to the ones that Shakespeare describes.

Challenge The poem presents the seven ages of life. What other processes might be divided into stages?

ANSWERS TO ANALYZING LITERATURE

1. Suggested Response: The poem is clear by itself because it does not refer to any specific action or character in the play. The idea it presents can stand by itself.
2. Suggested Response: The poem has a four-line introduction followed by a chronological description of each of the seven ages.

THINKING AND WRITING

Writing Transparency Students should use chronological order in developing their essays. Before they begin to write, you may wish to show them the *Chronological Order* Paragraph Exercise in the **Transparencies for Writing.**

LEARNING OPTIONS

1. Illustrating this poem will appeal to visual and kinesthetic learners. Extend the activity by having partners collaborate in creating a booklet depicting all seven ages.
2. Visual learners will enjoy this activity.

Closure and Extension

ANSWERS TO RESPONDING TO THE SELECTION
Your Response

1. Lead students to see that individual development varies from person to person.

Recalling

2. The seven ages are represented by a baby, a schoolboy, a lover, a soldier, a judge, an old man with spectacles, and an even older, now childish, man without teeth, sight, or taste.

Interpreting

3. Suggested Response: They represent infancy, school age, youth, adulthood, advanced middle age, old age, and senility.
4. Suggested Response: Entrance might be birth and exit death.
5. The soldier is a bearded man, very proud and quarrelsome, who acts bravely to gain fame. The judge is a fat man with a trim beard who likes to display his wisdom.
6. Suggested Response: During this last stage, humans resemble children again.
7. Suggested Response: The speaker seems to be expressing a detached, somewhat cynical, and ironical view of life. He seems to be laughing at the reluctance of the schoolchildren, the earnestness of the lover, and the soldier's pursuit of glory.

The Runaway

Robert Frost (1874–1963) was born in California and, as a struggling young poet, lived in England for a time. It is New England, however, that gave Frost the subjects of his finest poems—New England scenes, characters, and events that he depicted in clear, memorable verse. "The Runaway" presents a vivid picture of a little horse in a mountain pasture. The poem conveys affection, amusement, and compassion—feelings that run through many of Frost's memorable nature poems.

There Is a Longing . . .

Chief Dan George (1899–1981) was "discovered" at the age of sixty and became a television and movie actor. Teswahno (his Indian name) had already had careers as a longshoreman, a logger, and a musician. As a chief of the Squamish Band of Burrard Inlet in British Columbia, Canada, he was deeply concerned about developing mutual respect between Native Americans and North Americans of other descent. As an actor, he accepted only roles that presented Native Americans with dignity. As a writer and public speaker, he emphasized respect and understanding among people. His poem "There Is a Longing . . ." shows his concern for the dignity and recognition of his people.

George Gray

Edgar Lee Masters (1868–1950) was born in Kansas and raised in two small Illinois towns. His observations of life there are the basis of his masterpiece, *Spoon River Anthology.* This book is a collection of monologues by various characters—all of them dead—who speak honestly and with intense feeling about their lives. "George Gray" illustrates Masters's ability to condense the meaning of an entire life in a brief, powerful speech.

The Speaker

The **speaker** in a poem is the "voice" that talks to the reader. The voice may be that of the poet, or it may be that of a character. When speakers are characters, they express their own points of view—their own attitudes, backgrounds, and ways of looking at reality. Their thoughts and feelings may be similar to those of the author, or they may be entirely different. When the speaker is the author, he presents his own point of view.

Notice the speakers in the three poems that follow. In which poems are created characters speaking? In which poem is the author speaking? What do you learn about the lives and personalities of each speaker?

Focus

Write a brief letter to yourself from a well-known person whom you admire. Let the letter say whatever you wish this person would say to you in an actual letter. Then read your letter, imagining that person as the speaker. In the same way, as you read these poems, picture the speaker saying the words and giving the message.

Vocabulary

Knowing the following words will help you as you read these poems.

determination (dē tʉr′ mi nā′ shən) *n*.: Firm intention (p. 550, l. 11)

endurance (en dōōr′ əns) *n*.: Ability to withstand hardship and stress and to carry on (p. 550, l. 12)

furled (fʉrld) *v*.: Rolled up and tied (p. 552, l. 3)

disillusionment (dis′ i lōō′ zhən mənt) *n*.: Disappointment (p. 552, l. 6)

Literary Focus It will be easier for students to understand the concept of the speaker in poetry by comparing it to the first-person point of view in fiction. When a character narrates the action in a story, it is usually clear that the character is not the author. The narrator describes events from his or her own point of view.

Prereading Focus Ask for student volunteers to share their letters with the class. Compare several of the letters to identify differences among the "speakers" the students have chosen to imitate. Discuss the reasons why the speakers are so different from each other.

Vocabulary Have the **less advanced** students select a synonym for each of the words. Then ask them to write a sentence for each word that includes both the word and its synonym.

Spelling Tip Have students find the word *illusion* in *disillusionment*. Point out that *illusion* is spelled with one *s*, not two.

Motivation/Prior Knowledge
Ask students to explain why people become frightened by things
they have not experienced before. Then tell them that this
poem is about an animal that is
frightened by the unknown.

Master Teacher Note Although
Robert Frost most frequently
writes about simple New England countryside scenes, the
meanings of his poems are usually universal. Thus, the reader
can expect both a vivid and sensitive description and a theme
that cuts across class, locality,
and generations.

Purpose-Setting Question
What could have prevented the
young Morgan from running
away?

Thematic Focus Life's journey is
a voyage into the unknown. Discuss the human fear of the unknown. Ask students if they think
animals can experience similar
fear.

Making Connections Another
selection that deals with the universal conflict between the longing for freedom to explore and
the desire to stay with what is
familiar is the *Odyssey* by Homer, page 645.

1 Reading Strategy Ask students
to describe in their own words
the scene in the first part of this
poem. What prediction can they
make about what will happen to
the young Morgan?

2 Discussion Have students discuss the speaker's assessment
of the cause of the problem. Do
they agree or disagree? Why or
why not?

The Runaway

Robert Frost

1
5
    Once when the snow of the year was beginning to fall,
    We stopped by a mountain pasture to say, "Whose colt?"
    A little Morgan[1] had one forefoot on the wall,
    The other curled at his breast. He dipped his head
    And snorted at us. And then he had to bolt.
    We heard the miniature thunder where he fled,
    And we saw him, or thought we saw him, dim and gray,
    Like a shadow against the curtain of falling flakes.

2
10
    "I think the little fellow's afraid of the snow.
    He isn't winter-broken. It isn't play
    With the little fellow at all. He's running away.
    I doubt if even his mother could tell him, 'Sakes,
    It's only weather.' He'd think she didn't know!
    Where is his mother? He can't be out alone."

15
    And now he comes again with clatter of stone,

———————
1. Morgan (môr' gən) *n.*: A breed of saddle horse that originated in
New England.

ESL Teaching Strategy After
students have read the poem,
pair students who are native English speakers with students who
have limited English proficiency.
Provide the native speakers with
the following list of questions to
ask their partners:

    Why is the colt afraid?
    *He is experiencing snow for the
    first time.*
    How do you know the colt is afraid?

    *His eyes are showing white, his
    tail is up straight, and he is
    shuddering.*
    How many speakers are there in
    the poem?
    Two.

As soon as the tutors have made
certain that the poem was understood, allow the students to answer the Responding to the Selection questions.

Audiocassette Appreciation of poetry is enhanced
through hearing a poem. Play the
recording of "The Runaway" on
the **Listening to Literature**
Audiocassette, Side 4. Suggest
that students listen for the tone
that the reader conveys.

3

And mounts the wall again with whited eyes
And all his tail that isn't hair up straight.
He shudders his coat as if to throw off flies.
"Whoever it is that leaves him out so late,
20 When other creatures have gone to stall and bin,
Ought to be told to come and take him in."

3 **Discussion** Ask students to describe the scene in these lines. How is it similar to and different from the opening scene? What important details are added to this scene?

4 **Discussion** Who does the narrator believe is responsible for the plight of the Morgan?

Reader's Response Like animals, humans are also frightened by the unknown. Of what are you most frightened because it is unknown?

Thematic Response At what stage in life's journey is the colt? Which speaker is most aware of the colt's youth?

RESPONDING TO THE SELECTION

Your Response

1. Are you like the colt in any way? How?

Recalling

2. According to the person whose remarks are quoted, why is the colt acting as he is?

Interpreting

3. Find three descriptive phrases that suggest the colt's feelings and tell the feelings suggested.
4. Find two phrases that vividly suggest the sound of the running colt. Why are they especially effective as description?
5. The last three lines express disapproval of whoever has left the colt outside. Do you think these lines express the theme, or point, of the poem? Tell why you do or do not think so.

Applying

6. What is it about human beings that makes us want to aid creatures we see as helpless or in need of protection? Explain your answer.
7. How could the colt be a symbol for humanity in general?

ANALYZING LITERATURE

Understanding Point of View

In dramatic poetry, **point of view** refers to the speaker's attitudes, opinions, and ways of looking at reality or the situation presented in the poem. Even if the speaker's thoughts and feelings should be the same as the poet's, the speaker presents them in his or her own way and from within the situation presented in the poem. You should, therefore, not equate the speaker of a dramatic poem with the author of the poem.

1. The speaker of "The Runaway" twice quotes someone's remarks, once in lines 9–14 and again in lines 19–21. Are these two pairs of remarks uttered by the same person? Tell why you feel that they are or are not.
2. Do you think that the speaker of the entire poem is quoting himself or herself in these remarks? To answer this question, compare the tone of voice in the quoted lines with the tone of the rest of the poem.

LEARNING OPTION

Cross-curricular Connection. The horse in this poem is a Morgan. What other kinds of horses are common in the United States? What are they used for? Do research to gather information about types of horses, their appearance, and their uses. Deliver your report, with visuals, to the class.

The Runaway 549

ANSWERS TO ANALYZING LITERATURE

1. Answers will differ. Some students may view the two speeches as expressing the same concern, which indicates they are spoken by one person. Other students may notice the different emphasis in each speech—on the horse's youth in the first and the person responsible in the second—and take this as a clue that there are two different speakers.
2. Answers will differ. Some students may say that it is logical for the poet to give himself the final word, so the final speaker at least is the same as the narrator.

LEARNING OPTION

You may wish to have students focus on a single breed of horse, such as the Arabian, or a famous horse. Researching the famous Godolphin Arabian, for example, will provide students with the added benefit of a lesson in English history.

Closure and Extension

ANSWERS TO RESPONDING TO THE SELECTION

Your Response

1. Students may say that they, too, fear the unknown. Discuss the fact that most people feel unsure of themselves in new situations.

Recalling

2. The person says that the colt is frightened by the snow.

Interpreting

3. Suggested Response: The colt "mounts the wall . . . with whited eyes"—this description suggests the colt's fear. The phrase "his tail . . . up straight" suggests the colt's tenseness. The phrase "shudders his coat as if to throw off flies" suggests the colt's nervousness.
4. Suggested Response: "miniature thunder" and "clatter of stone" are effective descriptions of sounds.
5. Answers will differ, but most students will indicate that these lines express the theme—people should take care of those who depend on them.

Applying

6. Answers will differ, but most students will see that this impulse is a part of human nature.
7. Answers will differ, but most students will indicate that all humanity must face the unknown, and that the feeling of being unprotected in an unfamiliar and hostile environment is frightening.

Motivation/Prior Knowledge
Discuss with students the Native Americans' historical relationship with European Americans. Ask students why many Native Americans have become politically active on behalf of their people. Tell the students that this poem expresses a chief's yearning for a better life for young Native Americans.

Purpose-Setting Question How do the speaker's goals for his people differ from those of Native American leaders in the past?

1 **Discussion** Why might separation from home and family be very difficult for someone who was raised on a reservation?

2 **Discussion** To what two kinds of conflict does Chief Dan George refer when he uses the word *war*?

3 **Discussion** What does the speaker mean by "this new culture"?

There Is a Longing...

Chief Dan George

There is a longing in the heart of my people
to reach out and grasp that which is needed
for our survival. There is a longing among
the young of my nation to secure for them-
5 selves and their people the skills that will
provide them with a sense of worth and
purpose. They will be our new warriors.
Their training will be much longer and
more demanding than it was in olden days.
10 The long years of study will demand more
determination; separation from home and
family will demand endurance. But they
will emerge with their hand held forward,
not to receive welfare, but to grasp the
15 place in society that is rightly ours.

I am a chief, but my power to make war
is gone, and the only weapon left to me
is speech. It is only with tongue and speech
that I can fight my people's war.

20 Oh, Great Spirit![1] Give me back the courage
of the olden Chiefs. Let me wrestle with
my surroundings. Let me once again,
live in harmony with my environment.
Let me humbly accept this new culture
25 and through it rise up and go on. Like

---

1. Great Spirit: For many Native Americans, the greatest power or god.

Alternative Assessment Have your students complete this activity for assessment:

Assume the persona of Chief Dan George's grandson or granddaughter. You have fulfilled part of your grandfather's dream in that you have an education and are the "new warrior" that wants to help your people "grasp the place in society that is rightly [theirs]." You are preparing a speech to deliver to the members of the U.S. Congress. Based on your grandfather's hopes for his people and your own understanding of the plight of today's Native Americans, write a speech pleading for justice for your people.

WE THE PEOPLE
Kathy Morrow
Courtesy of the Artist

the thunderbird[2] of old, I shall rise again
out of the sea; I shall grab the instruments
of the white man's success—his
education, his skills. With these new tools
30   I shall build my race into the proudest
segment of your society. I shall see our
young braves and our chiefs sitting in
the houses of law and government, ruling
and being ruled by the knowledge and
35   freedoms of *our* great land.

---

2. thunderbird: A powerful supernatural creature that produces thunder
by flapping its wings and lightning by opening and closing its eyes. In the
folklore of some Native American nations, the thunderbird is in constant
warfare with the powers beneath the waters.

RESPONDING TO THE SELECTION

Your Response

1. What emotions do you feel as you read the
words of Chief Dan George? Why?

Interpreting

2. What sort of war is the speaker fighting?
3. What kind of "new warriors" does the speaker
wish to see?
4. How will living "in harmony with my environment" be different for the author from the way
it was for the "olden chiefs"?

Applying

5. Do you think that the speaker has selected the
best means for improving his people's lives?
Could his words apply to you? Explain.

CRITICAL THINKING AND READING

Inferring the Speaker's Meaning

Often facts are omitted in a work of literature.
The reader must infer information from whatever
the speaker says. In "There Is a Longing . . .", for
example, you can infer that the speaker feels a
great sense of responsibility for his people and
frequently speaks out on their behalf.

1. What lines in the poem allow you to infer something about the current status of many of the
speaker's people?
2. How do you know that the speaker's dream has
not yet been achieved?

There Is a Longing . . .   551

Humanities Note

Fine art, *We the People,* by Kathy
Morrow. Morrow grew up on
Apache and Sioux reservations
while her father trained and organized Native American police
forces. She developed a respect
for native spirituality and philosophy, and draws inspiration
for her work from her valuable
collection of Indian artifacts.
She learned beadwork from an
Apache woman and often uses it
on her scratchboard paintings. It
is not unusual for one of Morrow's
paintings to take 600 hours to
complete. The artist makes her
home in Las Cruces, New Mexico, with her husband (who also
had the experience of being a
white child raised on a reservation) and three children. The
painting *We the People* is on
scratchboard with hand-loomed
beadwork.

You might ask students:
1. How does this work convey
a sense of longing and determination?
2. How has the artist combined
Native American symbols with
symbols of contemporary
American society? What do
you think was her purpose in
doing so?
3. What does the title of the
painting suggest to you?

Closure and Extension

ANSWERS TO RESPONDING TO THE SELECTION
Your Response

1. Students may say that the poem
inspires feelings of hope and determination. Discuss how much of
their emotional response may be
due to the skill of the author in
communicating his own emotions
dramatically.

Interpreting

2. Suggested Response: He is fighting a social war in order to help his
people succeed.
3. He wants to see educated, skilled
people.
4. Suggested Response: The chief
lives in a modern, technologically
advanced society. That is his environment, and he must adapt
himself and his people to the demands of that society. The olden
chiefs had to deal with nature
alone as their environment.

Applying

5. Students may say that education
is the best means of improving
one's lot and that their own futures
will depend upon their education.

ANSWERS TO CRITICAL THINKING AND READING

1. "But they will emerge with their
hand held forward, not to receive
welfare, but to grasp the place in
society that is rightly ours."

2. There are few Native Americans
in the governments of North
America.

Motivation/Prior Knowledge
Have students imagine that they are invited to go on a great and potentially dangerous adventure. It could be mountain climbing in the Himalayas, a safari in deepest Africa, a voyage in a space shuttle into the unknown, or whatever else they might imagine. What would be the dangers involved? What would be the possible rewards? What would determine whether or not they would accept the invitation? Then tell them that this poem is spoken by a man who was afraid to take risks and strive for his goals.

Master Teacher Note Use the overhead projector to show students Art Transparency 12, *The Birthplace of Herbert Hoover,* by Grant Wood. Tell students that Hoover served as the thirty-first President of the United States (1929–1933). Ask students why we honor presidents and other famous figures by making their birthplaces into museums. Lead them to see that these figures, through their willingness to strive for their goals, can serve as role models for us. Then tell them that Masters's poem "George Gray" is about a person who was afraid to work for a goal.

Purpose-Setting Question
What are George Gray's main fear and main desire?

1 **Discussion** What feelings do you have when you see a sailboat running before the wind? What feelings does a boat with furled sails suggest?

2 **Discussion** What can you infer about his life from this comment?

3 **Discussion** How might his life be different if he could live it again? What is the effect of your knowledge that he will not have a second chance?

George Gray

Edgar Lee Masters

I have studied many times
The marble which was chiseled for me—
A boat with a furled sail at rest in a harbor.
In truth it pictures not my destination
5 But my life.
For love was offered me, and I shrank from its
    disillusionment;
Sorrow knocked at my door, but I was afraid;
Ambition called to me, but I dreaded the chances.
Yet all the while I hungered for meaning in my life
10 And now I know that we must lift the sail
And catch the winds of destiny
Wherever they drive the boat.
To put meaning in one's life may end in madness,
But life without meaning is the torture
15 Of restlessness and vague desire—
It is a boat longing for the sea and yet afraid.

RESPONDING TO THE SELECTION

Your Response

1. Have you let an important opportunity go by? If you had the chance again, how would you react differently?

Recalling

2. What did the speaker turn away from in life, yet what did he want?

Interpreting

3. Why is the carving on the speaker's tombstone a fitting image of his life?
4. Interpret the last three lines. What is "life without meaning"?

Applying

5. If you could ask the speaker "What should people do to put meaning in their lives?" what answer do you think he would give?

CRITICAL THINKING AND READING

Recognizing Assertions

An **assertion** is a positive statement made with great confidence but with little or no proof to support it. An assertion may be true or false, reasonable or unreasonable. In "George Gray" the speaker says, "And now I know that we must lift the sail/And catch the winds of destiny/Wherever they drive the boat."

1. What does this assertion mean? Rephrase it in plain, simple language.
2. Evaluate the assertion. Is it true and reasonable or not? Does it contain good advice? Give reasons for your opinion.

ANSWERS TO RESPONDING TO THE SELECTION
Your Response
1. Discuss the fact that often people do not recognize opportunity when it comes. Ask if students feel differently now about the lost opportunity than they did at the time.

Recalling
2. George Gray turned away from love, sorrow, and ambition. He wanted meaning in his life.

Interpreting
3. Suggested Response: The sails on the boat are furled, so it can go nowhere. This boat symbolizes the lack of adventure in his life.
4. Suggested Response: He now knows that to have meaning in one's life, one must take risks.

5. Suggested Response: The words "life without meaning" refer to a life in which nothing is risked, so a person experiences "vague desire" without fulfillment.

Applying
6. Most students will realize that the speaker would advise them to pursue love, risk sorrow, and work toward their ambition.

Lyric Poetry

QUINTET
Samuel Reindorf

Humanities Note

Fine art, *Quintet,* 1961, Samuel Reindorf. Samuel Reindorf, born in 1914, is a Mexican painter of Polish origins. He studied art at the Toronto School of Art in Canada and the American Artists School in New York City. He currently resides in Mexico.

Quintet is the artist's salute to jazz and the musicians who perform it. The harmonious colors of this abstract composition add to its lively charm.

Preparation

More About the Authors
Shakespeare's reputation as a lyric poet is also based on his series of sonnets—fourteen-line poems with a set rhythm and rhyme scheme. Scholars are still arguing about the identities of the young nobleman and the mysterious "dark lady" mentioned in these poems. Ask students what kind of detective work scholars might do to solve this puzzle.

Many people remember **Edwin Arlington Robinson** for his portraits of unfortunate people who led lives of tragedy and frustration. "Miniver Cheevy" and "Richard Cory" stand out as centerpieces of this poet's art. Ask students if a poet's choice of moral theme or subject matter clearly marks the type of person he or she is.

In addition to writing poetry, **Gordon Parks** has careers as an eminent photographer and motion picture director. He directed and wrote the score for the film *The Learning Tree*. Ask students for the names of other creative people who are or were multitalented. Also discuss the different ways in which creativity is manifested in people.

Christina Rossetti was the youngest child in a family of four children and was overshadowed by both her brothers. Ask students what a younger sibling who has older brothers or sisters with strong egos might do to assert her own identity.

Consider telling students that **James Joyce** seldom returned to Ireland once he had left. Ask them what factors might cause a writer to live and write in another country.

Winter

William Shakespeare (1564–1616) was a lyric poet as well as an author of poetic dramas. Among his most famous lyrics are his sonnets. Even Shakespeare's plays, however, contain lyric poems. "Winter," for example, appears at the end of the comedy *Love's Labor's Lost*. Like many of the lyrics in his plays, it was probably sung to music. The boy actors in the theater companies of the time were skilled singers, and many acting troupes had a variety of musical instruments.

The Dark Hills

Edwin Arlington Robinson (1869–1935) was considered the major poet of his time in America. He led a difficult life, plagued by ill health and money problems. These experiences probably contributed to the depiction of suffering in his poems about small-town life. Tilbury Town, the fictional small town of his work, was actually based on the place where he grew up—Gardiner, Maine. Robinson's lyric "The Dark Hills" reflects a yearning for the end of war and conflict.

The Funeral

Gordon Parks (1912–   ) achieved an important breakthrough as the first African American film director in the history of Hollywood. However, Parks is best known for his work as a photographer and writer. These two careers are summed up in the title of his book *A Poet and His Camera* (1968). In his poem "The Funeral," he writes about a universal theme—how the world you knew as a child seems different when you are older.

Uphill

Christina Rossetti (1830–1894) is considered by some critics to be the best female poet in English literature. She was the daughter of an Italian father (her mother is to the right in the picture), who had come to live in England, and her brother was the famous poet and painter Dante Gabriel Rossetti. Today Christina Rossetti's best-known work is the long poem "Goblin Market," a kind of supernatural fairy tale. Many of her other poems, however, reflect her concern with religion. A number of them, like "Uphill," deal with the theme of death.

554   Poetry

Objectives

1 To understand lyric poetry
2 To write a lyric poem
3 To interpret connotative meaning in a lyric poem
4 To write about a lyric poem
5 To interpret symbols in lyric poetry
6 To interpret sensory words
7 To write about fine art
8 To express individual interests and abilities through optional activities

Support Material

Teaching Portfolio
Teacher Backup, p. 689
Usage and Mechanics Worksheet, p. 695
Vocabulary Check, p. 696
Critical Thinking and Reading Worksheet, *Interpreting Symbols in Lyric Poetry*, p. 698
Language Worksheet, *Using General and Specific Words*, p. 699
Selection Test, p. 700
Art Transparency 13: *War Series: Casualty—The Secretary of War Regrets*, by Jacob Lawrence

I Hear an Army

James Joyce (1882–1941) was born in Dublin, Ireland. He was educated in Catholic schools and almost became a priest, but he chose to be a writer instead. Rebelling against traditional values, he left Ireland to live abroad after graduating from college. Joyce is primarily known for his daring, experimental works of fiction, such as *Portrait of the Artist as a Young Man* and *Ulysses*. However, he also published an excellent volume of lyrics, *Pomes Penyeach,* from which "I Hear an Army" comes.

Lyric Poetry

In **lyric poetry** writers express their thoughts and feelings about a subject in a brief but musical way. In ancient times lyric poetry was accompanied by an instrument called a lyre—which explains the term *lyric*. Today such poems still have a songlike quality.

Lyric poems can take many different forms. "The Dark Hills" uses rhymes and regular rhythms. "The Funeral," on the other hand, does not use these devices. Almost all lyric poems, however, convey the writer's thoughts and feelings in lively language.

Focus

In the following poems, the poets use words that appeal to the senses to communicate their observations and feelings. For example, in "Winter" Shakespeare vividly describes sights, sounds, and feelings associated with that season, making winter come alive for us. Choose your favorite season and list sights, sounds, feelings, tastes, and smells that conjure up that time of year for you. Then read the poems in this section, noticing the use of sensory words.

Vocabulary

Knowing the words below will help you as you read these poems.

brooding (brood′ iŋ) *v.*: Thinking about something in a troubled way (p. 556, l. 12)

legions (lē′ jǝnz) *n.*: Groups of soldiers (p. 558, l. 6)

whittled (hwit′ ′ld) *v.*: Reduced gradually, as if cut away in slices by a knife (p. 559, l. 2)

wayfarers (wā′ fer ǝrz) *n.*: Travelers (p. 560, l. 9)

arrogant (ar′ ǝ gǝnt) *adj.*: Proud; haughty (p. 561, l. 3)

disdaining (dis dān′ iŋ) *v.*: Rejecting with scorn (p. 561, l. 4)

cleave (klēv) *v.*: Split (p. 597, l. 7)

Guide for Reading 555

Literary Focus Readers of lyric poetry must be alert to the concentration of language in the poems they read. Authors of novels and stories and plays have many more words with which to create their effects, but the poet makes use of every word, connotation, syllable, and mark of punctuation. Because there is so much the poet does not say and so much the poet implies, the reader must be able to make inferences. Because the poet creates so many images, all the reader's sensory powers must be in gear. The reader must be active and alert to get the full experience and meaning from lyric poetry.

Prereading Focus You may want to prepare students for the activity by holding a class discussion in which students share sensations they associate with a single season of their choice. Students can then work on their own to list sensations associated with each of the other seasons.

Software If students have access to computers, you may have them use **Bank Street Writer** for the Focus activity. Using the program's cut and paste features, students can later incorporate material from the Focus activity into their compositions for the Thinking and Writing activity.

Vocabulary Ask less advanced students to create an analogy around each of the words on the list; for example, *brooding* is to *rejoicing* as *frowning* is to *smiling*.

Spelling Tip Point out that *arrogant* ends with an *ant,* not *ent*.

Listening to Literature
"The Funeral," "Uphill"

Prentice Hall Literature Writing Studio

Alternative Assessment To promote active reading, have students keep a reader's response journal as they read these five poems. Ask them to focus their observations on the vivid words in each poem that convey the feelings and thoughts of the poets. Encourage them to respond personally to each poem and to the lines that particularly impress them. What similarities in theme do they note in the poems?

Students' observations will enable you to assess their understanding of the poems.

Motivation/Prior Knowledge
Ask students to name their favorite season of the year. What associations do they have with that season? What is their least favorite season? What do they dislike about that time of year?

Master Teacher Note Students' reactions to the different seasons depend on their experiences. These experiences vary widely depending, in part, on where they have lived. Winter in one climate is very different from winter in another. For those who have never experienced winter in a northern climate, it would be of help to discuss vicarious experiences they might have had through motion pictures, television, or reading. Experience with the seasons also is different through the centuries. Establish with students the problems of coping with the weather 300 years ago compared with their experiences today.

Making Connections Other selections that you might use with "Winter" are "The Seven Ages of Man," page 543, a monologue from *As You Like It,* and Marchette Chute's essay from *Shakespeare of London,* page 497. This essay describes the training that Shakespeare received as an actor.

You might teach "The Raven," page 527, with "I Hear an Army." Both these poems deal with loss of love.

Purpose-Setting Question
What is the attitude of the poet toward winter?

1 **Discussion** Are Shakespeare's winter scenes realistic? Explain.

2 **Discussion** How do you think Shakespeare felt about the winter?

3 **Literary Focus** What is the effect of repetition in this poem?

Winter

William Shakespeare

1
> When icicles hang by the wall
>> And Dick the shepherd blows his nail[1]
> And Tom bears logs into the hall
>> And milk comes frozen home in pail,
5 When blood is nipp'd[2] and ways be foul,
Then nightly sings the staring owl,
>> Tu-whit;
> Tu-who, a merry note,
While greasy Joan doth keel the pot.[3]

10 When all around the wind doth blow
>> And coughing drowns the parson's saw[4]
2
> And birds sit brooding in the snow
>> And Marian's nose looks red and raw,
> When roasted crabs[5] hiss in the bowl,
15 Then nightly sings the staring owl,
>> Tu-whit;
3
> Tu-who, a merry note,
While greasy Joan doth keel the pot.

---

1. **blows his nail:** Blows on his fingernails to warm his hands.
2. **nipp'd:** Stung with cold.
3. **keel the pot:** Stir the pot to cool its contents.
4. **saw:** Sermon.
5. **crabs:** Here, crab apples.

Reader's Response How is your vision of winter similar to or different from that of Shakespeare?

Cooperative Learning Divide the class into groups of four. Ask each group to adapt Shakespeare's images in "Winter" to one other season. Give each group a sheet of paper. After group members select a season, have them take turns writing descriptions of objects and activities that reflect the characteristics of that season. Explain that each group should continue adding descriptions until you tell them to stop. Give students sufficient time to think of descriptions and write them down. Call on representatives from each group to read the group's description.

RESPONDING TO THE SELECTION

Your Response

1. Which of the images in this poem appealed to you most? Why?

Recalling

2. Identify four of the little winter scenes that Shakespeare depicts.

Interpreting

3. Why is the scene described in line 11 especially typical of the winter?
4. What is the mood of this poem?

Applying

5. Why do you think that lyric poets often write about a particular season?

ANALYZING LITERATURE

Understanding Lyric Poetry

In **lyric poetry** writers express their thoughts and feelings about a subject in a brief but musical way. Shakespeare's "Winter," like a number of his lyrics, was actually written as a song for a play. The repeated lines are similar to the repeated words and phrases you hear in popular songs.

1. Identify the refrain, or repeated lines, of this lyric poem.
2. What different senses does Shakespeare appeal to in his description? Explain.

THINKING AND WRITING

Writing a Lyric Poem

Recall the sights, sounds, tastes, and smells that you listed as you thought about your favorite season. Add to this list some of the thoughts and feelings that this season calls up in you. Using these notes, write a lyric poem about this season. It can present little scenes, as "Winter" does, but it does not have to use rhyme or definite rhythms. Read your first draft aloud. Then revise it to make your descriptions as vivid as possible.

Winter   557

Presentation

Motivation/Prior Knowledge
Ask students to compare their feelings about bright daylight with their feelings about the coming of evening. How does their mood change? Why? Then tell them that "The Dark Hills" focuses on evening.

Purpose-Setting Question Who is the poet speaking to in this poem?

1 **Discussion** Ask students to discuss in what ways the hovering of sunset could be like the sound of golden horns.

2 **Discussion** Point out to students that the last line gives the poem a more universal meaning. Have them discuss the poem's theme.

The Dark Hills

Edwin Arlington Robinson

1
Dark hills at evening in the west,
Where sunset hovers like a sound
Of golden horns that sang to rest
Old bones of warriors under ground,

2
5 Far now from all the bannered ways
Where flash the legions of the sun,
You fade—as if the last of days
Were fading, and all wars were done.

RESPONDING TO THE SELECTION

Your Response

1. How do sunsets affect you? Explain.

Recalling

2. Describe the scene at which the poet is looking.
3. What scene from the past does the sunset recall?
4. In the last two lines, what does the poet imagine is happening?

Interpreting

5. What is the main difference between the "bones of warriors under ground" and "the legions of the sun"?
6. How is the sunset "like a sound"?
7. Who or what is the "you" in line 7?
8. A critic has called this poem a wish for the end of war. Comment on this interpretation.

Applying

9. Why do you think that times of dramatic changes in light, like sunset, call up many thoughts and feelings in people?

CRITICAL THINKING AND READING

Interpreting Connotative Meaning

The **connotations** of words are the emotions and associations that they suggest, beyond their plain dictionary meaning. For example, the dictionary meaning of *dark,* which appears in the title and first line of Robinson's poem, is "the absence of light." However, this word also suggests peace, mystery, and even danger—these are some of its connotations. Poets use the connotations of words to create moods and reveal deeper meanings in their lyrics.

1. Explain how some of the connotations of *dark* contribute to the mood and meaning of "The Dark Hills."
2. What associations does the word "sunset" in line 2 bring to mind?
3. What are some of the connotations of the word "golden" in line 3?
4. What are some of the connotations of the word "sun" in line 6?
5. What do the connotations of these words add to the meaning of the poem?

Closure and Extension

ANSWERS TO RESPONDING TO THE SELECTION
Your Response

1. Encourage students to visualize how weather affects the appearance of sunsets. Have them discuss the ways in which these differences might alter their emotional response.

Recalling

2. The sun is setting behind hills in the west, which are now dark.
3. The sunset recalls the funerals of ancient warriors.
4. The speaker imagines that time itself is fading and all wars are done.

Interpreting

5. Suggested Response: When the warriors were bright looking,

young, and victorious, they were the "legions of the sun." Now they are dead and buried.
6. Suggested Response: The fading light from the sunset lingers for a moment like the sound of horns after a note has been sounded.
7. He is addressing the hills.
8. Answers will differ, but most students will realize that the poet seems to be wishing for the end of any kind of conflict.

Applying

9. Answers will differ, but most students will realize that such transitional times lift one out of the present and encourage meditation.

ANSWERS TO CRITICAL THINKING AND READING

1. Suggested Response: The word has connotations of peace and mystery that add to the end-of-conflict theme.

2. Suggested Response: The word *sunset* has connotations of a beautiful ending.
3. Suggested Response: Connotations of "golden" in this context are heavenly, rich, beautiful, and peaceful.
4. Suggested Response: The word *sun* has connotations of brightness and power.
5. Suggested Response: All these connotations give the poem an added dimension of feeling.

The Funeral

Gordon Parks

1
5

After many snows I was home again.
Time had whittled down to mere hills
The great mountains of my childhood.
Raging rivers I once swam trickled now like gentle streams.
And the wide road curving on to China or Kansas City or
    perhaps Calcutta,[1]
Had withered to a crooked path of dust
Ending abruptly at the county burying ground.

2
10

Only the giant who was my father remained the same.
A hundred strong men strained beneath his coffin
When they bore him to his grave.

---

1. **Calcutta** (kal kut′ ə) n.: A major city of India.

RESPONDING TO THE SELECTION

Your Response

1. Is there anyone in your life whom you view or once viewed as a giant? Explain.

Recalling

2. Identify three ways in which the place where the speaker grew up seems different to him.
3. What sole event occurs in this poem?

Interpreting

4. Why did the rivers seem "Raging" and the mountains "great" when he was a child?
5. Do the last three lines record a child's or an adult's perception? Explain.

Applying

6. Discuss one way in which your perception of familiar surroundings has changed as you have grown up. How do you account for the difference?

THINKING AND WRITING

Writing About a Lyric Poem

You can perform an experiment with Parks's poem "The Funeral" to show the effects of vivid language in a lyric. Rewrite the poem making the following changes: line 1—change "snows" to *years;* line 2—change "whittled" to *worn;* line 4—change "Raging" to *Wide* and "trickled" to *ran;* line 5—eliminate "wide" and change "curving" to *going;* line 6—change "withered" to *changed;* line 7—eliminate "abruptly." Compare and contrast the original poem with the one you have just created. Briefly note the differences between the two. Consider the effect of removing some of the vivid language. How do the descriptions and mood of the new poem compare with those of the original? Then, using your notes, write a comparison and contrast of the two poems.

The Funeral 559

Motivation/Prior Knowledge
Have students recall the longest trip they have taken. What was their feeling at the beginning of the journey? Ask them to contrast it with their feeling midway and just before they arrived at their destination. Tell them that this poem is about the longest possible journey.

Purpose-Setting Question
What is the destination of the journey in this poem?

Audiocassette Before students read "Uphill", play the reading of the poem on the **Listening to Literature** Audiocassettes. Ask how many people speak in the poem. How does the reader change inflections to indicate shifts from questions to answers?

1 Reading Strategy Have the students note that questions and answers alternate throughout the poem. Ask students to predict what the line of questioning will be.

2 Reading Strategy Have students summarize the literal description of the journey.

3 Discussion Ask students to discuss the possible figurative meaning of the journey. What is the final destination?

Closure and Extension

ANSWERS TO RESPONDING TO THE SELECTION
Your Response
1. Encourage students to share their perceptions of life within the context of a journey. Have them discuss the poet's implication that effort is rewarded in the end.

Recalling
2. The speaker learns that the road winds uphill; the trip takes a full day; there is an inn at the top where other wayfarers are staying;

Uphill
Christina Rossetti

1   Does the road wind uphill all the way?
         Yes, to the very end.
     Will the day's journey take the whole long day?
         From morn to night, my friend.

2 5   But is there for the night a restingplace?
         A roof for when the slow dark hours begin.
     May not the darkness hide it from my face?
         You cannot miss that inn.

   10   Shall I meet other wayfarers at night?
         Those who have gone before.
     Then must I knock, or call when just in sight?
         They will not keep you standing at that door.

         Shall I find comfort, travel-sore and weak?
         Of labor you shall find the sum.
3 15   Will there be beds for me and all who seek?
         Yea, beds for all who come.

RESPONDING TO THE **S**ELECTION

Your Response
1. Do you share the poet's view of life as described in this poem? Why or why not?

Recalling
2. Summarize what the questioner in this poem learns about the journey that he or she is taking.

Interpreting
3. What evidence is there that this journey is not just an ordinary trip?
4. Who do you think these speakers are?

Applying
5. If you were the questioner in this poem, how would you respond to the answers you received? Explain.

CRITICAL **T**HINKING AND **R**EADING

Interpreting Symbols in Lyric Poetry

A **symbol** is something that is itself and yet suggests or represents another thing as well. The advantage of a symbol is that it focuses a complex idea or experience onto an object or experience that can be readily understood. In "Uphill," for instance, Rossetti symbolizes life and death as a journey and rest. Once you understand this symbolism, the meaning of the poem becomes clear.

1. Why is a journey along a road a good symbol for life?
2. What might the uphill winding represent?
3. Explain what the "roof" and "slow dark hours" could symbolize.
4. Who are "Those who have gone before"?

---

one can see the inn after dark; it will be easy to get in; and beds are available for a good rest.

Interpreting
3. Suggested Response: The inn at the end of the journey is most unusual in that all who have gone before are still there, and yet there are beds available for all who come.
4. Suggested Response: The questioner is a person approaching death, and the answerer could be death itself.

Applying
5. Answers will differ, but students may have a difficult time identifying with an older person who is approaching the end of life.

ANSWERS TO CRITICAL THINKING AND READING

1. Suggested Response: In a sense life is a trip through many stages and experiences from birth to death.
2. Suggested Response: The struggles of life and its frustrations are symbolized by the winding uphill road.
3. Suggested Response: The roof may be the earth over the grave and the slow dark hours death itself.
4. Suggested Response: "Those who have gone before" are all the people who have lived and died.

I Hear an Army

James Joyce

1

I hear an army charging upon the land,
    And the thunder of horses plunging, foam about their
        knees:
Arrogant, in black armor, behind them stand,
    Disdaining the reins, with fluttering whips, the
        charioteers.

2

5 They cry unto the night their battle-name:
    I moan in sleep when I hear afar their whirling
        laughter.
They cleave the gloom of dreams, a blinding flame,
    Clanging, clanging upon the heart as upon an anvil.

3

They come shaking in triumph their long, green hair:
10   They come out of the sea and run shouting by the
        shore.
My heart, have you no wisdom thus to despair?
    My love, my love, my love, why have you left me alone?

I Hear an Army   561

ANSWERS TO RESPONDING TO THE SELECTION

Your Response

1. You might wish to have students describe the kinds of dreams they recall most vividly. Ask if they see a relationship between depth of emotion and intensity of dreams.

Recalling

2. An army of thundering horses and arrogant charioteers with green hair and black armor come charging out of the sea.
3. The speaker is sleeping and dreaming when he hears the army.
4. The speaker's love has departed and left the speaker alone.

Interpreting

5. Suggested Response: The army is not real. The charioteers have green hair and the horses come thundering from out of the sea.
6. Suggested Response: "Plunging," "fluttering," and "whirling" provide visual images of movement and force. The word "clanging" provides an aural image.

Applying

7. Answers will differ, but students may comment that heartbreak lends itself to images that are dramatic such as the ones in this poem. Happiness suggests images that are pleasant but not as exciting.

ANSWERS TO CRITICAL THINKING AND READING

1. Suggested Responses: You can hear the sounds of horses' hoofs and the splashing of water.
2. Suggested Response: You can hear the cracking of whips.
3. Suggested Response: The word that names this sound is *clanging.*

THINKING AND WRITING

Software If students have access to computers, have them use **Bank Street Writer** to complete the assignment. As students revise, they can use the program's on-line thesaurus to find specific words that describe the qualities of the subjects and moods of the two artistic works.

RESPONDING TO THE SELECTION

Your Response

1. How do moods influence your dreams?

Recalling

2. Describe the army that the poet hears.
3. What is the speaker doing when he hears this army?
4. What has the speaker's love done to him?

Interpreting

5. Is the army that the poet describes real? Explain your answer.
6. How do verbs like "plunging," "fluttering," "whirling," and "clanging" contribute to the mood of the poem?

Applying

7. A famous poet once said that it is easier to write about heartbreak than about happiness in love. Comment on this remark.

CRITICAL THINKING AND READING

Interpreting Sensory Words

Sensory words appeal to one or more of the five senses. Since Joyce's poem is called "I Hear an Army," many of the words he chose appeal to the sense of hearing.

1. What sounds do you hear when you read the words "charging upon the land"?
2. What sounds do you hear when you read of the "fluttering whips"?
3. Joyce uses onomatopoeia, or words that imitate sounds, to describe the army's effect on the heart. What word names this sound?

THINKING AND WRITING

Writing About Fine Art

Imagine that you are an editor working on a book of Joyce's poems. A fellow editor has suggested illustrating "I Hear an Army" with the painting *Horses of Neptune* (page 561). First, reread the poem and look carefully at the painting. Then list your reactions to this idea, considering whether the subject and mood of the picture are in harmony with the poem. Using your list, write a memo to your co-worker accepting or rejecting the proposal. In revising this memo, make sure that you have been specific in pointing out qualities of the picture that enhance or conflict with the poem. Share your memo with your classmates when you are finished.

LEARNING OPTIONS

1. **Writing.** In Joyce's poem the speaker seems to be describing a nightmare caused by his great despair. Dreams, and particularly nightmares, can leave a very strong impression. Write a poem about a vivid dream or nightmare. Use words that appeal to the senses to create vivid images. When you have finished your poem, share it with the class.
2. **Art.** Each poem you have read includes words that create vivid mental pictures. Draw or paint a picture to illustrate one of the poems in this section. Include in your picture as many of the details described in the poem as you can. When you have finished your artwork, display it in the classroom.

Alternative Assessment For Alternate Composition Assignments to assess students' learning on these five poems, see pages 773–735 of the **Teaching Portfolio.**

Publishing Student Writing You may want to display students' memos alongside a Xerox of the picture.

LEARNING OPTIONS

1. This activity will appeal to visual learners. You might extend the activity by having students illustrate their poems.
2. Kinesthetic learners will enjoy this activity. You might extend the activity for outgoing students by having them read aloud the poem they have illustrated.

Word Choice and Tone

ORION IN DECEMBER, 1959
Charles Burchfield
National Museum of American Art,
Smithsonian Institution

Humanities Note

Fine art, *Orion in December,* 1959, by Charles Burchfield. The American artist Charles Burchfield (1893–1967), was educated at the Cleveland institute of Art. His teacher there, Henry Keller, encouraged him to develop an individualistic style of painting. Burchfield worked at many things to finance his painting career, including designing wallpaper, illustrating, and teaching art classes. He eventually gained fame for his intense and imaginative paintings of nature and haunted buildings.

Orion in December is a mystical interpretation of a starry winter night. Energy seems to emanate from the natural forms, and the forces of nature vibrate through the elements of the painting. Burchfield wanted the viewer to experience looking at the stars on a cold, clear evening.

More About the Authors Robert Browning was a man of singularly strong and determined mind—even when it came to choosing a wife. Tell students about Browning's fabled love for the poet Elizabeth Barrett, about how he courted her despite her father's fierce opposition to the match, and about how he married her by eloping to Italy where they lived until Elizabeth's death. Ask students whether they think that it is important for a professional poet to be determined, even single-minded.

Consider telling students that, in addition to nonsense verse and fantasy, **Charles Dodgson** wrote books on logic—the study of correct reasoning. Ask students why a person interested in logic might also like to write silly and nonsensical verse.

T.S. Eliot, born and educated in America, decided in 1914, at the age of twenty-six, to live in England. Ask students to speculate about why Eliot moved to England. Why might he have wanted to leave America, and why would he choose England? Ask students what would make a certain country more desirable for a poet or an artist.

Wisława Szymborska, considered one of the best representatives of the rich tradition of Polish poetry, has won critical acclaim and popularity in her native land. Her poetry is known for its freshness, inventiveness, and originality. Ask students to see whether they agree with this assessment of Szymborska's work.

GUIDE FOR READING

Meeting at Night

Robert Browning (1812–1889) was one of the greatest English poets of the nineteenth century. Though he lacked a college education, his parents instilled in him a love of art and literature. Browning had a special fondness for Italy, where he lived for a time with his wife and fellow poet Elizabeth Barrett. That country is the setting for some of his most famous dramatic monologues, poems in which a character speaks to a silent listener. "Meeting at Night" is not a monologue, but it does show Browning's gift for vivid language.

Jabberwocky

Lewis Carroll (1832–1898) was the pen name of Charles Lutwidge Dodgson, a mathematics teacher at an English University. Dodgson wrote his most famous works, *Alice's Adventures in Wonderland* and *Through the Looking Glass,* for the young daughters of the dean of his college. One of the girls, Alice Liddell, was the model for Dodgson's Alice. In the course of her adventures in Wonderland, Alice encounters a poem that can only be read when held up to a mirror. Its name is "Jabberwocky."

Macavity: The Mystery Cat

T. S. Eliot (1888–1965) was born in St. Louis, Missouri, but went to England as a young man and lived there for most of his life. Eliot was an extremely influential poet and wrote one of the greatest poems of our time, "The Waste Land." Even on a first reading, this difficult poem conveys a sense of excitement. However, Eliot wrote humorous poems as well. His *Old Possum's Book of Practical Cats,* from which "Macavity: The Mystery Cat" comes, was the basis for the Broadway play *Cats*.

Astonishment

Wisława Szymborska (1923–   ) had her first poem published in 1945 in Cracow, Poland. Publication of her first collection of poems was canceled in 1948 when the Communist government decided that Szymborska's poems were not politically acceptable. Since then, however, she has earned critical praise as one of the greatest of the modern Polish poets.

564   Poetry

Objectives

1 To understand word choice in poetry
2 To understand made-up words in poetry
3 To write a poem using made-up words
4 To analyze the use of exaggeration in a poem

5 To write about a poem's tone
6 To understand an ironical tone
7 To express individual interests and abilities through optional activities

Support Material

Teaching Portfolio
Teacher Backup, p. 703
Grammar in Action Worksheet, *Using Coordinating Conjunctions,* p. 709
Usage and Mechanics Worksheet, p. 711
Analyzing Literature Worksheet, *Understanding Word Choice,* p. 712

Word Choice

What difference does it make whether a poet uses one or another of synonyms such as *bond, tie, link,* or *connection*? The answer is that it can matter a great deal. In addition to their denotations, or dictionary meanings, words have different connotations, or emotional associations, that result from their different histories. Choosing a word with the wrong connotation for your purposes is the same as singing a song out of tune. For example, would you describe a friendship as a *link* or *connection*? The word *bond* is better able to convey the warm feelings that friends have for each other.

As the poem "Jabberwocky" demonstrates, even made-up words have connotations. These emotional associations come mostly from the resemblance of these words to more familiar ones.

Mood and tone also depend on a poet's choice of words. **Mood** is the feeling that a poem creates, while **tone** is the attitude that a poet takes toward his or her subject and readers. If a poet calls a friendship a *connection,* he or she may be creating a tone of disapproval toward it. This choice of words may also call up a mood of coldness and a lack of caring. Other factors besides word choice, however, can influence mood and tone. If a poem has jingly rhymes and a bouncy rhythm, for instance, it is clear that the poet is not being serious.

Focus

Poets choose their words carefully to create the right mood and tone for a poem. For example, in "Jabberwocky," the made-up word *slithy* conveys a mood of mock horror and a tone of nonseriousness. It is a combination of two words, *slimy* and *lithe,* and it conveys the feel and the sense of both words. Lewis Carroll called such a combination of words a "portmanteau" word. (A portmanteau is a kind of suitcase.) In small groups think of words you can combine to make portmanteau words that create a certain mood or tone. Write a definition for each new word. Then read the poems in this section to see how the poets create mood and tone through their words.

Vocabulary

Knowing the following word will help you as you read these poems.
prow (prou) *n.*: Forward part of a ship (p. 566, l. 5)

Guide for Reading   565

Humanities Note

Fine art, *Moonlit Cove*, by Albert Pinkham Ryder. Ryder (1847–1917) was born in the whaling port of New Bedford, Massachusetts, and was deeply influenced by his boyhood contact with the sea.

You might want to use the following questions:
1. How does Ryder make the scene mysterious and inviting?
2. Does the picture show the type of beach you imagined while reading the poem? Explain.

Presentation

Motivation/Prior Knowledge Have students recall a time when they were outdoors at night. What sounds did they hear? How were familiar objects changed by the night? In what ways is the world different at night than it is during the day? Tell them that Browning's poem contains vivid nighttime images.

Master Teacher Note Use the overhead projector to show students Art Transparency 14, *The Voice*, by Edvard Munch. Ask students to describe the mood of this picture. Also ask them whom the girl might be waiting to meet. Then tell them that Browning's poem describes a rendezvous between lovers.

Making Connections Another selection that deals with anticipation is "Great Expectations," by Charles Dickens, page 723.

Purpose-Setting Question What mood does the poet create?

1 **Literary Focus** Poets create images with words that evoke responses from the five senses. The more vividly descriptive the poet's word choices are, the better the image is. Ask students to identify several images in "Meeting at Night" and explain to which senses these images appeal.

MOONLIT COVE, 1880–90
Albert Pinkham Ryder
The Phillips Collection, Washington D.C.

Meeting at Night

Robert Browning

I

The gray sea and the long black land;
And the yellow half-moon large and low;
And the startled little waves that leap
In fiery ringlets from their sleep,
5   As I gain the cove with pushing prow,
And quench its speed i' the slushy sand.

566   Poetry

II

2
10
> Then a mile of warm sea-scented beach;
> Three fields to cross till a farm appears;
> A tap at the pane, the quick sharp scratch
> And blue spurt of a lighted match,
> And a voice less loud, through its joys and fears,
> Than the two hearts beating each to each!

2 **Discussion** The first and second stanzas both describe different stages of the same journey, yet there is a subtle but noticeable difference between them. Have students contrast the two. Which offers a greater sense of warmth to the traveler? Why? Have students explain how the poem's last two lines are the culmination of the traveler's journey.

RESPONDING TO THE SELECTION

Your Response

1. Which words in this poem were especially effective in helping you imagine the scene? Explain.

Recalling

2. Describe the setting in each part of the poem.
3. Give a chronological account of the actions that occur in this poem.

Interpreting

4. Explain the title of this poem. What "Meeting at Night" does the poem describe?

Applying

5. Why do you think some poets try to appeal to as many of the reader's senses as possible?

ANALYZING LITERATURE

Understanding Word Choice

In choosing words poets pay as much attention to their connotations, or emotional associations, as to their denotations, or dictionary meanings. Poets also take into account the sounds of words and try to select words whose sounds harmonize with those of the words around them. You might wonder, for instance, why Browning chooses the word "black" rather than *dark* in line 1. The answer may be that the *l* and *a* sounds of "black" go better with similar sounds in "land." Also, the word *black* has a more vivid feeling than

dark. Browning may have been looking for a livelier word to contrast with "gray," which appears earlier in the line.

1. Explain why Browning might have chosen the word "pushing" rather than *moving* in line 5.
2. In line 7 why does "sea-scented" have better connotations for Browning's purposes than *salty-smelling*?

LEARNING OPTIONS

1. **Writing.** Write a brief story based on the poem "Meeting at Night." Tell the story from the point of view of one character who is traveling to see someone he or she loves dearly. Review the poem to familiarize yourself with its mood and tone. As you write your story, try to maintain the mood and tone of the poem. When you have finished your story, read it aloud to the class.

2. **Cross-curricular Connection.** As you read "Meeting at Night," you can feel the pace quicken and the excitement build. The effect is similar to a crescendo in music (an increase in volume and intensity). Find a piece of music in the library or elsewhere that fits the pacing and the mood of anticipation found in the poem. Then practice reading the poem aloud with the music playing in the background. When you are finished rehearsing, play the music while you read the poem aloud for your class.

Meeting at Night 567

Closure and Extension

ANSWERS TO RESPONDING TO THE SELECTION
Your Response

1. Lead students to see that the vivid images in this poem are created primarily through adjective/noun combinations. Encourage them to identify examples of these word groups to guide them in responding.

Recalling

2. The setting in the first stanza is an ocean cove at night, under a halfmoon. The setting in the second stanza is the countryside near the beach and the inside of a farmhouse.
3. The traveler sails into the cove; he beaches his boat; he walks up from the beach and crosses fields; he knocks on the window of a farmhouse; his love lights a match; the two people embrace.

Interpreting

4. Suggested Response: The poet is describing a romantic rendezvous, which is possibly secret.

Applying

5. Answers will differ, but students should demonstrate an understanding of the fact that poets try to create images through their use of language, and that images are more vivid and clear if the poet can make the reader sense what he or she is reading.

ANSWERS TO ANALYZING LITERATURE

1. Suggested Response: The word "pushing" creates a more specific image of the movement of the boat than the word "moving" would.
2. Suggested Response: "Sea-scented" has a much more pleasant connotation than does "salty-smelling." The smell Browning suggests is gentle and light. "Salty-smelling" has a rougher, heavier connotation than is appropriate here.

LEARNING OPTIONS

1. This activity will appeal to visual learners. You might want to extend the activity by having students add dialogue following the traveler's arrival.
2. Auditory learners will enjoy this activity. You might extend the activity by having students work with the music teacher to set the poem's words to music.

567

Motivation/Prior Knowledge
Ask students if they have ever read works by Lewis Carroll, such as *Alice in Wonderland*. What were their favorite characters or scenes? If students are not familiar with Carroll, explain that he is famous for his imaginative, often witty, fantasy stories. Tell them that "Jabberwocky" is from Carroll's book *Through the Looking Glass*. The poem is famous for its "nonsense" language.

Master Teacher Note Because of the nature of the created language used in "Jabberwocky," it would be most useful for the students to hear a recording of it. Have students listen to the recording once before they read the poem and then listen to it again as they read the selection themselves.

Purpose Setting Question What do you think a "Jabberwock" is?

1 Discussion You might want to remind students that rhyme is the repetition of the accented vowel and all subsequent sounds. Rhyme is usually found at the end of two or more lines; this is called end rhyme. However, rhyme can occur within a line, in which case it is called internal rhyme. Find examples of end rhyme and internal rhyme in "Jabberwocky."

2 Critical Thinking and Reading Who do students think might be speaking here and in stanza six?

3 Discussion Many descriptive words in this poem do not make literal sense. They are inventions or, as Carroll called them, "portmanteau words." For example, "slithy" is a combination of the words "lithe" and "slimy." Despite these inventions, we can still understand the poem. Why does the poet use made-up

THE JABBERWOCK, 1872
John Tenniel
The Granger Collection

Jabberwocky

Lewis Carroll

'Twas brillig, and the slithy toves
    Did gyre and gimble in the wabe;
All mimsy were the borogoves,
    And the mome raths outgrabe.

5 "Beware the Jabberwock, my son!
    The jaws that bite, the claws that
      catch!
Beware the Jubjub bird, and shun
    The frumious Bandersnatch!"

He took his vorpal sword in hand:
10   Long time the manxome foe he
      sought—
So rested he by the Tumtum tree,
    And stood awhile in thought.

And as in uffish thought he stood,
    The Jabberwock, with eyes of flame,
15 Came whiffling through the tulgey wood,
    And burbled as it came!

One, two! One, two! And through and
    through
    The vorpal blade went snicker-snack!
He left it dead, and with its head
20   He went galumphing back.

"And hast thou slain the Jabberwock?
    Come to my arms, my beamish boy!
O frabjous day! Callooh! Callay!"
    He chortled in his joy.

25 'Twas brillig, and the slithy toves
    Did gyre and gimble in the wabe;
All mimsy were the borogoves,
    And the mome raths outgrabe.

568   Poetry

words? What effect do these words have on the poem? What qualities might the poem lack if the poet had used ordinary language?

Reading Strategy Have the students explain the action in "Jabberwocky" using quotations from the text.

Reader's Response Do you like the poem "Jabberwocky?" Why or why not?

Humanities Note

Illustration, *The Jabberwock,* by John Tenniel. Tenniel (1820–1914) illustrated the original version of *Through the Looking Glass,* from which this poem comes.

You might want to use the following questions:
1. Describe what is happening in this picture.
2. Does Tenniel's version of the monster satisfy you? Explain.

RESPONDING TO THE SELECTION

Your Response

1. Do you think the poem would be as effective if the poet were to replace the made-up words with legitimate words? Why or why not?

Recalling

2. Reread lines 5–8. In your own words, express the warning that the hero receives.
3. Reread lines 9–20. Tell the key events that occur in this section of the poem.
4. Describe the reception that the hero receives from the person who warned him.

Interpreting

5. A critic has said that, despite its many strange words, the story of "Jabberwocky" is similar to many legends about knights and dragons. Comment on this remark.
6. You can often tell the part of speech of a word even if you do not understand it. Identify the part of speech of three of the made-up words in this poem. Explain how you arrived at each answer.
7. Explain how a real word that is part of the title is a clue to the poem's style.
8. What mood, or atmosphere, is created by the events in this poem? Explain your answer.

Applying

9. How can a poem like "Jabberwocky" give you a better understanding of language?

ANALYZING LITERATURE

Understanding Made-up Words

Lewis Carroll created the made-up words in "Jabberwocky" in several ways. Some are portmanteau words—a *portmanteau* is "a large, leather suitcase"—because they have "two meanings packed up into one word." *Mimsy* is such a word because it is made up of *flimsy* and *miserable* with some of the meaning of each. Other made-up words in the poem are parts of familiar words. For example, to "gyre" means "to go round and round like a gyroscope." Still other made-up words are just plain nonsense. Carroll says that "toves," for instance, are a combination of badgers, lizards, and corkscrews!

1. Fill in the missing half of the following portmanteau words and then figure out the meaning of each.
   a. *Chortled* is what word plus *snorted*? (Look this word up in the dictionary to check your answer. It became a part of our language as a result of this poem.)
   b. *Galumphing* is what word plus *triumph*?
2. A gimlet is a small tool. What do you think the word *gimble* means?

THINKING AND WRITING

Writing a Poem Using Made-up Words

Write a poem like Carroll's "Jabberwocky," using a combination of made-up words and ordinary words. The subject of your poem can also be the hunting of a strange monster. First, think of a name for your monster that will be as memorable as Carroll's Jabberwock. Some of your made-up words can be portmanteau words, while others can be parts of regular words, like *gyre* in Carroll's poem. You can also use words that are pure nonsense. However, write your poem so that your classmates can understand and enjoy it even if they cannot define each word. When you finish your first draft, read it aloud to several classmates. If they have trouble understanding it, try to make it clearer. Share your revised poem with the class.

LEARNING OPTION

Performance. Form a group of four students to perform the poem "Jabberwocky." Each person can choose one of the following parts: narrator, father, young man, and Jabberwock. Then divide the poem up according to speaker. Have the narrator read the first and last stanzas. Have the father read the second and sixth. Have the young man read the third and fifth, and have the Jabberwock read the fourth stanza. After you have rehearsed, perform the poem for your classmates.

Jabberwocky 569

ILLUSTRATION FROM
OLD POSSUM'S BOOK OF PRACTICAL CATS
Edward Gorey

Macavity: The Mystery Cat

T. S. Eliot

1

Macavity's a Mystery Cat: he's called the Hidden Paw—
For he's the master criminal who can defy the Law.
He's the bafflement of Scotland Yard,[1] the Flying Squad's[2] despair;
For when they reach the scene of crime—*Macavity's not there!*

---

1. Scotland Yard: The London police.
2. Flying Squad: A criminal-investigation department.

570 *Poetry*

570

5 Macavity, Macavity, there's no one like Macavity,
He's broken every human law, he breaks the law of gravity.
His powers of levitation[3] would make a fakir[4] stare,
And when you reach the scene of crime—*Macavity's not there!*
You may seek him in the basement, you may look up in the air—
10 But I tell you once and once again, *Macavity's not there!*

Macavity's a ginger cat, he's very tall and thin;
You would know him if you saw him, for his eyes are sunken in.
His brow is deeply lined with thought, his head is highly domed;
His coat is dusty from neglect, his whiskers are uncombed.
15 He sways his head from side to side, with movements like a snake;
And when you think he's half asleep, he's always wide awake.

Macavity, Macavity, there's no one like Macavity,
For he's a fiend in feline shape, a monster of depravity.
You may meet him in a by-street, you may see him in the square—
20 But when a crime's discovered, then *Macavity's not there!*

He's outwardly respectable. (They say he cheats at cards.)
And his footprints are not found in any file of Scotland Yard's.
And when the larder's looted, or the jewel-case is rifled,
Or when the milk is missing, or another Peke's[5] been stifled,
25 Or the greenhouse glass is broken, and the trellis past repair—
Ay, there's the wonder of the thing! *Macavity's not there!*

And when the Foreign Office[6] find a Treaty's gone astray,
Or the Admiralty[7] lose some plans and drawings by the way,
There may be a scrap of paper in the hall or on the stair—
30 But it's useless to investigate—*Macavity's not there!*
And when the loss has been disclosed, the Secret Service say:
"It *must* have been Macavity!"—but he's a mile away.
You'll be sure to find him resting, or a-licking of his thumbs,
Or engaged in doing complicated long-division sums.

---

3. levitation (lev′ ə tā′ shən) *n.:* Remaining in air with no physical
support.
4. fakir (fə kir′) *n.:* A Moslem or Hindu beggar who claims to
perform miracles.
5. Peke: Short for Pekingese, a small dog with long oilky hair and a
pug nose.
6. Foreign Office: The British equivalent of the U.S. Department of
State.
7. Admiralty: The British governmental department in charge of
naval affairs.

Macavity: The Mystery Cat 571

The conjunction joins two independent clauses, while *or* (used twice) joins three participles, two of them with modifiers.
Student Activity 1. Find four or more coordinating conjunctions in the poem. Tell what each joins.
Student Activity 2. Write four sentences about Macavity that include coordinating conjunctions. Use the conjunctions to join words, phrases, and clauses.

Electronic Handbook You might want students to review the use of coordinating conjunctions before completing the Grammar in Action activities. If students have access to the Language Master 6000, have them enter the access word *conjunction* and press the GRAMMAR key to get information on using coordinating conjunctions.

ILLUSTRATION FROM
OLD POSSUM'S BOOK OF PRACTICAL CATS
Edward Gorey

35 Macavity, Macavity, there's no one like Macavity,
    There never was a Cat of such deceitfulness and suavity.[8]
    He always has an alibi, and one or two to spare:
    At whatever time the deed took place—MACAVITY WASN'T THERE!
    And they say that all the Cats whose wicked deeds are widely known
40 (I might mention Mungojerrie, I might mention Griddlebone)
    Are nothing more than agents for the Cat who all the time
    Just controls their operations: the Napoleon of Crime!

---

8. suavity (swa′ və tē) *n.:* Graceful politeness.

RESPONDING TO THE SELECTION

Your Response

1. Did you find this poem amusing? Why or why not?

Recalling

2. Why is Macavity "a Mystery Cat"?
3. Describe his appearance.
4. Give four examples of his misdeeds.
5. Why can't the police charge him with a crime?
6. Why is Macavity known as "the Napoleon of Crime"?

Interpreting

7. Give three clues that indicate Eliot is taking a humorous tone in this poem.
8. What word in the name *Macavity* explains this cat's ability to evade the law? Explain.

Applying

9. What qualities do cats have that might humorously suggest criminal activities?

ANALYZING LITERATURE

Using Exaggeration

One technique that Eliot uses to create humor in "Macavity: The Mystery Cat" is **exaggeration.** For example, to call a naughty cat a "master criminal" or "the Napoleon of Crime" is to take an idea to ridiculous limits, which makes the reader laugh.

Review the poem for examples of exaggeration. Then answer the following questions:

1. Cite three examples of exaggeration, other than the two given above.
2. How do the realistic details that accurately describe a cat's behavior work with the exaggerated details to create humor?
3. Would the poem be funny if no realistic details were included? Why or why not?

THINKING AND WRITING

Writing About Tone

You have probably heard of people who are deaf to the tones in music. Imagine a reader who, in a similar way, cannot understand the tone that a writer is taking toward his or her subject. List some of the humorous *mistakes* that such a reader would make in trying to understand "Macavity: The Mystery Cat." Then, using your list, write an interpretation of the poem from this reader's point of view. (Of course, your tone will be ironic because you really understand Eliot's humor.) Try to make this reader's *mis*understandings of the tone as funny as possible. Show your first draft to several classmates and ask them for suggestions to make the misinterpretations of tone even more ridiculous. When you are finished, share your essay with the class.

LEARNING OPTIONS

1. **Speaking and Listening.** Form a group of four students to read aloud "Macavity: The Mystery Cat." Each person can choose among the first, third, fifth, and sixth verses to be read individually. Read aloud the second, fourth, and seventh verses of the poem as a group. Be sure to speak the italicized words with emphasis that increases as the poem progresses. When you have finished rehearsing, present your reading to the class.
2. **Language.** Antonyms are words that have opposite, or nearly opposite, meanings. For example, Macavity is described as a "fiend." The opposite of a *fiend* is an angel.

   Imagine that in a parallel world, Macavity has an opposite. Review the poem, and jot down key words that describe Macavity. Next to these words, write their antonyms. When you are finished, you will have a list of key words that describe Macavity's opposite.

Macavity: The Mystery Cat 573

---

8. Suggested Response: The word *cavity* in Macavity's name means "a hole" or "emptiness." This is appropriate for Macavity since he can never be found.

Applying

9. Answers will differ but might include the ideas that cats are quiet, appear sneaky, like to go out at night, seem aloof, and can never be found when something has been broken or when the curtains are torn.

ANSWERS TO ANALYZING LITERATURE

1. Three additional examples of exaggeration are "he breaks the law of gravity"; "his powers of levitation would make a fakir stare"; "a monster of depravity."
2. Suggested Response: The realistic details describe a docile animal oblivious to its surroundings. The exaggeration implies that this innocence is the pretense of a devious scoundrel who controls a far-flung criminal empire.
3. Answers will differ. Most will agree that realistic details add to the humor because they heighten the incongruity. Some may say a cat's behavior is so familiar that details are unnecessary.

THINKING AND WRITING

Writing Transparency Students often find it helpful to see a model of their writing assignment. Before students write, you may wish to show them Model 9: *Writing About Poetry* in the **Transparencies for Writing.**

LEARNING OPTIONS

1. This activity will appeal to auditory and kinesthetic learners. You might extend the activity by having students supply sound effects for such actions as "whiffling," "burbled," "galumphing," and "chortled," as well as the slaying of the Jabberwock.
2. This option will appeal to students who enjoy working within a structured framework, yet wish to express their creativity. A good way to extend the activity is to have students use their list to write a poem about Macavity's alter ego.

Closure and Extension

ANSWERS TO RESPONDING TO THE SELECTION

Your Response

1. Encourage students to share amusing experiences that they have had with cats or funny cartoons about cats. Ask them to compare these incidents or cartoons with the escapades of Macavity.

Recalling

2. Macavity is a "Mystery Cat" because he is never found at the scenes of his crimes.
3. Answers may differ but should include information from the third stanza of the poem.
4. Answers will differ, but students might include theft of jewels, milk, food, and treaties.

5. Macavity is never around after he commits his crimes; the police cannot catch him.
6. Macavity is a criminal mastermind, just as Napoleon was a military genius.

Interpreting

7. Answers will differ but might include the fact that Macavity can outwit Scotland Yard, that he can fly, or that he cheats at cards, all of which are beyond the capabilities of cats.

573

Presentation

Motivation/Prior Knowledge
Ask students whether they have ever wondered why they are here on earth or why they are who they are. Encourage students to discuss why we ask ourselves such unanswerable questions and whether anything positive comes of asking such questions.

Purpose-Setting Question As students read, have them ask themselves whether any of the poet's questions have ever occurred to them.

1 Reading Strategy To help students understand the poem, have them use their own words to rephrase the questions asked in the first six lines.

2 Discussion What are some possible answers to these questions? Are these answers satisfying? Why or why not?

3 Discussion What is the effect of the word *dog* at the end of the last line?

Closure and Extension

ANSWERS TO RESPONDING TO THE SELECTION
Your Response

1. You may wish to have students try to recall experiences from their childhood in which they struggled to understand some aspect of life. Encourage students to share their experiences and ideas in an informal discussion.

Recalling

2. The poet is sitting and staring in a dark corner.

Interpreting

3. The poet calls the time before she was born "epochs of absence," indicating the difficulty she has in imagining life without her own presence.
4. (a) By saving the word *dog* for the end, the poet maintains the tone of mystery and wonder without letting the banality of *dog* intrude.

574

Astonishment

Wisława Szymborska

translated from the Polish by Grażyna Drabik, Austin Flint, and Sharon Olds

1
Why as one person, and one only?
Why this one, not another? And why here?
On Tuesday? At home, not in a nest?
Why in skin, not scales? With a face, not a leaf?
5   And why do I come, I myself, only once?
On this earth? Near a small star?
After many epochs[1] of absence?
Instead of always, and as all?
As all insects, and all horizons?

2
10   And why right now? Why bone and blood?
Myself as myself with myself? Why—
not nearby or a hundred miles away,
not yesterday or a hundred years ago—
do I sit and stare into a dark corner,

3
15   just as it looks up, suddenly raising its head,
this growling thing that is called a dog?

---

1. **epochs** (epʹəks) *n*: Periods or spans of time.

RESPONDING TO THE SELECTION

Your Response

1. What astonishes you about your existence?

Recalling

2. What is the poet doing as she thinks these thoughts?

Interpreting

3. What does the poet mean by saying that she is on earth "After many epochs of absence"?
4. (a) Why does the poet save the name of the "growling thing" for the end? (b) How does holding back the name of the animal relate to the title of the poem?

Applying

5. Do you sometimes ask yourself questions that are not easily answered? Explain.

ANALYZING LITERATURE

Understanding Tone

The **tone** of a literary work is the writer's attitude toward the subject. You can infer a poet's attitude by paying close attention to the poet's choice of words or ways of expressing thoughts. You can usually describe the tone of a poem in a single word, such as formal, tragic, or ironic.

1. What is the tone of this poem? Explain.
2. How does the author convey this tone?

574   *Poetry*

(b) By sharing the poet's wonder about the creature only to find that it is a dog, the reader comes to understand that the poet finds life—in all its manifestations—astonishing.

Applying

5. Guide students to understand that many of the most interesting and most important philosophical questions cannot be answered in practical terms.

ANSWERS TO ANALYZING LITERATURE

1. The tone is one of wonder.
2. The poet indicates wonder by repeating the word *why* and by offering many examples of alternative possibilities that ask, "Why not this, instead?"

Alternative Assessment *Collaborative Assessment* Have a group of about four students

work together to prepare a presentation of one of the poems in this section. The presentation should include an interpretive choral reading of the poem, an illustration of the poem, and musical accompaniment. Have students study all four poems carefully in selecting one to present. Suggest that groups divide up the tasks according to students' interests. When all the groups

Imagery

PINK SHELL WITH SEAWEED, c. 1938
Georgia O'Keeffe
San Diego Museum of Art

Humanities Note

Fine art, *Pink Shell With Seaweed,* c. 1938, by Georgia O'Keeffe. Probably the best-known female American artist, Georgia O'Keeffe (1887–1986), acquired her formal art education at the Art Institute of Chicago and The Art Students League in New York City. She worked in commercial art and taught before deciding to devote her life to painting. O'Keeffe's work places her as a pioneer modern American artist. She was discovered by Alfred Stieglitz, a major exhibitor of "new" art in New York City.

O'Keeffe's hallmark in art is her abstraction of natural forms. *Pink Shell With Seaweed,* in pastels, is just that. Done while living in the desert in New Mexico, this work was perhaps inspired by the direct relationship between desert and ocean, the former being the remains of the latter. The gentle curve of the shell lends itself to the softness of the medium. The luminous colors recall the ocean. Taken out of context and viewed close up, the image of the shell assumes a greater importance and so becomes a symbol of the circular nature of life itself.

have presented their poems, have students respond in writing to each other's work.

In her volume *For My People,* **Margaret Walker** expresses disillusionment at discovering that racial prejudice was just as strong in the Midwest as in the South. Ask students how a writer's disillusionment with society could be turned into something positive.

You might want to tell students that **Theodore Roethke's** father raised plants and that, as a boy, Roethke played in and around his father's greenhouse. Later he wrote many excellent poems about growing plants. Ask students why childhood experience is often so important for a writer.

During most of her life, **Marge Piercy** has been politically active in civil rights, the antiwar movement, and the women's movement. In addition, she has contributed many articles and stories to underground newspapers and magazines. Currently she travels all over the country giving poetry readings, lectures, and writing workshops.

Gary Soto attended California State University. He is currently an associate professor at the University of California at Berkeley. He is an award-winning writer; his first collection of poems, *The Element of San Joaquin,* won the United States Award of the International Poetry Forum. Other awards include the Academy of American Poets Prize for his poem "The Discovery" and the American Book Award for *Living up the Street.*

576

GUIDE FOR READING

Memory

Margaret Walker (1915–   ) was born in Birmingham, Alabama. The daughter of a minister, she received her earliest education at Methodist Church schools. She earned degrees from Northwestern University and the State University of Iowa. She then taught college. Her first book of poetry won the Yale University Younger Poets competition. As an artist, she focuses on the experiences and hardships of black people in America. "Memory" is a powerful example of her artistic commitment to her people.

The Meadow Mouse

Theodore Roethke (1908–1963) was born in Saginaw, Michigan. He won a Pulitzer Prize, a National Book Award, and a Guggenheim Fellowship. He writes of the natural world and its creatures with precision, tenderness, and even, sometimes, poetic splendor. In some of his poems, the outer world of nature becomes an external representation of his own deepest feelings. "The Meadow Mouse" shows how sensitive, perceptive, and tender Roethke's best nature poetry is.

To be of use

Marge Piercy (1936–   ), who was born in Detroit, Michigan, is both a poet and a novelist. Her books of poetry include *Breaking Camp, Hard Loving,* and *Circles on the Water,* from which "To be of use" was taken. She also has a book of essays, short stories, and reviews entitled *Parti-Colored Blocks for a Quilt.*

The Space

Gary Soto (1952–   ) was born in Fresno, California. Both his poetry and prose exhibit a style and content influenced by his working-class Mexican American background. When he was a child, he worked as a migrant worker. Soto said, in an interview about his desire to become a poet, "I don't think I had any literary aspirations when I was a kid. . . . So my wanting to write poetry was a sort of fluke."

576   Poetry

Objectives

1 To write a poem entitled "Memory"
2 To understand imagery
3 To write about imagery
4 To appreciate the effects of imagery
5 To write a poem with imagery
6 To express individual interests and abilities through an optional activity

Support Material

Teaching Portfolio
Teacher Backup, p. 717
Grammar in Action Worksheet, *Using Commas,* p. 724
Usage and Mechanics Worksheet, p. 726
Vocabulary Check, p. 727
Analyzing Literature Worksheet, *Studying Imagery,* p. 728
Language Worksheet, *Appreciating Vivid Verbs,* p. 729

Selection Test, p. 730
Art Transparency 15: *Automat,* by Edward Hopper

Listening to Literature
"Memory," "The Space"

Prentice Hall Literature Writing Studio

The Creation

James Weldon Johnson (1871–1938) was born in Florida. He was a lawyer, a songwriter, a United States consul to Venezuela and Nicaragua, an executive secretary of the NAACP, and a college professor. "The Creation" is from his most famous book, *God's Trombones*. This volume is both a collection of poetry and a collection of folk sermons. It represents art drawn and shaped from the rich depths of African American spirituality.

Imagery

Imagery means a poet's use of words to create mental pictures, or images, that communicate experience. An image may appeal to any one of the five senses. When Theodore Roethke describes a meadow mouse as "Wriggling like a miniscule puppy," he is using visual imagery to give you a mental picture of the mouse. When Margaret Walker, in "Memory," speaks of "wind-swept streets of cities/on cold and blustery nights," she is using imagery that appeals to our sense of touch, or physical sensation. Imagery is one of the most important resources poets make use of to capture and express experience.

Focus

Choose a partner with whom you will experiment with the use of imagery. Create a series of images to describe an experience you remember vividly. Do not state what the experience was. For example, you might say that "someone was bowling strikes inside my head" to convey the idea of a headache. Your partner will have to guess what your image describes. Take turns creating images and guessing at their meanings. As you read the poems in this section, look for the images that the poets use to convey real and imagined experiences.

Vocabulary

Knowing the following words will help you as you read the poems in this section.

sinister (sin′ is tər) *adj.*: Threatening harm or evil (p. 578, l. 6)

paralytic (par ə lit′ ik) *n.*: A par

alyzed person (p. 580, l. 28)

forsaken (fər sāk′ ən) *adj.*: Abandoned; without hope (p. 580, l. 29)

Guide for Reading 577

James Weldon Johnson became a principal of a public school for African Americans, a newspaper publisher, an attorney, and U.S. Consul in Venezuela and Nicaragua. Ask students if this type of background is what they would expect of a man who wrote a poem about the creation. What might have led him to choose this subject?

Literary Focus To get a better idea of how imagery works, have students make a list of several events or items. Have the students create their own images for each of the events or items and share them with their classmates. Tell them the image must clearly express what is being discussed. Ask if they are able to imagine what their fellow students are describing with their images. Do the students imagine different things? Which images work best, and why?

Prereading Focus The purpose of this exercise is to give the students an opportunity to practice creating images. Lead students to see that the most striking images paint clear, precise pictures that relate to the reader's own experience.

Vocabulary Have the students use each of the vocabulary words in a sentence that creates an image.

Spelling Tip Students may have difficulty with the *cs* combination in *ecstatic*.

Making Connections Another selection you might want to use with "Memory" is "A Dream Deferred," page 594, by Langston Hughes. This poem deals with the same conditions described in Walker's lyric.

A selection you might use with "The Meadow Mouse" is "The Scarlet Ibis," page 181. Like the mouse, the central character in this story can be described as "innocent, hapless, forsaken."

Another selection you can teach with "To be of use" is "I Have a Dream," page 467. Both selections deal with the individual and society.

A selection you might use with "The Space" is "The Sound of the Sea," page 624. Both selections deal with a journey to personal fulfillment.

Alternative Assessment To promote active reading, have students keep a reader's response journal as they read these five poems. Encourage students to respond personally to each poem and to the images that particularly impress them.

Students' observations will enable you to assess their understanding of the poems.

Ask students what it might be like to live without hope of bettering oneself. Then tell them that, in this poem, Margaret Walker writes about the inhabitants of a black ghetto whose lives are bleak and hopeless.

Purpose-Setting Question How does the poet use adjectives to create a troubling mood?

Master Teacher Note Use the overhead projector to show students Art Transparency 15, *Automat,* by Edward Hopper. Ask students to describe the feelings that this scene calls up. Have them speculate about the thoughts and memories of the woman sitting at the table. Then tell them that Margaret Walker's poem "Memory" deals with recollections that are bitter and disturbing.

Vivid adjectives can help set the mood of a poem, and they are used skillfully here by Walker. Ask the students to point out the adjectives that they believe create a feeling of despair or distress in "Memory."

1 Discussion The poet recalls the despondency of the people she sees on the streets. She senses their dissatisfaction and resentment. Ask the students who these people are. Why might they be angry?

Closure and Extension

ANSWERS TO RESPONDING TO THE SELECTION
Your Response

1. Encourage students to select the specific words and phrases they found most vivid.

Recalling

2. Answers may differ but should include such things as memories of

Memory

Margaret Walker

I can remember wind-swept streets of cities
on cold and blustery nights, on rainy days;
heads under shabby felts[1] and parasols
and shoulders hunched against a sharp concern;
5   seeing hurt bewilderment on poor faces,
smelling a deep and sinister unrest
these brooding people cautiously caress;
hearing ghostly marching on pavement stones
and closing fast around their squares of hate.
10 I can remember seeing them alone,
at work, and in their tenements at home.
I can remember hearing all they said:
their muttering protests, their whispered oaths,
and all that spells their living in distress.

---

1. felts: Felt hats.

RESPONDING TO THE SELECTION

Your Response

1. What thoughts and feelings did this poem evoke in you? Explain.

Recalling

2. Describe in general terms the kind of memories the speaker presents in the poem.

Interpreting

3. What kind of lives do the people lead whom the poet remembers?
4. Pick out three phrases that suggest the feelings or spirit of these people. What do these phrases suggest?
5. Pick out three vivid images. Tell what each suggests to you.
6. Do you think that the imagery in the poem is primarily intended to create a picture of the external world—what you could see and hear if you were in it? Or is it intended to communicate the inner lives of the people there? Give reasons for your opinion.

Applying

7. Tell why you think that this poem is or is not a poem of social protest, that is, one that criticizes an injustice in society.

THINKING AND WRITING

Writing Your Own "Memory"

Freewrite about a moment in your life that is vivid in your memory. Then use this freewriting to write a poem titled "Memory." If you wish, imitate Walker's pattern. Her poem has fourteen lines. Most of the lines have five accented syllables. Three times she uses the phrase "I can remember." Try to fit your imagery into this or a similar pattern. When you revise, see if you can think of sharper or more vivid images to suggest your feelings about the experience you are treating.

the city, of poverty, of anger, and of the cold.

Interpreting

3. Answers will differ but should show that the students understand the difficulties of the people's lives and the anger and resentment they feel.
4. Answers will differ. Students should choose phrases that suggest hurt, anger, and suffering.

5. Answers will differ. Students should include vivid images that suggest anger or suffering.
6. Suggested Response: The poem contains descriptions of the outer world, but it mostly communicates feelings—with words such as "hurt," "brooding," and "hate."

Applying

7. Answers will differ. Most students will realize that the descriptions in the poem are an indirect form of protest.

THINKING AND WRITING

Software If students have access to computers, have them use **Bank Street Writer** to complete all stages of this assignment.

The Meadow Mouse

Theodore Roethke

I

In a shoe box stuffed in an old nylon stocking
Sleeps the baby mouse I found in the meadow,
Where he trembled and shook beneath a stick
Till I caught him up by the tail and brought him in,
5 Cradled in my hand,
A little quaker, the whole body of him trembling,
His absurd whiskers sticking out like a cartoon-mouse,
His feet like small leaves,
Little lizard-feet,
10 Whitish and spread wide when he tried to struggle away,
Wriggling like a miniscule[1] puppy.

Now he's eaten his three kinds of cheese and drunk from
  his bottle-cap watering-trough—
So much he just lies in one corner,
His tail curled under him, his belly big
15 As his head; his bat-like ears
Twitching, tilting toward the least sound.

Do I imagine he no longer trembles
When I come close to him?
He seems no longer to tremble.

II

20 But this morning the shoe-box house on the back porch is
  empty.
Where has he gone, my meadow mouse,
My thumb of a child that nuzzled in my palm?—
To run under the hawk's wing,
Under the eye of the great owl watching from the elm-tree,
25 To live by courtesy of the shrike,[2] the snake, the tom-cat.

---

1. **miniscule** (min′ ə skyōol′) adj.: Very small. The normal spelling
is *minuscule*, but the poet chose to use the spelling that appears
here.
2. **shrike** (shrīk) n.: A shrill-voiced bird that feeds on small
animals.

The Meadow Mouse 579

Presentation

Motivation/Prior Knowledge
Have students ever rescued and nursed a wild, baby animal? How did they feel about the animal while they were taking care of it? What did it feel like to return the animal to the wild? Tell them that this poem is about such a situation.

Purpose-Setting Question
What does the meadow mouse in the title symbolize?

1 **Literary Focus** How does the poet use comparisons to create an image of the little mouse? What words especially help the reader to visualize the mouse?

2 **Critical Thinking and Reading** What is the poet saying in this stanza? What is he hoping?

3 **Discussion** What feelings does the poet express here? How does he feel about the mouse?

---

the irony in this, and ask why they think mice are portrayed in fantasy so differently from the way they are viewed in reality.

Ask each student to pick a culture and research the folklore of that culture to find stories featuring mice. Have students tell the stories they find to the class. Discuss how mice are portrayed in different cultures.

Speaking and Listening After students discuss tone and imagery in "Memory," you may want to have them apply the principles they have learned to "The Meadow Mouse." After they read the poem silently, have them brainstorm for adjectives that describe the poem's images. Then you might select volunteers to read the poem to the class. Have them model their readings of "The Meadow Mouse" on the reading of "Memory."

Audiocassette To help students understand the relationship between tone and imagery, you may want to play the reading of "Memory" on the **Listening to Literature** audiocassettes. Discuss how the reader adapts her tone to suit the images.

Multicultural Focus Ask students to come up with stories, folk tales, or fables about mice. Possible responses include *Stuart Little*, by E. B. White, about a mouse born to human parents in New York City who leaves home to seek his fortune; *The Rescuers*, by Margery Sharp, about three mice who rescue a poet from a Norwegian prison; the classic cartoon Mighty Mouse.

You might also want to bring up the role of mice as rescuers in the Walt Disney movie version of Cinderella and in the *Chronicles of Narnia* by C. S. Lewis, which students may know. Discuss the cultural origins of any stories students bring up. Point out that most of these stories, regardless of origin, portray mice as strong and helpful, as well as clever and resourceful. Help students see

4 Discussion The poet has used his experience with the meadow mouse to illustrate a more universal issue, which he addresses in the final stanza. What is the "message" of this poem?

4 | I think of the nestling fallen into the deep grass,
The turtle gasping in the dusty rubble of the highway,
The paralytic stunned in the tub, and the water rising—
All things innocent, hapless,[3] forsaken.

---

3. hapless (hap′ lis) *adj.*: Unfortunate. luckless.

Closure and Extension

ANSWERS TO RESPONDING TO THE SELECTION
Your Response
1. Discuss with students the likely fate that will befall the innocent creatures depicted in the last stanza. Ask them why the disappearance of the mouse brings these images to the poet's mind.

Recalling
2. Answers may differ but should include some of the descriptive information found in the first stanza.
3. The meadow mouse escapes from the shoebox.

Interpreting
4. Suggested Response: The speaker is fond of the little mouse and cares about it. He hopes that the mouse has come to trust him. He is concerned about the mouse after it has gone.
5. Suggested Response: The speaker expresses fear for the mouse's safety after it has gone. He also expresses concern for all helpless creatures.
6. Suggested Response: The mouse is symbolic of all the innocent, gentle creatures, including humans, that exist alone and unprotected in the world.
7. Answers will differ, but students should fully explain why they think a particular image is the most effective.

Applying
8. Answers will differ, but students should be able to support their conclusions with evidence from the text, as well as their own opinions.

580

RESPONDING TO THE SELECTION
Your Response
1. What do you think the poet feels about "All things innocent, hapless, forsaken"?

Recalling
2. Briefly describe the meadow mouse that the speaker has found.
3. What happens to it?

Interpreting
4. Describe the speaker's feelings about the meadow mouse.
5. What new feelings are expressed in the second part of the poem?
6. What is the connection between the last four lines and the rest of the poem?
7. Pick out what you feel is the single most effective image used to describe the mouse. Why did you select this particular image?

Applying
8. Do you think that the speaker's feelings about the meadow mouse are in any way unusual or out of the ordinary? Or are they the feelings of any kind person taking care of a delicate little pet? Discuss this issue.

ANALYZING LITERATURE
Understanding Imagery
   Imagery is the use of words to create word pictures—images—that capture and communicate experience. Though visual imagery is the most common kind of imagery found in literature, a poet may use imagery that appeals to any of the five senses. Imagery may be used to communicate the sights, sounds, and sensations of the external world. It may also, however, be used to express the inner world of thought and emotion.

1. The speaker creates an image of the meadow mouse that appeals to the senses of sight and touch. He calls it "A little quaker, the whole body of him trembling" and describes it as "wriggling like a minuscule puppy." What feelings does this image arouse?
2. The word *nuzzled* in the second section also appeals to these senses. What feelings does it arouse?
3. What feelings are aroused by the images in the last four lines?

THINKING AND WRITING
Writing About Imagery
   Write an essay that begins with and develops the following sentence: In the second part of "The Meadow Mouse," the speaker never talks about his feelings, but he nevertheless expresses them forcefully through images. Develop your essay by pointing out the feelings implied in the various images. When you revise the essay, check your interpretations by asking, "If the speaker used this image, what must he have felt?" Compare your interpretations with those of other students.

580   Poetry

ANSWERS TO ANALYZING LITERATURE

1. Suggested Response: These images make the reader feel protective of the mouse.
2. Suggested Response: This word makes the reader feel as if the mouse is a little human baby.
3. Suggested Response: The images of the last four lines make the reader feel protective of all helpless creatures.

THINKING AND WRITING

Writing Transparency A model of the writing assignment might assist students in developing their essays. Before students begin, you might show them Model 9: *Writing About Poetry* in the **Transparencies for Writing.**

Publishing Student Writing You might want to divide the class into small groups and have students read their essays to their fellow group members.

To be of use

Marge Piercy

The people I love the best
jump into work head first
without dallying in the shallows
and swim off with sure strokes almost
    out of sight.
5 They seem to become natives of that
    element,
the black sleek heads of seals
bouncing like half-submerged balls.

I love people who harness themselves,
    an ox to a heavy cart,
who pull like water buffalo, with
    massive patience,
who strain in the mud and the muck to
10   move things forward,
who do what has to be done, again and
    again.
I want to be with people who submerge
in the task, who go into the fields to
    harvest
and work in a row and pass the bags
    along,

who are not parlor generals and field
15   deserters
but move in a common rhythm
when the food must come in or the fire be
    put out.

The work of the world is common as mud.
Botched, it smears the hands, crumbles to
    dust.
20 But the thing worth doing well done
has a shape that satisfies, clean and evident.
Greek amphoras[1] for wine or oil,
Hopi[2] vases that held corn, are put in
    museums
but you know they were made to be used.
25 The pitcher cries for water to carry
and a person for work that is real.

Marginal brackets: 2 (lines 14–15), 3 (lines 16–17), 4 (lines 20–22), 5 (lines 25–26)

---

1. **amphoras** (am′ fər əz) *n.*: Tall jars that have a narrow neck and base and two handles, used by the ancient Greeks and Romans.
2. **Hopi** (hō′ pē) *n.*: A Pueblo tribe of Indians in northeastern Arizona.

RESPONDING TO THE SELECTION

Your Response

1. Do you admire the qualities of the people who are celebrated in this poem? Why or why not?

Recalling

2. What kind of people does the speaker like?
3. Give two images the author uses to describe these people.

Interpreting

4. Why does the speaker like such people?

5. Explain the meaning of line 18. Do you agree with it? Why or why not?
6. Explain what lines 22–24 suggest. How do these lines relate to the title of the poem?

Applying

7. This poem suggests living and working according to a work ethic—an attitude about and a set of values one has toward work. What is your work ethic, or your attitude about work?

To be of use 581

Presentation

Motivation/Prior Knowledge
Write the following proverb on the blackboard: "The devil finds work for idle hands to do." Discuss what this proverb means. Then have students brainstorm about and discuss other sayings they have heard that reflect a work ethic.

Thematic Focus Poets often search for images that express their sense of self. Discuss with students the idea of finding oneself. What makes each person different from everyone else? Do we recognize ourselves in the people who have raised us and taught us?

Purpose-Setting Question
What is Piercy's attitude toward work in "To be of use"?

1 **Discussion** What is the meaning of this line?

2 **Discussion** To whom or to what type of people is Piercy referring in this line? What does this line suggest about her attitude toward those who do not share her work ethic?

3 **Literary Focus** What image does Piercy create in these lines? Why is this image important to the meaning of the poem? What about the workers is suggested in line 17?

4 **Discussion** What does this line mean? Do you agree with it? Why or why not?

5 **Discussion** Why does Piercy personify the pitcher? How does this line support the theme and title of the poem?

Thematic Response Marge Piercy uses several images to describe those who have influenced her sense of self. Which image do you think most clearly expresses her theme?

Closure and Extension

ANSWERS TO RESPONDING TO THE SELECTION
Your Response
1. Encourage students to compare the qualities of the people found in the poem with those of individuals they know.

Recalling
2. The speaker likes industrious, hard-working people.

3. The author compares these people with images of strong work animals, like the ox and water buffalo, and with field workers during the harvest season.

Interpreting
4. The speaker appreciates these people because of their patience and tenacity and because without them the world would crumble.
5. Answers will differ. This line suggests that all work is common and

is, therefore, equal. No work is better than any other.
6. Answers will differ. These lines suggest that although we exalt the beauty of the tools, we should not divorce them from their purpose.

Applying
7. Answers will differ. Most students will express their pride in their work and their desire to do a job well.

The Space

Gary Soto

West of town,
Near Hermosa's well,
I sleep sometimes—
In a hammock of course—
5 Among avocado trees,
Cane, spider-grass,
The hatchet-faced chula,[1]
The banana's umbrella
Of leaves.
10 It is here
In the spiny brush
Where cocks gabble,
Where the javelina[2]
Lies on its side
15 Like an overturned high-heel.
I say it is enough
To be where the smells
Of creatures
Braid like rope
20 And to know if
The grasses' rustle
Is only
A lizard passing.
It is enough, brother,
25 Listening to a bird coo
A leash of parables,[3]
Keeping an eye
On the moon,
The space
30 Between cork trees
Where the sun first appears.

---

1. chula (choo′ lə) *n*.: Prickly pear, the pear-shaped fruit of a cactus.
2. javelina (ha′ və lē′ nə) *n*.: A wild sow; literally a female mountain pig.
3. parables (par′ ə b'lz) *n*.: Short, simple stories that illustrate a moral or religious lesson.

582 Poetry

RESPONDING TO THE SELECTION

Your Response
1. Does the place that the speaker goes to sound appealing to you? Why or why not?

Recalling
2. Describe the place where the speaker sometimes likes to sleep.

Interpreting
3. Other than the physical space the speaker describes, what other meaning of space is suggested in the poem?
4. The speaker twice uses the phrase, "it is enough." What is the impact of repeating this statement?
5. What is the speaker's attitude about the space he describes?

Applying
6. Whether you live in the country or a city, you can have a space that is your own. Describe your special space and your attitude toward it. Then explain why it is important to have a private space.

CRITICAL THINKING AND READING

Appreciating the Effects of Imagery
An image is a word or phrase that appeals to one or more of the five senses. Writers use images to re-create sensory experiences with words and to aid the reader in understanding the poem. In "The Space," Soto creates images that appeal to four of the five senses: sight, sound, touch, and smell. For example, the line "In the spiny brush" appeals to the sense of touch; "spiny" suggests that the brush is prickly and full of thorns.

1. Name at least one image from the poem that appeals to each of the following senses: sight, sound, touch, and smell.
2. What effect do these images have on your understanding of the poem?

The Creation

James Weldon Johnson

And God stepped out on space,
And he looked around and said:
I'm lonely—
I'll make me a world.

5 And far as the eye of God could see
Darkness covered everything,
Blacker than a hundred midnights
Down in a cypress swamp.

Then God smiled,
10 And the light broke,
And the darkness rolled up on one side,
And the light stood shining on the other,
And God said: That's good!

Then God reached out and took the light in his hands,
15 And God rolled the light around in his hands
Until he made the sun;
And he set that sun a-blazing in the heavens.
And the light that was left from making the sun
God gathered it up in a shining ball
20 And flung it against the darkness,
Spangling the night with the moon and stars.
Then down between
The darkness and the light
He hurled the world;
25 And God said: That's good!

Then God himself stepped down—
And the sun was on his right hand,
And the moon was on his left;
The stars were clustered about his head,
30 And the earth was under his feet.
And God walked, and where he trod
His footsteps hollowed the valleys out
And bulged the mountains up.

The Creation   583

Fine art, *The Creation,* 1935, by Aaron Douglas. Aaron Douglas (1899–1979) was an African American painter who settled in Harlem in 1924 in search of a more meaningful outlet for his art than teaching. During his years there, he gave up his attachment to academic realism and devoted his painting to the expression of the black experience, using African motifs and a modern style. His example inspired many black artists of that time to turn toward their African roots.

The Creation shows the unique "synthetic cubist" style favored by Douglas. He divides his canvas geometrically—here with a circle—defined by flatly painted variations of color. An image of a man with recognizable black features dominates the stylized landscape, validating the place of blacks in God's creation of the human race.

You might ask students the following questions:

1. What feelings does this painting capture?
2. What shapes are important in this picture?
3. Why do you think Douglas did not choose to make his painting more realistic?
4. Does this picture go well with the poem? Explain.

3 Critical Thinking and Reading
What image of God does this stanza present?

THE CREATION
Aaron Douglas
Studio Museum of Harlem

<blockquote>

Then he stopped and looked and saw
35   That the earth was hot and barren.
So God stepped over to the edge of the world
And he spat out the seven seas—
He batted his eyes, and the lightnings flashed—
He clapped his hands, and the thunders rolled—
40   And the waters above the earth came down,
The cooling waters came down.

</blockquote>

3

584   Poetry

Grammar in Action

Commas are used to separate adjectives of equal rank. To test whether adjectives are of equal rank, you can insert *and* between them to see if the sentence still makes sense. Another test is to see whether the adjectives can be reversed.

> Sentence: The *rugged, jagged* incline was difficult to climb.

> Test 1: The *rugged and jagged* incline was difficult to climb. (makes sense)

> Test 2: The *jagged, rugged* incline was difficult to climb. (makes sense)

> Result: The adjectives are coordinate; use a comma between them.

Do not use commas between adjectives if they must stay in a specific order, if they do not make sense when joined by *and*, or if they are joined by *and* already.

> Sentence: After *several long* days, the job was finished.
> Nonsense: After *long several* days. . . .

Then the green grass sprouted,
And the little red flowers blossomed,
The pine tree pointed his finger to the sky,
45 And the oak spread out his arms,
The lakes cuddled down in the hollows of the ground,
And the rivers ran down to the sea;
And God smiled again,
And the rainbow appeared,
50 And curled itself around his shoulder.

Then God raised his arm and he waved his hand
Over the sea and over the land,
And he said: Bring forth! Bring forth!
And quicker than God could drop his hand,
55 Fishes and fowls
And beasts and birds
Swam the rivers and the seas,
Roamed the forests and the woods,
And split the air with their wings.
60 And God said: That's good!

Then God walked around,
And God looked around
On all that he had made.
He looked at his sun,
65 And he looked at his moon,
And he looked at his little stars;
He looked on his world
With all its living things,
And God said: I'm lonely still.

70 Then God sat down—
On the side of a hill where he could think;
By a deep, wide river he sat down;
With his head in his hands,
God thought and thought,
75 Till he thought: I'll make me a man!

Up from the bed of the river
God scooped the clay;
And by the bank of the river
He kneeled him down;
80 And there the great God Almighty
Who lit the sun and fixed it in the sky,

The Creation 585

4 Critical Thinking and Reading
Have the students explain what they imagine as they read this section. What makes Johnson's images work so well?

5 Discussion Ask the students why God was still dissatisfied after His immense acts of creation. Why was He still lonely?

Electronic Handbook You might want students to review the use of commas to separate adjectives before they complete the Grammar in Action activities. If students have access to the Language Master 6000, have them enter the access symbol , and press the GRAMMAR key to obtain information on this topic.

Nonsense: After *several and long* days. . . .
    Result: The adjectives are not coordinate; do not use a comma between them.

The following lines from "The Creation" show adjectives being used together:

. . . the earth was *hot and barren*. . . .

And the *little red* flowers blossomed. . . .

By a *deep, wide* river, he sat down. . . .

Student Activity 1. Explain whether or not Johnson followed these rules in the three lines quoted from "The Creation."

Student Activity 2. Write a short paragraph describing someone making something. Use at least two sentences in which adjectives are correctly combined.

585

6 Discussion What does this passage suggest about man's nature and being?

Reader's Response Which image in "The Creation" did you think was the most effective? Why?

Closure and Extension

ANSWERS TO RESPONDING TO THE SELECTION
Your Response

1. Suggest that students make a list of creative endeavors they enjoy and the reasons why.

Recalling

2. In "The Creation," God first creates the earth, then light—the sun, moon, and stars—the physical features of the earth, the oceans, thunderstorms and rain, plants, animals, and finally, mankind.
3. Answers will differ, but should express a logical reason for this chain of events.

Interpreting

4. Answers will differ but should include all the items from question 1. There is clearly a movement from inanimate to animate and also from creatures of lesser intelligence to man.
5. Answers will differ but may include impressions of strength, creativity, kindness, loneliness, power, majesty, or humanity.
6. Answers will differ, but students should include specific images found in the text to illustrate the impressions they described in question 4.

Applying

7. Answers will differ, but students will most likely feel that the poem would become more serious if it were presented as a sermon. Also, they may feel that the poet would then be more concerned with getting a message across in addition to capturing the imagination of the listener.

586

Who flung the stars to the most far corner of the night,
Who rounded the earth in the middle of his hand;
This Great God,
85 Like a mammy bending over her baby,
Kneeled down in the dust
Toiling over a lump of clay
Till he shaped it in his own image:

Then into it he blew the breath of life,
90 And man became a living soul.
Amen. Amen.

RESPONDING TO THE SELECTION

Your Response

1. (a) Why do you think that people like to create things? (b) What would you like to create? Why?

Recalling

2. Describe the progression God follows in creating the world. What did he create first, what next, and so on?
3. Why did he create the world and, finally, man?

Interpreting

4. After reviewing your answer to question 2, describe the system or kind of order God followed in creating the world.
5. Describe the impression of God created by the poem. Explain how specific images contributed to this impression.
6. Select one image applied to God that you consider especially imaginative and effective. What does this image suggest? Why do you consider it effective?

Applying

7. Johnson considered "The Creation" a sermon as well as a poem. Does the effect or meaning of "The Creation" change if it is read as a sermon? Give reasons for your opinion.

THINKING AND WRITING

Writing a Poem With Imagery

Write a brief poem that describes somebody doing or making something. Like Johnson and the other poets in this section, use vivid, imaginative images to make your subject come alive for the reader. When you have selected a subject, you might first write a clear description in prose. Then, when you describe the subject in verse, concentrate on using effective images. When you revise, see if you can improve the imagery in any way. Finally, share your completed poem with your classmates.

LEARNING OPTION

Art. Johnson creates clear, vivid images in this poem. Illustrate the poem either by drawing or painting pictures to represent selected images from "The Creation" or by creating a collage to represent the poem as a whole. When you are finished, display your artwork in the classroom.

586 Poetry

THINKING AND WRITING

Software If students have access to computers, have them use the *Develop a Paragraph* feature of **Writer's Helper** to write their prose descriptions.

Publishing Student Writing You might want to have volunteers read their poems to the class.

Alternative Assessment *Peer Review* In pairs or in groups of four, have students assess each other's stories by responding to the following questions:

What is the subject of the poem?

What vivid, imaginative images does the writer include in his or her poem?

What suggestions do you have for the writer to improve the imagery and enhance the presentation of the subject?

To validate the peer review, have students incorporate those suggestions they find helpful in a revision of their descriptions.

LEARNING OPTION

Visual and kinesthetic learners will find this activity exciting. Vary the activity by having students create booklets that display the pictures in an appropriate order.

Figurative Language

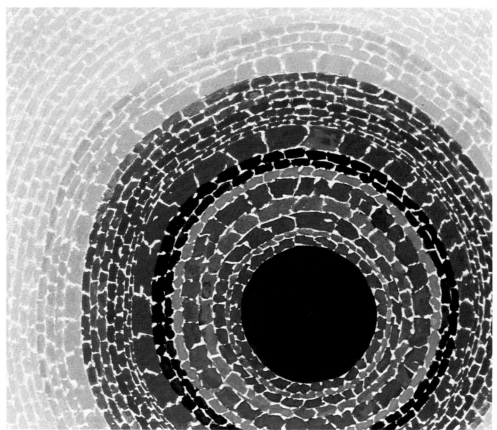

ECLIPSE, MARCH 1970
A. W. Thomas
National Museum of American Art,
Smithsonian Institution

Humanities Note

Fine art, *Eclipse,* by A.W. Thomas. The contemporary American artist A.W. Thomas has presented a decorative interpretation of a total eclipse. Concentric bands of color radiate from the black center of the sun. The fields of color are fragmented into a mosaiclike pattern. Thomas has rendered the simple observation of a natural phenomenon with dynamic energy.

Preparation

More About the Authors You might want to tell students that, of all nineteenth-century poets, **Alfred, Lord Tennyson,** was peraps the most familiar with science. He was familiar, for instance, with the latest discoveries in astronomy and geology. Ask students whether they believe breakthroughs in science today can be a source of inspiration for poets.

William Wordsworth is regarded as one of England's great nature poets. Ask students to name the authors and poets they have read whose love of and interest in nature has made an impression on them. Ask why some poets have affected them more than others.

Consider telling students that **Langston Hughes** was an excellent reciter of poetry and that he wrote many of his poems with public performance in mind. Ask students whether they have ever attended a poetry reading. Also, ask them why a reading might be a good introduction to a poet's work.

You might want to tell students that **Emily Dickinson** did not write for publication—only eight of her poems appeared in print during her lifetime. Have students consider the advantages and disadvantages of such a situation.

You may want to tell students that **Carl Sandburg** had a great deal of rough and ready experience. He served as a soldier and worked as a salesman, fireman, and newspaper reporter, to name only a few of the trades he followed. Have students consider whether such experience is necessary or helpful for a poet.

The Eagle

Alfred, Lord Tennyson (1809–1892) took an early interest in the classical literature of Greece and Rome. Later, he carefully studied the great English poets of the early nineteenth century. Their nature poetry inspired such impressive works as "The Eagle." This short lyric illustrates Tennyson's ability to re-create a natural scene so that it almost becomes the expression of a state of mind and feeling.

I Wandered Lonely as a Cloud

William Wordsworth (1770–1850) was born on the northern fringe of the Lake District of England. This rural area inspired most of his outstanding nature poetry, and his fame in turn transformed the area into the poetic center of England. Wordsworth thought of poetry as "emotion recollected in tranquility"—a concept perfectly illustrated in "I Wandered Lonely as a Cloud." Written in 1804, the poem is a recollection, or remembrance, of an experience the poet had two years earlier.

Dream Deferred, Dreams

Langston Hughes (1902–1967) was born in Joplin, Missouri. As a young man he held a variety of jobs—teacher, ranch hand, farmer, seaman, and night club cook, among others. He drew on all these experiences and, above all, on the experience of being an African American man to create his great body of literary work. "Dream Deferred" and "Dreams" illustrate his ability to express the spirit of black America.

The Sky Is Low

Emily Dickinson (1830–1886) was born and lived most of her life in Amherst, Massachusetts. Outwardly, her life was uneventful. The range and depth of her inner life, however, is suggested by the fact that she wrote at least 1,775 poems. The subjects of her poems—God, nature, love, death, and others—were conventional ones for her time. What makes the poems outstanding is her genius. "The Sky Is Low" illustrates the imaginative power with which Dickinson could describe a passing moment of New England weather.

588 *Poetry*

Objectives

1 To understand similes
2 To write a poem using a simile
3 To analyze a poem
4 To understand metaphors
5 To understand personification
6 To respond to literary criticism
7 To write a poem
8 To express individual interests and abilities through optional activities

Support Material

Teaching Portfolio
Teacher Backup, p. 733
Grammar in Action Worksheet, *Using Punctuation in Poetry*, p. 740
Usage and Mechanics Worksheet, p. 742
Vocabulary Check, p. 743
Analyzing Literature Worksheet, *Understanding Figurative Language*, p. 745

Splinter

Carl Sandburg (1878–1967) was born in Illinois to Swedish immigrants. Much of his poetry was inspired by the spirit and tempo of city life. "Splinter," however, shows the kind of poetry he wrote when inspired by the prairies of America. The brevity of the poem and the imaginative image of the last line show the influence of the Imagist poets, who relied on sharp, clear visual images to carry the meaning of a poem.

Figurative Language

Figurative language is language that uses figures of speech. A figure of speech is a way of saying one thing and meaning another. Three of the most important figures of speech are simile, metaphor, and personification. A **simile** compares one thing to another using the word *like* or *as;* for example, "This bread is like rubber." A **metaphor** compares one thing to another without using *like* or *as*— "Genius is a fountain." **Personification** gives human characteristics to an animal, object, or idea—"The sun's a wizard."

Focus

In small groups brainstorm to list experiences about which you have strong reactions. For each experience you have listed, work together to write a simile, a metaphor, or an example of personification that indicates your reaction. Here is an example of a simile: "Last Saturday was like a roller-coaster ride." When you have finished writing your figures of speech, share them with the other groups. As you read the poems in this section, notice how the figures of speech enrich meaning and add vividness and force to expression.

Vocabulary

Knowing the following words will help you as you read the poems in this section.

azure (azh′ ər) *adj.*: Blue (p. 591, l. 3)

host (hōst) *n.*: A great number (p. 592, l. 4)

glee (glē) *n.*: Joy; (p. 592, l. 14)

pensive (pen′ siv) *adj.*: Thinking deeply (p. 592, l. 20)

bliss (blis) *n.*: Great joy or happiness (p. 592, l. 22)

deferred (di furd′) *v.*: Put off until a future time (p. 594, l. 1)

fester (fes′ tər) *v.*: Form pus (p. 594, l. 4)

Literary Focus Tell students that using figurative language adds color and interest to our speech and writing. Ask them to consider the fact that they themselves probably use figurative language every day. We use figurative language most in descriptions. Have students ever described an item or an event to a friend by comparing it with something else? Have they ever thought of an inanimate object in human terms? Invite students to describe something, first using literal language, then using figurative language. What is the difference? How does the use of figurative language enhance their descriptions?

Prereading Focus You might want to lead into the activity by holding a class discussion in which students share examples of similes, metaphors, and personification. Which examples do students find most striking? Why?

Vocabulary Have the **less advanced** students read each of the words aloud in a sentence, so that you can be sure they understand their meanings and are able to pronounce them.

Spelling Tip Write the words *defer, deferred* on the board. Tell students that when a word ends with a consonant-vowel-consonant, usually we double the final consonant before adding a suffix beginning with a vowel.

Language Worksheet, *Using Context Clues,* p. 746
Selection Test, p. 747
Art Transparency 16: *The Thankful Poor,* by Henry O. Tanner

Listening to Literature
"The Eagle," "I Wandered Lonely as a Cloud," "Dreams," "Dream Deferred"

Prentice Hall Literature Writing Studio

Alternative Assessment To promote active reading, have your students keep a reader's response journal as they read these six poems. Ask students to focus their observations on the figurative language in each poem that impresses them as enriching the meaning and adding vividness to the poems. Encourage students to respond personally to each poem and to the examples of figurative language that have special impact on them. Which poems work best for them? Why?

Students' observations will enable you to assess their understanding of the poems.

Motivation/Prior Knowledge
Have students ever watched an eagle fly or dive? What are their images of eagles? Tell them that Tennyson expresses his impression of eagles in this poem.

Master Teacher Note This poem is written in rhymed verse. Ask students what end words they would substitute if they were to rewrite the poem in unrhymed verse. Would the poem be made more or less vivid by their changes?

Making Connections A contrasting selection that you may want to use with "The Eagle" is "The Meadow Mouse," page 579.

Purpose-Setting Question How successful is Tennyson in using language to create his image of the eagle?

1 Literary Focus Explain to students that a simile is a comparison between apparently unlike things using the words *like* or *as*. Point out the simile in line 6. How does the use of the simile here enhance the image of the eagle's dive?

2 Discussion What words in the poem give the eagle a majestic bearing? In the first stanza, how is it clear that the eagle rules the sky? in the second stanza, what is the reason for the very deliberate opposition of the words "crawls" and "falls"?

Humanitites Note

Fine art, *Eagle in a Snowstorm*, by Katsushika Hokusai (1760–1849). Tell students that Hokusai produced a tremendous number of works and that his landscapes are known for their sense of drama.

590

The Eagle
Alfred, Lord Tennyson

He clasps the crag with crooked hands;
Close to the sun in lonely lands,
Ring'd with the azure world, he stands.

The wrinkled sea beneath him crawls;
5 He watches from his mountain walls,
And like a thunderbolt he falls.

EAGLE IN A SNOWSTORM (detail)
Hokusai
*The Harari Collection of Japanese Paintings
and Drawings*

RESPONDING TO THE SELECTION

Your Response
1. If you were to attribute human traits to an eagle, what human traits would you say it had?

Recalling
2. Describe the scene "The Eagle" presents.

Interpreting
3. Since no spot on earth is literally "Close to the sun," how would you interpret this phrase figuratively?
4. Interpret the phrase "Ring'd with the azure world."

Applying
5. Compare "The Eagle" with the following excerpt from the *World Book Encyclopedia*. What does the poem express that the prose description does not?

> At close range, eagles look fierce and proud. As a result, they are pictured as fierce, courageous hunters. Some eagles soar high in the air hunting for food.

590 *Poetry*

Because of this, eagles have long been symbols of grace and power.

ANALYZING LITERATURE

Understanding Similes

A **simile** is a figure of speech in which one thing is compared to another using the word *like* or *as*. Like other figures of speech, similes enable poets to suggest a great deal in a very few words.

1. The last line of "The Eagle" consists of the simile "And like a thunderbolt he falls." Tell at least four qualities that a swooping eagle and a thunderbolt have in common.
2. In view to your answer to question 1, explain why this simile is an effective figure of speech.

LEARNING OPTION

Writing. Imagine that you are on a hike on a mountain trail and you spot an eagle. Write a brief journal entry of the sighting, describing in detail what you saw and how you felt about it.

You might want to ask students the following questions:
1. What is dramatic about Hokusai's eagle?
2. Compare and contrast this eagle with Tennyson's.

Closure and Extension

ANSWERS TO RESPONDING TO THE SELECTION
Your Response
1. Encourage students to share experiences in which they might have seen an eagle. Suggest that they examine the painting by Hokusai for additional inspiration.

Recalling
2. The eagle is perched on a high seaside cliff, watching for his prey. He then dives down to catch a small animal or fish.

Interpreting
3. Suggested Response: The eagle is perched high above everything else and is, therefore, "close to the sun" in relation to his surroundings.

MULTICULTURAL CONNECTION

The Symbolism of the Eagle

The eagle, the subject of Tennyson's poem, has long been one of the world's most recognizable symbols, representing such qualities as grace, power, and authority. Generally regarded as the "king of birds," the eagle has often been associated with royalty. For example, it was the symbol of King Charlemagne of France, of the Russian Romanov dynasty, and of the Hapsburgs, emperors of Austria. The eagle has also figured in the myths of South America, the South Pacific, India, Persia, and Greece.

Origins in the Middle East. Scholars think that the eagle was first used as a symbol in the Middle East—among the ancient Babylonians, Hittites, and Assyrians. The eagle was often depicted as a special companion to the gods and symbolized their divine power. Perhaps the eagle was chosen for this role because of the belief that it could gaze directly at the sun without being blinded—a sign of closeness to the gods. This association with divine strength and authority probably led ancient Sumerians, Egyptians, and Romans to use the eagle in decorating arms and banners.

Victorious over evil. In Babylon the image of an eagle fighting a snake represented victory over evil. This image also appears in the folklore of Native Americans, Melanesians, Polynesians, and peoples of New Zealand, where, oddly enough, snakes didn't exist. In addition, the much-loved *Arabian Nights* include the story of Roc, a giant eagle who is described as an enemy of snakes. Finally, the image of the eagle and the serpent can also be found on modern-day Mexico's official seal and flag, a reminder of an Aztec legend about the founding of their capital, Tenochtitlán (now Mexico City), on the site where an eagle was found devouring a snake.

Varied symbolic meanings. Throughout history the eagle has assumed a variety of symbolic meanings for people of different cultures. For example, the eagle was a bird of warning to the superstitious Romans. The ancient Hebrews and early Christians, on the other hand, saw it as representing the flight of the soul to heaven.

For many Native Americans, the eagle represents the living souls of their ancestors and is often featured on totem poles to commemorate them. Eagle feathers are prized by almost all Native American peoples in North America, and are used in ceremonial costumes and headdresses. For the Sioux, the feathers symbolize victory in battle. Such groups as the Iroquois and Delaware believe the feathers have magical healing powers.

An American symbol. In the United States, the eagle has assumed the role of a national symbol, representing freedom and courage. In fact, the eagle has been the central image on the American national seal since 1782. A deliberate effort seems to have been made to represent the nation as peace-loving but ready to fight if necessary: The eagle is clutching both an olive branch (symbolizing peace) and arrows, but it is looking toward the olive branch.

Exploring on Your Own

Find out which nations or organizations presently use the eagle as their symbol. Investigate more about the meaning of eagles and other birds used as symbols in various cultures.

Multicultural Connection   591

4. The "azure world" refers to the sky. The eagle is sitting very high on the top of a rocky cliff; there is nothing around him but the sky.

Applying

5. Answers will differ, but students should suggest that the poem appeals to the emotions and that it goes beyond the mere facts. The poem describes the eagle as a living, powerful animal, which the prose entry does not do. The poem also provides the reader with a much more vivid image of an eagle.

ANSWERS TO ANALYZING LITERATURE

1. Answers will differ but might include the ideas that a thunderbolt and an eagle are powerful, that they are both fast, that they both move through the sky, and that they can both be dangerous.

2. The simile is effective because the reader is provided with an instant sense of the eagle's nature, without having to read a literal list of all its qualities.

LEARNING OPTION

This activity will appeal to visual learners. You might vary the activity by having students describe their imaginary experience orally.

Motivation/Prior Knowledge
Have students ever seen anything in nature that was so beautiful that they wanted to talk or write about it? Tell them that a group of daffodils inspired such a feeling in Wordsworth.

Purpose-Setting Question What mood does the title suggest?

1 Literary Focus An effective use of figurative language adds to the meaning of a poem or to the vividness of the images. Figurative language needs to be original and clear. Have students find and evaluate the effectiveness of these uses of figurative language:
a. simile (an expressed comparison)
b. hyperbole (exaggeration for effect)
c. personification (giving human characteristics to inanimate objects)
   Ask students to point out other examples of figurative language as they read the rest of the poem.

2 Discussion The poet uses the image of the daffodils to establish the theme, or the message, of the poem. Ask students to paraphrase the last stanza so that they clearly express the theme of the poem.

Reader's Response If you were to wander "lonely as a cloud," what would you see?

I Wandered Lonely as a Cloud

William Wordsworth

I wandered lonely as a cloud
That floats on high o'er vales[1] and hills,
When all at once I saw a crowd,
A host, of golden daffodils;
5   Beside the lake, beneath the trees,
Fluttering and dancing in the breeze.

Continuous as the stars that shine
And twinkle on the milky way,
They stretched in never-ending line
10 Along the margin of a bay:
Ten thousand saw I at a glance,
Tossing their heads in sprightly dance.

The waves beside them danced; but they
Outdid the sparkling waves in glee;
15 A poet could not but be gay,
In such a jocund[2] company;
I gazed—and gazed—but little thought
What wealth the show to me had brought:

For oft,[3] when on my couch I lie
20 In vacant or in pensive mood,
They flash upon that inward eye
Which is the bliss of solitude;
And then my heart with pleasure fills,
And dances with the daffodils.

---

1. o'er vales: Over valleys.
2. jocund (jäk′ ənd) *adj.*: Cheerful.
3. oft: Often.

Grammar in Action

Poets sometimes take liberties with **punctuation** to clarify their meaning or to emphasize an idea. This practice can be effective if done carefully and with moderation. Poets, for instance, will use a comma at the end of a line where a comma would not appear in prose, or they will put a period at the end of a word group that is not a sentence.

Generally, in poetry, commas suggest a pause; semicolons, a longer pause; periods, full stops. Dashes usually set off items for emphasis, and colons show that an explanation follows. Study these lines from the Wordsworth poem:

13 The waves beside them danced; but they
14 Outdid the sparkling waves in glee;
15 A poet could not but be gay,
16 In such a jocund company;
17 I gazed—and gazed—but little thought
18 What wealth the show to me had brought:

Closure and Extension

ANSWERS TO RESPONDING TO THE SELECTION
Your Response

1. Before students begin, have them identify figures of speech in Wordsworth's poem. Encourage them to create similar devices for their own descriptions.

Recalling

2. The speaker sees many daffodils fluttering in the breeze beside a lake and underneath some trees.

Interpreting

3. Suggested Response: "I wandered lonely as a cloud" is a comparison of the poet's walk to a single cloud floating in the sky. The phrase "Continuous as the stars that shine" compares the many daffodils to the appearance of the stars in the Milky Way at night.
4. Suggested Response: The poet is amazed, surprised, and overcome by the beauty of the daffodils. He gazes at them and feels happy.
5. Suggested Response: "Wealth" refers to the fact that the poet now has a beautiful memory that he can use to cheer himself up when he is bored or unhappy.

Applying

6. Answers will differ, but most students will indicate that the beauty of such scenes can be inspiring.

THINKING AND WRITING

◆ **Software** If students have access to computers, you may have them use **Bank Street Writer** to complete all phases of the assignment.

RESPONDING TO THE SELECTION

Your Response
1. Describe a beautiful natural scene that made an impression on you.

Recalling
2. Describe the scene the speaker suddenly comes upon in his wandering.

Interpreting
3. Find two similes in which the comparison is indicated by the word *as*. In each simile, what is compared to what? What is suggested by each simile?
4. What effect does the scene have on the speaker while he is present?
5. What "wealth" is he later aware of?

Applying
6. Of what value to humans are natural scenes such as the one this poem presents?

THINKING AND WRITING

Writing a Poem Using a Simile
Review the list you made before reading "The Eagle." Select one of the experiences from it (or, if you wish, a different one). Write a short poem that leads up to a simile that suggests your view of or feeling about the experience. You might begin with a simple literal description of the experience, and then use the simile to convey its meaning. Be sure to let your imagination suggest an appropriate, effective simile. When you revise, remove unnecessary or ineffective details from the poem. Try to make each word count. Share your poem with your classmates.

I Wandered Lonely as a Cloud   593

The semicolons in lines 13, 14, and 16 separate four main clauses and show their equality. The comma at the end of line 15, though not required by punctuation rules, suggests a brief pause. The dashes in line 17, also not required by the rules, emphasize the repeated verb. Notice that Wordsworth always has a good reason for taking liberties with punctuation.

Student Activity 1. Examine other marks of punctuation in this poem. Which marks follow the rules and which are added by the poet to emphasize or clarify an idea?

Student Activity 2. Add a stanza of your own to Wordsworth's poem. Take liberties with punctuation to emphasize or clarify your meaning. Then write a brief paragraph justifying your violation of the rules.

594

Dream Deferred

Langston Hughes

Harlem

What happens to a dream deferred?

Does it dry up
like a raisin in the sun?
Or fester like a sore—
5 And then run?
Does it stink like rotten meat?
Or crust and sugar over—
like a syrupy sweet?

Maybe it just sags
10 like a heavy load.

Or does it explode?

RESPONDING TO THE SELECTION

Your Response
1. Describe what your life would be like if you were prevented from pursuing your dreams or goals.

Recalling
2. List the verbs used to indicate what can happen to "a dream deferred."

Interpreting
3. Harlem, in New York City, is one of the largest and most famous African American communities in the world. What does the mention of Harlem imply about the subject of this poem?
4. With what kind of dream do you think the poem is concerned?
5. In view of your answers to the preceding questions, interpret the five similes. What do you think the speaker is suggesting in each?

6. Interpret the last line.

Applying
7. Discuss why people need to feel they can fulfill their dreams.

THINKING AND WRITING

Analyzing a Poem
Write an essay for your school literary magazine in which you interpret the meaning of Hughes's poem. Since the poem is written entirely in figurative language, primarily similes, your interpretation should be based on a careful analysis of these figures of speech. When you have written a satisfactory first draft, revise it so that all your thoughts and suggestions support a single idea.

594   Poetry

Dreams

Langston Hughes

1
Hold fast to dreams
For if dreams die
Life is a broken-winged bird
That cannot fly.

2
5   Hold fast to dreams
For when dreams go
Life is a barren field
Frozen with snow.

RESPONDING TO THE SELECTION

Your Response

1. (a) What are your goals and dreams? (b) How does having these goals and dreams affect your life?

Recalling

2. To what does the speaker compare life in the first stanza and in the second stanza?

Interpreting

3. Interpret the metaphors. What does each suggest about life?

4. Restate in your own words the advice that this poem offers.

Applying

5. The American poet Delmore Schwartz once wrote, "In dreams begin responsibilities." How might Langston Hughes interpret this statement? Base your answer on the two poems you have just read.

ANALYZING LITERATURE

Understanding Metaphors

A **metaphor** is a comparison of one thing to another without the use of *like* or *as* or a similar word. In a metaphor, one thing is said *to be* another—for example, "Life *is* a broken-winged bird . . ."

1. Hughes might have written "Dreams" entirely in literal language, without the metaphors in lines 3–4 and 7–8. What do these metaphors contribute to the meaning of the poem?

2. Change the two metaphors into similes by adding *like*. Tell why this change does or does not alter the effect or meaning of "Dreams."

Dreams 595

595

The Sky Is Low

Emily Dickinson

The Sky is low—the Clouds are mean.
A Traveling Flake of Snow
Across a Barn or through a Rut
Debates if it will go—

5 A Narrow Wind complains all Day
How some one treated him.
Nature, like Us is sometimes caught
Without her Diadem.[1]

---

1. diadem (di′ ə dem) *n.*: Crown.

RESPONDING TO THE SELECTION

Your Response

1. Why do you think people so often interpret natural phenomena in terms of human emotions?

Recalling

2. Describe the scene.

Interpreting

3. What does "mean" suggest about the clouds?
4. What does "debates" suggest about the movement of the snowflake?
5. What impression of the wind do you get from lines 5–6?
6. Restate in your own words the meaning of lines 7–8.

Applying

7. How would you reply to someone who said that this poem is merely a weather report in rhyme?

ANALYZING LITERATURE

Understanding Personification

Personification is a figure of speech that represents nonhuman or lifeless things as if they had the qualities of living humans. When Wordsworth, in "I Wandered Lonely as a Cloud," describes the daffodils as "Tossing their heads in sprightly dance," he is using personification.

1. Point out at least two examples of personification in "The Sky Is Low," and explain how each fulfills the definition of this figure of speech.
2. Explain why Dickinson's use of personification is so effective. Could she have written an equally effective poem in plain, literal language?

CAP BON AMI, 1961 (detail)
Samuel Reindorf

Humanities Note

Fine Art, *Cap Bon Ami,* 1961 (detail), by Samuel Reindorf. Born in Poland in 1914, Reindorf immigrated to the United States and now lives in Mexico. He studied at the American Artists School, New York City, and has won many prizes for his work.

In *Cap Bon Ami,* Reindorf depicts a seaside scene, skillfully contrasting the textures of earth, water, stone, and sky.

You might want to use the following questions with this picture:

1. What kind of weather does the artist depict?
2. Does this picture go well with Dickinson's poem? Explain.

THINKING AND WRITING

Responding to Criticism

The poet and critic Conrad Aiken once wrote that Emily Dickinson's nature poems "are often superficial, a mere affectionate playing with the smaller things that give her delight . . ." Write an essay in which you explain why you think that Aiken's remark can or cannot be fairly applied to "The Sky Is Low." Before you write, decide whether or not the poem is superficial. Your reasons should be based squarely on the poem. Your first draft should consist of your judgment about the poem and your supporting reasons. When you revise the draft, check that you have not supported your opinion merely by restating it in different words. Compare your essay with those of your classmates. How many agreed with Aiken? How many disagreed?

LEARNING OPTION

Writing. Write a poem in which you describe an outdoor scene: You can describe a day in the park, a walk on the beach, or a stroll down a city street. Use personification in your poem. Review "I Wandered Lonely as a Cloud" and "The Sky Is Low" for examples of personification. When you have finished your first draft, choose a partner and read your drafts aloud to each other. After you have commented on each other's work, revise your poems. Then share your work with the class.

The Sky Is Low 597

ANSWERS TO ANALYZING LITERATURE

1. Answers will differ but might include the images of the mean clouds, the debating snowflake, and the complaining wind; all of these are examples of personification because they describe nonhuman things in terms of human behavior.
2. Answers will differ but should express the idea that the poem could not have been as effectively written without some use of figurative language, especially personification, because the poet is using the behavior of the weather to comment on the behavior of people.

THINKING AND WRITING

Writing Transparency Students might find it helpful to see a model of their writing assignment. Before students write, you may wish to show them Model 8: *Literary Analysis* in the **Transparencies for Writing.**

Publishing Student Writing You might want to collect the essays in a looseleaf book.

LEARNING OPTION

Visual learners will find this activity stimulating. To vary the activity, you might want students to illustrate their poems. ———

597

Closure and Extension

ANSWERS TO RESPONDING TO THE SELECTION
Your Response

1. You might want to have students brainstorm for natural phenomena and emotions associated with each.

Recalling

2. The scene is of an overcast, somewhat windy, winter day with snow flurries.

Interpreting

3. Suggested Response: "mean" suggests that the clouds are gray and threatening snow.
4. Suggested Response: "Debates" suggests that the snowflake is being tossed about by the wind before it settles.
5. Answers may differ but might include the concept that the wind is light but sharp and cold.
6. Answers will differ but should express the idea that Nature, like human beings, is not always perfect.

Applying

7. Answers will differ, but students should realize that there is another purpose to the poem besides the description of a winter day. Dickinson is also commenting on human behavior.

Motivation/Prior Knowledge
Ask students to tell how they know when the summer is over and the fall has begun. Is the first cold day a sign? Is it the first red leaves they see on the trees? How do they feel when seasons change? Tell them that this poem is about such a transition.

Purpose-Setting Question What images does the title of this poem bring to mind?

1 **Discussion** How does Sandburg capture the exact moment when one season ends and another begins? What is the literal meaning of the metaphor in the last line?

2 **Enrichment** Tell students that Japanese *haiku* often express images like the one in "Splinter." Explain to students that a *haiku* is made of three lines with a total of seventeen syllables arranged in a five-seven-five syllable pattern.

Closure and Extension

ANSWERS TO RESPONDING TO THE SELECTION
Your Response
1. Suggest that students close their eyes and visualize scenes from each season. Encourage them to focus on specific aspects of the scenes to recall accompanying sounds.
2. Lead students to see that there are positive as well as negative aspects to the coming of fall. Encourage them to share favorite fall activities.

Recalling
3. The poem is about the changing of the seasons from fall to winter.

Interpreting
4. Suggested Response: The cricket will die in the cold; his chirping is a farewell song.
5. Answers may differ, but one response might be that the cricket's song is like a thin splinter of wood.

Splinter

Carl Sandburg

The voice of the last cricket
1 across the first frost
2 is one kind of good-by.
It is so thin a splinter of singing.

RESPONDING TO THE SELECTION

Your Response
1. What sounds do you associate with summertime? With fall?
2. Describe how you feel as summer is ending and fall is just beginning.

Recalling
3. What real-life experience could be the basis of "Splinter"?

Interpreting
4. In what sense is the cricket's voice a "kind of good-by"?
5. Interpret the last line.

Applying
6. Does Sandburg in "Splinter" use personification in the same way Dickinson does in "The Sky Is Low"? Explain your answer.

THINKING AND WRITING

Writing a Poem
Sandburg provides one kind of good-by—"the voice of the last cricket." Brainstorm to list other images that make fitting pictures of good-by. Choose the one you consider most appropriate. Then, patterning Sandburg's poem, write a four-line poem describing this kind of good-by. When you revise, make sure you have ended your poem with a powerful descriptive sentence.

LEARNING OPTIONS

1. **Speaking and Listening.** Make a tape recording of many different sounds—loud and soft—and bring the cassette to class. Form a group of four or five students. Listen to the recorded sounds, and work together to write metaphors that describe each sound. Here is an example of such a metaphor: "The rain beating on the car roof was the rhythmic dance of a centipede's feet." When you are finished, play the recorded sounds and read your metaphors aloud for your classmates.
2. **Art.** Draw or paint a picture of the lonely cricket singing his slender song against a background of the chilly countryside. Display your artwork in the classroom.

598 Poetry

THINKING AND WRITING

◆ **Software** If students are working on computers, encourage them to use the **Writer's Helper** activity *Three Ways of Seeing* to generate ideas for their poems.

Alternative Assessment You might want to vary the Thinking and Writing assignment as follows. Ask students to work collaboratively and review the use of figurative language in these six poems. Then have them work together to create a poem modeled after one of the poems. Their poems might contain an extended metaphor, a simile, a symbol, and/or personification. They might find it easier to copy the pattern of the poem they choose to model.

Musical Devices

THREE MUSICIANS, 1921
Pablo Picasso
Collection, The Museum of Modern Art,
New York

Musical Devices 599

More About the Authors After leaving school at age sixteen **Walter de la Mare** had to earn a living and became a clerk in the offices of an oil company in London. Although he stayed there for eighteen years, he disliked his work and desperately hoped for literary success. Ask students why it is so difficult for a poet to earn a living as a poet and why it may be difficult for a poet to earn a living in another way.

Consider telling students that **Edgar Allan Poe** was particularly sensitive to the sounds of words and in poems like "The Bells" created suggestive patterns of sounds. Have students consider the similarities and differences between poetry and music.

Tell students that the work of translating the **Bible** was divided among about fifty translators. These translators circulated their drafts for mutual criticism. Then a special committee made further revisions. Ask students to consider some of the difficulties involved in such a task.

You may want to tell students that **Walt Whitman's** vision and sense of his audience may have been influenced by the journalistic writing he did for newspapers. Ask students to consider how media like television and radio might influence today's poets.

GUIDE FOR READING

The Listeners

Walter de la Mare (1873–1956) was born in Kent, England, and lived much of his life in and around London. Many of his poems are imaginative journeys into the shadowy world between the real and the unreal. His mastery of eerie moods and dreamlike situations is well illustrated by "The Listeners," one of his best-known poems.

The Bells

Edgar Allan Poe (1809–1849) lived a life marked by one misfortune after another. Ill health frequently afflicted him. Fortunately, Mrs. Marie Louise Shew, a woman with medical training, treated Poe. He expressed his gratitude by writing several poems to her. "The Bells" is one of these. Some scholars believe that this poem originated in an idea that Mrs. Shew suggested to him.

Ecclesiastes 3:1–8

The King James, or Authorized, Version of the Bible was published in 1611. It was the work of a committee of English churchmen led by Lancelot Andrewes. The language of the King James Version is so beautiful that the Bible is ranked in English literature with the works of Shakespeare. According to tradition, Ecclesiastes was written by Solomon, the Hebrew king who died around 932 B.C.

I Hear America Singing

Walt Whitman (1819–1892) was born on Long Island, near New York City. His ability to absorb and comprehend all that he observed of his growing country provided him with the subject matter of his major work, *Leaves of Grass*. Part of Whitman's mission as a poet was to inspire and vitalize the United States through the ecstatic vision of democratic life that *Leaves* projected. His expansive vision and spirit may be glimpsed in "I Hear America Singing."

600   Poetry

Objectives

1 To recognize alliteration
2 To recognize forms of repetition
3 To understand parallelism
4 To understand free verse
5 To respond to literary criticism
6 To express individual interests and abilities through optional activities

Support Material

Teaching Portfolio
Teacher Backup, p. 749
Grammar in Action Worksheets, *Using Precise Words,* p. 754; *Using Connotation and Denotation,* p. 756
Usage and Mechanics Worksheet, p. 758
Vocabulary Check, p. 759
Analyzing Literature Worksheet,

Recognizing Musical Devices and Parallelism, p. 760
Language Worksheet, *Identifying Synonyms,* p. 761
Selection Test, p. 762
Art Transparency 17: *Traveling Carnival, Santa Fe,* by John Sloan

Listening to Literature
"The Listeners," "The Bells," "I Hear America Singing"

Prentice Hall Literature Writing Studio

Musical Devices

The term **musical devices** refers to the various ways poets use the sound of words to enrich their poetry. One of the most frequently used musical devices is *alliteration,* the repetition of the same consonant sound, usually at the start of words. When De la Mare writes of the "*f*orest's *f*erny *f*loor," he is using this device. A similar device is *assonance,* the repetition of vowel sounds. Poe uses this device in line 3 of "The Bells": "What a world of merriment their melody foretells!" In the same poem, he uses another device, *onomatopoeia.* This is the use of a word whose sound imitates or suggests sound— "How they tinkle, tinkle, tinkle," he says of the bells.

Alliteration, assonance, and—often—onomatopoeia are forms of the most basic musical device of all: *repetition.* This device is found not only in particular words or sounds but also in the structure of entire lines of verse. In the passage from Ecclesiastes, all the lines after the first are structured the same way. Each has two pairs of contrasting phrases: "A time to be born, and a time to die; a time to plant and a time to pluck up that which is planted . . ." Such repetition of similarly structured lines is called *parallelism.* This device is fundamental to the kind of verse Whitman wrote, free verse.

Focus

Musical devices are found in song lyrics as well as poetry. For example, note the assonance, the repeated *o* sound, in this lyric from a popular folk song: "Michael row your boat ashore." In small groups brainstorm to list song lyrics that contain examples of alliteration, assonance, onomatopoeia, repetition, or parallelism. When your group has listed one example of each musical device, write your examples on the chalkboard to share with the rest of the class. Then, as you read the poems in this section, notice how the musical devices enhance the sound and meaning of the poetry.

Vocabulary

Knowing the following words will help you as you read the poems in this section.

thronging (throŋ′ iŋ) *v.:* Crowding into (p. 602, l. 17)

voluminously (və lōō′ mə nəs lē) *adv.:* Fully; in great volume (p. 604, l. 26)

palpitating (pal′ pə tāt′ iŋ) *v.:* Beating rapidly; throbbing (p. 606, l. 56)

paean (pē′ ən) *n.:* Song of joy, triumph, etc. (p. 607, l. 92)

Guide for Reading 601

Literary Focus The world is alive with sound. Birds sing, dogs bark, trains whistle and chug, and wheels click and clack. Even when we read, we listen to the sounds of letters and words that we see on the page. Poets have a number of sound effects they can use to help us hear the sounds in their poems. A poet chooses words not only to communicate, but also to create a distinct sound.

Prereading Focus You might want to expand the activity by encouraging students to bring in recordings of songs that contain sound devices. Have them play the recordings for the class. Then have the class discuss the effect of the sound devices in each recording.

Vocabulary Have less advanced students read the words aloud. Then have them use the words in sentences to reflect their meanings.

Electronic Handbook If students have access to the Language Master 6000, suggest that they listen to the pronunciation of each vocabulary word.

Spelling Tip Point out the *ae* combination in *paean.*

HET BLINDE HUIS
William Degouve de Nunques
State Museum, Kroller-Muller, Otterlo, The Netherlands

The Listeners
Walter de la Mare

'Is there anybody there?' said the Traveler,
    Knocking on the moonlit door;
And his horse in the silence champed[1]
    the grasses
    Of the forest's ferny floor:
5 And a bird flew up out of the turret,
    Above the Traveler's head:
And he smote[2] upon the door again a
    second time;
    'Is there anybody there?' he said.
But no one descended to the Traveler;
10   No head from the leaf-fringed sill
Leaned over and looked into his gray eyes,
    Where he stood perplexed and still.
But only a host of phantom listeners
    That dwelt in the lone house then
15 Stood listening in the quiet of the moonlight
    To that voice from the world of men:
Stood thronging the faint moonbeams on
    the dark stair,
    That goes down to the empty hall,
Hearkening in an air stirred and shaken
20   By the lonely Traveler's call.
And he felt in his heart their strangeness,
    Their stillness answering his cry,
While his horse moved, cropping the dark
    turf,
    'Neath the starred and leafy sky;
25 For he suddenly smote on the door, even
    Louder, and lifted his head:—
'Tell them I came, and no one answered,
    That I kept my word,' he said.
Never the least stir made the listeners,
30   Though every word he spake[3]

---

1. **champed** (champt) *v.:* Chewed.
2. **smote** (smōt) *v.:* Struck hard.
3. **spake** (spāk) *v.:* Spoke.

602   *Poetry*

Fell echoing through the shadowiness of
    the still house
From the one man left awake:
Ay, they heard his foot upon the stirrup,
    And the sound of iron on stone,
35 And how the silence surged softly backward,
    When the plunging hoofs were gone.

2

RESPONDING TO THE SELECTION

Your Response

1. Have you ever had an experience similar to the one described in this poem? If so, how did you react to this experience? If not, imagine that you are the Traveler and describe how you feel about what happened to you on that moonlit night.

Recalling

2. Briefly tell what happens in this poem.
3. Who are the listeners?

Interpreting

4. What details create the eerie, dreamlike atmosphere of the poem?
5. What unanswered questions does the poem leave you with?

Applying

6. What are some possible answers to these questions?

ANALYZING LITERATURE

Recognizing Alliteration

Alliteration is the repetition of the same consonant sound, usually at the start of words—as in the "*forest's ferny floor.*" In "The Listeners," the alliteration is light. Though you may have hardly noticed it, it contributes to the "music" and mood of the poem.

1. Find at least three lines with alliteration based on the *s* sound.
2. Find two lines with alliteration based on the *l* sound.
3. How important do you think such alliteration is to the mysterious mood of the poem?

LEARNING OPTIONS

1. **Speaking and Listening.** In a small group, take turns reading "The Listeners" aloud. Listen carefully to one another's readings, and offer suggestions on ways to improve your presentation. If possible, record your readings and listen to them together, stopping the tape at key points for comments. When group members have finished practicing, elect one representative to read the poem aloud for the class.
2. **Writing.** Write a brief story based on "The Listeners." Explain who the Traveler is, what he is doing at the house, who lives in the house, and why no one answers the door. Feel free to depart from the poem's plot line as you create your story. When you have finished your first draft, ask a classmate to read it and offer comments or suggestions. Then revise your story and share it with the class.

The Listeners   603

Recalling

2. A traveler comes to a house and knocks on the door. There seems to be no one in the house. When no one answers the door, the traveler tells whoever is listening to let someone know that he has kept his word.
3. It is not clear who the listeners are. Perhaps they are phantoms.

Interpreting

4. Answers will differ, but the following phrases might be suggested: "phantom listeners"; "lone house"; "empty hall"; "stillness answering his cry."
5. Answers will differ, but students might suggest that the questions left unanswered are: Who is the traveler? Why was he supposed to come to the house? Who had told him to come to the house? Who or what are the listeners?

Applying

6. Answers will differ, but the following might be suggested: The traveler could have been a person coming to pay off a debt or redeem a promise.

ANSWERS TO ANALYZING LITERATURE

1. Suggested Response: Lines 7, 25, and 28–29.
2. Suggested Response: Lines 11 and 26.
3. Answers will differ but might suggest that it helps to create a whispering eeriness.

LEARNING OPTIONS

1. Auditory learners will enjoy this activity. You might extend the activity for visual learners by having students write a poem from the viewpoint of the listeners in the house.
2. This activity will appeal to visual learners. You might extend this activity by having students illustrate their stories.

Audiocassette To help students appreciate the effect of sound devices, have them listen to the reading of "The Listeners" on the **Listening to Literature** Audiocassettes. Have them discuss how the sound devices contribute to the musical quality of the poem.

Closure and Extension

ANSWERS TO RESPONDING TO THE SELECTION
Your Response

1. Lead students to see that the traveler senses that someone is listening behind the closed door but will not respond.

The Bells

Edgar Allan Poe

I

Hear the sledges[1] with the bells—
　　　Silver bells!
What a world of merriment their melody foretells!
　　How they tinkle, tinkle, tinkle,
5　　　　In the icy air of night!
　　While the stars, that oversprinkle
　　All the heavens, seem to twinkle
　　　　With a crystalline delight;
　　　Keeping time, time, time,
10　　　In a sort of Runic[2] rhyme,
To the tintinnabulation[3] that so musically wells
　　From the bells, bells, bells, bells,
　　　Bells, bells, bells—
From the jingling and the tinkling of the bells.

II

15　　Hear the mellow wedding bells,
　　　　Golden bells!
What a world of happiness their harmony foretells!
　　Through the balmy air of night
　　How they ring out their delight!
20　　　From the molten golden-notes,
　　　　And all in tune,
　　What a liquid ditty[4] floats
To the turtle-dove[5] that listens, while she gloats
　　　　On the moon!
25　　　Oh, from out the sounding cells,
What a gush of euphony[6] voluminously wells!
　　　How it swells!
　　　How it dwells

---

1. sledges (slej' əz) *n.*: Sleighs.
2. Runic (r$\overline{oo}$' nik) *adj.*: Songlike; poetical.
3. tintinnabulation (tin ti nab y$\overline{oo}$ lā' sʰən) *n.*: The ringing of bells.
4. ditty (dit' ē) *n.*: A song.
5. turtle-dove: The turtle-dove is traditionally associated with love.
6. euphony (y$\overline{oo}$' fə nē) *n.*: Pleasing sound.

604　*Poetry*

Grammar in Action

Poetry is such a concentrated form that there is no room for words that don't quite do the jobs they are supposed to do. Poets must make every word count. Poets must always choose **precise words,** words that state exactly the idea being conveyed.

For a poet, the precise word might be one that imitates a particular sound. Using words that imitate sounds is called *onomatopoeia. (Buzz, murmur, hiss, hum* are onomatopoetic words.) Poe uses precise words and words that suggest sound to convey ideas about several different kinds of bells. Look at these lines:

　　While the stars that oversprinkle
　　All the heavens, seem to twinkle
　　　With a crystalline delight;
　　Keeping time, time, time,
　　In a sort of Runic rhyme,
To the tintinnabulation that so musically wells
　　From the bells, bells, bells, bells,
　　　Bells, bells, bells—
From the jingling and the tinkling of the bells.

In this passage, what words suggest that the poet is writing of

THE BELLS
Edmund Dulac
New York Public Library

The Bells 605

Fine art, *The Bells,* by Edmund Dulac (1882–1953). Dulac was a French illustrator known for the color and imagination of his work.

You might want to use the following questions:

1. Does the mood of the illustration suit that of the poem?
2. How else could this poem be illustrated?

Cooperative Learning Divide the class into small groups to examine and discuss the painting by Dulac and its relationship to the poem. Suggest using the Humanities Note questions as a guide. Ask each group to note differences between the painting and a realistic photograph. Have them discuss why the artist incorporated these changes. One member from each group should report its conclusions to the class.

sleigh bells and not the fire bells described in a later stanza? What examples of onomatopoeia do the lines contain?

Student Activity 1. Read aloud one of the stanzas to a partner, but begin the stanza after the poet has identified the kind of bell being described. Have your partner listen for words that precisely convey the kind of bell that is ringing. After the reading, discuss the words and the use of onomatopoeia in the passage.

Student Activity 2. In either a poem or a short paragraph, describe a place, an object, or an experience. Use precise words. Make use of onomatopoeia to convey the sound of what you are describing.

ESL Teaching Strategy You might wish to pair ESL students with native speakers to practice reading this poem aloud. Native speakers may explain the meanings of unusual words found in the work and assist with correct pronunciation.

30   On the future! how it tells
        Of the rapture that impels
        To the swinging and the ringing
        Of the bells, bells, bells,
        Of the bells, bells, bells, bells,
        Bells, bells, bells—
35   To the rhyming and the chiming of the bells!

III

        Hear the loud alarum[7] bells!
        Brazen[8] bells!
        What a tale of terror now their turbulency tells!
        In the startled ear of night
3   40   How they scream out their affright!
        Too much horrified to speak,
        They can only shriek, shriek,
        Out of tune,
        In a clamorous appealing to the mercy of the fire,
45   In a mad expostulation[9] with the deaf and frantic fire
        Leaping higher, higher, higher,
        With a desperate desire,
        And a resolute endeavor
        Now—now to sit or never,
50   By the side of the pale-faced moon.
        Oh, the bells, bells, bells!
        What a tale their terror tells
        Of Despair!
        How they clang, and clash, and roar!
55   What a horror they outpour
        On the bosom of the palpitating air!
        Yet the ear it fully knows,
        By the twanging
        And the clanging,
60   How the danger ebbs and flows;
        Yet the ear distinctly tells,
        In the jangling,
        And the wrangling,
        How the danger sinks and swells,
65   By the sinking or the swelling in the anger of the bells—
        Of the bells—

---

7. alarum (ə ler′ əm) *n.*: A sudden call to arms; alarm.
8. brazen (brā′ z′n) *adj.*: Made of brass; having the sound of brass.
9. expostulation (ik späs chə lā′ sh'n) *n.*: Objection; complaint.

Grammar in Action

Poets choose words carefully, not only for their denotation, but also for their connotation. The **denotation** of a word is its dictionary meaning; the **connotation** refers to a range of emotional and cultural associations that the word calls up. For instance, the words *home, house,* and *residence* all refer to a structure in which a family lives. That is their denotative meaning. The connotative meaning of *residence,* however, suggests something cold and impersonal, while *home* has connotations of warmth and comfort. The word *house* still emphasizes the structure rather than the people, but its connotative meaning is not so cold as *residence.*

Poe takes full advantage of connotative meanings, as this passage shows:

        Hear the *loud alarum* bells!
        Brazen bells!
        What a tale of *terror* now their *turbulency* tells!

Of the bells, bells, bells, bells,
Bells, bells, bells—
In the clamor and the clangor of the bells!

IV

70   Hear the tolling of the bells—
Iron bells!
What a world of solemn thought their monody[10] compels!
In the silence of the night,
How we shiver with affright
75 At the melancholy menace of their tone!
For every sound that floats
From the rust within their throats
Is a groan.
And the people—ah, the people—
80   They that dwell up in the steeple,
All alone,
And who tolling, tolling, tolling,
In that muffled monotone,
Feel a glory in so rolling
85   On the human heart a stone—
They are neither man nor woman—
They are neither brute nor human—
They are Ghouls:[11]
And their king it is who tolls;
90   And he rolls, rolls, rolls,
Rolls
A pæan from the bells!
And his merry bosom swells
With the pæan of the bells!
95   And he dances and he yells;
Keeping time, time, time,
In a sort of Runic rhyme,
To the pæan of the bells—
Of the bells:
100   Keeping time, time, time,
In a sort of Runic rhyme,
To the throbbing of the bells—
Of the bells, bells, bells—

---

10. monody (män′ ə dē) *n*.: A poem of mourning; a steady sound;
music in which one instrument or voice is dominant.
11. Ghouls (gōōlz) *n*.: Evil spirits that rob graves.

The Bells   607

In the *startled* ear of night
How they *scream* out their *affright*!

The italicized words have especially vivid connotative meanings. Poe chose them to call up in the reader feelings of danger, alarm, disturbance, and horror.

Student Activity 1. Reread the first six lines of section IV of "The Bells." Identify the words with especially vivid connotative meanings and explain the feelings and associations they call up.

Student Activity 2. Suppose you were planning to write a poem about the sound of an alarm clock. List three to five words with vivid connotations that would enhance your poem. Explain why each word would be effective.

To the sobbing of the bells;

105   Keeping time, time, time,
      As he knells, knells, knells,
      In a happy Runic rhyme,
      To the rolling of the bells—
    Of the bells, bells, bells—

110   To the tolling of the bells,
    Of the bells, bells, bells, bells,
       Bells, bells, bells—

To the moaning and the groaning of the bells.

Reader's Response One literary critic said that "The Bells" is a game of sounds and is not poetry. Which description do you think best fits Poe's poem? Explain.

Closure and Extension

ANSWERS TO RESPONDING TO THE SELECTION
Your Response
1. Encourage students to share personal experiences in which they might have heard the four different kinds of bells. Lead them to see that the alarum bells would be similar to firehouse sirens and the iron bells are those they may have heard at a funeral.

Recalling
2. Suggested Response: Each stanza begins with the same two words. The rhythm in the first five lines is the same in each stanza. The next-to-last line of each stanza is "Bells, bells, bells." There are other similarities as well.

Interpreting
3. Suggested Response: The first stanza suggests a sleigh ride on a winter night. The second suggests a wedding right after the ceremony. The third suggests a fire. The fourth suggests a nighttime scene.
4. Suggested Response: The mood varies. In the first stanza, the mood is merry; in the second stanza the mood is happy; in the third stanza the mood is turbulent; in the fourth stanza the mood is wild and sad.

Applying
5. Answers will differ, but students might suggest that what Eliot says can be applied to the poem "The Bells" because a person reading or listening to the poem gets caught up in its sounds and the moods it creates.

ANSWERS TO ANALYZING LITERATURE

1. Suggested Response: You can find assonance in lines 3 and 14 and alliteration in lines 3 and 10. Other forms of repetition are

---

RESPONDING TO THE SELECTION

Your Response
1. What feelings did each section of "The Bells" evoke in you?

Recalling
2. What similarities among the four sections do you see? Describe at least three.

Interpreting
3. What scene or situation is suggested in each of the sections?
4. Does the mood or spirit of the poem vary from one section to another, or is it basically the same throughout? Explain.

Applying
5. The poet T. S. Eliot once said that poetry can be enjoyed before it is understood. Could "The Bells" be used as evidence in support of this idea? Give reasons for your opinion.

ANALYZING LITERATURE

Recognizing Forms of Repetition
The **repetition** of sounds, patterns of rhythm, words, phrases, and so on is the primary source of the music of poetry. A number of different forms of repetition are found in "The Bells." Besides al-

---

literation, Poe uses *assonance* (the repetition of vowel sounds), as in the phrase "the mellow wedding bells . . ." He also uses repetition to achieve the effect of *onomatopoeia*, as in "How they tinkle, tinkle, tinkle . . ."

1. Point out all the different kinds of repetition you can find in the first section of "The Bells."
2. Compare any two stanzas of the poem. Point out two examples of Poe's repeating in one stanza words or phrases found in the other.
3. Usually, rhymes, which are a kind of repetition, are found at the ends of lines. Find examples of rhymes occurring within the lines of verse.

LEARNING OPTION

Speaking and Listening. "The Bells" is a perfect example of a poem that was meant to be read aloud. In fact, it is far more enjoyable read aloud than read silently. It is also a good example of a poem that must be gone over carefully before it can be recited smoothly and easily. Review the poem for its sense. Try to figure out just what the longer or more complex sentences are saying. Then go back to those parts you may have stumbled over when you first read them. Decide how they should be read. Finally, when you feel comfortable with the whole poem, read it aloud and notice how it comes alive.

---

rhyme and the repeating of words like *bells* and *time*.
2. Suggested Response: Comparison of stanzas 1 and 2—The poet repeats the word "delight," the phrases "air of night," and "what a world," and the word "wells." The word "bells" is also repeated in each stanza.
3. Suggested Response: Internal rhymes can be found in lines 31 and 35 of Stanza 2 and line 113 of Stanza 4.

LEARNING OPTION

Students who appreciate auditory experiences will enjoy this activity.

Ecclesiastes 3:1–8

(King James Version)

1 To every thing there is a season, and a time to every purpose under the heaven:
A time to be born, and a time to die; a time to plant, and a time to pluck up that
   which is planted;
A time to kill, and a time to heal; a time to break down, and a time to build up:

2 A time to weep, and a time to laugh; a time to mourn, and a time to dance:
5 A time to cast away stones, and a time to gather stones together; a time to
   embrace, and a time to refrain from embracing;
A time to get, and a time to lose; a time to keep, and a time to cast away;
A time to rend,[1] and a time to sew; a time to keep silence, and a time to speak:
A time to love, and a time to hate; a time of war, and a time of peace.

---

1. rend (rend) *v.*: Tear.

RESPONDING TO THE SELECTION

Your Response
1. Do you find this passage comforting? Why or why not?

Recalling
2. What verse contains the main idea of the passage?
3. How would you describe the way this passage is organized?

Interpreting
4. What activity is suggested by the words "A time to cast away stones, and a time to gather stones together . . ."?
5. Describe the tone or mood of this passage. Would you call it happy, sad, optimistic, calm? What other words might you use to describe it? Give reasons for your view.

Applying
6. What comfort or guidance can a person of to-day find in these verses written more than 2,200 years ago in ancient Israel?

ANALYZING LITERATURE

Understanding Parallelism

In poetry, **parallelism** is the use of similar grammatical structures in succeeding lines of verse. Often, as in Ecclesiastes, a single line of verse will contain balanced and coordinated phrases. The lines that follow will also contain such phrases. In line 2, for example, the phrase "A time to be born" is balanced with "a time to die," and "a time to plant" is balanced with "a time to pluck up that which is planted."

1. Read the passage aloud. Do all the lines have the same rhythm, or does the rhythm vary somewhat? Explain your answer.
2. "The Bells" represents one kind of poetic music; Ecclesiastes represents another kind. Which kind do you prefer, and why?

Ecclesiastes 3:1–8   609

Presentation

Motivation/Prior Knowledge
Ecclesiastes is a short book in the Old Testament. The word *Ecclesiastes* comes from the Greek word "ekklesia" which translated means "one who speaks in the assembly." Who might be the speaker of this poem?

Purpose-Setting Question
These lines are from the Bible. Is it justifiable to call them a poem? Why or why not?

1 **Discussion** What does "to every thing there is a season" mean?

2 **Literary Focus** Note the use of the phrase "a time" in these lines. What is the purpose of this repetition?

Recalling
2. The first verse contains the main idea.
3. The passage is organized through the repetitions of the phrase "a time to."

Interpreting
4. Answers will differ, but students might suggest that there is a time to destroy and a time to build.
5. Answers will differ, but students might suggest that the tone or mood suggests distance, objectivity, and finality.

Applying
6. Answers will differ, but students might suggest that a person can be comforted in knowing that if things are bad, there will come a time when things are good.

ANSWERS TO ANALYZING LITERATURE

1. Suggested Response: The rhythm varies. Line 5, for example, has more accented syllables than line 4.
2. Answers will differ. Accept any well-reasoned response.

Closure and Extension

ANSWERS TO RESPONDING TO THE SELECTION
Your Response

1. Lead students to see that the poet suggests that there is an underlying purpose for all that happens in a person's life. Ask how believing that all things happen for a reason might affect a person's reaction to adversity.

609

Fine Art, *Coal,* 1920, Thomas Hart Benton. Thomas Hart Benton (1889–1975) was an American painter and muralist. Benton attended the Art Institute of Chicago and Académie Julien in Paris; however, he said that his true education came from the years he spent roaming the United States. He became the primary force behind the American Regionalist movement in painting, a movement that glorified the hard-working farmers and laborers of the American heartland.

Coal is part of a series of murals glorifying contemporary America, done for the New School for Social Research in New York City. This vigorous, animated mural depicts the mining and industrial use of coal, showing the workers who make this whole process possible. Benton used an innovative montage of images separated by stylized architectural elements, a technique that revolutionized mural design in America.

You might want to use the following questions:
1. How does this mural depict the mining and use of coal?
2. What mood does Benton's mural call up?
3. Compare and contrast Benton's treatment of work with Whitman's.

Cooperative Learning You might want to have students work in small groups to illustrate this poem. Ask them to list each activity the poet describes. Explain that each group should draw colorful pictures depicting various scenes from the work. Suggest they arrange these pictures to form a collage. Display the artwork for the class.

COAL *(from America Today),* 1920
Thomas Hart Benton
Courtesy of The Equitable Life Assurance Society of the U.S.

Multicultural Focus Ask how Whitman's poem might be different if he were to write it today, and discuss the responses. Students might say, for example, that the occupations he describes would be different; that women would not be solely mothers, wives, and domestics; that Whitman might describe a diversity of racial and ethnic groups; that there might be disabled workers. Discuss the reasons for the social changes that students mention, including new inventions and the growth of new industries, the civil rights and women's movements, and new waves of immigration.

Have students find out more about social change in America in the last century. Assign specific topics for students to research, such as immigration, civil rights legislation, advancements for women, economic and industrial developments, and so forth. Alternatively, assign five- or ten-year periods to students and have them research social changes of all kinds during that period. Use their findings to make a timeline of social change on the bulletin board.

I Hear America Singing

Walt Whitman

I hear America singing, the varied carols I hear,
Those of mechanics, each one singing his as it should be
    blithe and strong,
The carpenter singing his as he measures his plank or
    beam,
The mason singing his as he makes ready for work, or
    leaves off work,
5 The boatman singing what belongs to him in his boat, the
    deckhand singing on the steamboat deck,
The shoemaker singing as he sits on his bench, the hatter[1]
    singing as he stands,
The wood-cutter's song, the ploughboy's on his way in the
    morning, or at noon intermission or at sundown,
The delicious singing of the mother, or of the young wife at
    work, or of the girl sewing or washing,
Each singing what belongs to him or her and to none else,
10 The day what belongs to the day—at night the party of
    young fellows, robust, friendly,
Singing with open mouths their strong melodious songs.

---

1. hatter: A person who makes, sells, or cleans hats.

I Hear America Singing   611

ANSWERS TO RESPONDING TO THE SELECTION

Your Response

1. Encourage students to share occasions that inspire them to sing.

Recalling

2. The people are mostly manual workers.

Interpreting

3. Suggested Response: Singing should be interpreted both literally and figuratively. In addition to literal song, singing refers to each worker's expression of himself or herself through work.

4. Suggested Response: The images of the various workers create a vision of what America is and represents. People can work at what they want. The poem implies that all of these individuals work for the common good.

5. Suggested Response: The spirit is one of togetherness. It is one of happiness and optimism.

Applying

6. Answers will differ, but students might suggest that Whitman was trying to depict a nation of individuals freely expressing themselves and yet working for the common good.

ANSWERS TO ANALYZING LITERATURE

1. Answers will differ. Students may respond that if another poet tried to treat the content of this poem with a regular rhythmic pattern, it might alter the free and expansive mood.

2. Suggested Response: Both poems use parallel structure. While the Biblical passage is distanced and unemotional, Whitman's poem is optimistic.

THINKING AND WRITING

Writing Transparency Organization affects clarity. Before students write, it may be helpful for them to see a model of the writing assignment. You might wish to show them Model 6: *Persuasive Essay* in the **Transparencies for Writing.**

RESPONDING TO THE SELECTION

Your Response

1. Have you ever found yourself "singing" as you were going about a task? If so, describe what you were doing and how you felt about it. If not, describe how you think the workers in the poem feel about what they are doing.

Recalling

2. In general, what are the various people mentioned in the poem doing?

Interpreting

3. Are the people literally singing, or should "singing" be interpreted figuratively? Explain.

4. Explain the title. In what sense does the speaker hear America singing?

5. Describe the tone and spirit of the poem.

Applying

6. What do you think Whitman was trying to express in this poem?

ANALYZING LITERATURE

Understanding Free Verse

Free verse is verse without a regular arrangement of accented and unaccented syllables. It is "free" of the restrictions of a set rhythmical pattern for each line. However, since free-verse poetry is divided into lines, the movement from one line to the next establishes a kind of rhythm. In the hands of a poet such as Whitman, free verse can be an instrument of rich and varied music.

1. Another poet might have treated the subject

---

matter of "I Hear America Singing" in rhymed verse with a regular rhythmic pattern. Tell why you think such a treatment would or would not have resulted in a more effective poem than Whitman's.

2. Compare the rhythm of Whitman's poem with that of Ecclesiastes 3:1–8. What similarities and what differences do you find?

THINKING AND WRITING

Responding to Criticism

The Whitman scholar James E. Miller, Jr., has written that "'I Hear America Singing' presents an image of America that America would like to believe true—an image of proud and healthy individualists engaged in productive and happy labor." Miller implies that Whitman's image of America may be untrue.

Do you think it is untrue? Write an essay in which you discuss this question. First gather evidence in support of your opinion. Then write it up in a well-organized first draft. When you revise, check that all your statements are relevant to your main idea. Compare your opinion and supporting arguments with those of your classmates.

LEARNING OPTION

Writing. Whitman's poem presents a vision of America from the 1800's. Consider what a modern version of Whitman's poem would be like. In a small group, brainstorm to list some modern occupations. Then work together to write a poem about the modern American worker. Elect a group member to read your poem aloud to the class.

Alternative Assessment You might vary the Thinking and Writing assignment as follows. Working collaboratively in groups of no more than four, have students prepare an oral presentation of one of these poems in which they share their illustration of it, the music they feel appropriate to the poem, and an interpretive choral reading of it for the class.

Have students select one member of the group to illustrate the poem and another to set it to music or to find appropriate background music. Students should present a written interpretation of the poem as well as their rationale for the music they chose. Divide the class so that each poem is presented by at least one group.

LEARNING OPTION

Visual learners will enjoy this activity. To extend the activity for students who enjoy research, suggest that students explore the classified section of the local newspaper to find additional information about various positions. Have them share their research with the class.

Structure

HARMONY IN RED, 1908–09
Henri Matisse
The Hermitage, Leningrad/Art Resource

More About the Authors Tell
students that, in many of her love
poems, **Sara Teasdale** left out
the specifics of who, when, and
why. She felt that the poems
would be more powerful without
this concrete information. Have
students discuss this device.

E.E. Cummings's method
of working was to sleep until
noon, work for hours on his writing, and then socialize in the
evening. Ask students if they
would enjoy a similar routine.

John Masefield was named
Poet Laureate of England because his poetic skills, insights,
and spirit were thought to carry
forward the British heritage and
to represent the concerns dearest to the British people. Ask
students whom they would
choose to be an American poet
laureate. How would this poet
echo the talent and ethos of our
nation?

Simon J. Ortiz earned his
master's degree at the University
of Iowa. Throughout his career,
Ortiz has been an influential
voice of Native Americans. Although he is also a short story
writer, essayist, and editor, Ortiz
is best known for his poetry. In
addition to his own writing, Ortiz
is currently an editor of the Navajo publication *Rough Rock News.*

Ask students which universal themes about Native Americans Ortiz might write about.

GUIDE FOR READING

"There Will Come Soft Rains"

Sara Teasdale (1884–1933) was born in St. Louis, Missouri. Success as a poet came early to her. Her first poems were published
when she was still a girl, and her first book appeared before she was
twenty-five. Her attachment to the well-known poet Vachel Lindsay
ended in grief when he committed suicide. Two years later she took
her own life. Many of Teasdale's poems, such as "There Will Come
Soft Rains," are sad, as her life was.

maggie and milly and molly and may

E. E. Cummings (1894–1962) was born in Cambridge, Massachusetts, and educated at Harvard. During World War I, he was an am-
bulance driver in France and spent three months in a detention camp.
The unusual typography of his poems is an expression of his quirky
individualism, which is squarely in the tradition of New England writers. The lyrical lightheartedness of "maggie and milly and molly and
may" is typical of much, though not all, of his verse.

Sea-Fever

John Masefield (1878–1967) was born in Herefordshire, England.
As a boy, he went to sea and for many years wandered the globe
working at odd jobs. His life at sea is the source of his best-known
poems. Of these "Sea-Fever" is the most famous. Masefield was the
twenty-second poet laureate of England.

My Father's Song

Simon J. Ortiz (1941–   )—an Acoma Pueblo Indian from New
Mexico—writes poems and stories about the universal experiences
of Native Americans. Embedded in his work are Indian history,
mythology, philosophy, and contemporary social concerns. In "My Father's Song," Ortiz pays tribute to and remembers his dead father.
Ortiz has a strong belief in the importance of education, and because of this he devotes much of his free time to educating fellow
Native Americans.

614   Poetry

Objectives

1 To understand structure in
poetry
2 To compare structures
3 To understand meter
4 To write a critical evaluation of a poem

Support Material

Teaching Portfolio
Teacher Backup, p. 765
Usage and Mechanics Work-
sheet, p. 771
Vocabulary Check, p. 772
Analyzing Literature Worksheet,
Understanding Structure, p.
773
Language Worksheet, *Recogniz-
ing Related Words,* p. 774

Selection Test, p. 775
Art Transparency 18: *Trees and
Rocks,* by Emile Branchard

Listening to Literature
"maggie and milly and molly and
may," "Sea-Fever," "My Father's Song," "Cradle Song
("Meciendo")

**Prentice Hall Literature Writing
Studio**

Meciendo ("Cradle Song")

Gabriela Mistral (1889–1957), whose real name is Lucila Godoy Alcayaga, was born in Vicuña, Chile. Mistral changed her name when she was a young teacher because she feared the content of her poetry might lead to the loss of her job. Her first name comes from the archangel Gabriel; her last name comes from the name of a sea wind. Mistral won the Nobel Prize for Literature in 1945; she was the first South American to receive this award. Mistral wrote many poems about children and motherhood, such as "Meciendo."

Structure

The **structure** of a poem may be described in terms of its stanza form and its meter. A *stanza* is a unit with a set number of lines. For example, the stanza form in a couplet is made up of two rhymed lines. A stanza of four lines is called a *quatrain*.

Meter is the pattern of accented and unaccented syllables that form the basis of a poem's rhythm. Meter signifies the number of rhythmic beats, or "feet," in a line and the arrangement of accented and unaccented syllables in each foot. For example, a line that has five beats, or feet, is called a pentameter. If each foot consists of an unaccented syllable followed by an accented one, it is called an iamb. The meter of the poem would then be iambic pentameter. A poem that does not have a regular meter is called free verse.

Focus

One example of poetry written in couplets and quatrains is the nursery rhyme. Brainstorm to list as many nursery rhymes as you can. Choose one nursery rhyme, and identify the meter. How many feet does each line have? Which syllables are accented? Look for examples of couplets and quatrains as you read the following poems. How do these examples compare with those written in free verse?

Vocabulary

Knowing the following words will help you as you read the poems in this section.

tremulous (trem′ yə ləs) *adj.*: Quivering (p. 616, l. 4)

languid (lan′ gwid) *adj.*: Drooping; weak (p. 617, l. 6)

spume (spyo͞om) *n.*: Foam; froth (p. 618, l. 8)

whetted (hwet′ əd) *v.*: Sharpened (p. 618, l. 11)

Guide for Reading 615

Motivation/Prior Knowledge
Ask students to imagine and describe Earth without its human inhabitants. Tell them that, in the poem they will read, Teasdale uses such an imagined scene to make an important point.

Master Teacher Note Use the overhead projector to show students Art Transparency 18, *Trees and Rocks,* by Emile Branchard. Ask students to describe the feelings that this picture calls up. Also ask them to comment on the lack of human figures. Do they think this is a spot to which people often come? Why or why not? Then tell them that Teasdale's poem describes what Earth would be like if humans vanished from it completely.

Thematic Focus In this poem, Teasdale imagines the effect our extinction might have on our living Earth. Ask students if life would go on for other species if humans were extinct. How would the environment be affected?

Making Connections Another suggestive, contrasting selection to use with Teasdale's poem about war is "The Charge of the Light Brigade," page 533.

Purpose Setting Question What is the theme of this poem?

Thematic Response Teasdale wrote this poem before the advent of nuclear weapons. Do you think she would draw the same conclusions today?

1 Discussion What kind of atmosphere is created in lines 1–6? How does this atmosphere contrast with the atmosphere created in lines 7–12?

"There Will Come Soft Rains"
(War Time)
Sara Teasdale

There will come soft rains and the smell of the ground,
And swallows circling with their shimmering sound;

And frogs in the pools singing at night,
And wild plum-trees in tremulous white;

5 Robins will wear their feathery fire
Whistling their whims on a low fence-wire;

And not one will know of the war, not one
Will care at last when it is done.

Not one would mind, neither bird nor tree
10 If mankind perished utterly;

And Spring herself, when she woke at dawn,
Would scarcely know that we were gone.

RESPONDING TO THE SELECTION

Your Response
1. What do *you* feel nature's attitude toward humans is? Explain your answer.

Recalling
2. What is the topic of this poem?

Interpreting
3. Describe nature's attitude, as the speaker imagines it, toward war.
4. What seem to be the speaker's feelings about the situation described in the poem?

Applying
5. Teasdale died in 1933. How might her poem be different had she written it in the age of nuclear weapons?

ANALYZING LITERATURE

Understanding Structure
Many poems have a **structure** that may be described in terms of *stanza, form,* and *meter,* or the pattern of accented and unaccented syllables. Teasdale's poem consists of *couplets*—that is, pairs of rhyming lines. Each line has four heavily accented syllables, or four feet. A line of four feet is called a tetrameter. So the structure of the poem may be described as tetrameter couplets.

1. Read the poem aloud. How does the structure of couplets and tetrameter lines affect the spirit or mood of what is said?
2. Change one of the rhymed words in each couplet (for example, change "ground" to "soil" in line 1). How does the absence of rhyme change the poem's overall effect?

Closure and Extension

ANSWERS TO RESPONDING TO THE SELECTION
Your Response
1. Lead students to draw their own conclusions about the practice of attributing human emotions to natural phenomena.

Recalling
2. This poem is about war.

Interpreting
3. Suggested Response: The speaker suggests that nature would be indifferent to human self-destruction.
4. Answers will differ, but students might suggest that the speaker seems to be melancholy.

Applying
5. Answers will differ, but students might suggest that the first three stanzas might not be about the beauties of nature but about its devastation.

ANSWERS TO ANALYZING LITERATURE
1. Answers will differ, but students may indicate that the first three couplets seem to be a regularly constructed nature poem. The regularity of the last three couplets, however, serves to contrast ironically with the theme of destruction.
2. Answers will differ, but students may indicate that the loss of rhyme weakens the structure and therefore the impact of the poem.

maggie and milly and molly and may

E. E. Cummings

maggie and milly and molly and may
went down to the beach(to play one day)

and maggie discovered a shell that sang
so sweetly she couldn't remember her troubles,and

5   milly befriended a stranded star
whose rays five languid fingers were;

and molly was chased by a horrible thing
which raced sideways while blowing bubbles:and

may came home with a smooth round stone
10   as small as a world and as large as alone.

For whatever we lose(like a you or a me)
it's always ourselves we find in the sea

RESPONDING TO THE SELECTION

Your Response
1. If you were to go to the sea, what would you find there that might represent you?

Recalling
2. Describe each girl's experience on the beach.

Interpreting
3. What creature did milly befriend?
4. Describe the tone and spirit of the poem.

Applying
5. Is this poem in any way serious, or is it just an amusement in verse? Discuss what you think the purpose of the poem might be.

THINKING AND WRITING

Comparing Structures

You are frequently asked on tests to write an essay of comparison and contrast. To practice for such a question, write a brief essay in which you compare and contrast the couplet structure of Cummings's poem and that of "There Will Come Soft Rains." Look closely at the two poems. What similarities do you see in the couplets, and what differences? Make sure you quote from the poems to support your judgments. When your essay is finished, see what some of your classmates had to say in their essays. Did anyone notice a similarity or difference that you missed?

maggie and milly and molly and may   617

Motivation/Prior Knowledge
When John Masefield was in the ninth grade, he was on board a ship that trained English boys for merchant service. Before his fifteenth birthday, he had sailed around Cape Horn on a windjammer. Masefield never returned to being a seaman, but his best-known poems are about the sea. Tell students that this poem expresses his love for a seafaring life.

Purpose-Setting Question
What is it about the sea that the speaker loves so much?

1 Discussion What images reflect the poet's love for the sea?

2 Discussion What does the poet mean by "the long trick"?

Reader's Response Do you have strong feelings about the sea? What are they?

Audiocassette Before students read the poem, you may wish to play the reading of it on the **Listening to Literature** Audiocassettes. To help students understand the role of meter in the poem, have them tap out the patterns of accented and unaccented syllables as they listen to the recording.

Sea-Fever

John Masefield

> I must go down to the seas again, to the lonely sea and the
>   sky,
> And all I ask is a tall ship and a star to steer her by,
> And the wheel's kick and the wind's song and the white
>   sail's shaking,
> And a gray mist on the sea's face and a gray dawn
>   breaking.
>
> 5 I must go down to the seas again, for the call of the
>   running tide
> Is a wild call and a clear call that may not be denied;
> And all I ask is a windy day with the white clouds flying,
> And the flung spray and the blown spume, and the seagulls
>   crying.
>
> I must go down to the seas again to the vagrant gypsy life,
> 10 To the gull's way and the whale's way where the wind's like
>   a whetted knife;
> And all I ask is a merry yarn from a laughing fellow-rover
> And quiet sleep and a sweet dream when the long trick's[1]
>   over.

---

1. trick: A shift of duty, as on a ship.

RESPONDING TO THE SELECTION

Your Response

1. What place calls to you the way the sea calls to the speaker in this poem? Explain.

Recalling

2. What reason does the speaker give for the statement, "I must go down to the seas again"?
3. Identify at least four of the things he asks for.

Interpreting

4. Explain the appeal the sea has for the speaker.
5. What figurative or symbolic meaning might the final line have?
6. Discuss the title. In particular, what is suggested by the word "fever"?

Applying

7. What other ways of life have a powerful hold on some people?

618   Poetry

ANSWERS TO RESPONDING TO THE SELECTION
Your Response
1. Encourage students to share the appeal of places they have actually visited and the lure of unseen vistas. Ask them to explain the attraction each holds.

618

Recalling
2. The call of the sea is wild and cannot be denied.
3. Answers might include a tall ship, a star, the wheel's kick, and the wind's song.

Interpreting
4. Answers will differ, but students might suggest that the sea's attraction is a strong one for someone who wants to wander.
5. Answers will differ, but students might suggest that the poet views life itself as a long sea voyage, with death the sleep at the end of it.
6. Answers will differ. A fever is a burning from a disease or restless excitement. The speaker burns with a desire to return to the sea and he cannot deny this desire.

Applying
7. Answers will differ, but students might include glamorous pursuits such as professional sports or entertainment.

ANSWERS TO ANALYZING LITERATURE

1. There are seven feet or beats in each line.
2. Suggested Response: The pattern of accented and unaccented syllables varies, but each line has seven stressed syllables.
3. Suggested Response: The rhythm is regular with small variations; it is an insistent rhythm that matches the call of the sea.

THE MUCH RESOUNDING SEA, 1884
Thomas Moran
National Gallery of Art, Washington, D.C.

ANALYZING LITERATURE

Understanding Meter

Meter is the pattern of accented and unaccented syllables that form the basis of a poem's rhythm. Here is the first line of "Sea-Fever" with the accented syllables indicated by an accent mark and the unaccented syllables indicated by a ˘. The separate feet are marked by vertical lines.

I must | go down | to the seas | again, | to the
lone | ly sea | and the sky . . .

Notice that the line has seven accented syllables. Such a line is called a heptameter. This particular heptameter has two different kinds of feet. Those made up of one unaccented syllable followed by an accented one are called iambs (for example, "I must"). Those made up of two unaccented syllables followed by one accented syllable are called anapests (for example, "to the seas"). This kind of analysis and identification of meter is called *scansion*.

1. Reread "Sea-Fever," noting the pattern of accented and unaccented syllables in each line. How many feet, or beats, do you find in each line?
2. Is the pattern of accented and unaccented syllables the same for all the lines, or does it vary? Explain.
3. How would you describe the connection between the meter or rhythm and the content of the poem?

Sea-Fever 619

Humanities Note

Fine art, *The Much Resounding Sea,* by Thomas Moran. Moran (1837–1926) was an American landscape painter. He went on an early expedition down the Colorado River and illustrated the report made by the explorers.

You might want to use the following questions:
1. What aspect of the sea does the painting express?
2. Does the painting express the same love of the sea that the poem does? Explain.

Multicultural Focus Ask students whether the feeling expressed in Masefield's poem is unique to the English or whether it might be a universal feeling that crosses lines of nationality and language. Look at a map of the world and locate areas where seafaring cultures may still thrive, such as islands like the British Isles, Indonesia, and the Aleutians, coastal areas, and harbors or bays. Discuss what people who live near the sea or make their living from the sea might have in common.

Ask students to find out more about seafaring cultures around the world. Students should choose one of the geographical areas discussed in class and research the culture of that area. Have students share their findings with the class.

Motivation/Prior Knowledge
Ask students to think about the one person whom they consider the most important to them. What do they remember about this person? What would they say to this person to express how they feel about him or her? Then tell students that in "My Father's Song" Ortiz expresses his feelings to the most important person to him—his father.

Purpose-Setting Question
What does the speaker of the poem learn from his father?

1 Discussion What might be preventing the speaker from saying things?

2 Discussion The speaker remembers the very specific characteristics of his father's voice. What might this suggest about the speaker? About the speaker's relationship with his father?

3 Clarification Students may be unfamiliar with the word *furrow*. A furrow is a narrow groove in the ground made by a plow.

4 Discussion What "things" might the father have said to his son?

Humanities Note

Fine art, *Año Siete (Seventh Year),* Amando M. Peña, Jr. Born on October 1, 1943, in Laredo, Texas. Peña is a reknowned artist of Mexican and Yaqui ancestry. Peña earned his bachelor's and master's degrees in art at Texas A & I University in Kingsville, Texas. In 1983 El Taller, Peña's private galleries in Sante Fe and Taos, New Mexico, opened.

Peña's paintings celebrate his Native American ancestry. Typical of his work are his use of bold color schemes and strong graphic lines.

Ask students in what ways the poem and this painting celebrate Native Americans.

620

My Father's Song

Simon J. Ortiz

Wanting to say things,
I miss my father tonight.
His voice, the slight catch,
the depth from his thin chest,
5   the tremble of emotion
in something he has just said
to his son, his song:

We planted corn one Spring at Acu—
we planted several times
10   but this one particular time
I remember the soft damp sand
in my hand.

My father had stopped at one point
to show me an overturned furrow;
15   the plowshare had unearthed
the burrow nest of a mouse
in the soft moist sand.

Very gently, he scooped tiny pink
animals
into the palm of his hand
20   and told me to touch them.
We took them to the edge
of the field and put them in the shade
of a sand moist clod.

I remember the very softness
of cool and warm sand and tiny alive
25   mice
and my father saying things.

AÑO SIETE (SEVENTH YEAR)
Amado Maurilio Peña, Jr.

RESPONDING TO THE SELECTION

Your Response
1. What special memory do you have of someone you love?

Recalling
2. What emotion does this poem express?

Interpreting
3. How are the first and last lines of this poem similar?
4. What values does the boy learn from his father?

Applying
5. Imagine that your children years in the future remember you "saying things." What understandings about life would you want them to remember?

Closure and Extension

ANSWERS TO RESPONDING TO THE SELECTION
Your Response
1. Encourage students to share their recollections of moments at which their affection for another seemed especially strong.

Recalling
2. The speaker appears to have written this poem out of his fondness and love for his father. The poem commemorates his father's life and the influence he had on the speaker.

Interpreting
3. Answers may vary. The first and last lines are similar, yet they suggest a difference between the speaker and his father. In the first line, the speaker expresses his desire to say something to or about his father. In the last line, the speaker remembers the words that his father was able to say.
4. The speaker learned to value the time he spent with his father. He also learned to appreciate life and the land on which they lived.

Applying
5. Answers will differ. Students should express their own personal feelings. Many students may express similar values as those expressed in this poem.

Meciendo ("Cradle Song")

Gabriela Mistral   translated by Langston Hughes (1957)

<table>
<tr><td>

El mar sus millares de olas
mece, divino
Oyendo a los mares amantes,
mezo a mi niño.

5   El viento errabundo en la noche
mece a los trigos.
Oyendo a los vientos amantes,
mezo a mi niño.

Dios Padre sus miles de mundos
10 mece sin ruido.
Sintiendo su mano en la sombra,
mezo a mi niño.

</td><td>

The sea cradles
its millions of stars divine.
Listening to the seas in love,
I cradle the one who is mine.

5   The errant[1] wind in the night
cradles the wheat.
Listening to the winds in love,
I cradle my sweet.

God Our Father cradles
10 His thousands of worlds without sound.
Feeling His hand in the darkness,
I cradle the babe I have found.

</td></tr>
</table>

1. **errant** (er′ ənt) *adj.*: Roving or wandering; shifting about.

RESPONDING TO THE SELECTION

Your Response

1. Do the images created in this poem appeal to you? Why or why not?

Recalling

2. Whom is the speaker cradling or rocking?
3. Which two lines in each stanza rhyme? What is the rhyme scheme of the poem?

Interpreting

4. Other poets have translated "Meciendo," the title of the poem, as "rocking"; Hughes translates it as "cradle song." What are the different connotations of each translation of the title? Which is a more appropriate title? Why?
5. What attitude about children and motherhood does Mistral convey in "Cradle Song"?

Applying

6. What universal truths about motherhood do you think Mistral is addressing in her poem?

THINKING AND WRITING

Writing a Critical Evaluation

Laurence Perrine, a notable teacher of poetry, once wrote, "Great poetry seeks not merely to entertain the reader but to bring him, along with pure pleasure, fresh insights . . . into the nature of human experience. Great poetry, we might say, gives its reader a broader and deeper understanding of life. . . ."

Which of the poems in this section best meets Perrine's requirement for great poetry? Write an essay in which you argue for the poem of your choice. Make sure you explain why you feel that the four other poems are less successful. Before you submit your work, review your arguments. Are they reasonable? Are they based on what is in the poems and not merely on personal preference? Revise your essay as necessary to strengthen your argument. Then compare your essay with those of your classmates.

Meciendo   621

Presentation

Motivation/Prior Knowledge
Tell students that love is a theme that runs through many works of literature, but each writer expresses his or her feelings of love in a different way. Have students imagine they were writing about the theme of love. How would they express this emotion? Then tell students that in "Cradle Song" Mistral expresses the love a mother has for her children.

Purpose-Setting   Question
What is the speaker's attitude about motherhood?

1 Discussion What images do these two stanzas create? Why are they appropriate for a cradle song?

2 Discussion What impact does this image of God cradling his people have? Why might Mistral have included this image in a song exalting motherhood?

Audiocassette To enhance students' appreciation of the poem, you may want to play the reading of the poem on the **Listening to Literature** Audiocassettes. Have students explore what qualities of the poem may have been lost in translation.

Closure and Extension

ANSWERS TO RESPONDING TO THE SELECTION

Your Response

1. Lead students to see the comparisons the poet draws. Discuss what images they would choose to express their feelings.

Recalling

2. The speaker is cradling her child.
3. The second and fourth lines in each stanza rhyme, giving the poem an *abcb* rhyme scheme.

Interpreting

4. Suggested Response: "Rocking" expresses a more distant feeling and connotation than the word "cradling." A mother can rock a child without actually holding the child. Cradling, on the other hand, expresses the physical closeness of the mother and child. "Cradle Song" is a more appropriate title because it has a gentle, motherly connotation. The title expresses the feeling that this poem is not just a poem, but a song of love a mother sings to her child as she is holding, rocking, and being close to her child.

5. Mistral has a positive attitude toward children and motherhood and is perhaps expressing her longing to be a mother.

Applying

6. Suggested Response: Mistral expresses the deep, caring, and loving relationship a mother has with her children. She compares this relationship with God's relationship to his people.

THINKING AND WRITING

Writing Transparency Before students write, they might benefit from viewing Model 5: *Expository Essay* in the **Transparencies for Writing**.

621

The Sound of the Sea

Henry Wadsworth Longfellow (1807–1882) was born in Portland, Maine, and educated at Bowdoin College. His knowledge of foreign languages gained him a professorship at Bowdoin and later at Harvard. The deaths of his first wife and child and of his second wife had a profound effect on his poetry. The thoughtful, serious brooding on life found in such poems as "The Sound of the Sea" is the result of these personal tragedies. Longfellow remains one of the most popular of American poets.

Sonnet 30

William Shakespeare (1564–1616) is revered not only for his thirty-seven plays but also for his 154 splendid sonnets. Taken together, the sonnets seem to tell a story. The "plot" is hard to follow, but it is clear that the main characters are a young nobleman, a lady, a poet (probably Shakespeare himself), and a rival poet. Some of the best sonnets, like Sonnet 30, are addressed to the young nobleman. In these, Shakespeare expresses his devotion to the man and urges him to marry and have children so that his virtues will live on in his offspring.

622   Poetry

The Sonnet

A **sonnet** is a lyric poem of fourteen lines with a set rhyme scheme. It is normally written in iambic pentameter, a line of ten syllables in which every second syllable is accented. This meter can be seen in the first line of Longfellow's sonnet.

The séa awoke at mídnight fróm its sleép . . .

Here the accented syllables are marked by ′, the unaccented by ˘. "The Sound of the Sea" is an example of a *Petrarchan sonnet,* named after the great Italian poet Petrarch. This kind of sonnet consists of an octave (eight lines of verse) and a sestet (six lines). The octave of a Petrarchan sonnet always uses two rhymes, in the pattern *abbaabba.* The rhyme scheme of the sestet can vary. The Shakespearean sonnet consists of three quatrains and a couplet. The rhyme scheme is *abab cdcd efef gg.*

Focus

The contents of a sonnet are divided into units that match the stanza structure. For example, a Shakespearean sonnet usually presents an idea or question in the first quatrain, explores it for the next two quatrains, and reaches a conclusion in the couplet at the end. To familiarize yourself with the pattern of a Shakespearean sonnet, write three short paragraphs, each with two or three sentences. Let the first paragraph begin with the word *Yesterday,* the second one with *Today,* the third with *Tomorrow.* Briefly describe your thoughts about the past, present, and future. Finally, write a sentence that reaches a conclusion about a point raised in your paragraphs. Then, as you read the sonnets in this section, notice how their contents are shaped by their structures.

Vocabulary

Knowing the following words will help you as you read Longfellow's and Shakespeare's sonnets.

cataract (kat′ ə rakt) n.; A large waterfall (p. 624, l. 7)

inaccessible (in ək ses′ ə b'l) *adj.*: Impossible to reach or enter (p. 624, l. 10)

deem (dēm) *v.*. Consider (p. 624, l. 12)

foreshadowing (fôr shad′ ō iŋ) *n.*: Sign of something to come (p. 624, l. 13)

Guide for Reading   623

Literary Focus The sonnet is a challenge to both poets and readers because of the controlled form of the poem. Both Longfellow and Shakespeare knew how to use this controlled form with ease and power. It takes a great deal of skill and thought to interpret a sonnet because a sonnet says a great deal in few words.

Prereading Focus The Longfellow and Shakespeare poems illustrate the two sonnet forms, Petrarchan and Shakespearean. The purpose of this exercise is to focus students' attention on the Shakespearean structure by adapting its format to a short prose work. To help students find ideas, you might suggest that they reread Shakespeare's "Seven Ages of Man" on page 543. You might also suggest that they recall previous discussions about personal dreams and goals.

Vocabulary Have your **less advanced** students discuss the meaning of each word and then use each word in a sentence reflecting its meaning.

Spelling Tip Point out the double *c* and double *s* in *inaccessible.*

624

The Sound of the Sea

Henry Wadsworth Longfellow

1   The sea awoke at midnight from its sleep,
      And round the pebbly beaches far and wide
      I heard the first wave of the rising tide
      Rush onward with uninterrupted sweep:
5   A voice out of the silence of the deep,
      A sound mysteriously multiplied
2   As of a cataract from the mountain's side,
      Or roar of winds upon a wooded steep.[1]
      So comes to us at times, from the unknown
10   And inaccessible solitudes of being,
      The rushing of the sea-tides of the soul;
3   And inspirations that we deem our own,
      Are some divine foreshadowing and foreseeing
      Of things beyond our reason or control.

---

1. steep (stēp) *n.*: A mountain slope.

RESPONDING TO THE SELECTION

Your Response
1. What thoughts and feelings do the sea and its sounds call up in you?

Recalling
2. Describe what the speaker sees and hears in the first four lines.
3. In lines 5–8, to what two things does he compare the sound he hears?

Interpreting
4. The word "so" at the start of the sestet signals a comparison between the octave and the sestet. What is being compared to what?
5. What are "the unknown/And inaccessible solitudes of being"?

6. What are the "sea-tides" of the soul?

Applying
7. Since the theme of this poem is contained in the sestet, what artistic purpose is served by the description of the sea in the octet?

ANALYZING LITERATURE

Understanding a Petrarchan Sonnet
    A **Petrarchan sonnet** consists of an octave (eight lines) and a sestet (six lines).
1. Using letters, describe the rhyme scheme of the sestet.
2. How does the content of the sonnet reflect the two-part structure of octave and sestet?

624   *Poetry*

Sonnet 30

William Shakespeare

When to the sessions of sweet silent thought
I summon up remembrance of things past,
I sigh the lack of many a thing I sought,
And with old woes' new wail my dear times waste:[1]
5 Then can I drown an eye, unused to flow,
For precious friends hid in death's dateless[2] night,
And weep afresh love's long since cancelled woe,
And moan the expense[3] of many a vanished sight:
Then can I grieve at grievances foregone,[4]
10 And heavily from woe to woe tell o'er[5]
The sad account of fore-bemoanèd moan,[6]
Which I new pay as if not paid before.
But if the while I think on thee, dear friend,
All losses are restored and sorrows end.

---

1. And . . . waste: And by grieving anew for past sorrows ruin the precious present.
2. dateless: Endless.
3. expense: Loss.
4. foregone: Past and done with.
5. tell o'er: Count up.
6. fore-bemoanèd moan: Sorrows suffered in the past.

RESPONDING TO THE SELECTION

Your Response

1. Would you like to have a friend like the one Shakespeare describes? Why or why not?

Recalling

2. In general, what are the speaker's feelings when he recalls the past?

Interpreting

3. What does "drown an eye" (line 5) mean?
4. What does line 7 mean?
5. In lines 10–12, the words "tell o'er" (count up), "account," "pay," and "paid" suggest someone going over bills. What action is the speaker describing through this metaphor?

Applying

6. What does this sonnet imply about the value of friendship?

ANALYZING LITERATURE

Understanding a Shakespearean Sonnet

Like a Petrarchan sonnet, a **Shakespearean sonnet** consists of fourteen lines.

1. Can the thought content of Sonnet 30 be divided into units that correspond to the divisions of three quatrains and a couplet? Give reasons for your opinion.
2. Where does the most obvious change in thought and feeling occur?

Sonnet 30 625

More About the Authors Haiku are usually poems of great delicacy in which a few key details suggest a scene or a mood. Ask students why the form of the haiku lends itself to this type of approach.

Richard Wright is best known for his book *Native Son,* which tells about a young black man living in the slums of Chicago. Wright is most famous for his contemporary realistic fiction. Ask students why he would also want to write haiku poetry, which is known for its subtle, descriptive beauty and its economy of words. Do the two genres have anything in common?

John Updike gained valuable experience as a staff writer for *The New Yorker,* a famous literary magazine. Ask students what other types of work might be helpful for a writer.

GUIDE FOR READING

Three Haiku

Bashō (bas h′ō) (1644–1694) was born near Kyoto, Japan. In his youth he was companion to the son of a lord. In later life he lived apart and devoted himself to the writing of haiku. Many of his best poems were inspired by travels in which he observed nature. His poem printed here illustrates his typical approach to poetry. He looks for a detail or two that will give the impression of an entire landscape.

Chiyojo (chē yō′ jē) (1703–1775) was the wife of a servant of a samurai. When her husband died, she became a nun. She also studied poetry with a well-known teacher of haiku. The two poems of hers printed here illustrate the lightness of spirit for which her work is valued by haiku scholars and critics.

Hokku Poems

Richard Wright (1908–1960) was born on a farm near Natchez, Mississippi. He left school early and worked at low-paying jobs. However, his interest in books prompted him to try writing, and in 1940 he published the novel *Native Son,* which describes the life of a boy raised in the Chicago slums. His wide knowledge of literature enabled him to experiment with different forms. In the two poems printed here, Wright shows how well he could write in the traditional haiku form.

Pendulum

John Updike (1932–   ) was born in Shillington, Pennsylvania. A Harvard graduate, Updike has a remarkable ability to absorb new knowledge and ideas and make them the basis of his short stories and novels. He often portrays the manners and morals of modern American families in his work. His perceptive interest in the contemporary social scene is the basis of "Pendulum," a little poem that is representative of the light verse Updike occasionally publishes in magazines.

626   Poetry

Objectives

1 To write haiku
2 To write a concrete poem
3 To understand concrete poetry
4 To express individual interests and abilities through optional activities

Support Material

Teaching Portfolio
Teacher Backup, p. 787
Usage and Mechanics Worksheet, p. 792
Analyzing Literature Worksheet, *Understanding Haiku,* p. 793
Language Worksheet, *Appreciating Concrete Words,* p. 794
Selection Test, p. 795

Prentice Hall Literature Writing Studio

Haiku and Concrete Poetry

Haiku is a Japanese form of poetry. A **haiku** consists of three lines of verse. The first and third lines have five syllables each. The second line has seven syllables. In this kind of poetry, a detail or two is presented and the reader is left to interpret what they suggest or imply.

Concrete poetry is poetry in which the words are arranged to look like, or suggest something about, the subject being presented. Updike's "Pendulum" is an example of the form.

Focus

Most haiku focus on subjects dealing with nature. These poems tend to capture one brief moment, observation, or impression. Consider what subject in nature you might like to write a haiku about. Create a word web of subjects that would be appropriate for the length and scope of haiku. Copy the web below and complete it. Once you have decided on a subject, read the haiku in this section to familiarize yourself with their structure. Notice the economical use of detail through which the poet creates the central image of the poem. Afterward you will have a chance to write your own haiku.

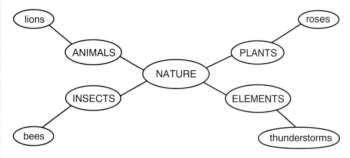

Vocabulary

In haiku the vocabulary is normally quite simple. The haiku poet chooses words for their vividness and their suggestive power.

Literary Focus Although the haiku looks as though it might be easy to write, it is a restrictive form of poetry. The word choice is dictated by the number of syllables necessary in a given line and by the descriptive, sensory nature of haiku. In concrete poetry, the poet arranges the words to form a picture related to the poem's subject.

Prereading Focus Haiku is one of the more challenging and rewarding poetic forms. The purpose of this exercise is to focus students' attention on the need for precision in creating the central image. Lead students to see that specific concrete objects are usually the best choice for a central image.

You might wish to have students work in small groups to complete the activity. Have each group brainstorm for words to complete the web. Tell each student to create his or her own word web, drawing on and adding to the group's suggestions.

Guide for Reading 627

Three Haiku

Temple bells die out.
The fragrant blossoms remain.
A perfect evening!

— BASHŌ

1
2
Dragonfly catcher,
How far have you gone today
In your wandering?

— CHIYOJO

Bearing no flowers,
I am free to toss madly
Like the willow tree.

— CHIYOJO

GIRL WITH LANTERN ON A BALCONY AT NIGHT, c. 1768
Suzuki Harunobu
The Metropolitan Museum of Art

Hokku Poems

Richard Wright

1

Make up your mind snail!
You are half inside your house
And halfway out!

In the falling snow
A laughing boy holds out his palms
Until they are white

Keep straight down this block
Then turn right where you will find
A peach tree blooming

2

Whose town did you leave
O wild and drowning spring rain
And where do you go?

RESPONDING TO THE SELECTION

Your Response

1. Of the haiku on pages 628–629, which do you like best? Why?

Recalling

2. If an artist were to paint the scene that Bashō's haiku suggests, what details might the painting include?
3. What scene do you think Chiyojo was observing in the first of her two haiku?
4. Describe the image presented in her second haiku.

Interpreting

5. Describe the kind of evening that you imagine inspired Bashō's haiku.
6. In Chiyojo's second haiku, what might the speaker be suggesting about herself?
7. What is the "house" in Wright's first haiku?
8. What feelings are stirred in you by the scene Wright depicts in his second haiku?

Applying

9. "Poetry," Robert Frost said, "is what gets lost in translation." Do the three Japanese poems seem less effective than Wright's two haiku? What do you suppose Bashō's and Chiyojo's haiku may have lost in translation?

THINKING AND WRITING

Writing Haiku

Using the details you listed before reading the poems in this section, write your own haiku. First decide what effect you want to create and what feelings you wish to suggest. Then select the details that will enable you to achieve your purpose. Follow the traditional haiku form: three lines of five, seven, and five syllables. When you revise, try to eliminate any unnecessary words.

You and your classmates might consider collecting your haiku and making them into a little volume of poetry.

Hokku Poems 629

Presentation

Motivation/Prior Knowledge Ask students whether they think an American writer could achieve the same effects in haiku as Japanese writers. Then have them read the poems by Richard Wright.

Purpose-Setting Question How are Richard Wright's poems similar to and different from traditional haiku?

1 **Literary Focus** Give examples of images that appeal to different senses.

2 **Discussion** Does Wright effectively describe the rain in just a few words? Why or why not?

Closure and Extension

ANSWERS TO RESPONDING TO THE SELECTION

Your Response

1. Encourage students to share the experiences, places, and emotions that their favorite haiku brings to mind.

Recalling

2. The painting might include a garden with flowers.
3. She was observing a bird that eats dragonflies.
4. She compares herself to a willow tree.

Interpreting

5. Answers will differ, but students might say that it was a warm summer or spring evening.
6. Answers will differ, but students will probably realize that she is expressing freedom to follow one's impulses.
7. The house is the shell of the snail.
8. Answers will differ, but students might say it gives them a happy, joyous feeling.

Applying

9. Answers will differ, but students might say that the haiku are a little less effective because, when you translate a poem, you cannot translate the meaning and the images that a poet had in mind. Since Wright's hokku were already in English, the meaning is not affected.

THINKING AND WRITING

◆ **Software** If students have access to computers, have them use **Bank Street Writer** to complete this assignment.

Publishing Student Writing When students have compiled their haiku, you might want to have volunteers illustrate the poems.

629

Pendulum

John Updike

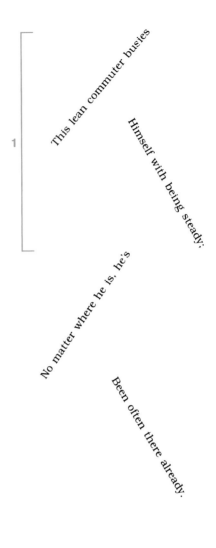

This lean commuter busies
Himself with being steady;
No matter where he is, he's
Been often there already.

1

RESPONDING TO THE SELECTION

Your Response

1. Do you think that the arrangement of lines in this poem helps or hinders your comprehension of the poem's message? Give reasons for your answer.

Recalling

2. Describe the scene that the speaker of the poem is observing.

Interpreting

3. What two meanings do you see in "lean"?
4. How do you interpret the last two lines?
5. Why are the lines arranged as they are?

Applying

6. In what way is a poet's choice of subject matter limited if he or she wishes to write concrete poetry?

ANALYZING LITERATURE

Understanding Concrete Poetry

A concrete poem uses the physical shape of the poem as well as the words to convey meaning. In "Pendulum" John Updike found the back-and-forth movement of a pendulum appropriate for picturing the daily movement of a commuter.

For each of the following items, find a shape that would be appropriate for conveying its meaning.

1. a typist
2. a rainstorm
3. a runner
4. a pilot
5. a rainbow
6. a doctor
7. a student
8. a computer expert
9. a rock-and-roll singer
10. a writer

THINKING AND WRITING

Writing a Concrete Poem

Create a sketch of an object such as an umbrella or a computer screen. Describe in words the object you drew, and arrange the words so that they resemble the drawing. (You might want to use one of the topics and pictures from the Analyzing Literature assignment.) When you revise your poem, try to make the language as expressive as it might be in a poem of the ordinary kind. You and your classmates might wish to mount your concrete poems on a bulletin board.

LEARNING OPTIONS

1. **Art.** Choose a poem from this section and illustrate it. If you choose a haiku, try to capture in your drawing or painting the precise moment or impression described in the poem. If you choose to illustrate Updike's poem, try to convey a feeling of motion and unsteadiness in your drawing or painting. Display your finished artwork in the classroom.
2. **Multicultural Activity.** Go to your public library or a music library and listen to recorded traditional Japanese music. If you can, bring the recording in to your class and listen to it as you read the Japanese haiku in this section. Familiarity with the music of a particular culture can enhance your appreciation of its poetry.

Pendulum   631

moves back and forth in the same way as the train or bus shifts.
5. Answers will differ, but students might argue that the appearance of the poem mimics the shifting of a person trying to stand still in a moving vehicle.

Applying

6. Answers will differ. Students will probably realize that there is a limit to the subjects that can be easily imitated by a poem's appearance.

ANSWERS TO ANALYZING LITERATURE

Answers will differ, but make sure students have selected shapes that will suitably illustrate the subject.

THINKING AND WRITING

Software If students have access to computers, you might have them use the **Writer's Helper** activity *Three Ways of Seeing* to generate ideas for their poems.

Publishing Student Writing

Have students submit their poems to the school newspaper to see if they can be published or publish them in a class newspaper.

LEARNING OPTIONS

1. This activity will appeal to visual learners. To extend this activity for kinesthetic learners, suggest that students create three-dimensional models.
2. Auditory learners will appreciate this activity. You might extend the activity by having students find and bring to class copies of traditional Japanese art to display as the class listens to the music.

Closure and Extension

ANSWERS TO RESPONDING TO THE SELECTION

Your Response

1. Encourage students to share experiences in which they have been in a crowd. Ask them to relate these experiences to the shape of Updike's concrete poem.

Recalling

2. The speaker is observing a commuter who has to stand while riding a train or bus.

Interpreting

3. *Lean* could mean "thin" or "bent slightly."
4. Answers will differ, but students might say that the commuter takes the same route to and from work every day. Also, the commuter

631

Preparation

Reading and Responding After reading many poems and studying the elements of poetry, students should be able to read a poem and recognize how the elements of poetry work together to convey a unified effect.

This lesson reviews the major elements of poetry, using the poem "A Red, Red Rose" as a model for "putting it together."

You may first want to review the elements of poetry, using the points suggested on this page. Then you can read "A Red, Red Rose" with students, discussing the annotations and having them make other critical comments.

To give students further practice in putting together the elements of a poem, use the poem "Our Fathers Had Powerful Songs," by Natalia Belting, following the Teacher Backup in the **Teaching Portfolio,** page 801, which students can annotate themselves.

READING AND RESPONDING

Poetry

Robert Frost has written, "A poem . . . begins in delight and ends in wisdom." Perhaps you experienced these feelings as you read and responded to the poems in this unit.

Poetry has qualities that set it apart from other forms of literature. The language is compact and musical, the structure may be specific to a standard poetic form, and the use of sound devices and sensory details is more common in poetry than in other forms of literature.

Use your active reading strategies to help you respond fully to poetry.

RESPONDING TO LANGUAGE Poets use language to create new ways of seeing things. They often use figures of speech, or figurative language—language that is not intended to be understood literally. Figures of speech enable you to see or think about something in a new and imaginative way. What thoughts and feelings do these figures of speech call up in you?

RESPONDING TO APPEARANCE Poetry can take a variety of forms. What does it look like on the page? Is its appearance related to the type of poetry it is, such as a sonnet or haiku? How does its appearance affect your expectations as you read it?

RESPONDING TO IMAGERY Poets appeal to your senses in creating images. Use your imagination and your five senses to respond to the images the poet has created.

RESPONDING TO SOUND The music of poetry is created by sound devices. Read poems aloud and listen to the rhythm and the rhyme. Listen to the repetition of consonant sounds and other devices. How do the effects of these devices contribute to the meaning of the poem?

RESPONDING TO THE SPEAKER AND TONE The speaker is the voice of the poem. The speaker may be a character or even an object. The tone is the attitude toward the subject that is conveyed throughout the poem. What effect does the tone of the poem have on you?

RESPONDING TO THEME Many poems convey an important idea or insight about life. What do you think is the message of the poem? What special meaning does the poem have for you?

On pages 633–634 you can see an example of active reading and responding by Jair Pinckney of Dwight Morrow High School in Englewood, New Jersey. The notes in the side column include Jair's thoughts and comments as he read "A Red, Red Rose." Your own thoughts as you read may be different because you bring your own experiences to your reading.

Objectives

1 To recognize musical devices in poetry
2 To analyze the effect of musical devices
3 To write a lyric poem
4 To express individual interests and abilities through an optional activity

Support Material

Teaching Portfolio
Teacher Backup, p. 797
Putting It Together, "Our Fathers Had Powerful Songs," by Natalia Belting, p. 801
Usage and Mechanics Worksheet, p. 803
Analyzing Literature Worksheet, *Analyzing Musical Devices,* p. 804

Language Worksheet, *Interpreting Dialect,* p. 805
Selection Test, p. 806

Prentice Hall Literature Writing Studio

A Red, Red Rose

Robert Burns

I

O, my love is like a red, red rose,
　That's newly sprung in June,
O, my love is like the melody,
　That's sweetly played in tune.

Imagery: *Red roses make me think of romance.*

Language: *The speaker is using similes to describe his love. The language is simple—it is easy to understand how the speaker feels.*

Sound: *There are a lot of "l" and "r" sounds. They give the poem a smooth quality.*

A Red, Red Rose 633

Presentation

Motivation/Prior Knowledge
Have students identify for themselves someone or something they love very much—a person, a pet, a thing, or even an activity. Then have them list items to which they might compare the loved person, pet, or thing. Then tell them that this love poem by Burns makes use of comparisons.

Thematic Focus This poem celebrates the poet's appreciation for his loved one. Discuss with students how necessary it is to express appreciation for those we love. Is a poem a good way to express appreciation for someone? Are there better ways to make someone feel appreciated? What are they?

Making Connections Another selection that deals with the endurance of love is *The Tragedy of Romeo and Juliet,* page 287.

Purpose-Setting Question Point out the model question with the title. Let it provide a purpose for reading.

Enrichment Burns's Scottish dialect may be unfamiliar to students. Before students read the poem, you might invite a guest from the school or community who is familiar with Scottish dialect to speak and read the poem to the class. You might ask the guest to entertain questions about Scottish culture.

Multicultural Focus Remind students that, in Western culture, roses symbolize love and red roses, romantic love. Talk about how such symbolism is manifested, for example, when a husband gives his wife roses on their anniversary or on Valentine's Day. Ask students whether this symbol is universal or whether it might be unique to Western culture. Have them give reasons for their opinions. They could answer that this symbol might not be universal because roses do not grow everywhere.

Have students do research to find out whether, in fact, the rose symbolizes love in non-Western cultures. If it does not, have them discover what the rose does symbolize. Also ask them to find out what flower or other object represents love in various cultures. Discuss their findings.

Clarification Students might have a little difficulty reading the dialect. To help them, point out that the apostrophes in *a', wi', o'* and *tho'* indicate letters that have been left out in speaking. If students can fill in the letters, it will help their comprehension.

More About the Author Robert Burns, sometimes known as the "national poet of Scotland," was an enthusiastic collector of Scottish folk songs throughout his life. Much of his poetry is an adaptation and imitation of these songs. Have students discuss folk music of today. Is it poetic? Why or why not?

Reader's Response If you were to write a poem similar to "A Red, Red Rose," to what would you compare love? Explain.

Thematic Response Do you think the poet's appreciation for his loved one is limited to her physical appearance? Explain.

Cooperative Learning You might divide the class into small groups to rewrite the poem using standard English. Have groups brainstorm for appropriate words that can be substituted for the dialect. Ask each group to select one member to read the revised poem to the class. You may consider combining this activity with the suggested Learning Option activity.

Speaker and Tone: *The speaker is deeply in love with the subject of the poem.*

Imagery: *The speaker uses different images—a rose, a melody, the seas—to describe his love.*

Appearance: *The poem looks like a song with four verses.*

Theme: *The speaker is expressing his total devotion to his love.*

II

5   As fair art thou, my bonny[1] lass,
    So deep in love am I,
And I will love thee still, my dear,
    Till a' the seas gang[2] dry.

III

Till a' the seas gang dry, my dear,
10   And the rocks melt wi' the sun!
And I will love thee still, my dear,
    While the sands o' life shall run.

IV

And fare thee weel,[3] my only love,
    And fare thee weel a while!
15   And I will come again, my love,
    Tho' it were ten thousand mile!

---

1. **bonny** (bän' ē) *adj.*: Pretty.
2. **gang** (gaŋ) *v.*: Go.
3. **weel** (wēl) *adv.*: Well.

Robert Burns (1759–1796) was born in southwestern Scotland. As a child he learned many traditional Scottish songs and stories, which he later used as material for his poetry. He first achieved success as a poet in 1786 when he published *Poems: Chiefly in Scottish Dialect*, a collection of poems that captured the essence of Scottish peasant life. Unfortunately, Burns's success was short-lived. He developed a serious heart condition and died at the early age of thirty-seven.

ANSWERS TO RESPONDING TO THE SELECTION

Your Response

1. Encourage students to brainstorm for qualities associated with a red rose. Ask students to express their feelings about these qualities.

Recalling

2. The speaker describes his love as

RESPONDING TO THE SELECTION

Your Response

1. Do you feel that love is like a red rose? If so, in what ways? If not, why not?

Recalling

2. How does the speaker describe his love in the first stanza?
3. According to the second and third stanzas, how long will the speaker love his "bonny lass"?
4. What does the speaker vow to do in the final stanza?

Interpreting

5. What do the similes, or explicit comparisons, in the first stanza suggest about the speaker's feelings?
6. How does the speaker use concrete images, or word pictures, to help express his feelings in the third stanza?
7. What does the vow that the speaker makes in the final stanza reveal about the depth of his love for his "bonny lass"?

Applying

8. Why do you think that a red rose is often used to symbolize, or represent, love?

ANALYZING LITERATURE

Musical Devices

Alliteration and assonance are two **musical devices** used in poetry. Alliteration is the repetition of similar sounds, usually consonants, at the beginnings of words or accented syllables. For example, Burns repeats the *r* sound in the first line of "A Red, Red Rose": "My love is like a *r*ed, *r*ed *r*ose." Assonance is the repetition of vowel sounds within words. Notice the repetition of the *ea* sound in line 9 of "A Red, Red Rose": "Till a' the s*ea*s gang dry, my d*ea*r."

1. Find two more examples of alliteration in "A Red, Red Rose."
2. Find two more examples of assonance.

CRITICAL THINKING AND READING

Analyzing the Effect of Musical Devices

Poets use musical devices to give their work a musical quality. The repetition of sounds can also reinforce the meaning of a poem by adding emphasis to important words. For example, Burns's use of alliteration in line 1 of "A Red, Red Rose" adds emphasis to the image of the rose.

1. Find two other instances in which Burns's use of alliteration or assonance adds emphasis to important words.
2. Explain how his use of musical devices helps to reinforce the overall meaning of the poem.

THINKING AND WRITING

Writing a Lyric

Write a lyric poem in which the speaker expresses his or her thoughts and feelings concerning a specific subject. Choose a subject. Then prepare a list of thoughts and feelings associated with this subject. When you write your poem, link these thoughts and feelings to concrete images. After you finish writing, revise and proofread your poem. Finally, share it with your classmates.

LEARNING OPTION

Speaking and Listening. Dialect is the colloquial language of people living in a certain region. Burns uses the dialect of Scottish peasants in "A Red, Red Rose." An example of this is the line, "Till a' the seas gang dry, my dear." Try reading the poem aloud, pronouncing the dialect expressions as a Scottish peasant would. Use the footnotes to help you with pronunciation. When you have practiced sufficiently, read the poem aloud for the class.

A Red, Red Rose 635

2. Suggested Response: Two examples of assonance are ". . . red, red rose" and "fare thee weel."

ANSWERS TO CRITICAL THINKING AND READING

1. Suggested Response: The repetition of *l* sounds throughout the first stanza gives it a liquid, lyrical quality that emphasizes his love. The assonance of the *ea* sound in line 9 emphasizes the extremity of seas going dry.
2. Suggested Response: Music has a lingering quality. A melody can remain in the mind after the song is over. The musical devices in this poem make it memorable, reinforcing the meaning—that the poet's love will continue through the years.

THINKING AND WRITING

Software If students have access to computers, have them use **Bank Street Writer** to complete all stages of the assignment. Using the program's cut and paste features, students will be able to reorganize their thoughts and feelings during the revision stage.

Alternative Assessment You might want to vary the Thinking and Writing assignment as follows. Have students work collaboratively in groups of four to develop a portfolio of original poems modeled after those in the poetry unit. Their portfolios should include at least one sonnet, one concrete poem, one haiku, one lyric, and one narrative poem. They may add illustrations to enhance their poetry collections.

LEARNING OPTION

This activity will appeal to auditory learners. You might wish to tape student presentations and replay them for everyone's appreciation.

---

a fresh, newly opened red rose in June and as a beautifully played melody.

3. The speaker will love his lass until the seas are dry, until rocks melt in the sun, and as long as he lives.
4. The speaker vows that he will return to his love no matter how far away he goes.

Interpreting

5. Suggested Response: The speaker is very much in love and believes his lass to be very beautiful.

6. Suggested Response: The poet's concrete images of the sea evaporating and rocks melting represent how long his love for his lass will continue. They effectively express the length and endurance of his love.

7. Suggested Response: The speaker's vow shows that neither time nor distance can affect his love for his lass.

Applying

8. Suggested Response: A rose is used to express love because of its beauty and its delicacy. Red is also the color associated with the heart.

ANSWERS TO ANALYZING LITERATURE

1. Suggested Response: Two examples of alliteration are ". . . *l*ove is *l*ike . . ." and ". . . *w*eel a *w*hile!"/

Preparation

Motivation/Prior Knowledge
You may wish to begin by playing some songs that demonstrate a variety of themes and styles. Ask students to share their observations on the relationship between the words, the melody, and the rhythm. Lead students to examine the lyrics for such literary devices as onomatopoeia, alliteration, internal rhyme, end rhyme, similes, and metaphors. Discuss how these devices enhance or detract from the overall effectiveness of the song.

Focus There will be a variety of purposes among your student songwriters. Some will aim only to entertain, others will be trying to evoke deep emotional responses, still others may wish to make a social or political statement. Summarize this variety of goals by pointing out that all the songwriters are trying to affect a listener through the use of poetic expression in a musical setting.

Presentation

Prewriting After students have created a list of topics, have them go back and jot down words, phrases, and images that they associate with each topic. The number and nature of the notes they make under each heading might be a determining factor in deciding on a topic and musical style.

◆ **Software** If students have access to computers, they can use the **Writer's Helper** activities *Idea Wheel* and *Associations* to generate further ideas about their topics.

Drafting Explain to students that their topics, particularly those related to their personal experiences and feelings, do not need to be expressed as literal truth. Many songwriters invent a story or a situation that will illustrate

"The poet is a liar who always speaks the truth."
Jean Cocteau

YOUR WRITING PROCESS

WRITING SONG LYRICS

Lyric poetry is often set to music, and many lyrics written by modern songwriters are actually poems. These lyrics are usually very personal and charged with emotion. When you write song lyrics, you often ask your audience to share in your own feelings or beliefs about your subject.

Focus

Assignment: Write the lyrics for a song.
Purpose: To entertain and perhaps to convey a message.
Audience: Teenagers.

Prewriting

1. Choose a subject. Brainstorm a list of topics that you might enjoy writing about. List as many different topics as you can under several different headings. Then select the one that most appeals to you.

Student Model

Song Subjects

Social Issues   *Personal Experiences*

racial injustice   school dances
dropping out   losing, failing
homeless people   relationships

---

2. Choose a style. You have many styles to choose from: rock, progressive, rap, pop, and others. Your choice will depend on what you want to say in your song.

Drafting

1. Make the lyrics match the style. Some subjects are especially appropriate for specific kinds of music. Progressive music, for example, tends to focus on social issues and personal experience. Country and western music often tells a story, whereas pop songs are about emotions like love.

2. Have a tune in mind. If you do not wish to write music for your song, choose a tune that you like and write the words of your song so that they can be sung to that tune.

their point. Call students' attention to the quotation from Jean Cocteau and discuss how it applies to songwriting.

Point out to students that the structure of their lyrics will be dictated by poetic and musical rhythms. The style of their expression should be appropriate for the subject and the audience. Consequently, some rules of grammar and mechanics may be suspended.

Revising and Editing You may wish to ask students to compose a single sentence that expresses the theme of their song and write it at the top of their work. This can be used as a reference point for the songwriters and the peer editors in reviewing the work for unity.

Encourage students to look for places where they can improve their work by using evoca-

tive language or a literary device. Caution the writers to avoid overworked images and clichés. A peer editor, looking at the work for the first time, might assist in spotting weaknesses that the writer has overlooked.

◆ **Software** If students have access to computers, have them use the **Writer's Helper** activity *Clichés* for help in avoiding this problem.

3. Make the language suitable. Remember that someone will sing your song. Avoid tongue-twisters. If you are writing for your fellow teenagers, your language may be informal and even include some slang expressions.

> **Student Model**
>
>   The Dance
> I would rather be sitting home alone
> Than to see that cracked gym wall right now
> And feel boredom and disgrace
> Wearing a phony smile on my face

Revising and Editing

1. Revise for unity. Read your song to see whether you have focused on a single idea. Eliminate any ideas or information that will distract your listener from what you are trying to say.

2. Use interesting language. Make sure that your lyrics flow and that the words are vivid and interesting.

> **Student Model**
>
>   The Dance *Lament*
>
> 'd
> I ~~would~~ rather be sitting home alone
>   *ing*
> Than ~~to~~ see that cracked gym wall right now
> *Feeling*   *fearing*
> ~~And feel waves of~~ boredom and disgrace
>   *plastic*
> Wearing a ~~phony~~ smile on my face
>   *that I can*
> I don't think I ~~want to~~ deal
>   *makes me*
> With the way it ~~always~~ feels
>   *that*
> I think they should ~~all~~ be repealed
>
> All of these high school dances—
>
> "Me? Of course I'd love to dance!"

3. Exchange lyrics with a partner. Begin your song-writing career with an audience of one. Have your partner read your song as you read his or hers. Ask yourself these questions as you read each other's lyrics:

- Did the writer stick to the subject?
- Do the lyrics convey a clear thought or message?
- Is the language appropriate for a song?

Grammar Tip
If you are careful about parallel structure, your song will be easier to sing.

Options for Publishing

- Form a group of four or five students. Rehearse your song. When you are ready, sing the song for the class.
- With your classmates, create books of songs for each of the musical styles that the members of the class have chosen.

Reviewing Your Writing Process

1. Did you find the experience of writing a song lyric very different from writing other kinds of poetry? Explain.

2. Do you have a new appreciation for the skills of songwriters? Why or why not?

Closure and Extension

Guidelines for Evaluation The following questions might assist you in assessing each student's song:

1. Do the lyrics focus consistently on a single theme?
2. Are the language and rhythm of the lyrics consistent with the topic?
3. Does the song effectively use imagery and other literary devices to achieve its purpose?
4. Did the student make constructive use of revision suggestions from peer editors?
5. Are the lyrics free of spelling errors?

Reviewing Your Writing Process The following questions will help students reflect on and internalize their own writing process:

1. What are the subject and purpose of your song lyrics?
2. For what kind of music are your lyrics appropriate?
3. For what tune did you write your lyrics?
4. Why was rhyming necessary or not necessary for your song?
5. What suggestions from your writing partner did you include to improve your lyrics?
6. What did you learn about writing song lyrics from this experience?

Publishing If possible, invite the music teacher to provide accompaniment and other assistance in creating an audio tape of students' songs.

Cross-Curricular Enrichment Bring the past to life! Work with the Social Studies teacher to show the class how the significant social and political changes of the 1960's are reflected in the music of that decade.

Preparation

Motivation/Prior Knowledge

The concept of poet as reporter has been with us for some time. Before the advent of published news, people looked to their poets, or bards, for accounts of significant events. These reports were usually given in verse, sometimes accompanied by music. As these poets were frequently called on to speak extemporaneously, they needed to organize their thoughts quickly, just as a modern reporter must do in order to meet deadlines. Unlike modern reporters, the poets were not constrained by space or time limitations. In fact, as they were sometimes the only entertainment at a banquet or an inn, they were encouraged to tell the story in elaborate language and at great length.

As time passed and published news reports became available, poet and reporter evolved into two distinct roles. Both continue to give accounts of significant events but from vastly different viewpoints.

Focus Ask students to contrast Tennyson's romanticized version of the Battle of Balaclava with objective news reports. Point out that poets may be inspired by actual events, but they usually relate them with some emotional or philosophical slant. Reporters aim to relate only the facts and leave readers to form their own opinions.

Emphasize the importance in this assignment of distinguishing between fact and opinion.

Presentation

Prewriting Encourage students to choose a poem that contains enough facts to give substance to their newspaper article. If the poem is based on an actual event, have students research any important facts omitted from the poem. If it is a fictional narra-

"Literature is news that stays news."
Ezra Pound

WRITING A NEWS STORY

"The Charge of the Light Brigade" was inspired by the newspaper account of the battle of Balaclava. Poets often write about people and events, and subject matter good for a news story is often appropriate for a poem as well.

Focus

Assignment: Write a newspaper article based on the events described in a poem.
Purpose: To inform.
Audience: Readers of a community newspaper.

Prewriting

1. Review the poems. Reread the poems in this unit to find one you like that might become a news story.

2. Organize the facts. Once you have selected the poem, jot down the facts. Remember that a news story answers the questions Who? What? When? Where? Why? and How?

Student Model

Who?	Macavity the Mystery Cat
What?	Looted larders, broken greenhouse glass
When?	Irregular intervals
Where?	Scattered locations in London
Why?	Unknown
How?	Unknown

Drafting

1. Start with the most essential information. The first paragraph of the news story is sometimes called the *lead* because it contains the leading facts in the story.

Student Model

A mysterious cat is the chief suspect in a series of baffling crimes, according to a source in Scotland Yard's Flying Squad. The source, a longtime veteran of the elite police unit, revealed today that underworld contacts have fingered Macavity as the cat burglar responsible for dozens of local crimes.

---

638 *Poetry*

tive, you may wish to allow students to invent facts to fill in significant gaps.

Drafting Students may need some assistance in organizing the information in order of importance. Be alert for students who are attempting to draft their story in chronological order. Point out that they must focus the readers' attention early and be aware of

the space limitations placed on newspaper articles.

Writing Transparency You might wish to use the Paragraph Exercise *Order of Importance* in **Transparencies for Writing** to demonstrate how the facts should be organized.

Revising and Editing Ask students to recall the differences they identified between poetry and news reports. Stress the difference in styles, and remind students that the elaborately descriptive language used in poetry is inappropriate in a news article. Direct students to use specific nouns and verbs where possible in place of modifying words and phrases.

2. Use the inverted pyramid format. A news story is constructed with the most important information first, followed by details of lesser importance. The result is an inverted pyramid of facts:

Student Model

Macavity fingered by underworld
contacts as mysterious cat burglar.
Unsolved cases: larder looted,
greenhouse glass broken.
Ginger cat is tall and thin.
Never seen at scene
of crimes.

The pyramid format allows the editor of the paper to eliminate less important paragraphs from the bottom of the story if space is needed in the paper for another story.

Revising and Editing

1. Keep it simple. Journalists write in a simple, direct style. Complicated sentence structure and elaborate language get in the way of telling the story.

Student Model

~~The eternally elusive~~ Macavity is a suspect in many ~~fiendish crimes because he is known throughout the~~ ~~civilized world as the Hidden Paw~~ and has been called ~~the Napoleon of crime; the furtive feline has also been~~ compared to the notorious Mungojerrie and Griddlebone.

---

2. Work with a partner. Exchange drafts with a partner. As you read each other's story, look for the answer to these questions:

• Is the information in the lead clear and understandable?
• Does the story answer the questions Who? What? When? Where? Why? and How?
• Is the important information at the beginning of the story, followed by less important details?

Your Writing Process 639

Grammar Tip

In order to avoid the possibility of writing sentence fragments, do not begin sentences with *and, but,* or *or.*

Options for Publishing

• Create the front page of a newspaper with some of your classmates. Use your stories, and illustrate them with pictures you have found in newspapers or magazines. Display your newspaper in the classroom.
• Form a group of five classmates to present *The Evening News* to the class. Take turns reading the

Reviewing Your Writing Process

1. Was it helpful to revise your work with a partner? Explain. What will you do differently the next time?
2. Did you find it easy to convert the poem into a news story? Explain.

3. Does the article answer the questions *Who? What? When? Where? Why?* and *How?*
4. Does the lead paragraph contain enough essential facts to stimulate the interest of the reader?
5. Is the information in the article presented in order of importance?
6. Does the article demonstrate economy of expression?
7. Is the article free of errors in spelling, punctuation, and grammar?

Reviewing Your Writing Process The following questions will help students reflect on and assess their own writing process:
1. What poem have you chosen as the basis for your news story?
2. What details from the poem do you include in your report?
3. What do you put in your lead? Why should this information be the most important or interesting to your readers?
4. What did you learn about writing news stories from this assignment?

Publishing You may wish to display the poems and articles together on a hall bulletin board under a title banner such as "In Other Words . . ." or "From Muse to News!" Encourage the writers to solicit comments from other students in the school.

Enrichment Students may enjoy reversing the process. Allow time for students to write poems based on current news items. The poems should communicate an emotional response, as well as relate the events.

You may wish to assign a limit to the number of words that may be used in the article. Tell students that real reporters must work within space limitations. The word limit will encourage students to identify the most essential information and express it concisely.

Software If students have access to computers, you might have them use the *Sentence Lengths* activity in **Writer's Helper** to assist them in revising complex sentences.

Closure and Extension

Guidelines for Evaluation You might consider the following questions as you evaluate each student's article:
1. Does the news article accurately report the factual information found in the poem?
2. Does the article exclude any opinions or judgments found in the poem?

Humanities Note

Fine art, *Ulysses Deriding Polyphemus,* J.M.W. Turner. Joseph Mallord William Turner (1775-1851), was a premier British landscape painter. His extreme talent was obvious at a very young age. At fifteen he exhibited a painting at the Royal Academy, well before he graduated from the Schools of the Royal Academy—an unusual occurrence. Today he is remembered for his landscape and marine paintings of poetic vision in which he studied the effects of light and atmosphere to the point of near abstraction.

Ulysses Deriding Polyphemus is one of Turner's complex mythological paintings. It was exhibited at the Royal Academy in 1829. The almost impressionistic treatment of this marine subject gives the scene the appearance of being painted in "colored steam." Turner's interest in the effects of light and weather result in the golden atmosphere, aglow with the rays of the setting sun. The romantic turmoil and grandeur of this scene won Turner critical acclaim.

ULYSSES DERIDING POLYPHEMUS
J. M. W. Turner
The National Gallery, London

THE EPIC

Have you ever said that a problem was of epic proportions? What are epics, and what do we mean when we describe something as having epic proportions?

An epic is a long narrative poem about the deeds of a hero. This epic hero often portrays the goals and values of the society. Typically, epics are based in part on historical fact, blending legend with truth. Gods and goddesses often play a part in epics, guiding the hero or thwarting his actions.

Two of the greatest epics are the *Iliad* and the *Odyssey*. Both arose from an oral tradition. They were passed down through word of mouth by wandering Greek minstrels until put into their final form, probably around 800 B.C. and possibly by the semi-legendary bard Homer.

Reading Strategies Point out that the *Odyssey* is a long narrative poem. You might have students review the section on narrative poetry beginning on page 519.

Emphasize that an epic is more difficult to read than a shorter narrative poem. Help students to read the lines as sentences rather than simply as lines. Encourage them to clarify and summarize regularly to ensure comprehension.

READING ACTIVELY

The Odyssey

BACKGROUND In primitive societies stories were passed from one person to another by word of mouth. Storytellers, arriving in a village, court, or camp, would entertain eager listeners with tales of the gods or great heroes. The longer stories, now called epics, might be told over a series of days. To help the storytellers remember these lengthy pieces, the tales were composed in poetic lines and were often recited to the accompaniment of stringed instruments. Although these stories were filled with fantastic deeds and exploits, many were based on historical events and were accepted as fact by the listeners. Two epics, the *Iliad* and the *Odyssey*, had their roots in the events of the Trojan War, which occurred about 1200 B.C. While legend credits the abduction of Helen, the wife of a Greek king, as the reason for the war, most probably economic conflict over control of trade in the Aegean Sea was the cause.

Although a major purpose for telling and retelling the myths and legends was entertainment, another goal was to teach important lessons about religion and society. Myths about Zeus, Athena, and Apollo were many, but there were also stories about great human heroes such as Hector, Odysseus, and Penelope, who served as examples of ideal human qualities. In fact, Alexander the Great credited Homer's *Iliad* as the source of his ideas about valor and nobility.

READING STRATEGIES As you read the *Odyssey*, remember you are reading an epic composed to be heard by an audience. You and your classmates might try reading the poem aloud. You may find a few areas that cause some difficulty when you read. The Greek names of the gods and humans might seem to be a problem at first. However, if you familiarize yourself with the names before you read, you will have less difficulty. The poetic form of the *Odyssey* might cause you a problem too. Try reading the sentences according to the punctuation, instead of line by line. Also remember that epics are written in an elevated style that includes epic similes, which are long, involved, and ornate comparisons. You might choose to skim through these on your first reading so that you do not lose the plot line. Later, reread the epic similes to appreciate their imagery. Finally, interact with the literature by using the active reading strategies: question, predict, visualize, connect, and respond.

CONCEPTS You will encounter the following concepts in the *Odyssey*:
• loyalty, devotion, and fortitude
• the Greek ideal of a strong body and a strong intellect
• the wandering hero
• the triumph of good over evil
• obedience to the laws of the gods

CHARACTERS The following characters appear in the *Odyssey*:

Alcinoüs (al sin′ ō əs)—king of the Phaeacians, to whom Odysseus tells his story
Odysseus (ō dis′ ē əs)—king of Ithaca
Calypso (kə lip′ so)—a sea goddess who loved Odysseus
Circe (sʉr′ sē)—an enchantress who helped Odysseus
Zeus (zo͞os)—king of the gods
Apollo (ə päl′ ō)—god of music, poetry, and medicine
Agamemnon (ag′ ə mem′ nän)—king and leader of Greek forces
Poseidon (pō sī′ d′n)—god of sea and earthquakes
Athena (ə thē′ nə)—goddess of wisdom, skills, and warfare
Polyphemus (päl′ ə fē′ məs)—the cyclops who imprisoned Odysseus
Laertes (lā ʉr′ tēz)—Odysseus' father
Cronus (krō′ nəs)—Titan ruler of the universe, father of Zeus
Perimedes (per′ ə mē′ dēz)—a member of Odysseus' crew
Eurylochus (yo͞o ril′ ə kəs)—another member of the crew
Tiresias (tī rē′ sē əs)—a blind prophet who advised Odysseus
Persephone (pər səf′ ə nē)—wife of Hades
Telemachus (tə lem′ ə kəs)—Odysseus and Penelope's son
Sirens (sī′ rənz)—creatures whose songs lure sailors to their deaths
Scylla (sil′ ə)—a sea monster of gray rock
Charybdis (ka rib′ dis)—an enormous and dangerous whirlpool
Lampetia (lam pē′ s hə)—a nymph
Hermes (hʉr′ mēz)—herald and messenger of the gods
Eumaeus (yo͞o mē′ əs)—an old swineherd and friend of Odysseus
Antinous (an tin′ ō əs)—a leader among the suitors
Eurynome (yo͞o rin′ ə mē)—a housekeeper for Penelope
Penelope (pə nel′ ə pē)—Odysseus' wife
Eurymachus (yo͞o ri′ mə kəs)—a suitor
Amphinomis (am fin′ ə məs)—a suitor

Homer

is thought to have been born sometime between 700 B.C. and 1000 B.C., possibly in western Asia Minor. According to tradition, he was blind. He did not write his two great epics, the *Iliad* and the *Odyssey*, as a modern novelist writes a novel. Rather, he composed them orally by assembling a number of earlier and shorter narrative songs. He probably traveled around the Greek-speaking world reciting them on many occasions. In later centuries the two epics were the basis of Greek and Roman education.

The Odyssey, Part 1

The Epic Hero

The **epic hero** is the central hero of an epic—a figure of great, sometimes larger-than-life stature. His importance is national, international, or even cosmic. He may be a character from history or from legend. His most remarkable traits are generally the ones most valued by the society in which the epic originated. Odysseus, the epic hero of the *Odyssey*, is probably the most famous of all epic heroes.

Focus

On his voyage home from war, Odysseus endures one extraordinary and dangerous adventure after another. Although he has a reputation for cleverness, this epic hero seems to have little control over his fate. What qualities do you think make a hero? Does a hero always need to exhibit superhuman traits? Can simple human qualities also contribute to heroism? Do the qualities of the ideal hero change over the course of history? With a small group of classmates, make a cluster of words, phrases, images, and actions you associate with the word *hero*. Discuss your responses. Then, as you read the *Odyssey*, compare your ideas about heroism with the traits that Odysseus displays in the epic.

Vocabulary

Knowing the following words will help you as you read Part 1 of the *Odyssey*.

plunder (plun′ dər) *n.*: Goods taken by force; loot (p. 647)

squall (skwôl) *n.*: A brief, violent storm (p. 649)

dispatched (dis pacht′) *v.*: Finished quickly (p. 654)

mammoth (mam′ əth) *adj.*: Enormous (p. 657)

bereft (bi reft′) *v.*: Left in a sad and lonely state (p. 667)

cherishes (cher′ ish əz) *v.*: Holds dear; feels love for (p. 674)

insidious (in sid′ ē əs) *adj.*: Characterized by treachery (p. 675)

644   The Epic

Preparation

More About the Author Oral poets like Homer composed their works from memory as they recited them to an audience. They organized narrative songs according to key themes or scenes —such as a wedding celebration, the arming of a hero for battle, and so forth—which they shortened, lengthened, and combined in different ways. Ask students to consider how the widespread use of writing may have affected this oral tradition of poetry.

Literary Focus Discuss with students the elevated and extraordinary qualities associated with an epic hero—for example, a national or international reputation for heroic deeds and a close relationship with the gods. In the opening lines of the poem, Homer describes two specific characteristics of Odysseus— his guile, during both peace and war, and his love of his native Greece. As students read, have them look for evidence of these characteristics in addition to others that emerge as the journey continues.

Prereading Focus To motivate students for the activity, you might want to hold a class discussion about contemporary heroes—both real and fictional. Why do students view these people as heroes? What traits do the heroes share?

Vocabulary Have more advanced students write a brief paragraph using five of the seven words.

Objectives

1 To understand the qualities of the epic hero
2 To interpret epithets
3 To write about the epic hero
4 To express individual interests and abilities through optional activities

Support Material

Teaching Portfolio
Teacher Backup, p. 829
Grammar in Action Worksheets: *Using Figurative Language,* p. 832; *Using Appositives and Appositive Phrases,* p. 834
Usage and Mechanics Worksheet, p. 836
Vocabulary Check, p. 837
Analyzing Literature Worksheet,

Understanding the Epic Hero, p. 838
Language Worksheet, *Recognizing Allusions,* p. 839
Selection Test, p. 840

Listening to Literature
"Sailing from Troy"

Prentice Hall Literature Writing Studio

The Odyssey

Homer

translated by Robert Fitzgerald

*In the opening verses, Homer addresses the muse
of epic poetry. He asks her help in telling the tale of
Odysseus.*

Sing in me, Muse,[1] and through me tell the story
of that man skilled in all ways of contending,
the wanderer, harried for years on end,
after he plundered the stronghold
5 on the proud height of Troy.[2]
                              He saw the townlands
and learned the minds of many distant men,
and weathered many bitter nights and days
in his deep heart at sea, while he fought only
to save his life, to bring his shipmates home.
10 But not by will nor valor could he save them,
for their own recklessness destroyed them all—
children and fools, they killed and feasted on
the cattle of Lord Helios,[3] the Sun,
and he who moves all day through heaven
15 took from their eyes the dawn of their return.

Of these adventures, Muse, daughter of Zeus,[4]
tell us in our time, lift the great song again.

1. Muse (myo͞oz): Any of
the nine goddesses of the
arts, literature, and the sciences.

2. Troy (troi): City in
northwest Asia Minor, site
of the Trojan War.

3. Helios (hē′ lē äs′): The
sun god.

4. Zeus (zo͞os): King of the
gods.

Note: In his translation of the *Odyssey*, Fitzgerald spelled Greek names in a
way that suggests the sound and flavor of the original Greek. In the excerpts
included here, more familiar spellings have been used. Where, for example,
Fitzgerald wrote "Kirkê," "Kyklops," and "Seirênês," you will here find
"Circe," "Cyclops," and "Sirens."

The Odyssey 645

Thematic Focus Odysseus' entire journey home is a series of
challenges to his character, his
intelligence, and his abilities as a
leader. Discuss with students the
idea that everyone faces such
challenges in life. What challenges do students themselves confront in their daily lives? Will the
challenges change as they grow
older?

Alternative Assessment To promote active reading, have students keep a reader's response
journal as they read the *Odyssey*. In the personal response
section of their journals, encourage students to react to Odysseus. How do they feel about him?
What do they believe to be his
strengths? His weaknesses?

Their observations will enable you to assess their understanding of the epic.

Presentation

Motivation/Prior Knowledge
Ask students what positive associations the word *home* calls up.
Have them explain how these
associations might affect them if
they were traveling in a foreign
country. Then tell them that
Odysseus, the hero of the epic
they are about to read, is strongly
motivated by thoughts of home.

Master Teacher Note You might
want to explain to students that
the *Iliad* and the *Odyssey* were
the keystones of Greek and Roman education. Ask students to
consider, as they read, what values and attitudes toward life this
epic teaches. Also, have students speculate about the values
that a modern epic might teach.

Making Connections Other selections that deal with ideas and
characters from the *Odyssey* are
the modern poems "Siren Song,"
page 711, "Ithaca," page 712.

Purpose-Setting Question The
Odyssey is rich with figurative
language. How does this language contribute to the story?

1 **Clarification** Scholars still debate whether or not the legendary Homer existed. They do
agree, however, that the *Iliad* and
the *Odyssey* were composed by
a poet or poets working in an oral
tradition.

2 **Reading Strategy** Have students summarize these lines.

3 **Clarification** This is probably a
reference to Calliope, the muse
of epic poetry.

Humanities Note

Fine art, *La Nef de Telemachus* (The Ship of Telemachus). This picture is an illustration for the *Odyssey* of Homer. The modern style of this rendering in no way interferes with its ancient flavor. The illustration was inspired by motifs from statues, urns, and frescoes of ancient Greece. The rich blue of the sea is a striking frame for the massive black ship. Powered by sail and oar, this craft is the kind on which Odysseus and his men would have sailed to and from Troy.

You might use these questions for discussion:

1. How do you think this ship compares in size with Columbus's vessels or with a modern ocean liner?
2. How do you think this ship would fare in a storm? Explain.

LA NEF DE TELEMACHUS
The New York Public Library
Picture Collection

646   *The Epic*

PART 1   THE ADVENTURES OF ODYSSEUS

Sailing from Troy

*Ten years after the Trojan War, Odysseus departs
from the goddess Calypso's island. He arrives in
Phaeacia, ruled by Alcinous. Alcinous offers a ship to
Odysseus and asks him to tell of his adventures.*

"I am Laertes'⁵ son, Odysseus.
                      Men hold me
formidable for guile in peace and war:
20 this fame has gone abroad to the sky's rim.

My home is on the peaked sea-mark of Ithaca⁶
under Mount Neion's wind-blown robe of leaves,
in sight of other islands—Dulichium,
Same, wooded Zacynthus—Ithaca
25 being most lofty in that coastal sea,
and northwest, while the rest lie east and south.
A rocky isle, but good for a boy's training;
I shall not see on earth a place more dear,
though I have been detained long by Calypso,⁷
30 loveliest among goddesses, who held me
in her smooth caves, to be her heart's delight,
as Circe of Aeaea,⁸ the enchantress,
desired me, and detained me in her hall.
But in my heart I never gave consent.
35 Where shall a man find sweetness to surpass
his own home and his parents? In far lands
he shall not, though he find a house of gold.

What of my sailing, then, from Troy?
                      What of those years
of rough adventure, weathered under Zeus?
40 The wind that carried west from Ilium⁹
brought me to Ismarus, on the far shore,
a strongpoint on the coast of Cicones.¹⁰
I stormed that place and killed the men who fought.
Plunder we took, and we enslaved the women,
45 to make division, equal shares to all—
but on the spot I told them: 'Back, and quickly!
Out to sea again!' My men were mutinous,
fools, on stores of wine. Sheep after sheep
they butchered by the surf, and shambling cattle,

5. Laertes (lā ûr′ tēz)

6. Ithaca (ith′ ə kə): An
island off the west coast of
Greece.

7. Calypso (kə lip′ sō)

8. Circe (sûr′ sē) of
Aeaea (ē′ ē ə)

9. Ilium (il′ ē əm): Troy.

10. Cicones (si kō′ nēz)

4 **Clarification** The *Iliad,* also attributed to Homer, is the epic
poem detailing the events of the
Trojan War.

5 **Enrichment** Hyperbole, or exaggeration, is used often throughout the poem.

6 **Discussion** Why did Odysseus
not give in to the charms of
Circe?

The Odyssey   647

ANSWERS TO RESPONDING TO THE SELECTION

Your Response

1. Discuss Odysseus' courage in battle. Ask if he is ruthless. Is there a softer side to his character? Encourage students to support their ideas with examples from the selection.

Recalling

2. Odysseus and his men attack the island—killing, plundering, and enslaving its women. When Odysseus orders his men to leave, they rebel (having had too much to drink) and continue slaughtering livestock. Survivors run to the main force of Cicones for help. This army soundly defeats Odysseus and his men, killing many of them.

Interpreting

3. Although Odysseus recognizes the beauty of Calypso and Circe, he is homesick for Ithaca.
4. The army of the Cicones is trained to fight on horseback or on foot; also it outnumbers Odysseus' army.

Applying

5. Answers will differ, but most students will include the influence of the gods in everyday life as the greatest difference.

---

50 feasting,—while fugitives went inland, running
to call to arms the main force of Cicones.
This was an army, trained to fight on horseback
or, where the ground required, on foot. They came
with dawn over that terrain like the leaves
55 and blades of spring. So doom appeared to us,
dark word of Zeus for us, our evil days.
My men stood up and made a fight of it—
backed on the ships, with lances kept in play,
from bright morning through the blaze of noon
60 holding our beach, although so far outnumbered;
but when the sun passed toward unyoking time,
then the Achaeans,[11] one by one, gave way.
Six benches were left empty in every ship
that evening when we pulled away from death.
65 And this new grief we bore with us to sea:
our precious lives we had, but not our friends.
No ship made sail next day until some shipmate
had raised a cry, three times, for each poor ghost
unfleshed by the Cicones on that field.

11. Achaeans (ə kē′ ənz): Greeks; here referring to Odysseus' men.

RESPONDING TO THE **S**ELECTION

Your Response

1. What is your first impression of Odysseus? Which of his qualities and values seem most admirable to you?

Recalling

2. Describe the events on Ismarus.

Interpreting

3. What were Odysseus' feelings when he was held captive by Calypso and Circe?
4. Why were Odysseus and his men defeated by the Cicones?

Applying

5. What impression do you have of the differences between the world of the *Odyssey* and our own world?

648   *The Epic*

The Lotus-Eaters

70 Now Zeus the lord of cloud roused in the north
a storm against the ships, and driving veils
of squall moved down like night on land and sea.
The bows went plunging at the gust; sails
cracked and lashed out strips in the big wind.
75 We saw death in that fury, dropped the yards,
unshipped the oars, and pulled for the nearest lee:[12]
then two long days and nights we lay offshore
worn out and sick at heart, tasting our grief,
until a third Dawn came with ringlets shining.
80 Then we put up our masts, hauled sail, and rested,
letting the steersmen and the breeze take over.

I might have made it safely home, that time,
but as I came round Malea the current
took me out to sea, and from the north
85 a fresh gale drove me on, past Cythera.
Nine days I drifted on the teeming sea
before dangerous high winds. Upon the tenth
we came to the coastline of the Lotus-Eaters,
who live upon that flower. We landed there
90 to take on water. All ships' companies
mustered alongside for the midday meal.
Then I sent out two picked men and a runner
to learn what race of men that land sustained.
They fell in, soon enough, with Lotus-Eaters,
95 who showed no will to do us harm, only
offering the sweet Lotus to our friends—
but those who ate this honeyed plant, the Lotus,
never cared to report, nor to return:
they longed to stay forever, browsing on
100 that native bloom, forgetful of their homeland.
I drove them, all three wailing, to the ships,
tied them down under their rowing benches,
and called the rest: 'All hands aboard;
come, clear the beach and no one taste
105 the Lotus, or you lose your hope of home.'
Filing in to their places by the rowlocks
my oarsmen dipped their long oars in the surf,
and we moved out again on our seafaring.

12. lee (lē) *n.*: An area
sheltered from the wind.

8 **Clarification** In this instance, *yards* means "thick poles used to support rigging."

9 **Discussion** Why did Odysseus not allow his men to eat "the sweet Lotus"?

The Odyssey 649

1. Discuss a variety of distractions with students. Ask if all the diversions have something in common, such as the desire for immediate gratification.

Recalling

2. Strong currents and a fierce storm drive Odysseus off course.
3. Crew members who eat the Lotus forget their homeland and want to remain in the land of the Lotus-Eaters forever.

Interpreting

4. Suggested Response: The imagery suggests that Dawn is like a person with beautiful hair.
5. Suggested Response: His men are easily swayed and distracted; they lack discipline.

Applying

6. Answers will differ, but students may respond that the notion of living a life of leisure without any cares has universal appeal.

---

10 Clarification Such indifference to a common set of laws would have been appalling to the Greeks, who were governed by an assembly.

11 Reading Strategy Ask students to keep this description in mind as they read on.

RESPONDING TO THE SELECTION

Your Response

1. Have you ever been diverted from achieving an important goal by something that temporarily seemed more attractive? What distracted you? What qualities did you need to overcome the distraction? Explain.

Recalling

2. What keeps Odysseus from reaching home?
3. What happens to the crew members who eat the Lotus?

Interpreting

4. The third dawn after the storm is described as coming "with ringlets shining." What impression of the dawn does this image give you?
5. What does this episode suggest about the kinds of problems Odysseus has with his men?

Applying

6. Brief as it is, the episode of the Lotus-Eaters is one of the most famous parts of the *Odyssey*. Why do you think readers have found it so interesting?

The Cyclops

In the next land we found were Cyclopes,[13]
110   giants, louts, without a law to bless them.
In ignorance leaving the fruitage of the earth in
      mystery
to the immortal gods, they neither plow
nor sow by hand, nor till the ground, though
      grain—
wild wheat and barley—grows untended, and
115   wine grapes, in clusters, ripen in heaven's rains.
Cyclopes have no muster and no meeting,
no consultation or old tribal ways,
but each one dwells in his own mountain cave
dealing out rough justice to wife and child,
120   indifferent to what the others do. . . .

As we rowed on, and nearer to the mainland,
at one end of the bay, we saw a cavern
yawning above the water, screened with laurel,
and many rams and goats about the place
125   inside a sheepfold—made from slabs of stone
earthfast between tall trunks of pine and rugged
towering oak trees.
                              A prodigious[14] man
slept in this cave alone, and took his flocks
to graze afield—remote from all companions,
130   knowing none but savage ways, a brute
so huge, he seemed no man at all of those
who eat good wheaten bread; but he seemed rather

13. Cyclopes (sī klō′ pēz) *n.*: Plural form of Cyclops (sī′ kläps), a race of giants with one eye in the middle of the forehead.

14. prodigious (prə dij′ əs) *adj.*: Enormous.

THE CYCLOPS (detail)
Odilon Redon
Rijksmuseum, Kroller Muller Otterloo

Humanities Note

Fine art, *The Cyclops* (detail), by Odilon Redon. Odilon Redon (1840-1916) was a French painter and lithographer. Critics have said that he was born too soon. Redon's visionary and highly imaginative work is a precursor to Surrealism, a revolutionary art movement which did not begin until after his death.

The painting *The Cyclops*, executed during the period 1898-1900, marks the beginning of a new phase in Redon's art. He discarded the sinister subjects in black and white that he had favored in previous years for bright, colorful paintings of mythological scenes and flowers. This radical change reflects the change in his life from an obscure unknown to a prominent, recognized artist. Reality is put aside in this dream-like interpretation of the Cyclops. The odd fusing of green and purple in the sky frame the countenance of the creature, whose single eye regards the viewer from an ochre-colored face. The purple vegetation in the foreground vibrates with a strange energy.

You might use these questions for class discussion:
1. How does Redon's interpretation of the Cyclops compare with that of N. C. Wyeth on page 660?
2. Which interpretation do you prefer? Explain your reasons.

12 **Clarification** The god Apollo, a son of Zeus, is associated with art, medicine, and the sun.

a shaggy mountain reared in solitude.
We beached there, and I told the crew
35 to stand by and keep watch over the ship;
as for myself I took my twelve best fighters
and went ahead. I had a goatskin full
of that sweet liquor that Euanthes' son,
Maron, had given me. He kept Apollo's[15]
40 holy grove at Ismarus; for kindness
we showed him there, and showed his wife and child,
he gave me seven shining golden talents[16]
perfectly formed, a solid silver winebowl,
and then this liquor—twelve two-handled jars
45 of brandy, pure and fiery. Not a slave
in Maron's household knew this drink; only
he, his wife and the storeroom mistress knew;

15. Apollo (ə päl′ ō): The god of music, poetry, prophecy, and medicine.

16. talents: Units of money in ancient Greece.

The Odyssey   651

13 Discussion What use would the wine and victuals be if they met a Cyclops?

14 Reading Strategy Based on what you know so far about Odysseus, predict whether he will honor his men's request.

15 Clarification The Greek laws of hospitality mandated an exchange of gifts. A host was expected to welcome his guests *and* give them gifts.

16 Enrichment Tell the students that the legendary Titan Atlas was so strong that he could support the world on his shoulders. Then ask students to recall some other literary characters renowned for their extraordinary strength.

and they would put one cupful—ruby-colored,
honey-smooth—in twenty more of water,
150 but still the sweet scent hovered like a fume
over the winebowl. No man turned away
when cups of this came round.
                    A wineskin full
I brought along, and victuals in a bag,
for in my bones I knew some towering brute
155 would be upon us soon—all outward power,
a wild man, ignorant of civility.

We climbed, then, briskly to the cave. But Cyclops
had gone afield, to pasture his fat sheep,
so we looked round at everything inside:
160 a drying rack that sagged with cheeses, pens
crowded with lambs and kids, each in its class:
firstlings apart from middlings, and the 'dewdrops,'
or newborn lambkins, penned apart from both.
And vessels full of whey[17] were brimming there—
165 bowls of earthenware and pails for milking.
My men came pressing round me, pleading:

                      'Why not
take these cheeses, get them stowed, come back,
throw open all the pens, and make a run for it?
We'll drive the kids and lambs aboard. We say
170 put out again on good salt water!'

                         Ah,
how sound that was! Yet I refused. I wished
to see the cave man, what he had to offer—
no pretty sight, it turned out, for my friends.
We lit a fire, burnt an offering,
175 and took some cheese to eat; then sat in silence
around the embers, waiting. When he came
he had a load of dry boughs on his shoulder
to stoke his fire at suppertime. He dumped it
with a great crash into that hollow cave,
180 and we all scattered fast to the far wall.
Then over the broad cavern floor he ushered
the ewes he meant to milk. He left his rams
and he-goats in the yard outside, and swung
high overhead a slab of solid rock
185 to close the cave. Two dozen four-wheeled wagons,
with heaving wagon teams, could not have stirred

17. whey (wā) *n.*: The thin, watery part of milk separated from the thicker curds.

652   *The Epic*

Grammar in Action

Figurative language is writing or speech that is not meant to be interpreted literally. Figurative expressions often involve comparisons between two basically unlike things. Look at this figurative expression in a speech by the Cyclops in the *Odyssey*:

   'Strangers,' he said, 'who are you? And where from?
      What brings you here by seaways—a fair traffic?
      Or are you wandering rogues, who cast their lives like
   dice, and ravage other folk by sea?'

Dice are thrown in games of chance or by gamblers. In asking whether Odysseus and his men cast their lives as people do the dice, in search of a quick fortune, the speaker uses figurative language, comparing the lives of pirates and other marauders to the behavior of gamblers.

    Writers use figurative language to create for the reader vivid impressions of what they are describing.

    Now look at this expression. What two things are being compared?

   . . . then two long days and nights we lay offshore tasting our grief,
      until a third Dawn came with ringlets shining.

the tonnage of that rock from where he wedged it
over the doorsill. Next he took his seat
and milked his bleating ewes. A practiced job
190 he made of it, giving each ewe her suckling;
thickened his milk, then, into curds and whey,
sieved out the curds to drip in withy[18] baskets,
and poured the whey to stand in bowls
cooling until he drank it for his supper.
195 When all these chores were done, he poked the fire,
heaping on brushwood. In the glare he saw us.

'Strangers,' he said, 'who are you? And where from?
What brings you here by seaways—a fair traffic?
Or are you wandering rogues, who cast your lives
200 like dice, and ravage other folk by sea?'

We felt a pressure on our hearts, in dread
of that deep rumble and that mighty man.
But all the same I spoke up in reply:

'We are from Troy, Achaeans, blown off course
205 by shifting gales on the Great South Sea;
homeward bound, but taking routes and ways
uncommon; so the will of Zeus would have it.
We served under Agamemnon,[19] son of Atreus—
the whole world knows what city
210 he laid waste, what armies he destroyed.
It was our luck to come here; here we stand,
beholden for your help, or any gifts
you give—as custom is to honor strangers.
We would entreat you, great Sir, have a care
215 for the gods' courtesy; Zeus will avenge
the unoffending guest.'

He answered this
from his brute chest, unmoved:

'You are a ninny,
or else you come from the other end of nowhere,
telling me, mind the gods! We Cyclops
220 care not a whistle for your thundering Zeus
or all the gods in bliss; we have more force by far.
I would not let you go for fear of Zeus—
you or your friends—unless I had a whim to.
Tell me, where was it, now, you left your ship—

18. withy (with' ē) *adj.:*
Tough, flexible twigs.

19. Agamemnon (ag'ə
mem' nän): The king who
led the Greek army during
the Trojan War.

The Odyssey 653

17 Discussion What kind of welcome does the Cyclops give Odysseus and his men?

18 Discussion What values could a Greek or Roman student have learned from this passage?

19 Clarification The word *ninny* means "a person who is a fool."

While the comparison in the first example is stated directly, the comparison in this one is implied, or suggested. Homer indirectly compares the dawn of day with a person by capitalizing the word as if it were a proper name and by alluding to Dawn's ringlets, or curly hair.

Student Activity 1. Find four other examples of figurative language in the epic and write these on your paper. Read your choices to the class, discussing the comparison in each expression as well as the effect of that expression on the reader.

Student Activity 2. Work with a partner to write five original figurative expressions. Share your work with the rest of the class.

Electronic Handbook You might want students to review figurative language before completing the Grammar in Action activities. If students have access to the Language Master 6000, have them enter the access words *figurative, simile, metaphor, personification, hyperbole,* or *irony* and press the GRAMMAR key to get information on the use of figurative language.

20 **Clarification** Poseidon is a brother of Zeus.

21 **Discussion** What does Odysseus' change of mind tell about his character?

22 **Clarification** Legend has it that Athena emerged, in full armor, from the head of Zeus. She was the goddess of wisdom and the special protector of Odysseus.

225   around the point, or down the shore, I wonder?'

He thought he'd find out, but I saw through this,
and answered with a ready lie:

                           'My ship?

20   Poseidon[20] Lord, who sets the earth a-tremble,
broke it up on the rocks at your land's end.
230   A wind from seaward served him, drove us there.
We are survivors, these good men and I.'

Neither reply nor pity came from him,
but in one stride he clutched at my companions
and caught two in his hands like squirming puppies
235   to beat their brains out, spattering the floor.
Then he dismembered them and made his meal,
gaping and crunching like a mountain lion—
everything: innards, flesh, and marrow bones.
We cried aloud, lifting our hands to Zeus,
240   powerless, looking on at this, appalled;
but Cyclops went on filling up his belly
with manflesh and great gulps of whey,
then lay down like a mast among his sheep.
My heart beat high now at the chance of action,
245   and drawing the sharp sword from my hip I went
along his flank to stab him where the midriff
holds the liver. I had touched the spot
when sudden fear stayed me: if I killed him
we perished there as well, for we could never
250   move his ponderous doorway slab aside.
So we were left to groan and wait for morning.

When the young Dawn with fingertips of rose
lit up the world, the Cyclops built a fire
and milked his handsome ewes, all in due order,
255   putting the sucklings to the mothers. Then,
his chores being all dispatched, he caught
another brace[21] of men to make his breakfast,
and whisked away his great door slab
to let his sheep go through—but he, behind,
260   reset the stone as one would cap a quiver.
There was a din of whistling as the Cyclops
rounded his flock to higher ground, then stillness.
And now I pondered how to hurt him worst,
22   if but Athena[22] granted what I prayed for.

20. Poseidon (pō sī' d'n): God of the sea and of earthquakes.

21. brace (brās) *n.*: A pair.

22. Athena (ə thē' nə): The goddess of wisdom, skills, and warfare.

265   Here are the means I thought would serve my turn:

a club, or staff, lay there along the fold—
an olive tree, felled green and left to season
for Cyclops' hand. And it was like a mast
a lugger[23] of twenty oars, broad in the beam—
270   a deep-sea-going craft—might carry:
so long, so big around, it seemed. Now I
chopped out a six foot section of this pole
and set it down before my men, who scraped it;
and when they had it smooth, I hewed again
275   to make a stake with pointed end. I held this
in the fire's heart and turned it, toughening it,
then hid it, well back in the cavern, under
one of the dung piles in profusion there.
Now came the time to toss for it: who ventured
280   along with me? whose hand could bear to thrust
and grind that spike in Cyclops' eye, when mild
sleep had mastered him? As luck would have it,
the men I would have chosen won the toss—
four strong men, and I made five as captain.

285   At evening came the shepherd with his flock,
his woolly flock. The rams as well this time,
entered the cave: by some sheepherding whim—
or a god's bidding—none were left outside.
He hefted his great boulder into place
290   and sat him down to milk the bleating ewes
in proper order, put the lambs to suck,
and swiftly ran through all his evening chores.
Then he caught two more men and feasted on them.
My moment was at hand, and I went forward
295   holding an ivy bowl of my dark drink,
looking up, saying:

                       'Cyclops, try some wine.
Here's liquor to wash down your scraps of men.
Taste it, and see the kind of drink we carried
under our planks. I meant it for an offering
300   if you would help us home. But you are mad,
unbearable, a bloody monster! After this,
will any other traveler come to see you?'

He seized and drained the bowl, and it went down
so fiery and smooth he called for more:

23. lugger (lug′ ər) *n.*: A ship equipped with a four-sided sail.

---

23 Clarification The "shepherd" is the Cyclops.

24 Discussion What does Odysseus hope to achieve by offering the Cyclops his wine?

Multicultural Focus Ask students to describe what makes the Cyclops such a dreadful monster. Discuss the feelings evoked by his gigantic size and his single eye. Ask whether these traits would be considered monstrous by people of any time and culture or whether they were horrible only to the ancient Greeks. Have students give reasons for their opinions.

Assign students to do research to find out more about the portrayal of monsters in different cultures. Ask them to do a multicultural literature search for examples of giants, one-eyed monsters, and other kinds of monsters. Discuss their findings, comparing their examples with the original Cyclops of Homer's *Odyssey*.

25 Clarification The word *fuddle* means "muddle or confusion."

26 Discussion What do you think Odysseus believed was the source of this "more than natural" strength?

27 Discussion What does this simile contribute to the description?

Cooperative Learning Have students work together in small groups to create a comic book version of Odysseus' escape from the Cyclops. They should meet first to brainstorm ideas and assign different tasks to each individual in the group. Tasks might include the following:

Art director—to supervise all facets of the visual portion of the strip including brainstorming ideas for art and approving sketches, coloring, and calligraphy

Artists—to sketch storyboard and do final outline drawings

Colorists—to color final drawings

Calligrapher—to transcribe narration and dialogue into each frame of the comic book

Writers—to write narration and copy for speech balloons

Editor—to supervise and revise written copy and to oversee continuity between art and written copy

Students will probably need to meet as a group several times as the project progresses. Between meetings, they should work individually to accomplish the tasks necessary to make future meetings productive.

In the first meeting, students can outline the steps they will need to accomplish and list the tasks needed to be assigned in order to create the comic book. They can plan a beginning storyboard by deciding together how much of the plot can be told with each picture.

Between meetings, the art director and his/her staff of artists, colorists, and calligraphers can develop sketches for the

main characters and thumbnail sketches as a storyboard for the entire story. Meanwhile, the editor and writers can write the first draft of the narration and some dialogue between the characters.

In the second meeting, artists and writers can share the ideas they have in sketch and first draft form and revise them as necessary. If there are disagreements about the art or the writ-ing, the group should try to arrive at a consensus, but if that is not possible, the art director should make final decisions about art, and the editor should make final continuity decisions as well as those concerning written material. Further meetings can be called as necessary.

305　'Give me another, thank you kindly. Tell me,
　　how are you called? I'll make a gift will please you.
　　Even Cyclopes know the wine grapes grow
　　out of grassland and loam in heaven's rain,
　　but here's a bit of nectar and ambrosia!'[24]
310　Three bowls I brought him, and he poured them
　　　down.
　　I saw the fuddle and flush come over him,
　　then I sang out in cordial tones:

　　　　　　　　　'Cyclops,
　　you ask my honorable name? Remember
　　the gift you promised me, and I shall tell you.
315　My name is Nohbdy: mother, father, and friends,
　　everyone calls me Nohbdy.'

　　　　　　　　　And he said:
　　'Nohbdy's my meat, then, after I eat his friends.
　　Others come first. There's a noble gift, now.'

　　Even as he spoke, he reeled and tumbled backward,
320　his great head lolling to one side; and sleep
　　took him like any creature. Drunk, hiccuping,
　　he dribbled streams of liquor and bits of men.

　　Now, by the gods, I drove my big hand spike
　　deep in the embers, charring it again,
325　and cheered my men along with battle talk
　　to keep their courage up: no quitting now.
　　The pike of olive, green though it had been,
　　reddened and glowed as if about to catch.
　　I drew it from the coals and my four fellows
330　gave me a hand, lugging it near the Cyclops
　　as more than natural force nerved them; straight
　　forward they sprinted, lifted it, and rammed it
　　deep in his crater eye, and I leaned on it
　　turning it as a shipwright turns a drill
335　in planking, having men below to swing
　　the two-handled strap that spins it in the groove.
　　So with our brand we bored that great eye socket
　　while blood ran out around the red-hot bar.
　　Eyelid and lash were seared; the pierced ball
340　hissed broiling, and the roots popped.

24. nectar (nek′ tər) **and ambrosia** (am brō′ zhə): Drink and food of the gods.

656　The Epic

                            In a smithy
one sees a white-hot axhead or an adze
plunged and wrung in a cold tub, screeching steam—
the way they make soft iron hale and hard—:
just so that eyeball hissed around the spike.

345 The Cyclops bellowed and the rock roared round him,
and we fell back in fear. Clawing his face
he tugged the bloody spike out of his eye,
threw it away, and his wild hands went groping;
then he set up a howl for Cyclopes

350 who lived in caves on windy peaks nearby.
Some heard him; and they came by divers[25] ways
to clump around outside and call:

                          'What ails you,
Polyphemus?[26] Why do you cry so sore
in the starry night? You will not let us sleep.

355 Sure no man's driving off your flock? No man
has tricked you, ruined you?

                          Out of the cave
the mammoth Polyphemus roared in answer:
'Nohbdy, Nohbdy's tricked me, Nohbdy's ruined me!'
To this rough shout they made a sage reply:

360 'Ah well, if nobody has played you foul
there in your lonely bed, we are no use in pain
given by great Zeus. Let it be your father,
Poseidon Lord, to whom you pray.'
                          So saying
they trailed away. And I was filled with laughter

365 to see how like a charm the name deceived them.
Now Cyclops, wheezing as the pain came on him,
fumbled to wrench away the great doorstone
and squatted in the breach with arms thrown wide
for any silly beast or man who bolted—

370 hoping somehow I might be such a fool.
But I kept thinking how to win the game:
death sat there huge; how could we slip away?
I drew on all my wits, and ran through tactics,
reasoning as a man will for dear life,

375 until a trick came—and it pleased me well.
The Cyclops' rams were handsome, fat, with heavy
fleeces, a dark violet.

25. divers (dī' vərz) *adj.*: Several, various.

26. Polyphemus (päl' ə fē məs)

---

28 Clarification The word *smithy* means "the forge of a black-smith."

29 Discussion How do you know that Odysseus anticipated this reply?

30 Discussion What personality trait is implied here? When else have we seen it displayed?

The Odyssey   657

I tied them silently together, twining
cords of willow from the ogre's bed

380 then slung a man under each middle one
to ride there safely, shielded left and right.
So three sheep could convey each man. I took
the woolliest ram, the choicest of the flock,

31 and hung myself under his kinky belly,

385 pulled up tight, with fingers twisted deep
in sheepskin ringlets for an iron grip.
So, breathing hard, we waited until morning.

32 When Dawn spead out her fingertips of rose
the rams began to stir, moving for pasture,

390 and peals of bleating echoed round the pens
where dams with udders full called for a milking.
Blinded, and sick with pain from his head wound,
the master stroked each ram, then let it pass,
but my men riding on the pectoral[27] fleece

395 the giant's blind hands blundering never found.

33 Last of them all my ram, the leader, came,
weighted by wool and me with my meditations.
The Cyclops patted him, and then he said:

'Sweet cousin ram, why lag behind the rest

400 in the night cave? You never linger so,
but graze before them all, and go afar
to crop sweet grass, and take your stately way
leading along the streams, until at evening
you run to be the first one in the fold.

405 Why, now, so far behind? Can you be grieving
over your Master's eye? That carrion rogue[28]
and his accurst companions burnt it out
when he had conquered all my wits with wine.

34 Nohbdy will not get out alive, I swear.

410 Oh, had you brain and voice to tell
where he may be now, dodging all my fury!
Bashed by this hand and bashed on this rock wall
his brains would strew the floor, and I should have
rest from the outrage Nohbdy worked upon me.'

415 He sent us into the open, then. Close by,
I dropped and rolled clear of the ram's belly,
going this way and that to untie the men.

658   The Epic

---

27. **pectoral** (pek′ tər əl)
adj.: Located on the chest.

28. **carrion** (kar′ ē ən)
rogue (rōg): Repulsive
scoundrel.

---

31 Clarification The word *kinky* means "tightly curled hair or fleece."

32 Discussion How does the reference to Dawn's "fingertips" contrast with the description of Odysseus' fingers in the previous passage?

33 Discussion Homer states that the ram is weighted down, in part by Odysseus' meditations. What does Homer mean?

34 Discussion How does the use of the double negative make this statement ironic?

With many glances back, we rounded up
his fat, stiff-legged sheep to take aboard,
420 and drove them down to where the good ship lay.
We saw, as we came near, our fellows' faces
shining; then we saw them turn to grief
tallying those who had not fled from death.
I hushed them, jerking head and eyebrows up,
425 and in a low voice told them: 'Load this herd;
move fast, and put the ship's head toward the
    breakers.'
They all pitched in at loading, then embarked
and struck their oars into the sea. Far out,
as far offshore as shouted words would carry,
430 I sent a few back to the adversary:
'O Cyclops! Would you feast on my companions?
Puny, am I, in a cave man's hands?
How do you like the beating that we gave you,
you damned cannibal? Eater of guests
435 under your roof! Zeus and the gods have paid you!'

The blind thing in his doubled fury broke
a hilltop in his hands and heaved it after us.
Ahead of our black prow it struck and sank
whelmed in a spuming geyser, a giant wave
440 that washed the ship stern foremost back to shore.
I got the longest boathook out and stood
fending us off, with furious nods to all
to put their backs into a racing stroke—
row, row, or perish. So the long oars bent
445 kicking the foam sternward, making head
until we drew away, and twice as far.
Now when I cupped my hands I heard the crew
in low voices protesting:

                    'Godsake, Captain!
Why bait the beast again? Let him alone!'

450 'That tidal wave he made on the first throw
all but beached us.'

                    'All but stove us in!'
'Give him our bearing with your trumpeting,
he'll get the range and lob a boulder.'

                    'Aye
He'll smash our timbers and our heads together!'

The Odyssey   659

35 **Clarification** Notice that Odysseus is especially furious at the Cyclops for violating the bond between host and guest.

36 **Clarification** The word *whelmed* means "submerged."

Humanities Note

Fine art, *Polyphemus, the Cyclops,* 1929, by N. C. Wyeth. Wyeth (1882-1945) was a renowned American illustrator, muralist, and painter. As a young man, he attended various art schools in his native Massachusetts but learned little that could help him. At the urging of a friend, Wyeth sent examples of his work to the elite Howard Pyle School of Art in Delaware. Acceptance by the school and subsequent contact with the artist and teacher Howard Pyle changed the course of N. C. Wyeth's life. Eventually, he came to be regarded as America's foremost illustrator.

The illustration *Polyphemus, the Cyclops* was done for a luxury edition of the *Odyssey* published in 1929. This illustrated book was very popular and has been reissued many times. The illustration demonstrates the skill with which Wyeth was able to depict fantastic creatures. The Cyclops he paints is fearsome and huge, yet believable.

You might use these questions for discussion:

1. What mood does this picture call up?
2. What details in this illustration contribute to this mood?
3. How does N. C. Wyeth's depiction of the Cyclops compare with the creature you imagined?

455 I would not heed them in my glorying spirit,
but let my anger flare and yelled:

                           'Cyclops,
if ever mortal man inquire
how you were put to shame and blinded, tell him
Odysseus, raider of cities, took your eye:
460 Laertes' son, whose home's on Ithaca!'

At this he gave a mighty sob and rumbled:

'Now comes the weird[29] upon me, spoken of old.
A wizard, grand and wondrous, lived here—Telemus,
a son of Eurymus; great length of days
465 he had in wizardry among the Cyclopes,

29. weird (wird) *n.*: Fate or destiny.

POLYPHEMUS, THE CYCLOPS
N. C. Wyeth
Delaware Art Museum

Grammar in Action

An **appositive** is a noun or pronoun placed next to another noun or pronoun to identify, rename, or explain it. An appositive phrase is an appositive with modifiers; it performs the same function as an appositive.

Appositives are used to develop the meaning of nouns and pronouns. In epic poetry, writers often use appositives to give brief but appropriate descriptions of gods and heroes. Notice how Homer adds information to his lines by using appositives:

"O hear me, lord, *blue girdler of the islands,*
if I am thine indeed, and thou art father:
grant that Odysseus, *raider of cities,* never
see his home. . . ."

Notice that the appositives in this example are set off by commas. These commas indicate that the appositives are nonessential to the sentence because they could be eliminated without changing the sentence's meaning. If an appositive is essential to the understanding of the sentence because it defines the noun before it, it is not separated by commas.

and these things he foretold for time to come:
my great eye lost, and at Odysseus' hands.
Always I had in mind some giant, armed
in giant force, would come against me here.
470 But this, but you—small, pitiful and twiggy—
you put me down with wine, you blinded me.
Come back, Odysseus, and I'll treat you well,
praying the god of earthquake[30] to befriend you—
his son I am, for he by his avowal
475 fathered me, and, if he will, he may
heal me of this black wound—he and no other
of all the happy gods or mortal men.'

Few words I shouted in reply to him:

'If I could take your life I would and take
480 your time away, and hurl you down to hell!
The god of earthquake could not heal you there!'

At this he stretched his hands out in the darkness
toward the sky of stars, and prayed Poseidon:

'O hear me, lord, blue girdler of the islands,
485 if I am thine indeed, and thou art father:
grant that Odysseus, raider of cities, never
see his home: Laertes' son, I mean,
who kept his hall on Ithaca. Should destiny
intend that he shall see his roof again
490 among his family in his father land,
far be that day, and dark the years between.
Let him lose all companions, and return
under strange sail to bitter days at home.'

In these words he prayed, and the god heard him.
495 Now he laid hands upon a bigger stone
and wheeled around, titanic for the cast,
to let it fly in the black-prowed vessel's track.
But it fell short, just aft the steering oar,
and whelming seas rose giant above the stone
500 to bear us onward toward the island.

                                    There
as we ran in we saw the squadron waiting,
the trim ships drawn up side by side, and all
our troubled friends who waited, looking seaward.

30. god of earthquake:
Poseidon.

The Odyssey   661

38 **Discussion** At this point, why would the Cyclops want to treat Odysseus well?

39 **Discussion** What is the implication of the phrase "and the god heard him"?

Student Activity 1. Find three other lines in which Homer uses appositives.

Student Activity 2. Write a brief addition to Odysseus' adventure with the Cyclops. Use appositives to identify or explain some of the nouns and pronouns. You may want to think of your own appositive phrases for Odysseus (like "raider of cities") or one of the gods.

Electronic Handbook You might want students to review appositives before completing the Grammar in Action activities. If students have access to the Language Master 6000, have them enter the access words *noun*, *appositive*, or *phrase* and press the GRAMMAR key to get information on the use of appositives.

We beached her, grinding keel in the soft sand,
505   and waded in, ourselves, on the sandy beach.
Then we unloaded all of Cyclops' flock
to make division, share and share alike,
only my fighters voted that my ram,
the prize of all, should go to me. I slew him
510   by the seaside and burnt his long thighbones
to Zeus beyond the stormcloud, Cronus[31] son,
who rules the world. But Zeus disdained my
      offering;
destruction for my ships he had in store
and death for those who sailed them, my
      companions.
515   Now all day long until the sun went down
we made our feast on mutton and sweet wine,
till after sunset in the gathering dark
we went to sleep above the wash of ripples.

When the young Dawn with fingertips of rose
520   touched the world, I roused the men, gave orders
to man the ships, cast off the mooring lines;
and filing in to sit beside the rowlocks
oarsmen in line dipped oars in the gray sea.
So we moved out, sad in the vast offing,[32]
525   having our precious lives, but not our friends.

31. Cronus (krō′ nəs): A Titan who was ruler of the universe until he was overthrown by his son Zeus.

32. offing (ôf′ iŋ) *n.*: The distant part of the sea visible from the shore.

■ RESPONDING TO THE SELECTION

Your Response

1. What do you think of Odysseus' plan for escaping from Polyphemus? How else could he have escaped?

Recalling

2. Describe Polyphemus and his home.
3. Why does Odysseus not kill Polyphemus when he first gets an opportunity to do so?

4. What does Odysseus do to blind Polyphemus and ultimately escape from him?

Interpreting

5. What survival qualities does Odysseus exhibit in his conflict with Polyphemus?

Applying

6. What might a young person in ancient Greece have learned from the Cyclops episode?

The Land of the Dead

Odysseus and his men sail to Aeolia, where Aeolus, king of the winds, sends Odysseus on his way with a gift: a sack containing all the winds except the favorable west wind. When they are near home, Odysseus' men open the sack, let-

662   The Epic

ting loose a storm that drives them back to Aeolia. Aeolus casts them out, having decided that they are detested by the gods. They sail seven days and arrive in the land of the Laestrygonians, a race of cannibals. These creatures destroy all of Odysseus' ships except the one he is sailing in. Odysseus and his reduced crew escape and reach Aeaea, the island ruled by the sorceress-goddess Circe. She transforms half of the men into swine. Protected by a magic herb, Odysseus demands that Circe change his men back into human form. Before Odysseus departs from the island a year later, Circe informs him that in order to reach home he must journey to the land of the dead, Hades, and consult the blind prophet Tiresias.

We bore down on the ship at the sea's edge
and launched her on the salt immortal sea,
stepping our mast and spar in the black ship;
embarked the ram and ewe and went aboard
530   in tears, with bitter and sore dread upon us.
But now a breeze came up for us astern—
a canvas-bellying land breeze, hale shipmate
sent by the singing nymph with sunbright hair;[33]
so we made fast the braces, took our thwarts,
535   and let the wind and steersman work the ship
with full sail spread all day above our coursing,
till the sun dipped, and all the ways grew dark
upon the fathomless unresting sea.
                              By night
our ship ran onward toward the Ocean's bourn,
540   the realm and region of the Men of Winter,
hidden in mist and cloud. Never the flaming
eye of Helios lights on those men
at morning, when he climbs the sky of stars,
nor in descending earthward out of heaven;
545   ruinous night being rove over those wretches.
We made the land, put ram and ewe ashore,
and took our way along the Ocean stream
to find the place foretold for us by Circe.
There Perimedes and Eurylochus,[34]
550   pinioned[35] the sacred beasts. With my drawn blade
I spaded up the votive[36] pit, and poured
libations[37] round it to the unnumbered dead:
sweet milk and honey, then sweet wine, and last
clear water; and I scattered barley down.
555   Then I addressed the blurred and breathless dead,

33. singing nymph ... hair.: Circe.

34. Perimedes (per' ə mē' dēz) **and Eurylochus** (yoo ril' ə kas)
35. pinioned (pin' yən'd) *v.*: Confined or shackled.
36. votive (vōt' iv) *adj.*: Done in fulfillment of a vow or pledge.
37. libations (lī bā' shənz) *n.*: Wine or other liquids poured upon the ground as a sacrifice.

The Odyssey   663

vowing to slaughter my best heifer for them
before she calved, at home in Ithaca,
and burn the choice bits on the altar fire;
44   as for Tiresias, I swore to sacrifice
560   a black lamb, handsomest of all our flock.
Thus to assuage the nations of the dead
I pledged these rites, then slashed the lamb and
     ewe,
letting their black blood stream into the wellpit.
Now the souls gathered, stirring out of Erebus,[38]
565   brides and young men, and men grown old in pain,
and tender girls whose hearts were new to grief;
many were there, too, torn by brazen lanceheads,

38. Erebus (er′ ə bəs): The dark region under the earth through which the dead pass before entering the realm of Hades.

ODYSSEUS IN THE LAND OF THE DEAD
N. C. Wyeth
Delaware Art Museum

battle-slain, bearing still their bloody gear.
From every side they came and sought the pit

570 with rustling cries; and I grew sick with fear.
But presently I gave command to my officers
to flay those sheep the bronze cut down, and make
burnt offerings of flesh to the gods below—
to sovereign Death, to pale Persephone.[39]

575 Meanwhile I crouched with my drawn sword to keep
the surging phantoms from the bloody pit
till I should know the presence of Tiresias.

One shade came first—Elpenor, of our company,
who lay unburied still on the wide earth

580 as we had left him—dead in Circe's hall,
untouched, unmourned, when other cares compelled us.
Now when I saw him there I wept for pity
and called out to him:

                              'How is this, Elpenor,
how could you journey to the western gloom

585 swifter afoot than I in the black lugger?'
He sighed, and answered:

                              'Son of great Laertes,
Odysseus, master mariner and soldier,
bad luck shadowed me, and no kindly power;
ignoble death I drank with so much wine.

590 I slept on Circe's roof, then could not see
the long steep backward ladder, coming down,
and fell that height. My neckbone, buckled under,
snapped, and my spirit found this well of dark.
Now hear the grace I pray for, in the name

595 of those back in the world, not here—your wife
and father, he who gave you bread in childhood,
and your own child, your only son, Telemachus,[40]
long ago left at home.

                              When you make sail
and put these lodgings of dim Death behind,

600 you will moor ship, I know, upon Aeaea Island;
there, O my lord, remember me, I pray,
do not abandon me unwept, unburied,
to tempt the gods' wrath, while you sail for home;
but fire my corpse, and all the gear I had,

605 and build a cairn[41] for me above the breakers—
an unknown sailor's mark for men to come.

39. Persephone (pər sɘf′ ə nē): Wife of Hades.

40. Telemachus (tə lem′ ə kəs)

41. cairn (kern) *n*.: A conical heap of stones built as a monument.

The Odyssey 665

45 Clarification The word *flay* means "to skin."

46 Discussion Why is Odysseus waiting for Tiresias?

47 Clarification The word *lugger* means "a small sailing vessel."

48 Enrichment To the ancients, it was a disgrace to die and not be buried or cremated with appropriate ceremony. Accordingly, it was customary to deny the rites of burial to traitors or enemies. In Sophocles' tragedy *Antigone*, Creon's denial of burial rites for Antigone's brother Polynices is the cause of the central conflict. Antigone defies Creon, her uncle, by performing this ceremony.

49 Clarification This word *barrow* means "a mound of stones covering the remains of the dead."

50 Clarification Recall from lines 362-363 that Cyclops is the son of Poseidon. Although Poseidon is best known as god of the sea, he also controlled thunder.

51 Reading Strategy Keep Tiresias' warning in mind as you read about the next stage of Odysseus' journey.

Heap up the mound there, and implant upon it
the oar I pulled in life with my companions.'

He ceased, and I replied:

'Unhappy spirit,
610 I promise you the barrow and the burial.'

So we conversed, and grimly, at a distance,
with my long sword between, guarding the blood,
while the faint image of the lad spoke on.
Now came the soul of Anticlea, dead,
615 my mother, daughter of Autolycus,
dead now, though living still when I took ship
for holy Troy. Seeing this ghost I grieved,
but held her off, through pang on pang of tears,
till I should know the presence of Tiresias.
620 Soon from the dark that prince of Thebes came
     forward
bearing a golden staff; and he addressed me:

'Son of Laertes and the gods of old,
Odysseus, master of landways and seaways,
why leave the blazing sun, O man of woe,
625 to see the cold dead and the joyless region?
Stand clear, put up your sword;
let me but taste the blood, I shall speak true.'

At this I stepped aside, and in the scabbard
let my long sword ring home to the pommel silver,
630 as he bent down to the somber blood. Then spoke
the prince of those with gift of speech:

'Great captain,
a fair wind and the honey lights of home
are all you seek. But anguish lies ahead;
the god who thunders on the land prepares it,
635 not to be shaken from your track, implacable,
in rancor for the son whose eye you blinded.
One narrow strait may take you through his blows:
denial of yourself, restraint of shipmates.
When you make landfall on Thrinacia first
640 and quit the violet sea, dark on the land
you'll find the grazing herds of Helios
by whom all things are seen, all speech is known.

666   *The Epic*

Avoid these kine,[42] hold fast to your intent,
and hard seafaring brings you all to Ithaca.

645 But if you raid the beeves, I see destruction
for ship and crew. Though you survive alone,
bereft of all companions, lost for years,
under strange sail shall you come home, to find
your own house filled with trouble: insolent men

650 eating your livestock as they court your lady.
Aye, you shall make those men atone in blood!
But after you have dealt out death—in open
combat or by stealth—to all the suitors,
go overland on foot, and take an oar,

655 until one day you come where men have lived
with meat unsalted, never known the sea,
nor seen seagoing ships, with crimson bows
and oars that fledge light hulls for dipping flight.
The spot will soon be plain to you, and I

660 can tell you how: some passerby will say,
'What winnowing fan is that upon your shoulder?'
Halt, and implant your smooth oar in the turf
and make fair sacrifice to Lord Poseidon:
a ram, a bull, a great buck boar; turn back,

665 and carry out pure hecatombs[43] at home
to all wide heaven's lords, the undying gods,
to each in order. Then a seaborne death
soft as this hand of mist will come upon you
when you are wearied out with rich old age,

670 your country folk in blessed peace around you.
And all this shall be just as I foretell.'

42. kine (kin) *n.pl.:* cattle.

43. hecatombs (hek' ə tōmz') *n.:* Large-scale sacrifices: often the slaughter of 100 cattle at one time.

RESPONDING TO THE SELECTION

Your Response
1. Do Tiresias' predictions and advice seem reasonable to you? Explain.

Recalling
2. What does the ghost of Elpenor request?
3. What does Tiresias foretell?
4. What directions and warnings does he give?

Interpreting
5. What character traits does Odysseus display in this episode that he did not reveal in his adventure with the Cyclops?
6. Describe Odysseus' reaction to the appearance of his mother's ghost

Applying
7. What events and adventures do you expect to read about in the remaining excerpts from the *Odyssey*?

The Odyssey 667

Humanities Note

Fine art, *"Circe Meanwhile Had Gone Her Ways . . ."* 1924, by William Russell Flint. The Scottish painter and illustrator William Russell Flint (1880-1969) was the son of landscape painter F. Wighton Flint. In 1900, the young artist became interested in the medium of watercolor. For many years this was his favorite medium, and his watercolors were exhibited in both England and Europe with great success. He also began to create designs to illustrate various literary works. His subsequent success as an illustrator added another dimension to his work.

The watercolor *"Circe Meanwhile Had Gone Her Ways . . ."* was executed in 1924 for an edition of the *Odyssey.* Combining his skill as a watercolorist with his narrative ability, Flint created a beautiful Circe who looks as if she has stepped from a Grecian urn. In keeping with this effect, the perspective of the painting is flat. The predominantly blue coloring creates an air of mystery.

You might use these questions for discussion:

1. What is the nature or personality of the woman in this painting?
2. What special abilities does she seem to have?

CIRCE MEANWHILE HAD GONE HER WAYS . . ., 1924
William Russell Flint
Collection of the New York Public Library,
Astor, Lenox and Tilden Foundations

668   *The Epic*

The Sirens

Odysseus returns to Circe's island. The goddess reveals his course to him and gives advice on how to avoid the dangers he will face: the Sirens, who lure sailors to their destruction; the Wandering Rocks, sea rocks that destroy even birds in flight; the perils of the sea monster Scylla and, nearby, the whirlpool Charybdis; and the cattle of the sun god, which Tiresias has warned Odysseus not to harm.

As Circe spoke, Dawn mounted her golden throne,
and on the first rays Circe left me, taking
her way like a great goddess up the island.
675 I made straight for the ship, roused up the men
to get aboard and cast off at the stern.
They scrambled to their places by the rowlocks
and all in line dipped oars in the gray sea.
But soon an offshore breeze blew to our liking—
680 a canvas-bellying breeze, a lusty shipmate
sent by the singing nymph with sunbright hair.
So we made fast the braces, and we rested,
letting the wind and steersman work the ship.
The crew being now silent before me, I
685 addressed them, sore at heart:

                                    'Dear friends,
more than one man, or two, should know those
      things
Circe foresaw for us and shared with me,
so let me tell her forecast: then we die
with our eyes open, if we are going to die,
690 or know what death we baffle if we can. Sirens
weaving a haunting song over the sea
we are to shun, she said, and their green shore
all sweet with clover; yet she urged that I
alone should listen to their song. Therefore
695 you are to tie me up, tight as a splint,
erect along the mast, lashed to the mast,
and if I shout and beg to be untied,
take more turns of the rope to muffle me.'

I rather dwelt on this part of the forecast,
700 while our good ship made time, bound outward
      down
the wind for the strange island of Sirens.
Then all at once the wind fell, and a calm

54 **Discussion** Compare and contrast the personifications of Dawn that Homer has included in the *Odyssey*.

55 **Discussion** Why does Odysseus not want to be the only man to know Circe's forecast?

56 **Clarification** The name Sirens comes from the Greek word *sirenes,* which means "entanglers." Today, the word refers to any woman who is dangerous and alluring.

Speaking and Listening You might wish to suggest to students that they work in small groups to prepare adaptations of the *Odyssey* in their own words to tell to younger students. The groups might wish to present the story in sections with each student being responsible for one section, or they might prefer to select a narrator and have other students play the roles of different characters. Students could then tell each section of the story from their own character's point of view. Students could make and include simple props or pieces of costuming to use as they tell the story.

57 **Enrichment** Homer refers to only two Sirens; later writers describe three.

58 **Discussion** What do the Sirens promise?

came over all the sea, as though some power
lulled the swell.

The crew were on their feet

705 briskly, to furl the sail, and stow it; then
each in place, they poised the smooth oar blades
and sent the white foam scudding by. I carved
a massive cake of beeswax into bits
and rolled them in my hands until they softened—
710 no long task, for a burning heat came down
from Helios, lord of high noon. Going forward
I carried wax along the line, and laid it
thick on their ears. They tied me up, then, plumb
amidships, back to the mast, lashed to the mast,
715 and took themselves again to rowing. Soon,
as we came smartly within hailing distance,
the two Sirens, noting our fast ship
off their point, made ready, and they sang:

> *This way, oh turn your bows,*
720 *   Achaea's glory,*
> *As all the world allows—*
> *   Moor and be merry.*

> *Sweet coupled airs we sing.*
> *   No lonely seafarer*
725 *Holds clear of entering*
> *   Our green mirror.*

> *Pleased by each purling note*
> *   Like honey twining*
> *From her throat and my throat,*
730 *   Who lies a-pining?*

> *Sea rovers here take joy*
> *   Voyaging onward,*
> *As from our song of Troy*
> *Graybeard and rower-boy*
735 *   Goeth more learnèd.*

> *All feats on that great field*
> *   In the long warfare,*
> *Dark days the bright gods willed,*
> *   Wounds you bore there,*

670   *The Epic*

740　　　　　Argos' old soldiery[44]
　　　　　　　On Troy beach teeming,
　　　　　　　Charmed out of time we see.
　　　　　　　No life on earth can be
　　　　　　　Hid from our dreaming.

745　　The lovely voices in ardor appealing over the water
　　　　made me crave to listen, and I tried to say
　　　　'Untie me!' to the crew, jerking my brows:
　　　　but they bent steady to the oars. Then Perimedes
　　　　got to his feet, he and Eurylochus,
750　　and passed more line about, to hold me still.
　　　　So all rowed on, until the Sirens
　　　　dropped under the sea rim, and their singing
　　　　dwindled away.
　　　　　　　　　　　　My faithful company
　　　　rested on their oars now, peeling off
755　　the wax that I had laid thick on their ears:
　　　　then set me free.

44. Argos' old soldiery:
Soldiers from Argos, a city
in ancient Greece.

Responding to the Selection

Your Response

1. Gods, goddesses, and other characters in mythology often represent basic human qualities. What do the Sirens represent to you?

Recalling

2. What does Odysseus have his crew do to him so that he can listen to the Sirens' song?

3. What does Odysseus do to protect his men?
4. How does he react to the song?

Interpreting

5. Summarize what the Sirens say in the song.
6. Compare and contrast the peril of the Sirens and the peril of the Lotus-Eaters.

Applying

7. Why do you think Homer decided to let only Odysseus hear the Sirens' song?

The Odyssey   671

60

Multicultural Focus Have the class examine a map of the Mediterranean Sea and ask students how geography might relate to the selection "Scylla and Charybdis." Discuss their responses. Point out that the monster Scylla is thought to have been located at what is today known as the Strait of Messina, the passage between Sicily and the toe of the boot of Italy. Suggest that, with such an abundance of islands in the Aegean and Mediterranean seas, treacherous sea straits probably inspired the notion of a ship passing between two deadly dangers. Then display a map of the world. Ask students to use their knowledge of geography to pinpoint other possibly dangerous sea passages, such as the Strait of Magellan, the Strait of Gibraltar, or the Bering Strait. List their ideas on the board.

Suggest that students do research to find out more about the places mentioned in class. Ask them to search fiction and nonfiction, historical accounts, and explorers' diaries, to find descriptions of these places. Have them share their findings with the class.

60 Discussion What qualities does Odysseus demonstrate here? Recall previous incidents where he displayed similar character traits.

Scylla and Charybdis

But scarcely had that island
faded in blue air than I saw smoke
and white water, with sound of waves in tumult—
a sound the men heard, and it terrified them.
760 Oars flew from their hands; the blades went
      knocking
wild alongside till the ship lost way,
with no oar blades to drive her through the water.

Well, I walked up and down from bow to stern,
trying to put heart into them, standing over
765 every oarsman, saying gently,

'Friends,
have we never been in danger before this?
More fearsome, is it now, than when the Cyclops
penned us in his cave? What power he had!
Did I not keep my nerve, and use my wits
770 to find a way out for us?

Now I say
by hook or crook this peril too shall be
something that we remember.

Heads up, lads!
We must obey the orders as I give them.
Get the oar shafts in your hands, and lay back
775 hard on your benches; hit these breaking seas.
Zeus help us pull away before we founder.
You at the tiller, listen, and take in
all that I say—the rudders are your duty;
keep her out of the combers and the smoke;
780 steer for that headland; watch the drift, or we
fetch up in the smother, and you drown us.'

That was all, and it brought them round to action.
But as I sent them on toward Scylla,[45] I
told them nothing, as they could do nothing.
785 They would have dropped their oars again, in panic,
to roll for cover under the decking. Circe's
bidding against arms had slipped my mind,
so I tied on my cuirass[46] and took up
two heavy spears, then made my way along
790 to the foredeck—thinking to see her first from there,
the monster of the gray rock, harboring

45. Scylla (sil´a)

46. cuirass (kwi ras´) *n.:* armor for the upper body.

672 *The Epic*

torment for my friends. I strained my eyes
upon the cliffside veiled in cloud, but nowhere
could I catch sight of her.

                                And all this time,
795 in travail, sobbing, gaining on the current,
we rowed into the strait—Scylla to port
and on our starboard beam Charybdis,[47] dire
gorge[48] of the salt-sea tide. By heaven! when she
vomited, all the sea was like a cauldron
800 seething over intense fire, when the mixture
suddenly heaves and rises.

                                The shot spume
soared to the landside heights, and fell like rain.

But when she swallowed the sea water down
we saw the funnel of the maelstrom,[49] heard
805 the rock bellowing all around, and dark
sand raged on the bottom far below.
My men all blanched against the gloom, our eyes
were fixed upon that yawning mouth in fear
of being devoured.

                                Then Scylla made her strike,
810 whisking six of my best men from the ship.
I happened to glance aft at ship and oarsmen
and caught sight of their arms and legs, dangling
high overhead. Voices came down to me
in anguish, calling my name for the last time.

815 A man surfcasting on a point of rock
for bass or mackerel, whipping his long rod
to drop the sinker and the bait far out,
will hook a fish and rip it from the surface
to dangle wriggling through the air:

                                        so these
820 were borne aloft in spasms toward the cliff.

She ate them as they shrieked there, in her den,
in the dire grapple, reaching still for me—
and deathly pity ran me through
at that sight—far the worst I ever suffered,
825 questing the passes of the strange sea.

                                We rowed on.
The Rocks were now behind; Charybdis, too,
and Scylla dropped astern. . . .

47. Charybdis (ka rib´ dis)
48. gorge (gôrj) *n.*: Voracious, consuming mouth.

49. maelstrom (māl´ strəm) *n.*: A large, violent whirlpool.

61 Enrichment Legend has it that Charybdis swallowed and threw up the sea three times a day.

62 Enrichment Artistic representations of Scylla show her with twelve feet and six heads, each with three rows of canine teeth.

63 Discussion To what does Homer compare the death of these men?

64 Discussion The expression "to pass between Scylla and Charybdis" is still used. What does it mean?

The Odyssey   673

ANSWERS TO RESPONDING TO THE SELECTION
Your Response
1. Answers will differ, but many students may agree with Odysseus' reasoning that the less the men knew about their destination, the less opportunity they would have to panic.

Recalling
2. They are terrified and lose control of the ship until Odysseus encourages them.
3. Scylla grabs them from the ship, hurls them into the air, and finally eats them.

Interpreting
4. Suggested Response: Despite the panic of his men, Odysseus is able to rally them back to their senses.
5. Suggested Response: He may have made the choice because Scylla looked less violent than Charybdis, and therefore he considered it the lesser of two evils.

Applying
6. The saying means that one is caught between two equally difficult or dangerous choices, or "between a rock and a hard place."

---

65 Enrichment The sacred cattle of Helios symbolized the days in one's life. Thus, it was believed that by killing them, Greeks cut short their own lives.

■ RESPONDING TO THE SELECTION

Your Response
1. Is Odysseus right to keep his decision to sail toward Scylla a secret from his men? Give reasons for your opinion.

Recalling
2. As Odysseus and his crew near Scylla and Charybdis, how do the men react?
3. Describe how Scylla kills six of the men.

Interpreting
4. How does Odysseus show himself to be an effective leader of men?
5. Why do you think Odysseus chooses to sail toward Scylla rather than Charybdis?

Applying
6. This episode inspired a famous saying: "caught between Scylla and Charybdis." What do you think it means?

The Cattle of the Sun God

In the small hours of the third watch, when stars
that shone out in the first dusk of evening
830 had gone down to their setting, a giant wind
blew from heaven, and clouds driven by Zeus
shrouded land and sea in a night of storm;
so, just as Dawn with fingertips of rose
touched the windy world, we dragged our ship
835 to cover in a grotto, a sea cave
where nymphs had chairs of rock and sanded floors.
I mustered all the crew and said:

            'Old shipmates,
our stores are in the ship's hold, food and drink;
the cattle here are not for our provision,
840 or we pay dearly for it.

                  Fierce the god is
who cherishes these heifers and these sheep:
Helios; and no man avoids his eye.'

To this my fighters nodded. Yes. But now
we had a month of onshore gales, blowing
845 day in, day out—south winds, or south by east.
As long as bread and good red wine remained

to keep the men up, and appease their craving,
they would not touch the cattle. But in the end,
when all the barley in the ship was gone,
850 hunger drove them to scour the wild shore
with angling hooks, for fishes and seafowl,
whatever fell into their hands; and lean days
wore their bellies thin.

                    The storms continued.
So one day I withdrew to the interior
855 to pray the gods in solitude, for hope
that one might show me some way of salvation.
Slipping away, I struck across the island
to a sheltered spot, out of the driving gale.
I washed my hands there, and made supplication
860 to the gods who own Olympus,[50] all the gods—
but they, for answer, only closed my eyes
under slow drops of sleep.

                  Now on the shore Eurylochus
made his insidious plea:

                    'Comrades,' he said,
'You've gone through everything; listen to what I say.
865 All deaths are hateful to us, mortal wretches,
but famine is the most pitiful, the worst
end that a man can come to.

                   Will you fight it?
Come, we'll cut out the noblest of these cattle
for sacrifice to the gods who own the sky;
870 and once at home, in the old country of Ithaca,
if ever that day comes—
we'll build a costly temple and adorn it
with every beauty for the Lord of Noon.[51]
But if he flares up over his heifers lost,
875 wishing our ship destroyed, and if the gods
make cause with him, why, then I say: Better
open your lungs to a big sea once for all
than waste to skin and bones on a lonely island!'

Thus Eurylochus; and they murmered 'Aye!'
880 trooping away at once to round up heifers.
Now, that day tranquil cattle with broad brows
were gazing near, and soon the men drew up
around their chosen beasts in ceremony.
They plucked the leaves that shone on a tall oak—

The Odyssey   675

50. Olympus (ō lim′ pəs):
Mount Olympus, home of
the gods.

51. Lord of Noon: Helios.

66 Discussion Why, at this point, does Odysseus pray to all the gods?

67 Discussion If you were one of Odysseus' men in this situation, would you take Eurylochus' advice? Why?

68 Discussion Is it a coincidence that Odysseus wakes up at this point? Explain.

69 Clarification This word *over-weening* means "arrogant and presumptuous."

70 Discussion Explain Helios' threat.

885 having no barley meal—to strew the victims,
performed the prayers and ritual, knifed the kine
and flayed each carcass, cutting thighbones free
to wrap in double folds of fat. These offerings,
with strips of meat, were laid upon the fire.
890 Then, as they had no wine, they made libation
with clear spring water, broiling the entrails first;
and when the bones were burnt and tripes shared,
they spitted the carved meat.

Just then my slumber
left me in a rush, my eyes opened,
895 and I went down the seaward path. No sooner
had I caught sight of our black hull, than savory
odors of burnt fat eddied around me;
grief took hold of me, and I cried aloud:

'O Father Zeus and gods in bliss forever,
900 you made me sleep away this day of mischief!
O cruel drowsing, in the evil hour!
Here they sat, and a great work they contrived.'

Lampetia[52] in her long gown meanwhile
had borne swift word to the Overlord of Noon:

905 'They have killed your kine.'

And the Lord Helios
burst into angry speech amid the immortals:

'O Father Zeus and gods in bliss forever,
punish Odysseus' men! So overweening,
now they have killed my peaceful kine, my joy
910 at morning when I climbed the sky of stars,
and evening, when I bore westward from heaven.
Restitution or penalty they shall pay—
and pay in full—or I go down forever
to light the dead men in the underworld.'

915 Then Zeus who drives the stormcloud made reply:

'Peace, Helios: shine on among the gods,
shine over mortals in the fields of grain.
Let me throw down one white-hot bolt, and make
splinters of their ship in the winedark sea.'

52. Lampetia (lam pē' shə): A nymph.

920 —Calypso later told me of this exchange,
as she declared that Hermes[53] had told her.
Well, when I reached the sea cave and the ship,
I faced each man, and had it out; but where
could any remedy be found? There was none.
925 The silken beeves of Helios were dead.
The gods, moreover, made queer signs appear:
cowhides began to crawl, and beef, both raw
and roasted, lowed like kine upon the spits.
Now six full days my gallant crew could feast
930 upon the prime beef they had marked for slaughter
from Helios' herd; and Zeus, the son of Cronus,
added one fine morning.
                          All the gales
had ceased, blown out, and with an offshore breeze
we launched again, stepping the mast and sail,
935 to make for the open sea. Astern of us
the island coastline faded, and no land
showed anywhere, but only sea and heaven,
when Zeus Cronion piled a thunderhead
above the ship, while gloom spread on the ocean.
940 We held our course, but briefly. Then the squall
struck whining from the west, with gale force,
      breaking
both forestays, and the mast came toppling aft
along the ship's length, so the running rigging
showered into the bilge.
                          On the afterdeck
945 the mast had hit the steersman a slant blow
bashing the skull in, knocking him overside,
as the brave soul fled the body, like a diver.
With crack on crack of thunder, Zeus let fly
a bolt against the ship, a direct hit,
950 so that she bucked, in reeking fumes of sulphur,
and all the men were flung into the sea.
They came up 'round the wreck, bobbing awhile
like petrels[54] on the waves.
                          No more seafaring
homeward for these, no sweet day of return;
955 the god had turned his face from them.
                          I clambered
fore and aft my hulk until a comber
split her, keel from ribs, and the big timber
floated free; the mast, too, broke away.

53. **Hermes** (hur′ mēz):
The herald and messenger
of the gods.

54. **petrels** (pet′ rəlz):
Small, dark sea birds.

71 Reading Strategy Ask students to predict what will happen.

72 Clarification The Greeks believed that, upon death, the soul departed the body.

73 Clarification A *comber* is "a long curling ocean wave."

The Odyssey 677

74 **Clarification** According to Homer, Charybdis lived under this enormous fig tree.

75 **Enrichment** According to classical mythology, Calypso kept Odysseus on the island for seven years and promised him eternal youth if he remained forever.

Reader's Response Which of Odysseus' adventures did you find most exciting or perilous? Explain.

Thematic Response Which of the many challenges faced by Odysseus was most difficult for him to overcome? Explain. How do Odysseus' challenges compare to challenges students have faced?

A backstay floated dangling from it, stout
960   rawhide rope, and I used this for lashing
mast and keel together. These I straddled,
riding the frightful storm.

                  Nor had I yet
seen the worst of it: for now the west wind
dropped, and a southeast gale came on—one more
965   twist of the knife—taking me north again,
straight for Charybdis. All that night I drifted,
and in the sunrise, sure enough, I lay
off Scylla mountain and Charybdis deep.
There, as the whirlpool drank the tide, a billow
970   tossed me, and I sprang for the great fig tree,
catching on like a bat under a bough.
Nowhere had I to stand, no way of climbing,
the root and bole[55] being far below, and far
above my head the branches and their leaves,
975   massed, overshadowing Charybdis pool.
But I clung grimly, thinking my mast and keel
would come back to the surface when she spouted.
And ah! how long, with what desire, I waited!
till, at the twilight hour, when one who hears
980   and judges pleas in the marketplace all day
between contentious men, goes home to supper,
the long poles at last reared from the sea.

Now I let go with hands and feet, plunging
straight into the foam beside the timbers,
985   pulled astride, and rowed hard with my hands
to pass by Scylla. Never could I have passed her
had not the Father of gods and men,[56] this time,
kept me from her eyes. Once through the strait,
nine days I drifted in the open sea
990   before I made shore, buoyed up by the gods,
upon Ogygia[57] Isle. The dangerous nymph
Calypso lives and sings there, in her beauty,
and she received me, loved me.

                But why tell
the same tale that I told last night in hall
995   to you and to your lady? Those adventures
made a long evening, and I do not hold
with tiresome repetition of a story."

55. bole (bōl) *n.*: A tree trunk.

56. Father . . . men: Zeus.

57. Ogygia (o jij' i a).

678   *The Epic*

Closure and Extension

ANSWERS TO RESPONDING TO THE SELECTION
Your Response
1. Stimulate discussion by having students recall the word clusters of heroic traits they created in the Focus exercise.

Recalling
2. Eurylochus convinces his shipmates that starvation is the worst form of death.
3. Zeus overrules Helios' plan for revenge, saying that he wants Helios to continue shining on earth and heaven. The destruction of Odysseus' ship will avenge the stolen cattle.

4. Odysseus clings to the fig tree above Charybdis and waits patiently for the pieces of the ship's mast and keel to resurface. Once Odysseus climbs back on his raft, Zeus helps him pass by Scylla unharmed.

Interpreting
5. Answers will differ; however, most students will see Odysseus' absence as a factor.
6. Suggested Response: It is Zeus who makes the final decisions.

RESPONDING TO THE SELECTION

Your Response

1. During which of his adventures do you think Odysseus acts most heroically? Explain.

Recalling

2. What does Eurylochus say to persuade Odysseus' men to slaughter and eat the cattle of Helios, the sun god?
3. What is Zeus' response to Helios' demand for revenge?
4. How does Odysseus manage to escape death?

Interpreting

5. Do the men obey Eurylochus because his speech is more persuasive than Odysseus' or because Odysseus is not present to stop them? Give reasons for your opinion.
6. What impression of the gods do you get from the conference between Helios and Zeus?

Applying

7. Tell why you do or do not think that the punishment Zeus inflicts on the men is the right one for their offense?

ANALYZING LITERATURE

Understanding the Epic Hero

The **epic hero** is the central character of an epic. He possesses qualities superior to those of most men, yet he remains recognizably human.

1. In what ways does Odysseus stand out from ordinary men?
2. At what points in the story does he seem more like an ordinary man with weaknesses?
3. Do you like and admire Odysseus? Tell why you do or do not.

CRITICAL THINKING AND READING

Interpreting Epithets

In epic poetry, an **epithet** is a word or phrase used repeatedly to characterize or describe someone or something. Odysseus, for example, is frequently described as "raider of cities" and "Laertes' son." Epithets are one of the distinctive aspects of epic style. They add formality and dignity to the poetry and emphasize basic qualities of the person or thing to which they are applied.

Describe the effect of each of the following frequently used epithets, and tell what quality it emphasizes.

1. "fingertips of rose" (applied to dawn)
2. "raider of cities" (applied to Odysseus)
3. "lord of cloud" (applied to Zeus)

THINKING AND WRITING

Writing About the Epic Hero

Write an essay on Odysseus that expresses how rich and complex his character is. First review your answers to the questions under the heading "Understanding the Epic Hero." Then select several traits to focus on. Refer to events in the *Odyssey* where the traits are displayed. When you revise your essay, concentrate on creating a sense of the living personality of Odysseus.

LEARNING OPTIONS

1. **Art.** Illustrate a scene in the *Odyssey*. Make your picture as authentic as possible by paying close attention to the details in the story. When you have completed your drawing, display it in the classroom.
2. **Speaking and Listening.** Odysseus is returning home from the Trojan War. Find out more about this ten-year conflict, as described by Homer and other ancient poets. In an oral report, share your findings with the class.
3. **Writing.** Imagine that you are a sailor aboard Odysseus' ship. Write a letter home, telling your family about the perilous encounters you have had on your voyage. If you wish, make up adventures not included in the *Odyssey*. When you have finished, share your letter with the class.

The Odyssey 679

THINKING AND WRITING

Writing Transparency Students often find it helpful to see a model of their writing assignment. Before students write, you may wish to show them Model 5: *Expository Essay* in the **Transparencies for Writing**.

Alternative Assessment *Protocol:* Ask students to assess their own work by responding to the following questions:

What traits of Odysseus do you discuss to demonstrate the complexity of his character?

What events do you select to support each trait?

What specific details do you include for each event?

What have you learned about Odysseus' personality from completing this assignment?

Have students use the information they have gained from their protocols as a guide for revising their compositions.

Publishing Student Writing
This assignment should produce an impressive variety of character studies. You might want to collect the finished assignments in a looseleaf notebook, so students can read them at their leisure.

LEARNING OPTIONS

1. This activity is appropriate for visual learners. To vary the activity, you might wish to have students incorporate their scenes into a mural depicting all the episodes in this selection.
2. To extend this activity, you might have students read aloud and explain excerpts from the *Iliad*.
3. Creative visual learners will enjoy this activity. You might vary the activity by having students imagine that they are other characters from the selection, such as Circe or the god Poseidon.

Applying

7. Answers will differ. Many students may think that the punishment is harsh.

ANSWERS TO ANALYZING LITERATURE

1. Answers will differ: Possible answers include that he is both protected and punished by the gods; he shows caution and restraint when ordinary men cannot; he survives extraordinary tests of courage. Also, he is exceptionally clever.
2. Suggested Response: Odysseus is more like ordinary men when he shows fear during his encounter with the dead; when he is proud of escaping from Polyphemus; and when he openly shows his emotions toward his family.
3. Answers will differ. However, many students will probably admire his courage and intelligence.

ANSWERS TO CRITICAL THINKING AND READING

1. Suggested Response: This epithet emphasizes the delicacy and beauty of dawn.
2. Suggested Response: This epithet emphasizes Odysseus' combative side. The effect is to characterize him as a merciless warrior.
3. Suggested Response: This epithet emphasizes the loftiness and majesty of Zeus.

Preparation

Literary Focus Point out that, although the plot of the *Odyssey* is episodic (that is, made up of a series of discrete incidents), it has definite recurring themes. As students read the poem, have them think about the themes that dominate, as well as the different ways Homer illustrates and dramatizes them.

Prereading Focus Before beginning the activity, ask if any of your students have been on an extended journey. If so, what was it like for these students to be away from home for a long period? Did they feel homesick? How did they feel when they returned home?

Vocabulary Ask less advanced students to give examples of situations where each of these words might apply. For example, a ballet or a gymnastics exhibition is a time when you would see people who are *lithe*.

Electronic Handbook You might want students to use the Language Master 6000 to hear the pronunciation of the vocabulary words.

GUIDE FOR READING

The Odyssey, Part 2

Plot in the Epic

The **plot** of an epic is made up of a series of stories. They are based on myths and legends that are central to the history and culture of a people. The plot of the *Odyssey* in its entirety has three broad divisions. The first consists of the adventures of Telemachus, Odysseus' son. The second presents the travels and adventures of Odysseus. The third is about the return of Odysseus to Ithaca. Homer, being a great poet, was able to weave all the separate stories of all three parts into a unified poem. Nevertheless, the plot of the *Odyssey* remains episodic—made up of distinct episodes.

Focus

The events you will read about in Part 2 of the *Odyssey* take place in Ithaca, Odysseus' homeland and the goal of all his voyaging. What does home mean to you? Make a list of the ideas and feelings you associate with the word *home*. What would you miss most if you were away from home for a long time? What might change while you were away? Share your ideas with a small group of classmates. Then briefly predict what you think will happen when Odysseus arrives home. Remember that his wife, Penelope, and his son, Telemachus, have not seen him in twenty years. As you read Part 2 of the *Odyssey,* compare your predictions with what actually happens.

Vocabulary

Knowing the following words will help you as you read Part 2 of the *Odyssey.*

dissemble (di sem' b'l) *v.*: Conceal with false appearances; disguise (p. 681)

lithe (li*th*) *adj.*: Supple; limber (p. 682)

incredulity (in' krǝ dōō' lǝ tē) *n.:* Inability to believe (p. 683)

bemusing (bi myōō' ziŋ) *v.*: Stupefying or muddling (p. 686)

glowering (glou' ǝr iŋ) *v.:* Staring with sullen anger; scowling (p. 689)

maudlin (môd' lin) *adj.*: Tearfully sentimental from too much liquor (p. 691)

contempt (kǝn tempt') *n.*: Actions or attitude of a person toward someone or something he or she considers low or worthless (p. 698)

680 The Epic

Objectives

1 To understand the plot of an epic
2 To read a map
3 To write an essay responding to literary criticism
4 To express individual interests and abilities through optional activities

Support Material

Teaching Portfolio
Teacher Backup, p. 843
Grammar in Action Worksheets, *Using Parenthetical Expressions,* p. 846; *Using Vivid Verbs,* p. 848
Usage and Mechanics Worksheet, p. 850
Vocabulary Check, p. 851
Critical Thinking and Reading

Worksheet, *Inferring Customs and Beliefs,* p. 852
Language Worksheet, *Interpreting Homeric Similes,* p. 853
Selection Test, p. 854
Art Transparency 19: *Odysseus and Penelope Reunited,* by Romare Bearden

Listening to Literature
Odysseus' Revenge

Prentice Hall Writing Studio

PART 2 THE RETURN OF ODYSSEUS

"Twenty years gone, and I am back again"

Odysseus has finished telling his story to the Phaeacians. The next day, young Phaeacian noblemen conduct him home by ship. He arrives in Ithaca after an absence of twenty years. The goddess Athena appears and informs him of the situation at home. Numerous suitors, believing Odysseus to be dead, have been continually seeking the hand of his wife, Penelope, in marriage, while overrunning Odysseus' palace and enjoying themselves at Penelope's expense. Moreover, they are plotting to murder Odysseus' son, Telemachus, before he can inherit his father's lands. Telemachus, who, like Penelope, still hopes for his father's return, has journeyed to Pylos and Sparta to learn what he can about his father's fate. Athena disguises Odysseus as a beggar and directs him to the hut of Eumaeus, his old and faithful swineherd. While Odysseus and Eumaeus are eating breakfast, Telemachus arrives. Athena then appears to Odysseus.

<blockquote>

. . . . From the air
she walked, taking the form of a tall woman,
handsome and clever at her craft, and stood

1000   beyond the gate in plain sight of Odysseus,
unseen, though, by Telemachus, unguessed,
for not to everyone will gods appear.
Odysseus noticed her; so did the dogs,
who cowered whimpering away from her. She only

1005   nodded, signing to him with her brows,
a sign he recognized. Crossing the yard,
he passed out through the gate in the stockade
to face the goddess. There she said to him:

"Son of Laertes and the gods of old,

1010   Odysseus, master of landways and seaways,
dissemble to your son no longer now.
The time has come: tell him how you together
will bring doom on the suitors in the town.
I shall not be far distant then, for I

1015   myself desire battle."

                    Saying no more,
she tipped her golden wand upon the man,
making his cloak pure white, and the knit tunic

</blockquote>

1

2

The Odyssey   681

Audiocassette To allow students to appreciate how the volume, pitch, stress, and pace of a reader's voice can convey feelings, you might wish to have them listen to "Odysseus' Revenge" on Side 6 of the **Listening to Literature** Audiocassettes.

fresh around him. Lithe and young she made him,
ruddy with sun, his jawline clean, the beard
1020 no longer gray upon his chin. And she
withdrew when she had done.

                Then Lord Odysseus
reappeared—and his son was thunderstruck.
Fear in his eyes, he looked down and away
as though it were a god, and whispered:

                      "Stranger,
1025 you are no longer what you were just now!
Your cloak is new; even your skin! You are
one of the gods who rule the sweep of heaven!
Be kind to us, we'll make you fair oblation[1]
and gifts of hammered gold. Have mercy on us!"

1. oblation (ä blā′ shən) *n.*: An offering to a god.

EUMAEUS, THE SWINEHERD
N. C. Wyeth
Delaware Art Museum

682   *The Epic*

1030 The noble and enduring man replied:

"No god. Why take me for a god? No, no.
I am that father whom your boyhood lacked
and suffered pain for lack of. I am he."

Held back too long, the tears ran down his cheeks
1035 as he embraced his son.
                        Only Telemachus,
uncomprehending, wild
with incredulity, cried out:

                              "You cannot
be my father Odysseus! Meddling spirits
conceived this trick to twist the knife in me!
1040 No man of woman born could work these wonders
by his own craft, unless a god came into it
with ease to turn him young or old at will.
I swear you were in rags and old,
and here you stand like one of the immortals!"

1045 Odysseus brought his ranging mind to bear
and said:

                        "This is not princely, to be swept
away by wonder at your father's presence.
No other Odysseus will ever come,
for he and I are one, the same; his bitter
1050 fortune and his wanderings are mine.
Twenty years gone, and I am back again
on my own island.
                        As for my change of skin,
that is a charm Athena, Hope of Soldiers,
uses as she will; she has the knack
1055 to make me seem a beggar man sometimes
and sometimes young, with finer clothes about me.
It is no hard thing for the gods of heaven
to glorify a man or bring him low."

When he had spoken, down he sat.
                        Then, throwing
1060 his arms around this marvel of a father
Telemachus began to weep. Salt tears
rose from the wells of longing in both men,
and cries burst from both as keen and fluttering

The Odyssey 683

4 **Discussion** Does this behavior make you think better or worse of Odysseus? Why?

5 **Clarification** Homer summarizes one of the underlying themes of the poem—the omnipotence of the gods.

6 **Discussion** Is this simile effective? Why?

7 **Discussion** This is one of the few instances of humor. Where else has Homer used humor?

6 │ 1065
as those of the great taloned hawk,
whose nestlings farmers take before they fly.
So helplessly they cried, pouring out tears,
and might have gone on weeping so till sundown,
had not Telemachus said:

7 │ 1070
                              "Dear father! Tell me
what kind of vessel put you here ashore
on Ithaca? Your sailors, who were they?
I doubt you made it, walking on the sea!"

Then said Odysseus, who had borne the barren sea:

"Only plain truth shall I tell you, child.
Great seafarers, the Phaeacians, gave me passage
1075 as they give other wanderers. By night
over the open ocean, while I slept,
they brought me in their cutter, set me down
on Ithaca, with gifts of bronze and gold
and stores of woven things. By the gods' will
1080 these lie all hidden in a cave. I came
to this wild place, directed by Athena,
so that we might lay plans to kill our enemies.
Count up the suitors for me, let me know
what men at arms are there, how many men.
1085 I must put all my mind to it, to see
if we two by ourselves can take them on
or if we should look round for help."

                                        Telemachus

replied:

                              "O Father, all my life your fame
as a fighting man has echoed in my ears—
1090 your skill with weapons and the tricks of war—
but what you speak of is a staggering thing,
beyond imagining, for me. How can two men
do battle with a houseful in their prime?
For I must tell you this is no affair
1095 of ten or even twice ten men, but scores,
throngs of them. You shall see, here and now.
The number from Dulichium alone
is fifty-two, picked men, with armorers,
a half dozen; twenty-four came from Same,

684   *The Epic*

Grammar in Action

A **parenthetical expression** is a word or phrase that is only loosely related to the rest of the sentence. Types of parenthetical expressions include names of people being addressed, certain nonessential adverbs, common expressions, and contrasting expressions. Here are some examples:

I'll go to the store, *Mom,* after I finish my other chores. (name of someone being addressed)
We bought the horse, *therefore,* with our savings. (adverb)

My new fountain pen, *not the old ball point,* was missing. (contrasting expression)

Notice that parenthetical expressions are separated from the rest of the sentence by commas.

Writers use parenthetical expressions to add interesting details, vary the length of their sentences, and add to the drama of their accounts. In the following passages from the *Odyssey,* for example, Homer's inclusion of the names of people addressed makes the story seem more urgent and emotional:

1100 twenty from Zacynthus; our own island
accounts for twelve, high-ranked, and their
    retainers,
Medon the crier, and the Master Harper,
besides a pair of handymen at feasts.
If we go in against all these
1105 I fear we pay in salt blood for your vengeance.
You must think hard if you would conjure up
the fighting strength to take us through."
                         Odysseus
who had endured the long war and the sea
answered:

                     "I'll tell you now.
1110 Suppose Athena's arm is over us, and Zeus
her father's, must I rack my brains for more?"

Clearheaded Telemachus looked hard and said:

"Those two are great defenders, no one doubts it,
but throned in the serene clouds overhead;
1115 other affairs of men and gods they have
to rule over."

                 And the hero answered:
"Before long they will stand to right and left of us
in combat, in the shouting, when the test comes—
our nerve against the suitors' in my hall.
1120 Here is your part: at break of day tomorrow
home with you, go mingle with our princes.
The swineherd later on will take me down
the port-side trail—a beggar, by my looks,
hangdog and old. If they make fun of me
1125 in my own courtyard, let your ribs cage up
your springing heart, no matter what I suffer,
no matter if they pull me by the heels
or practice shots at me, to drive me out.
Look on, hold down your anger. You may even
1130 plead with them, by heaven! in gentle terms
to quit their horseplay—not that they will heed you,
rash as they are, facing their day of wrath.
Now fix the next step in your mind.
                        Athena,
counseling me, will give me word, and I

8 **Discussion** What does this dialogue reveal about each man's experience with the gods?

9 **Reading Strategy** Summarize Odysseus' advice to his son. Where else has Odysseus given similar advice?

"Only plain truth shall I tell you, *child. . . .*" Telemachus replied:

    "*O Father,* all my life your fame. . . ."

Student Activity 1. Find five other lines in which Homer uses parenthetical expressions. Explain how each contributes to the story.

Student Activity 2. Write a brief scene in which the goddess Athena appears to Penelope before Odysseus returns to Ithaca. Use parenthetical expressions to heighten the drama.

Electronic Handbook You might want students to review parenthetical expressions before completing the Grammar in Action activities. If students have access to the Language Master 6000, have them enter the access word *parentheses* and press the GRAMMAR key to get information on the use of parenthetical expressions.

10 **Reading Strategy** Summarize the steps in Odysseus' plan for overpowering Penelope's suitors.

11 **Discussion** Why does Odysseus want Telemachus to keep his return a secret?

1135 shall signal to you, nodding: at that point
round up all armor, lances, gear of war
left in our hall, and stow the lot away
back in the vaulted storeroom. When the suitors
miss those arms and question you, be soft
1140 in what you say: answer:

               'I thought I'd move them
out of the smoke. They seemed no longer those
bright arms Odysseus left us years ago
when he went off to Troy. Here where the fire's
hot breath came, they had grown black and drear.
1145 One better reason, too, I had from Zeus:
suppose a brawl starts up when you are drunk,
you might be crazed and bloody one another,
and that would stain your feast, your courtship.
      Tempered
iron can magnetize a man.'
                     Say that
1150 But put aside two broadswords and two spears
for our own use, two oxhide shields nearby
when we go into action. Pallas Athena
and Zeus All-Provident will see you through,
bemusing our young friends.
                  Now one thing more.
1155 If son of mine you are and blood of mine,
let no one hear Odysseus is about.
Neither Laertes, nor the swineherd here,
nor any slave, nor even Penelope.
But you and I alone must learn how far
1160 the women are corrupted; we should know
how to locate good men among our hands,
the loyal and respectful, and the shirkers
who take you lightly, as alone and young."

RESPONDING TO THE SELECTION

Your Response
1. Is Telemachus' suspicion justified? Explain.

Recalling
2. What does Athena say and do to Odysseus?
3. Describe Telemachus' reactions when Odysseus reveals himself.
4. What does Odysseus direct his son to do in preparation for an attack on the suitors?

Interpreting
5. Compare Odysseus' emotions with Telemachus' when they are reunited.
6. What is Odysseus' relationship with Athena and Zeus?

Applying
7. When you look ahead to Odysseus' reunion with his wife, what scene do you imagine?

686 *The Epic*

Closure and Extension

ANSWERS TO RESPONDING TO THE SELECTION
Your Response
1. Discuss the fact that Telemachus has had little reason to hope that he will find his father. When the stranger appeared and was changed, Telemachus had reason to be suspicious.

Recalling
2. Athena disguises herself as a mortal, and she instructs Odysseus to reveal his identity to his son and prepare to kill Penelope's suitors.
3. Initially Telemachus does not believe that this man is really his father. However, after Odysseus explains his odd appearance, Telemachus is convinced and is overwhelmed with joy.
4. Odysseus tells his son to collect all the armor left in the great hall and stow it away in a storeroom. He is to tell the suitors that he put it away to move it out of the smoke and to keep the men from harming each other in case a brawl starts. Telemachus is also instructed to put aside certain gear for himself and his father to use when necessary.

Interpreting
5. Suggested Response: Telemachus and Odysseus are equally moved when they are reunited.
6. Suggested Response: Athena is Odysseus' protector at all times. Zeus sometimes helps him.

Applying
7. Answers may differ, but most students will anticipate an emotional reunion.

686

Argus

Odysseus heads for town with Eumaeus.[2] Outside the palace, Odysseus' old dog, Argus, is lying at rest as his long-absent master approaches.

2. **Eumaeus** (ū mē′ us)

While he spoke

an old hound, lying near, pricked up his ears
1165 and lifted up his muzzle. This was Argus,
trained as a puppy by Odysseus,
but never taken on a hunt before
his master sailed for Troy. The young men, afterward,
hunted wild goats with him, and hare, and deer,
1170 but he had grown old in his master's absence.
Treated as rubbish now, he lay at last
upon a mass of dung before the gates—
manure of mules and cows, piled there until
fieldhands could spread it on the king's estate.
1175 Abandoned there, and half destroyed with flies,
old Argus lay.

But when he knew he heard

Odysseus' voice nearby, he did his best
to wag his tail, nose down, with flattened ears,
having no strength to move nearer his master.
1180 And the man looked away,
wiping a salt tear from his cheek; but he
hid this from Eumaeus. Then he said:

"I marvel that they leave this hound to lie
here on the dung pile;
1185 he would have been a fine dog, from the look of
      him,
though I can't say as to his power and speed
when he was young. You find the same good build
in house dogs, table dogs landowners keep
all for style."

And you replied, Eumaeus:

1190 "A hunter owned him—but the man is dead
in some far place. If this old hound could show
the form he had when Lord Odysseus left him,
going to Troy, you'd see him swift and strong.
He never shrank from any savage thing
1195 he'd brought to bay in the deep woods; on the scent
no other dog kept up with him. Now misery
has him in leash. His owner died abroad,
and here the women slaves will take no care of him.

The Odyssey   687

---

12 Enrichment Argus' lying on the dung heap may symbolize the decay and ruin of Odysseus' kingdom.

13 Discussion Odysseus has wept several times. What kinds of things make him sad?

Multicultural Focus Begin an examination of cultural attitudes toward dogs by asking students what other famous dogs they can think of. Responses might include Lassie, Rin Tin Tin, Benji, and White Fang. Ask students why they think dogs are often called "man's best friend" and discuss their ideas. Point out that the bond between dogs and people may go back as far as 25,000 years, as evidenced by Paleolithic cave drawings of dogs.

Have students find out more about how dogs are viewed in different cultures. Since the dog has been portrayed in art from the Stone Age through all phases of Eastern and Western art, assign some students to find and bring in a variety of pictures of dogs in art and photography books. Assign other students to research the roles dogs have played in diverse societies, such as the hunting dog, farm dog, lap dog, sled dog, and even, in ancient Egypt, Dog God. Assign other students to do a multicultural literature search to find written portrayals of dogs. Have students share their findings with the class.

Your Response

1. Encourage students to relate experiences with their own pets to this episode.

Recalling

2. In his youth, Argus was a quick and fearless hunter.

Interpreting

3. Suggested Response: Odysseus doesn't want to risk the dog giving away his identity.
4. Answers will differ. If students accept that the dog's condition represents the ruin that has come to Odysseus' home, then they will probably think that his death is not a coincidence but a symbol of the end of bad times.

Applying

5. Answers will differ, but most students will recognize that Argus undoubtedly would have jumped up immediately to greet his old master, thus revealing his identity.

---

14 **Discussion** What is the purpose of this brief section?

15 **Discussion** What does this passage reveal about Antinous?

1200 You know how servants are: without a master
they have no will to labor, or excel.
For Zeus who views the wide world takes away
half the manhood of a man, that day
he goes into captivity and slavery."

14

1205 Eumaeus crossed the court and went straight
forward
into the megaron among the suitors:
but death and darkness in that instant closed
the eyes of Argus, who had seen his master,
Odysseus, after twenty years.

RESPONDING TO THE SELECTION

Your Response

1. Were you touched by this episode? Why or why not?

Recalling

2. What was Argus like in his youth?

Interpreting

3. Why doesn't Odysseus greet Argus?
4. Is Argus' death just when Odysseus returns a coincidence? Explain.

Applying

5. How would this scene be different if Argus were younger and more vigorous?

The Suitors

Still disguised as a beggar, Odysseus enters his home. He is confronted by the haughty suitor Antinous.

But here Antinous[3] broke in, shouting:

                                    "God!

15

1210 What evil wind blew in this pest?

                                    Get over,
stand in the passage! Nudge my table, will you?
Egyptian whips are sweet
to what you'll come to here, you nosing rat,
making your pitch to everyone!
1215 These men have bread to throw away on you
because it is not theirs. Who cares? Who spares
another's food, when he has more than plenty?"

With guile Odysseus drew away, then said:

3. Antinous (an tin' ō əs)

1220 "A pity that you have more looks than heart.
You'd grudge a pinch of salt from your own larder
to your own handyman. You sit here, fat
on others' meat, and cannot bring yourself
to rummage out a crust of bread for me!"

1225 Then anger made Antinous' heart beat hard,
and, glowering under his brows, he answered:

                              "Now!
You think you'll shuffle off and get away
after that impudence? Oh, no you don't!"

The stool he let fly hit the man's right shoulder
on the packed muscle under the shoulder blade—
1230 like solid rock, for all the effect one saw.
Odysseus only shook his head, containing
thoughts of bloody work, as he walked on,
then sat, and dropped his loaded bag again
upon the door sill. Facing the whole crowd
1235 he said, and eyed them all:

                              "One word only,
my lords, and suitors of the famous queen.
One thing I have to say.
There is no pain, no burden for the heart
when blows come to a man, and he defending
1240 his own cattle—his own cows and lambs.
Here it was otherwise. Antinous
hit me for being driven on by hunger—
how many bitter seas men cross for hunger!
If beggars interest the gods, if there are Furies[4]
1245 pent in the dark to avenge a poor man's wrong, then may
Antinous meet his death before his wedding day!"

Then said Eupeithes' son, Antinous:

                              "Enough.
Eat and be quiet where you are, or shamble
    elsewhere,
unless you want these lads to stop your mouth
1250 pulling you by the heels, or hands and feet,
over the whole floor, till your back is peeled!"

But now the rest were mortified, and someone
spoke from the crowd of young bucks to rebuke him:

4. Furies (fyoor′ēz):
Three terrible spirits who
punish those whose crimes
have not been avenged.

16

17

16 Clarification By enjoying the hospitality of Odysseus' home and refusing to help a beggar, Antinous is breaking the laws of hospitality. By law, Odysseus is justified in his remarks.

17 Reading Strategy What do you think will happen to Antinous?

The Odyssey 689

18 Critical Thinking Homer gives further evidence of how intimately involved the gods are in the everyday lives of the Greeks.

19 Discussion What does Homer accomplish by having Antinous mistreat Odysseus?

18

"A poor show, that—hitting this famished tramp—
1255 bad business, if he happened to be a god.
You know they go in foreign guise, the gods do,
looking like strangers, turning up
in towns and settlements to keep an eye
on manners, good or bad."

But at this notion
1260 Antinous only shrugged.

Telemachus,
after the blow his father bore, sat still
without a tear, though his heart felt the blow.
Slowly he shook his head from side to side,
containing murderous thoughts.

Penelope
1265 on the higher level of her room had heard
the blow, and knew who gave it. Now she murmured:

"Would god you could be hit yourself, Antinous—
hit by Apollo's bowshot!"

And Eurynome[5]
her housekeeper, put in:

"He and no other?
1270 If all we pray for came to pass, not one
would live till dawn!"

Her gentle mistress said:

"Oh, Nan, they are a bad lot; they intend
ruin for all of us; but Antinous
appears a blacker-hearted hound than any.
1275 Here is a poor man come, a wanderer,
driven by want to beg his bread, and everyone
in hall gave bits, to cram his bag—only
Antinous threw a stool, and banged his shoulder!"

So she described it, sitting in her chamber
1280 among her maids—while her true lord was eating.
Then she called in the forester and said:

"Go to that man on my behalf, Eumaeus,
and send him here, so I can greet and question him.
Abroad in the great world, he may have heard
1285 rumors about Odysseus—may have known him!"

5. Eurynome: (yo͞o rin′ ə mē)

Your Response

1. Was Odysseus right in not striking back at Antinous? Explain.

Recalling

2. Describe Antinous' treatment of Odysseus.
3. Why do the other suitors speak against Antinous?

Interpreting

4. Compare and contrast Telemachus' behavior and Odysseus'.
5. Compare Penelope's and Eurynome's reactions to the events in the hall below.

Applying

6. Dramatic irony consists of actions and speeches that readers understand in a way that characters cannot. Explain the dramatic irony in this scene.

Penelope

In the evening. Penelope questions the old beggar about himself.

"Friend, let me ask you first of all:
who are you, where do you come from, of what
    nation
and parents were you born?"

                And he replied:

20

"My lady, never a man in the wide world
1290 should have a fault to find with you. Your name
has gone out under heaven like the sweet
honor of some god-fearing king, who rules
in equity over the strong: his black lands bear
both wheat and barley, fruit trees laden bright,
1295 new lambs at lambing time—and the deep sea
gives great hauls of fish by his good strategy,
so that his folk fare well.
                 O my dear lady,

21

this being so, let it suffice to ask me
of other matters—not my blood, my homeland.
1300 Do not enforce me to recall my pain.
My heart is sore; but I must not be found
sitting in tears here, in another's house:
it is not well forever to be grieving.
One of the maids might say—or you might think—

22 1305 I had got maudlin over cups of wine."

And Penelope replied:

           "Stranger, my looks,
my face, my carriage, were soon lost or faded

The Odyssey   691

---

20 Clarification In complimenting Penelope, his hostess, Odysseus not only speaks from his heart but also abides by the Greek rules of hospitality.

21 Discussion What excuse does Odysseus give for not revealing his background?

22 Clarification The word *maudlin* as used here means "weak or sentimental."

Closure and Extension

ANSWERS TO RESPONDING TO THE SELECTION

Your Response

1. Encourage students to relate Odysseus' actions to experiences they have had in which they delayed immediate gratification for the sake of a greater goal.

Recalling

2. Antinous insults and abuses Odysseus.

3. The other suitors are embarrassed by his behavior. They are also afraid that Odysseus is one of the gods disguised as a mortal.

Interpreting

4. Suggested Response: Odysseus has more faith that the gods will help him defeat the suitors. Also, when Antinous attacks Odysseus, Telemachus thinks murderous thoughts, but Odysseus speaks up against his assailant.

5. Suggested Response: Penelope hopes that Antinous will be struck by Apollo's bow. Eurynome hopes that all suitors will die.

Applying

6. Answers will differ. One source of dramatic irony is that Penelope asks to speak to the beggar in hopes that he may have heard something about Odysseus. Another is that the abused beggar is really the master of the house.

when the Achaeans crossed the sea to Troy,
Odysseus my lord among the rest.
1310   If he returned, if he were here to care for me,
I might be happily renowned!
But grief instead heaven sent me—years of pain.
Sons of the noblest families on the islands,
Dulichium, Same, wooded Zacynthus,
1315   with native Ithacans, are here to court me,
against my wish; and they consume this house.
Can I give proper heed to guest or suppliant
or herald on the realm's affairs?

                    How could I?
wasted with longing for Odysseus, while here
1320   they press for marriage.

                 Ruses served my turn
to draw the time out—first a close-grained web
I had the happy thought to set up weaving
on my big loom in hall. I said, that day:
'Young men—my suitors, now my lord is dead,
1325   let me finish my weaving before I marry,
or else my thread will have been spun in vain.
It is a shroud I weave for Lord Laertes
when cold Death comes to lay him on his bier.
The country wives would hold me in dishonor
1330   if he, with all his fortune, lay unshrouded.'
I reached their hearts that way, and they agreed.
So every day I wove on the great loom,
but every night by torchlight I unwove it;
and so for three years I deceived the Achaeans.
1335   But when the seasons brought a fourth year on,
as long months waned, and the long days were spent,
through impudent folly in the slinking maids
they caught me—clamored up to me at night;
I had no choice then but to finish it.
1340   And now, as matters stand at last,
I have no strength left to evade a marriage,
cannot find any further way; my parents
urge it upon me, and my son
will not stand by while they eat up his property.
1345   He comprehends it, being a man full-grown,
able to oversee the kind of house
Zeus would endow with honor.

                    But you too
confide in me, tell me your ancestry.
You were not born of mythic oak or stone."

692   *The Epic*

PENELOPE
Henry Fuseli
*Courtesy of Stiftung für Kunst,
Kultur und Geschichte, Kusnacht*

Humanities Note

Fine art, *Penelope*, by Henry Fuseli. Fuseli (1741–1825), an English artist, was born in Switzerland. In the classic way of an artist of his time, Fuseli spent eight years in Rome studying the Italian masters. This study gave his painting a classic style, but his style was more admired for its emotional content than its artistic merit. His eccentric paintings appear to be almost surreal. He was fascinated by the strange, the romantic, and the psychologically complex. Psychological studies of figures from history and myth were among his subjects.

In the painting *Penelope,* Fuseli tries to capture the emotion of this moment in Penelope's life. The sorrow of Penelope is intensified by the dark, gloomy background of the painting.

You might use these questions for class discussion:
1. What is the overwhelming mood of this painting?
2. What physical, emotional, and psychological characteristics does this woman display?
3. How does Fuseli's portrayal of Penelope compare with Homer's.

25 Discussion Why does Odysseus take this oath?

Penelope again asks the beggar to tell about himself. He makes up a tale in which Odysseus is mentioned and declares that Penelope's husband will soon be home.

1350 You see, then, he is alive and well, and headed
homeward now, no more to be abroad
far from his island, his dear wife and son.
Here is my sworn word for it. Witness this,
god of the zenith, noblest of the gods,[6]
1355 and Lord Odysseus' hearthfire, now before me:
I swear these things shall turn out as I say.
Between this present dark and one day's ebb,
after the wane, before the crescent moon,
Odysseus will come."

6. god of the zenith, noblest of the gods: Zeus.

The Odyssey 693

RESPONDING TO THE SELECTION

Your Response

1. What feelings does this scene evoke in you?

Recalling

2. Describe the trick Penelope used to delay choosing a husband from among the suitors.

Interpreting

3. What emotions is Odysseus probably feeling during this scene?
4. What impression of Penelope do you get from her speech?

Applying

5. Why do you think Odysseus chooses not to reveal his identity to his wife?

The Challenge

Pressed by the suitors to choose a husband from among them, Penelope says she will marry whoever can string Odysseus' bow and shoot an arrow through twelve ax-handle sockets. The suitors try and fail. Still in disguise, Odysseus asks for a turn and gets it.

	. . . . And Odysseus took his time,
1360	turning the bow, tapping it, every inch,
	for borings that termites might have made
	while the master of the weapon was abroad.
	The suitors were now watching him, and some
	jested among themselves:

                         "A bow lover!"

1365   "Dealer in old bows!"

                    "Maybe he has one like it
at home!"

                "Or has an itch to make one for himself."

"See how he handles it, the sly old buzzard!"

And one disdainful suitor added this:

	"May his fortune grow an inch for every inch he
	bends it!"
1370	But the man skilled in all ways of contending,
	satisfied by the great bow's look and heft,

694   *The Epic*

THE TRIAL OF THE BOW
N. C. Wyeth
Delaware Art Museum

28

1375

like a musician, like a harper, when
with quiet hand upon his instrument
he draws between his thumb and forefinger
a sweet new string upon a peg: so effortlessly
Odysseus in one motion strung the bow.
Then slid his right hand down the cord and plucked it,
so the taut gut vibrating hummed and sang
a swallow's note.

The Odyssey   695

Humanities Note

Fine art, *The Trial of the Bow*, 1929, by N. C. Wyeth. The American illustrator N. C. Wyeth (1882–1945) was one of the most prolific artists of the century. In addition to painting many murals and canvases, he illustrated nearly 200 books.

The Trial of the Bow was executed for a 1929 edition of the *Odyssey*. The heroic portrayal of the figure and the historical accuracy of the costume and weapon are characteristic of Wyeth's art. Wyeth has also enhanced this illustration through his creative composition and rich colors.

You might ask your class these questions:
1. What does the picture of the central figure suggest to you?
2. What are the onlookers' attitudes?

28 Literary Focus Odysseus' gentleness and quiet strength contrast with the suitors' crudeness.

29 **Discussion** Why does Odysseus not laugh out loud at the thunder clap?

30 **Literary Focus** What is ironic about this statement?

In the hushed hall it smote the suitors
1380 and all their faces changed. Then Zeus thundered
overhead, one loud crack for a sign.

29 And Odysseus laughed within him that the son
of crooked-minded Cronus had flung that omen down.
He picked one ready arrow from his table
1385 where it lay bare: the rest were waiting still
in the quiver for the young men's turn to come.
He nocked[7] it, let it rest across the handgrip,
and drew the string and grooved butt of the arrow,
aiming from where he sat upon the stool.

Now flashed
1390 arrow from twanging bow clean as a whistle
through every socket ring, and grazed not one,
to thud with heavy brazen head beyond.

Then quietly

Odysseus said:

                    "Telemachus, the stranger
you welcomed in your hall has not disgraced you.
1395 I did not miss, neither did I take all day
stringing the bow. My hand and eye are sound,
not so contemptible as the young men say.

30 The hour has come to cook their lordships' mutton—
supper by daylight. Other amusements later,
1400 with song and harping that adorn a feast."

He dropped his eyes and nodded, and the prince
Telemachus, true son of King Odysseus,
belted his sword on, clapped hand to his spear,
and with a clink and glitter of keen bronze
1405 stood by his chair, in the forefront near his father.

7. nocked: Set an arrow against the bowstring.

RESPONDING TO THE SELECTION

Your Response
1. Predict what will happen next.

Recalling
2. What is the suitors' reaction when Odysseus, still in disguise, takes up the bow?

Interpreting
3. What does Odysseus mean when he says, "The hour has come to cook their lordships' mutton—/supper by daylight"?

Applying
4. Does Odysseus' success in the contest show that he is an extraordinary archer or merely that he has a god on his side? Give reasons for your opinion.

Closure and Extension

ANSWERS TO RESPONDING TO THE SELECTION
Your Response
1. Students' predictions will vary. Ask them to think about probable reactions of the suitors.

Recalling
2. At first the suitors are disdainful, but soon they are amazed at Odysseus' skill.

Interpreting
3. Suggested Response: Odysseus is referring to his imminent attack on the suitors—they will be the source of his feast.

Applying
4. Answers will differ, but students would be correct in answering that it shows both. Being an epic hero, Odysseus is undoubtedly a skilled archer, but it is also true that the gods often assist him.

Odysseus' Revenge

Now shrugging off his rags the wiliest fighter of the
    islands
leapt and stood on the broad doorsill, his own bow
    in his hand.
He poured out at his feet a rain of arrows from the
    quiver
and spoke to the crowd:
        "So much for that. Your clean-cut game is over.

1410 Now watch me hit a target that no man has hit
    before,
if I can make this shot. Help me, Apollo."

He drew to his fist the cruel head of an arrow for
    Antinous
just as the young man leaned to lift his beautiful
    drinking cup,
embossed, two-handled, golden: the cup was in his
    fingers:

1415 the wine was even at his lips: and did he dream of
    death?
How could he? In that revelry amid his throng of
    friends
who would imagine a single foe—though a strong foe
    indeed—
could dare to bring death's pain on him and
    darkness on his eyes?
Odysseus' arrow hit him under the chin

1420 and punched up to the feathers through his throat.

Backward and down he went, letting the winecup fall
from his shocked hand. Like pipes his nostrils jetted
crimson runnels, a river of mortal red,
and one last kick upset his table

1425 knocking the bread and meat to soak in dusty blood.
Now as they craned to see their champion where he lay
the suitors jostled in uproar down the hall,
everyone on his feet. Wildly they turned and scanned
the walls in the long room for arms; but not a shield,

1430 not a good ashen spear was there for a man to take
    and throw.
All they could do was yell in outrage at Odysseus:
"Foul! to shoot at a man! That was your last shot!"

"Your own throat will be slit for this!"
                    "Our finest lad is down!
You killed the best on Ithaca."
             "Buzzards will tear your eyes out!"

The Odyssey   697

31 **Discussion** Why do you think Homer includes this description of Antinous' life just before his death?

32 **Discussion** Why do you think Homer includes such vivid descriptions of death?

33 **Discussion** Why does Odysseus choose to reveal his identity under these circumstances?

34 **Reading Strategy** How do you think Odysseus will respond to Eurymachus' speech?

35 **Clarification** The word *glower* means "to frown with annoyance and anger."

1435 For they imagined as they wished—that it was a wild shot,
an unintended killing—fools, not to comprehend
they were already in the grip of death.
But glaring under his brows Odysseus answered:

33
"You yellow dogs, you thought I'd never make it
1440 home from the land of Troy. You took my house to plunder.
. . . You dared
bid for my wife while I was still alive.
Contempt was all you had for the gods who rule
    wide heaven,
contempt for what men say of you hereafter.
Your last hour has come. You die in blood."

1445 As they all took this in, sickly green fear
pulled at their entrails, and their eyes flickered
looking for some hatch or hideaway from death.
Eurymachus[8] alone could speak. He said:

8. Eurymachus (yoo ri′ mə kəs)

"If you are Odysseus of Ithaca come back,
1450 all that you say these men have done is true.
Rash actions, many here, more in the countryside.
But here he lies, the man who caused them all.
Antinous was the ringleader, he whipped us on
to do these things. He cared less for a marriage
1455 than for the power Cronion has denied him
as king of Ithaca. For that
he tried to trap your son and would have killed him.
He is dead now and has his portion. Spare
your own people. As for ourselves, we'll make
1460 restitution of wine and meat consumed,
and add, each one, a tithe of twenty oxen
with gifts of bronze and gold to warm your heart.
Meanwhile we cannot blame you for your anger."

34

35
Odysseus glowered under his black brows
1465 and said:

        "Not for the whole treasure of your fathers,
all you enjoy, lands, flocks, or any gold
put up by others, would I hold my hand.
There will be killing till the score is paid.
You forced yourselves upon this house. Fight your way out,
1470 or run for it, if you think you'll escape death.
I doubt one man of you skins by."

698 *The Epic*

Grammar in Action

Many verbs show action, and **vivid verbs** are ones that paint a particularly clear picture of that action. Look at some of the verbs Eurymachus uses to call his men to action in these lines from the *Odyssey:*

> *Fight,* I say,
> let's remember the joy of it. Swords out!
> *Hold* up your tables to *deflect* his arrows.
> After me, everyone, *rush* him where he *stands*.

If we *can budge* him from the door, if we *can pass* into the town, we'll *call out* men to *chase* him. This fellow with his bow *will shoot* no more.

Compare this with a similar passage that does not use these verbs:

> Move, I say,
> let's remember the joy of it. Swords out!
> Use your tables to shield you from his arrows.
> After me, everyone, get him where he is now.
> If we can move him from the door, if we then go
> into the town, we'll get men to go find him. This
> fellow with the bow will be no more.

They felt their knees fail, and their hearts—but heard
Eurymachus for the last time rallying them.

"Friends," he said, "the man is implacable.
1475 Now that he's got his hands on bow and quiver
he'll shoot from the big doorstone there
until he kills us to the last man.
                                    Fight, I say,
let's remember the joy of it. Swords out!
Hold up your tables to deflect his arrows.
1480 After me, everyone: rush him where he stands.
If we can budge him from the door, if we can pass
into the town, we'll call out men to chase him.
This fellow with his bow will shoot no more."

He drew his own sword as he spoke, a broadsword
      of fine bronze,
1485 honed like a razor on either edge. Then crying
      hoarse and loud
he hurled himself at Odysseus. But the kingly man
      let fly
an arrow at that instant, and the quivering
      feathered butt
sprang to the nipple of his breast as the barb stuck
      in his liver.
The bright broadsword clanged down. He lurched
      and fell aside,
1490 pitching across his table. His cup, his bread and meat,
were spilt and scattered far and wide, and his head
      slammed on the ground.
Revulsion, anguish in his heart, with both feet
      kicking out,
he downed his chair, while the shrouding wave of
      mist closed on his eyes.

Amphinomus now came running at Odysseus,
1495 broadsword naked in his hand. He thought to make
the great soldier give way at the door.
But with a spear throw from behind Telemachus hit him
between the shoulders, and the lancehead drove
clear through his chest. He left his feet and fell
1500 forward, thudding, forehead against the ground.
Telemachus swerved around him, leaving the long
      dark spear
planted in Amphinomus. If he paused to yank it out
someone might jump him from behind or cut him
      down with a sword

The Odyssey 699

36 **Discussion** What do you think of Eurymachus' plan? What is it motivated by?

37 **Discussion** What other metaphors for dying has Homer used?

38 **Discussion** What quality does Telemachus show here? Who else has demonstrated this same quality?

Notice how what began as a rousing speech becomes colorless and far less rousing when robbed of its vivid action words.

Student Activity 1. Find five other sentences in the epic that contain vivid verbs, and talk about these with your classmates.

Student Activity 2. Write four sentences about the illustration on page 700. Use vivid verbs in these.

Electronic Handbook You might want students to review verbs before completing the Grammar in Action activities. If students have access to the Language Master 6000, have them enter the access word *verb* and press the GRAMMAR key to get information on the use of verbs.

Fine art, *The Slaughter of the Suitors,* 1929, by N. C. Wyeth. N. C. Wyeth, America's foremost illustrator of children's books and of the classics, created this illustration for a 1929 edition of the *Odyssey.*

Wyeth's illustrations add elements of drama and imagination to this already exciting story. His animation of the figures in this illustration is a marvel of painterly skill. The intensity of the movement and the play of light and dark both serve to accentuate this dynamic composition.

You might use the following questions for discussion:
1. Which lines from the *Odyssey* does this scene illustrate?
2. Which details contribute to the realism of the scene?

39 Discussion Odysseus agrees with his son's plan. What does this suggest about Odysseus' confidence in his son?

THE SLAUGHTER OF THE SUITORS
N. C. Wyeth
Delaware Art Museum

at the moment he bent over. So he ran—ran from
    the tables
1505   to his father's side and halted, panting, saying:

"Father let me bring you a shield and spear,
a pair of spears, a helmet.
I can arm on the run myself; I'll give
outfits to Eumaeus and this cowherd.
1510   Better to have equipment."

               Said Odysseus:

39   "Run then, while I hold them off with arrows
as long as the arrows last. When all are gone
if I'm alone they can dislodge me."

                  Quick
upon his father's word Telemachus
1515   ran to the room where spears and armor lay.
He caught up four light shields, four pairs of spears,

700   *The Epic*

four helms of war high-plumed with flowing manes,
and ran back, loaded down, to his father's side.
He was the first to pull a helmet on
1520 and slide his bare arm in a buckler strap.
The servants armed themselves, and all three took
     their stand
beside the master of battle.
                    While he had arrows
he aimed and shot, and every shot brought down
one of his huddling enemies.
1525 But when all barbs had flown from the bowman's fist,
he leaned his bow in the bright entryway
beside the door, and armed: a four-ply shield
hard on his shoulder, and a crested helm,
horsetailed, nodding stormy upon his head,
1530 then took his tough and bronze-shod spears. . . .

    *Aided by Athena, Odysseus, Telemachus, Eu-
    maeus, and another faithful herdsman kill all the
    suitors.*

And Odysseus looked around him, narrow-eyed,
for any others who had lain hidden
while death's black fury passed.
                    In blood and dust
he saw that crowd all fallen, many and many slain.

1535 Think of a catch that fishermen haul in to a half-
     moon bay
in a fine-meshed net from the whitecaps of the sea:
how all are poured out on the sand, in throes for
     the salt sea,
twitching their cold lives away in Helios' fiery air:
so lay the suitors heaped on one another.

┃ RESPONDING TO THE SELECTION

Your Response
1. Is Odysseus' revenge justified? Explain.

Recalling
2. Describe the immediate reaction of the suitors to the killing of Antinous.
3. How does Telemachus aid his father in the battle?

Interpreting
4. Discuss Odysseus' judgment on the suitors. What are his reasons for slaying them all?

Applying
5. Compare justice at the hands of Odysseus with justice in a modern society.

The Odyssey 701

42 **Literary Focus** Odysseus is described as more godlike than human.

43 **Clarification** Athena was also the goddess of crafts and techniques that uphold civilization.

Penelope's Test

*Penelope tests Odysseus to prove that he really is
her husband.*

1540 Greathearted Odysseus, home at last,
was being bathed now by Eurynome
and rubbed with golden oil, and clothed again
in a fresh tunic and a cloak. Athena
lent him beauty, head to foot. She made him
1545 taller, and massive, too, with crisping hair
in curls like petals of wild hyacinth
but all red-golden. Think of gold infused
on silver by a craftsman, whose fine art
Hephaestus[9] taught him, or Athena: one
1550 whose work moves to delight: just so she lavished
beauty over Odysseus' head and shoulders.
He sat then in the same chair by the pillar,
facing his silent wife, and said:

"Strange woman,
the immortals of Olympus made you hard,
1555 harder than any. Who else in the world
would keep aloof as you do from her husband
if he returned to her from years of trouble,
cast on his own land in the twentieth year?

Nurse, make up a bed for me to sleep on.
1560 Her heart is iron in her breast."

Penelope
spoke to Odysseus now. She said:

"Strange man,
if man you are . . . This is no pride on my part
nor scorn for you—not even wonder, merely.
I know so well how you—how he—appeared
1565 boarding the ship for Troy. But all the same . . .

Make up his bed for him, Eurycleia.
Place it outside the bedchamber my lord
built with his own hands. Pile the big bed
with fleeces, rugs, and sheets of purest linen."

1570 With this she tried him to the breaking point,
and he turned on her in a flash raging:

9. **Hephaestus** (hi fes´
təs): God of fire and the
forge and of metalworking.

702   *The Epic*

"Woman, by heaven you've stung me now!
Who dared to move my bed?
No builder had the skill for that—unless
1575 a god came down to turn the trick. No mortal
in his best days could budge it with a crowbar.
There is our pact and pledge, our secret sign,
built into that bed—my handiwork
and no one else's!
                          An old trunk of olive
1580 grew like a pillar on the building plot,
and I laid out our bedroom round that tree,
lined up the stone walls, built the walls and roof,
gave it a doorway and smooth-fitting doors.
Then I lopped off the silvery leaves and branches,
1585 hewed and shaped that stump from the roots up
into a bedpost, drilled it, let it serve
as model for the rest. I planed them all,
inlaid them all with silver, gold and ivory,
and stretched a bed between—a pliant web
1590 of oxhide thongs dyed crimson.
                              There's our sign!
I know no more. Could someone else's hand
have sawn that trunk and dragged the frame away?"

Their secret! as she heard it told, her knees
grew tremulous and weak, her heart failed her.
1595 With eyes brimming tears she ran to him,
throwing her arms around his neck, and kissed
      him,
murmuring:

                          "Do not rage at me, Odysseus!
No one ever matched your caution! Think
what difficulty the gods gave: they denied us
1600 life together in our prime and flowering years,
kept us from crossing into age together.
Forgive me, don't be angry. I could not
welcome you with love on sight! I armed myself
long ago against the frauds of men,
1605 impostors who might come—and all those many
whose underhanded ways bring evil on! . . .
But here and now, what sign could be so clear
as this of our own bed?
No other man has ever laid eyes on it—
1610 only my own slave, Actoris, that my father

The Odyssey   703

45 **Reading Strategy** Compare and contrast this reunion with the reunion with Telemachus.

46 **Master Teacher Note** Use the overhead projector to show students Art Transparency 19 *Odysseus and Penelope Reunited*, by Romare Bearden. Ask students how this picture reflects the happy reunion of husband and wife in a peaceful kingdom. Also, how do they think Bearden's identity as a black artist has influenced his depiction of this scene?

47 **Enrichment** You might want to ask students to read Tennyson's "Ulysses," which presents Odysseus at the end of his life. Then have them compare Homer's hero with Tennyson's.

Reader's Response How would you have handled Odysseus' situation at home when he returns from war? Would you have acted differently? Explain.

Thematic Response Life's journey has been difficult for Odysseus, but the members of his family and kingdom have suffered as well. Who in this story do you believe had the most difficult journey through life? Explain.

sent with me as a gift—she kept our door.
You make my stiff heart know that I am yours."

Now from his breast into his eyes the ache
of longing mounted, and he wept at last,
1615   his dear wife, clear and faithful, in his arms,
longed for as the sunwarmed earth is longed for by a swimmer
spent in rough water where his ship went down
under Poseidon's blows, gale winds and tons of sea.
Few men can keep alive through a big surf
1620   to crawl, clotted with brine, on kindly beaches
in joy, in joy, knowing the abyss behind:
and so she too rejoiced, her gaze upon her husband,
her white arms round him pressed as though
     forever.

The Ending

Odysseus is reunited with his father. Athena commands that peace prevail between Odysseus and the relatives of the slain suitors. Odysseus has regained his family and his kingdom.

RESPONDING TO THE SELECTION

Your Response
1. Why do you think that Odysseus is one of the most famous epic heroes?

Recalling
2. Why is Odysseus displeased with Penelope?
3. What is her response to his complaint?
4. What is Penelope's test, and how does Odysseus pass it?

Interpreting
5. Since Odysseus has abandoned his disguise, why does Penelope doubt his identity?
6. Describe the mood of this scene. Is it altogether happy, or does it include some sadness? Give reasons for your opinion.

Applying
7. Some scholars believe the events that follow the reunion of Odysseus and Penelope were added to the *Odyssey* by someone other than Homer. Tell why you think that these events ("The Ending") do or do not make up an appropriate conclusion to the epic.

ANALYZING LITERATURE

Understanding the Plot of an Epic

The **plot** of an epic is made up of a series of episodes in which the hero performs extraordinary deeds. In classical epics such as the *Odyssey*, the outcomes of these episodes may depend on the influence of the gods as well as on the strengths and weaknesses of the human characters.

1. Give three examples of a god or goddess influencing the events of the *Odyssey*.
2. Do Odysseus' deeds seem less heroic because the gods sometimes assist him? Give reasons for your opinion.

704   *The Epic*

Closure and Extension

ANSWERS TO RESPONDING TO THE SELECTION
Your Response
1. As students discuss the question, have them think about the courage, intelligence, and talents Odysseus needed to face the various challenges in the story.

Recalling
2. Odysseus is displeased with Penelope's aloofness after such a long separation.
3. Penelope explains that she is still uncertain about Odysseus' identity and that she has had to guard against impostors.
4. Penelope tells her servant to move the bed, a suggestion that enrages Odysseus, who built the bed himself. He passes her test by describing the unique bed in detail.

3. In which episode in Odysseus' character most fully displayed? Tell what traits are revealed in it.

CRITICAL THINKING AND READING

Reading a Map

Understanding the geography of the Mediterranean region is crucial to understanding Homer's *Odyssey*. Although the adventures of Odysseus are fictional, many of the places mentioned in the story actually exist. Use the map below to answer the following questions.

1. Troy, or Ilium, the site of the Trojan War, was uncovered in what is now Turkey. Locate Turkey on the map. What body of water separates it from Greece?
2. The entrance to the Land of the Dead is believed to be the Strait of Gibraltar. Why might people in Homer's time have considered this location frightening?

THINKING AND WRITING

Responding to Criticism

The poet and critic W. H. Auden once made the following comment about Homer's heroes.

Though it would be unfair to describe the Homeric hero as a mere puppet of the gods, his area of free choice and responsibility is pretty circumscribed. In the first place he is born, not made . . . so that though he does brave deeds, he cannot be called brave in our sense of the word because he never feels fear.

Write an essay in which you tell why you agree or disagree with this comment. First find those episodes or parts of episodes that support your opinion. Refer to them when you write your draft. When you revise make sure that you have addressed the key questions about Odysseus that Auden's comment suggests: Does he act freely or not? Does he feel fear or not? Is he brave or not?

LEARNING OPTION

Writing. Imagine that Penelope kept a journal. Using her point of view, write three entries in which you describe her inner reactions to Odysseus' departure, long absence, and return home.

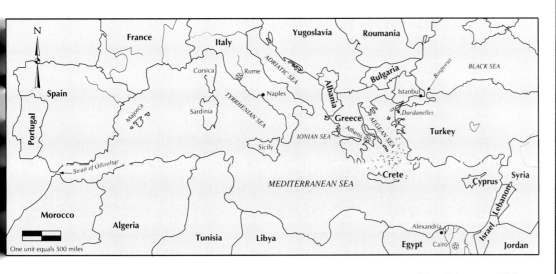

One unit equals 500 miles

The Odyssey 705

ANSWERS TO CRITICAL THINKING AND READING

1. The Aegean Sea separates Turkey from Greece.
2. Suggested Response: The Strait of Gibraltar is a narrow passage leading from the known world—the Mediterranean Sea—to the unknown and dangerous Atlantic Ocean.

THINKING AND WRITING

Software If students have access to computers, have them use **Bank Street Writer** to complete all stages of the assignment. Using the program's cut and paste features, students will be able to easily incorporate ideas from their prewriting work into their compositions.

Alternative Assessment *Peer Review* In pairs or in groups of four, have students assess each other's essays by responding to the following questions:

What position does the writer take?

What episodes does the writer cite to support his/her position?

What does the writer say about Odysseus' freedom of action?

What does the writer say about Odysseus' feelings of fear?

What conclusion does the writer arrive at about Odysseus' bravery?

What suggestions do you have for the writer to support his/her position more fully?

What, if anything, would you suggest the writer omit?

To validate the peer review, have students revise their work, incorporating those suggestions they believe will enhance their essays.

LEARNING OPTION

This activity will appeal to visual learners. You might vary the activity by suggesting that students write entries for a journal kept by Telemachus.

Interpreting

5. Suggested Response: She doubts his identity because he has changed so dramatically.
6. Suggested Response: The scene is one of conflicting emotions: suspicion, joy at being reunited, and sorrow for their long separation.

Applying

7. Answers will differ. Students should give reasons for their responses, indicating whether this ending is a satisfying climax.

ANSWERS TO ANALYZING LITERATURE

1. Suggested Response: Poseidon sinks Odysseus' ship; Athena tells Odysseus to reveal himself to his son; and Athena helps Odysseus kill the suitors.
2. Answers will differ. Some students might argue that the assistance of the gods does not detract from Odysseus' skill and courage. For example, he is obviously a skillful archer.
3. Answers will differ. Some students may argue that Odysseus' humanity is most clearly revealed in his sadness at seeing his mother's shade; his joy at being reunited with Telemachus; or his mixed joy, sadness, and anger in the reunion with Penelope. Other students may argue that the episode in which Odysseus blinds the Cy-

MULTICULTURAL CONNECTION
Great Epics of the World

What is an epic? Traditional epics like Homer's *Odyssey* and *Iliad* are long, narrative poems that describe great journeys, wars, or the founding of a nation. The stories are frequently based on myths in which human heroes interact with gods.

Epics also contain descriptions of historical events. For example, the Trojan War, described in the *Iliad*, might have actually occurred. The cause of the war, however, was probably not the kidnapping of a beautiful queen, as Homer asserts, but a struggle for economic or political advantage.

Before the invention of writing. The earliest epics, including Homer's, date back to a time before the invention of writing. Incredible as it may seem, poets made up and memorized poems consisting of thousands of lines. As a memory aid, they kept in mind certain typical situations that they could describe. For instance, a favorite type of scene was the arming of a hero for battle. When performing their epics, they would leave out a scene if the audience seemed bored or add one if the listeners were enthusiastic.

Living books in history. The bards who composed and sang these epics were a valuable source of entertainment and information. In an era without television, radio, newspapers, or books, they carried the histories of peoples in their heads.

The earliest epic. The earliest known epic is a long narrative poem about a Sumerian king named Gilgamesh, who lived between 2700 and 2500 B.C., an era about twenty-two times more distant from us than the Revolutionary War.

This epic tells how Gilgamesh, after the death of his closest friend, tries to discover the secret of immortal life. Although this poem is extremely ancient, its concerns are timeless and universal: how to become known and respected, how to cope with the loss of a dear friend, and how to accept one's own death.

European epics. The Gilgamesh epic, which comes from the ancient Middle East, is older even than the *Iliad* and the *Odyssey*. The European tradition of the epic, however, begins with these works by Homer. The Roman poet Virgil (70–19 B.C.) used Homer's epics as a model when he wrote the *Aeneid* (ē nē′ id), which tells how the city of Rome was founded.

During the Middle Ages, the Christian nations of Europe produced epics describing their wars with Muslim armies. For example, the French *Chanson de Roland,* which means "Song of Roland," commemorates an eighth-century battle between the French army and Muslim forces. Similarly, the twelfth-century Spanish epic *Poema del Cid* ("Poem of the Cid") describes the exploits of the warrior El Cid in his battles against the Muslim people known as Moors.

In the seventeenth century, the English poet John Milton wrote *Paradise Lost*, an epic poem based on the Bible. In many respects, however, he modeled his work after the epics written by Homer and Virgil.

The epic in India. Nations outside of Europe have their own traditions of epic poetry. A great national epic of India, for example, is the Ramayana (rä mä′ yə nə). It was written around 400 B.C. in Sanskrit, an ancient Indian language. Its hero, Rama, the son and heir of a Hindu king in northern India, is at the same time the earthly embodiment of the Indian god Vishnu.

Rama's father is forced to banish him to the forest, and Rama's wife, Sita, who accompanies him, is abducted by the demon king, Ravana. This demon takes Sita to his island kingdom of Lanka (modern-day Sri Lanka). Rama pursues her there and defeats the armies of Ravana in a furious battle. An ally of Rama's in this battle is the monkey Hanuman, who is able to leap from India to Lanka and spy on the demons in their kingdom.

A popular hero even today, Rama is regarded as a role model for Hindu men: He is handsome, brave, and devoted to duty and family.

An African epic. In Africa the literature conveyed by word of mouth includes stories, songs and chants, proverbs, riddles, and heroic tales. One African heroic tale is the epic *Sundiata*. Just as the *Aeneid* describes the founding of Rome by the Trojan warrior Aeneas, *Sundiata* tells about the founding of the African kingdom of Mali in the thirteenth century.

This tale has traditionally been recited by oral performers known as griots (grē′ ō). These men, like the bards of ancient Greece,

SCENE FROM THE *RAMAYANA* (detail), C. 1800
Victoria and Albert Museum

memorize thousands of lines of poetry and keep alive the history of their people.

Exploring on Your Own

Learn more about an epic that interests you and present your findings to the class.

Humanities Note

Fine art, scene from the *Ramayana,* 1800. This piece is a detail of a nineteenth-century Indian miniature or album painting. These paintings were small in size and very popular because of their portability. Learning to paint these miniatures was an educational requirement for children of Indian nobility. The epic *Ramayana* was a favorite theme for these paintings along with other sacred subjects.

This detail shows an exciting event from the *Ramayana* involving a monkey king and archers. The scene is bordered top and bottom by a floral band reminiscent of the intricate carvings that can be found on Indian temples. The stylized trees divide the picture plane so that scenes to the right and left are distinctly separate. The predominately warm coloration and the intricate details of the costumes of the characters make a highly decorative illustration for the epic.

This very lovely style of painting died out in India in the late eighteenth century when Indian artists adopted a Western influenced style of painting.

Use these questions to discuss the art:
1. Can you identify the god Rama in this painting?
2. What is the significance of the small monkey?

Preparation

More About the Author As a girl, Margaret Atwood grew up in a rural section of Canada. What advantages or disadvantages might a writer gain from growing up in the country rather than in a large city?

More About the Author Critics have commented on Cavafy's almost uncanny ability to make the past come alive. Even though he writes about people and events of long ago, he makes them seem as real as the newspaper stories of today. Ask students what factors might account for this ability.

More About the Author Derek Walcott considers himself, first and foremost, a Caribbean writer. Commenting that he yearns to see a stronger energy, discipline, and drive in West Indian poetry, he sees himself at the beginning, rather than at the end, of a new tradition of Caribbean poets.

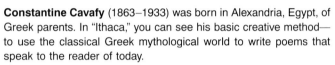

GUIDE FOR READING

Siren Song, Ithaca, and Homeric Chorus

Margaret Atwood (1939–   ) was born in Ottawa, Ontario, and has lived in Canada most of her life. She writes fiction, poetry, and screenplays. Her concern with what it means to be a woman in a period of social change is reflected in her startling re-creation of Homer's Sirens in "Siren Song."

Constantine Cavafy (1863–1933) was born in Alexandria, Egypt, of Greek parents. In "Ithaca," you can see his basic creative method—to use the classical Greek mythological world to write poems that speak to the reader of today.

Derek Walcott (1930–   ) was born on the Caribbean island of St. Lucia and grew up speaking both English and the island dialect. In addition to being a poet, Walcott is a playwright and director. He also teaches writing. Although much of his writing reflects his West Indian background, "Homeric Chorus" richly displays Walcott's eloquence concerning European traditions. In 1992 he was awarded the Nobel Prize for Literature.

Objectives

1 To understand interpretations of the *Odyssey*
2 To interpret the *Odyssey* creatively
3 To express individual interests and abilities through optional activities

Support Material

Teaching Portfolio
Teacher Backup, p. 857
Usage and Mechanics Worksheet, p. 860
Vocabulary Check, p. 861
Analyzing Literature Worksheet, *Understanding Interpretations of the Odyssey,* p. 862

Language Worksheet, *Recognizing Modern Allusions to the Odyssey,* p. 863
Selection Test, p. 864

Listening to Literature
"Siren Song," "Ithaca"

Audio Prose Library
Margaret Atwood Interview
Margaret Atwood Reading

Prentice Hall Literature Writing Studio

Modern Interpretations of the *Odyssey*

The characters and events of the *Odyssey* are timeless and universal in their interest and significance. They are so rich in meaning that every generation sees in them ideas and values relevant to the present. Hence countless writers have mined the *Odyssey* for material to create original poems, plays, novels, and essays. Though these "interpretations" differ widely in purpose, theme, and artistic method, they usually have two features in common. They present persons, places, and events whose origins are in Homer, but they use Homer's material in original ways to express contemporary thoughts, values, beliefs, and feelings.

Focus

If you were updating Homer's *Odyssey* for our own times, which episodes would you choose? Why? After answering these questions, read the poems by Atwood, Cavafy, and Walcott to see what material from the epic they chose to use. Also, decide whether or not they successfully adapted this material to our own times.

Vocabulary

Knowing the following words will help you as you read "Siren Song," "Ithaca," and "Homeric Chorus."

beached (bēc ht) *adj.*: Washed up and lying on a beach (p. 711) (usually a verb)

picturesque (pik′ chə resk′) *adj.*: Like or suggesting a picture (p. 711)

amber (am′ bər) *n.*: A yellowish resin used in jewelry (p. 712)

ebony (eb′ ə nē) *n.*: A hard, dark wood used for furniture (p. 712)

defrauded (di frôd′ əd) *v.*: Cheated (p. 713)

laurel (lôr′ əl) *n.*: Evergreen foliage used in wreaths by the ancient Greeks to crown contest winners (p. 714)

pliant (plī′ ənt) *adj.*: Flexible (p. 714)

incise (in cīz′) *v.*: Engrave; carve (p. 714)

Literary Focus "Ithaca" is based on Odysseus' return to his homeland. As students read it, have them note references from Homer's work that are familiar to them. "Siren Song" is also based on a particular incident from the *Odyssey.* In reading it, have students think about how Atwood's Siren is different from Homer's.

Thematic Focus Unlike Homer's Sirens, the siren in Atwood's poem experiences internal rather than external conflicts. Atwood's modern siren portrays ambivalence about her role as a seducer. Discuss with students the idea that internal conflicts can be as destructive as external ones. Have they ever experienced an internal conflict? How did they resolve it?

Prereading Focus Before having students complete this activity have a class discussion in which students share their favorite episodes of the *Odyssey.* For what reasons did they especially enjoy these episodes? How did they visualize the characters and events in the episodes?

Vocabulary Have **more advanced** students write a descriptive paragraph using as many of these words as possible.

Siren Song 709

Audiocassette To give students an appreciation of the tone of voice of a poem's speaker, you might wish to have them listen to the recordings of "Siren Song" and "Ithaca" on Side 6 of the **Listening to Literature** Audiocassettes.

Audiocassette As a closure activity, you might wish to have students listen to the recording of Margaret Atwood reading some of her own work and the interview with her in the **Audio Prose Library.**

Humanities Note

Fine art, *Ulysses and the Sirens,* by Pablo Picasso. The Spanish artist Pablo Picasso (1881–1973) was one of the greatest artists of the twentieth century. As the child of an artist and teacher, Picasso was given every encouragement when he showed an interest in drawing. When he was fifteen, he attended La Llonja Art School in Barcelona, where he studied painting and drawing under his father. He then worked as an illustrator and later as an art editor. In 1901, he settled in Paris. There he came into contact with the avant garde of the French art world. His role in influencing these artists and changing the face of twentieth century art cannot be overstated.

While figures from mythology are not a common subject in Picasso's work, they do recur throughout his working years. In *Ulysses and the Sirens,* Picasso does not let a strictly realistic approach limit his interpretation.

You might use these questions for discussion:

1. How does this work interpret Homer's Sirens?
2. How does the artist convey the reaction of Ulysses (Odysseus) to the Sirens?

ULYSSES AND THE SIRENS
Pablo Picasso
Musée Picasso

710   *The Epic*

Siren Song

Margaret Atwood

1   This is the one song everyone
would like to learn: the song
that is irresistible:

the song that forces men
5   to leap overboard in squadrons
even though they see the beached skulls

2   the song nobody knows
because anyone who has heard it
is dead, and the others can't remember.

10   Shall I tell you the secret
and if I do, will you get me
out of this bird suit?[1]

I don't enjoy it here
squatting on this island
15   looking picturesque and mythical

3   with these two feathery maniacs,
I don't enjoy singing
this trio, fatal and valuable.

I will tell the secret to you,
20   to you, only to you.
Come closer. This song

is a cry for help: Help me!
Only you, only you can,
you are unique

4   25   at last Alas
it is a boring song
but it works every time.

---

1. bird suit: The Sirens are usually represented as
half bird and half woman.

R ESPONDING TO THE SELECTION

Your Response

1. How effective is Atwood's modern rendition of
Homer's Sirens? Explain.

Recalling

2. What does the Siren reveal about the song?
3. What does she reveal about herself?

Interpreting

4. Who might the "others" be who have heard the
song but "can't remember"?
5. The Siren describes the song as "fatal and
valuable." In what sense is it valuable?
6. To whom might the Siren be speaking? Give
reasons for your opinion.

Applying

7. How much of "Siren Song" is based on Homer,
and how much is Atwood's original creation?

Presentation

Motivation/Prior Knowledge
Ask students how it might feel to
be one of the Sirens in the *Odyssey*. Then tell them that Atwood
offers an imaginative answer to
this question.

Master Teacher Note Although
Atwood's poem is based on well-
known figures from Homer's
classic, the poem offers a contemporary message. As students
read, ask them to consider the
effect of using a classical figure
to make a point about a contemporary issue.

Purpose-Setting   Question
What trick does the narrator of
Atwood's poem use to get men's
attention?

1 **Discussion** To whom do you
think "everyone" refers?

2 **Literary Focus** To what characteristics of Homer's Sirens
does this refer?

3 **Discussion** Why do you think the
speaker refers to the Sirens as
maniacs?

4 **Discussion** Notice Atwood's
play on words. How does it contribute to the meaning?

Thematic Response How do the
conflicts of Atwood's siren relate
to modern life?

---

who have not yet heard the Sirens
sing.
5. Suggested Response: It may be
valuable because it "is irresistible."
6. Answers will differ. Students may
even indicate that she is speaking
to herself.

Applying

7. Answers will differ. Most students
will realize that the character and
situation are Homeric but that the
modern speech and interpretation
are Atwood's.

Closure and Extension

ANSWERS TO RESPONDING TO THE SELECTION

Your Response

1. Discuss the style of language, the
impact of first person voice speaking directly to the reader, and the
idea that the siren is bored and
perhaps no longer wants to be a
siren.

Recalling

2. She says that the secret song is
irresistible and forces men to leap
overboard to their death.
3. The Siren reveals that she is unhappy in her role, "looking picturesque and mythical," that she
does not enjoy singing, and that
her song is a cry for help.

Interpreting

4. Answers will differ. Students may
respond that the "others" are men

Motivation/Prior Knowledge
Ask students what is enjoyable about a journey. Then ask them why life is sometimes compared to a journey. Tell them that Cavafy makes use of such a comparison.

Master Teacher Note Constantine Cavafy is described in *Twentieth-Century Literary Criticism* as "generally conceded to be the greatest Greek poet of the twentieth century." Discuss with students some of the qualities that may have earned this reputation for Cavafy.

Purpose-Setting Question To what audience might the poem be addressed?

1 **Reading Strategy** Restate lines 11 and 12 in your own words.

2 **Discussion** Why does the author encourage such extravagance?

3 **Discussion** This is the second time the poet suggests that we take our time on this journey. Why?

4 **Discussion** What might this "beautiful voyage" symbolize?

Ithaca

Constantine Cavafy

When you start on your journey to Ithaca,
then pray that the road is long,
full of adventure, full of knowledge.
Do not fear the Lestrygonians[1]
5 and the Cyclopes and the angry Poseidon.
You will never meet such as these on your path,
if your thoughts remain lofty, if a fine
emotion touches your body and your spirit.
You will never meet the Lestrygonians,
10 the Cyclopes and the fierce Poseidon,
if you do not carry them within your soul,
if your soul does not raise them up before you.

Then pray that the road is long.
That the summer mornings are many,
15 that you will enter ports seen for the first time
with such pleasure, with such joy!
Stop at Phoenician markets,
and purchase fine merchandise,
mother-of-pearl and corals, amber and ebony,
20 and pleasurable perfumes of all kinds,
buy as many pleasurable perfumes as you can:
visit hosts of Egyptian cities,
to learn and learn from those who have knowledge.

Always keep Ithaca fixed in your mind.
25 To arrive there is your ultimate goal.
But do not hurry the voyage at all.
It is better to let it last for long years;
and even to anchor at the isle when you are old,
rich with all that you have gained on the way,
30 not expecting that Ithaca will offer you riches.

Ithaca has given you the beautiful voyage.
Without her you would never have taken the road.
But she has nothing more to give you.

------

1. Lestrygonians (les trĭ gō′ nē ənz): Cannibals who destroy all of Odysseus' ships except his own and kill the crews.

And if you find her poor, Ithaca has not defrauded you.
With the great wisdom you have gained, with so much experience,
you must surely have understood by then what Ithacas mean.

Responding to the Selection

Your Response

1. Are you on your own "journey to Ithaca"? Explain.

Recalling

2. What benefits await the traveler to Ithaca if the road, or journey, is long?
3. What does the speaker say directly about the meaning and value of Ithaca?

Interpreting

4. What might the journey to Ithaca symbolize?
5. What might Ithaca symbolize?
6. What might the Lestrygonians, Cyclopes, and "fierce Poseidon" symbolize?

Applying

7. In what way could a person carry the Lestrygonians, Cyclopes, and angry Poseidon within his or her own soul?

Analyzing Literature

Understanding Interpretations

When modern writers interpret the *Odyssey* or some part of it creatively, they frequently use it to organize and express their own feelings, beliefs, and experiences. Atwood, for example, uses the Sirens to say something about women. Cavafy uses a basic plot thread of the *Odyssey*—the journey home of Odysseus—to say something about life and living. In the hands of these writers, Homer's subject matter takes on new meanings according to the special purpose of each artist.

1. What resemblance do you see between Atwood's Siren and some contemporary women?
2. Why is Odysseus' journey home such excellent material for a literary work concerned with the course of human life?

Thinking and Writing

Interpreting the *Odyssey* Creatively

Write a monologue in prose or poetry such as Telemachus or Penelope might utter after listening to Odysseus recount his adventures. Let the character you chose express some of your own thoughts and feelings about life. When you revise your monologue, try to make your speaker sound the way Telemachus or Penelope might sound. Compare your monologue with those of your classmates. In how many different ways was Homer's material used?

Learning Options

1. **Performance.** Both Atwood and Cavafy created modern versions of material from Homer's *Odyssey*. Choose a scene from the epic and adapt it for a contemporary audience. As you rewrite the scene, provide your own interpretation of Homer's material. Then perform your adaptation for the class.
2. **Art.** Notice Picasso's visual interpretation of Homer's Sirens on page 710. Now create your own painting, collage, or mobile to illustrate Atwood's or Cavafy's poem. Display your artwork in class.

Closure and Extension

ANSWERS TO RESPONDING TO THE SELECTION

Your Response

1. Encourage students to discuss both their short- and long-term goals as they respond to this question.

Recalling

2. Adventure and knowledge are the benefits of a long journey.
3. Ithaca has provided the opportunity for a journey, but once we arrive there, it will give nothing more.

Interpreting

4. Suggested Response: The journey probably represents the journey through life.
5. Suggested Response: Ithaca may be a metaphor for old age or death.
6. Suggested Response: These figures represent the obstacles and difficulties encountered in life.

Applying

7. Answers may differ. Students may respond that people create their own opportunities or difficulties, depending on how they respond to life.

ANSWERS TO ANALYZING LITERATURE

1. Suggested Response: Like many women today, Atwood's Siren is no longer content fulfilling the traditional female role.
2. Suggested Response: On his journey, Odysseus encountered a wide range of experiences—physical, emotional, and psychological. This journey therefore reflects the variety of experiences one encounters during a lifetime.

THINKING AND WRITING

Software If students have access to computers, have them use **Bank Street Writer** to complete all stages of the assignment. Using the program's cut and paste features, students will be able to easily incorporate ideas from their prewriting work into their monologues.

Publishing Student Writing You might ask volunteers to present their monologues to the class.

LEARNING OPTIONS

1. This activity will appeal to visual learners. You might vary the activity by offering students the option of writing their adaptations in the form of short stories, narrative poems, or plays for the stage or radio.
2. Visual learners will enjoy this activity. You may wish to extend the activity by having students illustrate episodes from Homer's *Odyssey*.

You might ask students if they have ever watched the Olympics on television. Have students who are familiar with the games describe them to those who are not. Tell students that they are about to read a poem about the Olympic games of ancient Greece.

Purpose-Setting Question
What is the poet's attitude toward the runners in the poem?

Thematic Focus Conflicts often present challenges that help us grow. Ask students to consider the value of formal competition in terms of the challenges it creates.

1 **Discussion** What is the speaker's attitude toward the runners?

2 **Clarification** Here, the speaker compares the runners to the laurel plant, an evergreen, whose leaves never turn brown with age. He wishes that the runners might stay youthful.

3 **Discussion** Have student volunteers share what they know about the modern Olympic games.

Humanities Note

Fine art, *The Olympic Experience,* by Ernie Barnes. Born in 1939 in Durham, North Carolina, Barnes received a full athletic scholarship to North Carolina Central University, where he studied art history and painting. He played football professionally until he decided to become an artist and "put all the violence and power [he] had felt on the field into [his] paintings." Not surprisingly, his subjects are often athletes. Barnes was honored as the official artist of the XXIII Olympiad.

THE OLYMPIC EXPERIENCE
Ernie Barnes
The Company of Art

Homeric Chorus

Derek Walcott

1
How fleet the bare feet of runners racing on the sand
As their ankles turn into hummingbirds towards the laurel
Extending their arms like swallows to reach the end
Their thighs are blurred ovals passing breakers of coral
What greater glory than what men win with their feet
Outdistancing friendly shadows in their short sun
Greater than poetry is the meter of the athlete
Since their glory is brief and swifter than any song
They turn into birds, they are stretching to leave the earth,
They vault like deer. They wrestle like lions with no wounds,
They're pliant as otters, their heads sleek from the surf
But their brightness is short, their names fade on the wind
2
But let them stay green as the Olympian laurel
In the kindest of wars, the games, the happiest quarrel
3
Kindle the torch, begin these Thaeician games
Then, on medals of gold, silver and bronze incise their names.

You might use the following questions for discussion.
1. Which words, phrases, or images from "Homeric Chorus" could be used to describe this painting?
2. What effect is created by the artist's exaggeration of certain physical characteristics?

RESPONDING TO THE SELECTION

Your Response

1. Do you agree with the author that "Greater than poetry is the meter of the athlete"? Explain your answer.

Recalling

2. What is the setting of the poem?
3. To what animals does the author compare the runners?
4. What does the author say about the runners' glory?

Interpreting

5. What is the significance of the laurel?
6. What does the author mean by the runners' "short sun"?
7. What is the effect of the author's comparisons of the athletes with animals?
8. (a) Why does the author call the games "the kindest of wars"? (b) What other metaphor suggests the same idea?
9. Does the last line contradict the author's earlier comment that the runners' "names fade on the wind"? Explain.

Applying

10. What qualities of the Olympic athlete would be valuable in any person's life?

ANALYZING LITERATURE

Understanding Historical Context

Works of literature often have a **historical context**; that is, a setting that reflects a specific society during a particular time in history. "Homeric Chorus," for example, celebrates the athletic achievements of runners at the original Olympic games in ancient Greece, and knowing some facts about these contests will enhance your understanding of the poem. The original Olympic games were barefoot races among athletes from different Greek city-states. When Walcott refers

to the glory that "men win with their feet," he is alluding to the fact that victory in the races was one of the highest honors in the Greek world.

1. What detail at the beginning of the poem suggests that the poet is speaking about ancient times?
2. What do you learn about the prize earned by the winning runner in ancient Greece?
3. (a) What does the poem tell you about the original name for the Olympic games? (b) Find out more about this term and share your findings with the class.

THINKING AND WRITING

Writing a Dialogue

Write a dialogue between a runner from ancient Greece and a modern Olympic athlete. You may wish to have them discuss their reasons for competing, the experience of the games, and rewards they will receive if they win. It may be helpful to do some library research on the ancient games before you begin. When you revise your dialogue, decide whether you have included details that accurately reflect the historical context of the original Olympic games.

LEARNING OPTIONS

1. **Speaking and Listening.** Walcott calls his poem a chorus, an element in many ancient Greek plays. Find out more about the function of the chorus in Greek plays, such as those by Euripides, Sophocles, or Aeschylus. Then give an oral presentation of your findings to the class.
2. **Multicultural Activity.** The Olympic games were originally competitions among only Greek athletes. They are now international events open to people from countries around the world. In a poem, song, poster, or other form, express your thoughts and feelings about the global nature of the games.

9. Students who feel that these lines are contradictory may say that the names will not fade because they are engraved on medals. Those who feel that the lines are not contradictory may say that "fade on the wind" can be understood figuratively to mean "fade from our memories."

Applying

10. Answers will differ but should include reference to qualities such as strength, endurance, discipline, and perseverance.

ANSWERS TO ANALYZING LITERATURE

1. Students may mention any of the following details: the runners are barefoot, they are racing on sand, they are running toward the laurel.
2. Suggested Response: The runners are running toward the Olympian laurel, indicating that this ancient symbol of victory is prized by the contestants.
3. a) The games are called "Thaeician games." b) Suggest that students ask their librarian to help them find out more about this term.

THINKING AND WRITING

Electronic Handbook If students have access to the Language Master 6000, have them review the punctuation of dialogue by entering the access word *quotation* and pressing the GRAMMAR key.

Publishing Student Writing Ask for student volunteers to read their dialogues aloud with a partner. Have students in the audience record their responses.

LEARNING OPTIONS

1. This option will appeal to students who enjoy public speaking. Assist less comfortable students by having them share their findings with small groups.
2. This option will appeal to the creative talents of students. Encourage students to use any medium of expression they wish.

Closure and Extension

ANSWERS TO RESPONDING TO THE SELECTION

Your Response

1. Students' answers will differ but should reflect the fact that the word *meter* refers both to the poem's meter and the beat of the runners' footsteps.

Recalling

2. The poem is set in the days of the original Olympic games of ancient Greece.
3. The runners are compared to hummingbirds, swallows, birds, deer, lions, and otters.
4. The author says that the runners' glory is "brief and swifter than any song."

Interpreting

5. The laurel signifies victory.
6. The runners' "short sun" refers to their brief time "in the sun," or moment of glory.

7. The runners are likened to animals known for their speed, grace, and strength, which serves to emphasize these physical qualities in the men.
8. Suggested Response: "The kindest of wars" suggests that the Olympic games are not battles of men against each other, but of each man against himself, striving to do his best. "The happiest quarrel" suggests the same idea.

Preparation

Motivation/Prior Knowledge

You might wish to begin by having students act out one of Odysseus' adventures. To help students identify with the feelings of the character they are portraying, suggest that they use their natural speech patterns and modern colloquial expressions. Urge the actors to speak the characters' thoughts out loud, as well as converse with other characters. Allow different groups of students to experiment with various adventures.

Ask each student actor to explain the actions and motivations of his or her character. Ask also what the character might think about the actions and motivations of other characters. Engage the class in a discussion about how different characters might perceive the events.

Focus Assist students in evaluating how a change in perspective might affect the interpretation of events. Advise students that the assignment does not ask them to change the story, only the manner in which it is told.

Presentation

Prewriting Some students may select a favorite adventure and choose their character based on who was there. Other students may be intrigued by a particular character and choose an episode in which that character was involved.

Urge students to consider some of the antagonists as potential narrators. Point out that such a choice will result in the most dramatic change in perspective, as the antagonist will become the protagonist of the new narration. Ask them to imagine how Polyphemus might tell his side of the story. Will telling the story from his viewpoint make him a sympathetic character?

WRITING FROM A DIFFERENT PERSPECTIVE

"There are no dull subjects. There are only dull writers."

H. L. Mencken

Most literature is written from a single perspective, usually that of the author or a participant in the story. What if a different person told the story? How would the *Odyssey* change if someone other than Odysseus were narrating?

> **Focus**
>
> **Assignment:** Rewrite an episode of the *Odyssey* from a perspective other than Odysseus'.
> **Purpose:** To entertain and to reveal another side to events.
> **Audience:** Fellow students.

Prewriting

1. Choose a character and an event. List the adventures in the *Odyssey*. Next to each, list the characters who participated in the episode. Decide which person might have had an interesting perspective on the events described.

2. Brainstorm about your character. Suppose that you wish to write from the point of view of one of Odysseus' men. Because Homer did not describe all the crew members, you would have to create your narrator's personality based on the information you have. Begin by listing what you know.

> **Student Model**
> Crew Member
>   survived the Cyclops
>   escaped from the land of the Lotus-Eaters
>   has been turned into a swine and back into a man

Include the crew member's feelings about his experiences.

3. Make a flowchart. Before you write, it is helpful to make a flowchart of the events in the adventure you have chosen.

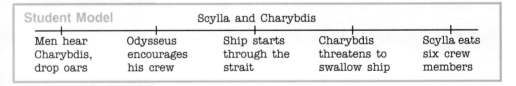

Student Model   Scylla and Charybdis

| Men hear Charybdis, drop oars | Odysseus encourages his crew | Ship starts through the strait | Charybdis threatens to swallow ship | Scylla eats six crew members |

716 The Epic

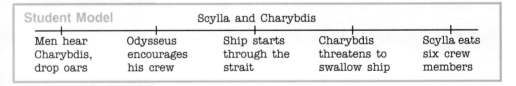 **Software** If students have access to computers, have them explore different perspectives by using the *Three Ways of Seeing* activity in **Writer's Helper**.

Drafting You might have students freewrite their characters' descriptions of themselves. These descriptions can later be revised to create an introductory paragraph.

Remind students to include their characters' remarks about the events they are relating. Each narrative should include some indications of what the narrator is thinking and feeling. Particular mention should be made of the character's reactions to Odysseus.

Writing Transparency You might use a graphic organizer to assist students in drafting their narrative. Use the *Story Map* in **Transparencies for Writing**.

Drafting

1. Establish your character first. Because your readers do not know your character, you need to provide enough details about the person so that his or her comments will seem natural and logical. You may introduce these details at the beginning of the story.

> **Student Model**
>
> It's not easy being one of Odysseus' men. We sail from one crisis to the next. You would not believe what has happened to me in the past years. A monster has tried to eat me, I've sailed to the land of the dead, and I've been turned into a swine. I'm certainly not safe with Odysseus in charge. He thinks that the shortest distance between two points is through the jaws of death! He's nice enough, but I think he's crazy.

2. Relate the plot accurately. You must be faithful to the details that the author has provided. You may, however, make up any details that do not affect the plot, such as what your character said to another minor character, or what your character ate or wore.

Revising and Editing

1. Work with a partner. Exchange stories with a classmate so that you can evaluate each other's work. As you read, ask yourself these questions:
- Are the details of the plot accurate?
- Does the narrator have a distinct point of view about the events?
- Is the narrator's character believable?
- Does the narrator stay in character?

2. Check for details. As you revise, keep your narrator's character in mind. Add any small details that will convince readers that the narrator actually experienced the events of the story. Remember that this is a personal account, and that the personality of the narrator is part of the story you are telling.

Options for Publishing
- Share your account of the adventure with the class in a dramatic reading.
- Join with classmates to make an *Odyssey* book telling about the events of the epic from all the different viewpoints that you and your class have chosen.

Reviewing Your Writing Process

1. Did writing this account from a different perspective add to your appreciation of the *Odyssey*? Why or why not?

2. Did you find it easier to establish your character or to tell about his or her adventures? Explain.

Revising and Editing The students can evaluate the accuracy of the narrative by using their prewriting flowchart as a checklist. Are all the events on the flowchart included in the draft? Are the events arranged in a logical order?

You might remind students, as they are checking their events, to make sure they have included enough comments and observations to establish the perspective of the narrator.

Software If students have access to computers, have them use the *Usage* activity in **Writer's Helper** as part of their final revision.

Grammar Tip Shifts in verb tense are likely to occur as students change back and forth from narrating events to reporting feelings and reactions. Caution students that this is a potential danger, and refer them to the Handbook of Grammar and Revising Strategies for guidance in correcting this problem.

Closure and Extension

Guidelines for Evaluation You might wish to consider the following questions as you evaluate each student's narrative:
1. Does the narrative include all the events from the original episode?
2. Are the events presented in a logical order?
3. Is the narrative told consistently from the new character's perspective?
4. Are the character's feelings and observations used to clarify the perspective?
5. Is the account free of errors in spelling, punctuation, grammar, and usage?

Enrichment Perspective is a factor not only in fictional works, but in historical accounts as well. Have students research some historical events and report back to the class how our understanding of these events might be affected by a change in perspective. The settling of the New World might be especially appropriate for this exercise.

Motivation/Prior Knowledge

Tell students to imagine themselves as Telemachus. Ask student volunteers to improvise a soliloquy in which Telemachus complains about his circumstances. Encourage the actors to free associate, allowing the speech to gravitate toward the problem that would most bother them, if they were in Telemachus' position.

Focus While students may sympathize with all of Telemachus' problems, they should not attempt to solve them all at once. Their letters will be disorganized and ineffective. Emphasize the importance of addressing only one problem, and offering viable solutions.

Presentation

Prewriting Suggest that students consider the problems brought out in the improvisations. Then ask students whether they feel they would have complained about these same issues or others. You might also ask students to take into account which problem they find most feasible to solve. For instance, some students may have several realistic suggestions for dealing with the lazy servants, but have no ideas on how Telemachus can solve the problem of Penelope's suitors.

Encourage students to offer solutions that advise positive constructive actions, rather than punitive actions with potentially harmful results.

Drafting Remind students that they are writing to a friend, and this should be reflected in the tone of the letter. Use the student model draft to illustrate how including comments and observations makes the letter sound personal and familiar. You might also suggest that students use contractions and informal language.

"Writing, like life itself, is a voyage of discovery."
Henry Miller

YOUR WRITING PROCESS

WRITING A PROBLEM-SOLVING LETTER

Odysseus' kingdom must have been in sorry shape during his absence. The suitors were living in his home and eating his food. Fields were left unplowed and fruit trees were neglected. Penelope was forced to waste her time weaving and unweaving the same shroud. Telemachus had no social life. Everyone guessed what would happen to him once Penelope settled on one of the suitors.

Focus

Assignment: Write a letter to Telemachus suggesting a solution to one of the problems in Odysseus' kingdom.
Purpose: To solve a problem.
Audience: Telemachus.

Prewriting

1. Choose a problem. The problem must be one that Telemachus would logically have faced, given his circumstances.
2. Brainstorm about some solutions. In order to be helpful, your suggestions must make sense. Telemachus must be able to carry out the advice you give him.

Student Model
Problem: Telemachus has very little social life.
Possible solutions:
1. He could borrow a boat and visit other islands.
2. He could persuade the suitors to allow him to have a feast for people his own age.
3. He could ask the suitors if any of them had younger sisters and brothers who could come to Ithaca.
4. He could petition one of the gods or goddesses to help him out.

Drafting

1. Use proper letter-writing form. Remember to begin your letter with a heading and a salutation. After you have written the body of the letter, end with a complimentary closing and your signature.
2. Establish the problem at the beginning. Begin your letter by stating the problem. Then make suggestions for solving the problem.

718   The Epic

Writing Transparency You might wish to review the correct format for this assignment by using Model 1: *Friendly Letter,* in **Transparencies for Writing.**

Student Model

Kingdom of Ionia
Spring, ───────────

Dear Telemachus,

I have not heard from you in a long while. Everyone here feels awful about the way you are being treated. Those suitors have a lot of nerve pestering your mom like that. I know you must be lonely with no one your own age to talk to.

Have you considered borrowing a boat and visiting some of the other kingdoms? I know that we are pretty far away here in Ionia, but some of the other kingdoms are within sailing distance. If you brought friends back with you to Ithaca, you would have some company for awhile. From what I hear, those suitors would just say, "The more, the merrier!"

Another possibility would be to ask the suitors to invite their younger brothers and sisters to visit Ithaca. They would probably go for that, since they don't seem to mind freeloading. I know that you might be reluctant to hang out with relatives of your enemies, but you don't have a lot of choices.

Let me know what you decide to do.

Sincerely yours,
Aristarchus

Revising and Editing

1. Revise for unity. Read your letter to make sure that you have stuck to the point. Have you stated the problem in the first paragraph? Does your letter contain at least two possible solutions to the problem? Are your solutions logical?

2. Get help from classmates. Edit your letter with the help of a small group of classmates. Read one another's work to see if the letters are convincing. As you read your classmates' letters, ask yourself these questions:
- Is the problem established at the beginning?
- Do the solutions to the problem make sense?
- Are the small details accurate? For example, has the writer used authentic Greek names for the people and places mentioned in the letter?
- Has the writer used the proper format for a friendly letter?

Options for Publishing
- Post your letter on a classroom bulletin board.
- Exchange letters with other members of a small group.
- Discuss whether or not the proposed solutions will work.
- Exchange letters with another classmate. Write a response as though you were Telemachus.

Reviewing the Writing Process

1. Did you enjoy solving a problem for someone who lived at the time of the Trojan War? Why or why not?

2. Do you think writing about a problem can help you to solve it? Explain.

Revising and Editing Instruct students to check over their paragraph divisions. Has each paragraph been logically developed around a controlling idea? Are transitions used to connect one paragraph to the next?

Software If students have access to computers, have them practice paragraph construction using the *Paragraph Coherence* and *Paragraph Development* activities in **Writer's Helper.**

You may wish to make copies of the questions for peer editors on student page 719. The students can jot down their answers and suggestions to the writer. The writers should carefully consider the peer recommendations as they revise their work.

Grammar Tip You might want to display a list of suggested complimentary closes. Prompt students to remember the comma by showing a comma after each sample on the list.

Closure and Extension

Guidelines for Evaluation The following questions might provide a framework for evaluating each student's letter:
1. Is the problem clearly stated in the introductory paragraph?
2. Does the letter offer at least two viable solutions?
3. Is the letter correctly divided into paragraphs?
4. Is each paragraph adequately developed around a topic sentence?
5. Is the assignment completed in the correct format for a friendly letter?
6. Is the letter free of errors in spelling, punctuation, and mechanics?

Enrichment The guest/host relationship in ancient Greece was governed by elaborate traditions that bordered on the sacred. In light of this cultural reverence for the proprieties, the behavior of the suitors must have been profanely offensive to Telemachus. If Telemachus were to pray to one of the gods for relief in this area, it would be Zeus, who was considered to be the guardian of guest/host relations.

THE APARTMENT OF MADAME SUNDHEIM
René Magritte

THE NOVEL

A novel is an extended fictional work written in prose. The novel presents plot, character, setting, theme, point of view, tone, symbol, and irony with greater breadth and freedom than does a short story. A novel can encompass a wide range of narratives and time spans, and can present more involved conflicts than a short story can. Although we are all familiar with novels, the novel is a relatively new form of literature. It has existed for only about three hundred years.

Novels provide us with a wealth of experience and understanding. The novelist William Styron has written, "A great book should leave you with many experiences, and slightly exhausted at the end. You live several lives while reading it."

721

Humanities Note

Fine art, *The Apartment of Madame Sundheim,* by René Magritte. Magritte (1898–1967) was a Belgian painter who is known for his contribution to Surrealism, a movement in art that juxtaposes images out of their ordinary context to express concepts that cannot be spoken and to create visual shock. Magritte had a natural affinity for the surreal and rendered his paintings of mysterious events, strange situations, and bizarre concepts in a precise, colorful, and highly realistic style.

At first glance the painting *The Apartment of Madame Sundheim* appears to be simply a view of a house at night with the windows lit to a rosy glow. On further study, the viewer is shocked to note that the entire house is inside a dark room. Here Magritte has achieved the surreal: Something that appears to be perfectly normal is not. The house has become extraordinary by its removal from a mundane context, such as a street, and its placement in an incongruous situation. Magritte's title for the painting causes further speculation: Is this house within a house the apartment of Madame Sundheim or is the house contained within her apartment? This ability to inspire wonder in the viewer has made René Magritte one of the most celebrated of the surrealist painters.

You might use these questions for discussion.

1. What is your explanation of this house within a room?
2. Do you think anyone lives in this house?
3. The piece of art causes you to think about different, unknown, and possibly strange places. In what ways does reading a novel give you a similar experience?

READING ACTIVELY

The Novel

Two novels are presented in this section: *Great Expectations* by Charles Dickens and *Dragonsong* by Anne McCaffrey. They are very different in tone, subject matter, and style. The settings and characters in each could not be more dissimilar. The following information will prepare you to read these novels.

Great Expectations

BACKGROUND Charles Dickens creates two worlds for his character Pip—a small village in the marshland and a prosperous London. Both these worlds existed as part of the industrial society of nineteenth-century England. Dickens uses this background to bring Pip into contact with a variety of characters and situations through which Dickens comments on good and evil in the world and Pip comes to self-discovery.

READING STRATEGIES When you read *Great Expectations*, you might encounter some difficulty with Dickens's vocabulary and sentence structure. His sentences can be complex, and occasionally his choice of words is difficult for the modern reader. Pay attention to the punctuation. Often, in long sentences, you can consider a semicolon to be a period. Dickens enjoyed using irony and caricature, so, as you read, be aware of these elements. Sometimes you will find them both in characters' names. Finally, interact with the literature by using active reading strategies: question, visualize, predict, connect, and respond.

Dragonsong

BACKGROUND The novel *Dragonsong* may be classified as science fiction or fantasy. It takes place in an imaginary world, on a planet called Pern. The main danger is from Thread, a destructive form of cellular life that falls on the planet. Thread is combated by dragons and their riders. Music plays an important role on Pern, especially for Menolly, whose musical gift must be acknowledged.

READING STRATEGIES Though *Dragonsong* takes place in an imaginary world, it still contains the elements of fiction as you know them: plot, character, setting, and theme. As you read, you will encounter objects, creatures, and procedures that are unfamiliar, yet you will be able to understand what they are from the context. Allow yourself to visualize the scenes and actions. Use all your active reading strategies—questioning, visualizing, predicting, connecting, and responding—to enrich your reading of this novel.

Great Expectations

MID-VICTORIAN FATHER READING
TO ENTIRE FAMILY

Humanities Note

Fine art, *Mid-Victorian Father Reading to Entire Family.* This work is a colored lithograph. Lithography, a process for printing unlimited multiple images, involves drawing a design on a smooth stone with a grease crayon, applying an oily ink that will adhere only to the crayon, and pressing paper onto the stone to transfer the design. This black and white image can then be hand-colored with transparent ink or watercolor. This process allowed inexpensive decorative pictures, such as this scene of the Victorian family, to become readily available to the public.

The father in this print might very well be reading a serialized novel of the Victorian period. Long novels, like those of Charles Dickens and others, were published in monthly installments, which were eagerly awaited by the reading public.

Master Teacher Note Use the overhead projector to show students Art Transparency 20, *St. Pancras Hotel and Pentonville Road,* by John Arthur O'Connor. This painting depicts a street scene from nineteenth-century London. You might tell students that much of *Great Expectations* takes place in nineteenth-century London. What impression of the city does this painting convey? Does the city seem large and crowded? What methods of transportation are people using? How are they dressed? How does the quality of the light affect the mood that the picture communicates?

Enrichment During the Victorian Age, novels were frequently published in serial form. In preparing a novel in this form, writers created short, self-contained episodes that usually ended without resolution, so that readers eagerly awaited the next installment to find out what happened. In this way, the authors sustained readers' interest from week to week or from month to month.

Reading Strategies Emphasize that novels are in many ways more difficult to read than short stories. When reading a novel, it is easy to lose track of events occurring earlier in the work. However, by pausing regularly to clarify and summarize, your students should be able to avoid this problem.

Master Teacher Note You may want to ask students to prepare a theme chart in their notebooks. Under each theme, have them jot down thoughts and comments as they read. They might also jot down quotations from the novel.

To help your students understand and appreciate the characters, you may want to suggest that they develop a list of personality traits for each of the main characters.

More About the Author Charles Dickens spent a happy childhood in Chatham, but this period was followed by an intensely sad one. His father was imprisoned for his debts, and Dickens had to go to work in a factory. Memories of this painful period inspired much of his fiction. Ask pupils to what extent early experiences affect an author's work.

Literary Focus Students will need to be aware of the subtle shifts between a child's and an adult's perspective that constantly occur in this novel. Pip may seem to be almost a "naive narrator" at the beginning of the novel, but his intense awareness of his motives discloses the older man who is looking through the child's eyes.

Prereading Focus *Great Expectations* begins with Pip's terrifying encounter with an escaped convict. The purpose of the brief writing exercise is to focus students' attention on Pip's emotional response. Encourage students to think of an experience that was truly frightening to them. Ask them if there are people, places, or things that remind them of a scary event in their lives. Encourage them to recall as many details as they can.

Vocabulary Even in a somewhat abridged text, Dickens's use of polysyllabic words may give some students difficulty. Encourage students to note any words that they do not understand. If possible, provide students with desk copies of a good dictionary.

GUIDE FOR READING

Charles Dickens

(1812–1870) is one of the greatest English novelists. He is known for creating lively works that are enjoyed by people of all ages and backgrounds. Dickens was raised in London and lived most of his life there. His passion for reading and his keen eye for observation prepared him for a career as a writer. Among his well-known novels are *Oliver Twist, David Copperfield, A Tale of Two Cities*, and *Great Expectations*. In these and other books, he created memorable characters and criticized the injustices of his time. His works continue to have special appeal to the reading public and are frequently transformed into plays and films.

724 The Novel

Great Expectations, Chapters 1–8

Point of View

Point of view is the perspective or angle from which the events of a story or novel are told. In a **first-person narrative,** a character in the novel tells you his or her story directly. This narrator refers to himself or herself as "I" or "me." What you learn immediately is limited to what that character observes or thinks. However, by reading between the lines, you may understand things the narrator does not.

The point of view in *Great Expectations* is that of the first-person narrator, Pip. You learn about the world of this novel through him.

Focus

At the opening of the novel, you meet the character Pip. He is a trusting young boy with an active imagination. Early in the story, he has a frightening encounter that has long-term results. What do you think might frighten a young child out alone by himself in a cemetery? Think of a scary experience you had as a child. Write about it, including as many details as you can remember. What sort of lasting effects did this experience have on you? Now read about Pip, and compare your experiences.

Vocabulary

Knowing the following words will help you as you read *Great Expectations.*

consternation (kän stər nā′ shən) *n.:* Great fear or shock that confuses or bewilders (p. 728)

imprecations (im′ prə kā′ shənz) *n.:* Curses (p. 732)

vicariously (vī ker′ ē əs lē) *adv.:* Experiencing something by imagined participation in another's experience (p. 733)

presentiment (prē zen′ tə mənt) *n.:* A feeling that something bad will occur (p. 733)

disdainfully (dis dān′ fəl lē) *adv.:* Scornfully (p. 737)

melancholy (mel′ ən käl′ ē) *adj.:* Sad; gloomy (p. 747)

Objectives

1 To understand point of view when reading a novel
2 To write from another point of view
3 To express individual interests and abilities through optional activities

Support Material

Teaching Portfolio
Teacher Backup, p. 877
Grammar in Action Worksheets, *Using Direct Quotations*, p. 882; *Using Gerunds*, p. 884
Usage and Mechanics Worksheet, p. 886
Vocabulary Check, p. 887
Analyzing Literature Worksheet, *Understanding Point of View*, p. 888

Language Worksheet, *Appreciating Word Histories*, p. 889
Selection Test, p. 890
Art Transparency 20: *St. Pancras Hotel and Pentonville Road*, by John Arthur O'Connor

Library of Video Classics
Great Expectations, The Changing World of Charles Dickens

Literature Videodisc
Scenes from Great Expectations

Great Expectations

Charles Dickens

Chapter 1

My father's family name being Pirrip, and my Christian name Philip, my infant tongue could make of both names nothing longer or more explicit than Pip. So I called myself Pip, and came to be called Pip.

I give Pirrip as my father's family name on the authority of his tombstone and my sister—Mrs. Joe Gargery, who married the blacksmith. As I never saw my father or my mother, and never saw any likeness of either of them (for their days were long before the days of photographs), my first fancies regarding what they were like were unreasonably derived from their tombstones. The shape of the letters on my father's gave me an odd idea that he was a square, stout, dark man, with curly black hair. From the character and turn of the inscription, "*Also Georgiana Wife of the Above*," I drew a childish conclusion that my mother was freckled and sickly. To five little stone lozenges,[1] each about a foot and a half long, which were arranged in a neat row beside their grave, and were sacred to the memory of five little brothers of mine—who gave up trying to get a living exceedingly early in that universal struggle—I am indebted for a belief I religiously entertained that they had all been born on their backs with their hands in their trousers pockets.

1. **lozenges** (läz´ ʹnj iz) *n.*: Diamond-shaped objects.

Ours was the marsh country, down by the river, within, as the river wound, twenty miles of the sea. My first most vivid and broad impression of the identity of things seems to me to have been gained on a memorable raw afternoon towards evening. At such a time I found out for certain that this bleak place overgrown with nettles was the churchyard; and that Philip Pirrip, Late of this Parish, and Also Georgiana Wife of the Above, were dead and buried; and that Alexander, Bartholomew, Abraham, Tobias, and Roger, infant children of the aforesaid, were also dead and buried; and that the dark flat wilderness beyond the churchyard, intersected with dikes and mounds and gates, with scattered cattle feeding on it, was the marshes; and that the low leaden line beyond was the river; and that the distant savage lair from which the wind was rushing was the sea; and that the small bundle of shivers growing afraid of it all and beginning to cry was Pip.

"Hold your noise!" cried a terrible voice, as a man started up from among the graves at the side of the church porch. "Keep still, you little devil, or I'll cut your throat!"

A fearful man, all in coarse gray, with a great iron on his leg. A man with no hat, and with broken shoes, and with an old rag tied around his head. A man who had been soaked in water, and smothered in mud, and lamed by stones, and cut by flints, and stung

Great Expectations **725**

Prentice Hall Literature Writing Studio

 Videocassette To provide additional background on Dickens's life and times, you might want to show students *The Changing World of Charles Dickens* in the **Prentice Hall Library of Video Classics.**

Thematic Focus Pip must deal with many conflicts in this part of the novel—conflicts between himself and his sister, between his ethics and the demands of the escaped convict, and between himself and Estella. Ask students if conflict is inevitable in life? What kinds of conflict have they experienced?

Making Connections You might want to contrast Pip's growth with the stages of life described in Shakespeare's "The Seven Ages of Man," page 543. Also, you might want to compare and contrast Pip's life journey with the maturing of Telemachus and journey home of Odysseus in the *Odyssey*, page 681.

Motivation/Prior Knowledge Ask students to imagine that they are exploring an isolated area when a person in prison garb suddenly grabs them and threatens to kill them unless they bring him, in secret, items he needs for escape. How would they react? Would they scream for help? Would they try to run away? Would they do exactly as the prisoner commands? Tell them that the narrator of this novel must face just such a situation.

Master Teacher Note Consider telling students that Dickens would have personally known the setting of this first section, since he lived for a part of his childhood in the marsh country by the sea. His understanding of how a child sees the world, feels, and acts might come in part from his own experiences as a sensitive child.

Purpose-Setting Question How does Pip change in this first section of the novel?

1 Reading Strategy The opening passages of a story are important in that they test the author's skill in capturing the reader's interest. Have students determine how effectively Dickens draws them into his story.

2 Discussion How does Dickens mix sadness and humor in this portrayal of a child's point of view?

3 Discussion What does Pip seem to realize for the first time? Why is the phrase "small bundle of shivers" an effective description?

4 Discussion Why does this image seem as if it comes from a nightmare?

5 Discussion Where do you think this man has come from? Why does he want a file?

 **Videodisc** To help students appreciate how Dickens develops the setting in the opening scene, you might want to show the segment of the *Scenes From Great Expectations* videodisc in which Pip visits his parents' grave.

Frames 1190 to 4492

Alternative Assessment To promote active reading, have students keep a reader's response journal as they read *Great Expectations*. Ask them to respond personally to Pip and his encounters with the convict and with Miss Havisham.

Their observations will enable you to assess their understanding of the issues in the story.

by nettles, and torn by briars; who limped, and shivered, and glared, and growled; and whose teeth chattered in his head, as he seized me by the chin.

"Oh! Don't cut my throat, sir," I pleaded in terror. "Pray don't do it, sir."

"Tell us your name!" said the man. "Quick!"

"Pip, sir."

"Once more," said the man, staring at me. "Give it mouth!"

"Pip. Pip, sir."

"Show us where you live," said the man. "Pint out the place!"

I pointed to where our village lay, on the flat in-shore among the alder trees and pollards,[2] a mile or more from the church.

The man, after looking at me for a moment, turned me upside down, and emptied my pockets. There was nothing in them but a piece of bread. When the church came to itself—for he was so sudden and strong that he made it go head over heels before me, and I saw the steeple under my feet—when the church came to itself, I say, I was seated on a high tombstone, trembling, while he ate the bread ravenously.

"You young dog," said the man, licking his lips, "what fat cheeks you ha' got."

I believe they were fat, though I was at that time undersized, for my years, and not strong.

"Darn me if I couldn't eat 'em," said the man, with a threatening shake of his head, "and if I han't half a mind to't!"

I earnestly expressed my hope that he wouldn't, and held tighter to the tombstone on which he had put me; partly to keep myself upon it; partly to keep myself from crying.

"Now lookee here!" said the man. "Where's your mother?"

"There, sir!" said I.

He started, made a short run, and stopped and looked over his shoulder.

"There, sir!" I timidly explained. "Also Georgiana. That's my mother."

"Oh!" said he, coming back. "And is that your father alonger your mother?"

"Yes, sir," said I; "him, too; late of this parish."

"Ha!" he muttered then, considering. "Who d'ye live with—supposin' ye're kindly let to live, which I han't made up my mind about?"

"My sister, sir—Mrs. Joe Gargery—wife of Joe Gargery, the blacksmith, sir."

"Blacksmith, eh?" said he. And looked down at his leg.

After darkly looking at his leg and at me several times, he came closer to my tombstone, took me by both arms, and tilted me back as far as he could hold me.

"Now lookee here," he said, "the question being whether you're to be let to live. You know what a file is?"

"Yes, sir."

"And you know what wittles[3] is?"

"Yes, sir."

After each question he tilted me over a little more, so as to give me a greater sense of helplessness and danger.

"You get me a file." He tilted me again. "And you get me wittles." He tilted me again. "You bring 'em both to me." He tilted me again. "Or I'll have your heart and liver out." He tilted me again.

I was dreadfully frightened, and so giddy that I clung to him with both hands.

"You bring me, to-morrow morning early, that file and them wittles. You bring the lot to me at that old battery[4] over yonder. You do it, and you never dare to say a word

---

2. **pollards** (päl' ərdz) *n.*: Trees with their top branches cut back to the trunk.

3. **wittles:** Victuals (vit' 'lz), food; some characters pronounce *v* as *w*.

4. **battery** (bat' ər ē) *n.*: Mound of earth on which cannons are placed.

or dare to make a sign concerning your having seen such a person as me, or any person sumever, and you shall be let to live. You fail, or you go from my words in any partickler, no matter how small it is, and your heart and your liver shall be tore out, roasted, and ate.

I said that I would get him the file, and I would get him what broken bits of food I could, and I would come to him at the battery, early in the morning.

"Say, Lord strike you dead if you don't!" said the man. I said so, and he took me down.

"Goo-good night sir," I faltered.

"Much of that!" said he, glancing about him over the cold wet flat. "I wish I was a frog. Or a eel!"

At the same time, he hugged his shuddering body in both his arms—clasping himself, as if to hold himself together—and limped towards the low church wall.

When he came to the low church wall, he got over it like a man whose legs were numbed and stiff, and then turned round to look for me. When I saw him turning, I set my face towards home, and made the best use of my legs.

Chapter 2

My sister, Mrs. Joe Gargery, was more than twenty years older than I, and had established a great reputation with herself and the neighbors because she had brought me up "by hand." Having at that time to find out for myself what the expression meant, and knowing her to have a hard and heavy hand, and to be much in the habit of laying it upon her husband as well as upon me, I supposed that Joe Gargery and I were both brought up by hand.

She was not a good-looking woman, my sister, and I had a general impression that she must have made Joe Gargery marry her

by hand. Joe was a fair man, with curls of flaxen hair on each side of his smooth face, and with eyes of such a very undecided blue that they seemed to have somehow got mixed with their own whites. He was a mild, good-natured, sweet-tempered, easy-going, foolish, dear fellow—a sort of Hercules[1] in strength, and also in weakness.

My sister, Mrs. Joe, with black hair and eyes, had such a prevailing redness of skin that I sometimes used to wonder whether it was possible she washed herself with a nutmeg-grater instead of soap. She was tall and bony, and almost always wore a coarse apron, fastened over her figure behind with two loops.

Joe's forge adjoined our house, which was a wooden house, as many of the dwellings in our country were—most of them, at that time. When I ran home from the churchyard, the forge was shut up, and Joe was sitting alone in the kitchen. Joe and I being fellow-sufferers, and having confidences as such, Joe imparted a confidence to me the moment I raised the latch of the door and peeped in at him.

"Mrs. Joe has been out a dozen times, looking for you, Pip. And she's out now, making it a baker's dozen."

"Is she?"

"Yes, Pip," said Joe; "and what's worse, she's got Tickler with her."

At this dismal intelligence,[2] I twisted the only button on my waistcoat round and round, and looked in great depression at the fire. Tickler was a wax-ended piece of cane, worn smooth by collision with my tickled frame.

"She sot down," said Joe, "and she got up, and she made a grab at Tickler, and she

---

1. **Hercules** (hŭr′ kyə lēz′): A character from Greek and Roman mythology, famous for his strength.
2. **intelligence** (in tel′ ə jəns) *n.*: Here, it means news.

Great Expectations 727

9 **Critical Thinking and Reading**
Why does Joe fence Pip up?

10 **Discussion** How do Mrs. Joe's mannerisms and gestures reveal her character?

ram-paged[3] out. That's what she did," said Joe, "she ram-paged out, Pip."

"Has she been gone long, Joe?" I always treated him as a larger species of child, and as no more than my equal.

"Well," said Joe, "she's been on the rampage, this last spell, about five minutes, Pip. She's a-coming! Get behind the door, old chap."

I took the advice. My sister, Mrs. Joe, throwing the door wide open, and finding an obstruction behind it, immediately divined the cause, and applied Tickler to its further investigation. She concluded by throwing me at Joe, who passed me on into the chimney and quietly fenced me up there with his great leg.

"Where have you been, you young monkey?" said Mrs. Joe, stamping her foot. "Tell me directly what you've been doing to wear me away with fret and fright and worrit, or I'd have you out of that corner if you was fifty Pips, and he was five hundred Gargerys."

"I have only been to the churchyard."

"Churchyard!" repeated my sister. "If it warn't for me, you'd have been to the churchyard long ago, and stayed there. Who brought you up by hand?"

"You did," said I.

"And why did I do it, I should like to know?"

I whimpered, "I don't know."

"*I* don't!" said my sister. "I'd never do it again! I know that. I may truly say I've never had this apron of mine off, since born you were. It's bad enough to be a blacksmith's wife (and him a Gargery) without being your mother."

My thoughts strayed from that question as I looked disconsolately at the fire. For the fugitive out on the marshes with the ironed

---

3. ram-paged: Rampaged (ram pāj'd'), rushed about in wild anger.

leg, the file, the food, and the dreadful pledge I was under to commit a larceny on those sheltering premises rose before me in the avenging coals.

"Hah!" said Mrs. Joe, restoring Tickler to his station. "Churchyard, indeed! You may well say churchyard, you two." One of us, by-the-bye, had not said it at all. "You'll drive *me* to the churchyard betwixt you, one of these days, and oh, a pr-r-recious pair you'd be without me!"

My sister had a trenchant way of cutting our bread-and-butter for us that never varied. First, with her left hand she jammed the loaf hard and fast against her bib. Then she took some butter (not too much) on a knife and spread it on the loaf, using both sides of the knife with a slapping dexterity, and trimming and molding the butter off round the crust. Then she gave the knife a final smart wipe and then sawed a very thick round off the loaf; which she finally, before separating from the loaf, hewed into two halves, of which Joe got one, and I the other.

On the present occasion, though I was hungry, I dared not eat my slice. I felt that I must have something in reserve for my dreadful acquaintance. Therefore I resolved to put my hunk of bread-and-butter down the leg of my trousers. I took advantage of a moment when Joe had just looked at me, and got my bread-and-butter down my leg.

When Joe saw that my bread-and-butter was gone, the wonder and consternation with which he stopped on the threshold of his bite and stared at me were too evident to escape my sister's observation.

"What's the matter now?" said she smartly, as she put down her cup.

"I say, you know!" muttered Joe, shaking his head at me in a very serious remonstrance. "Pip, old chap! You'll do yourself a mischief. It'll stick somewhere. You can't have chawed it, Pip."

Grammar in Action

Direct quotations represent a person's exact speech or thoughts and are enclosed in quotation marks. Only the actual words of a person or character can be used in a direct quotation. Sentences in which quotations appear often include expressions that indicate the speaker. These expressions can introduce, conclude, or interrupt a direct quotation. Use a comma or colon after an introductory expression. Use a comma, question mark, or exclamation mark after a quotation followed by a concluding expression. If an expression interrupts a quoted sentence, use another comma after the expression.

Authors use direct quotations in order to make their characters seem real to readers. Notice how Charles Dickens uses quotations in the following conversation among Pip, his sister, and Joe Gargery:

"Lord bless the boy!" exclaimed my sister, as if she didn't quite mean that, but rather the contrary. "From the Hulks!"
"Oh-h!" said I, looking at Joe. "Hulks!"

"What's the matter *now*?" repeated my sister more sharply than before.

"If you can cough any trifle on it up, Pip, I'd recommend you to do it," said Joe, all aghast. "Manners is manners, but still your 'elth's your 'elth."

By this time, my sister was quite desperate, so she pounced on Joe, and, taking him by the two whiskers, knocked his head for a little while against the wall behind him—while I sat in the corner, looking guiltily on.

"Now, perhaps you'll mention what's the matter," said my sister, out of breath, "you staring great stuck pig."

Joe looked at her in a helpless way, then took a helpless bite, and looked at me again.

"You know, Pip," said Joe, "you and me is always friends, and I'd be the last to tell upon you, any time. But such a—such a most uncommon bolt as that!"

"Been bolting his food, has he?" cried my sister.

"You know, old chap," said Joe, "I bolted, myself, when I was your age—frequent—and as a boy I've been among a many bolters; but I never see your bolting equal yet, Pip, and it's a mercy you ain't bolted dead."

My sister made a dive at me, and fished me up by the hair: saying nothing more than the awful words, "You come along and be dosed."

Some medical beast had revived tar-water in those days as a fine medicine, and Mrs. Joe always kept a supply of it in the cupboard, having a belief in its virtues correspondent to its nastiness. A pint of this mixture was poured down my throat, for my greater comfort, while Mrs. Joe held my head under her arm.

1 Conscience is a dreadful thing. The guilty knowledge that I was going to rob Mrs. Joe—I never thought I was going to rob Joe, for I never thought of any of the housekeeping property as his—united to the necessity of always keeping one hand on my bread-and-butter as I sat or when I was ordered about the kitchen on any small errand, almost drove me out of my mind.

It was Christmas Eve, and I had to stir the pudding for next day with a copper-stick, from seven to eight by the Dutch clock. I tried it with the load upon my leg (and that made me think afresh of the man with the load on *his* leg), and found the tendency of exercise to bring the bread-and-butter out at my ankle quite unmanageable. Happily I slipped away, and deposited that part of my conscience in my garret bedroom.

"Hark!" said I, when I had done my stirring, and was taking a final warm in the chimney-corner before being sent up to bed; "was that great guns, Joe?"

"Ah!" said Joe. "There's another conwict off."

"What does that mean, Joe?" said I.

Mrs. Joe, who always took explanations upon herself, said snappishly, "Escaped. Escaped," administering the definition like tar-water.

"There was a conwict off last night" said Joe, aloud, "after sunset-gun. And they fired warning of him. And now it appears they're firing warning of another."

"*Who's* firing?" said I.

"Drat that boy," interposed my sister, "what a questioner he is. Ask no questions, and you'll be told no lies."

"Mrs. Joe," said I, "I should like to know—if you wouldn't much mind—where the firing comes from."

"Lord bless the boy!" exclaimed my sister, as if she didn't quite mean that, but rather the contrary. "From the Hulks!"

"Oh-h!" said I, looking at Joe. "Hulks!"

Joe gave a reproachful cough, as much as to say, "Well, I told you so."

"And please, what's Hulks?" said I.

"That's the way with this boy!" exclaimed

Joe gave a reproachful cough, as much as to say, "Well, I told you so."

Student Activity 1. In the passage from *Great Expectations*, find an example of a quoted statement followed by a concluding expression. What punctuation mark separates the quotation from the concluding expression?

Student Activity 2. Write three direct quotations: one with an introductory expression, one with a concluding expression, and one with an interrupting expression.

Electronic Handbook You might want students to review quotation marks before completing the Grammar in Action activities. If students have access to the Language Master 6000, have them enter the access symbol " and press the GRAMMAR key to get information on the use of quotation marks.

11 **Critical Thinking and Reading** What can be inferred about Pip's moral values from his judgment of his own behavior?

12 **Reading Strategy** Ask students to predict how this new development will affect Pip.

my sister. "Answer him one question, and he'll ask you a dozen directly. Hulks are prison-ships, right 'cross th' meshes." We always used that name for marshes in our country.

"I wonder who's put into prison-ships, and why they're put there?" said I, in a general way, and with quiet desperation.

It was too much for Mrs. Joe, who immediately rose. "I tell you what, young fellow," said she, "I didn't bring you up by hand to badger people's lives out. People are put in the Hulks because they murder, and because they rob, and forge, and do all sorts of bad; and they always begin by asking questions. Now you get along to bed!"

I was never allowed a candle to light me to bed, and, as I went upstairs in the dark, I felt fearfully sensible of the great convenience that the Hulks were handy for me. I was clearly on my way there. I had begun by asking questions, and I was going to rob Mrs. Joe.

If I slept at all that night, it was only to imagine myself drifting down the river on a strong spring-tide, to the Hulks. As soon as the great black velvet pall outside my little window was shot with gray, I got up and went downstairs; every board upon the way, and every crack in every board, calling after me, "Stop thief!" and "Get up, Mrs. Joe!" I stole some bread, some rind of cheese, about half a jar of mincemeat, some brandy from a stone bottle (diluting the stone bottle from a jug in the kitchen cupboard), a meat bone with very little on it, and a beautiful round compact pork-pie.

There was a door in the kitchen communicating with the forge; I unlocked and unbolted that door, and got a file from among Joe's tools. Then I put the fastenings as I had found them, opened the door at which I had entered when I ran home last night, shut it, and ran for the misty marshes.

Chapter 3

It was a rimy morning, and very damp. On every rail and gate, wet lay clammy, and the marsh-mist was so thick that the wooden finger on the post directing people to our village—a direction which they never accepted, for they never came there—was invisible to me until I was quite close under it. However fast I went, I couldn't warm my feet, to which the damp cold seemed riveted, as the iron was riveted to the leg of the man I was running to meet. I had just crossed a ditch which I knew to be very near the battery, and had just scrambled up the mound beyond the ditch, when I saw the man sitting before me. His back was towards me, and he had his arms folded, and was nodding forward, heavy with sleep. I went forward softly and touched him on the shoulder. He instantly jumped up, and it was not the same man, but another man!

And yet this man was dressed in coarse gray, too, and had a great iron on his leg, and was lame, and hoarse, and cold, and was everything that the other man was; except that he had not the same face, and had a flat, broad-brimmed, low-crowned felt hat on. All this I saw in a moment, for I had only a moment to see it in: he swore an oath at me, made a hit at me—it was a round, weak blow that missed me and almost knocked himself down, for it made him stumble—and then he ran into the mist, stumbling twice as he went, and I lost him.

I was soon at the battery, after that, and there was the right man waiting for me. He was obviously cold, and his eyes looked awfully hungry. He did not turn me upside down, this time, to get at what I had, but left me right side upwards while I opened the bundle and emptied my pockets.

"What's in the bottle, boy?" said he.

"Brandy," said I.

THE STONE-BREAKER (1857–58)
Henry Wallis
Birmingham Museums and Art Gallery

He was already handing mincemeat down his throat in the most curious manner—more like a man who was putting it away somewhere in a violent hurry, than a man who was eating it—but he left off to take some of the liquor. He shivered all the while so violently that it was quite as much as he could do to keep the neck of the bottle between his teeth, without biting it off.

"I think you have got the ague,[1]" said I.

"I'm much of your opinion, boy," said he.

---

1. **ague** (ā′ gyōō) *n.*: Chills and fever.

"It's bad about here," I told him. "You've been lying out on the meshes."

"I'll eat my breakfast afore they're the death of me," said he. "I'd do that if I was going to be strung up to that there gallows as there is over there, directly arterwards. I'll beat the shivers so far, I'll bet you."

He was gobbling mincemeat, meatbone, bread, cheese, and pork pie all at once, staring distrustfully while he did so at the mist all round us, and often stopping—even stopping his jaws—to listen. Some real or fancied sound, some clink upon the river or breath-

Great Expectations 731

14 **Discussion** What qualities does Pip reveal in this exchange?

15 **Critical Thinking and Reading** What can you infer from this convict's eager interest in the other one?

ing of beast upon the marsh, now gave him a start, and he said suddenly:

"You're not a deceiving imp? You brought no one with you?"

"No, sir! No!"

"Nor giv' no one the office to follow you?"

"No!"

"Well," said he, "I believe you. You'd be but a fierce young hound indeed, if at your time of life you could help to hunt a wretched warmint,[2] hunted as near death and dunghill as this poor wretched warmint is!"

Something clicked in his throat as if he had works in him like a clock, and was going to strike. And he smeared his ragged rough sleeve over his eyes.

14 Pitying his desolation, and watching him as he gradually settled down upon the pie, I made bold to say, "I am glad you enjoy it."

"Did you speak?"

"I said, I was glad you enjoyed it."

"Thankee, my boy. I do."

"I am afraid you won't leave any of it for him," said I timidly.

"Leave any for him? Who's him?" said my friend, stopping in his crunching of pie-crust.

"The young man," said I, pointing; "over there, where I found him nodding asleep, and thought it was you."

He held me by the collar and stared at me so that I began to think his first idea about cutting my throat had revived.

"Dressed like you, you know, only with a hat," I explained, trembling; "and—and"—I was very anxious to put this delicately—"and with—the same reason for wanting to borrow a file. Didn't you hear the cannon last night?"

"Then, there *was* firing!" he said to himself.

_____
2. **warmint:** Varmint (vär′ mənt), an undesirable or troublesome person.

"This man"—he had said all the rest as if he had forgotten my being there—"did you notice anything in him?"

"He had a badly bruised face," said I, recalling what I hardly knew I knew.

"Not here?" exclaimed the man, striking his left cheek mercilessly with the flat of his hand.

"Yes, there!"

"Where is he?" He crammed what little food was left into the breast of his gray jacket. "Show me the way he went. I'll pull him down, like a bloodhound. Curse this iron on my sore leg! Give us hold of the file, boy."

I indicated in what direction the mist had shrouded the other man, and he looked up at it for an instant. But he was down on the rank wet grass, filing at his iron like a madman, and not minding me or minding his own leg, which had an old chafe upon it, and was bloody, but which he handled as roughly as if it had no more feeling in it than the file. I was very much afraid of him again, now that he had worked himself into this fierce hurry, and I was likewise very much afraid of keeping away from home any longer. I told him I must go, but he took no notice, so I thought the best thing I could do was to slip off. The last I saw of him, his head was bent over his knee and he was working hard at his fetter, muttering impatient imprecations at it and his leg. The last I heard of him, I stopped in the mist to listen, and the file was still going.

Chapter 4

I fully expected to find a constable in the kitchen, waiting to take me up. But not only was there no constable there, but no discovery had yet been made of the robbery.

"And where the deuce ha' *you* been?" was Mrs. Joe's Christmas salutation, when I and my conscience showed ourselves.

Commentary: More About Charles Dickens

Charles John Huffam Dickens was born in Portsea, Portsmouth on February 7, 1812. Dickens was a sickly child, but when his father, who was a clerk in the Navy Pay Office was transferred in 1817 to the government dockyard at Chatham, Dickens was able to enjoy a happy and carefree childhood that allowed him to grow strong and healthy. In 1822 his father was again transferred, this time to London, where Dickens was to spend the next thirty-eight years. In 1860 he moved near Chatham, where he died.

When Dickens was twelve, his father was imprisoned. As the oldest child, Dickens was pulled out of school to support his family. He worked in a blacking warehouse twelve hours a day and earned six shillings a week. Both his father's imprisonment and his experience in the factory affected Dickens deeply. His experience in the factory, however, provided him with knowledge about and experience with the lower class.

When Dickens was seventeen he worked as a court stenographer. His experience in this job aroused his contempt for law and the parliament. It, however, eventually led to and heightened his affection for journalism. From 1834 to 1836, Dickens worked as a reporter for the *Morning Chronicle*. Under the pen name

I said I had been down to hear the carols. "Ah! well!" observed Mrs. Joe. "You might ha' done worse."

We were to have a superb dinner, consisting of a leg of pickled pork and greens, and a pair of roast stuffed fowls. A handsome mince pie had been made yesterday morning (which accounted for the mincemeat not being missed), and the pudding was already on the boil.

My sister having so much to do, was going to church vicariously; that is to say, Joe and I were going. In his working clothes, Joe was a well-knit characteristic-looking blacksmith; in his holiday clothes, he was more like a scarecrow in good circumstances than anything else. Nothing that he wore then fitted him or seemed to belong to him. I was always treated as if I had insisted on being born in opposition to the dictates of reason, religion, and morality, and against the dissuading arguments of my best friends. Even when I was taken to have a new suit of clothes, the tailor had orders to make them like a kind of reformatory, and on no account to let me have the free use of my limbs.

Mr. Wopsle, the clerk[1] at church, was to dine with us; and Mr. Hubble, the wheelwright,[2] and Mrs. Hubble; and Uncle Pumblechook (Joe's uncle, but Mrs. Joe appropriated him), who was a well-to-do corn chandler[3] in the nearest town, and drove his own chaise-cart.[4] The dinner hour was half-past one. When Joe and I got home, we found the table laid, and Mrs. Joe dressed, and the dinner dressing, and the front door unlocked (it never was at any other time) for the company to enter by, and everything most splendid. And still, not a word of the robbery.

The time came, without bringing with it any relief to my feelings, and the company came. I opened the door—making believe that it was a habit of ours to open that door—and I opened it first to Mr. Wopsle, next to Mr. and Mrs. Hubble, and last of all to Uncle Pumblechook. N.B.[5] I was not allowed to call him uncle, under the severest penalties.

"Mrs. Joe," said Uncle Pumblechook—a large hard-breathing middle-aged slow man, with a mouth like a fish, dull staring eyes, and sandy hair standing upright on his head, so that he looked as if he had just been all but choked, and had that moment come to—"I have brought you as the compliments of the season—I have brought you, mum, a bottle of sherry wine—and I have brought you, mum, a bottle of port wine."

We dined on these occasions in the kitchen, and adjourned, for the nuts and oranges and apples, to the parlor. My sister was uncommonly lively on the present occasion, and indeed was generally more gracious in the society of Mrs. Hubble than in other company. When we sat down to dinner, Mr. Wopsle said grace with theatrical declamation and ended with the very proper aspiration that we might be truly grateful. Upon which my sister fixed me with her eye, and said, in a low reproachful voice, "Do you hear that? Be grateful."

"Especially," said Mr. Pumblechook, "be grateful, boy, of them which brought you up by hand."

Mrs. Hubble shook her head, and contemplating me with a mournful presentiment that I should come to no good, asked,

---

1. clerk (klʉrk) *n.*: Official who has minor duties in a church.
2. wheelwright (hwēl' rīt') *n.*: Person who makes and repairs wheels and wheeled vehicles.
3. corn chandler (chan' dlər): Corn merchant.
4. chaise-cart (shāz' kärt') *n.*: Lightweight carriage drawn by one or two horses.

---

5. N.B.: *Nota bene,* Latin for "note well."

16

16 Discussion Does Dickens give you a favorable or unfavorable impression of Uncle Pumblechook? Explain.

Boz, Dickens wrote brief descriptions of life in London. His sketches began appearing in periodicals, and by 1836 *Sketches by Boz* was a great success.

Dickens became the most popular English novelist in his day. He wrote his novels rapidly and sometimes worked on more than one book. He usually rushed his completed installment to his publishers just in the nick of time on the due date.

In Europe and the United States, Dickens's characters have become household names. References to such characters as Mr. Pickwick (*Pickwick Papers*), Uriah Heep (*David Copperfield*), Miss Havisham (*Great Expectations*), and Ebenezer Scrooge (*A Christmas Carol*) are heard even today. Despite his colorful and memorable characters, much of Dickens's success was from his ability to bring to life the sights, sounds, and smells of London and the customs of his day.

17 **Enrichment** Speech characteristics—choice of wording, grammar, pronunciation, intonation, and so forth—reflect social and regional differences. Dickens had a keen ear for speech patterns, which he imitated with great skill. If students "listen" as they read, they may be able to tell much about characters from the way they speak.

18 **Discussion** How does Dickens heighten the suspense and tension?

17 "Why is it that the young are never grateful?" This moral mystery seemed too much for the company until Mr. Hubble tersely solved it by saying, "Naterally wicious." Everybody then murmured "True!" and looked at me in a particularly unpleasant and personal manner.

Joe's station and influence were something feebler (if possible) when there was company than when there was none. But he always aided and comforted me when he could, in some way of his own, and he always did so at dinner-time by giving me gravy, if there were any. There being plenty of gravy to-day, Joe spooned into my plate, at this point, about half a pint.

The guests continued discussing how ungrateful I was and how much trouble I had been to my sister as they finished the main course. Then my sister offered some brandy to Uncle Pumblechook, and I was sure my time had come. He would find it was weak, he would say it was weak, and I was lost! I held tight to the leg of the table under the cloth, with both hands, and awaited my fate.

My sister went for the stone bottle, came back with the stone bottle, and poured his brandy out; no one else taking any. The wretched man trifled with his glass—took it up, looked at it through the light, put it down—prolonged my misery. All this time Mrs. Joe and Joe were briskly clearing the table for the pie and pudding.

I watched the miserable creature finger his glass playfully, take it up, smile, throw his head back, and drink the brandy off. Instantly afterwards, the company were seized with unspeakable consternation, owing to his springing to his feet, turning round several times in an appalling spasmodic whooping-cough dance, and rushing out at the door; he then became visible through the window, violently plunging and expectorating,[6] making the most hideous faces and apparently out of his mind.

I held on tight, while Mrs. Joe and Joe ran to him. I didn't know how I had done it, but I had no doubt I had murdered him somehow. In my dreadful situation, it was a relief when he was brought back, and, surveying the company all round as if *they* had disagreed with him, sank down into his chair with the one significant gasp, "Tar!"

I had filled up the bottle from the tar-water jug. I knew he would be worse by-and-by.

"Tar!" cried my sister, in amazement. "Why, how ever could tar come there?"

But Uncle Pumblechook, who was omnipotent in that kitchen, wouldn't hear the word, wouldn't hear of the subject, imperiously waved it all away with his hand, and asked for hot gin-and-water. My sister, who had begun to be alarmingly meditative, had to employ herself actively in getting the gin, the hot water, the sugar, and the lemon-peel, and mixing them. For the time at least, I was saved.

All partook of pudding. The course terminated, and Mr. Pumblechook had begun to beam under the genial influence of gin-and-water. I began to think I should get over the day, when my sister said to Joe, "Clean plates—cold."

I clutched the leg of the table again immediately, and pressed it to my bosom as if it had been the companion of my youth and friend of my soul. I foresaw what was coming, and I felt that this time I really was gone.

"You must taste," said my sister, addressing the guests with her best grace, "You must taste, to finish with, such a delightful and delicious present of Uncle Pumblechook's!"

---

6. expectorating (ik spek′ tə rāt′ iŋ) *v*.: Spitting.

Must they! Let them not hope to taste it!

"You must know," said my sister, rising, "it's a pie—a savory pork pie."

My sister went out to get it. I heard her steps proceed to the pantry. I heard Joe say, "You shall have some, Pip." I have never been absolutely certain whether I uttered a shrill yell of terror, merely in spirit, or in the bodily hearing of the company. I felt that I could bear no more, and that I must run away. I released the leg of the table, and ran for my life.

But I ran no further than the house door, for there I ran head foremost into a party of soldiers with their muskets; one of whom held out a pair of handcuffs to me, saying, "Here you are, look sharp, come on!"

Chapter 5

The apparition of a file of soldiers ringing down the butt-ends of their loaded muskets on our doorstep caused the dinner party to rise from the table in confusion, and caused Mrs. Joe, reentering the kitchen empty-handed, to stop short and stare, in her wondering lament of "Gracious goodness me, what's gone—with the—pie!"

"Excuse me, ladies and gentlemen," said the sergeant, "but as I have mentioned at the door to this smart young shaver"—which he hadn't—"I am on a chase in the name of the King, and I want the blacksmith."

"You see, blacksmith," continued the sergeant, who had by this time picked out Joe with his eye, "we have had an accident with these, and I find the lock of one of 'em goes wrong, and the coupling don't act pretty. As they are wanted for immediate service, will you throw your eye over them?"

Joe threw his eye over them, and pronounced that the job would necessitate the lighting of his forge fire, and would take nearer two hours than one. "Will it? Then will you set about it at once, blacksmith?" said the off-hand sergeant, "as it's on his Majesty's service. And if my men can bear a hand anywhere, they'll make themselves useful." With that he called to his men, who came trooping into the kitchen one after another, and piled their arms in a corner.

I was in an agony of apprehension. But, beginning to perceive that the handcuffs were not for me, and that the military had so far got the better of the pie as to put it in the background, I collected a little more of my scattered wits.

"How far might you call yourselves from the marshes, hereabouts?" asked the sergeant, reflecting. "Not above a mile, I reckon?"

"Just a mile," said Mrs. Joe.

"That'll do. We begin to close in upon 'em about dusk. A little before dusk, my orders are. That'll do."

"Convicts, sergeant?" asked Mr. Wopsle.

"Aye!" returned the sergeant, "two. They're pretty well known to be out on the marshes still, and they won't try to get clear of 'em before dusk. Anybody here seen anything of any such game?"

Everybody, myself excepted, said no, with confidence. Nobody thought of me.

"Well," said the sergeant, "they'll find themselves trapped in a circle, I expect, sooner than they count on. Now, blacksmith! If you're ready, his Majesty the King is."

Joe had got his coat and waistcoat and cravat[1] off, and his leather apron on, and passed into the forge. One of the soldiers opened its wooden windows, another lighted the fire, another turned to at the bellows, the rest stood round the blaze, which was soon roaring. Then Joe began to hammer and clink, hammer and clink, and we all looked on.

---

1. **cravat** (krə vat′) *n.*: Necktie.

Great Expectations 735

19 **Enrichment** This story, like others Dickens wrote, appeared first as a serial in a monthly magazine. As is common with serial stories, each installment ended at a particularly suspenseful moment in order to hold the reader's interest until the next installment. The first installment of the story ended here. Tell students that critics disagree about the effectiveness of this device—some consider it melodramatic. Then ask students to express their opinions of this technique.

20 **Critical Thinking and Reading** Why did Pip assume that the handcuffs were for him?

When Joe's job was done, the ringing and roaring stopped. As Joe got on his coat, he mustered courage to propose that some of us should go down with the soldiers and see what came of the hunt. Mr. Pumblechook and Mr. Hubble declined, on the plea of a pipe and ladies' society; but Mr. Wopsle said he would go, if Joe would. Joe said he was agreeable, and would take me.

The sergeant took a polite leave of the ladies, and parted from Mr. Pumblechook as from a comrade.

His men resumed their muskets and fell in. Mr. Wopsle, Joe, and I received strict charge to keep in the rear, and to speak no word after we reached the marshes. When we were all out in the raw air and were steadily moving towards our business, I treasonably whispered to Joe, "I hope, Joe, we sha'n't find them." And Joe whispered to me, "I'd give a shilling if they had cut and run, Pip."

We struck out on the open marshes, through the gate at the side of the churchyard. A bitter sleet came rattling against us here on the east wind, and Joe took me on his back.

Now that we were out upon the dismal wilderness where they little thought I had been within eight or nine hours, and had seen both men hiding, I considered for the first time, with great dread, if we should come upon them, would my particular convict suppose that it was I who had brought the soldiers there? He had asked me if I was a deceiving imp, and he said I should be a fierce young hound if I joined the hunt against him. Would he believe that I was both imp and hound in treacherous earnest, and had betrayed him?

With my heart thumping like a blacksmith at Joe's broad shoulder, I looked all about for any sign of the convicts. I could see none, I could hear none. The soldiers were moving on in the direction of the old battery, and we were moving on a little way behind them, when, all of a sudden, we all stopped. For, there had reached us, on the wings of the wind and rain, a long shout. It was repeated. It was at a distance towards the east, but it was long and loud.

The sergeant, a decisive man, ordered that the sound should not be answered, but that the course should be changed, and that his men should make towards it "at the double." So we started to the right (where the east was), and Joe pounded away so wonderfully that I had to hold on tight to keep my seat.

It was a run indeed now, and what Joe called, in the only two words he spoke all the time, "a winder." Down banks and up banks, and over gates, and splashing into dikes, and breaking among coarse rushes: no man cared where he went. As we came nearer to the shouting, it became more and more apparent that it was made by more than one voice. After a while, we had so run it down that we could hear one voice calling "Murder!" and another voice, "Convicts! Runaways! Guard! This way for the runaway convicts!" Then both voices would seem to be stifled in a struggle, and then would break out again. And when it had come to this, the soldiers ran like deer, and Joe too.

The sergeant ran in first, when we had run the noise quite down, and two of his men ran in close upon him. Their pieces[2] were cocked and leveled when we all ran in.

"Here are both men!" panted the sergeant, struggling at the bottom of a ditch. "Surrender, you two! And confound you for two wild beasts! Come asunder!"

Water was splashing, and mud was flying, and oaths were being sworn, and blows were being struck, when some more men went down into the ditch to help the sergeant; and dragged out, separately, my convict and the other one. Both were bleeding

---

2. **pieces** *n.*: Rifles.

Grammar in Action

A **gerund** is a verb form that ends in *ing* and is used as a noun:

When Joe's job was done, the *ringing* and *roaring* stopped.

Use of gerunds allows writers to vary sentence style within a work of literature.

These forms of the verb can be used anywhere that nouns are. Notice that in this sentence from the novel, the two gerunds act as the compound subject of the verb *stopped*.

Don't confuse gerunds with other verb forms that end in *ing*.

Participle: He asked me if I was a *deceiving* imp, and he said I would be a fierce young hound if I joined the hunt against him.

Verb phrase: The soldiers were *moving* on in the direction of the old battery, and we were *moving* on a little way behind them.

Gerund: As we came nearer to the *shouting,* it became more and more apparent that it was made by more than one voice.

In the first sentence the *deceiving* acts as an adjective modifying *imp;* it is a participle, not a gerund. In the second sentence, *moving* is part of a verb phrase. In the last sentence,

and panting and execrating and struggling; but of course I knew them both directly.

"Mind!" said my convict, wiping blood from his face with his ragged sleeves, and shaking torn hair from his fingers; "*I* took him! *I* give him up to you! Mind that!"

"It's not much to be particular about," said the sergeant; "it'll do you small good, my man, being in the same plight yourself. Handcuffs there!"

"I don't expect it to do me any good. I don't want it to do me more good than it does now," said my convict, with a greedy laugh. "I took him. He knows it. That's enough for me."

The other convict was livid to look at, and, in addition to the old bruised left side of his face, seemed to be bruised and torn all over. He could not so much as get his breath to speak until they were both separately handcuffed, but leaned upon a soldier to keep himself from falling.

"Take notice, guard—he tried to murder me," were his first words.

"Tried to murder him?" said my convict disdainfully. "Try, and not do it? I took him, and giv' him up; that's what I done. I not only prevented him getting off the marshes, but I dragged him here—dragged him this far on his way back. He's a gentleman, if you please, this villain. Now, the Hulks has got its gentleman again, through me. Murder him? Worth my while, too, to murder him, when I could do worse and drag him back!"

The other one still gasped, "He tried—he tried—to—murder me. Bear—bear witness."

"Lookee here!" said my convict to the sergeant. "Single-handed I got clear of the prison-ship; I made a dash and I done it. I could ha' got clear of these death-cold flats likewise—look at my leg: you won't find much iron on it—if I hadn't made discovery that *he* was here. Let *him* go free? Let *him* profit by the means as I found out? Let *him* make a tool of me afresh and again? Once

more? No, no, no. If I had died at the bottom there"—and he made an emphatic swing at the ditch with his manacled hands—"I'd have held to him with that grip, that you should have been safe to find him in my hold."

The other fugitive, who was evidently in extreme horror of his companion, repeated, "He tried to murder me. I should have been a dead man if you had not come up."

"He lies!" said my convict, with fierce energy. "He's a liar born, and he'll die a liar. Look at his face; ain't it written there? Let him turn those eyes of his on me. I defy him to do it."

The other, with an effort at a scornful smile, looked at the soldiers, and looked about at the marshes and at the sky, but certainly did not look at the speaker.

"Do you see him?" pursued my convict. "Do you see what a villain he is? Do you see those groveling and wandering eyes? That's how he looked when we were tried together. He never looked at me."

The other, always working and working his dry lips and turning his eyes restlessly about him far and near, did at last turn them for a moment on the speaker, with the words, "You are not much to look at," and with a half-taunting glance at the bound hands. At that point, my convict became so frantically exasperated that he would have rushed upon him but for the interposition of the soldiers. "Didn't I tell you," said the other convict then, "that he would murder me, if he could?"

"Enough of this parley," said the sergeant. "Light those torches."

As one of the soldiers, who carried a basket in lieu[3] of a gun, went down on his knee to open it, my convict looked round him for the first time, and saw me. I had alighted from Joe's back on the brink of the ditch

---

3. in lieu (lōō): Instead.

Great Expectations 737

22 Critical Thinking and Reading What can you infer from the behavior of the first convict toward the second one?

23 Reading Strategy Have students summarize the events in the story of the escape and capture of the convicts.

24 Critical Thinking and Reading Why do you think the first convict is so set on vengeance that he forfeits his own freedom in order to see the second convict returned to prison?

shouting acts as the object of a preposition. In this sentence, *shouting* is a gerund.

Student Activity 1. Find and copy three more examples of Dickens's use of gerunds. Share and discuss these with a partner.

Student Activity 2. Write five sentences containing gerunds. Discuss these with a group of classmates, noting what part of speech the gerund functions as in each sentence.

Electronic Handbook You might want students to review conjugation of verbs and verbal phrases before completing the Grammar in Action activities. If students have access to the Language Master 6000, have them enter the access words *tense* and *gerund* and press the GRAMMAR key to get information on verb tenses and gerunds.

when we came up, and had not moved since. I looked at him eagerly when he looked at me, and slightly moved my hands and shook my head. He gave me a look that I did not understand, and it all passed in a moment. But if he had looked at me for an hour or for a day, I could not have remembered his face ever afterwards as having been more attentive.

The soldier with the basket soon got a light, and lighted three or four torches. Before we departed from that spot, four soldiers standing in a ring fired twice into the air. Presently we saw other torches kindled at some distance behind us, and others on the marshes on the opposite bank of the river. "All right," said the sergeant. "March."

We had not gone far when three cannon were fired ahead of us with a sound that seemed to burst something inside my ear. "You are expected on board," said the sergeant to my convict; "they know you are coming. Don't straggle, my man. Close up here."

The two were kept apart, and each walked surrounded by a separate guard. I had hold of Joe's hand now, and Joe carried one of the torches. Mr. Wopsle had been for going back, but Joe was resolved to see it out, so we went on with the party. When I looked round, I could see the other lights coming in after us. Our lights warmed the air about us with their pitchy blaze, and the two prisoners seemed rather to like that, as they limped along in the midst of the muskets. We could not go fast because of their lameness; and they were so spent that two or three times we had to halt while they rested.

After an hour or so of this traveling, we came to a rough wooden hut and a landing place. There was a guard in the hut, and they challenged, and the sergeant answered. Then, we went into the hut. The sergeant made some kind of report, and some entry in a book, and then the convict whom I call the other convict was drafted off with his guard, to go on board first.

My convict never looked at me, except that once. While we stood in the hut, he turned to the sergeant, and remarked:

"I wish to say something respecting this escape. It may prevent some persons laying under suspicion alonger me."

"You can say what you like," returned the sergeant, "but you have no call to say it here. You'll have opportunity enough to say about it, and hear about it, before it's done with, you know."

"I know, but this is another pint, a separate matter. A man can't starve; at least *I* can't. I took some wittles, up at the willage over yonder."

"You mean stole," said the sergeant.

"And I'll tell you where from. From the blacksmith's."

"Halloa!" said the sergeant, staring at Joe.

"Halloa, Pip!" said Joe, staring at me.

"It was some broken wittles—that's what it was—and a dram of liquor, and a pie."

"Have you happened to miss such an article as a pie, blacksmith?" asked the sergeant confidentially.

"My wife did, at the very moment when you came in. Don't you know, Pip?"

"So," said my convict, turning his eyes on Joe in a moody manner, and without the least glance at me; "so you're the blacksmith, are you? Then I'm sorry to say I've eat your pie."

"God knows you're welcome to it—so far as it was ever mine," returned Joe, with a saving remembrance of Mrs. Joe. "We don't know what you have done, but we wouldn't have you starved to death for it, poor miserable fellow-creatur. Would us, Pip?"

The something that I had noticed before clicked in the man's throat again, and he turned his back. The boat had returned, and his guard were ready, so we followed him to

738   *The Novel*

the landing-place made of rough stakes and stones, and saw him put into the boat, which was rowed by a crew of convicts like himself. No one seemed surprised to see him, or interested in seeing him, or glad to see him, or sorry to see him, or spoke a word, except that somebody in the boat growled as if to dogs, "Give way, you!" which was the signal for the dip of the oars. By the light of the torches, we saw the black Hulk lying out a little way from the mud of the shore, like a wicked Noah's ark. We saw the boat go alongside, and we saw him taken up the side and disappear. Then, the ends of the torches were flung hissing into the water, and went out, as if it were all over with him.

Chapter 6

I do not recall that I felt any tenderness of conscience in reference to Mrs. Joe, when the fear of being found out was lifted off me. But I loved Joe—perhaps for no better reason in those early days than because the dear fellow let me love him—and as to him my inner self was not so easily composed. It was much upon my mind (particularly when I first saw him looking about for his file) that I ought to tell Joe the whole truth. Yet I did not. The fear of losing Joe's confidence, and of thenceforth sitting in the chimney-corner at night staring drearily at my for ever lost companion and friend, tied up my tongue. I was too cowardly to do what I knew to be right, as I had been too cowardly to avoid doing what I knew to be wrong.

By that time, I was staggering on the kitchen floor, through having been newly set upon my feet, and through having been fast asleep, and through waking in the heat and lights and noise of tongues. As I came to myself I found Joe telling them about the convict's confession, and all the visitors sug-

gesting different ways by which he had got into the pantry.

This was all I heard that night before my sister clutched me, as a slumberous offense to the company's eyesight, and assisted me up to bed with such a strong hand that I seemed to have fifty boots on, and to be dangling them all against the edges of the stairs.

Chapter 7

When I was old enough, I was to be apprenticed to Joe, and until I could assume that dignity I was not to be what Mrs. Joe called "pompeyed," or (as I render it) pampered. Therefore, I was not only odd-boy about the forge, but if any neighbor happened to want an extra boy to frighten birds, or pick up stones, or do any such job, I was favored with the employment. In order, however, that our superior position might not be compromised thereby, a money-box was kept on the kitchen mantel shelf, into which it was publicly made known that all my earnings were dropped. I have an impression that they were to be contributed eventually towards the liquidation of the national debt, but I know I had no hope of any personal participation in the treasure.

Mr. Wopsle's great-aunt kept an evening school in the village. She rented a small cottage, and Mr. Wopsle had the room upstairs, where we students used to overhear him reading aloud in a most dignified and terrific manner, and occasionally bumping on the ceiling. There was a fiction that Mr. Wopsle "examined" the scholars once a quarter. What he did on those occasions was to turn up his cuffs, stick up his hair, and give us Mark Antony's oration over the body of Caesar.[1]

---

1. give us . . . Caesar: Recite a famous speech from Shakespeare's play *Julius Caesar.*

26 **Discussion** Why is this image effective?

27 **Literary Focus** Explain how this passage might reflect an adult's point of view as well as a child's.

28 **Discussion** How does this comment reveal the nature of Pip's relationship with his sister?

29 **Enrichment** Dickens often wrote about inadequate schools and incompetent or cruel teachers. He describes such schools, for example, in *Nicholas Nickleby*, *David Copperfield*, and *Hard Times*.

30 **Discussion** What do these details reveal about Biddy?

31 **Discussion** What does Pip mean by this statement?

29 Mr. Wopsle's great-aunt, besides keeping this educational institution, kept in the same room—a little general shop. She had no idea what stock she had, or what the price of anything in it was; but here was a little greasy memorandum book kept in a drawer which served as a catalogue of prices, and by this oracle[2] Biddy arranged all the shop transactions. Biddy was Mr. Wopsle's great-aunt's granddaughter; I confess myself quite unequal to the working out of the problem, what relation she was to Mr. Wopsle. She was an orphan like myself; like me, too, had been brought up by hand. She was **30** most noticeable, I thought, in respect of her extremities; for her hair always wanted brushing, her hands always wanted washing, and her shoes always wanted mending and pulling up at heel.

Much of my unassisted self, and more by the help of Biddy than of Mr. Wopsle's great-aunt, I struggled through the alphabet as if it had been a bramble bush, getting considerably worried and scratched by every letter. After that, I fell among those thieves, the **31** nine figures, who seemed every evening to do something new to disguise themselves and baffle recognition. But, at last I began, in a purblind groping way, to read, write, and cipher[3] on the very smallest scale.

One night, I was sitting in the chimney corner with my slate, expending great efforts on the production of a letter to Joe. I think it must have been a full year after our hunt upon the marshes, for it was a long time after, and it was winter and a hard frost. With an alphabet on the hearth at my feet for reference, I contrived in an hour or two to print and smear this epistle:

"MI deEr JO i opE U r krWitE wEll i opE i shAl soN B haBelL 4 2 teeDge U JO AN theN wE shOrl b sO glOdd AN wEn i M PreNgtD 2 u JO woT larX AN blEvE ME inF xn PiP."

There was no indispensable necessity for my communicating with Joe by letter, inasmuch as he sat beside me and we were alone. But I delivered this written communication (slate and all) with my own hand, and Joe received it as a miracle of erudition.

"I say, Pip, old chap!" cried Joe, opening his blue eyes wide, "what a scholar you are! Ain't you?"

"I should like to be," said I, glancing at the slate as he held it—with a misgiving that the writing was rather hilly.

"Why, here's a J," said Joe, "and a O equal to anythink! Here's a J and a O, Pip, and a J-O, Joe."

I had never heard Joe read aloud to any greater extent than this monosyllable, and I had observed at church last Sunday, when I accidentally held our prayer book upside down, that it seemed to suit his convenience quite as well as if it had been all right. Wishing to embrace the present occasion of finding out whether, in teaching Joe, I should have to begin quite at the beginning, I said, "Ah! But read the rest, Joe."

"The rest, eh, Pip?" said Joe, looking at it with a slowly searching eye, "One, two, three. Why, here's three Js, and three Os, and three J-O, Joes, in it, Pip!"

I leaned over Joe, and, with the aid of my forefinger, read him the whole letter.

"Astonishing!" said Joe, when I had finished. "You ARE a scholar."

"How do you spell Gargery, Joe?" I asked him, with a modest patronage.[4]

"I don't spell it at all," said Joe.

"But supposing you did?"

"It *can't* be supposed," said Joe. "Tho' I'm oncommon fond of reading, too."

"Are you, Joe?"

---

2. oracle (ôr′ ə k'l) *n.*: Source of wisdom.
3. cipher (sī′ fər) *v.*: Do arithmetic.

4. patronage (pā′ trən ij) *n.*: Encouragement shown to someone inferior.

RUSTIC GIRL SEATED
John Constable

"Oncommon. Give me," said Joe, "a good book, or a good newspaper, and sit me down afore a good fire, and I ask no better. Lord!" he continued, after rubbing his knees a little "when you *do* come to a J and a O, and says you, 'Here, at last, is a J-O, Joe,' how interesting reading is!"

I derived from this last that Joe's education, like steam, was yet in its infancy. Pursuing the subject, I inquired:

32

Great Expectations 741

"Didn't you ever go to school, Joe, when you were as little as me?"

"No, Pip."

"Why didn't you ever go to school, Joe, when you were as little as me?"

"Well, Pip," said Joe, taking up the poker, and settling himself to his usual occupation when he was thoughtful, of slowly raking the fire between the lower bars, "I'll tell you. My father, Pip, he were given to drink, and when he were overtook with drink, he hammered away at my mother most onmerciful. It were a'most the only hammering he did, indeed, 'xcepting at myself. And he hammered at me with a wigor only to be equaled by the wigor with which he didn't hammer at his anwil. You're a-listening and understanding, Pip?"

"Yes, Joe."

" 'Consequence, my mother and me we ran away from my father several times; and then my mother she'd go out to work, and she'd say, 'Joe,' she'd say, 'now, please God, you shall have some schooling, child,' and she'd put me to school. But my father were that good in his hart that he couldn't a-bear to be without us. So, he'd come with a most tremenjous crowd and make such a row at the doors of the houses where we was that they used to be obligated to have no more to do with us and to give us up to him. And then he took us home and hammered us. Which, you see, Pip," said Joe, pausing in his meditative raking of the fire, and looking at me, "were a drawback on my learning."

"Certainly, poor Joe!"

"Though mind you, Pip," said Joe, with a judicial touch or two of the poker on the top bar, "rendering unto all their doo, and maintaining equal justice betwixt man and man, my father were that good in his hart, don't you see?"

I didn't see, but I didn't say so.

"Well!" Joe pursued, "somebody must keep the pot a-biling, Pip, or the pot won't bile, don't you know?"

I saw that, and said so.

" 'Consequence, my father didn't make objections to my going to work; so I went to work at my present calling, which were his, too, if he would have followed it, and I worked tolerable hard, I assure *you*, Pip. In time I were able to keep him, and I kep him till he went off in a purple 'leptic fit.[5] Then all the money that could be spared were wanted for my mother. She were in poor 'elth, and quite broke. She waren't long of following, poor soul, and her share of peace came round at last."

"It were but lonesome then," said Joe, "living here alone, and I got acquainted with your sister. Now, Pip"—Joe looked firmly at me, as if he knew I was not going to agree with him—"your sister is a fine figure of a woman."

I could not help looking at the fire, in an obvious state of doubt.

"Whatever family opinions, or whatever the world's opinions, on that subject may be, Pip, your sister is"—Joe tapped the top bar with the poker after every word following—"a—fine—figure—of—a—woman!"

I could think of nothing better to say than, "I am glad you think so, Joe."

"So am I," returned Joe, catching me up. "*I* am glad I think so, Pip. When I got acquainted with your sister," said Joe, "it were the talk how she was bringing you up by hand. Very kind of her, too, all the folks said, and I said, along with all the folks. As to you, if you could have been aware how small and flabby and mean you was, dear me, you'd have formed the most contemptible opinions of yourself!"

---

5. purple 'leptic fit: Joe means an apoplectic (ap' ə plek' tik) fit, a sudden paralysis and partial or complete loss of consciousness.

Not exactly relishing this, I said, "Never mind me, Joe."

"But I did mind you, Pip," he returned, with tender simplicity. "When I offered to your sister to keep company, and to be asked in church, at such times as she was willing and ready to come to the forge, I said to her, 'And bring the poor little child. God bless the poor little child,' I said to your sister, 'there's room for *him* at the forge!' "

I broke out crying and begging pardon, and hugged Joe round the neck: who dropped the poker to hug me, and to say, "Ever the best of friends; ain't us, Pip? Don't cry, old chap!"

When this little interruption was over, Joe resumed:

"Well, you see, Pip, and here we are! That's about where it lights; here we are! Now, when you take me in hand in my learning, Pip (and I tell you beforehand I am awful dull, most awful dull), Mrs. Joe mustn't see too much of what we're up to. It must be done, as I may say, on the sly. And why on the sly? I'll tell you why, Pip. Your sister is given to government."

"Given to government, Joe?"

"Given to government," said Joe. "Which I meantersay the government of you and myself."

"Oh!"

"And she ain't over partial to having scholars on the premises," Joe continued, "and in partickler would not be over partial to my being a scholar, for fear as I might rise. Like a sort of rebel."

"Your sister is a mastermind. And I ain't a mastermind. And last of all, Pip—and this I want to say very serous to you, old chap—I see so much in my poor mother, of a woman drudging and slaving and breaking her honest hart and never getting no peace in her mortal days, that I'm dead afeerd of going wrong in the way of not doing what's right by a woman, and I'd fur rather of the two go wrong the t'other way, and be a little ill-conwenienced myself. I wish it was only me that got put out, Pip; I wish there warn't no Tickler for you, old chap; I wish I could take it all on myself; but this is the up-and-down-straight on it, Pip, and I hope you'll overlook shortcomings."

Young as I was, I believe that I dated a new admiration of Joe from that night. We were equals afterwards, as we had been before; but, afterwards at quiet times when I sat looking at Joe and thinking about him, I had a new sensation of feeling conscious that I was looking up to Joe in my heart.

"However," said Joe, rising to replenish the fire, "here's the Dutch clock a-working himself up to being equal to strike eight of 'em, and she's not come home yet! I hope Uncle Pumblechook's mare mayn't have set a fore-foot on a piece o' ice, and gone down."

Mrs. Joe made occasional trips with Uncle Pumblechook on market days, to assist him in buying such household stuffs and goods as required a woman's judgment; Uncle Pumblechook being a bachelor and reposing no confidences in his domestic servant. This was market day, and Mrs. Joe was out on one of these expeditions.

Joe made the fire and swept the hearth, and then we went to the door to listen for the chaise-cart. "Here comes the mare," said Joe, "ringing like a peal of bells!"

Mrs. Joe was soon landed, and Uncle Pumblechook was soon down too, covering the mare with a cloth, and we were soon all in the kitchen, carrying so much cold air with us that it seemed to drive all the heat out of the fire.

"Now," said Mrs. Joe, unwrapping herself with haste and excitement, and throwing her bonnet back on her shoulders where it hung by the strings, "if this boy ain't grateful this night, he never will be!"

35 **Discussion** Why would Mrs. Joe object to Pip's teaching Joe to read and write?

35

I looked as grateful as any boy possibly could who was wholly uninformed why he ought to assume that expression.

"It's only to be hoped," said my sister, "that he won't be pompeyed. But I have my fears."

"She ain't in that line, mum," said Mr. Pumblechook. "She knows better."

She? I looked at Joe, making the motion with my lips and eyebrows, "She?" Joe looked at me, making the motion with *his* lips and eyebrows, "She?" My sister catching him in the act, he drew the back of his hand across his nose with his usual conciliatory air on such occasions, and looked at her.

"Well?" said my sister, in her snappish way. "What are you staring at? Is the house afire?"

"—Which some individual," Joe politely hinted, "mentioned she."

"And she is a she, I suppose?" said my sister. "Unless you call Miss Havisham a he. And I doubt if even you'll go so far as that."

"Miss Havisham up town?" said Joe.

"Is there any Miss Havisham down town?" returned my sister. "She wants this boy to go and play there. And of course he's going. And he had better play there," said my sister, "or I'll work him."

I had heard of Miss Havisham up town as an immensely rich and grim lady who lived in a large and dismal house barricaded against robbers, and who led a life of seclusion.

"Well, to be sure!" said Joe, astounded. "I wonder how she comes to know Pip!"

"Noodle!" cried my sister. "Who said she knew him?"

"—Which some individual," Joe again politely hinted, "mentioned that she wanted him to go and play there."

"And couldn't she ask Uncle Pumblechook if he knew of a boy to go and play there? Isn't it just barely possible that Uncle Pumblechook may be a tenant of hers, and that he may sometimes go there to pay his rent? And couldn't she then ask Uncle Pumblechook if he knew of a boy to go and play there? And couldn't Uncle Pumblechook, being always considerate and thoughtful for us—though you may not think it, Joseph," in a tone of the deepest reproach, "then mention this boy that I have for ever been a willing slave to?"

"Uncle Pumblechook, being sensible that for anything we can tell, this boy's fortune may be made by his going to Miss Havisham's, has offered to take him into town tonight in his own chaise-cart, and to keep him tonight, and to take him with his own hands to Miss Havisham's tomorrow morning. And Lor-a-mussy me!" cried my sister, casting off her bonnet in sudden desperation, "here I stand talking to mere mooncalfs, with Uncle Pumblechook waiting, and the mare catching cold at the door, and the boy grimed with crock and dirt from the hair of his head to the sole of his foot!"

With that, she pounced on me, like an eagle on a lamb, and my face was squeezed into wooden bowls in sinks, and my head was put under taps of water-butts, and I was soaped, and kneaded, and toweled, and thumped, and harrowed, and rasped, until I really was quite beside myself.

When my ablutions were completed, I was put into clean linen of the stiffest character, like a young penitent into sackcloth, and was trussed up in my tightest and fearfullest suit. I was then delivered over to Mr. Pumblechook, who formally received me as if he were the sheriff, and who let off upon me the speech that I knew he had been dying to make all along: "Boy, be for ever grateful to all friends, but especially unto them which brought you up by hand!"

"Good-bye, Joe!"

"God bless you, Pip, old chap!"

I had never parted from him before, and what with my feelings and what with soapsuds, I could at first see no stars from the chaise-cart. But they twinkled out one by one, without throwing any light on the questions why on earth I was going to play at Miss Havisham's, and what on earth I was expected to play at.

Chapter 8

Mr. Pumblechook's premises in the High Street of the market town were of a peppercorny and farinaceous character, as the premises of a corn chandler and seedsman should be.

Mr. Pumblechook and I breakfasted at eight o'clock in the parlor behind his shop. I considered Mr. Pumblechook wretched company. Besides being possessed by my sister's idea that a mortifying and penitential character ought to be imparted to my diet—besides giving me as much crumb as possible in combination with as little butter, and putting such a quantity of warm water into my milk that it would have been more candid to have left the milk out altogether—his conversation consisted of nothing but arithmetic. On my politely bidding him good morning, he said pompously, "Seven times nine, boy?" And how should *I* be able to answer, dodged in that way, in a strange place, on an empty stomach! I was hungry, but before I had swallowed a morsel, he began a running sum that lasted all through the breakfast. "Seven?" "And four?" "And eight?" "And six?" "And two?" "And ten?" And so on.

For such reasons I was very glad when ten o'clock came and we started for Miss Havisham's. Within a quarter of an hour we came to Miss Havisham's house, which was of old brick, and dismal, and had a great many iron bars to it. Some of the windows had been walled up; of those that remained, all the lower were rustily barred. There was a courtyard in front, and that was barred; so, we had to wait, after ringing the bell, until some one should come to open it. While we waited at the gate, I peeped in and saw that at the side of the house there was a large brewery.[1] No brewing was going on in it, and none seemed to have gone on for a long time.

A window was raised, and a clear voice demanded "What name?" To which my conductor replied, "Pumblechook." The voice returned, "Quite right," and the window was shut again, and a young lady came across the courtyard, with keys in her hand.

"This," said Mr. Pumblechook, "is Pip."

"This is Pip, is it?" returned the young lady, who was very pretty and seemed very proud; "come in, Pip."

Mr. Pumblechook was coming in also, when she stopped him with the gate.

"Oh!" she said. "Did you wish to see Miss Havisham?"

"If Miss Havisham wished to see me," returned Mr. Pumblechook, discomfited.

"Ah!" said the girl; "but you see, she don't."

She said it so finally that Mr. Pumblechook, though in a condition of ruffled dignity, could not protest. But he eyed me severely—as if *I* had done anything to him!—and departed with the words reproachfully delivered: "Boy! Let your behavior here be a credit unto them which brought you up by hand!"

My young conductress locked the gate, and we went across the courtyard. It was paved and clean, but grass was growing in every crevice. The brewery buildings had a little lane of communication with it; and the wooden gates of that lane stood open, and all

---

1. brewery (broo′ ər ē) *n.*: Establishment where beer and similar beverages are made.

37 Discussion How do you think Pip feels as he leaves Joe?

38 Discussion What mood does this description call up?

Speaking and Listening You might want to have students volunteer to read aloud portions of Pip's encounter with Miss Havisham and Estella. If you wish, individual students may read the parts of Pip (as the narrator), Pip (when quoted directly), Miss Havisham, and Estella.

39 Discussion What is the irony in the name Satis House?

40 Discussion How does Pip view the girl? How does he view himself in relationship to her?

41 Reading Strategy Have students summarize Pip's impressions of Miss Havisham's room.

42 Discussion What does this passage reveal about Miss Havisham?

Multicultural Focus Point out that Miss Havisham's wedding finery—long white dress with white veil and flowers—is not very different from the kind of wedding dress an American woman might wear today. Ask female students what kind of wedding dresses they might someday wear. Compare their responses to see how many envision a white dress and a veil. Explain that this type of garb is typical of many Western cultures, but that other cultures, especially non-Western cultures, have very different modes of dressing for a wedding.

Have students do research to find out how people dress for weddings in other cultures. Ask them to bring in drawings, photographs, or reproductions of paintings if possible, to share with the class.

the brewery beyond stood open, away to the high enclosing wall; and all was empty and disused.

"What is the name of this house, miss?"

"Its name was Satis; which is Greek, or Latin, or Hebrew, or all three—or all one to me—for enough."

"Enough House!" said I; "that's a curious name, miss."

"Yes," she replied; "but it meant more than it said. It meant, when it was given, that whoever had this house could want nothing else. They must have been easily satisfied in those days, I should think. But don't loiter, boy."

Though she called me "boy" so often, and with a carelessness that was far from complimentary, she was of about my own age. She seemed much older than I, of course, being a girl, and beautiful and self-possessed; and she was as scornful of me as if she had been one-and-twenty, and a queen.

We went into the house by a side door—the great front entrance had two chains across it outside—and the first thing I noticed was that the passages were all dark, and she had left a candle burning there. She took it up, and we went through more passages and up a staircase, and still it was all dark, and only the candle lighted us.

At last we came to the door of a room, and she said, "Go in."

I answered, more in shyness than politeness, "After you, miss."

To this, she returned: "Don't be ridiculous, boy; I am not going in." And scornfully walked away, and—what was worse—took the candle with her.

This was very uncomfortable, and I was half-afraid. However, the only thing to be done being to knock at the door, I knocked, and was told from within to enter. I entered, therefore, and found myself in a pretty large room, well lighted with wax candles. No glimpse of daylight was to be seen in it. It was a dressing room, as I supposed from the furniture, though much of it was of forms and uses then quite unknown to me. But prominent in it was a draped table with a gilded looking glass, and that I made out at first sight to be a fine lady's dressing-table.

Whether I should have made out this object so soon if there had been no fine lady sitting at it, I cannot say. In an arm-chair, with an elbow resting on the table and her head leaning on that hand, sat the strangest lady I have ever seen, or shall ever see.

She was dressed in rich materials—satins, and lace, and silks—all of white. Her shoes were white. And she had a long white veil dependent from her hair, and she had bridal flowers in her hair, but her hair was white. Some bright jewels sparkled on her neck and on her hands, and some other jewels lay sparkling on the table. Dresses less splendid than the dress she wore, and half-packed trunks, were scattered about. She had not quite finished dressing, for she had but one shoe on—the other was on the table near her hand—her veil was but half arranged, her watch and chain were not put on, and some lace for her bosom lay with those trinkets, and with her handkerchief, and gloves, and some flowers, and a prayer book, all confusedly heaped about the looking glass.

I saw that everything within my view which ought to be white, had been white long ago, and had lost its luster, and was faded and yellow. I saw that the bride within the bridal dress had withered like the dress, and like the flowers, and had no brightness left but the brightness of her sunken eyes. I saw that the dress had been put upon the rounded figure of a young woman, and that the figure upon which it now hung loose had shrunk to skin and bone.

"Who is it?" said the lady at the table.

"Pip, ma'am."

"Pip?"

"Mr. Pumblechook's boy, ma'am. Come—to play."

"Come nearer; let me look at you. Come close."

It was when I stood before her, avoiding her eyes, that I took note of the surrounding objects in detail, and saw that her watch had stopped at twenty minutes to nine, and that a clock in the room had stopped at twenty minutes to nine.

"Look at me," said Miss Havisham. "You are not afraid of a woman who has never seen the sun since you were born?"

I regret to state that I was not afraid of telling the enormous lie comprehended in the answer "No."

"Do you know what I touch here?" she said, laying her hands, one upon the other, on her left side.

"Yes, ma'am."

"What do I touch?"

"Your heart."

"Broken!"

She uttered the word with an eager look, and with strong emphasis, and with a weird smile that had a kind of boast in it. Afterwards, she kept her hands there for a little while, and slowly took them away as if they were heavy.

"I am tired," said Miss Havisham. "I want diversion, and I have done with men and women. Play."

I think it will be conceded by my most disputatious reader that she could hardly have directed an unfortunate boy to do anything in the wide world more difficult to be done under the circumstances.

"I sometimes have sick fancies," she went on, "and I have a sick fancy that I want to see some play. There, there!" with an impatient movement of the fingers of her right hand; "play, play, play!"

I had a desperate idea of starting round the room in the assumed character of Mr. Pumblechook's chaise-cart. But I felt myself so unequal to the performance that I gave it up, and stood looking at Miss Havisham in what I suppose she took for a dogged manner, inasmuch as she said, when we had taken a good look at each other: "Are you sullen and obstinate?"

"No, ma'am, I am very sorry for you, and very sorry I can't play just now. If you complain of me I shall get into trouble with my sister, so I would do it if I could; but it's so new here, and so strange, and so fine—and melancholy—" I stopped, fearing I might say too much, or had already said it, and we took another look at each other.

"So new to him," she muttered, "so old to me; so strange to him, so familiar to me; so melancholy to both of us! Call Estella."

I thought she was still talking to herself, and kept quiet.

"Call Estella," she repeated, flashing a look at me. "You can do that. Call Estella. At the door."

To stand in the dark in a mysterious passage of an unknown house, bawling Estella to a scornful young lady neither visible nor responsive, and feeling it a dreadful liberty so to roar out her name, was almost as bad as playing to order. But she answered at last, and her light came along the dark passage like a star.

Miss Havisham beckoned her to come close, and took up a jewel from the table, and tried its effect against her pretty brown hair. "Your own, one day, my dear, and you will use it well. Let me see you play cards with this boy."

"With this boy! Why, he is a common laboring boy!"

I thought I overheard Miss Havisham answer—only it seemed so unlikely, "Well? You can break his heart."

43

43 Critical Thinking and Reading What does Estella say about Pip that makes her opinion of him very clear? What does Miss Havisham's response mean? Is there a relationship between her response and her disclosure about her own broken heart?

Humanities Note

Fine art, *Miss Cicely Alexander: Harmony in Grey and Green*, 1872–1874, by James McNeill Whistler. James McNeill Whistler (1834–1903) was an American artist who lived and worked in England, where he became known for his distinctive landscapes and portraits.

This particular portrait was commissioned by a wealthy British patron. The simplicity of form and subtle blending of color suggest the influence of Japanese prints. Whistler often included musical references in his titles—like *Harmony in Grey and Green*—to stress the lyricism of his work.

You might want to use the following questions in a class discussion:

1. What is the personality and social status of this young girl?
2. Which details in the picture reveal this information?
3. Do you think the subject of this portrait resembles Estella? Explain.

MISS CICELY ALEXANDER:
HARMONY IN GREY AND GREEN
James McNeill Whistler
The Tate Gallery, London

"What do you play, boy?" asked Estella of myself, with the greatest disdain.

"Nothing but Beggar my Neighbor, miss."

"Beggar him," said Miss Havisham to Estella. So we sat down to cards.

It was then I began to understand that everything in the room had stopped, like the watch and the clock, a long time ago. As Estella dealt the cards, I glanced at the dressing table again, and saw that the shoe upon it, once white, now yellow, had never been worn. I glanced down at the foot from which the shoe was absent, and saw that the silk stocking on it, once white, now yellow, had been trodden ragged.

"He calls the knaves, jacks, this boy!" said Estella with disdain, before our first game was out. "And what coarse hands he has! And what thick boots!"

I never thought of being ashamed of my hands before; but I began to consider them a very indifferent pair. Her contempt for me was so strong that it became infectious, and I caught it.

She won the game, and I dealt. I misdealt, as was only natural, when I knew she was lying in wait for me to do wrong; and she denounced me for a stupid, clumsy laboring boy.

"You say nothing of her," remarked Miss Havisham to me, as she looked on. "She says many hard things of you, yet you say nothing of her. What do you think of her?"

"I don't like to say," I stammered.

"Tell me in my ear," said Miss Havisham, bending down.

"I think she is very proud," I replied, in a whisper.

"Anything else?"

"I think she is very pretty."

"Anything else?"

"I think she is very insulting." (She was looking at me then with a look of supreme aversion.)

"Anything else?"

"I think I should like to go home."

"And never see her again, though she is so pretty?"

"I am not sure that I shouldn't like to see her again, but I should like to go home now."

"You shall go soon," said Miss Havisham aloud. "Play the game out."

I played the game to an end with Estella, and she beggared me. She threw the cards down on the table when she had won them all, as if she despised them for having been won of me.

"When shall I have you here again?" said Miss Havisham. "Let me think."

I was beginning to remind her that today was Wednesday when she checked me with her former impatient movement of the fingers of her right hand.

"There, there! I know nothing of the days of the week; I know nothing of the weeks of the year. Come again after six days. You hear?"

"Yes, ma'am."

"Estella, take him down. Let him have something to eat, and let him roam and look about him while he eats. Go, Pip."

I followed the candle down, as I had followed the candle up, and she stood it in the place where we had found it. Until she opened the side entrance, I had fancied, without thinking about it, that it must necessarily be nighttime. The rush of daylight quite confounded me, and made me feel as if I had been in the candlelight of the strange room many hours.

"You are to wait here, you boy," said Estella, and disappeared and closed the door.

I took the opportunity of being alone in the courtyard to look at my coarse hands and my common boots. My opinion of those accessories was not favorable. They had never troubled me before, but they troubled me now. I determined to ask Joe why he had ever taught me to call those picture cards

Great Expectations 749

44 Discussion How does the name of the card game take on extra meaning?

45 Discussion What is it about Estella that would make Pip want to see her again, although she has scorned and insulted him?

46 Discussion How has this visit affected Pip's opinion of himself?

47

47 Reading Strategy Have students predict how Pip's life will change as a result of this visit.

Reader's Response Pip was threatened by the convict and forced to steal food for him. Do you think this justifies Pip's actions and frees him from blame? Explain.

Thematic Response Pip had many conflicts in this part of the novel. Which conflict do you think will have the greatest effect on his life?

---

jacks which ought to be called knaves. I wished Joe had been rather more genteelly brought up, and then I should have been so, too.

She came back with some bread and meat and a little mug of beer. She put the mug down on the stones of the yard, and gave me the bread and meat without looking at me, as insolently as if I were a dog in disgrace. I was so humiliated, hurt, spurned, offended, angry, sorry—I cannot hit upon the right name for the smart—God knows what its name was—that tears started to my eyes. The moment they sprang there, the girl looked at me with a quick delight in having been the cause of them. This gave me power to keep them back and to look at her: so, she gave a contemptuous toss—but with a sense, I thought, of having made too sure that I was so wounded—and left me.

But, when she was gone, I looked about me for a place to hide my face in, and got behind one of the gates in the brewery lane, and leaned my sleeve against the wall there, and leaned my forehead on it and cried. As I cried, I kicked the wall, and took a hard twist at my hair.

I got rid of my injured feelings for the time by kicking them into the brewery wall, and twisting them out of my hair, and then I smoothed my face with my sleeve, and

came from behind the gate. The bread and meat were acceptable, and I was soon in spirits to look about me.

Then I saw Estella approaching with the keys, to let me out. She gave me a triumphant glance in passing me, as if she rejoiced that my hands were so coarse and my boots were so thick, and she opened the gate, and stood holding it. I was passing out without looking at her, when she touched me with a taunting hand.

"Why don't you cry?"

"Because I don't want to."

"You do," said she. "You have been crying till you were half-blind, and you are near crying again now."

She laughed contemptuously, pushed me out, and locked the gate upon me. I went straight to Mr. Pumblechook's, and was immensely relieved to find him not at home. So, leaving word with the shopman on what day I was wanted at Miss Havisham's again, I set off on the four-mile walk to our forge, pondering, as I went along, on all I had seen, and deeply revolving that I was a common laboring boy; that my hands were coarse; that my boots were thick; that I had fallen into a despicable habit of calling knaves jacks; that I was much more ignorant than I had considered myself last night; and generally that I was in a low-lived bad way.

47

![R]ESPONDING TO THE SELECTION

Your Response

1. How would you respond if you had an encounter like Pip's in the cemetery?
2. What do you think of Pip's opinion of himself at the end of Chapter 8?

Recalling

3. In what two ways does Pip help the convict?
4. Describe Miss Havisham and her house.

Interpreting

5. Explain why the convict claims to have taken the items that Pip actually took.

Closure and Extension

ANSWERS TO RESPONDING TO THE SELECTION
Your Response

1. Encourage students to relate Pip's encounter with the convict to frightening experiences in their own lives. Ask students if they responded in real life as Pip did in the novel.

2. Discuss self-esteem with the students. Ask if Pip was overly impressed with Estella. Suggest that Estella's need to make Pip feel bad about himself was a sign that she herself had poor self-esteem.

Recalling

3. Pip steals food and drink from Mrs. Joe's larder and a file from the forge, and he brings them to the convict.
4. Miss Havisham is an old lady dressed in a yellowed bridal

gown, with faded flowers in her hair, a tattered veil, and bright jewels on her neck and fingers. Her bright eyes shine from sunken sockets. She is the strangest person Pip has ever seen.

The house is a decaying mansion of brick behind a high wall, with many barred or walled-up windows. There is a barred courtyard in front and an abandoned brewery at the side. The front doors are heavily chained.

Interpreting

5. Suggested Response: Since Pip probably saved the convict's life, the convict wants to protect him from the punishment that will follow the knowledge of the theft.
6. Suggested Response: Pip has a warm relationship with Joe; however, they are more like equals than adult and child. Both are under the thumb of Mrs. Joe, Pip's sister and Joe's wife. She is a hot-tempered and domineering person.

6. Explain the relationship between Pip and Joe. Explain the relationship that they have with Pip's sister.
7. How would you characterize Estella's behavior toward Pip? What does her behavior indicate about her?

Applying

8. Based on the conversation between Joe and Pip in Chapter 7, what conclusions do you draw about education in England at the time of this novel?
9. Pip shows great determination and a growing ambition to change. How does determination play a role in change? Give examples.

ANALYZING LITERATURE

Understanding Point of View

Point of view is the angle or perspective from which a story is told. *Great Expectations* is told in the **first person.** The narrator is Pip, an orphan being raised by his sister and her husband in a small, nineteenth-century English town. However, Pip is not telling the events at the time they happen. He tells them as an adult looking back on his past. From his adult perspective, he is able to have insight into his childhood actions.

1. Why is the meeting with the convict more effective in a first-person narrative than it would be if it were told by the author?
2. How does Pip as narrator get the reader's sympathy? Would you feel as sympathetic to him if another character were telling the story? Explain your answer.
3. Give an example in which Pip judges his own behavior.

4. Explain how the novel would be different if Pip were writing about events at the time they occurred.

THINKING AND WRITING

Writing From Another Point of View

We have Pip's point of view on his meeting with Estella. Put yourself in the place of Estella meeting Pip. What does she think of him? How does she feel playing cards with him? Rewrite the incident from Estella's point of view. When you have written a draft, revise it, making sure you have used "I" as Estella. Add details that would be known only by Estella.

LEARNING OPTIONS

1. **Writing.** Pip has had two important things happen to him so far. Imagine that you are Pip's age and that you keep a journal. Describe how you feel about these two new experiences. In order to re-create the way Pip writes, you may wish to consult the example of his writing in Chapter 7.
2. **Art.** On page 746 Dickens provides a very detailed description of Miss Havisham and her dressing room. Use this information to produce the scene visually. Draw it, paint it, or create a diorama. Display your artwork for your classmates.
3. **Art.** Charles Dickens is known for his complex plots with many subplots. Devise a way to map out the main plot and the subplots as you read the novel. It might take the form of a flow chart, for example, or a tree diagram.

THINKING AND WRITING

Writing Transparency Students often find it helpful to see a model of their writing assignment. Before students write, you may wish to show them Model 2: Autobiography in **Transparencies for Writing.**

Alternative Assessment *Protocol:* Have students assess their own work by responding to the questions that follow:

What do you say Estella thought of Pip?

How does your narrative reveal Estella's personality?

Which details do you include in your version of the scene, and which do you leave out because Estella would not know them?

Have students use information from their protocols when they revise their work.

LEARNING OPTIONS

1. This activity will appeal to visual learners. You might wish to extend this activity by having students write a version of the journal entries using standard spelling and punctuation.
2. This activity is particularly appropriate for visual learners, but students with other learning styles will find it interesting. You might wish to give students a choice of scenes to illustrate.
3. Analytic learners will find this activity interesting. You might wish to vary the activity by having students make predictions on their flow charts or diagrams before reading each section of the novel.

7. Suggested Response: Estella is proud and haughty. She assumes she is better than Pip and treats him cruelly.

Applying

8. Answers will differ; however, many students will probably respond that village schools were private establishments and therefore not available to every child. Books were scarce, primary-grade children wrote on slates instead of paper, and reading and basic

arithmetic were taught. Children from wealthy backgrounds were probably privately tutored.
9. Answers will differ, but most students will realize that change is difficult and determination is required to overcome obstacles.

ANSWERS TO ANALYZING LITERATURE

1. Suggested Response: The first-person narrative allows us to feel more powerfully the fear that Pip experiences.

2. Suggested Response: Pip gets our sympathy because he is bright, perceptive, good-hearted, and oppressed. We would probably not feel quite as sympathetic toward him if the story were narrated by another character because we would not know as much about Pip's thoughts and feelings.
3. Suggested Response: Pip feels guilty about stealing Joe's file.
4. Suggested Response: If Pip were writing as a child, he would not be able to explain his conflicts and feelings as well.

Preparation

Literary Focus You might want to tell students that Dickens created a whole world of memorable characters in his novels. His major characters, like Pip, are convincing, complex, and round. But Dickens also created many flat characters—eccentric, fascinating, near-caricatures who are essential to the plot.

Prereading Focus The purpose of the brief writing exercise is to focus students' attention on the things Pip does to impress Estella as he awakens to his yearning to rise above his station in life. Ask students to think of someone who triggered their desire to be something more than they are. Suggest that the person might have been a relative, a new acquaintance, or even a teacher. Encourage them to describe the changes that were effected because of this person.

Vocabulary Have less advanced students identify the prefixes and suffixes of the polysyllabic words. Then have them find additional words in these chapters with these same prefixes and suffixes.

Electronic Handbook You might suggest that students use the Language Master 6000 to hear the pronunciations of *felicitous* and *superciliously.*

GUIDE FOR READING

Great Expectations, Chapters 9–15

Characterization

Characterization refers to the methods by which writers reveal the personalities of their fictional characters. When writers use **direct characterization,** they openly tell you about the traits of their characters. **Indirect characterization** is the technique of revealing characters' personalities through their own words or actions or what others say about them. In *Great Expectations,* Dickens cannot tell you directly about the characters because Pip is narrating the story. Although Pip is sensitive and intelligent, his information is limited, and he himself changes over the course of the book. Yet you learn a great deal about Pip because you know how he responds and what he thinks in given situations.

In novels as well as short stories, **round characters** are those who have many traits and are capable of growth. Pip is a good example of a round character. Dickens also uses **flat characters,** with only one or two traits, to contrast with the round ones. Mr. Pumblechook, for example, is little more than a bundle of bullying self-importance.

Focus

As the story proceeds, Pip works hard on improving himself to impress Estella. Have you ever tried to improve or change yourself to impress someone? Write a few sentences about your experience. What were some of the things you did? Were your efforts worth it in the end? Now continue reading and see how Pip's relationship with Miss Havisham and Estella changes as he grows.

Vocabulary

Knowing the following words will help you as you read Chapters 9–15 of *Great Expectations.*

felicitous (fə lis′ ə təs) *adj.*: Suitable to the occasion (p. 755)

superciliously (soo′ pər sil′ ē əs lē) *adv.*: Haughtily (p. 757)

plaintively (plān′ tiv lē) *adv.*: Sadly (p. 761)

condescend (kän′ də send′) *v.*: Lower oneself to another's level (p. 762)

alluded (ə lood′ id) *v.*: Referred to indirectly (p. 765)

unscrupulous (un skroo′ yə ləs) *adj.*: Without principles (p. 771)

Objectives

1 To understand characterization
2 To draw conclusions about characters
3 To write about art

Support Material

Teaching Portfolio
Teacher Backup, p. 893
Grammar in Action Worksheets, *Writing Dialogue,* p. 896; *Appreciating Details of Setting that Suggest Time,* p. 898
Usage and Mechanics Worksheet, p. 900
Vocabulary Check, p. 901
Analyzing Literature Worksheet, *Understanding Characterization,* p. 902
Language Worksheet, *Understanding Context Clues,* p. 903
Selection Test, p. 904

Library of Video Classics
The Changing World of Charles Dickens, Great Expectations

Literature Videodisc
Scenes From Great Expectations

Prentice Hall Literature Writing Studio

Chapter 9

When I reached home, my sister was very curious to know all about Miss Havisham's, and asked a number of questions. And I soon found myself getting heavily bumped from behind in the nape of the neck and the small of the back, and having my face ignominiously shoved against the kitchen wall, because I did not answer those questions at sufficient length.

I felt convinced that if I described Miss Havisham's as my eyes had seen it, I should not be understood. Not only that, but I felt convinced that Miss Havisham, too, would not be understood; and although she was perfectly incomprehensible to me, I entertained an impression that there would be something coarse and treacherous in my dragging her as she really was (to say nothing of Miss Estella) before the contemplation of Mrs. Joe. Consequently, I said as little as I could, and had my face shoved against the kitchen wall.

The worst of it was that that bullying old Pumblechook, preyed upon by a devouring curiosity to be informed of all I had seen and heard, came gaping over in his chaise-cart at tea-time to have the details divulged to him. "Well, boy," Uncle Pumblechook began, "how did you get on up town?"

I answered, "Pretty well, sir," and my sister shook her fist at me.

"Pretty well?" Mr. Pumblechook repeated. "Pretty well is no answer. Tell us what you mean by pretty well, boy."

"I mean pretty well."

My sister with an exclamation of impatience was going to fly at me—I had no shadow of defense, for Joe was busy in the forge—when Mr. Pumblechook interposed with "No! Don't lose your temper. Leave this lad to me, ma'am; leave this lad to me." Mr. Pumblechook then turned me towards him as if he were going to cut my hair, and said:

"Boy! What like is Miss Havisham?"

"Very tall and dark," I told him.

"Is she, Uncle?" asked my sister.

Mr. Pumblechook winked assent; from which I at once inferred that he had never seen Miss Havisham, for she was nothing of the kind.

"Good!" said Mr. Pumblechook conceitedly.

"I am sure, Uncle," returned Mrs. Joe, "I wish you had him always: you know so well how to deal with him."

"Now, boy! What was she a-doing of, when you went in today?" asked Mr. Pumblechook.

"She was sitting," I answered, "in a black velvet coach."

Mr. Pumblechook and Mrs. Joe stared at one another—as they well might—and both repeated, "In a black velvet coach?"

"Was anybody else there?" asked Mr. Pumblechook.

"Four dogs," said I.

"Large or small?"

"Immense," said I. "And they fought for veal-cutlets out of a silver basket."

Mr. Pumblechook and Mrs. Joe stared at one another again, in utter amazement. I was perfectly frantic—a reckless witness under the torture—and would have told them anything.

"Where *was* this coach, in the name of gracious?" asked my sister.

"In Miss Havisham's room." They stared again. "But there weren't any horses to it." I added this saving clause, in the moment of rejecting four richly caparisoned coursers,[1] which I had had wild thoughts of harnessing.

"Did you ever see her in it, Uncle?" asked Mrs. Joe.

---

1. **caparisoned** (kə par′ ə s′nd) **coursers:** Horses with ornamented coverings.

Great Expectations 753

Videocassette You might wish to present the portions of the film dramatization of *Great Expectations* that show the importance of common sense, such as Joe Gargery's advice to Pip or the scene in which Pip uses a common-sense method of fighting the pale young boy.

Alternative Assessment To promote active reading, have students continue their reader's response journals as they read chapters 9 through 15. Encourage students to respond to Pip's growing discontent.

Their observations will enable you to assess their understanding of the issues in the story.

4 Critical Thinking and Reading
Why does Pip feel penitent only
with regard to Joe?

"How could I," he returned, forced to the admission, "when I never see her in my life?"

"Goodness, Uncle! And yet you have spoken to her?"

"Why, don't you know," said Mr. Pumblechook testily, "that when I have been there, I have been took up to the outside of her door, and the door has stood ajar, and she has spoken to me that way. Don't say you don't know *that*, mum. Howsever, the boy went there to play. What did you play at, boy?"

"We played with flags," I said.

"Flags!" echoed my sister.

"Yes," said I. "Estella waved a blue flag, and I waved a red one, and Miss Havisham waved one sprinkled all over with little gold stars, out at the coach-window. And then we all waved our swords and hurrahed."

"Swords!" repeated my sister. "Where did you get swords from?"

"Out of the cupboard," said I. "And I saw pistols in it—and jam—and pills. And there was no daylight in the room, but it was all lighted up with candles."

"That's true, mum," said Mr. Pumblechook, with a grave nod. "That's the state of the case, for that much I've seen myself." When Joe came in, they were occupied in discussing the marvels I had already presented for their consideration. More for the relief of her own mind than for the gratification of his, my sister related my pretended experiences to Joe.

4 Now when I saw Joe open his blue eyes and roll them all round the kitchen in helpless amazement, I was overtaken by penitence; but only as regarded him—not in the least as regarded the other two. Towards Joe, and Joe only, I considered myself a young monster, while they sat debating what results would come to me from Miss Havisham's acquaintance and favor.

After Mr. Pumblechook had driven off,

and when my sister was washing up, I stole into the forge to Joe, and remained by him until he had done for the night. Then I said, "Before the fire goes out, Joe, I should like to tell you something."

"Should you, Pip?" said Joe, drawing his shoeing-stool near the forge. "Then tell us. What is it, Pip?"

"Joe," said I, taking hold of his rolled-up shirt-sleeve, and twisting it between my finger and thumb, "you remember all that about Miss Havisham's?"

"Remember?" said Joe. "I believe you! Wonderful!"

"It's a terrible thing, Joe; it ain't true."

"What are you telling of, Pip?" cried Joe, falling back in the greatest amazement. "You don't mean to say it's—"

"Yes, I do; it's lies, Joe."

As I fixed my eyes hopelessly on Joe, Joe contemplated me in dismay. "Pip, old chap! This won't do, old fellow! I say! Where do you expect to go to?"

"It's terrible, Joe; ain't it?"

"Terrible?" cried Joe. "Awful! What possessed you?"

"I don't know what possessed me, Joe," I replied, letting his shirt-sleeve go, and sitting down in the ashes at his feet, hanging my head; "but I wish you hadn't taught me to call knaves at cards jacks; and I wish my boots weren't so thick nor my hands so coarse."

And then I told Joe that I felt very miserable, and that I hadn't been able to explain myself to Mrs. Joe and Pumblechook, who were so rude to me, and that there had been a beautiful young lady at Miss Havisham's who was dreadfully proud, and that she had said I was common, and that I knew I was common, and that I wished I was not common, and that the lies had come of it somehow, though I didn't know how.

"There's one thing you may be sure of,

Pip," said Joe, after some rumination, "namely, that lies is lies. Howsever they come, they didn't ought to come. Don't you tell no more of 'em, Pip. *That* ain't the way to get out of being common, old chap. And as to being common, I don't make it out at all clear. You are oncommon in some things. You're oncommon small. Likewise you're a oncommon scholar."

"No, I am ignorant and backward, Joe."

"Why, see what a letter you wrote last night! Wrote in print even! I've seen letters—ah! and from gentlefolks!—that I'll swear weren't wrote in print," said Joe.

"I have learnt next to nothing, Joe. You think much of me. It's only that."

"Well, Pip," said Joe, "be it so, be it son't, you must be a common scholar afore you can be a oncommon one, I should hope!"

There was some hope in this piece of wisdom, and it rather encouraged me.

"If you can't get to be oncommon through going straight," pursued Joe, "you'll never get to do it through going crooked. So don't tell no more on 'em, Pip, and live well and die happy."

"You are not angry with me, Joe?"

"No, old chap. But bearing in mind that them were which I meantersay of a stunning and outdacious sort—alluding to them which bordered on weal-cutlets and dog-fighting—a sincere well-wisher would advise, Pip, their being dropped into your meditations, when you go upstairs to bed. That's all, old chap, and don't never do it no more."

When I got up to my little room and said my prayers, I did not forget Joe's recommendation, and yet my young mind was in that disturbed and unthankful state that I thought long after I laid me down, how common Estella would consider Joe, a mere blacksmith: how thick his boots, and how coarse his hands.

Chapter 10

The felicitous idea occurred to me a morning or two later when I woke that the best step I could take towards making myself uncommon was to get out of Biddy everything she knew. In pursuance of this luminous conception, I mentioned to Biddy when I went to Mr. Wopsle's great-aunt's at night that I had a particular reason for wishing to get on in life, and that I should feel very much obliged to her if she would impart all her learning to me. Biddy, who was the most obliging of girls, immediately said she would, and indeed began to carry out her promise within five minutes.

Biddy entered on our special agreement by imparting some information from her little catalogue of prices under the head of moist sugar, and lending me, to copy at home, a large old English D which she had imitated from the heading of some newspaper, and which I supposed, until she told me what it was, to be a design for a buckle.

Of course there was a public house[1] in the village, and of course Joe liked sometimes to smoke his pipe there. I had received strict orders from my sister to call for him at the Three Jolly Bargemen that evening, on my way from school, and bring him home at my peril. To the Three Jolly Bargemen, therefore, I directed my steps.

I wished the landlord good evening and passed into the common room at the end of the passage, where there was a bright large kitchen fire, and where Joe was smoking his pipe in company with Mr. Wopsle and a stranger. Joe greeted me as usual with "Halloa, Pip, old chap!" and the moment he said that, the stranger turned his head and looked at me.

He was a secret-looking man whom I had

---

1. **public house:** Bar or inn.

5 **Literary Focus** What new aspects of Joe's character do these statements reveal?

6 **Literary Focus** Explain the inner conflict that Pip experiences.

7 **Discussion** What is Pip's reason for wanting to "get on"?

Great Expectations 755

8 Critical Thinking and Reading
What conclusions do you draw
from the odd behavior of the
stranger?

never seen before. His head was all on one
side, and one of his eyes was half-shut up, as
if he were taking aim at something with an
invisible gun. He had a pipe in his mouth,
and he took it out, and, after slowly blowing
all his smoke away and looking hard at me
all the time, nodded. So, I nodded, and then
he nodded again, and made room on the settle[2] beside him that I might sit down there.

But, as I was used to sit beside Joe
whenever I entered that place of resort, I said
"No, thank you, sir," and fell into the space
Joe made for me on the opposite settle. The
strange man, after glancing at Joe, and seeing that his attention was otherwise engaged, nodded to me again when I had taken
my seat, and then rubbed his leg—in a very
odd way, as it struck me.

"You was saying," said the strange man,
turning to Joe, "that you was a blacksmith."

"Yes. I said it, you know," said Joe.

8 | The stranger, with a comfortable kind of
grunt over his pipe, put his legs up on the
settle that he had to himself. He wore a
flapping broad-brimmed traveler's hat, and
under it a handkerchief tied over his head in
the manner of a cap, so that he showed no
hair. As he looked at the fire, I thought I saw
a cunning expression, followed by a half-
laugh, come into his face.

"I am not acquainted with this country,
gentlemen, but it seems a solitary country
towards the river."

"Most marshes is solitary," said Joe.

"No doubt, no doubt. Do you find any
gypsies, now, or tramps, or vagrants of any
sort, out there?"

"No," said Joe; "none but a runaway convict now and then. And we don't find *them*,
easy. Eh, Mr. Wopsle?"

Mr. Wopsle, with a majestic remem-

brance of old discomfiture, assented, but not
warmly.

"Seems you have been out after such?"
asked the stranger.

"Once," returned Joe. "Not that we
wanted to take them, you understand; we
went out as lookers on; me and Mr. Wopsle,
and Pip. Didn't us, Pip?"

"Yes, Joe."

The stranger looked at me again—still
cocking his eye, as if he were expressly taking aim at me with his invisible gun—and
said, "He's a likely young parcel of bones
that. What is it you call him?"

"Pip," said Joe.

"Christened Pip?"

"No, not christened Pip."

"Surname Pip?"

"No," said Joe; "It's a kind of family
name what he gave himself when an infant,
and is called by."

"Son of yours?"

"Well," said Joe, "well, no. No, he ain't."

"Nevvy?"[3] said the strange man.

"Well," said Joe, "he is not—no, not to
deceive you, he is *not* —my nevvy."

"What the blue blazes is he?" asked the
stranger.

Mr. Wopsle struck in upon that—and ex-
pounded the ties between me and Joe. Having his hand in, Mr. Wopsle finished off with
a most terrifically snarling passage from
Richard the Third,[4] and seemed to think he
had done quite enough to account for it
when he added, "as the poet says."

All this while, the strange man looked at
nobody but me, and looked at me as if he
were determined to have a shot at me at last,
and bring me down. But he said nothing after offering his blue blazes observation, until
the glasses of rum-and-water were brought:

---

2. settle (set´ 'l) *n*.: Bench.

3. nevvy: Nephew.
4. *Richard the Third*: Play by William Shakespeare.

and then he made his shot, and a most extraordinary shot it was.

It was not a verbal remark, but a proceeding in dumb show, and was pointedly addressed to me. He stirred his rum-and-water pointedly at me, and he tasted his rum-and-water pointedly at me. And he stirred it and he tasted it: not with a spoon that was brought to him, but *with a file.*

He did this so that nobody but I saw the file; and when he had done it, he wiped the file and put it in a breast-pocket. I knew it to be Joe's file, and I knew that he knew my convict, the moment I saw the instrument. I sat gazing at him, spell-bound. But he now reclined on his settle, taking very little notice of me, and talking principally about turnips.

Joe got up to go, and took me by the hand. "Stop half a moment, Mr. Gargery," said the strange man. "I think I've got a bright new shilling somewhere in my pocket, and if I have, the boy shall have it."

He looked it out from a handful of small change, folded it in some crumpled paper, and gave it to me. "Yours!" said he. "Mind! Your own."

I thanked him, staring at him far beyond the bounds of good manners, and holding tight to Joe. He gave Joe good night, and he gave Mr. Wopsle good night (who went out with us), and he gave me only a look with his aiming eye—no, not a look, for he shut it up, but wonders may be done with an eye by hiding it.

My sister was not in a very bad temper when we presented ourselves in the kitchen, and Joe was encouraged by that unusual circumstance to tell her about the bright shilling. "A bad un, I'll be bound," said Mrs. Joe triumphantly, "or he wouldn't have given it to the boy. Let's look at it."

I took it out of the paper, and it proved to be a good one. "But what's this?" said Mrs. Joe, throwing down the shilling and catching up the paper. "Two one-pound notes?"[5]

Nothing less than two fat sweltering one-pound notes that seemed to have been on terms of the warmest intimacy with all the cattle markets in the county. Joe caught up his hat again, and ran with them to the Jolly Bargmen to restore them to their owner. While he was gone I sat down on my usual stool and looked vacantly at my sister, feeling pretty sure that the man would not be there.

Presently, Joe came back, saying that the man was gone, but that he, Joe, had left word at the Three Jolly Bargemen concerning the notes. Then my sister sealed them up in a piece of paper, and put them under some dried rose-leaves in an ornamental tea-pot on the top of a press in the state parlor. There they remained a nightmare to me many and many a night and day.

Chapter 11

At the appointed time I returned to Miss Havisham's, and my hesitating ring at the gate brought out Estella. She locked it after admitting me, as she had done before, and again preceded me into the dark passage where her candle stood. She took no notice of me until she had the candle in her hand, when she looked over her shoulder, superciliously saying, "You are to come this way to-day," and took me to quite another part of the house.

The passage was a long one, and seemed to pervade the whole square basement of the Manor House. We traversed but one side of the square, however, and at the end of it she stopped and put her candle down and opened a door. Here, the daylight reap-

---

5. two one-pound notes: The pound is the basic unit of British currency, equal to twenty shillings.

9 Discussion Why is Pip sure that the man will not be there? What was the purpose of the man's visit?

10 Discussion Why do you think Pip's ring is "hesitating"?

peared, and I found myself in a small paved courtyard, the opposite side of which was formed by a detached dwelling house that looked as if it had once belonged to the manager or head clerk of the extinct brewery. There was a clock in the outer wall of this house. Like the clock in Miss Havisham's room, and like Miss Havisham's watch, it had stopped at twenty minutes to nine.

We went in at the door, which stood open, and into a gloomy room with a low ceiling, on the ground floor at the back. There was some company in the room, and Estella said to me as she joined it, "You are to go and stand there, boy, till you are wanted." "There" being the window, I crossed to it, and stood "there" in a very uncomfortable state of mind, looking out.

It opened to the ground, and looked into a most miserable corner of the neglected garden, upon a rank ruin of cabbage-stalks, and one box-tree that had been clipped round long ago, like a pudding, and had a new growth at the top of it, out of shape and of a different color, as if that part of the pudding had stuck to the saucepan and got burnt.

I divined that my coming had stopped conversation in the room, and that its other occupants were looking at me. There were three ladies in the room and one gentleman. Before I had been standing at the window five minutes, they somehow conveyed to me that they were all toadies and humbugs[1], but that each of them pretended not to know that the others were toadies and humbugs, because the admission that he or she did know it would have made him or her out to be a toady and humbug.

They all had a listless and dreary air of waiting somebody's pleasure, and the most talkative of the ladies had to speak quite rigidly to suppress a yawn. This lady, whose name was Camilla, very much reminded me of my sister, with the difference that she was older.

"Poor dear soul!" said this lady, with an abruptness of manner quite my sister's. "Nobody's enemy but his own!"

"It would be much more commendable to be somebody else's enemy," said the gentleman; "far more natural."

"Cousin Raymond," observed another lady, "we are to love our neighbor."

"Sarah Pocket," returned Cousin Raymond, "if a man is not his own neighbor, who is?"

"Poor soul!" Camilla presently went on (I knew they had all been looking at me in the meantime), "he is so very strange! Would any one believe that when Tom's wife died, he actually could not be induced to see the importance of the children's having the deepest of trimmings to their mourning? 'Good Lord!' says he, 'Camilla, what can it signify so long as the poor bereaved little things are in black?' So like Matthew! The idea!"

"Good points in him, good points in him," said Cousin Raymond; "Heaven forbid I should deny good points in him; but he never had, and he never will have, any sense of the proprieties."[2]

The ringing of a distant bell, combined with the echoing of some cry or call along the passage by which I had come, interrupted the conversation and caused Estella to say to me, "Now, boy!" On my turning round, they all looked at me with the utmost contempt, and, as I went out, I heard Sarah Pocket say, "Well I am sure! What next!" and Camilla add, with indignation, "Was there ever such a fancy! The i-de-a!"

As we were going with our candle along the dark passage, Estella stopped all of a

---

1. **toadies** (tōd′ ēz) **and humbugs:** Flatterers and deceivers.

2. **proprieties** (prə prī′ ə tēz) *n.:* Proper manners or behavior.

Grammar in Action

Dialogue is direct conversation between two or more people. When writing dialogue for a story or essay, most authors use a new paragraph to indicate a change of speaker. Notice that by beginning new paragraphs as he changes speakers, Dickens makes it easier for the reader to follow the conversation between Estella and Pip:

"Now?" said she. "You little coarse monster, what do you think of me now?"

"I shall not tell you."

"Because you are going to tell upstairs. Is that it?"

"No," said I, "that's not it."

"Why don't you cry again, you little wretch?"

"Because I'll never cry for you again," said I.

In addition to changing paragraphs with speakers, Dickens punctuates each sentence according to the rules governing direct quotations.

THE SCHOOLMASTER'S DAUGHTER
James Sant, R.A.
Royal Academy of Arts, London

Humanities Note

Fine art, *The Schoolmaster's Daughter,* 1871, by James Sant. James Sant (1820–1916) was an English painter known for his genre paintings—depictions of scenes and subjects of everyday life—and portraits. His successful portraits of children won him the praise of Queen Victoria and appointment as "Principal Painter . . . to the Queen."

The Schoolmaster's Daughter is both a genre painting and a portrait. Sant's own son was the model for the boy.

You might want to ask students the following questions:
1. What action is taking place in this picture?
2. What mood does the picture call up?
3. Would you choose this picture to illustrate a scene between Biddy and Pip? Explain.

12 Discussion Why does Estella slap Pip?

sudden, and, facing round, said in her taunting manner, with her face quite close to mine:

"Well?"

"Well, miss," I answered, almost falling over her and checking myself.

She stood looking at me, and of course I stood looking at her.

"Am I pretty?"

"Yes, I think you are very pretty."

"Am I insulting?"

"Not so much so as you were last time," said I.

"Not so much so?"

"No."

She fired when she asked the last question, and she slapped my face with such force as she had, when I answered it.

"Now?" said she. "You little coarse monster, what do you think of me now?"

"I shall not tell you."

"Because you are going to tell upstairs. Is that it?"

"No," said I, "that's not it."

"Why don't you cry again, you little wretch?"

"Because I'll never cry for you again," said I. Which was, I suppose, as false a declaration as ever was made; for I was inwardly crying for her then, and I know what I know of the pain she cost me afterwards.

We went on our way upstairs after this

Great Expectations 759

Student Activity. Read again several other passages of dialogue in this chapter. Then use one you like as a model and write your own conversation between two of Dickens's characters. It should have at least five changes of speaker.

Electronic Handbook You might want students to review quotation marks before completing the Grammar in Action activities. If students have access to the Language Master 6000, have them enter the access symbol " or the access word *quotation* and press the GRAMMAR key to obtain information on the punctuation of dialogue.

13 **Literary Focus** What inferences can you make about the personality of this new character?

14 **Critical Thinking and Reading** What does the state of this room reveal about Miss Havisham?

episode, and as we were going up, we met a gentleman groping his way down.

"Whom have we here?" asked the gentleman, stopping and looking at me.

"A boy," said Estella.

He was a burly man of an exceedingly dark complexion, with an exceedingly large head and a corresponding large hand. He took my chin in his large hand and turned up my face to have a look at me by the light of the candle. He was prematurely bald on the top of his head, and had bushy black eyebrows that wouldn't lie down, but stood up bristling. His eyes were set very deep in his head, and were disagreeably sharp and suspicious. He was nothing to me, and I could have had no foresight then that he ever would be anything to me, but it happened that I had this opportunity of observing him well.

"Boy of the neighborhood? Hey?" said he.

"Yes, sir," said I.

"How do *you* come here?"

"Miss Havisham sent for me, sir," I explained.

13 "Well! Behave yourself. I have a pretty large experience of boys, and you're a bad set of fellows. Now mind!" said he, biting the side of his great forefinger as he frowned at me, "you behave yourself!"

With these words he released me—which I was glad of, for his hand smelt of scented soap—and went his way downstairs. We were soon in Miss Havisham's room, where she and everything else were just as I had left them. Estella left me standing near the door, and I stood there until Miss Havisham cast her eyes upon me from the dressing table.

"So!" she said, without being startled or surprised; "the days have worn away, have they?"

"Yes, ma'am. Today is—"

"There, there, there!" with the impatient movement of her fingers. "I don't want to know. Are you ready to play?"

"I don't think I am, ma'am."

"Not at cards again?" she demanded with a searching look.

"Yes, ma'am; I could do that, if I was wanted."

"Since this house strikes you old and grave, boy," said Miss Havisham impatiently, "and you are unwilling to play, are you willing to work?"

I said I was quite willing.

"Then go into that opposite room," said she, pointing at the door behind me with her withered hand, "and wait there till I come."

I crossed the staircase landing, and entered the room she indicated. From that room too, the daylight was completely excluded, and it had an airless smell that was oppressive. A fire had been lately kindled in the damp old-fashioned grate, and it was more disposed to go out than to burn up, and the reluctant smoke which hung in the room seemed colder than the clearer air—like our own marsh mist. Certain wintry branches of candles on the high chimney piece faintly lighted the chamber, or, it would be more expressive to say, faintly troubled its darkness. It was spacious, and I dare say had once been handsome, but every discernible thing in it was covered with dust and mold, and dropping to pieces. The most prominent object was a long table with a tablecloth spread on it, as if a feast had been in preparation when the house and the clocks all stopped together. An épergne or centerpiece of some kind was in the middle of this cloth; it was so heavily overhung with cobwebs that its form was quite undistinguishable; and, as I looked along the yellow expanse out of which I remember its seeming to grow, like a black fungus, I saw speckled-legged spiders with blotchy bodies running home to it, and running out from

14

it, as if some circumstance of the greatest public importance had just transpired in the spider community.

But, the black beetles took no notice of the agitation, and groped about the hearth in a ponderous elderly way, as if they were shortsighted and hard of hearing, and not on terms with one another.

These crawling things had fascinated my attention, and I was watching them from a distance, when Miss Havisham laid a hand upon my shoulder. In her other hand she had a crutch-headed stick on which she leaned, and she looked like the witch of the place.

"This," said she, pointing to the long table with her stick, "is where I will be laid when I am dead. They shall come and look at me here."

"What do you think that is?" she asked me, again pointing with her stick; "that, where those cobwebs are?"

"I can't guess what it is, ma'am."

"It's a great cake. A bride-cake. Mine!"

She looked all round the room in a glaring manner, and then said, leaning on me while her hand twitched my shoulder, "Come, come, come! Walk me, walk me!"

I made out from this that the work I had to do was to walk Miss Havisham round and round the room. Accordingly, I started at once, and she leaned upon my shoulder, and we went away at a pace that might have been an imitation (founded on my first impulse under that roof) of Mr. Pumblechook's chaise-cart.

After a while she said, "Call Estella!" so I went out on the landing and roared that name as I had done on the previous occasion. When her light appeared, I returned to Miss Havisham, and we started away again round and round the room.

If only Estella had come to be a spectator of our proceedings, I should have felt suffi-ciently discontented; but, as she brought with her the three ladies and the gentleman whom I had seen below, I didn't know what to do.

"Dear Miss Havisham," said Miss Sarah Pocket. "How well you look!"

"I do not," returned Miss Havisham. "I am yellow skin and bone."

Camilla brightened when Miss Pocket met with this rebuff; and she murmured, as she plaintively contemplated Miss Havisham, "Poor dear soul! Certainly not to be expected to look well, poor thing. The idea!" | 15

"And how are *you*?" said Miss Havisham to Camilla. As we were close to Camilla then, I would have stopped as a matter of course, only Miss Havisham wouldn't stop.

"Thank you, Miss Havisham," she returned, "I am as well as can be expected."

"Why, what's the matter with you?" asked Miss Havisham, with exceeding sharpness.

"Nothing worth mentioning," replied Camilla. "I don't wish to make a display of my feelings, but I have habitually thought of you more in the night than I am quite equal to."

"Then don't think of me," retorted Miss Havisham.

"Very easily said!" remarked Camilla, amiably repressing a sob, while a hitch came into her upper lip, and her tears overflowed. "It's a weakness to be so affectionate, but I can't help it."

Miss Havisham and I kept going round and round the room; now brushing against the skirts of the visitors, now giving them the whole length of the dismal chamber.

"There's Matthew!" said Camilla. "Never mixing with any natural ties, never coming here to see how Miss Havisham is!"

When Matthew was mentioned, Miss Havisham stopped me and herself, and stood looking at the speaker.

"Matthew will come and see me at last,"

---

15 **Discussion** Why does Camilla brighten when Miss Havisham rebuffs Sarah Pocket?

16 **Critical Thinking and Reading**
What does Miss Havisham mean when she speaks of "sharper teeth than teeth of mice"?

17 **Discussion** Why does Miss Havisham want Pip to notice Estella's beauty?

said Miss Havisham sternly, "when I am laid on that table. That will be his place—there," striking the table with her stick, "at my head! And yours will be there! And your husband's there! And Sarah Pocket's there! And Georgiana's there! Now you all know where to take your stations when you come to feast upon me.[3] And now go!"

At the mention of each name, she had struck the table with her stick in a new place. She now said, "Walk me, walk me!" and we went on again.

"I suppose there's nothing to be done," exclaimed Camilla, "but comply and depart. It's something to have seen the object of one's love and duty, even for so short a time. I shall think of it with a melancholy satisfaction when I wake up in the night. I wish Matthew could have that comfort, but he sets it at defiance."

While Estella was away lighting them down, Miss Havisham still walked with her hand on my shoulder, but more and more slowly. At last she stopped before the fire, and said, after muttering and looking at it some seconds:

"This is my birthday, Pip."

I was going to wish her many happy returns, when she lifted her stick.

"I don't suffer it to be spoken of. I don't suffer those who were here just now, or any one, to speak of it. They come here on the day, but they dare not refer to it."

Of course *I* made no further effort to refer to it.

"On this day of the year, long before you were born, this heap of decay," stabbing with her crutched stick at the pile of cobwebs on the table, but not touching it, "was brought here. It and I have worn away together. The mice have gnawed at it, and sharper teeth than teeth of mice have gnawed at me."

---

3. feast upon me: Claim your inheritance when I die.

"When the ruin is complete," said she, with a ghastly look, "and when they lay me dead, in my bride's dress on the bride's table—which shall be done, and which will be the finished curse upon him—so much the better if it is done on this day!"

She stood looking at the table as if she stood looking at her own figure lying there. I remained quiet. Estella returned, and she, too, remained quiet. It seemed to me that we continued thus a long time.

At length, not coming out of her distraught state by degrees, but in an instant, Miss Havisham said, "Let me see you two play at cards; why have you not begun?" With that we returned to her room, and sat down as before; I was beggared, as before; and again, as before, Miss Havisham watched us all the time, directed my attention to Estella's beauty, and made me notice it the more by trying her jewels on Estella.

Estella, for her part, likewise treated me as before; except that she did not condescend to speak. When we had played some half-dozen games, a day was appointed for my return, and I was taken down into the yard to be fed in the former dog-like manner. There, too, I was again left to wander about as I liked.

When I had exhausted the garden and a greenhouse with nothing in it but a fallen-down grape-vine and some bottles, I found myself in the dismal corner upon which I had looked out of the window. Never questioning for a moment that the house was now empty, I looked in at another window, and found myself, to my great surprise, exchanging a broad stare with a pale young gentleman with red eyelids and light hair.

This pale young gentleman quickly disappeared, and reappeared beside me.

"Halloa!" said he, "young fellow!"

I said "Halloa!" politely omitting young fellow.

"Who let *you* in?" said he.

JOHN RANDOLPH
Gilbert Stuart
National Gallery of Art, Washington

"Miss Estella."

"Who gave you leave to prowl about?"

"Miss Estella."

"Come and fight," said the pale young gentleman.

What could I do but follow him? I have often asked myself the question since; but what else could I do? His manner was so final, and I was so astonished, that I followed where he led, as if I had been under a spell.

"Stop a minute, though," he said, wheeling round before we had gone many paces. "I ought to give you a reason for fighting, too. There it is!" In a most irritating manner he instantly slapped his hands against one another, daintily flung one of his legs up behind him, pulled my hair, slapped his hands again, dipped his head, and butted it into my stomach.

I hit out at him, and was going to hit out again, when he said, "Aha! Would you?" and began dancing backwards and forwards in a manner quite unparalleled within my limited experience.

"Laws of the game!" said he. Here, he skipped from his left leg on to his right. "Regular rules!" Here, he skipped from his right leg on to his left. "Come to the ground, and go through the preliminaries!" Here, he dodged backwards and forwards, and did all sorts of things while I looked helplessly at him.

Great Expectations 763

Fine art, *John Randolph,* 1805, by Gilbert Stuart. Gilbert Stuart (1755–1828) was the premier portraitist of the new American Republic. Stuart painted nearly one thousand portraits in his lifetime, the most famous of which is the picture of George Washington that is reproduced on the one-dollar bill.

John Randolph (1805) is a charming study of a young man in a casual pose. The background is left sketchy in the manner of Reynolds or Gainsborough, directing the focus of the viewer to the sitter.

You may want to use the following questions to prompt a discussion:

1. To which social class do you think this young man belongs?
2. Describe his personality, as the artist reveals it.
3. Do you think he resembles the "pale young gentleman" whom Pip sees? Why or why not?

18 **Discussion** Does Dickens intend that readers take this character seriously? Explain.

Videodisc To further introduce students to the "pale young gentleman", you might want to show the segment of the *Scenes From Great Expectations* videodisc in which Pip first encounters him. What does the video segment add to their impressions of the "pale young gentleman"?

Frames 18468 to 21618

19 **Critical Thinking and Reading**
What do you think accounts for
this change in Estella's behavior
toward Pip?

20 **Discussion** When else has Pip
shown signs of guilt?

I was secretly afraid of him when I saw him so dexterous, but I followed him, without a word, to a retired nook of the garden. On his asking me if I was satisfied with the ground, and on my replying Yes, he begged my leave to absent himself for a moment, and quickly returned with a bottle of water and a sponge dipped in vinegar. "Available for both," he said, placing these against the wall. And then fell to pulling off, not only his jacket and waistcoat, but his shirt too, in a manner at once light-hearted, business-like, and bloodthirsty.

My heart failed me when I saw him squaring at me with every demonstration of mechanical nicety, and eyeing my anatomy as if he were minutely choosing his bone. I never have been so surprised in my life as I was when I let out the first blow, and saw him lying on his back, looking up at me with a bloody nose and his face exceedingly foreshortened.

But, he was on his feet directly, and after sponging himself with a great show of dexterity, began squaring again. The second greatest surprise I have ever had in my life was seeing him on his back again, looking up at me out of a black eye.

His spirit inspired me with great respect. He seemed to have no strength, and he never once hit me hard, and he was always knocked down; but, he would be up again in a moment sponging himself or drinking out of the water bottle, with the greatest satisfaction in seconding himself according to form, and then came at me with an air and a show that made me believe he really was going to do for me at last. He got heavily bruised, for I am sorry to record that the more I hit him, the harder I hit him; but, he came up again and again and again, until at last he got a bad fall with the back of his head against the wall. Even after that crisis in our affairs, he got up and turned round and round confusedly a few times, not know-

ing where I was; but finally went on his knees to his sponge and threw it up: at the same time panting out, "That means you have won."

He seemed so brave and innocent that, although I had not proposed the contest, I felt but a gloomy satisfaction in my victory. However, I got dressed, darkly wiping my sanguinary face at intervals, and, I said, "Can I help you?" and he said, "No thankee," and I said, "Good afternoon," and *he* said, "Same to you."

When I got into the courtyard, I found Estella waiting with the keys. But she neither asked me where I had been, nor why I had kept her waiting; and there was a bright flush upon her face, as though something had happened to delight her. Instead of going straight to the gate too, she stepped back into the passage, and beckoned me.

"Come here! You may kiss me if you like."

I kissed her cheek as she turned it to me. I think I would have gone through a great deal to kiss her cheek. But I felt that the kiss was given to the coarse common boy as a piece of money might have been, and that it was worth nothing.

What with the birthday visitors, and what with the cards, and what with the fight, my stay had lasted so long that, when I neared home, the light on the spit of sand off the point on the marshes was gleaming against a black night sky, and Joe's furnace was flinging a path of fire across the road.

Chapter 12

My mind grew very uneasy on the subject of the pale young gentleman. The more I thought of the fight, and recalled the pale young gentleman on his back, the more certain it appeared that something would be done to me. I felt that the pale young gentle-

Primary Source

Much has been written about Charles Dickens. He is, in fact, one of the authors most often written about among biographers and literary critics. Much is now known about Dickens, his work, and his life in London. In what is considered the most comprehensive and authoritative biography of Charles Dickens, *Charles Dickens: His Tragedy and Triumph*, Edgar Johnson states this about Dickens's character and his life:

Dickens was himself a Dickens character, bursting with an inordinate and fantastic vitality. The world in which his spirit dwelt was identical with the world of his novels, brilliant in hue, violent in movement, crammed with people all furiously alive and with places as alive as the people. 'The Dickens world' was his everyday world. He found his own intimates as funny as Mr. Micawber [(*David Copperfield*)], Mr. Toots [(*Dombey and Son*)], and Flora Finching [(*Little Dorrit*)], and felt their joys and sorrows as deeply as he did those of the characters in his fictions. His adventures and misadventures were as hilarious or painful as those of Mr. Pickwick or David Copperfield or Pip. And Dickens was not

man's blood was on my head, and that the law would avenge it.

When the day came round for my return to the scene of the deed of violence, my terrors reached their height. However, go to Miss Havisham's I must, and go I did. And behold! nothing came of the late struggle. It was not alluded to in any way, and no pale young gentleman was to be discovered on the premises.

On the broad landing between Miss Havisham's own room and that other room in which the long table was laid out, I saw a garden chair—a light chair on wheels, that you pushed from behind. It had been placed there since my last visit, and I entered, that same day, on a regular occupation of pushing Miss Havisham in this chair (when she was tired of walking with her hand upon my shoulder) round her own room, and across the landing, and round the other room. Over and over and over again, we would make these journeys, and sometimes they would last as long as three hours at a stretch. I insensibly fall into a general mention of these journeys as numerous, because it was at once settled that I should return every alternate day at noon for these purposes, and because I am now going to sum up a period of at least eight or ten months.

As we began to be more used to one another, Miss Havisham talked more to me, and asked me such questions as what had I learnt and what was I going to be? I told her I was going to be apprenticed to Joe, I believed; and I enlarged upon my knowing nothing and wanting to know everything, in the hope that she might offer some help towards that desirable end. But she did not; on the contrary, she seemed to prefer my being ignorant. Neither did she ever give me any money or anything but my daily dinner—nor even stipulate that I should be paid for my services.

Estella was always about, and always let me in and out, but never told me I might kiss her again. Miss Havisham would often ask me in a whisper, or when we were alone, "Does she grow prettier and prettier, Pip?" And when I said Yes (for indeed she did), would seem to enjoy it greedily. Also, when we played at cards, Miss Havisham would look on, with a miserly relish of Estella's moods, whatever they were. And sometimes, when her moods were so many and so contradictory of one another that I was puzzled what to say or do, Miss Havisham would embrace her with lavish fondness, murmuring something in her ear that sounded like, "Break their hearts, my pride and hope, break their hearts and have no mercy!"

Perhaps I might have told Joe about the pale young gentleman, if I had not previously been betrayed into those enormous inventions to which I had confessed. Under the circumstances, I felt that Joe could hardly fail to discern in the pale young gentleman an appropriate passenger to be put into the black velvet coach; therefore, I said nothing of him. I reposed complete confidence in no one but Biddy; but I told poor Biddy everything. Why, it came natural for me to do so, and why Biddy had a deep concern in everything I told her, I did not know then, though I think I know now.

Meanwhile, councils went on in the kitchen at home. Pumblechook used often to come over of a night for the purpose of discussing my prospects. He and my sister would pair off in such nonsensical speculations about Miss Havisham, and about what she would do with me and for me, that I used to want—quite painfully—to burst into spiteful tears. In these discussions, Joe bore no part. But he was often talked at, while they were in progress, by reason of Mrs. Joe's perceiving that he was not favorable to my being taken from the forge.

We went on in this way for a long time, and it seemed likely that we should continue

21 Discussion Do you think Pip is correct in thinking that Miss Havisham would prefer him to remain ignorant? If so, what explains her attitude?

22 Critical Thinking and Reading What can you infer about the relationship between Miss Havisham and Estella?

23 Discussion What do you think provokes Biddy's concern?

one of those frugal authors who save all their good things for their books. In the profusion of his creativity, in his prodigal exuberance, he poured out through his thousands of letters a wealth of psychological observation and comic episode, a depth of feeling and a vividness of language, that might have enriched a dozen more novels. . . .

766

24 Clarification The indenture system was a means of training young men for a trade or occupation. The master, or teacher, would usually be paid a fee and he would specify the number of years it would take to complete the training. The indenture papers were a binding contract.

25 Critical Thinking and Reading Why is Mrs. Joe so upset?

26 Discussion Why do you think Joe refuses to address Miss Havisham directly?

to go on in this way for a long time, when, one day, Miss Havisham stopped short as she and I were walking—she leaning on my shoulder—and said, with some displeasure:

"You are growing tall, Pip!"

She said no more at the time; but she presently stopped and looked at me again; and presently again; and after that, looked frowning and moody. On the next day of my attendance, she stayed me with a movement of her impatient fingers:

"Tell me the name again of that blacksmith of yours."

"Joe Gargery, ma'am."

"Meaning the master you were to be apprenticed to?"

"Yes, Miss Havisham."

24 "You had better be apprenticed at once. Would Gargery come here with you, and bring your indentures,[1] do you think?"

I signified that I had no doubt he would take it as an honor to be asked.

"Then let him come."

"At any particular time, Miss Havisham?"

"There, there! I know nothing about times. Let him come soon, and come alone with you."

25 When I got home at night, and delivered this message for Joe, my sister "went on the rampage" in a more alarming degree than at any previous period.

Chapter 13

It was a trial to my feelings, on the next day but one, to see Joe arraying himself in his Sunday clothes to accompany me to Miss Havisham's. However, as he thought his court suit necessary to the occasion, it was not for me to tell him that he looked far better in his working dress; the rather, because

---

1. indentures (in den' chərz) *n.*: A contract binding an apprentice to a master.

I knew he made himself so dreadfully uncomfortable entirely on my account, and that it was for me he pulled up his shirt-collar so very high behind that it made the hair on the crown of his head stand up like a tuft of feathers.

At breakfast-time, my sister declared her intention of going to town with us, and being left at Uncle Pumblechook's, and called for "when we had done with our fine ladies." The forge was shut up for the day, and Joe inscribed in chalk upon the door (as it was his custom to do on the very rare occasions when he was not at work) the monosyllable HOUT, accompanied by a sketch of an arrow supposed to be flying in the direction he had taken.

When we came to Pumblechook's, my sister bounced in and left us. As it was almost noon, Joe and I held straight on to Miss Havisham's house. Estella opened the gate as usual, and, the moment she appeared, Joe took his hat off and stood weighing it by the brim in both his hands.

Estella took no notice of either of us, but led us the way that I knew so well. I followed next to her, and Joe came last. Estella told me we were both to go in, so I took Joe by the coat cuff and conducted him into Miss Havisham's presence. She was seated at her dressing table, and looked round at us immediately.

"Oh!" said she to Joe. "You are the husband of the sister of this boy?"

I could hardly have imagined dear old Joe looking so unlike himself or so like some extraordinary bird, standing, as he did, speechless, with his tuft of feathers ruffled, and his mouth open as if he wanted a worm.

"You are the husband," repeated Miss Havisham, "of the sister of this boy?"

It was very aggravating; but, throughout the interview, Joe persisted in addressing me instead of Miss Havisham.

2

"Which I meantersay, Pip," Joe now

observed, in a manner that was at once expressive of forcible argumentation, strict confidence, and great politeness, "as I hup and married your sister, and I were at the time what you might call (if you was any ways inclined) a single man."

"Well!" said Miss Havisham. "And you have reared the boy, with the intention of taking him for your apprentice; is that so, Mr. Gargery?"

"You know, Pip," replied Joe, "as you and me were ever friends, and it were looked for'ard to betwixt us, as being calc'lated to lead to larks.[1] Not but what, Pip, if you had ever made objections to the business—such as its being open to black and sut, or suchlike—not but what they would have been attended to, don't you see?"

"Has the boy," said Miss Havisham, "ever made any objection? Does he like the trade?"

"Which it is well beknown to yourself, Pip," returned Joe, "that it were the wish of your own hart."

It was quite in vain for me to endeavor to make him sensible that he ought to speak to Miss Havisham. The more I made faces and gestures to him to do it, the more confidential, argumentative, and polite he persisted in being to me.

"Have you brought his indentures with you?" asked Miss Havisham.

"Well, Pip, you know," replied Joe, as if that were a little unreasonable, "you yourself see me put 'em in my 'at, and therefore you know as they are here." With which he took them out, and gave them, not to Miss Havisham, but to me. I am afraid I was ashamed of the dear good fellow—I *know* I was ashamed of him—when I saw that Estella stood at the back of Miss Havisham's chair, and that her eyes laughed mischievously. I took the indentures out of his hand and gave them to Miss Havisham.

---

1. larks: Fun.

"You expected," said Miss Havisham, as she looked them over, "no premium[2] with the boy?"

"Joe!" I remonstrated; for he made no reply at all. "Why don't you answer—"

"Pip," returned Joe, cutting me short as if he were hurt, "which I meantersay that were not a question requiring a answer betwixt yourself and me, and which you know the answer to be full well No. You know it to be No, Pip, and wherefore should I say it?"

Miss Havisham glanced at him as if she understood what he really was better than I had thought possible, seeing what he was there, and took up a little bag from the table beside her.

"Pip has earned a premium here," she said, "and here it is. There are five-and-twenty guineas[3] in this bag. Give it to your master, Pip."

As if he were absolutely out of his mind with the wonder awakened in him by her strange figure and the strange room, Joe, even at this pass, persisted in addressing me.

"This is very liberal on your part, Pip," said Joe, "and it is as such received and grateful welcome, though never looked for, far nor near nor nowheres. And now, old chap," said Joe, "and now, old chap, may we do our duty! May you and me do our duty, both on us by one and another, and by them which your liberal present—have—conweyed—to be—for the satisfaction of mind—of—them as never—" here Joe showed that he felt he had fallen into frightful difficulties, until he triumphantly rescued himself with the words, "and from myself far be it!"

"Good-bye, Pip!" said Miss Havisham. "Let them out, Estella."

---

2. premium (prē' mē əm) n.: A fee paid by an apprentice to a master.
3. guineas (gin' ēz) n.: Gold coins worth about one pound each.

27 Discussion There have been many indications that Pip's views of "common" people are changing. How do you think Pip's association with Miss Havisham and Estella has influenced his reaction to Joe's awkward behavior?

28 Literary Focus How are Pumblechook and Mrs. Joe similar?

29 Discussion Why is Pip no longer pleased at the thought of becoming a blacksmith?

"Am I to come again, Miss Havisham?" I asked.

"No. Gargery is your master now. Gargery! One word!"

Thus calling him back as I went out of the door, I heard her say to Joe, in a distinct emphatic voice, "The boy has been a good boy here, and that is his reward. Of course, as an honest man, you will expect no other and no more."

In another minute we were outside the gate, and it was locked, and Estella was gone. Joe backed up against a wall, and said to me, "Astonishing!" And there he remained so long, saying "Astonishing" at intervals so often that I began to think his senses were never coming back. At length, he prolonged his remark into "Pip, I assure *you* this is as-TON-ishing!" and so, by degrees, became conversational and able to walk away.

I have reason to think that Joe's intellects were brightened by the encounter they had passed through, and that on our way to Pumblechook's, he invented a subtle and deep design. My reason is to be found in what took place in Mr. Pumblechook's parlor: where, on our presenting ourselves, my sister sat in conference with that detested seedsman.

"Well!" cried my sister, "what did Miss Havisham give young Rantipole[4] here?"

"She giv' him," said Joe, "nothing."

Mrs. Joe was going to break out, but Joe went on.

"What she giv'," said Joe, "she giv' to his friends. 'And by his friends,' were her explanation, 'I mean into the hands of his sister, Mrs. J. Gargery.' "

"And how much have you got?" asked my sister, laughing. Positively, laughing!

"Five-and-twenty pound," said Joe, de-lightedly handing the bag to my sister.

"It's five-and-twenty pound, mum," echoed that basest of swindlers, Pumblechook, rising to shake hands with her; "and it's no more than your merits (as I said when my opinion was asked), and I wish you joy of the money!"

"Goodness knows, Uncle Pumblechook," said my sister (grasping the money), "we're deeply beholden to you."

"Never mind me, mum," returned that diabolical corn chandler. "A pleasure's a pleasure all the world over. But this boy, you know; we must have him bound. I said I'd see to it—to tell you the truth."

The justices were sitting in the Town Hall near at hand, and we at once went over to have me bound apprentice to Joe in the magisterial presence. I say, we went over, but I was pushed over by Pumblechook, exactly as if I had that moment picked a pocket or fired a rick.[5] My indentures were duly signed and attested, and I was "bound," Mr. Pumblechook holding me all the while as if we had looked in on our way to the scaffold[6] to have those little preliminaries disposed of.

When I got into my little bedroom that night, I was truly wretched, and had a strong conviction on me that I should never like Joe's trade. I had liked it once, but once was not now.

Chapter 14

Once it had seemed to me that when I should at last roll up my shirt-sleeves and go into the forge, Joe's 'prentice, I should be distinguished and happy. Now the reality was in my hold, I only felt that I was dusty with the dust of the small coal, and that I had a weight upon my daily remembrance to

---

4. rantipole (ran′ tē pōl) *n.*: Wild and reckless person.

5. fired a rick: Set fire to a stack of hay or straw.
6. scaffold (skaf′ ′ld) *n.*: Raised platform on which criminals are executed.

which the anvil was a feather. There have been occasions in my later life (I suppose as in most lives) when I have felt for a time as if a thick curtain had fallen on all its interest and romance, to shut me out from anything save dull endurance any more. Never has that curtain dropped so heavy and blank as when my way in life stretched out straight before me through the newly-entered road of apprenticeship to Joe.

I was dejected on the first working day of my apprenticeship; but I am glad to know that I never breathed a murmur to Joe while my indentures lasted. It is about the only thing I *am* glad to know of myself in that connection.

For, though it includes what I proceed to add, all the merit of what I proceed to add was Joe's. It was not because I was faithful, but because Joe was faithful, that I never ran away and went for a soldier or a sailor. It is not possible to know how far the influence of any amiable honest-hearted duty-doing man flies out into the world, but it is very possible to know how it has touched one's self in going by, and I know right well that any good that intermixed itself with my apprenticeship came of plain contented Joe, and not of restless aspiring discontented me.

What I wanted, who can say? How can *I* say, when I never knew? What I dreaded was that in some unlucky hour I, being at my grimiest and commonest, should lift up my eyes and see Estella looking in at one of the wooden windows of the forge. I was haunted by the fear that she would, sooner or later, find me out, with a black face and hands, doing the coarsest part of my work, and would exult over me and despise me.

Chapter 15

As I was getting too big for Mr. Wopsle's great-aunt's room, my education under that preposterous female terminated. Not, how-ever, until Biddy had imparted to me everything she knew, from the little catalogue of prices. In my hunger for information, I also made proposals to Mr. Wopsle to bestow some intellectual crumbs upon me; with which he kindly complied.

Whatever I acquired, I tried to impart to Joe. This statement sounds so well that I cannot in my conscience let it pass unexplained. I wanted to make Joe less ignorant and common, that he might be worthier of my society and less open to Estella's reproach.

The old battery out on the marshes was our place of study, and a broken slate and a short piece of slate pencil were our educational implements: to which Joe always added a pipe of tobacco. I never knew Joe to remember anything from one Sunday to another, or to acquire, under my tuition, any piece of information whatever. Yet he would smoke his pipe at the battery with a far more sagacious air than anywhere else—even with a learned air—as if he considered himself to be advancing immensely. Dear fellow, I hope he did.

It was pleasant and quiet, out there with the sails on the river passing beyond the earth-work, and sometimes, when the tide was low, looking as if they belonged to sunken ships that were still sailing on at the bottom of the water. Whenever I watched the vessels standing out to sea with their white sails spread, I somehow thought of Miss Havisham and Estella. One Sunday I resolved to mention a thought concerning them that had been much in my head.

"Joe," said I, "don't you think I ought to pay Miss Havisham a visit?"

"Well, Pip," returned Joe, slowly considering. "What for?"

"What for, Joe? What is any visit made for?"

"There is some wisits p'r'aps," said Joe, "as for ever remains open to the question,

30 **Critical Thinking and Reading**
How does this statement reveal the perspective of the adult Pip as well as the boy?

Pip. But in regard of wisiting Miss Havisham. She might think you wanted something—expected something of her."

"Don't you think I might say that I did not, Joe?"

"You might, old chap," said Joe. "And she might credit it. Similarly, she mightn't."

Joe felt, as I did, that he had made a point there, and he pulled hard at his pipe to keep himself from weakening it by repetition.

"You see, Pip," Joe pursued, as soon as he was past that danger,"Miss Havisham done the handsome thing by you. When Miss Havisham done the handsome thing by you, she called me back to say to me as that were all."

"Yes, Joe. I heard her."

"Which I meantersay, Pip, it might be that her meaning were—Make a end on it!—As you was!—Me to the North, and you to the South!—Keep in sunders!"

I had thought of that too, and it was very far from comforting to me to find that he had thought of it; for it seemed to render it more probable.

"But, Joe."

"Yes, old chap."

"Here am I, getting on in the first year of my time, and, since the day of my being bound I have never thanked Miss Havisham, or asked after her, or shown that I remembered her."

"That's true, Pip; and unless you were to turn her out a set of shoes all four round—and which I meantersay as even a set of shoes all four round might not act acceptable as a present in a total wacancy of hoofs—"

"I don't mean that sort of remembrance, Joe; I don't mean a present."

But Joe had got the idea of a present in his head and must harp upon it."Or even," said he, "if you was helped to knocking her

up a new chain for the front door—or say a gross or two of shark-headed screws for general use—or some light fancy article, such as a toasting-fork when she took her muffins."

"My dear Joe," I cried in desperation, taking hold of his coat, "don't go on in that way. I never thought of making Miss Havisham any present."

"No, Pip," Joe assented, as if he had been contending for that all along, "and what I say to you is, you are right, Pip."

"Yes, Joe; but what I wanted to say was that, as we are rather slack just now, if you would give me a half-holiday tomorrow, I think I would go up town and make a call on Miss Est—Havisham."

"Which her name," said Joe gravely, "ain't Estavisham, Pip, unless she have been rechris'ended."

"I know, Joe, I know. It was a slip of mine. What do you think of it, Joe?"

In brief, Joe thought that if I thought well of it, he thought well of it. But, he was particular in stipulating that if I were not received with cordiality, then this experimental trip should have no successor. By these conditions I promised to abide.

Now Joe kept a journeyman[1] at weekly wages whose name was Orlick. He was a broad-shouldered loose-limbed swarthy fellow of great strength, never in a hurry, and always slouching. He never even seemed to come to his work on purpose, but would slouch in as if by mere accident; and when he went to the Jolly Bargemen to eat his dinner, or went away at night, he would slouch out as if he had no idea where he was going, and no intention of ever coming back. He lodged at a sluice-keeper's[2] out on the marshes, and on working days would come

---

1. journeyman (jʉr′ nē mən) *n*.: Person who has learned a trade but still works for a master.
2. sluice (sloos)**-keeper:** Person in charge of regulating the flow of water in an artificial stream.

Grammar in Action

When reading a work of literature, look for specific details that help determine the time in which that work takes place. Details of setting that indicate time suggest to the reader the general historical period of a work. Look at these details from *Great Expectations*:

"Or even," [said Joe] "—or some light fancy article, such as a toasting fork when she took her muffins."

Joe, a blacksmith, is suggesting that he and Pip make a toasting fork for Miss Havisham to spear muffins in order to toast them over an open flame. Today, blacksmiths devote their time to shoeing horses for riding stables or mounted police, and most toast is made in an electric toaster or a gas or electric oven. This detail from the novel indicates that it takes place in an earlier time.

What does the following passage tell you about the historical time of the setting?

He [Orlick] and Joe had got a piece of hot iron between them, and I was at the bellows.

slouching from his hermitage,[3] with his hands in his pockets and his dinner loosely tied in a bundle round his neck and dangling on his back. He always slouched, locomotively, with his eyes on the ground; and, when accosted or otherwise required to raise them, he looked up in a half-resentful, half-puzzled way.

This morose journeyman had no liking for me. When I became Joe's 'prentice, Orlick was perhaps confirmed in some suspicion that I should displace him.

Orlick was at work and present, next day, when I reminded Joe of my half-holiday. He said nothing at the moment, for he and Joe had just got a piece of hot iron between them, and I was at the bellows;[4] but by-and-by he said, leaning on his hammer:

"Now, master! Sure you're not a going to favor only one of us. If young Pip has a half-holiday, do as much for Old Orlick." I suppose he was about five-and-twenty, but he usually spoke of himself as an ancient person.

"Why, what'll you do with a half-holiday, if you get it?" said Joe.

"What'll *I* do with it? What'll *he* do with it? I'll do as much with it as *him*," said Orlick.

"As to Pip, he's going up town," said Joe.

"Well, then, as to Old Orlick, *he's* a-going up town," retorted that worthy. "Two can go up town. Tain't only one wot can go up town."

"Don't lose your temper," said Joe.

"Shall if I like," growled Orlick. "Some and their up towning! Now, master! Come. No favoring in this shop. Be a man!"

"All right, as in general you stick to your work as well as most men," said Joe, "let it be a half-holiday for all."

My sister had been standing silent in the yard, within hearing—she was a most unscrupulous spy and listener—and she instantly looked in at one of the windows.

"Like you, you fool!" said she to Joe, "giving holidays to great idle hulkers like that. You are a rich man, upon my life, to waste wages in that way. I wish *I* was his master!"

"You'd be everybody's master if you durst," retorted Orlick, with an ill-favored grin.

("Let her alone," said Joe.)

"I'd be a match for all noodles and all rogues," returned my sister, beginning to work herself into a mighty rage. "And I couldn't be a match for the noodles without being a match for your master, who's the dunderheaded king of the noodles. And I couldn't be a match for the rogues without being a match for you, who are the blackest-looking and the worst rogue between this and France. Now!"

"You're a foul shrew, Mother Gargery," growled the journeyman. "If that makes a judge of rogues, you ought to be a good 'un."

("Let her alone, will you?" said Joe.)

"What did you say?" cried my sister, beginning to scream. "What did you say? What did that fellow Orlick say to me, Pip? What did he call me, with my husband standing by? Oh! Oh! Oh!" Each of these exclamations was a shriek. "What was the name that he gave me before the base man who swore to defend me? Oh! Hold me! Oh!"

"Ah-h-h!" growled the journeyman, between his teeth, "I'd hold you, if you was my wife. I'd hold you under the pump, and choke it out of you."

("I tell you, let her alone," said Joe.)

"Oh! To hear him!" cried my sister, with a clap of her hands and a scream together—which was her next stage. "To hear the

---

3. **hermitage** (hur′ mit ij) *n.*: Secluded and solitary dwelling.
4. **bellows** (bel′ ōz) *n.*: Device for blowing air on a fire.

32 Discussion Why is Mrs. Joe so upset by Joe's decision?

Knowledge of details of setting that suggest the period will add to your understanding and enjoyment of a work of literature.

Student Activity 1. Find three or four more passages that contain details that suggest the time period in which the novel is set. Explain what you learned from each passage for your classmates and teacher.

Student Activity 2. With a partner or small group of classmates, decide on a time period other than the present and brainstorm a list of details that suggest that period. Discuss how you might work such details of setting into a short story set at the time you chose.

Software If students are working on computers, you might want to have them use the **Writer's Helper** activity Brainstorms to help them generate details about the temporal setting of a short story.

Humanities Note

Fine art, *Pat Lyon at the Forge,* 1826–1827, by John Neagle. Neagle (1796–1865) was an American portrait painter trained by the famous painter of presidents, Gilbert Stuart. John Neagle and his father-in-law Thomas Sully were the most fashionable portrait painters in Philadelphia.

There is an interesting story connected with *Pat Lyon at the Forge.* Lyon, a Philadelphia blacksmith, was imprisoned for a bank robbery he did not commit. Released after three months, he sued the city and won a great deal of money. He immediately commissioned John Neagle to paint his portrait, not as a gentleman but as a working man.

You might ask students the following questions:
1. Which details reveal the trade and social status of the subject?
2. Do you think Pat Lyon resembles Dickens's character Joe Gargery? Why or why not?

PAT LYON AT THE FORGE 1826–27
John Neagle
The Museum of Fine Arts, Boston

772   *The Novel*

names he's giving me! That Orlick! In my own house! Me, a married woman! With my husband standing by! Oh! Oh!"

What could the wretched Joe do now, after his disregarded parenthetical interruptions, but stand up to his journeyman? Old Orlick felt that the situation admitted of nothing less than coming on, and was on his defense straightway, so, without so much as pulling off their singed and burnt aprons, they went at one another, like two giants. But if any man in that neighborhood could stand up long against Joe, I never saw the man. Orlick, as if he had been of no more account than the pale young gentleman, was very soon among the coal dust, and in no hurry to come out of it. Then Joe unlocked the door and picked up my sister, who had dropped insensible at the window (but who had seen the fight first I think), and who was carried into the house.

I went upstairs to dress myself. When I came down again, I found Joe and Orlick sweeping up, without any other traces of discomposure than a slit in one of Orlick's nostrils.

33 With what absurd emotions (for we think the feelings that are very serious in a man quite comical in a boy) I found myself again going to Miss Havisham's matters little here. Nor how I passed and repassed the gate many times before I could make up my mind to ring.

Miss Sarah Pocket came to the gate. No Estella.

"How, then? You here again?" said Miss Pocket. "What do you want?"

When I said that I only came to see how Miss Havisham was, Sarah evidently deliberated whether or no she should send me about my business. But, unwilling to hazard the responsibility, she let me in, and presently brought the sharp message that I was to "come up."

Everything was unchanged, and Miss Havisham was alone. "Well!" said she, fixing her eyes upon me. "I hope you want nothing? You'll get nothing."

"No, indeed, Miss Havisham. I only wanted you to know that I am doing very well in my apprenticeship, and am always much obliged to you."

"There, there!" with the old restless fingers. "Come now and then; come on your birthday. Aye!" she cried suddenly, turning herself and her chair towards me, "You are looking round for Estella? Hey?"

I had been looking round—in fact, for Estella—and I stammered that I hoped she was well.

"Abroad," said Miss Havisham; "educating for a lady. Do you feel that you have lost her?"

There was such a malignant enjoyment in her utterance of the last words, and she broke into such a disagreeable laugh that I was at a loss what to say. She spared me the trouble of considering, by dismissing me. When the gate was closed upon me by Sarah of the walnut-shell countenance, I felt more than ever dissatisfied with my home and with my trade and with everything.

As I was loitering along the High Street, looking in disconsolately at the shop windows, and thinking what I would buy if I were a gentleman, who should come out of the bookshop but Mr. Wopsle. Mr. Wopsle had in his hand the affecting tragedy of George Barnwell, in which he had that moment invested sixpence, with the view of heaping every word of it on the head of Pumblechook, with whom he was going to drink tea. No sooner did he see me than he appeared to consider that a special Providence had put a 'prentice in his way to be read at; and he laid hold of me, and insisted on my accompanying him to the Pumblechookian parlor. As I knew it would be miserable at

Great Expectations 773

33 Discussion What do you think the "absurd emotions" were?

Critical Thinking and Reading
Why do you think Dickens ends the chapter with this dramatic incident?

Reader's Response Do you think Pip's "great expectations" are too great and beyond his abilities? Explain.

Thematic Response Pip is awakened to what he considers flaws in himself and in those close to him. Do you admire Pip's tolerance of and attitude toward his flaws? What about his attitude toward Joe's shortcomings?

home, and as the nights were dark and the way was dreary, and almost any companionship on the road was better than none, I made no great resistance; consequently, we turned into Pumblechook's just as the street and the shops were lighting up.

It was a very dark night when it was all over, and when I set out with Mr. Wopsle on the walk home. Beyond town, we found a heavy mist out, and it fell wet and thick. The turnpike lamp was a blur, and its rays looked solid substance on the fog. We were noticing this, when we came upon a man, slouching under the lee of the turnpike house.

"Halloa!" we said, stopping. "Orlick there?"

"Ah!" he answered, slouching out. "I was standing by, a minute, on the chance of company."

"You are late," I remarked.

Orlick not unnaturally answered, "Well? And *you're* late."

"We have been," said Mr. Wopsle, exalted with his late performance, "we have been indulging, Mr. Orlick, in an intellectual evening."

Old Orlick growled, as if he had nothing to say about that, and we all went on together. I asked him presently whether he had been spending his half-holiday up and down town?

"Yes," said he, "all of it. I come in behind yourself. I didn't see you, but I must have been pretty close behind you. By-the-bye, the guns is going again."

"At the Hulks?" said I.

"Aye! There's some of the birds flown from the cages. The guns have been going since dark, about. You'll hear one presently."

In effect, we had not walked many yards further, when the well-remembered boom came towards us, deadened by the mist.

"A good night for cutting off in," said Orlick. "We'd be puzzled how to bring down a jailbird on the wing tonight."

We came to the village. The way by which we approached it took us past the Three Jolly Bargemen, which we were surprised to find—it being eleven o'clock—in a state of commotion, with the door wide open, and unwonted lights that had been hastily caught up and put down scattered about. Mr. Wopsle dropped in to ask what was the matter (surmising that a convict had been taken), but came running out in a great hurry.

"There's something wrong," said he, without stopping, "up at your place, Pip. Run all!"

"What is it?" I asked, keeping up with him. So did Orlick, at my side.

"I can't quite understand. The house seems to have been violently entered when Joe Gargery was out. Supposed by convicts. Somebody has been attacked and hurt."

We were running too fast to admit of more being said, and we made no stop until we got into our kitchen. It was full of people; the whole village was there, or in the yard; and there was a surgeon, and there was Joe, and there was a group of women, all on the floor in the midst of the kitchen. The unemployed bystanders drew back when they saw me, and so I became aware of my sister—lying without sense or movement on the bare boards where she had been knocked down by a tremendous blow on the back of the head, dealt by some unknown hand when her face was turned towards the fire—destined never to be on the rampage again while she was the wife of Joe.

Closure and Extension

ANSWERS TO RESPONDING TO THE SELECTION
Your Response

1. Discuss with students what they think Pip's goals are. Ask what Pip must do to reach those goals.

Recalling

2. Pip cannot bring himself to tell the truth because he does not think that Pumblechook and Mrs. Joe would understand him. Also, he thinks that it would be "treacherous" to reveal information about Miss Havisham to Mrs. Joe.

3. Pip plans to be educated, and he asks Biddy to teach him everything she knows.

4. For his meeting with Miss Havisham, Joe dresses in his Sunday best, looking stiff and uncomfortable, his hair tousled and his mouth open as he faces her. Her purpose is to ask Joe whether he intends to apprentice Pip as a blacksmith. Joe will not answer her questions directly, but persists in turning to Pip and giving the answers to him, much to Pip's annoyance and embarrassment.

Interpreting

5. Suggested Response: The stranger wants Pip to know that he has been sent by "Pip's convict," and feeling assured that Pip has understood, he slips Pip a shilling wrapped in two one-pound notes.

6. Suggested Response: We learn from the meeting that Joe is very fond of Pip, is looking forward to working with him, and is not motivated by greed.

7. Suggested Response: Pip is no longer content to be a black-

RESPONDING TO THE SELECTION

Your Response

1. What advice would you give Pip in planning for his future?

Recalling

2. Why does Pip lie to Mrs. Joe and Pumblechook about Miss Havisham?
3. How does Pip plan to make himself "uncommon"?
4. Describe Miss Havisham's meeting with Joe. What is its purpose?

Interpreting

5. What does the visitor to the Three Jolly Bargemen want to communicate to Pip?
6. What does Joe's meeting with Miss Havisham reveal about his feelings for Pip?
7. Explain how Pip changes after his visit to Miss Havisham. What do you predict about his future based on this change?
8. Why does Miss Havisham take satisfaction in Estella's beauty and arrogance?
9. Based on what you know of Miss Havisham, what role do you think she will play in Pip's achieving his expectations?

Applying

10. Pip's determination to impress Estella drives him to improve himself. Comment on situations in which people pursue an admirable goal but for reasons that may not be so admirable.

ANALYZING LITERATURE

Understanding Characterization

Direct characterization refers to statements by the writer about the characters. **Indirect characterization** is the method by which the writer reveals the characters' personalities through what they say or do or what others say about them. Since Pip rather than Dickens is the narrator of *Great Expectations,* all of the characterization in this novel is indirect.

Pip is a **round** rather than a **flat character** because he displays many traits and is capable of changing. He begins to change, in fact, as a result of his visit to Satis House.

1. How does this visit cause him to change?
2. Identify three of Pip's traits and indicate whether you learned about each through his words or actions, or what others say.
3. Name a flat character besides Mr. Pumblechook and explain your choice.

CRITICAL THINKING AND READING

Drawing Conclusions About Characters

You must often reach conclusions about characters based on what they say or do or what others say about them. For example, Pip does not mind lying to Mrs. Joe and Mr. Pumblechook about his visit to Miss Havisham, but he feels guilty about deceiving Joe. These different reactions indicate that he has less respect for Mrs. Joe and Pumblechook than he does for Joe.

Explain what conclusions the following facts suggest about each of the characters.

1. Miss Havisham has allowed her bridal feast to become a "heap of decay."
2. The young gentleman that Pip meets provokes a fight but proves to be a terrible boxer.

THINKING AND WRITING

Writing About Art

Look at the fine art on any of the following pages: 759, 763, or 772. Choose one of these paintings and write a characterization of the person in the art. First, examine carefully the painting you choose and list outstanding points or details about the person in it. Then make inferences about the traits or qualities of that person based on the details you see. Finally, if you think the portrait resembles one of the characters in *Great Expectations,* tell which character and give your reasons. Revise your draft, adding specific detail about the art to support your points.

cause he wants to improve his education (revealed through his words and actions); and he is self-divided because his contact with Estella leads him to think of himself as "common" (revealed through his thoughts).

3. Suggested Response: Sarah Pocket is another flat character. There is little to her personality besides her hypocrisy and greed. She is one of the greedy hangers-on at Satis House.

ANSWERS TO CRITICAL THINKING AND READING

1. Suggested Response: The decayed bridal feast symbolizes Miss Havisham's decay and withdrawal from life. It also symbolizes the death of her hopes caused by her fiancé's betrayal.
2. Suggested Response: The young gentleman is not very objective about his own skills and abilities.

THINKING AND WRITING

Writing Transparency Students often find it helpful to see a model of their writing assignment. Before students write, you may wish to show them Model 2: Autobiography in the **Transparencies for Writing.**

Alternative Assessment For alternative Composition assignments to assess students' learning, see page 936 of the **Teaching Portfolio.**

---

smith and wants to rise in life. He will probably find some way to obtain more education.

8. Suggested Response: Estella's beauty will attract men, and her arrogance will break their hearts. Miss Havisham may want to use Estella as a means for revenging herself on men.
9. Answers will differ. Some students may respond that Miss Havisham is a self-centered person. She says that there will be no more money coming to Pip

after she has paid his indenture fee. It is not probable, therefore, that she will help him further.

Applying

10. Answers will differ. Some students might advise Pip to go to London and work as a junior clerk, while continuing to study on his own.

Challenge Do you think Pip will meet Estella again? Explain.

ANSWERS TO ANALYZING LITERATURE

1. Suggested Response: Pip is ashamed of his appearance and ignorance. He wants to rise in life so that he can be with Estella.
2. Suggested Response: Pip is conscientious because he cares deeply about how he behaves toward others and often says how guilty he feels about some action or thought (revealed through his thoughts); he is ambitious, be-

Preparation

Literary Focus You might want to point out to students that the various subplots include Abel Magwitch's conflict with Compeyson and Biddy's rise from servant to Joe's wife. Have students explain how these and other subplots are related to the main plot.

Prereading Focus Pip is about to learn that he is to have "great expectations," that is, he is to become a gentleman. The purpose of making the list is to focus on the changes that Pip must face in his passage from being a "coarse and common" blacksmith to being an educated gentleman. Tell students that education sometimes makes changes in a person's social status. Discuss the benefits of such change as well as the costs.

Vocabulary Have less advanced students find the vocabulary words in the text and replace each one with an appropriate synonym.

GUIDE FOR READING

Great Expectations, Chapters 16–23

Plot and Subplot

The **plot** is the sequence of interrelated events in a work of fiction. It often centers on one or more **conflicts,** the struggles between opposing forces. Since a novel is longer than a short story, novelists can develop their plots more fully. They can take more time to introduce the characters and conflicts, and they can build suspense more gradually. There may be both external and internal conflicts. Dickens does not resolve the main conflict of *Great Expectations,* Pip's internal conflict, until the book is nearly over.

A novel may contain **subplots,** which are minor, secondary plots running through the novel. Subplots are related to the main plot through the characters, who have parts in both. Subplots are also based on conflicts that must be resolved. For example, one subplot involves the career of "the pale young gentleman," whom Pip meets again in London.

Focus

In these chapters, a huge change occurs in Pip's life. It seems that a great wish has been granted, but this change in circumstances causes him to leave everyone he knows and loves. Think about the effects of a major change in your life. In a list like the following, jot down the positive and negative effects of the change. Then read the following chapters and see how Pip reacts to his new situation.

Positive effects	Negative effects

Vocabulary

Knowing the following words will help you as you read Chapters 16–23 of *Great Expectations.*

corroborated (kə räb′ ə rāt′ əd) *v.*: Confirmed (p. 777)

extract (ek strakt′) *v.*: Draw out with special effort (p. 777)

aberration (ab′ ər ā shən) *n.*: Mental derangement (p. 778)

latent (lāt′ 'nt) *adj.*: Hidden (p. 780)

audacious (ô dā′ shəs) *adj.*: Brave; without fear (p. 788)

alleviated (ə lē′ vē āt əd) *v.*: Lessened; relieved (p. 794)

languor (laŋ′ gər) *n.*: Weakness; sluggishness (p. 787)

perplexity (pər plek′ sə tē) *n.*: State of being confused (p. 799)

776   The Novel

Objectives

1 To understand plot and subplot in a novel
2 To predict outcomes
3 To extend the story of a novel
4 To express individual interests and abilities through optional activities

Support Material

Teaching Portfolio
Teacher Backup, p. 907
Grammar in Action Worksheets, *Using Who and Whom,* p. 911; *Using Participial Phrases,* p. 913
Usage and Mechanics Worksheet, p. 915
Vocabulary Check, p. 916
Critical Thinking and Reading Worksheet, *Predicting Outcomes,* p. 918

Language Worksheet, *Understanding the Latin Root spect,* p. 919
Selection Test, p. 920

Library of Video Classics
The Changing World of Charles Dickens, Great Expectations

Literature Videodisc
Scenes from *Great Expectations*

Prentice Hall Literature Writing Studio

Chapter 16

Joe had been at the Three Jolly Bargemen, smoking his pipe, from a quarter after eight o'clock to a quarter before ten. While he was there, my sister had been seen standing at the kitchen door and had exchanged good night with a farm laborer going home. When Joe went home at five minutes before ten, he found her struck down on the floor, and promptly called in assistance. The fire had not then burnt unusually low, nor was the snuff[1] of the candle very long; the candle, however, had been blown out.

Nothing had been taken away from any part of the house. But, there was one remarkable piece of evidence on the spot. She had been struck with something blunt and heavy, on the head and spine; after the blows were dealt, something heavy had been thrown down at her with considerable violence, as she lay on her face. And on the ground beside her, when Joe picked her up, was a convict's leg iron which had been filed asunder.

Now, Joe, examining this iron with a smith's eye, declared it to have been filed asunder some time ago. The hue and cry going off to the Hulks, and people coming thence to examine the iron, Joe's opinion was corroborated. They did not undertake to say when it had left the prison ships to which it undoubtedly had once belonged, but they claimed to know for certain that that particular manacle had not been worn by either of two convicts who had escaped last night. Further, one of those two was already retaken, and had not freed himself of his iron.

Knowing what I knew, I set up an inference of my own here. I believed the iron to be my convict's iron—the iron I had seen and heard him filing at, on the marshes—but my mind did not accuse him of having put it to its latest use. For, I believed one of two other persons to have become possessed of it, and to have turned it to this cruel account. Either Orlick, or the strange man who had shown me the file.

Now, as to Orlick; he had gone to town exactly as he told us when we picked him up at the turnpike, he had been seen about town all the evening, he had been in divers[2] companies in several public houses, and he had come back with myself and Mr. Wopsle. There was nothing against him, save the quarrel; and my sister had quarrelled with him, and with everybody else about her, ten thousand times. As to the strange man, if he had come back for his two bank notes, there could have been no dispute about them, because my sister was fully prepared to restore them. Besides, there had been no altercation; the assailant had come in so silently and suddenly that she had been felled before she could look round.

The constables, and the Bow Street men from London—for, this happened in the days of the extinct red-waistcoated police—were about the house for a week or two, and did pretty much what I have heard and read of like authorities doing in other such cases. They took up several obviously wrong people, and they ran their heads very hard against wrong ideas, and persisted in trying to fit the circumstances to the ideas, instead of trying to extract ideas from the circumstances.

Long after these constitutional powers had dispersed, my sister lay very ill in bed. Her sight was disturbed, so that she saw objects multiplied, and grasped at visionary

---

1. **snuff** *n.*: Charred end of the candlewick.

2. **divers** (dī′ vərz) *adj.*: Several, various.

Presentation

Motivation/Prior Knowledge Ask students how they would react if someone offered them a great deal of money on the condition that they leave their homes and move to a new city. Would they accept the offer? Tell students that Pip must face a similar choice.

Master Teacher Note You might want to tell students that the novel's title, *Great Expectations,* has several meanings in the story. In this section, for example, Pip is literally told that he has "great expectations." An unknown benefactor gives him the means to become a gentleman. In still another sense of the phrase, however, Pip's own expectations change as his way of life is altered. Have students keep in mind the various meanings of the word *expectations*.

Purpose-Setting Question How do Pip's expectations affect his life?

1 Critical Thinking and Reading Pip tries to think as a detective would. Evaluate his reasoning and conclusions.

2 Enrichment Students might be interested to know that Dickens could be regarded as one of the founders of the modern detective novel. The last section of *Bleak House,* for example, focuses on the activities of a skillful detective. Ask students how Dickens's humorous criticisms of "the Bow Street Men" reveal his understanding of detective work.

Videocassette You might wish to show the portion of the film adaptation of *Great Expectations* in which Pip prepares to leave for London so that students can visualize the conflict between Pip's love for his family and his desire to be gentleman.

Thematic Focus Growing up, everyone experiences rites of passage. Pip's rites of passage include parting from those he loves. Ask students which rites of passage they have experienced. Do rites of passage always change the person who experiences them?

Alternative Assessment To promote active reading, have students continue their reader's response journal. Encourage students to make predictions about what will happen next in the novel.

Their observations will enable you to assess their understanding of the issues in the story.

teacups and wineglasses instead of the realities; her hearing was greatly impaired; her memory also; and her speech was unintelligible. When, at last, she came round so far as to be helped downstairs, it was still necessary to keep my slate always by her, that she might indicate in writing what she could not indicate in speech. As she was (very bad handwriting apart) a more than indifferent speller, and as Joe was a more than indifferent reader, extraordinary complications arose between them, which I was always called in to solve.

However, her temper was greatly improved, and she was patient. A tremulous uncertainty of the action of all her limbs soon became a part of her regular state, and afterwards, at intervals of two or three months, she would often put her hands to her head, and would then remain for about a week at a time in some gloomy aberration of mind. We were at a loss to find a suitable attendant for her, until a circumstance happened conveniently to relieve us. Mr. Wopsle's great-aunt conquered a confirmed habit of living into which she had fallen,[3] and Biddy became a part of our establishment.

It may have been about a month after my sister's reappearance in the kitchen when Biddy came to us with a small speckled box containing the whole of her worldly effects, and became a blessing to the household. Above all she was a blessing to Joe, for the dear old fellow was sadly cut up by the constant contemplation of the wreck of his wife, and had been accustomed, while attending on her of an evening, to turn to me every now and then and say, with his blue eyes moistened, "Such a fine figure of a woman as she once were, Pip!" Biddy instantly taking the cleverest charge of her as though she

3

---

3. conquered . . . fallen: Died.

had studied her from infancy, Joe became able in some sort to appreciate the greater quiet of his life, and to get down to the Jolly Bargemen now and then for a change that did him good.

Biddy's first triumph in her new office was to solve a difficulty that had completely vanquished me. I had tried hard at it, but had made nothing of it. Thus it was:

Again and again and again, my sister had traced upon the slate a character that looked like a curious T, and then with the utmost eagerness had called our attention to it as everything she particularly wanted. I had in vain tried everything producible that began with a T, from tar to toast and tub. At length it had come into my head that the sign looked like a hammer, and on my lustily calling that word in my sister's ear, she had begun to hammer on the table and had expressed a qualified assent. Thereupon, I had brought in all our hammers, one after another, but without avail.

When my sister found that Biddy was very quick to understand her, this mysterious sign reappeared on the slate. Biddy looked thoughtfully at it, heard my explanation, looked thoughtfully at my sister, looked thoughtfully at Joe (who was always represented on the slate by his initial letter), and ran into the forge, followed by Joe and me.

"Why, of course!" cried Biddy, with an exultant face. "Don't you see? It's *him*!"

Orlick, without a doubt! She had lost his name, and could only signify him by his hammer. We told him why we wanted him to come into the kitchen, and he slowly laid down his hammer, wiped his brow with his arm, took another wipe at it with his apron, and came slouching out.

I confess that I expected to see my sister denounce him, and that I was disappointed by the different result. She manifested the greatest anxiety to be on good terms with him, was evidently much pleased by his being at length produced, and motioned that she would have him given something to drink. After that day, a day rarely passed without her drawing the hammer on her slate, and without Orlick's slouching in and standing doggedly before her, as if he knew no more than I did what to make of it.

Chapter 17

I now fell into a regular routine of apprenticeship life, which was varied, beyond the limits of the village and the marshes, by no more remarkable circumstance than the arrival of my birthday and my paying another visit to Miss Havisham. I found Miss Havisham just as I had left her, and she spoke of Estella in the very same way, if not in the very same words. The interview lasted but a few minutes, and she gave me a guinea when I was going, and told me to come again on my next birthday. I may mention at once that this became an annual custom.

So unchanging was the dull old house that I felt as if the stopping of the clocks had stopped time in that mysterious place. It bewildered me, and under its influence I continued at heart to hate my trade and to be ashamed of home.

Imperceptibly I became conscious of a change in Biddy, however. Her shoes came up at the heel, her hair grew bright and neat, her hands were always clean. She was not beautiful—she was common, and could not be like Estella—but she was pleasant and wholesome and sweet-tempered. I observed to myself one evening that she had curiously thoughtful and attentive eyes; eyes that were very pretty and very good.

It came of my lifting up my own eyes from a task I was poring at—writing some passages from a book, to improve myself in two ways at once by a sort of stratagem—and seeing Biddy observant of what I was about. I laid down my pen, and Biddy stopped in her needlework without laying it down.

"How do you manage, Biddy," said I, "to learn everything that I learn, and always to keep up with me?" I was beginning to be rather vain of my knowledge, for I spent my birthday guineas on it, and set aside the greater part of my pocket-money for similar investment; though I have no doubt, now, that the little I knew was extremely dear at the price.

"I might as well ask you," said Biddy, "how *you* manage?"

"No; because when I come in from the forge of a night anyone can see me turning to at it. But you never turn to at it, Biddy."

"I suppose I must catch it—like a cough," said Biddy, quietly, and went on with her sewing.

Pursuing my idea as I leaned back in my wooden chair and looked at Biddy sewing away with her head on one side, I began to think her rather an extraordinary girl. For, I called to mind now that she was equally accomplished in the terms of our trade, and the names of our different sorts of work, and our various tools. In short, whatever I knew, Biddy knew. Theoretically, she was already as good a blacksmith as I, or better.

"You are one of those, Biddy," said I, "who make the most of every chance. You never had a chance before you came here, and see how improved you are!"

Biddy looked at me for an instant, and went on with her sewing. "I was your first teacher though, wasn't I?" said she, as she sewed.

I recalled the hopeless circumstances by which she had been surrounded in the miserable little shop and the miserable little

4 **Critical Thinking and Reading** What might motivate Mrs. Joe's behavior?

5 **Critical Thinking and Reading** How much of this change results from a real change in Biddy and how much from an alteration in Pip's perception of her? Explain.

6 **Discussion** Why is the word *you* emphasized? Who else might Pip have in mind?

7 **Discussion** Why is this an insightful question?

noisy evening school, with that miserable old bundle of incompetence always to be dragged and shouldered. I reflected that even in those untoward times there must have been latent in Biddy what was now developing, for, in my first uneasiness and discontent, I had turned to her for help as a matter of course. Biddy sat quietly sewing, and while I looked at her and thought about it all, it occurred to me that perhaps I had not been sufficiently grateful to Biddy.

"Yes, Biddy," I observed, "you were my first teacher, and that at a time when we little thought of ever being together like this, in this kitchen. Let us have a quiet walk on the marshes next Sunday, Biddy, and a long chat."

My sister was never left alone now; but Joe more than readily undertook the care of her on that Sunday afternoon, and Biddy and I went out together. When we came to the riverside and sat down on the bank, I resolved that it was a good time and place for the admission of Biddy into my inner confidence.

"Biddy," said I, after binding her to secrecy, "I want to be a gentleman."

"Oh, I wouldn't, if I was you!" she returned. "I don't think it would answer."

"Biddy," said I, with some severity, "I have particular reasons for wanting to be a gentleman."

"You know best, Pip; but don't you think you are happier as you are?"

"Biddy," I exclaimed impatiently, "I am not at all happy as I am. I am disgusted with my calling and with my life. I have never taken to either since I was bound. Don't be absurd."

"Was I absurd?" said Biddy, quietly raising her eyebrows; "I am sorry for that; I didn't mean to be. I only want you to do well, and be comfortable."

"Well, then, understand once for all that I never shall or can be comfortable—or anything but miserable—there, Biddy!—unless I can lead a very different sort of life from the life I lead now."

"That's a pity!" said Biddy, shaking her head with a sorrowful air.

"If I could have settled down," I said to Biddy, "and been but half as fond of the forge as I was when I was little, I know it would have been much better for me. You and I and Joe would have wanted nothing then, and Joe and I would perhaps have gone partners when I was out of my time, and I might even have grown up to keep company with you, and we might have sat on this very bank on a fine Sunday, quite different people. I should have been good enough for *you*; shouldn't I, Biddy?"

Biddy sighed as she looked at the ships sailing on, and returned for answer, "Yes, I am not over-particular." It scarcely sounded flattering, but I knew she meant well.

"Instead of that," said I, "see how I am going on. Dissatisfied, and uncomfortable, and—what would it signify to me, being coarse and common, if nobody had told me so?"

"It was neither a very true nor a very polite thing to say," she remarked. "Who said it?"

"The beautiful young lady at Miss Havisham's, and she's more beautiful than anybody ever was, and I admire her dreadfully, and I want to be a gentleman on her account."

"Do you want to be a gentleman to spite her or to gain her over?" Biddy quietly asked me, after a pause.

"I don't know," I moodily answered.

"Because, if it is to spite her," Biddy pursued, "I should think—but you know best—that might be better and more independently done by caring nothing for her words. And if it is to gain her over, I should think—but you know best—she was not worth gaining over."

8

Exactly what I myself had thought, many times. Exactly what was perfectly manifest to me at the moment. But how could I, a poor dazed village lad, avoid that wonderful inconsistency into which the best and wisest of men fall every day?

"It may be all quite true," said I to Biddy, "but I admire her dreadfully."

Biddy was the wisest of girls, and she tried to reason no more with me. She softly patted my shoulder in a soothing way, while with my face upon my sleeve I cried a little—exactly as I had done in the brewery-yard—and felt vaguely convinced that I was very much ill-used by somebody, or by everybody; I can't say which.

"I am glad of one thing," said Biddy, "and that is that you have felt you could give me your confidence, Pip."

"Biddy," I cried, getting up, putting my arm around her neck, and giving her a kiss, "I shall always tell you everything."

"Till you're a gentleman," said Biddy.

"You know I never shall be, so that's always."

Chapter 18

It was in the fourth year of my apprenticeship to Joe, and it was a Saturday night. There was a group assembled round the fire at the Three Jolly Bargemen, attentive to Mr. Wopsle as he read the newspaper aloud. Of that group, I was one.

A highly popular murder had been committed, and Mr. Wopsle was imbrued in blood to the eyebrows. He gloated over every abhorrent adjective in the description, and identified himself with every witness at the inquest. He enjoyed himself thoroughly, and we all enjoyed ourselves, and were delightfully comfortable. In this cozy state of mind we came to the verdict of willful murder.

Then, and not sooner, I became aware of a strange gentleman leaning over the back of the settle opposite me, looking on. There was an expression of contempt on his face, and he bit the side of a great forefinger as he watched the group of faces.

9

"Well!" said the stranger to Mr. Wopsle, when the reading was done, "you have settled it all to your own satisfaction, I have no doubt?"

The strange gentleman, with an air of authority not to be disputed, and with a manner expressive of knowing something secret about every one of us that would effectually do for each individual if he chose to disclose it, left the back of the settle, and came into the space between the two settles, in front of the fire.

"From information I have received," said he, looking round at us as we all quailed before him, "I have reason to believe there is a blacksmith among you, by name Joseph—or Joe—Gargery. Which is the man?"

"Here is the man," said Joe.

The strange gentleman beckoned him out of his place, and Joe went.

"You have an apprentice," pursued the stranger, "commonly known as Pip? Is he here?"

"I am here!" I cried.

The stranger did not recognize me, but I recognized him as the gentleman I had met on the stairs on the occasion of my second visit to Miss Havisham. I had known him the moment I saw him looking over the settle, and now that I stood confronting him with his hand upon my shoulder, I checked off again in detail, his large head, his dark complexion, his deep-set eyes, his bushy black

Great Expectations   781

8 Discussion Why is Pip unable to follow advice he knows to be true?

9 Critical Thinking and Reading How does the description of the strange gentleman looking contemptuously at the unpretentious villagers suggest the ideas that Pip and Biddy discussed in the previous chapter?

Humanities Note

Fine art, *Mortlake Terrace,* 1827, J.M.W. Turner. The British painter J.M.W. Turner (1775–1851) developed a unique style to convey the effects of light and atmosphere.

Mortlake Terrace was painted on a commission from the owner of the garden, William Moffat, Esq., but the work is far more than a record of a pretty place. This picture is a study of sunlight filtering through an evening mist, and the canvas glows with a radiance that had not been seen in painting before.

You might use the following questions to prompt a discussion:
1. What is unusual about the way Turner shows the effects of light?
2. What mood does this painting call up?

MORTLAKE TERRACE
J. M. W. Turner
National Gallery of Art, Washington

eyebrows, his large watch chain, his strong black dots of beard and whisker, and even the smell of scented soap on his great hand.

"I wish to have a private conference with you two," said he, when he had surveyed me at his leisure. "It will take a little time. Perhaps we had better go to your place of residence."

Amidst a wondering silence, we three walked out of the Jolly Bargemen, and in a wondering silence walked home.

Our conference began with the strange gentleman's sitting down at the table, drawing the candle to him, and looking over some entries in his pocket book. He then put up the pocket book and set the candle a little aside, after peering round it into the darkness at Joe and me to ascertain which was which.

10

"My name," he said, "is Jaggers, and I am a lawyer in London. I am pretty well known. I have unusual business to transact with you, and I commence by explaining that it is not of my originating. If my advice had been asked, I should not have been here. It was not asked, and you see me here. What I have to do as the confidential agent of another, I do. No less, no more.

"Now, Joseph Gargery, I am the bearer of an offer to relieve you of this young fellow, your apprentice. You would not object to cancel his indentures at his request and for his good? You would want nothing for so doing?"

"Lord forbid that I should want anything for not standing in Pip's way," said Joe, staring.

"Lord forbidding is pious, but not to the purpose," returned Mr. Jaggers. "The question is, would you want anything? Do you want anything?"

11

"The answer is," returned Joe sternly, "No."

I thought Mr. Jaggers glanced at Joe as if he considered him a fool for his disinterestedness. But I was too much bewildered between breathless curiosity and surprise to be sure of it.

"Very well," said Mr. Jaggers. "Recollect the admission you have made, and don't try to go from it presently."

"Who's a-going to try?" retorted Joe.

"I don't say anybody is. Do you keep a dog?"

"Yes, I do keep a dog."

"Bear in mind then, that Brag is a good dog, but that Holdfast is a better. Bear that in mind, will you?" repeated Mr. Jaggers, shutting his eyes and nodding his head at Joe, as if he were forgiving him something. "Now, I return to this young fellow. And the communication I have got to make is that he has great expectations."

Joe and I gasped, and looked at one another.

"I am instructed to communicate to him," said Mr. Jaggers, throwing his finger at me sideways, "that he will come into a handsome property. Further, that it is the desire of the present possessor of that property that he be immediately removed from his present sphere of life and from this place, and be brought up as a gentleman—in a word, as a young fellow of great expectations."

My dream was out; my wild fancy was surpassed by sober reality; Miss Havisham was going to make my fortune on a grand scale.

12

"Now, Mr. Pip," pursued the lawyer, "I address the rest of what I have to say to you. You are to understand, first, that it is the request of the person from whom I take my instructions that you always bear the name of Pip. You will have no objection, I dare say, to your great expectations being encumbered with that easy condition. But if you have any objection, this is the time to mention it."

My heart was beating so fast, and there was such a singing in my ears, that I could scarcely stammer I had no objection.

"I should think not! Now you are to understand, secondly, Mr. Pip, that the name of the person who is your liberal benefactor remains a profound secret, until the person chooses to reveal it. I am empowered to mention that it is the intention of the person to reveal it at first hand by word of mouth to yourself. When or where that intention may be carried out, I cannot say; no one can say. It may be years hence. Now, you are distinctly to understand that you are most posi-

---

10 **Discussion** What does Mr. Jaggers's opening statement reveal about him?

11 **Discussion** Compare and contrast Mr. Jaggers and Joe.

12 **Critical Thinking and Reading** What makes Pip believe Miss Havisham is his benefactress? Is this a reasonable assumption? Explain.

13 Discussion Why is it important that Pip be better educated?

14 Discussion How has Mr. Jaggers's profession influenced the way he talks?

15 Discussion How does Mr. Jaggers's mention of Matthew Pocket as tutor support Pip's belief that Miss Havisham is the benefactress?

tively prohibited from making any inquiry on this head, in all the communications you may have with me. Your acceptance of this, and your observance of it as binding, is the only remaining condition that I am charged with by the person from whom I take my instructions, and for whom I am not otherwise responsible. That person is the person from whom you derive your expectations, and the secret is solely held by that person and by me. Again, not a very difficult condition with which to encumber such a rise in fortune; but if you have any objection to it, this is the time to mention it. Speak out."

Once more, I stammered with difficulty that I had no objection.

"I should think not! Now, Mr. Pip, I have done with stipulations. We come next to mere details of arrangement. You must know that although I use the term 'expectations' more than once, you are not endowed with expectations only. There is already lodged in my hands a sum of money amply sufficient for your suitable education and maintenance. You will please consider me your guardian. Oh!" for I was going to thank him, "I tell you at once, I am paid for my services, or I shouldn't render them. It is considered that you must be better educated, in accordance with your altered position, and that you will be alive to the importance and necessity of at once entering on that advantage."

I said I had always longed for it.

"Never mind what you have always longed for, Mr. Pip," he retorted; "keep to the record. If you long for it now, that's enough. Am I answered that you are ready to be placed at once under some proper tutor? Is that it?"

I stammered yes, that was it.

"Good. Now, your inclinations are to be consulted. I don't think that wise, mind, but it's my trust. Have you ever heard of any tutor whom you would prefer to another?"

I had never heard of any tutor but Biddy, and Mr. Wopsle's great-aunt, so I replied in the negative.

"There is a certain tutor, of whom I have some knowledge, who I think might suit the purpose," said Mr. Jaggers. "I don't recommend him, observe; because I never recommended anybody. The gentleman I speak of is one Mr. Matthew Pocket."

Ah! I caught at the name directly. Miss Havisham's relation. The Matthew whom Mr. and Mrs. Camilla had spoken of. The Matthew whose place was to be at Miss Havisham's head, when she lay dead, in her bride's dress on the bride's table.

"You know the name?" said Mr. Jaggers, looking shrewdly at me, and then shutting up his eyes while he waited for my answer.

My answer was that I had heard of the name.

"Oh!" said he. "You have heard of the name! But the question is, what do you say of it?"

I said, or tried to say, that I was much obliged to him for his mention of Matthew Pocket, and that I would gladly try that gentleman.

"Good. You had better try him in his own house. The way shall be prepared for you, and you can see his son first, who is in London. When will you come to London?"

I said (glancing at Joe, who stood looking on, motionless), that I supposed I could come directly.

"First," said Mr. Jaggers, "you should have some new clothes to come in, and they should not be working clothes. Say this day week.[1] You'll want some money. Shall I leave you twenty guineas?"

---

1. this day week: One week from today.

Grammar in Action

In informal speech and often in informal writing, the pronouns *who* and *whoever* are frequently used for *whom* and *whomever*.

Who is this?
Who did you call?
Whoever left the ice cream out?
Whoever did you give that information to?

In more formal written or spoken English, however, a distinction is made between these pronouns:

The way will be prepared for you, and you will see his son first, *who* is in London.

Your acceptance of this, and your observation of it as binding, is the only remaining condition that I am charged with by the person from *whom* I take my instructions, and for *whom* I am not otherwise responsible.

In these examples from *Great Expectations,* the formal rules for using these pronouns apply: *Who* is in the nominative case, and so is used as subject and subject complement. *Whom* is in the objective case, and so is used as direct object and object of a preposition. In the first sentence above, *who* is the subject of the verb *is.* In the second sentence, both examples of *whom* are

He produced a long purse, with the greatest coolness, and counted them out on the table and pushed them over to me.

"Well, Joseph Gargery? You look dumb-founded!"

"I *am*!" said Joe, in a very decided manner.

"It was understood that you wanted nothing for yourself, remember?"

"It were understood," said Joe. "And it are understood. And it ever will be similar according."

"But what," said Mr. Jaggers, swinging his purse, "what if it was in my instructions to make you a present, as compensation?"

"As compensation what for?" Joe demanded.

"For the loss of his services."

Joe laid his hand upon my shoulder with the touch of a woman. "Pip is that hearty welcome," said Joe, "to go free with his services, to honor and fortun', as no words can tell him. But if you think as money can make compensation to me for the loss of the little child—what come to the forge—and ever the best of friends!—"

Oh, dear good Joe, whom I was so ready to leave and so unthankful to, I see you again, with your muscular blacksmith's arm before your eyes, and your broad chest heaving, and your voice dying away.

But I encouraged Joe at the time. I was lost in the mazes of my future fortunes, and could not retrace the bypaths we had trodden together. I begged Joe to be comforted, for (as he said) we had ever been the best of friends, and (as I said) we ever would be so. Joe scooped his eyes with his disengaged wrist, as if he were bent on gouging himself, but said not another word.

Mr. Jaggers had looked on at this as one who recognized in Joe the village idiot, and in me his keeper. When it was over, he said, weighing in his hand the purse he had ceased to swing:

"Now, Joseph Gargery, I warn you this is your last chance. No half-measures with me. If you mean to take a present that I have it in charge to make you, speak out, and you shall have it. If on the contrary you mean to say—" Here, to his great amazement, he was stopped by Joe's suddenly working round him with every demonstration of a fell pugilistic purpose.[2]

"Which I meantersay," cried Joe, "that if you come into my place bull-baiting and badgering me, come out! Which I meantersay as sech if you're a man, come on! Which I meantersay that what I say, I meantersay and stand or fall by!"

I drew Joe away, and he immediately became placable, merely stating to me, in an obliging manner and as a polite expostulatory notice to any one whom it might happen to concern, that he were not a-going to be bull-baited and badgered in his own place. Mr. Jaggers had risen when Joe demonstrated, and had backed near the door. Without evincing any inclination to come in again, he there delivered his valedictory remarks. They were these:

"Well, Mr. Pip, I think the sooner you leave here—as you are to be a gentleman—the better. Let it stand for this day week, and you shall receive my printed address in the meantime. You can take a hackney coach at the stagecoach office in London, and come straight to me. Understand that I express no opinion, one way or other, on the trust I undertake. I am paid for undertaking it, and I do so. Now, understand that finally. Understand that!"

---

2. **pugilistic** (pyŏŏ′ jəl is′ tik) **purpose:** Intention to start a fistfight.

16 **Discussion** How does this passage reflect two different perspectives on the same events?

17 **Discussion** Why do you think Joe is so angry?

---

objects of prepositions; therefore, the objective case is necessary.

Student Activity 1. Find five other examples of sentences using *who* and *whom* in the novel, and copy these. Share the sentences with a small group, discussing how the pronouns are used in each.

Student Activity 2. Write three sentences containing *who* and three containing *whom*. Trade papers with a partner and discuss your sentences.

Electronic Handbook You might wish to have students review the use of *who* and *whom* before completing the Grammar in Action activities. If students have access to the Language Master 6000, assist them in the use of the LM-6000 Dictionary to obtain information on the use of *who* and *whom*.

18 **Clarification** A comment by Jesus in the gospels indicates that it will be more difficult for a rich man to enter the kingdom of heaven than for a camel to pass through the eye of a needle. What does Pip's reaction to this statement reveal about his state of mind?

He was throwing his finger at both of us, and I think would have gone on, but for his seeming to think Joe dangerous, and going off.

Chapter 19

The next morning, after breakfast, Joe brought out my indentures from the press in the best parlor, and we put them in the fire, and I felt that I was free. With all the novelty of my emancipation on me, I went to church with Joe, and thought perhaps the clergyman wouldn't have read that about the rich man and the kingdom of Heaven, if he had known all.

After our early dinner, I strolled out alone, proposing to finish off the marshes at once, and get them done with. As I passed the church, I felt (as I had felt during service in the morning) a sublime compassion for the poor creatures who were destined to go there, Sunday after Sunday, all their lives through, and to lie obscurely at last among the low green mounds. I promised myself that I would do something for them one of these days, and formed a plan in outline for bestowing a dinner of roast beef and plum pudding, a pint of ale, and a gallon of condescension upon everybody in the village.

I made my exultant way to the old battery, and, lying down there to consider the question whether Miss Havisham intended me for Estella, fell asleep. When I awoke, I was much surprised to find Joe sitting beside me, smoking his pipe. He greeted me with a cheerful smile on my opening my eyes, and said:

"As being the last time, Pip, I thought I'd foller."

"And Joe, I am very glad you did so."

"Thankee, Pip."

"You may be sure, dear Joe," I went on, after we had shaken hands, "that I shall never forget you."

"No, no, Pip!" said Joe, in a comfortable tone, "I'm sure of that. Aye, aye, old chap! Bless you, it were only necessary to get it well round in a man's mind to be certain on it. But it took a bit of time to get it well round, the change come so oncommon plump; didn't it?"

I made no remark on Joe's first head, merely saying as to his second that the tidings had indeed come suddenly, but that I had always wanted to be a gentleman, and had often and often speculated on what I would do if I were one.

"Have you though?" said Joe. "Astonishing!"

"It's a pity now, Joe," said I, "that you did not get on a little more, when we had our lessons here; isn't it?"

"Well, I don't know," returned Joe. "I'm so awful dull. I'm only master of my own trade. It were always a pity as I was so awful dull; but it's no more of a pity now, than it was—this day twelvemonth[1]—don't you see!"

What I had meant was that when I came into my property and was able to do something for Joe, it would have been much more agreeable if he had been better qualified for a rise in station. He was so perfectly innocent of my meaning, however, that I thought I would mention it to Biddy in preference.

So, when we had walked home and had had tea, I took Biddy into our little garden by the side of the lane, and, after throwing out in a general way for the elevation of her spirits, that I should never forget her, said I had a favor to ask of her.

"And it is, Biddy," said I, "that you will not omit any opportunity of helping Joe on, a little."

---

1. **this day twelvemonth:** One year ago today.

"How helping him on?" asked Biddy.

"Well! Joe is a dear good fellow—in fact, I think he is the dearest fellow that ever lived—but he is rather backward in some things. For instance, Biddy, in his learning and his manners."

Although I was looking at Biddy as I spoke, and although she opened her eyes very wide when I had spoken, she did not look at me.

"Oh, his manners! Won't his manners do, then?" asked Biddy.

"My dear Biddy, they do very well here—"

"Oh! They *do* very well here?" interrupted Biddy.

"Hear me out—but if I were to remove Joe into a higher sphere, as I shall hope to remove him when I fully come into my property, they would hardly do him justice."

"And don't you think he knows that?" asked Biddy.

It was such a provoking question (for it had never in the most distant manner occurred to me) that I said snappishly, "Biddy, what do you mean?"

Biddy said, "Have you never considered that he may be proud?"

"Proud?" I repeated, with disdainful emphasis.

"Oh, there are many kinds of pride," said Biddy, looking full at me and shaking her head; "pride is not all of one kind—"

"Well? What are you stopping for?" said I.

"Not all of one kind," resumed Biddy. "He may be too proud to let any one take him out of a place that he is competent to fill, and fills well and with respect. To tell you the truth, I think he is—though it sounds bold in me to say so, for you must know him far better than I do."

"Now, Biddy," said I, "I am very sorry to see this in you. You are envious, Biddy, and grudging. You are dissatisfied on account of my rise in fortune, and you can't help showing it."

"If you have the heart to think so," returned Biddy, "say so. Say so over and over again, if you have the heart to think so."

"If you have the heart to be so, you mean, Biddy," said I, in a virtuous and superior tone; "don't put it off upon me. I am very sorry to see it, and it's a—it's a bad side of human nature. I did intend to ask you to use any little opportunities you might have after I was gone of improving dear Joe. But after this, I ask you nothing. I am extremely sorry to see this in you, Biddy," I repeated. "It's a—it's a bad side of human nature."

"Whether you scold me or approve of me," returned poor Biddy, "you may equally depend upon my trying to do all that lies in my power, here, at all times. And whatever opinion you take away of me shall make no difference in my remembrance of you. Yet a gentleman should not be unjust neither," said Biddy, turning away her head.

I again warmly repeated that it was a bad side of human nature, and I walked down the little path away from Biddy, and Biddy went into the house, and I went out at the garden gate and took a dejected stroll until suppertime.

But morning once more brightened my view, and I extended my clemency to Biddy, and we dropped the subject. Putting on the best clothes I had, I went into town as early as I could hope to find the shops open, and presented myself before Mr. Trabb, the tailor; who was having his breakfast in the parlor behind his shop, and who did not think it worth his while to come out to me, but called me in to him.

"Well!" said Mr. Trabb, in a hail-fellow-well-met kind of way. "How are you, and what can I do for you?"

"Mr. Trabb," said I, "it's an unpleasant

Great Expectations 787

19 Discussion How would you describe Pip's attitude toward Joe? How might Pip's attitude have been influenced by his "expectations"?

20 Critical Thinking and Reading Do you agree with Pip? Why or why not?

21 Discussion How has Trabb's behavior toward Pip changed? What does this change indicate about Trabb's character?

22 Discussion What does this memory suggest about Pip's state of mind at the time?

Cooperative Learning Arrange the class in groups of four. Assign each group member a number from 1 to 4. Tell students that they are to work together to find examples of the struggle between love and intolerance that is going on inside Pip. (You might want to suggest that they read the scenes with Biddy, in particular.) When students have had sufficient time to look in the text for specific examples, call a number for each group and ask for the group's responses.

thing to have to mention, because it looks like boasting, but I have come into a handsome property."

A change passed over Mr. Trabb. He got up from the bedside and wiped his fingers on the table-cloth, exclaiming, "Lord bless my soul!"

"I am going up to my guardian in London," said I, casually drawing some guineas out of my pocket and looking at them; "and I want a fashionable suit of clothes to go in. I wish to pay for them," I added—otherwise I thought he might only pretend to make them—"with ready money."

21 "My dear sir," said Mr. Trabb, "don't hurt me by mentioning that. May I venture to congratulate you? Would you do me the favor of stepping into the shop?"

Mr. Trabb's boy was the most audacious boy in all that countryside. When I had entered he was sweeping the shop, and he had sweetened his labors by sweeping over me. He was still sweeping when I came out into the shop with Mr. Trabb, and he knocked the broom against all possible corners and obstacles to express (as I understood it) equality with any blacksmith, alive or dead.

"Hold that noise," said Mr. Trabb, with the greatest sternness, "or I'll knock your head off! Do me the favor to be seated, sir."

I selected the materials for a suit, with the assistance of Mr. Trabb's judgment, and reentered the parlor to be measured. When he had at last done and had appointed to send the articles to Mr. Pumblechook's on the Thursday evening, he said, with his hand upon the parlor lock, "I know, sir, that London gentlemen cannot be expected to patronize local work, as a rule; but if you would give me a turn now and then in the quality of a townsman, I should greatly esteem it. Good morning, sir, much obliged. Door!"

The last word was flung at the boy, who

had not the least notion what it meant. But I saw him collapse as his master rubbed me out with his hands, and my first decided experience of the stupendous power of money was that it had morally laid upon his back, Trabb's boy.

After this memorable event, I went to the hatter's, and the bootmaker's, and the hosier's. I also went to the coach office and took my place for seven o'clock on Saturday morning. When I had ordered everything I wanted, I directed my steps towards Pumblechook's, and, as I approached that gentleman's place of business, I saw him standing at his door.

He was waiting for me with great impatience. He had been out early with the chaise-cart, and had called at the forge and heard the news. He had prepared a collation[2] for me in the Barnwell parlor, and he too ordered his shopman to "come out of the gangway" as my sacred person passed.

"To think," said Mr. Pumblechook, after snorting admiration at me for some moments, "that I should have been the humble instrument of leading up to this is a proud reward."

I begged Mr. Pumblechook to remember that nothing was to be ever said or hinted on that point.

I mentioned to him that I wished to have my new clothes sent to his house, and he was ecstatic on my so distinguishing him. I mentioned my reason for desiring to avoid observation in the village, and he lauded it to the skies. There was nobody but himself, he intimated, worthy of my confidence. Then he asked me tenderly if I remembered our boyish games at sums, and how we had gone together to have me bound apprentice, and, in effect, how he had ever been my favorite fancy and my chosen friend? I remember **2**

---

2. collation (kä lā′ shən) *n.*: Light meal.

feeling convinced that I had been much mistaken in him, and that he was a sensible practical good-hearted prime fellow.

So Tuesday, Wednesday, and Thursday passed; and on Friday morning I went to Mr. Pumblechook's, to put on my new clothes and pay my visit to Miss Havisham. Mr. Pumblechook's own room was given up to me to dress in, and was decorated with clean towels expressly for the event. My clothes were rather a disappointment, of course. Probably every new and eagerly expected garment ever put on since clothes came in fell a trifle short of the wearer's expectation. But after I had had my new suit on some half an hour, it seemed to fit me better.

I went circuitously to Miss Havisham's by all the back ways, and rang at the bell. Sarah Pocket came to the gate, and positively reeled back when she saw me so changed.

"You?" said she. "You? Good gracious! What do you want?"

"I am going to London, Miss Pocket," said I, "and want to say good-bye to Miss Havisham."

I was not expected, for she left me locked in the yard, while she went to ask if I were to be admitted. After a very short delay, she returned and took me up, staring at me all the way.

Miss Havisham was taking exercise in the room with the long spread table, leaning on her crutch stick. The room was lighted as of yore, and at the sound of our entrance, she stopped and turned. She was then just abreast of the rotted bride-cake.

"Don't go, Sarah," she said. "Well, Pip?"

"I start for London, Miss Havisham, tomorrow," I was exceedingly careful what I said, "and I thought you would kindly not mind my taking leave of you."

"This is a gay figure, Pip," said she, making her crutch stick play round me, as if she, the fairy godmother who had changed me, were bestowing the finishing gift.

"I have come into such good fortune since I saw you last, Miss Havisham," I murmured. "And I am so grateful for it, Miss Havisham!"

"Aye, aye!" said she, looking at the discomfited and envious Sarah, with delight. "I have seen Mr. Jaggers. I have heard about it, Pip. So you go tomorrow?"

"Yes, Miss Havisham."

"And you are adopted by a rich person?"

"Yes, Miss Havisham."

"Not named?"

"No, Miss Havisham."

"And Mr. Jaggers is made your guardian?"

"Yes, Miss Havisham."

She quite gloated on these questions and answers, so keen was her enjoyment of Sarah Pocket's jealous dismay. "Well!" she went on; "you have a promising career before you. Be good—deserve it—and abide by Mr. Jaggers's instructions." She looked at me, and looked at Sarah, and Sarah's countenance wrung out of her watchful face a cruel smile. "Good-bye, Pip! You will always keep the name of Pip, you know."

"Yes, Miss Havisham."

"Good-bye, Pip!"

She stretched out her hand, and I went down on my knee and put it to my lips. I had not considered how I should take leave of her; it came naturally to me at the moment, to do this. She looked at Sarah Pocket with triumph in her weird eyes, and so I left my fairy godmother, with both her hands on her crutch stick, standing in the midst of the dimly lighted room beside the rotten bride-cake that was hidden in cobwebs.

And now those six days which were to have run out so slowly had run out fast and

23 **Discussion** Why does he refer to Miss Havisham as his "fairy godmother"?

Speaking and Listening You might want to have students volunteer to read aloud the two key scenes that show Pip's inner conflict between love and intolerance. Both are scenes between Pip and Biddy. The first forms Chapter 17, and the second is toward the beginning of Chapter 19. Individual students may read the parts of Pip (as the narrator), Pip (when quoted directly), and Biddy.

23

24 Discussion What is the source of Pip's inner conflict?

25 Clarification Joe and Biddy throw old shoes after Pip as a way of wishing him good luck.

were gone, and tomorrow looked me in the face more steadily than I could look at it. As the six evenings had dwindled away to five, to four, to three, to two, I had become more and more appreciative of the society of Joe and Biddy. On this last evening, I dressed myself out in my new clothes for their delight, and sat in my splendor until bedtime. We had a hot supper on the occasion, graced by the inevitable roast fowl. We were all very low, and none the higher for pretending to be in spirits.

I was to leave our village at five in the morning, and I had told Joe that I wished to walk away all alone. I am afraid—sore afraid—that this purpose originated in my sense of the contrast there would be between me and Joe, if we went to the coach together. I had pretended with myself that there was nothing of this taint in the arrangement; but when I went up to my little room on this last night, I felt compelled to admit that it might be done so, and had an impulse upon me to go down again and entreat Joe to walk with me in the morning. I did not.

Biddy was astir so early to get my breakfast that, although I did not sleep at the window an hour, I smelt the smoke of the kitchen fire when I started up with a terrible idea that it must be late in the afternoon. But long after that, and long after I heard the clinking of the teacups and was quite ready, I wanted the resolution to go downstairs. After all, I remained up there, repeatedly unlocking and unstrapping my small portmanteau and locking and strapping it up again, until Biddy called to me that I was late.

It was a hurried breakfast with no taste in it. I got up from the meal, saying with a sort of briskness, as if it had only just occurred to me, "Well! I suppose I must be off!"

and then I kissed my sister, who was laughing, and nodding and shaking in her usual chair, and kissed Biddy, and threw my arms around Joe's neck. Then I took up my little portmanteau and walked out. The last I saw of them was when I presently heard a scuffle behind me, and looking back, saw Joe throwing an old shoe after me and Biddy throwing another old shoe. I stopped then, to wave my hat, and dear old Joe waved his strong right arm above his head, crying huskily, "Hooroar!" and Biddy put her apron to her face.

I walked away at a good pace, thinking it was easier to go than I had supposed it would be. I whistled and made nothing of going. But the village was very peaceful and quiet, and the light mists were solemnly rising, as if to show me the world, and I had been so innocent and little there, and all beyond was so unknown and great, that in a moment with a strong heave and sob I broke into tears. It was by the finger-post at the end of the village, and I laid my hand upon it, and said, "Good-bye, O my dear, dear friend!"

So subdued I was by those tears, and by their breaking out again in the course of the quiet walk, that when I was on the coach, and it was clear of the town, I deliberated with an aching heart whether I would not get down when we changed horses and walk back, and have another evening at home, and a better parting.

We changed again, and yet again, and it was now too late and too far to go back, and I went on. And the mists had all solemnly risen now, and the world lay spread before me.

THIS IS THE END OF THE FIRST STAGE OF
PIP'S EXPECTATIONS

Grammar in Action

Certain verb forms, called verbals, can function as other parts of speech. One of these verbals is the **participle.** Participles function as adjectives to modify nouns or pronouns. Participles usually end in *-ing* or *-ed,* but some also have irregular endings. Because participles are verb forms, they can have modifiers and complements. When this occurs, the entire **participial phrase** acts as an adjective.

Using participles and participial phrases adds variety to your sentences and helps hold the reader's interest. Participles and participial phrases are especially useful for adding details to sentences. Notice Dickens's use of participial phrases in the following passage:

Then I stepped outside and turned into a street where I saw the great black dome of Saint Paul's *bulging at me* from behind a grim stone building which a bystander said was

Chapter 20

The journey from our town to the metropolis was a journey of about five hours. It was a little past midday when the four-horse stagecoach by which I was a passenger got into the ravel of traffic frayed out about the Cross Keys, Wood Street, Cheapside, London.

Mr. Jaggers had duly sent me his address; it was Little Britain, and he had written after it on his card, "just out of Smithfield, and close by the coach-office." Nevertheless, a hackney coachman, who seemed to have as many capes to his greasy greatcoat as he was years old, packed me up in his coach and hemmed me in with a folding and jingling barrier of steps, as if he were going to take me fifty miles.

I had scarcely had time to enjoy the coach and to think how like a straw yard it was, and yet how like a rag shop, and to wonder why the horses' nose bags were kept inside, when I observed the coachman beginning to get down, as if we were going to stop presently. And stop we presently did, in a gloomy street, at certain offices with an open door, whereon was painted MR. JAGGERS.

I went into the front office with my little portmanteau in my hand, and asked, was Mr. Jaggers at home?

"He is not," returned the clerk. "He is in court at present. Am I addressing Mr. Pip?"

I signified that he was addressing Mr. Pip.

"Mr. Jaggers left word would you wait in his room. He couldn't say how long he might be, having a case on. But it stands to reason, his time being valuable, that he won't be longer than he can help."

With those words, the clerk opened a door, and ushered me into an inner chamber at the back. Mr. Jaggers's room was lighted by a skylight only, and was a most dismal place. I sat down in the cliental chair placed over against Mr. Jaggers's chair. After I had sat wondering and waiting in Mr. Jaggers's close room for some time, I got up and went out.

I told the clerk that I would take a turn in the air while I waited. Then I stepped outside and turned into a street where I saw the great black dome of Saint Paul's[1] bulging at me from behind a grim stone building which a bystander said was Newgate Prison. Following the wall of the jail, I found the roadway covered with straw to deaden the noise of passing vehicles; and from this, and from the quantity of people standing about, I inferred that the trials were on.

I dropped into the office to ask if Mr. Jaggers had come in yet, and I found he had not, and I strolled out again. This time I made the tour of Little Britain, and now I became aware that other people were waiting about for Mr. Jaggers, as well as I. There were two men of secret appearance lounging, and thoughtfully fitting their feet into the cracks of the pavement as they talked together, one of whom said to the other when they first passed me that "Jaggers would do it if it was to be done." There was a knot of three men and two women standing at a corner, and one of the women was crying on her dirty shawl, and the other comforted her by saying, as she pulled her own shawl over her shoulders, "Jaggers is for him, 'Melia, and what more *could* you have?" These testimonies to the popularity of my guardian made a deep impression on me, and I admired and wondered more than ever.

At length, I saw Mr. Jaggers coming across the road towards me. All the others who were waiting saw him at the same time,

26

---

1. **Saint Paul's:** Famous cathedral in London.

Great Expectations 791

26 **Discussion** What does the overheard conversation suggest about Jaggers?

Videodisc To help students appreciate how Pip's life changes, you might want to show them the segment of the *Scenes From Great Expectations* videodisc in which Pip arrives in London.

Frames 29558 to 33328

Electronic Handbook You might want students to review the use of participial phrases before they complete the Grammar in Action activities. If students have access to the Language Master 6000, have them enter the access words *tense, phrase,* or *verbal* and press the GRAMMAR key to obtain information on these topics.

Newgate Prison. *Following the wall of the jail,* I found the roadway *covered with straw* to deaden the noise of *passing vehicles;* and from the quantity of people *standing about,* I inferred that the trials were on.

In addition to adding details, participles and participial phrases can furnish you with a variety of sentence openers. Notice Dickens's use of a participial phrase to begin the final sentence in the paragraph.

Student Activity 1. What details does Dickens add to the paragraph by using participles and participial phrases?

Student Activity 2. Write an original paragraph describing a place you have visited. Use five participles or participial phrases to add details to your description.

Humanities Note

Fine art, *Ludgate Hill,* by Gustave Doré. Gustave Doré (1832–1883) was a French painter, engraver, and lithographer. He learned to draw without a teacher, and at age 16 he was employed as a caricaturist by a Paris newspaper—an achievement that won him the nickname "child genius" from older artists. His work for the newspaper, combined with his study of engravings and etchings at the National Library, made him a superb wood engraver. Wood engraving is a printing technique in which lines are incised into a wooden block and then the block is inked and pressed onto paper to record the image.

Ludgate Hill is from a series of engravings by Doré entitled *The City of London in the 1860's.* Have students note the mire of people and animals—the sheep sharing the same roadway as the coaches, wagons, and carts. The intense crowding is heightened by the stone buildings framing and defining the flow of traffic, as though making everyone march through a vise-like canyon, and by the vast numbers of people coming from beyond the arched roadway, on which the train moves.

You might want to use the following questions to provoke a discussion:

1. What impression of London does this engraving convey?
2. Which details contribute to this impression?
3. How would such a scene affect a young man like Pip, who had never been to the city before?

LUDGATE HILL
Gustave Doré
Reproduced by courtesy of the Trustees of The British Museum

792   *The Novel*

and there was quite a rush at him. Mr. Jaggers, putting a hand on my shoulder and walking me on at his side without saying anything to me, addressed himself to his followers.

First, he took the two secret men.

"Now, I have nothing to say to *you*," said Mr. Jaggers, throwing his finger at them. "I want to know no more than I know. As to the result, it's a toss-up. I told you from the first it was a toss-up. Have you paid Wemmick?"

"Yes, sir," said both the men together.

"Very well; then you may go. Now, I won't have it!" said Mr. Jaggers, waving his hand at them to put them behind him. "If you say a word to me, I'll throw up the case."

"We thought, Mr. Jaggers—" one of the men began, pulling off his hat.

"That's what I told you not to do," said Mr. Jaggers. "*You* thought! I think for you; that's enough for you.

"And now *you*!" said Mr. Jaggers, suddenly stopping, and turning on the two women with the shawls. "Once for all. If you don't know that your Bill's in good hands, I know it. And if you come here bothering about your Bill, I'll make an example of both your Bill and you, and let him slip through my fingers. Have you paid Wemmick?"

"Oh, yes, sir!"

"Very well. Then you have done all you have got to do. Say another word—one single word—and Wemmick shall give you your money back."

This terrible threat caused the two women to fall off immediately. Without further interruption, we reached the front office.

My guardian then took me into his own room, and while he lunched, standing, from a sandwich-box, informed me what arrangements he had made for me. I was to go to "Barnard's Inn," to young Mr. Pocket's rooms, where a bed had been sent in for my accommodation; I was to remain with young Mr. Pocket until Monday; on Monday I was to go with him to his father's house on a visit, that I might try how I liked it. Also, I was told what my allowance was to be—it was a very liberal one—and had handed to me from one of my guardian's drawers the cards of certain tradesmen with whom I was to deal for all kinds of clothes, and such other things as I could in reason want. "You will find your credit good, Mr. Pip," said my guardian, "but I shall by this means be able to check your bills, and to pull you up if I find you outrunning the constable. Of course you'll go wrong somehow, but that's no fault of mine."

After I had pondered a little over this encouraging sentiment, I asked Mr. Jaggers if I could send for a coach. He said it was not worthwhile, I was so near my destination; Wemmick should walk round with me, if I pleased.

I then found that Wemmick was the clerk in the next room. Another clerk was rung down from upstairs to take his place while he was out, and I accompanied him into the street, after shaking hands with my guardian. We found a new set of people lingering outside, but Wemmick made a way among them by saying coolly yet decisively, "I tell you it's no use; he won't have a word to say to one of you"; and we soon got clear of them, and went on side by side.

Chapter 21

Casting my eyes on Mr. Wemmick as we went along, to see what he was like in the light of day, I found him to be a dry man, rather short in stature, with a square wooden face, whose expression seemed to have been imperfectly chipped out with a dull-edged chisel. There were some marks in it that might have been dimples, if the mate-

Great Expectations 793

27 **Discussion** What does Mr. Jaggers's attitude toward his clients reveal about him?

28 **Critical Thinking and Reading** What inferences can you make about Mr. Wemmick based on this description?

rial had been softer and the instrument finer, but which, as it was, were only dints. He had glittering eyes—small, keen, and black—and thin wide mottled lips. He had had them, to the best of my belief, from forty to fifty years.

"Do you know where Mr. Matthew Pocket lives?" I asked Mr. Wemmick.

"Yes," said he, nodding in the direction. "At Hammersmith, west of London."

"Is that far?"

"Well! Say five miles."

"Do you know him?"

"Why, you are a regular cross-examiner!" said Mr. Wemmick, looking at me with an approving air. "Yes, I know him. *I* know him!"

There was an air of toleration or depreciation about his utterance of these words that rather depressed me; and I was still looking sideways at his block of a face in search of any encouraging note to the text, when he said here we were at Barnard's Inn. My depression was not alleviated by the announcement, for I had supposed that establishment to be a hotel kept by Mr. Barnard, to which the Blue Boar in our town was a mere public house. Whereas I now found Barnard to be a disembodied spirit, or a fiction, and his inn the dingiest collection of shabby buildings ever squeezed together in a rank corner as a club for tomcats.

So imperfect was this realization of the first of my great expectations that I looked in dismay at Mr. Wemmick. "Ah!" said he, mistaking me, "the retirement reminds you of the country. So it does me."

He led me into a corner and conducted me up a flight of stairs—which appeared to me to be slowly collapsing into sawdust, so that one of those days the upper lodgers would look out at their doors and find themselves without the means of coming down—to a set of chambers on the top floor. MR.

POCKET, JUN., was painted on the door, and there was a label on the letter box, "Return shortly."

"He hardly thought you'd come so soon," Mr. Wemmick explained. "You don't want me any more?"

"No, thank you," said I.

"As I keep the cash," Mr. Wemmick observed, "we shall most likely meet pretty often. Good day."

"Good day."

When he was gone, I opened the staircase window and had nearly beheaded myself, for the lines had rotted away, and it came down like the guillotine.[1] After this escape, I was content to take a foggy view of the Inn through the window's encrusting dirt, and to stand dolefully looking out, saying to myself that London was decidedly overrated.

Mr. Pocket, Junior's, idea of shortly was not mine, for I had nearly maddened myself with looking out for half an hour, and had written my name with my finger several times in the dirt of every pane in the window, before I heard footsteps on the stairs. Gradually there arose before me the hat, head, neckcloth, waistcoat, trousers, boots, of a member of society of about my own standing. He had a paper bag under each arm and a pottle[2] of strawberries in one hand, and was out of breath.

"Mr. Pip?" said he.

"Mr. Pocket?" said I.

"Dear me!" he exclaimed. "I am extremely sorry; but I knew there was a coach from your part of the country at midday, and I thought you would come by that one. The fact is, I have been out on your account—not that that is any excuse—for I thought, com-

---

1. guillotine (gil′ ə tēn′) *n.*: Instrument that beheads a victim with a falling blade.
2. pottle (pät′l) *n.*: Pot that holds two quarts.

COVENT GARDEN, LONDON
John Wykeham Archer
British Library, London

Humanities Note

Fine art, *Covent Garden, London,* by John Wykeham Archer. John Wykeham Archer (1808–1864) was a British etcher and painter. A student of the celebrated engraver, John Scott, Archer devoted most of his life to print making. He did many etchings of London life and architecture, which he used to illustrate the books he wrote on that subject.

In *Covent Garden, London,* his constant study and drawing of the London scene served him well in capturing the raucous flavor of this busy produce market.

You might want to use the following questions to help students appreciate the picture:
1. Which details indicate that Covent Garden was a produce market?
2. Compare and contrast this London scene with the one shown in Gustave Doré's *Ludgate Hill,* page 792.

30 **Discussion** How is this remark in keeping with Herbert's character, as it was previously revealed?

ing from the country, you might like a little fruit after dinner, and I went to Covent Garden Market to get it good."

For a reason that I had, I felt as if my eyes would start out of my head. I began to think this was a dream.

As I stood opposite to Mr. Pocket, Junior, I saw the starting appearance come into his own eyes that I knew to be in mine, and he said, falling back:

"Lord bless me, you're the prowling boy!"

"And you," said I, "are the pale young gentleman!"

Chapter 22

The pale young gentleman and I stood contemplating one another in Barnard's Inn, until we both burst out laughing. "The idea of its being you!" said he. "The idea of its being *you!*" said I. And then we contemplated one another afresh, and laughed again. "Well!" said the pale young gentleman, reaching out his hand good-humoredly, "it's all over now, I hope, and it will be magnanimous in you if you'll forgive me for having knocked you about so."

30

Great Expectations 795

I derived from this speech that Mr. Herbert Pocket (for Herbert was the pale young gentleman's name) still rather confounded his intention with his execution. But I made a modest reply, and we shook hands warmly.

"You hadn't come into your good fortune at that time?" said Herbert Pocket.

"No," said I.

"No," he acquiesced. "I heard it had happened very lately. *I* was rather on the lookout for good fortune then."

"Indeed?"

"Yes. Miss Havisham had sent for me, to see if she could take a fancy to me. But she couldn't—at all events, she didn't."

I thought it polite to remark that I was surprised to hear that.

"Bad taste," said Herbert, laughing, "but a fact. Yes, she had sent for me on a trial visit, and if I had come out of it successfully, I suppose I should have been provided for, perhaps I should have been what-you-may-called it to Estella."

"What's that?" I asked, with sudden gravity.

He was arranging his fruit in plates while we talked, which divided his attention, and was the cause of his having made this lapse of a word. "Affianced," he explained, still busy with the fruit. "Betrothed. Engaged. What's-his-named. Any word of that sort."

"How did you bear your disappointment?" I asked.

"Pooh!" said he, "I didn't care much for it. *She's a Tartar.*"[1]

"Miss Havisham?"

"I don't say no to that, but I meant Estella. That girl's hard and haughty and capricious to the last degree, and has been brought up by Miss Havisham to wreak revenge on all the male sex."

"What relation is she to Miss Havisham?"

"None," said he. "Only adopted."

"Why should she wreak revenge on all the male sex? What revenge?"

"Lord, Mr. Pip!" said he. "Don't you know?"

"No," said I.

"Dear me! It's quite a story, and shall be saved till dinner time. And now let me take the liberty of asking you a question. How did you come there, that day?"

I told him, and he was attentive until I had finished, and then burst out laughing again, and asked me if I was sore afterwards? I didn't ask him if *he* was, for my conviction on that point was perfectly established.

"Mr. Jaggers is your guardian, I understand?" he went on.

"Yes."

"You know he is Miss Havisham's man of business and solicitor,[2] and has her confidence when nobody else has?"

This was bringing me (I felt) towards dangerous ground. I answered with a constraint I made no attempt to disguise, that I had seen Mr. Jaggers in Miss Havisham's house on the very day of our combat, but never at any other time, and that I believed he had no recollection of having ever seen me there.

"He was so obliging as to suggest my father for your tutor, and he called on my father to propose it. Of course he knew about my father from his connection with Miss Havisham. My father is Miss Havisham's

31

----

1. Tartar (tär′ tər) *n.*: Ferocious, unmanageable person.

2. solicitor (sə lis′ it ər) *n.*: British lawyer who can assist clients but cannot plead cases in the higher courts.

Primary Source

Much of Dickens's life has been revealed through his letters, which he wrote frequently and which were detailed accounts of his life, current events, and his social philosophy. Dickens kept up a continual correspondence with family and friends, which are now in print; his letters were published in a three-volume collection, comprising twenty-five hundred pages and over a million words. He wrote more than five hundred letters to Miss Angela Burdett Coutts, the wife of Sir Francis Burdett, in which he discussed his involvement in charities, slum improvements, and reform movements. He also often wrote about his work and the ideas that were brewing in his mind. The following letter, which is published in *The Heart of Charles Dickens* by Edgar Johnson, was written to Angela Burdett Coutts on November 12, 1842. In it Dickens wrote about his state of mind as he embarked on the writing of a new book:

Your most kind note found me in the agonies of plotting and contriving a new book [*Martin Chuzzlewit*], in which stage of the tremendous process, I am accustomed to walk up and down the house, smiting my forehead dejectedly; and to be so horribly cross and surly, that the boldest fly at my

cousin; not that that implies familiar inter-course between them, for he is a bad court-ier and will not propitiate her."

Herbert Pocket had a frank and easy way with him that was very taking. I had never seen any one then, and I have never seen any one since, who more strongly expressed to me, in every look and tone, a natural inca-pacity to do anything secret and mean. There was something wonderfully hopeful about his general air, and something that at the same time whispered to me he would never be very successful or rich. I don't know how this was.

He was still a pale young gentleman, and had a certain conquered languor about him in the midst of his spirits and briskness, that did not seem indicative of natural strength. He had not a handsome face, but it was better than handsome, being extremely amiable and cheerful.

I told him my small story, and laid stress on my being forbidden to inquire who my benefactor was. I further mentioned that as I had been brought up by a blacksmith in a country place, and knew very little of the ways of politeness, I would take it as a great kindness in him if he would give me a hint whenever he saw me at a loss or going wrong.

"With pleasure," said he, "though I ven-ture to prophesy that you'll want very few hints. Will you do me the favor to begin at once to call me by my Christian name, Her-bert?"

I thanked him, and said I would. I in-formed him in exchange that my Christian name was Philip.

"I don't take to Philip," said he, smiling, "for it sounds like a moral boy out of the spelling book. I tell you what I should like. We are so harmonious, and you have been a blacksmith. Would you mind Handel for a fa-miliar name? There's a charming piece of music by Handel[3] called 'The Harmonious Blacksmith.' "

"I should like it very much."

"Then, my dear Handel," said he, turn-ing round as the door opened, "here is the dinner."

We had made some progress in the din-ner when I reminded Herbert of his promise to tell me about Miss Havisham.

"True," he replied. "I'll redeem it at once. Let me introduce the topic, Handel, by men-tioning that in London it is not the custom to put the knife in the mouth—for fear of ac-cidents—and that while the fork is reserved for that use, it is not put further in than necessary. It is scarcely worth mentioning, only it's as well to do as other people do. Also, the spoon is not generally used over-hand, but under. This has two advantages. You get at your mouth better (which after all is the object), and you save a good deal of the attitude of opening oysters on the part of the right elbow."

He offered these friendly suggestions in such a lively way that we both laughed and I scarcely blushed.

"Now," he pursued, "concerning Miss Havisham. Miss Havisham, you must know, was a spoiled child. Her mother died when she was a baby, and her father denied her nothing. Her father was a country gentleman down in your part of the world, and was a brewer. Well! Mr. Havisham was very rich and very proud. So was his daughter."

"Miss Havisham was an only child?" I hazarded.

"Stop a moment, I am coming to that. No, she was not an only child; she had a

---

3. Handel (han' d'l): George Frederick Handel (1685–1759), a German-born English composer.

32 **Discussion** Why do you think Pip believes Herbert will not be successful?

33 **Discussion** Why do you think Pip allows Herbert to rename him?

approach. At such times, even the Postman knocks at the door with a mild feebleness, and my publishers always come two together, lest I should fall upon a single invader and do murder on his intrusive body. . . .

. . . In starting a work which is to last for twenty months, there are so many little things to attend to, which require my personal superintendence, that I am obliged to be constantly on the watch; and I may add seriously, that unless I were to shut myself up, obstinately and sullenly in my own room for a great many days without writing a word, I don't think I ever should make a beginning. . . .

half-brother. Her father privately married again—his cook, I rather think."

"I thought he was proud," said I.

"My good Handel, so he was. He married his second wife privately because he was proud, and in course of time *she* died. When she was dead, I apprehend he first told his daughter what he had done, and then the son became a part of the family, residing in the house you are acquainted with. As the son grew a young man, he turned out riotous, extravagant, undutiful—altogether bad. At last his father disinherited him; but he softened when he was dying, and left him well off, though not nearly so well off as Miss Havisham.

"Miss Havisham was now an heiress, and you may suppose was looked after as a great match. Her half-brother had now ample means again, but what with debts and what with new madness, wasted them again. There were stronger differences between him and her than there had been between him and his father, and it is suspected that he cherished a deep and mortal grudge against her as having influenced the father's anger. Now, I come to the cruel part of the story.

"There appeared upon the scene a certain man who made love to Miss Havisham. I have heard my father mention that he was a showy man, and the kind of man for the purpose. But he was not to be, without ignorance or prejudice, mistaken for a gentleman. Well! This man pursued Miss Havisham closely, and professed to be devoted to her. I believe she had not shown much susceptibility up to that time, but all the susceptibility she possessed certainly came out then, and she passionately loved him. There is no doubt that she perfectly idolized him. He got great sums of money from her, and he induced her to buy her brother out of a share in the brewery (which had been weakly left him by his father) at an immense price,

on the plea that when he was her husband he must hold and manage it all. Your guardian was not at that time in Miss Havisham's councils, and she was too haughty and too much in love to be advised by any one. Her relations were poor and scheming, with the exception of my father; he was poor enough, but not time-serving or jealous. The only independent one among them, he warned her that she was doing too much for this man, and was placing herself too unreservedly in his power. She took the first opportunity of angrily ordering my father out of the house, in his presence, and my father has never seen her since."

I thought of her having said, "Matthew will come and see me at last when I am laid dead upon that table."

"To return to the man and make an end of him. The marriage day was fixed, the wedding dresses were bought, the wedding tour was planned out, the wedding guests were invited. The day came, but not the bridegroom. He wrote a letter—"

"Which she received," I struck in, "when she was dressing for her marriage? At twenty minutes to nine?"

"At the hour and minute," said Herbert, nodding, "at which she afterwards stopped all the clocks. What was in it, further than that it most heartlessly broke the marriage off, I can't tell you, because I don't know. When she recovered from a bad illness that she had, she laid the whole place waste, as you have seen it, and she has never since looked upon the light of day."

"Is that all the story?" I asked, after considering it.

"All I know of it. But I have forgotten one thing. It has been supposed that the man to whom she gave her misplaced confidence acted throughout in concert with her half-brother; that it was a conspiracy between them; and that they shared the profits."

798   The Novel

"What became of the two men?" I asked, after again considering the subject.

"They fell into deeper shame and degradation—if there can be deeper—and ruin."

"Are they alive, now?"

"I don't know."

"You said just now that Estella was not related to Miss Havisham, but adopted. When adopted?"

Herbert shrugged his shoulders. "There has always been an Estella, since I have heard of a Miss Havisham. I know no more."

"And all I know," I retorted, "you know."

"I fully believe it. So there can be no competition or perplexity between you and me. And as to the condition on which you hold your advancement in life—namely, that you are not to inquire or discuss to whom you owe it—you may be very sure that it will never be encroached upon, or even approached, by me."

He said this with so much meaning that I felt he as perfectly understood Miss Havisham to be my benefactress as I understood the fact myself.

We were very gay and sociable, and I asked him, in the course of conversation, what he was? He replied, "A capitalist—an insurer of ships. However, I shall not rest satisfied with merely employing my capital in insuring ships. I think I shall trade," said he, leaning back in his chair, "to the East Indies, for silks, shawls, spices, dyes, drugs, and precious woods. It's an interesting trade."

"I think I shall trade, also," said he, putting his thumbs in his waistcoat pockets, "to the West Indies, for sugar, tobacco, and rum. Also to Ceylon, especially for elephants' tusks."

"You will want a good many ships," said I.

"A perfect fleet," said he.

Quite overpowered by the magnificence of these transactions, I asked him where the ships he insured mostly traded to at present?

"I haven't begun insuring yet," he replied. "I am looking about me."

Somehow that pursuit seemed more in keeping with Barnard's Inn. I said (in a tone of conviction), "Ah-h!"

"Yes. I am in a countinghouse,[4] and looking about me."

"Is a countinghouse profitable?" I asked.

"Why, n-no; not to me. Not directly profitable. That is, it doesn't pay me anything, and I have to—keep myself. But the thing is that you look about you. *That's* the grand thing. You are in a countinghouse, you know, and you look about you."

This was very like his way of conducting that encounter in the garden; very like. His manner of bearing his poverty, too, exactly corresponded to his manner of bearing that defeat. It seemed to me that he took all blows and buffets now with just the same air as he had taken mine then. It was evident that he had nothing around him but the simplest necessaries, for everything that I remarked upon turned out to have been sent in on my account from the coffee-house or somewhere else.

Yet, having already made his fortune in his own mind, he was so unassuming with it that I felt quite grateful to him for not being puffed up. It was a pleasant addition to his naturally pleasant ways, and we got on famously.

On Monday, we took coach for Hammersmith. We arrived there at two or three o'clock in the afternoon, and had very little way to walk to Mr. Pocket's house. Lifting the latch of a gate, we passed direct into a

---

4. **countinghouse** (koun' tiŋ hous') *n.*: Office where a firm keeps business records and handles correspondence.

Great Expectations 799

35 Critical Thinking and Reading Do you agree with Pip's reasoning? Explain.

36 Critical Thinking and Reading What do Herbert Pocket's dreams reveal about him?

Reader's Response If you suddenly acquired a great deal of wealth, how do you think you would change? How would you spend your time and money?

Thematic Response Pip had to face many difficulties in his passage toward becoming a gentleman. Which problem do students think was the most difficult for Pip?

little garden overlooking the river, where Mr. Pocket's children were playing about. And, unless I deceive myself on a point where my interests or prepossessions are certainly not concerned, I saw that Mr. and Mrs. Pocket's children were not growing up or being brought up, but were tumbling up.

Mrs. Pocket was sitting on a garden chair under a tree, reading, with her legs upon another garden chair, and Mrs. Pocket's two nursemaids were looking about them while the children played. "Mamma," said Herbert, "this is young Mr. Pip." Upon which Mrs. Pocket received me with an appearance of amiable dignity.

37 | Mr. Pocket came out to make my acquaintance, and I was not much surprised to find that Mr. Pocket was a gentleman with a rather perplexed expression of face, and with his very gray hair disordered on his head, as if he didn't quite see his way to putting anything straight.

Chapter 23

Mr. Pocket said he was glad to see me, and he hoped I was not sorry to see him. "For, I really am not," he added, with his son's smile, "an alarming personage." He was a young-looking man, in spite of his perplexities and his very gray hair, and his manner seemed quite natural.

Mr. Pocket took me into the house and showed me my room, which was a pleasant one. He then knocked at the doors of two other similar rooms, and introduced me to their occupants, by name Drummle and Startop. Drummle, an old-looking young man of a heavy order of architecture, was whistling. Startop, younger in years and appearance, was reading and holding his head, as if he thought himself in danger of exploding it with too strong a charge of knowledge.

By degrees I learned, and chiefly from Herbert, that Mr. Pocket had been educated at Harrow and at Cambridge,[1] where he had distinguished himself. He had come to London, and after gradually failing in loftier hopes, he had turned his acquirements to the account of literary compilation[2] and correction.

In the evening there was rowing on the river. As Drummle and Startop had each a boat, I resolved to set up mine, and to cut them both out. I was pretty good at most exercises in which country boys are adepts, but, as I was conscious of wanting elegance of style for the Thames[3]—not to say for other waters—I at once engaged to place myself under the tuition of the winner of a prize wherry[4] who plied at our stairs, and to whom I was introduced by my new allies.

---

1. Harrow and Cambridge: A famous English preparatory school and university, respectively.
2. compilation (käm′ pə lā′ shən) *n.*: Making collections or anthologies.
3. Thames (temz): River that flows through London into the North Sea.
4. wherry (hwer′ ē) *n.*: Light rowboat used on rivers.

Closure and Extension

ANSWERS TO RESPONDING TO THE SELECTION
Your Response

1. Have students consider the motivations for the actions and the attitudes that these new characters have toward Pip. Ask them to predict how much help Pip would receive from each were he in trouble.

Recalling

2. Pip learns that an unknown benefactor has left him a fortune, on the following conditions: that he bear the name of Pip, that the name of his benefactor remain a secret until his benefactor chooses to reveal it, that Pip never ask Mr. Jaggers to reveal any information about this benefactor, and that Jaggers act as his guardian.

3. Mr. Jaggers is Pip's "man of business" and his guardian. Wemmick makes out the drafts of money for Pip and gives him advice. Herbert is Pip's best friend and confidant.

4. Pip learns from Herbert that Miss Havisham was the daughter of a wealthy father and her mother died when Miss Havisham was still a baby. When Miss Havisham grew up, she was courted by a handsome man with whom she fell in love, but he abandoned her on their wedding day. Jaggers was Miss Havisham's lawyer, and Miss Havisham adopted Estella as a baby.

Interpreting

5. Suggested Response: Pip leaves with mixed feelings of regret for the past and longing for his future expectations. Pip attempts to instill in Joe and Biddy the idea that they should get more education and raise their station. Joe tolerates him placidly, but Biddy is offended by his presumed superiority.

RESPONDING TO THE SELECTION

Your Response

1. What are your initial impressions of the new characters Pip has encountered? Why?

Recalling

2. What does Pip learn from Mr. Jaggers about his "great expectations"? What conditions are attached?
3. Summarize the roles that Jaggers, Wemmick, and Herbert each play in Pip's new life.
4. What important facts does Pip learn about Miss Havisham?

Interpreting

5. What are Pip's conflicting feelings about his good fortune? How do Pip's "expectations" affect his relationship with Biddy and Joe?
6. On what basis does Pip believe that Miss Havisham is his benefactor?

Applying

7. Why do sudden wealth or good luck often change people?

ANALYZING LITERATURE

Understanding Plot and Subplot

The **plot** is the sequence of interrelated events in a work of fiction. These events are often based on a **conflict.** A long novel may also have **subplots,** or secondary plots, to complicate and mirror the action of the main plot.

The plot of *Great Expectations* focuses on Pip's conflict about the importance of money and success compared to love and devotion. Various subplots—involving Orlick, Herbert, and Wemmick—introduce conflicts involving Pip.

1. Which feelings seem to be gaining in the conflict that Pip is experiencing? Explain.
2. One subplot concerns the "expectations" of Herbert Pocket. Contrast the attitudes, background, and prospects of Pip and Herbert.
3. Identify another subplot of the novel.

CRITICAL THINKING AND READING

Predicting Outcomes

Once the central conflict is clear and certain situations and relationships are established in a novel, you can make predictions about the outcome. For example, you know that Pip is experiencing two opposite feelings: wanting to embrace Joe, Biddy, and his old life and wanting to reject them as "coarse and common." The outcome of the story will depend, in part, on which of these two feelings becomes stronger.

1. How do you think Pip will resolve his inner conflict? Support your answer with details.
2. What does this resolution suggest about the life that Pip will lead?

THINKING AND WRITING

Extending the Story

Recall the predictions you made about the outcome of the central conflict. List additional details that you would include if you were finishing the story based on your prediction. Then, using your notes, write an ending to the story that resolves the conflict. Discuss your first draft with classmates. Use their ideas to revise your work.

LEARNING OPTIONS

1. **Art.** Pip sometimes goes with Joe to the Three Jolly Bargemen, where the townsmen take refreshment and socialize. Such establishments were identified by a signboard outside, which illustrated their name and advertised their offerings. Design a sign for the Three Jolly Bargemen. Show it to your classmates.
2. **Writing.** When Pip arrives in London, he experiences many new sights, although he does say at one point that he considers the place "overrated." Pretend you are Pip and write a letter home describing your first day in town. Include your impressions about the people you have met as well as what you've seen.

Great Expectations 801

Preparation

Literary Focus Consider pointing out to students that Victorian England is so vivid for us today in part because novelists described it. Dickens is particularly famous for his descriptions of London, a city whose streets he walked incessantly.

Prereading Focus The purpose of preparing this chart is to focus student attention on Dickens's expert use of sensory detail to create accurate, detailed pictures of his settings in the reader's mind. Encourage students to list as many sensory details as possible and to share their work with classmates.

Software If students have access to computers, you might want to have them use **Bank Street Writer** for the Focus activity. Using the program's cut and paste features, students can later incorporate material from the Focus activity into their compositions for the Thinking and Writing activity.

Vocabulary You might want to call out vocabulary words from the first four sections and have students give synonyms and antonyms for them.

Spelling Tip Point out that three words in this list—*cupidity, incongruity,* and *disparity*—have the same ending sound spelled *ity*.

GUIDE FOR READING

Great Expectations, Chapters 24–31

Setting and Atmosphere

The **setting** of a novel refers to the time and place of the events, as well as the clothing, customs, and occupations that reflect this time and place. *Great Expectations,* for example, is set in England during the nineteenth century. More specifically, the events of the novel alternate between Pip's small town in the marsh country and the great city of London. The stagecoach that journeys between these two places, the blacksmith's forge, and Jaggers's law office are all part of the setting.

Through careful description of details such as these, Dickens creates an **atmosphere,** or mood, which gives a special flavor to each part of the story. The description of the cemetery near the marsh, for instance, calls up a feeling of mystery and fear. This atmosphere prepares you for the first appearance of the convict.

Focus

Dickens uses specific details to make the various settings come alive. In doing so, he creates a distinct atmosphere that affects the characters. Recall a place that you have visited that had a definite atmosphere. Prepare a sensory-language chart modeled on the one below. Fill it in with details that create the atmosphere, such as the quality of light, certain colors or sounds, or even a particular odor. Then notice how Dickens's details create atmosphere.

Sights	Sounds	Smells	Tastes	Touch

Vocabulary

Knowing the following words will help you as you read Chapters 24–31 of *Great Expectations.*

discomfiture (dis kum′ fi chər) *n.*: Unease; confusion (p. 803)
cupidity (kyōō pid′ ə tē) *n.*: Greed (p. 804)
dexterously (deks′ tər əs lē) *adv.*: With skillful use of the hands (p. 809)

incongruity (in′ kən grōō′ ə tē) *n.*: Quality of being out of place (p. 809)
lethargic (li thär′ jik) *adj.*: Drowsy; without energy (p. 813)
disparity (dis par′ ə tē) *n.*: Condition of inequality (p. 816)

Objectives

1 To understand setting and atmosphere
2 To identify details that create setting
3 To compare and contrast settings
4 To express individual interests and abilities through optional activities

Support Material

Teaching Portfolio
Teacher Backup, p. 923
Grammar in Action Worksheets, *Using Prepositional Phrases,* p. 927; *Using Parallelism,* p. 929
Usage and Mechanics Worksheet, p. 931
Vocabulary Check, p. 932
Analyzing Literature Worksheet, *Understanding Setting and Atmosphere,* p. 933

Language Worksheet, *Exploring Connotations,* p. 934
Selection Test, p. 935

Library of Video Classics
The Changing World of Charles Dickens, Great Expectations

Literature Videodisc
Scenes from Great Expectations

Prentice Hall Literature Writing Studio

Chapter 24

After two or three days, when I had established myself in my room and had gone backwards and forwards to London several times, and had ordered all I wanted of my tradesmen, Mr. Pocket and I had a long talk together. He knew more of my intended career than I knew myself, for he referred to his having been told by Mr. Jaggers that I was not designed for any profession, and that I should be well enough educated for my destiny if I could "hold my own" with the average of young men in prosperous circumstances.

When I had begun to work in earnest, it occurred to me that if I could retain my bedroom in Barnard's Inn, my life would be agreeably varied, while my manners would be none the worse for Herbert's society. Mr. Pocket did not object to this arrangement, but urged that before any step could possibly be taken in it, it must be submitted to my guardian. I felt that his delicacy[1] arose out of the consideration that the plan would save Herbert some expense, so I went off to Little Britain and imparted my wish to Mr. Jaggers.

"If I could buy the furniture now hired for me," said I, "and one or two other little things, I should be quite at home there."

"Go it!" said Mr. Jaggers, with a short laugh. "I told you you'd get on. Well! How much do you want?"

I said I didn't know how much.

"Come!" retorted Mr. Jaggers. "How much? Fifty pounds?"

"Oh, not nearly so much."

"Five pounds?" said Mr. Jaggers.

This was such a great fall that I said in discomfiture, "Oh! more than that."

---

1. **delicacy** (del′ i kə sē) *n*.: Regard for what is proper.

"More than that, eh!" retorted Mr. Jaggers. "How much more?"

"It is so difficult to fix a sum," said I, hesitating.

"Come!" said Mr. Jaggers. "Let's get at it. Twice five; will that do? Three times five; will that do? Four times five; will that do?"

I said I thought that would do handsomely.

"Four times five will do handsomely, will it?" said Mr. Jaggers, knitting his brows. "Now, what do you make of four times five?"

"Twenty pounds, of course."

"Wemmick!" said Mr. Jaggers, opening his office door. "Take Mr. Pip's written order, and pay him twenty pounds."

This strongly marked way of doing business made a strongly marked impression on me, and that not of an agreeable kind. As Mr. Jaggers happened to go out now, and as Wemmick was brisk and talkative, I said to Wemmick that I hardly knew what to make of Mr. Jaggers's manner.

"Tell him that, and he'll take it as a compliment," answered Wemmick; "he don't mean that you *should* know what to make of it. Oh!" for I looked surprised, "it's not personal; it's professional, only professional."

Then he went on to say in a friendly manner:

"If at any odd time when you have nothing better to do, you wouldn't mind coming over to see me at Walworth, I could offer you a bed, and I should consider it an honor. I have not much to show you; but such two or three curiosities as I have got, you might like to look over; and I am fond of a bit of garden and a summer house."

I said I should be delighted to accept his hospitality.

"Thankee," said he; "then we'll consider that it's to come off, when convenient to you. Have you dined with Mr. Jaggers yet?"

"Not yet."

Great Expectations 803

Videocassette You might wish to show students the scene from *Great Expectations* in the **Library of Video Classics,** in which Pip first visits Miss Havisham. Have students compare the language Dickens uses to describe the scene and the details and techniques used by the director and set designer of the film.

Alternative Assessment To promote active reading, have students continue their reader's response journals as they read chapters 24 through 31. Encourage them to respond personally to the events. How do they feel about the possibility of a romance between Pip and Estella? Does this situation remind them of anything in their own lives?

Their observations will enable you to assess their understanding of the issues in the story.

Presentation

Motivation/Prior Knowledge Ask students whether they think Pip will meet Estella again. Have them speculate about this question.

Thematic Focus As Pip continues through life's journey, he discovers that his experiences are causing changes in his relationships with the people who have claims on his love and loyalty. Does this often happen when people grow up? Does a person's life experience alter his or her relationships as time goes on?

Master Teacher Note In *Great Expectations*, Dickens has written a first-person narrative; Pip is telling his story. From the start, readers are engaged with the character Pip. There is also an optimism the reader feels—since it is Pip's story—that things will work out, that Pip will achieve his goals. Have students note the use of first-person narrative as they read and consider its impact on the story and on the reader.

Purpose-Setting Question How does Pip's change in status modify or change his relationships with others?

1 Discussion What is the motive behind Herbert's "delicacy"?

2 Discussion What is Mr. Wemmick's explanation of Mr. Jaggers's "strongly marked" manner of doing business?

3 **Discussion** How does Wemmick's comment add to the suspense of the story?

4 **Discussion** What is the irony in the description of how Bentley Drummle reads a book? How does Dickens compare his reading a book and meeting a new acquaintance?

5 **Discussion** Consider what has already been noted about Mr. Wemmick. Although putting his key "down his back" appears to be unusual behavior, how does it fit in with his already portrayed personality?

3   "Well," said Wemmick, "I'll tell you something. When you go to dine with Mr. Jaggers, look at his housekeeper."

"Shall I see something very uncommon?"

"Well," said Wemmick, "you'll see a wild beast tamed. It won't lower your opinion of Mr. Jaggers's powers. Keep your eye on it."

I told him I would do so, with all the interest and curiosity that his preparation awakened.

Chapter 25

4   Bentley Drummle, who was so sulky a fellow that he even took up a book as if its writer had done him an injury, did not take up an acquaintance in a more agreeable spirit. Heavy in figure, movement, and comprehension, he was idle, proud, niggardly, reserved, and suspicious.

Startop had been spoiled by a weak mother, and kept at home when he ought to have been at school, but he was devotedly attached to her, and admired her beyond measure. He had a woman's delicacy of feature, and was—"as you may see, though you never saw her," said Herbert to me—"exactly like his mother." It was but natural that I should take to him much more kindly than to Drummle, and that, even in the earliest evenings of our boating, he and I should pull homeward abreast of one another conversing from boat to boat, while Bentley Drummle came up in our wake alone.

Herbert was my intimate companion and friend. I presented him with a half share in my boat, which was the occasion of his often coming down to Hammersmith; and my possession of a half share in his chambers often took me up to London. We used to walk between the two places at all hours.

When I had been in Mr. Pocket's family a month or two, Mr. and Mrs. Camilla turned up. Camilla was Mr. Pocket's sister. Georgi-

ana, whom I had seen at Miss Havisham's on the same occasion, also turned up. These people hated me with the hatred of cupidity and disappointment. As a matter of course, they fawned upon me in my prosperity with the basest meanness.

These were the surroundings among which I settled down, and applied myself to my education. I soon contracted expensive habits, and began to spend an amount of money that within a few short months I should have thought almost fabulous; but through good and evil I stuck to my books.

5   I had not seen Mr. Wemmick for some weeks, when I thought I would write him a note and propose to go home with him on a certain evening. He replied that it would give him much pleasure, and that he would expect me at the office at six o'clock. Thither I went, and there I found him, putting the key of his safe down his back as the clock struck.

"Did you think of walking down to Walworth?" said he.

"Certainly," said I, "if you approve."

"Very much," was Wemmick's reply, "for I have had my legs under the desk all day, and shall be glad to stretch them. Now I'll tell you what I've got for supper, Mr. Pip. I have got a stewed steak—which is of home preparation—and a cold roast fowl—which is from the cook's shop. You don't object to an aged parent, I hope?"

I really thought he was still speaking of the fowl, until he added, "Because I have got an aged parent at my place." I then said what politeness required.

"So you haven't dined with Mr. Jaggers yet?" he pursued, as we walked along.

"Not yet."

"He told me so this afternoon when he heard you were coming. I expect you'll have an invitation tomorrow. He's going to ask your pals, too."

Primary Source

According to Edgar Johnson in *The Heart of Charles Dickens:*
During the opening dozen years of Dickens's career his rise was rapid and dazzling. Almost every novel he wrote represented an advance over its predecessors in structural skill and intellectual grasp. With his glowing enjoyment of all the rich variety of existence, his delight in the varicolored aspects of human nature, and his zeal for the welfare of mankind, he developed as both a literary artist of brilliant genius and social reformer of penetrating insight. In long explorations through London's slums and in repeated journeys through the manufacturing towns of England he learned how an industrial civilization was affecting the lives of the poor, and in innumerable parliamentary blue books he studied its consequences in child labor, conditions in mines and factories, filth and disease in people's homes, illiteracy, brutality, and crime in their lives.

His knowledge made him both a compassionate advocate of social betterment in all his written works and a man of action, laboring persistently to help all victims of misfor-

DAVID JOHNSTON
Pierre-Paul Prud'hon
National Gallery of Art, Washington, D.C.

Humanities Note

Fine art, *David Johnston,* by Pierre-Paul Prud'hon. The French painter Pierre-Paul Prud'hon (1758–1823) taught himself the elements of oil painting. A prize won in a competition enabled him to go to Italy where he studied the old masters, particularly da Vinci. Prud'hon drew illustrations, designed stationery, and painted portraits to support his family. He attributed the grace and emotional quality of his paintings to his study of da Vinci. Pierre-Paul Prud'hon gained recognition late in life and was given the honor of painting a ceiling in the Louvre.

David Johnston shows Prud'hon's considerable skill as a portraitist. The clean lines and sensitivity of the rendering show the classicism of his style. You might want to use the following questions:

1. How would you describe the personality of this subject?
2. Which details convey his personality?
3. Do you think this subject is similar to Bentley Drummle in *Great Expectations?* Why or why not?

6 **Literary Focus** Mr. Wemmick has something in common with Pip when it comes to living in a fantasy world. What are the details of his home that create this special atmosphere?

Mr. Wemmick and I beguiled the time and the road, until he gave me to understand that we had arrived in the district of Walworth.

It appeared to be a collection of black lanes, ditches, and little gardens, and to present the aspect of a rather dull retirement. Wemmick's house was a little wooden cottage in the midst of plots of garden, and the top of it was cut out and painted like a battery mounted with guns.

"My own doing," said Wemmick. "Looks pretty, don't it?"

I highly commended it. I think it was the smallest house I ever saw, with the queerest Gothic[1] windows, and a Gothic door, almost too small to get in at.

"That's a real flagstaff, you see," said Wemmick, "and on Sundays I run up a real flag. Then look here. After I have crossed this bridge, I hoist it up—so—and cut off the communication."

The bridge was a plank, and it crossed a chasm about four feet wide and two deep. But it was very pleasant to see the pride with

---

1. **Gothic** (gäth' ik) *adj.*: Style of architecture that makes use of pointed arches.

tune upon whom he came, seeking out still others, and tirelessly devising ways of dealing with specific evils to which he devoted hours of effort beyond those he spent at his desk. [The letters he wrote to Miss Burdett Coutts] reveal Dickens in action, moved by a most warmhearted social conscience to the most practical efforts, not only in behalf of individuals but in striking at the ignorance and dirt that degraded the lives of whole classes of the poor and fostered every social evil.

7 **Discussion** What do you infer about Mr. Wemmick's character from his manner with his father?

8 **Clarification** "Proud as Punch" is a familiar expression that refers to the character in a favorite puppet show in Dickens's day—*Punch and Judy.*

9 **Critical Thinking and Reading** Why does Mr. Wemmick tell Pip he wants to keep his private life totally separate from his business life at Mr. Jaggers's office?

10 **Critical Thinking and Reading** Why does the nightly entertainment appeal to the Aged? Have students cite examples from the story that support their responses.

which he hoisted it up, and made it fast; smiling as he did so, with a relish, and not merely mechanically.

"At nine o'clock every night, Greenwich time,"[2] said Wemmick, "the gun fires. There he is, you see! And when you hear him go, I think you'll say he's a stinger."

The piece of ordnance referred to was mounted in a separate fortress, constructed of latticework. It was protected from the weather by an ingenious little tarpaulin contrivance in the nature of an umbrella.

"Then, at the back," said Wemmick, "there's a pig, and there are fowls and rabbits; then I knock together my own little frame, you see, and grow cucumbers; and you'll judge at supper what sort of a salad I can raise. So, sir," said Wemmick, "if you can suppose the little place besieged, it would hold out a devil of a time in point of provisions.

"I am my own engineer, and my own carpenter, and my own plumber, and my own gardener, and my own jack of all trades," said Wemmick. "Well, it's a good thing, you know. It brushes the Newgate[3] cobwebs away, and pleases the Aged. You wouldn't mind being at once introduced to the Aged, would you? It wouldn't put you out?"

I expressed the readiness I felt, and we went into the castle. There, we found sitting by a fire, a very old man in a flannel coat—clean, cheerful, comfortable, and well cared for, but intensely deaf.

"Well, aged parent," said Wemmick, shaking hands with him in a cordial and jocose way, "how am you?"

"All right, John; all right!" replied the old man.

---

2. **Greenwich** (gren′ ich) **time:** Solar time at Greenwich, England, is the basis for standard time throughout most of the world.
3. **Newgate:** Newgate Prison in London.

"Here's Mr. Pip, aged parent," said Wemmick, "and I wish you could hear his name. Nod away at him, Mr. Pip; that's what he likes. Nod away at him, if you please."

"This is a fine place of my son's, sir," cried the old man, while I nodded as hard as I possibly could.

"You're as proud of it as Punch; ain't you, Aged?" said Wemmick, contemplating the old man, with his hard face really softened. "*There's* a nod for you"—giving him a tremendous one. "You like that, don't you? If you're not tired, Mr. Pip—though I know it's tiring to strangers—would you tip him one more? You can't think how it pleases him."

I tipped him several more, and he was in great spirits. We left him bestirring himself to feed the fowls, and we sat down to our punch in the arbor, where Wemmick told me as he smoked a pipe that it had taken him a good many years to bring the property up to its present pitch of perfection.

"Is it your own, Mr. Wemmick?"

"Oh, yes," said Wemmick.

"Is it, indeed? I hope Mr. Jaggers admires it?"

"Never seen it," said Wemmick. "Never heard of it. Never seen the Aged. Never heard of him. No; the office is one thing, and private life is another. When I go into the office, I leave the castle behind me, and when I come into the castle, I leave the office behind me. If it's not in any way disagreeable to you, you'll oblige me by doing the same. I don't wish it professionally spoken about."

Of course I felt my good faith involved in the observance of his request. The punch being very nice, we sat there drinking it and talking, until it was almost nine o'clock. "Getting near gun-fire," said Wemmick then, as he laid down his pipe; "it's the Aged's treat."

Proceeding into the castle again, we found the Aged heating the poker, with expectant eyes, as a preliminary to the performance of this great nightly ceremony. Wemmick stood with his watch in his hand until the moment was come for him to take the red-hot poker from the Aged, and repair to the battery. He took it, and went out, and presently the stinger went off with a bang that shook the crazy little box of a cottage as if it must fall to pieces, and made every glass and tea-cup in it ring. Upon this the Aged—who I believed would have been blown out of his armchair but for holding on by the elbows—cried out exultingly, "He's fired! I heerd him!" and I nodded at the old gentleman until I absolutely could not see him.

The supper was excellent, and I was heartily pleased with my whole entertainment. Nor was there any drawback on my little turret bedroom.

Our breakfast was as good as the supper, and at half-past eight precisely we started for Little Britain. By degrees, Wemmick got dryer and harder as we went along. At last, when we got to his place of business and he pulled out his key from his coat collar, he looked as unconscious of his Walworth property as if the castle and the drawbridge and the arbor and the lake and the fountain and the Aged had all been blown into space together by the last discharge of the stinger.

Chapter 26

It fell out, as Wemmick had told me it would, that I had an early opportunity of comparing my guardian's establishment with that of his cashier and clerk. My guardian was in his room, washing his hands with his scented soap, when I went into the office from Walworth; and he called me to him, and gave me the invitation for myself and friends which Wemmick had prepared me to receive. "No ceremony," he stipulated, "and no dinner dress, and say tomorrow."

When I and my friends repaired[1] to him at six o'clock next day, he conducted us to Gerrard Street, Soho, to a house on the south side of that street, rather a stately house of its kind, but dolefully in want of painting, and with dirty windows. He took out his key and opened the door, and we all went into a stone hall, bare, gloomy, and little used. So up a dark brown staircase into a series of three dark brown rooms on the first floor.

As he had scarcely seen my three companions until now—for he and I had walked together—he stood on the hearth rug, after ringing the bell, and took a searching look at them. To my surprise, he seemed at once to be principally, if not solely, interested in Drummle.

"Pip," said he, putting his large hand on my shoulder and moving me to the window, "I don't know one from the other. Who's the spider?"

"The spider?" said I.

"The blotchy, sprawly, sulky fellow."

"That's Bentley Drummle," I replied; "the one with the delicate face is Startop."

Not making the least account of "the one with the delicate face," he returned, "Bentley Drummle is his name, is it? I like the look of that fellow."

He immediately began to talk to Drummle. I was looking at the two, when there came between me and them, the housekeeper, with the first dish for the table.

She was a woman of about forty, I supposed—but I may have thought her younger than she was. Rather tall, of a lithe nimble figure, extremely pale, with large faded eyes, and a quantity of streaming hair. She set the dish on, touched my guardian quietly on the arm with a finger to notify that dinner was ready, and vanished.

---

1. **repaired** (ri perd') *v*.: Went.

Great Expectations 807

11

11 **Critical Thinking and Reading**
Drummle's attitudes and qualities are not portrayed as appealing ones. Why, then, might Mr. Jaggers select him from among the others for his special attention?

Speaking and Listening You might want to have students volunteer to read aloud from Chapter 25, in which Pip visits Mr. Wemmick's home, in order to see the different methods Dickens uses to plant description in narrative, dialogue, and expository sections of his work. If you wish, individual students may read the parts of Pip (as the narrator), Pip (when quoted directly), Wemmick, and the Aged Parent.

12 **Discussion** Why does Jaggers revel in his control over Molly? What important aspects of his character are revealed in this scene?

13 **Discussion** How does Mr. Jaggers's behavior toward Drummle relate to his behavior toward Molly?

14 **Reading Strategy** Have students note Drummle's behavior at the dinner party. What action indicates that there might be further trouble from him in a later chapter?

Induced to take particular notice of the housekeeper, both by her own striking appearance and by Wemmick's preparation, I observed that whenever she was in the room, she kept her eyes attentively on my guardian. I fancied that I could detect in his manner a consciousness of this, and a purpose of always holding her in suspense.

Dinner went off gaily, and, although my guardian seemed to follow rather than originate subjects, I knew that he wrenched the weakest part of our dispositions out of us. It was not then, but when we had got to the cheese, that our conversation turned upon our rowing feats, and that Drummle was rallied for coming up behind of a night in that slow amphibious way of his. Drummle, upon this, informed our host that he much preferred our room to our company, and that as to skill he was more than our master, and that as to strength he could scatter us like chaff. By some invisible agency, my guardian wound him up to a pitch little short of ferocity about this trifle, and he fell to baring and spanning his arm to show how muscular it was, and we all fell to baring and spanning our arms in a ridiculous manner.

Now the housekeeper was at that time clearing the table; my guardian, taking no heed of her, but with the side of his face turned from her, was leaning back in his chair, biting the side of his forefinger and showing an interest in Drummle that, to me, was quite inexplicable. Suddenly, he clapped his large hand on the housekeeper's, like a trap, as she stretched it across the table.

"If you talk of strength," said Mr. Jaggers, "*I'll* show you a wrist. Molly, let them see your wrist."

Her entrapped hand was on the table, but she had already put her other hand behind her waist: "Master," she said, in a low voice, "don't."

"*I'll* show you a wrist," repeated Mr. Jag-

gers, with an immovable determination to show it. "Molly, let them see your wrist."

"Master," she again murmured. "Please!"

"Molly," said Mr. Jaggers, "let them see *both* your wrists. Show them. Come!"

He took his hand from hers, and turned that wrist up on the table. She brought her other hand from behind her, and held the two out side by side. The last wrist was much disfigured—deeply scarred and scarred across and across. When she held her hands out, she took her eyes from Mr. Jaggers, and turned them watchfully on every one of the rest of us in succession.

"There's power here," said Mr. Jaggers, coolly tracing out the sinews with his forefinger. "Very few men have the power of wrist that this woman has. It's remarkable what mere force of grip there is in these hands. I have had occasion to notice many hands; but I never saw stronger in that respect, man's or woman's, than these."

"That'll do, Molly," said Mr. Jaggers, giving her a slight nod; "you have been admired, and can go." She withdrew her hands and went out of the room.

"At half-past nine, gentlemen," said he, "we must break up. Pray make the best use of your time. I am glad to see you all. Mr. Drummle, I drink to you."

If his object in singling out Drummle were to bring him out still more, it perfectly succeeded. In a sulky triumph, Drummle showed his morose depreciation of the rest of us in a more and more offensive degree, until he became downright intolerable. Through all his stages, Mr. Jaggers followed him with the same strange interest.

We became particularly hot upon some boorish sneer of Drummle's to the effect that we were too free with our money. It led to my remarking, with more zeal than discretion, that it came with a bad grace from him, to whom Startop had lent money in my pres-

Grammar in Action

A **prepositional phrase** is a group of words that includes a preposition, a noun or pronoun, and any modifiers. Writers use such phrases to add descriptive details and create longer, more interesting sentences.

Notice the use that Dickens makes of prepositional phrases in the following passage from *Great Expectations:*

Now the housekeeper was *at that time* clearing the table;

my guardian, taking no heed *of her,* but *with the side of his face* turned *from her,* was leaning back *in his chair,* biting the side *of his forefinger* and showing an interest *in Drummle* that, *to me,* was quite inexplicable. Suddenly, he clapped his large hand *on the housekeeper's* like a trap, as she stretched it *across the table.*

As you can see, the prepositional phrases add many details that make the description lively and specific. Some prepositions, like *across* in the final line, almost seem as if they were action verbs.

ence but a week or so before. Startop tried to turn the discussion aside with some small pleasantry that made us all laugh. Resenting this little success more than anything, Drummle, without any threat or warning, pulled his hands out of his pockets, dropped his round shoulders, swore, took up a large glass, and would have flung it at his adversary's head, but for our entertainer's dexterously seizing it at the instant when it was raised for that purpose.

"Gentlemen," said Mr. Jaggers, deliberately putting down the glass, "I am exceedingly sorry to announce that it's half-past nine."

On this hint we all rose to depart. Before we got to the street door, Startop was cheerily calling Drummle "old boy," as if nothing had happened. But the old boy was so far from responding that he would not even walk to Hammersmith on the same side of the way, so Herbert and I, who remained in town, saw them going down the street on opposite sides; Startop leading, and Drummle lagging behind in the shadow of the houses, much as he was wont to follow in his boat.

In about a month after that, the spider's time with Mr. Pocket was up for good, and, to the great relief of all the house but Mrs. Pocket, he went home to the family hole.

Chapter 27

My dear Mr. Pip,

I write this by request of Mr. Gargery, for to let you know that he is going to London in company with Mr. Wopsle and would be glad if agreeable to be allowed to see you. He would call at Barnard's Hotel Tuesday morning at nine o'clock, when if not agreeable please leave word. Your

poor sister is much the same as when you left. We talk of you in the kitchen every night, and wonder what you are saying and doing. If now considered in the light of a liberty, excuse it for the love of poor old days. No more, dear Mr. Pip, from

Your ever obliged, and affectionate servant,

Biddy.

P.S. He wishes me most particular to write *what larks.* He says you will understand. I hope and do not doubt it will be agreeable to see him even though a gentleman, for you had ever a good heart, and he is a worthy worthy man. I have read him all excepting only the last little sentence, and he wishes me most particular to write again *what larks.*

I received this letter by post on Monday morning, and therefore its appointment was for the next day. Let me confess exactly with what feelings I looked forward to Joe's coming.

Not with pleasure, though I was bound to him by so many ties; no; with considerable disturbance, some mortification, and a keen sense of incongruity. If I could have kept him away by paying money, I certainly would have paid money. My greatest reassurance was that he was coming to Barnard's Inn, not the Hammersmith. I had little objection to his being seen by Herbert or his father, for both of whom I had a respect, but I had the sharpest sensitiveness as to his being seen by Drummle, whom I held in contempt. So throughout life our worst weaknesses and meannesses are usually committed for the sake of the people whom we most despise.

I had got on so fast of late that I had even

Great Expectations 809

15 **Critical Thinking and Reading** Pip has been to two dinner parties, one at Wemmick's house and the other at Mr. Jaggers's. Compare and contrast the atmosphere and events at each.

16 **Discussion** What is Pip's reaction to the letter from Biddy, and what are his reasons for feeling as he does?

Student Activity 1. Identify four other prepositional phrases that Dickens uses in this chapter.

Student Activity 2. Write a one-paragraph description of a sudden or surprising occurrence. Use prepositional phrases to make your description more detailed and dramatic.

Electronic Handbook You might want students to review prepositions and phrases before they complete the Grammar in Action activities. If students have access to the Language Master 6000, have them enter the access words *preposition* or *phrase* and press the GRAMMAR key to obtain information on these topics related to prepositional phrases.

started a boy in boots[1]—top boots—and had clothed him with a blue coat, canary waistcoat, white cravat, creamy breeches, and the boots already mentioned, I had to find him a little to do and a great deal to eat; and with both of these horrible requirements he haunted my existence.

I came into town on the Monday night to be ready for Joe, and I got up early in the morning, and caused the sitting room and breakfast table to assume their most splendid appearance.

As the time approached I should have liked to run away, but presently I heard Joe on the staircase. I knew it was Joe by his clumsy manner of coming upstairs. When at last he stopped outside our door, I could hear his finger tracing over the painted letters of my name. Finally he gave a faint single rap, and Pepper—such was the compromising name of the boy—announced "Mr. Gargery!"

"Joe, how are you, Joe?"

"Pip, how AIR you, Pip?"

With his good honest face all glowing and shining, and his hat put down on the floor between us, he caught both my hands and worked them straight up and down.

"I am glad to see you, Joe. Give me your hat."

But Joe, taking it up carefully with both hands, like a bird's-nest with eggs in it, wouldn't hear of parting with that piece of property.

"Which you have that growed," said Joe, "and that swelled and that gentle-folked"—Joe considered a little before he discovered this word—"as to be sure you are a honor to your king and country."

"And you, Joe, look wonderfully well."

"Thank God," said Joe, "I'm ekerval to most. And your sister, she's no worse than she were. And Biddy, she's ever right and ready. And all friends is no backerder, if not no forarder. 'Ceptin' Wopsle; he's had a drop."

All this time (still with both hands taking great care of the bird's-nest), Joe was rolling his eyes round and round the room, and round and round the flowered pattern of my dressing-gown.

"Had a drop, Joe?"

"Why, yes," said Joe, lowering his voice, "he's left the Church and went into the play-acting. Which the play-acting have likewise brought him to London along with me. And his wish were," said Joe, getting the bird's-nest under his left arm for the moment, and groping in it for an egg with his right, "if no offense, as I would 'and you that."

I took what Joe gave me, and found it to be the crumpled playbill of a small metropolitan theater, announcing the first appearance, in that very week, of "the celebrated provincial amateur, whose unique performance in the highest tragic walk of our national bard[2] has lately occasioned so great a sensation in local dramatic circles."

"Were you at his performance, Joe?" I inquired.

"I *were*," said Joe, with emphasis and solemnity.

"Was there a great sensation?"

"Why," said Joe, "yes, there certainly were a peck of orange-peel. Partickler when he see the ghost."

A ghost-seeing effect in Joe's own countenance informed me that Herbert had entered the room. So, I presented Joe to Herbert, who held out his hand; but Joe backed from it, and held on by the bird's-nest.

Joe, being invited to sit down to table, looked all round the room for a suitable spot

---

1. **started a boy in boots:** Hired a servant.

2. **our national bard:** William Shakespeare.

on which to deposit his hat and ultimately stood it on an extreme corner of the chimney piece, from which it ever afterwards fell off at intervals.

"Do you take tea, or coffee, Mr. Gargery?" asked Herbert, who always presided of a morning.

"Thankee, sir," said Joe, stiff from head to foot, "I'll take whichever is most agreeable to yourself."

"What do you say to coffee?"

"Thankee, sir," returned Joe, evidently dispirited by the proposal, "since you *are* so kind as make chice of coffee, I will not run contrairy to your own opinions. But don't you never find it a little 'eating?"

"Say tea, then," said Herbert, pouring it out.

Here Joe's hat tumbled off the mantlepiece, and he started out of his chair and picked it up, and fitted it to the same exact spot.

"When did you come to town, Mr. Gargery?"

"Were it yesterday afternoon?" said Joe. "No, it were not. Yes, it were. Yes. It were yesterday afternoon."

"Have you seen anything of London yet?"

"Why, yes, sir," said Joe, "me and Wopsle went off straight to look at the Blacking Ware'us. But we didn't find that it come up to its likeness in the red bills at the shop doors."

Then he fell into such unaccountable fits of meditation, with his fork midway between his plate and his mouth; had his eyes attracted in such strange directions; was afflicted with such remarkable coughs; sat so far from the table, and dropped so much more than he ate, and pretended that he hadn't dropped it; that I was heartily glad when Herbert left us for the City.

I had neither the good sense nor the good feeling to know that this was all my fault, and that if I had been easier with Joe, Joe would have been easier with me. I felt impatient of him and out of temper with him.

"Us two being now alone, sir"—began Joe.

"Joe," I interrupted, pettishly, "how can you call me sir?"

Joe looked at me for a single instant with something faintly like reproach. Utterly preposterous as his cravat was, and as his collars were, I was conscious of a sort of dignity in the look.

"Us two being now alone," resumed Joe, "and me having the intentions and abilities to stay not many minutes more, I will now conclude—leastways begin—to mention what have led to my having had the present honor.

"Well, sir," pursued Joe, "this is how it were. I were at the Bargemen t'other night, Pip"—whenever he subsided into affection, he called me Pip, and whenever he relapsed into politeness he called me sir—"when there come up in his shay cart Pumblechook. Which that same identical come to me at the Bargemen, and his word were, 'Joseph, Miss Havisham she wish to speak to you.'"

"Miss Havisham, Joe?"

"'She wished,' were Pumblechook's word, 'to speak to you.'" Joe sat and rolled his eyes at the ceiling.

"Yes, Joe? Go on, please."

"Next day, sir," said Joe, "having cleaned myself, I go and I see Miss A."

"Miss A., Joe? Miss Havisham?"

"Which I say, sir," replied Joe, "Miss A., or otherways Havisham. Her expression air then as follering: 'Mr. Gargery. You air in correspondence with Mr. Pip?' Having had a letter from you, I were able to say 'I am.' 'Would you tell him, then,' said she, 'that which Estella has come home, and would be glad to see him.'"

19 **Enrichment** Joe reports that he and Mr. Wopsle have gone walking in London and visited the Blacking Ware'us. This could be a reference to the factory where Dickens worked as a child. Dickens was ashamed of having worked in such a factory. Years afterward Dickens avoided the smells and sights of blacking corks because they reminded him of this experience.

20 **Discussion** Why does Pip reproach himself for Joe's obvious discomfort during his visit?

Great Expectations 811

21 Discussion Joe's sound judgments on human relationships are disclosed in this passage. How does he explain to Pip that he will not prolong his visit or try to visit Pip again?

22 Discussion Pip, too, understands what Joe is saying, but cannot bring himself to act to make theirs a more satisfactory parting. Why?

23 Critical Thinking and Reading When Pip returns to the village in response to Miss Havisham's request, what reasons does he give for not staying with Joe at the forge on the visit? Basing your answer on what you know about Pip, why do you think he does not want to stay at the forge?

I felt my face fire up as I looked at Joe. I hope one remote cause of its firing, may have been my consciousness that if I had known his errand, I should have given him more encouragement.

"Biddy," pursued Joe, "when I got home and asked her fur to write the message to you, a little hung back. Biddy says, 'I know he will be very glad to have it by word of mouth, it is holiday time, you want to see him, go!' I have now concluded, sir," said Joe, rising from his chair, "and, Pip, I wish you ever well and ever prospering to a greater and greater height."

"But you are not going now, Joe?"

"Yes, I am," said Joe.

"But you are coming back to dinner, Joe?"

"No, I am not," said Joe.

Our eyes met, and all the "sir" melted out of that manly heart as he gave me his hand.

"Pip, dear old chap, life is made of ever so many partings welded together, as I may say, and one man's a blacksmith, and one's a whitesmith,[3] and one's a goldsmith, and one's a coppersmith. Diwisions among such must come, and must be met as they come. If there's been any fault at all today, it's mine. You and me is not two figures to be together in London; nor yet anywheres else but what is private, and beknown, and understood among friends. It ain't that I am proud, but that I want to be right, as you shall never see me no more in these clothes. I'm wrong in these clothes. I'm wrong out of the forge, the kitchen, or off th' meshes. You won't find half so much fault in me if you think of me in my forge dress, with my hammer in my hand, or even my pipe. You won't find half so much fault in me if, supposing as you should ever wish to see me, you come and put your head in at the forge window

---

3. whitesmith (hwīt' smith') *n*.: Tinsmith.

and see Joe the blacksmith there at the old anvil, in the old burnt apron, sticking to the old work. I'm awful dull, but I hope I've beat out something nigh the rights of this at last. And so GOD bless you, dear old Pip, old chap, GOD bless you!"

I had not been mistaken in my fancy that there was a simple dignity in him. The fashion of his dress could no more come in its way when he spoke these words than it could come in its way in Heaven. He touched me gently on the forehead, and went out. As soon as I could recover myself sufficiently, I hurried out after him and looked for him in the neighboring streets, but he was gone.

Chapter 28

It was clear that I must repair to our town next day, and in the first flow of my repentance it was equally clear that I must stay at Joe's. But when I had secured my box place by tomorrow's coach, and had been down to Mr. Pocket's and back, I was not by any means convinced on the last point, and began to invent reasons and make excuses for putting up at the Blue Boar. I should be an inconvenience at Joe's; I was not expected, and my bed would not be ready; I should be too far from Miss Havisham's, and she was exacting and mightn't like it. All other swindlers upon earth are nothing to the self-swindlers, and with such pretenses did I cheat myself. I settled that I must go to the Blue Boar.

At that time it was customary to carry convicts down to the dockyards by stagecoach. As I had often heard of them in the capacity of outside passengers, and had more than once seen them on the high road dangling their ironed legs over the coach roof, I had no cause to be surprised when

Herbert, meeting me in the yard, came up and told me there were two convicts going down with me. But I had a reason that was an old reason now for constitutionally faltering whenever I heard the word convict.

"You don't mind them, Handel?" said Herbert.

"Oh, no!"

"I thought you seemed as if you didn't like them."

"I can't pretend that I do like them, and I suppose you don't particularly. But I don't mind them."

"See! There they are," said Herbert, "coming out of the tap. What a degraded and vile sight it is!"

The two convicts were handcuffed together, and had irons on their legs—irons of a pattern that I knew well. They wore the dress that I likewise knew well. One was a taller and stouter man than the other, and appeared to have had allotted to him the smaller suit of clothes. His attire disguised him absurdly; but I knew his half-closed eye at one glance. There stood the man whom I had seen on the settle at the Three Jolly Bargemen on a Saturday night.

But this was not the worst of it. It came out that the whole of the back of the coach had been taken by a family removing from London, and that there were no places for the two prisoners but on the seat in front, behind the coachman. The convict I had recognized sat behind me with his breath on the hair of my head.

24

"Good-bye, Handel!" Herbert called out as we started. I thought what a blessed fortune it was that he had found another name for me than Pip.

The weather was miserably raw, and the two cursed the cold. It made us all lethargic before we had gone far, and when we had left the Half-way House behind, we habitually dozed and shivered and were silent. I dozed off, myself, in considering the question whether I ought to restore a couple of pounds sterling to this creature before losing sight of him, and how it could best be done. In the act of dipping forward, as if I were going to bathe among the horses, I woke in a fright and took the question up again.

Cowering forward for warmth and to make me a screen against the wind, the convicts were closer to me than before. The very first words I heard them interchange as I became conscious were the words of my own thought, "Two one-pound notes."

"How did he get 'em?" said the convict I had never seen.

"How should I know?" returned the other. "He had 'em stowed away somehows. Giv him by friends, I expect."

"I wish," said the other, "that I had 'em here."

"Two one-pound notes, or friends?"

"Two one-pound notes. I'd sell all the friends I ever had, for one, and think it a blessed good bargain. Well? So he says—?"

"So he says," resumed the convict I had recognized, "—it was all said and done in half a minute, behind a pile of timber in the dockyard—'You're a-going to be discharged!' Yes, I was. Would I find out that boy that had fed him and kep' his secret, and give him them two one-pound notes? Yes I would. And I did."

"More fool you," growled the other. "I'd have spent 'em on a man, in wittles and drink. He must have been a green one. Mean to say he knowed nothing of you?"

"Not a ha'porth.[1] Different gangs and different ships. He was tried again for prison breaking, and got made a lifer.[2]"

25

---

1. **Not a ha'porth:** Not a half-penny's worth.
2. **got made a lifer:** Was given a life sentence in prison.

24 Discussion What reason does Pip have for being grateful to Herbert for calling him by another name?

25 Discussion Pip is astonished at the news the convict he knows is revealing to the other convict. What is this news and how does it solve a mystery?

Humanities Note

Fine art, *Omnibus Life in London,* 1859, by William Maw Egley. William Maw Egley (1826–1916) was a British painter of genre and historical scenes. A genre scene shows common or everyday activities. William Egley is especially remembered for anecdotal scenes of London life, which show his fine touch and sense of humor.

The influence of the Pre-Raphaelites is apparent in the detail, realism and intense color of the painting *Omnibus Life in London.*

You might want to use the following questions:

1. What impression of this mode of travel does the picture convey?
2. Compare and contrast this omnibus with a modern bus or train.

OMNIBUS LIFE IN LONDON, 1859
William Maw Egley
The Tate Gallery, London

814   The Novel

"And was that—Honor!—the only time you worked out, in this part of the country?"

"The only time."

"What might have been your opinion of the place?"

"A most beastly place. Mudbank, mist, swamp, and work: work, swamp, mist, and mudbank."

They both execrated the place in very strong language, and gradually growled themselves out, and had nothing left to say.

After overhearing this dialogue, I resolved to alight as soon as we touched the town. This device I executed successfully. As to the convicts, they went their way with the coach, and I knew at what point they would be spirited off to the river. In my fancy, I saw the boat with its convict crew waiting for them at the slime-washed stairs; again heard the gruff "Give way, you!" like an order to dogs; again saw the wicked Noah's Ark lying out on the black water.

Chapter 29

Betimes in the morning I was up and out. It was too early yet to go to Miss Havisham's, so I loitered into the country on Miss Havisham's side of town—which was not Joe's side; I could go there tomorrow—thinking about my patroness, and painting brilliant pictures of her plans for me.

I so shaped out my walk as to arrive at the gate at my old time. When I had rung at the bell with an unsteady hand, I turned my back upon the gate. I heard the side door open, and steps come across the courtyard; but I pretended not to hear, even when the gate swung on its rusty hinges.

Being at last touched on the shoulder, I started and turned. I started much more naturally, then, to find myself confronted by a man in a sober gray dress. The last man I should have expected to see in that place of porter at Miss Havisham's door.

"Orlick!"

"Ah, young master, there's more changes than yours. But come in, come in. It's opposed to my orders to hold the gate open."

I entered, and he swung it, and locked it, and took the key out. "Yes!" said he, facing round, after doggedly preceding me a few steps towards the house. "Here I am!"

"How did you come here?"

"I come here," he retorted, "on my legs."

"Are you here for good?"

"I ain't here for harm, young master, I suppose."

"Then you have left the forge?" I said.

"Do this look like a forge?" replied Orlick.

By this time we had come to the house, where I found his room to be one just within the side door, with a little window in it looking on the courtyard.

"I never saw this room before," I remarked; "but there used to be no porter here."

"No," said he, "not till it got about that there was no protection on the premises, and it come to be considered dangerous, with convicts and tag and rag and bobtail going up and down. And then I was recommended to the place as a man who could give another man as good as he brought, and I took it. It's easier than bellowsing and hammering. That's loaded, that is."

My eye had been caught by a gun with a brass-bound stock over the chimney piece, and his eye had followed mine.

"Well," said I, not desirous of more conversation, "shall I go up to Miss Havisham?"

"Burn me, if I know!" he retorted, first stretching himself and then shaking himself; "my orders ends here, young master. I give this here bell a rap with this here ham-

26 **Discussion** Why does Pip turn his back and pretend not to hear the footsteps approach the gate?

26

27 Clarification The colors *green* and *yellow* are used symbolically here to describe Sarah Pocket's feelings. Green and yellow together stand for *jealousy* or *envy*, and also *bitterness* or *spite*.

28 Discussion What surprise awaits Pip when he is ushered into Miss Havisham's room?

29 Discussion Although greatly attracted by Estella's beauty, Pip begins to feel awkward with her. Why?

30 Discussion What changes do both Pip and Estella see in each other?

mer, and you go on along the passage till you meet somebody."

Upon that I turned down the long passage which I had first trodden in my thick boots, and he made his bell sound. At the end of the passage, I found Sarah Pocket, who appeared to have now become constitutionally green and yellow by reason of me.

"Oh!" said she. "You, is it, Mr. Pip?"

"It is, Miss Pocket. I am glad to tell you that Mr. Pocket and family are all well."

"Are they any wiser?" said Sarah, with a dismal shake of the head; "they had better be wiser than well. Ah, Matthew, Matthew! You know your way, sir?"

Tolerably, for I had gone up the staircase in the dark, many a time. I ascended it now, in lighter boots than of yore, and tapped in my old way at the door of Miss Havisham's room. "Pip's rap," I heard her say immediately; "come in, Pip."

She was in her chair near the old table, in the old dress, with her two hands crossed on her stick, her chin resting on them, and her eyes on the fire. Sitting near her, with the white shoe that had never been worn in her hand, and her head bent as she looked at it, was an elegant lady whom I had never seen.

"Come in, Pip," Miss Havisham continued to mutter, without looking round or up; "come in, Pip; how do you do, Pip?"

"I heard, Miss Havisham," said I, "that you were so kind as to wish me to come and see you, and I came directly."

The lady whom I had never seen before lifted up her eyes and looked archly at me, and then I saw that the eyes were Estella's eyes. But she was so much changed, was so much more beautiful, so much more womanly, in all things winning admiration had made such wonderful advance, that I seemed to have made none. I fancied, as I looked at her, that I slipped hopelessly back into the

coarse and common boy again. Oh, the sense of distance and disparity that came upon me, and the inaccessibility that came about her!

"Do you find her much changed, Pip?" asked Miss Havisham.

"When I came in, Miss Havisham, I thought there was nothing of Estella in the face or figure; but now it all settles down so curiously into the old—"

"What? You are not going to say into the old Estella?" Miss Havisham interrupted. "She was proud and insulting, and you wanted to go away from her. Don't you remember?"

I said confusedly that that was long ago, and that I knew no better then, and the like. Estella smiled with perfect composure, and said she had no doubt of my having been quite right, and of her having been very disagreeable.

"Is *he* changed?" Miss Havisham asked her.

"Very much," said Estella, looking at me.

"Less coarse and common?" said Miss Havisham, playing with Estella's hair.

Estella laughed, and looked at the shoe in her hand, and laughed again, and looked at me, and put the shoe down. She treated me as a boy still, but she lured me on.

We sat in the dreamy room among the old strange influences which had so wrought upon me, and I learned that she had but just come home from France, and that she was going to London.

It was settled that I should stay there all the rest of the day, and return to the hotel at night, and to London tomorrow. When we had conversed for a while, Miss Havisham sent us two out to walk in the neglected garden.

The garden was too overgrown and rank for walking in with ease, and after we had made the round of it twice or thrice, we

Grammar in Action

Parallelism is the arrangement of equal ideas in equivalent grammatical structures. A writer's careful use of parallelism adds balance, emphasis, and clarity to sentences and paragraphs. Look at this example of parallelism from *Great Expectations.*

Estella smiled with perfect composure, and said she had no doubt *of my having been quite right,* and *of her having been very disagreeable.* [parallel prepositional phrases

with gerunds as objects]

Parallelism may also extend through more than one sentence:

I have not bestowed my tenderness anywhere. I have never had any such thing. [parallel sentences made up of subject-verb-direct object, beginning with *I have*]

Parallel structure adds a dignity and a pleasant rhythm to many passages but it may also help clarify long and involved sentences:

I verily believe that her *not remembering* and *not minding* in the least, made me cry again inwardly—and that is the sharpest crying of all.

came out again into the brewery yard. I showed her to a nicety where I had seen her walking on the casks that first old day, and she said with a cold and careless look in that direction, "Did I?" I reminded her where she had come out of the house and given me my meat and drink, and she said, "I don't remember." "Not remember that you made me cry?" said I. "No," said she, and shook her head and looked about her. I verily believe that her not remembering and not minding in the least, made me cry again, inwardly—and that is the sharpest crying of all.

"You must know," said Estella, condescending to me as a brilliant and beautiful woman might, "that I have no heart—if that has anything to do with my memory."

I got through some jargon to the effect that I took the liberty of doubting that. That I knew better. That there could be no such beauty without it.

"I am serious," said Estella, not so much with a frown (for her brow was smooth) as with a darkening of her face; "if we are to be thrown much together, you had better believe it at once. No!" imperiously stopping me as I opened my lips. "I have not bestowed my tenderness anywhere. I have never had any such thing."

We went back into the house, and there I heard, with surprise, that my guardian had come down to see Miss Havisham on business, and would come back to dinner. The old wintry branches of chandeliers in the room where the moldering table was spread had been lighted while we were out, and Miss Havisham was in her chair and waiting for me.

It was like pushing the chair itself back into the past, when we began the old slow circuit round about the ashes of the bridal feast. The time so melted away that our early dinner-hour drew close at hand, and Estella left us to prepare herself.

Then, Estella being gone and we two left alone, she turned to me and said in a whisper:

"Is she beautiful, graceful, well-grown? Do you admire her?"

"Everybody must who sees her, Miss Havisham."

She drew an arm round my neck, and drew my head close down to hers as she sat in the chair. "Love her, love her, love her! How does she use you?"

Before I could answer (if I could have answered so difficult a question at all), she repeated, "Love her, love her, love her! If she favors you, love her. If she wounds you, love her. If she tears your heart to pieces—and as it gets older and stronger it will tear deeper—love her, love her, love her!"

"I'll tell you," said she, in the same hurried passionate whisper, "what real love is. It is blind devotion, unquestioning self-humiliation, utter submission, trust and belief against yourself and against the whole world, giving up your whole heart and soul to the smiter[1]—as I did!"

When she came to that, and to a wild cry that followed that, I caught her round the waist. For she rose up in the chair, in her shroud of a dress, and struck at the air as if she would as soon have struck herself against the wall and fallen dead.

All this passed in a few seconds. As I drew her down into her chair, I was conscious of a scent that I knew, and turning, saw my guardian in the room.

Miss Havisham had seen him as soon as I, and was (like everybody else) afraid of him. She made a strong attempt to compose herself, and stammered that he was as punctual as ever.

"As punctual as ever," he repeated, coming up to us. "And so you are here, Pip?"

---

1. smiter (smīt' ər) *n.:* One who hurts you.

31 **Reading Strategy** Summarize the interaction between Estella and Pip.

32 **Discussion** What reply of Estella's makes Pip want to cry all over again, as he did when a child?

33 **Discussion** Miss Havisham is virtually unchanged since the beginning of the novel. How does her conversation with Pip indicate this and how is her attitude toward her adopted daughter, Estella, unchanged?

34 **Discussion** What is Miss Havisham's definition of love? How does it reflect her own experiences?

We sat in the dreamy room among the old strange influences which had so wrought upon me, and I learned *that she had but just come home from France* and *that she was going to London.*

Student Activity 1. Find five other examples of parallelism in the novel, and copy these. Share them with the class, explaining why they are parallel.

Student Activity 2. Use the passages you copied as models for writing five passage of your own, each passage containing an example of parallelism. Exchange papers with a partner and discuss improvements.

Electronic Handbook You might wish students to review parallel structure before completing the Grammar in Action activities. If students have access to the Language Master 6000, have them enter the access word *parallel* and press the GRAMMAR key to obtain information on parallel structure.

I told him when I had arrived, and how Miss Havisham wished me to come and see Estella. To which he replied, "Ah! Very fine young lady!"

"Well, Pip! How often have you seen Miss Estella before?" said he.

"How often?"

"Ah! How many times? Ten thousand times?"

"Oh! Certainly not so many."

"Twice?"

"Jaggers," interposed Miss Havisham, much to my relief, "leave my Pip alone, and go with him to your dinner."

He complied, and we groped our way down the dark stairs together.

"Pray, sir," said I, "may I ask you a question?"

"You may," said he, "and I may decline to answer it. Put your question."

"Estella's name, is it Havisham or—?" I had nothing to add.

"Or what?" said he.

"Is it Havisham?"

"It is Havisham."

This brought us to the dinner table, where she and Sarah Pocket awaited us. Mr. Jaggers presided, Estella sat opposite to him, I faced my green and yellow friend. We dined very well, and were waited on by a maidservant whom I had never seen in all my comings and goings, but who, for anything I know, had been in that mysterious house the whole time.

35 Anything to equal the determined reticence of Mr. Jaggers under that roof I never saw elsewhere, even in him. He kept his very looks to himself, and scarcely directed his eyes to Estella's face once during dinner. When she spoke to him, he listened, and in due course, answered, but never looked at her that I could see. On the other hand, she often looked at him with interest and curiosity, if not distrust, but his face never showed the least consciousness. Throughout dinner, he took a dry delight in making Sarah Pocket greener and yellower by often referring in conversation with me to my expectations.

I think Miss Pocket was conscious that the sight of me involved her in the danger of being goaded to madness. She did not appear when we afterwards went up to Miss Havisham's room, and we four played at whist.[2] We played until nine o'clock, and then it was arranged that when Estella came to London I should be forewarned of her coming and should meet her at the coach; and then I took leave of her, and touched her, and left her.

My guardian lay at the Boar in the next room to mine. Far into the night, Miss Havisham's words, "Love her, love her, love her!" sounded in my ears. I adapted them for my own repetition, and said to my pillow, "I love her, I love her, I love her!" hundreds of times.

Ah me! I thought those were high and great emotions. But I never thought there was anything low and small in my keeping away from Joe, because I knew she would be contemptuous of him. It was but a day gone, and Joe had brought the tears into my eyes; they had soon dried—God forgive me!—soon dried.

Chapter 30

After well considering the matter while I was dressing at the Blue Boar in the morning, I resolved to tell my guardian that I doubted Orlick's being the right sort of man to fill a post of trust at Miss Havisham's. "Why, of course he is not the right sort of man, Pip," said my guardian, comfortably

---

2. whist (hwist) *n.*: A card game like bridge.

THE WHITE GIRL
(SYMPHONY IN WHITE NO. 1)
James McNeill Whistler
National Gallery of Art, Washington, D.C.

Humanities Note

Fine art, *The White Girl: Symphony in White, No. 1,* by James McNeill Whistler. The American artist James McNeill Whistler (1834–1903) lived and worked in London. His eccentric and controversial style resulted from the influence of French painters in Paris, Japanese prints, and his own radical views of painting.

The White Girl: Symphony in White, No. 1 is a portrait of Joanna Heffernan, a friend of Whistler's. Shown at a French exhibition in 1863, it was derided by the public and highly praised by critics. The sensation it created established Whistler as the first American painter to gain recognition in Europe.

Point out to students how the dark hair falling on the right shoulder frames and contrasts with the face, heightening its beauty. Then ask students the following questions:

1. What is the personality of this young woman?
2. Compare and contrast her with Estella.

36 Discussion Why does Pip choose to walk along the London road and let the coach catch up with him instead of going to the station with Mr. Jaggers?

37 Discussion When Pip confesses his love for Estella to Herbert, how does Herbert prove to be a true friend?

satisfied beforehand on the general head, "because the man who fills the post of trust never is the right sort of man." It seemed quite to put him in spirits to find that this particular post was not exceptionally held by the right sort of man, and he listened in a satisfied manner while I told him what knowledge I had of Orlick. "Very good, Pip," he observed, when I had concluded, "I'll go round presently, and pay our friend off." Rather alarmed by this summary action, I was for a little delay, and even hinted that our friend himself might be difficult to deal with. "Oh, no, he won't," said my guardian, with perfect confidence: "I should like to see him argue the question with *me*."

As we were going back together to London by the midday coach, and as I breakfasted under such terrors of Pumblechook that I could scarcely hold my cup, this gave me an opportunity of saying that I wanted a walk, and that I would go on along the London road while Mr. Jaggers was occupied, if he would let the coachman know that I would get into my place when overtaken.

The coach, with Mr. Jaggers inside, came up in due time, and I took my box seat again, and arrived in London safe—but not sound, for my heart was gone. As soon as I arrived, I sent a penitential codfish and barrel of oysters to Joe (as reparation for not having gone myself), and then went on to Barnard's Inn.

I found Herbert delighted to welcome me back, and I felt that I must open my breast that very evening to my friend and chum.

Dinner done and we sitting with our feet upon the fender, I said to Herbert, "My dear Herbert, I have something very particular to tell you."

"My dear Handel," he returned, "I shall esteem and respect your confidence."

"Herbert," said I, laying my hand upon his knee, "I love—I adore—Estella."

Instead of being transfixed, Herbert replied in an easy matter-of-course way, "Exactly. Well?"

"Well, Herbert. Is that all you say? Well?"

"What next, I mean?" said Herbert. "Of course I know *that*."

"How do you know it?" said I.

"How do I know it, Handel? Why, from you."

"I never told you."

"Told me! You have never told me when you have got your hair cut, but I have had senses to perceive it. You have always adored her, ever since I have known you. Have you any idea yet of Estella's views on the adoration question?"

I shook my head gloomily. "Oh! She is thousands of miles away from me," said I.

"Patience, my dear Handel—time enough, time enough. But you have something more to say?"

"I am ashamed to say it," I returned, "and yet it's no worse to say it than to think it. You call me a lucky fellow. Of course I am. I was a blacksmith's boy but yesterday; I am—what shall I say I am today?"

"Say, a good fellow, if you want a phrase," returned Herbert, smiling, and clapping his hand on the back of mine: "a good fellow, with impetuosity and hesitation, boldness and diffidence, action and dreaming curiously mixed in him."

"When I ask what I am to call myself today, Herbert," I went on, "I suggest what I have in my thoughts. You say I am lucky. I know I have done nothing to raise myself in life, and that fortune alone has raised me; that is being very lucky. And yet, when I think of Estella—

"—Then, my dear Herbert, I cannot tell you how dependent and uncertain I feel, and how exposed to hundreds of chances. Avoiding forbidden ground, as you did just now, I may still say that on the constancy of one person (naming no person) all my expectations depend. And at the best, how indefinite and unsatisfactory only to know so vaguely what they are!"

"Now, Handel," Herbert replied, in his gay hopeful way, "it seems to me that in the despondency of the tender passion, we are looking into our gift horse's mouth with a magnifying glass. Didn't you tell me that your guardian, Mr. Jaggers, told you in the beginning that you were not endowed with expectations only? And even if he had not told you so—though that is a very large if, I grant—could you believe that of all men in London, Mr. Jaggers is the man to hold his present relations towards you unless he was sure of his ground?"

I said I could not deny that this was a strong point.

"I should think it *was* a strong point," said Herbert. "You'll be one-and-twenty before you know where you are, and then perhaps you'll get some further enlightenment. At all events, you'll be nearer getting it, for it must come at last."

"What a hopeful disposition you have!" said I.

"I ought to have," said Herbert, "for I have not much else. And now, I want to make myself seriously disagreeable to you for a moment—positively repulsive."

"You won't succeed," said I.

"Oh, yes, I shall!" said he. "Handel, my good fellow, I have been thinking since we have been talking with our feet on this fender that Estella cannot surely be a condition of your inheritance, if she was never referred to by your guardian. Am I right in so understanding what you have told me, as that he never referred to her, directly or indirectly, in any way? Never even hinted, for instance, that your patron might have views as to your marriage ultimately?"

"Never."

"Now, Handel, I am quite free from the flavor of sour grapes, upon my soul and honor! Not being bound to her, can you not detach yourself from her? I told you I should be disagreeable."

I turned my head aside and there was silence between us for a little while.

"Yes; but my dear Handel," Herbert went on, as if we had been talking instead of silent, "think of her bringing-up, and think of Miss Havisham. Think of what she is herself. This may lead to miserable things."

"I know it, Herbert," said I, with my head still turned away, "but I can't help it."

"Well!" said Herbert, getting up with a lively shake as if he had been asleep, and stirring the fire; "now I'll endeavor to make myself agreeable again! I was going to say a word or two, Handel, concerning my father and my father's son. May I ask you if you have ever had an opportunity of remarking, down in your part of the country, that the children of not exactly suitable marriages are always most particularly anxious to be married?"

This was such a singular question that I asked him, in return, "Is it so?"

"I don't know," said Herbert; "that's what I want to know. Because it is decidedly the case with us. I think we are all engaged, except the baby."

"Then you are?" said I.

"I am," said Herbert; "but it's a secret."

I assured him of my keeping the secret, and begged to be favored with further particulars. He had spoken so sensibly and feelingly of my weakness that I wanted to know something about his strength.

"May I ask the name?" I said.

"Name of Clara," said Herbert.

"Live in London?"

"Yes. Perhaps I ought to mention," said Herbert, "that she is rather below my mother's nonsensical family notions. Her fa-

Great Expectations 821

39 Reading Strategy Ask students to predict whether Pip will continue to be frustrated by Estella.

Reader's Response If you were Pip, how would you feel when you found out that a convict had given you the two one-pound notes? Why?

Thematic Response Pip's journey through life takes him to many new places in this part of the novel, but he returns to familiar settings, too. In which setting is Pip most comfortable? Which is most important to him?

ther had to do with the victualling[1] of passenger-ships. I think he was a species of purser."

"What is he now?" said I.

"He's an invalid now," replied Herbert.

"Living on—?"

"On the first floor," said Herbert. Which was not at all what I meant, for I had intended my question to apply to his means. "I have never seen him, for he has always kept his room overhead, since I have known Clara. But I have heard him constantly. He makes tremendous rows—roars, and pegs at the floor with some frightful instrument."

"Don't you expect to see him?" said I.

"Oh, yes, I constantly expect to see him," returned Herbert, "because I never hear him without expecting him to come tumbling through the ceiling. But I don't know how long the rafters may hold."

When he had once more laughed heartily, he became meek again, and told me that the moment he began to realize capital,[2] it was his intention to marry this young lady. He added as a self-evident proposition, engendering low spirits, "But you *can't* marry, you know, while you're looking about you."

---

1. **victualling** (vit' 'l iŋ) *v.*: Supplying victuals, or food.
2. **realize capital:** Make money.

Chapter 31

One day when I was busy with my books and Mr. Pocket, I received a note by the post. It had no set beginning, as Dear Mr. Pip, or Dear Pip, or Dear Sir, or Dear Anything, but ran thus:

I am to come to London the day after tomorrow by the midday coach. I believe it was settled you should meet me? At all events Miss Havisham has that impression, and I write in obedience to it. She sends you her regard.

Yours,
ESTELLA.

My appetite vanished instantly, and I knew no peace or rest until the day arrived. Not that its arrival brought me either, for then I was worse than ever, and began haunting the coach office in Wood Street, Cheapside, before the coach had left the Blue Boar in our town. For all that I knew this perfectly well, I still felt as if it were not safe to let the coach office be out of my sight longer than five minutes at a time.

The coach came quickly after all, and I saw her face at the coach window and her hand waving to me.

RESPONDING TO THE SELECTION

Your Response

1. Pip continues to have mixed feelings about Joe. Have you ever been embarrassed by old friends in front of newer acquaintances? Explain why.

Recalling

2. What is remarkable about Mr. Jaggers's housekeeper?

3. What does Pip learn from the two convicts he overhears on the stagecoach?

4. Explain how Pip's relationship with Estella continues to disappoint him.

Interpreting

5. Compare and contrast Wemmick's home life with that of Jaggers.

6. How do Pip's mixed feelings about Joe's visit reveal an inner conflict?

7. Why does Estella say she has "no heart"? Do

Closure and Extension

ANSWERS TO RESPONDING TO THE SELECTION
Your Response

1. Encourage students to discuss the reasons why Pip has mixed feelings about Joe Gargery. Are Pip's feelings related to his new standards as a gentleman or to his guilt about his new attitudes?

Recalling

2. Her wrist is scarred and powerful. Wemmick says she is an example of Jagger's powers.

3. Pip learns that the convict whom he had helped in the cemetery was the one who had sent him the two one-pound bank notes.

4. Whenever Pip and Estella are together and Estella turns cool toward him, he is unhappy. When he leaves her at Richmond, realizing she will attract many admirers, he

is jealous and wretched. He also realizes that he has never been happy in their relationship.

Interpreting

5. Suggested Response: Mr. Wemmick lives in a tiny wooden cottage, which he has built to look like a miniature castle. He lives comfortably with his aged father, who is cared for by a young girl. Mr. Wemmick caters to his father's needs. There is a warm, cheerful atmosphere in the house. By con-

you agree with her judgment of herself? Find evidence that supports your answer.

Applying

8. Miss Havisham says that "real love is . . . blind devotion, unquestioning self-humiliation. . . ." Comment on this remark.

ANALYZING LITERATURE

Understanding Setting and Atmosphere

Setting refers to the time and place in which the events of a work of fiction occur. **Atmosphere** is the mood that a setting calls up. In *Great Expectations* the story unfolds in a number of places and over a period of years. Each of these places has its own atmosphere. Satis House, for instance, is haunted and decaying, whereas Mr. Jaggers's office is cold and businesslike.

What atmosphere is suggested by each of the following settings?

a. the marshes	c. Pip's rooms
b. Wemmick's house	d. London

CRITICAL THINKING AND READING

Identifying Details That Create Setting

Even in a long novel, writers do not have the space to describe every aspect of a setting. They must therefore sketch in a few details and leave the rest to your imagination. By observing which details they choose to describe, you can learn how they create an atmosphere or reveal character. If a writer stresses the pleasant colors in an apartment, for instance, he or she may be trying to create a joyful mood. These colors may also reveal that the person who lives there is happy. Dickens makes a definite association between certain characters and the settings in which they are found.

What do the following settings reveal about the characters associated with them?

1. Satis House—Miss Havisham
2. Jaggers's office—Jaggers
3. Wemmick's house—Wemmick

THINKING AND WRITING

Comparing and Contrasting Settings

Comparing settings means showing how they are similar, while **contrasting** them means indicating how they are different. Compare and contrast Satis House with Wemmick's home. List the details that Dickens uses to describe each. Briefly note the atmosphere of each house and the way it reveals its owner's personality. Using your notes, write a comparison and contrast of these two settings, with an introduction and a conclusion. In your introduction tell whether the houses are mostly similar or different. Support your view in the body of your paper. When you revise, make sure you have discussed both houses for each point of comparison or contrast.

LEARNING OPTIONS

1. **Art.** Wemmick's house and its surroundings are one of the sources of amusement in this novel. Draw or sketch them, showing the many features Dickens describes on pages 805–806.
2. **Art.** Some details of setting are a result of the time in which a story occurs. Dickens lived in the period we call Victorian. What does Victorian architecture look like? Find out about the elements and details commonly used in Victorian architecture. Use sketches or some other illustrations to share your findings with your class.

whimsical, warm, peaceful, and orderly atmosphere.
c. Pip's rooms seem to be a comfortable, pleasant apartment for two bachelors.
d. London is dense with people. Its atmosphere is lively and exciting, though much of it is also dingy and poor.

ANSWERS TO CRITICAL THINKING AND READING

1. Suggested Response: The Satis House setting reveals Miss Havisham's own state of decay and withdrawal.
2. Suggested Response: Jaggers's office setting reveals his single-minded devotion to business and his coldness.
3. Suggested Response: Wemmick's house reveals the pleasant and whimsical nature he hides beneath his business exterior. It also reveals his devotion to his father.

THINKING AND WRITING

◆ **Software** If students used the **Bank Street Writer** to do the Focus activity, have them incorporate the material they generated for that activity into their Thinking and Writing composition.

Alternative Assessment For Alternative Composition assignments to assess your students' learning, see pages 966–967 of the Teaching Portfolio.

LEARNING OPTIONS

1. This activity will appeal to visual learners. You might wish to extend the activity for kinesthetic learners by having some students build a model based on their drawing.
2. Visual learners will appreciate this activity.

trast, Mr. Jaggers's home is rather dignified and much larger than Mr. Wemmick's but is badly in need of paint, has dirty windows, a bare and cold stone hallway, and a dark-brown staircase; all these features produce a gloomy atmosphere. He is cared for by an efficient housekeeper, Molly, whom he bullies.
6. Suggested Response: Pip is both devoted to Joe and ashamed of him. These divided feelings reflect his inner conflict regarding the

worth of advancement and status versus that of love.
7. Suggested Response: Estella says she has "no heart" because she never bestows affection on anyone. Estella made Pip cry on his first visit to Satis House. When she is asked if she remembers making Pip cry on that visit, she replies in such a casual way that Pip feels hurt.

Applying

8. Answers will differ. Most students

will respond that Miss Havisham's definition of love is unrealistic and distorted, reflecting her own unfortunate experience.

ANSWERS TO ANALYZING LITERATURE

Suggested Responses:
a. The marshes suggest an atmosphere of melancholy, brooding, and romance.
b. Wemmick's house suggests a

Preparation

Literary Focus In *Great Expectations*, the central theme concerns Pip's resolution of the conflicts in his life, trapped as he is between Miss Havisham's vindictiveness and Magwitch's gratitude. As always in Dickens, the abstract concepts are personified in larger-than-life figures of good and evil, with good ultimately prevailing.

Prereading Focus Students might require some prompting to think of events that did not turn out as they expected. Suggest some possibilities—a birthday present that was not what they wanted, a test score that was drastically different from what they anticipated, a meeting with someone who turned out to look and sound different from their expectations. Remind students to write about how they had come to misinterpret the information they had, and how they felt about their miscalculations.

Vocabulary Have more advanced students write original sentences using each of the vocabulary words in this section. Ask them to imitate Dickens's style.

Electronic Handbook You might want students to use the Language Master 6000 to find synonyms of *feign*.

GUIDE FOR READING

Great Expectations, Chapters 32–44

Theme

A **theme** is the central idea or insight into life revealed in a work of literature. Sometimes writers will state the theme directly, but often you must read between the lines to find it. A good clue to the theme of a novel is its main conflict. Imagine, for example, a novel that describes a woman's attempt to climb a steep and dangerous mountain. If she succeeds against all odds, the theme of the book might be the importance of facing challenges with courage.

Short stories and novels can have equally important themes. The size of a work does not limit its ability to treat matters of universal concern. The theme of a novel, however, may have a greater emotional effect than that of a short story. In reading a novel, you have more time to become involved with the characters and therefore may be more receptive to the insight that their struggles reveal.

Focus

These next chapters of the novel are exciting because they contain the climax. Pip finally meets his benefactor, whose identity is something of a shock to him. This causes even greater inner conflict for Pip. Think of a time when you learned that something was not what you expected. Write a few sentences describing the way you thought events would turn out and the reasons why you thought this. Then explain what actually happened and your reaction to the situation. Now read the following chapters and see how Pip reacts to the changes in his life.

Vocabulary

Knowing the following words will help you as you read Chapters 32–44 of *Great Expectations*.

chronic (krön′ ik) *adj.*: Constant (p. 827)

pacific (pə sif′ ik) *adj.*: Peaceful (p. 834)

sundry (sun′ drē) *adj.*: Various; several (p. 836)

abhorrence (əb hôr′ əns) *n.*: Hatred and disgust (p. 844)

dubiously (do͞o′ bē əs lē) *adv.*: Uncertainly; doubtfully (p. 848)

extricate (eks′ trə kāt) *v.*: Free or disentangle (p. 853)

feign (fān) *v.*: Pretend (p. 857)

haggard (hag′ ərd) *adj.*: Worn; gaunt (p. 859)

Objectives

1 To understand theme when reading a novel
2 To paraphrase key statements when reading a novel
3 To respond to the theme of a novel
4 To express individual interests and abilities through optional activities

Support Material

Teaching Portfolio
Teacher Backup, p. 937
Grammar in Action Worksheets, *Using Subordination*, p. 942; *Appreciating Dialect*, p. 944
Usage and Mechanics Worksheet, p. 946
Vocabulary Check, p. 947
Critical Thinking and Reading Worksheet, *Paraphrasing Key Statements*, p. 949

Language Worksheet, *Completing Analogies*, p. 950
Selection Test, p. 951

Library of Video Classics
The Changing World of Charles Dickens, Great Expectations

Literature Videodisc
Scenes from Great Expectations

Prentice Hall Literature Writing Studio

Chapter 32

In her furred traveling-dress, Estella seemed more delicately beautiful than she had ever seemed yet, even in my eyes. Her manner was more winning than she had cared to let it be to me before, and I thought I saw Miss Havisham's influence in the change.

We stood in the inn yard while she pointed out her luggage to me, and when it was all collected I remembered—having forgotten everything but herself in the meanwhile—that I knew nothing of her destination.

"I am going to Richmond," she told me. "The distance is ten miles. I am to have a carriage, and you are to take me. This is my purse, and you are to pay my charges out of it. Oh, you must take the purse! We have no choice, you and I, but to obey our instructions. We are not free to follow our own devices, you and I."

As she looked at me in giving me the purse, I hoped there was an inner meaning in her words. She said them slightingly, but not with displeasure.

"A carriage will have to be sent for, Estella. Will you rest here a little?"

"Yes, I am to rest here a little, and I am to drink some tea, and you are to take care of me the while."

She drew her arm through mine, as if it must be done, and I requested a waiter to show us a private sitting-room. He led us to the black hole of the establishment: fitted up with a diminishing mirror, an anchovy sauce cruet, and somebody's pattens.[1] On my objecting to this retreat, he took us into another room with a dinner table for thirty. Then he took my order—which, proving to be merely "Some tea for the lady," sent him out of the room in a very low state of mind.

I was sensible that the air of this chamber, in its strong combination of stable with soup stock, might have led one to infer that the coaching department was not doing well, and that the enterprising proprietor was boiling down the horses for the refreshment department. Yet the room was all in all to me, Estella being in it. I thought that with her I could have been happy there for life. (I was not at all happy there at the time, observe, and I knew it well.)

"Where are you going to at Richmond?" I asked Estella.

"I am going to live," said she, "at a great expense, with a lady there, who has the power—or says she has—of taking me about, and introducing me, and showing people to me and showing me to people. How do you thrive with Mr. Pocket?"

"I live quite pleasantly there; at least—" It appeared to me that I was losing a chance.

"At least?" repeated Estella.

"As pleasantly as I could anywhere, away from you."

"You silly boy," said Estella quite composedly, "how can you talk such nonsense? Your friend Mr. Matthew, I believe, is superior to the rest of his family?"

"Very superior indeed."

"He really is disinterested, and above small jealousy and spite, I have heard?"

"I am sure I have every reason to say so."

"You have not every reason to say so of the rest of his people," said Estella, "for they beset Miss Havisham with reports and insinuations to your disadvantage. They watch you, misrepresent you, write letters about you (anonymous sometimes), and you are the torment and occupation of their lives. You can scarcely realize to yourself the hatred those people feel for you."

"They do me no harm, I hope?"

---

1. **an anchovy sauce cruet . . . pattens:** A bottle for anchovy sauce; thick, wooden sandals.

Great Expectations 825

Presentation

Motivation/Prior Knowledge Explain to students that knowing characters and their traits can help in predicting the outcome of a story. In this segment of *Great Expectations*, Dickens reveals who is responsible for Pip's wealth, who Miss Havisham's fiancé was, and who Estella's prospective husband is. Each of these is a character students have already met. Have students make predictions about these unsolved mysteries and verify their predictions as they read.

Master Teacher Note Up to this point, Dickens has woven an intricate web of characters, events, and settings. In these chapters the plot becomes even more interwoven and complex. It may be helpful for students to summarize the major events of the story thus far, noting the main characters and their involvement in the major events.

Purpose-Setting Question Describe the changing relationships between Pip and each of the following characters: Estella, Miss Havisham, Joe, and Magwitch.

1 Reading Strategy In this chapter, Pip and Estella are alone together as they travel to Richmond. Pip alternates between hope and despair in his desire to have Estella love him. As students read, have them identify Pip's emotional reactions and use this information to predict his future success with Estella.

2 Discussion What is Estella's attitude toward Pip as they start off on their journey?

3 Discussion Why does Estella refuse to take Pip's statement seriously?

Videocassette You might wish to show the part of the film adaptation of *Great Expectations* in the **Library of Video Classics** that records Pip's reactions to his new knowledge. Students should be able to identify Pip's responses—from shock to firmness of purpose—as he tries to help his benefactor.

Thematic Focus Pip must face many difficult issues because of the choices he has made. Ask students if they have ever made choices that led to unfortunate consequences. Discuss whether an informed choice is safer than one made in ignorance of all the facts.

Alternative Assessment To promote active reading, have students continue their reader's response journals. How do they feel about Pip at this point? Why do they think Estella has decided to marry Drummle?

Students' observations will enable you to assess their understanding of the issues in the novel.

4 **Discussion** What information does Pip learn from Estella that might raise his hopes?

5 **Discussion** What does Estella try to make Pip understand about her when she says, ". . . will you never take warning"? Why does Pip not understand?

6 **Reading Strategy** Summarize Pip's account of his relationship with Estella.

Instead of answering, Estella burst out laughing.

"I hope I may suppose that you would not be amused if they did me any harm?"

"No, no, you may be sure of that," said Estella. "You may be certain that I laugh because they fail. It is not easy for even you to know what satisfaction it gives me to see those people thwarted. For you were not brought up in that strange house from a mere baby—I was. You had not your little wits sharpened by their intriguing against you, suppressed and defenseless, under the mask of sympathy and pity and what not that is soft and soothing—I had. You did not gradually open your round childish eyes wider and wider to the discovery of that impostor of a woman who calculates her stores of peace of mind for when she wakes up in the night—I did.

"Two things I can tell you. First, these people never will—never would in a hundred years—impair your ground with Miss Havisham, in any particular, great or small. Second, I am beholden to you as the cause of their being so busy and so mean in vain, and there is my hand upon it."

As she gave it me playfully—for her darker mood had been but momentary—I held it and put it to my lips. "You ridiculous boy," said Estella, "will you never take warning? Or do you kiss my hand in the same spirit in which I once let you kiss my cheek?"

"What spirit was that?" said I.

"A spirit of contempt for the fawners and plotters."

"If I say yes, may I kiss the cheek again?"

"You should have asked before you touched the hand. But, yes, if you like."

I leaned down, and her calm face was like a statue's. "Now," said Estella, gliding away the instant I touched her cheek, "you are to take care that I have some tea, and you are to take me to Richmond."

Her reverting to this tone, as if our association were forced upon us and we were mere puppets, gave me pain; but everything in our intercourse did give me pain. Whatever her tone with me happened to be, I could put no trust in it, and build no hope on it; and yet I went on against trust and against hope.

I rang for the tea, and the waiter brought in by degrees some fifty adjuncts to that refreshment, but of tea not a glimpse. Then, after a prolonged absence, he at length came back with a casket of precious appearance containing twigs. These I steeped in hot water, and so from the whole of these appliances extracted one cup of I don't know what for Estella.

The bill paid, and the waiter remembered, we got into our post coach and drove away.

When we passed through Hammersmith, I showed her where Mr. Matthew Pocket lived, and said it was no great way from Richmond, and that I hoped I should see her sometimes.

"Oh, yes, you are to see me; you are to come when you think proper; you are to be mentioned to the family; indeed, you are already mentioned."

I inquired, was it a large household she was going to be a member of?

"No, there are only two; mother and daughter. The mother is a lady of some station, though not averse to increasing her income."

"I wonder Miss Havisham could part with you again so soon."

"It is a part of Miss Havisham's plans for me, Pip," said Estella, with a sigh, as if she were tired; "I am to write to her constantly and see her regularly, and report how I go on—I and the jewels—for they are nearly all mine now."

It was the first time she had ever called me by my name. Of course she did so pur-

THE SEAT OF MAJOR NORICE, MAIDSTONE
George Sidney Shepherd
Maidstone Museums and Art Gallery

posely, and knew that I should treasure it up.

We came to Richmond all too soon, and our destination there was a house by the green—a staid old house, where hoops and powder and patches, embroidered coats, rolled stockings, ruffles, and swords had had their court days many a time. Some ancient trees before the house were still cut into fashions as formal and unnatural as the hoops and wigs and stiff skirts.

Two cherry-colored maids came fluttering out to receive Estella. The doorway soon absorbed her boxes, and she gave me her hand and a smile, and said good night, and was absorbed likewise. And still I stood looking at the house, thinking how happy I should be if I lived there with her, and knowing that I never was happy with her, but always miserable.

Chapter 33

As I had grown accustomed to my expectations, I had insensibly begun to notice their effect upon myself and those around me. Their influence on my own character I disguised from my recognition as much as possible, but I knew very well that it was not all good. I lived in a state of chronic uneasiness respecting my behavior to Joe. My conscience was not by any means comfortable

Great Expectations   827

Humanities Note

Fine art, *The Seat of Major Norice, Maidstone,* by George Sidney Shepherd. George Sidney Shepherd (active 1821–1861) was a British topographical painter. Topographical painting includes views of estates, country homes, churches, antiquities, sporting events, and fairs. Painters such as George Sidney Shepherd were hired by wealthy patrons to paint these subjects.

The picture entitled *The Seat of Major Norice, Maidstone* was commissioned by such a patron. Painted in watercolor, it is a charming example of this successful topographer's work.

You might want to ask students the following questions:
1. What is the social status of the owner of this house?
2. Why do you think the owner wanted this picture painted?
3. Do you think this house resembles the one in Richmond to which Estella travels? Why or why not?

7 Discussion Dickens gives a description of the house where Estella will be living. What details convey its setting and atmosphere?

8 Reading Strategy In this chapter, Pip reflects on how his "great expectations" have affected the lives of the people close to him, as well as his relationships with them. Have students keep Pip's reflections in mind as they read the chapter.

9 Discussion In his unhappy mood, how does Pip's conscience bother him with respect to Joe?

10 Discussion What depresses Pip when he thinks about what might have been had he never met Miss Havisham?

11 Discussion What is ironic about Herbert's estimate of Pip's business ability?

about Biddy. When I woke up in the night, I used to think, with a weariness of my spirits, that I should have been happier and better if I had never seen Miss Havisham's face, and had risen to manhood content to be partners with Joe in the honest old forge. Many a time of an evening, when I sat alone looking at the fire, I thought, after all, there was no fire like the forge fire and the kitchen fire at home.

Now, concerning the influence of my position on others, I perceived that it was not beneficial to anybody, and above all, that it was not beneficial to Herbert. My lavish habits led his easy nature into expenses that he could not afford, corrupted the simplicity of his life, and disturbed his peace with anxieties and regrets.

In my confidence in my own resources, I would willingly have taken Herbert's expenses on myself; but Herbert was proud, and I could make no such proposal to him. So, he got into difficulties in every direction, and continued to look about him. When we gradually fell into keeping late hours and late company, I noticed that he looked about him with a desponding eye at breakfast-time; that he began to look about him more hopefully about midday; that he drooped when he came into dinner; that he seemed to descry[1] capital in the distance, rather clearly, after dinner; that he all but realized capital towards midnight; and that about two o'clock in the morning, he became so deeply despondent again as to talk of buying a rifle and going to America, with a general purpose of compelling buffaloes to make his fortune.

At certain times I would say to Herbert, as if it were a remarkable discovery:

"My dear Herbert, we are getting on badly."

"My dear Handel," Herbert would say to

---

1. **descry** (di skrī′) v.: Catch sight of.

me, in all sincerity, "if you will believe me, those very words were on my lips, by a strange coincidence."

"Then, Herbert," I would respond, "let us look into our affairs."

We always derived profound satisfaction from making an appointment for this purpose. I always thought this was business, this was the way to confront the thing.

I would then take a sheet of paper, and write across the top of it, in a neat hand, the heading, "Memorandum of Pip's debts," with Barnard's Inn and the date very carefully added. Herbert would also take a sheet of paper, and write across it with similar formalities, "Memorandum of Herbert's debts."

Each of us would then refer to a confused heap of papers at his side. The sound of our pens going refreshed us exceedingly, insomuch that I sometimes found it difficult to distinguish between this edifying business proceeding and actually paying the money.

When we had written a little while, I would ask Herbert how he got on.

"They are mounting up, Handel," Herbert would say, "upon my life, they are mounting up."

"Be firm, Herbert," I would retort. "Look the thing in the face. Look into your affairs. Stare them out of countenance."

"So I would, Handel, only they are staring *me* out of countenance."

However, my determined manner would have its effect, and Herbert would fall to work again. After a time he would give up once more, on the plea that he had not got Cobbs's bill, or Lobbs's, or Nobbs's, as the case might be.

"Then, Herbert, estimate; estimate it in round numbers, and put it down."

"What a fellow of resource you are!" my friend would reply, with admiration. "Really, your business powers are very remarkable."

Grammar in Action

Subordination is the process by which writers connect two unequal but related ideas to form a complex sentence. The main clause of such a sentence should be able to stand by itself, but the subordinate clause—which includes a conjunction like *although*, *because*, or *while*—cannot function as an independent sentence:

Although we went to bed early, we could not fall asleep.

Because he left school without a degree, he had trouble finding a job.

While I want to help you, I won't be able to drive to your house tomorrow.

Writers use subordination to vary the structure and length of their sentences and to clarify the relationship between ideas. The less important idea is placed in the subordinate clause.

Notice how Dickens uses subordinate clauses in the following sentences from *Great Expectations*:

I thought so, too. I established with myself, on these occasions, the reputation of a first-rate man of business—prompt, decisive, energetic, clear, coolheaded. When I had got all my responsibilities down upon my list, I compared each with the bill, and ticked it off. My self-approval when I ticked an entry was quite a luxurious sensation. When I had no more ticks to make, I folded all my bills up uniformly, docketed[2] each on the back, and tied the whole into a symmetrical bundle. Then I did the same for Herbert, and felt that I had brought his affairs into a focus for him.

There was a calm, a rest, a virtuous hush consequent on these examinations of our affairs that gave me, for the time, an admirable opinion of myself. Soothed by my exertions, my method, and Herbert's compliments, I would sit with his symmetrical bundle and my own on the table before me among the stationery, and feel like a bank of some sort, rather than a private individual.

We shut our outer door on these solemn occasions in order that we might not be interrupted. I had fallen into my serene state one evening, when we heard a letter dropped through the slit in the said door, and fall on the ground. "It's for you, Handel," said Herbert, going out and coming back with it, "and I hope there is nothing the matter." This was in allusion to its heavy black seal and border.

The letter was signed TRABB & CO., and its contents were simply that I was an honored sir, and that they begged to inform me that Mrs. J. Gargery had departed this life on Monday last at twenty minutes past six in the evening, and that my attendance was requested at the interment[3] on Monday next at three o'clock in the afternoon.

2. **docketed** (däk′ it əd) *v.*: Labeled.
3. **interment** (in tʉr′ mənt) *n.*: Burial.

Chapter 34

It was the first time that a grave had opened in my road of life, and the gap it made in the smooth ground was wonderful.[1] The figure of my sister in her chair by the kitchen fire haunted me night and day. That the place could possibly be without her was something my mind seemed unable to compass, and whereas she had seldom or never been in my thoughts of late, I had now the strangest idea that she was coming towards me in the street, or that she would presently knock at the door.

Whatever my fortunes might have been, I could scarcely have recalled my sister with much tenderness. But I suppose there is a shock of regret which may exist without much tenderness.

Having written to Joe to offer him consolation, and to assure him that I would come to the funeral, I passed the intermediate days in the curious state of mind I have glanced at.[2] I went down early in the morning, and alighted at the Blue Boar in good time to walk over to the forge.

At last I came within sight of the house, and saw that Trabb & Co. had put in a funereal execution and taken possession. Poor dear Joe, entangled in a little black cloak tied in a large bow under his chin, was seated apart at the upper end of the room; where, as chief mourner, he had evidently been stationed by Trabb. When I bent down and said to him, "Dear Joe, how are you?" he said, "Pip, old chap, you know'd her when she were a fine figure of a—" and clasped my hand and said no more.

Biddy, looking very neat and modest in her black dress, went quietly here and there,

1. **wonderful** (wun′ dər fəl) *adj.*: In this case, it means "amazing."
2. **curious state . . . glanced at:** Strange state of mind I have briefly mentioned.

Great Expectations 829

12 **Discussion** How does this system of handling bills affect Pip's spirits?

13 **Reading Strategy** Ask students to predict the changes that will result from this event.

14 **Critical Thinking and Reading** What is the strange experience that Pip has as he thinks about his relationship with his sister and tries to acknowledge the reality of her death? How does this reflect the emotional atmosphere of the funeral?

15 **Discussion** What expression is Joe's way of communicating his feeling about his first wife?

The sounds of our pens going refreshed us exceedingly, *insomuch that I sometimes found it difficult to distinguish between this edifying business and actually paying the money.*
Whatever my fortunes might have been, I could scarcely have recalled my sister with much tenderness.
The somewhat old-fashioned sounding subordinate conjunction *insomuch that* means "to the degree that."

Student Activity. Write a one-paragraph description of the most exciting sports event you ever witnessed or heard about. Use subordination in at least two sentences.

Electronic Handbook You might want students to review the skills related to using subordination before they complete the Grammar in Action activities. If students have access to the Language Master 6000, have them enter the access words *conjunction, complex,* or *clause* and press the GRAMMAR key to obtain information on these topics related to subordination.

16 **Discussion** Why is this simile effective?

17 **Discussion** How does Pip help restore his old relationship with Joe?

18 **Discussion** In his talk with Biddy after the funeral, what attitude does Pip adopt that temporarily strains their relationship?

and was very helpful. When I had spoken to Biddy, as I thought it not a time for talking, I went and sat down near Joe.

"Pocket-handkerchiefs out, all!" cried Mr. Trabb at this point, in a depressed business-like voice. "Pocket-handkerchiefs out! We are ready!"

So, we all put our pocket-handkerchiefs to our faces, as if our noses were bleeding, and filed out two and two: Joe and I: Biddy and Pumblechook; Mr. and Mrs. Hubble. The remains of my poor sister had been brought round by the kitchen door, and it being a point of undertaking ceremony that the six bearers must be stifled and blinded under a horrible black velvet housing with a white border, the whole looked like a blind monster with twelve human legs, shuffling and blundering along under the guidance of two keepers—the post-boy and his comrade. The neighborhood, however, highly approved of these arrangements, and we were much admired as we went through the village.

And now the range of marshes lay clear before us, with the sails of the ships on the river growing out of it; and we went into the churchyard, close to the graves of my unknown parents, Philip Pirrip, Late of this Parish, and Also Georgiana, Wife of the Above. And there my sister was laid quietly in the earth while the larks sang high above it, and the light wind strewed it with beautiful shadows of clouds and trees.

Soon afterwards, Biddy, Joe, and I had a cold dinner together; but we dined in the best parlor, not in the old kitchen, and Joe was so exceedingly particular what he did with his knife and fork and the saltcellar and what not that there was great restraint upon us. But after dinner, when I made him take his pipe, and when I had loitered with him about the forge, and when we sat down together on the great block of stone outside it, we got on better.

He was very much pleased by my asking if I might sleep in my own little room, and I was pleased, too, for I felt that I had done rather a great thing in making the request. When the shadows of evening were closing in, I took an opportunity of getting into the garden with Biddy for a little talk.

"Biddy," said I, "I think you might have written to me about these sad matters."

"Do you, Mr. Pip?" said Biddy. "I should have written if I had thought that."

She was so quiet, and had such an orderly, good, and pretty way with her that I did not like the thought of making her cry again. After looking a little at her downcast eyes as she walked beside me, I gave up that point.

"I suppose it will be difficult for you to remain here now, Biddy, dear?"

"Oh! I can't do so, Mr. Pip," said Biddy, in a tone of regret, but still of quiet conviction. "I have been speaking to Mrs. Hubble, and I am going to her tomorrow. I hope we shall be able to take some care of Mr. Gargery, together, until he settles down."

"How are you going to live, Biddy? If you want any mo—"

"How am I going to live?" repeated Biddy, striking in, with a momentary flush upon her face. "I'll tell you, Mr. Pip. I am going to try to get the place of mistress in the new school nearly finished here. I can be well recommended by all the neighbors, and I hope I can be industrious and patient, and teach myself while I teach others. The new schools are not like the old, but I learned a good deal from you after that time, and have had time since then to improve."

"I think you would always improve, Biddy, under any circumstances."

Then I thought I would give up that point, too. So, I walked a little further with Biddy, looking silently at her downcast eyes.

"I have not heard the particulars of my sister's death, Biddy."

"They are very slight, poor thing. She

had been in one of her bad states for four days when she came out of it in the evening, just at tea-time, and said quite plainly, 'Joe.' As she had never said any word for a long while, I ran and fetched in Mr. Gargery from the forge. She made signs to me that she wanted him to sit down close to her, and wanted me to put her arms round his neck. So I put them round his neck, and she laid her head down on his shoulder quite content and satisfied. And so she presently said 'Joe' again, and once 'Pardon,' and once 'Pip.' And so she never lifted her head up any more, and it was just an hour later when we laid it down on her own bed, because we found she was gone."

Biddy cried; the darkening garden, and the lane, and the stars that were coming out were blurred in my own sight.

"Nothing was ever discovered, Biddy?"

"Nothing."

"Do you know what is become of Orlick?"

"I should think from the color of his clothes that he is working in the quarries."

"Of course you have seen him then? Why are you looking at that dark tree in the lane?"

"I saw him there, on the night she died."

"That was not the last time either, Biddy?"

"No, I have seen him there since we have been walking here. It is of no use," said Biddy, laying her hand upon my arm, as I was for running out, "you know I would not deceive you; he was not there a minute, and he is gone."

It revived my utmost indignation to find that she was still pursued by this fellow, and I felt inveterate against him. I told her so, and told her that I would spend any money or take any pains to drive him out of that country. By degrees she led me into more temperate talk, and she told me how Joe loved me, and how Joe never complained of anything—she didn't say of me; she had no

need; I knew what she meant—but ever did his duty in his way of life, with a strong hand, a quiet tongue, and a gentle heart.

"Indeed, it would be hard to say too much for him," said I; "and, Biddy, we must often speak of these things, for of course I shall be often down here now. I am not going to leave poor Joe alone."

"Are you quite sure, then, that you *will* come to see him often?" asked Biddy, stopping in the narrow garden walk, and looking at me under the stars with a clear and honest eye.

"Oh, dear me!" said I, as I found myself compelled to give up Biddy in despair. "This really is a very bad side of human nature! Don't say any more, if you please, Biddy. This shocks me very much."

For which cogent reason I kept Biddy at a distance during supper, and when I went up to my own old little room, took as stately a leave of her as I could. As often as I was restless in the night, and that was every quarter of an hour, I reflected what an unkindness, what an injury, what an injustice Biddy had done me.

Early in the morning, I was to go. Early in the morning, I was out, and looking in, unseen, at one of the wooden windows of the forge. There I stood for minutes looking at Joe, already at work with a glow of health and strength upon his face that made it show as if the bright sun of the life in store for him were shining on it.

"Good-bye, dear Joe! No, don't wipe it off—for God's sake, give me your blackened hand! I shall be down soon and often."

"Never too soon, sir," said Joe, "and never too often, Pip!"

Biddy was waiting for me at the kitchen door, with a mug of new milk and a crust of bread. "Biddy," said I, when I gave her my hand at parting, "I am not angry, but I am hurt."

"No, don't be hurt," she pleaded quite

19 Discussion What do you infer from the information that Biddy imparts about Orlick?

20 Discussion Is her view of Joe accurate? Explain.

21 Discussion How does Pip react to Biddy's implied criticism of him?

832

22 Discussion What does Pip reveal about future events?

23 Reading Strategy Pip's twenty-first birthday is a milestone in his life. As students read this chapter, have them review the state of Pip's "great expectations," his financial situation, and his relationships with those who are important to him.

24 Discussion What tone does Mr. Jaggers use to wring a confession from Pip and make him face up to his careless spending habits? Why has Pip squandered his money?

22 pathetically; "let only me be hurt, if I have been ungenerous."

Once more, the mists were rising as I walked away. If they disclosed to me, as I suspect they did, that I should *not* come back, and that Biddy was quite right, all I can say is—they were quite right, too.

Chapter 35

23 Herbert and I went on from bad to worse, in the way of increasing our debts. But we looked forward to my one-and-twentieth birthday, for we had both considered that my guardian could hardly help saying something definite on that occasion.

I had taken care to have it well understood in Little Britain when my birthday was. On the day before it, I received an official note from Wemmick, informing me that Mr. Jaggers would be glad if I would call upon him at five in the afternoon of the auspicious day. This convinced us that something great was to happen, and threw me into an unusual flutter when I repaired to my guardian's office, a model of punctuality.

In the outer office Wemmick offered me his congratulations, and incidentally rubbed the side of his nose with a folded piece of tissue paper that I liked the look of. It was November, and my guardian was standing before his fire leaning his back against the chimneypiece, with his hands under his coat-tails.

"Well, Pip," said he, "I must call you Mr. Pip today. Congratulations, Mr. Pip."

We shook hands—he was always a remarkably short shaker—and I thanked him.

"Take a chair, Mr. Pip," said my guardian.

As I sat down, I felt at a disadvantage, which reminded me of that old time when I had been put upon a tombstone.

24 "Now, my young friend," my guardian began, as if I were a witness in the box, "I am going to have a word or two with you."

"If you please, sir."

"What do you suppose," said Mr. Jaggers, "you are living at the rate of?"

"At the rate of, sir?"

"At," repeated Mr. Jaggers, "the—rate—of?"

Reluctantly, I confessed myself quite unable to answer the question. This reply seemed agreeable to Mr. Jaggers, who said, "I thought so!"

"Now, I have asked *you* a question, my friend," said Mr. Jaggers. "Have you anything to ask *me*?"

"Of course it would be a great relief to me to ask you several questions, sir; but I remember your prohibition."

"Ask one," said Mr. Jaggers.

"Is my benefactor to be made known to me today?"

"No. Ask another."

"Is that confidence to be imparted to me soon?"

"Waive that, a moment," said Mr. Jaggers, "and ask another."

"Have—I—anything to receive, sir?" On that, Mr. Jaggers said triumphantly, "I thought we should come to it!" and called to Wemmick to give him that piece of paper. Wemmick appeared, handed it in, and disappeared.

"Now, Mr. Pip," said Mr. Jaggers, "attend if you please. You have been drawing pretty freely here; your name occurs pretty often in Wemmick's cash book: but you are in debt, of course?"

"I am afraid I must say yes, sir."

"You know you must say yes, don't you?" said Mr. Jaggers.

"Yes, sir."

"I don't ask you what you owe, because you don't know; and if you did know, you wouldn't tell me; you would say less. Yes, yes, my friend," cried Mr. Jaggers, waving his forefinger to stop me, as I made a show of protesting, "it's likely enough that you think you wouldn't, but you would. You'll excuse me, but I know better than you. Now, take this piece of paper in your hand. You have got it? Very good. Now, unfold it and tell me what it is."

"This is a bank note," said I, "for five hundred pounds."

"You consider it, undoubtedly, a handsome sum of money. Now, that handsome sum of money, Pip, is your own. It is a present to you on this day, in earnest of your expectations. And at the rate of that handsome sum of money per annum,[1] and at no higher rate, you are to live until the donor of the whole appears. That is to say, you will now take your money affairs entirely into your own hands, and you will draw from Wemmick one hundred and twenty-five pounds per quarter, until you are in communication with the fountainhead,[2] and no longer with the mere agent."

After a pause, I hinted:

"There was a question just now, Mr. Jaggers, which you desired me to waive for a moment. I hope I am doing nothing wrong in asking it again?"

"What is it?" said he.

"Is it likely," I said, after hesitating, "that my patron, the fountainhead you have spoken of, Mr. Jaggers, will soon come to London, or summon me anywhere else?"

"Now here," replied Mr. Jaggers, fixing me for the first time with his dark deep-set eyes, "we must revert to the evening when we first encountered one another in your village. What did I tell you then, Pip?"

"You told me, Mr. Jaggers, that it might be years hence when that person appeared."

"Just so," said Mr. Jaggers; "that's my answer."

---

1. **per annum:** Latin for "yearly."
2. **fountainhead** (foun′ t'n hed′) *n.*: Source.

"Do you suppose it will still be years hence, Mr. Jaggers?"

"Come!" said Mr. Jaggers, "I'll be plain with you, my friend Pip. That's a question I must not be asked. You'll understand that better when I tell you it's a question that might compromise *me*. When that person discloses, you and that person will settle your own affairs. When that person discloses, my part in this business will cease and determine. And that's all I have got to say."

We looked at one another until I withdrew my eyes, and looked thoughtfully at the floor. From this last speech I derived the notion that Miss Havisham, for some reason or no reason, had not taken him into her confidence as to her designing me for Estella; that he resented this, and felt a jealousy about it; or that he really did object to that scheme, and would have nothing to do with it.

"If that is all you have to say, sir," I remarked, "there can be nothing left for me to say."

He nodded assent and asked me where I was going to dine. I replied at my own chambers, with Herbert. As a necessary sequence, I asked him if he would favor us with his company, and he promptly accepted the invitation. But he insisted on walking home with me, in order that I might make no extra preparation for him, and first he had a letter or two to write. So, I said I would go into the outer office and talk to Wemmick.

The fact was that when the five hundred pounds had come into my pocket, a thought had come into my head which had been often there before, and it appeared to me that Wemmick was a good person to advise[3] with, concerning such thought.

"Mr. Wemmick," said I, "I want to ask your opinion. I am very desirous to serve a

---

3. **advise** (əd vīz′) *v.*: Consult.

25

Great Expectations 833

26 Discussion Do you think this advice represents all that Wemmick has to say on the subject? Explain.

friend. This friend," I pursued, "is trying to get on in commercial life, but has no money, and finds it difficult and disheartening to make a beginning. Now, I want somehow to help him to a beginning."

"With money down?" said Wemmick, in a tone drier than any sawdust.

"With *some* money down," I replied, for an uneasy remembrance shot across me of that symmetrical bundle of papers at home; "with *some* money down, and perhaps some anticipation of my expectations."

26 "Choose a bridge, Mr. Pip," returned Wemmick, "and take a walk upon your bridge, and pitch your money into the Thames over the center arch of your bridge, and you know the end of it. Serve a friend with it, and you may know the end of it, too—but it's a less pleasant and profitable end."

"And that," said I, "is your deliberate opinion, Mr. Wemmick?"

"That," he returned, "is my deliberate opinion in this office."

"Ah!" said I, pressing him, for I thought I saw him near a loophole here. "But would that be your opinion at Walworth?"

"Mr. Pip," he replied with gravity, "Walworth is one place, and this office is another. Much as the Aged is one person, and Mr. Jaggers is another. They must not be confounded together. My Walworth sentiments must be taken at Walworth; none but my official sentiments can be taken in this office."

"Very well," said I, much relieved, "then I shall look you up at Walworth, you may depend upon it."

"Mr. Pip," he returned, "you will be welcome there, in a private and personal capacity."

We had held this conversation in a low voice, well knowing my guardian's ears to be the sharpest of the sharp. As he now appeared in his doorway, toweling his hands,

Wemmick got on his greatcoat and stood by to snuff out the candles. We all three went into the street together, and from the doorstep Wemmick turned his way, and Mr. Jaggers and I turned ours.

Chapter 36

Deeming Sunday the best day for taking Mr. Wemmick's Walworth sentiments, I devoted the next ensuing Sunday afternoon to a pilgrimage to the castle. On arriving before the battlements, I found the Union Jack flying and the drawbridge up, but undeterred by this show of defiance and resistance, I rang at the gate, and was admitted in a most pacific manner by the Aged.

"My son, sir," said the old man, after securing the drawbridge, "left word that he would soon be home from his afternoon's walk."

I nodded at the old gentleman as Wemmick himself might have nodded, and we went in and sat down by the fireside.

"You made acquaintance with my son, sir," said the old man in his chirping way, while he warmed his hands at the blaze, "at his office, I expect?" I nodded. "Hah! I have heerd that my son is a wonderful hand at his business, sir?" I nodded hard. "Yes, so they tell me. His business is the law?" I nodded harder.

I was startled by a sudden click in the wall on one side of the chimney, and the ghostly tumbling open of a little wooden flap with "JOHN" upon it. The old man, following my eyes, cried with great triumph, "My son's come home!" and we both went out to the drawbridge.

It was worth any money to see Wemmick waving a salute to me from the other side of the moat, when we might have shaken hands across it with the greatest ease. The Aged was so delighted to work the draw-

Primary Source

Literary critics have both praised and criticized Dickens's work. It has fallen under harsh criticism by critics who have claimed that Dickens's characters are flat and can be described in one sentence. Other critics state that although Dickens ought to be considered bad, there is something compelling and appealing about his work. Still others, such as is illustrated in the following example, highly praise Dickens's talent and works. In "The Great Inimitable," one of the essays in *Charles Dickens 1812–1870, a Centennial Volume* edited by E.W.F. Tomlin, J. B. Priestley quotes literary critic G. K. Chesterton as follows:

The art of Dickens was the most exquisite of arts: it was the art of enjoying everybody. Dickens, being a very human writer, had to be a very human being; he had his faults and sensibilities in a strong degree; and I do not for a moment maintain that he enjoyed everybody in his daily life. But he enjoyed everybody in his books; and everybody has enjoyed everybody in those books even till today. His books are full of baffled villains stalking out or cowardly bullies kicked downstairs. But the villains and the cowards

bridge that I made no offer to assist him, but stood quiet until Wemmick had come across, and had presented me to Miss Skiffins, a lady by whom he was accompanied.

Miss Skiffins was of a wooden appearance. The cut of her dress from the waist upward, both before and behind, made her figure very like a boy's kite, and I might have pronounced her gown a little too decidedly orange, and her gloves a little too intensely green. But she seemed to be a good sort of fellow, and showed a high regard for the Aged. I was not long in discovering that she was a frequent visitor at the castle.

While Miss Skiffins was taking off her bonnet, Wemmick invited me to take a walk with him round the property, and see how the island looked in wintertime. Thinking that he did this to give me an opportunity of taking his Walworth sentiments, I seized the opportunity as soon as we were out of the castle.

I informed Wemmick that I was anxious in behalf of Herbert Pocket, and I told him how we had first met, and how we had fought. I alluded to the advantages I had derived in my first rawness and ignorance from his society, and I confessed that I feared I had but ill repaid them, and that he might have done better without me and my expectations. For all these reasons (I told Wemmick), and because he was my young companion and friend, and I had a great affection for him, I wished my own good fortune to reflect some rays upon him, and therefore I sought advice from Wemmick's experience and knowledge of men and affairs, how I could best try with my resources to help Herbert to some present income—say of a hundred a year, to keep him in good hope and heart—and gradually to buy him on to some small partnership. I begged Wemmick, in conclusion, to understand that my help must always be rendered without Her-bert's knowledge or suspicion, and that there was no one else in the world with whom I could advise. I wound up by laying my hand upon his shoulder, and saying, "I can't help confiding in you, though I know it must be troublesome to you; but that is your fault, in having ever brought me here."

"I'll put on my considering cap," said Wemmick "and I think all you want to do may be done by degrees. Skiffins (that's her brother) is an accountant and agent. I'll look him up and go to work for you."

After a little further conversation to the same effect, we returned into the castle, where we found Miss Skiffins preparing tea. The responsible duty of making the toast was delegated to the Aged, and that excellent old gentleman prepared such a haystack of buttered toast that I could scarcely see him over it.

We ate the whole of the toast, and drank tea in proportion, and it was delightful to see how warm and greasy we all got after it. Then we drew round the fire, and Wemmick said, "Now, Aged Parent, tip us the paper."

Wemmick explained to me while the Aged got his spectacles out that this was according to custom, and that it gave the old gentleman infinite satisfaction to read the news aloud. "I won't offer an apology," said Wemmick, "for he isn't capable of many pleasures—are you, Aged P.?"

"All right, John, all right," returned the old man, seeing himself spoken to.

"Only tip him a nod every now and then when he looks off his paper," said Wemmick, "and he'll be as happy as a king. We are all attention, Aged One."

After awhile the Aged read himself into a light slumber. Then we all had something warm to drink, including the Aged, who was soon awake again. Miss Skiffins mixed, and I observed that she and Wemmick drank out of one glass. Of course I knew better than to

Great Expectations 835

27 **Critical Thinking and Reading** Compare and contrast Miss Skiffins with Biddy, Estella, or Mrs. Joe in appearance and manner. Also compare and contrast the professional Mr. Wemmick with the private Mr. Wemmick.

28 **Discussion** What is Pip's purpose in visiting Mr. Wemmick?

are such delightful people that the reader always hopes the villain will put his head through a side window and make a last remark; or that the bully will say one thing more, even from the bottom of the stairs. . . . Though Mr Pecksniff [(*Martin Chuzzlewit*)] fell to be a borrower of money, and Mr Mantalini [(*Nicholas Nickleby*)] to turning a mangle, the human race has the comfort of thinking they are still alive: and one might have the rapture of receiving a begging letter from Mr Pecksniff, or even of catching Mr Mantalini collecting the washing, if one always lurked about on Monday mornings. . . .

29 **Discussion** How does Mr. Wemmick arrange to improve Herbert's prospects while keeping Pip's part in the scheme anonymous?

30 **Discussion** What effect does Pip's plan have on Herbert and on Pip?

31 **Discussion** Pip becomes aware of Estella's many admirers and her attitude toward them. What effect does this awareness have on Pip?

offer to see Miss Skiffins home, and under the circumstances I thought I had best go first—which I did, taking a cordial leave of the Aged, and having passed a pleasant evening.

Before a week was out, I received a note from Wemmick, dated Walworth, stating that he hoped he had made some advance in that matter appertaining to our private and personal capacities. The upshot was that we found a worthy young merchant or shipping broker, not long established in business, who wanted intelligent help, and who wanted capital, and who in due course of time and receipt would want a partner. Between him and me, secret articles were signed of which Herbert was the subject, and I paid him half of my five hundred pounds down, and engaged for sundry other payments: some, to fall due at certain dates out of my income; some contingent on my coming into my property. Miss Skiffins's brother conducted the negotiation. Wemmick pervaded it throughout, but never appeared in it.

The whole business was so cleverly managed that Herbert had not the least suspicion of my hand being in it. I never shall forget the radiant face with which he came home one afternoon, and told me as a mighty piece of news, of his having fallen in with one Clarriker (the young merchant's name), and of Clarriker's having shown an extraordinary inclination towards him, and of his belief that the opening had come at last. Day by day as his hopes grew stronger and his face brighter, he must have thought me a more and more affectionate friend, for I had the greatest difficulty in restraining my tears of triumph when I saw him so happy.

At length, the thing being done, and he having that day entered Clarriker's House, and he having talked to me for a whole evening in a flush of pleasure and success, I did really cry in good earnest when I went to bed, to think that my expectations had done some good to somebody.

A great event in my life, the turning point of my life, now opens on my view. But before I proceed to narrate it, and before I pass on to all the changes it involved, I must give one chapter to Estella. It is not much to give to the theme that so long filled my heart.

Chapter 37

The lady with whom Estella was placed, Mrs. Brandley by name, was a widow, with one daughter several years older than Estella. They were in what is called a good position, and visited, and were visited by, numbers of people.

In Mrs. Brandley's house and out of Mrs. Brandley's house, I suffered every kind and degree of torture that Estella could cause me. She made use of me to tease other admirers, and she turned the very familiarity between herself and me to the account of putting a constant slight on my devotion to her.

She had admirers without end. No doubt my jealousy made an admirer of every one who went near her, but there were more than enough of them without that.

I saw her often at Richmond, I heard of her often in town, and I used often to take her and the Brandleys on the water; there were picnics, fête days, plays, operas, concerts, parties, all sorts of pleasures, through which I pursued her—and they were all miseries to me. I never had one hour's happiness in her society, and yet my mind all round the four-and-twenty hours was harping on the happiness of having her with me unto death.

Throughout this part of our intercourse, she habitually reverted to that tone which expressed that our association was forced

ONLY A LOCK OF HAIR
Sir John Everett Millais
City of Manchester Art Galleries

upon us. There were other times when she would come to a sudden check in this tone and in all her many tones, and would seem to pity me.

"Pip, Pip," she said one evening, coming to such a check, when we sat apart at a darkening window of the house in Richmond; "will you never take warning?"

"Of what?"

"Of me."

"Warning not to be attracted by you, do you mean, Estella?"

"Do I mean! If you don't know what I mean, you are blind."

"At any rate," said I, "I have no warning given me just now, for you wrote to me to come to you, this time."

"That's true," said Estella, with a cold careless smile that always chilled me. "The time has come round when Miss Havisham

Great Expectations   837

Humanities Note

Fine art, *Only a Lock of Hair*, 1859, by Sir John Everett Millais. John Everett Millais (1829–1896) was a British painter. Extremely precocious, Millais entered the Royal Academy at age eleven and won a gold medal for his paintings at seventeen. This exceptionally talented portrait painter worked in the Pre-Raphaelite style, which can be characterized as true to nature, romantic, and emotional.

Only a Lock of Hair is a portrait of Ellen Petrie. This lovely painting of a young woman is a study in contrasts: the creamy white of her skin against the dark background and the silky texture of her hair against the dark background and the silky texture of her hair against the velvet of her gown. The white lace collar and cuffs add a demure note to this otherwise sensuous portrait, which is a romantic salute to this young woman's beauty.

You might want to ask students the following questions:

1. Why do you think Millais chose to focus on his subject's face and hands?
2. How do the contrasts between light and dark areas enhance the picture?
3. What overall impression does this portrait convey?

32 Discussion Estella has warned Pip on several occasions to use caution in respect to his feelings for her. Why does Pip repeatedly refuse to heed Estella's warnings about herself?

33 Discussion How does Miss Havisham intensify her efforts to enchant Pip with Estella's beauty? How does Pip judge Miss Havisham as a result?

34 Discussion Why does Estella draw away from Miss Havisham, causing a quarrel?

35 Discussion Describe the setting and atmosphere of this scene. What effect do they have on the characters present?

36 Clarification The phrase *stock and stone* means "as heartless as an inanimate object."

wishes to have me for a day at Satis. You are to take me there, and bring me back, if you will. She would rather I did not travel alone, and objects to receiving my maid, for she has a sensitive horror of being talked of by such people. Can you take me?"

"Can I take you, Estella!"

"You can then? The day after tomorrow, if you please. You are to pay all charges out of my purse. You hear the condition of your going?"

"And must obey," said I.

This was all the preparation I received for that visit, or for others like it: Miss Havisham never wrote to me, nor had I ever so much as seen her handwriting. We went down on the next day but one, and we found her in the room where I had first beheld her.

She was even more dreadfully fond of Estella than she had been when I last saw them together; I repeat the word advisedly, for there was something positively dreadful in the energy of her looks and embraces. She hung upon Estella's beauty, hung upon her words, hung upon her gestures, and sat mumbling her own trembling fingers while she looked at her, as though she were devouring the beautiful creature she had reared.

From Estella she looked at me, with a searching glance that seemed to pry into my heart and probe its wounds. "How does she use you, Pip, how does she use you?" she asked me again, with her witch-like eagerness, even in Estella's hearing. But, when we sat by her flickering fire at night, she was most weird; for then, keeping Estella's hand drawn through her arm and clutched in her own hand, she extorted from her by dint of referring back to what Estella had told her in her regular letters, the names and conditions of the men whom she had fascinated.

I saw in this that Estella was set to wreak Miss Havisham's revenge on men, and that

she was not to be given to me until she had gratified it for a term. I saw in this a reason for her being beforehand assigned to me. Sending her out to attract and torment and do mischief, Miss Havisham sent her with the malicious assurance that she was beyond the reach of all admirers. I saw in this, that I, too, was tormented by a perversion of ingenuity, even while the prize was reserved for me. I saw in this the reason for my being staved off so long, and the reason for my late guardian's declining to commit himself to the formal knowledge of such a scheme.

It happened on the occasion of this visit that some sharp words arose between Estella and Miss Havisham. It was the first time I had ever seen them opposed.

We were seated by the fire, and Miss Havisham still had Estella's arm drawn through her own, and still clutched Estella's hand in hers, when Estella gradually began to detach herself.

"What!" said Miss Havisham, flashing her eyes upon her, "are you tired of me?"

"Only a little tired of myself," replied Estella, disengaging her arm, and moving to the great chimneypiece, where she stood looking down at the fire.

"Speak the truth, you ingrate!" cried Miss Havisham, passionately striking her stick upon the floor; "you are tired of me."

Estella looked at her with perfect composure, and again looked down at the fire. Her graceful figure and her beautiful face expressed a self-possessed indifference to the wild heat of the other that was almost cruel.

"You stock and stone!" exclaimed Miss Havisham. "You cold, cold heart!"

"What!" said Estella. "Do you reproach me for being cold? You?"

"Are you not?" was the fierce retort.

"You should know," said Estella. "I am what you have made me."

"Oh, look at her, look at her!" cried Miss

Havisham bitterly. "Look at her, so hard and thankless, on the hearth where she was reared!"

"You have been very good to me," said Estella "and I owe everything to you. What would you have?"

"Love," replied the other.

"You have it."

"I have not," said Miss Havisham.

"Mother by adoption," retorted Estella, "I have said that I owe everything to you. All I possess is freely yours. All that you have given me is at your command to have again. Beyond that, I have nothing. And if you ask me to give you what you never gave me, my gratitude and duty cannot do impossibilities."

"Did I never give her love!" cried Miss Havisham, turning wildly to me. "Let her call me mad!"

"Why should I call you mad," returned Estella, "I, of all people? Does any one live who knows what set purposes you have half as well as I do? I who have sat on this same hearth on the little stool that is even now beside you there, learning your lessons and looking up into your face."

"Soon forgotten!" moaned Miss Havisham.

"No, not forgotten," retorted Estella. "Not fogotten, but treasured up in my memory. When have you found me false to your teaching? When have you found me unmindful of your lessons?"

"So proud, so proud!" moaned Miss Havisham.

"Who taught me to be proud?" returned Estella.

"So hard, so hard!" moaned Miss Havisham.

"Who taught me to be hard?" returned Estella.

"But to be proud and hard to *me*!" Miss Havisham quite shrieked, as she stretched out her arms. "Estella, Estella, Estella, to be proud and hard to *me*!"

Estella looked at her for a moment with a kind of calm wonder, but was not otherwise disturbed; when the moment was past, she looked down at the fire again.

Miss Havisham settled down, I hardly knew how, upon the floor, among the faded bridal relics with which it was strewn. I took advantage of the moment to leave the room, after beseeching Estella's attention to her with a movement of my hand.

It was with a depressed heart that I walked in the starlight for an hour and more, about the courtyard, and about the ruined garden. When I at last took courage to return to the room, I found Estella sitting at Miss Havisham's knee, taking up some stitches in one of those old articles of dress that were dropping to pieces. Afterwards, Estella and I played at cards, as of yore—only we were skillful now, and played French games—and so the evening wore away, and I went to bed.

Before we left next day, there was no revival of the difference between her and Estella, nor was it ever revived on any similar occasion.

It is impossible to turn this leaf of my life without putting Bentley Drummle's name upon it; or I would, very gladly.

On a certain occasion when the Finches[1] were assembled in force, the presiding Finch called the Grove to order, forasmuch as Mr. Drummle had not yet toasted a lady. What was my indignant surprise when he called upon the company to pledge him to "Estella!"

This was no light thing to me. For I cannot adequately express what pain it gave me to think that Estella should show any favor

---

1. Finches: Finches of the Grove, a social club to which Drummle, Herbert, and Pip belong.

Great Expectations 839

37 Discussion Why is Estella unable to love Miss Havisham? What has Estella offered her instead?

Critical Thinking and Reading
Why does Estella ignore Pip's warnings about Drummle?

Speaking and Listening You might want to have students volunteer to read aloud from Chapter 38 to demonstrate the different techniques Dickens uses to inform Pip and his readers of his benefactor's identity and to depict Pip's reaction. If you wish, individual students may read the parts of Pip (as the narrator), Pip (when quoted directly), and Magwitch.

to a contemptible, clumsy, sulky booby, so very far below the average.

It was easy for me to find out, and I did soon find out, that Drummle had begun to follow her closely, and that she allowed him to do it. A little while, and he was always in pursuit of her. He held on, in a dull persistent way, and Estella held him on; now with encouragement, now with discouragement, now almost flattering him, now openly despising him, now knowing him very well, now scarcely remembering who he was.

The Spider, as Mr. Jaggers had called him, was used to lying in wait, however, and had the patience of his tribe.

At a certain Assembly Ball at Richmond, this blundering Drummle so hung about her, and with so much toleration on her part, that I resolved to speak to her concerning him. I took the next opportunity, which was when she was waiting for Mrs. Brandley to take her home.

"Estella," said I, "look at that fellow in the corner yonder who is looking over here at us."

"Why should I look at him?" returned Estella, with her eyes on me instead. "What is there in that fellow in the corner yonder that I need look at?"

"Indeed, that is the very question I want to ask you," said I. "For he has been hovering about you all night."

"Moths, and all sorts of ugly creatures," replied Estella, with a glance towards him, "hover about a lighted candle. Can the candle help it?"

"No," I returned: "but cannot the Estella help it?"

"Well!" said she, "perhaps. Yes. Anything you like."

"But, Estella, do hear me speak. It makes me wretched that you should encourage a man so generally despised as Drummle. You know he is despised."

"Well?" said she.

"You know he is a deficient, ill-tempered, lowering, stupid fellow."

"Well?" said she.

"You know he has nothing to recommend him but money, don't you?"

"Well?" said she again.

"Well! Then, that is why it makes me wretched."

"Pip," said Estella, "don't be foolish about its effect on you. It may have its effect on others, and may be meant to have. It's not worth discussing."

"Yes it is," said I, "because I cannot bear that people should say, 'She throws away her graces and attractions on a mere boor,[2] the lowest in the crowd.'"

"I can bear it," said Estella.

"Oh, don't be so proud, Estella, and so inflexible."

"Calls me proud and inflexible in this breath!" said Estella. "And in his last breath reproached me for stooping to a boor!"

"There is no doubt you do," said I something hurriedly, "for I have seen you give him looks and smiles this very night, such as you never give to—me."

"Do you want me then," said Estella, turning suddenly with a fixed and serious, if not angry look, "to deceive and entrap you?"

"Do you deceive and entrap him, Estella?"

"Yes, and many others—all of them but you. Here is Mrs. Brandley. I'll say no more."

Chapter 38

I was three-and-twenty years of age. Not another word had I heard to enlighten me on the subject of my expectations. We had left Barnard's Inn more than a year, and lived in the Temple.[1] Our chambers were in Garden

---

2. boor (bŏŏr) *n.*: A rude, unpleasant person.
1. Temple: Buildings near the Thames River for people associated with the court system.

Court, down by the river. Mr. Pocket and I had for some time parted company as to our original relations, though we continued on the best terms.

Business had taken Herbert on a journey to Marseilles.[2] I was alone, and had a dull sense of being alone. Dispirited and anxious, I sadly missed the cheerful face and ready response of my friend.

It was wretched weather; stormy and wet, stormy and wet; mud, mud, mud, deep in all the streets. Day after day, a vast heavy veil had been driving over London from the east, and it drove still, as if in the east there were an eternity of cloud and wind.

Alterations have been made in that part of the Temple since that time, and it has not now so lonely a character as it had then, nor is it so exposed to the river. We lived at the top of the last house, and the wind rushing up the river shook the house that night, like discharges of cannon, or breakings of a sea. I saw that the lamps in the court were blown out, and that the lamps on the bridges and the shore were shuddering, and that the coal fires in barges on the river were being carried away before the wind like red-hot splashes in the rain.

I read with my watch upon the table, purposing to close my book at eleven o'clock. As I shut it, Saint Paul's, and all the many church-clocks in the City struck that hour. The sound was curiously flawed by the wind; and I was listening, and thinking how the wind assailed and tore it, when I heard a footstep on the stair.

Remembering, then, that the staircase lights were blown out, I took up my reading-lamp and went out to the stair-head. Whoever was below had stopped on seeing my lamp, for all was quiet.

---

2. **Marseilles** (mär se′ y′): Seaport in southeast France.

"There is some one down there, is there not?" I called out, looking down.

"Yes," said a voice from the darkness beneath.

"What floor do you want?"

"The top. Mr. Pip."

"That is my name. There is nothing the matter?"

"Nothing the matter," returned the voice. And the man came on.

I stood with my lamp held out over the stair-rail, and he came slowly within its light. I saw a face that was strange to me, looking up with an incomprehensible air of being touched and pleased by the sight of me.

Moving the lamp as the man moved, I made out that he was substantially dressed, but roughly, like a voyager by sea. That he had long iron-gray hair. That his age was about sixty. That he was a muscular man, strong on his legs, and that he was browned and hardened by exposure to weather. As he ascended the last stair or two, and the light of my lamp included us both, I saw, with a stupid kind of amazement, that he was holding out both his hands to me.

"Pray what is your business?" I asked him.

"My business?" he repeated, pausing. "Ah! Yes. I will explain my business, by your leave."

"Do you wish to come in?"

"Yes," he replied, "I wish to come in, master."

I took him into the room I had just left, and, having set the lamp on the table, asked him as civilly as I could to explain himself.

He looked about him with the strangest air—an air of wondering pleasure, as if he had some part in the things he admired—and he pulled off a rough outer coat, and his hat. Then, I saw that his head was furrowed and bald, and that the long iron-gray hair grew only on its sides. But I saw nothing

Great Expectations 841

39 Literary Focus Foreshadowing is a literary device by which writers hint at events to come. How might weather foreshadow future events?

Videodisc To bring to life Provis's appearance at Pip's home, you might want to show the appropriate segment of the *Scenes From Great Expectations* videodisc. Based on Provis's speech and physical appearance, what are students' impressions of his character? Why?

Frames 48837 to 52555

that in the least explained him. On the contrary, I saw him next moment once more holding out both his hands to me.

"What do you mean?" said I, half-suspecting him to be mad.

He stopped in his looking at me and slowly rubbed his right hand over his head. "It's disappointing to a man," he said, in a coarse broken voice, "arter having looked for'ard so distant, and come so fur; but you're not to blame for that—neither on us is to blame for that. I'll speak in half a minute. Give me half a minute, please."

He sat down on a chair that stood before the fire, and covered his forehead with his large brown veinous hands. I looked at him attentively then, and recoiled a little from him; but I did not know him.

"There's no one nigh," said he, looking over his shoulder, "is there?"

"Why do you, a stranger coming into my rooms at this time of the night, ask that question?" said I.

"You're a game one," he returned. "I'm glad you've grow'd up a game one! But don't catch hold of me. You'd be sorry arterwards to have done it."

40 I relinquished the intention he had detected, for I knew him! Even yet I could not recall a single feature, but I knew him! If the wind and the rain had driven away the intervening years, had scattered all the intervening objects, had swept us to the churchyard where we first stood face to face on such different levels, I could not have known my convict more distinctly than I knew him now, as he sat in the chair before the fire. No need to take a file from his pocket and show it to me; no need to take the handkerchief from his neck and twist it round his head; no need to hug himself with both his arms, and take a shivering turn across the room, looking back at me for recognition. I knew him before he gave me one of those aids, though, a mo-

ment before, I had not been conscious of remotely suspecting his identity.

He came back to where I stood, and again held out both his hands. Not knowing what to do—for, in my astonishment I had lost my self-possession—I reluctantly gave him my hands. He grasped them heartily, raised them to his lips, kissed them, and still held them.

"You acted nobly, my boy," said he. "Noble Pip! And I have never forgot it!"

At a change in his manner as if he were even going to embrace me, I laid a hand upon his breast and put him away.

"Stay!" said I. "Keep off! If you are grateful to me for what I did when I was a little child, I hope you have shown your gratitude by mending your way of life. If you have come here to thank me, it was not necessary. Still, however, you have found me out, there must be something good in the feeling that has brought you here, and I will not repulse you; but surely you must understand—I—"

My attention was so attracted by the singularity of his fixed look at me that the words died away on my tongue.

"You was a-saying," he observed, when we had confronted one another in silence, "that surely I must understand. What, surely must I understand?"

"That I cannot wish to renew that chance intercourse with you of long ago, under these different circumstances. I am glad to believe you have repented and recovered yourself. I am glad to tell you so. I am glad that, thinking I deserve to be thanked, you have come to thank me. But our ways are different ways, none the less. You are wet, and you look weary. Will you drink something before you go?"

He had replaced his neckerchief loosely, and had stood, keenly observant of me, biting a long end of it. "I think," he answered, still with the end at his mouth and still observant of me, "that I *will* drink (I thank you) afore I go." I made him some hot rum-and-water. When I put the glass to him, I saw with amazement that his eyes were full of tears.

"I hope," said I, "that you will not think I spoke harshly to you just now. I had no intention of doing it, and I am sorry for it if I did. I wish you well, and happy!"

As I put my glass to my lips, he stretched out his hand. I gave him mine, and then he drank, and drew his sleeve across his eyes and forehead.

"How are you living?" I asked him.

"I've been a sheep-farmer, stock-breeder, other trades besides, away in the New World,[3] said he, "many a thousand mile of stormy water off from this."

"I hope you have done well."

"I've done wonderful well. No man has done nigh as well as me. I'm famous for it."

"I am glad to hear it."

"I hope to hear you say so, my dear boy."

Without stopping to try to understand those words or the tone in which they were spoken, I turned off to a point that had just come into my mind.

"Have you ever seen a messenger you once sent to me," I inquired, "since he undertook that trust?"

"Never set eyes upon him. I warn't likely to it."

"He came faithfully, and he brought me the two one-pound notes. I was a poor boy then, as you know, and to a poor boy they were a little fortune. But, like you, I have done well since, and you must let me pay them back. You can put them to some other poor boy's use." I took out my purse.

He watched me as I laid my purse upon the table and opened it, and he watched me as I separated two one-pound notes from its

3. **New World:** Australia.

contents. They were clean and new, and I spread them out and handed them over to him. Still watching me, he laid them one upon the other, folded them long-wise, gave them a twist, set fire to them at the lamp, and dropped the ashes into the tray.

"May I make so bold," he said then, "as ask you *how* you have done well, since you and me was out on them lone shivering marshes?"

He emptied his glass, got up, and stood at the side of the fire, with his heavy brown hand on the mantelshelf. He put a foot up to the bars, to dry and warm it, and the wet boot began to steam; but he neither looked at it, nor at the fire, but steadily looked at me. It was only now that I began to tremble.

When my lips had parted, I forced myself to tell him that I had been chosen to succeed to some property.

"Might a mere warmint ask what property?" said he.

I faltered, "I don't know."

"Might a mere warmint ask whose property?" said he.

I faltered again, "I don't know."

"Could I make a guess, I wonder," said the convict, "at your income since you come of age! As to the first figure, now. Five?"

With my heart beating like a heavy hammer of disordered action, I rose out of my chair, and stood with my hand upon the back of it, looking wildly at him.

"Concerning a guardian," he went on. "There ought to have been some guardian or such-like, whiles you was a minor. Some lawyer, maybe. As to the first letter of that lawyer's name, now. Would it be J?"

All the truth of my position came flashing on me, and its disappointments, dangers, disgraces, consequences of all kinds rushed in in such a multitude that I was borne down by them and had to struggle for every breath I drew. "Put it," he resumed, "as the employer of that lawyer whose name begun with a J, and might be Jaggers—put it as he had come over sea to Portsmouth,[4] and had landed there, and had wanted to come on to you. 'However, you have found me out,' you says just now. Well, however, did I find you out? Why, I wrote from Portsmouth to a person in London for particulars of your address. That person's name? Why, Wemmick."

I could not have spoken one word, though it had been to save my life. I stood, with a hand on the chair-back and a hand on my breast, where I seemed to be suffocating—I stood so, looking wildly at him, until I grasped at the chair, when the room began to surge and turn. He caught me, drew me to the sofa, put me up against the cushions, and bent on one knee before me; bringing the face that I now well remembered, and that I shuddered at, very near to mine.

"Yes, Pip, dear boy, I've made a gentleman on you! It's me wot has done it! I swore that time, sure as ever I earned a guinea, that guinea should go to you. I swore arterwards, sure as ever I spec'lated and got rich, you should get rich. I lived rough, that you should live smooth; I worked hard that you should be above work. What odds, dear boy? Do I tell it fur you to feel a obligation? Not a bit. I tell it fur you to know as that there hunted dunghill dog wot you kep life in got his head so high that he could make a gentleman—and, Pip, you're him!"

The abhorrence in which I held the man, the dread I had of him, the repugnance with which I shrank from him could not have been exceeded if he had been some terrible beast.

"Look'ee here, Pip. I'm your second father. You're my son—more to me nor any son. I've put away money, only for you to spend. When I was a hired-out shepherd in a solitary hut, not seeing no faces but faces of sheep till I half-forgot wot men's and women's faces wos like, I see yourn. I drops my knife many a time in that hut when I was a-eating my dinner or my supper, and I says, 'Here's the boy again, a-looking at me whiles I eats and drinks!' I see you there a many times as plain as ever I see you on them misty marshes. 'Lord strike me dead!' I says each time—and I goes out in the open air to say it under the open heavens—'but wot, if I gets liberty and money, I'll make that boy a gentleman!' And I done it. Why, look at you, dear boy! Look at these here lodgings of yourn, fit for a lord! A lord? Ah! You shall show money with lords for wagers, and beat 'em!"

Again he took both my hands and put them to his lips, while my blood ran cold within me.

"Don't you mind talking, Pip," said he, "You ain't looked slowly forward to this as I have; you wosn't prepared for this, as I wos. But didn't you never think it might be me?"

"Oh, no, no, no," I returned. "Never, never!"

"Well, you see it wos me, and single-handed. Never a soul in it but my own self and Mr. Jaggers."

"Was there no one else?" I asked.

"No," said he, with a glance of surprise. "Who else should there be? And, dear boy, how good-looking you have growed! There's bright eyes somewheres—eh? Isn't there bright eyes somewheres, wot you love the thoughts on?"

O Estella, Estella!

"They shall be yourn, dear boy, if money can buy 'em. Not that a gentleman like you, so well set up as you, can't win 'em off of his own game; but money shall back you! Let me finish wot I was a-telling you, dear boy. From that there hut and that there hiring-out, I

---

4. **Portsmouth:** Seaport in south England.

got money left me by my master (which died, and had been the same as me), and got my liberty and went for myself. In every single thing I went for, I went for you. 'Lord strike a blight upon it,' I says, wotever it was I went for, 'if it ain't for him!' It all prospered wonderful. As I giv' you to understand just now, I'm famous for it. It was the money left me, and the gains of the first few year, wot I sent home to Mr. Jaggers—all for you—when he first come arter you, agreeable to my letter."

O that he had never come! That he had left me at the forge—far from contented, yet, by comparison, happy!

"And then, dear boy, I held steady afore my mind that I would for certain come one day and see my boy, and make myself known to him, on his own ground."

He laid his hand on my shoulder. I shuddered at the thought that for anything I knew, his hand might be stained with blood.

"Where will you put me?" he asked presently. "I must be put somewheres, dear boy."

"To sleep?" said I.

"Yes. And to sleep long and sound," he answered, "for I've been sea-tossed and sea-washed, months and months."

"My friend and companion," said I, rising from the sofa, "is absent; you must have his room."

"He won't come back tomorrow, will he?"

"No," said I, answering almost mechanically, "not tomorrow."

"Because, look'ee here, dear boy," he said, dropping his voice, and laying a long finger on my breast in an impressive manner, "caution is necessary."

"How do you mean, caution?"

"It's death!"

"What's death?"

"I was sent for life. It's death to come back. There's been overmuch coming back of late years, and I should of a certainty be hanged if took."

Nothing was needed but this; the wretched man, after loading me with his wretched gold and silver chains for years, had risked his life to come to me, and I held it there in my keeping!

My first care was to close the shutters, so that no light might be seen from without, and then to close and make fast the doors. While I did so, he stood at the table drinking rum and eating biscuit.

When I had gone into Herbert's room, and had shut off any other communication between it and the staircase than through the room in which our conversation had been held, I asked him if he would go to bed. He said yes, but asked me for some of my "gentleman's linen" to put on in the morning. I brought it out, and laid it ready for him, and my blood again ran cold when he again took me by both hands to give me good night.

I got away from him, without knowing how I did it, and mended the fire in the room where we had been together, and sat down by it, afraid to go to bed. For an hour or more, I remained too stunned to think; and it was not until I began to think that I began fully to know how wrecked I was.

Miss Havisham's intentions towards me, all a mere dream; Estella not designed for me; I only suffered in Satis House as a convenience, a sting for the greedy relations, a model with a mechanical heart to practice on when no other practice was at hand; those were the first smarts I had. But, sharpest and deepest pain of all—it was for the convict, guilty of I knew not what crimes, that I had deserted Joe.

In every rage of wind and rush of rain, I heard pursuers. Twice I could have sworn there was a knocking and whispering at the outer door. With these fears upon me, I began either to imagine or recall that I had had mysterious warnings of this man's ap-

43 Discussion Although not part of the action of this novel, the tale Pip's benefactor tells about his life is a dramatic story in itself. What are some important details in this account? What is Pip's reaction to the story?

44 Discussion Why would the convict risk death by coming to see Pip?

45 Discussion Why is Pip so distressed by what he has learned?

46 Discussion What is the "sharpest and deepest pain of all" when Pip realizes that Miss Havisham is not his benefactor?

ESL Teaching Strategy Explain to students that the nonstandard English spoken by many of Dickens's characters is unfamiliar to modern readers. Suggest that students use the techniques of looking for context clues to find the meanings of unfamiliar words.

Write these sentences on the chalkboard:
1. "You'll be sorry arterwards to have done it." (page 842)
2. "Might a mere warmint ask what property?" (page 843)
3. "Isn't there bright eyes somewheres, wot you love the thoughts on?" (page 844)
4. "There's been overmuch coming back of late years, and I should of a certainty be hanged if took." (page 845)

Ask students to locate the sentences in the text and to read them in context. Question students about the meaning of each sentence, and about the meanings of such words as *arterwards*, *wot*, and *warmint*. Ask what clues in the text helped them find the meanings of these sentences.

Humanities Note

Fine art, *Adeline, Seventh Countess of Cardigan,* 1858–1868, by Richard Buckner. The British painter Richard Buckner (active 1840–1879) specialized in full-length portraits.

Adeline, Seventh Countess of Cardigan is an unusual portrait of a young woman in an evening dress. With her graceful hands, tiny feet, lacy gown, and shy demeanor, she is the embodiment of youthful loveliness. The romance of the balcony setting is accentuated by moonlight.

You might want to use the following questions:

1. Is this young woman as cold and callous as Estella? Explain.
2. Compare and contrast this young woman with the subject of Whistler's *The White Girl: Symphony in White, No. 1,* page 819.

ADELINE, SEVENTH COUNTESS OF CARDIGAN
Richard Buckner
From the collection of Edmund Brudenell, Esq.

proach. That for weeks gone by I had passed faces in the streets which I had thought like his.

Then came the reflection that I had seen him with my childish eyes to be a desperately violent man; that I had heard that other convict reiterate that he had tried to murder him. Out of such remembrances I brought into the light of the fire, a half-formed terror that it might not be safe to be shut up there with him in the dead of the wild solitary night. This dilated until it filled the room, and impelled me to take a candle and go in and look at my dreadful burden.

He had rolled a handkerchief round his head, and his face was set and lowering in his sleep. But he was asleep, and quietly, too, though he had a pistol lying on the pillow. Assured of this, I softly removed the key to the outside of his door, and turned it on him before I again sat down by the fire. Gradually I slipped from the chair and lay on the floor. When I awoke without having parted in my sleep with the perception of my wretchedness, the clocks of the eastward churches were striking five, the candles were wasted out, the fire was dead, and the wind and rain intensified the thick black darkness.

THIS IS THE END OF THE SECOND STAGE
OF PIP'S EXPECTATIONS

Chapter 39

The impossibility of keeping my dreaded visitor concealed in the chambers was self-evident. It could not be done, and the attempt to do it would inevitably engender suspicion. True, I had no one in my service now, but I was looked after by an inflammatory old female, assisted by an animated rag-bag whom she called her niece, and to keep a room secret from them would be to invite curiosity and exaggeration. So I resolved to announce in the morning that my uncle had unexpectedly come from the country.

This course I decided on while I was yet groping about in the darkness for the means of getting a light. Then in groping my way down the black staircase, I fell over something, and that something was a man crouching in a corner.

As the man made no answer when I asked him what he did there, but eluded my touch in silence, I ran to the lodge and urged the watchman to come quickly, telling him of the incident on the way back. We examined the staircase from the bottom to the top and found no one there.

It troubled me that there should have been a lurker on the stairs, on that night of all nights in the year, and I asked the watchman whether he had admitted at his gate any gentleman who had perceptibly been dining out?

"The night being so bad, sir," said the watchman, "uncommon few have come in at my gate. Besides them three gentlemen that I have named, I don't call to mind another since about eleven o'clock, when a stranger asked for you."

"My uncle," I muttered. "Yes."

"You saw him, sir?"

"Yes. Oh, yes."

"Likewise the person with him?"

"Person with him!" I repeated. "What sort of person?"

The watchman had not particularly noticed; he should say a working person; to the best of his belief, he had a dust-colored kind of clothes on, under a dark coat.

My mind was much troubled by these two circumstances taken together. I lighted my fire, which burnt with a raw pale flare at that time of the morning, and fell into a doze

47 **Discussion** At the end of the second stage of Pip's "great expectations," what new incidents does he dread?

48 **Critical Thinking and Reading** What is Pip's reaction on learning that there was a man "with" his uncle? What might be the significance of this information?

before it. I seemed to have been dozing a whole night when the clocks struck six. As there was full an hour and a half between me and daylight, I dozed again; now waking up uneasily, with prolix conversations about nothing, in my ears; now making thunder of the wind in the chimney; at length falling off into a profound sleep from which the daylight woke me with a start.

The old woman and the niece came in and testified surprise at sight of me and the fire. To whom I imparted how my uncle had come in the night and was then asleep, and how the breakfast preparations were to be modified accordingly.

By-and-by, his door opened and he came out. I could not bring myself to bear the sight of him, and I thought he had a worse look by daylight.

"I do not even know," said I, speaking low as he took his seat at the table, "by what name to call you. I have given out that you are my uncle."

"That's it, dear boy! Call me uncle."

"You assumed some name, I suppose, on board ship?"

"Yes, dear boy. I took the name of Provis."

"Do you mean to keep that name?"

"Why, yes, dear boy, it's as good as another—unless you'd like another."

"What is your real name?" I asked him in a whisper.

"Magwitch," he answered, in the same tone; "chrisen'd Abel."

"What were you brought up to be?"

"A warmint, dear boy."

He answered quite seriously, and used the words as if it denoted some profession.

"When you came in at the gate and asked the watchman the way here, had you any one with you?"

"With me? No, dear boy."

"But there was some one there?"

"I didn't take particular notice," he said dubiously, "not knowing the ways of the place. But I think there *was* a person, too, come in alonger me."

"Are you known in London?"

"I hope not!" said he.

"Were you known in London, once?"

"Not over and above, dear boy. I was in the provinces mostly."

"Were you—tried—in London?"

"Which time?" said he, with a sharp look.

"The last time."

He nodded. "First knowed Mr. Jaggers that way. Jaggers was for me."

It was on my lips to ask him what he was tried for, but he took up a knife, gave it a flourish, and with the words, "And what I done is worked out and paid for!" fell to at his breakfast.

I found that I was beginning slowly to settle down to the contemplation of my condition. What I was chained to, and how heavily, became intelligible to me, as I heard his hoarse voice, and sat looking up at his furrowed bald head with its iron-gray hair at the sides.

He took out of his pocket a great thick pocketbook, bursting with papers, and tossed it on the table.

"There's something worth spending in that there book, dear boy. It's yourn. All I've got ain't mine; it's yourn. Don't you be afeered on it. There's more where that come from. I've come to the old country fur to see my gentleman spend his money *like* a gentleman. That'll be my pleasure. *My* pleasure 'ull be fur to see him do it."

"Stop!" said I, almost in a frenzy of fear and dislike, "I want to speak to you. I want to know what is to be done. I want to know how you are to be kept out of danger, how long you are going to stay, what projects you have."

"Look'ee here, Pip," said he, "I forgot myself half a minute ago. What I said was low; that's what it was; low. Look'ee here, Pip. Look over it. I ain't a-going to be low."

"First," I resumed, half-groaning, "what precautions can be taken against your being recognized and seized?"

"Well, dear boy, the danger ain't so great. Without I was informed agen, the danger ain't so much to signify. There's Jaggers, and there's Wemmick, and there's you. Who else is there to inform?"

"Is there no chance person who might identify you in the street?" said I.

"Well," he returned, "there ain't many. Still, look'ee here, Pip. If the danger had been fifty times as great, I should ha' come to see you, mind you, just the same."

"And how long do you remain?"

"How long?" said he. "I'm not a-going back. I've come for good."

"Where are you to live?" said I. "What is to be done with you? Where will you be safe?"

"Dear boy," he returned, "there's disguising wigs can be bought for money, and there's hair powder, and spectacles, and black clothes—shorts and what not. As to the where and how of living, dear boy, give me your own opinions on it."

It appeared to me that I could do no better than secure him some quiet lodging hard by, of which he might take possession when Herbert returned—whom I expected in two or three days. That the secret must be confided to Herbert as a matter of unavoidable necessity, even if I could have put the immense relief I should derive from sharing it with him out of the question, was plain to me. But it was by no means so plain to Mr. Provis (I resolved to call him by that name), who reserved his consent to Herbert's participation until he should have seen him and formed a favorable judgment of his physiognomy. "And even then, dear boy," said he, pulling a greasy little clasped black Testament out of his pocket, "we'll have him on his oath."

There being to my knowledge a respectable lodginghouse in Essex Street, the back of which looked into the Temple, and was almost within hail of my windows, I first of all repaired to that house, and was so fortunate as to secure the second floor for my uncle, Mr. Provis. I then went from shop to shop, making such purchases as were necessary to a change in his appearance. This business transacted, I turned my face, on my own account, to Little Britain. Mr. Jaggers was at his desk, but, seeing me enter, got up immediately and stood before his fire.

"Now, Pip," said he, "be careful."

"I will, sir," I returned.

"Don't commit yourself," said Mr. Jaggers, "and don't commit any one. You understand—any one. Don't tell me anything; I don't want to know anything; I am not curious."

Of course I saw that he knew the man was come.

"I merely want, Mr. Jaggers," said I, "to assure myself what I have been told, is true."

Mr. Jaggers nodded. "But did you say 'told' or 'informed'?" he asked me. "Told would seem to imply verbal communication. You can't have verbal communication with a man in New South Wales,[1] you know."

"I will say informed, Mr. Jaggers."

"Good."

"I have been informed by a person named Abel Magwitch that he is the benefactor so long unknown to me."

---

1. **New South Wales:** A state in southeast Australia.

Great Expectations 849

50 **Discussion** What does Provis believe will be an effective disguise?

51 **Reading Strategy** Summarize the discussion between Mr. Jaggers and Pip.

50

51

52 Discussion What is the admission Pip makes to Mr. Jaggers about his "mistake"?

53 Discussion What advice does Mr. Jaggers give in regard to "appearance" versus "reality" after Pip explains his mistaken conviction that Miss Havisham was his benefactress?

54 Discussion What were the cautions Mr. Jaggers told Pip he had communicated to Provis in Australia?

55 Discussion How did Provis know how to find Pip's lodgings in London?

"That is the man," said Mr. Jaggers, "—in New South Wales."

"And only he?" said I.

"And only he," said Mr. Jaggers.

52 "I am not so unreasonable, sir, as to think you at all responsible for my mistakes and wrong conclusions, but I always supposed it was Miss Havisham."

"As you say, Pip," returned Mr. Jaggers, "I am not at all responsible for that."

"And yet it looked so like it, sir," I pleaded with a downcast heart.

53 "Not a particle of evidence, Pip," said Mr. Jaggers. "Take nothing on its looks; take everything on evidence. There's no better rule."

"I have no more to say," said I. "I have verified my information, and there's an end."

"And Magwitch—in New South Wales—having at last disclosed himself," said Mr. Jaggers, "you will comprehend, Pip, how rigidly throughout my communication with you I have always adhered to the strict line of fact.

54 "I communicated to Magwitch—in New South Wales—when he first wrote to me—from New South Wales—the caution that he must not expect me ever to deviate from the strict line of fact. I also communicated to him another caution. He appeared to me to have obscurely hinted in his letter at some distant idea of seeing you in England here. I cautioned him that I must hear no more of that; that he was not at all likely to obtain a pardon; that he was expatriated[2] for the term of his natural life; and that his presenting himself in this country would be an act of felony, rendering him liable to the extreme penalty of the law. I gave Magwitch that caution," said Mr. Jaggers, looking hard at me; "I wrote it to New South Wales. He guided himself by it, no doubt."

---

2. expatriated (eks pā′ trē āt′ əd) v.: Exiled.

"No doubt," said I.

"I have been informed by Wemmick," pursued Mr. Jaggers, "that he has received a letter, under date Portsmouth, from a colonist of the name of Purvis, or—"

"Or Provis," I suggested.

"Or Provis—thank you, Pip. Perhaps it *is* Provis? Perhaps you know it's Provis?"

"Yes," said I.

55 "You know it's Provis. A letter, under date Portsmouth, from a colonist of the name of Provis, asking for the particulars of your address, on behalf of Magwitch. Wemmick sent him the particulars, I understand, by return of post. Probably it is through Provis that you have received the explanation of Magwitch—in New South Wales?"

"It came through Provis," I replied.

"Good day, Pip," said Mr. Jaggers, offering his hand; "glad to have seen you. In writing by post to Magwitch—in New South Wales—or in communicating with him through Provis, have the goodness to mention that the particulars and vouchers of our long account shall be sent to you, together with the balance; for there is still a balance remaining. Good day, Pip!"

We shook hands, and he looked hard at me as long as he could see me. Wemmick was out, and though he had been at his desk he could have done nothing for me. I went straight back to the Temple, where I found the terrible Provis.

Next day the clothes I had ordered all came home, and he put them on. Whatever he put on became him less (it dismally seemed to me) than what he had worn before. To my thinking there was something in him that made it hopeless to attempt to disguise him. The more I dressed him, and the better I dressed him, the more he looked like the slouching fugitive on the marshes.

Words cannot tell what a sense I had of the dreadful mystery that he was to me.

HENRY, LORD MONTAGUE OF BROUGHTON
Sir Francis Grant
National Galleries of Scotland

Great Expectations   851

Humanities Note

Fine art, *Henry, Lord Montague of Broughton,* by Sir Francis Grant. The British painter Sir Frances Grant (1803–1878) was the fourth son of the Laird of Kilgraston. He took lessons from painter John Ferneley and exhibited his first picture at the age of thirty-six. Immediately successful, he was soon in demand as a fashionable portrait painter. He was named the President of the Royal Academy in 1866.

This portrait of *Henry, Lord Montague of Broughton* is painted with the style and naturalness that characterize Grant's work.

You might want to have students consider the following questions:

1. What qualities do you see in young Lord Montague's face?
2. Do you think that Pip has come to resemble an upper-class gentleman like this one? Why or why not?

56 Discussion What nagging thought prevents Pip from trusting Provis?

57 Discussion How is Provis prepared to protect himself against intruders?

When he fell asleep of an evening, with his knotted hands clenching the sides of the easy chair, and his bald head tattooed with deep wrinkles falling forward on his breast, I would sit and look at him, wondering what he had done, and loading him with all the crimes in the calendar, until the impulse was powerful on me to start up and fly from him. Every hour so increased my abhorrence of him that I even think I might have yielded to this impulse in the first agonies of being so haunted, notwithstanding all he had done for me and the risk he ran, but for the knowledge that Herbert must soon come back.

One evening when dinner was over and I had dropped into a slumber quite worn out—for my nights had been agitated and my rest broken by fearful dreams—I was roused by the welcome footstep on the staircase. Provis, who had been asleep, too, staggered up at the noise I made, and in an instant I saw his jackknife shining in his hand.

"Quiet! It's Herbert!" I said, and Herbert came bursting in.

"Handel, my dear fellow, how are you, and again how are you, and again how are you? I seem to have been gone a twelvemonth! Why, so I must have been, for you have grown quite thin and pale! Handel, my—Halloa! I beg your pardon."

He was stopped in his running on and in his shaking hands with me, by seeing Provis. Provis, regarding him with a fixed attention, was slowly putting up his jackknife, and groping in another pocket for something else.

"Herbert, my dear friend," said I, shutting the double doors, while Herbert stood staring and wondering, "something very strange has happened. This is—a visitor of mine."

"It's all right, dear boy!" said Provis, coming forward, with his little clasped black book, and then addressing himself to Herbert. "Take it in your right hand. Lord strike you dead on the spot, if ever you split[3] in any way sumever. Kiss it!"

"Do so, as he wishes it," I said to Herbert. So Herbert, looking at me with a friendly uneasiness and amazement, complied, and Provis immediately shaking hands with him, said, "Now, you're on your oath, you know. And never believe me on mine, if Pip sha'n't make a gentleman on you!"

Chapter 40

In vain should I attempt to describe the astonishment and disquiet of Herbert when he and I and Provis sat down before the fire, and I recounted the whole of the secret. Enough that I saw my own feelings reflected in Herbert's face, and, not least among them, my repugnance towards the man who had done so much for me.

"Look'ee here, Pip's comrade," Provis said to Herbert, after having discoursed for some time, "I know very well that once since I come back—for half a minute—I've been low. I said to Pip I knowed as how I had been low. But don't you fret yourself on that score. I ain't made Pip a gentleman, and Pip ain't a-goin to make you a gentleman, not fur me not to know what's due to ye both."

Herbert said, "Certainly," but looked as if there were no specific consolation in this, and remained perplexed and dismayed. We were anxious for the time when he would go to his lodging, and leave us together, but he was evidently jealous of leaving us together, and sat late. It was midnight before I took him round to Essex Street, and saw him

---

3. split: Slang for "tell."

safely in at his own dark door. When it closed upon him, I experienced the first moment of relief I had known since the night of his arrival.

Herbert received me with open arms, and I had never felt before so blessedly what it is to have a friend. When he had spoken some sound words of sympathy and encouragement, we sat down to consider the question, What was to be done?

"My poor dear Handel," said Herbert, "I am too stunned to think."

"So was I, Herbert, when the blow first fell. Still, something must be done. He is intent upon various new expenses—horses, and carriages, and lavish appearances of all kinds. He must be stopped somehow."

"You mean that you can't accept—"

"How can I?" I interposed, as Herbert paused. "Think of him! Look at him!"

An involuntary shudder passed over both of us.

"Then," said I, "after all, stopping short here, never taking another penny from him, think what I owe him already! Then again, I am heavily in debt—very heavily for me, who have now no expectations—and I have been bred to no calling, and I am fit for nothing."

"Well, well, well!" Herbert remonstrated. "Don't say fit for nothing."

"What am I fit for? I know only one thing that I am fit for, and that is to go for a soldier."

"My dear Handel," said he presently, "soldiering won't do. You would be infinitely better in Clarriker's house, small as it is. I am working up towards a partnership, you know."

Poor fellow! He little suspected with whose money.

I said to Herbert that even if Provis were recognized and taken, I should be wretched as the cause, however innocently. Yes; even though I was so wretched in having him at large and near me, and even though I would far rather have worked at the forge all the days of my life than I would ever have come to this!

But there was no staving off the question, What was to be done?

"The first and the main thing to be done," said Herbert, "is to get him out of England. You will have to go with him, and then he may be induced to go."

"But get him where I will, could I prevent his coming back?"

"My good Handel, is it not obvious that, with Newgate in the next street, there must be far greater hazard in your breaking your mind to him and making him reckless here than elsewhere. If a pretext to get him away could be made out of that other convict, or out of anything else in his life, now."

Herbert got up, and linked his arm in mine, and we slowly walked to and fro together, studying the carpet.

"Handel," said Herbert, stopping, "you feel convinced that you can take no further benefits from him, do you?"

"Fully. Surely you would, too, if you were in my place?"

"And you feel convinced that you must break with him?"

"Herbert, can you ask me?"

"Then you must get him out of England before you stir a finger to extricate yourself. That done, extricate yourself, in Heaven's name, and we'll see it out together, dear old boy."

It was a comfort to shake hands upon it, and walk up and down again, with only that done.

"Now Herbert," said I, "with reference to gaining some knowledge of his history. There is but one way that I know of. I must ask him point-blank."

58 Discussion How does Herbert assist Pip?

59 Discussion What does Pip plan to do about the riches Provis has offered him?

60 Discussion What plans do Pip and Herbert make to extricate Pip from his dilemma?

Clarification The phrase "coming out strong" means "spending lavishly."

62 Discussion As Provis starts his story, he keeps repeating a certain phrase. What is the phrase? What is the effect of this repetition?

63 Clarification "Epsom races" refers to a famous race track, Epsom Downs, in Surrey, England, where the Derby is held annually.

64 Discussion What kind of revenge would Provis take if he could get his hands on Compeyson?

"Yes. Ask him," said Herbert, "when we sit at breakfast in the morning." For, he had said, on taking leave of Herbert, that he would come to breakfast with us.

61 — He came round at the appointed time, took out his jackknife, and sat down to his meal. He was full of plans "for his gentleman's coming out strong, and like a gentleman," and urged me to begin speedily upon the pocketbook, which he had left in my possession. When he had made an end of his breakfast, and was wiping his knife on his leg, I said to him, without a word of preface:

"After you were gone last night, I told my friend of the struggle that the soldiers found you engaged in on the marshes, when we came up. You remember?"

"Remember!" said he. "I think so!"

"We want to know something about that man—and about you. It is strange to know no more about either, and particularly you, than I was able to tell last night. Is not this as good a time as another for our knowing more?"

"Well!" he said, after consideration. "You're on your oath, you know, Pip's comrade?"

"Assuredly," replied Herbert.

"And look'ee here! Wotever I done is worked out and paid for," he insisted again.

"So be it."

He spread a hand on each knee, and, after turning an angry eye on the fire for a few silent moments, looked around at us and said what follows.

Chapter 41

"Dear boy and Pip's comrade. I am not a-going fur to tell you my life, like a song or a storybook. But to give it you short and handy, I'll put it at once into a mouthful of 62 ⌐ English. In jail and out of jail, in jail and out of jail, in jail and out of jail. There, you've got it. That's *my* life pretty much, down to such times as I got shipped off, arter Pip stood my friend.

"When I was a ragged little creetur as much to be pitied as ever I see, I got the name of being hardened. 'This is a terrible hardened one,' they says to prison wisitors, picking out me. 'May be said to live in jails, this boy.' They always went on agen me about the devil. But what the devil was I to do? I must put something into my stomach, mustn't I?—Howsomever, I'm a-getting low, and I know what's due. Dear boy and Pip's comrade, don't you be afeerd of me being low.

"Tramping, begging, thieving, working sometimes when I could—though that warn't as often as you may think, till you put the question whether you would ha' been over-ready to give me work yourselves—a bit of a poacher,[1] a bit of a laborer, a bit of a waggoner, a bit of a haymaker, a bit of a hawker,[2] a bit of most things that don't pay and lead to trouble, I got to be a man. A deserting soldier in a traveler's rest, what lay hid up to the chin under a lot of taturs, learnt me to read; and a traveling giant what signed his name at a penny a time learnt me to write. I warn't locked up often now as formerly, but I wore out my good share of key metal still.

"At Epsom races, a matter of over twenty 63 year ago, I got acquainted wi' a man whose skull I'd crack wi' this poker, like the claw of a lobster, if I'd got it on this hob. His right 64 name was Compeyson; and that's the man, dear boy, what you see me a-pounding in the ditch.

"He set up fur a gentleman, this Compey-

---

1. poacher (pōch′ ər) *n.*: Person who hunts or fishes illegally on someone else's property.
2. hawker (hôk′ ər) *n.*: Peddler.

854 *The Novel*

son, and he'd been to a public boarding school and had learning. He was a smooth one to talk, and was a dab at the ways of gentlefolks. He was good-looking, too.

"Compeyson took me on to be his man and pardner. And what was Compeyson's business in which we was to go pardners? Compeyson's business was the swindling, handwriting forging, stolen bank note passing, and such-like. All sorts of traps as Compeyson could set with his head, and keep his own legs out of and get the profits from and let another man in for, was Compeyson's business!

"There was another in with Compeyson, as was called Arthur—not as being so chrisen'd, but as a surname. Him and Compeyson had been in a bad thing with a rich lady some years afore, and they'd made a pot of money by it; but Compeyson betted and gamed, and he'd have run through the king's taxes. So Arthur was a-dying and a-dying poor and with the horrors on him, and Compeyson's wife (which Compeyson kicked mostly) was a-having pity on him when she could, and Compeyson was a-having pity on nothing and nobody.

"I mighta took warning by Arthur, but I didn't; and I won't pretend I was partick'ler—for where 'ud be the good on it, dear boy and comrade? So I begun wi' Compeyson, and a poor tool I was in his hands. Arthur lived at the top of Compeyson's house (over nigh Brentford, it was), and Compeyson kept a careful account agen him for board and lodging, in case he should ever get better to work it out. But Arthur soon settled the account. The second or third time as ever I see him, he come a-tearing down into Compeyson's parlor late at night, in only a flannel gown, with his hair all in a sweat, and he says to Compeyson's wife, 'Sally, she really is upstairs alonger me, now, and I can't get rid of her. She's all in white,' he says, 'wi' white flowers in her hair, and she's awful mad, and she's got a shroud hanging over her arm, and she says she'll put it on me at five in the morning.'

"Compeyson's wife and me took him up to bed agen, and he raved most dreadful. 'Why look at her!' he cries out. 'She a-shaking the shroud at me!'

"Compeyson's wife, being used to him, give him something to get the horrors off, and by-and-by he quieted. 'Oh, she's gone! Has her keeper been for her?' he says. 'Yes,' says Compeyson's wife.

"He rested pretty quiet till it might want a few minutes of five, and then he starts up with a scream, and screams out, 'Here she is! She's got the shroud again. Don't let her throw it over my shoulders. Don't let her lift me up to get it round me. She's lifting me up. Keep me down!' Then he lifted himself up hard, and was dead.

"Compeyson took it easy as a good riddance for both sides, and him and me was soon busy.

"Not to go into the things that Compeyson planned, and I done—which 'ud take a week—I'll simply say to you, dear boy, and Pip's comrade, that that man got me into such nets as made me his slave. I was always in debt to him, always under his thumb, always a-working, always a-getting into danger. He was younger than me, but he'd got craft, and he'd got learning, and he overmatched me five hundred times told and no mercy. My missis as I had the hard time wi'—Stop though! I ain't brought *her* in—

"There ain't no need to go into it," he said, looking round. "The time wi' Compeyson was a'most as hard a time as ever I had; that said, all's said. Did I tell you as I was tried, alone, for misdemeanor,[3] while with Compeyson?"

---

3. misdemeanor (mis' di mēn' ər) *n.*: Minor offense.

65 Clarification A "public boarding school" in England would be a private boarding school in America.

66 Discussion According to Provis, what kind of man is Compeyson?

67 Discussion How does Provis describe his relationship with Compeyson?

Discussion What strategy did Compeyson use to implicate Provis as the mastermind of the crime?

I answered, No.

"Well!" he said, "I *was*, and got convicted. As to took up[4] on suspicion, that was twice or three times in the four or five year that it lasted; but evidence was wanting. At last, me and Compeyson was both committed for felony—on a charge of putting stolen notes in circulation—and there was other charges behind. Compeyson says to me, 'Separate defenses, no communication,'[5] and that was all. And I was so miserable poor that I sold all the clothes I had, except what hung on my back, afore I could get Jaggers.

"When we was put in the dock,[6] I noticed first of all what a gentleman Compeyson looked, wi' his curly hair and his black clothes and his white pocket handkercher, and what a common sort of a wretch I looked. When the evidence was giv in the box,[7] I noticed how it was always me that had come for'ard, and could be swore to, how it was always me that the money had been paid to, how it was always me that had seemed to work the thing and get the profit. But, when the defense come on, then I see the plan plainer; for, says the counselor for Compeyson, 'My lord and gentlemen, here you has afore you, side by side, two persons as your eyes can separate wide; one, the younger, well brought up, who will be spoke to as such; one, the elder, ill brought up, who will be spoke to as such; one, the younger, seldom if ever seen in these here transactions, and only suspected; t'other, the elder, always seen in 'em and always wi' his guilt brought home.' And such-like. And warn't it me as had been tried afore, and as

---

4. **took up:** Arrested.
5. **separate . . . communication:** They would use different lawyers and not speak to each other about the trial.
6. **dock** *n.*: Place where the accused stands or sits in court.
7. **box** *n.*: Witness stand.

---

had been know'd up hill and down dale in Bridewells and Lockups? And when it come to speechmaking, warn't it Compeyson as could speak to 'em wi' his face dropping every now and then into his white pocket handkercher! and wi' verses in his speech, too—and warn't it me as could only say, 'Gentlemen, this man at my side is a most precious rascal'? And when the verdict come, warn't it Compeyson as was recommended to mercy on account of good character and bad company, and giving up all the information he could agen me, and warn't it me as got never a word but guilty? And when I says to Compeyson, 'Once out of this court, I'll smash that face of yourn!' ain't it Compeyson as prays the judge to be protected. And when we're sentenced, ain't it him as gets seven year, and me fourteen?

"I had said to Compeyson that I'd smash that face of his, and I swore Lord smash mine! to do it. We was in the same prison ship, but I couldn't get at him for long, though I tried. At last I come behind him and hit him on the cheek to turn him round and get a smashing one at him, when I was seen and seized. The black hole of that ship warn't a strong one, to a judge of black holes that could swim and dive. I escaped to the shore, and I was a-hiding among the graves there, envying them as was in 'em and all over, when I first see my boy!

"By my boy, I was giv to understand as Compeyson was out on them marshes, too. Upon my soul, I half-believe he escaped in his terror, to get quit of me, not knowing it was me as had got ashore. I hunted him down. I smashed his face. 'And now,' says I, 'as the worst thing I can do, caring nothing for myself, I'll drag you back.' And I'd have swum off, towing him by the hair, if it had come to that, and I'd a-got him aboard without the soldiers."

"Is he dead?" I asked after a silence.

Grammar in Action

The term *dialect* refers to the speech of a particular group or class of people or of people from a particular region. Dialect differs from standard speech, the speech of the majority of educated people in a particular time or place. Read these examples from the novel. Which passage is written in dialect? How do you know?

"When I was a ragged little creetur as much to be pitied as ever I see, I got the name of being hardened. 'This is a terrible hardened one,' they says to prison wisitors, picking out me. 'May be said to live in jails, this boy.' They went on agen me about the devil."

"Then you must get him out of England before you stir a finger to extricate yourself. That done, then extricate yourself, in Heaven's name, and we'll see it out together, dear old boy."

Notice that in the first passage, which is written in dialect, the author makes use of a number of techniques to convey the speech of the character. Word choice, grammar, sentence structure, spelling, and pronunciation are all different from those

"Is who dead, dear boy?"

"Compeyson."

"He hopes *I* am, if he's alive, you may be sure," with a fierce look. "I never heard no more of him."

Herbert had been writing with his pencil in the cover of a book. He softly pushed the book over to me, and I read in it:

Young Havisham's name was Arthur. Compeyson is the man who professed to be Miss Havisham's lover.

Chapter 42

A new fear had been engendered in my mind by his narrative. If Compeyson were alive and should discover his return, I could hardly doubt the consequence. Compeyson stood in mortal fear of him and would release himself for good from a dreaded enemy by the safe means of becoming an informer.

Never had I breathed, and never would I breathe—or so I resolved—a word of Estella to Provis. But I said to Herbert that before I could go abroad, I must see both Estella and Miss Havisham. This was when we were left alone on the night of the day when Provis told us his story. I resolved to go out to Richmond next day, and I went.

On my presenting myself at Mrs. Brandley's, Estella's maid was called to tell me that Estella had gone into the country. Where? To Satis House, as usual. Not as usual, I said, for she had never yet gone there without me; when was she coming back? The answer was that her maid believed she was only coming back at all for a little while. I could make nothing of this, and I went home again in complete discomfiture.

Next day, I had the meanness to feign that I was under a binding promise to go down to Joe; but I was capable of almost any

meanness towards Joe or his name. Provis was to be strictly careful while I was gone, and Herbert was to take charge of him.

Having thus cleared the way for my expedition to Miss Havisham's, I set off by the early morning coach before it was yet light, and was out in the open country road when the day came creeping on, halting and whimpering and shivering, and wrapped in patches of cloud and rags of mist, like a beggar. When we drove up to the Blue Boar after a drizzly ride, whom should I see come out under the gateway, toothpick in hand, to look at the coach, but Bentley Drummle!

As he pretended not to see me, I pretended not to see him. It was a very lame pretense on both sides; the lamer because we both went into the coffee-room, where he had just finished his breakfast, and where I had ordered mine. It was poisonous to me to see him in the town, for I very well knew why he had come there.

I sat at my table while he stood before the fire. By degrees it became an enormous injury to me that he stood before the fire. And I got up, determined to have my share of it. I had to put my hands behind his legs for the poker when I went up to the fireplace to stir the fire, but still pretended not to know him. "Is this a cut?"[1] said Mr. Drummle.

"Oh?" said I, poker in hand; "it's you, is it? How do you do? I was wondering who it was, who kept the fire off."

"You have just come down?" said Mr. Drummle.

"Yes," said I.

"Beastly place," said Drummle. "Your part of the country, I think?"

"Yes," I assented. "I am told it's very like your Shropshire."

"Not in the least like it," said Drummle.

"Do you stay here long?"

---

1. **cut** *n.*: Act of snubbing someone.

70

69 **Discussion** What is the significance of this news?

70 **Critical Thinking and Reading** What metaphor does Dickens use to describe the dawn? Why do you think he chose to use such a figure of speech at this point in the story?

found in standard English. These are not mistakes, but rather part of a deliberate effort by the author to convey a particular type of speech.

Dialect adds realism, liveliness, color, and often humor to language. Try to imagine this novel without the dialect. What would be lost?

Student Activity 1. Find another passage of dialect in the novel and practice reading it aloud. Read your example aloud to a classmate and discuss ways to improve it.

Student Activity 2. Listen as volunteers read aloud their choices of passages written in dialect. After each reading discuss with your classmates and teacher what the passage contributes to characterization and plot.

Electronic Handbook You might wish students to review the use of idioms and informal language before completing the Grammar in Action activities. If students have access to the Language Master 6000, have them enter the access words *informal* or *idiom* and press the GRAMMAR key to obtain information related to dialect.

71 Discussion Pip has an unexpected encounter with Drummle. How do they act toward each other?

72 Reading Strategy The plot becomes more and more entangled as characters reappear in different situations. As students read this chapter, have them predict what will happen.

73 Discussion Why does Pip believe that Estella has guessed his news before he has disclosed it?

Speaking and Listening You might want to have students volunteer to read aloud from Chapter 43 where Pip's most difficult confrontation takes place. Dickens's hero will make what he considers to be the correct choice when his basic code of ethics is challenged. Pip, now dealing with basic truths, must clear away the lies, deceptions, and incorrect deductions to face the facts, no matter how unpleasant they may be.

"Can't say," answered Mr. Drummle. "Do you?"

"Can't say," said I.

"I am going out for a ride in the saddle," said Drummle. "I mean to explore those marshes for amusement. Out-of-the-way villages there, they tell me. Curious little public houses—and smithies—and that. Waiter!"

"Yes, sir."

"Is that horse of mine ready?"

"Brought round to the door, sir."

"I say. Look here, you sir. The lady won't ride today; the weather won't do."

"Very good, sir."

"And I don't dine, because I am going to dine at the lady's."

"Very good, sir."

Then Drummle glanced at me, with an insolent triumph on his great-jowled face that cut me to the heart.

After Drummle had left the room, I saw him through the window, seizing his horse's mane, and mounting in his blundering brutal manner, and sidling and backing away.

Too heavily out of sorts to touch the breakfast, I washed the weather and the journey from my face and hands, and went out to the memorable old house that it would have been so much the better for me never to have entered, never to have seen.

Chapter 43

In the room where the dressing table stood, and where the wax candles burnt on the wall, I found Miss Havisham and Estella; Miss Havisham seated on a settee[1] near the fire, and Estella on a cushion at her feet. Estella was knitting, and Miss Havisham was looking on. They both raised their eyes as I went in, and both saw an alteration in me. I

---

1. settee (se tē′) *n.*: Small or medium-sized sofa.

derived that from the look they interchanged.

"And what wind," said Miss Havisham, "blows you here, Pip?"

Though she looked steadily at me, I saw that she was rather confused. Estella, pausing a moment in her knitting with her eyes upon me, and then going on, I fancied that I read in the action of her fingers, as plainly as if she had told me in the dumb alphabet, that she perceived I had discovered my real benefactor.

"Miss Havisham," said I, "I went to Richmond yesterday, to speak to Estella; and finding that some wind had blown *her* here, I followed.

"What I had to say to Estella, Miss Havisham, I will say before you, presently—in a few moments. It will not surprise you, it will not displease you. I am as unhappy as you can ever have meant me to be."

Miss Havisham continued to look steadily at me. I could see in the action of Estella's fingers as they worked that she attended to what I said—but she did not look up.

"I have found out who my patron is. It is not a fortunate discovery, and is not likely ever to enrich me in reputation, station, fortune, anything. There are reasons why I must say no more of that. It is not my secret, but another's."

As I was silent for a while, looking at Estella and considering how to go on, Miss Havisham repeated, "It is not your secret, but another's. Well?"

"When you first caused me to be brought here, Miss Havisham; when I belonged to the village over yonder, that I wish I had never left; I suppose I did really come here, as any other chance boy might have come—as a kind of servant, to gratify a want or a whim, and to be paid for it?"

"Aye, Pip," replied Miss Havisham, "you did."

"And that Mr. Jaggers—"

"Mr. Jaggers," said Miss Havisham, taking me up in a firm tone, "had nothing to do with it, and knew nothing of it. His being my lawyer, and his being the lawyer of your patron, is a coincidence. He holds the same relation towards numbers of people, and it might easily arise. Be that as it may, it did arise, and was not brought about by anyone."

Anyone might have seen in her haggard face that there was no suppression or evasion so far.

"But when I fell into the mistake I have so long remained in, at least you led me on?" said I.

"Yes," she returned, "I let you go on."

"Was that kind?"

"Who am I," cried Miss Havisham, striking her stick upon the floor, and flashing into wrath so suddenly that Estella glanced up at her in surprise, "who am I, for God's sake, that I should be kind?"

Waiting until she was quiet again, I went on.

"I have been thrown among one family of your relations, Miss Havisham, and have been constantly among them since I went to London. I know them to have been as honestly under my delusion as I myself. And I should be false and base if I did not tell you that you deeply wrong both Mr. Matthew Pocket and his son Herbert, if you suppose them to be otherwise than generous, upright, open, and incapable of anything designing or mean."

"They are your friends," said Miss Havisham.

"They made themselves my friends," said I, "when they supposed me to have superseded them; and when Sarah Pocket, Miss Georgiana, and Mistress Camilla were not my friends, I think."

This contrasting of them with the rest seemed, I was glad to see, to do them good with her. She looked at me keenly for a little while, and then said quietly:

"What do you want for them?"

"Miss Havisham, if you could spare the money to do my friend Herbert a lasting service in life, but which from the nature of the case must be done without his knowledge, I could show you how."

"Why must it be done without his knowledge?" she asked.

"Because," said I, "I began the service myself, more than two years ago, without his knowledge, and I don't want to be betrayed. Why I fail in my ability to finish it I cannot explain. It is a part of the secret which is another person's and not mine."

She gradually withdrew her eyes from me, and turned them on the fire. "Estella," said I turning to her now, and trying to command my trembling voice, "you know I love you. You know that I have loved you long and dearly."

She raised her eyes to my face on being thus addressed, and her fingers plied their work, and she looked at me with an unmoved countenance. I saw that Miss Havisham glanced from me to her and from her to me.

"I should have said this sooner, but for my long mistake. It induced me to hope that Miss Havisham meant us for one another. While I thought you could not help yourself, as it were, I refrained from saying it. But I must say it now."

With her fingers still going, Estella shook her head.

"I know," said I, in answer to that action; "I know. I have no hope that I shall ever call you mine, Estella. I am ignorant what may become of me very soon, how poor I may be, or where I may go. Still, I love you. I have loved you ever since I first saw you in this house."

Great Expectations 859

74 Discussion How does Miss Havisham react to Pip's outspoken support of the Matthew Pocket family and the suggestion that she help his friend Herbert financially?

75 Discussion What can you infer from Estella's silent response to Pip when he declares his love for her openly?

76 Discussion What symbolic action does Miss Havisham perform when Pip refers to her personal tragedy? What does the action signify?

77 Discussion Why has Estella encouraged Drummle? How will having a relationship with him accomplish two goals: harming herself (through the love of such a coarse person) and harming Pip? Of the two, which goal is the more important to her? Why?

Looking at me perfectly unmoved and with her fingers busy, she shook her head again.

"It would have been cruel in Miss Havisham, horribly cruel, to practice on the susceptibility of a poor boy, and to torture me through all these years with a vain hope and an idle pursuit, if she had reflected on the gravity of what she did. But I think she did not. I think that in the endurance of her own trial, she forgot mine, Estella."

I saw Miss Havisham put her hand to her heart and hold it there, as she sat looking by turns at Estella and at me.

"It seems," said Estella very calmly, "that there are sentiments, fancies—I don't know how to call them—which I am not able to comprehend. When you say you love me, I know what you mean as a form of words, but nothing more. I don't care for what you say at all. I have tried to warn you of this, now, have I not?"

I said, in a miserable manner, "Yes."

"Yes. But you would not be warned, for you thought I did not mean it. Now, did you not think so?"

"I thought and hoped you could not mean it. You, so young, untried, and beautiful, Estella! Surely it is not in nature."

"It is in *my* nature," she returned.

"Is it not true," said I, "that Bentley Drummle is in town here, and pursuing you?"

"It is quite true," she replied, referring to him with the indifference of utter contempt.

"You cannot love him, Estella?"

Her fingers stopped for the first time, as she retorted rather angrily, "What have I told you? Do you still think, in spite of it, that I do not mean what I say?"

"You would never marry him, Estella?"

She looked towards Miss Havisham. Then she said, "Why not tell you the truth? I am going to be married to him."

I dropped my face into my hands, but was able to control myself better than I could have expected, considering what agony it gave me to hear her say those words. When I raised my face again, there was such a ghastly look upon Miss Havisham's that it impressed me, even in my passionate hurry and grief.

"Estella, dearest, dearest Estella, do not let Miss Havisham lead you into this fatal step. Put me aside for ever—you have done so, I well know—but bestow yourself on some worthier person than Drummle. Miss Havisham gives you to him as the greatest slight and injury that could be done to the many far better men who admire you, and to the few who truly love you."

My earnestness awoke a wonder in her that seemed as if it would have been touched with compassion, if she could have rendered me at all intelligible to her own mind.

"I am going," she said again, in a gentler voice, "to be married to him. The preparations for my marriage are making, and I shall be married soon."

"Such a mean brute, such a stupid brute!" I urged in despair.

"Don't be afraid of my being a blessing to him," said Estella; "I shall not be that. Come! Here is my hand. Do we part on this, you visionary boy—or man?"

"Oh, Estella," I answered, as my bitter tears fell fast on her hand, do what I would to restrain them; "even if I remained in England and could hold my head up with the rest, how could I see you Drummle's wife?"

"Nonsense," she returned, "nonsense. This will pass in no time."

"Never, Estella!"

"You will get me out of your thoughts in a week."

"Out of my thoughts! You are part of my existence, part of myself. You have been in every line I have ever read, since I first came here, the rough common boy whose poor heart you wounded even then. You have been in every prospect I have ever seen since—on the river, on the sails of the ships, on the marshes, in the clouds, in the light, in the darkness, in the wind, in the woods, in the sea, in the streets. You have been the embodiment of every graceful fancy that my mind has ever become acquainted with. Estella, to the last hour of my life, you cannot choose but remain part of my character, part of the little good in me, part of the evil. But, in this separation I associate you only with the good and I will faithfully hold you to that always, for you must have done me far more good than harm, let me feel now what sharp distress I may. O God bless you, God forgive you!"

I held her hand to my lips some lingering moments, and so I left her. But ever afterwards, I remembered—and soon afterwards with stronger reason—that while Estella looked at me merely with incredulous wonder, the spectral figure of Miss Havisham, her hand still covering her heart, seemed all resolved into a ghastly stare of pity and remorse.

All done, all gone! So much was done and gone that when I went out at the gate, the light of day seemed of a darker color than when I went in. For a while, I hid myself among some lanes and bypaths, and then struck off to walk all the way to London. For, I had by that time come to myself so far as to consider that I could not go back to the inn and see Drummle there; that I could not bear to sit upon the coach and be spoken to; that I could do nothing half so good for myself as tire myself out.

It was past midnight when I crossed London Bridge. I was not expected till tomorrow, but I had my keys, and, if Herbert were gone to bed, could get to bed myself without disturbing him.

I came in at that Whitefriars gate after the Temple was closed. The night-porter examined me with much attention as he held the gate a little way open for me to pass in. To help his memory I mentioned my name.

"I was not quite sure, sir, but I thought so. Here's a note, sir. The messenger that brought it said, Would you be so good as read it by my lantern?"

Much surprised by the request, I took the note. It was directed to Philip Pip, Esquire, and on the top of the superscription were the words, "PLEASE READ THIS HERE." I opened it, the watchman holding up his light, and read inside, in Wemmick's writing:

"DON'T GO HOME."

Chapter 44

Turning from the Temple gate as soon as I had read the warning, I made the best of my way to Fleet Street, and there got a late hackney chariot[1] and drove to the Hummums in Covent Garden. In those times a bed was always to be got there at any hour of the night.

What a doleful night! How anxious, how dismal, how long! There was an inhospitable smell in the room of cold soot and hot dust.

I had left directions that I was to be called at seven, for it was plain that I must see Wemmick before seeing any one else, and equally plain that this was a case in which his Walworth sentiments only could be taken. It was a relief to get out of the room where the night had been so miserable, and I needed no second knocking at the door to startle me from my uneasy bed.

The castle battlements arose upon my view at eight o'clock. The little servant hap-

---

1. **hackney chariot:** Coach for hire.

78 Discussion When Pip hears the news that Estella is going to marry Drummle, how does his speech toward Estella change?

79 Discussion After his last impassioned speech to Estella, Pip realizes that he is left with two different impressions of Miss Havisham's and Estella's responses to his words. What are the two impressions that he has?

80 Discussion When Pip returns home, what new development takes his mind off his misery and turns it in another direction?

81 Reading Strategy A new twist in the plot increases the tension. Have students predict what will happen and follow the story carefully. What action does Pip take to clarify the message he received?

Fine art, *February Fill Dyke*, by Benjamin William Leader. Benjamin William Leader (1831–1923) was a Victorian painter. Born Benjamin Williams, he added the surname Leader to give distinction to his name. Leader was educated at the Royal Academy and influenced by the Pre-Raphaelites. He gained a reputation as a landscape painter devoted to truth in nature.

In *February Fill Dyke*, Leader depicts the puddles left after a rainy day, as they reflect the colors of the flamboyant sunset.

You might want to have students discuss the following questions:

1. Describe the quality of light in this painting.
2. What mood does the painting call up?

FEBRUARY FILL DYKE
Benjamin William Leader
Published by permission of the Birmingham Museum and Art Gallery

pening to be entering the fortress with two hot rolls, I passed through the postern[2] and crossed the drawbridge in her company, and so came without announcement into the presence of Wemmick as he was making tea for himself and the Aged. An open door afforded a perspective view of the Aged in bed.

"Halloa, Mr. Pip!" said Wemmick. "You did come home, then?"

"Yes," I returned; "but I didn't go home."

"That's all right," said he, rubbing his hands. "I left a note for you at each of the Temple gates, on the chance. Which gate did you come to?"

I told him.

"I'll go round to the others in the course of the day and destroy the notes," said Wemmick. "*Would* you mind toasting this sausage for the Aged P.?"

I said I should be delighted to do it.

"Then you can go about your work, Mary Anne," said Wemmick to the little servant, "which leaves us to ourselves, don't you see, Mr. Pip?" he added, winking, as she disappeared.

"I heard by chance, yesterday morning,"

---

2. **postern** (pōs′ tərn) *n.*: Back gate.

said Wemmick, "that a certain person not altogether of uncolonial pursuits, and not unpossessed of portable property—I don't know who it may really be had made some little stir in a certain part of the world by disappearing from such place, and being no more heard of thereabouts. From which conjectures had been raised and theories formed, I also heard that you at your chambers in Garden Court Temple, had been watched, and might be watched again."

"By whom?" said I.

"I wouldn't go into that," said Wemmick evasively; "it might clash with official responsibilities."

"You have heard of a man of bad character whose true name is Compeyson?" I asked.

He answered with a nod.

"Is he living?"

One other nod.

"Is he in London?"

He gave me one last nod, and went on with his breakfast.

"Now," said Wemmick, "questioning being over"—which he emphasized and repeated for my guidance—"I come to what I did, after hearing what I heard. I went to Garden Court to find you; not finding you, I went to Clarriker's to find Mr. Herbert."

"And him you found?" said I, with great anxiety.

"And him I found. Without mentioning any names or going into any details, I gave him to understand that if he was aware of anybody—Tom, Jack, or Richard—being about the chambers, or about the immediate neighborhood, he had better get Tom, Jack, or Richard out of the way while you were out of the way.

"Mr. Herbert, after being all of a heap for half an hour, struck out a plan. He mentioned to me as a secret that he is courting a young lady who has, as no doubt you are aware, a bedridden pa. Which pa lies a-bed in a bow window[3] where he can see the ships sail up and down the river. You are acquainted with the young lady, most probably?"

"Not personally," said I.

The truth was that she had objected to me as an expensive companion who did Herbert no good, and that, when Herbert had first proposed to present me to her, she had received the proposal with such very moderate warmth that Herbert had felt himself obliged to confide the state of the case to me, with a view to the lapse of a little time before I made her acquaintance.

"The house with the bow window," said Wemmick, "being by the riverside, down the Pool there between Limehouse and Greenwich; and being kept, it seems, by a very respectable widow, who has a furnished upper floor to let, Mr. Herbert put it to me, what did I think of that as a temporary tenement for Tom, Jack, or Richard. Now, I thought very well of it, for three reasons I'll give you. That is to say, firstly, it's altogether out of all your beats. Secondly, without going near it yourself, you could always hear of the safety of Tom, Jack, or Richard through Mr. Herbert. Thirdly, after a while, and when it might be prudent, if you should want to slip Tom, Jack, or Richard on board a foreign packet boat,[4] there he is—ready."

Much comforted by these considerations, I thanked Wemmick again and again, and begged him to proceed.

"Well, sir! Mr. Herbert threw himself into the business with a will, and by nine o'clock last night he housed Tom, Jack, or Richard—whichever it may be—you and I don't

---

3. bow window: Rounded window projecting out from a house.
4. packet boat: Boat that travels a regular route, carrying passengers, freight, and mail.

82 **Discussion** What news does Wemmick have for Pip?

83 **Discussion** "Tom, Jack, or Richard" is the equivalent of the familiar "Tom, Dick, and Harry," meaning everybody or nobody in particular. Why does Wemmick refer to Magwitch in such a roundabout way, as if his identity were not known?

84 **Discussion** How does Herbert plan to hide Magwitch until Herbert and Pip are ready for his escape out of London?

85 **Discussion** What objection does Herbert's fiancée, Clara, have regarding Pip's invitation to her house?

86 **Discussion** What are Wemmick's three reasons for approving of Herbert's plan?

87 Discussion What is Wemmick's final advice to Pip?

88 Reading Strategy Ask students to summarize the events of this section. Also ask them to evaluate Pip's behavior in this crisis.

Reader's Response In the struggle between the love of others and material wealth and success, which do you value more? Why?

Thematic Response Pip had many difficult choices to make in this part of the novel. Which do you think was the most difficult for him, and what effect do you think it will have on his life?

Closure and Extension

ANSWERS TO RESPONDING TO THE SELECTION
Your Response
1. Encourage students to name all the possible benefactors and to tell why they chose each of these characters. Ask why Magwitch was or was not included.

Recalling
2. Pip receives five hundred pounds from his benefactor, but does not learn that person's identity.
3. He consults Mr. Wemmick, who, through connections, finds a young shipping merchant needing capable help and capital for his business. The affair is managed so smoothly that Herbert does not know that a new job has been arranged for him with Pip's money and Mr. Wemmick's assistance.

want to know—quite successfully. At the old lodgings it was understood that he was summoned to Dover, and in fact he was taken down the Dover road and cornered out of it. Now, another great advantage of all this is that it was done without you, and when, if any one was concerning himself about your movements, you must be known to be ever so many miles off, and quite otherwise engaged.

"And now, Mr. Pip, I have probably done the most I can do; but if I can ever do more—from a Walworth point of view, and in a strictly private and personal capacity—I shall be glad to do it. Here's the address. There can be no harm in your going here tonight and seeing for yourself that all is well with Tom, Jack, or Richard before you go home. But after you have gone home, don't go back here. And let me finally impress one important point upon you. Avail yourself of this evening to lay hold of his portable property. You don't know what may happen to him. Don't let anything happen to the portable property.

"I must be off. If you had nothing more pressing to do than to keep here till dark, that's what I should advise. You look very much worried, and it would do you good to have a perfectly quiet day with the Aged—he'll be up presently.

I soon fell asleep before Wemmick's fire, and the Aged and I enjoyed one another's society by falling asleep before it more or less all day. We had loin of pork for dinner, and greens grown on the estate, and I nodded at the Aged with a good intention whenever I failed to do it drowsily. When it was quite dark, I left the Aged preparing the fire for toast.

87

88

RESPONDING TO THE SELECTION

Your Response
1. Who did you think Pip's benefactor was? Why?

Recalling
2. Why is Pip's twenty-first birthday significant?
3. How does Pip secretly help Herbert?
4. Describe Pip's reaction when he discovers his benefactor.
5. Summarize the story that Provis tells Pip.
6. Why is Pip's visit to Miss Havisham so painful?
7. What fear leads Pip to plan Provis's escape from the country?

Interpreting
8. What causes Pip to regret that he has ever "seen Miss Havisham's face"?

9. How has Miss Havisham's upbringing of Estella affected Estella, Pip, and Miss Havisham herself?
10. How are Provis and Joe similar? Explain the role each plays in Pip's life.
11. What is similar about the way that Pip relates to Provis and to Joe?

Applying
12. Pip is disappointed by Provis's arrival. Why is a person's reaction to disappointment a good sign of his or her character?

ANALYZING LITERATURE

Understanding Theme
A **theme** is the central idea or insight into life revealed in a work of literature. When a writer does not state the theme directly, you can often

4. The revelation shocks and repels him. Pip is also afraid of this exconvict, having seen the knife he carries and how ready he was to use it when they heard footsteps approaching their door. He is afraid, too, that the money might have been obtained by some criminal act. Pip is too worried to sleep until he and Herbert can find another place for the man to stay.
5. Provis tells Pip how he fell under the spell of Compeyson, a master criminal, and was imprisoned in Compeyson's stead.
6. Pip learns that Estella is betrothed to Bentley Drummle.
7. Pip learns that Compeyson knows that Magwitch is in England, has been watching the Garden Court apartment, and has been following him (Pip). The fear that Compeyson might learn the whereabouts of Magwitch and expose him to the police makes it imperative to get him out of the country.

Interpreting
8. Suggested Response: Pip feels guilty about his treatment of Joe and Biddy.
9. Suggested Response: Estella has been used by Miss Havisham to seek revenge on all men for being jilted by her lover. Her training toward this end has made Estella cold, haughty, and unable to love anyone. Pip has been deeply hurt, having misinterpreted Miss Havisham's motive in bringing Estella and him

discover it by considering the main conflict. In *Great Expectations,* Pip is divided between his love for himself and others and his longing for material success.

Keeping this conflict in mind, write a statement that you think expresses the theme of the novel.

CRITICAL THINKING AND READING

Paraphrasing Key Statements

Paraphrasing means expressing another person's statements in your own words. By paraphrasing key statements in a novel, you will gain a better insight into the main conflict and the theme. For example, reread Pip's statement beginning "It would have been cruel. . . ." (p. 860). Pip is saying that Miss Havisham would not have deceived him about his expectations if she had realized the seriousness of what she was doing. He says that her own sufferings kept her blind to his. This speech indicates that, in his willingness to forgive Miss Havisham, Pip is beginning to overcome his own conflict.

1. Paraphrase the speech beginning "Estella, dearest. . . ." (p. 860).
2. Explain how this speech relates to Pip's conflict and the book's theme.

THINKING AND WRITING

Responding to the Theme of a Novel

Suppose a friend of yours has argued that Dickens's theme is old-fashioned. Jot down some reasons why the theme is as relevant today as it was in Dickens's time. Try to imagine current situations to which this theme would apply. Use the ideas you have gathered to write a composition

answering your friend's argument. In revising, make sure you have clearly stated Dickens's theme and shown how it applies to at least one modern situation. When you are finished, share your composition with your classmates.

LEARNING OPTIONS

1. **Art.** Dickens had a genius for creating memorable characters. Occasionally his characters lend themselves to caricature—a rendering in which distinctive features are exaggerated or distorted. Choose a character to draw as a caricature or cartoon. Deliberately exaggerate those features that Dickens emphasizes. Display your work in your classroom.
2. **Writing.** As Pip travels about London, he refers to various places such as Little Britain, Whitefriar Gate, and the Temple. Prepare a brief guidebook to Pip's London. Identify, locate, and describe the particular places Pip mentions as well as any others of importance to this novel.
3. **Cross-curricular Connection.** Magwitch reveals that he has been in New South Wales, Australia. Investigate the colonization of Australia. Who went there, and why? Share your findings in a brief report, either oral or written, with your classmates.
4. **Art.** Imagine that you are a designer for a publishing company that is preparing a new edition of *Great Expectations.* Design the book jacket. Include both the art and the text for the front and back covers. Display your work in your classroom.
5. **Art.** Prepare a collage representing great expectations. You may decide whether to represent Pip's expectations or your own. When you have finished it, present it to your classmates, explaining what each item in the collage represents and why you chose it.

Great Expectations 865

1. Suggested Response: Do not marry Drummle at the urging of Miss Havisham. Do not even consider my love for you. However, choose someone who is more worthy of you.
2. Suggested Response: Pip is beginning to overcome his inner conflict. He realizes that his dream of having wealth, status, and Estella is an illusion. Even at his own expense, he advises Estella to do something for her own good.

THINKING AND WRITING

◈ **Software** If students are working on computers, have them use *Debating an Issue* from the **Writer's Helper** activities to help them organize their compositions.

Alternative Assessment *Protocol:* Ask students to assess their own work by responding to these questions:

What theme do you discuss?

What relevance to the modern world do you cite?

How do you try to convince your audience that the theme is not old-fashioned?

Tell students to use information from their protocols to help them revise their compositions.

LEARNING OPTIONS

1. Visual and kinesthetic learners will like this activity. You can vary the activity by having students accompany their drawings with the lines from the text on which they are based.
2. Analytic learners will find this activity enjoyable.
3. Visual learners will enjoy doing research. You may want to extend the activity by having students illustrate their reports with drawings of the unique flora and fauna of Australia.
4. Visual learners will find this activity appealing. You can extend the activity by having students write a short biography of Dickens for a flyleaf of the cover.
5. Kinesthetic and auditory learners will enjoy this activity.

together and in encouraging Estella to bewitch him so that she could later break his heart. Miss Havisham herself has failed as a human being since her obsession with revenge blinded her to the damage she inflicted on Estella and Pip.

10. Suggested Response: Both men have been kind and generous toward Pip. They are also similar in that they come from the lower classes and are not educated.
11. Suggested Response: Pip experiences an inner conflict with

regard to each of these men. He knows they deserve his devotion, but he also wants to reject them.

Applying

12. Answers will differ, but most students will realize that dealing with disappointment in a constructive way is a sign of character.

ANSWERS TO ANALYZING LITERATURE

Answers will differ, but students' responses should reflect the idea that love and devotion are worth more than material goods and status.

Preparation

Literary Focus Remind students that a traditional novel aims to represent reality. Its characters must seem real, its actions probable, its setting realistic. Consequently, the novel differs from a fairy tale or legend, where the writer may create a totally unreal world. The novelist's greatest gift is to actualize people and settings of other times and places and make them come alive for us, as Dickens does in *Great Expectations*.

Prereading Focus Remind students that in the last few chapters Pip began to recognize the truth about himself and others. Suggest that students consider the past behavior and the personalities of the main characters before making their predictions.

Vocabulary Have all students work in groups to create a crossword puzzle or a word game using the vocabulary words from this and previous sections of the novel.

Electronic Handbook You might want students to use the Language Master 6000 to hear the pronunciations of *truculent*, *obdurate*, *querulous*, and *assiduity*.

Spelling Tip Point out that the ending of *indelible* is spelled *ible*, not the more common *able*.

GUIDE FOR READING

Great Expectations, Chapters 45–58

The Novel as a Whole

You have learned how a novelist uses point of view, characterization, plot, setting, and theme to construct a narrative. The first-person narrative in *Great Expectations*, for example, leads you to depend on Pip's view of events and characters. Similarly, the descriptions of settings often reveal important character traits. Also, your involvement in the events of the plot makes you more receptive to the theme of the story. You will better understand the novel as a whole by continuing to consider how its elements reinforce each other.

Focus

Elizabeth Bowen has written: "For people who live on expectations, to face up to their realizations is something of an ordeal." Until now it seems as though Pip's assumptions have caused him to be deceived by several people, and it is easy to sympathize with him. Pip may also be at fault, however, for wanting to believe something that was not true. Pip must now face up to his situation. Sit with a partner and predict what will happen to Pip in the concluding chapters of *Great Expectations*. Consider also the fates of other major characters.

Vocabulary

Knowing the following words will help you as you read Chapters 45–58 of *Great Expectations*.

truculent (truk′ yoo lənt) *adj.*: Savage; cruel (p. 867)

averse (ə vʉrs′) *adj.*: Opposed to (p. 869)

tremulous (trem′ yoo ləs) *adj.*: Shaking; unsteady (p. 873)

vivacity (vi vas′ ə tē) *n.*: Liveliness (p. 876)

obdurate (äb′ door ət) *adj.*: Stubborn; unbending (p. 879)

proffered (präf′ ərd) *adj.*: Offered (usually a verb) (p. 882)

irresolute (i rez′ ə loot) *adj.*: Unsure; indecisive (p. 883)

tumult (too′ mult) *n.*: Great noise or disturbance (p. 884)

querulous (kwer′ ə ləs) *adj.*: Complaining (p. 891)

indelible (in del′ ə bəl) *adj.*: Cannot be erased (p. 893)

diffidence (dif′ ə dəns) *n.*: Shyness; uncertainty (p. 898)

assiduity (as′ ə dyoo′ ə tē) *n.*: Hard work and perseverance (p. 900)

avarice (av′ ə ris) *n.*: Greed (p. 905)

Objectives

1 To understand a novel as a whole
2 To use criteria to evaluate a novel
3 To write an evaluation of a novel

Support Material

Teaching Portfolio
Teacher Backup, p. 953
Grammar in Action Worksheets, *Using Repetition*, p. 957; *Understanding Referent*, p. 959
Usage and Mechanics Worksheet, p. 961
Vocabulary Check, p. 962
Critical Thinking and Reading Worksheet, *Using Criteria to Evaluate the Novel*, p. 964

Language Worksheet, *Recognizing Dialect*, p. 966
Selection Test, p. 967

Library of Video Classics
The Changing World of Charles Dickens, Great Expectations

Literature Videodisc
Scenes From Great Expectations

Prentice Hall Literature Writing Studio

Eight o'clock had struck before I got into the air that was scented, not disagreeably, by the chips and shavings of the longshore boat builders, and mast, oar, and block[1] makers. All that waterside region was unknown ground to me, and when I struck down by the river, I found that the spot I wanted was not where I had supposed it to be, and was anything but easy to find.

Selecting from the few queer houses upon Mill Pond Bank, a house with a wooden front and three stories of bow window, I looked at the plate upon the door, and read there Mrs. Whimple. That being the name I wanted, I knocked, and an elderly woman of a pleasant and thriving appearance responded. She was immediately deposed, however, by Herbert, who silently led me into the parlor and shut the door. It was an odd sensation to see his very familiar face established quite at home in that very unfamiliar room and region.

"All is well, Handel," said Herbert, "and he is quite satisfied, though eager to see you. My dear girl is with her father; and if you'll wait till she comes down, I'll make you known to her, and then we'll go upstairs. *That's* her father."

I had become aware of an alarming growling overhead, and had probably expressed the fact in my countenance.

"I am afraid he is a sad old rascal," said Herbert, smiling, "but I have never seen him."

While he thus spoke, the growling noise became a prolonged roar, and then died away.

"To have Provis for an upper lodger is quite a godsend to Mrs. Whimple," said Herbert, "for of course people in general won't

---
1. **block** (bläk) *n*.: Pulley.

stand that noise. A curious place, Handel, isn't it?"

It was a curious place, indeed, but remarkably well kept and clean.

"Mrs. Whimple," said Herbert, when I told him so, "is the best of housewives, and I really do not know what my Clara would do without her motherly help. For Clara has no mother of her own, Handel, and no relation in the world but old Gruffandgrim."

"Surely that's not his name, Herbert?"

"No, no," said Herbert, "that's my name for him. His name is Mr. Barley."

As we were thus conversing in a low tone while Old Barley's sustained growl vibrated in the beam that crossed the ceiling, the room door opened, and a very pretty, slight, dark-eyed girl of twenty or so came in with a basket in her hand: whom Herbert tenderly relieved of the basket, and presented blushing, as "Clara." She really was a most charming girl, and might have passed for a captive fairy whom the truculent ogre, Old Barley, had pressed into his service.

Clara returned soon afterwards, and Herbert accompanied me upstairs to see our charge. In his two cabin rooms at the top of the house, I found Provis comfortably settled. He expressed no alarm, and seemed to feel none that was worth mentioning, but it struck me that he was softened.

When Herbert and I sat down with him by his fire, I asked him first of all whether he relied on Wemmick's judgment and sources of information.

"Aye, aye, dear boy!" he answered, with a grave nod, "Jaggers knows."

"Then, I have talked with Wemmick," said I, "and have come to tell you what caution he gave me and what advice."

I told him how Wemmick had heard that he was under some suspicion, and that my chambers had been watched; how Wemmick had recommended his keeping close for a

Motivation/Prior Knowledge
Discuss with students what they believe influences change and growth. Tell them that in this last part of the novel, Pip comes to understand a new meaning of "great expectations." He changes and grows, and in doing so, he discovers an important new purpose in life.

Thematic Focus As people grow in self-awareness and in maturity, they learn to appreciate others. Pip learns this lesson in the denouement of the novel. Ask students if immature people can appreciate others. Discuss the idea that they cannot appreciate others until they know and understand themselves.

Master Teacher Note *Great Expectations* ends with Pip's growth and enlightenment. The theme of the novel—that goodness comes from within a person, not from external sources like wealth—is articulated through the experiences of Pip. The novel conveys the importance of love and true friendship.

Purpose-Setting Question
What changes had to occur in Pip's character before he could recognize his new purpose?

1 **Discussion** What is the atmosphere of the Mill Pond Bank neighborhood?

2 **Discussion** What fanciful picture does Pip draw of the relationship between Clara and her father, based on his observation of both?

Alternative Assessment To promote active reading, have students continue their reader's response journals. Encourage students to respond personally to the conclusions. How satisfactory do they find the reliance on coincidence?

Their observations will enable you to assess their understanding of the issues in the novel.

3 Discussion What plan does Herbert suggest for getting Provis safely out of London?

4 Discussion What uneasy thought occurs to Pip as he leaves the Mill Pond Bank area?

time, and my keeping away from him; and what Wemmick had said about getting him abroad. I added that, of course, when the time came, I should go with him, or should follow close upon him, as might be safest in Wemmick's judgment.

Herbert, who had been looking at the fire and pondering, here said that something had come into his thoughts arising out of Wemmick's suggestion, which it might be worthwhile to pursue. "We are both good watermen, Handel, and could take him down the river ourselves when the right time comes. No boat would then be hired for the purpose, and no boatmen; that would save at least a chance of suspicion, and any chance is worth saving. Never mind the season; don't you think it might be a good thing if you began at once to keep a boat at the Temple stairs and were in the habit of rowing up and down the river? You fall into that habit, and then who notices or minds? Do it twenty or fifty times, and there is nothing special in your doing it the twenty-first or fifty-first."

I liked this scheme, and Provis was quite elated by it. We agreed that it should be carried into execution, and that Provis should never recognize us if we came below Bridge and rowed past Mill Pond Bank. But we further agreed that he should pull down the blind in that part of his window which gave upon the east, whenever he saw us and all was right.

Our conference being now ended, and everything arranged, I rose to go, remarking to Herbert that he and I had better not go home together, and that I would take half an hour's start of him. "I don't like to leave you here," I said to Provis, "though I cannot doubt your being safer here than near me. Good-bye!"

"Dear boy," he answered, clasping my hands, "I don't know when we may meet again, and I don't like good-bye. Say good night!"

"Good night! Herbert will go regularly between us, and when the time comes you may be certain I shall be ready. Good night, good night!"

All things were as quiet in the Temple as ever I had seen them. The windows of the rooms of that side lately occupied by Provis were dark and still, and there was no lounger in Garden Court.

Next day, I set myself to get the boat. It was soon done, and the boat was brought round to the Temple stairs, and lay where I could reach her within a minute or two. Then, I began to go out as for training and practice—sometimes alone, sometimes with Herbert. At first, I kept above Blackfriars Bridge; but as the hours of the tide changed, I took towards London Bridge. The first time I passed Mill Pond Bank, Herbert and I were pulling a pair of oars; and, both in going and returning, we saw the blind towards the east come down. Herbert was rarely there less frequently than three times in a week, and he never brought me a single word of intelligence that was at all alarming. Still, I knew that there was cause for alarm, and I could not get rid of the notion of being watched. Once received, it is a haunting idea; how many undesigning persons I suspected of watching me it would be hard to calculate.

Chapter 46

Some weeks passed without bringing any change. We waited for Wemmick, and he made no sign.

My wordly affairs began to wear a gloomy appearance, and I was pressed for money by more than one creditor. Even I myself began to know the want of money (I mean of ready money in my own pocket), and to relieve it by converting some easily spared articles of jewelry into cash. But I had quite determined that it would be a heartless fraud to take more money from my patron in the existing state of my uncertain thoughts and plans.

As the time wore on, an impression settled heavily upon me that Estella was married. Fearful of having it confirmed, though it was all but a conviction, I avoided the newspapers, and begged Herbert (to whom I had confided the circumstances of our last interview) never to speak of her to me.

It was an unhappy life that I lived. Condemned to inaction and a state of constant restlessness and suspense, I rowed about in my boat, and waited, waited, waited, as I best could.

There were states of the tide when, having been down the river, I could not get back through the eddy-chafed arches and starlings of Old London Bridge; then I left my boat at a wharf near the Custom House, to be brought up afterwards to the Temple stairs. I was not averse to doing this, as it served to make me and my boat a commoner incident among the waterside people there. From this slight occasion sprang two meetings that I have now to tell of.

One afternoon, late in the month of February, I came ashore at the wharf at dusk. Both in going and returning, I had seen the signal in his window, All well.

As it was a raw evening and I was cold, I

MOONLIGHT. A STUDY AT MILLBANK
J. M. W. Turner
The Tate Gallery, London

5 Discussion What is Pip's state of mind as they wait for a sign from Wemmick? What causes this state of mind?

6 Clarification The phrase "eddy-chafed arches and starlings" refers to the erosion of the supporting structure of the bridge caused by the tidal-river currents. The word *starlings* means "pilings."

Humanities Note

Fine art, *Moonlight, A Study at Millbank,* by J.M.W. Turner. The British painter J.M.W. Turner (1775–1851) was educated at the Royal Academy. His approach to landscape painting, characterized by a study of the effects of light and atmosphere, was unique for its time.

Moonlight, A Study at Millbank shows that Turner did not confine his exploration of light to daytime. Here he shows the hauntingly beautiful effects of moonlight on the sky and water.

You might want to use the following questions:
1. Describe the quality of light in this painting.
2. What mood does Turner create through his depiction of moonlight?
3. Is this picture an appropriate accompaniment to the action in this section of the novel? Why or why not?

thought I would comfort myself with dinner at once; and as I had hours of dejection and solitude before me if I went home to the Temple, I thought I would afterwards go to the play. The theater where Mr. Wopsle was performing was in that waterside neighborhood, and to that theater I resolved to go.

When I came out of the theater after the play, I found Mr. Wopsle waiting for me near the door.

"How do you do?" said I, shaking hands with him as we turned down the street together. "I saw that you saw me."

"Saw you, Mr. Pip?" he returned. "Yes, of course I saw you. But who else was there?"

"Who else?"

"It is the strangest thing," said Mr. Wopsle, drifting into his lost look again, "and yet I could swear to him."

Becoming alarmed, I entreated Mr. Wopsle to explain his meaning.

"Whether I should have noticed him at first but for your being there," said Mr. Wopsle, "I can't be positive; yet I think I should."

Involuntarily I looked round me.

"Oh! He can't be in sight," said Mr. Wopsle. "He went out before I went off. I saw him go. I had a ridiculous fancy that he must be with you, Mr. Pip, till I saw that you were quite unconscious of him, sitting behind you there like a ghost."

"I dare say you wonder at me, Mr. Pip; indeed, I see you do. But it is so very strange! You'll hardly believe what I am going to tell you. I could hardly believe it myself, if you told me."

"Indeed?" said I.

"No, indeed. Mr. Pip, you remember in old times a certain Christmas Day, when you were quite a child, and I dined at Gargery's, and some soldiers came to the door to get a pair of handcuffs mended?"

"I remember it very well."

"And you remember that there was a chase after two convicts, and that we joined in it, and that Gargery took you on his back? And you remember that we came up with the two in a ditch, and that there was a scuffle between them, and that one of them had been severely handled and much mauled about the face by the other?"

"I see it all before me."

"And that the soldiers lighted torches, and put the two in the center, and that we went on to see the last of them, over the black marshes, with the torchlight shining on their faces—I am particular about that—with the torchlight shining on their faces, when there was an outer ring of dark night all about us?"

"Yes," said I. "I remember all that."

"Then, Mr. Pip, one of those two prisoners sat behind you tonight. I saw him over your shoulder."

"Steady!" I thought. I asked him then, "Which of the two do you suppose you saw?"

"The one who had been mauled," he answered readily, "and I'll swear I saw him! The more I think of him, the more certain I am of him."

"This is very curious!" said I, with the best assumption I could put on of its being nothing more to me. "Very curious indeed!"

I cannot exaggerate the enhanced disquiet into which this conversation threw me, or the special and peculiar terror I felt at Compeyson's having been behind me "like a ghost."

When Mr. Wopsle had imparted to me all that he could recall or I extract, and when I had treated him to a little appropriate refreshment after the fatigues of the evening, we parted. It was between twelve and one o'clock when I reached the Temple, and the gates were shut. No one was near me when I went in and went home.

Herbert had come in, and we held a very serious council by the fire. But there was

7

nothing to be done, saving to communicate to Wemmick what I had that night found out, and to remind him that we waited for his hint. As I thought that I might compromise him if I went too often to the castle, I made this communication by letter. I wrote it before I went to bed and went out and posted it; and again no one was near me. Herbert and I agreed that we could do nothing else but be very cautious.

Chapter 47

The second of the two meetings referred to in the last chapter occurred about a week after the first. I had strolled up into Cheapside, and was strolling along it, surely the most unsettled person in all the busy concourse, when a large hand was laid upon my shoulder by some one overtaking me. It was Mr. Jaggers's hand, and he passed it through my arm.

"As we were going in the same direction, Pip, we may walk together. Where are you bound for?"

"For the Temple, I think," said I.

"Don't you know?" said Mr. Jaggers.

"Well," I returned, glad for once to get the better of him in cross-examination, "I do *not* know, for I have not made up my mind."

"You are going to dine?" said Mr. Jaggers. "You don't mind admitting that, I suppose?"

"No," I returned, "I don't mind admitting that."

"And are not engaged?"

"I don't mind admitting also that I am not engaged."

"Then," said Mr. Jaggers, "come and dine with me."

I was going to excuse myself, when he added, "Wemmick's coming." So I changed my excuse into an acceptance.

We went to Gerrard Street, all three together, in a hackney coach, and as soon as we got there, dinner was served.

"Did you send that note of Miss Havisham's to Mr. Pip, Wemmick?" Mr. Jaggers asked, soon after we began dinner.

"No, sir," returned Wemmick; "it was going by post, when you brought Mr. Pip into the office. Here it is." He handed it to his principal, instead of to me.

"It's a note of two lines, Pip," said Mr. Jaggers, handing it on, "sent up to me by Miss Havisham, on account of her not being sure of your address. She tells me that she wants to see you on a little matter of business you mentioned to her. You'll go down?"

"Yes," said I.

"When do you think of going down?"

"I have an impending engagement," said I, glancing at Wemmick, who was putting fish into the post office, "that renders me rather uncertain of my time. At once, I think."

"If Mr. Pip has the intention of going at once," said Wemmick to Mr. Jaggers, "he needn't write an answer, you know."

Receiving this as an intimation that it was best not to delay, I settled that I would go tomorrow, and said so.

"So, Pip! Our friend the Spider," said Mr. Jaggers, "has played his cards. He has won the pool." | 8

It was as much as I could do to assent.

"So, here's to Mrs. Bentley Drummle," said Mr. Jaggers, "and may the question of supremacy be settled to the lady's satisfaction! To the satisfaction of the lady *and* the gentleman, it never will be. Now, Molly, Molly, Molly, Molly, how slow you are today!"

She was at his elbow when he addressed her, putting a dish upon the table. As she withdrew her hands from it, she fell back a step or two, nervously muttering some excuse. And a certain action of her fingers as she spoke arrested my attention.

Great Expectations 871

8 **Discussion** What does Mr. Jaggers mean? What conflict has now been resolved?

9 Critical Thinking and Reading
As Molly serves Pip dinner, what does he notice about her that seems significant to him? What conclusion can you draw about his particular interest in this subject?

10 Reading Strategy Pip makes an important discovery about Molly that prompts him to question Mr. Jaggers and Wemmick about Estella's history. Predict what the outcome will be for Pip.

11 Discussion What crime was Molly charged with? How did Mr. Jaggers get her acquitted?

The action of her fingers was like the action of knitting. She stood looking at her master. Her look was very intent. Surely, I had seen exactly such eyes and such hands on a memorable occasion very lately!

He dismissed her, and she glided out of the room. But she remained before me, as plainly as if she were still there. I looked at those hands, I looked at those eyes, I looked at that flowing hair, and I compared them with other hands, other eyes, other hair, that I knew of, and with what those might be after twenty years of a brutal husband and a stormy life. I looked again at those hands and eyes of the housekeeper, and thought of the inexplicable feeling that had come over me when I last walked—not alone—in the ruined garden, and through the deserted brewery. And I felt absolutely certain that this woman was Estella's mother.

Wemmick and I took our leave early, and left together. "Well!" said Wemmick, "that's over!"

I asked him if he had ever seen Miss Havisham's adopted daughter, Mrs. Bentley Drummle? He said no.

"Wemmick," said I, "do you remember telling me, before I first went to Mr. Jaggers's private house, to notice that housekeeper?"

"Did I?" he replied. "Ah, I dare say I did."

"A wild beast tamed, you called her?"

"And what did *you* call her?"

"The same. How did Mr. Jaggers tame her, Wemmick?"

"That's his secret. She has been with him many a long year."

"I wish you would tell me her story. I feel a particular interest in being acquainted with it. You know that what is said between you and me goes no further."

"Well!" Wemmick replied, "I don't know her story—that is, I don't know all of it. But what I do know, I'll tell you.

"A score or so of years ago, that woman was tried at the Old Bailey[1] for murder and was acquitted. She was a very handsome young woman.

"Mr. Jaggers was for her and worked the case in a way quite astonishing. It was a desparate case, and it was comparatively early days with him then, and he worked it to general admiration; in fact, it may almost be said to have made him. The murdered person was a woman; a woman, a good ten years older, very much larger, and very much stronger. It was a case of jealousy. This woman in Gerrard Street here had been married very young and was a perfect fury in point of jealousy. The murdered woman—more a match for the man, certainly, in point of years—was found dead in a barn near Hounslow Heath. There had been a violent struggle. She was bruised and scratched and torn, and had been held by the throat at last and choked. Now, there was no reasonable evidence to implicate any person but this woman, and, on the improbabilities of her having been able to do it, Mr. Jaggers principally rested his case. You may be sure that he never dwelt upon the strength of her hands then, though he sometimes does now."

I had told Wemmick of his showing us her wrists that day of the dinner party.

"Well, sir!" Wemmick went on, "it happened—happened, don't you see?—that this woman was so very artfully dressed from the time of her apprehension that she looked much slighter than she really was; in particular, her sleeves are always remembered to have been so skillfully contrived that her arms had quite a delicate look.

"It was attempted to be set up in proof of her jealousy that she was under strong suspicion of having, at about the time of the

---

1. **Old Bailey:** Criminal court on Old Bailey Street in London.

Grammar in Action

The **repetition** of words and phrases is a device that is usually associated with poetry. Great prose writers, however, often use repetition to create a musical rhythm, emphasize certain words, or imitate a circling, repetitive pattern of thought.

Read the following passage from *Great Expectations* and notice the repeated words and phrases in italics:

He dismissed her, and she glided out of the room. But she remained before me, as plainly as if she were still there. *I looked at* those hands, *I looked at* those eyes, *I looked at* that flowing hair, and I compared them with *other hands, other eyes, other hair,* that I knew of, and with what those might be after twenty years of a brutal husband and a stormy life. *I looked again at* those *hands* and *eyes* of the housekeeper. . . . And I felt absolutely certain that this woman was Estella's mother.

Pip is looking, again and again, at the hands and eyes of the housekeeper, comparing them with Estella's hands and eyes.

murder, frantically destroyed her child by this man—some three years old—to revenge herself upon him. But Mr. Jaggers was altogether too many for the jury, and they gave in."

"Has she been in his service ever since?"

"Yes; but not only that," said Wemmick; "she went into his service immediately after her acquittal, tamed as she is now. She has since been taught one thing and another in the way of her duties, but she was tamed from the beginning."

"Do you remember the sex of the child?"

"Said to have been a girl."

"You have nothing more to say to me tonight?"

"Nothing. I got your letter and destroyed it. Nothing."

We exchanged a cordial good night, and I went home with new matter for my thoughts, though with no relief from the old.

Chapter 48

Putting Miss Havisham's note in my pocket, that it might serve as my credentials for so soon reappearing at Satis House, in case her waywardness should lead her to express any surprise at seeing me, I went down again by the coach next day. But I alighted at the Halfway House, and breakfasted there, and walked the rest of the distance, for I sought to get into the town quietly by the unfrequented ways, and to leave it in the same manner.

The best light of the day was gone when I passed along the quiet echoing courts behind the High Street. An elderly woman, whom I had seen before as one of the servants who lived in the supplementary house across the back courtyard, opened the gate. The lighted candle stood in the dark passage within, as of old, and I took it up and ascended the staircase alone. Miss Havisham was not in her own room, but was in the larger room across the landing. Looking in at the door, after knocking in vain, I saw her sitting on the hearth in a ragged chair, close before, and lost in the contemplation of, the ashy fire.

Doing as I had often done, I went in, and stood, touching the old chimneypiece, where she could see me when she raised her eyes. There was an air of utter loneliness upon her that would have moved me to pity though she had willfully done me a deeper injury than I could charge her with.

"It is I, Pip. Mr. Jaggers gave me your note yesterday, and I have lost no time."

"Thank you. Thank you."

As I brought another of the ragged chairs to the hearth and sat down, I remarked a new expression on her face, as if she were afraid of me.

"I want," she said, "to pursue that subject you mentioned to me when you were last here, and to show you that I am not all stone. But perhaps you can never believe, now, that there is anything human in my heart?"

When I said some reassuring words, she stretched out her tremulous right hand, as though she was going to touch me.

"You said, speaking for your friend, that you could tell me how to do something useful and good. Something that you would like done, is it not?"

"Something that I would like done very very much."

"What is it?"

I began explaining to her that secret history of the partnership and told her how I had hoped to complete the transaction out of my means, but how in this I was disappointed. That part of the subject (I reminded her) involved matters which could form no

---

12 **Discussion** What further important information does Pip learn from Wemmick? What further insight into Mr. Jaggers's character does this story give?

13 **Reading Strategy** As students read this chapter, have them look for the dramatic changes in the relationship between Miss Havisham and Pip. When they have completed the chapter, have students summarize the changes.

14 **Discussion** What conflicting feelings does Pip have when he sees the changes in Miss Havisham?

15 **Discussion** What evidence indicates that Miss Havisham has had a change of heart?

Dickens captures the emotional intensity of this moment and the movement from one memory to another by repeating the phrase *I looked at.* He also repeats the traits that he observed—*hands, eyes,* and *hair.* Dickens uses repetition to imitate the searching of thought as it reaches for an idea.

Student Activity. Using this paragraph from *Great Expectations* as a model, write a paragraph of your own about a gradual discovery. Use repetition to create a distinctive rhythm, emphasize important words, and add to the drama of your description.

Software If students are working on computers, you might wish them to use the **Writer's Helper** revision tool Word Frequency to help them revise their paragraphs.

part of my explanation, for they were the weighty secrets of another.

"So!" said she, assenting with her head, but not looking at me. "And how much money is wanting to complete the purchase?"

I was rather afraid of stating it, for it sounded a large sum. "Nine hundred pounds."

"If I give you the money for this purpose, will you keep my secret as you have kept your own?"

"Quite as faithfully."

"And your mind will be more at rest?"

"Much more at rest."

"Are you very unhappy now?"

She asked this question, still without looking at me, but in an unwonted tone of sympathy. I could not reply at the moment, for my voice failed me. She put her left arm across the head of her stick, and softly laid her forehead on it.

"I am far from happy, Miss Havisham, but I have other causes of disquiet than any you know of. They are the secrets I have mentioned."

After a little while, she raised her head, and looked at the fire again.

" 'Tis noble in you to tell me that you have other causes of unhappiness. Is it true?"

"Too true."

"Can I only serve you, Pip, by serving your friend? Regarding that as done, is there nothing I can do for you yourself?"

"Nothing. I thank you for the question. I thank you even more for the tone of the question. But there is nothing."

She presently rose from her seat, and looked about the blighted room for the means of writing. There were none there, and she took from her pocket a yellow set of ivory tablets, mounted in tarnished gold, and wrote upon them with a pencil in a case

of tarnished gold that hung from her neck.

"You are still on friendly terms with Mr. Jaggers?"

"Quite. I dined with him yesterday."

"This is an authority to him to pay you that money, to lay out at your irresponsible discretion for your friend. I keep no money here; but if you would rather Mr. Jaggers knew nothing of the matter, I will send it to you."

"Thank you, Miss Havisham; I have not the least objection to receiving it from him."

She read me what she had written, and it was direct and clear, and evidently intended to absolve me from any suspicion of profiting by the receipt of the money. I took the tablets from her hand, and it trembled.

"My name is on the first leaf. If you can ever write under my name, 'I forgive her,' though ever so long after my broken heart is dust, pray do it!"

"Oh, Miss Havisham," said I, "I can do it now. There have been sore mistakes; and my life has been a blind and thankless one; and I want forgiveness and direction far too much to be bitter with you."

She turned her face to me for the first time since she had averted it, and to my amazement, I may even add to my terror, dropped on her knees at my feet.

To see her, with her white hair and her worn face, kneeling at my feet, gave me a shock through all my frame. I entreated her to rise, and got my arms about her to help her up, but she only pressed that hand of mine which was nearest to her grasp, and hung her head over it, and wept.

"Oh!" she cried, despairingly. "What have I done! What have I done!"

"If you mean, Miss Havisham, what have you done to injure me, let me answer. Very little. I should have loved her under any circumstances. Is she married?"

"Yes!"

17 It was a needless question, for a new desolation in the desolate house had told me so.

"What have I done! What have I done!" She wrung her hands, and crushed her white hair, and returned to this cry over and over again. "What have I done!"

Miss Havisham looked distractedly at me for a while, and then burst out again. What had she done!

"If you knew all my story," she pleaded, "you would have some compassion for me, and a better understanding of me."

"Miss Havisham," I answered, as delicately as I could, "I believe I may say that I do know your story. And I hope I understand it and its influences. Does what has passed between us give me any excuse for asking you a question relative to Estella?"

She looked full at me when I said this, and replied, "Go on."

"Whose child was Estella?"

She shook her head.

"But Mr. Jaggers brought her here, or sent her here?"

"Brought her here."

"Will you tell me how that came about?"

She answered in a low whisper and with caution: "I had been shut up in these rooms a long time when I told him that I wanted a little girl to rear and love, and save from my fate. He told me that he would look about him for such an orphan child. One night he brought her here asleep, and I called her Estella."

"Might I ask her age then?"

"Two or three. She herself knows nothing, but that she was left an orphan and I adopted her."

So convinced I was of that woman's being her mother that I wanted no evidence to establish the fact in my mind.

What more could I hope to do by prolonging the interview? I had succeeded on behalf of Herbert, Miss Havisham had told me all she knew of Estella, I had said and done what I could to ease her mind. No matter with what other words we parted; we parted.

Twilight was closing in when I went downstairs into the natural air. I called to the woman who had opened the gate when I entered that I would not trouble her just yet, but would walk round the place before leaving.

After I had finished my walk, I hesitated whether to call the woman to let me out at the locked gate, or first go upstairs and assure myself that Miss Havisham was as safe and well as I had left her. I took the latter course and went up.

I looked into the room where I had left her, and I saw her seated in the ragged chair upon the hearth close to the fire, with her back towards me. In the moment when I was withdrawing my head to go quietly away, I saw a great flaming light spring up. In the same moment I saw her running at me, shrieking, with a whirl of fire blazing all about her, and soaring at least as many feet above her head as she was high.

18 I had a double-caped greatcoat on, and over my arm another thick coat. That I got them off, closed with her, threw her down, and got them over her; that I dragged the great cloth from the table for the same purpose, and with it dragged down the heap of rottenness in the midst, and all the ugly things that sheltered there; that we were on the ground struggling like desperate enemies, and that the closer I covered her, the more wildly she shrieked and tried to free herself; that this occurred I knew through the result, but not through anything I felt, or thought, or knew I did. I knew nothing until I knew that we were on the floor by the great table, and that patches of tinder yet alight were floating in the smoky air, which a moment ago had been her faded bridal dress.

Then I looked round and saw the dis-

17 Discussion How does Pip describe the mood in Satis House?

18 Discussion What occurrence shocks Pip into action and changes the role he has played in this house?

876

19 Discussion What scene does Pip recall when he sees Miss Havisham lying on the large table in her room?

20 Critical Thinking and Reading What can you infer about Pip's motive for wanting to communicate only with Matthew Pocket?

21 Literary Focus How does the fire relate to the theme of the novel?

Cooperative Learning Use the Roundtable structure to create a summary of chapters 45 through 48. Arrange students in groups of four. Have one student in each group write a brief description of an event at the beginning of chapter 45, such as "Pip visits Mrs. Whimple's house, and Herbert introduces him to Clara." Tell students to pass the paper containing the first entry on to a second student in the group. Each student will add a significant fact—in story sequence—to the paper until the summary is complete.

To ensure that all students have participated, you might want to have each student in a group write in different colored ink or sign his or her entries.

When the summaries are complete, call on representatives from several of the groups to read the group's summary aloud.

turbed beetles and spiders running away over the floor, and the servants coming in with breathless cries at the door.

She was insensible, and I was afraid to have her moved, or even touched. Assistance was sent for, and I held her until it came. When I got up, on the surgeon's coming to her with other aid, I was astonished to see that both my hands were burnt, for I had no knowledge of it through the sense of feeling.

On examination it was pronounced that she had received serious hurts, but that they of themselves were far from hopeless; the danger lay mainly in the nervous shock. By the surgeon's directions, her bed was carried into that room and laid upon the great table.

19 When I saw her again, an hour afterwards, she lay indeed where I had seen her strike her stick, and had heard her say she would lie one day.

Though every vestige of her dress was burnt, she still had something of her old ghastly bridal appearance, for they had covered her to the throat with white cotton-wool, and as she lay with a white sheet loosely overlying that, the phantom air of something that had been and was changed was still upon her.

20 I found, on questioning the servants, that Estella was in Paris, and I got a promise from the surgeon that he would write by the next post. Miss Havisham's family I took upon myself, intending to communicate with Matthew Pocket only, and leave him to do as he liked about informing the rest.

There was a stage, that evening, when she spoke collectedly of what had happened, though with a certain terrible vivacity. Towards midnight she began to wander in her speech, and after that it gradually set in that she said innumerable times in a low solemn voice, "What have I done!" And then, "Take the pencil and write under my name, 'I forgive her!'"

Chapter 49

My hands had been dressed twice or thrice in the night, and again in the morning. My left arm was a good deal burned to the elbow, and, less severely, as high as the shoulder; it was very painful, but the flames had set in that direction, and I felt thankful it was no worse. **21**

Herbert was the kindest of nurses, and at stated times took off the bandages, and steeped them in the cooling liquid that was kept ready, and put them on again, with a patient tenderness that I was deeply grateful for.

Neither of us spoke of the boat, but we both thought of it. That was made apparent by our avoidance of the subject, and by our agreeing—without agreement—to make my recovery of the use of my hands a question of so many hours, not of so many weeks.

My first question when I saw Herbert had been, of course, whether all was well down the river. As he replied in the affirmative, with perfect confidence and cheerfulness, we did not resume the subject until the day was wearing away. But then, as Herbert changed the bandages, more by the light of the fire than by the outer light, he went back to it spontaneously.

"I sat with Provis last night, Handel, two good hours. He was very communicative, and told me more of his life. You remember his breaking off here about some woman that he had had great trouble with. The woman was a young woman, and a jealous woman, and a revengeful woman; revengeful, Handel, to the last degree."

"To what last degree?"

"Murder—does it strike too cold on that sensitive place?"

"I don't feel it. How did she murder? Whom did she murder?"

"Why, the deed may not have merited

quite so terrible a name," said Herbert, "but she was tried for it, and Mr. Jaggers defended her, and the reputation of that defense first made his name known to Provis. It was another and a stronger woman who was the victim, and there had been a struggle—in a barn."

"Was the woman brought in guilty?"

"No, she was acquitted."

"Yes? What else?"

"This acquitted young woman and Provis had a little child, a little child of whom Provis was exceedingly fond. On the evening of the very night when the object of her jealousy was strangled as I tell you, the young woman presented herself before Provis for one moment, and swore that she would destroy the child (which was in her possession), and he should never see it again; then she vanished. . . ."

"Did the woman keep her oath?"

"There comes the darkest part of Provis's life. She did."

"That is, he says she did."

"Why, of course, my dear boy," returned Herbert, in a tone of surprise, and bending forward to get a nearer look at me. "He says it all. I have no other information."

"No, to be sure."

"Now, whether," pursued Herbert, "he had used the child's mother ill, or whether he had used the child's mother well, Provis doesn't say; but she had shared some four or five years of the wretched life he described to us at this fireside, and he seems to have felt pity for her, and forbearance towards her. Therefore, fearing he should be called upon to depose[1] about this destroyed child, and so be the cause of her death, he hid himself, kept himself dark, as he says, out of the way and out of the trial, and was only vaguely talked of as a certain man called Abel, out of

---
1. depose (di pōz') v.: Testify.

whom the jealousy arose. After the acquittal she disappeared, and thus he lost the child and the child's mother."

"I want to know," said I, and "particularly, Herbert, whether he told you when this happened?"

"How old were you when you came upon him in the little churchyard?"

"I think in my seventh year."

"Aye. It had happened some three or four years, then, he said, and you brought into his mind the little girl so tragically lost, who would have been about your age."

"Herbert," said I, after a short silence, "the man we have in hiding down the river is Estella's father."

Chapter 50

Early next morning we went out together, and at the corner of Giltspur Street by Smithfield, I left Herbert to go his way into the City, and took my way to Little Britain.

There were periodical occasions when Mr. Jaggers and Mr. Wemmick went over the office accounts, and checked off the vouchers, and put all things straight. On these occasions Wemmick took his books and papers into Mr. Jaggers's room, and one of the upstairs clerks came down into the outer office. Finding such clerk on Wemmick's post that morning, I knew what was going on; but I was not sorry to have Mr. Jaggers and Wemmick together, as Wemmick would then hear for himself that I said nothing to compromise him.

My appearance, with my arm bandaged and my coat loose over my shoulders, favored my object. Although I had sent Mr. Jaggers a brief account of the accident as soon as I had arrived in town, yet I had to give him all the details now. While I described the disaster, Mr. Jaggers stood before the fire. Wemmick

22 **Discussion** What does Pip know that Herbert does not?

23 **Reading Strategy** Have students summarize what clues point to the identity of Estella's father.

Humanities Note

Fine art, *Little London Model,* 1896, by James McNeill Whistler. The American-English artist James McNeill Whistler (1834–1903) did not confine his art to painting. He produced drawings, etchings, and lithographs as well.

Little London Model is a lithograph, an image produced by drawing on a smooth stone slab with a grease crayon, applying an oily ink that adheres only to the crayon, and then pressing paper onto the stone to transfer the drawing. This view of the Thames River demonstrates the same rhythm of line and simplicity of composition that characterizes Whistler's paintings.

You might want to use the following questions:

1. How does Whistler suggest a busy city without drawing in every detail?

2. Why is Whistler's lithograph an appropriate accompaniment to this section of the novel?

24 Discussion Does Pip share Wemmick's philosophy? Explain.

25 Discussion What is the "theme" that is so dear to Pip's heart? What connection does it have with the theme of the novel?

LITTLE LONDON MODEL
James McNeill Whistler
Frank S. Benson Funds
The Brooklyn Museum

leaned back in his chair, staring at me, with his hands in the pockets of his trousers.

My narrative finished, I then produced Miss Havisham's authority to receive the nine hundred pounds for Herbert. "I am sorry, Pip," said Mr. Jaggers, "that we do nothing for *you.*"

"Miss Havisham was good enough to ask me," I returned, "whether she could do nothing for me, and I told her no."

"Everybody should know his own business," said Mr. Jaggers.

24 "Every man's business," said Wemmick, "is 'portable property.' "

25 As I thought the time was now come for pursuing the theme I had at heart, I said, turning on Mr. Jaggers:

"I did ask something of Miss Havisham, however, sir. I asked her to give me some information relative to her adopted daughter, and she gave me all she possessed."

"Did she?" said Mr. Jaggers.

"I know more of the history of Miss Havisham's adopted child than Miss Havisham herself does, sir. I know her mother."

Mr. Jaggers looked at me inquiringly, and repeated "Mother?"

"I have seen her mother within these three days."

"Yes?" said Mr. Jaggers.

"And so have you sir. And you have seen her still more recently."

"Yes?" said Mr. Jaggers.

"Perhaps I know more of Estella's history than even you do," said I. "I know her father, too."

A certain stop that Mr. Jaggers came to in his manner assured me that he did not know who her father was.

"So! You know the young lady's father, Pip?" said Mr. Jaggers.

26 "Yes," I replied, "and his name is Provis—from New South Wales."

Even Mr. Jaggers started when I said those words.

"And on what evidence, Pip," asked Mr. Jaggers, "does Provis make this claim?"

"He does not make it," said I, "and has never made it, and has no knowledge or belief that his daughter is in existence."

Mr. Jaggers folded his arms and looked with stern attention at me, though with an immovable face.

Then I told him all I knew, and how I knew it, with the one reservation that I left him to infer that I knew from Miss Havisham what I in fact knew from Wemmick.

"Hah!" said Mr. Jaggers at last, as he moved towards the papers on the table. "—What item was it you were at, Wemmick, when Mr. Pip came in?"

But I could not submit to be thrown off in that way, and I made a passionate, almost an indignant appeal to him to be more frank and manly with me. And seeing that Mr. Jaggers stood quite still and silent, and apparently quite obdurate, under this appeal, I turned to Wemmick, and said, "Wemmick, I know you to be a man with a gentle heart. I have seen your pleasant home, and your old father, and all the innocent cheerful playful ways with which you refresh your business life. And I entreat you to say a word for me to Mr. Jaggers, and to represent to him that,

all circumstances considered, he ought to be more open with me!"

I have never seen two men look more oddly at one another than Mr. Jaggers and Wemmick did after this apostrophe.

"What's all this?" said Mr. Jaggers. "You with an old father, and you with pleasant and playful ways?"

"Well!" returned Wemmick. "If I don't bring 'em here, what does it matter?"

Mr. Jaggers nodded his head retrospectively two or three times, and actually drew a sigh. "Pip," said he, "I'll put a case to you. Mind! I admit nothing."

He waited for me to declare that I quite understood that he expressly said that he admitted nothing.

"Now, Pip," said Mr. Jaggers, "put this case. Put the case that a woman, under such circumstances as you have mentioned, held her child concealed, and was obliged to communicate the fact to her legal adviser. Put the case that at the same time he held a trust to find a child for an eccentric rich lady to adopt and bring up."

"I follow you, sir."

"Put the case that he lived in an atmosphere of evil, and that he often saw children solemnly tried at a criminal bar,[1] where they were held up to be seen; put the case that he habitually knew of their being imprisoned, whipped, transported,[2] neglected, and cast out."

"I follow you, sir."

"Put the case, Pip, that here was one pretty little child out of the heap who could be saved; whom the father believed dead, and dared make no stir about; as to whom, over the mother, the legal adviser had this power: 'I know what you did, and how you

---

1. **bar** *n.*: Court.
2. **transported** (trans pôrt′ əd) *v.*: Sent out of the country to a colony for prisoners.

26 **Discussion** Why is there a change here in the usual relationship between Pip and Mr. Jaggers?

27 **Enrichment** As a newspaper reporter in his early career, Dickens was familiar with the extreme punishments handed down by criminal courts, and in this passage he is voicing his criticism of the system.

28 **Discussion** What hold does Mr. Jaggers have over Molly that keeps her "tamed"?

29 **Discussion** Why does Pip believe Estella should not be told about her origins? What does this reveal about Pip's character?

30 **Discussion** What new direction in Herbert's life will affect Pip?

31 **Clarification** The phrase "driving with the wind and waves" describes Pip's feeling that he has no control over his life.

32 **Discussion** What is Wemmick telling Pip?

Speaking and Listening You might want to have students volunteer to read aloud selected sections from Chapters 47 through 50, in which Dickens allows Pip to deduce the identity of Jaggers's servant Molly. If you wish, individual students may read the parts of Pip (as the narrator), Pip (when quoted directly), Wemmick, Miss Havisham, Herbert Pocket, and Jaggers. As the reading progresses, you might want to question the class as a whole about Dickens's technique in having Pip learn seemingly disconnected facts about Molly before certifying her identity.

did it. Give the child into my hands, and I will do my best to bring you off. If you are saved, your child will be saved, too; if you are lost, your child is still saved.' Put the case that this was done, and that the woman was cleared."

"I understand you perfectly."

"But that I make no admissions?"

"That you make no admissions." And Wemmick repeated, "No admissions."

"Put the case, Pip, that passion and the terror of death had a little shaken the woman's intellects, and that when she was set at liberty, she was scared out of the ways of the world and went to him to be sheltered. Put the case that he took her in, and that he kept down the old wild violent nature, whenever he saw an inkling of its breaking out, by asserting his power over her in the old way. Do you comprehend the imaginary case?"

"Quite."

"Put the case that the child grew up, and was married for money. That the mother was still living. That the father was still living. That the mother and father, unknown to one another, were dwelling within so many miles, furlongs, yards if you like, of one another. That the secret was still a secret, except that you had got wind of it. Put that last case to yourself very carefully."

"I do."

"I ask Wemmick to put it to *himself* very carefully."

And Wemmick said, "I do."

"For whose sake would you reveal the secret? For the father's? I think he would not be much the better for the mother. For the mother's? I think if she had done such a deed, she would be safer where she was. For the daughter's? I think it would hardly serve her to establish her parentage for the information of her husband, and to drag her back to disgrace, after an escape of twenty years, pretty secure to last for life."

I looked at Wemmick, whose face was very grave. He gravely touched his lips with his forefinger. I did the same. Mr. Jaggers did the same. "Now, Wemmick," said the latter then, resuming his usual manner, "what item was it you were at when Mr. Pip came in?"

Chapter 51

From Little Britain, I went, with my check in my pocket, to Miss Skiffins's brother, the accountant; and Miss Skiffins's brother, the accountant, going straight to Clarriker's and bringing Clarriker to me, I had the great satisfaction of concluding that arrangement.

Clarriker informing me on that occasion that the affairs of the house were steadily progressing, that he would now be able to establish a small branch-house in the East and that Herbert in his new partnership capacity would go out and take charge of it, I found that I must have prepared for a separation from my friend, even though my own affairs had been more settled. And now indeed I felt as if my last anchor were loosening its hold, and I should soon be driving with the winds and waves.

On a Monday morning, when Herbert and I were at breakfast, I received the following letter from Wemmick by the post.

Walworth. Burn this as soon as read. Early in the week, or say Wednesday, you might do what you know of, if you felt disposed to try it. Now, burn.

When I had shown this to Herbert and had put it in the fire—but not before we had both got it by heart—we considered what to do. For, of course, my being disabled could now be no longer kept out of view.

"I have thought it over, again and

again," said Herbert, "and I think I know a better course than taking a Thames waterman. Take Startop. A good fellow, a skilled hand, fond of us, and enthusiastic and honorable."

"But how much would you tell him, Herbert?"

"It is necessary to tell him very little. Let him suppose it a mere freak, but a secret one, until the morning comes—then let him know that there is urgent reason for your getting Provis aboard and away. You go with him?"

"No doubt."

"Where?"

It had seemed to me, in the many anxious considerations I had given the point, almost indifferent what port we made for—the place signified little, so that he was out of England. Any foreign steamer that fell in our way and would take us up would do. As foreign steamers would leave London at about the time of high water, our plan would be to get down the river by a previous ebb tide,[1] and lie by in some quiet spot until we could pull off to one. The time when one would be due where we lay could be calculated pretty nearly, if we made inquiries beforehand.

Herbert assented to all this, and we went out immediately after breakfast to pursue our investigations. We found that a steamer for Hamburg[2] was likely to suit our purpose best, and we directed our thoughts chiefly to that vessel. We then separated for a few hours, and did what we had to do without any hindrance, and when we met again at one o'clock reported it done. I, for my part, was prepared with passports; Herbert had seen Startop, and he was more than ready to join.

Those two would pull a pair of oars, we settled, and I would steer: our charge would be sitter, and keep quiet; as speed was not our object, we should make way enough. We arranged that Herbert should not come home to dinner before going to Mill Pond Bank that evening; that he should not go there at all tomorrow evening, Tuesday; that he should prepare Provis to come down to some stairs hard by the house, on Wednesday, when he saw us approach, and not sooner; that all the arrangements with him should be concluded that Monday night; and that he should be communicated with no more in any way, until we took him on board.

These precautions well understood by both of us, I went home.

On opening the outer door of our chambers with my key, I found a letter in the box, directed to me; a very dirty letter, though not ill-written. It had been delivered by hand (of course since I left home), and its contents were these.

> If you are not afraid to come to the old marshes tonight or tomorrow night at nine, and to come to the little sluice house by the limekiln,[3] you had better come. If you want information regarding *your Uncle Provis*, you had much better come and tell no one and lose no time. *You must come alone.* Bring this with you.

I had had load enough upon my mind before the receipt of this strange letter. What to do now, I could not tell. And the worse was that I must decide quickly, or I should miss the afternoon coach, which would take me down in time for tonight. Tomorrow night I

---

1. **ebb tide:** The outgoing or falling tide.
2. **Hamburg** (ham′ bərg): Seaport in northwest Germany.

3. **limekiln** (līm′ kiln′) *n.*: Furnace in which limestone is burned to make lime, a substance used in mortar and cement.

33 Discussion How do Pip and Herbert alter their plan as a result of Pip's injury?

34 Clarification Information about the tides would be necessary to Herbert and Pip's calculations. To row against an incoming tide would tire them and slow them down.

35 Discussion How do Pip and Herbert plan to make contact with an outgoing steamer so that Pip and Provis can escape safely?

882

36 Discussion When Pip receives a mysterious letter, why does he decide to comply with it?

37 Literary Focus Pip goes to the limekiln alone. What character traits are indicated by this action?

could not think of going, for it would be too close upon the time of the flight. And again, for anything I knew, the proffered information might have some important bearing on the flight itself.

36 Having hardly any time for consideration, I resolved to go. I should certainly not have gone but for the reference to my Uncle Provis. That, coming on Wemmick's letter and the morning's busy preparation, turned the scale.

The journey seemed long and dreary to me who could see little of it inside, and who could not go outside in my disabled state. Avoiding the Blue Boar, I put up at an inn of minor reputation down the town, and ordered some dinner. While it was preparing, I went to Satis House and inquired for Miss Havisham; she was still very ill, though considered something better.

My inn had once been a part of an ancient ecclesiastical[4] house, and I dined in a little octagonal common room, like a font.[5] As I was not able to cut my dinner, the old landlord with a shining bald head did it for me. This bringing us into conversation, he was so good as to entertain me with my own story—of course with the popular feature that Pumblechook was my earliest benefactor and the founder of my fortunes.

I had never been struck at so keenly for my thanklessness to Joe, as through the brazen impostor Pumblechook. The falser he, the truer Joe; the meaner he, the nobler Joe.

My heart was deeply and most deservedly humbled as I mused over the fire for an hour or more. The striking of the clock aroused me, but not from my dejection or remorse, and I got up and had my coat fastened round

my neck, and went out. I had previously sought in my pockets for the letter, that I might refer to it again, but I could not find it, and was uneasy to think that it must have been dropped in the coach. I knew very well, however, that the appointed place was the little sluice house by the limekiln on the marshes, and the hour nine. Towards the marshes I now went straight, having no time to spare.

Chapter 52

37 It was a dark night, though the full moon rose as I left the enclosed lands, and passed out upon the marshes. Beyond their dark line there was a ribbon of clear sky, hardly broad enough to hold the red large moon.

The direction that I took was not that in which my old home lay, nor that in which we had pursued the convicts. My back was turned towards the distant Hulks as I walked on, and, though I could see the old lights away on the spits of sand, I saw them over my shoulder. I knew the limekiln as well as I knew the old battery, but they were miles apart, so that if a light had been burning at each point that night, there would have been a long strip of the blank horizon between two bright specks.

It was another half-hour before I drew near to the kiln. The lime was burning with a sluggish stifling smell, but the fires were made up and left, and no workmen were visible.

Coming up again to the marsh level out of this excavation, I saw a light in the old sluice house. I quickened my pace, and knocked at the door with my hand. There was no answer, and I knocked again. No answer still, and I tried the latch.

It rose under my hand, and the door yielded. Looking in, I saw a lighted candle on

---

4. ecclesiastical (e klē′ zē as′ ti kəl) *adj.*: Associated with the church.
5. font *n.*: Basin for holy water in a church.

a table, a bench, and a mattress on a truckle bedstead.[1] As there was a loft above, I called, "Is there any one here?" but no voice answered. Then, I looked at my watch, and finding that it was past nine, called again, "Is there any one here?" There being still no answer, I went out at the door, irresolute what to do.

It was beginning to rain fast. Seeing nothing save what I had seen already, I turned back into the house, and stood just within the shelter of the doorway, looking out into the night. While I was considering that some one must have been there lately and must soon be coming back, or the candle would not be burning, it came into my head to look if the wick were long. I turned round to do so, and had taken up the candle in my hand, when it was extinguished by some violent shock, and the next thing I comprehended was that I had been caught in a strong running noose, thrown over my head from behind.

"Now," said a suppressed voice with an oath, "I've got you!"

"What is this?" I cried, struggling. "Who is it? Help, help, help!"

Not only were my arms pulled close to my sides, but the pressure on my bad arm caused me exquisite pain. I struggled ineffectually in the dark, while I was fastened tight to the wall. "And now," said the suppressed voice with another oath, "call out again, and I'll make short work of you!"

After groping about for a little, he found the flint and steel he wanted, and began to strike a light. Presently I saw his blue lips again, breathing on the tinder, and then a flare of light flashed up, and showed me Orlick.

He lighted the candle from the flaring match with great deliberation, and dropped the match, and trod it out. Then, he put the candle away from him on the table, so that he could see me, and sat with his arms folded on the table and looked at me. I made out that I was fastened to a stout perpendicular ladder a few inches from the wall.

"Now," said he, when we had surveyed one another for some time, "I've got you."

"Unbind me. Let me go!"

"Ah!" he returned, "I'll let you go. I'll let you go to the moon, I'll let you go to the stars. All in good time."

"Why have you lured me here?"

"Don't you know?" said he, with a deadly look.

"Why have you set upon me in the dark?"

"Because I mean to do it all myself. One keeps a secret better than two. Oh, you enemy, you enemy!"

As I watched him in silence, he put his hand into the corner at his side, and took up a gun with a brass-bound stock.

"Do you know this?" said he. "Do you know where you saw it afore?"

'Yes," I answered.

"You cost me that place.[2] You did. Speak!"

"What else could I do?"

"You did that, and that would be enough, without more. It was you as always give Old Orlick a bad name.

"What are you going to do to me?"

"I'm a-going," said he, bringing his fist down upon the table with a heavy blow, and rising as the blow fell, to give it greater force, "I'm a-going to have your life!

"More than that, I won't have a rag of you, I won't have a bone of you, left on earth. I'll put your body in the kiln and let people

---

1. **truckle bedstead:** Low bed on wheels that can be rolled underneath another bed.

2. **that place:** His position as watchman for Miss Havisham.

38 **Discussion** Why does Orlick consider himself Pip's enemy?

39 **Clarification** Lime dissolves bone as well as flesh, so there would be no trace of Pip's body if it were put in the limekiln.

suppose what they may of you, they shall never know nothing."

My mind, with inconceivable rapidity, followed out all the consequences of such a death. Estella's father would believe I had deserted him, would be taken, would die accusing me; even Herbert would doubt me. Joe and Biddy would never know how sorry I had been that night, none would ever know what I had suffered, how true I had meant to be, what an agony I had passed through. The death close before me was terrible, but far more terrible than death was the dread of being misremembered after death. And so quick were my thoughts that I saw myself despised by unborn generations—Estella's children, and their children—while the wretch's words were yet on his lips.

"Wolf!" said he, folding his arms, "Old Orlick's a-going to tell you somethink. It was me as did for your shrew sister. I come upon her from behind, as I come upon you tonight. I giv' it her! I left her for dead, and if there had been a limekiln as nigh her as there is now nigh you, she shouldn't have come to life again.

"Wolf, I'll tell you something more," he continued. "It was Old Orlick as you tumbled over on your stairs that night."

I saw the staircase with its extinguished lamps. I saw the shadows of the heavy stair-rails, thrown by the watchman's lantern on the wall. I saw the rooms that I was never to see again, here a door half-open, there a door closed, all the articles of furniture around.

"And why was Old Orlick there? Old Orlick says to himself, 'Somehow or another I'll have him!' What! When I looks for you, I finds your Uncle Provis, eh? And when Old Orlick come for to hear that your Uncle Provis had mostlike wore the leg-iron wot Old Orlick had picked up, filed asunder, on these meshes ever so many year ago, and wot he

kep by him till he dropped your sister with it, like a bullock, as he means to drop you—hey?—when he come for to hear that—hey?—

"Old Orlick knowed you was a-smuggling your Uncle Provis away. Old Orlick's a match for you and know'd you'd come tonight! Now I'll tell you something more, wolf, and this ends it. There's them that's as good a match for your Uncle Provis as Old Orlick has been for you. There's them that can't and that won't have Magwitch—yes, *I* know the name!—alive in the same land with them, and that's had such sure information of him when he was alive in another land, as that he couldn't and shouldn't leave it unbeknown and put them in danger."

There was a clear space of a few feet between the table and the opposite wall. Within this space, he now slouched backwards and forwards. His great strength seemed to sit stronger upon him than ever before, as he did this with his hands hanging loose and heavy at his sides, with his eyes scowling at me. I had no grain of hope left.

I shouted out with all my might, and struggled with all my might. It was only my head and my legs that I could move, but to that extent I struggled with all the force, until then unknown, that was within me. In the same instant I heard responsive shouts, saw figures and a gleam of light dash in at the door, heard voices and tumult, and saw Orlick emerge from a struggle of men, as if it were tumbling water, clear the table at a leap, and fly out into the night!

After a blank, I found that I was lying unbound, on the floor, in the same place, with my head on some one's knee. Too indifferent at first even to look round and ascertain who supported me, I was lying looking at the ladder when there came between me and it, a face. The face of Trabb's boy!

"I think he's all right!" said Trabb's boy, in a sober voice, "but ain't he just pale though!"

At these words, the face of him who supported me looked over into mind, and I saw my supporter to be—

"Herbert! Great Heaven!"

"Softly," said Herbert. "Gently, Handel. Don't be too eager."

"And our old comrade, Startop!" I cried, as he too bent over me.

"Remember what he is going to assist us in," said Herbert, "and be calm."

The allusion made me spring up, though I dropped again from the pain in my arm. "The time has not gone by, Herbert, has it? What night is tonight? How long have I been here?" For, I had a strange and strong misgiving that I had been lying there a long time—a day and a night—two days and nights—more.

"The time has not gone by. It is still Monday night."

"Thank God!"

"And you have all tomorrow, Tuesday, to rest in," said Herbert. "But you can't help groaning, my dear Handel. What hurt have you got? Can you stand?"

"Yes, yes," said I, "I can walk. I have no hurt but in this throbbing arm."

Entreating Herbert to tell me how he had come to my rescue, I learned that I had in my hurry dropped the letter, open, in our chambers, where he, coming home to bring with him Startop, whom he had met in the street on his way to me, found it very soon after I was gone. Its tone made him uneasy, so he set off for the coach office with Startop to make inquiry when the next coach went down. Finding that the afternoon coach was gone, and finding that his uneasiness grew into positive alarm, as obstacles came in his way, he resolved to follow in a post-chaise.

So he and Startop arrived at the Blue Boar, fully expecting there to find me, or tidings of me but finding neither. Among the loungers under the Boar's archway happened to be Trabb's boy, and Trabb's boy had seen me passing from Miss Havisham's in the direction of my dining place. Thus, Trabb's boy became their guide.

When I told Herbert what had passed within the house, he was for our immediately going before a magistrate in the town, late at night as it was, and getting out a warrant. But I had already considered that such a course, by detaining us there, or binding us to come back, might be fatal to Provis.

Wednesday being so close upon us, we determined to go back to London that night, three in the post-chaise. It was daylight when we reached the Temple, and I went at once to bed, and lay in bed all day.

They kept me very quiet all day, and kept my arm constantly dressed, and gave me cooling drinks. About midnight I got out of bed and went to Herbert, with the conviction that I had been asleep for four-and-twenty hours, and that Wednesday was past. It was the last self-exhausting effort of my fretfulness, for after that I slept soundly.

Wednesday morning was dawning when I looked out of window. The winking lights upon the bridges were already pale, the coming sun was like a marsh of fire on the horizon. The river, still dark and mysterious, was spanned by bridges that were turning coldly gray. As I looked along the clustered roofs, with church towers and spires shooting into the unusually clear air, the sun rose up, and a veil seemed to be drawn from the river, and millions of sparkles burst out upon its waters. From me, too, a veil seemed to be drawn, and I felt strong and well.

Herbert lay asleep in his bed, and our old fellow-student lay asleep on the sofa. I could

41

41 **Discussion** How do Pip's injury and exhaustion add to the suspense of the attempt to rescue Provis?

THE YORK-LONDON MAIL COACH
Gilbert S. Wright
© *Three Lions*

not dress myself without help, but I made up the fire which was still burning, and got some coffee ready for them. In good time they too started up strong and well, and we admitted the sharp morning air at the windows, and looked at the tide that was still flowing towards us.

"When it turns at nine o'clock," said Herbert cheerfully, "look out for us, and stand ready, you over there at Mill Pond Bank!"

Chapter 53

It was one of those March days when the sun shines hot and the wind blows cold—when it is summer in the light, and winter in the shade. We had our peacoats[1] with us, and I took a bag. Of all my worldly posses-

---

1. **peacoats** (pē′ kōts′) *n.:* Heavy woolen jackets, often worn by sailors.

sions I took no more than the few necessaries that filled the bag. Where I might go, what I might do, or when I might return were questions utterly unknown to me.

We loitered down to the Temple stairs. Of course I had taken care that the boat should be ready, and everything in order. After a little show of indecision, we went on board and cast off. It was then about high water—half-past eight.

Our plan was this. The tide beginning to run down at nine, and being with us until three, we intended still to creep on after it had turned, and row against it until dark. We should then be well in those long reaches below Gravesend, where lone public houses are scattered here and there, of which we could choose one for a resting-place. There we meant to lie all night. The steamer for Hamburg, and the steamer for Rotterdam,[2] would start from London at about nine on Thursday morning. We should know at what time to expect them, according to where we were, and would hail the first, so that if by any accident we were not taken aboard, we should have another chance.

Old London Bridge was soon passed, and old Billingsgate market with its oyster boats and Dutchmen, and the White Tower and Traitor's Gate, and we were in among the tiers of shipping. And now, I, sitting in the stern,[3] could see with a faster beating heart Mill Pond Bank and Mill Pond stairs.

"Is he there?" said Herbert.

"Not yet."

"Right! He was not to come down till he saw us. Can you see his signal?"

"Not well from here; but I think I see it. Now I see him! Pull both. Easy, Herbert. Oars!"

We touched the stairs lightly for a single moment, and he was on board and we were off again. He had a boat-cloak with him, and a black canvas bag, and he looked as like a river pilot[4] as my heart could have wished.

"Dear boy!" he said, putting his arm on my shoulder, as he took his seat. "Faithful dear boy, well done. Thankye, thankye!"

The air felt cold upon the river, but it was a bright day, and the sunshine was very cheering. The tide ran strong, I took care to lose none of it, and our steady stroke carried us on thoroughly well. By imperceptible degrees, as the tide ran out, we lost more and more of the nearer woods and hills, and dropped lower and lower between the muddy banks, but the tide was yet with us when we were off Gravesend.

Our oarsmen were so fresh, by dint of having occasionally let her drive with the tide for a minute or two, that a quarter of an hour's rest proved full as much as they wanted. We got ashore among some slippery stones while we ate and drank what we had with us, and looked about. It was like my own marsh country, flat and monotonous, and with a dim horizon.

We pushed off again, and made what way we could. It was much harder work now, but Herbert and Startop persevered, and rowed, and rowed, and rowed, until the sun went down.

As the night was fast falling, and as the moon, being past the full, would not rise early, we held a little council—a short one, for clearly our course was to lie by at the first lonely tavern we could find. So they plied

---

2. Rotterdam (rät′ ər dam′): Seaport in the Netherlands.

3. stern *n*.: Rear end of the boat.

4. river pilot: Person who directs or steers ships on a river.

42 Discussion Have students discuss or list the items *they* would pack in a bag if they were going abroad for an indefinite stay.

43 Discussion Do you think their plan is a good one? Explain.

44 Discussion Why do you think Provis selected this particular costume?

45 Discussion What news do Pip, Herbert, Provis, and Startop hear that increases their uneasiness?

their oars once more, and I looked out for anything like a house. Thus we held on, speaking little, for four or five dull miles.

At this dismal time we were evidently all possessed by the idea that we were followed. As the tide made, it flapped heavily at irregular intervals against the shore; and whenever such a sound came, one or other of us was sure to start and look in that direction.

At length we descried a light and a roof, and presently afterwards ran alongside a little causeway[5] made of stones that had been picked up hard by. Leaving the rest in the boat, I stepped ashore, and found the light to be in the window of a public house. It was a dirty place enough, and I dare say not unknown to smuggling adventures, but there was a good fire in the kitchen, and there were eggs and bacon to eat. No other company was in the house than the landlord, his wife, and a grizzled male creature, the "jack"[6] of the little causeway.

With this assistant, I went down to the boat again, and we all came ashore, and brought out the oars, and rudder, and boathook, and all else, and hauled her up for the night.

While we were comforting ourselves by the fire after our meal, the jack asked me if we had seen a four-oared galley[7] going up with the tide. When I told him no, he said she must have gone down then, and yet she "took up too," when she left there.

"They must ha' thought better on't for some reason or another," said the Jack, "and gone down."

"A four-oared galley did you say?" said I.

"A four," said the Jack, "and two sitters."

"He thinks," said the landlord, "he thinks they was what they wasn't."

"*I* knows what I thinks," observed the jack.

"*You* thinks custom-'us,[8] Jack?" said the landlord.

"I do," said the Jack.

"Why, what do you make out that they done with their buttons, then, Jack?" asked the landlord.

"A custom-'us officer knows what to do with his buttons," said the jack. "A four and two sitters don't go hanging and hovering, up with one tide and down with another, and both with and against another, without there being custom-'us at the bottom of it."

This dialogue made us all uneasy, and me very uneasy. A four-oared galley hovering about in so unusual a way as to attract this notice was an ugly circumstance that I could not get rid of. When I had induced Provis to go up to bed, I went outside with my two companions (Startop by this time knew the state of the case), and held another council. We decided to lie where we were, until within an hour or so of the steamer's time, and then to get out in her track, and drift easily with the tide. Having settled to do this, we returned into the house and went to bed.

When I awoke, the wind had risen, and the sign of the house (the Ship) was creaking and banging about, with noises that startled me. Rising softly, for my charge lay fast asleep, I looked out of the window. It commanded the causeway where we had hauled up our boat, and, as my eyes adapted themselves to the light of the clouded moon, I saw two men looking into her. They passed by under the window, looking at nothing else, and struck across the marsh in the direction of the Nore.

---

5. causeway (kôz' wā) *n.*: Raised path or road across wet ground.
6. "jack": Sailor.
7. galley (gal' ē) *n.*: Large rowboat.

---

8. custom-'us: Customs officers, who inspect passengers and goods entering or leaving the country.

888 *The Novel*

My first impulse was to call up Herbert, and show him the two men going away. But, reflecting that he and Startop had had a harder day than I, and were fatigued, I forbore. Going back to my window, I could see the two men moving over the marsh. In that light, however, I soon lost them, and feeling very cold, lay down to think of the matter, and fell asleep again.

We were up early. As we walked to and fro, all four together, before breakfast, I deemed it right to recount what I had seen. I proposed that Provis and I should walk away together to a distant point we could see, and that the boat should take us aboard there.

We got aboard easily, and rowed out into the track of the steamer. By that time it wanted but ten minutes of one o'clock, and we began to look out for her smoke.

But it was half-past one before we saw her smoke, and soon after we saw behind it the smoke of another steamer. As they were coming on at full speed, we got the two bags ready, and took that opportunity of saying good-bye to Herbert and Startop. We had all shaken hands cordially, and neither Herbert's eyes nor mine were quite dry, when I saw a four-oared galley shoot out from under the bank but a little way ahead of us, and row out into the same track.

A stretch of shore had been as yet between us and the steamer's smoke, by reason of the bend and wind of the river; but now she was visible coming head on. I called to Herbert and Startop to keep before the tide, that she might see us lying by for her, and adjured Provis to sit quite still, wrapped in his cloak. He answered cheerily, "Trust to me, dear boy," and sat like a statue. Meantime the galley, which was skilfully handled, had crossed us, let us come up with her, and fallen alongside. Leaving just room enough for the play of the oars, she kept alongside, drifting when we drifted, and pulling a stroke or two when we pulled. Of the two sitters, one held the rudder lines, and looked at us attentively—as did all the rowers; the other sitter was wrapped up, much as Provis was, and seemed to shrink, and whisper some instruction to the steerer as he looked at us. Not a word was spoken in either boat.

Startop could make out, after a few minutes, which steamer was first, and gave me the word "Hamburg," in a low voice as we sat face to face. She was nearing us very fast, and the beating of her paddles grew louder and louder. I felt as if her shadow were absolutely upon us, when the galley hailed us. I answered.

"You have a returned transport there," said the man who held the lines. "That's the man, wrapped in the cloak. His name is Abel Magwitch, otherwise Provis. I apprehend that man, and call upon him to surrender, and you to assist."

At the same moment, without giving any audible direction to the crew, he ran the galley aboard of us. They had pulled one sudden stroke ahead, had got their oars in, had run athwart us, and were holding on to our gunwale,[9] before we knew what they were doing. This caused great confusion on board of the steamer, and I heard them calling to us, and heard the order given to stop the paddles, and heard them stop, but felt her driving down upon us irresistibly. In the same moment, I saw the steersman of the galley lay his hand on his prisoner's shoulder, and saw that both boats were swinging round with the force of the tide, and saw that all hands on board the steamer were running forward quite frantically. Still in the same moment, I saw the prisoner start up, lean across his captor, and pull the cloak from the neck of the shrinking sitter in the galley.

_____

9. gunwale (gun'l) _n._: Upper edge of the side of a boat.

46 **Discussion** How does Dickens heighten the suspense of this moment?

47 Discussion Why does Magwitch swim back to the boat when he might have escaped?

48 Discussion Do you believe this account of events? Explain.

Still in the same moment, I saw that the face disclosed was the face of the other convict of long ago. Still in the same moment, I saw the face tilt backward with a white terror on it that I shall never forget, and heard a great cry on board the steamer and a loud splash in the water, and felt the boat sink from under me.

It was but for an instant that I seemed to struggle with a thousand mill-weirs[10] and a thousand flashes of light; that instant passed, I was taken on board the galley. Herbert was there, and Startop was there, but our boat was gone, and the two convicts were gone.

What with the cries aboard the steamer, and the furious blowing off of her steam, and her driving on, and our driving on, I could not at first distinguish sky from water or shore from shore; but the crew of the galley righted her with great speed, and, pulling certain swift strong strokes ahead, lay upon their oars, every man looking silently and eagerly at the water astern. Presently a dark object was seen in it, bearing towards us on the tide. No man spoke, but the steersman held up his hand, and all softly backed water, and kept the boat straight and true before it. As it came nearer, I saw it to be Magwitch, swimming, but not swimming freely. He was taken on board, and instantly manacled at the wrists and ankles.

The galley was kept steady, and the silent eager look-out at the water was resumed. But the Rotterdam steamer now came up, and apparently not understanding what had happened, came on at speed. By the time she had been hailed and stopped, both steamers were drifting away from us, and we were rising and falling in a troubled wake of water. The look-out was kept, long after all

10. **mill-weirs** (mil′ wirz′) *n.*: Low dams to back up or divert water for a mill.

was still again and the two steamers were gone, but everybody knew that it was hopeless now.

At length we gave it up, and pulled under the shore towards the tavern we had lately left, where we were received with no little surprise. Here I was able to get some comforts for Magwitch—Provis no longer—who had received some very severe injury in the chest and a deep cut in the head.

He told me that he believed himself to have gone under the keel of the steamer, and to have been struck on the head in rising. The injury to his chest (which rendered his breathing extremely painful) he thought he had received against the side of the galley. He added that he did not pretend to say what he might or might not have done to Compeyson, but, in that moment of his laying his hand on his cloak to identify him, that villain had staggered up and staggered back, and they had both gone overboard together; when the sudden wrenching of him (Magwitch) out of our boat, and the endeavor of his captor to keep him in it, had capsized us. He told me in a whisper that they had gone down, fiercely locked in each other's arms, and that there had been a struggle under water, and that he had disengaged himself, struck out, and swam away.

I never had any reason to doubt the exact truth of what he had told me. The officer who steered the galley gave the same account of their going overboard.

When I asked this officer's permission to change the prisoner's wet clothes, he gave it readily, merely observing that he must take charge of everything his prisoner had about him. So the pocketbook which had once been in my hands passed into the officer's. He further gave me leave to accompany the prisoner to London.

We remained at the public house until the tide turned, and then Magwitch was car-

890 *The Novel*

ried down to the galley and put on board. Herbert and Startop were to get to London by land, as soon as they could. We had a doleful parting, and when I took my place by Magwitch's side, I felt that that was my place henceforth while he lived.

For now my repugnance to him had all melted away, and in the hunted wounded shackled creature who held my hand in his, I only saw a man who had meant to be my benefactor, and who had felt affectionately, gratefully, and generously towards me with great constancy through a series of years. I only saw in him a much better man than I had been to Joe.

His breathing became more difficult and painful as the night drew on, and often he could not repress a groan. I tried to rest him on the arm I could use, in any easy position, but it was dreadful to think that I could not be sorry at heart for his being badly hurt, since it was unquestionably best that he should die.

As we returned towards the setting sun we had yesterday left behind us, and as the stream of our hopes seemed all running back, I told him how grieved I was to think he had come home for my sake.

"Dear boy," he answered, "I'm quite content to take my chance. I've seen my boy, and he can be a gentleman without me."

No. I had thought about that while we had been there side by side. No. Apart from any inclinations of my own, I understand Wemmick's hint now. I foresaw that, being convicted, his possessions would be forfeited to the Crown.[11]

"Lookee here, dear boy," said he. "It's best as a gentleman should not be knowed to belong to me now. Only come to see me as if

11. **forfeited to the Crown:** Seized by the government.

you come by chance alonger Wemmick. Sit where I can see you when I am swore to, for the last o' many times, and I don't ask no more."

"I will never stir from your side," said I, "when I am suffered to be near you."

I felt his hand tremble as it held mine, and he turned his face away as he lay in the bottom of the boat, and I heard that old sound in his throat—softened now, like all the rest of him. It was a good thing that he had touched this point, for it put into my mind what I might not otherwise have thought of until too late: that he need never know how his hopes of enriching me had perished.

Chapter 54

He was taken to the police court next day, and would have been immediately committed for trial but that it was necessary to send down for an old officer of the prison ship from which he had once escaped, to speak to his identity. Nobody doubted it; but Compeyson, who had meant to depose to it, was tumbling on the tides, dead, and it happened that there was not at that time any prison officer in London who could give the required evidence. I had gone direct to Mr. Jaggers at his private house, on my arrival over night, to retain his assistance, and Mr. Jaggers on the prisoner's behalf would admit nothing. It was the sole resource, for he told me that the case must be over in five minutes when the witness was there, and that no power on earth could prevent its going against us.

I imparted to Mr. Jaggers my design of keeping him in ignorance of the fate of his wealth. Mr. Jaggers was querulous and angry with me for having "let it slip through my fingers," and said we must memorialize

to regard them as human; his heart could explain them only as monsters. The evil that they did he fought with unwavering hostility, attacking them with the weapons of caricature and burlesque, or melodrama and unabashed sentiment. His spontaneous sympathy with the fruitful and the creative enabled him to understand how human nature was crippled by exploitation and selfishness, and he fought his way steadily to an understanding of all those dark forces in society that blight men's health and happiness. The great roll call of Dickens's work on every page is a celebration of the true wealth of life.

49 **Discussion** How has Pip's attitude toward Magwitch changed?

50 **Literary Focus** Why does Pip think it better that Magwitch not know that his dream has "perished"? How does Pip's attitude reflect the theme of the novel?

51 **Discussion** Why does Mr. Jaggers tell Pip that no power on earth can save Magwitch from a sentence of death?

by-and-by, and try at all events for some of it. But he did not conceal from me that although there might be many cases in which forfeiture would not be exacted, there were no circumstances in this case to make it one of them.

There appeared to be reason for supposing that the drowned informer had hoped for a reward out of this forfeiture, and had obtained some accurate knowledge of Magwitch's affairs. When his body was found, many miles from the scene of his death, and so horribly disfigured that he was only recognizable by the contents of his pockets, notes were still legible, folded in a case he carried. Among these were the name of a banking house in New South Wales where a sum of money was, and the designation of certain lands of considerable value. Both those heads of information were in a list that Magwitch, while in prison, gave to Mr. Jaggers, of the possessions he supposed I should inherit. His ignorance, poor fellow, at last served him; he never mistrusted but that my inheritance was quite safe, with Mr. Jaggers's aid.

After three days' delay, the witness came, and completed the easy case. He was committed to take his trial at the next session, which would come on in a month.

It was at this dark time of my life that Herbert returned home one evening, a good deal cast down, and said:

"My dear Handel, I fear I shall soon have to leave you."

His partner having prepared me for that, I was less surpised than he thought.

"We shall lose a fine opportunity if I put off going to Cairo,[1] and I am very much afraid I must go, Handel, when you most need me."

---

1. **Cairo** (kī′ rō): Capital of Egypt.

"Herbert, I shall always need you, because I shall always love you, but my need is no greater now than at another time."

"My dear fellow," said Herbert, "let the near prospect of our separation—for, it is very near—be my justification for troubling you about yourself. Have you thought of your future?"

"No, for I have been afraid to think of any future."

"But yours cannot be dismissed; indeed, my dear, dear Handel, it must not be dismissed. I wish you would enter on it now, as far as a few friendly words go, with me."

"I will," said I.

"In this branch-house of ours, Handel, we must have a—"

I saw that his delicacy was avoiding the right word, so I said, "A clerk."

"A clerk. And I hope it is not at all unlikely that he may expand (as a clerk of your acquaintance has expanded) into a partner. Now, Handel—in short, my dear boy, will you come to me?"

I thanked him heartily, but said I could not yet make sure of joining him as he so kindly offered.

"But if you thought, Herbert, that you could, without doing any injury to your business, leave the question open for a little while—"

"For any while," cried Herbert. "Six months, a year!"

"Not so long as that," said I. "Two or three months at most."

Herbert was highly delighted when we shook hands on this arrangement, and said he could now take courage to tell me that he believed he must go away at the end of the week.

On the Saturday in that same week, I took my leave of Herbert—full of bright hope, but sad and sorry to leave me—as he sat on one of the seaport mail coaches.

Back at the Temple, I encountered Wemmick, who was coming down, after an unsuccessful application of his knuckles to my door. I had not seen him alone since the disastrous issue of the attempted flight, and he had come, in his private and personal capacity, to say a few words of explanation in reference to that failure.

"The late Compeyson," said Wemmick, "had by little and little got at the bottom of half of the regular business now transacted, and it was from the talk of some of his people in trouble that I heard what I did. I kept my ears open, seeming to have them shut, until I heard that he was absent, and I thought that would be the best time for making the attempt. I can only suppose now that it was a part of his policy, as a very clever man, habitually to deceive his own instruments. You don't blame me, I hope, Mr. Pip? I'm sure I tried to serve you, with all my heart."

"I am as sure of that, Wemmick, as you can be, and I thank you most earnestly for all your interest and friendship."

"Thank you, thank you very much. It's a bad job," said Wemmick, scratching his head, "and I assure you I haven't been so cut up for a long time. What I look at is the sacrifice of so much portable property. Dear me!"

"What _I_ think of, Wemmick, is the poor owner of the property."

"Yes, to be sure," said Wemmick. "Of course there can be no objection to your being sorry for him, and I'd put down a five-pound note myself to get him out of it. But what I look at is this. The late Compeyson having been beforehand with him in intelligence of his return, and being so determined to bring him to book, I do not think he could have been saved. Whereas the portable property certainly could have been saved. That's the difference between the property and the owner, don't you see?"

Chapter 55

He lay in prison very ill, during the whole interval between his committal for trial, and the coming round of the sessions. He had broken two ribs, they had wounded one of his lungs, and he breathed with great pain and difficulty, which increased daily.

Being far too ill to remain in the common prison, he was removed, after the first day or so, into the infirmary. This gave me opportunities of being with him that I could not otherwise have had.

The trial was very short and very clear. Such things as could be said for him were said—how he had taken to industrious habits, and had thriven lawfully and reputably. But nothing could unsay the fact that he had returned, and was there in presence of the judge and jury. It was impossible to try him for that, and do otherwise than find him guilty.

At that time it was the custom to devote a concluding day to the passing of sentences, and to make a finishing effect with the sentence of death. But for the indelible picture that my remembrance now holds before me, I could scarcely believe that I saw two-and-thirty men and women put before the judge to receive that sentence together.

Among the wretched creatures before the judge whom he must single out for special address was one who almost from his infancy had been an offender against the laws; who, after repeated imprisonments and punishments, had been at length sentenced to exile for a term of years; and who, under circumstances of great violence and daring, had made his escape and been resentenced to exile for life. That miserable man would seem for a time to have become convinced of his errors, when far removed from the scenes of his old offenses, and to have lived a peaceable and honest life. But in a fatal

54 **Discussion** How do Wemmick's thoughts contrast with Pip's?

55 **Discussion** What is the effect of summarizing Magwitch's life in terms that the judge uses? Compare and contrast this summary with your own knowledge of his life.

56 **Discussion** In his reply to the court, what character trait does Magwitch reveal?

57 **Discussion** Why does Pip pray that Magwitch will die?

56

moment, he had quitted his haven of rest and repentance, and had come back to the country where he was proscribed.[1] The appointed punishment for his return to the land that had cast him out being death, and his case being this aggravated case, he must prepare himself to die. Rising for a moment, a distinct speck of face in this way of light, the prisoner said, "My Lord, I have received my sentence of death from the Almighty, but I bow to yours," and sat down again.

57

I earnestly hoped and prayed that he might die before the recorder's report was made, but, in the dread of his lingering on, I began that night to write out a petition to the Home Secretary of State, setting forth my knowledge of him, and how it was that he had come back for my sake. I wrote it as fervently and pathetically as I could, and when I had finished it and sent it in, I wrote out other petitions to such men in authority as I hoped were the most merciful, and drew up one to the Crown itself. For several days and nights after he was sentenced I took no rest, except when I fell asleep in my chair, but was wholly absorbed in these appeals.

The daily visits I could make him were shortened now, and he was more strictly kept. The officer always gave me the assurance that he was worse, and some other sick prisoners in the room always joined in the same report.

As the days went on, I noticed more and more that he would lie placidly looking at the white ceiling, with an absence of light in his face, until some word of mine brightened it for an instant, and then it would subside again.

The number of the days had risen to ten, when I saw a greater change in him than I had seen yet. His eyes were turned towards the door, and lighted up as I entered.

---

1. **proscribed** (prō skrīb'd') *v*.: Banished.

"Dear boy," he said, as I sat down by his bed: "I thought you was late. But I knowed you couldn't be that."

"It is just the time," said I. "I waited for it at the gate."

"You always waits at the gate, don't you, dear boy?"

"Yes. Not to lose a moment of the time."

"Thank'ee, dear boy, thank'ee. God bless you! You've never deserted me, dear boy."

I pressed his hand in silence, for I could not forget that I had once meant to desert him.

"Are you in much pain today?"

"I don't complain of none, dear boy."

"You never do complain."

He had spoken his last words. He smiled, and I understood his touch to mean that he wished to lift my hand, and lay it on his breast. I laid it there, and he smiled again, and put both his hands upon it.

The allotted time ran out, while we were thus; but, looking round, I found the governor of the prison standing near me, and he whispered, "You needn't go yet." I thanked him gratefully, and asked, "Might I speak to him, if he can hear me?"

The governor stepped aside, and beckoned the officer away. The change, though it was made without noise, drew back the film from the placid look at the white ceiling, and he looked most affectionately at me.

"Dear Magwitch, I must tell you, now at last. You understand what I say?"

A gentle pressure on my hand.

"You had a child once, whom you loved and lost."

A stronger pressure on my hand.

"She lived and found powerful friends. She is living now. She is a lady and very beautiful. And I love her!"

With a last faint effort, which would have been powerless but for my yielding to it, and assisting it, he raised my hand to his lips.

Then he gently let it sink upon his breast again, with his own hands lying on it. The placid look at the white ceiling came back, and passed away, and his head dropped quietly on his breast.

Chapter 56

Now that I was left wholly to myself, I gave notice of my intention to quit the chambers in the Temple as soon as my tenancy could legally determine, and in the meanwhile to underlet them.[1] I was in debt, and had scarcely any money, and began to be seriously alarmed by the state of my affairs. I ought rather to write that I should have been alarmed if I had had energy and concentration enough to help me to the clear perception of any truth beyond the fact that I was falling very ill.

For a day or two, I lay on the sofa, or on the floor—anywhere, according as I happened to sink down—with a heavy head and aching limbs, and no purpose, and no power. Then there came one night which appeared of great duration, and which teemed with anxiety and horror; and when in the morning I tried to sit up in my bed and think of it, I found I could not do so.

Whether I really had been down in Garden Court in the dead of the night, groping about for the boat that I supposed to be there; whether I had two or three times come to myself on the staircase with great terror, not knowing how I had got out of bed; whether I had been inexpressibly harassed by the distracted talking, laughing, and groaning of some one, and had half-suspected those sounds to be of my own making; whether there had been a closed iron furnace in a dark corner of the room, and a voice had called out over and over again that Miss Havisham was within it; these were things that I tried to settle with myself and get into some order, as I lay that morning on my bed. But the vapor of a lime-kiln would come between me and them, disordering them all, and it was through the vapor at last that I saw two men looking at me.

"What do you want?" I asked, starting; "I don't know you."

"Well, sir," returned one of them, "this is a matter that you'll soon arrange, I dare say, but you're arrested."

"What is the debt?"

"Hundred and twenty-three pound, fifteen, six. Jeweler's account, I think."

"What is to be done?"

"You had better come to my house," said the man. "I keep a very nice house."

I made some attempt to get up and dress myself. When I next attended to them, they were standing a little off from the bed, looking at me. I still lay there.

"You see my state," said I. "I would come with you if I could; but indeed I am quite unable. If you take me from here, I think I shall die by the way."

Perhaps they replied, or argued the point, or tried to encourage me to believe that I was better than I thought. Forasmuch as they hang in my memory by only this one slender thread, I don't know what they did, except that they forbore to remove me.

After I had turned the worse point of my illness, I began to notice that while all its other features changed, this one consistent feature did not change. Whoever came about me, settled down into Joe. I opened my eyes in the night, and I saw in the great chair at the bedside, Joe. I opened my eyes in the day, and, sitting on the window seat, still I saw Joe. I asked for cooling drink, and the

---

1. **gave ... underlet them:** Gave notice that I would leave my apartment as soon as the lease could be terminated, and in the meantime, sublet my rooms.

Great Expectations 895

58 **Discussion** What is the relationship between Pip and Magwitch at the end of Magwitch's life?

59 **Discussion** What episodes from Pip's past are incorporated into his hallucinations?

Humanities Note

Fine art, *Waiting for the Verdict*, 1857, by Abraham Solomon. Abraham Solomon (1824–1862) was a British painter of the Victorian era who specialized in anecdotal subjects.

A student of the Royal Academy, Solomon exhibited *Waiting for the Verdict* there in 1857. This intense and pathetic portrayal of a family awaiting the result of an accused son's trial was very well received by the public. *Waiting for the Verdict*, together with its sequel *Not Guilty*, established Solomon's reputation as a narrative painter.

You might want to use the following questions to prompt a discussion:
1. What story does this painting suggest?
2. How is this painting a good accompaniment to this section of the novel?

WAITING FOR THE VERDICT, 1857
Abraham Solomon
From the collection of Barbara and Norman S. Namerow,
Beverly Hills, California

dear hand that gave it me was Joe's. I sank back on my pillow after drinking, and the face that looked so hopefully and tenderly upon me was the face of Joe.

At last, one day, I took courage, and said, "*Is* it Joe?"

And the dear old home-voice answered, "Which it air, old chap."

"Oh, Joe, you break my heart! Look angry at me, Joe. Strike me, Joe. Tell me of my ingratitude. Don't be so good to me!"

For Joe had actually laid his head down on the pillow at my side, and put his arm round my neck, in his joy that I knew him.

"Which dear old Pip, old chap," said Joe, "you and me was ever friends. And when you're well enough to go out for a ride—what larks!"

After which, Joe withdrew to the window, and stood with his back towards me, wiping his eyes. And as my extreme weakness prevented me from getting up and going to him, I lay there, penitently whispering, "O God bless him! O God bless this gentle Christian man!"

Joe's eyes were red when I next found him beside me, but I was holding his hand and we both felt happy.

"How long, dear Joe?"

"Which you meantersay, Pip, how long have your illness lasted, dear old chap?"

"Yes, Joe."

"It's the end of May, Pip. Tomorrow is the first of June."

"And have you been here all the time, dear Joe?"

"Pretty nigh, old chap. For, as I says to Biddy when the news of your being ill were brought by letter, which it were brought by the post that how you might be amongst strangers, and that how you and me having been ever friends, a wisit at such a moment might not prove unacceptabobble. And Biddy, her word were, 'Go to him, without loss of time.' That," said Joe, summing up with his judicial air, "were the word of Biddy. 'Go to him,' Biddy say, 'without loss of time.' "

There Joe cut himself short, and informed me that I was to be talked to in great moderation, and that I was to take a little nourishment at stated frequent times, whether I felt inclined for it or not, and that I was to submit myself to all his orders. So I kissed his hand, and lay quiet, while he proceeded to indite a note to Biddy, with my love in it.

Evidently Biddy had taught Joe to write. As I lay in bed looking at him, it made me, in my weak state, cry again with pleasure to see the pride with which he set about his letter.

Not to make Joe uneasy by talking too much, even if I had been able to talk much, I deferred asking him about Miss Havisham until next day. He shook his head when I then asked him if she had recovered.

"Is she dead, Joe?"

"Why, you see, old chap," said Joe, "I wouldn't go so far as to say that, for that's a deal to say; but she ain't living."

"Dear Joe, have you heard what becomes of her property?"

"Well, old chap," said Joe, "it do appear that she had settled the most of it, which I meantersay tied it up, on Miss Estella. But she had wrote out a little coddleshell[2] in her own hand a day or two afore the accident, leaving a cool four thousand to Mr. Matthew Pocket. And why, do you suppose, above all things, Pip, she left that cool four thousand unto him? 'Because of Pip's account of him the said Matthew.' I am told by Biddy that air the writing," said Joe, repeating the legal turn as if it did him infinite good, " 'account of him the said Matthew.' And a cool four thousand, Pip!"

This account gave me great joy, as it perfected the only good thing I had done.

"And now," said Joe, "you ain't that strong yet, old chap, that you can take in more nor one additional shovel-full today. Old Orlick he's been a-bustin' open a dwelling'ouse."

"Whose?" said I.

"Not, I grant you, but what his manners is given to blusterous," said Joe apologetically; "still, a Englishman's 'ouse is his castle, and castles must not be busted 'cept when done in wartime. And wotsome'er the failings on his part, he were a corn and seedsman in his hart."

---

2. coddleshell: Joe means codicil (käd' i s'l), an addition to a will.

60 Discussion How does Joe help restore Pip to life after the worst of his illness has passed? In what way is Joe unchanged?

61 Discussion Why does Matthew Pocket's good fortune make Pip so happy?

62 Discussion How has Uncle Pumblechook met with misfortune?

63 Discussion What is significant about this particular memory?

64 Discussion As Pip's health improves and as he becomes stronger, what change does he notice in Joe's attitude toward him? How does the change affect Pip?

62 "Is it Pumblechook's house that has been broken into, then?"

"That's it, Pip," said Joe: "and they took his till, and they took his cashbox, and they slapped his face, and they pulled his nose, and they tied him up to his bed-pust. But he knowed Orlick, and Orlick's in the county jail."

We looked forward to the day when I should go out for a ride, as we had once looked forward to the day of my apprenticeship. And when the day came, and an open carriage was got into the lane, Joe wrapped me up, took me in his arms, carried me down to it, and put me in, as if I were still the small helpless creature to whom he had so abundantly given of the wealth of his great nature.

And Joe got in beside me, and we drove away together into the country, where the rich summer growth was already on the trees and on the grass, and sweet summer scents filled all the air.

63 When we got back again and he lifted me out, and carried me—so easily!—across the court and up the stairs, I thought of that eventful Christmas Day when he had carried me over the marshes. We had not yet made any allusion to my change of fortune, nor did I know how much of my late history he was acquainted with. I was so doubtful of myself now, and put so much trust in him, that I could not satisfy myself whether I ought to refer to it when he did not.

"Have you heard, Joe," I asked him that evening, upon further consideration, "who my patron was?"

"I heerd," returned Joe, "as it were not Miss Havisham, old chap."

"Did you hear who it was, Joe?"

"Well! I heerd as it were a person what sent the person what giv' you the banknotes at the Jolly Bargemen, Pip."

"So it was."

"Astonishing!" said Joe, in the placidest way.

"Did you hear that he was dead, Joe?" I presently asked, with increasing diffidence.

"I think," said Joe, after meditating a long time, and looking rather evasively at the window-seat, "as I *did* hear tell that how he were something or another in a general way in that direction."

"Did you hear anything of his circumstances, Joe?"

"Not partickler, Pip."

"If you would like to hear, Joe—" I was beginning, when Joe got up and came to my sofa.

"Look'ee here, old chap," said Joe, bending over me. "Ever the best of friends; ain't us, Pip?"

I was ashamed to answer him.

"Werry good, then," said Joe, as if I *had* answered; "that's all right; that's agreed upon. Then why go into subjects, old chap, which as betwixt two sech must be for ever onnecessary?"

Another thing in Joe that I could not understand when it first began to develop itself, but which I soon arrived at a sorrowful comprehension of, was this: as I became stronger and better, Joe became a little less easy with me.

6 It was on the third or fourth occasion of my going out walking in the Temple gardens, leaning on Joe's arm, that I saw this change in him very plainly. We had been sitting in the bright warm sunlight, looking at the river, and I chanced to say as we got up:

"See, Joe! I can walk quite strongly. Now, you shall see me walk back by myself."

"Which do not overdo it, Pip," said Joe; "but I shall be happy fur to see you able, sir."

The last word grated on me, but how could I remonstrate! I walked no further

Grammar in Action

Think of how awkward writing and speaking would be if we had to always refer to something by its name. To avoid that, writers will use pronouns that refer to the noun previously mentioned. A **referent** is the person, thing, idea, or condition to which a word refers. Referents must agree with the noun to which it refers in gender and number. Look at the lines from the novel:

"Is it Pumblechook's house that has been broken into, then?"

"That's it, Pip," said Joe, "and they took his till, and they took his cashbox, and they slapped his face, and they pulled his nose, and they tied him to his bed-post."

The referents of pronouns may be at times difficult to figure out. Context can help determine for what each pronoun stands. In this passage, *it* in the first sentence has its referent, *house,* in that sentence. When Joe uses *it* in the second sentence, he refers to the entire statement that Pip has just made. In Joe's statement, to whom does *they* refer? To whom does *he* refer?

than the gate of the gardens, and then pretended to be weaker than I was, and asked Joe for his arm. Joe gave it me, but was thoughtful.

It was a thoughtful evening with both of us. But before we went to bed, I had resolved that I would wait over tomorrow, tomorrow being Sunday, and would begin my new course with the new week. On Monday morning I would speak to Joe about this change, I would lay aside this last vestige of reserve, I would tell him what I had in my thoughts (that secondly, not yet arrived at), and why I had not decided to go out to Herbert, and then the change would be conquered for ever.

We had a quiet day on the Sunday, and we rode out into the country, and then walked in the fields.

"I feel thankful that I have been ill, Joe," I said.

"Dear old Pip, old chap, you're a'most come round, sir."

"It has been a memorable time for me, Joe."

"Likeways for myself, sir," Joe returned.

"We have had a time together, Joe, that I can never forget. There were days once, I know, that I did for a while forget; but I never shall forget these."

"Pip," said Joe, appearing a little hurried and troubled, "there has been larks. And, dear sir, what have been betwixt us—have been."

At night, when I had gone to bed, Joe came into my room, as he had done all through my recovery. He asked me if I felt sure that I was as well as in the morning.

"Yes, dear Joe, quite."

"And are always a-getting stronger, old chap?"

"Yes, dear Joe, steadily."

Joe patted the coverlet on my shoulder with his great good hand, and said, in what I thought a husky voice, "Good night!"

When I got up in the morning, refreshed and stronger yet, I was full of my resolution to tell Joe all, without delay. I hurried then to the breakfast-table, and on it found a letter. These were its brief contents.

Not wishful to intrude I have departured fur you are well again dear Pip and will do better without Jo. P.S. Ever the best of friends.

Enclosed in the letter was a receipt for the debt and costs on which I had been arrested. Down to that moment I had vainly supposed that my creditor had withdrawn or suspended proceedings until I should be quite recovered. I had never dreamed of Joe's having paid the money; but Joe had paid it, and the receipt was in his name.

What remained for me now, but to follow him to the dear old forge, and there to have out my disclosure to him, and my penitent remonstrance with him, and there to relieve my mind and heart of that reserved secondly, which had begun as a vague something lingering in my thoughts, and had formed into a settled purpose?

The purpose was that I would go to Biddy, that I would show her how humbled and repentant I came back, that I would tell her how I had lost all I once hoped for, that I would remind her of our old confidences in my first unhappy time. Then, I would say to her, "Biddy, I think you once liked me very well, when my errant heart, even while it strayed away from you, was quieter and better with you than it ever has been since. If you can like me only half as well once more, if you can take me with all my faults and disappointments on my head, if you can receive me like a forgiven child, I hope I am a little

Great Expectations 899

65 **Discussion** What inspires Pip's new purpose?

65

Student Activity 1. Find another passage in the novel that contains at least four different pronouns. Read the passage aloud to a small group of classmates as they follow in their texts.

Student Activity 2. Explain the referent of each pronoun in the passage you just read, discussing each one with the group.

Student Activity 3. Write a brief summary of *Great Expectations* so far. In your description, be sure to use referents. Exchange papers with another classmate and underline the nouns and their referents.

Electronic Handbook You might want students to review pronouns before allowing them to complete the Grammar in Action activities. If students have access to the Language Master 6000, have them enter the access word *pronoun* and press the GRAMMAR key to obtain information relating to pronoun referents.

66 **Reading Strategy** Have students summarize the events of this chapter, as they affect the following characters: Pip, Joe, Matthew, Pocket, and Mr. Pumblechook.

67 **Discussion** How does Pip learn that news of his change in fortune has reached the village ahead of him?

68 **Discussion** Pip returns to "the old place." What is familiar about "the old place" and what is different?

worthier of you than I was—not much, but a little. And, Biddy, it shall rest with you to say whether I shall work at the forge with Joe, or whether I shall try for any different occupation down in this country, or whether we shall go away to a distant place where an opportunity awaits me which I set aside when it was offered, until I knew your answer. And now, dear Biddy, if you can tell me that you will go through the world with me, you will surely make it a better world for me, and me a better man for it, and I will try hard to make it a better world for you."

Such was my purpose. After three days more of recovery, I went down to the old place, to put it in execution.

Chapter 57

The tidings of my high fortunes had a heavy fall, had got down to my native place and its neighborhood before I got there. I found the Blue Boar in possession of the intelligence, and I found that it made a great change in the Boar's demeanor. Whereas the Boar had cultivated my good opinion with warm assiduity when I was coming into property, the Boar was exceedingly cool on the subject now that I was going out of property.

It was evening when I arrived, much fatigued by the journey I had so often made so easily. The Boar could not put me into my usual bedroom, which was engaged (probably by some one who had expectations), and could only assign me a very indifferent chamber among the pigeons and post-chaises up the yard. But I had as sound a sleep in that lodging as in the most superior accommodation the Boar could have given me, and the quality of my dreams was about the same as in the best bedroom.

Early in the morning while my breakfast was getting ready, I strolled round by Satis House. There were printed bills on the gate and on bits of carpet hanging out of the windows, announcing a sale by auction of the household furniture and effects, next week. The house itself was to be sold as old building materials, and pulled down.

The schoolhouse where Biddy was mistress, I had never seen, but the little round-about lane by which I entered the village for quietness' sake, took me past it. I was disappointed to find that the day was a holiday; no children were there, and Biddy's house was closed. Some hopeful notion of seeing her, busily engaged in her daily duties, before she saw me, had been in my mind and was defeated.

But the forge was a very short distance off, and I went towards it under the sweet green limes, listening for the clink of Joe's hammer. Long after I ought to have heard it, and long after I had fancied I heard it and found it but a fancy, all was still. The limes were there, and the white thorns were there, and the chestnut trees were there, and their leaves rustled harmoniously when I stopped to listen, but the clink of Joe's hammer was not in the midsummer wind.

Almost fearing, without knowing why, to come in view of the forge, I saw it at last, and saw that it was closed. No gleam of fire, no glittering shower of sparks, no roar of bellows; all shut up, and still.

But the house was not deserted, and the best parlor seemed to be in use, for there were white curtains fluttering in its window, and the window was open and gay with flowers. I went softly towards it, meaning to peep over the flowers, when Joe and Biddy stood before me, arm in arm.

At first Biddy gave a cry, as if she thought it was my apparition, but in another moment she was in my embrace. I wept to see her, and she wept to see me; I because she looked so fresh and pleasant; she because I looked so worn and white.

"But, dear Biddy, how smart you are!"

"Yes, dear Pip."

"And Joe, how smart *you* are!"

"Yes, dear old Pip, old chap."

I looked at both of them, from one to the other, and then—

"It's my wedding-day," cried Biddy, in a burst of happiness, "and I am married to Joe!"

They had taken me into the kitchen, and I had laid my head down on the old deal table. Biddy held one of my hands to her lips, and Joe's restoring touch was on my shoulder. "Which he warn't strong enough, my dear, fur to be surprised," said Joe. And Biddy said, "I ought to have thought of it, dear Joe, but I was too happy." They were both so overjoyed to see me, so proud to see me, so touched by my coming to them, so delighted that I should have come by accident to make their day complete!

69 My first thought was one of great thankfulness that I had never breathed this last baffled hope to Joe. How often, while he was with me in my illness, had it risen to my lips. How irrevocable would have been his knowledge of it, if he had remained with me but another hour!

"Dear Biddy," said I, "you have the best husband in the whole world, and if you could have seen him by my bed you would have—But no, you couldn't love him better than you do."

"No, I couldn't indeed," said Biddy.

"And, dear Joe, you have the best wife in the whole world, and she will make you as happy as even you deserve to be, you dear, good, noble Joe!"

Joe looked at me with a quivering lip, and fairly put his sleeve before his eyes.

"And Joe and Biddy both, as you have been to church today and are in charity and love with all mankind, receive my humble thanks for all you have done for me, and all I have so ill-repaid! And when I say that I am going away within the hour, for I am soon going abroad, and that I shall never rest until I have worked for the money with which you have kept me out of prison, and have sent it to you, don't think, dear Joe and Biddy, that if I could repay it a thousand times over, I suppose I could cancel a farthing[1] of the debt I owe you, or that I would do so if I could!"

They were both melted by these words, and both entreated me to say no more.

"But I must say more. Dear Joe, I hope you will have children to love, and that some little fellow will sit in this chimney corner, of a winter night, who may remind you of another little fellow gone out of it for ever. Don't tell him, Joe, that I was thankless; don't tell him, Biddy, that I was ungenerous and unjust; only tell him that I honored you both, because you were both so good and true, and that, as your child, I said it would be natural to him to grow up a much better man than I did." 70

"I ain't a-going," said Joe, from behind his sleeve, "to tell him nothink o' that natur, Pip. Nor Biddy ain't. Nor yet no one ain't."

"And now, though I know you have already done it in your own kind hearts, pray tell me, both, that you forgive me! Pray let me hear you say the words, that I may carry the sound of them away with me, and then I shall be able to believe that you can trust me, and think better of me, in the time to come!"

"Oh, dear old Pip, old chap," said Joe. "God knows as I forgive you, if I have anything to forgive!"

---

1. **farthing** (fär′ thiŋ) *n.:* Small British coin equal to one fourth of a penny.

69 **Discussion** Why is Pip thankful?

70 **Discussion** In what way does Pip hope Joe and Biddy will be reminded of him in time to come? What is Joe's attitude toward this idea?

71 **Literary Focus** How does this summary of later events relate to the theme of the novel?

72 **Discussion** What changes have eleven years of marriage made in the lives of Joe and Biddy?

Cooperative Learning Use the Numbered Heads cooperative learning structure. Arrange the class in groups of four. Assign a number from 1 to 4 to each member of each group. Tell students to work together to find examples of ways in which Herbert Pocket helped Pip. When the students have had sufficient time to find examples, call a number for each group to hear the group's response.

"Amen! And God knows I do!" echoed Biddy.

'Now let me go up and look at my old little room, and rest there a few minutes by myself. And then when I have eaten and drunk with you, go with me as far as the finger post,[2] dear Joe and Biddy, before we say goodbye!"

I sold all I had, and put aside as much as I could, for a composition with my creditors—who gave me ample time to pay them in full—and I went out and joined Herbert. Within a month, I had quitted England, and within two months I was clerk to Clarriker & Co., and within four months I assumed my first undivided responsibility. For the beam across the parlor ceiling at Mill Pond Bank had then ceased to tremble under old Bill Barley's growls and was at peace, and Herbert had gone away to marry Clara, and I was left in sole charge of the Eastern branch until he brought her back.

Many a year went round, before I was a partner in the house; but I lived happily with Herbert and his wife, and lived frugally, and paid my debts, and maintained a constant correspondence with Biddy and Joe. It was not until I became third in the firm that Clarriker betrayed me to Herbert; but he then declared that the secret of Herbert's partnership had been long enough upon his conscience, and he must tell it. So, he told it, and Herbert was as much moved as amazed, and the dear fellow and I were not the worse friends for the long concealment. I must not leave it to be supposed that we were ever a great house, or that we made mints of money. We were not in a grand way of business, but we had a good name, and worked for our profits, and did very well.

_____
2. **finger post:** Signpost.

Chapter 58

For eleven years I had not seen Joe nor Biddy with my bodily eyes—though they had both been often before my fancy in the East—when, upon an evening in December, an hour or two after dark, I laid my hand softly on the latch of the old kitchen door. I touched it so softly that I was not heard, and I looked in unseen. There, smoking his pipe in the old place by the kitchen firelight, as hale and as strong as ever, though a little gray, sat Joe; and there, fenced into the corner with Joe's leg, and sitting on my own little stool looking at the fire, was—I again!

"We giv' him the name of Pip for your sake, dear old chap," said Joe, delighted when I took another stool by the child's side (but I did _not_ rumple his hair), "and we hoped he might grow a little bit like you, and we think he do."

I thought so, too, and I took him out for a walk next morning, and we talked immensely, understanding one another to perfection. And I took him down to the churchyard, and set him on a certain tombstone there, and he showed me from that elevation which stone was sacred to the memory of Philip Pirrip, Late of this Parish, and Also Georgiana Wife of the Above.

"Biddy," said I, when I talked with her after dinner, as her little girl lay sleeping in her lap, "you must give Pip to me, one of these days; or lend him, to all events."

"No, no," said Biddy gently. "You must marry."

"So Herbert and Clara say, but I don't think I shall, Biddy. I have so settled down in their home that it's not at all likely. I am already quite an old bachelor."

Biddy looked down at her child, and put its little hand to her lips, and then put the good matronly hand with which she had touched it into mine. There was something in the action and in the light pressure of Biddy's wedding ring that had a very pretty eloquence in it.

"Dear Pip," said Biddy, "you are sure you don't fret for her?"

"Oh, no—I think not, Biddy."

"Tell me as an old friend. Have you quite forgotten her?"

"My dear Biddy, I have forgotten nothing in my life that ever had a foremost place there, and little that ever had any place there. But that poor dream, as I once used to call it, has all gone by, Biddy, all gone by!"*

Nevertheless, I knew that while I said those words that I secretly intended to revisit the sight of the old house that evening alone, for her sake. Yes, even so. For Estella's sake.

I had heard of her as leading a most unhappy life, and as being separated from her husband, who had used her with great cruelty, and who had become quite renowned as a compound of pride, avarice, brutality, and meanness. And I had heard of the death of her husband from an accident consequent on his ill-treatment of a horse. This release had befallen her some two years before; for anything I knew, she was married again.

The early dinner-hour at Joe's left me abundance of time, without hurrying my talk with Biddy, to walk over to the old spot before dark. But what with loitering on the way to look at old objects and to think of old times, the day had quite declined when I came to the place.

There was no house now, no brewery, no building whatever left, but the wall of the old garden. The cleared space had been enclosed with a rough fence, and looking over it, I saw that some of the old ivy had struck root

---

*The original ending of the book followed this paragraph. See the explanation on page 905.

anew, and was growing green on low quiet mounds of ruin. A gate in the fence standing ajar, I pushed it open, and went in.

A cold silvery mist had veiled the afternoon, and the moon was not yet up to scatter it. But the stars were shining beyond the mist, and the moon was coming, and the evening was not dark. I could trace out where every part of the old house had been, and where the brewery had been, and where the gates, and where the casks. I had done so, and was looking along the desolate garden-walk, when I beheld a solitary figure in it.

The figure showed itself aware of me as I advanced. It had been moving towards me, but it stood still. As I drew nearer, I saw it to be the figure of a woman. As I drew nearer yet, it was about to turn away, when it stopped, and let me come up with it. Then it faltered as if much surprised, and uttered my name, and I cried out:

"Estella!"

"I am greatly changed. I wonder you know me."

The freshness of her beauty was indeed gone, but its indescribable majesty and its indescribable charm remained. Those attractions in it I had seen before; what I had never seen before was the saddened, softened light of the once proud eyes; what I had never felt before was the friendly touch of the once insensible hand.

We sat down on a bench that was near, and I said, "After so many years, it is strange that we should thus meet again, Estella, here where our first meeting was! Do you often come back?"

"I have never been here since."

"Nor I."

The moon began to rise, and I thought of the placid look at the white ceiling, which had passed away. The moon began to rise,

Great Expectations 903

---

73 Discussion What has changed Pip's attitude toward marriage?

74 Discussion What mood does this description create?

75 Discussion How has Estella changed in appearance?

Speaking and Listening You might want to have students read aloud from Chapter 58 the two endings of *Great Expectations* so that they might compare them. If you wish, individual students may read the parts of Pip (as the narrator), Pip (when quoted directly), and Estella.

Humanities Note

Fine art, *The Proposal,* 1877, by William Powell Frith. The British painter William Powell Frith (1819–1909) vowed to devote his art to the description of scenes of ordinary life. Upon graduating from the Royal Academy school, Frith did just that and so became a favorite of the Victorians. He painted what the public wanted to see and received high prices for his works.

The Proposal is the second painting of this title and theme done by Frith. The story-telling skill of this artist allows the title and the scene itself to inform the viewer of the situation. The woman seems demure and the man shows a protective concern.

You might want to ask students the following questions:

1. Explain what is occurring in this picture.
2. Describe the different attitudes of the man and woman.
3. Is this picture an appropriate accompaniment to the final meeting of Pip and Estella? Explain.

THE PROPOSAL, 1877
William Powell Frith
Lady Scott, Boughton House, Kettering

904   *The Novel*

and I thought of the pressure on my hand when I had spoken the last words he had heard on earth.

Estella was the next to break the silence that ensued between us.

"I have very often hoped and intended to come back, but have been prevented by many circumstances. Poor, poor old place!"

The silvery mist was touched with the first rays of the moonlight, and the same rays touched the tears that dropped from her eyes. Not knowing that I saw them, and setting herself to get the better of them, she said quietly:

"Were you wondering, as you walked along, how it came to be left in this condition?"

"Yes, Estella."

"The ground belongs to me. It is the only possession I have not relinquished. Everything else has gone from me, little by little, but I have kept this. It was the subject of the only determined resistance I made in all the wretched years."

"Is it to be built on?"

"At last it is. I came here to take leave of it before its change. And you," she said, in a voice of touching interest to a wanderer, "you live abroad still."

"Still."

"And do well, I am sure?"

"I work pretty hard for a sufficient living, and therefore—Yes, I do well!"

"I have often thought of you," said Estella.

"Have you?"

"Of late, very often. There was a long hard time when I kept far from me the remembrance of what I had thrown away when I was quite ignorant of its worth. But since my duty has not been incompatible with the admission of that remembrance, I have given it a place in my heart."

"You have always held your place in *my* heart," I answered.

And we were silent again until she spoke.

"I little thought," said Estella, "that I should take leave of you in taking leave of this spot. I am very glad to do so."

"Glad to part again, Estella? To me, parting is a painful thing. To me, the remembrance of our last parting has been ever mournful and painful."

"But you said to me," returned Estella very earnestly, " 'God bless you, God forgive you!' And if you could say that to me then, you will not hesitate to say that to me now— now, when suffering has been stronger than all other teaching, and has taught me to understand what your heart used to be. I have been bent and broken, but—I hope—into a better shape. Be as considerate and good to me as you were, and tell me we are friends."

"We are friends," said I, rising and bending over her, as she rose from the bench.

"And will continue friends apart," said Estella.

I took her hand in mine, and we went out of the ruined place; and as the morning mists had risen long ago when I first left the forge, so the evening mists were rising now, and in all the broad expanse of tranquil light they showed to me, I saw no shadow of another parting from her.

The passage below, which once followed the asterisk on page 903, made up the original ending of Great Expectations. *Just before the book was published, however, Dickens substituted the ending you have already read.*

It was two years more before I saw herself. I had heard of her as leading a most unhappy life, and as being separated from

Great Expectations   905

76 **Reading Strategy** Summarize the discussion between Estella and Pip. How has each of them changed?

77 **Discussion** Why does Estella say this?

78 **Critical Thinking and Reading** After students read the original ending, ask: Which ending do you prefer? Explain.

her husband, who had used her with great cruelty, and who had become quite renowned as a compound of pride, brutality, and meanness. I had heard of the death of her husband from an accident consequent on ill-treating a horse, and of her being married again to a Shropshire doctor who, against his interest, had once very manfully interposed on an occasion when he was in professional attendance upon Mr. Drummle, and had witnessed some outrageous treatment of her. I had heard that the Shropshire doctor was not rich, and that they lived on her own personal fortune. I was in England again—in London, and walking along Piccadilly with little Pip—when a servant came running after me to ask would I step back to a lady in a carriage who wished to speak to me. It was a little pony carriage which the lady was driving, and the lady and I looked sadly enough on one another.

"I am greatly changed, I know, but I thought you would like to shake hands with Estella, too, Pip. Lift up that pretty child and let me kiss it!" (She supposed the child, I think, to be my child.) I was very glad afterwards to have had the interview, for in her face and in her voice, and in her touch, she gave me the assurance that suffering had been stronger than Miss Havisham's teaching, and had given her a heart to understand what my heart used to be.

MULTICULTURAL CONNECTION
Coming of Age and Expectations

The journey from childhood to adulthood is filled with events that affect adult life. There is no doubt that the journey to adulthood is significant all over the world, as many societies mark it with special ceremonies. These rites of passage differ from one culture to another, often depending on what is expected of the young people by their elders.

Bar Mitzvah and Bas Mitzvah. In the Jewish religion, boys and girls are declared adults at age thirteen. The ceremony that marks this occasion is a *bar mitzvah* for boys and *bas mitzvah* for girls. The words mean "son or daughter of the commandment," referring to God's law for his people.

A Tlingit tradition. Among the Tlingit Indians of southeastern Alaska, the tradition calls for girls to be isolated from the rest of the community upon reaching puberty. For eight days they fast and pass the time being taught traditional crafts that have been handed down through their culture for many generations. They may learn how to make jewelry and festive headdresses, how to weave elaborate baskets of long, dry grasses that grow on Alaskan beaches, or how to sew parkas and make mukluks (boots) especially suited to their rugged climate. When the time is up, their hair is washed with blueberry juice, an ancient custom believed to bring good luck. Then the girls' clothes are burned and the ashes put in an old tree stump, to assure them of a long life. Afterward, their mothers give them new clothes and jewelry, symbolizing their new adult status in the community.

Ancient traditions in Africa. Boys in many African societies are also separated from the community before coming of age. In some cultures they are sent out into the wild for an appointed number of days, armed only with a spear, and told to live off the land and find their own food. Among the !Kung, nomadic hunters of the Kalahari Desert in southwestern Africa where hunting is an essential means of providing food for the family, young men aged fifteen to eighteen must kill a large animal before returning home. Because the !Kung people depend on hunting for their livelihood, they believe that a man cannot support a family without good hunting skills. He is not permitted to marry until he has passed this test.

A Hispanic tradition. In Hispanic cultures a girl's fifteenth birthday is very important. The occasion is celebrated with a large party and gifts to honor *la quinceañera* (the fifteen-year-old). Guests include the extended family: grandparents, aunts, uncles, and cousins, as well as godparents, who may give her a special gift of jewelry. In some countries the event is announced in a local newspaper.

Moving forward. All societies around the world have coming-of-age rituals. Some of these rituals are such an integral part of our culture that we may not even be aware of them. School graduation day is one example. Dressed in cap and gown, graduates receive their diplomas and leave school, ready to face the adult world and pursue a career.

Sharing Your Experiences

Have you taken part in ceremonies or celebrations marking the coming of age? What was special about the ceremony? Tell the class about the event.

Multicultural Connection 907

ANSWERS TO RESPONDING TO THE SELECTION

Your Response

1. Encourage students to discuss the double ending thoroughly. Ask students why they think Dickens provided the second ending to the novel after he wrote the original ending.

Recalling

2. Pip realizes that she is Estella's mother.
3. Miss Havisham agrees to continue Pip's plan of assisting Herbert, begs Pip's forgiveness, and gives him more information about Estella.
4. Pip helps Magwitch by hiding him from his pursuers, and then he attempts an escape. After the attempt fails, Pip stays close to the dying man, comforting him until the end.
5. The key events include the following: Pip becomes ill and is nursed to health by Joe. Pip learns that Miss Havisham has died and left her estate to Estella, with a small provision for Matthew Pocket. Orlick is jailed for robbing Pumblechook. Pip decides to return to the forge and marry Biddy, but arrives on her and Joe's wedding day. Pip works for Clarriker and eventually becomes a partner. He returns to England and finds another little Pip sitting by the chimney corner.
6. Pip and Estella are now middle-aged. He has long since given up his dream of marrying her. Estella has lost her youthful beauty.

Interpreting

7. Suggested Response: Pip tells Miss Havisham about the suffering she has caused him, and she is shocked into looking at herself realistically.
8. Suggested Response: Pip is devoted to his benefactor even though he knows that such devotion will not bring him wealth or status. He therefore affirms the value of love.
9. Answers will differ. Students may respond that Dickens believed

---

RESPONDING TO THE SELECTION

Your Response

1. Which of Dickens's two endings do you prefer? Why?

Recalling

2. What does Pip realize about Mr. Jaggers's housekeeper?
3. Explain the discussion between Pip and Miss Havisham before her accident and death.
4. In what ways does Pip show loyalty to Magwitch before and after his capture?
5. What key events occur between Magwitch's death and Pip's meeting with Estella?
6. How are Pip and Estella changed when they meet again?

Interpreting

7. What accounts for Miss Havisham's change of heart?
8. How does Pip's loyalty to Magwitch relate to the theme of the novel?
9. Why do you think Dickens altered the original ending of *Great Expectations?*

Applying

10. What would happen to Pip if the novel continued? Give reasons for your answer.

ANALYZING LITERATURE

Understanding the Novel as a Whole

By considering how the elements in *Great Expectations* work together, you will better appreciate the novel as a whole.

1. Find three examples of how the first-person narrative adds to the drama of the plot.
2. Show how the changes that Pip, Estella, and Miss Havisham experience relate to the theme of the novel.
3. Identify two passages where the setting creates a mood that enhances the action.

---

4. Why is the surprise return of Pip's benefactor valuable in pointing up the theme?
5. Choose a scene from the book and show how all the literary elements contribute to it.
6. Explain what this novel reveals about expectations and happiness.

CRITICAL THINKING AND READING

Using Criteria to Evaluate the Novel

Criteria are the standards by which a work is judged. You can develop criteria for evaluating a novel by answering the following questions about its elements. (You should think of additional questions as well.) Does the point of view involve you in the events of the story? Are the characters interesting and believable? Does the writer pace events so they do not move too quickly or too slowly? Does the writer describe the setting vividly? Is the central idea about life important? Does this idea flow naturally from the story?

Create a chart with the headings *Criteria, Opinions,* and *Evidence.* Under *Criteria,* list the above questions and some of your own. Briefly note your answers in the next column, *Opinions.* Then, under *Evidence,* list passages from the book that support your answers.

THINKING AND WRITING

Evaluating the Novel

Using your chart, write an evaluation of *Great Expectations.* Your chart should support your overall opinion of the book. If you liked the novel, for instance, most of the opinions on the chart should be positive. Begin your essay with an introduction briefly stating your general opinion of the novel. In the body of the essay, evaluate each of the elements based on your criteria. Conclude with a summary and restatement of your opinion. In revising, make sure you have discussed how the elements work together. Share your essay with your classmates when you have finished.

---

his audience would prefer a happier ending and that Pip had earned happiness through his suffering.

Applying

10. Answers will differ. Some students may feel that Pip will marry Estella, and they will then live near Joe, Biddy, and little Pip.

ANSWERS TO ANALYZING LITERATURE

1. Suggested Response: The first-person narrative contributes to the intensity, suspense, and emotion of such scenes as Pip's first encounter with Magwitch, the convict's encounter with Pip many years later, and Pip's last interview with Miss Havisham.
2. Suggested Response: The theme of the novel concerns the impor-

tance of love and devotion. Pip realizes that love is more important than wealth, advancement, or status. Estella is eventually able to sympathize with and respond to others' feelings. She is no longer the cruel beauty that Miss Havisham used to revenge herself on men. Before she dies, Miss Havisham sees that her plans for revenge have hurt herself, Estella, and Pip. She is genuinely sorry for what she has done.

Dragonsong

NATURE WALK
Rolland Dingman
Courtesy of the Artist

Humanities Note

Fine art, *Nature Walk,* by Rolland Dingman. Dingman, born in 1946, has been a wildlife painter, a cartoonist, and a commercial artist. Now, as a priest in the Orthodox Christian Church, he paints icons. Dingman lives with his family in the redwoods on the San Lorenzo River in California.

He describes *Nature Walk,* done in watercolor in 1984, as a "doodle that got out of hand." It appears to be a strange jungle planet where every plant and animal is a product of the artist's imagination.

You might use these questions for discussion:
1. Imagine you have traveled in time and space and have just landed in the scene depicted in this art. How would you describe what you are seeing to the people back home?
2. Are there environments besides your own that you would like to explore? Explain.
3. This work of art introduces the novel *Dragonsong,* which takes place in an imaginary world, though not the world depicted in this scene. What might be some features of setting or environment in a novel that takes place on an imaginary planet?

have a model. Before students write, you might wish to show them Model 8: Literary Analysis in the **Transparencies for Writing.**

Alternative Assessment You might vary the Thinking and Writing assignment as follows: Ask students to review their reader's response journals and write an essay defending or attacking the new ending. They should analyze each ending and then discuss why they think Dickens chose to end his novel happily. Have them consider whether or not that ending is as logical a resolution of all the issues raised in the story as is the original ending.

3. Suggested Response: At the start of the novel, the graveyard creates an atmosphere of mystery and fear. When Pip falls into Orlick's trap, the marshes create a similar atmosphere, adding to the suspense.
4. Suggested Response: The surprise return of Pip's benefactor shocks Pip out of his mistaken assumptions and brings him face-to-face with reality. This painful experience shows him that love is more important than wealth.

5. Answers will differ. Students should note how point of view, events, mood, setting, and characterization contribute to the scene.
6. Answers will differ. Students may respond that true happiness comes from devotion to others, not through a selfish pursuit of wealth or status.

ANSWERS TO CRITICAL THINKING AND READING

Answers will differ. Make sure that students have created a chart with three headings and have filled in material under each of these categories.

THINKING AND WRITING

Writing Transparency Students often write better if they

Motivation/Prior Knowledge
Have students speculate on the subject of this novel by thinking about the title, reviewing the illustrations, and looking at this map. In observing that the location and creatures are not real, they should conclude that the novel may be considered fantasy or science fiction.

Reading Strategy Half-Circle Sea Hold and Benden Weyr are the two main settings of *Dragonsong*. Have students locate the two places on the map before they begin reading the novel. Suggest that they refer to the map periodically while reading the novel.

Dragonsong
Foreword

Rukbat, in the Sagittarian Sector, was a golden G-type star. It had five planets, two asteroid belts, and a stray planet it had attracted and held in recent millennia. When men first settled on Rukbat's third world and called it Pern, they had taken little notice of the stranger planet, swinging about its adopted primary in a wildly erratic elliptical orbit. For two generations, the colonists gave the bright red star little thought, until the path of the wanderer brought it close to its stepsister at perihelion.[1]

Then, the spore life,[2] which proliferated at an incredible rate on the Red Star's wild surface, spun off into space and bridged the gap to Pern. The spores fell as thin threads on the temperate, hospitable planet, and devoured anything organic in their way, seeking to establish burrows in Pern's warm earth from which to set out more voracious[3] Threads.

The colonists suffered staggering losses in terms of people scored to death,[4] and in crops and vegetation wiped out completely. Only fire killed Thread on land: only stone and metal stopped its progress. Fortunately it drowned in water, but the colonists could scarcely live on the seas.

The resourceful men cannibalized their transport ships and, abandoning the open southern continent where they had touched down, set about making the natural caves in the northern continent habitable.[5] They evolved a two-phase plan to combat Thread. The first phase involved breeding a highly specialized variety of a life-form indigenous[6] to their new world. The "dragons" (named for the mythical Terran beast they resembled) had two extremely useful characteristics: they could get from one place to another instantly by teleportation, and when they had chewed a phosphine-bearing rock, they could emit a flaming gas. Thus the flying dragons could char Thread to ash midair and escape its ravages themselves.

Men and women with high empathy ratings[7] or some innate telepathic ability[8] were trained to use and preserve these unusual animals, partnering them in a lifelong and intimate relationship.

The original cave-Fort, constructed in the eastern face of the great West Mountain range, soon became too small to hold either the colonists or the great "dragons." Another settlement was started slightly to the north, by a great lake, conveniently nestled near a cave-filled cliff. Ruatha Hold, too, became overcrowded in a few generations.

Since the Red Star rose in the East, it was decided to start a holding in the eastern mountains, provided suitable accommodations could be found. The ancient cave-

---

1. In this imaginary galaxy, the people of Pern begin to notice that the irregular orbit of a wandering planet is bringing it close to Pern.
2. spore life: Tiny, single-celled bodies capable of reproducing themselves.
3. voracious (vô rā′ shəs) *adj.*: Greedy in eating; devouring large quantities of food.
4. scored to death: Cut or eaten into so severely as to cause death.

5. habitable (hab′ it ə bəl) *adj.*: Suitable to live in.
6. indigenous (in dij′ ə nəs) *adj.*: Existing naturally in an area.
7. high empathy (em′ pə thē) **ratings:** Measures of the depth of understanding of the feelings and thoughts of another being.
8. innate telepathic (tel ə path′ ik) **ability:** An inborn ability to communicate through transference of thoughts.

Reading Strategy The Foreword contains information about the setting. In order to best understand and appreciate many aspects of the story, students should be familiar with the history of Pern. You may wish to question them about the details concerning dragons, Thread, and Pernese society.

Teaching to Ability Levels Your **less advanced** students may skip the Foreword and begin with Chapter 1. Though the Foreword gives some background details, it is possible for students to read and enjoy the novel without complete comprehension of this background information.

ESL Teaching Strategy Use the chalkboard to depict the relationship between the Red Star and Pern: Draw the two planets—the Red Star is actually a planet, not a star. Using arrows and a dotted ellipse, show the path of the Red Star as it approaches and leaves Pern's space. Indicate the passage of Thread from the Red Star to the surface of Pern. Discuss with students what makes Thread so dangerous.

pocked cones of extinct volcanoes in the Benden mountains proved so suitable to the dragonmen and women that they searched and found several more throughout Pern, and left Fort Hold and Ruatha Hold for the pastoral colonists, the holders.

However, such projects took the last of the fuel for the great stonecutters, originally thought to be used for the most diffident mining since Pern was light on metals, and any subsequent Holds and Weyrs were hand-hewn.

The dragons and their riders in their Weyrs, and the people in the cave holdings, went about their separate tasks and each developed habits that became custom, which solidified into tradition as incontrovertible as law.

By the Third Pass of the Red Star, a complicated social, political and economic structure had developed to deal with the recurrent evil of Thread. There were now six Weyrs, pledged to protect all Pern, each Weyr having a geographical section of the northern continent literally under its wings. The rest of the population, the Holds, agreed to tithe to support the Weyrs, since these fighters, these dragonmen, did not have any arable land in their volcanic homes, nor did they have time for farming while protecting the planet from Passes of the Thread.

Holds developed wherever natural caves could be found: some, of course, were extensive or strategically placed near good water and grazing; others were smaller and less well placed. It took a strong man to keep frantic, terrified people in control in the Holds during Thread attacks: it took wise administration to conserve food supplies for times when nothing could be safely grown. Extraordinary measures controlled population, keeping its number healthy and useful until such time as the Thread should pass. And often children from one Hold were raised in another Hold, to spread the genetic pool and keep the Holds from dangerous inbreeding. Such a practice was called "fostering" and was used in both Holds and Crafthalls, where special skills such as metalworking, animal breedings, farming, fishing and mining (such as there was) were preserved. So that one Lord Holder could not deny the products of a Crafthall situated in his Hold to others, the Crafts were decreed independent of a Hold affiliation, each craftmaster at a hall owing allegiance only to the Master of that particular craft who, as the need arose, took likely students in as fosterlings.

Except for the return of the Red Star approximately every two hundred years, life was pleasant on Pern.

There came a time when the Red Star, due to the conjunction of Rukbar's five natural satellites, did not pass close enough to Pern to drop the dreadful spores. And the Pernese forgot about the danger. The people prospered, spreading out across the rich land, carving more Holds out of solid rock and becoming so busy with their pursuits, that they did not realize that there were only a few dragons in the skies, and only one Weyr of dragonriders left on Pern. In a few generations, the descendants of the Holders began to wonder if the Red Star would ever return. The dragonriders fell into disfavor: why should all Pern support these people and their hungry beasts? The legends of past braveries, and the very reason for such courage, became dishonored.

But, in the natural course of events, the Red Star again spun close to Pern, winking with a baleful red eye on its intended victim. One man, F'lar, rider of the bronze dragon, Mnementh, believed that the ancient tales had truth in them. His half brother, F'nor, rider of brown Canth, listened to his arguments and came to believe. When the last golden egg of a dying queen dragon lay hardening on the Benden Weyr Hatching Ground, F'lar and F'nor seized the opportunity to gain control of the Weyr. Searching Ruatha Hold, they found a strong woman, Lessa, the only surviving member of the proud bloodline of Ruatha Hold. She Impressed[9] young Ramoth, the new queen, and became Weyrwoman of Benden Weyr. And F'lar's bronze Mnementh became the new queen's mate.

The three young riders, F'lar, F'nor and Lessa, forced the Lord Holders and the Craftsmen to recognize their imminent danger and prepare the almost defenseless planet against Thread. But it was distressingly obvious that the scant two hundred dragons of Benden Weyr could not defend the wide-spread and sprawling settlements. Six full Weyrs had been needed in the olden days when the settled land had been much less extensive. In learning to direct her queen *between* one place and another, Lessa discovered that dragons could teleport *between* times as well. Risking her life as well as Pern's only queen, Lessa and Ramoth went back in time, four hundred Turns, to the days before the mysterious disappearance of the other five Weyrs, just after the last Pass of the Red Star had been completed.

The five Weyrs, seeing only the decline of their prestige and bored with inactivity after a lifetime of exciting combat, agreed to help Lessa, and Pern, and came forward to her time.

Dragonsong begins seven Turns after the Five Weyrs came forward.

---

9. Impressed: Created a deep bond enabling unspoken communication.

At Half-Circle Sea Hold, in Benden Hold

Yanus (yä' nəs), Sea Holder
Mavi (mä' vē), Sea Holder's Lady
Menolly (men' əl ē), their youngest child and daughter
Sella (sel' ə), the next oldest daughter
Alemi (ə lem' ē), the third son of six

Petiron (pet' i rôn), the old Harper
Elgion (el' gē ôn), the new Harper

Soreel (sō rēl'), wife of First Holder
Old Uncle, Menolly's great-grandfather

At Benden Weyr

F'lar (f' lär'), Weyrleader—bronze Mnementh (ne menth')
Lessa (les' ə), Weyrwoman—queen Ramoth (ram' oth)
N'ton (n' tôn), a wingleader—bronze Lioth (lē' oth)
T'gellan (t' gel' ən), a wingleader for Half-Circle Sea Hold—bronze Monarth (môn' ärth)
T'gran (t' gran'), dragonrider—brown Branth
T'sel (t' sel'), dragonrider—green Trenth, bronze fire lizard Rill

F'nor (f' nōr'), wing-second—brown Canth, gold fire lizard Grall
Brekke (brek' ē), queenrider—queen Wirenth (wir' ənth), killed, bronze fire lizard Berd

Manora (man ōr' ə), Headwoman of the Weyr's Lower Caverns
Felena (fə lēn' ə), her second in charge
Oharan (o här' ən), Weyr Harper
Mirrim (mi' rim), fosterling of Brekke, (3 fire lizards) green Reppa
                                                                  Lok
                                                          brown Tolly
Sanra, in charge of children in living cavern

Masterharper Robinton (rô' bin t'n)
Masterminer Nicat (nē' cat)

Menolly's fire lizards: gold   Beauty
                           bronze Rocky
                                   Diver
                           brown   Lazybones
                                   Mimic
                                   Brownie
                           blue   Uncle
                           green   Auntie One
                                   Auntie Two

McCaffrey studied voice for nine years. Her interest in music led to a career as a stage director for operas and operettas. Her interest in writing led to her next career, that of a full-time writer of novels and short stories. Ask students whether they think the author's background influenced her choice of a main character and a plot when she wrote this novel.

Literary Focus The details about the setting of an imaginary or fantasy novel are much more important to the reader than similar details in a realistic work of fiction. The author must help the reader to recognize the familiar elements in the setting as well as to identify and understand the unusual aspects of the time and place. Tell students to notice as they read how the author blends familiar activities with imaginary details.

Prereading Focus You might wish to select some of the more creative students to head each group. Remind students that they have seen and read about many imaginary places on television and in novels. You might wish to have the groups create planets with different physical characteristics: a desert planet with little water, a water planet with little or no land, a frigid planet, a tropical planet. Display students' maps so that they may share their creations with the class.

◆ **Software** If students have access to computers, you might have them use **Bank Street Writer** for the Focus activity.

Vocabulary Many students will find these words challenging. You might use the Vocabulary Check in the Teaching Portfolio, page 978, as a practice sheet before students read the novel.

914

GUIDE FOR READING

Anne McCaffrey

(1926–   ) lives in Ireland with her children and a large menagerie. She has been writing about the inhabitants of Pern since the mid-1960's. Ever since *Dragonflight* was published in 1968, readers have eagerly awaited each new story in the series. *Dragonsong, Dragonsinger,* and *The White Dragon* are among the bestsellers that McCaffrey has written about her imaginary planet. McCaffrey says of the exotic animals of Pern: "Dragons are not horses, but I do believe that fire lizards must be the interstellar equivalent of cats. There is no doubt that my fondness for furred people of all sorts accounts for the fun I have in 'creating' believable aliens."

Dragonsong, Chapters 1–3

Imaginary Setting

In most novels the setting reflects reality as you already know it. The times and places are familiar to you, even when the novels are set in previous centuries. Novels like *Dragonsong,* however, do not draw on the familiar places. The setting is an imaginary place. The author creates details that allow you to see the setting. Such details often include a map that helps you visualize distance and direction. The author may also describe foods, animals, and natural phenomena that would be probable in such a world. When the author creates a successful imaginary setting, you feel at home in the author's made-up universe.

Focus

Suppose that you were a descendant of a group of people who left Earth hundreds of years ago to settle on another planet. What would your everyday life be like? Working with a group of four or five students, create a picture of life on your imaginary planet. Draw a map showing the geography of the planet, and indicate where your people have settled. Describe the animals, the plants, and the weather. Explain how you communicate with other settlements on the planet. Share your work with the rest of the class. As you read *Dragonsong,* compare your planet with the world of Pern.

Vocabulary

Knowing the following terms will help you as you read Chapters 1–3 of *Dragonsong.*

palisades (pal′ ə sadz) *n.:* A line of steep cliffs (p. 916)

querulous (kwer′ yoo ləs) *adj.:* Inclined to find fault or complain; peevish (p. 919)

belligerent (bə lij′ ər ənt) *adj.:* Ready to fight or quarrel (p. 920)

incredulity (in krə doo′ lə tē) *n.:* Unwillingness to believe (p. 922)

cubicle (kyoo′ bi kəl) *n.:* A small compartment (p. 924)

deviation (dē vē ā′ shən) *n.:* A turning aside from normal behavior (p. 926)

aghast (ə gast′) *adj.:* Feeling horror or dismay (p. 934)

imperious (im pir′ ē əs) *adj.:* Arrogant or domineering; overbearing (p. 934)

Objectives

1 To understand setting
2 To infer the meanings of words
3 To write a description of an imaginary place
4 To express individual interests and abilities through optional activities

Support Material

Teaching Portfolio
Teacher Backup, p. 969
Grammar in Action Worksheets, *Varying Sentence Beginnings,* p. 973; *Using Phrases in a Series,* p. 975
Usage and Mechanics Worksheet, p. 977
Vocabulary Check, p. 978
Analyzing Literature Worksheet, *Understanding Setting,* p. 979

Critical Thinking and Reading Worksheet, *Inferring the Meanings of Words,* p. 980
Selection Test, p. 981

Prentice Hall Literature Writing Studio

Dragonsong

Anne McCaffrey

Chapter 1

1

> *Drummer, beat, and piper, blow*
> *Harper, strike, and soldier, go*
> *Free the flame and sear the grasses*
> *Till the dawning Red Star passes.*

Almost as if the elements, too, mourned the death of the gentle old Harper, a south-easter blew for three days, locking even the burial barge in the safety of the Dock Cavern.

The storm gave Sea Holder Yanus too much time to brood over his dilemma. It gave him time to speak to every man who could keep rhythm and pitch, and they all gave him the same answer. They couldn't properly honor the old Harper with his Deathsong, but Menolly could.

2 To which answer Yanus would grunt and stamp off. It rankled in his mind that he couldn't give voice to his dissatisfaction with that answer, and his frustration. Menolly was only a girl: too tall and lanky to be a proper girl at that. It galled him to have to admit that, unfortunately, she was the only person in the entire Half-Circle Sea Hold who could play any instrument as well as the old Harper. Her voice was true, her fingers clever on string, stick or pipe, and she knew the Deathsong. For all Yanus could be certain, the aggravating child had been practicing that song ever since old Petiron started burning with his fatal fever.

"She will have to do the honor, Yanus," his wife, Mavi, told him the evening the storm began to slacken. "The important

thing is that Petiron is properly sung to rest. One does not have to record who did the 3 singing."

"The old man knew he was dying. Why didn't he instruct one of the men?"

"Because," replied Mavi with a touch of sharpness in her voice, "you would never spare him a man when there was fishing."

"There was young Tranilty . . ."

"Whom you sent fostering to Ista Sea Hold."

"Couldn't that young lad of Forolt's . . ."

"His voice is changing. Come, Yanus, it'll have to be Menolly."

Yanus grumbled bitterly against the inevitable as he climbed into the sleeping furs.

"That's what everyone else has told you, haven't they? So why make so much of a necessity?"

Yanus settled himself, resigned.

"The fishing will be good tomorrow," his wife said, yawning. She preferred him fishing to stomping around the Hold, sullen and critical with enforced inactivity. She knew he was the finest Sea Holder Half-Circle had ever had: the Hold was prospering, with plenty for bartering[1] set by in the storage caves; they hadn't lost a ship or a man in several Turns either, which said much for his weather-wisdom. But Yanus, at home on a heaving deck in foul weather, was very much adrift when taxed with the unexpected on land.

---

1. **bartering:** Trading.

Dragonsong 915

Presentation

Motivation/Prior Knowledge
Ask students to recall what they have learned about feudalism. Discuss the fact that ordinary people in the Middle Ages lived on land that was protected from invaders by knights who served a feudal lord. In exchange, people supplied the lord and his knights with foods and services. Ask what might be the advantages and disadvantages of such a system. Tell students to look for similarities between the feudal society of the Middle Ages and the society on Pern.

Purpose-Setting Question In what ways is Menolly not typical of the teenagers in her Hold?

1 **Reading Strategy** If students have not read the Foreword, summarize the background for them. To what does this verse refer?

2 **Discussion** Why is Yanus unhappy about his daughter's talents?

3 **Discussion** What do you infer about the traditions of these people?

Master Teacher Note You might wish to discuss with students the fact that this novel is science fiction, not fantasy. Explain that the Foreword indicates that the dragons—often found in fantasy novels—are in this case bioengineered creatures. Their ability to teleport and their telepathic relationship with the dragonriders are not magic. Such abilities are often treated in science fiction.

Note: Science fiction fans regard the term *sci-fi* as derogatory. The term *SF* is preferred.

Making Connections You might want to have students compare Menolly's situation and character with that of the young girl in "Rules of the Game," page 39. Both selections are about a girl in conflict with her family's expectations of her.

"'If I Forget Thee, O Earth . . . ,'" p. 157, is a science fiction story. Students might compare and contrast the elements of science fiction found in that story and *Dragonsong*.

Thematic Focus Menolly, the main character in *Dragonsong,* finds herself in conflict with her parents and with the customs and beliefs of the small society in which she lives. Ask students if it is unusual for teenagers to experience such conflict. Ask why a person might feel "out of step" with his or her world.

4 Discussion Why is a Harper necessary in a Hold?

5 Discussion What does Petiron's burial reveal about his position in the Hold?

6 Reading Strategy Have students locate Half-Circle Sea Hold and Nerat on the map on page 910.

7 Discussion What do you infer about roles and positions of men and women, boys and girls? What is valued in each?

Master Teacher Note This novel contains numerous invented terms. You might want to remind students to use context clues to determine their meanings. Point out to students that the meaning of an unfamiliar word is often provided in the sentence in which it occurs or in nearby sentences. You may want to locate some of these invented terms in the text and work with students to determine by what method the authors conveys the meaning of each term. Explain that writers are careful when inventing terminology to provide sufficient clues to enable readers to understand the terms. Tell students to be aware that such clues are sometimes given in apposition following the term. Sometimes the meaning of a term can be inferred from its use. Klah, for example, is a hot beverage served with meals and as a refreshment. It is clear from the references to its use that klah is similar to tea or coffee.

Mavi was keenly aware that Yanus was displeased with his youngest child. Mavi found the girl exasperating, too. Menolly worked hard and was very clever with her fingers: two clever by half when it came to playing any instrument in the Harper Craft. Perhaps, Mavi thought, she had not been wise to permit the girl to linger in the old Harper's constant company once she had learned all the proper Teaching Songs. But it had been one less worry to let Menolly nurse the old Harper, and Petiron had wished it. No one begrudged a Harper's requests. Ah well, thought Mavi, dismissing the past, there'd be a new Harper soon, and Menolly could be put to tasks proper to a young girl.

The next morning, the storm had cleared off: the skies were cloudless, the sea, calm. The burial barge had been outfitted in the Dock Cavern, Petiron's body wrapped in harper-blue on the tilter board. The entire Fleet and most of the Sea Hold followed in the wake of the oar-driven barge, out into the faster-moving current above Nerat Deep.

Menolly, on the barge prow, sang the elegy:[2] her clear strong voice carrying back to the Half-Circle Fleet; the men chanting the descant[3] as they rowed the barge.

On the final chord, Petiron went to his rest. Menolly bowed her head, and let drum and stock slide from her fingers into the sea. How could she ever use them again when they had beaten Petiron's last song? She'd held back her tears since the Harper had died because she knew she had to be able to sing his elegy and you couldn't sing with a throat closed from crying. Now the tears ran down her cheeks, mingled with sea spray: her sobs punctuated by the soft chant of the steersman, setting about.

---

2. elegy (el' ə jē) *n.*: A song of lament and praise for the dead.
3. descant (des' kant) *n.*: A melody sung or chanted above the main melodic line.

Petiron had been her friend, her ally and mentor. She had sung from the heart as he'd taught her: from the heart and the gut. Had he heard her song where he had gone?

She raised her eyes to the palisades of the coast: to the white-sanded harbor between the two arms of Half-Circle Hold. The sky had wept itself out in the past three days: a fitting tribute. And the air was cold. She shivered in her thick wherhide jacket. She would have some protection from the wind if she stepped down into the cockpit with the oarsmen. But she couldn't move. Honor was always accompanied by responsibility, and it was fitting for her to remain where she was until the burial barge touched the stones of Dock Cavern.

Half-Circle Hold would be lonelier than ever for her now. Petiron had tried so hard to live long enough for his replacement to arrive. He'd told Menolly he wouldn't last the winter. He'd dispatched a message to Masterharper Robinton to send a new Harper as soon as possible. He'd also told Menolly that he'd sent two of her songs to the Masterharper.

"Women can't be Harpers," she'd said to Petiron, astonished and awed.

"One in ten hundred have perfect pitch,"[4] Petiron had said in one of his evasive replies, "One in ten thousand can build an acceptable melody with meaningful words. Were you only a lad, there'd be no problem at all."

"Well, we're stuck with me being a girl."

"You'd make a fine big strong lad, you would," Petiron had replied exasperatingly.

"And what's wrong with being a fine big strong girl?" Menolly had been half-teasing, half-annoyed.

"Nothing, surely. Nothing." And Petiron had patted her hands, smiling up at her.

---

4. perfect pitch: A sense of musical tone so sharp that it can produce or identify any note.

She'd been helping him eat his dinner, his hands so crippled even the lightest wooden spoon left terrible ridges in the swollen fingers.

"And Masterharper Robinton's a fair man. No one on Pern can say he isn't. And he'll listen to me. He knows his duty, and I am, after all, a senior member of the Crafthall, being taught up in the Craft before him himself. And I'll require him to listen to you."

"Have you really sent him those songs you made me wax down on slates?"

"I have. Sure I have done that much for you, dear child."

He'd been so emphatic that Menolly had to believe that he'd done what he'd said. Poor old Petiron. In the last months, he'd not remembered the time of Turn much less what he'd done the day before.

He was timeless now, Menolly told herself, her wet cheeks stinging with cold, and she'd never forget him.

The shadow of the two arms of Half-Circle's cliffs fell across her face. The barge was entering the home harbor. She lifted her head. High above, she saw the diminutive outline of a dragon in the sky. How lovely! And how had Benden Weyr known? No, the dragonrider was only doing a routine sweep. With Thread falling at unexpected times, dragons were often flying above Half-Circle, isolated as it was by the bogs at the top of Nerat Bay. No matter, the dragon was awing above Half-Circle Hold at this appropriate moment and that was, to Menolly, the final tribute to Petiron the Harper.

The men lifted the heavy oars out of the water, and the barge glided slowly to its mooring at the far end of the dock. Fort and Tillek might boast of being the oldest Sea Holds, but only Half-Circle had a cavern big enough to dock the entire fishing fleet and keep it safe from Threadfall and weather.

Dock Cavern had moorings for thirty boats; storage space for all the nets, traps and lines; airing racks for sail; and a shallow ledge where hulls could be scraped free of seagrowths and repaired. At the very end of the immense cavern was a shelf of rock where the Hold's builders worked when there was sufficient timber for a new hull. Beyond was the small inner cave where priceless wood was stored, dried on high racks or warped into frames.

The burial barge lightly touched its pier.

"Menolly?" The first oarsman held out a hand to her.

Startled by the unexpected courtesy to a girl her age, she was about to jump down when she saw in his eyes the respect due her at this moment. And his hand, closing on hers, gave silent approval for her singing of the Harper's elegy. The other men stood, too, waiting for her to disembark first. She straightened her shoulders, although her throat felt tight enough for more tears, and she stepped proudly down to the solid stone.

As she turned to walk back to the landside of the cavern, she saw that the other boats were discharging their passengers quickly and quietly. Her father's boat, the biggest of the Half-Circle Fleet, had already tacked back into the harbor. Yanus's voice carried across the water, above the incidental sounds of creaking boats and muted voices.

"Quickly now, men. We've a good breeze rising and the fish'll be biting after three days of storm."

The oarsmen hurried past her, to board their assigned fishing boats. It seemed unfair to Menolly that Petiron, after a long life's dedication to Half-Circle Hold, was dismissed so quickly from everyone's mind. And yet . . . life did go on. There were fish to be caught against winter's hungry months. Fair days during the cold months of the Turn were not to be squandered.

Dragonsong 917

8 **Critical Thinking and Reading** What does Menolly mean by "wax down on slates"?

9 **Reading Strategy** Have students visualize this scene and imagine its impact on Menolly.

10 **Literary Focus: Setting** What do you know about the setting that explains why wood is "priceless" in the Sea Hold?

Commentary: Prizes for Science Fiction

The genre of science fiction has developed largely in this century. Imaginative literature set in other times, places, and universes has had a growing popular appeal. Science fiction describes events that could actually occur, while fantasy—a similar genre—discusses the impossible.

Anne McCaffrey has written many novels about Pern and similar places. A very popular science fiction writer, she has received the two most prestigious awards given for science fiction writing, the Hugo and the Nebula awards.

The Hugo is named after Hugo Gernsback, a publisher and editor of science fiction in the early twentieth century. Gernsback is notable for many reasons, among them the fact that he coined the term *science fiction*. Hugos are awarded at World Science Fiction Conventions, called worldcons by SF fans. Science fiction readers who attend the conventions vote each year for the new science fiction works they have most enjoyed during the year.

The Nebula has been given by the Science Fiction Writers of America (SFWA) since 1966. Unlike the Hugo, the Nebula award is voted on by professional writers and editors. The voting is done by SFWA members, who select the winners from five categories: novel (over 40,000 words); novella (17,500–40,000 words); nov-

She quickened her pace. She'd far to go around the rim of the Dock Cavern and she was cold. Menolly also wanted to get into the Hold before her mother noticed that she didn't have the drum. Waste wasn't tolerated by Mavi any more than idleness by Yanus.

While this was an occasion, it had been a sad one and the women and children and also the men too old to sea-fish observed a decorous pace out of the Cavern, making smaller groups as they headed towards their own Holds in the southern arc of Half-Circle's sheltering palisade.

Menolly saw Mavi organizing the children into work groups. With no Harper to lead them in the Teaching Songs and Ballads, the children would be kept occupied in clearing the storm debris from the white-sanded beaches.

There might be sun in the sky, and the dragonrider still circling on his brown, but the wind was frigid and Menolly began to shiver violently. She wanted to feel the warmth of the fire on the great Hold's kitchen hearth and a cup of hot klah inside her.

She heard her sister Sella's voice carrying to her on the breeze.

"She's got nothing to do now, Mavi, why do I have to . . ."

Menolly ducked behind a group of adults, avoiding her mother's searching glance. Trust Sella to remember that Menolly no longer had the excuse of nursing the ailing Harper. Ahead of her, one of the old aunts tripped, her querulous voice raised in a cry for help. Menolly sprinted to her side, supporting her and receiving loud protestations of gratitude.

"Only for Petiron would I have dragged these old bones out on the cold sea this morning. Bless the man, rest the man," the old woman went on, clinging with unexpected strength to Menolly. "You're a good child, Menolly, so you are. It is Menolly, isn't it?"

The old one peered up at her. "Now you just give me a hand up to Old Uncle and I'll tell him the whole of it, since he hasn't legs to leave his bed."

So Sella had to supervise the children and Menolly got to the fire: at least long enough to stop shivering. Then old auntie would have it that the Uncle would be grateful for some klah, too, so when Mavi entered her kitchen, her eyes searching for her youngest daughter, she found Menolly dutifully occupied serving the oldster.

"Very well then, Menolly, while you're up there, see that you set the old man comfortably. Then you can start on the glows."

Menolly had her warming cup with the Old Uncle and left him comfortable, mournfully exchanging tales of other burials with the aunt. Checking the glows had been her task ever since she had grown taller than Sella. It had meant climbing up and down the different levels to the inner and outer layers of the huge Sea Hold, but Menolly had established the quickest way to finish the job so that she'd have some free time to herself before Mavi started looking for her. She had been accustomed to spending those earned minutes practicing with the Harper. So Menolly was not surprised to find herself, eventually, outside Petiron's door.

She was surprised, however, to hear voices in his room. She was about to charge angrily through the half-open door and demand an accounting when she heard her mother's voice clearly.

"The room won't need much fixing for the new Harper, so it won't."

Menolly stepped back into the shadow of the corridor. The new Harper?

"What I want to know, Mavi, is who is to keep the children up in their learning until he comes?" That voice was Soreel's, the wife of the First Holder and therefore spokeswoman for the other Hold women to Mavi as

elette (7,500–17,500 words); short story (under 7,500 words); and the best dramatic presentation.

If students are interested in science fiction, you might direct them to other Anne McCaffrey novels or to the works of other respected science fiction writers, such as Isaac Asimov, Paul Anderson, Robert Heinlein, Lester del Ray, or Ursula K. Le Guin.

11 **Discussion** What can you infer about the everyday life of a child in the Hold? Does it seem pleasant or hard?

12 **Literary Focus: Setting** What does the description of "checking the glows" reveal about the setting?

13 Discussion Schooling in the Hold is obviously very different from education on Earth. Have students explain how. Why must Hold children be taught by means of the Teaching Ballads?

14 Discussion What does Soreel mean by "his mind was ranging back in time"?

15 Reading Strategy Summarize the responsibilities of the Harper. How is the position of Harper viewed?

16 Discussion Why does Yanus consider Menolly's tendency "distressing"?

Sea Holder's lady. "She did well enough this morning. You have to give her that, Mavi."

"Yanus will send the message ship."

"Not today, nor tomorrow he won't. I don't fault Sea Holder, Mavi, but it stands to reason that the boats must fish and the sloop's crew can't be spared. That means four, five days before the messenger gets to Igen Hold. From Igen Hold, if a dragonrider obliges by carrying the message—but we all know what the Oldtimers at Igen Weyr are like so let's say, Harper drums to the Masterharper Hall at Fort is another two–three days. A man has to be selected by Masterharper Robinton and sent overland and by ship. And with Thread falling any time it pleases, no one travels fast or far in a day. It'll be spring before we see another Harper. Are the children to be left without teaching for months?"

Soreel had punctuated her comments with brushing sounds, and there were other clatters in the room, the swishing of bed rushes being gathered up. Now Menolly could hear the murmur of two other voices supporting Soreel's arguments.

"Petiron has taught well . . ."

"He taught *her* well, too," Soreel interrupted Mavi.

"Harpering is a man's occupation . . ."

"Fair enough if Sea Holder'll spare a man for it." Soreel's voice was almost belligerent because everyone knew the answer to that. "Truth be told, I think the girl knew the Sagas[5] better than the old man this past Turn. You know his mind was ranging back in time, Mavi."

"Yanus will do what's proper." The finality in Mavi's tone firmly ended that discussion.

Menolly heard footsteps crossing the old Harper's room, and she ducked down the

5. **Sagas** (sä′ gəz) *n.*: Long narrative songs recounting historical and legendary events.

hall, around the nearest bend and down into the kitchen level.

It distressed Menolly to think of anyone, even another Harper, in Petiron's room. Obviously it distressed others that there was no Harper. Usually such a problem didn't arise. Every Hold could boast one or two musically able men and every Hold took pride in encouraging *these* talents. Harpers liked to have other instrumentalists to share the chore of entertaining their Holds during the long winter evenings. And it was also the better part of wisdom to have a substitute available for just such an emergency as Half-Circle was experiencing. But fishing was hard on the hands: the heavy work, the cold water, the salt and fish oils thickened joints and calloused fingers in the wrong places. Fishermen were often away many days on longer hauls. After a Turn or two at net, trap and sail line, young men lost their skill at playing anything but simple tunes. Harper Teaching Ballads required deft quick fingers and constant practice.

By putting to sea to fish so quickly after the old Harper's burial, Yanus thought to have time enough to find an alternative solution. There was no doubt that the girl could sing well, play well, and she'd not disgraced Hold or Harper that morning. It was going to take time to send for and receive a new Harper, and the youngsters must not lose all progress in the learning of the basic Teaching Ballads.

But Yanus had many strong reservations about putting such a heavy responsibility on the shoulders of a girl not fifteen Turns old. Not the least of these was Menolly's distressing tendency toward tune-making. Well enough and amusing now and again in the long winter evenings to hear her sing them, but old Petiron had been alive to keep her to rights. Yanus wasn't sure that he could trust her not to include her trivial little whistles in the lessons. How were the young to know that hers weren't proper songs for their learning? The trouble was, her melodies were the sort that stayed in the mind so a man found himself humming or whistling them without meaning to.

By the time the boats had profitably trawled the Deep and tacked for home, Yanus had found no compromise. It was no consolation to know that he wouldn't have any argument from the other Holders. Had Menolly sung poorly that morning . . . but she hadn't.

17 As Sea Holder for Half-Circle, he was obliged to bring up the young of the Hold in the traditions of Pern: knowing their duty and how to do it. He counted himself very lucky to be beholden to Benden Weyr, to have F'lar, bronze Mnementh's rider, as Weyrleader and Lessa as Ramoth's Weyrwoman. So Yanus felt deeply obliged to keep tradition at Half-Circle: and the young would learn what they needed to know, even if a girl had the teaching.

That evening, after the day's catch had been salted down, he instructed Mavi to bring her daughter to the small room off the Great Hall where he conducted Hold business and where the Records were stored. Mavi had put the Harper's instruments on the mantel for safekeeping.

Appropriately Yanus handed Menolly Petiron's gitar. She took the instrument in a properly reverential manner, which reassured Yanus that she appreciated the responsibility.

"Tomorrow you'll be excused from your regular morning duties to take the youngsters for their teaching," he told her. "But I'll have no more of those finger-twiddlings of yours."

"I sang my songs when Petiron was alive and you never minded them . . ."

Yanus frowned down at his tall daughter.

"Petiron *was* alive. He's dead now, and you'll obey me in this . . ."

Over her father's shoulders, Menolly saw her mother's frowning face, saw her warning headshake and held back a quick reply.

"You bear in mind what I've said!" And Yanus fingered the wide belt he wore. "No tuning!"

"Yes, Yanus."

"Start tomorrow then. Unless, of course, there's Threadfall, and then everyone will bait longlines."

Yanus dismissed the two women and began to compose a message to the Masterharper to go when he could next spare the sloop's crew. They'd sail it to Igen Hold. About time Half-Circle had some news of the rest of Pern anyway. And he could ship some of the smoked fish. The journey needn't be a wasted trip. 18

Once in the hallway, Mavi gripped her daughter's arm hard. "Don't disobey him, girl."

"There's no harm in my tunes, mother. You know what Petiron said . . ."

"I'll remind you that the old man's dead. And that changes everything that went on during his life. Behave yourself while you stand in a man's place. No tuning! To bed now, and mind you turn the glowbaskets. No sense wasting light no eye needs."

Chapter 2

Honor those the dragons heed
In thought and favor, word and deed.
Worlds are lost or worlds are saved
From those dangers dragon-braved.

Dragonman, avoid excess:
Greed will bring the Weyr distress:
To the ancient Law adhere,
Prospers thus the Dragonweyr. 19

It was easy enough, at first, for Menolly to forget her tuning during the Teachings. She wanted to do Petiron proud so that when the new Harper came, he'd find no fault in the 20

17 Discussion What kind of person is Yanus? Is he a good leader? Explain.

18 Discussion What is Yanus's highest priority?

19 Discussion Which advice in the verses is intended for Holders and which is intended for dragonriders? Why is such advice necessary?

20 Reading Strategy From what you have read so far, what subjects do you think the children were taught in the Teaching Ballads?

Speaking and Listening You might wish to have student volunteers read aloud the verses of the Teaching Ballad at the beginning of each chapter. If there are students with a musical background in the class, you may wish to have them set the words of the verses to an appropriate melody —folk music, for example. After the verses have been read or sung, discuss with students how the verses relate to life on Pern, why the verses were composed, and who composed them.

Dragonsong 921

Multicultural Focus Menolly is adept at playing a "gitar." Later she creates a reed pipe, a wind instrument made from hollow reeds. Point out that the guitar and wind instruments, which are variations on the flute, are two of the oldest musical instruments known and that they appear, with variations, in cultures all over the world. Ask students how many different kinds of guitars or flutes they know of, and list their responses on the board. Discuss the various kinds of music students may be familiar with that utilize guitar or flute, such as rock, blues, jazz, Reggae, or classical.

Have students do research to find out more about guitars and flutes. Ask some students to research the history of the guitar and the flute and find out how sound is produced by each instrument. Ask others to research the different varieties of guitars and flutes and in what cultures they are widely used. Still other students can bring in records or cassettes of music from different cultures that feature the guitar or the flute. Have students share their findings.

21 **Reader's Response** Do you think Menolly has a right to know the contents of the Masterharper's message?

22 **Discussion** What does the author mean by the statement that the Aunties would "find good out of any bad and the worst of any blessing"?

23 **Reading Strategy** Visualize the flame-crewing activities. Does it seem dangerous? Exciting? Explain.

children's recitations. The children were attentive: the Teaching was always better than gutting and preserving fish, or net mending, and longline baiting. Then, too, winter storms, the severest in many Turns, kept the fishing fleet docked and the Teaching eased the boredom.

When the Fleet was in, Yanus would stop by the Little Hall where Menolly held her class. He'd scowl at her from the back of the Hall. Fortunately, he'd only stay a little while because he made the children nervous. Once she actually saw his foot tapping the beat; he scowled when he realized what he was doing and then he left.

He had sent the message sloop to Igen Hold three days after the burial. The crew brought back news of no interest to Menolly but the adults went around looking black: something about the Oldtimers and Menolly wasn't to worry her head, so she didn't. The crew also brought back a message slate addressed to Petiron and signed with the imprint of Masterharper Robinton.

"Poor old Petiron," one of the aunties told Menolly, sighing and dabbing affectedly at her eyes. "He always looked forward to slates from Masterharper. Ah well, it'll keep till the new Harper comes. He'll know what to do with it."

It took Menolly a while to find out where the slate was: propped up conspicuously on the mantel in her father's Records room. Menolly was positive that the message had something to do with her, with the songs that Petiron had said he'd sent to the Masterharper. The notion so obsessed her that she got bold enough to ask her mother why Yanus didn't open the message.

"Open a sealed message from the Masterharper to a man dead?" Mavi stared at her daughter in shocked incredulity. "Your father would do no such thing. Harpers' letters are for Harpers."

"I only remembered that Petiron had sent a slate to the Masterharper. I thought it might be about a replacement coming. I mean . . ."

"I'll be glad when the new Harper does come, m'girl. You've been getting above yourself with this Teaching."

The next few days were full of apprehension for Menolly: she conceived the idea that her mother would make Yanus replace her as Teacher. That was, of course, impossible for the same reasons that had forced Yanus to make her the Teacher in the first place. But it was a fact that Mavi found all the smelliest, most boring or tedious jobs for Menolly once her teaching duty was done. And Yanus took it into his head to appear in the Little Hall more frequently.

Then the weather settled down into a clear spell and the entire Sea Hold was kept at a run with fish. The children were excused from the Teaching to gather seaweeds blown up by the high tides and all the Hold women set to boiling the weed for the thick juice in the stalks: juice that kept back many sicknesses and bone ailments. Or so the old aunties said. But they'd find good out of any bad and the worst of any blessing. And the worst of the seaweed was its smell, thought Menolly, who had to stir the huge kettles.

Threadfalls came and added some excitement: the fear in being holdbound while the dragons swept the skies with their fiery breath, charring Thread to impotence. (Menolly wanted to see that grand sight one day, instead of just singing about it, or knowing it was taking place outside the thick walls and heavy metal shutters of the Hold's windows.) Afterward she joined the flamethrower crews that checked for any possible Thread that might have escaped dragon flame. Not that there was much for Thread to eat on the windswept bare marshes and bogs around Half-Circle Sea Hold. The barren rock palisades that made Half-Circle bore no greenery at all, winter or summer, but it was wise to check the marshes and beaches. Thread could burrow into the seagrass stalks, or slide down the marshberry and seabeachplum bushes, burrow into the roots, multiply and eat anything green and growing until the coast was as bare as rock.

Flame-crewing was cold work, but it was a distinct pleasure for Menolly to be out of the Hold, in the rough air. Her team got as far as the Dragon Stones to the south. Petiron had told her that those stones, standing offshore in the treacherous waters, had once been part of the palisade, probably hollowed with caves like all this stretch of cliff.

The crowning treat for Menolly was when the Weyrleader, F'lar, himself, on bronze Mnementh, circled in for a chat with Yanus. Of course, Menolly wasn't near enough to hear what the two men said, but she was close enough to smell the fire-stone reek of the giant bronze dragon. Close enough to see his beautiful eyes catching all colors in the pale wintry sunlight: to see his muscles knot and smooth under the soft hide. Menolly stood, as was properly respectful, with the other flame-thrower crews. But once, when the dragon turned his head in a lazy fashion to peer in her direction, his eyes whirled slowly with their changing colors and she was certain that Mnementh looked at *her*. She didn't dare breathe, he was so beautiful!

24 **Reading Strategy** What might these lines foreshadow?

25 **Discussion** What is the relationship between F'lar and Yanus? What reason does F'lar have to talk with the Holder?

26 **Literary Focus: Setting** Have students note the richness of the sensory details in this passage. What details appeal to sight? Smell? Touch?

Then, suddenly, the magic moment was over. F'lar gave a graceful leap to the dragon's shoulder, caught the fighting straps and pulled himself into place on the neck ridges. Air whooshed around Menolly and the others as the great bronze opened his fragile-looking wings. The next moment, he seemed to be in the air, catching the updraft, beating steadily higher. Abruptly the dragon winked from view. Menolly was not the only one to sigh deeply. To see a dragonrider in the sky was always an occurrence: to be on the same ground with a dragon and his rider, to witness his graceful takeoff and exit *between* was a marvel.

All the songs about dragonriders and dragons seemed inadequate to Menolly. She stole up to the little cubicle in the women's dormitory that she shared with Sella. She wanted to be alone. She'd a little pipe among her things, a soft, whispery reedpipe, and she began to play it: a little whistle composed of her excitement and her response to the day's lovely event.

"So there you are!" Sella flounced into the room, her face reddened, her breath rough. She'd obviously run up the steep stairs. "Told Mavi you'd be here." Sella grabbed the little pipe from Menolly's fingers. "And tuning, too."

"Oh, Sella. It's an old tune!" Menolly said mendaciously and grabbed her pipe back.

Sella's jaw worked with anger. "Old, my foot! I know your ways, girl. And you're dodging work. You get back to the kitchen. You're needed now."

"I am not dodging work. I taught this morning during Threadfall and then I had to go with the crews."

"Your crew's been in this past half-day or more and you still in smelly, sandy clothes, mucking up the room I have to sleep in. You get below or I'll tell Yanus you've been tuning."

"Ha! You wouldn't know a tune if you had your nose rubbed in it."

But Menolly was shedding her work clothes as fast as she could. Sella was just likely to slip the word to Mavi (her sister was as wary of Yanus as Menolly) about Menolly piping in her room—a suspicious action on its own. Though Menolly hadn't sworn not to tune at all; only not to do it in front of people.

However, everyone was in a good mood that night: Yanus, because he'd spoken to F'lar the Weyrleader and because there'd be good fishing on the morrow if the weather held. Fish always rose to feed from drowned Thread, and half the Fall had been over Nerat Bay. The Deep would be thick with schools. With Yanus in a good mood, the rest of the Sea Holders could also rejoice because there'd been no Thread on the ground at all.

So it wasn't any wonder that they called on Menolly to play for them. She sang two of the longer Sagas about dragons and then did the Name-Song for the current wingleaders of Benden Weyr so her Sea Hold would know their dragonmen. She wondered if there'd been a recent Hatching that Half-Circle mightn't have heard about, being so isolated. But she was certain that F'lar would have told Yanus if that were so. But would Yanus have told Menolly? She wasn't the Harper to be told such things as courtesy.

The Sea Holders wanted more singing, but her throat was tired. So she played them a song they could sing, bellowing out the words in voices roughened by wind and salt. She saw her father scowling at her, though he was singing along with the rest of them, and she wondered if he didn't want her—a mere girl—to play men's songs. It galled her because she'd played them often enough when Petiron was alive. She sighed at this injustice. And then wondered what F'lar would have said if he'd known that Half-Circle Sea Hold was dependent on a mere girl for their harpering. She'd heard everyone say that F'lar was a fair man, a farseeing man, and a fine dragonrider. There were even songs about him and his Weyrwoman, Lessa.

So she sang them, in honor of the Weyrleader's visit, and her father's expression lightened. She sang on until her throat was so tight that not a squeak would come out. She wished that someone else could play to give her a rest but, as she scanned the faces of the Holders, there wasn't any of them who could beat a drum properly, much less finger a gitar or pipe.

That was why the next day it seemed only logical for her to start one of the children learning the drum rolls. Plenty of songs could be sung just to drumbeat. And one of Soreel's two children still in Teaching was sensitive enough to learn to pipe.

Someone, Sella perhaps, Menolly thought bitterly, informed Mavi of Menolly's activity.

"You were told no tuning . . ."

"Teaching someone drum beats is not tuning . . ."

"Teaching anyone to play is Harper business, not yours, m'girl. Just your good fortune Sea Holder is out in the Deep or you'd have the belt across your shoulders, so you would. No more nonsense."

"But it's not nonsense, Mavi. Last night another drummer or piper would have . . ."

Her mother raised her hand in warning, and Menolly bit shut her lips.

"No tuning, Menolly!"

And that was that.

"Now girl, see to the glows before the Fleet gets back."

That job took Menolly inexorably to the Harper's room: swept clean of everything that had been personal to Petiron. She was also reminded of the sealed message on the Record room mantel. What if the Masterharper were expecting a message from Petiron about the songmaker? Menolly was so very sure

that part of that unopened message was about her. Not that thinking about it did Menolly any good. Even knowing it for a fact would be no help, Menolly decided gloomily. But that didn't stop her from going past Yanus's Record room and peering in at the tempting package on the mantel.

She sighed, turning from the room. By now the Masterharper would have heard of Petiron's death and be sending a new Harper. Maybe the new man would be able to open the message, and maybe, if it was about her, maybe if it said that the songs she'd sent were good ones, Yanus and her mother wouldn't put such restrictions on her about tuning and whistling and everything.

As the winter spun itself out, Menolly found that her sense of loss when she thought of Petiron deepened. He had been the only person in the Sea Hold who had ever encouraged her in anything: and most especially in that one thing that she was now forbidden to do. Melodies don't stop growing in the mind, tapping at fingers, just because they're forbidden. And Menolly didn't stop composing them—which, she felt, was not precisely disobeying.

What seemed to worry Yanus and Mavi most, Menolly reasoned to herself, was the fact that the children, whom she was supposed to teach only the proper Ballads and Sagas, might think Menolly's tunes were Harper-crafted. (If her tunes were that good in her parents' ears, what was the harm of them?) Basically they didn't want her to play her songs aloud where they would be heard and perhaps repeated at awkward times.

Menolly could, therefore, see no harm in writing down new tunes. She played them softly in the empty Little Hall when the children had left, before she began her afternoon chores, carefully hiding her notations among the Harper records in the rack of the Hall. Safe enough, for no one but herself, till the

31

31 **Discussion** Menolly thinks there is no harm in writing down new tunes. How do you think her parents would feel about it?

32 Reading Strategy Have students summarize the reasons for Menolly's loneliness.

33 Discussion What "lapse" has Menolly fallen into? Why is it a problem?

34 Discussion Is Yanus justified in giving Menolly a beating?

35 Discussion What unspoken hope has Menolly lost?

new Harper came, would discover them there.

32 This mild deviation from the absolute obedience to her father's restriction about tuning did much to ease Menolly's growing frustration and loneliness. What Menolly didn't realize was that her mother had been watching her closely, having recognized the signs of rebellion in her. Mavi didn't want the Hold to be disgraced in any way, and she feared that Menolly, her head turned by Petiron's marked favor, was not mature enough to discipline herself. Sella had warned her mother that Menolly was getting out of hand. Mavi put some of that tale down to sisterly envy. But, when Sella had told Mavi that Menolly had actually started to teach another how to play an instrument, Mavi had been obliged to intervene. Let Yanus get one whisper of Menolly's disobedience and there'd be real trouble in the Hold for the girl.

Spring was coming and with spring, the quieter seas. Perhaps the new Harper would arrive soon.

And then spring did come, a first glorious day. The sweet scents of seabeachplum and marshberry filled the seaward breezes and came in through the opened shutters of the Little Hall. The children were singing loudly, as if shouting got them through the learning faster. True, they were singing one of the longer Sagas, word perfect, but with far more exuberance than was strictly needed. Perhaps it was that exuberance that infected Menolly and reminded her of a tune she'd tried to set down the day before.

33 She did not consciously disobey. She certainly was unaware that the fleet had returned from an early catch. She was equally unaware that the chords she was strumming were not—officially—of the Harper's craft. And it was doubly unfortunate that this lapse occurred just as the Sea Holder passed the open windows of the Hall.

926 *The Novel*

He was in the Little Hall almost at once, summarily dismissing the youngsters to help unload the heavy catch. Then he silently, which made the anticipation of the punishment worse, removed his wide belt, signaled Menolly to raise her tunic over her head and to bend over the high Harper's stool. **34**

When he had finished, she had fallen to her knees on the hard stone flags, biting her lips to keep back the sobs. He'd never beaten her so hard before. The blood was roaring in her ears so fiercely that she didn't hear Yanus leave the Little Hall. It was a long while before she could ease the tunic over the painful weals on her back. Only when she'd got slowly to her feet did she realize that he'd taken the gitar, too. She knew then that his judgment was irrevocable and harsh. **35**

And unjust! She'd only played the first few bars . . . hummed along . . . and that only because the last chords of the Teaching Ballad had modified into the new tune in her head. Surely that little snitch wouldn't have done any lasting harm! And the children knew all the Teaching Ballads they were supposed to know. She hadn't *meant* to disobey Yanus.

"Menolly?" Her mother came to the class-hall door, the carrying thong of an empty skin in her hand. "You dismissed them early? Is that wise . . ." Her mother stopped abruptly and stared at her daughter. An expression of anger and disgust crossed her face. "So you've been the fool after all? With so much at stake, and you had to tune . . ."

"I didn't do it on purpose, Mavi. The song . . . just came into my mind. I'd played no more than a measure . . ."

There wasn't any point in trying to justify the incident to her mother. Not now. The desolation Menolly had felt when she realized her father had taken the gitar intensified in the face of her mother's cold displeasure.

"Take the sack. We need fresh greens," Mavi said in an expressionless voice. "And any of the yellow-veined grass that might be up. There should be some."

Resignedly, Menolly took the sack and, without thinking, looped the thong over her shoulder. She caught her breath as the unwieldy sack banged against her scored back.

36

Before Menolly could avoid it, her mother had flipped up the loose tunic. She gave an inarticulate exclamation. "You'll need numbweed on some of those."

Menolly pulled away. "What good's a beating then, if it's numbed away first chance?" And she dashed out of the Hall.

Much Mavi cared if she hurt, anyhow, except that a sound body works harder and longer and faster.

Her thoughts and her misery spurred her out of the Hold, every swinging stride she took jarring her sore back. She didn't slow down because she'd the whole long track in front of the Hold to go. The faster she went, the better, before some auntie wanted to know why the children were out of lessons so soon, or why Menolly was going greenpicking instead of Teaching.

Fortunately she encountered no one. Everyone was either down at the Dock Cave, unloading, or making themselves scarce to the Sea Holder's eyes so they wouldn't have to. Menolly charged past the smaller holds, down aways on the marshroad, then up the righthand track, south of the Half-Circle. She'd put as much distance between herself and Sea Hold as she could: all perfectly legitimate, in search of greenery.

As she jogged along the sandy footpath, she kept her eyes open for fresh growth, trying to ignore the occasional rough going when she'd jar her whole body. Her back began to smart. She gritted her teeth and paced on.

Her brother, Alemi, had once said that she could run as well as any boy of the Hold and outdistance the half of them on a long race. If only she had been a boy . . . Then it wouldn't have mattered if Petiron had died and left them Harperless. Nor would Yanus have beaten a boy for being brave enough to sing his own songs.

The first of the low marsh valleys was pink and yellow with blooming seabeach-plum and marshberry, slightly blackened here and there: more from the low-flying queens catching the odd Thread that escaped the main wings. Yes, and there was the patch that the flame-thrower had charred: the one Thread infestation that had gotten through. One day, Menolly told herself, she'd just throw open a window's steel shutters and *see* the dragons charring Thread in the sky. What a sight that must be for certain!

37

Fearful, too, she reckoned, having seen her mother treat men for Threadburn. Why, the mark looked as if someone had drawn a point-deep groove with a red-hot poker on the man's arm, leaving the edges black with singed skin. Torly would always bear that straight scar, puckered and red. Threadscore never healed neatly.

She had to stop running. She'd begun to sweat heavily and her back was stinging. She loosened her tunic belt, flapping the soft runner-beast hide to send cooling drafts up between her shoulder blades.

Past the first marsh valley, up over the rocky hump hill into the next valley. Cautious going here: this was one of the deep, boggy places. No sign of yellow-veined grasses. There had been a stand last summer two humpy hills over.

She heard them first, glancing up with a stab of terror at the unexpected sounds above. Dragons? She glanced wildly about for the telltale gray glitter of sky-borne Thread in the east. The greeny blue sky was clear of that dreaded fogging, but not of dragonwings.

36 Discussion What is Menolly's real reason for refusing to let Mavi treat the cuts with numbweed?

37 Discussion Why has Menolly never seen Thread?

38 **Discussion** Judging from Menolly's surprise, what can you infer about the Pernians' beliefs about the fire lizards?

39 **Critical Thinking and Reading** Ask students how they would paraphrase Petiron's statement: "People've been trying to since the first shell was cracked."

40 **Discussion** How did Petiron feel about riding a dragon? How do you know?

She heard dragons? It couldn't be! They didn't swarm like that. Dragons always flew in ordered wings, a pattern against the sky. These were darting, dodging, then swooping and climbing. She shaded her eyes. Blue flashes, green, the odd brown and then . . . Of course, sun glinted golden off the leading, dartlike body. A queen! A queen that tiny?

She expelled the breath she'd been holding in her amazement. A fire lizard queen? It had to be. Only fire lizards could be that small and look like dragons. Whers certainly didn't. And whers didn't mate midair. And that's what Menolly was seeing: the mating flight of a fire lizard queen, with her bronzes in close pursuit.

So fire lizards weren't boy talk! Awed, Menolly watched the swift, graceful flight. The queen had led her swarm so high that the smaller ones, the blues and greens and browns, had been forced down. They circled now at a lower altitude, struggling to keep the same direction as the high fliers. They dipped and dashed in mimicry of the queen and bronzes.

They had to be fire lizards! thought Menolly, her heart almost stopping at the beauty and thrill of the sight. Fire lizards! And they *were* like dragons. Only much, much smaller. She didn't know all the Teachings for nothing. A queen dragon was gold: she mated with the bronze who could outfly her. Which was exactly what was happening right now with the fire lizards.

Oh, they were beautiful to behold! The queen had turned sunward and Menolly, for all her eyes were very longsighted, could barely pick out that black mote and trailing cluster.

She walked on, following the main group of fire lizards. She'd bet anything that she'd end up on the coastline near the Dragon Stones. Last fall her brother, Alemi, had claimed he'd seen fire lizards there at dawn, feeding on fingertails in the shallows. His report had set off another rash of what Petiron had called "lizard-fever." Every lad in the Sea Hold had burned with plans to trap a fire lizard. They'd plagued Alemi to repeat his sighting.

It was just as well that the crags were unapproachable. Not even an experienced boatman would brave those treacherous currents. But, if anyone had been *sure* there were fire lizards there . . . Well no one would know from her.

Even if Petiron had been alive, Menolly decided, she would not have told him. He'd never seen a fire lizard, though he'd admitted to the children that the Records allowed that fire lizards did exist.

"They're seen," Petiron had told her later, "but they can't be captured." He gave a wheezing chuckle. "People've been trying to since the first shell was cracked."

"Why can't they be caught?"

"They don't want to. They're smart. They just disappear . . ."

"They go *between* like dragons?"

"There's no proof of that," said Petiron, a trifle cross, as if she'd been too presumptuous in suggesting a comparison between fire lizards and the great dragons of Pern.

"Where else can you disappear to?" Menolly had wanted to know. "What is *between*?"

"Some place that isn't." Petiron had shuddered. "You're neither here nor there," and he gestured first to one corner of the Hall and then towards the Sea Dock on the other side of the harbor. "It's cold, and it's nothing. No sight, no sound, no sensations."

"You've ridden dragonback?" Menolly had been impressed.

"Once. Many Turns ago." He shuddered again in remembrance. "Now, since we're touching on the subject, sing me the Riddle Song."

"It's been solved. Why do we have to know it now?"

"Sing it for me so I'll know that you know it, girl," Petiron had said testily. Which was no reason at all.

But Petiron had been very kind to her, Menolly knew, and her throat tightened with remembered regret for his passing. (Had he gone *between*? The way dragons did when they lost their riders or grew too infirm to fly? No, one left nothing behind, going *between*. Petiron had left his body to be slipped into the deeps.) And Petiron had left more behind than his body. He'd left her every song he'd ever known, every lay, every ballad, saga, every fingering, chord and strum, every rhythm. There wasn't any way a stringed instrument could be played that she didn't know, nor any cadence on the drums at which she wasn't time-perfect. She could whistle double-trills as well as any wherry with her tongue or on the reeds. But there had been some things Petiron wouldn't—or perhaps couldn't—tell her about her world. Menolly wondered if this was because she was a girl and there were mysteries that only the male mind could understand.

"Well," as Mavi had once told Menolly and Sella, "there are feminine puzzles that no mere man could sort, so that score is even."

"And one more for the feminine side," said Menolly as she followed the fire lizards. A mere girl had seen what all the boys—and men—of the Sea Hold had only dreamed of seeing, fire lizards at play.

They'd ceased following the queen and her bronzes and now indulged in mock air battles, swooping now and then to the land itself. And seemingly under it. Until Menolly realized that they must be over the beaches. The sand was slipping under her feet. An unwary step could plunge her into the holes and dips. She could hear the sea. She changed her course, keeping to the thicker patches of coarse marsh grasses. The ground would be firmer there, and she'd be less visible to the fire lizards.

She came to a slight rise, before the bluff broke off into a steep dive onto the beaches. The Dragon Stones were beyond in the sea, slightly hidden by a heat haze. She could hear fire lizards chirping and chattering. She crouched in the grasses and then, dropping to her full length, crept to the bluff edge, hoping for another glimpse of the fire lizards.

They were quite visible—delightfully so. The tide was out, and they were exceedingly busy in the shallows, picking rockmites from

41 **Clarification** Menolly uses a number of music terms in this passage. For students who are unfamiliar with music terminology, here are the meanings:

lay: a simple ballad

ballad: a traditional narrative song, with a slight instrumental accompaniment

saga: a long narrative song recording historical and legendary events

fingering: the method of applying fingers to the strings, holes, or keys of a musical instrument

chord: three or four notes sounded together

strum: playing by running the fingers or a pick across the strings

rhythm: the regularized pattern of notes with respect to time and emphasis

cadence: a progression of chords moving to a harmonic close or point of rest

trill: the rapid alternation of a note with the note above

42 **Reader's Response** Is it true that there are "mysteries" that only a male—or a female—can understand?

the tumbled exposed boulders, or wallowing on the narrow edging of red and white sand, bathing themselves with great enthusiasm in the little pools, spreading their delicate wings to dry. There were several flurries as two fire lizards vied for the same choice morsel. In that alone, she decided, they must differ from dragons; she'd never heard of dragons fighting amongst themselves for anything. She'd heard that dragons feeding among herds of runner-beasts and wherries were something horrible to behold. Dragons didn't eat that frequently, which was as well, or not all the resources of Pern could keep the dragons fed.

Did dragons like fish? Menolly giggled, wondering if there were any fish in the sea big enough to satisfy a dragon's appetite. Probably those legendary fish that always eluded the Sea Hold nets. Her Sea Hold sent their tithe[6] of sea produce, salted, pickled or smoked, to Benden Weyr. Occasionally a dragonrider came asking for fresh fish for a special feasting, like a Hatching. And the women of the Weyr came every spring and fall to berry or cut withies and grasses. Menolly had once served Manora, the Headwoman of Benden Lower Caverns, and a very pleasant gentle woman she'd been, too. Menolly hadn't been allowed to stay in the room long because Mavi shooed her daughters out, saying that she had things to discuss with Manora. But Menolly had seen enough to know she liked her.

The whole flock of lizards suddenly went aloft, startled by the return of the queen and the bronze who had flown her. The pair settled wearily in the warm shallow waters, wings spread as if both were too exhausted to fold them back. The bronze tenderly twined his neck about his queen's and they floated so, while blues excitedly offered the resting pair fingertails and rockmites.

6. **tithe** (tīth) *n.*: A contribution of one tenth of whatever they produce.

Entranced, Menolly watched from her screen of seagrass. She was utterly engrossed by the small doings of eating, cleaning and resting. By and by, singly or in pairs, the lesser fire lizards winged up to the first of the sea-surrounded bluffs, lost quickly from Menolly's sight as they secreted themselves in tiny creviced weyrs.

With graceful dignity, the queen and her bronze rose from their bathing. How they managed to fly with their glistening wings so close together, Menolly didn't know. As one, they seemed to dart aloft, then glided in a slow spiral down to the Dragon Stone, disappearing on the seaside and out of Menolly's vision.

Only then did she become conscious of discomfort; of the hot sun on her welted back, sand in the waistband of her trousers, seeping into her shoes, dried as sweaty grit on her face and hands.

Cautiously, she wriggled back from the edge of the bluff. If the fire lizards knew they'd been overseen, they might not return to this cove. When she felt she'd crawled far enough, she got to a crouching position and ran for a way.

She felt as rarely privileged as if she'd been asked to Benden Weyr. She kicked up her heels in an excess of joy and then, spotting some thick marsh grass canes in the bog, snicked one off at the waterline. Her father may have taken her gitar away, but there were more materials than strings over a sounding box to make music.

She measured the proper length barrel and cut off the rest. She deftly made six holes top and two bottom, as Petiron had taught her, and in moments, she was playing her reedpipe. A saucy tune, bright and gay because she was happy inside. A tune about a little fire lizard queen, sitting on a rock in the lapping sea, preening herself for her adoring bronze.

Grammar in Action

Varying sentence beginnings is a technique writers use to make a narrative passage interesting. Instead of beginning every sentence with the subject of a main clause, writers may use introductory phrases, subordinate clauses, and verbals. Look at how the Anne McCaffrey has begun these sentences from *Dragonsong:*

Entranced, Menolly watched from her screen of seagrass. (Past participle)

By and by, singly or in pairs, the fire lizards winged up to the first of the sea-surrounded bluffs . . . (Adverb phrases)

With graceful dignity, the queen and her bronze rose from bathing. (Prepositional phrase)

How they managed to fly with their glistening wings so close together, Menolly didn't know. (Noun clause)

The variety of sentence beginnings promotes a smooth flow and helps enhance meaning by emphasizing certain details. Usually, introductory expressions are separated from the main clause by a comma.

Student Activity 1. Rewrite these sentences varying the beginnings.

She'd a bit of trouble with the obligatory runs and found herself changing keys, but when she'd rehearsed the tune several times, she decided she liked it. It sounded so different from the sort of melody Petiron had taught her, different from the traditional form. Furthermore, it sounded like a fire lizard song: sprightly, cunning, secretive.

She stopped her piping, puzzled. Did the dragons know about fire lizards?

Chapter 3

> *Holder, watch; Holder, learn*
> *Something new in every Turn.*
> *Oldest may be coldest, too.*
> *Sense the right: find the true!*

When Menolly finally got back to the Sea Hold, the sky was darkening. The Hall was bustling with the usual end-of-day activity. The oldsters were setting the dinner tables, tidying the Great Hall and chattering away as if they hadn't met for Turns instead of only that morning.

With luck, thought Menolly, she could get her sack down to the water rooms . . .

"Where did you go for those greens, Menolly? Nerat?" Her mother appeared in front of her.

"Almost."

Immediately Menolly saw that her pert words were ill-timed. Mavi roughly grabbed the sack and peered inside critically.

"If you'd not made the trip worth the while . . . Sail's been sighted."

"Sail?"

Mavi closed the sack and shoved it back into Menolly's hands. "Yes, sail. You should have been back hours ago. Whatever possessed you to take off so far with Thread . . ."

"There weren't any greens nearer . . ."

"With Thread due to fall anytime? You're a fool twice over."

"I was safe enough. I saw a dragonrider doing his sweep . . ."

That pleased Mavi. "Thank heavens we're beholden to Benden. They're a proper Weyr." Mavi gave her daughter a shove towards the kitchen level. "Take those, and be sure the girls wash every speck of sand off. Who knows who's sailing in?"

Menolly slipped through the busy kitchen, countering orders flung at her by various other women who saw in her a capable assistant at their own tasks. Menolly merely brandished the sack and proceeded down to the water rooms. There some of the older but still able women were busily sandscouring the best metal plates and trays.

"I must have one basin for the greens, auntie," said Menolly, pushing up to the rank of stone sinks.

"Greens is easier on old skin than sand," said one of the women in a quavering, long-suffering voice and promptly deposited her pile of plates into the sink beside her and pulled her plug.

"More sand in greens than cleaning," another woman remarked in an acid tone.

"Yes, but take it *off* greens," said the obliging one. "Oh, what a lovely mess of yellow-veins, too. Where did you find them this time of year, daughter?"

"Halfway to Nerat." Menolly suppressed her grin at their startled shrieks of dismay. The furthest they'd stir from the Hold was the ledge in front on a sunny day.

"With Thread falling? You naughty girl!" "Did you hear about the sail?" "Who do you suppose?" "The new Harper, who else?" There was a wild chorus of cackling laughs and great wonderings about the appearance of the new Harper.

"They always send a young one here."

"Petiron was old!"

"He got *that* way. Same as we did!"

"How would you remember?"

"Why not? I've lived through more Harpers than you have, my girl."

Dragonsong 931

44 Discussion This verse from the Teaching Ballad advises Holders to learn something new every Turn. Using evidence from the story, would you say that Yanus heeded this advice? Why or why not?

45 Reading Strategy Do you think the new Harper will be able to help Menolly? Predict why or why not.

---

1. Menolly heard the fire lizards as she ran along the beach.
2. The queen soared high and was followed by a bronze.
3. Menolly watched the fire lizards from a hiding place.
4. Menolly composed a tune about the fire lizards as she watched them.

Student Activity 2. Provide commas where needed in the following sentences:
1. On the final chord Petiron went to his rest.
2. When the fleet was in Yanus would stop by the little Hall where Menolly held her class.
3. Then suddenly the magic moment was over.
4. Even if Petiron had been alive Menolly would not have told him.

Student Activity 3. Write four related sentences, each with a different beginning. You may model them after the examples in this activity or after other sentences in this novel.

Electronic Handbook You might wish to have students review phrases and clauses before completing the Grammar in Action activities. If students have access to the Language Master 6000, have them enter *phrase, clause, prepositional,* or *verbal* and press the GRAMMAR key to review sentence elements that may be used as introductory expressions.

"You have not! I came here from Red Sands in Ista . . ."

"You were born at Half-Circle, you old fool, and I birthed you!"

"Ha!"

Menolly listened to the four old women arguing back and forth until she heard her mother demanding to know if the greens had been washed. And where were the good plates and how was she to get anything done with all the gossip?

Menolly found a sieve large enough to hold the washed greens and brought them up for her mother's inspection.

"Well, that'll be enough for the head table," Mavi said, poking at the glistening mound with her fork. Then she stared at her daughter. "You *can't* appear like that. Here you, Bardie, take the greens and put the dressing on them. The one in the brown flask on the fourth shelf in the cool room. You, Menolly, have the goodness to get yourself sandfree and decently dressed. You're to attend Old Uncle. The moment he opens his mouth, shove something into it or we'll be hearing him all night long."

Menolly groaned. Old Uncle smelled almost as much as he chattered.

"Sella's much better handling him, Mavi . . ."

"Sella's to attend head table. You do as you're told and be grateful!" Mavi fixed her rebellious daughter with a stern eye, tacitly reminding her of her disgrace. Then Mavi was called away to check a sauce for the baking fish.

Menolly went off to the bathing rooms, trying to convince herself that she was lucky she hadn't been banished completely from the Hall this evening. Though tending Old Uncle came as close as could be to banishment. Honor obliged the Sea Holder to have all his household there to greet the new Harper.

Menolly shucked off the dirty tunic and breeches, and slipped into the warm bathing pool. She swung her shoulders this way and that for the water to wash the sand and sweat as painlessly as possible from her sore back. Her hair was all gritty with sea sand, too, so she washed that. She was quick because she'd have her hands full with Old Uncle. It'd be much better to have him all arranged in his hearth seat before everyone else assembled for dinner.

Draping her dirty clothes around her, Menolly took the calculated risk that few people would be in the High Hold at this hour and charged up the dimly lit steps from the bathing pools to the sleeping level. Every glow in the main corridor was uncovered, which meant that the Harper, if such it were, would have a guided tour of the Hold later. She dashed down to the narrow steps leading to the girls' dormitories, and got into her cubicle without a soul the wiser.

When she got to Old Uncle's room, later, she had to clean his face and hands and slip a clean tunic over his bony shoulders. All the while he was chattering about new blood in the Hold and hee-hee who was the new Harper going to marry? He'd a thing or two to tell the Harper, give him the chance, and why did she have to be so rough? His bones ached. Must be a change in the weather because his old legs never failed to give warning. Hadn't he warned them about the big storm a while back? Two boats had been lost with all crew. If they'd paid attention to his warning, it wouldn't have happened. His own son was the worst one for not listening to what his father said and why was she hurrying him so? He liked to take his time. No, couldn't he have the blue tunic? The one his daughter had made him, matching his eyes, she'd said. And why hadn't Turlon come to see him today as he'd asked and asked and asked, but who paid him any heed anymore?

Grammar in Action

Writers often use **phrases in a series** as a way of expressing many ideas smoothly and effectively in a single sentence. Adjective, adverb, and noun phrases may be used in a series, as well as the verbal forms (participle, gerund, and infinitive phrases). When phrases are used in a series, they are parallel in structure. Look at this example from *Dragonsong:*

There was so much bustle, *putting food on the tables,* *pouring the welcoming cups of wine,* all the Hold *arranging itself to meet the guests,* no one noticed what Menolly was or wasn't doing.

This series of participial phrases reads smoothly and effectively describes a number of activities. When three or more phrases occur in a series, they are separated by commas, as in this example:

Thread fell over the Hold, along the beach, and into the sea.

Student Activity 1. Write three sentences about the characters or events in *Dragonsong.* Use a series of phrases in each. You may do this activity with a partner.

The old man was so frail that he was no burden to a strong girl like Menolly. She carried him down the steps, he complaining all the way about people who'd been dead before she was born. Old Uncle's notion of time was distorted, that's what Petiron had told her. Brightest in Uncle's memory were his earlier days, when he'd been Sea Holder of Half-Circle, before a tangled trawler line had sliced off his legs below the knee. The great Hall was almost ready for guests when Menolly entered with him.

"They're tacking into Dock," someone was saying as Menolly arranged Old Uncle in his special seat by the fire. She wrapped him well in the softened wherhides and tied the strap that would keep him upright. When he got excited, Old Uncle had a tendency to forget he had no feet.

"Who's tacking into Dock? Who's coming? What's all the hubblebubble about?"

Menolly told him, and he subsided, moments later wanting to know in a querulous tone of voice if anyone was going to feed him or was he supposed to sit here dinnerless?

47 Sella, in the gown she'd spent all winter making, swirled past Menolly, pressing a small packet into her hand.

"Feed him these if he gets difficult!" And she skimmed away before Menolly could say a word.

Opening the packet, Menolly saw balls of a sweet made from seaweed, flavored with purple grass seed. One could chew these for hours, keeping the mouth fresh and moist. Small wonder Sella'd been able to keep Old Uncle happy. Menolly giggled and then wondered why Sella was being so helpful. It must have pleased Sella no end to learn Menolly had been displaced as Harper. Or would she know? Mavi wouldn't have mentioned it. Ah, but the Harper was here now, anyhow.

Now that she had Old Uncle settled,

Menolly's curiosity got the better of her and she slipped over to the windows. There was no sign of the sail in the harbor now, but she could see the cluster of men, glows held high, as they walked around the shore from the Dock to the Hold proper. Keen though her eyes were, Menolly could not pick out the new faces and that was that.

Old Uncle began one of his monologues in a high-pitched voice, so Menolly scooted back to his side before her mother could notice she'd left her post. There was so much bustle, putting food on the tables, pouring the welcoming cups of wine, all the Hold arranging itself to meet the guests, no one noticed what Menolly was or wasn't doing.

Just then, Old Uncle came to himself again, eyes bright and focused on her face. "What's the stir today, girl? Good haul? Someone getting spliced? What's the lay?"

"There's a new Harper coming, everyone thinks, Old Uncle."

"Not another one?" Old Uncle was disgusted. "Harpers ain't what they used to be when I was Sea Holder, not by a long crack. I mind myself of one Harper we had . . ."

His voice fell clearly in the suddenly quiet Hall.

"Menolly!" Her mother's voice was low, but the urgency was unmistakable.

Menolly fumbled in her skirt pocket, found two sweetballs and popped them into Old Uncle's mouth. Whatever he'd been about to say was stopped by the necessity of dealing with two large round objects. He mumbled contentedly to himself as he chewed and chewed and chewed.

All the food had been served and everyone seated before Menolly got so much as a glimpse of the new arrivals. There had been a new Harper. She heard his name before she ever saw his face. Elgion, Harper Elgion. She heard that he was young and good-looking and had brought two gitars, two wooden

Dragonsong 933

47 **Discussion** Sella and Menolly have different reasons for welcoming the arrival of a new Harper. How do their reasons differ?

Student Activity 2. Punctuate these sentences correctly.
1. Menolly was busy tending Old Uncle avoiding her sister and watching for the Harper's arrival.
2. Yanus wanted Menolly to stop tuning to avoid whistling and to behave like the other girls.
3. Sea Holders often had klah for breakfast soup for lunch and baked fish for dinner.
4. Flaming dragons darting fire lizards and falling Thread were all part of life on Pern.

Electronic Handbook You might wish to have students review the use of commas before completing the Grammar in Action activity. If students have access to the Language Master 6000, have them enter the access symbol #, and press the GRAMMAR key for information on punctuating items in series.

48 **Critical Thinking and Reading**
Why would Igen Hold have "urgent" need for fish?

49 **Critical Thinking and Reading**
Why does the Harper ask whether the Hold is rocking?

50 **Discussion** The Harper is obviously a man with a sense of humor. Why, then, does he refuse Old Uncle's request for a funny song?

pipes and three drums, each carried separately in its own case of stiffened wherhide. She heard that he'd been very seasick across Keroon Bay and wasn't doing justice to the lavish dinner spread in his honor. With him had come a Craftmaster from the Smithcrafthall to do the metal work required on the new ship and other repairs beyond the metalman in the Sea Hold. She heard that there was urgent need at Igen Hold for any salted or smoked fish the Sea Hold might have to spare on the return voyage.

From where Menolly sat with Old Uncle, she could see the backs of heads at the high table and occasionally a profile of one of the visitors. Very frustrating. So were Old Uncle and the other elderly relatives whose old bones rated them a spot near the fire. The aunts were, as usual, squabbling over who had received the choicer portions of fish, and then Old Uncle decided to call them to order, only his mouth was full at that moment and he choked. So the aunts turned on Menolly for trying to stuff him to an early death. Menolly could hear nothing over their babble. She tried to content herself with the prospect of hearing the Harper sing, as he surely would once the interminable meal was ended. But it was hot so close to the big fire and the heat made Old Uncle smell worse than ever, and she was very tired after the day's exertions.

She was roused from a half-doze by a sudden hallwide thudding of heavy seaboots. She jerked fully awake to see the tall figure of the new Harper rising at the head table. He had his gitar ready and was taking an easy stance, one foot on the stone bench.

"You're sure this Hall isn't rocking?" he asked, strumming a few chords to test the instrument's pitch. He was assured that the Hall had been steady for many, many Turns, never known to rock at all. The Harper affected not to be reassured as he tuned the

G-string slightly higher (to Menolly's relief). He made the gitar moan then, like a seasick soul.

As laughter rippled through the eager audience, Menolly strained to see how her father was taking this approach. The Sea Holder had little humor. A Harper's welcome was a serious occasion, and Elgion did not appear to realize this. Petiron had often told Menolly how carefully Harpers were chosen for the Hold they were assigned to. Hadn't anyone warned Elgion about her father's temperament?

Suddenly Old Uncle cut across the gentle strumming with a cackle of laughter. "Ha! A man with humor! That's what we need in this Hold—some laughter. Some music! Been missing it. Let's have some rollicking tunes, some funny songs. Give us a good rib-popping ditty, Harper. You know the ones I like."

Menolly was aghast. She fumbled in her skirt pocket for some of the sweetballs as she shushed Old Uncle. This was exactly the sort of incident that she was supposed to prevent.

Harper Elgion had turned at the imperious order, bowing with good respect to the old gentleman by the hearth.

"I would that I could, Old Uncle," he said most courteously, "but these are serious times," and his fingers plucked deep somber notes, "very serious times and we must put lightness and laughter behind us. Square our backs to the problems that face us . . ." and with that he swung into a new exhortation to obey the Weyr and honor the dragonrider.

The sticky sweetballs had got warmed and stuck to the fabric of her pocket, but Menolly finally got some out and into Old Uncle's mouth. He chewed angrily, fully aware that his mouth was being plugged and resenting it. He chewed as fast as he could, swallowing to clear his mouth for more com-

51 Discussion Why does it seem that everything Menolly does is not right? How does she behave or think differently from others?

52 Clarification Tell students that *sequestering* means "withdrawing into seclusion." What connotation does it have here?

plaints. Menolly was only just aware that the new tune was forceful, the words stirring. Harper Elgion had a rich tenor voice, strong and sure. Then Old Uncle began to hiccup. Noisily, of course. And to complain, or try to, through the hiccups. Menolly hissed at him to hold his breath, but he was furious at not being allowed to talk, at getting hiccups, and he started to pound the arm of his chair. The thumps made an out-of-tempo counterpoint to the Harper's song and brought her furious glances from the head table.

One of the aunts gave her some water for the old man, which he overturned on Menolly. The next thing, Sella was beside her, gesturing that they were to take the old man back to his quarters instantly.

He was still hiccuping as they put him back to bed, and still beating the air with punctuated gestures and half-uttered complaints.

"You'll have to stay with him until he calms down, Menolly, or he'll fall out of bed. Whyever didn't you give him the sweetballs? They always shut him up," Sella said.

"I did. They're what started him hiccuping."

"You can't do anything right, can you?"

"Please, Sella. You stay with him. You manage him so well. I've had him all evening and not heard a word . . ."

"*You* were told to keep him quiet. *You* didn't. *You* stay." And Sella swept out of the room, leaving Menolly to cope.

That was the end of the first of Menolly's difficult days. It took hours for the old man to calm down and go to sleep. Then, as Menolly wearily got to her cubicle, her mother arrived to berate her soundly for the inattention that had given Uncle a chance to embarrass the entire Hold. Menolly was given no chance to explain.

The next day, Thread fell, sequestering them all within the Hold for hours. When the Fall was over, she had to go with the flame-thrower crews. The leading edge of Thread had tipped the marshes, which meant hours of plodding through sticky marsh mud and slimy sand.

She was tired enough when she returned from that task, but then they all had to help load the big nets and ready the boats for a night trawl. The tide was right then.

She was roused before sunrise the next

Dragonsong 935

53 Discussion What do you think are the answers to these questions?

54 Reader's Response How do you think Menolly feels at this remark?

55 Discussion Menolly thinks she is being singled out for much misunderstanding. Is she justified in her belief, or has she brought her troubles on herself? Explain.

56 Reader's Response Do you think that Menolly is treated unjustly?

morning to gut and salt the phenomenal catch. That took all the livelong day and sent her to bed so early she just stripped off her dirty clothes, and dropped into her sleeping furs.

The next day was devoted to net-mending, normally a pleasant task because the Hold women would chat and sing. But her father was anxious for the net to be repaired quickly so that he could take the evening tide again for another deep-sea cast. Everyone bent to his work without time for talk or singing while the Sea Holder prowled among them. He seemed to watch Menolly more often than anyone else, and she felt clumsy.

It was then that she began to wonder if perhaps the new Harper had found fault with the way the youngsters had been taught their Ballads and Sagas. Time and again Petiron had told her that there was only one way to teach them and, as she had learned properly from him, she must have passed on the knowledge correctly. Why then did her father seem to be so annoyed with her? Why did he glare at her so much? Was he still angry with her for letting Old Uncle babble?

She worried enough to ask her sister about it that evening when the ships had finally set sail and everyone else could relax a little.

"Angry about Old Uncle?" Sella shrugged. "What on earth are you talking about, girl? Who remembers that? You think entirely too much about yourself, Menolly, that's your biggest problem. Why should Yanus care one way or another about *you*?"

The scorn in Sella's voice reminded Menolly too acutely that she was only a girl, too big for a proper girl, and the youngest of a large family, therefore of least account. It was in no way a consolation to be insignificant, even if her father was, for that reason, less likely to notice her. Or remember her misdeeds. Except that he'd remembered

about her singing her own songs to the youngsters. Or had Sella forgotten that? Or did Sella even know that?

Probably, thought Menolly as she tried to find a comfortable spot in the old bed rushes for her weary body. But then, what Sella said about Menolly thinking only of herself applied even more to Sella, who was always thinking about her appearance and her self. Sella was old enough to be married to some advantage to the Hold. Her father had only three fosterlings at that moment, but four of Menolly's six brothers were out at other Sea Holds, learning their trade. Now, with a Harper to speak for them all again, perhaps there'd be some rearrangements.

The next day the Hold women spent in washing clothes. With Threadfall past, and a good clear sunny day, they could count on fast drying. Menolly hoped for a chance to speak to her mother to find out if the Harper had faulted her teaching, but the opportunity never arose. Instead, Menolly came in for another scolding from Mavi for the state of her clothes, unmended; her bed furs, unaired; her hair, her sloppy appearance and her slothfulness in general. That evening Menolly was quite content to take a bowl of soup and disappear into a shadowy corner of the big kitchen rather than be noticed again. She kept wondering why she was being singled out for so much misunderstanding.

Her thoughts kept returning to the sin of having strummed a few bars of her own song. That, and being a girl and the only one who could teach or play in the absence of a real Harper.

Yes, she finally decided, that was the reason for her universal disfavor. No one wanted the Harper to know that the youngsters had been schooled by a girl. But, if she hadn't taught them right, then Petiron had taught her all wrong. That didn't hold water. And, if the old man had really written the Masterharper about her, wouldn't the new Harper have been curious, or sought her out? Maybe her songs hadn't been as good as old Petiron had thought. Probably Petiron had never sent them to the Masterharper. And that message hadn't said anything about her. At any rate, the packet was now gone from the mantel in the Records room. And, the way things were going, Menolly would never get close enough to Elgion to introduce herself.

Sure as the sun came up, Menolly could guess what she'd have to do the next day— gather new grasses and rushes to repack all the beds in the Hold. It was just the sort of thing her mother would think of for someone so out of favor.

She was wrong. The ships came back to port just after dawn, their holds packed with yellow-stripe and packtails. The entire Hold was turned out to gut, salt and start the smoke-cave.

Of all the fish in the sea, Menolly detested packtails the most. An ugly fish, with sharp spines all over, it oozed an oily slime that ate into the flesh of your hands and made the skin peel off. Packtails were more head and mouth than anything else but hack the front end off and the rounded, blunt tail could be sliced off the backbone. Grilled fresh it was succulent eating: smoked it would be softened later for baking or boiling and be as tasty as the day it was caught. But packtails were the messiest, hardest, toughest, smelliest fish to gut.

Halfway through the morning, Menolly's knife slipped across the fish she was slicing, gashing her left palm wide open. The pain and shock were so great that Menolly just stood, stupidly staring at her hand bones, until Sella realized that she wasn't keeping pace with the others.

"Menolly, just dreaming . . . Oh, for the love of . . . Mavi! Mavi!" Sella could be irritating, but she could keep her wits. As she did now, grabbing Menolly's wrist and stopping the spurt of blood from the severed artery.

As Mavi came and led her past the furiously working Holders, Menolly was seized with a sense of guilt. Everyone glared at her as if she'd deliberately wounded herself to get out of working. The humiliation and silent accusations brought tears to her eyes, not the pain nor the sick feeling in her hand.

"I didn't do it on purpose," Menolly blurted out to her mother as they reached the Hold's infirmary.

Her mother stared at her. "Who said that you did?"

"No one! They just looked it!"

"My girl, you think entirely too much about yourself. I assure you that no one was thinking any such thing. Now hold your hand, so, for a moment."

The blood spurted up as Mavi released the pressure on the tendon in Menolly's wrist. For one instant Menolly thought she might faint, but she was determined not to think of herself again. She pretended that she didn't own the hand that Mavi was going to have to fix.

Mavi now deftly fastened a tourniquet and then laved the wound with a pungent herbal lotion. Menolly's hand began to numb, increasing her detachment from the injury. The bleeding ceased, but somehow Menolly couldn't bring herself to look into the wound. Instead she watched the intent expression on her mother's face as she quickly stitched the severed blood vessel and closed the long slice. Then she slathered quantities of salve on the cut and bound the hand in soft cloths.

"There! Let's hope I got all that packtail slime out of the wound."

Concern and doubt caused Mavi to frown, and Menolly became fearful. Suddenly she remembered other things: women losing fingers and . . .

"My hand will be all right, won't it?"

Dragonsong 937

57 **Discussion** Why would Menolly feel guilty?

58 **Discussion** Does Menolly think too much about herself and her problems? Explain.

Reader's Response Menolly has been the victim of both injustice and bad luck. In her place, would you have reacted as she did, or would you have behaved differently? Explain.

Thematic Response Menolly is in conflict with her family and the customs of the Hold. Out of conflict often comes a challenge. What challenge does Menolly face?

Multicultural Connection As you discuss this feature, you may wish to compare the historical songs of *Dragonsong* to the intergenerational oral history in the well-known TV mini-series *Roots*. You might discuss what could be perceived as problems in this method of disseminating information: sometimes names, dates, and other factual data were lost. Have students offer opinions about the effectiveness and validity of oral histories.

"We'll hope so."

Mavi never lied, and the small hard ball of sick fear began to unknot in Menolly's stomach.

"You should have some use of it. Enough for all practical purposes."

"What do you mean? Practical purposes? Won't I be able to play again?"

"Play?" Mavi gave her daughter a long, hard stare, as if she'd mentioned something forbidden. "Your playing days are over, Menolly. You're way past the teaching . . ."

"But the new Harper has new songs . . . the Ballad he sang the first night . . . I never heard all of it. I don't know the chording. I want to learn . . ." She broke off, horribly frightened by the closed look on her mother's face, and the shine of pity in her eyes.

"Even if your fingers will work after that slice, you won't be playing again. Content yourself that Yanus was so indulgent while old Petiron was dying . . ."

"But Petiron . . ."

"That's enough *buts*. Here, drink this. I want you in your bed before it puts you to sleep. You've lost a lot of blood, and I can't have you fainting away on me."

Stunned by her mother's words, Menolly barely tasted the bitter wine and weed. She stumbled, even with her mother's help, up the stone steps to her cubicle. She was cold despite the furs, cold in spirit. But the wine and weed had been liberally mixed, and she couldn't fight the effect. Her last conscious thought was of misery, of being cheated of the one thing that had made her life bearable. She knew now what a dragonless rider must feel.

MULTICULTURAL CONNECTION

Literature in the Oral Tradition

It is hard to imagine a culture in which all learning, literature, and wisdom is communicated by the spoken word—the method of education seen in *Dragonsong*. This practice is not found only in fiction. Indeed, there have been many people who compose and pass on their heritage orally.

Oral literature in African cultures. The rich tradition of African oral literature includes heroic legends, histories of entire peoples, fables, proverbs, riddles, and songs. This literature serves several purposes: It preserves the past and teaches the traditions and morals of the culture to its youth.

In West Africa traveling storytellers called *griots* tell, chant, or sing their tales to large groups of people in each village they visit. The griot may bring along a chorus, and the listeners clap and join in the storytelling.

When they were brought against their will to America as slaves, many Africans brought their oral literature with them. Such familiar African characters as Anansi the Spider were transformed into the wily Br'er Rabbit, made famous in the southern stories of Joel Chandler Harris.

Native American legends. Among Native Americans, fathers handed down the legends of their ancestors to their sons. Many of these legends explain how the world and people were created, and they often formed the basis of tribal ceremonies.

Exploring and Sharing

Were any examples of oral literature passed on to you from your parents or grandparents? What is your favorite family story?

Closure and Extension

ANSWERS TO RESPONDING TO THE SELECTION
Your Response
1. Encourage students to explore the various courses of action open to a person. Ask if it would be necessary to do something drastic.
2. Discuss the reasons why Menolly wants to keep the fire lizards a secret. Ask whether telling everyone might have bad results for the fire lizards and for Menolly.

Recalling
3. Yanus knew that Menolly was the only person who could sing the song.

Interpreting
4. Yanus is very traditional. He would be humiliated if anyone suggested that his daughter would do something as "unfeminine" as tuning.
5. Suggested Response: The Hold is probably quite a distance from

RESPONDING TO THE SELECTION

Your Response

1. How would you feel if someone prevented you from using your talents?
2. Would you have kept the existence of the fire lizards a secret, as Menolly did?

Recalling

3. Why does Yanus allow Menolly to sing the Deathsong at Petiron's burial?

Interpreting

4. Why is Yanus so opposed to Menolly's tuning?
5. Why is there so little contact between Half-Circle Sea Hold and the other Holds on Pern?
6. What do you infer about the values of the Hold from their treatment of Old Uncle?
7. What does the author mean when she says that Menolly "knew now what a dragonless rider must feel"?

Applying

8. Menolly is the victim of an injustice created by the rules of her society. What can a person in a situation like Menolly's do to obtain justice?

ANALYZING LITERATURE

Understanding Imaginary Settings

In a novel with an **imaginary setting,** the author makes an unfamiliar world seem familiar to the reader by creating realistic, believable details. In *Dragonsong,* for example, the details of everyday living are perfectly familiar.

1. Give three details of the world of Pern that tell you it is imaginary.
2. Give three details of daily life on Pern that could have come from your own daily life.

CRITICAL THINKING AND READING

Inferring the Meanings of Words

When writers create an imaginary setting, they often make up words and terms to describe objects or phenomena that are not familiar to us. In order to understand these words, you must depend upon context clues. Sometimes the author describes the object to which the word refers. Often you can deduce the meaning from the function of the object in the story. The *glows* in the story, for example, are tended to at night. You can assume that they are some form of light source. What are the meanings of these words from *Dragonsong?*

1. between   4. Harper
2. Turns   5. tuning
3. klah   6. teleportation

THINKING AND WRITING

Creating an Imaginary Place

Write a description of an imaginary world. You may wish to describe the one your group created before beginning to read. Explain how the people in this world obtain food and clothing and how they travel from one place to another. Discuss the customs of the world and how those customs affect the men and women who live there. Share your draft with a response group for feedback. Revise details according to their suggestions.

LEARNING OPTIONS

1. **Writing.** In this novel, Menolly is punished for tuning, but it is perfectly acceptable here on Earth. Write a song about the fire lizards. Use the words and terms from the novel wherever possible. The lines of your song need not rhyme. Set the words to a familiar piece of music and choose some classmates to join you in performing your song for the class.
2. **Art.** Draw a picture of some aspect of Pern. It may be a scene from the novel or some objects that are used by the characters, such as the gitar and pipes that Harper Elgion brought with him to Half-Circle Sea Hold. Display your drawing in the classroom.

Dragonsong 939

Literary Focus In science fiction stories, motivation can be quite unusual. In the Pern novels, for example, the dragonriders are often motivated by their telepathic relationship with their dragons. Science fiction authors have un-limited possibilities in creating motives for alien creatures. Tell students to be aware of the un-usual or unexpected motives of the animal characters as well as the human ones in *Dragonsong*.

Prereading Focus You might want to ask students about their experiences in training a pet. Ask if they can imagine any differenc-es between training a dog and training a fire lizard. Dogs might be easier to train because they do not go "between." Fire lizards might be easier to train because they are so intelligent. Ask stu-dents, as they read, to evaluate the way Menolly handles this task.

Vocabulary Have students ex-amine these words and their meanings. What impression about the events in the novel are conveyed by the words *writhing, dour, obliterated,* and *recalcitrant*?

Spelling Tip Because many of these words are multisyllabic, urge students to pronounce the words carefully when spelling them to be sure to include all the syllables. Also note that three words contain the *ous* combina-tion: *precariously, audacious,* and *scrupulously.*

Dragonsong, Chapters 4–6

Motivation

Motivation is the reason that a character behaves or thinks in a certain way. When characters have different motives, conflict often results, usually spurred by an outside force or event. For example, the death of Petiron, which allows Menolly to take up teaching du-ties, spurs a conflict between her and her father. In this conflict, Menolly is motivated by a desire for freedom and creativity, while her father wishes to preserve traditional forms.

Focus

Taming a wild animal is not an easy task. How would you go about winning the trust of a fire lizard? Working with a partner or a small group, write a brief description of the steps you would take to tame one of the beasts. Explain any particular obstacles that might stand in your way, such as the fire lizard's ability to go *between.* You might end your writing by completing this simile: Taming a fire lizard is like _____." When you have finished, compare your ideas with those of your classmates. As you read the next chapters, note how Menolly deals with the problem.

Vocabulary

Knowing the following words will help you as you read Chapters 4–6 of *Dragonsong.*

gratified (grat′ i fid) *v.*: Pleased or satisfied (p. 941)

writhing (riŧh′ iŋ) *v.*: Suffering great emotional distress; twist-ing, contorting (p. 942)

dour (dour) *adj.*: Stern; severe; gloomy (p. 943)

daunted (dônt′ əd) *v.*: Fright-ened or disheartened (p. 945)

precariously (prē ker′ ē əs lē) *adv.*: In a dangerous, risky way (p. 948)

obliterated (ə blit′ ər āt əd) *v.*: Destroyed without leaving any traces (p. 950)

audacious (ô dā′ shəs) *adj.*: Bold; daring (p. 951)

scrupulously (skrōō′ pyə ləs lē) *adv.*: Marked by precision and extreme conscientiousness (p. 953)

myriad (mir′ ē əd) *adj.*: Nu-merous (p. 954)

recalcitrant (ri kal′ si trənt) *adj.*: Refusing to obey authority; hard to handle (p. 960)

Objectives

1 To understand motivation
2 To recognize cause and effect
3 To write about cause and effect
4 To express individual in-terests and abilities through optional activities

Support Material

Teaching Portfolio
Teacher Backup, p. 983
Grammar in Action Worksheets, *Recognizing Infinitive Phrases,* p. 987; *Recognizing Participial Phrases,* p. 989
Usage and Mechanics Work-sheet, p. 991
Vocabulary Check, p. 992
Analyzing Literature Worksheet, *Understanding Motivation,* p. 993

Critical Thinking and Reading Worksheet, *Recognizing Cause and Effect,* p. 994
Selection Test, p. 995

Prentice Hall Literature Writing Studio

Chapter 4

Black, blacker, blackest
And cold beyond frozen things.
Where is between when there is naught
To Life but fragile dragons' wings?

Despite her mother's care in cleaning the wound, Menolly's hand was swollen by evening and she was feverish with pain. One of the old aunts sat with her, placing cool cloths on her head and face, and gently crooning what she thought would be a comforting song. The notion was misplaced since, even in her delirium,[1] Menolly was aware that music had now been forbidden her. She became more irritated and restless. Finally Mavi dosed her liberally with fellis juice and wine, and she fell into a deep slumber.

This proved to be a blessing because the hand had so swollen that it was obvious some of the packtail slime had gotten in the bloodstream. Mavi called in one of the other Hold women deft in such matters. Luckily for Menolly, they decided to release the coarse stitches, to allow better drainage of the infection. They kept Menolly heavily dosed and hourly changed the hot poulticing[2] of her hand and arm.

Packtail infection was pernicious, and Mavi was dreadfully afraid that they might have to remove Menolly's arm to prevent a further spread. She was constantly by her daughter's side, an attention that Menolly would have been surprised, and gratified, to receive, but she remained unconscious. Fortunately the angry red lines faded on the girl's swollen arm on the evening of the fourth day. The swelling receded, and the edges of the terrible gash assumed the healthier color of healing flesh.

Throughout her delirium, Menolly kept begging "them" to let her play just once more, just once again, pleading in such a pitiful tone that it all but broke Mavi's heart to realize that unkind fortune had made that impossible. The hand would always be crippled. Which was as well since some of the new Harper's questions were provoking Yanus. Elgion very much wanted to know who had drilled the youngsters in their Teaching Songs and Ballads. At first, thinking that Menolly had been nowhere near as skilled as everyone had assumed, Yanus had told Elgion that a fosterling had undertaken the task and he'd returned to his own Hold just prior to the Harper's arrival.

"Whoever did has the makings of a good Harper then," Elgion told his new Holder. "Old Petiron was a better teacher than most."

The praise unexpectedly disturbed Yanus. He couldn't retract his words, and he didn't want to admit to Elgion that the person was a girl. So Yanus decided to let matters stand. No girl could be a Harper, any way the road turned. Menolly was too old now to be in any of the classes, and he'd see that she was busy with other things until she came to think of her playing as some childish fancy. At least she hadn't disgraced the Hold.

He was, of course, sorry that the girl had cut herself so badly, and not entirely because she was a good worker. Still it kept her out of the Harper's way until she forgot her silly tuning. Once or twice though, while Menolly was ill, he missed her clear sweet voice in counter-song, the way she and Petiron used to sing. Yet he dismissed the matter from his mind. Women had more to do than sit about singing and playing.

There were exciting doings in the Holds and Weyrs, according to Elgion's private report to him. Troubles, too, deep and

---

1. delirium (di lir′ ē əm) *n*.: A temporary state of mental confusion often caused by fever and marked by restlessness and confused speech.
2. poulticing (pōl′ tis iŋ) *n*.: A soft mass of an adhesive substance applied to a sore or inflamed part of the body.

Dragonsong   941

4 Discussion Do you think the mutual interdependence between the Hold and the Weyr is good? Explain.

5 Discussion Masterharper Robinton wants more from his journeymen than teaching children and entertaining the Hold. Explain what he wants, and discuss whether it is a good idea.

Multicultural Focus Explain that the singer/storyteller, or Harper as he is called in *Dragonsong*, is a very important person in traditional societies. Long before people used written language, the singer/storyteller was the person who remembered and told family and community history and passed it on, in the form of stories, to a new generation. Even after written language developed, many people could not read or write, so storytelling and singing continued to be a vital source of entertainment and historical recordkeeping.

Have students do research to find out more about the role of the singer/storyteller in different cultures. They might explore the role of the griot in certain African cultures, for example. Have them present their findings to the class.

Speaking and Listening You might want to ask a student to read the paragraph beginning "If the Harper. . . ." Discuss with students the role of Harpers in general and the role of Elgion in particular in influencing the fate of Pern.

worrisome enough to take his mind from the minor matter of a wounded girl.

One of the questions that Harper Elgion often posed concerned the Sea Hold's attitude towards their Weyr, Benden. Elgion was curious as to how often they came in contact with the Oldtimers at Ista Weyr. How did Yanus and his Holders feel about dragonriders? About the Weyrleader and Weyrwoman of Benden? If they resented dragonmen going on Search for young boys and girls of the Holds and Crafthalls to become dragonriders? Had Yanus or any of his Hold ever attended a Hatching?

Yanus answered the questions with the fewest possible words, and at first this seemed to satisfy the Harper.

"Half-Circle's always tithed to Benden Weyr, even before Thread fell. We know our duty to our Weyr, and they do theirs by us. Not a single burrow of Thread since the Fall started seven or more Turns ago."

"Oldtimers? Well, with Half-Circle beholden to Benden Weyr, we don't much see any of the other Weyrs, not as the people in Keroon or Nerat might when the Fall overlaps two Weyrs' boundaries. Very glad we were that the Oldtimers would come *between* so many hundreds of Turns to help our time out."

"Dragonmen are welcome any time at Half-Circle. Come spring and fall, the women are here anyway, gathering seabeachplums and marshberries, grasses and the like. Welcome to all they want."

"Never met Weyrwoman Lessa. I see her on her queen Ramoth in the sky after a Fall now and then. Weyrleader F'lar's a fine fellow."

"Search? Do they find any likely lad at Half-Circle, it will be to our honor, and he's our leave to go."

Although the problem had never worried the Sea Holder; no one from Half-Circle had

answered a Search. Which was as well, Yanus thought privately. If a lad happened to be chosen, every other lad in the Hold would take to grumbling that he should have been picked. And on the seas of Pern, you had to keep your mind on your work, not on dreams. Bad enough to have those pesky fire lizards appearing now and then by the Dragon Stones. But as no one could get near enough to the stones to catch a fire lizard, no harm was done.

If the new Harper found his Holder an unimaginative man, hardworking and hidebound, he had been well prepared for it by his training. His problem was that he must provoke a change, subtle at first, in what he found; for Masterharper Robinton wanted each of his journeymen to get every Holder and Craftmaster to think beyond the needs of their own lands, Hall and people. Harpers were not simply tellers of tales and singers of songs; they were arbiters of justice,[3] confidants of Holders and Craftmasters, and molders of the young. Now, more than ever, it was necessary to alter hidebound thinking, to get everyone, starting with the young and working on the old, to consider more of Pern than the land they kept Threadfree or the problems of their particular area. Many old ways needed shaking up, revising. If F'lar of Benden Weyr hadn't done some shaking up, if Lessa hadn't made her fantastic ride back four hundred Turns to bring up the missing five Weyrs of dragonriders, Pern would be writhing under Thread, with nothing green and growing left on the surface. The Weyrs had profited and so had Pern. Similarly the Holds and Crafts would profit if they only were willing to examine new ideas and ways.

Half-Circle could expand, Elgion thought. The present quarters were becoming

---

3. arbiters (är′ bət ərz) **of justice:** Those selected to judge disputed issues.

cramped. The children had told him that there were more caves in the adjacent bluffs. And the Dock Cavern could accommodate more than the thirty-odd craft now anchored so safely there.

By and large, though, Elgion was rather relieved at his situation, since this was his first post as Harper. He had his own well-furnished apartments in the Hold, enough to eat, though the diet of fish might soon pall on a man accustomed to red meat, and the Sea Holders were generally pleasant people, if a little dour.

Only one thing puzzled him: who had drilled the children so perfectly? Old Petiron had sent word to the Harper that there was a likely songmaker at Half-Circle, and he had included two scored melodies that had greatly impressed the Masterharper. Petiron had also said that there'd be some difficulty in the Sea Hold about the songmaker. A new Harper, for Petiron had known that he was dying when he wrote the Masterharper, would have to go carefully. This was a Hold that had kept much to itself and observed all the old ways.

So Elgion had kept his counsel on the matter of the songmaker, certain that the lad would make himself known. Music was hard to deny and, based on the two songs Elgion had been shown, this lad was undeniably musical. However, if the chap were a fosterling and away from the Hold, he'd have to await his return.

Elgion had soon managed to visit all the different smaller holds in the Half-Circle palisade and gotten to know most people by name. The young girls would flirt with him or gaze at him with sorrowful eyes and sighs when he played in the evenings at the Great Hall.

There was really no way in which Elgion would have realized that Menolly was the person he wanted. The children had been told by the Sea Holder that the Harper would not like to know that they'd been drilled by a girl, so they were not to bring disgrace on the Hold by telling him. After Menolly cut her hand so badly, it was rumored that she'd never use it again, so everyone was told that it would be heartless to ask her to sing in the evenings.

When Menolly was well of the infection and her hand healed but obviously stiff, no one was thoughtless enough to remind her of her music. She herself stayed away from the singing in the Great Hall. And since she could not use her hand well and so many occupations in the Hold required two, she was frequently sent away in the day to gather greens and fruits, usually alone.

If Mavi was perplexed by the quietness and passivity of her youngest child, she put it down to the long and painful recovery, not to loss of her music. Mavi knew that all manner of pain and trouble could be forgotten in time, and so she did her best to keep her daughter occupied. Mavi was a very busy woman, and Menolly kept out of her way.

Gathering greens and fruit suited Menolly perfectly. It kept her out in the open and away from the Hold, away from people. She would have her morning drink, bread and fish quietly in the great kitchen when everyone was dashing around to feed the men of the Hold, either going out to fish or coming back in from a night's sailing. Then Menolly would wrap up a fishroll and take one of the nets or skin slings. She'd tell the old aunt in charge of the pantry that she was going out for whatever it was, and since the old aunt had a memory like a seine net, she wouldn't remember that Menolly had done the same thing the day before or realize that she would do the same the day after.

When spring was fully warming the air and making the marshes brilliant with green and blossom color, spiderclaws began to walk in from the sea to lay their eggs in the

Dragonsong 943

6 **Discussion** What is the danger in the Sea Hold keeping its old ways?

7 **Discussion** Why do you think that no one reminded Menolly of her music?

8 **Reader's Response** In your opinion, which of the two dangers, Thread or high water, makes the Holders more apprehensive?

9 **Connection** Have students cite parallels with Earth.

10 **Discussion** What do you think Menolly means by the "last day . . . of her trusting childhood"?

shallower cove waters. As these plump shell-fish were a delicacy in themselves, besides adding flavor to every dish when dried or smoked, the young people of the Hold—Menolly with them—were sent off with traps, spades and nets. Within four days the nearby coves were picked clear of spiderclaws and the young harvesters had to go farther along the coast to find more. With Thread due to fall any time, it was unwise to stray too far from the Hold, so they were told to be very careful.

There was another danger that concerned the Sea Holder considerably: tides had been running unusually high and full this Turn. Much higher water in the harbor and they'd not get the two big sloops in or out of the cavern unless they unstepped the masts. Due notice was taken of the high-tide lines, and there was much shaking of heads when it was observed that the line was two full hands higher than ever before recorded.

The lower caverns of the Hold were checked against possible seepage. Bags of sand were filled and placed along the lower portions of the seawalls around the harbor.

A good storm and the causeways would be awash. Yanus was concerned enough to have a long chat with Old Uncle to see if he remembered anything from his earlier and clearer days of Sea Holding. Old Uncle was delighted to talk and ranted on about the influence of the stars, but when Yanus, Elgion and two of the other older shipmasters had sifted through what he'd said, it was not to any great increase in knowledge. Everyone knew that the two moons affected the tides, not the three bright stars in the sky.

They did, however, send a message about these curious tides to Igen Hold to be forwarded with all possible speed to the main Seacraft Hold at Fort. Yanus didn't want to have his biggest boats caught out in the open, so he kept careful check on the tides,

determined to leave them within the Dock Cavern if the tide rose another hand higher.

When the youngsters went out to gather spiderclaws, they were told to keep their eyes open and report back anything unusual, especially new high-water marks on the coves. Only Thread deterred the more adventurous lads from using this as an excuse for ranging far down the coast. Menolly, who preferred to explore the more distant places alone, mentioned Thread to them as often as possible.

Then, after the next Threadfall, when everyone was sent out for spiderclaws, Menolly made certain that she got a headstart on the boys, making good use of her long legs.

It was fine to run like this, Menolly thought, putting yet another rise between her and her nearest pursuers. She altered her stride for uneven ground. It wouldn't do to break an ankle now. Running was something even a girl with a crippled hand could do well.

Menolly closed her mind to that thought. She'd learned the trick of not thinking about anything: she counted. Right now she counted her strides. She ran on, her eyes sweeping ahead of her to save her feet. The boys would never catch her now, but she was running for the sheer joy of the physical effort, chanting a number to each stride. She ran until she got a stitch in her side and her thighs felt the strain.

She slowed, turning her face into the cool breeze blowing offshore, inhaling deeply of its freshness and sea odors. She was somewhat surprised to see how far she had come down the coast. The Dragon Stones were visible in the clear air, and it was only then that she recalled the little queen. Unfortunately, she also remembered the tune she'd made up that day: that last day, Menolly now realized, of her trusting childhood.

She walked on, following the line of the bluffs, peering down to see if she could spot

Grammar in Action

English allows writers to express ideas with certain structures, called verbals, that function as a single part of speech in a sentence. One type of verbal is the infinitive. An **infinitive** is the present tense verb form preceded by the word *to: to run, to sing, to teach.* An infinitive phrase is made of the infinitive form plus words that complete an idea: *to sing the teaching ballads,* for example. Infinitives can function in sentences as nouns, adjectives, or adverbs. Notice how Anne McCaffrey uses infinitive phrases in these sentences:

When the youngsters went out, they were told *to keep their eyes open.* [The infinitive phrase is used as a noun—the direct object in this sentence.]

It was fine *to run like this,* Menolly thought, putting yet another rise between her and her nearest pursuers. [The infinitive phrase is used as an adverb, modifying *fine.*]

Student Activity 1. Locate the infinitive phrases in these sentences.

1. She was somewhat surprised to see how far she had come down the coast.

new high-water marks on the stone escarpments.[4] Tide was halfway in now, Menolly decided. And yes, she could see the lines of sea debris from the last tide, in some places right up against the cliff face. And this had been a cove with a deep beach.

A movement above, a sudden blotting of the sun, made her gaze upwards. A sweep rider. Knowing perfectly well that he couldn't see her, she waved vigorously anyhow, watching the graceful glide as the pair dwindled into the distance.

Sella had told her one evening when they were preparing for bed that Elgion had flown on dragons several times. Sella had given a quiver of delighted terror, vowing that she wouldn't have the courage to ride a dragon.

Privately Menolly thought that Sella wouldn't likely have the opportunity. Most of Sella's comments, and probably thoughts, were centered on the new Harper. Sella was not the only one, Menolly knew. If Menolly could think how silly all the Hold girls were being about Harper Elgion, it didn't hurt so much to think about Harpers in general.

Again she heard the fire lizards before she saw them. Their excited chirpings and squeals indicated something was upsetting them. She dropped to a crouch and crept to the edge of the bluff, overlooking the little beach. Only there wasn't much beach left, and the fire lizards were hovering over a spot on the small margin of sand, almost directly below her.

She inched up to the edge, peering down. She could see the queen darting at the incoming waves as if she would stop them with her violently beating wings. Then she'd streak back, out of Menolly's line of sight, while the rest of the creatures kept milling and swooping, rather like frightened herd-beasts running about aimlessly when wild

wherries circled their herd. The queen was shrieking at the top of her shrill little voice, obviously trying to get them to do something. Unable to imagine what the emergency could be, Menolly leaned just a little further over the edge. The whole lip of the cliff gave way.

Clutching wildly at seagrasses, Menolly tried to prevent her fall. But the seagrass slipped cuttingly through her hand and she slid over the edge and down. She hit the beach with a force that sent a shock through her body. But the wet sand absorbed a good deal of the impact. She lay where she'd fallen for a few minutes, trying to get her breath into her lungs and out again. Then she scrambled to her feet and crawled away from an incoming wave.

She looked up the side of the bluff, rather daunted by the fact that she'd fallen a dragon length or more. And how was she going to climb back up? But, as she examined the cliff face, she could see that it was not so unscalable as she'd first thought. Almost straight up, yes, but pocked by ledges and holds, some fairly large. If she could find enough foot and handholds, she'd be able to make it. She dusted the sand from her hands and started to walk towards one end of the little cove, to begin a systematic search for the easiest way up.

She'd gone only a few paces when something dove at her, screeching in fury. Her hands went up to protect her face as the little queen came diving down at her. Now Menolly recalled the curious behavior of the fire lizards. The little queen acted as if she were protecting something from Menolly as well as the encroaching sea, and she looked about her. She was within handspans of stepping into a fire lizard clutch.[5]

"Oh, I'm sorry. I'm sorry. I wasn't looking! Don't be mad at me," Menolly cried as the

---

4. **escarpments** (e skärp′ mәntz) *n*.: Steep slopes formed by erosion.

5. **clutch** *n*.: A nest of eggs.

11 Discussion Why does it hurt Menolly so much to think about Harpers?

12 Discussion What do you think a dragon length is equivalent to in standard English or metric measurements?

---

2. Sella had given a quiver of delighted terror, vowing that she wouldn't have the courage to ride a dragon.
3. Menolly was delighted to find herself ahead in the race.
4. It wouldn't do to break an ankle now, she thought.
5. Yanus was concerned enough to have a long chat with Old Uncle.

Student Activity 2. In each sentence that follows, identify the infinitive phrase and explain whether it is used as a noun, an adjective, or an adverb.
1. It was exhilarating to ride on a dragon.
2. Menolly thought it was a good day to hunt for spiderclaws.
3. To be able to sing and play music was all Menolly wanted.
4. Menolly climbed the cliff to help the fire lizard queen.

Electronic Handbook You might wish to have students review verbals before completing the Grammar in Action activities. If students have access to the Language Master 6000, have them enter the access word *verbal* and press the GRAMMAR key for a review of verbals.

13 Discussion Why does Menolly have to prove her sincerity?

14 ESL Teaching Strategy You might wish to have a student read this sentence and explain the meanings of *materialized* and *worriedly*.

little fire lizard came at her again. "Please! Stop! I won't hurt them!"

To prove her sincerity, Menolly backtracked to the far end of the beach. There she had to duck under a small overhang. When she looked around, there wasn't a sign of the little queen. Menolly's relief was short-lived, for how was she to find a way up the cliff if the little fire lizard kept attacking her every time she approached the eggs. Menolly hunched down, trying to get comfortable in her cramped refuge.

Maybe if she kept away from the eggs? Menolly peered up the cliff directly above her. There were some likely looking holds. She eased herself out the far side, keeping one eye on the clutch, basking in the hot sun, and reached for the first ledge.

Immediately the fire lizard came at her. "Oh, leave me alone! Ow! Go away. I'm trying to."

The fire lizard's talons had raked her cheek.

"Please! I won't hurt your eggs!"

The little queen's next pass just missed Menolly, who ducked back under the ledge.

Blood oozed from the long scratch, and Menolly dabbed at it with the edge of her tunic.

"Haven't you got any sense?" Menolly demanded of her now invisible attacker. "What would I want with your silly eggs? Keep 'em. I just want to get home. Can't you understand? I just want to go home."

Maybe if I sit very still, she'll forget about me, Menolly thought and pulled her knees up under the chin, but her toes and elbows protruded from under the overhang.

Suddenly a bronze fire lizard materialized above the clutch, squeaking worriedly. Menolly saw the queen swooping to join him, so the queen must have been on the top of the ledge, waiting, just waiting for Menolly to break cover.

And to think I made up a pretty tune about you, Menolly thought as she watched the two lizards hovering over the eggs. The last tune I ever made up. You're ungrateful, that's what you are!

Despite her discomfort, Menolly had to laugh. What an impossible situation! Held under a cramped ledge by a creature no bigger than her forearm.

At the sound of her laughter, the two fire lizards disappeared.

Frightened, were they? Of laughter?

"A smile wins more than a frown," Mavi was fond of saying.

Maybe if I keep laughing, they'll know I'm friendly? Or get scared away long enough for me to climb up? Saved by a laugh?

Menolly began to chuckle in earnest, for she had also seen that the tide was coming in rather quickly. She eased out of her shelter, flung the carry-sack over her shoulder, and started to climb. But it proved impossible to chuckle and climb. She needed breath for both.

Abruptly both the little queen and the bronze were back to harry her, flying at her head and face. The fragile-looking wings were dangerous when used as a weapon.

No longer laughing, Menolly ducked back under her ledge, wondering what to do next.

If laughter had startled them, what about a song? Maybe if she gave that pair a chorus of her tune, they'd let her go. It was the first time she'd sung since she'd seen the lizards, so her voice sounded rough and uncertain. Well, the lizards would *know* what she meant, she hoped, so she sang the saucy little song. To no one.

"Well, so much for that notion," Menolly muttered under her breath. "Which makes the lack of interest in your singing absolutely unanimous."

No audience? Not a fire lizard's whisker in sight?

As fast as she could, Menolly slipped from her shelter and came face to face, for a split second, with two fire lizard faces. She ducked down, and they evidently disappeared because when she cautiously peered again, the ledge where they'd been perched was empty.

She had the distinct impression that their expressions had registered curiosity and interest.

"Look, if wherever you are, you can hear me . . . will you stay there and let me go? Once I'm on the top of the cliff, I'll serenade you till the sun goes down. Just let me get up there!"

She started to sing a dutiful dragonsong, as she once again emerged from her refuge. She was about five steps upward when the queen fire lizard emerged, with help. With squeaks and squeals she was driven back down. She could even hear claws scraping on the rock above her. She must have quite an audience by now. When she didn't need one!

Cautiously she looked up, met the fascinated whirling of ten pairs of eyes.

"Look, a bargain! One long song and then let me up the cliff? Is that agreed?"

Fire lizard eyes whirled.

Menolly took it that the bargain was made and sang. Her voice started a flutter of surprised and excited chirpings, and she wondered if by any possible freak they actually understood that she was singing about grateful Holds honoring dragonriders. By the last verse she eased out into the open, awed by the sight of a queen fire lizard and nine bronzes entranced by her performance.

"Can I go now?" she asked and put one hand on the ledge.

The queen dived for her hand, and Menolly snatched it back.

"I thought we'd struck a bargain."

The queen chirped piteously, and Menolly realized that there had been no menace in the

17

15 **Critical Thinking and Reading** What do you think are Menolly's thoughts as she remembers her mother's phrase?

16 **Discussion** Why does Menolly think that a song might affect the fire lizards?

17 **Literary Focus: Motivation** What might be the motives of the fire lizards first for attacking Menolly and now for watching her with curiosity?

18 **Literary Focus: Motivation** The little queen seems to have made a choice. What seems to have motivated her?

19 **Discussion** Explain Menolly's mixed feelings of admiration and pity for the little queen.

queen's action. She simply wasn't allowed to climb.

"You don't want me to go?" Menolly asked.

The queen's eyes seemed to glow more brightly.

"But I have to go. If I stay, the water will come up and drown me." And Menolly accompanied her words with explanatory gestures.

Suddenly the queen let out a shrill cry, seemed to hold herself midair for a moment and then, her bronzes in close pursuit, she glided down the sandy beach to her clutch. She hovered over the eggs, making the most urgent and excited sounds.

If the tide was coming in fast enough to endanger Menolly, it was also frighteningly close to swamping the nest. The little bronzes began to take up the queen's plaint and several, greatly daring, flew about Menolly's head and then circled back to the clutch.

"I can come there now? You won't attack me?" Menolly took a few steps forward.

The tone of the cries changed, and Menolly quickened her step. As she reached the nest, the little queen secured one egg from the clutch. With a great laboring of her wings, she bore it upward. That the effort was great was obvious. The bronzes hovered anxiously, squeaking their concern but, being much smaller, they were unable to assist the queen.

Now Menolly saw that the base of the cliff at this point was littered with broken shells and the pitiful bodies of tiny fire lizards, their wings half-extended and glistening with egg fluid. The little queen now had raised the egg to a ledge, which Menolly had not previously noticed, about a half-dragon length up the cliff face. Menolly could see the little queen deposit the egg on the ledge and roll it with her forelegs towards what must be a hold in the cliff. It was a long moment before the queen reappeared again. Then she dove to-

wards the sea, hovering over the foamy crest of a wave that rolled in precariously close to the endangered clutch. With a blurred movement, the queen was hovering in front of Menolly and scolding like an old aunt.

Although Menolly couldn't help grinning at the thought, she was filled with a sense of pity and admiration for the courage of the little queen, single-handedly trying to rescue her clutch. If the dead fire lizards were that fully formed, the clutch was near to hatching. No wonder the queen could barely move the eggs.

"You want me to help you move the eggs, right? Well, we'll see what I can do!"

Ready to jump back if she had mistaken the little queen's imperious command, Menolly very carefully picked up an egg. It was warm to the touch and hard. Dragon eggs, she knew, were soft when first laid but hardened slowly on the hot sands of the Hatching Grounds in the Weyrs. These definitely must be close to hatching.

Closing the fingers of her damaged hand carefully around the egg, Menolly searched for and found foot and hand holds, and reached the queen's ledge. She carefully deposited the egg. The little queen appeared, one front talon resting proprietarily on the egg, and then she leaned forward, towards Menolly's face, so close that the fantastic motion of the many-faceted eyes were clearly visible. The queen gave a sort of sweet chirp and then, in a very businesslike manner, began to scold Menolly as she rolled her egg to safety.

Menolly managed three eggs in her hand the next time. But it was obvious that between the onrushing tide and the startling number of eggs in the clutch, there'd be quite a race.

"If the hole were bigger," she told the little queen as she deposited three eggs, "some of the bronzes could help you roll."

The queen paid her no attention, busy

Grammar in Action

Another verbal that writers use to build ideas into sentences is the participial phrase. **Participial phrases** are formed from either the present participal of the verb, which is the form that ends in *ing*, or the past participle, which is the form that usually ends in *ed*. Participial phrases act as adjectives in a sentence. Notice how Anne McCaffrey has used participial phrases in these sentences from *Dragonsong*.

Clutching wildly at sea grasses, Menolly tried to prevent her fall. (The participial phrase modifies *Menolly*.)

She looked up the side of the bluff, rather *daunted by the fact that she'd fallen a dragon length or more*. (The participial phrase modifies *she*.)

Notice that the participle *daunted* in the second sentence is modified by the adverb *rather*, just as adjectives can be modified in sentences by adverbs.

Student Activity 1. Locate the participial phrases in these sentences.

1. She had gone only a few paces when something dove at her, screeching in fury.

20 Discussion Do you think the little queen's hysterics are warranted? Explain.

pushing the three eggs, one at a time, to safety.

Menolly peered into the opening, but the fire lizard's body obscured any view. If the hole was bigger and the ledge consequently broader, Menolly could bring the rest of the eggs up in her carry-sack.

Hoping that she wouldn't pull down the cliff side and bury the queen, clutch and all, Menolly prodded cautiously at the mouth of the opening. Loose sand came showering down.

The queen took to scolding frantically as Menolly brushed the rubble from the ledge. Then she felt around the opening. There seemed to be solid stone just beyond. Menolly yanked away at the looser rock, until she had a nice tunnel exposed with a slightly wider opening.

Ignoring the little queen's furious complaints, Menolly climbed down, unslinging her sack when she reached the ground. When the little queen saw Menolly putting the eggs in the sack, she began to have hysterics, beating at Menolly's head and hands.

"Now, look here," Menolly said sternly, "I am not stealing your eggs. I am trying to get them all to safety in jig time. I can do it with the sack but not by the handful."

Menolly waited a moment, glaring at the little queen who hovered at eye level.

"Did you understand me?" Menolly pointed to the waves, more vigorously dashing up the small beach. "The tide is coming in. Dragons couldn't stop it now." Menolly put another egg carefully in the sack. As it was she'd have to make two, maybe three trips or risk breaking eggs. "I take this," and

Dragonsong 949

2. Menolly, running as fast as she could, reached the cave.
3. Looking all around her, Menolly could see the little queen.
4. Swooping to reach her, the little queen darted at Menolly.

Student Activity 2. Add a participial phrase to each of these sentences.

1. Menolly ran along the cliff.
2. The fire lizards ate.
3. The people of the Sea Hold watched the skies.
4. The dragonriders patrolled their sector.

Electronic Handbook You might wish to have students review participial phrases before completing the Grammar in Action activities. If students have access to the Language Master 6000, have them enter the access word *participial* and press the GRAMMAR key for a review of participial phrases.

21 **Discussion** What evidence is there that the little queen understands Menolly's actions?

22 **Discussion** Why does Menolly question the authenticity of her own adventure?

she gestured up to the ledge, "up there. Do you understand, you silly beast?"

Evidently, the little creature did because, crooning anxiously, she took her position on the ledge, her wings half-extended and twitching as she watched Menolly's progress up to her.

Menolly could climb faster with two hands. And she could, carefully, roll the eggs from the mouth of the sack well down the tunnelway.

"You'd better get the bronzes to help you now, or we'll have the ledge stacked too high."

It took Menolly three trips in all, and as she made the last climb, the water was a foot's width from the clutch. The little queen had organized her bronzes to help, and Menolly could hear her scolding tones echoing in what must be a fair-sized cave beyond the tunnel. Not surprising since these bluffs were supposed to be riddled with caverns and passages.

Menolly gave a last look at the beach, water at least ankle deep on both ends of the little cove. She glanced upward, past the ledge. She was a good halfway up the cliff now, and she thought she could see enough hand and foot holds ahead.

"Good-bye!" She was answered by a trill of chirps, and she chuckled as she imagined the scene: the queen marshalling her bronzes to position her eggs just right.

Menolly did not make the cliff top without a few anxious moments. She was exhausted when she finally flopped on the seagrasses at the summit, and her left hand ached from unaccustomed gripping and effort. She lay there for some time, until her heart stopped thudding in her ribs and her breath came more easily. An inshore breeze dried her face, cooling her; but that reminded her of the emptiness of her stomach. Her exertions had reduced the rolls in her pouch to crumby fragments, which she gobbled as fast as she could find them.

All at once the enormity of her adventure struck her, and she was torn between laughter and awe. To prove to herself that she'd actually done what she remembered, she crept cautiously to the bluff edge. The beach was completely underwater. The sandy wallow where the fire lizard eggs had baked was being tideswept smooth. The rubble that had gone over the edge with her had been absorbed or washed away. When the tide retreated, all evidence of her energies to save herself and the clutch would be obliterated. She could see the protuberance of rock down which the queen had rolled her eggs but not a sign of a fire lizard. The waves crashed with firm intent against the Dragon Stones when she gazed out to sea, but no bright motes of color flitted against the somber crags.

Menolly felt her cheek. The fire lizard's scratch was crusted with dried blood and sand.

"So it did happen!"

However did the little queen know I could help her? No one had ever suggested that fire lizards were stupid. Certainly they'd been smart enough for endless Turns to evade every trap and snare laid to catch them. The creatures were so clever, indeed, that there was a good deal of doubt about their existence, except as figures of overactive imaginations. However, enough trustworthy men had actually seen the creatures, at a distance, like her brother, Alemi, when he'd spotted some about the Dragon Stones, that most people did accept their existence as fact.

Menolly could have sworn that the little queen had understood her. How else could Menolly have helped her? That proved how smart the little beast was. Smart enough certainly to avoid the boys who tried to capture them . . . Menolly was appalled. Capture a fire lizard? Pen it up? Not, Menolly supposed with relief, that the creature would stay caught long. It only had to pop *between*.

Now why hadn't the little queen just gone *between* with her eggs, instead of arduously transporting them one by one? Oh, yes, *between* was the coldest place known. Any cold would do the eggs harm. At least it did dragon eggs harm. Would the clutch be all right now in the cold cavern? Hmmm. Menolly peered below. Well, if the queen had as much sense as she'd already shown, she'd get all her followers to come lie on the eggs and keep them warm until they did hatch.

Menolly turned her pouch inside out, hoping for some crumbs. She was still hungry. She'd find enough early fruits and some of the succulent reeds to eat, but she was curiously loath to leave the bluff. Though, it was unlikely that the queen, now her need was past, would reappear.

Menolly rose finally and found herself stiff from the unaccustomed exercise. Her hand ached in a dull way, and the long scar was red and slightly swollen. But, as Menolly flexed her fingers, it seemed that the hand opened more easily. Yes, it did. She could almost extend the fingers completely. It hurt, but it was a stretchy-hurt. Could she open her hand enough to play again? She folded her fingers as if to chord. That hurt, but again, it was a stretchy-hurt. Maybe if she worked her hand a lot more . . . She had been favoring it until today when she hadn't given it a thought. She'd used it to climb and carry and everything.

"Well, you did me a favor, too, little queen," Menolly called, speaking into the breeze and waving her hands high. "See? My hand is better."

There was no answering chirp or sound, but the soft whistle of the seaborne breeze and the lapping of the waves against the bluff. Yet Menolly liked to think that her words had been heard. She turned inland,

feeling considerably relieved and rather pleased with the morning's work.

She'd have to scoot now and gather what she could of greens and early berries. No point in trying for spiderclaws with the tide so high.

Chapter 5

*Oh, Tongue, give sound to joy and sing
Of hope and promise on dragonwing.*

No one, as usual, noticed Menolly when she got back to the Hold. Dutifully she saw the harbormaster and told him about the tides.

"Don't you go so far, girl," he told her kindly. "Thread's due any day now, you know. How's the hand?"

She mumbled something, which he didn't hear anyway, as a shipmaster shouted for his attention.

The evening meal was hurried since all the masters were going off to the Dock Cavern to check tide, masts and ships. In the bustle Menolly could keep to herself.

And she did—seeking the cubicle and the safety of her bed as soon as possible. There she hugged to herself the incredible experience of the morning. She was certain that the queen had understood her. Just like the dragons, fire lizards knew what was in the mind and heart of a person. That's why they disappeared so easily when boys tried to trap them. They'd liked her singing, too.

Menolly gave herself a squeeze, ignoring the spasm of pain in her now stiff hand. Then she tensed, remembering that the bronzes had been waiting to see what the queen would do. She was the clever one, the audacious one. What was it Petiron was always quoting? "Necessity breeds solution."

Did fire lizards really understand people, even when they kept away from them, then, Menolly puzzled again. Of course, dragons understood what their riders were thinking,

---

23 **Literary Focus: Motivation** What would motivate Menolly to remain on the bluff?

24 **Discussion** Why does Menolly "dutifully" tell the harbormaster about the tides?

25 **Discussion** What does this imply about the bond between dragons and their riders?

26 **Reader's Response** Menolly cannot decide what to do—to go back to the cave immediately or wait a few days. What do you think she should do?

27 **Discussion** Why do you think Mavi is so harsh with Menolly?

but dragons Impressed at Hatching to their riders. The link was never broken, and the dragon would only hear that one person, or so Petiron had said. So *how* had the little queen understood her?

"Necessity?"

Poor queen! She must have been frantic when she realized that the tide was going to cover her eggs! Probably she'd been depositing her clutches in that cove for who knows how long! How long did fire lizards live? Dragons lasted the life of their rider. Sometimes that wasn't so long, now that Thread was dropping. Quite a few riders had been so badly scored they'd died and so had their dragons. Would the little fire lizards have a longer life, being smaller and not in so much danger? Questions darted through Menolly's mind, like fire lizards' flashing, she thought, as she cuddled into the warmth of her sleeping fur. She'd try to go back tomorrow, maybe, with food. She rather thought fire lizards would like spiderclaws, too, and maybe then she'd get the queen's trust. Or maybe it would be better if she didn't go back tomorrow? She should stay away for a few days. Then, too, with Thread falling so often, it was dangerous to go so far from the safety of the Hold.

What would happen when the fire lizard eggs hatched? What a sight that would be! Ha! All the lads in the Sea Hold talking about catching fire lizards and she, Menolly, had not only seen but talked to them and handled their eggs! And if she were lucky, she might even see them hatching, too. Why, that would be as marvelous as going to a dragon Hatching at one of the Weyrs! And no one, not even Yanus, had been to a Hatching!

Considering her exciting thoughts, it was a wonder that Menolly was able to sleep.

The next morning her hand ached and throbbed, and she was stiff from the fall and the climbing. Her half-formed notion of going back to the Dragon Stones' cove was thwarted by the weather, of all things. A storm had blown in from the sea that night, lashing the harbor with pounding waves. Even the Dock Cavern waters were turbulent, and a wind whipped with such whimsical force that walking from Hold to Cavern was dangerous.

The men gathered in the Great Hall in the morning, mending gear and yarning.[6] Mavi organized her women for an exhaustive cleaning of some of the inner Hold rooms. Menolly and Sella were sent down to the glow storage so often that Sella vowed she didn't need light to show her the way anymore.

Menolly worked willingly enough, checking glows in every single room in the Hold. It was better to work than to think. That evening she couldn't escape the Great Hall. Since everyone had been in all day, everyone needed entertainment and was going. The Harper would surely play. Menolly shuddered. Well, there was no help for it. She had to hear music sometime. She couldn't avoid it forever. And at least she could sing along with the others. But she soon found she couldn't even have that pleasure. Mavi gestured to her when the Harper began to tune his gitar. And when the Harper beckoned for everyone to join in the choruses, Mavi pinched Menolly so hard that she gasped.

"Don't roar. You may sing softly as befits a girl your age," Mavi said. "Or don't sing at all."

Across the Hall, Sella was singing, not at all accurately and loud enough to be heard in Benden Hold; but when Menolly opened her mouth to protest, she got another pinch.

So she didn't sing at all but sat there by her mother's side, numb and hurt, not even able to enjoy the music and very conscious

---

6. yarning (yärn' iŋ): Telling yarns—long, complicated tales that seem exaggerated or hard to believe.

that her mother was being monstrously unfair.

Wasn't it bad enough she couldn't play anymore—yet—but not to be allowed to sing? Why, everyone had encouraged her to sing when old Petiron had been alive. And been glad to hear her. Asked her to sing, time and again.

Then Menolly saw her father watching her, his face stern, one hand tapping not so much to the time of the music but to some inner agitation. It was her father who didn't want her to sing! It wasn't fair! It just wasn't fair! Obviously they knew and were glad she hadn't come before. They didn't want her here.

She wrenched herself free from her mother's grip and, ignoring Mavi's hiss to come back and behave herself, she crept from the Hall. Those who saw her leave thought sadly that it was such a pity she'd hurt her hand and didn't even want to sing anymore.

Wanted or not, creeping out like that would send Mavi looking for her when there was a pause in the evening's singing. So Menolly took her sleeping furs and a glow and went to one of the unused inner rooms where no one would find her. She brought her clothes, too. If the storm cleared, she'd be away in the morning to the fire lizards. *They* liked her singing. They liked *her!*

Before anyone else was up, she had risen. She gulped down a cold klah and ate some bread, stuffed more in her pouch and was almost away. Her heart beat fast while she struggled with the big metal doors of the Hold entrance. She'd never opened them before and hadn't appreciated how very solid they were. She couldn't, of course, bar them again, but there was scarcely any need.

Sea mist was curling up from the quiet harbor waters, the entrances to the Dock Cavern visible as darker masses in the gray. But the sun was beginning to burn through the fog, and Menolly's weather-sense told her that it would soon be clear.

As she strode down the broad holdway, mist swirled up and away from her steps. It pleased Menolly to see something give way before her, even something as nebulous as fog. Visibility was limited, but she knew her path by the shape of the stones along the road and was soon climbing through the caressing mists to the bluff.

She struck somewhat inland, towards the first of the marshes. One cup of klah and a hunk of bread was not enough food, and she remembered some unstripped marshberry bushes. She was over the first humpy hill and suddenly the mist had left the land, the brightness of the spring sun almost an ache to the eyes.

She found her patch of marshberry and picked one handful for her face, then one for the pouch.

Now that she could see where she was going, she jogged down the coast and finally dropped into the cove. The tide was just right to catch spiderclaws. These should be a pleasant offering to the fire lizard queen she thought as she filled her bag. Or could fire lizards hunt in fog?

When Menolly had carried her loaded sack through several long valleys and over humpy hills, she was beginning to wish she'd waited a while to do her netting. She was hot and tired. Now that the excitement of her unorthodox behavior had waned, she was also depressed. Of course, it was quite likely that no one had noticed she'd left. No one would realize it was she who had left the Hold doors unbarred, a terrible offense against the Hold safety rules. Menolly wasn't sure why—because who'd want to enter the Sea Hold unless he had business there? Come all that dangerous way across the marshes? For what? There were quite a few precautions scrupulously observed in the Sea Hold that

28 **Discussion** Menolly feels that the only ones who like her are the fire lizards. Why does she feel this way?

29 **Reading Strategy** Predict what might happen to Menolly if it's discovered that she is the one who left the doors unbarred.

Multicultural Focus Remind students that much of Menolly's conflict is due to the fact that she is a girl and girls are not allowed to be harpers. Ask students if they can think of any occupations today that are closed either to women or to men. Discuss their responses. Help students realize that while virtually all occupations are legally open to both sexes, tradition still dictates many roles for men and women, even in contemporary society. Discuss some of the traditional and nontraditional roles of men and women today. For example, it is common for women who are mothers to work outside the home. It is less common for fathers to stay at home and raise children, though it does happen.

Have students find out more about how men and women are redefining their roles in society today. Ask each student to choose a profession or occupation and do research to find out the following: how many people in that field are men and how many are women, whether the current gender balance has changed over the years, and if so, how and why.

30 **Literary Focus: Motivation**
What does Menolly consider when she makes her choice not to return to the Hold?

31 **ESL Teaching Strategy** Does the author give any clues to what is disturbing Menolly?

didn't make much sense to Menolly: like the Hold doors being barred every night, and unshielded glows never being left in an unused room, although it was all right in corridors. Glows wouldn't burn anything, and think of all the barked shins that would be saved by leaving a few room glows unshielded.

No, no one was likely to notice that she was gone until there was some unpleasant or tedious job for a one-handed girl to do. So they wouldn't assume that *she'd* opened the Hold door. And since Menolly was apt to disappear during the day, no one would think anything about her until evening. Then someone might just wonder where Menolly was.

That was when she realized that she didn't plan to return to the Hold. And the sheer audacity of that thought was enough to make her halt in her tracks. Not return to the Hold? Not go back to the endless round of tedious tasks? Of gutting, smoking, salting, pickling fish? Mending nets, sails, clothes? Cleaning dishes, clothes, rooms? Gathering greens, berries, grasses, spiderclaws? Not return to tend old uncles and aunts, fires, pots, looms, glowbaskets? To be able to sing or shout or roar or play if she so chose? To sleep . . . ah, now where would she sleep? And where would she go when there was Thread in the skies?

Menolly trudged on more slowly up the sand dunes, her mind churning with these revolutionary ideas. Why, everyone had to return to the Hold at night! The Hold, any hold or cot or weyr. Seven Turns had Thread been dropping from the skies, and no one traveled far from shelter. She remembered vaguely from her childhood that there used to be caravans of traders coming through the marshlands in the spring and the summer and early fall. There'd been gay times, with lots of singing and feasting. The Hold doors had not been barred then. She sighed, those had been happier times . . . the good old days that Old Uncle and the aunties were always droning on about. But once Thread started falling, everything had changed . . . for the worse . . . at least that was the overall impression she had from the adults in the Hold.

Some stillness in the air, some vague unease caused Menolly to glance about her apprehensively. There was certainly no one else about at this early hour. She scanned the skies. The mist banking the coast was rapidly dispersing. She could see it retreating across the water to the north and west. Towards the east the sky was brilliant with sunrise, except for what were probably some traces of early morning fog in the northeast. Yet something disturbed Menolly. She felt she should know what it was.

She was nearly to the Dragon Stones now, in the last marsh before the contour of the land swept gently up towards the seaside bluff. It was as she traversed the marsh that she identified the odd quality: it was the stillness. Not of wind, for that was steady seaward, blowing away the fog, but a stillness of marsh life. All the little insects and flies and small wrigglers, the occasional flights of wild wherries who nested in the heavier bushes were silent. Their myriad activities and small noises began as soon as the sun was up and didn't cease until just before dawn, because the nocturnal insects were as noisy as the daytime ones.

It was this quiet, as if every living thing was holding its breath, that was disturbing Menolly. Unconsciously she began to walk faster and she had a strong urge to glance over her right shoulder, towards the northeast—where a smudge of gray clouded the horizon . . .

A smudge of gray? Or silver?

Menolly began to tremble with rising fear, with the dawning knowledge that she was too far from the safety of the Hold to reach it before Thread reached her. The heavy metal doors, which she had so negligently left ajar, would soon be closed and barred against her, and Thread. And, even if she were missed, no one would come for her.

She began to run, and some instinct directed her towards the cliff edge before she consciously remembered the queen's ledge. It wasn't big enough, really. Or she could go into the sea? Thread drowned in the sea. So would she, for she couldn't keep under the water for the time it would take Thread to pass. How long would it take the leading edge of a Fall to pass over? She'd no idea.

She was at the edge now, looking down at the beach. She could see her ledge off to the right. There was the lip of the cliff that had broken off under her weight. That was the quick way down, to be sure, but she couldn't risk it again, and didn't want to.

32 She glanced over her shoulder. The grayness was spreading across the horizon. Now she could see flashes against that gray. Flashes? Dragons! She was seeing dragons fighting Thread, their fiery breath charring the dreaded stuff midair. They were so far away that the winking lights were more like lost stars than dragons fighting for the life of Pern.

Maybe the leading edge wouldn't reach this far? Maybe she was safe. "Maybes seldom are" as her mother would say.

In the stillness of the air, a new sound made itself heard: a soft rhythmic thrumming, something like the tuneless humming of small children. Only different. The noise seemed to come from the ground. 33

She dropped, pressing one ear to a patch of bare stone. The sound was coming from within.

Of course! The bluff was hollow . . . that's why the queen lizard . . .

On hands and knees, Menolly scooted to the cliff edge, looking for that halfway ledge of the queen's.

Menolly had enlarged the entry once. There was every chance she could make it big enough to squirm through. The little queen would certainly be hospitable to someone who had saved her clutch!

And Menolly didn't come empty-handed as a guest! She swung the heavy sack of spiderclaws around to her back. Grabbing handfuls of the grasses on the lip of the cliff, she began to let herself slowly down. Her feet

32 Reading Strategy Ask students to visualize this scene. What is Menolly feeling?

33 Reading Strategy Predict the source of the sound Menolly hears. What does *thrumming* mean?

34 Literary Focus: Motivation
What is motivating Menolly to seek this shelter—fear or curiosity?

35 ESL Teaching Strategy Ask students to visualize this scene and describe the steps Menolly is taking to ensure her safety.

fumbled for support; she found one toehold and dug half that foot in, the other foot prodding for another place.

34 She slithered badly once, but a rock protrusion caught her in the crotch before she'd slipped far. She laid her face against the cliff, gulping to get back her breath and courage. She could feel the thrumming through the stone, and oddly, that gave her heart. There was something intensely exciting and stimulating about that sound.

Sheer luck guided her foot to the queen's ledge. She'd risked only a few glances beneath her—the aspect was almost enough to make her lose her balance completely. She was trembling so much with her exertions that she had to rest then. Definitely the humming came from the queen's cavern.

She could get her head into the original opening. No more. She began to tear at the sides with her bare hands until she thought of her belt knife. The blade loosened a whole section all at once, showering her with sand and bits of rock. She had to clean her eyes and mouth of grit before she could continue. Then she realized that she'd gotten to sheer rock.

35 She could get herself into the shelter only up to her shoulders. No matter how she turned and twisted, there was an outcropping that she could not pass. Once again she wished she were as small as a girl ought to be. Sella would have had no trouble crawling through that hole. Resolutely, Menolly began to chip at the rock with her knife, the blows jarring her hand to the shoulder, and making no impression at all on the rock.

She wondered frantically how long it had taken her to get down the cliff. How long did she have before Thread would be raining down on her unprotected body?

Body? She might not get past the bobble in the wall with her shoulders . . . but . . . She reversed her position, and feet, legs,

hips, all right up to the shoulders passed into the safety of solid rock. Her head was covered, but only just, by the cliff overhang.

Did Thread *see* where it was going when it fell? Would it notice her, crowded into this hole as it flashed by? Then she saw the thong of the carry-sack where she'd looped it over the ledge to keep it handy but out of her way. If Thread got into the spiderclaws. . . .

She pulled herself far enough out of the hole to cast an eye above. No silver yet! No sound but the steadily increasing thrumming. That wouldn't have anything to do with Thread, would it?

The carry-sack thong had bitten into the ledge and she had a job freeing it, having to yank rather hard. The next thing she knew the sack came free, the force of her pull threw her backwards, cracking her head on the roof of her tunnel, and then the surface beneath her buttocks started to slide, out and down. Menolly clawed her way into the tunnel, as the ledge slowly detached itself from the face of the cliff and tumbled down onto the beach.

Menolly scrambled back quickly, afraid more of the entrance would go, and suddenly she was in a cave, wide, high, deep, clutching the carry-sack and staring at the greatly widened mouth.

The thrumming was behind her and, startled at what she could only consider to be an additional threat, she whirled.

Fire lizards were perched around the walls, clinging to rock spur and ledge. Every eye glinted at the mound of eggs in the sandy center of the cave. The thrumming came from the throats of all the little fire lizards, and they were far too intent on what was happening to the eggs to give any heed to her abrupt appearance.

Just as Menolly realized that she was witnessing a Hatching, the first egg began to rock and cracks appeared in its shell.

It rocked itself off the mound of the clutch

36 Discussion What is the importance of this scene Menolly is witnessing?

37 Discussion Why is the baby bronze angry?

36 and, in hitting the ground, split. From the two parts emerged a tiny creature, not much bigger than Menolly's hand, glistening brown and creeling[7] with hunger, swaying its head back and forth and tottering forward a few awkward steps. The transparent brown wings unfolded, flapping weakly to dry, and the creature's balance improved. The creel turned to a hiss of displeasure, and the little brown peered about defensively.

37 The other fire lizards crooned, encouraging it to some action. With a tiny shriek of anger, the little brown launched itself to-

---

7. creeling (krē liŋ): Making a crying and squealing sound.

wards the cave opening, passing so close to Menolly she could have touched it.

The brown fire lizard lurched off the eroded lip of the cave, pumping its wings frantically to achieve flight. Menolly gasped as the creature dropped, and then sighed with relief as it came into sight briefly, airborne, and flew off, across the sea.

More creeling brought her attention back to the clutch. Other fire lizards had begun to hatch in that brief period, each one shaking its wings and then, encouraged by the Weyrmates, flopping and weaving towards the cave mouth, defiantly independent and hungry.

Several greens and blues, a little bronze and two more browns hatched and passed

Dragonsong 957

38 Critical Thinking and Reading Why is the queen encouraging the little fire lizards to escape from the cave?

39 Reading Strategy Visualize the spiderclaws. What do you think they look like?

Cooperative Learning Arrange the class in groups of four. Hand each group a sheet of paper. Ask students to take turns writing a response to this question: What vivid words does the author use on pages 954–958 to create excitement and a sense of urgency? Have each member of each group write a response on the paper. When students have had sufficient time to write their responses, have a representative of each group read the group's responses.

Menolly. And then, as she watched a little blue launch itself, Menolly screamed. No sooner had the blue emerged from the safety of the cliff than she saw the thin, writhing silver of Thread descending. In a moment, the blue was covered with the deadly filaments. It uttered one hideous shriek and disappeared. Dead? Or *between*? Certainly badly scored.

Two more little fire lizards passed Menolly, and she reacted now.

"No! No! You can't! You'll be killed." She flung herself across their path.

The angry fire lizards pecked at her unprotected face and while she covered herself, made their escape. She cried aloud when she heard their screams.

"Don't let them go!" She pleaded with the watching fire lizards. "You're older. You know about Thread. Tell them to stop!" She half-crawled, half-ran to the rock where the golden queen was perched.

38

"Tell them not to go! There's Thread out there! They're being killed!"

The queen looked at her, the many-faceted eyes whirling violently. The queen chuckled and chirped at her, and then crooned as yet another fledgling spread its wings and began to totter towards sure death.

"Please, little queen! Do something! Stop them!"

The thrill of being the witness to a Hatching of fire lizards gave way to horror. Dragons had to be protected because they protected Pern. In Menolly's fear and confusion, the little fire lizards were linked to their giant counterparts.

She turned to the other lizards now, begging them to do something. At least until the Threadfall was over. Desperately she plunged back to the cave mouth and tried to turn the little fire lizards back with her hands, blocking their progress with her body. She was

overwhelmed with pangs of hunger, belly-knotting, gut-twisting hunger. It took her only a moment to realize that the driving force in these fire lizards was that sort of hunger: that was what was sending them senselessly forth. They had to eat. She remembered that dragons had to eat, too, when they first Hatched, fed by the boys they Impressed.

Menolly wildly grabbed for her carry-sack. With one hand she snatched a fire lizard back from the entrance, and with the other, a spiderclaw from the sack. The little bronze screeched once and then bit the spiderclaw behind the eye, neatly killing it. Wings beating, the bronze lifted itself free of Menolly's grasp and with more strength than Menolly would have thought the newborn creature could possess flew its prey to a corner and began tearing it apart.

39

Menolly reached out randomly now and, with some surprise, found herself holding the one queen in the clutch. She snagged two spiderclaws from the sack in her other hand, and deposited them and the queen in another corner. Finally realizing she couldn't handfeed the whole clutch, she upended the sack, spilling the shellfish out.

Newly hatched fire lizards swarmed over and after the spiderclaws. Menolly caught two more lizards before they could reach the cave mouth and put them squarely in the center of their first meal. She was busy trying to make sure that each new fire lizard had a shellfish when she felt something pricking her shoulder. Surprised, she looked up to find the little bronze clinging to her tunic. His round eyes were whirling and he was still hungry. She gave him an unclaimed spiderclaw and put him back in his corner. She tossed the little queen another and snared several other spiderclaws for her "specials."

Not many more of the newly hatched got

out, not with a source of food so nearby. She'd had a fair haul in the sack, but it didn't take long for the hungry fire lizards to devour every last morsel. The poor things were still sounding starved as they creeled about, tipping over claws and body shells, trying to find any scraps overlooked. But they stayed in the cave and now the older fire lizards joined them, nuzzling or stroking, making affectionate noises.

Utterly exhausted, Menolly leaned back against the wall, watching their antics. At least they'd not all died. She glanced apprehensively at the entrance and saw no more writhing lengths of Thread falling past. She peered further. There wasn't even a trace of the menacing gray fog on the horizon. Threadfall must be over.

And not a moment too soon. Now she was experiencing hunger thoughts from all the fire lizards. Rather overpoweringly, in fact. Because she realized how hungry she herself was.

The little queen, the old queen, began to hover in the cave, squeaking an imperious command to her followers. Then she darted out and the old clutch began to follow her. The fledglings, moving awkwardly, made their virgin flight, and within moments, the cave was empty of all but Menolly, her torn sack, and a pile of empty spiderclaw and fire lizard shells.

With their exit, some of Menolly's hunger eased and she remembered the bread she'd tucked in her pocket. Feeling a bit guilty at this belated discovery, she gratefully ate every crumb.

Then she made herself a hollow in the sand, pulled the torn carry-sack over her shoulders, and went to sleep.

Chapter 6

*Lord of the Hold, your charge is sure
In thick walls, metal doors, and no verdure.*

Threadfall was well past, the flame-thrower crews safely back in Half-Circle Hold before anyone missed Menolly. Sella did because she didn't want to have to tend Old Uncle. He had had another seizure, and someone had to stay by his bedside.

"That's about all she's good for now anyway," Sella told Mavi and then hastily demurred at her mother's stern look. "Well, all she does is drag about, cradling that hand of hers as if it were precious. She gets off all the *real* work . . ." Sella let out a heavy sigh.

"We've enough trouble this morning what with someone leaving the Hold doors unfastened and Thread falling . . ." Mavi shuddered at the thought of that brace of horrors; the mere notion of Thread cascading down, able to wriggle within the Hold, turned her stomach. "Go find Menolly and see that she knows what to do in case the old man has another fit."

It took Sella the better part of an hour to realize that Menolly was neither in the Hold nor among those baiting longlines. She hadn't been among the flame-thrower crews. In fact, no one could remember having seen or spoken to her all day.

"She couldn't have been out hunting greens like she usually does," said an old auntie thoughtfully, pursing her lips. "Threadfall was on directly we'd our morning klah. Didn't see her in the kitchen then, either. And she's usually so good about helping, one-handed and all that she is, poor dear."

At first Sella was just annoyed. So like Menolly to be absent when needed. Mavi was a good deal too lenient with the child. Well, if she'd not been in the Hold in the morning, she'd been caught out in the Thread. And that served her right.

Then Sella wasn't so sure. She began to feel the first vestige of fright. If Menolly had been out during Threadfall, surely there'd be

Dragonsong 959

40 **Discussion** After reading about the "poor things," which are still sounding starved, what do you think Menolly's feelings toward the fire lizards are?

41 **Discussion** How can she experience hunger thoughts from the fire lizards?

42 **Reading Strategy** Ask students to explain what is meant by the two-line song at the beginning of Chapter 6. Who is referred to in the song? What does the advice mean?

43 **Discussion** What is Alemi's opinion of Menolly? On what do you base your answer?

44 **Literary Focus: Motivation** Why is Sella pleased to inform Mavi that Menolly is missing? What are her motives?

45 **Discussion** What are Yanus's feelings about Menolly being missing?

. . . something . . . left that Thread couldn't eat.

Gulping back nausea at that thought, she sought out her brother, Alemi, who was in charge of the flame-throwers.

"Alemi, you didn't see anything . . . unusual . . . when you were ground checking?"

"What do you mean by 'unusual'?"

"You know, traces . . ."

"Of what? I've no time now for riddles, Sella."

"I mean, if someone were caught out during Threadfall, how would you know?"

"Whatever are you tacking around?"

"Menolly's nowhere in the Hold, or the Dock, or anywhere. She wasn't on any of the teams . . ."

Alemi frowned. "No, she wasn't, but I thought Mavi needed her in the Hold for something."

". . . There! And none of the aunties remember seeing her this morning. *And* the Hold doors were unbarred!"

"You think Menolly left the Hold early?" Alemi realized that a strong, tall girl like Menolly could very easily have managed the door bars.

"You know how she's been since she hurt her hand: creeping away every chance she gets."

Alemi did know, for he was fond of his gawky sister, and he particularly missed her singing. He didn't share Yanus's reservations about Menolly's ability. And he didn't honestly agree with Yanus's decision to keep knowledge of it from the Harper, especially now that there was a Harper in the Hold to keep her in line.

"Well?" Sella's prompting irritated him out of his thoughts.

"I saw nothing unusual."

"Would there *be* something? If Thread did get her?"

Alemi gave Sella a long hard look. She sounded as if she'd be glad if Menolly did get Threaded.

"There'd be nothing left if she'd been caught by Thread. But no Thread got through the Benden wings."

With that he turned on his heel and left his sister, mouth agape. His reassurance was curiously no consolation to Sella. However, since Menolly was so obviously missing, Sella could take some pleasure in informing Mavi of this fact, adding her theory that Menolly had committed the enormous crime of leaving the Hold door unbarred.

"Menolly?" Mavi was handing out sea salt and spiceroot to the head cook when Sella imparted her news. "Menolly?"

"Yes, Menolly. She's gone. Not been seen, and she's the one left the Hold doors unbarred. With Thread falling!"

"Thread wasn't falling when Yanus discovered the doors open," Mavi corrected Sella mechanically. She shuddered at the thought of anyone, even a recalcitrant daughter, caught out in the silvery rain of Thread.

"Alemi said no Thread got through the dragons, but how can he be sure?"

Mavi said nothing as she locked up the condiment press and spun the rollers. "I'll inform Yanus. And I'll have a word with Alemi, too. You'd better take care of Old Uncle."

"Me?"

"Not that that's real work, but it is suited to your temperament and ability."

Yanus was silent for a long moment when he heard of Menolly's disappearance. He didn't like untoward things happening, such as the Hold doors being left unbarred. He'd worried about that all during the Fall and the fishing after the Fall. It wasn't good for a Sea Holder to have his mind diverted from the task at hand. He felt some relief that the mystery had been solved, and a keen annoyance and anxiety about the girl. Foolish thing for her to have done—leave the Hold that early. She'd been sulking ever since that beating. Mavi hadn't kept her busy enough to make her forget the nonsense of tuning.

"I've heard that there're plenty of caves in the cliffs along the coast," Elgion said. "The girl probably took shelter in one."

"She probably did," said Mavi briskly, grateful to the Harper for such a sensible suggestion. "Menolly knows the coast very well. She must know every crevice by now."

"She'll be back then," Yanus said. "Give her time to get over the fright of being out during Threadfall. She'll be back." Yanus found relief in his theory and turned to less distressing business.

"It *is* spring," said Mavi, more to herself than to the others. Only the Harper caught the anxious note in her voice.

Two days later Menolly had not returned, and the entire Sea Hold was alerted to her disappearance. No one remembered seeing her on the day of Threadfall. No one had seen her since. Children sent out for berries or spiderclaws had encountered no trace of her, nor had she been in any of the caves they knew.

"Not much point in sending out a search," said one of the shipmasters, mindful that there was more surety of catching fish than finding any trace of a foolish girl. Particularly one with a crippled hand. "Either she's safe and doesn't choose to come back, or . . ."

"She could be hurt . . . Threadscored, a broken leg or arm . . ." said Alemi, "unable to make her way back."

"Shouldn't've been out anyway without letting someone know where she'd gone." The shipmaster's eyes moved towards Mavi, who did not catch this implied negligence on her part.

"She was used to going out for greens first thing in the morning," Alemi said. If no one else would defend Menolly, he would speak up.

"Did she carry a belt knife? Or a metal buckle?" asked Elgion. "Thread doesn't touch metal."

"Aye. We'd find that much of her," said Yanus.

"If Thread got her," said the shipmaster darkly. He rather favored the notion that she'd fallen into a crevice or over the edge of the bluff, in terror at finding herself out during Threadfall. "Her body'd wash up around the Dragon Stones. Current throws up a lot of sea trash down that way."

Mavi caught her breath in a sound very like a sob.

"I don't know the girl," Elgion said quickly, seeing Mavi's distress. "But if she did, as you say, stay out a good deal of the time, she'd know the land too well to go over the edge of a cliff."

"Threadfall's enough to rattle anyone's wits . . ." said the shipmaster.

"Menolly is not stupid," said Alemi with such feeling that everyone looked at him in surprise. "And she knew her Teaching well enough to know what to do if she were caught out."

"Right enough, Alemi," said Yanus sharply and rose to his feet. "If she were able and of a mind to return, she'd have done so. Everyone who is abroad is to keep a sharp eye for any trace of her. That includes sea as well as land. As Sea Holder, I cannot in conscience do more than that, under the circumstances. And the tide is making. To the boats now."

While Elgion did not actually expect the Sea Holder to institute an intensive search for a lost girl, he was surprised at the decision. Mavi, even, accepted it, almost as if she were glad of an excuse, as if the girl were an embarrassment. The shipmaster was obviously pleased by his Sea Holder's impartiality. Only Alemi betrayed resentment. The

46 **Discussion** What Hold attitude is the shipmaster expressing?

47 **Discussion** Why does the shipmaster imply that Mavi is negligent?

48 **Discussion** Why does Yanus say that he "cannot in conscience do more than that"? Is he being irresponsible?

49 Discussion Alemi feels that Menolly is still alive. Why do you think he feels this way?

50 Discussion Why does Elgion think that Yanus is keeping the identity of the musically gifted "lad" a secret?

Harper motioned to the young man to hang back as the others filed out.

"I've some time. Where would you suggest I look?"

Hope flashed in Alemi's eyes, then as suddenly wariness clouded them.

"I'd say it's better if Menolly remains where she is . . ."

"Dead or hurt?"

"Aye." Alemi sighed deeply. "And I wish her luck and long life."

"Then you think she's alive and chooses to be without Hold?"

Alemi regarded the Harper quickly. "I think she's alive and better off wherever she is than she would be in Half-Circle." Then the young Sea Man strode after the others, leaving the Harper with some interesting reflections.

He was not unhappy at Half-Circle Hold. But the Masterharper had been correct in thinking that Elgion would have to make quite a few adjustments to life in this Sea Hold. It would be a challenge, Robinton had told Elgion, to try to broaden the narrow outlook and straitened thinking of the isolated group. At the moment Elgion wondered if the Masterharper had not vastly overrated his abilities when he was unable to get the Sea Holder, or his family, to even try to rescue a blood relation.

Then, shifting through the tones of voices, rather than the words spoken, Elgion came to realize that this Menolly posed some sort of problem to her Hold beyond the crippled hand. For the life of him, Elgion couldn't remember seeing the girl, though he thought he could recognize every member of the Hold. He'd spent considerable time now with every family unit, with the children in the Little Hall, with the active fishermen, with the honorably retired old people.

He tried to recall when he'd seen a girl with an injured hand and had only the fleetingest recollection of a tall, gawky figure hurrying out of the Hall one evening when he'd been playing. He hadn't seen the girl's face, but he'd recall her slumping figure if he saw it again.

It was regrettable that Half-Circle Hold was so isolated that there was no way to send a drum-message. He could signal the next dragonrider he saw, as an alternative, and get word to Benden Weyr. The sweep riders could keep their eyes open for the girl, and alert any Holds beyond the marshes and down the coast. How she could have gotten that far with Thread falling, Elgion didn't know, but he'd feel better taking some measures to find her.

He had also made no headway in discovering the identity of the songmaker. And Masterharper had charged him to have that lad in the Harpercrafthall for training as soon as possible. Gifted songmakers were a rare commodity. Something to be sought and cherished.

By this time Elgion understood why the old Harper had been so cautious about identifying the lad. Yanus thought only of the sea, of fishing, of how to use every man, woman and child of his Sea Hold to the Hold's best advantage. He had them all well trained. Yanus would certainly have looked askance at any able-bodied lad who spent too much time tuning. There was, in fact, no one to help Elgion with the evening task of entertainment. One likely lad had a fair sense of rhythm, and Elgion had already started him on the drum, but the majority of his students were thick-fingered. Oh, they knew their Teachings, spot-on, but they were passive musically. No wonder Petiron had been so effusive about the one really talented child among so many deadheads. Too bad the old man had died before he received Robinton's

962 *The Novel*

message. That way the boy would have known that he was more than acceptable as a candidate to the Harpercrafthall.

Elgion watched the fishing fleet out of the harbor and then rounded up several lads, got meatrolls from an auntie in the Hold kitchen, and set off on, ostensibly, a food-gathering mission.

As Harper he was acquainted with them; but mindful that he was the Harper, the boys regarded him with respect and kept him at a distance. The moment he told them that they should keep their eyes open for Menolly, for her belt knife, if they knew it, or belt buckle, the distance widened inexplicably. They all seemed to know, though Elgion doubted that the adults had told them, that Menolly had been missing from the Hold for some days. They all seemed equally reluctant to look for her, or to suggest to him possible areas in which to search. It was as if, Elgion told himself with frustrated anger, they were *afraid* the Harper would find her. So he tried to regain their confidence by telling them that Yanus had suggested that everyone who went outside the Hold should keep their eyes open for the lost girl.

He came back with his charges to the Hold, with sacksful of berries, greens and some spiderclaws. The only information the boys had volunteered about Menolly during the entire morning was that she could catch more spiderclaws than anyone.

As it turned out, Elgion didn't have to signal for a dragonrider. The next day a bronze wingleader came circling down to the beach at Half-Circle, greeting Yanus affably and asking if he might have a few words with the Harper.

"You'll be Elgion," said the young man, raising his hand in greeting. "I'm N'ton, rider of Lioth. I heard you were settling in."

"What can I do for you, N'ton?" and El-

gion tactfully walked the bronze rider out of Yanus's earshot.

"You've heard of fire lizards?"

Elgion stared at N'ton in surprise for a moment before he laughed. "That old myth!"

"Not really a myth, friend," said N'ton. Despite the laughing mischief in his eyes, he was speaking in earnest.

"Not a myth?"

"Not at all. Would you know if the lads here have spotted any along the coast? They tend to leave their clutches in beach sands. It's the eggs we want."

"Really? Actually it isn't the lads who've seen them, but the Sea Holder's son, not the fanciful sort, although I didn't really credit . . . he saw some around some rock crags

Dragonsong 963

51 **Discussion** Why do the boys of the Hold regard Elgion with such respect?

52 **Discussion** Why would Elgion take N'ton out of earshot?

53 Critical Thinking and Reading Why does N'ton feel that Yanus will not look for fire lizards?

54 Discussion What is N'ton implying in this statement?

Reader's Response At this point Menolly can still return to the Hold instead of remaining in the cave with the fire lizards. What choice would you make in her place?

Thematic Response Menolly made a difficult choice that will affect her future. Do you think she made a good decision?

known as the Dragon Stones. Down the coast some ways." Elgion pointed the direction.

"I'll go have a look myself. But this is what has happened. F'nor, brown Canth's rider, has been injured." N'ton paused. "He's been convalescing at Southern Hold. He found, and Impressed," and again N'ton paused significantly to emphasize his last word, "a fire lizard queen . . ."

"Impressed? I thought only dragons . . ."

"Fire lizards are much like dragons, only smaller."

"But this would mean . . ." And Elgion was lost in the wonder of that meaning.

"Yes, precisely, Harper," said N'ton with a wide grin. "And now everyone wants a fire lizard. I can't imagine Yanus Sea Holder wasting the time and energy of his men looking for fire lizard clutches. But if fire lizards have been seen, any cove with warm sand might just hide a clutch."

"The high tides this spring have been flooding most of the coves."

"Too bad. See if you can't organize the Hold youngsters to search. I don't think you'd have much resistance . . ."

"None at all." And Elgion realized that N'ton, dragonrider though he now was, must have been susceptible to the same boyhood designs on fire lizards that Elgion had once planned. "When we find a clutch, what do we do?"

"*If* you find one," N'ton said, "fly the signal banner and the sweep rider will report. If the tide is threatening, put the clutch in either warm sand or warmed hides."

"If they should hatch, you did mention they can be Impressed . . ."

"I hope you're that lucky, Harper. Feed the fledglings. Stuff their faces with as much as they can eat, talking all the time. That's how you Impress. But then, you've been to a Hatching, haven't you? So, you know how to go about it. Same principle involved."

"Fire lizards." Elgion was enchanted with the prospect.

"Don't Impress them all, Harper. I'd like one of the little beasties myself."

"Greedy?"

"No, they're engaging little pets. Nothing as intelligent as my Lioth there," and N'ton grinned indulgently at his bronze who was scrubbing one cheek in the sand. As he turned back to Elgion, N'ton noticed the line of awed children, lining the seawall, all eyes on Lioth's action. "You'll have no lack of help, I suspect."

"Speaking of help, Wingleader, a young girl of the Sea Hold is missing. She went out the morning of the last Fall and hasn't been seen since."

N'ton whistled softly and nodded sympathetically. "I'll tell the sweep riders. She probably took shelter, if she'd any sense. Those palisades are riddled with caves. How far have you searched?"

"That's it. No one has bothered to."

N'ton scowled and glanced towards the Sea Holder. "How old a girl?"

"Come to think of it, I don't know. His youngest daughter, I believe."

N'ton snorted. "There are other things in life than fish."

"So I used to believe."

"Don't be so sour so young, Elgion. I'll see you come to the next Hatching at Benden."

"I'd appreciate that."

"I suspect so." With a farewell wave, N'ton strode back to his bronze dragon, leaving Elgion with an easier conscience and the prospect of some relief from the monotony of the Sea Hold.

Closure and Extension

ANSWERS TO RESPONDING TO THE SELECTION
Your Response

1. Encourage students to discuss the choices open to Menolly. Is she being responsible? Is she hurting anyone with her actions?

RESPONDING TO THE SELECTION

Your Response

1. Do you feel that Menolly was right to leave the Hold without telling anyone? Explain.
2. Do you think that Yanus was justified in not searching for Menolly? Explain.

Recalling

3. What natural danger threatens both the Hold and the fire lizard eggs? Describe it.
4. How does Menolly stop the baby fire lizards from flying to certain death?

Interpreting

5. Explain why Mavi implies that Menolly's injury would not allow her to play her music again.
6. Why does Menolly feel that the day she first saw the fire lizards was the "last day . . . of her trusting childhood"?
7. What evidence indicates that the fire lizards are intelligent animals?

Applying

8. Menolly avoids her problem with the Hold by running away. Does running away from problems solve them? How else might Menolly have reacted to her conflict with the Hold?

ANALYZING LITERATURE

Understanding Motivation

Motivation is the reason that characters act as they do. Motivation springs from characters' thoughts, beliefs, desires, and needs. Understanding a character's motivation gives you deeper insight into a story.

1. Explain Yanus's motives for (a) beating Menolly and (b) denying to Elgion that Menolly taught the children.
2. What motivates Menolly to leave Half-Circle Sea Hold?

CRITICAL THINKING AND READING

Recognizing Cause and Effect

In a novel, the characters' motives cause them to act in a certain way. Their actions are the effects. An effect can then be the cause of another action. This series of causes and effects moves the plot along.

1. What is the cause of Menolly's unhappiness at Half-Circle Sea Hold?
2. What causes Menolly to seek shelter in the fire lizards' cave? What is the effect on the newly hatched fire lizards?

THINKING AND WRITING

Writing About Cause and Effect

Write a short paper about the effects of Thread on the lives of the people of Pern. Begin with a topic sentence that states the cause. The developing sentences should detail the effects of the cause. End with a summary statement.

LEARNING OPTIONS

1. **Writing.** Thread falls from the sky and devours all living things, ultimately burrowing into the ground. Write a concrete poem about this strange natural phenomenon of Pern. Remember that a concrete poem has a shape that suggests its subject visually.
2. **Writing.** Pretend that you are Menolly. You have just awakened in the fire lizards' cave. Write a letter to your family explaining why you have decided to leave Half-Circle Sea Hold forever. Consider whether or not you wish to tell them about the fire lizards.
3. **Cross-curricular Connection.** After Menolly's first meeting with the fire lizards, she makes a reed pipe. Find some information about this instrument. How does it work? Then make a reed pipe or some other simple instrument and demonstrate how it is played.

Dragonsong   965

Literary Focus Often, details about the setting will convey atmosphere. In some writers' hands, a cavern will become a threatening, damp, claustrophobia-inducing place. The caverns of Pern, however, are busy and productive. Nonetheless, each cavern has its own personality, its own atmosphere. Students will notice that the atmosphere of Benden Weyr is very different from that of Half-Circle Sea Hold.

Prereading Focus You might want to help students by telling them that contrasting means explaining how things are different. If they know that Half-Circle Holders are fish eaters and Benden Weyr residents are meat eaters, they have then discovered a contrast. If they feel that the dragonriders are brave fighting men and the Holders at Half-Circle are fishermen, they have another contrast.

As the students continue reading, they will be able to find and note more of these differences in the lives of the two groups.

Vocabulary You might wish to point out that all of these terms have negative connotations. Ask students to think of situations in which each of the words might be used. For example, *lacerated* might be used in a description of an accident, and *wistfulness* could describe the look on the face of a child in a toy store.

Electronic Handbook You might suggest that students use the Language Master 6000 to hear the pronunciations of the vocabulary words.

Spelling Tip Have students note that in two of the vocabulary words, *lacerated* and *grimaced,* the s sound is spelled with a c.

GUIDE FOR READING

Dragonsong, Chapters 7–10

Atmosphere

Atmosphere is the feeling or mood that a literary work or passage creates in the reader. Many different factors in a novel contribute to atmosphere. Most writers use descriptive language to communicate the mood. Words like *grim* or *bustling* suggest the atmosphere of a place effectively. The behavior of the characters contributes to atmosphere as well. For example, a place described as *gloomy* will seem gloomier if the people there never sing or laugh or speak optimistically about the future.

Focus

In the chapters you are about to read, Menolly will experience a drastic change in her circumstances. She will find herself in Benden Weyr, the place that is home to the dragons and dragonriders who defend Pern from the dreaded Thread. Benden Weyr is presented in contrast to Half-Circle Hold. What sort of place do you think the Weyr will be? How do you think the behavior of the dragonriders will differ from that of the Holders at Half-Circle Hold? With a group of two or three classmates, create a description of life at Benden Weyr. As you read the next chapters, compare your description to the author's.

Vocabulary

Knowing the following words will help you as you read Chapters 7–10 of *Dragonsong.*

lacerated (las′ ər āt əd) *v.*: Cut or torn jaggedly (p. 982)

wistfulness (wist′ fəl nes) *n.*: Expression of vague yearnings (p. 983)

apprehensions (ap rē hen′ shənz) *n.*: Fears; anxieties (p. 983)

derision (di rizh′ ən) *n.*: Ridicule (p. 985)

grimaced (grim′ ist) *v.*: Dis

torted the face, as in expressing pain (p. 989)

insatiable (in sā′ shə bəl) *adj.*: Constantly wanting more; incapable of being satisfied (p. 991)

pique (pēk) *n.*: Resentment at being slighted (p. 929)

officious (ə fish′ əs) *adj.*: Offering unwanted and unnecessary advice; meddlesome (p. 993)

Objectives

1 To recognize atmosphere
2 To compare and contrast atmospheres
3 To write a description of a specific atmosphere
4 To express individual interests and abilities through optional activities

Support Material

Teaching Portfolio
Teacher Backup, p. 997
Grammar in Action Worksheets
  Using Adverb Clauses, p. 1001;
  Using Noun Clauses, p. 1003
Usage and Mechanics Worksheet, p. 1005
Vocabulary Check, p. 1006
Analyzing Literature Worksheet, *Recognizing Atmosphere,* p. 1007

Critical Thinking and Reading Worksheet, *Comparing and Contrasting Atmospheres,* p. 1008
Selection Test, p. 1009

Prentice Hall Literature Writing Studio

Chapter 7

Who wills,
Can.
Who tries,
Does.
Who loves,
Lives.

It took Menolly four days to find the right sort of rocks to spark a fire. She'd had plenty of time before that to dry seaweeds and gather dead marshberry bushes for fuel, and to build a little hearth in the side of the big cavern where a natural chimney took the smoke up. She'd gathered a generous pile of sweet marsh grasses for bedding and picked out the seam of the carry-sack to make herself a rug. It wasn't quite long enough unless she curled up under it, but the fire lizards insisted on sleeping about and around her and their bodies made up the lack. In fact, she was quite comfortable at night.

With fire, she was very comfortable. She found a stand of young klahbark trees, and though the resultant brew was harsh, it woke her up very well. She went to the clay deposits that Half-Circle Hold used and got sufficient clay to make herself several cups, plates and rude containers for storage, which she hardened in the ashes of her fire. And she filled in the holes of a dishlike porous rock in which she could boil water. With all the fish she needed in the sea in front of her, she ate as well as, if not better than, she would have in the Hold. Although, she did miss bread.

She even made herself a sort of path down the cliff face. She carved out footrests and staked in some handholds, to make both ascent and descent safer.

And she had company. Nine fire lizards were constantly in attendance.

The morning after her hectic adventure, Menolly had been absolutely stunned to wake with the unaccustomed weight of warm bodies about her. Scared, too, until the little creatures roused, with strong thoughts of renewed hunger and love and affection for her. Driven by their need, she had climbed down the treacherous rock face to the sea and gathered fingertails, trapped in the shallow tidal pools. She wasn't quite able to dig rockmites, but when she showed her charges where they could get them out with their long, agile tongues, the creatures found their instinct adequate for the job. Having fed her friends, Menolly was too tired to go in search of sparking rocks and had eaten a flat fish raw. Then she and the fire lizards had crept back into the cavern and slept again.

As the days went by their appetite drove Menolly to lengths she wouldn't have attempted for her own comfort. The result was that she was kept entirely too busy to feel either sorry for or apprehensive about herself. Her friends had to be fed, comforted and amused. She also had to supply her own needs—as far as she was able—and she was able to do a lot more than she'd suspected she could. In fact, she began to wonder about a lot of things the Hold took for granted.

She had automatically assumed, as she supposed everyone did, that to be caught without shelter during Threadfall was tantamount to dying. No one had ever correlated the fact that the dragonriders cleared most of the Thread from the skies before it fell—that was the whole point of having dragons—with the idea that as a result there was very little Thread to fall on the unsheltered. Hold thinking had hardened into an inflexible rule—to have no shelter during Threadfall was to experience death.

In spite of her increasing independence, however, had Menolly been alone, she might have regretted her foolishness and crept back to the Sea Hold. But the company and wonder of the fire lizards gave her all the diversion she needed. And they loved her music.

Dragonsong 967

4 It was no great trick at all to make one reedpipe, and a lot more fun to put five together so she could play a counter-tune. The fire lizards adored the sounds and would sit listening, their dainty heads rocking in time with the music she played. When she sang, they'd croon, at first off-key; but gradually, she thought, their "ear" improved, and she had a soft chorus. Menolly sang, in amused duty, all the Teaching Ballads, particularly the ones about dragons. The fire lizards might understand less than a child three Turns old, but they responded with small cries and flapping wings to any of the dragon songs, as if they appreciated the fact that she was singing about their kin.

5 There was no doubt in Menolly's mind that these lovely creatures were related to the huge dragons. How, she didn't know and didn't really care. But if you treated them the way Weyrmen treated their dragons, the fire lizards responded. She, in turn, began to understand their moods and needs, and insofar as she was able, supplied them.

They grew quickly, those first days. So quickly that she was hard pressed to keep their mouths full. Menolly didn't see too much of the other hatchlings, the ones she hadn't fed or had fed only casually. She saw them now and again, smaller creatures, as the entire Weyr fed on the rockmites at low tide. The little queen and her bronze mate would often hover, watching Menolly and her small group. The queen sometimes scolded Menolly or perhaps berated the fire lizard Menolly was holding. Menolly wasn't sure which. And occasionally the queen would even fly at one of the fledglings, beating it soundly with her wings. For what reason, Menolly could never figure out, but the little ones meekly submitted to her discipline.

Occasionally Menolly offered food to one of the others, but they'd never take it if she remained near. Nor would any of the older fire lizards, including the queen. Menolly concluded that that was as well; otherwise she'd have to spend every single waking moment feeding lazy fire lizards. The nine she'd Impressed were quite enough to keep sated.

When she saw the first skin lesion[1] on the little queen, Menolly wondered where she would find oil. They'd all need it. Cracks in the skin would be deadly for the young fire lizards if they had to go *between*. And with natural enemies around, like wherries and eager boys from nearby Holds, *between* was a needed refuge.

The closest source of oil swam in the sea. But she'd no boat to catch the deep-sea oily fishes, so she searched the coast for dead fish and found a packtail washed up during the night. She slit the carcass, carefully, always working the knife blade away from her, and squeezed the oil from the skin into a cup. Not the most pleasant of jobs; and by the time she'd finished, she had a bare cupful of unpleasantly fishy yellow oil. Yet it did work. The queen might not smell very pleasant, but the oil did coat the crack. For good measure, she smeared all her friends.

The stench in the cavern that night was almost more than she could endure, and she fell asleep trying to think of alternatives. By morning the possibilities had narrowed down to one: sweetening the fish oil with certain marsh grasses. She couldn't get the pure sweet oil they used in the Hold because that was traded from Nerat; it was pressed from the flesh of a hot-climate fruit that grew abundantly in the rain forests there. The oily seed pod that grew from a sea bush would not be available until fall; and while she could get some oil from black marshberries, it would take immense quantities, which she'd prefer to eat.

---

1. skin lesion (lē zhən): Injury or skin disease.

With her fire lizards as winged escort, she made her way south and inland, towards country little penetrated by the Sea Holders as being too far, these days, from shelter.

Menolly set out as soon as the sun was up and varied her pace between a striding walk and an easy jog. She decided to go on as far as she could until the sun was mid-heaven; she couldn't risk being too far from her cave when night fell.

The fire lizards were excited, darting about until she scolded them for wasting their energy. They took enough feeding without all that flying and all they could count on in this flat marsh area were berries and a few early sour plums. They took turns clinging to her shoulders and hair, then, until the little brown pulled at her once too often, and she shooed them all off.

She was soon past any familiar terrain and began to proceed more slowly. It wouldn't do to be bogged down. Midday found her deep in the marshes, gathering berries for herself, her friends and her basket. She'd managed to harvest some of the aromatic grasses she wanted, but not enough for her purpose. She had decided to sweep in a wide circle back towards her cliff cave when she heard distant cries.

The little queen heard them, too, landing on Menolly's shoulder and adding her agitated comments.

Menolly told her to be quiet so she could hear, and to her surprise, the little queen instantly obeyed. The others subsided, and all seemed to wait expectantly. Without diversion Menolly recognized the distinctive and frantic noise of a distressed wherry.

Following the sound, Menolly crossed the slight rise into the next bog valley and saw the creature, wings flapping, head jerking but its legs and body firmly captured by treacherous sinking sands.

Oblivious to the excitement of the fire liz-

ards who recognized the wherry as an enemy, Menolly ran forward, drawing her knife. The bird had been eating berries from the bushes edging the boggy sands and stupidly stepped into the mire. Menolly approached the sands cautiously, making certain that she was stepping on firm land. She got close enough—the frightened bird not even aware of her proximity—and plunged her knife into its back, at the base of the neck.

One more frightened squawk and the thing was dead, limp wings settling on the surface and rapidly submerging.

Menolly unbuckled her belt to make a loop of the buckle end. Grabbing the tough branches of a berry bush, she leaned out just far enough to snap the loop around the head of the bird. She tightened the loop and slowly began to pull.

Not only was there wherry meat here to feed herself and the fire lizards, but the layer of fat under its tough hide would provide her with the best possible grease for her friends' fragile skins.

Again, to Menolly's surprise, the fire lizard queen appeared to understand the situation. She sank her tiny talons into a wherry wing and pulled the tip out of the mud. She

9 **Discussion** Menolly's concern reflects the common medieval myth that red meat "fired the blood" and made animals vicious. What do you think about this?

10 **Clarification** Tell students that *refuge* means "shelter or protection from danger." To what does the word refer?

11 **Literary Focus: Atmosphere** What feeling does Menolly have about this cave as her home?

squeaked shrilly at the others, and before Menolly realized it, all of them had seized some tenable part of the wherry and were exerting their efforts to pull it from the bog-sand.

It took a lot of pulling and shrill fire lizard orders, but they managed to get the wherry out of the sands and onto firm ground.

The rest of her day was spent in sawing through the tough outer hide to disembowel and dress the carcass. The fire lizards made an enthusiastic meal of the entrails and the blood that flowed from the wherry's neck. The sight somewhat nauseated Menolly, but she set her jaw and tried to ignore the voracity with which her otherwise gentle companions attacked the unexpected delicacy.

She hoped the taste of hot raw meat wouldn't change their temperaments, but she reckoned that dragons didn't become savage from their diet of live meat so it was fair to assume that the fire lizards wouldn't. At least, they were well fed for the day.

The wherry had been a good-sized bird, doubtless feeding somewhere in the lower reaches of Nerat for its fatty layer was juicy. It couldn't be a northern bird. Menolly skinned it, stopping twice to hone her knife sharp. She carved the meat from the bones, stuffing it into the hide to carry home. When she had finished, she had a hefty burden, and the bones were by no means stripped clean. Too bad she couldn't tell the old queen where they were.

She was rigging a forehead sling of her belt and the leg skin when suddenly the air was alive with fire lizards. With creels of shrill delight, the old queen and her bronzes settled on the bones. Menolly backed hastily away before the fire lizards decided to attack her for the meat she carried.

She had plenty of time on her long and tiring march back to the sea cave to wonder about their appearance. She could easily believe that the little queen could understand what she was thinking, and the others she had been taking care of. But had the young queen told the others? Or had Menolly some tenuous contact with the old queen, too?

Her special group showed no inclination to remain with the others, but kept her company, sometimes disappearing or making lazy figures in the sky. Sometimes the little queen sat on her shoulder for a few dragon lengths, chirruping sweetly.

It was fully dark long before Menolly reached her refuge. Only the moonlight and familiarity with the access route helped her down the cliff face. Her hearth fire was sullen embers, which she wearily coaxed into a cheery blaze. She was too tired to do more than wrap a piece of wherry meat in a few leaves of seaweed and stick it in the heated sands by the fire to cook for the morning. Then she wrapped herself up in her carry-sack and fell asleep.

She rendered the fat over the next several days, wishing time and again for one decent cooking pot. She heaped aromatic herbs into the hot fat and poured the mixture into clay pots for cooling. The wherry meat had a slightly fishy taste, which suggested that the stupid bird had been of a seaside flock rather than an inland or mountain group. But the cooled grease smelled of the herbs. Not, Menolly supposed, that the fire lizards minded how they smelled so long as their itching skin was soothed.

They loved to be oiled, lying on their backs, their wings spread for balance, curling around her hand as she spread oil on their softer belly hide. They hummed with delight at the attention, and when she had finished each one, the creature would stroke her cheek with its small triangular head, the glistening eyes sparkling with brilliant colors.

She was beginning to find individual

Grammar in Action

An **adverb clause** is a subordinate clause that is used in a sentence the same way an adverb is used. It begins with a subordinating conjunction, such as *after, although, as, because, before, if, since, though, unless, until, when, where, whether,* and *while*. Writers use adverb clauses to show how why, when, where, under what conditions, or with what results something happens. Notice how Anne McCaffrey uses adverb clauses to show the relationships between ideas in these sentences:

When she had finished each one, the creature would stroke her cheek with its small triangular head. (The adverb clause tells *when* the creature would stroke her cheek.)

She'd peck them fast enough *if they disobeyed her.* (The adverb clause tells *under what conditions* she would peck them.)

Student Activity 1. Identify the adverb clause in each sentence.

1. Later she spoke with them because they understood what she was saying.
2. When Menolly gave the fire lizards the food, they ate it quickly.
3. The fire lizards responded to the dragon songs as if they understood their relationship to the great beasts.
4. If you treated fire lizards kindly, they responded.

traits among her nine charges. The little queen was exactly as she should be: into everything, bossing everyone else, as imperious and demanding as a Sea Holder. She'd listen, however, very quietly to Menolly. And she'd listen to the old queen, too. But she paid no heed to any of the others, although they were expected to obey anything she said. She'd peck them fast enough if they disobeyed her.

There were two bronzes, three browns, a blue and two greens. Menolly felt a little sorry for the blue. He seemed to be left out or picked upon by the others. The two greens were always scolding him. She named him Uncle, and the greens became Auntie One and Auntie Two. Two was slightly smaller than One. Because one of the bronzes preferred to hunt for rockmites while the other was deft at diving into pools for fingertails, they became Rocky and Diver. The browns were so much alike that for a long time they remained nameless, but gradually she found that the largest of the trio usually fell asleep, given any opportunity to do so, so she called him Lazybones. The second was Mimic because he always did what he saw the other doing; and the third was Brownie for lack of any other distinguishing feature.

The little queen was Beauty because she was and because she took such elaborate pains with her grooming and required much more attention and oiling than the others. She was forever digging at her talons with her teeth, spreading them to clean between the toes, or licking any specks of dust from her tail, burnishing her neck ridges in the sand or grass.

At first Menolly talked to her creatures to hear the sound of her own voice. Later she spoke with them because they seemed to understand what she was saying. They certainly gave every indication of intelligent listening, humming or crooning an encouraging response when she paused. And they never seemed to get enough of her singing to them, or playing her pipes. She couldn't exactly say that they harmonized with her, but they did hum softly in tune as she played.

Chapter 8

Wheel and turn
Or bleed and burn.
Fly between,
Blue and green.
Soar, dive down,
Bronze and brown.
Dragonmen must fly
When Threads are in the sky.

As it turned out, Alemi sailed Elgion to the Dragon Stones to search there for the elusive fire lizards. One windy day, not long after the visit of N'ton, the young Sea Man broke a leg bone when the rough seas tossed him against the pilot house of his ship. They were coming into harbor and the high tide made for heavier waters there than he'd expected. Yanus grumbled a good deal about Alemi being too experienced a Sea Man to get injured, but his grumbling subsided when Mavi pointed out that here was a chance to see if Alemi's first mate would be capable of assuming command of the ship being finished in the building cavern.

Alemi tried to take the injury in good part, but after four days in bed, with the swelling eased, he was heartily bored and restless. He plagued Mavi so constantly that she handed him the crutch she had not meant to give him for a full sevenday more, and suggested that if he broke his neck, too, he would have only himself to blame.

Alemi had more sense than that and navigated the inner stairways, narrow and dark, slowly and carefully; he kept to the wider outer stairs and the Sea Hold's main rooms and the holdway whenever possible.

While he had some mobility, he didn't

Dragonsong 971

12 Reading Strategy Summarize the "personality" of the little queen.

13 Discussion Can you think of any reasons why the greens were always scolding the little blue?

14 Discussion What is the message of the song at the beginning of the chapter? How would you express it in prose?

Student Activity 2. Add an adverb clause to each sentence.
1. Menolly enjoyed singing.
2. The fire lizards needed much food.
3. Dragons protected the Holds.
4. The children learned from the Teaching Ballads.

Electronic Handbook You may want students to review adverbs and clauses before completing the Grammar in Action activities. If students have access to the Language Master 6000, have them enter the access words *adverb* and *clause* and press the GRAMMAR key to get information on these topics.

15 Discussion What does Alemi mean when he says he'll have a "weather-wise" ache?

16 Discussion What does the sentence "Alemi was torn between duty to the Hold and love of his sister" tell you about him?

17 Discussion Why is Alemi surprised to hear that the songs are so good? What Hold belief is reflected in his surprise?

have much activity if the Fishing Fleet was out, so he was soon attracted by the sound of the children learning a new Ballad from the Harper. He caught Elgion's eye and received a courteous wave to enter the Little Hall. If the children were startled to hear a baritone suddenly take up the learning, they had too much respect for the Harper to do more than hazard a quick peek and the class progressed.

To Alemi's pleasure he found himself as quick to memorize the new words and tune as the youngsters, and he thoroughly enjoyed the session; he was almost sorry when Elgion excused them.

"How's the leg, Alemi?" the Harper asked when the room had emptied.

15 "I'll have a weather-wise ache now for sure."

"Is that why you did it?" Elgion said with a broad grin. "I'd heard you wanted to be sure Tilsit got a chance at command."

Alemi let out a snort of laughter. "Nonsense. I haven't had a rest since the last five-day gale. That's a fine Ballad you're teaching."

"That's a fine voice you were singing it with, too. Why don't you sound out more often? I was beginning to think the sea wind snatches the voice of everyone at about twelve Turns."

"You should have heard my sis . . ." and Alemi stopped, flushed, and clamped his lips tight.

"Which reminds me: I took the liberty of asking N'ton, Lioth's rider, to spread the word at Benden Weyr that she's missing. She may still be alive, you know."

Alemi nodded slowly.

"You Sea Holders are full of surprises," said Elgion, thinking to switch to a less painful topic. He went to the racks of wax tablets and removed the two he sought. "These must have been done by that fosterling who took over when Petiron died. The other slates are all in the older script notations, which the old Harper used. But these . . . A lad who can do this sort of work is needed in the Harper's craft. You don't know where the boy is now, do you?"

16 Alemi was torn between duty to the Hold and love of his sister. But she wasn't in the Hold anymore, and common sense told Alemi that she must be dead if, in this length of time, with dragonriders looking for her, she hadn't been found. Menolly was only a girl, so what good did it do that her songs found favor with the Harper? Alemi was also reluctant to put the lie to his father. So, despite the fact that Elgion was impressed by the songs, since the songmaker was beyond them, Alemi answered truthfully that he didn't know where "he" was.

Elgion wrapped the waxed slates carefully, and with a noticeable sigh of regret. "I'll send them on to the Harpercrafthall anyway. Robinton will want to use them."

17 "Use them? They're that good?" Alemi was startled and regretted the lies still more.

"They're cracking good. Maybe if the lad hears them, he'll come forward on his own." Elgion gave Alemi a rueful smile. "Since it's obvious there's some reason you can't name him." He chuckled at the Sea Man's reaction. "Come now, man, the lad was sent away in some sort of disgrace, wasn't he? That happens, as any Harper worth his salt knows— and understands. Hold honor and all that. I won't tease you anymore. He'll surface to the sound of his own music."

They talked of other things then, until the Fishing Fleet returned—two men of the same age but different backgrounds: one with an inquisitive interest in the world beyond his Sea Hold, and the other quite willing to satisfy it. Elgion was, in fact, delighted to find none of Yanus's denseness and inflexibility in Alemi, and the Harper began to feel that after all he might be able to follow Master

972   *The Novel*

Robinton's ambitious plan of broadening understanding beyond the limits of this Sea Hold.

Alemi was back the following day after the children had been dismissed, with more questions. He stopped midsentence finally, apologizing profusely for taking so much of Elgion's time.

"I tell you what, Alemi, I'll teach you what you'd like to know if you'll teach me how to sail."

"Teach you to sail?"

Elgion grinned. "Yes, teach me to sail. The smallest child in my class knows more about that than I do, and my professional standing is in jeopardy. After all, a Harper is supposed to know everything.

"I may be wrong but I don't imagine that you need both legs to sail one of those little skiffs the children use."

Alemi's face lit up, and he pounded the Harper on the back with enthusiasm.

"Of course I can. By the First Shell, man, I'd be glad to do it. Glad."

And nothing would satisfy Alemi but to take the Harper down to the Dock Cavern immediately and give him the fundamentals of seamanship. In his own subject, Alemi was as good an instructor as the Harper; and Elgion was able to tack across the harbor by himself by the end of the first lesson. Of course, as Alemi remarked, the wind was from the right quarter and the sea calm, ideal sailing conditions.

"Which rarely prevail?" asked Elgion; and he was rewarded by Alemi's tolerant chuckle. "Well, practice makes perfect, and I'd better learn the practical."

"And the theory."

So their friendship was cemented by mutual exchanges of knowledge and long visits together. Although their conversation touched many subjects, Elgion hesitated to bring up the subject of fire lizards, or the fact that the Weyr had asked him to search for traces of the elusive little creatures. He had, however, searched as much of the accessible coastline as he could on foot. There were some beaches that should be checked now from the seaside. With Alemi teaching him how to handle the skiff, he hoped he'd soon be able to do it himself. Elgion knew with certainty that Yanus would be completely scornful of any search for fire lizards, and the Harper didn't want to implicate Alemi in any plan that would bring Yanus's anger down on his head. Alemi was in bad enough straits over breaking his leg.

One clear bright morning, Elgion decided to put his solution to the test. He dismissed the children early, then sought out Alemi and suggested that today was not only a fine day but the sea was rough enough to test his ability. Alemi laughed, cast a wise eye at the clouds, and said that it would be mild as a bathing pool by afternoon but that the practice now would be useful to Elgion's progress.

Elgion wheedled a large package of fish rolls and spicecakes from a kitchen auntie, and the two men set off. Alemi was agile enough now with his crutch and splint-bound leg on land, but he was glad of any excuse to be on the sea.

Once beyond the protecting arms of the Half-Circle cliffs, the sea was choppy with crosscurrent and wind; Elgion's skill would be well tested. Alemi, disregarding an occasional wetting as the skiff plunged in and out of the wave troughs, played silent passenger while the Harper fought tiller and sheet to keep them on the course Alemi had set down the coast. The Sea Man became aware of the windshift some moments before Elgion, but it was the mark of his abilities as a teacher that Elgion was quick enough to notice the change.

"Wind's slacking off."

Alemi nodded, adjusting his cap slightly

for the wind's new direction. They sailed on, the wind slackening to a gentle pressure against the sail, the skiff's speed aided more by the deep current than the wind.

"I'm hungry," Alemi announced as he and Elgion saw the stumpy violet crags of the Dragon Stones to leeward.[2]

Elgion released the sheet line, and Alemi pulled the sail down, furling it with absent skill against the boom. At his direction, Elgion lashed the tiller so that the current carried them idly downcoast.

"Don't know why," Alemi said through a mouthful of fish roll, "food always tastes better on the sea."

Elgion contented himself with a nod since his mouth was full. He also had a good appetite; not, he qualified to himself, that he had been working overhard, just hanging on to the tiller and adjusting the said sheet now and then.

"Come to think, don't often have time to eat on the sea," Alemi added. He gestured to include their leisurely bobbing, the skiff itself and the informal meal. "Haven't been this lazy on a sail since I was old enough to haul a net." He stretched and then adjusted his splinted leg slightly, grimacing against the awkwardness and discomfort. Suddenly he leaned away from the bulwark, to reach into the small locker fitted against the curve of the hull. "Thought so." Grinning, he held up fishline, hook and dry worm.

"Can't you leave off?"

"What? And have Yanus give out about unproductive hands?" Alemi deftly threaded line to hook and baited it. "Here. You might as well try hook line and bait. Or does the Masterharper object to cross-crafting?"

"The more crafts the better, says Master Robinton."

---

2. to leeward (lē´wərd): On the side toward which the wind is blowing.

Alemi nodded, his eyes on the current. "Aye, sending lads away to other Sea Holds for fostering doesn't quite answer, does it?" Deftly he threw the line from him, watched the cast carry it well away from the drifting skiff and sink.

Elgion gave a fair imitation of that cast and settled himself, as Alemi had, to wait for results.

"What would we be catching out here?"

Alemi drew his mouth up in a grimace of indifference. "Probably nothing. Tide's full, current's strong, midday. Fish feed at dawn, unless there's Thread."

"Is that why you use the dry worm? Because it resembles Thread?" Elgion couldn't suppress the shudder that went down his spine at the thought of loose Thread.

"You're right."

The silence that often grips fishermen settled comfortably in the boat.

"Yellow-stripe, if anything," Alemi finally said in answer to the question that Elgion had almost forgotten he'd asked. "Yellow-stripe or a very hungry packtail. They'll eat anything."

"Packtail? That's good eating."

"Line'll break. Packtail's too heavy for this."

"Oh."

The current was inexorably drawing them closer to the Dragon Stones. But, although he wanted to get Alemi talking about them, Elgion couldn't find the proper opening. At about the point where Elgion felt he'd better speak or they'd be pulled by the current into the Stones, Alemi casually glanced around. They were only several dragon lengths from the most seaward of the great crags. The water now lapped peacefully against the base, exposing occasionally the jagged points of submerged rock, eddying around others. Alemi unfurled the sail and hauled on the sheet line.

"We need more sea room near those. Dangerous with sunken rock. When the tide's making, current can pull you right in. If you sail this way by yourself, and you'll soon be able to, make sure you keep your distance."

"The lads say you saw fire lizards there once." Elgion found the words out of his mouth before he could censor them.

Alemi shot him a long amused look. "Let's say I can't think what else it could've been. They weren't wherries: too fast, too small, and wherries can't maneuver that way. But fire lizards?" He laughed and shrugged his shoulders, indicating his own skepticism.

"What if I told you that there are such things? That F'nor, Canth's rider, Impressed one in Southern and so did five or six other riders? That the Weyrs are looking for more fire lizard clutches, and I've been asked to search the beaches?"

Alemi stared at the Harper. Then the skiff rocked in the subtle crosscurrents. "Mind now, pull the tiller hard aport. No, to your left, man!"

They had the looming Dragon Stone comfortably abaft[3] before further conversation.

"You can Impress fire lizards?" If Alemi's voice was incredulous, an eager light sparkled in his eyes, and Elgion knew he'd made an ally; he told as much as he, himself, knew.

"Well, that would explain why you rarely see grown ones, and why they evade capture so cleverly. They *hear* you coming." Alemi laughed, shaking his head. "When I think of the times . . ."

"Me, too." Elgion grinned broadly, remembering his boyhood attempts to rig a successful trap.

"We're to look on beaches?"

"That's what N'ton suggested. Sandy beaches, sheltered places, preferably hard for

---

3. abaft (ə baft′): in the rear; behind.

small active boys to find. There're plenty of places where a fire lizard queen could hide a clutch around here."

"Not with the tides so high this season."

"There must be some beaches deep enough." Elgion felt impatient with Alemi's arguments.

The Sea Man motioned Elgion out of the tiller seat, and deftly tacked about.

"I saw fire lizards about the Dragon Stones. And those crags'd be right good weyrs. Not that I think we'd have a chance of seeing them today. They feed at dawn: that's when I saw them. Only," and Alemi chuckled, "I thought my eyes were deceiving me since it was the end of a long watch and a man's eyes can play tricks with him at dawn."

Alemi sailed the little skiff far closer to the Dragon Stones than Elgion would have dared. In fact the Harper found himself gripping the weatherboard very hard and edging his body away from the towering crags as the skiff breezed lightly by. There was no doubt that the crags were riddled with holes, likely weyrs for fire lizards.

"I wouldn't try this tack except when the tide is full, Elgion," said Alemi as they sailed between the innermost crag and the tide-washed land. "There's a right mess of bottom-reaming rocks here even at half-tide."

It was quiet, too, with the waves softly caressing the narrow verge of sand between sea and cliff. Quiet enough for the unmistakable sound of piping to carry across the water to Elgion.

"Did you hear that?" Elgion grabbed Alemi's arm.

"Hear what?"

"The music!"

"What music?" Alemi wondered briefly if the sun were strong enough to give the Harper a stroke. But he sharpened his ears for any unusual sound, following the line of Elgion's stare to the cliffs. His heart leaped

22 Discussion Why is Alemi amused at Elgion's words?

23 Discussion How do you think the Dragon Stones got their name?

976   The Novel

for a moment, but he said, "Music? Nonsense! Those cliffs are riddled with caves and holes. All you hear is the wind . . ."

"There isn't any wind now . . ."

Alemi had to admit that because he'd let the boom out and was even beginning to wonder if they had enough wind to come about on a tack that would clear the northern side of the stones.

"And look," said Elgion, "there's a hole in the cliff face. Big enough for a person to get into, I'd wager. Alemi, can't we go inshore?"

"Not unless we walk home, or wait for high tide again."

"Alemi! That's music! Not wind over blow holes! That's someone playing pipes."

An unhappy furtive thought crossed Alemi's face so plainly that Elgion jumped to a conclusion. All at once, all the pieces fell into place.

"Your sister, the one who's missing. *She* wrote those songs. She taught the children, not that conveniently dismissed fosterling!"

"Menolly's not playing any pipes, Elgion. She sliced her left hand, gutting packtail, and she can't open or close her fingers."

Elgion sank back to the deck, stunned but still hearing the clear tone of pipes. Pipes? You'd need two whole hands to play multiple pipes. The music ceased and the wind, rising as they tacked past the Dragon Stones, covered his memory of that illusive melody. It could have been the land breeze, sweeping down over the cliffs, sounding into holes.

"Menolly did teach the children, didn't she?"

Slowly Alemi nodded. "Yanus believed the Sea Hold disgraced to have a girl taking the place of a Harper."

"Disgraced?" Once again Elgion was appalled at the obtuseness of the Sea Holder. "When she taught so well? When she can turn a tune like the ones I've seen?"

"She can play no more, Elgion. It would be cruel to ask now. She wouldn't even sing in the evenings. She'd leave as soon as you started to play."

So he'd been right, thought Elgion, the tall girl had been Menolly.

"If she's alive, she's happier away from the Hold! If she's dead . . ." Alemi didn't continue.

In silence they sailed on, the Dragon Stones falling away, back into violent indefiniteness as each man avoided the other's gaze.

Now Elgion could understand many things about Menolly's disappearance and the general reluctance at the Hold to discuss her or find her. There was no doubt in his mind that her disappearance was deliberate. Anyone sensitive enough to compose such melodies must have found life in the Sea Hold intolerable: doubly so with Yanus as Sea Holder and father. And then to be considered a disgrace! Elgion cursed Petiron for not making the matter plain. If only he had told Robinton that the promising musician were a girl, she might have been at the Harperhall before that knife had a chance to slip.

"There'd be no clutches on the Dragon Stones' cove," Alemi said, breaking into Elgion's rueful thoughts. "Water's right up to the bluff at high tide. There is one place . . . I'll take you there after the next Threadfall is past. A good long day's sail down the coast. You *can* Impress a fire lizard, you say?"

"I'll set the signal for N'ton to talk to you after Fall." Elgion was happy enough to use any subject to break the restraint that had fallen between them. "Evidently you or I can Impress, though lowly Harpers and young Sea Men may be far down on the list for available eggs."

"By the dawn star, when I think of the hours I spent as a small fellow . . ."

"Who hasn't?" Elgion grinned back, eager too for the chance.

This time their silence was companion-

Dragonsong 977

24 Discussion Why is Alemi looking unhappy?

25 Discussion Why does Alemi stop talking at this point?

26 **Discussion** Why is Alemi so adamant about keeping secret the fact that Menolly did the teaching?

27 **Discussion** Why is Elgion happy at not having to teach for a day?

able, and when they exchanged glances, it was for remembered boyish fancies of capturing the elusive and much-desired fire lizard.

As they tacked into the Dock Cavern late that afternoon, Alemi had a final word for Elgion.

26 "You understand why you're not to know it was Menolly who did the teaching?"

"The Sea Hold is not disgraced." Elgion felt Alemi's hand tighten on his arm so he nodded. "But I would never betray that confidence."

If his solemn response reassured the Sea Man, it reinforced Elgion's determination to find out who had made that pipe music. Was it possible to play multiple pipes with one hand? He was convinced that he'd heard music, not wind over blow holes. Somehow, whether on the pretext of searching for fire lizards or not, he must get close enough to examine that cave in the Dragon Stones' cove.

The next day was rainy, a thin soft drizzle that did not deter the fishermen but that made both Elgion and Alemi unwilling to take a long and possibly fruitless journey in an open boat.

That same evening Yanus asked Elgion to excuse the children from lessons the following morning as they'd be needed to gather **27** seaweed for the smoke-cave. Elgion granted considered permission, masterfully suppressing a desire to thank the Sea Holder for a free day, and determined to rise early and be off to seek the answer to the music mystery. He was up as soon as the sun, first in the Great Hall, so that he had to unbar the metal doors, little realizing as he did so that he would be following an unnerving precedent. With fish rolls and dried fruit in his pouch, his own pipe slung across his back, a stout rope about his middle (for he rather thought he might need it climbing down that cliff face), Elgion was away.

Chapter 9

*Oh, Tongue, give sound to joy and sing
Of hope and promise on dragonwing.*

The hunger of the fire lizards roused Menolly from sleep. There was nothing in the cave to eat because the previous day had been wet enough to keep them all inside. She saw that the tide was well out, and the day was clear.

"If we scramble, we can get downcoast and pick us up a nice lot of spiderclaws. They'll be gone soon," she told her friends. "Or we can look for rockmites. So come along, Beauty." The little queen hummed from her warm nest in the rushes, and the others began to stir. Menolly reached down and tickled Lazy's neck where he lay by her feet. He slapped at her, rousing enough to let out a huge yawn. His eyelids peeled back and his eyes sparkled faintly red.

"Now, don't you all start in on me. I got you up so we could be off. You won't be hungry long if we all stir smartly."

As she descended agilely to the beach, her friends swooping gracefully from the cave, some of the other fire lizards were feeding in the shallows. Menolly called out a greeting to them. She wondered, as she often did, if the other fire lizards, with the notable exception of the queen, were at all aware of her. She felt it rude not to acknowledge their presence whether they responded or not. Maybe one day they would have grown so used to her that they'd answer.

She slipped on the wet rocks at the far end of the cove, wincing as a sharp edge made itself painfully felt through the thinning soles of her boots. *That* was a matter she'd have to attend to soon, new boot soles. With such rough surfaces, she couldn't go barefoot. And she certainly couldn't climb barefooted, not if she had toes like a watchwher. She'd have to get another

Grammar in Action

In most cases, writers use nouns as the subject of a sentence, a direct or indirect object of a verb, or as the object of a preposition. However, when a noun cannot convey enough information, writers use noun clauses. **Noun clauses** are subordinate clauses that are used in a sentence as if they were nouns. Noun clauses are often introduced by the words *who, whose, whom, which, what, whoever, whichever, that, when, where, why,* *how, whether,* or *if.* Notice how Anne McCaffrey uses the noun clauses in these sentences:

> She could concentrate on *where she was putting her feet.* (The noun clause is the object of the preposition.)

> The fellis juice acted so quickly that she wondered *how she could possibly stay awake.* (The noun clause is the direct object of the predicate *wondered.*)

Student Activity 1. Identify the noun clauses in the following sentences.
1. Menolly thought about how she could stand up with such pain.
2. Whoever Impresses the most fire lizards will be considered the most successful.

wherry, tan its leg hide to a proper tough-ness. But how could she sew the new leather to her old boot sole? She looked down at her feet, placing them carefully, as much to save the leather as her feet.

She took her band to the furthest cove they'd yet explored, far enough down the coast for the Dragon Stones to be knobs on the horizon. But the long walk was worth the effort for spiderclaws scurried wildly up and down the wide, gently curving beach. The bluff had dwindled to a height just above her head in some places, and at the far end of the crescent sands, a stream fed into the sea.

Beauty and the others were soon playing havoc with[4] the spiderclaws, diving down on their intended prey, then darting up to the cliffs to eat. When her net was full, Menolly searched for enough sea wreckage to start a fire. That was how she found the clutch, cov-ered as it was and almost level with the beach surface. But she saw the faint outline of a mound, suspiciously circular. She brushed away enough sand to expose the mottled shell of a hardening fire lizard egg. She glanced around carefully, wondering if the queen was anywhere about; but she saw only her own nine. She put a gentle finger on the exposed egg: it was softish. Quickly she patted the sand back into place and hurried from the clutch. The high-tide mark on this beach was a long way from threatening the eggs. It pleased her to realize that this beach was a long way from any Hold so these fire lizard eggs were safe.

She gathered sufficient wood, made a rude hearth, started her fire, killed the spiderclaws deftly and laid them on a conve-niently flat stone and went exploring while they baked.

The stream flowed broad into the sea; sand banks had formed and re-formed to

---

4. playing havoc (hav' ek) **with:** Destroying or ruining.

judge by the myriad channels. Menolly fol-lowed the stream inland, looking for the sweet cresses that often grew where the water freshened. Submarine bodies moved up-stream, too, and she wondered if she could catch one of the big specklers. Alemi often boasted that he could tickle them into his grasp as they fought the current. Thinking of the spiderclaws roasting on her fire, Menolly decided to leave that exercise until another day. She did want some greens; succulent cresses with their odd tangy aftertaste would make a good addition to spiderclaws.

She found the greens well above the tide-water, where the stream was fed by tiny trick-les from the flat marshy lands through which it looped. She was greedily stuffing a handful of greens into her mouth before she really took in her surroundings. In the distance, low on the horizon, were lightning flashes against a gray sky.

Thread! Fear rooted her to the ground; she nearly choked on the half-chewed mouth-ful of greens. She tried to talk herself out of terror by counting the flashes of dragon fire that made a pattern across the sky: a wide, long pattern. If the dragonriders were already at work, the Thread wouldn't get as far as here. She was a long way from it.

But how far away was safe? She'd just made it to the cave before that other Fall. She was too far away, run as fast as ever she could, to reach the cave's safety now. She'd the sea behind her. Water! She'd the stream beside her. Thread drowned in water. But how deep did it fall before it drowned?

She told herself firmly that now was not the time to panic. She forced herself to swal-low the last of the cress juices. Then she had no control over her legs; they took off with her and she was running, towards the sea and towards the rock safety of her cave.

Beauty appeared above her head, swoop-ing and chittering as she caught Menolly's

Dragonsong 979

---

28 Discussion Menolly tests the egg with her finger. Why does she do this?

29 Critical Thinking and Reading What does Menolly consider, and then finally conclude, when she sees the lightning flashes in the sky?

---

3. When the dragons hatch does indeed matter to the inhabi-tants of Benden Weyr.
4. The food goes to whoever is the hungriest.
5. The fire lizards thought about how they could protect Menolly.

Student Activity 2. Complete each sentence with a noun clause.
1. Menolly did not know _____.
2. _____ was a mystery.
3. The greatest danger of Threadfall was _____.
4. Menolly fed a spiderclaw to _____.

Electronic Handbook You might wish to review noun clauses with students before completing this activity. If students have access to the Language Master 6000, have them enter the access words *noun* and *clause* and press the GRAMMAR key to get information on these topics.

fear. Rocky and Diver arrived with Mimic popping in a half-breath later. They experienced her alarm, circling around her head as she ran, calling out with the piercingly sweet tenor bugle of challenge. Then they all disappeared. Which made running easier for Menolly. She could concentrate on where she was putting her feet.

She made diagonally for the beaches, wondering briefly if it wouldn't be smarter to go along the shore line. She'd be that much nearer the dubious safety of the water. She hurdled a ditch; managed to keep her balance as her left foot twisted on landing; staggered a few paces before she found her stride again. No, there'd be more rocks on the shore, cutting down her speed and increasing the danger of a badly twisted ankle.

Two queens gleamed golden in the air above her, and Rocky and Diver were back, with Lazybones, Mimic and Brownie. The two queens chittered angrily, and the males, to Menolly's surprise, flew ahead of her now, and high enough not to be a nuisance. She ran on.

She came to a height, and the incline robbed her of breath so that she staggered to the summit and had to drop to a walk, clutching her right side against the nagging stitch, but somehow moving forward. Ahead of her the Dragon Stones were more than knobs but too distant to reassure. One look over her shoulder at the sky bursts of dragon fire told her that the Thread was gaining on her.

She broke into a run again, the two queens gliding right over her head, and she felt oddly protected. She had her second wind now, and her stride, and felt as if she could run forever. If she could only run fast enough to stay beyond the reach of Thread . . . She kept her eyes on the Dragon Stones, refusing to look over her shoulder: that unnerving sight caught the breath she needed for running.

She ran as close to the bluff edge as she dared. She'd slithered down one cliff without desperate damage to herself: she'd risk it again to get into the water if she had to.

She ran, one eye on the Dragon Stones, one for the ground ahead of her feet.

She heard the whoosh, heard the fire lizards' startled chirrups, saw the shadow and fell to the ground, covering her head instinctively with her hands, her body taut for the first feel of flesh-scoring Thread. She smelt fire-stone, and felt the air heavy against her body.

"Get on your feet, you silly fool! And hurry. Leading edge is nearly on us!"

Incredulous, Menolly looked up, right into the whirling eyes of a brown dragon. He cocked his head and hummed urgently.

"Get up!" said his rider.

Menolly wasted no time after a frantic look at the fire blossoms and the sight of a line of dragons swooping and disappearing. She scrambled to her feet, dove for the brown rider's extended hand and one of the fighting strap ends, and got herself firmly astride the brown's neck behind his rider.

"Hang on to me tightly. And don't be afraid. I'm to take you *between* to Benden. It'll be cold and dark, but I'll be with you."

The relief of being rescued when she was fearing injury or death was too overwhelming for speech. The brown dragon half-ran to the bluff edge, dropped down briefly to get wing room, and then surged up. Menolly felt herself pressed against the soft warm flesh and burrowed into the hide-clad back of her rescuer, struggling for a lungful of air to ease her tight chest. She had one brief glimpse of her little fire lizards trying vainly to follow when the dragon winked into *between*.

Sweat froze on her forehead and cheeks, down her back, on her calves, her wet and ragged boots and her sore feet. There was no air to breathe and she felt she would suf-

Commentary: Teleportation

The talented dragons and fire lizards in this story are among Anne McCaffrey's most original contributions to science fiction. Their ability to go between is teleportation, moving oneself instantaneously from one place to another. The dragons take teleportation a step further than the definition suggests; they can also move from one time to another. Although "timing it" is frowned upon by responsible dragonriders, such heroic characters as Lessa (in *Dragonflight*) and Jaxom (in *The White Dragon*

and in *All the Weyrs of Pern*) have used this draconic ability to achieve noble ends.

Although McCaffrey makes clever use of the dragons' ability to teleport, she is not the first writer to deal with the subject. One of the earliest and best teleportation stories is *The Stars My Destination* (1956) by Alfred Bester. In this novel, the hero, Jaunte, discovers the ability to teleport and uses it to remove himself from perilous situations. Remarkably, teleportation, called *jaunting,* can be taught to others. The novel depicts an interesting future in which the customary means of transportation become obsolete.

Teleportation is but one of many "psi" (short for psionic) powers that became popular in science fiction in the 1950's. SF

writers created characters who could manipulate the minds of others, levitate, and create hallucinations. The ability to start fires, pyrotics, is a psi power used most notably by Stephen King in his novel *Fire Starter*. Among such an array of exotic talents, mere ESP seems like child's play.

32 **Discussion** Can you recall (from the Foreword) the importance of the Red Star to the people of Pern?

33 **Critical Thinking and Reading** What was Menolly's first impression of Benden?

focate. She tightened her hands convulsively on the dragonrider, but she couldn't feel him or the dragon she knew she was riding.

Now, she thought with that part of her mind that wasn't frozen in panic, she fully understood that Teaching Song. In terror, she fully understood it.

Abruptly, sight, sound, feeling, and breath returned. They were spiralling down at a dizzying height above Benden Weyr. As big as Half-Circle was, this place of dragons and dragonmen was bigger by half again as much. Why, the immense harbor of Half-Circle would have fitted with dragon lengths to spare in the Bowl of the Weyr.

32 As the dragon circled, she saw the giant Star Stones, and the Eye Rock, which told when the Red Star would make its fateful Passes. She saw the watch dragon beside the Stones, heard him trumpet a greeting to the brown she rode. Between her legs she felt the rumble of response in the brown's throat. As they glided down, she saw several dragons on the Bowl floor, with people gathered about **33** them; saw the steps leading to the queen's Weyr, and the yawning maw[5] of the Hatching Ground. Benden was vaster than she'd imagined.

The brown landed near the other dragons, and Menolly now realized that the dragons had been Threadscored and were being treated. The brown dragon half-folded his wings, craning his neck around to the two on his back.

"You can relax your death hold, lad," said the brown rider with tolerant amusement as he unfastened the fighting straps from his belt.

Menolly jerked her hands free with a muttered apology. "I can't thank you enough for finding me. I thought Thread would get me."

"Whoever let you out of your Hold so near to Threadfall?"

---

5. maw (mô) *n.*: A large gaping opening.

"I was catching spiderclaws. Went out early."

He accepted that hurried explanation, but now Menolly wondered how she could make it plausible. She couldn't remember the name of the nearest Hold on the Nerat side of Half-Circle.

"Down you go, lad, I've got to rejoin my wing to mop up."

That was the second time he'd called her "lad."

"You've a fine pace on you. Ever think of going for a Hold runner?"

The brown rider swung her forward so she could slide down the brown's shoulder. The moment her feet touched the ground, she thought she'd faint with the pain. She grabbed frantically at the brown's foreleg. He nuzzled her sympathetically, humming to his rider.

"Branth says you're hurt?" The man slid down quickly beside her.

"My feet!" She'd run the boots to uppers without knowing it, and her lacerated feet were bloody from toe to heel.

"I'll tell the world. Here we go!"

He grabbed her by the wrist, gave a practiced yank and laid her over his shoulder. As he made for the entrance to the lower caverns, he called out for someone to bring a pot of numbweed.

She was uprighted into a chair, the blood singing in her ears. Someone was propping her damaged feet onto a stool while women converged on her from several sides.

"Hey, Manora, Felena," yelled the brown rider urgently.

"Just look at his feet! He's run them raw!"

"T'gran, wherever . . ."

"Saw him trying to outrun Thread down Nerat way. Bloody near did!"

"Bloody's quite accurate. Manora, could you spare a moment, please?"

"Should we wash the feet first or . . ."

"No, a cup of weed first," was T'gran's

suggestion. "You'll have to cut the boots off . . ."

Someone was holding a cup against her lips, bidding her drink it all down. On a stomach empty of anything but a few blades of cress, the fellis juice acted so quickly that the circle of faces about her became a confused blur.

"Good heavens, the Holders have gone mad, going out in Threadfall." Menolly thought the speaker sounded like Manora. "This is the second one we've rescued today."

After that, voices became indistinguishable mumbles. Menolly was unable to focus her eyes. She seemed to be floating a few handspans off the ground. Which suited her because she didn't want to use her feet anyway.

Seated at a table on the other side of the kitchen cavern, Elgion at first thought the boy had fainted with relief at being rescued. He could appreciate the feeling certainly, having been sighted by a dragonrider as he was pelting back towards Half-Circle, fully winded and despairing of life. Now, with his stomach full of good weyr stew, his wits and breath restored, he was forced to face his folly in going outside the Hold so close to a Fall. And, more daunting to contemplate, the reception on his return to Half-Circle. Talk about disgracing the Sea Hold! And his explanation that he was searching for fire lizard eggs would not go down well with Yanus. Even Alemi, what would he think? Elgion sighed and watched as several Weyrwomen carried the boy off towards the living caverns. He half-rose, wondering if he should have volunteered to help. Then he saw his first fire lizard and forgot everything else.

It was a little golden queen, swooping into the cavern, calling piteously. She seemed to hover motionless in midair, then winked out of sight. A moment later, she was diving into the kitchen cavern again, less agitated but looking for something or someone.

A girl emerged from the living cavern, saw the fire lizard and held up her arm. The little queen delicately landed, stroking the girl's face with her tiny head while the girl evidently reassured her. The two walked out into the Bowl.

"You've never seen one, Harper?" asked an amused voice, and Elgion came out of his trance to attend the Weyrwoman who'd been serving him food.

"No, I hadn't."

She laughed at the wistfulness in his voice. "That's Grall, F'nor's little queen," Felena told him. Then abruptly she asked Elgion if he'd like more stew.

He politely declined because he'd already had two platefuls: food being the Weyr's way of reassuring those they rescued.

"I really should be finding out if I can get back to Half-Circle Sea Hold. They'll have discovered my absence and . . ."

"Don't worry on that account, Harper, for word was passed back through the fighting wings. They'll let Half-Circle know you're safely here."

Elgion expressed proper gratitude, but he couldn't help fretting over Yanus's displeasure. He would simply have to make it clear that he'd been following Weyr orders, and Yanus was nothing if not obedient to his Weyr. Nonetheless, Elgion did not relish his return to the Sea Hold. He also couldn't politely insist on going when he chose because the dragons were tired as they returned to their Weyr, Thread successfully obliterated on this Fall.

Some of the young Harper's worst apprehensions were relieved by T'gellan, the bronze wingleader in charge of that Fall.

"I myself told them you were safe, and a good thing, too. They were all ready to mount a Search. Which, for old Yanus, is a remarkable concession."

Elgion grimaced. "I suppose it wouldn't look well to lose two Harpers in a short time."

Dragonsong 983

34 **Discussion** What effect did the fellis juice have on Menolly? Why?

35 **Discussion** Why does Elgion feel that he disgraced the Sea Hold?

36

"Nonsense. Already Yanus prizes you above fish! Or so Alemi said."

"Was he angry?"

"Who? Yanus?"

"No, Alemi."

"Why? I'd say he was better pleased than Yanus to hear you were safe and scoreless at Benden. More important, *did* you see any signs of fire lizard clutches?"

"No."

37

T'gellan sighed, stripping off his wide riding belt and opening the heavy wherhide jacket. "How we need the silly creatures."

"Are they that useful?"

T'gellan gave him a long look. "Possibly not. Lessa thinks them a real nuisance; but they look, and act, like dragons. And they give those narrow-minded, hidebound, insensitive Lord Holders just that necessary glimpse of what it is to ride a dragon. *That* is going to make life . . . and progress . . . easier for us in the Weyrs."

Elgion rather hoped that this had been made plain to Yanus; and he was going to tactfully suggest that he was ready to go back to the Sea Hold when the bronze rider was called away to check a dragon's wing injury.

Elgion found the additional delay instructive. He decided he would put his observations to good use in getting back into Yanus's favor—for he had an opportunity to see Weyr life as unsung in Saga and Ballad. An injured dragon cried as piteously as a child until his wounds were salved with numbweed. A dragon also cried distressingly if his rider was injured. Elgion watched the touching sight of a green dragon crooning anxiously at her rider as he leaned against her forearm, while the Weyrwomen dressed his Thread-scored arm. Elgion saw the weyrlings bathing and oiling their young beasts, the Weyr's several fire lizards assisting. He saw the youngsters of the Weyr refilling fire-stone sacks for

the next Fall, and couldn't fail to notice that they made less work of the onerous chore than Sea Hold lads would have done. He even ventured to peer into the Hatching Ground where golden Ramoth lay curled protectively around her eggs. He ducked out of sight, hoping she hadn't seen him.

Time passed so quickly that Elgion was surprised to hear the kitchen women calling everyone in to eat. He hovered at the entrance, wondering what to do, when T'gellan grabbed him by the arm and propelled him to an empty table.

"G'sel, come over here with that bronze nuisance of yours. I want the Half-Circle Harper to see him. G'sel has one of the original clutch F'nor discovered in Southern," T'gellan said in an undertone as they watched the stocky young man weaving his way through the tables towards them, balancing a bronze fire lizard on his forearm.

"This is Rill, Harper," G'sel said, extending his arm to Elgion. "Rill, be courteous; he's a Harper."

With great dignity the fire lizard extended his wings, executing what Elgion construed to be a bow, while the jeweled eyes regarded him intently. Not knowing how one saluted a fire lizard, Elgion tentatively extended his hand.

"Scratch his eye ridges," G'sel suggested. "They all love that."

To Elgion's delight and amazement, the fire lizard accepted the caress, and as Elgion's stroking eased an itch, Rill's eyelids began to close in sensuous pleasure.

"He's another convert," said T'gellan, laughing and pulling out his chair. The noise roused the fire lizard from somnolence and he hissed softly at T'gellan. "They're bold creatures, too, you'll notice, Harper, with no respect for degree."

This was evidently an old jibe, for G'sel,

seating himself, paid it no heed, but coaxed Rill to step onto a padded shoulder rest so he could eat the dinner now being served.

"How much do they understand?" Elgion asked, taking the chair opposite G'sel so he could see Rill better.

"To hear Mirrim talk about her three, everything."

T'gellan snorted with good-natured derision.

"I can ask Rill to carry a message to any place he's already been. No, to a *person* he knows at another Hold or Weyr I've taken him to. He follows me no matter where I go. Even during Threadfall." At T'gellan's snort, G'sel added, "I told you to watch today, T'gellan. Rill was with us."

"Yes, so tell Elgion how long it takes Rill to come back from delivering a message."

"All right, all right," said G'sel with a laugh as he stroked Rill affectionately. "And when you've one of your own, T'gellan . . ."

"Possibly, possibly," the bronze rider said easily. "Unless Elgion here finds us another clutch, we'll just have to stay jealous of you."

T'gellan changed the subject then to ask about Half-Circle Hold, general questions that did not embarrass or compromise Elgion. T'gellan evidently knew Yanus's reputation.

"If you feel too isolated there, Harper, don't fail to fly the signal and we'll pop you up for an evening here."

"Hatching's soon," G'sel suggested, grinning and giving Elgion a wink.

"He'll be here for that certainly," T'gellan agreed.

Then Rill creeled for a bite to eat while the bronze rider chided G'sel for turning the lizard into an importunate beggar. Elgion noticed T'gellan, himself, finding a tidbit for the little bronze, however, and he, too, offered Rill some meat, which the creature daintily accepted from the knife.

By the end of the meal Elgion was ready to brave Yanus's worst displeasure and wrath to find a fire lizard clutch and Impress a fire lizard of his own. That prospect made his inevitable return easier.

"I'd better do you the honors, Elgion," T'gellan said, rising at last from the table. "And I'd also better get you back early. No sense aggravating Yanus more than necessary."

Elgion wasn't certain how to take that remark or the wink that accompanied it, particularly as it was now full dark and for all he knew, the Hold doors were already barred for the night. Too late now to wish he'd gone back as soon as the dragonriders had returned from the Fall. But then he wouldn't have met Rill.

They were aloft, Elgion reveling in the experience, craning his head to see as much as possible in the clear night air. He had only a glimpse of the Higher Benden Range hills before T'gellan asked Monarth to take them *between.*

Suddenly, it was no longer full dark: the sun was a handspan above the glowing sea as they burst into the air above Half-Circle Harbor.

"Told you I'd get you back early," T'gellan said, turning to grin at the Harper's startled exclamation. "We're not supposed to time it, but all in a good cause."

Monarth circled down lazily so that everyone in the Sea Hold was gathered on the holdway when they landed. Yanus strode a few paces ahead of the others while Elgion searched the faces for Alemi's.

T'gellan leaped from the bronze's shoulder and made a show of assisting Elgion as the entire Hold cheered loudly for their Harper's safe return.

"I'm neither crippled nor old," Elgion muttered under his breath, aware of Yanus's approach. "Don't overdo it."

T'gellan laid his arm across Elgion's

38 Discussion Once again, Yanus is mentioned, and not in a complimentary way. What exactly is his reputation?

39 Discussion Why does the author use such measurements as "handspan" and "dragon length" instead of such terms as inches, feet, miles, or meters?

shoulders in a comradely fashion, beaming at the oncoming Sea Holder. "Not at all," he said out of the corner of his mouth. "The Weyr approves!"

"Sea Holder, I am profoundly embarrassed at the inconvenience . . ."

"No, Harper Elgion," T'gellan interrupted him, "any apologies are the Weyr's. You were adamant in wishing to return to Half-Circle immediately. But Lessa needed to have his report, Yanus, so we had to wait."

Whatever Yanus had been about to say to his erring Harper was neatly blocked by T'gellan's obvious approval. The Sea Holder rocked a bit on his feet, blinking as he reorganized his thoughts.

"Any fire lizard sign you discover must be made known to the Weyr as soon as possible," T'gellan continued blithely.

"Then that tale is true?" Yanus asked in a grumble of disbelief. "Those . . . those creatures do exist?"

"They do indeed, sir," Elgion replied warmly. "I have seen, touched and fed a bronze fire lizard; his name is Rill. He's about as big as my forearm . . ."

"You did? He is?" Alemi had pushed through the crowd, breathless from excitement and the exercise of hobbling as fast as he could down the holdway. "Then you did find something in the cave?"

"The cave?" Elgion had forgotten all about his original destination that morning.

"What cave?" demanded T'gellan.

"The cave . . ." and Elgion gulped and then boldly embroidered on the lie T'gellan had begun, "I told Lessa about. Surely you were in the room then."

"What cave?" demanded Yanus, stepping close to the younger men, his voice half-angry because he was being excluded from the conversation.

"The cave that Alemi and I spotted on the shore near the Dragon Stones," Elgion said, trying to give the proper cues. "Alemi," Elgion had to address T'gellan now, "is the Sea Man who saw the fire lizards last spring near the Dragon Stones. Two–three days back, we sailed down the coast and saw the cave. That's where I think it's likely we'll find fire lizard eggs."

41 "Well, then, since you're now safely in your Hold, Harper Elgion, I will leave you." T'gellan couldn't wait to get back to Monarth. And the cave.

"You'll let us know if you find anything, won't you?" Elgion called after him and received only a wild arm gesture before the bronze rider swung himself up to Monarth's back.

"We offered him no hospitality for his trouble in returning you," Yanus said, worried and somewhat aggrieved by the bronze rider's precipitous departure.

"He'd just eaten," Elgion replied, as the bronze dragon beat his way upward above the sunset-lit waters of the harbor.

"So early."

"Ah, he'd been fighting Thread. And he's wingleader, so he must be back at the Weyr."

That did impress Yanus.

Rider and dragon winked out, drawing a startled exclamation of delight from everyone. Alemi caught Elgion's eye, and the Harper had to suppress his grin: he'd share the full jest with Alemi later. Only would the joke be on himself if after all the half-truths T'gellan found fire lizard eggs . . . or a piper . . . in the cave?

"Harper Elgion," said Yanus firmly, waving the rest of the Holders away from them as he pointed to the Hold door. "Harper Elgion, I'd be grateful for a few words of explanation."

"Indeed, sir, and I've much to report to you of happenings in the Weyr." Elgion respectfully followed the Sea Holder. He knew now how to deal with Yanus with no further recourse to evasions or lies.

42

Chapter 10

Then my feet took off and my legs went, too,
So my body was obliged to follow
Me with my hands and my mouth full of cress
And my throat too dry to swallow.

43

When Menolly roused, she was in a quiet dark place and something crooned comfortingly in her ear. She knew it was Beauty, but she wondered how she could be so warm all over. She moved, and her feet felt big, stuffed and very sore.

She must have made some sound because she heard a soft movement and then the glow in the corner of the room was half-unshielded.

"Are you comfortable? Are your feet painful?"

The warmth beside Menolly's ear disappeared. Clever Beauty, Menolly thought with approval after an instant's fear of discovery.

Someone was bending over Menolly now, securing the sleeping furs about her shoulders; someone whose hands were gentle, soothing, who smelled of clean herbs and faintly of numbweed.

Dragonsong 987

41 **Discussion** Why do you think T'gellan is anxious to leave the Sea Hold?

42 **Discussion** How does Elgion now know how to deal with Yanus with "no further recourse to evasions and lies"?

43 **Discussion** Whose song is at the beginning of Chapter 10?

Speaking and Listening You might wish to tell students that the songs at the beginning of each chapter represent the history of the people. Songs were often used in place of written language when the society had only an oral tradition. You might want to have a student read the songs from the beginning of each chapter and then ask them to work in small groups to discuss how the songs might be transformed into a written history.

44 **Reading Strategy** When Manora says that Menolly's not "just" a girl, what insight do you get into the kind of a person Manora is? As you read, look for other evidence of this kind of thinking in the people of Benden Weyr.

45 **Discussion** Why do you think Menolly is concerned about her little pets?

46 **Critical Thinking and Reading** What details in this passage indicate an atmosphere different from that of Half-Circle Sea Hold?

"They only hurt a little," Menolly replied untruthfully because her feet had taken to throbbing so hard she was afraid the woman could hear them.

Her soft murmur and her gentle hands denied Menolly's stoicism.

"You must surely be hungry. You've slept all day."

"I have?"

"We gave you fellis juice. You'd run your feet to ribbons . . ." There was a slight hesitation in the woman's voice. "They'll be fine in a sevenday. No serious cuts." The quiet voice held a ripple of amusement. "T'gran is convinced you're the fastest . . . runner in Pern."

"I'm not a runner. I'm just a girl."

"Not 'just' a girl. I'll get you something to eat. And then it's best if you sleep again."

Alone, Menolly tried not to think of her throbbing feet and a body which felt stone-heavy, immobile. She worried for fear Beauty or some of the others would come and be discovered by the Weyrwoman, and what would happen to Lazy with no one to make him hunt for himself and . . .

"I'm Manora," the woman said as she returned with a bowl of steaming stew and a mug. "You realize that you're at Benden Weyr? Good. You may stay here, you know, as long as you wish."

"I can?" A relief as intense as the pain in her feet flooded Menolly.

"Yes, you can," and the firmness of that reply made that right inalienable.

"Menolly is my name . . ." She hesitated because Manora was nodding. "How did you know?"

Manora motioned for her to continue eating. "I've seen you at Half-Circle, you know, and the Harper asked the wingleader to keep Search for you . . . after you disappeared. We won't discuss that now, Menolly, but I do assure you that you can stay at Benden."

"Please don't *tell* them . . ."

"As you wish. Finish your stew and take all the drink. You must sleep to heal."

She left as noiselessly as she'd come, but Menolly was reassured. Manora was Headwoman at Benden Weyr, and what she said was so.

The stew was delicious, thick with meat chunks and satisfying with herb flavors. She'd almost finished it when she heard a faint rustle and Beauty returned, piteously broadcasting hunger. With a sigh, Menolly pushed the bowl under the little queen's nose. Beauty licked it dry, then hummed softly and rubbed her face against Menolly's cheek.

"Where are the others?" Menolly asked, worriedly.

The little queen gave another hum and began to curl herself up in a ball by Menolly's shoulder. She wouldn't have been so relaxed if the others were in trouble, Menolly thought, as she sipped the fellis juice.

"Beauty," Menolly whispered, nudging the queen, "if anyone comes, you go. You mustn't be seen here. Do you understand?"

The queen rustled her wings irritably.

"Beauty, you mustn't be seen." Menolly spoke as sternly as she could, and the queen opened one eye, which whirled slowly. "Oh, dear, won't you understand?" The queen gave a soft reassuring croon and then closed both lids.

The fellis juice was already melting Menolly's limbs into weightlessness. The dreadful throb of her feet eased. As her eyes relentlessly closed, Menolly had one last thought: how had Beauty known where she was?

When Menolly woke, it was to hear faint sounds of children laughing, an infectious laughter that made her grin and wonder what caused such happiness. Beauty was

47 Discussion The author tells us that at a certain moment the girls' friendship began. What does she mean?

gone but the space where she'd lain by Menolly's head was warm to the touch. The curtain across the cubicle parted and a figure was silhouetted against the light beyond.

"What's the matter with you all of a sudden, Reppa?" the girl said softly to someone Menolly couldn't see. "Oh, all right. I'm well rid of you for now." She turned and saw Menolly looking at her. "How do you feel today?" As she adjusted the glow for full light, Menolly saw a girl about her own age, dark hair tied primly back from a face that was sad, tired and oddly mature. Then she smiled, and the impression of maturity dissolved. "Did you really run across Nerat?"

"I really didn't, although my feet feel as if *they* had."

"Imagine it! And you holdbred and out during a Fall!" There was a grudging respect in her voice.

"I was running for shelter," Menolly felt obliged to say.

"Speaking of running, Manora couldn't come to see you herself right now so you're in my charge. She's told me exactly what to do," and the girl grimaced with such feeling that Menolly had a swift vision of Manora delivering her precise and careful instructions, "and I've had a lot of experience . . ." An expression of pain and anxiety crossed her face.

"Are you Manora's fosterling?" asked Menolly politely.

The expression deepened for a moment, and then the girl erased all expression from her face, drawing her shoulders up with pride. "No, I'm Brekke's. My name is Mirrim. I used to be in the Southern Weyr."

She made the statement as if that should make all plain to Menolly.

"You mean, in the Southern Continent?"

"Yes," and Mirrim sounded irritated.

"I didn't know anyone lived there." The words were no sooner out of her mouth than Menolly remembered some snippet of information overheard in conversations between Petiron and her father.

"Where have you *been* all your life?" demanded Mirrim, exasperated.

"In Half-Circle Sea Hold," Menolly replied meekly because she didn't wish to offend the girl.

Mirrim stared at her.

"Haven't you ever heard of it?" It was Menolly's turn to be condescending. "We have the biggest Dock Cavern on Pern."

Mirrim caught her eye, and then both girls began to laugh, the moment in which their friendship began.

"Look, let me help you to the necessary, you must be bursting . . ." and Mirrim

47

Dragonsong 989

48 Clarification What word or words could be used instead of *longsighted*?

49 Discussion Why did Menolly feel that she had to defend her Hold?

briskly threw back the sleeping fur. "You just lean on me."

Menolly had to because her feet were incredibly sore, even with Mirrim supporting most of her weight. Fortunately the necessary was no more than a few steps beyond the sleeping cubicle. By the time Menolly crawled back into her bed, she was shaking all over.

"Stay on your stomach, Menolly; it'll be easier to change your bandages," Mirrim said. "I haven't had to do many feet, it's true; but if you don't have to see what's going on, that makes it easier. Everyone at Southern said my hands are gentle, and I'll drown your feet in numbweed. Or would you want some more fellis juice? Manora said you could."

Menolly shook her head.

"Brekke . . ." and here Mirrim's voice faltered briefly, "Brekke taught me how to change sticky bandages because I . . . Oh, dearie me, your feet look just like raw meat. Ooops, that's not the right thing to say, but they do. They *will* be all right, Manora said," and there was such confidence in that statement that Menolly preferred to believe it, too. "Now Threadscore . . . that's nasty. You've just lost all the skin on your feet, that's all, but I expect you feel that's quite enough. Sorry. Caught you there. Anyway, you'll not even have scars once the new skin grows, and it's really amazing how quickly skin does grow. Or so I've observed. Now Threadscore, that's nasty for healing. Never quite fades. Lucky for you T'gran's Branth spotted you running. Dragons are very longsighted, you know. There, now, this should help . . ."

Menolly gasped involuntarily as Mirrim slathered cool numbweed on her right foot. She'd been biting her lips against the pain while Mirrim, with very gentle hands indeed, had removed the blood-caked bandages but the relief from pain was almost a shock. If she'd only lost the skin from her feet, why did they hurt so much more than her hand had?

"Now, we've only the left foot to go. The numbweed does help, doesn't it? Did you ever have to boil it?" Mirrim asked with a groan and, as usual, didn't wait for an answer. "For three days I just grit my teeth and close my nose and firmly remind myself that it would be so *much* worse if we *didn't* have numbweed. I suppose that's the bad with the good Manora's always saying we have to have. But you'll be relieved to know that there's no sign of infection . . ."

"Infection?" Menolly jerked herself up on her elbows, craning her head about.

"Will you keep still?" Mirrim glared so authoritatively that Menolly forced herself to relax. All she could see of her feet were salve-smeared heels. "And you're very, very lucky there isn't any infection. After all, you'd been running shoeless over sand, dirt and goodness knows what. It took us forever to wash the grit off." Mirrim made a sympathetic sound. "Just as well we'd dosed you good."

"You're sure there's no infection this time?"

"This time? You haven't done this before, have you?" Mirrim's voice was shocked.

"No, not my feet. My hand," and Menolly turned on her side, holding out her scarred hand. She was considerably gratified by the concerned pity in Mirrim's face as she examined the wound.

"However did you do that?"

"I was gutting packtail, and the knife slipped."

"You were lucky to miss the tendons."

"Miss?"

"Well, you are using those fingers. A bit drawn that scar, though." Mirrim clucked her tongue with professional dismay. "Don't think much of your Hold's nursing if that's any sample."

"Packtail slime is difficult, as bad as Threadscore in its own way," Menolly muttered, perversely defending her Hold.

"Be that as it may," and Mirrim gave the foot bandage a final twitch, "we'll see you don't have any such trouble with your feet. Now, I'll bring you something to eat. You must be starved . . ."

Now that the worst of the dressing was over and the numbweed had deadened the pain in her feet, Menolly was definitely aware of the emptiness in her stomach.

"So I'll be right back, Menolly, and if you need anything after that, just shout for Sanra. She's below on the Floor, minding the little ones, and she knows she's to listen for you."

As Menolly worked her way through the generous meal Mirrim brought, she reflected on some harsh truths. Definitely Mavi had given her the distinct impression that she'd never be able to use her hand again. Yet Mavi was too skilled a healer not to have known that the knife had missed the finger tendons. She had deliberately let the hand heal with drawn flesh. It was painfully clear to Menolly that Mavi, as well as Yanus, had not wanted her to be able to play again.

Grimly Menolly vowed that she'd never, never return to Half-Circle. Her reflections made her doubt Manora's assurance that she could stay at Benden Weyr. No matter, she could run away again. Run she could, and live holdless. And that's what she'd do. Why, she'd run across all Pern . . . And why not? Menolly became pleased with the notion. Indeed, there was nothing to stop her running right to the Masterharperhall in Fort Hold. Maybe Petiron *had* sent her songs to Masterharper Robinton. Maybe they were more than just twiddles. Maybe . . . but there was no maybe about returning to Half-Circle Hold! That she would not do.

The issue did not arise over the next few days while her feet itched—Mirrim said that was a good sign of healing—and she found herself beginning to fret with impatience at her disability.

She also worried about her fire lizards now she wasn't able to forage for them. But the first evening when Beauty reappeared, her little eyes darting about the chamber to be sure Menolly was alone, there was nothing of hunger in her manner. She daintily accepted the morsels that Menolly had carefully saved from her supper. Rocky and Diver appeared just as she was drifting off to sleep. However, they promptly curled themselves up to sleep against the small of her back, which they wouldn't have done if they'd been hungry.

They were gone the next morning, but Beauty lingered, stroking her head against Menolly's cheek until she heard footsteps in the corridor. Menolly shooed her away, telling her to stay with the others.

"I know it's boring to stay abed," Mirrim agreed the third morning with a weary sigh that told Menolly Mirrim would gladly have swapped places, "but it's kept you out of Lessa's way. Since the . . . well," and Mirrim censored what she'd been about to say. "With Ramoth broody over those eggs, we're all treading hot sands until they hatch, so it's better you're here."

"There must be something I can do, now that I'm better. I'm good with my hands . . ." and then Menolly, too, halted uncertainly.

"You could help Sanra with the little ones if you would. Can you tell any stories?"

"Yes, I . . ." and Menolly all but blurted out what she'd done at the Sea Hold, ". . . can at least keep them amused."

Weyrbred children were not like Hold children, Menolly discovered: they were more active physically, possessed of insatiable curiosity for every detail she cared to tell them about fishing and sailing. It was only when she taught them to fashion tiny boats of sticks and wide root leaves and sent them off to sail the skiffs in the Weyr lake that she had any rest the first morning.

50 **Discussion** What is Mirrim implying here when she tells Menolly that she (Menolly) won't have any trouble with her feet?

51 **Literary Focus: Atmosphere** Menolly "grimly" decides never to return to Half-Circle Hold again. What aspects of the Benden Weyr atmosphere might have influenced this decision?

52 **Discussion** Why is Menolly hesitant to reveal what she'd done at the Sea Hold?

53 Discussion Why is Thread not as horrifying to Weyr children as it is to Holders' children?

54 Critical Thinking and Reading Why does no one in the Hold "ever tell girls anything"?

53 In the afternoon, she amused the younger ones by recounting how T'gran had rescued her. Thread was not as automatically horrifying to Weyr children as it would be to Holders, and they were far more interested in her running and rescue than in what she was running from. Unconsciously she fell into a rhyming pattern and caught herself up sharply just before she'd conceived a tune. The children didn't seem to notice, fortunately, and then it was time to peel tubers for the evening meal.

It was difficult to subdue that little tune as she worked. Really it had exactly the cadence of her running stride . . .

"Oh!"

"Did you cut yourself?" asked Sanra from the other side of the table.

"No," replied Menolly, and she grinned with great good humor. She had just realized something very important. She wasn't in the Sea Hold any longer. And no one here knew about her harpering. Likewise no one would know if it were her own songs she hummed when she felt like humming. So she began to hum her running song, and was doubly pleased with herself because the tune matched her paring strokes, too.

"It's a relief to hear someone happy," remarked Sanra, smiling encouragingly at Menolly.

Menolly realized then that she'd been vaguely aware all day of the fact that the atmosphere in the living cavern reminded her of those times when the Fishing Fleet was overdue in a storm and everyone was "waiting." Mirrim was very worried about Brekke but she wouldn't say why, and Menolly was reluctant to broach the girl's sad reserve.

"I'm happy because my feet are healing," she told Sanra and then hurried on, "but I wish someone would tell me what's wrong with Brekke. I know Mirrim's worried sick about her . . ."

Sanra stared at Menolly for a moment. "You mean, you haven't heard about . . ." she lowered her voice and glanced about to make sure they weren't overheard, ". . . about the queens?"

54 "No. No one tells girls anything in the Sea Hold."

Sanra looked surprised but accepted the explanation. "Well, Brekke used to be at Southern, you did know that? Good. And when F'lar banished all the rebellious Old-timers to Southern, the Southerners had to go somewhere. T'bor became Weyrleader at Fort Hold, Kylara . . ." and Sanra's usually gentle voice became hard, "Kylara was Weyrwoman for Prideth, with Brekke and Wirenth . . ." Sanra was having enough trouble telling the tale so Menolly was very glad she hadn't asked Mirrim. "Wirenth rose to mate, but Kylara . . ." and the name was spoken with intense hatred, "Kylara hadn't taken Prideth far enough away. She was close to mating, too, and when Wirenth flew the bronzes, she rose, and . . ."

There were tears in Sanra's eyes, and she shook her head, unable to continue.

"Both queens . . . died?"

Sanra nodded.

"Brekke's alive, though . . . Isn't she?"

"Kylara lost her mind, and we're desperately afraid that Brekke will lose hers . . ." Sanra mopped the tears from her face, sniffing back her sorrow.

"Poor Mirrim. And she's been so good to me!"

Sanra sniffed again, this time from pique.

"Mirrim likes to think she's got the cares of the Weyr on her shoulders."

"Well, I've a lot more respect for her the way she keeps on going when she's worried sick than if she crept off someplace and just felt sorry for herself."

Sanra stared at Menolly. "No need to bristle at me, girl, and if you keep on stabbing your knife that way, you will cut yourself."

"Will Brekke be all right?" asked Menolly after a few minutes' strict attention to her peeling.

"We hope so," but Sanra didn't sound confident. "No, we do. You see, Ramoth's clutch is about to hatch, and Lessa is certain that Brekke could Impress the queen. You see, she can speak to any of the dragons, the way Lessa can, and Grall and Berd are always with her . . . Here comes Mirrim."

55

Menolly had to admit that Mirrim, who only numbered the same Turns as she did, did assume an officious manner. She could understand that an older woman like Sanra might not take kindly to it. Yet Menolly had no fault to find with Mirrim's ministrations. And she let the girl bustle her off to her cubicle to change the bandages.

"You've been on them all day, and I want to be sure no dirt's in the scabs," she said, briskly.

Menolly obediently lay on her stomach in the bed and then tentatively suggested that perhaps tomorrow she could change her own bandages and save Mirrim some work.

"Don't be silly. Feet are very awkward, but *you're* not. You should just hear C'tarel complain. He got Threadscored during the last Fall. You'd think he was the only one ever in the world scored. And besides, Manora *said* I was to take care of you. You're easy, you don't moan, groan, complain, *and* swear like C'tarel. Now, these *are* healing nicely. In spite of the way it might feel to you. Manora says that feet hurt worse than any part of your body, but hands. That's why it seems much worse to you, I expect."

Menolly had no argument and breathed a sigh of relief that the painful session was now over.

"*You* taught the weyrlings how to make those little boats, didn't you?"

Menolly flipped over, startled, and wondering if she'd done wrong, but Mirrim was grinning.

"You should have *seen* the dragons snorting them about the lake." Mirrim giggled. "Having the grandest time. I haven't laughed so much in weeks. There you are!" And Mirrim bustled away on some other errand.

56

The following day Mirrim hovering beside her, Menolly walked slowly and not too painfully through the living cavern and into the main kitchen cavern for the first time.

"Ramoth's eggs are just about to hatch," Mirrim told her as she placed Menolly at one of the worktables along the back side of the huge cave. "There's nothing wrong with your hands, and we'll need all the help we can get for the feast . . ."

"And maybe your Brekke will be better?"

"Oh, she's got to be, Menolly, she's got to be." Mirrim scrubbed her hands together anxiously. "If she isn't, I don't know what will become of her and F'nor. He cares so much. Manora's as worried about him as she is about Brekke . . ."

"It'll all come right, Mirrim. I'm sure it will," Menolly said, putting all the confidence she could muster into her voice.

"Oh, do you really think so?" Mirrim dropped her pose of bustling efficiency and was briefly a young, bewildered girl in need of reassurance.

"I most certainly do!" And Menolly was angry with Sanra's unkind statements of the day before. "Why, when I thought I'd be scored to death, T'gran appeared. And when I thought they'd all be Threaded . . ." Menolly hastily shut her mouth, frantically trying to think of something to fill that gap. She'd almost told Mirrim about saving the fire lizards.

"They must belong to somebody," a man said in a loud, frustrated tone of voice.

Dragonsong 993

55 Reader's Response Do you think Menolly approves of officious people?

56 Literary Focus: Atmosphere Knowing Menolly's background, what do you think her reaction is to all this lightheartedness in Benden Weyr?

Two dragonriders entered the kitchen cavern, slapping dusty gloves against sandy boots and loosening their riding belts.

"They could be attracted by the ones we have, T'gellan."

"Considering how badly we need the creatures . . ."

"In the egg . . ."

"It's a raking nuisance to have a whole flaming fair that no one will claim!"

The next thing Menolly knew, Beauty appeared over her head, gave a terrified squawk and landed on Menolly's thinly clad shoulder. Beauty wrapped her tail, choking tight, about Menolly's neck and buried her face into her hair. Rocky and Diver seized the cloth of her shirt in their claws, struggling to burrow into her arms. The air was full of frightened fire lizards, diving at her; and Mirrim, who made no attempt to defend herself, stared with utter amazement at Menolly.

"Mirrim? Do they belong to you after all?"

cried T'gellan as he strode towards their table.

"No, they're not mine." Mirrim pointed to Menolly. "They're hers."

Menolly was speechless, but she managed to contain Rocky and Diver. The others took refuge on ledges above her, broadcasting fear and uncertainty. She was just as confused as the fire lizards, because why were they in the Weyr? And the Weyr seemed to know about fire lizards, and . . .

"We'll soon know whose they are," said a woman's angry voice, carrying clearly in the pause. A small, slim woman in riding gear came striding purposefully into the main section of the kitchen cavern. "I asked Ramoth to speak to them . . ."

She was followed by another rider.

"Over here, Lessa," T'gellan said, beckoning, but his gaze did not leave Menolly's.

At the sound of that name, she struggled out of the chair, with the fire lizards squawk-

ing and trying to retain their balance and hold on her. All Menolly could think of was to keep out of Lessa's way, but she got tangled up in the chairs about the table and painfully stubbed her toes. Mirrim grabbed her arm, trying to make her sit down, and there seemed to be more fire lizards than Menolly could claim circling over her head and chittering wildly.

"Will someone quiet this lot?" demanded the small, dark woman, confronting Menolly, her fists on her riding belts, her eyes snapping with anger. "Ramoth! If you would . . ."

Abruptly, complete silence reigned in the huge kitchen cavern. Menolly felt Beauty trembling more violently than ever against her neck, and the talons of the two bronzes dug into her arms and sides.

"That's better," said Lessa, her eyes brilliant. "And who are you? Are these all yours?"

"My name is Menolly, please and," Menolly glanced up nervously at all the fire lizards perched silently with whirling eyes on ledges and hanging from the ceiling, "not all of these are mine."

"Menolly?" Some of Lessa's anger abated in her perplexity. "Menolly?" She was trying to place the name.

"Manora told you about her, Lessa," said Mirrim, which Menolly thought greatly daring and very much appreciated. "T'gran rescued her from Threadfall. She'd run her feet raw."

"Ah, yes. So, Menolly, how many fire lizards do look to you?"

Menolly was trying to figure out whether Lessa was annoyed or pleased, and if she had too many fire lizards would she be sent back to Half-Circle. She felt Mirrim prod her in the ribs.

"These," Menolly indicated the three clinging to her and felt Mirrim dig her again, "and only six of those up there."

"Only six of those up there?"

Menolly saw Lessa's fingers drumming on her wide riding belt; she heard one of the dragonriders muffling a sound; and glancing up saw that he had his hand over his mouth. But his eyes were dancing with laughter. Then she dared look at Lessa's face and saw the slight smile on the Weyrwoman's face.

"That makes nine, I think," Lessa said. "Just how did you contrive to Impress nine fire lizards, Menolly?"

"I didn't contrive. I was in the cave when they hatched, and they were hungry, you see. I'd a sackful of spiderclaws so I fed them . . ."

"Cave? Where?" Lessa's words were crisp but not unkind.

"On the coast. Above Nerat, by the Dragon Stones."

T'gellan uttered an exclamation. "You were living in that cave? I found jars and pots . . . no sign of fire lizard shells."

"I didn't think fire lizards clutched in caves," Lessa remarked.

"It was only because the tide was high and the clutch would have been washed away. I helped the queen put them into the cave."

Lessa regarded Menolly steadily for a long moment. "You helped the fire lizard?"

"Yes, you see I'd fallen over the cliff, and they—the queen and her bronzes, from the old clutch, not these here," and Menolly jerked her chin at Beauty, Rocky and Diver, "they wouldn't let me get off the beach until I helped them."

T'gellan was staring at her, but the other two riders were grinning broadly. Then Menolly saw that Mirrim, too, was smiling with delight. More unbelievable to Menolly in her confusion was the fact that a little brown fire lizard was perched on Mirrim's shoulder, intently staring at Beauty who wouldn't take her head out of Menolly's hair.

"I'd like to hear the whole story, in sequence, one day," Lessa said. "Right now,

60 Discussion Very obviously Menolly does not want to return to the Sea Hold. What do you think would happen to her there if she did?

61 Discussion What is Menolly thinking when she refers to Lessa's size?

will you please keep your lot under control and with you? They're upsetting Ramoth and all the others. Nine, eh?" And Lessa sighed, turning away. "When I think where I could use nine eggs to good purpose . . ."

"Please . . . do you need more fire lizard eggs?"

Lessa whirled so fast that Menolly took an involuntarily backward step.

"Of course we need fire lizard eggs! Where have you been that you don't know?" She turned on T'gellan.

"You're wingleader. Didn't you inform all the Sea Holds?"

"Yes, I did, Lessa," and T'gellan looked straight at Menolly now, "just about the time Menolly first disappeared from her Hold. Right, Menolly? The sweep riders have been on the lookout for her ever since, but she was holed up snug as you please in that cave, with nine fire lizards."

Menolly hung her head in despair.

60 "Please, Weyrwoman, don't send me back to Half-Circle Hold!"

"A girl who can Impress nine fire lizards," said Lessa in a sharp rippling tone that made Menolly look up, "does not belong in a Sea Hold. T'gellan, find out from Menolly where that clutch is and secure it for us immediately. Let us fervently hope it hasn't hatched." To Menolly's intense relief, Lessa actually smiled at her, obviously in a much-improved temper. "Remember to keep those pesky creatures away from Ramoth. Mirrim can help you train them. Hers are quite useful now."

She swept away, leaving the entire cavern breathless. Activity suddenly picked up on all sides of the kitchen. Menolly felt Mirrim pressing her into a chair; she sank weakly down. She found a cup of klah in her hands and heard T'gellan urging her to take a few sips.

"One's first encounter with Lessa is apt to be unnerving."

"She's . . . she's so small," Menolly said dazedly.

"Size is irrelevant."

Menolly turned anxiously to Mirrim. "Did she really mean it? I can stay, Mirrim?"

"If you can Impress nine fire lizards, you belong here. But why didn't you tell me about them? Didn't you see mine? I've only the three . . ."

T'gellan clicked his tongue at Mirrim, who stuck hers out at him.

"I told mine to stay in the cave . . ."

"And here we've been wracking our brains," Mirrim went on, "accusing riders of hoarding eggs . . ."

"I didn't *know* you people needed fire lizards . . ."

"Mirrim, stop teasing her; she's unnerved. Menolly, drink your klah and relax," T'gellan told her.

Menolly obediently sipped her klah, but she felt obliged to explain about the boys in her Sea Hold who could think of nothing but snaring fire lizards; and she felt so strongly that that was wrong that she hadn't even mentioned seeing them mating.

"Under the circumstances, you did just as you should, Menolly," said T'gellan. "But let's get to that clutch and rescue it. Where did you see it? How close do you think it is to hatching?"

"The eggs were still pretty soft when I found them the day T'gran rescued me. And it's about a half-morning's walk from the Dragon Stones."

"A few minutes' glide by dragonback; but south? north? Where?"

"Well, south, where a stream feeds into the sea."

T'gellan raised his eyes in exasperation. "That describes too many places. You'd better come with me."

"T'gellan," Mirrim sounded shocked. "Menolly's feet are in shreds . . ."

"So is Lessa's temper. We'll wrap her feet in hides, but we must get those eggs. And you're not Headwoman yet, my girl," T'gellan said, waggling a finger at Mirrim.

It didn't take long to outfit Menolly. Mirrim, as if to make up for her officiousness, brought her own wherhide riding jacket and headgear and a pair of vastly oversized boots. They were eased over Menolly's sore and bandaged feet and fastened tightly around her legs with leather strips.

Rocky and Diver were reassured by tidbits of meat, but Beauty refused to unwrap her tail from Menolly's neck. She chattered angrily at T'gellan when he half-carried Menolly to Monarth, waiting patiently just outside the kitchen cavern.

T'gellan threw Menolly up the dragon's shoulder. She hauled herself up to his neck ridges by the fighting straps, giving her feet one or two painful knocks.

T'gellan started to settle himself in front of Menolly, but Beauty came alive, hissing menacingly and lashing out at the dragonrider with one foreleg, talons unsheathed.

"She's never been so bad mannered," Menolly said apologetically.

"Monarth, will you speak to her?" asked T'gellan good-naturedly.

The next instant, Beauty stopped midhiss, chirped experimentally, her eyes whirling less frantically, and her tail relaxed from its choke hold on Menolly's throat.

"That's a sight better. She does have a baleful stare!"

"Oh dear!"

"I'm teasing you, Menolly. Now, look, I shall have Monarth tell your fair of fire lizards exactly what we're going to do so they don't go mad when we take off."

"Oh, would you?"

"I would, and I . . ." T'gellan paused, "I have. We're away!"

This time Menolly could enjoy the sensations of flying. She couldn't imagine why Petiron had found the experience so horrible. She didn't even fear the lack of all sensation as they went *between*. She did feel the bitter, bitter cold in the soles of her half-healed feet, but the pain lasted such a fleeting second. Abruptly, they were low over the Dragon Stones, coming in from the sea. The sheer thrill of the flight took Menolly's breath away.

"There is a chance that the first queen might lay another clutch in that cave," T'gellan said over his shoulder. "But it should be cleared of your things."

So they landed on the beach with Monarth peering rather disapprovingly at the little cove while the water lapped gently on his feet.

Her group arrived, carolling in wild delight at coming home. A single fire lizard appeared above and to one side of them.

"Look, T'gellan, that's the old queen!"

But she'd gone when T'gellan looked up.

"I'm sort of sorry she saw us here. I was hoping . . . Where was the clutch when you rescued it?"

"We're standing on the place."

Monarth moved to one side.

"Does he hear what I'm telling you?" Menolly whispered anxiously in T'gellan's ear.

"Yes, so be careful how you speak of him. He's very sensitive."

"I haven't said anything, have I, that would hurt his feelings?"

"Menolly!" T'gellan looked back at her, grinning. "I was teasing you."

"Oh!"

"Hmmm. Yes. Well, so you managed to climb that cliff face?"

"It wasn't so hard. If you'll look, you'll see there're plenty of hand and footholds, even before I made a regular path."

"A regular path? Hmmm. Yes. Monarth, can you get us a bit closer, please?"

62 Discussion T'gellan compares Menolly's feet to Lessa's temper. Why does he do this, and why is it important to him to please Lessa?

63 Discussion What influence do you think Monarth has on Beauty?

Discussion If you were in Menolly's place, what would you be thinking at this point?

Reader's Response Menolly is rescued from a dangerous situation by a rider on a brown dragon. At this point, she is too overwhelmed to speak. If you were in her place, do you think that you would have had anything to say? If so, what would it have been?

Thematic Response Menolly's search for self has brought her very far from home—literally, as well as figuratively. Do you think this escape from the Hold will help her to realize her potential?

Closure and Extension

ANSWERS TO RESPONDING TO THE SELECTION
Your Response

1. You may wish to discuss with students the characteristics, attributes, and peculiarities of a fire lizard. You might ask students to explain how they feel about their more conventional pets.

2. Have students discuss what Benden Weyr is like, its atmosphere, its people. You might ask students to discuss the advantages and disadvantages of living in such a place.

Recalling

3. Elgion wants to search for fire lizards.

Interpreting

4. Elgion assumes that the "boy" was sent away in disgrace because it is the only explanation for the reluctance of the Holders to tell the Harper his name. It does not occur to him that the "boy" could be a girl.

5. Dragonriders live in such close telepathic contact with their dragons that losing the dragons is like losing a part of themselves.

6. Suggested Response: T'gellan has obviously had contact with the Hold and knows Yanus's reputation. Outsiders would see the Hold as a place where sensitivity of any kind would not be encouraged.

998

Monarth obligingly angled against the cliff face and raised himself to his haunches; Menolly was amazed to see that they could step off his shoulders right into the cave.

Her nine came arrowing into the opening, trumpeting and squealing, their bugles abruptly amplified by the vaulting height of the inner cavern. Just as she and T'gellan reached it, the light was suddenly blocked. Turning, she saw Monarth's head in the opening, his great eyes whirling idly.

"Monarth, get your great, bloody, big head out of the light, will you?" asked T'gellan.

Monarth blinked, gave a little wistful rumble, but removed his great head.

"Why didn't anyone find you on Search, young lady?" T'gellan asked, and she saw that he'd been watching her intently.

"No one's ever been Searched at Half-Circle Sea Hold."

"That shouldn't surprise me. Now, where did the old queen have her clutch?"

"Right where you're standing."

T'gellan jumped sideways, giving her a second admonitory look, which she couldn't interpret. He knelt, running his fingers through the sand, making pleased noises in his throat.

"You tossed out the old shells?"

"Yes. Was that wrong?"

"I don't think so."

"Would she come back here again?"

"She might. If the cove waters remain high the next time she mates. D'you happen to remember when you saw her mating flight?"

"Yes, I do. Because we had Threadfall just after. The one when the leading edge hit the marshes halfway to Nerat."

"Good girl!" T'gellan tipped his head back, pressing his lips together, and Menolly thought he was doing some rapid mental calculations. Alemi had a similar habit when he

998   The Novel

---

was charting a course. "Yes. And when did these hatch?"

"I lost track of my sevendays, but they hatched five Falls ago."

"That's great. She may mate before high summer, if fire lizards follow the same sort of cycle the dragons do during a Pass." He glanced around him at the bits and pieces with which she had made the cave livable. "D'you want any of these things?"

"Not many," Menolly said and dove for her sleeping rug. Her pipes were still there, so he hadn't seen them in his first visit to the cave. She bundled the rug round the pipes again. "My oil . . ." she said, grabbing up the pot. "I'll need that."

"Not really," said T'gellan with a grin, "but bring it along. Manora's always interested in such things."

She took her dried herbs, too, and made a neat package, which she could tie on her back. Ruthlessly then she began to chuck her homemade crockery out of the cave entrance.

"Oh!" Aghast, she rushed to the mouth, looking about for Monarth.

"You missed him! He's got more sense than to stay around when there's a cleaning." With that T'gellan launched her boiling pot into the air.

"That's everything, I think," she said. "Let's go!"

At the entrance, Menolly turned for one last look at the cave and smiled to herself. She'd never thought to leave it, certainly not to step to the shoulders of a dragon. But then, she'd never thought she'd live in a cave like this at all, much less ride a dragon. Nothing now marked that anyone had ever sheltered in this cave. Even the dry sand was falling back into the depressions their feet had made. T'gellan held out his hand to help her to Monarth's back, and then they were away to find the fire lizard's clutch.

Applying

7. Discuss with students the idea that having an open mind is important for inventiveness and creativity.

ANSWERS TO ANALYZING LITERATURE

1. (a) The atmosphere is grim and cheerless in Half-Circle. (b) Fishing is considered more important than searching for Menolly. Musical ability is not encouraged, and

girls and women are considered second-class citizens.

2. (a) The atmosphere at Benden Weyr is warm and caring with very outgoing, friendly people. (b) The living area is filled with humming fire lizards and cheerful people going about their business.

ANSWERS TO CRITICAL THINKING AND READING

Students' charts might include the following information:

Comparison: The Hold and the Weyr are physically similar, with specific areas for working, sleeping, and eating. People live and work communally, like a large family. Both places have a specific function in the Pern economy. The children learn from the Teaching Ballads taught by the Harper, and the children have chores they must perform regularly.

RESPONDING TO THE SELECTION

Your Response

1. How would you feel if you impressed a fire lizard? Explain your answer.
2. Would you like to live in Benden Weyr? Explain.

Recalling

3. What is Elgion's reason for wanting to learn how to sail?

Interpreting

4. Why does Elgion assume that the "boy" who wrote the songs on Petiron's tablets has been sent away from the Hold in disgrace?
5. The deaths of Prideth and Wirenth, the queen dragons, affect their riders drastically. Why?
6. T'gellan is not surprised to hear that no one has ever been Searched at Half-Circle Sea Hold. What does this tell you about how outsiders perceive the Hold?

Applying

7. Yanus, the leader of Half-Circle Sea Hold, is very traditional and closed-minded, a situation that Harper Elgion would like to change. Why is it important to be open to new ideas and new ways of doing things?

ANALYZING LITERATURE

Recognizing Atmosphere

The **atmosphere** of a story refers to its mood or spirit. The places where stories occur can have atmospheres of their own. The author's descriptive language and the behavior of the characters create the special mood of each place. In *Dragonsong*, Mcnolly finds that two different places can feel almost like two different worlds.

1. (a) Describe the atmosphere in Half-Circle Sea Hold. (b) Which details create this atmosphere?
2. (a) Describe the atmosphere at Benden Weyr. (b) How does the author create it?

CRITICAL THINKING AND READING

Comparing and Contrasting Atmospheres

Comparing is finding similarities between two things. **Contrasting** is pointing out differences. When you compare and contrast Half-Circle Sea Hold and Benden Weyr, you will find many physical similarities. However, the atmospheres are very different. Make a chart like the following in which to compare and contrast the Hold and the Weyr.

Points to compare	Hold	Benden Weyr

THINKING AND WRITING

Describing Atmosphere

Think about a place you have been. Write a descriptive paragraph about the place, creating a specific atmosphere. You want your readers to feel the mood of the place. Use vivid language to evoke this mood and to draw an emotional response from the reader. If you wish to write in the first person, you may reveal the effect of the place on your own mood.

LEARNING OPTIONS

1. **Writing.** Suppose that Benden Weyr has a newspaper. Form a group of four students. Each of you chooses a different news item to write about for the paper. You may choose from any of the events related to the Weyr, such as the rescues of Menolly and Harper Elgion, the imminent hatching of Ramoth's eggs, or the discovery of Menolly's fire lizards. When you have finished your story, work with your group to create the first page of the *Benden Weekly Chronicle*.
2. **Art.** Create a collage that depicts life on Pern. In addition to illustrating some of the objects and daily activities, you might also try to reflect the atmosphere there.

1. Both visual and kinesthetic learners will enjoy the fun of creating a group newspaper. You may wish to extend the activity by having a student artist do a sketch for each article.
2. Visual learners will appreciate this activity. You might extend the activity for extroverted learners by having them present their collage to the class and describe it orally.

Contrast: The Hold is a cheerless place where the emphasis on fishing seems to preclude pleasant diversions. The Weyr is active and bustling, and even worries about Brekke do not prevent people from being happy and caring. The children of the Weyr are more physically active than the Hold children, and their exuberance is encouraged by their elders. The Weyr children do their chores cheerfully and promptly, unlike the more repressed children of the Sea Hold. The attitude of the Hold toward Menolly's singing is that it is shameful. In the Weyr, her singing is encouraged.

THINKING AND WRITING

Writing Transparency A graphic organizer may be useful to students with their descriptive paragraphs. You might want to work with students as they use the Sensory Language Chart graphic organizer in the **Transparencies for Writing** before they begin to write.

Students might also find it useful to review descriptive paragraphs. You will find practice sheets in the Writing Process Activities section of Volume II of the Teaching Portfolio.

GUIDE FOR READING

Dragonsong, Chapters 11–13

Universal Themes

A good novel has at least one **universal theme** around which the plot is built. Many novels have multiple themes. These universal themes are basic and recognizable. They are a part of the reader's own life experience. The search for self, choices and consequences, and the need for love, for example, are all parts of the fabric of human life. When the plot reveals such themes, your appreciation of the novel is enhanced by a recognition of familiar experiences. No matter how strange the setting may be, if the theme is familiar the reader will accept what is happening to the characters.

Focus

In the past chapters, it became clear that Menolly is very happy to be at Benden Weyr. She is treated well, and both her singing and her fire lizards are accepted without reservation by the dragonriders. What about her tuning, though? Will she ever play again? Menolly has many unresolved issues in her life. With a group of three of four classmates, discuss what you think will happen to Menolly. Draw up a list of predictions about her fate. As you read the conclusion of *Dragonsong*, compare your predictions to the actual story events.

Vocabulary

Knowing the following words will help you as you read Chapters 11–13 of *Dragonsong*.

condescension (kän′ di sen′ shən) *n.*: Dealing with others as if to do so were beneath one's dignity (p. 1003)
obtrusive (əb trōō′ siv) *adj.*: Calling attention to oneself (p. 1005)
zealous (zel′ əs) *adj.*: Very eager (p. 1007)
resurgence (ri sur′ jens) *n.*: The condition of having risen again (p. 1009)

unprecedented (un pres′ ə dent əd) *adj.*: Not done or known before (p. 1010)
irascible (i ras′ ə bəl) *adj.*: Easily angered; hot-tempered (p. 1011)
deference (def′ ər əns) *n.*: Courteous respect (p. 1012)
· **chagrin** (sha grin′) *n.*: Embarrassment and annoyance due to failure; disappointment (p. 1013)

1000 The Novel

Literary Focus Without universal themes neither prose nor poetry could have been written. In fact, the theme is the message of every story, song, or rhyme. How this theme is presented and explained is the job of the author. Discuss with students the theme of awakening and personal fulfillment that runs through *Dragonsong*. Point out that the author uses this theme to involve the reader with Menolly and to make the reader an understanding partner in Menolly's search for self.

Prereading Focus Menolly has to be wondering what her place in Benden Weyr will be. Could she be thinking that she might even become a harper? Could she be hoping that she might work in the Mastercrafthall? You might wish to ask students what they would be hoping for if they were in Menolly's place. You might also wish to tell them that some of their predictions will undoubtedly be accurate since they know Menolly fairly well at this point.

Vocabulary As students read the chapters, have them locate the words on the vocabulary list. Then have them use a thesaurus —or the Language Master 6000 —to find synonyms for the vocabulary words.

Electronic Handbook You might suggest that your students use the Language Master 6000 to hear the pronunciation of the vocabulary words.

Spelling Tip Point out that *irascible* has a silent *c* after the *s* in the second syllable.

Objectives

1 To understand universal themes
2 To evaluate a novel
3 To write a critique
4 To express individual interests and abilities through optional activities

Support Materials

Teacher Portfolio
Teacher Backup, p. 1011
Grammar in Action Worksheets *Using Adjective Clauses*, p. 1015; *Using Prepositional Phrases*, p. 1017
Usage and Mechanics Worksheet, p. 1019
Vocabulary Check, p. 1020
Analyzing Literature Worksheet,

Understanding Universal Themes, p. 1021
Critical Thinking and Reading Worksheet, *Evaluating a Novel*, p. 1022
Selection Test, p. 1023

Prentice Hall Literature Writing Studio

The little queen, all golden
Flew hissing at the sea.
To keep it back,
To turn it back
She flew forth bravely.

Menolly and T'gellan brought the thirty-one eggs of the clutch safely to Benden Weyr without so much as cracking a shell in the double, furred sack that had been provided for the journey *between*. Their return caused a flurry of excitement, the Weyrfolk crowding around to examine the eggs. Duly informed, Lessa arrived, imperiously ordering a basket of warm sand from the Hatching Ground; directing it to be placed by the small sauce hearth and scrupulously turned at intervals to distribute the heat evenly. She judged that the eggs were a good sevenday from hatching hardness.

"As well," she said in her dry fashion. "One hatching at a time is enough. Better still, we can present the worthies with their eggs at the Impression." She seemed inordinately pleased with that solution and smiled on Menolly. "Manora says that your feet aren't healed yet, so you're in charge of the clutch. And, Felena, get this child out of those ridiculous boots and into some decent clothes. Surely we have something in stores that'll make her look less disreputable."

Lessa departed, leaving Menolly the object of intense scrutiny. Felena, a tall, willowy woman with very beautiful, curved black eyebrows and green eyes, gave her a long appraisal, sent one helper off for clothing from a special press, another to get the tanner to take Menolly's measure for footwear, a child for her shears because Menolly's hair must be trimmed. Who had hacked it off? They must have used a knife. And such pretty hair, too. Was Menolly hungry? T'gellan had snatched her out of the cavern without a nay—yea or maybe. Bring that chair here and push that small table over! Don't stand there gawking, get the girl something to eat.

"How many Turns do you have?" Felena asked on the end of that long series of orders.

"I've fifteen, please," answered Menolly, dazed and trying very hard not to cry. Her throat ached and her chest was tight and she couldn't believe what was happening to her: people fussing over how she looked and what she wore. Above all, Lessa had smiled at her because she was so pleased about the clutch. And it seemed as if she didn't have to worry about being sent back to Half-Circle. Not if the Weyrfolk were ordering her shoes and giving her clothes. . . .

"Fifteen? Well, you wouldn't need much more fostering, would you?" Felena sounded disappointed. "We'll see what Manora has in mind for you. I'd like you as mine."

Menolly burst into tears. That provoked more confusion because her fire lizards began swooping dangerously close to people's faces. Beauty pecked at Felena, who was only trying to offer comfort.

"Let us have some order here," said a fresh, authoritative voice. Everyone, except the fire lizards, obediently subsided, and room was made for Manora. "And you be quiet, too," she said to squealing Beauty. "Go on," and she waved at the others, "go sit quietly somewhere. Now, why is Menolly crying?"

"She just burst into tears, Manora," said Felena, as perplexed as everyone else.

"I'm happy, I'm happy, I'm happy," Menolly managed to blurt out, each repetition punctuated by a heaving sob.

"Of course you are," said Manora understandingly, and made gestures to one of the women. "It's been a very exciting and tiring day. Now you just drink this." The woman had returned with a mug. "Now, everyone will go about their duties and let you catch your breath. There, that's better."

Dragonsong 1001

Presentation

Motivation/Prior Knowledge
You might wish to ask students to recall from previous chapters what life is like at the Sea Hold and how closely related the lifestyle is to a feudal society. Although Benden Weyr is part of that same society, the citizens' outlook is completely different. The Weyrmen and Weyrwomen could be compared to the lords and ladies of the feudal system. The Sea Holders are similar to the feudal vassals. Ask students if there are any advantages to being a Sea Holder and any disadvantages to being a Weyr person.

Purpose-Setting Question
What is left to make Menolly's happiness complete?

1 **Reading Strategy** Menolly seems to be doing well in Benden Weyr, even though she is still in pain from her injuries. You may wish to ask students to predict, as they read, what the future will bring to Menolly. You might also ask if they have any ideas on what might be going on back at the Sea Hold.

2 **ESL Teaching Strategy** You might ask students to describe an outfit that Menolly might wear.

3 **Discussion** Why is Menolly trying hard not to cry?

4 **Discussion** What does the statement "Now everyone will go about their duties" tell you about Benden Weyr society?

Thematic Focus Menolly, the main character, has had her "awakening." She has realized that there is a better life outside the Sea Hold and that she can find a place in it. She has also matured and has learned that she can take care of herself. You may wish to ask students if they can relate in any way to Menolly's awakening. Have they ever become suddenly aware of their capabilities?

5 Discussion Why does Menolly find it easy to talk to Manora?

6 Discussion Menolly becomes uneasy when she hears Manora mention Mavi's name. Why is this?

Speaking and Listening You might ask three students to read the paragraph beginning "Menolly's ease disappeared . . ." to ". . . We'll talk again later." One student can read the part of the narrator, the others, Menolly and Manora, respectively. When they have finished, you might have them give their views on Menolly's statements. Ask them to explain their views.

Menolly obediently sipped the drink. It wasn't fellis juice, but there was a slightly bitter taste. Manora urged her to drink deeply, and gradually Menolly felt her chest loosen, her throat stop aching and she began to relax.

She looked up to see that Manora was the only one at the little table, sitting with her hands folded serenely in her lap, her aura of calm patience very soothing.

"Feel more like yourself? Now, you just sit quietly and eat. We don't take in many new people, so there's bound to be a fuss about you. Soon enough to do everything else. How many fire lizard eggs did you find in that clutch?"

5 Menolly found it easy to talk to Manora, and soon she was showing the Headwoman the oil and explaining how she'd made it.

"I think you did wonderfully well all on your own, Menolly, not but what I'd expect it of someone Mavi has trained."

6 Menolly's ease disappeared at the sound of her mother's name. Involuntarily she clenched her left hand, feeling the scar tissue pull painfully from the intensity of her grip.

"You wouldn't like me to send a message to Half-Circle?" asked Manora. "To say that you're safely here?"

"I don't want you to, please! I'm no use to them there." She held up her scarred hand. "And . . ." she halted, she'd been about to add "a disgrace." "I seem to be useful here," she said quickly, pointing to the basket of fire lizard eggs.

"So you are, Menolly, so you are." Manora rose. "Now eat your meat, and we'll talk again later."

When she had finished her food, Menolly felt much better. She was content to sit in her hearth corner, watching the industry of others. And in a little while, Felena came over with her shears and trimmed Menolly's hair. Then someone watched the fire lizard eggs while Menolly changed into the first brand-new garments she'd ever had, being the youngest in a large family. The tanner came and not only measured her feet for proper boots but by evening he'd also made up some soft hide slippers that fit loosely over her bandaged feet.

She was so changed in appearance that Mirrim, passing her table just before the evening meal, almost failed to recognize her. Menolly had been worrying that Mirrim was deliberately avoiding her because Menolly had Impressed nine fire lizards, but there was no restraint in Mirrim's manner. Flopping into a chair across the table, she heartily approved the hair trim, the clothing and the slippers.

"I heard all about the clutch, but I've been so busy, up, down, in, out, running errands for Manora that I simply haven't had a moment."

Menolly suppressed a grin. Mirrim sounded exactly like Felena.

Then Mirrim cocked her head at Menolly. "You know, you look so much nicer in proper clothes that I didn't recognize you. Now, if we can only get you to smile once in a while . . ."

Just then a little brown lizard glided in to land on Mirrim's shoulder, snuggling affectionately up to her neck, and peering at Menolly from under her chin.

"Is he yours?"

"Yes, this is Tolly, and I have two greens, Reppa and Lok. And I'll make it very plain that three is quite enough for me. How ever did you manage to feed nine? They're so ravenous all the time!"

The last of Menolly's awkwardness with her friend disappeared as she recounted how she had coped with her fair of fire lizards.

The evening meal was then ready, and Mirrim, ignoring Menolly's protests that she was able to fetch her own, served them both. T'gellan joined their table and managed to coax Beauty, much to Menolly's amazement, to accept some food from his knife.

"Don't be surprised," Mirrim told Menolly with just a touch of condescension. "These greedy guts will eat what's offered from anyone. But that doesn't mean that they'll *look* to whoever feeds them. Besides, with nine . . ." She rolled her eyes so expressively that T'gellan chuckled.

"She's jealous, so she is, Menolly."

"I am not. There's quite enough, though . . . I would've liked a queen. Let's see if Beauty will come to me. Grall does."

Mirrim concentrated on coaxing Beauty to accept a piece of meat while T'gellan teased her, rather unfairly Menolly thought; but Mirrim returned his jibes with a few tart remarks of her own in a way that Menolly would never have dared address an older man, much less a dragonrider.

She was very tired, but it was pleasant to sit in the big kitchen cavern, listening to T'gellan, watching Mirrim coax Beauty, though it was Lazybones who finally ate from her hand. There were other small groups, chatting late over their evening meal, the women pairing with dragonriders. Menolly noticed wineskins being passed. She was surprised, at first, because the Sea Hold served wine only on very special occasions. T'gellan sent one of the Weyrboys to get him cups and a skin and insisted that Menolly, as well as Mirrim, have a cup.

"Good Benden wine is not to be refused," he told her, filling her cup. "There, now, isn't that the best you've ever tasted?"

Menolly forebore to mention that, barring wine laced with fellis juice, it was the first. Living was certainly conducted on different rules in the Weyr.[1]

When the Weyr Harper began to play

---

1. **different rules in the Weyr:** Menolly's having wine is an acceptable custom in Benden Weyr, but not in her Hold.

softly, more for his own pleasure than to entertain anyone in the cavern, Menolly did not restrain her fingers from tapping the rhythm. It was a song she liked, though she felt his chords were dull, which was why she began to hum her harmony when it did not discord with his. She wasn't even aware of what she was doing until Mirrim looked up with a smile on her face.

"That was just lovely, Menolly. Oharan? Come over here; Menolly has a new harmony for that one."

"No, no, I couldn't."

"Why not?" demanded T'gellan, and poured a bit more wine in her glass. "A little music would give us all heart. There're faces around here as long as a wet Turn."

Timidly at first, because of the older injunction against singing in front of people, Menolly joined her voice to Harper Oharan's baritone.

"Yes, I like it, Menolly. You've got a sure sense of pitch," said Oharan so approvingly that she started to worry again.

If Yanus knew she was singing at the Weyr . . . But Yanus wasn't here and he would never know.

"Say, can you harmonize to this one?" And Oharan broke into one of the older Ballads, one in which she had always sung a counter-tune against Petiron's melody.

Suddenly there were other voices humming along, softly but surely. Mirrim looked around, stared suspiciously at T'gellan, and then pointed at Beauty.

"She's humming in tune. Menolly, how ever did you teach her to do that? And the others . . . some of them are singing, too!" Mirrim was wide-eyed with amazement.

Oharan kept on playing, nodding at Mirrim to be quiet so they could all hear the fire lizards while T'gellan craned his head and cocked his ears, first at Beauty, then at Rocky and Diver and Brownie who were near him.

Dragonsong 1003

7 **Discussion** Why does Menolly feel that T'gellan is being unfair to Mirrim? What does this tell you about Menolly's background?

8 **ESL Teaching Strategy** Ask students: What do you think the expression "faces as long as a wet Turn" means? Have students paraphrase the expression.

9 **Discussion** Mirrim "fusses" at T'gellan and Oharan, calling them names. Why did she do this?

10 **Discussion** From your previous reading, why do you think the Hatching is such an important event in Pern?

"I don't believe it," said T'gellan.

"Don't scare them! Just let them do it," said Oharan in a low voice as he modulated his chords into another verse.

They finished the song with the fire lizards humming obediently along with Menolly. Mirrim demanded then to know how on earth Menolly had gotten her lizards to sing with her.

"I used to play and sing for them in the cave, you know, to keep us company. Just little twiddles."

"Just little twiddles! I've had my three much longer, and I never even knew they liked music."

"Just shows that you don't know all there is to know, doesn't it, young Mirrim?" teased T'gellan.

"Now that isn't fair," Menolly interceded and then hiccuped. To her embarrassment she hiccuped again.

"How much wine have you been giving her, T'gellan?" demanded Mirrim, frowning at the bronze rider.

"Certainly not enough to put her in her cups."

Menolly hiccuped again.

"Get her some water!"

"Hold your breath," Oharan suggested.

T'gellan brought water and, with quick sips, Menolly managed to stop her hiccuping. She kept insisting that she didn't feel the wine, but she was very tired. If someone would watch the eggs . . . it was so late . . . With solicitous help, T'gellan and Oharan supported her to her sleeping chamber, Mirrim fussing at them that they were two great big numbwits who hadn't a lick of sense between them.

Menolly was very glad to lie down and let Mirrim remove the slippers and the new clothes and cover her. She was asleep before the fire lizards had disposed themselves about her for the night.

Chapter 12

Dragonman, dragonman,
Between thee and thine,
Share me that glimpse of love
Greater than mine.

Mirrim roused Menolly early the next morning, impatiently shushing the fire lizards who hissed at her rough shaking of their mistress.

"Menolly, wake up. We need every hand in the kitchen. The eggs will hatch today and half Pern's invited. Turn over. Manora's coming to look at your feet."

"Ouch! You're too rough!"

"Tell Beauty . . . ouch . . . I'm *not* hurting you. Beauty! Behave or I'll tell Ramoth!"

To Menolly's surprise, Beauty stopped diving at Mirrim and retreated with a squeak to the far corner of the room.

"You were hurting me," said Menolly, too sleepy to be tactful.

"Well, I said I was sorry. Hmmm. Your feet really do look a lot better."

"We won't use such heavy bandages today," said Manora, entering at that moment. "The slippers give enough protection."

Menolly craned her head about as she felt Manora's strong gentle fingers turn first one foot and then the other.

"Yes, lighter bandages today, Mirrim, and salve. Tonight, no bandages at all. Wounds must have fresh air, too, you know. But you've done a good job. The fire lizard eggs are fine this morning, Menolly."

With that she left, and Mirrim quickly set about dressing the feet. When she'd finished and Menolly rose to put on her clothes, her fingers lingering in the soft folds of the overshirt, Mirrim sank onto the bed with an exaggerated sigh.

"What's the matter with you?" Menolly asked.

"I'm getting all the rest I can while I can,"

Mirrim replied. "You don't know what a Hatching is like, with all those Holders and crafters stumbling about the Weyr, poking here and there where they're NOT supposed to be and getting scared of and scaring the dragons and the weyrlings and the hatchlings. And the way they eat!" Mirrim rolled her eyes expressively. "You'd think they'd never seen food and . . ." Mirrim flopped over on the bed and started to sob wildly.

"Mirrim, what's the matter? Oh, it's Brekke! Isn't she all right? I mean, won't she re-Impress? Sanra said that's what Lessa hoped . . ."

Menolly bent to comfort her friend, herself upset by those heart-rending sobs. Mirrim's words were garbled by her weeping, although Menolly gathered that Mirrim didn't want her foster-mother to re-Impress and the reason was obscure. Brekke didn't want to live, and they had to find some way to make her. Losing her dragon was like losing half herself, and it hadn't been Brekke's fault. She was so gentle and sensible, and she loved F'nor, and for some reason that was unwise, too.

Menolly just let Mirrim cry, knowing how much relief she had felt the day before when she'd wept, and hoping deep in her heart that there might be joyful tears, too, for Mirrim later that day. There had to be. She forgave Mirrim all her little poses and attitudes, aware that that was how Mirrim had masked her intense anxiety and grief.

There was a rattling of the cubicle's curtain, a squabble of fire lizard protest, and then Mirrim's Tolly crawled under the curtain, his eyes whirling with indignation and worry. He saw Menolly stroking Mirrim's hair and, raising his wings, made as if to launch himself at her when Beauty warbled sharply from the corner. Tolly sort of shook his wings, but when he leaped to the bed, he landed gently on the edge and remained there, his eyes first on Mirrim, then on Menolly. A moment later the two greens entered. They settled themselves on the stool, watchful but not obtrusive.

Beauty, in her corner, kept an eye on them all.

"Mirrim? Mirrim?" It was Sanra's voice from the living cavern. "Mirrim, haven't you finished Menolly's feet yet? We need both of you! Now!"

As Menolly rose obediently, Mirrim caught her hand and squeezed it. Then she rose, shook her skirts out and marched from the cubicle, Menolly following more slowly behind her.

Mirrim had by no means exaggerated the amount of work to be done. It was just past sunrise, but obviously the main cooks had already been up for hours, judging by the breads—sweet, spiced and sour—cooling on long tables. Two Weyrmen were trussing a huge herdbeast for the main spit and at the smaller hearths, wild wherries were being cleaned and stuffed for roasting later.

For added protection in the busy kitchen, someone had placed the small table over her fire lizard egg basket. They were doing fine, the sand nice and warm all around. Felena caught sight of her, told her to feed herself quickly from the sauce hearth and did she know anything flavorful to do with dried fish? Or would she prefer to help pare roots?

Menolly instantly elected to cook fish, so Felena asked what ingredients she'd need. Menolly was a little dismayed to learn the quantity she'd have to prepare. She had had no idea that so many people came to a Hatching: the number coming was more than *lived* at Half-Circle Sea Hold.

The knack in making the fish stew tasty was in the long baking so Menolly applied herself to prepare the huge pots quickly, to give them enough time to simmer into succulence. She did so with such dispatch

11 **Literary Focus: Theme** Menolly stops thinking of herself as she tries to comfort her friend. What does this tell us about Menolly?

12 **ESL Teaching Strategy** You might wish to ask students to visualize the kitchen scene and describe it in their own words.

13 Discussion Why does the woman express sympathy for Brekke?

14 Discussion What do you think a spiced cake is? What might the list of ingredients include?

that there were still plenty of roots left to pare.

Excitement filled the air of the kitchen cavern. The mound of root vegetables in front of Menolly melted away as she listened to the chatter of the other girls and women. There was great speculation as to which of the boys, and the girls for the queen egg, would Impress the dragons to be hatched that day.

"No one has ever re-Impressed a dragon," said one woman wistfully. "D'you think Brekke will?"

"No one's ever been given the chance before."

"Is it a chance we should take?" asked someone else.

"*We* weren't asked," said Sanra, glaring at the last speaker. "It's Lessa's idea, but it wasn't F'nor's or Manora's . . ."

13 "Something has to help her," said the first woman. "It tears my heart to see her lying there, just lying, like the undead. I mind me of the way D'namal went. He sort of . . . well . . . faded completely away."

"If you'll finish that root quickly, we can put this kettle on," said Sanra, briskly rising.

"Will all of this be eaten?" asked Menolly of the woman beside her.

"Yes, indeed, and there'll be some looking for more," she said with a complacent smile. "Impression Days are good days. I've a fosterling and a blood son on the Hatching Ground today!" she added with understandable pride. "Sanra!" she turned her head to shout over her shoulder, "just one more largish kettle will take what's left."

Then white roots had to be sliced finely, covered with herbs and placed in clay pots to bake. The succulent odors of Menolly's fish concoction aroused compliments from Felena, who was in charge of the various hearths and ovens. Then Menolly, who was told to keep off her poor feet, helped decorate **14** the spiced cakes. She giggled with the rest when Sanra distributed pieces of one cake

about, saying they had to be certain the bake had turned out well, didn't they?

Menolly did not forget to turn the fire lizard eggs, or to feed her friends. Beauty stayed within sight of Menolly, but the others had been seen bathing in the lake and sunning themselves, scrupulously avoiding Ramoth, whose bugles punctuated the morning.

"She's always like that on Impression Day," T'gellan told Menolly as he grabbed a quick bite to eat at her table. "Say, will you get your fire lizards to hum along with you again this evening? I've been called a liar because I said you'd taught them to sing."

"They might turn difficult and shy in front of a lot of people, you know."

"Well, we'll wait till things get quiet, and then we'll give it a try, huh. Now, I'm to see you get to the Hatching. Midafternoon, I'd say, so be ready."

As it happened, she wasn't. She felt the thrumming before she heard it. She and everyone else in the cavern stopped working as one-by-one they became aware of the intensely exciting noise. Menolly gasped, because she recognized it as the same sort of sound the fire lizards had made when their eggs had hatched.

There was suddenly no time for her to return to her cubicle and change. T'gellan appeared at the cavern entrance, gesturing urgently to her. She made as much speed as her feet would permit because she could see Monarth waiting outside the entrance. T'gellan had already taken her hand when she exclaimed over the cooking stains and wet marks on her overshirt.

"I told you to be ready. I'll put you in a corner, pet, not that anyone will notice stains today," T'gellan reassured her.

A trifle resentful, Menolly noticed that he was dressed in new dark trousers, a handsomely overstitched tunic, a belt worked with metal and jewels, but she didn't resist.

"I have to get you in place first, because

1006   The Novel

I'm to collect some visitors," T'gellan said, climbing nimbly into place in front of her on Monarth's neck ridges. "F'lar's filling the Hatching Ground with anyone who'll ride a dragon *between*."

Monarth was awing, slanting up from the Bowl floor to an immense opening, high up on the Weyr wall, which Menolly had not noticed before. Other dragons were angling towards it, too. Menolly gasped as they entered the mouth, with a dragon before them and one abaft, so close that she had momentary fears of collision. The dark core of the tunnel was lit at the far end, and abruptly they were in the gigantic Hatching Ground.

The whole north quadrant of the Weyr must be hollow, thought Menolly, awed. Then she saw the gleaming clutch of dragon eggs and gasped. Slightly to one side was a larger egg, and hovering over it was the zealous golden form of Ramoth, her eyes incredibly brilliant with the coming of Impression.

Monarth dropped with distressing abruptness, then backwinged to land neatly on a ledge.

"Here you are, Menolly. Best seat in the Ground. I'll be back for you afterwards."

Menolly was only too glad to sit still after that incredible ride. She was in the third tier, by the outer wall, so she had a perfect view of the Hatching Ground and the entrance through which people were beginning to file. They were all so elegantly dressed that she brushed vainly at the stains and crossed her arm over her chest. At least the clothes were new.

Other dragons were arriving from the upper entrance, depositing their passengers, often three and four at a time. She watched the now steady stream of visitors coming in from the ground entrance. It was amusing to watch the elegant, and sometimes overdressed, ladies having to pick up their heavy skirts and run in awkward little steps across the hot sands. The tiers filled rapidly, and the excited thrumming of the dragons increased in pitch so that Menolly found it difficult to sit quietly.

A sudden cry announced the rocking of some of the eggs. Late arrivals began to hurry across the sands, and the seats beyond Menolly were filled with a group of minecraftsmen, to judge from their red-brown tunic devices. She crossed her arms again and then uncrossed them because she had to lean forward to see around the minecraftsmen's stocky bodies.

More eggs were rocking, all of them except the smallish gray egg that had somehow got shoved back against the inside wall.

Another rush of wings, and this time bronze dragons entered, depositing the girls who were candidates for the queen egg. Menolly tried to figure out which one was Brekke, but they all looked very aware and healthy. Hadn't the Weyrwomen remarked that morning how Brekke just lay like someone dead? The girls formed a loose but incomplete semicircle about the queen egg while Ramoth hissed softly behind it.

Young boys marched in now from the Bowl, their expressions purposeful, their shoulders straight in the white tunics as they approached the main clutch.

Menolly did not see Brekke's entrance because she was trying to figure out which of the violently rocking eggs would hatch first. Then one of the miners exclaimed and pointed towards the entrance, to the slender figure, stumbling, halting, then moving onward, apparently insensitive to the hot sands underfoot.

"That would be the one. That would be Brekke," he told his comrades. "Dragonrider said she'd be put to the egg."

Yes, thought Menolly, she walks as if she's asleep. Then Menolly saw Manora and a man she didn't recognize standing by the entrance, as if they had done all they could in bringing Brekke to the Hatching Ground.

Dragonsong   1007

15 **Discussion** What is the significance of Ramoth hovering over a large egg?

16 **Discussion** What modern event could be compared to the Hatching?

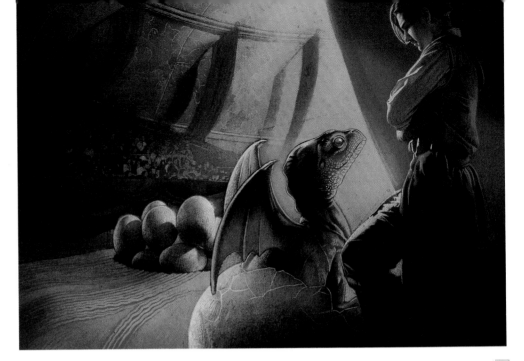

Suddenly Brekke straightened her shoulders with a shake of her head. She walked slowly but steadily across the sands to join the five girls who waited by the golden egg. One girl turned and gestured for her to take the space that would complete the semicircle.

The humming ceased so abruptly that a little ripple of reaction ran through those assembled. In the expectant silence, the faint crack of a shell was clear, and the pop and shatter of others.

First one dragonet, then another, awkward, ugly, glistening creatures, flopped and rolled from their casings, squawking and creeling, their wedge-shaped heads too big for the thin, sinuous short necks.

Menolly noticed how very still the boys were standing, as stunned as she'd been in that very little cave with those tiny fire lizards crawling from their shells, voracious with hunger.

Now the difference became apparent; the fire lizards had expected no help at their hatching; their instinct was to get food into their churningly empty stomachs as fast as possible. But the dragons looked expectantly about them. One staggered beyond the first boy who sidestepped its awkward progress. It fell, nose first at the feet of a tall, black-haired boy. The boy knelt, helped the dragonet balance on his shaky feet, looked into the rainbow eyes.

Emotion like a fist squeezed Menolly's heart. Yes, she'd her fire lizards, but to Impress a dragon . . . Startled, she wondered where Beauty, Rocky, Diver and the others were. She missed them acutely, wanted Beauty's affectionate nuzzling, even the choke-tight twist of the little queen's tail about her neck.

The crack of the golden egg was a summons for all attention to be centered on it. The egg split right down the center, and its

17

inmate, protesting her abrupt birth, fell to the sand on her back. Three of the girls moved to assist it. They got the little queen to her four legs and then stepped back. Menolly held her breath as they all turned towards Brekke. She was unaware of anything. Whatever strength had sustained her to walk across the sands had now left her. Her shoulders sagged pathetically, her head listed to one side as if too heavy to hold upright. The queen dragonet turned her head towards Brekke, the glistening eyes enormous in the outsize skull. Brekke shook her head as if aware of the scrutiny. The dragonet lurched forward one step.

Menolly saw a bronze blur out of the corner of her right eye and for an unnerving moment thought it must be Diver. But it couldn't be, because the little bronze just hung above the dragonet's head, screaming defiantly. He was so close to her head that she reared back with a startled shriek and bit at the air, instinctively spreading her wings forward as protection for her vulnerable eyes.

Dragons bugled warnings from their perches at the top of the Hatching Ground, and Ramoth spread her wings, rising to her haunches as if to strike at the invader. One of the girls interposed her body between the queen and her small attacker.

"Berd! Don't!" Brekke, too, moved, her arm extended towards the irate bronze.

The dragonet queen creeled and hid her face in the girl's skirt. The two women faced each other for a moment, tense, worried. Then the other stretched her hand out to Brekke, and Menolly could see her smile. The gesture lasted only a moment because the young queen butted imperiously, and the girl knelt, her arms reassuringly encircling the dragonet's shoulders.

At the same instant, Brekke turned, no longer a somnolent figure, immersed in grief. She walked back to the entrance of the cavern, the little bronze fire lizard whirring around her head, making noises that went from scolding to entreaty, just like Beauty when Menolly was doing something that had upset her.

Menolly didn't realize that she was weeping until tears dropped onto her arms. She glanced hastily to see if the miners had noticed, but they were concentrating on the main clutch. From their comments it seemed that a boy had been found on Search in one of their craftholds, and they were impatiently waiting for him to Impress. For a fleeting moment, Menolly was angry with them; hadn't they seen Brekke's deliverance? Didn't they realize how marvelous that was? Oh, think how happy Mirrim would be now!

Menolly sank wearily back against the stones, depleted by the emotionally laden miracle. And the look on Brekke's face as she passed under the arched entrance! Manora was there, her face radiant, her arms outstretched in a joyful gesture. The man, who was surely F'nor, swept Brekke up in his arms, his tired face mirroring his relief and gladness.

A cheer from the miners beside her indicated that their lad had Impressed, although Menolly couldn't be certain which of the boys he was. There were so many now paired off with wobbly-legged hatchlings, all creeling with hunger, lurching and falling towards the entrance. The miners were urging their favorite on; and when a curly-haired, skinny lad passed by, with a grin for their cheering, she saw that he had done rather well, Impressing a brown. When the exultant miners turned to her to share their triumph, she managed to respond properly, but she was relieved when they scrambled down the tiers to follow the pair out of the Hatching Ground.

She sat there, glowing over the resurgence of Brekke, the determination and fierceness of bronze Berd, his courage in braving Ramoth's ire at such a moment.

Dragonsong 1009

18 **Discussion** Why is the bronze angry?

19 **Discussion** What is the cause of Brekke's change in attitude?

20 **Discussion** Why does Menolly guess that the man was F'nor?

21 **Reading Strategy** Do you have any thoughts as to why Jaxom's Impression was not considered a good thing?

22 **Discussion** What problem did Menolly have when T'gellan did not return?

Now, why, Menolly wondered, didn't Berd want Brekke to Impress the new queen? At all events, the experiment had successfully roused Brekke from her lethargy.

The dragons were returning, landing in the Hatching Ground so that their riders could help the Weyrlings, or to escort guests outside. The tiers were emptying. Soon there was only a man in Holder colors on the first tier with two boys. The man looked as tired as she felt. Then one of the boys rose, pointing to the little egg on the sand that wasn't even rocking.

Idly Menolly thought that it might not hatch, remembering the uncracked egg left in the fire lizard's sand nest the morning after her fire lizards had hatched. She'd shaken it and something hard had rattled within. Sometimes Hold babies were born dead, so she'd supposed that it could happen to other creatures, too.

The boy was running along the tier now. To Menolly's astonishment, he jumped to the Hatching Ground and began kicking at the little egg. His cries and his actions attracted the notice of the Weyrleader and the small knot of candidates who had not Impressed. The Holder half rose, one hand extended in a cautionary gesture. The other boy was shouting at his friend.

"Jaxom, what are you doing?" shouted the Weyrleader.

The egg fractured then, and the boy began tearing at the shell, ripping out sections and kicking until Menolly could see the small body pushing at the thick inner membrane.

Jaxom cut at the membrane with his belt knife, and a small white body, not much larger than the boy's torso, fell from the sac. The boy reached out to help the creature to his feet.

Menolly saw the little white dragon lift his head, his eyes, brilliant with greens and yellows, fastened on the boy's face.

1010   The Novel

"He says his name is Ruth!" the boy cried in amazed delight.

With a strangled exclamation, the older man sank back to the stone seat, his face a mask of grief. The Weyrleader and the others who had rushed to prevent what had just occurred halted. To Menolly it was all too obvious that Jaxom's Impression of the little white dragon was unprecedented and unwelcome. And she couldn't imagine why: the boy and the dragon looked so radiant, who could deny them their joyous union?

Chapter 13

Harper, your song has a sorrowful sound,
Though the tune was written as gay.
Your voice is sad and your hands are slow
And your eye meeting mine turns away.

When it became obvious to Menolly that T'gellan had forgotten his promise to return, she slowly climbed down from the tiers and made her way out of the deserted Hatching Ground, over the hot sand.

Beauty met her at the entrance, demanding caresses and reassurance. She was swiftly followed by the others, all chittering nervously and with many anxious dartings to the entrance to see if Ramoth was about.

Although Menolly had not had far to walk on the sands, the heat had quickly penetrated the soles of her slippers. Her discomfort was acute by the time she stepped onto the cooler earth of the Bowl. She edged to one side of the entrance and sank down, her fire lizards grouping themselves about her while she waited for the pain to subside.

As everyone was on the kitchen cavern side of the Bowl, no one noticed her, for which she was grateful since she felt useless and foolish. It would be a long walk across the Bowl to the kitchens. Well, she'd just take it in small sections.

She heard the faint cries of the herdbeasts at the farthest end of the Bowl

Grammar in Action

Writers often use adjective clauses to provide more information about a noun or pronoun. An **adjective clause** is a subordinate clause that begins with a relative pronoun and modifies a noun or pronoun. The most common relative pronouns are *who, whose, which,* and *that.* **Adjective clauses** always modify nouns and pronouns, just as single adjectives do. Notice how Anne McCaffrey uses adjective clauses in these sentences.

Auntie One and Two came sweeping down to her, chittering about something *that had excited them* and ducking their heads at her for reassurance. (The adjective clause modifies *something*.)

Felena's voice, raised above the conversational babble, brought Menolly's gaze back to the kitchen cavern *where tables were being erected for the evening's feasting.* (The adjective clause describes the *cavern*.)

Student Activity 1. Identify the adjective clauses in the following sentences.
1. She caressed the little fire lizard, who crooned and closed her eyelids in appreciation.

valley and saw Ramoth hovering for a kill. The Weyrwomen had said that Ramoth hadn't eaten for the past ten days, which was partly the cause of her irascible temper.

By the lakeside, hatchlings were being fed and bathed, and their riders shown how to oil the fragile skin. Their white tunics stood out among the gleaming green, blue, brown and bronze hides. The little queen was slightly removed from the others, with two of the bronze dragons in attendance. She couldn't see where the white dragon was.

On the Weyr ledges dotting the Bowl's face, some dragons were curled in what remained of the afternoon sun. Above and to the left of her, Menolly saw great bronze Mnementh on the ledge of the queen's Weyr. He was seated on his haunches, watching his mate choose her meal. Menolly saw him move slightly, glancing over his left shoulder. Then Menolly caught a glimpse of a man's head as he descended the stairs from the queen's Weyr.

Felena's voice, raised above the conversational babble, brought Menolly's gaze back to the kitchen cavern where tables were being erected for the evening's feasting. The dragonriders were doing it, for the bright colors of their best tunics were conspicuous, moving about while the soberer colors of Holder and Craft seemed to stay in stationary clumps at a polite distance from the workers.

The man had reached the Bowl floor now from the queen's weyr, and Menolly idly watched him start across. Auntie One and Two came sweeping down to her, chittering about something that had excited them and ducking their heads at her for reassurance. They needed to be oiled, and she felt guilty for not taking better care of them.

"Do you have *two* greens?" asked an amused voice, and the tall man was standing in front of her, his eyes friendly and interested.

"Yes, they're mine," she said and held up Two for him to inspect, responding to the kindness and good humor in his long face. "They like their eye ridges scratched, gently, like this," she added, showing him.

He dropped to one knee in the sand and obligingly caressed Two, who crooned and closed her eyelids in appreciation. Auntie One whistled at Menolly for attention, digging a jealous claw into her hand.

"Stop that, you naughty creature."

Beauty roused, and Rocky and Diver reacted as well, all three scolding Auntie One so fiercely that she took flight.

"Don't tell me the queen *and* the two browns are yours as well?" the man asked, startled.

"I'm afraid so."

"Then you must be Menolly," he said, rising to his feet and making such an elaborate bow that she blushed. "Lessa has just told me that I may have two eggs of that clutch *you* discovered. I'm rather partial to browns, you know, though I wouldn't actually object to a bronze. Of course the greens, like this lady here," and he smiled such a winning smile to the watching Two that she crooned responsively, "are such delicate darlings. That doesn't mean that I would object to a blue, however."

"Don't you want the queen?"

"Ah, now that would be greedy of me, wouldn't it?" He rubbed his face thoughtfully and gave her a wry half-smile. "All things considered, though, I'd be heartily embarrassed if Sebell—my Journeyman is to have possession of the other egg—secured a queen instead. But . . . " and he threw his long-fingered hand upwards to signify his submission to chance. "Are you waiting here for some purpose? Or is the confusion on the other side of the Bowl too much for all your friends?"

"I should be there. The clutch must be turned; the eggs are in warm sand by the hearth; but T'gellan brought me into the Hatching Cavern and told me to wait . . . "

23
24

23 Discussion At this point, are there any clues to the man's identity? Can you guess why the author is taking time revealing his name?

24 Clarification Tell students that Pern's guilds reflect the structure of Earth's medieval guilds. A *journeyman* is a worker who has learned a trade and works for another person. A journeyman is a step above an *apprentice*, who is learning a trade. After years of working as a journeyman, a person might become a *master*, if the person is skilled enough. Tell the students that to become a master, a person must demonstrate his or her skills by creating a *masterpiece*, a piece of work worthy of a master.

2. Menolly was happy in Benden Weyr, which was the finest weyr in Pern.
3. The queen looked at Ramoth, who hadn't eaten in ten days.
4. Menolly heard Lessa's voice, which was loud and clear.

Student Activity 2. Add an adjective clause to each of the following sentences.
1. Lessa was a fine dragonwoman.
2. Beauty was the prettiest fire lizard.
3. On Pern Thread was a danger.
4. The songs were written by Menolly.

Electronic Handbook You might want students to review phrases and clauses before completing the Grammar in Action activities. If students have access to the Language Master 6000, have them enter the access words *adjective* and *clause* and press the GRAMMAR key to get information.

25 **Discussion** Why does the man decide after "sober reflection" that he wants greens?

26 **Discussion** What additional clues suggest the man's identity?

"And seems to have forgot you. Not surprising, considering today's surprises." The man hastily cleared his throat and extended his hand to her.

She accepted his aid because she couldn't have risen without it. He had taken three strides when he realized that she wasn't keeping up with him. Politely he turned. Menolly tried to walk normally, a feat she managed for about three strides when her heel came down so painfully on a patch of pebbles that she involuntarily cried out. Beauty whirled, scolding fiercely, and Rocky and Diver added their antics, which were of no help to anyone.

"Here's my arm, girl. Were you too long on the hot sand? Ah now, wait. You're a long child, but there's no meat on your bones."

Before Menolly could protest, he'd swung her up into his arms and was carrying her across the Bowl.

"Tell that queen of yours I'm helping you," he asked when Beauty disordered his silvering hair, diving at him. "After sober reflection, be sure you give me green eggs."

Beauty was too excited to harken to Menolly, so she had to wave her arms about his head and face to protect him. It was not astonishing then that their approach to the kitchen caverns attracted attention; but people made way so politely, bowing to them with such deference, that Menolly began to wonder who the man was. His tunic was a gray cloth with just a band of blue, so he must be a Harper of some sort; probably weyrbound to Fort Weyr to judge by the yellow arm device.

"Menolly, did you hurt your feet?" Felena appeared before them, curious at the flurry of excitement. "Didn't T'gellan remember you? He's got no memory, drat the man. How good of you to rescue her, sir!"

"Think nothing of it, Felena. I discovered she was custodian of the fire lizard eggs. However, if you happened to have a cup of wine . . . This is thirsty work."

"I can stand, really I can, sir," Menolly protested, for something in Felena's manner told her that this man was too important to be toting sore-footed girls. "Felena, I couldn't stop him."

"I'm only being my usual ingratiating self," the man told her, "and do stop struggling. You're too heavy!"

Felena was laughing at his exaggeration as she led the way to Menolly's table above the egg basket.

"You're a terrible fellow, Master Robinton, indeed you are. But you'll have your wine while Menolly picks out the best of the clutch. Have you spotted the queen egg, Menolly?"

"After the way Menolly's queen has been attacking me, I'd be safer with any other color, Felena. Now do get that wine for me, there's a good woman. I'm utterly parched."

As he gently settled her into her chair, Menolly heard Felena's teasing remark, " . . . terrible fellow, Master Robinton . . . terrible fellow, Master Robinton . . . " She stared at him, disbelieving.

"Now, what's the matter, Menolly? Did my exercise bring out spots on my face?" He mopped at his cheeks and brow and examined his hand. "Ah, thank you, Felena. You've saved my life. My tongue was quite stuck to the roof of my mouth. And here's to you, young queen, and thank you for your courtesy." He raised his cup to Beauty, who was perched on Menolly's shoulder, her tail firmly entwined as she glared at him. "Well?" he asked kindly of Menolly.

"You're the Masterharper?"

"Yes, I'm Robinton." He sounded quite casual about it. "And I think you need some wine, too."

"No, I couldn't." Menolly held up her hands in refusal. "I get hiccups. And go to sleep." She hadn't meant to say that either, but she had to explain why she was discourteous enough to refuse his cup. She was also acutely aware now of her stained overshirt,

Commentary

Several of Anne McCaffrey's Pern novels began as short stories and developed into full-length novels. The plots of many of the stories and novels overlap, and a character who appears briefly in one novel may well be the central character in another. Such is the case with Jaxom, the young boy who impresses Ruth, the white dragon.

Jaxom's story begins in *Dragonflight,* the first of McCaffrey's Pern novels. Jaxom's father is Fax, the vicious Lord of High

Reaches who invaded Ruatha and murdered the rightful lord and his family, except for one daughter, Lessa, who survives. Fax dies in combat with F'lar, and Jaxom's mother, the Lady Gemma, dies giving birth to him.

Lessa, by now the Benden Weyrwoman, gives up her claim to Ruatha. Lessa and F'lar choose Lytol as Jaxom's guardian. Once known as the dragonrider L'tol, Lytol still grieves the death of his green dragon, but he devotes all his energy to raising Jaxom. Jaxom is to be Lord of Ruatha, not a mere dragonrider. Thus, when the boy Impresses Ruth, Lytol is in despair. He feels that Jaxom cannot be both a dragonrider and a Lord Holder.

27

her sandy clothes and slippers, her complete disarray. This wasn't how she imagined her first meeting with the Masterharper of Pern, and she hung her head in embarrassment.

"I always advise eating *before* drinking," remarked Master Robinton in the nicest possible way. "I shouldn't wonder but that's half the problem right now," he added and then raised his voice. "This child is faint with hunger, Felena."

Menolly shook her head, denying his suggestion and trying to forestall Felena, but she was already ordering one of the lads to bring klah, a basket of breads, and a dish of sliced meats. When she was served, just as if she were one of the Weyrwomen, she kept her head bent over her cup, blowing to cool the contents.

"Do you think there's enough here for a starving man?" asked Masterharper Robinton, his voice so plaintive and faint with his pretended hunger that Menolly was startled into glancing up at him. His expression was at once so wistful, appealing and kind that, despite her deep chagrin, she smiled in response to his foolishness. "I'll need strength for this evening's work, and a base for my drinking," he added in a very quiet, worried voice.

She had the feeling that he had let her share his responsibilities, but she wondered at the sadness and anxiety. Surely everyone in the Weyr was happy today?

"A few slices of meat on a slab of that good bread," and Robinton made his voice quaver like a peevish old uncle's. "And . . . " his voice returned to his normal baritone range, "a cup of good Benden wine to wash it down . . . "

To her consternation, he rose then, bread and meat in one hand, the wine mug in the other. He bowed to her with great dignity and, with a smile, was off.

"But, Masterharper, your fire lizard eggs . . . "

"Later, Menolly. I'll come back later for them."

His tall figure, his head visible above the bustling activity, retreated across the cavern, away from her. She watched until he was out of sight amid the visitors, bewildered, and all too keenly aware that there was no way in which she would be able to ask Masterharper Robinton about her songs. Twiddles they were, as Yanus and Mavi had always said: too insignificant to be presented for serious consideration to such a man as Masterharper Robinton.

28

Beauty crooned softly and headstroked Menolly's cheek. Rocky hopped down from his wall perch to her shoulder. He nuzzled her ear, humming in a consoling tone.

Mirrim found her that way, and she roused from her apathy to rejoice with her friend.

Dragonsong 1013

27 **Discussion** Why is Menolly so embarrassed?

28 **Discussion** How does Menolly reveal her feelings about herself and her abilities when she refers to her songs as "twiddles"?

Fortunately for Pern, Jaxom does manage to blend both roles. As the protagonist of both *The White Dragon* and *All the Weyrs of Pern*, Jaxom, along with his beloved dragon Ruth, becomes one of the great heroes of Pern.

29 **ESL Teaching Strategy** What does "all mischievous girl, not Mirrim-Felena or Mirrim-Manora" mean? Have students explain in their own words.

30 **Discussion** This is another reference to an earlier statement made by Menolly. What did Menolly say about girls being told things at the Sea Hold?

"Oh, I'm so very happy for you, Mirrim. You see it did come right!" If Mirrim, with all her worries, had been able to keep a good face, surely Menolly, with much to be grateful for, could manage to follow her example.

"Did you see it? You *were* in the Hatching Ground? I was so terrified that I didn't dare watch," Mirrim said, no trace of terror now in her radiant face. "I made Brekke eat, the first food she's taken in just days. And she smiled at me, Menolly. She smiled at me, and she knew me. She's going to be perfectly all right. And F'nor ate every speck of the roast wherry I brought him." She giggled, all mischievous girl, not Mirrim-Felena, or Mirrim-Manora. "I snitched the best slices of the spiced wherry breast, too. And you know, he ate every bit of it! He'll probably eat himself sick at the Feast as well. Then I told him to take poor Canth down to feed because that dragon's just about transparent with hunger." Her voice dropped in awe. "Canth tried to protect Wirenth from Prideth, you know. Can you imagine that? A brown protecting a queen! It's because F'nor loves Brekke so. And now it's all right. It's well and truly all right. So tell me."

"Tell you? What?"

Irritation flashed across Mirrim's face. "Tell me exactly what happened when Brekke got on the Hatching Ground. I told you I didn't dare look myself."

So Menolly told her. And told her again until she ran out of answers to all the detailed questions Mirrim found to ask her.

"Now you tell me why everyone's so upset about this Jaxom Impressing the little white dragon. He saved his life, you know. The dragon would have died if Jaxom hadn't broken the shell and cut the sac."

"Jaxom Impressed a dragon? I didn't know!" Mirrim's eyes widened with consternation. "Oh! Now why would that kid do such a dreadful thing?"

"Why is it dreadful?"

"Because he's got to be Lord Holder of Ruatha Hold, that's why."

Menolly was a bit annoyed with Mirrim's impatience and said so.

"Well, he can't be Lord Holder *and* dragonrider. Didn't you learn anything in that Sea Hold of yours? And, by the way, I saw the Half-Circle Harper, I think his name is Elgion. Shall I tell him you're here?"

"No!"

"Well, no need to bite my head off." And with that Mirrim flounced off in a huff.

"Menolly, will you forgive me? I completely forgot to come back for you," T'gellan said, striding up to the table before Menolly had a chance to catch her breath. "Look, the Masterminer is supposed to have two eggs. He can't stay for the whole Feast, so we've got to fix something for him to carry the eggs home in. And the rest of the eggs as well. No, don't get up. Here, you, come be feet for Menolly," he ordered, beckoning to one of the Weyrboys.

So Menolly spent most of that evening in the kitchen cavern sewing furry bags to carry eggs safely *between*. But she could hear all the jollity outside; and with no small effort, she made herself enjoy the singing. Five Harpers, two drummers and three pipers made music for the Impression Feast. She thought she recognized Elgion's strong tenor in one song, but it was unlikely he'd look for her at the back of the kitchen cavern.

His voice made her briefly homesick for seawinds and the taste of salty air; briefly, too, she longed for the solitude of her cave. Only briefly; this Weyr was the place for her. Her feet would heal soon; she'd no longer be Old-Auntie-Sit-by-the-Fire. So how would she make her place in the Weyr? Felena had enough cooks, and how often would the Weyr, used to meat when it wished, want to eat fish? Even if she knew more ways of preparing it than anyone else? When she came down to it, the only thing in which she excelled was gutting fish. No, she would not think about harpering anymore. Well, there had to be something she could do.

"Are you Menolly?" asked a man tentatively.

She looked up to see one of the minercraftsmen who'd shared her tier at the Impression.

"I'm Nicat, Masterminer of Crom Hold. Weyrwoman Lessa said that I was to have two fire lizard eggs."

Beyond his stiff manner, Menolly could see he was restraining an eager impatience to hold fire lizard eggs of his own.

"Indeed I have sir, right here," she said, smiling warmly at him and indicating the table-protected basket.

"Well, my word," and his manner thawed visibly, "you're taking no chances, are you."

He helped her move the table and watched anxiously as she brushed back the top layer of sand and exposed the first of the eggs.

"Could I have a queen egg?" he asked.

"Master Nicat, Lessa explained to you that there's no way of telling which is which among the fire lizard eggs," said T'gellan, joining them to Menolly's intense relief. "Of course, Menolly might have a way of telling . . ."

"She might?" Masterminer Nicat regarded her with surprise.

"She's Impressed nine, you know."

31 "Nine?" Master Nicat frowned at her now, and she could practically read his mind: nine for a child, and only two for the Masterminer?

"Pick Master Nicat two of the best, Menolly! We don't want him to be disappointed." Although T'gellan's face was sober, Menolly caught the expression in his eyes.

She managed to conduct herself with property dignity and made a play of picking out just the right eggs for Masterminer Nicat, all the while being certain in her own mind that the queen egg was going to Masterharper Robinton only.

"Here you are, sir," she said, handing Masterminer Nicat the furry pouch with its precious contents. "You'd best carry them in your riding jacket, against your skin, on the way home."

"Then what do I do?" Master Nicat asked with humility as he held the sack in both hands against his chest.

Menolly looked at T'gellan, but both men were looking at her. She gulped.

"Well, I'd do exactly what we're doing here. Keep them near the hearth in a strong basket with either hot sand or furs. The Weyrwoman said they'd be hatching in about a sevenday. Feed them as soon as they break their shells, as much as they can eat, and talk to them all the time. It's important to . . ." She faltered; how could she tell this hard-faced man that you had to be affectionate and kind . . .

"You must reassure them constantly. They're nervous when they're first hatched. You saw the dragons today. Touch them and stroke them . . ." The Masterminer was nodding as he catalogued her instructions. "They must be bathed daily, and their skins must be oiled. You can always tell when a crack is developing from scaly patches on the hide. And they keep scratching themselves . . ."

Master Nicat turned questioningly to T'gellan.

"Oh, Menolly knows what to do. Why, she has her fire lizards singing tunes along with her and all . . ."

T'gellan's airy assurance did not sit too well with the Masterminer.

"Yes, but how do you get them to come to you?" he asked pointedly.

"You make them *want* to come back to you," Menolly said so firmly that she rated one of the Miner's daunting frowns.

"Kindness and affection, Master Nicat, are the essential ingredients," T'gellan said

Dragonsong 1015

31 **Discussion** How can Menolly "practically read" Master Nicat's mind?

32 **Discussion** What accounts for the change in Master Nicat's attitude as he continues to speak to Menolly?

33 Discussion What opinions about the Half-Circle and Yanus does Elgion now hold?

34 Discussion What does Elgion decide to do on his return to the Sea Hold?

with equal force. "Now I see that T'gran is waiting to escort you, and your fire lizards, back to Crom." And he led the Masterminer off.

When T'gellan returned to Menolly, his eyes were dancing.

"I'll wager you my new tunic that one won't keep a fire lizard. Cold clod, that's what he is. Numbwit!"

"You shouldn't have said that about my fire lizards singing with me."

"Why not?" T'gellan was surprised at her criticism. "Mirrim hasn't done that much with her three, and she's had them longer. I told . . . Ah, yes, Craftmaster, F'lar did indeed say that you're to have a fire lizard egg."

And so the evening went, with lucky eager Holders and craftsmen arriving to collect the precious fire lizard eggs. By the time only Masterharper Robinton's eggs remained in the warm sands of the basket, Menolly had become resigned to hearing T'gellan's wheeze that she had taught her fair of fire lizards to sing. Fortunately no one asked her to put it to the test, since her weary friends were curled up on their wall perches. They hadn't roused from sleep for all the singing and laughter at the merry tables in the Bowl.

33 Harper Elgion was thoroughly enjoying the Impression Feast. He hadn't realized how dour Half-Circle Hold was until this evening. Yanus was a good man, a fine Sea Holder to judge by the respect his Holders accorded him, but he certainly knew how to take the joy out of living.

34 When Elgion had sat in the Hatching Ground, watching the young boys Impress, he'd determined that he'd find a fire lizard clutch of his own. That would alleviate the gloom at Half-Circle. And he'd see that Alemi got an egg, too. He'd heard from his neighbors in the tiers that the clutch being distributed this evening to the fortunate had been found down the coast from Half-Circle Sea Hold by T'gellan. Elgion had promised himself a chat with the bronze dragonrider; but T'gellan had had two passengers aboard Monarth when he'd collected Elgion at Half-Circle so there'd been no opportunity to talk. Elgion hadn't seen the man since the Hatching. But he'd bide his time.

Meanwhile, Oharan, the Weyr Harper, had Elgion playing guitar with him to amuse the visitors.

Elgion had just finished another tune with Oharan and some of the other visiting Harpers when he caught sight of T'gellan, assisting a craftsman to mount a green dragon. It was then that Elgion noticed that the visitors were thinning out and this rare evening was drawing to a close. He'd speak with T'gellan, and then seek out the Masterharper, too.

"Over here, man," he said, beckoning to the bronze rider.

"Oh, Elgion, a cup of wine, please. I'm parched with talking. Not that it'll do those cold clods much good. They've no feeling for fire lizards at all."

"I heard you found the clutch. It wasn't in that cave by the Dragon Stones, was it?"

"By the Dragon Stones? No. Way down the coast in fact."

"Then there wasn't anything there?" Elgion was so bitterly disappointed that T'gellan gave him a long look.

"Depends on what you were expecting. Why? What did you think would be in that cave if it didn't hold fire lizard eggs?"

Elgion wondered briefly if he would be betraying Alemi's confidence. But it had become a matter of his professional honor to know if the sounds he'd heard from that cave had been made by pipes.

"The day Alemi and I saw the cave from the boat, I could have sworn I heard pipes. Alemi insisted it was wind over blow holes in the cliff, but there wasn't that much wind that day."

1016   The Novel

Grammar in Action

Writers use **prepositional phrases** as modifiers. Prepositional phrases can be used in the same ways as individual adverbs and adjectives. Notice how Anne McCaffrey uses prepositional phrases in these sentences from *Dragonsong*.

He had not realized how dour Half-Circle Hold was *until this evening*. (The prepositional phrase is used as an adverb telling *when* he had *realized*.)

Elgion had promised himself a chat *with the bronze dragonrider*. (The prepositional phrase is used as an adjective to describing the *chat*.)

Note: Sometimes a word is used both as a preposition and as an adverb.

The harper walked *by*. (adverb)
The harper walked *by* the dragon cave. (preposition)

The word *to* is a preposition. However, the word *to* also begins infinitive phrases.

The fire lizard flew *to* the top of the wall. (prepositional phrase)
The fire lizard flew *to* escape Thread. (infinitive phrase)

"No," T'gellan said, seeing a chance to tease the Harper, "you heard pipes. I saw 'em when I searched the place."

"You found pipes? Where was the player?"

"Sit down. Why're you so excited?"

"Where's that player?"

"Oh, here at Benden Weyr."

Elgion sat down again, so deflated and disappointed that T'gellan forbore to tease him further.

"Remember the day we rescued you from Thread?" T'gran brought someone in as well."

"The lad?"

"That was no lad. That was a girl. Menolly. She'd been living in the cave . . . Now, what's the matter?"

"Menolly? Here? Safe? Where's the Masterharper? I've got to find Master Robinton. Come, T'gellan, help me find him!"

35 Elgion's excitement was contagious and though he was mystified, T'gellan joined the search. Taller than the young Harper, T'gellan spotted Master Robinton in deep conversation with Manora at a quiet table in the Bowl.

"Sir, sir, I've found her," Elgion cried, dashing up to them.

"Have you now? The love of your life?" asked Master Robinton amiably.

"No, sir. I've found Petiron's apprentice."

"Her? The old man's apprentice was a girl?"

Elgion was gratified by the Masterharper's surprise and grabbed at his hand, quite prepared to drag the man after him to search.

"She ran away from the Sea Hold, because they wouldn't let her make music, I think. She's Alemi's sister . . . "

"What's this about Menolly?" asked Manora, obstructing Elgion's flight with the Harper.

"Menolly?" Robinton raised his hand to silence Elgion. "That lovely child with the nine fire lizards?"

"What do you want of Menolly, Master Robinton?" Manora's voice was so stern that the Harper was brought up sharp.

He took a deep breath. "My much respected Manora, old Petiron sent me two songs written by his 'apprentice'; two of the loveliest melodies I've heard in all my Turns of harpering. He asked were they any good . . . " Robinton raised his eyes heavenward for patience, "I sent word back immediately, but the old man had died. Elgion found my message unopened when he got to the Sea Hold, and then he couldn't find the apprentice. The Sea Holder gave him some folderol about a fosterling who'd returned to his own Hold. What's distressing you, Manora?"

"Menolly. I knew something had broken that girl's heart, but not what. She may not be able to play, Master Robinton. Mirrim says there's a dreadful scar on her left hand."

"She can, too, play," said T'gellan and Elgion together.

"I heard the sound of multiple pipes coming from that cave," Elgion said hurriedly.

"I saw her hide those pipes when we cleared out her cave," T'gellan added. "And furthermore, she's taught her fire lizards to sing, too."

"She has!" Bright sparks lit the Masterharper's eyes, and he turned purposefully towards the kitchen cavern.

"Not so fast, Masterharper," said Manora. "Go softly with that child." 36

"Yes, I saw that, too, when we were chatting this evening, and now I understand what was inhibiting her. So how to proceed cautiously?" The Masterharper frowned and gazed at T'gellan so long that the bronze rider wondered what he'd done wrong. "How do you know she's taught her fire lizards to sing?"

"Why, they were singing along with her and Oharan last night."

Dragonsong   1017

35 Discussion For what reason is T'gellan so mystified?

36 Discussion Why does Manora tell the Masterharper to "go softly" with Menolly?

Student Activity 1. Identify the prepositional phrase in each sentence that follows. Tell whether each phrase is used as an adjective or an adverb.
1. Oharan had Elgion playing the guitar with him to amuse the visitors.
2. The Masterharper spoke to Manora about Menolly's songs.
3. Menolly had been living in a cave with the fire lizards.
4. Master Robinton was a man with a rich voice and many talents.

Student Activity 2. Add a prepositional phrase to each of the sentences that follow.
1. Elgion was worried.
2. T'gellan told Elgion some welcome news.
3. Robinton was surprised.
4. Menolly was shy.

Electronic Handbook You might want students to review facts about prepositional phrases, adjectives, and adverbs before completing the Grammar in Action activities. If students have access to the Language Master 6000, have them enter the access words *preposition, phrase, adjective,* or *adverb* and press the GRAMMAR key to find information on these topics.

37 **Discussion** What do you think of Oharan's plan to "trap" Menolly?

38 **Discussion** What reasons does Menolly give for not being able to play?

"Hmmm, now that's very interesting. Here's what we shall do."

Menolly was tired now, and most of the visitors had left. Still the Masterharper did not appear to collect his fire lizard eggs. She wouldn't leave until she'd seen him again. He'd been so kind; she hugged to herself the memory of their meeting. It was hard for her to believe that the Masterharper of Pern had carried her, Menolly of . . . Menolly of the Nine Fire Lizards. She propped her elbows up on the table and rested her head on her hands, feeling the rough scar against her left cheek and not even minding that at the moment.

She didn't hear the music at first; it was soft, as if Oharan was playing to himself at a nearby table.

"Would you sing along with me, Menolly?" asked Oharan softly, and she looked up to see him taking a place at the table.

Well, no harm in singing. It would help keep her awake until the Masterharper arrived. So she joined in. Beauty and Rocky roused at the sound of her voice, but Rocky went back to sleep after a peevish complaint. Beauty, however, dropped down to Menolly's shoulder, her sweet soprano trill blending with Menolly's voice.

"Do sing another verse, Menolly," said Manora, emerging from the shadows of the darkened cavern.

She took the chair opposite Menolly, looking weary, but sort of peaceful and pleased. Oharan struck the bridging chords and started the second verse.

"My dear, you have such a restful voice," Manora said when the last chord died away. "Sing me another one and then I'm away."

Menolly could scarcely refuse, and she glanced at Oharan to see what she should sing.

"Sing this one along with me," the Weyr Harper said, his eyes intent on Menolly's as his fingers struck an opening chord. Menolly knew the song, which had such an infectious rhythm that she began to sing before she realized why it was so familiar. She was also tired and not expecting to be trapped, not by Oharan and certainly not by Manora. That's why she didn't realize at first what Oharan was playing. It was one of the two songs she'd jotted down for Petiron: the ones he'd said he'd sent to the Masterharper.

She faltered.

"Oh, don't stop singing, Menolly," Manora said, "it's such a lovely tune."

"Maybe she should *play* her own song," said someone standing just behind Menolly in the shadow; and the Masterharper walked forward, holding out his own gitar to her.

"No! no!" Menolly half-rose, snatching her hands behind her back. Beauty gave a startled squawk and twined her tail about Menolly's neck.

"Won't you please play it . . . for me?" asked the Harper, his eyes entreating her.

Two more people emerged from the darkness: T'gellan, grinning fit to crack his face wide open, and Elgion! How did he know? From the gleam of his eyes and his smile, he was pleased and proud. Menolly was frightened and hid her face in confusion. How neatly she had been tricked!

"Don't be afraid now, child," said Manora quickly, catching Menolly's arm and gently pressing her back into the chair. "There's nothing for you to fear now: for yourself or your rare gift of music."

"But I can't play . . . " She held up her hand. Robinton took it in both of his, gently fingering the scar, examining it.

"You can play, Menolly," he said quietly, his kind eyes on hers, as he continued to stroke her hand, much as she would have caressed her frightened Beauty. "Elgion heard you when you were playing the pipes in the cave."

"But I'm a girl . . . " she said. "Yanus told me . . . "

39 **Discussion** Why does Master Robinton want Menolly's fire lizards in the Harperhall?

Reader's Response Menolly's encounter with Master Robinton is certainly serendipitous. In her place, how would you have felt and acted when you realized who he was?

Thematic Response Menolly's awakening is certainly to a different and more wonderful world. She is about to realize a wonderful ambition. Do you think that there are more "awakenings" in store for Menolly?

"As to that," replied the Masterharper somewhat impatiently, though he smiled as he spoke, "if Petiron had had sense enough to tell me that that was the problem, you might have been spared a great deal of anguish: and I certainly would have been spared a great deal of trouble searching all Pern for you. Don't you *want* to be a Harper?" Robinton ended on such a wistful, distressed note that Menolly had to reassure him.

"Oh yes, yes. I want music more than anything else in the world . . . " On her shoulder, Beauty trilled sweetly and Menolly caught her breath sharply in distress.

"Now what's the matter?" asked Robinton.

"I've got fire lizards. Lessa said I belong in the Weyr."

"Lessa will not tolerate *nine singing* fire lizards in her Weyr," said the Harper in a voice that brooked no contradiction. "And they *do* belong in my Harperhall. You've a trick or two to teach me, my girl." He grinned down at her with such mischief dancing in his eyes that she smiled timorously back at him. "Now," and he waggled a finger at her, in mock seriousness, "before you can think of any more obstacles, arguments or distractions, will you kindly bundle up my fire lizard eggs, get whatever you have, and let us be off to the Harperhall? This has been a day of many tiring impressions."

His hand pressed hers reassuringly, and his kind eyes urged her acquiescence. All Menolly's doubts and fears dissolved in an instant.

Beauty bugled, releasing the stranglehold of her tail about Menolly's neck. Beauty called again, rousing the rest of the fair, her voice echoing Menolly's joy. She rose slowly to her feet, her hand clinging to the Harper's for support and confidence.

"Oh, gladly will I come, Master Robinton," she said, her eyes blurred by happy tears.

And nine fire lizards bugled a harmonious chorus of accord!

Dragonsong   1019

ANSWERS TO RESPONDING TO THE SELECTION

Your Response

1. You might want to ask the students to recall the many different aspects of life in the Weyr, such as the existence of dragons and dragonriders.
2. You might ask students to consider both human and animal characters and to remember some facts about them.

Recalling

3. He is the Masterharper of Pern.

Interpreting

4. (a) The Hatching supplies Pern with the dragons needed to fight Thread. (b) The girl or woman who Impresses the queen dragon becomes the Weyrwoman, who is the partner of the Weyrleader and the most important woman in the Weyr.
5. Menolly is afraid that Elgion will tell her parents where she is and that they will take her back to the Hold.
6. Menolly does not realize how good her songs are.
7. Oharan knows that Menolly is too shy to sing the songs without his tricking her.

Applying

8. Discuss with students the idea that Menolly can now settle down to the task of developing her talent. Ask students if it is important to know your talents—and your limitations—before setting goals for yourself.

ANSWERS TO ANALYZING LITERATURE

1. Menolly is searching for personal fulfillment throughout the novel because she wants to be able to sing and play her music.
2. Other themes include the struggle for survival against nature [Thread], the search for happiness, longing for a true home, and many others.

RESPONDING TO THE SELECTION

Your Response

1. What aspect of life in the Weyr do you find most interesting? Explain your answer.
2. Which character in the novel would you like as a friend? Why?

Recalling

3. Who is Master Robinton?

Interpreting

4. (a) Why is the Hatching such an important event on Pern? (b) What is the significance of Impressing a queen dragon?
5. Explain why Menolly tries to avoid being seen by Harper Elgion.
6. Why does Menolly feel that she cannot ask Master Robinton about her songs?
7. Why does Oharan feel it necessary to trick Menolly into singing her own song?

Applying

8. What do you think will happen to Menolly at Harperhall? Explain your answer.

ANALYZING LITERATURE

Understanding Universal Themes

Universal themes are the ideas in a literary work that embody basic human experience. Everyone struggles for survival, searches for love, and longs for personal fulfillment. When you encounter such themes in literature, they are familiar because they are a reflection of your own personal experience.

1. In what way is the search for personal fulfillment a theme of *Dragonsong*?
2. What other themes have you found in this novel?

CRITICAL THINKING AND READING

Evaluating a Novel

In order to evaluate a novel, you must have standards, or criteria, against which to judge the

---

author's work. You must ask yourself: Are the characters interesting? Do I believe in their motivation? Is the plot well paced and does it involve me, the reader? Has the author made the setting believable? Given the setting, are the events that take place *probable*? (In an imaginative setting, the events need not be scientifically *possible*. They must only follow the rules that the author sets forth.) Are the details consistent?

1. Which details make Menolly's behavior at Half-Circle Sea Hold believable?
2. How does the author make the behavior of fire lizards seem logical and natural?

THINKING AND WRITING

Writing a Critique

Write a critique of the novel based on the criteria mentioned in the Critical Thinking and Reading activity. The first paragraph of your critique should present your general impression of the novel. The following paragraphs should present examples to support your statements. The last paragraph should summarize your statements and restate the ideas in the opening paragraph.

LEARNING OPTIONS

1. **Writing.** Menolly has many reasons to be happy now that she is going to live at Harperhall. Write a song that Menolly might write to express her happiness. Set your song to some familiar piece of music. When you have finished writing your song, ask some classmates to join you in performing the song for your fellow students.
2. **Writing.** Reading *Dragonsong* has given you many pointers on how to raise dragons. Write a *Guide to the Care and Training of Dragons*. Include details from the story, and make up any information that you consider appropriate. Illustrate your guide with helpful pictures and diagrams, and design an appealing cover. When your guide is complete, display it in the classroom.

ANSWERS TO CRITICAL THINKING AND READING

1. Her behavior is believable because of the repressive nature of Yanus and the willingness of Mavi to carry out her husband's wishes.
2. The author establishes that dragons are telepathic. Once the reader accepts that, the fire lizards behave consistently with the author's premise. Also they are physically similar to Earth lizards [eggs, warm sand for hatching, etc.]

THINKING AND WRITING

Software If students are working on computers, you may wish to have them use the **Writer's Helper** activity *Paragraph Development* to help them revise their critiques.

Alternative Assessment *Collaborative Assessment:* Ask students to review the questions in Responding to the Selection and

Critical Thinking and Reading. Have them meet in groups of three to discuss the themes they found in the novel. In their groups they should brainstorm for the specifics of how the author develops that theme. Have each group then write one essay. Encourage students to include specific incidents as well as relevant quotes from the story. Students should exchange essays with other groups for peer reviews before revising.

MULTICULTURAL CONNECTION
The Dragon Myth Throughout the World

Strange creatures? Perhaps the most unusual thing about these creatures that never existed is that they seem to be part of the folklore of nearly every culture in the world. Such different people as the Vikings and the Chinese, for example, carved the heads of dragons on the front of their ships. Dragon myths apparently go back to a time well before recorded history. They may have begun in the Middle East and traveled from there. The Babylonians' *Creation Epic* held that one of the two original elements from which the earth was formed was dragon-like.

Symbol of evil. The Old Testament makes several references to the dragon. By the Middle Ages, European Christians had come to associate dragons with Satan and viewed them as symbols of sin and evil. Many angels and saints were represented as battling dragons.

Symbols of good fortune. At the same time, in some cultures dragons were believed to offer valuable benefits to humans. Invincibility was one. According to legend, after the Germanic hero Siegfried slew the dragon Fafnir, he became invincible by bathing in the dragon's blood. In Germany dragon's blood was also believed to cure a variety of ills, including blindness and kidney stones.

Dragons in different cultures. The Chinese *Lung Wang*, or Dragon Kings, were believed to live in the heavens and the oceans and to be responsible for rain. The dragon is one of the twelve animals in the Chinese Zodiac: Every twelfth year is called the Year of the Dragon. It is the Chinese symbol of strength and goodness and, according to Chinese custom, is featured each year at the head of the traditional New Year's parade.

The dragon is also part of the Vietnamese Mid-Autumn Festival, the biggest holiday for children in Vietnam. Dragons made of paper and silk are carried through the streets by dancers, who are accompanied by children.

The dragon reached Japan from China and, just as in China, is believed to govern rainfall. In Japan it is considered to be the most important mythological beast and often appears in legends and fairy tales. Featured extensively in Japanese art, the dragon is also often used in ornamentation.

Although in China and Japan dragons were thought to control water, in other cultures they were depicted as fire-breathing creatures and were linked to volcanoes. St. Brendan of Ireland, a traveler who is believed to have visited America long before Columbus, reported that there were many dragons along the coast of Iceland, an area with many volcanoes. Some traditions suggest a connection between dragons and earthquakes. For example, according to a Native American tale, California was formed when the Earth Dragon traveled south under the coastal waters. Legend has it that the dragon then lay down upon the land and was covered with earth. California earthquakes were thought to be caused by the stirring of this dragon.

Exploring on your own

Do you know any legends that include dragons? Which country do these legends come from? Are the dragons a symbol of good or evil? Share these stories with your classmates.

Multicultural Connection 1021

1. This activity will be challenging to both auditory and kinesthetic learners. You may extend this activity by asking some students to illustrate some scenes to explain the lyrics.
2. Visual learners will enjoy this activity as they draw on their imaginations. Kinesthetic learners will enjoy making the book. You might want to extend the activity by having students insert songs in appropriate places, much as the author of *Dragonsong* did at the beginning of chapters.

Presentation

As students read this feature, suggest that they make a chart comparing and contrasting the traits of dragons in myths and stories that come from different parts of the world.

Suggest that they compare the dragons in historical myths and stories to the dragons in *Dragonsong*.

Motivation/Prior Knowledge

Ask students to share ideas they had about dragons before they read *Dragonsong*. Why is it that myths and stories about a creature that never existed are pervasive throughout the world? Why have diverse people invented a similar creature?

Closure and Extension

Have students research for reports of contemporary "sightings" of dragons. The giant Loch Ness monster in Scotland, for example, is spotted occasionally in the lake by people who believe that it may be a dragon.

ONE WRITER'S PROCESS

Anne McCaffrey and Dragonsong

PREWRITING

The Persistent Character Years ago, when Anne McCaffrey tried to make Menolly the main character in a short story, she ran into a problem. "The story plain wouldn't *write*," says McCaffrey. She went on to other projects. Then her publisher requested a novel about a young girl growing up on Pern. "I bethought myself of Menolly, and took out my notes," relates McCaffrey. "I recast the story in a new framework and the story took off. . . . Stories do this now and then and the author knows this is a run."

Dragonsong is set on Pern, the planet that McCaffrey had created in her previous novels *Dragonflight* and *Dragonquest*. Because of this, McCaffrey says, "I had my background, my rules, all the parameters necessary to write about a girl of a Hold, an isolated Hold where people might be more 'sot' in their ways and inflexible. Under those circumstances, Menolly's excellence as a musician would not be recognized, nor would she be encouraged. Conflict develops character and 'compulsion' motivates. If Menolly had not had a true gift, she would have knuckled under to her parents' demands. She did not. Therefore I have a plot and a story line."

Creating a Character McCaffrey modeled Menolly after two Irish teenagers she knew. One young woman served as the model for Menolly's appearance, the other for Menolly's personality and determination. McCaffrey says that her young friends "have always been very well pleased about their association with Menolly."

Creating a Plot McCaffrey asserts that "the situations in *Dragonsong* develop natu-

rally from Menolly's compulsion to compose and sing, and her unhappiness in a situation where she is unable to do so. "I don't *plan* novels, but I choose to start at a point where the characters are in contention with each other or with their society. In this case, it was Menolly in conflict with her immediate social group."

DRAFTING

Getting Started Anne McCaffrey claims that sitting in front of a computer keyboard is "a trigger for me to write." Writing is not always easy, though. "Sometimes," she admits, "I have to wind myself up to get on with the work in hand when it is being difficult and the story won't *write*."

"I've come to understand," she says, "that there are people who can put words together well but not all of these people can inject into words that special quality that makes readers want to continue reading. I use *emotion* as a tool of writing. Because I *believe* so strongly in what I am putting down on paper, it endures through all the mechanical phases which a book undergoes, and then hits the reader between the eyes with the emotion I was feeling when I first typed that scene.

"Most of all," says McCaffrey, "*I'm telling a story!*"

The Writer's Attitude McCaffrey believes that being overconfident while writing is not a good idea. She says that doubt "is a form of self-criticism and very useful if used constructively. I'm always sure I'm writing a good novel until I revise it and then I'm positive this is the worst novel I've ever written. This is a good attitude to take. I'm learning this craft with every new book or story I write. It's an ongoing process. I hope!"

Writing Scenes Like many authors, McCaffrey has her own techniques to help her to create a scene. "I do picture scenes as I write them: a spin-off from having done opera stage direction. . . . I know where everyone is in a particular scene, and if I don't, I make sure I visualize the 'stage' at some point so I know where 'I' am."

REVISING

Revising Every Day "To revise," relates McCaffrey, "I reread the previous day's work, even further back in the novel, to be sure I've details correctly. Basically, I revise as I go along—and then again when I'm [checking the spelling] at the end of a project. Mostly I revise dialogue, tighten scenes, and make sure phrases are in proper order."

Because McCaffrey no longer has the manuscript of *Dragonsong* in her possession (she donated the manuscript and rough draft to a library), she hasn't any notes of her revisions. She gives the excerpt that follows, however, as an example of her revision process. The paragraph is from a novel on which McCaffrey collaborated with fellow-writer Elizabeth Ann Scarborough. The novel is about a planet that has been terraformed—given an Earth-type environment. McCaffrey says: "In this particular section, our editor at Del Rey asked us to be more specific in our explanations."

McCaffrey revised the sentence this way:

PUBLISHING

Response to Dragonsong McCaffrey feels that *Dragonsong* is one of her better novels. She reread it recently for an audio book and decided it "wasn't half-bad, and stood up well."

McCaffrey says: "The comments I have received from readers are generally complimentary, but then people with objections to novels rarely write the author about them. I have letters from young girls identifying strongly with Menolly and suggesting they could play the part in a movie. Other youngsters have found that they could 'escape' to Pern . . . and reread the novels frequently for fun. That's [what] I like to hear."

THINKING ABOUT THE PROCESS

1. Why does McCaffrey find visualizing a scene so helpful? Do you think that visualizing could help you with your writing? Explain.
2. Why do you think that Menolly's story was easier to write in the form of a novel than it was as a short story? Explain.
3. **Cooperative Learning.** Anne McCaffrey places great emphasis on emotion in her writing. In a small group, look through the novel to find examples of the many different emotions Menolly feels. Make a chart that lists each emotion and the reason Menolly experiences it. Tell how McCaffrey creates these emotions. Share your chart with the class.

Since he [Dr. Fiske] understands the brief evolution of the planet better than anyone, he's decided to ~~personally~~ conduct *a personal* ~~an~~ investigation to rule out any malfunction ~~in this planet's development resulting from~~ *of* the terraforming process *on this planet* as a cause for the *aberrations* ~~aberrant circumstances~~ you mention.

ANSWERS TO THINKING ABOUT THE PROCESS

1. McCaffrey finds it useful to visualize a scene so that her descriptions of characters and their actions are logical and realistic.
2. Suggested Response: Menolly's situation is complicated. It requires some length to develop properly. A short story is too condensed to develop Menolly's situation and show her emotional growth.
3. After students have prepared and shared their charts, suggest that they keep the information in mind and apply it when they do their own writing.

Enrichment Point out to students that McCaffrey has written other novels about Pern. Have them speculate about other problems or situations that might provide a good conflict for a novel. Suggest that interested students read another Pern novel by McCaffrey and report on it to the class. You might consider assigning different McCaffrey novels to small groups.

Preparation

Motivation/Prior Knowledge

Students are probably familiar with eyewitness accounts from the television news. Courtroom dramas also use eyewitness accounts, which students may have seen in movies or on television programs. Elicit from students some comments about the manner in which eyewitnesses relate events. Are they objective? Are they specific about all the details, or do they recall some better than others? Do they share their emotional reactions? Do they offer their opinions about the causes of the events they have witnessed?

Focus Point out to students that in this assignment the writer is also the audience. While their diary entries will relate the facts, they will also be a tool by which the eyewitnesses clarify the events they have seen. They will draw some conclusions based on their information.

Presentation

Prewriting Making a map of the area where the episode occurred may help students to organize and describe the events. They can use the map to establish the vantage point from which the events were viewed and place numbers on the map to show the location of each event in sequence.

Writing Transparency You may use the paragraph exercise *Spatial Order* in **Transparencies for Writing** to demonstrate how students can organize their drafts to show the relationships between the events and locations.

Call students' attention to the Cause and Effect chart in the Graphic Organizers section of **Transparencies for Writing.** Assist them in discovering that all the entries in the Effect column are objective observations. Any

YOUR WRITING PROCESS

WRITING AN EYEWITNESS ACCOUNT

"The wastepaper basket is the writer's best friend."
Isaac Bashevis Singer

Imagine that you had witnessed an event in a novel you have read and then recorded your impressions in a diary. Certainly you would have reflected on the cause of the event and on its results. Why did these people act as they did? What was the outcome? These are the questions you would have tried to answer as you wrote your account of the events.

> **Focus**
>
> **Assignment:** As an eyewitness to an incident in a novel you have read, write a diary entry telling what you observed.
> **Purpose:** To describe the causes and effects of the characters' actions.
> **Audience:** Yourself.

Prewriting

1. Choose an event and an observer. Are there any episodes from the novel that are so vivid that they stay in your mind? One of these might be good to write about. Choose the character from whose perspective you will be writing. You may choose a major character or a minor character. You may even want to make up a character who was not mentioned by the author but who managed to witness the events.

2. Make a cause-and-effect chart. When you are writing about a chain of causes and effects, it is helpful to organize your thoughts.

> **Student Model**
>
> Observer: A man walking nearby when the two convicts were recaptured by soldiers (*Great Expectations*)
>
> | **Effect** | **Probable Cause** |
> | --- | --- |
> | Soldiers are running through the marsh. | They are chasing convicts. |
> | Soldiers capture two convicts who are fighting. | They might have escaped if they had not fought. |
> | Other convict claims first man was trying to kill him. | First man has a reason for beating the second. |

1024   The Novel

inferences that the observer makes are listed under Probable Cause. Instruct students to follow this model in organizing their own facts and opinions.

Drafting Encourage students to include all the information and opinions that occur to them. Stress the importance of getting it all down on paper. They can later revise the draft for clarity.

Software If students have access to computers, allow them to create their draft using **Bank Street Writer.** They can use the program's Cut and Paste features to rearrange their sentences in the revision stage.

Revising and Editing Instruct students to check for unity as well as accuracy. As students review their drafts, they may find that some sentences need to be moved to improve the coherence of paragraphs.

Once students have revised the structure of their account, they can enhance the style and tone by adding modifying words and phrases.

3. Remember, you are not all-knowing. Whichever character you choose, keep in mind that this character won't know everything about the events. He or she will only be able to observe and to make inferences about these observations.

Drafting

1. Use your cause-and-effect chart. When you are describing a series of events, many of the sentences you write will contain both a cause and an effect. As you write, be sure that you have explained what happened in a logical sequence.

2. Mention your own reactions. This is an eyewitness account. As a participant in the action, you will naturally have personal reactions to what has occurred. Because you are writing in a diary, you will want to indicate your feelings. Were you afraid or excited as the events unfolded? What did you think of the other participants?

Revising and Editing

1. Check for accuracy. Compare your account with the author's description in the novel. Have you recorded the events in the proper sequence?

2. Add details and words to show cause and effect. Have you included enough personal details to make the account seem as though it were written by an eyewitness? You might even want to make up details so that your diarist seems like a real person. Also, make sure you have included words that show cause-and-effect relationships.

Student Model

Because ~~^~~ As I was crossing the marsh, _to visit George's farm_ some armed soldiers _I was in the right place to see_ ~~ing~~ rushed past me. _I guessed they were chasing convicts and sure enough_ They found the two convicts in a ditch.

One convict was beating the other.

3. Exchange accounts with a partner. Ask yourselves the following questions:
- Is the account in the proper sequence?
- Is it consistently told from the point of view of one observer?
- Has the writer added personal details?
- Are causes and effects clearly indicated?

Remember to mention the good things about the account in addition to making helpful criticisms.

Closure and Extension

Guidelines for Evaluation You may consider the following questions as you evaluate each student's eyewitness account:

1. Does the student give an accurate account of the events as they are described in the novel?

2. Are details used to give a vivid impression of the setting and action?

3. Does the student write consistently from the perspective of the observer?

4. Does the character make inferences based on the facts?

5. Does the writer communicate the character's emotional and intellectual reactions to the events?

6. Is the account dated and in the form of a diary entry?

7. Is the diary entry free of errors in spelling, punctuation, and grammar?

Reviewing Your Writing Process The following Protocol will help students reflect on and internalize their own writing process:

1. What incident from what novel have you written about in a diary?

2. From whose perspective do you record the events? Is your character mentioned by the author or created by you just to witness events?

3. Of the events you record, which are from the book and which are ones you have created to make you as the observer diarist seem more real?

Student Portfolios You may wish to have students keep their diary entries in the Writing Portfolios.

Enrichment Encourage students to keep journals that they use each day to record an observation and their reactions to the event they record. Ask students to share their reflections on the writing process, but allow the sharing of journal entries to remain optional.

Preparation

Motivation/Prior Knowledge

Distribute samples of various travel brochures. Use the samples to illustrate how pictures and text are used to communicate a message about the location. Elicit student comments on how colors, images, language, and overall design affect their impressions of the setting featured in the brochure.

Focus Call students' attention to the purpose of this assignment. Ask them to provide suggestions about the kinds of information that might induce them to visit a particular place. Suggestions may include climate, accommodations, unique customs, exciting events, and beautiful or unusual landscapes.

Presentation

Prewriting Prompt students to jot down adjectives as they list details in each of their categories. You may allow students to refer to the sample brochures for ideas.

Writing Transparency The *Sensory Language Chart* in **Transparencies for Writing** may help generate further ideas for descriptive language.

Assist students in assessing which categories in their notes will require the most space in their travel brochure. Show students how to use the book map to indicate where information will appear in the brochure.

Drafting Have students draft blocks of text on separate pieces of paper. They should create illustrations and headings independently. Students may experiment with these pieces to explore the visual impact of different arrangements.

Software If students have access to computers, allow time for them to try different type sizes

YOUR WRITING PROCESS

WRITING A TRAVEL BROCHURE

"The idea is to get the pencil moving quickly."
Bernard Malamud

Sometimes an author can make a setting sound so interesting that you wish you could visit it yourself. What features of the setting interest you? What attractions would you mention in a travel brochure to make tourists want to visit that time and place.

Focus

Assignment: Write a travel brochure for a place described in a novel.
Purpose: To encourage people to visit.
Audience: The general public.

Prewriting

1. Review the author's description of the setting. Skim the novel for any situations in which the setting is important. Remember that your brochure is not limited to a description of the scenery. The brochure will include references to food, special events, and atmosphere as well.

2. List the information you find. Make lists in various categories of all the details about the setting.

Student Model

For a brochure about Benden Weyr in *Dragonsong*:
Physical appearance: rocky mountainside, huge caverns, rooms carved out of rock, lit by glows.
Food: klah; wherry meat; sweet, spiced, and sour breads; meat stew; fish stew; vegetables; fruit.
Animals: dragons, fire lizards.
Special events: Hatching Day, fighting Thread.
Atmosphere: friendly, exciting, full of danger.

3. Design your brochure. Most travel brochures have four to six pages. In addition to writing text, you will have to plan your illustrations and decide on the appearance of the project. You may wish to make a book map of your brochure.

to create their blocks of text.

Instruct students to identify a word or phrase for each section of text that conveys the controlling idea of the block. The word or words can be displayed in large colorful letters to draw the reader's attention to the information in the text.

Revising and Editing Ask students to consider the power of their language. Encourage them to look for places where a stronger or more specific word can replace a neutral or general one.

Peer editors can help identify the most effective sections of the brochure. The editors should offer specific reasons why these sections are successful, so that the techniques can be incorporated into other areas. Students should solicit reactions to the design from peer editors as well.

Student Model

Page 1	Page 2	Page 3	Page 4
Main reasons to visit	Special events	Atmosphere: dragons, danger	Food, places to stay

Drafting

1. Begin with the main points. A brochure should get to the point right away. You may wish to begin with questions or statements that will invite the reader to look inside for more information. The first page of your brochure should provide a good notion of the place you are advertising.

Student Model

BENDEN WEYR
FOR THE EXPERIENCE OF A LIFETIME!
Watch dragons hatch and be Impressed!
See brave dragonmen and dragonwomen fight deadly Thread!
Eat and sleep in caverns that house the mighty dragons of Benden Weyr.

2. Follow your book map. Use your plan as a guide to developing the rest of your brochure. On your first page, include all the details that you think a potential tourist would find exciting or interesting.

Revising and Editing

1. Add descriptive language. You want your reader to almost taste and feel the experience. As you edit your brochure, look for places to add sensory language.

2. Exchange brochures with a partner. As you read each other's work, ask yourselves these questions:
- Does the first page tell what the place is like?
- Do the pages that follow develop the ideas presented in the first page?
- Is the information provided in the brochure accurate?
- Is any important information missing?
- Did the writer use sensory language in the descriptions?

Grammar Tip

Remember that the comparative degree of adjectives is used to describe two things. The superlative degree is used when describing three or more things.

Options for Publishing

- Read your brochure aloud to the class.
- Post your illustrated brochure on a bulletin board in the classroom.
- Create a classroom travel agency. Put all your brochures on a table or shelf so that class members can examine them.

Reviewing Your Writing Process

1. Did you find it easy or difficult to convey a sense of the place you were describing? Explain.

2. Did working with a partner help you to improve your description? Why or why not?

Closure and Extension

Guidelines for Evaluation The following questions may help you evaluate each student's travel brochure:

1. Does the brochure demonstrate a knowledge of the setting as described in the novel?
2. Is the information organized into appropriate categories?
3. Does the layout achieve an appealing balance among text, illustrations, and headings?
4. Are the main points highlighted to focus the reader's attention?
5. Is the language powerfully descriptive?
6. Is the brochure free of errors in spelling and usage?

Reviewing Your Writing Process The following Protocol will help students reflect on and assess their own writing process:

1. What place from which novel do you describe in your travel brochure?
2. What details of the setting do you describe to intrigue a potential tourist?
3. What references to food, special events, atmosphere, etc. do you include?
4. What sensory language do you use to make the place you describe seem inviting and wonderful?
5. What reactions did your writing partner have to your brochure? What in your description made him or her want to visit this place?

Student Portfolios You may wish to have students keep their travel brochures in the writing portfolios.

Enrichment Take a tour! You might want to use the sample travel brochures to stimulate students' interest in different cultures and countries. Allow students with similar interests to form "tour groups." The groups should research their chosen city or country and prepare a presentation about their imaginary tour. Students might report their observations on the different customs, food, language, living conditions, and so on.

HANDBOOK OF THE WRITING PROCESS

Lesson 1: Prewriting

Writing is a process that involves several stages:

1. *Prewriting:* planning the work to be done
2. *Drafting:* putting ideas down on paper
3. *Revising:* reworking the written draft
4. *Proofreading:* checking for errors in spelling, mechanics, and manuscript form
5. *Publishing* (or sharing): giving others the opportunity to experience the writing

This lesson will explain the steps to be taken during the prewriting stage.

STEP 1: ANALYZE THE SITUATION

When you *analyze* something, you divide it into parts and then study these parts. When you have a piece of writing to do, begin by analyzing the writing situation into the following parts:

1. *Topic* (the subject you will be writing about): What, exactly, is this subject? Can you state it in a sentence? Is your subject too broad or too narrow?
2. *Purpose* (what you want the writing to accomplish): Is your purpose to explain? to describe? to persuade? to tell a story? What do you want the reader to take away from the writing?
3. *Audience* (the people who will be reading or listening to your work): What are the backgrounds of these people? Do they already know a great deal about your subject, or will you have to provide basic information?
4. *Voice* (the way the writing will sound to the reader): What impression do you want to make on your readers? What tone should the writing have? Should it be formal or informal? Should it be cool and reasoned or charged with emotion?
5. *Content* (the subject and all the information provided about the subject): How much do you already know about the subject? What will you have to find out? Will you have to do some research? What people, books, magazines, newspapers, or other sources can you consult?
6. *Form* (the shape that the writing will take, including its organization and its length): What will the final piece of writing look like? How long will it be? Will it be a single paragraph or several paragraphs? Will it take some special form such as verse or drama? In what order will the content be presented?

When you begin your prewriting, try to answer all these questions. Doing so will help you to clarify your goals. Some of the answers may already be provided for you. For example, a teacher might have given you a topic or a form to follow. However, many of the answers will be up to you. Writing always involves making decisions and choices.

STEP 2: MAKE A PLAN

When you have analyzed the writing situation and examined your goals, you will usually find that some of your questions remain unanswered or that some of your answers are incomplete. Therefore, the next step is to make a plan for answering all your questions completely. For example, if you are unsure about your topic, you might want to do some general reading about the topic, perhaps in an encyclopedia. If you are unsure about what content you want to include, you will have to make a plan for gathering the information you need.

STEP 3: GATHER INFORMATION

The content of a piece of writing—the ideas and information presented—can come from many different sources. Use the following methods to gather ideas and information:

1. *Freewriting:* Write out everything that comes to your mind when you think about the topic. Don't pause to punctuate or to think about spelling or proper form. Simply write, fast and furiously, for one to five minutes. Then study the freewriting for ideas that you can use.

2. *Clustering:* Write your topic in the middle of a piece of paper. Circle the topic. Then think about your topic and write down any other ideas that occur to you. Circle these ideas and draw lines connecting your ideas to the center circle. Continue in this manner until the page is full.

3. *Analyzing:* Break your subject down into parts. Study each part and describe it in your notes. Then look for relationships between the parts and between the parts and the whole.

4. *Questioning:* Make a list of questions about your topic. Begin the questions with *who, what, where, when, why,* and *how.* Then find the answers to your questions.

5. *Using outside sources:* Consult other people, books, and reference works.

6. *Making charts or lists:* Prepare charts or lists of information. For example, for a persuasive paragraph you might make a pros-and-cons chart. For a story you might make a time line or a list of events.

Note that all these techniques for gathering information can also be used to identify a topic in the first place.

STEP 4: ORGANIZE YOUR NOTES

Once you have gathered enough information, you'll need to organize your information logically. Often people organize their notes in *chronological order,* in *spatial order,* by *degree* (less to more or more to less), or in *order of importance, value,* or *familiarity.* Sometimes the topic itself suggests a possible organization. After organizing your notes, make a rough outline.

CASE STUDY: PREWRITING

George's English teacher asked the class to write a paragraph on some aspect of modern media. George decided to write about television. Here are some of his prewriting notes:

- Topic: television

- Purpose: to inform

- Audience: my English teacher and my classmates

- Voice: fairly formal, knowledgeable

- Content: not sure. Television is a pretty broad topic. I should be able to use a lot of my own knowledge about television.

- Form: single paragraph

George looked over his notes and decided that he would need a plan of action. First, his topic was too broad. Therefore, he made the following clustering chart to narrow his topic:

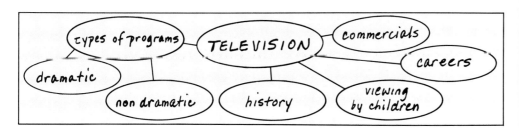

George decided to use the subject "nondramatic television programs" as the main topic of his paragraph. His purpose would be to explain the types of nondramatic programs. To gather the information he needed, George looked at a weekly programming directory. There he found several types of nondramatic programs—newscasts, interview programs, talk shows, game shows, educational children's programs, and specials of various kinds. Next, George made a chart with the headings "Type of Program," "Description," and "Example." Finally, he used the programming directory and his own knowledge to complete the chart.

George looked over his chart and decided that in his paragraph he would first introduce his topic—nondramatic television programs. Then he would use topic organization, describing each type of program in turn.

ACTIVITIES AND ASSIGNMENTS

A. Answer the following questions about the case study:

1. Find the section of George's notes in which he analyzed the writing situation. Which of his initial notes needed more fleshing out? Which were sufficient?
2. Why did George make a clustering diagram? Why did he make a chart? What purposes did these serve?

B. Choose one of the following topics or one of your own:

Mexico	computers
wild animals	games

Prepare to write a paragraph about your topic. Follow these steps:

1. Make notes about the topic, purpose, audience, voice, content, and form of your paragraph.
2. Look over your notes and decide what additional planning or research you need to do. Use prewriting techniques such as freewriting, clustering, analyzing, questioning, using outside sources, and making charts or lists to narrow your topic and to gather ideas.
3. Organize your notes and make a rough outline. Save your notes in your portfolio.

Lesson 2: Drafting and Revising

CHOOSING A METHOD FOR DRAFTING

After a writer has completed his or her prewriting notes, the next step is to begin drafting, or putting ideas on paper in rough form. When you draft, keep the following points in mind:

1. Choose a drafting method that you are comfortable with. Some writers like to plan very carefully, make a thorough outline, and then write slowly, correcting and polishing the work as they go. Other writers like simply to get all their ideas down on paper quickly and then to go back and worry about details. Either method—the slow draft or the quick one—is fine. The choice is up to you.

2. Whichever method you choose, don't worry about getting everything perfect at the drafting stage. A rough draft is not meant to be perfect. It is simply another step toward the final product. Concentrate on getting your ideas down. At this stage in the writing process, you needn't be overly concerned about proper spelling, punctuation, capitalization, and the like. You can take care of these matters later.

3. As you write, work from your prewriting notes and keep your audience and purpose in mind.

4. Do not be afraid to change your original plans during drafting. Some of the best ideas are ones that were not planned ahead of time. Feel free to add, delete, or change ideas as you write.

5. Write as many drafts as you like. As the writer Neil Simon once observed, writing is not like baseball, in which you have only three chances and then you're out. The nice thing about writing is that you can do it over and over until you've got it the way you want it.

CHECKLIST FOR REVISION

Topic and Purpose
- [ ] Is my topic clear?
- [ ] Does the writing have a specific purpose?
- [ ] Does the writing achieve its purpose?

Audience
- [ ] Will everything that I have written be clear to my audience?
- [ ] Will my audience find the writing interesting?
- [ ] Will my audience respond in the way I would like?

Voice, Word Choice
- [ ] Is the impression that my writing conveys the one that I intended it to convey?
- [ ] Is my language appropriately formal or informal?
- [ ] Have I avoided vague, undefined terms?
- [ ] Have I used vivid, specific nouns, verbs, and adjectives?
- [ ] Have I avoided jargon that my audience will not understand?
- [ ] Have I avoided clichés?
- [ ] Have I avoided slang, odd connotations, euphemisms, and gobbledygook (except for novelty or humor)?

Content/Development
- [ ] Have I avoided including unnecessary or unrelated ideas?
- [ ] Have I developed my topic completely?
- [ ] Have I supplied examples or details that support the statements that I have made?
- [ ] Are my sources of information unbiased, up-to-date, and authoritative?

Form
- [ ] Have I followed a logical method of organization?
- [ ] Have I used transitions, or connecting words, to make the organization clear?
- [ ] Does the writing have a clear introduction, body, and conclusion?

Drafting and Revising 1031

REVISING YOUR DRAFT

Once you have finished drafting, you are ready to revise. Revising is the process of re-working what you have written to make it as good as it can be. When revising your draft, ask yourself the questions in the Checklist for Revision on the previous page.

EDITORIAL SYMBOLS

When revising a rough draft, it is helpful to use the editorial symbols in the chart at the right.

CASE STUDY: DRAFTING AND REVISING

George used his notes from the preceding lesson to begin writing a rough draft of his paragraph. Here is the beginning of his uncorrected rough draft:

> There are many different types of nondra-matic programs. There are non-dramatic pro-grams that deal with current events. Including news reports, interview programs and specials of various kinds. There are also entertainment pro-grams such as talk shows and game shows. And there are also educational programs and spe-cials. First, about current events programs:

George stopped writing for a moment and looked at his draft. He observed that he had al-ready written quite a bit and that he had a lot more to say. At this rate, George thought, my par-agraph will be a hundred sentences long! He de-cided to narrow his topic and to include only cur-rent events programs. His topic would be "Nondramatic Television Programs Dealing With Current Affairs." He wrote a new rough draft based on this topic. Then he made revisions using the standard editorial symbols. George's rough draft with his corrections and revisions is shown on the next page.

ACTIVITIES AND ASSIGNMENTS

A. Answer the following questions about the revised rough draft shown on the next page:

1. Why did George delete material from his first two sentences?
2. In what places did George add new informa-tion to his draft?
3. Why did George add the words "in the" be-fore the word "nation"? What two phrases in

SYMBOL	MEANING	EXAMPLE
↶↷	move text	Never! shall never forget.
ℓ or ⟋	delete	for the the winter
∧	insert	too ∧ money (much)
⌒	close up; no space	space walk
⊙	insert period	few people⊙ She
⋏	insert comma	lions, tigers⋏ and bears
⌄	add apostrophe	dogs ⌄ tails
⌄⌄ ⌄⌄	add quotation marks	"The Necklace"
∼	transpose	to boldly go
¶	begin paragraph	him. When
/	make lower case	the new Principal
≡	capitalize	principal Marion Ohman

George's paragraph are parallel because of this change?

4. Why did George change the word "folks" to "viewers"?

5. What transitional word did George add to indicate that he was about to tell about the last of the types of programs?

6. Why did George change "are also good" to "serve a variety of purposes"?

7. Why did George delete "and things"?

8. Why did George change "things happening" to "situations of significance"?

9. What other revisions did George make? Why did he make them?

10. What errors still need to be corrected in George's paragraph?

B. Using your notes from the preceding lesson, draft a paragraph on your topic. Then revise your draft. Follow these steps in drafting and revising your paragraph.

1. If you haven't already done so, make a rough outline that shows how you will organize your paragraph. Your outline should include your main topic and two or three subtopics, or parts of the main topic. Under each subtopic, you should list the specific information, or details, that you will include in your paragraph.

2. Write an introductory sentence that presents your topic.

3. Based on your rough outline and your prewriting notes, quickly write out the body of your paragraph.

4. Write a conclusion of one or two sentences.

5. Use the checklist in this lesson to revise your draft. Make sure that you can answer "yes" to each of the questions. If your answer to a question is "no," use editorial symbols to make the necessary corrections.

Television keeps the American public informed by means of ~~special programs. These programs are~~ (nondramatic programs that deal with current events.) Including news reports, interview programs and specials of various kinds. News reports provide information about the daily events in the world and nation. Interview programs such as the Barbara Walters Specials, give ~~folks~~ *viewers* a chance to ~~see~~ *observe close up* the people who make the news. *Finally* Specials about current events ~~are also good. They~~ *serve a variety of purposes. Some* bring political candidates together for debates ~~and things.~~ *Others* ~~They~~ describe in depth political ~~things~~ *situations* *of significance* ~~happening~~ around the Globe. *Still others probe* ~~They tell about~~ controvershul issues facing ~~people~~ *voters and lawmakers*. Without programs such as these ~~where would we be?~~ *Americans would doubtless be less able to make informed, intelligent political decisions.*

Lesson 3: Proofreading and Publishing

PROOFREADING YOUR FINAL DRAFT

After you finish your final draft, the last step is to proofread the draft to make it ready for a reader. When you proofread the final draft, use the following checklist:

CHECKLIST FOR PROOFREADING

Grammar and Usage
- ☐ Are all of my sentences complete? That is, have I avoided sentence fragments?
- ☐ Do all of my sentences express only one complete thought? That is, have I avoided run-on sentences?
- ☐ Do the verbs I have used agree with their subjects?
- ☐ Have all the words in my paper been used correctly? Am I sure about the meanings of all of these words?
- ☐ Is the thing being referred to by each pronoun (I, me, this, each, etc.) clear?
- ☐ Have I used adjectives and adverbs correctly?

Punctuation
- ☐ Does every sentence end with a punctuation mark?
- ☐ Have I used commas, semicolons, colons, hyphens, dashes, parentheses, quotation marks, and apostrophes correctly?

Spelling
- ☐ Am I absolutely sure that each word has been spelled correctly?

Capitalization
- ☐ Have I capitalized any words that should not be capitalized?
- ☐ Should I capitalize any words that I have not capitalized?

Manuscript Form
- ☐ Have I indented the first line(s) of my paragraph(s)?
- ☐ Have I written my name and the page number in the top right-hand corner of each page?
- ☐ Have I double-spaced the manuscript?

If your answer to any of these questions is "no," make the necessary corrections on your paper. Refer to a dictionary, writing textbook, or handbook of style as necessary.

PUBLISHING, OR SHARING YOUR WORK

After you have proofread your final copy, it is ready to be shared with other people. Of course, much of the writing you do for school will be submitted by teachers. However, there are many other ways to share or publish your writing. The following are a few of these many ways:

1. Share your work in a small group.
2. Read your work aloud to the class.
3. Make copies for your parents, other relatives, or friends.
4. Have your work put on a class bulletin board.
5. Save your writing in your portfolio and, at the end of the year, bind the copies together into a booklet.
6. Submit your writing to the school literary magazine or start a literary magazine for your school or for your class.
7. Submit your writing to your school or community newspaper.
8. Enter your writing in literary contests for student writers.
9. Submit your writing to a magazine that publishes work by young people.

CASE STUDY: PROOFREADING AND PUBLISHING

After revising his final draft, George made a fresh, clean copy. Then he read the Checklist for Proofreading and applied each question to his revised draft. While doing this, he found some errors he had overlooked when revising. Look at

¶ Television keeps the American public informed by means of non-dramatic programs that deal
Such programs
with current events. *Including* news reports, interview programs, and specials of various kinds. News reports, such as the Macneil, Lerer News Hour, provide information about daily events in the world and in the nation. Interview programs such as the Barbara Walters Specials, give viewers a chance to observe, close up, the people who make the news. Finally, specials about current events serve a variety of purposes. Some bring political candidates together for debates. Others describe, in depth, political situations of significance around the globe. Still others
controversial
probe ~~controvershul~~ issues facing voters and lawmakers. Without programs such as these, Americans would doubtless be less able to make informed, intelligent political decisions.

George's paragraph with the proofreading corrections that he made (in the left-hand column).

George made a clean final copy of his paragraph. Then he shared his paragraph with other students in a small group discussion.

ACTIVITIES AND ASSIGNMENTS

A. Answer the following questions about the case study in this lesson:

1. What errors in spelling did George correct during proofreading?
2. What corrections on George's paper indicate the importance of checking the spellings of proper nouns such as names of people and places?
3. Which sentence fragment did he correct? How did he do this?
4. What punctuation errors did George correct?
5. What error in manuscript form did George correct?
6. Are there any changes that you think should still be made in George's paragraph? Explain.

B. Make a clean copy of your revised draft from the preceding lesson. Then use the Checklist for Proofreading to correct any errors that remain in your draft.

Share your proofread draft with your teacher and classmates.

HANDBOOK OF GRAMMAR AND REVISING STRATEGIES

STRATEGIES FOR REVISING PROBLEMS IN GRAMMAR AND USAGE
Problems of Sentence Structure

■ Run-on Sentences

GUIDE FOR REVISING: A run-on sentence results when no punctuation or coordinating conjunction separates two or more independent clauses. A run-on sentence also occurs when only a comma is used to join two or more independent clauses.

Strategy 1:	**Use a period to separate independent clauses, forming two sentences.**
First Draft	Much of Carl Sandburg's poetry is about the American worker, he also wrote a six-volume biography of Abraham Lincoln.
Revision	Much of Carl Sandburg's poetry is about the American worker. He also wrote a six-volume biography of Abraham Lincoln.

Strategy 2:	**Use a semicolon to separate independent clauses.**
First Draft	Clarke is a terrific science fiction writer he can present ordinary objects in a context that makes them seem unfamiliar.
Revision	Clarke is a terrific science fiction writer; he can present ordinary objects in a context that makes them seem unfamiliar.
Model From Literature	I should be an inconvenience at Joe's; I was not expected, and my bed would not be ready; . . . —*Dickens, p. 812*

Strategy 3:	**Join the sentences with a comma and a coordinating conjunction** *(and, but, or, for, yet, so).*
First Draft	The *Iliad* is a stirring tale, I prefer reading the *Odyssey*.
Revision	The *Iliad* is a stirring tale, but I prefer reading the *Odyssey*.
Model From Literature	That is his main fault, but on the whole he's a good worker. —*Conan Doyle, p. 74*

Strategy 4:	**Join the sentences with a semicolon and a conjunctive adverb.**
First Draft	Della loved Jim she gave him a thoughtful Christmas present.
Revision	Della loved Jim; consequently, she gave him a thoughtful Christmas present.

Handbook of Grammar and Revising Strategies   1037

Strategy 5:	**Make one clause subordinate by adding a subordinating conjunction.**
First Draft	She had practiced and prepared for many weeks she was nervous when the curtain went up.
Revision	Although she had practiced and prepared for many weeks, she was nervous when the curtain went up.
Model From Literature	When I shot some of his prize turkeys with it, he did not punish me; . . . *—Connell, p. 19*

■ Fragments

GUIDE FOR REVISING: A sentence fragment is an incomplete sentence. Although a fragment begins with a capital letter and ends with a period, it lacks a subject or a verb and does not express a complete thought.

Strategy 1:	**Add a subject and verb when necessary.**
First Draft	Mark Twain had an interesting past. Printer's apprentice, riverboat pilot, journalist, humorist, and author.
Revision	Mark Twain had an interesting past. He was a printer's apprentice, riverboat pilot, journalist, humorist, and author.

Strategy 2:	**If possible, omit the subordinating conjunction, or connect the fragment to an independent clause.**
First Draft	Because Sherlock Holmes was observant and rational. He was a brilliant detective.
Revision	Sherlock Holmes was observant and rational. He was a brilliant detective.
	or
	Because Sherlock Holmes was observant and rational, he was a brilliant detective.

■ Illogical Combination of Subject and Predicate

GUIDE FOR REVISING: The predicate of a sentence must be logically related to its subject.

Strategy 1:	**Rewrite the sentence so that the subject and predicate are logically related and compatible in meaning.**
First Draft	Reading "Sea-Fever" aloud is a sense of enjoyment.
Revision	Reading "Sea-Fever" aloud provides a sense of enjoyment.

Strategy 2:	Change an adverb clause to a noun clause or a noun phrase.
First Draft	A great expectation is when one is looking forward to something important.
Revision	A great expectation is a keen anticipation of something important.

Problems of Clarity and Coherence

■ Effective Transition

GUIDE FOR REVISING: Transitions are words or phrases that help the reader by signaling connections between words, sentences, and even paragraphs.

Strategy 1:	Use transitions to show logical relationships. Transitions may be used to introduce another item in a series, an illustration or an example, a result or a cause, a restatement, a conclusion or a summary, or an opposing point.
First Draft	I don't usually enjoy poetry. I liked "Casey at the Bat."
Revision	I don't usually enjoy poetry. Nevertheless, I liked "Casey at the Bat."
Model From Literature	Paradoxically, some of the victims with the worst injuries eventually recovered, while others who appeared unscathed suddenly died. —Anderson, p. 132

Strategy 2:	Use transitions to indicate time relationships, such as sequence or progression in time. Translations may be used to indicate frequency, duration, a particular time, the beginning, the middle, the end, and beyond.
First Draft	Skelton watches for the Loch Ness monster.
Revision	Day after day, Skelton watches for the Loch Ness monster.
Model From Literature	Afterward we left our people crying there, for we were going very far across the big water. —Black Elk, p. 422

Strategy 3:	Use transitions to indicate relationships in space. Transitions may be used to indicate closeness, distance, and direction.
First Draft	He reads Shakespeare's plays.
Revision	Under the sycamore tree, he reads Shakespeare's plays.
Model From Literature	Outside the church, as the procession was forming to go to the graveyard, Dr. Frazier came up to his grandmother and asked how she was. —Moss, p. 113

Handbook of Grammar and Revising Strategies 1039

■ Incomplete and Illogical Comparisons

GUIDE FOR REVISING: When something is left out of a comparison or only implied, the comparison is incomplete and illogical.

Strategy 1: **Be sure that a comparison contains only items of a similar kind.**

First Draft   The report of a journalist is likely to be more factual than a poet.

Revision   The report of a journalist is likely to be more factual than a poet's.

Strategy 2: **Be sure to include the words *other* or *else* in comparisons that compare one of a group with the rest of the group.**

First Draft   Julia found *Great Expectations* more satisfying than any Dickens novel she'd read.

Revision   Julia found *Great Expectations* more satisfying than any other Dickens novel she'd read.

Strategy 3: **Check to see if the words *better, less, more,* and *worse* and words formed with the suffix *-er* signal the need for a fully stated comparison; if so, use *than* and explain the comparison completely.**

First Draft   Odysseus' revenge was more complete.

Revision   Odysseus' revenge was more complete than I had anticipated.

Model From Literature   Lau Po, as he allowed me to call him, turned out to be a much better player than my brothers. —*Tan, p. 43*

■ Pronoun-Antecedent Agreement

GUIDE FOR REVISING: A personal pronoun must agree with its antecedent in number (singular or plural), person (first, second, or third), and gender (masculine, feminine, or neuter).

Strategy 1: **When you use a pronoun to stand for a noun that appears somewhere else in the sentence, check to see that it agrees in number (singular or plural) with that noun.**

First Draft   Suspense and the supernatural fascinate Joan Aiken, and it often appears in her writing.

Revision	Suspense and the supernatural fascinate Joan Aiken, and they often appear in her writing.
Model From Literature	The creature swims with remarkable speed, as much as ten or fifteen knots when it is really moving. —*McPhee, p. 462*

Strategy 2:	**(a) When you use a pronoun to stand for two or more singular nouns joined by *or* or *nor*, make sure it is singular.**
First Draft	Neither Tonya nor Lynn gave their report on Christina Rossetti today.
Revision	Neither Tonya nor Lynn gave her report on Christina Rossetti today.
	(b) When you use a pronoun to stand for two or more nouns joined by *and*, make sure it is plural.
First Draft	T. S. Eliot and James Joyce did some of his best work in the years between the world wars.
Revision	T. S. Eliot and James Joyce did some of their best work in the years between the world wars.
Model From Literature	The king and his court were in their places, opposite the twin doors —those fateful portals, so terrible in their similarity! —*Stockton, p. 51*

Strategy 3:	**When you use a personal pronoun to stand for a singular indefinite pronoun, make sure it is also singular.**
First Draft	Joan Didion and Ellen Harkins Wheat are noted American writers; each has chosen an American painter as the subject of their essay.
Revision	Joan Didion and Ellen Harkins Wheat are noted American writers; each has chosen an American painter as the subject of her essay.
Model From Literature	Each had a rifle in his hand, . . . —*Saki, p. 34*

■ Dangling Modifiers

GUIDE FOR REVISING: A prepositional phrase or a participial phrase should clearly modify some word in the sentence in which it appears. If there is no word in the sentence that the modifier can logically modify, it is called a dangling modifier or dangler.

Strategy 1:	**Reword the main part of the sentence to include a word that the dangler can modify.**

First Draft	Entering the forest, a light snow covered the ground.
Revision	Entering the forest, the two men found that a light snow covered the ground.
Model From Literature	Frightened, everyone in the village fled into the canes. —*Marshall, p. 148*

Strategy 2:	**Reword the dangling modifier as a subordinate clause. Choose a subordinator that reflects the relationship of the main idea in the modifier to the main idea of the sentence.**
First Draft	Sheltering his brother, his sense was of desperate loss.
Revision	As he sheltered his brother, he had the sense of desperate loss.
Model From Literature	After we had drifted a long way, I put the oars in place and made Doodle row back against the tide.　　—*Hurst, p. 189*

■ Misplaced Modifiers

GUIDE FOR REVISING: A misplaced modifier appears to modify the wrong word in a sentence.

Strategy:	**Move the modifying word, phrase, or clause closer to the word it should logically modify.**
First Draft	Used on Mississippi River steamboats, Mark Twain took his pen name from a sounding cry.
Revision	Mark Twain took his pen name from a sounding cry used on Mississippi River steamboats.
Model From Literature	Then he could see them as they crossed the yard to the gate, where Dr. Frazier's horse and buggy stood. —*Moss, p. 108*

Problems of Consistency

■ Subject-Verb Agreement

GUIDE FOR REVISING: A verb must agree in number with its subject. A singular subject requires a singular verb, and a plural subject requires a plural verb.

Strategy 1:	**Check to see that if the subject is singular (it names only one thing), then the verb must also be singular. If the subject is plural (it names two or more things), then the verb must be plural.**
First Draft	His favorite hobby are hunting.

Revision	His favorite hobby is hunting.
First Draft	The proposals for park improvement has been completed.
Revision	The proposals for park improvement have been completed.
Model From Literature	Ten thousand eyes were on him as he rubbed his hands with dirt, . . . *—Thayer, p. 522*

Strategy 2:	**Use a plural verb with two singular subjects joined by *and*.**
First Draft	Legnani and Kchessinska was famous ballerinas.
Revision	Legnani and Kchessinska were famous ballerinas.

Strategy 3:	**Make sure that when a singular subject and a plural subject are joined by *or*, *either/or*, or *neither/nor*, the verb agrees in number with the subject closest to it.**
First Draft	Neither the crypt nor the catacombs gives me the creeps.
Revision	Neither the crypt nor the catacombs give me the creeps.

Strategy 4:	**Be aware that in sentences in which the subject comes after the verb, the subject and verb must agree in number.**
First Draft	Despite all the warnings, there is many athletes and dancers who use steroids.
Revision	Despite all the warnings, there are many athletes and dancers who use steroids.
Model From Literature	There was then a long and obstinate silence. *—Poe, p. 8*

Strategy 5:	**Make sure that when a word group that includes one or more nouns comes between the subject and the verb, the verb agrees with its subject and not with a noun in the word group.**
First Draft	All the men, including Odysseus, was frightened by Cyclops.
Revision	All the men, including Odysseus, were frightened by Cyclops.
Model From Literature	Lawrence's painstakingly crafted works, characteristically executed in water-base media, are notable for their vivid pure color and compelling designs and pattern. *—Wheat, p. 401*

■ **Confusion of Adjectives and Adverbs**

GUIDE FOR REVISING: Adjectives modify nouns and pronouns. Adverbs modify verbs, adjectives, and other adverbs; they may also modify phrases and clauses.

Handbook of Grammar and Revising Strategies   **1043**

Strategy 1:	Change an adverb to its adjective form when it is used as a subject complement after a sensory verb or the verb *to be*.
First Draft	Pet owners tend to feel proudly when their pets win awards.
Revision	Pet owners tend to feel proud when their pets win awards.

Strategy 2:	Make sure that you make the correct use of troublesome adjective and adverb pairs such s *bad/badly* and *good/well*.
First Draft	The baking bread smells well.
Revision	The baking bread smell good.
Model From Literature	At night he didn't sleep well, . . . —*Hurst, p. 195*

■ Inconsistencies in Verb Tense

GUIDE FOR REVISING: Verb tenses should not shift unnecessarily from sentence to sentence or within a single sentence.

Strategy 1:	Make certain that the main verbs in a single sentence or in a group of sentences are in the same tense.
First Draft	Juliet enjoyed the music and was unaware that Romeo watches her secretly.
Revision	Juliet enjoyed the music and was unaware that Romeo watched her secretly.
Model From Literature	She told adults that she wanted to be an artist and was embarrassed when they asked her what kind of artist she wanted to be: . . . —*Didion, p. 484*

Strategy 2:	In sentences describing two actions that occurred at different times in the past, the past perfect tense is used for the earlier action.
First Draft	The defendant confessed that he lied at the time of his arrest.
Revision	The defendant confessed that he had lied at the time of his arrest.
Model From Literature	When she had caught her breath she sniffed the air, enjoying the tangy scent that made her think of dry crackling leaves and wood-burning stoves—the heady smell of Autumn in New England. —*Anderson, p. 127*

Problems With Incorrect Words or Phrases

■ Nonstandard Pronoun Cases

GUIDE FOR REVISING: When a pronoun is either the subject of a sentence or a predicate nominative, use the nominative case. Use the objective case when a pronoun is a direct object, an indirect object, or the object of a preposition.

Strategy 1:	**Take special care to identify the case of a pronoun correctly when the pronoun is part of a compound construction. You will often find it helpful to reword the sentence mentally.**
First Draft	The winners of the oral interpretation contest were Rory and me.
Revision	The winners of the oral interpretation contest were Rory and I. [Could be reworded as follows: Rory and I were the winners . . .]
Model From Literature	Each singing what belongs to him or her and to none else, . . . —*Whitman, p. 611*

Strategy 2:	**Pronouns in the possessive case show possession before nouns. The possessive case is also regularly used when a pronoun precedes a gerund.**
First Draft	She losing the necklace led to years of hard work for Madame Loisel and her husband.
Revision	Her losing the necklace led to years of hard work for Madame Loisel and her husband.

■ Wrong Words or Phrases

GUIDE FOR REVISING: Words or phrases that are appropriate in one context may be inappropriate in another.

Strategy 1:	**Check whether you have mistaken one word for another because they sound alike, are spelled similarly, or are easily confused.**
First Draft	O'Keeffe found some of her male critics contemptuous.
Revision	O'Keeffe found some of her male critics contemptible.

Strategy 2: Check that the connotations of a word or phrase express exactly the meaning you have in mind.

First Draft People commented unfavorably on his boyish behavior.

Revision People commented unfavorably on his juvenile behavior.

■ Double Negatives

GUIDE FOR REVISING: A double negative is the use of two or more negative words in one clause to express a negative meaning.

Strategy: Use only one negative word to give a sentence a negative meaning.

First Draft Doodle couldn't hardly walk.

Revision Doodle could hardly walk.

Problems of Readability

■ Sentence Variety

GUIDE FOR REVISING: Varying the lengths and structures of your sentences will help you hold your readers' attention.

Strategy 1: Expand short sentences by adding details.

First Draft Lincoln's papers contain information about the war.

Revision Lincoln's speeches, letters, telegrams, and official messages during the war provide much information and many insights into the causes of the Civil War.

Model From Literature He was probably in his fifties then, a ruddy-faced man whose hair, already turning white, was parted carefully in the center. —*Uchida, p. 415*

Strategy 2: Break up lengthy, overly complicated sentences into simpler, shorter sentences.

First Draft For three days the men on board the *Kon-Tiki* drifted across the sea, were tossed by the waves, and were carried by unseen tides, without sighting land.

Revision For three days the men on board the *Kon-Tiki* drifted across the sea, without sighting land. They were tossed by the waves and carried by unseen tides.

1046 *Handbook of Grammar and Revising Strategies*

Strategy 3:	**Use coordination to join simple sentences.**
First Draft	Sarah was fascinated by "Across the Big Water." She did some extra research on the subject.
Revision	Sarah was fascinated by "Across the Big Water," so she did some extra research on the subject.
Model From Literature	A door beneath the royal party opened, and the lover of the princess walked into the arena. —*Stockton, p. 51*

Stragegy 4:	**Use the subordination to join simple sentences to form complex or compound-complex sentences.**
First Draft	The existence of the Loch Ness monster is questionable. Many people have tried to catch a glimpse of the monster. Some swear they have seen it.
Revision	Although its existence is questionable, many people have tried to catch a glimpse of the Loch Ness monster, and some swear they have seen it.
Model From Literature	Night fell with a shocking abruptness as they crossed the shadow line and the sun dropped below the crest of the plateau. —*Clarke, p. 159*

Problems of Conciseness

■ Wordy Phrases

GUIDE FOR REVISING: Wordy phrases and clauses can weaken your writing by causing ideas to lose their sharpness and impact.

Strategy:	**Shorten wordy phrases and clauses when you can do so without changing the meaning of a sentence.**
First Draft	In "The Red-headed League," Doyle places clues throughout in a very careful manner.
Revision	In "The Red-headed League," Doyle carefully places clues throughout.

■ Redundancy

GUIDE FOR REVISING: Redundancy is the unnecessary repetition of an idea. Redundancy makes writing heavy and dull.

Strategy:	**Eliminate redundant modifiers in your sentences.**
First Draft	"Casey at the Bat" is a narrative poem that tells a story.
Revision	"Casey at the Bat" is a narrative poem.

Handbook of Grammar and Revising Strategies   1047

GUIDE FOR REVISING: Intensifiers such as *really, very, truly,* and *of course* should be used to strengthen statements. Overuse of these words may, however, weaken a sentence.

Strategy: **Eliminate unnecessary intensifiers from your writing.**

First Draft I really think that Annie Sullivan was a very remarkable person.

Revision I think that Annie Sullivan was a remarkable person.

First Draft Mark Twain was, of course, a very extraordinary writer.

Revision Mark Twain was an extraordinary writer.

Problems of Appropriateness

■ **Inappropriate Diction**

GUIDE FOR REVISING: Problems of inappropriate diction occur when words or phrases that are generally accepted in informal conversation or writing are inappropriately included in formal writing.

Strategy: **Choose the appropriate level of diction based on the audience for which you are writing, as well as the subject.**

First Draft "The Scarlet Ibis" is a neat story about the fragility of the individual in society.

Revision "The Scarlet Ibis" is a profound story about the fragility of the individual in society.

■ **Clichés**

GUIDE FOR REVISING: Clichés are expressions that were once fresh and vivid but through overuse now lack force and appeal.

Strategy: **When you recognize a cliché, you should substitute a fresh expression of your own.**

First Draft Holmes is as smart as a tack.

Revision Holmes is perspicacious.

SUMMARY OF GRAMMAR

Nouns A **noun** is the name of a person, place, or thing.

A **common noun** names any one of a class of people, places, or things. A **proper noun** names a specific person, place, or thing.

Common nouns	Proper nouns
city	Brighton, Washington, D.C.

Pronouns **Pronouns** are words that stand for nouns or for words that take the place of nouns.

Personal pronouns refer to (1) the person speaking, (2) the person spoken to, or (3) the person, place, or thing spoken about.

	Singular	Plural
First Person	I, me, my, mine	we, us, our, ours
Second Person	you, your, yours	you, your, yours
Third Person	he, him, his, she, her, hers it, its	they, them, their, theirs

A **reflexive pronoun** ends in -*self* or -*selves* and adds information to a sentence by pointing back to a noun or pronoun earlier in the sentence.

. . . I found *myself* hanging on to a slack line outside the raft. —*Heyerdahl, p. 436*

An **intensive pronoun** ends in -*self* or -*selves* and simply adds emphasis to a noun or pronoun in the same sentence.

The anchor *itself* consisted of empty water cans . . . —*Heyerdahl, p. 432*

Demonstrative pronouns direct attention to specific people, places, or things.

this   these   that   those
These are the juiciest pears I've ever tasted.

A **relative pronoun** begins a subordinate clause and connects it to another idea in the sentence.

The poet *who* wrote "The Runaway" is Robert Frost.
The president *whom* Sandburg admired was Lincoln.

Indefinite pronouns refer to people, places, or things, often without specifying which ones.

Some of the flowers were in bloom.
Everybody chose something.

Verbs A **verb** is a word that expresses time while showing an action, a condition, or the fact that something exists.

An **action verb** is a verb that tells what action someone or something is performing.

An action verb is **transitive** if it directs action toward someone or something named in the same sentence.

Then God *raised* his arm and he *waved* his hand . . . —*Johnson, p. 585*

An action verb is **intransitive** if it does not direct action toward something or someone named in the same sentence.

Then he *stooped* and *looked* and *saw* . . . —*Johnson, p. 584*

A **linking verb** is a verb that connects a word at or near the beginning of a sentence with a word at or near the end. All linking verbs are intransitive.

Life *is* a broken-winged bird . . . —*Hughes, p. 595*

Helping verbs are verbs that can be added to another verb to make a single verb phrase.

Nor *did* I *suspect* that these experiences could be part of a novel's meaning.

Adjectives An **adjective** is a word used to describe a noun or pronoun or to give a noun or pronoun a more specific meaning. Adjectives answer these questions:

What kind?	*blue* lamp, *large* tree
Which one?	*this* table, *those* books
How many?	*five* stars, *several* buses
How much?	*less* money, *enough* votes

The articles *the, a,* and *an* are adjectives. *An* is used before a word beginning with a vowel sound.

A noun may sometimes be used as an adjective.
diamond necklace   *summer* vacation

Adverbs An **adverb** is a word that modifies a verb, an adjective, or another adverb. Adverbs answer the questions *Where? When? In what manner? To what extent?*

He could stand *there.* (modifies verb *stand*)
He was *blissfully* happy. (modifies adjective *happy*)
It ended *too* soon. (modifies adverb *soon*)

Prepositions A **preposition** is a word that relates a noun or pronoun that appears with it to another word in the sentence. Prepositions are almost always followed by nouns or pronouns.

before the end   *near* me   *inside* our fence

Conjunctions A **conjunction** is a word used to connect other words or groups of words.

Handbook of Grammar and Revising Strategies   1049

Coordinating conjunctions connect similar kinds or groups of words.

mother *and* father   simple *yet* stylish

Correlative conjunctions are used in pairs to connect similar words or groups of words.

both Sue *and* Meg   *neither* he *nor* I

Subordinating conjunctions connect two complete ideas by placing one idea below the other in rank or importance.

You would know him *if you saw him.*

Interjections An **interjection** is a word that expresses feeling or emotion and functions independently of a sentence.

"Oh, my poor, poor Mathilde!"
—*Maupassant, p. 198*

Sentences A **sentence** is a group of words with two main parts: a complete subject and a complete predicate. Together these parts express a complete thought.

We have all felt time stand still. —*Anaya, p. 448*
Her face was drowned in the shadow of an ugly hat. . . .   —*Marshall, p. 139*

A **fragment** is a group of words that does not express a complete thought.

The Swan Theatre in London

Subject-Verb Agreement To make a subject and verb agree, make sure that both are singular or both are plural.

Either the *cats* or the *dog is* hungry.
Neither *Angie* nor her *sisters were* present.
The *conductor,* as well as the soloists, *was applauded.*
Many *storms are* the cause of beach erosion.

Phrases A **phrase** is a group of words, without a subject and verb, that functions in a sentence as one part of speech.

A **prepositional phrase** is a group of words that includes a preposition and a noun or pronoun.

outside my window   below the counter

An **adjective phrase** is a prepositional phrase that modifies a noun or pronoun by telling what kind or which one.

The wooden gates *of that lane* stood open.

An **adverb phrase** is a prepositional phrase that modifies a verb, an adjective, or an adverb by pointing out where, when, in what manner, or to what extent.

Mr. Pumblechook and I breakfasted *at eight o'clock in the parlor* . . .   —*Dickens, p. 745*

An **appositive phrase** is a noun or pronoun with modifiers, placed next to a noun or pronoun to add information and details.

"It is a very great pleasure and honor to welcome Mr. Sanger Rainsford, *the celebrated hunter,* to my home."   —*Connell, p. 17*

A **participial phrase** is a participle modified by an adjective or an adverb phrase or accompanied by a complement. The entire phrase acts as an adjective.

"Try the settee," said Holmes, *relapsing into his armchair* . . .   —*Doyle, p. 71*
Finally I went back and found him huddled beneath a red nightshade bush beside the road.
—*Hurst, p. 190*

A **gerund phrase** is a gerund with modifiers or a complement, all acting together as a noun.

The baying of the hounds drew nearer, . . .
—*Connell, p. 17*
This was the king's semibarbaric method of *administering justice.*   —*Stockton, p. 50*

An **infinitive phrase** is an infinitive with modifiers, complements, or a subject, all acting together as a single part of speech.

I continued, as was my wont, *to smile in his face,* . . .   —*Poe, p. 3*

Clauses A **clause** is a group of words with its own subject and verb.

An **independent clause** can stand by itself as a complete sentence.

A **subordinate clause** cannot stand by itself as a complete sentence; it can only be part of a sentence.

An **adjective clause** is a subordinate clause that modifies a noun or pronoun by telling what kind or which one.

Walter Mitty stopped the car in front of the building *where his wife went to have her hair done.*
—*Thurber, p. 202*

Subordinate **adverb clauses** modify verbs, adjectives, adverbs, or verbals by telling *where, when, in what manner, to what extent, under what condition,* or *why.*

The hunter shook his head several times, *as if he was puzzled.*   —*Connell, p. 28*

A **noun clause** is a subordinate clause that acts as a noun.

. . . he knew *that Sam Carr was puzzled by his mother.*   —*Callaghan, p. 59*

SUMMARY OF CAPITALIZATION AND PUNCTUATION

CAPITALIZATION

Capitalize the first word in sentences. Also capitalize the first word in a quotation if the quotation is a complete sentence.

Mr. Carr, turning the latch, said crisply, "Come in, Mrs. Higgins." —*Callaghan, p. 59*

Capitalize all proper nouns and adjectives.

O. Henry   Ganges River   Great Wall of China

Capitalize a person's title when it is followed by the person's name or when it is used in direct address.

Madame   Dr. Mitty   General Zaroff

Capitalize titles showing family relationships when they refer to a specific person, unless they are preceded by a possessive noun or pronoun.

Gran'ther Pendleton   Bennie's grandmother

Capitalize the first word and all other key words in the titles of books, periodicals, poems, stories, plays, paintings, and other works of art.

Great Expectations   "Before the End of Summer"

PUNCTUATION

End Marks   Use a **period** to end a declarative sentence, an imperative sentence, an indirect question, and most abbreviations.

I did not know what they wanted.
"Let me introduce you to Mr. Merryweather . . ."
—*Doyle, p. 83*

Use a **question mark** to end a direct question, an incomplete question, or a statement that is intended as a question.

Shall I meet other wayfarers at night?
—*Rossetti, p. 596*

Use an **exclamation mark** after a statement showing strong emotion, an urgent imperative sentence, or an interjection expressing strong emotion.

No wonder the princess loved him!
—*Stockton, p. 52*

Commas   Use a comma before the conjunction to separate two independent clauses in a compound sentence.

All at once . . . she came upon a superb diamond necklace, and her heart started beating with overwhelming desire. —*Maupassant, p. 195*

Use commas to separate three or more words, phrases, or clauses in a series.

My brothers and I would peer into the medicinal herb shop, watching old Li dole out onto a stiff sheet of white paper the right amount of insect shells, saffron-colored seeds, and pungent leaves for his ailing customers. —*Tan, p. 39*

Use commas to separate adjectives of equal rank. Do not use commas to separate adjectives that must stay in a specific order.

The big cottonwood tree stood apart from a small group of winterbare cottonwoods which grew in the wide, sandy arroyo. —*Silko, p. 151*
The gray sea and the long black land; . . .
—*Browning, p. 566*

Use a comma after an introductory word, phrase, or clause.

When Marvin was ten years old, his father took him through the long, echoing corridors . . .
—*Clarke, p. 157*

Use commas to set off parenthetical and nonessential expressions.

"Tell me, Doctor, I can stand it."   —*Moss, p. 107*

Use commas with places, dates, and titles.
Poe was raised in Richmond, Virginia.
On September 1, 1939, World War II began.
Dr. Martin Luther King, Jr., was born in 1929.

Use a comma to indicate words left out of an elliptical sentence, to set off a direct quotation, and to prevent a sentence from being misunderstood.

In the *Odyssey*, the Cyclops may symbolize brutishness; the Sirens, knowledge.
As the rockets fired, Sally Ride remained calm.

Semicolons   Use a semicolon to join independent clauses that are not already joined by a conjunction.

The lights of cities sparkle; on nights when there was no moon, it was difficult for me to tell the Earth from the sky. . . . —*Ride, p. 489*

Use a semicolon to join independent clauses separated by either a conjunctive adverb or a transitional expression.

Edward Way Teale wrote nearly thirty books; moreover, he was also an artist and a naturalist.

Use semicolons to avoid confusion when independent clauses or items in a series already contain commas.

Handbook of Grammar and Revising Strategies   **1051**

Unable to afford jewelry, she dressed simply; but she was as wretched as a *declassée,* for women have neither caste nor breeding—in them beauty, grace, and charm replace pride of birth.
—*Maupassant, p. 193*

Colons Use a colon before a list of items following an independent clause.
The authors we are reading include a number of poets: Robert Frost, Lewis Carroll, and Margaret Walker.

Use a colon to introduce a formal quotation.
I have a dream that one day this nation will rise up and live out the true meaning of its creed: "We hold these truths to be self-evident; . . ."
—*King, p. 467*

Use a colon to introduce a sentence that summarizes or explains the sentence before it.
And the difference is enormous: Space flight moves the traveler another giant step farther away.
—*Ride, p. 487*

Quotation Marks A **direct quotation** represents a person's exact speech or thoughts and is enclosed in quotation marks.
"Where I was born and where and how I have lived is unimportant," Georgia O'Keeffe told us in the book of paintings and words published in her ninetieth year on earth.   —*Didion, p. 481*

An **indirect quotation** reports only the general meaning of what a person said or thought and does not require quotation marks.
He told me he was raised in a one-hundred-fifty-year-old cabin still standing in one of the hollows.   —*Least Heat Moon, p. 443*

Always place a comma or a period inside the final quotation mark.
It was in Paris, from late 1918 until early 1920, that there was a glut . . . of "You said it" and "You can say that again," and an American Marine I knew, from Montana, could not speak any sentence . . . without saying "It *is,* you *know.*"
—*Thurber, p. 494*

Place a question mark or an exclamation mark inside the final quotation mark if the end mark is part of the quotation; if it is not part of the quotation, place it outside the final quotation mark.
"Look at the raft—she's holding!"
—*Heyerdahl, p. 434*

Have you ever read the poem "Dreams"?

Use single quotation marks for a quotation within a quotation.
"I said to Thurmond, 'Thurmond, unless you want shut of me, call the doctor.' "
—*Least Heat Moon, p. 443*

Use quotation marks around the titles of short written works, episodes in a series, songs, and titles of works mentioned as parts of collections.
"A Red, Red Rose"   "Penny Lane"

Dashes Use dashes to indicate an abrupt change of thought, a dramatic interrupting idea, or a summary statement.
James happened to be, as well, the founder of the Loch Ness Phenomena Investigation Bureau—phenomena, because, for breeding purposes, there would have to be at least two monsters living in the lake at any one time; . . .
—*McPhee, p. 468*

Parentheses Use parentheses to set off asides and explanations only when the material is not essential or when it consists of one or more sentences.
At 58 minutes and 43 seconds past 11:00 p.m. (just 1 minute and 17 seconds before the end) will come the beginning of the Christian era.
—*Rettie, p. 478*

Hyphens Use a hyphen with certain numbers, after certain prefixes, with two or more words used as one word, and with a compound modifier coming before a noun.
seventy-six   post-Modernist

Apostrophes Add an apostrophe and *-s* to show the possessive case of most singular nouns.
Thurmond's wife   the playwright's craft

Add an apostrophe to show the possessive case of plural nouns ending in *-s* and *-es.*
the sailors' ships   the Wattses' daughter

Add an apostrophe and *-s* to show the possessive case of plural nouns that do not end in *-s* or *-es.*
the children's games   the people's friend

Use an apostrophe in a contraction to indicate the position of the missing letter or letters.

"'Oh no, you'd freeze to death. . . .'"
—*Marshall, p. 144*

GLOSSARY OF COMMON USAGE

among, between

Among is usually used with three or more items. *Between* is generally used with only two items.

Among the *poems* we read this year, Margaret Walker's "Memory" was my favorite.

Mark Twain's "The Invalid's Story" includes a humorous encounter *between* the *narrator* and a *character* named Thompson.

amount, number

Amount refers to a mass or a unit, whereas *number* refers to individual items that can be counted. Therefore, *amount* generally appears with a singular noun, and *number* appears with a plural noun.

Annie Sullivan's work with Helen Keller must have required a huge *amount* of *patience*.

In her poem "Uphill," Christina Rossetti uses a *number* of intriguing *symbols*.

any, all

Any should not be used in place of *any other* or *all*.

Rajika liked Amy Tan's "Rules of the Game" better than *any other* short story.

Of *all* O. Henry's short stories, "The Gift of the Magi" is one of the most famous.

around

In formal writing *around* should not be used to mean *approximately* or *about*. These usages are allowable, however, in informal writing or in colloquial dialogue.

Shakespeare's Romeo and Juliet had its first performance in *approximately* 1595.

Shakespeare was *about* thirty when he wrote this play.

as, because, like, as to

The word *as* has several meanings and can function as several parts of speech. To avoid confusion, use *because* rather than *as* when you want to indicate cause and effect.

Because Cyril was interested in the history of African American poetry, he decided to write his report on Paul Laurence Dunbar.

Do not use the preposition *like* to introduce a clause that requires the conjunction *as*.

Dorothy Parker conversed *as* she wrote—wittily.

The use of *as to* for *about* is awkward and should be avoided.

Rosa has an interesting theory *about* E. E. Cummings's unusual typography in his poems.

bad, badly

Use the predicate adjective *bad* after linking verbs such as *feel, look,* and *seem*. Use *badly* whenever an adverb is required.

Sara Teasdale's poem "There Will Come Soft Rains" shows clearly that the author felt *bad* about the destruction of war.

In O. Henry's "The Gift of the Magi," Della *badly* wants to buy a wonderful Christmas present for her husband, Jim.

because of, due to

Use *due to* if it can logically replace the phrase *caused by*. In introductory phrases, however, *because of* is better usage than *due to*.

The popularity of Frank Stockton's "The Lady or the Tiger?" is largely *due to* the story's open ending.

Because of her feeling that Bennie's mother has enough to worry about already, Bennie's grandmother keeps the doctor's conclusions to herself.

being as, being that

Avoid these expressions. Use *because* or *since* instead.

Because the protagonist of James Hurst's "The Scarlet Ibis" is a dynamic character, he changes significantly in the course of the story.

Since Romeo and Juliet were from feuding families, their relationship involved secrecy and risk.

beside, besides

Beside is a preposition meaning "at the side of" or "close to." Do not confuse *beside* with *besides*, which means "in addition to." *Besides* can be a preposition or an adverb.

When our group discussed William Least Heat Moon's "Nameless, Tennessee," Luis sat *beside* Eileen.

Besides "The Bells," can you think of any other poems by Edgar Allan Poe?

John Updike is a celebrated novelist; he is a gifted poet and essayist, *besides*.

can, may

The verb *can* generally refers to the ability to do something. The verb *may* generally refers to permission to do something.

The mysterious listeners in Walter de la Mare's poem *can* hear the words of the lonely traveler.

May I tell you why I admire Edgar Lee Masters's "George Gray"?

compare, contrast

The verb *compare* can involve both similarities and differences. The verb *contrast* always involves differences. Use *to* or *with* after *compare*. Use *with* after *contrast*.

> Theo's paper *compared* James Weldon Johnson's style in "The Creation" *with* the style of African American sermons of the same period.
>
> The opening lines of famous speech in Shakespeare's *As You Like It compare* the word *to* a stage and men and women *to* actors or players.
>
> The speaker's tone of hysteria in the closing stanzas of Poe's "The Raven" *contrasts with* the quiet opening of the poem.

different from, different than

The preferred usage is *different from*.

> The structure of "The Meadow Mouse" is quite *different from* that of "I Wandered Lonely as a Cloud."

farther, further

Use *farther* when you refer to distance. Use *further* when you mean "to a greater degree" or "additional."

> The *farther* Rainsford traveled in the jungle in "The Most Dangerous Game," the nearer the baying of the hounds sounded.
>
> Despite his men's advice, Odysseus *further* insults the Cyclops and provokes the monster's curse.

fewer, less

Use *fewer* for things that can be counted. Use *less* for amounts or quantities that cannot be counted.

> Poetry often uses *fewer words* than prose to convey ideas and images.
>
> T. S. Eliot's humorous poems have received *less critical attention* than his serious verse has.

good, well

Use the adjective *good* after linking verbs such as *feel, look, smell, taste,* and *seem.* Use *well* whenever you need an adverb.

> In Walt Whitman's "I Hear America Singing," the "varied carols" sound *good* to the speaker.
>
> Dickens wrote especially *well* when he described eccentric characters.

hopefully

You should not loosely attach this adverb to a sentence, as in "Hopefully, the rain will stop by noon." Rewrite the sentence so that *hopefully* modifies a specific verb. Other possible ways of revising such sentences include using the adjective *hopeful* or a phrase like *everyone hopes that.*

> Dr. Martin Luther King, Jr., wrote and spoke *hopefully* abut his dream of racial harmony.
>
> Akko was *hopeful* that he could find some of the unusual words from Lewis Carroll's "Jabberwocky" in an unabridged dictionary.
>
> *Everyone hopes that* the class production of *Romeo and Juliet* will be a big success.

its, it's

Do not confuse the possessive pronoun *its* with the contraction *it's,* standing for "it is" or "it has."

> Ancient Greek society must have recognized many of *its* ideal values in the *Odyssey.*
>
> In Walter de la Mare's "The Listeners," the traveler thinks *it's* strange that no one replies to his call.

just, only

When you use *just* as an adverb meaning "no more than," be sure you place it directly before the word it logically modifies. Likewise, be sure you place *only* before the word it logically modifies.

> Shakespeare's "Sonnet 30" offers *just* one remedy for the speaker's grief and depression: the thought of a dear friend.
>
> A stereotyped character exhibits *only* those traits or behavior patterns that are assumed to be typical.

kind of, sort of

In formal writing you should not use these colloquial expressions. Instead, use a word such as *rather* or *somewhat.*

> Alfred is *rather* irresponsible in Morley Callaghan's story "All the Years of Her Life."
>
> In "The Secret Life of Walter Mitty," James Thurber characterizes Mitty as *somewhat* absent-minded.

lay, lie

Do not confuse these verbs. *Lay* is a transitive verb meaning "to set or put something down." Its principal parts are *lay, laying, laid, laid. Lie* is an intransitive verb meaning "to recline." Its principal parts are *lie, lying, lay, lain.*

> In Heyerdahl's *Kon-Tiki* the narrator says that after the ship hit the reef, Herman *lay* pressed flat across the ridge of the cabin roof.
>
> Homer describes the slaughtered suitors *lying* dead in a heap on the floor of Odysseus' hall.

leave, let

Be careful not to confuse these verbs. *Leave* means "to go away" or "to allow to remain." *Let* means "to permit."

> In Tennyson's "The Eagle," the bird *leaves* the crag and plunges like a thunderbolt toward the sea.

The love-sick Romeo asks his friends to *leave* him alone while they go to Capulet's party.

"*Let* wantons light of heart / Tickle the senseless rushes with their heels," he says.

literally, figuratively

Literally means "word for word" or "in fact." The opposite of *literally* is *figuratively*, meaning "metaphorically." Be careful not to use *literally* as a synonym for *nearly*, as in informal expressions like this: "He was literally beside himself with rage."

Certain specific details in "I Hear an Army" show that James Joyce does not intend us to interpret the army *literally*; instead, the army and the speaker's nightmare are meant *figuratively* to suggest his despair at his abandonment by his love.

of, have

Do not use *of* in place of *have* after auxiliary verbs like *would, could, should, may,* or *might.*

Sir Arthur Conan Doyle *might have* continued to practice medicine, but soon after the publication of his first Sherlock Holmes stories, he decided to write full time.

raise, rise

Raise is a transitive verb that usually takes a direct object. *Rise* is an intransitive verb and never takes a direct object.

In "Casey at the Bat," Ernest Lawrence Thayer suspensefully *raises* the reader's expectations throughout the poem, only to end the narrative with a mighty anticlimax.

Jorge *rose* to the challenge of interpreting Gabriel García Márquez's story "A Very Old Man With Enormous Wings."

set, sit

Do not confuse these verbs. *Set* is a transitive verb meaning "to put (something) in a certain place." Its principal parts are *set, setting, set, set. Sit* is an intransitive verb meaning "to be seated." Its principal parts are *sit, sitting, sat, sat.*

The opening sentence of Saki's "The Interlopers" *sets* a tone of tension and conflict for the story.

While Walter Mitty *sat* in a big leather chair in the hotel lobby, he picked up a copy of a magazine.

so, so that

Be careful not to use the coordinating conjunction *so* when your context requires *so that. So* means "accordingly" or "therefore" and expresses a cause-and-effect relationship. *So that* expresses purpose.

He wanted to check the clues, *so* he read "The Red-headed League" again.

The priest wanted to locate Teofilo's body *so that* he could give him the Last Rites.

than, then

The conjunction *than* is used to connect the two parts of a comparison. Do not confuse *than* with the adverb *then,* which usually refers to time.

I enjoyed reading "Jacob Lawrence: American Painter" more *than* "Autumn Gardening."

Sally Ride earned a doctorate in physics and *then* became the first American woman in space.

that, which, who

Use the relative pronoun *that* to refer to things or people. Use *which* only for things and *who* only for people.

The phrase *that* James Thurber dislikes is "you know."

Donald Justice wrote "Incident in a Rose Garden," *which* is a dramatic poem.

The sea goddess *who* loved Odysseus was Calypso.

unique

Because *unique* means "one of a kind," you should not use it carelessly to mean "interesting" or "unusual." Avoid such illogical expressions as "most unique," "very unique," and "extremely unique."

Homer occupies a *unique* position in the history of Western literature.

when, where

Do not directly follow a linking verb with *when* or *where.* Also be careful not to use *where* when your context requires *that.*

Faulty: Foreshadowing *is when* an author uses clues to suggest future events.

Revised: In foreshadowing an author uses clues to suggest future events.

Faulty: Ithaca *was where* Penelope awaited Odysseus.

Revised: Penelope awaited Odysseus on Ithaca.

who, whom

In formal writing remember to use *who* only as a subject in clauses and sentences and *whom* only as an object.

Richard Wright, *who* is widely admired for his novel *Native Son,* also wrote haiku verse.

Leslie Marmon Silko, *whom* Mark quoted in his oral report, was raised on the Laguna Pueblo reservation in New Mexico.

HANDBOOK OF LITERARY TERMS
AND TECHNIQUES

ACT   See *Drama.*

ALLITERATION   *Alliteration* is the repetition of initial consonant sounds. Writers use alliteration to give emphasis to words, to imitate sounds, and to create musical effects. Notice, in the following lines from Walter de la Mare's "The Listeners," how the *s* sound imitates a whisper:

> Never the least *s*tir made the listeners,
>   Though every word he *s*pake
> Fell echoing through the *s*hadowiness of the
>   *s*till house
> From the one man left awake:
> Ay, they heard his foot upon the *s*tirrup,
>   And the *s*ound of iron on *s*tone,
> And how the *s*ilence *s*urged *s*oftly backward,
>   When the plunging hoofs were gone.

The title of Langston Hughes's poem "*Dream Deferred*," on page 594, uses alliteration, as does E. E. Cummings's "*m*aggie and *m*illy and *m*olly and *m*ay," on page 617.

Prose writers use alliteration too, but not as frequently as poets do. Jane Austen used the technique for the titles of her novels *Pride and Prejudice* and *Sense and Sensibility*. Notice, too, that alliteration is the basis of tongue twisters: *She sells sea shells by the seashore.*
See *Repetition.*

ALLUSION   An *allusion* is a reference to a well-known person, place, event, literary work, or work of art. In "The Gift of the Magi," on page 175, O. Henry writes about a young couple and the Christmas gifts they give each other. At the end of the story, the narrator explains the Biblical allusion in the title: "The Magi, as you know, were wise men—wonderfully wise men—who brought gifts to the Babe in the manger. They invented the art of giving Christmas presents. Being wise, their gifts were no doubt wise ones. . . ."

The broader your reading experiences, the easier it will be for you to spot and understand allusions. When you have read the *Odyssey,* on page 645, for example, you will have become familiar with a great many mythological characters, places, and events. Then poems like Margaret Atwood's "Siren Song," on page 711, will have more meaning for you.

ANECDOTE   An *anecdote* is a brief story about an interesting, amusing, or strange event. Anecdotes are told to entertain or to make a point. In "A Lincoln Preface," on page 405, Carl Sandburg tells anecdotes about Abraham Lincoln.
See *Narrative.*

ANTAGONIST   An *antagonist* is a character or force in conflict with a main character, or protagonist. In Thurber's "The Secret Life of Walter Mitty," on page 201, Mitty's wife is the antagonist.
See *Protagonist.*

ASIDE   An *aside* is a short speech delivered by an actor in a play, expressing the character's thoughts. Traditionally, the aside is directed to the audience and is presumed to be inaudible to the other actors.

ASSONANCE   *Assonance* is the repetition of vowel sounds followed by different consonants in two or more stressed syllables. Assonance is found in the phrase "w*ea*k and w*ea*ry" in Edgar Allan Poe's "The Raven," on page 527.
See *Consonance.*

ATMOSPHERE   See *Mood.*

AUTOBIOGRAPHY An *autobiography* is a form of nonfiction in which a person tells his or her own life story. It may tell about the person's whole life or only a part of it. Both autobiographies and biographies are nonfiction. In most libraries they are shelved in a special section, arranged alphabetically by subject.
See *Biography* and *Nonfiction.*

BIOGRAPHY A *biography* is a form of nonfiction in which a writer tells the life story of another person. Biographies have been written about many famous people, historical and contemporary, but they can also be written about "ordinary" people. Nicholas Gage's biography of his mother, *Eleni,* includes this passage in which he states the key idea he wants readers to understand about her:

> [She] was one of 600,000 Greeks who were killed during the years of war that ravaged the country from 1940 to 1949. Like many of the victims, she died because her home lay in the path of the opposing armies, but she would have survived if she hadn't defied the invaders of her village to save her children.

A *biographical essay* is shorter than a biography. In "Georgia O'Keeffe," on page 481, Joan Didion writes about the independent spirit of the famous painter.

Like autobiographies, biographies are usually shelved in a special section of the library, arranged alphabetically by subject.
See *Autobiography* and *Nonfiction.*

BLANK VERSE *Blank verse* is poetry written in unrhymed iambic pentameter lines. This verse form was widely used by Elizabethan dramatists like William Shakespeare.
See *Meter.*

CHARACTER A *character* is a person or an animal who takes part in the action of a literary work. The *main character* is the most important character in a story. This character often changes in some important way as a result of the story's events. The princess is the main character in Frank R. Stockton's "The Lady or the Tiger?" on page 49. It is her heart the story explores. In the same story, other major characters are the king and the young man. They contribute to the events that lead to the princess's conflict. *Protagonist* is another word for the main character. The *antagonist* is a major character who opposes the protagonist. In Richard Connell's "The Most Dangerous Game," on page 13, Rainsford is the protagonist and General Zaroff is the antagonist.

Characters are sometimes classified as round or flat, dynamic or static. A *round character* shows many different traits—faults as well as virtues. Walter Mitty, in James Thurber's "The Secret Life of Walter Mitty," on page 201, is a round character. We know him not only as a mousy husband but also as a man who has a means of escape: his fantasies. His wife is a *flat character.* We see her only as a shrew. A *dynamic character* develops and grows during the course of the story, as does Doodle's brother in "The Scarlet Ibis," on page 181. A *static character* does not change. Walter Mitty, for example, is neither less mousy nor less inclined to fantasize at the end of the story than he was at the beginning.
See *Characterization, Hero/Heroine,* and *Motivation.*

CHARACTERIZATION *Characterization* is the act of creating and developing a character. In *direct characterization,* the author directly states a character's traits. In "Uncle Marcos," for example, a character states that "Uncle Marcos's manners were those of a cannibal."

In *indirect characterization,* an author tells what a character looks like, does, and says and how other characters react to him or her. It is up to the reader to draw conclusions about the character based on this indirect information. Toni Cade Bambara describes Granny Cain indirectly in the following passages from her story "Blues Ain't No Mockin Bird," on page 91.

"I don't know about the thing, the it, and the stuff," said Granny, still talkin with her eyebrows. "Just people here is what I tend to consider."

Me and Cathy were waitin, too, cause Granny always got somethin to say. She teaches steady with no letup.

The most effective indirect characterizations usually result from showing characters acting or speaking. In Saki's "The Interlopers," on page 33, two enemies lie trapped under a fallen tree. When one of them, Ulrich, suddenly offers a drink of wine to the other, the reader knows that Ulrich is beginning to change his mind about the old feud.
See *Character.*

CINQUAIN   See *Stanza.*

CLIMAX   The *climax* of a story, novel, or play is the high point of interest or suspense. The events that make up the rising action lead up to the climax. The events that make up the falling action follow the climax.
See *Conflict* and *Plot.*

CONCRETE POEM   A *concrete poem* is one with a shape that suggests its subject. William Burford's "A Christmas Tree" is a concrete poem:

Star,
If you are
A Love compassionate,
You will walk with us this year.
We face a glacial distance, who are here
Huddl'd
At your feet.

The lines of the poem appear on the page in the shape of a tree, and the words *star* and *at your feet* appear in appropriate positions, at the top and at the bottom.

CONFLICT   A *conflict* is a struggle between opposing forces. Characters in conflict form the basis of stories, novels, and plays.

There are two kinds of conflict: external and internal. In an *external conflict,* the main charac-
ter struggles against an outside force. This force may be another character, as in Richard Connell's "The Most Dangerous Game," on page 13, in which Rainsford struggles with General Zaroff. The outside force may be the standards or expectations of a group, such as the family prejudices that Romeo and Juliet struggle against. Their story, on page 287, shows them in conflict with society. The outside force may be nature itself, a person-against-nature conflict. The two men trapped by a fallen tree in Saki's "The Interlopers," on page 33, face such a conflict.

An *internal conflict* involves a character in conflict with himself or herself. An example is Frank R. Stockton's "The Lady or the Tiger?" on page 49, in which the princess struggles "beneath the combined fires of despair and jealousy." The story, as the author says, "involves a study of the human heart."

A story may have more than one conflict. In addition to the person-against-nature conflict of "The Interlopers," there is also a person-against-person conflict between the two men and an internal conflict for the main character, who must decide whether he should forgive his enemy.
See *Plot.*

CONNOTATION   The *connotation* of a word is the set of associations that occur to people when they hear or read that word. Paul Laurence Dunbar, in his poem "Sympathy," on page 517, does not speak of a canary or of a parakeet, either of which suggests a pet and thus has positive connotations. Instead, he speaks of a "caged bird," which connotes a sad, trapped creature. The connotation of a word can be personal, based on individual experiences, but cultural connotations—those recognizable by most people in a group—most often determine a writer's word choices.
See *Denotation.*

CONSONANCE   *Consonance* is the repetition in two or more words of final consonants in

stressed syllables. These consonants are preceded by different vowel sounds. An example is the word pair *a*dd-*rea*d.
See *Assonance.*

COUPLET   A *couplet* is a pair of rhyming lines, usually of the same length and meter. A couplet generally expresses a single idea. In the following couplet from a poem by William Shakespeare, the speaker comforts himself with the thought of his love:

> For thy sweet love remember'd such wealth
> brings
> That then I scorn to change my state with
> kings.

See *Stanza.*

DENOTATION   The *denotation* of a word is its dictionary meaning, independent of other associations that the word calls up. The denotation of the word *lake,* for example, is an inland body of water. "Vacation spot" and "place where the fishing is good" are connotations of the word *lake.*
See *Connotation.*

DENOUEMENT   See *Plot.*

DESCRIPTION   A *description* is a portrait in words of a person, place, or object. Descriptive writing uses sensory details, those that appeal to the senses: sight, hearing, taste, smell, and touch. Description can be found in all types of writing. Rudolfo Anaya's essay "A Celebration of Grandfathers," on page 447, contains descriptive passages, and John Masefield's poem "Sea-Fever," on page 618, is a description of those things that the speaker loves about the sailing life:

> And all I ask is a tall ship and a star to
> steer her by,
> And the wheel's kick and the wind's song and
> the white sail's shaking.
> And a gray mist on the sea's face and a gray
> dawn breaking.

See *Image.*

DEVELOPMENT   See *Plot.*

DIALECT   *Dialect* is the form of a language spoken by people in a particular region or group. Pronunciation, vocabulary, and sentence structure are affected by dialect. In "A Red, Red Rose," on page 633, the poet Robert Burns uses a Scottish dialect:

> And I will love thee still, my dear,
> Till a' the seas gang dry.

The word *a'* represents the Scottish pronunciation of *all,* and *gang* is the local word for *go.*

DIALOGUE   A *dialogue* is a conversation between characters. It is used to reveal character and to advance action. In a story or novel, quotation marks are generally used to indicate a speaker's exact words. A new paragraph usually indicates a change of speaker. Look at an example from Charles Dickens's *Great Expectations,* on page 726. The narrator is a young boy who is confronted by a fearful-looking man:

> "Oh! Don't cut my throat, sir," I pleaded in terror. "Pray don't do it, sir."
> "Tell us your name!" said the man. "Quick!"
> "Pip, sir."
> "Once more," said the man, staring at me. "Give it mouth!"
> "Pip. Pip, sir."

A drama, of course, depends entirely on dialogue and actions. Quotation marks are not used in the *script,* which is the printed version of a play. Instead, the dialogue follows the name of the speaker. Here is an example from *The Miracle Worker,* on page 232:

> **KELLER.** [*Very courtly*] Welcome to Ivy Green, Miss Sullivan. I take it you are Miss Sullivan—
> **KATE.** My husband, Miss Annie, Captain Keller.
> **ANNIE.** [*Her best behavior*] Captain, how do you do?
> **KELLER.** A pleasure to see you, at last. I trust you had an agreeable journey?

DICTION   *Diction* is word choice. To discuss a writer's diction is to consider the vocabulary used, the appropriateness of the words, and the vividness of the language. Both the *denotation,* or literal meaning, and the *connotation,* or associations, of words contribute to the overall effect. Diction can be quite formal, as in this sentence from Charles Dickens's *Great Expectations,* which begins on page 725.

> I had heard of her as leading a most unhappy life, and as being separated from her husband, who had used her with great cruelty, and who had become quite renowned as a compound of pride, brutality, and meanness.

Diction can also be informal and conversational, as in these lines from Ernest Lawrence Thayer's ''Casey at the Bat,'' on page 521:

> It looked extremely rocky for the Mudville nine
>   that day;
> The score stood two to four, with but an
>   inning left to play.
> So, when Cooney died at second, and Burrows
>   did the same,
> A pallor wreathed the features of the patrons
>   of the game.

See *Connotation* and *Denotation.*

DIRECT CHARACTERIZATION See *Characterization.*

DRAMA A *drama* is a story written to be performed by actors. The script of a drama is made up of dialogue, which is the words the actors say, and stage directions, which are comments on how and where action happens.

The drama's *setting* is the place where the action occurs. It is indicated by one or more sets that suggest interior or exterior scenes. *Props* are objects, such as a sword or a cup of tea, that are used onstage.

At the beginning of most plays, a brief exposition gives the audience some background information about the characters and the situation. Just as in a story or novel, the plot of a drama is built around characters in conflict.

Dramas are divided into large units called *acts* and into smaller units called *scenes.* A long play may include many sets that change with the scenes, or it may indicate a change of scene with lighting. Look at these stage directions from William Gibson's *The Miracle Worker,* which begins on page 219:

> *The room dims out quickly.*
> *Time, in the form of a slow tune or distant belfry chimes which approaches in a crescendo and then fades, passes; the light comes up again on a day five years later, on three kneeling children and an old dog outside around the pump.*

See *Genre, Stage Directions,* and *Tragedy.*

DRAMATIC DIALOGUE See *Dramatic Poetry.*

DRAMATIC IRONY See *Irony.*

DRAMATIC MONOLOGUE See *Dramatic Poetry.*

DRAMATIC POETRY *Dramatic poetry* is poetry that involves the techniques of drama. The dialogue used in Donald Justice's ''Incident in a Rose Garden,'' on page 539, makes it a *dramatic dialogue.* A *dramatic monologue* is a poem spoken by one person.

END RHYME See *Rhyme.*

EPIC An *epic* is a long narrative poem about the deeds of gods or heroes. Homer's the *Odyssey,* on page 645, is an example of epic poetry. It tells the story of the Greek hero Odysseus, the king of Ithaca.

An epic is elevated in style and usually follows certain patterns. The poet begins by announcing the subject and asking a Muse, one of the nine goddesses of the arts, literature, and sciences, to help. Early on, the poet asks an epic question. The epic itself is the answer. Odysseus asks,

Where shall a man find sweetness to surpass his own home and his parents? In far lands he shall not, though he find a house of gold. What of my sailing, then, from Troy?

　　　What of those years
of rough adventure, weathered under Zeus?

See *Homeric Simile* and *Narrative Poem.*

EPIC SIMILE See *Homeric Simile.*

ESSAY An *essay* is a short nonfiction work about a particular subject. While classification is difficult, four types of essays are sometimes identified. A *descriptive essay* seeks to convey an impression about a person, place, or object. In "A Celebration of Grandfathers," on page 447, Rudolfo Anaya describes the cultural values that his grandfather and other "old ones" from his childhood passed down.

A *narrative essay* tells a true story. In "Nameless, Tennessee," on page 441, William Least Heat Moon tells about his visit to a small town called "Nameless."

An *expository essay* gives information, discusses ideas, or explains a process. In "The Loch Ness Monster," page 457, John McPhee tells about an organization that gathers data on a 40-foot monster living in a Scottish lake.

A *persuasive essay* tries to convince readers to do something or to accept the writer's point of view. Martin Luther King, Jr.'s "'I Have a Dream'" speech, delivered during the days of the civil rights movement, makes an impassioned appeal for freedom and equality.

This classification of essays is loose at best. Most essays contain passages that could be classified differently from the essay as a whole. For example, a descriptive passage may be found in a narrative essay, or a factual, expository section may be used to support a persuasive argument.
See *Description, Exposition, Genre, Narration, Nonfiction,* and *Persuasion.*

EXPOSITION *Exposition* is writing or speech that explains a process or presents information. In the plot of a story or drama, the exposition is the part of the work that introduces the characters, the setting, and the basic situation. In William Gibson's *The Miracle Worker,* on page 219, the opening scene serves as an exposition, revealing that the infant Helen has had a serious fever that has left her blind and deaf.
See *Essay, Nonfiction,* and *Plot.*

EXTENDED METAPHOR In an *extended metaphor,* as in regular metaphor, a subject is spoken or written of as though it were something else. However, extended metaphor differs from regular metaphor in that several comparisons are made. All extended metaphor sustains the comparison for several lines or for an entire poem. The "caged bird" of Paul Laurence Dunbar's "Sympathy," on page 517, is an extended metaphor for a person who is not free. In the poem below, Robert Frost's "In a Glass of Cider," the speaker identifies himself as a "mite of sediment," or a speck of matter that settles in the bottom:

> It seemed I was a mite of sediment
> That waited for the bottom to ferment
> So I could catch a bubble in ascent.
> I rode up on one till the bubble burst,
> And when that left me to sink back reversed
> I was no worse off than I was at first.
> I'd catch another bubble if I waited.
> The thing was to get now and then elated.

The poet extends the metaphor to show the highs and lows of life. The last line expresses the theme of the poem.
See *Figurative Language* and *Metaphor.*

FALLING ACTION See *Plot.*

FANTASY A *fantasy* is highly imaginative writing that contains elements not found in real life. Examples of fantasy include stories that deal with possible or supernatural elements, stories that resemble fairy tales, and stories that deal with imaginary places and creatures, like Anne McCaffrey's *Dragonsong,* on page 915.

Some writers consider science fiction a type of fantasy. Other writers make a distinction between the two kinds of writing.
See *Science Fiction.*

FICTION   *Fiction* is prose writing that tells about imaginary characters and events. The term is usually used for novels and short stories, but it also applies to dramas and narrative poetry. Some writers rely on their imaginations alone to create their works of fiction. Others base their fiction on actual events and people, to which they add invented characters, dialogue, and plot situations.
See *Genre, Narrative,* and *Nonfiction.*

FIGURATIVE LANGUAGE   *Figurative language* is writing or speech not meant to be interpreted literally.

Figurative language is often used to create vivid impressions by setting up comparisons between dissimilar things. Notice, for example, how vivid the image is in the excerpt from D. C. Berry's "On Reading Poems to a Senior Class at South High":

> Before
> I opened my mouth
> I noticed them sitting there
> as orderly as frozen fish
> in a package.

Though such figures of speech are especially important in poetry, they are used in prose as well. Look, for example, at this description from James Hurst's "The Scarlet Ibis," on page 181:

> . . . the oriole nest in the elm was untenanted and rocked back and forth like an empty cradle. The last graveyard flowers were blooming, and their smell drifted across the cotton field and through every room of our house, speaking softly the names of our dead.

Some frequently used figures of speech are *metaphors, similes,* and *personifications.*
See *Literal Language.*

FLASHBACK   A *flashback* is a section of a literary work that interrupts the sequence of events to relate an event from an earlier time. Normally, events are told in chronological order, the order in which they happen in time. A flashback, however, interrupts chronological order to go back to an earlier time. A flashback may be a short part of the story, or the story may be built around a flashback. Mark Twain's "The Invalid's Story," on page 99, starts when the narrator is forty-one but feels sixty. Then the narrator jumps back in time to "One winter's night, two years ago," when the events happened that ruined his health.

FLAT CHARACTER   See *Character.*

FOIL   A *foil* is a character who is contrasted with another character. In Richard Connell's "The Most Dangerous Game," on page 13, General Zaroff surrounds himself with the trappings of civilization, but we see Rainsford as the more civilized man because of the contrast between the two men's views on hunting. Thus Rainsford serves as a foil for Zaroff, and Zaroff serves as a foil for Rainsford.

FOOT   See *Meter.*

FORESHADOWING   *Foreshadowing* is the use in a literary work of clues that suggest events that have yet to occur. Use of this technique helps to create suspense, keeping readers wondering and speculating about what will happen next. Both the title of Grant Moss, Jr.'s "Before the End of Summer," on page 107, and this brief bit of dialogue from early in the story tell readers that something important will happen before the end of summer:

"How long will it be?" he heard his grandmother say.

"Before the end of summer."

See *Suspense.*

FRAMEWORK STORY   A *framework story* is one that contains a story within another story. A famous example of a framework story is Chaucer's *Canterbury Tales,* an account of a group of pilgrims who, on their way to Canterbury, take turns telling tales. In Toni Cade Bambara's "Blues Ain't No Mockin Bird," on page 91, the framing story is the main story about the Cain family's reactions to and attitude about the men who want to film them for the county. The story within a story is the one Granny Cain tells the children about the filming of a man who attempts suicide.

FREE VERSE   *Free verse* is poetry not written in a regular rhythmical pattern, or meter. Free verse seeks to capture the rhythms of speech. It is the dominant form of contemporary poetry, as in these lines from Leroy V. Quintana's "piñones":

> when i was young
> we would sit by
> an old firewood stove
> watching my grandmother make candy,
> listening to the stories
> my grandparents would tell
> about "the old days"
> and eat piñones

See *Meter.*

GENRE   A *genre* is a division or type of literature. Literature is commonly divided into three major genres: poetry, prose, and drama. Each major genre is in turn divided into smaller genres, as follows:

1. Poetry: Lyric Poetry, Concrete Poetry, Dramatic Poetry, Narrative Poetry, and Epic Poetry

2. Prose: Fiction (Novels and Short Stories) and Nonfiction (Biography, Autobiography, Letters, Essays, and Reports)
3. Drama: Serious Drama and Tragedy, Comic Drama, Melodrama, and Farce

See *Drama, Poetry,* and *Prose.*

HAIKU   The *haiku* is a three-line Japanese verse form. The first and third lines of a haiku have five syllables. The second line has seven syllables. A haiku seeks to convey a single vivid emotion by means of images from nature. The poems on page 628 are haiku. In the example below, the poet Shiki conveys loneliness through the image of wild geese in the fall:

> Railroad tracks; a flight
> of wild geese close above them
> in the moonlit night.

Translators of Japanese haiku try to maintain the syllabic requirements. Western writers, however, sometimes use the form more loosely.

HEPTAMETER   See *Meter.*

HERO/HEROINE   A *hero* or *heroine* is a character whose actions are inspiring or noble. In ancient stories and myths, the hero or heroine is usually morally, physically, and intellectually superior. In modern literature the main character is usually an ordinary human being.

See *Character.*

HEXAMETER   See *Meter.*

HOMERIC SIMILE   A *Homeric simile,* also called an *epic simile,* is an elaborate comparison of unlike subjects. In this example from the *Odyssey,* on page 645, Homer compares the bodies of men killed by Odysseus to a fisherman's catch heaped up on the shore:

> Think of a catch that fishermen haul in to a
>   half-moon bay

in a fine-meshed net from the whitecaps of the
    sea:
how all are poured out on the sand, in throes
    for the salt sea,
twitching their cold lives away in Helios'
    fiery air;
so lay the suitors heaped on one another.

See *Figurative Language* and *Simile.*

IAMB   See *Meter.*

IMAGE   An *image* is a word or phrase that appeals to one or more of the five senses—sight, hearing, touch, taste, or smell. Writers use images to re-create sensory experiences in words. See *Description.*

INCITING INCIDENT   See *Plot.*

INDIRECT CHARACTERIZATION   See *Characterization.*

INTERNAL RHYME   See *Rhyme.*

IRONY   *Irony* is the general name given to literary techniques that involve differences between appearance and reality, expectation and result, or meaning and intention. In *verbal irony* words are used to suggest the opposite of what is meant. In *dramatic irony* there is a contradiction between what a character thinks and what the reader or audience knows to be true. In *irony of situation,* an event occurs that directly contradicts the expectations of the characters, the reader, or the audience. The humor in Ernest Lawrence Thayer's "Casey at the Bat," on page 521, derives in part from irony of situation. The speaker creates the expectation that Casey will save the day. However, at the end of the poem "there is no joy in Mudville" because "Mighty Casey has struck out."

IRONY OF SITUATION   See *Irony.*

LITERAL LANGUAGE   *Literal language* uses words in their ordinary senses. It is the opposite of *figurative language.* If you tell someone standing on a diving board to jump in, you are speaking literally. If you tell someone standing on the street corner to go jump in the lake, you are speaking figuratively.
See *Figurative Language.*

LYRIC POEM   A *lyric poem* is a highly musical verse that expresses the observations and feelings of a single speaker. In ancient times lyric poems were sung to the accompaniment of the lyre, a type of stringed instrument. Modern lyric poems are not usually sung. However, they still have a musical quality that is achieved through rhythm and other devices such as alliteration and rhyme. Alfred, Lord Tennyson's "The Eagle," on page 590, is a lyric poem expressing the speaker's feeling of wonder as he watches an eagle dive from a cliff.

MAIN CHARACTER   See *Character.*

METAPHOR   A *metaphor* is a figure of speech in which one thing is spoken of as though it were something else. Unlike a simile, which compares two things using *like* or *as,* a metaphor states a comparison directly. In "Dreams," on page 595, Langston Hughes uses a metaphor to show what happens to a life without dreams:

Hold fast to dreams
For if dreams die
Life is a broken-winged bird
That cannot fly.

Metaphors are especially important to poets, but prose writers use them as well. In *The Great Gatsby,* F. Scott Fitzgerald, a twentieth-century American novelist, described age thirty with a metaphor:

Thirty—the promise of a decade of loneliness, a thinning list of single men to know, *a thinning briefcase of enthusiasm,* thinning hair.

Note that people often use metaphoric language in everyday speech, as in the expression "He's got an eagle eye."
See *Extended Metaphor* and *Figurative Language*.

METER The *meter* of a poem is its rhythmical pattern. This pattern is determined by the number and types of stresses, or beats, in each line. To describe the meter of a poem, you must *scan* its lines. *Scanning* involves marking the stressed and unstressed syllables, as shown with the following two lines from "The Charge of the Light Brigade" by Alfred, Lord Tennyson, on page 533:

Hálf ă leăgue, | hálf ă leăgue
Hálf ă leăgue, | ŏnwaŕd

As you can see, each strong stress is marked with a slanted line (·) and each unstressed syllable with a horseshoe symbol (˘). The stressed and unstressed syllables are then divided by vertical lines (|) into groups called *feet*. The following types of feet are common in English poetry:

1. *Iamb:* a foot with one unstressed syllable followed by a stressed syllable, as in the word "ăgáin"
2. *Trochee:* a foot with a stressed syllable followed by an unstressed syllable, as in the word "wónděr"
3. *Anapest:* a foot with two unstressed syllables followed by one strong stress, as in the phrase "ŏn thĕ béach"
4. *Dactyl:* a foot with one strong stress followed by two unstressed syllables, as in the word "wónděrfŭl"
5. *Spondee:* a foot with two strong stresses, as in the word "spácewálk"
6. *Pyrrhic:* a foot with two unstressed syllables, as in the last foot of the line "ănd súd|děnlў"
7. *Amphibrach:* a foot with an unstressed syllable, followed by a stressed syllable, and another unstressed syllable, as in "thăt márvěl|ŏus músĭc"

8. *Amphimacer:* a foot with a stressed syllable, an unstressed syllable, and a stressed syllable, as in "hére ănd góne"

Depending on the type of foot that is most common in them, lines of poetry are described as *iambic, trochaic, anapestic,* and so forth.

Lines are also described in terms of the number of feet that occur in them, as follows:
1. *Monometer:* verse written in one-foot lines

Aĺl thíngs
Mŭst páss
Ăwáy.

2. *Dimeter:* verse written in two-foot lines

Thŏmas | Jéffĕrsŏn
Whăt dŏ | yŏu sáy
Ŭndĕr thĕ | grávestŏne
Híddĕn | ăwáy?
　　—Rosemary and Stephen Vincent Benét,
　　"Thomas Jefferson 1743–1826"

3. *Trimeter:* verse written in three-foot lines

Ĭ knów | nŏt whŏm | Ĭ méet
Ĭ knów | nŏt whĕre | Ĭ ǵo.

4. *Tetrameter:* verse written in four-foot lines
5. *Pentameter:* verse written in five-foot lines
6. *Hexameter:* verse written in six-foot lines
7. *Heptameter:* verse written in seven-foot lines

A complete description of the meter of a line tells the kinds of feet each line contains, as well as how many feet of each kind of foot is most common. Thus the lines quoted under the head "Monometer" in this entry would be described as *iambic monometer. Blank verse* is poetry written in unrhymed iambic pentameter. Poetry that does not have a regular meter is called *free verse.*

MONOLOGUE A *monologue* is a speech by one character in a play, story, or poem. An example from Shakespeare's *Romeo and Juliet,* on page 287, is the speech in which the Prince of Verona commands the Capulets and Montagues to cease feuding (Act I, Scene i, lines 62–84). See *Dramatic Poetry* and *Soliloquy.*

Handbook of Literary Terms and Techniques 1065

MONOMETER See *Meter.*

MOOD *Mood,* or *atmosphere,* is the feeling created in the reader by a literary work or passage. The mood is often suggested by descriptive details. Often the mood can be described in a single word such as lighthearted, frightening, or despairing. The mood of Alfred, Lord Tennyson's "The Charge of the Light Brigade," on page 533, can be described as grand or heroic:

Half a league, half a league
Half a league onward,
All in the valley of Death
    Rode the six hundred.
"Forward the Light Brigade!
Charge for the guns!" he said.
Into the valley of Death
    Rode the six hundred.

See *Tone.*

MORAL A *moral* is a lesson taught by a literary work. A fable usually ends with a moral that is directly stated.

MOTIVATION *Motivation* is a reason that explains or partially explains a character's thoughts, feelings, actions, or behavior. Motivation results from a combination of the character's personality and the circumstances he or she must deal with. Mrs. Higgins, in Morley Callaghan's "All the Years of Her Life," on page 57, is motivated by fear for her son together with her own embarrassment at his being caught stealing.

When the motives of a main character are not clear and logical, neither that character nor the story seems believable. Adventure stories often do not concern themselves much with the character's motivations. In contrast, serious fiction usually explores motivations in depth.
See *Character* and *Characterization.*

MYTH A *myth* is a fictional tale that explains the actions of gods or the causes of natural phenomena. Unlike legends, myths have little histori-

cal truth and involve supernatural elements. Every culture has its collections of myths. Among the most familiar are the myths of the ancient Greeks and Romans. The *Odyssey,* on page 645, is a mythical story, attributed to the ancient Greek poet Homer.
See *Oral Tradition.*

NARRATION *Narration* is writing that tells a story. The act of telling a story is also called narration. Novels and short stories are fictional narratives. Nonfiction works such as news stories, biographies, and autobiographies are also narratives. A narrative poem tells a story in verse.
See *Anecdote, Essay, Narrative Poem, Nonfiction, Novel,* and *Short Story.*

NARRATIVE A *narrative* is a story told in fiction, nonfiction, poetry, or drama.
See *Narration.*

NARRATIVE POEM A *narrative poem* is one that tells a story. "Casey at the Bat," on page 521, is a humorous narrative poem about the last inning of a baseball game. Edgar Allan Poe's "The Raven," on page 527, is a serious narrative poem about a man's grief over the loss of a loved one.
See *Dramatic Poetry, Epic,* and *Narration.*

NARRATOR A *narrator* is a speaker or character who tells a story. The narrator may be either a character in the story or an outside observer. The writer's choice of narrator determines the story's *point of view,* which in turn determines the type and amount of information the writer can reveal.

When a character in the story tells the story, that character is a *first-person narrator.* This narrator may be a major character, a minor character, or just a witness. Readers see only what this character sees, hear only what he or she hears, and so on. The first-person narrator may or may not be reliable. We have reason, for example, to be suspicious of the first-person narrator of Edgar Allan Poe's "The Cask of Amontillado," on page 3.

When a voice outside the story narrates, the story has a *third-person narrator*. An *omniscient,* or all-knowing, third-person narrator can tell readers what any character thinks and feels. For example, in Guy de Maupassant's "The Necklace," on page 193, we know the feelings of both Monsieur and Madame Loisel. A *limited* third-person narrator, on the other hand, sees the world through one character's eyes and reveals only that character's thoughts, no one else's. For example, in Siu Wai Anderson's "Autumn Gardening," on page 127, readers share only Mariko's experiences and feelings.
See *Speaker.*

NONFICTION *Nonfiction* is prose writing that presents and explains ideas or that tells about real people, places, objects, or events. Nonfiction narratives are about actual people, places, and events, unlike fictional narratives, which present imaginary characters and events. To be classed as nonfiction, a work must be true. Arthur C. Clarke's "If I Forget Thee, Oh Earth . . . ," on page 157, presents a fictional account of the Earth as viewed from space. "Single Room, Earth View," on page 487, presents a nonfictional account of the same subject.

Among nonfiction forms are essays, newspaper and magazine articles, journals, travelogues, biographies, and autobiographies. Historical, scientific, technical, political, and philosophical writings are also nonfiction.
See *Autobiography, Biography,* and *Essay.*

NOVEL A *novel* is a long work of fiction. Like a short story, a novel has a plot that explores characters in conflict. However, a novel is much longer than a short story and may have one or more subplots, or minor stories, and several themes.

The novel has its roots in ancient storytelling traditions, but it became an especially important literary form in the late nineteenth and early twentieth centuries. The subject matter of a novel can range form the fantasy of Anne McCaffrey's *Dragonsong,* on page 915, to the realistic detail of Charles Dickens's *Great Expectations,* on page 725.

OCTAVE See *Stanza.*

ONOMATOPOEIA *Onomatopoeia* is the use of words that imitate sounds. *Whirr, thud, sizzle,* and *hiss* are typical examples. Writers can deliberately choose words that contribute to a desired sound effect. In the following lines, from Edgar Allan Poe's "The Bells," on page 604, *clang, crash, roar,* and *twang* are onomatopoeic:

Oh, the bells, bells, bells!
What a tale their terror tells
Of Despair!
How they clang, and clash, and roar!
What a horror they outpour
On the bosom of the palpitating air!
Yet the ear it fully knows,
By the twanging
And the clanging,
How the danger ebbs and flows

ORAL TRADITION The *oral tradition* is the passing of songs, stories, and poems from generation to generation by word of mouth. Many folk songs, ballads, fairy tales, legends, and myths originated in the oral tradition.
See *Myth.*

PARODY A *parody* is a work done in imitation of another, usually in order to mock it, but sometimes just in fun. The following lines are Lewis Carroll's parody of the familiar children's rhyme, "Twinkle, Twinkle, Little Star":

Twinkle, twinkle, little bat!
How I wonder what you're at!
Up above the world you fly,
Like a teatray in the sky.

PENTAMETER See *Meter.*

PERSONIFICATION *Personification* is a type of figurative language in which a nonhuman subject is given human characteristics. When Edgar Lee Masters says on page 552 that "Sorrow knocked at my door, but I was afraid;/Ambition called to me, but I dreaded the chances," he is personifying the abstract qualities of sorrow and ambition. In the poem below, "Soft Snow," William Blake personifies both the snow and winter:

> I walked abroad in a snowy day;
> I asked the soft snow with me to play;
> She played and she melted in all her
>   prime,
> And the winter called it a dreadful crime.

See *Figurative Language.*

PERSUASION *Persuasion* is writing or speech that attempts to convince the reader to adopt a particular opinion or course of action. A newspaper editorial that says a city council decision was wrong is an example of persuasive writing attempting to mold opinion. A television commercial showing the benefits of a new toothpaste is meant to move viewers to act, in this case to buy toothpaste.

PLOT *Plot* is the sequence of events in a literary work. In most novels, dramas, short stories, and narrative poems, the plot involves both characters and a central conflict. The plot usually begins with an *exposition* that introduces the setting, the characters, and the basic situation. This is followed by the *inciting incident,* which introduces the central conflict. The conflict then increases during the *development* until it reaches a high point of interest or suspense, the *climax.* All the events leading up to the climax make up the *rising action.* The climax is followed by the *falling action,* which leads to the *resolution,* or end, of the central conflict. Any events that occur after the resolution make up the *denouement.*

POETRY *Poetry* is one of the three major types of literature, the others being prose and drama. Most poems make use of highly concise, musical, and emotionally charged language. Many also make use of imagery, figurative language, and special devices of sound such as rhyme. Poems are often divided into lines and stanzas and often employ regular rhythmical patterns, or meters. However, some poems are written out just like prose, and some are written in free verse. See *Genre.*

POINT OF VIEW See *Narrator.*

PROSE *Prose* is the ordinary form of written language. Most writing that is not poetry, drama, or song is considered prose. Prose is one of the major genres of literature and occurs in two forms: fiction and nonfiction. See *Fiction, Genre,* and *Nonfiction.*

PROTAGONIST The *protagonist* is the main character in a literary work. In "The Secret Life of Walter Mitty," on page 201, Walter Mitty is the protagonist. See *Antagonist.*

PUN A *pun* is a play on words based on different meanings of words that sound alike. Here is an example:

> Question: Define *wise.*
> Answer: It's what little kids are always asking, as in "Wise the sky blue?"

QUATRAIN A *quatrain* is a stanza or poem made up of four lines, usually with a definite rhythm and rhyme scheme. The following quatrain is from Stephen Vincent Benét's "The Ballad of William Sycamore":

> My father, he was a mountaineer,
> His fist was a knotty hammer;
> He was quick on his feet as a running deer,
> And he spoke with a Yankee stammer.

See *Stanza.*

REFRAIN A *refrain* is a repeated line or group of lines in a poem or song. For example, in "The Charge of the Light Brigade," by Alfred, Lord Tennyson, on page 533, the line "Rode the six hundred" is repeated with variations at the ends of each stanza.
See *Repetition.*

REPETITION *Repetition* is the use, more than once, of any element of language—a sound, a word, a phrase, a clause, or a sentence. In his famous civil rights speech, on page 467, Martin Luther King, Jr. repeats the words "I have a dream" eight times, each time in connection with a different image.

Poets use many kinds of repetition. Alliteration, assonance, rhyme, and rhythm are repetitions of certain sounds and sound patterns. A refrain is a repeated line or group of lines. In both prose and poetry, repetition is used for musical effects and for emphasis.
See *Alliteration, Assonance, Consonance, Refrain, Rhyme,* and *Rhythm.*

RESOLUTION See *Plot.*

RHYME *Rhyme* is the repetition of sounds at the ends of words. *End rhyme* occurs when the rhyming words come at the ends of lines, as in "The Desired Swan Song," by Samuel Taylor Coleridge:

Swans sing before they die—'twere no bad
  thing
Should certain persons die before they sing.

Internal rhyme occurs when the rhyming words appear in the same line, as in lines 1 and 3 of Edgar Allan Poe's "The Raven," on page 527:

Once upon a midnight d*reary,* while I pondered,
  weak and w*eary,*
Over many a quaint and curious volume of
  forgotten lore,
While I nodded, nearly n*apping,* suddenly there
  came a t*apping,*

See *Repetition* and *Rhyme Scheme.*

RHYME SCHEME A *rhyme scheme* is a regular pattern of rhyming words in a poem. The rhyme scheme of a poem is indicated by using different letters of the alphabet for each new rhyme. In an *aabb* stanza, for example, line 1 rhymes with line 2 and line 3 rhymes with line 4. William Wordsworth's poem on page 592 uses an *ababcc* rhyme pattern:

I wandered lonely as a cloud	*a*
That floats on high o'er vales and hills,	*b*
When all at once I saw a crowd,	*a*
A host, of golden daffodils;	*b*
Beside the lake, beneath the trees,	*c*
Fluttering and dancing in the breeze.	*c*

Many poems use the same pattern of rhymes, though not the same rhymes, in each stanza. The next stanza of Wordsworth's poem, for example, has this rhyme scheme: *dedeff.*
See *Rhyme.*

RHYTHM *Rhythm* is the pattern of *beats,* or stresses, in spoken or written language. Some poems have a very specific pattern, or meter, whereas prose and free verse use the natural rhythms of everyday speech.
See *Meter.*

RISING ACTION See *Plot.*

ROUND CHARACTER See *Character.*

SATIRE *Satire* is a style of writing that uses humor—sometimes gentle and sometimes biting—to criticize people, ideas, or institutions in hopes of improving them. In "The Spreading 'You Know,'" on page 493, James Thurber mocks people's tendency to use a careless phrase. Clearly, he would prefer they didn't.

SCENE See *Drama.*

SCIENCE FICTION *Science fiction* is writing that tells about imaginary events that involve science or technology. Many science-fiction stories are set in the future. The setting can be on Earth,

in space, on other planets, or in a totally imaginary place. Arthur C. Clarke's "If I Forget Thee, Oh Earth . . . ," on page 157, is a science-fiction story set on the moon after a nuclear disaster on Earth.
See *Fantasy.*

SENSORY LANGUAGE   *Sensory language* is writing or speech that appeals to one or more of the senses.
See *Image.*

SESTET   See *Stanza.*

SETTING   The *setting* of a literary work is the time and place of the action. Time can include not only the historical period—past, present, or future—but also a specific year, season, or time of day. Place may involve not only the geographical place—a region, country, state, or town—but also the social, economic, or cultural environment.

In some stories setting serves merely as a backdrop for action, a context in which the characters move and speak. In others, however, setting is a crucial element. Both the desert and Native American culture are important in Leslie Marmon Silko's "The Man to Send Rain Clouds," on page 151, and the lunar landscape and the future are important in Arthur C. Clarke's "If I Forget Thee, Oh Earth . . . ," on page 157.

Description of the setting often helps establish the mood of a story. For example, in Edgar Allan Poe's "The Cask of Amontillado," on page 3, the setting contributes to the growing horror.
See *Mood.*

SHORT STORY   A *short story* is a brief work of fiction. A novel, by contrast, is a long work of fiction. In most short stories, one main character faces a conflict that is worked out in the plot of the story. Great craftsmanship must go into the writing of a good story, for it has to accomplish its purpose in very few words.

The short story as a distinct literary form emerged in the nineteenth century. The American writers Edgar Allan Poe and Nathaniel Hawthorne were especially important in the development of the short story.
See *Fiction* and *Genre.*

SIMILE   A *simile* is a figure of speech in which *like* or *as* is used to make a comparison between two basically unlike ideas. "Claire is as fighty as Roger" is a comparison, not a simile. "Claire is as flighty as a sparrow" is a simile.

Poets often use similes. The following example is from Donald Justice's "Incident in a Rose Garden," on page 539:

> Sir, I encountered Death
> Just now among our roses.
> *Thin as a scythe* he stood there.

Prose writers also use similes. Here is one from Paule Marshall's "To Da-duh, in Memoriam," on page 139:

> . . . her eyes were alive . . . with a sharp light that flicked out of the dim clouded depths like a lizard's tongue to snap up all in her view.

See *Figurative Language.*

SOLILOQUY   A *soliloquy* is a long speech expressing the thoughts of a character alone on stage. In William Shakespeare's *Romeo and Juliet,* on page 287, Romeo gives a soliloquy after the servant has fled and Paris has died (Act V, Scene iii, lines 74–120).
See *Monologue.*

SONNET   A *sonnet* is a fourteen-line lyric poem, usually written in rhymed iambic pentameter. The *English,* or *Shakespearean, sonnet* consists of three quatrains (four-line stanzas) and a couplet (two lines), usually rhyming *abab cdcd efef gg.* The couplet usually comments on the ideas contained in the preceding twelve lines. The sonnet is usually not printed with the stanzas divided, but a reader can see distinct ideas in each. See the English sonnet by William Shakespeare on page 625.

The *Italian*, or *Petrarchan, sonnet* consists of an octave (eight-line stanza) and a sestet (six-line stanza). Often the octave rhymes *abbaabba* and the sestet rhymes *cdecde*. The octave states a theme or asks a question. The sestet comments on or answers the question. Henry Wadsworth Longfellow's "The Sound of the Sea," on page 624, is a Petrarchan sonnet.

The Petrarchan sonnet took its name from Petrarch, a fourteenth-century Italian poet. Once the form was introduced in England, it underwent change. The Shakespearean sonnet is, of course, named after William Shakespeare. See *Lyric Poem, Meter,* and *Stanza.*

SPEAKER   The *speaker* is the imaginary voice assumed by the writer of a poem. In many poems the speaker is not identified by name. When reading a poem, remember that the speaker and the poet are not the same person, no more than an actor is the playwright. The speaker within the poem may be a person, an animal, a thing, or an abstraction. The speaker in the following stanza by Emily Dickinson is a person who has died:

Because I could not stop for Death—
He kindly stopped for me—
The Carriage held but just Ourselves—
And Immortality.

STAGE DIRECTIONS   *Stage directions* are notes included in a drama to describe how the work is to be performed or staged. These instructions are printed in italics and are not spoken aloud. They are used to describe sets, lighting, sound effects, and the appearance, personalities, and movements of characters.
See *Drama.*

STANZA   A *stanza* is a formal division of lines in a poem, considered as a unit. Often the stanzas in a poem are separated by spaces.

Stanzas are sometimes named according to the number of lines found in them. A *couplet,* for example, is a two-line stanza. A *tercet* is a stanza with three lines. Other types of stanzas include the following:

1. *Quatrain:* a four-line stanza
2. *Cinquain:* a five-line stanza
3. *Sestet:* a six-line stanza
4. *Heptastich:* a seven-line stanza
5. *Octave:* an eight-line stanza

Sonnets, limericks, and haiku all have distinct stanza forms. A *sonnet* is a fourteen-line poem that is made up either of three quatrains and a couplet or of an octave followed by a sestet. A *limerick* consists of a single five-line stanza with a particular pattern of rhymes. A *haiku* is made up of a single three-line stanza.
See *Haiku* and *Sonnet.*

STATIC CHARACTER   See *Character.*

SURPRISE ENDING   A *surprise ending* is a conclusion that violates the expectations of the reader but in a way that is both logical and believable. O. Henry's "The Gift of the Magi," on page 175, and Guy de Maupassant's "The Necklace," on page 193, have surprise endings. Both authors were masters of the form.

SUSPENSE   *Suspense* is a feeling of curiosity or uncertainty about the outcome of events in a literary work. Writers create suspense by raising questions in the minds of their readers. Suspense may stem from the physical danger faced by a character or from psychological tension, as in the battle of wills between Annie and Helen in William Gibson's *The Miracle Worker.*

SYMBOL   A *symbol* is anything that stands for or represents something else. An object that serves as a symbol has its own meaning, but it also represents abstract ideas. Marks on paper can symbolize spoken words. A flag symbolizes a country. A flashy car may symbolize wealth. Writers sometimes use such conventional symbols in their work, but they also sometimes create symbols of their own through emphasis or repetition.

In James Hurst's "The Scarlet Ibis," on page 181, the ibis symbolizes the character named Doodle. Doodle and the ibis have many traits in common. Both are beautiful and otherworldly. Both struggle against great odds. Both meet an unfortunate fate. Since a story says something about life or people in general, the ibis, in a larger sense, becomes a symbol for all those who struggle.

TETRAMETER   See *Meter.*

THEME   A *theme* is a central message or insight into life revealed through the literary work. The theme is not a condensed summary of the plot. Instead, it is a generalization about human beings or about life that the literary work communicates.

The theme of a literary work may be stated directly or implied. In James Hurst's "The Scarlet Ibis," on page 181, the narrator directly states one theme of the story: ". . . pride is a wonderful, terrible thing, a seed that bears two vines, life and death."

When the theme of a work is implied, readers think about what the work seems to say about the nature of people or about life. The story or poem can be viewed as a specific example of the generalization the writer is trying to communicate.

Note that there is usually no single correct statement of a work's theme, though there can be incorrect ones. Also, a long work, like a novel or a full-length play, may have several themes. Finally, not all literary works have themes. A work meant only to entertain may have no theme at all.

TONE   The *tone* of a literary work is the writer's attitude toward his or her audience and subject. The tone can often be described by a single adjective such as *formal* or *informal, serious* or *playful, bitter,* or *ironic.* When O. Henry discusses the young married couple in "The Gift of the Magi," on page 175, he uses a sympathetic tone. By contrast, Margaret Walker uses a grieving tone in her poem "Memory," on page 578. See *Mood.*

TRAGEDY   A *tragedy* is a work of literature, especially a play, that results in a catastrophe for the main character. In ancient Greek drama, the main character was always a significant person, a king or a hero, and the cause of the tragedy was a tragic flaw, or weakness, in his or her character. In modern drama the main character can be an ordinary person, and the cause of the tragedy can be some evil in society itself. The purpose of tragedy is not only to arouse fear and pity in the audience, but also, in some cases, to convey a sense of the grandeur and nobility of the human spirit.

Shakespeare's *Romeo and Juliet,* on page 287, is a tragedy. Romeo and Juliet both suffer from the tragic flaw of impulsiveness. This flaw ultimately leads to their deaths.
See *Drama.*

TRIMETER   See *Meter.*

VERBAL IRONY   See *Irony.*

VERISIMILITUDE   *Verisimilitude,* which literally means "similar to the truth," is the appearance of truth or reality in a work of fiction. A writer creates verisimilitude by giving characters realistic traits, mannerisms, speech, and so on, and by describing realistic settings or situations. For example, in "Blues Ain't No Mockin Bird," beginning on page 91, Toni Cade Bambara creates characters who are believable and true to life.

GLOSSARY

READING THE GLOSSARY ENTRIES

The words in this glossary are from selections appearing in your textbook. Each entry in the glossary contains the following parts:

1. Entry Word. This word appears at the beginning of the entry, in boldface type.

2. Pronunciation. The symbols in parentheses tell how the entry word is pronounced. If a word has more than one possible pronunciation, the most common of these pronunciations is given first.

3. Part of Speech. Appearing after the pronunciation, in italics, is an abbreviation that tells the part of speech of the entry word. The following abbreviations have been used:

n. noun   **p.** pronoun   **v.** verb

adj. adjective   **adv.** adverb   **conj.** conjunction

4. Definition. This part of the entry follows the part-of-speech abbreviation and gives the meaning of the entry word as used in the selection in which it appears.

KEY TO PRONUNCIATION SYMBOLS USED IN THE GLOSSARY

The following symbols are used in the pronunciations that follow the entry words:

Symbol	Key Words	Symbol	Key Words
a	asp, fat, parrot	b	bed, fable, dub
ā	ape, date, play	d	dip, beadle, had
ä	ah, car, father	f	fall, after, off
		g	get, haggle, dog
e	elf, ten, berry	h	he, ahead, hotel
ē	even, meet, money	j	joy, agile, badge
		k	kill, tackle, bake
i	is, hit, mirror	l	let, yellow, ball
ī	ice, bite, high	m	met, camel, trim
		n	not, flannel, ton
ō	open, tone, go	p	put, apple, tap
ô	all, horn, law	r	red, port, dear
o͞o	ooze, tool, crew	s	sell, castle, pass
oo	look, pull, moor	t	top, cattle, hat
yo͞o	use, cute, few	v	vat, hovel, have
yoo	united, cure, globule	w	will, always, swear
oi	oil, point, toy	y	yet, onion, yard
ou	out, crowd, plow	z	zebra, dazzle, haze
u	up, cut, color	ch	chin, catcher, arch
ur	urn, fur, deter	sh	she, cushion, dash
		th	thin, nothing, truth
ə	a in ago	th	then, father, lathe
	e in agent	zh	azure, leisure
	i in sanity	ŋ	ring, anger, drink
	o in comply	'	[indicates that a
	u in focus		following l or n is a
ər	perhaps, murder		syllabic consonant, as in
			able (ā' b'l)]

FOREIGN SOUNDS

à This symbol, representing the a in French *salle*, can best be described as intermediate between (a) and (ä).

ë This symbol represents the sound of the vowel cluster in french *coeur* and can be approximated by rounding the lips as for (ō) and pronouncing (e).

ö This symbol variously represents the sound of *eu* in French *feu* or of ö or *oe* in German *blöd* or *Goethe* and can be approximated by rounding lips as for (ō) and pronouncing (ā).

ô This symbol represents a range of sounds between (ô) and (u); it occurs typically in the sound of the o in French *tonne* or German *korrekt;* in Italian *poco* and Spanish *torero*, it is almost like English (ô), as in *horn.*

ü This symbol variously represents the sound of *u* in French *duc* and in German *grun* and can be approximated by rounding the lips as for (ō) and pronouncing (ē).

kh This symbol represents the voiceless velar or uvular fricative as in the *ch* of German *doch* or Scots English *loch.* It can be approximated by placing the tongue as for (k) but allowing the breath to escape in a stream, as in pronouncing (h).

r This symbol represents any of various sounds used in languages other than English for the consonant *r.* It may represent the tongue-point trill or uvular trill of the *r* in French *reste* or *sur*, German *Reuter,* Italian *ricotta,* Russian *gorod,* etc.

ƀ This symbol represents the sound made by the letter *v* between vowels. It is pronounced like a *b* sound but without letting the lips come together.

This pronunciation key is from *Webster's New World Dictionary*, Second College Edition. Copyright © 1986 by Simon & Schuster. Used by permission.

A

abashed (ə basht') *adj.* Ill-at-ease; ashamed

aberration (ab' ər ā' shən) *n.* Mental derangement

abhor (əb hôr') *v.* Detest; intensely dislike

abhorrence (əb hôr' əns) *n.* Hatred and disgust

abolitionist (ab' ə lish' ən ist) *n.* Person in favor of doing away with slavery in the United States

abstracted (ab strak' tid) *adj.* Absent-minded

adjure (ə joor') *v.* To appeal to

admonition (ad' mə nish' ən) *n.* A warning

advent (ad' vent') *n.* A coming or arrival

advise (əd vīz') *v.* To consult

aesthetic (es thet' ik) *adv.* Sensitive to art and beauty

aghast (ə gast') *adj.* Feeling horror or dismay

agile (aj′ əl) *adj.* Quick and easy of movement

ague (ā′ gyōō) *n.* Chills and fever

alleviate (ə lē′ vē āt) *v.* To lessen; relieve

allotted (ə lät′ id) *adj.* Assigned; apportioned

allude (ə lōōd′) *n.* To refer to indirectly

allusion (ə lōō′ zhən) *n.* An indirect reference

altimeter (al tim′ ə tər) *n.* An instrument for measuring the height of an aircraft above the surface of the earth or the sea

amber (am′ bər) *n.* A yellowish resin used in jewelry

ambiguity (am′ bə gyōō′ ə tē) *n.* A statement or event whose meaning is unclear

ambrosia (am brō′ zhə) *n.* Food of the gods

ambrosial (am brō′ zhəl) *adj.* Like ambrosia, the delicious food of the Greek and Roman gods

amphitheater (am′ fə thē′ ə ter) *n.* An open space surrounded by rising rings of seats

anathema (ə nath′ ə mə) *n.* Something greatly detested

anguish (an′ gwish) *n.* Great suffering, as from worry or pain

animate (an′ i mit) *adj.* Having life, particularly animal life

anomalous (ə näm′ ə ləs) *adj.* Departing from the usual situation

aphorism (af′ ə rizm) *n.* A short, pointed sentence expressing a wise or clever observation or truth

apprehension (ap′ rē hen′ shən) *n.* Fear; anxiety

aquatic (ə kwat′ ik) *adj.* Growing or living in or upon water

ardor (är′ dər) *n.* Emotional warmth; passion

arpeggio (är pej′ ō) *n.* The notes of a chord played one after the other instead of together

arrogant (ar′ ə gant) *adj.* Proud; haughty

arroyo (ə roi′ ō) *n.* A dry gully

articulate (är tik′ yə lit) *adj.* Expressing oneself well

asafetida (as′ ə fet′ ə də) *n.* A bad-smelling substance from certain plants, used as medicine

assiduity (as′ ə dyōō′ ə tē) *n.* Hard work and perseverance

asthma (az′ mə) *n.* A disease accompanied by difficulty in breathing

astrakhan (as′ trə kan′) *n.* Fur made from young lambs

astutely (ə stōōt′ lē) *adv.* Cleverly or cunningly

astuteness (ə stōōt′ nis) *n.* Shrewdness

atoll (a′ tōl) *n.* A ring-shaped coral island

audacious (ô dā′ shəs) *adj.* Bold; daring

augment (ôg ment′) *v.* To enlarge; increase

aura (ô′rə) *n.* Atmosphere

authentic (ô then′ tik) *adj.* Genuine; of true value

avail (ə vāl′) *v.* To be of help

avarice (av′ ə ris) *n.* Greed

averse (ə vʉrs′) *adj.* Opposed to

aversion (ə vʉr′ zhən) *n.* An intense dislike

awe (ô) *n.* A mixed feeling of fear and wonder

azure (azh′ ər) *adj.* Blue

B

balalaika (bal′ ə līk′ ə) *n.* A Russian stringed instrument somewhat like a guitar

bamboozle (bam bōō′ z'l) *v.* To trick

baritone (bar′ ə tōn′) *n.* A deep-toned male voice between a bass and a tenor

barre (bär) *n.* A handrail held onto while doing ballet exercises

bask (bask) *v.* To warm oneself pleasantly as in sunlight

battery (bat′ ə rē) *n.* A mound of earth on which cannons are placed

beached (bēcht) *adj.* Washed up and lying on a beach

beguile (bi gīl′) *v.* To trick

belligerent (bə lij′ ər ənt) *adj.* Ready to fight or quarrel

bellows (bel′ ōz) *n.* A device for blowing air on a fire

bemuse (bi myōōz′) *v.* To stupefy or muddle

benevolently (bə nev′ ə lənt lē) *adv.* Kindly; charitably

benison (ben′ ə z'n) *n.* A blessing

bereft (bi reft′) *adj.* Left in a sad and lonely state

billet (bil′ it) *n.* A position, job

bizarre (bi zär′) *adj.* Odd in appearance

bland (bland) *adj.* 1. Pleasantly smooth; agreeable 2. In a mild and soothing manner

blight (blīt) *n.* 1. Anything that destroys 2. Plant diseases that result in the death of leaves or whole plants

bliss (blis) *n.* Great joy or happiness

block (bläk) *n.* A pulley

bluebottle (blōō bät′ 'l) *n.* A kind of fly

bluster (blus′ tər) *v.* To speak in a noisy, swaggering manner

bodice (bäd′ is) *n.* The upper part of a woman's dress

bole (bōl) *n.* A tree trunk

bonny (bän′ ē) *adj.* Pretty

boor (bōōr) *n.* A rude, unpleasant person

bowler (bōl′ ər) *n.* A derby hat

brace (brās) *n.* A pair

bravado (brə vä′ dō) *n.* Pretended courage

brazen (brā′ z'n) *adj.* Made of brass: having the sound of brass

brewery (brōō′ ər ē) *n.* An establishment where beer and similar beverages are made

bristle (bris′ 'l) *v.* To become tense with fear or anger

brood (brōōd) *v.* To think about something in a troubled way

brougham (brōōm) *n.* A horse-drawn carriage

brusquely (brusk′ lē) *adv.* In an abrupt and curt manner

Byronic (bī rän′ ik) *adj.* Romantic, like the dashing British poet Lord Byron (1788–1824)

C

cairn (kern) *n.* A conical heap of stones built as a monument

capon (kā′ pän) *n.* A roasted chicken

carboy (kär′ boi) *n.* A large glass bottle enclosed in basketwork to prevent it from breaking

caress (kə res′) *v.* To touch or stroke lovingly or affectionately

cascade (kas kād′) *n.* A waterfall

cashier (kash ir′) *v.* To dishonorably discharge

catacomb (kat′ ə kōm′) *n.* Any of a series of vaults or passages in an underground burial place

cataract (kat′ ə rakt) *n.* A large waterfall

caul (kôl) *n.* The membrane enclosing a baby at birth

causeway (kôz′ wā) *n.* A raised path or road across wet ground

celestial (sə les′ chəl) *adj.* Of heaven; divine

cellulose (sel′ yoo lōs′) *n.* The chief substance composing the cell walls or fibers of all plant tissue

censer (sen′ sər) *n.* A container for burning incense

censure (sen′ shər) *n.* Strong disapproval

chagrin (shə grin′) *n.* Annoyance at a disappointment

chalice (chal′ is) *n.* A cup or goblet

challis (shal′ ē) *n.* A soft, lightweight fabric, usually printed with a design

chaste (chāst) *adj.* Pure or clean in style; not ornate

chattel (chat′ ′l) *n.* A movable item of personal property

cherish (cher′ ish) *v.* To hold dear; feel love for

chic (shēk) *n.* Fashionable

chronic (krän′ ik) *adj.* Constant

cipher (sī′ fər) *v.* To do arithmetic

cirrus (sir′ əs) *adj.* Feathery

cleave (klēv) *v.* Split

clerk (klʉrk) *n.* An official who has minor duties in a church

cloister (klois′ tər) *n.* A place devoted to religious seclusion

coarse (kôrs) *adj.* Rough; crude; unrefined

collaborate (kə lab′ ə rāt′) *v.* To work together

collaborator (kə lab′ ə rāt′ ər) *n.* A person who helps an enemy invader of his or her country

collation (kä lā′ shən) *n.* A light meal

combatant (käm′ bə tənt) *adj.* Prepared for fighting

compel (kəm pel′) *v.* To force

compilation (käm′ pə lā′ shən) *n.* Making collections or anthologies

complacent (kəm plās′ ′nt) *adj.* Self-satisfied

comply (kəm plī′) *v.* To act as requested

concession (kən sesh′ ən) *n.* An act of yielding

condescend (kän′ də send′) *v.* To lower oneself to another's level

condescending (kän′ də sen′ diŋ) *adj.* Characterized by looking down on someone

condescension (kän′ di sen′ shən) *n.* Dealing with others as if doing a thing regarded as beneath one's dignity

condolence (kən dō′ ləns) *n.* An expression of sympathy with a grieving person

confidant (kän′ fə dant′) *n.* A close friend to whom one tells secrets

conglomerate (kən gläm′ ə rāt′) *adj.* Whole made up of parts (usually a noun)

conjecture (kən jek′ chər) *n.* A guess based on incomplete information

connoisseurship (kän′ ə sʉr′ ship) *n.* Expert judgment

conspire (kən spīr′) *v.* To plan and act together secretly, especially to commit a crime

consternation (kän stər nā′ shən) *n.* Great fear or shock that confuses or bewilders

contempt (kən tempt′) *n.* 1. The feeling or attitude toward a person one considers unworthy 2. Scorn; disrespect

contrail (kän′ trāl) *n.* The white trail of condensed water vapor that sometimes forms in the wake of aircraft

conundrum (kə nun′ drəm) *n.* A puzzling question or problem

cornice (kôr′ nis) *n.* A horizontal projection along the top of a wall or building

corroborate (kə räb′ ə rāt′) *v.* To confirm

cosmopolite (käz mäp′ ə līt′) *n.* A person at home in all parts of the world

countenance (koun′ tə nəns) *n.* Facial appearance

countinghouse (koun′ tiŋ hous′) *n.* An office where a firm keeps business records and handles correspondence

cowling (kou′ liŋ) *n.* A detachable metal cover for an airplane engine

cravat (krə vat′) *n.* A necktie

craven (krā′ vən) *n.* A coward (usually an adjective)

credential (kri den′ shəl) *n.* A paper that shows a person's credits and qualifications

creditor (kred′ it ər) *n.* A person to whom money is owed

creed (krēd) *n.* A statement of belief

crepe (krāp) *n.* A thin, black cloth worn to show mourning

crepitation (krep′ ə tā shən) *n.* A crackling sound

crochet (krō shā′) *n.* A kind of needlework

cubicle (kyoo′ bi kəl) *n.* A small compartment

cuirass (kwi ras′) *n.* Armor for the upper body

cunning (kun′ iŋ) *n.* Cleverness; slyness

cupidity (kyoo pid′ ə tē) *n.* Greed

cynical (sin′ i kəl) *adj.* Sneering

D

dainty (dan′ te) *adj.* Delicately pretty

daunt (dônt) *v.* To frighten or dishearten

dauntless (dônt′ lis) *adj.* Unable to be intimidated

deacon (dēk′ ′n) *n.* A church officer who helps the minister

debacle (di bäk′ ′l) *n.* A bad defeat

déclassé (dā′ klä sā′) *adj.* Lowered in social status

declivity (di kliv′ ə tē) *n.* A downward slope

deem (dēm) *v.* To consider

defer (di fur') *v.* To put off until a future time

deference (def' ər əns) *n.* Courteous respect

deferential (def ə ren' sh'l) *adj.* Very respectful

defraud (di frôd) *v.* To cheat

dejection (di jek' shən) *n.* Lowness of spirits; depression

deleterious (del' ə tir' ē əs) *adj.* Injurious; harmful to health or well-being

delicacy (del' i kə sē) *n.* A regard for what is proper

delirious (di lir' ē əs) *adj.* In a state of temporary mental confusion, characterized by delusions and incoherence

dell (del) *n.* A small secluded valley

deportment (di pôrt' mənt) *n.* A way of holding oneself or behaving

depose (di pōz') *v.* To testify

depot (dē' pō) *n.* A railroad or bus station

depreciate (di prē' shē āt') *v.* To reduce in value

derision (di rizh' ən) *n.* Ridicule

derisive (di rī' siv) *adj.* Scornful; mocking

descant (des' kant) *n.* In two-part singing, the added melody sung above the main theme

descry (di skrī') *v.* To catch sight of

desiccate (des' i kāt') *v.* To dry up

desolate (des' ə lit) *adj.* Deserted, abandoned

despotic (de spät' ik) *adj.* Absolute; unlimited

desultory (des'l tôr' ē) *adj.* Random

determinate (di tur' mi nit) *adj.* Final

determination (de tur' mi na' shən) *n.* Firm intention

deviation (dē vē ā' shən) *n.* A turning aside from normal behavior

dexterous (dek' strəs) *adj.* With skillful use of the hands

diadem (dī' ə dem) *n.* A crown

diffidence (dif' ə dəns) *n.* Shyness; uncertainty

diffuse (di fyooz') *v.* To spread out

diffuse (di fyoos') *adj.* Spread out; not concentrated

dilapidated (də lap' ə dat' id) *adj.* Broken down; shabby and neglected

dire (dīr) *adv.* Dreadful; terrible

discomfiture (dis kum' fi chər) *n.* Unease; confusion

disconsolately (dis kän' sə lit lē) *adj.* Unhappily; sadly

discreet (dis krēt') *adj.* Tactful; respectful

disdain (dis dān') *v.* To reject with scorn

disdainful (dis dān' fəl) *adj.* Scornful

disheveled (di shev' 'ld) *adj.* Disarranged and untidy; tousled

disillusionment (dis i loo' zhən mənt) *n.* Disappointment

dismal (diz' m'l) *adj.* Gloomy; depressing

dismay (dis mā') *v.* To discourage; make afraid

disparity (dis par' ə tē) *n.* Condition of inequality

dispatch (dis pach') *v.* To finish quickly

dissemble (di sem' b'l) *v.* To conceal with false appearances; disguise

dissolution (dis' ə loo' shən) *n.* Disintegration; death

ditty (dit' ē) *n.* A song

divers (dī' vərz) *adj.* Several, various

divining (də vīn' iŋ) *v.* Guessing

docket (däk' it) *v.* To label

doff (däf) *v.* To lift

doggerel (dôg' ər əl) *adj.* Dull verse that sounds like a jingle

domesticate (dō mes' ti kāt) *v.* To tame wild animals and breed for human use

dour (door) *adj.* Stern; severe; gloomy

dowdy (dou' dē) *adj.* Shabby

dowry (dou' rē) *n.* The property that a woman brings to her husband at marriage

droll (drōl) *adj.* Comic and amusing in an odd way

dubious (doo' bē əs) *adj.* Uncertain; doubtful

E

ebb (eb) *v.* To lessen; weaken

ebony (eb' ə nē) *n.* A hard dark wood used for furniture

ecclesiastical (i klē' zē as' ti k'l) *adj.* Associated with the church

echo (e' kō) *n.* The repetition of a sound caused by reflection of sound waves

ecstatic (ek stat' ik) *adj.* In a state of extreme emotion

eddy (ed' ē) *n.* A circular current

eerie (ir' ē) *adj.* Mysterious

elation (i lā' shən) *n.* A feeling of great joy

elegy (el' ə jē) *n.* A song of mourning

eloquence (el' ə kwəns) *n.* Speech that is vivid, forceful, graceful and persuasive

emanate (em' ə nāt) *v.* To come from a source, as fragrance

embryo (em' brē ō') *n.* An animal in the earliest stages of its development

emergence (ē mur' jens) *n.* The development or evolution as something new, improved

eminence (em' ə nəns) *n.* A high or lofty place

encroaching (in krōch' iŋ) *adj.* Intruding in a gradual or sneaking way

endurance (en door' əns) *n.* Ability to stand hardship and stress and to carry on

enigmatic (en' ig mat' ik) *adj.* Baffling; perplexing

enjoin (in join') *v.* To order

entrails (en' trālz) *n.* Internal organs, specifically intestines; guts

enzyme (en' zīm) *n.* Any of various proteinlike substances, formed in plant and animal cells, that act to start or speed up specific chemical reactions

epiphany (ē pif'ə nē) *n.* A moment of sudden understanding

euphony (yoo' fə nē) *n.* Pleasing sound

evanesce (ev ə nes') *v.* To fade away

ewer (yoo' ər) *n.* A large water pitcher

exacting (ig zakt' iŋ) *adj.* Demanding

exalt (ig zôlt') *v.* To lift up

exhilarated (ig zil' ə rāt' əd) *adj.* Lively

exile   (eg′ zīl)   *n.* Enforced removal from one's native land

exorbitant   (ig zôr′ bə tənt)   *adj.* Exceeding the appropriate limits

expatriate   (eks pā′ trē āt)   *v.* To exile

expectorate   (ik spek′ tə rāt)   *v.* To spit

expediency   (ik spē′ dē ən sē)   *n.* Practicality

expostulation   (ik späs chə lā′ sh'n)   *n.* Objection; complaint

extract   (ik strakt′)   *v.* To draw out with special effort

extrapolate   (ik strap′ ə lāt)   *v.* To arrive at a conclusion by making inferences based on known facts

extricate   (eks′ trə kāt)   *v.* To free or disentangle

exuberant   (ig zōō′ bər ənt)   *adj.* Very great; extreme

F

fain   (fān)   *adj.* Gladly; eagerly

fakir   (fə kir′)   *n.* A Moslem or Hindu beggar who claims to perform miracles

fanatical   (fə nat′ ik'l)   *adj.* Unreasonably enthusiastic

fandango   (fan daŋ′ gō)   *n.* A lively Spanish dance

farthing   (fär′ *th*iŋ)   *n.* A small British coin equal to one fourth of a penny

feign   (fān)   *v.* To pretend

felicitous   (fə lis′ ə təs)   *adj.* Suitable to the occasion

fervent   (fʉr′ vənt)   *adj.* Burning; passionate

fester   (fes′ tər)   *v.* To form pus

fetid   (fet′ id)   *adj.* Rancid; rank; smelly

fetter   (fet′ ər)   *v.* To encircle with metal fasteners

fickle   (fik′ əl)   *adj.* Changeable

flag   (flag)   *v.* To grow weak or tired

flagon   (flag′ ən)   *n.* A pitcher for water or wine

flirt   (flʉrt)   *n.* A quick, uneven movement

flout   (flout)   *v.* To show scorn or contempt for

fond   (fänd)   *adj.* Tender and affectionate, with a possible meaning of foolish as well

foreshadowing   (fôr shad′ ō iŋ)   *n.* A sign of something to come

formality   (fôr mal′ ə tē)   *n.* Established rules or customs

formidable   (fôr′ mə də b'l)   *adj.* 1. Awe-inspiring 2. Causing fear or dread

forsaken   (fər sāk′ ən)   *adj.* Abandoned; without hope

fortnight   (fôrt′ nīt′)   *n.* Two weeks

fountainhead   (foun′ t'n hed′)   *n.* Source

fray   (frā)   *n.* A noisy fight

fungus   (fun′ gəs)   *n.* A parasite such as mold, mildew, and mushroom, which feeds on dead organic material and lacks chlorophyll

furl   (fʉrl)   *v.* To roll up and tie

furtive   (fʉr′ tiv)   *adv.* Preventing observation; sneaky

futile   (fyōōt′'l)   *adj.* Useless; hopeless

G

gallant   (gal′ ənt)   *adj.* Brave and noble

galley   (gal′ ē)   *n.* A large rowboat

galliard   (gal′ yərd)   *n.* A lively French dance

garbling   (gär′ b'liŋ)   *n.* Confusion, mix-up

gargoyle   (gär′ goil)   *n.* A strange and distorted animal form projecting from a building

gaunt   (gônt)   *adj.* Looking grim, forbidding, or desolate; thin and bony

gemmary   (jem′ ə rē′)   *n.* Knowledge of precious stones

genesis   (jen′ ə sis)   *n.* Birth; origin; beginning

genus   (jē′ nəs)   *n.* Main subdivision of a family of closely related species

ghoul   (gōōl)   *n.* An evil spirit that robs graves

glided   (glid′ əd)   *adj.* Overlaid with gold; made bright and attractive

gingham   (giŋ′ əm)   *adj.* A cotton cloth, usually woven in stripes, checks, or plaids (most often, a noun)

glee   (glē)   *n.* Lively joy; merriment

glisten   (glis′ 'n)   *v.* To shine or sparkle with reflected light

glower   (glou′ər)   *v.* To stare with sullen anger; scowl

gorge   (gôrj)   *n.* A voracious, consuming mouth

gossamer   (gäs′ ə mər)   *adj.* Light, thin, and delicate

Gothic   (gäth′ ik)   *adj.* A style of architecture that makes use of pointed arches

gratify   (grat′ i fī)   *v.* To please or satisfy

grievance   (grē′ vəns)   *n.* An injustice; complaint

grimace   (grim′ is)   *v.* To distort the face, as in expressing pain

grotesque   (grō tesk′)   *adj.* Having a fantastic design

guillotine   (gil′ lə tēn′)   *n.* An instrument that beheads a victim with a falling blade

guinea   (gin′ ē)   *n.* A gold coin worth about one pound

gunwale   (gun′'l)   *n.* The upper edge of the side of a boat

guy   (gī)   *adj.* Used for steadying or guiding

H

haggard   (hag′ ərd)   *adj.* Worn, as from lack of sleep; gaunt

hamlet   (ham′ lit)   *n.* A very small village

hapless   (hap′ lis)   *adj.* Unfortunate; luckless

harrow   (har′ ō)   *v.* To break up and to level by a harrow, a frame with spikes or sharp-edged disks, drawn by a horse or tractor

haughty   (hôt′ ē)   *adj.* Arrogant

hawker   (hôk′ ər)   *n.* A peddler

hecatomb   (hek′ ə tōm)   *n.* A large-scale sacrifice; often the slaughter of 100 cattle at one time

heifer   (hef′ ər)   *n.* A young cow

heliotrope   (hē′ lē ə trōp′)   *n.* A sweet-smelling plant

hellions   (hel′ yənz)   *n.* Mischievous troublemakers

herculean   (hʉr′ kyə lē′ ən)   *adj.* Of or relating to Hercules or his feats

heretic   (her′ ə tik)   *n.* One who holds to a belief opposed to the established teachings of a church

hermitage   (hʉr′ mit ij)   *n.* A secluded and solitary dwelling

hieroglyph   (hī′ ər ə glif′)   *n.* A mark that looks like those used in the ancient Egyptian writing system

hoax   (hōks)   *n.* A deceitful trick; fraud

hose (hōz) *n.* Stockings
host (hōst) *n.* A great number
humility (hyōō mil' ə tē) *n.* Humbleness; lack of pride
hypothetical (hī pə thet' i k'l) *adj.* Assumed; supposed
hydroplane (hī' drə plān) *n.* A seaplane

I

idyll (ī' d'l) *n.* A romantic scene, usually in the country
idyllic (ī dil' ik) *adj.* Pleasing and simple; peaceful
imminent (im' ə nent) *adj.* Likely to happen soon
immolation (im' ə lā' shən) *n.* Sacrifice
immutable (i myōōt' ə b'l) *adj.* Never changing
impassively (im pas' iv lē) *adv.* In an unfeeling or unemotional manner
impediment (im ped' ə mənt) *n.* An obstruction; hindrance
imperious (im pir' ē əs) *adj.* Overbearing; arrogant; domineering
impertinence (im pʉrt''n əns) *n.* Examples of insolence or lack of respect
impoverishment (im päv' ər ish mənt) *n.* Deprivation of strength, resources
imprecation (im' prə kā' shən) *n.* A curse
improvised (im' prə vīz'd) *adj.* Made at the spur of the moment with materials at hand
impudence (im' pyōō dəns) *n.* Disrespect
impunity (im pyōō' nə tē) *n.* Freedom from punishment
inaccessible (in ək ses' ə b'l) *adj.* Impossible to reach or enter
inarticulate (in är tik' yə lit) *adj.* Not able to speak well
incantation (in' kan tā shən) *n.* A spell
incise (in sīz') *v.* To cut into with a sharp tool
incongruity (in' kən grōō' ə tē) *n.* The quality of being out of place
incredulity (in' krə dōō' lə tē) *n.* The inability to believe
incredulous (in krej' oo ləs) *adj.* Disbelieving
indelible (in del' ə b'l) *adj.* Cannot be erased
indenture (in den' chər) *n.* A contract binding an apprentice to a master
indignation (in' dig nā' shən) *n.* Anger resulting from injustice
indolently (in' də lənt lē) *adj.* Lazily; idly
indulge (in dulj') *v.* To accept in a belittling way
inexplicable (in eks' pli kə b'l) *adj.* Unexplainable
inexplicably (in eks' pli kə blē) *adv.* In an incomprehensible manner; mysteriously
infallibility (in fal' ə bil' ə tē) *n.* The condition of being unable to fail
in lieu of (in lōō əv) *adj.* Instead of
insatiable (in sā' shə bəl) *adj.* Constantly wanting more; incapable of being satisfied
insidious (in sid' ē əs) *adj.* Characterized by treachery
instigate (in' stə gāt') *v.* To urge on; stir up

integrity (in teg' rə tē) *n.* The state of being of sound moral principle; uprightness; honesty; sincerity
interment (in tʉr' mənt) *n.* Burial
interminable (in tʉr' mi nə b'l) *adj.* Lasting or seeming to last forever
intimate (in' tə māt) *v.* To hint or imply
intricate (in' tri kit) *adj.* Complex
introspective (in' trə spekt' iv) *adj.* Causing one to look into one's own thoughts and feelings
inviolable (in vī' ə lə b'l) *adj.* Not to be changed
irascible (i ras' ə bel) *adj.* Easily angered; hot-tempered
ire (īr) *n.* Anger
iridescent (ir' ə des' 'nt) *adj.* Having shifting, rainbowlike colors
irresolute (i rez' ə lōōt) *adj.* Unsure; indecisive

J

jerkin (jʉr' kin) *n.* A short, closefitting jacket
jocund (jak' ənd) *adj.* Cheerful
journeyman (jʉr' nē mən) *n.* A person who has learned a trade but still works for a master
judicious (jōō dish' əs) *adj.* Showing good judgment

K

kimono (kə mō' nə) *n.* A loose-fitting gown, part of the traditional costume of Japanese men and women
kindling (kin' dliŋ) *n.* Bits of dry wood for starting a fire
kine (kīn) *n.* cattle
kinsman (kinz' mən) *n.* A relative
knouter (nout' ər) *n.* Someone who beats criminals with a leather whip, or knout
kvass (kväs) *n.* A Russian drink made from rye or barley

L

lacerate (las' ər āt) *v.* To cut or tear jaggedly
laconic (lə kän' ik) *adj.* Not speaking much
lagoon (la gōōn') *n.* Water enclosed by a circular coral reef
lament (lə ment') *n.* A song of mourning
lamentable (lam' ən tə b'l) *adj.* Distressing; sad
lampetia (lam pē' shə) *n.* A nymph
languid (laŋ' gwid) *adj.* Drooping; weak
languor (laŋ' gər) *n.* A lack of vigor; weakness; sluggishness
lascar (läs' kər) *n.* An Oriental sailor, especially a native of India
lasso (las' ō) *v.* Wrap around
latent (lāt''nt) *adj.* Hidden
lateral (lat' ər əl) *adj.* On the side
lattice (lat' is) *n.* A framework of wood or metal
laurel (lôr' əl) *n.* Any of a genus of evergreen trees or shrubs of the laurel family
league (lēg) *n.* Three miles
lee (lē) *n.* An area sheltered from the wind
legion (lē' jən) *n.* A group of soldiers

lend (lend) *v.* To pass along, as from parent to child

lenticular (len tik′ yoo lər) *adj.* Shaped like a lentil bean

lethargic (li thär′ jik) *adj.* Drowsy; without energy

lethe (lē′ thē) *n.* Oblivion; forgetfulness

levitation (lev′ ə tā′ shən) *n.* Remaining in air with no physical support

libation (lī bā′ shən) *n.* Wine or other liquids poured upon the ground as a sacrifice

lift (lift) *n.* British for "elevator"

limekiln (līm′ kiln′) *n.* A furnace in which limestone is burned to make lime, a substance used in mortar and cement

lithe (līth) *adj.* Supple; limber

livery (liv′ ər ē) *n.* Servants' uniforms

loathsome (lōth′ səm) *adj.* Disgusting

lore (lôr) *n.* Knowledge of a particular subject

lozenge (läz′′nj) *n.* A diamond-shaped object

lugger (lug′ ər) *n.* A ship equipped with a four-sided sail

M

maelstrom (māl′ strəm) *n.* A large violent whirlpool

magnanimous (mag nan′ ə məs) *adj.* Noble in mind; high-souled, especially in overlooking injury or insult

malaria (mə ler′ ē ə) *n.* A disease associated with the tropics that causes chills and fever

malodorous (mal′ ō′ dər əs) *adj.* Having a bad odor; stinking

mammoth (mam′ əth) *adj.* Enormous

marauder (mə rôd′ ər) *n.* A raider; one who takes goods by force

martial (mär′ shəl) *adj.* Military

masochistic (mas′ ə kis′ tik) *adj.* Getting pleasure from pain

maudlin (môd′ lin) *adj.* Tearfully sentimental from too much liquor

maunder (môn′ dər) *v.* To talk in an unconnected way

medley (med′ lē) *n.* A mixture of things not usually found together

melancholy (mel′ ən käl′ ē) *adj.* Sad; gloomy

melodramatically (mel′ ə drə mat′ ik lē) *adv.* In an extravagantly emotional manner

meretricious (mer′ ə trish′ əs) *adj.* Attractive in a cheap, flashy way

mewling (myool′ iŋ) *v.* Whimpering; crying like a baby

milieu (mēl yoo′) *n.* Environment; setting

mill-weir (mil′ wir′) *n.* A low dam to back up or divert water for a mill

minuscule (min′ nus kyool) *adj.* Tiny; very small

misdemeanor (mis′ di mēn′ ər) *n.* A minor offense

molder (mold′ ər) *v.* To crumble into dust; decay

monody (män′ ə dē) *n.* A poem of mourning; a steady sound; music in which one instrument or voice is dominant

mooncalf (moon′ kaf′) *n.* A foolish young man

Morgan (môr′ gən) *n.* A breed of saddle horse that originated in New England

motley (mät′ lē) *n.* A clown's multicolored costume

multitudinous (mul′ tə tood′ 'n əs) *adj.* Very numerous

muster (mus′ tər) *n.* An assembly, especially of soldiers

muted (myoot′ əd) *adj.* Weaker; less intense

myriad (mir′ ē əd) *adj.* Numerous

N

naive (nä ēv′) *adj.* Unsophisticated

narcissism (när′ sə siz′m) *n.* Egoism; overevaluation of one's own attributes or achievements or those of one's group

nectar (nek′ tər) *n.* Drink of the gods

newt (noot) *n.* A salamander

niche (nich) *n.* A recess in a wall

niter (nīt′ ər) *n.* A white or gray mineral

nocturnal (näk tur′ n'l) *adj.* Happening in the night

noncommissioned (nän kə mish′ ənd) *adj.* Referring to enlisted soldiers of a rank no higher than sergeant major

novice (näv′ is) *adj.* A beginner

nurturing (nur′ chər iŋ) *n.* The act or process of raising or guiding

O

oasis (ō ā′sis) *n.* A fertile place in the desert

obdurate (äb′door ət) *adj.* Stubborn; unbending

obeisance (ō bā′ s′ns) *n.* A bow or another sign of respect

oblation (ä blā′ shən) *n.* An offering to a god

obliterate (ə blit′ ər at′) *v.* To destroy without leaving any traces

oblivion (ə bliv′ ē ən) *n.* Forgetfulness

obsession (əb sesh′ ən) *n.* A compulsive preoccupation with an idea

obstinate (äb′ stə nit) *adj.* Stubborn

obtrusive (əb troo′ siv) *adj.* Calling attention to oneself

oculist (äk′ yə list) *n.* An old-fashioned term for an eye specialist

officious (ə fish′əs) *adj.* Offering unwanted and unnecessary advice; meddlesome

offing (ôf′ iŋ) *n.* The distant part of the sea visible from the shore

ominous (äm′ ə nəs) *adj.* Threatening; dangerous

oppression (ə presh′ ən) *n.* Keeping others down by the unjust use of power

oracle (ôr′ ə k′l) *n.* A source of wisdom

ovipositor (ō′ vi päz′ i tər) *n.* A tubular structure of many female insects, usually at the end of the abdomen, for depositing eggs

ozone (ō′ zōn) *n.* A form of oxygen with a sharp odor

P

pacific (pə sif′ ik) *adj.* Peaceful

paean (pē′ ən) *n.* A song of joy or triumph

pagan (pā′ gən)   *n.* One who is not a Christian, a Moslem, or a Jew

painstakingly (pānz′ tā′ kiŋ lē)   *adj.* Acting very carefully

palazzo (pä lät′ sō)   *n.* A palace

palisades (pal′ ə sadz′)   *n.* A line of steep cliffs

pallid (pal′ id)   *adj.* Pale

pallor (pal′ ər)   *n.* Paleness

palpable (pal′ pə b′l)   *adj.* Able to be touched or felt

palpitate (pal′ pə tāt′)   *v.* To beat rapidly; throb

panorama (pan′ ə ram′ ə)   *n.* An unlimited view in all directions

pantaloon (pan′ t′l ōōn′)   *n.* A thin, foolish old man—originally a character in old comedies

pantomime (pan′ tə mīm′)   *n.* Wordless actions or gestures as a means of expression

paradox (par′ ə däks)   *n.* A contradiction

paradoxically (par′ ə däk′ si k′lē)   *adv.* In a way that seems opposite or contradictory

paralytic (par ə lit′ ik)   *n.* A paralyzed person

pard (pärd)   *n.* A leopard or panther

parry (par′ ē)   *v.* To ward off a sword-thrust

patronage (pā′ trən ij)   *n.* Encouragement shown to someone inferior

peacoat (pē′ kōt′)   *n.* A heavy woolen jacket, often worn by sailors

pectoral (pek′ tər əl)   *adj.* Located on the chest

pensive (pen′ siv)   *adj.* Thinking deeply

penury (pen′ yə rē)   *n.* Extreme poverty

perennial (pə ren′ ē əl)   *adj.* Lasting through the year or for a long time

perfunctory (pə fuŋk′ tər ē)   *adj.* Routine; superficial

peridot (per′ ə dät′)   *n.* A yellowish-green gem

permeate (pʉr′ mē āt′)   *v.* To spread or flow throughout

pernicious (pər nish′ əs)   *adj.* Causing great injury or ruin

perplex (pər pleks′)   *v.* To confuse or make hard to understand

perplexity (pər plek′ sə tē)   *n.* State of being confused

pertly (pʉrt′ lē)   *adv.* In a saucy manner

peruse (pə rōōz′)   *v.* To examine in detail

pervasive (pər vā′ siv)   *adj.* Spread throughout

perverse (pər vʉrs′)   *adj.* Persisting in error

petrel (pet′ rəl)   *n.* A small, dark sea bird

phosphorescence (fäs′ fə res′ ′ns)   *n.* An emission of light resulting from exposure to radiation

picturesque (pik′ chə resk′)   *adj.* Like or suggesting a picture

pilgrimage (pil′ grəm ij)   *n.* A journey to a sacred place or shrine; a special trip to a place of personal signifiance

pinion (pin′ yən)   *v.* To confine or shackle

pipe (pīp)   *n.* A large barrel

pique (pēk)   *n.* Resentment at being slighted

pirouette (pir′ oo wet)   *n.* A rapid turn on one foot or the point of the toe

placidly (plas′ id lē)   *adv.* Calmly; quietly

plaintively (plān′ tiv lē)   *adj.* Sadly

plait (plāt)   *n.* A braid

plaiting (plāt′ iŋ)   *n.* Braiding

pliant (plī′ ənt)   *adj.* Easily bent; pliable

plunder (plun′ dər)   *n.* Goods taken by force; loot

poacher (pōch′ ər)   *n.* A person who hunts or fishes illegally on someone else's property

poise (poiz)   *v.* To balance, suspend

pollard (päl′ ərd)   *n.* A tree with its top branches cut back to the trunk

postern (pōs′ tərn)   *n.* Back gate

pottle (pät′′l)   *n.* A pot that holds two quarts

precarious (prē ker′ ē əs)   *adj.* Dependent upon circumstances

precariously (prē ker′ ē əs lē)   *adv.* In a dangerous, risky way

precipitous (pri sip′ ə təs)   *adj.* Steep; sheer

preclude (pri klōōd′)   *v.* To make impossible in advance

premium (prē′ mē əm)   *n.* A fee paid by an apprentice to a master

presentiment (pri zen′ tə mənt)   *n.* A feeling that something bad will occur

procedure (prō sē′ jər)   *n.* The method of carrying out an action

procure (prō kyōōr′)   *v.* To get; obtain

prodigious (prə dij′ əs)   *adj.* 1. Enormous 2. Wonderful; of great size

prodigy (präd′ ə jē)   *n.* A person, thing, or act so extraordinary as to inspire wonder

proffered (präf′ ərd)   *adj.* Offered (usually a verb)

profoundly (prə found′ lē)   *adv.* Deeply and intensely

proliferate (prō lif′ ər āt′)   *v.* Grow rapidly

promissory (präm′ i sōr′ ē) **notes**   *n.* Written promises to pay back borrowed money

propriety (prə prī′ ə tē)   *n.* Proper manner or behavior

proscribe (prō skrīb′)   *v.* To banish

prostrate (präs′ trāt)   *adj.* Lying face downward

protozoa (prōt′ ə zo′ ə)   *n.* Microscopic animals

protracted (prō trakt′ id)   *adj.* Lengthy; prolonged

providential (präv′ ə den′ shəl)   *adj.* As if decreed by God

prow (prou)   *n.* The forward part of a ship

prudence (prōōd′′ns)   *n.* Practical and sound judgment

pugilist (pyōō′ jə ləst)   *n.* A fighter; boxer

pulverized (pul′ vər īzd′)   *adj.* Crushed or ground into a powder or dust

pungent (pun′ jənt)   *adj.* Producing a sharp sensation of taste and smell; acrid

pyre (pīr)   *n.* A pile of wood on which a body is burned at a funeral

Q

quaff (kwäf)   *v.* To drink

quaint (kwānt)   *adj.* Strange; unusual

qualmish (kwäm′ ish)   *adj.* Slightly ill

querulous (kwer′ ə lis)   *adj.* Complaining

R

raillery (rāl′ ər ē) *n.* Good-natured teasing

rampage (ram pāj′) *v.* To rush about in wild anger

rancor (raŋ′ kər) *n.* Hatred; spite

rantipole (ran′ tē pōl) *n.* A wild and reckless person

rapier (rā′ pē ər) *n.* A slender, two-edged sword with cuplike handle

ravage (rav′ ij) *n.* Ruin; devastating damage

raveled (rav′'ld) *adj.* Untwisted; unwoven

rawboned (rô′ bond′) *adj.* Having little flesh or fat covering the bones; lean

recalcitrant (ri kal′ si trənt) *adj.* Refusing to obey authority; hard to handle

reciprocate (ri sip′ rə kāt′) *v.* Give or feel in return

reconcile (rek′ ən sil′) *v.* To make compatible; bring into harmony

reel (rēl) *v.* To fall back; stagger

reiteration (rē it′ ə rā′ shən) *n.* Repetition

reminisce (rem′ə nis′) *v.* To think about remembered events or experiences

remnant (rem′ nənt) *n.* Remaining person or thing

rend (rend) *v.* To tear

repository (ri päz′ ə tôr′ ē) *n.* A place for safekeeping

repress (ri pres′) *v.* To keep down; hold back

resiliency (ri zil′ yen sē) *n.* The ability to bounce or spring back

respite (res′ pit) *n.* Rest; relief

resplendent (ri splen′ dənt) *adj.* Shining brightly; full of splendor

resurgence (ri sur′ jens) *n.* The condition of having risen again

retort (ri tôrt′) *n.* Sharp or clever reply

retribution (ret′ rə byōō′ shən) *n.* Deserved punishment

reverence (rev′ ər əns) *n.* A curtsy or bow

rivalry (rī′ v'l rē) *n.* Competition

roan (rōn) *n.* A horse of a solid color such as reddish brown or black with a thick sprinkling of white hair

roebuck (rō′ buk′) *n.* A male deer

rogue (rōg) *n.* A repulsive scoundrel

romanticize (rō man′ tə sīz′) *v.* To treat or regard in an ideal way rather than a realistic one

row (rou) *n.* A noisy quarrel

ruble (rōō′ b'l) *n.* A Russian coin

rueful (rōō′ fəl) *adj.* Causing sorrow or pity

S

sallow (sal′ ō) *adj.* Of a sickly pale-yellowish complexion

salve (sav) *n.* An ointment that soothes or heals skin irritations, burns, or wounds

samurai (sam′ ə rī′) *n.* A member of a military class in feudal Japan who wore two swords

sanitarium (san′ ə ter′ ē əm) *n.* A place where people go to rest and regain their health

sans (sanz) *prep.* Without; lacking

sash (sash) *n.* A sliding window-frame

saturnalia (sat′ ər nā′ lē ə) *n.* An ancient Roman holiday marked by wild celebration

scaffold (skaf′ 'ld) *n.* A raised platform on which criminals are executed

scruple (skrōō′ p'l) *n.* A misgiving about something one feels is wrong

scrupulously (skrōō pyə ləs lē) *adv.* Marked by precision and extreme conscientiousness

scrutiny (skrōōt′ 'n ē) *n.* Close examination or inspection

scythe (sīth) *n.* A tool used for cutting down tall grass

sedative (sed′ ə tiv) *n.* Something that soothes or quiets

sentimental (sen′ tə men′ t'l) *adj.* Foolishly emotional

sepulcher (sep′ 'l kər) *n.* A tomb

serpentine (sur′ pən tēn) *n.* A coil of thin paper that unwinds as it is thrown

settee (se tē′) *n.* A small sofa

settle (set′ 'l) *n.* A bench

shank (shank) *n.* A leg

shard (shärd) *n.* A fragment or broken piece

shrike (shrīk) *n.* A shrill-voiced bird that feeds on small animals

singular (siŋ′ gyə lər) *adj.* Extraordinary; rare

sinister (sin′ is tər) *adj.* Threatening harm or evil

sleight (slīt) **of hand** *n.* Skill in deceiving onlookers

slouching (slouch′ iŋ) *adj.* Drooping (usually a verb)

smiter (smīt′ ər) *n.* One who hurts you

solace (säl′ is) *v.* To comfort

solemnity (sə lem′ nə tē) *n.* Solemn feeling, character, or appearance; serious or awesome quality; gravity

solicitor (sə lis′ it ər) *n.* A British lawyer who can assist clients but cannot plead cases in the higher courts

speculation (spek yə lā′ shən) *n.* Consideration of some subject or idea

speculatively (spek′ yə lə tiv lē) *adv.* In a meditative way

spume (spyōōm) *n.* Foam; froth

squall (skwôl) *n.* A brief, violent storm

stay (stā) *n.* A heavy rope or cable used for support

stateroom (stāt′ rōōm) *n.* A private cabin on a ship

steep (stēp) *n.* A mountain slope

steward (stōō′ ərd) *n.* The manager of an estate

stifling (stī′ fliŋ) *adj.* Suffocating

strenuous (stren′ yoo wəs) *adj.* Requiring great effort

suavity (swa′ və tē) *n.* Graceful politeness

sublunary (sub′ loo ner′ ē) *adj.* Earthly

subterfuge (sub′ tər fyōōj′) *n.* A deceptive action

subtle (sut′ 'l) *adj.* 1. Not obvious; delicately suggestive 2. Small

succession (sək sesh′ ən) *n.* The act of succeeding or coming after another in order or sequence

succor (suk′ ər) *n.* Aid; help; relief

suffused (sə fyōōzd′) *adj.* Filled with; spread throughout

suitor (sōōt′ ər) *n.* A man courting a woman

sullen (sul′ ən) *adj.* Showing resentment

sunder (sun′ dər) *v.* To break apart

sundry (sun′ drē) *adj.* Various; several

superciliously (soō′ pər sil′ ē əs lē) *adv.* In a contemptuous or haughty manner

supple (sup′ ′l) *adj.* Flexible; adaptable

surcease (sʉr′ sēs) *n.* End

surfeited (sʉr′ fit id) *adj.* Supplied to excess

surreal (sə rē′ əl) *adj.* Strange

surrey (sʉr′ ē) *n.* A light, horse-drawn carriage

susceptible (sə sep′ tə b′l) *adj.* Receptive

T

tambour (tam′ boor) *n.* A drum

tantalizingly (tan′ tə līz′ iŋ lē) *adv.* In a teasing or tormenting way

tartar (tär′ tər) *n.* A ferocious, unmanageable person

tedious (tē′ dē əs) *adj.* Tiresome and boring

tenor (ten′ ər) *n.* A singer with voice ranging about an octave, or eight full notes, above and below middle C.

tentative (ten′ tə tiv) *adj.* Done with hesitation

terrestrial (tə res′ trē əl) *adj.* Of this world; earthly; mundane

throng (throŋ) *v.* To crowd into

tintinnabulation (tin ti nab yoō la′ shən) *n.* The ringing of bells

token (tō′ k′n) *n.* A sign

tonic (tän′ ik) *adj.* Stimulating; invigorating

trachoma (trə kō′ mə) *n.* A disease of the eyelid and eyeball

transgression (trans gresh′ ən) *n.* Wrongdoing; sin

transport (trans′ pôrt) *n.* A strong emotion of joy or delight

transport (trans port′) *v.* To send out of the country to a colony for prisoners

treble (treb′ ′l) *n.* A high-pitched voice

tremulous (trem′ yə ləs) *adj.* Quivering; trembling; shaking; unsteady

tribunal (trī byoō′ n′l) *n.* Court

trifle (trī′ fəl) *n.* A small, unimportant thing

trimmer (trim′ ər) *n.* A person who changes his opinion to suit the circumstances

truculent (truk′ yoō lənt) *adj.* Savage; cruel

tumult (toō′ mult) *n.* A great noise or disturbance; noisy commotion

tycoon (tī koōn′) *n.* A wealthy and powerful person

typhoon (tī foōn′) *n.* A violent tropical storm

U

undulate (un′ joo lāt′) *v.* To move in waves

unprecedented (un pres′ ə den′ tid) *adj.* Not done or known before

unpretentious (un prē ten′ shəs) *adj.* Not ostentatious; modest

unredressed (un ri drest′) *adj.* Not set right

unrequited (un ri kwīt′ id) *adj.* Not returned; unreciprocated

unscrupulous (un skroōp′ yə ləs) *adj.* Without principles

unwieldy (un wēl′ dē) *adj.* Awkward; clumsy

V

vanquish (vaŋ′ kwish) *v.* Defeat; conquer

variable (ver′ ē ə b′l) *adj.* Changeable; inconstant

varmint (vär′ mənt) *n.* An undesirable or troublesome person

veery (vir′ ē) *n.* A brown and cream-colored thrush

venerable (ven′ ər ə b′l) *adj.* Old and respected

vex (veks) *v.* To annoy

vial (vī′ əl) *n.* A small bottle containing medicine or other liquids

vicarious (vī ker′ ē əs) *adj.* Experiencing something by imagined participation in another's experience

vigil (vij′ əl) *n.* A watchful staying awake

vile (vīl) *adj.* Worthless; cheap; low

visage (viz′ ij) *n.* Face

vivacious (vi vā′ shəs) *adj.* Lively

vivacity (vi vas′ ə tē) *n.* Liveliness

volley (väl′ ē) *v.* To fire at the same time

voluminously (və loō′ mə nəs lē) *adv.* Fully; in great volume

vortex (vôr′ teks) *n.* The center of a situation, which draws all that surrounds it

votive (vōt′ iv) *adj.* Done in fulfillment of a vow or pledge

W

waverer (wā′ vər ər) *n.* One who changes or is unsteady

wayfarer (wā′ fər ər) *n.* A traveler

weird (wird) *n.* Fate or destiny

wheelwright (hwēl′ rīt′) *n.* A person who makes and repairs wheels and wheeled vehicles

wherry (hwer′ ē) *n.* A light rowboat used on rivers

whet (hwet) *v.* To sharpen

whey (hwā) *n.* The thin, watery part of milk separated from the thicker curds

whin (hwin) *n.* A prickly, evergreen shrub

whist (hwist) *n.* A card game like bridge

whitesmith (hwit′ smith′) *n.* A tinsmith

whittle (hwit′ ′l) *v.* To reduce gradually, as if to cut away in slices by a knife

wistfulness (wist′ fəl nis) *n.* Expression of vague yearnings

withy (with′ ē) *adj.* Tough, flexible twigs

woeful (wō′ fəl) *adj.* Full of sorrow

wrath (rath) *n.* Intense anger

wreathe (rēth) *v.* To curl around

writhe (rith) *v.* To twist; turn

writhing (rith′ iŋ) *v.* Suffering great emotional distress; twisting; contorting

Z

zealous (zel′ əs) *adj.* Very eager

INDEX OF FINE ART

INDEX OF SKILLS

CRITICAL THINKING AND READING

LEARNING OPTIONS

READING IN THE ARTS AND SCIENCES

THINKING AND WRITING

INDEX OF TITLES BY THEMES

INDEX OF AUTHORS AND TITLES

Page numbers in *italics* refer to biographical information.

Index of Authors and Titles 1093

ACKNOWLEDGMENTS (continued)

Atheneum Publishers, an imprint of Macmillan Publishing Company
Reprinted with the permission of Atheneum Publishers, an imprint of Macmillan Publishing Company from *The Miracle Worker* by William Gibson. Copyright © 1956, 1957 by William Gibson. Copyright © 1959, 1969 Tamarack Productions, Ltd., and George S. Klein and Leo Garel as trustees under three separate deeds of trust, renewed © 1977 by William Gibson. No performance of any kind may be given without permission in writing from the author's agent, Samuel French, Inc., 45 West 25th Street, New York, NY 10010. *Dragonsong* by Anne McCaffrey, copyright © 1976 by Anne McCaffrey. Reprinted by permission.

Margaret Atwood and Oxford University Press Canada
"Siren Song" from *You Are Happy* by Margaret Atwood. Copyright © 1974 by Margaret Atwood. Reprinted by permission of Margaret Atwood.

D. C. Berry
Lines from "On Reading Poems to a Senior Class at South High" by D. C. Berry. Reprinted by permission of the author, D. C. Berry, c/o The Center for Writers at the University of Southern Mississippi.

Brandt & Brandt Literary Agents, Inc.
Lines from "Thomas Jefferson 1743–1826" from *A Book of Americans* by Rosemary & Stephen Vincent Benét. Copyright 1933 by Rosemary & Stephen Vincent Benét; Copyright © renewed 1961 by Rosemary Carr Benét. "The Most Dangerous Game" by Richard Connell. Copyright 1924 by Richard Connell; copyright renewed 1952 by Louise Fox Connell. Reprinted by permission of Brandt & Brandt Literary Agents, Inc.

Calyx Books
"Autumn Gardening" by Siu Wai Anderson, first published in *The Forbidden Stitch: An Asian American Women's Anthology,* edited by Shirley Lim et al., published by Calyx Books © 1989. Reprinted by permission of the editors and publisher.

Arthur C. Clarke and Scott Meredith Literary Agency, Inc.
"If I Forget Thee, Oh Earth . . . " from *Expedition to Earth* by Arthur C. Clarke. Copyright © 1953, 1970 by Arthur C. Clarke; copyright 1951 by Columbia Publications, Inc. Reprinted by permission of the author and the author's agents, Scott Meredith Literary Agency, Inc., 845 Third Avenue, New York, NY 10022.

Don Congdon Associates, Inc.
"All the Years of Her Life" by Morley Callaghan, published in *The New Yorker,* 1935. Copyright 1935 by Morley Callaghan; renewed © 1962 by Morley Callaghan. Reprinted by permission of Don Congdon Associates, Inc.

Joan Daves Agency
"I Have a Dream" by Martin Luther King, Jr., from *The Words of Martin Luther King, Jr.* Copyright © 1963 by Martin Luther King, Jr. "Cradle Song" from *Selected Poems of Gabriela Mistral* by Gabriela Mistral, translated by Langston Hughes. Copyright © 1957 by Indiana University Press. Reprinted by permission of Joan Daves Agency.

Doubleday, a division of Bantam, Doubleday, Dell Publishing Group, Inc.
"The New and the Old" by Shiki, excerpts from *An Introduction to Haiku* by Harold G. Henderson. Copyright © 1958 by Harold G. Henderson. "The Gift of the Magi" by O. Henry from *The Complete Works of O. Henry.* Copyright 1905 by Press Publications Company. "The Invalid's Story" by Mark Twain from *The Comic Mark Twain Reader* edited by Charles Neider. Copyright © 1977 by Charles Neider. "The Meadow Mouse" by Theodore Roethke, copyright © 1963 by Beatrice Roethke, Administratrix of the Estate of Theodore Roethke. from *The Collected Poems of Theodore Roethke* by Theodore Roethke. Reprinted by permission of Doubleday, a division of Bantam, Doubleday, Dell Publishing Group, Inc.

E.P. Dutton, an imprint of New American Library, a division of Penguin Books USA Inc.
From *Shakespeare of London* by Marchette Chute. Copyright 1949, renewed © 1977 by Marchette Chute. Reprinted by permission of the publisher.

Farrar, Straus & Giroux, Inc.
Excerpt from "Pieces of the Frame" (titled, "The Loch Ness Monster") in *Pieces of the Frame* by John McPhee. Copyright © 1970, 1975 by John McPhee. "Georgia O'Keeffe" from *The White Album* by Joan Didion. Copyright © 1976, 1979, 1989 by Joan Didion. "Homeric Chorus" from *Homer's Odyssey* by Derek Walcott. Copyright © 1992 by Derek Walcott. First appeared in *The New York Times,* January 1, 1992. Reprinted by permission of Farrar, Straus & Giroux, Inc.

The Feminist Press
"To Da-duh, in Memoriam" from *Reena and Other Stories* by Paule Marshall. Copyright © 1967, 1983 by Paule Marshall. Published by The Feminist Press at The City University of New York. All rights reserved. Reprinted by permission of The Feminist Press.

Harcourt Brace Jovanovich, Inc.
"Ithaca" from *The Complete Poems of Cavafy* translated by Rae Dalven, copyright © 1948 and renewed 1976 by Rae Dalven. "A Lincoln Preface" from *The Sandburg Range* by Carl Sandburg, copyright 1953 by Carl Sandburg; renewed 1985 by Margaret Sandburg, Janet Sandburg, and Helga Sandburg Crile. "Splinter" from *Good Morning, America,* copyright 1928, renewed 1956 by Carl Sandburg. Reprinted by permission of Harcourt Brace Jovanovich, Inc.

Harcourt Brace Jovanovich, Inc. and Faber and Faber Ltd.
"Macavity: The Mystery Cat" from *Old Possum's Book of*

Practical Cats, copyright 1939 by T. S. Eliot; renewed 1967 by Esme Valerie Eliot. Reprinted by permission.

HarperCollins Publishers Inc.
"A Very Old Man with Enormous Wings" from *Leaf Storm and Other Stories* by Gabriel García Márquez. Copyright © 1971 by Gabriel García Márquez. "But a Watch in the Night" by James C. Rettie, from *Forever the Land* by Russell and Kate Lord. Copyright 1950 by Harper & Row, Publishers, Inc. Copyright renewed 1978 by Russell and Kate Lord. Reprinted by permission of HarperCollins Publishers Inc.

Harvard University Press
Lines from "Because I could not stop for Death" reprinted by permission of the publishers and the Trustees of Amherst College from *The Poems of Emily Dickinson* edited by Thomas H. Johnson, Cambridge, Mass.: The Belknap Press of Harvard University Press, copyright 1951 © 1955, 1979, 1983 by The President and Fellows of Harvard College.

John Hawkins & Associates, Inc.
"Make up your mind, snail! . . . ," "In the falling snow . . . ," "Keep straight down this block . . . ," and "Whose town did you leave . . . " by Richard Wright. Reprinted by permission of John Hawkins & Associates, Inc.

Henry Holt and Company, Inc.
"The Runaway" and "In a Glass of Cider" from *The Poetry of Robert Frost* edited by Edward Connery Lathem. Copyright © 1969 by Holt, Rinehart and Winston, Inc. Copyright © 1962 by Robert Frost. Copyright © 1975 by Lesley Frost Ballantine. Reprinted by permission of Henry Holt and Company, Inc.

Evelyn Tooley Hunt
Lines from "Taught Me Purple" by Evelyn Tooley Hunt, from *Negro Digest,* February 1964. Used by permission of the author.

James R. Hurst
"The Scarlet Ibis" by James Hurst, published in *The Atlantic Monthly,* July 1960. Copyright *The Atlantic Monthly,* July 1960. Reprinted by permission of the author.

Japan Publications, Inc.
"Temple Bells die out" by Bashō; and "Dragonfly catcher" and "Bearing no flowers" by Chiyojo, reprinted from *One Hundred Famous Haiku* by Daniel C. Buchanan, with permission from Japan Publications, © 1973.

Heirs of the Estate of Martin Luther King Jr.
Excerpt from the first draft of "I Have a Dream" by Martin Luther King, Jr., from *The Words of Martin Luther King, Jr.* Reprinted by arrangement with the Heirs of the Estate of Martin Luther King Jr., c/o Joan Daves Agency as agent for the proprietor. Copyright 1963 by Martin Luther King, Jr., copyright renewed 1991 by Coretta Scott King.

Alfred A. Knopf, Inc.
"Uncle Marcos" from *The House of the Spirits* by Isabel Allende, translated by Magda Bogin. Translation copyright © 1985 by Alfred A. Knopf, Inc. "Dream Deferred" copyright 1951 by Langston Hughes. Reprinted from *The Panther and the Lash* by Langston Hughes. "Dreams" from *The Dream Keeper and Other Poems* by Langston Hughes. Copyright 1932 by Alfred A. Knopf, Inc. and renewed 1960 by Langston Hughes. "Pendulum" copyright © 1982, by John Updike. Reprinted from *The Carpentered Hen and Other Tame Creatures* by John Updike. "To be of use" from *Circles on the Water* by Marge Piercy. Copyright © 1982 by Marge Piercy. Reprinted by permission of Alfred A. Knopf, Inc.

The Literary Trustees of Walter de la Mare and The Society of Authors as their representative
"The Listeners" from *The Complete Poems of Walter de la Mare* by Walter de la Mare. Reprinted by permission.

Little, Brown and Company, in association with The Atlantic Monthly Press
"Nameless, Tennessee" from *Blue Highways* by William Least Heat Moon. Copyright © 1982 by William Least Heat Moon. By permission of Little, Brown and Company, in association with The Atlantic Monthly Press.

Liveright Publishing Corporation
"maggie and milly and molly and may" is reprinted from *Complete Poems, 1913–1962,* by E. E. Cummings, by permission of Liveright Publishing Corporation. Copyright © 1923, 1925, 1931, 1935, 1938, 1939, 1940, 1944, 1945, 1946, 1947, 1948, 1949, 1950, 1951, 1952, 1953, 1954, 1955, 1956, 1957, 1958, 1959, 1960, 1961, 1962 by the Trustees for the E. E. Cummings Trust. Copyright © 1961, 1963, 1968 by Marion Morehouse Cummings.

Macmillan Publishing Company
"Jabberwocky" from *The Collected Verse of Lewis Carroll* (New York: Macmillan, 1933). "The Dark Hills" reprinted with permission of Macmillan Publishing Company from *Collected Poems* by Edwin Arlington Robinson. Copyright 1920 by Edwin Arlington Robinson, renewed 1948 by Ruth Nivison. "Uphill" from *The Poetical Works of Christina G. Rossetti* (New York: Macmillan, 1924). "There Will Come Soft Rains" reprinted with permission of Macmillan Publishing Company from *Collected Poems* by Sara Teasdale. Copyright 1920 by Macmillan Publishing Company, renewed 1948 by Mamie T. Wheless.

Ellen C. Masters
"George Gray" from *Spoon River Anthology* by Edgar Lee Masters, Macmillan Publishing Co. Reprinted by permission.

New American Library, a division of Penguin Books USA Inc.
"The Necklace" from *Boule de Suif and Selected Stories* by Guy de Maupassant, translated by Andrew MacAndrew. Translation Introduction copyright © 1964 by New American Library. Copyright © 1964 by Andrew MacAndrew. From *The Tragedy of Romeo and Juliet* by William Shakespeare, edited by J. A. Bryant, Jr., copyright © 1964 by J. A. Bryant, Jr. Reprinted by permission of New American Library, a division of Penguin Books USA Inc.

Acknowledgments 1095

The New Yorker
"Before the End of Summer" by Grant Moss, Jr., from *The New Yorker*, October 15, 1960; copyright © 1960, reprinted by permission of The New Yorker Magazine, Inc.

Simon J. Ortiz
"My Father's Song" by Simon J. Ortiz, from *New Worlds of Literature* by Jerome Beaty and J. Paul Hunter. Copyright 1989 by W. W. Norton & Company, Inc. Reprinted by permission of the author.

Putnam Publishing Group
"Rules of the Game" by Amy Tan. Reprinted by permission of the Putnam Publishing Group from *The Joy Luck Club* by Amy Tan. Copyright © 1989 by Amy Tan.

Quarterly Review of Literature
"Astonishment" by Wisława Szymborska, translated by Grazyna Drabik, Austin Flint, and Sharon Olds. Copyright *Quarterly Review of Literature Poetry Series*, Volume XXIII, edited by T. and R. Weiss. Reprinted by permission.

Rand McNally & Company and Unwin Hyman Ltd.
Adapted from *Kon-Tiki: Across the Pacific by Raft* by Thor Heyerdahl, copyright © 1984, 1978, 1950 by Thor Heyerdahl. Published in the U.S.A. by Rand McNally & Company. Reprinted by permission.

Random House, Inc.
"Blues Ain't No Mockin Bird," copyright © 1971 by Toni Cade Bambara. Reprinted from *Gorilla, My Love,* by Toni Cade Bambara, by permission of Random House, Inc.

Andrea Reynolds, attorney-in-fact for André Milos
"The Red-headed League" by Sir Arthur Conan Doyle. Reprinted by permission.

Dr. Sally K. Ride
"Single Room, Earth View" by Sally Ride, published in the April/May 1986 issue of *Air & Space/Smithsonian Magazine*, published by The Smithsonian Institution. Reprinted by permission of the author.

Leslie Marmon Silko
"The Man to Send Rain Clouds" from *Storyteller* by Leslie Marmon Silko. Reprinted by permission of the author.

Simon & Schuster, Inc.
Pronunciation key from *Webster's New World Dictionary,* Second College Edition. Copyright © 1984 by Simon & Schuster, Inc. Reprinted by permission of Simon & Schuster.

The Society of Authors as the Literary representative of the Estate of John Masefield
"Sea-Fever" from *Salt-Water Poems and Ballads* by John Masefield. Reprinted by permission.

Southern Methodist University Press
"A Christmas Tree" by William Burford from *Man Now,* 1954, Southern Methodist University Press. Reprinted by permission of the publisher and William S. Burford.

The Sterling Lord Literistic, Inc.
"The Funeral" from *Whispers of Intimate Things* by Gordon Parks. Copyright © 1971, 1987 by Gordon Parks. Reprinted by permission of Sterling Lord Literistic, Inc.

Summit Books, a division of Simon & Schuster, Inc. and George Borchardt, Inc.
"Butch Cassidy" from *In Patagonia* by Bruce Chatwin. Copyright 1977 by Bruce Chatwin. Reprinted by permission of Summit Books, a division of Simon & Schuster and George Borchardt, Inc.

Rosemary A. Thurber
"The Secret Life of Walter Mitty" copyright 1942 James Thurber; copyright © 1970 Helen W. Thurber and Rosemary A. Thurber. From *My World—And Welcome To It,* published by Harcourt Brace Jovanovich, Inc. "The Spreading 'You Know'" copyright © 1961 James Thurber. From *Lanterns and Lances,* published by Harper & Row. Reprinted by permission.

Yoshiko Uchida
"Of Dry Goods and Black Bow Ties" by Yoshiko Uchida. Copyright 1979 by Yoshiko Uchida. Reprinted by permission of the author.

University of Pittsburgh Press
"The Space" reprinted from *The Tale of Sunlight* by Gary Soto, by permission of the University of Pittsburgh Press. Copyright © 1978 by Gary Soto.

University of Washington Press
"Jacob Lawrence: American Painter" adapted from the Introduction to *Jacob Lawrence, American Painter* by Ellen Harkins Wheat, copyright 1986, University of Washington Press. Reprinted with permission of University of Washington Press.

University Press of New England
"Incident in a Rose Garden" copyright © 1967 by Donald Justice, reprinted from *The Orb Weaver: Night Light* by permission of University Press of New England.

Viking Penguin, a division of Penguin Books USA Inc.
"The Creation" from *God's Trombones* by James Weldon Johnson. Copyright 1927 by The Viking Press, Inc.; copyright renewed 1955 by Grace Nail Johnson. "I Hear an Army" (Poem XXXVI) from *Collected Poems* by James Joyce. Copyright 1918 by B. W. Huebsch; copyright 1927, 1936 by James Joyce; copyright renewed 1946 by Nora Joyce. "The Interlopers" from *The Complete Short Stories of Saki* by Saki (H. H. Munro). Copyright 1930, renewed 1958 by The Viking Press, Inc. Reprinted by permission of Viking Penguin Inc.

Vintage Books, a division of Random House, Inc.
From *The Odyssey,* translated by Robert Fitzgerald. Copyright © 1961, 1963 by Robert Fitzgerald and renewed 1989 by Benedict R. C. Fitzgerald. Reprinted by permission of Vintage Books, a division of Random House, Inc.

Note: Every effort has been made to locate the copyright owner of material reprinted in this book. Omissions brought to our attention will be corrected in subsequent editions.

ART CREDITS

Boldface numbers refer to the page on which the art is found.

Cover and Title Page: *Overseas Highway,* 1939, Oil on canvas, 28 x 45 inches, Ralston Crawford, The Regis Collection, Minneapolis, MN; **v:** *Farmworker de Califas,* Tony Ortega, Monotype, Courtesy of the artist; **vii:** *Harriet Tubman Series No. 4* (detail), Jacob Lawrence, Hampton University Museum, Hampton, Virginia; **ix:** *Polyphemous, the Cyclops* from Homer's *The Odyssey,* N. C. Wyeth, Delaware Art Museum, Photo by Jon MacDowell; **xii:** *The Gulf Stream,* 1899, Winslow Homer, The Metropolitan Museum of Art, Wolfe Fund, 1906, Catherine Lorillard Wolfe Collection, Copyright © 1980 by The Metropolitan Museum of Art; **6:** *Keying Up—The Court Jester,* 1875, William Merritt Chase, Courtesy of the Pennsylvania Academy of the Fine Arts, Philadelphia, Gift of the Chapellier Galleries; **11:** *Angst,* Edvard Munch, Superstock; **20:** *Hat, Knife, and Gun in Woods,* David Mann, Sal Barracca & Associates; **23:** *Peering Through the Jungle,* Larry Noble, Sal Barracca & Associates; **27:** *The Red Cedar,* Emily Carr, The Vancouver Art Gallery; **34:** *Winter in the Rockies,* Thomas Moran, Superstock; **43:** *Chess Mates,* 1992, Pamela Chin Lee, Courtesy of the artist, Photo by John Lei/Omni-Photo Communications, Inc.; **48:** *Frank R. Stockton* (detail), J. W. Alexander, The Bettmann Archive; **50:** *Tiger, Woodward Gardens, San Francisco,* Samuel Marsden Brookes, The Oakland Museum, Kahn Collection; **51:** Original Illustration by Edmund Dulac for "The Story of the King of the Ebony Isles" from *Stories From the Arabian Nights,* Retold by Lawrence Housman (Hodder & Stoughton, 1907), Photograph by John Lei/Omni-Photo Communications, Inc.; **55:** *Passing By,* 1924, E. Martin Hennings, The Museum of Fine Arts, Houston, Gift of the Henry W. Ranger Fund, National Academy of Design; **58:** *Self-Portrait,* 1944–1945, Charley Toorop, Stedelijk Van Abbedmuseum, Eindhoven; **70:** *Sir Arthur Conan Doyle* (detail), 1927, H. L. Gates, By courtesy of the National Portrait Gallery, London; **93:** *Sharecropper,* 1970, Elizabeth Catlett, Courtesy Evans-Tibbs Collection; **97:** *Open Doorway on the Beach,* K. Rodko, Superstock; **98:** *Samuel Langhorne Clemens* (detail), 1935, Frank Edwin Larson, The National Portrait Gallery, Smithsonian Institution; **109:** *Negro Boy,* Eastman Johnson, National Academy of Design, New York; **114:** *Anna Washington Derry,* 1927, Laura Wheeler Waring, National Museum of American Art, Smithsonian Institution, Gift of the Harmon Foundation; **122:** *Farmworker de Califas,* Tony Ortega, Monotype, Courtesy of the artist; **124:** *Campesino,* 1976, Oil on canvas, 50 1/2 x 58 1/2 inches, Daniel DeSiga, Courtesy of the Wight Art Gallery, University of California, Los Angeles, Collection of Alfredo Aragon, Photo by Grey Crawford; **129:** *Laundryman's Daughter,* 1988, Tomie Arai, Silkscreen, mixed media, Courtesy of the artist, Photo by D. James Dee; **132:** *Fallout Shelter,* Silkscreen, Akemi Takeda, Courtesy of the Trustees of the British Museum, Photo by John Lei/Omni-Photo Communications, Inc.; **137:** *Sunken Forest,* Rebecca Grutzik, Student, Stevens Point, Wisconsin, Courtesy of the artist; **141:** *Grandmother and Child,* Carlton Murrell, Courtesy of the artist; **142:** *Selling Fruit, Highway 1,*

Barbados, Jill Walker, Courtesy of Savacou Gallery, New York; **145:** *Going Home,* Carlton Murrell, Courtesy of the artist, Photo by John Lei/Omni-Photo Communications, Inc.; **147:** *Classon Ave., Brooklyn,* Carlton Murrell, Courtesy of the artist; **153:** *Feast Day, San Juan Pueblo,* 1921, William Penhallow Henderson, National Museum of American Art, Smithsonian Institution; Given in memory of Joshua C. Taylor; **163:** *Men Exist for the Sake of One Another. Teach Them Then or Bear With Them,* Jacob Lawrence, 1984.124.171, National Museum of American Art, Washington, D.C./Art Resource, New York; **174:** *O. Henry,* Artist unknown, UPI/Bettmann Archive; **185:** *Two Boys in a Punt,* N. C. Wyeth, Courtesy of Dr. and Mrs. William A. Morton, Jr., Photograph from Brandywine River Museum; **188:** *Scarlet Ibis,* John James Audubon, Courtesy of The New York Historical Society, New York; **195:** *The New Necklace,* 1910, William McGregor Paxton, American, 1869–1941, Oil on canvas, 35 1/2 x 28 1/2 in. (90.2 x 72.3 cm), Zoe Oliver Sherman Collection, Courtesy, Museum of Fine Arts, Boston; **202:** *The Man With Three Masks,* John Rush, Courtesy of the artist; **205:** *New Orleans Fantasy,* 1985, Max Papart, Lithograph, Courtesy of Nahan Galleries, New York; **207:** *Untitled,* John P. Maggard III, Courtesy of the artist; **214:** *The Sheridan Theatre,* 1937, Edward Hopper, Collection of the Newark Museum; **285:** *The Swan Theater, London,* c. 1596, Johannes de Witt, The Granger Collection, New York; **286:** *William Shakespeare* (detail), Artist unknown, By courtesy of the National Portrait Gallery, London; **394:** *Office in a Small City,* 1953, Edward Hopper, The Metropolitan Museum of Art, George A. Hearn Fund, Copyright © 1979 by The Metropolitan Museum of Art; **399:** *The Studio,* 1977, Jacob Lawrence, Seattle Art Museum, Gift of Gull Industries, John H. and Ann H. Hauberg, Links, Seattle, and by exchange from the estate of Mark Tobey, 90.27, Photo by Paul Macapia; **400:** *Harriet Tubman Series No. 4,* Jacob Lawrence, Hampton University Museum, Hampton, Virginia; **403:** *My Wife, Sackville River, Nova Scotia,* 1918, Arthur Lismer, Art Gallery of Ontario, Toronto, Gift of Arthur Lismer, 1951; **404:** *Carl Sandburg* (detail), 1962, Miriam Svet, The National Portrait Gallery, Smithsonian Institution; **406:** *Lincoln Proclaiming Thanksgiving,* Dean Cornwell, Louis A. Warren Lincoln Library and Museum, Fort Wayne, Indiana; **409:** *Peculiarsome Abe,* N. C. Wyeth, The Free Library of Philadelphia; **423:** *Distinguished Visitors to Buffalo Bill's Wild West, London,* 1887, Original color lithograph poster, Buffalo Bill Historical Center, Cody, Wyoming; **427:** *Black Elk Under the Tree of Life* from *Black Elk Speaks,* Standing Bear, an Oglala Sioux, Courtesy of the Western Historical Manuscript Collection Columbia and the John C. Neihardt Trust; **439:** *Music and Literature,* 1878, William Harnett, Albright-Knox Art Gallery, Buffalo, New York, Gift of Seymour H. Knox, 1941; **449:** *Farm Worker,* Armando Hinojosa, Courtesy of DagenBela Graphics, Inc.; **451:** *Don Nemesio,* 1977, Esperanza Martinez, Courtesy of the artist; **473:** *Woman With Violin,* Henri Matisse, Paris, Musee de l'Orangerie, Scala/Art Resource, New York; **481:** *The White*

Trumpet Flower, 1932, Georgia O'Keeffe, San Diego Museum of Art, Gift of Inez Grant Parker in memory of Earle W. Grant; **483:** Cow's Skull: Red, White and Blue, 1931, Georgia O'Keeffe, The Metropolitan Museum of Art, The Alfred Stieglitz Collection, 1949, Copyright © 1984 by The Metropolitan Museum of Art, Photograph by Malcolm Varon; **493, 494:** Illustrations from "The Spreading 'You Know,'" Copyright © 1961 James Thurber, From Lanterns and Lances published by Harper & Row; **498:** Reconstruction of the Second Globe Theatre in London, Artist unknown, The Granger Collection, New York; **514:** Mist Fantasy, 1922, J. E. H. MacDonald, Art Gallery of Ontario, Toronto, Gift of Mrs. S. J. Williams in memory of F. Elinor Williams, 1927; **517:** Paul Laurence Dunbar, Artist unknown, The Granger Collection, New York; **519:** Buffalo Chase With Bows and Lances, George Catlin, Oil on canvas, 24 x 29", National Museum of American Art, Smithsonian Institution, Gift of Mrs. Joseph Harrison, Jr.; **523:** Baseball Players Practicing, 1875, Thomas Eakins, Museum of Art, Rhode Island School of Design, Jesse Metcalf Fund and Walter H. Kimball Fund; **529:** The Raven, Edouard Manet, Gift of W. G. Russell Allen, Courtesy, Museum of Fine Arts, Boston; **532:** Baron Alfred, Lord Tennyson (detail), c. 1840, S. Laurence, By courtesy of the National Portrait Gallery, London; **534:** Charge of the Light Brigade at the Battle of Balaklava, 1854, Artist unknown, Superstock; **536:** Beinecke Rare Book and Manuscript Library, Yale University; **537:** Portrait of Mme. Matisse, Henri Matisse, The Hermitage, Leningrad, Bridgeman/Art Resource, New York; **539:** The Race Track or Death on a Pale Horse, Albert Pinkham Ryder, The Cleveland Museum of Art, Purchase from J. H. Wade Fund; **542:** William Shakespeare (detail), Artist unknown, By courtesy of the National Portrait Gallery, London; **544:** Seven Ages of Man, Stained glass window, Folger Shakespeare Library, Washington, D.C., Photo by Julie Ainsworth; **546:** Edgar Lee Masters (detail), 1946, Francis J. Quirk, The National Portrait Gallery, Smithsonian Institution, Gift of the artist; **550:** We the People, Kathy Morrow, Original scratchboard painting with handloomed beadwork, Courtesy of the artist; **553:** Quintet, 1961, Samuel Reindorf, Courtesy of the artist; **554:** William Shakespeare (detail), Artist unknown, By courtesy of the National Portrait Gallery, London; Edwin Arlington Robinson (detail), 1933, Thomas Richard Hood, The National Portrait Gallery, Smithsonian Institution; Christina Rossetti (detail), D. G. Rossetti, By courtesy of the National Portrait Gallery, London; **555:** James Joyce, Jacques-Emile Blanche, The Granger Collection, New York; **561:** Horses of Neptune, 1892, Walter Crane, Bayerische Staatsgemaldesammlungen, Photo from Arthothek; **563:** Orion in December, 1959, Charles Burchfield, National Museum of American Art, Smithsonian Institution, Gift of S. C. Johnson & Sons, Inc.; **564:** Robert Browning, M. Gordigiani, The Granger Collection, New York; T. S. Eliot, Artist unknown, The Granger Collection, New York; **566:** Moonlit Cove, 1880–1890, Albert Pinkham Ryder, The Phillips Collection, Washington, D.C.; **568:** The Jabberwock, 1872, John Tenniel, The Granger Collection, New York; **570, 572:** From Old Possum's Book of Practical Cats, Copyright 1939 by T. S. Eliot; renewed 1967 by Esme Valerie Eliot, Reproduced by permission of Harcourt Brace Jovanovich, Inc., Illustration by Edward Gorey; **575:** Pink Shell With Seaweed, c. 1938, Georgia O'Keeffe, San Diego Museum of Art; **577:** James Weldon Johnson (detail), c. 1925, Winold Reiss, The National Portrait Gallery, Smithsonian Institution, Gift of Lawrence A. Fleischman and Howard Garfinkle with a matching grant from the National Endowment of the Arts; **584:** The Creation, Aaron Douglas, The Studio Museum in Harlem, Photo by John Lei/Omni-Photo Communications, Inc.; **587:** The Eclipse, March 1970, Alma Woodsey Thomas, Acrylic on canvas, 62 x 49 3/4", National Museum of American Art, Smithsonian Institution, Gift of Alma W. Thomas; **588:** Baron Alfred Tennyson (detail), c. 1840, S. Laurence, By courtesy of the National Portrait Gallery, London; William Wordsworth, Artist unknown, The Granger Collection, New York; Langston Hughes (detail), c. 1925, Winold Reiss, The National Portrait Gallery, Smithsonian Institution, Gift of H. Tjark Reiss, in memory of his father, Winold Reiss; Emily Dickinson, Artist unknown, The Granger Collection, New York; **589:** Carl Sandburg (detail), 1962, Miriam Svet, The National Portrait Gallery, Smithsonian Institution; **590:** Eagle in a Snowstorm (detail), Hokusai, Reproduced from The Harai Collection of Japanese Paintings and Drawings, Edited by J. Hiller, Published by Lund Humphries, London; **596:** Cap Bon Ami (detail), 1961, Samuel Reindorf, Courtesy of the artist; **599:** Three Musicians, 1921, Pablo Picasso, Oil on canvas, 6'7" x 7'3 3/4", Collection, The Museum of Modern Art, New York, Mrs. Simon Guggenheim Fund; **600:** Walt Whitman, UPI/Bettmann Newsphotos; **602:** Het Blinde Huis, William Degouve de Nunques, State Museum, Kröller-Müller, Otterlo, The Netherlands; **605:** The Bells, Edmund Dulac, New York Public Library; Astor, Lenox and Tilden Foundations; **610:** Coal (from America Today), 1920, Thomas Hart Benton, Courtesy of The Equitable Life Assurance Society of the U.S.; **613:** Harmony In Red, 1908–1909, Henri Matisse, The Hermitage, Leningrad/Art Resource, New York; **614:** Self-Portrait (detail), 1958, E. E. Cummings, The National Portrait Gallery, Smithsonian Institution, Washington; **618:** The Much Resounding Sea, 1884, Thomas Moran, National Gallery of Art, Washington, Gift of the Avalon Foundation; **620:** Año Siete, Amado Peña, 21st Century Art Investment; **622:** Henry Wadsworth Longfellow (detail), Thomas B. Read, The National Portrait Gallery, Smithsonian Institution; William Shakespeare, Artist unknown, By courtesy of the National Portrait Gallery, London; **626:** (top) Girl With Lantern on a Balcony at Night (detail), c. 1768, Suzuki Harunobu, The Metropolitan Museum of Art, Fletcher Fund, 1929; **626:** (center) Richard Wright (detail), 1949, Miriam Troop, The National Portrait Gallery, Smithsonian Institution, Washington, D.C.; **628:** Girl With Lantern on a Balcony at Night, c. 1768, Suzuki Harunobu, The Metropolitan Museum of Art, Fletcher Fund, 1929; **634:** Robert Burns (detail), A. Nasmyth, By courtesy of the National Portrait Gallery, London; **640:** Ulysses Deriding Polyphemus, 1819, J.M.W. Turner, The National Gallery, London; **644:** Homer, Artist Unknown, The New York Public Library Picture Collection; **646:** La Nef De Telemachus (The Ship of Telemachus), New York Public Library Picture Collection; **651:** The Cyclops (detail), Odilon Redon, Rijksmuseum,

Kröller-Müller, Otterlo, Bridgeman/Art Resource, New York; **660:** *Polyphemous, the Cyclops* from Homer's *The Odyssey*, N. C. Wyeth, Delaware Art Museum, Photo by Jon MacDowell; **664:** *Odysseus in the Land of the Dead* from Homer's *The Odyssey*, N. C. Wyeth, Delaware Art Museum, Photo by Jon MacDowell; **668:** *Circe Meanwhile Had Gone Her Ways . . . ,* 1924, William Russell Flint, Collection of the New York Public Library; Astor, Lenox, and Tilden Foundations; **682:** *Eumaeus, the Swineherd* from Homer's *The Odyssey*, N. C. Wyeth, Delaware Art Museum, Photo by Jon MacDowell; **693:** *Penelope,* Henry Fuseli, Courtesy of Stiftung für Kunst, Kultur und Geschichte, Küsnacht; **695:** *The Trial of The Bow* from Homer's *The Odyssey*, N. C. Wyeth, Delaware Art Museum, Photo by Jon MacDowell; **700:** *The Slaughter of the Suitors* from Homer's *The Odyssey*, N. C. Wyeth, Delaware Art Museum, Photo by Jon MacDowell; **707:** Scene from the *Ramayana* (detail), c.1800, Gouache on paper, Murshidabad, Bengal, By courtesy of the Board of Trustees of the Victoria and Albert Museum; **710:** *Ulysses and the Sirens,* Pablo Picasso, Musée Picasso; **714:** *The Olympic Experience,* Copyright © Ernie Barnes, Courtesy of The Company of Art, Photo by John Lei/Omni-Photo Communications, Inc.; **720:** *The Apartment of Madame Sundheim,* René Magritte, Superstock; **723:** *Mid-Victorian Father Reading to Entire Family,* Artist unknown, Superstock; **724:** *Charles Dickens,* Artist unknown, The Granger Collection, New York; **731:** *The Stone-Breaker,* 1857–1858, Henry Wallis, By courtesy of the Birmingham Museums and Art Gallery; **741:** *Rustic Girl Seated,* John Constable, Victoria and Albert Museum Trustees, London; **748:** *Miss Cicely Alexander: Harmony in Grey and Green,* James McNeill Whistler, The Tate Gallery, London; **759:** *The School Master's Daughter,* James Sant, R.A., Royal Academy of Arts, London; **763:** *John Randolph,* 1805; Gilbert Stuart, National Gallery of Art, Washington, Andrew W. Mellon Collection; **772:** *Pat Lyon at the Forge,* 1826–1827, John Neagle, Henry H. and Zoe Oliver Sherman Fund, 1975, Courtesy, Museum of Fine Arts, Boston; **782:** *Mortlake Terrace,* J. M. W. Turner, National Gallery of Art, Washington, Scala/Art Resource, New York; **792:** *Ludgate Hill,* Gustave Dore, Reproduced by courtesy of the Trustees of the British Museum; **795:** *Covent Garden, London,* John Wykeham Archer, British Library, London, Bridgeman/Art Resource, New York; **805:** *David Johnston,* 1808, Pierre-Paul Prud'hon, National Gallery of Art, Washington, Samuel H. Kress Collection; **814:** *Omnibus Life in London,* 1859, William Maw Egley, The Tate Gallery, London; **819:** *The White Girl (Symphony in White No. 1),* 1862, James McNeill Whistler, Canvas, 2.147 x 1.080, National Gallery of Art, Washington, Harry Whittemore Collection; **827:** *The Seat of Major Norice, Maidstone,* 1837, George Sidney Shepherd, Maidstone Museums and Art Gallery; **837:** *Only a Lock of Hair,* Sir John Everett Millais, Manchester City Art Galleries; **846:** *Adeline, Seventh Countess of Cardigan,* Richard Buckner, From the collection of Edmund Brudenell, Esq.; **851:** *Henry, Lord Montague of Broughton,* Sir Francis Grant, National Galleries of Scotland, Tom Scott of Edinburgh; **862:** *February Fill Dyke,* Benjamin William Leader, By courtesy of the Birmingham Museums and Art Gallery; **869:** *Moonlight, a Study at Millbank,* J. M. W. Turner, The Tate Gallery, London; **878:** *Little London Model,* James McNeill Whistler, Frank S. Benson Funds, The Brooklyn Museum; **886:** *The York-London Mail Coach,* Gilbert S. Wright, Superstock; **896:** *Waiting for the Verdict,* 1857, Abraham Solomon, From the collection of Barbara and Norman S. Namerow, Beverly Hills, California; **904:** *The Proposal,* 1877, William Powell Frith, Lady Scott, Boughton House, Kettering; **909:** *Nature Walk,* Rolland Dingman, Courtesy of the artist.

PHOTOGRAPH CREDITS

vi: Photofest; **2:** Courtesy of Scott Reilly; **9:** The Bettmann Archive; **12:** New York Times Pictures; **32:** The Granger Collection, New York; **38:** G. P. Putnam's Sons; **56:** AP/Wide World Photos; **62:** Inge Morath/Magnum Photos, Inc.; **90:** Nikky Finney; **120:** Courtesy of Arte Publico Press, University of Houston; **126:** Shelley Rotner/Omni-Photo Communications, Inc.; **130:** Shunkichi Kikuchi/Magnum Photos Inc.; **138:** AP/Wide World Photos; **150:** Thomas Victor; **156:** UPI/Bettmann Newsphotos; **161:** NASA; **164:** The Bettmann Archive; **178:** Memory Shop; **180:** Wardene Weisser/Bruce Coleman, Inc.; **192:** The Bettmann Archive; **200:** Courtesy of Mark Devine; **208:** UPI/Bettmann Newsphotos; **281:** Culver Pictures, Inc.; **288, 295:** Photofest; **302:** Culver Pictures, Inc.; **304:** Photofest; **307:** Culver Pictures, Inc.; **309:** Photofest; **316:** Culver Pictures, Inc.; **325, 332:** Photofest; **339:** Memory Shop; **346:** Culver Pictures, Inc.; **355, 367:** Memory Shop; **379:** Photofest; **381:** Memory Shop; **384:** Photofest; **396:** Courtesy of Brendan Lippman; **401:** Courtesy of Ellen Wheat; **414, 416:** Nippon Kan Heritage Society; **420:** Courtesy of the John G. Neihardt Trust; **428:** The Granger Collection, New York; **431, 435:** From the book, *Kon-Tiki* by Thor Heyerdahl, © 1984, 1960, 1950, Used by permission of the publisher, Prentice Hall Press, Simon & Schuster, New York; **440:** AP/Wide World Photos; **442:** From *Blue Highways: A Journey Into America* by William Least Heat Moon, Copyright © 1982 William Least Heat Moon, By permission of Little, Brown, and Company in association with the Atlantic Monthly Press; **446:** Courtesy of Rudolfo Anaya; **456:** Thomas Victor; **457:** Academy of Applied Sciences, Boston/Photo Trends; **462:** Everett C. Johnson/Folio, Inc.; **466:** UPI/Bettmann Newsphotos; **468:** The Bettmann Archive; **480:** Thomas Victor; **486, 488, 490:** NASA; **492:** UPI/Bettmann Newsphotos; **496:** The Bettmann Archive; **502:** Courtesy of Stephanie Huang; **506:** Utah State Historical Society; **509:** Viking Penguin, Inc.; **516:** Courtesy of Tuan Quoc Pham; **526:** UPI/Bettmann Newsphotos; **538:** Thomas Victor; **546:** (top) Dmitri Kessel/*Life* Magazine, © Time, Inc.; (center) Globe Photos, Inc.; **548:** Stephanie Pfriender/The Stock Market; **554:** AP/Wide World Photos;

556: Harvey Lloyd/The Stock Market; 564: New York Public Library Picture Collection; 576: (center) AP/Wide World Photos; (bottom) Dianne Trejo; 592: AP/Wide World Photos; 600: (top) The Bettmann Archive; (center) UPI/Bettmann Newsphotos; 614: (top, center) The Bettmann Archive; (bottom) Marlene Fostor; 615: The Bettmann Archive; 616: Runk/Schoenberger/Grant Heilman Photography; (bottom) Thomas Victor; 632: Courtesy of Jair Pinckney; 633: John Scheirer/The Stock Market; 708: (top) Thomas Victor; (bottom) Eugene Richards/Magnum Photos, Inc.; 914: Edmund Ross.

ILLUSTRATION CREDITS

pp. 14–15: Chet Jezerski/Jeff Cavaty; pp. 72, 76, 81, 86, 100–101, 102–103: The Art Source; pp. 166–167, 178–179; Carlos Ochagavia/Frank and Jeff Cavaty & Associates; p. 437: Mapping Specialists Limited, Don Larson; p. 477: Ray Smith; pp. 910, 918, 923, 929, 935, 946, 949, 955, 957, 963, 969, 976, 981, 986, 989, 994, 1008, 1013, 1019: Robert Rodriguez.